AUSTRALIAN
STUDENT'S
THE FUTURE OF AUSTRALIAN ENGLISH
OXFORD
DICTIONARY

FOURTH EDITION

EDITED BY
MARK GWYNN

OXFORD
UNIVERSITY PRESS
AUSTRALIA & NEW ZEALAND

OXFORD
UNIVERSITY PRESS

Oxford University Press is a department of the University of Oxford.
It furthers the University's objective of excellence in research,
scholarship, and education by publishing worldwide. Oxford is a
registered trademark of Oxford University Press in the UK and in certain
other countries.

Published in Australia by
Oxford University Press
253 Normanby Road, South Melbourne, Victoria 3205, Australia

© Oxford University Press 1997

The moral rights of the author have been asserted.

Second edition 1997
Third edition 2005
Fourth edition 2010
Reprinted 2011, 2012, 2013

This dictionary is based on *The Oxford Study Dictionary*
compiled by Joyce M. Hawkins, John Weston, and Julia Swannell
(first published 1991, redesigned impression 1994). *The Australian
Student's Dictionary* (first edition) was published as *The Australian
Secondary Dictionary* in 1986.

National Library of Australia Cataloguing-in-Publication data

Gwynn, Mark.
Australian student's Oxford dictionary/edited by Mark Gwynn.

4th ed.

ISBN 978 0 19 557391 6 (hbk.).

English language—Dictionaries.
English language—Australia—Dictionaries.

423

Reproduction and communication for educational purposes
The Australian *Copyright Act 1968* (the Act) allows a maximum of one chapter
or 10% of the pages of this work, whichever is the greater, to be reproduced
and/or communicated by any educational institution for its educational purposes
provided that the educational institution (or the body that administers it) has
given a remuneration notice to Copyright Agency Limited (CAL) under the Act.

For details of the CAL licence for educational institutions contact:

Copyright Agency Limited
Level 15, 233 Castlereagh Street
Sydney NSW 2000
Telephone: (02) 9394 7600
Facsimile: (02) 9394 7601
Email: info@copyright.com.au

Proofread by Greg Alford
Typeset by diacriTech, Chennai, India
Printed in China by Sheck Wah Tong Printing Press Ltd

*Links to third party websites are provided by Oxford in good faith and for information only.
Oxford disclaims any responsibility for the materials contained in any third party website
referenced in this work.*

¯ased on the *Australian Student's Colour Dictionary* edited by Anne Knight
˙ ˘ assistance of George Turner, © Oxford University Press

OWLS
OXFORD
DICTIONARY
WORD AND
LANGUAGE
SERVICE

Do you have a query about
words, their origin, meaning,
use, spelling, pronunciation, or
any other aspect of international
English? Then write to OWLS at
the Australian National Dictionary
Centre, Australian National
University, Canberra ACT 0200
(email ANDC@anu.edu.au). All
queries will be answered using
the full resources of *The Australian
National Dictionary* and *The
Oxford English Dictionary*.
The Australian National Dictionary
Centre and Oxford University
Press also produce *Ozwords*, a
biannual newsletter which contains
interesting items about Australian
words and language. Subscription
is free–please contact the
Ozwords subscription manager
at Oxford University Press, GPO
Box 2784, Melbourne, VIC
3001, or ozwords.au@oup.com

AUSTRALIAN STUDENT'S

THE FUTURE OF AUSTRALIAN ENGLISH

OXFORD DICTIONARY

FOURTH EDITION

EDITED BY
MARK GWYNN

OXFORD
UNIVERSITY PRESS
AUSTRALIA & NEW ZEALAND

OXFORD
UNIVERSITY PRESS

Oxford University Press is a department of the University of Oxford.
It furthers the University's objective of excellence in research,
scholarship, and education by publishing worldwide. Oxford is a
registered trademark of Oxford University Press in the UK and in certain
other countries.

Published in Australia by
Oxford University Press
253 Normanby Road, South Melbourne, Victoria 3205, Australia

© Oxford University Press 1997

The moral rights of the author have been asserted.

Second edition 1997
Third edition 2005
Fourth edition 2010
Reprinted 2011, 2012, 2013

This dictionary is based on *The Oxford Study Dictionary*
compiled by Joyce M. Hawkins, John Weston, and Julia Swannell
(first published 1991, redesigned impression 1994). *The Australian
Student's Dictionary* (first edition) was published as *The Australian
Secondary Dictionary* in 1986.

National Library of Australia Cataloguing-in-Publication data

Gwynn, Mark.
Australian student's Oxford dictionary/edited by Mark Gwynn.

4th ed.

ISBN 978 0 19 557391 6 (hbk.).

English language—Dictionaries.
English language—Australia—Dictionaries.

423

Reproduction and communication for educational purposes
The Australian *Copyright Act 1968* (the Act) allows a maximum of one chapter
or 10% of the pages of this work, whichever is the greater, to be reproduced
and/or communicated by any educational institution for its educational purposes
provided that the educational institution (or the body that administers it) has
given a remuneration notice to Copyright Agency Limited (CAL) under the Act.

For details of the CAL licence for educational institutions contact:

Copyright Agency Limited
Level 15, 233 Castlereagh Street
Sydney NSW 2000
Telephone: (02) 9394 7600
Facsimile: (02) 9394 7601
Email: info@copyright.com.au

Proofread by Greg Alford
Typeset by diacriTech, Chennai, India
Printed in China by Sheck Wah Tong Printing Press Ltd

*Links to third party websites are provided by Oxford in good faith and for information only.
Oxford disclaims any responsibility for the materials contained in any third party website
referenced in this work.*

Based on the *Australian Student's Colour Dictionary* edited by Anne Knight
with the assistance of George Turner, © Oxford University Press

OWLS
**OXFORD
DICTIONARY
WORD AND
LANGUAGE
SERVICE**

Do you have a query about
words, their origin, meaning,
use, spelling, pronunciation, or
any other aspect of international
English? Then write to OWLS at
the Australian National Dictionary
Centre, Australian National
University, Canberra ACT 0200
(email ANDC@anu.edu.au). All
queries will be answered using
the full resources of *The Australian
National Dictionary* and *The
Oxford English Dictionary*.
The Australian National Dictionary
Centre and Oxford University
Press also produce *Ozwords*, a
biannual newsletter which contains
interesting items about Australian
words and language. Subscription
is free—please contact the
Ozwords subscription manager
at Oxford University Press, GPO
Box 2784, Melbourne, VIC
3001, or ozwords.au@oup.com

Contents

Preface

This dictionary is an authoritative guide to English as used in Australia, especially for use by students in secondary schools and colleges, but with continuing usefulness in adult life. Its authority comes from the ultimate authority in Oxford dictionaries, the twenty volumes of the *Oxford English Dictionary,* now updated and available online, and its even vaster database of quotations recording the senses in which words have been used by speakers and writers of English. For Australian English this is augmented by the database of Australian English at the Australian National Dictionary Centre in Canberra. Over the years, various derivative dictionaries have been compiled to meet the needs of particular age groups or levels of difficulty.

As with its predecessors, this dictionary's compilation has been based on a survey of current textbooks to ensure thorough coverage of words encountered in the school curriculum. It is intended to be easy to use, with straightforward definitions, examples showing how words are used in context, and notes on points of usage.

The previous edition included many entries for people, places, and institutions. This edition updates these entries, including countries and their capital cities, major geographical features (such as mountains and seas), and biographical entries for major historical and cultural figures.

Supplementing these encyclopedic entries is a new appendix section for quick and easy reference by students. The appendices include a grammar and reference guide, the countries of the world (with their capital cities, units of currency, and Internet domain name suffixes), a list of Australian, UK, and US leaders, the chemical elements, and a conversion guide for units of measurement.

Following an Oxford tradition, we have included etymologies where the derivation sheds light on a word's meaning, or to show how a meaning has changed, to demonstrate the connection between related words and to help with recognition of word elements (e.g. in *attract, contract, extract, subtract, traction,* and *tractor*), and occasionally for general interest in the history of a word (e.g. *apron, budget, carnival,* and *deadline*). Of particular interest are the words derived from Aboriginal languages (e.g. *kangaroo, koala, and kookaburra*).

This edition includes a range of new entries that reflect changes in contemporary technology, culture, and society. Words emerging from developments in technology and electronic communications (often being new senses of established words) include: *avatar, cloud computing, defriend, photoshop, tweet,* and *twitter*. Other new words include: *alcopop, bromance, carbon footprint, identity theft, intelligent design,* and *taser*.

I would like to thank all the people who helped in the planning, preparation, and production of this dictionary, particularly Dr Bruce Moore, Director of the Australian National Dictionary Centre.

Mark Gwynn

How to use this dictionary

The words defined (headwords) are printed in blue, and are listed in alphabetical order.

Alternative spellings of the headword are given before the definition.

Words with the same spelling but different meanings or origins have different raised numbers and are treated as separate entries.

Pronunciation is given where it is not obvious.

The part of speech is printed in italics.

If a word is used as more than one part of speech, these are defined separately.

Meanings are given in ordinary type. If a word has more than one meaning, these meanings are listed separately and numbered.

Example phrases help to clarify the meaning or show how a word is used.

Plurals are given if there might be doubt about their spelling.

Comparative and superlative forms of adjectives are given if they are irregular or their spelling is not obvious.

Derivatives are included without their definition if their meaning can easily be worked out from the meaning of the headword.

soggy *adjective* **1** sodden. **2** moist and heavy in texture. **soggily** *adverb*, **sogginess** *noun*

soigné (**swahn**-yay) *adjective* (of a woman, **soignée**) well-groomed and sophisticated. [French. = taken care of]

soil¹ *noun* **1** the loose upper layer of earth in which plants grow. **2** grounds as territory, *on native soil*.

soil² *verb* to make or become dirty.

soirée (**swah**-ray) *noun* a social gathering in the evening, e.g. for music. [French, = evening]

sojourn (**soh**-jern *or* **soj**-ern) *noun* a temporary stay. **sojourn** *verb* to stay at a place temporarily.

solace (**sol**-ăs) *noun* comfort in distress; something that gives this. **solace** *verb* to give solace to. [from Latin *solari* = to console]

solar (**soh**-ler) *adjective* **1** of or derived from the sun, *solar energy*. **2** reckoned by the sun, *solar time*. □ **solar battery** or **cell** a device converting solar radiation into electricity. **solar heating** heating derived from solar energy. **solar plexus** the network of nerves at the pit of the stomach; this area. **solar system** the sun with the heavenly bodies that revolve round it. [from Latin *sol* = sun]

solarium (sŏ-**lair**-ree-ŭm) *noun* (*plural* **solaria**) a room or balcony, often enclosed with glass, where sunlight can be enjoyed for medical purposes or for pleasure.

icy *adjective* (**icier**, **iciest**) **1** very cold, as cold as ice, *icy winds*. **2** covered with ice, *icy roads*. **3** very cold and unfriendly in manner, *an icy voice*. **icily** *adverb*, **iciness** *noun*

pawky *adjective* (**pawkier**, **pawkiest**) drily humorous. **pawkily** *adverb*, **pawkiness** *noun*

eat *verb* (**ate, eaten, eating**) **1** to take food into the mouth and swallow it for nourishment; to have a meal, *when do we eat?* **2** to chew and swallow (food). **3** to destroy gradually, *acids eat into metals.* **4** to consume. **eats** *plural noun* (*informal*) food. □ **eat one's heart out** to suffer greatly with vexation or longing. **eat one's words** to be obliged to withdraw what one has said. **what's eating you?** (*informal*) why are you annoyed? **eater** *noun*

lend *verb* (**lent, lending**) **1** to give or allow the use of (a thing) temporarily on the understanding that it or its equivalent will be returned. **2** to provide (money) temporarily in return for payment of interest. **3** to contribute as a temporary help or effect etc., *lend dignity to the occasion.* □ **lend a hand** to help. **lend an ear** to listen. **lend itself to** to be suitable for. **lender** *noun*

pawn[2] *verb* to deposit (a thing) with a pawnbroker as security for money borrowed. – **pawn** *noun* something deposited as a pledge. □ **in pawn** deposited as a pawn. **pawn ticket** a receipt for a thing deposited with a pawnbroker. [from Old French *pan* = pledge]

pawnbroker *noun* a person licensed to lend money on the security of personal property deposited with him or her.

paw *noun* **1** the foot of an animal that has claws. **2** (*informal*) a person's hand. – **paw** *verb* **1** to strike with a paw. **2** to scrape (the ground) with a hoof. **3** (*informal*) to touch awkwardly or rudely with the hands.

Usage *Proscribe* is sometimes confused with *prescribe*. A doctor *prescribes* medicine to make you better, whereas the use of heroin is *proscribed*.

prosecute *verb* **1** to take legal proceedings against (a person etc.) for a crime. **2** to carry on or conduct, *prosecuting their trade.* **prosecutor** *noun* [from Latin *prosecutus* = pursued]

Rubicon (roo-bĭ-kŏn) *noun* **cross the Rubicon** to take a decisive step that commits one to an enterprise. (¶ The river Rubicon, in NE Italy, was the ancient boundary between Gaul and Italy; by crossing it into Italy Julius Caesar committed himself to war against the Senate and Pompey.)

Peking (pee-**king**) *see* Beijing.

vii

Pronunciation

A guide to pronunciation is given for any word that is difficult to pronounce, or difficult to recognise when read, or spelt the same as another word but pronounced differently. The pronunciation given represents that used in standard Australian speech. It is shown in brackets, usually just after the word itself. Alternative pronunciations are given where there is more than one in common use.

The letters *pr.* (= pronounced) are sometimes put in to make clear that it is the pronunciation that follows, not an alternative spelling.

Words are broken up into small units, usually of one syllable. The syllable that is spoken with the most stress in a word of two or more syllables is shown in heavy letters, like **this**.

The sounds represented are as follows:

a	*as in* c**a**t
ă	*as in* **a**go
ah	*as in* c**a**lm
air	*as in* h**air**
ar	*as in* b**ar**
aw	*as in* l**aw**
ay	*as in* s**ay**
b	*as in* **b**at
ch	*as in* **ch**in
d	*as in* **d**ay
e	*as in* b**e**d
ě	*as in* tak**e**n
ee	*as in* m**ee**t
eer	*as in* b**eer**
er	*as in* h**er**
ew	*as in* f**ew**
ewr	*as in* dem**ure**
f	*as in* **f**at
g	*as in* **g**et
h	*as in* **h**at
i	*as in* p**i**n
ĭ	*as in* penc**i**l
I	*as in* **e**ye
j	*as in* **j**am

k	*as in* **k**ing
l	*as in* **l**eg
m	*as in* **m**an
n	*as in* **n**ot
ng	*as in* si**ng**
nk	*as in* tha**nk**
o	*as in* t**o**p
ŏ	*as in* lem**o**n
oh	*as in* m**o**st
oi	*as in* j**oi**n
oo	*as in* s**oo**n
oor	*as in* p**oor**
or	*as in* **for**
ow	*as in* c**ow**
p	*as in* **p**en
r	*as in* **r**ed
s	*as in* **s**it
sh	*as in* **sh**op
t	*as in* **t**op
th	*as in* **th**in
th	*as in* **th**is
u	*as in* c**u**p
ŭ	*as in* circ**u**s
uu	*as in* b**oo**k
v	*as in* **v**an
w	*as in* **w**ill
y	*as in* **y**es (before a vowel); otherwise = I as *in* b**y**
yoo	as in **u**nit
yoor	*as in* end**ure**
yr	*as in* **fire**
z	*as in* **z**ebra
zh	*as in* vi**si**on

A consonant is sometimes doubled to help show that the vowel just before it is short (like the vowels in *cat, bed, pin, top, cup*), or when without this the combination of letters might suggest a wrong pronunciation through looking misleadingly like a familiar word. Similarly, an apostrophe is sometimes used to break up a confusing combination of letters. The pronunciation of a word (or part of a word) is sometimes indicated by giving a well-known word that rhymes with it.

Abbreviations

Amer.	American
Austral.	Australian
Brit.	British
Gk.	Greek
myth.	mythology
pr.	pronounced
Rom.	Roman
Scand.	Scandinavian

Abbreviations that are in general use (such as mm, RC, NZ, and WA) appear in the dictionary itself.

Proprietary terms

This dictionary includes some words that are, or are asserted to be, proprietary names or trademarks. Their inclusion does not imply that they have acquired for legal purposes a non-proprietary or general significance, nor is any other judgment implied concerning their legal status. In cases where the editor has some evidence that a word is used as a proprietary name or trademark this is indicated by the label *trademark*, but no judgment concerning the legal status of such words is made or implied thereby.

Aa

A the first letter of the alphabet. □ **A1, A2, A3, A4** standard paper sizes, each half of the previous one, e.g. A4 = 297 × 210 mm. **from A to Z** from beginning to end.

A *abbreviation* ampere(s).

Å *abbreviation* ångström(s).

a *adjective* (called the *indefinite article*) **1** one person or thing but not any specific one, *I need a knife*. **2** per, *we pay $40 a year*; *twice a day*.

a-¹ *prefix* **1** on; to; towards (as in *afoot, ashore, aside*). **2** in the process of (as in *a-hunting*).

a-² *prefix* (**an-** is used before a vowel sound) not; without (as in *asymmetrical, anarchy*). [from Greek *a-* = not]

aardvark (**ard**-vark) *noun* an African termite-eating animal with a bulky piglike body and a thick tail. [from Afrikaans *aarde* = earth, + *vark* = pig]

Aaron (**air**-rŏn) brother of Moses and traditional founder of the Jewish priesthood.

ab- *prefix* (changing to **abs-** before *c* and *t*) away; from (as in *abduct, abnormal, abstract*). [from Latin *ab-* = away]

aback *adverb* **taken aback** disconcerted.

abacus (**ab**-ă-kŭs) *noun* (*plural* **abacuses**) a frame containing parallel rods with beads that slide along them, used for counting.

abalone (ab-ă-**loh**-nee) *noun* an edible mollusc with an ear-shaped shell lined with mother-of-pearl.

abandon *verb* **1** to go away from (a person or thing or place) without intending to return; *abandon ship*, leave a sinking ship. **2** to give up, to cease work on, *abandon the attempt*. **3** to yield completely to an emotion or impulse, *abandoned himself to despair*. **–abandon** *noun* careless freedom of manner. **abandonment** *noun*

abandoned *adjective* (of behaviour) showing abandon, lacking restraint, depraved.

abase *verb* to humiliate, to degrade. **abasement** *noun*

abashed *adjective* embarrassed, ashamed.

abate *verb* to make or become less; *the storm abated*, died down. **abatement** *noun*

abattoir (**ab**-ă-twar) *noun* a place where animals are killed for food, a slaughterhouse. [French]

abbess (**ab**-ess) *noun* a woman who is head of an abbey of nuns.

abbey *noun* **1** a building occupied by monks or nuns living as a community. **2** the community itself. **3** a church or house that was formerly an abbey, *Westminster Abbey*.

abbot *noun* a man who is head of an abbey of monks.

abbreviate *verb* to shorten (especially a word or title).

abbreviation *noun* **1** abbreviating, being abbreviated. **2** a shortened form of a word or title.

ABC *noun* **1** the alphabet. **2** the elementary facts of a subject, *the ABC of music*. **3** an alphabetically arranged guide. **–ABC** *abbreviation* Australian Broadcasting Corporation.

abdicate *verb* to resign from a throne or other high office; to give up (office, responsibility, etc.). **abdication** *noun*

abdomen (**ab**-dŏ-měn) *noun* **1** the part of the body below the chest and diaphragm, containing most of the digestive organs. **2** the hindmost section of the body of an insect, spider, or crustacean, *head, thorax, and abdomen*. **abdominal** (ăb-**dom**-ĭ-năl) *adjective*, **abdominally** *adverb*

abduct *verb* to carry off (a person) illegally by force or fraud. **abduction** *noun*, **abductor** *noun* [from *ab-*, + Latin *ductum* = led]

Abelian (ă-**bee**-lee-ăn) *adjective* (of a mathematical group) in which the operation applied to the elements is commutative, as in (4 + 3) and (3 + 4), which are equal.

aberrant (ab-e-**rănt**) *adjective* deviating from the normal type or accepted standard. [from *ab-*, + Latin *errare* = wander]

aberration (ab-ĕ-**ray**-shŏn) *noun* **1** a deviation from what is normal. **2** a mental or moral lapse. **3** distortion, e.g. of an image produced through an imperfect lens.

1

abet *verb* (abetted, abetting) to encourage or assist in committing an offence. abetter (*or*, in legal use) abettor *noun*, abetment *noun*

abeyance (ă-**bay**-ăns) *noun* in abeyance (of a right or rule or problem etc.) suspended for a time.

abhor (ăb-**hor**) *verb* (abhorred, abhorring) to detest. [from Latin *abhorrere* = shrink in fear]

abhorrent (*rhymes with torrent*) *adjective* detestable. abhorrence *noun* detestation.

abide *verb* (abided (in sense 1 abode), abiding) 1 (*old use*) to remain, to dwell. 2 to bear, to endure, *can't abide opera*. □ abide by to act in accordance with; *abide by a promise*, keep it; *abide by the consequences*, accept them.

abiding *adjective* long-lasting, permanent.

Abidjan (ab-ĭ-**jahn**) the capital and chief port of the Ivory Coast.

ability *noun* 1 the quality that makes an action or process possible, the capacity or power to do something. 2 cleverness, talent.

abiotic (ay-by-**ot**-ik) *adjective* not having life. [from *a-*², + Greek *bios* = life]

abject (**ab**-jekt) *adjective* 1 wretched, without resources, *abject poverty*. 2 lacking all pride, *an abject coward; an abject apology*, a very humble one. abjectly *adverb* [from *ab-*, + Latin *-jectum* = thrown]

abjure (ăb-**joor**) *verb* to renounce; to repudiate. abjuration *noun* [from *ab-*, + Latin *jurare* = take an oath]

Abkhazia (ab-**kah**-zee-ă) a self-governing republic in NW Georgia, south of the Caucasus mountains on the Black Sea.

ablative (**ab**-lă-tiv) *noun* the grammatical case (especially in Latin) that indicates the agent, instrument, or location of an action.

ablaze *adjective* blazing.

able *adjective* 1 having the ability to do something. 2 having great ability, competent. □ able-bodied *adjective* fit and strong. ably *adverb*

ablution (ă-**bloo**-shŏn) *noun* ceremonial washing of hands, vessels, etc. ablutions *plural noun* (*informal*) 1 washing of the body, *perform one's ablutions*. 2 a place for doing this.

ABN *abbreviation* Australian business number.

abnegation (ab-nĕ-**gay**-shŏn) *noun* renunciation; self-denial.

abnormal *adjective* different from what is normal. abnormally *adverb*, abnormality *noun*

aboard *adverb* & *preposition* on or into a ship or aircraft or train.

abode¹ *noun* (*old use*) a dwelling place.

abode² *see* abide.

abolish *verb* to put an end to, *abolish slavery*. abolition (abŏ-**lish**-ŏn) *noun*

abolitionist *noun* a person who favours abolishing slavery or capital punishment.

abominable *adjective* 1 detestable, loathsome. 2 very bad or unpleasant. □ Abominable Snowman a large manlike or bearlike animal said to exist in the Himalayas, a yeti. abominably *adverb*

abominate *verb* to detest, to loathe.

abomination *noun* 1 loathing. 2 something loathed.

aboriginal *adjective* 1 indigenous, inhabiting a land from the earliest times, *aboriginal inhabitants* or *plants*. 2 Aboriginal of Aborigines. –aboriginal *noun* 1 an aborigine. 2 Aboriginal an Aborigine. 3 Aboriginal (*informal*) an Aboriginal language. Aboriginality *noun*

aborigine (ab-ŏ-**rij**-ĭ-nee) *noun* 1 an aboriginal inhabitant. 2 Aborigine an aboriginal Australian. [from Latin *ab origine* = from the beginning]

Usage *Aborigine(s)* and *Aboriginal(s)* can both be used as nouns to refer to the indigenous peoples of Australia. Many Aboriginal people prefer to use the word for 'person' from their particular language. *Koori* is used in much of SE Australia; *Murri* in most of south and central Queensland; *Bama* in north Queensland; *Nunga* in southern SA, *Yura* in SA, *Nyoongah* around Perth; *Mulba* in the Pilbara region; *Wongi* in the Kalgoorlie region; *Yammagi* in the Murchison River region; *Yolngu* in Arnhem Land; *Anangu* in central Australia; and *Yuin* on the south coast of NSW.

abort (ă-**bort**) *verb* 1 to cause an abortion of or to; to suffer abortion. 2 to end or cause to end prematurely and unsuccessfully.

abortion *noun* 1 the expulsion (either spontaneous or induced) of a foetus from the womb before it is able to survive, especially in the first 28 weeks of pregnancy. 2 a misshapen creature or thing.

abortionist *noun* a person who practises abortion, especially illegally.

abortive *adjective* **1** producing abortion.
2 unsuccessful, *an abortive attempt*.
abortively *adverb*

abound *verb* **1** to be plentiful, *fish abound
in the river*. **2** to have in great quantities, *the
river abounds in fish*.

about *preposition* & *adverb* **1** approximately,
about $10. **2** in connection with, on the subject
of, *what is he talking about?* **3** all around,
look about you. **4** somewhere near, not far
off, *he's somewhere about*. **5** here and there in
(a place), *papers were lying about* or *about the
room*. **6** on the move, in circulation, *will soon
be about again*. **7** so as to face in the opposite
direction, *put the ship about*. **8** in rotation,
on duty week and week about. □ **about-face**,
about-turn *nouns* a complete reversal of
previous actions or opinions. **be about to** to
be on the point or verge of doing something.

above *adverb* **1** at or to a higher point;
overhead; in heaven. **2** in addition. **3** earlier in
a book or article, *mentioned above*. –**above**
preposition **1** over; higher than; more than.
2 upstream from. **3** beyond the level or reach
of, *she is above suspicion*; *above himself*,
carried away by high spirits or conceit. **4** more
important than, *this above all*. □ **above board**
without deception or concealment, done
honourably.

abracadabra (ab-ră-kă-**dab**-ră) *noun*
1 a supposedly magic formula or spell.
2 gibberish.

abrade (ă-**brayd**) *verb* to scrape or wear away
by rubbing.

Abraham the Hebrew patriarch from whom
all Jews trace their descent.

abrasion (ă-**bray**-zhŏn) *noun* abrading; an
abraded place.

abrasive (ă-**bray**-siv) *adjective* **1** causing
abrasion. **2** capable of polishing surfaces by
rubbing or grinding. **3** harsh, causing angry
feelings, *an abrasive personality*. –**abrasive**
noun an abrasive substance.

abreast *adverb* **1** side by side and facing the
same way. **2** keeping up, not behind, *keep
abreast of modern developments*.

abridge *verb* to shorten by using fewer words.
abridgement *noun* [from Old French *abregier*
= shorten]

abroad *adverb* **1** away from one's own
country. **2** far and wide, everywhere, *scattered
the seeds abroad*. **3** out and about, *no one was
abroad*.

abrogate (**ab**-rŏ-gayt) *verb* to cancel, to
repeal, *abrogate a law*. **abrogation** *noun* [from
ab-, + Latin *rogare* = ask]

abrupt *adjective* **1** sudden, *came to an abrupt
stop*. **2** disconnected, not smooth, *short abrupt
sentences*. **3** curt. **4** (of a slope) very steep.
abruptly *adverb*, **abruptness** *noun* [from *ab-*,
+ Latin *ruptum* = broken]

ABS *abbreviation* **1** anti-lock braking system.
2 Australian Bureau of Statistics.

abs- *prefix see* **ab-**.

abscess (**ab**-sĕs) *noun* a collection of pus
formed in the body.

abscissa (ab-**sis**-ă) *noun* (*plural* **abscissae**) (in
mathematics) the first member of an ordered
pair, a coordinate measured parallel to the
horizontal or x-axis.

abscond (ăb-**skond**) *verb* to go away secretly,
especially after wrongdoing. **absconder** *noun*

abseil (**ab**-sayl) *verb* to descend a rock face
using a doubled rope that is fixed at a higher
point. –**abseil** *noun* this process.

absence *noun* **1** being away; the period of
this. **2** lack, non-existence, *in the absence of
proof*. **3** inattention, *absence of mind*.

absent (**ab**-sĕnt) *adjective* **1** not present.
2 non-existent. **3** with one's mind on other
things. –**absent** (ăb-**sent**) *verb* **absent oneself**
to stay away. **absently** *adverb*

absentee *noun* a person who is absent from
work etc.; *absentee landlord*, one who seldom
visits the premises he lets.

absenteeism *noun* frequent absence from
work or school.

absent-minded *adjective* with one's mind
on other things; forgetful. **absent-mindedly**
adverb, **absent-mindedness** *noun*

absolute *adjective* **1** complete, *absolute
silence*. **2** unrestricted, *absolute power*.
3 independent, not relative, *there is no
absolute standard for beauty*. **4** (*informal*)
utter, out-and-out, *it's an absolute miracle*.
□ **absolute majority** a majority over all
rivals combined. **absolute pitch** the ability to
recognise or reproduce exactly the pitch of a
note in music; a fixed standard of pitch defined
by the rate of vibration. **absolute temperature**
that measured in kelvins from absolute zero.
absolute zero the lowest possible temperature
(−273.15°C). [same origin as *absolve*]

absolutely *adverb* **1** completely. **2** without
restrictions, unconditionally. **3** (*informal*) quite
so, yes.

absolution (ab-sŏ-**loo**-shŏn) *noun* a priest's formal declaration of the forgiveness of penitents' sins.

absolutism *noun* **1** being absolute. **2** the principle of having a rule etc. that must apply in all cases.

absolve *verb* **1** to clear of blame or guilt. **2** to give absolution to (a person). **3** to free from an obligation. [from *ab-*, + Latin *solvere* = set free]

absorb *verb* **1** to take in, to soak up; to combine or merge into itself or oneself, *sponges absorb water*; *absorb knowledge*; *the large firm absorbed the smaller ones*. **2** to reduce the effect of, *buffers absorbed most of the shock*. **3** to occupy the attention or interest of; *an absorbing book*, holding one's interest. absorber *noun*, absorption *noun*

absorbent *adjective* able to absorb moisture etc. absorbency *noun*

absorptive *adjective* **1** able to absorb liquids etc. **2** engrossing.

abstain *verb* **1** to keep oneself from some action or indulgence, especially from drinking alcohol. **2** to refrain from using one's vote. abstainer *noun*, abstention *noun*

abstemious (ăb-**steem**-ee-ŭs) *adjective* sparing in one's taking of food and drink, not self-indulgent. abstemiously *adverb*, abstemiousness *noun*

abstinence (**ab**-stĭ-něns) *noun* abstaining, especially from food or alcohol. abstinent *adjective*

abstract (**ab**-strakt) *adjective* **1** having no material existence, *beauty is an abstract quality*. **2** theoretical rather than practical. –abstract (**ab**-strakt) *noun* **1** an abstract quality or idea. **2** a summary. **3** an example of abstract art. –abstract (ăb-**strakt**) *verb* **1** to take out; to separate; to remove. **2** to make a written summary. ☐ abstract art art that does not represent things pictorially but expresses the artist's ideas or sensations. abstract noun a noun denoting a quality or state. in the abstract regarded theoretically, *he favours economy in the abstract but refuses to economise*. abstractly *adverb*, abstractness *noun*, abstractor *noun* [from *abs-*, + Latin *tractum* = pulled]

abstracted *adjective* with one's mind on other things, not paying attention.

abstraction *noun* **1** abstracting, removing. **2** an abstract idea. **3** being abstracted.

abstruse (ăb-**strooss**) *adjective* hard to understand, profound. abstruseness *noun*

absurd *adjective* **1** not in accordance with common sense, very unsuitable. **2** ridiculous, foolish. absurdly *adverb*, absurdity *noun* [from Latin *absurdus* = out of tune]

Abu Dhabi (ab-oo **dah**-bee) **1** a sheikhdom that is a member of the United Arab Emirates. **2** the capital city of this sheikhdom and of the United Arab Emirates.

Abuja (ă-**boo**-jă) the capital of Nigeria.

abundance *noun* a quantity that is more than enough, plenty.

abundant *adjective* **1** more than enough, plentiful. **2** having plenty of something, rich, *a land abundant in minerals*. abundantly *adverb*

abuse (ă-**bewss**) *noun* **1** a misuse. **2** an unjust or corrupt practice. **3** abusive words, insults. **4** maltreatment of a person, physically, emotionally, or sexually, *child abuse*. –abuse (ă-**bewz**) *verb* **1** to make a bad or wrong use of, *abuse one's authority*. **2** to ill-treat. **3** to attack in words, to utter insults to or about. [from *ab-* + *use*]

abusive (ă-**bew**-siv) *adjective* insulting, criticising harshly or angrily. abusively *adverb*

abut (ă-**but**) *verb* (abutted, abutting) to have a common boundary; to touch at one side, *their land abuts on ours*.

abutment *noun* a structure supporting the end of a bridge, arch, etc.

abysmal (ă-**biz**-măl) *adjective* **1** extreme and deplorable, *abysmal ignorance*. **2** (*informal*) extremely bad, *their taste is abysmal*. abysmally *adverb*

abyss (ă-**biss**) *noun* a hole so deep that it appears bottomless.

Abyssinia a former name of Ethiopia. Abyssinian *adjective* & *noun*

AC *abbreviation* **1** (also ac) alternating current. **2** Companion of the Order of Australia.

ac- *prefix* see ad-.

acacia (ă-**kay**-shă) *noun* **1** a leguminous tree or shrub, including Australian wattles. **2** a tree resembling a wattle.

academic (ak-ă-**dem**-ik) *adjective* **1** of a school, college, or university. **2** scholarly as opposed to technical or practical, *academic subjects*. **3** of theoretical interest only, with no practical application. –academic *noun* an academic person. academically *adverb*

academician (ă-kad-ĕ-**mish**-ăn) *noun*
a member of an Academy.

academy *noun* **1** a school, especially for
specialised training, *a military academy*.
2 Academy a society of scholars or artists.
□ Academy award any of the awards of the
Academy of Motion Picture Arts and Sciences
(Hollywood, USA) given annually for success
in the film industry.

a cappella (ah kă-**pel**-ă) *adjective* & *adverb*
(of choral music) unaccompanied.

ACCC *abbreviation* Australian Competition and
Consumer Commission.

accede (ăk-**seed**) *verb* **1** to take office, to
become monarch. **2** to agree to what is
proposed. [from *ac-*, + Latin *cedere* = go]

accelerate *verb* **1** to move faster or happen
earlier or more quickly. **2** to cause to do this.
3 to increase the speed of a motor vehicle.
acceleration *noun* [from *ac-*, + Latin *celer* =
swift]

accelerator *noun* **1** a device for increasing
speed; a pedal operating this in a motor
vehicle. **2** an apparatus for causing charged
particles to move at high speeds.

accelerometer *noun* an instrument for
measuring acceleration or vibrations.

accent (**ak**-sĕnt) *noun* **1** emphasis on a syllable
or word. **2** a mark indicating such emphasis
or the quality of a vowel sound. **3** a national,
local, or individual way of pronouncing
words. **4** the emphasis given to something, *the
accent is on quality*. –accent (ăk-**sent**) *verb*
1 to pronounce with an accent. **2** to emphasise.

accentuate (ăk-**sen**-tew-ayt) *verb* to
emphasise. accentuation *noun*

accept *verb* **1** to take (a thing offered)
willingly; to say yes to an offer or invitation.
2 to undertake (a responsibility). **3** to treat as
welcome, *they were never really accepted by
their neighbours*. **4** to be willing to agree to,
we accept the proposed changes. **5** to take
as true, *we do not accept your conclusions*.
acceptance *noun*, acceptor *noun*

acceptable *adjective* **1** worth accepting,
welcome. **2** tolerable, *an acceptable risk*.
acceptably *adverb*, acceptability *noun*

acceptor *noun* **1** one who accepts something.
2 an atom or molecule able to receive an extra
electron or proton etc.

access (**ak**-sess) *noun* **1** a way in, a means
of approaching or entering. **2** the right or
opportunity of reaching or using, *students
need access to books*. **3** an attack of emotion, *a
sudden access of rage*. –access *verb* to retrieve
(information stored in a computer). □ direct
or random access the process of storing or
retrieving information in a computer without
having to read through items stored previously
(contrasted with *sequential* or *serial access*).

accessible *adjective* able to be reached or
used. accessibly *adverb*, accessibility *noun*

accession (ăk-**sesh**-ŏn) *noun* **1** reaching a
rank or position, *the Queen's accession to
the throne*. **2** an addition, being added, *recent
accessions to the library*.

accessory (ăk-**sess**-ŏ-ree) *adjective*
additional, extra. –accessory *noun* **1** a thing
that is extra or useful or decorative but not
essential, a minor fitting or attachment.
2 a person who helps another in a crime.

acciaccatura (ă-chah-kă-**toor**-ră) *noun* (in
music) a grace note played quickly before the
primary note. [Italian]

accidence (**ak**-sĭ-dĕns) *noun* the part of
grammar that deals with the way words are
inflected.

accident *noun* **1** an unexpected or undesirable
event, especially one causing injury or
damage. **2** chance, fortune, *we met by
accident*. □ accident-prone *adjective* more
than usually likely to have accidents. [from
ac-, + Latin *cadens* = falling]

accidental *adjective* happening or done by
accident. –accidental *noun* a sign attached to
a single note in music, showing temporary
departure from the key signature. accidentally
adverb

acclaim (ă-**klaym**) *verb* to welcome with
shouts of approval; to applaud enthusiastically.
–acclaim *noun* a shout of welcome; applause.
acclamation (ak-lă-**may**-shŏn) *noun* [from *ac-*,
+ Latin *clamare* = to shout]

acclimatise *verb* (also -ize) to make or
become used to a new climate or new
conditions. acclimatisation *noun*

accolade (ak-ŏ-**layd**) *noun* **1** a ceremonial tap
on the shoulder with the flat of a sword, given
when a knighthood is conferred. **2** praise,
approval.

accommodate *verb* **1** to provide lodging
or room for. **2** to provide or supply, *the bank
will accommodate you with a loan*. **3** to adapt,
to harmonise, *I will accommodate my plans
to yours*.

accommodating *adjective* willing to do as
one is asked.

accommodation *noun* 1 lodgings, living-premises. 2 the process of accommodating or adapting. 3 provision.

accompaniment *noun* 1 an instrumental part supporting a solo instrument or voice or a choir. 2 an accompanying thing.

accompanist *noun* a person who plays a musical accompaniment.

accompany *verb* (accompanied, accompanying) 1 to go with, to travel with as a companion or helper. 2 to be present with. 3 to provide in addition. 4 to play a musical accompaniment to.

accomplice (ă-**kum**-plĭs) *noun* a partner in wrongdoing.

accomplish (ă-**kum**-plish) *verb* to succeed in doing, to fulfil.

accomplished *adjective* skilled, having many accomplishments.

accomplishment *noun* 1 skill in a social or domestic art. 2 accomplishing, completion. 3 a thing accomplished.

accord *noun* consent, agreement. –accord *verb* 1 to be in harmony or consistent. 2 (*formal*) to give or grant, *he was accorded this privilege*. □ **of one's own accord** without being asked or compelled.

accordance *noun* agreement, conformity. accordant *adjective*

according *adverb* according as in proportion as; in a manner depending on whether, *he was praised or blamed according as his work was good or bad*. according to as stated by or in, *according to the Bible*; in a manner consistent with or in proportion to, *grouped according to size*.

accordingly *adverb* 1 according to what is known or stated, *ask what they want and act accordingly*. 2 therefore.

accordion *noun* a portable musical instrument with bellows, metal reeds, and keys (like those of a piano) or buttons. accordionist *noun*

accost (ă-**kost**) *verb* to approach and speak to.

account *noun* 1 a statement of money paid or owed for goods or services. 2 a credit arrangement with a bank or firm. 3 importance, *that is of no account*. 4 a description, a report. –account *verb* to regard as, *a person is accounted innocent until proved guilty*. account for to give a reckoning of (money received); to explain the cause of; to be the explanation of; to bring about the death or destruction etc. of; to supply or

constitute (an amount). give a good account of oneself to perform well. on account as an interim payment, *here is $10 on account*; debited to be paid for later, *bought it on account*. on account of because of. on no account under no circumstances, never. on one's own account for one's own purposes and at one's own risk. take into account to make allowances for. turn to account to use profitably.

accountable *adjective* 1 obliged to give a reckoning or explanation for one's actions etc., responsible. 2 able to be explained. accountability *noun*

accountant *noun* one whose profession is to keep and examine business accounts. accountancy *noun* this profession.

accounting *noun* keeping or examining accounts; accountancy.

accoutrements (ă-**koo**-trě-měnts) *plural noun* equipment, a soldier's outfit other than weapons and clothes. [French]

Accra (ă-**krah**) the capital of Ghana.

accredited (ă-**kred**-ĭ-těd) *adjective* 1 officially recognised, *our accredited representative*. 2 generally accepted or believed. 3 certified as being of a prescribed quality.

accretion (ă-**kree**-shŏn) *noun* 1 a growth or increase by means of gradual additions. 2 the growing of separate things into one.

accrue (ă-**kroo**) *verb* to come as a natural increase or advantage, to accumulate, *interest accrues on investments*. accrual *noun*

acculturate *verb* to adapt to or adopt a different culture. acculturation *noun*

accumulate *verb* 1 to acquire an increasing quantity of. 2 to increase in quantity or amount. accumulation *noun*, accumulative *adjective* [from *ac-*, + Latin *cumulus* = heap]

accumulator *noun* 1 a rechargeable battery. 2 a storage register in a computer.

accurate *adjective* 1 free from error, conforming exactly to a standard or to truth. 2 careful and exact, showing precision. accurately *adverb*, accuracy *noun*

accursed (ă-**ker**-sĕd *or* ă-**kerst**) *adjective* 1 under a curse. 2 (*informal*) detestable, hateful.

accusation *noun* 1 accusing; being accused. 2 a statement accusing a person of a fault or crime or wrongdoing.

accusative (ă-**kew**-ză-tiv) *noun* & *adjective* the accusative case, the grammatical case used for the object of a verb etc., e.g. *him* in *'we saw him'*.

accusatory (ă-**kew**-ză-tŏ-ree) *adjective* of or implying accusation.

accuse *verb* to state that one lays blame for a fault, crime, or wrongdoing etc. upon (a named person). □ the accused the person accused in a court of law. accuser *noun*, accusingly *adverb*

accustom *verb* to make or become used (to something). accustomed *adjective* usual, customary, *in his accustomed seat*. [from *ac-*, + *custom*]

ace *noun* 1 a playing card with one spot. 2 a person who excels at something, *an ace pilot*. 3 (in tennis) a service stroke that is too good for the opponent to touch. –ace *adjective* (*informal*) excellent. □ within an ace of on the verge of.

acerbity (ă-**ser**-bĭ-tee) *noun* sharpness of speech or manner.

acetate (**ass**-ĕ-tayt) *noun* 1 a compound derived from acetic acid. 2 a fabric made from cellulose acetate.

acetic (ă-**see**-tik) *adjective* of vinegar. □ acetic acid the acid that gives vinegar its characteristic taste and smell, also called *ethanoic acid*. [from Latin *acetum* = vinegar]

acetone (**ass**-ĕ-tohn) *noun* a colourless liquid used as a solvent.

acetylene (ă-**set**-ĭ-leen) *noun* a gas that burns with a bright flame, used in cutting and welding metal.

ache *verb* 1 to suffer a dull continuous physical or mental pain. 2 to yearn. –ache *noun* a dull continuous pain. achy *adjective*

achieve *verb* to accomplish, to gain or reach by effort, *we achieved success at last*. achievable *adjective*, achievement *noun* [from Old French *a chief* = to a head]

Achilles (ă-**kil**-eez) (*Gk. legend*) a Greek hero who could not be wounded except in his heel. □ Achilles heel a weak or vulnerable point. Achilles tendon the tendon connecting the heel with the calf muscles.

acicular *adjective* needle-shaped. [from modern Latin *acicula* = small needle]

acid *adjective* 1 sharp-tasting, sour. 2 looking or sounding bitter, *acid remarks*. –acid *noun* 1 a sour substance. 2 any of a class of substances containing hydrogen that can be replaced by a metal to form a salt. 3 (*informal*) the drug LSD. □ acid rain rain made acid by contamination, especially by waste gases from power stations, factories, etc. acid test a severe or conclusive test. (¶ Acid is applied to a metal to test whether it is gold or not.) acidly *adverb*

acidic (ă-**sid**-ik) *adjective* of or like an acid.

acidify (ă-**sid**-ĭ-fy) *verb* (acidified, acidifying) to make or become acid.

acidity (ă-**sid**-ĭ-tee) *noun* 1 being acid. 2 an over-acid condition of the stomach.

acidophilus (as-ĭ-**do**-fĭ-lŭs) *noun* a bacterium used to make yoghurt and to supplement the bacteria naturally inhabiting the intestines.

acknowledge *verb* 1 to admit that something is true or valid. 2 to report that one has received, *acknowledge his letter*. 3 to express thanks for, *acknowledge his services*. 4 to indicate that one has noticed or recognised. acknowledgement *noun*

acme (**ak**-mee) *noun* the highest point, the peak of perfection. [from Greek *akme* = highest point]

acne (**ak**-nee) *noun* inflammation of the oil glands of the skin, producing red pimples.

acolyte (**ak**-ŏ-lyt) *noun* 1 a person who assists a priest in certain church services. 2 an attendant.

acorn *noun* the fruit of the oak tree, with a cuplike base.

acoustic (ă-**koo**-stik) *adjective* 1 of sound or the sense of hearing; of acoustics. 2 (of a musical instrument) not electrically amplified. acoustics *plural noun* the properties of sound; the qualities of a hall etc. that make it good or bad for carrying sound. acoustical *adjective*, acoustically *adverb* [from Greek *akouein* = hear]

acquaint *verb* to make aware or familiar, *acquaint him with the facts*. be acquainted with to know slightly.

acquaintance *noun* 1 being acquainted. 2 a person one knows slightly.

acquiesce (ak-wee-**ess**) *verb* to agree without protest, to assent. acquiesce in to accept as an arrangement.

acquiescent (ak-wee-**ess**-ĕnt) *adjective* acquiescing. acquiescence *noun*

acquire *verb* to gain possession of. □ acquired immune deficiency syndrome = AIDS. acquired taste a liking gained gradually.

acquirement *noun* [from *ac-*, + Latin *quaerere* = seek]

acquisition (ak-wĭ-**zish**-ŏn) *noun* 1 acquiring. 2 something acquired.

acquisitive (ă-**kwiz**-ĭ-tiv) *adjective* keen to acquire things. acquisitively *adverb*, acquisitiveness *noun*

acquit *verb* (acquitted, acquitting) to declare (a person) to be not guilty of the crime etc. with which he or she was charged. □ acquit oneself to conduct oneself, to perform, *she acquitted herself well in the test*.

acquittal (ă-**kwit**-ăl) *noun* acquitting; a verdict acquitting a person.

acre (**ay**-ker) *noun* 1 a measure of land, 4840 sq. yds. (0.405 ha). 2 a stretch of land, *broad acres*.

acreage (**ay**-kĕ-rij) *noun* the total number of acres; the extent of a piece of land.

acrid (**ak**-rĭd) *adjective* 1 having a bitter smell or taste. 2 bitter in temper or manner. acridity (ă-**krid**-ĭ-tee) *noun*

acrimony (**ak**-rĭ-mŏnee) *noun* bitterness of manner or words. acrimonious (ak-rĭ-**moh**-nee-ŭs) *adjective*, acrimoniously *adverb*

acrobat *noun* a performer of spectacular gymnastic feats. acrobatics *plural noun* acrobatic feats. acrobatic *adjective*, acrobatically *adverb* [from Greek *akrobatos* = walking on tiptoe]

acromion *noun* the outer extremity of the shoulder blade forming the bony part at the top of the shoulder.

acronym (**ak**-rŏ-nim) *noun* a word formed from the initial letters of other words, e.g. *Anzac*, *ASEAN*. [from Greek *akros* = top, + *onoma* = name]

acrophobia (ak-rŏ-**foh**-bee-ă) *noun* an abnormal fear of heights. [from Greek *akros* = top, + *phobos* = fear]

acropolis (ă-**krop**-ŏ-lĭs) *noun* 1 the citadel or upper fortified part of an ancient Greek city. 2 the Acropolis that of Athens.

across *preposition* & *adverb* 1 from one side of a thing to the other. 2 to or on the other side of. 3 so as to be understood or accepted, *got his points across to the audience*. 4 so as to form a cross or intersect, *laid across each other*. □ across the board applying to all members or groups.

acrostic (ă-**kros**-tik) *noun* a word puzzle or poem in which the first or last letters of each line form a word or words.

acrylic (ă-**kril**-ik) *adjective* of a synthetic material made from an organic acid. –acrylic *noun* an acrylic fibre, plastic, or resin.

ACT *abbreviation* Australian Capital Territory.

act *noun* 1 something done. 2 the process of doing something, *caught in the act*. 3 a decree or law made by a parliament. 4 each of the main divisions of a play. 5 each of a series of short performances in a program, *a circus act*. 6 (*informal*) a pose or pretence, *put on an act*. –act *verb* 1 to perform actions, to behave, *you acted wisely*. 2 to do what is required, to function, *act as umpire*; *the brakes did not act*. 3 to have an effect on, *acid acts on metal*. 4 to portray by actions; to perform a part in a play etc.; *act the fool*, to clown. □ Act of God the operation of uncontrollable natural forces. Acts (of the Apostles) the fifth book of the New Testament, relating the early history of the Church in the time of St Peter and St Paul. [from Latin *actum* = done]

acting *adjective* serving temporarily, especially as a substitute, *the acting principal*.

actinide (**ak**-tĭ-nyd) *noun* any of fifteen metallic elements from actinium to lawrencium on the periodic table. All are radioactive, the heavier members being very unstable and only occurring artificially.

actinium (ak-**tin**-ee-ŭm) *noun* a radioactive metallic element of the actinide series (symbol Ac).

action *noun* 1 the process of doing something, the exertion of energy or influence, *go into action*; *the action of acid on metal*, the way it affects metal. 2 a thing done, *generous actions*. 3 a series of events in a story or play, *the action is set in Spain*. 4 a way or manner of moving or functioning, the mechanism of an instrument. 5 a lawsuit. 6 a battle, *was killed in action*. □ action painting abstract painting in which the artist applies paint by random actions. action replay a playback (at normal or reduced speed) of a televised incident in a sports event. out of action not working. take action to do something in response to what has happened.

actionable *adjective* 1 giving cause for legal action. 2 able to be done or acted upon.

activate *verb* to make active. activation *noun*, activator *noun*

active *adjective* 1 moving about, characterised by energetic action. 2 taking part in activities. 3 functioning, in operation; *an active volcano*, one that erupts occasionally. 4 having an effect,

the active ingredients. **5** radioactive. **–active**
noun the form of a verb used when the subject
of the sentence is the doer of the action, e.g.
saw in *'we saw him'*. **actively** *adverb*

activist *noun* one who follows a policy of
vigorous action, especially in politics. **activism**
noun

activity *noun* **1** being active, the exertion
of energy. **2** energetic action, being busy.
3 actions, occupations, *outdoor activities.*

actor *noun* a performer in a stage play or a
film. **actress** *feminine noun*

ACTU *abbreviation* Australian Council of Trade
Unions.

actual *adjective* existing in fact, real; current.
actually *adverb*

actuality (ak-tew-**al**-ĭ-tee) *noun* reality.
actualities *plural noun* existing conditions.

actuary (**ak**-choo-ă-ree) *noun* an expert in
statistics who calculates insurance risks and
premiums. **actuarial** (ak-choo-**air**-ree-ăl)
adjective

actuate *verb* **1** to activate (a movement or
process). **2** to be a motive for (a person's
actions). **actuation** *noun*, **actuator** *noun*

acuity (ă-**kew**-ĭ-tee) *noun* sharpness,
acuteness.

acumen (**ak**-yŭ-měn) *noun* sharpness of
mind, shrewdness. [Latin, = a point]

acupuncture (**ak**-yŭ-punk-cher) *noun*
pricking the tissues of the body with fine
needles as medical treatment or to relieve
pain. **acupuncturist** *noun* [from Latin *acu* =
with a needle, + *puncture*]

acute *adjective* **1** very perceptive, having a
sharp mind. **2** sharp or severe in its effect,
acute pain; *an acute shortage.* **3** (of an illness)
coming sharply to a crisis of severity, *acute
appendicitis.* □ **acute accent** a mark over a
vowel, as over *e* in *café.* **acute angle** an angle
of less than 90°. **acutely** *adverb*, **acuteness**
noun

AD *abbreviation* (in dates) of the Christian era.
[short for Latin *anno domini* = in the year of
Our Lord]

ad *noun* (*informal*) an advertisement.

ad- *prefix* (changing to **ac-**, **af-**, **ag-**, **al-**, **an-**,
ap-, **ar-**, **as-**, **at-** before certain consonants)
to; towards (as in *adapt, admit*). [from Latin
ad- = to]

adage (**ad**-ij) *noun* a proverb, a saying.

adagio (ă-**dah**-zhee-oh) *adverb* (in music)
in slow time. **–adagio** *noun* (*plural* **adagios**)
a movement to be played in this way. [Italian]

Adam (in the Bible) the first man.
□ **Adam's apple** the projection of cartilage at
the front of the neck, especially in men.

adamant (**ad**-ă-mănt) *adjective* unyielding to
requests, quite firm.

adapt *verb* to make or become suitable for a
new use or situation. **adaptation** *noun* [from
ad-, + Latin *aptus* = fitted]

adaptable *adjective* **1** able to be adapted.
2 able to adapt oneself. **adaptability** *noun*

adaptor *noun* a device that connects pieces of
equipment that were not originally designed to
be connected.

ADD *abbreviation* attention deficit disorder;
a condition with symptoms such as
hyperactivity and poor concentration.

add *verb* **1** to join (one thing to another) as
an increase or supplement; *this adds to the
expense*, increases it. **2** to put numbers or
amounts together to get a total. **3** to make a
further remark.

addendum *noun* (*plural* **addenda**)
something added at the end of a book etc.
[from Latin, = thing to be added]

Usage The word *addenda* is used as a plural,
and also as a collective noun with a singular
verb, as in *the addenda contains new
information.*

adder *noun* a small poisonous snake, a viper.
[originally called *a nadder*, which became *an
adder*]

addict (**ad**-ikt) *noun* a person who is addicted
to something, especially to drugs. [from
Latin *addictus* = person given as a servant to
someone to whom he owes money]

addicted (ă-**dik**-těd) *adjective* **1** doing or
using something as a habit or compulsively.
2 devoted to something as a hobby or interest.
addiction *noun*

addictive *adjective* causing addiction.

Addis Ababa (adĭs-**a**-bă-bă) the capital of
Ethiopia.

addition *noun* **1** adding, being added.
2 a thing added to something else.
□ **in addition** as an extra thing or
circumstance.

additional *adjective* added, extra.
additionally *adverb*

additive (**ad**-ĭ-tiv) *adjective* involving addition. –**additive** *noun* a substance added in small amounts for a special purpose, e.g. as a colouring agent or preservative.

addle *verb* **1** to become rotten and produce no chick after being brooded, *addled eggs*. **2** to muddle or confuse, *addle one's brains*.

address *noun* **1** the place where a person lives; particulars of where mail should be delivered to a person or firm. **2** a speech delivered to an audience. **3** the part of a computer instruction that specifies the location of a piece of stored information. –**address** *verb* **1** to write directions for delivery on (an envelope or parcel). **2** to make a speech to. **3** to direct a remark or written statement to. **4** to use a particular word or words in speaking or writing to, *how to address a bishop*. **5** to apply (oneself) to a task or problem, to direct one's attention to (a problem). **6** to take aim at (the ball) in golf. **7** to store or retrieve (a piece of information) by using an address (see *noun* sense 3). □ **forms of address** words (such as *Mr*, *Sir*, *Your Majesty*) used in addressing a person.

addressee (ad-ress-**ee**) *noun* a person to whom a letter etc. is addressed.

adduce (ă-**dewss**) *verb* to cite as an example or proof. **adducible** *adjective* [from *ad-*, + Latin *ducere* = to lead]

Adelaide the capital of South Australia.

Adélie Land (ă-**day**-lee) (also **Adélie Coast**) French territory in the coastal region of Antarctica, south of Australia.

Aden (**ay**-d'n) a port in Yemen, the capital of South Yemen until 1990. □ **Gulf of Aden** an arm of the Indian Ocean at the entrance to the Red Sea.

adenoids (**ad**-ĕ-noidz) *plural noun* enlarged spongy tissue between the back of the nose and the throat, often hindering breathing. **adenoidal** *adjective*

adenovirus *noun* any of a group of DNA viruses first discovered in adenoidal tissue, most of which cause respiratory diseases.

adept (**ad**-ept) *adjective* very skilful. –**adept** *noun* a skilful person, especially at a craft.

adequate *adjective* **1** sufficient, satisfactory. **2** passable but not outstandingly good. **adequately** *adverb*, **adequacy** *noun*

adhan *noun* = azan.

ADHD *abbreviation* attention deficit hyperactivity disorder.

adhere (ăd-**heer**) *verb* **1** to stick when glued or by suction, or as if by these. **2** to remain faithful, to continue to give one's support (to a person or cause). **3** to keep to and not alter, *we adhered to our plan*. [from *ad-*, + Latin *haerere* = to stick]

adherent *adjective* sticking, adhering. –**adherent** *noun* a supporter of a party or doctrine. **adherence** *noun*

adhesion (ăd-**hee**-zhŏn) *noun* **1** adhering. **2** tissue formed when normally separate tissues of the body grow together as a result of inflammation or injury.

adhesive *adjective* causing things to adhere, sticky. –**adhesive** *noun* an adhesive substance. □ **adhesive tape** a strip of paper or transparent material coated with adhesive. **adhesiveness** *noun*

ad hoc for a specific purpose, *an ad hoc arrangement*. [Latin, = for this]

adieu (ă-**dew**) *interjection* & *noun* (*plural* **adieus**) goodbye. [from French *à* = to, + *Dieu* = God]

Adi Granth (ah-dee **grunt**) the sacred scripture of Sikhism.

ad infinitum (in-fĭ-**ny**-tŭm) without limit, for ever. [Latin, = to infinity]

adipose (**ad**-ĭ-pohs) *adjective* of animal fat, fatty. **adiposity** (ad-ĭ-**poss**-ĭ-tee) *noun* [from Latin *adiposus* = fatty]

adit *noun* a horizontal entrance or passage in a mine.

adjacent *adjective* lying near, adjoining. [from *ad-*, + Latin *jacens* = lying]

adjective (**aj**-ĕk-tiv) *noun* a word added to a noun to describe a quality or modify a meaning, e.g. *old*, *tall*, *rural*, *my*, *this*. **adjectival** (aj-ĕk-**ty**-văl) *adjective*, **adjectivally** *noun*

adjoin *verb* to be next or nearest to.

adjourn (ă-**jern**) *verb* **1** to postpone, to break off temporarily. **2** to break off and go elsewhere. **adjournment** *noun* [from Latin, = to another day]

adjudge *verb* to decide or award judicially, *he was adjudged to be guilty*.

adjudicate (ă-**joo**-dĭ-kayt) *verb* **1** to act as judge in a court, tribunal, or competition. **2** to judge and pronounce a decision upon. **adjudication** *noun*, **adjudicator** *noun* [from *ad-*, + Latin *judicare* = to judge]

adjunct (**ad**-junkt) *noun* **1** something added or attached but subordinate. **2** (in grammar) a word, phrase, or clause used to modify a part of a sentence. [from *ad-*, + Latin *junctum* = joined]

adjure (ă-**joor**) *verb* to command or urge solemnly. adjuration *noun* [from *ad-*, + Latin *jurare* = take an oath]

adjust *verb* 1 to arrange, to put into the proper position. 2 to alter by a small amount so as to fit or be right for use, *the brakes need adjusting*. 3 to be able to be adjusted. 4 to adapt or adapt oneself to new circumstances. 5 to assess (loss or damage) in settlement of an insurance claim. adjustable *adjective*, adjuster *noun*, adjustment *noun*

adjutant (**aj**-ŭ-tănt) *noun* an army officer assisting a superior officer with administrative work. adjutancy *noun*

ad lib *adverb* as one pleases, without restraint. –ad lib *adjective* said or done impromptu. –ad lib *verb* (ad libbed, ad libbing) (*informal*) to speak impromptu, to improvise (remarks or actions). [from the Latin *ad libitum*, according to pleasure]

admin *noun* (*informal*) administration.

administer *verb* 1 to manage (business affairs), to be an administrator. 2 to give or hand out formally, to provide, *administer the sacrament*; *administer comfort* or *a rebuke*; *administer the oath to a person*, hear him swear it officially.

administrate *verb* to act as administrator (of).

administration *noun* 1 administering. 2 the management of public or business affairs. 3 the people who administer an organisation etc.; the government.

administrative *adjective* of or involving administration.

administrator *noun* 1 a person responsible for administration; one who has a talent for this. 2 a person appointed to administer an estate.

admirable *adjective* worthy of admiration, excellent. admirably *adverb*

admiral *noun* 1 a naval officer of high rank, commander of a fleet or squadron. 2 a boldly patterned butterfly, *Australian admiral*; *red admiral*. [from Arabic *amir* = commander]

admire *verb* 1 to regard with pleasure or satisfaction, to think highly of. 2 to express admiration of, *don't forget to admire her cat*. admiration *noun*, admirer *noun* [from *ad-*, + Latin *mirari* = wonder at]

admissible *adjective* capable of being admitted; allowed to be included, *admissible evidence*. admissibly *adverb*, admissibility *noun*

admission *noun* 1 admitting; being admitted. 2 the charge for this. 3 a statement admitting something, a confession.

admit *verb* (admitted, admitting) 1 to allow to enter. 2 to accept into a school etc. as a pupil or into a hospital as a patient. 3 to accept as true or valid. 4 to state reluctantly, *we admit that the task is difficult*. [from *ad-*, + Latin *mittere* = send]

admittance *noun* being allowed to enter, especially into a private place.

admittedly *adverb* as an acknowledged fact.

admixture *noun* something added as an ingredient.

admonish (ăd-**mon**-ish) *verb* 1 to advise or urge seriously. 2 to reprove mildly but firmly. admonition (ad-mŏ-**nish**-ŏn) *noun*, admonitory (ăd-**mon**-ĭ-tŏ-ree) *adjective*

ad nauseam (**naw**-see-ăm *or* -zee-) *adverb* to a sickening extent. [Latin, = to sickness]

Adnyamathanha (**ad**-nyă-mud-ă-nă) 1 a member of an Aboriginal people of central South Australia. 2 their language.

ado (ă-**doo**) *noun* fuss, trouble, excitement. [originally in *much ado* = much to do]

adobe (ă-**doh**-bee) *noun* 1 a sun-dried clay brick. 2 the clay for making this.

adolescent (ad-ŏ-**less**-ĕnt) *adjective* between childhood and maturity. –adolescent *noun* an adolescent person. adolescence *noun*

Adonis (ă-**doh**-nĭs) (*Gk. myth.*) a beautiful youth, loved by Aphrodite.

adopt *verb* 1 to take into one's family as a relation, especially as one's child with legal guardianship. 2 to take (a person) as one's heir or representative, *adopt a candidate*. 3 to take and use as one's own, *adopted this name* or *custom*. 4 to approve or accept (a report or financial accounts). adoption *noun* [from *ad-*, + Latin *optare* = choose]

adoptive *adjective* related by adoption, *his adoptive parents*.

adorable *adjective* 1 very lovable. 2 (*informal*) delightful. adorably *adverb*

adore *verb* 1 to love deeply. 2 to worship as divine. 3 (*informal*) to like very much. adoration *noun*, adorer *noun* [from Latin *ad-*, + Latin *orare* = pray]

adorn *noun* 1 to decorate with ornaments. 2 to be an ornament to. adornment *noun*

ADP *abbreviation* adenosine diphosphate (*see* ATP).

adrenal (ă-**dree**-năl) *noun* an adrenal gland, either of two ductless glands on top of the kidneys, secreting adrenalin. [from *ad-*, + Latin *renes* = kidneys]

adrenalin (ă-**dren**-ă-lĭn) *noun* a hormone that stimulates the nervous system, secreted by a part of the adrenal glands or prepared synthetically.

Adriatic (ay-dree-**at**-ik) *adjective* of the Adriatic Sea, between Italy on the west and the Balkans on the east. –Adriatic *noun* the Adriatic Sea.

adrift *adverb* & *adjective* 1 drifting. 2 (*informal*) unfastened, loose.

adroit (ă-**droit**) *adjective* skilful, ingenious. adroitly *adverb*, adroitness *noun* [from French *à droit* = according to right]

ADSL *abbreviation* asymmetric digital subscriber line, a technology for transmitting digital information over standard telephone lines.

adsorb *verb* (of a solid) to hold (particles of a gas or liquid) to its surface. adsorption *noun*

adulation (ad-yŭ-**lay**-shŏn) *noun* excessive flattery. adulatory (**ad**-yŭ-lay-tŏ-ree) *adjective*

adult (**ad**-ult *or* ă-**dult**) *adjective* grown to full size or strength, mature. –adult *noun* an adult person. adulthood *noun*

adulterant *noun* a substance added in adulterating something.

adulterate *verb* to make impure or poorer in quality by adding another substance, especially an inferior one. adulteration *noun* [from Latin *adulterare* = to corrupt]

adulterer *noun* a person who commits adultery. adulteress *feminine noun*

adultery *noun* the act of being unfaithful to one's wife or husband by voluntarily having sexual intercourse with someone else. adulterous *adjective*

adumbrate *verb* to indicate faintly, to outline; to foreshadow. adumbration *noun*

advance *verb* 1 to move or put forward; to make progress. 2 to help the progress of, *advance someone's interests*. 3 to bring forward or make, *advance a suggestion*. 4 to bring (an event) to an earlier date. 5 to lend (money), to pay before a due date, *advance her a month's salary*. –advance *noun*

1 a forward movement, progress. 2 an increase in price or amount. 3 a loan, payment beforehand. –advance *adjective* going before others, done or provided in advance, *the advance party*; *advance bookings*. advances *plural noun* attempts to establish a friendly relationship or a business agreement. □ in advance ahead in place or time.

Advance Australia Fair the national anthem of Australia, composed by P. D. McCormick *c.* 1878.

advanced *adjective* 1 far on in progress or in life, *an advanced age*. 2 not elementary, *advanced studies*. 3 (of ideas etc.) new and not yet generally accepted.

advancement *noun* progress; promotion.

advantage *noun* 1 a favourable condition or circumstance. 2 benefit, profit; *the treaty is to their advantage*, benefits them; *turn it to your advantage*, use it profitably. 3 the next point won after deuce in tennis. □ take advantage of to make use of; to exploit. to advantage making a good effect, *the painting shows to advantage here*.

advantageous (ad-van-**tay**-jŭs) *adjective* profitable, beneficial. advantageously *adverb*

Advent *noun* 1 the coming of Christ; *Second Advent*, his coming at the Last Judgment. 2 the season (with four Sundays) before Christmas Day. –advent *noun* an important arrival. [from *ad-*, + Latin *ventum* = arrived]

Adventist *noun* a member of a sect believing that Christ's second coming is very near.

adventitious (ad-ven-**tish**-ŭs) *adjective* 1 accidental, casual. 2 (of roots etc.) occurring in an unusual place. adventitiously *adverb*

adventure *noun* 1 an exciting or dangerous experience. 2 willingness to take risks, *the spirit of adventure*. adventurous *adjective*, adventurously *adverb*

adventurer *noun* 1 a person who seeks adventures. 2 a person who is ready to make gains by risky or unscrupulous methods.

adverb *noun* a word that qualifies a verb, adjective, or other adverb and indicates how, when, or where, e.g. *softly*, *fully*, *soon*. adverbial *adjective*, adverbially *adverb* [from *ad-*, + Latin *verbum* = word]

adversary (**ad**-ver-să-ree) *noun* an opponent, an enemy.

adverse (**ad**-vers) *adjective* 1 unfavourable, *an adverse report*. 2 bringing misfortune or harm, *the drug has no adverse effects*.

adversely *adverb* [from Latin *adversus* = opposite (*ad* = to, *versus* = turned)]

adversity (ăd-**vers**-ĭ-tee) *noun* misfortune, trouble.

advert *noun* (*informal*) an advertisement.

advertise *verb* 1 to make generally or publicly known, *advertise a meeting*. 2 to praise publicly in order to encourage people to buy or use something, *advertise soap*. 3 to ask or offer by public notice, *advertise for a secretary*. **advertiser** *noun*

advertisement *noun* 1 advertising. 2 a public notice advertising something.

advice *noun* 1 an opinion given about what to do or how to behave. 2 a piece of information.

advisable *adjective* worth recommending as a course of action. **advisability** *noun*

advise *verb* 1 to give advice to, to recommend. 2 to inform, to notify. **adviser** *noun*

advisory *adjective* giving advice, having the power to advise, *an advisory committee*.

advocacy (**ad**-vŏ-kă-see) *noun* 1 the advocating of a policy etc. 2 the function of an advocate.

advocate (**ad**-vŏ-kayt) *verb* to recommend, to be in favour of, *I advocate caution.* – **advocate** (**ad**-vŏ-kăt) *noun* 1 a person who advocates a policy, *an advocate of reform*. 2 a person who pleads on behalf of another, a lawyer presenting a client's case in a lawcourt.

adze (*rhymes with* lads) *noun* a kind of axe with a blade at right angles to the handle, used for trimming large pieces of wood.

aedile (**ee**-dyl) *noun* either of two magistrates in ancient Rome who were responsible for public buildings. [from Latin *aedes* = a building]

Aegean (ĕ-**jee**-ăn) *adjective* of the Aegean Sea, between Greece and Turkey. – **Aegean** *noun* the Aegean Sea.

aegis (**ee**-jĭs) *noun* protection, sponsorship, *under the aegis of the United Nations*. [from Greek *aigis* = magical shield of the god Zeus]

Aeneas (ĕ-**nee**-ăs) (*Gk. & Rom. legend*) a Trojan leader, regarded by the Romans as the founder of their State.

Aeneid (**ee**-nee-ĭd) a Latin epic poem by Virgil, which relates the wanderings of Aeneas after the fall of Troy.

aeolian (ee-**oh**-lee-ăn) *adjective* moved by the wind, *aeolian sands*. □ **aeolian harp** a stringed instrument giving musical sounds when exposed to wind. [from the name of Aeolus, god of the winds in Greek mythology]

aeon (**ee**-ŏn) *noun* an immense time.

aerate (**air**-rayt) *verb* 1 to expose to the chemical action of air, *aerate the soil by forking it*. 2 to add carbon dioxide to (a liquid) under pressure, *aerated water*. **aeration** *noun*, **aerator** *noun*

aerial (**air**-ree-ăl) *adjective* 1 of or like air. 2 existing in the air, suspended overhead, *an aerial railway*. 3 by or from aircraft, *aerial bombardment*. – **aerial** *noun* a device (usually a wire, rod, or dish) for transmitting or receiving radio waves.

aero- *prefix* of air or aircraft (as in *aeronautics*). [from Greek *aer* = air]

aerobatics *plural noun* spectacular feats of flying aircraft, especially for display. **aerobatic** *adjective* [from *aero-* + *acrobatics*]

aerobic (air-**roh**-bik) *adjective* 1 using oxygen from the air. 2 (of exercises) designed to strengthen the heart and lungs. **aerobics** *plural noun* exercises of this kind.

aerodrome *noun* an airfield. [from *aero-*, + Greek *dromos* = running track]

aerodynamics *noun* (also as *plural noun*) interaction between airflow and the movement of solid bodies (e.g. aircraft, bullets) through air. **aerodynamic** *adjective* [from *aero-* + *dynamic*]

aerofoil *noun* a body (e.g. an aircraft wing or fin or tailplane) shaped to produce a desired aerodynamic reaction (e.g. lift) when it passes through air.

aerogramme *noun* an airmail letter in the form of a single sheet folded and sealed.

aeronautics *noun* the scientific study of the flight of aircraft. **aeronautic** *adjective*, **aeronautical** *adjective* [from *aero-* + *nautical*]

aeroplane *noun* a powered flying vehicle with fixed wings and a weight greater than that of the air it displaces. [from *aero-* + *plane*²]

aerosol *noun* 1 a substance sealed in a container under pressure, with a device for releasing it as a fine spray. 2 the container itself. [from *aero-* + *solution*]

aerospace *noun* 1 earth's atmosphere and space beyond it. 2 the technology of aviation in this region.

Aeschylus (**ees**-kĭ-lŭs) (525–456 BC) Greek dramatist, regarded as the founder of Greek tragic drama.

Aesop (**ee**-sop) (6th century BC) Greek teller of animal fables with a moral.

aesthete (ees-theet *or* **ess-**) *noun* a person who claims great understanding and appreciation of what is beautiful, especially in the arts.

aesthetic (ees-**thet**-ik *or* ess-) *adjective* **1** belonging to the appreciation of beauty, *the aesthetic standards of the times*. **2** having or showing such appreciation. **3** artistic, tasteful. **aesthetics** *noun* a branch of philosophy dealing with the principles of beauty and tastefulness. **aesthetically** *adverb* [from Greek, = perceiving]

aetiology (ee-tee-**ol**-ŏ-jee) *noun* **1** the study of causes or reasons. **2** a scientific account of the causes of any disease. **aetiological** *adjective*, **aetiologically** *adverb*

af- *prefix* see **ad-**.

afar *adverb* far off, far away.

affable *adjective* polite and friendly. **affably** *adverb*, **affability** *noun*

affair *noun* **1** a thing done or to be done, a matter, a concern. **2** (*informal*) an event; a thing, *this camera is a complicated affair*. **3** a temporary sexual relationship between two people who are not married to each other. **affairs** *plural noun* public or private business, *put your affairs in order*. [from French *à faire* = to do]

affect *verb* **1** to have an effect on, *the new tax laws affect us all*. **2** to arouse sadness or sympathy in, *the news of his death affected us deeply*. **3** (of a disease) to attack or infect, *tuberculosis affected his lungs*. **4** to pretend to have or feel; *she affected ignorance*, pretended she did not know.

Usage *Affect* should not be confused with *effect* which means 'to bring about, to accomplish', as in *to effect a cure*. *Effect* is also commonly used as a noun, as in *music has a good effect on her*.

---

affectation *noun* behaviour that is put on for display and not natural or genuine, pretence.

affected *adjective* **1** full of affectation. **2** pretended.

affecting *adjective* having an effect upon one's emotions, *an affecting appeal*.

affection *noun* **1** love, a liking. **2** a disease or diseased condition.

affectionate *adjective* showing affection, loving. **affectionately** *adverb*

afferent (**af**-ĕ-rĕnt) *adjective* **1** (of nerves) carrying impulses towards the brain. **2** (of blood vessels) carrying blood from the heart towards an organ of the body. [from *af-*, + Latin *ferre* = carry]

affiance (ă-**fy**-ăns) *verb* (*formal*) to betroth.

affidavit (af-ĭ-**day**-vĭt) *noun* a written statement for use as legal evidence, sworn on oath to be true. [Latin, = he or she has stated on oath]

affiliate (ă-**fil**-ee-ayt) *verb* to connect as a subordinate member or branch, *the club is affiliated to a national society*. **affiliation** *noun* [from Latin *affiliatum* = adopted (from *af-*, + *filius* = son)]

affinity (ă-**fin**-ĭ-tee) *noun* **1** a strong natural liking or attraction. **2** relationship (especially by marriage) other than blood relationship. **3** similarity, close resemblance or connection. **4** the tendency of certain substances to combine with others.

affirm *verb* **1** to assert, to state as a fact. **2** to make an affirmation instead of an oath.

affirmation (af-er-**may**-shŏn) *noun* **1** affirming. **2** a solemn declaration made instead of an oath by a person who has conscientious objections to swearing an oath or who has no religion.

affirmative (ă-**ferm**-ă-tiv) *adjective* affirming, agreeing; *an affirmative reply*, answering 'yes'. –**affirmative** *noun* an affirmative word or statement; *the answer is in the affirmative*, answer is 'yes'.
□ **affirmative action** action (especially in employment) favouring those who tend to suffer from discrimination, particularly women. **affirmatively** *adverb*

affix (ă-**fiks**) *verb* **1** to stick on, to attach. **2** to add in writing, *affix your signature*. –**affix** (**af**-iks) *noun* a prefix or suffix.

afflict *verb* to distress physically or mentally; *he is afflicted with rheumatism*, suffers from it. [from *af-* + Latin *flictum* = struck]

affliction *noun* **1** pain, distress, misery. **2** something that causes this.

affluent (**af**-loo-ĕnt) *adjective* rich; *the affluent society*, in which most people are relatively wealthy. **affluently** *adverb*, **affluence** *noun* [from Latin *affluens* = overflowing (see *fluent*)]

afford *verb* **1** to have enough money, means, or time for a specified purpose, *we can afford to pay $50*. **2** to be in a position to do something, *we can't afford to be critical*.

3 (*formal*) to provide, *her diary affords no information*. affordable *adjective*

afforest *verb* to plant with trees to form a forest. afforestation *noun*

affray (ă-**fray**) *noun* a breach of the peace by fighting or rioting in public. [from Old French *esfreer* = to riot]

affront (ă-**frunt**) *verb* to insult deliberately, to offend or embarrass. –affront *noun* a deliberate insult or show of disrespect.

Afghan (**af**-gan) *noun* **1** a native of Afghanistan. **2** the language spoken there, Pashto. **3** (*historical*) an immigrant to Australia from Afghanistan, Pakistan, etc., engaged especially in camel driving in the outback. **4 afghan** a loose sheepskin coat with shaggy fleece lining. □ **Afghan hound** a tall breed of dog with long silky hair.

Afghanistan (af-gan-ĭ-**stahn**) a republic in central Asia, to the west of Pakistan.

aficionado (ă-fis-yŏ-**nah**-doh) *noun* (*plural* aficionados) a devotee of a particular sport or pastime. [Spanish]

afield *adverb* far away from home, to or at a distance.

afire *adverb* & *adjective* on fire.

AFL *abbreviation* Australian Football League.

aflame *adverb* & *adjective* in flames, burning.

afloat *adverb* & *adjective* **1** floating. **2** at sea, on board ship, *enjoying life afloat*. **3** flooded.

aflutter *adjective* in a state of tremulous excitement.

afoot *adverb* & *adjective* progressing, in operation, *there's a scheme afoot to raise taxes*.

aforesaid *adjective* mentioned previously.

aforethought *adjective* premeditated, planned in advance, *with malice aforethought*.

a fortiori (ay for-tee-**or**-ry) *adverb* & *adjective* with yet stronger reason than a conclusion already accepted. [Latin, = with stronger (reason)]

afraid *adjective* **1** alarmed, frightened, anxious about consequences. **2** politely regretful, *I'm afraid there's none left*.

afresh *adverb* anew, beginning again.

Africa a continent south of the Mediterranean Sea between the Atlantic and Indian Oceans.

African *adjective* of Africa or its people or languages. –African *noun* a native of Africa, especially a Black person. □ **African violet** an East African plant with purple, pink, or white flowers, grown as an indoor plant.

Africanise *verb* (also -ize) to make African, to place under the control of African Blacks. Africanisation *noun*

African National Congress a South African political party and Black nationalist organisation that came to power in the country's first democratic elections in 1994.

Afrikaans (af-ri-**kahns**) *noun* a language developed from Dutch, used in South Africa. [from Dutch, = African]

Afrikaner (af-ri-**kah**-ner) *noun* a White person in South Africa whose native language is Afrikaans.

Afro (**af**-roh) *adjective* (of a hairstyle) tightly curled and bushy, as naturally grown by some Blacks.

Afro- *prefix* African, *Afro-Asian*; *Afro-Caribbean*.

aft *adverb* in or near or towards the stern of a ship or the tail of an aircraft.

after *preposition* **1** behind in place or order. **2** at a later time than. **3** in spite of, *after all I did for him he still ignored me*. **4** as a result of, *after what he did, I hate him*. **5** in pursuit or search of, *run after him*. **6** about, concerning; *he asked after you*, asked how you were. **7** in imitation of, *painted after the manner of Picasso*; *named after a person*. –after *adverb* **1** behind, *Jill came tumbling after*. **2** later, *twenty years after*. –after *conjunction* at or in a time later than, *they came after I left*. –after *adjective* **1** later, following, *in after years*. **2** nearer the stern in a boat, *the after cabins*. **afters** *plural noun* (*informal*) a course following the main course at a meal; dessert. □ **after-effect** *noun* an effect that arises or persists after its cause has gone.

afterbirth *noun* the placenta and foetal membrane discharged from the womb after childbirth.

aftercare *noun* further care or treatment of a patient who has left hospital, rehabilitation of a discharged prisoner.

afterlife *noun* life in a later part of a person's lifetime or after death.

aftermath *noun* events or circumstances that follow and are a consequence of an event etc., *the aftermath of war*.

afternoon *noun* the time from noon to about 6 p.m. or sunset (if this is earlier).

aftershave *noun* a lotion for use after shaving.

aftershock *noun* a lesser quake or shock following an earthquake.

aftertaste *noun* a taste that remains after something has been swallowed.

afterthought *noun* something thought of or added later.

afterwards *adverb* at a later time.

ag- *prefix* see **ad-**.

again *adverb* 1 another time, once more, *try again*. 2 as before, to or in the original place or condition, *you'll soon be well again*. 3 furthermore, besides. 4 on the other hand, *I might, and again I might not*.

against *preposition* 1 in opposition to; *his age is against him*, is a disadvantage to him. 2 in contrast to, *against a dark background*. 3 in preparation for, in anticipation of, *saved against a rainy day*. 4 opposite, so as to cancel or lessen, *allowances to be set against income*. 5 into collision or contact with, *lean against the wall*. □ **against the clock** in order to finish by a certain time.

Aga Khan (ah- gă **kahn**) the spiritual leader of Ismaili Muslims.

Agamemnon (ag-ă-**mem**-nŏn) (*Gk. legend*) king of Mycenae and leader of the Greek expedition against Troy.

agape¹ (ă-**gayp**) *adjective* gaping, open-mouthed.

agape² (**ag**-ă-pay) *noun* 1 (in the New Testament) love. 2 a religious meal held by the early Christians in connection with the Eucharist. [Greek, = love]

agar (**ay**-gah) *noun* (also **agar-agar**) a gelatinous substance obtained from seaweed, used in cooking and as a microbiological medium. [Malay]

agaric (**ag**-ă-rik) *noun* a fungus with a cap and stalk, e.g. the common mushroom. [Greek *agarikon*]

agate (**ag**-ăt) *noun* a very hard stone with patches or concentric bands of colour.

age *noun* 1 the length of time a person has lived or a thing has existed. 2 the later part of life, old age. 3 a historical period, a time with special characteristics or events, *the Elizabethan Age; the atomic age*. 4 (*informal*) a very long time, *it was ages* or *an age before he came*. –**age** *verb* (**aged, ageing**) 1 to grow old, to show signs of age. 2 to become mature, *heavy wines age slowly*. 3 to cause to become

old, *worry aged him rapidly*. 4 to allow to mature. □ **age-long, age-old** *adjectives* having existed for a very long time. **of age** having reached the age at which one has an adult's legal rights and obligations. **under age** not yet of age.

aged *adjective* 1 (*pr.* ayjd) of the age of, *aged 10*. 2 (*pr.* **ay**-jĕd) very old, *an aged man*.

ageless *adjective* not growing or appearing old.

agency *noun* 1 the business or place of business of an agent, *a travel agency*. 2 the means of action through which something is done, *fertilised by the agency of bees*.

agenda (ă-**jen**-dă) *noun* (*plural* **agendas**) a program of items of business to be dealt with at a meeting. [Latin, = things to be done]

> Usage This word is by origin a Latin plural, but is now always used with a singular verb, e.g. *the agenda is rather long*.

agent *noun* 1 a person who does something or instigates some activity, *he is a mere instrument, not an agent*. 2 one who acts on behalf of another, *write to our agents in New York*. 3 something that produces an effect or change, *soda is the active agent*. 4 a secret agent (*see* **secret**). □ **agent orange** a chemical defoliant used in the Vietnam War. [from Latin *agens* = doing things]

agent provocateur (**ah**-*zh*ahn prŏ-vok-ă-**ter**) *noun* (*plural* **agents provocateurs**) a person employed to detect suspects by tempting them to do something illegal openly. [French, = provocative agent]

agglomerate (ă-**glom**-ĕ-rayt) *verb* to collect or become collected into a mass. –**agglomerate** (ă-**glom**-ĕ-răt) *noun* something composed of clustered fragments. **agglomeration** *noun* [from *ag-*, + Latin *glomus* = mass]

agglutinate (ă-**gloo**-tĭ-nayt) *verb* to stick or fuse together. **agglutination** *noun*, **agglutinative** *adjective* [from *ag-*, + Latin *glutinare* = to glue]

agglutinin (ă-**gloo**-tĭ-nin) *noun* a substance that causes agglutination of bacteria or red blood cells.

aggrandise (ă-**gran**-dyz) *verb* (also **-ize**) to increase the power, wealth, or importance of. **aggrandisement** *noun*

aggravate *verb* 1 to make worse or more serious. 2 (*informal*) to annoy. **aggravation**

noun [from *ag-*, + Latin *gravare* = load heavily]

aggregate (**ag**-rĕ-găt) *adjective* combined, total, *the aggregate amount*. –**aggregate** (**ag**-rĕ-găt) *noun* **1** a total, a mass or amount brought together. **2** hard substances (sand, gravel, broken stone, etc.) mixed with cement to make concrete. –**aggregate** (**ag**-rĕ-gayt) *verb* **1** to collect or form into an aggregate, to unite. **2** (*informal*) to amount to (a total). **aggregation** *noun* [from *ag-*, + Latin *gregatum* = herded together]

aggression *noun* **1** unprovoked attacking. **2** a hostile action, hostile behaviour. [from *ag-* = against, + Latin *gressum* = gone]

aggressive *adjective* **1** apt to make attacks, showing aggression. **2** self-assertive, forceful, *an aggressive salesperson*. **aggressively** *adverb*, **aggressiveness** *noun*

aggressor *noun* a person or country that attacks first or begins hostilities.

aggrieved (ă-**greevd**) *adjective* made resentful by unfair treatment.

aggro (*informal*) *noun* deliberate trouble-making. –**aggro** *adjective* aggressive, hostile.

aghast (ă-**gahst**) *adjective* filled with consternation.

agile *adjective* nimble, quick-moving. **agilely** *adverb*, **agility** (ă-**jil**-ĭ-tee) *noun*

Agincourt (**aj**-ĭn-kor *or* **ahzh**-) a village in N France, scene of a great English victory (1415) by an invading army under Henry V.

agist (ă-**jist**) *verb* to pasture livestock for a fee. **agistment** *noun*

agitate *verb* **1** to shake or move briskly. **2** to disturb, to cause anxiety to. **3** to stir up public interest or concern. **agitation** *noun*, **agitator** *noun* [from Latin *agitare* = shake]

aglow *adjective* glowing. –**aglow** *adverb* glowingly.

AGM *abbreviation* annual general meeting.

agnail (**ag**-nail) *noun* = **hangnail**.

Agni (in Hinduism) the Vedic god of fire.

agnostic (ag-**nos**-tik) *noun* a person who believes that nothing can be known about the existence of God or of anything except material things. **agnosticism** *noun* [from *a-*² = not, + Greek *gnostikos* = knowing]

ago *adverb* in the past. [from an old word *agone* = gone by]

agog (ă-**gog**) *adjective* eager, expectant.

agonise *verb* (also -**ize**) **1** to cause agony, to pain greatly; *agonised shrieks*, expressing agony. **2** to suffer agony, to worry intensely, *agonising over decisions*. **agonisingly** *adverb*

agony *noun* extreme mental or physical suffering. [from Greek *agon* = a struggle]

agoraphobia (ag-ŏ-ră-**foh**-bee-ă) *noun* abnormal fear of open spaces or public places. **agoraphobic** *noun* a person who suffers from agoraphobia. [from Greek *agora* = market place, + *phobia*]

Agra (**ah**-gră) a city on the River Jumna in northern India, the site of the Taj Mahal.

agrarian (ă-**grair**-ree-ăn) *adjective* of agricultural land or its cultivation; of landed property. ☐ **agrarian revolution** the change from medieval to modern methods of farming begun in the 18th century. [from Latin *ager* = field]

agree *verb* (**agreed**, **agreeing**) **1** to hold a similar opinion; *we are agreed*, we have reached a similar opinion. **2** to consent, to say that one is willing; *agree to differ*, agree to cease trying to convince each other. **3** to decide by mutual consent, *we agreed on a time*. **4** to get on well together. **5** to be consistent, to harmonise, *your story agrees with his*. **6** to suit a person's health or digestion, *curry doesn't agree with me*. **7** to correspond in grammatical case, number, gender, or person, *the pronoun 'she' agrees with the noun 'woman'*; *'he' agrees with 'man'*.

agreeable *adjective* **1** pleasing, giving pleasure, *an agreeable voice*. **2** willing to agree, *we'll go if you are agreeable*. **agreeably** *adverb*

agreement *noun* **1** agreeing. **2** harmony in opinion or feeling. **3** an arrangement agreed between people.

Agricola (ă-**grik**-ŏ-lă) (40–93), Roman senator, governor of Britain from 78.

agriculture *noun* the science or practice of cultivating land on a large scale and rearing livestock. **agricultural** *adjective*, **agriculturally** *adverb* [from Latin *agri* = of a field, + *culture*]

Agrippa (ă-**grip**-ă) (64–12 BC) the right-hand man of Augustus during the latter's rise to power.

agronomy (ă-**gron**-ŏ-mee) *noun* the science of soil management and crop production. [from Greek *agros* = field, + *-nomia* = management]

aground *adverb & adjective* upon or touching the bottom in shallow water, *the ship is aground* or *ran aground*.

ague (**ay**-gew) *noun* malarial fever; a fit of shivering.

AH *abbreviation* (in dates) of the Muslim era. [short for Latin *anno Hegirae* = in the year of the Hegira]

ah *interjection* an exclamation of surprise, pity, admiration, etc.

aha *interjection* an exclamation of surprise, triumph, or mockery.

ahead *adverb* further forward in space, time, or progress; *try to plan ahead*, plan for the future; *full speed ahead!*, go forward at full speed.

ahem *interjection* the noise made when clearing one's throat, used to call attention or express doubt.

ahimsa (ă-**him**-să) *noun* (in Hinduism, Buddhism, Jainism) the doctrine of non-violence or non-killing.

ahistorical *adjective* lacking historical perspective or context.

ahoy *interjection* a cry used by sailors to call attention.

Ahriman (**ah**-ri-măn) the evil spirit in Zoroastrianism.

Ahura Mazda (ă-hoor-ră **maz**-dă) (later called *Ormuzd*) the creator god in Zoroastrianism, the force for good.

aid *verb* to help.–**aid** *noun* 1 help. 2 something that helps, *a hearing aid*. 3 food, money, etc., sent to a country to help it, *overseas aid*.

aide *noun* 1 an aide-de-camp. 2 an assistant. [French]

aide-de-camp (ayd-dĕ-**kahn**) *noun* (*plural* aides-de-camp, *pr.* aydz) a naval or military officer acting as assistant to a senior officer.

Aids *abbreviation* (also **AIDS**) a condition caused by a virus that breaks down a person's natural defences against illness. [from the initials of 'acquired immune deficiency syndrome']

aikido (I-**kee**-doh) *noun* a Japanese form of self-defence and martial art.

ail *verb* (*old use*) to make ill or uneasy, *what ails him?*; to be in poor health.

aileron (**ail**-ĕ-rŏn) *noun* a hinged flap on an aeroplane wing, used to control balance. [from French *aile* = wing]

ailing *adjective* unwell; in poor condition.

ailment *noun* a slight illness.

aim *verb* 1 to point or send towards a target; to direct (a blow, missile, remark, etc.) towards a specified object or goal; *aiming at a scholarship*, trying to win one; *aim high*, be ambitious. 2 to attempt, to try, *we aim to please the customers*.–**aim** *noun* 1 the act of aiming; *take aim*, aim a weapon. 2 purpose, intention; *what is his aim?*, what does he want to achieve?

aimless *adjective* without a purpose. **aimlessly** *adverb*, **aimlessness** *noun*

ain't = am not, is not, are not, has not, have not.

Usage This word is avoided in standard speech except in humorous use, e.g. *things ain't what they used to be*.

---

air *noun* 1 the mixture of gases surrounding the earth and breathed by all land animals and plants. 2 the earth's atmosphere; open space in this. 3 the earth's atmosphere as the place where aircraft operate; *air travel*, travel in aircraft. 4 a light wind. 5 an impression given, *an air of mystery*. 6 an impressive manner, *he does things with such an air*; *put on airs*, behave in an affected haughty manner. 7 a melody, a tune.–**air** *verb* 1 to expose to the air, to ventilate (a room etc.) so as to cool or freshen it. 2 to put (clothes etc.) into a warm place to finish drying. 3 to express publicly, *air one's opinions*. □ **air bag** a safety device in a vehicle that fills with air on impact to protect the occupants in a collision. **air-bed** *noun* an inflatable mattress. **air brake** a brake worked by compressed air. **air-conditioned** *adjective* supplied with **air-conditioning**, a system controlling the humidity and temperature of the air in a room or building. **air force** a branch of the armed forces equipped for attacking and defending by means of aircraft. **air hostess** a female flight attendant in a passenger aircraft. **air letter** an aerogramme. **air pocket** a partial vacuum in the air causing aircraft in flight to drop suddenly. **air raid** an attack by aircraft dropping bombs. **by air** in or by aircraft. **in the air** current, exerting an influence, *dissatisfaction is in the air*; uncertain, *these plans are still in the air*. **on the air** broadcast or broadcasting by radio or television.

airbase *noun* a base for military aircraft.

airborne *adjective* 1 transported by the air, *airborne pollen*. 2 in flight after taking off. 3 transported by aircraft, *airborne troops*.

aircraft *noun* (*plural* aircraft) **1** a machine or structure capable of flight in the air and regarded as a vehicle or carrier. **2** such craft collectively, including aeroplanes, gliders, and helicopters. □ aircraft carrier a ship that carries and acts as a base for aeroplanes.

aircrew *noun* the crew of an aircraft.

airfield *noun* an area of open level ground equipped with hangars and runways for aircraft.

airflow *noun* a flow of air.

airgun *noun* a gun in which compressed air propels the missile.

airless *adjective* **1** stuffy. **2** without a breeze, calm and still. **airlessness** *noun*

airlift *noun* large-scale transport of troops or supplies by aircraft, especially in an emergency. −airlift *verb* to transport thus.

airline *noun* a regular service of air transport for public use; a company providing this.

airliner *noun* a large passenger aircraft.

airlock *noun* **1** a stoppage of the flow in a pump or pipe, caused by an air bubble. **2** a compartment with an airtight door at each end, providing access to a pressurised chamber.

airmail *noun* mail carried by air. −airmail *verb* to send by airmail.

airman *noun* (*plural* airmen) **1** a male member of an air force. **2** a male aviator.

airport *noun* an airfield with facilities for passengers and goods.

airship *noun* a power-driven aircraft that is lighter than air.

airsick *adjective* made sick or queasy by the motion of an aircraft. **airsickness** *noun*

airspace *noun* the atmosphere above a country and subject to its control.

airstrip *noun* a strip of ground prepared for aircraft to land and take off.

airtight *adjective* not allowing air to enter or escape.

airwaves *plural noun* (*informal*) radio waves used in broadcasting.

airway *noun* **1** a regular route for aircraft. **2** a passage for air into the lungs; a device to secure this.

airwoman *noun* (*plural* airwomen) **1** a female member of an air force. **2** a female aviator.

airworthy *adjective* (of an aircraft) fit to fly. **airworthiness** *noun*

airy *adjective* (airier, airiest) **1** well-ventilated. **2** light as air. **3** careless and light-hearted, *an airy manner*. □ airy-fairy *adjective* fanciful, impractical. **airily** *adverb*, **airiness** *noun*

aisle (*rhymes with* mile) *noun* **1** a side part of a church. **2** a gangway between rows of pews or seats.

ajar *adverb* & *adjective* slightly open.

Ajax (*Gk. legend*) a Greek hero of the Trojan War.

Akbar, Jalaludin Muhammad (1542–1605), Mogul emperor of India from 1556.

AK-47 *noun* a type of assault rifle originally made in the Soviet Union. [abbreviation of Russian *Avtomat Kalashnikov 1947*, the designation of the original model designed by Mikhail T. Kalashnikov (born 1919)]

akhand path (ă-kand put) the continuous reading of the complete Sikh scriptures. [Punjabi, = unbroken reading]

akimbo (ă-**kim**-boh) *adverb* with hands on hips and elbows pointed outwards.

akin *adjective* related, similar, *a feeling akin to envy*.

Akubra (ă-**koo**-bră) *noun* (*trademark*) a wide-brimmed Australian felt hat.

al- *prefix* see ad-.

Alabama (al-ă-**bam**-ă) a State of the SE USA, on the Gulf of Mexico.

alabaster (**al**-ă-bas-ter) *noun* a translucent usually white form of gypsum, often carved into ornaments.

à la carte (ah lah **kart**) *adverb* & *adjective* (of a restaurant meal) ordered as separate items from a menu. [French]

alacrity (ă-**lak**-rĭ-tee) *noun* prompt and eager readiness.

Aladdin's cave a room or box etc. filled with wonderful things. [named after the hero of an Oriental tale]

Alamein *see* El Alamein.

à la mode (ah lah **mohd**) *adverb* & *adjective* in fashion, fashionable. [French]

Alaric (**al**-ă-rik) (c. 370–410), king of the Visigoths from 395, who in 410 captured and sacked Rome.

alarm *noun* **1** a warning sound or signal, an apparatus giving this. **2** an alarm clock. **3** fear caused by expectation of danger. −alarm *verb* to arouse to a sense of danger, to frighten.

☐ **alarm clock** a clock with a device that rings or bleeps at a set time. [from Italian *all'arme!* = to arms!]

alarmist *noun* a person who raises unnecessary or excessive alarm.

alas *interjection* an exclamation of sorrow.

Alaska (ă-**las**-kă) a State of the USA, extending into the Arctic Circle. **Alaskan** *adjective* & *noun*

alb *noun* a white robe reaching to the feet, worn by some Christian priests at church ceremonies.

Alban (**awl**-băn), St (3rd century), the first British martyr. Feast day, 20 June.

Albania a republic in SE Europe, bordering on the Adriatic Sea. **Albanian** *adjective* & *noun*

albatross *noun* 1 a long-winged sea bird related to the petrel. 2 a constant burden or encumbrance (¶ an allusion to Coleridge's *The Rime of the Ancient Mariner*).

albeit (awl-**bee**-it) *conjunction* (*literary*) although.

albino (al-**bee**-noh) *noun* (*plural* albinos) a person or animal with no colouring pigment in the skin and hair (which are white) and the eyes (which are pink). [from Latin *albus* = white]

Albion (**al**-bee-ŏn) (*poetic*) Britain.

album *noun* 1 a book in which a collection of autographs, photographs, postage stamps, etc., can be kept. 2 a recording containing several items, usually by the same performer(s). [Latin, = white piece of stone etc. on which to write things]

albumen (**al**-bew-měn) *noun* the white of an egg. [from Latin *albus* = white]

albumin (**al**-bew-mĭn) *noun* any of a group of proteins found in egg white, milk, and blood.

alchemy (**al**-kĕ-mee) *noun* a medieval form of chemistry, the chief aim of which was to discover how to turn ordinary metals into gold. **alchemist** *noun* [from Arabic *alkimiya* = the art of changing metals]

Alcheringa (al-chĕ-**ring**-gă) [*see* **Dreamtime**. from Aranda *aljerre-nge* = in the Dreamtime]

alcohol *noun* 1 a colourless inflammable liquid, the intoxicant present in wine, beer, whisky, etc. 2 any liquor containing this. 3 a chemical compound of this type. [from Arabic *al-kuhl*]

alcoholic *adjective* 1 of or containing alcohol. 2 caused by drinking alcohol. –**alcoholic** *noun* a person suffering from alcoholism.

alcoholism *noun* a diseased condition caused by continual heavy drinking of alcohol.

alcopop *noun* a ready-mixed soft drink containing alcohol.

alcove *noun* 1 a recess in a wall. 2 a recess forming an extension of a room etc. [from Arabic *al-kubba* = the arch]

aldehyde (**al**-dĕ-hyd) *noun* 1 a fluid with a suffocating smell, obtained from alcohol. 2 a compound with the same structure.

alder (**awl**-der) *noun* a tree of the birch family.

alderman (**awl**-der-măn) *noun* (*plural* aldermen) an elected member of a local government body. **alderwoman** *feminine noun* [from Old English *aldor* = older, + *man*]

Alderney (**awl**-der-nee) one of the Channel Islands. –**Alderney** *noun* a breed of small dairy cattle that originated in Alderney.

ale *noun* beer.

aleatory (**ay**-lee-ă-tŏ-ree) *adjective* depending on random choice. [from Latin *alea* = dice]

alert *adjective* watchful, observant. –**alert** *noun* 1 a state of watchfulness or readiness. 2 a warning of danger, notice to stand ready. –**alert** *verb* to warn of danger, to make alert. ☐ **on the alert** on the lookout, watchful. **alertly** *adverb*, **alertness** *noun* [from Italian *all'erta!* = to the watchtower]

Aleutian Islands (ă-**lew**-shăn) (also **Aleutians**) a group of islands in US possession, extending south-west from Alaska.

Alexander 'the Great' (356–323 BC), king of Macedon from 336 BC, whose conquests extended from Greece in the west to Bactria and the Punjab in the east.

alexandrine (al-ĕg-**zan**-dryn) *noun* a verse of six iambic feet or twelve syllables.

alfalfa (al-**fal**-fă) *noun* lucerne. [from Arabic *al-fasfasa* = a green fodder]

Alfred 'the Great' (849–99), king of Wessex from 871, who defeated the Danes and encouraged learning and literature.

alfresco (al-**fres**-koh) *adjective* & *adverb* in the open air.

alga (**al**-gă) *noun* (*plural* algae, *pr.* **al**-jee *or* -gee) a water plant with no true stems or leaves. **algal** *adjective*

algebra (**al**-jĕ-bră) *noun* a branch of mathematics in which letters and symbols are used to represent quantities. **algebraic** (al-jĕ-**bray**-ik) *adjective*, **algebraically** *adverb* [from Arabic *al-jabr* = putting together broken parts]

Algeria a republic in North Africa on the Mediterranean coast. **Algerian** *adjective* & *noun*

Algiers (al-**jeerz**) the capital of Algeria.

Algonquian (al-**gong**-kwee-ăn) *noun* (also **Algonkian**) 1 a large family of indigenous languages of North America. 2 a speaker of any of these languages. – **Algonquian** *adjective* of or relating to this family of languages or its speakers.

algorithm (**al**-gŏ-ri*th*m) *noun* a procedure or set of rules for solving a problem, especially by computer.

Alhambra a magnificent Moorish palace, built in 1248–1354 at Granada in Spain.

alias (**ay**-lee-ăs) *noun* (*plural* **aliases**) a false name, an assumed name, *Brown had several aliases*. – **alias** *adverb* also falsely called, *John Brown, alias Peter Harrison*. [Latin, = at another time]

Ali Baba (al-ee **bah**-bă) the hero of a story from the *Arabian Nights*, who discovered the magic formula ('Open, Sesame!') which opened the robbers' treasure cave.

alibi (**al**-ĭ-by) *noun* 1 evidence that an accused person was elsewhere when the crime was committed. 2 (*incorrect use*) an excuse, an answer to an accusation. – **alibi** *verb* (**alibied**, **alibiing**) to provide an alibi for. [Latin, = at another place]

Alice Springs a town on the Todd River in the Northern Territory, informally called *Alice* or *The Alice*.

alien (**ay**-lee-ĕn) *noun* 1 a person who is not a subject of the country in which he is living. 2 a being from another world. – **alien** *adjective* 1 foreign, not one's own, unfamiliar, *alien customs*. 2 different in nature, contrary, *cruelty is alien to her character*. [from Latin *alius* = other]

alienate (**ay**-lee-ĕ-nayt) *verb* to cause to become unfriendly or hostile. **alienation** *noun*

alight[1] *verb* 1 to get down from a horse or a vehicle. 2 to descend and settle, *the bird alighted on a branch*. [from *a-*[1] + *light*[2]]

alight[2] *adjective* on fire, lit up. [from *a-*[1] + *light*[1]]

align (ă-**lyn**) *verb* 1 to place in line, to bring into line. 2 to join as an ally, *they aligned themselves with the Liberals*.

☐ **out of alignment** not in line. **alignment** *noun* [from French *à ligne* = into line]

alike *adjective* & *adverb* like one another, in the same way.

alimentary canal (alĭ-**ment**-ă-ree) *noun* the tubular passage through which food passes from mouth to anus in the process of being digested and absorbed by the body. [from Latin *alimentum* = food]

alimony (**al**-ĭ-mŏnee) *noun* (now called *maintenance*) an allowance payable to a spouse (usually by a man to his wife or former wife) pending or after a legal separation or divorce. [from Latin *alimonia* = nourishment]

aliphatic (al-ĭ-**fat**-ik) *adjective* (of chemical compounds) in which carbon atoms form open chains.

aliquot (**al**-ĭ-kwot) *adjective* that produces a quotient without a fraction when a given larger number is divided by it. – **aliquot** *noun* 1 an aliquot part. 2 a representative portion of a substance. [Latin, = some, so many]

alive *adjective* 1 living. 2 alert, *he is alive to the possible dangers*. 3 active, lively. 4 full of living or moving things, *the river was alive with boats*.

alkali (**al**-kă-ly) *noun* (*plural* **alkalis**) any of a class of substances (such as caustic soda, potash, and ammonia) that neutralise and are neutralised by acids, and form caustic or corrosive solutions in water. ☐ **alkali metal** any of the reactive metals lithium, sodium, potassium, rubidium, and caesium, whose hydroxides are alkalis. **alkaline earth** any of the reactive metals beryllium, magnesium, calcium, strontium, barium, and radium. **alkaline** (**al**-kă-lyn) *adjective*, **alkalinity** (al-kă-**lin**-ĭ-tee) *noun* [from Arabic *al-kily* = the ashes]

alkaloid (**al**-kă-loid) *noun* any of a large group of nitrogen-containing substances derived from plants, many of which are used as drugs, e.g. morphine, quinine.

alkane *noun* any of a series of saturated aliphatic hydrocarbons (the *paraffin series*) including methane, ethane, and propane.

alkene *noun* any of a series of unsaturated aliphatic hydrocarbons containing a double bond (the *olefin series*) including ethylene and propene.

alkyd (**al**-kĭd) *noun* any of a group of synthetic resins derived from various alcohols and acids.

alkyl (**al**-kĭl *or* -kyl) *adjective* derived from an alkane by removing a hydrogen atom or replacing it by another atom or group.

alkyne (**al**-kyn) *noun* any of a series of unsaturated aliphatic hydrocarbons containing a triple bond (the *acetylene series*) including acetylene.

all *adjective* the whole amount or number or extent of, *waited all day*; *beyond all doubt*, beyond any doubt whatever. −**all** *noun* all persons concerned, everything, *all are agreed*; *all is lost*; *the score is four all*, four games or goals to each side. −**all** *adverb* entirely, quite, *dressed all in white*; *an all-powerful dictator*; *ran all the faster*, even faster. ☐ **All Blacks** the New Zealand international rugby football team, so called from the colour of their uniforms. **all but** very little short of, *it is all but impossible*. **all-clear** *noun* a signal that a danger is over. **all ears** listening intently. **all for** (*informal*) much in favour of. **all in** (*informal*) exhausted. **all-in** *adjective* including everything, *the all-in price*; *all-in wrestling*, freestyle wrestling. **all in all** everything considered. **all one to** a matter of indifference to. **all ordinaries index** the weighted average share price on the Australian stock exchange of a selected group of companies. **all out** using all possible strength, energy, or speed. **all right** as desired, satisfactorily; in good condition, safe and sound; yes, I consent. **all-round** *adjective* general, not specialised. **all-rounder** *noun* a versatile person, especially in sport. **All Saints' Day** 1 November. **all set** (*informal*) ready to start. **All Souls' Day** 2 November. **all there** (*informal*) mentally alert; *not quite all there*, mentally deficient. **all the same** in spite of this; making no difference. **all-time** *adjective* unsurpassed, *an all-time record*. **on all fours** on hands and knees.

Allah (**al**-ă) the name of God among Muslims and Arab Christians.

Allahabad (al-ă-hă-**bahd**) an Indian city at the confluence of the River Jumna with the Ganges; a place of pilgrimage for Hindus.

allay (ă-**lay**) *verb* (**allayed**, **allaying**) to calm, to put at rest, *to allay suspicion*.

allegation (alĕ-**gay**-shŏn) *noun* a statement made without proof.

allege (ă-**lej**) *verb* to declare (especially to those doubting one's truthfulness) without being able to prove, *alleging that he was innocent*; *he alleged illness as the reason for his absence*; *the alleged culprit*, the person said to be the culprit.

allegedly (ă-**lej**-ĕd-lee) *adverb* according to allegation.

allegiance (ă-**lee**-jăns) *noun* support of a government or sovereign or cause, etc.

allegory (**al**-ĕ-gŏ-ree) *noun* a story or description in which the characters and events symbolise some deeper underlying meaning. **allegorical** (al-ĕ-**go**-ri-kăl) *noun*, **allegorically** *adverb*

allegretto (alĕ-**gret**-oh) *adverb* (in music) in fairly brisk time. −**allegretto** *noun* (*plural* **allegrettos**) a movement to be played in this way. [Italian]

allegro (ă-**lay**-groh) *adverb* (in music) fast and lively. −**allegro** *noun* (*plural* **allegros**) a movement to be played in this way. [Italian]

allele (ă-**leel**) *noun* (also **allelomorph**) any of the alternative forms of a particular gene.

alleluia *interjection* & *noun* praise to God. [from Hebrew]

Allen *noun* (*trademark*) **Allen key** a kind of spanner designed to fit and turn an **Allen screw**, a screw with a hexagonal socket in the head.

allergenic (al-er-**jen**-ik) *adjective* causing an allergic reaction.

allergic (ă-**ler**-jik) *adjective* **1** having an allergy. **2** caused by an allergy, *an allergic reaction*. **3** (*informal*) having a strong dislike, *allergic to hard work*.

allergy (**al**-er-jee) *noun* an adverse immune response by the body to a particular food, pollen, etc. to which it has become hypersensitive.

alleviate (ă-**lee**-vee-ayt) *verb* to lessen, to make less severe, *to alleviate pain*. **alleviation** *noun* [from *al*-, + Latin *levis* = light]

alley *noun* (*plural* **alleys**) **1** (also **alleyway**) a narrow passage or street between houses or other buildings. **2** a path bordered by hedges or shrubbery. **3** a long channel for balls in games such as tenpin bowling. **4** a marble of excellent quality. [from French *aller* = go]

alliance *noun* a union or association formed for mutual benefit, especially of countries by treaty or families by marriage.

allied *see* **ally**. −**allied** *adjective* of the same general kind, similar.

alligator *noun* a reptile of the crocodile family, found especially in the rivers of tropical America and China. [from Spanish *el lagarto* = the lizard]

alliteration (ă-lit-ĕ-**ray**-shŏn) *noun* the occurrence of the same letter or sound at the beginning of several words in succession, e.g. *sing a song of sixpence*. alliterative (ă-**lit**-ĕ-ră-tiv) *adjective* [from *al-*, + Latin *littera* = letter]

allocate (**al**-ŏ-kayt) *verb* to allot. allocation *noun*, allocator *noun*, allocable *adjective* [from *al-*, + Latin *locus* = a place]

allot (ă-**lot**) *verb* (allotted, allotting) to distribute officially, to give as a share of things available or tasks to be done.

allotment *noun* 1 allotting. 2 a share allotted. 3 a small area of land; a building block.

allotrope (**al**-ŏ-trohp) *noun* one of the forms of an element that exists in different physical forms, *diamond and graphite are allotropes of carbon*.

allotropy (ă-**lot**-rŏ-pee) *noun* the existence of several forms of a chemical element in the same state (gas, liquid, or solid) but with different physical or chemical properties. allotropic (al-ŏ-**trop**-ik) *adjective* [from Greek *allos* = other, + *tropos* = manner]

allow *verb* 1 to permit. 2 to permit to have, to give a limited quantity or sum, *allow him $200 a year*. 3 to add or deduct in estimating, *allow 10% for inflation*. 4 to agree that something is true or acceptable, *I allow that you have been patient*; *the judge allowed their claim for expenses*. allowable *adjective*

allowance *noun* 1 allowing. 2 an amount or sum allowed. □ **make allowances for** to be lenient towards or because of, *make allowances for him* or *for his youth*.

alloy (**al**-oi) *noun* 1 a metal formed of a mixture of metals or of metal and another substance. 2 an inferior metal mixed with one of greater value. –alloy (ă-**loi**) *verb* (alloyed, alloying) 1 to mix with metal(s) of lower value. 2 to weaken or spoil by something that reduces value or pleasure.

allspice *noun* 1 spice made from the dried and ground berries of the pimento. 2 this berry.

allude (ă-**lood** *or* -**lewd**) *verb* to refer briefly or indirectly in speaking. allusion *noun*

allure (ă-**loor** *or* -**lyoor**) *verb* to entice, to attract. –allure *noun* attractiveness. allurement *noun* [from French *à* = to, + *lure*]

alluring *adjective* attractive, charming.

allusive (ă-**loo**-siv) *adjective* containing allusions. allusively *adverb*

alluvial (ă-**loo**-vee-ăl) *adjective* made of alluvium. □ **alluvial fan** a fan-shaped mass

of alluvium deposited by a stream where it begins to flow less swiftly.

alluvium (ă-**loo**-vee-ŭm) *noun* a deposit of soil and sand left by rivers or floods.

ally (**al**-I) *noun* 1 a country in alliance with another. 2 a person who cooperates with another in some project. –ally (ă-**ly**) *verb* (allied, allying) to form an alliance. □ **the Allies** the nations allied in opposition to Germany and its supporters in each of the two World Wars.

Alma-Ata (al-mă **ah**-tă) the capital of Kazakhstan.

almanac (**awl**-mă-nak *or* **al**-) (also almanack) *noun* 1 an annual publication containing a calendar with times of sunrise and sunset, astronomical data, dates of anniversaries, and sometimes other information. 2 a yearbook of sport, theatre, etc.

almighty *adjective* 1 all-powerful. 2 (*informal*) very great. □ **the Almighty** God.

almond (**ah**-mŏnd) *noun* 1 the kernel of the fruit of a tree related to the peach. 2 this tree. □ **almond-eyed** *adjective* having eyes that appear to narrow and slant upwards at the outer corners.

almost *adverb* all but, as the nearest thing to.

alms (*pr.* ahmz) *noun* (*old use*) money and gifts given to the poor.

aloe *noun* a plant with thick sharp-pointed leaves and bitter juice. aloes *noun* this juice. □ **aloe vera** a kind of aloe, the leaves of which yield a juice used in cosmetics etc.

aloft *adverb* high up, up in the air.

alone *adjective* not with others, without the company or help of others or other things. –alone *adverb* only, exclusively, *you alone can help me*. [from *all one*]

along *adverb* 1 onward, *push it along*. 2 beside or through part or the whole of a thing's length, *along by the fence*; *knew it all along*, from the beginning. 3 in company with oneself, in addition, *brought my sister along*; *I'll be along soon*, will come and join you. –along *preposition* close to or parallel with the length of something, *along the wall*.

alongside *adverb* close to the side (of a ship, wharf, etc.). –alongside *preposition* beside.

aloof *adverb* apart; *keep* or *hold aloof from*, deliberately take no part in. –aloof *adjective* unconcerned, cool and remote in character, not friendly. aloofly *adverb*, aloofness *noun*

aloud *adverb* in a voice loud enough to be heard, not silently or in a whisper.

ALP *abbreviation* Australian Labor Party.

alp *noun* 1 a high mountain. 2 pastureland on mountains in Switzerland. **Alps** *plural noun* a high range of mountains, especially the Alps in Switzerland and adjacent countries; the Australian Alps, in SE Australia; the Southern Alps, in New Zealand.

alpaca (al-**pak**-ă) *noun* 1 a South American llama with long wool. 2 its wool; fabric made from this.

alpha (**al**-fă) *noun* the first letter of the Greek alphabet, = a. □ Alpha and Omega the beginning and the end. alpha particles or rays helium nuclei emitted by radioactive substances (originally regarded as rays).

alphabet *noun* 1 the letters used in writing a language. 2 a list of these in a set order. 3 symbols or signs indicating letters but not written, *the Morse alphabet*. [from *alpha, beta*, the first two letters of the Greek alphabet]

alphabetical *adjective* in the order of the letters of the alphabet. alphabetically *adverb*

alphabetise *verb* (also -**ize**) to put into alphabetical order. alphabetisation *noun*

alphanumeric (al-fă-new-**me**-rik) *adjective* containing letters of the alphabet and numerals.

alpine *adjective* of high mountains; growing on these; Alpine of the Alps. –alpine *noun* a plant suited to mountain regions or grown in rock gardens. [from the *Alps*]

Al Qaeda (al-**ky**-dă) a militant Islamic fundamentalist group. [from Arabic, = 'the base']

already *adverb* 1 before this time, *had already gone*. 2 as early as this, *is he back already?*

alright *adverb* a form of *all right* widely regarded as incorrect.

Alsatian (al-**say**-shăn) *noun* a dog of a large strong smooth-haired breed (also called *German shepherd*). [from Latin *Alsatia* = Alsace (a region of eastern France)]

also *adverb* in addition, besides. □ also-ran *noun* a horse or dog not among the first three to finish in a race; a person who fails to win distinction.

Altamira (al-tă-**meer**-ră) the site of a cave in northern Spain with palaeolithic paintings.

altar *noun* 1 the table on which bread and wine are consecrated in the Communion service. 2 any structure on which offerings are made to a god.

alter *verb* to make or become different, to change in character, position, or setting. alteration *noun* [from Latin *alter* = other]

altercation (awl-ter-**kay**-shŏn or ol-) *noun* a noisy dispute or quarrel.

alter ego (al-ter **ee**-goh or awl-) *noun* 1 one's hidden or second self. 2 an intimate friend. [Latin, = other self]

alternate (awl-**ter**-năt or ol-) *adjective* happening or following in turns, first the one and then the other; *on alternate days*, every second day. –alternate (**awl**-ter-nayt or ol-) *verb* 1 to arrange or perform or occur alternately. 2 to consist of alternate things. □ alternate angles angles positioned like those in the Z shape (or reversed Z) formed when one line intersects two others. alternating current electric current that reverses its direction at regular intervals. alternately *adverb*, alternation *noun*

Usage See the note under alternative.

alternative (awl-**ter**-nă-tiv or ol-) *adjective* 1 available in place of something else. 2 different or unconventional, *alternative lifestyle*; *alternative medicine*, unconventional treatments such as homoeopathy and hypnosis. –alternative *noun* one of two or more possibilities. alternatively *adverb*

Usage The use of *alternative* with reference to more than two options is well established. Some people object to it, however, on the basis that the Latin word *alter* from which it is derived means 'one or other of two'. *Alternative* should be distinguished from *alternate*; *alternative colours* means that one colour can be chosen instead of another or others, *alternate colours* means that there is first one colour then another.

alternator (**awl**-ter-nay-ter or ol-) *noun* a dynamo giving alternating current.

although *conjunction* though.

altimeter (**al**-tǐ-mee-ter) *noun* an instrument used especially in aircraft for showing the height above sea level. [from Latin *altus* = high, + *meter*]

altitude *noun* 1 the height above sea level. 2 the distance of a star etc. above the horizon, measured as an angle. **3** the height of a triangle as measured by a line drawn from a vertex perpendicular to the opposite side. [from Latin *altus* = high]

alto (**al**-toh) *noun* (*plural* altos) **1** a contralto. **2** the highest adult male singing voice. **3** a singer with such a voice, a part written for it. **4** a musical instrument with the second or third highest pitch in its group, *alto-saxophone*. [Italian, = high]

altocumulus (al-toh-**kewm**-yǔ-lǔs) *noun* clouds resembling cumulus but higher in the sky. [from Latin *altus* = high, + *cumulus*]

altogether *adverb* **1** entirely, totally. **2** on the whole. –altogether *noun* (*informal*) a state of nudity; *in the altogether*, nude.

***

Usage Distinguish *altogether* meaning 'in total' from *all together* meaning 'all at once' or 'all in one place', as in *The party guests arrived all together*; *There were ten altogether*.

***

altostratus (al-toh-**strah**-tǔs) *noun* clouds in a continuous layer at medium altitude. [from Latin *altus* = high, + *stratus*]

altruism (**al**-troo-izm) *noun* unselfishness. altruist *noun* an unselfish person. altruistic *adjective*, altruistically *adverb* [from Italian *altrui* = somebody else]

alum (**al**-ǔm) *noun* a white mineral salt used in medicine and in dyeing.

alumina (ǎ-**loo**-mǐ-nǎ) *noun* an oxide of aluminium, e.g. corundum.

aluminise (ǎ-**loo**-mǐ-nyz) *verb* (also -ize) to coat with aluminium.

aluminium *noun* a chemical element (symbol Al), a lightweight silvery metal used either pure or as an alloy for making utensils or fittings where lightness is an advantage.

alumnus (ǎ-**lum**-nǔs) *noun* (*plural* alumni, *pr.* -ny) a former student of a university, college, or school. alumna *feminine noun* (*plural* alumnae, *pr.* -nee).

alveolus (al-vee-ǒ-lǔs *or* al-vee-**oh**-lǔs) *noun* (*plural* alveoli, *pr.* -ly) **1** a small cavity such as a tooth socket or a cell in a honeycomb. **2** any of the tiny air-filled sacs in the lungs from which oxygen passes into the blood and through which carbon dioxide is removed from it. alveolar *adjective* [Latin, = small cavity]

always *adverb* **1** at all times, on all occasions. **2** whatever the circumstances, *you can always leave*. **3** repeatedly, *he is always grizzling*.

alyssum (ǎ-**liss**-ǔm) *noun* a plant with small usually yellow or white flowers.

Alzheimer's disease (**alts**-hy-merz) *noun* a brain disorder causing premature senility. [named after Alois Alzheimer (1864–1915), German neurologist]

AM *abbreviation* **1** Member of the Order of Australia. **2** amplitude modulation.

am *see* be.

a.m. *abbreviation* before noon. [short for Latin *ante meridiem*]

amalgam *noun* **1** an alloy of mercury and another metal, used especially in dental fillings. **2** any soft pliable mixture.

amalgamate *verb* to mix, to combine. amalgamation *noun*

amanuensis (ǎ-man-yoo-**en**-sǐs) *noun* (*plural* amanuenses) a literary assistant, especially one who writes from dictation.

amaryllis (am-ǎ-**ril**-ǐss) *noun* a lily-like plant growing from a bulb.

amass (ǎ-**mass**) *verb* to heap up, to collect, *amassed a large fortune*.

amateur (**am**-ǎ-ter) *noun* a person who does something as a pastime rather than as a profession. [from Latin *amator* = lover]

amateurish (**am**-ǎ-tě-rish) *adjective* inexpert, lacking professional skill. amateurishly *adverb*, amateurishness *noun*

amatory (**am**-ǎ-tǒ-ree) *adjective* showing sexual love.

amaze *verb* to overwhelm with wonder. amazement *noun*

Amazon **1** (*Gk. myth.*) a woman of a race of female warriors. **2** a great river in South America. –amazon *noun* a tall and strong or athletic woman. amazonian *adjective*

ambassador *noun* **1** a diplomat sent by one country as a permanent representative or on a special mission to another. **2** an official messenger.

amber *noun* **1** a hardened clear yellowish-brown resin used for making ornaments. **2** a yellow traffic light shown as a cautionary signal between red (= stop) and green (= go). –amber *adjective* **1** made of amber. **2** coloured like amber.

ambergris (**am**-ber-grees) *noun* a waxlike substance found floating in tropical seas and present in the intestines of sperm whales, used as a fixative in perfumes.

ambi- *prefix* both; on both sides (as in *ambidextrous*). [from Latin *ambo* = both]

ambidextrous (am-bee-**deks**-trŭs) *adjective* able to use either hand equally well. [from *ambi-*, + Latin *dexter* = right-handed]

ambience (**am**-bee-ĕns) *noun* environment, surrounding. **ambient** *adjective* [from French]

ambiguous (am-**big**-yoo-ŭs) *adjective* **1** having two or more possible meanings. **2** doubtful, uncertain. **ambiguously** *adverb*, **ambiguity** (am-bĭ-**gew**-ĭ-tee) *noun*

ambit *noun* the bounds, scope, or extent of something.

ambition *noun* **1** a strong desire to achieve something. **2** the object of this.

ambitious (am-**bish**-ŭs) *adjective* full of ambition. **ambitiously** *adverb*

ambivalent (am-**biv**-ă-lĕnt) *adjective* with mixed feelings towards a certain object or situation. **ambivalently** *adverb*, **ambivalence** *noun* [from *ambi-*, + Latin *valens* = strong]

amble *verb* to walk at a slow easy pace. –**amble** *noun* a slow easy pace. **ambler** *noun* [from Latin *ambulare* = to walk]

ambo *noun* (*Austral. informal*) an ambulance officer.

ambrosia (am-**broh**-zee-ă) *noun* **1** (*Gk. & Rom. myth.*) the food of the gods. **2** something delicious. **ambrosial** *adjective* [from Greek, = elixir of life]

ambulacrum (am-bew-**lay**-krŭm) *noun* (*plural* **ambulacra**) each of the bands (usually five) on an echinoderm, from which its tube-feet grow. **ambulacral** *adjective*

ambulance *noun* a vehicle equipped to carry sick or injured people.

ambulatory (**am**-bew-lă-tŏ-ree) *adjective* **1** of or for walking. **2** able to walk. –**ambulatory** *noun* a place for walking, as in a cloister.

ambuscade (am-bŭs-**kayd**) *noun* an ambush.

ambush *noun* **1** the placing of troops etc. in a concealed position to make a surprise attack on an approaching enemy or victim. **2** such an attack. –**ambush** *verb* to lie in wait for, to attack from an ambush.

ameliorate (ă-**mee**-lee-ŏ-rayt) *verb* to make or become better. **amelioration** *noun* [from *ad-*, + Latin *melior* = better]

amen (ah-**men** *or* ay-**men**) *interjection* (in prayers) so be it. [from Hebrew, = certainly]

amenable (ă-**meen**-ă-bŭl) *adjective* **1** willing to be guided or controlled by some influence, *she is not amenable to discipline*. **2** subject to a legal authority, *we are all amenable to the law*. **amenably** *adverb*, **amenability** *noun* [from French *amener* = to lead]

amend *verb* to correct an error in; to make minor alterations in, *they amended the agreement*. □ **make amends** to compensate or make up for something. **amendment** *noun*

amenity (ă-**men**-ĭ-tee *or* -**meen**-) *noun* **1** pleasantness of a place or circumstance. **2** a feature of a place etc. that makes life there easy or pleasant. **amenities** *plural noun* public toilets.

America 1 a continent of the western hemisphere (also called **the Americas**) consisting of the two great land masses **North America** and **South America** joined by the narrow isthmus of **Central America**. **2** the USA. □ **America's Cup** an international yachting trophy named after the yacht *America*, which won it in 1851.

American *adjective* **1** of the continent of America. **2** of the USA. –**American** *noun* **1** a native of America. **2** a citizen of the USA. **3** the English language as spoken in the USA. □ **American football** (also called *gridiron*) a form of football played in the USA with an oval ball on a field marked out as a gridiron. **American Indian** *see* **Indian**.

Americanism *noun* a word or phrase of American origin or usage.

americium (am-ĕ-**ris**-ee-ŭm) *noun* an artificial radioactive metallic element of the actinide series (symbol Am).

Amerindian *adjective* & *noun* = **American Indian**.

amethyst (**am**-ĕ-thĭst) *noun* a precious stone, purple or violet quartz.

Amharic (am-**ha**-rik) *noun* the official and trade language of Ethiopia.

amiable (**aym**-ee-ă-bŭl) *adjective* feeling and inspiring friendliness, good-tempered. **amiably** *adverb*, **amiability** *noun*

amicable (**am**-ik-ă-bŭl) *adjective* friendly. **amicably** *adverb*, **amicability** *noun* [from Latin *amicus* = friend]

amid, amidst *prepositions* in the middle of, during, *amid shouts of dismay*.

amide (**am**-yd) *noun* a compound in which an acid radical or metal atom replaces a hydrogen atom of ammonia.

amidships *adverb* in the middle of a ship.

amine (**ay**-meen) *noun* a compound in which an alkyl or other non-acidic radical replaces a hydrogen atom of ammonia.

amino acid (ă-**mee**-noh) *noun* an organic acid found in proteins.

amir (ă-**meer**) *noun* a title used by various Muslim rulers. [Arabic, = ruler]

amirate (ă-**meer**-răt) *noun* the territory of an amir.

amiss *adjective* wrong, out of order, *what is amiss with it?* –**amiss** *adverb* wrongly, faultily; *don't take his criticism amiss*, do not be offended by it.

amity *noun* friendship.

Amman (ă-**mahn**) the capital of Jordan.

ammeter (**am**-ee-ter) *noun* an instrument that measures electric current, usually in amperes.

ammo *noun* (*informal*) ammunition.

ammonia *noun* **1** a colourless gas with a strong smell. **2** a solution of this in water.

ammonite (**am**-ŏ-nyt) *noun* the fossil of a coil-shaped shell.

ammonium *noun* a radical present in ammonia salts.

ammonoid (**am**-ŏ-noid) *noun* a member of a group of fossils, including ammonites, showing coil-shaped shells.

ammunition *noun* **1** projectiles (bullets, shells, grenades, etc.) and their propellants. **2** facts and reasoning used to prove a point in an argument. [from French *la munition*, wrongly taken as *l'ammunition*]

amnesia (am-**nee**-zee-ă) *noun* loss of memory. **amnesiac** *adjective & noun* [from *a-²* = without, + Greek *-mnesis* = memory]

amnesty (**am**-něs-tee) *noun* a general pardon, especially for offences against the State.

Amnesty International an international organisation supporting human rights and working for the release of people imprisoned for their political or religious beliefs.

amnion (**am**-nee-ŏn) *noun* (*plural* **amnia**) the membrane enclosing the foetus and the fluid that surrounds it before birth. **amniotic** (am-nee-**ot**-ik) *adjective*

amniocentesis (am-nee-oh-sen-**tee**-sĭs) *noun* a prenatal test to obtain information about the foetus by inserting a hollow needle into the womb and withdrawing a sample of the fluid there (**amniotic fluid**) for analysis.

amoeba (ă-**mee**-bă) *noun* (*plural* **amoebae** (*pr*. ă-**mee**-bee) *or* **amoebas**) a microscopic organism consisting of a single cell that changes shape constantly. **amoebic** *adjective*

amok *adverb* (also **amuck**) on the rampage in murderous frenzy, *to run amok*. [from Malay, = fighting mad]

among, amongst *prepositions* **1** in an assembly of, surrounded by, *poppies amongst the corn*. **2** in the number of, *this is reckoned among his best works*. **3** within the limits of, between, *have only $5 amongst us*; *quarrelled among themselves*, with one another. [from Old English *ongemang* = in a crowd]

amoral (ay-**mo**-răl) *adjective* not based on moral standards, neither moral nor immoral. [from *a-²* = not, + *moral*]

amorous (**am**-ŏ-rŭs) *adjective* of, showing, or readily feeling sexual love. **amorously** *adverb*, **amorousness** *noun* [from Latin *amor* = love]

amorphous (ă-**mor**-fŭs) *adjective* having no definite shape or form. [from *a-²* = not, + Greek *morphe* = form]

amortise (ă-**mor**-tyz) *verb* (also **-ize**) **1** to pay off (a debt) gradually by money regularly put aside. **2** to write off the initial costs of (assets) gradually. **amortisation** *noun*

Amos (**ay**-moss) **1** a Hebrew minor prophet (c. 760 BC). **2** the book of the Old Testament containing his prophecies.

amount *noun* **1** the total of anything. **2** a quantity, *a small amount of salt*. –**amount** *verb* **amount to 1** to add up to. **2** to be equivalent to. [from Latin *ad montem* = to the mountain, upwards]

amp *noun* **1** an ampere. **2** (*informal*) an amplifier.

amperage (**am**-pě-rij) *noun* the strength of electric current, measured in amperes.

ampere (**am**-pair) *noun* a unit for measuring electric current (symbol A). [named after the French physicist A. M. Ampère (1775–1836)]

ampersand *noun* the sign & (= and).

amphetamine (am-**fet**-ă-meen) *noun* a drug used as a stimulant or to relieve congestion.

amphi- *prefix* both; on both sides; in both places (as in *amphibian*). [from Greek *amphi-* = around]

amphibian (am-**fib**-ee-ăn) *noun* **1** an animal able to live both on land and in water.

2 a vehicle that can move on both land and water. [from *amphi-*, + Greek *bios* = life]

amphibious (am-**fib**-ee-ŭs) *adjective*
1 living or operating both on land and in water. **2** involving both sea and land forces, *amphibious operations*.

amphibole (**am**-fi-bohl) *noun* any of a group of minerals including hornblende.

amphitheatre *noun* an oval or circular unroofed building with tiers of seats surrounding a central arena. (¶ This is not the same as a Greek or Roman *theatre*, which is semicircular.) [from Greek *amphi* = all round, + *theatre*]

amphora (**am**-fŏ-ră) *noun* (*plural* **amphorae**, -ree) an ancient Greek or Roman jar with two handles and a narrow neck.

amphoteric (am-fŏ-**te**-rik) *adjective* (of a substance) able to react chemically as an acid or as a base.

ample *adjective* **1** plentiful, quite enough, *ample evidence*. **2** large, of generous proportions. **amply** *adverb*

amplifier *noun* a device that increases the loudness of sounds or the power of audio or radio signals.

amplify *verb* (**amplified**, **amplifying**)
1 to increase the strength of, *to amplify sound*. **2** to make fuller, to add details to, *please amplify your story*. **amplification** *noun* [from Latin *amplificare* = make more ample]

amplitude *noun* **1** breadth. **2** largeness, abundance. **3** the maximum extent of vibration from the equilibrium position; the largest amount by which an alternating current or electromagnetic wave can vary from its average. □ **amplitude modulation** the systematic variation of wave amplitude, leaving the frequency unaltered; used especially in broadcasting (abbreviation **AM**).

ampoule (**am**-pool) *noun* a small sealed container holding a liquid, especially for injection. [from Latin *ampulla*]

amputate *verb* to cut off by surgical operation. **amputation** *noun*

amputee *noun* a person who has had a limb amputated.

Amritsar (am-**rit**-ser) a city in Punjab in NW India that is the centre of the Sikh faith and the site of its holiest temple.

Amsterdam the capital of the Netherlands.

amuck *adverb* = **amok**.

amulet (**am**-yŭ-lĕt) *noun* a thing worn as a charm against evil.

Amundsen (**ah**-muund-sĕn), Roald (1872–1928), Norwegian polar explorer, the first to reach the South Pole (December 1911).

amuse *verb* **1** to cause to laugh or smile. **2** to make time pass pleasantly for. **amusement** *noun*, **amusingly** *adverb* [from French *amuser* = distract]

amygdale (ă-**mig**-dayl) *noun* a small cavity in an igneous rock, filled with another mineral such as quartz. [from Greek, = almond]

amygdaloid (ă-**mig**-dă-loid) *noun* an igneous rock containing amygdales.

amylase (**am**-ĭ-layz) *noun* diastase.

an *adjective* the form of *a* used before vowel sounds, as in *an apple*, *an hour*, *an MA*, *an umbrella*.

an-¹ *prefix* see **a-²**.

an-² *prefix* see **ad-**.

ana- *prefix* up; back (as in *analysis*); again. [from Greek *ana* = up]

Anabaptist *noun* a member of any of various Protestant religious groups (especially in the 16th century) holding that only believing adults should be baptised.

anabolic (an-ă-**bol**-ik) *adjective* of anabolism. □ **anabolic steroid** a steroid hormone used to build up tissue.

anabolism (ă-**nab**-ŏ-lizm) *noun* the chemical changes in living organisms when complex substances are formed from simpler ones.

anabranch (**an**-ă-branch) *noun* (*Austral.*) a branch stream leaving a river and re-entering it lower down.

anachronism (ă-**nak**-rŏ-nizm) *noun*
1 a mistake in placing something into a particular historical period. **2** the thing wrongly placed. **3** a person, custom, or idea regarded as out of date. **anachronistic** (ă-nak-rŏ-**nis**-tik) *adjective* [from *ana-*, + Greek *khronos* = time]

anaconda (an-ă-**kon**-dă) *noun* a large South American boa.

anacrusis (an-ă-**kroo**-sĭs) *noun* (*plural* **anacruses**) (in music) an unstressed note or notes before the first bar line.

anaemia (ă-**nee**-mee-ă) *noun* lack of red corpuscles, or of their haemoglobin in blood. [from *an-¹* = without, + Greek *haima* = blood]

anaemic (ă-**nee**-mik) *adjective* **1** suffering from anaemia. **2** pale, weak in colour. **3** lacking vigour or positive characteristics.

anaerobic (an-air-**roh**-bik) *adjective* not using oxygen from the air, *anaerobic bacteria*. anaerobically *adverb*

anaesthesia (an-ĕs-**theez**-ee-ă) *noun* loss of sensation, especially that induced by anaesthetics.

anaesthetic (an-ĕs-**thet**-ik) *noun* a substance that produces loss of sensation and the ability to feel pain. – anaesthetic *adjective* having this effect. [from *an-*[1] = without, + Greek *aisthesis* = sensation]

anaesthetise (ă-**nees**-thĕ-tyz) *verb* (also -ize) to administer an anaesthetic to (a person etc.). anaesthetisation *noun*

anaesthetist (ă-**nees**-thĕ-tĭst) *noun* a person trained to administer anaesthetics.

anagram (**an**-ă-gram) *noun* a word or phrase formed from the rearranged letters of another word or phrase (*stripe* is an anagram of *priest*). [from *ana*, + Greek *gramma* = letter]

anal *adjective* of the anus.

analgesia (an-ăl-**jeez**-ee-ă) *noun* loss of ability to feel pain while still conscious.

analgesic (an-ăl-**jee**-zik) *adjective* relieving pain. – analgesic *noun* a drug that relieves pain. [from *an-*[1] = without, + Greek *algesis* = pain]

analog *adjective* (also analogue) using signals or information represented by a continuous usually variable quantity (compare *digital*). □ analog clock or watch one with hands or pointers which move continuously to show the time on a clock face (compare a *digital clock or watch* where the time changes by discrete jumps). analog signal one in which the size of the signal, e.g. voltage, represents the value transmitted.

analogous (ă-**nal**-ŏ-gŭs) *adjective* similar in certain respects. analogously *adverb*

analogue (**an**-ă-log) *noun* something that is analogous to something else. – analogue *adjective* = analog.

analogy (ă-**nal**-ŏ-jee) *noun* partial likeness between two things that are compared, *the analogy between the human heart and a pump*.

analyse *verb* **1** to separate (a substance etc.) into its parts in order to identify it or study its structure. **2** to examine and interpret, *tried to analyse the causes of their failure.*

3 to psychoanalyse. analysable *adjective* [from *ana-*, + Greek *lusis* = loosening]

analysis *noun* (*plural* analyses, *pr.* ă-**nal**-ĭ-seez) **1** analysing. **2** a statement of the result of this. **3** psychoanalysis.

analyst (**an**-ă-lĭst) *noun* **1** a person who is skilled in (especially chemical) analysis. **2** a psychoanalyst.

analytic (an-ă-**lit**-ik) *adjective* (also analytical) of or using analysis. analytically *adverb*

Anangu (**ah**-nah-ngoo) *noun* (*plural* same) an Aboriginal person from central Australia. [Western Desert Language, = person]

Usage see aborigine.

---

anapaest (**an**-ă-pest) *noun* a metrical foot with two short or unstressed syllables followed by one long or stressed syllable (as in the word *cigarette*).

anaphora (ă-**naf**-ŏ-ră) *noun* the use of a short word (such as *it* or *do*) to refer to a word recently used, e.g. in *Do you clean your oven regularly? I do it every Friday.*

anarchist (**an**-ă-kĭst) *noun* a person who believes that government is undesirable and should be abolished. anarchism *noun*, anarchistic (an-ă-**kis**-tik) *adjective*

anarchy (**an**-ă-kee) *noun* **1** absence of government or control, resulting in lawlessness. **2** disorder, confusion. anarchic (ă-**nar**-kik) *adjective*, anarchical *adjective* [from *an-*[1] = without, + Greek *arkhe* = rule]

anastigmatic (an-ă-stig-**mat**-ik) *adjective* free from astigmatism.

anathema (ă-**nath**-ĕ-mă) *noun* **1** a formal curse of the Church, excommunicating someone or condemning something as evil. **2** a detested person or thing, *conscription is anathema to him.*

Anatolia (an-ă-**toh**-lee-ă) = Asia Minor. Anatolian *adjective* & *noun*

anatomy *noun* **1** the scientific study of bodily structures. **2** the bodily structure of an animal or plant. anatomical (an-ă-**tom**-i-kăl) *adjective*, anatomically *adverb* [from *ana-*, + Greek *tome* = cutting]

ANC *abbreviation* African National Congress.

ancestor *noun* any of the persons from whom a person is descended, especially those more remote than grandparents. ancestral *adjective*

ancestry *noun* a line of ancestors.

anchor *noun* **1** a heavy metal structure used to moor a ship to the sea bottom or a balloon etc. to the ground; *at anchor*, moored by an anchor. **2** anything that gives stability or security. –**anchor** *verb* **1** to lower an anchor, to make secure with an anchor. **2** to fix firmly.

anchorage *noun* **1** a place where ships may anchor safely. **2** the charge for this.

anchorite (**ang**-kŏ-ryt) *noun* a hermit, a religious recluse. **anchoretic** *adjective*, **anchoress** *feminine noun*

anchorman *noun* **1** a person who plays a vital part (e.g. at the back of a tug-of-war team). **2** a person who coordinates activities, especially the compère in a TV or radio program. **anchorwoman** *feminine noun*

anchovy (**an**-chŏ-vee) *noun* a small rich-flavoured fish of the herring family.

ancient *adjective* **1** belonging to times long past; *the ancients*, people who lived in ancient times. **2** having lived or existed for a long time. ☐ **ancient history** history of the period before the end of the Western Roman Empire in AD 476.

ancillary (an-**sil**-ă-ree) *adjective* helping in a subsidiary way, *ancillary services*. [from Latin *ancilla* = servant]

and *conjunction* **1** together with, *bacon and eggs*. **2** then again repeatedly or increasingly, *gets better and better*; *goes on and on*. **3** added to, *two and two make four*. **4** (*informal*) to, *try and come*. **5** with this consequence; *move and I shoot*, if you move I shall shoot. ☐ **and/or** together with or as an alternative. (¶ This should be used only in technical, legal, commercial, or official documents.)

Andalusian (an-dă-**loo**-see-ăn) *adjective* of or relating to Andalusia in southern Spain.

andante (an-**dan**-tay) *adverb* (of music) in moderately slow time. –**andante** *noun* a movement to be played in this way. [Italian]

andantino (an-dan-**tee**-noh) *adverb* (of music) rather quicker than andante. –**andantino** *noun* a movement to be played in this way.

Andes a range of mountains in western South America. **Andean** (an-**dee**-ăn) *adjective*

andesite (**an**-dě-zyt) *noun* a fine-grained brown or greyish volcanic rock.

Andorra (an-**dor**-ră) a small autonomous principality in the southern Pyrenees, between France and Spain. **Andorran** *adjective* & *noun*

Andorra-la-Vella the capital of Andorra.

Andrew, St (1st century) an Apostle, the patron saint of Scotland. Feast day, 30 November.

andro- *prefix* men; male. [Greek]

android *noun* (in science fiction) a robot with human form. [from Greek *andros* = of a man]

Andromeda (an-**drom**-ĕ-dă) **1** (*Gk. legend*) a king's daughter who was fastened to a rock as a sacrifice to a sea monster, and was rescued by Perseus. **2** a northern constellation.

anecdotal (an-ĕk-**doh**-tăl) *adjective* in the nature of an anecdote; *anecdotal evidence*, hearsay evidence. [from Greek *anekdota* = things unpublished]

anecdote (**an**-ĕk-doht) *noun* a short amusing or interesting story about a real person or event.

anemometer (an-ĕ-**mom**-ĕ-ter) *noun* an instrument for measuring the force of wind. [from Greek *anemos* = wind, + *meter*]

anemone (ă-**nem**-ŏ-nee) *noun* a plant related to the buttercup, with white or brightly coloured flowers. ☐ **anemone fish** a small fish that lives in sea anemones. [from Greek, = wind-flower]

aneroid barometer (**an**-ĕ-roid) *noun* a barometer that measures air pressure by the action of air on the lid of a box containing a vacuum.

aneurysm (**an**-yŭ-rizm) *noun* (also **aneurism**) an abnormal enlargement of an artery. [from Greek *aneuruno* = to widen out]

anew *adverb* again; in a new or different way.

angel *noun* **1** an attendant or messenger of God, usually pictured as a being in human form with wings and dressed in long white robes. **2** a very beautiful or kind person. [from Greek *angelos* = messenger]

angelfish *noun* a fish with winglike fins.

angelic *adjective* of or like an angel. **angelically** *adverb*

angelica (an-**jel**-i-kă) *noun* **1** a fragrant plant used in cookery and medicine. **2** its candied stalks.

angelus (**an**-jě-lŭs) *noun* (in the RC Church) **1** a prayer to the Virgin Mary commemorating the Incarnation, said at morning, noon, and sunset. **2** a bell rung as a signal for this.

anger *noun* the strong feeling caused by extreme displeasure. –**anger** *verb* to make angry.

angina (an-**jy**-nă) *noun* (also angina pectoris) sharp pain in the chest caused by exertion when the heart is diseased. [Latin, = spasm (of the chest)]

angiosperm (**an**-jee-ŏ-sperm) *noun* a member of the group of flowering plants that have seeds enclosed in an ovary. [from Greek *angeion* = vessel, + *sperma* = seed]

Angkor (**ang**-kor) the capital of the ancient kingdom of Khmer, in NW Cambodia.

Angle *noun* a member of a North German tribe who came to England in the 5th century, founded kingdoms, and finally gave their name to England and the English.

angle¹ *noun* 1 the space between two lines or surfaces that meet. 2 a point of view. –angle *verb* 1 to move or place in a slanting position. 2 to present (news etc.) from a particular point of view.

angle² *verb* 1 to fish with hook and bait. 2 to try to obtain by hinting, *angling for an invitation*. angler *noun*

Anglican *adjective* of the Church of England or other Church in communion with it. –Anglican *noun* a member of the Anglican Church. Anglicanism *noun*

anglicise (**ang**-glĭ-syz) *verb* (also -ize) to make English in form or character.

Anglo- *prefix* English, British; *an Anglo-French agreement*, one between Britain and France. [from *Angle*]

Anglo-Catholic *adjective* of the section of the Anglican Church that stresses its unbroken connection with the early Christian Church and objects to being called Protestant. –Anglo-Catholic *noun* a member of this section of the Church.

Anglo-Celtic *adjective* descended from English or Celtic inhabitants of the British Isles. Anglo-Celt *noun*

Anglo-Saxon *noun* 1 an English person of the period before the Norman Conquest. 2 the English language of this period, also called *Old English*. 3 a person of English descent. –Anglo-Saxon *adjective* of the Anglo-Saxons or their language.

Angola (an-**goh**-lă) a republic on the west coast of Africa. Angolan *adjective* & *noun*

angophora (ang-**gof**-ŏ-ră) *noun* an Australian tree, closely related to eucalyptus, bearing white flowers.

angora *noun* 1 yarn or fabric made from the hair of angora goats or rabbits. 2 a long-haired variety of cat, goat, or rabbit.

angry *adjective* (angrier, angriest) 1 feeling or showing anger. 2 inflamed, *an angry sore*. angrily *adverb*

angst *noun* anxiety; a feeling of guilt or remorse.

ångström (**ang**-ström) *noun* a unit of length used in measuring wavelengths. [named after A. J. Ångström (1814–74), Swedish physicist]

Anguilla (ang-**gwil**-ă) an island in the West Indies, a self-governing dependency of the UK. Anguillan *adjective* & *noun*

anguish *noun* severe physical or mental pain.

anguished *adjective* feeling anguish.

angular *adjective* 1 having angles or sharp corners. 2 lacking plumpness or smoothness. 3 measured by angle; *angular distance*, the distance between two objects measured as an angle from a given point. angularity (ang-gew-**la**-rĭ-tee) *noun*

anhydrous *adjective* (in chemistry) without water.

aniline (**an**-ĭ-leen) *noun* an oily liquid obtained from nitrobenzene, used in the manufacture of dyes and plastics.

animadvert (an-ĭ-mad-**vert**) *verb* to make hostile criticisms. animadversion *noun*

animal *noun* 1 a living thing that can feel and move voluntarily. 2 such a being other than a human being. 3 a four-footed animal distinguished from a bird or fish or reptile or insect. 4 a brutish or uncivilised person. –animal *adjective* of, from, or relating to animal life.□ animal liberation a movement aiming to free animals from exploitation by humans, especially in scientific research. [from Latin *animalis* = having breath]

animalcule (an-ĭ-**mal**-kewl) *noun* a microscopic animal.

animalism *noun* 1 the nature and activity of animals. 2 the belief that humans are not superior to other animals. 3 concern with physical matters; sensuality.

animate (**an**-ĭ-măt) *adjective* living. –animate (**an**-ĭ-mayt) *verb* 1 to give life or movement to, to make lively, *an animated discussion*. 2 to motivate, *he was animated by loyalty*. 3 to produce as an animated cartoon. □ animated cartoon a film made by photographing a series of drawings, giving an illusion of movement. animator *noun*

animation *noun* **1** animating. **2** liveliness. **3** a technique of film-making by photographing a sequence of drawings etc. to create the illusion of movement; the manipulation of electronic images using a computer to create moving images.

anime (**an**-ĭ-may) *noun* Japanese animation, often intended for mature audiences.

animism *noun* belief that all beings and things such as rocks, streams, and winds have a living soul. **animistic** *adjective*

animosity (an-ĭ-**mos**-ĭ-tee) *noun* a spirit of hostility.

animus (**an**-ĭ-mŭs) *noun* animosity shown in speech or action.

anion (**an**-I-ŏn) *noun* an ion with a negative charge. **anionic** (an-I-**on**-ik) *adjective*

aniseed *noun* the sweet-smelling seed of the plant anise, used for flavouring.

Ankara (**ang**-kă-ră) the capital of Turkey.

ankle *noun* **1** the joint connecting the foot with the leg. **2** the slender part between this and the calf.

anklet *noun* an ornamental chain or band worn around the ankle.

annals (**an**-ălz) *plural noun* a history of events year by year, historical records. **annalistic** (an-ă-**lis**-tik) *adjective* [from Latin *annales* = yearly books]

Annapurna (an-ă-**per**-nă) a ridge of the Himalayas, in north central Nepal; rising to 8078 metres.

Anne[1] (1665–1714) queen of Great Britain and Ireland 1702–14.

Anne[2], St (in Christian tradition) the mother of the Virgin Mary. Feast day, 26 July.

Anne Boleyn *see* Boleyn.

Anne of Cleves (1515–57) the fourth wife of Henry VIII.

anneal (ă-**neel**) *verb* to toughen (glass or metal) by heating it and then cooling it slowly.

annelid (**an**-ĕ-lid) *noun* a worm (such as an earthworm) with a segmented body.

annex (ă-**neks**) *verb* **1** to add or join to a larger thing. **2** to take possession of, *to annex territory*. **annexation** *noun* [from *an-*[2], + Latin *nexum* = tied]

annexe (**an**-eks) *noun* a supplementary building or one attached to a larger one or forming a subordinate part of a main building.

annihilate (ă-**ny**-ĭ-layt) *verb* to destroy completely. **annihilation** *noun*, **annihilator** *noun* [from *an-*[2], + Latin *nihil* = nothing]

anniversary *noun* the yearly return of the date of an event; a celebration of this. [from Latin *annus* = year, + *versum* = turned]

Anno Domini (an-oh **dom**-ĭ-ny) *adverb* in the year of Our Lord (usually shortened to AD). [Latin]

annotate (**an**-ŏ-tayt) *verb* to add notes of explanation to. **annotation** *noun*

announce *verb* **1** to make known publicly or to an audience. **2** to make known the presence or arrival of. **announcement** *noun* [from *an-*[2] + Latin *nuntius* = messenger]

announcer *noun* a person who announces items in a broadcast.

annoy *verb* **1** to cause slight anger to. **2** to be troublesome to, to harass. **annoyance** *noun* [from Latin *in odio* = hateful]

annoyed *adjective* slightly angry.

annual *adjective* **1** coming or happening once every year. **2** of one year, reckoned by the year, *her annual income*. **3** lasting only one year or season, *annual plants*. –**annual** *noun* **1** a plant that lives for one year or one season. **2** a book or periodical published in yearly issues. **annually** *adverb* [from Latin *annus* = year]

annualised *adjective* (also -**ized**) (of rates of interest, inflation, etc.) calculated on an annual basis from information about figures given for a shorter period.

annuity (ă-**new**-ĭ-tee) *noun* a fixed annual allowance, especially one provided by a form of investment. [same origin as *annual*]

annul (ă-**nul**) *verb* (**annulled**, **annulling**) to make null and void, to destroy the validity of, *to annul a marriage*. [from *an-*[2], + Latin *nullus* = none]

annular (**an**-yŭ-ler) *adjective* ring-like.

annulus (**an**-yŭ-lŭs) *noun* (*plural* annuli, *pr.* -ly *or* -lee) the ring-shaped space between two concentric circles.

Annunciation *noun* **1** the announcement by the angel Gabriel to the Virgin Mary that she was to be the mother of Christ. **2** the festival commemorating this (25 March; also called *Lady Day*).

anode (**an**-ohd) *noun* the electrode by which current enters a device. [from *ana-* = up, + Greek *hodos* = way]

anodise (**an**-ŏ-dyz) *verb* (also **-ize**) to coat (metal) with a protective layer by electrolysis.

anodyne (**an**-ŏ-dyn) *noun* **1** a drug that relieves pain. **2** anything that relieves pain or distress.

anoint *verb* **1** to apply ointment or oil to, especially as a sign of consecration. **2** to smear or rub with grease.

anomaly (ă-**nom**-ă-lee) *noun* something that deviates from the general rule or the usual type, an irregularity or inconsistency, *anomalies in our tax system.* **anomalous** *adjective* [from *an-*[1] = not, + Greek *homalos* = even]

anon (ă-**non**) *adverb* (*old use*) soon, presently, *I will say more of this anon.*

anon. *abbreviation* anonymous (author).

anonymity (an-ŏ-**nim**-ĭ-tee) *noun* being anonymous.

anonymous (ă-**non**-ĭ-mŭs) *adjective* **1** with a name that is not known or not made public, *an anonymous donor.* **2** written or given by such a person, *an anonymous gift*; *an anonymous letter*, one that is not signed. **anonymously** *adverb* [from *an-*[1] = not, + Greek *onoma* = name]

anopheles (ă-**nof**-ĕ-leez) *noun* a species of mosquito that can carry the malaria parasite. [from Greek, = unprofitable]

anorak (**an**-ŏ-rak) *noun* a jacket (usually with a hood attached), worn as a protection against rain, wind, and cold. [from an Eskimo word]

anorexia (an-ŏ-**reks**-ee-ă) *noun* lack of appetite for food, especially (in full **anorexia nervosa**) a medical condition characterised by an obsessive desire to lose weight and refusal to eat normally. **anorexic** *adjective* & *noun* [from *an-*[1] = not, + Greek *orexis* = appetite]

another *adjective* **1** additional, one more; *he is another Solomon*, one like him. **2** different, *fit another pipe, this one leaks.* **3** some or any other, *will not do another man's work.* –**another** *pronoun* another person or thing.

answer *noun* something said or written or needed or done to deal with a question, accusation, or problem. –**answer** *verb* **1** to make an answer to; to say, write, or do something in return; *answer the door*, go to it in response to a signal; *he answers to the name of Thomas*, is so called. **2** to suffice or be suitable for, *this will answer the purpose.* **3** to take responsibility, to vouch, *I will answer for his honesty*; *they must answer for their crimes*, must justify them or pay the penalty.

4 to correspond, *this bag answers to the description of the stolen one.* □ **answer back** to answer a rebuke cheekily. **answering machine** a machine that answers telephone calls by repeating a recorded message and recording the caller's reply.

answerable *adjective* **1** able to be answered. **2** having to account for something.

ant *noun* a very small insect of which there are many species, all of which form and live in highly organised groups.

ant- *prefix* see **anti-**.

antacid (an-**tass**-ĭd) *noun* a substance that prevents or corrects acidity.

antagonise *verb* (also **-ize**) to arouse antagonism in.

antagonism (an-**tag**-ŏ-nizm) *noun* active opposition, hostility. [from *ant-*, + Greek *agon* = struggle]

antagonist (an-**tag**-ŏ-nĭst) *noun* an opponent, one who is hostile to something.

antagonistic (an-tag-ŏ-**nis**-tik) *adjective* **1** showing or feeling antagonism. **2** (of a muscle) producing a movement opposite to that of another. **antagonistically** *adverb*

Antananarivo (an-tă-nan-ă-**ree**-voh) the capital of Madagascar.

Antarctic *adjective* of the regions round the South Pole. –**Antarctic** *noun* **1** these regions. **2** the Southern Ocean, the sea surrounding Antarctica. □ **Antarctic Circle** the line of latitude 66° 33′ S.

Antarctica the continent mainly within the Antarctic Circle.

ante (**an**-tee) *noun* a stake put up by a poker player before drawing new cards. –**ante** *verb* to put up an ante, to pay up.

ante- (**an**-tee) *prefix* before (as in *ante-room*). [from Latin]

anteater *noun* an animal that feeds on ants and termites, including the echidna (= spiny anteater) and the numbat (= banded anteater).

antecedent (an-tĕ-**see**-dĕnt) *noun* **1** a preceding thing or circumstance, *the war and its antecedents*; *I know nothing of his antecedents*, of his ancestry or past life. **2** a noun or clause or sentence to which a following pronoun refers (in *the book which I have*, 'book' is the antecedent of 'which'). –**antecedent** *adjective* previous. [from *ante-*, + Latin *cedere* = go]

antechamber *noun* an ante-room.

antechinus (an-tee-**ky**-nŭs) *noun* (*plural* antechinuses) an Australian marsupial mouse.

antedate *verb* **1** to put an earlier date on (a document) than that on which it was issued. **2** to precede in time.

antediluvian (an-tee-dĭ-**loo**-vee-ăn) *adjective* **1** of the time before Noah's Flood. **2** (*informal*) utterly out of date. [from *ante-*, + Latin *diluvium* = deluge]

antelope *noun* a swift-running animal (e.g. chamois, gazelle) resembling a deer, found especially in Africa.

antenatal *adjective* **1** before birth. **2** before giving birth; *antenatal clinic*, for pregnant women.

antenna *noun* **1** (*plural* antennae, *pr.* an-**ten**-ee) each of a pair of flexible sensitive projections on the heads of insects, crustaceans, etc., a feeler. **2** (*plural* antennas) an aerial.

antepenultimate (an-tee-pĕ-**nul**-tĭ-măt) *adjective* last but two.

anterior *adjective* coming before in position or time. [Latin, = further forward]

ante-room *noun* a room leading to a more important one.

anthem *noun* **1** a short musical composition to be sung in religious services, often with words taken from the Bible. **2** a solemn song of praise or loyalty identified with a country, organisation, etc., *national anthem*.

anther *noun* the part of a flower's stamen that contains pollen.

anthill *noun* a mound over an ants' nest.

anthology (an-**thol**-ŏ-jee) *noun* a collection of passages from literature, especially poems. anthologist *noun* [from Greek *anthos* = flower, + *-logia* = collection]

anthracite *noun* a hard form of coal that burns with little flame or smoke.

anthrax *noun* a disease of sheep and cattle that can be transmitted to people.

anthropoid (**an**-thrŏ-poid) *adjective* human in form. –anthropoid *noun* an anthropoid ape such as a gorilla or chimpanzee. [from Greek *anthropos* = human being]

anthropologist *noun* an expert in anthropology.

anthropology (an-thrŏ-**pol**-ŏ-jee) *noun* the scientific study of mankind, especially of human origins, development, customs, and beliefs. anthropological (an-thrŏ-pŏ-**loj**-i-kăl)

adjective, anthropologically *adverb* [from Greek *anthropos* = human being, + *-logy*]

anthropomorphic (an-thrŏ-pŏ-**mor**-fik) *adjective* attributing human form or personality to a god or animal or object. anthropomorphism *noun*

anthropomorphous (an-thrŏ-pŏ-**mor**-fŭs) *adjective* in human form.

anti *noun* (*plural* antis) a person who opposes a certain policy etc. –anti *preposition* opposed to.

anti- *prefix* (changing to ant- before a vowel) **1** against, opposed to, *anti-slavery*. **2** preventing, counteracting, *antiperspirant*. [from Greek *anti* = against]

anti-aircraft *adjective* used against enemy aircraft.

antibiotic (an-tee-by-**ot**-ik) *noun* a substance capable of destroying or preventing the growth of bacteria. –antibiotic *adjective* functioning in this way. [from *anti-*, + Greek *bios* = life]

antibody (**an**-tee-bod-ee) *noun* a protein formed in the blood in reaction to certain substances, which it then attacks and destroys.

antic *noun* **1** an absurd movement intended to cause amusement. **2** odd or foolish behaviour.

Antichrist *noun* an enemy of Christ.

anticipate *verb* **1** to deal with or use before the proper time; *anticipate one's income*, spend it before receiving it. **2** to take action before someone else has had time to do so, *others may have anticipated Columbus in the discovery of America*. **3** to notice what needs doing and take action in advance; *anticipate someone's needs*, provide for them in advance; *the boxer anticipated the blow*, saw it coming and blocked it. **4** to expect, *we anticipate that it will rain*. anticipation *noun* [from *ante-*, + Latin *capere* = take]

Usage The use of *anticipate* in sense 4 is common in informal use, but some people regard it as incorrect.

---

anticipatory (an-tiss-ĭ-**pay**-tŏ-ree) *adjective* showing anticipation.

anticlimax *noun* a disappointing ending or outcome of events where a climax was expected.

anticline *noun* a land formation in which strata are folded so that they slope down on opposite sides of a ridge (contrasting with a *syncline*). anticlinal *adjective*

34

anticlockwise *adverb* & *adjective* moving in a curve from right to left, as seen from the centre of the circle.

anticyclone *noun* an area in which atmospheric pressure is high, producing fine settled weather, with an outward flow of air.

antidote (an-tee-doht) *noun* **1** a substance that counteracts the effects of a poison or a disease. **2** anything that counteracts unpleasant effects. [from *anti-*, + Greek *dotos* = given]

antifreeze *noun* a substance added to water to lower its freezing point and therefore make it less likely to freeze.

antigen (**an**-tĭ-jĕn) *noun* a substance (e.g. a toxin) that causes the body to produce antibodies. [from *anti-*, + Greek *-genes* = born]

Antigone (an-**tig**-ŏ-nee) (*Gk. legend*) the daughter of Oedipus and Jocasta, condemned to death for burying the body of her brother against King Creon's order.

Antigua and Barbuda (an-**tee**-gă, bar-**boo**-dă) a country consisting of two of the Leeward Islands in the West Indies. **Antiguan** *adjective* & *noun*, **Barbudan** *adjective* & *noun*

anti-hero *noun* a central character in a story or drama who noticeably lacks conventional heroic attitudes.

antihistamine (an-tee-**hiss**-tă-meen) *noun* a substance that counteracts the effects of histamine, used in treating allergies.

Antilles (an-**til**-eez) a group of islands forming the greater part of the West Indies.

antilogarithm *noun* the number to which a given logarithm belongs.

antimacassar (an-tee-mă-**kas**-er) *noun* a small protective cover for the backs or arms of chairs etc. [originally a protection against the Macassar oil that was used on hair]

antimony (**an**-tĭ-mŏ-nee) *noun* a chemical element (symbol Sb), a brittle silvery metal used in alloys.

antinode *noun* a point where the amplitude is greatest in a vibrating string etc.

antioxidant *noun* **1** an agent that inhibits oxidation. **2** a substance (e.g. vitamin C or E) that removes potentially damaging oxidising agents in an organism.

antiparticle *noun* an elementary particle having the same mass as a given particle but an opposite electric charge or magnetic effect.

antipasto (an-tee-**pah**-stoh) *noun* (*plural* **antipasti**) an Italian hors d'oeuvre. [from Italian *anti* = before, + *pasto* = food]

antipathy (an-**tip**-ă-thee) *noun* **1** a strong and settled dislike. **2** the object of this. [from *anti-*, + Greek *pathos* = feeling]

antiperspirant (an-tee-**per**-spĭ-rănt) *noun* a substance that prevents or reduces sweating.

antipodes (an-**tip**-ŏ-deez) *plural noun* places on opposite sides of the earth; **the Antipodes** the Australasian regions, almost diametrically opposite Europe. **antipodean** (an-tip-ŏ-**dee**-ăn) *adjective* [from Greek, = having the feet opposite (*pod-* = foot)]

antipope *noun* a person set up as pope in opposition to one held by his supporters to be rightfully elected.

antiquary (**an**-tĭ-kwă-ree) *noun* one who studies or collects antiques or antiquities. **antiquarian** (an-tĭ-**kwair**-ree-ăn) *adjective* & *noun*

antiquated (**an**-tĭ-kway-tĕd) *adjective* old-fashioned, out of date.

antique (an-**teek**) *adjective* belonging to the distant past, in the style of past times. **–antique** *noun* an antique object, especially furniture or a decorative object of a kind sought by collectors. [from Latin *antiquus* = ancient]

antiquity (an-**tik**-wĭ-tee) *noun* ancient times, especially before the Middle Ages; *it is of great antiquity*, is very old. **antiquities** *plural noun* objects dating from ancient times.

anti-Semitic (an-tee-sĕ-**mit**-ik) *adjective* hostile to Jews. **anti-Semitism** (an-tee-**sem**-ĭ-tizm) *noun* hostility to Jews.

antiseptic *adjective* **1** preventing the growth of bacteria etc. that cause things to become septic. **2** thoroughly clean and free from germs. **–antiseptic** *noun* a substance with an antiseptic effect. **antiseptically** *adverb*

antisocial *adjective* **1** opposed to the social institutions and laws of an organised community. **2** interfering with amenities enjoyed by others. **3** unsociable, withdrawing oneself from others. **antisocially** *adverb*

antistatic *adjective* counteracting the effects of static electricity.

antistrophe (an-**tiss**-trŏ-fee) *noun* the second of a group of three stanzas (*strophe, antistrophe, epode*) sung by the chorus in ancient Greek drama.

antithesis (an-**tith**-ĕ-sĭs) *noun* (*plural* **antitheses**) **1** the direct opposite of something, opposition or contrast, *slavery is the antithesis of freedom*. **2** contrast of ideas emphasised by the choice of words or by their arrangement. **antithetic** (an-tĭ-**thet**-ik) *adjective*, **antithetical** *adjective*, **antithetically** *adverb* [from *anti*-, + Greek *thesis* = placing]

antitoxin *noun* a substance that neutralises a toxin and prevents it from having a harmful effect. **antitoxic** *adjective*

antitrade *adjective* & *noun* an **antitrade wind**, a wind blowing in the opposite direction to a trade wind and at a higher altitude.

antivenin *noun* (also **antivenene** or **antivenom**) a blood serum containing antibodies against specific poisons in the venom of snakes, spiders, etc.

antivivisectionist *noun* a person who is opposed to making experiments on live animals.

antler *noun* a branched horn, one of a pair of these on a stag or other deer. **antlered** *adjective*

Antony, Mark (c. 83–30 BC), Roman general and politician, a supporter of Julius Caesar.

antonym (**an**-tŏ-nim) *noun* a word that is opposite in meaning to another. [from *ant*-, + Greek *onoma* = name]

Anubis (ă-**new**-bĭs) the ancient Egyptian god of mummification, protector of tombs, usually represented as a seated dog or with a dog's head.

anus (**ay**-nŭs) *noun* the opening at the end of the alimentary canal, through which waste matter passes out of the body.

anvil *noun* **1** a block of iron on which a smith hammers metal into shape. **2** a bone in the middle ear. [from Old English *an* = on, + *filt*- = beat]

anxiety *noun* **1** the state of being anxious. **2** something causing this.

anxious *adjective* **1** troubled and uneasy in mind. **2** causing worry, filled with such feeling, *an anxious moment*. **3** eager, *anxious to please*. **anxiously** *adverb*

any *adjective* **1** one or some (but no matter which) from three or more or from a quantity. **2** every, whichever you choose, *any fool knows that*. **3** in a significant amount, *did not stay any length of time*. –**any** *pronoun* any person or thing or amount, *can't find any of them*; *we haven't any*. –**any** *adverb* at all, in

some degree, *isn't any better*. □ **any amount** or **any number** much, many.

anybody *noun* & *pronoun* **1** any person. **2** a person of importance, *is he anybody?*

anyhow *adverb* **1** anyway. **2** not in an orderly manner, *work was done all anyhow*.

anyone *noun* & *pronoun* anybody.

anything *noun* & *pronoun* any thing, *anything will do*; *as easy as anything*, very easy. □ **anything but** far from being, *it's anything but cheap*. **like anything** with great intensity.

anyway *adverb* in any case.

Usage Where the sense is 'in any way or manner', *any way* is written as two separate words, as in *do it any way you like*.

---

anywhere *adverb* in or to any place. –**anywhere** *pronoun* any place.

Anzac *noun* **1** a member of the Australian and New Zealand Army Corps (1914–18). **2** an Australian or a New Zealand soldier or ex-soldier. □ **Anzac biscuit** a biscuit whose ingredients include rolled oats, golden syrup, and coconut. **Anzac Day** 25 April, a public holiday in Australia and New Zealand commemorating the anniversary of the Anzac landing at Gallipoli in 1915. [from the initial letters of the Corps]

ANZUS Treaty an alliance formed in 1951 of Australia, New Zealand, and the USA for the security of the Pacific region. New Zealand withdrew from ANZUS in 1985 when it refused to allow visits by nuclear armed or powered war ships. [named from the initials of these countries]

AO *abbreviation* Officer of the Order of Australia.

aorist (**ay**-ŏ-rist) *noun* a past tense (especially in Greek) that does not specify how long the action of the verb continued.

aorta (ay-**or**-tă) *noun* the great artery through which blood is carried from the left side of the heart. **aortic** *adjective*

ap-¹ *prefix* see **ad**-.

ap-² *prefix* see **apo**-.

apace *adverb* swiftly, *work proceeded apace*.

Apache (ă-**pach**-ee) *noun* **1** a member of an indigenous North American people inhabiting the south-western part of the USA. **2** their language.

apart *adverb* **1** aside, separately, to or at a distance; *cannot tell them apart*, cannot distinguish one from the other. **2** into pieces, *it came apart*. □ **apart from** independently of, other than. [from French *à* = to, + *part* = side]

apartheid (ă-**pah**-tayt) *noun* a policy or system (especially formerly in South Africa) of racial segregation. [Afrikaans, = being apart]

apartment *noun* **1** a set of rooms. **2** a private residence that is one of several in a building; a home unit or flat.

apathy (**ap**-ă-thee) *noun* lack of interest or concern. **apathetic** (apă-**thet**-ik) *adjective*, **apathetically** *adverb* [from *a-²* = without, + Greek *pathos* = feeling]

apatosaurus (ă-pah-tŏ-**saw**-rŭs) *noun* (*plural* **apatosauruses**) a large plant-eating dinosaur, formerly called *brontosaurus*. [from Greek *apatē* = deceit, + *sauros* = lizard]

ape *noun* any of the four primates (gorilla, chimpanzee, orang-utan, gibbon) most closely related to man. –**ape** *verb* to imitate, to mimic.

APEC *abbreviation* Asia-Pacific Economic Cooperation.

apeman *noun* a supposed extinct creature intermediate between apes and men.

Apennines (**ap**-ĕ-nynz) a mountain range in Italy.

aperient (ă-**peer**-ree-ĕnt) *adjective* laxative. –**aperient** *noun* a laxative medicine. [from Latin *aperiens* = opening]

aperitif (ă-**pe**-rĭ-teef) *noun* an alcoholic drink taken as an appetiser. [French]

aperture *noun* an opening, especially one that admits light. [from Latin *aperire* = to open]

apex (**ay**-peks) *noun* (*plural* **apexes**) the tip or highest point, the pointed end, *the apex of a triangle*.

aphelion (ap-**hee**-lee-ŏn *or* ă-**fee**-lee-ŏn) *noun* (*plural* **aphelia**) the point in a planet's or comet's orbit when it is furthest from the sun (contrasts with *perihelion*).

aphid (**ay**-fĭd) *noun* a plant louse such as a greenfly or blackfly.

aphis (**ay**-fĭss) *noun* (*plural* **aphides**, *pr.* **ay**-fĭ-deez) an aphid.

aphorism (**af**-ŏ-rizm) *noun* a short wise saying, a maxim.

aphrodisiac (af-rŏ-**diz**-ee-ak) *adjective* arousing sexual desire. –**aphrodisiac** *noun* an aphrodisiac substance.

Aphrodite (af-rŏ-**dy**-tee) (*Gk. myth.*) the goddess of beauty, fertility, and sexual love, identified by the Romans with Venus.

Apia (**ah**-pee-ă) the capital of Samoa.

apiary (**ay**-pee-ă-ree) *noun* a place with a number of hives where bees are kept. **apiarist** *noun* [from Latin *apis* = bee]

apiece *adverb* to each, for or by each one of a group, *cost a dollar apiece*.

aplomb (ă-**plom**) *noun* dignity and confidence. [from French, = straight as a plumb line]

apo- *prefix* (changing to **ap-** before a vowel or *h*) from; out or away (as in *Apostle*). [from Greek *apo* = away from]

Apocalypse (ă-**pok**-ă-lips) *noun* the *Revelation of St John the Divine*, the last book in the New Testament, containing a prophetic description of the end of the world. –**apocalypse** *noun* great and dramatic events like those in the Apocalypse.

apocalyptic (ă-pok-ă-**lip**-tik) *adjective* of or like an apocalypse; prophesying events of this kind. **apocalyptically** *adverb*

Apocrypha (ă-**pok**-rĭ-fă) *noun* those books of the Old Testament that were not accepted by Jews as part of the Hebrew Scriptures and were excluded from the Protestant Bible at the Reformation. **Apocryphal** *adjective*

apocryphal (ă-**pok**-rĭ-făl) *adjective* unlikely to be true, *an apocryphal account of his travels*. **apocryphally** *adverb* [from the *Apocrypha*]

apodosis (ă-**pod**-ŏ-sĭs) *noun* (*plural* **apodoses**) the clause that indicates the consequence in a sentence expressing a condition, e.g. 'I shall fire' in *if you move, I shall fire*. [from Greek *apodidonai* = give back]

apogee (**ap**-ŏ-jee) *noun* **1** the point in the orbit of the moon or any planet when it is at its furthest point from earth. **2** the highest or most distant point, a climax. [from *apo-*, + Greek *ge* = earth]

apolitical (ay-pŏ-**lit**-i-kăl) *adjective* not political, not concerned with politics.

Apollo **1** (*Gk. myth.*) a god associated with the sun, music, and prophecy, represented in art as the ideal type of manly beauty. **2** the American space program for landing men on the moon, which ended in 1974 after several successful landings.

apologetic *adjective* making an apology. **apologetics** *plural noun* a reasoned defence, especially of Christianity. **apologetically** *adverb*

apologise *verb* (also **-ize**) to make an apology.

apologist *noun* a person who explains or defends a doctrine by reasoned argument.

apology *noun* 1 a statement of regret for having done wrong or hurt someone's feelings. 2 an explanation or defence of one's beliefs. 3 a poor or scanty specimen, *this feeble apology for a meal*. [from Greek *apologia* = a speech in your own defence]

apophthegm (**ap**-ŏ-them) *noun* a terse or pithy saying.

apoplectic (ap-ŏ-**plek**-tik) *adjective* 1 of apoplexy. 2 suffering from apoplexy. 3 (*informal*) liable to fits of rage in which the face becomes very red. **apoplectically** *adverb*

apoplexy (**ap**-ŏ-plek-see) *noun* sudden inability to feel and move, caused by a blockage or rupture of an artery in the brain; a stroke. [from Greek, = a stroke]

apostate (ă-**poss**-tayt) *noun* a person who renounces his or her former belief, principles, or party. **apostasy** (ă-**poss**-tă-see) *noun* [from Greek *apostates* = deserter]

apostatise (ă-**poss**-tă-tyz) *verb* (also **-ize**) to become apostate.

a posteriori (ay pos-teer-ree-**or**-ry) *adjective* (of reasoning) inductive; proceeding from effect to cause. [Latin, = from what comes after.]

Apostle *noun* any of the twelve men sent forth by Christ to preach the Gospel. –**apostle** *noun* a leader or teacher of a new faith or movement. □ **apostle bird** an Australian bird that builds its nest of mud, and is found in flocks of about twelve. [from Greek *apostellein* = send out]

apostolic (ap-ŏ-**stol**-ik) *adjective* 1 of the Apostles or their teaching. 2 of the pope as successor to St Peter. □ **apostolic succession** transmission of spiritual authority from the Apostles through successive popes and bishops.

apostrophe (ă-**pos**-trŏ-fee) *noun* 1 the sign (') used to show that letters or numbers have been omitted (as in *can't* = cannot; '05 = 1905), or showing the possessive case (*the boy's book*, *the boys' books*), or the plurals of letters (*there are two l's in 'Bell'*). 2 a part of a speech or a poem etc. addressed to an absent person or an abstract idea. [from *apo-*, + Greek *strophe* = turning]

apostrophise (ă-**pos**-trŏ-fyz) *verb* (also **-ize**) to address in an apostrophe.

apothecary (ă-**poth**-ĕ-kă-ree) *noun* (*old use*) a pharmaceutical chemist.

apotheosis (ă-poth-ee-**oh**-sĭs) *noun* 1 deification. 2 a thing's highest development; a sublime example. [from *apo-*, + Greek *theos* = god]

appal (ă-**pawl**) *verb* (**appalled**, **appalling**) to fill with horror or dismay, to shock deeply. [from Old French *apalir* = become pale]

appalling *adjective* (*informal*) shocking, unpleasant.

apparatus *noun* 1 the equipment used for doing something; the instruments etc. used in scientific experiments. 2 the equipment (e.g. vaulting horse, parallel bars, etc.) used in gymnastics. 3 a group of bodily organs by which some natural process is carried out, *the digestive apparatus*. 4 a complex (especially political) organisation.

apparel *noun* (*formal*) clothing.

apparent (ă-**pa**-rĕnt) *adjective* 1 clearly seen or understood; *it became apparent*, became obvious. 2 seeming but not real, *his reluctance was only apparent*. □ **heir apparent** *see* **heir**. **apparently** *adverb* [same origin as *appear*]

apparition (ap-ă-**rish**-ŏn) *noun* 1 an appearance; something that appears, especially something remarkable or unexpected. 2 a ghost.

appeal *verb* (**appealed**, **appealing**) 1 to make an earnest or formal request, *appealed for contributions*. 2 to ask a person or go to a recognised authority for an opinion, *appealed to the chairman*; (in cricket) to ask the umpire to declare a batsman 'out'. 3 to take a case to a higher court for judicial review of a lower court's decision, to take (a case) in this way. 4 to offer attraction, to seem pleasing, *dogs don't appeal to him*. –**appeal** *noun* 1 the act of appealing. 2 the referral of a case to a higher court. 3 attraction, pleasantness. 4 a request for public donations to a cause.

appear *verb* 1 to become or be visible. 2 to present oneself, especially formally or publicly, *the school choir appeared at the Town Hall*. 3 to act as counsel in a lawcourt, *I appear for the defendant*. 4 to be published, *the story appeared in the newspapers*. 5 to give a certain impression, *you appear to* *have forgotten.* [from Latin *apparere* = come in sight]

appearance *noun* 1 appearing; *made its appearance*, appeared. 2 an outward sign, what something appears to be, *has an appearance of prosperity*.
□ keep up appearances to keep an outward show of prosperity or good behaviour.

appease *verb* to make calm or quiet by making concessions and by satisfying demands. appeasement *noun* [from French *à* = to, + *paix* = peace]

appellant (ă-**pel**-ănt) *noun* a person making an appeal to a higher court.

appellation (ap-ĕ-**lay**-shŏn) *noun* 1 naming. 2 a name or title.

append *verb* 1 to attach. 2 to add at the end, *append one's signature*. [from *ap-*¹, + Latin *pendere* = hang]

appendage (ă-**pen**-dij) *noun* a thing added to or forming a natural part of something larger or more important.

appendicitis *noun* inflammation of the appendix of the intestine.

appendix *noun* 1 (*plural* appendices) a section with supplementary information at the end of a book or document. 2 (*plural* appendixes) a small blind tube of tissue forming an outgrowth of the intestine. [same origin as *append*]

appertain (ap-er-**tayn**) *verb* to pertain.

appetiser *noun* (also -izer) something eaten or drunk to stimulate the appetite.

appetising *adjective* (also -izing) stimulating the appetite, *an appetising smell.* appetisingly *adverb*

appetite *noun* 1 physical desire, especially for food. 2 a desire or liking, *an appetite for power.* [from *ap-*¹, + Latin *petere* = seek]

applaud *verb* 1 to show approval of (a thing) by clapping one's hands. 2 to praise, *we applaud your decision.* [from *ap-*¹, + Latin *plaudere* = clap hands]

applause *noun* 1 hand-clapping by people applauding. 2 warm approval.

apple *noun* 1 a round fruit with firm juicy flesh. 2 the tree that bears this.
□ apple of one's eye a cherished person or thing. apple-pie bed a bed made (as a joke) with the sheets folded short, so that the legs do not fit. apple-pie order perfect order. she's apples (*Austral. informal*) everything's all

right. upset the apple cart to spoil carefully laid plans.

applet *noun* a small computer program.

appliance *noun* a device, an instrument.

applicable (**ap**-lik-ă-bŭl) *adjective* able to be applied, appropriate. applicability (ă-plik-ă-**bil**-ĭ-tee) *noun*

applicant (**ap**-lĭ-kănt) *noun* a person who applies, especially for a job.

application *noun* 1 applying something, putting one thing on another, *ointment for external application only.* 2 the thing applied. 3 making a formal request; the request itself, *his application was refused.* 4 bringing a rule into use; putting something to practical use; relevance. 5 the ability to apply oneself. 6 a computer program or set of programs designed for a particular purpose.

applicator *noun* a device for applying something.

applied *see* apply. – applied *adjective* put to practical use; *applied science, applied mathematics*, these subjects used in a practical way (e.g. in engineering), not merely theoretical.

appliqué (**ap**-lĭ-kay) *noun* 1 a piece of cut-out material sewn or fixed ornamentally to another. 2 needlework of this kind. – appliqué *verb* (appliquéd, appliquéing) to ornament with appliqué. [French, = put on]

apply *verb* (applied, applying) 1 to put (a thing) into contact with another; to spread on a surface. 2 to bring into use or action, *apply economic sanctions*; *this name was applied to them*, was used in describing or referring to them. 3 to put into effect, to be relevant, *the rules must be applied in every case*; *what I said does not apply to you.* 4 to make a formal request, *to apply for a job.* □ apply oneself to give one's attention and energy to a task.

appoggiatura (ă-poj-ă-**toor**-ră) *noun* a grace note played or sung on the beat, taking time from the main note and so delaying it. [Italian]

appoint *verb* 1 to choose (a person) for a job; to set up by choosing members, *appoint a committee.* 2 to fix or decide by authority, *they appointed a time for the next meeting.*
□ well-appointed *adjective* well equipped or furnished.

appointee *noun* the person appointed.

appointment *noun* 1 an arrangement to meet or visit at a particular time. 2 appointing

a person to a job; the person appointed.
3 the job or position itself. **appointments**
plural noun equipment, furniture.

apportion (ă-**por**-shŏn) *verb* to divide into
shares, to allot. **apportionment** *noun*

apposite (**ap**-ŏ-zĭt) *adjective* (of a remark)
appropriate. **appositely** *adverb*

apposition (ap-ŏ-**zish**-ŏn) *noun* **1** placing
side by side. **2** a grammatical relationship in
which a word or phrase is placed with another
that it describes, e.g. in 'Canberra, Australia's
capital', *Australia's capital* is in apposition to
Canberra. [from *ap-*[1] + *position*]

appraise *verb* to estimate the value or quality
of. **appraisal** *noun*

appreciable (ă-**pree**-shă-bŭl) *adjective* able
to be seen or felt, considerable, *an appreciable
change in temperature*. **appreciably** *adverb*

appreciate *verb* **1** to value greatly, to
be grateful for. **2** to enjoy intelligently,
to appreciate poetry. **3** to understand, *we
appreciate their reluctance to give details*.
4 to rise or raise in value, *the investments have
appreciated*. **appreciation** *noun* [from *ap-*[1], +
Latin *pretium* = price]

appreciative (ă-**pree**-shă-tiv) *adjective*
feeling or showing appreciation.
appreciatively *adverb*

apprehend (ap-rĕ-**hend**) *verb* **1** to seize,
to arrest. **2** to grasp the meaning of, to
understand. **3** to expect with fear or anxiety.
[from *ap-*[1], + Latin *prehendere* = to grasp]

apprehension (ap-rĕ-**hen**-shŏn) *noun*
1 a feeling of fear about a possible danger or
difficulty. **2** understanding. **3** arrest.

apprehensive (ap-rĕ-**hen**-siv) *adjective*
feeling apprehension, anxious. **apprehensively**
adverb, **apprehensiveness** *noun*

apprentice *noun* **1** a person learning a trade
etc. by working in it for an agreed period.
2 a novice. –**apprentice** *verb* to bind (a person)
legally as an apprentice. **apprenticeship** *noun*
[from French *apprendre* = learn]

apprise (ă-**pryz**) *verb* (*formal*) to inform.

approach *verb* **1** to come near or nearer in
space or time. **2** to set about doing or tackling,
approach the problem in a practical way.
3 to go to with a request or offer. **4** to be
similar to, *his liking for it approaches
infatuation*. –**approach** *noun* **1** approaching,
watched their approach. **2** a way of reaching
a place. **3** the final part of an aircraft's flight
before landing. **4** a method of doing or

tackling something. **5** an effort to establish
an agreement or friendly relations. **6** an
approximation, *his nearest approach to a
smile*.

approachable *adjective* able to be
approached; *he is very approachable*, is
friendly and easy to talk to. **approachability**
noun

approbation (ap-rŏ-**bay**-shŏn) *noun* approval.

appropriate (ă-**proh**-pree-ăt) *adjective*
suitable, proper. –**appropriate** (ă-**proh**-pree-
ayt) *verb* **1** to take and use as one's own.
2 to set aside for a special purpose, *$500 was
appropriated to the sports fund*. **appropriately**
adverb, **appropriateness** *noun*, **appropriation**
noun, **appropriator** *noun*

approval *noun* feeling, showing, or saying
that one considers something to be good or
acceptable. □ **on approval** (of goods) taken by
a customer for examination without obligation
to buy unless satisfied.

approve *verb* **1** to say or feel that something
is good or suitable. **2** to sanction, to agree to,
the committee approved the expenditure.

approximate (ă-**prok**-sĭ-măt) *adjective*
almost exact or correct but not completely so.
–**approximate** (ă-**prok**-sĭ-mayt) *verb* **1** to be
almost the same, *a story that approximated to
the truth*. **2** to make approximately the same.
approximately *adverb*, **approximation** *noun*
[from *ap-*[1], + Latin *proximus* = very near]

appurtenance (ă-**per**-tĕ-năns) *noun* a minor
piece of property, or a right or privilege, that
goes with a more important one.

après-ski (ap-ray-**skee**) *adjective* of or
suitable for the evening period after skiing,
at a resort. –**après-ski** *noun* this period.
[French]

apricot *noun* **1** a juicy stone fruit related to
the plum and peach, orange-pink when ripe.
2 this colour.

April *noun* the fourth month of the year. **April
fool** a person who is hoaxed on **April Fool's
Day** (1 April). [from Latin *Aprilis*]

a priori (ay pry-**or**-ry *or* ay pree-**or**-ree)
adjective **1** (of reasoning) deductive; from
cause to effect. **2** (of concepts) not derived
from experience. **3** assumed without
investigation. [Latin, = from what is before.]

apron *noun* **1** a garment worn over the front
part of the body to protect the wearer's
clothes. **2** a similar garment worn as part of
official dress (e.g. by a bishop or freemason).

3 anything resembling such a garment in shape or function; an extension of a theatre stage in front of the curtain. **4** a hard-surfaced area on an airfield, where aircraft are manoeuvred or loaded and unloaded. **5** the part of a lathe enclosing the gears operated by the lead screw. [originally *a naperon*, from French *nappe* = tablecloth]

apropos (ap-rŏ-**poh**) *adverb* appropriately, to the point. –**apropos** *adjective* suitable or relevant to what is being said or done. ☐ **apropos of** concerning, with reference to. [from French *à propos* = to the purpose]

apse *noun* a recess usually with an arched or domed roof, especially in a church.

apt *adjective* **1** suitable, appropriate, *an apt quotation*. **2** having a certain tendency, likely, *he is apt to be careless*. **3** quick at learning. **aptly** *adverb*, **aptness** *noun* [from Latin *aptus* = fitted]

aptitude *noun* a natural ability or skill.

aqua *noun* the colour aquamarine.

aquaculture *noun* the cultivation or rearing of aquatic plants or animals.

aqualung *see* scuba [from Latin *aqua* = water, + *lung*]

aquamarine (ak-wă-mă-**reen**) *noun* **1** a bluish-green beryl. **2** its colour. [from Latin *aqua marina* = sea water]

aquaplane *noun* a board on which a person stands to be towed by a speedboat. –**aquaplane** *verb* **1** to ride on such a board. **2** to glide uncontrollably on the wet surface of a road.

aquarium (ă-**kwair**-ree-ŭm) *noun* (*plural* **aquariums**) **1** an artificial pond or tank for keeping living fish and water animals and plants. **2** a building containing such ponds or tanks. [same origin as *Aquarius*]

Aquarius (ă-**kwair**-ree-ŭs) a sign of the zodiac, the Water-carrier, which the sun enters about 21 January. **Aquarian** *adjective* & *noun* [Latin, = of water]

aquatic (ă-**kwat**-ik) *adjective* **1** growing or living in or near water, *aquatic plants*. **2** taking place in or on water; *aquatic sports*, rowing, swimming, etc. [from Latin *aqua* = water]

aquatint *noun* an etching made on copper by using nitric acid.

aqueduct (**ak**-wĕ-dukt) *noun* an artificial channel carrying water across country, especially one built like a bridge above a

valley or low ground. [from Latin *aqua* = water, + *ducere* = to lead]

aqueous (**ay**-kwee-ŭs) *adjective* **1** of or like water. **2** produced by water. ☐ **aqueous humour** clear fluid in the eye between the lens and the cornea.

aquifer (**ak**-wĭ-fer) *noun* a layer of rock that can hold or transmit a large amount of water. [from Latin *aqua* = water, + *ferre* = bring]

aquiline (**ak**-wĭ-lyn) *adjective* hooked like an eagle's beak, *an aquiline nose*. [from Latin *aquila* = eagle]

Aquinas (ă-**kwy**-năs), St Thomas (1225–74), Italian theologian, a Dominican friar. Feast day, 7 March.

ar- *prefix* see ad-.

Arab *noun* **1** a member of a Semitic people originally inhabiting the Arabian peninsula and neighbouring countries, now also other parts of the Middle East and North Africa. **2** a horse of a breed native to Arabia. –**Arab** *adjective* of Arabs.

Arabana (u-ră-**bun**-ă) *noun* **1** a member of an Aboriginal people of central Australia. **2** their language.

arabesque (a-ră-**besk**) *noun* **1** an elaborate design with intertwined leaves, branches, and scrolls. **2** a ballet dancer's posture poised on one leg with the other stretched backwards horizontally. **3** a florid musical composition.

Arabia a peninsula in the Middle East between the Red Sea and the Persian Gulf.

Arabian *adjective* of Arabia. ☐ **Arabian Nights** the popular title of a collection of Oriental folk tales.

Arabic *adjective* of the Arabs or their language. –**Arabic** *noun* the language of the Arabs. ☐ **arabic figures** or **numerals** the symbols 1, 2, 3, 4, 5, etc.

arable (**a**-ră-bŭl) *adjective* (of land) suitable for growing crops. –**arable** *noun* arable land. [from Latin *arare* = to plough]

arachnid (ă-**rak**-nĭd) *noun* a member of the class of animals including spiders, scorpions, and mites. [from Greek *arachne* = spider]

Arafura Sea a sea lying between the northern coast of Australia and Irian Jaya.

Aral Sea an inland sea in central Asia, east of the Caspian Sea.

Aramaic (a-ră-**may**-ik) *noun* a Semitic language spoken in Syria and Palestine in New Testament times.

Aran *adjective* made in the knitted patterns traditional to the Aran Islands, off the west coast of Ireland, *an Aran sweater*.

Aranda (ă-**run**-tă *or* a-**răn**-dă) *noun*
1 a member of an Aboriginal people of central Australia. 2 their language.

Ararat (a-ră-rat) either of two mountain peaks in eastern Turkey, where Noah's ark is said to have rested after the Flood.

arbiter (**ar**-bǐ-ter) *noun* 1 a person who has the power to decide what shall be done or accepted, one with entire control, *French designers are no longer the arbiters of fashion*. 2 an arbitrator.

arbitrary (**ar**-bǐ-tră-ree) *adjective* 1 based on random choice or impulse, not on reason, *an arbitrary selection*. 2 despotic, unrestrained, *arbitrary powers*. arbitrarily *adverb*, arbitrariness *noun*

arbitrate *verb* to act as an arbitrator.

arbitration *noun* settlement of a dispute by a person or persons acting as arbitrators. □ **arbitration court** a tribunal resolving industrial disputes, determining industrial awards, etc. [from Latin *arbitrari* = to judge]

arbitrator *noun* an impartial person chosen to settle a dispute between two parties.

arbor *noun* an axle or spindle on which a wheel etc. revolves in mechanism.

Arbor Day a day dedicated in certain countries for public tree-planting. [from Latin *arbor* = tree]

arboreal (ar-**bor**-ree-ăl) *adjective* 1 of trees. 2 living in trees. [from Latin *arbor* = tree]

arboretum (ar-bŏ-**ree**-tŭm) *noun* (*plural* arboreta) a place where trees are grown for study and display. [from Latin *arbor* = tree]

arbour (**ar**-ber) *noun* a shady place among trees, often made in a garden with climbing plants growing over a framework.

arc *noun* 1 part of the circumference of a circle or other curve. 2 anything shaped like this. 3 a luminous electric current passing across a gap between two terminals. –arc *verb* (arced, arcing) to form an arc. □ **arc lamp**, **arc light** lighting using an electric arc. **arc welding** welding by means of an electric arc. [same origin as *archer*]

arcade *noun* 1 a covered passage or area, usually with shops on both sides. 2 a series of arches supporting or along a wall.

Arcadia (ar-**kay**-dee-ă) a mountainous area in the central Peloponnese in Greece, in poetic fantasy the idyllic home of song-loving shepherds. Arcadian *noun* & *adjective*

arcane (ar-**kayn**) *adjective* mysterious, secret.

arch[1] *noun* 1 a curved structure supporting the weight of what is above it or used ornamentally. 2 something shaped like this. 3 the curved underpart of the foot. –arch *verb* to form into an arch. [same origin as *archer*]

arch[2] *adjective* consciously or affectedly playful, *an arch smile*. archly *adverb*, archness *noun*

arch- *prefix* 1 chief. 2 extreme. [from Greek]

archaeologist *noun* an expert in archaeology.

archaeology (ar-kee-**ol**-ŏ-jee) *noun* the scientific study of civilisations through their material remains. archaeological *adjective* [from Greek *arkhaios* = old, + -*logy*]

archaic (ar-**kay**-ik) *adjective* belonging to former or ancient times. [from Greek *arkhe* = beginning]

archaism (**ar**-kay-izm) *noun* an archaic word or expression.

archangel *noun* an angelic being ranking above an angel.

archbishop *noun* a bishop ranking above other bishops in a province of the Church. archbishopric *noun* the office or diocese of an archbishop.

archdeacon *noun* an Anglican priest ranking next below a bishop. archdeaconry *noun*

archduke *noun* (*historical*) chief duke, especially as the title of a son of an Austrian Emperor.

arch-enemy *noun* the chief enemy.

archer *noun* a person who shoots with bow and arrows. [from Latin *arcus* = a bow or curve]

archery *noun* the sport of shooting with bows and arrows, toxophily.

archetype (**ar**-kě-typ) *noun* an original model from which others are copied. archetypal *adjective* [from *arch-* + *type*]

Archibald Prize an annual prize for a portrait by an Australian artist, preferably of a person distinguished in art, letters, or politics. [named after Jules François Archibald (1856–1919), Australian journalist and co-founder of the Sydney *Bulletin*, under whose will the prize was established in 1921]

archiepiscopal (ar-kee-ě-**pis**-kŏ-păl) *adjective* of an archbishop or archbishopric.

archimandrite (ar-kee-**man**-dryt) *noun* the head of a large monastery in the Orthodox Church.

Archimedean screw (ar-kĭ-**mee**-dee-ăn) *noun* a device consisting of a large spiral screw in a tube, rotated by a handle, used for raising water. Its principle is used in other devices (e.g. a mincing machine).

Archimedes (ar-kĭ-**mee**-deez) (3rd century BC) Greek mathematician and inventor. □ Archimedes' principle the law that a body immersed in a fluid is subject to an upward force equal in magnitude to the weight of fluid it displaces.

archipelago (ar-kĭ-**pel**-ă-goh) *noun* (*plural* archipelagos) a group of many islands; a sea containing such a group. [from *arch-*, + Greek *pelagos* = sea]

architect *noun* a designer of buildings. [from *arch-*, + Greek *tekton* = builder]

architecture *noun* 1 the art or science of designing buildings. 2 the design or style of a building or buildings. architectural *adjective*, architecturally *adverb*

architrave (**ar**-kĭ-trayv) *noun* 1 the horizontal piece resting on the columns of a building. 2 the surround of a doorway or window.

archive (**ar**-kyv) *noun* (also archives *plural noun*) 1 the records or historical documents of an institution, community, etc. 2 the place where these are kept. –archive *verb* 1 place or store in an archive. 2 transfer (computer data) to a less frequently used file etc. [from Greek *arkheia* = public records]

archivist (**ar**-kĭ-vĭst) *noun* a person trained to deal with archives.

archway *noun* a passageway under an arch.

Arctic *adjective* of the regions round the North Pole. –arctic *adjective* very cold, *the weather was arctic*. –Arctic *noun* 1 the Arctic regions. 2 the Arctic Ocean, the ocean surrounding the North Pole. □ Arctic Circle the line of latitude 66° 33′ N.

arcuate *adjective* arc-shaped.

ardent (**ar**-děnt) *adjective* full of ardour, enthusiastic. ardently *adverb* [from Latin *ardens* = burning]

ardour (**ar**-der) *noun* great warmth of feeling.

arduous (**ar**-dew-ŭs) *adjective* needing much effort, laborious. arduously *adverb* [from Latin *arduus* = steep]

are[1] *see* be.

are[2] (*pr.* ar) *noun* an area of 100 square metres.

area *noun* 1 the extent or measurement of a surface. 2 a region; *picnic area*, a space set aside for this use. 3 the field of an activity or subject, *in the area of computing*.

areca *noun* a tropical Asian palm. areca nut its astringent seed, also called *betel nut*.

areg *see* erg[2].

arena (ă-**ree**-nă) *noun* the level area in the centre of an amphitheatre or a sports stadium. [Latin, = sand]

arenaceous (a-rě-**nay**-shŭs) *adjective* 1 like sand, sandy. 2 (of plants) growing in sand.

aren't (*informal*) = are not.

Usage The phrase *aren't I?* is a recognised colloquialism for *am I not?*

---

areola (a-ree-**oh**-lă) *noun* (*plural* areolae) a circular coloured area, especially around a nipple.

Ares (**air**-reez) (*Gk. myth.*) the god of war, identified by the Romans with Mars.

arête (ă-**ret**) *noun* a sharp ridge on a mountain. [French]

Argentina (ar-jěn-**tee**-nă) a republic in the southern part of South America. Argentine (**ar**-jěn-tyn) *adjective* & *noun*, Argentinian (ar-jěn-**tin**-ee-ăn) *adjective* & *noun*

Argentine ant *noun* a destructive brown ant.

argillaceous (ar-gĭ-**lay**-shŭs) *adjective* of or like clay.

argon *noun* a chemical element (symbol Ar), an inert gas used in electric lamps etc. [from Greek *argos* = idle]

Argonauts (**ar**-gŏ-nawts) *plural noun* (*Gk. legend*) the heroes who accompanied Jason on the ship *Argo* in quest of the Golden Fleece.

argosy (**ar**-gŏ-see) *noun* (*poetic*) a merchant ship; a fleet of such ships.

arguable *adjective* 1 able to be asserted. 2 open to doubt or dispute. arguably *adverb*

argue *verb* 1 to express disagreement, to exchange angry words. 2 to give reasons for or against something, to debate. 3 to persuade by talking, *argued him into going*.

argument *noun* 1 a discussion involving disagreement, a quarrel. 2 a reason put forward. 3 a theme or chain of reasoning. 4 (in mathematics) an independent variable determining the value of a function.

argumentation *noun* arguing.

argumentative (arg-yŭ-**men**-tă-tiv) *adjective* fond of arguing. **argumentatively** *adverb*

Argus (*Gk. myth.*) a monster with many eyes, slain by Hermes.

arhat *noun* (in Buddhism and Jainism) a saint of one of the highest ranks. [from Sanskrit, literally 'meritorious']

aria (**ah**-ree-ă) *noun* an operatic song for one voice. [Italian]

Ariadne (a-ree-**ad**-nee) (*Gk. legend*) the daughter of Minos, who provided Theseus with a thread to guide him out of the Cretan labyrinth.

arid (**a**-rĭd) *adjective* **1** dry, parched; *arid regions*, deserts etc. **2** uninteresting, *an arid discussion*. **aridly** *adverb*, **aridness** *noun*, **aridity** (ă-**rid**-ĭ-tee) *noun*

Aries (**air**-reez) *noun* a sign of the zodiac, the Ram, which the sun enters about 20 March. **Arian** (**air**-ree-ăn) *adjective* & *noun*

aright *adjective* rightly.

arise *verb* (**arose**, **arisen**) **1** to come into existence, to come to people's notice, *problems arose*. **2** (*old use*) to get up, to stand up; to rise from the dead.

aristocracy (a-rĭ-**stok**-răsee) *noun* **1** the hereditary upper classes of people in a country, the nobility. **2** a country ruled by these. [from Greek *aristos* = best, + -*cracy*]

aristocrat (**a**-rĭs-tŏ-krat) *noun* a member of the aristocracy, a noble.

aristocratic (a-rĭs-tŏ-**krat**-ik) *adjective* **1** of the aristocracy. **2** noble in style. **aristocratically** *adverb*

Aristophanes (a-rĭ-**stof**-ă-neez) (c. 450–c. 385 BC), Greek comic playwright.

Aristotle (384–322 BC), Greek philosopher, whose systematic analysis of logic, science, and philosophy influenced Islamic philosophy and, through that, medieval Western thought. **Aristotelian** *adjective* & *noun*

arithmetic (ă-**rith**-mĕ-tik) *noun* the science of numbers, calculating by means of numbers. –**arithmetic** (a-rith-**met**-ik) *adjective* (also **arithmetical**) of arithmetic. ☐ **arithmetic-logic unit** the part of a computer where data are processed (as distinct from storage or control units). **arithmetic mean** *see* **mean³**. **arithmetic progression** a series of numbers (such as 1, 3, 5, 7) that increase or decrease by the same amount each time. **arithmetically** *adverb* [from Greek *arithmos* = number]

Arizona (a-rĭ-**zoh**-nă) a State of the SW USA.

Arjuna a Kshatriya prince in the Mahabharata, one of the two main characters of the Bhagavadgita.

ark *noun* Noah's boat or a model of this. ☐ **Ark of the Covenant** a wooden chest in which the writings of Jewish Law were kept. [from Latin *arca* = box]

Arkansas (**ar**-kăn-saw) a State of the S central USA.

arm¹ *noun* **1** either of the two upper limbs of the human body, from the shoulder to the hand. **2** a sleeve. **3** something shaped like an arm or projecting from a main part, *an arm of a sea*; *the arms of a chair*, the raised side parts supporting a sitter's arms.

arm² *verb* **1** to supply or fit with weapons; *the enemy is arming*, is preparing as if for war. **2** to make (a bomb etc.) ready to explode, *the device was not yet armed*. –**arm** *noun* **1** each of the kinds of troops of which an army etc. is composed, *the Fleet Air Arm*. **2** (usually in *plural*) a weapon; a firearm. **arms** *plural noun* a coat of arms (*see* **coat**). ☐ **armed forces** or **services** military forces. **arms race** competition among nations in accumulating weapons. **up in arms** protesting vigorously. [from Latin *arma* = weapons]

armada (ar-**mah**-dă) *noun* a fleet of warships. **the (Spanish) Armada** an armada sent from Spain to invade England in 1588. [Spanish, = navy]

armadillo (ar-mă-**dil**-oh) *noun* (*plural* **armadillos**) a small burrowing animal of South America with a body covered with a shell of bony plates.

Armageddon 1 (in the Bible) the scene of the final conflict between the forces of good and evil at the end of the world. **2** any decisive conflict.

armament *noun* **1** the weapons with which an army or a ship, aircraft, or fighting vehicle is equipped. **2** the process of equipping for war.

armature (**ar**-mă-choor) *noun* **1** the wire-wound core of a dynamo or electric motor. **2** a bar placed in contact with the poles of a magnet to preserve its power or transmit force to support a load. **3** a framework round which a clay or plaster sculpture is modelled.

armband *noun* a band worn round the arm or sleeve.

armchair *noun* a chair with arms or raised sides; *armchair sportsmen*, those who watch sport on television rather than participate.

Armenia (ar-**mee**-nee-ă) a republic between the Black and Caspian Seas, south of the Caucasus, east of Turkey. **Armenian** *adjective & noun*

armful *noun* (*plural* **armfuls**) as much as the arm can hold.

armhole *noun* an opening in a garment through which the arm is inserted.

armistice *noun* an agreement during a war or battle to stop fighting for a time.
□ **Armistice Day** the anniversary of the armistice of 11 November 1918, ending the First World War (now usually called *Remembrance Day*). [from Latin *arma* = weapons, + *sistere* = to stop]

armless *adjective* without arms.

armlet *noun* an armband.

armour *noun* **1** a protective covering for the body, formerly worn in fighting. **2** metal plates covering a warship, car, or tank to protect it from missiles. **3** armoured fighting vehicles collectively. [same origin as *arm²*]

armoured *adjective* **1** covered or protected with armour, *an armoured car*. **2** equipped with armoured vehicles, *armoured divisions*.

armoury (**ar**-mŏ-ree) *noun* a place where weapons and ammunition are stored.

armpit *noun* the hollow under the arm below the shoulder.

arms *plural noun see* arm².

army *noun* **1** an organised force equipped for fighting on land. **2** a vast group, *an army of locusts*. **3** a body of people organised for a particular purpose, *an army of helpers*.

Arnhem Land (**ar**-něm) the eastern half of the large peninsula on the north coast of the Northern Territory, an Aboriginal Reserve. [named by Matthew Flinders in 1803 after one of the Dutch ships that discovered this coast in 1623]

aroma (ă-**roh**-mă) *noun* a smell, especially a pleasant one.

aromatherapy *noun* the use of essential plant oils in massage or other treatment.

aromatic *adjective* **1** fragrant, spicy. **2** (of organic compounds) having an unsaturated ring of atoms, especially containing a benzene ring. – **aromatic** *noun* an aromatic substance or plant.

arose *see* arise.

around *adverb & preposition* **1** all round, on every side, in every direction. **2** about, here and there; *he's somewhere around*, close at hand; *we shopped around*, going from place to place. **3** about, approximately at, *be here around five o'clock*.

arouse *verb* **1** to wake. **2** to cause (a reaction, feeling, etc.); to stimulate. **arousal** *noun*

arpeggio (ar-**pej**-ee-oh) *noun* (*plural* **arpeggios**) the notes of a musical chord played in succession instead of simultaneously. [from Italian *arpa* = harp]

arraign *verb* to accuse; to find fault with. **arraignment** *noun*

arrange *verb* **1** to put into a certain order, to adjust; *arrange flowers*, place them attractively, especially in a vase. **2** to form plans, to settle the details of, to prepare, *arrange to be there*; *arrange a meeting*. **3** to adapt (a musical composition) for voices or instruments other than those for which it was written; to adapt (a play etc.) for broadcasting. **arrangement** *noun*, **arranger** *noun*

arrant (**a**-rănt) *adjective* downright, out-and-out, *this is arrant nonsense!*

arras (**a**-răs) *noun* a richly decorated tapestry or wall hanging.

array *verb* **1** to arrange in order, *arrayed his forces along the river*. **2** to dress, *arrayed in her coronation dress*. – **array** *noun* **1** an imposing series, a display, *a fine array of tools*. **2** an ordered arrangement, often in a rectangular form of rows and columns. **3** an arrangement of data in a computer, so constructed that a program can extract the items by means of a key. [from *ar-*, + old form of *ready*]

arrears *plural noun* **1** money that is owing and ought to have been paid earlier, *arrears of rent*. **2** work that should have been finished but is still waiting to be dealt with, *arrears of correspondence*. □ **in arrears** behindhand with payment or work, not paid or done when it was due, *he is in arrears with his rent*; *the rent is in arrears*.

arrest *verb* **1** to stop or check (a process or movement); *arrest attention*, catch and hold it. **2** to seize by authority of the law. – **arrest** *noun* **1** stoppage. **2** seizure, legal arresting of an offender; *he is under arrest*, has been arrested.

arris (**a**-rĭs) *noun* the sharp edge formed where two surfaces meet to form an angle, especially in architecture and carpentry.

arrival *noun* **1** arriving. **2** a person or thing that has arrived.

arrive *verb* **1** to reach one's destination or a certain point on a journey; *arrived at an agreement*, reached it after discussion. **2** to come at last, to make an appearance; *the great day arrived.* **3** to be recognised as having achieved success in the world.

arrogant (**a**-rŏ-gănt) *adjective* proud and overbearing through an exaggerated feeling of one's superiority. **arrogantly** *adverb*, **arrogance** *noun*

arrogate (**a**-rŏ-gayt) *verb* **1** to claim or seize without having the right to do so. **2** to attribute or assign to another person etc. unjustly. **arrogation** *noun*

arrow *noun* **1** a straight thin pointed shaft to be shot from a bow. **2** a line with an outward-pointing V at the end, used to show direction or position.

arrowhead *noun* the head of an arrow.

arrowroot *noun* an edible starch prepared from the root of an American plant.

arroyo (ă-**roi**-oh) *noun* (*plural* **arroyos**) (especially *Amer.*) a usually dry river bed in a desert region, which becomes a temporary watercourse after rain. [Spanish]

arsenal *noun* a place where weapons and ammunition are stored or manufactured. [from Arabic, = workshop]

arsenic (**ar**-sĕ-nik) *noun* **1** a chemical element (symbol As), a brittle steel-grey substance. **2** a violently poisonous white compound of this. **arsenical** (ar-**sen**-i-kăl) *adjective* [from Persian *zar* = gold]

arson *noun* the act of setting fire to a house or other property intentionally and unlawfully.

arsonist *noun* a person who is guilty of arson.

art[1] *noun* **1** the production of something beautiful; skill or ability in such work. **2** works such as paintings or sculptures produced by skill. **3** any practical skill, a knack, *the art of sailing.* **4** cunning, artfulness. **arts** *plural noun* subjects (e.g. languages, literature, history) in which sympathetic understanding plays a great part, as opposed to sciences where exact measurements and calculations are used. □ **art house** a cinema which specialises in showing films that are artistic or experimental rather than merely entertaining. **arts and crafts** decorative design and handicraft.

art[2] (*old use*) the present tense of **be**, used with *thou.*

art deco (**dek**-oh) *noun* a style of decorative art and architecture in the 1920s and 1930s, characterised by geometric patterns, sharp edges, and bright colours.

artefact (**ar**-tĕ-fakt) *noun* a man-made object, a simple prehistoric tool or weapon. [from Latin *arte* = by art, + *factum* = made]

Artemis (**ar**-tĕ-miss) (*Gk. myth.*) a goddess, sister of Apollo, identified by the Romans with Selene and Diana.

arterial (ar-**teer**-ree-ăl) *adjective* of an artery; *an arterial road*, an important main road.

arteriole *noun* a small artery.

arteriosclerosis (ar-teer-ree-oh-sklĕ-**roh**-sĭs) *noun* a condition in which the walls of arteries become thicker and less elastic so that blood circulation is hindered.

artery *noun* **1** any of the tubes carrying blood away from the heart to all parts of the body. **2** an important transport route.

artesian bore (ar-**tee**-zhăn) (also **bore**) a well that is bored vertically into a place where a constant supply of water will rise to the earth's surface with little or no pumping.

artful *adjective* crafty, cunningly clever at getting what one wants. **artfully** *adverb*, **artfulness** *noun*

arthritis (arth-**ry**-tĭss) *noun* a condition in which there is pain and stiffness in the joints. **arthritic** (arth-**rit**-ik) *adjective* & *noun* [from Greek *arthron* = joint]

arthropod (**arth**-rŏ-pod) *noun* an animal of the group that includes insects, spiders, and crustaceans, having segmented bodies and jointed limbs. [from Greek *arthron* = joint, + *podos* = of a foot]

Arthur reputed king of the Britons (perhaps 5th or 6th century), leader of the Knights of the Round Table at his court at Camelot. **Arthurian** (ar-**thew**-ree-ăn) *adjective* & *noun*

artichoke *noun* a plant related to the thistle, with a flower consisting of thick leaflike scales used as a vegetable. **Jerusalem artichoke** a kind of sunflower with tubers that are used as a vegetable.

article *noun* **1** a particular or separate thing; *articles of clothing, toilet articles*, things of the kind named. **2** a piece of writing, complete in itself, in a newspaper or periodical, *an article on immigration.* **3** a separate clause or item in an agreement, *articles of apprenticeship.* **4** a word used before a noun to identify what it refers to. −**article** *verb* to bind by articles of apprenticeship; *articled clerk*, a trainee solicitor. □ **articles of association** regulations for the business of a registered company. **definite article** the word 'the', **indefinite article** 'a' or 'an' (or their equivalents in another language).

articulate (ar-**tik**-yŭ-lăt) *adjective* **1** spoken clearly, in words. **2** able to express ideas clearly. –**articulate** (ar-**tik**-yŭ-layt) *verb* **1** to say or speak distinctly, *articulating each word with care*. **2** to form a joint, to connect by joints, *this bone articulates* or *is articulated with another*. □ **articulated vehicle** one that has sections connected by a flexible joint or joints. **articulately** *adverb*, **articulation** *noun*

artifice (**ar**-tĭ-fĭss) *noun* trickery; a clever trick intended to mislead someone. [same origin as *artificial*]

artificer (ar-**tif**-ĭ-ser) *noun* a skilled worker or mechanic.

artificial *adjective* not originating naturally, made by human skill in imitation of something natural. □ **artificial insemination** injection of semen into the womb artificially so that conception may take place without sexual intercourse. **artificial respiration** the process of forcing air into and out of the lungs to start or stimulate natural breathing. **artificially** *adverb*, **artificiality** (ar-tĭ-fish-ee-**al**-ĭ-tee) *noun* [from Latin *ars* = art, + *facere* = make]

artillery *noun* **1** large guns used in fighting on land. **2** a branch of an army that uses these. **artilleryman** *noun*

artisan (ar-tĭ-**zan**) *noun* a skilled worker in industry or trade, a mechanic.

artist *noun* **1** a person who produces works of art, especially paintings. **2** a person who does something with exceptional skill. **3** a professional entertainer.

artiste (ar-**teest**) *noun* a professional entertainer.

artistic *adjective* **1** showing or done with skill and good taste. **2** of art or artists. **artistically** *adverb*

artistry *noun* artistic skill.

artless *adjective* free from artfulness, simple and natural. **artlessly** *adverb*, **artlessness** *noun*

art nouveau (art noo-**voh**) *noun* a style of art developed in the late 19th century, with ornamental and flowing designs.

artwork *noun* **1** illustrations and diagrams in a printed work. **2** a work or works of art, *the children's artwork was on display*.

arty *adjective* (*informal*) with an exaggerated and often affected display of artistic style or interests. **artiness** *noun*

arty-crafty *adjective* (*informal*) of arts and crafts.

arum (**air**-rŭm) *noun* a plant with a flower consisting of a single petal-like part surrounding a central spike. □ **arum lily** a cultivated white arum.

arvo *noun* (*Austral. informal*) afternoon.

Aryan (**air**-ree-ăn) *adjective* **1** of the original Indo-European language; of its speakers or their descendants. **2** (in Nazi Germany) of non-Jewish Caucasian descent. –**Aryan** *noun* an Aryan person.

as *adverb* **1** in the same degree, equally; *I thought as much*, I thought so. **2** similarly, like. **3** in the character of, *Olivier as Hamlet*. –**as** *conjunction* **1** at the same time that, *they came as I left*. **2** because, for the reason that, *as he refuses, we can do nothing*. **3** in the way in which, *do as I do*. –**as** *relative pronoun* that, who, which, *I had the same trouble as you*; *he was a foreigner, as I knew from his accent*. □ **as for** with regard to, *as for you, I despise you*. **as from** from the date stated, *your salary will be increased as from 1 July*. **as if** as it would be if, *he said it as if he meant it*. **as it was** in the actual circumstances. **as it were** as if it was actually so, *he became, as it were, a man without a country*. **as of** at the date mentioned, *that was the position as of last Monday*. **as though** as if. **as to** with regard to, *she said nothing as to holidays*. **as well** in addition, too; desirable, *it might be as well to go*; desirably, *we might as well go*. **as well as** in addition to. **as yet** up to this time. **as you were!** return to the previous position.

as- *prefix* see **ad-**.

asafoedita (as-ă-fŏ-**dee**-tă) *noun* a strong-smelling spice used in Indian cooking.

asbestos *noun* a soft fibrous mineral substance, made into fireproof material or used for heat insulation. [Greek, = unquenchable]

asbestosis (ass-best-**oh**-sĭs) *noun* a lung disease caused by inhaling asbestos particles.

ascend *verb* to go or come up. □ **ascend the throne** to become king or queen. [from Latin *ascendere* = climb up]

ascendancy (ă-**sen**-dăn-see) *noun* the state of being dominant; *gain ascendancy*, win control.

ascendant *adjective* ascending, rising.
□ **in the ascendant** rising in power or influence.

ascension (ă-**sen**-shŏn) *noun* ascent.
□ **the Ascension** the taking up of Christ into heaven, witnessed by the Apostles. **Ascension Day** the Thursday on which this is commemorated, the 40th day after Easter.

Ascension Island a small island in the South Atlantic, incorporated with St Helena.

ascent *noun* **1** ascending. **2** a way up, an upward slope or path.

ascertain (ass-er-**tayn**) *verb* to find out by making enquiries. **ascertainable** *adjective*

ascetic (ă-**set**-ik) *adjective* self-denying, not allowing oneself pleasures and luxuries. –**ascetic** *noun* a person who leads a severely simple life without ordinary pleasures, often for religious reasons. **ascetically** *adverb*, **asceticism** (ă-**set**-ĭ-sizm) *noun* [from Greek *asketes* = hermit]

ASCII (**as**-kee) *abbreviation* American Standard Code for Information Interchange, a code assigning a different character to each letter, number, and character for computing purposes.

Asclepius (ă-**sklee**-pee-ŭs) (*Gk. myth.*) a hero and god of healing, often represented bearing a staff with a serpent round it.

ascorbic acid (ă-**skor**-bik) *noun* vitamin C.

ascribe (ă-**skryb**) *verb* to attribute. **ascribable** *adjective*, **ascription** (ă-**skrip**-shŏn) *noun*

ASEAN (**az**-ee-ăn) *abbreviation* Association of South East Asian Nations, promoting stability and economic cooperation in South East Asia.

aseptic (ay-**sep**-tik) *adjective* free from bacteria that cause something to become septic, surgically clean. **aseptically** *adverb* [from *a-²* = not, + *septic*]

asexual (ay-**sek**-shoo-ăl) *adjective* without sex, sex organs, or sexuality. **asexually** *adverb* [from *a-²* = not, + *sexual*]

ash¹ *noun* **1** a tree with silver-grey bark and close-grained wood. **2** this wood.

ash² *noun* the powder that remains after something has burnt. □ **the Ashes** a trophy awarded as the symbol of victory in a season of Anglo-Australian cricket matches. **Ash Wednesday** the first day of Lent (¶ from the ritual of the priest marking the foreheads of churchgoers with blest ashes on that day).

ashamed *adjective* feeling shame.

ashen *adjective* **1** of ashes. **2** pale as ashes.

Ashkhabad (ash-kă-**bad**) the capital of Turkmenistan.

Ashkenazi (ash-kĕ-**nah**-zee) *noun* (*plural* **Ashkenazim**) a Jew of northern and eastern Europe, as distinct from a Sephardi.

ashlar *noun* square-cut stones; masonry made of these.

ashore *adverb* to or on shore.

ashram *noun* an Indian place of religious learning or retreat. [from Sanskrit *ashrama* = hermitage]

ashrama (**ash**-ră-mă) *noun* (in Hinduism) any of the four stages of an ideal life.

ashtray *noun* a receptacle for tobacco ash.

ashy *adjective* **1** ashen. **2** covered with ash.

Asia (**ay**-zhă) the largest of the continents, extending from Europe to the Pacific Ocean, divided from Europe by the Ural Mountains and the Caspian Sea. **Asian** *adjective* & *noun*

Asia Minor the western peninsula of Asia between the Mediterranean and the Black Sea, including most of Turkey.

Asiatic (ay-zee-**at**-ik) *adjective* of Asia. –**Asiatic** *noun* an Asian.

Usage *Asian* is the preferred word when used of people.

aside *adverb* **1** to or on one side, away from the main part or group, *pull it aside*; *step aside*. **2** away from one's thoughts or from consideration. **3** in reserve, *put money aside for a holiday*. –**aside** *noun* words spoken so that only certain people will hear. □ **aside from** apart from.

asinine (**ass**-ĭ-nyn) *adjective* silly, stupid. **asininity** (ass-ĭ-**nin**-ĭ-tee) *noun* [same origin as *ass*]

ASIO (**ay**-zee-oh) *abbreviation* Australian Security Intelligence Organisation.

ASIS (**ay**-sĭs) *abbreviation* Australian Secret Intelligence Service.

ask *verb* **1** to call for an answer to or about, to address a question to (a person). **2** to seek to obtain from another person, *ask a favour of him*; *asked $9 for the book*. **3** to invite, *ask him to dinner*. □ **ask for** to ask to be given, or to see or speak to, or to be directed to. **ask for it, ask for trouble** to behave in such a way that trouble is likely. **asking price** the price at which something is offered for sale.

askance (ă-**skanss**) *adverb* sideways.
look askance at to regard with distrust or
disapproval.

askew *adverb* & *adjective* not straight or level.

asleep *adverb* & *adjective* **1** in or into a state
of sleep. **2** numbed, *my foot is asleep.*

asp *noun* a small poisonous snake.

asparagus (ă-**spa**-ră-gŭs) *noun* **1** a plant
whose young shoots are cooked and eaten as a
vegetable. **2** these shoots.

aspect *noun* **1** the look or appearance of
a person or thing, *the forest had a sinister
aspect*; *this aspect of the problem*, this feature
of it. **2** the direction a thing faces, a side facing
this way, *the house has a southern aspect.*
3 the set of forms of a verb (e.g. in Russian)
that indicate the quality of an action, such as
whether it is complete or incomplete. [from
as-, + Latin *specere* = to look]

aspen *noun* a kind of poplar with leaves that
move in the slightest wind.

Asperger's syndrome *noun* a mild autistic
disorder characterised by awkwardness in
social interaction etc. [named after Hans
Asperger, Austrian psychiatrist (died 1980)]

asperity (ă-**spe**-rĭ-tee) *noun* harshness or
severity, especially of manner. [from Latin
asper = rough]

aspersions (ă-**sper**-shŏnz) *plural noun*
an attack on someone's reputation, *casting
aspersions on his rivals.*

asphalt (**ash**-felt *or* **ass**-felt) *noun* **1** a black
sticky substance like coal tar. **2** a mixture of
this with gravel etc. used for paving. –**asphalt**
verb to surface with asphalt.

asphyxia (ăs-**fiks**-ee-ă) *noun* a condition
caused by lack of air in the lungs, suffocation.
[Greek, = stopping of the pulse]

asphyxiate (ăs-**fiks**-ee-ayt) *verb* to suffocate.
asphyxiation *noun* [from *asphyxia*]

aspic *noun* a savoury jelly used for coating
meats, eggs, etc.

aspidistra *noun* a plant with broad tapering
leaves, grown as a house plant. [from Greek
aspis = a shield]

aspirant (**ass**-pĭ-rănt) *noun* a person who
aspires to something.

aspirate (**ass**-pĭ-răt) *noun* the sound of *h.*
–**aspirate** (**ass**-pĭ-rayt) *verb* to pronounce with
an *h.*

aspiration (ass-pĭ-**ray**-shŏn) *noun*
1 ambition, strong desire. **2** aspirating.
3 the drawing of breath.

aspire *verb* to have a high ambition, *he
aspires to become president* or *aspires to
the presidency.* [from *as-*, + Latin *spirare* =
breathe]

aspirin *noun* a medicinal drug used to relieve
pain and reduce fever; a tablet of this.

ass *noun* **1** a donkey. **2** (*informal*) a stupid
person. [from *asinus* = donkey]

assail (ă-**sayl**) *verb* **1** to attack violently and
persistently. **2** to begin (a task) resolutely.
[from Latin *assilire* = leap upon]

assailant *noun* an attacker.

assassin *noun* a person, especially one hired
by others, who assassinates another. [from
Arabic, = hashish-takers, Muslim fanatics
who murdered people during the time of the
Crusades]

assassinate *verb* to kill (an important
person) by violent means, usually from
political or religious motives. **assassination**
noun

assault *noun* **1** a violent attack. **2** an unlawful
personal attack on another person, even if only
with menacing words. –**assault** *verb* to make
an assault upon. □ **assault course** an obstacle
course used for training soldiers etc. [same
origin as *assail*]

assay (ă-**say**) *noun* a test of metal or ore
(especially of gold or silver used for coin or
bullion) for quality. –**assay** *verb* to make an
assay of. [from French *essai* = trial]

assegai (**ass**-ĕ-gy) *noun* a light iron-tipped
spear of South African peoples. [from Arabic
alzagayah = the spear]

assemblage *noun* **1** assembling.
2 an assembly. **3** things assembled.

assemble *verb* **1** to bring or come together.
2 to fit or put together. **3** to translate by using
an assembler.

assembler *noun* a computer program that
translates instructions from a low-level
language into a form that can be understood
and executed by the computer.

assembly *noun* **1** assembling. **2** an assembled
group, especially of people meeting for a
specific purpose. □ **assembly language** a
low-level computer language for translation
by an assembler. **assembly line** a sequence of
machines and workers through which parts of

a product move to be assembled in successive stages.

assent *verb* to consent, to express agreement. –**assent** *noun* (official) consent or approval.

assert *verb* **1** to declare as true, to state, *asserted his innocence*. **2** to enforce a claim to (rights etc.), *asserted his authority*. □ **assert itself** to become active, to make its effect felt. **assert oneself** to take effective action; to use one's authority; to insist on one's rights.

assertion *noun* **1** asserting. **2** a statement that something is a fact.

assertive *adjective* asserting oneself, self-assertive. **assertively** *adverb*, **assertiveness** *noun*

assess *verb* **1** to decide or fix the amount or value of. **2** to estimate the worth or quality or likelihood of. **assessment** *noun* [from Latin *assessor* = an assistant judge]

asset (**ass**-et) *noun* **1** any property that has money value, especially that which can be used or sold to pay debts. **2** a useful or valuable quality or skill; a person regarded as useful.

assiduous (ă-**sid**-yoo-ŭs) *adjective* diligent and persevering. **assiduously** *adverb*, **assiduity** (ass-i-**dew**-ĭ-tee) *noun*

assign *verb* **1** to allot, *rooms were assigned to us*. **2** to appoint or designate to perform a task etc., *assign your best investigator to the job*. **3** to ascribe, to regard as belonging to, *we cannot assign an exact date to the document*. **4** (*Austral. historical*) to allocate a convict to a free settler as a servant or labourer. **assignable** *adjective* [from *as*-, + Latin *signare* = mark out]

assignation (ass-ig-**nay**-shŏn) *noun* **1** assigning; being assigned. **2** an arrangement to meet, an appointment.

assignee *noun* (*Austral. historical*) an assigned convict.

assignment *noun* **1** assigning; being assigned. **2** a thing or task that is assigned to a person etc., *a history assignment*. **3** (*Austral. historical*) the system of assigning convicts.

assimilate *verb* **1** to absorb into the body or into a group or system; to become absorbed into something. **2** to absorb into the mind as knowledge. **3** to change (a sound in a word) so that it resembles another sound near to it (as in *cupboard*, where p is assimilated to b). **assimilation** *noun*

Assisi (ă-**see**-see) a town in central Italy, famous as the birthplace of St Francis.

assist *verb* to help. **assistance** *noun* [from Latin *assistere* = stand by]

assistant *noun* **1** a person who assists, a helper. **2** a person who serves customers in a shop. –**assistant** *adjective* assisting, helping and ranking next below a senior person, *the assistant manager*.

associate (ă-**soh**-see-ayt *or* -shee-) *verb* **1** to join or cause to join as a companion, colleague, or supporter. **2** to have frequent dealings, to be often in a certain company, *he associates with dishonest dealers*. **3** to connect in one's mind, *we associate pyramids with Egypt*. –**associate** (ă-**soh**-see-ăt *or* -shee-) *noun* **1** a partner, colleague, or companion. **2** one who has been admitted to a lower level of membership of an association without the status of a full member. –**associate** (ă-**soh**-see-ăt *or* -shee-) *adjective* **1** associated. **2** having subordinate membership. **3** of lower status, *associate professor*. [from *as*-, + Latin *socius* = an ally]

association *noun* **1** associating; being associated; companionship. **2** a group of people organised for some common purpose. **3** a mental connection between ideas.

associative (ă-**soh**-see-ă-tiv *or* ă-**soh**-shă-tiv) *adjective* **1** involving association. **2** (of a mathematical operation) producing the same result regardless of the way the elements are grouped, e.g. $(3 + 4) + 5 = 12$, just as $3 + (4 + 5) = 12$.

assonance (**ass**-ŏ-năns) *noun* similarity of vowel sounds in syllables that do not form a complete rhyme, as in *vermin/furnish*. [from *as*-, + Latin *sonus* = sound]

assorted *adjective* of different sorts put together, *assorted chocolates*; *an ill-assorted couple*, not well matched.

assortment *noun* **1** a collection composed of several sorts. **2** classification.

assuage (ă-**swayj**) *verb* to soothe, to make less severe; *to assuage one's thirst*, to satisfy it. [from *as*-, + Latin *suavis* = pleasant]

assume *verb* **1** to take as true or sure to happen before there is proof, *we assume that we shall win*. **2** to take on, to undertake, *he assumed the extra responsibility*. **3** to put on, *assumed a serious expression*. [from *as*-, + Latin *sumere* = take]

assuming *adjective* presumptuous.

assumption *noun* **1** assuming. **2** something taken for granted, something assumed but not proved; *on this assumption*, assuming this to be true or sure to happen. **–the Assumption** the reception of the Virgin Mary in bodily form into heaven; the festival commemorating this (15 August).

assurance *noun* **1** a formal declaration or promise given to inspire confidence. **2** life insurance. **3** self-confidence.

assure (ă-**shoor**) *verb* **1** to declare confidently, to promise, *I assure you there is no danger*. **2** to cause to know for certain, *tried the door to assure himself that it was locked*. **3** to make certain, to ensure, *this will assure your success*. **4** to insure by means of an assurance policy.

assured (ă-**shoord**) *adjective* **1** sure. **2** confident, *has an assured manner*. **3** payable under an assurance policy, *the sum assured*.

assuredly (ă-**shoor**-rĕd-lee) *adverb* certainly.

Assyria an ancient country in what is now northern Iraq. **Assyrian** *adjective* & *noun*

astatine (**as**-tă-teen) *noun* a radioactive element, a member of the halogen group (symbol At).

aster *noun* a garden plant with daisy-like flowers of various colours. [from Greek *aster* = star]

asterisk *noun* a star-shaped symbol (*) used in writing or printing to call attention to something or as a reference mark. **–asterisk** *verb* to mark with an asterisk. [from Greek *asteriskos* = little star]

astern *adverb* **1** in or at or towards the stern of a ship or the tail of an aircraft, behind. **2** backwards, *full speed astern!*

asteroid (**ass**-tĕ-roid) *noun* any of the small planets revolving round the sun, especially between the orbits of Mars and Jupiter. [same origin as *aster*]

asthma (**ass**-mă) *noun* a chronic condition causing difficulty in breathing.

asthmatic (ass-**mat**-ik) *adjective* **1** of asthma. **2** suffering from asthma. **–asthmatic** *noun* an asthmatic person. **asthmatically** *adverb*

astigmatism (ă-**stig**-mă-tizm) *noun* a defect in an eye or lens, preventing proper focusing. **astigmatic** (ass-tig-**mat**-ik) *adjective*, **astigmatically** *adverb* [from *a-²* = not, + Greek *stigma* = a point]

astir *adverb* & *adjective* in motion, moving.

astonish *verb* to surprise very greatly. **astonishment** *noun*

astound *verb* to shock with surprise.

astrakhan (ass-tră-**kan**) *noun* the dark tightly-curled fleece of lambs from Astrakhan in Russia; fabric imitating this.

astral (**ass**-trăl) *adjective* of or from the stars.

astray *adverb* & *adjective* away from the right path. **go astray** to be led into error or wrongdoing; (of things) to be mislaid. **lead astray** to lead into error or wrongdoing.

astride *adjective* **1** with legs wide apart. **2** with one leg on either side of something. **–astride** *preposition* astride of; extending across.

astringent (ă-**strin**-jĕnt) *adjective* **1** causing skin or body tissue to contract. **2** harsh, severe. **–astringent** *noun* an astringent substance, used medically or in cosmetics. **astringency** *noun* [from *as-*, + Latin *stringere* = bind tightly]

astrolabe (**ass**-trŏ-layb) *noun* an instrument formerly used for measuring the altitudes of stars. [from Greek *astrolabos* = star-taking]

astrologer *noun* an expert in astrology.

astrology (ă-**strol**-ŏ-jee) *noun* study of the supposed influence of stars on human affairs. **astrological** *adjective*, **astrologically** *adverb* [from Greek *astron* = star, + *-logy*]

astronaut *noun* a person trained to operate a spacecraft in which he or she travels. [from Greek *astron* = star, + *nautes* = sailor]

astronautics *noun* the scientific study of space travel and its technology.

astronomer *noun* an expert in astronomy.

astronomical *adjective* **1** of astronomy. **2** enormous in amount, *an astronomical sum of money*. **astronomically** *adverb*

astronomy (ă-**stron**-ŏ-mee) *noun* the scientific study of the stars and planets and their movements. [from Greek *astron* = star, + *-nomia* = arrangement]

astrophysics (as-troh-**fiz**-iks) *noun* the branch of astronomy concerned with the physics and chemistry of the heavenly bodies. **astrophysical** *adjective*, **astrophysicist** *noun*

astute (ă-**stewt**) *adjective* shrewd, quick at seeing how to gain an advantage. **astutely** *adverb*, **astuteness** *noun*

Asunción (ă-suun-see-**ohn**) the capital of Paraguay.

asunder (ă-**sun**-der) *adverb* apart, into pieces, *torn asunder*.

asura (ă-**syoor**-ră) *noun* a member of a class of divine beings in the Vedic period, which in Indian mythology are evil (opposed to *devas*) and in Zoroastrianism are benevolent.

Aswan (**as**-wahn) a city in southern Egypt near which are two dams across the Nile.

ASX *abbreviation* Australian Stock Exchange.

asylee *noun* a person who has left their native country to seek political asylum in another.

asylum *noun* 1 refuge and safety; a place of refuge. 2 (*old use*) a mental institution. [from Greek, = refuge]

asymmetry (ay-**sim**-ĕ-tree) *noun* lack of symmetry. **asymmetrical** *adjective*

asymptote (**as**-im-toht) *noun* a line that continuously approaches a curve but never touches it. **asymptotic** (a-sim-**tot**-ik) *adjective* [from Greek *asumptotos* = not falling together]

at *preposition* expressing position or state. 1 of place, order, or time of day, *at the top*; *came at midnight*. 2 of condition or occupation, *at ease*; *they are at dinner*. 3 of price, amount, or age, etc., *sold at $1 each*; *left school at 15*. 4 of cause, *was annoyed at his failure*. 5 of direction towards, *aimed at the target*. □ **at all** in any way, to any extent, of any kind. **at home** *see* **home**. **at-home** *noun* a reception for visitors between certain hours. **at it** engaged in some activity, working. **at once** immediately; simultaneously. **at one** in agreement or in harmony with someone. **at risk** undergoing a risk; in danger. **at that** at that point; moreover.

at- *prefix see* **ad-**.

Atalanta (at-ă-**lan**-tă) (*Gk. legend*) a fleet-footed maiden who refused to marry anyone who could not defeat her in a race.

Atatürk (**at**-ă-terk), Kemal (1881–1938), Turkish general and statesman, the founder of Turkey as a modern state.

atavism (**at**-ă-vizm) *noun* likeness to remote ancestors rather than to parents; reversion to an earlier type. [from Latin *atavus* = great-grandfather's grandfather]

atavistic (at-ă-**vis**-tik) *adjective* like a remote ancestor.

ataxia *noun* loss of full control of bodily movements.

ate *see* **eat**.

Atharda Veda *noun* one of the Vedas, a collection of hymns and ritual utterances. [from Sanskrit *Atharvan* (the name of Brahma's eldest son, said to be the author of the collection) + *veda*,'(sacred) knowledge']

atheist (**ay**-thee-ĭst) *noun* a person who does not believe in the existence of God or gods. **atheism** *noun*, **atheistic** (ay-thee-**ist**-ik) *adjective* [from *a-*[2] = not, + Greek *theos* = god]

Athene (ă-**thee**-nee) (*Gk. myth.*) the patron goddess of ancient Athens, goddess of wisdom, identified by the Romans with Minerva.

Athens the capital of Greece.

Atherton Tableland a high plateau in NE Queensland, west of Cairns.

athlete *noun* a person who is good at athletics. □ **athlete's foot** a fungal foot condition.

athletic *adjective* 1 of athletes. 2 physically strong and active, muscular in build. **athletics** *noun* or *plural noun* physical exercises and sports, especially competitions in running, jumping, etc. **athletically** *adverb*, **athleticism** *noun*

athwart *adverb* & *preposition* across from side to side.

Atlantic *adjective* of the Atlantic Ocean. –**Atlantic** *noun* the **Atlantic Ocean**, the ocean lying between the Americas and Europe/Africa.

Atlantis (*Gk. legend*) a beautiful and prosperous island in the Atlantic Ocean, overwhelmed by the sea.

Atlas (*Gk. myth.*) one of the Titans, who was punished for his part in their revolt against Zeus by being made to support the heavens.

atlas *noun* a book of maps. [named after Atlas]

Atlas Mountains a range of mountains in N Africa extending from Morocco to Tunis.

ATM *abbreviation* automated (or automatic) teller machine.

atm. *abbreviation* atmosphere(s).

atman *noun* (in Hinduism) the individual self; the supreme principle of life in the universe, Brahman. [Sanskrit, = essence, breath]

atmosphere *noun* 1 the mixture of gases surrounding the earth or any star or planet. 2 the air in any place. 3 a psychological environment, a feeling or tone conveyed by

something, *an atmosphere of peace and calm*.
4 a unit of pressure, equal to the pressure
of the atmosphere at sea level. **atmospheric**
adjective [from Greek *atmos* = vapour, +
sphere]

atmospherics *plural noun* electrical
disturbances in the atmosphere;
crackling sounds or other interference in
telecommunications caused by these.

atoll (**at**-ol) *noun* a ring-shaped coral reef
enclosing a lagoon.

atom *noun* **1** the smallest particle of a
chemical element. **2** this as a source of
atomic energy. **3** a very small quantity or
thing, *there's not an atom of truth in it*.
☐ **atom bomb** an atomic bomb. [from Greek
atomos = indivisible]

atomic *adjective* of an atom or atoms.
☐ **atomic bomb** a bomb that derives its
destructive power from atomic energy. **atomic
energy** energy obtained as the result of nuclear
fission. **atomic mass** the mass of an atom
measured in atomic mass units. **atomic mass
unit** a unit of mass used to express atomic and
molecular weights, equal to one-twelfth of the
mass of an atom of carbon-12. **atomic number**
the number of protons in the nucleus of an
atom. **atomic theory** the theory that all matter
consists of atoms. **atomic weight** = **relative
atomic mass**.

atomise *verb* (also **-ize**) to reduce to atoms or
fine particles. **atomisation** *noun*

atomiser *noun* (also **-izer**) a device for
reducing liquids to a fine spray.

atonal (ay-**toh**-năl) *adjective* (of music) not
written in any particular key or scale system.
[from *a-²* + *tonal*]

atone *verb* to make amends, to make up for
some error or deficiency. [from *at one*]

atonement *noun* **1** atoning. **2 the Atonement**
the expiation of man's sin by Christ.
☐ **Day of Atonement** Yom Kippur, the most
solemn religious fast of the Jewish year, eight
days after the Jewish New Year.

ATP *abbreviation* adenosine triphosphate, a
substance in living cells that provides energy
on being converted into ADP.

atrium (**ay**-tree-ŭm) *noun* (*plural* **atria** *or*
atriums) **1** the central court of an ancient
Roman house. **2** either of the two upper
cavities in the heart that receive blood from
the veins.

atrocious (ă-**troh**-shŭs) *adjective* **1** extremely
wicked, brutal. **2** (*informal*) very bad or

unpleasant. **atrociously** *adverb* [from Latin
atrox = cruel]

atrocity (ă-**tross**-ĭ-tee) *noun* **1** wickedness, a
wicked or cruel act. **2** a repellent thing.

atrophy (**at**-rŏ-fee) *noun* wasting away
through undernourishment or lack of use.
–**atrophy** *verb* (**atrophied**, **atrophying**)
1 to cause atrophy in. **2** to suffer atrophy.
[from *a-²*, + Greek *-trophia* = nourishment]

attach *verb* **1** to fix to something else. **2** to
join as a companion or member; to assign (a
person) to a particular group. **3** to attribute,
we attach no importance to the matter. **4** to
be ascribed, to be attributable, *no blame
attaches to the company*. **5** to make a legal
attachment of (money or goods). **attachable**
adjective

attaché (ă-**tash**-ay) *noun* a person who is
attached to the staff of an ambassador in
some specific field of activity, *the military
attaché*. ☐ **attaché case** a small rectangular
case for carrying documents etc. [French, =
attached]

attached *adjective* **1** fastened on. **2** bound by
affection or loyalty.

attachment *noun* **1** attaching; being
attached. **2** something attached; an extra part
that fixes on. **3** affection, devotion. **4** legal
seizure.

attack *verb* **1** to act violently against; to start a
fight. **2** to criticise strongly. **3** to act harmfully
on, *rust attacks metals*. **4** to begin vigorous
work on. –**attack** *noun* **1** a violent attempt to
hurt, overcome, or defeat. **2** strong criticism.
3 a sudden onset of illness, *an asthma attack*.
attacker *noun*

attain *verb* to succeed in doing or getting.
attainable *adjective*

attainment *noun* **1** attaining. **2** something
attained, a personal achievement.

attar (**at**-er) *noun* fragrant oil obtained from
flowers, *attar of roses*.

attempt *verb* **1** to make an effort to
accomplish, *that's attempting the impossible*.
2 to try to climb or master (a mountain etc.).
–**attempt** *noun* **1** an effort to accomplish
something. **2** an attack, an effort to overcome
or surpass something. [from *at-*, + Latin
temptare = try]

attend *verb* **1** to be present at; to go regularly
to, *to attend school*. **2** to apply one's mind,
to give care and thought; *attend to the
matter*, deal with it. **3** to take care of, to

look after, *which doctor is attending you?*
4 to accompany as an attendant.

attendance *noun* **1** attending. **2** the number of people present.

attendant *noun* a person who is present as a companion or whose function is to provide service. –**attendant** *adjective* accompanying.

attention *noun* **1** applying one's mind to something, mental concentration; *the drain needs attention*, needs to be repaired. **2** awareness, *it attracts attention*. **3** consideration, care, *she shall have every attention*. **4** a soldier's erect attitude of readiness with feet together and arms stretched downwards, *stand at attention*. –**attention** *interjection* an exclamation used to call people to take notice or to assume an attitude of attention. **attentions** *plural noun* small acts of kindness or courtesy.

attentive *adjective* **1** paying attention, watchful. **2** devotedly showing consideration or courtesy to another person. **attentively** *adverb*, **attentiveness** *noun*

attenuate (ă-**ten**-yoo-ayt) *verb* **1** to make slender or thin. **2** to make weaker, to reduce the force or value of. **attenuation** *noun*

attest (ă-**test**) *verb* **1** to provide clear proof of. **2** to declare to be true or genuine. **attestation** (at-ess-**tay**-shŏn) *noun* [from *at-*, + Latin *testari* = be a witness]

Attic *adjective* of Athens or Attica.

attic *noun* a room in the top storey of a house, immediately below the roof.

Attica the easternmost part of central Greece, in ancient times the territory of Athens (its chief city).

Attila (**at**-il-ă *or* ă-**til**-ă) king of the Huns 434–53, who inflicted great devastation on much of the Roman Empire.

attire *noun* (*formal*) clothes. –**attire** *verb* (*formal*) to clothe.

attitude *noun* **1** a position of the body or its parts. **2** a way of thinking or behaving.

attorney (ă-**ter**-nee) *noun* (*plural* **attorneys**) **1** a person who is appointed to act on behalf of another in business or legal matters; *power of attorney*, authority to act as attorney. **2** (*Amer.*) a lawyer, especially one qualified to act for clients in legal proceedings.

□ **attorney-general** (*plural* **attorney-generals** *or* **attorneys-general**) *noun* the chief legal officer in some countries or states, appointed by the Government holding office.

attract *verb* **1** to draw towards itself by unseen force. **2** to get the attention of. **3** to arouse the interest or pleasure of. [from *at-*, + Latin *tractum* = pulled]

attraction *noun* **1** attracting. **2** the ability to attract. **3** something that attracts by arousing interest or pleasure.

attractive *adjective* able to attract, pleasing in appearance or effect. **attractively** *adverb*, **attractiveness** *noun*

attribute (ă-**trib**-yoot) *verb* to regard as belonging to or caused by or originated by; *this play is attributed to Shakespeare*, people say that he wrote it. –**attribute** (**at**-rĭ-byoot) *noun* **1** a quality that is characteristic of a person or thing, *kindness is one of his attributes*. **2** an object regularly associated with a person or thing, *keys are an attribute of St Peter*; *a pair of scales is an attribute of Justice*. **attributable** (ă-**trib**-yŭ-tă-bŭl) *adjective*, **attribution** (at-rĭ-**byoo**-shŏn) *noun* [from *at-*, + Latin *tribuere* = allot]

attributive (ă-**trib**-yŭ-tiv) *adjective* expressing an attribute and placed before the word it describes, e.g. 'old' in *the old dog* (but not in *the dog is old*). (Compare *predicative*.) **attributively** *adverb*

attrition (ă-**trish**-ŏn) *noun* **1** wearing something away by rubbing. **2** a gradual wearing down of strength and morale by continuous harassment, *a war of attrition*. **3** loss of employees other than by redundancy.

attune *verb* to adapt (one's mind etc.) to a situation or idea.

atypical (ay-**tip**-ikăl) *adjective* not typical; not conforming to a type. [from *a-²* + *typical*]

aubergine (**oh**-ber-*zh*een) *noun* = **eggplant**.

aubrietia (aw-**bree**-shă) *noun* a low-growing perennial rock plant, flowering in spring. [named after Claude Aubriet, French botanist (1668–1743)]

auburn (**aw**-bern) *adjective* (of hair) reddish-brown.

AUC *abbreviation* (in dates) ab urbe condita. [Latin, = from the founding of the city, i.e. Rome, taken as 753 BC]

Auckland the largest city and chief seaport of New Zealand.

auction *noun* a public sale in which articles are sold to the highest bidder. –**auction** *verb* to sell by auction. [from Latin *auctum* = increased]

auctioneer *noun* a person who conducts an auction.

audacious (aw-**day**-shŭs) *adjective* bold, daring. **audaciously** *adverb*, **audacity** (aw-**dass**-ĭ-tee) *noun* [from Latin *audax* = bold]

audible *adjective* loud enough to be heard. **audibly** *adverb*, **audibility** *noun* [from Latin *audire* = hear]

audience *noun* 1 people who have gathered to hear or watch something. 2 people within hearing. 3 the people for whom a book or speech etc. is intended. 4 a formal interview with a ruler or other important person. [from Latin *audire* = hear]

audio *noun* (*plural* **audios**) 1 audible sound reproduced mechanically. 2 its reproduction. □ **audio book** a recording on cassette or compact disc of a reading of a book. **audio frequency** a frequency audible to the human ear (about 20 Hz to 20 kHz). **audio typist** one who types from a recording.

audiology *noun* the science of hearing. **audiologist** *noun*

audiotape *noun* magnetic tape for recording sound; a recording on this.

audio-visual *adjective* (of teaching aids etc.) involving both sight and sound.

audit *noun* an official examination of accounts to see that they are in order. – **audit** *verb* (**audited**, **auditing**) to make an audit of.

audition *noun* a trial to test the ability of a prospective performer. – **audition** *verb* 1 to hold an audition. 2 to be tested in an audition. [same origin as *audience*]

auditor *noun* 1 a person who makes an audit. 2 a listener.

auditorium (aw-dĭ-**tor**-ree-ŭm) *noun* (*plural* **auditoriums**) the part of a theatre or hall in which the audience sits.

auditory (**aw**-dĭ-tŏ-ree) *adjective* of or concerned with hearing.

au fait (oh **fay**) *adjective* well acquainted (with a subject). [French, = to the fact]

Augean (aw-**jee**-ăn) *adjective* 1 of the legendary king Augeus or his filthy stables, which Hercules cleaned in a day by diverting a river through them. 2 filthy.

auger (**awg**-er) *noun* a tool for boring holes in wood, like a gimlet but larger.

aught (*pr.* awt) *noun* (*old use*) anything, *for aught I know*.

augment (awg-**ment**) *verb* to add to, to increase. – **augment** (**awg**-ment) *noun* a vowel that is prefixed to the past tense of verbs in certain languages. **augmentation** *noun* [from Latin *augere* = increase]

augmented *adjective* 1 (of a musical interval) one semitone greater than the corresponding major or perfect interval. 2 (of a chord) containing such an interval.

au gratin (oh gră-**tan**) *adjective* cooked with a crisp crust of breadcrumbs or grated cheese or both. [French]

augur (**awg**-er) *verb* to foretell, to be a sign of; *this augurs well for your future*, is a favourable sign. – **augur** *noun* a religious official in ancient Rome who foretold future events by interpreting omens. [from Latin *augur* = prophet]

August *noun* the eighth month of the year. [named after Augustus Caesar]

august (aw-**gust**) *adjective* majestic, imposing. [from Latin *augustus* = majestic]

Augustan (aw-**gus**-tăn) *adjective* 1 of the reign of Augustus, especially as the period when Latin literature flourished. 2 (of any national literature) classical, stylish. – **Augustan** *noun* a writer of an Augustan period.

Augustine¹ (aw-**gus**-tĭn), St (of Canterbury, died c. 604), the first archbishop of Canterbury. Feast day, 26 May.

Augustine², St (of Hippo in North Africa, 354–430). Feast day, 28 August.

Augustinian (aw-gŭs-**tin**-ee-ăn) *adjective* of St Augustine of Hippo. – **Augustinian** *noun* a member of any of the Roman Catholic religious orders which observe a rule based on his writings.

Augustus¹ (aw-**gus**-tŭs) (63 BC–AD 14), the first Roman emperor, grand-nephew of Julius Caesar.

Augustus², Mount a large monolith in WA, rising to 1105 m.

auk *noun* a northern seabird with small narrow wings.

auld lang syne days of long ago, the title of a song written by Robert Burns. [Scots, = old long since]

aunt *noun* 1 a sister or sister-in-law of one's father or mother. 2 (*informal*) an unrelated woman friend of a child's parents, *Aunt Jane*.

☐ **Aunt Sally** a figure used as a target in a throwing game; a target of general abuse or criticism.

auntie *noun* (*informal*) **1** an aunt. **2 Auntie** an institution considered to be conservative or cautious, especially the ABC.

au pair (oh **pair**) *noun* a young person, usually a woman, from overseas helping with housework and receiving board and lodging in return. [French]

aura (**aw**-ră) *noun* a distinctive atmosphere surrounding a person or thing, *an aura of happiness*. [Greek, = breeze]

aural (**aw**-răl) *adjective* of the ear or hearing. **aurally** *adverb* [from Latin *auris* = ear]

Aurelius (aw-**ree**-lee-ŭs), Marcus (121–80), Roman emperor from 161, whose *Meditations* express his Stoic views.

aureole (**aw**-ree-ohl) *noun* (also **aureola**) **1** a celestial crown or halo, especially on a painting etc. of a divine figure. **2** a corona round the sun or moon.

au revoir (oh ră-**vwar**) *interjection* goodbye for the moment. [French]

auricle (**aw**-ri-kŭl) *noun* **1** the external part of the ear. **2** an atrium of the heart; a small appendage to this.

auriferous (aw-**rif**-ĕ-rŭs) *adjective* yielding gold.

Aurora (ă-**ror**-ră) (*Rom. myth.*) the goddess of the dawn, corresponding to the Greek Eos.

aurora (ă-**ror**-ră) *noun* bands of coloured light appearing in the sky at night and probably caused by electrical radiation from the north and south magnetic poles, **aurora australis** (o-**stray**-lĭs), also called the southern lights, in the southern hemisphere; **aurora borealis** (bor-ree-**ay**-lĭs), also called the northern lights, in the northern hemisphere. [from Latin *aurora* = dawn]

Auschwitz (**owsh**-vits) a town in Poland, site of a Nazi concentration camp in the Second World War.

auspice (**aw**-spĭs) *noun* an omen. **auspices** *plural noun* patronage, *under the auspices of the Red Cross*.

auspicious (aw-**spish**-ŭs) *adjective* showing signs that promise success. **auspiciously** *adverb*

AUSSAT *noun* Australia's domestic satellite system.

Aussie (**oz**-ee) *noun* (*informal*) **1** an Australian. **2** Australia. –**Aussie** *adjective*

(*informal*) Australian. ☐ **Aussie Rules** = **Australian Rules**.

Austen, Jane (1775–1817), English novelist, whose works include *Pride and Prejudice*, *Emma*, and *Persuasion*.

austere (os-**teer**) *adjective* severely simple and plain without ornament or comfort. **austerely** *adverb* [from Greek, = severe]

austerity (o-**ste**-rĭ-tee) *noun* being austere, an austere condition; *the austerities of wartime*, the shortages and hardships of wartime.

Australasia (os-tră-**lay**-*zh*ă) Australia, New Zealand, New Guinea, and neighbouring islands in the S Pacific. **Australasian** *adjective* & *noun*

Australia (o-**stray**-lee-ă) a country and continent in the southern hemisphere bounded by the Indian, Southern, and Pacific Oceans. ☐ **Australia Day** a public holiday commemorating the landing of Governor Phillip at Sydney Cove on 26 January 1788 and the beginning of British settlement in Australia. **Australia Felix** the name given by the explorer Thomas Mitchell in 1836 to the region now known as Victoria.

Australian (o-**stray**-lee-ăn) *noun* **1** a native or national of Australia. **2** a person of Australian descent. –**Australian** *adjective* of or relating to Australia. ☐ **Australian Antarctic Territory** an area of Antarctica administered by Australia as an external territory. **Australian Broadcasting Corporation** Australia's national and international television and radio broadcaster. **Australian Capital Territory** federal territory in SE Australia comprising two areas, one containing Canberra, and the other containing Jervis Bay. **Australian crawl** an overarm swimming stroke. **Australian Democrats** a centre political party (abbreviated to **Democrats**). **Australian Football League** the regulating body for Australian Rules Football; the national competition run by this organisation. **Australian Inland Mission Aerial Medical Service** an organisation, later known as the Royal Flying Doctor Service, founded by John Flynn in 1928 to provide medical services to people in remote outback areas. **Australian Labor Party** a social-democratic political party, formed to represent the interests of working people (abbreviated to **Labor** or **ALP**). **Australian Rules** a form of football played with an oval ball by teams of eighteen (also called *Aussie Rules* or *Australian National Football*). **Australian silky**

terrier a small terrier with long silky bluish hair (also called a *Sydney silky*).

Australiana (o-stray-lee-**ah**-nă) *noun* objects relating to or characteristic of Australia.

Australianise *verb* (also -ize) to make Australian in form or character.

Australianism *noun* a distinctively Australian word or phrase.

australite *noun* a small piece of dark meteoric glass found in Australia.

Australopithecus (os-tră-lŏ-**pith**-ĕ-kŭs) *noun* an extinct form of primitive man from the Lower Pleistocene era. **Australopithecine** *adjective* & *noun*

Austria (**os**-tree-ă) a republic in central Europe. **Austrian** *adjective* & *noun*

AUSTUDY *noun* a financial assistance scheme for Australian secondary and tertiary students.

aut- *prefix* see **auto-**.

autarchy (**aw**-tar-kee) *noun* a system of government with unrestricted powers; autocracy.

autarky (**aw**-tar-kee) *noun* self-sufficiency, especially in economic affairs.

authentic *adjective* genuine, known to be true. **authentically** *adverb*, **authenticity** *noun*

authenticate *verb* to prove the truth or authenticity of. **authentication** *noun*, **authenticator** *noun*

author *noun* 1 the writer of a book or books etc. 2 the originator of a plan or policy; the originator of anything, *the author of her woes*. **authoress** *feminine noun*, **authorship** *noun* [from Latin *auctor* = originator]

Usage The word *author* applies to both male and female writers, and is generally preferred to *authoress*.

---

authorise *verb* (also -ize) 1 to give authority to. 2 to give authority for, to sanction, *I authorised this payment*. ☐ **Authorised Version** the English translation of the Bible (1611) made by order of King James I (also called the *King James Bible*). **authorisation** *noun*

authoritarian (aw-tho-rĭ-**tair**-ree-ăn) *adjective* favouring complete obedience to authority as opposed to individual freedom. –**authoritarian** *noun* a holder of such principles.

authoritative (aw-**tho**-rĭ-tă-tiv) *adjective* having or using authority. **authoritatively** *adverb*

authority *noun* 1 the power or right to give orders and make others obey, or to take specific action. 2 a person or group with such power. 3 a person with specialised knowledge, a book etc. that can supply reliable information. [same origin as *author*]

autistic (aw-**tiss**-tik) *adjective* having a form of mental illness that causes a person to withdraw into a private world and be unable to communicate with others or respond to the real environment. **autism** (**aw**-tizm) *noun* this condition. [from *auto-*]

auto *noun* (*informal*) a motor car. [short for *automobile*]

auto- *prefix* (changing to **aut-** before a vowel). 1 self; own. 2 of or by oneself or itself, automatic. [from Greek *autos* = self]

autobiography *noun* the story of a person's life written by that person himself or herself. **autobiographical** *adjective* [from *auto-*, + *biography*]

autochthonous (aw-**tok**-thŏ-nŭs) *adjective* aboriginal, indigenous.

autocracy (aw-**tok**-ră-see) *noun* despotism. [from *auto-*, + *-cracy*]

autocrat (**aw**-tŏ-krat) *noun* a person with unlimited power, a dictatorial person. **autocratic** (aw-tŏ-**krat**-ik) *adjective*, **autocratically** *adverb*

autocrine *adjective* denoting or relating to a cell-produced substance that has an effect on the cell by which it is secreted.

Autocue *noun* (*trademark*) a device from which a television speaker may read the script.

auto-da-fé (aw-toh-da-**fay**) *noun* 1 the ceremonial judgment of heretics by the Spanish Inquisition. 2 the execution of heretics by public burning. [Portuguese, = act of the faith]

autogiro (aw-toh-**jy**-roh) *noun* (*plural* **autogiros**) an aircraft resembling a helicopter but with wings that are not powered and rotate in the slipstream. [Spanish]

autograph *noun* 1 a person's signature, his or her handwriting. 2 a manuscript in an author's own handwriting. 3 a document signed by its author. –**autograph** *verb* to write one's name on or in, *the author will autograph copies of her book tomorrow*. [from *auto-*, + *-graph*]

automate *verb* to control or operate by automation, *the process is fully automated.* □ **automated teller machine** a machine at which customers may conduct their banking using a personalised plastic card.

automatic *adjective* **1** working of itself without direct human control, self-regulating. **2** firing repeatedly until pressure on the trigger is released, *an automatic pistol.* **3** done without thought, done from habit or routine. –**automatic** *noun* **1** an automatic machine or tool or firearm. **2** a vehicle with a system for automatic gear change. □ **automatic pilot** a device in an aircraft or ship to keep it on a set course. **automatic teller machine** = automated teller machine. **automatically** *adverb* [from Greek *automatos* = self-operating]

automation *noun* the use of automatic equipment to save mental and manual labour.

automaton (aw-**tom**-ă-tŏn) *noun* a robot; a person who seems to act like one, mechanically and without thinking.

automobile (**aw**-tŏ-mŏ-beel) *noun* (especially *Amer.*) a motor car. [from *auto-*, + *mobile*]

automotive (aw-tŏ-**moh**-tiv) *adjective* concerned with motor vehicles.

autonomic (aw-tŏ-**nom**-ik) *adjective* functioning or occurring involuntarily. □ **autonomic nervous system** that part of the nervous system that controls involuntary functions such as digestion and heartbeats.

autonomous (aw-**ton**-ŏ-mŭs) *adjective* self-governing. **autonomy** *noun* self-government, independence. [from *auto-*, + Greek *nomos* = law]

autopilot *noun* an automatic pilot.

autopsy (**aw**-top-see) *noun* a post-mortem. [from Greek *autopsia* = seeing with your own eyes]

autosome *noun* a chromosome other than a sex chromosome.

auto-suggestion *noun* a self-induced or subconscious suggestion affecting reaction, behaviour, etc.

autotrophic (aw-toh-**troh**-fik) *adjective* self-nourishing; able to find nutritional organic substances from simple inorganic substances. □ **autotrophic bacteria** bacteria that obtain energy from light and that can assimilate carbon dioxide. [from *auto-*, + Greek *trophos* = feeder]

autumn *noun* the season between summer and winter. **autumnal** (aw-**tum**-năl) *adjective*, **autumnally** *adverb*

auxiliary (awg-**zil**-yă-ree) *adjective* giving help or support, *auxiliary services*; *an auxiliary verb*, one used in forming parts of other verbs, e.g. *have* in *I have finished.* –**auxiliary** *noun* a helper. **auxiliaries** *plural noun* auxiliary troops, foreign or allied troops employed by a country at war. [from Latin *auxilium* = help]

auxin (**awk**-sĭn) *noun* a hormone or similar substance that stimulates the growth of plants.

avail *verb* to be of help or advantage, *nothing availed against the storm.* –**avail** *noun* effectiveness, advantage, *it was of no avail.* □ **avail oneself of** to make use of. [from Latin *valere* = be strong]

available *adjective* ready or able to be used, obtainable. **availability** *noun*

avalanche (**av**-ă-lahnsh *or* -lansh) *noun* **1** a mass of snow or rock pouring down a mountainside. **2** a great onrush, *an avalanche of letters.* [French, from *avaler* = descend]

Avalon (**av**-ă-lŏn) **1** (in Arthurian legend) the place to which King Arthur was conveyed after death. **2** (*Welsh myth.*) an island paradise of the blessed dead.

avant-garde (av-ahn **gard**) *adjective* using or favouring an ultra-modern style, especially in art or literature. –**avant-garde** *noun* an avant-garde group. [French, = vanguard]

avarice (**av**-ă-rĭss) *noun* greed for gain. **avaricious** (av-ă-**rish**-ŭs) *adjective*, **avariciously** *adverb* [from Latin *avarus* = greedy]

avatar (**av**-ă-tar) *noun* **1** (in Hinduism) the descent to earth of a deity in human, animal, or superhuman form. **2** a movable icon representing a person in cyberspace etc.

Ave (**ah**-vay) *noun* (in full **Ave Maria**, *pr.* mă-**ree**-ă) Hail Mary. [Latin]

avenge *verb* to take vengeance for. **avenger** *noun*

avenue *noun* **1** a street or road, especially a wide one lined with trees. **2** a way of approaching or making progress, *other avenues to fame.*

aver (ă-**ver**) *verb* (**averred**, **averring**) to assert.

average *noun* **1** the value arrived at by adding several quantities together and dividing the total by the number of quantities.

2 the standard or level regarded as usual. **3** (in Law) sharing out of losses made on a ship or cargo. –average *adjective* **1** found by making an average. **2** of the ordinary or usual standard, *people of average intelligence*. –average *verb* **1** to amount to or produce as an average, *we averaged 90 kilometres an hour*. **2** to calculate the average of.

averse (ă-**verss**) *adjective* unwilling, disinclined, *he is averse to hard work*. [same origin as *avert*]

aversion (ă-**ver**-zhŏn) *noun* **1** a strong dislike. **2** something disliked.

avert (ă-**vert**) *verb* **1** to turn away, *people averted their eyes*. **2** to prevent, to ward off, *managed to avert disaster*. [from *ab-* = away, + Latin *vertere* = turn]

Avesta (ă-**vest**-ă) *noun* the sacred writings of Zoroastrianism.

aviary (**ayv**-yă-ree) *noun* a large cage or building for keeping birds. [from Latin *avis* = bird]

aviation (ay-vee-**ay**-shŏn) *noun* the practice or science of flying aircraft.

aviator (**ay**-vee-ay-ter) *noun* a pilot or member of an aircraft crew in the early days of aviation.

avid (**av**-ĭd) *adjective* eager, greedy. avidly *adverb*, avidity (ă-**vid**-ĭ-tee) *noun*

avionics (ay-vee-**on**-iks) *noun* the application of electronics in aviation.

AVO *abbreviation* apprehended violence order.

avocado (av-ŏ-**kah**-doh) *noun* (*plural* avocados) a pear-shaped tropical fruit with a dark leathery skin and pale green edible flesh.

avocet (**av**-ŏ-set) *noun* a wading bird with long legs and an upturned bill.

Avogadro (av-ŏ-**gahd**-roh), Amadeo (1776–1856), Italian physicist, noted for his work on gases. □ Avogadro's constant or number the number of atoms or molecules in a mole of a substance, equal to 6.023×10^{23}.

avoid *verb* **1** to keep oneself away from (something or someone dangerous or undesirable). **2** to refrain from, *avoid making rash promises*. avoidable *adjective*, avoidance *noun*

avoirdupois (av-er-dew-**poiz**) *noun* a system of weights based on the pound of 16 ounces or 7,000 grains. [from French, = goods of weight]

avow *verb* (*formal*) to admit, to declare openly. avowal *noun*, avowedly (ă-**vow**-ĕd-lee) *adverb*

avuncular (ă-**vunk**-yŭ-ler) *adjective* of or like a kindly uncle.

Awabakal (ă-**wub**-ă-kul) *noun* **1** a member of an Aboriginal people of eastern NSW north of Sydney. **2** their language.

AWACS (**ay**-waks) *abbreviation* (also Awacs) airborne warning and control system, an airborne long-range radar system.

await *verb* **1** to wait for, *I await your reply*. **2** to be waiting for, *a surprise awaits you*.

awake *verb* (awoke, awoken) **1** to wake, to cease to sleep. **2** to become active. **3** to rouse from sleep. –awake *adjective* **1** not yet asleep, no longer asleep. **2** alert, aware.

awaken *verb* to awake. awakening *noun*

award *verb* to give by official decision as a payment, penalty, or prize. –award *noun* **1** a decision of this kind. **2** a thing awarded. □ award wage (*Austral.*) a wage fixed by an industrial tribunal etc., payable by law in a particular occupation, industry, etc.

aware *adjective* having knowledge or realisation. awareness *noun*

awash *adjective* washed over by water or waves.

away *adverb* **1** to or at a distance. **2** out of existence, *the water has boiled away*. **3** constantly, persistently, *we worked away at it*. –away *adjective* played or playing on an opponent's ground, *an away match*. –away *noun* an away match.

awe *noun* respect combined with fear and wonder. –awe *verb* to fill with awe.

aweigh (ă-**way**) *adverb* hanging just clear of the sea bottom, *the anchor is aweigh*.

awesome *adjective* **1** causing awe. **2** (*informal*) excellent.

awestricken *adjective* (also awestruck) suddenly filled with awe.

awful *adjective* **1** extremely bad or unpleasant, *an awful accident*. **2** (*informal*) extreme, very great. awfully *adverb* [from *awe* + *full*]

awhile *adverb* for a short time.

awkward *adjective* **1** difficult to handle, use, or deal with. **2** clumsy, having little skill. **3** inconvenient, *came at an awkward time*. **4** embarrassed, *feel awkward about it*. awkwardly *adverb*, awkwardness *noun* [from Old Norse *afugr* = turned the wrong way]

awl *noun* a small pointed tool for making holes, especially in leather or wood.

awning *noun* a roof-like shelter of canvas etc., erected as a protection against sun or rain.

awoke, awoken *see* awake.

AWOL (**ay**-wol) *abbreviation* absent without leave.

awry (ă-**ry**) *adverb* 1 twisted towards one side. 2 amiss, *plans went awry*. –**awry** *adjective* crooked, wrong.

axe *noun* 1 a chopping tool. 2 (*informal*) removal, dismissal (of employees etc.); abandonment of a project etc. –**axe** *verb* to remove by abolishing or dismissing, *the project was axed*. □ **have an axe to grind** to have some personal interest involved and be anxious to take care of it.

axial *adjective* 1 of or forming an axis. 2 round an axis, *axial rotation*. □ **axial trace** the central line of a fold of land from which the strata slope up or down. **axially** *adverb*

axil *noun* the angle where a leaf joins a stem.

axillary (**aks**-il-ă-ree) *adjective* 1 of the armpit. 2 of or growing from an axil. [from Latin *axilla* = armpit]

axiom (**aks**-ee-ŏm) *noun* an accepted general truth or principle.

axiomatic (aks-ee-ŏ-**mat**-ik) *adjective* 1 of or like an axiom. 2 self-evident.

axis *noun* (*plural* **axes**) 1 an imaginary line through the centre of an object, round which it rotates when spinning. 2 a line about which a regular figure is symmetrically arranged. 3 a reference line for the measurement of coordinates etc. □ **the Axis** the alliance between Germany and Italy (and later Japan) in the Second World War. [Latin, = axle]

axle *noun* the bar or rod on which a wheel or wheels turn.

axolotl (ak-sŏ-**lot**-ŭl) *noun* a newtlike amphibian from Mexico.

ay (*pr*. I) *adverb & noun* (*plural* **ayes**) = aye[1].

ayatollah (I-ă-**tol**-ă) *noun* a Shi'ite Muslim religious leader in Iran. [Persian, = token of God]

aye[1] (*pr*. I) *adverb* yes. –**aye** *noun* a vote in favour of a proposal; *the ayes have it*, those in favour are in the majority.

aye[2] (*pr*. ay) *adverb* (*old use*) always.

Ayers Rock (*pr*. airz) *see* Uluru.

azalea (ă-**zay**-lee-ă) *noun* a flowering shrub.

azan *noun* (also adhan) the Muslim call to prayer made by the muezzin from the minaret of a mosque. [Arabic]

Azerbaijan (az-er-by-**jahn**) a republic of Eastern Europe on the western side of the Caspian Sea, north of Iran. **Azerbaijani** *adjective & noun*

azimuth (**az**-ĭ-mŭth) *noun* 1 an arc of the sky from the zenith to the horizon. 2 the angle between this arc and the meridian.

Azores (ă-**zorz**, the) a group of volcanic islands in the N Atlantic, in Portuguese possession but partly self-governing.

Azrael (**az**-rayl) (in Judaism and Islam) the angel who severs the soul from the body at death.

Aztec *noun* 1 a member of an indigenous people dominant in Mexico before the Spanish conquest (1521). 2 the language of this people. –**Aztec** *adjective* of the Aztecs or their language.

azure (**ay**-zher) *adjective & noun* sky-blue.

Bb

BA *abbreviation* Bachelor of Arts.

baa *noun* the cry of a sheep or lamb.

Baal (*pr.* bayl) an ancient Semitic male fertility god.

baba (**bah**-bah) *noun* a kind of sponge cake served soaked in flavoured syrup.

Babbage, Charles (1791–1871), English mathematician and inventor, pioneer of machine computing.

babble *verb* **1** to chatter in a thoughtless or confused way. **2** to make a continuous murmuring sound, *a babbling brook*. **–babble** *noun* babbling talk or sound.

babe *noun* **1** (*formal*) a baby. **2** (*informal*) a sexually attractive young man or woman. □ **babes and sucklings** very inexperienced people.

babel (**bay**-běl) *noun* a confused noise or scene. □ **tower of Babel** (in the Old Testament) a high tower built in an attempt to reach heaven, which God frustrated by confusing the languages of its builders so that they could not understand one another.

baboon *noun* a large African or Arabian monkey.

Babur (**bah**-boor) (1483–1530), the first Mogul emperor, who invaded India c. 1525.

baby *noun* **1** a very young child or animal. **2** a babyish or timid person. **3** something small of its kind. **4** (*informal*) something that is one's creation or in one's care. **–baby** *verb* (**babied, babying**) to treat like a baby, to pamper. □ **baby boom** a period with a high birth rate. **baby boomer** a person born in a baby boom, especially in the years immediately following the Second World War. **baby grand** the smallest kind of grand piano. **be left holding the baby** (*informal*) to be left with an unwelcome responsibility. **babyhood** *noun*

babyish *adjective* like a baby.

Babylon the capital of Babylonia.

Babylonia the ancient name for S Mesopotamia (now part of Iraq), a powerful kingdom until 538 BC. **Babylonian** *adjective & noun*

babysit *verb* to look after a child or children while the parents are out. **babysitter** *noun*

baccalaureate (bak-ă-**lor**-ree-ăt) *noun* (in full **international baccalaureate**, abbreviated **IB**) an international course of study and examination intended to qualify successful candidates for higher education.

Bacchanalia (bak-ă-**nay**-lee-ă) *noun* the festival of Bacchus, the god of wine, in ancient Rome. **Bacchanalian** *adjective*

Bacchus (**bak**-ŭs) (*Gk. myth*) another name for Dionysus.

Bach (*pr.* bahk), Johann Sebastian (1685–1750), German composer, the greatest of a large family of musicians, noted for his choral and keyboard music.

bachelor *noun* an unmarried man. **–Bachelor** *noun* a person who holds a university degree below that of Master, *Bachelor of Science*.

bacillus (bă-**sil**-ŭs) *noun* (*plural* **bacilli**, *pr.* bă-**sil**-I) a rod-like bacterium.

back *noun* **1** the hinder surface of the human body from neck to hip; the corresponding part of an animal's body. **2** that part of a chair etc. against which a seated person's back rests. **3** the part or surface of an object that is less used or less important; the part furthest from the front. **4** the part of a garment covering the back. **5** a defensive player near the goal in football etc.; his position. **–back** *adjective* **1** situated behind, *the back teeth*; *back streets*, remote and inferior. **2** of or for a past time, *back pay*. **–back** *adverb* **1** at or towards the rear, away from the front or centre. **2** in check, *hold it back*. **3** in or into a previous time or position or condition; *I'll be back at six*, shall return then. **4** in return, *pay it back*. **–back** *verb* **1** to go or cause to go backwards. **2** (of wind) to change gradually in an anticlockwise direction. **3** to give one's support to, to assist. **4** to give financial support to, *he is backing the play*. **5** to lay a bet on. **6** to cover the back of, *the rug is backed with canvas*. □ **at the back of** giving (a person) help and support; being the underlying cause or motive of (a thing). **back burner** a burner at the back of a stove; *put a problem on the back burner*, to delay dealing with it. **back**

cross a cross between a hybrid plant or animal and one of the same genetic type as one of its parents. **back-door** *adjective* underhand, secret, *back-door methods*. **back down** to give up a claim; to withdraw one's argument. **back number** an old issue of a periodical. **back of beyond** a very remote place. **back of Bourke** *see* Bourke². **back out** to withdraw from an agreement. **back seat** a seat at the back; *take a back seat*, to take a less prominent position; *back-seat driver*, a person who has no responsibility but is eager to give orders to one who has. **back to front** with the back placed where the front should be. **back up** to give one's support to; to confirm (a statement); to make a copy of (a computer record) to be stored in safety separately from the original. **have one's back to the wall** to be fighting for survival in a desperate situation. **backer** *noun*

backache *noun* a pain in one's back.

backbencher *noun* an MP who does not hold a senior office, and is therefore not entitled to sit on the front benches in parliament (*see* frontbencher).

backbiting *noun* spiteful talk, especially about a person who is not present.

backblocks *plural noun* (*Austral.*) land in the remote interior.

backbone *noun* 1 the column of small bones down the centre of the back, the spine. 2 strength of character.

backchat *noun* (*informal*) impudent repartee.

backdate *verb* to declare that (a thing) is to be regarded as valid from some date in the past.

backdrop *noun* 1 a flat painted curtain at the back of a stage set. 2 the setting or background for a scene or event.

backfire *verb* 1 to ignite or explode prematurely, especially in an internal combustion engine. 2 to produce an undesired effect, especially upon the originators, *their original plan backfired*. –**backfire** *noun* an instance of backfiring.

backflip *noun* a backward somersault in the air.

backgammon *noun* a game played on a double board with draughts and dice. [from *back* (because sometimes pieces must go back to the start), + Old English *gamen* = game]

background *noun* 1 the back part of a scene or picture, the setting for the chief objects or people; *he was kept in the background*, in an inconspicuous position; *background music*,

used as an accompaniment to a play or film etc. 2 the conditions and events surrounding and influencing something; *a person's background*, his or her family life, education, experience, etc.

backhand *adjective* (of a stroke or blow) made with the back of the hand turned outwards. –**backhand** *noun* a backhand stroke or blow.

backhanded *adjective* 1 backhand. 2 indirect; ambiguous; *a backhanded compliment*, one made with underlying sarcasm so that it is not a compliment at all.

backhander *noun* 1 a backhanded stroke or blow or remark. 2 (*informal*) a bribe, a reward for services rendered.

backing *noun* 1 help, support; *he has a large backing*, many supporters. 2 material used to support or line a thing's back. 3 a musical accompaniment to a singer.

backlash *noun* 1 a violent and usually hostile reaction to some event or development. 2 a recoil in machinery; excessive play between parts.

backless *adjective* 1 without a back. 2 (of a dress) cut low at the back.

backlog *noun* arrears of work.

backpack *noun* a bag worn slung by straps from both shoulders and resting on the back, used especially by hikers, a rucksack. **backpacker** *noun*

back-pedal *verb* (back-pedalled, back-pedalling) 1 to work a pedal backwards. 2 to back down from an argument or policy. 3 to reverse one's previous action.

backside *noun* (*informal*) the buttocks.

backslide *verb* to slip back from good behaviour into bad.

backspace *verb* to cause a typewriter carriage or computer cursor to move one space back.

backstage *adjective* & *adverb* behind the stage of a theatre, in the wings or dressing rooms.

backstitch *verb* to sew by inserting the needle each time in a line behind the place where it has just been brought out. –**backstitch** *noun* a stitch made in this way.

backstroke *noun* a swimming stroke done lying on the back.

backtrack *verb* 1 to go back the same way that one came. 2 to back down from an argument or policy, to reverse one's previous action.

backup *noun* 1 support. 2 a spare or reserve. 3 (in computing) the copying of data for safety; the copy itself. –**backup** *adjective* spare, reserve, supporting.

backward *adjective* 1 directed towards the back or the starting point. 2 having made less than normal progress. 3 diffident, not putting oneself forward. –**backward** *adverb* backwards. **backwardness** *noun*

backwards *adverb* 1 away from one's front, towards the back. 2 with the back foremost; in a reverse direction or order. □ **backwards and forwards** in each direction alternately.

backwash *noun* 1 a backward flow of water. 2 the after-effects of an action or event.

backwater *noun* 1 a stretch of stagnant water joining a stream. 2 a place unaffected by progress or new ideas.

backwoods *noun* 1 remote uncleared forest, as in North America. 2 a remote or backward area. **backwoodsman** *noun*

backyard *noun* a yard or garden at the back of a house. –**backyard** *adjective* done by an untrained person, or under primitive conditions, *backyard abortion*.

bacon *noun* salted or smoked meat from back or sides of a pig. □ **bring home the bacon** (*informal*) to achieve something successfully. **save one's bacon** (*informal*) to escape death or injury.

bactericide (bak-**teer**-rĭ-syd) *noun* a substance that kills bacteria. **bactericidal** *adjective* [from *bacterium*, + Latin *caedere* = kill]

bacteriology *noun* the scientific study of bacteria. **bacteriological** *adjective*, **bacteriologist** *noun* [from *bacterium* + -*logy*]

bacterium (bak-**teer**-ree-ŭm) *noun* (*plural* **bacteria**) a microscopic organism. **bacterial** *adjective* [from Greek *bakterion* = little stick]

Bactrian camel *noun* a two-humped camel, native to central Asia.

bad *adjective* (**worse**, **worst**) 1 wicked, evil. 2 unpleasant. 3 serious, severe. 4 inferior, of poor quality, worthless, incorrect; *the meat went bad*, decayed; *a bad business*, an unfortunate affair. 5 hurtful, unsuitable, *sweets are bad for the teeth*. 6 in ill health, diseased. –**bad** *adverb* (*Amer. informal*) badly, *is he hurt bad?* □ **bad blood** ill feeling, enmity. **bad debt** one that will not be repaid. **bad language** swear words. **bad luck** misfortune; an expression of real or mock sympathy at a misfortune. **bad-tempered** *adjective* having or showing bad temper. **not bad** (*informal*) quite good. **badness** *noun*

baddy *noun* (*informal*) a villain.

bade *see* bid².

badge *noun* a thing worn to show one's rank, occupation, membership of an organisation, support of a cause, etc.

badger *noun* an animal of the weasel family that burrows in the ground. –**badger** *verb* to pester. (¶ From the old sport of tormenting badgers.)

badinage (**bad**-ĭ-nah*zh*) *noun* banter. [French]

badlands *plural noun* a barren eroded region.

badly *adverb* (**worse**, **worst**) 1 in an inferior, unsuitable, or defective way. 2 so as to inflict much injury, severely. 3 (*informal*) very much.

badminton *noun* a game played with racquets and shuttlecocks across a high net. [named after Badminton in England where it was invented in about 1870]

Baffin Bay the strait between **Baffin Island** (the largest island in the Canadian Arctic) and Greenland, named after the English explorer William Baffin (c. 1584–1622) who discovered the island in 1616.

baffle *verb* 1 to puzzle, to perplex. 2 to frustrate, *baffled their attempts*. –**baffle** *noun* a screen placed so as to hinder or control the passage of sound, light, or fluid. **bafflement** *noun*

bag *noun* 1 a container made of flexible material with an opening at the top, used for holding or carrying things. 2 this with its contents; the amount it contains. 3 something resembling a bag; *bags under the eyes*, folds of loose skin. 4 the amount of game shot by a hunter. 5 (*informal, offensive*) a woman, especially an unattractive or unpleasant one. –**bag** *verb* (**bagged**, **bagging**) 1 to put into a bag or bags. 2 to kill or capture, *bagged a pheasant*. 3 (also **bags**) (*informal*) to stake a claim to, *I bags the front seat*. 4 to hang loosely. 5 (*Austral. informal*) to criticise or disparage. **bags** *plural noun* (*informal*) plenty, *bags of room*. □ **be in the bag** (*informal*) to be secured as one wished. **bagful** *noun* (*plural* **bagfuls**).

bagatelle (bag-ă-**tel**) *noun* 1 a board game in which small balls are struck into holes. 2 something small and unimportant. 3 a short piece of music.

bagel (**bay**-gĕl) *noun* a hard bread roll in the shape of a ring. [Yiddish]

baggage *noun* 1 luggage. 2 portable equipment. 3 (*humorous* or *derogatory*) a girl or woman.

baggy *adjective* (**baggier**, **baggiest**) hanging in loose folds. **baggily** *adverb*, **bagginess** *noun*

Baghdad (bag-**dad**) the capital of Iraq.

bagpipe *noun* (also **bagpipes**) a musical instrument with air stored in a bag and pressed out through pipes.

bahada *noun* = **bajada**.

Baha'i (bah-**hah**-ee) *noun* 1 a religion founded in Persia in the 19th century by Baha'ullah (1817–92) and his son, whose quest is for the peace and unification of mankind. 2 a follower of this religion. **Baha'ism** *noun*

Bahamas (bă-**hah**-măz) a country consisting of a group of islands in the West Indies. **Bahamian** *adjective* & *noun*

Bahasa (bă-**hah**-să) 1 **Bahasa Indonesia** the form of Malay used as the official language of Indonesia. 2 **Bahasa Malaysia** the form of Malay used as the official language of Malaysia.

Bahrain (bah-**rayn**) a sheikhdom consisting of a group of islands on the Persian Gulf. **Bahraini** *adjective* & *noun*

baht *noun* (*plural* **baht**) the unit of money in Thailand.

bail¹ *noun* 1 money or property pledged as security that a person accused of a crime will return, if he is released temporarily, to stand trial. 2 permission for a person's release on such security. –**bail** *verb* 1 to obtain or allow (a person's) release on bail. 2 to relieve by financial help in an emergency, *bail the firm out*. □ **go bail** to pledge money etc. as bail. **out on bail** released after bail is pledged.

bail² *noun* 1 either of the two crosspieces resting on the three stumps in cricket. 2 a bar separating horses in an open stable. 3 a stall in a milking shed. 4 a bar holding paper against the roller of a typewriter. –**bail** *verb* **bail up** (*Austral.*) 1 to drive (a cow) into a stall in a milking shed. 2 to hold up and rob (a traveller). 3 to buttonhole (a person).

bail³ *verb* to scoop out (water that has entered a boat); to clear (a boat) in this way. [from French *baille* = bucket]

bailey *noun* the outer wall of a castle, a courtyard enclosed by this.

Bailey bridge *noun* a temporary bridge made in prefabricated sections designed for rapid assembly. [named after its designer Sir Donald Bailey (1901–85)]

bailiff *noun* a law officer who helps a sheriff, serving writs and performing arrests.

bailiwick *noun* 1 the authority or territory of a bailiff. 2 a person's particular interest or sphere.

Bairam (by-**rahm**) *noun* either of two annual Muslim festivals, **Lesser Bairam** (which follows Ramadan) in the tenth month and **Greater Bairam** in the twelfth month of the Islamic year.

bairn *noun* (*Scottish*) a child.

Baisakhi (**by**-sa-kee) *noun* a major Sikh festival, commemorating the formation of the Khalsa in 1699. [from Sanskrit]

bait *noun* 1 food (real or sham) placed to attract prey. 2 an enticement. –**bait** *verb* 1 to place bait on or in, *bait the trap*. 2 to torment by jeering.

baize *noun* thick green woollen cloth, used especially for covering billiard tables and card tables.

bajada (bă-**hah**-dă) *noun* (also **bahada**) a sloping area at the base of a mountain range, formed by several alluvial fans joining together.

bake *verb* 1 to cook or be cooked by dry heat. 2 to expose to great heat; to harden or be hardened by heat.

bakehouse *noun* a building or room for baking bread.

bakelite (**bay**-kĕ-lyt) *noun* a kind of plastic. [named after its Belgian-American inventor L.H. Baekeland (died 1944)]

baker *noun* one who bakes and sells bread. □ **baker's dozen** thirteen. (¶ From the former custom of giving the customer an extra loaf free for each twelve paid for.)

bakery *noun* a place where bread is baked for sale.

baking powder *noun* a mixture of powders (including sodium bicarbonate) used as a raising agent for cakes etc.

baking soda *noun* sodium bicarbonate, used in baking.

baklava (**bak**-lă-vă) *noun* a rich cake of flaky pastry, honey, and nuts. [Turkish]

Baku (ba-**koo**) the capital of Azerbaijan.

Balaclava (bal-ă-**klah**-vă) a Crimean village, scene of a battle (1854) in the Crimean War. –balaclava *noun* a woollen garment covering the head and neck.

balalaika (bal-ă-**ly**-kă) *noun* a musical instrument like a guitar with a triangular body. [Russian]

balance *noun* 1 a weighing apparatus with two scales or pans hanging from a crossbar. 2 a balance wheel. 3 an even distribution of weight or amount, a steady position; *the balance of one's mind*, one's sanity. 4 the difference between credits and debits. 5 money remaining after payment of a debt. –balance *verb* 1 to consider by comparing, *balance one argument against another*. 2 to be or put or keep (a thing) in a state of balance. 3 to compare the debits and credits of an account and make the entry needed to equalise these; to have these equal. □ balance of payments the difference between the amount paid to foreign countries for imports and services and the amount received from them for exports etc. in a given period. balance of power a situation in which the chief States of the world have roughly equal power; the power to decide events, held by a small group when the larger groups are of equal strength to each other. balance of trade the difference in value between imports and exports. balance sheet a written statement of assets and liabilities. balance wheel a wheel regulating the speed of a clock or watch. in the balance with the outcome still uncertain. off balance in danger of falling. on balance taking everything into consideration. [from Latin *bilanx* = having two scale-pans]

Balboa, Vasco Núñez de (1475–1517), Spanish explorer, especially of Central America; the first European to see the Pacific Ocean.

balcony (**bal**-kŏ-nee) *noun* 1 a platform with a rail or parapet, projecting outside an upper storey of a building. 2 an upper floor of seats in a cinema or above the dress circle in a theatre. balconied *adjective*

bald *adjective* 1 with the scalp wholly or partly hairless. 2 (of animals) lacking the usual hair or feathers of the species. 3 (of tyres) with the tread worn away. 4 bare, without details, *bald facts*. baldly *adverb*, baldness *noun*

Balder (**bawl**-der) (*Scand. myth.*) a son of Odin and god of the summer sun, who could not be wounded by anything except mistletoe.

balderdash *noun* nonsense.

balding *adjective* becoming bald.

bale[1] *noun* 1 a large bundle of straw etc. bound with cord or wire. 2 a large package of goods. –bale *verb* to make into a bale. baler *noun*

bale[2] *verb* bale out to make a parachute descent from an aircraft in an emergency.

baleen (bă-**leen**) *noun* whalebone. □ baleen whale a whale having plates of baleen in its mouth for straining plankton from the water.

baleful *adjective* menacing, destructive, *a baleful influence*. balefully *adverb* [from Old English *balu* = evil]

Bali (**bah**-lee) an island of Indonesia. Balinese *adjective* & *noun*

balk (*pr.* bawk) *verb* & *noun* = baulk.

Balkan (**bawl**-kăn) *adjective* of the peninsula in SE Europe bounded by the Adriatic, Aegean, and Black Seas, or of its people or countries. –the Balkans the Balkan countries.

ball[1] *noun* 1 a solid or hollow sphere. 2 such a sphere used in games. 3 a single delivery of the ball by the bowler in cricket or by the pitcher in baseball. 4 material gathered or wound into a round mass, *a ball of string*. 5 a rounded part; *the ball of the foot*, that under the foot at the base of the big toe. –ball *verb* 1 to squeeze or wind so as to form a ball. 2 to form a lump or lumps. □ ball bearing a bearing using small steel balls; one of these balls. on the ball (*informal*) alert, competent. start the ball rolling to start a discussion or activity.

ball[2] *noun* a social assembly for dancing. [same origin as *ballet*]

ballad *noun* a simple song or poem, especially one telling a story.

ballade (ba-**lahd**) *noun* a poem with sets of three verses each ending with the same refrain line.

ballast (**bal**-ăst) *noun* 1 heavy material placed in a ship's hold to improve its stability; *ship is in ballast*, laden with ballast only. 2 coarse stones etc. forming the bed of a railway or road.

ballcock *noun* a device with a floating ball controlling the water level in a cistern.

ballerina (ba-lĕ-**ree**-nă) *noun* a female ballet dancer.

ballet (**bal**-ay) *noun* a form of dancing and mime to music; a performance of this. [from Old French *baler* = to dance]

ballistic (bă-**lis**-tik) *adjective* **1** of projectiles such as bullets and missiles. **2** (*informal*) wildly angry. **ballistics** *plural noun* the scientific study of projectiles or of firearms. [from Greek *ballein* = to throw]

balloon *noun* **1** a small inflatable rubber pouch with a neck, used as a child's toy or a decoration. **2** a large usually round envelope inflated with hot air or light gases to make it rise in the air, often carrying a basket etc. in which passengers may ride. **3** a balloon-shaped line enclosing the words or thoughts of a character in a comic strip or cartoon. –**balloon** *verb* **1** to swell like a balloon. **2** to travel by balloon. **3** to kick or hit high in the air.

balloonist *noun* a person who travels by balloon.

ballot *noun* **1** the process of (usually secret) voting by means of papers or tokens. **2** a paper or token used in this. **3** the number of such votes recorded. –**ballot** *verb* (**balloted**, **balloting**) **1** to vote by ballot. **2** to cause to do this, *balloting their members*. □ **ballot box** a container for ballot papers. **ballot paper** a paper used in voting by ballot, usually having the names of candidates etc. printed on it. [from Italian *ballotta* = little ball (because originally this kind of voting was by dropping balls into a box)]

ballpark *noun* (*Amer.*) a baseball ground. –**ballpark** *adjective* (*informal*) approximate, *a ballpark figure*.

ballpoint *noun* (in full **ballpoint pen**) a pen with a tiny ball as its writing point.

ballroom *noun* a large room where dances are held.

ballyhoo *noun* **1** loud noise, fuss. **2** extravagant publicity.

balm (*pr.* bahm) *noun* **1** = balsam (sense 1). **2** a fragrant ointment. **3** a healing or soothing influence. **4** an aromatic herb.

Balmain bug *noun* an edible marine shellfish, a shovel-nosed lobster.

balmy (**bah**-mee) *adjective* (**balmier**, **balmiest**) **1** like balm, fragrant. **2** soft and warm, *balmy air*. **3** (*informal*) barmy.

balsa (**bawl**-să) *noun* (also **balsa wood**) very lightweight wood from a tropical American tree, used for making rafts, models, etc.

balsam (**bawl**-săm) *noun* **1** a soothing oil. **2** a kind of flowering plant.

balsamic vinegar *noun* a dark sweet vinegar, matured in wooden barrels.

Baltic (**bawl**-tik) *adjective* of the **Baltic Sea**, an almost landlocked sea of NE Europe. –**Baltic** *noun* the Baltic Sea.

baluster (**bal**-ŭster) *noun* each of the short stone pillars in a balustrade.

balustrade (bal-ŭs-**trayd**) *noun* a row of short posts or pillars supporting a rail or stone coping round a balcony or terrace.

Bama (**bah**-mă) *noun* an Aboriginal person from north Queensland.

Usage see **aborigine**.

Bamako (**bam**-ă-koh) the capital of Mali.

bamboo (bam-**boo**) *noun* a giant tropical grass with hollow stems. [from Malay word]

bamboozle *verb* (*informal*) **1** to hoax, to cheat. **2** to mystify. **bamboozlement** *noun*

ban *verb* (**banned**, **banning**) to forbid officially. –**ban** *noun* an order that bans something.

banal (bă-**nahl**) *adjective* commonplace, uninteresting. **banality** *noun*

banana *noun* **1** the finger-shaped fruit of a tropical tree. **2** this tree. □ **banana republic** (*derogatory*) a small country dependent on its fruit exports and regarded as economically unstable. **go bananas** (*informal*) to go crazy.

band[1] *noun* **1** a narrow strip, hoop, or loop. **2** a range of values, wavelengths, etc. within a series. –**band** *verb* to put a band on or round.

band[2] *noun* **1** an organised group of people with a common purpose. **2** a set of people playing music together, especially on wind or percussion instruments. –**band** *verb* to unite in an organised group, *band together*.

bandage *noun* a strip of material for binding up a wound. –**bandage** *verb* to bind up with this.

band-aid *adjective* temporary; makeshift, *a band-aid solution to the problem*. [from *Band-Aid* (*trademark*) a type of sticking plaster with a gauze pad]

bandanna (ban-**dan**-ă) *noun* a large coloured handkerchief typically worn as clothing.

Bandar Seri Begawan (**ban**-dah se-ree bě-**gah**-wăn) the capital of Brunei.

B. & B. *abbreviation* bed and breakfast.

bandeau (**ban**-doh) *noun* (*plural* bandeaux, *pr.* **ban**-doh) a strip of material worn round the head. [French]

bandicoot *noun* a marsupial of Australia and New Guinea with a long pointed head.

bandit *noun* a member of a band of robbers. banditry *noun* [from Italian *bandito* = outlawed or banned]

bandmaster *noun* the conductor of a musical band.

bandolier (band-ŏ-**leer**) *noun* a shoulder-belt with loops for ammunition. [from Dutch *bandelier*]

bandsaw *noun* a power saw consisting of a toothed steel belt running over wheels.

bandsman *noun* (*plural* bandsmen) a member of a musical band.

bandstand *noun* a covered outdoor platform for a musical band.

bandwagon *noun* 1 (*Amer.*) a wagon for a band of musicians to ride on, as in a parade. 2 an imaginary vehicle thought of as carrying a thing that is heading for success. □ climb or jump on the bandwagon to seek to join a successful enterprise or follow its example.

bandwidth *noun* a range of frequencies in telecommunications etc.

bandy[1] *verb* (bandied, bandying) to pass to and fro, *the story was bandied about*; *bandy words*, exchange remarks in quarrelling.

bandy[2] *adjective* (bandier, bandiest) curving apart at the knees. bandiness *noun*

bane *noun* a cause of trouble, misery, or anxiety. baneful *adjective*, banefully *adverb*

bang *verb* 1 to make a sudden loud noise like an explosion. 2 to strike or shut noisily. 3 to collide. –bang *noun* 1 the sudden loud noise of or like an explosion. 2 a sharp blow. –bang *adverb* 1 with a bang, abruptly; *bang go my chances*, they are suddenly destroyed. 2 (*informal*) exactly, *bang in the middle*; *his estimate was bang on*, was exactly right. □ go with a bang (*informal*) to be very successful or impressive.

bangalay (**bang**-gă-lay) *noun* a shady gumtree of eastern Australia. [probably from Dharawal]

bangalow (**bang**-gă-loh) *noun* a tall eastern Australian palm with arching feather-like fronds. [from Dharawal, probably *banggala*]

banger *noun* 1 a firework made to explode noisily. 2 (*informal*) a sausage.

Bangkok (bang-**kok**) the capital of Thailand.

Bangladesh (bang-glă-**desh**) a republic in SE Asia bordering on northern India. Bangladeshi *adjective* & *noun* (*plural* Bangladeshis).

bangle *noun* a bracelet of rigid material. [from Hindi *bangri*]

Bangui (**bang**-gee) the capital of the Central African Republic.

banian *noun* = banyan.

banish *verb* 1 to condemn to exile. 2 to dismiss from one's presence or one's mind, *banish fears*. banishment *noun*

banister *noun* each of the uprights supporting the handrail of a stair. banisters *plural noun* these uprights and the rail together.

banjo (**ban**-joh) *noun* (*plural* banjos) a stringed instrument rather like a guitar.

Banjul (ban-**jool**) the capital of the Gambia.

bank[1] *noun* 1 a slope, especially at the side of a river. 2 a raised mass of sand etc. in a river bed. 3 a long mass of cloud, snow, or other soft substance. 4 a row or series of lights, switches, etc. –bank *verb* 1 to build or form a bank; *bank up the fire*, heap on coal dust etc. so that it burns slowly. 2 to tilt or be tilted sideways in rounding a curve.

bank[2] *noun* 1 an establishment for keeping people's money etc. safely and paying it out on a customer's order. 2 the money held by the keeper of a gaming table. 3 a place for storing a reserve supply, *a blood bank*. –bank *verb* 1 to place or keep money in a bank. 2 to base one's hopes, *we are banking on your success*. □ bank book a book recording a customer's deposits and withdrawals, interest payments, bank fees, etc.; a passbook.

banker[1] *noun* 1 a person who runs a bank. 2 the keeper of a gaming bank.

banker[2] *noun* (*Austral.*) a river in flood, flowing as high as its banks.

banking *noun* the business of running a bank.

banknote *noun* a small strip of paper or plastic issued by a bank to serve as currency, printed with the amount for which it is valid.

bankrupt *noun* a person who is unable to pay his debts in full and whose estate is administered and distributed for the benefit of his creditors. –bankrupt *adjective* 1 declared by a lawcourt to be a bankrupt. 2 financially ruined and in debt. –bankrupt *verb* to make bankrupt. bankruptcy *noun* [from *bank*[2], + Latin *ruptum* = broken]

Banks, Sir Joseph (1743–1820), English naturalist who accompanied Cook on his expedition to Australia (1768–71).

banksia *noun* an Australian shrub with yellowish cylindrical heads of flowers. [named after Sir Joseph Banks]

banner *noun* **1** a flag. **2** a strip of cloth bearing an emblem or slogan, hung up or carried on a crossbar or between two poles in a procession etc. **3** an advertisement on a website in the form of a bar or box.

banns *plural noun* a public announcement in church of a forthcoming marriage between two named people. [from *ban* = proclamation]

banquet *noun* an elaborate ceremonial public meal. –**banquet** *verb* (**banqueted**, **banqueting**) to give or take part in a banquet. [from Old French *banquet* = little bench]

banshee (**ban**-shee) *noun* (*Irish & Scottish*) a female spirit whose wail is superstitiously believed to foretell a death in a house. [from Irish *bean sídhe* = woman of the fairies]

bantam *noun* a kind of small domestic fowl. [named after Bantan, in Java]

bantamweight *noun* a boxing weight between featherweight and flyweight, in amateur boxing 51–54 kg.

banter *noun* good-humoured teasing. –**banter** *verb* to joke in a good-humoured way.

Bantu (ban-**too**) *noun* (*plural* Bantu *or* Bantus) one of a group of Black African peoples or their languages. [Bantu word, = people]

banyan (**ban**-yăn) *noun* a tropical fig tree with spreading branches from which roots grow downwards to the ground and form new trunks. [Portuguese]

baobab (**bay**-ŏ-bab) *noun* (also **boab**, *pr.* **boh**-ab) a northern Australian and African tree with a massive trunk and large edible pulpy fruit.

bap *noun* a soft flat bread roll.

baptise *verb* (also **-ize**) to perform baptism on. [from Greek *baptizein* = to dip]

baptism *noun* the religious rite of sprinkling water on the forehead or immersing a person in water to symbolise purification and admission to the Christian Church. **baptismal** *adjective*

Baptist *noun* a member of a Protestant religious denomination believing that baptism should be by immersion and performed at an age when the person is old enough to affirm

his or her own faith before witnesses. –**the Baptist** St John, who baptised Christ.

baptistery (**bap**-tĭst-eree) *noun* **1** a building or part of a church used for baptism. **2** a tank used in a Baptist chapel for baptism by immersion.

bar[1] *noun* **1** a long piece of solid material. **2** a narrow strip, *bars of colour*; a strip of silver below the clasp of a medal, given as an additional award of an honour. **3** any barrier or obstacle; a sandbank; a restriction. **4** each of the vertical lines dividing a piece of music into equal units; a unit contained by these. **5** a partition (real or imaginary) across a court of justice separating the judge, jury, and certain lawyers from the public; **the Bar** barristers. **6** a counter or room where alcohol is served. **7** a place where refreshments are served across a counter, *a coffee bar*. **8** a shop counter selling a single type of commodity or service. –**bar** *verb* (**barred**, **barring**) **1** to fasten with a bar or bars. **2** to keep in or out by this. **3** to obstruct, *barred the way*. **4** to prevent or prohibit. –**bar** *preposition* except, *all over bar the shouting*. □ **bar chart** a graph on which quantities are represented by bars of equal width but varying height. **bar code** a pattern of stripes (on packaging or on a library book etc.) containing information for processing by a computer. **bar-coded** *adjective* marked with a bar code. **not have a bar of** (*Austral. informal*) to reject utterly; to be unable to tolerate. **to be called to the Bar** to become a barrister. **behind bars** in prison.

bar[2] *noun* a unit of pressure used in meteorology. [from Greek *baros* = weight]

Barabbas (bă-**rab**-ăs) the robber whom Pontius Pilate released from prison to the Jews instead of Jesus Christ.

barathea (ba-răth-**ee**-ă) *noun* a kind of fine woollen cloth.

barb *noun* **1** the backward-pointing part of an arrowhead or fish hook etc. that makes it difficult to withdraw from what it has pierced. **2** a wounding remark. **3** a small pointed projecting part or filament. [from Latin *barba* = beard]

Barbados (bar-**bay**-dos) an island nation in the West Indies. **Barbadian** *adjective* & *noun*

barbarian *noun* an uncivilised person. –**barbarian** *adjective* of barbarians. [from Greek *barbaros* = babbling, not speaking Greek]

barbaric (bar-**ba**-rik) *adjective* suitable for barbarians, rough and wild. **barbarically** *adverb*

barbarism (**bar**-bă-rizm) *noun* an uncivilised condition or practice.

barbarity (bar-**ba**-rĭ-tee) *noun* savage cruelty; a savagely cruel act.

Barbarossa the nickname of the Holy Roman Emperor Frederick I (reigned 1152–90). [Italian, = Redbeard]

barbarous (**bar**-bă-rŭs) *adjective* uncivilised, cruel. **barbarously** *adverb*

Barbary an old name for the W part of N Africa. □ **Barbary ape** a macaque of N Africa and Gibraltar.

barbecue (**bar**-bĕ-kew) *noun* (also **barbeque**) **1** an appliance for cooking food out of doors, consisting of a grill or metal plate heated by any of various means; a fireplace containing such an appliance. **2** an open-air party at which food is cooked on this. **3** the food itself. –**barbecue** *verb* to cook on a barbecue.

barbed *adjective* having a barb or barbs. □ **barbed wire** wire with short sharp points at intervals.

barber *noun* a men's hairdresser. [from Latin *barba* = beard]

barbican *noun* an outer defence of a castle or city, especially a double tower over a gate or bridge.

barbie *noun* (*Austral. informal*) a barbecue.

barbiturate (bar-**bich**-ŭ-răt) *noun* a kind of sedative drug.

Barbuda *see* **Antigua and Barbuda.**

barcarole (bar-kă-**rohl**) *noun* **1** a gondolier's song. **2** a piece of music with a steady lilting rhythm. [from Italian *barca* = boat]

Barcelona (bar-sĕ-**loh**-nă) a city and province of Catalonia in NE Spain.

barchan (**bar**-kăn) *noun* a crescent-shaped sand dune.

bard *noun* **1** a Celtic minstrel. **2** (*formal*) a poet. □ **the Bard of Avon** Shakespeare. **bardic** *adjective*

bardie *noun* (*Austral.*) an edible grub found in the bark of some trees. [Nyungar and other Aboriginal languages]

bardo *noun* (in Tibetan Buddhism) a state of existence between death and rebirth, varying in length according to one's conduct in life. [Tibetan]

bare *adjective* **1** without clothing or covering; *trees were bare*, leafless; *with one's bare hands*, without tools or weapons. **2** exposed, undisguised, *lay bare the truth*. **3** plain, without detail, *the bare facts*. **4** empty of stores, *the cupboard was bare*. **5** only just sufficient, *the bare necessities of life*. –**bare** *verb* to uncover, to reveal, *bared its teeth in a snarl*. **bareness** *noun*

bareback *adjective* & *adverb* on a horse without a saddle.

barefaced *adjective* shameless, undisguised.

barefoot *adjective* & *adverb* without shoes or socks etc. on the feet.

bareheaded *adjective* not wearing a hat.

barely *adverb* **1** scarcely, only just. **2** scantily, *barely furnished*.

Barents Sea (**ba**-rĕnts) a part of the Arctic Ocean, north of Russia, named after the Dutch explorer Willem Barents (died 1597).

bargain *noun* **1** an agreement made with obligations on both or all sides. **2** something obtained as a result of this; a thing got cheaply. –**bargain** *verb* to discuss the terms of an agreement. □ **bargain for** or **on** to be prepared for, to expect, *didn't bargain on his arriving so early*; *got more than he bargained for*, was unpleasantly surprised. **bargain on** to rely on. **into the bargain** in addition to other things.

barge *noun* a large flat-bottomed boat for use on canals or rivers, especially for carrying goods. –**barge** *verb* to move clumsily or heavily. □ **barge in** to intrude.

bargee (bar-**jee**) *noun* a person in charge of a barge, a member of its crew.

barista (bă-**ris**-tă) *noun* a person who operates an espresso machine in a cafe etc. [from Italian, = bartender]

barite (**bair**-ryt) *noun* barium sulphate.

baritone *noun* **1** a male voice between tenor and bass. **2** a singer with such a voice; a part written for this. [from Greek *barus* = heavy, + *tone*]

barium (**bair**-ree-ŭm) *noun* **1** a chemical element (symbol Ba), a soft silvery-white metal. **2** a chemical substance swallowed or injected into the digestive tract when this is to be X-rayed.

bark[1] *noun* the outer layer of tree trunks and branches. –**bark** *verb* **1** to peel bark from. **2** to scrape the skin off accidentally, *barked my knuckles*.

bark² *noun* the sharp harsh sound made by a dog or fox. –**bark** *verb* **1** to make this sound. **2** to speak in a sharp commanding voice, *barked out orders*.

barley *noun* a kind of cereal plant; its grain. □ **barley sugar** a sweet made of boiled sugar. **barley water** a drink made from pearl barley.

barmaid *noun* a female attendant at a bar serving alcohol.

barman *noun* (*plural* **barmen**) a male attendant at a bar serving alcohol.

bar mitzvah (**mits**-vă) *noun* **1** a Jewish boy aged 13 when he takes on the responsibilities of an adult under Jewish law. **2** the ceremony at which he does this. [Hebrew, = son of commandment]

barmy *adjective* (*informal*) crazy.

barn *noun* a simple roofed building for storing grain or hay etc. on a farm. □ **barn owl** an owl that often breeds and roosts in barns and other buildings. [from Old English *bere ern* = barley house]

Barnabas, St (1st century), a Cypriot Levite, who accompanied St Paul on missionary journeys. Feast day, 11 June.

barnacle *noun* a kind of shellfish that attaches itself to objects under water.

Barnardo, Thomas John (1845–1905), British philanthropist, founder of a chain of homes for destitute children.

barney *noun* (*informal*) a noisy dispute.

barnyard *noun* a yard beside a barn.

barograph (**ba**-rŏ-grahf) *noun* a barometer that produces a graph showing the atmospheric pressure. [from Greek *baros* = weight, + *graph*]

barometer (bă-**rom**-ĕ-ter) *noun* an instrument measuring atmospheric pressure, used for forecasting the weather. **barometric** (barŏ-**met**-rik) *adjective* [from Greek *baros* = weight, + *meter*]

baron *noun* **1** a member of the lowest rank of the nobility in Britain and certain other countries. **2** (in the Middle Ages in Britain) a man who held lands etc. from the king. **3** an important businessman, a magnate; *a newspaper baron*, one controlling many newspapers. **baroness** *feminine noun*

baronet *noun* a holder of a British hereditary title ranking below a baron but above a knight, having the title 'Sir'. **baronetcy** *noun* the rank of a baronet.

baronial (bă-**roh**-nee-ăl) *adjective* of or suitable for a baron, *a grand baronial hall*.

barony *noun* the rank or lands of a baron.

baroque (bă-**rok** *or* -**rohk**) *adjective* of the ornate architectural style of the 17th and 18th centuries, or of comparable musical developments c. 1600–1750. –**baroque** *noun* this style of ornamentation.

Barossa Valley a wine-producing region north-east of Adelaide in SA, settled in 1838 by German immigrants.

barouche (bă-**roosh**) *noun* **1** a four-wheeled horse-drawn carriage with seats for two couples facing each other. **2** a metal trolley with a rubber mattress used for transporting hospital patients between wards.

barrack *verb* **1** to shout protests or jeer at. **2** barrack for (*Austral.*) to cheer on, to encourage, *they barracked for their school's team*.

barracks *noun* a large building or group of buildings for soldiers to live in. [from Spanish *barraca* = soldier's tent]

barracouta *noun* a long slender sea fish of southern oceans (called *snoek* in South Africa). [from *barracuda*]

barracuda (ba-ră-**koo**-dă) *noun* a large and voracious tropical sea fish. [Spanish]

barrage (**ba**-rah*z*h) *noun* **1** an artificial barrier, especially one damming a river. **2** a heavy continuous bombardment by artillery. **3** a rapid fire of questions or comments. □ **barrage balloon** a large balloon anchored to the ground as part of a barrier against aircraft. [from French *barre* = a bar]

barramundi (ba-ră-**mun**-dee) *noun* a large Australian freshwater fish, especially a tropical fish of the perch kind.

barre *noun* a horizontal bar used by dancers to steady themselves while exercising. [French]

barred *see* **bar¹**.

barrel *noun* **1** a large round container with flat ends. **2** the amount this contains, (as a measure of mineral oil) 35 gallons (about 160 litres), or 42 US gallons. **3** a tube-like part, especially of a gun. –**barrel** *verb* (**barrelled**, **barrelling**) to put into barrels. □ **barrel organ** an automatic pipe organ in which projections on a cylinder turned by a handle open pipes to produce a predetermined tune; a street instrument from which music is produced by turning a handle. **over a barrel** in a helpless position.

barren *adjective* 1 not fertile enough to produce crops, *barren land*. 2 not producing fruit or seeds, *a barren tree*. 3 unable to have offspring. 4 unproductive, *a barren discussion*. **barrenness** *noun*

barricade *noun* a barrier, especially one hastily erected as a defence. **–barricade** *verb* to block or defend with a barricade.

barrier *noun* something that prevents or controls advance, access, or progress. □ **barrier cream** a cream used to protect a person's skin from damage or infection. **barrier reef** a coral reef with a channel between it and the land (*see also* **Great Barrier Reef**).

barrister (**ba**-rĭs-ter) *noun* a lawyer entitled to represent clients in the courts.

barrow¹ *noun* 1 a wheelbarrow. 2 a small cart with two wheels, pulled or pushed by hand. [from Old English *bearwe* = carrier]

barrow² *noun* a prehistoric burial mound. [from Old English *beorg* = hill]

bartender *noun* a barman or barmaid.

barter *verb* to trade by exchanging goods etc. for other goods, not for money. **–barter** *noun* trading by exchange.

Bartholomew, St (1st century), one of the twelve Apostles. Feast day, 12 August.

Barton, Sir Edmund (1849–1920), Australia's first Prime Minister (1901–03).

Baruch (**bar**-ruuk) a book of the Apocrypha, attributed in the text to Baruch, the scribe of Jeremiah.

baryon (**ba**-ree-on) *noun* a heavy elementary particle (nucleon or hyperon). [from Greek *barus* = heavy]

barysphere (**ba**-rĭ-sfeer) *noun* the core of heavy material at the centre of the earth. [from Greek *barus* = heavy, + *sphere*]

BAS *abbreviation* business activity statement.

basal (**bay**-săl) *adjective* of, at, or forming the base or the lowest level of something. □ **basal metabolism** *see* **metabolism**.

basalt (**ba**-sawlt) *noun* a kind of dark rock of volcanic origin. **basaltic** (bă-**sawl**-tik) *adjective*

base¹ *noun* 1 the lowest part of anything, the part on which it rests or is supported. 2 a starting point. 3 the headquarters of an expedition or other enterprise, where its supplies are stored. 4 a substance into which other things are mixed, *some paints have an oil base*. 5 a cream or liquid applied to the skin as a foundation for make-up. 6 a substance (e.g. an alkali) capable of combining with an acid to form a salt. 7 the number on which a system of counting and calculation is based, e.g. 10 in conventional notation, 2 in the binary system. 8 the middle terminal of a transistor, between the emitter and the collector. 9 each of the four stations to be reached by a runner in baseball. **–base** *verb* to use as a base or foundation or as evidence for a forecast. □ **base rate** the rate of interest that a bank uses as a basis for fixing the rates it charges to borrowers or pays to investors. [from Greek *basis* = stepping]

base² *adjective* 1 dishonourable, *base motives*. 2 of inferior value, *base metals*. 3 debased, not of acceptable quality, *base coins*. **basely** *adverb*, **baseness** *noun* [from French *bas* = low]

baseball *noun* a team game in which runs are scored by hitting a ball and running round a series of four bases.

baseless *adjective* without foundation, *baseless rumours*.

baseline *noun* 1 a line used as a base or starting point. 2 the line at each end of a tennis court.

basement *noun* the lowest storey of a building, below ground level.

bash *verb* 1 to strike violently. 2 to attack with blows or words or hostile actions. **–bash** *noun* a violent blow or knock. □ **have a bash** (*informal*) to have a try.

bashful *adjective* shy and self-conscious. **bashfully** *adverb*, **bashfulness** *noun* [from *abashed*]

BASIC *noun* a high-level computer language designed to be easy to learn. [from the initials of Beginners' All-purpose Symbolic Instruction Code]

basic *adjective* forming a base or starting point, fundamental, *basic principles*; *basic rates of pay*, calculated without including overtime etc. **basics** *plural noun* basic facts or principles etc. □ **basic slag** a by-product formed in steel manufacture, containing phosphates and used as a fertiliser. **basic wage** the statutory minimum wage for any worker. **basically** *adverb* [from *base¹*]

basil *noun* a sweet-smelling herb.

basilica (bă-**zil**-ikă) *noun* a large oblong hall or church with two rows of columns and an apse at one end.

basilisk (**baz**-ĭ-lisk) *noun* **1** a small tropical American lizard. **2** a mythical reptile said to cause death by its glance or breath.

basin *noun* **1** a round open dish for holding liquids or soft substances. **2** this with its contents, the amount it contains. **3** a washbasin. **4** a sunken place where water collects; *a river basin*, the area drained by a river. **5** an almost landlocked harbour, *a yacht basin*. **basinful** *noun* (*plural* **basinfuls**).

basis *noun* (*plural* **bases**) a foundation or support, a main principle. [same origin as *base*[1]]

bask *verb* **1** to expose oneself comfortably to a pleasant warmth. **2** to enjoy someone's approval.

basket *noun* **1** a container for holding or carrying things, made of interwoven flexible material or wire. **2** this with its contents. **3** the ring with net attached through which players try to throw the ball in basketball; a point scored in this way. **4** an assorted set, *a basket of currencies*. □ **basket weave** a weave resembling basketwork.

basketball *noun* a game between two teams of five, in which goals are scored by putting the ball through a high hooped net at each end of a court; the ball used in this game.

basketry *noun* basketwork.

basketwork *noun* **1** a structure of interwoven osiers etc. **2** the art of making this.

basmati *noun* a kind of long-grain Indian rice with a delicate fragrance. [Hindi, = fragrant]

Basque (*pr*. bahsk) *noun* **1** a member of a people living in the western Pyrenees area of Spain and France. **2** their language.

bas-relief (**bas**-rĕ-leef) *noun* sculpture or carving in low relief. [from French *bas* = low]

Bass (*pr*. bas), George (1711–c. 1803), English naval surgeon and explorer. With Flinders he circumnavigated Van Diemen's Land (1798–99). **Bass Strait** a stretch of ocean separating Tasmania from mainland Australia.

bass[1] (*pr*. bas) *noun* (*plural* **bass**) a fish of the perch family.

bass[2] (*pr*. bayss) *adjective* deep-sounding; of the lowest pitch in music. –**bass** *noun* **1** the lowest male voice; a singer with such a voice; a part written for this. **2** the lowest-pitched member of a group of similar musical instruments. **3** (*informal*) a double bass; a bass guitar. [from *base*[2] meaning 'low']

basset (**bas**-ĕt) *noun* (also **basset hound**) a short-legged hound used for hunting hares etc. [from French *bas* = low]

Basseterre (bas-**tair**) the capital of St Kitts and Nevis.

bassinet *noun* a basket for a baby to lie in.

bassoon (bă-**soon**) *noun* a deep-toned woodwind instrument. **bassoonist** *noun*

bastard *noun* **1** (*old use*, often *offensive*) an illegitimate child. **2** (*informal*, *derogatory*) an unpleasant or despicable person. **3** (*informal*, often *affectionate*) a person, *poor bastard*. –**bastard** *adjective* **1** of illegitimate birth. **2** hybrid. **3** (of plants and animals) resembling the species whose name is taken. **bastardy** *noun*

baste[1] (*pr*. bayst) *verb* to sew together temporarily with long loose stitches.

baste[2] (*pr*. bayst) *verb* **1** to moisten with fat during cooking. **2** to thrash.

Bastille (bas-**teel**) a fortress in Paris used in the 17th–18th centuries as a prison until its storming on 14 July 1789 marked the start of the French Revolution.

bastinado (bas-tĭ-**nay**-doh) *noun* torture by caning on the soles of the feet.

bastion (**bas**-tee-ŏn) *noun* **1** a projecting part of a fortification. **2** a fortified place near hostile territory. **3** something serving as a stronghold, *a bastion of democracy*.

bat[1] *noun* **1** a shaped wooden implement for striking the ball in games. **2** a batsman, *he's a good bat*. –**bat** *verb* (**batted**, **batting**) **1** to use a bat. **2** to strike with a bat, to hit. □ **off one's own bat** without prompting or help from another person.

bat[2] *noun* a flying mammal with membranous wings.

bat[3] *verb* (**batted**, **batting**) to flutter, *it batted its wings*; *didn't bat an eyelid*, did not show any surprise.

batch[1] *noun* **1** a number of things produced at the same time. **2** a number of people or things dealt with as a group. –**batch** *verb* to group (items) for batch processing. □ **batch processing** the processing by a computer etc. of similar transactions in batches in order to make economical use of time.

batch[2] *verb* (*Austral.*) to live alone; to provide for oneself without the usual domestic conveniences. [from *bachelor*]

bated (**bay**-tĕd) *adjective* lessened.

☐ **with bated breath** with breath held anxiously. [from *abate*]

bath *noun* **1** washing of the whole body by immersing it in water. **2** water for this. **3** a large container for water, in which one sits to wash all over. **4** a liquid in which something is immersed; its container. –**bath** *verb* to wash in a bath. **baths** *plural noun* **1** a building with rooms where baths may be taken. **2** a public swimming pool.

bathe *verb* **1** to apply liquid to; to immerse in liquid. **2** to make wet or bright all over, *fields were bathed in sunlight*. **3** to swim for pleasure. –**bathe** *noun* a swim. ☐ **bathing suit** a garment worn for swimming.

bather *noun* a person who bathes. **bathers** *plural noun* (*Austral. informal*) a swimming costume.

batholith (**ba**-thŏ-lith) *noun* a huge mass of igneous rock extending from near the earth's surface to an unknown depth. [from *bathos*, + Greek *lithos* = stone]

bathos (**bay**-thoss) *noun* an anticlimax, descent from something important to something trivial. [Greek, = depth]

bathroom *noun* a room containing a bath, shower, etc.

Bathurst Island an island north of Darwin. Together with Melville Island it is the homeland of the Tiwi people.

bathyscaphe (**ba**-thĭ-skaf) *noun* a manned vessel for deep-sea diving, with special buoyancy gear. [from *bathos*, + Greek *skaphos* = ship]

bathysphere (**ba**-thĭ-sfeer) *noun* a spherical diving-vessel for deep-sea observation. [from *bathos* + *sphere*]

batik (**bah**-tik) *noun* **1** a method (originating in Java) of printing coloured designs on textiles by waxing the parts not to be dyed. **2** fabric treated in this way.

batiste (bă-**teest**) *noun* a very soft fine woven fabric.

Batman, John (1801–39), Australian farmer and pioneer, a founder of Melbourne.

batman *noun* (*plural* **batmen**) a soldier acting as an officer's personal servant.

bat mitzvah (**mits**-vă) *noun* the religious initiation of a Jewish girl at the age of 12 years and one day old. [from Hebrew, = 'daughter of commandment']

baton (**bat**-ŏn) *noun* **1** a short thick stick, especially one serving as a symbol of authority; a truncheon. **2** a thin stick used by the conductor of an orchestra for beating time. **3** a short stick or tube carried in relay races. ☐ **baton round** a rubber or plastic bullet, as used by police dealing with riots.

batsman *noun* (*plural* **batsmen**) a player who is batting in cricket or baseball; one who is good at this.

battalion *noun* an army unit made up of several companies and forming part of a regiment. [from Italian *battaglia* = battle]

batten[1] *noun* a strip of wood or metal fastening or holding something in place. –**batten** *verb* to fasten with battens; *batten down the hatches*, close them securely.

batten[2] *verb* to feed greedily, to thrive or prosper at the expense of others or so as to injure them, *corellas battening on the crops*.

batter[1] *verb* to hit hard and often; *battered babies*, *battered wives*, those subjected to repeated violence. –**batter** *noun* a beaten mixture of flour, eggs, and milk, for cooking. [from Latin *battuere* = to beat]

batter[2] *noun* a batsman in baseball.

battering ram *noun* an iron-headed beam formerly used in war to breach walls or gates.

battery *noun* **1** a group of big guns on land or on a warship. **2** an artillery unit of guns, men, and vehicles. **3** a set of similar or connected units of equipment, or of cages for poultry etc. **4** an electric cell or group of cells supplying current. **5** unlawful blows or a menacing touch on a person. [same origin as *batter*[1]]

battle *noun* **1** a fight between large organised forces. **2** any contest, *a battle of wits*. **3** victory, success; *confidence is half the battle*, a help towards success. –**battle** *verb* to engage in battle, to struggle. ☐ **battle cry** a war cry, a slogan. [same origin as *batter*[1]]

battleaxe *noun* **1** a heavy axe used as a weapon in ancient times. **2** (*informal*) a formidable aggressive woman. ☐ **battleaxe block** a block of land behind one with a street frontage having narrow (usually driveway) access to the street.

battledore *noun* a small racquet used with a shuttlecock in the volleying game **battledore and shuttlecock**.

battledress *noun* the everyday uniform of a soldier etc.

battlefield *noun* a place where a battle is or was fought.

battleground *noun* a battlefield.

battlements *plural noun* **1** a parapet with gaps at intervals, originally for firing from. **2** the roof within this.

battler *noun* (*Austral.*) a person who struggles against difficulties and does not give up.

battleship *noun* the most heavily armed kind of warship.

batty *adjective* (*informal*) crazy. **battiness** *noun* [from *bat²*]

bauble *noun* a showy but valueless ornament or fancy article.

baud (*rhymes with* code) *noun* a unit for measuring speed in telegraphic signalling and computers, corresponding to one dot or other signal per second. [named after J. M. E. Baudot, French engineer (died 1903)]

Baudin (**boh**-dan), Nicolas Thomas (1754–1803), French cartographer who charted the southern Australian coast.

Bauhaus (**bow**-hows) a German school of architecture and design established by Walter Gropius in 1919.

baulk (*pr.* bawk) *verb* **1** to shirk, to jib at, *baulked the problem*; *the horse baulked at the gate*. **2** to frustrate, *it baulked him of his prey*. –**baulk** *noun* **1** the area of a billiard table within which the cue balls are placed at the start of a game. **2** a stumbling block, a hindrance. **3** a roughly squared timber beam.

bauxite (**bawk**-syt) *noun* the clay-like substance from which aluminium is obtained.

Bavaria a State of south Germany. **Bavarian** *adjective* & *noun*

bawdy *adjective* (**bawdier**, **bawdiest**) humorous in a coarse or indecent way. **bawdily** *adverb*, **bawdiness** *noun*

bawl *verb* to shout or cry loudly.

bay¹ *noun* a kind of laurel with deep green leaves that are dried and used for seasoning.

bay² *noun* part of the sea or of a large lake within a wide curve of the shore.

bay³ *noun* **1** each of a series of compartments in a building, structure, or area, *a parking bay*. **2** a recess in a room or building. □ **bay window** a window projecting from the outside wall of a house.

bay⁴ *noun* the deep drawn-out cry of a large dog or of hounds in pursuit of a hunted animal. –**bay** *verb* to make this sound. □ **at bay** forced to face attackers and showing defiance in a desperate situation. **hold at bay** to ward off.

bay⁵ *adjective* reddish-brown. –**bay** *noun* a bay horse.

Bayeux Tapestry (by-**er**) a long strip of Anglo-Saxon embroidery (11th century) depicting the Norman Conquest, kept at Bayeux in Normandy, France.

bayonet (**bay**-ŏ-nĕt) *noun* a dagger-like blade that can be fixed to the muzzle of a rifle and used in hand-to-hand fighting. –**bayonet** *verb* (**bayoneted**, **bayoneting**) to stab with a bayonet. □ **bayonet cap** an electrical or light fitting engaged by being pushed into a socket and twisted. [named after *Bayonne* in France, where it was first made]

Bayreuth (**by**-roit) a town in Bavaria, Germany, associated with Wagner, holding regular performances of his *Ring* Cycle.

bazaar *noun* **1** a series of shops or stalls in an Oriental country. **2** a sale of goods to raise funds. **3** a large shop selling a variety of cheap goods. [from Persian *bazar*]

bazooka (bă-**zoo**-kă) *noun* a portable weapon for firing anti-tank rockets. [the word originally meant a musical instrument rather like a trombone]

BBQ *abbreviation* barbecue.

BC¹ *abbreviation* British Columbia.

BC² *abbreviation* (in dates) before Christ.

BCE *abbreviation* (in dates) before the Common Era.

be *verb* (**am**, **are**, **is**; **was**, **were**; **been**, **being**) **1** to exist, to occur, to live; to occupy a position, *she has never been to Bali*, visited it. **2** to have a certain identity, quality, or condition; *how much is it?*, what does it cost? **3** to become, *he wants to be a pilot*. –**be** *auxiliary verb*, used to form parts of other verbs, e.g. *it is rising*; *he was killed*; *I am to inform you*, it is my duty to inform you. □ **be-all and end-all** the supreme purpose or essence. **be that as it may** no matter what the facts about it may be. **let it be** do not disturb it.

be- *prefix* used to form verbs (as in *befriend*, *belittle*) or to strengthen (as in *begrudge*).

beach *noun* the shore between high- and low-water mark, usually covered with sand. –**beach** *verb* to bring on shore, *beach a boat*; *a beached whale*.

beachcomber (**beech**-koh-mer) *noun* **1** a person who salvages stray articles along a beach. **2** a long wave rolling in from the sea. **beachcombing** *noun*

beachhead *noun* a fortified position established on a beach by an invading army.

beacon *noun* 1 a fire or light on a hill or tower used as a signal or warning. 2 a signal station such as a lighthouse.

bead *noun* 1 a small shaped piece of hard material pierced for threading with others on a string or wire, or for sewing on to fabric. 2 a drop or bubble of liquid on a surface. 3 a small knob forming the front sight of a gun. **beads** *plural noun* 1 a necklace of beads. 2 a rosary. □ **draw a bead on** to take aim at.

beaded *adjective* 1 decorated with beads. 2 forming or covered with beads of moisture etc.

beading *noun* 1 a decoration of beads. 2 a moulding or carving like a series of beads. 3 a strip of material with one side rounded, used as a trimming on edges of wood.

beady *adjective* like beads; (of eyes) small and bright. **beadily** *adverb*

beagle *noun* a small hound used for hunting hares.

beak *noun* 1 a bird's horny projecting jaws. 2 any similar projection. 3 (*informal*) a magistrate. **beaked** *adjective*

beaker *noun* 1 a small open glass vessel with straight sides and a lip for pouring liquids, used in laboratories. 2 a tall narrow cup, often without a handle.

beam *noun* 1 a long piece of squared timber or other solid material, supported at both ends and carrying the weight of part of a building or other structure. 2 a ship's breadth at its widest part. 3 the crosspiece of a balance, from which the scales hang. 4 a ray or stream of light or other radiation; a radio signal used to direct the course of an aircraft. 5 a bright look, a radiant smile. **–beam** *verb* 1 to send out (light or other radiation). 2 to look or smile radiantly. □ **broad in the beam** (*informal*) wide at the hips. **off beam** (*informal*) mistaken. **on one's beam-ends** near the end of one's resources.

bean *noun* 1 a leguminous plant with long pods used as a vegetable. 2 its usually kidney-shaped edible seeds. 3 a similar seed of coffee and other plants. □ **bean sprout** the edible sprout of a bean seed, especially a mung bean. **full of beans** (*informal*) in high spirits. **not a bean** (*informal*) no money.

beanbag *noun* 1 a small bag filled with dried beans and used for throwing or carrying in games. 2 a large bag with a circular base, filled with plastic granules and used as a seat.

beanfeast *noun* a festive meal.

beanie *noun* a small close-fitting knitted cap.

beanpole *noun* (*informal*) a tall thin person.

bear[1] *noun* 1 a large heavy animal with thick fur. 2 a child's toy like this animal. 3 a rough ill-mannered person. □ **bear market** (*Stock Exchange*) a situation where share prices are falling rapidly (contrasting with *bull market*). **Great Bear, Little Bear** constellations near the North Pole.

bear[2] *verb* (**bore**, **borne**, **bearing**; ¶ see the note under **borne**) 1 to carry, to support; *bear oneself bravely*, to behave bravely. 2 to have or show a certain mark or characteristic, *he still bears the scar*; *bears the same name*. 3 to have in one's heart or mind, *bear a grudge*; *I will bear it in mind*, will remember it. 4 to bring, to provide. 5 to endure, to tolerate, *grin and bear it*. 6 to be fit for, *his language won't bear repeating*. 7 to produce, to give birth to, *land bears crops*; *she had borne him two sons*. 8 to turn, to diverge, *bear right when the road forks*. 9 to exert pressure, to thrust. □ **bear down on** to move rapidly or purposefully towards. **bear on** to be relevant to, *information bearing on the case*. **bear out** to confirm. **bear up** to be strong enough not to give way or despair. **bear with** to tolerate patiently. **bear witness to** to provide evidence of the truth of.

bearable *adjective* able to be borne, endurable. **bearably** *adverb*

beard *noun* 1 hair on and round a man's chin. 2 a similar hairy or bristly growth of hair on an animal or plant. **–beard** *verb* to confront boldly; *beard the lion in his den*, confront and oppose someone in his own stronghold. **bearded** *adjective*

beardie *noun* (*Austral.*) an edible sea fish, a ling.

bearer *noun* 1 one who carries or bears something; *cheque is payable to bearer*, to the person who presents it at a bank. 2 one who helps to carry something (e.g. a coffin to the grave, a stretcher).

beargarden *noun* a scene of uproar.

bearing *noun* 1 deportment, behaviour, *soldierly bearing*. 2 relationship, relevance, *it has no bearing on this problem*. 3 a compass direction; *get one's bearings*, find out where one is by recognising landmarks etc. 4 a device reducing friction in a part of a machine where another part turns.

Béarnaise sauce (**bair**-nayz) *noun* a rich sauce thickened with egg yolks.

bearskin *noun* a tall black fur headdress worn by some regiments on ceremonial occasions.

beast *noun* **1** a large four-footed animal. **2** a cruel or disgusting person. **3** (*informal*) a disliked person or thing; something difficult.

beastly *adjective* (**beastlier, beastliest**) **1** like a beast or its ways. **2** (*informal*) abominable, very unpleasant. **–beastly** *adverb* (*informal*) unpleasantly, *it was beastly cold*.

beat *verb* (**beat, beaten, beating**) **1** to hit repeatedly, especially with a stick; *we heard the drums beating*, being beaten. **2** to strike; *the sun beat down*, shone with great heat. **3** to shape or flatten by blows; *beat a path*, make it by trampling things down. **4** to mix vigorously to a frothy or smooth consistency, *beat the eggs*. **5** (of the heart) to expand and contract rhythmically. **6** to overcome, to do better than; *someone beat me to it*, got there first; *it beats me*, is too difficult for me. **7** to sail towards the direction from which the wind is blowing, by tacking in alternate directions. **–beat** *noun* **1** a regular repeated stroke, a sound of this. **2** recurring emphasis marking rhythm in music or poetry; the strongly marked rhythm of pop music. **3** the appointed course of a sentinel or policeman, the area covered by this. □ **beat about the bush** to discuss a subject without coming to the point. **beat a retreat** to go away defeated. **beat down** to bargain with (a seller) to lower the price. **beaten track** a well-worn path. **beat it** (*informal*) to go away. **beat off** to drive off by fighting. **beat time** to mark or follow the rhythm of music by waving a stick or by tapping. **beat up** to assault violently.

beater *noun* an implement for beating things.

beatific (bee-ă-**tif**-ik) *adjective* showing great happiness, *a beatific smile*. **beatifically** *adverb*

beatification *noun* the pope's official statement that a dead person is among the Blessed, the first step towards canonisation.

beatify (bee-**at**-ĭ-fy) *verb* (**beatified, beatifying**) to honour by beatification. [from Latin *beatus* = blessed]

beating *noun* **1** the process of hitting or being hit with a stick etc. **2** a defeat.

beatitude (bee-**at**-ĭ-tewd) *noun* blessedness. **the Beatitudes** the declarations made by Christ in the Sermon on the Mount, beginning 'Blessed are …'. [same origin as *beatify*]

beau (*pr.* boh) *noun* (*plural* **beaux**) **1** a boyfriend. **2** a dandy.

Beaufort scale (**boh**-fert) *noun* a scale and description of wind velocity ranging from 0 (calm) to 12 (hurricane). [named after its inventor Sir F. Beaufort, English admiral (died 1857)]

Beaujolais (**boh**-zhŏ-lay) *noun* a red or white burgundy wine from Beaujolais, France.

beaut *adjective* (*Austral. informal*) excellent.

beautician (bew-**tish**-ăn) *noun* a person whose job is to give beautifying treatments to the face or body.

beautiful *adjective* **1** having beauty, giving pleasure to the senses or the mind. **2** very satisfactory. **beautifully** *adverb*

beautify *verb* (**beautified, beautifying**) to make beautiful. **beautification** *noun*

beauty *noun* **1** a combination of qualities that give pleasure to the sight or other senses or to the mind. **2** a person or thing having this; a beautiful woman. **3** a fine specimen, *here's a beauty*. **4** a beautiful feature; *that's the beauty of it*, the point that gives satisfaction. □ **beauty parlour** or **salon** an establishment for giving beautifying treatments to the face, body, etc. **beauty spot** a place with beautiful scenery; a birthmark or artificial patch on the face, said to heighten beauty.

beaver *noun* **1** an animal with soft fur and strong teeth that lives both on land and in water. **2** its brown fur. **–beaver** *verb* to work hard.

bebop *noun* a kind of jazz music.

becalmed (bĕ-**kahmd**) *adjective* unable to move because there is no wind.

became *see* **become.**

because *conjunction* for the reason that, *did it because I was asked*. **–because** *adverb* **because of** by reason of, on account of, *because of his age*.

béchamel sauce (besh-ă-mel) *noun* a kind of white sauce.

beck *noun* (*old use*) a gesture. □ **at someone's beck and call** always ready and waiting to obey that person's orders. [from *beckon*]

Becket, St Thomas (c. 1118–70), Archbishop of Canterbury and Chancellor under Henry II, murdered in Canterbury Cathedral. Feast day, 29 December.

Beckett, Samuel Barclay (1906–89), Irish dramatist, novelist, and poet, author of the play *Waiting for Godot*.

beckon *verb* (beckoned, beckoning) to signal or summon by a gesture.

become *verb* (became, become, becoming) 1 to come or grow to be, to begin to be, *he became a doctor*; *ask what has become of it*, ask what happened to it, or where it is. 2 to suit, to be becoming to.

becoming *adjective* giving a pleasing appearance or effect, suitable. becomingly *adverb*

becquerel (**bek**-ĕ-rĕl) *noun* a unit of radioactivity. [named after A. H. Becquerel (1852–1908), French physicist]

bed *noun* 1 a thing to sleep or rest on, a piece of furniture with a mattress and coverings. 2 a mattress, *a feather bed*. 3 the use of a bed, being in bed, *price includes bed and breakfast*. 4 a flat base on which something rests, a foundation. 5 the bottom of the sea or a river etc. 6 a layer, *a bed of clay*. 7 a garden plot for plants. –bed *verb* (bedded, bedding) 1 to provide with a place to sleep, to put or go to bed. 2 to place or fix in a foundation, *the bricks are bedded in concrete*. 3 to plant in a garden bed, *he was bedding out seedlings*.

bedaub *verb* to smear all over.

bedbug *noun* a bug infesting beds.

bedclothes *plural noun* sheets and blankets etc.

bedding *noun* mattresses and bedclothes.

bedfellow *noun* 1 a person who shares one's bed. 2 an associate; *it makes strange bedfellows*, obliges unlikely people to associate.

bedevil *verb* (bedevilled, bedevilling) to trouble or vex.

bedizen (bĕ-**dy**-zĕn) *verb* to deck gaudily.

bedlam (**bed**-lăm) *noun* uproar. [from 'Bedlam', the popular name of the Hospital of St Mary of Bethlehem, a London mental institution in the 14th century]

Bedouin (**bed**-oo-ĭn) *noun* (*plural* Bedouin) a member of an Arab people living in tents in the desert. [from Arabic *badawi* = desert dweller]

bedpan *noun* a pan for use as a toilet by a person confined to bed.

bedpost *noun* one of the upright supports of a bedstead.

bedraggled (bĕ-**drag**-ŭld) *adjective* hanging in a limp untidy way, especially when wet.

bedridden *noun* confined to bed through illness or weakness, especially permanently.

bedrock *noun* 1 solid rock beneath loose soil. 2 basic facts or principles.

bedroom *noun* a room for sleeping in.

bedside *noun* a position by a bed; *a bedside table*, one for placing by a bed.

bedsitter *noun* (also bedsit) a room used for both living and sleeping in.

bedsore *noun* a sore caused by pressure, developed by lying in bed for a long time.

bedspread *noun* a covering spread over a bed.

bedstead *noun* a framework supporting the springs and mattress of a bed.

bedtime *noun* the hour for going to bed.

bee *noun* a four-winged stinging insect that produces wax and honey after gathering nectar from flowers. □ have a bee in one's bonnet to have a particular idea that occupies one's thoughts continually.

beech *noun* 1 a kind of tree with smooth bark and glossy leaves. 2 its wood.

beef *noun* 1 the flesh of an ox, bull, or cow used as meat. 2 (*informal*) muscular strength, brawn. 3 (*informal*) a grumble. –beef *verb* (*informal*) to grumble. □ beef road (*Austral.*) an all-weather road for trucking cattle from remote areas. beef tea the juice from stewed beef, for invalids. beef up (*informal*) to strengthen, to reinforce.

beefburger *noun* a flat round cake of minced beef, served fried or grilled.

beefeater *noun* a warder in the Tower of London, officially called a *Yeoman Warder*.

beefwood *noun* an Australian tree yielding a dark red close-grained timber.

beefy *adjective* (beefier, beefiest) having a solid muscular body. beefiness *noun*

beehive *noun* a hive.

beeline *noun* make a beeline for to go straight or rapidly towards.

Beelzebub (**beel**-zĕ-bub) (in the New Testament) the Devil; (in the Old Testament) a Philistine god.

been *see* be.

beep *noun* a short high-pitched sound of a car horn etc. –**beep** *verb* to (cause to) emit a beep; to summon with a beep. **beeper** *noun*

beer *noun* an alcoholic drink made from malt and flavoured with hops. **beery** *adjective*

beeswax *noun* a yellowish substance secreted by bees, used for polishing wood.

beet *noun* a plant with a fleshy root used as a vegetable or for making sugar.

Beethoven (**bayt**-hoh-věn), Ludwig van (1770–1827), German composer, whose works crowned the classical age of music and heralded the Romantic.

beetle[1] *noun* an insect with hard wing-covers.

beetle[2] *noun* a heavy-headed tool for crushing or ramming things.

beetle-browed *adjective* with brows projecting.

beetling *adjective* overhanging, projecting, *beetling brows*.

beetroot *noun* the fleshy dark red root of beet, used as a vegetable.

befall (bě-**fawl**) *verb* (**befell**, **befallen**, **befalling**) (*formal*) to happen, to happen to.

befit (bě-**fit**) *verb* (**befitted**, **befitting**) to be right and suitable for.

before *adverb*, *preposition*, & *conjunction* **1** at an earlier time; earlier than. **2** ahead; ahead of; in front of; *they sailed before the wind*, under its impulse, with the wind behind them. **3** rather than, in preference to, *death before dishonour!* □ **before Christ** (of dates) reckoned backwards from the year of the birth of Christ (usually shortened to BC).

beforehand *adverb* in advance, in readiness.

befriend *verb* to act as a friend to, to be kind and helpful to.

befuddle *verb* to stupefy, to make confused.

beg *verb* (**begged**, **begging**) **1** to ask for as charity or as a gift, to obtain a living in this way. **2** to request earnestly or humbly. **3** to ask for formally, *I beg your pardon*; *beg to differ*, take the liberty of disagreeing. **4** (of a dog) to sit up expectantly, as it has been trained, with forepaws off the ground. □ **beg the question** to assume the truth of something that needs to be proved. **go begging** (of things) to be available but unwanted.

began *see* **begin**.

beget (bě-**get**) *verb* (**begot**, **begotten**, **begetting**) **1** to be the father of. **2** to give rise to, *war begets misery and ruin*.

beggar *noun* **1** a person who lives by begging, a very poor person. **2** (*informal*) a person, *you lucky beggar!* –**beggar** *verb* **1** to reduce to poverty. **2** to make seem poor or inadequate; *the scenery beggars description*, is so magnificent that any description is inadequate. **beggary** *noun*

beggarly *adjective* mean and insufficient.

begin *verb* (**began**, **begun**, **beginning**) **1** to perform the earliest or first part of (some activity); to start speaking; to be the first to do something. **2** to come into existence, to arise. **3** to have its first element or starting point.

beginner *noun* a person who is just beginning to learn a skill.

beginning *noun* **1** the first part. **2** the starting point, the source or origin.

begone (bee-**gon**) *verb* to go away immediately, *begone dull care!*

begonia (bě-**goh**-nee-ǎ) *noun* a garden plant with brightly coloured leaves and flowers.

begot, **begotten** *see* **beget**.

begrudge *verb* to grudge.

beguile (bě-**gyl**) *verb* **1** to win the attention or interest of, to amuse. **2** to deceive. **beguilement** *noun*

beguine (bě-**geen**) *noun* a West Indian dance.

begum (**bay**-gŭm) *noun* (in Pakistan and India) **1** the title of a Muslim married woman, = Mrs. **2** a Muslim woman of high rank. [from Urdu *begam*]

begun *see* **begin**.

behalf *noun* **on behalf of** in aid of; as the representative of, *speaking on behalf of his client*.

behave *verb* **1** to act or react in some specified way. **2** to function, *the car is behaving well*. **3** to show good manners, *they behaved* or *behaved themselves*.

behaviour *noun* a way of behaving, treatment of others, manners. **behavioural** *adjective*

behead *verb* to cut the head from, to execute (a person) in this way.

beheld *see* **behold**.

behest *noun* (*formal*) a command, a request.

behind *adverb* **1** in or to the rear. **2** remaining after others have gone. **3** behindhand. –**behind** *preposition* **1** in the rear of, on the further side of; *put the past behind you*, recognise that it is over and done with. **2** causing. **3** supporting. **4** having made less progress than, *some countries are behind others in development*. **5** later than, *we are behind schedule*. –**behind** *noun* **1** (*informal*) the buttocks. **2** (in Australian Rules) a score of one point when a ball is sent over a line between a goalpost and an outer post. ☐ **behind a person's back** without a person's knowledge. **behind the scenes** backstage; hidden from public view or knowledge. **behind time** late, unpunctual. **behind the times** having out-of-date ideas or practices.

behindhand *adverb* & *adjective* **1** in arrears. **2** late, behind time; out of date.

behold *verb* (**beheld**, **beholding**) (*old use*) to see, to observe. **beholder** *noun*

beholden *adjective* owing thanks, *we don't want to be beholden to anybody*.

behove *verb* (*literary*) to be incumbent on, to befit, *it ill behoves him to complain*.

beige (*pr.* bay*zh*) *noun* a light fawn colour. –**beige** *adjective* of this colour.

Beijing (bay-**jing**) the capital of China, formerly called **Peking**.

being *noun* **1** existence. **2** essence or nature, constitution. **3** something that exists and has life, especially a person.

Beirut (bay-**root**) the capital of Lebanon.

bejewelled *adjective* adorned with jewels.

Bel = Baal. ☐ **Bel and the Dragon** a book of the Apocrypha.

belabour *verb* **1** to attack with blows or words. **2** to labour (a subject).

belah (bě-**lah**) *noun* a casuarina of inland Australia with slender jointed branches and woody cones. [Wiradjuri *bilaarr*]

Belarus (bel-ă-**ruuss**) (also **Belorussia**) a republic in eastern Europe to the west of Russia. **Belarussian** *adjective* & *noun*

belated (bě-**lay**-těd) *adjective* coming very late or too late. **belatedly** *adverb*

belay *verb* to secure (a rope) by winding it round a peg or rock. –**belay** *noun* the securing of a rope in this way.

belch *verb* **1** to send out wind from the stomach noisily through the mouth. **2** to send out from an opening or funnel, to gush. –**belch** *noun* an act or sound of belching.

beleaguer (bě-**leeg**-er) *verb* **1** to besiege. **2** to harass, to oppress. [from Dutch *belegeren* = camp round]

Belfast the capital of Northern Ireland.

belfry *noun* a bell tower, a space for bells in a tower.

Belgium a kingdom in western Europe. **Belgian** *adjective* & *noun*

Belgrade the capital of Serbia.

belie *verb* (**belied**, **belying**) **1** to fail to confirm, to show to be untrue. **2** to give a false idea of.

belief *noun* **1** the feeling that something is real and true; trust, confidence. **2** something accepted as true, what one believes. **3** acceptance of the teachings of a religion etc.; these teachings.

believable *adjective* able to be believed.

believe *verb* **1** to accept as true or as speaking or conveying the truth. **2** to think, to suppose, *I believe it's raining*. **3** to have religious faith. ☐ **believe in** to have faith in the existence of; to feel sure of the value or worth of. **believer** *noun*

belittle *verb* to imply that (a thing) is unimportant or of little value. **belittlement** *noun*

Belize (bě-**leez**) a country in Central America, on the Caribbean coast. **Belizean** (bě-**lee**-*zhă*n) *adjective* & *noun*

Bell, Alexander Graham (1847–1922), Scottish-American inventor of the telephone.

bell *noun* **1** a cup-shaped metal instrument that makes a ringing sound when struck; a device making a ringing or buzzing sound to attract attention in a house etc. **2** the sound of this, especially as a signal; *one to eight bells*, the strokes of a ship's bell, indicating the half-hours of each four-hour watch. **3** a bell-shaped thing. **4** (*informal*) a telephone call. ☐ **bell-bottomed** *adjective* (of trousers) widening from knee to ankle.

belladonna *noun* **1** deadly nightshade. **2** a medicinal drug prepared from this.

bellbird *noun* a bird with a clear ringing note.

belle (*pr.* bel) *noun* a beautiful woman. [French]

belles-lettres (bel-**letr**) *plural noun* literary writings or studies.

bellicose (**bel**-ĭ-kohs) *adjective* eager to fight, warlike. **bellicosity** (bel-ĭ-**koss**-ĭ-tee) *noun* [from Latin *bellum* = war]

belligerent (bĕ-**lij**-ĕ-rĕnt) *adjective* **1** waging a war, *the belligerent nations*. **2** aggressive, showing eagerness to fight, *a belligerent reply*. **belligerently** *adverb*, **belligerence** *noun* [from Latin *bellum* = war, *gerens* = waging]

bellow *noun* **1** the loud deep sound made by a bull. **2** a deep shout. –**bellow** *verb* to utter a bellow.

bellows *plural noun* **1** an apparatus for driving air into or through something; *a pair of bellows*, two-handled bellows for blowing air into a fire. **2** a device or part that can be expanded or flattened in a series of folds.

belly *noun* **1** the abdomen. **2** the stomach. **3** a bulging or rounded part of something. –**belly** *verb* (**bellied**, **bellying**) to swell out, *the sails bellied out*; *wind bellied out the sails*. □ **belly button** (*informal*) the navel. **belly dance** an oriental dance by a woman, with erotic movement of the belly.

bellyflop *noun* an awkward dive in which the body hits the water almost horizontally.

bellyful *noun* (*informal*) as much as one wants or rather more.

Belmopan (**bel**-moh-pan) the capital of Belize.

belong *verb* **1** to be rightly assigned as property or as a part or appendage or inhabitant etc., *the house belongs to me*; *that lid belongs to this jar*. **2** to be a member, *we belong to the club*. **3** to have a rightful or usual place, *the pans belong in the kitchen*.

belongings *plural noun* personal possessions.

Belorussia (bel-oh-**rush**-ă) the former name for **Belarus**.

beloved *adjective* (*pr.* bĕ-**luvd**) dearly loved, *she was beloved by all*. –**beloved** *adjective* & *noun* (*pr.* bĕ-**luv**-ĕd) darling, *my beloved wife*.

below *adverb* **1** at or to a lower position, downstream. **2** at the foot of a page, further on in a book or article, *see chapter 6 below*. –**below** *preposition* **1** lower in position, amount, or rank etc. than. **2** downstream from.

Belsen a village in Germany, site of a Nazi concentration camp in the Second World War.

Belshazzar (in the Old Testament) the last king of Babylon, son of Nebuchadnezzar.

belt *noun* **1** a strip of cloth or leather etc. worn round the waist. **2** a continuous moving strap passing over pulleys and so driving machinery, *a fan belt*. **3** a long narrow region or strip, *a belt of rain will move eastwards*. **4** (*informal*)

a heavy blow. –**belt** *verb* **1** to put a belt round. **2** to attach with a belt. **3** to thrash with a belt, (*informal*) to hit. **4** (*informal*) to hurry, to rush. □ **below the belt** unfair, unfairly. **belt out** (*informal*) to sing or play loudly. **belt up** (*informal*) to wear a seat belt; (*informal*) to be quiet. **under one's belt** (*informal*) eaten; obtained or achieved.

beluga (bĕ-**loo**-gă) *noun* **1** a large sturgeon; caviar from this. **2** a white whale.

bema (**bee**-mă) *noun* a raised platform for the reading desk in a synagogue. [Greek]

bemused (bĕ-**mewzd**) *adjective* **1** bewildered. **2** lost in thought.

Benares (bĕ-**nah**-reez) the former name of Varanasi.

bench *noun* **1** a long seat of wood or stone. **2** a long work table in certain trades or in a kitchen or a laboratory. **3** a lawcourt. **4** the judges or magistrates hearing a case.

benchmark *noun* **1** a surveyor's mark used as a reference point in measuring altitudes. **2** a standard or point of reference.

bend[1] *verb* (**bent**, **bending**) **1** to force out of straightness, to make curved or angular. **2** to become curved or angular. **3** to turn downwards, to stoop. **4** to turn in a new direction, *they bent their steps homeward*; *bend your mind to this*, give it your attention. **5** (*informal*) to corrupt, to make dishonest. –**bend** *noun* a curve or turn. **bends** *plural noun* sickness due to too rapid decompression, e.g. after diving. □ **bend the rules** to interpret them loosely to suit oneself. **round the bend** (*informal*) crazy.

bend[2] *noun* any of various knots. –**bend** *verb* (**bent**, **bending**) to attach (a rope or sail etc.) with a knot.

bender *noun* (*informal*) a wild drinking spree.

bene- *prefix* well (as in *benefit*, *benevolent*). [from Latin *bene* = well]

beneath *adverb* & *preposition* **1** below, under, underneath. **2** not worthy of, not befitting; *beneath contempt*, not even worth despising.

Benedict, St (c. 480–c. 550), a hermit, living in Italy, who drew up a code of discipline for monks and nuns. Feast day, 21 March.

Benedictine (*pr.* ben-ĕ-**dik**-tĭn) *noun* a monk or nun following the code of St Benedict. –**Benedictine** *adjective* of St Benedict or the Benedictines.

benediction (ben-ĕ-**dik**-shŏn) *noun* a spoken blessing. **benedictory** *adjective* [from *bene-*, + Latin *dicere* = to say]

benefactor *noun* a person who gives financial or other help. **benefactress** *feminine noun* [from *bene-*, + Latin *factor* = doer]

benefice (**ben**-ĕ-fĭss) *noun* the position of being in charge of a parish or parishes, for which a member of the clergy is paid.

beneficial *adjective* having a helpful or useful effect. **beneficially** *adverb*

beneficiary (ben-ĕ-**fish**-ă-ree) *noun* a person who receives a benefit; one who is left a legacy under someone's will.

benefit *noun* **1** something helpful, favourable, or profitable. **2** an allowance of money etc. to which a person is entitled from an insurance policy or government funds. **3** a performance or game held in order to raise money for a particular player, *a benefit match*. –**benefit** *verb* (**benefited**, **benefiting**) **1** to do good to. **2** to receive benefit. □ **benefit of the doubt** the assumption that a person is innocent (or right) rather than guilty (or wrong) when nothing can be fully proved either way. [from *bene-*, + Latin *facere* = do]

Benelux (**ben**-ĕ-luks) Belgium, the Netherlands, and Luxembourg, considered as a group.

benevolent *adjective* **1** wishing to do good to others; kindly and helpful. **2** charitable, *a benevolent fund*. **benevolently** *adverb*, **benevolence** *noun* [from *bene-*, + Latin *volens* = wishing]

Bengal (ben-**gawl**) a former province of NE India, now divided into West Bengal (a State of India) and Bangladesh. **Bay of Bengal** the part of the Indian Ocean lying between India and Burma. **Bengali** *adjective* & *noun* (*plural* **Bengalis**).

benighted *adjective* **1** overtaken by night. **2** intellectually or morally ignorant.

benign (bĕ-**nyn**) *adjective* **1** kindly. **2** mild and gentle in its effect; *a benign tumour*, one that is not malignant. **benignly** *adverb* [from Latin *benignus* = kind-hearted]

benignant (bĕ-**nig**-nănt) *adjective* kindly.

benignity (bĕ-**nig**-nĭ-tee) *noun* kindliness.

Benin (ben-**een**) a republic in West Africa. **Beninese** *adjective* & *noun*

Bennelong (died 1813), an Australian Aborigine captured on Governor Phillip's orders in 1789 and brought to live at Government House. Later he lived at what is now Bennelong Point (the site of the Sydney Opera House).

Ben Nevis (**nev**-ĭs) the highest mountain in the British Isles (1343 m), in Scotland.

bent *see* bend¹. –**bent** *noun* a natural skill or liking, *she has a bent for needlework*. –**bent** *adjective* (*informal*) dishonest. □ **bent on** determined or seeking to do something, *bent on mischief*.

Bentham (**ben**-tăm *or* **ben**-thăm), Jeremy (1748–1832), English philosopher, who upheld the theory that society should try to achieve the greatest happiness of the greatest number of people.

bentwood *noun* wood that has been artificially bent into a permanent curve, used for making chairs etc.

benzene (**ben**-zeen) *noun* a colourless liquid obtained from petroleum and coal tar, used as a solvent, as fuel, and in the manufacture of plastics. □ **benzene ring** a hexagonal ring of carbon atoms characteristic of the structure of benzene and most aromatic compounds.

benzine (**ben**-zeen) *noun* a colourless liquid mixture of hydrocarbons obtained from petroleum and used as a solvent in dry-cleaning.

Beowulf (**bay**-ŏ-wuulf) a legendary Swedish hero (6th century) celebrated in the Anglo-Saxon poem 'Beowulf'.

bequeath (bĕ-**kweeth**) *verb* to leave as a legacy.

bequest (bĕ-**kwest**) *noun* a legacy.

berate (bĕ-**rayt**) *verb* to scold.

Berber *noun* **1** a member of a group of North African peoples. **2** their language.

bereave *verb* to deprive, especially of a relative, by death; *the bereaved husband*, the man whose wife died. **bereavement** *noun* [from *reave* = take forcibly]

bereft *adjective* deprived; *bereft of reason*, driven mad.

beret (**be**-ray) *noun* a round flat cap with no peak.

berg *noun* an iceberg.

bergamot (**ber**-gă-mot) *noun* a fragrant herb.

beriberi (*pr. as* berry-berry) *noun* a disease affecting the nervous system, caused by lack of vitamin B_1. [from a Sinhalese word]

Bering Sea (**bair**-ring) the northernmost part of the Pacific Ocean, between Alaska and Siberia. [named after the Danish explorer V. J. Bering (1681–1741)]

Berkeley (**bark**-lee), George (1685–1753), Irish-born philosopher and bishop, who held that material objects exist only by being perceived.

berkelium (ber-**kee**-lee-ŭm) *noun* an artificially made radioactive metallic element (symbol Bk).

berley *noun* (*Austral.*) chopped or ground fish bait.

Berlin the capital of Germany.

Bermuda a group of islands in the West Atlantic, a self-governing British dependency. □ **Bermuda Triangle** an area of the Atlantic between Bermuda and Florida, associated with a number of unexplained disappearances of ships and aircraft. **Bermudian** *adjective*

Bernadette, St (1844–79), French peasant girl (Marie Bernadette Soubirous) who claimed to have had visions of the Virgin Mary at Lourdes in SW France in 1858.

Bernard, St (c. 996–c. 1081), priest who founded two hospices in the Alps to aid travellers. St Bernard dogs are named after him.

Berne (*pr.* bern) the capital of Switzerland.

berry *noun* **1** a small round juicy stoneless fruit. **2** (in botanical use) a fruit with seeds enclosed in pulp (e.g. gooseberry, tomato, banana). **3** an egg in the roe of fish or lobster.

berserk (ber-**zerk**) *adjective* frenzied. □ **go berserk** to go into an uncontrollable and destructive rage. [from Icelandic *berserkr* = wild warrior (*ber-* = bear, *serkr* = coat)]

berth *noun* **1** a bunk or sleeping-place in a ship or train. **2** a place for a ship to swing at anchor or tie up at a wharf. **3** (*informal*) a job, employment. –**berth** *verb* to moor at a berth. □ **give a wide berth to** to keep at a safe distance from.

beryl *noun* a transparent usually green precious stone.

beryllium (bě-**ril**-ee-ŭm) *noun* a very light hard greyish-white metallic element (symbol Be), used in alloys where lightness and a high melting-point are important.

beseech *verb* (**besought**, **beseeching**) to implore. [from *be-* + *seek*]

beset *verb* (**beset**, **besetting**) to hem in, to surround; to attack persistently; *the temptations that beset people*, that face them on all sides.

besetting *adjective* habitually affecting or troubling a person, *laziness is his besetting sin*.

beside *preposition* **1** at the side of, close to. **2** compared with, *his work looks poor beside yours*. □ **be beside oneself** to be at the end of one's self-control. **beside the point** having nothing to do with the point, irrelevant.

besides *preposition* in addition to, other than, *he has no income besides his pension*. –**besides** *adverb* also.

besiege *verb* **1** to lay siege to. **2** to crowd round with requests or questions.

besom (**bee**-zǒm) *noun* a broom made by tying a bundle of twigs to a long handle.

besotted (bě-**sot**-ĕd) *adjective* infatuated.

besought *see* **beseech**.

bespeak *verb* (**bespoke**, **bespoken**, **bespeaking**) **1** to engage beforehand. **2** to order (goods). **3** to be evidence of.

bespectacled *adjective* wearing spectacles.

bespoke *see* **bespeak**. –**bespoke** *adjective* (of clothes) made to order; (of a tailor etc.) making such clothes.

Bessemer process (**bes**-ě-mer) *noun* a process formerly much used for converting pig iron into a material suitable for steel-making, devised by Sir Henry Bessemer (1813–98). Compressed air is forced through the iron in order to remove carbon, silicon, and other impurities.

best *adjective* of the most excellent kind; most satisfactory. –**best** *adverb* **1** in the best manner, to the greatest degree. **2** most usefully; *we had best go*, would find it wisest to go. –**best** *noun* **1** that which is best; the chief merit or advantage; *dressed in her Sunday best*, in her best clothes. **2** victory in a fight or argument; *the best of three games*, the winning of two out of three; *give a person best*, admit that he or she has won. –**best** *verb* (*informal*) to defeat, to outdo, to outwit. □ **at best** taking the most hopeful view. **best end** the rib end of lamb's neck for cooking, with more meat than scrag end. **best man** the bridegroom's chief attendant at a wedding. **best part of** most of. **do one's best** to do all one can. **make the best of** to be as contented as possible with; to do what one can with. **to the best of one's ability** using all one's ability. **with the best of them** as well as anyone.

bestial (**best**-ee-ăl) *adjective* of or like a beast, savage. **bestiality** (best-ee-**al**-ĭ-tee) *noun* [from Latin *bestia* = beast]

bestir *verb* (**bestirred, bestirring**) **bestir oneself** to rouse or exert oneself.

bestow *verb* to present as a gift. **bestowal** *noun*

bestrew *verb* **1** to strew. **2** to lie scattered over. **bestrewn** *adjective*

bestride *verb* (**bestrode, bestridden, bestriding**) to sit or stand astride over.

bet *noun* **1** an agreement pledging something that will be forfeited if one's forecast of some event proves to have been wrong. **2** the money etc. pledged. **3** a person or thing considered likely to be successful in something; *your best bet is to call tomorrow*, this is your best course of action. **4** (*informal*) a prediction, *my bet is that he won't come*. –**bet** *verb* (**bet or betted, betting**) **1** to make a bet, to pledge in a bet. **2** (*informal*) to predict, to think most likely. □ **you bet** (*informal*) you may be sure.

beta (**bee-tă**) *noun* **1** the second letter of the Greek alphabet, = b. **2** a second-class mark in an examination. **3** (in names of stars) the second-brightest in a constellation. □ **beta blocker** a drug used to prevent increased cardiac activity. **beta particles** (or **rays**) fast-moving electrons emitted by radioactive substances (originally regarded as rays).

betake *verb* (**betook, betaken, betaking**) **betake oneself** to go.

betatron *noun* an apparatus for accelerating electrons in a circular path.

betel (**bee-těl**) *noun* a leaf chewed in Asian and Pacific countries with **betel nut** (the areca nut).

bête noire (bayt **nwar**) (*plural* **bêtes noires**, *pr.* bayt **nwar**) a thing or person that one dislikes very much. [French, = black beast]

Bethlehem a small town near Jerusalem, the birthplace of Jesus Christ.

betide *verb* to happen to; *woe betide him*, trouble will come to him. [from *be-*, + an old word *tide* = befall]

betimes *adverb* (*old use*) in good time, early.

betoken *verb* to be a sign of.

betook *see* **betake**.

betray *verb* **1** to give up or reveal disloyally to an enemy. **2** to be disloyal to. **3** to show unintentionally. **betrayal** *noun*, **betrayer** *noun* [from *be-*, + Latin *tradere* = hand over]

betroth (bě-**troh***th*) *verb* (*formal*) to engage with a promise to marry. **betrothal** *noun*

better¹ *adjective* **1** of a more excellent kind; more satisfactory; *one's better feelings*, more charitable feelings, conscience; *it's against my better judgment*, I feel it may be unwise. **2** partly or fully recovered from an illness. –**better** *adverb* in a better manner, to a better degree; more usefully; *we had better go*, would find it wiser to go. –**better** *noun* that which is better. –**better** *verb* to improve, to do better than. **betters** *plural noun* people who are of higher status than oneself. □ **better half** (*humorous*) one's spouse. **better oneself** to get a better social position or status. **better part** more than half. **get the better of** to overcome.

better² *noun* a person who bets.

betterment *noun* making or becoming better.

bettong *noun* a short-nosed rat kangaroo. [from Dharuk *bidung*]

between *preposition & adverb* **1** in the space bounded by two or more points, lines, or objects. **2** intermediate to, especially in time or quantity or quality etc. **3** separating, *the difference between right and wrong*. **4** to and from, *the shuttle operates between Sydney and Canberra*. **5** connecting, *the great love between them*. **6** shared by, *divide the money between you*. **7** taking one and rejecting the other, *choose between them*. □ **between you and me, between ourselves** in confidence; to be kept secret.

betwixt *preposition & adverb* (*old use*) between. **betwixt and between** midway.

bevel (**bev-ĕl**) *noun* **1** a sloping edge or surface. **2** a tool for making such slopes. –**bevel** *verb* (**bevelled, bevelling**) to give a sloping edge to.

beverage (**bev-ĕ-rij**) *noun* any drink.

bevy (**bev-ee**) *noun* a company, a large group.

bewail *verb* to wail over, to mourn for.

beware *verb* to be on one's guard. [from *be-*, + *ware* = wary]

bewilder *verb* to puzzle, to confuse. **bewilderment** *noun* [from *be-*, + an old word *wilder* = lose your way]

bewitch *verb* **1** to put under a magic spell. **2** to delight very much.

beyond *adverb & preposition* **1** at or to the further side of; further on. **2** outside; outside the range of, *this is beyond repair*; *it is beyond me*, too difficult for me to do or to understand;

he lives beyond his income, spends more than he earns. **3** besides, except.

b/f *abbreviation* brought forward.

Bhagavadgita (bah-gǎ-vahd-**gee**-tǎ) *noun* the 'Song of the Lord' (i.e. Krishna), the most famous religious text of Hinduism.

bhakti (**bahk**-tee) *noun* (in Hinduism) worship directed to one supreme deity, usually Vishnu or Siva.

bhang (*pr.* bang) *noun* the dried leaves and flower-tops of Indian hemp smoked or chewed as a narcotic and intoxicant.

bhikkhu *noun* a Buddhist monk or devotee. [Pali]

Bhutan (boo-**tahn**) a kingdom between India and Tibet. **Bhutanese** *adjective* & *noun* (*plural* **Bhutanese**).

bi *adjective* (*informal*) bisexual. –**bi** *noun* (*informal*) a bisexual person.

bi- *prefix* two (as in *bicycle*); twice (as in *biannual*). [from Latin *bis* = twice]

biannual *adjective* appearing or happening twice a year. **biannually** *adverb*

bias *noun* **1** an opinion or feeling or influence that strongly favours one side in an argument or one item in a group or series. **2** the slanting direction across threads of woven material; *skirt is cut on the bias*, cut with the threads running diagonally across the up-and-down line of the garment. **3** the tendency of a ball in the game of bowls to swerve because of the way it is weighted. **4** a steady voltage, applied to an electronic device, that can be adjusted to change the way the device operates. –**bias** *verb* (**biased**, **biasing**) to give a bias to, to influence. □ **bias binding** a strip of fabric cut on the bias and used to bind edges.

bib *noun* **1** a cloth or plastic covering put under a young child's chin to protect the front of its clothes, especially while it is feeding; any similar covering. **2** the front part of an apron, above the waist.

Bible *noun* the Christian scriptures; the Jewish scriptures. –**bible** *noun* **1** a copy of either of these. **2** a book regarded as authoritative. [from Greek *biblia* = books (originally = rolls of papyrus from Byblos, a port now in Lebanon]

biblical *adjective* of or in the Bible.

bibliography (bib-lee-**og**-rǎ-fee) *noun* **1** a list of books or articles about a particular subject or by a particular author. **2** the study of the history of books and

their production. **bibliographer** *noun*, **bibliographical** *adjective* [from Greek *biblion* = book, + -*graphy*]

bicameral (**by**-kam-ě-rǎl) *adjective* having two legislative chambers. [from *bi-*, + Latin *camera* = chamber]

bicarbonate *noun* any acid salt of carbonic acid. □ **bicarbonate of soda** (also **bicarb soda**) sodium bicarbonate, used as an antacid or in baking powder.

bicentenary (by-sěn-**tee**-nǎ-ree) *noun* a 200th anniversary.

bicentennial (by-sěn-**ten**-ee-ǎl) *adjective* of a bicentenary. –**bicentennial** *noun* a bicentenary.

biceps (**by**-seps) *noun* the large muscle at the front of the upper arm, which bends the elbow. [Latin, = two-headed (because its end is attached at two points)]

bicker *verb* to quarrel constantly about unimportant things.

bickie *noun* (also **bikkie**) (*informal*) a biscuit. □ **big bickies** a large sum of money.

biconcave (by-**kon**-kayv) *adjective* (of a lens) having both its surfaces concave.

biconvex (by-**kon**-veks) *adjective* (of a lens) having both its surfaces convex.

bicuspid (by-**kusp**-ǐd) *adjective* having two cusps. –**bicuspid** *noun* a bicuspid tooth. [from *bi-*, + Latin *cuspis* = sharp point]

bicycle *noun* a two-wheeled vehicle driven by pedals. –**bicycle** *verb* to ride on a bicycle. □ **bicycle clip** a clip for securing a trouser leg at the ankle while cycling.

bicyclist *noun* a person who rides a bicycle.

bid[1] *noun* **1** an offer of a price in order to buy something, especially at an auction. **2** a statement of the number of tricks a player proposes to win in a card game. **3** an effort to obtain something, *made a bid for popular support*. –**bid** *verb* (**bid**, **bidding**) to make a bid. **bidder** *noun*

bid[2] *verb* (**bid**, *old use* **bade** (*pr.* bad); **bid** or **bidden**, **bidding**) **1** to command, *do as you are bid* or **bidden**. **2** to say as a greeting or farewell, *bidding them good night*.

biddable *adjective* willing to obey.

bidding *noun* a command. **do a person's bidding** to do what he or she commands.

bide *verb* to wait. □ **bide one's time** to wait for a good opportunity.

bidet (**bee**-day) *noun* a low narrow washbasin that one can sit astride for washing the genital regions. [from French *bidet* = a pony]

biennial (by-**en**-ee-ăl) *adjective* **1** lasting or living for two years. **2** happening every second year. –**biennial** *noun* **1** a plant that lives for two years, flowering and dying in the second. **2** a festival taking place every second year, *Brisbane Biennial*. **biennially** *adverb* [from *bi-*, + Latin *annus* = year]

bier *noun* a movable stand on which a coffin or a dead body is placed before burial.

biff *verb* (*informal*) to hit. –**biff** *noun* (*informal*) a blow.

bifocal (by-**foh**-kăl) *adjective* having two foci. **bifocals** *plural noun* spectacles with each lens made in two sections, the upper part for looking at distant objects and the lower part for reading and other close work.

bifurcate (**by**-fŭ-kayt) *verb* to divide into two branches. **bifurcation** *noun*

big *adjective* (**bigger**, **biggest**) **1** large in size, amount, or intensity. **2** more grown up, elder, *my big brother*. **3** important, *the big match*. **4** boastful, pretentious, *big talk*. **5** (*informal*) generous, *that's big of you*. –**big** *adverb* (*informal*) **1** on a large scale; *think big*, plan ambitiously. **2** successfully, *it went over big*. □ **Big Apple** (*informal*) New York City. **big bang theory** the theory that our universe originated when a fireball of radiation expanded suddenly and then cooled. **Big Ben** the great bell (or loosely, the clock or tower) of the Houses of Parliament in London. **Big Brother** an all-powerful dictator who exercises close supervision and control of everything while pretending to be kindly. **big business** commerce on a large financial scale. **big deal!** (*informal*) I am not impressed. **big dipper** a roller coaster. **big end** the end of a connecting rod that encircles the crankshaft. **big game** the larger animals hunted for sport. **big gun** (*informal*) a bigwig. **big-head** *noun* (*informal*) a conceited person. **big-hearted** *adjective* very kind, generous. **big-note** *verb* (*Austral. informal*) to exalt (oneself). **big shot** (*informal*) a bigwig. **big smoke** a large town or city. **big toe** the first and largest toe. **big top** the main tent at a circus. **have big ideas** to be ambitious. **too big for one's boots** (*informal*) conceited.

bigamist *noun* a person guilty of bigamy.

bigamy *noun* the crime of marrying when already married to another person. **bigamous**

adjective, **bigamously** *adverb* [from *bi-*, + Greek *gamos* = marriage]

bight (*rhymes with* kite) *noun* **1** a long inward curve in a coast, *the Great Australian Bight*. **2** a loop of rope.

bigot (**big**-ŏt) *noun* a person who holds an opinion or belief obstinately and is intolerant towards those who think differently. **bigoted** *adjective*, **bigotry** *noun*

bigwig *noun* (*informal*) an important person.

bijou (**bee**-zhoo) *adjective* small and elegant. [French, = jewel]

bike *noun* (*informal*) a bicycle or motorcycle. –**bike** *verb* (*informal*) to travel on a bike.

biker *noun* a motorcyclist.

bikie *noun* (*Austral. informal*) a motorcyclist, especially a member of a gang.

bikini *noun* a woman's two-piece swimsuit consisting of bra and briefs. [named after Bikini, an atoll in the West Pacific, where an atomic bomb was tested in 1946]

bilateral (by-**lat**-erăl) *adjective* of or on two sides; having two sides; *a bilateral agreement*, one made between two persons or groups. □ **bilateral symmetry** symmetry in which the left and right sides are mirror images of each other. **bilaterally** *adverb* [from *bi-* + *lateral*]

bilberry *noun* **1** a northern European shrub with small round dark blue berries. **2** the fruit of this shrub.

bilby *noun* an Australian nocturnal burrowing marsupial with blue-grey fur. [Yuwaalaraay *bilbi*]

bile *noun* a bitter yellowish liquid produced by the liver and stored in the gall bladder, aiding digestion of fats.

bilge (*pr.* bilj) *noun* **1** a ship's bottom, inside and outside. **2** the water that collects there. **3** (*informal*) worthless ideas or talk.

bilingual (by-**ling**-gwăl) *adjective* **1** written in two languages. **2** able to speak two languages. [from *bi-*, + Latin *lingua* = language]

bilious (**bil**-yŭs) *adjective* **1** affected by sickness assumed to be caused by too much bile. **2** of a sickly yellowish colour or shade, *a bilious green*. **biliousness** *noun* [from *bile*]

bilk *verb* to escape paying one's debts to, to defraud.

bill[1] *noun* **1** a written statement of charges for goods supplied or services rendered. **2** a poster or placard. **3** a program of entertainment. **4** the draft of a proposed law, to be discussed by a parliament (and called an *Act* when passed). **5** a banknote, *a five-dollar bill*. **6** a certificate; *a clean bill of health*, a declaration that there is no disease or defect. –**bill** *verb* **1** to announce in a bill or poster. **2** to send a note of charges to. □ **bill of exchange** a written order to pay a specified sum of money on a particular date to a named person or to the bearer. **bill of fare** a menu. **bill of lading** a list giving details of a ship's cargo. **fill the bill** to be or do what is required.

bill² *noun* a bird's beak. –**bill** *verb* (of doves) to stroke each other with their bills.

billabong *noun* (*Austral.*) a river branch forming a backwater or stagnant pool. [Wiradjuri *bilabang*]

billboard *noun* a hoarding for advertisements.

billet¹ *noun* **1** a lodging for troops, evacuees, sports teams, etc., especially in a private house. **2** (*informal*) a position, a job. –**billet** *verb* (**billeted**, **billeting**) to place in a billet.

billet² *noun* a thick piece of firewood.

billet-doux (bil-ay-**doo**) *noun* (*plural* **billets-doux**, *pr.* bil-ay-**doo**) a love letter. [French, = sweet note]

billhook *noun* a long-handled tool with a curved blade for lopping trees.

billiards *noun* a game played with cues and three balls on a cloth-covered table. [from French *billard* = cue]

billion *noun* **1** a thousand million. **2** (now less often) a million million. **billionth** *adjective* & *noun* [from *bi-* + *million*]

Usage The sense 'a thousand million' was originally used in the USA but is now common elsewhere.

---

billionaire *noun* a person who has over a billion dollars etc.

billow *noun* a great wave. –**billow** *verb* to rise or roll like waves, *smoke billowed forth*.

billy *noun* (also **billycan**) (*Austral.*) a tin can or enamelled container with a lid and wire handle, used by campers etc. as a kettle or cooking pot. [From Scottish *billy-pot* = cooking utensil]

billycart *noun* (*Austral.*) a simple four-wheeled structure for a child to play on (also called a *go-cart*).

billy goat *noun* a male goat. [from the name *Billy*]

billy-o *noun* (*informal*) **like billy-o** vigorously.

bimah *noun* = **bema**.

bimbo *noun* (*plural* **bimbos**) (*informal*, usually *derogatory*) an attractive but empty-headed young woman.

bimetallic (by-mĕ-**tal**-ik) *adjective* of two metals. □ **bimetallic strip** a device used in thermostats, made of two bands of metals that expand at different rates when heated, so that the whole strip bends. [from *bi-* + *metal*]

bimonthly *adjective* **1** happening every second month. **2** happening twice a month.

bin *noun* **1** a large rigid container or enclosed space, usually with a lid, used for storing coal, grain, flour, etc. **2** a receptacle for rubbish or litter.

binary (**by**-nă-ree) *adjective* of a pair or pairs. –**binary** *noun* a binary star. □ **binary digit** or **number** either of the two digits, 0 and 1, used in the binary system. **binary fission** division of a cell or organism into two in reproduction. **binary notation** or **scale** a system of numbers using only the two digits 0 and 1. **binary operation** (in mathematics) an operation that combines two elements of a set to produce a third. **binary star** two stars that revolve round each other. **binary system** a system using the numbers 0 and 1 to code information, especially in computing. [from Latin *bini* = two together]

bind *verb* (**bound**, **binding**) **1** to tie or fasten; to tie up. **2** to hold together; to unite, *bound by ties of friendship*. **3** to encircle with a strip or band of material; *bind up the wound*, bandage it. **4** to cover the edge of (a thing) in order to strengthen it or as a decoration. **5** to fasten the pages of (a book) into a cover. **6** to stick together in a solid mass, *bind the mixture with egg yolk*. **7** to place under an obligation or a legal agreement. –**bind** *noun* (*informal*) a bore, a nuisance. □ **bind over** to put under a legal obligation to keep the peace.

binder *noun* **1** a person or thing that binds. **2** a bookbinder. **3** a machine that binds harvested corn into sheaves or straw into bales. **4** a loose cover for papers.

bindery *noun* a workshop where books are bound.

bindi-eye *noun* **1** a small Australian plant bearing barbed fruits. **2** the fruit of these plants. [Kamilaroi and Yuwaalaraay *bindayaa*]

binding *noun* **1** fabric used for binding edges. **2** the strong covering holding the leaves of a book together. **–binding** *adjective* making a legal obligation, *the agreement is binding on both parties*.

bindweed *noun* a wild convolvulus.

bine (*rhymes with* mine) *noun* the flexible stem of a climbing plant, especially of hops.

binge (*pr.* binj) *noun* (*informal*) a spree, eating and drinking and making merry.

bingo *noun* a gambling game with cards on which numbered squares are covered as the numbers are called at random.

binnacle (**bin**-ă-kŭl) *noun* a non-magnetic stand for a ship's compass.

binocular (bǐ-**nok**-yŭ-ler) *adjective* for or using both eyes. **binoculars** *plural noun* an instrument with lenses for both eyes, making distant objects seem nearer. [from Latin *bini* = two together, + *oculus* = eye]

binomial (by-**noh**-mee-ăl) *noun* an algebraic expression consisting of two terms linked by a plus or minus sign. ☐ **binomial theorem** a formula for finding any power of a binomial without doing the series of multiplications. [from *bi-*, + Greek *nomos* = part]

bio- *prefix* life (as in *biology*). [from Greek *bios* = life]

biochemistry *noun* chemistry of living organisms. **biochemical** *adjective*, **biochemist** *noun*

biodegradable (by-oh-dĕ-**gray**-dă-bŭl) *adjective* able to be broken down by bacteria in the environment, *some plastics are not biodegradable*. **biodegradability** *noun*, **biodegradation** *noun*

biodiesel *noun* biofuel intended as a substitute for diesel.

bioengineering *noun* the application of engineering techniques to biological processes.

bioethics *noun* the ethics of medical and biological research.

biofuel *noun* fuel derived immediately from living matter.

biogas *noun* gaseous fuel, especially methane, produced by fermentation of organic matter.

biographer *noun* a person who writes a biography.

biography *noun* the story of a person's life written by someone else. **biographical** *adjective* [from *bio-* + *-graphy*]

biology *noun* the scientific study of the life and structure of living things. ☐ **biological clock** an internal mechanism controlling the rhythmic pattern of activities of a living thing. **biological control** the control of pests by introducing natural predators. **biological warfare** the deliberate use of organisms to spread disease amongst an enemy. **biological** *adjective*, **biologically** *adverb*, **biologist** *noun* [from *bio-* + *-logy*]

biomass (**by**-oh-mas) *noun* the total quantity or weight of living things in a particular area.

biome (**by**-ohm) *noun* **1** a large naturally occurring community of fauna and flora adapted to the particular conditions in which they occur, e.g. a rainforest. **2** the geographical region containing such a community.

bionic (by-**on**-ik) *adjective* **1** of bionics. **2** (of a person or his or her faculties) operated by electronic means, not naturally. **bionics** *noun* the study of mechanical systems that function like parts of living beings. [from *bio-* + electro*nic*]

biophysics *noun* the scientific study of the properties of physics in living organisms, and investigation of biological matters by means of modern physics. **biophysical** *adjective*, **biophysicist** *noun*

biopsy (**by**-op-see) *noun* examination of tissue cut from a living body. [from *bio-* + auto *psy*]

biorhythm (**by**-ŏ-ri*th*m) *noun* any of the recurring cycles of physical, emotional, and intellectual activity said to occur in people's lives.

biosecurity *noun* measures taken to protect the population against harmful biological or biochemical substances.

biosphere (**by**-ŏ-sfeer) *noun* the regions of the earth's crust and atmosphere occupied by living things.

biotechnology *noun* the use of living microorganisms and biological processes in industrial and commercial production.

bioterrorism *noun* the use of infectious agents or other harmful biological or biochemical substances as weapons of terrorism.

biotic (by-**ot**-ik) *adjective* of life or living things.

biotope *noun* an area with a particular habitat that supports a particular community of flora and fauna.

bipartisan (by-par-tǐ-**zan**) *adjective* of or involving two political or other parties.

bipartite (by-**par**-tyt) *adjective* having two parts, shared by or involving two groups.

biped (**by**-ped) *noun* a two-footed animal. [from *bi*-, + Latin *pedis* = of a foot]

biplane (**by**-playn) *noun* a type of aeroplane with two sets of wings, one above the other.

bipolar *adjective* having two poles or extremities. □ **bipolar disorder** a mental illness characterised by manic and depressive episodes. **bipolarity** *noun*

birch *noun* 1 a deciduous tree with smooth bark and slender branches. 2 its wood. 3 a bundle of birch twigs used for flogging. –**birch** *verb* to flog with a birch.

bird *noun* 1 a feathered animal with two wings and two legs. 2 (*informal*) a person, *he's a cunning old bird*. 3 (*informal*) a young woman. □ **bird of paradise** a New Guinean bird with brightly coloured plumage. **bird's-eye view** a general view from above.

birdie *noun* 1 (*informal*) a little bird. 2 a score of one stroke under par for a hole at golf.

birdseed *noun* special seed used as food for caged birds.

Birdsville Track a 500 km stockroute from Birdsville in SW Queensland to Marree in SA.

biretta (bǐ-**ret**-ǎ) *noun* a square cap worn by (especially Roman Catholic) priests.

biriani (bi-ree-**ah**-nee) *noun* an Indian dish made with rice and meat, fish, or vegetables. [Urdu]

biro *noun* (*trademark*) a kind of ballpoint pen. [named after its Hungarian inventor L. Biró (1900–85)]

birth *noun* 1 the emergence of young from the mother's body. 2 origin, parentage, *he is of noble birth*. □ **birth certificate** an official document giving the date and place of a person's birth. **birth control** prevention of unwanted pregnancy. **birth rate** the number of births in one year for every 1000 persons. **give birth to** to produce as young from the body; to cause to begin.

birthday *noun* an anniversary of the day of one's birth. □ **birthday suit** a state of nakedness as at birth.

birthmark *noun* an unusual coloured mark on a person's skin at birth.

birthplace *noun* the house or district where one was born.

birthright *noun* a privilege or property to which a person has a right through being born into a particular family (especially as the eldest son) or country.

bis *adverb* (in music) to be repeated. [Latin, = twice]

Biscay (**bis**-kay), **Bay of** part of the North Atlantic between the N coast of Spain and the W coast of France, notorious for storms. □ **Bay of Biscay soil** an unstable clayey soil in parts of Adelaide, SA.

biscuit (**bis**-kǐt) *noun* 1 a flat, thin, crisp, savoury or sweet, unleavened cake. 2 fired unglazed pottery. 3 light-brown colour. [from Latin *bis* = twice, + *coctus* = cooked]

bisect (by-**sekt**) *verb* to divide into two equal parts. **bisection** *noun*, **bisector** *noun* [from *bi*-, + Latin *sectum* = cut]

bisexual (by-**sek**-shoo-ǎl) *adjective* 1 of two sexes. 2 having both male and female sexual organs in one individual. 3 sexually attracted by members of both sexes. –**bisexual** *noun* a bisexual person. **bisexuality** *noun*

Bishkek the capital of Kyrgyzstan.

bishop *noun* 1 a senior member of the Christian clergy with authority over the work of the Church in a city or district (a *diocese*). 2 a chess piece shaped like a mitre.

bishopric *noun* the office or diocese of a bishop.

Bismarck (**biz**-mark), Otto Eduard Leopold, Prince von (1815–98), German statesman.

Bismarck Archipelago a group of over 200 islands to the north-east of Papua New Guinea.

bismillah (bis-**mil**-ǎ) *interjection* in the name of God (an invocation used by Muslims at the beginning of an undertaking).

bismuth (**biz**-mǔth) *noun* 1 a chemical element (symbol Bi), a greyish-white metal used in alloys. 2 a compound of this used in medicines.

bison (**by**-sǒn) *noun* (*plural* **bison**) a wild humpbacked ox of N America (also called *buffalo*) or of Europe.

Bissau (bis-**ow**) the capital of Guinea-Bissau.

bistable (by-**stay**-bǔl) *adjective* (in computers) having two stable states that can be used to represent 0 and 1.

bistro (**bis**-troh) *noun* (*plural* **bistros**) a small restaurant. [French]

bit¹ *noun* **1** a small piece, quantity, or portion of anything; *I'm a bit puzzled*, slightly puzzled; *it's a bit of a nuisance*, rather a nuisance; *it takes a bit of doing*, is quite difficult. **2** a short time or distance, *wait a bit*. □ **bit by bit** gradually. **bit part** (*informal*) a small part in a play or film. **do one's bit** (*informal*) to do one's due share.

bit² *noun* **1** a metal bar forming the mouthpiece of a bridle. **2** the part of a tool that cuts or grips when twisted; the boring-piece of a drill. □ **take the bit between one's teeth** to take decisive action.

bit³ *noun* (in computers) a unit of information expressed as a choice between two possibilities. [from *b*inary dig*it*]

bit⁴ *see* bite.

bitch *noun* **1** a female dog; a female fox, wolf, otter, etc. **2** (*offensive*) a spiteful woman. –**bitch** *verb* (*informal*) to speak spitefully; to complain. **bitchy** *adjective*, **bitchiness** *noun*

bite *verb* (**bit**, **bitten**, **biting**) **1** to cut into or nip with the teeth; *this dog bites*, is in the habit of biting people. **2** (of an insect) to sting; (of a snake) to pierce with its fangs. **3** to accept bait, *the fish are biting*. **4** to grip or act effectively, *wheels can't bite on a slippery surface*. **5** (*Austral. informal*) to cadge, to borrow from. –**bite** *noun* **1** an act of biting. **2** a wound made by this. **3** a mouthful cut off by biting. **4** food to eat, a small meal. **5** the taking of bait by a fish. **6** a firm grip or hold. **7** the way the teeth close in biting. **8** sharpness, effectiveness. **biter** *noun*

biting *adjective* **1** causing a smarting pain, *a biting wind*. **2** (of remarks) sharp and critical.

bitser *noun* (*informal*) **1** a mongrel dog. **2** anything made of miscellaneous parts.

bitten *see* bite.

bitter *adjective* **1** tasting sharp, not sweet. **2** unwelcome to the mind, causing sorrow. **3** showing, feeling, or caused by mental pain or resentment, *bitter remarks*. **4** piercingly cold, *a bitter wind*. –**bitter** *noun* beer strongly flavoured with hops and tasting bitter. **bitters** *plural noun* liquor flavoured with bitter herbs. □ **bitter-sweet** *adjective* sweet but with a bitter taste at the end; pleasant but with a mixture of something unpleasant. **to the bitter end** until all that is possible has been done. **bitterly** *adverb*, **bitterness** *noun*

bittern *noun* a wading bird related to the heron, especially the kind known for the male's booming note.

bitty *adverb* made up of unrelated bits.

bitumen (**bich**-ŭ-měn) *noun* **1** a black sticky substance obtained from petroleum, used for covering roads etc. **2** (*Austral.*) a tarred road. **bituminous** (bĭ-**choo**-mĭ-nŭs) *adjective*

bivalve (**by**-valv) *noun* a shellfish with a hinged double shell.

bivouac (**biv**-oo-ak) *noun* a temporary camp without tents or other cover. –**bivouac** *verb* (**bivouacked**, **bivouacking**) to camp in a bivouac.

bi-weekly *adjective* **1** happening every second week. **2** happening twice a week.

bizarre (biz-**ar**) *adjective* strikingly odd in appearance or effect.

blab *verb* (**blabbed**, **blabbing**) to talk indiscreetly, to let out a secret.

blabber *verb* to talk (especially at length) about trivial things.

blabbermouth *noun* a person who blabs.

black *adjective* **1** of the very darkest colour, like coal or soot. **2** having a black skin, *a black snake*. **3** Black of or relating to the human group with dark-coloured skin, especially of Aboriginal or African descent. **4** soiled with dirt. **5** dismal, sullen, hostile; *things look black*, not hopeful; *a black day*, disastrous. **6** evil, wicked. **7** not to be handled by trade unionists while others are on strike, *declared the cargo black*. –**black** *noun* **1** a black colour. **2** a black substance or material; black clothes. **3** the black ball in snooker etc. **4** the black men in chess etc.; the player using these. **5** the credit side of an account; *in the black*, having a credit balance. **6** Black a member of a dark-skinned race, especially of Aboriginal or African descent. –**black** *verb* **1** to make black. **2** to polish with blacking. **3** to declare goods or work to be 'black'. □ **black armband** a black band worn around the arm to indicate mourning. **black ban** a refusal to supply or provide goods or services, usually as part of an industrial dispute or protest; a prohibition (especially as imposed by a trade union) preventing work (on a site etc.) from proceeding. **black belt** the highest grade of proficiency in judo, karate, etc.; the holder of this. **black box** an electronic device in an aircraft recording information about its flight. **black comedy** comedy presenting a tragic theme or situation in comic terms. **black eye** an eye with the skin round it darkened by a bruise. **black hole** a region in outer space with a gravitational field so intense that no matter or radiation can escape from it. black ice hard thin transparent ice on roads. black magic magic involving the invocation of devils. black mark a mark of disapproval placed against a person's name. black market the illegal buying and selling of goods or currencies. black marketeer one who trades in the black market. black out to cover windows etc. so that no light can penetrate; to suffer temporary loss of consciousness or sight or memory. black pudding a large dark sausage containing blood, suet, etc. black sheep a bad character in an otherwise well-behaved group. black spot a place where conditions are dangerous or difficult, one that has a bad record. black stump (*Austral.*) a distant edge of settlement; *beyond the black stump*, in the remote outback. black tie a man's black bow tie worn with a dinner jacket; (*informal*) formal evening dress. black widow a poisonous spider found in tropical and subtropical regions (the female of a North American species devours its mate). in a person's black books having earned his or her disapproval. in black and white consisting of extremes only, oversimplified. blackish *adjective*, blackly *adverb*, blackness *noun*

blackball *verb* to prevent (a person) from being elected as a member of a club by voting against him at a secret ballot.

blackberry *noun* 1 the bramble. 2 its small dark berry. blackberrying *noun* picking blackberries.

blackbird *noun* a common European thrush, the male of which is black; introduced into Australia.

blackbirding *noun* (*historical*) the practice of kidnapping Pacific Islanders and selling them as slave labour, mainly for the Queensland cotton and sugar plantations. blackbirder *noun*

blackboard *noun* a board usually coloured black, for writing on with chalk in front of a class in school etc.

blackboy *noun* an Australian tree with a black trunk, a head of grasslike leaves, and a tall spearlike flower head. Also called a *grass-tree*.

blackbutt *noun* a eucalypt with blackish bark on its lower trunk.

Black Death an epidemic of plague in Europe during the 14th century.

blacken *verb* 1 to make or become black. 2 to say unpleasant things about, *blackened his character*.

blackfish *noun* a bass-like Australian sea or freshwater fish.

blackfly *noun* a kind of insect infesting plants.

Black Forest a hilly wooded region of SW Germany. Black Forest cake a chocolate cake with layers of morello cherries and cream.

Black Friars Dominicans, so called from their black cloaks.

blackguard (**blag**-erd) *noun* a scoundrel. blackguardly *adverb*

blackhead *noun* a small hard lump blocking a pore in the skin.

blacking *noun* black polish for shoes.

blacklead *noun* graphite.

blackleg *noun* a person who works while fellow workers are on strike. –blackleg *verb* (blacklegged, blacklegging) to act as a blackleg.

blacklist *noun* a list of persons who are disapproved of. –blacklist *verb* to put on a blacklist.

blackmail *verb* to demand payment or action from (a person) by threats especially of revealing a discreditable secret. –blackmail *noun* the crime of demanding payment in this way; the money itself. blackmailer *noun*

blackout *noun* 1 a loss of electric power. 2 the extinguishing of all lights. 3 a compulsory period of darkness during wartime. 4 a temporary loss of consciousness or sight or memory. 5 a temporary suppression of the release of information.

Black Power a militant movement supporting civil rights, political power, etc., for Blacks.

Black Prince the name given in the 16th century to Edward Plantagenet (1330–76), eldest son of Edward III of England.

Black Rod the usher of the Australian Senate, so called from the ebony rod of office.

Black Sea a tideless sea bounded by Turkey, Bulgaria, Romania, Ukraine, Russia, and Georgia.

blackshirt *noun* a member of a Fascist organisation.

blacksmith *noun* a smith who works in iron.

blackwood *noun* a tall Australian acacia with reddish-brown wood.

blackwork *noun* a kind of embroidery done in black silk on fine linen.

bladder *noun* 1 a sac in which urine collects in human and animal bodies. 2 an inflatable bag, e.g. in a football. □ bladder worm the larva of a tapeworm, which forms a protective capsule round itself.

bladderwrack *noun* a seaweed with air-filled swellings among its fronds.

blade *noun* 1 the flattened cutting part of a knife, sword, chisel, etc. 2 the flat wide part of an oar, spade, propeller, etc. 3 a flat narrow leaf, especially of grass and cereals. 4 a broad flattish bone, *shoulder blade*. 5 a rollerblade. –**blade** *verb* (*informal*) skate using rollerblades.

Blake, William (1757–1827), English artist and poet.

blame *verb* to hold responsible and criticise for a fault; *I don't blame you*, I feel your action was justified. –**blame** *noun* responsibility for a fault, criticism for doing wrong.

blameless *adjective* deserving no blame, innocent.

blanch *verb* 1 to make or become white or pale; *blanch the almonds*, peel them. 2 to immerse (fruit or vegetables) briefly in boiling water.

blancmange (blă-**monj**) *noun* a flavoured jelly-like pudding made with milk. [from French *blanc* = white, + *manger* = eat]

bland *adjective* 1 mild in flavour, *bland foods*. 2 gentle and casual in manner, not irritating or stimulating. **blandly** *adverb*, **blandness** *noun* [from Latin *blandus* = soothing]

blandish *verb* to flatter, to coax. **blandishment** *noun* [same origin as *bland*]

blank¹ *adjective* 1 not written or printed on, unmarked; *a blank wall*, without ornament or opening. 2 without interest or expression; without result; *look blank*, to appear puzzled. –**blank** *noun* 1 a blank space or paper; an empty surface; *his mind was a blank*, he could not remember anything. 2 a blank cartridge. □ **blank cartridge** one that contains no bullet. **blank cheque** one with the amount left blank, to be filled in by the payee. **blank verse** verse written in lines of usually ten syllables, without rhyme. **blankly** *adverb*, **blankness** *noun* [from French *blanc* = white]

blank² *verb* **blank off** to seal (an opening). **blank out** to cross out, to obscure.

blanket *noun* a thick covering made of woollen or other fabric; *a blanket of fog*, a thick covering mass. –**blanket** *adjective* inclusive, covering all cases, *a blanket agreement*. –**blanket** *verb* (**blanketed**, **blanketing**) to cover with a blanket.

□ **blanket bath** a body wash given to a bedridden patient. **blanket stitch** an embroidery stitch suitable for finishing a raw edge.

blare *noun* a harsh loud sound like that of a trumpet. –**blare** *verb* to make such a sound.

blarney *noun* smooth talk that flatters and deceives people. [named after a castle in Ireland where there is a stone said to give anyone who kisses it the ability to talk persuasively]

blasé (**blah**-zay) *adjective* bored or unimpressed by things because one has already experienced or seen them so often. [French]

blaspheme *verb* to utter blasphemies. **blasphemer** *noun* [from Greek *blasphemos* = evil-speaking]

blasphemy (**blas**-fĕ-mee) *noun* contemptuous or irreverent talk about God or sacred things. **blasphemous** *adjective*, **blasphemously** *adverb*

blast *noun* 1 a sudden strong rush of wind or air, a wave of air from an explosion. 2 a single emission of sound by a wind instrument or whistle or car horn etc. 3 (*informal*) a severe reprimand. –**blast** *verb* 1 to blow up with explosives. 2 to cause to wither, to blight, to destroy. 3 (*informal*) to reprimand severely. □ **at full blast** at maximum power. **blast furnace** a furnace for smelting ore, with compressed hot air driven in. **blast off** to be launched by firing of rockets. **blast-off** *noun* the launching of a spacecraft.

blatant (**blay**-tănt) *adjective* attracting attention in a very obvious way; *a blatant lie*, very obvious and unashamed. **blatantly** *adverb* [from an old word meaning 'noisy']

Blaxland, Gregory (1778–1853), English-born farmer who, with William Lawson and W. C. Wentworth, crossed the Blue Mountains in 1813.

blaze¹ *noun* 1 a bright flame or fire. 2 a bright light, a brightly coloured display. 3 an outburst, *a blaze of anger*. –**blaze** *verb* 1 to burn or shine brightly. 2 to have an outburst of intense feeling or anger.

blaze² *noun* 1 a white mark on an animal's face. 2 a mark chipped in the bark of a tree to mark a route. –**blaze** *verb* to mark (a tree or route) with blazes. □ **blaze a trail** to make such marks; to pioneer and show the way for others to follow.

blaze³ *verb* to proclaim, *blazed the news abroad*.

blazer *noun* a loose-fitting jacket, often in the colours or bearing the badge of a school, club, or team. [from *blaze¹*]

blazon (**blay**-zŏn) *noun* a heraldic shield, a coat of arms. [from *blaze³*]

bleach *verb* to whiten by sunlight or chemicals. –**bleach** *noun* a bleaching substance.

bleak *adjective* cold and cheerless; *the future looks bleak*, unpromising. **bleakly** *adverb*, **bleakness** *noun*

bleary *adjective* watery and seeing indistinctly, *bleary eyes*. **blearily** *adverb*, **bleariness** *noun*

bleat *noun* the cry of a sheep, goat, or calf. –**bleat** *verb* **1** to make this cry. **2** to speak or say plaintively.

bleed *verb* (**bled**, **bleeding**) **1** to leak blood or other fluid; *some dyes bleed*, come out in water. **2** to draw blood or fluid from. **3** to extort money from.

bleep *noun* a short high-pitched sound used as a signal. –**bleep** *verb* to make this sound. **bleeper** *noun*

blemish *noun* a flaw that spoils a thing's perfection. –**blemish** *verb* to spoil with a blemish.

blench *verb* to flinch.

blend *verb* **1** to mix in order to get a certain quality. **2** to mingle, to become a mixture. **3** to have no sharp or unpleasant contrast, *the colours blend well*. –**blend** *noun* a mixture of different sorts, *a blend of tea*.

blender *noun* **1** something that blends things. **2** an electric mixing machine for blending, liquidising, or chopping foods.

blenny *noun* a small scaleless sea fish with spiny fins.

bless *verb* **1** to make sacred or holy with the sign of the Cross. **2** to call holy, to praise, *to bless God*. **3** to call God's favour upon, *Christ blessed the children*; *bless his heart!*, an exclamation of affection; *bless my soul!*, an exclamation of surprise. **4** (*informal*) to curse, *she'll bless you for breaking that!* □ **be blessed with** to be fortunate in having, *be blessed with good health*.

blessed (**bles**-ĕd) *adjective* **1** holy, sacred; *the Blessed Virgin*, the Virgin Mary. **2** in paradise; *the Blessed*, people who are in paradise. **3** (*old use*) fortunate, *blessed are the meek*. **4** (*ironic*)

wretched, *a blessed nuisance*. **blessedness** *noun*

blessing *noun* **1** God's favour; a prayer for this. **2** a short prayer of thanks to God before or after a meal, grace. **3** something one is glad of; *a blessing in disguise*, something unwelcome at the time but which later turns out to have a good effect.

blest *adjective* (*old use*) blessed, *our blest Redeemer*. □ **well, I'm blest!** an exclamation of surprise. **I'm blest if I know** I do not know at all.

blew *see* **blow¹**.

Bligh, William (1754–1817), British naval officer, commander of HMS *Bounty* whose crew mutinied in 1789, later Governor of NSW (1806–8).

blight *noun* **1** a disease that withers plants. **2** a fungus or insect causing this disease. **3** a malignant influence. **4** an unsightly area. –**blight** *verb* **1** to affect with blight. **2** to spoil.

blighter *noun* (*informal*) a person or thing, especially an annoying one.

blimp *noun* a small non-rigid airship; a barrage balloon.

blind *adjective* **1** without sight; *a blind corner*, where road users cannot see what is approaching. **2** without foresight or understanding, without adequate information, *blind obedience*. **3** concealed, *blind hemming*. **4** (in cookery) without filling, *bake it blind*. **5** (of a passage or road) closed at one end. –**blind** *adverb* blindly. –**blind** *verb* **1** to make blind; to dazzle with bright light. **2** to take away the power of judgment; *blinded with science*, overawed by a display of knowledge. –**blind** *noun* **1** a screen, especially on a roller, for a window. **2** a pretext. □ **blind alley** an alley that is closed at one end; a job with no prospects of advancement. **blind date** a date between people who have not met before. **blind Freddy** (*Austral. informal*) an imaginary person of minimum perception, *even blind Freddy could see that*. **blind man's buff** a game in which a blindfolded player tries to catch others who push him or her about. **blind spot** a point on the eye that is insensitive to light; an area where understanding is lacking; an area cut off from a motorist's vision. **turn a blind eye** to pretend not to notice. **blindly** *adverb*, **blindness** *noun*

blindfold *adjective* & *adverb* with the eyes covered with a cloth to block one's

sight. **–blindfold** *noun* a cloth used for this.
–blindfold *verb* to cover the eyes with a cloth.

bling *noun* (also **bling-bling**) (*informal*)
expensive, ostentatious clothing and jewellery,
or the wearing of them.

blink *verb* **1** to open and shut the eyes rapidly.
2 to shine unsteadily. **3** to ignore, to refuse
to consider; *there's no blinking these facts*,
we must consider them. **–blink** *noun* **1** an act
of blinking. **2** a quick gleam. ☐ **on the blink**
(*informal*) not working properly.

blinker *verb* to obstruct the sight or
understanding of. **–blinker** *noun* a small
signal-light on a motor vehicle, flashing
to indicate a change of direction of travel.
blinkers *plural noun* leather pieces fixed
on a bridle to prevent a horse from seeing
sideways.

blip *noun* **1** a spot of light on a radar screen.
2 a quick popping sound. **–blip** *verb* (**blipped**,
blipping) to make a blip.

bliss *adjective* perfect happiness. **blissful**
adjective, **blissfully** *adverb*

blister *noun* **1** a bubble-like swelling on the
skin, filled with watery liquid. **2** a raised
swelling, e.g. on a painted surface. **–blister**
verb **1** to cause a blister on; to be affected with
blisters. **2** to criticise severely. ☐ **blister pack** a
bubble pack.

blithe (*rhymes with* scythe) *adjective* casual
and carefree. **blithely** *adverb*

blithering *adjective* (*informal*) absolute,
contemptible, *blithering idiot*.

blitz *noun* (also **blitzkrieg**) **1** a sudden
violent attack, especially from aircraft; **the
Blitz** the German air raids on London in
1940. **2** an intensive attack, *a police blitz on
speeding*. **–blitz** *verb* **1** to attack or damage in
a blitz. **2** (in competition) beat soundly; defeat
by a large margin. [short for German *blitzkrieg*
(*blitz* = lightning, *krieg* = war)]

blizzard *noun* a severe snowstorm.

bloated *adjective* **1** swollen with fat, gas, or
liquid. **2** puffed up with pride of wealth or
with self-indulgence etc.

bloater *noun* a salted smoked herring.

blob *noun* a drop of liquid; a round mass or
spot.

bloc *noun* a group of parties or countries who
unite to support a particular interest.

block *noun* **1** a solid piece of wood or stone
or other hard substance. **2** a log of wood.
3 a large piece of wood for chopping or

hammering on; *the block*, that on which
condemned people were beheaded. **4** the
main part of a petrol engine, consisting of
the cylinders. **5** a compact mass of buildings
bounded by streets. **6** a large building divided
into separate flats or offices. **7** (*Austral.*)
an area of land divided for settlement; an
allotment of land for building, fruit growing,
etc. **8** a pad of paper for drawing or writing
on. **9** an obstruction; *a mental block*, failure
to understand etc., caused by emotional
tension. **10** (*informal*) the head. **–block** *verb*
1 to obstruct, to prevent the movement or use
of. **2** to stop (a bowled ball) with the bat.
☐ **block and tackle** a system of pulleys and
ropes used for lifting things. **block diagram** a
diagram showing the general arrangement of
parts in an apparatus. **block graph** a bar chart
on which the bars are divided into equal units
(blocks). **block in** to sketch in roughly. **block
letters** plain capital letters. **block mountain**
a mountain formed when a block of land
bounded by faults is pushed upwards. **do one's
block** (*Austral. informal*) to lose one's temper.

blockade *noun* the blocking of access to a
place in order to prevent the entry of goods
etc. **–blockade** *verb* to set up a blockade of.

blockage *noun* **1** something that blocks.
2 the state of being blocked.

blockbuster *noun* (*informal*) **1** a huge
bomb. **2** something very large, powerful, or
successful.

blocker *noun* (also **blockie**) (*Austral.*) the
owner of a smallholding.

blockhead *noun* (*informal*) a stupid person.

blog *noun* a weblog. **–blog** *verb* (**blogs**,
blogging, **blogged**) add new material to or
regularly update a weblog.

blogosphere *noun* personal websites and
weblogs collectively.

bloke *noun* (*informal*) a man.

blond (of a woman or her hair **blonde**)
adjective fair-haired; (of hair) fair. **–blond**
noun, **blonde** *feminine noun* a fair-haired
person. [from medieval Latin *blondus* =
yellow]

blood *noun* **1** the red oxygen-bearing
liquid circulating in the bodies of animals.
2 bloodshed; the guilt for this. **3** temper,
courage; *his blood is up*, he is in a fighting
mood; *there's bad blood between them*,
hatred. **4** race, descent, parentage; *new
blood*, new members admitted to a family
or group; *they are my own blood*, relatives.

–blood *verb* to give a first taste of blood to (a hound); to initiate. □ **blood-curdling** *adjective* horrifying. **blood group** any of the classes or types of human blood. **blood orange** an orange with red-streaked pulp. **blood poisoning** the condition that results when the bloodstream is infected with harmful microorganisms that have entered the body, especially through a cut or wound. **blood pressure** the pressure of blood within the arteries and veins; abnormally high pressure of this kind. **blood-red** *adjective* as red as blood. **blood sports** sports involving killing. **blood test** an examination of a specimen of blood in medical diagnosis. **blood vessel** a vein, artery, or capillary tube carrying blood.

bloodbath *noun* a massacre.

bloodhound *noun* a large keen-scented dog formerly used in tracking.

bloodless *adjective* 1 having no blood; looking pale, drained of blood. 2 without bloodshed. 3 without vitality.

bloodletting *noun* violence during a conflict; bloodshed.

bloodshed *noun* the killing or wounding of people.

bloodshot *adjective* (of eyes) red from dilated veins.

bloodstain *noun* a stain made by blood.

bloodstained *adjective* 1 stained with blood. 2 disgraced by bloodshed.

bloodstock *noun* thoroughbred horses.

bloodstream *noun* the blood circulating in the body.

bloodsucker *noun* 1 a creature that sucks blood. 2 a person who extorts money.

bloodthirsty *adjective* eager for bloodshed.

bloodwood *noun* any of various Australian eucalypts with red sap.

bloody *adjective* 1 bloodstained. 2 with much bloodshed, *a bloody battle*. 3 (in strong language) damned, very great. –**bloody** *adverb* (as an intensifier) very, *bloody good*. –**bloody** *verb* (**bloodied**, **bloodying**) to stain with blood. □ **bloody-minded** (*informal*) deliberately uncooperative. **bloodily** *adverb*, **bloodiness** *noun*

Usage The use of *bloody* to mean 'very' or 'very great' is offensive to some people.

bloom *noun* 1 a flower; *in bloom*, in flower. 2 beauty, perfection, *in the bloom of youth*. 3 fine powder on fresh ripe grapes etc. –**bloom** *verb* 1 to bear flowers, to be in bloom. 2 to be in full beauty.

bloomer *noun* (*informal*) a blunder.

bloomers *plural noun* (*informal*) knickers with legs. [named after Mrs A. Bloomer, American social reformer (died 1894), who wore loose-fitting trousers]

blossom *noun* 1 a flower, especially of a fruit tree. 2 a mass of such flowers. –**blossom** *verb* 1 to open into flowers. 2 to develop and flourish.

blot *noun* 1 a spot of ink etc. 2 something ugly, *a blot on the landscape*. 3 a fault, a disgraceful act or quality. –**blot** *verb* (**blotted**, **blotting**) 1 to make a blot or blots on. 2 to dry with blotting paper, to soak up. □ **blot one's copybook** to spoil one's good record. **blot out** to cross out thickly; to obscure, *mist blotted out the view*; to destroy completely. **blotting paper** absorbent paper for drying ink.

blotch *noun* a large irregular mark. **blotched** *adjective*, **blotchy** *adjective*

blotter *noun* a pad of blotting paper, a device holding this.

blouse *noun* 1 a shirt-like garment worn by women and children. 2 a waist-length coat forming part of a military uniform. –**blouse** *verb* 1 to make (a top etc.) loose like a blouse. 2 to swell or hang loosely like a blouse.

blow¹ *verb* (**blew**, **blown**, **blowing**) 1 to send out a current of air or breath; to move or propel by this; *blow one's nose*, clear it by breathing out through it; *blow the whistle*, sound it. 2 to move or flow as a current of air does. 3 to shape (molten glass) by blowing into it. 4 to be moved or carried by air, *door blew open*. 5 to puff and pant. 6 to swell; *the tin of fruit has blown*, swollen from gas pressure inside. 7 to melt with too strong an electric current, *blow the fuse*; *a fuse has blown*. 8 to break with explosives. 9 (*informal*) to reveal; *the spy's cover was blown*, became known to the enemy. 10 (*informal*) to spend recklessly. 11 (*informal*) to bungle. 12 (*Austral. informal*) to boast. –**blow** *noun* 1 an act of blowing. 2 exposure to fresh air. □ **blow in** (*informal*) to arrive casually or unexpectedly. **blow-in** *noun* (*Austral. informal*) a casual visitor or newcomer. **blow one's own trumpet** to praise oneself. **blow one's top** (*informal*) to show great anger. **blow over** to die down without serious

consequences. **blow the gaff** *see* gaff².
blow the mind to produce hallucinations, or
a very pleasurable or shocking sensation, in
the mind. **blow up** to inflate; to exaggerate;
to make an enlargement of (a photograph);
to explode; to shatter by an explosion; to
lose one's temper; to reprimand severely; to
become a crisis, *this problem has blown up
recently.* **blow-up** *noun*

blow² *noun* **1** a stroke with a hand or weapon.
2 a shock, a disaster. □ **blow-by-blow**
adjective telling all the details of an event in
their order of occurrence.

blow-dry *verb* to use a hand-held dryer to
style (washed hair) while drying it.

blower *noun* **1** a person or thing that blows.
2 (*informal*) a telephone.

blowfly *noun* a fly that lays its eggs on meat.

blowhole *noun* **1** the nostril of a whale.
2 a hole in a coastal cave through which air
or water rushes in response to the action
of waves. **3** (in inland Australia) a vent
through which air passes out forcefully from
an underground reservoir of air. **4** a hole
(especially in ice) for breathing or fishing
through.

blowlamp *noun* a portable burner producing
a very hot flame that can be directed on a
selected spot.

blown *see* blow¹.

blow-out *noun* **1** a burst tyre. **2** a melted fuse.
3 a rapid uncontrolled upward rush of oil or
gas from a well. **4** (*informal*) a large meal.

blowpipe *noun* **1** a tube through which air is
blown. **2** a tube for sending out darts or pellets
by blowing.

blowtorch *noun* = blowlamp.

blowy *adjective* windy.

blowzy (*rhymes with* drowsy) *adjective* red-
faced and coarse-looking.

blubber *noun* whale fat. – **blubber** *verb* to
weep noisily. – **blubbery** *adjective* (of lips)
thick, swollen.

bludge (*Austral. informal*) *verb* **1** to avoid
work or responsibility. **2** to impose on other
people. – **bludge** *noun* **1** an act or instance
of bludging. **2** an easy or undemanding task.
bludger *noun*

bludgeon (**bluj**-ĕn) *noun* a short stick with a
thickened end, used as a weapon. – **bludgeon**
verb **1** to strike with a bludgeon. **2** to compel
forcefully.

blue *adjective* **1** of the colour of the sky
on a cloudless day. **2** unhappy, depressed.
3 indecent, obscene, *blue jokes.* – **blue** *noun*
1 blue colour. **2** a blue substance or material;
blue clothes. **3** *the blue*, the clear sky; the sea.
4 (*Austral. informal*) an argument, a fight.
5 (*Austral. informal*) a mistake, a blunder.
6 (*Austral.*, as a nickname) a redhead.
– **blue** *verb* (**blued**, **blueing**) **1** to make blue.
2 (*informal*) to spend recklessly. **blues** *noun*
melancholy jazz melodies. **the blues** a state of
depression. □ **blue blood** aristocratic descent.
blue cheese cheese with veins of blue mould.
blue-chip *adjective* (of shares) fairly reliable
as an investment though less secure than
gilt-edged. (¶ So called from the high-valued
blue chips in the game of poker.) **blue-collar
worker** a manual or industrial worker. **blue
flyer** an adult female red kangaroo. **blue gum**
a eucalypt with smooth bluish-grey bark
or bluish foliage. **blue heeler** an Australian
cattle dog with a blue or red-flecked coat.
blue-pencil *verb* to cross out with a blue
pencil; to censor. **Blue Peter** a blue flag with a
white square, hoisted by a ship about to sail.
blue pointer a large bluish shark of southern
Australian waters. **blue-ribbon** *adjective*
prize-winning; (of an electorate) held by
a very comfortable margin by a particular
political party. **blue-screen** a special-effects
technique used in films in which scenes shot
against a blue background are superimposed
on other scenes. **blue-tongue** an Australian
lizard with a cobalt-blue tongue. **blue whale**
a rorqual, the largest known living animal.
once in a blue moon very rarely. **out of the
blue** unexpectedly. **true blue** faithful, loyal.
blueness *noun*, **bluish** *adjective*

bluebell *noun* a plant with blue bell-shaped
flowers.

blueberry *noun* **1** a shrub with edible blue
berries. **2** its fruit.

bluebottle *noun* **1** a large fly with a bluish
body. **2** (*Austral.*) a jellyfish with a painful
sting.

bluebush *noun* an Australian saltbush with
bluish foliage.

bluefin *noun* the commonest large tuna,
which occurs worldwide in warm seas.

bluegrass *noun* a style of instrumental
music influenced by American folk and
country music.

Blue Mountains a plateau on the eastern
side of the Great Dividing Range, west of
Sydney.

blueprint *noun* 1 a blue photographic print of building plans. 2 a detailed plan or scheme.

bluestocking *noun* a learned woman. [named after the 'Blue Stocking Club', a London literary group, many of whose male members wore grey or 'blue' stockings]

bluestone *noun* 1 copper sulphate. 2 a building stone.

Bluetooth *noun* (*trademark*) wireless technology for interconnecting mobile phones, computers, etc. [said to be named after King Harold *Bluetooth* (910–85), credited with uniting Denmark and Norway]

bluey *adjective* rather blue, *bluey-green*. – bluey *noun* (*Austral.*) a bushman's swag.

bluff¹ *adjective* 1 with a broad steep front, *a bluff headland*. 2 abrupt, frank, and hearty in manner. – bluff *noun* a bluff headland or cliff. bluffness *noun*

bluff² *verb* to deceive someone by making a pretence, especially of strength. – bluff *noun* bluffing, a threat intended to get results without being carried out. [from Dutch *bluffen* = boast]

blunder *verb* 1 to move clumsily and uncertainly. 2 to make a blunder. – blunder *noun* a mistake made especially through ignorance or carelessness. blunderer *noun*

blunderbuss *noun* an old type of hand-held gun firing many balls at one shot. [from Dutch *donderbus* = thunder gun]

blunt *adjective* 1 with no sharp edge or point, not sharp. 2 speaking or expressed in plain terms, *a blunt refusal*. – blunt *verb* to make or become blunt. bluntly *adverb*, bluntness *noun*

blur *noun* 1 a confused or indistinct appearance. 2 a smear. – blur *verb* (blurred, blurring) 1 to make or become indistinct. 2 to smear.

Blu-ray *noun* (*trademark*) a very high-definition optical disk for video, storage of data, etc.

blurb *noun* a description of something praising it, e.g. in advertising matter.

blurt *verb* to utter abruptly or tactlessly, *he blurted it out before he had time to think*.

blush *verb* to become red in the face from shame or embarrassment. – blush *noun* such reddening of the face.

blusher *noun* a reddish powder or cream for colouring the cheeks, rouge.

bluster *verb* 1 to be windy, to blow in gusts. 2 to talk aggressively, especially with empty threats. – bluster *noun* such talk. blustery *adjective*

BMI *abbreviation* body mass index.

BMX *noun* 1 organised bicycle racing on a dirt track. 2 a kind of bicycle for use in this. [short for 'bicycle moto-cross']

BO *abbreviation* (*informal*) body odour.

boa (**boh**-ă) *noun* a large non-poisonous South American snake that squeezes its prey so as to suffocate it. □ **boa constrictor** a Brazilian species of boa.

boab *noun see* baobab.

Boadicea = Boudicca.

boar *noun* 1 a wild pig. 2 an uncastrated domestic male pig.

board *noun* 1 a thin flat piece of sawn timber, usually long and narrow. 2 a flat piece of wood or stiff material for a special purpose, e.g. a blackboard, a diving board, a chessboard. 3 thick stiff paper used for book covers. 4 daily meals obtained in return for payment or services, *board and lodging*. 5 a committee. 6 (*Austral.*) the part of the floor of a shearing shed where the shearers work. – board *verb* 1 to cover with boards. 2 to go on board (a ship, aircraft, etc.). 3 to receive or provide with meals and accommodation for payment. □ **go by the board** to be ignored or rejected. **on board** on or in a ship, aircraft, etc. **take on board** to accept (a new idea etc.) and consider or act upon it.

boarder *noun* 1 a person who boards with someone. 2 a resident pupil at a boarding school.

boardies *plural noun* (*Austral. informal*) boardshorts.

boarding *noun* 1 boards. 2 material from which these are cut; a structure or covering made of this.

boarding house *noun* a house at which board and lodging may be obtained for payment.

boarding school *noun* a school in which pupils receive board and lodging.

boardroom *noun* a room where the meetings of the board of a company etc. are held.

boardshorts *plural noun* long shorts, originally as used by surfboard riders.

boast *verb* 1 to speak with great pride and try to impress people, especially about oneself. 2 to possess as something to be proud of,

the town boasts a fine park. –boast *noun*
1 a boastful statement. **2** something one is
proud of. **boaster** *noun*

boastful *adjective* boasting frequently, full
of boasting. **boastfully** *adverb*, **boastfulness**
noun

boat *noun* **1** a small vessel for travelling on
water, propelled by paddle, oars, sails, or
an engine; (loosely) a ship. **2** a boat-shaped
serving dish for sauce or gravy. □ **boat people**
refugees leaving a country by sea. **boat train**
a train timed to carry passengers to or from a
ship's docking place. **in the same boat** in the
same predicament.

boater *noun* a hard flat straw hat.

boathouse *noun* a shed at the water's edge
for housing boats.

boating *noun* rowing or sailing for pleasure.

boatman *noun* (*plural* **boatmen**) a person
who rows or sails boats or who rents out boats.

boatswain (**boh**-sŭn) *noun* a ship's officer in
charge of rigging, boats, anchors, etc.

bob[1] *verb* (**bobbed**, **bobbing**) **1** to make a
jerky movement, to move quickly up and
down; *bob up*, to appear suddenly, to become
active or conspicuous again. **2** to cut (hair)
short so that it hangs loosely. –bob *noun*
1 a bobbing movement. **2** the style of bobbed
hair.

bob[2] *noun* (*plural* **bob**) (*informal, historical*)
a shilling (= 10c).

bobbin *noun* a small spool holding thread or
wire in a machine.

bobble *noun* a small ornamental woolly ball.

bobby *noun* (*Brit. informal*) a police officer.
[named after Sir Robert Peel, founder of the
metropolitan police force]

bobby pin *noun* a hairpin.

Bobcat *noun* (*trademark*) a small four-
wheeled earth-moving machine.

bob-sleigh (**bob**-slay) *noun* (also
bob-sled) a sledge with two sets of runners,
especially with mechanical steering, used for
tobogganing. **bob-sleighing** *noun*

bobtail *noun* a docked tail; a horse or dog
having this.

Boccaccio (bok-**ah**-chee-oh), Luigi
(1313–75), Italian novelist, poet, and
humanist, author of the *Decameron*.

bocce (bo-chay) *noun* an Italian game similar
to bowls.

bode *verb* to be a sign of, to promise, *it boded
well for their future*.

bodgie *noun* (*Austral. informal*) a male youth
of the 1950s who conformed to American
fashions and antisocial behaviour. –bodgie
adjective (*informal*) worthless; flawed;
inferior; false. [from British dialect *bodge* =
'work clumsily']

bodhisattva (bod-ĭ-**saht**-vă) *noun*
(in Mahayana Buddhism) one who is able to
reach nirvana, but delays doing so in order to
help other suffering beings.

bodice (**bod**-ĭss) *noun* the upper part of a
woman's dress, down to the waist.

bodily *adjective* of the human body or
physical nature. –bodily *adverb* **1** in person,
physically. **2** as a whole, *the bridge was moved
bodily 50 metres downstream*.

bodkin *noun* a blunt thick needle with a large
eye, for drawing tape etc. through a hem.

body *noun* **1** the structure of bones, flesh,
etc., of a human being or animal, living or
dead. **2** a corpse, a carcass. **3** the trunk, the
main part of the body apart from the head and
limbs. **4** the main part of anything; *a car body*,
bodywork; *the body of a concert hall*, the
central part where the seats are. **5** (*informal*) a
person, *she's a cheerful old body*. **6** a group or
quantity of people, things, or matter, regarded
as a unit. **7** a distinct piece of matter; an object
in space. **8** thick texture, strong quality, *this
fabric has more body*; *this wine has no body*.
□ **body blow** a severe setback. **body-building**
noun strengthening of the body by exercises.
body language involuntary movements or
attitudes by which a person communicates his
or her feelings or moods etc. **body mass index**
an approximate measure of whether someone
is over- or underweight, calculated by dividing
their weight in kilograms by the square of
their height in metres (abbreviation **BMI**).
body odour the smell of the human body,
especially when unpleasant. **body surfing**
surfing without a surfboard. **in a body** all
together. **keep body and soul together** to have
just enough food etc. to remain alive.

bodyguard *noun* an escort or personal guard
of an important person.

bodywork *noun* the shell of a motor vehicle.

Boer (**boh**-er *or* boor) *noun* **1** an Afrikaner.
2 (*old use*) an early Dutch inhabitant of the
Cape. –Boer *adjective* of Boers.

☐ **Boer War** either of two wars fought by Britain in South Africa, 1880–1 and 1899–1902. [from Dutch, = farmer]

boffin *noun* (*informal*) a person engaged in technical research.

bog *noun* an area of ground that is permanently wet and spongy, formed of decayed plants etc. –**bog** *verb* (**bogged**, **bogging**) to be stuck fast in wet ground; to cause to be stuck and unable to make progress. **boggy** *adjective*

bogey[1] *noun* (*plural* **bogeys**) (in golf) a score of one stroke over par at a hole.

bogey[2] (*Austral.*) *noun* a swim or bathe. –**bogey** *verb* to swim or bathe. [from Dharuk *bugi*]

boggle *verb* to hesitate in alarm or consternation, to raise objections, *the mind boggles at the idea*. [from dialect *bogle* = bogy]

bogie (**boh**-gee) *noun* an undercarriage fitted below a railway vehicle, pivoted at the end for going round curves.

bogong (**boh**-gong) *noun* a large brown Australian moth. [Ngarigo *bugung*]

Bogotá (bog-ŏ-**tah**) the capital of Colombia.

bogus *adjective* sham, counterfeit.

bogy *noun* **1** an evil spirit. **2** something that causes fear. [originally *Old Bogey* = the Devil]

bogyman *noun* (*plural* **bogymen**) an imaginary person feared by children, especially in the dark.

Bohemia (boh-**hee**-mee-ă) an area that forms the western part of the Czech Republic.

Bohemian *adjective* **1** of Bohemia. **2** very informal in one's way of living. –**Bohemian** *noun* **1** a native or inhabitant of Bohemia. **2** a person of Bohemian habits.

Bohr (*pr.* bor), Niels Hendrik David (1885–1962), Danish physicist, influential in the field of quantum physics.

bohrium (**bor**-ee-ŭm) *noun* a very unstable artificial element (symbol Bh).

boil[1] *verb* **1** to bubble up and change into vapour through being heated. **2** to heat (a liquid or its container) so that the liquid boils; to cook or wash or process in this way; to be heated or cooked etc. in this way. **3** to seethe like boiling liquid; to be hot with anger. –**boil** *noun* boiling point; *on the boil*, boiling; *off the boil*, having just ceased to boil. ☐ **boil down** to reduce or be reduced in quantity by boiling; (*informal*) to express or be expressed in fewer words. **boiling hot** (*informal*) very hot. **boiling**

point the temperature at which a liquid boils; a state of great anger or excitement. **boil over** to overflow when boiling. [from Latin *bulla* = a bubble]

boil[2] *noun* an inflamed swelling under the skin, producing pus.

boiler *noun* **1** a container in which things are boiled, especially a closed metal tub for boiling laundry. **2** a container in which water is heated, especially to supply hot water for a heating system, or steam to drive an engine etc. **3** a fowl too tough to roast but suitable for boiling. ☐ **boiler suit** a one-piece garment combining overalls and shirt, worn for rough work.

boilermaker *noun* **1** a person who makes boilers. **2** a metalworker in heavy industry.

boisterous *adjective* **1** noisy and cheerful, *boisterous children*. **2** windy, *boisterous weather*. **boisterously** *adverb*

bolar *noun* (*Austral.*) a cut of beef adjacent to the blade.

bold *adjective* **1** confident and courageous. **2** without feelings of shame, impudent. **3** (of colours) strong and vivid. **4** (also **boldface**) printed in thick black typeface. **boldly** *adverb*, **boldness** *noun*

bole *noun* the trunk of a tree.

bolero *noun* (*plural* **boleros**) **1** (bŏ-**lair**-roh) a Spanish dance, the music for this. **2** (*pr.* bol-ĕ-roh) a woman's short jacket with no front fastening. [Spanish]

Boleyn (bŏ-**lin**), Anne (1507–36), the second wife of Henry VIII, and mother of Elizabeth I.

Bolivia (bŏ-**liv**-ee-ă) a landlocked republic in South America. **Bolivian** *adjective* & *noun* [named after the Venezuelan statesman Simón Bolívar (1783–1830), who did much to free South America from Spanish rule]

boll *noun* the round seed vessel of the cotton or flax plant etc.

bollard (**bol**-erd) *noun* **1** a short thick post to which a ship's mooring-rope may be tied. **2** a short post for keeping traffic off a path etc.

boloney (bŏ-**loh**-nee) *noun* (*informal*) nonsense.

Bolshevik *noun* **1** a member of the extremist faction of the Russian socialist party that was renamed the (Russian) Communist Party in 1918. **2** (*loosely*) any socialist extremist. **Bolshevism** *noun*, **Bolshevist** *noun*

Bolshie *adjective* (*informal*) **1** Bolshevik, left-wing. **2** (also **bolshie**) rebellious, uncooperative. **bolshiness** *noun*

Bolshoi Ballet (**bol**-shoi) a Moscow ballet company dating from 1776. [Russian, = great]

bolson (**bohl**-sŏn) *noun* (*Amer.*) a large depression in the ground surrounded by mountains, in south-western USA and Mexico.

bolster *noun* a long pillow for the head of a bed. **–bolster** *verb* to support, to prop.

bolt *noun* **1** a sliding bar for fastening a door. **2** the sliding part of a rifle-breech. **3** a strong metal pin for fastening things together. **4** a shaft of lightning. **5** a roll of fabric. **6** an arrow shot from a crossbow. **7** the act of bolting. **–bolt** *verb* **1** to fasten with a bolt or bolts. **2** to run away, (of a horse) to run off out of control. **3** (of plants) to run to seed. **4** to gulp down (food) hastily. □ **a bolt from the blue** a complete (usually unwelcome) surprise. **bolt-hole** *noun* a place into which one can escape. **bolt upright** quite upright.

bolus (**boh**-lŭs) *noun* a quantity of food, chewed and mixed with saliva, as it is swallowed. [from Greek *bolus* = clod]

bomb *noun* **1** a container filled with explosive or incendiary material to be set off by impact or by a timing device. **2 the bomb** an atomic or hydrogen bomb, regarded as the supreme weapon. **3** (*informal*) a large sum of money. **4** (*Austral.*) a dilapidated old car. **–bomb** *verb* to attack with bombs. □ **bomb out** (*informal*) to fail badly, *bombed out in physics*. [from Greek *bombos* = loud humming]

bombard *verb* **1** to attack with many missiles, especially from big guns. **2** to send a stream of high-speed particles against. **3** to attack with questions or complaints. **bombardment** *noun*

bombardier *noun* a non-commissioned officer in the artillery.

bombast (**bom**-bast) *noun* pompous words or speech. **bombastic** (bom-**bas**-tik) *adjective*

bomber *noun* **1** an aircraft that carries and drops bombs. **2** a person who throws or plants bombs. □ **bomber jacket** a waist-length jacket gathered into a band at waist and cuffs.

bomblet *noun* a small bomb.

bombora (bom-**bor**-ră) *noun* (*Austral.*) a dangerous stretch of water where waves break over a submerged reef or rock; the reef or rock itself. [perhaps Dharuk *bumbora*]

bombshell *noun* something that comes as a great surprise and shock.

bona fide (**boh**-nă **fy**-dee) *adjective* genuine, without fraud, *bona fide customers*. [Latin, = with good faith]

bona fides (**boh**-nă **fy**-deez) *noun* honest intention, sincerity. [Latin, = good faith]

bonanza (bŏ-**nan**-ză) *noun* a source of sudden great wealth or luck, a windfall.

Bonaparte (**bohn**-ă-part) the name of a Corsican family including the three French rulers named Napoleon.

bon-bon *noun* **1** a paper cylinder pulled apart with a sharp noise and releasing a hat, toy, etc. **2** a lolly, a sweet.

bond *noun* **1** something that binds, attaches, or restrains, e.g. a rope. **2** something that unites people. **3** the linkage between atoms in a molecule. **4** a binding agreement; a document containing this. **5** money deposited as a guarantee. **6** a document issued by a government or public company acknowledging that money has been lent to it and will be repaid usually with interest. **7** writing paper of high quality. **–bond** *verb* **1** to connect or unite with a bond, to link with an emotional bond. **2** to put into a Customs warehouse. **3** to insure a contract etc. by means of a financial bond. □ **in bond** stored in a Customs warehouse until duties are paid.

bondage *noun* slavery, captivity.

bonded *adjective* **1** stored in bond. **2** storing in bond, *a bonded warehouse*.

bone *noun* **1** any of the hard parts (other than teeth, nails, horns, and cartilage) of an animal's body. **2** a piece of bone with meat on it, as food. **3** the substance from which such parts are made; a similar hard substance. **–bone** *verb* to remove the bones from. □ **bone china** fine china made of clay mixed with bone ash. **bone dry** quite dry. **bone idle** very lazy. **bone of contention** the subject of a dispute. **bone up** to study (a subject) intensively, *boned up on history*. **have a bone to pick** to have something to argue or complain about. **make no bones about** to raise no objection to; to speak frankly about. **point the bone at** (*Austral.*) to cast a fatal spell on. **to the bone** thoroughly, completely; to the bare minimum.

bonehead *noun* a stupid person.

bonemeal *noun* crushed powdered bones used as a fertiliser.

bonfire *noun* a large fire built in the open air to destroy rubbish or as a celebration. [originally *bone fire* = a fire to dispose of people's or animals' bones]

bong *noun* (*informal*) a water pipe used for smoking marijuana or other drugs.

bongo *noun* (*plural* bongos) each of a pair of small drums played with the fingers.

bonhomie (**bon**-ŏmee) *noun* a genial manner. [French]

bonkers *adjective* (*informal*) crazy.

Bonn a city in Germany, the former capital of West Germany.

bonnet *noun* 1 a hat with strings that tie under the chin. 2 a hinged cover over the engine etc. of a motor vehicle.

bonny *adjective* (bonnier, bonniest) 1 healthy-looking. 2 (*Scottish & N. England*) good-looking. [from French *bon* = good]

bonsai (**bon**-sy) *noun* 1 a plant or tree grown in miniature form in a pot by artificially restricting its growth. 2 the method of cultivating this. [Japanese]

bonus *noun* (*plural* bonuses) a payment or benefit in addition to what is usual or expected. [from Latin *bonus* = good]

bon voyage (bawn vwah-**yahzh** *or* bon voi-**ahzh**) *interjection & noun* an expression of good wishes to someone starting a journey. [French]

bony *adjective* (bonier, boniest) 1 like bones. 2 having large or prominent bones, having bones with little flesh. 3 full of bones. boniness *noun*

bonze (*pr.* bonz) *noun* a Buddhist priest in Japan or adjacent countries.

bonzer *adjective* (*Austral. informal*) excellent.

boo *interjection* 1 a sound made to show disapproval or contempt. 2 an exclamation used to startle someone. –boo *verb* to show disapproval by shouting 'boo'.

boob[1] *noun* (*informal*) 1 a foolish person. 2 a stupid mistake. –boob *verb* (*informal*) to make a stupid mistake.

boob[2] *noun* (*informal*) a woman's breast.

boobialla (boo-bee-**al**-ă) *noun* 1 any of several Australian shrubs having pale flowers and globular fruits. 2 a small coastal wattle. [from the Aboriginal language of SE Tasmania *bubiala*]

boobook (**boo**-buuk) *noun* a small brown spotted owl of Australia and New Zealand. [from Dharuk *bubug*]

booby *noun* a foolish person. □ **booby prize** a prize given as a joke to the competitor with the lowest score. **booby trap** a hidden trap rigged up for a practical joke; a hidden bomb placed so that it will explode when some apparently harmless object is touched or moved. **booby-trap** *verb* to place a booby trap in or on.

boogie-woogie *noun* a style of playing blues on the piano, marked by a persistent bass rhythm.

book *noun* 1 a series of written or printed or plain sheets of paper fastened together at one edge and enclosed in a cover. 2 a literary work that would fill such a book or books if printed, *he is working on his book*. 3 a number of cheques, stamps, tickets, matches, etc. fastened together in the shape of a book. 4 each of the main divisions of a written work. 5 a libretto; the script of a play. –book *verb* 1 to enter in a book or list; *the police booked him for speeding*, recorded a charge against him; *we booked in at the hotel*, registered our names there as guests. 2 to reserve (a seat or accommodation etc.); to buy (tickets) in advance. □ **booking office** an office where tickets are sold. **bring to book** to make (a person) answer for his or her conduct. **by the book** in accordance with the correct procedure. **in a person's good** (or **bad**) **books** in favour (or disfavour) with a person.

bookable *adjective* able to be booked.

bookbinding *noun* binding books professionally. **bookbinder** *noun*

bookcase *noun* a piece of furniture with shelves for books.

bookends *plural noun* a pair of supports for keeping a row of books upright.

Booker Prize (in full **Man Booker Prize**) an annual money prize established in 1969, and awarded to the best novel by a British or Commonwealth citizen published in the previous 12 months.

bookie *noun* (*informal*) a bookmaker.

bookish *adjective* fond of reading.

bookkeeping *noun* the systematic recording of business transactions. **bookkeeper** *noun*

booklet *noun* a small thin usually paper-covered book.

bookmaker *noun* a person whose business is taking bets.

bookmark *noun* 1 a strip of paper or other material placed between the pages of a book to mark a place. 2 (in computing) a record of the address of a file, Internet page, etc., enabling quick access by a user. –**bookmark** *verb* (in computing) make a bookmark.

bookplate *noun* a decorative label in a book bearing the owner's name.

bookseller *noun* a person whose business is selling books.

bookshop *noun* a shop selling only (or chiefly) books.

bookworm *noun* 1 a grub that eats holes in books. 2 a person who is very fond of reading.

Boole, George (1815–64), English mathematician, who developed an algebraic system of reasoning, known as Boolean algebra.

boom¹ *verb* 1 to make a hollow deep resonant sound. 2 to have a period of prosperity or rapid economic growth. –**boom** *noun* 1 a booming sound. 2 a period of increased growth, prosperity, or value.

boom² *noun* 1 a long pole used to keep the bottom of a sail stretched. 2 a floating barrier or a heavy chain across a river or a harbour entrance. 3 a long horizontal pole that can be raised or lowered to control traffic. 4 a long pole carrying a microphone etc.

boomer *noun* (*Austral.*) 1 a large adult male kangaroo. 2 anything large or outstanding of its kind, *a boomer nugget*. 3 a large wave.

boomerang *noun* 1 a curved wooden missile used by Australian Aborigines, especially one that can be thrown so that it returns to the thrower if it fails to hit anything. 2 something that causes unexpected harm to its originator. –**boomerang** *verb* to act as a boomerang. [from Dharuk *bumaring*]

boon¹ *noun* a benefit. [from Old Norse *bón* = prayer]

boon² *adjective* boon companion a favourite sociable companion. [from French *bon* = good]

boor *noun* an ill-mannered person. boorish *adjective*, boorishly *adverb*, boorishness *noun*

boost *verb* 1 to push upwards. 2 to increase the strength, value, or good reputation of; to promote. –**boost** *noun* 1 an upward thrust. 2 an increase. booster *noun*

boot¹ *noun* 1 a shoe or outer covering for the foot and ankle or leg. 2 a compartment for luggage in a car. 3 the boot (*informal*) dismissal. –**boot** *verb* 1 to kick. 2 (usually followed by *up*) put (a computer) in a state of readiness. □ **boot out** (*informal*) to dismiss or eject forcefully. boots and all (*Austral. informal*) wholeheartedly; with no holds barred.

boot² *noun* to boot as well, in addition.

bootee *noun* a baby's knitted or crocheted boot.

booth *noun* 1 a small temporary shelter at a market or fair. 2 an enclosure for a public telephone. 3 a compartment in a large room, e.g. for voting at elections.

bootleg *verb* (bootlegged, bootlegging) 1 to smuggle (alcohol). 2 to make and sell illicitly. –**bootleg** *adjective* smuggled or sold illicitly. bootlegger *noun*

booty *noun* loot.

booze *verb* (*informal*) to drink alcohol, especially in large quantities. –**booze** *noun* (*informal*) alcoholic drink. □ **booze-up** *noun* a drinking session. boozer *noun*, boozy *adjective*

bop *noun* = bebop.

bora *noun* a cold, usually dry, NE wind blowing in the upper Adriatic, chiefly in winter.

boracic *adjective* = boric.

borage (**bo**-rij) *noun* a plant with blue flowers and hairy leaves, used as flavouring.

borak *noun* (*Austral.*) nonsense, rubbish. □ **poke borak at** make fun of. [Wathawurung *burag* = no, not]

borax *noun* a soluble white powder that is a compound of boron, used in making glass, enamels, and detergents.

Bordeaux (bor-**doh**) *noun* a red or white wine from Bordeaux in France.

border *noun* 1 an edge or boundary, the part near this. 2 the line dividing two countries or States, the area near this. 3 an edging. 4 a strip of ground round a garden or a part of it. –**border** *verb* to put or be a border to. □ **border on** to be next to; to come close to, *it borders on the absurd*.

borderland *noun* the district near a boundary.

borderline *noun* the line that marks a boundary. –**borderline** *adjective* on the borderline between different groups or categories.

bore¹ *verb* **1** to make (a hole or well etc.) with a revolving tool or by digging out soil. **2** to pierce or penetrate in this way; *bore one's way*, get through by pushing. **–bore** *noun* **1** the hollow inside of a gun barrel or engine cylinder, its diameter. **2** a hole made by boring. **3** (*Austral.*) an artesian bore.

bore² *verb* to make (a person) feel tired or uninterested by being dull or tedious. **–bore** *noun* a boring person or thing. **boredom** *noun*, **boring** *adjective*

bore³ *noun* a tidal wave with a steep front that moves up some estuaries.

bore⁴ see bear².

boreal *adjective* of the North or northern regions, *boreal forest*.

boree (**bor**-ree) *noun* any of several Australian wattles. [Wiradjuri and Kamilaroi *burrii*]

borer *noun* **1** an insect, insect larva, worm, mollusc, etc., which bores into wood, other plant material, or rock. **2** a tool for boring.

boric (**bor**-rik) *adjective* of boron. **boric acid** a substance derived from boron, used as a mild antiseptic.

born (⁋ See the note under **borne**.) **be born** to be brought forth by birth; *born to suffer*, destined for this by birth; *their courage was born of despair*, originated from this. **–born** *adjective* **1** having a certain order, status, or place of birth, *first-born*; *well-born*; *French-born*. **2** having a certain natural quality or ability, *a born leader*. □ **born-again** *adjective* converted (to Christianity) in a life-changing way; enthusiastic in a newly adopted cause.

borne see bear². **–borne** *adjective* (in *combinations*) carried by, *airborne*. □ **it was borne in upon him** he became convinced.

Usage The word *borne* is used as part of the verb *to bear* when it comes before *by* or after *have*, *has*, or *had*, e.g. *children* (*who were*) *borne by Eve*, *she had borne him a son*. The word *born* is used in *a son was born*.

Borneo a large island of the Malay Archipelago, comprising Kalimantan (a region of Indonesia), Sabah and Sarawak (now parts of Malaysia), and Brunei.

boron (**bor**-ron) *noun* a chemical element (symbol B) that is very resistant to high temperatures, used in metal-working and in nuclear reactors.

boronia (bŏ-**rohn**-ee-ă) *noun* a fragrant Australian shrub. [from Francesco Borone, Italian botanist (died 1794)]

borough (**bu**-ră) *noun* **1** (in Britain) a town with a corporation and with privileges conferred by royal charter or defined by statute. **2** (in Australia) an urban local government area in Victoria. **3** an administrative area in London, New York, or Alaska. [from Old English *burg* = fortress or fortified town]

borrow *verb* **1** to get the temporary use of, on the understanding that the thing received is to be returned; to obtain money thus. **2** to use without being the inventor; *borrow their methods*, copy them. **3** to take (a word etc.) into a language from a foreign source. □ **borrowed time** an extension of one's life beyond an illness or crisis that could have ended it. **borrower** *noun*

bortsch (*pr.* borch) *noun* (also **borsch**, *pr.* borsh) a Russian or Polish beetroot soup.

borzoi (**bor**-zoi) *noun* a large hound with a narrow head and silky coat. [from Russian *borzyi* = swift]

bosh *noun* & *interjection* (*informal*) nonsense.

Bosnia (**boz**-nee-ă) a region in the Balkans forming the larger, northern part of the country of **Bosnia-Herzegovina**. **Bosnian** *adjective* & *noun*

bosom *noun* **1** a person's breast. **2** the part of a garment covering this. **3** the centre or inmost part; *returned to the bosom of his family*, to a loving family circle. □ **bosom friend** one who is dear and close.

Bosporus a strait connecting the Black Sea and the Sea of Marmara, with Istanbul at its south end.

boss¹ *noun* a person who controls or gives orders to workers. **–boss** *verb* to be the boss of, to give orders to, *boss about*; *boss around*. [from Dutch *baas* = master]

boss² *noun* a round projecting knob or stud.

boss-eyed *adjective* (*informal*) **1** blind in one eye; cross-eyed. **2** crooked. [from dialect *boss* = miss, bungle]

bossy *adjective* (**bossier**, **bossiest**) (*informal*) fond of ordering people about; doing this continually. **bossily** *adverb*, **bossiness** *noun*

bo'sun (**boh**-sŭn) *noun* (also **bo's'n**) = **boatswain**.

botanical (bŏ-**tan**-ikăl) *adjective* (also botanic) of botany.

botanist *noun* an expert in botany.

botany *noun* the scientific study of plants. [from Greek *botane* = a plant]

Botany Bay a bay near Sydney, NSW, which was the site of James Cook's landing in 1770 (so called because of the many botanical specimens collected there by Joseph Banks). **Botany wool** wool from merino sheep, especially from Australia.

botch *verb* to spoil by poor or clumsy work. –botch *noun* a piece of spoilt work.

both *adjective*, *pronoun*, & *adverb* the two, not only the one.

bother *verb* 1 to cause trouble, worry, or annoyance to, to pester. 2 to take trouble, to feel concern. –bother *interjection* an exclamation of annoyance. –bother *noun* 1 worry; minor trouble. 2 a person or thing causing this.

botheration *interjection* & *noun* bother.

bothersome *adjective* causing bother.

Botox *noun* (*trademark*) a drug prepared from botulin, used medically to treat certain muscular conditions and cosmetically to remove wrinkles by temporarily paralysing facial muscles.

bo tree *noun* a species of Indian fig tree, sacred to Buddhists, the Buddha's enlightenment having occurred beneath such a tree. [from Sinhalese *bo gaha* tree of knowledge]

Botswana (bot-**swah**-nă) an inland republic of southern Africa.

Botticelli (bot-ĭ-**chel**-ee), Alessandro ('Sandro') (1445–1510), Florentine painter.

bottle *noun* 1 a narrow-necked glass or plastic container for storing liquid. 2 the amount contained in this. 3 a baby's feeding bottle; milk from this. 4 a hot water bottle. 5 (*informal*) courage. –bottle *verb* 1 to store in bottles. 2 to preserve in glass jars, *bottled fruit*. □ **bottle green** dark green. **bottle shop** a shop selling bottles of alcoholic drinks for consumption off the premises. **bottle tree** an Australian tree with a swollen bottle-shaped trunk. **bottle up** to restrain or suppress (a feeling).

bottlebrush *noun* 1 a cylindrical brush for washing bottles. 2 an Australian plant with flowers shaped like a bottlebrush.

bottleneck *noun* 1 a narrow stretch of road where traffic cannot flow freely. 2 anything similarly obstructing progress.

bottom *noun* 1 the lowest part of anything, the part on which it rests; the lowest place; *the bottom of the garden*, the end furthest from the house; *the bottom fell out of the market*, trade fell dramatically. 2 the buttocks, the part of the body on which one sits. 3 the ground under a stretch of water. 4 bottom or first gear. 5 a ship's keel or hull; a ship. –bottom *adjective* lowest in position, rank, or degree. –bottom *verb* 1 to provide with a bottom. 2 to reach or touch bottom. □ **at bottom** basically, really. **be at the bottom of** to be the underlying cause or originator of. **bottom line** the amount of total assets after profit and loss etc. have been calculated; the basic essential requirement; the ultimate truth. **bottom out** to reach the lowest level. **from the bottom of one's heart** with deep feeling, sincerely. **get to the bottom of** to find out the cause or origin of.

bottomless *adjective* extremely deep; *a bottomless purse*, an inexhaustible supply of money.

bottommost *adjective* lowest.

botulin *noun* the bacterial toxin involved in botulism.

botulism (**bot**-yŭ-lizm) *noun* a kind of food poisoning. [from Latin *botulus* = sausage]

bouclé (**boo**-klay) *noun* 1 yarn with one of its strands looped at intervals. 2 fabric made from this.

Boudicca (**boo**-dik-ă) (popularly known as Boadicea, died AD 62), a queen of the ancient Britons in eastern England who led her forces against the Romans.

boudoir (**boo**-dwar) *noun* a woman's private room. [from French, = place to sulk in]

Bougainville (**boh**-găn-vil) an island at the northern end of the Solomon Islands, a province of Papua New Guinea.

bougainvillea (boo-găn-**vil**-ee-ă *or* boh-) *noun* a tropical shrub with red or purple bracts. [named after the French explorer L. A. de Bougainville (1729–1811)]

bough *noun* a large branch coming from the trunk of a tree.

bought *see* buy.

bouillon (**boo**-yawn) *noun* clear soup, broth. [French, from *bouiller* = to boil]

boulder (**bohl**-der) *noun* a large stone or rock rounded by water or weather.

boulevard (**boo**-lĕ-vard) *noun* a wide street, often with trees on each side. [French]

bounce *verb* 1 to spring back when sent against something hard; to cause to do this. 2 (*informal*, of a cheque) to be sent back by the bank as worthless. 3 to jump suddenly; to move in a lively manner. 4 (also **bounce back**) (of an email) be returned to its sender after failing to reach its destination. **–bounce** *noun* 1 bouncing; the power of bouncing. 2 a strongly self-confident manner.

bouncer *noun* 1 (in cricket) a bowled ball that bounces forcefully. 2 (*informal*) a person employed to expel troublesome people from a gathering.

bouncing *adjective* big and healthy, boisterous.

bouncy *adjective* full of bounce.

bound¹ *verb* to limit, to be the boundary of. **bounds** *plural noun* limits. □ **out of bounds** outside the areas one is allowed to enter.

bound² *verb* to jump or spring; to run with jumping movements. **–bound** *noun* a bounding movement.

bound³ *adjective* going or heading towards, *bound for Tasmania*; *northbound traffic*.

bound⁴ *see* **bind**. **–bound** *adjective* obstructed or hindered by, *snowbound*. □ **bound to** certain to. **bound up with** closely associated with. **I'll be bound** I feel certain.

boundary *noun* 1 a line that marks a limit. 2 a hit to or over the boundary of the field in cricket. □ **boundary rider** a person employed to ride round the fences of a cattle or sheep station and keep them in good order. [from *bound¹*]

bounden *adjective* obligatory. □ **one's bounden duty** a duty dictated by one's conscience. [from *bind*]

bounder *noun* (especially *Brit. informal*) a person who behaves dishonourably, a cad.

boundless *adjective* without limits.

bountiful *adjective* 1 giving generously. 2 abundant.

bounty *noun* 1 generosity in giving. 2 a generous gift. 3 a reward or payment given as an inducement. [from Latin *bonitas* = goodness]

bouquet (boo-**kay** *or* boh-) *noun* 1 a bunch of flowers for carrying in the hand. 2 a compliment, praise. 3 the perfume of wine. □ **bouquet garni** (gar-**nee**) a bunch of herbs used for flavouring. [French, = group of trees]

Bourbon (**boor**-bŏn) the name of a branch of the French royal family whose members ruled in France from 1589 (Henry IV) until 1848 (Louis Philippe), Spain (1700–1931), and Naples (1734–1806, 1815–60).

bourbon (**ber**-bŏn) *noun* whisky made mainly from maize.

Bourdon gauge (**boor**-dŏn gayj) *noun* a device for measuring pressure, using a curled tube that begins to uncurl as pressure increases inside it.

bourgeois (**boor**-*zh*wah) *adjective* (often *derogatory*) of the middle class; having conventional ideas and tastes.

bourgeoisie (**boor**-*zh*wah-zee) *noun* the bourgeois class.

Bourke¹, Sir Richard (1777–1855), Irish military officer, Governor of NSW 1831–7, founder of Melbourne.

Bourke² □ **back of Bourke** the outback. [*Bourke* a town in north-west NSW]

bout *noun* 1 a period of exercise or work or illness. 2 a boxing contest.

boutique (boo-**teek**) *noun* a small shop selling clothes etc. of the latest fashion. [French]

bovine (**boh**-vyn) *adjective* 1 of or like an ox. 2 dull and stupid. □ **bovine spongiform encephalopathy** *see* **BSE**. [from Latin *bovis* = of an ox]

bow¹ (*rhymes with* go) *noun* 1 a piece of wood curved by a tight string joining its ends, used as a weapon for shooting arrows. 2 a rod with horsehair stretched between its ends, used for playing the violin etc. 3 a knot made with a loop or loops; ribbon etc. tied in this way. □ **bow-legged** *adjective* having **bow-legs**, bandy legs. **bow tie** a man's necktie tied into a bow. **bow window** a curved bay window.

bow² (*rhymes with* cow) *noun* bending of the head or body in greeting, respect, agreement, etc. **–bow** *verb* 1 to make a bow; to bend in greeting etc. 2 to bend downwards under a weight. 3 to submit or give in, *must bow to the inevitable*. □ **bow and scrape** to be obsequiously polite.

bow³ (*rhymes with* cow) *noun* **1** the front or forward end of a boat or ship. **2** the rower nearest the bow.

bowdlerise (**bowd**-lĕ-ryz) *verb* (also **-ize**) to censor words or scenes considered improper. [named after T. Bowdler who in 1818 produced a censored version of Shakespeare's plays]

bowel *noun* the intestine. **bowels** *plural noun* the intestines; the innermost parts. [from Latin *botellus* = little sausage]

bower (*rhymes with* flower) *noun* a leafy shelter.

bowerbird *noun* **1** an Australian and New Guinean bird, the male of which constructs bowers decorated with feathers, shells, etc. **2** (*Austral. informal*) a person who collects and hoards things.

bowie knife (**boh**-ee) *noun* a long hunting-knife with a double-edged point. [named after J. Bowie, American soldier (died 1836)]

bowl¹ *noun* **1** a basin for holding food or liquid. **2** this with its contents; the amount it contains. **3** a deep-sided container shaped like a bowl, *toilet bowl*. **4** the hollow rounded part of a spoon, tobacco pipe, etc. **5** a bowl-shaped building, an amphitheatre.

bowl² *noun* **1** a heavy ball that is slightly asymmetrical, so that it rolls in a curve, used in the game of bowls. **2** a large heavy ball with indents for gripping, used in tenpin bowling. **3** a spell or turn of bowling in cricket. **–bowl** *verb* **1** to send rolling along the ground. **2** to be carried fast and smoothly by car etc. **3** to send a ball to be played by a batsman; to dismiss by knocking down a wicket with this. **4** to play bowls or tenpin bowling. **bowls** *noun* a game played indoors (**indoor bowls** or **carpet bowls**) or on grass (**lawn bowls**), in which the bowls are rolled towards a small ball (the *jack*). □ **bowl over** to knock down; to overwhelm with surprise or emotion.

bowler¹ *noun* **1** a person who plays bowls. **2** a person who bowls in cricket.

bowler² *noun* (in full **bowler hat**) a stiff felt hat with a rounded top.

bowline (**boh**-lĭn) *noun* a simple knot for forming a non-slipping loop at the end of a rope.

bowling *noun* the game of tenpin bowling, or a similar game using skittles. **–bowling** *adjective* of or relating to bowls or bowling.

□ **bowling alley** a long enclosure for playing tenpin bowling etc. **bowling green** a lawn for playing bowls.

Bowman's capsule *noun* the dilated end of a urine duct in the kidney. [named after Sir William Bowman, English surgeon]

bowser (**bow**-zer) *noun* (*trademark*) a petrol pump.

bowsprit (**boh**-sprit) *noun* a long pole projecting from the stem of a ship, to which ropes from the front mast and sails are fastened.

bowyang (**boh**-yang) *noun* (*Austral.*) a band or strap tied round a trouser leg below the knee.

box¹ *noun* **1** a container with a flat base and usually a lid, for holding solids. **2** the amount it contains. **3** a boxlike receptacle, a money box, letterbox, etc. **4** a compartment, e.g. with seats for several persons in a theatre, for a horse in a stable or vehicle, for the jury or witnesses in a lawcourt. **5** a small hut or shelter, *sentry box*. **6** a receptacle at a newspaper office for replies to an advertisement. **7 the box** (*informal*) television. **–box** *verb* to put into a box. □ **box in** or **up** to shut into a small space, preventing free movement. **box jellyfish** a very poisonous jellyfish with a box-shaped body and stinging tentacles. **box kite** a kite with an open boxlike frame. **box number** a number used to identify a box in a newspaper office or post office to which letters may be sent. **box office** an office for booking seats at a theatre etc. **box pleat** an arrangement of parallel pleats folding in alternate directions, forming a raised strip. **box spring** each of a set of vertical springs in a mattress. **out of the box** (*Austral.*) excellent.

box² *verb* to fight with the fists; to engage in boxing. **–box** *noun* a slap with the open hand. □ **box a person's ears** to slap them.

box³ *noun* **1** a small evergreen European shrub. **2** its hard wood. **3** an Australian tree having similar wood.

Boxer *noun* a member of a fanatical Chinese secret organisation in the 19th century.

boxer *noun* **1** a person who engages in boxing. **2** a dog of a breed resembling the bulldog. □ **boxer shorts** short shorts; loose underpants or pyjama pants like shorts.

boxing *noun* the sport of fighting with the fists. □ **boxing gloves** a pair of padded leather mittens worn in boxing.

Boxing Day *noun* the first day after Christmas Day. [from the old custom of giving presents (Christmas boxes) to tradesmen and servants on that day]

boy *noun* **1** a male child. **2** a young man. **3** a young male employee, *a delivery boy*. **4** (in some countries) a male servant. **–boy** *interjection* an exclamation of surprise or joy. ☐ **Boy Scout = scout** (sense 3). **boyhood** *noun*

boycott (**boy**-kot) *verb* to refuse to have anything to do with; *boycotted the goods*, refused to handle or buy them. **–boycott** *noun* boycotting, treatment of this kind. [from the name of Captain Boycott, a harsh landlord in Ireland whose tenants in 1880 refused to deal with him]

Boyd the name of an Australian family notable as artists and writers, including the artist Arthur Merric Bloomfield Boyd (1920–99).

boyfriend *noun* a person's regular male companion or lover.

boyish *adjective* like a boy. **boyishly** *adverb*, **boyishness** *noun*

Boyle, Robert (1627–91), English scientist. ☐ **Boyle's law** the volume of a fixed quantity of gas at constant temperature is inversely proportional to its pressure.

Boyne a river in the Republic of Ireland, scene of the victory of a Protestant army under William III over the Catholic forces of the deposed James II in 1690.

BP *abbreviation* (in geology) before the present.

bra *noun* a woman's undergarment worn to support the breasts, a brassière.

brace *noun* **1** a device that clamps things together or holds and supports them in position. **2** (*plural* **brace**) a pair, *five brace of partridge*. **3** a connecting mark {or} used in printing. **–brace** *verb* to support, to give firmness to. **braces** *plural noun* straps used to keep trousers up, fastened to the waistband and passing over the shoulders; a wire device for straightening the teeth. ☐ **brace and bit** a revolving tool for boring holes, with a D-shaped central handle. **brace oneself** to steady oneself in order to meet a blow or shock. [from Latin *brachia* = arms]

bracelet *noun* an ornamental band or chain worn on the arm.

brachia *see* **brachium**.

brachiopod (**brak**-ee-ŏ-pod) *noun* any of a group of small sea creatures with an upper and lower shell and brachia fringed with cilia that by their movement send water bearing microscopic food to the mouth. [from *brachium*, + Greek *podos* = of a foot]

brachium (**bray**-kee-ŭm) *noun* (*plural* **brachia**) an arm or arm-like part of an animal. **brachial** *adjective* [Latin, = an arm]

bracing *adverb* invigorating, stimulating.

bracken *noun* a large fern that grows on waste land; a mass of such ferns.

bracket *noun* **1** a support projecting from an upright surface. **2** any of the marks used in pairs for enclosing words or figures, ( ), [ ], { }, < >. **3** a group bracketed together as similar or falling between certain limits, *an income bracket*. **–bracket** *verb* (**bracketed**, **bracketing**) **1** to enclose or join by brackets. **2** to put together to imply connection or equality. **3** to place shots both short of the target and beyond it in order to find the range.

brackish *adjective* slightly salty, *brackish water*.

bract *noun* a leaflike part of a plant, often highly coloured, e.g. in bougainvillea and poinsettia.

bradawl *noun* a small boring-tool.

Bradman, Sir Donald George (1908–2001), Australian cricketer, considered to be Australia's finest batsman, whose career extended from 1927 to 1949.

brae (*pr.* bray) *noun* (*Scottish*) a hillside.

brag *verb* (**bragged**, **bragging**) to boast. **–brag** *noun* a boast.

braggart *noun* a person who brags.

Brahma (in Hinduism) the creator god, who forms a triad with Siva and Vishnu.

Brahman the supreme divine reality underlying all phenomena, often identified with the inner core of the individual (*atman*), personified in Hindu mythology as the male creator god Brahma. **–brahman** *noun* = **Brahmin**.

Brahmaputra (brah-mă-**poo**-tră) a river that flows from Tibet through the Himalayas and NE India to join the Ganges at its delta (in Bangladesh) on the Bay of Bengal.

Brahmin (**brah**-mǐn) *noun* a member of the Hindu priestly class. **Brahminical** *adjective*, **Brahminism** *noun* [from Sanskrit *brahman* = priest]

Brahms, Johannes (1833–97), German composer and pianist.

braid *noun* **1** a woven ornamental trimming.
2 a plait of hair. **–braid** *verb* **1** to plait.
2 to trim with braid.

Braille (*pr.* brayl) *noun* a system of
representing letters etc. by raised dots that
blind people can read by touch. [named after
its inventor, Louis Braille, who perfected it
in 1834]

brain *noun* **1** the organ that is the centre of
the nervous system in animals, a mass of soft
grey matter in the skull. **2** (often **brains**) the
mind or intellect, intelligence. **3** an intelligent
person; (also **brains**) one who originates a
complex plan or idea. **–brain** *verb* to kill by a
heavy blow on the head. □ **brain drain** the loss
of clever and skilled people by emigration. **on
the brain** obsessively in one's thoughts.

brainchild *noun* a person's invention or plan.

brainless *adjective* stupid.

brainpower *noun* mental ability,
intelligence.

brainstorm *noun* **1** a sudden violent mental
disturbance. **2** (*informal*) a sudden bright idea.
brainstorming *noun* a spontaneous discussion
in search of new ideas.

brainwash *verb* to force (a person) to reject
old beliefs and accept new ones by subjecting
him or her to great mental pressure.

brainwave *noun* **1** an electrical impulse in
the brain. **2** (*informal*) a sudden bright idea.

brainy *adjective* (**brainier**, **brainiest**) clever,
intelligent. **braininess** *noun*

braise *verb* to cook slowly with very little
liquid in a closed container. [from French
braise = burning coals]

brake *noun* **1** a device for reducing the speed
of something or stopping its motion. **2** the
pedal etc. operating this. **–brake** *verb* to
slow down by means of this. □ **brake drum**
a cylinder attached to a wheel, on which
the brake shoe presses. **brake horsepower**
the power of an engine measured by the
force needed to brake it. **brake shoe** a
long curved block acting on a wheel to
brake it.

bramble *noun* a rough shrub with long
prickly shoots, a blackberry bush.

bran *noun* coarse meal consisting of the
ground inner husks of grain, sifted out from
flour.

branch *noun* **1** an arm-like part of a tree.
2 a similar part of anything; a lateral extension
of a river, road, railway, etc. **3** a subdivision of
a family or a group of languages or a subject.
4 a local shop or office etc. belonging to a
larger organisation. **–branch** *verb* to send out
branches; to divide into branches. □ **branch
off** to leave a main route and take a minor one.
branch out to begin a new line of activity.
branch stacking (*Austral.*) the process of
improperly increasing the membership of
a local branch of a political party in order
to ensure the pre-selection of a particular
candidate. [from Latin *branca* = a paw]

brand *noun* **1** a trademark; a particular make
of goods. **2** a mark of identification made with
a hot iron; the iron used for this. **3** a piece
of burning or charred wood. **–brand** *verb*
1 to mark with a hot iron; to label with a
trademark. **2** to give a bad name to, *he was
branded as a troublemaker.* **3** to impress on
the memory. □ **brand new** completely new.

brandish *verb* to wave (a thing) in display or
threateningly.

brandling *noun* a red earthworm with rings
of brighter colour, used as bait.

brandy *noun* a strong alcoholic spirit distilled
from wine or from fermented fruit juice.
□ **brandy snap** a thin crisp curled wafer of
gingerbread. [from Dutch *brandewijn* = burnt
(distilled) wine]

Braque (*pr.* brahk), Georges (1882–1963),
French painter who, with Picasso, inaugurated
cubism.

brash *adjective* **1** vulgarly self-assertive.
2 reckless. **brashly** *adverb*, **brashness** *noun*

Brasilia the capital of Brazil.

brass *noun* **1** a yellow alloy of copper and zinc.
2 a thing or things made of this. **3** the brass
wind instruments of an orchestra. **4** a brass
memorial tablet in a church. **5** (*informal*)
money. **6** (*informal*) impudence. **7** (*informal*)
high-ranking officers or officials, *the top
brass.* **–brass** *adjective* made of brass.
□ **brass band** a band playing brass and
percussion instruments only. **brass rubbing**
taking an impression of brass memorial
tablets; an impression produced from one of
these. **get down to brass tacks** (*informal*) to
start to consider the basic facts or practical
details (¶ rhyming informal *brass tacks* =
facts).

brasserie (**bras**-ĕ-ree) *noun* a bar where food
can be obtained as well as drinks. [French, =
brewery]

brassière (**bras**-ee-air) *noun* a bra. [French,
= child's vest]

brassy *adjective* (**brassier**, **brassiest**) **1** like brass in appearance or sound. **2** bold and vulgar. **brassiness** *noun*

brat *noun* (*derogatory*) a child.

Bratislava (brat-i-**slah**-vă) the capital of Slovakia.

bravado (bră-**vah**-doh) *noun* a show of boldness. [from Spanish *bravata*]

brave *adjective* **1** able to face and endure danger or pain. **2** (*formal*) spectacular, *a brave show of peonies.* –**brave** *noun* (*old use*) a warrior of a North American indigenous people. –**brave** *verb* to face and endure with bravery. **bravely** *adverb*, **bravery** *noun*

bravo *interjection* & *noun* (*plural* **bravos**) a cry of 'well done!'

bravura (bră-**voor**-ră) *noun* **1** a brilliant or ambitious performance. **2** a style of music requiring brilliant technique. [Italian]

brawl *noun* a noisy quarrel or fight. –**brawl** *verb* to take part in a brawl.

brawn *noun* **1** muscular strength. **2** meat from a pig's or calf's head boiled, chopped, and pressed in a mould.

brawny *adjective* (**brawnier**, **brawniest**) strong and muscular.

bray *noun* the cry of a donkey; a sound like this. –**bray** *verb* to make this cry or sound.

braze *verb* to cement (metal parts) together, with an alloy of brass and zinc.

brazen (**bray**-zěn) *adjective* **1** made of brass, like brass. **2** shameless, impudent. –**brazen** *verb* **brazen it out** to behave, after doing wrong, as if one has nothing to be ashamed of.

brazier (**bray**-zee-er) *noun* a basket-like stand for holding burning coals.

Brazil a republic in NE South America. –**Brazil** *noun* a Brazil nut. ☐ **Brazil nut** a large three-sided nut. **Brazilian** *adjective* & *noun*

Brazzaville the capital and major port of the Congo.

breach *noun* **1** the breaking or neglect of a rule of agreement etc. **2** an estrangement. **3** a broken place, a gap. –**breach** *verb* to break through, to make a gap in. ☐ **step into the breach** to give help in a crisis.

bread *noun* **1** a food made of flour and liquid, usually leavened by yeast, and baked. **2** (*informal*) money.

breadboard *noun* **1** a board for cutting bread etc. on. **2** a board for making experimental models of an electric circuit etc.

breadcrumbs *plural noun* bread crumbled for use in cooking.

breaded *adjective* coated with breadcrumbs.

breadfruit *noun* the fruit of a tropical tree, with white pulp, which when baked becomes soft like new bread.

breadline *noun* **on the breadline** living in extreme poverty.

breadth *noun* width, broadness.

breadwinner *noun* the member of a family who earns the money to support the others.

break *verb* (**broke**, **broken**, **breaking**) **1** to fall into pieces; to cause to do this; *she broke her leg*, broke the bone in it. **2** to damage, to make or become unusable. **3** to fail to keep (a promise). **4** to stop for a time, to make or become discontinuous, *broke the silence*; *we broke for coffee*; *broke into a run*, began to run; *broke the strike*, forced it to end by a means other than bargaining. **5** to make a way suddenly or violently; *broke prison*, escaped from prison. **6** to emerge or appear. **7** to reveal (news etc.); to become known, *the story broke*. **8** to surpass, *broke the world record*. **9** to make or become weak; to overwhelm with grief etc.; to destroy, *the scandal broke him*. **10** (of a voice) to change its even tone, either with emotion or (of a boy's voice) by becoming suddenly deeper at puberty. **11** (of a ball) to change direction after touching the ground. **12** (of waves) to fall in foam. **13** (of boxers) to come out of a clinch. –**break** *noun* **1** breaking. **2** an escape; a sudden dash. **3** a gap, a broken place. **4** an interval, e.g. between periods of work or exercise. **5** points scored continuously in billiards or snooker. **6** (*informal*) a piece of luck; *a bad break*, bad luck. **7** a fair chance; *give him a break*, an opportunity. ☐ **break-dancing** *noun* an energetic and acrobatic style of street dancing. **break down** to demolish; to cease to function because of mechanical failure; (of a person's health) to collapse; to give way to emotion; to act upon chemically and reduce to constituent parts; to analyse, *break down the costs*. **break even** to make gains and losses that balance exactly. **break-even point** the stage when revenue exactly matches costs. **break in** to force one's way into a building; to interrupt; to accustom to a new routine. **break-in** *noun* a forcible entry, especially by a thief. **break in on** to disturb, to interrupt. **break of day** dawn. **break off** to detach by breaking; to bring to an end; to stop speaking. **break out** to begin suddenly; to exclaim; to force one's way out; to become covered (in a rash etc.). **break service** to win a game at tennis when one's opponent is serving. **break the bank** to use up all its resources. **break the heart of** to overwhelm with grief. **break the ice** to overcome formality. **break up** to break into small pieces; to bring or come to an end; to become weaker; to separate, (of schoolchildren) to begin holidays when school closes at the end of term. **break with** to give up; to end one's friendship with.

breakable *adjective* able to be broken.

breakage *noun* **1** breaking. **2** something broken.

breakaway *noun* **1** becoming separate or free. **2** an outside second-row forward in rugby football. **3** (*Austral.*) a stampede of cattle, especially at the sight of water. –**breakaway** *adjective* that breaks or has broken away.

breakbeat *noun* (in dance music etc.) a sample of a syncopated drum beat forming a rhythm.

breakdown *noun* **1** mechanical failure. **2** weakening. **3** a collapse of health or mental stability. **4** an analysis of statistics.

breaker *noun* a heavy wave that breaks on the coast or over a reef.

breakfast *noun* the first meal of the day. –**breakfast** *verb* to eat breakfast. [from *break* + *fast²*]

breakneck *adjective* (of speed) dangerously fast.

breakthrough *noun* **1** breaking through an obstacle etc. **2** a major advance in knowledge.

breakup *noun* breaking up; collapse; dispersal.

breakwater *noun* a wall built out into the sea to protect a harbour or coast against heavy waves.

breakwind *noun* a temporary shelter.

bream *noun* **1** (*pr.* brim) an edible Australian sea fish. **2** (*pr.* breem) a freshwater or sea fish of northern waters.

breast *noun* **1** either of the two milk-producing organs on the upper front of a woman's body; the corresponding part of a man's body. **2** the upper front part of the human body or of a garment covering this. **3** the corresponding part in animals. **4** the breast as a source of emotion. –**breast** *verb* to face and advance against, *breasted the waves*.

breastbone *noun* the flat vertical bone in the chest or breast, joined to the ribs; the sternum.

breastfeed *verb* (**-fed**, **-feeding**) to feed (a baby) by allowing it to suck at the mother's breast.

breastplate *noun* a piece of armour covering the breast.

breaststroke *noun* a swimming stroke performed face downwards, with sweeping movements of the arms.

breath (*pr.* breth) *noun* **1** air drawn into and sent out of the lungs. **2** breathing in, *take six deep breaths*. **3** a gentle blowing, *a breath of wind*. **4** a hint or slight rumour, *not a breath of scandal*. □ **in the same breath** immediately after saying something else. **out of breath** panting after violent exercise. **under one's breath** in a whisper.

breathalyse *verb* to test with a breathalyser.

breathalyser *noun* a device that measures the amount of alcohol in a person's breath as he or she breathes out. [from *breath* + *analyse*]

breathe (*pr.* bree*th*) *verb* **1** to draw air into the lungs and send it out again; (of plants) to respire. **2** to take in or send out of the lungs, *breathing cigar smoke*. **3** to utter; *don't breathe a word of it*, keep it secret. □ **breathe again** to feel relieved of fear or anxiety. **breathing-space** *noun* room to breathe; a pause to recover from effort.

breather *noun* **1** a pause for rest. **2** a short period in the fresh air.

breathless *adjective* **1** out of breath, panting. **2** holding one's breath with excitement. **breathlessly** *adverb*, **breathlessness** *noun*

breathtaking *adjective* very exciting, spectacular.

breathy (**breth**-ee) *adjective* with a noticeable sound of breathing.

breccia (**brech**-ă) *noun* rock consisting of rough stones cemented together by lime etc.

Brecht (*pr.* brekt), Bertolt (1898–1956), German dramatist and producer.

bred *see* **breed**.

breech *noun* **1** the back part of a gun barrel. **2** (*old use*) the buttocks. □ **breech birth** a birth in which the baby's buttocks or feet appear first.

breeches (**brich**-ĕz) *plural noun* trousers reaching to just below the knee.

breed *verb* (**bred**, **breeding**) **1** to produce offspring. **2** to keep (animals) for the purpose of producing young. **3** to train, to bring up. **4** to give rise to. –**breed** *noun* a variety of animals etc. within a species, having similar appearance.

breeder *noun* a person who breeds animals. □ **breeder reactor** a nuclear reactor that produces more fissile material than it uses in operating.

breeding *noun* **1** the production of young from animals, propagation. **2** good manners resulting from training or background.

breeze *noun* **1** a light wind. **2** (*informal*) an easy task. –**breeze** *verb* (*informal*) to move in a lively manner, *they breezed in*.

breeze block *noun* a lightweight building block made of sand, cinders, and cement.

breezy *adjective* (**breezier**, **breeziest**) **1** exposed to wind. **2** pleasantly windy. **3** lively, jovial. **breezily** *adverb*, **breeziness** *noun*

Bren gun *noun* a lightweight machine gun. [from *Br*no in the Czech Republic and *En*field in England, the two places where Bren guns were made]

brethren *plural noun* (*old use*) brothers.

Breton (**bret**-ŏn) *adjective* of Brittany or its people or language. –**Breton** *noun* **1** a native of Brittany. **2** the Celtic language of Brittany.

Breughel = **Bruegel**, **Brueghel**.

breve (*pr.* breev) *noun* **1** a mark placed over a short or unstressed vowel (ŏ). **2** a note in music, equal to two semibreves.

breviary (**breev**-yă-ree) *noun* a book of prayers to be said daily by Roman Catholic priests.

brevity (**brev**-ĭ-tee) *noun* shortness, briefness.

brew *verb* **1** to make (beer) by boiling and fermentation, to make (tea) by infusion. **2** to be being prepared in this way, *the tea is brewing*. **3** to bring about; to develop, *trouble is brewing*. –**brew** *noun* **1** liquid made by brewing. **2** an amount brewed.

brewer *noun* a person whose trade is brewing beer.

brewery *noun* a building in which beer is brewed.

briar *noun* = **brier**.

bribe *noun* something offered in order to influence a person to act in favour of the giver.

–**bribe** *verb* to persuade by a bribe. **bribable** *adjective*, **bribery** *noun*

bric-à-brac (**brik**-ă-brak) *noun* odd items of furniture, ornaments, etc., of no great value.

brick *noun* **1** a block of baked or dried clay or other substance used to build walls; building work consisting of such blocks. **2** a child's toy building block. **3** a rectangular block of something. **4** (*informal*) a kind-hearted person. –**brick** *adjective* **1** built of brick. **2** brick-red. –**brick** *verb* to block with brickwork. □ **brick-red** *adjective* of the red colour of bricks. **brick veneer** (a house with) a timber frame and a brick exterior that is not part of the structure. **drop a brick** (*informal*) to say something tactless or indiscreet.

brickbat *noun* **1** a piece of brick, especially one used as a missile. **2** an uncomplimentary remark.

bricklayer *noun* a person who builds with bricks.

brickwork *noun* a structure made of bricks.

bricolage (**bri**-kŏ-lahzh) *noun* (*plural* **bricolage**) **1** construction or creation from what is immediately available for use. **2** an assemblage of haphazard or incongruous elements.

bridal *adjective* of a bride or wedding.

bride *noun* a woman on her wedding day; a newly married woman. [from Old English *bryd*]

bridegroom *noun* a man on his wedding day; a newly married man.

brideprice *noun* (especially in tribal societies) the money and goods given by the bridegroom's relatives to those of the bride.

bridesmaid *noun* an unmarried woman or girl attending the bride at a wedding (compare **matron of honour**).

bridge¹ *noun* **1** a structure providing a way across something or carrying a road or railway etc. across. **2** the raised platform on a ship from which the captain and officers direct its course. **3** the bony upper part of the nose. **4** something that joins, connects, or supports other parts. **5** (also **bridgework**) a dental structure used to cover a gap, joined to the teeth on either side. –**bridge** *verb* to make or form a bridge over. □ **bridging loan** a loan given for the period between two transactions, e.g. between buying a new house and selling one's own.

bridge² *noun* a card game developed from whist.

bridgehead *noun* a fortified area established in enemy territory, especially on the far side of a river.

Bridgetown the capital of Barbados.

bridle *noun* **1** the part of a horse's harness that goes on its head. **2** a joint used in woodwork, in which the end of one piece of wood is cut to fit into a groove cut in the end of another. –**bridle** *verb* **1** to put a bridle on. **2** to restrain, to keep under control. **3** to draw one's head up in pride or scorn.

brie (*pr.* bree) *noun* a kind of soft cheese, originally from Brie in N France.

brief¹ *adjective* **1** lasting only for a short time. **2** concise. **3** short in length. **briefs** *plural noun* very short close-fitting pants or knickers. □ **in brief** in a few words. **briefly** *adverb*, **briefness** *noun*

brief² *noun* **1** a summary of the facts of a case, drawn up for a barrister. **2** a case given to a barrister. **3** instructions and information given in advance. –**brief** *verb* **1** to give a brief to. **2** to instruct or inform concisely in advance. □ **hold no brief for** not to be obliged to support. [from Latin *brevis* = short]

briefcase *noun* a flat case for carrying documents etc.

brier¹ *noun* a thorny bush, the wild rose.

brier² *noun* **1** a European heath plant with a hard woody root. **2** a tobacco pipe made from this root.

brig *noun* a square-rigged sailing vessel with two masts.

brigade *noun* **1** an army unit forming part of a division. **2** a group of people organised for a particular purpose. [from Italian *brigata* = a troop]

brigadier *noun* an officer commanding a brigade; a staff officer of similar status.

brigalow (**brig**-ă-loh) *noun* an Australian wattle with dark furrowed bark and silver foliage. [perhaps from Kamilaroi *burriigal*]

brigand (**brig**-ănd) *noun* a member of a band of robbers. **brigandage** *noun*, **brigandry** *noun*

bright *adjective* **1** giving out or reflecting much light, shining. **2** cheerful. **3** quick-witted, clever. –**bright** *adverb* brightly. **brightly** *adverb*, **brightness** *noun*

brighten *verb* to make or become brighter.

brilliant *adjective* **1** very bright or sparkling. **2** very clever. **3** (*informal*) excellent. –**brilliant** *noun* a cut diamond with many facets. **brilliantly** *adverb*, **brilliance** *noun*, **brilliancy** *noun* [from Italian *brillare* = shine]

brim *noun* **1** the edge of a cup or hollow or channel. **2** the projecting edge of a hat. –**brim** *verb* (**brimmed**, **brimming**) to fill or be full to the brim. □ **brim-full** *adjective* (also **brimful**) full to the brim. **brim over** to overflow.

brimstone *noun* (*old use*) sulphur.

brindled (**brin**-d'ld) *adjective* brown with streaks of other colour, *the brindled cow*.

brine *noun* salt water.

bring *verb* (**brought**, **bringing**) **1** to cause to come, especially with oneself by carrying, leading, or attracting. **2** to produce as profit or income. **3** to result in, to cause, *war brought famine*. **4** to put forward (charges etc.) in a lawcourt, *they brought an action for libel*. **5** to cause to arrive at a particular state, *bring it to the boil*. □ **bring about** to cause to happen. **bring down** to cause to fall; *bring the house down*, to get loud applause in a theatre etc. **bring forth** to give birth to; to cause; (*old use*) to produce. **bring forward** to arrange for (a thing) to happen earlier than was intended; to call attention to (a matter); to transfer from a previous page or account. **bring in** to initiate, to introduce; to produce as profit or income; to pronounce as a verdict in court. **bring into being** to cause to exist. **bring off** to do successfully. **bring on** to cause to develop rapidly. **bring out** to cause to appear, to show clearly; to publish. **bring to bear** to direct and concentrate (forces), *pressure was brought to bear on the strikers*. **bring up** to look after and train (growing children); to vomit; to mention for discussion; to cause to stop suddenly. **bring up the rear** to come last in a line.

brink *noun* **1** the edge of a steep place or of a stretch of water. **2** the verge, the edge of something unknown, dangerous, or exciting.

brinkmanship *noun* the art of pursuing a dangerous policy to the brink of war etc. before stopping.

briny *adjective* salty. –**briny** *noun* (*humorous*) the sea.

brio (**bree**-oh) *noun* vivacity. [Italian]

brioche (**bree**-osh) *noun* a small sweetened bread roll, circular in shape. [French]

briquette (brik-**et**) *noun* a block of compressed coal dust. [French, = little brick]

bris *noun* the ceremony in which a Jewish baby boy is circumcised.

Brisbane the capital and main port of Queensland.

brisk *adjective* active, lively, moving quickly. **briskly** *adverb*, **briskness** *noun*

brisket (**brisk**-ĕt) *noun* a joint of beef cut from the breast.

brisling (**briz**-ling) *noun* a small herring or sprat, processed like sardines. [Norwegian]

bristle *noun* **1** a short stiff hair. **2** any of the stiff pieces of hair or wire etc. in a brush. –**bristle** *verb* **1** (of an animal) to raise the bristles in anger or fear. **2** to show indignation. **3** to be thickly set with bristles. □ **bristle with** to be full of, *the plan bristled with difficulties*.

bristly *adjective* full of bristles.

Brit *noun* (*informal*) a British person.

Britain (in full **Great Britain**) England, Wales, and Scotland.

Britannia the personification of Britain, shown as a woman with a shield, helmet, and trident.

Britannic *adjective* of Britain, *Her Britannic Majesty*.

Briticism (**brit**-ĭ-sizm) *noun* an English word or idiom used mainly in Britain.

British *adjective* of Great Britain or its inhabitants. –**the British** British people.

British Isles Britain and Ireland with the islands near their coasts.

Briton *noun* **1** a native or inhabitant of southern Britain before the Roman conquest. **2** a British person.

Brittany a district of NW France.

brittle *adjective* hard but easily broken.

broach *verb* **1** to make a hole in and draw out liquid. **2** to begin a discussion of, *broached the subject*.

broad *adjective* **1** large across, wide. **2** measuring from side to side, *20 metres broad*. **3** full and complete, *broad daylight*; *a broad Australian accent*; *a broad hint*, strong and unmistakable. **4** in general terms, not detailed; *in broad outline*, without details. **5** rather coarse, *broad humour*. –**broad** *noun* the broad part. □ **broad bean** an edible bean with large flat seeds. **broad-minded** *adjective* having tolerant views.

broadband *adjective* using signals over a broad range of frequencies, especially in high-capacity telecommunications.

–**broadband** *noun* a high-speed network for the transmission of a range of frequencies including video, audio, etc.

broadcast *verb* (**broadcast**, **broadcasting**) **1** to send out by radio or television. **2** to speak or appear in a radio or television program. **3** to make generally known. **4** to sow (seed) by scattering, not in drills. –**broadcast** *noun* a broadcast program. –**broadcast** *adverb* scattered freely. **broadcaster** *noun*

broaden *verb* to make or become broad.

broadloom *adjective* woven in broad widths.

broadly *adverb* **1** in a broad way. **2** in a general way, *broadly speaking*.

broadside *noun* **1** the firing of all guns on one side of a ship. **2** a strong attack in words. □ **broadside on** sideways.

broadsword *noun* a sword with a broad blade, used for cutting rather than thrusting.

Broadway a long street in New York City, famous for its theatres.

brocade (brŏ-**kayd**) *noun* fabric woven with raised patterns. **brocaded** *adjective*

broccoli (**brok**-ŏ-ly *or* -lee) *noun* (*plural* **broccoli**) a vegetable with tightly packed green flower heads. [Italian, = cabbage heads]

brochure (**broh**-shoor) *noun* a booklet or pamphlet containing information. [from French, = stitching]

broderie anglaise (broh-dĕ-ree ahn-**glayz**) *noun* fabric with a kind of open-work embroidery. [French, = English embroidery]

brogue (*rhymes with* rogue) *noun* **1** a strong shoe with ornamental perforated bands. **2** a dialectal accent, especially Irish.

broil *verb* **1** to cook (meat) on a fire or gridiron. **2** to make or be very hot, especially from sunshine. [from French *brûler* = to burn]

broiler *noun* a young chicken suitable or specially reared for broiling or roasting.

broke *see* **break**. –**broke** *adjective* (*informal*) having spent all one's money, bankrupt.

broken *see* **break**. –**broken** *adjective* **1** having been broken; out of order. **2** reduced to despair; beaten. **3** (of language) imperfectly spoken, as by a foreigner, *broken English*. **4** interrupted; *broken sleep*. □ **broken chord** *see* **chord**[1]. **broken-down** *adjective* worn out; not functioning. **broken-hearted** *adjective* crushed by grief. **broken home** a family lacking one parent through divorce or separation. **broken reed** a person or thing too weak to be depended upon. **brokenly** *adverb*

Broken Hill a city (nicknamed the Silver City) in western NSW, the centre of a major silver-lead-zinc mining district.

broker *noun* **1** an agent who buys and sells things on behalf of others. **2** a member of the Stock Exchange dealing in stocks and shares.

brokerage *noun* a broker's fee or commission.

brolga *noun* an Australian crane having grey feathers and a red patch on the head. Also called *native companion*. [Kamilaroi (and other languages) *burralga*]

brolly *noun* (*informal*) an umbrella.

bromance *noun* (*informal*) an intimate non-sexual relationship between two men.

bromide (**broh**-myd) *noun* **1** a compound of bromine, used in medicine to calm the nerves. **2** a trite remark. **3** a reproduction on paper coated with silver bromide emulsion.

bromine (**broh**-meen) *noun* a dark red liquid chemical element (symbol Br), compounds of which are used in medicine and photography.

bronchial (**bronk**-ee-ăl) *adjective* of the branched tubes (*bronchi*) into which the windpipe divides before entering the lungs. [from Greek *bronchos* = windpipe]

bronchitis (brong-**ky**-tĭss) *noun* inflammation of the mucous membrane inside the bronchial tubes.

bronchus (**brong**-kŭs) *noun* (*plural* **bronchi**, *pr.* **brong**-ky) either of the two main tubes into which the windpipe divides, leading to the lungs.

bronco (**brong**-koh) *noun* (*plural* **broncos**) a wild or half-tamed horse of western North America.

Brontë (**bron**-tee), Charlotte (1816–55), Emily (1818–48), and Anne (1820–49), English novelists, three sisters.

brontosaurus (bront-ŏ-**saw**-rŭs) *noun* = **apatosaurus**. [from Greek *bronte* = thunder, + *sauros* = lizard]

bronze *noun* **1** a brown alloy of copper and tin. **2** a thing made of this; a bronze medal (awarded as third prize). **3** its colour. –**bronze** *adjective* made of bronze; bronze-coloured. –**bronze** *verb* to make or become tanned by sun. □ **Bronze Age** the period when weapons and tools were made of bronze. **bronze-wing** *noun* an Australian pigeon with bronze markings on the wings.

brooch (*rhymes with* coach) *noun* an ornamental hinged pin fastened with a clasp.

brood *noun* **1** the young birds or other animals produced at one hatching or birth. **2** a family of children. –**brood** *verb* **1** to sit on eggs to hatch them. **2** to think long and deeply or resentfully. □ **brood mare** a mare kept for breeding.

broody *adjective* **1** (of a hen) wanting to brood. **2** thoughtful and depressed.

brook¹ *noun* a small stream.

Usage In Australia *brook* is mainly used as an element in place names, e.g. *Glenbrook, Crystal Brook*.

---

brook² *verb* to tolerate, *he would brook no interference*.

broom *noun* **1** a shrub with yellow or white flowers. **2** a long-handled brush for sweeping floors. □ **new broom** a newly appointed official who gets rid of old methods etc., *a new broom sweeps clean* (proverb).

broomstick *noun* a broom handle.

Bros *abbreviation* Brothers.

broth *noun* the water in which meat or fish has been boiled; soup made with this.

brothel (**broth**-ĕl) *noun* a house where prostitutes work.

brother *noun* **1** a son of the same parents as another person. **2** a man who is a fellow member of a Church, trade union, or other association. **3** a monk who is not a priest; **Brother** his title. □ **brother-in-law** *noun* (*plural* **brothers-in-law**) the brother of one's husband or wife; the husband of one's sister. **brotherly** *adjective* [from Old English *brothor*]

brotherhood *noun* **1** the relationship of brothers. **2** brotherliness, comradeship. **3** an association of men; its members. □ **Brotherhood of St Lawrence** a social welfare organisation connected with the Anglican Church.

brought *see* **bring**.

brougham (**broo**-ăm) *noun* **1** a four-wheeled closed carriage drawn by one horse or electrically driven. **2** a former type of motor car with the driver's seat open. [named after Lord Brougham (died 1858), who designed the carriage]

brow *noun* **1** an eyebrow. **2** the forehead. **3** a projecting or overhanging part; *the brow of the hill*, the ridge at the top.

browbeat *verb* (**browbeat**, **browbeaten**, **browbeating**) to intimidate.

brown *adjective* **1** of a colour between orange and black. **2** having skin of this colour; suntanned. **3** (of bread) brown in colour, especially through being made with wholemeal flour. –**brown** *noun* **1** brown colour. **2** a brown substance, material, or thing; brown clothes. **3** the brown ball in snooker etc. –**brown** *verb* to make or become brown. □ **brown coal** a kind of coal, brownish in colour, in which the original plant or wood structures can usually be seen. **browned off** (*informal*) bored, fed up. **brown rice** unprocessed rice with only the outer husk of the grain removed. **brown sugar** sugar that is only partly refined. **in a brown study** deep in thought. **brownish** *adjective*

Brownian motion *noun* (also **movement**) the irregular movements of microscopic particles (e.g. of smoke or pollen) in a liquid or gas, caused by molecules of the liquid or gas striking against them. [named after R. Brown, Scottish botanist (1773–1858)]

brownie *noun* **1** a benevolent elf. **2** a small square chocolate cake. –**Brownie** *noun* a member of a junior branch of the Guides. □ **earn brownie points** (*informal*) to do good deeds in order to earn recognition.

Brownlow Medal a medal awarded annually to the best and fairest player of the season in the Australian Football League. [named after Charles Brownlow (1861–1924), captain and coach of the Geelong team]

browse (*rhymes with* cows) *verb* **1** to feed as animals do, on leaves or grass etc. **2** to look through a book, or examine items for sale, in a casual leisurely way. **3** (in computing) read or survey (data files), typically via a network.

browser *noun* **1** a person or animal that browses. **2** (in computing) a program used to search for and access documents on the World Wide Web.

brucellosis (broo-sĕ-**loh**-sĭs) *noun* a disease caused by bacteria, affecting cattle and causing fever in humans consuming their products.

Bruegel (**brer**-gĕl), Pieter (c. 1525–69), Flemish artist, known as 'Peasant Bruegel' and 'Pieter Bruegel the Elder'.

Brueghel (**brer**-gĕl), Pieter (1564–1638), Flemish artist, and Jon ('Velvet') (1568–1623), a celebrated still-life and mythological painter, sons of Bruegel.

bruise (*pr.* brooz) *noun* an injury caused by a knock or by pressure that discolours the skin without breaking it. –**bruise** *verb* **1** to cause a bruise or bruises on. **2** to show the effects of a knock etc.; to be susceptible to bruises.

bruit (*pr.* broot) *noun* (*old use*) to spread (a report).

brumby *noun* (*Austral.*) a wild or unbroken horse.

brunch *noun* (*informal*) a meal combining breakfast and lunch. □ **brunch coat** a lightweight dressing gown.

Brunei Darussalam (**broo**-ny dah-roo-sah-**lahm**) (also **Brunei**) a sultanate on the north coast of Borneo. **Bruneian** *adjective*

Brunelleschi (broo-nĕ-**lesk**-ee) (1377–1446), Florentine architect, who designed the dome of Florence cathedral and is often credited with the 'discovery' of perspective.

brunette (broo-**net**) *noun* a woman with dark brown hair. [from French *brun* = brown]

brunt *noun* the chief stress or strain, *bore the brunt of the attack.*

Bruny Island an island off SE Tasmania.

brush *noun* **1** an implement with bristles of hair, wire, or nylon, etc., set in a solid base, used for cleaning or painting things, dressing the hair, etc. **2** a brushlike piece of carbon or metal for making a good electrical connection. **3** a fox's bushy tail. **4** each of a pair of thin sticks with long wire bristles for striking a drum, cymbal, etc. **5** a short sharp encounter, *a brush with the law.* **6** brushing, *give it a brush.* **7** (*Austral.*) brushwood. **8** (*Austral.*) scrub; dense forest. –**brush** *verb* **1** to use a brush on, to remove with a brush or by passing something lightly over the surface of. **2** to touch lightly in passing. □ **brush aside** to reject casually or curtly. **brush fence** a fence made of sections of brushwood wired together. **brush off** to reject curtly, to snub. **brush-off** *noun* a curt rejection, a snub. **brush turkey** a large mound-building bird of eastern Australia. **brush up** to smarten; to study and revive one's former knowledge of. **brush-up** *noun*

brushed *adjective* (of cloth) with raised nap.

brushtail *noun* (also **brush-tailed possum**) the most common Australian possum, having a bushy tail.

brushwood *noun* **1** undergrowth. **2** cut or broken twigs.

brushwork *noun* the style of the strokes made with a painter's brush.

brusque (*pr.* bruusk) *adjective* curt and offhand in manner. **brusquely** *adverb*, **brusqueness** *noun* [from Italian *brusco* = sour]

Brussels the capital of Belgium.
□ **Brussels sprout** a plant of the cabbage family with small cabbage-like buds growing thickly on the stem; the bud eaten as a vegetable.

brutal *adjective* very cruel, merciless. **brutally** *adverb*, **brutality** *noun*

brutalise *verb* (also **-ize**) **1** to make or become brutal. **2** to treat brutally. **brutalisation** *noun*

brute *noun* **1** an animal other than man. **2** a brutal person; *brute force*, cruel and unthinking force. **2** (*informal*) an unpleasant or difficult person or thing. **brutish** *adjective* [from Latin *brutus* = stupid]

Brutus (**broo**-tŭs), Marcus Junius (85–42 BC), Roman senator, one of the assassins of Julius Caesar in 44 BC.

bryony (**bry**-ŏ-nee) *noun* a climbing plant with black or white berries.

bryophyte (**bry**-ŏ-fyt) *noun* any of the group of plants that consists of mosses and liverworts.

BSc *abbreviation* Bachelor of Science.

BSE *abbreviation* bovine spongiform encephalopathy, a usually fatal disease of cattle, affecting the nervous system (also known as *mad cow disease*).

bubble *noun* **1** a thin ball of liquid enclosing air or gas. **2** a small ball of air in a liquid or in a solidified liquid, such as glass. **3** a transparent domed cover. **–bubble** *verb* **1** to send up bubbles; to rise in bubbles; to make the sound of these. **2** to show great liveliness. □ **bubble chamber** a device containing superheated liquid in which the paths of charged particles, X-rays, and gamma rays can be observed by the trail of bubbles that they produce. **bubble gum** chewing gum that can be blown into large bubbles. **bubble pack** a package enclosing goods in a transparent domed cover on a backing. **bubble wrap** sheets of transparent, flexible plastic containing bubbles of air, used for packaging.

bubbler *noun* (*Austral.*) a drinking fountain.

bubbly *adjective* full of bubbles. **–bubbly** *noun* (*informal*) champagne, or similar sparkling wine.

bubonic (bew-**bon**-ik) *adjective* **bubonic plague** a contagious disease with inflamed swellings (*buboes*) in the groin or armpit. [from Latin *bubo* = a swelling]

buccaneer *noun* a pirate, an unscrupulous adventurer. **buccaneering** *adjective* & *noun*

Bucharest (buuk-ă-**rest**) the capital of Romania.

Buchenwald (**buuk**-ĕn-vahlt) a village in eastern Germany, site of a Nazi concentration camp in the Second World War.

buck[1] *noun* the male of a deer, hare, or rabbit. **–buck** *verb* **1** (of a horse) to jump with the back arched. **2** (*informal*) to resist or oppose, *bucking the system*. □ **buck's night** or **party** a party for males only given for a bridegroom, usually on the eve of his wedding, by his male friends. **buck-tooth** *noun* an upper front tooth that sticks out. **buck up** (*informal*) to hurry up; to make or become more cheerful.

buck[2] *noun* an article placed as a reminder before the person whose turn it is to deal at poker. □ **pass the buck** (*informal*) to shift responsibility (and possible blame) to someone else. **buck-passing** *noun*

buck[3] *noun* (*Amer.* & *Austral. informal*) a dollar.

buck[4] *noun* a small vaulting horse without pommels.

bucked *adjective* cheered and encouraged.

bucket *noun* **1** a round open container usually with a handle, used for holding or carrying liquids or substances that are in small pieces. **2** this with its contents; the amount it contains. **–bucket** *verb* **1** to move along fast and bumpily. **2** to pour heavily, *rain was bucketing down*. **3** (*Austral.*) to criticise, to condemn. □ **bucket seat** a seat with a rounded back, for one person, especially in a car. **bucketful** *noun* (*plural* **bucketfuls**).

Buckingham Palace the London residence of the British sovereign.

buckle *noun* a device usually with a hinged tongue, through which a belt or strap is threaded to secure it. **–buckle** *verb* **1** to fasten with a buckle. **2** to crumple under pressure; to cause to do this. □ **buckle down to** to set about doing. **buckle to** to make a vigorous start on work.

buckler *noun* a small round shield with a handle.

Buckley's chance *noun* (also **Buckley's**) (*Austral. informal*) no chance at all.

buckram (**buk**-răm) *noun* stiffened cloth, especially that used for binding books.

buckshee *adjective & adverb* (*informal*) free of charge.

buckshot *noun* coarse shot.

buckthorn *noun* a kind of thorny shrub.

bucolic (bew-**kol**-ik) *adjective* characteristic of country life. [from Greek *boukolos* = herdsman]

bud *noun* **1** a small knob that will develop into a branch, leaf-cluster, or flower. **2** a flower or leaf not fully open; *in bud*, putting forth such buds. **3** a projecting finger-like growth that forms on the body of certain organisms (e.g. polyps) and develops into a new individual. **–bud** *verb* (**budded**, **budding**) **1** to be in bud. **2** to graft a bud of (a plant) on to another.

Budapest (boo-dă-**pest**) the capital of Hungary.

Buddha (**buud**-ă) *noun* **1** the title (often treated as a name) of the Indian philosopher Gautama (5th century BC), and of a series of teachers of Buddhism. **2** a statue or carving representing Gautama Buddha. [from Sanskrit *buddha* = enlightened one]

Buddhism (**buud**-izm) *noun* an Asian religion based on the teachings of the Buddha. **Buddhist** *adjective & noun*

budding *adjective* beginning to develop, *a budding poet*. **–budding** *noun* asexual reproduction by formation of a bud (*see* **bud sense 3**).

buddleia (**bud**-lee-ă) *noun* a shrub or tree with fragrant lilac or yellow flowers.

buddy *noun* (*informal*) a friend.

budge *verb* **1** to move slightly. **2** to cause to alter a position or opinion.

budgerigar (**buj**-ĕ-ree-gar) *noun* a kind of Australian parakeet, often kept in a cage. [possibly from Kamilaroi *gijirrigaa*]

budget *noun* **1** an estimate or plan of income and expenditure; **the Budget** that made annually by the Federal and State governments. **2** the amount allotted for a particular purpose. **–budget** *verb* (**budgeted**, **budgeting**) to plan or allot in a budget. **budgetary** *adjective* [from French *bouge* = leather bag]

budgie *noun* (*informal*) a budgerigar.

budo *noun* martial arts, and the code on which they are based.

Buenos Aires (bwayn-ŏs **I**-reez) the capital of Argentina.

buff *noun* **1** strong velvety dull yellow leather. **2** the colour of this. **3** the bare skin, *stripped to the buff*. **4** (*informal*) an enthusiast, *tennis buffs*. (¶ Originally, an enthusiast for going to fires, from the buff-coloured uniforms once worn by New York volunteer firemen.) **–buff** *adjective* **1** dull yellow. **2** (*informal*) in good physical shape; muscular. **–buff** *verb* to polish with soft material. [from *buff leather* = leather of buffalo hide]

buffalo *noun* (*plural* **buffaloes** *or* **buffalo**) **1** a wild ox found in Asia and Africa, domesticated in parts of Asia, and introduced into northern Australia. **2** a North American bison. ◻ **buffalo grass** a coarse lawn grass.

buffer *noun* **1** something that lessens the effect of an impact; a device for this purpose on a railway engine or at the end of a track. **2** a temporary store in a computer system between two devices that work at different speeds. **3** (*informal*) a fellow. **–buffer** *verb* to act as a buffer to. ◻ **buffer state** a small country between two powerful ones, thought to reduce the chance of war between these.

buffet[1] (**buf**-ay *or* **buu**-fay) *noun* **1** a counter where food and drink may be bought and consumed. **2** provision of food where guests serve themselves, *buffet lunch*. **3** a sideboard. ◻ **buffet car** a railway coach serving light meals. [from French, = stool]

buffet[2] (**buff**-ĕt) *noun* a blow, especially with the hand. **–buffet** *verb* (**buffeted**, **buffeting**) to give a buffet to. [from Old French *buffe* = a blow]

buffoon (buf-**oon**) *noun* a person who plays the fool. **buffoonery** *noun* clowning. [from medieval Latin *buffo* = clown]

bug *noun* **1** a flat evil-smelling insect infesting dirty houses and beds. **2** (*informal*) any small insect. **3** (*informal*) a microorganism, especially one causing disease. **4** (*informal*) an enthusiasm or obsession, *she's got the travel bug*. **5** (*informal*) a very small hidden microphone installed secretly. **6** (*informal*) a defect in a computer program or system. **7** a marine shellfish, a Balmain bug or Moreton Bay bug. **–bug** *verb* (**bugged**, **bugging**) (*informal*) **1** to fit with a hidden microphone secretly so that conversations etc. can be overheard from a distance. **2** to annoy. ◻ **bug-eyed** *adjective* with bulging eyes.

bugbear *noun* something feared or disliked. [from an old word *bug* = bogy]

buggy *noun* **1** (*old use*) a light horse-drawn carriage. **2** a small sturdy vehicle, *beach buggy*.

bugle *noun* a brass instrument like a small trumpet, used for sounding military signals. **bugler** *noun*

bugloss (**bew**-gloss) *noun* a wild plant with bristly leaves and blue flowers.

build *verb* (**built**, **building**) to construct by putting parts or material together. **–build** *noun* bodily shape, *of slender build*. ☐ **build on** to rely on; to add (an extension etc.). **build up** to accumulate; to establish gradually; to fill in with buildings; to boost with praise or flattering publicity. **build-up** *noun*

builder *noun* one who builds, one whose trade is building houses etc.

building *noun* **1** the constructing of houses etc. **2** a permanent built structure that can be entered. ☐ **building society** an organisation that accepts deposits and lends out money especially for buying houses.

built *see* **build**. **–built** *adjective* having a specified build, *sturdily built*. ☐ **built-in** *adjective* incorporated as part of a structure. **built-up** *adjective* filled in with buildings; *built-up area*, an urban area.

Bujumbura (boo-jŭm-**boor**-ră) the capital of Burundi.

bulb *noun* **1** a thick rounded mass of scale-like leaves from which a stem grows up and roots grow down. **2** a plant grown from this. **3** a bulb-shaped object. **4** = **light bulb**.

bulbous (**bul**-bŭs) *adjective* **1** growing from a bulb. **2** shaped like a bulb.

Bulgar (**bul**-gar) *adjective* & *noun* = Bulgarian.

Bulgaria a republic in SE Europe, on the Black Sea. **Bulgarian** *adjective* & *noun*

bulge *noun* a rounded swelling, an outward curve. **–bulge** *verb* to form a bulge, to cause to swell out.

bulimia (bŭ-**lim**-ee-ă) *noun* (in full **bulimia nervosa**) a psychological condition causing bouts of compulsive overeating followed by self-induced vomiting, purging, or fasting. [from Greek, = hunger of an ox]

bulk *noun* **1** size or magnitude, especially when great. **2** the greater part, the majority. **3** a large shape or body or person. **–bulk** *verb* to increase the size or thickness of, *bulk it out*. ☐ **bulk-bill** *verb* (of a doctor) to bill (Medicare) directly for the fees for treating a number of patients (who pay nothing). **bulk billing** *noun*. **bulk buying** buying a large quantity at one time; the buying of all or most of a producer's output by one purchaser. **bulk large** to seem important. **in bulk** in large amounts; in a mass, not packaged.

bulkhead *noun* an upright partition in a ship, aircraft, or vehicle.

bulky *adjective* (**bulkier**, **bulkiest**) taking up much space.

bull¹ *noun* **1** an uncastrated male of any animal of the ox family. **2** the male of the whale, elephant, and other large animals. **3** the bullseye of a target. ☐ **bull ant** (also **bulldog ant**) an Australian ant with a vicious sting. **bull market** (*Stock Exchange*) a situation where share prices are rising rapidly. **bull-nosed** *adjective* with a rounded front end. **bull terrier** a dog of a breed originally produced by crossing a bulldog and a terrier.

bull² *noun* an official edict issued by the pope.

bull³ *noun* (*informal*) an obviously absurd statement; lies, nonsense. ☐ **bull artist** (*informal*) a person who boasts, exaggerates, or lies.

bullbar *noun* a strong metal bar or grill mounted to the front of a vehicle to protect it in a collision with an animal. (Also called a *roo bar* or *kangaroo bar*).

bulldog *noun* a dog of a powerful courageous breed with a short thick neck. ☐ **bulldog clip** a spring clip that closes very strongly.

bulldoze *verb* **1** to clear with a bulldozer. **2** (*informal*) to force or intimidate, *he bulldozed them into accepting it*.

bulldozer *noun* a powerful tractor with a broad steel sheet mounted in front, used for shifting earth or clearing ground.

bulldust *noun* (*Austral.*) **1** fine dust on outback roads. **2** (*informal*) nonsense.

bullet *noun* **1** a small round or conical missile used in a rifle or revolver. **2** (in printing) a small solid circle used to introduce a line or an item in a list. ☐ **get the bullet** (*informal*) to be dismissed.

bulletin *noun* a short official statement of news or of the condition of a patient etc. ☐ **bulletin board** a noticeboard; a computer-based storage system for sending and receiving messages.

bulletproof *adjective* able to keep out bullets.

bullfight *noun* the sport of baiting and killing bulls for public entertainment, as in Spain. **bullfighter** *noun*, **bullfighting** *noun*

bullfrog *noun* a large frog with a bellowing cry.

bullion *noun* gold or silver in bulk or bars, before coining or manufacture.

bullock *noun* a bull after castration.

bullocky *noun* (*Austral. informal*) a driver of a team of bullocks. □ **bullocky's joy** treacle or golden syrup.

bullring *noun* an arena for bullfights.

bullroarer *noun* a flat strip of wood on a string making a whirring noise when whirled around, used especially in Aboriginal religious rites.

bullseye *noun* 1 the centre of a target. 2 a large hard round peppermint sweet. 3 a hemisphere or thick disc of glass as a window.

bully¹ *noun* a person who uses his or her strength or power to hurt or frighten others. –**bully** *verb* (**bullied, bullying**) to behave as a bully towards, to intimidate. □ **bully for you!** (*informal*) bravo!

bully² *verb* (**bullied, bullying**) **bully off** to start play in hockey, where two opposing players tap the ground and each other's stick alternately three times before hitting the ball. **bully-off** *noun* this procedure.

bulrush *noun* a kind of tall rush with a thick velvety head.

bulwark (**buul**-werk) *noun* 1 a wall of earth built as a defence. 2 something that acts as a protection or defence. **bulwarks** *plural noun* a ship's side above the level of the deck.

bum¹ *noun* (*informal*) the buttocks.

bum² *noun* (*informal*) a beggar, a loafer. –**bum** *verb* to loaf, to wander around, *spent the holidays bumming around*.

bumble *verb* 1 to move or act in a blundering way. 2 to ramble in speaking.

bumble-bee *noun* a large bee with a loud hum.

bump *verb* 1 to knock with a dull-sounding blow; to hurt by this. 2 to travel with a jolting movement. –**bump** *noun* 1 a bumping sound, knock, or movement. 2 a raised mark left by a blow. 3 a swelling or lump on a surface. □ **bump into** (*informal*) to meet by chance. **bump off** (*informal*) to kill. **bump up** (*informal*) to raise, *bumped up the price*.

bumper *noun* 1 something unusually large or plentiful, *a bumper crop*. 2 (in full **bumper bar**) a horizontal bar attached to the front or back of a motor vehicle to lessen the effect of a collision. 3 a ball in cricket that rises high after pitching.

bumpkin *noun* a country person with awkward manners.

bumptious (**bump**-shŭs) *noun* conceited. **bumptiously** *adverb*, **bumptiousness** *noun*

bumpy *adjective* (**bumpier, bumpiest**) full of bumps; causing jolts. **bumpiness** *noun*

bun *noun* 1 a small round sweet cake, often with dried fruit. 2 a soft flattish bread roll. 3 hair twisted into a bun shape at the back of the head.

bunch *noun* 1 a cluster, *a bunch of grapes*. 2 a number of small similar things held or fastened together, *a bunch of keys*. 3 (*informal*) a mob, a gang. –**bunch** *verb* to come or bring together into a bunch or in folds.

bunchy *adjective* gathered in clumsy folds.

Bundjalung (**bun**-jă-lung) *noun* 1 a member of an Aboriginal people of NE New South Wales and SE Queensland. 2 their language.

bundle *noun* 1 a collection of things loosely fastened or wrapped together; a set of sticks or rods tied together. 2 (*informal*) a large amount of money. –**bundle** *verb* 1 to make into a bundle; *bundled up in thick clothes*, cumbersomely dressed in these. 2 to put away hastily and untidily, to push hurriedly, *bundled him into a taxi*. □ **drop one's bundle** (*informal*) to go to pieces mentally; to give up hope. **go a bundle on** (*informal*) to like immensely.

bundu (**buun**-doo) *noun* (in southern Africa) the bush (**bush¹** sense 3).

bung¹ *noun* a stopper for closing a hole in a barrel or jar. –**bung** *verb* 1 to close with a bung. 2 (*informal*) to throw or toss, *bung it over here*. □ **bunged up** blocked.

bung² *adjective* (*Austral. informal*) broken down; useless. □ **go bung** to break down; to go bankrupt.

bungalow *noun* a one-storeyed house. [from Hindi *bangla* = of Bengal]

bungee (**bun**-jee) *noun* an elasticated rope used for securing baggage and in bungee jumping. □ **bungee jumping** the sport of jumping from a height attached to a bungee.

bungle *verb* to spoil by lack of skill; to tackle clumsily and without success. **–bungle** *noun* a bungled attempt. **bungler** *noun*

bunion *noun* a swelling at the base of the big toe, with thickened skin.

bunk¹ *noun* a built-in shelf-like bed, e.g. on a ship. □ **bunk beds** a pair of small single beds mounted one above the other as a unit.

bunk² *verb* (*informal*) to run away. □ **do a bunk** (*informal*) to run away.

bunk³ *noun* (*informal*) bunkum.

bunker *noun* **1** a container for fuel. **2** a sandy hollow forming a hazard on a golf course. **3** a reinforced underground shelter. **–bunker** *verb* to put fuel into the bunkers of (a ship).

bunkum *noun* nonsense.

bunny *noun* (*informal*) **1** a rabbit. **2** (*Austral.*) a victim or dupe. [from dialect *bun* = rabbit]

Bunsen, Robert Wilhelm Eberhard (1811–99), German chemist, a pioneer of spectral analysis in chemistry. □ **Bunsen burner** a laboratory instrument devised by Bunsen, with a vertical tube burning a mixture of air and gas to produce great heat.

bunting *noun* **1** flags and streamers for decorating streets and buildings. **2** a loosely-woven fabric used for making these.

bunya *noun* (also **bunya-bunya**) a Queensland tree whose cones contain edible seeds; the seed of this tree. [Yagara *bunya-bunya*]

bunyip *noun* a mythical Australian monster of swamps and billabongs. [Wemba-wemba *banib*]

buoy (*pr.* boi) *noun* an anchored floating object marking a navigable channel or showing the position of submerged rocks etc. **–buoy** *verb* **1** to mark with a buoy or buoys. **2** to keep (a thing) afloat; *buoyed up with new hope*, encouraged.

buoyant (**boi**-ănt) *adjective* **1** able to float. **2** light-hearted, cheerful. **buoyantly** *adverb*, **buoyancy** *noun*

bur *noun* = **burr** sense 4.

burble *verb* **1** to make a gentle murmuring sound. **2** to speak lengthily.

burden *noun* **1** something carried, a heavy load. **2** something difficult to support, *the heavy burden of taxation*. **3** the chief theme of a speech etc. **–burden** *verb* **1** to load, to put a burden on. **2** to oppress.

□ **beast of burden** an animal that carries packs on its back. **the burden of proof** the obligation to prove what one says.

burdensome *adjective* troublesome, tiring.

bureau (bew-roh) *noun* (*plural* **bureaux**) **1** a piece of furniture with drawers and a hinged flap for use as a desk. **2** an office or department, *a travel bureau*. [French, = desk]

bureaucracy (bew-**rok**-ră-see) *noun* **1** government by State officials not by elected representatives. **2** these officials. **3** excessive official routine, especially because there are too many offices or departments. [from *bureau* + *-cracy*]

bureaucrat (**bew**-rŏ-krat) *noun* **1** an official who works in a government office. **2** one who applies the rules of a department without exercising much judgment.

bureaucratic (bew-rŏ-**krat**-ik) *adjective* **1** of bureaucracy. **2** of or like bureaucrats.

burette (bew-**ret**) *noun* a graduated glass tube with a tap, used for measuring out small quantities of liquid.

burgeon (**ber**-jŏn) *verb* to begin to grow rapidly.

burger *noun* a hamburger or food resembling this, *chicken burger*.

burgess (**ber**-jĕs) *noun* (in the UK) a citizen of a town or borough.

burgher *noun* **1** a citizen, especially of a town in continental Europe. **2** a descendant of a Dutch or Portuguese colonist in Sri Lanka.

burghul (**berg**-ŭl) *noun* wheat crushed into tiny pieces, cracked wheat.

burglar *noun* a person who enters a building illegally, especially in order to steal. **burglary** *noun*

burgle *verb* to rob as a burglar.

burgomaster (**berg**-ŏ-mah-ster) *noun* the mayor of a Dutch or Flemish town.

burgundy *noun* **1** a red or white wine from Burgundy in France; a similar wine from elsewhere. **2** dark purplish red.

burial *noun* burying; being buried; a funeral.

burin (**bew**-rĭn) *noun* an engraving tool.

burka (**ber**-kă) *noun* (also **burqa**) a long enveloping garment worn in public by some Muslim women.

Burke, Robert O'Hara (1821–61), Irish-born Australian explorer who, with W. J. Wills and others, successfully crossed Australia from south to north, but died on the return journey.

Burkina (ber-**keen**-ǎ) (also **Burkina Faso**) an inland republic of western Africa. **Burkinan** *adjective & noun*

burlesque (ber-**lesk**) *noun* a mocking imitation.

burly *adjective* (**burlier**, **burliest**) with a strong heavy body, sturdy. **burliness** *noun*

Burma (since 1989 officially called **Myanmar**) a republic of SE Asia, on the Bay of Bengal.

Burmese *noun* (*plural* **Burmese**) 1 a person from Burma. 2 the language of Burma. –**Burmese** *adjective* of Burma or its people or language. ☐ **Burmese cat** a cat of a breed with short fur.

burn¹ *verb* (**burned** *or* **burnt** (¶ see note at end of entry), **burning**) 1 to blaze or glow with fire. 2 to produce heat or light; to be alight. 3 to damage, hurt, or destroy by fire, heat, or the action of acid; to be injured or damaged in this way; to produce (a mark etc.) by heat or fire; *money burns a hole in his pocket*, makes him eager to spend it. 4 to use as fuel. 5 to be able to be set on fire. 6 to feel or cause to feel hot; *my ears are burning*, they feel hot, jokingly supposed to be a sign that one is being talked about elsewhere. 7 to make or become brown from heat or light. 8 produce (a CD, DVD, etc.) by copying from an original or master copy. –**burn** *noun* 1 a mark or sore made by burning. 2 the firing of a spacecraft's rocket(s). ☐ **burn one's boats** or **bridges** to do something deliberately that makes retreat impossible. **burn-out** *noun* physical or emotional exhaustion. **burn the midnight oil** to study or work far into the night. **have money to burn** to have so much that one does not need to take care of it.

Usage The form *burnt* (not *burned*) is always used when an adjective is required, e.g. in *a burnt offering*. As parts of the verb, either *burned* or *burnt* may be used.

---

burn² *noun* (*Scottish*) a small stream.

burner *noun* the part of a lamp or stove that emits and shapes the flame.

Burnet, Sir (Frank) Macfarlane (1899–1985), Australian medical scientist, noted for his studies of viruses (which assisted in the development of vaccines), and for his work in immunology.

burning *see* **burn¹**. –**burning** *adjective* 1 intense, *a burning desire*. 2 hotly discussed, vital, *a burning question*.

burnish *verb* to polish by rubbing.

burnous (ber-**noos**) *noun* an Arab or Moorish hooded cloak. [from Arabic *burnus*]

burnt *see* **burn¹**. –**burnt** *adjective* of a deep shade, *burnt sienna*, *burnt umber*.

burp *noun* (*informal*) a belch, a belching sound. –**burp** *verb* (*informal*) 1 to belch. 2 to cause (a baby) to bring up wind from the stomach.

burr *noun* 1 a whirring sound. 2 the strong pronunciation of 'r' a soft country accent, especially one using this. 3 a small drill. 4 (also **bur**) a plant's seed case or flower that clings to hair or clothing; the plant itself. –**burr** *verb* to make a whirring sound.

burrow *noun* a hole or tunnel dug by a wombat or rabbit etc. as a dwelling. –**burrow** *verb* 1 to dig a burrow, to tunnel. 2 to form by tunnelling. 3 to search deeply, to delve.

bursar (**ber**-ser) *noun* 1 a person who manages the finances and other business of a school or college. 2 a student who holds a bursary. [from Latin *bursa* = a bag]

bursary (**ber**-sǎ-ree) *noun* a grant given to a student.

burst *verb* (**burst**, **bursting**) 1 to force or be forced open; to fly violently apart because of pressure inside; *buds are bursting*, opening out. 2 to appear or come suddenly and forcefully, *burst into flame*. 3 to let out a violent expression of feeling, *burst into tears*, *burst out laughing*; *she burst into song*, suddenly began to sing. –**burst** *noun* 1 a bursting, a split. 2 an explosion or outbreak; a series of shots, *a burst of gunfire*, *of applause*. 3 a brief violent effort; a spurt.

bursting *adjective* full to breaking point, *sacks bursting with grain*; *we are bursting to tell you*, very eager.

Burundi (bǔ-**ruun**-dee) a republic in central Africa. **Burundian** *adjective & noun*

bury *verb* (**buried**, **burying**) 1 to place (a dead body) in the earth, a tomb, or the sea. 2 to put underground, to hide in earth etc.; to cover up; *buried themselves in their books*, gave all their time and attention to reading. ☐ **bury the hatchet** to cease quarrelling and become friendly.

bus *noun* (*plural* **buses**) 1 a long-bodied passenger vehicle. 2 a busbar. 3 a set of conductors carrying data and control signals within a computer. **–bus** *verb* (**bussed**, **bussing**) **1** to travel by bus. **2** to transport by bus. □ **bus station** an area where a number of (especially long-distance) buses stop, with facilities for passengers etc. as at a railway station. **bus stop** a regular stopping place of a bus. [short for *omnibus*]

busbar *noun* an electrical conductor or set of conductors for collecting and distributing electric current.

busby (**buz**-bee) *noun* a tall fur cap worn by members of certain cavalry regiments.

bush[1] *noun* **1** a shrub. **2** a thick growth or clump, *a bush of hair*. **3** wild uncultivated land, especially in Australia and Africa. **4** (*Austral.*) rural areas as opposed to the city. □ **bush lawyer** (*Austral.*) a person claiming legal knowledge but with no legal qualifications. **bush medicine** (*Austral.*) traditional Aboriginal medicine. **bush telegraph** (*Austral.*) a way in which news is passed on unofficially. **bush tucker** (*Austral.*) food naturally available in the bush. **go bush** (*Austral.*) to disappear from one's usual surroundings; to leave the city to settle in the country; to visit the country; (of Aborigines) to return to traditional life.

bush[2] *noun* **1** a metal lining for a round hole in which something fits or revolves. **2** an electrically insulating sleeve. **–bush** *verb* to fit with a bush.

bushcraft *noun* knowledge of how to live or survive in the bush.

bushed *adjective* (*Austral. informal*) **1** lost in the bush. **2** tired out, exhausted. **3** bewildered.

bushel *noun* a measure for grain and fruit (8 gallons or 36.4 litres). □ **hide one's light under a bushel** to conceal one's abilities.

bushfire *noun* (*Austral.*) a fire in scrub or forest land, often spreading widely.

bushido (boo-**shee**-doh) *noun* the strict ethical code of the Japanese samurai, involving military skill, fearlessness, and obedience.

bushman *noun* (*plural* **bushmen**) a dweller or traveller in the Australian bush. **–Bushman** *noun* (*plural* **Bushmen**) a member or the language of an aboriginal people in southern Africa. **bushmanship** *noun*

bushranger *noun* (in former times) an outlaw living in the bush as a highwayman.

bushwalking *noun* hiking in the bush, often including camping out. **bushwalker** *noun*

bushy *adjective* (**bushier**, **bushiest**) **1** covered with bushes. **2** growing thickly. **bushiness** *noun*

business *noun* **1** a trade, a profession; a person's usual occupation. **2** buying and selling, trade. **3** a commercial firm, a shop, *they own a grocery business*. **4** a thing one is concerned about or needs to deal with; the agenda. **5** a difficult matter, *what a business it is!* **6** an affair, subject, or device. □ **have no business to** to have no right to (do something).

businesslike *adjective* practical, systematic.

businessman *noun* a man engaged in trade or commerce, especially at a senior level.

businesswoman *noun* a woman engaged in trade or commerce, especially at a senior level.

busk *verb* to perform in the street etc. for voluntary donations. **busker** *noun* [from an old word *busk* = be a pedlar]

buskin *noun* a thick-soled boot worn by actors in tragedy in ancient Greece.

busman *noun* (*plural* **busmen**) the driver of a bus (now usually called a *bus driver*). □ **busman's holiday** leisure time spent doing something similar to one's usual work.

bust[1] *noun* **1** a sculpture of the head, shoulders, and chest. **2** the bosom. **3** the measurement round a woman's body at the bosom.

bust[2] *verb* (**busted** *or* **bust**, **busting**) (*informal*) **1** to burst. **2** to raid, to search; to arrest. **–bust** *noun* (*informal*) **1** a failure. **2** a police raid. **–bust** *adjective* (*informal*) **1** burst, broken. **2** bankrupt, *go bust*. □ **bust up** (*informal*) to collapse, to explode; (of a couple) to separate. **bust-up** *noun* (*informal*) a quarrel.

bustard *noun* a large swift-running bird.

buster *noun* **1** (*informal*) a fellow. **2** (*informal*) a fall, *come a buster*. **3** a strong wind, *the southerly buster*.

bustle[1] *verb* **1** to make a show of hurrying. **2** to cause to hurry. **–bustle** *noun* excited activity.

bustle[2] *noun* padding used to puff out the top of a woman's skirt at the back.

busy *adjective* (**busier**, **busiest**) **1** working, occupied; having much to do; *get busy*, start doing things. **2** full of activity, *a busy day*; *telephone line is busy*, is engaged. **3** (of a picture or design) too full of detail. **–busy** *verb* (**busied**, **busying**) to keep busy, *busy oneself*. **busily** *adverb*, **busyness** *noun*

Usage *Busyness* (*pr.* **biz**-ee-něss) meaning 'a state of being busy' should be distinguished from *business* (*pr.* **biz**-něss).

busybody *noun* a meddlesome person.

but *adverb* only, no more than, *we can but try*. –**but** *preposition* & *conjunction* **1** however; on the other hand. **2** except, otherwise than, *there's no one here but me*; *I'd have drowned but for you*, if you had not helped me. –**but** *noun* an objection, *ifs and buts*.

butane (**bew**-tayn) *noun* an inflammable gas produced from petroleum, used in liquid form as a fuel.

butanol (**bew**-tă-nol) *noun* an inflammable alcohol used as a solvent and in the manufacture of plastics.

butch *adjective* (*informal*) tough-looking; masculine, mannish.

butcher *noun* **1** a person whose trade is to slaughter animals for food; one who cuts up and sells animal flesh. **2** a person who kills or has people killed needlessly or brutally. –**butcher** *verb* **1** to slaughter or cut up (an animal) for meat. **2** to kill needlessly or brutally.

butcherbird *noun* an Australian grey or black and white bird, noted for impaling its prey on thorns.

butchery *noun* **1** a butcher's trade. **2** needless or brutal killing.

butler *noun* the chief servant of a household, usually a man, especially one in charge of the wine cellar. [from Old French *bouteillier* = bottler]

butt[1] *noun* a large cask or barrel. [from Latin *buttis* = cask]

butt[2] *noun* **1** the thicker end of a tool or weapon. **2** a short remnant, a stub, *cheque butt*; *cigarette butt*. [from Dutch *bot* = stumpy]

butt[3] *noun* **1** the mound of earth behind the targets on a shooting range. **2** a person or thing that is frequently a target for ridicule or teasing. **butts** *plural noun* a shooting range. [from Old French *but* = goal]

butt[4] *verb* **1** to push with the head like a ram or goat. **2** to meet or place edge to edge, *the strips should be butted against each other, not overlapping*. –**butt** *noun* **1** an act of butting. **2** a butted join. □ **butt in** to interrupt; to meddle. **butt out** (*informal*) to cease to interfere. [from French *buter* = to hit]

butte (*pr.* bewt) *noun* an isolated hill with steep sides and a flat top, smaller than a mesa; found especially in western USA. [French, = mound]

butter *noun* **1** a fatty food substance made from cream by churning. **2** a similar substance made from other materials, *peanut butter*. –**butter** *verb* to spread, cook, or serve with butter (or a substitute). □ **butter bean** a pale yellow-podded haricot bean; a dried lima bean. **butter-fingers** *noun* a person likely to drop things. **butter up** (*informal*) to flatter. **buttery** *adjective*

buttercup *noun* a wild plant with bright yellow cup-shaped flowers.

butterfish *noun* any of several fish with a coating of mucus.

butterfly *noun* **1** an insect with four often brightly coloured wings and knobbed feelers. **2** a swimming stroke in which both arms are lifted at the same time. □ **butterfly nut** a kind of wing nut. **have butterflies in the stomach** to feel nervous tremors.

buttermilk *noun* the slightly acid liquid left after butter has been churned from milk.

butternut *noun* a variety of pumpkin, shaped like an elongated pear.

butterscotch *noun* a kind of hard toffee.

buttock *noun* either of the two fleshy rounded parts at the lower or rear end of the back of the human or an animal body.

button *noun* **1** a knob or disc sewn on a garment as a fastener or ornament. **2** a small rounded object. **3** a knob or switch pressed to operate equipment. **4** a buttonlike image on a computer display selected by clicking (*see* click). –**button** *verb* (**buttoned**, **buttoning**) to fasten with a button or buttons. □ **button-through** *adjective* fastening by buttons down its whole length.

buttonhole *noun* **1** a slit through which a button is passed to fasten clothing. **2** a flower worn in the buttonhole of a coat lapel. –**buttonhole** *verb* to accost and detain with conversation.

buttress *noun* **1** a support built against a wall. **2** a thing that supports or reinforces something, *buttress roots*. –**buttress** *verb* to prop up. [same origin as *butt*[4]]

butyl (**bew**-til) *noun* the monovalent alkyl radical C_4H_9. □ **butyl rubber** a synthetic rubber used to make tyre inner tubes.

buxom *adjective* plump and healthy-looking.

buy *verb* (**bought, buying**) **1** to obtain in exchange for money or by some sacrifice. **2** to win over by bribery. **3** (*informal*) to believe, to accept the truth of, *no one would buy that excuse*. –**buy** *noun* a purchase; *a good buy*, a useful purchase, a bargain. □ **buy into** (*Austral. informal*) to choose to become involved in. **buy off** to get rid of by payment. **buy out** to obtain full ownership by paying (another person) to give up his or her share. **buy up** to buy all or as much as possible of.

buyer *noun* **1** a person who buys something. **2** an agent choosing and buying stock for a large shop. □ **buyers' market** a state of affairs when goods are plentiful and prices are low.

buzz *noun* **1** a vibrating humming sound. **2** a rumour. **3** (*informal*) a telephone call, *give me a buzz*. **4** (*informal*) a thrill. –**buzz** *verb* **1** to make a buzz. **2** to be filled with a buzzing noise. **3** to go about quickly and busily. **4** to threaten (an aircraft) by flying close to it. □ **buzz off** (*informal*) to go away.

buzzard *noun* a kind of hawk.

buzzer *noun* a device that produces a buzzing note as a signal.

buzzword *noun* (*informal*) a piece of fashionable jargon; a catchword.

by *preposition* **1** near, beside; *north by east*, between north and north-north-east. **2** along; via; past. **3** during, *came by night*. **4** through the agency or means of; (of an animal) having as its sire. **5** (of members or measurements) taking it together with, *multiply six by four*; *it measures twelve centimetres by eight*, with eight centimetres as a second dimension. **6** not later than. **7** according to, *judging by appearances*; *sold by the kilo*. **8** after, succeeding, *bit by bit*. **9** to the extent of, *better by far*; *beat him by ten seconds*. **10** in respect of, *a tailor, Jones by name*; *pull it up by the roots*. **11** in the belief of, *swear by God*. –**by** *adverb* **1** near, *lives close by*. **2** in reserve, *puts $50 by every week*. **3** past, *drove by*. –**by** *adjective* additional; less important, *a byroad*; *by-product*. □ **by and by** before long. **by and large** on the whole, considering everything. **by oneself** alone; without help. **by the bye** or **by** incidentally.

bye *noun* **1** a run scored in cricket from a ball that passes the batsman without being hit. **2** a hole or holes remaining unplayed when a golf match is ended. **3** the status of having no opponent for one round in a tournament and so advancing to the next as if having won.

bye-bye *interjection* (*informal*) goodbye.

by-election *noun* an election of an MP to fill a single vacancy, caused by the death or resignation of a member.

bygone *adjective* belonging to the past. **bygones** *plural noun* things belonging to the past; *let bygones be bygones*, forgive and forget past offences.

by-law *noun* a law or regulation made by a local government authority or corporation.

byline *noun* **1** the goal line or touch line of a soccer pitch. **2** a line in a newspaper etc. naming the writer of an article.

BYO *abbreviation* bring your own. –**BYO** *adjective* **1** (of a restaurant) to which diners may bring their own liquor. **2** (of a barbecue, party, etc.) to which people bring their own drinks and sometimes food.

bypass *noun* **1** a road taking traffic round a congested area. **2** a secondary channel allowing something to flow when the main route is blocked, *heart bypass*. –**bypass** *verb* **1** to avoid by means of a bypass. **2** to omit or ignore (procedures, regulations, etc.) in order to act quickly.

byplay *noun* action, usually without speech, of minor characters in a play etc.

by-product *noun* a substance produced during the making of something else.

byre *noun* a cowshed.

byroad *noun* a minor road.

Byron, George Gordon, 6th Baron (1788–1824), English Romantic poet.

bystander *noun* a person standing near but taking no part when something happens.

byte (*rhymes with* kite) *noun* a fixed number of bits (= binary digits) in a computer, often representing a single character.

byway *noun* a byroad.

byword *noun* **1** a person or thing spoken of as a notable example, *the firm became a byword for mismanagement*. **2** a familiar saying.

Byzantine (bǐ-**zan**-tyn) *adjective* **1** of Byzantium or the Eastern Roman Empire. **2** complicated, devious, underhand.

Byzantium (bǐ-**zan**-tee-ŭm *or* by-) an ancient Greek city on the Bosporus, refounded by Constantine the Great as Constantinople (modern Istanbul).

Cc

C *abbreviation* **1** Celsius, centigrade.
2 coulomb(s).

© *symbol* copyright.

c *abbreviation* **1** century. **2** (also **c.**) circa.
3 cent(s).

cab *noun* **1** a taxi. **2** a compartment for the
driver of a train, truck, or crane.

cabal (kǎ-**bal**) *noun* a secret plot; the people
engaged in it.

cabaret (**kab**-ǎ-ray) *noun* an entertainment
provided in a restaurant or nightclub. [French,
= tavern]

cabbage *noun* a vegetable with green or
purple leaves usually forming a round head.
☐ **cabbage tree** an Australian palm with large
fan-shaped leaves.

cabbala *noun* = **kabbalah**.

cabby *noun* (*informal*) a taxi driver.

caber (**kay**-ber) *noun* a roughly-trimmed tree
trunk used in the Scottish sport of **tossing the
caber**.

Cabernet (**kab**-er-nay) *noun* (in full **Cabernet
Sauvignon**, *pr.* **soh**-vin-yon) a black grape
used in wine-making; the red wine made
from it.

cabin *noun* **1** a small dwelling or shelter,
especially of wood. **2** a compartment in a ship
or aircraft or spacecraft. **3** a driver's cab.

cabinet *noun* a cupboard or container with
drawers or shelves for storing or displaying
articles, or containing a radio or television
set etc. –**Cabinet** *noun* the group of
ministers chosen by the Prime Minister to be
responsible for government policy.

cabinetmaker *noun* a skilled joiner.

cable *noun* **1** a thick rope of fibre or wire.
2 an anchor chain. **3** a set of insulated wires
for carrying electricity or electronic signals.
4 a telegram sent abroad. **5** a knitted pattern
(*cable stitch*) looking like twisted rope. –**cable**
verb to send a telegram to (a person) abroad,
to transmit (money or information) in this
way. ☐ **cable car** any of the cars in a **cable
railway**, a railway with cars drawn by an
endless cable by means of a stationary engine.

cable television transmission of television
programs by cable to subscribers.

caboodle (kǎ-**boo**-d'l) *noun* (*informal*)
the whole caboodle or **the whole kit and
caboodle** the whole lot.

Cabot (**kab**-ŏt), John (died c. 1498), Venetian
explorer and navigator who, with his son
Sebastian, sailed from Bristol in 1497 and
discovered the mainland of North America a
year before Columbus.

cabriole (**kab**-ree-ohl) *noun* a curved leg on
furniture.

cacao (kǎ-**kay**-oh) *noun* (*plural* **cacaos**)
1 a tropical tree producing a seed from which
cocoa and chocolate are made. **2** its seed.

cache (*pr.* kash) *noun* **1** a hiding place for
treasure or stores. **2** hidden treasure or stores.
3 (*pr.* kaysh) (in computing) an auxiliary
memory from which high-speed retrieval is
possible. –**cache** *verb* put in a cache. [from
French *cacher* = to hide]

cachet (**kash**-ay) *noun* **1** a distinguishing mark
or seal. **2** prestige.

cachou (**kash**-oo) *noun* a scented lozenge.

cackle *noun* **1** the loud clucking noise a hen
makes after laying. **2** a loud silly laugh.
3 noisy chatter. –**cackle** *verb* **1** to give a cackle.
2 to chatter noisily.

cacophony (kǎ-**kof**-ŏ-nee) *noun* a harsh
discordant sound. **cacophonous** *adjective*
[from Greek *kakos* = bad, + *phone* = sound]

cactus *noun* (*plural* **cacti**, *pr.* **kak**-ty) a plant
from a hot dry climate, with a fleshy stem and
usually prickles but no leaves.

CAD *abbreviation* computer-assisted design.

cad *noun* a person (especially a man) who
behaves dishonourably. **caddish** *adjective*

cadaverous (kǎ-**dav**-ě-rŭs) *adjective* gaunt
and pale. [from Latin *cadaver* = corpse]

caddie *noun* (also **caddy**) a person who carries
a golfer's clubs during a game. –**caddie** *verb*
(also **caddy**) (**caddied**, **caddying**) to act as
caddie.

caddis fly *noun* a four-winged insect living
near water.

caddy[1] *noun* a small container, especially a box for holding tea.

caddy[2] *see* caddie.

cadence (**kay**-dĕns) *noun* **1** rhythm in sound. **2** the rise and fall of the voice in speaking. **3** the end of a musical phrase.

cadential (kă-**den**-shăl) *adjective* of a cadence or cadenza.

cadenza (kă-**den**-ză) *noun* an elaborate passage for a solo instrument or voice, showing off the performer's skill.

cadet (kă-**det**) *noun* a young trainee for the armed forces, police, journalism, etc.

cadge *verb* to ask for as a gift; to go about begging. **cadger** *noun*

cadmium (**kad**-mee-ŭm) *noun* a chemical element (symbol Cd) that looks like tin.

cadre (**kah**-der) *noun* a group forming a nucleus of trained persons round which a military or political unit can be formed.

caecilian (sĕ-**sil**-ee-ăn) *noun* a member of a group of amphibians, mainly tropical and wormlike.

caecum (**see**-kŭm) *noun* (*plural* caeca) a tubular pouch forming the first part of the large intestine.

Caesar = Julius Caesar. –**Caesar** *noun* a title of the Roman emperors.

Caesarean (sĕ-**zair**-ree-ăn) *noun* (*informal*) a Caesarean section, a surgical operation by which a child is taken from the womb by cutting through the wall of the abdomen and into the womb. [from the name of Julius Caesar, who was said to have been born in this way]

caesium (**see**-zee-ŭm) *noun* a soft silver-white metallic element (symbol Cs).

caesura (sĕz-**yoor**-ră) *noun* a short pause in a line of verse.

café (**kaf**-ay) *noun* (also cafe) a small coffee house or restaurant. [French, = coffee]

cafeteria (kaf-ĕ-**teer**-ree-ă) *noun* a café where customers serve themselves from a counter.

caffeine (**kaf**-een) *noun* a stimulant found in tea and coffee.

caftan (**kaf**-tan) *noun* **1** a long coat-like garment worn by men in the Middle East. **2** a woman's long loose dress.

cage *noun* **1** a framework with wires or bars in which birds or animals are kept. **2** any similar structure; the enclosed platform in which

people travel in a lift or the shaft of a mine. –**cage** *verb* to put or keep in a cage.

cagey *adjective* (cagier, cagiest) (*informal*) cautious about giving information, secretive. **cagily** *adverb*, **caginess** *noun*

cahoots (kă-**hoots**) *plural noun* (*informal*) □ **in cahoots with** in league with, conspiring with.

Cain the eldest son of Adam, and murderer of his brother Abel. □ **raise Cain** *see* raise.

Cainozoic = Cenozoic.

cairn *noun* a pyramid of rough stones set up as a landmark or a monument.

Cairo the capital of Egypt.

caisson (**kay**-sŏn) *noun* a watertight box or chamber inside which work can be carried out on underwater structures. [French]

cajole (kă-**johl**) *verb* to coax. **cajolery** *noun*

Cajun (**kay**-jŭn) *adjective* of or relating to the French-speaking people of southern Louisiana in the US, *Cajun cooking*; *Cajun music*.

cake *noun* **1** a baked sweet bread-like food made from a mixture of flour, fats, sugar, eggs, etc. **2** a mixture cooked in a round flat shape, *fish cakes*. **3** a shaped or hardened mass, *a cake of soap*. –**cake** *verb* **1** to harden into a compact mass. **2** to encrust with a hardened mass.

Calabria (kă-**lab**-ree-ă) the SW promontory of Italy.

calamari (kal-ă-**mah**-ree) *noun* (*plural* calamari) a squid used as food.

calamine *noun* a pink powder, chiefly zinc carbonate or oxide, used in skin lotions.

calamity *noun* a disaster. **calamitous** *adjective*

calcareous (kal-**kair**-ree-ŭs) *adjective* of or containing calcium carbonate.

calcify (**kal**-sĭ-fy) *verb* (calcified, calcifying) to harden by a deposit of calcium salts. **calcification** *noun*

calcite *noun* natural crystalline calcium carbonate.

calcium *noun* a greyish-white chemical element (symbol Ca), present in bones and teeth and forming the basis of lime. □ **calcium carbonate** a white insoluble solid occurring as chalk, marble, etc. [from Latin *calcis* = of lime]

calculable *adjective* able to be calculated.

calculate *verb* **1** to find out by using mathematics, to count. **2** to plan deliberately; to intend. □ **calculated risk** a risk taken deliberately with full knowledge of the dangers. calculation *noun*

calculating *adjective* shrewd, scheming.

calculator *noun* **1** a device used in making calculations, especially a small electronic one. **2** one who calculates.

calculus (**kal**-kew-lŭs) *noun* (*plural* calculi *or* calculuses) **1** a stone formed in the body. **2** a branch of mathematics that deals with problems involving rates of variation. [from Latin *calculus* = small stone (used on an abacus)]

caldera (kahl-**dair**-ră) *noun* a saucer-shaped depression formed where part of a volcano has collapsed.

Caledonian (kal-ĕ-**doh**-nee-ăn) *adjective* of Scotland.

calendar *noun* **1** a chart showing the days, weeks, and months of a particular year. **2** a device displaying the date. **3** a list of dates or events of a particular kind, *the School Calendar*. **4** the system by which time is divided into fixed periods, *the Gregorian calendar*.

calender *noun* a machine in which cloth or paper is pressed by rollers to glaze or smooth it. –calender *verb* to press in a calender.

calends *plural noun* the first day of the month in the ancient Roman calendar.

calf¹ *noun* (*plural* calves) **1** the young of cattle, also of the seal, whale, and certain other animals. **2** calfskin. □ calf love adolescent romantic love.

calf² *noun* (*plural* calves) the fleshy back part of the leg below the knee.

calfskin *noun* leather made from the skin of a calf.

calibrate (**kal**-ĭ-brayt) *verb* **1** to mark or correct units of measurement on a gauge. **2** to measure the calibre of. calibration *noun*, calibrator *noun*

calibre (**kal**-ĭ-ber) *noun* **1** the diameter of the inside of a tube or gun barrel. **2** the diameter of a bullet or shell. **3** ability, importance, *we need someone of your calibre*. [from Arabic *kalib* = mould]

calicivirus (kă-**lee**-see-**vy**-rŭs) *noun* (in full rabbit calicivirus) a virus which kills rabbits.

calico *noun* a kind of cotton cloth. [from Calicut, a town in India]

California a state of the USA, on the Pacific coast. Californian *adjective & noun*

californium (ka-lĭ-**for**-nee-ŭm) *noun* a radioactive metallic element of the actinide series (symbol Cf).

Caligula (kă-**lig**-yŭ-lă) the nickname of Gaius, Roman emperor 37–41.

caliph (**kay**-lĭf) *noun* the former title of certain Muslim leaders seen as successors to Muhammad in being defenders of the faith. caliphate *noun* [from Arabic *khalifa* = successor of Muhammad]

call *noun* **1** a shout or cry. **2** the characteristic cry of a bird. **3** a signal on a bugle etc. **4** a short visit. **5** a summons; an invitation; *the call of the wild*, its attraction. **6** a demand, a claim, *I have many calls on my time*. **7** a need, an occasion, *there's no call for you to worry*. **8** a declaration of trumps etc. in card games. **9** an act of telephoning, a conversation on the telephone. –call *verb* **1** to shout or speak loudly in order to attract attention etc. **2** to utter a call. **3** to pay a short visit. **4** to name; to describe or address as, *I call that cheating*. **5** to declare (a trump suit etc.) in card games. **6** to rouse deliberately; to summon to get up. **7** to summon, *call the fire brigade*. **8** to command or invite. **9** to communicate with by telephone or radio. **10** (*Austral.*) to describe (a horse race etc.) for radio or television as it is being run. □ call a person's bluff to challenge him or her to carry out a threat. call for to demand, to require; to come and collect. call girl a prostitute who accepts appointments by telephone. call in to pay a casual visit; to seek advice or help from; to order the return of, to take out of circulation. call off to call away; to cancel, *the strike was called off*. call on to make a short visit to (a person); to appeal to, to request. call out to summon to action; to order to come out on strike. call sign, call signal a signal identifying a radio transmitter, *the call sign is Alpha Alpha*. call the tune to control the proceedings. call to mind to remember. call up to telephone to; to bring back to one's mind; to summon for military service. call-up *noun* a summons for military service. on call available to be called out on duty. within call near enough to be summoned by calling. caller *noun*

calligraphy (kă-**lig**- răfee) *noun* **1** beautiful handwriting; the art of producing this. **2** handwriting. calligrapher *noun* [from Greek *kalos* = beautiful, + *-graphy*]

calling *noun* an occupation, a profession or trade; a vocation.

Calliope (kă-**ly**-ŏ-pee) (*Gk. & Rom. myth.*) the Muse of epic poetry.

calliper (**kal**-ĭ-per) *noun* a metal support for a weak or injured leg. **callipers** *plural noun* compasses for measuring the diameter of tubes or of round objects.

callistemon (kă-**lis**-tĕ-mŏn) *noun* an Australian shrub or small tree, popularly called a *bottlebrush*.

callisthenics *plural noun* exercises to develop elegance and grace of movement.

callop *noun* an Australian edible freshwater fish, also called *golden perch* or *yellowbelly*.

callosity (kă-**loss**-ĭ-tee) *noun* **1** abnormal hardness of the skin. **2** a callus.

callous (**kal**-ŭs) *adjective* **1** unsympathetic. **2** (also **calloused**) hardened, having calluses. **callously** *adverb*, **callousness** *noun*

callow (*rhymes with* shallow) *adjective* immature and inexperienced. **callowly** *adverb*, **callowness** *noun*

callus (**kal**-ŭs) *noun* (*plural* **calluses**) an area of thick hardened skin or tissue.

calm *adjective* **1** quiet and still, not windy. **2** not excited or agitated. **3** casual and confident. – **calm** *noun* a calm condition or period, lack of strong winds. – **calm** *verb* to make or become calm. **calmly** *adverb*, **calmness** *noun*

calorie *noun* a unit for measuring a quantity of heat: **1** (in full **small calorie**) the energy needed to raise the temperature of one gram of water by 1°C. **2** (in full **large calorie**) the energy needed to raise the temperature of one kilogram of water by 1°C, often used to measure the energy value of foods. **caloric** *adjective* [from Latin *calor* = heat]

Usage The energy value of foods is now generally measured in *kilojoules*.

---

calorific *adjective* producing heat.

calorimeter (kal-ŏ-**rim**-ĕ-ter) *noun* a device used in the measurement of thermal constants such as specific heat.

calumny (**kal**-ŭm-nee) *noun* **1** slander. **2** a slanderous statement.

Calvary the place (just outside ancient Jerusalem) where Christ was crucified.

calve *verb* to give birth to a calf.

Calvin, John (1509–64), French Protestant religious reformer, living in Switzerland.

Calvinism *noun* the teachings of John Calvin and of his followers. **Calvinist** *noun*, **Calvinistic** *adjective*

calx *noun* (*plural* **calces**, *pr.* **kal**-seez) the powdery or crumbling substance left after the burning of a metal or mineral.

calypso *noun* (*plural* **calypsos**) a West Indian song with a variable rhythm and topical usually improvised lyrics.

calyx (**kay**-liks) *noun* (*plural* **calyces**) **1** a ring of leaves (*sepals*) enclosing an unopened flower bud. **2** a cuplike cavity or organ.

cam *noun* a projecting part on a wheel or shaft, shaped or mounted so that its circular motion transmits an up-and-down or back-and-forth motion to another part.

camaraderie (kam-ă-**rah**-dĕ-ree) *noun* comradeship. [French]

camber *noun* a slight arch or upward curve given to a surface, especially of a road. **cambered** *adjective*

cambium *noun* (in woody plants) a layer of tissue in stems and roots that increases their girth by new tissue produced by division of its cells. [Latin, = an exchange]

Cambodia (kam-**boh**-dee-ă) a monarchy in SE Asia between Thailand and the south of Vietnam; formerly called Kampuchea. **Cambodian** *adjective* & *noun*

Cambrian *adjective* **1** Welsh. **2** of the first period of the Palaeozoic era. – **Cambrian** *noun* this period.

cambric *noun* thin linen or cotton cloth.

Cambridge a city in England, seat of a major university.

camcorder *noun* a combined video camera and sound recorder.

came *see* **come**.

camel *noun* **1** a long-necked animal with either one or two humps on its back, used in the desert for riding and for carrying goods. (See also **dromedary**.) **2** fawn colour.

camellia (kă-**mee**-lee-ă) an evergreen shrub native to eastern Asia, with shiny leaves and showy flowers.

Camelot (**kam**-ĕ-lot) (in legend) the place where King Arthur held his court.

camembert (**kam**-ĕm-bair) *noun* a soft rich cheese originally made in Normandy, France.

cameo (**kam**-ee-oh) *noun* (*plural* **cameos**) **1** a small piece of hard stone carved with a raised design, especially with two coloured layers cut so that one serves as a background to the design. **2** something small but well executed, e.g. a short description or a part in a play.

camera *noun* an apparatus for taking photographs, moving pictures, or television pictures. □ **camera obscura** a darkened box or room with a hole at one end to admit rays of light that cast an image of distant objects on to the opposite wall. **in camera** (of the hearing of evidence or lawsuits) in the judge's private room; in private, in secret. [Latin, = a room]

cameraman *noun* (*plural* **cameramen**) a person whose job is to operate a film camera or television camera.

Cameroon (kam-ĕ-**roon**) a republic on the west coast of Africa. **Cameroonian** *adjective* & *noun*

camisole (**kam**-ĭ-sohl) *noun* a woman's garment or undergarment for the upper part of the body, usually with shoulder straps.

camomile (**kam**-ŏ-myl) a sweet-smelling plant with daisy-like flowers which are dried for use in medicine as a tonic.

camouflage (**kam**-ŏ-flah*zh*) *noun* a method of disguising or concealing objects by colouring or covering them so that they look like part of their surroundings. –**camouflage** *verb* to conceal in this way. [from French *camoufler* = to disguise]

camp¹ *noun* **1** a place where people live temporarily in tents, huts, or similar shelters; a place where troops are lodged or trained. **2** the occupants of such a place. **3** a group of people with the same ideals. –**camp** *verb* **1** to make or live in a camp. **2** to live temporarily as if in a camp. □ **camp bed** a folding portable bed. [same origin as *campus*]

camp² *adjective* **1** effeminate, homosexual. **2** exaggerated in style, especially for humorous effect. –**camp** *noun* such a style or manner.

campaign *noun* **1** a series of military operations with a set purpose, usually in one area. **2** a similar series of planned activities, *an advertising campaign*. –**campaign** *verb* to take part in a campaign. **campaigner** *noun*

campanology (kam-pă-**nol**-ŏ-jee) *noun* the study of bells (their ringing, founding, etc.). **campanologist** *noun*

campanula (kăm-**pan**-yŭ-lă) *noun* a plant with bell-shaped usually blue or white flowers.

camper *noun* **1** a person who is camping. **2** (in full **campervan**) a large motor vehicle with beds, stove, etc.

camphor *noun* a strong-smelling white substance used in medicine and mothballs and in making plastics.

camphorated *adjective* containing camphor.

campion *noun* a wild plant with pink or white flowers.

campsite *noun* a place for camping, especially one equipped for holidaymakers.

campus *noun* (*plural* **campuses**) the grounds and buildings of a university, college, or school. [Latin, = field]

camshaft *noun* a shaft carrying cams.

can¹ *noun* **1** a metal or plastic container for liquids. **2** a sealed tin in which food or drink is preserved. **3** either of these with its contents; the amount it contains. –**can** *verb* (**canned, canning**) to preserve in a sealed can. □ **carry the can** (*informal*) to bear the responsibility or blame. **canner** *noun*

can² *auxiliary verb* expressing ability or knowledge of how to do something (*he can play the violin*) or permission (*you can go*) or desire or liberty to act (*we cannot allow this*). [from an old word meaning 'know']

Usage To ask or give permission in more formal speech use *may*, as in *May I go?* and *You may go*.

Canaan the land (later known as Palestine) that the Israelites gradually conquered and occupied in Old Testament times.

Canada a country in North America, a member of the Commonwealth. **Canadian** *adjective* & *noun*

canal *noun* **1** a channel cut through land for navigation or irrigation. **2** a tubular passage through which food or air passes in a plant or animal body, *the alimentary canal*. [same origin as *channel*]

canalise (**kan**-ă-lyz) *verb* (also **-ize**) to channel. **canalisation** *noun*

canapé (**kan**-ă-pay) *noun* a small piece of bread or pastry spread with savoury food.

canary *noun* a small yellow songbird.

Canary Islands (also **Canaries**) a group of islands, provinces of Spain, off the NW coast of Africa.

canasta (kă-**nas**-tă) *noun* a card game played with two packs of cards including jokers. [Spanish, = basket]

Canberra (**kan**-bě-ră) the capital of Australia and of the Australian Capital Territory.

cancan *noun* a lively stage dance involving high kicking, performed by women in long skirts and petticoats.

cancel *verb* (**cancelled**, **cancelling**) **1** to say that (something already decided upon or arranged) will not be done or take place. **2** to order (a thing) to be discontinued. **3** to neutralise, *forgot to cancel my indicator*. **4** to cross out. **5** to divide (the numerator and denominator of a fraction) by the same factor; to remove (a common factor) from two sides of an equation etc., usually by crossing it out. **6** to mark (a stamp or ticket) in order to prevent further use. □ **cancel out** to counterbalance, to neutralise (each other). **cancellation** *noun*

Cancer a sign of the zodiac, the Crab, which the sun enters about 21 June. □ **tropic of Cancer** *see* tropic. **Cancerian** (kan-**seer**-ree-ăn) *adjective* & *noun*

cancer *noun* **1** any malignant growth or tumour from an abnormal or uncontrolled division of body cells. **2** a disease caused by this. **3** something evil that spreads destructively. **cancerous** *adjective* [from Latin *cancer* = crab]

candelabrum (kandě-**lab**-rŭm) *noun* (*plural* **candelabra**) a large branched candlestick or holder for lights. [from Latin *candela* = candle]

candid *adjective* frank, not hiding one's thoughts. **candidly** *adverb*, **candidness** *noun* [from Latin *candidus* = white]

candidate *noun* **1** a person who seeks or is nominated for appointment to an office or position or membership. **2** a person taking an examination. **candidacy** (**kan**-did-ă-see) *noun*, **candidature** (**kan**-did-ă-cher) *noun* [from Latin *candidus* = white (because Roman candidates for office had to wear a pure white toga)]

candied (**kan**-deed) *adjective* encrusted with sugar, preserved in sugar. □ **candied peel** peel of citrus fruits candied for use in cooking. [from *candy*]

candle *noun* a stick of wax with a wick through it, giving light when burning. □ **cannot hold a candle to** is very inferior to. **the game is not worth the candle** the result does not justify the trouble or cost.

candlelight *noun* the light of a candle or candles. **candlelit** *adjective*

Candlemas *noun* the feast of the Purification of the Virgin Mary, when candles are blessed (2 February).

candlestick *noun* a holder for one or more candles.

candlewick *noun* **1** a fabric with a raised tufted pattern worked in soft cotton yarn. **2** this yarn.

candour (**kan**-der) *noun* candid speech or quality, frankness.

candy *noun* **1** (in full **sugar candy**) sugar crystallised by repeated boiling and slow evaporation. **2** (*Amer.*) sweets, a sweet. –**candy** *verb* to preserve (fruit etc.) in candy. □ **candy stripes** alternate stripes of white and colour. **candy-striped** *adjective* [from Arabic *kand* = sugar]

candyfloss (*Brit.*) = fairy floss.

cane *noun* **1** the hollow jointed stem of tall reeds and grasses (e.g. bamboo, sugar cane), the solid stem of slender palms (e.g. Malacca). **2** the material of these used for making furniture etc. **3** a stem or a length of it, or a slender rod, used as a walking stick or to support a plant etc., or as a stick for use in corporal punishment. **4** a raspberry or blackberry plant. –**cane** *verb* **1** to punish by beating with a cane. **2** to weave cane into (a chair etc.). □ **cane sugar** sugar obtained from the juice of sugar cane. **cane toad** a large toad introduced into Queensland to control insects in sugar cane plantations, but spreading more widely.

canine (**kay**-nyn) *adjective* of dogs; of the animal family that includes dogs, dingoes, wolves, foxes, etc. –**canine** *noun* **1** a dog. **2** a **canine tooth**, a strong pointed tooth next to the incisors. [from Latin *canis* = dog]

canister *noun* **1** a metal box or other container. **2** a cylinder, filled with shot or tear gas, that bursts and releases its contents when fired from a gun or thrown.

canker *noun* **1** a disease that destroys the wood of plants and trees. **2** a disease that causes ulcerous sores in animals. **3** a corrupting influence.

cannabis (**kan**-ă-bĭs) *noun* **1** a hemp plant. **2** a preparation of this for smoking or chewing as an intoxicant drug; marijuana. [the Latin name of the hemp plant, used as its botanical name]

canned *see* can¹. –**canned** *adjective* **1** recorded for reproduction, *canned music*. **2** tinned, *canned fruit*.

129

cannelloni (kan-ĕ-**loh**-nee) *plural noun* rolls of pasta containing meat and seasoning. [Italian]

cannery *noun* a canning-factory.

cannibal *noun* a person who eats human flesh; an animal that eats its own kind. **cannibalism** *noun*, **cannibalistic** *adjective* [named after the Caribs, a supposedly man-eating nation in the West Indies]

cannibalise *verb* (also -**ize**) to dismantle (a machine etc.) in order to provide spare parts for others. **cannibalisation** *noun*

cannon *noun* 1 (*plural* **cannon**) an old type of large heavy gun firing solid metal balls. 2 an automatic shell-firing gun used in aircraft. 3 a shot in billiards in which the player's ball hits the two other balls in succession. – **cannon** *verb* (**cannoned**, **cannoning**) 1 to collide heavily. 2 to make a cannon at billiards. □ **cannon fodder** soldiers regarded merely as material to be expended in war.

cannonade *noun* continuous heavy gunfire.

cannot = can not.

canny *adjective* (**cannier**, **canniest**) shrewd. **cannily** *adverb*, **canniness** *noun*

canoe *noun* a light narrow boat propelled by paddles. – **canoe** *verb* (**canoed**, **canoeing**) to paddle or travel in a canoe. **canoeist** *noun*

canon *noun* 1 a general principle. 2 a set of writings accepted as genuinely by a particular author; sacred writings included in the Bible. 3 a member of the clergy with duties in a cathedral. 4 a member of certain Roman Catholic religious orders. 5 the central unchanging part of the Roman Catholic mass. 6 a passage or piece of music in which a theme is taken up by two or more parts in succession. □ **canon law** Church law. [from Greek *kanon* = rule]

canonical (kă-**non**-ikăl) *adjective* 1 ordered by canon law. 2 included in the canon of Scripture. 3 standard, accepted. **canonicals** *plural noun* the canonical dress of clergy. **canonically** *adverb*

canonise *verb* (also -**ize**) to declare officially to be a saint. **canonisation** *noun*

canopied *adjective* having a canopy.

canopy *noun* 1 a hanging cover forming a shelter above a throne, bed, or person etc. 2 any similar covering. 3 the part of a parachute that spreads in the air. 4 the uppermost layers of leaves etc. in a forest.

cant¹ *verb* to slope, to tilt. – **cant** *noun* a tilted or sloping position. [from a Dutch word meaning 'edge']

cant² *noun* 1 insincere talk. 2 jargon. [from Latin *cantare* = sing]

can't (*informal*) = cannot.

cantaloupe (**kan**-tă-loop) *noun* (also **cantaloup**) a small round melon with orange-coloured flesh, a rockmelon.

cantankerous (kan-**tank**-ĕ-rŭs) *adjective* bad-tempered. **cantankerously** *adverb*, **cantankerousness** *noun*

cantata (kan-**tah**-tă) *noun* a musical composition, like an oratorio but shorter. [from Italian *cantare* = sing]

canteen *noun* 1 a restaurant or cafeteria for the employees of a factory, office, etc. 2 a school shop selling lunches and snack food, a tuck shop. 3 a case or box containing a set of cutlery. 4 a soldier's or camper's water flask.

canter *noun* a slow easy gallop. – **canter** *verb* to ride at a canter, to gallop gently. [short for 'Canterbury gallop', the gentle pace at which pilgrims were said to travel to Canterbury in the Middle Ages]

Canterbury a city in SE England, seat of the archbishop who is Primate of All England.

canticle (**kan**-ti-kŭl) *noun* a song or chant with words taken from the Bible, e.g. the Magnificat. [from Latin, = little song]

cantilever (**kan**-tĭ-lee-ver) *noun* a projecting beam or girder supporting a balcony or similar structure.

canto *noun* (*plural* **cantos**) each of the sections into which a long poem is divided. [Italian, = song]

canton *noun* a division of a country, especially of Switzerland.

Cantonese *noun* 1 (*plural* **Cantonese**) a native or inhabitant of the city of Canton in China. 2 a Chinese language spoken in southern China and in Hong Kong. – **Cantonese** *adjective* of Canton or its people or language.

cantor *noun* 1 the leader of the singing of a church choir in a religious service. 2 the leader of the prayers in a synagogue. [from Latin *canere* = sing]

Canute = Cnut.

canvas *noun* 1 strong coarse cloth used for making tents and sails etc. and by artists for painting on. 2 a piece of canvas for painting on, especially in oils, an oil painting. [from

Latin *cannabis* = hemp, from whose fibres cloth was made]

canvass *verb* **1** to visit in order to ask for votes, orders for goods etc., or opinions. **2** to propose (a plan). –**canvass** *noun* canvassing. **canvasser** *noun*

canyon (**kan**-yŏn) *noun* a deep gorge, usually with a river flowing through it. [from Spanish *cañón* = tube]

cap *noun* **1** a soft head covering without a brim but often with a peak. **2** an academic headdress, a mortarboard. **3** a cap-like cover or top. **4** = percussion cap. –**cap** *verb* (**capped**, **capping**) **1** to put a cap on; to cover the top or end of. **2** to excel, to outdo; *cap a joke*, to tell another, usually a better one. **3** to set a limit to (expenditure etc.). □ **cap and trade** a system in which a government sets a limit on carbon emissions, and any company exceeding its quota must buy credits from companies which are below their quota.

capable *adjective* **1** competent. **2** having a certain ability or capacity, *quite capable of lying*. **capably** *adverb*, **capability** *noun*

capacious (kă-**pay**-shŭs) *adjective* roomy, able to hold much. **capaciously** *adverb*, **capaciousness** *noun*

capacitance *noun* **1** ability to store an electric charge. **2** the measure of this; the ratio of the change in the electric charge in a system to a corresponding change in its potential.

capacitor (kă-**pas**-ĭ-ter) *noun* a device storing a charge of electricity.

capacity *noun* **1** the ability to contain or accommodate, the amount that can be contained; *full to capacity*, completely full. **2** ability, capability; *working at full capacity*, as intensively as possible. **3** a position or function, *signed it in his capacity as chairman*.

cape¹ *noun* **1** a cloak. **2** a very short similarly shaped part of a coat etc., covering the shoulders.

cape² *noun* a coastal promontory. □ **the Cape** the Cape of Good Hope; the province containing it, Cape Province.

Cape Horn the southernmost point of South America, on an island south of Tierra del Fuego, belonging to Chile.

Cape of Good Hope a mountainous promontory near the southern extremity of South Africa, south of Cape Town.

Cape Province the southern province of the Republic of South Africa.

caper¹ *verb* to jump or run about playfully. –**caper** *noun* **1** capering. **2** (*informal*) an activity, an occupation, an escapade.

caper² *noun* **1** a bramble-like shrub. **2** one of its buds, which are pickled for use as a flavouring.

Cape Town the legislative capital and chief port of South Africa.

Cape Verde Islands (kayp **verd**) a republic consisting of a group of islands off the west coast of Africa. **Cape Verdean** *adjective* & *noun*

Cape York the northernmost point of mainland Australia at the tip of the Cape York Peninsula in Queensland.

capillary (kă-**pil**-ă-ree) *noun* any of the very fine branching blood vessels that connect veins and arteries. –**capillary** *adjective* of or like a hair; of hairlike diameter. □ **capillary action** (also **capillarity**) the rise or fall of a liquid through surface tension when in contact with the walls of a narrow tube, or in absorbent material such as wicks or blotting paper. [from Latin *capillus* = hair]

capital *adjective* **1** principal, most important; *capital city*, the chief town of a country. **2** (*informal*) excellent. **3** involving the death penalty, *a capital offence*; *capital punishment*. **4** very serious, fatal, *a capital error*. **5** (of letters) of the form and size used to begin a name or a sentence, *a capital A*. –**capital** *noun* **1** a capital city. **2** a capital letter. **3** the head or top part of a pillar. **4** wealth or property that is used or invested to produce more wealth; the money with which a business etc. is started. □ **capital gain** profit from the sale of investments or property. **capital goods** goods such as ships, railways, machinery, etc., used in producing consumer goods. **capital sum** a lump sum of money, especially that payable to an insured person. **make capital out of** to use (a situation etc.) to one's own advantage. [from Latin *caput* = head]

capitalise (**kap**-ĭ-tă-lyz) *verb* (also -ize) **1** to write or print as a capital letter. **2** to convert into capital, to provide with capital. □ **capitalise on** to profit by, to use (a thing) to one's advantage. **capitalisation** *noun*

capitalism (**kap**-ĭ-tă-lizm) *noun* an economic system in which trade and industry are controlled by private owners for profit.

capitalist (**kap**-ĭ-tă-list) *noun* **1** one who has much capital invested, a rich person. **2** one who favours capitalism. –**capitalist** *adjective* of or favouring capitalism. **capitalistic** *adjective*

capitation *noun* a tax or fee levied per person.

Capitol 1 the building in Washington DC in which the Congress of the USA meets. **2** the temple of Jupiter in ancient Rome.

capitulate *verb* to surrender. **capitulation** *noun*

capo (**ka**-poh) *noun* (*plural* **capos**) a device fitted across the strings of a guitar, banjo, etc. to raise their pitch equally. [from Italian *capo tasto* = head stop]

capon (**kay**-pŏn) *noun* a domestic cock castrated and fattened for eating.

cappuccino (kah-pŭ-**chee**-noh) *noun* (*plural* **cappuccinos** *or* **cappuccini**) espresso coffee topped with milk made frothy with pressurised steam. [Italian]

Capri (kă-**pree**) an island off the west coast of Italy, in the Bay of Naples.

caprice (kă-**prees**) *noun* **1** a whim. **2** a piece of music in a lively fanciful style.

capricious (kă-**prish**-ŭs) *adjective* **1** guided by caprice, impulsive. **2** changeable, *a capricious breeze*. **capriciously** *adverb*, **capriciousness** *noun*

Capricorn *noun* a sign of the zodiac, the Goat, which the sun enters about 22 December. □ **tropic of Capricorn** *see* **tropic**. **Capricornian** *adjective* & *noun* [from Latin *caper* = goat + *cornu* = horn]

capsicum (**kap**-sĭ-kŭm) *noun* **1** a plant with hollow edible fruits, especially varieties of sweet pepper. **2** the fruits themselves, usually red, green, or yellow, used as a vegetable. □ **capsicum spray** an oil extracted from cayenne pepper, used especially by police to ward off attackers etc.

capsize *verb* to overturn, *a wave capsized the boat*; *the boat capsized*.

capstan (**kap**-stăn) *noun* **1** a thick revolving post used to pull in a rope or cable that winds round it as it turns, e.g. for raising a ship's anchor. **2** a revolving spindle on a tape recorder. □ **capstan lathe** a lathe with a revolving tool holder.

capsule *noun* **1** a small soluble case in which a dose of medicine is enclosed for swallowing. **2** a plant's seed case that splits open when ripe. **3** a detachable compartment of a spacecraft.

captain *noun* **1** a person given authority over a group or team. **2** an army officer ranking below a major and above a lieutenant. **3** a naval officer ranking below a rear admiral and above a commander. **4** the person commanding a ship. **5** the pilot of a civil aircraft. –**captain** *verb* to act as captain of. **captaincy** *noun* [same origin as *capital*]

caption (**kap**-shŏn) *noun* **1** a short title or heading. **2** a description or explanation printed with an illustration etc. **3** words shown on a cinema or television screen.

captious (**kap**-shŭs) *adjective* fond of finding fault or raising objections about trivial matters. **captiously** *adverb*, **captiousness** *noun*

captivate *verb* to capture the fancy of, to charm. **captivation** *noun*

captive *adjective* **1** taken prisoner. **2** kept as a prisoner, unable to escape. –**captive** *noun* a captive person or animal. □ **captive audience** people who cannot get away easily and therefore cannot avoid being addressed.

captivity *noun* the state of being held captive. –**the Captivity** the exile of the Jews in Babylon in the 6th century BC.

captor *noun* one who captures a person or animal.

capture *verb* **1** to make a prisoner of. **2** to take or obtain by force, trickery, attraction, or skill. **3** to put (data) into a form accessible by computer. **4** to record on film etc; to portray in permanent form. **5** (of a river) to divert the upper course of (another river) into its own waters by encroaching on the other's basin. –**capture** *noun* **1** capturing. **2** a person or thing captured. [from Latin *capere* = take]

Capuchin (**kap**-yŭ-chĭn) *noun* a friar of a branch of the Franciscan order.

car *noun* **1** a motor car. **2** a carriage of a specified type, *dining car*; *jaunting car*. **3** the passenger compartment of an airship, balloon, cable railway, or lift. □ **car park** an area for parking cars. [from Latin *carrus* = wagon]

Caracas (kă-**rak**-ăs) the capital of Venezuela.

carafe (kă-**raf**) *noun* a glass bottle in which wine or water is served at the table. [from Arabic *gharrafa*]

caramel *noun* **1** burnt sugar used for colouring and flavouring food. **2** a kind of toffee tasting like this.

caramelise *verb* (also **-ize**) to turn or be turned into caramel. **caramelisation** *noun*

carapace (**ka**-ră-payss) *noun* the shell on the back of a tortoise or crustacean.

carat (**ka**-răt) *noun* **1** a unit of weight for precious stones, 200 milligrams. **2** a measure of the purity of gold, pure gold being 24 carat.

Caravaggio (ka-ră-**vah**-jee-oh), Michelangelo Merisi da (1573–1610), Italian painter, noted for his realistic depiction of traditional religious subjects.

caravan *noun* **1** an enclosed carriage equipped for living in, able to be towed by a vehicle; a covered cart used similarly, towed by a horse. **2** a company of people (e.g. merchants) travelling together across desert country. caravanning *noun* travelling by caravan, especially on holiday. [from Persian *karwan*]

caraway *noun* a plant with spicy seeds that are used for flavouring cakes etc.

carbide (**kar**-byd) *noun* a compound of carbon and one other element; the compound used in making acetylene gas.

carbine (**kar**-byn) *noun* a short light rifle.

carbohydrate *noun* an organic compound, such as the sugars and starches, composed of carbon, oxygen, and hydrogen. carbohydrates *plural noun* starchy foods.

carbolic *noun* (in full carbolic acid) phenol, especially when used as a disinfectant.

carbon *noun* **1** a chemical element (symbol C) that is present in all living matter and occurs in its pure form as diamond and graphite. **2** a rod of carbon in an arc lamp. **3** carbon paper; a copy made with this. ☐ carbon copy a copy made with carbon paper; an exact copy. carbon cycle the series of processes in which carbon dioxide from the air is converted by plants into more complex substances, which are eaten by animals, and is finally released again into the air by their respiration or when organic substances decay. carbon dating a method of deciding the age of prehistoric objects by measuring the decay of radiocarbon in them. carbon dioxide a colourless odourless gas formed by the burning of carbon or breathed out by animals in respiration. carbon fibre a carbon filament used to strengthen other fibres etc. carbon footprint the amount of carbon dioxide produced by a particular person, group, etc. carbon monoxide a very poisonous gas formed when carbon burns incompletely, occurring e.g. in the exhaust of motor engines. carbon paper thin paper coated with pigment, placed between sheets of writing paper for making copies of what is

written or typed on the top sheet. carbon sink a part of the environment viewed in terms of its ability to absorb carbon dioxide from the atmosphere.

carbonate *noun* a compound that releases carbon dioxide when mixed with acid.

carbonated *adjective* charged with carbon dioxide; *carbonated drinks*, made fizzy with this. carbonation *noun*

carbonic acid *noun* a weak acid formed from carbon dioxide and water.

carboniferous (kar-bŏ-**nif**-ĕ-rŭs) *adjective* producing coal. –Carboniferous *adjective* of the geological period in the Palaeozoic era when many coal deposits were created. –Carboniferous *noun* this period. [from *carbon*, + Latin *ferre* = to bear]

carbonise *verb* (also -ize) **1** to convert (a substance that contains carbon) into carbon alone, e.g. by heating or burning it. **2** to coat with carbon. carbonisation *noun*

carborundum (kar-bŏ-**run**-dŭm) *noun* a hard compound of carbon and silicon used for polishing and grinding things.

carboy (**kar**-boi) *noun* a large round bottle surrounded by a protecting framework, used for transporting liquids safely.

carbuncle *noun* **1** a severe abscess in the skin. **2** a bright red gem cut in a knoblike shape.

carburettor *noun* an apparatus for mixing fuel and air in an internal-combustion engine.

carcass *noun* (also carcase) **1** the dead body of an animal, especially one prepared for cutting up as meat. **2** the bony part of the body of a bird before or after cooking. **3** a framework (of a building, ship, etc.); the foundation structure of a tyre.

carcinogen (kar-**sin**-ŏ-jĕn) *noun* a cancer-producing substance. [from *carcinoma*, + Greek *-genes* = born]

carcinogenic (kar-sĭ-nŏ-**jen**-ik) *adjective* producing cancer.

carcinoma (kar-sĭ-**noh**-mă) *noun* (*plural* carcinomas or carcinomata) a cancerous growth. [from Greek *karkinos* = crab]

card[1] *noun* **1** thick stiff paper or thin cardboard; a small piece of this used e.g. to send messages or greetings, or to record information. **2** a small flat usually rectangular piece of thin pasteboard, plastic, etc., recording membership or identifying the bearer; a cash or credit card. **3** a playing card. **4** (*informal*) an odd or amusing person. cards noun card-playing, card games. □ **be on the cards** to be likely or possible. **card-carrying member** a registered member of a political party, trade union, etc. **card game** a game using playing cards. **card index** an index in which each item is entered on a separate card. **card-sharp**, **card-sharper** nouns a person who makes a living by cheating others at card games. **put one's cards on the table** to be frank about one's resources and intentions.

card² noun a wire brush or toothed instrument for cleaning or combing wool. –**card** verb to clean or comb with this.

cardamom (**kar**-dă-mŏm) noun an aromatic plant of the ginger family from Sri Lanka and India; its seed pods used as a spice.

cardboard noun pasteboard, especially for making into boxes.

cardiac (**kar**-dee-ak) adjective of the heart. [from Greek kardia = heart]

Cardiff the capital of Wales.

cardigan noun a knitted jacket. [named after the 7th Earl of Cardigan (died 1868)]

cardinal adjective 1 chief, most important, the cardinal virtues. 2 deep scarlet. –**cardinal** noun a member of the Sacred College of the Roman Catholic Church, which elects the Pope. □ **cardinal numbers** the whole numbers, 1, 2, 3, etc. **cardinal points** the four main points of the compass, North, East, South, and West.

cardiogram noun an electrocardiogram. [from Greek kardia = heart, + -gram]

cardiograph noun a device recording heart movements; an electrocardiograph. [from Greek kardia = heart, + -graph]

cardioid noun a heart-shaped curve.

cardiology (kar-dee-**ol**-ŏjee) noun the scientific study of diseases and abnormalities of the heart. **cardiological** adjective, **cardiologist** noun [from Greek kardia = heart, + -logy]

cardiovascular adjective of the heart and blood vessels.

care noun 1 serious attention and thought, planned with care. 2 caution to avoid damage or loss, handle with care. 3 protection, charge, supervision, left the child in her sister's care. 4 worry, anxiety, freedom from care. –**care** verb 1 to feel concern or interest. 2 to feel affection or liking, don't care for cheese. 3 to feel willing, would you care to try one?

□ **care for** to have in one's care; to take care of. **care of, c/o** to the address of (someone who will deliver or forward things), write to him care of his bank. **take care** to be cautious. **take care of** to take charge of; to see to the safety or well-being of; to deal with. [from Old English caru = sorrow]

careen (kă-**reen**) verb 1 to tilt or keel over to one side. 2 to swerve.

career noun 1 progress through life, especially in a profession. 2 an occupation, a way of making a living, especially one with opportunities for advancement or promotion. 3 quick or violent forward movement; stopped him in mid-career, as he was rushing. –**career** verb to move swiftly or wildly.

carefree adjective light-hearted through being free from anxiety or responsibility.

careful adjective 1 giving serious attention and thought, painstaking, a careful worker. 2 done with care, careful work. 3 cautious, avoiding damage or loss. **carefully** adverb, **carefulness** noun

caregiver noun a person who cares for a child or an elderly or disabled person.

careless adjective 1 not taking care. 2 done without care. 3 unthinking, insensitive. 4 casual and light-hearted. **carelessly** adverb, **carelessness** noun

carer noun a person who looks after a sick, disabled, or elderly person at home.

caress (kă-**ress**) noun a loving touch, a kiss. –**caress** verb to touch lovingly, to kiss.

caret (**ka**-rĕt) noun a mark (^) indicating a proposed insertion in printing or writing. [Latin, = it is lacking]

caretaker noun a person employed to look after a house or building. □ **caretaker government** one holding office temporarily until another can be elected.

careworn adjective showing signs of prolonged worry.

Carey, Peter (born 1944), Australian novelist and writer of short stories, whose novels include Oscar and Lucinda, Bliss, and Illywhacker.

cargo noun (plural cargoes) goods carried on a ship or aircraft. □ **cargo cult** a belief that ancestral spirits will come one day bringing cargoes of food and other goods.

Carib (**ka**-rib) noun 1 an indigenous inhabitant of the southern West Indies or the adjacent coasts. 2 their language.

Caribbean (ka-rĭ-**bee**-ăn) *noun* the Caribbean Sea, the part of the Atlantic between the southern West Indies and Central America. –Caribbean *adjective* **1** of this region. **2** of the Caribs.

caribou (**ka**-rĭ-boo) *noun* (*plural* caribou) a North American reindeer.

caricature (**ka**-rik-ă-tyoor *or* -choor) *noun* a picture, description, or imitation of a person or thing that exaggerates certain characteristics, especially for comic effect. –caricature *verb* to make a caricature of. caricaturist *noun* [from Italian *caricare* = exaggerate]

caries (**kair**-reez) *noun* (*plural* caries) decay in bones or teeth, *dental caries*. [Latin]

carillon (kă-**ril**-yŏn) *noun* a set of bells sounded either from a keyboard or mechanically.

caring *adjective* **1** kind, compassionate. **2** concerned with looking after people; *caring professions*, those that give professional social or medical care.

Carmelite (**kar**-mĕ-lyt) *noun* a member of an order of friars (also called *White Friars*) or of a corresponding order of nuns. [named after Mount Carmel in Palestine where the order was founded in the 12th century]

carmine (**kar**-myn) *adjective* & *noun* deep red.

carnage (**kar**-nij) *noun* the killing of many people.

carnal (**kar**-năl) *adjective* of the body or flesh, not spiritual, *carnal desires*. □ carnal knowledge (*Law*) sexual intercourse. carnally *adverb* [from Latin *carnis* = of flesh]

carnassial (kar-**nas**-ee-ăl) *noun* a carnassial tooth, each of the cutting-teeth in carnivorous animals, positioned before the molars. [from French *carnassier* = carnivore]

carnation *noun* a cultivated clove-scented pink with showy flowers.

carnelian *noun* = cornelian.

carnival *noun* **1** festivities and public merrymaking, usually with a procession, especially in the period between Epiphany and Lent. **2** a series of sporting events, *swimming carnival*. [named from the practice of giving up meat (Latin *carnis* = of flesh) during Lent]

carnivore (**kar**-nĭ-vor) *noun* a carnivorous animal.

carnivorous (kar-**niv**-ŏ-rŭs) *adjective* feeding on flesh or other animal matter. [from Latin *carnis* = of flesh, + *vorare* = devour]

carob (**ka**-rŏb) *noun* the bean-shaped edible pod of a Mediterranean evergreen tree, sometimes used as a substitute for chocolate.

carol *noun* a joyful song, especially a Christmas hymn. –carol *verb* (carolled, carolling) **1** to sing carols. **2** to sing joyfully.

Caroline Islands (also Carolines) a group of islands in the western Pacific Ocean, the majority forming the Federated States of Micronesia.

Carolingian *adjective* of the Frankish dynasty founded by Charlemagne. –Carolingian *noun* a member of this dynasty.

carotene (**ka**-rŏ-teen) *noun* an orange or red substance in plants that is a source of vitamin A.

carotid (kă-**rot**-ĭd) *noun* either of the carotid arteries, the two great arteries (one on either side of the neck) carrying blood to the head. –carotid *adjective* of these arteries.

carouse (kă-**rowz**) *verb* to drink and be merry. carousal *noun*

carousel (ka-rŭ-**sel**) *noun* **1** a merry-go-round. **2** a rotating conveyor or delivery system especially for luggage at an airport.

carp[1] *noun* (*plural* carp) an edible freshwater fish that lives in lakes and ponds.

carp[2] *verb* to keep finding fault, to raise petty objections.

carpal (**kar**-păl) *adjective* of the wrist joint. –carpal *noun* any of the wrist bones.

carpel (**kar**-pĕl) *noun* the female reproductive organ of a flower, the part in which the seeds develop.

Carpentaria, Gulf of a large indentation in the north coast of Australia between Arnhem Land and Cape York. [named in 1623 after Pieter de Carpentier, Governor-General of the Dutch East Indies]

carpenter *noun* a person who makes or repairs wooden objects and structures.

carpentry *noun* a carpenter's work.

carpet *noun* **1** a thick textile covering for floors. **2** a thick layer underfoot, *a carpet of leaves*. –carpet *verb* (carpeted, carpeting) **1** to cover with a carpet. **2** (*informal*) to reprimand. □ carpet shark a slow-moving eastern Australian shark with a variegated skin, a wobbegong. carpet snake a large non-venomous Australian python with a variegated skin. carpet sweeper a household device with revolving brushes for sweeping carpets. on the carpet (*informal*) being reprimanded.

carpeting *noun* 1 material for carpets.
2 (*informal*) a reprimand.

carport *noun* an open-sided shelter for a car, projecting from the side of a house.

carriage *noun* 1 a wheeled vehicle, usually horse-drawn, for carrying passengers. 2 a railway vehicle for passengers. 3 the carrying of goods from place to place; the cost of this. 4 a gun carriage. 5 a moving part carrying or holding something in a machine; the roller of a typewriter. 6 the posture of the body when walking. ☐ **carriage clock** a portable clock in a rectangular case with a handle on top.

carriageway *noun* the part of the road on which vehicles travel.

carrier *noun* 1 a person or thing that carries something. 2 a person or company that transports goods or people for payment. 3 a support for luggage or a seat for a passenger on a bicycle etc. 4 a person or animal that transmits a disease to others without being affected by it. 5 an aircraft carrier. ☐ **carrier pigeon** a homing pigeon used to carry messages tied to its leg or neck. **carrier wave** a high-frequency electromagnetic wave modulated either in amplitude or frequency to convey a signal.

carrion (**ka**-ree-ŏn) *noun* dead and decaying flesh. ☐ **carrion crow** a black crow that lives on carrion and small animals. [same origin as *carnal*]

Carroll, Lewis (pseudonym of Charles Lutwidge Dodgson, 1832–98), English writer, author of *Alice's Adventures in Wonderland* and *Through the Looking Glass*.

carrot *noun* 1 a plant with a tapering orange-coloured root. 2 this root, used as a vegetable. 3 a means of enticing someone to do something; *the carrot and the stick*, bribes and threats. **carrots** *noun* (*informal*) red hair; a red-haired person.

carroty *adjective* orange-red.

carry *verb* (**carried, carrying**) 1 to take from one place to another. 2 to have on one's person, *he is carrying a gun*. 3 to conduct, to take, *wires carry electric current*. 4 to support the weight of, to bear. 5 to involve, to entail, *the crime carries a life sentence*. 6 to extend; *don't carry modesty too far*, do not be too modest. 7 to reckon in the next column when adding figures. 8 to win, to capture; *the motion was carried*, was approved. 9 (of a newspaper or broadcast) to contain, *they all carried the story*. 10 to hold and move (the

body) in a certain way. 11 to be transmitted clearly, *sound carries across water*. 12 to be the driving force behind or mainstay of, *she carries the department*. ☐ **be carried away** to be very excited. **carry all before one** to be very successful. **carry conviction** to sound convincing. **carry-cot** *noun* a baby's portable cot. **carry forward** to transfer to a new page of accounts in bookkeeping. **carry off** (of a disease) to cause the death of; to win (a prize); to deal with (a situation) successfully. **carry on** to continue; to take part in (a conversation); to manage or conduct (a business etc.); (*informal*) to behave excitedly, to complain lengthily; (*informal*) to flirt, to have an affair. **carry-on** *noun* (also **carryings-on**) (*informal*) a fuss; excitement; questionable behaviour. **carry out** to put into practice, to accomplish. **carry over** to carry forward in bookkeeping. **carry weight** to be influential or important. [same origin as *car*]

carsick *adjective* made sick or queasy by the motion of a car. **carsickness** *noun*

cart *noun* 1 a two-wheeled vehicle used for carrying loads, pulled by a horse etc. 2 a light vehicle with a shaft, pushed or drawn by hand. –**cart** *verb* 1 to carry in a cart, to transport. 2 (*informal*) to carry laboriously, to lug. ☐ **put the cart before the horse** to put a thing first when it should logically come second.

cartage (**kar**-tij) *noun* 1 carting goods. 2 the cost of this.

carte blanche (kart **blahnsh**) *noun* full power to act as one thinks best. [French, = blank paper]

cartel (kar-**tel**) *noun* a combination of business firms to control production, marketing, etc. and avoid competing with one another.

carter *noun* 1 a person whose job is driving carts. 2 one whose trade is transporting goods.

Cartesian (kar-**tee**-zhăn) *adjective* of the philosopher Descartes (17th century) or his theories. ☐ **Cartesian coordinates** coordinates measured from straight axes that intersect.

Carthage an ancient Phoenician city on the north coast of Africa, near Tunis.

carthorse *noun* a strong horse fit for heavy work.

Carthusian (kar-**thew**-zee-ăn) *noun* a member of an order of monks founded at La Grande Chartreuse near Grenoble, France, in 1084.

cartilage *noun* 1 tough white flexible tissue attached to the bones of animals. 2 a structure made of this. **cartilaginous** (kar-tĭ-**laj**-ĭ-nŭs) *adjective*

cartography (kar-**tog**-răfee) *noun* map-drawing. **cartographer** *noun*, **cartographic** (kar-tŏ-**graf**-ik) *adjective* [from French *carte* = map, + -*graphy*]

carton *noun* **1** a cardboard or plastic container. **2** the amount it contains.

cartoon *noun* **1** an amusing drawing in a newspaper etc., especially as a comment on public matters. **2** a sequence of these telling a comic or serial story. **3** an animated cartoon. **4** a drawing made by an artist as a preliminary sketch for a painting etc. – **cartoon** *verb* to draw cartoons, to represent in a cartoon.

cartoonist *noun* a person who draws cartoons.

cartouche (kar-**toosh**) *noun* **1** a scroll-like ornamentation in architecture etc. **2** an oval emblem of an ancient Egyptian king.

cartridge *noun* **1** a tube or case containing explosive for firearms or blasting, with bullet or shot if for a rifle etc. **2** a sealed case holding film, recording-tape, etc., put into apparatus and removed from it as a unit. **3** the detachable head of a pickup on a record player, holding the stylus. □ **cartridge paper** thick strong paper.

cartwheel *noun* **1** the wheel of a cart. **2** a handspring in which the body turns with limbs spread like spokes of a wheel, balancing on each hand in turn.

cartwright *noun* a maker of carts.

carve *verb* **1** to form or produce or inscribe by cutting solid material. **2** to cut (cooked meat) into slices for eating. **3** to make by great effort, *carved out a career for himself.* □ **carve up** to divide into parts or shares. **carver** *noun*

carving *noun* a carved object or design.

caryatid (ka-ree-**at**-ĭd) *noun* a sculptured female figure used as a supporting pillar in a building.

Casanova (kas-ă-**noh**-vă) *noun* a man with a reputation for having many love affairs. [named after an 18th-century Italian]

cascade (kas-**kayd**) *noun* **1** a waterfall. **2** something falling or hanging like this. – **cascade** *verb* to fall as or like a cascade.

cascara (kas-**kar**-ă) *noun* the bark of a North American buckthorn, used as a laxative. [Spanish, *cascara sagrada* = sacred bark]

case¹ *noun* **1** an instance or example of the occurrence of something; an actual state of affairs. **2** a condition of disease or injury; a person suffering from this, *two cases of measles*. **3** something being investigated by police etc., *a murder case*. **4** a lawsuit. **5** a set of facts or arguments supporting something. **6** the form of a noun or pronoun that shows its relationship to another word, e.g. in *Mary's hat*, *'s* shows the possessive case. □ **in any case** whatever the facts are; whatever may happen. **in case** lest something should happen. **in case of** in the event of; *in case of fire*, if there should be a fire. [from Latin *casus* = occasion]

case² *noun* **1** a container or protective covering. **2** this with its contents, the amount it contains. **3** a suitcase. – **case** *verb* **1** to enclose in a case. **2** (*informal*) to reconnoitre (a house etc.) before committing a robbery. □ **case-harden** *verb* to harden the surface of (metal) by carbonising it; to make unfeeling or unsympathetic. **case-sensitive** differentiating between upper and lower case letters. [from Latin *capsa* = box]

casebook *noun* a record of legal or medical cases.

casein (**kay**-seen) *noun* a protein found in milk, the basis of cheese. [from Latin *caseus* = cheese]

casement *noun* a window that opens on hinges at the side, like a door.

casework *noun* social work that involves dealing with people who have problems. **caseworker** *noun*

cash *noun* **1** money in coin or notes. **2** immediate payment for goods, as opposed to credit. **3** (*informal*) money, wealth, *they're short of cash*. – **cash** *verb* to give or get cash for, *cashed a cheque*. □ **cash card** a plastic card enabling the holder to draw money from a bank account especially using an automated teller machine. **cash crop** a crop grown for selling. **cash flow** the movement of money out of and into a business as goods are bought and sold, affecting its ability to make cash payments. **cash in on** to make a large profit from; to turn to one's advantage. **cash on delivery** payment to be made when goods are delivered, not at the time of purchase. **cash register** a machine in a shop etc. with a drawer for money and a mechanism for recording the amount of each sale. **cashable** *adjective*, **cashless** *adjective*

cashew (**kash**-oo) *noun* **1** the small edible kidney-shaped nut of a tropical tree. **2** this tree.

cashier[1] *noun* a person employed to receive and pay out money in a bank, shop etc.

cashier[2] *verb* to dismiss from service, especially with disgrace.

cashmere *noun* **1** a very fine soft wool, especially that from the Kashmir goat. **2** fabric made from this. [old spelling of *Kashmir* in Asia]

casing *noun* **1** a protective covering. **2** the material from which this is made.

casino *noun* (*plural* **casinos**) a public building or room for gambling and other amusements.

cask *noun* **1** a barrel, especially for alcoholic drinks. **2** its contents. **3** (*Austral.*) a cardboard box enclosing a plastic or foil bag fitted with a tap, used for storing and serving wine or juice.

casket *noun* a small usually ornamental box for holding valuables etc.

Caspian Sea a landlocked sea between SE Europe and Asia, the world's largest inland sea.

Cassandra (kă-**san**-dră) *noun* a person who prophesies disaster. [named after a prophetess in Greek legend who foretold evil events but was doomed never to be believed]

cassata (kă-**sah**-tă) *noun* ice cream containing fruit and nuts. [Italian]

cassava (kă-**sah**-vă) *noun* a tropical plant with starchy roots from which tapioca is obtained.

casserole *noun* **1** a covered dish in which meat etc. is cooked and served. **2** food cooked in this. – **casserole** *verb* to cook (meat etc.) in a casserole. [French from Greek, = little cup]

cassette (kă-**set**) *noun* a small sealed case containing a reel of film or magnetic tape. □ **cassette player** an apparatus for playing audio cassettes. [French, = little case]

cassia *noun* **1** any of various Australian shrubs or trees with golden flowers. **2** a plant yielding senna. **3** a kind of cinnamon, the bark of an unrelated tree.

cassock *noun* a long garment worn by certain clergy and members of a church choir.

cassowary (**kas**-ŏ-wă-ree) *noun* a large flightless Australasian bird. [from Malay *kasuari*]

cast *verb* (**cast**, **casting**) **1** to throw, to emit, *cast a net*; *cast a shadow*, cause there to be one. **2** to shed. **3** to turn or send in a particular direction; *cast your eye over this*, examine it. **4** to record or register (one's vote). **5** to make (an object) by pouring metal etc. into a mould and letting it harden. **6** to calculate, *cast a horoscope*. **7** to select actors for a play etc.; to assign a role to. – **cast** *noun* **1** an act of casting; the throwing of a missile, dice, fishing line or net, etc. **2** something made by putting soft material into a mould to harden; a plaster cast (*see* plaster). **3** a set of actors cast for parts in a play. **4** the form, type, or quality (of features, the mind, etc.). **5** a tinge of colour. **6** a slight squint. □ **cast about for** to search or look for. **cast down** to depress, to cause dejection in. **cast iron** a hard alloy of iron made by casting in a mould. **cast-iron** *adjective* made of cast iron; very strong, *a cast-iron alibi*. **cast off** to release a ship from its moorings; (in knitting) to loop stitches off a needle. **cast-offs** *plural noun* clothes that the owner will not wear again. **cast on** (in knitting) to loop stitches on to a needle.

castanets (kast-ă-**nets**) *plural noun* a pair of shell-shaped pieces of wood or ivory etc., struck together with the fingers, especially as an accompaniment to a Spanish dance. [from Spanish *castañetas* = little chestnuts]

castaway *noun* a shipwrecked person.

caste (*pr.* kahst) *noun* **1** each of the hereditary Hindu social divisions, varna. **2** any exclusive social class. **3** a social insect with a particular function, e.g. drones, workers, and queen, amongst bees. [from Spanish *casta* = descent from ancestors]

castellated (**kas**-tĕ-lay-tĕd) *adjective* having turrets or battlements like a castle.

caster *noun* (also **castor**) **1** a small container for sugar or salt, with a perforated top for sprinkling from. **2** a small swivelled wheel (usually one of a set) fixed to a leg or underside of furniture so that it can be moved easily. □ **caster sugar** finely granulated white sugar. [from *cast*]

castigate (**kas**-tĭ-gayt) *verb* to punish with blows; to criticise severely. **castigation** *noun*, **castigator** *noun* [from Latin *castigare* = punish]

Castile (kas-**teel**) the central plateau of the Iberian peninsula, a former Spanish kingdom. **Castilian** *adjective* & *noun*

casting vote *noun* a vote that decides the issue when votes on each side are equal.

castle *noun* **1** a large fortified building or group of buildings. **2** a chess piece also called a *rook*. – **castle** *verb* (in chess) to move the king two squares towards a rook and the rook to the square the king has crossed. □ **castles in the air** daydreams. [from Latin *castellum* = fort]

Castor 1 (*Gk. myth.*) the twin brother of **Pollux**. 2 a bright star in the constellation Gemini.

castor *noun see* **caster**.

castor oil *noun* oil from the seeds of a tropical plant, used as a purgative and as a lubricant.

castrate (kas-**trayt**) *verb* to remove the testicles of, to geld. **castration** *noun*

castrato *noun* (*plural* **castrati**) (*historical*) a male singer castrated before puberty so as to retain a pure soprano or alto voice. [Italian]

Castries (kas-**treess**) the capital of St Lucia.

casual *adjective* 1 happening by chance, *a casual encounter*. 2 made or done without forethought, not serious, *a casual remark*; not methodical, *a casual inspection*. 3 informal, for informal occasions, *casual clothes*. 4 irregular, not permanent, *casual work*; *casual labourers*, doing such work. **casuals** *plural noun* casual clothes; casual shoes. **casually** *adverb*, **casualness** *noun*

casualty *noun* 1 a person who is killed or injured in war or in an accident. 2 a thing lost or destroyed. 3 (in full **casualty department**) a hospital department dealing with accident victims or emergencies.

casuarina (kaz-yoo-ă-**ree**-nă) *noun* a tree with jointed branches that resemble gigantic horsetails.

casuistry (**kaz**-yoo-ĭ-stree) *noun* clever but often false reasoning, especially about moral issues. **casuistic** *adjective*

CAT *abbreviation* (in full **computerised axial tomography**) an X-ray scanner providing a series of cross-sectional pictures of the internal organs; a scan made with this.

cat *noun* 1 a small furry domesticated animal often kept as a pet. 2 a wild animal related to this; *the great cats*, lion, tiger, leopard, etc. 3 (*informal*) a spiteful or malicious woman. 4 the cat-o'-nine-tails. □ **cat-and-dog life** a life with perpetual quarrels. **cat-and-mouse game** the practice of taking slight action repeatedly against a weaker party. **cat burglar** a burglar who enters by climbing a wall or drainpipe etc. **cat-o'-nine-tails** *noun* a whip with nine knotted lashes, formerly used for flogging people. **cat's cradle** a game with string forming looped patterns between the fingers. **cat's paw** a person who is used by another to do something risky. (¶ From the fable of the monkey who used the paw of his friend the cat to rake hot chestnuts out of the fire.) **let the cat out of the bag** to give away a secret.

cata- *prefix* (becoming **cat-** before a vowel; combining with an *h* to become **cath-**) 1 down (as in *catapult*). 2 thoroughly (as in *catalogue*). [from Greek *kata* = down]

catabolism (kă-**tab**-ŏ-lizm) *noun* destructive metabolism, the breaking down of complex substances in the body. **catabolic** (kat-ă-**bol**-ik) *adjective* [from Greek *katabole* = descent]

cataclysm (**kat**-ă-klizm) *noun* a violent upheaval or disaster. **cataclysmic** (kată-**kliz**-mik) *adjective*

catacombs (**kat**-ă-koomz) *plural noun* a series of underground galleries with side recesses for tombs.

catafalque (**kat**-ă-falk) *noun* a decorated platform on which the coffin of a distinguished person stands during the funeral or lying in state, or on which it is drawn in procession.

Catalan *adjective* of Catalonia or its people or language. –**Catalan** *noun* 1 a native or inhabitant of Catalonia. 2 a language (closely related to Provençal) used in Catalonia, Andorra, the Balearic Islands, and some parts of southern France.

catalepsy (**kat**-ă-lepsee) *noun* a condition in which a person becomes rigid and unconscious. **cataleptic** (kată-**lep**-tik) *adjective* [from *cata-* = down, + Greek *lepsis* = seizure]

catalogue *noun* a list of items, usually in systematic order and with a description of each. –**catalogue** *verb* (**catalogued**, **cataloguing**) to list in a catalogue. **cataloguer** *noun* [from Greek *katalogos* = list]

Catalonia a district of NE Spain.

catalyse (**kat**-ă-lyz) *verb* to accelerate or produce by catalysis.

catalysis (kă-**tal**-ĭ-sĭs) *noun* (*plural* **catalyses**) the action of a catalyst.

catalyst (**kat**-ă-lĭst) *noun* 1 a substance that aids or speeds up a chemical reaction while remaining unchanged itself. 2 a person or thing that precipitates a change. [from *cata-*, + Greek *lusis* = loosening]

catalytic (kat-ă-**lit**-ik) *adjective* of or using a catalyst. □ **catalytic converter** a device in the exhaust system of a motor vehicle that converts polluting gases into harmless products.

catamaran (**kat**-ă-mă-ran) *noun* a boat with twin hulls. [from Tamil *kattumaram* = tied wood]

catapult *noun* **1** a device with elastic for shooting small stones. **2** an ancient military weapon for hurling large stones etc. **3** a device for launching a glider, or an aircraft from the deck of a carrier. –**catapult** *verb* **1** to hurl from a catapult; to fling forcibly. **2** to rush violently. [from *cata*-, + Greek *pellein* = to throw]

cataract *noun* **1** a large waterfall; a rush of water. **2** a condition in which the lens of the eye becomes cloudy and obscures sight; this opaque area.

catarrh (kă-**tar**) *noun* inflammation of mucous membrane, especially of the nose and throat, accompanied by a watery discharge. **catarrhal** *adjective* [from *cata*-, + Greek *rhein* = to flow]

catastrophe (kă-**tas**-trŏfee) *noun* a sudden great disaster. **catastrophic** (kat-ă-**strof**-ik) *adjective*, **catastrophically** *adverb*

catcall *noun* a shrill whistle of disapproval. **catcalling** *noun* making catcalls.

catch *verb* (**caught**, **catching**) **1** to capture in a net or snare or after a chase. **2** to overtake. **3** to grasp something moving and hold it; (in cricket) to cause (a batsman) to be 'out' by catching the ball after it leaves the bat and before it touches the ground. **4** to come unexpectedly upon; to take by surprise; to detect; to trap into a mistake or contradiction etc. **5** to be in time for and get on (a train etc.). **6** (*informal*) to hear (a broadcast); to watch (a film). **7** to get briefly, *caught a glimpse of it*; *you have caught the likeness well*, seen and reproduced it in painting etc.; *try and catch his eye*, make him notice you. **8** to become or cause to become fixed or prevented from moving. **9** to hit, *the blow caught him on the nose*. **10** to begin to burn. **11** to become infected with, *caught a cold*. –**catch** *noun* **1** the act of catching. **2** something caught or worth catching; *he's a good catch*, worth getting as a husband. **3** a concealed difficulty or disadvantage. **4** a device for fastening something. **5** a round for singing by three or more voices. □ **catch-as-catch-can** wrestling in which few or no holds are barred. **catch crop** a crop that grows quickly and is harvested while the main crop is growing. **catch hold of** to seize in the hand(s). **catch it** (*informal*) to be scolded or punished. **catch on** (*informal*) to become popular; to understand what is meant.

catch out to detect in a mistake. **catch up** to come abreast with; to do arrears of work.

catcher *noun* **1** one who catches. **2** a baseball fielder who stands behind the batter.

catching *adjective* infectious.

catchment area 1 an area from which rainfall drains into a river or reservoir. **2** an area from which a hospital draws its patients or a school its pupils.

catchphrase *noun* a phrase in frequent current use, a catchword or slogan.

catch-22 *noun* (*informal*) a dilemma where the victim is bound to suffer, no matter which course of action is chosen. [the phrase is the title of a comic novel by J. Heller (1961), set in the Second World War, in which the hero wishes to avoid flying any more missions and decides to go crazy, only to be told that anyone who wants to get out of combat duty is not really crazy]

catchweight *adjective* & *noun* (in sports) accepting a contestant at the weight he happens to be, not at one fixed for that sport.

catchword *noun* a memorable word or phrase that is often used, a slogan.

catchy *adjective* (**catchier**, **catchiest**) **1** pleasant and easy to remember, *a catchy tune*. **2** tricky, involving a catch.

catechise (**kat**-ĕ-kyz) *verb* (also **-ize**) to put a series of questions to (a person).

catechism (**kat**-ĕ-kizm) *noun* **1** a summary of the principles of a religion in the form of questions and answers. **2** a series of questions.

categorical (kat-ĕ-**go**-ri-kăl) *adjective* absolute, unconditional, *a categorical refusal*. **categorically** *adverb*

categorise (**kat**-ĕ-gŏ-ryz) *verb* (also **-ize**) to place in a particular category. **categorisation** *noun*

category (**kat**-ĕ-gŏ-ree) *noun* a class of things.

catenary (kă-**teen**-eree) *noun* a curve formed by a chain that hangs from two points. [from Latin *catena* = a chain]

cater (**kay**-ter) *verb* to provide what is needed or wanted, especially food or entertainment, *cater for 50 people*. □ **cater to** to pander to (people's bad inclinations).

caterer *noun* one whose trade is to supply food for social events.

Caterpillar *noun* (*trademark*) a steel band passing round two wheels of a tractor or tank, enabling it to travel over very rough ground, *Caterpillar track* or *tread*.

caterpillar *noun* the larva of a butterfly or moth. [from Old French *chatepelose* = hairy cat]

caterwaul *verb* to make a cat's howling cry.

catfish *noun* a large usually freshwater fish with whisker-like feelers round the mouth.

catgut *noun* a fine strong cord made from the dried intestines of animals, used for the strings of musical instruments and for sewing up surgical incisions.

catharsis (kă-**thar**-sĭs) *noun* relief of strong feelings or tension, e.g. by giving vent to them in drama or art etc. **cathartic** *adjective*

Cathay (kă-**thay**) (*poetical*) the name by which China was known in medieval Europe.

cathead *noun* a small Australian plant with spiny fruits.

cathedral *noun* the principal church of a diocese. [from Greek *kathedra* = seat]

Catherine II 'the Great' (1729–96), Russian empress, reigned 1762–96.

Catherine of Aragon (1485–1536), Spanish princess, first wife of Henry VIII and mother of Mary I.

Catherine wheel *noun* a rotating firework. [named after St Catherine, who was martyred on a spiked wheel]

catheter (**kath**-ĕ-ter) *noun* a tube for insertion into a body cavity for introducing or removing fluid. [from Greek *kathienai* = send down]

cathode (**kath**-ohd) *noun* the electrode by which current leaves a device. □ **cathode ray tube** a vacuum tube in which beams of electrons are directed against a fluorescent screen where they produce a luminous image, e.g. the picture tube of a television set. [from *cata-* = down, + Greek *hodos* = way]

Catholic *adjective* **1** of all Churches or Christians. **2** Roman Catholic. –**Catholic** *noun* a Roman Catholic. **Catholicism** (kă-**thol**-ĭ-sizm) *noun*

catholic *adjective* universal, including many or most things, *his tastes are catholic*. **catholicity** (kath-ŏ-**liss**-ĭ-tee) *noun* [from Greek *katholikos* = universal]

cation (**kat**-I-ŏn) *noun* an ion with a positive charge. **cationic** (kat-I-**on**-ik) *adjective*

catkin *noun* a spike of small soft flowers hanging from trees such as willow and hazel. [from Dutch *katteken* = kitten]

catmint *noun* a plant with a strong smell that is attractive to cats.

catnap *noun* a short nap. –**catnap** *verb* (**catnapped**, **catnapping**) to have a catnap.

catnip *noun* catmint.

Catseye *noun* (*trademark*) each of a line of reflector studs marking the centre, lanes, or edges of a road.

cattery *noun* a place where cats are bred or boarded.

cattle *plural noun* large ruminant animals with horns and □ cloven hoofs, bred for their milk or meat. □ **cattle cake** concentrated food for cattle, in cake form. **cattle dog** a dog bred and trained for droving cattle. **cattle grid** a grid covering a ditch so that vehicles can pass but not cattle or sheep etc.

catty *adjective* (**cattier**, **cattiest**) spiteful, speaking spitefully. **cattily** *adverb*, **cattiness** *noun*

Catullus (kă-**tul**-ŭs), Gaius Valerius (c. 84– c. 54 BC), Roman poet, best known for his love poems.

catwalk *noun* a raised narrow pathway, used in fashion parades.

Caucasian (kaw-**kay**-zhăn) *adjective* **1** of the Caucasus. **2** of the white or light-skinned race of mankind. –**Caucasian** *noun* a Caucasian person.

Caucasus (**kaw**-kă-sŭs) a mountain range in south-west Asia, between the Black Sea and the Caspian Sea.

caucus (**kaw**-kŭs) *noun* **1** (in Australia) the parliamentary members of a political party; a meeting of these. **2** (often *contemptuous*) a small group within a larger organisation or party, making plans, decisions, etc.; a meeting of such a group.

caudal (**kaw**-dăl) *adjective* of or at the tail. [from Latin *cauda* = tail]

caudate *adjective* having a tail.

caught *see* catch.

caul (*pr.* kawl) *noun* a membrane enclosing a foetus in the womb.

cauldron *noun* a large deep pot for boiling things in. [from Latin *caldarium* = hot bath]

cauliflower *noun* a cabbage with a large white flower head. [from French *chou fleuri* = flowered cabbage]

caulk (*pr.* kawk) *verb* to make watertight by filling seams or joints with waterproof material, or by driving edges of plating together. **caulking** *noun* material used to caulk seams etc.

causal *adjective* of or forming a cause. **causally** *adverb*

causality (kaw-**zal**-ĭ-tee) *noun* the relationship between cause and effect.

causation *noun* **1** the act of causing. **2** causality.

causative (**kaw**-ză-tiv) *adjective* **1** acting as a cause. **2** expressing a cause.

cause *noun* **1** a person or thing that makes something happen or produces an effect. **2** a reason, *there is no cause for alarm*. **3** a purpose or aim for which efforts are made, a movement or charity. **4** a lawsuit; *pleading his cause*, his case. – **cause** *verb* to be the cause of, to produce, to make happen.

cause célèbre (kohz say-**lebr**) *noun* a lawsuit or other issue that rouses great interest. [French]

causeway *noun* a raised road across low or wet ground.

caustic (**kos**-tik) *adjective* **1** able to burn or corrode things by chemical action. **2** sarcastic. – **caustic** *noun* a caustic substance. □ **caustic soda** sodium hydroxide, strongly alkaline in solution and used in the making of soap and paper. **caustically** *adverb*, **causticity** (kos-**tiss**-ĭ-tee) *noun* [from Greek *kaustikos* = capable of burning]

cauterise *verb* (also **-ize**) to burn the surface of (living tissue) with a caustic substance or a hot iron in order to destroy infection or stop bleeding. **cauterisation** *noun*, **cautery** *noun* [from Greek *kauterion* = branding iron]

caution *noun* **1** avoidance of rashness, attention to safety. **2** a warning against danger etc. **3** a warning and reprimand, *let him off with a caution*. – **caution** *verb* **1** to warn. **2** to warn and reprimand.

cautionary *adjective* conveying a warning.

cautious *adjective* having or showing caution. **cautiously** *adverb*, **cautiousness** *noun*

cavalcade (kav-ăl-**kayd**) *noun* a procession, especially of people on horseback or in cars etc. [from Italian *cavalcare* = to ride]

Cavalier *noun* a supporter of Charles I in the English Civil War. – **cavalier** *noun* a courtly gentleman, especially as a lady's escort. – **cavalier** *adjective* arrogant, offhand, *a cavalier attitude*. [from French *chevalier* = knight, from Latin *caballus* = horse]

cavalry *noun* troops who fight on horseback or in armoured vehicles. [from Latin *caballus* = horse]

cave *noun* a natural hollow in the side of a hill or cliff, or underground. – **cave** *verb* **cave in 1** to fall inwards, to collapse. **2** to cause to do this. **3** to withdraw one's opposition. [from Latin *cavus* = hollow]

caveat (**kav**-ee-ăt) *noun* a warning. [Latin, = let him beware]

caveat emptor *noun* the principle that the buyer alone is responsible if dissatisfied. [Latin, = let the buyer beware]

caveman *noun* (*plural* **cavemen**) a person of prehistoric times living in caves.

cavern *noun* a large cave. **cavernous** *adjective*

caviar (**kav**-ee-ar) *noun* (also **caviare**) the pickled roe of sturgeon or other large fish.

cavil *verb* (**cavilled**, **cavilling**) to raise petty objections. – **cavil** *noun* a petty objection.

caving *noun* the sport of exploring caves.

cavitation *noun* the making of cavities in a structure or bubbles in a liquid.

cavity *noun* **1** a hollow within a solid body. **2** a decayed part of a tooth. □ **cavity wall** a double wall with a cavity between.

cavort (kă-**vort**) *verb* to caper about excitedly.

caw *noun* the harsh cry of a crow etc. – **caw** *verb* to make this sound.

Cayenne the capital of French Guiana.

cayenne pepper (kay-**en**) *noun* a hot red powdered pepper.

cayman *noun* (*plural* **caymans**) a reptile similar to an alligator, found in South America.

Cayman Islands (also **Caymans**) three islands in the Caribbean Sea, a British dependency.

CB *abbreviation* citizens' band (*see* citizen).

CBD *abbreviation* central business district.

cc *abbreviation* **1** carbon copy. **2** cubic centimetre(s).

CCTV *abbreviation* closed-circuit television.

CD *abbreviation* compact disc. □ **CD-ROM** *noun* a compact disc storing data for use as a read-only memory (for display on a computer screen).

CE *abbreviation* Common Era.

cease *verb* to come or bring to an end, to stop. – **cease** *noun* ceasing.

ceasefire *noun* a signal to stop firing guns in war; a truce.

ceaseless *adjective* not ceasing, going on continually. **ceaselessly** *adverb*

Cecilia (sĕ-**see**-lee-ă), St (2nd or 3rd century), a martyr in the early Roman Church, patron saint of church music. Feast day, 22 November.

cedar (**see**-der) *noun* **1** an evergreen tree with hard sweet-smelling wood. **2** its wood.

cede (*pr.* seed) *verb* to give up one's rights to or possession of, *they were compelled to cede certain territories.* [from Latin *cedere* = to yield]

cedilla (sĕ-**dil**-ă) *noun* a mark written under *c* in certain languages to show that it is pronounced as *s*, as in *façade*. [from Spanish, = a little *z*]

ceilidh (**kay**-lee) *noun* (*Scottish* & *Irish*) an informal gathering for traditional music and dancing etc. [Gaelic]

ceiling *noun* **1** the undersurface of the top of a room. **2** the maximum altitude at which a particular aircraft can fly. **3** an upper limit or level, *wage ceilings.*

celebrant *noun* a person who performs a rite, especially a priest at Mass, or a secular person authorised to conduct civil marriages or funerals.

celebrate *verb* **1** to do something to show that a day or event is important; to honour with festivities; to make merry on such an occasion. **2** to officiate at (a religious ceremony). **celebration** *noun*

celebrated *adjective* famous.

celebrity (sĕ-**leb**-rĭ-tee) *noun* **1** a well-known person. **2** fame, being famous.

celeriac (sĕ-**le**-ree-ak) *noun* a kind of celery with a turnip-like root.

celerity (sĕ-**le**-rĭ-tee) *noun* swiftness.

celery *noun* a garden plant with crisp juicy stems used in salads or as a vegetable.

celestial *adjective* **1** of the sky; *celestial bodies*, stars etc. **2** of heaven, divine.

celibate (**sel**-ĭ-băt) *adjective* remaining unmarried or abstaining from sexual intercourse, especially for religious reasons. **celibacy** (**sel**-ĭ-bă-see) *noun*

cell *noun* **1** a very small room, e.g. for a monk in a monastery or for confining a prisoner. **2** a compartment in a honeycomb. **3** a device for producing electric current by chemical action.

4 a microscopic unit of living matter. **5** a small group of people forming a centre or nucleus of political activities. [from Latin *cella* = storeroom]

cellar *noun* **1** an underground room used for storing things. **2** a room in which wine is stored, a stock of wine. [same origin as *cell*]

cellist (**chel**-ĭst) *noun* a person who plays the cello.

cello (**chel**-oh) *noun* (*plural* **cellos**) a violoncello, an instrument like a large violin, played by a seated player who sets it upright between the knees. [short for *violoncello* (same origin as *violin*)]

cellophane (**sel**-ŏ-fayn) *noun* (*trademark*) thin moisture-proof transparent material used for wrapping things.

cellphone *noun* a mobile phone.

cellular (**sel**-yŭ-ler) *adjective* **1** of cells, composed of cells. **2** woven with an open mesh, *cellular blankets.* **cellular radio** or **telephone** a system of mobile radio-telephone transmission with an area divided into cells, each served by a small transmitter.

cellulite (**sel**-yŭ-lyt) *noun* a lumpy form of fat, especially on the hips, thighs, and buttocks of some women, producing puckering of the skin.

celluloid (**sel**-yŭ-loid) *noun* a plastic made from cellulose nitrate and camphor.

cellulose (**sel**-yŭ-lohs) *noun* **1** an organic substance found in all plant tissues and in textile fibres derived from these; this used in making plastics. **2** paint or lacquer made from this. **cellulosic** *adjective*

Celsius (**sel**-see-ŭs) *adjective* centigrade. [named after A. Celsius, Swedish astronomer (1701–44), who devised the centigrade scale]

Celt (*pr.* kelt) *noun* a member of an ancient European people who settled in Britain before the coming of the Romans, or of their descendants especially in Ireland, Wales, Cornwall, Scotland, and Brittany.

Celtic (**kelt**-ik) *adjective* of the Celts. –**Celtic** *noun* a group of languages spoken by the Celts.

cement *noun* **1** a grey powder, made by burning lime and clay, that sets to a stone-like mass when mixed with water and is used for building. **2** any similar soft substance that sets firm. –**cement** *verb* **1** to put cement on or in, to join with cement. **2** to unite firmly.

cemetery *noun* a burial ground. [from Greek *koimeterion* = dormitory]

cenotaph (**sen**-ŏ-tahf) *noun* a tomblike monument to a person or people buried elsewhere. [from Greek *kenos* = empty, + *taphos* = tomb]

Cenozoic (see-nŏ-**zoh**-ik) *adjective* (also **Cainozoic**) of the third and most recent geological era, lasting from about 65 million years ago (following the Mesozoic era) to the present day. –**Cenozoic** *noun* this era.

censer (**sen**-ser) *noun* a container in which incense is burnt, swung on chains in a religious ceremony to disperse its fragrance. [same origin as *incense*]

censor (**sen**-ser) *noun* a person authorised to examine letters, books, films, etc. and remove or ban anything regarded as harmful. –**censor** *verb* to subject to such examination or removal. **censorship** *noun* [Latin, = magistrate with power to ban unsuitable people from ceremonies]

censorious (sen-**sor**-ree-ŭs) *adjective* severely critical. **censoriously** *adverb*, **censoriousness** *noun*

censure (**sen**-sher) *noun* strong criticism or condemnation. –**censure** *verb* to blame or rebuke.

Usage *Censure* should not be confused with *censor*.

---

census (**sen**-sŭs) *noun* an official count of the population or of things (e.g. traffic). [from Latin *censere* = to estimate]

cent *noun* one 100th of a dollar or of certain other metric units of currency, a coin of this value. [from Latin *centum* = 100]

Centaur (**sen**-tor) *noun* (*Gk. myth.*) a member of a tribe of wild creatures with a man's upper body, head, and arms on a horse's body and legs. –**the Centaur** the southern constellation Centaurus.

centenarian (sen-tĕ-**nair**-ree-ăn) *noun* a person who is 100 years old or more.

centenary (sen-**teen**-ă-ree) *noun* a 100th anniversary.

centennial (sen-**ten**-ee-ăl) *adjective* of a centenary.

center *noun* & *verb* (*Amer.*) = **centre**.

centi- (sent-ee) *prefix* one 100th. [from Latin *centum* = 100]

centigrade (**sent**-ĭ-grayd) *adjective* of or using a temperature scale divided into 100 degrees, 0° being the freezing point and 100° the boiling point of water. [from *centi-*, + Latin *gradus* = step]

centigram *noun* one 100th of a gram.

centilitre *noun* one 100th of a litre.

centimetre *noun* one 100th of a metre, about 0.4 inch.

centipede *noun* a small crawling creature with a long thin segmented body and many legs, one pair on each segment. [from *centi-*, + Latin *pedes* = feet]

central *adjective* **1** of or at or forming the centre. **2** chief, most important, *the central character in this novel*. □ **central bank** a national (not commercial) bank, issuing currency. **central heating** a system of heating a building from one source by circulating hot water or hot air or steam in pipes or by linked radiators. **central nervous system** the brain and spinal cord. **central processing unit** (also **central processor**) the principal operating part of a computer (abbreviation **CPU**). **centrally** *adverb*, **centrality** (sen-**tral**-ĭ-tee) *noun*

Central African Republic a country in central Africa.

Central America the narrow southern part of North America, south of Mexico.

centralise *verb* (also **-ize**) to bring under the control of one central authority. **centralisation** *noun*

centralism *noun* a centralising policy, especially in administration. **centralist** *noun*

centre *noun* **1** the middle point or part. **2** a point towards which interest is directed or from which administration etc. is organised. **3** a place where certain activities or facilities are concentrated, *a shopping centre*. **4** a political party or group holding moderate opinions between two extremes. **5** the player occupying the position in the centre of the field or in the middle of a line in various games. –**the Centre** the central part of Australia. –**centre** *adjective* of or at the centre. –**centre** *verb* (**centred**, **centring**) **1** to place in or at the centre. **2** to concentrate or be concentrated at one point, *centre in* or *on* (¶ avoid *centre round* or *around*, which are regarded as illogical). **3** to kick or hit (the ball) from the side towards the middle of the field in football or hockey. □ **centre of gravity** *see* **gravity**. **centre square** a device for marking the centre of a circular object. **centric** *adjective* [from Greek *kentron* = sharp point]

centricity (sen-**tris**-ĭ-tee) *noun* being central or a centre.

centrifugal (sen-**tri**-few-găl *or* sen-trĭ-**few**-găl) *adjective* **1** moving away from the centre or axis. **2** using **centrifugal force**, a force that appears to cause a body that is travelling round a centre to fly outwards and off its circular path. **centrifugally** *adverb* [from Latin *centrum* = centre, + *fugere* = flee]

centrifuge (**sen**-trĭ-fewj) *noun* a machine using centrifugal force to separate substances, e.g. milk and cream. –**centrifuge** *verb* to separate by centrifuge.

centripetal (sen-**trip**-ĕt'l) *adjective* moving towards the centre or axis. [from Latin *centrum* = centre, + *petere* = seek]

centurion (sen-**tew**-reeŏn) *noun* an officer in the ancient Roman army, originally one commanding 100 infantrymen. [from Latin *centum* = 100]

century *noun* **1** a period of 100 years; one of these periods reckoned from the birth of Christ. **2** 100 runs made by a batsman in one innings in cricket. **3** a unit of 100 men in the army of ancient Rome. [from Latin *centum* = 100]

CEO *abbreviation* chief executive officer.

cephalic (sĕ-**fal**-ik) *adjective* of or in the head.

cephalon (**sef**-ă-lon) *noun* (*plural* **cephala**) the head-part of a trilobite.

cephalopod (**sef**-ă-lŏ-pod) *noun* a mollusc (such as the octopus) that has a distinct head with a ring of tentacles round the mouth. [from Greek *kephale* = head, + *podos* = of a foot]

ceramic (sĕ-**ram**-ik) *adjective* of pottery or similar substances. –**ceramic** *noun* a ceramic substance. **ceramics** *noun* the art of making pottery.

Cerberus (**ser**-bĕ-rŭs) (*Gk. myth.*) the monstrous three-headed watchdog guarding the entrance to Hades.

cereal *noun* **1** a grass, such as wheat, rye, oats, or rice, producing an edible grain. **2** its seed. **3** a breakfast food made from such grain. [from the name of Ceres, Roman goddess of the corn]

cerebellum (se-rĕ-**bel**-ŭm) *noun* a small part of the brain, located in the back of the skull, which coordinates and regulates muscular activity. [Latin, = little brain]

cerebral (se-rĕ-**brăl**) *adjective* **1** of the brain. **2** intellectual rather than emotional. ☐ **cerebral palsy** a condition resulting from brain damage before or at birth, involving muscle spasms and involuntary movements.

cerebrum (se-rĕ-**brŭm**) *noun* the principal part of the brain, located in the front of the skull. [Latin, = brain]

ceremonial *adjective* of a ceremony, used in ceremonies, formal. –**ceremonial** *noun* **1** ceremony. **2** a system of rules for ceremonies. **ceremonially** *adverb*

ceremonious *adjective* full of ceremony, elaborately performed. **ceremoniously** *adverb*

ceremony *noun* **1** a set of formal acts, especially those used on religious or public occasions. **2** formal politeness.

Ceres (**seer**-reez) (*Rom. myth.*) a corn goddess, usually identified with Demeter.

cerise (sĕ-**rees**) *adjective* & *noun* light clear red. [French, = cherry]

cerium (**seer**-ee-ŭm) *noun* a silvery-white metallic element, the most abundant of the lanthanide elements (symbol Ce).

cert *noun* (*informal*) a certainty, something sure to happen or to be successful.

certain *adjective* **1** feeling sure, convinced. **2** known without doubt. **3** able to be relied on to come or happen or be effective. **4** specific but not named or stated for various reasons. **5** small in amount but definitely there, *I feel a certain reluctance*. **6** existing but not well known, *a certain John Smith*. ☐ **for certain** without doubt, as a certainty. **make certain** to make sure.

certainly *adverb* **1** without doubt. **2** yes.

certainty *noun* **1** being certain. **2** something that is certain; *that horse is a certainty*, is certain to win.

certifiable *adjective* able to be certified; deserving to be certified as insane. **certifiably** *adverb*

certificate *noun* an official written or printed statement giving certain facts. **certificated** *adjective*

certify *verb* (**certified**, **certifying**) to declare formally; to show on a certificate or other document. ☐ **certified mail** a postal service in which the despatch and receipt of an item are recorded. **certification** *noun*

certitude (**ser**-tĭ-tewd) *noun* a feeling of certainty.

cerulean (sĕ-**roo**-lee-ăn) *adjective* sky-blue.

Cervantes (ser-**van**-teez), Miguel de (1547–1616), Spanish novelist and dramatist, author of *Don Quixote*.

cervical (ser-**vy**-kăl *or* **ser**-vik-ăl) *adjective* 1 of the neck, *cervical vertebrae*. 2 of a cervix, of the cervix of the womb.

cervix (**ser**-viks) *noun* (*plural* **cervices**) 1 the neck. 2 a necklike structure, the neck of the womb. [Latin, = neck]

cessation (sess-**ay**-shŏn) *noun* ceasing.

cession (**sesh**-ŏn) *noun* ceding, giving up.

cesspit *noun* (also **cesspool**) a covered pit where liquid waste or sewage is stored temporarily.

cetacean (sĕ-**tay**-shăn) *noun* a member of the order of animals that contains whales, dolphins, and porpoises. – **cetacean** *adjective* of this order.

Ceylon the former name of Sri Lanka.

Cézanne (say-**zan**), Paul (1839–1906), French painter, a forerunner of cubism.

cf. *abbreviation* compare. [short for the Latin *confer*]

c.f. *abbreviation* carried forward.

CFC *abbreviation* chlorofluorocarbon.

CGI *abbreviation* computer-generated imagery.

chablis (**shab**-lee *or* shă-**blee**) *noun* a dry white wine. [from *Chablis* in France, where it is produced]

Chad a republic in North Africa. **Chadian** *adjective* & *noun*

chador (**chah**-der) *noun* a large piece of cloth worn as a cloak, leaving one side of the face exposed, by Muslim women in some countries. [Persian]

chafe (*pr.* chayf) *verb* 1 to warm by rubbing. 2 to make or become sore from rubbing. 3 to become irritated or impatient. [from French *chauffer* = make warm]

chaff *noun* 1 husks separated from the seed of cereals by threshing or winnowing. 2 hay or straw cut up as food for cattle. 3 good-humoured teasing or joking. – **chaff** *verb* to tease or joke in a good-humoured way.

chafing dish (**chay**-fing dish) *noun* a pan with a heater under it for cooking food or keeping it warm at the table.

Chagall (shă-**gal**), Marc (1887–1985), French painter, born in Russia.

chagrin (**shag**-rĭn) *noun* a feeling of annoyance and embarrassment or disappointment. **chagrined** *adjective* [French]

Chain, Sir Ernst Boris (1906–79), British biochemist (*see* **Florey**).

chain *noun* 1 a series of connected metal links, used for hauling or supporting weights or for restraining things or as an ornament. 2 a connected series or sequence, *chain of mountains*, *chain of events*. 3 a number of shops or hotels etc. owned by the same company. 4 a unit of length for measuring land, 22 yards (= 20.12 metres, the length of a cricket pitch); a jointed metal rod for measuring this. – **chain** *verb* to make fast with a chain or chains. □ **chain gang** (*historical*) a team of convicts in Australia chained together to work out of doors. **chain letter** a letter of which the recipient is asked to make copies and send these to other people, who will do the same. **chain reaction** a chemical or other change forming products that themselves cause more changes; a series of events each of which causes or influences the next. **chain-smoke** *verb* to smoke many cigarettes in a continuous succession. **chain-smoker** *noun* a person who chain-smokes. **chain stitch** a looped stitch that looks like a chain, in crochet or embroidery. **chain store** one of a series of similar shops owned by one firm.

chainsaw *noun* a saw with teeth set on an endless chain.

chair *noun* 1 a movable seat, with a back, for one person. 2 a position of authority at a meeting; a chairperson. 3 a professorship. 4 (*Amer.*) the electric chair. – **chair** *verb* 1 to seat in a chair of honour. 2 to carry in triumph on the shoulders of a group. 3 to act as chairperson of.

chairlift *noun* a series of chairs suspended from an endless cable, for carrying people up and down a mountain.

chairman *noun* 1 a person who presides over a meeting or a committee. 2 the president of a board of directors. **chairmanship** *noun*, **chairwoman** *feminine noun*

Usage The word *chairman* may be used of persons of either sex, a man being formally addressed as *Mr Chairman* and a woman as *Madam Chairman* or *Madam Chair*. However, many people prefer to use the terms *chair* or *chairperson*.

chairperson *noun* a chairman or chairwoman.

chaise longue (shayz **lawng**) *noun* a chair with a very long seat on which the sitter can stretch out his or her legs. [French, = long chair]

chalet (**shal**-ay) *noun* **1** a Swiss mountain hut or cottage with overhanging eaves; a house in a similar style. **2** a small house or hut at a ski resort etc.

chalice (**chal**-iss) *noun* a large goblet for holding wine; one from which consecrated wine is drunk at the Eucharist. [from Latin *calix* = cup]

chalk *noun* **1** a soft white limestone used for burning into lime. **2** a piece of this or of similar substance, white or coloured, used in crayons for drawing. –**chalk** *verb* to write, draw, or mark with chalk, to rub with chalk. □ **by a long chalk** by far. **chalk-stripe** *noun* a pattern of thin white stripes on a dark background. **chalk-striped** *adjective* **chalk up** to record, to register, *chalked up another victory*. **chalky** *adjective*

chalkie *noun* (*Austral. informal*) a schoolteacher.

challenge *noun* **1** a call to demonstrate one's ability or strength. **2** a call or demand to respond; a sentry's call for a person to identify himself or herself. **3** a formal objection, e.g. to a juror. **4** a difficult or demanding task. –**challenge** *verb* **1** to issue a challenge to. **2** to raise a formal objection to. **3** to question the truth or rightness of. **challenger** *noun*

challenged *adjective* lacking a physical or mental attribute.

challenging *adjective* offering problems that test one's ability, stimulating.

chamber *noun* **1** an assembly hall; the hall used for meetings of a parliament etc.; the members of the group using it. **2** a cavity or compartment in the body of an animal or plant, or in machinery. **3** (*old use*) a room, a bedroom. **chambers** *plural noun* rooms used by a barrister or group of barristers; a judge's room for hearing cases that do not need to be taken in court. □ **chamber music** music written for a small number of players, suitable for performance in a room or small hall. **Chamber of Commerce** an association to promote local commercial interests. **chamber pot** a receptacle for urine etc., used in the bedroom.

chamberlain (**chaym**-ber-lin) *noun* an official who manages the household of a sovereign or a great noble.

chambermaid *noun* a woman employed to clean and take care of bedrooms in a hotel.

chambray (**shom**-bray) *noun* a linen-finished cotton cloth with a white weft and a coloured warp.

chameleon (kă-**mee**-lee-ŏn) *noun* a small lizard that can change colour according to its surroundings.

chamfer (**cham**-fer) *verb* to bevel the edge or corner of. –**chamfer** *noun* a chamfered part.

chamois *noun* (*plural* **chamois**) **1** (*pr.* **sham**-wah) a small wild antelope found in the mountains of Europe and Asia. **2** (*pr.* **sham**-ee) a piece of **chamois leather**, soft yellowish leather made from the skin of sheep, goats, and deer and used for washing and polishing things. [French]

chamomile (**kam**-ŏ-myl) *noun* = **camomile**.

champ[1] *verb* **1** to munch noisily, to make a chewing action or noise. **2** to show impatience.

champ[2] *noun* (*informal*) a champion.

champagne *noun* **1** a sparkling white wine from Champagne in France. **2** (loosely) a similar wine from elsewhere. **3** a pale straw colour.

Usage Officially, only a wine from the Champagne region of France can be called a *champagne*.

---

champion *noun* **1** a person or thing that has defeated all others in a competition. **2** a person who fights, argues, or speaks in support of another or of a cause. –**champion** *adjective* & *adverb* (*informal*) splendid, splendidly. –**champion** *verb* to support as a champion.

championship *noun* **1** a contest to decide the champion in a sport etc. **2** the position of champion.

chance *noun* **1** the way things happen through no known cause or agency, luck, fate; *games of chance*, those decided by luck not skill. **2** a possibility, likelihood. **3** an opportunity, an occasion when success seems very probable. –**chance** *verb* **1** to happen without plan or intention. **2** (*informal*) to risk, *let's chance it*. –**chance** *adjective* coming or happening by chance, *a chance meeting*. □ **by chance** as it happens or happened, without being planned. **chance on** to come upon or find by chance. **take a chance** to take a risk, to act in the hope that a particular thing will (or will not) happen. **take chances** to behave riskily. **take one's chance** to trust to luck.

chancel (**chahn**-sĕl *or* **chan**-) *noun* the part of a church near the altar, used by the clergy and choir.

chancellery (**chahn**-sĕl-ree *or* **chan**-) *noun* **1** a chancellor's position, department, or official residence. **2** = chancery (sense 2).

chancellor *noun* **1** (especially in the UK) a government or legal official of various kinds; *Chancellor of the Exchequer*, the UK finance minister. **2** the head of government in some European countries, e.g. Germany. **3** the honorary head of a university. **chancellorship** *noun*

chancery *noun* **1** Chancery (in the UK) a division of the High Court of Justice. **2** an office attached to an embassy or consulate.

chancy *adjective* (**chancier**, **chanciest**) risky, uncertain.

chandelier (shan-dĕ-**leer**) *noun* an ornamental hanging fixture with supports for several lights. [from French *chandelle* = candle]

chandler *noun* a dealer in ropes, canvas, and other supplies for ships. [same origin as *chandelier*]

change *verb* **1** to make or become different. **2** to pass from one form or phase into another. **3** to take or use another instead of. **4** to put fresh clothes or coverings etc. on; *change the baby*, put a clean nappy on it. **5** to go from one to another, *change trains*. **6** to exchange; *can you change $5?*, give small money in change, or give different currency for it. **–change** *noun* **1** changing, alteration; *a change of the moon*, a fresh phase. **2** a substitution of one thing for another; variety. **3** a fresh occupation or surroundings. **4** money in small units. **5** money returned as the balance when the price is less than the amount offered in payment. □ **change hands** to pass into another person's possession. **change of heart** a great alteration in one's attitude or feelings. **the change (of life)** the menopause. **change over** to change from one system or position to another. **change-ringing** *noun* ringing a peal of bells in a series of different sequences. **for a change** for the sake of variety, to vary one's routine.

changeable *adjective* **1** able to be changed. **2** altering frequently, *changeable weather*.

changeling (**chaynj**-ling) *noun* a child or thing believed to have been substituted secretly for another.

changeover *noun* a change from one system or position to another.

Changi (**chang**-ee) an area in eastern Singapore used by the Japanese during the Second World War as a prisoner-of-war camp.

channel *noun* **1** the sunken bed of a stream of water. **2** the navigable part of a waterway, deeper than the parts on either side. **3** a stretch of water, wider than a strait, connecting two seas. **4** a passage along which a liquid may flow, a sunken course or line along which something may move. **5** any course by which news or information etc. may travel. **6** a band of broadcasting frequencies reserved for a particular set of programs. **7** a circuit for transmitting electrical signals. **8** a lengthwise section of recording tape. **–channel** *verb* (**channelled**, **channelling**) **1** to form a channel or channels in. **2** to direct through a channel or desired route. □ **the Channel** the English Channel. [from Latin *canalis* = canal]

Channel Islands a group of islands in the English Channel off the NW coast of France, including Jersey, Guernsey, and Alderney.

chant *noun* **1** a tune to which the words of psalms or other works with irregular rhythm are fitted by singing several syllables or words to the same note. **2** a monotonous song. **3** a rhythmic call or shout. **–chant** *verb* **1** to sing, especially a chant. **2** to call or shout rhythmically. [from Latin *cantare* = sing]

chanter *noun* **1** a person who chants. **2** the melody-pipe of bagpipes.

chantry *noun* a chapel founded for priests to sing masses for the founder's soul.

chaos (**kay**-oss) *noun* great disorder. **chaotic** (kay-**ot**-ik) *adjective*, **chaotically** *adverb* [Greek, = bottomless pit]

chap[1] *noun* (*informal*) a man; a fellow. [short for *chapman*, an old word for a pedlar]

chap[2] *verb* (**chapped**, **chapping**) (of skin) to split or crack, to become cracked. **–chap** *noun* a crack in the skin.

chap[3] *noun* the lower jaw or half of the cheek, especially of a pig, as food.

chaparral (shap-ă-**ral** *or* **chap**-) *noun* (*Amer.*) dense tangled brushwood, especially in the southwestern USA and Mexico. [from Spanish *chaparra* = evergreen oak]

chapati (chă-**pah**-tee) *noun* (also **chupatty**) a small flat disc of coarse unleavened bread. [from Hindi]

chapbook *noun* (*old use*) a small pamphlet of tales, ballads, etc., sold by chapmen.

chapel *noun* **1** a place used for Christian worship, other than a cathedral or parish church, e.g. in a school or hospital. **2** a service in this, *go to chapel*. **3** a place with a separate altar within a church or cathedral.

chaperone (**shap**-ĕ-rohn) *noun* (also **chaperon**) a person who takes charge of especially young people in public. –**chaperone** *verb* to act as chaperone to.

chaplain (**chap**-lĭn) *noun* a member of the clergy attached to a private chapel, school, hospital, ship, military unit, etc.

chaplet (**chap**-lĕt) *noun* **1** a wreath for the head. **2** a short rosary.

chapman *noun* (*plural* **chapmen**) (*old use*) a pedlar.

chaps *plural noun* long leather leggings worn by cowboys. [short for Spanish *chaparajos*]

chapter *noun* **1** a division of a book, usually numbered. **2** the canons of a cathedral or members of a monastic order; a meeting of these. □ **chapter and verse** an exact reference to a passage or authority. **chapter house** the building used for meetings of a cathedral chapter. **chapter of accidents** a series of misfortunes.

char *verb* (**charred**, **charring**) to make or become black by burning. [from *charcoal*]

charabanc (**sha**-ră-bank) *noun* an early form of bus with bench seats, used for outings.

character *noun* **1** all those qualities that make a person, group, or thing what he, she, or it is and different from others. **2** a person's moral nature. **3** moral strength. **4** a person, especially a noticeable or eccentric one. **5** a person in a novel or play etc. **6** a description of a person's qualities, a testimonial. **7** a letter, sign, or mark used in a system of writing or printing etc. **8** a physical characteristic of a plant or animal. □ **in character** appropriate to a person's general character. **out of character** not appropriate.

characterise *verb* (also **-ize**) **1** to describe the character of. **2** to be a characteristic of. **characterisation** *noun*

characteristic *adjective* forming part of the character of a person or thing, showing a distinctive feature. –**characteristic** *noun* **1** a characteristic feature. **2** the part of the logarithm before the decimal point (contrasted with *mantissa*). **characteristically** *adverb*

characterless *adjective* lacking any positive character.

charade (shă-**rahd**) *noun* **1** a scene acted as a clue in **charades**, a game that involves guessing a word from a series of acted clues. **2** an absurd pretence.

charcoal *noun* a black substance made by burning wood slowly in an oven with little air, used as a filtering material or as fuel or for drawing. □ **charcoal grey** very dark grey.

chard *noun* a kind of beet with edible leaves and stalks, silver beet.

chardonnay (**shar**-dŏ-nay) *noun* a variety of white grape; the wine made from this.

charge *noun* **1** the price asked for goods or services. **2** the quantity of material that an apparatus holds at one time; the amount of explosive needed for one explosion. **3** the electricity contained in a substance; energy stored chemically for conversion into electricity; the electrical property (positive or negative) of a particle of matter. **4** a task or duty; custody. **5** a person or thing entrusted. **6** formal instructions about one's duty or responsibility. **7** an accusation, especially of having committed a crime. **8** a rushing attack. –**charge** *verb* **1** to ask as a price. **2** to record as a debt, *charge it to my account*. **3** to load or fill; to put a charge into. **4** to give an electric charge to, to store energy in. **5** to give as a task or duty; to entrust. **6** to accuse formally. **7** to rush forward in attack; *charge in*, to act impetuously. □ **charge card** a kind of credit card. **in charge** in command. **take charge** to take control. **chargeable** *adjective*

chargé d'affaires (shar-*zh*ay da-**fair**) *noun* (*plural* **chargés d'affaires**) **1** an ambassador's deputy. **2** an envoy to a minor country.

charger *noun* **1** a cavalry horse. **2** an apparatus for charging a battery.

chariot *noun* a two-wheeled horse-drawn carriage used in ancient times in battle and in racing.

charioteer *noun* the driver of a chariot.

charisma (kă-**riz**-mă) *noun* **1** the power to inspire devotion and enthusiasm; great charm. **2** a power or talent conferred by God. [Greek, = divine favour]

charismatic (ka-rĭz-**mat**-ik) *adjective* **1** having charisma. **2** (of Christian groups and worship) emphasising spiritual gifts (e.g. prophecy, speaking in tongues, healing), *the charismatic movement*.

charitable *adjective* **1** generous in giving to the needy. **2** of or belonging to charities, *charitable institutions.* **3** unwilling to think badly of people or acts. **charitably** *adverb*

charity *noun* **1** leniency or tolerance in judging people or acts. **2** generosity in giving to the needy. **3** an institution or fund for helping the needy. **4** loving kindness towards others. [from Latin *caritas* = love]

charlatan (**shar**-lă-tăn) *noun* a person who falsely claims to be an expert, especially in medicine. [from Italian, = babbler]

Charlemagne (**shar**-lĕ-mayn) (742–814), ruler of the Franks in northern Europe from 768, and emperor from 800.

Charles the name of two kings of Britain: Charles I (reigned 1625–49), Charles II (reigned 1660–85).

charleston *noun* (also **Charleston**) a lively dance of the 1920s, with side-kicks from the knee.

charlotte (**shar**-lŏt) *noun* a pudding made of stewed fruit with a covering or layers of crumbs, biscuits, etc.

charm *noun* **1** attractiveness, the power of arousing love or admiration. **2** an act or object or words believed to have magic power. **3** a small ornament worn on a chain or bracelet. –**charm** *verb* **1** to give pleasure to. **2** to influence by personal charm. **3** to influence as if by magic. **charmer** *noun* [from Latin *carmen* = song or spell]

charming *adjective* delightful.

charnel house (**char**-nĕl) *noun* a place in which the bodies or bones of the dead are kept.

Charon (**kair**-rŏn) (*Gk. myth.*) the aged ferryman who conveyed the souls of the dead across the river of the Underworld to Hades.

chart *noun* **1** a map designed for navigators on water or in the air. **2** an outline map for showing special information, *a weather chart*. **3** a diagram, graph, or table giving information in an orderly form, *a temperature chart*; *the charts*, those listing the recordings that are currently most popular. –**chart** *verb* to make a chart of, to map. [from Latin *charta* = card]

charter *noun* **1** a document from a ruler or government granting certain rights or defining the form of an institution. **2** the chartering of a ship, aircraft, or vehicle. –**charter** *verb* **1** to grant a charter to, to found by charter. **2** to let or hire a ship, aircraft, or vehicle. □ **charter flight** a flight by chartered aircraft. **charterer** *noun*

chartered *adjective* qualified according to the rules of a professional association that has a royal charter, *chartered accountant*.

Chartism *noun* a popular movement in Britain for electoral and social reform, 1837–48, whose principles were set out in a manifesto called *The People's Charter*. **Chartist** *noun*

chartreuse (shar-**trerz**) *noun* **1** a fragrant green or yellow liqueur. **2** its green colour.

charwoman *noun* (*plural* **charwomen**) (*Brit.*) a woman employed to do cleaning.

chary (**chair**-ree) *adjective* **1** cautious, wary. **2** sparing; *chary of giving praise*, seldom praising people.

Charybdis (kă-**rib**-dĭs) (*Gk. legend*) a dangerous whirlpool in a narrow channel, opposite the cave of Scylla.

chase¹ *verb* **1** to go quickly after in order to capture, overtake, or drive away. **2** to hurry, *chasing round the shops*. **3** (*informal*) to try to attain. –**chase** *noun* **1** chasing, pursuit. **2** hunting, especially as a sport. **3** a steeplechase. **4** unenclosed parkland, originally for hunting, *Ku-ring-gai Chase*.

chase² *verb* to engrave or emboss (metal).

chasm (**kaz**-ŭm) *noun* a deep opening or gap, especially in earth or rock. [Greek, = wide hollow]

chassis (**sha**-see) *noun* (*plural* **chassis**, *pr.* **sha**-seez) a base frame, especially of a vehicle on which other parts are mounted.

chaste (*pr.* chayst) *adjective* **1** virgin, celibate. **2** not having sexual intercourse except with the person to whom one is married. **3** simple in style, not ornate. **chastely** *adverb* [from Latin *castus* = pure]

chasten (**chay**-sĕn) *verb* **1** to discipline, to punish by inflicting suffering. **2** to subdue the pride of.

chastise (chas-**tyz**) *verb* to punish severely, especially by beating. **chastisement** *noun*

chastity *noun* **1** being chaste, virginity, celibacy. **2** simplicity of style.

chasuble (**chaz**-yŭ-bŭl) *noun* a loose garment worn over all other vestments by a priest celebrating Mass or the Eucharist.

chat¹ *noun* a friendly informal conversation. –**chat** *verb* (**chatted**, **chatting**) to have a chat. □ **chat up** to chat to (a person) flirtatiously or with a particular motive. [from *chatter*]

chat² *noun* a small bird with a ringing or chattering call, *crimson chat*, *gibber chat*, etc.

château (**shat**-oh) *noun* (*plural* **châteaux**, *pr.* **shat**-ohz) a castle or large country house in France. [French]

chatelaine (**shat**-ĕ-layn) *noun* the mistress of a large house.

chattel *noun* a movable possession (as opposed to a house or land).

chatter *verb* **1** to talk or converse quickly and continuously about unimportant matters. **2** to make sounds like this, as some birds and animals do. **3** to make a repeated clicking or rattling sound. –**chatter** *noun* **1** chattering talk. **2** a chattering sound. **chatterer** *noun*

chatterbox *noun* a talkative person.

chatty *adjective* (**chattier**, **chattiest**) **1** fond of chatting. **2** resembling chat, *a chatty description*. **chattily** *adverb*, **chattiness** *noun*

Chaucer, Geoffrey (c. 1342–1400), English poet, whose best-known work is *The Canterbury Tales*.

chauffeur (**shoh**-fer) *noun* a person employed to drive a car. –**chauffeur** *verb* to drive as chauffeur. **chauffeuse** (**shoh**-ferz) *feminine noun* [French, = stoker]

chauvinism (**shoh**-vĭ-nizm) *noun* **1** exaggerated patriotism. **2** excessive or prejudiced support or loyalty to one's group or sex, *male chauvinism*. **chauvinist** *noun*, **chauvinistic** *adjective* [from the name of Nicolas Chauvin, a French soldier under Napoleon, noted for his extreme patriotism]

cheap *adjective* **1** low in price, worth more than it cost; *cheap money*, available at a low rate of interest. **2** charging low prices, offering good value. **3** poor in quality, of low value. **4** showy but worthless, silly. **5** costing little effort, or acquired by discreditable means, and hence of little worth. –**cheap** *adverb* cheaply, *we got it cheap*. **cheaply** *adverb*, **cheapness** *noun* [from Old English *ceap* = a bargain]

cheapen *verb* to make or become cheap; depreciate, degrade.

cheapskate *noun* (*informal*) a mean stingy person.

cheat *verb* **1** to act dishonestly or unfairly in order to win some profit or advantage. **2** to trick, to deceive; to deprive by deceit. –**cheat** *noun* **1** a person who cheats, an unfair player. **2** a deception.

Chechnya an autonomous region of southern Russia seeking independence. **Chechen** *adjective* & *noun*

check¹ *verb* **1** to stop or slow the motion of suddenly, to restrain. **2** to make a sudden stop. **3** to threaten (an opponent's king) at chess. **4** to test or examine in order to make sure that something is correct or in good condition; *check the items off*, mark them when you find they are correct. **5** (*Amer.*) to correspond when compared. –**check** *noun* **1** a stopping or slowing of motion, a pause. **2** a restraint. **3** a control to secure accuracy; a test or examination to check that something is correct or in good working order. **4** (*Amer.*) a receipt for something handed over; a bill in a restaurant. **5** (*Amer.*) a cheque. **6** (in chess) exposure of a king to possible capture. □ **check in** to register on arrival, e.g. as a passenger at an airport. **check on** or **up** or **up on** to examine or investigate the correctness of. **check out** to register on departure or dispatch; to check on. **check-up** *noun* a thorough examination, especially a medical one. **keep in check** to keep under control. **checker** *noun* [from Persian *shah* = king]

check² *noun* a pattern of squares like a chessboard, or of crossing lines. **checked** *adjective* having a check pattern. [from *chequered*]

checkmate *noun* **1** in chess, = **mate²**. **2** a complete defeat. –**checkmate** *verb* **1** to put into checkmate in chess. **2** to defeat finally, to foil. [from Persian *shah mat* = the king is dead]

checkout *noun* **1** checking out. **2** a place where goods are paid for by customers in a supermarket.

checkpoint *noun* a place where documents, vehicles, etc. are checked or inspected.

cheddar *noun* a firm cheese of a kind originally made at Cheddar in England.

cheek *noun* **1** either side of the face below the eye. **2** impudent speech, quiet arrogance. –**cheek** *verb* to address cheekily. □ **cheek by jowl** close together, in close association.

cheeky *adjective* (**cheekier**, **cheekiest**) **1** showing bold or cheerful lack of respect. **2** coquettish. **cheekily** *adverb*, **cheekiness** *noun*

cheep *noun* a weak shrill cry like that made by a young bird. –**cheep** *verb* to make such a cry.

cheer *noun* **1** a shout of encouragement or applause; *give three cheers*, three shouts of 'hurray'. **2** cheerfulness. –**cheer** *verb* **1** to utter a cheer; to encourage or applaud with cheers. **2** to comfort, to gladden. **cheers** *plural noun* (as *interjection*) (*informal*) an expression of good wishes before drinking; (especially *Brit.*) an expression of thanks, or of good wishes on leaving. □ **cheer up** to make or become more cheerful.

cheerful *adjective* **1** visibly happy, contented, in good spirits. **2** pleasantly bright, *cheerful colours*. **cheerfully** *adverb*, **cheerfulness** *noun*

cheerio[1] *interjection* (*informal*) goodbye.

cheerio[2] *noun* (*Austral.*) a small frankfurt.

cheerless *adjective* gloomy, dreary.

cheery *adjective* exuberantly happy. **cheerily** *adverb*

cheese *noun* **1** a food made from milk curds. **2** a shaped mass of this. **3** thick stiff jam, *lemon cheese*. □ **cheese-paring** *adjective* stingy; (*noun*) stinginess.

cheeseburger *noun* a hamburger with cheese in or on it.

cheesecake *noun* a tart with a filling of sweetened cream or cottage cheese.

cheesecloth *noun* a thin loosely-woven cotton fabric.

cheesed *adjective* (*informal*) **cheesed off** fed up, exasperated.

cheesy *adjective* **1** like cheese in taste, smell, appearance, etc. **2** (*informal*) inferior, cheap and nasty. **3** (*informal*) (of a smile etc) forced, artificial, *he had a cheesy grin*. **4** (*informal*) hackneyed and trite.

cheetah (**chee**-tă) *noun* a very swift feline with leopard-like spots.

chef (*pr.* shef) *noun* a professional cook, the chief cook in a restaurant etc. [French, = chief]

chef-d'œuvre (shay-**dervr**) *noun* (*plural* **chefs-d'œuvre**, *pr.* shay-**dervr**) a masterpiece. [French, = chief work]

chemical *adjective* of, using, or produced by chemistry. –**chemical** *noun* a substance obtained by or used in a chemical process. □ **chemical engineering** engineering concerned with processes that involve chemical change and with the equipment needed for these. **chemical warfare** warfare using poison gas and other chemicals. **chemically** *adverb*

chemise (shě-**meez**) *noun* **1** a loose-fitting undergarment formerly worn by women, hanging straight from the shoulders. **2** a dress of similar shape. [from Latin *camisia* = shirt]

chemist *noun* **1** a person or firm dealing in medicinal drugs; a shop where medicines are

dispensed and that usually also sells other medical goods and toiletries. **2** a scientist skilled in chemistry.

chemistry *noun* **1** the scientific study of substances and their elements and of how they react when combined or in contact with one another. **2** chemical structure, properties, and reactions. [same origin as *alchemy*]

chemotherapy (kee-moh-th'**e**-ră-pee *or* kem-ŏ-) *noun* treatment of disease by medicinal drugs and other chemical substances.

chenille (shě-**neel**) *noun* a fabric with a long velvety pile, used for furnishings.

cheque *noun* **1** a written order to a bank to pay out money from an account. **2** the printed form on which this is written. □ **cheque book** a book of printed cheques. [from *check*[1]]

chequer (**chek**-er) *noun* a pattern of squares, especially of alternate squares of colour.

chequerboard *noun* a board marked in a pattern of squares, a chessboard.

chequered *adjective* marked with a pattern of squares or irregularly. □ **chequered career** one marked by frequent changes of fortune.

cherish *verb* **1** to look after lovingly. **2** to be fond of. **3** to keep in one's heart, *we cherish hopes of his return*. [from French *cher* = dear]

Chernobyl (**cher**-nŏ-bĭl) a city near Kiev in Ukraine, where in 1986 explosions at a nuclear power station resulted in a serious escape of radioactivity which spread to a number of countries in Europe.

chernozem (**chair**-nŏ-zem) *noun* a fertile black soil found in southern Russia and elsewhere.

Cherokee *noun* **1** a member of an indigenous North American people of the southern USA. **2** their language.

cheroot (shě-**root**) *noun* a cigar with both ends open.

cherry *noun* **1** a small soft round fruit with a stone. **2** a tree producing this or grown for its ornamental flowers. **3** the wood of this tree. **4** deep red. –**cherry** *adjective* deep red. □ **cherry picker** a crane for raising and lowering people. **cherry tomato** a miniature tomato.

chert *noun* a flintlike form of quartz.

cherub *noun* **1** (*plural* **cherubim**) any of the angelic beings usually grouped with the seraphim. **2** a representation (in art) of a chubby infant with wings. **3** an angelic child. [from Hebrew]

cherubic (chĕ-**roo**-bik) *adjective* like a cherub, with a plump innocent face.

chervil *noun* a herb used for flavouring.

cheshire *noun* a kind of firm crumbly cheese, originally made in Cheshire in England.
□ **like a Cheshire cat** with a broad fixed grin.

chess *noun* a game for two players played on a chessboard, chequered with 64 squares, and using 32 chessmen (16 each). [same origin as *check*[1]]

chest *noun* **1** a large strong box for storing or shipping things in. **2** the upper front surface of the body; the part containing the heart and lungs. **3** a small cabinet for medicines etc. □ **chest of drawers** a piece of furniture with drawers for storing clothes etc. **get it off one's chest** (*informal*) to reveal what one is anxious about.

chesterfield *noun* a sofa with a padded back, seat, and ends.

chestnut *noun* **1** a tree with hard brown nuts, those of the Spanish or sweet chestnut being edible. **2** the wood of this tree. **3** its nut. **4** deep reddish-brown. **5** a horse of reddish-brown or yellowish-brown colour. **6** an old joke or story. **–chestnut** *adjective* deep reddish-brown or (of horses) yellowish-brown.

chevalier (shev-ă-**leer**) *noun* a member of certain orders of knighthood or other groups.

chevron (**shev**-rŏn) *noun* a V-shaped line or stripe or bar, especially one worn on the sleeve to show rank.

chew *verb* to work or grind between the teeth; to make this movement. **–chew** *noun* **1** the act of chewing. **2** something for chewing. □ **chewing gum** a sticky substance sweetened and flavoured for prolonged chewing.

chewy *adjective* **1** suitable for chewing. **2** needing to be chewed, not soft.

chiack (**chy**-ak) *verb* (*Austral. informal*) to tease, to jeer at.

chiaroscuro (kee-ah-rŏ-**skoor**-roh) *noun* **1** treatment of the light and dark parts in a painting. **2** light and shade effects in nature. **3** use of contrast in literature etc. [from Italian *chiaro* = clear, + *oscuro* = dark]

chic (*pr.* sheek) *adjective* stylish and elegant. **–chic** *noun* stylishness and elegance. [French]

chicane (shĭ-**kayn**) *noun* **1** chicanery. **2** an artificial barrier or obstacle on a motor racing course.

chicanery (shĭ-**kayn**-ĕ-ree) *noun* trickery used to gain an advantage. [from French *chicaner* = to quibble]

chick *noun* **1** a young bird before or after hatching. **2** (*informal*) a young woman.

chicken *noun* **1** a young bird, especially of the domestic fowl. **2** the flesh of domestic fowl as food. **3** a young person, *she's no chicken* or *no spring chicken*. **4** (*informal*) a coward. **5** (*informal*) a game testing courage in the face of danger, *to play chicken*. **–chicken** *adjective* (*informal*) afraid to do something, cowardly. **–chicken** *verb* **chicken out** (*informal*) to withdraw through cowardice. □ **chicken feed** food for poultry; (*informal*) something that is small in amount. **chicken wire** light wire netting.

chickenpox *noun* a disease, especially of children, with red spots on the skin.

chickpea *noun* a dwarf pea with yellow seeds used as a vegetable.

chicory *noun* a blue-flowered plant, cultivated for its salad leaves and for its root, which is roasted, ground, and used with or instead of coffee.

chide *verb* (**chided** *or* **chid**, **chidden**, **chiding**) (*old use*) to scold.

chief *noun* **1** a leader or ruler. **2** a person with the highest authority. **–chief** *adjective* **1** highest in rank or authority. **2** most important. **chiefly** *adverb*

chieftain (**cheef**-tăn) *noun* the chief of a tribe, clan, or other group.

chiffon (**shif**-on) *noun* **1** a thin almost transparent fabric of silk or nylon etc. **2** a very light-textured dessert made with beaten egg white, *lemon chiffon*. [French]

chiffonier (shif-ŏ-**neer**) *noun* **1** a movable low cupboard with a top used as a sideboard. **2** a tall chest of drawers.

chignon (**sheen**-yawn) *noun* a knot or roll of long hair, worn at the back of the head by women. [French]

chigoe *noun* (also **chigger**) a tropical flea that burrows into the skin.

chihuahua (chĭ-**wah**-wă) *noun* a very small smooth-haired dog. [from the name of a city and State in Mexico]

chilblain *noun* a painful swelling on the hand, foot, or ear, caused by exposure to cold and by poor circulation. [from *chill* + *blain* = a sore]

child *noun* (*plural* children) **1** a young human being below the age of puberty; a boy or girl. **2** a son or daughter. □ **child abuse** maltreatment of a child, especially by physical or emotional violence or sexual molestation. **child care** the care of preschool children while parents are at work etc. **child's play** something very easy to do. **with child** pregnant.

childbearing *noun* pregnancy and childbirth.

childbirth *noun* the process of giving birth to a child.

childhood *noun* the condition or period of being a child.

childish *adjective* like a child, unsuitable for a grown person. **childishly** *adverb*, **childishness** *noun*

childless *adjective* having no children.

childlike *adjective* having the good qualities of a child, simple and innocent.

children *see* **child**.

Chile (**chil**-ee) a republic in South America, on the Pacific coast. **Chilean** *adjective* & *noun*

chill *noun* **1** unpleasant coldness. **2** an illness with feverish shivering. **3** a feeling of discouragement. –**chill** *adjective* chilly. –**chill** *verb* **1** to cool (food or drink); to preserve at a low temperature without freezing. **2** to horrify.

chilli *noun* (*plural* **chillies**) a small hot-tasting green or red pod of a variety of capsicum, used fresh or dried in cooking. □ **chilli con carne** (*pr.* **kar**-nee) a chilli-flavoured stew of minced beef and kidney beans.

chilly *adjective* (**chillier**, **chilliest**) **1** rather cold, unpleasantly cold. **2** cold and unfriendly in manner. **chilliness** *noun*

chime *noun* a tuned set of bells; a series of notes sounded by these. –**chime** *verb* **1** (of bells) to ring. **2** (of a clock) to show the hour by chiming. □ **chime in** to insert a remark when others are talking.

chimera (kĭ-**meer**-ră) *noun* **1** (*Gk. myth.*) a monster with a lion's head, goat's body, and serpent's tail. **2** a wild or fantastic product of the imagination. **chimeric**, **chimerical** *adjectives* [from Greek *khimaira* = female goat]

chimney *noun* (*plural* **chimneys**) a structure carrying off smoke or gases from a fire. □ **chimney pot** a pipe fitted to the top of a chimney. **chimney sweep** a person whose job is removing soot from inside chimneys.

chimp *noun* (*informal*) a chimpanzee.

chimpanzee *noun* an African ape, smaller than a gorilla.

chin *noun* the front of the lower jaw. □ **keep one's chin up** to remain cheerful.

China a republic in eastern Asia. **China Sea** a part of the Pacific Ocean off the coast of China, divided by the island of Taiwan into the **East China Sea** in the north and the **South China Sea** in the south.

china *noun* **1** fine earthenware porcelain. **2** articles made of this, *household china*. □ **china clay** kaolin.

chinchilla (chin-**chil**-ă) *noun* **1** a small squirrel-like South American animal. **2** its soft grey fur. **3** a breed of cat or rabbit.

chine *noun* **1** an animal's backbone; a joint of meat containing part of this. **2** a mountain ridge. –**chine** *verb* to cut along and separate the backbone in (a joint of meat).

Chinese *adjective* of China or its people or language. –**Chinese** *noun* **1** (*plural* **Chinese**) a native of China, a person of Chinese descent. **2** the language of China. □ **Chinese lantern** a collapsible paper lantern; a plant with an orange-coloured calyx resembling this.

Ch'ing the name of the Manchu dynasty of China, 1644–1912.

chink[1] *noun* a narrow opening or slit.

chink[2] *noun* a sound like glasses or coins being struck together. –**chink** *verb* to make or cause to make this sound.

Chinook (chĭ-**nuuk**) *noun* (*plural* **Chinook**) **1** a member of an indigenous North American people of the Pacific coast. **2** their language.

chintz *noun* a cotton cloth with a printed pattern, usually glazed, used for furnishings. [from Hindi]

chinwag *noun* (*informal*) a chat. –**chinwag** *verb* (**chinwagged**, **chinwagging**) to chat, to have a gossip.

chip *noun* **1** a thin piece cut or broken off something hard. **2** a fried oblong strip of potato. **3** a potato crisp. **4** a place from which a chip has been broken. **5** a counter used to represent money, especially in gambling. **6** a microchip. –**chip** *verb* (**chipped**, **chipping**) **1** to cut or break at the surface or edge; to shape or carve by doing this. **2** to make (potatoes) into chips. **3** (*informal*) to tease. □ **a chip off the old block** a child who resembles a parent. **a chip on one's shoulder** something about which one feels bitter or resentful. **chip heater** (*Austral.*) a domestic water heater that burns woodchips. **chip in** (*informal*) to interrupt with a remark when someone is speaking; to contribute money.

chipboard *noun* thin material made of compressed woodchips and resin.

chipmunk *noun* a small striped squirrel-like animal of North America.

chipolata (chip-ŏ-**lah**-tă) *noun* a small spicy sausage.

Chippendale *noun* an 18th-century style of English furniture, named after its designer Thomas Chippendale (died 1779).

chiropody (kĭ-**rop**-ŏ-dee) *noun* the treatment of ailments of the feet. **chiropodist** *noun* [from Greek *kheir* = hand, + *pod-* = foot]

Usage *Podiatry* and *podiatrist* are now the more usual terms.

chiropractic (**ky**-rŏ-prak-tik) *noun* treatment of certain disorders by manipulation of the joints, especially those of the spine, not by medicinal drugs or surgery. **chiropractor** *noun* a practitioner of this. [from Greek *kheir* = hand, + *prattein* = to do]

chirp *noun* the short sharp note made by a small bird or a grasshopper. –**chirp** *verb* to make this sound.

chirpy *adjective* lively and cheerful.

chirrup *noun* a series of chirps. –**chirrup** *verb* to make this sound.

chisel *noun* a tool with a bevelled edge for shaping wood, stone, or metal. –**chisel** *verb* (**chiselled, chiselling**) 1 to cut or shape with a chisel. 2 (*informal*) to treat unfairly, to swindle. **chiseller** *noun*

Chisholm (**chiz**-ŏm), Caroline (1808–77), English-born philanthropist who founded a Female Immigrants' Home in Sydney and helped new immigrants find employment.

Chisinau (**chis**-now) (also **Kishinev**) the capital of Moldova.

chit[1] *noun* (often *derogatory*) a young child, a small young woman, *only a chit of a girl.*

chit[2] *noun* 1 a short written note. 2 a note containing an order or statement of money owed.

chit-chat *noun* chat, gossip.

chitin (**ky**-tĭn) *noun* a substance forming the horny constituent in the hard outer covering of certain insects, spiders, and crustaceans. **chitinous** *adjective* [from Greek *khiton* = tunic]

chiton (**ky**-tŏn) *noun* 1 a long woollen tunic worn by ancient Greeks. 2 a sea mollusc with a shell of eight overlapping plates.

chitterlings *plural noun* the small intestines of a pig, cooked as food.

chivalry (**shiv**-ăl-ree) *noun* courtesy and considerate behaviour, especially towards weaker persons. **chivalrous** *adjective* [= like a perfect knight (same origin as *Cavalier*)]

chive (*rhymes with* hive) *noun* a small herb with onion-flavoured leaves.

chivvy *verb* (**chivvied, chivvying**) (*informal*) to keep urging (a person) to hurry; to harass.

chlamydia (klă-**mid**-ee-ă) *noun* (*plural* **chlamydiae**) a parasitic bacterium that can cause diseases such as trachoma, and can be sexually transmitted.

chloral (**klor**-răl) *noun* (also **chloral hydrate**) a white crystalline compound used as a sedative or anaesthetic.

chlorate *noun* a salt of chloric acid.

chlorella (klor-**rel**-ă) *noun* a kind of green alga consisting of a single cell.

chloric (**klor**-rik) *adjective* of or containing chlorine.

chloride (**klor**-ryd) *noun* a compound of chlorine and one other element.

chlorinate (**klor**-rĭ-nayt) *verb* to treat or sterilise with chlorine. **chlorination** *noun*

chlorine (**klor**-reen) *noun* a chemical element (symbol Cl), a poisonous gas used in sterilising water and in industry. [from Greek *khloros* = green]

chlorofluorocarbon *noun* any gas that is a compound of carbon, hydrogen, chlorine, and fluorine, used in refrigerators, aerosols, etc. and harmful to the ozone layer.

chloroform (**klo**-rŏ-form) *noun* a liquid that gives off vapour that causes unconsciousness when breathed in. –**chloroform** *verb* to make unconscious by this.

chlorophyll (**klo**-rŏ-fil) *noun* the green colouring matter in most plants, responsible for the absorption of light to provide energy for photosynthesis. [from Greek *khloros* = green, + *phullon* = leaf]

chloroplast (**klo**-rŏ-plahst) *noun* any of the small structures in a plant cell that contain chlorophyll and use this in photosynthesis.

chock *noun* a block or wedge used to prevent something from moving. –**chock** *verb* to wedge with a chock or chocks. □ **chock-a-block** *adverb* & *adjective* crammed or crowded together. **chock-full** *adjective* crammed full.

chocolate *noun* **1** a powdered or solid food made from roasted cacao seeds. **2** a drink made with this. **3** a sweet made of or covered with this. **4** dark brown colour. –**chocolate** *adjective* **1** flavoured or coated with chocolate. **2** dark brown. [from Mexican *chocolatl*]

choice *noun* **1** choosing; the right of choosing; *I have no choice*, no alternative. **2** a variety from which to choose, *a wide choice of holidays*. **3** a person or thing chosen, *this is my choice*. –**choice** *adjective* of the best quality. □ **for choice** preferably.

choir (*pr.* kwyr) *noun* **1** an organised band of singers, especially leading the singing in church. **2** the part of a cathedral or church where the choir and clergy sit. [from Latin *chorus* = choir]

choirboy, **choirgirl** *nouns* a boy or girl who sings in a church choir, a chorister.

choke *verb* **1** to cause to stop breathing by squeezing or blocking the windpipe or (of smoke etc.) by being unfit to breathe. **2** to be unable to breathe from such causes. **3** to make or become speechless from emotion. **4** to clog, to smother, *the garden is choked with weeds*. –**choke** *noun* **1** choking; a choking sound. **2** a valve controlling the flow of air into a petrol engine. □ **choke off** (*informal*) to silence or discourage, usually by snubbing.

choker *noun* **1** a high stiff collar, a clerical collar. **2** a close-fitting necklace.

choko *noun* a succulent green pear-shaped vegetable.

choler (kol-er) *noun* (*old use*) **1** one of the four humours. **2** anger, bad temper.

cholera (kol-ĕ-ră) *noun* an infectious and often fatal disease causing severe diarrhoea. [from Greek *khole* = bile]

choleric (kol-ĕ-rik) *adjective* easily angered, often angry.

cholesterol (kŏ-lest-ĕ-rol) *noun* a fatty substance found in animal tissues, thought to cause hardening of the arteries. [from Greek *khole* = bile, + *stereos* = stiff]

chomp *verb* to munch noisily.

chook (*pr.* chuuk) *noun* (*Austral. informal*) a chicken or fowl.

choose *verb* (**chose**, **chosen**, **choosing**) **1** to select out of a greater number of things. **2** to decide, to prefer, to desire; *there is nothing to choose between them*, they are about equal. **chooser** *noun*

choosy *adjective* (*informal*) careful and cautious in choosing, hard to please.

chop[1] *verb* (**chopped**, **chopping**) **1** to cut by a blow with an axe or knife. **2** to hit with a short downward stroke or blow. –**chop** *noun* **1** a cutting stroke, especially with an axe. **2** a chopping blow. **3** a thick slice of meat, usually including a rib. □ **get the chop** (*informal*) to be dismissed; (of a project etc.) to be cancelled; to be murdered.

chop[2] *verb* (**chopped**, **chopping**) **chop and change** to keep changing.

chop[3] *noun* **not much chop** (*Austral. informal*) no good.

chop[4] *noun* (usually in *plural*) the jaw of an animal.

Chopin (**shoh**-pan), Fryderyk (Frédéric) (1810–49), Polish composer, whose works are chiefly for the piano.

chopper *noun* **1** a chopping tool; a short axe. **2** (*informal*) a helicopter.

choppy *adjective* **1** full of short broken waves. **2** jerky, not smooth. **choppiness** *noun*

chopstick *noun* each of a pair of sticks used for eating especially Chinese and Japanese food.

chop suey (chop-**soo**-ee) *noun* a Chinese dish made with small pieces of meat fried with vegetables and served with rice.

choral (**kor**-răl) *adjective* written for a choir or chorus; sung or spoken by these. **chorally** *adverb*

chorale (kŏ-**rahl**) *noun* a choral composition, using the words of a hymn.

chord[1] (*pr.* kord) *noun* a combination of notes sounded together in harmony. □ **broken chord** an arpeggio. [from *accord*]

chord[2] (*pr.* kord) *noun* a straight line joining two points on a curve. [from *cord*]

chore (*pr.* chor) *noun* a routine task, a tedious task.

choreograph (**ko**-ree-ŏ-grahf) *verb* to provide choreography for.

choreography (ko-ree-**og**-ră-fee) *noun* the composition of ballets or stage dances. **choreographer** *noun*, **choreographic** *adjective* [from Greek *khoreia* = dance, + *-graphy*]

chorister (**ko**-rĭs-ter) *noun* a member of a choir.

choroid *noun* a membrane in the eye between the retina and the iris.

chortle *noun* a loud gleeful chuckle. –**chortle** *verb* to utter a chortle. [a mixture of *chuckle* and *snort*]

chorus *noun* **1** a group of singers. **2** a piece of music for these. **3** something spoken or sung by many people together, *a chorus of approval*. **4** the refrain or main part of a song. **5** a group of singing dancers in a musical comedy. –**chorus** *verb* (**chorused**, **chorusing**) to sing, speak, or say in chorus. □ **in chorus** speaking or singing all together. [from Greek]

chose, **chosen** *see* **choose**.

chough (*pr.* chuf) *noun* **1** an eastern Australian bird that builds a mud nest. **2** a red-legged European crow.

choux pastry (*pr.* shoo) *noun* very light pastry enriched with eggs.

chow (*rhymes with* cow) *noun* **1** a long-haired dog of a Chinese breed. **2** (*informal*) food.

chowchilla *noun* a dark-coloured perching bird of eastern Australia, also called a *log runner*. [Dyirbal and Yidiny *jawujala*]

chowder *noun* a thick soup of clams, fish, or corn with vegetables.

chow mein (*pr.* min) *noun* a Chinese dish of fried noodles with shredded meat and vegetables.

chrism *noun* consecrated oil.

Christ the title of Jesus (= 'the anointed one'), now treated as a name.

Christadelphian (kristă-**del**-fee-ăn) *noun* a member of a religious sect rejecting the doctrine of the Trinity and expecting the second coming of Christ.

christen *verb* **1** to admit to the Christian Church by baptism. **2** to give a name or nickname to.

Christendom (**kris**-ĕn-dŏm) *noun* all Christians, all Christian countries.

christening *noun* the ceremony of baptising or naming.

Christian *adjective* **1** of the doctrines of Christianity; believing in or based on these. **2** of Christians. **3** showing the qualities of a Christian; kindly, humane. –**Christian** *noun* **1** one who believes in Christianity. **2** a kindly or humane person. □ **Christian era** the period from the birth of Christ onwards. **Christian name** a name given at a christening, a person's given name. **Christian Science** a religious system claiming that health and healing can be achieved through the mental effect of the Christian faith, without medical treatment.

Christian Scientist one who believes in this system.

Christianity *noun* **1** the religion based on the belief that Jesus Christ was the incarnate Son of God, and on his teachings. **2** being a Christian.

Christmas *noun* (*plural* **Christmases**) the Christian festival (celebrated on 25 December) commemorating Christ's birth; the period about this time. □ **Christmas beetle** any of several Australian scarab beetles which appear in summer. **Christmas bush** (*Austral.*) any of various shrubs that flower or fruit at Christmas. **Christmas Day** 25 December. **Christmas Eve** 24 December. **Christmas Island** an island in the Indian Ocean, NW of Australia, administered by Australia. **Christmas pudding** a rich dark plum pudding eaten at Christmas. **Christmas tree** an evergreen (or artificial) tree decorated at Christmas; a Western Australian tree with golden flowers in summer. [from *Christ* + *mass*²]

Christmassy *adjective* looking festive, typical of Christmas.

Christopher, St, legendary martyr, adopted as the patron saint of travellers.

chromatic (krŏ-**mat**-ik) *adjective* of colour, in colours. □ **chromatic scale** (in music) a scale that ascends or descends by semitones. [from Greek *khroma* = colour]

chromaticism (krŏ-**mat**-ĭ-sizm) *noun* **1** the use of chromatic scales in music. **2** an example of this.

chromatin (**kroh**-mă-tin) *noun* the substance in the nucleus of a cell that can be stained very easily.

chromatography (kroh-mă-**tog**-ră-fee) *noun* separation of a mixture into its component substances by passing it over material that absorbs these at different rates so that they appear as layers, often of different colours. **chromatographic** *adjective*

chrome (*pr.* krohm) *noun* **1** chromium. **2** yellow colouring matter obtained from a compound of chromium. [from Greek *khroma* = colour (because its compounds have brilliant colours)]

chroming *noun* (*Austral. informal*) the inhaling of fumes from chrome-based spray-paint.

chromium (**kroh**-mee-ŭm) *noun* a chemical element (symbol Cr), a hard metal used in making stainless steel and for coating other metals, *chromium-plated*. [from *chrome*]

chromosome (**kroh**-mŏ-sohm) *noun* one of the tiny threadlike structures in animal and plant cells, carrying genes. [from Greek *khroma* = colour, + *soma* = body]

chronic *adjective* 1 (of a disease etc.) affecting a person for a long time, constantly recurring. 2 having an illness or a habit for a long time, *a chronic invalid*. 3 (*informal*) very unpleasant or bad. **chronically** *adverb* [from Greek *khronikos* = of time]

chronicle (**kron**-ikŭl) *noun* a record of events in the order in which they happened. –**chronicle** *verb* to record in a chronicle. **chronicler** *noun* [same origin as *chronic*]

Chronicles either of two books of the Old Testament recording the history of Israel and Judah.

chronological (kron-ŏ-**loj**-ikăl) *adjective* arranged in the order in which things occurred. **chronologically** *adverb*

chronology (krŏ-**nol**-ŏ-jee) *noun* the arrangement of events in the order in which they occurred, e.g. in history or geology. [from Greek *khronos* = time, + -*logy*]

chronometer (krŏ-**nom**-ĕ-ter) *noun* a time-measuring instrument with special mechanism for keeping exact time, used especially in navigation. [from Greek *khronos* = time, + *meter*]

chrysalis (**kris**-ă-lĭs) *noun* (*plural* **chrysalises**) the stage in an insect's life when it forms a sheath inside which it changes from a grub to an adult insect, especially a butterfly or moth. [from Greek *khrusos* = gold (the colour of its covering)]

chrysanthemum *noun* a garden plant with bright flowers, blooming in autumn, commonly given on Mother's Day. [from Greek *khrusos* = gold, + *anthemon* = flower]

chubby *adjective* (**chubbier**, **chubbiest**) round and plump. **chubbiness** *noun*

chuck¹ *verb* 1 (*informal*) to throw carelessly or casually. 2 (*informal*) to give up, to resign. 3 to touch playfully under the chin. 4 (*informal*) to vomit. –**chuck** *noun* 1 a playful touch. 2 **the chuck** (*informal*) dismissal, *get the chuck*. □ **chuck in** (*informal*) to give up, to resign, *he chucked in the job*; to contribute, *we all chucked in $5*. **chuck off at** (*Austral. informal*) to ridicule. **chuck out** (*informal*) to throw away; to expel (a troublesome person).

chuck² *noun* 1 the part of a lathe that grips the drill; the part of a drill that holds the bit. 2 a cut of beef from the neck to the ribs, *chuck steak*.

chuckle *noun* a quiet or half-suppressed laugh. –**chuckle** *verb* to give a chuckle.

chuddar *noun* = **chador**.

chuffed *adjective* (*informal*) pleased.

chug *verb* (**chugged**, **chugging**) to make a dull short repeated sound, like an engine running slowly. –**chug** *noun* this sound.

chukka *noun* (also **chukker**) each of the 7-minute periods of play in a game of polo. [from Hindi]

chum *noun* (*informal*) a close friend. –**chum** *verb* (**chummed**, **chumming**) **chum up** (*informal*) to form a close friendship. **chummy** *adjective*

chump *noun* (*informal*) a foolish person. □ **chump chop** a chop from the thick end of a loin of lamb or mutton.

chunder (*Austral. informal*) *verb* to vomit. –**chunder** *noun* vomit.

chunk *noun* 1 a thick piece of something. 2 a substantial amount.

chunky *adjective* 1 short and thick. 2 in chunks, containing chunks.

church *noun* 1 a building for public Christian worship. 2 a religious service in this, *will see you after church*. –**the Church** the whole body of Christian believers; a particular group of these; the clergy, the clerical profession. □ **Church of England** the English branch of the Western Christian Church, rejecting the pope's supremacy and having the monarch as its head. Also called the *Anglican Church*. (¶ The Church of England in Australia is officially called the *Anglican Church of Australia*.) **Church of Rome** the branch of the Christian Church having the pope as its head. Also called the *Roman Catholic Church*. [from Greek *kuriakon* = Lord's house]

churchgoer *noun* a person who goes to church, especially regularly.

Churchill, Sir Winston Leonard Spencer (1874–1965), British Conservative statesman, Prime Minister 1940–5, 1951–55.

churchwarden *noun* a layperson who helps with the business of the church.

churchyard *noun* the enclosed land round a church, in some places used for burials.

churinga (chŭ-**ring**-gă) *noun* an Aboriginal sacred object, normally carved or painted.

[Aranda *jwerrenge* = object from the Dreaming]

churlish *adjective* ill-mannered, surly. **churlishly** *adverb*, **churlishness** *noun*

churn *noun* **1** a machine in which milk is beaten to make butter. **2** a large can in which milk is carried from a farm. – **churn** *verb* **1** to beat (milk) or make (butter) in a churn. **2** to stir or swirl violently. □ **churn out** to produce in quantity. **churn up** to break up the surface of; to upset.

chute (*pr.* shoot) *noun* **1** a sloping or vertical channel down which things can slide or be dropped. **2** (*informal*) a parachute. [French, = a fall]

chutney *noun* a highly seasoned mixture of fruit or vegetables, vinegar, spices, etc. [from Hindi *catni*]

chyme (*pr.* kym) *noun* partly digested food as it leaves the stomach.

CIA *abbreviation* Central Intelligence Agency, a federal agency of the USA responsible for coordinating government intelligence activities abroad.

CIB *abbreviation* (in Australia) Criminal Investigation Branch.

cicada (sĭ-**kah**-dă) *noun* a grasshopper-like insect that makes a shrill chirping sound.

cicatrice (**sik**-ă-trĭss) *noun* the scar left by a healed wound.

Cicero (**sis**-ĕ-roh), Marcus Tullius (106–43 BC), Roman statesman, orator, and writer.

cider *noun* a drink made from fermented or crushed apples.

cigar *noun* a roll of tobacco leaves for smoking. [from Spanish *cigarro*]

cigarette *noun* a roll of shredded tobacco enclosed in thin paper for smoking. [French, = little cigar]

ciliate (**sil**-ee-ăt) *adjective* having cilia. – **ciliate** *noun* an organism with cilia.

cilium (**sil**-ee-ŭm) *noun* (*plural* **cilia**) **1** each of the minute hairs fringing a leaf, an insect's wing, etc. **2** an eyelash. **3** a hairlike vibrating organ on animal or vegetable tissue. **ciliary** *adjective* [Latin, = eyelash]

cinch (*pr.* sinch) *noun* (*informal*) a certainty, an easy task.

cinder *noun* a small piece of partly burnt coal or wood. **cinders** *plural noun* ashes.

Cinderella *noun* a person or thing that is persistently neglected in favour of others. [the name of a character in a fairy tale by Perrault]

cine (**sin**-ee) *prefix* cinematographic, *cine-camera*, *cine-film*, *cine-projector*.

cinema *noun* **1** a theatre where motion-picture films are shown. **2** films as an art form or an industry. [from Greek *kinema* = movement]

cinematographic (sĭnĕ-mat-ŏ-**graf**-ik) *adjective* for taking or projecting motion pictures.

cinematography (sĭnĕ-mă-**tog**-ră-fee) *noun* the art of making motion-picture films. [from *cinema* + -*graphy*]

cineraria (sin-ĕ-**rair**-ree-ă) *noun* a plant with bright daisy-like flowers.

cinerary urn (**sin**-ĕ-ră-ree) *noun* an urn for holding a person's ashes after cremation. [from Latin *cineris* = of ashes]

cinnabar (**sin**-ă-bar) *noun* **1** red mercuric sulphide; the pigment obtained from this, vermilion. **2** a moth with red wing markings.

cinnamon (**sin**-ă-mŏn) *noun* **1** an aromatic spice made from the inner bark of a SE Asian tree. **2** its colour, yellowish brown.

Cinque Ports (*pr.* sink) a group of ports (originally five) on the SE coast of England, with ancient privileges.

cipher (**sy**-fer) *noun* **1** the symbol 0, representing nought or zero. **2** any Arabic numeral. **3** a person or thing of no importance. **4** a set of letters or symbols representing others, used to conceal the meaning of a message etc. – **cipher** *verb* to write in cipher. [from Arabic *sifr* = nought]

circa (**ser**-kă) *preposition* about, *a vase from circa 1850*. [Latin]

circadian (ser-**kay**-dee-ăn) *adjective* occurring about once a day. [from *circa*, + Latin *dies* = day]

Circe (**ser**-see) (*Gk. legend*) an enchantress who detained Odysseus on her island and changed his companions into pigs.

circle *noun* **1** a perfectly round plane figure. **2** the line enclosing it, every point on which is the same distance from the centre. **3** something shaped like this, a ring. **4** curved rows of seats rising in tiers at a theatre etc. above the lowest level. **5** a number of people bound together by similar interests, *in business circles*. – **circle** *verb* to move in a circle, to form a circle round.

circlet (**ser**-klĕt) *noun* a circular band worn as an ornament, especially round the head.

circuit (**ser**-kĭt) *noun* **1** a line, route, or distance round a place; a motor racing track. **2** a closed path for an electric current; an apparatus with conductors, valves, etc., through which electric current passes. **3** the journey of a judge round a particular district to hold courts; the district itself. **4** a group of churches in an area served by an itinerant minister. **5** a sequence of sporting events, *the tennis circuit*; a sequence of athletic exercises. □ *circuit-breaker noun* a device for interrupting an electric current. [from Latin *circum* = round, + *itum* = gone]

circuitous (ser-**kew**-ĭ-tŭs) *adjective* roundabout, indirect. **circuitously** *adverb*

circuitry (**ser**-kĭ-tree) *noun* circuits; the equipment forming these.

circular *adjective* **1** shaped like a circle. **2** moving round a circle; *a circular tour*, one by a route that brings travellers back to the starting point. **3** (of reasoning) using as evidence for its conclusion the very thing that it is trying to prove. **4** addressed to a circle of people, *a circular letter*. –**circular** *noun* a circular letter or advertising leaflet. **circularity** (serk-yŭ-**la**-rĭ-tee) *noun*

circularise *verb* (also **-ize**) to send a circular to.

circulate *verb* **1** to go round continuously. **2** to pass from place to place. **3** to cause to move round, to send round, *we will circulate this letter*. **4** to circularise, *we will circulate these people*.

circulation *noun* **1** circulating, being circulated. **2** the movement of blood round the body, pumped by the heart. **3** the number of copies sold or distributed, especially of a newspaper.

circulatory (serk-yŭ-**layt**-ŏ-ree) *adjective* of the circulation of blood.

circum- *prefix* around (as in *circumference*). [from Latin *circum* = around]

circumcise *verb* to cut off the foreskin of (a male person), or the clitoris (of a female), as a religious rite or surgically. **circumcision** *noun* [from *circum-*, + Latin *caedere* = to cut]

circumference (ser-**kum**-fĕ-rĕns) *noun* the boundary of a circle, the distance round this. [from *circum-*, + Latin *ferens* = carrying]

circumflex accent (**ser**-kŭm-fleks) *noun* a mark over a vowel, as over *e* in *fête*.

circumlocution (ser-kŭm-lŏ-**kew**-shŏn) *noun* **1** use of many words where a few would do. **2** evasive talk.

circumnavigate *verb* to sail completely round. **circumnavigation** *noun* [from *circum-* + *navigate*]

circumscribe *verb* **1** to draw a line round. **2** to mark the limits of, to restrict. **circumscription** *noun* [from *circum-*, + Latin *scribere* = write]

circumspect (**ser**-kŭm-spekt) *adjective* cautious and watchful, wary. **circumspection** *noun* [from *circum-*, + Latin *specere* = to look]

circumstance *noun* **1** any of the conditions or facts connected with an event, person, or action; *he was a victim of circumstances*, the conditions affecting him were beyond his control; *what are his circumstances?*, what is his financial position?; *they live in reduced circumstances*, in poverty that contrasts with their former prosperity. **2** ceremony, *pomp and circumstance*. □ **in** or **under the circumstances** owing to or making allowances for them. **under no circumstances** certainly not, whatever happens. [from *circum-*, + Latin *stans* = standing]

circumstantial (ser-kŭm-**stan**-shăl) *adjective* **1** giving full details. **2** consisting of facts that strongly suggest something but do not provide direct proof, *circumstantial evidence*. **circumstantially** *adverb*

circumvent (ser-kŭm-**vent**) *verb* to evade, to find a way round, *managed to circumvent the rules*. **circumvention** *noun* [from *circum-*, + Latin *ventum* = come]

circus *noun* **1** a travelling show with performing animals, acrobats, clowns, etc. **2** (*informal*) a group of people performing in sports or a series of lectures etc. either together or in succession. **3** (*informal*) a scene of lively action or disorganisation. **4** (in ancient Rome) a round or oval arena used for chariot races etc. [Latin, = ring]

cirque (*pr.* serk) *noun* a bowl-shaped hollow on a mountain.

cirrhosis (si-**roh**-sĭs) *noun* a chronic disease in which the liver hardens.

cirrocumulus (si-roh-**kewm**-yŭ-lŭs) *noun* rows of small fleecy high clouds.

cirrostratus (si-roh-**strah**-tŭs) *noun* a layer of thin hazy high clouds.

cirrus (**si**-rŭs) *noun* light wispy high clouds. [Latin, = a curl]

CIS the Commonwealth of Independent States, a group of countries most of which used to be republics of the USSR.

cissy *noun* = sissy.

Cistercian (sis-**ter**-shăn) *noun* a member of a religious order that was founded as a branch of the Benedictines.

cistern (**sis**-tern) *noun* a tank or other vessel for storing water, the tank above a toilet bowl.

citadel (**sit**-ă-del) *noun* **1** a fortress overlooking a city. **2** a meeting hall of the Salvation Army.

cite (*pr. as* sight) *verb* **1** to quote or mention as an example or to support an argument. **2** to mention in an official dispatch. **citation** *noun*

citizen *noun* **1** an inhabitant of a city. **2** a person who has full rights in a country or commonwealth by birth or by naturalisation. □ **citizens' band** radio frequencies to be used by private persons for local communication. **citizenship** *noun* [same origin as *city*]

citizenry *noun* citizens collectively.

citric acid (**sit**-rik) *noun* the acid in the juice of lemons, limes, etc.

citrus (**sit**-rŭs) *noun* any of a group of related trees including lemon, orange, and grapefruit. □ **citrus fruit** fruit from such a tree.

city *noun* **1** a large and important town. **2** an urban or rural area meeting the population requirements for city status (which vary from State to State in Australia). **3** the business centre of a city. **4** the people who live in a city. □ **city slicker** (usually *derogatory*) a smart and sophisticated city dweller. [from Latin *civitas* = city]

civet (**siv**-ĕt) *noun* **1** (also **civet cat**) a catlike animal of central Africa. **2** a musky-smelling substance obtained from its glands, used in making perfumes.

civic (**siv**-ik) *adjective* of or proper to a city or town, of citizens or citizenship. **civics** *noun* the study of municipal government and the rights and duties of citizens. □ **civic centre** an area containing municipal offices and other public buildings. [from Latin *civis* = citizen]

civil *adjective* **1** belonging to citizens; *civil liberty*, liberty restricted only by those laws established for the good of the community. **2** of the general public, not the armed forces or the Church; *civil aviation*, non-military; *civil marriage*, with a civil ceremony not a religious one. **3** involving civil law not

criminal law, *a civil dispute*. **4** polite and obliging. □ **civil defence** an organisation for protecting and assisting civilians in an air raid or other enemy action or in a natural disaster. **civil engineering** the designing and construction of roads, bridges, canals, etc. **civil law** law dealing with the private rights of citizens, not with crime. **civil rights** the rights of a citizen. **civil servant** a public servant. **civil war** war between groups of citizens of the same country. **civilly** *adverb*

civilian *noun* a person not serving in the armed forces.

civilisation *noun* (also **-ization**) **1** making or becoming civilised. **2** a stage in the evolution of organised society; a particular type of this, *ancient civilisations*. **3** civilised conditions or society, *far from civilisation*.

civilise *verb* (also **-ize**) **1** to cause to improve from a savage or primitive stage of human society to a more developed one. **2** to improve the behaviour of.

civility *noun* politeness; an act of politeness.

civvies (**siv**-eez) *plural noun* (*informal*) civilian clothes.

cl *abbreviation* centilitre(s).

clack *noun* **1** a short sharp sound like that made by plates struck together. **2** the noise of chatter. –**clack** *verb* to make a clack.

clad *adjective* clothed, *warmly clad*; *iron-clad*, protected with iron.

cladding *noun* a metal or other material applied to the surface of another as a protective covering.

clade *noun* a group of organisms that have evolved from a common ancestor. [from Greek *klados* = a branch]

claim *verb* **1** to request as one's right or due; *the floods claimed many lives*, people died as a result. **2** to declare that something is true or has been achieved; to state without being able to prove. –**claim** *noun* **1** a request for something as one's right; *lay claim to* (see **lay**[3]). **2** the right to something, *a widow has a claim on her deceased husband's estate*. **3** a statement claiming that something is true, an assertion. **4** a thing (especially land) claimed. [same origin as *clamour*]

claimant *noun* a person who makes a claim, especially in law.

clairvoyance (klair-**voy**-ăns) *noun* the supposed power of seeing in the mind either future events or things that are happening or existing out of sight. **clairvoyant** *noun* a person said to have this power. [from French *clair* = clear, + *voyant* = seeing]

clam *noun* a large shellfish with a hinged shell. –**clam** *verb* (**clammed**, **clamming**) **clam up** (*informal*) to refuse to talk.

clamber *verb* to climb with some difficulty.

clammy *adjective* unpleasantly moist and sticky. **clammily** *adverb*, **clamminess** *noun*

clamour *noun* **1** a loud confused noise, especially of shouting. **2** a loud protest or demand. –**clamour** *verb* to make a loud protest or demand. **clamorous** *adjective* [from Latin *clamare* = call out]

clamp *noun* a device for holding things tightly, often with a screw. –**clamp** *verb* to grip with a clamp; to fix firmly. ☐ **clamp down on** to become stricter about; to put a stop to. **clamp-down** *noun*

clan *noun* **1** a group with a common ancestor, *the Scottish clans*. **2** a large family forming a close group.

clandestine (klan-**dest**-ĭn) *adjective* kept secret, done secretly. **clandestinely** *adverb*

clang *noun* a loud ringing sound. –**clang** *verb* to make a clang.

clanger *noun* (*informal*) a blunder; *drop a clanger*, to make a blunder.

clangour (**klang**-ger) *noun* a clanging noise.

clank *noun* a metallic sound like that of metal striking metal. –**clank** *verb* to make a clank.

clannish *adjective* showing clan feeling, clinging together and excluding others.

clap *noun* **1** the sharp noise of thunder. **2** the sound of the palms of the hands being struck together, especially in applause. **3** a friendly slap, *gave him a clap on the shoulder*. –**clap** *verb* (**clapped**, **clapping**) **1** to strike the palms loudly together, especially in applause. **2** to flap (wings) audibly. **3** to put or place quickly, *clapped him into gaol*. ☐ **clapped out** (*informal*) worn out; exhausted.

clapper *noun* the tongue or striker of a bell.

claptrap *noun* pretentious talk or ideas used only to win applause.

Clare, St (1194–1253), founder of the 'Poor Clares', an order of Franciscan nuns.

claret (**kla**-rĕt) *noun* a dry red wine.

clarify *verb* (**clarified**, **clarifying**) **1** to make or become clear or easier to understand. **2** to remove impurities from (fats), e.g. by heating. **clarification** *noun* [from Latin *clarus* = clear]

clarinet (kla-rĭ-**net**) *noun* a woodwind instrument with a single-reed mouthpiece, finger holes, and keys.

clarinettist *noun* a person who plays the clarinet.

clarion (**kla**-ree-ŏn) *noun* **1** a loud clear rousing sound. **2** (*old use*) a shrill war trumpet.

clarity *noun* clearness.

clash *verb* **1** to strike making a loud harsh sound like that of cymbals. **2** to conflict; to disagree. **3** to take place inconveniently at the same time as something else. **4** (of colours) to produce an unpleasant visual effect by not being harmonious. –**clash** *noun* **1** a sound of clashing. **2** a conflict; a disagreement. **3** a clashing of colours.

clasp *noun* **1** a device for fastening things, with interlocking parts. **2** a grasp, a handshake. –**clasp** *verb* **1** to fasten; to join with a clasp. **2** to grasp; to hold or embrace closely. ☐ **clasp knife** a folding knife with a catch for fixing it open.

clasper *noun* a clasping organ of certain fishes, insects, crustaceans, etc., especially for holding the female during mating.

class *noun* **1** people, animals, or things with some characteristics in common. **2** people of the same social or economic level, *the working class*. **3** a set of students taught together; a session when these are taught. **4** a division according to quality, *first class*; *tourist class*. **5** distinction, high quality, *a tennis player with class*. –**class** *verb* to place in a class, to classify. ☐ **class interval** (in mathematics) each of the groups into which a range of values is divided. **in a class of its own** much superior to everything else of its kind. [from Latin *classis* = a social division of the Roman people]

classic *adjective* **1** having a high quality that is recognised and unquestioned, *Hardy's classic novel*. **2** very typical, *a classic case of malnutrition*. **3** having qualities like those of classical art, simple and harmonious; *classic clothes*, plain and conventional in style. **4** famous through being long established. –**classic** *noun* **1** a classic author or work etc., *'Pride and Prejudice' is a classic*. **2** a garment in classic style. **classics** *noun* the study of ancient Greek and Roman literature, culture, etc. [from Latin *classicus* = of the highest class]

classical *adjective* **1** model or first-class, especially in literature. **2** of ancient Greek and

Roman art, literature, and culture; *a classical scholar*, an expert in these. **3** simple and harmonious in style. **4** traditional and standard in style, *classical music*. **classically** *adverb*

classicism *noun* following of the classic style.

classicist *noun* a classical scholar.

classified *adjective* **1** (of advertisements) arranged according to subject matter. **2** (of information) designated as officially secret and available only to specified people.

classify *verb* (**classified**, **classifying**) to arrange systematically in classes or groups, to put into a particular class. **classifiable** *adjective*, **classification** *noun*

classless *adjective* without distinctions of social class.

classroom *noun* a room where a class of students is taught.

classy *adjective* (*informal*) stylish, superior. **classily** *adverb*, **classiness** *noun*

clatter *noun* **1** a sound like that of plates rattled together. **2** noisy talk. –**clatter** *verb* to make or cause to make a clatter.

Claudius (10 BC–AD 54), Tiberius Claudius Nero Germanicus, Roman emperor 41–54.

clause *noun* **1** a single part in a treaty, law, or contract. **2** a part of a complex sentence, with its own finite verb.

claustrophobia (klos-trŏ-**foh**-bee-ă) *noun* abnormal fear of being in an enclosed space. **claustrophobic** *adjective* [from Latin *claustrum* = enclosed space, + *phobia*]

clave *see* **cleave²**.

claves *plural noun* a pair of sticks that make a hollow sound when struck together, used as a musical instrument.

clavichord (**klav**-ĭ-kord) *noun* a stringed keyboard instrument with a very soft tone.

clavicle (**klav**-ikŭl) *noun* the collarbone.

clavier (**klav**-ee-er) *noun* **1** a musical instrument played from a keyboard. **2** this keyboard.

claw *noun* **1** the pointed nail on an animal's or bird's foot; a foot with such nails. **2** the pincers of a shellfish, *a lobster's claw*. **3** a device like a claw, used for grappling and holding things. –**claw** *verb* to grasp, scratch, or pull with a claw or with the hands. ☐ **claw hammer** a hammer with one side of the head forked for pulling out nails.

clay *noun* stiff sticky earth that becomes hard when baked, used for making bricks and

pottery. ☐ **clay pigeon** a breakable disc thrown up as a target for shooting. **clayey** *adjective*

claymore *noun* a Scottish two-edged broadsword.

claypan *noun* (*Austral.*) a natural hollow in clay soil, retaining water after rain.

Clayton's *adjective* (*Austral. informal*) imitation, sham; lacking an element normally considered essential. [from the proprietary name of a non-alcoholic drink marketed as 'the drink you have when you're not having a drink']

clean *adjective* **1** free from dirt or impurities, not soiled, not yet used. **2** (of a nuclear bomb) producing relatively little fallout. **3** with nothing dishonourable in it; (of a licence) with no endorsements. **4** without projections or roughness, smooth and even. **5** keeping to the rules; not unfair, *a clean fighter*. –**clean** *adverb* completely, entirely, *I clean forgot*; *clean bowled*, bowled out directly, without the ball touching the bat. –**clean** *verb* **1** to make clean. **2** to dry-clean. **3** to remove the innards of before cooking, to gut, *clean the fish*. –**clean** *noun* cleaning, *give it a clean*. ☐ **clean-cut** *adjective* sharply outlined, *clean-cut features*. **clean-shaven** *adjective* with beard, moustache, and whiskers shaved off. **clean up** to make clean and tidy; to rid of crime and corruption; (*informal*) to make a gain or profit; (*informal*) to defeat thoroughly. **come clean** (*informal*) to confess. **make a clean breast of** to confess fully. **cleanness** *noun*

cleaner *noun* **1** a device or substance used for cleaning things. **2** a person employed to clean rooms. **cleaners** *plural noun* a dry-cleaning establishment.

cleanly¹ (**kleen**-lee) *adverb* **1** in a clean way, *make the break cleanly*. **2** efficiently; without difficulty.

cleanly² (**klen**-lee) *adjective* attentive to cleanness, with clean habits. **cleanliness** *noun*

cleanse (*pr.* klenz) *verb* to make thoroughly clean. **cleanser** *noun* a cleansing substance.

cleanskin *noun* (*Austral.*) **1** an unbranded animal. **2** an unlabelled bottle of wine.

clear *adjective* **1** transparent, *clear glass*; *clear water*, not muddy or cloudy; *clear soup*, not thickened. **2** free from blemishes. **3** free from guilt, *a clear conscience*. **4** easily seen, heard, or understood; distinct. **5** evident, *a clear case of cheating*. **6** free from doubt, not confused. **7** free from obstruction or from something undesirable. **8** net, without deductions, complete, *a clear $1000*; *give 3 clear days' notice.* –**clear** *adverb* **1** clearly. **2** completely. **3** apart, not in contact, *stand clear!* –**clear** *verb* **1** to make or become clear. **2** to free (one's throat) of phlegm or huskiness by a slight cough. **3** to get past or over, especially without touching. **4** to get approval or authorisation for; *clear goods through customs*, satisfy official requirements there. **5** to pass (a cheque) through a clearing house. **6** to make as net gain or profit. ☐ **clear away** to remove; to remove used crockery etc. after a meal. **clear-cut** *adjective* very distinct; not open to doubt. **clear off** (*informal*) to go away. **clear the decks** to clear away hindrances and prepare for action. **clear up** to tidy up; to become better or brighter; *clear up the mystery*, solve it. **in the clear** free of suspicion or difficulty. **clearly** *adverb*, **clearness** *noun* [from Latin *clarus* = clear]

clearance *noun* **1** clearing. **2** authorisation, permission. **3** the space left clear when one object moves past another.

clearing *noun* an open space from which trees have been cleared in a forest.

clearing house *noun* **1** an office at which banks exchange cheques and settle the balances. **2** an agency that collects and distributes information etc.

clearway *noun* a road on which vehicles must not stop between certain hours.

cleat *noun* **1** a short piece of wood or metal with projecting ends round which a rope may be fastened. **2** a strip or other projecting piece fixed to a gangway etc. or to footwear, to prevent slipping. **3** a wedge.

cleavage *noun* **1** a split, a division made by cleaving. **2** the hollow between a woman's breasts, exposed by a low-cut garment.

cleave[1] *verb* **1** to divide by chopping, to split or become split. **2** to make a way through.

Usage The past tense may be either *cleaved* or *clove* or *cleft*, or *has cloven* or *has cleft*. The adjectives *cloven* and *cleft* are used of different objects (*see* **cleft** and **cloven**).

---

cleave[2] *verb* (**cleaved** *or* **clave**, **cleaved**, **cleaving**) (*old use*) to adhere, to cling.

cleaver *noun* a butcher's chopper.

clef *noun* a symbol on a stave in a musical score, showing the pitch of the notes (e.g. treble, bass). [French, = key]

cleft *see* **cleave**[1]. –**cleft** *adjective* split, partly divided; *a cleft chin*, with a V-shaped hollow. –**cleft** *noun* a split, a cleavage. ☐ **cleft palate** a defect in the roof of the mouth where two sides of the palate failed to join before birth. **in a cleft stick** in a difficult dilemma.

clematis (**klem**-ă-tĭss *or* klĕ-**may**-tĭss) *noun* a climbing plant with white or purplish flowers.

clemency (**klem**-ĕn-see) *noun* **1** mildness, especially of weather. **2** mercy. **clement** *adjective*

clench *verb* **1** to close (the teeth or fingers) tightly. **2** to grasp tightly. **3** to fasten (a nail or rivet) by hammering the point sideways after it is driven through. –**clench** *noun* a clenching action; a clenched state.

Cleopatra (69–30 BC) ruler of Egypt from 51 BC, famous for her liaisons with Julius Caesar and Mark Antony.

clerestory (**kleer**-stŏ-ree *or* -stor-ree) *noun* **1** an upper row of windows in a large church, above the level of the roofs of the aisles. **2** a raised section of the roof of a house or other building with windows to admit light.

clergy *noun* the people who have been ordained as priests or ministers of the Christian Church. **clergyman**, **clergywoman** *nouns*

cleric (**kle**-rik) *noun* a member of the clergy.

clerical *adjective* **1** of clerks; *a clerical error*, one made in copying or writing something out. **2** of the clergy.

clerihew (**kle**-rĭ-hew) *noun* a short witty verse in four lines of unequal length, rhyming in couplets. [named after E. Clerihew Bentley, who invented it]

clerk (*pr.* klark) *noun* **1** a person employed to keep records or accounts etc. in an office. **2** an official who keeps the records of a court or council etc.

clever *adjective* **1** quick at learning and understanding things, skilful; *he was too clever for us*, he outwitted us. **2** showing skill, *a clever plan*. **cleverly** *adverb*, **cleverness** *noun*

cliché (**klee**-shay) *noun* a phrase or idea that has lost its meaning or impact through overuse. [French, = stereotyped]

click *noun* a short sharp sound, *the click of a switch.* –**click** *verb* **1** to make or cause to make a click; to fasten with a click. **2** (*informal*) to be a success. **3** (*informal*) to become understood. **4** (*informal*) to get on well, to become friendly. **5** (in computing) to press and release (a button on a mouse); to select (an item represented on a screen) by positioning the pointer on the item and then pressing and releasing the mouse button. clicky *adjective*

client *noun* **1** a person using the services of a professional person such as a lawyer, architect, etc. **2** a customer.

clientele (kly-ĕn-**tel** *or* klee-) *noun* clients, customers.

cliff *noun* a steep rock face, especially on a coast.

cliffhanger *noun* a story or contest full of suspense.

climacteric (kly-**mak**-tĕ-rik) *noun* the period of life when physical powers begin to decline.

climactic (kly-**mak**-tik) *adjective* of a climax.

climate *noun* **1** the regular weather conditions of an area. **2** an area with certain weather conditions, *living in a hot climate*. **3** a general attitude or feeling, an atmosphere, *a climate of hostility*. climatic (kly-**mat**-ik) *adjective*

climax *noun* **1** the event or point of greatest interest or intensity. **2** the point at which a community of plants has reached its fully developed form and continues to reproduce itself without further change. –climax *verb* to reach or bring to a climax. [from Greek *klimax* = ladder]

climb *verb* **1** to go up or over by effort. **2** to move upwards, to go higher. **3** to grow up a support, *a climbing rose*. –climb *noun* an ascent made by climbing. ☐ climb down to go downwards by effort; to retreat from a position taken up in argument. climbing frame a structure of joined poles and bars for children to climb on.

climber *noun* **1** one who climbs, a mountaineer. **2** a climbing plant.

clime *noun* (*literary*) **1** a region. **2** a climate.

clinch *verb* **1** to fasten securely; to clench (a nail or rivet). **2** (in boxing) to be too close together for a full-arm blow. **3** to settle conclusively, *clinched the deal*. –clinch *noun* **1** a clinching position in boxing. **2** (*informal*) an embrace. [from *clench*]

clincher *noun* a decisive point that settles an argument, proposition, etc.

cling *verb* (clung, clinging) **1** to hold on tightly. **2** to become attached, to stick. **3** to remain close or in contact; to be emotionally attached or dependent. **4** to refuse to abandon, *clinging to hopes of rescue*. ☐ cling film a very thin

clinging kind of polythene used as a wrapping, especially for food. cling peach *or* clingstone *noun* a kind of peach or nectarine in which the stone is difficult to separate from the flesh.

clinic *noun* **1** a private or specialised hospital. **2** a place or session at which specialised treatment or advice is given to visiting persons, *antenatal clinic*; *tennis clinic*. [from Greek *klinikos* = of a bed]

clinical *adjective* **1** of a clinic. **2** of or used in the treatment of patients, *clinical thermometer*. **3** of or based on observed signs and symptoms, *clinical medicine*. **4** looking bare and hygienic. **5** unemotional, cool and detached. clinically *adverb*

clink¹ *noun* a thin sharp sound like glasses striking together. –clink *verb* to make or cause to make this sound.

clink² *noun* (*informal*) prison, *in the clink*.

clinker *noun* a mass of slag or lava; rough stony material left after coal has burnt; a piece of this.

Clio (**kly**-oh) (*Gk. & Rom. myth.*) the Muse of history.

clip¹ *noun* **1** a device for holding things tightly or together; a paper clip. **2** a magazine for a firearm. **3** an ornament fastened by a clip. –clip *verb* (clipped, clipping) to fix or fasten with a clip.

clip² *verb* (clipped, clipping) **1** to cut or trim with shears or scissors. **2** to punch a small piece from (a ticket) to show that it has been used. **3** (*informal*) to hit sharply, *clipped his ear*. –clip *noun* **1** the act or process of clipping; a piece clipped off or out. **2** the wool cut from a sheep or flock at one shearing. **3** an extract from a film; a video clip. **4** (*informal*) a sharp blow.

clipboard *noun* **1** a portable board with a spring clip at the top for holding papers. **2** a temporary storage area in a computer where text or other data cut or copied from a file is kept until it is pasted into another file.

clipper *noun* a fast horse or ship.

clippers *plural noun* an instrument for clipping hair.

clipping *noun* a piece clipped off or out.

clique (*pr.* kleek) *noun* a small exclusive group. cliquey *adjective*, cliquish *adjective*

clitoris (**klit**-ŏ-rĭss) *noun* a small erectile part of the female genitals, at the upper end of the vulva. clitoral *adjective* [from Greek *kleitoris*]

cloaca (kloh-**ay**-kǎ) *noun* the excretory opening at the end of the intestinal canal in birds, reptiles, etc. [Latin, = sewer]

cloak *noun* **1** a loose sleeveless outdoor garment. **2** something that conceals, *under the cloak of darkness*. –**cloak** *verb* to cover or conceal. ☐ **cloak-and-dagger** *adjective* involving dramatic adventures in spying.

cloakroom *noun* a room where outdoor clothes and bags etc. may be left temporarily.

clobber[1] *noun* (*informal*) clothing and equipment.

clobber[2] *verb* (*informal*) **1** to hit repeatedly. **2** to defeat. **3** to criticise severely.

cloche (*pr.* klosh *or* klohsh) *noun* **1** a portable glass or plastic cover for outdoor plants. **2** a woman's close-fitting bell-shaped hat. [French, = a bell]

clock[1] *noun* **1** an instrument (other than a watch) for measuring and showing the time. **2** a measuring device with a dial or displayed figures, e.g. a taximeter, an odometer. **3** the seed-head of a dandelion. –**clock** *verb* **1** to time (a race or competitor). **2** (*informal*) to achieve as a speed, *he clocked* or *clocked up 10 seconds for the 100 metres*. **3** (*informal*) to hit. ☐ **clock arithmetic** modulo arithmetic. **clock in** or **on** to register one's arrival for work. **clock out** or **off** to register one's departure from work. **round the clock** all day and night. [from Latin *clocca* = bell]

clock[2] *noun* an ornamental pattern on the side of a stocking or sock.

clockwise *adverb* & *adjective* moving in a curve from left to right, as seen from the centre of the circle. [from *clock* + *-wise*[2]]

clockwork *noun* a mechanism with wheels and springs, like that of a clock. ☐ **like clockwork** with perfect regularity and precision.

clod *noun* a lump of earth or clay.

clodhopper *noun* (*informal*) a large heavy shoe.

clog *noun* a wooden-soled shoe. –**clog** *verb* (**clogged**, **clogging**) **1** to cause an obstruction in. **2** to become blocked.

cloister *noun* **1** a covered walk along the side of a church or other building, looking on a courtyard. **2** a monastery or convent; life in this. **cloistral** *adjective* [from Latin *claustrum* = enclosed place]

cloistered *adjective* sheltered, secluded.

clone *noun* **1** a group of plants or organisms produced asexually from one ancestor; a member of this group. **2** a person or thing regarded as identical with another. –**clone** *verb* to propagate or become propagated as a clone.

close[1] (*pr.* klohs) *adjective* **1** near in space or time. **2** near in relationship, *a close relative*. **3** dear to each other, *close friends*. **4** nearly alike, *a close resemblance*. **5** in which the competitors are nearly equal, *a close contest*. **6** dense, compact, with only slight intervals, *a close texture*. **7** detailed; leaving no gaps or weaknesses; concentrated. **8** secretive. **9** stingy. **10** stuffy, humid, without fresh air. –**close** *adverb* closely, in a near position, *they live close by*. –**close** *noun* a cul-de-sac. ☐ **at close quarters** very close together. **close-fisted** *adjective* (*informal*) stingy. **close-knit** *adjective* tightly interlocked; closely united in friendship. **a close shave** *see* shave. **close-up** *noun* a photograph giving a detailed view of something; a close view. **closely** *adverb*, **closeness** *noun*

close[2] (*pr.* klohz) *verb* **1** to shut, to block up. **2** to be or declare to be not open to the public. **3** to bring or come to an end. **4** to bring or come closer or into contact, *close ranks*. **5** to make (an electric circuit) continuous. **6** to come within striking distance, to grapple. –**close** *noun* a conclusion, an end. ☐ **closed book** a subject one has never studied. **closed-circuit television** that transmitted by wires, not waves, to a restricted number of screens. **closed curve** a curve whose end is connected to its beginning, such as a circle or an ellipse. **closed season** the season when killing of game etc. is forbidden by law. **closed shop** the system whereby membership of a trade union (or of a specified one) is a condition of employment in a certain establishment. **close in (on)** to approach from all sides (so as to shut in or entrap). **close with** to accept (an offer); to accept the offer made by (a person). [from *clausum* = shut]

closet *noun* **1** a cupboard. **2** a small room. **3** (used as *adjective*) secret, *a closet drinker*. –**closet** *verb* (**closeted**, **closeting**) to shut away in private conference or study.

closure (kloh-*zh*er) *noun* **1** closing; a closed condition. **2** a decision in Parliament to take a vote without further debate.

clot *noun* **1** a small thickened mass formed from blood or other liquid. **2** (*informal*) a stupid person. –**clot** *verb* (**clotted**, **clotting**) to form clots. ☐ **clotted cream** cream thickened by being scalded.

cloth *noun* **1** woven or felted material. **2** a piece of this for a special purpose; a dishcloth, tablecloth, etc. **3** clerical clothes, the clergy, *respect for the cloth*.

clothe *verb* (**clothed** *or* **clad, clothing**) **1** to put clothes upon; to provide with clothes. **2** to cover as with clothes.

clothes *plural noun* **1** things worn to cover the body and limbs. **2** bedclothes. □ **clothes horse** a frame with bars over which clothes etc. are hung to air. **clothes line** a rope or wire or hoist etc. on which washed clothes are hung to dry. **clothes peg** a clip or forked device for securing clothes to a clothes line.

clothier (**kloh**-*thee*-er) *noun* a seller of men's clothes.

clothing *noun* clothes, garments.

cloud *noun* **1** a visible mass of condensed watery vapour, floating in the sky. **2** a mass of smoke or mist etc. **3** a mass of things moving in the air, *a cloud of insects*. **4** a state of gloom, trouble, or suspicion. –**cloud** *noun* **1** to cover or darken with clouds or gloom or trouble. **2** to become overcast or indistinct or gloomy. □ **cloud chamber** a device containing vapour in a state such that the paths of charged particles, X-rays, and gamma rays can be observed by the trail of tiny drops of condensed vapour that they produce. **cloud computing** the use of Internet-based servers rather than local servers. **under a cloud** out of favour; under suspicion; in disgrace.

cloudburst *noun* a sudden violent rainstorm.

cloudless *adjective* free from clouds.

cloudy *adjective* (**cloudier, cloudiest**) **1** covered with clouds. **2** not transparent, *a cloudy liquid*. **cloudiness** *noun*

clout *noun* (*informal*) **1** a blow. **2** power of effective action, *trade unions with clout*. –**clout** *verb* (*informal*) to hit.

clove[1] *see* **cleave**[1].

clove[2] *noun* one of the small bulbs making up a compound bulb, *a clove of garlic*.

clove[3] *noun* the dried unopened flower bud of tropical myrtle, used as a spice.

clove hitch *noun* a knot used to secure a rope round a spar or pole.

cloven *see* **cleave**[1]. □ **cloven hoof** one that is divided, like those of oxen or sheep.

clover *noun* a fodder plant with usually three-lobed leaves (¶ the rare *four-leaved clover* is often thought to bring luck to the finder). □ **in clover** in ease and luxury.

clown *noun* **1** a performer, especially in a circus, who does comical tricks and actions. **2** a person who is always behaving comically. –**clown** *verb* to perform as a clown, to behave comically. **clownish** *adjective*

cloy *verb* to sicken by glutting with sweetness or pleasure, *cloy the appetite*.

cloying *adjective* sickeningly sweet.

club *noun* **1** a heavy stick with one end thicker than the other, used as a weapon. **2** a stick with a shaped head used to hit the ball in golf. **3** a playing card of the suit (*clubs*) marked with black (three-leaved) clovers. **4** a society of people who subscribe to provide themselves with sport or entertainment etc.; their premises. **5** an organisation offering subscribers certain benefits, *a Christmas club*; *a book club*. –**club** *verb* (**clubbed, clubbing**) **1** to strike with a club. **2** to join in subscribing, *we clubbed together to buy a boat*. □ **club foot** a deformed foot.

clubbable *adjective* sociable, likely to be a good member of a social club.

clubhouse *noun* the premises used by a club.

cluck *noun* the throaty cry of a hen. –**cluck** *verb* to utter a cluck.

clucky *adjective* **1** (of a hen) sitting on eggs. **2** (*Austral. informal*) (of a woman) wanting to have a baby.

clue *noun* **1** a fact or idea that gives a guide to the solution of a problem; *hasn't a clue*, (*informal*) is stupid or incompetent. **2** a word or words indicating what is to be inserted in a crossword puzzle. –**clue** *verb* to provide with a clue. □ **clue up** (*informal*) to inform.

clueless *adjective* **1** without a clue. **2** (*informal*) stupid or incompetent.

cluey *adjective* (*informal*) well informed, aware.

clump *noun* **1** a cluster or mass. **2** a clumping sound. –**clump** *verb* **1** to form a clump; to arrange in a clump. **2** to walk with a heavy tread. **3** (*informal*) to hit.

clumsy *adjective* (**clumsier, clumsiest**) **1** heavy and ungraceful in movement or shape. **2** large and difficult to handle or use. **3** done without tact or skill, *a clumsy apology*. **clumsily** *adverb*, **clumsiness** *noun*

clung *see* **cling**.

clunk *noun* a dull sound like thick metal objects striking together. –**clunk** *verb* to make this sound.

cluster *noun* a small close group. –**cluster** *verb* to bring or come together in a cluster.

clutch¹ *verb* to grasp tightly; *clutch at*, to try to grasp. –**clutch** *noun* **1** a tight grasp; a clutching movement. **2** a device for connecting and disconnecting certain working parts in machinery; the pedal or other device operating this.

clutch² *noun* **1** a set of eggs for hatching. **2** the chickens hatched from these.

clutter *noun* **1** things lying about untidily. **2** a crowded untidy state. –**clutter** *verb* to fill with clutter, to crowd untidily.

Clydesdale *noun* a draughthorse of a heavily-built breed.

cm *abbreviation* centimetre.

CND *abbreviation* Campaign for Nuclear Disarmament.

Cnut (k-**noot**) (c. 994–1035), Danish king of England 1017–35.

CO *abbreviation* Commanding Officer.

Co. *abbreviation* Company.

c/o *abbreviation* care of (*see* **care**).

co- *prefix* together with, jointly, *co-author*; *co-pilot*; *coexistence*.

coach *noun* **1** a large four-wheeled horse-drawn carriage. **2** a railway carriage. **3** a chartered or long-distance bus. **4** an instructor in sports. **5** a teacher giving private specialised tuition. –**coach** *verb* to train or teach.

coachwood *noun* an Australian tree with light tough wood used in boat-building, cabinetmaking, etc.

coagulant (koh-**ag**-yŭ-lănt) *noun* a substance that causes coagulation.

coagulate (koh-**ag**-yŭ-layt) *verb* to change from liquid to semi-solid, to clot. **coagulation** *noun*

coal *noun* **1** a hard black mineral used for burning to supply heat. **2** a piece of this; one that is burning, *a live coal*. ☐ **carry coals to Newcastle** to take a thing to a place where it is already plentiful. **coal tar** tar produced when gas is made from coal. **haul over the coals** to reprimand severely. **heap coals of fire** to cause remorse by returning good for evil.

coalesce (koh-ă-**less**) *verb* to combine and form one whole. **coalescence** *noun*

coalface *noun* the exposed surface of coal in a mine.

coalfield *noun* an area where coal occurs.

coalification (koh-lĭ-fik-**ay**-shŏn) *noun* the process by which vegetable matter in the earth is converted into coal.

coalition (koh-ă-**lish**-ŏn) *noun* **1** union. **2** a temporary union between political parties. –**Coalition** *noun* (in Australia) the alliance of the Liberal Party and the National Party.

coarse *adjective* **1** composed of large particles, rough or loose in texture. **2** rough or crude in manner or behaviour, not refined. **coarsely** *adverb*, **coarseness** *noun*

coarsen *verb* to make or become coarse.

coast *noun* the seashore and the land near it; its outline. –**coast** *verb* **1** to sail along a coast. **2** to ride down a hill or slope without using power. ☐ **the coast is clear** there is no chance of being seen or hindered.

coastal *adjective* of or near the coast.

coaster *noun* **1** a ship that trades between ports on the same coast. **2** a small mat or tray for a glass or decanter.

coastguard *noun* **1** a public organisation that keeps watch on the coast to report passing ships, prevent or detect smuggling, etc. **2** any of its members.

coastline *noun* the shape or outline of a coast.

coat *noun* **1** an outdoor garment with sleeves. **2** an animal's hair or fur covering its body. **3** a covering layer, *a coat of paint*. –**coat** *verb* to cover with a layer; to form a covering to. ☐ **coat of arms** a design on a shield, used as an emblem by a family, city, or institution.

coating *noun* **1** a covering layer. **2** material for coats.

coax *verb* **1** to persuade gently or gradually. **2** to obtain in this way, *coaxed a smile*.

coaxial (koh-**aks**-ee-ăl) *adjective* having an axis in common. **coaxial cable** an electric cable in which there are two conductors arranged so that one is inside the other with a layer of insulating material between. [from *co-* + *axis*]

cob¹ *noun* **1** a male swan. **2** a sturdy short-legged horse for riding. **3** a large kind of hazelnut. **4** a round domed loaf of bread. **5** the central part of an ear of maize, on which the corn grows.

cob² *noun* a building material of earth, clay, or chalk reinforced with straw.

cobalt (**koh**-bolt) *noun* **1** a chemical element (symbol Co), a hard white metal used in many alloys and with radioactive forms used in medicine and industry. **2** colouring matter made from this; its deep blue colour.

Cobb & Co. an Australian coaching company operating from 1853–1924 in the eastern colonies.

cobber *noun* (*Austral. informal*) a friend, a mate.

cobble¹ *noun* (in full **cobblestone**) a rounded stone used for paving. **–cobble** *verb* to pave with cobblestones.

cobble² *verb* to put together or mend roughly.

cobbler *noun* **1** a shoe repairer. **2** (*Austral.*) a sheep that is difficult to shear and therefore the last to be shorn. **3** a dessert of stewed fruit topped with a crust.

cobra (**koh**-brǎ *or* **kob**-rǎ) *noun* a poisonous snake of Asia and Africa that can rear up.

cobweb *noun* the fine network spun by a spider; a strand of this. **cobwebby** *adjective* [from an old word *coppe* = spider, + *web*]

coca (**koh**-kǎ) *noun* a South American shrub with leaves that are chewed as a stimulant; its leaves.

cocaine (kǒ-**kayn**) *noun* a drug made from coca, used as a local anaesthetic or as a stimulant.

coccyx (**kok**-siks) *noun* a small triangular bone at the base of the spine. [from Greek *kokkux* = cuckoo (the bone looks like a cuckoo's beak)]

cochineal (koch-ĭ-**neel**) *noun* bright red colouring matter made from the dried bodies of certain insects.

cochlea (**kok**-lee-ǎ) *noun* the spiral cavity of the inner ear. [Latin, = snail shell]

cock¹ *noun* **1** a male bird, especially of the domestic fowl. **2** a tap or spout for controlling the flow of a liquid. **3** a lever in a gun, raised ready to be released by the trigger; *at half cock*, only half ready for something. **–cock** *verb* **1** to tilt or turn upwards; *the dog cocked his ears*, raised them attentively. **2** to raise the cock of (a gun) ready for firing; to set (the shutter of a camera) ready for release. ☐ **cock-a-doodle-doo** *interjection* the sound of a cock crowing. **cock-a-hoop** *adjective* & *adverb* pleased and triumphant. **cock and bull story** a foolish story that one should not believe. **cock a snook** *see* **snook**. **cock-crow** *noun* dawn, when cocks begin to crow. **cock of the walk** the most influential person.

cock² *noun* a cone-shaped pile of straw or hay. **–cock** *verb* to pile in cocks.

cockade (kok-**ayd**) *noun* a rosette of ribbon worn on a hat as a badge.

cockatiel *noun* a small Australian crested parrot.

cockatoo *noun* (*plural* **cockatoos**) **1** a crested parrot. **2** (*Austral. informal*) a farmer with a small holding. **3** (*Austral. informal*) a lookout posted to protect an illegal activity. [from Malay *kakatua*]

Cockatoo Island an island in the mouth of the Parramatta River, near Sydney Harbour, used as a convict prison and later as a dockyard.

cockchafer (**kok**-chay-fer) *noun* a large flying beetle.

cocked hat *noun* a triangular hat worn with some uniforms.

cockerel *noun* a young domestic cock.

cocker spaniel *noun* a small spaniel with a golden-brown coat.

cock-eyed *adjective* (*informal*) **1** slanting, not straight. **2** absurd, impractical.

cockfight *noun* a fight between cocks as sport. **cockfighting** *noun*

cockle *noun* **1** an edible shellfish. **2** a small shallow boat. **3** a pucker or bulge. **–cockle** *verb* to pucker (a stiff substance); to become puckered. ☐ **warm the cockles of one's heart** to make one rejoice.

cockney *noun* (*plural* **cockneys**) **1** a native of East London. **2** the dialect or accent of this area. **–cockney** *adjective* of cockneys or cockney.

cockpit *noun* **1** a place made for cockfighting. **2** the compartment for the pilot and crew of an aircraft. **3** the well where the wheel is situated in certain small yachts etc. **4** the driver's seat in a racing car.

cockroach *noun* a beetle-like insect.

cocksure *adjective* **1** quite convinced, very positive. **2** overconfident of oneself.

cocktail *noun* **1** a mixed alcoholic drink. **2** an appetiser containing shellfish or fruit, *prawn* or *grapefruit cocktail*. **3** a mixture or concoction. ☐ **cocktail dress** a usually short evening dress. **cocktail frankfurt** a small frankfurt.

cocky¹ *adjective* (**cockier, cockiest**) conceited and arrogant. **cockily** *adverb*, **cockiness** *noun*

cocky² *noun* (*Austral. informal*) a farmer with a small property. ☐ **cocky's joy** treacle or golden syrup.

cocoa *noun* **1** powder made from crushed cacao seeds. **2** a drink made from this. [an alteration of *cacao*]

coconut *noun* **1** the hard-shelled nut of the coconut palm, containing a sweet juice. **2** its edible white lining. □ **coconut matting** matting made from the tough fibre of the coconut's outer husk. [from Spanish *coco* = grinning face (the base of the nut looks like a monkey's face)]

cocoon (kŏ-**koon**) *noun* **1** the silky sheath round a chrysalis. **2** a protective wrapping. –**cocoon** *verb* to protect by wrapping completely.

Cocos Islands (koh-kŏs) (also **Keeling Islands**) a group of 27 small islands in the Indian Ocean, administered by Australia.

COD *abbreviation* cash on delivery.

cod *noun* (*plural* **cod**) any of several sea and freshwater fish used as food, e.g. *Atlantic cod*, *Murray cod*, etc. □ **cod liver oil** oil obtained from cod livers, rich in vitamins A and D.

coda (koh-dă) *noun* the concluding passage of a piece of music, after the main part. [Italian]

coddle *verb* **1** to cherish and protect carefully. **2** to cook (eggs) in water just below boiling point.

code *noun* **1** a pre-arranged word or phrase representing a message, for secrecy. **2** a system of words, letters, or symbols used to represent others, especially in order to send messages by machine (e.g. the *Morse code*). **3** a set of laws or rules, *a code of practice for advertisers*. **4** a set of program instructions for use in a computer. –**code** *verb* to put into code.

codeine (koh-deen) *noun* a white substance made from opium, used to relieve pain or induce sleep. [from Greek *kodeia* = poppy-head]

codger *noun* (*informal*) a fellow.

codicil (koh-dĭ-sil) *noun* an addition to a will.

codify (koh-dĭ-fy) *verb* (**codified**, **codifying**) to arrange (laws or rules) systematically into a code. **codification** *noun*, **codifier** *noun*

codling[1] *noun* (also **codlin**) **1** a kind of cooking apple. **2** a **codling moth**, a moth whose larva feeds on apples.

codling[2] *noun* a small cod.

codomain *noun* (in mathematics) the set into which a mapping leads; the set that contains the range in use in all its possible expressions.

co-dominant *adjective* being one of the two or more dominant species in an area.

–**co-dominant** *noun* a co-dominant species. **co-dominance** *noun*

codpiece *noun* a bag or flap at the front of men's breeches in 15th- and 16th-century dress.

co-driver *noun* a person who takes turns in driving a vehicle in a rally.

codswallop *noun* (*informal*) nonsense, humbug.

coed *adjective* (*informal*) coeducational.

coeducation *noun* education of boys and girls together. **coeducational** *adjective*

coefficient (koh-ĕ-**fish**-ĕnt) *noun* a multiplier, a mathematical factor.

coelacanth (seel-ă-kanth) *noun* a kind of sea fish that is extinct except for one species.

coelenterate (sĕ-**len**-tĕ-răt) *noun* a member of the group of aquatic animals (including sea anemones, hydras, jellyfish, and corals) with a simple tube-shaped or cup-shaped body and a digestive system with a single opening surrounded by a ring of tentacles.

co-enzyme *noun* an organic compound with which an enzyme needs to combine to become active.

coequal *adjective* equal to one another.

coerce (koh-**erss**) *verb* to compel by threats or force. **coercion** (koh-**er**-shŏn) *noun*, **coercive** (koh-**er**-siv) *adjective*

coeval (koh-ee-văl) *adjective* having the same age; existing at the same epoch. [from *co-*, + Latin *aevum* = age]

coexist *verb* to exist together, especially in mutual tolerance. **coexistence** *noun*, **coexistent** *adjective*

coextensive *adjective* extending over the same space or time.

C. of E. *abbreviation* Church of England.

coffee *noun* **1** the beanlike seeds of a tropical shrub, roasted and ground for making a drink. **2** this drink. **3** light brown colour. □ **coffee bar** or **shop** a place serving coffee and light refreshments from a counter. **coffee table** a small low table. [from Arabic *kahwa*]

coffer *noun* a large strong box for holding money and valuables. **coffers** *plural noun* funds, financial resources. □ **coffer dam** a temporary watertight structure built or placed round an area of water that can then be pumped dry to allow building work etc. to be done within.

coffin *noun* a box in which a dead body is placed for burial or cremation.

cog *noun* each of a series of teeth on the edge of a wheel, fitting into and pushing those on another wheel.

cogent (**koh**-jěnt) *adjective* convincing, compelling belief. **cogently** *adverb*, **cogency** *noun*

cogitate (**koj**-ĭ-tayt) *verb* to think deeply. **cogitation** *noun*

cognac (**kon**-yak) *noun* a high-quality brandy made in Cognac in France; (loosely) any brandy, especially a French brandy.

cognate (**kog**-nayt) *adjective* having the same source or origin; (of things) related. –**cognate** *noun* 1 a relative. 2 a cognate word, e.g. English *fish*, Latin *pisce*, German *Fisch*. □ **cognate object** one closely related in meaning or derivation to the verb governing it, e.g. *life* in 'he lives a hectic life'. [from *co-*, + Latin *natus* = born]

cognisant (**kog**-nĭ-zǎnt) *adjective* (also -**izant**) aware, having knowledge. **cognisance** *noun*

cognition (kog-**ni**-shŏn) *noun* the faculty of knowing or perceiving things. **cognitive** (**kog**-nĭ-tiv) *adjective* [from Latin *cognoscere* = know]

cogwheel *noun* a wheel with cogs.

cohabit *verb* to live together as man and wife (especially if a couple who are not married to each other). **cohabitation** *noun*

cohere (koh-**heer**) *verb* 1 to stick together, to remain united in a mass, *the particles cohere*. 2 to be logical or consistent. [from *co-*, + Latin *haerere* = to stick]

coherent (koh-**heer**-rěnt) *adjective* 1 cohering. 2 connected logically, not rambling in speech or in reasoning. 3 (in physics, of waves) having a constant phase relationship. **coherently** *adverb*, **coherence** *noun*

cohesion (koh-**hee**-zhŏn) *noun* cohering, a tendency to stick together. **cohesive** *adjective*

cohort *noun* 1 a division of the ancient Roman army, one-tenth of a legion. 2 persons grouped together; a group having a common statistical characteristic.

coiffure (kwahf-**yoor**) *noun* a hairstyle. [French]

coil *verb* to wind into rings or a spiral. –**coil** *noun* 1 something coiled. 2 one ring or turn in this. 3 a length of wire wound in a spiral

to conduct electric current. 4 a contraceptive device for insertion into the womb.

coin *noun* a small stamped piece of metal as official money; coins collectively. –**coin** *verb* 1 to make (coins) by stamping metal. 2 (*informal*) to make (money) in large quantities as profit. 3 to invent (a word or phrase).

coinage *noun* 1 coining. 2 coins; the system of coins in use. 3 a coined word or phrase.

coincide (koh-ĭn-**syd**) *verb* 1 to occur at the same time, *his holidays don't coincide with hers*. 2 to occupy the same portion of space. 3 to agree; *our tastes coincide*, are the same. [from *co-*, + Latin *incidere* = fall on]

coincidence (koh-**in**-sĭ-děnss) *noun* 1 coinciding. 2 a remarkable occurrence of similar or corresponding events at the same time by chance.

coincident (koh-**in**-sĭ-děnt) *adjective* coinciding.

coincidental (koh-in-sĭ-**den**-t'l) *adjective* happening by coincidence. **coincidentally** *adverb*

coir (**koi**-er) *noun* fibre from the outer husk of the coconut, used for ropes, matting, etc.

coition (koh-**ish**-ŏn) *noun* sexual intercourse. [from *co-*, + Latin *itum* = gone]

coitus (**koh**-ĭ-tŭs) *noun* coition. **coital** *adjective*

coke¹ *noun* the solid substance left after coal gas and coal tar have been extracted from coal, used as fuel. □ **coking coal** coal suitable for being converted into coke.

coke² *noun* (*informal*) cocaine.

Col. *abbreviation* Colonel.

col *noun* 1 a depression in a range of mountains. 2 a region of low pressure between two anticyclones. [French, = neck]

col- *prefix* see **com-**.

colander (**kol**-ǎn-der) *noun* a bowl-shaped container with holes for straining water from foods.

cold *adjective* 1 at or having a low temperature, especially when compared with the human body. 2 not heated, having cooled after being heated or cooked, *cold meat*. 3 (*informal*) unconscious, *knocked him cold*. 4 without friendliness, affection, or enthusiasm, *got a cold reception*. 5 (of colours) suggesting coldness. 6 (of the scent in hunting) faint because no longer fresh. 7 (in children's games) far from finding or guessing what is sought. –**cold** *adverb* in a cold state.

–**cold** *noun* **1** lack of heat or warmth; low temperature. **2** an infectious illness causing catarrh and sneezing. ☐ **cold-blooded** *adjective* having a body temperature that varies with the temperature of surroundings, as fish have; unfeeling, deliberately ruthless, *a cold-blooded killer*. **cold case** an unsolved criminal investigation. **cold chisel** a very strong steel chisel. **cold comfort** poor consolation. **cold cream** ointment for cleansing and softening the skin. **cold front** the forward edge of an advancing mass of cold air. **cold shoulder** deliberate unfriendliness. **cold-shoulder** *verb* to treat with deliberate unfriendliness. **cold sore** inflammation and blistering around the mouth, caused by the *herpes simplex* virus. **cold storage** storage in a refrigerated place; *in cold storage*, (of plans etc.) postponed but available when required. **cold turkey** (*informal*) sudden withdrawal of addictive drugs. **cold war** intense hostility between nations without actual fighting. **get cold feet** to become afraid or reluctant. **in cold blood** without passion, deliberately and ruthlessly. **leave cold** to fail to affect or impress, *their promises leave me cold*. **throw** or **pour cold water on** to make discouraging remarks about. **coldly** *adverb*, **coldness** *noun*

coleopterous (kol-ee-**op**-tĕ-rŭs) *adjective* of the group of animals (Coleoptera) consisting of beetles and weevils, insects with front wings serving as sheaths for the hinder wings. [from Greek *koleon* = sheath, + *pteron* = wing]

coleoptile (kol-ee-**op**-tyl) *noun* the first leaf to emerge from the seed in grasses, forming a protective sheath round the young shoot. [from Greek *koleon* = sheath, + *ptilon* = feather]

Coleridge, Samuel Taylor (1772–1834), English Romantic poet whose works include *Kubla Khan* and *The Rime of the Ancient Mariner*.

coleslaw *noun* finely shredded raw cabbage and carrot coated in dressing, as a salad.

coleus (**koh**-lee-ŭs) *noun* a plant grown for its variegated leaves.

colic *noun* severe spasmodic abdominal pain. **colicky** *adjective*

colitis (kŏ-**ly**-tĭs) *noun* inflammation of the lining of the colon.

collaborate *verb* to work in partnership. **collaboration** *noun*, **collaborator** *noun* [from *col-*, + Latin *laborare* = to work]

collage (kol-**ahzh**), *noun* **1** an artistic composition made by fixing bits of paper, cloth, string, etc. to a surface. **2** a collection of unrelated things. [French, = gluing]

collagen (**kol**-ă-jĕn) *noun* a protein substance found in bone and tissue.

collapse *verb* **1** to fall down or in suddenly. **2** to lose strength or force or value suddenly, *enemy resistance collapsed*. **3** to fold or be foldable. **4** to cause to collapse. –**collapse** *noun* collapsing; a breakdown. [from *col-*, + Latin *lapsum* = slipped]

collapsible *adjective* made so as to fold together compactly, *a collapsible bed*.

collar *noun* **1** an upright or turned-over band round the neck of a garment. **2** a band of leather etc. put round the neck of an animal. **3** a band, ring, or pipe holding part of a machine. –**collar** *verb* (*informal*) to seize, to take for oneself. [from Latin *collum* = neck]

collarbone *noun* the bone joining the breastbone and shoulder blade, the clavicle.

collarless *adjective* without a collar.

collate (kŏ-**layt**) *verb* **1** to compare in detail. **2** to collect and arrange systematically, *collate information*. **collator** *noun*

collateral (kŏ-**lat**-ĕ-răl) *adjective* **1** side by side, parallel. **2** additional but subordinate, *collateral evidence*. **3** descended from the same ancestor but by a different line, *a collateral branch of the family*. –**collateral** *noun* a collateral person or security.

collation *noun* **1** the process of collating; something collated. **2** a light meal.

colleague *noun* a fellow official or worker, especially in a business or profession.

collect[1] (**kol**-ekt) *noun* a short prayer of the Anglican or the Catholic Church.

collect[2] (kŏ-**lekt**) *verb* **1** to bring or come together. **2** to get from a number of people; to ask for (payment or contributions) from people. **3** to seek and obtain specimens of, especially as a hobby or for study. **4** to fetch. **5** to gather (one's thoughts) into systematic order or control; *collect oneself*, to regain control of oneself.

collectable *adjective* (also **collectible**) worth collecting; suitable for being collected as a hobby etc. –**collectable** *noun* an item sought by collectors.

collected *adjective* calm and self-controlled. **collectedly** *adverb*

172

collection *noun* 1 collecting. 2 money collected for a charity etc., e.g. at a church service. 3 objects collected systematically. 4 a number of things that have come or been placed together.

collective *adjective* of a group taken as a whole, *our collective impression of the new plan*. –**collective** *noun* a collective farm. □ **collective bargaining** bargaining by an organised group of employees. **collective farm** a farm or group of smallholdings organised and run by its workers, usually under State control. **collective noun** a noun that is singular in form but denotes many individuals, e.g. *army, cattle, committee, herd*. **collective ownership** ownership of land etc. by all and for the benefit of all. **collectively** *adverb*

collector *noun* 1 a person who collects things. 2 the terminal of a transistor from which the output signal is normally taken.

colleen (**kol**-een *or* kol-**een**) *noun* (*Irish*) a girl.

college *noun* 1 an educational establishment for further, higher, or professional education. 2 a residential part of a university. 3 a school, especially a private school, or (in some states) a senior secondary school. 4 the buildings of any of these. 5 an organised body of professional people with common purposes and privileges, *the Royal Australian College of General Practitioners*.

collegiate (kŏ-**lee**-jee-ăt) *adjective* of or belonging to a college; constituted as a college.

collide *verb* 1 (of a moving object) to strike violently against something, to meet and strike. 2 (of interests or opinions) to conflict.

collie *noun* a dog with a long pointed muzzle and shaggy hair.

collier *noun* 1 a coal miner. 2 a ship that carries coal as its cargo.

colliery *noun* a coal mine and its buildings.

collinear *adjective* lying in the same straight line. [from *col-* + *linear*]

collision *noun* colliding, the striking of one body against another. □ **collision course** a set course bound to end in a collision.

collocate *verb* 1 to place together or side by side. 2 to bring together for purposes of comparison. **collocation** *noun*, **collocator** *noun* [from *col-* + *locate*]

colloid *noun* 1 a gluey substance. 2 a non-crystalline substance with very large

molecules and a gluey texture, with special properties. 3 a substance consisting of many very fine particles suspended in a gas, liquid, or solid. **colloidal** *adjective*

colloquial (kŏ-**loh**-kwee-ăl) *adjective* suitable for ordinary conversation but not for formal speech or writing. **colloquially** *adverb* [from *col-*, + Latin *loqui* = speak]

colloquialism *noun* a colloquial word or phrase.

colloquy (**kol**-ŏ-kwee) *noun* (*formal*) a conversation.

collude *verb* to conspire together.

collusion (kŏ-**loo**-*zh*ŏn) *noun* an agreement between two or more people for a deceitful or fraudulent purpose. **collusive** *adjective* [from *col-*, + Latin *ludere* = to play]

collywobbles *plural noun* (*informal*) 1 stomach ache. 2 nervousness.

cologne (kŏ-**lohn**) *noun* eau de Cologne or other lightly scented liquid, used to cool and scent the skin.

Colombia (kŏ-**lum**-bee-ă) a republic in South America. **Colombian** *adjective* & *noun*

Colombo (kŏ-**lum**-boh) the capital of Sri Lanka.

colon[1] (**koh**-lŏn) *noun* the lower and greater part of the large intestine. **colonic** *adjective*

colon[2] (**koh**-lŏn) *noun* the punctuation mark (:) used (1) to show that what follows is an example or list or summary of what precedes it, or a contrasting idea, (2) between numbers that are in proportion, e.g. 1:2 = 2:4.

colonel (**ker**-nĕl) *noun* an army officer commanding a regiment, ranking next below a brigadier. [from French]

colonial *adjective* of a colony or colonies. –**colonial** *noun* an inhabitant of a colony.

colonialism *noun* the policy of acquiring or maintaining colonies.

colonisation *noun* (also **-ization**) 1 colonising. 2 the establishment of particular animals or plants in an area.

colonise *verb* (also **-ize**) to establish a colony in.

colonist *noun* a pioneer settler in a colony.

colonnade (kol-ŏn-**ayd**) *noun* a row of columns.

colony *noun* 1 an area of land settled or conquered by a distant State and controlled by it. 2 its inhabitants. 3 a group of colonists. 4 people of one nationality or occupation etc.

living in a particular area, the area itself, *the artists' colony*. **5** a number of animals or plants that live as a group or close together.

Colorado (kol-ŏ-**rah**-doh) a State of the central USA.

coloration *noun* colouring.

coloratura (kol-ŏ-ră-**toor**-ră) *noun*
1 elaborate ornamentation of a vocal melody.
2 a soprano skilled in singing this.

colossal *adjective* **1** immense. **2** (*informal*) remarkable, splendid. **colossally** *adverb*

Colosseum (kol-ŏ-**see**-ŭm) a vast amphitheatre in Rome, begun c. AD 75.

Colossians (kŏ-**losh**-ănz) the *Epistle to the Colossians*, a book of the New Testament, an epistle of St Paul to the Church at Colossae in Asia Minor.

colossus (kŏ-**los**-ŭs) *noun* (*plural* colossi, *pr.* kŏ-**los**-I) **1** an immense statue. **2** a person of immense importance and influence. [from the bronze statue of Apollo at Rhodes, the *Colossus of Rhodes*]

colostrum (kŏ-**lost**-rŭm) *noun* the clear fluid that appears in the breasts of mammals before milk is produced.

colour *noun* **1** the sensation produced by rays of light of different wavelengths; a particular variety of this. **2** the use of all colours, not only black and white; *in colour*, using all colours; *a colour film*, producing photographs that are in colour. **3** ruddiness of complexion; *she has no colour*, looks pale. **4** the pigmentation of the skin, especially if dark. **5** pigment, paint, or dye. **6** the flag of a ship or regiment. –**colour** *verb* **1** to put colour on; to paint, stain, or dye. **2** to change colour; to blush. **3** to give a special character or bias to, *his political opinions colour his writings*. **colours** *plural noun* an award given to regular or leading members of a sports team.
☐ **colour bar** racial discrimination against non-White people. **colour-blind** *adjective* unable to see the difference between certain colours. **colour-fast** *adjective* not liable to lose its colour when washed. **give** or **lend colour to** to give an appearance of truth to. **in its true colours** with its real characteristics revealed.

colourant *noun* colouring matter.

coloured *adjective* **1** having colour. **2** (often *offensive*) wholly or partly of non-White descent. **3** Coloured (often *offensive*) (in South Africa) of mixed White and non-White descent. –**coloured** *noun* (often *offensive*)
1 a coloured person. **2** Coloured (in South

Africa) a person of mixed White and non-White descent.

colourful *adjective* **1** full of colour. **2** with vivid details, *a colourful account of his journey*. **colourfully** *adverb*

colouring *noun* **1** the way in which something is coloured. **2** a substance used to colour things.

colourless *adjective* without colour.

colt *noun* a young male horse.

Columba, St (c. 521–97), Irish missionary, who established a monastery on the island of Iona, off Scotland, and lived there for 34 years, evangelising the mainland. Feast day, 9 June.

Columbia, **District of** a district of the USA coextensive with the city of Washington.

Columbine a character in Italian comedy, the mistress of Harlequin.

columbine *noun* a garden flower with slender pointed projections on its petals.

Columbus, Christopher (1451–1506), Italian explorer, in the service of Spain, who in 1492 discovered the New World.

column *noun* **1** a round pillar. **2** something shaped like this, *a column of smoke*; *the spinal column*, the backbone. **3** a vertical section of a page, *there are two columns on this page*. **4** a regular feature in a newspaper, devoted to a special subject. **5** a long narrow formation of troops or vehicles etc. **columnar** (kŏ-**lum**-ner) *adjective*

columnist (**kol**-ŭm-nĭst) *noun* a journalist who regularly writes a column of comments.

com- *prefix* (becoming **col-** before *l*, **cor-** before *r*, **con-** before many other consonants) with; together (as in *combine*, *connect*). [from Latin *cum* = with]

coma (**koh**-mă) *noun* a state of deep unconsciousness. [from Greek, = deep sleep]

Comanche (kŏ-**man**-chee) *noun* **1** a North American indigenous people of Texas and Oklahoma. **2** their language.

comatose (**koh**-mă-tohs) *adjective* **1** in a coma. **2** drowsy.

comb *noun* **1** a strip of bone or plastic etc. with teeth, used for tidying the hair or holding it in place. **2** something shaped or used like this, e.g. for separating strands of wool or cotton. **3** the fleshy crest of a fowl. **4** a honeycomb. –**comb** *verb* **1** to tidy or untangle with a comb. **2** to search thoroughly.

combat *noun* a fight or contest. **–combat** *verb* (**combated, combating**) to strive against; to counter, *to combat the effects of alcohol*.

combatant (**kom**-bă-tănt) *adjective* engaged in fighting. **–combatant** *noun* one who is engaged in fighting.

combative (**kom**-bă-tiv) *adjective* eager to fight, aggressive.

combe (*pr.* koom) *noun* = **coomb**.

comber *noun* **1** a person or thing that combs. **2** a long curling wave; a breaker.

combination *noun* **1** combining, being combined. **2** a number of people or things that are combined. **3** a sequence of numbers or letters used in opening a combination lock. □ **combination lock** a lock that can be opened only by turning one or more dials into a particular series of positions, indicated by numbers or letters.

combine (kŏm-**byn**) *verb* to join or be joined into a group, set, or mixture. **–combine** (**kom**-byn) *noun* **1** a combination of people or firms acting together in business. **2** a **combine harvester**, a combined reaping and threshing machine. [from *com-*, + Latin *bini* = pair]

combustible (kŏm-**bust**-ĭ-bŭl) *adjective* capable of catching fire and burning, used for burning. **–combustible** *noun* a combustible substance. **combustibility** *noun*

combustion (kŏm-**bus**-chŏn) *noun* the process of burning, a chemical process (accompanied by heat) in which substances combine with oxygen in air.

come *verb* (**came, come, coming**) **1** to move or be brought towards the speaker or a place or point. **2** (of an illness) to begin to develop. **3** to arrive, to reach a point, condition, or result, *when winter comes*; *for several years to come*, in the future. **4** to take or occupy a specified position, *what comes next?* **5** to be available, *the dress comes in three sizes*. **6** to happen, *how did you come to lose it?* **7** to occur as a result, *that's what comes of being too confident*. **8** to be descended, *she comes from a rich family*. **–come** *interjection* think again, don't be hasty, *oh come, it's not that bad!* □ **come about** to happen. **come across** (*informal*) to find or meet unexpectedly; to give a specified impression, *comes across as a bit arrogant*. **come along** to make progress, to thrive, *coming along nicely*; *come along!*, hurry up. **come at** (*Austral. informal*) to accept, *wouldn't come at my idea*. **come by** to obtain (a thing). **come clean** (*informal*) to confess fully. **come down**

to collapse; to fall, to become lower. **come down on** to rebuke or punish. **come from** to have as one's birthplace or as a place of origin. **come in** to take a specified position in a race or competition, *he came in third*; to become seasonable or fashionable; to be received as income; to have a part to play, to serve a purpose, *it will come in useful*; *where do I come in?*, what is my role?, where is my advantage? **come in for** to receive a share of. **come into** to inherit. **come of age** to reach adult status. **come off** to become detached or separated, to be detachable; to fall from, *she came off her bicycle*; to fare, to acquit oneself, *they came off well*; to succeed. **come off it!** (*informal*) stop talking or behaving like that. **come on** to make progress, to thrive; to appear on the stage, in a filmed scene etc.; to find or meet unexpectedly. **come on!** hurry up. **come out** to go on strike; to become visible in a photograph, *the house has come out well*; to become known, *the truth came out*; to be published; to be solved; to erupt, to become covered (in a rash); to declare one's opinions publicly, *came out in favour of the plan*; to declare openly that one is homosexual; (of stains etc.) to be removed. **come out with** to utter. **come over** to affect, *what has come over you?*; (*informal*) to be affected with a feeling, *she came over faint*. **come round** to make a casual or informal visit; to recover from faintness or bad temper; to be converted to another person's opinion; to recur. **come to** to amount to, to be equivalent to; to regain consciousness. **come to pass** to happen. **come up** to arise for discussion etc., to occur, *a problem has come up*. **come upon** to find or meet unexpectedly. **come-uppance** *noun* (*informal*) a punishment or rebuke that one deserves. **come up to** to equal, *it doesn't come up to our expectations*. **come up with** to contribute (a suggestion etc.). **come what may** whatever may happen.

comeback *noun* **1** a return to one's former successful position. **2** (*informal*) a reply or retort. **3** (*Austral.*) a sheep bred from cross-bred and pure-bred parents for both wool and meat.

comedian *noun* **1** an actor who plays comic parts. **2** a humorous entertainer. **3** a person who behaves humorously.

comedienne (kŏ-mee-dee-**en**) *noun* a female comedian.

comedown *noun* **1** a fall in status. **2** an anticlimax; a disappointment.

comedy *noun* **1** a light amusing play or film. **2** the branch of drama that consists of such plays. **3** an amusing incident. **4** humour. [from Greek *komos* = merrymaking, + *oide* = song]

comely (**kum**-lee) *adjective* good-looking. **comeliness** *noun*

comer (**kum**-er) *noun* one who comes, *the first comers*; *all comers*, anyone who comes or challenges or applies.

comestibles (kŏ-**mest**-ĭ-bŭlz) *plural noun* (*formal*) things to eat.

comet (**kom**-ĕt) *noun* a hazy object that moves round the sun, usually with a star-like centre and a tail pointing away from the sun. [from Greek *kometes* = long-haired]

comfort *noun* **1** a state of ease and contentment. **2** relief of suffering or grief. **3** a person or thing that gives this. –**comfort** *verb* to give comfort to. **comforter** *noun*

comfortable *adjective* **1** giving ease and contentment. **2** not close or restricted, *won by a comfortable margin*. **3** feeling at ease, in a state of comfort. **comfortably** *adverb*

comfrey (**kum**-free) *noun* a tall plant with rough leaves and purple or white flowers.

comfy *adjective* (*informal*) comfortable.

comic *adjective* **1** causing amusement or laughter. **2** of comedy. –**comic** *noun* **1** a comedian. **2** a magazine (usually for children) with series of comic strips. ▢ **comic strip** a sequence of drawings telling a story. **comical** *adjective*, **comically** *adverb*

coming *see* **come**. –**coming** *adjective* **1** approaching, next, *the coming week*. **2** likely to be important in the near future, *a coming man*. –**coming** *noun* arriving, *comings and goings*.

comma *noun* the punctuation mark (,) indicating a slight pause or break between parts of a sentence, or separating words or figures in a list. [from Greek *komma* = clause]

command *noun* **1** a statement, given with authority, that some action must be performed. **2** an instruction to a computer. **3** the right to control others, authority. **4** ability to use something, mastery, *a great command of languages*. **5** a body of troops or staff, *Bomber Command*. –**command** *verb* **1** to give a command or order to. **2** to have authority over. **3** to have at one's disposal, *the firm commands great resources*. **4** to deserve and get, *they command our respect*. **5** to look down over or dominate. ▢ **command module** the control compartment in a spacecraft.

commandant (kom-ăn-**dant**) *noun* the officer in command of a fortress or other military establishment.

commandeer *verb* **1** to seize for military purposes. **2** to seize for one's own purposes.

commander *noun* **1** the person in command. **2** a naval officer ranking next below a captain. ▢ **commander-in-chief** *noun* the supreme commander.

commandment *noun* a divine command. –**Commandment** *noun* any of the ten laws given by God to Moses.

commando *noun* (*plural* **commandos**) a member of a military unit specially trained for making raids and assaults.

commemorate *verb* **1** to keep in the memory by means of a celebration or ceremony. **2** to be a memorial to, *a plaque commemorates the victory*. **commemoration** *noun*, **commemorative** *adjective* [compare *memory*]

commence *verb* to begin. **commencement** *noun*

commend *verb* **1** to praise. **2** to recommend. **3** to entrust, to commit, *commending his soul to God*. **commendation** *noun*

commendable *adjective* worthy of praise. **commendably** *adverb*

commensal (kŏ-**men**-săl) *adjective* living in or with another plant or animal (without harming it) and so obtaining food. **commensalism** *noun* [from *com-*, + Latin *mensa* = table]

commensurable (kŏ-**men**-shŭ-ră-bŭl) *adjective* able to be measured by the same standard.

commensurate (kŏ-**men**-shŭ-răt) *adjective* **1** of the same size or extent. **2** proportionate. [from *com-*, + Latin *mensum* = measured]

comment *noun* an opinion given briefly about an event or in explanation or criticism. –**comment** *verb* to utter or write comments.

commentary *noun* **1** a series of descriptive comments on an event or performance. **2** a collection (usually a book) of explanatory comments, *a new commentary on the Bible*.

commentate *verb* to act as commentator.

commentator *noun* a person who broadcasts or writes a commentary.

commerce (**kom**-erss) *noun* all forms of trade and the services that assist trading, e.g. banking and insurance. [from *com-*, + Latin *merx* = merchandise]

commercial *adjective* **1** of or engaged in commerce; *commercial vehicles*, those carrying goods or fare-paying passengers; *commercial art*, art used in advertising etc.; *produced on a commercial scale*, in amounts suitable for marketing widely. **2** financed by firms etc. whose advertisements are included, *commercial radio*. **3** intended to produce profits rather than to be of artistic or scholarly merit. – **commercial** *noun* a broadcast advertisement. ☐ **commercial traveller** a business firm's representative who visits shops etc. to show samples and get orders. **commercially** *adverb*, **commercialism** *noun*

commercialise *verb* (also **-ize**) to make commercial, to alter in order to make profitable, *Easter has been commercialised with the selling of Easter eggs.* **commercialisation** *noun*

commingle *verb* (*literary*) to mingle together.

comminute *verb* to reduce to small fragments. **comminution** *noun*

commiserate (kŏ-**miz**-ĕ-rayt) *verb* to express pity for, to sympathise. **commiseration** *noun* [from *com-*, + Latin *miserari* = to pity]

commissar (**kom**-ĭ-sar) *noun* the head of a government department in the former USSR before 1946.

commissariat (kom-ĭ-**sair**-ree-ăt) *noun* **1** a stock of food. **2** a military etc. department supplying this.

commission *noun* **1** the giving of authority to someone to perform a certain task or duty. **2** the task etc. given, *a commission to paint a portrait*. **3** the body of people to whom such authority is given. **4** a warrant conferring authority especially on officers above a certain rank in the armed forces. **5** performance, committing, *the commission of a crime*. **6** payment to an agent for selling goods or services etc. often calculated in proportion to the amount sold. – **commission** *verb* **1** to give a commission to. **2** to place an order for, *commissioned a portrait*. ☐ **in commission** (of a warship etc.) manned and ready for service. **out of commission** not in commission; not in working order. **Royal Commission** *see* **royal**.

commissionaire (kŏ-mish-ŏ-**nair**) *noun* a uniformed attendant at the entrance to a theatre, large shop, or offices etc.

commissioner *noun* **1** a person appointed by commission (e.g. the head of a police force).

2 a member of a commission. **3** a government official in charge of a department.

commit *verb* (**committed**, **committing**) **1** to do, to perform, *commit a crime*. **2** to entrust for safe keeping or treatment; *commit a prisoner for trial*, send him or her to prison pending trial; *commit a body to the earth*, bury it with a formal ceremony. **3** to pledge, to bind with an obligation; *she did not commit herself*, gave no definite statement or opinion. ☐ **commit to memory** memorise.

committed *adjective* dedicated or pledged, especially to support a doctrine or cause.

commitment *noun* **1** committing. **2** the state of being involved in an obligation. **3** an obligation or pledge.

committal *noun* **1** committing to prison or other place of confinement. **2** committing a body at burial or cremation. ☐ **committal hearing** proceedings before a magistrate to determine whether a case should go for trial.

committee *noun* a group of people appointed to attend to special business or to manage the business of a club etc.

commode (kŏ-**mohd**) *noun* **1** a chamber pot mounted in a chair or box with a cover. **2** a chest of drawers.

commodious (kŏ-**moh**-dee-ŭs) *adjective* roomy.

commodity *noun* a useful thing, an article of trade, a product. [from Latin *commodus* = convenient]

commodore (**kom**-ŏ-dor) *noun* **1** a naval officer ranking above a captain and below a rear admiral. **2** the commander of a squadron or other division of a fleet.

common *adjective* **1** of or affecting the whole community; *it was common knowledge*, was known to most people. **2** belonging to or shared by two or more people or things; *common ground*, something on which two or more people agree or in which they share an interest. **3** occurring frequently, familiar, *a common weed*. **4** without special distinction, ordinary, *the common house spider*. **5** ill-bred, not refined in behaviour or style. – **common** *noun* (chiefly in Britain) an area of unfenced grassland for all to use. ☐ **common denominator** *see* **denominator**. **Common Era** the Christian era. **common factor** a factor that is common to two or more numbers, e.g. the common factors of 8 and 12 are 1, 2, 4. **common law** unwritten law based on custom and usage and on former court decisions. **common-law husband** or **wife** one recognised by common law without an official ceremony, usually after a period of living together, a de facto spouse. **Common Market** the European Economic Community (now superseded by the European Union). **common multiple** a number that is a multiple of each of two or more numbers, e.g. 15 and 30 are common multiples of 3 and 5. **common noun** a name denoting a class of objects or a concept, not a particular individual. **common or garden** (*informal*) ordinary. **common room** a room shared for social purposes by pupils or students or teachers of a school or college. **common sense** normal good sense in practical matters, gained by experience of life not by special study. **common-sense** *adjective* showing common sense. **common time** (in music) two or four beats (especially four crotchets) in the bar. **in common** shared by two or more people or things. **commonly** *adverb*, **commonness** *noun* [from Latin *communis* = common]

commoner *noun* one of the common people, not a member of the nobility.

commonplace *adjective* ordinary, usual; *a few commonplace remarks*, lacking originality. –**commonplace** *noun* something commonplace, *air travel is now a commonplace*.

commonwealth *noun* 1 an independent State or community, especially a democratic republic. 2 a federation of States, *the Commonwealth of Australia*. ☐ **the Commonwealth** an association of the UK and various independent States (formerly subject to Britain) and dependencies; (in history) the republican government of Britain between the execution of Charles I (1649) and the Restoration (1660). **Commonwealth Games** a competition for members of Commonwealth countries, modelled on the Olympic Games and held every four years midway between Olympics. **Commonwealth of Independent States** *see* **CIS**. **New Commonwealth** those countries that have achieved self-government within the British Commonwealth since 1945.

commotion *noun* uproar, fuss and disturbance.

communal (**kom**-yŭ-năl *or* kŏ-**mew**-năl) *adjective* shared between members of a group or community, *a communal bathroom*. **communally** *adverb* [same origin as *common*]

commune[1] (**kom**-yoon) *noun* 1 a group of people, not all of one family, sharing accommodation and goods; a communal settlement. 2 a small district of local government in France and certain other European countries.

commune[2] (kŏ-**mewn**) *verb* to communicate mentally or spiritually.

communicable *adjective* able to be communicated or passed on, *communicable diseases*.

communicant *noun* 1 a person who receives Holy Communion; one who does this regularly. 2 a person who communicates information.

communicate *verb* 1 to make known, *communicate the news to your friends*. 2 to transfer, to transmit, *communicated the disease to others*. 3 to pass news and information to and fro; to have social dealings. 4 to be connected, *the passage communicates with the hall and stairs*.

communication *noun* 1 communicating. 2 something that communicates information from one person to another, a letter or message. 3 a means of communicating, e.g. a road, railway, telegraph line, radio, or other link between places. ☐ **communication cord** a cord or chain inside a train, to be pulled to stop the train in an emergency.

communicative (kŏ-**mew**-nĭ-kă-tiv) *adjective* ready and willing to talk and give information.

communion *noun* 1 fellowship, having ideas or beliefs in common; *Churches in communion with each other*, those that accept each other's doctrines and sacraments. 2 social dealings between people. 3 a body of Christians belonging to the same denomination, *the Anglican communion*. –**Communion** *or* **Holy Communion** the Christian sacrament in which bread and wine are consecrated and consumed, the Eucharist.

communiqué (kŏ-**mew**-nĭ-kay) *noun* an official communication giving a report of a meeting or a battle etc. [French, = communicated]

communism *noun* a social system in which property is owned by the community and each member works for the common benefit. –**Communism** *noun* a political doctrine or movement seeking to overthrow capitalism and establish a form of communism; such a system established in the former USSR and elsewhere. [from French *commun* = common]

communist *noun* a supporter of communism. –Communist *noun* a member of the Communist Party, a political party supporting Communism. communistic *adjective*

community *noun* 1 a group of people living in one place or district or country and considered as a whole. 2 a group with common interests or origins, *the student community*. 3 fellowship, being alike in some way, *community of interests*. 4 a group of animals or plants living or growing together in the same area. ☐ community centre a place providing social, recreational, and educational facilities for a neighbourhood. community service performance of specified unpaid services to the community as an alternative to serving a prison sentence.

commutable *adjective* 1 exchangeable, able to be exchanged for money. 2 (of a punishment) able to be commuted.

commutate (**kom**-yŭ-tayt) *verb* to regulate the direction of (electric current), especially so as to make it a direct current. commutation *noun*

commutative (kŏ-**mew**-tă-tiv) *adjective* (of a mathematical operation) producing the same result regardless of the order in which the quantities are taken, e.g. $3 + 4 = 7$, $4 + 3 = 7$. ☐ commutative group an Abelian group.

commutator (**kom**-yŭ-tay-ter) *noun* a device that commutates electric current.

commute *verb* 1 to travel regularly by bus, train, or car to and from one's daily work in a city. 2 to exchange for something else. 3 to change (a punishment) into something less severe. commutation *noun* [from *com-*, + Latin *mutare* = to change]

commuter *noun* a person who commutes to and from work.

Comoros (**kom**-ŏ-rohz) a republic consisting of a group of islands in the Indian Ocean north of Madagascar. Comoran *adjective* & *noun*

compact[1] (**kom**-pakt) *noun* an agreement, a contract. [from *com-* + *pact*]

compact[2] (kŏm-**pakt**) *adjective* 1 closely or neatly packed together. 2 concise. –compact (kŏm-**pakt**) *verb* to make compact; to join or press firmly together or into a small space. –compact (**kom**-pakt) *noun* a small flat container for face powder. ☐ compact disc a disc without grooves, on which information or sound is recorded digitally for reproduction

by means of a laser beam directed on to it. compactly *adverb*, compactness *noun* [from Latin *compactum* = put together]

companion *noun* 1 a person who accompanies another or who shares in his or her work, pleasures, or misfortunes etc. 2 the title of a member of certain orders, *Companion of the Order of Australia*. 3 a person employed to live with and accompany another. 4 each of two things that match or go together. 5 a handbook or reference book, *a companion to literature*. [from *com-*, + Latin *panis* = bread, = 'person who eats bread with another']

companionable *adjective* friendly, sociable. companionably *adverb*

companionship *noun* the state of being companions, the friendly feeling of being with another or others.

companionway *noun* a staircase from a ship's deck to the saloon or cabins.

company *noun* 1 companionship. 2 a number of people assembled, guests. 3 the people with whom one spends one's time, *got into bad company*. 4 people working together or united for business purposes, a firm; *the ship's company*, the officers and crew. 5 a subdivision of an infantry battalion. ☐ keep a person company to accompany him or her, especially for the sake of companionship.

comparable (**kom**-pă-răbŭl) *adjective* able or suitable to be compared, similar. comparably *adverb*, comparability *noun*

comparative *adjective* 1 involving comparison, *a comparative study of the output of two firms*. 2 estimated by comparison; *living in comparative comfort*, comfortably when compared against a previous standard or that of others. 3 of a grammatical form used in comparing, expressing 'more', e.g. *bigger*, *greater*, *worse*. –comparative *noun* a comparative form of a word. comparatively *adverb*

compare *verb* 1 to judge the similarity between (one thing and another). 2 to form the comparative and superlative of (an adjective or adverb). –compare *noun* comparison. ☐ compare notes to exchange ideas or conclusions. compare to to liken, to declare to be similar. compare with to consider (things or people) together so as to judge their similarities and differences; to be worthy of comparison. [from Latin *comparare* = match with each other]

comparison *noun* comparing. ☐ **beyond comparison** not comparable because one is so much better than the other(s).

compartment *noun* **1** one of the spaces into which a structure or other object is divided, separated by partitions. **2** such a division of a railway carriage. **compartmental** *adjective* [from *com-*, + Latin *partiri* = to share]

compartmentalise (kom-part-**ment**-ă-lyz) *verb* (also -**ize**) to divide into compartments or categories.

compass *noun* **1** a device for determining direction, with a needle that points to the magnetic north; *a radio compass*, a similar device using radio. **2** circumference, boundary; range, scope. **–compass** *verb* to encompass. **compasses** *plural noun* (also **compass** *noun*) an instrument used for drawing circles, measuring distances, etc., usually with two legs joined at one end.

compassion *noun* a feeling of pity that makes one want to help or show mercy. **compassionate** *adjective*, **compassionately** *adverb* [from *com-*, + Latin *passum* = suffered]

compatible (kŏm-**pat**-ĭ-bŭl) *adjective* **1** capable of living together harmoniously. **2** able to exist or be used together, *at a speed compatible with safety*. **compatibly** *adverb*, **compatibility** *noun*

compatriot (kŏm-**pat**-ree-ŏt) *noun* a person from the same country as another.

compel *verb* (**compelled, compelling**) **1** to use force or influence to cause (a person) to do something; to allow no choice of action. **2** to arouse irresistibly, *his courage compels admiration*. [from *com-*, + Latin *pellere* = to drive]

compendious (kŏm-**pen**-dee-ŭs) *adjective* giving much information concisely.

compendium (kŏm-**pen**-dee-ŭm) *noun* (*plural* **compendia**) **1** a concise and comprehensive summary. **2** a collection or set of things. [Latin, = a saving]

compensate *verb* **1** to make a suitable payment in return for (a loss or damage etc.). **2** to serve as a counterbalance, *our present success compensates for earlier failures*. **compensation** *noun*, **compensatory** *adjective*

compère (**kom**-pair) *noun* a person who introduces the performers in a variety show etc. **–compère** *verb* to act as compère to. [French, = a godfather]

compete *verb* to take part in a competition or other contest.

competence (**kom**-pĕ-tĕns) *noun* (also **competency**) **1** the state of being competent, ability; a skill. **2** the legal capacity (of a court etc.) to deal with a matter. **3** an adequate income to live on.

competent (**kom**-pĕ-tĕnt) *adjective* **1** having the ability or authority to do what is required. **2** adequate, satisfactory, *a competent knowledge of French*. **competently** *adverb*

competition *noun* **1** a friendly contest in which people try to do better than their rivals. **2** competing, *competition for export markets*. **3** those competing with oneself, *we have strong foreign competition*.

competitive *adjective* of or involving competition, *competitive sports*; *competitive prices*, prices that compare favourably with those of rivals. **competitively** *adverb*, **competitiveness** *noun*

competitor *noun* one who competes.

compile *verb* **1** to collect and arrange (information) into a list or book. **2** to make up (a book, e.g. a dictionary) in this way. **compilation** (kom-pĭ-**lay**-shŏn) *noun*

compiler *noun* **1** a person who compiles information into a list or book. **2** a computer program that translates instructions from a high-level language into a form that can be understood by the computer with little or no further translation.

complacent (kŏm-**play**-sĕnt) *adjective* self-satisfied. **complacently** *adverb*, **complacency** *noun* [from *com-*, + Latin *placens* = pleasing]

complain *verb* to say that one is dissatisfied, to protest that something is wrong. ☐ **complain of** to state that one is suffering from (a pain etc.); to state a grievance concerning.

complaint *noun* **1** a statement saying that one is dissatisfied, a protest. **2** a cause of dissatisfaction, *a list of complaints*. **3** an illness.

complaisant (kŏm-**play**-zĕnt) *adjective* willing to do what pleases others. **complaisance** *noun* [from French *complaire* = acquiesce]

Usage *Complaisant* should not be confused with *complacent*.

complement (**kom**-plĕ-mĕnt) *noun* **1** that which makes a thing complete. **2** the number or quantity needed to fill something, *the bus* *had its full complement of passengers.* **3** a word or words used after verbs meaning 'to be' or 'become' (sometimes also 'to make' or 'create'), completing what is said about the subject, e.g. *happy* in the sentence *we are happy.* **4** the number obtained by altering all the zeros in a number expressed in binary notation to ones and vice versa (e.g. the complement of 100101 is 011010). **–complement** *verb* to make complete, to form a complement to, *the hat complements the outfit.* □ **complement of an angle** another angle that when added to the first makes 90°. **complement of a set** (in mathematics) another set that when added to that set makes a specified larger set. [same origin as *complete*]

Usage *Complement* should not be confused with *compliment.*

complementary *adjective* completing, forming a complement. □ **complementary angles** angles that add up to 90°. **complementary colours** two colours of light that when mixed have the appearance of white light (e.g. blue and yellow).

Usage *Complementary* should not be confused with *complimentary.*

complementation *noun* (in mathematics) finding the complement of a set.

complete *adjective* **1** having all its parts, not lacking anything. **2** finished, *the work is now complete.* **3** thorough, in every way, *a complete stranger.* **–complete** *verb* **1** to add what is lacking to (a thing) and make it complete. **2** to finish (a piece of work etc.). **3** to add what is required to (a thing). **completely** *adverb*, **completeness** *noun* [from Latin *completum* = filled up]

completion (kŏm-**plee**-shŏn) *noun* completing, being completed.

complex (**kom**-pleks) *adjective* **1** made up of parts. **2** complicated. **–complex** *noun* **1** a complex whole. **2** a connected group of feelings or ideas that influence a person's behaviour or mental attitude, *a persecution complex.* **3** (in general use) a preoccupation; a feeling of inadequacy, *has a complex about his big ears.* **4** a set of buildings. □ **complex number** (in mathematics) a number containing real and imaginary parts. **complexity** (kŏm-**pleks**-ĭ-tee) *noun* [from Latin *complexum* = embraced, plaited]

complexion *noun* **1** the colour, texture, and appearance of the skin of the face. **2** the general character or nature of things; *that puts a different complexion on the matter*, makes it seem different.

compliant (kŏm-**ply**-ănt) *adjective* complying, obedient. **compliance** *noun*

complicate *verb* to make complex or complicated. [from *com-*, + Latin *plicare* = to fold]

complicated *adjective* made up of many parts, difficult to understand or use because of this.

complication *noun* **1** complicating; being made complicated. **2** a complex combination of things. **3** something that complicates or adds difficulties. **4** an illness or condition that arises during the course of another and makes it worse.

complicity (kŏm-**plis**-ĭ-tee) *noun* partnership or involvement in wrongdoing.

compliment *noun* an expression of praise or admiration either in words or by action. **–compliment** *verb* to pay a compliment to, to congratulate. **compliments** *plural noun* formal greetings conveyed in a message.

Usage Distinguish *compliment* from *complement.*

complimentary *adjective* **1** expressing a compliment. **2** given free of charge.

Usage Distinguish *complimentary* from *complementary.*

compline (**kom**-plĭn) *noun* the last service of the day in the Roman Catholic and High Anglican Church.

comply (kŏm-**ply**) *verb* (**complied**, **complying**) to do as one is asked or ordered; *comply with the rules*, obey them.

compo *noun* (*Austral. informal*) compensation, especially for an injury at work.

component (kŏm-**poh**-nĕnt) *noun* each of the parts of which a thing is composed. **–component** *adjective* being a component.

comport *verb* **comport oneself** (*literary*) to behave. **comport with** to suit, to befit. **comportment** *noun*

compose *verb* **1** to form, to make up, *the group was composed of 20 students.* **2** to create in music or literature. **3** to arrange into good order. **4** to make calm. [from Latin *compositum* = put together]

composed *adjective* calm, with one's feelings under control. **composedly** (kŏm-**pohz**-ĕd-lee) *adverb*

composer *noun* a person who composes music etc.

composite (kom-pŏ-zĭt) *adjective* **1** made up of a number of parts or styles. **2** (of a plant, e.g. a daisy or dandelion) having a flower head made up of many individual flowers which together look like one bloom. **3** (of a number) able to be divided exactly by one or more whole numbers as well as by itself and 1 (compare *prime*). [same origin as *compose*]

composition *noun* **1** putting together into a whole, composing. **2** something composed; a piece of music or writing; a short essay written as a school exercise. **3** the parts of which something is made up, *the composition of the soil*. **4** the arrangement of parts of a picture. **5** a compound artificial substance.

compositor *noun* a person who sets up type for printing.

compos mentis *adjective* in one's right mind, sane. [Latin]

compost *noun* **1** a mixture of decaying substances used as a fertiliser. **2** a mixture usually of soil and other ingredients for growing seedlings, cuttings, etc. –**compost** *verb* to treat with compost; to make into compost. [same origin as *compose*]

composure *noun* calmness of mind or manner.

compote (kom-poht) *noun* fruit preserved or cooked in syrup.

compound¹ (**kom**-pownd) *adjective* made up of several parts or ingredients. –**compound** (**kom**-pownd) *noun* **1** something formed from a combination of two or more parts or ingredients. **2** (*Chemistry*) a substance formed from two or more elements chemically united in fixed proportions. –**compound** (kŏm-**pownd**) *verb* **1** to put together to form a whole, to combine. **2** to agree to refrain from revealing (a crime), *compounding a felony*. □ **compound fraction** a number that is made up of a whole number and a fraction, e.g. $5\frac{3}{4}$. **compound fracture** one where the fractured bone has pierced the skin. **compound interest** interest paid on the original capital and on the interest that has been added to it. **compound time** (in music) that with a subdivision of

the unit into three, six, or nine. [from Latin *componere* = put together]

compound² (**kom**-pownd) *noun* a fenced-in enclosure; (in India, China, etc.) an enclosure in which a house or factory stands. [Malay *kampung*]

comprehend *verb* **1** to grasp mentally, to understand. **2** to include.

comprehensible *adjective* able to be understood. **comprehensibly** *adverb*, **comprehensibility** *noun*

comprehension *noun* **1** understanding. **2** an exercise consisting of reading a passage of text and answering questions designed to test understanding of it. **3** inclusion.

comprehensive *adjective* inclusive; including much or all; *comprehensive car insurance*, providing protection against most risks. **comprehensively** *adverb*, **comprehensiveness** *noun*

compress (kŏm-**press**) *verb* to squeeze together, to force into less space. –**compress** (**kom**-press) *noun* a pad or cloth pressed on the body to stop bleeding or to cool inflammation etc. **compressible** *adjective*, **compression** *noun*

compressor *noun* a machine for compressing air or other gases.

comprise (kŏm-**pryz**) *verb* to include; to consist of, *the flat comprises three rooms*.

compromise (**kom**-prŏ-myz) *noun* **1** making a settlement by each side giving up part of its demands. **2** a settlement made in this way. **3** something that is halfway between opposite opinions or courses of action etc. –**compromise** *verb* **1** to settle a dispute by a compromise. **2** to expose to danger or suspicion or scandal etc. by unwise action.

compulsion *noun* **1** compelling, being compelled. **2** an irresistible urge.

compulsive *adjective* **1** compelling. **2** acting as if from compulsion, *a compulsive gambler*. **compulsively** *adverb*

Usage See the note under **compulsory**.

compulsory *adjective* that must be done, required by the rules etc. **compulsorily** *adverb*

Usage *Compulsory* is sometimes confused with *compulsive*. An action is *compulsory* if rules or a law require it to be done, *compulsive* if the doer feels an irresistible urge to do it.

compunction *noun* the pricking of conscience, a slight regret or scruple. [from *com-*, + Latin *punctum* = pricked (by conscience)]

compute *verb* to reckon mathematically, to calculate. **computable** *adjective*, **computation** *noun*

computer *noun* an electronic machine for making calculations, storing and analysing information fed into it, or controlling machinery automatically. □ **computer-assisted design** the use of a computer to plan, record, display, test, and modify the design of a product. **computer-assisted manufacture** the computerised integration of all processes of production. **computer graphics** the use of computers to generate and manipulate visual images; visual images produced by computer processing. **computer-literate** *adjective* able to use computers efficiently. **computer science** the study of the principles and practice of computers.

computerise *verb* (also **-ize**) **1** to process or store (information) by means of a computer. **2** to convert (a process or machinery etc.) so that it can make use of or be controlled by a computer. **computerisation** *noun*

comrade *noun* **1** a companion who shares one's activities. **2** a fellow socialist or Communist. **comradeship** *noun* [from Spanish *camarada* = room mate]

con¹ *verb* (**conned**, **conning**) (*informal*) to persuade or swindle after winning a person's confidence. **–con** *noun* (*informal*) a confidence trick. □ **con man** (*informal*) a confidence trickster. [short for *confidence trick*]

con² *see* **pros and cons**.

con- *prefix see* **com-**.

Conakry (**kon**-ă-kree) the capital of Guinea.

concatenate (kŏn-**kat**-ĕ-nayt) *verb* to link together, to form a sequence or combination of. **concatenation** *noun* [from *con-*, + Latin *catena* = chain]

concave *adjective* curving like the surface of a ball as seen from the inside. **concavity** (kŏn-**kav**-ĭ-tee) *noun* [from *con-*, + Latin *cavus* = hollow]

conceal *verb* to keep secret or hidden. **concealment** *noun*

concede (kŏn-**seed**) *verb* **1** to admit to be true. **2** to grant, to allow, to yield. **3** to admit defeat in, especially before the official end of the contest.

conceit *noun* **1** too much pride in oneself. **2** (*literary*) a far-fetched comparison; a fanciful metaphor.

conceited *adjective* being too proud of oneself. **conceitedly** *adverb*

conceivable *adjective* able to be imagined or believed. **conceivably** *adverb*

conceive *verb* **1** to become pregnant. **2** to form (an idea or plan etc.) in the mind; to think.

concentrate *verb* **1** to employ all one's thought, attention, or effort on something. **2** to bring or come together to one place. **3** to make less dilute. **–concentrate** *noun* a concentrated substance or solution. [from *con-* + *centre*]

concentrated *adjective* **1** (of a solution etc.) having a large proportion of effective elements, not dilute. **2** intense, *concentrated hatred*.

concentration *noun* **1** concentrating, being concentrated. **2** the ability to concentrate. **3** the mass or amount of a substance contained in a specified amount of a solvent or in a mixture. □ **concentration camp** a place where civilian political prisoners are brought together and confined.

concentric (kŏn-**sen**-trik) *adjective* having the same centre, *concentric circles*.

concept (**kon**-sept) *noun* an idea, a general notion, *the concept of freedom*.

conception *noun* **1** conceiving, being conceived. **2** an idea.

conceptual *adjective* of mental concepts. **conceptually** *adverb*

conceptualise *verb* (also **-ize**) to form a concept or idea of. **conceptualisation** *noun*

concern *verb* **1** to be about, to have as its subject. **2** to be of importance to, to affect. **3** to take up the time or attention of; *she concerned herself about it*, gave it her care and attention. **–concern** *noun* **1** something of interest or importance, a responsibility; *it's no concern of mine*, I have nothing to do with it. **2** a connection, a share, *he has a concern in industry*. **3** worry, anxiety. **4** a business, a firm, *a going concern*. **5** (*informal*) a thing, *smashed the whole concern*.

concerned *adjective* **1** worried, anxious. **2** involved, interested.

concerning *preposition* about, in regard to.

concert *noun* a musical entertainment of usually several separate compositions.

☐ concert pitch (in music) the pitch internationally agreed whereby A above middle C = 440 Hz; a state of unusually great readiness, efficiency, keenness (for action etc.). in concert in combination, together.

concerted (kŏn-**sert**-ĕd) *adjective* **1** arranged by mutual agreement, done in cooperation. **2** (of music) arranged in parts for voices or instruments.

concertina *noun* a portable musical instrument with hexagonal ends and bellows, played by squeezing while pressing studs at each end. –concertina *verb* (concertinaed, concertinaing) to fold or collapse like the bellows of a concertina.

concerto (kŏn-**sher**-toh *or* -**cher**-) *noun* (*plural* concertos *or* concerti) a musical composition for one or more solo instruments and an orchestra. [Italian]

concession *noun* **1** conceding. **2** something conceded. **3** a right given by the owners of land to extract minerals etc. from it or to sell goods there, *an oil concession*. **4** a reduction in price for certain categories of person. concessionary *adjective*

conch *noun* the spiral shell of a kind of shellfish, sometimes used as a horn.

concierge (kon-see-**air***zh*) *noun* **1** (especially in France) a doorkeeper or porter, especially in a block of flats. **2** a hotel employee who assists guests in making reservations, booking tours, etc.

conciliate *verb* **1** to overcome the anger or hostility of, to win the goodwill of. **2** to reconcile (people who disagree). conciliation *noun*, conciliator *noun*, conciliatory (kŏn-**sil**-yă-tree) *adjective*

concise (kŏn-**syss**) *adjective* brief, giving much information in few words. concisely *adverb*

conclave (**kon**-klayv) *noun* **1** a private meeting for discussing something, *in conclave*. **2** an assembly of cardinals of the Roman Catholic Church for the election of a pope.

conclude *verb* **1** to bring or come to an end. **2** to arrange, to settle finally, *they concluded a treaty*. **3** to arrive at a belief or opinion by reasoning. [from *con-*, + Latin *claudere* = to shut]

conclusion *noun* **1** ending, an end. **2** arrangement, settling, *conclusion of the treaty*. **3** a belief or opinion based on reasoning.

conclusive *adjective* ending doubt, completely convincing. conclusively *adverb*

concoct (kŏn-**kokt**) *verb* **1** to prepare by putting ingredients together. **2** to invent, *concocted an excuse*. concoction *noun* [from *con-*, + Latin *coctum* = cooked]

concomitant (kŏn-**kom**-ĭ-tănt) *adjective* accompanying. –concomitant *noun* an accompanying thing. concomitance *noun* [from *con-*, + Latin *comitis* = of a companion]

concord *noun* agreement or harmony between people or things. concordant (kŏn-**kor**-dănt) *adjective* [from *con-*, + Latin *cor* = heart]

concordance (kŏn-**kor**-dănss) *noun* an index of the words used in a book or an author's writings, *a concordance to the Bible*.

concordat *noun* an agreement made, especially between the Roman Catholic Church and a State.

concourse (**kon**-korss *or* **kong**-) *noun* **1** a crowd, a gathering. **2** an open area through which people pass e.g. at a railway terminus. [same origin as *concur*]

concrete (**kon**-kreet *or* **kong**-) *noun* a mixture of cement with sand and gravel, used for building and paving. –concrete *adjective* **1** existing in material form, able to be touched and felt. **2** definite, positive, *concrete evidence*. –concrete *verb* **1** to cover with or embed in concrete. **2** to form into a solid mass, to solidify.

concretion (kŏn-**kree**-shŏn) *noun* a hard solid mass.

concubine (**kong**-kew-byn) *noun* a secondary wife in countries where polygamy is customary. concubinage (kŏn-**kew**-bĭ-nij) *noun*

concur (kŏn-**ker**) *verb* (concurred, concurring) **1** to agree in opinion. **2** to happen together, to coincide. [from *con-*, + Latin *currere* = run]

concurrence (kŏn-**ku**-rĕns) *noun* **1** agreement, *concurrence of opinion*. **2** simultaneous occurrence of events.

concurrent (kŏn-**ku**-rĕnt) *adjective* existing or occurring at the same time. concurrently *adverb*

concuss (kŏn-**kus**) *verb* to affect with concussion.

concussion (kŏn-**kush**-ŏn) *noun* injury to the brain caused by a hard blow. [from Latin *concussum* = shaken violently]

condemn *verb* **1** to express strong disapproval of. **2** to pronounce guilty, to convict. **3** to sentence, *was condemned to death*. **4** to destine to an unhappy fate. **5** to declare unfit for use or uninhabitable, *condemned houses*. **condemnation** (kon-dem-**nay**-shŏn) *noun* [from *con-*, + Latin *damnare* = condemn]

condense *verb* **1** to make denser or more concentrated. **2** to change or be changed from gas or vapour into liquid. **3** to express in fewer words. ☐ **condensed milk** milk made thick by evaporation and sweetened. **condenser** *noun*, **condensation** (kon-den-**say**-shŏn) *noun*

Conder, Charles (1868–1909), English-born Australian painter, a member of the Heidelberg School.

condescend *verb* to behave in a way that shows (pleasantly or unpleasantly) one's feeling of dignity or superiority. **condescension** *noun*

condign (kŏn-**dyn**) *adjective* (of punishment) severe and well-deserved. [from *con-*, + Latin *dignus* = worthy]

condiment (**kon**-dĭ-měnt) *noun* a seasoning (such as salt or pepper) for food.

condition *noun* **1** the state in which a person or thing is with regard to characteristics and circumstances. **2** a state of physical fitness or (of things) fitness for use, *get into condition*; *out of condition*, not fully fit. **3** an abnormality, *she has a heart condition*. **4** something required as part of an agreement. **– condition** *verb* **1** to bring into a desired condition; to make physically fit; to put into a proper state for work or use. **2** to have a strong effect on. **3** to train, to accustom. **conditions** *plural noun* the facts or situations or surroundings that affect something, *working conditions are good*. ☐ **conditioned reflex** or **response** a reaction produced by training, not a natural one. **on condition that** on the understanding that (a thing will be done).

conditional *adjective* not absolute, containing a condition or stipulation, *a conditional agreement*. **– conditional** *noun* a word or clause, or a form of a verb, expressing a condition. **conditionally** *adverb*

conditioner *noun* an agent that brings something into good condition, especially an agent applied to the hair.

condole (kŏn-**dohl**) *verb* to express sympathy, *they condoled with her over the death of her husband*. **condolence** *noun* [from *con-*, + Latin *dolere* = grieve]

condom (**kon**-dom) *noun* a sheath for wearing on the penis during sexual intercourse as a contraceptive or to prevent infection.

condominium (kon-dŏ-**min**-ee-ŭm) *noun* **1** joint control of a State's affairs by two or more other States. **2** (especially *Amer.*) a building containing individually owned flats or home units; such a unit.

condone (kŏn-**dohn**) *verb* to forgive or overlook (wrongdoing) without punishment. **condonation** (kon-dŏ-**nay**-shŏn) *noun*

condor *noun* a very large vulture of South America.

conduce (kŏn-**dewss**) *verb* to help to cause or produce.

conducive (kŏn-**dew**-siv) *adjective* helping to cause or produce, *an atmosphere that is conducive to work*.

conduct (kŏn-**dukt**) *verb* **1** to lead or guide; *conducted tour*, escorted by a guide. **2** to be the conductor of (a choir or orchestra or music). **3** to manage or direct (business or negotiations etc., or an experiment). **4** to have the property of allowing heat, light, sound, or electricity to pass along or through. **– conduct** (**kon**-dukt) *noun* **1** a person's behaviour. **2** managing or directing affairs; *the conduct of the war*, the way it is being conducted. ☐ **conduct oneself** to behave. [from *con-*, + Latin *ducere* = to lead]

conductance *noun* the power of a specified body to conduct electricity.

conduction *noun* the transmission or conducting of heat or electricity etc.

conductive *adjective* able to conduct heat or electricity. **conductivity** *noun*

conductor *noun* **1** a person who directs the performance of an orchestra or choir etc. by gestures. **2** a person who collects the fares in a bus etc. **3** a substance that conducts heat or electricity etc.

conduit (**kon**-dit *or* **kon**-joo-ĭt) *noun* **1** a pipe or channel for conveying liquids. **2** a tube or trough protecting insulated electric wires.

cone *noun* **1** a solid body that narrows to a point from a round flat base. **2** something shaped like this; a cone-shaped part of the retina in the eye, sensitive to coloured light. **3** a cone-shaped wafer etc. holding ice cream. **4** the dry fruit of certain evergreen trees, consisting of woody scales arranged in a shape suggesting a cone.

confection *noun* something made of various things, especially sweet ones, put together.

confectioner *noun* a maker or retailer of confectionery.

confectionery *noun* lollies, chocolates, cakes, etc.

confederacy *noun* a union of States, a confederation.

confederate *adjective* allied, joined by agreement or treaty. –**confederate** *noun* 1 a member of a confederacy. 2 an ally, an accomplice. □ **Confederate States** the 11 southern States that seceded from the United States in 1860–1 and formed a confederacy of their own (thus precipitating the American Civil War), which was overthrown in 1865. [from *con-*, + Latin *foederatum* = allied]

confederated *adjective* united by agreement or treaty.

confederation *noun* 1 joining in an alliance. 2 a confederated group of people or organisations or States.

confer *verb* (**conferred**, **conferring**) 1 to grant, to bestow. 2 to hold a conference or discussion. **conferrable** *adjective*

conference *noun* a meeting for discussion.

conferment (kŏn-**fer**-mĕnt) *noun* granting, bestowing.

confess *verb* 1 to state formally that one has done wrong or has a weakness, *he confessed* or *confessed his crime* or *confessed to the crime*. 2 to state one's attitude or reaction reluctantly, *I must confess that I am puzzled*. 3 to declare one's sins formally, especially to a priest. 4 (of a priest) to hear the confession of.

confession *noun* 1 confessing. 2 a thing confessed, a statement of one's wrongdoing. 3 a declaration of one's religious beliefs or one's principles.

confessional *noun* an enclosed stall in a church, where a priest sits to hear confessions.

confessor *noun* 1 a priest who hears confessions and gives spiritual counsel. 2 a person who keeps to the Christian faith in the face of danger, *King Edward the Confessor*.

confetti *noun* bits of coloured paper thrown over the bride and bridegroom at a wedding. [Italian]

confidant (kon-fĭ-**dant**) *noun* a person in whom one confides. **confidante** *feminine noun*

confide *verb* 1 to tell confidentially; *confided in his friend*, told him things confidentially.

2 to entrust. [from *con-*, + Latin *fidere* = to trust]

confidence *noun* 1 firm trust. 2 a feeling of certainty, self-reliance, boldness. 3 something told confidentially. □ **confidence man** one who defrauds people by means of a **confidence trick**, a swindle in which the victim is persuaded to trust the swindler. **in confidence** as a secret. **in a person's confidence** trusted with his or her secrets.

confident *adjective* feeling confidence, bold. **confidently** *adverb*

confidential *adjective* 1 spoken or written in confidence, to be kept secret. 2 entrusted with secrets, *a confidential secretary*. 3 confiding, *spoke in a confidential tone*. **confidentially** *adverb*, **confidentiality** *noun*

configuration *noun* 1 a method of arrangement (e.g. of apparatus or parts of a computer system). 2 a shape or outline.

confine (kŏn-**fyn**) *verb* 1 to keep or restrict within certain limits. 2 to keep shut up. **confines** (**kon**-fynz) *plural noun* the limits or boundaries of an area. [from *con-*, + Latin *finis* = limit, end]

confined *adjective* narrow, restricted, *a confined space*.

confinement *noun* 1 confining; being confined. 2 the time during which a woman is giving birth to a baby.

confirm *verb* 1 to provide supporting evidence for the truth or correctness of, to prove. 2 to establish more firmly, *it confirmed him in his fear of dogs*. 3 to make definite or valid formally, *bookings by telephone must be confirmed in writing*. 4 to administer the rite of confirmation to.

confirmation *noun* 1 confirming. 2 something that confirms. 3 a religious rite confirming a baptised person as a member of the Christian Church. 4 a ceremony confirming a person in the Jewish faith.

confirmatory (kŏn-**ferm**-ă-tŏ-ree) *adjective* confirming, *we found confirmatory evidence*.

confiscate (**kon**-fis-kayt) *verb* to take or seize by authority. **confiscation** *noun*

conflagration (kon-flă-**gray**-shŏn) *noun* a great and destructive fire. [same origin as *flagrant*]

conflate *verb* to fuse or blend together (especially two variant texts into one). **conflation** *noun*

conflict (**kon**-flikt) *noun* **1** a fight, a struggle. **2** disagreement between people with different ideas or beliefs. –**conflict** (kŏn-**flikt**) *verb* **1** to fight, to struggle. **2** to be in opposition or disagreement. [from *con-* = together, + Latin *flictum* = struck]

confluence (**kon**-floo-ĕns) *noun* the place where two rivers unite. [from *con-*, + Latin *fluens* = flowing]

conform *verb* **1** to keep to rules or general custom, *she refuses to conform*. **2** to make or be consistent. ☐ **conform to** to act or be in accordance with. [from Latin *conformare* = shape evenly]

conformation *noun* **1** the way a thing is formed, its structure. **2** conforming.

conformist (kŏn-**form**-ĭst) *noun* a person who readily conforms to established rules or standards etc. **conformism** *noun*

conformity *noun* conforming to established rules or standards etc.

confound *verb* **1** to astonish and perplex, to bewilder. **2** to confuse. **3** (*old use*) to defeat, to overthrow. –**confound** *interjection* an exclamation of annoyance, *confound it!*

confounded *adjective* (*informal*) damned.

confront (kŏn-**frunt**) *verb* **1** to be or come face to face with, *the problems confronting us*. **2** to face boldly as an enemy or in defiance. **3** to bring face to face, *we confronted him with his accusers*. **confrontation** (kon-frun-**tay**-shŏn) *noun*

Confucianism (kŏn-**few**-shă-nizm) *noun* the moral and religious system founded by Confucius.

Confucius (kŏn-**few**-shŭs) (551–479 BC), the most influential Chinese philosopher. **Confucian** *adjective* & *noun*

confuse *verb* **1** to throw into disorder, to mix up. **2** to throw the mind or feelings of (a person) into disorder; to destroy the composure of. **3** to mix up in the mind, to fail to distinguish between. **4** to make unclear. **confusable** *adjective*, **confusion** *noun*

confute (kŏn-**fewt**) *verb* to prove (a person or argument) to be wrong. **confutation** (kon-few-**tay**-shŏn) *noun*

conga *noun* a dance in which people form a long winding line.

congeal (kŏn-**jeel**) *verb* to become semi-solid instead of liquid. **congelation** (kon-jĕ-**lay**-shŏn) *noun* [from Latin *congelare* = freeze]

congenial (kŏn-**jeen**-ee-ăl) *adjective* **1** pleasant because similar to oneself in character or tastes, *a congenial companion*. **2** suited or agreeable to oneself, *a congenial climate*.

congenital (kŏn-**jen**-ĭt'l) *adjective* **1** existing since a person's birth, *a congenital deformity*. **2** born in a certain condition, *a congenital idiot*. **congenitally** *adverb* [from *con-*, + Latin *genitus* = born]

conger (**kong**-ger) *noun* a large sea eel.

congested *adjective* **1** too full, overcrowded. **2** (of an organ or tissue of the body) abnormally full of blood.

congestion (kŏn-**jes**-chŏn) *noun* a congested condition.

conglomerate (kŏn-**glom**-ĕ-răt) *adjective* **1** gathered into a mass. **2** (of rocks) made up of small stones cemented together. –**conglomerate** (kŏn-**glom**-ĕ-răt) *noun* **1** a conglomerate mass. **2** a group formed by merging several different firms. **3** a conglomerate rock. –**conglomerate** (kŏn-**glom**-ĕ-rayt) *verb* to gather into a mass. **conglomeration** *noun* [from *con-*, + Latin *glomus* = mass]

Congo **1** (also **Zaïre**) a major river in central Africa. **2** (also **the Congo**) a republic in central Africa with a short Atlantic coastline. **3** (in full **Democratic Republic of Congo**) a republic, formerly known as Zaïre, to the east of the Congo. **Congolese** *adjective* & *noun*

congratulate *verb* to praise and tell (a person) that one is pleased about his or her achievement or good fortune. [from *con-*, + Latin *gratulari* = show joy]

congratulation *noun* **1** congratulating. **2** (usually **congratulations**) an expression of this.

congratulatory (kŏn-**grat**-yŭ-lă-tŏ-ree) *adjective* expressing congratulations.

congregate *verb* to flock together. [from *con-*, + Latin *gregatum* = herded]

congregation *noun* a group of people gathered together to take part in religious worship. **congregational** *adjective*

Congregationalism *noun* a form of church organisation in which each local church is independent. **Congregational** *adjective*, **Congregationalist** *noun*

congress *noun* a formal meeting of representatives, for discussion. –**Congress** *noun* the law-making body of a country,

especially of the USA. **congressional** *adjective*
[from *con-*, + Latin *gressus* = going]

congruent (**kong**-groo-ĕnt) *adjective*
1 suitable, consistent. 2 (of geometrical
figures) having exactly the same shape and
size. **congruence** *noun*, **congruency** *noun*

conic (**kon**-ik) *adjective* of a cone. □ **conic
section** a geometric figure (e.g. circle, ellipse,
parabola) formed by the intersection of a cone
and a plane.

conical *adjective* cone-shaped. **conically**
adverb

conifer (**kon**-ĭ-fer) *noun* a coniferous tree,
e.g. pine, cedar, fir. [from *cone* + Latin *ferens*
= bearing]

coniferous (kŏ-**nif**-ĕ-rŭs) *adjective* bearing
cones.

conjectural *adjective* based on conjecture.

conjecture *verb* to guess. –**conjecture** *noun*
a guess.

conjoin *verb* join, combine. □ **conjoined
twins** technical term for *Siamese twins*.

conjugal (**kon**-jŭ-găl) *adjective* of marriage,
of the relationship between husband and wife.

conjugate (**kon**-jŭ-gayt) *verb* 1 to give the
different forms of (a verb), e.g. *get*, *gets*.
2 to unite, to become fused.

conjugation *noun* 1 conjugating. 2 any of
the different sets of inflected forms of verbs
in a language. 3 the fusion of gametes in
reproduction.

conjunction *noun* 1 a word that joins
words or phrases or sentences, e.g. *and*, *but*.
2 combination, union, *the four countries acted
in conjunction*. 3 the occurrence of events
etc. at the same time. [from Latin *conjunctum*
= yoked together]

conjunctivitis *noun* inflammation of the
surface of the eyeball or inner eyelid.

conjure (**kun**-jer) *verb* 1 to perform tricks
that appear to be magical, especially by
movements of the hands, *conjuring tricks*. 2 to
summon (a spirit) to appear. 3 to produce as if
from nothing, *managed to conjure up a meal*.
4 to produce in the mind, *mention of the Arctic
conjures up visions of snow and ice*. □ **a name
to conjure with** a name of great importance.

conjuror *noun* a person who performs
conjuring tricks.

conk *noun* (*informal*) the nose, the head.
–**conk** *verb* (*informal*) to hit on the head.

□ **conk out** (*informal*, of a machine) to
break down, to fail; (of a person) to become
exhausted and give up, to faint, to die.

conker *noun* the fruit of the horse chestnut
tree. [from a dialect word, = snail shell]

connect *verb* 1 to join or be joined. 2 (of
a train etc.) to be timed to arrive so that
passengers from one train etc. can catch
another in which to continue their journey.
3 to put into communication by telephone.
4 to think of (things or persons) as being
associated with each other. [from *con-*, + Latin
nectere = bind]

Connecticut (kŏ-**net**-ĭ-kŭt) a State of the
USA.

connection *noun* 1 connecting, being
connected. 2 a place where things connect; a
connecting part. 3 a train etc. timed to connect
with another; transfer between such trains.
4 a link, especially by telephone. 5 a link or
relationship between ideas. 6 a relative or
associate, especially one with influence, *he
has connections*. □ **in connection with this** or
in this connection on this subject.

connective *adjective* connecting.

connector *noun* a thing that connects others.

conning tower *noun* 1 a raised structure on
a submarine, containing the periscope. 2 an
armoured pilot house on a warship.

connive (kŏ-**nyv**) *verb* **connive at** to take
no notice of (wrongdoing), thus seeming to
consent to it. **connive with** to conspire with,
connived with his friend to steal the money.
connivance *noun* [from Latin *connivere* = shut
the eyes]

connoisseur (kon-ŏ-**ser**) *noun* a person with
expert understanding of artistic and similar
subjects. [French, = one who knows]

connote (kŏ-**noht**) *verb* to imply in addition
to the primary or literal meaning. (Compare
denote.) **connotation** *noun*

connubial (kŏ-**new**-bee-ăl) *adjective* of
marriage, of the relationship between husband
and wife. [from *con-*, + Latin *nubere* = marry]

conoid (**koh**-noid) *adjective* of or shaped like
a cone. –**conoid** *noun* a conoid object.

conquer *verb* 1 to overcome in war, to win.
2 to overcome by effort. **conqueror** *noun*

conquest *noun* 1 conquering; **the Conquest**
or **Norman Conquest**, conquest of England
by the Normans in 1066. 2 something got by
conquering.

conquistador (kon-**kwis**-tă-dor) *noun* a conqueror, especially one of the Spanish soldiers and adventurers who conquered South America in the 16th century.

Conrad, Joseph (1857–1924), Polish-born British novelist, author of *Heart of Darkness* and *Nostromo*.

consanguinity (kon-sang-**gwin**-ĭ-tee) *noun* relationship by descent from the same ancestor. **consanguineous** *adjective* [from *con-*, + Latin *sanguis* = blood]

conscience *noun* 1 a person's sense of what is right and wrong, especially in his or her own actions or motives. 2 a feeling of remorse, *I have no conscience about leaving them*. □ **conscience-stricken** *adjective* filled with remorse. **on one's conscience** causing one to feel guilty or remorseful. [from *con-*, + Latin *sciens* = knowing]

conscientious (kon-shee-**en**-shŭs) *adjective* showing or done with careful attention. □ **conscientious objector** one who refuses to do something (especially to serve in the armed forces in a war) because he or she believes it is morally wrong. **conscientiously** *adverb*, **conscientiousness** *noun*

conscious *adjective* 1 with one's mental faculties awake, aware of one's surroundings. 2 aware, *he was conscious of his guilt*; *fashion-conscious*. 3 realised by oneself, intentional, *a conscious insult*. **consciously** *adverb*, **consciousness** *noun*

conscript (kŏn-**skript**) *verb* to call up for compulsory military service. –**conscript** (**kon**-skript) *noun* a conscripted recruit. **conscription** *noun* [from *con-*, + Latin *scriptus* = written in a list, enlisted]

consecrate *verb* to make or declare sacred, to dedicate formally to the service or worship of God. **consecration** *noun*

consecutive (kŏn-**sek**-yŭ-tiv) *adjective* 1 following continuously, in unbroken order. 2 (in grammar) expressing a consequence, *a consecutive clause*. **consecutively** *adverb* [from Latin *consecutum* = following]

consensus (kŏn-**sen**-sŭs) *noun* general agreement in opinion. [same origin as *consent*]

consent *verb* to say that one is willing to do or allow what someone wishes. –**consent** *noun* agreement to what someone wishes, permission. [from *con-*, + Latin *sentire* = feel]

consequence *noun* 1 a result produced by some action or condition. 2 importance, *a person of consequence*; *of no consequence*, not important. □ **in consequence** as a result. **take the consequences** to accept whatever results from one's choice or action.

consequent *adjective* following as a result. [same origin as *consecutive*]

consequential (kon-sĕ-**kwen**-shăl) *adjective* 1 following as a result. 2 self-important. **consequentially** *adverb*

consequently *adverb* as a result, therefore.

conservation *noun* 1 conserving, being conserved. 2 preservation, especially of the natural environment.

conservationist *noun* a person who supports conservation.

conservatism *noun* a conservative attitude, conservative principles (general or political).

conservative *adjective* 1 disliking or opposed to great or sudden change. 2 moderate, avoiding extremes; *a conservative estimate*, a low one. –**conservative** *noun* 1 a conservative person. 2 a person with conservative political views. –**Conservative** *noun* a member of the **Conservative Party**, a British political party favouring private enterprise and freedom from State control, also informally called the *Tories*. **conservatively** *adverb*

conservatorium (kŏn-serv-ă-**tor**-ree-ŭm) *noun* (*Austral*.) a school of music.

conservatory *noun* a greenhouse, especially one attached to a house.

conserve (kŏn-**serv**) *verb* to keep from harm, decay, or loss, for future use. –**conserve** (**kon**-serv) *noun* jam. [from *con-*, + Latin *servare* = keep safe]

consider *verb* 1 to think about, especially in order to make a decision; to weigh the merits of. 2 to make allowances for, *consider people's feelings*. 3 to think to be, to suppose, *consider yourself lucky*.

considerable *adjective* fairly great in amount or extent etc., *of considerable importance*. **considerably** *adverb*

considerate *adjective* taking care not to inconvenience or hurt others. **considerately** *adverb*

consideration *noun* 1 careful thought. 2 being considerate, kindness. 3 a fact that must be kept in mind, *time is now an important consideration*. 4 payment given as a reward, *he will do it for a consideration*. □ **in consideration of** in return for; on account of. **on no consideration** (not do something) no matter what the circumstances may be. take into consideration to allow for. under consideration being considered.

considering *preposition* taking into consideration, *her skin is very good, considering her age*. –considering *adverb* (*informal*) taking everything into account, *you've done very well, considering*.

consign *verb* 1 to hand over or deliver formally. 2 to give into someone's care.

consignee (kon-sy-**nee**) *noun* the person to whom goods etc. are consigned.

consignment *noun* 1 consigning. 2 a batch of goods etc. consigned.

consignor (kŏn-**sy**-nor) *noun* one who consigns goods etc. to another.

consist *verb* consist of to be made up of, *the flat consists of three rooms*. consist in to have as its basis or essential feature, *their happiness consists in hoping*.

consistency *noun* 1 the degree of thickness, firmness, or solidity, especially of a liquid or soft mixture, *mix it to the consistency of thick cream*. 2 being consistent.

consistent *adjective* 1 conforming to a regular pattern or style, unchanging, *they have no consistent policy*. 2 not contradictory. consistently *adverb*

consolable *adjective* able to be consoled.

consolation *noun* consoling; being consoled. ☐ consolation prize a prize given to a competitor who has just missed winning one of the main prizes.

console[1] (kŏn-**sohl**) *verb* to comfort in time of sorrow or disappointment. [from *con*-, + Latin *solari* = to comfort]

console[2] (**kon**-sohl) *noun* 1 a bracket to support a shelf. 2 a frame containing the keyboards and stops etc. of an organ. 3 a panel holding the controls of electrical or other equipment. 4 (also games console) a small machine for playing computerised video games etc. 5 a cabinet containing a television etc., designed to stand on the floor. [French]

consolidate *verb* 1 to make or become secure and strong, *consolidating his position as leader*. 2 to combine or become combined, to merge. consolidation *noun*

consommé (kŏn-**som**-ay *or* **kon**-sŏ-may) *noun* clear meat soup. [French]

consonance (**kon**-sŏ-năns) *noun* 1 agreement, harmony, especially of a combination of notes in music. 2 a recurrence of similar-sounding consonants.

consonant *noun* 1 a letter of the alphabet other than a vowel. 2 the speech sound it represents. –consonant *adjective* consistent, harmonious. [from *con*-, + Latin *sonans* = sounding]

consort[1] (**kon**-sort) *noun* 1 a husband or wife, especially of a monarch. 2 a ship sailing with another. –consort (kŏn-**sort**) *verb* to associate, to keep company, *consorting with criminals*. [from Latin *consors* = sharer]

consort[2] (**kon**-sort) *noun* a group of musicians who perform together.

consortium (kŏn-**sort**-ee-ŭm) *noun* (*plural* consortia) a combination of countries, companies, or other groups acting together.

conspicuous *adjective* 1 easily seen, attracting attention. 2 worthy of notice. conspicuously *adverb*, conspicuousness *noun*

conspiracy *noun* 1 conspiring. 2 a plan made by conspiring.

conspirator *noun* a person who conspires. conspiratorial *adjective*, conspiratorially *adverb*

conspire *verb* 1 to plan secretly with others, especially for some unlawful purpose. 2 (of events) to seem to combine, *events conspired to bring about his downfall*. [from *con*-, + Latin *spirare* = breathe]

Constable (**kun**-stă-bŭl), John (1776–1837), English painter of landscapes.

constable *noun* a police officer of the lowest rank. [from Latin, originally = officer in charge of the stable]

constabulary (kŏn-**stab**-yŭ-lă-ree) *noun* a police force.

constancy *noun* 1 the quality of being constant and unchanging. 2 faithfulness.

constant *adjective* 1 happening or continuing all the time; happening repeatedly. 2 unchanging, faithful, *remained constant to his principles*. –constant *noun* 1 something that is constant and does not vary. 2 a number expressing a physical property or relationship and remaining the same in all circumstances (e.g. the *constant of gravitation*) or for the same substance in the same conditions. constantly *adverb* [from *con*-, + Latin *stans* = standing]

Constantine (died 337), Roman emperor from 306, during whose reign toleration and imperial favour were given to the Christian faith.

Constantinople the former name of Istanbul.

constellation *noun* a group of fixed stars. [from *con-*, + Latin *stella* = star]

consternation *noun* great surprise and anxiety or dismay.

constipate *verb* to affect with constipation.

constipation *noun* difficulty in emptying the bowels.

constituency *noun* a body of voters who elect a representative, especially as a Member of Parliament; a district thus represented (in Australia usually called *an electorate*).

constituent *adjective* forming part of a whole, *its constituent parts.* – **constituent** *noun* 1 a constituent part. 2 a member of a constituency.

constitute *verb* 1 to make up, to form, *12 months constitute a year.* 2 to appoint, *they constituted him chief adviser.* 3 to establish or be, *this does not constitute a precedent.* [from *con-*, + Latin *statuere* = to set up]

constitution *noun* 1 constituting. 2 composition. 3 the principles according to which a country is organised. 4 general condition and character, especially of a person's body, *she has a strong constitution.*

constitutional *adjective* 1 of a country's constitution; established, permitted, or limited by this. 2 of or produced by a person's physical or mental constitution, *a constitutional weakness.* – **constitutional** *noun* a walk taken for the sake of one's health. **constitutionally** *adverb*

constrain *verb* to compel, to oblige.

constrained *adjective* (of the voice, manner, etc.) strained, showing constraint.

constraint *noun* 1 constraining, being constrained; compulsion. 2 a strained manner caused by holding back one's natural feelings.

constrict *verb* to tighten by making narrower, to squeeze. **constriction** *noun* [from *con-*, + Latin *strictum* = bound]

constrictor *noun* 1 a snake (e.g. a boa) that kills by squeezing its prey. 2 a muscle that contracts an organ or part of the body.

construct *verb* to make by placing parts together. **constructor** *noun* [from *con-*, + Latin *structum* = built]

construction *noun* 1 constructing; being constructed. 2 something constructed. 3 two or more words put together to form a phrase or clause or sentence. 4 an interpretation, *put a bad construction on their refusal.* **constructional** *adjective*

constructive *adjective* offering helpful suggestions, *they made constructive criticisms.* **constructively** *adverb*

construe (kŏn-**stroo**) *verb* 1 to interpret, to explain. 2 to analyse the syntax of. 3 to translate word for word.

consubstantiation *noun* the doctrine, associated especially with Luther, that in the Eucharist, after the consecration of the elements, the body and blood of Christ are present along with the bread and wine. [from *con-*, + Latin *substantia* = essence]

consul *noun* 1 either of the two chief magistrates in ancient Rome. 2 an official appointed to live in a foreign city in order to assist and protect his or her countrymen who live or visit there and to help commercial relations between the two countries. **consular** (**kons**-yŭ-ler) *adjective* [Latin]

consulate *noun* 1 the official premises of a consul. 2 a consul's position.

consult *verb* 1 to seek information or advice from; *a consulting engineer*, one who acts as a consultant. 2 to confer. **consultation** *noun*

consultant *noun* a person qualified to give expert professional advice, especially a specialist in a branch of medicine or surgery.

consultative (kŏn-**sult**-ă-tiv) *adjective* for consultation, *a consultative committee.*

consumable *adjective* able to be consumed.

consume *verb* 1 to use up, *much time was consumed in waiting.* 2 to eat or drink up, especially in large quantities. 3 to destroy completely, *fire consumed the buildings.* [from *con-*, + Latin *sumere* = take up]

consumer *noun* a person who buys or uses goods or services. ☐ **consumer goods** those bought and used by individual consumers rather than used for producing other goods (*see* **capital goods**). **consumer price index** (*Austral.*) a measure of the cost of living based on a standard set of prices.

consumerism *noun* 1 the protection of consumer's interests. 2 high consumption of goods etc.; belief in this.

consuming *adjective* overwhelming, dominating, *a consuming ambition.*

consummate (**kon**-sŭ-mayt) *verb* to accomplish, to make complete. – **consummate** (kŏn-**sum**-ăt) *adjective* supremely skilled, *a consummate artist.* **consummation** *noun* [from *con-*, + Latin *summus* = highest]

consumption *noun* 1 consuming, using up, destruction. 2 the amount consumed. 3 (*old use*) tuberculosis of the lungs.

consumptive *adjective* suffering from tuberculosis of the lungs.

contact (**kon**-takt) *noun* 1 touching, coming together. 2 being in touch, communication. 3 a connection for the passage of electric current. 4 a person who has recently been near someone with a contagious disease and may carry infection. 5 an acquaintance who may be contacted when one needs information or help. –**contact** *verb* to get in touch with (a person). □ **contact lens** a very small lens worn in contact with the eyeball. [from *con-*, + Latin *tactum* = touched]

contagion (kŏn-**tay**-jŏn) *noun* 1 the spreading of disease by contact or close association. 2 a disease spread in this way.

contagious (kŏn-**tay**-jŭs) *adjective* 1 able to be spread by contact or close association, *a contagious disease*. 2 capable of spreading disease in this way, *all these children are now contagious*.

contain *verb* 1 to have within itself, *the packet contains five pens*; *whisky contains alcohol*. 2 to consist of, to be equal to, *a litre contains 1000 mls*. 3 to restrain, *try to contain your laughter*. 4 to keep within limits, *enemy troops were contained in the valley*. [from *con-*, + Latin *tenere* = hold]

container *noun* 1 a box or bottle etc. designed to contain a substance or goods. 2 a large boxlike receptacle of standard design for transporting goods.

containerise *verb* (also **-ize**) to transport by container; to convert to this method of transporting goods. **containerisation** *noun*

containment *noun* the policy of preventing the expansion of a hostile country or influence.

contaminate *verb* to pollute. **contaminant** *noun*, **contamination** *noun*, **contaminator** *noun*

contemplate (**kon**-těm-playt) *verb* 1 to gaze at thoughtfully. 2 to consider. 3 to intend, to have in view as a possibility, *she is contemplating an overseas trip*. 4 to meditate. **contemplation** *noun*

contemplative (kŏn-**tem**-plă-tiv) *adjective* thoughtful, fond of contemplation; devoted to religious contemplation. –**contemplative** *noun* a contemplative person.

contemporaneous *adjective* existing or occurring at the same time.

contemporary (kŏn-**tem**-pŏ-ră-ree) *adjective* 1 belonging to the same period; *Dickens was contemporary with Thackeray*, lived at the same time. 2 modern, *contemporary designs*. –**contemporary** *noun* 1 a person contemporary with another, *Dickens and his contemporaries*. 2 one who is approximately the same age as another. [from *con-*, + Latin *tempus* = time]

contempt *noun* 1 the process or feeling of despising a person or thing. 2 the condition of being despised, disrespect.

contemptible *adjective* deserving contempt. **contemptibly** *adverb*, **contemptibility** *noun*

contemptuous *adjective* feeling or showing contempt. **contemptuously** *adverb*, **contemptuousness** *noun*

contend *verb* 1 to strive or fight or struggle, especially in competition or against difficulties. 2 to assert, to argue, *the defendant contends that he is innocent*. **contender** *noun* [from *con-*, + Latin *tendere* = strive]

content[1] (kŏn-**tent**) *adjective* contented, satisfied with what one has. –**content** *noun* being contented, satisfaction. –**content** *verb* to make content, to satisfy. □ **to one's heart's content** as much as one desires. [from Latin *contentum* = restrained]

content[2] (**kon**-tent) *noun* what is contained in something, *the contents of the barrel*; *butter has a high fat content*, contains much fat; *the table of contents*, the list of chapter-headings etc. showing the subject matter of a book. [from Latin *contenta* = things contained]

contented *adjective* happy with what one has, satisfied. **contentedly** *adverb*

contention *noun* 1 contending; quarrelling, arguing. 2 an assertion made in arguing.

contentious (kŏn-**ten**-shŭs) *adjective* 1 quarrelsome. 2 likely to cause contention. **contentiously** *adverb*

contentment *noun* a contented state.

contest (**kon**-test) *noun* 1 a struggle for superiority or victory. 2 a competition, a test of skill or ability etc. between rivals. –**contest** (kŏn-**test**) *verb* 1 to compete for or in, *contest a seat at an election*; *contest an election*. 2 to dispute, to challenge.

contestant *noun* one who takes part in a contest, a competitor.

context *noun* 1 the words that come before and after a particular word or phrase and help to fix its meaning. 2 the circumstances

192

in which an event occurs, *shortages were tolerated in the context of war*. □ **out of context** without the surrounding words and therefore giving a false impression of the meaning. [from *con-*, + Latin *textum* = woven]

contiguous (kŏn-**tig**-yoo-ŭs) *adjective* adjoining, neighbouring. **contiguity** (kon-tig-**yoo**-ĭ-tee) *noun*

continent[1] *noun* any of the main land masses of the earth (Europe, Asia, Africa, North and South America, Australia, Antarctica). □ **the Continent** the mainland of Europe as distinct from the British Isles. [from Latin, = continuous land]

continent[2] *adjective* able to control the excretion of one's urine and faeces. **continence** *noun*

continental *adjective* of a continent; **Continental** of the Continent. –**Continental** *noun* an inhabitant of the Continent. □ **Continental breakfast** a light breakfast of coffee and rolls etc. **continental drift** the slow drift of the continents on the earth's surface to their present positions, above a layer of dense molten rock lying very deep within the earth. **continental quilt** a quilt filled with down, feathers, or other materials, used instead of blankets. **continental shelf** the shallow seabed bordering a continent.

contingency (kŏn-**tin**-jĕn-see) *noun* 1 something unforeseen. 2 a possibility, something that may occur at a future date; *contingency plans*, plans made in case something happens.

contingent (kŏn-**tin**-jĕnt) *adjective* 1 happening by chance. 2 possible, liable to occur but not certain. 3 depending on something that may or may not happen, *an advantage that is contingent on the success of the expedition*. –**contingent** *noun* 1 a body of troops or ships etc. contributed to form part of a force. 2 a group of people forming part of a gathering.

continual *adjective* constantly or frequently recurring; always happening. **continually** *adverb*

Usage *Continual* and *continuous* are often confused. *Continual* is used of something that happens frequently, but with breaks between each occurrence (e.g. *the tennis was interrupted by continual brief showers*), while *continuous* is used of something that happens without a break (e.g. *continuous rain all morning caused the match to be abandoned*).

continuance *noun* continuing.

continuation *noun* 1 continuing, starting again after ceasing. 2 a thing that continues something else.

continue *verb* 1 to keep up (an action etc.), to do something without ceasing, *continue to eat*; *continue the struggle*. 2 to remain in a certain place or condition, *he will continue as chairman*. 3 to go further, *the road continues beyond the bridge*. 4 to begin again after stopping. [same origin as *contain*]

continuity (kon-tĭ-**new**-ĭ-tee) *noun* 1 being continuous. 2 the uninterrupted succession of things. 3 linkage between broadcast items.

continuo *noun* (*plural* **continuos**) a bass accompaniment in Baroque music, usually played on a keyboard instrument, e.g. a harpsichord.

continuous *adjective* 1 continuing, without a break. 2 (of a mathematical set) such that any number, point, etc., that lies between any two elements of the set is also a member of that set. **continuously** *adverb*

Usage See note at **continual**.

continuum (kŏn-**tin**-yoo-ŭm) *noun* (*plural* **continua**) something that extends continuously.

contort (kŏn-**tort**) *verb* to force or twist out of the usual shape. **contortion** (kŏn-**tor**-shŏn) *noun* [from *con-*, + Latin *tortum* = twisted]

contortionist (kŏn-**tor**-shŏ-nĭst) *noun* a performer who can twist his or her body into unusual postures.

contour (**kon**-toor) *noun* 1 a line (on a map) joining the points that are the same height above sea level. 2 an outline. □ **contour ploughing** ploughing along contour lines in order to reduce the erosion of soil.

contra- *prefix* against. [Latin]

contraband *noun* 1 smuggled goods. 2 smuggling. [from *contra-*, + Italian *bando* = a ban]

contraception (kon-trǎ-**sep**-shŏn) *noun* the prevention of conception; the use of contraceptives. [from *contra-*, + *conception*]

contraceptive (kon-trǎ-**sep**-tiv) *adjective* preventing conception. –**contraceptive** *noun* a contraceptive drug or device.

contract (**kon**-trakt) *noun* 1 a formal agreement between people or groups or countries. 2 a document setting out the terms of such an agreement. –**contract** (kŏn-**trakt**) *verb* **1** to make or become smaller or shorter. **2** to arrange or undertake by contract, *they contracted to supply oil to the factory*; *the job was contracted out to a private firm*. **3** to catch (an illness), to form or acquire (a habit, a debt, etc.). □ **contract out** to choose to withdraw or not to enter a scheme or commitment. [from *con-*, + Latin *tractum* = pulled]

contractable *adjective* (of a disease) able to be contracted.

contractile *adjective* able to contract or to produce contraction. **contractility** *noun*

contraction *noun* **1** contracting. **2** shortening a word or words by combination or by elision or omission of a syllable etc.

contractor *noun* one who makes a contract, especially for constructing a building.

contractual (kŏn-**trakt**-yoo-ăl) *adjective* of a contract. **contractually** *adverb*

contradict *verb* **1** to state that (what is said) is untrue or that (a person) is wrong. **2** to state the opposite of, to be contrary to, *these rumours contradict previous ones*. □ **a contradiction in terms** a statement that contradicts itself. **contradiction** *noun*, **contradictory** *adjective* [from *contra-*, + Latin *dicere* = say]

contradistinction *noun* in **contradistinction to** as distinct from.

contralto (kŏn-**trahl**-toh) *noun* (*plural* **contraltos**) **1** the lowest female singing voice. **2** a singer with such a voice; a part written for it. [Italian, from *contra-* + *alto*]

contraption *noun* (*informal*) an odd-looking gadget or machine.

contrapuntal *adjective* of or in counterpoint. [from Italian *contrappunto* = counterpoint]

contrariwise (kŏn-**trair**-ree-wyz) *adverb* on the other hand, in the opposite way.

contrary (**kon**-tră-ree) *adjective* **1** opposite in nature, opposed, *contrary to expectation*. **2** opposite in direction; *contrary winds*, unfavourable ones. **3** (*pr.* kŏn-**trair**-ree) doing the opposite of what is expected or advised, wilful. –**contrary** *noun* the opposite. –**contrary** *adverb* in opposition, against, *acting contrary to instructions*. □ **on the contrary** in denial of what has just been said or implied and stating that the opposite is true. **contrariness** *noun* [from Latin *contra* = against]

contrast (**kon**-trahst) *noun* **1** the act of contrasting. **2** a difference clearly seen

when things are put together. **3** something showing such a difference. **4** the degree of difference between tones or colours. –**contrast** (kŏn-**trahst**) *verb* **1** to compare or oppose two things so as to show their differences. **2** to show a striking difference when compared. [from *contra-*, + Latin *stare* = to stand]

contravene (kon-tră-**veen**) *verb* to act in opposition to, to conflict with, *contravening the law*. **contravention** (kontră-**ven**-shŏn) *noun* [from *contra-*, + Latin *venire* = come]

contretemps (**kawn**-trĕ-tahn) *noun* an unfortunate happening. [French, = out of time (in music)]

contribute (kŏn-**trib**-yoot) *verb* **1** to give jointly with others, especially to a common fund. **2** to supply for publication in a newspaper or magazine or book. **3** to help to bring about, *drink contributed to his ruin*. **contribution** *noun*, **contributor** *noun* [from *con-*, + Latin *tribuere* = bestow]

contributory (kŏn-**trib**-yŭ-tŏ-ree) *adjective* **1** contributing to a result; *contributory negligence*, failure to have taken proper precautions against an accident etc. in which one becomes involved. **2** involving contributions to a fund.

contrite (**kon**-tryt) *adjective* penitent, feeling guilty. **contritely** *adverb*, **contrition** (kŏn-**trish**-ŏn) *noun*

contrivance (kŏn-**try**-văns) *noun* **1** contriving. **2** something contrived, a plan. **3** a mechanical device.

contrive *verb* to plan cleverly; to achieve in a clever or resourceful way; to manage. **contriver** *noun*

control *noun* **1** the power to give orders or to restrain something. **2** a means of restraining or regulating; a device such as a switch or knob by which a machine is operated. **3** restraint, self-restraint. **4** a standard of comparison for checking the results of an experiment. **5** a place where cars taking part in a race must stop for inspection etc. **6** a personality said to direct the actions of a spiritualist medium. **7** a control unit. –**control** *verb* (**controlled**, **controlling**) **1** to have control of, to regulate. **2** to restrain. □ **control technology** the use of programmed devices to monitor a process or environment and make changes to it in response to data collected. **control tower** a tall building from which air traffic is controlled at an airport. **control unit** that part of a computer which controls the operation of the other units.

in control controlling. out of control no longer able to be controlled. under control controlled, in proper order. controllable *adjective*, controller *noun*

controversial (kon-trŏ-**ver**-shăl) *adjective* causing controversy.

controversy (**kon**-trŏ-ver-see *or* kŏn-**trov**-er-see) *noun* a prolonged argument or dispute. [from *contra-*, + Latin *versum* = turned]

controvert (**kon**-trŏ-vert) *verb* to deny the truth of, to contradict. controvertible *adjective*

contumely (**kon**-tewm-lee) *noun* 1 an insult. 2 a disgrace. [from Latin *contumelia*]

contusion (kŏn-**tew**-zhŏn) *noun* a bruise.

conundrum (kŏ-**nun**-drŭm) *noun* a hard question, or a riddle.

conurbation (kon-er-**bay**-shŏn) *noun* a large urban area formed where towns have spread and merged. [from *con-*, + Latin *urbs* = city]

convalesce *verb* to regain health after illness. convalescence *noun*, convalescent *adjective* & *noun* [from *con-*, + Latin *valescere* = grow strong]

convection *noun* the transmission of heat within a liquid or gas by movement of the heated parts. convective *adjective* [from *con-*, + Latin *vectum* = carried]

convector *noun* a heating appliance that circulates warmed air.

convene *verb* to assemble, to cause to assemble. convener (also convenor) *noun* [from *con-*, + Latin *venire* = come]

convenience *noun* 1 the quality of being convenient. 2 something that is convenient. 3 a toilet, *public conveniences*. □ at your convenience whenever or however you find convenient. convenience foods those that are convenient to use because they need little preparation. make a convenience of someone to use his or her services to an unreasonable extent.

convenient *adjective* 1 easy to use or deal with, not troublesome. 2 available or occurring at a suitable time or place; with easy access, *convenient for the bus*. conveniently *adverb* [from Latin *convenire* = to suit]

convent *noun* 1 a religious community of nuns. 2 a building in which they live. 3 a convent school, a school run by members of a convent.

convention *noun* 1 a formal assembly. 2 a formal agreement, especially between

countries, *the Geneva Convention*. 3 an accepted custom.

conventional *adjective* done according to conventions, traditional; *conventional weapons*, non-nuclear. conventionally *adverb*

converge *verb* to come to or towards the same point. convergence *noun*, convergent *adjective* [from *con-*, + Latin *vergere* = to turn]

conversant (kŏn-**ver**-sănt) *adjective* conversant with having a knowledge of. [from *converse*[1]]

conversation *noun* informal talk between people. conversational *adjective*, conversationally *adverb*

conversationalist *noun* a person who is good at conversation.

converse[1] (kŏn-**verss**) *verb* to hold a conversation. [from Latin, = keep company]

converse[2] (**kon**-verss) *adjective* opposite, contrary. –converse *noun* an idea or statement that is the opposite of another. conversely *adverb* [same origin as *convert*]

convert (kŏn-**vert**) *verb* 1 to change from one form, use, or character to another. 2 to be able to be changed, *the sofa converts into a bed*. 3 to cause (a person) to change his or her attitude or beliefs. 4 to score a goal from (a try in rugby football). –convert (**kon**-vert) *noun* a person who is converted, especially to a religious faith. conversion *noun* [from *con-*, + Latin *vertere* = to turn]

converter *noun* 1 a device for converting something, e.g. for converting electric current from AC to DC or vice versa. 2 a large vessel used in steelmaking in which molten metal is subjected to the Bessemer or a similar process.

convertible *adjective* able to be converted. –convertible *noun* a car with a roof that can be folded down or removed.

convex (**kon**-veks) *adjective* curving like the surface of a ball as seen from the outside. convexly *adverb*, convexity (kŏn-**veks**-ĭ-tee) *noun*

convey *verb* 1 to carry or transport or transmit. 2 to communicate as an idea or meaning. conveyable *adjective*

conveyance *noun* 1 conveying. 2 a means of transporting people, a vehicle. 3 transfer of the legal ownership of land etc.; a document effecting this.

conveyancing *noun* the business of transferring the legal ownership of land etc.

conveyor *noun* a person or thing that conveys. □ **conveyor belt** a continuous moving belt for conveying objects in a factory etc.

convict (kŏn-**vikt**) *verb* to prove or declare (a person) to be guilty of a crime. –**convict** (**kon**-vikt) *noun* a convicted person in prison or (in former times) transported for a crime. [from *con-*, + Latin *victum* = conquered]

conviction *noun* 1 convicting; being convicted. 2 being convinced. 3 a firm opinion or belief. □ **carry conviction** to be convincing.

convince *verb* to make (a person) feel certain that something is true. [from *con-*, + Latin *vincere* = conquer]

convivial (kŏn-**viv**-ee-ăl) *adjective* sociable and lively. **convivially** *adverb*, **conviviality** (kŏn-viv-ee-**al**-ĭ-tee) *noun* [from Latin *convivium* = feast]

convocation *noun* 1 convoking. 2 an assembly convoked.

convoke *verb* to summon (people) to assemble. [from *con-*, + Latin *vocare* = to call]

convoluted (kon-vŏ-**loo**-tĕd) *adjective* 1 coiled, twisted. 2 complicated, involved. [from *con-*, + Latin *volutum* = rolled]

convolution (kon-vŏ-**loo**-shŏn) *noun* 1 a coil, a twist. 2 complexity.

convolvulus *noun* a twining plant with trumpet-shaped flowers.

convoy (**kon**-voi) *verb* to escort and protect, especially with an armed force or warships. –**convoy** *noun* a group of ships or vehicles travelling under escort or together.

convulse *verb* 1 to cause violent movement in. 2 to cause to double up with laughter. [from *con-*, + Latin *vulsum* = pulled]

convulsion *noun* 1 a violent movement of the body, especially one caused by muscles contracting involuntarily. 2 a violent upheaval.

convulsive *adjective* like a convulsion; producing upheaval. **convulsively** *adverb*

cony *noun* (also **coney**) rabbit skin or fur used in making clothes.

coo *verb* to make a soft murmuring sound. –**coo** *noun* a cooing sound.

Coober Pedy (**koo**-ber **pee**-dee) an opal-mining town in northern SA.

cooee *interjection* a cry to attract someone's attention. –**cooee** *verb* to utter a cooee. □ **within cooee** near, within earshot. [Dharuk *guuu-wi* = come here]

Cook, James (1728–79), English explorer, who circumnavigated and charted New Zealand and charted the east coast of Australia, landing at Botany Bay in 1770. He also charted much of the Pacific coast of North America.

Cook, **Mount** the highest mountain in New Zealand, in the South Island (3754 m).

cook *verb* 1 to prepare (food) for eating, by using heat. 2 to undergo this preparation, *lunch is cooking*. 3 (*informal*) to alter or falsify in order to produce a desired result, *cook the books*. –**cook** *noun* a person who cooks, especially as a job. □ **cook a person's goose** to ruin his or her chances. **cook up** (*informal*) to concoct; to invent, *cook up an excuse*.

cooker *noun* a container or stove for cooking food.

cookery *noun* the art and practice of cooking; *a cookery book*, one containing recipes.

cookie *noun* 1 a sweet biscuit. 2 a packet of data sent by an Internet server to a browser and used to identify the user or track their access to the server.

Cook Islands a group of 15 islands in the South Pacific between Tonga and French Polynesia.

cool *adjective* 1 moderately cold, not hot or warm. 2 (of colours) suggesting coolness. 3 calm and unexcited. 4 not enthusiastic, *got a cool reception*. 5 casual and confident; calmly audacious. 6 full in amount, *cost me a cool thousand*. 7 (*informal*, as a general term of approval) good; excellent; trendy, *the present was really cool*; *her parents are cool*. –**cool** *noun* 1 coolness; cool air, a cool place, *the cool of the evening*. 2 (*informal*) calmness, composure, *keep your cool*. –**cool** *verb* to make or become cool. □ **cooling-off period** an interval to allow for a change of mind before action. **cooling tower** a tower for cooling hot water in an industrial process so that it can be reused. **cool it** (*informal*) to calm down. **cool one's heels** to be kept waiting. **coolly** *adverb*, **coolness** *noun*

coolamon (**kool**-ă-mŏn) *noun* (*Austral*.) a wooden or bark dish used for carrying liquids. [Kamilaroi and nearby languages *gulaman*]

coolant *noun* a fluid used for cooling machinery etc.

coolibah (**kool**-ĭ-bah) *noun* (also **coolabah**) an Australian eucalypt found along rivers. [Yuwaalaraay and nearby languages *gulabaa*]

coolie *noun* (*old use*) an unskilled native labourer in some Asian countries.

coomb *noun* a valley on the side of a hill; a short valley running up from the coast; a cirque.

coop *noun* a cage for poultry. –**coop** *verb* **coop up** to confine or shut in.

co-op *noun* (*informal*) **1** a cooperative society. **2** a shop belonging to such a society.

cooper *noun* a person whose job is making and repairing barrels and tubs.

cooperate *verb* to work with another or others. **cooperation** *noun*, **cooperator** *noun*

cooperative *adjective* **1** of or providing cooperation. **2** willing to cooperate. **3** owned and run jointly by its members with profits shared between them. –**cooperative** *noun* a farm, society, or business organised on a cooperative basis. **cooperatively** *adverb*

Cooper Creek a river flowing seasonally from SW Queensland to the north-east of SA and, in very wet seasons, reaching to Lake Eyre.

co-opt *verb* to appoint to become a member of a group by the invitation of its existing members. **co-option** *noun*, **co-optive** *adjective* [from *co-*, + Latin *optare* = choose]

coordinate (koh-**ord**-ĭ-năt) *adjective* equal in importance. –**coordinate** (koh-**ord**-ĭ-năt) *noun* **1** a coordinate thing. **2** any of the magnitudes used to give the position of a point etc., e.g. latitude and longitude. –**coordinate** (koh-**ord**-ĭ-nayt) *verb* to bring (parts etc.) into a proper relationship; to work or cause to work together efficiently. **coordinately** *adverb*, **coordination** *noun*, **coordinator** *noun* [from *co-*, + Latin *ordinare* = arrange]

coot *noun* **1** a kind of waterbird, especially one with a horny white plate on the forehead. **2** (*informal*) a stupid person.

cop¹ *verb* (**copped**, **copping**) (*informal*) **1** to catch (an offender). **2** to receive, to suffer, *copped a heavy blow*; *copped a lot of flak*. –**cop** *noun* (*informal*) **1** a police officer. **2** capture, *it's a fair cop*. □ **cop it** (*informal*) to get into trouble, to be punished. **cop it sweet** (*Austral. informal*) to accept a setback with equanimity; to be lucky. **cop out** (*informal*) to back out; to fail to do what one promised. **cop-out** *noun* (*informal*) an evasion or failure of this kind.

cop² *noun* a spool (of yarn).

cope¹ *verb* to manage successfully. **cope with** to deal successfully with.

cope² *noun* a long loose cloak worn by clergy in certain ceremonies and processions.

Copenhagen (koh-pĕn-**hay**-gĕn) the capital of Denmark.

copernicium *noun* an artificial radioactive element (symbol Cn).

Copernicus (kŏ-**per**-nik-ŭs), Nicolaus (1473–1543), Polish astronomer, a pioneer of the idea that planets orbit the sun.

copier *noun* a copying machine, a photocopier.

co-pilot *noun* a second pilot in an aircraft.

coping (**koh**-ping) *noun* the top row of masonry (usually sloping) in a wall. **coping stone** a stone used in this. [from *cope²*]

copious *adjective* existing in large amounts, plentiful. **copiously** *adverb*

coplanar *adjective* (in mathematics) lying in the same plane.

copper¹ *noun* **1** a chemical element (symbol Cu), a reddish-brown metal. **2** a coin made of copper or a copper alloy. **3** a reddish-brown colour. **4** a large metal vessel for boiling things, especially laundry. –**copper** *adjective* **1** made of copper. **2** reddish-brown. □ **copper sulphate** a blue crystalline solid used in electroplating, dyeing, and plant sprays. [from Latin *cuprum* = Cyprus metal (because the Romans got most of their copper from Cyprus)]

copper² *noun* (*informal*) a police officer. [from *cop¹*]

copperhead *noun* **1** a venomous Australian snake. **2** a venomous North American viper.

copperplate *noun* neat clear handwriting.

coppice *noun* an area of undergrowth and small trees, grown for periodic cutting.

copra *noun* the dried kernels of the coconut.

copse *noun* a coppice.

Copt *noun* **1** an Egyptian of the period from the mid 4th century BC onwards. **2** a member of the Coptic Church.

Coptic *adjective* of the Copts or their language. –**Coptic** *noun* the language of the Copts, now used only as the liturgical language of the Coptic Church in Egypt.

copula *noun* a connecting word, especially a part of the verb *to be* connecting the predicate with the subject.

copulate (**kop**-yŭ-layt) *verb* to come together sexually as in the act of mating. **copulation** *noun* [from Latin *copulare* = join together]

copy *noun* 1 a thing made to look like another.
2 one specimen of a book or document or
newspaper. 3 material for printing. –copy *verb*
(copied, copying) 1 to make a copy of. 2 to try
to do the same as, to imitate.

copybook *noun* a book containing models of
handwriting for learners to imitate. –copybook
adjective 1 very good, model. 2 boringly
conventional.

copycat *noun* (*informal*) a person who copies
another's actions.

copyist *noun* a person who makes copies of
documents etc.

copyright *noun* the sole legal right to
print, publish, perform, film, or record a
literary, artistic, or musical work, or a piece
of computer software. –copyright *adjective*
(of material) protected by copyright.

copywriter *noun* a person who writes or
prepares advertising material for publication.

coquette (kŏ-**ket**) *noun* a woman who flirts.
coquettish *adjective* [French]

cor- *prefix* see com-.

coracle (**ko**-ră-kŭl) *noun* a small wickerwork
boat covered with watertight material. [from
Welsh *corwgl*]

coral *noun* 1 a hard red, pink, or white
substance built by tiny sea creatures; *coral
reef*, one formed by coral. 2 reddish-pink
colour. –coral *adjective* reddish-pink.

coralline *adjective* of or like coral. –coralline
noun 1 a seaweed with a hard jointed stem.
2 a coral-like growth.

Coral Sea a part of the Pacific lying between
Australia, New Guinea, and Vanuatu, and
including the waters of Torres Strait and the
Great Barrier Reef.

cor anglais (kor **ahn**-glay) *noun* an alto
woodwind instrument of the oboe family.
[French, = English horn]

corbel (**kor**-bĕl) *noun* a stone or timber
projection from a wall, to support something.
corbelled *adjective*

cord *noun* 1 long thin flexible material made
from twisted strands; a piece of this; electric
flex. 2 a similar structure in the body, *the
spinal cord*. 3 corduroy material. 4 a measure
of cut wood (usually 128 cubic feet, 3.6 cubic
metres). –cord *verb* to fasten or bind with
cord. cords *plural noun* corduroy trousers.

corded *adjective* (of fabric) with raised ridges.

cordial *noun* a syrup flavoured with fruit etc.,
diluted to make a drink. –cordial *adjective*

warm and friendly, *cordial greetings*. cordially
adverb, cordiality (kor-dee-**al**-ĭ-tee) *noun*
[from Latin *cordis* = of the heart]

cordite (**kor**-dyt) *noun* a smokeless explosive
used as a propellant in bullets and shells.

cordless *adjective* (of a telephone or item of
electrical equipment) not connected by a flex
to a telephone or mains circuit.

cordon *noun* 1 a ring of people or military
posts etc. enclosing or guarding something.
2 an ornamental cord or braid worn as a badge
of honour. 3 a fruit tree with its branches
pruned so that it grows as a single stem,
usually against a wall or along wires. –cordon
verb to enclose with a cordon.

cordon bleu (kor-dawn **bler**) *adjective* of
the highest degree of excellence in cookery.
–cordon bleu *noun* a cook of this class.
[French, = blue ribbon]

corduroy *noun* cotton cloth with velvety
ridges.

core *noun* 1 the horny central part of certain
fruits, containing the seeds. 2 the central or
most important part of something. 3 a unit in
the structure of a computer memory storing
one bit of data. 4 the part of a nuclear reactor
that contains the fissile material. 5 a piece of
soft iron along the middle of an electromagnet
or induction coil. –core *verb* to remove the
core from. corer *noun*

corella (kŏ-**rel**-ă) *noun* a predominantly white
Australian cockatoo. □ corella pear a South
Australian pear with red skin. [Wiradjuri]

co-respondent (koh-rĕ-**spon**-dĕnt) *noun*
the person with whom the person proceeded
against in a divorce suit (the *respondent*) is
said to have committed adultery.

Corfu an island off the west coast of Greece.

corgi *noun* (*plural* corgis) a dog of a small
Welsh breed with a foxlike head. [from Welsh
cor = dwarf, + *ci* = dog]

coriander (ko-ree-**and**-er) *noun* a plant with
aromatic leaves and seeds used for flavouring.

Corinthian (kŏ-**rinth**-ee-ăn) *adjective* 1 of
Corinth, a city of ancient Greece. 2 of the
Corinthian order, the most ornate of the five
classical orders of architecture. –Corinthians
the *Epistle to the Corinthians*, either of two
books of the New Testament, epistles of St
Paul to the Church at Corinth in Greece.

Coriolanus (ko-ree-ŏ-**lay**-nŭs), Gnaeus
Marcius (5th c. BC), Roman general, said to
have led an army against Rome after being

charged with tyrannical conduct, and to have been turned back by the pleas of his wife and mother.

cork *noun* 1 a light tough substance, the thick outer bark of a kind of south European oak. 2 a piece of this used as a float. 3 a bottle stopper made of this or other material. –**cork** *verb* to close or stop up with a cork.

corkage *noun* a charge made by a restaurant for serving wine brought by the customers.

corker *noun* (*informal*) an excellent person or thing.

corkscrew *noun* 1 a tool for extracting corks from bottles. 2 a spiral thing.

corm *noun* a rounded underground base of a stem, from the top of which buds sprout.

cormorant *noun* a large black diving seabird.

corn[1] *noun* 1 maize; its grains used as a vegetable. 2 (especially *Brit.*) any cereal plant before or after harvesting, e.g. wheat, oats, etc. 3 a single grain of a cereal plant or a seed of pepper etc.

corn[2] *noun* a small tender area of horny hardened skin on the foot.

corncrake *noun* a bird with a harsh cry.

cornea (**korn**-ee-ă) *noun* the tough transparent outer covering of the eyeball. **corneal** *adjective*

corned *adjective* preserved in salt, *corned beef.*

cornelian *noun* a reddish or white semi-precious stone.

corner *noun* 1 the angle or area where two lines or sides meet or where two streets join. 2 a hidden or remote place. 3 a difficult position, one with no escape. 4 a free hit or kick from the corner of the field in hockey or soccer. 5 a virtual monopoly of a certain type of goods or services, enabling the holder to control the price. –**corner** *verb* 1 to drive into a corner; to force into a position from which there is no escape. 2 to obtain (all or most of something) for oneself; to establish a monopoly of. 3 to move round a corner, *the car had cornered too fast.* □ **turn the corner** to begin to improve; to start recovering.

cornerstone *noun* 1 a stone in the projecting angle of a wall. 2 a basis, a vital foundation.

cornet *noun* a brass musical instrument like a small trumpet. [from Latin *cornu* = horn, trumpet]

cornflakes *plural noun* a breakfast cereal of toasted maize flakes.

cornflour *noun* flour made from maize or rice, used to thicken sauces.

cornflower *noun* a plant (especially a blue-flowered kind) that often grows wild among corn or is cultivated as a garden plant.

cornice (**korn**-iss) *noun* a band of ornamental moulding round the wall of a room just below the ceiling or crowning a building.

Cornish *adjective* of Cornwall or its people or language. –**Cornish** *noun* the ancient language of Cornwall. □ **Cornish pasty** a mixture of meat and vegetables in pastry.

cornucopia (korn-yŭ-**koh**-pee-ă) *noun* 1 a symbol of plenty consisting of a horn-shaped container overflowing with fruit and flowers. 2 an abundant supply. [from Latin *cornu* = horn, + *copiae* = of plenty]

Cornwall a county of SW England.

corny *adjective* (**cornier, corniest**) (*informal*) hackneyed, repeated so often that people are tired of it, over-sentimental. **corniness** *noun* [from *corn*[1]]

corolla (kŏ-**rol**-ă) *noun* the part of a flower consisting of petals, especially when these are joined at the base. [Latin, = small crown]

corollary (kŏ-**rol**-ă-ree) *noun* a natural consequence or result, something that follows logically after something else is proved.

corona (kŏ-**roh**-nă) *noun* 1 a small circle or glow of light round something. 2 a crownlike outgrowth from the corolla of a flower such as a daffodil. [Latin, = crown]

coronary (**ko**-rŏ-nă-ree) *adjective* of the arteries supplying blood to the heart. –**coronary** *noun* 1 a coronary artery. 2 a **coronary thrombosis**, blockage of a coronary artery by a clot of blood.

coronation *noun* the ceremony of crowning a king, queen, or consort. [same origin as *corona*]

coroner (**ko**-rŏ-ner) *noun* an officer who holds an inquiry into the cause of a death thought to be from violence or unnatural causes, or in cases of treasure trove. **coronial** (kŏ-**roh**-nee-ăl) *adjective*

coronet *noun* 1 a small crown. 2 a band of gold or jewels etc. for the head.

corporal[1] *adjective* of the body. □ **corporal punishment** punishment by whipping or beating. **corporality** *noun* [from Latin *corpus* = body]

corporal[2] *noun* a non-commissioned officer ranking just below sergeant.

corporate (**kor**-pŏ-răt) *adjective* **1** shared by members of a group, *corporate responsibility*. **2** united in one group, *a corporate body*; *the body corporate*. □ **corporate memory** employees' knowledge of the history of an organisation, especially its undocumented procedures.

corporation *noun* a group of people authorised to act as an individual, especially in business.

corporeal (kor-**por**-ree-ăl) *adjective* bodily, physical; material. **corporeality** *noun*, **corporeally** *adverb*

corposant (**kor**-pŏ-zănt) *noun* a luminous electrical discharge (also known as *St Elmo's fire*) sometimes seen on a ship or aircraft during a storm. [from Italian *corpo santo* = holy body]

corps (*pr.* kor) *noun* (*plural* **corps**, *pr.* korz) **1** a military force, an army unit. **2** a body of people engaged in a special activity, *the diplomatic corps*.

corpse *noun* a dead body. [from Latin *corpus* = body]

corpulent (**korp**-yŭ-lĕnt) *adjective* having a bulky body, fat. **corpulence** *noun*

corpus *noun* (*plural* **corpora**) a large collection of writings etc. □ **corpus luteum** (*pr.* **loo**-tee-ŭm) a structure developing in the ovary from a Graafian follicle after the ovum has been released.

Corpus Christi a Christian festival in honour of the Eucharist, celebrated on the Thursday after Trinity Sunday.

corpuscle (**kor**-pŭ-sŭl) *noun* any of the red or white cells in the blood. [from Latin, = little body]

corral (kŏ-**rahl**) *noun* an enclosure for horses, cattle, etc. –**corral** *verb* (**corralled**, **corralling**) to put into a corral.

corrasion *noun* erosion caused by solid material being carried over the earth's surface by water, ice, etc.

correa *noun* an Australian flowering shrub.

correct *adjective* **1** true, accurate. **2** proper, in accordance with an approved way of behaving or working. –**correct** *verb* **1** to make correct, to set right by altering or adjusting. **2** to mark the errors in. **3** to point out faults in (a person); to punish (a person or a fault). **correctly** *adverb*, **correctness** *noun*, **correctable** *adjective* [from *cor-*, + Latin *rectus* = straight]

correction *noun* **1** correcting; being corrected. **2** an alteration made to something that was incorrect.

corrective *adjective* correcting what is bad or harmful. –**corrective** *noun* something that corrects.

correlate (**ko**-rĕ-layt) *verb* **1** to compare or connect systematically. **2** to have systematic connection. **correlation** *noun* [from *cor-* + *relate*]

correlative (kŏ-**rel**-ă-tiv) *adjective* **1** corresponding, having a systematic connection. **2** (of words) regularly used together, e.g. *either* and *or*.

correspond *verb* **1** to be in harmony or agreement, *this corresponds with what I've heard*. **2** to be similar or equivalent, *an assembly that corresponds to our parliament*. **3** to write letters to each other. □ **corresponding angles** the equal angles that are formed on the same side of a straight line by parallel lines cutting it. [from *cor-* + *respond*]

correspondence *noun* **1** corresponding; harmony. **2** communicating by writing letters; the letters themselves. □ **correspondence course** instruction by means of materials sent by post.

correspondent *noun* **1** a person who writes letters. **2** a person who is employed to gather news and contribute reports to a newspaper, radio or television station, etc.

corridor *noun* a long narrow passage, especially one from which doors open into rooms or compartments.

corrigendum (ko-rĭ-**jen**-dŭm) *noun* (*plural* **corrigenda**) an error, especially in a printed book, for which a correction is printed. [Latin, = thing to be corrected]

corroborate (kŏ-**rob**-ŏ-rayt) *verb* to get or give supporting evidence. **corroboration** *noun*, **corroborative** (kŏ-**rob**-ŏ-ră-tiv) *adjective*, **corroborator** *noun*, **corroboratory** (kŏ-**rob**-ŏ-ră-tŏ-ree) *adjective*

corroboree (kŏ-**rob**-ŏ-ree) *noun* (*Austral.*) an Aboriginal dance ceremony with song and rhythmical music. [from Dharuk *garabari* = a style of dancing]

corrode *verb* to destroy gradually by chemical action, *rust corrodes metal*. **corrosion** *noun*, **corrosive** *adjective* & *noun*, **corrodable** *adjective* [from *cor-*, + Latin *rodere* = gnaw]

corrugated *adjective* shaped into alternate ridges and grooves, *corrugated iron*.

corrugation *noun* [from *cor-*, + Latin *ruga* = wrinkle]

corrupt *adjective* **1** dishonest, accepting bribes. **2** immoral, wicked. **3** decaying. –**corrupt** *verb* **1** to cause to become dishonest or immoral, to persuade to accept bribes. **2** to spoil, to taint. **3** to introduce errors into (computer files). **corruption** *noun* [from *cor-*, + Latin *ruptum* = broken]

corruptible *adjective* able to be corrupted. **corruptibility** *noun*

corsage *noun* a small bouquet of flowers worn by a woman.

corsair (**kor**-sair) *noun* (*old use*) **1** a pirate ship. **2** a pirate.

corset *noun* a close-fitting undergarment worn to shape or support the body.

Corsica an island off the west coast of Italy, belonging to France, birthplace of Napoleon I. **Corsican** *adjective & noun*

cortège (kor-**tairzh** *or* -**tayzh**) *noun* a funeral procession. [French]

Cortés (**kor**-tez), Hernando (1485–1547), Spanish conqueror of Mexico.

cortex *noun* (*plural* **cortices**, *pr.* **kor**-tĭ-seez) **1** an outer layer of tissue (e.g. of a kidney or a plant stem); the bark of a tree. **2** the outer grey matter of the brain. **cortical** *adjective* [Latin, = bark of a tree]

cortisone (**kor**-tĭ-zohn) *noun* a hormone produced by the adrenal glands or made synthetically, used against inflammation and allergy.

corundum (kŏ-**run**-dŭm) *noun* extremely hard alumina, used especially as an abrasive.

coruscate (**ko**-rŭ-skayt) *verb* to sparkle.

corvette (kor-**vet**) *noun* a small fast gunboat designed for escorting merchant ships.

cos[1] (*pr.* koss) *noun* a kind of lettuce with long leaves. [from Kos, a Greek island]

cos[2] (*pr.* koz *or* koss) *abbreviation* cosine.

'cos (*pr.* koz) *adverb & conjunction* (*informal*) because.

cosec (**koh**-sek) *abbreviation* cosecant.

cosecant (koh-**see**-kănt *or* -**sek**-) *noun* the secant of the complement of a given angle.

cosh *noun* a weighted weapon for hitting people. –**cosh** *verb* to hit with a cosh.

cosine (**koh**-syn) *noun* (in a right-angled triangle) the ratio of the length of a side adjacent to one of the acute angles to the length of the hypotenuse.

cosmetic *noun* a substance for beautifying the body, especially the face. –**cosmetic** *adjective* for beautifying or improving the appearance, *cosmetic surgery*.

cosmic *adjective* of the universe. □ **cosmic rays** or **radiation** high-energy radiation that reaches the earth from outer space. [from *cosmos*]

cosmonaut *noun* a Russian astronaut. [from *cosmos + astronaut*]

cosmopolitan *adjective* **1** of or from many parts of the world, containing people from many countries, *a cosmopolitan city*. **2** free from national prejudices and at home in all parts of the world, *a cosmopolitan outlook*. –**cosmopolitan** *noun* a cosmopolitan person. [from *cosmos* + Greek *polites* = citizen]

cosmos[1] (**koz**-moss) *noun* the universe. [from Greek *kosmos* = the world]

cosmos[2] *noun* a garden plant with purple, pink, or white flowers.

Cossack (**koss**-ak) *noun* a member of a people of south Russia, famous as horsemen.

cosset (**koss**-ĕt) *verb* (**cosseted, cosseting**) to pamper.

cossie (**koz**-ee) *noun* (*Austral. informal*) a swimming costume.

cost *noun* **1** an amount given or required as payment. **2** an expenditure of time or labour; a loss suffered in achieving something, *succeeded at the cost of his life*. –**cost** *verb* (**cost** (in sense 3 **costed**), **costing**) **1** to be obtainable at a certain price. **2** to require a certain effort or loss etc. **3** to estimate the cost involved; *a costing clerk*, one who does this for a firm. **costs** *plural noun* the expenses involved in having something settled in a lawcourt. □ **at all costs** no matter what the risk or loss involved may be. **at cost** at cost price. **cost accountant** one employed to supervise a firm's expenditure. **cost-effective** *adjective* producing useful results in relation to its cost. **cost of living** the general level of prices. **cost price** the price at which a thing is bought by someone who intends to re-sell or process it. **to one's cost** involving bitter experience.

co-star *noun* a stage or cinema star performing with another or others of equal or greater importance. –**co-star** *verb* (**co-starred, co-starring**) to perform or include as a co-star.

Costa Rica (**ree**-kă) a Central American republic. **Costa Rican** *adjective & noun*

costermonger (**kost**-er-mung-ger) *noun* (*Brit.*) a person who sells fruit etc. from a barrow in the street. [from old words *costard* = large apple, + *monger* = trader]

costly *adjective* (**costlier**, **costliest**) costing much, expensive. **costliness** *noun*

costume *noun* **1** a style of clothes belonging to a particular place, period, or group, or suitable for a particular activity. **2** special garments worn by an actor; *costume plays*, in which the actors wear historical costume. □ **costume jewellery** jewellery made of inexpensive materials.

cosy *adjective* (**cosier**, **cosiest**) warm and comfortable. –**cosy** *noun* a cover placed over a teapot or boiled egg to keep it hot. **cosily** *adverb*, **cosiness** *noun*

cot[1] *noun* a child's bed with high sides. □ **cot death** = **sudden infant death syndrome**. [from Hindi *khat* = bedstead]

cot[2] *abbreviation* cotangent.

cotangent (koh-**tan**-jĕnt) *noun* the tangent of the complement of a given angle.

coterie (**koh**-tĕ-ree) *noun* an exclusive group of people.

cottage *noun* a small simple one-storeyed house, especially in the country. □ **cottage cheese** soft white cheese made from curds without pressing. **cottage industry** one that can be carried on at home, e.g. knitting. **cottage pie** a dish of minced meat topped with mashed potato, also called *shepherd's pie*.

cotter *noun* a bolt or wedge for securing parts of machinery etc. □ **cotter pin** a cotter; a split pin put through a cotter to keep it in place.

cotton *noun* **1** a soft white substance round the seeds of a tropical plant. **2** the plant itself. **3** thread made from this. **4** fabric made from this thread. –**cotton** *verb* **cotton on (to)** (*informal*) to understand; to form a liking for. □ **cotton bush** an Australian downy shrub providing fodder during drought. **cotton wool** fluffy wadding of a kind originally made from raw cotton.

cotyledon (kot-ĭ-**lee**-dŏn) *noun* the first leaf growing from a seed.

couch[1] (*pr.* kowch) *noun* **1** a sofa or settee. **2** a piece of furniture like a sofa but with the back extending along half its length and only one raised end. **3** a bed-like structure on which a doctor's patient can lie for examination. –**couch** *verb* **1** to express in words of a certain kind, *the request was couched in polite terms*. **2** to lay as on a couch. **3** to lie in a lair etc. or in ambush. **4** (in embroidery) to stitch down (one or more threads) with another thread

at intervals. □ **couch potato** (*informal*) a person who likes lazing, especially watching television.

couch[2] (*pr.* kooch) *noun* (in full **couch grass**) a kind of grass with long creeping roots.

couchant (**cow**-chănt) *adjective* (in heraldry, of an animal) lying with the body resting on the legs and the head raised.

couchette (koo-**shet**) *noun* a sleeping berth in a railway compartment that can be converted to form an ordinary compartment with seats during the day.

cougar (**koog**-er) *noun* a puma.

cough *verb* to send out air or other matter from the lungs with a sudden sharp sound. –**cough** *noun* **1** an act or sound of coughing. **2** an illness causing frequent coughing.

could *auxiliary verb* **1** used as the past tense of can[2]. **2** to feel inclined to, *I could scream with the pain*. **3** might, *you could be right*.

couldn't (*informal*) = could not.

coulis (**koo**-lee) *noun* a fruit purée of pouring consistency. [French from *couler* = to flow]

coulomb (**koo**-lom) *noun* a unit of electric charge. [named after C. A. de Coulomb (1736–1806), French engineer]

council *noun* **1** an assembly of people to advise on, discuss, or organise something. **2** an administrative body of a local government area, district, town, city, etc. [from Latin *concilium* = assembly]

Usage Distinguish *council* and *councillor* from *counsel* and *counsellor*.

---

councillor *noun* a member of a council.

counsel *noun* **1** advice, suggestions, *give counsel*. **2** (*plural* **counsel**) a barrister or group of barristers giving advice in a legal case. –**counsel** *verb* (**counselled**, **counselling**) **1** to advise, to recommend. **2** to give professional guidance to (a person in need of psychological help). □ **keep one's own counsel** to keep one's views or plans secret. **take counsel with** to consult. [from Latin *consulere* = consult]

counsellor *noun* an adviser; a person giving professional guidance on personal, social, or psychological matters.

count[1] *verb* **1** to find the total of. **2** to say or name the numbers in order. **3** to include or be included in a reckoning, *six for dinner, counting the baby*; *this will count against him*, will be a disadvantage to his reputation.

4 to be important, to be worth reckoning; *fine words count for nothing*, are of no value. **5** to regard or consider, *I should count it an honour.* –**count** *noun* **1** counting, a calculation. **2** a number reached by counting, a total. **3** any of the points being considered; each of the charges against an accused person, *he was found guilty on all counts.* ☐ **count down** to count numerals backwards to zero, as in the procedure before launching a spacecraft etc. **count noun** one which names something that can be counted, and can form a plural or be used with 'a' or 'an', e.g. *two books*, *a deed*, etc. **count on** to rely on; to expect confidently. **keep** or **lose count** to know or not know how many there have been. **out for the count** defeated in a boxing match by failing to rise within ten seconds after being knocked to the floor; (*informal*) out of action. **countable** *adjective*

count² *noun* (in some European countries) a nobleman.

countdown *noun* counting numerals backwards to zero, as in the procedure for launching a spacecraft etc.; the final preparations before a great event.

countenance *noun* **1** the expression of the face. **2** an appearance of approval, *lending countenance to their plan.* –**countenance** *verb* to give approval to.

counter¹ *noun* **1** a flat-topped fitment over which goods are sold or served or business is transacted with customers. **2** a small disc used for keeping account in table games. **3** a token representing a coin. **4** an apparatus for counting things. ☐ **under the counter** sold or transacted in an underhand way.

counter² *adverb* in the opposite direction. –**counter** *adjective* opposed. –**counter** *verb* **1** to oppose, to contradict. **2** to hinder or defeat by an opposing action.

counter- *prefix* **1** against; opposing; done in return (as in *counter-attack*). **2** corresponding (as in *countersign*). [from Latin *contra* = against]

counteract *verb* to reduce or prevent the effects of. **counteraction** *noun*

counter-attack *noun* an attack directed against an enemy who has already attacked or invaded. –**counter-attack** *verb* to make a counter-attack (on).

counterbalance *noun* a weight or influence that balances another. –**counterbalance** *verb* to act as a counterbalance to.

counterblast *noun* a powerful retort.

countercheck *noun* **1** an obstruction checking movement or operating against another. **2** a second test for verifying another. –**countercheck** *verb* to verify by a second test.

counter-clockwise *adjective* & *adverb* anticlockwise.

counter-culture *noun* a culture or way of life based on different values from the established or conventional ones of society.

counter-espionage (es-pee-ŏ-**nah***zh*) *noun* action taken to uncover and counteract enemy espionage.

counterfeit (**cown**-ter-fĭt) *adjective* fake. –**counterfeit** *noun* a fake. –**counterfeit** *verb* to fake. [from Old French *countrefait* = made in opposition]

counterfoil *noun* a detachable section of a cheque or receipt etc. kept by the sender as a record.

counter-intelligence *noun* counter-espionage.

countermand *verb* to cancel (a command or order). –**countermand** *noun* a command or order cancelling a previous one.

countermeasure *noun* action taken to counteract a threat or danger etc.

counter-offensive *noun* a large-scale counter-attack.

counterpane *noun* a bedspread.

counterpart *noun* a person or thing corresponding to another in position or use.

counterpoint *noun* **1** a melody added as an accompaniment to another. **2** a method of combining melodies according to fixed rules.

counterpoise *noun* a counterbalance. –**counterpoise** *verb* to counterbalance.

counter-productive *adjective* having the opposite of the desired effect.

Counter-Reformation *noun* the reformation in the Church of Rome following on the Protestant Reformation (mid-16th–mid-17th century).

countersign *noun* a password; a mark of identification. –**countersign** *verb* to add another signature to (a document) to give it authority. **countersignature** *noun*

countersink *verb* (**countersunk**, **countersinking**) to enlarge the top of (a hole) so that the head of a screw or bolt will lie level with or below the surface; to sink (a screw etc.) in such a hole.

counterstroke *noun* a stroke made in return.

counter-tenor *noun* a male singing voice higher than tenor but with its quality; a singer with this; a part written for it.

counterterrorism *noun* political or military activities designed to prevent or thwart terrorism.

counterweight *noun* a counterbalancing weight or influence. –**counterweight** *verb* **1** to counterbalance. **2** to fit with a counterweight.

countess *noun* **1** the wife or widow of a count or earl. **2** a woman holding the rank of count or earl.

countless *adjective* too many to be counted.

countrified *adjective* having the characteristics of the country or country life.

country *noun* **1** a nation or State; the land it occupies. **2** less densely settled districts outside of cities, *moved from the city to the country*; *a country town*. **3** an area of land with certain features, *mulga country*. **4** the territory or traditional territory of a people. **5** the people of a country. ☐ **across country** across fields etc., not keeping to main roads or to a direct road. **country and western** (also **country music**) a type of rural folk music (which originated in the US), usually sung to a guitar etc. **Country Party** the former name of the National Party of Australia. **Country Women's Association** (abbreviation **CWA**) an Australian organisation which aims to improve the welfare of country women and children.

countryman *noun* (*plural* **countrymen**) **1** a person living in the country, as opposed to the city. **2** a person of one's own country, a compatriot. **countrywoman** *feminine noun* (*plural* **countrywomen**).

countryside *noun* country areas; the land in the country.

countrywide *adjective* extending throughout a nation.

county *noun* a territorial division in some countries, usually forming the chief unit of local administration. [originally = the land of a count (*count²*)]

coup (*pr.* koo) *noun* (*plural* **coups**, *pr.* kooz) a sudden action taken to obtain power or achieve a desired result. [French, = a blow]

coup de grâce (koo dě **grahs**) *noun* a stroke or blow that puts an end to something. [French, = mercy-blow]

coup d'état (koo day-**tah**) *noun* the sudden overthrowing of a government by force or by unconstitutional means. [French, = blow of State]

coupe (*pr.* koop) *noun* an area of forest set aside for felling.

coupé (**koo**-pay) *noun* a closed two-door car with a sloping back.

couple *noun* **1** two people or things considered together; (loosely) about two, *I'll just be a couple of minutes*. **2** a married, engaged, or similar pair. –**couple** *verb* **1** to fasten or link together; to join by a coupling. **2** to copulate.

couplet (**kup**-lĕt) *noun* two successive lines of verse, especially when these rhyme and have the same metre.

coupling *noun* a device for connecting two railway carriages or parts of machinery.

coupon *noun* a detachable ticket or part of a document etc. that entitles the holder to receive something or that can be used as an application form. [French, = piece cut off]

courage *noun* the ability to control fear when facing danger or pain, bravery. ☐ **have the courage of one's convictions** to be brave enough to do what one believes to be right. [from Latin *cor* = heart]

courageous (kŏ-**ray**-jŭs) *adjective* having or showing courage. **courageously** *adverb*

courgette (koor-**zhet**) *noun* = zucchini.

courier (**kuu**-ree-er) *noun* **1** a messenger carrying news; a person who collects and delivers documents, parcels, etc. **2** a person employed to guide and assist a group of tourists. [from Latin *currere* = to run]

course *noun* **1** an onward movement in space or time, *in the ordinary course of events*. **2** the direction taken or intended, *the course of the river*; *the ship was off course*. **3** a series of things one can do to achieve something, *your best course is to start again*. **4** a series of talks, lessons, or treatment etc. **5** a golf course; a stretch of land or water over which a race takes place. **6** a continuous layer of brick or stone etc. in a wall. **7** each of the successive parts of a meal. –**course** *verb* **1** to follow a course. **2** to move or flow freely, *blood coursed through his veins*. **3** to hunt (especially hares) with hounds that follow game by sight not by scent. ☐ **in course of** in the process of, *the bridge is in course of construction*. **in the course of** during; in the course of nature, as part of the normal sequence of events; *in the course of time*, after some time has passed. **of course** without a doubt, as was to be expected; admittedly. [from Latin *cursus* = running]

court *noun* 1 a courtyard. 2 a cul-de-sac. 3 an enclosed area for certain games, e.g. squash, tennis. 4 a sovereign's establishment with attendants, councillors, etc. 5 a lawcourt; the judges in this. –**court** *verb* 1 to try to win the favour or support of. 2 to try to win the affection of, especially in order to marry. 3 (of animals) to try to attract sexually. 4 to behave as though trying to provoke something harmful, *courting danger*. □ **court card** the king, queen, or jack in playing cards. **court shoe** a woman's light strapless shoe with a low-cut upper.

courteous (**ker**-tee-ŭs) *adjective* polite. **courteously** *adverb*

courtesan (kor-tě-**zan**) *noun* (*old use*) a prostitute with wealthy or upper-class clients.

courtesy (**ker**-tě-see) *noun* courteous behaviour. □ **by courtesy of** by the permission or favour of. **courtesy light** a light (in a motor vehicle) that is switched on by opening the door.

courtier (**kor**-tee-er) *noun* (*old use*) one of a sovereign's companions at court.

courtly (**kort**-lee) *adjective* dignified and polite. **courtliness** *noun*

court martial *noun* (*plural* **courts martial**) 1 a court for trying offences against military law. 2 trial by such a court. –**court-martial** *verb* (**court-martialled**, **court-martialling**) to try by a court martial.

courtroom *noun* a room in which a court of law meets.

courtship *noun* courting; the period during which this takes place.

courtyard *noun* a space enclosed by walls or buildings.

couscous (**kuus**-kuus) *noun* 1 a type of semolina. 2 a North African dish of this steamed over a spicy meat and vegetable stew with which it is served.

cousin *noun* (also **first cousin**) a child of one's uncle or aunt. □ **first cousin once removed** a child of one's first cousin; one's parent's first cousin. **second cousin** a child of one's parent's first cousin. **cousinly** *adverb*

couture (koo-**tewr**) *noun* the design and making of high-class fashionable clothes. [French, = sewing]

couturier (koo-**tew**-ree-ay) *noun* a designer of high-class fashionable clothes. **couturière** (koo-tew-ree-**air**) *feminine noun*

covalency *noun* 1 the linking of atoms by a covalent bond. 2 the number of pairs of electrons an atom can share with another.

covalent *adjective* (of a chemical bond) in which pairs of electrons are shared by two atoms in a molecule.

cove[1] *noun* 1 a small bay or inlet on a coast. 2 a curved moulding at a junction of a ceiling and a wall.

cove[2] *noun* (*informal*) 1 a fellow, a chap. 2 (in early Australia) a manager or overseer.

coven (**kuv**-ěn) *noun* an assembly, especially of witches.

covenant (**kuv**-ě-nănt) *noun* a formal agreement, a contract. –**covenant** *verb* to undertake by covenant. **covenanter** *noun*

Coventry (**kov**-ěn-tree) *noun* **send a person to Coventry** to refuse to speak to or associate with a person. [from *Coventry*, a city in England]

cover *verb* 1 to place a thing over or in front of; to conceal or protect in this way. 2 to spread over. 3 to lie or extend over, to occupy the surface of; *a covering letter*, an explanatory letter sent with a document or goods. 4 to travel over (a distance), *we covered thirty kilometres a day*. 5 to guard; to protect by dominating the approach to; to have within range of one's gun(s); to keep a gun aimed at. 6 to protect by providing insurance or a guarantee, *covering you against fire or theft*. 7 to be enough money to pay for, *$10 will cover the taxi fare*. 8 to include, to deal with (a subject). –**cover** *noun* 1 a thing that covers. 2 the binding of a book etc.; either half of this. 3 a wrapper or envelope. 4 a place or area giving shelter or protection, *there was no cover*. 5 a supporting force etc. protecting another from attack, *fighter cover*. 6 a screen or pretence, *under cover of friendship*. 7 insurance against loss or damage etc. □ **cover charge** an extra charge per person in a restaurant. **cover for** to deputise temporarily for. **cover much ground** to travel far; to deal with a variety of topics. **cover point** (in cricket) a fielder on the off side and halfway to the boundary; this position. **cover up** to conceal (a thing or fact). **cover-up** *noun* concealment, especially of facts. **under separate cover** in a separate envelope or packet.

coverage *noun* **1** the act or fact of covering. **2** the area or amount covered.

coverlet *noun* a bedspread.

covert (**koh**-vert *or* **kuv**-ert) *noun* **1** an area of thick undergrowth in which animals hide. **2** a bird's feather covering the base of another. –**covert** *adjective* concealed, done secretly, *covert glances*. **covertly** *adverb*

covet (**kuv**-ĕt) *verb* (**coveted**, **coveting**) to desire eagerly, especially something belonging to another person.

covetous (**kuv**-ĕ-tŭs) *adjective* coveting. **covetously** *adverb*, **covetousness** *noun*

covey (**kuv**-ee) *noun* (*plural* **coveys**) **1** a brood or small flock of partridges. **2** a small group of people or things.

cow[1] *noun* **1** the fully-grown female of cattle or of certain other large animals (e.g. elephant, whale, seal). **2** (*Austral. informal, derogatory*) an unpleasant person or thing.

cow[2] *verb* to subdue by frightening with threats or force.

coward *noun* **1** a person who lacks courage. **2** one who attacks only those who cannot retaliate. **cowardly** *adjective*, **cowardliness** *noun*

cowardice *noun* cowardly feelings or actions.

cowboy *noun* **1** a cowhand, especially in fiction. **2** (*informal*) a person who uses reckless or unscrupulous methods in business.

cowcatcher *noun* a fender at the front of a locomotive for pushing aside obstacles on the line.

cower *verb* to crouch or shrink back in fear.

cowhand *noun* a person in charge of grazing cattle on a ranch in the western USA.

cowhide *noun* **1** a cow's hide. **2** leather made from this.

cowl *noun* **1** a monk's hood or hooded robe. **2** a hood-shaped covering, e.g. on a chimney.

cowlick *noun* a lock of hair that stands out over the forehead.

cowling *noun* a removable metal cover over an engine.

cowpat *noun* a flat, round piece of cow dung.

cowrie *noun* **1** a mollusc found in tropical seas, with a glossy often brightly-coloured shell. **2** its shell, especially when used as money in parts of Africa and S Asia. [from Urdu *kauri*]

cowshed *noun* a shed where cattle are milked or (in cold climates) kept when not at pasture.

cowslip *noun* a wild plant with small fragrant yellow flowers.

cox *noun* a coxswain. –**cox** *verb* to act as cox of a racing boat.

coxcomb *noun* a conceited young man; a dandy.

coxswain (**kok**-sŭn *or* -swayn) *noun* **1** a person who steers a rowing boat. **2** a sailor in charge of a ship's boat. **3** a senior petty officer on certain naval vessels.

coy *noun* pretending to be shy or embarrassed, bashful. **coyly** *adverb*, **coyness** *noun*

coyote (ky-**oh**-tee *or* **koi**-oht) *noun* a North American wolflike wild dog.

coypu (**koi**-poo) *noun* a beaver-like water animal, originally from South America.

cozen (**kuz**-ĕn) *verb* (*literary*) to cheat; to act deceitfully. **cozenage** *noun*

CPI *abbreviation* Consumer Price Index.

CPU *abbreviation* central processing unit.

crab *noun* **1** a ten-footed shellfish. **2** its flesh as food. ☐ **catch a crab** to get an oar jammed under the water by a faulty stroke in rowing. **crab apple** a kind of small sour apple.

crabbed (*pr.* krabd) *adjective* **1** bad-tempered. **2** (of writing) difficult to read or decipher.

crabby *adjective* bad-tempered. **crabbily** *adverb*, **crabbiness** *noun*

crabhole *noun* (*Austral.*) a hole or shallow depression in the ground.

crack *noun* **1** a sudden sharp explosive noise. **2** a sharp blow. **3** (*informal*) a wisecrack, a joke. **4** a chink. **5** a line of division where something is broken but has not come completely apart. **6** a very strong form of cocaine used as a stimulant. –**crack** *adjective* (*informal*) first-rate. –**crack** *verb* **1** to make or cause to make a sudden sharp explosive sound. **2** to tell (a joke). **3** to break with a sharp sound. **4** to break into (a safe etc.). **5** to find the solution to (a code or problem). **6** to break without coming completely apart. **7** (of a voice) to become suddenly harsh, especially with emotion. **8** to collapse under strain, to cease to resist. **9** to break down (heavy oils) in order to produce lighter ones. ☐ **crack-brained** *adjective* (*informal*) crazy. **crack down on** (*informal*) to take severe measures against (something illegal or against rules). **crack of dawn** daybreak. **crack up** (*informal*) to praise highly; to have a physical or mental breakdown. **get cracking** (*informal*) to get busy on work that is waiting to be done. **have a crack at** (*informal*) to attempt.

crackdown *noun* (*informal*) severe measures taken against something.

cracked *adjective* (*informal*) crazy. □ **cracked wheat** wheat crushed into tiny pieces, burghul.

cracker *noun* 1 a firework that explodes with a sharp crack. 2 a small paper toy made so as to explode harmlessly when the ends are pulled. 3 a thin dry biscuit. **crackers** *adjective* (*informal*) crazy.

cracking *adjective* (*informal*) 1 very good. 2 fast, *a cracking pace*.

crackle *verb* to make or cause to make a series of slight cracking sounds. **– crackle** *noun* these sounds.

crackling *noun* crisp skin on roast pork.

crackpot *adjective* (*informal*) crazy, unpractical. **– crackpot** *noun* a person with such ideas.

-cracy *suffix* forming nouns meaning 'ruling' or 'government' (e.g. *democracy*). [from Greek *-kratia* = rule]

cradle *noun* 1 a small bed or cot for a baby, usually on rockers. 2 a place where something originates, *the cradle of civilisation*. 3 a supporting framework or structure. **– cradle** *verb* to place in a cradle; to hold or support as if in a cradle.

craft *noun* 1 an occupation in which skill is needed. 2 such a skill or technique. 3 cunning, deceit. 4 (*plural* **craft**) a ship or boat or raft, an aircraft or spacecraft.

craftsman *noun* (*plural* **craftsmen**) a person who is skilled in a craft. **craftsmanship** *noun*

crafty *adjective* (**craftier**, **craftiest**) cunning, using underhand methods; ingenious. **craftily** *adverb*, **craftiness** *noun*

crag *noun* a steep or rugged rock. **craggy** *adjective*, **cragginess** *noun*

cram *verb* (**crammed**, **cramming**) 1 to force into too small a space so that the container is overfull. 2 to overfill in this way. 3 to study intensively for an examination.

cramp *noun* 1 sudden painful involuntary tightening of a muscle. 2 a metal bar with bent ends for holding masonry etc. together. 3 a clamp. **– cramp** *verb* 1 to affect with cramp. 2 to keep within too narrow limits. 3 to fasten with a cramp.

cramped *adjective* 1 put or kept in too narrow a space, without room to move. 2 (of a space)

too narrow. 3 (of writing) small and with letters close together.

crampon (**kram**-pŏn) *noun* an iron plate with spikes, worn on boots for walking or climbing on ice.

cranberry *noun* 1 the small acid red berry of a kind of shrub, used for making jelly and sauce. 2 the shrub itself.

crane *noun* 1 an apparatus for moving heavy objects, usually by suspending them from a jib by ropes or chains. 2 a large wading bird with long legs, neck, and bill. **– crane** *verb* to stretch (one's neck) in order to see something.

cranium (**kray**-nee-ŭm) *noun* (*plural* **crania**) the bones enclosing the brain; the skull. **cranial** *adjective* [from Greek *kranion* = skull]

crank[1] *noun* an L-shaped part for converting to-and-fro motion into circular motion. **– crank** *verb* to cause to move by means of a crank.

crank[2] *noun* a person with very strange ideas.

crankshaft *noun* a shaft turned by a crank.

cranky *adjective* 1 bad-tempered. 2 eccentric; strange, *has cranky ideas*. 3 working badly; shaky. **crankiness** *noun*

cranny *noun* a crevice. **crannied** *adjective*

crash[1] *noun* 1 a sudden violent noise like that of something breaking by impact. 2 a violent collision or fall. 3 a sudden drop or failure; a financial collapse. **– crash** *verb* 1 to make a crash; to move or go with a crash. 2 to cause (a vehicle or aircraft) to have a collision; to be involved in a crash. 3 (*informal*) to enter without permission, to gatecrash. 4 to drop or fail suddenly; to collapse financially. 5 (*informal*) to go to sleep, especially on a floor etc. **– crash** *adjective* involving intense effort to achieve something rapidly, *a crash diet*. □ **crash barrier** a protective fence erected where there is danger of vehicles leaving a road. **crash-dive** *noun* a sudden dive by an aircraft or submarine, especially in an emergency; (*verb*) to dive in this way. **crash helmet** a padded helmet worn to protect the head in case of a crash. **crash-land** *verb* to land (an aircraft) in an emergency, especially with damage to it; to be landed in this way. **crash landing** *noun*

crash[2] *noun* a kind of coarse linen or cotton fabric.

crass *adjective* 1 gross, *crass stupidity*. 2 very stupid. **crassly** *adverb*, **crassness** *noun* [from Latin *crassus* = thick]

crate *noun* **1** a wickerwork or slatted wooden packing case. **2** a divided container for holding bottles. **3** (*informal*) an old aircraft or car. –**crate** *verb* to pack into a crate.

crater *noun* a bowl-shaped cavity or hollow.

cravat (krǎ-**vat**) *noun* **1** a short scarf. **2** a broad necktie.

crave *verb* **1** to long for, to have a strong desire. **2** to ask earnestly for, *crave mercy* (*for*) *mercy*.

craven *adjective* cowardly.

craving *noun* a strong desire, a longing.

crawl *verb* **1** to move with the body close to the ground etc. or on hands and knees. **2** to move slowly or with difficulty. **3** (*informal*) to seek favour by behaving in a servile way. **4** to be covered with crawling things. **5** to feel as if covered with crawling things. –**crawl** *noun* **1** a crawling movement. **2** a very slow pace, *at a crawl*. **3** a swimming stroke with an overarm movement of each arm alternately. **crawler** *noun*

cray *noun* = crayfish.

crayfish *noun* (*plural* **crayfish**) **1** a small freshwater lobster-like shellfish, e.g. marron, yabby. **2** (*Austral*.) a marine lobster.

crayon *noun* a stick or pencil of coloured wax etc. for drawing. –**crayon** *verb* to draw or colour with crayons.

craze *noun* **1** a great but often short-lived enthusiasm for something. **2** the object of this.

crazed *adjective* driven insane, *crazed with grief*.

crazy *adjective* (**crazier**, **craziest**) **1** insane. **2** very foolish, not sensible, *this crazy plan*. □ **like crazy** (*informal*) like mad, very much. **crazily** *adverb*, **craziness** *noun*

creak *noun* a harsh squeak like that of an unoiled hinge. –**creak** *verb* to make such a sound.

cream *noun* **1** the fatty part of milk. **2** its colour, yellowish white. **3** a food containing or like cream, *chocolate cream*. **4** a soft creamlike substance, especially as a cosmetic. **5** the best part of something, *the cream of society*. –**cream** *adjective* cream-coloured. –**cream** *verb* **1** to remove the cream from. **2** to make creamy; to beat (ingredients) to a creamy consistency. **3** to apply a cream to. **4** to form cream, froth, or scum. □ **cream cheese** a soft cheese made from unskimmed milk and cream. **cream off** to remove (the

best or a required part). **cream of tartar** a compound of potassium used in cookery.

creamery *noun* a place where milk and milk products are processed or sold.

creamy *adjective* (**creamier**, **creamiest**) **1** rich in cream. **2** like cream. **creaminess** *noun*

crease *noun* **1** a line caused by crushing, folding, or pressing. **2** a line marking the limit of the bowler's or batsman's position in cricket. –**crease** *verb* **1** to make a crease or creases in. **2** to develop creases.

create *verb* **1** to bring into existence; to originate. **2** to give rise to; to produce by what one does, *create a good impression*. **3** to give a new rank or position to. **4** (*informal*) to make a fuss, to grumble.

creation *noun* **1** the act of creating. **2** something created. □ **the Creation** God's creating of the universe; **Creation** the universe; all things.

creationism *noun* a theory attributing all matter, biological species, etc., to separate acts of creation by God, rather than to evolution. **creationist** *noun*

creative *adjective* **1** having the power or ability to create things. **2** showing imagination and originality as well as routine skill, *creative work*. **creatively** *adverb*

creator *noun* one who creates something. □ **the Creator** God.

creature *noun* **1** a living being, especially an animal. **2** a person; *a poor creature*, someone who is pitied or despised. □ **creature comforts** things that make one's life comfortable, e.g. good food.

crèche (*pr*. kresh) *noun* a place where young children and babies are minded. [French]

Crécy (**kress**-ee) a village in northern France, scene (1346) of the first great English victory in the Hundred Years War.

credence (**kree**-děns) *noun* belief; *give credence to the story*, believe it. [from Latin *credere* = believe]

credentials (krě-**den**-shǎlz) *plural noun* letters or papers showing that a person is who or what he or she claims to be. [same origin as *credit*]

credibility *noun* the quality of being credible or believable.

credible *adjective* that can be believed, convincing. **credibly** *adverb* [same origin as *credit*]

Usage *Credible*, *credulous*, and *creditable* are sometimes confused. A *credible excuse* is one which is 'able to be believed', a *creditable performance*, is one which is 'worthy of praise', and a *credulous victim of a con man* is one who is 'gullible or too ready to believe'.

credit *noun* **1** honour or acknowledgement given for some achievement or good quality. **2** a source of honour, *a credit to the firm*. **3** credibility, confidence in a person or his or her actions etc. **4** a system of doing business by trusting that a person will pay at a later date for goods or services supplied. **5** the power to buy in this way. **6** the amount of money in a person's bank account or entered in an account book as paid to the holder. **– credit** *verb* (**credited**, **crediting**) **1** to believe. **2** to attribute; *credit Strauss with this waltz*, say that he wrote it. **3** to enter as credit in an account book. **credits** *plural noun* a list of acknowledgements shown at the end of a film or television program. □ **credit card** a card authorising a person to buy on credit. **credit note** a document crediting a sum of money to a customer, e.g. for goods returned. **credit rating** an estimate of a person's suitability for credit or a loan. **credit union** a financial institution like a bank, usually for a group of employees. **do credit to** to bring credit upon. [from Latin *credere* = believe, trust]

creditable *adjective* deserving praise. **creditably** *adverb*

creditor *noun* a person to whom money is owed.

credo (**kree**-doh) *noun* (*plural* **credos**) a creed. [Latin, = I believe]

credulous (**kred**-yŭ-lŭs) *adjective* too ready to believe things. **credulously** *adverb*, **credulity** (krĕ-**dew**-lĭ-tee) *noun*

Usage See note under **credible**.

creed *noun* **1** a formal summary of Christian beliefs. **2** a set of beliefs or principles. [from *credo*]

creek *noun* **1** a small stream, especially an intermittent one, or a tributary of a river. **2** (in the UK) a narrow coastal inlet. □ **up the creek** (*informal*) in difficulties; crazy.

creel *noun* a fisherman's wicker basket for carrying fish.

creep *verb* (**crept**, **creeping**) **1** to move with the body close to the ground. **2** to move

timidly, slowly, or stealthily; to come on gradually. **3** (of plants) to grow along the ground or other surface. **4** to feel as if covered with crawling things; *it will make your flesh creep*, have this effect by causing fear or dislike. **– creep** *noun* **1** creeping. **2** (*informal*) a person one dislikes; one who seeks favour by behaving in a servile way. □ **the creeps** (*informal*) a nervous feeling produced by fear or dislike.

creeper *noun* **1** a person or thing that creeps. **2** a creeping plant.

creepy *adjective* (**creepier**, **creepiest**) making one's flesh creep; feeling this sensation. □ **creepy-crawly** *noun* (*informal*) a crawling insect. **creepily** *adverb*, **creepiness** *noun*

cremate *verb* to dispose of (a corpse) by burning it to ashes. **cremation** *noun*

crematorium (krem-ă-**tor**-ree-ŭm) *noun* (*plural* **crematoria**) a place where corpses are cremated.

crème de la crème *noun* the best part; the elite. [French, = cream of the cream]

crenellated (**kren**-ĕ-lay-tĕd) *adjective* having battlements. **crenellation** (kren-ĕ-**lay**-shŏn) *noun*

Creole (**kree**-ohl) *noun* **1** a descendant of European settlers in the West Indies or Central or South America; a white descendant of French settlers in the southern USA. **2** a person of mixed European and Black descent. **3** a language formed from a European language and another (especially African) language. **– Creole** *adjective* of Creole or Creoles. **– creole** *adjective* of local origin or descent.

creosote (**kree**-ŏ-soht) *noun* **1** a thick brown oily liquid obtained from coal tar, used as a preservative for wood. **2** a colourless liquid obtained from wood tar, used as an antiseptic. **– creosote** *verb* to treat with creosote. [from Greek, = flesh-preserver]

crêpe (*pr.* krayp) *noun* **1** a fine fabric with a wrinkled surface. **2** rubber with a wrinkled texture, used for the soles of shoes. **3** a thin pancake usually with a sweet or savoury filling. □ **crêpe paper** thin crinkled paper. **crêpey** (also **crêpy**) *adjective*

crept *see* **creep**.

crepuscular (krĕ-**pusk**-yŭ-ler) *adjective* of twilight; appearing or active at dusk or dawn, not at night or in full daylight. [from Latin *crepusculum* = twilight]

crescendo (krě-**shen**-doh) *adjective & adverb* gradually becoming louder. **–crescendo** *noun* (*plural* **crescendos**) a gradual increase in loudness. [Italian]

crescent *noun* 1 the waxing moon, seen as a narrow curved shape tapering to a point at each end. 2 something shaped like this. 3 a curved street. [from Latin *crescens* = growing]

cress *noun* any of various plants with hot-tasting leaves used in salads.

crest *noun* 1 a tuft or fleshy outgrowth on a bird's or animal's head. 2 a plume on a helmet. 3 the top of a slope or hill; the white top of a large wave. 4 the highest point in one cycle of an electromagnetic or sound wave. 5 a design above the shield on a coat of arms, or used separately on a seal or notepaper etc.

crested *adjective* having or bearing a crest.

crestfallen *adjective* downcast, disappointed at failure.

cretaceous (krě-**tay**-shŭs) *adjective* of or like chalk. **–Cretaceous** *adjective* of the geological period in the Mesozoic era when chalk was deposited. **–Cretaceous** *noun* this period. [from Latin *creta* = chalk]

Crete a Greek island in the eastern Mediterranean. **Cretan** *adjective & noun*

cretin (**kret**-ĭn) *noun* 1 (*old use*) a person who is deformed and mentally undeveloped through lack of thyroid hormone. 2 (*informal*) a stupid person. **cretinism** *noun*, **cretinous** *adjective*

cretonne (kre-**ton**) *noun* heavy cotton cloth with a printed pattern, used in furnishings.

crevasse (krě-**vass**) *noun* a deep open crack, especially in the ice of a glacier.

crevice (**krev**-ĭss) *noun* a narrow opening or crack, especially in a rock or wall.

crew[1] *see* crow[2].

crew[2] *noun* 1 the people working a ship or aircraft. 2 all these except the officers. 3 a group of people working together, *the camera crew*. 4 a gang. **–crew** *verb* 1 to act as crew (for). 2 to supply a crew for. □ **crew cut** a closely cropped style of haircut. **crew neck** a closely fitting round neckline of a knitted garment.

crewel (**kroo**-ěl) *noun* 1 fine worsted yarn used for tapestry and embroidery. 2 an embroidery needle with a long eye able to take several strands of thread.

crib *noun* 1 a wooden framework from which animals can pull out fodder. 2 a baby's cot. 3 a model of the manger scene at Bethlehem. 4 the cards given by other players to the dealer at cribbage. 5 (*informal*) cribbage. 6 something copied from another person's work. 7 a literal translation (for use by students) for something written in a foreign language. **–crib** *verb* (**cribbed**, **cribbing**) to copy unfairly or without acknowledgement.

cribbage *noun* a card game in which the dealer scores also from cards in the crib (*see* crib sense 4).

Crick, Francis Henry Compton (1916–2004), British biophysicist, who together with J. D. Watson proposed a structure for the DNA molecule.

crick *noun* a painful stiffness in the neck or back. **–crick** *verb* to cause a crick in.

cricket[1] *noun* an outdoor game played with a ball, bats, and wickets, between two sides of eleven players. □ **not cricket** (*informal*) not fair play. **cricketer** *noun*

cricket[2] *noun* a brown grasshopper-like insect that makes a shrill chirping sound.

crime *noun* 1 a serious offence, one for which there is punishment by law. 2 such offences, serious law-breaking, *the detection of crime*. 3 (*informal*) a shame, a senseless act.

Crimea (kry-**mee**-ă) a peninsula in southern Ukraine. □ **Crimean War** a war fought mainly in the Crimea in 1853–6, between Russia and an alliance of Great Britain, France, Sardinia, and Turkey. **Crimean** *adjective*

criminal *noun* a person who is guilty of crime. **–criminal** *adjective* 1 of or involving crime, *a criminal offence*. 2 concerned with crime and its punishment, *criminal law*.

criminologist *noun* an expert in criminology.

criminology *noun* the scientific study of crime. [from Latin *crimen* = offence, + *-logy*]

crimp *verb* to press into small folds or ridges.

crimson *adjective & noun* deep red.

cringe *verb* 1 to shrink back in fear or embarrassment, to cower. 2 to behave obsequiously. **–cringe** *noun* an act or instance of cringing, *cultural cringe*.

crinkle *verb* to make or become wrinkled. **–crinkle** *noun* a wrinkle, a crease. **crinkly** *adjective*

crinoid *adjective* lily-shaped. **–crinoid** *noun* any of a class of echinoderms with feathery arms, e.g. sea lilies. [from Greek *krinos* = lily]

crinoline (**krin**-ŏ-lĭn) *noun* a light framework formerly worn to make a long skirt stand out; a skirt shaped by this.

cripple *noun* a person who is permanently lame. **–cripple** *verb* **1** to make a cripple of. **2** to disable; to weaken or damage seriously, *crippled by lack of money*.

crisis *noun* (*plural* **crises**, *pr.* **kry**-seez) **1** a decisive time. **2** a time of acute difficulty or danger.

crisp *adjective* **1** brittle, breaking with a snap, *crisp pastry*. **2** slightly stiff, *a crisp $5 note*. **3** cold and bracing, *a crisp winter morning*. **4** brisk and decisive, *a crisp manner*. **–crisp** *noun* a thin fried slice of potato (usually sold in packets). **–crisp** *verb* to make or become crisp. □ **burnt to a crisp** burnt until it is crisp, badly burnt. **crisply** *adverb*, **crispness** *noun*

crispy *adjective* (**crispier, crispiest**) crisp.

criss-cross *noun* a pattern of crossing lines. **–criss-cross** *adjective* with crossing lines. **–criss-cross** *verb* to mark or form or move in this pattern.

criterion (kry-**teer**-ree-ŏn) *noun* (*plural* **criteria**) a standard of judgment. [from Greek *kriterion* = means of judging]

Usage Note that *criteria* is a plural; it is incorrect to speak of *a criteria* or *this criteria*, or of *criterias*.

critic *noun* **1** a person who finds fault with something. **2** a person who forms and expresses judgments about books, art, musical works, etc. [from Greek *krites* = judge]

critical *adjective* **1** looking for faults. **2** expressing criticism, *critical remarks*. **3** of or at a crisis; *the critical moment*, one when there will be a decisive change; *the patient's condition is critical*, he is dangerously ill. **3** (of a nuclear reactor) having reached the stage of maintaining a self-sustaining chain reaction. □ **critical path analysis** the study of a complex set of operations (e.g. in building a ship) to decide in what order these should be carried out in order to complete the work as quickly and efficiently as possible. **critically** *adverb*

criticise *verb* (also **-ize**) **1** to find fault (with). **2** to examine critically; to express judgments about.

criticism *noun* **1** finding fault; a remark pointing out a fault. **2** the work of a critic; judgments about books, art, music, etc.

critique (kri-**teek**) *noun* a critical essay or review.

croak *noun* a deep hoarse cry or sound, like that of a frog. **–croak** *verb* **1** to utter or speak with a croak. **2** (*informal*) to die; to kill.

Croat (**kroh**-at) *noun* **1** a native or inhabitant of Croatia. **2** the language of the Croats.

Croatia (kroh-**ay**-shă) a republic in SE Europe on the eastern side of the Adriatic Sea, formerly part of Yugoslavia. **Croatian** *adjective* & *noun*

crochet (**kroh**-shay) *noun* a kind of needlework in which thread is looped into a pattern of connected stitches by means of a hooked needle. **–crochet** *verb* (**crocheted, crocheting**) to do this needlework; to make (an article) by this. [French, = little hook]

crock[1] *noun* **1** an earthenware pot or jar. **2** a broken piece of this.

crock[2] *noun* (*informal*) an old or worn-out person, horse, vehicle, etc.

crockery *noun* household china.

crocket *noun* a small ornamental carving on the sloping side of a pinnacle etc.

crocodile *noun* **1** a large tropical amphibious reptile with a thick skin, long tail, and huge jaws. **2** its skin, used to make bags, shoes, etc. **3** a long line of schoolchildren walking in pairs. □ **crocodile tears** insincere sorrow (¶ so called from the belief that the crocodile wept while devouring its victim or to allure it).

crocus *noun* (*plural* **crocuses**) a small plant growing from a corm, with yellow, purple, or white flowers.

Croesus (**kree**-sŭs) (6th century BC) the last king of Lydia in Asia Minor, proverbial for his wealth.

croissant (**krwass**-ahn) *noun* a rich crescent-shaped bread roll. [French, = crescent]

Cro-Magnon (kroh-**man**-yon) *adjective* of a tall broad-faced European race of late palaeolithic times. [from the name of a hill in France where remains were found in 1868]

cromlech (**krom**-lek) *noun* **1** = **dolmen**. **2** a circle of upright prehistoric stones. [from Welsh *crom* = bent, + *llech* = flat stone]

Cromwell, Oliver (1599–1658), English general and statesman, Puritan leader during the English Civil War, who became Lord

Protector of the Commonwealth after the execution of Charles I.

crone *noun* a withered old woman.

Cronus (**kron**-ŭs) (*Gk. myth.*) a Titan who ruled the universe until his son Zeus dethroned him.

crony *noun* a close friend or companion.

crook *noun* **1** a hooked stick or staff, that used by a shepherd. **2** something bent or curved, *carried it in the crook of her arm*. **3** (*informal*) a person who makes a living dishonestly. –**crook** *adjective* (*Austral. informal*) **1** unsatisfactory, unpleasant. **2** ailing, injured; out of order. **3** angry. –**crook** *verb* to bend into the shape of a crook. □ **go crook** (*Austral. informal*) to become angry, to lose one's temper.

crooked *adjective* **1** not straight or level; having curves, bends, or twists. **2** dishonest, not straightforward. **crookedly** *adverb*, **crookedness** *noun*

croon *verb* to sing softly and gently. –**croon** *noun* singing of this kind. **crooner** *noun*

crop *noun* **1** a batch of plants grown for their produce. **2** the harvest from this. **3** a group or quantity appearing or produced at one time. **4** the baglike part of a bird's throat where food is broken up for digestion before passing into the stomach. **5** the handle of a whip; a whip with a loop instead of a lash. **6** a very short haircut. –**crop** *verb* (**cropped**, **cropping**) **1** to cut or bite off, *sheep crop the grass closely*. **2** to cut (hair) very short. **3** to bear a crop. □ **crop dusting** the spraying of insecticide or fertiliser on crops, especially from the air. **crop up** to occur unexpectedly.

cropper *noun* a plant producing a crop of a specified quality. □ **come a cropper** (*informal*) to fall heavily; to fail badly.

croquet (**kroh**-kay) *noun* a game played on a lawn with wooden balls that are driven through hoops with mallets.

croquette (krŏ-**ket**) *noun* a fried ball or roll of potato, meat, or fish.

crosier (**kroh**-zee-er) *noun* a hooked staff carried by a bishop as a symbol of office.

cross *noun* **1** a mark made by drawing one line across another, × or +. **2** an upright post with another piece of wood across it, used in ancient times for crucifixion; **the Cross** that on which Christ died. **3** a model of this as a Christian emblem; a monument in this form. **4** an affliction, an annoying thing one has to bear. **5** a cross-shaped emblem or medal, *the*

Victoria Cross. **6** an animal or plant produced by cross-breeding. **7** a mixture of two different things. –**cross** *verb* **1** to go or extend across. **2** to place crosswise. **3** draw a line across, *cross the t's*; *cross a cheque*, mark it with two parallel lines so that it must be paid into a bank. **4** to make the sign of the Cross on or over; *cross oneself*, as a sign of religious awe or to call upon God for protection. **5** to frustrate, to oppose the wishes or plans of. **6** to cross-breed (animals); to cross-fertilise (plants). –**cross** *adjective* **1** passing from side to side. **2** annoyed, showing bad temper. **3** contrary, opposed; reciprocal. □ **at cross purposes** misunderstanding or conflicting with each other. **crossed line** a faulty telephone connection in which another conversation can be heard. **cross off** to cross out. **cross one's mind** to come briefly into one's mind. **cross out** to draw a line through (an item on a list) to show that it is no longer valid. **cross stitch** a stitch formed by two crossing stitches. **cross swords** to have an argument or disagreement. **keep one's fingers crossed** to hope that nothing unfortunate will happen, crooking one finger over another to bring good luck. **on the cross** crosswise, on the bias. **crossly** *adverb*, **crossness** *noun*

crossbar *noun* a horizontal bar.

crossbow *noun* a powerful bow with mechanism for drawing and releasing the string.

cross-breed *verb* (**cross-bred**, **cross-breeding**) to produce by mating an animal with one of a different kind. –**cross-breed** *noun* an animal produced in this way.

cross-check *verb* to check by a different method.

cross-country *adjective* & *adverb* across fields or open country, not keeping to main roads or to a direct road.

cross-dresser *noun* a person who dresses in the clothes of the opposite sex, a transvestite. **cross-dress** *verb*

crosse *noun* a stick with a triangular net at the end, used in lacrosse.

cross-examine *verb* to cross-question, especially in a lawcourt. **cross-examination** *noun*

cross-eyed *adjective* having one or both eyes turned towards the nose.

cross-fertilise *verb* (also -**ize**) to fertilise (an animal or plant) from one of a different kind. **cross-fertilisation** *noun*

crossfire *noun* the firing of guns from two or more points so that the lines of fire cross.

cross-grained *adjective* **1** (of wood) with the grain in crossing directions. **2** bad-tempered.

cross-halving *noun* fitting together crossing pieces of wood by cutting out half the thickness of each.

crossing *noun* **1** a journey across water, *we had a smooth crossing*. **2** a place where things cross. **3** a place at which one may cross; a specially marked place for pedestrians to cross a road. □ crossing over an interchange of genes between corresponding parts of a pair of chromosomes.

cross-legged *adjective* & *adverb* with the ankles crossed and knees apart.

cross-multiply *verb* to multiply the numerator of one fraction by the denominator of another and vice versa. cross-multiplication *noun*

crosspatch *noun* a bad-tempered person.

crosspiece *noun* a transverse beam, bar, section, etc.

cross-ply *adjective* (of tyres) having fabric layers with cords lying crosswise (compare *radial-ply*).

cross-pollinate *verb* to pollinate (a plant) from another. cross-pollination *noun*

cross-question *verb* to question closely in order to test answers given to previous questions.

cross-reference *noun* a note directing people to another part of a book or index for further information.

crossroads *noun* a place where two or more roads intersect.

cross-section *noun* **1** a diagram showing the internal structure of something as though it has been cut through. **2** a representative sample.

cross-slide *noun* the part of a lathe or planing machine on which the tool-holder is mounted and can slide horizontally.

crosstalk *noun* **1** conversation heard on a crossed telephone line. **2** dialogue, especially between two comedians in an entertainment. **3** leakage of an electronic signal from one channel to another, especially in a stereo system.

crossways *adverb* & *adjective* in the form of a cross, with one crossing another.

crosswind *noun* a wind blowing across the direction of travel.

crosswise *adjective* & *adverb* crossways.

crossword *noun* a puzzle in which intersecting words, indicated by clues, have to be inserted into blank squares in a diagram.

crotch *noun* **1** a place where things fork. **2** the part of the body or of a garment where the legs fork.

crotchet (**kroch**-ĕt) *noun* a note in music, lasting half as long as a minim.

crotchety *adjective* peevish.

crouch *verb* to lower the body with the limbs bent and close to it; to be in this position.

croup (*pr.* kroop) *noun* a children's disease in which inflammation of the windpipe causes a hard cough and difficulty in breathing.

croupier (**kroop**-ee-er) *noun* a person who rakes in the money at a gambling table and pays out winnings.

croûton (**kroo**-tawn) *noun* a small piece of fried or toasted bread served with soup etc.

crow[1] *noun* a large black bird of a family that includes the jackdaw, raven, and rook. □ as the crow flies in a straight line. crow's-feet *plural noun* wrinkles in the skin at the side of the eyes. crow's-nest *noun* a protected lookout platform high on the mast of a ship.

crow[2] *verb* (crowed *or* crew, crowing) **1** (of a cock) to make a loud shrill cry. **2** (of a baby) to make sounds of pleasure. **3** to express gleeful triumph. –crow *noun* a crowing cry or sound.

crowbar *noun* a bar of iron with a flattened or beak-like end, used as a lever.

crowd *noun* **1** a large group of people gathered together. **2** (*informal*) a particular set of people, *doesn't belong to their crowd*. –crowd *verb* **1** to come together in a crowd. **2** to fill or occupy fully; to cram with people or things. □ crowd out to keep out by crowding. crowded *adjective*

croweater *noun* (*Austral. informal*) a South Australian.

crown *noun* **1** an ornamental headdress worn by a monarch. **2** (often Crown) the sovereign; his or her authority; the supreme governing power in a monarchy; *Crown land*, government-owned land. **3** a wreath worn on the head, especially as a symbol of victory. **4** a crown-shaped object or ornament. **5** the top part of something (e.g. of the head or a hat or a tooth); the highest part of something arched, *the crown of the road*. **6** a former coin worth 5 shillings. –crown *verb* **1** to place a crown on as a symbol of royal power or victory; *the* crowned heads of Europe, kings and queens. **2** to form, cover, or ornament the top part of. **3** to make a successful conclusion to, *our efforts were crowned with success*. **4** to put an artificial top on (a tooth). **5** (*informal*) to hit on the head. □ **Crown Colony** a colony subject to direct control by the British government. **crown jewels** the sovereign's crown, sceptre, orb, etc. used at coronations. **crown of thorns starfish** a spiny coral-eating starfish. **Crown Prince** or **Princess** the heir to the throne. [from Latin *corona* = garland or crown]

crucial (**kroo**-shăl) *adjective* decisive, critical; deciding an important issue. **crucially** *adverb* [from Latin *crucis* = of a cross]

Usage *Crucial* is sometimes used loosely to mean simply 'very important', but this use is best avoided.

---

crucible (**kroo**-sĭ-bŭl) *noun* a pot in which metals are melted.

crucifer (**kroo**-sĭ-fer) *noun* **1** a cruciferous plant. **2** the cross-bearer in church ceremonies.

cruciferous (kroo-**sif**-ĕ-rŭs) *adjective* of the family of plants bearing flowers with four equal petals arranged crosswise. [from Latin *crucis* = of the cross, + *ferre* = to carry]

crucifix *noun* a model of the Cross or of Christ on the Cross. [from Latin, = fixed to a cross]

crucifixion *noun* crucifying, being crucified. □ **the Crucifixion** that of Christ.

cruciform (**kroo**-sĭ-form) *adjective* cross-shaped.

crucify *verb* (**crucified, crucifying**) **1** to put to death by nailing or binding to a cross. **2** to cause extreme mental pain to; to destroy in argument etc.

crude *adjective* **1** in a natural state, not refined, *crude oil*. **2** not well finished or worked out, rough, *a crude attempt*. **3** without good manners, vulgar. –**crude** *noun* crude oil. **crudely** *adverb*, **crudity** *noun* [from Latin *crudus* = raw, rough]

cruel *adjective* (**crueller, cruellest**) **1** feeling pleasure in another's suffering. **2** causing pain or suffering, *this cruel war*. –**cruel** *verb* (*Austral. informal*) to thwart, to spoil. **cruelly** *adverb*, **cruelty** *noun*

cruet *noun* **1** a small stoppered glass bottle for holding oil or vinegar for use at the table. **2** a stand holding this and salt, pepper, etc.

cruise *verb* **1** to sail about for pleasure or on patrol. **2** (of a vehicle or aircraft) to travel at a moderate speed that is economical of fuel. **3** to drive at moderate speed, or at random when looking for passengers etc. –**cruise** *noun* a cruising voyage. □ **cruise missile** a missile that is able to fly at low altitude and guide itself by reference to the features of the region traversed.

cruiser *noun* **1** a fast warship. **2** a yacht or motor boat for cruising.

crumb *noun* **1** a small fragment, especially of bread or other food. **2** the soft inner part of bread. –**crumb** *verb* **1** to cover with breadcrumbs. **2** to crumble (bread). **crumby** *adjective*

crumble *verb* to break or fall into small fragments. –**crumble** *noun* fruit cooked with a crumbly topping, *apple crumble*.

crumbly *adjective* easily crumbled.

crummy *adjective* (**crummier, crummiest**) (*informal*) inferior, worthless; squalid. **crumminess** *noun*

crumpet *noun* a soft cake of yeast mixture, baked on a griddle and eaten toasted and buttered.

crumple *verb* **1** to crush or become crushed into creases. **2** to collapse loosely.

crunch *verb* **1** to crush noisily with the teeth. **2** to walk or move with a sound of crushing; to make such a sound. **3** (especially of a computer) process (large quantities of information). –**crunch** *noun* **1** crunching; a crunching sound. **2** (*informal*) a decisive event, a showdown.

crupper *noun* a strap for holding a harness back, passing under a horse's tail.

Crusade (kroo-**sayd**) *noun* any of the military expeditions made by Europeans in the Middle Ages to recover the Holy Land from the Muslims. –**crusade** *noun* a campaign for a cause. –**crusade** *verb* to take part in a crusade. **crusader** *noun*

cruse *noun* (*old use*) an earthenware pot or jar.

crush *verb* **1** to press so as to break, injure, or wrinkle; to squeeze tightly. **2** to pound into small fragments. **3** to become crushed. **4** to defeat or subdue completely. –**crush** *noun* **1** a crowd of people pressed together. **2** (*Austral.*) a narrow passage in a stockyard through which animals can pass only in single file. **3** a drink made from crushed fruit. **4** (*informal*) an infatuation. **crushable** *adjective*

crust *noun* **1** the hard outer layer of something especially bread. **2** the rocky outer portion of the earth. **3** (*Austral. informal*) a living, *what do you do for a crust?*

crustacean (krus-**tay**-shăn) *noun* an animal that has a hard shell (e.g. crab, lobster, prawn).

crusty *adjective* (**crustier**, **crustiest**) **1** having a crisp crust. **2** having a harsh manner. **crustily** *adverb*, **crustiness** *noun*

crutch *noun* **1** a support for a lame person, usually fitting under the armpit. **2** the crotch of the body or of a garment. **–crutch** *verb* to remove wool from a sheep's hindquarters to prevent blowfly strike.

crux *noun* (*plural* **cruces**, *pr.* **kroo**-seez) the vital part of a problem. [Latin, = a cross]

cry *noun* **1** a loud wordless sound expressing pain, grief, joy, etc. **2** a shout. **3** the call of a bird or animal. **4** an appeal, a demand. **5** a battle cry. **6** a spell of weeping. **–cry** *verb* (**cried**, **crying**) **1** to shed tears. **2** to call out loudly in words. **3** to appeal, to demand; *a crying shame*, one demanding attention. **4** (of an animal) to utter its cry. **5** to announce for sale, *crying their wares*. □ **cry-baby** *noun* a person who weeps easily without good cause. **cry off** to withdraw from a promise or arrangement. **in full cry** giving tongue in hot pursuit.

cryogenics (kry-ŏ-**jen**-iks) *noun* the scientific study of very low temperatures and their effects. [from Greek *kruos* = frost, + *-genes* = born]

crypt (*pr.* kript) *noun* a room below the floor of a church; a vault used as a burial place.

cryptic (**krip**-tik) *adjective* concealing its meaning in a puzzling way. **cryptically** *adverb* [from Greek *kruptos* = hidden]

cryptogam (**krip**-tŏ-gam) *noun* a flowerless plant such as a fern, moss, or fungus. [from Greek *kruptos* = hidden, + *gamos* = marriage]

cryptogram (**krip**-tŏ-gram) *noun* something written in cipher. [from Greek *kruptos* = hidden, + *-gram*]

cryptography (krip-**tog**-ră-fee) *noun* the art of writing in codes or ciphers or of deciphering these. **cryptographer** *noun* [from Greek *kruptos* = hidden, + *-graphy*]

crystal *noun* **1** a clear transparent colourless mineral. **2** a piece of this. **3** very clear glass of high quality. **4** each of the pieces into which certain substances solidify, *crystals of ice*. **–crystal** *adjective* made of crystal; like or clear as crystal. □ **crystal ball** a globe of glass used in crystal-gazing. **crystal-gazing** *noun* looking

into a crystal ball in an attempt to see future events pictured there.

crystalline (**krist**-ă-lyn) *adjective* **1** like or containing crystals. **2** transparent, very clear.

crystallise *verb* (also **-ize**) **1** to form crystals. **2** (of ideas or plans) to become clear and definite in form. □ **crystallised fruit** fruit preserved in and coated with sugar. **crystallisation** *noun*

Crystal Palace a large building of iron and glass, designed by (Sir) Joseph Paxton for the Great Exhibition in London (1851).

CSIRO *abbreviation* Commonwealth Scientific and Industrial Research Organisation.

CT scan *noun* see **CAT**.

cu. *abbreviation* cubic.

cub *noun* the young of certain animals, e.g. fox, bear, lion. **–cub** *verb* (**cubbed**, **cubbing**) **1** to bring forth (cubs). **2** to hunt foxcubs. □ **Cub** or **Cub Scout** a member of the junior branch of the Scout Association.

Cuba a Caribbean republic, the largest of the islands in the West Indies. **Cuban** *adjective* & *noun*

cubby *noun* **1** (in full **cubby hole**) a small compartment. **2** (in full **cubby house**) a child's playhouse.

cube *noun* **1** a solid body with six equal square faces. **2** a block shaped like this. **3** the product of a number multiplied by itself twice, *the cube of 4 is 64 (4 × 4 × 4 = 64)*. **–cube** *verb* **1** to cut (food) into small cubes. **2** to find the cube of (a number). □ **cube root** the number that produces a given number when cubed, *the cube root of 64 is 4*.

cubic *adjective* of three dimensions. □ **cubic metre** etc., the volume of a cube with sides one metre etc. long (used as a unit of measurement for volume).

cubical *adjective* cube-shaped.

cubicle *noun* a small division of a large room; an enclosed space screened for privacy.

cubism *noun* an early 20th century art movement in which objects are often represented geometrically. **cubist** *noun*

cubit (**kew**-bĭt) *noun* an ancient measure of length, approximately equal to the length of the arm from elbow to fingertips. [from Latin *cubitum* = elbow]

cuboid (**kew**-boid) *adjective* cube-shaped, like a cube. **–cuboid** *noun* a solid body with rectangular sides.

cuckold (**kuk**-ŏld) *noun* a man whose wife has committed adultery during their marriage.

cuckoo *noun* a bird with a call that is like its name, which lays its eggs in the nests of other birds. □ cuckoo clock a clock that strikes the hours with a sound like a cuckoo's call.

cucumber *noun* 1 a usually long green-skinned fleshy fruit, eaten in salads or pickled. 2 the plant producing this.

cud *noun* the food that cattle etc. bring back from the stomach into the mouth and chew again. □ chew the cud (*informal*) to meditate.

cuddle *verb* 1 to hold closely and lovingly in one's arms. 2 to nestle. –cuddle *noun* an affectionate hug.

cuddlesome, **cuddly** *adjectives* pleasant to cuddle.

cudgel (**kuj**-ĕl) *noun* a short thick stick used as a weapon. –cudgel *verb* (cudgelled, cudgelling) to beat with a cudgel. □ cudgel one's brains to think hard about a problem. take up the cudgels for to defend vigorously.

cue[1] *noun* something said or done that serves as a signal for something else to be done, e.g. for an actor to speak in a play. –cue *verb* (cued, cueing) to give a cue to.

cue[2] *noun* a long rod for striking the ball in snooker, billiards, and similar games. [from *queue*]

cuff[1] *noun* 1 a doubled strip of cloth forming a band round the end part of a sleeve; a separate band worn similarly. 2 the part of a glove covering the wrist. 3 a trouser turn-up. □ cuff link each of a pair of fasteners for shirt cuffs, used instead of buttons. off the cuff without rehearsal or preparation.

cuff[2] *verb* to strike with the open hand. –cuff *noun* a cuffing blow.

cuirass (kwĭ-**ras**) *noun* 1 a piece of armour consisting of a breastplate and a similar plate protecting the back. 2 something shaped like this, especially a device for artificial respiration.

cuisine (kwĭ-**zeen**) *noun* a style of cooking. [French]

cul-de-sac (**kul**-dĕ-sak) *noun* (*plural* culs-de-sac) a street with an opening at one end only. [French, = bottom of a sack]

culinary (**kul**-ĭ-nă-ree) *adjective* 1 of a kitchen or cooking. 2 used in cooking, *culinary herbs*.

cull *verb* 1 to pick (flowers). 2 to select. 3 to pick out and kill (surplus animals from a flock or herd). –cull *noun* culling; thing(s) culled.

Culloden (kŭ-**lod**-ĕn) a moor in NE Scotland, site of a Jacobite defeat in 1746.

culminate *verb* to reach its highest point or degree. culmination *noun* [from Latin *culmen* = summit]

culottes (kŭ-**lots**) *plural noun* women's trousers or shorts styled to look like a skirt.

culpable (**kul**-pă-bŭl) *adjective* deserving blame. culpably *adverb*, culpability *noun* [from Latin *culpare* = to blame]

culprit *noun* a person who has committed a slight offence.

cult *noun* 1 a system of religious worship. 2 devotion to or admiration of a person or thing; a popular fashion especially followed by a particular group, *cult movie*.

cultivar *noun* a variety of plant produced by cultivation.

cultivate *verb* 1 to prepare and use (land) for crops. 2 to produce (crops) by tending them. 3 to spend time and care in developing (a thing, person, friendship, etc.). cultivation *noun*

cultivator *noun* 1 a device for breaking up ground for cultivation. 2 a person who cultivates.

cultural *adjective* of culture. □ Cultural Revolution a political upheaval in China (1966–8) in support of the theories of Mao Zedong. culturally *adverb*

culture *noun* 1 the appreciation and understanding of literature, arts, music, etc. 2 the customs and civilisation of a particular people or group, *Japanese culture*. 3 improvement by care and training, *physical culture*. 4 the cultivating of plants; the rearing of bees, silkworms, etc. 5 a quantity of bacteria grown for study. –culture *verb* to grow (bacteria) for study. □ culture shock confusion and discomfort felt when subjected to an unfamiliar way of life.

cultured *adjective* educated to appreciate literature, arts, music, etc. □ cultured pearls pearls formed by an oyster when a foreign body is inserted artificially into its shell.

culvert (**kul**-vert) *noun* a drain that crosses under a road or railway etc.

cum *preposition* with; also used as, *a sofa-cum-bed*. [Latin]

cumbersome (**kum**-ber-sŏm) *adjective* clumsy to carry, wear, or manage.

216

cumin (**kum**-ĭn) *noun* (also **cummin**) a plant with fragrant seeds that are used for flavouring.

cummerbund *noun* a sash worn round the waist.

cumquat (**kum**-kwot) *noun* (also **kumquat**) a small orange-like fruit used in preserves etc.

cumulative (**kewm**-yŭ-lă-tiv) *adjective* increasing in amount by one addition after another. **cumulatively** *adverb* [from Latin *cumulus* = heap]

cumulonimbus (kewm-yŭ-loh-**nim**-bŭs) *noun* a tall dense mass of cloud present during thunderstorms. [from *cumulus*, + Latin *nimbus* = cloud]

cumulus *noun* (*plural* **cumuli**) a form of cloud consisting of rounded masses heaped on a horizontal base. [Latin, = a heap]

cuneiform (**kew**-nĭ-form) *adjective* of or written in the wedge-shaped strokes used in the inscriptions of ancient Assyria, Persia, etc. –**cuneiform** *noun* cuneiform writing. [from Latin *cuneus* = a wedge]

cunjevoi[1] (**kun**-jĕ-voy) *noun* an Australian sea squirt used as bait.

cunjevoi[2] *noun* a kind of arum, found in rainforests of eastern Australia.

cunning *adjective* 1 skilled at deceiving people, crafty. 2 ingenious, *a cunning device*. –**cunning** *noun* craftiness.

cup *noun* 1 a small open container for drinking from, usually bowl-shaped and with a handle, used with a saucer. 2 its contents; the amount it contains (used as a measure in cookery, 250 ml). 3 something shaped like a cup. 4 an ornamental goblet-shaped vessel awarded as a prize. –**cup** *verb* (**cupped**, **cupping**) 1 to form into a cuplike shape, *cupped his hands*. 2 hold as if in a cup, *with her chin cupped in her hands*. □ **not one's cup of tea** (*informal*) not what one likes or what suits one. **cupful** *noun* (*plural* **cupfuls**).

cupboard *noun* a recess or piece of furniture with a door, in which things may be stored. □ **cupboard love** a display of affection put on in the hope of obtaining a reward.

cupcake *noun* a small cake baked in a cup-shaped paper or foil container.

Cupid the Roman god of love. –**cupid** *noun* a picture or statue of a beautiful boy with wings and a bow and arrows.

cupidity (kew-**pid**-ĭ-tee) *noun* greed for gain. [from Latin *cupido* = desire]

cupola (**kew**-pŏ-lă) *noun* a small dome on a roof.

cupro-nickel *noun* an alloy of copper and nickel.

cur *noun* a bad-tempered or worthless dog.

curable *adjective* able to be cured.

curacy *noun* the position of a curate.

curare (kew-**rah**-ree) *noun* a bitter substance obtained from certain South American plants, used by some indigenous peoples there to poison their arrows.

curate *noun* a member of the clergy who assists a parish priest. □ **curate's egg** a thing that is partly good and partly bad. [same origin as *cure*]

curative (**kew**-ră-tiv) *adjective* helping to cure illness.

curator (kew-**ray**-ter) *noun* 1 a person in charge of a museum or other collection. 2 a person who organises an art collection etc. [same origin as *cure*]

curb *noun* 1 something that restrains, *put a curb on spending*. 2 a chain or strap passing under a horse's lower jaw, used to restrain it. –**curb** *verb* to restrain. [from Latin *curvare* = to curve]

curd *noun* 1 (often **curds**) the thick soft substance formed when milk turns sour. 2 a substance with a similar consistency, *lemon curd*; *bean curd*. 3 the edible head of a cauliflower.

curdle *verb* to form or cause to form curds. □ **make one's blood curdle** to fill one with horror.

cure *verb* 1 to restore to health. 2 to rid (of a disease or troublesome condition); to eliminate (a disease etc.). 3 to preserve (meat, fruit, tobacco, or skins) by salting, drying, etc. 4 to vulcanise (rubber). –**cure** *noun* 1 curing, being cured, *cannot guarantee a cure*. 2 a substance or treatment that cures a disease, a remedy. [from Latin *curare* = take care of something]

curette (kew-**ret**) *noun* a surgeon's small scraping-instrument. –**curette** *verb* to clean or scrape with this.

curfew *noun* a signal or time after which people must remain indoors until the next day.

Curia *noun* the papal court, the government department of the Vatican.

Curie, Marie (1867–1934) and Pierre (1859–1906), French pioneers of the study of radioactivity.

curie *noun* **1** a unit of radioactivity. **2** a quantity of radioactive substance having this. [named after Pierre Curie]

curio *noun* (*plural* **curios**) an object that is interesting because it is rare or unusual.

curiosity *noun* **1** a desire to find out and know things. **2** something that is of interest because it is rare or unusual.

curious *adjective* **1** eager to learn or know something. **2** strange, unusual. **curiously** *adverb* [from Latin, = careful (compare *cure*)]

curium (**kyoo**-ree-ŭm) *noun* an artificial radioactive metallic element of the actinide series (symbol Cm).

curl *verb* **1** to bend, to coil into a spiral. **2** to move in a spiral form, *smoke curled upwards*. –**curl** *noun* **1** something curved inwards or coiled. **2** a coiled lock of hair. **3** a curling movement.

curler *noun* a device for curling the hair.

curlew (**kerl**-yoo) *noun* a wading bird with a long slender curved bill.

curlicue (**ker**-lee-kew) *noun* a curly ornamental line.

curling *noun* a game played with large flat round stones that are sent along ice towards a mark.

curly *adjective* (**curlier**, **curliest**) curling, full of curls. **curliness** *noun*

curmudgeon (ker-**muj**-ŏn) *noun* a bad-tempered person.

currant *noun* **1** the dried fruit of a small seedless grape, used in cookery. **2** a small round red, white, or black berry; the shrub that produces it.

currawong *noun* an Australian bird like a crow with a loud ringing call. [probably from Yagara or Dharuk]

currency *noun* **1** money in actual use in a country. **2** the state of being in common or general use; *the rumour gained currency*, became generally known and believed. □ **currency lad** or **lass** (*historical*) a native-born Australian (as opposed to a British-born immigrant). [from *current*]

current *adjective* **1** belonging to the present time, happening now, *current events*. **2** in general circulation or use. –**current** *noun* **1** water or air etc. moving in a certain direction; a running stream. **2** the flow of electricity through something or along a wire or cable. **3** a general tendency or course, *the current of opinion*. □ **current account** a bank

account offering instant access to one's money and the use of a cheque book; transactions in goods etc. that make up a part of a country's balance of payments. [from Latin *currens* = running]

currently *adverb* at the present time.

curricle *noun* an old type of light open two-wheeled carriage drawn by two horses abreast.

curriculum (kŭ-**rik**-yŭ-lŭm) *noun* (*plural* **curricula**) a course of study. □ **curriculum vitae** (*pr.* **vee**-ty) a brief account of one's previous career. [Latin, = course of life]

curry[1] *noun* a dish of meat, vegetables, etc. cooked with hot-tasting spices. –**curry** *verb* (**curried**, **currying**) to cook (meat etc.) in a curry sauce. [from Tamil *kari* = sauce]

curry[2] *verb* (**curried**, **currying**) to groom (a horse) with a **curry-comb**, a pad with rubber or plastic projections. □ **curry favour** to win favour by flattery.

curse *noun* **1** a call for evil to come upon a person or thing. **2** the evil produced by this. **3** a violent exclamation of anger. **4** something that causes evil or harm. –**curse** *verb* **1** to utter a curse against. **2** to exclaim violently in anger. □ **be cursed with** to have as a burden or source of harm.

cursed (**ker**-sĕd or kerst) *adjective* damnable.

cursive *adjective* (of writing) done with joined letters. –**cursive** *noun* cursive writing.

cursor *noun* **1** an indicator (usually a flashing light) on a VDU screen, showing a specific position in the matter displayed. **2** the transparent slide, bearing the reference line, on a slide rule. [Latin, = runner (compare *current*)]

cursory (**ker**-sŏ-ree) *adjective* hasty and not thorough, *a cursory inspection*. **cursorily** *adverb* [from Latin, = of a runner]

curt *adjective* noticeably or rudely brief. **curtly** *adverb*, **curtness** *noun*

curtail *verb* to cut short, to reduce. **curtailment** *noun*

curtain *noun* **1** a piece of cloth or other material hung up as a screen, especially at a window or between the stage and auditorium of a theatre. **2** the fall of a stage curtain at the end of an act or scene. **3** a curtain call. –**curtain** *verb* to provide or shut off with a curtain or curtains. **curtains** *plural noun* (*informal*) the end. □ **curtain call** applause calling for an actor etc. to take a bow after the curtain has been lowered. **curtain-raiser** *noun* an introductory item; a preliminary event.

curtsy *noun* a movement of respect made by women and girls, bending the knees and lowering the body with one foot forward. – **curtsy** *verb* (**curtsied**, **curtsying**) to make a curtsy. [= *courtesy*]

curvature (**ker**-vǎ-cher) *noun* curving; a curved form, *the curvature of the earth*.

curve *noun* 1 a line of which no part is straight. 2 a smooth continuous surface of which no part is flat. 3 a curved form or thing. – **curve** *verb* to bend or shape so as to form a curve. **curvy** *adjective*

curvet (ker-**vet**) *noun* a horse's short frisky leap. – **curvet** *verb* (**curvetted**, **curvetting**) to make a curvet.

cuscus (**kus**-kus) *noun* a tree-dwelling possum-like marsupial (phalanger) of northern Australia and New Guinea.

cushion *noun* 1 a bag of cloth or other fabric filled with soft or firm or springy material, used to make a seat etc. more comfortable. 2 a soft pad or other means of support or of protection against jarring; a means of protection against shock. 3 the padded border round a billiard table, from which the balls rebound. 4 the body of air supporting a hovercraft etc. – **cushion** *verb* 1 to furnish with a cushion or cushions. 2 to lessen the impact of (a blow or shock). 3 to protect from the effects of something harmful.

cushy *adjective* (**cushier**, **cushiest**) (*informal*) pleasant and easy, *a cushy job*. [from Hindi *khush* = pleasant]

cusp *noun* a pointed end where two curves meet, e.g. the horn of a crescent moon. [from Latin *cuspis* = point]

cuss *verb* (*informal*) to curse. – **cuss** *noun* (*informal*) 1 a curse. 2 a difficult person, *an awkward cuss*.

cussed (**kus**-ĕd) *adjective* (*informal*) awkward and stubborn. **cussedness** *noun*

custard *noun* 1 a dish or sauce made with beaten eggs and milk. 2 a sweet sauce made with milk and flavoured cornflour. □ **custard apple** a tropical fruit with a custard-like pulp.

custodian (kus-**toh**-dee-ǎn) *noun* a guardian or keeper, especially of a public building.

custody *noun* 1 the right or duty of taking care of something, guardianship; *in safe custody*, safely guarded. 2 imprisonment.

□ **take into custody** to arrest. **custodial** *adjective* [from Latin *custos* = guardian]

custom *noun* 1 a usual way of behaving or of doing something. 2 the regular support given to a business by customers. **customs** *noun* (see separate entry). □ **custom-built**, **custom-made** *adjectives* made according to a customer's order.

customary *adjective* in accordance with custom, usual. **customarily** *adverb*

customer *noun* 1 a person who buys goods or services from a shop or business. 2 a person one has to deal with, *an awkward customer*.

customise *verb* (also **-ize**) to make or modify to individual requirements.

customs *noun* duty charged on goods imported from other countries. – **Customs** *noun* or *plural noun* 1 the government department dealing with this. 2 the area at a port or airport where Customs officials examine goods and baggage brought into a country.

cut *verb* (**cut**, **cutting**) 1 to divide, wound, or detach with an edged instrument; *the knife won't cut*, is blunt. 2 to shape, make, or shorten in this way. 3 to be able to be cut, *the steak cuts easily*. 4 to have (a tooth) appear through the gum. 5 to cross, to intersect; to go (through or across), especially as a shorter way. 6 to reduce by removing part, *cut taxes*; *two scenes were cut by the censor*. 7 to go directly to another shot in a film. 8 to switch off (electric power, an engine, etc.). 9 to lift and turn up part of a pack of cards, e.g. in deciding who is to deal. 10 to hit a ball with a chopping movement in cricket etc. 11 (*informal*) to stay away deliberately from, *cut classes*. 12 to ignore (a person) deliberately. – **cut** *noun* 1 the act of cutting; a division or wound made by this. 2 a stroke with a sword, whip, or cane. 3 a stroke made by cutting a ball in cricket etc. 4 a piece of meat cut from the carcass of an animal. 5 the way a thing is cut; the style in which clothes are made by cutting. 6 a cutting remark. 7 a reduction, *tax cuts*; *power cut*, a temporary reduction or stoppage of electric current. 8 the cutting out of part of a play or film etc. 9 (*informal*) a share of profits, commission. □ **a cut above** noticeably superior to. **cut across** to go beyond, *cuts across political divisions*. **cut and dried** completely decided, inflexible; planned or prepared in advance. **cut back** to reduce; to prune. **cut both ways** to have both a good and a bad effect; to support both sides of an argument etc. **cut a corner** to go across

it rather than round it. **cut corners** to fail to
do something properly, especially to save
time. **cut a dash** to make a brilliant show in
appearance and behaviour. **cut glass** glass
with patterns cut in it. **cut in** to interrupt; to
return too soon to one's own side of the road,
obstructing the path of an overtaking vehicle;
to give a share of the profits to. **cut it out!**
(*informal*) stop doing that. **cut lunch** (*Austral.*)
a packed lunch, usually sandwiches. **cut no ice**
(*informal*) to have no influence or effect. **cut
off** to prevent from continuing; to keep from
union or contact. **cut one's losses** to abandon
an unprofitable scheme before one loses too
much. **cut out** to shape by cutting; to outdo (a
rival); to cease or cause to cease functioning,
the engine cut out; to omit, to stop doing
or something); (*Austral.*) to separate
(animals) from a herd. **cut-out** *noun* a shape
cut out of paper etc.; a device that disconnects
something automatically. **cut out for** having
the qualities and abilities needed for. **cut-price**
adjective for sale at a reduced price. **cut work**
a kind of embroidery in which holes are cut
in material and ornamental patterns of threads
are worked in these.

cutaneous (kew-**tay**-nee-ŭs) *adjective* of the
skin. [from Latin *cutis* = skin]

cutaway *adjective* (of a diagram, model, etc.)
with parts of the outside missing to reveal the
interior.

cutback *noun* a reduction, especially in
expenditure.

cute *adjective* (*informal*) 1 attractive, pretty.
2 ingenious, clever. **cutely** *adverb*, **cuteness**
noun [from *acute*]

cuticle (**kew**-ti-kŭl) *noun* skin at the base of a
fingernail or toenail. [from Latin *cutis* = skin]

cutlass *noun* a short sword with a slightly
curved blade.

cutler *noun* a maker of cutlery.

cutlery *noun* knives, forks, and spoons used in
eating and serving food.

cutlet *noun* 1 a rib-chop of meat, especially of
lamb. 2 a slice of veal etc. for frying. 3 a fish
steak.

cutter *noun* 1 a person or thing that cuts; a
tailor who takes measurements and cuts cloth.
2 a small fast sailing ship. 3 a small boat
carried by a large ship.

cutthroat *noun* a person who cuts throats, a
murderer. –**cutthroat** *adjective* 1 intense and
merciless, *cutthroat competition*. 2 (of card

games) three-handed. 3 (of a razor) having a
long blade set in a handle.

cutting *see* cut. –**cutting** *adjective* (of words)
hurtful, *cutting remarks*. –**cutting** *noun*
1 a piece cut from something; a section
cut from a newspaper etc. and kept for
reference. 2 an excavation through high
ground for a road or railway. 3 a piece cut
from a plant for replanting to form a new
plant. □ **cutting edge** an edge that cuts; the
forefront (of an activity etc.).

cuttlefish *noun* a sea creature (a mollusc)
similar to a squid that sends out a black liquid
when attacked.

CV *abbreviation* curriculum vitae.

CWA *abbreviation* Country Women's
Association.

cwt *abbreviation* hundredweight.

cyan (**sy**-ăn) *adjective* & *noun* (in
photography) greenish-blue.

cyanide (**sy**-ă-nyd) *noun* any of the very
poisonous salts or esters of hydrocyanic acid.

Cybele (si-**bee**-lee) a mother-goddess in
ancient mythology.

cyber- *prefix* of or relating to electronic
communication and virtual reality, *cyberspace*;
cyberaccess.

cybernetics (sy-ber-**net**-iks) *noun* the science
of communication and control in animals
(e.g. by the nervous system) and in machines
(e.g. computers). **cybernetic** *adjective* [from
Greek *kubernetes* = steersman]

cycad *noun* a tall palmlike tropical plant.

Cyclades (**sik**-lă-deez) a group of Greek
islands in the Aegean Sea.

cyclamate (**sy**-klă-mayt) *noun* an artificial
sweetening substance.

cyclamen (**sy**-klă-měn) *noun* a plant with
pink, purple, or white flowers with petals that
turn back.

cycle *noun* 1 a series of events or operations
that are regularly repeated in the same order,
the cycle of the seasons. 2 the time needed for
one such series. 3 one complete occurrence
of a continually recurring process such as
electrical oscillation or alternation of electric
current. 4 a complete set or series, e.g. of
songs or poems. 5 a bicycle or motorcycle.
6 (in graph theory) a path through a network
of edges and vertices in which the first vertex
is the same as the last. –**cycle** *verb* to ride a
bicycle etc. [from Greek *kuklos* = circle]

cyclic (**sy**-klik) *adjective* **1** recurring in cycles or series. **2** forming a cycle. ☐ cyclic quadrilateral a quadrilateral such that a circle can be drawn round it passing through all four corners. cyclical *adjective*, cyclically *adverb*

cyclist *noun* a person who rides a cycle.

cyclo-cross *noun* cross-country racing on bicycles.

cycloid (**sy**-kloid) *noun* the curve traced by a point on a circle rolling along a straight line.

cyclone (**sy**-klohn) *noun* **1** a system of winds rotating round a calm central area of low barometric pressure; a depression. **2** (in full tropical cyclone) a violent destructive form of this. ☐ cyclone fence (*trademark*) a fence made with interlocking wire in a metal frame. Cyclone Tracy a severe cyclone that caused extensive damage to Darwin on 25 December 1974. cyclonic (sy-**klon**-ik) *adjective*

Cyclops (**sy**-klops) (*plural* Cyclopes) (*Gk. myth.*) a member of a race of one-eyed giants.

cyclotron (**sy**-klŏ-tron) *noun* an apparatus for accelerating charged particles by making them move spirally in a magnetic field.

cygnet (**sig**-nĕt) *noun* a young swan.

cylinder *noun* **1** a solid or hollow object with straight sides and circular ends. **2** a machine-part shaped like this; the chamber in which a piston moves in an engine. cylindrical *adjective* [from Greek *kulindein* = to roll]

cymbal *noun* a percussion instrument consisting of a brass plate struck with another or with a stick. cymbalist *noun*

Cynic (**sin**-ik) *noun* a member of a school of ancient Greek philosophers who despised ease and wealth.

cynic (**sin**-ik) *noun* a person who believes people's motives are bad or selfish. cynical *adjective*, cynically *adverb*

cynicism (**sin**-ĭ-sizm) *noun* the attitude of a cynic.

cynosure (**sin**-ŏ-shoor) *noun* a centre of attraction or admiration.

cypress *noun* a coniferous evergreen tree with dark feathery leaves. ☐ cypress pine any of several Australian trees of the *Callitris* genus; the wood of these trees, often termite-resistant.

Cyprus an island in the eastern Mediterranean. Cypriot (**sip**-ree-ŏt) *adjective* & *noun*

Cyrillic (sĭ-**ril**-ik) *adjective* of the alphabet used by Slavonic peoples of the Eastern Church, named after St Cyril (9th c.), Greek missionary, who is said to have introduced it; now used especially for Russian, Serbian, and Bulgarian.

Cyrus king of Persia 559–529 BC, who conquered Asia Minor and a large part of the Middle East.

cyst (*pr.* sist) *noun* an abnormal sac formed in or on the body, containing fluid or semi-solid matter.

cystic (**sis**-tik) *adjective* **1** of the bladder. **2** like a cyst. ☐ cystic fibrosis a hereditary disease affecting the exocrine glands, usually resulting in respiratory infections. [from Greek *kustis* = bladder]

cystitis (sis-**ty**-tĭss) *noun* inflammation of the bladder.

cytology (sy-**tol**-ŏ-jee) *noun* the scientific study of biological cells. cytological *adjective*, cytologist *noun* [from Greek *kutos* = vessel, + *-logy*]

cytoplasm (**sy**-tŏ-plazm) *noun* the content of a biological cell other than the nucleus. cytoplasmic *adjective*

czar (*pr.* zar) *noun* = tsar.

Czech (*pr.* chek) *noun* **1** a native or the language of the Czech Republic. **2** (*historical*) a Czechoslovak. –Czech *adjective* of or relating to the Czechs or their language.

Czechoslovakia a former country in central Europe which divided in 1993 into the independent Czech and Slovak Republics. Czechoslovak (chek-ŏ-**sloh**-vak) *or* Czechoslovakian *adjectives* & *nouns*

Czech Republic, the a country in central Europe made up of the provinces of Bohemia and Moravia, which once formed western Czechoslovakia.

Dd

d. *abbreviation* (in pre-decimal currency) penny, pence. [short for the Latin *denarius*]

dab¹ *noun* **1** a light or feeble blow, a tap. **2** quick gentle pressure on a surface with something soft. **3** a small amount of a soft substance applied to a surface. –**dab** *verb* (**dabbed**, **dabbing**) **1** to strike lightly or feebly. **2** to press quickly and lightly.

dab² *noun* (also **dab hand**) (*informal*) an adept.

dabble *verb* **1** to wet by splashing or by putting in and out of water. **2** to move the feet, hands, or bill lightly in water or mud. □ **dabble in** to study or work at casually not seriously. **dabbler** *noun*

dabchick *noun* a small waterbird of the grebe family.

Dachau (**dak**-ow) a city in southern Germany, site of a Nazi concentration camp in the Second World War.

dachshund (**daks**-huund) *noun* a small dog of a breed with a long body and very short legs. [German, = badger dog]

dactyl (**dak**-til) *noun* a metrical foot with one long or stressed syllable followed by two short or unstressed syllables, as in the word *corporal*. **dactylic** (dak-**til**-ik) *adjective*

dad *noun* (*informal*) father.

Dada (**dah**-dah) *noun* an international movement in art and literature about 1915–20, intended to shock people.

daddy *noun* (*informal*) father.

daddy-long-legs *noun* a spider with long thin legs.

dado (**day**-doh) *noun* (*plural* **dados**) the lower part of the wall of a room or corridor when it is coloured or faced differently from the upper part.

daffodil *noun* a yellow flower with a trumpet-shaped central part, growing from a bulb.

daft *adjective* (*informal*) silly, foolish, crazy.

dag¹ *noun* (*Austral.*) a lock of wool clotted with dung on a sheep. □ **rattle one's dags** (*informal*) to hurry up.

dag² *noun* (*Austral. informal*) **1** an unfashionable or socially awkward person.

2 (*old use*) an eccentric; a character. **daggy** *adjective*

da Gama *see* Gama.

dagger *noun* a short pointed two-edged weapon used for stabbing. □ **at daggers drawn** hostile and on the point of quarrelling. **look daggers** to stare angrily.

daguerreotype (dă-**ge**-rŏ-typ) *noun* an early kind of photograph taken on a silver-coated copper plate, giving an image of white on silver. [named after its French inventor, Louis Daguerre (died 1851)]

dahlia (**day**-leeă) *noun* a garden plant with large richly coloured flowers and tuberous roots. [named after a Swedish botanist, A. Dahl]

Dáil (*pr.* doil) *noun* (in full **Dáil éireann**, *pr.* doil **air**-răn) the lower house of parliament in the Republic of Ireland.

daily *adjective* happening or appearing on every day (or every weekday). –**daily** *adverb* **1** once a day. **2** progressively. –**daily** *noun* a daily newspaper.

Daintree an area of tropical NE Queensland, where coastal rainforest is fringed by a coral reef.

dainty *adjective* (**daintier**, **daintiest**) **1** small and pretty, delicate. **2** fastidious, especially about food. **dainties** *plural noun* choice foods, delicacies. **daintily** *adverb*, **daintiness** *noun*

dairy *noun* a room or building where milk and milk products are processed, distributed, or sold. –**dairy** *adjective* of milk or milk products; **dairy cattle**, cattle kept for milk production.

dais (**day**-ĭss) *noun* a low platform, especially at one end of a room or hall.

daisy *noun* a flower with many petal-like rays surrounding a centre. □ **daisy wheel** a printing head used in a kind of typewriter or computer printer, having characters arranged round the circumference of a segmented disc. [from *day's eye*]

Dakar (**dak**-ar) the capital of Senegal.

Dalai Lama (dal-I **lah**-mă) the spiritual leader of Tibetan Buddhists.

dale *noun* a valley, especially in north England, *we travelled up hill and down dale.*

dalgite *noun* a Western Australian name for the bilby. [Nyungar *dalgaj*]

Dali (**dah**-lee), Salvador (1904–89), Spanish surrealist painter.

dally *verb* (**dallied**, **dallying**) 1 to idle, to dawdle. 2 to amuse oneself; to flirt. **dalliance** *noun*

Dalmatian (dal-**may**-shăn) *adjective* of Dalmatia, a region of Croatia including a coastal strip and offshore islands. – **Dalmatian** *noun* a large white dog with dark spots.

Dalton (**dawl**-tŏn), John (1766–1844), English chemist, founder of the modern atomic theory. He also described colour-blindness, from which he suffered, which became known as **Daltonism**.

dam¹ *noun* 1 a barrier built across a river etc. to hold back water and control its flow or form a reservoir. 2 (*Austral.*) an artificial pond or reservoir. – **dam** *verb* (**dammed**, **damming**) 1 to hold back with a dam. 2 to obstruct (a flow).

dam² *noun* the mother of a four-footed animal. [from *dame*]

damage *noun* 1 something done or suffered that reduces the value or usefulness of the thing affected or spoils its appearance. 2 (*informal*) the cost or charge, *what's the damage?* – **damage** *verb* to cause damage to. **damages** *plural noun* money claimed or paid as compensation for an injury.

Damascus the capital of Syria.

damask (**dam**-ăsk) *noun* silk or linen material woven with a pattern that is visible on either side. □ **damask rose** an old sweet-scented variety of rose.

dame *noun* 1 Dame the title of a woman who has been awarded an order of knighthood (corresponding to the title of *Sir* for a knight). 2 (*old use* or *Amer. informal*) a woman. 3 a comic female character in pantomime, usually played by a man. [from Latin *domina* = lady]

damn *verb* 1 to condemn to eternal punishment in hell; *I'll be damned*, (*informal*) I am astonished. 2 to condemn as a failure. 3 to swear at, to curse. – **damn** *interjection* an exclamation of anger or annoyance; *let's go, and damn the expense*, never mind the expense. [from Latin *damnare* = condemn]

damnable *adjective* hateful, annoying. **damnably** *adverb*

damnation *noun* being damned or condemned to hell. – **damnation** *interjection* an exclamation of anger or annoyance.

Damocles (**dam**-ŏ-kleez) *noun* sword of Damocles imminent danger. [from the story of Damocles, a Greek of the 4th century BC, above whose head a sword was once hung by a hair while he ate]

damp *noun* 1 moisture in the air or on a surface or throughout something. 2 foul or explosive gas in a mine. – **damp** *adjective* slightly or moderately wet. – **damp** *verb* 1 to make damp. 2 to make sad or dull, to discourage, *damped their enthusiasm*. 3 to reduce the vibration of (a string in music). □ **damp course** a layer of waterproof material built into a wall near the ground to prevent damp from rising. **damp down** to heap ashes on (a fire) to make it burn more slowly. **damply** *adverb*, **dampness** *noun*

dampen *verb* to damp.

damper *noun* 1 a movable metal plate that regulates the flow of air into the fire in a stove or furnace. 2 an influence that damps or discourages enthusiasm, *cast a damper over the proceedings*. 3 a felt pad that presses against a piano string to stop it vibrating. 4 (*Austral.*) an unleavened bread often baked in ashes.

Dampier, William (1652–1715), English explorer and buccaneer who twice sailed round the world; the first Englishman known to have set foot on Australian soil (on the north-west coast).

damsel (**dam**-zĕl) *noun* (*old use*) a young woman.

damson *noun* 1 a small dark purple plum. 2 the tree that bears this. 3 dark purple.

dan *noun* 1 a degree of proficiency in judo, karate, etc. 2 one who reaches this.

Danaë (**dan**-ă-ee) (*Gk. myth.*) the mother of Perseus by Zeus, who visited her in the form of a shower of gold.

dance *verb* 1 to move with rhythmical steps or movements, usually to music; to perform in this way. 2 to move in a quick or lively way; to bob up and down. – **dance** *noun* 1 a piece of dancing. 2 a piece of music for dancing to. 3 a social gathering for the purpose of dancing. **dancer** *noun*

dandelion *noun* a wild plant with bright yellow flowers. [from French *dent-de-lion* = tooth of a lion]

dandle *verb* to dance (a child) in one's arms or on one's knee.

dandruff *noun* flakes of scurf on the scalp and amongst the hair.

dandy *noun* a man who pays excessive attention to the smartness of his appearance and clothes. –**dandy** *adjective* (*informal*) smart; very satisfactory. ☐ **dandy brush** a stiff brush for cleaning horses.

Dane *noun* 1 a native of Denmark. 2 a Scandinavian invader of England in the 9th–11th centuries.

Danegeld *noun* a land tax levied in Anglo-Saxon England, originally to bribe the invading Danes to go away. [from *Dane*, + Old Norse *gjald* = payment]

Danelaw *noun* the north-eastern part of England that was settled or held by the Danes from the late 9th century until after the Norman Conquest.

danger *noun* 1 liability or exposure to harm or death. 2 a thing that causes this.

dangerous *adjective* involving or causing danger. **dangerously** *adverb*

dangle *verb* 1 to hang loosely. 2 to hold or carry (a thing) so that it swings loosely. 3 to hold out (hopes) to a person temptingly.

Daniel 1 a Hebrew prophet saved by God when he was thrown into the lions' den. 2 the book of the Old Testament named after him.

Danish *adjective* of Denmark or its people or language. –**Danish** *noun* the language of Denmark.

dank *adjective* unpleasantly damp and cold.

Dante (**dan**-tay) (1265–1321) Italian poet and philosopher, author of the *Divine Comedy*.

Danube a river in central and SE Europe, that rises in the Black Forest and flows into the Black Sea.

daphne (**daf**-nee) *noun* a kind of flowering shrub.

dapper *noun* neat and smart in dress and appearance, *a dapper little man*.

dapple *verb* to mark with spots or patches of shade or a different colour. ☐ **dapple-grey** *adjective* grey with darker markings.

Dardanelles (dar-dǎ-**nelz**) a narrow strait between Europe and Asiatic Turkey, called

the Hellespont in ancient times, the scene, on Gallipoli Peninsula, of the unsuccessful campaign against Turkey by Anzac and other forces in 1915.

dare *verb* 1 to have the courage or impudence to do something, to be bold enough, *he didn't dare go* or *dare to go*. 2 to take the risk of, to face as a danger. 3 to challenge (a person) to do something risky. –**dare** *noun* a challenge to do something risky. ☐ **I dare say** I am prepared to believe; it is very likely, I do not deny it.

daredevil *noun* a recklessly daring person.

daren't = dare not.

daring *noun* boldness. –**daring** *adjective* 1 bold, taking risks boldly. 2 boldly dramatic or unconventional. **daringly** *adverb*

dariole (**da**-ree-ohl) *noun* 1 a savoury or sweet dish cooked in a small mould. 2 the mould itself.

Darius (dǎ-**ry**-ŭs) king of Persia 521–486 BC.

dark *adjective* 1 with little or no light. 2 (of colour) of a deep shade closer to black than to white, *dark grey*; *a dark suit*. 3 (of people) having a brown or black skin; having dark hair. 4 gloomy, cheerless, dismal, *the long dark years of the war*. 5 secret, *keep it dark*. 6 mysterious, remote and unexplored, *in darkest Africa*. –**dark** *noun* 1 absence of light. 2 a time of darkness, night or nightfall, *out after dark*. 3 a dark colour. ☐ **Dark Ages** the early part of the Middle Ages in Europe (about 500–1100), when learning and culture had declined. **Dark Continent** Africa, at the time when the continent was little known to Europeans. **dark horse** a competitor of whose abilities little is known before the contest. **in the dark** having no information about something. **darkly** *adverb*, **darkness** *noun*

darken *verb* to make or become dark or darker. ☐ **never darken a person's door** to stay away from him or her because one is unwelcome.

darkroom *noun* a room where light is excluded so that photographs can be processed.

Darling a river of SE Australia, flowing into the Murray. ☐ **Darling shower** a dust storm.

Darling Downs a fertile low-lying area in SE Queensland.

darling *noun* 1 a dearly loved or lovable person or thing, a favourite. 2 (*informal*) something charming. –**darling** *adjective* dearly loved, (*informal*) charming. [from Old English *deorling* = little dear]

darmstadtium (dahm-**stat**-ee-ŭm) *noun*
a radioactive element produced artificially
(symbol Ds).

darn *verb* to mend by weaving yarn across a
hole. –**darn** *noun* a place mended by darning.
darning *noun* **1** a piece of such mending.
2 things to be darned.

dart *noun* **1** a small pointed missile. **2** a small
metal-tipped object thrown in the game of
darts. **3** a darting movement. **4** a tapering
stitched tuck in a garment. –**dart** *verb*
1 to spring or move suddenly and rapidly in
some direction. **2** to send out rapidly, *darted
an angry look at him.* **darts** *noun* an indoor
game in which darts are thrown at a dartboard.

dartboard *noun* a circular board used as a
target in the game of darts.

darter *noun* a large waterbird having a narrow
head and long thin neck.

Dartmoor 1 a moorland district in SW
England. **2** a prison near Princetown in this
district.

Darwin[1] the capital of the Northern Territory.
[named after Charles Darwin]

Darwin[2], Charles Robert (1809–82), English
naturalist who put forward the theory (known
as the **Darwinian theory** or **Darwinism**) of
evolution by natural selection.

dash *verb* **1** to run rapidly, to rush. **2** to knock
or drive or throw (a thing) with force against
something, to shatter (a thing) in this way; *our
hopes were dashed*, were destroyed. **3** to write
hastily, *dashed off a letter*. –**dash** *noun*
1 a short rapid run, a rush. **2** a small amount
of liquid or flavouring added. **3** a dashboard.
4 energy, vigour. **5** lively spirit or appearance.
6 the punctuation mark (–) used to show a
break in sense. **7** the longer of the two signals
used in the Morse code.

dashboard *noun* a board below the
windscreen in a motor vehicle, carrying
various instruments and controls.

dashing *adjective* spirited, showy.

dastardly *adjective* contemptible and
cowardly.

dasyure (**das**-ee-yoor *or* **daz**-) *noun* a small
carnivorous catlike marsupial, an Australian
native cat. [from Greek *dasus* = rough, + *oura*
= tail]

data (**day**-tă *or* **dah**-tă) *plural noun* facts
or information to be used as a basis for
discussing or deciding something, or prepared
for being processed by a computer etc.

☐ **data bank** a large store of computerised
data. **data capture** the process of putting data
into a form that is accessible by computer.
data processing the performance of operations
on data, especially using a computer, to obtain
information, solutions to problems, etc. **data
protection** the process of ensuring that data
held in computer storage cannot be accessed
except by legally authorised persons.

Usage This word is now often used with a
singular verb (like 'information'), especially in
the context of computers, e.g. *the data is entered
here*, but it is by origin a Latin plural (the
singular is *datum*) and in other contexts should
be used (like 'facts') with a plural verb, *these
data are from official sources*.

---

database *noun* a structured store of
computerised data, usually comprising a
number of files.

datable *adjective* able to be dated.

date[1] *noun* **1** the day on which something
happened or was written or is to happen etc.;
a statement of this in terms of day, month, and
year (or any of these). **2** the period to which
something belongs, *objects of prehistoric
date*. **3** (*informal*) an appointment to meet
socially. **4** (*informal*) a person of the opposite
sex with whom one has a social engagement.
–**date** *verb* **1** to mark with a date. **2** to assign
a date to. **3** to originate from a particular
date, *the custom dates from Victorian times*.
4 to show up the age of, to show signs of
becoming out of date, *dated fashions*; *some
fashions date quickly*. **5** (*informal*) to make a
social engagement (with). ☐ **Date Line** (in full
International Date Line) a line from north to
south roughly along the meridian 180° from
Greenwich, east of which the date is one day
earlier than it is to the west. **out of date** *see
out*. **to date** until now, *here are our sales
figures to date*. **up to date** *see up*. [from Latin
data = given (at a certain time)]

date[2] *noun* the small brown sweet edible fruit
of the **date palm**, a palm tree of N Africa and
SW Asia.

dative *noun* the grammatical case of a word
expressing the indirect object or a recipient,
e.g. *me* in 'give me the book'. [same origin
as *datum*]

datum (**day**-tŭm *or* **dah**-tŭm) *noun* **1** (*plural*
data; see the entry for **data**) an item of
information; a unit of data. **2** (*plural* **datums**)
the starting point from which something is

measured or calculated. ☐ **datum line** a set horizontal line from which measurements are taken. [Latin, = thing given]

daub *verb* to cover or smear roughly with a soft substance; to paint clumsily. –**daub** *noun* **1** a clumsily-painted picture. **2** a covering or smear of something soft.

daughter *noun* **1** a female child in relation to her parents. **2** a female descendant. ☐ **daughter-in-law** *noun* (*plural* **daughters-in-law**) a son's wife.

daunt *verb* to make afraid or discouraged; *nothing daunted*, not discouraged.

dauntless *adjective* brave, not to be daunted. **dauntlessly** *adverb*

dauphin (**daw**-fĭn) *noun* the title borne by the eldest son of the king of France in the days when France was ruled by a king.

David¹ king of the Hebrews after Saul.

David², St 6th century, the patron saint of Wales, Feast day, 1 March.

da Vinci *see* Leonardo da Vinci.

Davis an Australian Antarctic research base.

Davis Cup an annual award for a men's international tennis team competition, donated by a leading American player, Dwight F. Davis, in 1900.

davit (**dav**-ĭt) *noun* a kind of small crane on board ship.

Davy, Sir Humphry (1778–1829), English chemist. ☐ **Davy lamp** a type of safety lamp for miners, invented by Davy in 1816.

Davy Jones (*informal*) the evil spirit of the sea. ☐ **Davy Jones's locker** the bottom of the sea thought of as the graveyard of those who are drowned or buried at sea.

dawdle *verb* to walk slowly and idly, to take one's time. **dawdler** *noun*

dawn *noun* **1** the first light of day. **2** the beginning, *the dawn of civilisation*. –**dawn** *verb* **1** to begin to grow light. **2** to begin to appear or become evident.

day *noun* **1** the time during which the sun is above the horizon. **2** the time for one rotation of the earth; a period of 24 hours, especially from one midnight to the next. **3** the hours given to work, *an eight-hour day*. **4** a specified or appointed day, *their wedding day*. **5** a period, time, or era, *in the days of steam engines*; *in my young days*, when I was young. **6** a period of success; *colonialism has had its day*, its successful period is over. **7** victory in a contest, *win the day*.

☐ **day boy**, **day girl** a pupil travelling daily from home to school, especially to a boarding school. **day by day** each day; progressively. **day care** care of preschool children during the day. **day centre** a place where social and other facilities are provided for elderly or handicapped people during the day. **day in, day out** every day, unceasingly. **day school** a school where the pupils live at home, not a boarding school.

daybook *noun* a book in which sales are noted as they take place, being transferred later to a ledger.

daybreak *noun* the first light of day, dawn.

daydream *noun* idle and pleasant thoughts. –**daydream** *verb* to have daydreams.

daylight *noun* **1** the light of day. **2** dawn. ☐ **daylight saving** the system of putting forward the time shown by clocks to give longer evening daylight in summer. **see daylight** to begin to understand what was previously puzzling.

daytime *noun* the time of daylight.

daze *verb* to make (a person) feel stunned or bewildered. –**daze** *noun* a dazed state.

dazzle *verb* **1** to make (a person) unable to see clearly because of too much bright light. **2** to amaze and impress or confuse (a person) by a splendid display. –**dazzle** *noun* bright confusing light.

dB *abbreviation* decibels.

DC *abbreviation* **1** (also **dc**) direct current. **2** District of Columbia (as in *Washington DC*).

D-Day *noun* **1** the day (6 June 1944) on which British, American, and other allied forces invaded northern France in the Second World War. **2** the date on which an important operation is planned to begin.

DDT *noun* a white chlorinated hydrocarbon used as an insecticide.

de- *prefix* **1** removing (as in *defrost*). **2** down, away (as in *descend*). **3** completely (as in *denude*). [from Latin *de* = away from]

deacon *noun* **1** a member of the clergy ranking below a priest. **2** (in Nonconformist churches) a lay person attending to church business. **deaconess** *noun* a woman with certain similar duties. [from Greek *diakonos* = servant]

dead *adjective* **1** no longer alive. **2** numb, without feeling. **3** no longer used, *a dead language*. **4** lifeless and without lustre, resonance, or warmth; *a dead match*, already struck and burnt out. **5** no longer active or functioning, *the microphone went dead*. **6** dull; without interest, movement, or activity, *the city is dead on Sundays*. **7** (of a ball in games) out of play. **8** complete, abrupt, exact, *dead silence*; *a dead stop*; *dead centre*; *he is a dead shot*, shoots very accurately. **–dead** *adverb* completely, exactly, *dead drunk*; *dead level*. **–dead** *noun* an inactive or silent time, *the dead of night*. □ **dead cat bounce** a temporary recovery in share prices after a substantial fall. **dead end** the closed end of a road or passage, a blind alley. **dead-end job** a job with no prospects of advancement. **dead heat** the result of a race in which two or more competitors finish exactly even. **dead-heat** *verb* to finish in a dead heat. **dead letter** a rule or law that is no longer observed; an unclaimed or undelivered letter. **dead loss** (*informal*) a useless person or thing; a complete loss or failure. **dead man's handle** a controlling device (on a train etc.) that disconnects the driving power if it is released. **dead march** a funeral march. **dead reckoning** calculating a ship's position by log and compass etc. when observations are impossible. **dead set** a determined attack; *make a dead set at a person*, try to attract him or her. **dead weight** a heavy inert weight.

deaden *verb* to deprive of or lose vitality, loudness, feeling, etc.

deadline *noun* a time limit. [originally this meant the line round a military prison beyond which a prisoner was liable to be shot]

deadlock *noun* a complete standstill or lack of progress. **–deadlock** *verb* to reach a deadlock; to cause to do this.

deadly *adjective* (**deadlier**, **deadliest**) **1** causing or capable of causing fatal injury, death, or serious damage. **2** deathlike, *a deadly silence*. **3** (*informal*) very dreary. **–deadly** *adverb* **1** as if dead, *deadly pale*. **2** extremely, *deadly serious*. □ **deadly nightshade** a plant with poisonous black berries. **the seven deadly sins** those that result in damnation for a person's soul (traditionally pride, covetousness, lust, envy, gluttony, anger, sloth). **deadliness** *noun*

deadpan *adjective* & *adverb* with an expressionless face.

Dead Sea an inland salt lake in the Jordan valley on the Israel-Jordan border. □ **Dead Sea scrolls** a collection of ancient Hebrew and Aramaic manuscripts discovered (chiefly in fragments) in caves near the Dead Sea between 1947 and 1956.

deaf *adjective* **1** wholly or partly without the sense of hearing, unable to hear. **2** refusing to listen, *deaf to all advice*. □ **deaf mute** a person who is both deaf and dumb. **deafness** *noun*

deafen *verb* to make deaf or unable to hear by a very loud noise.

deal[1] *verb* (**dealt**, **dealing**) **1** to distribute among several people; to hand out (cards) to players in a card game. **2** to give, to inflict, *dealt him a severe blow*. **3** to do business, to trade. **–deal** *noun* **1** dealing; a player's turn to deal; a round of play after dealing. **2** a business transaction, *the deal fell through*; *it's a deal*, I agree to this. **3** treatment, *didn't get a fair deal*. **4** (*informal*) a large amount. □ **a good deal**, **a great deal** a large amount. **deal with** to do business with; to take action about or be what is needed by (a problem etc.); to discuss (a subject) in a book or speech etc. **dealer** *noun*

deal[2] *noun* sawn fir or pine timber.

dealings *plural noun* a person's transactions with another.

dean *noun* **1** a member of the clergy who is head of a cathedral chapter. **2** a college or university official, responsible for the organisation of studies or for discipline; the head of a university faculty, department, or medical school.

deanery *noun* **1** the position of dean. **2** a dean's official residence.

dear *adjective* **1** much loved, cherished. **2** esteemed; *Dear Sir*, a polite phrase beginning a letter. **3** costing more than it is worth, not cheap. **–dear** *noun* a dear person. **–dear** *adverb* dearly, at a high price. **–dear** *interjection* an exclamation of surprise or distress. **dearly** *adverb*, **dearness** *noun*

dearth (*pr.* derth) *noun* a scarcity.

death *noun* **1** the process of dying, the end of life; final cessation of vital functions. **2** the state of being dead. **3** a cause of death, *drink was the death of him*. **4** the ending or destruction of something, *the death of our hopes*. □ **at death's door** close to death. **death adder** a venomous Australian snake. **death certificate** an official statement of the date, place, and cause of a person's death. **death duty** tax levied on property after the owner's death. **death penalty** punishment for a crime by being put to death. **death rate** the number of deaths in one year for every 1000 persons. **death row** a prison area housing prisoners sentenced to death. **death toll** the number of those killed in an accident, battle, etc. **death trap** a dangerous place. **death warrant** an order for the execution of a condemned person; something that causes the end of an established practice etc. **death-watch beetle** a beetle whose larva bores holes in old wood and makes a ticking sound formerly supposed to be a sign of an imminent death. **death wish** a desire (usually unconscious) for the death of oneself or another person. **put to death** to kill, to execute. **to death** extremely, to the utmost limit, *bored to death*. **to the death** until one or other is killed, *a fight to the death*.

deathbed *noun* the bed on which a person dies or is dying.

deathless *adjective* immortal.

deathly *adjective & adverb* like death, *a deathly hush; deathly pale*.

debacle (day-**bahkl**) *noun* (also **débâcle**) a sudden disastrous collapse. [from French *débâcler* = unbar]

debar *verb* (**debarred**, **debarring**) to exclude, to prohibit.

debark *verb* to disembark. **debarkation** *noun*

debase *verb* to lower in quality or value; to reduce the value of (coins) by using an alloy or inferior metal. **debasement** *noun*

debatable *adjective* questionable, open to dispute. **debatably** *adverb*

debate *noun* a formal discussion. –**debate** *verb* **1** to hold a debate about. **2** to discuss, to consider.

debauch (dĕ-**bawch**) *verb* to make dissolute, to lead into debauchery.

debauchery (dĕ-**bawch**-ĕ-ree) *noun* over-indulgence in harmful or immoral pleasures.

debenture (dĕ-**ben**-cher) *noun* a certificate or bond acknowledging a debt on which fixed interest is being paid. [from Latin *debentur* = they are owed]

debilitate *verb* to cause debility in.

debility *noun* feebleness, weakness.

debit *noun* **1** an entry in an account book of a sum owed by the holder. **2** the sum itself; the total of such sums. –**debit** *verb* (**debited**, **debiting**) to enter as a debit in an account. □ **debit card** a card enabling funds to be transferred electronically from the holder's bank account to another, e.g. when making

a purchase. [from Latin *debitum* = what is owed]

debonair (deb-ŏ-**nair**) *adjective* having a carefree self-confident manner. [from French *de bon air* = of good disposition]

debrief *verb* (*informal*) to question (a person) in order to obtain information about a mission just completed.

debris (**deb**-ree) *noun* scattered broken pieces. [from French *débris* = broken down]

debt *noun* something owed by one person to another. □ **in debt** owing something. [same origin as *debit*]

debtor *noun* a person who owes money to another.

debug *verb* (**debugged**, **debugging**) **1** to free from bugs (= insects). **2** (*informal*) to remove concealed listening devices from (a room etc.) or defects from (a machine, computer program or system, etc.).

debunk *verb* (*informal*) to show up (a claim or theory, or a good reputation) as exaggerated or false.

Debussy (dĕ-**bew**-see), Achille-Claude (1862–1918), French composer.

debut (**day**-bew) *noun* (also **début**) a first public appearance. [from French *débuter* = begin]

debutante (**deb**-yŭ-tont) *noun* (also **débutante**) a young woman making her first appearance in society.

deca- *prefix* ten (as in *decathlon*). [from Greek *deka* = ten]

decade (**dek**-ayd) *noun* a period of ten years.

decadent (**dek**-ă-dĕnt) *adjective* **1** becoming less worthy, deteriorating in standard. **2** self-indulgent. **decadence** *noun* [same origin as *decay*]

decaffeinated (dee-**kaf**-ĭ-nayt-ĕd) *adjective* with the caffeine removed or reduced.

decagon *noun* a geometric figure with ten sides. **decagonal** (dĕ-**kag**-ŏ-năl) *adjective* [from *deca-*, + Greek *gonia* = angle]

Decalogue (**dek**-ă-log) *noun* the Ten Commandments. [from *deca-*, + Greek *logos* = word]

decamp *verb* **1** to break up camp; to leave camp. **2** to go away suddenly or secretly.

decant (dĕ-**kant**) *verb* **1** to pour (liquid) gently from one container to another without disturbing the sediment. **2** (*informal*) to transfer from one place to another.

decanter (dĕ-**kant**-er) *noun* a stoppered glass bottle into which wine etc. may be decanted before serving.

decapitate (dĕ-**kap**-ĭ-tayt) *verb* to behead. **decapitation** *noun* [from *de-*, + Latin *caput* = head]

decapod (**dek**-ă-pod) *noun* a crustacean with ten feet, e.g. a crab. [from *deca-*, + Greek *podos* = of the foot]

decarbonise *verb* (also **-ize**) to remove the carbon deposit from (an engine etc.). **decarbonisation** *noun*

decathlon (dĕ-**kath**-lŏn) *noun* an athletic contest in which each competitor takes part in the ten events it includes. [from *deca-*, + Greek *athlon* = contest]

decay *verb* 1 to become rotten; to cause to rot. 2 to lose quality or strength. 3 (of a substance) to undergo change by radioactivity; (of an atomic nucleus or particle) to change spontaneously into another or others. **–decay** *noun* 1 decaying, rot. 2 decayed tissue. 3 radioactive decay. [from *de-*, + Latin *cadere* = to fall]

decease (dĕ-**seess**) *noun* (*formal*) death.

deceased *adjective* dead; *the deceased*, the person(s) who died recently.

deceit *noun* deceiving, a deception.

deceitful *adjective* deceiving people. **deceitfully** *adverb*, **deceitfulness** *noun*

deceive *verb* 1 to cause (a person) to believe something that is not true. 2 to be sexually unfaithful to. ☐ **deceive oneself** to persist in a mistaken belief. **deceiver** *noun*

decelerate (dee-**sel**-ĕ-rayt) *verb* to cause to slow down; to decrease one's speed. **deceleration** *noun*

December *noun* the twelfth month of the year. [from Latin *decem* = ten, because it was the tenth month of the ancient Roman calendar]

decency *noun* being decent. ☐ **the decencies** the requirements of respectable behaviour in society.

decent *adjective* 1 conforming to the accepted standards of what is proper, not immodest or obscene. 2 respectable, *ordinary decent people*. 3 (*informal*) quite good, *earns a decent salary*. 4 (*informal*) kind, generous, obliging. **decently** *adverb*

decentralise *verb* (also **-ize**) to divide and distribute (powers etc.) from a central authority to places or branches away from the centre. **decentralisation** *noun*

deception *noun* 1 deceiving; being deceived. 2 something that deceives people.

deceptive *adjective* deceiving; easily mistaken for something else. **deceptively** *adverb*

deci- (dess-ee) *prefix* one tenth part, as in *decigram, decilitre*. [same origin as *decimal*]

decibel (**dess**-ĭ-bĕl) *noun* a unit for measuring the relative loudness of sound. [originally one-tenth of the unit called a *bel*]

decide *verb* 1 to think about and make a choice or judgment; to come to a decision. 2 to settle by giving victory to one side, *this goal decided the match*. 3 to cause to reach a decision, *that decided me*. **decider** *noun*

decided *adjective* 1 having clear opinions; determined. 2 clear, definite, *a decided difference*. **decidedly** *adverb*

deciduous (dĕ-**sid**-yoo-ŭs) *adjective* 1 (of a tree) shedding its leaves annually. 2 falling off or shed after a time, *a deer has deciduous antlers*. [from Latin *decidere* = fall off]

decile (**dess**-I'l) *noun* 1 any of the points at which a range of statistical data is divided to make ten equal groups. 2 any of these groups.

decimal (**dess**-ĭ-măl) *adjective* reckoned in tens or tenths. **–decimal** *noun* a decimal fraction. ☐ **decimal currency** currency in which each unit is ten or one hundred times the value of the one next below it. **decimal fraction** a fraction whose denominator is a power of ten, expressed in figures after a dot (the **decimal point**), e.g. $0.5 = \frac{5}{10}$, $0.52 = \frac{52}{100}$. **decimal places** the number of figures after the decimal point in a decimal fraction. **decimal system** a system of weights and measures with each unit ten times that immediately below it. [from Latin *decimus* = tenth]

decimalise *verb* (also **-ize**) 1 to express as a decimal. 2 to convert to a decimal system. **decimalisation** *noun*

decimate (**dess**-ĭ-mayt) *verb* to destroy one-tenth of; (loosely) to destroy a large proportion of. **decimation** *noun* [Latin, from the practice of putting to death one in every ten of a body of soldiers guilty of mutiny or other crime–a practice in the ancient Roman army, sometimes followed in later times]

decipher (dĕ-**sy**-fer) *verb* to make out the meaning of (a coded message, bad handwriting, or something difficult to interpret). **decipherment** *noun*

decision *noun* **1** deciding, making a reasoned judgment about something. **2** the judgment itself. **3** the ability to form clear opinions and act on them.

decisive (dĕ-**sy**-siv) *adjective* **1** settling something conclusively, *a decisive battle*. **2** showing decision and firmness. **decisively** *adverb*

deck *noun* **1** any of the horizontal floors in a ship. **2** a similar floor or platform, especially one of two or more, *a sun deck*; *the top deck of a bus*. **3** a component of a sound system for playing discs or tapes, or for making recordings. **4** a pack of cards. –**deck** *verb* **1** to decorate, to dress up, *decked with flags*; *decked out in her finest clothes*. **2** (*informal*) knock (a person) to the ground; punch.

deckchair *noun* a portable folding chair of canvas on a wood or metal frame.

declaim (dĕ-**klaym**) *verb* to speak or say impressively or dramatically. **declamation** (dek-lă-**may**-shŏn) *noun* [from *de-*, + Latin *clamare* = to shout]

declare *verb* **1** to make known; to announce openly, formally, or explicitly. **2** to state firmly, *he declares that he is innocent*. **3** to inform customs officials that one has (goods) on which duty may be payable. **4** to choose to close one's side's innings at cricket before ten wickets have fallen. ☐ **declare war** to announce that a state of war exists. **declaration** *noun*, **declarative** *adjective*, **declaratory** *adjective* [from *de-*, + Latin *clarare* = make clear]

declension *noun* **1** variation of the form of a noun, adjective, or pronoun to give its grammatical case; the class by which a noun etc. is declined. **2** decrease, deterioration. [same origin as *decline*]

declination (dek-li-**nay**-shŏn) *noun* **1** a downward turn or bend. **2** the angle between the true north and the magnetic north. **3** the angle between the direction of a star etc. and the celestial equator.

decline *verb* **1** to refuse. **2** to slope downwards. **3** to decrease, to lose strength or vigour; *one's declining years*, old age. **4** to give the forms of (a noun or adjective) corresponding to the grammatical cases. –**decline** *noun* a gradual decrease or loss of strength. ☐ **in decline** decreasing. [from *de-*, + Latin *clinare* = to bend]

declivity (dĕ-**kliv**-ĭ-tee) *noun* a downward slope.

decoction *noun* boiling down to extract an essence; the extract itself. [from *de-*, + Latin *coctum* = cooked]

decode *verb* to put (a coded message) into plain language; (in computing, engineering, etc.) to reverse an encoding procedure in order to retrieve the original information.

decoder *noun* a person or device that decodes messages, signals, etc.

décolleté (day-**kol**-tay) *adjective* having a low neckline. **décolletage** (day-**kol**-tah*zh*) *noun* [French]

decompose *verb* **1** to decay; to cause to decay. **2** to separate (a substance) into its elements. **decomposition** *noun*

decompress *verb* to subject to decompression.

decompression *noun* **1** release from compression. **2** the gradual and safe reduction of air pressure on a person who has been in compressed air. ☐ **decompression chamber** an enclosed space where this can be done.

decongestant (dee-kŏn-**jest**-ănt) *noun* a medicinal substance that relieves congestion.

deconstruct *verb* to dismantle (especially literary text) to reveal its inner tensions. **deconstruction** *noun*, **deconstructionism** *noun*, **deconstructionist** *adjective* & *noun*

decontaminate *verb* to rid of radioactive or other contamination. **decontamination** *noun*

decontrol *verb* (**decontrolled**, **decontrolling**) to release from government control. –**decontrol** *noun* decontrolling.

decor (**day**-kor) *noun* (also **décor**) the style of furnishings and decoration used in a room etc. [French (compare *decorate*)]

decorate *verb* **1** to make (a thing) look attractive or striking or festive with objects or details added for this purpose. **2** to put fresh paint or paper on the walls etc. of. **3** to confer a medal or other award upon. [from Latin *decor* = beauty]

decoration *noun* **1** decorating. **2** something that decorates. **3** a medal etc. awarded and worn as an honour. **decorations** *plural noun* flags and other decorative objects put up on festive occasions.

decorative (**dek**-ŏ-rătiv) *adjective* ornamental, pleasing to look at. **decoratively** *adverb*

decorator *noun* a person who decorates, especially one whose job is to paint and paper houses.

decorous (**dek**-ŏ-rŭs) *adjective* showing decorum; polite and well-behaved, decent. **decorously** *adverb*

decorum (dĕ-**kor**-rŭm) *noun* correctness and dignity of behaviour or procedure etc.

decoy (**dee**-koi) *noun* something used to lure an animal or person into a trap or situation of danger. –**decoy** (dĕ-**koi**) *verb* to lure by means of a decoy.

decrease *verb* to make or become shorter, smaller, or fewer. –**decrease** *noun* 1 decreasing. 2 the amount by which something decreases. [from *de-*, + Latin *crescere* = grow]

decree *noun* 1 an order given by a government or other authority and having the force of a law. 2 a judgment or decision of certain lawcourts. –**decree** *verb* (**decreed, decreeing**) to order by decree. □ **decree nisi** (*pr.* **ny**-sy) a provisional order for divorce, made absolute unless cause to the contrary is shown within a fixed period.

decrepit (dĕ-**krep**-ĭt) *adjective* made weak by old age or hard use, dilapidated. [from Latin, = creaking]

decrepitude *noun* the state of being decrepit.

decriminalise *verb* (also -ize) to pass a law causing (an action etc.) to cease to be treated as a crime. **decriminalisation** *noun*

decry (dĕ-**kry**) *verb* (**decried, decrying**) to disparage.

dedicate *verb* 1 to devote to a sacred person or use, *this church is dedicated to St Peter*. 2 to devote (one's time, energy, and loyalty) to a special purpose. 3 (of an author etc.) to address (a book or piece of music etc.) to a person as a compliment, putting his or her name at the beginning. **dedication** *noun*, **dedicator** *noun*

dedicated *adjective* 1 devoted to a vocation, cause, etc., *a dedicated scientist*. 2 having single-minded loyalty.

dedicatory (**ded**-ĭ-kayt-ŏ-ree) *adjective* making a dedication, *a dedicatory inscription*.

deduce (dĕ-**dewss**) *verb* to arrive at (knowledge or a conclusion) by reasoning from observed facts. **deducible** *adjective* [from *de-*, + Latin *ducere* = to lead]

deduct *verb* to take away (an amount or quantity), to subtract. **deductible** *adjective*

deduction *noun* 1 deducting; something that is deducted. 2 deducing; a conclusion reached by reasoning. 3 logical reasoning that something must be true because it is a particular case of a general law that is known to be true.

deductive *adjective* based on reasoning.

deed *noun* 1 something done, an act. 2 a written or printed legal agreement, especially one giving ownership or rights, bearing the giver's signature and seal. □ **deed box** a strongbox for holding deeds and other documents. **deed poll** a deed made by one party only, making a formal declaration, especially to change a name.

deem *noun* (*formal*) to believe, to consider, to judge.

deep *adjective* 1 going or situated far down or back or in, *a deep cut*; *deep cupboards*; *a deep sigh*, coming from far down. 2 (in cricket) distant from the batsman. 3 intense, extreme, *a deep sleep*; *deep colours*, strong in tone. 4 low-pitched and resonant, not shrill, *a deep voice*. 5 fully absorbed or overwhelmed, *deep in thought*. 6 heartfelt, *deep sympathy*. 7 difficult to understand, obscure, *that's too deep for me*; *he's a deep one*, (*informal*) he is secretive and not easy to know. –**deep** *adverb* deeply, far down or in. –**deep** *noun* a deep place or state; *the deep*, the sea. □ **deep-fry** *verb* to fry (food) in fat that covers it. **deep-seated** *adjective* firmly established, not superficial, *a deep-seated fear*. **Deep South** the States in the south-eastern USA. **deep space** the far distant regions beyond the earth's atmosphere or those beyond the solar system. **go off the deep end** (*informal*) to give way to emotion or anger. **deeply** *adverb*, **deepness** *noun*

deepen *verb* to make or become deep or deeper.

deep-freeze *noun* a freezer. –**deep-freeze** *verb* (**deep-froze, deep-frozen, deep-freezing**) to store in a deep-freeze.

deer *noun* (*plural* **deer**) a ruminant swift-footed animal, the male of which usually has antlers.

deerskin *noun* leather made from a deer's skin.

deerstalker *noun* a soft cloth cap with one peak in front and another at the back.

deface *verb* to spoil or damage the surface of. **defacement** *noun*

de facto (dee **fak**-toh) *adjective* existing in fact (whether by right or not). –**de facto** *noun* a person living with another as if married. [Latin]

defalcation (dee-fal-**kay**-shǒn) *noun* misappropriation of funds; a breach of trust concerning money. **defalcator** *noun*

defamatory (dě-**fam**-ǎ-tǒ-ree) *adjective* defaming.

defame (dě-**faym**) *verb* to attack the good reputation of, to speak ill of. **defamation** (def-ǎ-**may**-shǒn) *noun*

default *verb* to fail to fulfil one's obligations. –**default** *noun* failure to fulfil an obligation or to appear; *they won by default*, because the other side did not appear; *in default of this*, if this does not take place; since it is not here. **defaulter** *noun*

defeat *verb* **1** to win a victory over. **2** to cause to fail, to frustrate, *this defeats our hopes for reform*. **3** to baffle, *the problem defeats me*. –**defeat** *noun* **1** defeating others. **2** being defeated; a lost battle or contest.

defeatist *noun* a person who expects to be defeated or accepts defeat too easily. **defeatism** *noun*

defecate (**def**-ě-kayt) *verb* to discharge waste matter from the bowels. **defecation** *noun*

defect (**dee**-fekt) *noun* a deficiency, an imperfection. –**defect** (dě-**fekt**) *verb* to desert one's country; to abandon one's allegiance to a cause. **defection** *noun*, **defector** *noun*

defective *adjective* **1** having defects, imperfect, incomplete. **2** mentally deficient. **defectively** *adverb*, **defectiveness** *noun*

defence *noun* **1** defending from or resistance against attack. **2** something that defends or protects against attack. **3** a justification put forward in response to an accusation. **4** the defendant's case in a lawsuit; the lawyer(s) representing an accused person. **5** the players in a defending position in a game. **defensible** *adjective*, **defensibly** *adverb*

defenceless *adjective* having no defence, unable to defend oneself.

defend *verb* **1** to protect by warding off an attack. **2** to try to preserve; *the champion is defending his title*, trying to defeat one who challenges him. **3** to uphold by argument, to put forward a justification of. **4** to represent the defendant in a lawsuit.

defendant *noun* a person accused or sued in a lawsuit.

defender *noun* a person who defends something. ☐ **Defender of the Faith** a title (translation of Latin *Fidei defensor*) conferred by the Pope on Henry VIII in 1521 and borne by all subsequent sovereigns.

defensive *adjective* used or done for defence, protective. ☐ **on the defensive** in an attitude of defence; ready to defend oneself against criticism. **defensively** *adverb*

defer[1] *verb* (**deferred**, **deferring**) to put off to a later time, to postpone. ☐ **deferred shares** shares on which dividends are paid only after they have been paid on all other shares. **deferment** *noun* [same origin as *differ*]

defer[2] *verb* (**deferred**, **deferring**) to give way to a person's wishes, judgment, or authority, to yield. [from Latin *deferre* = to grant]

deference (**def**-ě-rěns) *noun* polite respect; compliance with another person's wishes. ☐ **in deference to** out of respect for.

deferential (def-ě-**ren**-shǎl) *adjective* showing deference. **deferentially** *adverb*

defiance *noun* defying, open disobedience, bold resistance.

defiant *adjective* showing defiance. **defiantly** *adverb*

deficiency (dě-**fish**-ěn-see) *noun* **1** being deficient. **2** a lack or shortage; a thing lacking; the amount by which something falls short of what is required. ☐ **deficiency disease** a disease caused by lack of vitamins or other essential elements in food.

deficient (dě-**fish**-ěnt) *adjective* **1** not having enough, *deficient in vitamins*; *mentally deficient*, see **mental**. **2** insufficient or not present at all.

deficit (**def**-ĭ-sĭt) *noun* **1** the amount by which a total falls short of what is required. **2** the excess of expenditure over income, or of liabilities over assets.

defile[1] (dě-**fyl**) *verb* to make dirty, to pollute. **defilement** *noun* [from an old word *defoul*]

defile[2] (dě-**fyl**) *noun* (also *pr*. **dee**-fyl) a narrow pass through which troops etc. can pass only in file. –**defile** *verb* to march in file.

define *verb* **1** to give the exact meaning of (a word etc.). **2** to state or explain the scope of, *customers' rights are defined by the law*. **3** to outline clearly, to mark out the boundary of. **definable** *adjective* [from *de-*, + Latin *finis* = limit]

definite *adjective* **1** having exact limits. **2** clear and unmistakable, not vague, *I want a* *definite answer.* **3** certain, settled, *is it definite that we are to move?* ☐ **definite article** the word 'the'. **definitely** *adverb*

Usage See the note under **definitive**.

definition *noun* **1** a statement of the exact meaning of a word or phrase, or of the nature of a thing. **2** making or being distinct; clearness of outline.

definitive (dĕ-**fin**-ĭ-tiv) *adjective* finally fixing or settling something, conclusive.

Usage This word is sometimes confused with *definite*. A *definite* offer is one that is clearly stated. A *definitive* offer is one that must be accepted or refused without trying to alter its terms. A *definitive edition* is one with authoritative status.

deflate *verb* **1** to let out air or gas from (an inflated tyre etc.). **2** to cause (a person) to lose confidence or self-esteem. **3** to counteract inflation in (a country's economy), e.g. by reducing the amount of money in circulation. **4** to become deflated. [from *de-* + *inflate*]

deflation *noun* **1** deflating, being deflated. **2** the movement of fine particles of dust or sand (e.g. from sand dunes) by wind.

deflationary *adjective* causing deflation.

deflect *verb* to turn or cause to turn aside. **deflection** *noun*, **deflector** *noun* [from *de-*, + Latin *flectere* = to bend]

deflower *verb* **1** to deprive of virginity. **2** to spoil the perfection of, to ravage.

Defoe (dĕ-**foh**), Daniel (1660–1731), English novelist, author of *Robinson Crusoe* (1719).

defoliant (dĕ-**foh**-lee-ănt) *noun* a chemical substance that destroys foliage.

defoliate (dĕ-**foh**-lee-ayt) *verb* to strip of leaves, to destroy the foliage of by chemical means. **defoliation** *noun* [from *de-*, + Latin *folium* = leaf]

deforest *verb* to clear of trees. **deforestation** *noun*

deform *verb* to spoil the form or appearance of, to put out of shape. **deformation** (dee-for-**may**-shŏn) *noun*

deformed *adjective* badly or abnormally shaped.

deformity *noun* **1** being deformed. **2** a deformed part of the body.

defrag *verb* (**defragged**, **defragging**) short for defragment.

defragment *verb* (in computing) reduce the fragmentation of (a file) by concatenating parts stored in separate locations. **defragmentation** *noun*, **defragmenter** *noun*

defraud *verb* to deprive by fraud.

defray *verb* to provide money to pay (costs or expenses). **defrayal** *noun*

defriend *verb* (*informal*) to delete (someone) from a list of friends or contacts associated with a weblog etc.

defrost *verb* **1** to remove frost or ice from. **2** to unfreeze.

deft *adjective* skilful, handling things neatly. **deftly** *adverb*, **deftness** *noun*

defunct (dĕ-**funkt**) *adjective* **1** dead. **2** no longer existing or used or functioning.

defuse *verb* **1** to remove the fuse of, to make (an explosive) unable to explode. **2** to reduce the dangerous tension in (a situation).

defy *verb* (**defied**, **defying**) **1** to resist openly, to refuse to obey. **2** to challenge (a person) to try and do something that one believes he or she cannot or will not do, *I defy you to prove this.* **3** to offer difficulties that cannot be overcome by, *the door defied all attempts to open it.*

degauss (dee-**gowss**) *verb* to demagnetise. [from *de-*, + the name of K. Gauss, German mathematician]

degenerate (dĕ-**jen**-ĕ-rayt) *verb* to become worse or lower in standard; to lose good qualities. –**degenerate** (dĕ-**jen**-ĕ-răt) *adjective* having degenerated. **degeneracy** *noun*, **degeneration** *noun*

degradable *adjective* able to be broken down by chemical or biological processes.

degrade *verb* **1** to reduce to a lower rank or status. **2** to bring disgrace or contempt on. **3** to decompose. **degradation** (deg-ră-**day**-shŏn) *noun*

degrading *adjective* shaming, humiliating.

degree *noun* **1** a step or stage in an ascending or descending series. **2** a stage in intensity or amount, *a high degree of skill.* **3** an academic rank awarded to a person who has successfully completed a course of study or as an honour. **4** a unit of measurement for angles or arcs, indicated by the symbol °, e.g. 45°. **5** a unit of measurement in a scale e.g. of temperatures. ☐ **by degrees** step by step, gradually.

degustation *noun* **1** tasting something carefully to appreciate it fully. **2** (of a menu) providing a wide variety of foods in small quantities.

dehisce (dĕ-**hiss**) *verb* (especially of seed vessels) to gape, to burst open when ripe. **dehiscence** *noun*, **dehiscent** *adjective* [from *de-*, + Latin *hiscere* = begin to gape]

dehumanise *verb* (also **-ize**) to take away human qualities from; to make impersonal.

dehydrate *verb* **1** to remove the moisture content from. **2** to lose moisture. **dehydration** *noun* [from *de-*, + Greek *hudor* = water]

deify (**dee**-ĭ-fy) *verb* (**deified**, **deifying**) to make a god of; to treat as a god. **deification** *noun*

deign (*pr.* dayn) *verb* to condescend, to be kind or gracious enough to do something, *she did not deign to reply.*

deindustrialisation *noun* (also **-ization**) a decline in the amount of manufacturing industry in a country or area.

deism (**dee**-izm) *noun* belief in the existence of a god (creator of the world) without accepting revelation (see **theism**). **deist** *noun*

deity (**dee**-ĭ-tee) *noun* **1** a god or goddess, *Roman deities*; **the Deity** God. **2** divinity. [from Latin *deus* = god]

déjà vu (day-*zh*a **vew**) *noun* a feeling of having experienced the present situation before. [French, = already seen]

dejected *adjective* in low spirits, depressed. **dejectedly** *adverb* [from *de-*, + Latin *-jectum* = thrown]

dejection *noun* lowness of spirits, depression.

de jure (day **joor**-ray) *adjective & adverb* rightful, by right. [Latin]

Delaware a State of the eastern USA.

delay *verb* **1** to make or be late, to hinder. **2** to put off until later, to postpone. **3** to wait, to linger. – **delay** *noun* **1** delaying, being delayed. **2** the amount of time for which something is delayed. □ **delayed-action** *adjective* operating after an interval of time.

delectable *adjective* delightful, enjoyable. **delectably** *adverb*

delectation (dee-lek-**tay**-shŏn) *noun* enjoyment, delight, *for your delectation.*

delegate (**del**-ĕ-găt) *noun* a person who represents others and acts according to their instructions. – **delegate** (**del**-ĕ-gayt) *verb* **1** to entrust (a task, power, or responsibility)

to an agent. **2** to appoint or send as a representative. [from Latin *delegare* = entrust]

delegation (del-ĕ-**gay**-shŏn) *noun* **1** delegating. **2** a body of delegates.

delete (dĕ-**leet**) *verb* to remove or strike out (something written or printed); to remove a computer record or item of data. **deletion** *noun*

deleterious (del-ĕ-**teer**-ree-ŭs) *adjective* harmful to the body or mind.

delft *noun* (also **delftware**) a kind of glazed earthenware, usually decorated in blue, made at Delft in Holland.

Delhi (**del**-ee) **1** a state in north central India. **2** the capital of India (New Delhi).

deli *noun* (*informal*) **1** a delicatessen. **2** a shop selling sandwiches, drinks, confectionery, newspapers, etc.

deliberate (dĕ-**lib**-ĕ-răt) *adjective* **1** done or said on purpose, intentional. **2** slow and careful, unhurried, *entered with deliberate steps.* – **deliberate** (dĕ-**lib**-ĕ-rayt) *verb* to think over or discuss carefully before reaching a decision. **deliberately** *adverb*

deliberation *noun* **1** careful consideration or discussion. **2** careful slowness.

deliberative (dĕ-**lib**-ĕ-rătiv) *adjective* for the purpose of deliberating or discussing things, *a deliberative assembly.*

delicacy *noun* **1** delicateness. **2** avoidance of what is immodest or offensive or hurtful to others. **3** a choice food.

delicate *adjective* **1** fine in texture, soft, slender. **2** of exquisite quality or workmanship. **3** (of colour or flavour) pleasant and not strong or intense. **4** easily injured, liable to illness, (of plants) unable to withstand cold. **5** requiring careful handling. **6** skilful and sensitive, *has a delicate touch.* **7** taking great care to avoid what is immodest or offensive or hurtful to others. **delicately** *adverb*, **delicateness** *noun*

delicatessen (del-ĭ-kă-**tess**-ĕn) *noun* a shop (or section of a shop) selling smallgoods, cheeses, prepared delicacies, etc. [from German, = delicacies to eat]

delicious *adjective* delightful, especially to the senses of taste or smell. – **delicious** *noun* a variety of apple with red skin. **deliciously** *adverb*

delight *verb* **1** to please greatly. **2** to be greatly pleased, to feel great pleasure, *she delights in giving parties.* – **delight** *noun* **1** great pleasure. **2** something that causes this.

delightful *adjective* giving delight.
  delightfully *adverb*

Delilah (dĕ-**ly**-lă) *noun* a seductive and treacherous woman. [named after a woman in the Bible, who betrayed her husband Samson to the Philistines]

delimit (dee-**lim**-ĭt) *verb* to fix the limits or boundaries of. **delimitation** *noun*

delineate (dĕ-**lin**-ee-ayt) *verb* to show by drawing or by describing. **delineation** *noun*

delinquent (dĕ-**link**-wĕnt) *adjective* committing an offence; failing to perform a duty. **–delinquent** *noun* a delinquent person, especially a young offender against the law. **delinquency** *noun*

deliquesce (del-ĭ-**kwess**) *verb* to become liquid, to melt; to dissolve in moisture absorbed from the air. **deliquescence** *noun*

delirious (dĕ-**li**-ree-ŭs) *adjective* **1** affected with delirium, raving. **2** wildly excited.
  deliriously *adverb*

delirium (dĕ-**li**-ree-ŭm) *noun* **1** a disordered state of mind, especially during feverish illness. **2** wild excitement or emotion. □ **delirium tremens** (**trem**-ĕnz) a form of delirium with tremors and hallucinations, caused by heavy drinking.

deliver *verb* **1** to take (letters or goods etc.) to the addressee or purchaser. **2** to transfer, to hand over, to present. **3** to utter (a speech). **4** to aim or launch (a blow, an attack); to bowl (a ball) in cricket etc. **5** to rescue, to save or set free. **6** to assist at the birth of or in giving birth; *she was delivered of a child*, gave birth to it. **7** to give birth to. **deliverer** *noun* [from *de-*, + Latin *liberare* = to set free]

deliverance *noun* rescue, setting free.

delivery *noun* **1** delivering; being delivered. **2** a periodical distribution of letters or goods etc. **3** the manner of delivering a speech. **4** the manner of bowling or sending a ball in cricket etc.

dell *noun* a small wooded hollow or valley.

Delos (**dee**-loss) a small Greek island regarded as the centre of the Cyclades, legendary birthplace of Apollo and Artemis.

Delphi (**del**-fee) an ancient Greek city on the southern slopes of Mount Parnassus, site of the most famous oracle of Apollo.

Delphic *adjective* of or like the ancient Greek oracle at Parnassus, which often gave obscure and enigmatic prophecies.

delphinium *noun* a garden plant with tall spikes of flowers, usually blue.

delta *noun* **1** the fourth letter of the Greek alphabet, = d (written Δ). **2** a triangular patch of land accumulated at the mouth of a river between two or more of its branches, *the Nile Delta*. **deltaic** *adjective*

delude (dĕ-**lood**) *verb* to deceive.

deluge (**del**-yooj) *noun* **1** a great flood, a heavy fall of rain. **2** anything coming in a heavy rush, *a deluge of questions*. **–deluge** *verb* to flood, to come down on like a deluge. **–the Deluge** the flood in Noah's time.

delusion *noun* **1** a false belief or opinion. **2** a persistent false belief that is a symptom or form of madness.

delusive *adjective* deceptive, raising vain hopes.

deluxe *adjective* of very high quality, luxurious. [French, = of luxury]

delve *verb* **1** (*old use*) to dig. **2** to search deeply for information.

demagnetise *verb* (also **-ize**) to remove the magnetisation of. **demagnetisation** *noun*

demagogue (**dem**-ă-gog) *noun* a leader or agitator who wins support by appealing to people's feelings and prejudices rather than by reasoning. **demagogic** *adjective* [from Greek *demos* = people, + *agogos* = leading]

demand *noun* **1** a request made imperiously or as if one had a right. **2** a desire for goods or services by people who wish to buy or use these. **3** an urgent claim, *there are many demands on my time*. **–demand** *verb* **1** to make a demand for. **2** to need, *the work demands great skill*. □ **in demand** sought after. **on demand** as soon as the demand is made, *payable on demand*. [from *de-*, + Latin *mandare* = to order]

demanding *adjective* **1** making many demands. **2** requiring skill or effort, *a demanding job*.

demarcation (dee-mar-**kay**-shŏn) *noun* marking of the boundary or limits of something. □ **demarcation dispute** a dispute between trade unions about work they consider to belong to different trades.

demean *verb* to lower the dignity of, *I wouldn't demean myself to ask for it*.

demeanour *noun* the way a person behaves.

demented *adjective* driven mad, crazy. [from *de-*, + Latin *mentis* = of the mind]

dementia (dĕ-**men**-shă) *noun* a chronic disorder of the mental processes marked by memory loss, personality changes, etc.

demerara (dem-ĕ-**rair**-ră) *noun* brown raw cane sugar. [named after Demerara in South America]

demerit *noun* a fault, a defect; a mark awarded against an offender.

demersal (dĕ-**mer**-săl) *adjective* (of fish etc.) living at or near the bottom of the sea or of a lake. [from *de-*, + Latin *mersum* = plunged]

demesne (dĕ-**meen**) *noun* **1** a domain. **2** a landed estate.

Demeter (dĕ-**mee**-ter) (*Gk. myth*) the corn goddess, mother of Persephone.

demi- *prefix* half (as in *demisemiquaver*).

demilitarise *verb* (also -**ize**) to remove military installations or forces from (an area). **demilitarisation** *noun*

demise (dĕ-**myz**) *noun* (*formal*) death.

demisemiquaver *noun* a note in music, lasting half as long as a semiquaver.

demist *verb* to clear mist from (a windscreen etc.). **demister** *noun*

demo *noun* (*plural* **demos**) (*informal*) a demonstration.

demob *verb* (**demobbed**, **demobbing**) (*informal*) to demobilise. –**demob** *noun* (*informal*) demobilisation.

demobilise *verb* (also -**ize**) to release from military service. **demobilisation** *noun*

democracy *noun* **1** government by the whole people of a country, especially through representatives whom they elect. **2** a country governed in this way. [from Greek *demos* = people, + *-cracy*]

democrat *noun* a person who favours democracy. –**Democrat** *noun* a member of the Australian Democrats; a member of the Liberal Democrats in the UK; a member of the Democratic Party in the USA.

democratic *adjective* **1** of, like, or supporting democracy. **2** in accordance with the principle of equal rights for all, *a democratic decision*. –**Democratic** *adjective* of the **Democratic Party**, one of the two main political parties in the USA. **democratically** *adverb*

democratise (dĕ-**mok**-ră-tyz) *verb* (also -**ize**) to make democratic. **democratisation** *noun*

demodulation *noun* the process of extracting a modulating radio signal from a modulated wave etc.

demography (dĕ-**mog**-răfee) *noun* the study of statistics of births, deaths, diseases, etc., as illustrating the conditions of life in communities. **demographic** *adjective* [from Greek *demos* = people, + *-graphy*]

demolish *verb* **1** to pull or knock down (a building). **2** to destroy (a person's argument or theory etc.); to put an end to (an institution). **3** (*informal*) to eat up. **demolition** (dem-ŏ-**lish**-ŏn) *noun* [from *de-*, + Latin *moliri* = build]

demon *noun* **1** a devil or evil spirit. **2** a cruel or forceful person. **demonic** (dĕ-**mon**-ik) *adjective* [from Greek *daimon* = a spirit]

demoniac (dĕ-**moh**-nee-ak) *adjective* **1** of or like a demon. **2** possessed by an evil spirit.

demonstrate *verb* **1** to show evidence of, to prove. **2** to describe and explain by the help of specimens or examples; *demonstrate the machine to customers*, show them how it works. **3** to take part in a public demonstration. **demonstrable** *adjective*, **demonstrator** *noun*

demonstration *noun* **1** demonstrating. **2** a show of feeling. **3** an organised gathering or procession to express the opinion of a group publicly. **4** a display of military force.

demonstrative (dĕ-**mon**-stră-tiv) *adjective* **1** showing or proving. **2** expressing one's feelings openly. **3** (in grammar, of an adjective or pronoun) indicating the person or thing referred to (*this*, *that*, *these*, and *those*). **demonstratively** *adverb*, **demonstrativeness** *noun*

demoralise *verb* (also -**ize**) to weaken the morale of, to dishearten. **demoralisation** *noun*

Demosthenes (dĕ-**moss**-thĕ-neez) (384–322 BC), the greatest Athenian orator.

demote (dee-**moht**) *verb* to reduce to a lower rank or category. **demotion** *noun* [from *de-* + *promote*]

demur (dĕ-**mer**) *verb* (**demurred**, **demurring**) to raise objections, *they demurred at working on Sundays*. –**demur** *noun* an objection raised, *they went without demur*.

demure (dĕ-**mewr**) *adjective* quiet and serious or pretending to be so. **demurely** *adverb*, **demureness** *noun*

den *noun* **1** a wild animal's lair. **2** a place where people gather for some illegal activity, *an opium den*; *a den of vice*. **3** a small room in which a person shuts himself or herself away to work or relax.

denarius (dĕ-**nair**-ree-ŭs) *noun* (*plural* **denarii**, *pr.* dĕ-**nair**-ree-I) an ancient Roman silver coin.

denary (**dee**-nă-ree) *adjective* of ten, decimal.

denationalise *verb* (also **-ize**) to transfer (an industry) from national to private ownership. **denationalisation** *noun*

denature *verb* 1 to change the natural qualities of. 2 to make (alcohol) unfit for drinking (but usable for other purposes).

dendrite *noun* 1 any of the short (usually branched) outgrowths from a nerve cell, carrying signals into it. 2 a stone or mineral with a treelike or mosslike marking. 3 this marking. **dendritic** *adjective* [from Greek *dendron* = tree]

dendrochronology *noun* a system of dating timber by studying the annual growth rings of trees.

dene (*pr.* deen) *noun* a narrow wooded valley. (In Australia the word is used only as an ending in place names, e.g. *Hawthorndene*.)

dengue (**deng**-gee) *noun* an infectious tropical disease, transmitted by mosquitoes, causing fever and acute pain in the joints.

deniable *adjective* able to be denied.

denial *noun* 1 denying. 2 a statement that a thing is not true. 3 refusal of a request or wish.

denier (**den**-yer) *noun* a unit of weight by which the fineness of silk, rayon, or nylon yarn is measured.

denigrate (**den**-ĭ-grayt) *verb* to blacken the reputation of, to sneer at. **denigration** *noun*

denim *noun* a strong twilled cotton fabric used for making clothes, especially jeans. [from *serge de Nim* = fabric of Nîmes (a town in southern France)]

Denis, St (c. 250), the patron saint of France. Feast day, 9 October.

denitrify (dee-**ny**-trĭ-fy) *verb* to remove nitrates or nitrites from (soil etc.). **denitrification** *noun*

denizen (**den**-ĭ-zĕn) *noun* a person, animal, or plant living or often present in a particular place, *denizens of the desert*.

Denmark a kingdom in northern Europe.

denomination *noun* 1 a name or title. 2 a distinctively named Church or religious sect, *Baptists and other Protestant denominations*. 3 a unit of measurement; a unit of money, *coins of small denomination*.

denominational *adjective* of a particular religious denomination.

denominator *noun* the number written below the line in a fraction, e.g. 4 in $\frac{3}{4}$, showing how many parts the whole is divided into. ☐ **common denominator** a number that is a multiple of each of the denominators of two or more fractions; the feature that members of a group have in common.

denote (dĕ-**noht**) *verb* 1 to be the sign, symbol, or name of, to indicate, *in road signs, P denotes a parking place*. 2 (of a word) to have as its literal or basic meaning, without additional implications. (Compare *connote*.) **denotation** (dee-noh-**tay**-shŏn) *noun*

denouement (day-**noo**-mahn) *noun* (also **dénouement**) the clearing up, at the end of a play or story, of the complications of the plot. [French, = unravelling]

denounce *verb* 1 to speak publicly against. 2 to give information against, *denounced him as a spy*. 3 to announce that one is ending (a treaty or agreement). [from *de-*, + Latin *nuntiare* = announce]

dense *adjective* 1 thick, not easy to see through, *dense fog*. 2 massed closely together, *dense crowds*. 3 stupid. **densely** *adverb*

density *noun* 1 a dense or concentrated condition, *the density of the fog*. 2 stupidity. 3 the relation of mass to volume.

dent *noun* a depression left by a blow or by pressure. **–dent** *verb* 1 to make a dent in. 2 to become dented.

dental *adjective* 1 of or for the teeth. 2 of dentistry, *a dental practice*. ☐ **dental floss** strong thread used for cleaning between the teeth. **dental surgeon** a dentist. [from Latin *dentis* = of a tooth]

dentifrice (**dent**-ĭ-friss) *noun* toothpaste or tooth powder. [from Latin *dentis* = of a tooth, + *fricare* = to rub]

dentine (**den**-teen) *noun* the hard dense tissue forming the main part of teeth.

dentist *noun* a person who is qualified to treat the teeth, extract them, fit artificial ones, etc.

dentistry *noun* the work or profession of a dentist.

dentition *noun* 1 the type and arrangement of teeth in a species etc. of animals. 2 teething.

D'Entrecasteaux (don-trĕ-kas-**toh**), Joseph-Antoine Raymond de Bruni (1739–93), French navigator who in 1791–3 charted Australian waters, especially around Tasmania.

denture *noun* a set of artificial teeth.

denude *verb* **1** to make naked or bare, to strip the cover from, *the trees were denuded of their leaves*. **2** to expose (a formation or layer of rock) by removing what lies above it. **3** to take all of something away from (a person), *creditors denuded him of every cent*. **denudation** (dee-new-**day**-shŏn) *noun*

denunciation (dĕ-nun-see-**ay**-shŏn) *noun* denouncing. **denunciatory** *adjective*

deny *verb* (**denied**, **denying**) **1** to say that (a thing) is not true or does not exist. **2** to disown, to refuse to acknowledge, *Peter denied Christ*. **3** to refuse to give what is asked for or needed, to prevent from having, *no one can deny you your rights*. □ **deny oneself** to restrict one's food, drink, or pleasure.

deodar (**dee**-ŏ-dar) *noun* the Himalayan cedar. [from Sanskrit *devadaru* = divine tree]

deodorant (dee-**oh**-dŏ-rănt) *noun* a substance that removes or conceals unwanted odours. – **deodorant** *adjective* deodorising.

deodorise *verb* (also -**ize**) to destroy the odour of. [from *de-*, + Latin *odor* = a smell]

de-oxygenate *verb* to remove oxygen from.

deoxyribonucleic acid *see* DNA.

depart *verb* **1** to go away, to leave. **2** (of trains or buses) to start, to begin a journey. **3** to cease following a particular course, *departing from our normal procedure*.

departed *adjective* **1** bygone, *departed glories*. **2 the departed** a dead person or dead people.

department *noun* any of the units, each with a specialised function, into which a business, shop, or organisation is divided. □ **department store** a large shop in which there are various departments each dealing in a separate type of goods.

departmental (dee-part-**men**-tăl) *adjective* of a department. **departmentally** *adverb*

departure *noun* **1** departing, going away. **2** setting out on a new course of action or thought.

depend *verb* **depend on 1** to be controlled or determined by, *whether we can picnic depends on the weather*. **2** to be unable to do without, *she depends on my help*. **3** to trust confidently,

to feel certain about, *you can depend on John to be there when he's needed*. [from *de-*, + Latin *pendere* = hang]

dependable *adjective* able to be relied on. **dependably** *adverb*, **dependability** *noun*

dependant *noun* one who depends on another for support, *he has four dependants*.

Usage Australian and British spelling is *-ant* for the noun and *-ent* for the adjective; in the USA *-ent* is used for both.

---

dependence *noun* depending, being dependent.

dependency *noun* a country that is controlled by another.

dependent *adjective* **1** depending, conditioned, *promotion is dependent on ability*. **2** needing the help of, unable to do without, *he is dependent on drugs*. **3** maintained at another's cost; controlled by another, not independent, *our dependent territories*. **4** (of a clause, phrase, or word) in a subordinate relation to a sentence or word.

Usage See the note under **dependant**.

---

depict *verb* **1** to show in the form of a picture. **2** to describe in words. **depiction** *noun* [from *de-*, + Latin *pictum* = painted]

depilatory (dĕ-**pil**-ă-tŏ-ree) *noun* a substance that removes superfluous hair. – **depilatory** *adjective* removing hair. [from *de-*, + Latin *pilus* = hair]

deplete (dĕ-**pleet**) *verb* to use up large quantities of, to reduce in number or quantity. **depletion** *noun* [from *de-*, + Latin *-pletum* = filled]

deplorable *adjective* **1** regrettable. **2** exceedingly bad, shocking. **deplorably** *adverb*

deplore *verb* **1** to regret deeply, *we deplore his death*. **2** to find deplorable, *we deplore their incompetence*. [from *de-*, + Latin *plorare* = weep]

deploy *verb* to spread out, to bring or come into action systematically, *deploying his troops* or *resources*; *the ships deployed into line*. **deployment** *noun*

deponent (dĕ-**poh**-nĕnt) *adjective* (of certain verbs in Latin and Greek)

conjugated in the passive or middle voice
but active in meaning.

depopulate *verb* to reduce the population of.
depopulation *noun*

deport *verb* to remove (a person) from a
country. **deportation** *noun*, **deportee** *noun*
[from *de-*, + Latin *portare* = carry]

deportment *noun* behaviour, a person's way
of holding himself or herself in standing and
walking.

depose *verb* 1 to remove from power, *the
king was deposed*. 2 to testify or bear witness,
especially on oath in court.

deposit *noun* 1 a thing deposited for safe
keeping. 2 a sum of money paid into a
bank. 3 a sum paid as a guarantee or a first
instalment. 4 a layer of matter deposited
or accumulated naturally, *new deposits of
copper were found.* –**deposit** *verb* (**deposited,
depositing**) 1 to lay or put down, *she
deposited the books on the desk.* 2 to store
or entrust for safe keeping, to pay (money)
into a bank. 3 to pay as a guarantee or first
instalment. 4 to leave as a layer or covering of
matter, *floods deposited mud on the land.*
□ **on deposit** in a bank account. [from *de-*,
+ Latin *positum* = placed]

deposition *noun* 1 deposing or being
deposed from power. 2 a statement made on
oath. 3 depositing. 4 the taking down of Christ
from the Cross.

depositor *noun* a person who deposits money
or property.

depository *noun* a storehouse.

depot (**dep**-oh) *noun* 1 a storehouse,
especially for military supplies. 2 the
headquarters of a regiment. 3 a place where
goods are deposited or from which goods,
vehicles, etc. are dispatched. 4 a place where
buses, trams, and trains are parked and
serviced. [same origin as *deposit*]

deprave (dĕ-**prayv**) *verb* to make morally
bad, to corrupt. **depravation** (dep-ră-**vay**-
shŏn) *noun*

depraved *adjective* 1 immoral, wicked.
2 made bad, perverted, *depraved tastes.*

depravity (dĕ-**prav**-ĭ-tee) *noun* moral
corruption, wickedness.

deprecate (**dep**-rĕ-kayt) *verb* 1 to feel and
express disapproval of. 2 to try to turn aside
(praise or blame etc.) politely. **deprecation**
noun, **deprecatory** (**dep**-rĕ-kay-tŏ-ree)

adjective [from Latin *deprecari* = to keep
away misfortune by prayer]

Usage Distinguish *deprecate* from *depreciate*.

---

depreciate (dĕ-**pree**-shee-ayt) *verb* 1 to make
or become lower in value. 2 to belittle, to
disparage. **depreciatory** (dĕ-**pree**-shă-tŏ-ree)
adjective [from *de-*, + Latin *pretium* = price]

depreciation *noun* a decline in value,
especially the reduction in the value of a fixed
asset charged as an expense when calculating
profit and loss.

depredation (dep-rĕ-**day**-shŏn) *noun*
plundering; damage.

depress *verb* 1 to make sad, to lower the
spirits of. 2 to make less active; *the stock
market is depressed*, values are low. 3 to press
down, *depress the lever.*

depressant *noun* a substance that reduces the
activity of the nervous system, a sedative.

depression *noun* 1 a state of excessive
sadness or hopelessness, often with physical
symptoms. 2 a long period of inactivity
in business and trade, with widespread
unemployment; **the Depression** the severe
worldwide economic depression of 1929–34.
3 a lowering of atmospheric pressure, an
area of low pressure which may bring rain.
4 a sunken place or hollow on a surface.
5 pressing down. □ **angle of depression**
the angle a descending line makes with the
horizontal.

depressive *adjective* 1 depressing.
2 involving mental depression. –**depressive**
noun a person suffering from mental
depression.

deprival (dĕ-**pry**-văl) *noun* depriving; being
deprived.

deprivation (dep-rĭ-**vay**-shŏn) *noun*
1 deprival. 2 a keenly felt loss.

deprive *verb* to take a thing away from, to
prevent from using or enjoying something, *the
prisoner had been deprived of food.*
□ **deprived child** one who has been prevented
from having a normal home life. [from *de-*, +
Latin *privare* = rob]

Dept *abbreviation* Department.

depth *noun* 1 being deep. 2 the distance from
the top down, or from the surface inwards, or
from front to back. 3 deep learning or thought
or feeling. 4 intensity of colour or darkness.
5 lowness of pitch in a voice or sound.
6 the deepest or most central part, *living in the*

depths of the country. □ **depth charge** a bomb that will explode under water, for use against submarines etc. **in depth** with thorough and intensive investigations, *studied it in depth*; *defence in depth*, a system of successive areas of resistance. **in-depth** *adjective* thorough and intensive. **out of one's depth** in water that is too deep to stand in; attempting something that is beyond one's ability.

deputation *noun* a body of people appointed to go on a mission on behalf of others.

depute (dĕ-**pewt**) *verb* **1** to delegate (a task) to a person. **2** to appoint (a person) to act as one's representative.

deputise *verb* (also **-ize**) to act as deputy.

deputy *noun* **1** a person appointed to act as substitute for another. **2** a member of a parliament in certain countries, *the Chamber of Deputies*.

deracinate *verb* **1** to tear up by the roots. **2** to uproot (someone) from their natural environment.

derail *verb* (**derailed, derailing**) to cause (a train) to leave the rails. **derailment** *noun*

derange *verb* **1** to throw into confusion, to disrupt. **2** to make insane. **derangement** *noun*

derate *verb* to abolish or lower the rates on.

derby (**dar**-bee) *noun* **1** a horse race for three-year-olds. **2** a sporting contest. [from the name of an annual English horse race for three-year-olds, founded in 1780 by the 12th Earl of Derby]

deregulate *verb* to free from regulations or controls. **deregulation** *noun*

derelict *adjective* abandoned, deserted and left to fall into ruin. –**derelict** *noun* **1** an abandoned property, especially a ship. **2** a person who is abandoned by society or who does not fit into a normal social background. [from *de-* = completely, + Latin *relictum* = left behind]

dereliction (derrĕ-**lik**-shŏn) *noun* **1** neglect of duty. **2** abandoning; being abandoned.

derestrict *verb* to remove restrictions from; *a derestricted road*, one where a special speed limit has been removed or has not been imposed. **derestriction** *noun*

deride (dĕ-**ryd**) *verb* to laugh at scornfully, to treat with scorn. [from *de-*, + Latin *ridere* = to laugh]

de rigueur (dĕ rig-**er**) *adjective* required by custom or etiquette, *evening dress is de rigueur*. [French, = of strictness]

derision (dĕ-**rizh**-ŏn) *noun* scorn, ridicule.

derisive (dĕ-**ry**-siv) *adjective* scornful, showing derision, *derisive cheers*. **derisively** *adverb*

derisory (dĕ-**ry**-zŏ-ree) *adjective* **1** showing derision. **2** deserving derision; too insignificant for serious consideration, *a derisory offer*.

derivation (derrĭ-**vay**-shŏn) *noun* **1** deriving. **2** origin.

derivative (dĕ-**riv**-ă-tiv) *adjective* derived from a source. –**derivative** *noun* **1** a thing that is derived from another. **2** (in mathematics) a quantity measuring the rate of change of another.

derive *verb* **1** to obtain from a source, *he derived great pleasure from music*; *some English words are derived from Latin*, are formed from Latin words. **2** to show or assert that something is derived from (a source). □ **derived function** (in mathematics) a derivative of a function. [from *de-*, + Latin *rivus* = a stream]

dermatitis (der-mă-**ty**-tĭss) *noun* inflammation of the skin.

dermatologist *noun* a specialist in dermatology.

dermatology (der-mă-**tol**-ŏ-jee) *noun* the scientific study of the skin and its diseases. [from Greek *derma* = skin, + *-logy*]

dermis *noun* the layer of skin below the epidermis.

derogatory (dĕ-**rog**-ă-tŏ-ree) *adjective* disparaging, contemptuous.

derrick *noun* **1** a kind of crane with an arm pivoted to the base of a central post or to a floor. **2** a framework over an oil well or borehole, holding the drilling machinery etc. [this word originally meant 'a gallows', named after Derrick, a London hangman in about 1600]

derring-do *noun* (*literary*) heroic courage or action.

derris *noun* **1** a tropical climbing plant. **2** an insecticide made from its powdered root.

derry *noun* (*Austral. informal*) a down, a grudge, *the teacher has a derry on him*.

derv *noun* fuel oil for diesel engines. [from the initials of *d*iesel-*e*ngined *r*oad *v*ehicle]

dervish *noun* a member of a Muslim religious order, vowed to poverty. [from Persian *darvish* = poor]

Derwent a river of Tasmania, at the mouth of which is the city of Hobart.

desalinate *verb* to remove the salt from (sea water etc.). **desalination** *noun*

descant *noun* a melody sung or played in accompaniment to the main melody. [from *dis-*, + Latin *cantus* = song]

Descartes (day-**kart**), René (1596–1650), French philosopher, mathematician, and scientist.

descend *verb* 1 to come or go down. 2 to slope downwards. 3 to make a sudden attack or visit. 4 to sink or stoop to unworthy behaviour, to lower oneself. 5 to be passed down by inheritance, *the title descended to his son*. □ **be descended from** to come by descent from (a specified person, family, or people).

descendant *noun* a person who is descended from another.

descent *noun* 1 descending. 2 a way by which one may descend. 3 a downward slope. 4 a sudden attack or invasion. 5 lineage, family origin, *of French descent*.

describe *verb* 1 to set forth in words; to say what something is like. 2 to mark out or draw the outline of, to move in a certain pattern, *described a complete circle*. [from *de-*, + Latin *scribere* = write]

description *noun* 1 describing. 2 an account or picture in words. 3 a kind or class of thing, *there's no food of any description*.

descriptive *adjective* 1 giving a description. 2 (of grammatical rules etc.) describing what is actually used, not prescriptive.

desecrate (dess-ĕ-krayt) *verb* to treat (a sacred thing) with irreverence or disrespect. **desecration** *noun*, **desecrator** *noun* [from *de-* + *consecrate*]

desegregate *verb* to end segregation of (groups, races, etc.). **desegregation** *noun*

desert[1] (**dez**-ert) *noun* a dry barren often sand-covered area of land. – **desert** *adjective* 1 barren and uncultivated. 2 uninhabited, *a desert island*.

desert[2] (dĕ-**zert**) *verb* 1 to abandon, to leave without intending to return, to forsake. 2 to leave service in the armed forces without permission. **deserter** *noun*, **desertion** *noun*

deserts (dĕ-**zerts**) *plural noun* what one deserves. [from *deserve*]

deserve *verb* to be worthy of or entitled to (a thing) because of actions or qualities.

deservedly (dĕ-**zerv**-ĕd-lee) *adverb* according to what is deserved, justly.

deserving *adjective* worthy, worth rewarding or supporting, *a deserving charity*.

desiccate *verb* (**dess**-ĭ-kayt) to dry out the moisture from; to dry (solid food) in order to preserve it, *desiccated coconut*. **desiccation** *noun*, **desiccator** *noun*

desideratum (dĕ-zid-ĕ-**rah**-tŭm) *noun* (*plural* **desiderata**) something that is lacking but needed or desired.

design *noun* 1 a drawing that shows how something is to be made. 2 the art of making such drawings, *she studied design*. 3 the general form or arrangement of something, *the design of the building is good*. 4 a combination of lines or shapes to form a decoration. 5 a mental plan, a purpose. – **design** *verb* 1 to prepare a drawing or design for (a thing). 2 to plan, to intend for a specific purpose, *the book is designed for students*. □ **have designs on** to plan to get possession of. [from *de-*, + Latin *signare* = mark out]

designate (**dez**-ig-nayt) *verb* 1 to mark or point out clearly, to specify, *the river was designated as the western boundary*. 2 to describe as; to give a name or title to. 3 to appoint to a position, *designated Smith as his successor*. – **designate** (**dez**-ig-năt) *adjective* (placed after the noun) appointed but not yet installed in office, *the bishop designate*. [same origin as *design*]

designation (dez-ig-**nay**-shŏn) *noun* 1 designating. 2 a name or title.

designedly *adverb* intentionally.

designer *noun* a person who designs things, e.g. clothing, sets, etc. □ **designer drug** a synthetic drug that is designed for its stimulating or other effects.

designing *adjective* crafty, scheming.

desirable *adjective* 1 arousing desire, worth desiring. 2 advisable, worth doing. **desirably** *adverb*, **desirability** *noun*

desire *noun* 1 a feeling that one would get pleasure or satisfaction by obtaining or possessing something. 2 an expressed wish, a request, *at the desire of her late father*. 3 an object of desire, *all your heart's desires*. – **desire** *verb* 1 to have a desire for. 2 to ask for. □ **leave much to be desired** to be very imperfect.

desirous *adjective* having a desire, desiring.

desist (dĕ-**zist**) *verb* to cease (from an action etc.).

desk *noun* **1** a piece of furniture with a flat or sloped top and often drawers, used when reading or writing etc. **2** a counter behind which a cashier or receptionist etc. sits, *ask at the information desk*. **3** the section of a newspaper office dealing with specified topics.

desktop *noun* **1** the working surface of a desk. **2** (in full **desktop computer**) a computer suitable for use at a desk. ☐ **desktop publishing** the preparation of text for publication etc. by the use of a desktop computer and printer.

desolate (**dess**-ŏ-lăt) *adjective* **1** solitary, lonely. **2** deserted, uninhabited, barren, dismal, *a desolate landscape*. **3** forlorn and unhappy.

desolated (**dess**-ŏ-lay-tĕd) *adjective* feeling lonely and wretched.

desolation *noun* **1** a desolate or barren condition. **2** loneliness. **3** grief, wretchedness.

despair *noun* **1** complete loss or lack of hope. **2** a thing that causes this. **–despair** *verb* to lose all hope. [from *de-*, + Latin *sperare* = to hope]

desperado (dess-pĕ-**rah**-doh) *noun* (*plural* **desperadoes**) a reckless criminal.

desperate *adjective* **1** leaving little or no hope, extremely serious. **2** made reckless by despair or urgency. **3** done or used in a nearly hopeless situation. **desperately** *adverb* [same origin as *despair*]

desperation *noun* **1** hopelessness. **2** being desperate; recklessness caused by despair.

despicable (dĕ-**spik**-ăbŭl) *adjective* deserving to be despised, contemptible. **despicably** *adverb*

despise *verb* to regard as inferior or worthless, to feel disrespect for. [from *de-*, + Latin *-spicere* = to look]

despite *preposition* in spite of.

despoil *verb* (*literary*) to plunder, to rob. **despoliation** *noun*

despondent *adjective* in low spirits, dejected. **despondently** *adverb*, **despondency** *noun*

despot (**dess**-pot) *noun* a tyrant, a ruler who has unrestricted power.

despotic (dĕs-**pot**-ik) *adjective* having unrestricted power. **despotically** *adverb*

despotism (**dess**-pŏ-tizm) *noun* **1** tyranny, government by a despot. **2** a country ruled by a despot.

dessert (dĕ-**zert**) *noun* the sweet or fruit course at the end of a meal. [from French *desservir* = clear the table]

dessertspoon *noun* **1** a medium-sized spoon used for eating dessert, smaller than a tablespoon and larger than a teaspoon. **2** the amount held by this. **dessertspoonful** *noun* (*plural* **dessertspoonfuls**).

destination *noun* the place to which a person or thing is going.

destine (**dess**-tĭn) *verb* to settle or determine the future of, to set apart for a purpose; *he was destined to become President*, this was his destiny.

destiny *noun* **1** fate considered as a power. **2** that which happens to a person or thing, thought of as determined in advance by fate.

destitute *adjective* **1** penniless, without the necessaries of life. **2** lacking in something, *a landscape destitute of trees*.

destitution *noun* being destitute; extreme poverty.

destroy *verb* **1** to pull or break down; to reduce to a useless form; to spoil completely. **2** to kill (a sick or unwanted animal) deliberately, *the dog had to be destroyed*. **3** to put out of existence, *it destroyed our chances*. [from *de-*, + Latin *struere* = build]

destroyer *noun* **1** a person or thing that destroys. **2** a fast warship designed to protect other ships.

destructible *adjective* able to be destroyed. **destructibility** *noun*

destruction *noun* **1** destroying, being destroyed. **2** a cause of destruction or ruin.

destructive *adjective* destroying; causing destruction; frequently destroying things.

desuetude (dĕs-**yoo**-ĕ-tewd) *noun* a state of disuse, *fall into desuetude*.

desultory (**des**-ŭl-tŏ-ree) *adjective* going constantly from one subject to another, not systematic. **desultorily** *adverb*

detach *verb* to release or remove from something else or from a group.

detachable *adjective* able to be detached.

detached *adjective* **1** (of a house) not joined to another. **2** (of the mind or opinions) free from bias or emotion.

detachment *noun* **1** detaching; being detached. **2** freedom from bias or emotion, aloofness, lack of concern. **3** a group of people or ships etc. detached from a larger group for a special duty.

detail *noun* **1** an individual item; a small or subordinate particular. **2** a number of such particulars, *the description is full of detail*. **3** the minor decoration in a building or picture etc., *look at the detail in the carvings*. **4** a small military detachment assigned to special duty. –**detail** *verb* **1** to give particulars of, to describe fully. **2** to assign to special duty. □ **in detail** describing the individual parts or events etc. fully.

detailed *adjective* giving many details.

detain *verb* **1** to keep in confinement or under restraint. **2** to keep waiting; to cause delay to; to keep from proceeding. [from *de-*, + Latin *tenere* = to hold]

detainee (dee-tayn-**ee**) *noun* a person who is detained by the authorities.

detect *verb* **1** to discover the existence or presence of. **2** to find (a person) doing something bad or secret. **detectable** *adjective* [from *de-*, + Latin *tectum* = covered]

detection *noun* **1** detecting, being detected. **2** the work of a detective.

detective *noun* a person, especially a member of the police force, whose job is to investigate crimes. –**detective** *adjective* detecting. □ **detective story** a story that tells of crime and the detection of criminals.

detector *noun* a device for detecting the presence of something, *a smoke detector*.

détente (day-**tont**) *noun* the easing of strained relations between countries. [French, = relaxation]

detention *noun* **1** detaining; being detained. **2** being kept in custody. **3** being kept in school after hours as a punishment. □ **detention centre** an institution where people, in particular refugees and people awaiting trial, are detained for short periods.

deter *verb* (**deterred**, **deterring**) to discourage or prevent from doing something through fear or dislike of the consequences. **determent** *noun* [from *de-*, + Latin *terrere* = frighten]

detergent *noun* a cleansing substance, especially a synthetic substance other than soap. –**detergent** *adjective* having a cleansing effect.

deteriorate *verb* to become worse. **deterioration** *noun* [from Latin *deterior* = worse]

determinable *adjective* able to be settled or calculated, *its age is not determinable*.

determinant *adjective* determining, decisive. –**determinant** *noun* **1** a decisive factor. **2** the quantity obtained by adding the products of the elements of a square matrix according to a certain rule.

determinate (dĕ-**ter**-mĭ-năt) *adjective* limited, of fixed and definite scope or nature.

determination *noun* **1** firmness of purpose. **2** the process of deciding, determining, or calculating.

determine *verb* **1** to find out or calculate precisely. **2** to settle, to decide. **3** to be the decisive factor or influence on, *income determines one's standard of living*. **4** to decide firmly. [from *de-*, + Latin *terminare* = set a limit]

determined *adjective* showing determination, firm and resolute. **determinedly** *adverb*

determinism *noun* the theory that human action is not free but is determined by external forces acting on the will. **determinist** *noun*, **deterministic** *adjective*

deterrent (dĕ-**te**-rĕnt) *adjective* deterring. –**deterrent** *noun* a thing that deters; a nuclear weapon that deters countries from attacking the one who has it. **deterrence** *noun*

detest *verb* to dislike intensely, to loathe. **detestation** *noun*

detestable *adjective* intensely disliked, hateful. **detestably** *adverb*

dethrone *verb* to remove from a throne, to depose. **dethronement** *noun*

detonate (**det**-ŏ-nayt) *verb* to explode or cause to explode loudly. **detonation** *noun* [from *de-* = thoroughly, + Latin *tonare* = to thunder]

detonator *noun* a device for detonating an explosive.

detour (**dee**-toor) *noun* a deviation from one's direct or intended course, a roundabout route, *make a detour*. [from French *détourner* = turn away]

detract *verb* **detract from** to take away a part or amount from, to lessen (a quantity, value, etc.), *it will not detract from our pleasure*. **detraction** *noun* [from *de-*, + Latin *tractum* = pulled]

detractor *noun* a person who criticises something unfavourably.

detriment (det-rĭ-mĕnt) *noun* 1 harm, damage. 2 something causing this.

detrimental (det-rĭ-**men**-tăl) *adjective* causing harm. **detrimentally** *adverb*

detritus (dĕ-**try**-tŭs) *noun* debris; loose matter (e.g. gravel) produced by erosion. [from *de-*, + Latin *tritum* = worn]

de trop (dĕ **troh**) *adjective* not wanted, in the way. [French, = too much]

deuce[1] *noun* 1 (in tennis) the score of 40 all. 2 the two on dice.

deuce[2] *noun* (*informal*, in exclamations of surprise or annoyance) the Devil.

deus ex machina (**day**-ŭs eks **mak**-ĭ-nă) *noun* an unexpected power or event that saves a seemingly impossible situation. [Latin, = god from the machinery, with reference to the machinery by which, in ancient Greek theatre, gods were shown in the air]

deuterium (dew-**teer**-ree-ŭm) *noun* a heavy form of hydrogen (symbol D or ^{2}H). [from Greek *deuteros* = second]

deuteron (**dew**-tĕ-ron) *noun* the nucleus of a deuterium atom.

Deuteronomy (dew-tĕ-**ron**-ŏmee) the fifth book of the Old Testament, containing a restatement of the Mosaic Law. [from Greek *deuteros* = second, + *nomos* = law]

Deutschmark (**doich**-mark) *noun* the former unit of money in Germany.

deva (**day**-vă) *noun* a member of a class of divine beings in the Vedic period, which in Indian mythology are benevolent and in Zoroastrianism are evil. (See also **asura**.)

devalue *verb* to reduce the value of (currency) in relation to other currencies or to gold. **devaluation** *noun*

devastate *verb* to lay waste, to cause great destruction to. **devastation** *noun*

devastating *adjective* 1 causing destruction. 2 overwhelming, *a devastating handicap*.

develop *verb* (**developed**, **developing**) 1 to make or become larger, fuller, or more mature or organised. 2 to bring or come gradually into existence, *a storm developed*. 3 to begin to exhibit or suffer from, to acquire gradually, *develop measles*; *develop bad habits*. 4 to convert (land) to a new purpose so as to use its resources; to use (an area) for the building of houses, shops, factories, etc. 5 to treat (a photographic film or plate etc.) so as to make the picture visible. □ **developing**

country a poor country that is developing better economic and social conditions.

developer *noun* 1 one who develops. 2 a person or firm that develops land. 3 a substance used for developing photographic film etc.

development *noun* 1 developing; being developed. 2 something that has developed or been developed, *the latest developments in foreign affairs*. 3 the middle section of a movement in sonata form in which the themes (stated in the exposition) are developed.

Devi (**day**-vee) the supreme Hindu goddess, often identified with Parvati and Sakti.

deviant (**dee**-vee-ănt) *adjective* deviating from what is accepted as normal or usual. –**deviant** *noun* a person who deviates from accepted standards in beliefs or behaviour.

deviate (**dee**-vee-ayt) *verb* to turn aside or diverge from a course of action, a rule, truth, etc. **deviation** *noun*, **deviator** *noun* [from *de-*, + Latin *via* = way]

device *noun* 1 a thing that is made or used for a particular purpose, *a device for opening tins*. 2 a plan or scheme for achieving something. 3 a design used as a decoration or emblem. □ **leave a person to his** or **her own devices** to leave a person to do as he or she wishes without help or advice.

devil *noun* 1 **the Devil** (in Jewish and Christian teaching) the supreme spirit of evil and enemy of God. 2 an evil spirit. 3 a wicked, cruel, or annoying person. 4 a person of great energy or cleverness. 5 (*informal*) something difficult or hard to manage. 6 (*informal*) a person, *poor devil*; *lucky devil*. □ **devil's advocate** one who tests a theory by putting forward possible objections to it. **devilish** *adjective*

devilment *noun* mischief.

devilry *noun* 1 wickedness. 2 devilment.

devious (**dee**-vee-ŭs) *adjective* 1 winding, roundabout. 2 not straightforward, underhand. **deviously** *adverb*, **deviousness** *noun*

devise (dĕ-**vyz**) *verb* 1 to think out, to plan, to invent. 2 to leave (real estate) by will.

devoid (dĕ-**void**) *adjective* lacking or free from something, *devoid of merit*.

devolution (dee-vŏ-**loo**-shŏn) *noun* 1 the delegation or transference of work or power from a central administration to a local or regional one. 2 the handing down of property etc. to an heir.

devolve *verb* to pass or be passed on to a deputy or successor, *this work will devolve on the new manager*.

devon *noun* (*Austral.*) a large bland sausage eaten cold and sliced.

Devonian (dĕ-**voh**-nee-ăn) *adjective* of the fourth period of the Palaeozoic era. –**Devonian** *noun* this period.

Devonshire tea *noun* a cup or pot of tea served with scones, jam, and cream. [from *Devonshire*, the former name for the English county of Devon]

devote *verb* to give or use for a particular activity or purpose, *devoted himself* or *his time to sport*.

devoted *adjective* showing devotion, very loyal or loving. **devotedly** *adverb*

devotee (dev-ŏ-**tee**) *noun* a person who is devoted to something, an enthusiast.

devotion *noun* **1** great love or loyalty; enthusiastic zeal. **2** religious worship. **devotions** *plural noun* prayers.

devotional *adjective* used in religious worship.

devour *verb* **1** to eat hungrily or greedily. **2** to destroy completely, to consume, *fire devoured the forest*. **3** to take in greedily with the eyes or ears, *they devoured the story*. **4** to absorb the attention of, *she was devoured by curiosity*. [from *de-* = completely, + Latin *vorare* = to swallow]

devout *adjective* **1** earnestly religious. **2** earnest, sincere, *a devout supporter*. **devoutly** *adverb*, **devoutness** *noun*

dew *noun* **1** small drops of moisture that condense on cool surfaces during the night from water vapour in the air. **2** moisture in small drops on a surface. □ **dew point** the temperature at which vapour condenses into dew.

dewar flask *noun* a double-walled flask with a vacuum between the walls to reduce heat transfer. [named after Sir James Dewar, British physicist (died 1923)]

dewclaw *noun* a small claw on the inner side of a dog's leg.

dewdrop *noun* a drop of dew.

Dewey system *noun* a decimal system for classifying books in libraries. [named after Melville Dewey (died 1931), the American librarian who devised it]

dewlap *noun* a fold of loose skin that hangs from the throat of cattle and other animals.

dewy *adjective* wet with dew. □ **dewy-eyed** *adjective* innocently trusting or sentimental.

dexter *adjective* (in heraldry) of or on the righthand side (the observer's left) of a shield etc.

dexterity (deks-**te**-rĭ-tee) *noun* skill in handling things. [from Latin *dexter* = on the righthand side]

dextrose *noun* a form of glucose.

dextrous (**deks**-trŭs) *adjective* showing dexterity. **dextrously** *adverb*

Dhaka (**dak**-ă) the capital of Bangladesh.

dhal *noun* a purée of pulse, a common food in India.

Dharawal (**du**-ră-wol) *noun* **1** a member of an Aboriginal people of the south coast of NSW. **2** their language.

dharma (**dar**-mă) *noun* the eternal law of the Hindu cosmos, what is and what should be. [Sanskrit, = decree]

Dharuk (**du**-ruuk) *noun* **1** a member of an Aboriginal people of the Sydney region. **2** their language.

dhikr *noun* (in Islam) a form of devotion, associated chiefly with Sufism, in which the worshipper is absorbed in the rhythmic repetition of the name of God or his attributes. [Arabic]

dhoti (**doh**-tee) *noun* (*plural* **dhotis**) a loincloth worn by male Hindus.

dhow (*pr.* dow) *noun* a ship of the Arabian Sea, with a triangular sail on a slanting yard.

di-¹ *prefix* two; double (as in *dioxide*). [from Greek *dis* = twice]

di-² *prefix* see **dis-**.

dia- *prefix* through (as in *diarrhoea*); across (as in *diagonal*); apart (as in *diaeresis*). [from Greek *dia* = through]

diabetes (dy-ă-**bee**-teez) *noun* a disease in which sugar and starch are not properly absorbed by the body.

diabetic (dy-ă-**bet**-ik) *adjective* of diabetes. –**diabetic** *noun* a person suffering from diabetes.

diabolic (dy-ă-**bol**-ik) *adjective* of the Devil; cruel, wicked.

diabolical (dy-ă-**bol**-ikăl) *adjective* **1** like a devil, very cruel or wicked. **2** fiendishly clever, cunning, or annoying. **diabolically** *adverb*

diadem (**dy**-ă-dem) *noun* a crown or headband worn as a sign of sovereignty.

diaeresis (dy-**eer**-rĕ-sĭs) *noun* (*plural*
diaereses) a mark placed over a vowel to
show that it is sounded separately, as in *naïve*.
[from Greek *diairesis* = separation]

diagnose (dy-ăg-nohz) *verb* to make a
diagnosis of, *typhoid fever was diagnosed in
six patients.*

diagnosis (dy-ăg-**noh**-sĭs) *noun* (*plural*
diagnoses) a statement of the nature of
a disease or other condition made after
observing its signs and symptoms.

diagnostic (dy-ăg-**noss**-tik) *adjective* of or
used in diagnosis, *diagnostic procedures.*

diagonal (dy-**ag**-ŏ-năl) *adjective* slanting,
crossing from corner to corner. –**diagonal**
noun a straight line joining two opposite
corners. **diagonally** *adverb* [from *dia-*,
+ Greek *gonia* = angle]

diagram *noun* **1** an outline drawing that
shows the parts of something or how it works.
2 a stylised drawing showing the course or
results of a process etc. or representing a series
of quantities. **3** (in geometry etc.) a drawing
composed of lines, used in demonstrating a
theorem etc. [from *dia-* + *-gram*]

diagrammatic (dy-ă-gră-**mat**-ik) *adjective*
in the form of a diagram. **diagrammatically**
adverb

dial *noun* **1** the face of a clock or watch.
2 a similar flat plate marked with a scale for
the measurement of something and having
a movable pointer that indicates the amount
registered. **3** a plate or disc etc. on a radio
or television set showing the wavelength
or channel selected. **4** a movable disc with
finger-holes over a circle of numbers or letters,
turned in order to connect one telephone
with another. –**dial** *verb* (**dialled**, **dialling**)
1 to select or regulate by means of a dial.
2 to make a telephone connection by using a
dial or numbered buttons; to ring up (a number
etc.) thus. □ **dial-up** (of a computer system or
service) used remotely via a telephone line.

dialect (**dy**-ă-lekt) *noun* the words and
pronunciation that are used in a particular area
and differ from what is regarded as standard in
the language as a whole.

dialectic (dy-ă-**lek**-tik) *noun* investigation
of truths in philosophy etc. by systematic
reasoning.

dialectical (dy-ă-**lek**-tik-ăl) *adjective* of
dialectic. □ **dialectical materialism** the theory,
put forward by Marx and Engels, that political
and social conditions result from a conflict of

social forces (the 'class struggle') produced by
economic factors.

dialogue (**dy**-ă-log) *noun* **1** a conversation or
discussion. **2** the words spoken by characters
in a play or story.

dialysis (dy-**al**-ĭ-sĭs) *noun* purification of
the blood by causing it to flow through a
suitable membrane. [from *dia-*, + Greek *lusis*
= loosening]

diamanté (dee-ă-**mahn**-tay) *adjective*
decorated with fragments of crystal or other
sparkling substance. [French]

diameter (dy-**am**-ĕ-ter) *noun* **1** a straight line
passing from side to side through the centre of
a circle or sphere. **2** the length of this. [from
Greek, = measuring across]

diametrical (dy-ă-**met**-rik-ăl) *adjective* of or
along a diameter; *the diametrical opposite*, the
exact opposite. **diametrically** *adverb*

diamond *noun* **1** a very hard brilliant precious
stone of pure crystallised carbon. **2** a figure or
shape with four equal sides and with angles
that are not right angles. **3** a playing card of
the suit (*diamonds*) marked with red figures
of this shape. –**diamond** *adjective* made of
or set with diamonds. □ **diamond wedding**
the 60th (or 75th) anniversary of a wedding.
[from Greek *adamas* = adamant (= a very hard
stone)]

Diana (*Rom. myth.*) an early Italian goddess
identified with Artemis.

diapason (dy-ă-**pay**-zŏn) *noun* **1** the entire
range of a musical instrument or a voice.
2 a fixed standard of musical pitch. **3** either of
the two main organ stops extending through
the whole range.

diaper (**dy**-ă-per) *noun* a baby's nappy.

diaphanous (dy-**af**-ă-nŭs) *adjective* (of
fabric) light, delicate, and almost transparent.

diaphragm (**dy**-ă-fram) *noun* **1** the midriff,
the internal muscular partition that separates
the chest from the abdomen and is used in
breathing. **2** a vibrating disc in a microphone
or telephone receiver etc. **3** a device for
varying the aperture of a camera lens. **4** a thin
contraceptive cap fitting over the neck of the
womb.

diarist (**dy**-ă-rĭst) *noun* one who keeps a diary.

diarrhoea (dy-ă-**ree**-ă) *noun* a condition in
which bowel movements are very frequent
and fluid. [from *dia-*, + Greek *rhoia* = a flow]

diary *noun* **1** a daily record of events or thoughts. **2** a book for this or for noting engagements. [from Latin *dies* = day]

Diaspora (dy-**ass**-pŏ-ră) *noun* the Dispersion of the Jews (see dispersion).

diastase (**dy**-ă-stayss) *noun* the enzyme (important in digestion) that converts starch into sugar.

diastole (dy-**ass**-tŏ-lee) *noun* the rhythmical dilatation of the chambers of the heart, alternating with the systole to form the pulse. diastolic (dy-ă-**stol**-ik) *adjective*

diatom (**dy**-ă-tŏm) *noun* a one-celled microscopic alga found as plankton and forming fossil deposits. [from *dia-*, + Greek *tome* = cutting]

diatomic (dy-ă-**tom**-ik) *adjective* **1** consisting of two atoms. **2** having two replaceable atoms or radicals. [from *di-*[1] + *atom*]

diatonic (dy-ă-**tonn**-ik) *adjective* (in music) using the notes of the major or minor scale only, not of the chromatic scale.

diatribe (**dy**-ă-tryb) *noun* a violent attack in words, abusive criticism.

dibber *noun* a hand tool used to make holes in the ground for seeds or young plants.

dibbler *noun* a small spotted marsupial mouse, now almost extinct. [from a dialect of Nyungar, probably *dibala*]

dice *noun* **1** (properly the plural of die[2], but often used as a singular, *plural* dice) a small cube marked on each side with a number of spots (1–6), used in games of chance. **2** a game played with these. –dice *verb* **1** to gamble using dice. **2** to take great risks, *dicing with death*. **3** to cut into small cubes, *diced carrots*. **4** (*Austral. informal*) to reject, to abandon.

dicey *adjective* (*informal*) risky, unreliable.

dichotomy (dy-**kot**-ŏmee) *noun* division into two parts or kinds. [from Greek *dicho-* = apart, + *tome* = cutting]

dichromate (dy-**kroh**-mayt) *noun* a salt of an acid whose ions contain two chromium atoms.

Dickens, Charles Huffham (1812–70), English novelist, whose works include *A Tale of Two Cities*, *David Copperfield*, and *Oliver Twist*. Dickensian *adjective*

dickens *noun* (*informal*, in exclamations of surprise or annoyance) deuce, the Devil, *what the dickens were you doing*.

Dickinson, Emily (Elizabeth) (1830–86), American poet.

dicky *adjective* (*informal*) unsound, likely to collapse or fail, *a dicky heart*.

dicotyledon (dy-kot-ĭ-**lee**-dŏn) *noun* a flowering plant that has two cotyledons.

dictate *verb* **1** to say or read aloud (words) to be written down by a person or recorded by a machine. **2** to state or order with the force of authority, *dictate terms to a defeated enemy*. **3** to give orders officiously, *I will not be dictated to*. dictation *noun* [from Latin *dictare* = keep saying]

dictates (**dik**-tayts) *plural noun* authoritative commands, *the dictates of conscience*.

dictator *noun* **1** a ruler who has unrestricted authority, especially one who has taken control by force. **2** a person with supreme authority in any sphere; one who dictates what is to be done. **3** a domineering person. dictatorial *adjective*, dictatorship *noun*

diction (**dik**-shŏn) *noun* a person's manner of uttering or pronouncing words.

dictionary *noun* a book that lists and explains the words of a language or the words and topics of a particular subject, or that gives their equivalents in another language, usually in alphabetical order. [from Latin *dictio* = word]

dictum *noun* (*plural* dicta) **1** a formal expression of opinion. **2** a saying.

did *see* do.

didactic (dy-**dak**-tik) *adjective* **1** giving instruction. **2** having the manner of one who is lecturing pupils. didactically *adverb* [from Greek *didaktikos* = teaching]

diddle *verb* (*informal*) to cheat, to swindle.

didgeridoo (dij-ĕ-ree-**doo**) *noun* an Aboriginal musical instrument in the form of a long wooden tube.

didn't (*informal*) = did not.

Dido (**dy**-doh) (*Rom. legend*) queen of Carthage, who fell in love with the shipwrecked Aeneas and killed herself when he deserted her.

die[1] *verb* (died, dying) **1** to cease to be alive; to have one's vital functions cease finally. **2** to cease to exist. **3** to cease to function, to stop, *the engine sputtered and died*. **4** (of a fire or flame) to go out. **5** to become exhausted, *we were dying with laughter*. **6** to feel an intense longing, *we are dying to go*; *dying for a drink*.

□ **die away** to become fainter or weaker and then cease, *the noise died away*. **die back** (of plants) to decay from the tip towards the root. **die down** to become less loud or less violent, *the excitement died down*. **die off** to die one by one. **die out** to pass out of existence.

die² *noun* a dice (see **dice**). □ **the die is cast** a step has been taken and its consequences must follow.

die³ *noun* an engraved device that stamps a design on coins or medals etc.; a device that stamps or cuts or moulds material into a particular shape. □ **as straight as a die** quite straight; very honest. **die-cast** *adjective* made by casting metal in a mould. **die-casting** *noun* this process. **die-stamping** *noun* stamping with a die that leaves an embossed design.

diehard *noun* a person who obstinately refuses to abandon old theories or policies, one who resists change.

dielectric *adjective* that does not conduct electricity. – **dielectric** *noun* a dielectric substance usable for insulating things.

diesel (**dee**-zĕl) *noun* **1** a diesel engine; a vehicle driven by this. **2** fuel for a diesel engine. □ **diesel-electric** *adjective* driven by electric current from a generator driven by a diesel engine. **diesel engine** an oil-burning engine in which ignition is produced by the heat of highly compressed air. [named after the German engineer Rudolf Diesel (1858–1913)]

diet¹ *noun* **1** the sort of foods usually eaten by a person or animal or community. **2** a selection of food to which a person is restricted. – **diet** *verb* (**dieted**, **dieting**) **1** to restrict oneself to a special diet, especially in order to control one's weight. **2** to restrict (a person) to a special diet. **dieter** *noun* [from Greek *diaita* = way of life]

diet² *noun* a congress, a parliamentary assembly in certain countries, e.g. Japan. [from Latin *dieta* = day's business]

dietary (**dy**-ĕ-tă-ree) *adjective* of or involving diet.

dietetic (dy-ĕ-**tet**-ik) *adjective* of diet and nutrition. **dietetics** *plural noun* the scientific study of diet and nutrition.

dietitian (dy-ĕ-**tish**-ăn) *noun* an expert in dietetics.

dif- *prefix* see **dis-**.

differ *verb* **1** to be unlike, to be distinguishable from something else. **2** to disagree in opinion.

difference *noun* **1** the state of being different or unlike. **2** the point in which things differ; the amount or degree of unlikeness. **3** the quantity by which amounts differ; the remainder left after subtraction, *the difference between 8 and 5 is 3*. **4** a disagreement in opinion, a quarrel.

different *adjective* **1** unlike, of other nature or form or quality, *different from others*. **2** separate, distinct, *several different people*. **3** unusual, *try Antarctica for a holiday that's different*. **differently** *adverb*

Usage In sense 1 *different from* is the preferred phrase; *different to* is acceptable in informal use; *different than* is common in American use.

---

differential (dif-ĕ-**ren**-shăl) *adjective* **1** of, showing, or depending on a difference. **2** (in mathematics) relating to infinitesimal differences. – **differential** *noun* **1** an agreed difference in wages between industries or between different classes of workers in the same industry. **2** a differential gear. □ **differential calculus** a method of calculating rates of change, maximum and minimum values, etc. **differential gear** an arrangement of gears that allows a motor vehicle's driven wheels to revolve at different speeds in rounding corners.

differentiate (dif-ĕ-**ren**-shee-ayt) *verb* **1** to be a difference between, to make different, *the features that differentiate one breed from another*. **2** to recognise as different, to distinguish, to discriminate. **3** to develop differences, to become different. **4** (in mathematics) to calculate the derivative of. **differentiation** *noun*

difficult *adjective* **1** needing much effort or skill, not easy to do or practise. **2** troublesome, perplexing, *these are difficult times*. **3** not easy to please or satisfy, *a difficult employer*.

difficulty *noun* **1** being difficult. **2** a difficult problem or thing; a hindrance to action. **3** a difficult state of affairs, trouble; *in financial difficulties*, short of money. □ **make difficulties** to raise objections, to put obstacles in the way of progress. **with difficulty** not easily.

diffident (**dif**-ĭ-dĕnt) *adjective* lacking self-confidence, hesitating to put oneself or one's ideas forward. **diffidently** *adverb*, **diffidence** *noun* [from *dif-* = not, + Latin *fidere* = to trust]

diffract *verb* **1** to break up (a beam of light) into a series of dark and light bands or the coloured bands of the spectrum. **2** to break up (a beam of radiation or particles) into a series of high and low intensities. **diffraction** *noun* [from *dif-* = apart, + Latin *fractum* = broken]

diffuse (dǐ-**fewss**) *adjective* **1** spread out, diffused, not concentrated, *diffuse light*. **2** wordy, not concise, *a diffuse style*. –**diffuse** (dǐ-**fewz**) *verb* **1** to spread widely or thinly throughout something, *to diffuse knowledge* or *light* or *heat*. **2** to mix (liquids or gases) slowly, to become intermingled. □ **diffused lighting** lighting that is spread or filtered so that there is no glare. **diffusely** *adverb*, **diffuseness** *noun*, **diffuser** *noun*, **diffusion** *noun* [from *dif-* = apart, + Latin *fusum* = poured]

diffusible *adjective* able to be diffused.

diffusive *adjective* diffusing.

dig *verb* (**dug**, **digging**) **1** to break up and move (ground) with a tool or machine or claws etc.; to make (a way or a hole) by doing this. **2** to obtain or remove by digging, *dig potatoes*. **3** to excavate archaeologically. **4** to seek or discover by investigation, *dug up some useful information*. **5** to thrust, to plunge, *dig a knife into it*. **6** (*informal, old use*) to appreciate, to enjoy; to understand, *they don't dig opera*; *I don't dig it*. –**dig** *noun* **1** a piece of digging. **2** an archaeological excavation. **3** a thrust, a poke, *a dig in the ribs*. **4** a cutting remark; *that was a dig at me*, a remark directed against me. □ **dig in** (*informal*) to begin eating. **dig oneself in** to dig a defensive trench or pit; to establish oneself securely. **dig one's heels in** to become obstinate, to refuse to give way.

digest (dy-**jest**) *verb* **1** to dissolve (food) in the stomach etc. so that it can be absorbed by the body. **2** to think over, to absorb into the mind, *digesting the information*. **3** to summarise methodically. –**digest** (**dy**-jest) *noun* **1** a methodical summary. **2** a periodical publication giving excerpts and summaries of news, writings, etc.

digestible *adjective* able to be digested.

digestion *noun* **1** the process of digesting. **2** the power of digesting food, *has a good digestion*.

digestive *adjective* **1** of or aiding digestion. **2** having the function of digesting food, *the digestive system*. –**digestive** *noun* a **digestive biscuit**, a kind of wholemeal biscuit.

digger *noun* **1** one who digs. **2** a mechanical excavator. **3** a miner, especially a gold digger.

4 (*informal*) an Australian or New Zealand soldier, originally in the First World War.

digit (**dij**-ǐt) *noun* **1** any numeral from 0 to 9, especially when forming part of a number. **2** a finger or toe. [from Latin *digitus* = finger or toe]

digital (**dij**-ǐ-tǎl) *adjective* relating to or using signals or information represented by discrete values of physical quantity such as voltage or magnetic polarisation. Often contrasted with *analog*. □ **digital clock** or **watch** one that shows the time by displaying a row of figures. **digitally** *adverb*

digitalin (dij-ǐ-**tay**-lǐn) *noun* a poisonous substance extracted from foxglove leaves.

digitalis (dij-ǐ-**tay**-lǐs) *noun* a drug prepared from dried foxglove leaves, used as a heart stimulant.

digitiser *noun* (also **-izer**) a device for converting analog signals (e.g. video) to digital ones for computer processing.

dignified *adjective* having or showing dignity.

dignify *verb* (**dignified**, **dignifying**) **1** to give dignity to. **2** to make (a thing) sound more important than it is, *they dignified the creek with the name of 'river'*.

dignitary (**dig**-nǐ-tǎ-ree) *noun* a person holding a high rank or position.

dignity *noun* **1** a calm and serious manner or style, showing suitable formality or indicating that one deserves respect. **2** worthiness, *the dignity of labour*. **3** a high rank or position. [from Latin *dignus* = worthy]

digraph (**dy**-grahf) *noun* a union of two letters representing one sound (as *ph*, *ea*). [from *di-*[1] + *-graph*]

digress (dy-**gress**) *verb* to depart from the main subject temporarily in speaking or writing. **digression** *noun* [from *di-*[2] = away, + Latin *gressum* = gone]

digs *plural noun* (*informal*) lodgings.

dike *noun* = **dyke**.

dilapidated *adjective* falling to pieces, in a state of disrepair.

dilapidation *noun* a state of disrepair; bringing or being brought into this state.

dilatation (dy-lǎ-**tay**-shǒn) *noun* dilation.

dilate (dy-**layt**) *verb* **1** to make or become wider or larger. **2** to speak or write at length. **dilation** *noun*, **dilator** *noun* [from *di-*[2] = apart, + Latin *latus* = wide]

dilatory (**dil**-ă-tŏ-ree) *adjective* **1** slow in doing something, not prompt. **2** designed to cause delay. **dilatorily** *adverb*, **dilatoriness** *noun*

dilemma (dil-**em**-ă) *noun* **1** a perplexing situation, in which a choice has to be made between alternatives that are equally undesirable. **2** a problem or difficult choice, *what to do with one's spare time is a modern dilemma.* [from Greek, = double proposal]

Usage Many people regard the use in sense 2 as unacceptable.

---

dilettante (dil-ĕ-**tan**-tee) *noun* a person who dabbles in a subject for enjoyment and without serious study.

Dili the capital of East Timor.

diligent (**dil**-ĭ-jĕnt) *adjective* **1** hard-working, putting care and effort into what one does. **2** done with care and effort, *a diligent search.* **diligently** *adverb*, **diligence** *noun* [from Latin *diligens* = conscientious]

dill[1] *noun* a yellow-flowered herb with spicy seeds used for flavouring pickles.

dill[2] *noun* (*Austral. informal*) a fool or simpleton.

dillybag *noun* (*Austral.*) a small bag, originally of plaited grass or fibre. [Yagara *dili* = (a bag woven of) coarse grass]

dilly-dally *verb* (*informal*) to dawdle, to waste time by not making up one's mind.

dilute (dy-**lewt**) *verb* **1** to thin down, to make a liquid less concentrated by adding water or other liquid. **2** to weaken or reduce the forcefulness of. **–dilute** *adjective* diluted, *a dilute acid.* **dilution** *noun*

dim *adjective* (**dimmer, dimmest**) **1** faintly lit, luminous but not bright. **2** indistinct, not clearly seen or heard or remembered. **3** not seeing clearly, *eyes dim with tears.* **4** (*informal*) stupid. **–dim** *verb* (**dimmed, dimming**) to make or become dim. ☐ **take a dim view of** (*informal*) to disapprove of; to feel gloomy about. **dimly** *adverb*, **dimness** *noun*

dime *noun* a ten-cent coin of the USA.

dimension (dy-**men**-shŏn) *noun* **1** a measurable extent such as length, breadth, thickness, area, or volume. **2** size; *of great dimensions,* very large. **3** extent, scope, *gave the problem a new dimension.* **dimensional** *adjective*

diminish *verb* to make or become smaller or less.

diminuendo (dĭ-min-yoo-**en**-doh) *adjective & adverb* (in music) gradually becoming quieter. [Italian]

diminution (dim-ĭn-**yoo**-shŏn) *noun* **1** diminishing; being diminished. **2** a decrease.

diminutive (dĭ-**min**-yŭ-tiv) *adjective* remarkably small. **–diminutive** *noun* a word for a small specimen of something (e.g. *booklet, duckling*), or an affectionate form of a name etc. (e.g. *dearie, Johnnie*).

dimity *noun* a cotton fabric woven with checks or stripes of heavier thread.

dimmer *noun* a device for reducing the brightness of lights.

dimple *noun* a small hollow or dent, especially a natural one on the skin of the cheek or chin. **–dimple** *verb* **1** to produce dimples in. **2** to show dimples.

dimwit *noun* (*informal*) a stupid person. **dimwitted** *adjective*

din *noun* a loud resonant and annoying noise. **–din** *verb* (**dinned, dinning**) **1** to make a din. **2** to force (information) into a person by continually repeating it, *din it into him.*

dinar (**dee**-nar) *noun* a unit of currency in the states of the former Yugoslavia and various countries of the Middle East and North Africa.

dine *verb* **1** to eat dinner. **2** to entertain to dinner, *we were wined and dined.*

diner *noun* **1** a person who dines. **2** a dining car on a train. **3** a small dining room.

ding[1] *verb* to make a ringing sound. **–ding** *noun* a ringing sound.

ding[2] (*informal*) *noun* **1** a dent (in a car, surfboard, etc.). **2** a minor collision of motor vehicles etc. **–ding** *verb* to dent, smash, or damage (a car etc.).

dingbat *noun* (*informal*) a stupid or eccentric person. **dingbats** *adjective* peculiar; crazy.

ding-dong *noun* the sound of a clapper bell or alternate strokes of two bells. **–ding-dong** *adjective & adverb* with vigorous and alternating action, *a ding-dong argument.*

dinghy (**ding**-gee *or* **ding**-ee) *noun* (*plural* **dinghies**) **1** a small open boat driven by oars or sails. **2** a small inflatable rubber boat. [from Hindi, = Indian riverboat]

dingo (**ding**-goh) *noun* (*plural* **dingoes**) an Australian native dog. [Dharuk *din-gu* or *dayn-gu* = domesticated dingo]

dingy (**din**-jee) *adjective* (**dingier**, **dingiest**) dirty-looking, not fresh or cheerful. **dingily** *adverb*, **dinginess** *noun*

dining room *noun* a room in which meals are eaten.

dink (*Austral. informal*) *noun* a lift on a bicycle ridden by another person. –**dink** *verb* to give (someone) a dink.

dinkum (*Austral. informal*) *adjective* true, genuine. –**dinkum** *adverb* really, truly. [probably from British dialect, = 'work, a due share of work']

dinky *adjective* (*informal*) attractively small and neat.

dinky-di *adjective* (*Austral. informal*) = **dinkum**.

dinner *noun* **1** the chief meal of the day, whether at midday or in the evening. **2** a formal evening meal in honour of a person or event. □ **dinner jacket** a man's short (usually black) jacket for evening wear.

dinosaur (**dy**-nŏ-sor) *noun* an extinct lizard-like creature of the Mesozoic era, often of enormous size. [from Greek *deinos* = terrible, + *sauros* = lizard]

dint *noun* a dent. –**dint** *verb* to mark with dints. □ **by dint of** by means of.

diocese (**dy**-ŏ-sĕs) *noun* a district under the pastoral care of a bishop. **diocesan** (dy-**oss**-ĕ-săn) *adjective*

Diocletian (dy-ŏ-**klee**-shăn) (died 316), Roman emperor 284–305, noted for his persecution of the Christians.

diode (**dy**-ohd) *noun* a rectifier made of semiconducting materials and having two terminals. [from *di-*[1] + *electrode*]

Diogenes (dy-**oj**-ĕ-neez) (4th c. BC), founder of the Cynics, noted for his ostentatious disregard of conventions.

Dionysus (dy-ŏ-**ny**-sŭs) (*Gk. myth.*) the god of wine and vegetation, also known as Bacchus.

diorama (dy-ŏ-**rah**-mă) *noun* **1** a small model of a scene with three-dimensional figures, viewed through a window etc. **2** a small-scale model or miniature film set. **3** a scenic painting in which changing lighting simulates sunrise etc.

dioxide (dy-**ok**-syd) *noun* an oxide with two atoms of oxygen to one of a metal or other element. [from *di-*[1] + *oxide*]

dip *verb* (**dipped**, **dipping**) **1** to put or lower into liquid; *dip sheep*, wash them in a vermin-killing liquid; *dip fabrics*, dye them in liquid. **2** to go under water and emerge quickly. **3** to go down, *the sun dipped below the horizon*. **4** to put a hand or ladle etc. into something in order to take something out; *dip into one's pocket* or *reserves*, take out money etc. and use it. **5** to lower for a moment, *dip the flag*; *dip headlights*, lower their beam to avoid dazzling other drivers. **6** to slope or extend downwards, *the path dips down to the river*. **7** to read short passages here and there in a book, *we've dipped into 'Middlemarch'*. –**dip** *noun* **1** dipping; being dipped. **2** a quick plunge; (*informal*) a short bathe. **3** a downward slope. **4** a liquid into which something is dipped, *sheep dip*. **5** a creamy mixture or sauce into which food is dipped before eating. **dipper** *noun*

diphtheria (dif-**theer**-reeă) *noun* an acute infectious disease causing severe inflammation of a mucous membrane, especially in the throat. [from Greek, = leather (because a tough skin forms)]

diphthong (**dif**-thong) *noun* a compound vowel sound produced by combining two simple ones, e.g. *oi* in *point*, *ou* in *loud*. [from *di-*[1], + Greek *phthoggos* = sound]

diplodocus (dip-**lod**-ŏ-kŭs) *noun* a giant Jurassic plant-eating dinosaur with a long neck and tail.

diploid (**dip**-loid) *adjective* **1** (of a cell) having its chromosomes in pairs, with half of each pair coming from each parent. **2** (of an organism) having diploid cells. –**diploid** *noun* a diploid cell or organism. **diploidy** *noun* [from Greek *diplous* = double]

diploma *noun* a certificate awarded by a college etc. to a person who has successfully completed a course of study. [from Greek, = folded paper]

diplomacy (dĭ-**ploh**-mă-see) *noun* **1** the handling of international relations; skill in this. **2** tact.

diplomat (**dip**-lŏ-mat) *noun* **1** a member of the diplomatic service. **2** a tactful person.

diplomatic (dip-lŏ-**mat**-ik) *adjective* **1** of or engaged in diplomacy; *the diplomatic service*, the officials engaged in diplomacy on behalf of their country. **2** tactful, *a diplomatic person* or *reply*. **diplomatically** *adverb*

dipole *noun* **1** an object with an opposite magnetisation or electrical charge at two points or poles. **2** a molecule in which positive and negative charges are separated.

diprotodon (dy-**proh**-tŏ-don) *noun* an extinct, very large, herbivorous, Australian quadruped marsupial having two prominent incisors in the lower jaw.

dipsomania (dip-sŏ-**may**-neeǎ) *noun* an uncontrollable craving for alcohol. **dipsomaniac** *noun* a person suffering from this.

dipstick *noun* **1** a rod for measuring the depth of a liquid. **2** a foolish or inept person.

dipterous (**dip**-tě-rŭs) *adjective* **1** (of insects) having two wings. **2** (of seeds) having two winglike parts. [from *di-*[1], + Greek *pteron* = wing]

dire *adjective* **1** dreadful, terrible, *in dire peril*. **2** ominous, predicting trouble, *dire warnings*. **3** extreme and urgent, *in dire need*.

direct *adjective* **1** going in a straight line, not curved or crooked or roundabout, *the direct route*. **2** with nothing or no one in between, in an unbroken line, *in direct contact*. **3** straightforward, frank, going straight to the point, *a direct way of speaking*. **4** exact, complete, *the direct opposite*. –**direct** *adverb* by a direct route, *travelled to Bangkok direct*. –**direct** *verb* **1** to tell or show how to do something or get somewhere, *can you direct me to the station?* **2** to address (a letter or parcel etc.). **3** to cause to have a specified direction or target. **4** to control, to manage, *there was no one to direct the workmen*; *direct a film*, supervise the acting and filming of it. **5** to command, to order, *directed his men to advance*. □ **direct access** *see* **access**. **direct current** electric current flowing in one direction only. **direct debit** an arrangement for the regular debiting of a bank account at the request of the payee. **directed number** a number with a plus or minus sign. **direct object** *see* **object**. **direct question** or **speech** etc., words quoted in the form in which they were actually spoken (e.g. 'Has he come?'), not altered by being reported (e.g. 'she asked whether he had come'). **direct taxes** taxes (such as income tax) that are levied on the actual person who pays them, not on goods etc. that he or she buys. **directness** *noun* [from Latin *directum* = kept straight]

direction *noun* **1** directing, aiming, guiding, managing. **2** the line along which something moves or faces, *in the direction of Melbourne*. **directions** *plural noun* instructions for finding a place or doing something. □ **sense of direction** a person's ability to get his or her bearings without guidance.

directional *adjective* **1** of or indicating direction. **2** operating or sending radio signals in one direction only.

directive *noun* a general instruction issued by authority.

directly *adverb* **1** without delay. **2** very soon. **3** in a direct line, *lives directly opposite the park*. **4** in a direct manner, frankly. –**directly** *conjunction* (*informal*) as soon as, *I went directly I knew*.

director *noun* **1** a person who supervises or manages things, especially a member of the board managing a business company on behalf of shareholders. **2** a person who directs a film or play. **directorship** *noun*

directorate *noun* **1** the position of director. **2** a board of directors.

directory *noun* a book containing a list of telephone subscribers, inhabitants of a district, members of a profession, business firms, etc.

directrix *noun* (*plural* **directrices**, *pr.* di-**rek**-trĭ-seez) a fixed straight line used in drawing parabolas and certain other curves.

dirge (*pr.* derj) *noun* a slow mournful song, a lament for the dead.

dirigible (**di**-rij-ĭbŭl) *adjective* capable of being guided. –**dirigible** *noun* a balloon or airship that can be steered in flight.

dirk *noun* a kind of dagger, especially of a Scottish highlander.

dirndl (**dern**-d'l) *noun* a full skirt gathered into a tight waistband.

dirt *noun* **1** unclean matter that soils something. **2** earth, soil. **3** anything worthless or not deserving respect. **4** foul words or talk, scandal.

dirty *adjective* (**dirtier**, **dirtiest**) **1** soiled, unclean; *a dirty job*, causing the doer to become dirty. **2** not having clean habits. **3** dishonourable, mean, unfair, *a dirty trick*; *a dirty fighter*. **4** (of weather) rough and stormy. **5** lewd, obscene, *dirty jokes*. –**dirty** *verb* (**dirtied**, **dirtying**) to make or become dirty. □ **dirty bomb** a bomb dispersed by conventional explosives but containing radioactive material. **dirtily** *adverb*, **dirtiness** *noun*

dis- *prefix* (changing to **dif-** before *f*, **di-** before some consonants). **1** not; the reverse of (as in *dishonest*). **2** apart, separated (as in *disarm*, *disperse*). [from Latin, = not; away]

disability *noun* something that disables or disqualifies a person; an incapacity, either congenital or caused by injury or disease etc.

disable *verb* to deprive of some ability, to make unfit or useless. **disablement** *noun*

disabled *adjective* having a physical or mental disability.

disabuse (dis-ă-**bewz**) *verb* to disillusion, to free from a false idea, *he was soon disabused of this notion*.

disaccharide (dy-**sak**-ă-ryd) *noun* any sugar whose molecule consists of two simple sugar molecules linked together.

disadvantage *noun* 1 an unfavourable condition or circumstance; *at a disadvantage*, in an unfavourable position. 2 damage to one's interest or reputation; *to our disadvantage*, causing us loss or inconvenience etc. – disadvantage *verb* to put at a disadvantage.

disadvantaged *adjective* suffering from unfavourable conditions of life.

disadvantageous (dis-ad-văn-**tay**-jŭs) *adjective* causing disadvantage.

disaffected *adjective* discontented, having lost one's feelings of loyalty. **disaffection** *noun*

disagree *verb* (disagreed, disagreeing) 1 to have a different opinion. 2 to be unlike, to fail to correspond. 3 to quarrel. □ **disagree with** to differ in opinion from; (of food or climate) to have bad effects on. **disagreement** *noun*

disagreeable *adjective* 1 unpleasant. 2 bad-tempered. **disagreeably** *adverb*

disallow *verb* to refuse to allow or accept as valid, *the judge disallowed the claim*.

disappear *verb* to cease to be visible, to pass from sight or from existence. **disappearance** *noun*

disappoint *verb* to fail to do or be equal to what was hoped or desired or expected by. □ **disappointed** *adjective* feeling disappointment, *we were disappointed at the failure* or *in* or *with a thing*. **disappointment** *noun*

disapprobation (dis-ap-rŏ-**bay**-shŏn) *noun* disapproval.

disapprove *verb* to have or express an unfavourable opinion. **disapproval** *noun*

disarm *verb* 1 to deprive of weapons or of the means of defence. 2 to disband or reduce armed forces. 3 to defuse (a bomb). 4 to make it difficult for a person to feel (anger or suspicion or doubt), *his friendliness disarmed their hostility*.

disarmament *noun* reduction of a country's armed forces or weapons of war.

disarrange *verb* to put into disorder, to disorganise. **disarrangement** *noun*

disarray *noun* disorder. – disarray *verb* to disarrange.

disassociate *verb* = dissociate.

disaster *noun* 1 a sudden great misfortune. 2 a complete failure. **disastrous** *adjective*, **disastrously** *adverb* [literally 'an unlucky star', from *dis-*, + Latin *astrum* = star]

disavow *verb* to disclaim. **disavowal** *noun*

disband *verb* to break up, to separate, *disbanded the choir*; *the troops disbanded*. **disbandment** *noun*

disbelieve *verb* to refuse or be unable to believe. **disbeliever** *noun*, **disbelief** *noun*

disburse *verb* to pay out (money), *disbursing large sums*. **disbursal** *noun*, **disbursement** *noun*

disc *noun* 1 a thin circular plate of any material. 2 something shaped or looking like this, *the sun's disc*. 3 a layer of cartilage between vertebrae; *a slipped disc*, one that has become displaced, causing pain from pressure on nerves. 4 a gramophone record. 5 a compact disc. 6 (in computing) = disk. □ **disc brake** one in which a flat plate presses against a plate at the centre of a wheel. **disc jockey** (*informal*) the compère of a broadcast program of records of light and popular music. [from Latin *discus* = disc]

discard (dis-**kard**) *verb* to throw away, to put aside as useless or unwanted. – discard (**dis**-kard) *noun* something discarded.

discern (dĭ-**sern**) *verb* to perceive clearly with the mind or senses. **discernible** *adjective*, **discernment** *noun*

discerning (dĭ-**sern**-ing) *adjective* perceptive, showing good judgment.

discharge (dis-**charj**) *verb* 1 to give or send out (fluid etc.); to pour out. 2 to give out an electric charge; to cause to do this. 3 to fire (a missile or gun). 4 to dismiss from employment, *a discharged servant*. 5 to allow to leave, *the patient was discharged from hospital*; *a discharged bankrupt*, a bankrupt who has done what the court required and is now freed from its control. 6 to pay (a debt); to perform or fulfil (a duty or contract). – discharge (dis-**charj** or **dis**-charj) *noun*

1 discharging; being discharged. 2 something that is discharged, *the discharge from the wound.* 3 the release of an electric charge, especially with a spark. 4 a written certificate of release or dismissal etc.

disciple (dĭ-**sy**-pŭl) *noun* 1 any of the original followers of Christ. 2 a person who follows the teachings of another whom he or she accepts as a leader. [from Latin *discipulus* = learner]

disciplinarian (dis-ĭ-plĭ-**nair**-ree-ăn) *noun* one who enforces or believes in strict discipline.

disciplinary (**dis**-ĭ-plin-ă-ree) *adjective* of or for discipline.

discipline (**dis**-ĭ-plĭn) *noun* 1 training that produces obedience, self-control, or a particular skill. 2 controlled behaviour produced by such training. 3 punishment given to correct a person or enforce obedience. 4 a branch of instruction or learning.
–**discipline** *verb* 1 to train to be obedient and orderly. 2 to punish. [from Latin *disciplina* = training]

disclaim *verb* to disown; *they disclaim responsibility for the accident*, say that they are not responsible.

disclaimer *noun* a statement disclaiming something.

disclose *verb* to expose to view, to reveal, to make known. **disclosure** *noun*

disco *noun* (*plural* **discos**) (*informal*) a discothèque.

discolour *verb* 1 to spoil the colour of, to stain. 2 to become changed in colour or stained. **discoloration** *noun*

discomfit (dis-**kum**-fĭt) *verb* (**discomfited**, **discomfiting**) to disconcert; to thwart. **discomfiture** (dis-**kum**-fĭ-cher) *noun*

discomfort *noun* 1 being uncomfortable in body or mind. 2 something that causes this.

discompose *verb* to disturb the composure of, to agitate. **discomposure** *noun*

disconcert (dis-kŏn-**sert**) *verb* to upset the self-possession of, to fluster.

disconnect *verb* to break the connection of; to put out of action by disconnecting certain parts. **disconnection** *noun*

disconnected *adjective* lacking orderly connection between its parts.

disconsolate (dis-**kon**-sŏ-lăt) *adjective* unhappy at the loss of something, disappointed. **disconsolately** *adverb*

discontent *noun* dissatisfaction, lack of contentment. **discontentment** *noun*

discontented *adjective* not contented, feeling discontent.

discontinue *verb* to put an end to, to come to an end. **discontinuance** *noun*

discontinuous *adjective* not continuous. **discontinuity** (dis-kon-tĭn-**yoo**-ĭ-tee) *noun*

discord (**dis**-kord) *noun* 1 disagreement, quarrelling. 2 a combination of musical notes producing a harsh or unpleasant sound. **discordance** *noun*, **discordant** (dis-**kor**-dănt) *adjective*, **discordantly** *adverb* [from *dis-* = not, + Latin *cordis* = of the heart]

discothèque (**dis**-kŏ-tek) *noun* 1 a club or party etc. where amplified recorded music is played for dancing. 2 the equipment used at a discothèque. [French, = record library]

discount (**dis**-kownt) *noun* an amount of money taken off the full price or total.
–**discount** (dis-**kownt**) *verb* 1 to disregard partly or wholly, *we cannot discount this possibility.* 2 to reduce the price of.
☐ **at a discount** below the nominal or usual price; not valued as it used to be, *is honesty at a discount nowadays?*

discourage *verb* 1 to dishearten. 2 to dissuade. 3 to deter. **discouragement** *noun*

discourse (**dis**-korss) *noun* 1 a speech or lecture. 2 a written treatise on a subject.
–**discourse** (dis-**korss**) *verb* to utter or write a discourse.

discourteous (dis-**ker**-tee-ŭs) *adjective* lacking courtesy. **discourteously** *adverb*, **discourtesy** *noun*

discover *verb* 1 to obtain sight or knowledge of, especially by searching or other effort. 2 to be the first to do this. **discoverer** *noun* [from *dis-* = apart, + *cover*]

discovery *noun* 1 discovering; being discovered. 2 something that is discovered.

discredit *verb* (**discredited**, **discrediting**) 1 to damage the good reputation of. 2 to refuse to believe. 3 to cause to be disbelieved.
–**discredit** *noun* 1 damage to reputation. 2 something that causes this. 3 doubt, lack of credibility.

discreditable *adjective* bringing discredit, shameful. **discreditably** *adverb*

discreet *adjective* 1 showing caution and good judgment in what one does; not giving away secrets. **2** not showy or obtrusive. **discreetly** *adverb*

Usage Distinguish *discreet* from *discrete*.

---

discrepancy (dĭs-**krep**-ăn-see) *noun* difference, failure to tally, *there were discrepancies between the two accounts*. **discrepant** *adjective* [from Latin, = discord]

discrete (dis-**kreet**) *adjective* **1** discontinuous, individually distinct. **2** (of a mathematical set) such that between any two elements of the set there is a number, point, etc. that is not a member of that set. **discretely** *adverb*

Usage Distinguish *discrete* from *discreet*.

---

discretion (dĭs-**kresh**-ŏn) *noun* **1** being discreet in one's speech, keeping secrets. **2** good judgment, *he acted with discretion*. **3** freedom or authority to act according to one's judgment, *the treasurer has full discretion*. □ **at a person's discretion** in accordance with his or her decision. **years** or **age of discretion** the age at which a person is considered capable of managing his or her own affairs.

discretionary (dĭs-**kresh**-ŏ-nă-ree) *adjective* done or used at a person's discretion.

discriminate *verb* **1** to have good taste or judgment. **2** to make a distinction; to give unfair treatment, especially because of prejudice. **discrimination** *noun*, **discriminatory** *adjective* [from Latin *discrimen* = separator]

discursive *adjective* rambling from one subject to another.

discus *noun* a heavy thick-centred disc, thrown in contests of strength.

discuss *verb* to examine by means of argument; to talk or write about. **discussion** *noun*

disdain *noun* scorn, contempt. **–disdain** *verb* **1** to regard with disdain, to treat as unworthy of notice. **2** to refrain because of disdain, *she disdained to reply*. **disdainful** *adjective*, **disdainfully** *adverb* [from *dis-* = not, + Latin *dignus* = worthy]

disease *noun* an unhealthy condition caused by infection or diet or by faulty functioning of a bodily process. [from *dis-* = not, + *ease*]

diseased *adjective* affected with disease.

disembark *verb* to put or go ashore. **disembarkation** *noun*

disembodied *adjective* (of the soul or spirit) freed from the body.

disembowel *verb* (**disembowelled**, **disembowelling**) to take out the bowels of.

disenchant *verb* to free from enchantment, to disillusion. **disenchantment** *noun*

disencumber *verb* to free from an encumbrance.

disenfranchise (dis-ĕn-**fran**-chyz) *verb* **1** to deprive of the right to vote. **2** to deprive of rights etc. or of a franchise. **disenfranchisement** *noun*

disengage *verb* to free from engagement, to detach. **disengagement** *noun*

disengaged *adjective* not engaged in attending to another person or to business, free.

disentangle *verb* to free from tangles or confusion, to extricate. **disentanglement** *noun*

disestablish *verb* to end the established state of; to deprive (the Church) of its official connection with the State. **disestablishment** *noun*

disfavour *noun* dislike, disapproval.

disfigure *verb* to spoil the appearance of. **disfigurement** *noun*

disgorge *verb* **1** to throw out from the gorge or throat, *the whale swallowed Jonah and then disgorged him*. **2** to pour forth, *the river disgorges itself into the sea*. **3** (*informal*) to hand over, *made him disgorge the stolen property*. [from *dis-* + *gorge* = throat]

disgrace *noun* **1** loss of favour or respect. **2** something that causes this. **–disgrace** *verb* to bring disgrace upon, to humiliate.

disgraceful *adjective* causing disgrace. **disgracefully** *adverb*

disgruntled *adjective* discontented, resentful.

disguise *verb* **1** to conceal the identity of. **2** to conceal; *there's no disguising the fact*, it cannot be concealed. **–disguise** *noun* **1** something worn or used for disguising. **2** disguising; a disguised condition.

disgust *noun* a strong feeling of dislike; finding a thing very unpleasant or against one's principles. **–disgust** *verb* to cause disgust in. [from *dis-* = not, + Latin *gustare* = to taste]

disgusted *adjective* feeling disgust.

dish *noun* **1** a shallow flat-bottomed container for holding or serving food; *wash the dishes*, wash all the crockery and utensils after use at a meal. **2** the amount a dish contains. **3** the food itself; a particular kind of food. **4** a shallow concave object. **5** a concave dish-shaped aerial used for receiving satellite communications and in radio astronomy. **6** (*informal*) an attractive person. –**dish** *verb* to make dish-shaped. □ **dish out** (*informal*) to distribute. **dish up** to put food into dishes ready for serving; (*informal*) to serve up as facts etc., *dished up the usual excuses.*

disharmony *noun* lack of harmony.

dishcloth *noun* a cloth for washing dishes.

dishdasha *noun* (also **dishdash**) a long robe with long sleeves worn by men from the Arabian peninsula. [Arabic]

dishearten *verb* to cause to lose hope or confidence. **disheartenment** *noun*

dishevelled (dish-**ev**-ĕld) *adjective* ruffled and untidy. **dishevelment** *noun* [from *dis-* = apart, + Old French *chevel* = hair]

dishonest *adjective* not honest. **dishonestly** *adverb*, **dishonesty** *noun*

dishonour *noun* **1** loss of honour or respect, disgrace. **2** something that causes this. –**dishonour** *verb* **1** to bring dishonour upon, to disgrace. **2** to refuse to honour (a cheque etc.).

dishonourable *adjective* not honourable, shameful. **dishonourably** *adverb*

dishwasher *noun* a machine for washing dishes etc. automatically.

dishwater *noun* water in which used dishes have been washed. □ **dull as dishwater** *see* **ditchwater**.

dishy *adjective* (**dishier**, **dishiest**) (*informal*) very attractive.

disillusion *verb* to set free from pleasant but mistaken beliefs. –**disillusion** *noun* the state of being disillusioned. **disillusionment** *noun*

disincentive *noun* something that discourages an action or effort.

disinclination *noun* reluctance, unwillingness; a slight dislike.

disincline *verb* to make (a person) feel reluctant or unwilling to do something.

disinfect *verb* to cleanse by destroying bacteria that may cause disease. **disinfection** *noun*

disinfectant *noun* a substance used for disinfecting things.

disinflation *noun* the process of counteracting inflation without causing deflation. **disinflationary** *adjective*

disinformation *noun* deliberately false information.

disingenuous (dis-in-**jen**-yoo-ŭs) *adjective* insincere, not frank. **disingenuously** *adverb*

disinherit *verb* to deprive (a person) of an inheritance by making a will naming another or others as one's heir(s).

disintegrate *verb* **1** to break or cause to break into small parts or pieces. **2** (of an atomic nucleus or particle) to decay (*see* **decay** *verb* sense 3), to change in a similar way when bombarded. **disintegration** *noun*

disinter (dis-in-**ter**) *verb* (**disinterred**, **disinterring**) to dig up (something buried), to unearth.

disinterested *adjective* **1** impartial, unbiased, not influenced by self-interest. **2** (*informal*) uninterested, uncaring. **disinterestedly** *adverb*

Usage Although the use in sense 2 is common informally, it is widely regarded as incorrect and is best avoided because it obscures a useful distinction between *disinterested* and *uninterested*.

---

disjoin *verb* to separate.

disjointed *adjective* (of talk) disconnected.

disjunctive *adjective* (of conjunctions such as *or* and *but*) introducing an alternative or contrast. □ **disjunctive pronouns** the pronouns in French (*moi, toi, lui,* etc.) that are used instead of nominative forms (*je, tu, il,* etc.) after the verb *to be* etc. [from *dis-*, + Latin *junctum* = joined]

disk *noun* (also **disc**) **1** a computer storage device consisting of one or more circular plates, coated with magnetic material on which data can be recorded. (*See also* **floppy disk** and **hard disk**.) **2** *see* **CD-ROM**. □ **disk drive** a mechanism that turns the disk on a computer etc. while data are recorded or retrieved.

diskette *noun* a floppy disk.

dislike *noun* **1** a feeling of not liking some person or thing. **2** the object of this. –**dislike** *verb* to feel dislike for.

dislocate *verb* **1** to put (a thing) out of place in relation to connecting parts; to displace (a bone) from its proper position in a joint. **2** to put out of order, to disrupt, *the power failure dislocated business*. **dislocation** *noun*

dislodge *verb* to move or force from an established position. **dislodgement** *noun*

disloyal *adjective* not loyal. **disloyally** *adverb*, **disloyalty** *noun*

dismal *adjective* **1** causing or showing gloom, dreary. **2** (*informal*) feeble, *a dismal attempt at humour*. **dismally** *adverb* [from Latin *dies mali* = unlucky days]

dismantle *verb* to take away fittings or furnishings from, to take to pieces.

dismay *noun* a feeling of surprise and discouragement. −**dismay** *verb* to fill with dismay.

dismember *verb* **1** to remove the limbs of. **2** to divide into parts; to partition (a country etc.). **dismemberment** *noun*

dismiss *verb* **1** to send away from one's presence or employment. **2** to put out of one's thoughts; to mention or discuss only briefly. **3** to reject without further hearing, *the case was dismissed for lack of evidence*. **4** to put (a batsman or side) out in cricket, *dismissed him for six runs*. **dismissal** *noun*, **dismissive** *adjective* [from *dis-*, + Latin *missum* = sent]

dismount *verb* **1** to get off or down from something on which one is riding. **2** to cause to fall off, to unseat.

disobedient *adjective* not obedient. **disobediently** *adverb*, **disobedience** *noun*

disobey *verb* (**disobeyed**, **disobeying**) to disregard orders, to fail to obey.

disorder *noun* **1** lack of order, untidiness. **2** a disturbance of public order, a riot. **3** disturbance of the normal working of the body or mind, *a nervous disorder*. −**disorder** *verb* to throw into disorder, to upset. **disorderly** *adjective*

disorganise *verb* (also **-ize**) to throw into confusion, to upset the orderly system or arrangement of. **disorganisation** *noun*

disorganised *adjective* (also **-ized**) lacking organisation or an orderly system.

disorientate (dis-**o**-ree-ĕn-tayt) *verb* to confuse (a person) and make him lose his bearings. **disorientation** *noun*

disown *verb* to refuse to acknowledge as one's own, to reject all connection with.

disparage (dĭs-**pa**-rij) *verb* to speak of in a slighting way, to belittle. **disparagingly** *adverb*, **disparagement** *noun*

disparate (**dis**-pă-răt) *adjective* different in kind.

disparity (dis-**pa**-rĭ-tee) *noun* inequality, difference.

dispassionate *adjective* free from emotion, calm, impartial. **dispassionately** *adverb*

dispatch *verb* **1** to send off to a destination or for a purpose. **2** to give the death blow to, to kill. **3** to complete or dispose of quickly. −**dispatch** *noun* **1** dispatching; being dispatched. **2** promptness, speed, *he acted with dispatch*. **3** an official message or report sent with speed. **4** a news report sent to a newspaper or news agency etc.

dispel *verb* (**dispelled**, **dispelling**) to drive away, to scatter, *the doctor dispelled her fears*. [from *dis-* = apart, + Latin *pellere* = to drive]

dispensable *adjective* not essential.

dispensary *noun* a place where medicines are dispensed, *the hospital dispensary*.

dispensation *noun* **1** dispensing, distributing. **2** ordering or management, especially of the world by Providence. **3** exemption from a penalty, rule, or duty.

dispense *verb* **1** to distribute, to deal out; *dispense justice*, to administer it. **2** to prepare and give out (medicines etc.) according to prescriptions. □ **dispense with** to do without; to make unnecessary. [from *dis-* = separately, + Latin *pensum* = weighed]

dispenser *noun* **1** a person who dispenses medicines. **2** a device that deals out a quantity of something, *a soap dispenser*.

dispersant *noun* a substance that disperses something.

disperse *verb* to scatter, to go or drive or send in different directions. **dispersal** *noun* [from Latin *dispersum* = scattered]

dispersion *noun* dispersing; being dispersed. −**the Dispersion** the scattering of Jews among Gentiles from the time of the Captivity in Babylon (6th century BC) onwards.

dispirited *adjective* depressed, disheartened.

displace *verb* **1** to shift from its place. **2** to take the place of, to oust, *weeds tend to displace other plants*.

displacement *noun* **1** displacing, being displaced. **2** the distance something is shifted. **3** the amount or weight of fluid displaced by something floating or immersed in it.

display *verb* **1** to show, to arrange (a thing) so that it can be seen. **2** (of birds and animals) to make a display (see sense 3 below).

–**display** *noun* **1** displaying; being displayed. **2** something displayed conspicuously. **3** a special pattern of behaviour used by birds and animals as a means of visual communication. **4** the presentation of signals or data on a visual display unit; the information presented; a VDU. [from *dis-* = separately, + Latin *plicare* = to fold]

displease *verb* to offend, to arouse the disapproval or anger of.

displeasure *noun* a displeased feeling, dissatisfaction.

disport *verb* (*formal*) to play, to amuse oneself, *disporting themselves on the beach*. [from *dis-*, + Latin *portare* = carry]

disposable *adjective* **1** able to be disposed of. **2** at one's disposal; *disposable income*, the amount left after taxes have been deducted. **3** designed to be thrown away after being used once. –**disposable** *noun* a disposable article, e.g. a disposable nappy.

disposal *noun* disposing of something. □ **at one's disposal** available for one's use.

dispose *verb* **1** to place suitably or in order, *disposed the troops in two lines*. **2** to determine the course of events, *man proposes, God disposes*. **3** to make willing or ready to do something, to incline, *their friendliness disposed us to accept the invitation*; *we felt disposed to accept*. □ **be well disposed towards** to be friendly towards, to favour. **dispose of** to get rid of; to deal with. [from *dis-* = away, + French *poser* = to place]

disposition *noun* **1** setting in order, arrangement, *the disposition of troops*. **2** a person's natural qualities of mind and character, *has a cheerful disposition*. **3** a natural tendency or inclination, *a disposition to spite*.

dispossess *verb* to deprive (a person) of the possession of something. **dispossession** *noun*

disproof *noun* disproving; a refutation.

disproportionate *adjective* out of proportion, relatively too large or too small. **disproportionately** *adverb*, **disproportion** *noun*

disprove *verb* to show to be false or wrong.

disputable (dis-**pewt**-ăbŭl) *adjective* able to be disputed, questionable.

disputant (dis-**pew**-tănt) *noun* a person engaged in a dispute.

disputation *noun* argument, debate.

dispute (dĭs-**pewt**) *verb* **1** to argue, to debate. **2** to quarrel. **3** to question the truth or validity of, *dispute a claim; the disputed territory*, that which is the subject of a dispute. –**dispute** (dĭs-**pewt** *or* **dis**-pewt) *noun* **1** an argument or debate. **2** a quarrel. □ **in dispute** being argued about. [from *dis-* = apart, + Latin *putare* = consider]

disqualify *verb* (**disqualified**, **disqualifying**) **1** to debar from a competition because of an infringement of the rules. **2** to make unsuitable or ineligible, *flat feet disqualified him for military service*. **disqualification** *noun*

disquiet *noun* uneasiness, anxiety. –**disquiet** *verb* to cause disquiet to. **disquietude** *noun*

disquieting *adjective* causing disquiet.

disquisition (dis-kwĭ-**zish**-ŏn) *noun* a long elaborate spoken or written account of something. [from *dis-*, + Latin *quaesitum* = sought]

disregard *verb* to pay no attention to, to treat as of no importance. –**disregard** *noun* lack of attention to something, treating it as of no importance, *complete disregard for his own safety*.

disrepair *noun* a bad condition caused by lack of repairs, *in a state of disrepair*.

disreputable (dis-**rep**-yŭ-tăbŭl) *adjective* having a bad reputation, not respectable in character or appearance. **disreputably** *adverb*

disrepute (dis-rĕ-**pewt**) *noun* lack of good repute, discredit, *fell into disrepute*.

disrespect *noun* lack of respect, rudeness. **disrespectful** *adjective*, **disrespectfully** *adverb*

disrobe *verb* to take off official or ceremonial robes; to undress.

disrupt *verb* to cause to break up, to throw into disorder, to interrupt the flow or continuity of, *party quarrels disrupted the coalition*; *rain disrupted play*. **disruption** *noun* [from *dis-* = apart, + Latin *ruptum* = broken]

disruptive *adjective* causing disruption.

dissatisfaction *noun* lack of satisfaction or of contentment.

dissatisfied *adjective* not satisfied, feeling dissatisfaction.

dissect *verb* **1** to cut into pieces, especially in order to examine internal structure. **2** to examine (a theory etc.) part by part. **dissection** *noun*, **dissector** *noun* [from *dis-* = apart, + Latin *sectum* = cut]]

dissemble *verb* to conceal (one's feelings).

disseminate (dĭ-**sem**-ĭ-nayt) *verb* to spread (ideas etc.) widely. **dissemination** *noun* [from *dis-* = apart, + Latin *seminare* = sow (scatter seeds)]

dissension *noun* disagreement that gives rise to strife.

dissent *verb* to have or express a different opinion. –**dissent** *noun* a difference in opinion. **dissenter** *noun* [from *dis-* = apart, + Latin *sentire* = feel]

dissentient (dĭ-**sen**-shĕnt) *adjective* dissenting. –**dissentient** *noun* one who dissents.

dissertation *noun* a spoken or written discourse.

disservice *noun* a harmful action done by a person who intended to help.

dissident (**dis**-ĭ-dĕnt) *adjective* disagreeing. –**dissident** *noun* one who disagrees; one who opposes the authorities. **dissidence** *noun*

dissimilar *adjective* unlike. **dissimilarity** *noun*

dissimulation *noun* dissembling.

dissipate (**dis**-ĭ-payt) *verb* **1** to dispel, to disperse. **2** to squander or fritter away. [from Latin *dissipare* = scatter]

dissipated *adjective* indulging one's vices, living a dissolute life.

dissipation *noun* **1** dissipating; being dissipated. **2** dissipated living.

dissociate (dis-**soh**-see-ayt *or* -shee-) *verb* to separate in one's thoughts; *dissociate oneself from a thing*, to declare that one has no connection with it. **dissociation** *noun*

dissoluble *adjective* able to be disintegrated, loosened, or disconnected.

dissolute (**dis**-ŏ-loot) *adjective* lacking moral restraint or self-discipline.

dissolution *noun* **1** the dissolving of an assembly or partnership. **2** death. **3** the ending of the existence of monasteries in the reign of Henry VIII.

dissolve *verb* **1** to make or become liquid; to disperse or cause to be dispersed in a liquid. **2** to cause to disappear; to disappear gradually. **3** to dismiss or disperse (an assembly, e.g. parliament); to annul or put an end to (a partnership, e.g. a marriage). **4** to give way to emotion, *she dissolved into tears*. [from *dis-* = separate, + Latin *solvere* = loosen]

dissonant (**dis**-ŏ-nănt) *adjective* discordant. **dissonance** *noun* [from *dis-*, + Latin *sonare* = to sound]

dissuade *verb* to discourage or persuade against a course of action, *dissuaded her from going*. **dissuasion** *noun* [from *dis-* = apart, + Latin *suadere* = advise]

dissuasive *adjective* dissuading.

distaff (**dis**-tahf) *noun* a cleft stick holding wool etc. for spinning. ☐ **on the distaff side** on the mother's side of a family.

distance *noun* **1** the length of space between one point and another. **2** a distant part, *in the distance*. **3** being distant, remoteness. –**distance** *verb* to outdistance in a race. ☐ **at a distance** far off, not very near; *keep someone at a distance*, to avoid becoming too friendly. **keep one's distance** to remain at a safe distance; to behave aloofly, to be not very friendly.

distant *adjective* **1** at a specified or considerable distance away, *three kilometres distant*. **2** remote, much apart in space, time, or relationship etc., *the distant past*. **3** not friendly, aloof. **distantly** *adverb* [from *dis-* = apart, + Latin *stans* = standing]

distaste *noun* dislike.

distasteful *adjective* unpleasant, arousing distaste. **distastefully** *adverb*

distemper[1] *noun* a disease of dogs and certain other animals, with coughing and weakness.

distemper[2] *noun* a paint made from powdered colouring matter mixed with glue or size. –**distemper** *verb* to paint with this.

distend *verb* to swell or become swollen by pressure from within. **distension** *noun* [from *dis-* = apart, + Latin *tendere* = stretch]

distil *verb* (**distilled**, **distilling**) **1** to treat by distillation; to make or produce or purify in this way. **2** to undergo distillation. [from *dis-* = apart, + Latin *stillare* = drip down]

distillate *noun* a substance produced by distillation.

distillation *noun* **1** the process of turning a substance to vapour by heat, then cooling the vapour so that it condenses and collecting the resulting liquid in order to purify it or separate its constituents or extract an essence. **2** something distilled.

distiller *noun* a person who distils; one who makes alcoholic liquors by distillation.

distillery *noun* a place where alcoholic liquor is distilled.

distinct *adjective* **1** able to be perceived clearly by the senses or the mind, definite

and unmistakable, *a distinct improvement*.
2 different in kind, separate. **distinctly** *adverb*,
distinctness *noun*

distinction *noun* **1** seeing or making a
difference between things. **2** a difference
seen or made. **3** a thing that differentiates
one thing from another. **4** a mark of honour.
5 excellence, *a person of distinction*.

distinctive *adjective* characteristic, serving
to distinguish a thing by making it different
from others.

Usage *Distinctive* is sometimes confused with
distinct. A *distinct* sign is one that can be seen
clearly; a *distinctive* sign is one not commonly
found elsewhere.

distinguish *verb* **1** to see or point out a
difference between, to draw distinctions,
we must distinguish fact from opinion.
2 to make different, to be a characteristic
mark or property of, *speech distinguishes
man from animals*. **3** to make out by listening
or looking, *unable to distinguish distant
objects*. **4** to make notable, to bring honour
to, *he distinguished himself by his bravery*.
distinguishable *adjective* [from Latin
distinguere = to separate]

distinguished *adjective* **1** showing
excellence. **2** famous for great achievements.
3 having an air of distinction and dignity.

distort *verb* **1** to pull or twist out of its
usual shape. **2** to misrepresent (facts etc.).
3 to transmit (sound etc.) inaccurately.
distortion *noun* [from *dis-* = apart, + Latin
tortum = twisted]

distract *verb* **1** to draw away the attention of.
2 to confuse, to bewilder. [from *dis-* = apart,
+ Latin *tractum* = pulled]

distracted *adjective* distraught, *distracted
by grief*.

distraction *noun* **1** something that distracts
the attention and prevents concentration.
2 an amusement or entertainment. **3** mental
upset or distress. ☐ **to distraction** almost to a
state of madness.

distraught (dĭs-**trawt**) *adjective* greatly
upset, nearly crazy with grief or worry.

distress *noun* **1** suffering caused by pain,
worry, illness, or exhaustion. **2** the condition
of being damaged or in danger and requiring
help, *a ship in distress*. –**distress** *verb* to cause
distress to.

distributary *noun* a branch of a river or
glacier that does not return to it after leaving
the main stream (e.g. in a delta).

distribute (dĭs-**trib**-yoot) *verb* **1** to divide
and give a share to each of a number, to
deal out. **2** to spread or scatter, to place at
different points. **distribution** *noun* [from *dis-* =
separate, + Latin *tributum* = given]

distributive *adjective* **1** of or concerned with
distribution. **2** (of a mathematical operation
applied to a sum of elements) producing the
same result whether it is performed before or
after the elements are added, e.g. $5(3 + 4) =
(5 \times 3) + (5 \times 4) = 35, 5(3 + 4) = 5 \times 7 = 35$.

distributor *noun* **1** one who distributes
things, an agent who markets goods.
2 a device for passing current to each of
the spark plugs in an engine.

district *noun* an area or region having a
particular feature or regarded as a unit for a
special purpose; a rural local government area
in South Australia.

distrust *noun* lack of trust, suspicion.
–**distrust** *verb* to feel distrust in. **distrustful**
adjective

disturb *verb* **1** to break the rest, quiet, or
calm of. **2** to cause to move from a settled
position. [from *dis-* = thoroughly, + Latin
turbare = confuse, upset]

disturbance *noun* **1** disturbing; being
disturbed. **2** a commotion; an outbreak of
social or political disorder.

disturbed *adjective* emotionally or mentally
unstable or abnormal.

disunion *noun* **1** separation, lack of union.
2 discord.

disunite *verb* **1** to remove unity from.
2 to cause to separate. **3** to experience
separation. **disunity** *noun*

disuse *noun* the state of not being used, *rusty
from disuse*. **disused** *adjective*

ditch *noun* a trench to hold or carry off
water or to serve as a boundary. –**ditch** *verb*
1 to make or repair ditches. **2** to drive (a
vehicle) into a ditch. **3** (*informal*) to make a
forced landing on the sea; to bring (an aircraft)
down thus. **4** (*informal*) to abandon, to discard,
to leave in the lurch, *ditched his girlfriend*.
☐ **dull as ditchwater** very dull.

dither *verb* **1** to tremble, to quiver. **2** to
hesitate indecisively. –**dither** *noun* a state of
dithering, nervous excitement or fear, *all of
a dither*.

ditto *noun* (used in lists to avoid repeating something) the same again. □ **ditto marks** two small marks placed under the item to be repeated.

ditty *noun* a short simple song.

diurnal (dy-**ern**-ăl) *adjective* **1** of the day, not nocturnal. **2** occupying one day. [from Latin *diurnus* = of a day]

divalent (dy-**vay**-lĕnt) *adjective* having a valence of two.

divan (dĭ-**van**) *noun* a low couch without a raised back or ends; a bed resembling this. [Persian, = cushioned bench]

dive *verb* **1** to plunge head first into water. **2** (of an aircraft) to plunge steeply downwards. **3** (of a submarine or diver) to go under water. **4** to go down or out of sight suddenly; to rush headlong, *dived into a shop*. **5** to move (a thing, e.g. one's hand) quickly downwards into something. –**dive** *noun* **1** an act of diving. **2** a sharp downward movement or fall. □ **dive-bomb** *verb* to drop bombs from a diving aircraft.

diver *noun* **1** one who dives. **2** a person who works underwater in a diving suit. **3** a diving bird.

diverge (dy-**verj**) *verb* **1** to go in different directions from a common point or from each other; to become further apart. **2** to go aside from a path; *diverge from the truth*, depart from it. **divergent** *adjective*, **divergence** *noun* [from *di-²* = apart, + Latin *vergere* = to slope]

divers (**dy**-verz) *adjective* (*old use*) several, various.

diverse (dy-**verss**) *adjective* of different kinds.

diversify *verb* (**diversified**, **diversifying**) **1** to introduce variety into, to vary. **2** to expand one's range of products or services etc. **diversification** *noun*

diversion *noun* **1** diverting something from its course. **2** diverting of attention; *create a diversion*, do something to divert attention. **3** a recreation, an entertainment. **4** an alternative route when a road is temporarily closed to traffic. **diversionary** *adjective*

diversity (dy-**vers**-ĭ-tee) *noun* variety.

divert *verb* **1** to turn (a thing) from its course; *divert traffic*, cause it to go by a different route; *divert attention*, distract it. **2** to entertain or amuse with recreations. [from *di-²* = apart, + Latin *vertere* = to turn]

diverting *adjective* entertaining, amusing.

divest (dy-**vest**) *verb* **1** to strip of clothes, *divested himself of his robes*. **2** to take away, to deprive, *divested him of his power*.

divide *verb* **1** to separate into parts, to split or break up. **2** to separate from something else, *the Murray divides New South Wales from Victoria*. **3** to arrange in separate groups, to classify. **4** to cause to disagree, *this controversy divided the party*. **5** (in Parliament) to part or cause to part in order to vote, *the House divided*; *they decided not to divide the House*, not to ask for a vote to be taken. **6** to find how many times one number contains another, *divide 12 by 3*. **7** to be able to be divided. –**divide** *noun* a dividing line, a watershed. □ **divided road** a road with a dividing strip between traffic flowing in opposite directions, a dual carriageway.

dividend *noun* **1** a number that is to be divided. **2** a share of profits paid to shareholders or winners in a totalisator pool. **3** a benefit from an action.

divider *noun* something that divides; *a room divider*, a screen or piece of furniture to divide a room into two parts. **dividers** *plural noun* measuring compasses.

divination (div-ĭ-**nay**-shŏn) *noun* divining, foretelling future events or discovering hidden knowledge.

divine *adjective* **1** of, from, or like God or a god. **2** (*informal*) excellent, very beautiful, *the food was divine*. –**divine** *noun* a theologian; a member of the clergy. –**divine** *verb* to discover or learn about future events by what are alleged to be magical means, or by inspiration or guessing. **divinely** *adverb*, **diviner** *noun*

diving *see* dive. □ **diving bird** one that dives for its food. **diving board** a board for diving from. **diving suit** a watertight suit worn for working underwater.

divinity *noun* **1** being divine. **2** a god. **3** the study of religion; theology.

divisible (dĭ-**viz**-ĭbŭl) *adjective* able to be divided. **divisibility** *noun*

division *noun* **1** dividing; being divided. **2** (in Parliament) separation of members into two sections for counting votes. **3** a dividing line, a partition. **4** one of the parts into which a thing is divided. **5** a major unit of an organisation, *our export division*. □ **division of labour** giving different parts of a task to different workers, so as to improve efficiency. **division sign** the sign ÷ (as in 12 ÷ 4) indicating that one quantity is to be divided by another. **divisional** *adjective*

divisive (dĭ-**vy**-siv) *adjective* tending to cause disagreement among members of a group.

divisor (dĭ-**vy**-zer) *noun* a number by which another is to be divided.

divorce *noun* 1 the legal termination of a marriage. 2 the separation of things that were together. –**divorce** *verb* 1 to end a marriage with (one's husband or wife) by divorce. 2 to separate, especially in thought or organisation.

divorcee (dĭ-vor-**see**) *noun* a divorced person.

divot (**div**-ŏt) *noun* a piece of turf cut out by a golf club in making a stroke.

divulge (dy-**vulj**) *verb* to reveal (information).

divvy *noun* (*informal*) a dividend. –**divvy** *verb* (**divvied**, **divvying**) (*informal*) to share out, *divvy up the takings*.

Diwali (dĭ-**wah**-lee) *noun* a Hindu religious festival at which lamps are lit, held in October or November. [from Sanskrit, = row of lamps]

Dixie *noun* the southern States of the USA.

dixie *noun* 1 (*Austral.*) a small carton of ice cream. 2 a large iron pot in which stew or tea is made by campers etc. [from Hindi *degchi* = cooking pot]

Dixieland *noun* 1 Dixie. 2 a kind of jazz.

DIY *abbreviation* do-it-yourself.

Diyari (**deer**-ree) *noun* 1 a member of an Aboriginal people of east central SA. 2 their language.

dizzy *adjective* (**dizzier**, **dizziest**) 1 giddy, feeling confused. 2 causing giddiness, *dizzy heights*. **dizzily** *adverb*, **dizziness** *noun*

DJ *abbreviation* disc jockey.

Djakarta = Jakarta.

Djibouti (jĭ-**boo**-tee) 1 a republic on the NE coast of Africa. 2 its capital city.

DNA *abbreviation* deoxyribonucleic acid, a substance in chromosomes that stores genetic information.

DNS *abbreviation* 1 domain name server, the system that automatically translates Internet addresses to the numeric machine addresses that computers use. 2 domain name system, the hierarchical method by which Internet addresses are constructed.

do *verb* (**did**, **done**, **doing**) 1 to perform, to carry out, to fulfil or complete (a work, duty, etc.). 2 to produce, to make, *do five copies*; *we do meals*, provide them. 3 to have a specified

effect on; to be the cause of, *swimming did her good*. 4 to deal with, to set in order, to solve, *do a crossword*. 5 to cover (a distance) in travelling. 6 to visit, to see the sights of, *we did England last year*. 7 to undergo; *did time for robbery*, was in prison. 8 to act or proceed, *do as you like*. 9 to fare, to get on. 10 to be suitable or acceptable, to suffice, to serve a purpose, *it doesn't do to worry*; *that will do!*, stop it. 11 (*informal*) to swindle, to rob. 12 (*informal*) to take (a drug). –**do** *auxiliary verb* 1 used to indicate present or past tense, *what does he think?*, *what did he think?* 2 used for emphasis, *I do like nuts*. 3 used to avoid repetition of a verb just used, *we work as hard as they do*. –**do** *noun* (*plural* **dos** *or* **do's**) 1 a statement of what should be done, *dos and don'ts*. 2 (*informal*) an entertainment, a party. ☐ **do away with** to abolish, to get rid of. **do for** (*informal*) (especially in *passive*) to ruin, to destroy, to kill, *she knew she was done for*. **do-gooder** *noun* a person who is well-meaning but unrealistic or officious in trying to promote social work or reform. **do in** (*informal*) to ruin, to kill; (*informal*) to tire out. **do-it-yourself** *adjective* for use or making etc. by an amateur at home. **do up** to fasten, to wrap up; to repair or redecorate. **do with** to need or want. **do without** to manage without.

dob *verb* (**dobbed**, **dobbing**) (*Austral. informal*) ☐ **dob in** to inform on; to commit (a person) to a task; to contribute. **dob on** to inform on. **dobber** *noun*

Dobell, Sir William Smith (1899–1970), Australian portrait painter.

Dobermann pinscher *noun* a large dog of a German breed with a smooth coat. [named after L. Dobermann, German dog breeder, + German *Pinscher* = terrier]

docile (**doh**-syl) *adjective* willing to obey. **docilely** *adverb*, **docility** (dŏ-**sil**-ĭ-tee) *noun* [from Latin *docilis* = easily taught]

dock¹ *noun* a weed with broad leaves.

dock² *verb* 1 to cut short (an animal's tail). 2 to reduce or take away part of (wages etc.).

dock³ *noun* an artificially enclosed body of water where ships are admitted for loading, unloading, or repair. –**dock** *verb* 1 to bring or come into dock. 2 to join (two or more spacecraft) together in space; to become joined thus. **docks** *plural noun* a dockyard.

dock⁴ *noun* an enclosure in a criminal court for a prisoner on trial. [from Flemish *dok* = cage]

docker *noun* a labourer who loads and unloads ships in a dockyard.

docket *noun* a document or label listing goods delivered or the contents of a package, or recording payment of customs dues etc. –**docket** *verb* (**docketed**, **docketing**) to enter on a docket; to label with a docket.

dockland *noun* the district near a dockyard.

dockyard *noun* an area with docks and equipment for building and repairing ships.

doctor *noun* **1** a person who is qualified to be a practitioner of medicine, a physician. **2** a person who holds a doctorate, *Doctor of Philosophy*. –**doctor** *verb* **1** to treat medically. **2** to castrate or spay. **3** to patch up (machinery etc.). **4** to tamper with or falsify, *doctored the evidence*. [from Latin *doctor* = teacher]

doctorate (**dok**-tŏ-răt) *noun* the highest degree at a university, entitling the holder to the title of 'doctor'.

doctrinaire (dok-tri-**nair**) *adjective* applying theories or principles without regard for practical considerations, *doctrinaire socialism*.

doctrine (**dok**-trǐn) *noun* a principle or set of principles and beliefs held by a religious or political or other group. **doctrinal** (dok-**try**-năl) *adjective* [same origin as *doctor*]

document *noun* a piece of written, printed, or electronic matter that provides information or evidence or that serves as an official record. –**document** *verb* to prove or provide with documents; *a heavily documented report*, supporting its statements by many references to evidence. **documentation** *noun*

documentary (dok-yŭ-**ment**-ă-ree) *adjective* **1** consisting of documents, *documentary evidence*. **2** giving a factual filmed report of a subject or activity. –**documentary** *noun* a documentary film.

dodder *verb* to tremble or totter because of age or frailty. **dodderer** *noun*, **doddery** *adjective*

dodeca- *prefix* twelve. [from Greek *dodeka* = twelve]

dodecagon (doh-**dek**-ă-gŏn) *noun* a geometric figure with twelve sides. [from *dodeca-*, + Greek *gonia* = angle]

dodecahedron (doh-dekă-**hee**-drŏn) *noun* a solid body with twelve faces. [from *dodeca-*, + Greek *hedra* = base]

Dodecanese (doh-dekă-**neez**) a group of twelve Greek islands in the south-east Aegean, of which the largest is Rhodes. [from *dodeca-*, + Greek *nesos* = island]

dodecaphonic (doh-dekă-**fon**-ik) *adjective* (of music) using the twelve chromatic notes of the octave arranged in a chosen order, without a conventional key. [from *dodeca-*, + Greek *phone* = sound]

dodge *verb* **1** to move quickly to one side; to change position or direction in order to avoid something. **2** to evade by cunning or trickery, *dodged military service*. –**dodge** *noun* **1** a quick movement to avoid something. **2** (*informal*) a clever trick, an ingenious way of doing something. **dodger** *noun*

dodgem (**doj**-ĕm) *noun* (in full **dodgem car**) a small electrically-driven car in an enclosure at a funfair etc., in which each driver tries to bump other similar cars and dodge those trying to bump his car.

dodgy *adjective* (**dodgier**, **dodgiest**) (*informal*) **1** cunning, artful. **2** awkward, difficult; unreliable.

dodo (**doh**-doh) *noun* (*plural* **dodos**) **1** a large non-flying bird that formerly lived in Mauritius but has been extinct since the 18th century. **2** (*informal*) a stupid person. [from Portuguese *doudo* = fool]

Dodoma (dŏ-**doh**-mă) the capital of Tanzania.

doe *noun* the female of the kangaroo, fallow deer, reindeer, hare, or rabbit.

doer *noun* a person who does something, one who takes action rather than thinking or talking about things.

doesn't (*informal*) = does not.

doff *verb* to take off (one's hat etc.). [from *do off*; compare *don*¹]

dog *noun* **1** a four-legged carnivorous animal, commonly kept as a pet or trained for use in hunting etc. **2** the male of this or of the wolf or fox. **3** a mechanical device for gripping things. –**dog** *verb* (**dogged**, **dogging**) to follow closely or persistently, *dogged his footsteps*; *dogged by financial problems*. □ **the dogs** (*informal*) greyhound racing. **dog box** (*Austral.*) a compartment in a railway carriage without a door. **dog collar** (*informal*) a clerical collar. **dog-eared** *adjective* (of a book) having the corners of the pages turned down through use. **dog fence** (*Austral.*) a fence to keep out dingoes. **dog in the manger** a person who selfishly keeps something of no personal use, in order to prevent others from having it. **dog-paddle** *noun* a simple swimming stroke with short quick movements of the arms and legs. **dog's life** a life of misery or harassment. **Dog Star** Sirius. **dog-tired** *adjective* tired out. **dog whistle politics** the use of political statements which seem unexceptional to a general audience but which contain coded messages (often controversial) directed at a target audience. **go to the dogs** (*informal*) to become worthless, to be ruined. **doglike** *adjective*

dogcart *noun* a light horse-drawn two-wheeled vehicle.

doge (*pr.* dohj) *noun* the title of the former ruler of Venice or of Genoa. [from Latin *dux* = leader]

dogfight *noun* **1** a fight between dogs. **2** a battle between fighter aircraft.

dogged (**dog**-ĕd) *adjective* determined, not giving up easily. **doggedly** *adverb*

doggerel (**dog**-ĕ-rĕl) *noun* bad verse.

doggo *adverb* **lie doggo** (*informal*) to lie motionless or hidden, making no sign.

doggy *adjective* **1** of dogs. **2** (*informal*) fond of dogs. ☐ **doggy bag** a bag containing leftovers taken home from a restaurant.

doghouse *noun* (*Amer.*) a dog's kennel. ☐ **in the doghouse** (*informal*) in disgrace.

dogleg *noun* (also **dog's leg**) a sharp bend like that in a dog's hind leg. ☐ **dogleg fence** a fence of logs in a zigzag pattern.

dogma *noun* a doctrine or doctrines put forward by some authority, especially the Church, to be accepted as true without question.

dogman *noun* (*plural* **dogmen**) (*Austral.*) a worker directing the operation of a crane, often while riding on its load.

dogmatic (dog-**mat**-ik) *adjective* **1** of or like dogmas. **2** putting forward statements in a very firm authoritative way. **dogmatically** *adverb*, **dogmatism** *noun* [from *dogma*]

dogsbody *noun* (*informal*) a drudge.

dogwatch *noun* each of the two-hour watches on a ship (4–6 or 6–8 p.m.).

doh *noun* a name for the keynote of a scale in music, or the note C.

Doha (**doh**-hă) the capital of Qatar.

doily *noun* a small ornamental mat of paper, lace, etc. placed under a dish or under cake etc. on a dish.

doings *plural noun* **1** things done or being done. **2** (*informal*) things needed.

doldrums *plural noun* **1** the ocean regions near the equator where there is little or no wind. **2** a period of inactivity. ☐ **in the doldrums** in low spirits.

dole *verb* to distribute, *dole it out.* –**dole** *noun* (*informal*) a government payment to people who are unable to find employment; *on the dole,* receiving this.

doleful *adjective* mournful, sad. **dolefully** *adverb* [from an old word *dole* = grief]

doll *noun* **1** a small model of a human figure, especially as a child's toy. **2** a ventriloquist's dummy. –**doll** *verb* (*informal*) to dress smartly, *dolled herself up.*

dollar *noun* the unit of money in Australia, New Zealand, the USA, and certain other countries. [from German *thaler* = a silver coin]

dollop *noun* (*informal*) **1** a mass or quantity. **2** a shapeless lump of something soft.

dolly *noun* **1** (*informal*) a doll. **2** a movable platform for a cine-camera.

dolma *noun* (*plural* **dolmas** or **dolmades**, *pr.* dol-**mah**-deez) a delicacy consisting of spiced rice or meat etc. wrapped in a vine or cabbage leaf. [modern Greek]

dolman sleeve *noun* a loose sleeve cut in one piece with the body of a garment.

dolmen (**dol**-měn) *noun* a prehistoric structure with a large flat stone laid on upright ones.

dolomite (**dol**-ŏ-myt) *noun* a mineral or rock of calcium magnesium carbonate.

Dolomite Mountains (also **Dolomites**) a rocky mountain range in north Italy.

dolour (**dol**-er) *noun* (*literary*) sorrow, distress. **dolorous** *adjective* [from Latin *dolor* = pain]

dolphin *noun* a sea animal like a porpoise but larger and with a beaklike snout.

dolt *noun* a stupid person.

domain (dŏ-**mayn**) *noun* **1** a district or area under someone's control; a range of influence. **2** a field of thought or activity, *the domain of science.* **3** the set of input values for a mathematical function. **4** a distinct subset of the Internet with addresses sharing a common suffix. ☐ **domain name** (in computing) part of a network address which identifies it as belonging to a particular domain.

dome *noun* **1** a rounded roof with a circular base. **2** something shaped like this. **domed** *adjective* having a dome; shaped like a dome.

Dome of the Rock an Islamic shrine in Jerusalem.

Domesday Book (**doomz**-day) a record of the ownership of lands in England made in 1086 by order of William the Conqueror.

domestic *adjective* **1** of the home or household or family affairs. **2** of one's own country, not foreign or international, *domestic air services*. **3** (of animals) kept by man, not wild. –**domestic** *noun* a servant in a household. □ **domestic science** the study of household management. **domestically** *adverb* [from Latin *domus* = home]

domesticated *adjective* **1** (of animals) trained to live with and be kept by people. **2** (of people) enjoying household work and home life.

domesticity (dom-es-**tiss**-ĭ-tee) *noun* being domestic; domestic or home life.

domicile (**dom**-ĭ-syl) *noun* a person's place of residence. **domiciled** *adjective* dwelling (in a place).

domiciliary (dom-ĭ-**sil**-yă-ree) *adjective* **1** of a dwelling place. **2** visiting a patient etc. at home, *domiciliary nurse*.

dominant *adjective* **1** dominating. **2** (of a species of plant or animal) most widespread in a particular area and influencing the type and abundance of other species. **3** (of a gene or inherited characteristic) appearing in offspring even if a contrary gene or characteristic is also inherited. –**dominant** *noun* **1** a dominant species, characteristic, or gene. **2** (in music) the fifth note of a diatonic scale. **dominance** *noun*

dominate *verb* **1** to have a commanding influence over. **2** to be the most influential or conspicuous person or thing. **3** (of a high place) to tower over, *the mountain dominates the whole valley*. **domination** *noun* [from Latin *dominus* = master]

domineer *verb* to behave in a forceful way, making others obey.

Dominica (dom-i-**nee**-kă) an island in the West Indies, an independent republic within the Commonwealth. **Dominican** (dom-i-**nee**-kăn) *adjective* & *noun*

Dominican (dŏ-**min**-i-kăn) *noun* a member of an order of friars (also called *Black Friars*) founded by a Spanish priest, St Dominic (died 1221), or of a corresponding order of nuns.

Dominican Republic (dŏ-**min**-i-kăn) a country in the West Indies. **Dominican** *adjective* & *noun*

dominion *noun* **1** authority to rule, control. **2** territory controlled by a ruler or government; a domain.

domino *noun* (*plural* **dominoes**) each of the small oblong pieces marked with 0–6 (or 0–9) dots on each half, used in the game of **dominoes**. □ **domino effect** an effect compared to a row of dominoes falling, when a political or other event in one place seems to cause similar events elsewhere.

Don *noun* a Spanish title put before a man's forename.

don¹ *verb* (**donned**, **donning**) to put on. [from *do on*; compare *doff*]

don² *noun* a university teacher.

donate *verb* to give as a donation.

Donatello (don-ă-**tel**-oh), Donato di Niccolo (1386–1466), Florentine sculptor.

donation *noun* **1** an act of donating. **2** a gift of money etc. to a fund or institution.

done *see* do. –**done** *adjective* **1** cooked sufficiently; *done to a turn*, cooked perfectly. **2** (*informal*) tired out. **3** (*informal*) socially acceptable, *the done thing; it isn't done*. –**done** *interjection* (in reply to an offer) I accept. □ **done for** (*informal*) in trouble; ruined. **done in** (*informal*) tired out. **done with** finished with, *it's over and done with*.

dong¹ *verb* **1** to make the deep sound of a bell. **2** (*Austral. informal*) to hit or punch. –**dong** *noun* **1** the deep sound of a bell. **2** (*Austral. informal*) a heavy blow.

dong² *noun* the chief unit of money in Vietnam.

donga *noun* **1** (*Austral.* & *South African*) a dry watercourse. **2** (*Austral.*) **the donga** the bush, the outback.

donjon *noun* the great tower or keep of a castle. [an old spelling of *dungeon*]

Don Juan (**joo**-ăn) legendary Spanish nobleman of dissolute life, whose name is used as a heartless seducer of women.

donkey *noun* (*plural* **donkeys**) an animal of the horse family, with long ears. □ **donkey engine** a small auxiliary engine. **donkey's years** (*informal*) a very long time. **donkey vote** a vote recorded by allocating preferences according to the order in which candidates are listed on the ballot paper; such votes viewed collectively. **donkey work** drudgery, the laborious part of a job.

Donna *noun* the title of an Italian, Spanish, or Portuguese lady.

Donne (*pr*. dun), John (1572–1631), English poet and cleric.

donor *noun* **1** one who gives or donates something. **2** one who provides blood for transfusion or semen for insemination or tissue for transplantation.

Don Quixote *see* quixotic.

don't (*informal*) = do not. –**don't** *noun* a prohibition, *do's and don'ts*.

doodle *verb* to scribble while thinking about something else. –**doodle** *noun* a drawing or marks made by doodling.

doom *noun* a grim fate, death or ruin. –**doom** *verb* to destine to a grim fate.

doomsday *noun* the day of the Last Judgment, the end of the world.

doona *noun* (*trademark Austral*.) a thick soft quilt, used instead of a top sheet and blankets.

door *noun* **1** a hinged, sliding, or revolving barrier that closes an entrance or exit. **2** a doorway. **3** a means of obtaining or approaching something; *closed the door to any reconciliation*, made it impossible.
□ *door-to-door adjective* (of selling etc.) done at each house in turn.

doorbell *noun* a bell inside a house, rung from outside by visitors as a signal.

doorknob *noun* a knob for turning to release the latch of a door.

doorknock *noun* (*Austral*.) a fundraising, vote soliciting, etc. campaign conducted by going from house to house. –**doorknock** *verb* to conduct a doorknock.

doormat *noun* **1** a mat placed at a door, for wiping dirt from shoes. **2** a very submissive person.

doorstep *noun* a step or area just outside a door; (*informal*) a thick slice of bread; *on one's doorstep*, very close.

doorstop *noun* a device for keeping a door open or preventing it from striking a wall when it opens.

doorway *noun* an opening filled by a door.

dope *noun* **1** (*informal*) a medicine or drug; a narcotic; a drug given to an athlete, horse, or greyhound to affect performance. **2** (*informal*) information. **3** (*informal*) a stupid person. –**dope** *verb* **1** to treat with dope. **2** to give a narcotic or stimulant to. **3** to take drugs that cause addiction. **4** to add an impurity to (a semiconductor) to achieve a specific electrical property. [from Dutch *doop* = sauce]

dopey *adjective* (*informal*) **1** half asleep, stupefied by a drug. **2** stupid. **dopiness** *noun*

doppelgänger (**dop**-ĕl-geng-er) *noun* an apparition or double of a living person. [German, = double-goer]

Doppler effect *noun* the apparent increase (or decrease) in the frequency of light or other radiation, e.g. the pitch of sound, as the source and the observer approach or recede from each other. [named after the Austrian physicist C. J. Doppler (1803–53)]

Doric (*rhymes with* historic) *adjective* of the Doric order, the oldest and simplest of the five classical orders of architecture.

dork *noun* (*informal*) a stupid or ineffectual person.

dormant *adjective* **1** sleeping, lying inactive as if in sleep. **2** (of plants) alive but not actively growing. **3** temporarily inactive, *a dormant volcano*. **dormancy** *noun* [from French, = sleeping]

dormer window *noun* an upright window under a small gable built out from a sloping roof.

dormitory *noun* a room with a number of beds, especially in a school or institution. [from Latin *dormire* = to sleep]

dormouse *noun* (*plural* dormice) a mouselike animal that hibernates in winter.

Dorothy Dix (also Dorothy Dixer) *noun* (*Austral*. *informal*) a pre-arranged parliamentary question asked to allow a minister to deliver a prepared speech. [named after a US writer of question-and-answer columns]

dorsal *adjective* of or on the back of an animal or plant, *a dorsal fin*. **dorsally** *adverb* [from Latin *dorsum* = the back]

dory *noun* an edible sea fish, especially John Dory.

DOS *noun* an operating system for personal computers. [abbreviation of *disk operating system*]

dosage *noun* **1** the giving of medicine in doses. **2** the size of a dose.

dose *noun* **1** an amount of medicine to be taken at one time. **2** an amount of radiation received by a person or thing. **3** (*informal*) an amount of flattery or punishment etc. –**dose** *verb* to give a dose or doses of medicine to; to treat by this.

doss *verb* (*informal*) to sleep, especially in a dosshouse. □ **doss down** (*informal*) to sleep on a makeshift bed. **dosser** *noun*

dosshouse *noun* a cheap lodging house.

dossier (**dos**-ee-er) *noun* a set of documents containing information about a person or event.

Dostoevsky (dost-oi-**ef**-skee), Fedor Mikhailovich (1821–81), Russian novelist, whose novels include *Crime and Punishment* and *The Brothers Karamazov*.

dot *noun* **1** a small round mark, a point. **2** the shorter of the two signals used in the Morse code. –**dot** *verb* (**dotted**, **dotting**) **1** to mark with a dot or dots, to place a dot over a letter. **2** to scatter here and there, *the sea was dotted with ships*. **3** (*informal*) to hit, *dotted him one*. □ **dot matrix printer** a printer in which each printed letter or number is made up of dots printed by the tips of small wires selected from a rectangular array. **dotted line** a line of dots showing where a signature etc. is to be entered on a document. **dot the i's and cross the t's** to be minutely accurate and explicit about details. **on the dot** exactly on time. **the year dot** (*informal*) a very long time ago.

dotage (**doh**-tij) *noun* a state of weakness of mind caused by old age, *in his dotage*.

dotard (**doh**-terd) *noun* a person who is in his dotage.

dote *verb* to show great fondness, *a doting husband*. **dote on** to be very fond of.

doth (*old use*) does.

dotterel *noun* a small plover.

dottle *noun* unburnt tobacco left in a pipe.

dotty *adjective* (**dottier**, **dottiest**) (*informal*) feeble-minded, eccentric, silly. **dottiness** *noun*

double *adjective* **1** consisting of two things or parts that form a pair. **2** twice as much or as many; *a double whisky*, twice the standard portion. **3** designed for two persons or things, *a double bed*. **4** combining two things or qualities, *it has a double meaning*. **5** (of flowers) having more than one circle of petals. –**double** *adverb* **1** twice the amount or quantity, *it costs double what it cost last year*. **2** in twos; *see double*, to see two things where there is only one. –**double** *noun* **1** a double quantity or thing. **2** a person or thing that looks very like another. **3** a hit between the two outer circles of the board in darts, scoring double. –**double** *verb* **1** to make or become twice as much or as many. **2** to bend or fold in two. **3** to turn sharply back from a course, *the mouse doubled back on its tracks*. **4** to sail round, *the ship doubled the Cape*. **5** to act two parts in the same play; to have two functions, *the*

umbrella doubles as a sunshade. **6** (*Austral.*) to dink. **doubles** *plural noun* a game between two pairs of players. □ **at the double** running, hurrying. **double agent** one who spies for two rival countries. **double-barrelled** *adjective* (of a gun) having two barrels; (of a surname) having two parts. **double bass** the lowest-pitched instrument of the violin family. **double-breasted** *adjective* (of a coat) having fronts that overlap to fasten across the breast. **double-check** *verb* to verify twice or in two ways. **double chin** a chin with a fold of loose flesh below it. **double-cross** *verb* to deceive or cheat a person with whom one pretends to be collaborating. **double-dealing** *noun* deceit, especially in business. **double-decker** *noun* a bus or train with two decks; (*informal*) anything having two layers. **double dissolution** the simultaneous dissolution of the upper and lower houses of a parliament preparatory to an election. **double Dutch** unintelligible talk. **double entry** a system of bookkeeping in which each transaction is entered as a debit in one account and a credit in another. **double figures** any number from 10 to 99 inclusive. **double helix** a pair of parallel helices with a common axis, esp. in the structure of a DNA molecule. **double-jointed** *adjective* having very flexible joints that allow the fingers, arms, or legs to bend in unusual ways. **double-pole switch** a switch that opens or closes two electrical circuits, or two sides of one circuit, simultaneously. **double-quick** *adjective & adverb* very quick, very quickly. **double standard** a rule or principle applied more strictly to some people than to others (or to oneself). **double take** a delayed reaction to a situation etc., coming immediately after one's first reaction. **double time** payment of an employee at twice the normal rate. **doubly** *adverb*

double entendre (doobl ahn-**tahndr**) *noun* a phrase with two meanings, one of which is usually indecent. [French, = double understanding]

doublespeak *noun* a kind of talk that means something very different from its apparent meaning.

doublet (**dub**-lĕt) *noun* **1** a man's close-fitting jacket, with or without sleeves, worn in the 15th–17th centuries. **2** either of a pair of similar things. **3** a combination of two simple lenses.

doubletalk *noun* doublespeak.

doubloon (dub-**loon**) *noun* a former Spanish gold coin.

doubt *noun* **1** a feeling of uncertainty about something, an undecided state of mind. **2** a feeling of disbelief. **3** an uncertain state of affairs. –**doubt** *verb* **1** to feel uncertain or undecided about. **2** to hesitate to believe. □ **doubting Thomas** a person who (like St Thomas) refuses to believe something until it has been fully proved. **doubter** *noun* [from Latin *dubitare* = hesitate]

doubtful *adjective* **1** feeling doubt. **2** causing doubt; *a doubtful ally*, unreliable; *a doubtful reputation*, not a good one. **doubtfully** *adverb*

doubtless *adverb* no doubt.

douche (*pr.* doosh) *noun* **1** a jet of liquid applied to a part of the body to cleanse it or for medical purposes. **2** a device for applying this. –**douche** *verb* to treat with a douche; to use a douche. [from Italian *doccia* = a pipe]

dough (*rhymes with* go) *noun* **1** a thick mixture of flour etc. and liquid, to be baked as bread, cake, or pastry. **2** (*informal*) money. **doughy** *adjective*

doughnut *noun* (also **donut**) **1** a small fried cake of sweetened dough, usually in the shape of a ball or ring. **2** a tight 360° turn in a vehicle.

doughty (**dow**-tee) *adjective* (*old use* or *humorous*) valiant, stout-hearted.

dour (*rhymes with* poor) *adjective* stern, severe, gloomy-looking. **dourly** *adverb*, **dourness** *noun* [from Gaelic *dur* = dull, obstinate]

douse (*rhymes with* mouse) *verb* **1** to put into water, to throw water over. **2** to extinguish, *douse the light*.

dove *noun* **1** a kind of bird with short legs, a small head, and a thick body, that makes a cooing sound. **2** a person who favours a policy of peace and negotiation.

dovecote *noun* a shelter for domesticated pigeons.

dovetail *noun* a wedge-shaped joint interlocking two pieces of wood. –**dovetail** *verb* **1** to join by such a joint. **2** to fit closely together, to combine neatly, *my plans dovetailed with hers*.

dowager (**dow**-ă-jer) *noun* **1** a woman who holds a title or property from her dead husband, *the dowager duchess*. **2** (*informal*) a dignified elderly woman.

dowdy *adjective* (**dowdier**, **dowdiest**) **1** (of clothes) unattractively dull, not stylish.

2 dressed in dowdy clothes. **dowdily** *adverb*, **dowdiness** *noun*

dowel (*rhymes with* fowl) *noun* a headless wooden or metal pin for holding two pieces of wood or stone together by fitting into a corresponding hole in each. –**dowel** *verb* (**dowelled**, **dowelling**) to fasten with a dowel.

dowelling *noun* round rods for cutting into dowels.

dower *noun* a widow's share of her husband's estate.

Dow-Jones index (also **Dow-Jones average**) a figure indicating the relative price of shares on the New York Stock Exchange, based on the average price of selected stocks. [named after C. H. Dow (died 1902) and E. D. Jones (died 1920), American economists]

down[1] *adverb* **1** from an upright position to a horizontal one, *fell down*. **2** to, in, or at a lower place, level, value, or condition; to a smaller size; further south. **3** away from a central place or major city, *he is down from headquarters*. **4** so as to be less active, *quieten down*. **5** incapacitated by illness, *is down with flu*; (of a computer) out of action. **6** from an earlier to a later time, *down to the present day*. **7** in writing, *note it down; he is down to speak*, is listed in the program. **8** to the source or the place where something is, *track it down*. **9** as a payment at the time of purchase, *paid $10 down*. –**down** *preposition* **1** downwards along or through or into, along, from top to bottom of. **2** at a lower part of (a river etc.). –**down** *adjective* **1** directed downwards, *a down draught*. **2** travelling away from a central place, *a down train; the down platform*, one for such a train. –**down** *verb* (*informal*) **1** to knock or bring down; *down tools*, to cease work for the day or in a strike. **2** to swallow. –**down** *noun* **1** misfortune, *ups and downs*. **2** a throw in wrestling. **3** (*informal*) a dislike, a grudge against someone, *has a down on him*. □ **down and out** completely destitute. **down-and-out** *noun* a destitute person. **down at heel** shabby. **down beat** an accented beat in music, when the conductor's baton moves downwards. **down-hearted** *adjective* in low spirits. **down in the mouth** looking unhappy. **down on** disapproving or hostile towards, *she is down on smoking*. **down payment** a partial initial payment. **down stage** at or towards the front of a theatre stage. **down to** attributable to; the responsibility of. **down-to-earth** *adjective* sensible and practical. **down**

under (in or to) Australia or other countries of the antipodes (as seen from the Northern Hemisphere).

down² *noun* very fine soft furry feathers or short hairs.

down³ *noun* (usually in *plural*) an area of open rolling land, *Darling Downs*.

downcast *adjective* **1** looking downwards, *downcast eyes*. **2** (of a person) dejected.

downfall *noun* a fall from prosperity or power; something that causes this.

downfold *noun* a syncline.

downgrade *verb* to reduce to a lower grade or rank.

downhill *adverb* in a downward direction; further down a slope. **–downhill** *adjective* going or sloping downwards. ☐ **go downhill** to deteriorate.

Downing Street a street in London containing the official residence of the British Prime Minister and those of other members of the government.

download *verb* (in computing) to transfer (software or data) from one storage device or system to another (especially a smaller remote one). **–download** *noun* a computer file transferred in such a way, *he got the game as a download from the Internet*.

downmarket *adjective* & *adverb* towards or relating to the cheaper or less affluent sector of the market.

downpipe *noun* a pipe for carrying rainwater from a roof to a drain.

downpour *noun* a great fall of rain.

downright *adjective* **1** frank, straightforward. **2** thorough, complete, *a downright lie*. **–downright** *adverb* thoroughly, *felt downright scared*.

downs *see* down³.

downside *noun* a negative or adverse aspect of a situation etc.

downsize *verb* to reduce in size.

downstairs *adverb* down the stairs; to or on a lower floor. **–downstairs** *adjective* situated downstairs.

downstream *adjective* & *adverb* in the direction in which a stream or river flows.

Down syndrome *noun* an abnormal congenital condition in which a person has a broad flattened skull, slanting eyes, and mental deficiency. [named after J. L. H. Down, English physician (died 1896)]

downthrow *noun* the side of a geological fault that appears to have moved downwards in relation to the other side.

downtown (especially *Amer.*) *adjective* of a lower or more central part of a town or city. **–downtown** *adverb* in or into this part. **–downtown** *noun* a downtown area.

downtrodden *adjective* trampled underfoot; oppressed.

downturn *noun* a decline, especially in economic or business activity.

downward *adjective* moving or leading or pointing towards what is lower or less important or later, *a downward movement*. **–downward** *adverb* downwards. **downwards** *adverb* towards what is lower etc., *moved downwards*.

downwind *adjective* & *adverb* in the direction towards which the wind is blowing.

downy *adjective* (**downier, downiest**) like or covered with soft down.

dowry (*rhymes with* floury) *noun* property or money brought by a bride to her husband.

dowse (*rhymes with* cows) *verb* to search for underground water or minerals by using a Y-shaped stick or rod. **dowser** *noun*

doxology *noun* a formula of praise to God used in prayer. [from Greek *doxa* = glory, + *logos* = word]

doyen (**doy-**ĕn) *noun* (**doyenne** *feminine noun, pr.* **doy-**en) the senior member of a staff, profession, etc. [French]

Doyle, Sir Arthur Conan (1859–1930), Scottish-born novelist, creator of Sherlock Holmes and Dr Watson.

doze *verb* to sleep lightly. **–doze** *noun* a short light sleep. ☐ **doze off** to fall into a doze.

dozen *noun* a set of twelve, *six dozen*; *pack them in dozens*; *dozens of things*, very many.

dozy *adjective* **1** drowsy. **2** (*informal*) stupid; lazy.

DPP *abbreviation* director of public prosecutions.

Dr *abbreviation* **1** Doctor. **2** debtor. **3** Drive.

drab *adjective* **1** dull, uninteresting. **2** of dull greyish-brown colour. **–drab** *noun* drab colour. **drably** *adverb*, **drabness** *noun*

drachm (*pr.* dram) *noun* one-eighth of an ounce or of a fluid ounce.

drachma (**drak-**mă) *noun* (*plural* **drachmas** *or* **drachmae**, *pr.* **drak-**mee) the former unit of money in Greece.

drack *adjective* (*Austral. informal*) unattractive, dreary.

draconian (dră-**koh**-nee-ăn) *adjective* very harsh, *draconian laws*. [named after *Draco*, who is said to have established severe laws in ancient Athens in the 6th century BC]

Dracula, **Count** the chief of the vampires in Bram Stoker's novel *Dracula* (1897), partly set in a lonely castle in Transylvania.

draft *noun* **1** a rough preliminary written version, *a draft of a speech*. **2** a written order for the payment of money by a bank; the drawing of money by this. **3** a group detached from a larger group for special duty; the selection of these. **4** (*Amer.*) conscription. –**draft** *verb* **1** to prepare a written draft of. **2** to select for a special duty, *he was drafted to the Perth branch*. **3** (*Amer.*) to conscript. **4** (*Austral.*) to separate sheep or cattle from a flock or herd for some special purpose.

draftsman *noun* **1** a person who drafts documents. **2** = **draughtsman** (sense 1).

drag *verb* (**dragged**, **dragging**) **1** to pull along with effort or difficulty. **2** to trail or allow to trail along the ground; to move slowly and with effort. **3** to search the bottom of water with grapnels, nets, etc., *drag the river*. **4** to continue slowly in a dull manner, *the speeches dragged on*. –**drag** *noun* **1** something that is made for pulling along the ground, e.g. a heavy harrow, a dragnet. **2** something that slows progress; something boring. **3** (*informal*) women's clothes worn by men. ☐ **drag in** to bring in (a subject) unnecessarily or in an artificial way. **drag one's feet** or **heels** to be deliberately slow or reluctant. **drag out** to prolong unnecessarily. **drag race** a race between cars to see which can accelerate fastest from a standstill. **drag up** (*informal*) to rear (a child) roughly and without proper training; to revive (a forgotten scandal etc.).

dragnet *noun* **1** a net drawn through a river or across ground to trap fish or game, or to find a drowned person, etc. **2** a systematic hunt for criminals etc.

dragon *noun* **1** a mythical monster resembling a reptile, usually with wings and able to breathe out fire. **2** any of various lizards, often having crests, spines, and neck frills, *Komodo dragon*; *bearded dragon*. **3** a fierce person. [from Greek *drakon* = serpent]

dragonfly *noun* a long-bodied insect with wings that spread while it is resting.

dragoon *noun* a cavalryman (originally a mounted infantryman). –**dragoon** *verb* to force into doing something.

dragster *noun* a car built or modified to take part in drag races.

drain *verb* **1** to draw off (liquid) by means of channels or pipes etc. **2** to flow or trickle away. **3** to dry or become dried when liquid flows away. **4** (of a river) to carry off the superfluous water from (a district). **5** to deprive gradually of (strength or resources). **6** to drink, to empty (a glass etc.) by drinking its contents. –**drain** *noun* **1** a channel or pipe through which liquid or sewage is carried away. **2** something that drains one's strength or resources.

drainage *noun* **1** draining. **2** a system of drains. **3** what is drained off.

drainpipe *noun* a pipe used in a system of drains.

Drake, Sir Francis (c. 1540–96), Elizabethan sailor and explorer.

drake *noun* a male duck.

dram *noun* **1** a drachm. **2** a small drink of spirits.

drama (**drah**-mă) *noun* **1** a play for acting on the stage or for broadcasting. **2** plays as a branch of literature; their composition and performance. **3** a dramatic series of events. **4** dramatic quality, *the drama of the situation*.

dramatic *adjective* **1** of drama. **2** exciting, impressive, *a dramatic change*. **dramatics** *plural noun* the performance of plays; exaggerated behaviour. **dramatically** *adverb*

dramatise *verb* (also **-ize**) **1** to make (a story etc.) into a play. **2** to make (a thing) seem dramatic. **dramatisation** *noun*

dramatist *noun* a writer of dramas.

drank *see* **drink**.

drape *verb* **1** to cover loosely or decorate with cloth etc. **2** to arrange loosely or in graceful folds. **drapes** *plural noun* curtains; drapery.

draper *noun* a retailer of cloth or clothing.

drapery *noun* **1** a draper's trade or fabrics. **2** fabric arranged in loose folds.

drastic *adjective* having a strong or violent effect. **drastically** *adverb*

drat *interjection* (*informal*) expresing anger or annoyance. **dratted** *adjective*

draught (*rhymes with* craft) *noun* **1** a current of air in an enclosed place. **2** pulling. **3** the pulling in of a net of fish; the fish caught in this. **4** the depth of water needed to float a ship. **5** the drawing of liquor from a cask etc. **6** one continuous process of swallowing liquid; the amount swallowed. **draughts** *plural noun* a game for two players using twenty-four round pieces, played on a **draughtboard** (the same as a chessboard). □ **draught beer** beer drawn from a cask, not bottled.

draughthorse *noun* a horse used for pulling heavy loads.

draughtsman (*rhymes with* craftsman) *noun* (*plural* **draughtsmen**) **1** a person who makes drawings or plans or sketches. **2** a piece used in the game of draughts. **draughtsmanship** *noun*

draughty (*rhymes with* crafty) *adjective* (**draughtier**, **draughtiest**) letting in sharp currents of air. **draughtiness** *noun*

Dravidian (dră-**vid**-ee-ăn) *noun* a member of a dark-skinned people of southern India and Sri Lanka.

draw *verb* (**drew**, **drawn**, **drawing**) **1** to pull; *draw a bow*, pull back its string; *draw the curtains*, pull them across the window. **2** to attract, *draw attention*. **3** to take in, *draw breath*; *he drew at his pipe*, sucked smoke from it; *chimney draws well*, has a good draught. **4** to take out, *drew the cork*; *draw water*; *draw teeth*, extract them; *draw $10*, withdraw it from one's account; *draw a salary*, receive it from one's employer; *draw an abscess*, cause blood or pus to concentrate; *draw a fowl*, take out its inside before cooking it; *draw on one's imagination*, use it as a source. **5** to draw lots; to obtain in a lottery. **6** to get information from, *tried to draw him about his plans*. **7** to finish a contest with neither side winning. **8** to require (a certain depth of water) in which to float, *the ship draws 3 metres*. **9** to produce a picture or diagram by making marks on a surface. **10** to formulate, *draw a conclusion*. **11** to write out (a cheque etc.) for encashment. **12** to search (a covert) for game. **13** to make one's way, *draw near*. **14** (of tea) to infuse. –**draw** *noun* **1** the act of drawing; *quick on the draw*, quick at drawing a gun. **2** a person or thing that draws custom, an attraction. **3** the drawing of lots. **4** a drawn game. □ **draw a blank** to get no response or result. **draw in** (of the time of daylight) to become shorter. **draw out** to prolong (a discussion etc.); to encourage (a person) to talk; (of the time of daylight) to become longer. **draw rein** to check a horse by pulling the reins. **draw sheet** one that can be taken from under a patient

without remaking the bed. **draw the line at** to refuse to do or tolerate. **draw up** to come to a halt; to compose (a contract etc.); *draw oneself up*, to make oneself stiffly erect.

drawback *noun* a disadvantage.

drawbridge *noun* a bridge over a moat, hinged at one end so that it can be drawn up.

drawcard *noun* a person, event, etc. that attracts a large audience.

drawee *noun* the person who is required to pay the sum of money specified in a bill of exchange.

drawer *noun* **1** a person who draws something; one who draws (= writes out) a cheque. **2** a boxlike compartment without a lid, that can be slid horizontally in and out of a piece of furniture. **drawers** *plural noun* knickers; underpants.

drawing *noun* a picture etc. drawn but not coloured. □ **drawing board** a flat board on which paper is stretched while a drawing is made; *back to the drawing board*, we must begin planning afresh. **drawing pin** a flat-headed pin for fastening paper etc. to a surface. **drawing room** a room in which guests are received in a private house, a sitting room.

drawl *verb* to speak lazily or with drawn-out vowel sounds. –**drawl** *noun* a drawling manner of speaking.

drawn *see* draw. –**drawn** *adjective* (of a person's features) looking strained from tiredness or worry. □ **drawn-thread-work** *noun* needlework in which threads are drawn from fabric that is then stitched ornamentally.

drawstring *noun* a string that can be pulled to tighten an opening.

dray *noun* a strong low flat cart for heavy loads.

dread *noun* **1** great fear. **2** a Rastafarian; one who wears dreadlocks. –**dread** *verb* to fear greatly. –**dread** *adjective* (*old use*) dreaded.

dreadful *adjective* **1** causing dread. **2** (*informal*) troublesome, boring, very bad, *dreadful weather*. **dreadfully** *adverb*

dreadlocks *plural noun* hair worn in many ringlets or plaits, as worn by Rastafarians.

dream *noun* **1** a series of pictures or events in a sleeping person's mind. **2** the state of mind of one dreaming or daydreaming, *goes round in a dream*. **3** an ambition, an ideal. **4** a beautiful person or thing. –**dream** *verb* (**dreamt** (*pr.* dremt) *or* **dreamed**, **dreaming**) **1** to have a dream or dreams while sleeping.

2 to have an ambition, *dreamt of being champion*. **3** to think of as a possibility, *never dreamt it would happen*; *wouldn't dream of allowing it*, will certainly not allow it. □ **dream up** to imagine, to invent. **like a dream** (*informal*) easily, effortlessly. **dreamer** *noun*

Dreamtime *noun* (also **Dreaming**) in Aboriginal belief, events beyond living memory that shaped the physical, spiritual, and moral world. Also called *tjukurpa*. [translation of *alcheringa*]

dreamy *adjective* **1** daydreaming. **2** (*informal*) wonderful. **dreamily** *adverb*, **dreaminess** *noun*

dreary *adjective* (**drearier**, **dreariest**) dull, boring; (of places etc.) gloomy. **drearily** *adverb*, **dreariness** *noun*

dredge[1] *noun* an apparatus for scooping things from the bottom of a river or the sea. **–dredge** *verb* to bring up or clean out with a dredge.

dredge[2] *verb* to sprinkle with flour or sugar etc.

dredger[1] *noun* a dredge; a boat with a dredge.

dredger[2] *noun* a container with a perforated lid, used for sprinkling things.

dregs *plural noun* **1** bits of worthless matter that sink to the bottom of a liquid. **2** the worst and most useless part, *the dregs of society*.

drench *verb* to make wet through.

dress *noun* **1** clothing, especially the visible part of it. **2** a woman's or girl's garment with a bodice and skirt. **–dress** *verb* **1** to put clothes upon; to put on one's clothes; to provide clothes for. **2** to put on evening dress, *they dress for dinner*. **3** to decorate; to arrange decoratively. **4** to put a dressing on (a wound etc.). **5** to groom and arrange (hair). **6** to finish or treat the surface of, *to dress leather*. **7** to prepare (poultry, crab, etc.) for cooking or eating; to coat (salad) with dressing. □ **dress circle** the first gallery in theatres, where evening dress was formerly required. **dress rehearsal** a rehearsal in full costume. **dress shirt** a shirt suitable for wearing with evening dress. **dress up** to put on special clothes; to make (a thing) look more interesting.

dressage (**dress**-ah*zh*) *noun* the management of a horse to show its obedience and deportment. [French, = training]

dresser[1] *noun* **1** one who dresses a person or thing. **2** a person who dresses in a specified way, *a smart dresser*.

dresser[2] *noun* a sideboard with shelves for dishes etc.

dressing *noun* **1** a sauce (especially of oil, vinegar, etc.) for food. **2** manure etc. spread over land. **3** a bandage, ointment, etc. for a wound. **4** a substance used to stiffen fabrics during manufacture. □ **dressing down** a scolding. **dressing gown** a loose gown worn when one is not fully dressed. **dressing room** a room for dressing or changing one's clothes. **dressing table** a piece of bedroom furniture with a mirror and usually drawers.

dressmaker *noun* a person who makes clothes, especially for a living. **dressmaking** *noun*

dressy *adjective* **1** wearing stylish clothes. **2** (of clothes) elegant, elaborate.

drew *see* **draw**.

dribble *verb* **1** to allow saliva to flow from the mouth. **2** to flow or allow to flow in drops. **3** to move the ball forward in soccer or hockey with slight touches of the feet or stick. **–dribble** *noun* **1** an act of dribbling. **2** a dribbling flow.

driblet *noun* a small amount.

dribs and drabs *noun* (*informal*) small amounts.

dried *see* **dry**. **–dried** *adjective* (of foods) preserved by drying, *dried apples*.

drier *noun* = **dryer**.

drift *verb* **1** to be carried by or as if by a current of water or air. **2** to move casually or aimlessly. **3** to be piled into drifts by wind, *the sand had drifted*. **4** to cause to drift. **–drift** *noun* **1** a drifting movement. **2** a mass of snow or sand piled up by wind. **3** deviation from a set course. **4** the general tendency or meaning of a speech etc. **5** fragments of rock carried and deposited by wind or water or a glacier. □ **drift net** a large net for catching fish, allowed to drift with the tide.

drifter *noun* **1** a boat used for fishing with a drift net. **2** an aimless person.

driftwood *noun* wood floating on the sea or washed ashore by it.

drill[1] *noun* **1** a pointed tool or a machine used for boring holes or sinking wells. **2** training in military exercises. **3** thorough training through practical exercises, usually with much repetition. **4** (*informal*) a routine procedure to be followed, *what's the drill?* **–drill** *verb* **1** to use a drill; to make (a hole) with a drill. **2** to train or be trained by means of drill.

drill² *noun* **1** a furrow. **2** a machine for making furrows or for sowing seed in furrows. **3** a row of seeds sown in this way. – **drill** *verb* to plant in drills.

drill³ *noun* strong twilled linen or cotton cloth.

drily *adverb* in a dry way.

drink *verb* (**drank**, **drunk**, **drinking**) **1** to swallow (liquid). **2** (of plants, the soil, etc.) to take in or absorb liquid. **3** to take alcoholic liquors, especially in excess. **4** to pledge good wishes to by drinking, *drank his health*. – **drink** *noun* **1** liquid for drinking. **2** alcoholic liquor; excessive use of this. **3** a portion of liquid for drinking. **4** (*informal*) the sea. □ **drink-drive** *verb* to drive having drunk more than the legal limit of alcohol. **drink in** to watch or listen to with delight or eagerness. **drinker** *noun*

drip *verb* (**dripped**, **dripping**) to fall or let fall in drops. – **drip** *noun* **1** liquid falling in drops; each of these drops. **2** the sound of this. **3** a device that drips liquid into a vein. **4** (*informal*) a weak or dull person.

drip-dry *verb* (**drip-dried**, **drip-drying**) **1** (of fabric) to dry without creases when hung up wet. **2** to leave to dry in this way. – **drip-dry** *adjective* made of fabric that will drip-dry.

dripping *noun* fat melted from roasted meat.

drive *verb* (**drove**, **driven**, **driving**) **1** to urge or send in some direction by blows, threats, violence, etc. **2** to push, send, or carry along. **3** to strike and propel (a ball etc.) forcibly. **4** to force to penetrate, *drove a stake into the ground*; *drove a tunnel through the hill*, dug it. **5** to operate (a vehicle or locomotive) and direct its course. **6** to travel or convey in a private vehicle. **7** (of steam or other power) to keep (machinery) going. **8** to cause, to compel, *was driven by hunger to steal*; *he drives himself too hard*, overworks; *drove him mad*, forced him into this state. **9** to rush, to move or be moved rapidly, *driving rain*. – **drive** *noun* **1** a journey in a vehicle. **2** a stroke made by driving in cricket or golf etc. **3** the transmission of power to machinery, *front-wheel drive*; *left-hand drive*, having the steering wheel on the left of the vehicle. **4** = **disk drive**. **5** energy, persistence; a psychological urge. **6** an organised effort to achieve something, to raise money, etc., *a sales drive*; *a lamington drive*. **7** a social gathering to play card games etc., changing partners and tables. **8** a street or road, especially a scenic one. **9** a road or track

leading to a house. □ **drive a hard bargain** to conclude one without making concessions. **drive at** to intend to convey as a meaning, *what was he driving at?* **drive-in** *adjective* (of a cinema, bank, food outlet, etc.) able to be used without getting out of one's car; (*noun*) such a cinema, bank, etc.

drivel *noun* silly talk, nonsense. – **drivel** *verb* (**drivelled**, **drivelling**) to talk or write drivel.

driven *see* **drive**.

driver *noun* **1** a person who drives. **2** a golf club for driving from a tee. **3** (in computing) a piece of software controlling the operation of a device.

driveway *noun* = **drive** *noun* sense 9.

drizzle *noun* very fine rain. – **drizzle** *verb* to rain in very fine drops. **drizzly** *adjective*

drogue (*pr.* drohg) *noun* a funnel-shaped piece of fabric used as a windsock, brake, target, etc.

droid *noun* **1** (in science fiction) a robot. **2** (in computing) a program that automatically collects information from remote systems.

droll (*pr.* drohl) *adjective* amusing in an odd way. **drolly** *adverb*

drollery (**drohl**-ĕ-ree) *noun* droll humour.

dromedary (**drom**-ĕ-dă-ree) *noun* a light one-humped camel bred for riding. [from Greek *dromas* = runner]

drone *noun* **1** a male honey bee. **2** an idler. **3** a deep humming sound. **4** a pipe, especially of a bagpipe, sounding a continuous low-pitched note; this note. **5** a remote-controlled pilotless aircraft or missile. – **drone** *verb* **1** to make a deep humming sound. **2** to speak or utter monotonously.

drongo *noun* (*plural* **drongos**) **1** a black bird with elongated tail feathers like a fish's tail. **2** (*Austral. informal*) a fool or simpleton.

drool *verb* **1** to water at the mouth, to dribble. **2** to show gushing appreciation.

droop *verb* to bend or hang downwards through tiredness or weakness. – **droop** *noun* a drooping attitude. **droopy** *adjective*

drop *noun* **1** a small rounded or pear-shaped portion of liquid. **2** something shaped like this, e.g. a sweet or a hanging ornament. **3** a very small quantity. **4** the act of dropping. **5** a fall, *a drop in prices*. **6** a steep or vertical descent; the distance of this. **7** the length of a hanging curtain. **8** a thing that drops or is dropped. – **drop** *verb* (**dropped**, **dropping**) **1** to fall by force of gravity through not being held; to allow to fall. **2** to sink from exhaustion. **3** to form a steep or vertical descent, *the cliff drops sharply to the sea.* **4** to lower, to become lower or weaker. **5** to allow oneself to move to a position further back, *dropped behind the others.* **6** to utter or send casually, *drop a hint; drop me a note.* **7** to omit, to fail to pronounce or insert, *drop one's h's.* **8** to set down (a passenger or parcel etc.). **9** to fell with an axe, blow, or bullet. **10** to give up, to reject, to cease to associate with; *drop the subject,* cease talking about it. **11** to score by a drop kick. **drops** *plural noun* liquid medicine to be measured by drops. ☐ **drop by** or **drop in** to pay a casual visit. **drop kick** a kick made by dropping a football and kicking it as it falls to the ground. **drop off** to fall asleep; to set down (a passenger or parcel etc.). **drop out** to cease to participate. **drop-out** *noun* one who drops out from a course of study or from conventional society. **drop scone** a pikelet. **drop shot** (in tennis, badminton, etc.) a shot that drops abruptly just over the net.

droplet *noun* a small drop of liquid.

dropper *noun* a device for releasing liquid in drops.

droppings *plural noun* dung of animals or birds.

dropsy *noun* a disease in which watery fluid collects in the body. **dropsical** *adjective*

drosophila (drŏ-**soff**-ĭ-lă) *noun* a small fruit fly much used in research on genetics. [from Greek *drosos* = dew, + *philos* = loving]

dross *noun* **1** scum on molten metal. **2** impurities, rubbish.

drought (*rhymes with* out) *noun* continuous dry weather.

drove *see* drive. –**drove** *noun* **1** a moving herd or flock. **2** a moving crowd, *droves of people.*

drover *noun* a person who herds cattle or sheep to market or pasture, especially over a long distance. ☐ **drover's dog** a person who earns no respect; a drudge.

drown *verb* **1** to kill or be killed by suffocating in water or other liquid. **2** to flood, to drench. **3** to overpower (a sound) with greater loudness. **4** to deaden (grief etc.) with drink, *drown one's sorrows.* ☐ **drowned valley** a valley that has become partly or wholly submerged by the sea or a lake.

drowse (*rhymes with* cows) *verb* to be half asleep.

drowsy *adjective* (**drowsier, drowsiest**) half asleep. **drowsily** *adverb*, **drowsiness** *noun*

drub *verb* (**drubbed, drubbing**) **1** to thrash. **2** to defeat thoroughly. **drubbing** *noun*

drudge *noun* a person who does dull, laborious, or menial work. –**drudge** *verb* to do such work. **drudgery** *noun*

drug *noun* **1** a substance used in medicine. **2** a substance that acts on the nervous system, e.g. a narcotic or stimulant, especially one causing addiction. –**drug** *verb* (**drugged, drugging**) **1** to add a drug to (food or drink). **2** to give drugs to, to stupefy.

drugget (**drug**-ĕt) *noun* coarse woven fabric used for floor coverings.

druggie *noun* (*informal*) a drug addict.

druggist *noun* a pharmaceutical chemist.

drugstore *noun* (*Amer.*) a chemist's shop also selling many kinds of goods.

Druid (**droo**-ĭd) *noun* a priest of an ancient Celtic religion. **Druidism** *noun*, **Druidic** *adjective*

drum *noun* **1** a percussion instrument consisting of a skin or sheet of plastic stretched tightly across a round frame. **2** the sound of this being struck; a similar sound. **3** a cylindrical structure or object or container. **4** the eardrum. **5** (*Austral.*) a swagman's bundle of possessions. **6** (*Austral. informal*) a reliable piece of information. –**drum** *verb* (**drummed, drumming**) **1** to play a drum or drums. **2** to make a drumming sound; to tap or thump continuously or rhythmically. **3** to drive (facts etc.) into a person's mind by constant repetition. ☐ **drum brake** one in which curved pads on a vehicle press against the inner cylindrical part of a wheel. **drum up** to obtain through vigorous effort, *drum up support.*

drumlin *noun* a long oval hill or ridge formed from material deposited by a glacier and shaped by its movement.

drummer *noun* a person who plays a drum or drums.

drumstick *noun* **1** a stick for beating a drum. **2** the lower part of a cooked fowl's leg.

drunk *see* drink. –**drunk** *adjective* **1** excited, stupefied, or rendered incapable by alcohol. **2** overcome or elated (with power, success, etc.), *drunk with success.* –**drunk** *noun* a drunken person.

Usage See the note under **drunken**.

drunkard *noun* a person who is often drunk.

drunken *adjective* **1** drunk. **2** happening during or because of drunkenness, *a drunken brawl*. **3** frequently drunk. **drunkenly** *adverb*, **drunkenness** *noun*

Usage This word is used before a noun (e.g. *a drunken man*), whereas *drunk* is usually used after a verb (e.g. *he is drunk*).

drupe (*pr.* droop) *noun* a fruit with juicy flesh round a stone with a kernel, e.g. a peach. [from Greek *druppa* = olive]

Druse *noun* a member of a political and religious sect of Muslim origin, concentrated in Lebanon, considered heretics by the general Muslim community.

dry *adjective* (**drier**, **driest**) **1** without water or moisture; *dry land*, not under water; *a dry cough*, without phlegm. **2** eaten without butter etc., *dry bread*. **3** thirsty. **4** (of wine) not sweet. **5** uninteresting, *a dry book*. **6** expressed with pretended seriousness, *dry humour*. **7** not allowing the sale of alcohol. **8** (of cows) not producing milk. **9** (*informal*) of, or being, a political 'dry'. **1** to make or become dry. **2** to preserve (food) by removing its moisture. **–dry** *noun* **1** **the dry** (in northern and central Australia) the rainless season. **2** (*informal*) a politician who advocates individual responsibility, free trade, and economic stringency, and opposes high government spending on social welfare etc. □ **dry battery**, **dry cell** an electric battery or cell in which the electrolyte is absorbed in a solid. **dry-clean** *verb* to clean (clothes etc.) by a solvent that evaporates very quickly, not by water. **dry dock** a dock that can be emptied of water, used for repairing ships. **dry ice** solid carbon dioxide used as a refrigerant. **dry measure** a measure of capacity for dry goods. **dry rot** decay of wood that is not well ventilated; the fungi that cause this; any moral or social decay. **dry run** (*informal*) a dummy run. **dry up** to dry washed dishes; (*informal*) to cease talking; (of an actor) to forget one's lines; (of supplies) to run out. **dry valley** a valley in which the stream or river that formed it has disappeared. **dryness** *noun*

dryad *noun* a wood nymph.

dryer *noun* (also **drier**) a device for drying things.

Drysdale, Sir (George) Russell (1912–81), English-born Australian artist, best known for his paintings of the outback.

drystone *adjective* (of a stone wall) built without mortar.

dual *adjective* composed of two parts, double. □ **dual carriageway** *see* **divided road**. **dual control** two linked sets of controls, enabling either of two persons to operate a car or aircraft. **duality** (dew-**al**-ĭ-tee) *noun* [from Latin *duo* = two]

dub[1] *verb* (**dubbed**, **dubbing**) **1** to make (a man) a knight by touching him on the shoulder with a sword. **2** to give a nickname to. **3** to smear (leather) with grease. [from an old French word, = make a person a knight]

dub[2] *verb* (**dubbed**, **dubbing**) **1** to replace the soundtrack of (a film), especially in a different language. **2** to add (sound effects or music) to a film or broadcast. **3** to impose (additional sounds) on to a recording. **4** to copy (a recording). [short for *double*]

Dubai (doo-**by**) an emirate belonging to the federation of United Arab Emirates.

dubbin *noun* thick grease for softening and waterproofing leather.

dubious (**dew**-bee-ŭs) *adjective* doubtful. **dubiously** *adverb* [from Latin *dubium* = doubt]

Dublin the capital of the Republic of Ireland.

dubnium (**dub**-nee-ŭm) *noun* a very unstable artificial element (symbol Db). See also **hahnium**.

ducal *adjective* of or like a duke.

ducat (**duk**-ăt) *noun* a gold coin formerly current in most European countries.

duchess *noun* **1** a duke's wife or widow. **2** a woman whose rank is equal to that of a duke.

duchy *noun* the territory of a duke or duchess.

duck[1] *noun* **1** a swimming bird of various kinds. **2** the female of this (¶the male is the *drake*). **3** its flesh as food. **4** (*informal*) dear. **5** (in cricket) a batsman's score of 0. **6** a ducking movement. **–duck** *verb* **1** to dip the head under water and emerge; to push (a person) under water. **2** to bob down, especially to avoid being seen or hit. **3** to dodge, to avoid (a task etc.). □ **duck into** or **out** (*informal*) to go into (or out) briefly.

duck[2] *noun* strong linen or cotton cloth. **ducks** *plural noun* trousers made of this.

duckboards *plural noun* boards forming a narrow path in a trench or over mud.

duckling *noun* a young duck.

duckshove *verb* (*Austral. informal*) to evade (responsibility); to avoid (an issue). **duckshover** *noun*

duckweed *noun* a plant that grows on the surface of ponds etc.

duct *noun* **1** a tube or channel for conveying liquid, gas, air, cable, etc. **2** a tube in the body through which fluid passes, *tear ducts*. –**duct** *verb* to convey through a duct. [from Latin *ductum* = conveyed]

ductile *adjective* **1** (of metal) able to be drawn out into fine strands. **2** (of a substance) easily moulded. **ductility** *noun*

ductless *adjective* without a duct. ☐ **duct-less glands** glands that pour their secretions directly into the blood, not through a duct.

dud *noun* (*informal*) something that is useless or counterfeit or that fails to work. –**dud** *adjective* (*informal*) useless, defective.

dude (*pr.* dood) *noun* (*informal*) **1** a person, a guy, *a cool dude*. **2** (as a form of address) mate, *Hey dude!*

dudgeon (**duj**-ŏn) *noun* resentment, indignation, *in high dudgeon*.

due *adjective* **1** owed as a debt or obligation. **2** payable immediately, *it has become due*. **3** that ought to be given to a person, rightful, adequate, *with due respect*. **4** scheduled to do something or to arrive. –**due** *adverb* exactly, *sailed due east*. –**due** *noun* a person's right, what is owed to him or her; *give the Devil his due*, give a disliked person credit for one of his good qualities or actions. **dues** *plural noun* a fee, *union dues*. ☐ **in due course** in the proper order, at the appropriate time. **due to** caused by.

Usage The use of *due to* in sentences such as *Play was stopped, due to rain* is regarded by many people as unacceptable, and can be avoided by using *because of* or *owing to* instead. *Due to* is used after a noun as in *an absence due to illness*, or after the verb *to be*, as in *The stoppage was due to rain*.

---

duel *noun* **1** a fight with weapons between two persons. **2** a contest between two persons or sides. –**duel** *verb* (**duelled**, **duelling**) to fight a duel. **duellist** *noun*

duet *noun* a musical composition for two performers. [from Latin *duo* = two]

duff *verb* (*Austral.*) to steal and alter brands on (horses or cattle).

duffel *noun* (also **duffle**) heavy woollen cloth with a thick nap. ☐ **duffel bag** a cylindrical canvas bag closed by a drawstring. **duffel coat** a hooded overcoat made of duffel, fastened with toggles. [named after Duffel, a town in Belgium]

duffer[1] *noun* (*informal*) an inefficient or stupid person.

duffer[2] *noun* (*Austral.*) **1** a person who duffs cattle or horses. **2** an unproductive mine.

dug[1] *see* dig.

dug[2] *noun* an udder, a teat.

dugite (**doo**-gyt) *noun* a highly venomous Australian snake. [Nyungar, probably *dugaj*]

dugong (**doo**-gong) *noun* (*plural* **dugong** or **dugongs**) an Asian sea mammal; a sea cow. [Malay]

dugout *noun* **1** an underground shelter. **2** a canoe made by hollowing a tree trunk.

duke *noun* **1** a nobleman of the highest hereditary rank. **2** the male ruler of a duchy or of certain small countries. [from Latin *dux* = leader]

dukedom *noun* the position or lands of a duke.

dulcet (**dul**-sĕt) *adjective* sweet-sounding. [from Latin *dulcis* = sweet]

dulcimer (**dul**-sĭ-mer) *noun* a musical instrument with strings stretched over a sounding board or box, played by being struck with two hammers.

dull *adjective* **1** not bright or clear. **2** slow in understanding, stupid. **3** not sharp, (of pain) not felt sharply, (of sound) not resonant. **4** not interesting or exciting, boring. –**dull** *verb* to make or become dull. **dully** *adverb*, **dullness** *noun*

dullard *noun* a mentally dull person.

duly (**dew**-lee) *adverb* in a correct or suitable way.

dumb *adjective* **1** unable to speak. **2** temporarily silent; *was struck dumb*, speechless from surprise etc. **3** (*informal*) stupid. ☐ **dumb-bell** *noun* a short bar with a weight at each end, lifted to exercise the muscles. **dumb down** *verb* (*informal*) simplify or reduce the intellectual content (of something) so as to make it accessible to a larger audience. **dumb show** gestures without words. **dumb waiter** a small lift for conveying food between floors. **dumbly** *adverb*, **dumbness** *noun*

dumbfound *verb* to astonish, to strike dumb with surprise. [from *dumb* + *confound*]

dumdum bullet *noun* a soft-nosed bullet that expands on impact. [named after Dum-Dum in India, where it was first produced]

dummy *noun* **1** a sham article. **2** a model of the human figure, used to display clothes. **3** a rubber teat for a baby to suck. **4** (in card games) a player whose cards are placed upwards on the table and played by his partner. **5** (*informal*) a stupid person. **6** (in football) a pretended pass or kick. –**dummy** *adjective* sham. –**dummy** *verb* (in football) make a pretend pass or kick etc. □ **dummy run** a trial run, a practice. [from *dumb*]

dump *verb* **1** to deposit as rubbish. **2** to put down carelessly. **3** to get rid of (something unwanted). **4** to market goods abroad at a lower price than is charged in the home market. –**dump** *noun* **1** a rubbish heap; a place where rubbish may be deposited. **2** a temporary store, *ammunition dump*. **3** (*informal*) a dull or unattractive place.

dumpling *noun* **1** a ball of dough cooked in stew etc. or baked with fruit inside it. **2** a small fat person.

dumps *plural noun* (*informal*) low spirits, *down in the dumps*.

dumpy *adjective* short and fat. **dumpiness** *noun*

dun¹ *adjective* & *noun* greyish-brown.

dun² *verb* (**dunned**, **dunning**) to ask persistently for payment of a debt.

dunce *noun* a person who is slow at learning. [from Duns Scotus, a Scottish philosopher in the Middle Ages, whose followers were said by their opponents to be unable to understand new ideas]

dune (*pr.* dewn) *noun* a sand dune (*see* **sand**).

dung *noun* animal excrement. □ **dung beetle** a beetle whose larvae develop in dung.

dungarees (dung-gǎ-**reez**) *plural noun* overalls or trousers of coarse cotton cloth. [from Hindi *dungri*]

dungeon (**dun**-jŏn) *noun* a strong underground cell for prisoners.

dunk *verb* to dip into liquid.

Dunkirk a seaport in northern France from which British troops were evacuated in 1940.

dunnart *noun* a narrow-footed marsupial mouse. [Nyungar *dunard*]

dunny *noun* (*Austral. informal*) a toilet, especially one detached from a residence.

Dunstan, St (c. 909–88), Benedictine abbot of Glastonbury and Archbishop of Canterbury, who restored monastic life in England. Feast day, 19 May.

duo (**dew**-oh) *noun* (*plural* **duos**) **1** a pair of performers. **2** a piece of music for these.

duodecagon *noun* = **dodecagon**.

duodecimal (dew-ŏ-**dess**-ĭ-măl) *adjective* based on 12; reckoning by twelves. [from Latin *duodecim* = twelve]

duodenum (dew-ŏ-**deen**-ŭm) *noun* the first part of the small intestine, immediately below the stomach. **duodenal** *adjective*

duologue (**dew**-ŏ-log) *noun* a dialogue between two persons. [from *duo*, + Greek *logos* = word]

dupe *noun* a person who is deceived or tricked. –**dupe** *verb* to deceive, to trick.

duple (**dew**-pŭl) *adjective* of or having two parts. □ **duple time** (in music) that with two beats to the bar.

duplex (**dew**-pleks) *adjective* having two parts. –**duplex** *noun* either of two semi-detached houses or home units.

duplicate (**dew**-plĭ-kǎt) *noun* **1** one of two or more things that are exactly alike. **2** an exact copy. –**duplicate** (**dew**-plĭ-kǎt) *adjective* exactly like another thing; being a duplicate. –**duplicate** (**dew**-plĭ-kayt) *verb* **1** to make or be an exact copy of. **2** to repeat or do something twice. □ **in duplicate** as two identical copies. **duplication** *noun* [from Latin *duplex* = double]

duplicator *noun* a machine for making copies of documents.

duplicity (dew-**pliss**-ĭ-tee) *noun* double-dealing, deceitfulness. [from Latin *duplex* = double]

durable *adjective* likely to last, not wearing out or decaying quickly. **durables** *plural noun* durable goods. **durably** *adverb*, **durability** *noun* [from Latin *durare* = endure]

duration *noun* the time during which a thing continues.

duress (dew-**ress**) *noun* the use of force or threats to procure something.

Durga a fierce Hindu goddess (often identified with Kali), wife of Siva.

during *preposition* throughout or at a point in the continuance of.

Dushanbe (doo-**shan**-bay) the capital of Tajikistan.

dusk *noun* the darker stage of twilight.

dusky *adjective* (**duskier**, **duskiest**) **1** shadowy, dim. **2** dark-coloured. **duskiness** *noun*

dust *noun* fine particles of earth or other matter. –**dust** *verb* **1** to sprinkle with dust or powder. **2** to clear of dust by wiping; to clear furniture etc. of dust. ☐ **dust bowl** an arid or unproductive dry region. **dust cover**, **dust jacket** a decorated paper cover on a hardback book. **dust storm** a dry storm raising dust. **dust-up** *noun* (*informal*) a noisy argument, a fight.

duster *noun* **1** a cloth for dusting furniture etc. **2** a wooden block with a thick pad of felt, used to clean a blackboard.

dustpan *noun* a pan into which dust is brushed from a floor.

dusty *adjective* (**dustier**, **dustiest**) **1** full of dust; covered with dust. **2** like dust. **3** (of a colour) greyish, *dusty pink*. **dustiness** *noun*

Dutch *adjective* of the Netherlands or its people or language. –**Dutch** *noun* the Dutch language. –**Dutch** Dutch people. ☐ **Dutch auction** one in which the price asked is gradually reduced until a buyer is found. **Dutch cap** a contraceptive diaphragm. **Dutch courage** that obtained by drinking alcohol. **Dutch oven** a large cooking pot with a lid for braising, etc. **Dutch treat** an outing where people pay for themselves. **Dutch uncle** a person giving advice with benevolent firmness. **go Dutch** to share expenses on an outing. **Dutchman**, **Dutchwoman** *nouns*

dutiable (**dew**-tee-ăbŭl) *adjective* on which customs or other duties must be paid.

dutiful *adjective* doing one's duty, showing due obedience. **dutifully** *adverb* [from *duty* + -*ful*]

duty *noun* **1** a moral or legal obligation. **2** a task that must be done, action required from a particular person. **3** a tax charged on certain goods or on imports. ☐ **do duty for** to serve as (something else). **in duty bound**, **duty-bound** *adjective* obliged by duty. **duty-free** *adjective* (of goods) on which duty is not charged. **on** or **off duty** actually engaged in or not engaged in one's regular work.

duvet (**doo**-vay) *noun* a thick soft quilt used instead of a top sheet and blankets. [French]

dux *noun* the top pupil in a class or in a school.

DVD *abbreviation* digital versatile (or video) disc, a data storage medium for audio, video, etc.

Dvořák (**dvor**-*zh*ak), Antonin (1841–1904), Czech composer.

dwarf *noun* (*plural* **dwarfs**) **1** a person, animal, or plant much below the usual size. **2** (in fairy tales) a small being with magic powers. –**dwarf** *adjective* of a kind that is very small in size. –**dwarf** *verb* **1** to stunt. **2** to make seem small by contrast or distance. ☐ **dwarf planet** a planet-like object that orbits the sun, but is not large or solid enough to be designated a planet.

dwell *verb* (**dwelt**, **dwelling**) to live as an inhabitant. ☐ **dwell on** to think or speak or write lengthily about. **dweller** *noun*

dwelling *noun* a house etc. to live in.

dwindle *verb* to become gradually less or smaller.

Dyak (**dy**-ak) *noun* a member of the native non-Muslim inhabitants of Borneo.

dye *verb* (**dyed**, **dyeing**) **1** to colour, especially by dipping in a liquid. **2** to be able to be dyed, *this fabric dyes well*. –**dye** *noun* **1** a substance used for dyeing. **2** a colour given by dyeing. ☐ **dyed-in-the-wool** *adjective* unchangeable, confirmed in one's beliefs. **dyer** *noun*

dying *see* **die**[1].

Dyirbal (**jeer**-bahl) *noun* **1** a member of an Aboriginal people of northern Queensland. **2** their language (with dialectal variants).

dyke *noun* **1** a long wall or embankment to keep back water and prevent flooding. **2** a ditch for draining water from land. **3** (*informal*) a toilet.

dynamic *adjective* **1** (of force) producing motion (as opposed to *static*). **2** (of a person) energetic, having force of character. **dynamics** *plural noun* **1** (usually treated as *singular*) a branch of physics that deals with matter in motion. **2** varying degrees of loudness in musical performance. **3** the forces affecting behaviour in any sphere, *group dynamics*. **dynamically** *adverb* [from Greek *dunamis* = power]

dynamite *noun* **1** a powerful explosive made of nitroglycerine. **2** something likely to cause violent or dangerous reactions, *the frontier question is dynamite*. **3** a person or thing with great vitality or effectiveness. –**dynamite** *verb* to fit with a charge of dynamite, to blow up with dynamite. [same origin as *dynamic*]

dynamo *noun* (*plural* dynamos) a generator producing electric current; *a human dynamo*, a dynamic person.

dynasty (**din**-ă-stee) *noun* a line of hereditary rulers. dynastic *adjective* [same origin as *dynamic*]

dyne *noun* the force required to give a mass of one gram an acceleration of one centimetre per second per second.

dys- *prefix* bad; difficult. [from Greek]

dysentery (**dis**-ĕn-tree) *noun* a disease with inflammation of the intestines, causing severe diarrhoea. [from *dys-*, + Greek *entera* = bowels]

dysfunction (dis-**funk**-shŏn) *noun* failure to function normally.

dyslexia (dis-**leks**-ee-ă) *noun* abnormal difficulty in reading and spelling, caused by a brain condition. dyslexic *adjective* & *noun* [from *dys-*, + Greek *lexis* = speech]

dyspepsia (dis-**pep**-see-ă) *noun* indigestion. [from *dys-*, + Greek *peptikos* = able to digest]

dyspeptic *adjective* (dis-**pep**-tik) suffering from dyspepsia or the resulting irritability.

dysprosium (dis-**proh**-zee-ŭm) *noun* a soft silver-white metallic element of the lanthanide series (symbol Dy).

dystrophy (**dis**-trŏ-fee) *noun* a hereditary condition causing progressive weakening of the muscles, *muscular dystrophy*. [from *dys-*, + Greek *-trophia* = nourishment]

Ee

E *abbreviation* (also **E.**) east; eastern.

e- *prefix* **1** involving electronic communication. **2** see **ex-**.

each *adjective* every one of two or more, *each child*. –**each** *pronoun* each person or thing, *each of them*; *give them two each*; *we see each other*, each of us sees the other, we meet.

eager *adjective* full of strong desire, enthusiastic. **eagerly** *adverb*, **eagerness** *noun*

eagle *noun* **1** a large bird of prey. **2** a score of two strokes under par or bogey for a hole at golf. □ **eagle eye** very sharp eyesight; keen watchfulness. **eagle-eyed** *adjective*. **eagle hawk = wedge-tailed eagle**.

eaglet *noun* a young eagle.

ear¹ *noun* **1** the organ of hearing in man and certain animals; the external part of this. **2** the ability to distinguish sounds accurately; *has an ear for music*, enjoys it. **3** listening, attention; *lend an ear*, listen; *have a person's ear*, to have his or her favourable attention. **4** an ear-shaped thing. □ **be all ears** to listen attentively. **have one's ear to the ground** to be alert to rumours or trends of opinion.

ear² *noun* the seed-bearing part of corn.

earache *noun* a pain in the eardrum.

eardrum *noun* a membrane inside the ear that vibrates when sound waves strike it.

earl *noun* a British nobleman ranking between marquis and viscount.

earldom *noun* the position or lands of an earl.

early *adjective* & *adverb* (**earlier**, **earliest**) **1** before the usual or expected time. **2** not far on in a period of time or development or a series, *his early years*. □ **early bird** a person who gets up early or arrives early. **early on** at an early stage. **earliness** *noun*

earmark *noun* a distinguishing mark. –**earmark** *verb* **1** to put a distinguishing mark on. **2** to set aside for a particular purpose. [from the custom of marking an animal's ear to identify it]

earn *verb* (**earned**, **earning**) **1** to get or deserve as a reward for one's work or merit.

2 (of money lent or invested) to gain as interest.

earnest¹ *adjective* showing serious feeling or intentions. □ **in earnest** seriously, not jokingly; with determination, intensively. **earnestly** *adverb*, **earnestness** *noun*

earnest² *noun* **1** money paid as an instalment or to confirm a contract etc. **2** a foretaste or token, *an earnest of what is to come*.

earnings *plural noun* money earned.

earphone *noun* a device applied to the ear to aid hearing or receive radio or telephone communications.

earplug *noun* a plug inserted in the ear to keep out noise or water.

earring *noun* an ornament worn on the ear.

earshot *noun* range of hearing, *within earshot*.

earth *noun* **1** (also **Earth**) the planet on which we live; the world in which we live. **2** its surface, dry land, the ground, *it fell to earth*. **3** (*informal*) a huge amount of money, *it cost the earth*. **4** soil. **5** the hole of a fox or badger. **6** an oxide with little taste or smell. **7** connection to the ground as completion of an electrical circuit. –**earth** *verb* **1** to cover roots of plants with heaped-up earth, *earth them up*. **2** to connect an electrical circuit to earth. □ **on earth** in existence, in this world (as distinct from a future life). **run a thing to earth** to find it after a long search.

earthen *adjective* **1** made of earth. **2** made of baked clay.

earthenware *noun* pottery made of coarse baked clay.

earthly *adjective* of this earth, of man's life on it. □ **no earthly use** (*informal*) no use at all. **not an earthly** (*informal*) no chance at all.

earthquake *noun* a violent natural movement of a part of the earth's crust.

earthwork *noun* an artificial bank of earth.

earthworm *noun* a common worm that lives in the soil.

earthy *adjective* **1** like earth or soil. **2** gross, coarse, *earthy humour*. **earthiness** *noun*

earwig *noun* a small insect with pincers at the end of its body. [so called because it was formerly thought to enter the head through the ear]

ease *noun* 1 freedom from pain, trouble, or anxiety. 2 relief from pain. 3 absence of painful effort, *did it with ease*. –**ease** *verb* 1 to relieve from pain or anxiety. 2 to make less tight, forceful, or burdensome. 3 to move gently or gradually, *ease it in*. 4 to slacken, to reduce in severity or pressure etc., *it will ease off* or *up*. □ **at ease** free from anxiety, in comfort; standing relaxed with feet apart. **at one's ease** relaxed, not feeling awkward or embarrassed.

easel *noun* a wooden frame to support a painting or a blackboard etc. [from Dutch *ezel* = donkey (which carries a load)]

easement *noun* a legal right of way or similar right over another's land.

easily *adverb* 1 in an easy way, with ease. 2 by far, *easily the best*.

east *noun* 1 the point on the horizon where the sun rises; the direction in which this point lies. 2 the eastern part of something. 3 **the East** the part of the world lying east of Europe; the former bloc of Communist countries of eastern Europe. –**east** *adjective* & *adverb* towards or in the east; *an east wind*, blowing from the east.

Easter *noun* the Christian festival (celebrated on the first Sunday after the first full moon on or after 21 March) commemorating Christ's resurrection; the period about this time. □ **Easter egg** a painted or imitation egg given at Easter.

Easter Island an island in the SE Pacific west of Chile, famous for its monolithic statues of human heads.

easterly *adjective* in or towards the east; *an easterly wind*, blowing from the east (approximately). –**easterly** *noun* an easterly wind.

eastern *adjective* of or in the east. □ **Eastern Church** the Orthodox Church. **Eastern States** the Australian states to the east of South Australia, or sometimes Western Australia.

easterner *noun* a native or inhabitant of the east.

easternmost *adjective* furthest east.

East India Company a company, formed in 1600 to trade in the East Indies, which administered British India until the Indian Mutiny (1857).

East Indies the many islands off the SE coast of Asia, now often called the Malay Archipelago.

easting *noun* 1 a distance travelled or measured eastward. 2 an easterly direction.

East Timor see **Timor**.

eastward *adjective* towards the east. **eastwards** *adverb*

easy *adjective* (**easier**, **easiest**) 1 not difficult, done or obtained without great effort. 2 free from pain, trouble, or anxiety, *with an easy mind*; *easy manners*, relaxed and pleasant; *in easy circumstances*, with enough money to live comfortably. –**easy** *adverb* in an easy way, with ease. □ **easy chair** a large comfortable chair. **go easy with** to be careful with; *go easy on the butter*, do not use too much. **stand easy** stand at ease. **take it easy** to proceed comfortably or carefully; to rest or relax. **easiness** *noun*

easygoing *adjective* placid and tolerant, not strict.

eat *verb* (**ate**, **eaten**, **eating**) 1 to take food into the mouth and swallow it for nourishment; to have a meal, *when do we eat?* 2 to chew and swallow (food). 3 to destroy gradually, *acids eat into metals*. 4 to consume. **eats** *plural noun* (*informal*) food. □ **eat one's heart out** to suffer greatly with vexation or longing. **eat one's words** to be obliged to withdraw what one has said. **what's eating you?** (*informal*) why are you annoyed? **eater** *noun*

eatable *adjective* fit to be eaten (because of its condition). **eatables** *plural noun* food.

eatery *noun* (*plural* **eateries**) (*informal*) a place at which to eat, a restaurant.

eau de Cologne (oh-dĕ-kŏ-**lohn**) *noun* a delicate perfume originally made at Cologne.

eaves *plural noun* the overhanging edge of a roof.

eavesdrop *verb* (**eavesdropped**, **eavesdropping**) to listen secretly to a private conversation. **eavesdropper** *noun* [as if outside a wall, where water drops from the eaves]

ebb *noun* 1 the outward movement of the tide, away from the land. 2 a condition of lowness or decline. –**ebb** *verb* 1 (of tides) to flow away from the land. 2 to become lower, to weaken, *his strength ebbed*.

ebonite *noun* vulcanite.

ebony *noun* the hard black wood of a tropical tree. –**ebony** *adjective* black as ebony.

ebullient (ĕ-**bul**-ee-ĕnt) *adjective* exuberant, bubbling over with high spirits. **ebullience** *noun*, **ebulliency** *noun*, **ebulliently** *adverb* [from *e-*, + Latin *bullire* = to boil]

EC *abbreviation* European Community.

ecad (**ee**-kad) *noun* an organism modified by its environment.

eccentric *adjective* **1** unconventional in appearance or behaviour. **2** (of circles) not concentric; (of orbits) not circular; (of a pivot) not placed centrally. –**eccentric** *noun* **1** an eccentric person. **2** a disc fixed off centre on a revolving shaft, for changing rotary motion to to-and-fro motion. **eccentrically** *adverb*, **eccentricity** *noun* [from Greek *ekkentros* = away from the centre]

Ecclesiastes (ĕ-kleez-ee-**ast**-eez) a book of the Old Testament traditionally ascribed to Solomon.

ecclesiastical (ĕ-kleez-ee-**ast**-ikăl) *adjective* of the Church or the clergy. [from Greek *ekklesia* = church]

Ecclesiasticus (ĕ-kleez-ee-**ast**-ikŭs) a book of the Apocrypha containing moral and practical maxims.

ecdysis (**ek**-dĭ-sĭss) *noun* the casting off of a shell or outer skin. [from Greek *ekdusis* = putting off]

ECG *abbreviation* electrocardiogram.

echelon (**esh**-ĕ-lŏn) *noun* **1** a formation of troops or aircraft etc. like a series of steps, with each unit to the right (or left) of the one in front. **2** a level of rank or authority, *the upper echelons of the Public Service*. [from French *échelle* = ladder]

echidna (ĕ-**kid**-nă) *noun* an insectivorous monotreme found in Australia and New Guinea. Also called *spiny anteater*.

echinacea (ek-ĭ-**nay**-shă) *noun* a North American plant of the daisy family, used in herbal medicine.

echinoderm (ĕ-**ky**-nŏ-derm) *noun* an invertebrate sea animal of the group that includes starfish and sea urchins.

echinoid (ĕ-**ky**-noid) *noun* a sea urchin. [from Greek *echinos* = hedgehog]

echo *noun* (*plural* **echoes**) **1** repetition of sound by the reflection of sound waves; a secondary sound produced in this way. **2** a reflected radio or radar beam. **3** a close imitation or imitator. –**echo** *verb* (**echoed**,

echoing) **1** to repeat (sound) by echo, to resound. **2** to repeat or imitate. □ **echo sounder** a sounding apparatus for finding the depth of the sea beneath a ship by measuring the time taken for an echo to be received. **echo-sounding** *noun*

echolocation *noun* location of objects by means of reflected sound.

eclair (ĕ-**klair** *or* ay-**klair**) *noun* (also **éclair**) a finger-shaped cake of choux pastry with cream filling.

eclectic (ĕ-**klek**-tik) *adjective* choosing or accepting from various sources. **eclectically** *adverb*, **eclecticism** *noun* [from Greek *eklegein* = pick out]

eclipse *noun* **1** the blocking of light from one heavenly body by another. **2** a loss of brilliance, power, or reputation. –**eclipse** *verb* **1** to cause an eclipse of. **2** to outshine, to throw into obscurity.

ecliptic (ĕ-**klip**-tik) *noun* the sun's apparent path among stars during the year.

eclogue (**ek**-log) *noun* a pastoral poem.

ecologist (ĕ-**kol**-ŏ-jĭst) *noun* an expert in ecology.

ecology (ĕ-**kol**-ŏjee) *noun* **1** the scientific study of living things in relation to each other and to their environment. **2** this relationship. □ **ecological footprint** the amount of land required to sustain a particular person or society. **ecological** (ee-kŏ-**loj**-ik-ăl) *adjective*, **ecologically** *adverb* [from Greek *oikos* = house, + *-logy*]

economic (ee-kŏ-**nom**-ik *or* ek-ŏ-) *adjective* **1** of economics, *the government's economic policies*. **2** sufficient to give a good return for the money or effort laid out, *an economic rent*. **economics** *noun* **1** the science concerned with the production and consumption or use of goods and services. **2** (as *plural noun*) the financial aspects of something, *the economics of farming*.

economical (ee-kŏ-**nom**-ikăl *or* ek-ŏ-) *adjective* thrifty, avoiding waste. **economically** *adverb*

economise *verb* (also **-ize**) to be economical, to use or spend less than before, *economise on fuel*.

economist (ĕ-**kon**-ŏmĭst) *noun* an expert in economics.

economy *noun* **1** being economical, *practise economy*. **2** an instance of this, a saving, *make economies*. **3** a community's system of using its resources to produce wealth; *an agricultural economy*, one where agriculture is the chief industry. **4** the state of a country's prosperity. [from Greek *oikos* = house, + *-nomia* = management]

ecosystem (ee-koh-sis-tĕm *or* ek-oh-) *noun* the group of plants and animals that interact with each other and form an ecological unit.

ecotourism (ee-koh-toor-rizm *or* ek-oh-) *noun* a form of tourism that supports conservation efforts in ecologically sensitive areas.

ecru (**ay**-kroo) *noun* light fawn colour. [French *écru* = unbleached]

ecstasy *noun* **1** a feeling of intense delight. **2** (*informal*) a stimulant and hallucinatory drug. **ecstatic** *adjective*, **ecstatically** *adverb* [from Greek, = standing outside yourself]

ECT *abbreviation* electroconvulsive therapy.

ectopic (ek-**top**-ik) *adjective* in an abnormal place; *ectopic pregnancy*, one occurring outside the womb. [from Greek *ektopos* = out of place]

ectoplasm (**ek**-tŏ-plazm) *noun* **1** the outer portion of the matter of an animal or vegetable cell. **2** a substance supposed to be exuded from a spiritualist medium during a trance.

Ecuador (**ek**-wă-dor) a republic in South America, on the Pacific coast. **Ecuadorean** *adjective* & *noun*

ecumenical (ee-kew-**men**-ikăl *or* ek-yoo-) *adjective* **1** of the whole Christian Church, not only of separate denominations. **2** seeking worldwide Christian unity, *the ecumenical movement*. [from Greek *oikoumenikos* = of the inhabited world]

eczema (**ek**-sĕ-mă) *noun* a skin disease causing scaly itching patches.

edam (**ee**-dam) *noun* a round Dutch cheese, usually with a red rind.

edaphic (ĕ-**daf**-ik) *adjective* of the soil. [from Greek *edaphos* = floor]

Edda (**ed**-ă) a body of ancient Icelandic literature compiled in the 13th century.

eddy *noun* a swirling patch of water, air, or fog etc. –**eddy** *verb* (**eddied**, **eddying**) to swirl in eddies. □ **eddy current** a current of electricity induced where such currents are undesirable and cause waste of energy.

edelweiss (**ay**-dĕl-vys) *noun* an alpine plant with woolly white bracts round the flowers.

Eden (also **the Garden of Eden**) the place where Adam and Eve lived at their creation. –**Eden** *noun* a delightful place.

edge *noun* **1** the sharpened side of a blade. **2** its sharpness, *has lost its edge*. **3** the line where two surfaces meet at an angle. **4** a rim, the narrow surface of a thin or flat object. **5** the outer limit or boundary of an area. –**edge** *verb* **1** to supply with a border; to form the border of. **2** to move gradually, *edging towards the door*. □ **be on edge** to be tense and irritable. **have the edge on** (*informal*) to have an advantage over. **set a person's teeth on edge** to upset his or her nerves by causing an unpleasant sensation. **take the edge off** to dull or soften; *take the edge off one's appetite*, to make one's hunger less acute.

edgeways *adverb* with the edge forwards or outwards. □ **get a word in edgeways** to manage to break into a lengthy talk.

edging *noun* something placed round an edge to define or strengthen or decorate it.

edgy *adjective* with nerves on edge, irritable. **edginess** *noun*

edible *adjective* fit to be eaten (because of its nature). **edibility** *noun*

edict (**ee**-dikt) *noun* an order proclaimed by an authority. [from *e*-, + Latin *dictum* = said]

edifice (**ed**-ĭ-fĭs) *noun* a large building.

edify (**ed**-ĭ-fy) *verb* (**edified**, **edifying**) to be an uplifting influence on the mind of (a person). **edification** *noun*

Edinburgh (**ed**-ĭn-bu-ră) the capital of Scotland.

Edison, Thomas Alva (1847–1931), American inventor of apparatus for telephony, sound recording, and lighting etc.

edit *verb* (**edited**, **editing**) **1** to act as editor of (a newspaper etc.). **2** to prepare (written material) for publication. **3** to reword for a purpose. **4** to prepare (data) for processing by computer. **5** to prepare (a film or recording) by selecting individual sections and arranging them in sequence.

edition *noun* **1** the form in which something is published, *a pocket edition*. **2** the copies of a book or newspaper in one particular form, formerly printed from one set of type.

editor *noun* **1** a person who is responsible for the content and writing of a newspaper etc. or a section of this. **2** one who edits written material for publication. **3** one who edits cinema film or recording tape. **4** a computer program enabling the user to enter and alter text.

editorial *adjective* of an editor, *editorial work.* – **editorial** *noun* a newspaper article giving the editor's comments on current affairs.

educable *adjective* able to be educated.

educate *verb* to train the mind and abilities of, to provide education for. **educator** *noun* [from Latin *educare* = bring up, train]

education *noun* systematic training and instruction designed to impart knowledge and develop skill. **educational** *adjective*, **educationally** *adverb*

educationist *noun* (also **educationalist**) an expert in educational methods.

educative (ed-yŭ-kă-tiv) *adjective* educating.

Edward the name of six kings of England since the Norman Conquest and two of the United Kingdom, who reigned as Edward I 1272–1307, II 1307–27, III 1327–77, IV 1461–83, V 1483, VI 1547–53, VII 1901–10, VIII 1936.

Edwardian (ed-**wor**-deeăn) *adjective* of the time of King Edward VII's reign (1901–10). – **Edwardian** *noun* a person living at this time.

Edward the Confessor king of England 1042–66.

EEC *abbreviation* European Economic Community.

EEG *abbreviation* electroencephalogram.

eel *noun* a snakelike fish.

eerie *adjective* (**eerier**, **eeriest**) causing a feeling of mystery and fear. **eerily** *adverb*, **eeriness** *noun*

ef- *prefix* see **ex-**.

efface *verb* to rub out, to obliterate. □ **efface oneself** to make oneself inconspicuous. **effacement** *noun*

effect *noun* 1 a change produced by an action or cause, a result; *have an effect*, to produce such a change. 2 an impression produced on a spectator or hearer etc. 3 a state of being operative, *the law came into effect last week*. – **effect** *verb* to bring about, to accomplish, *effect one's purpose*; *effect a cure*; *effect an insurance policy*, obtain one. **effects** *plural noun* 1 property, *personal effects*. 2 sounds and lighting etc. provided to accompany a broadcast or film. □ **in effect** in fact, really, *it is, in effect, a refusal*. **take effect** to produce its effect(s); to become operative. **to that effect** with that implication. **with effect from**

coming into operation at (a stated time). [from *ef-*, + Latin *-fectum* = done]

Usage See the note under **affect**.

effective *adjective* 1 producing an effect, powerful in its effect. 2 making a striking impression. 3 actual, existing. 4 operative, *the law is effective from 1 April*. **effectively** *adverb*, **effectiveness** *noun*

effector *adjective* (of an organ of the body, e.g. a muscle) performing actions in response to impulses from motor nerves. – **effector** *noun* an organ of this kind.

effectual *adjective* answering its purpose, sufficient to produce an effect. **effectually** *adverb*

effeminate (ĕ-**fem**-ĭ-năt) *adjective* unmanly, having qualities associated with women. **effeminately** *adverb*, **effeminacy** *noun*

efferent (**ef**-ĕ-rĕnt) *adjective* 1 (of nerves) carrying impulses from the brain. 2 (of blood vessels) carrying blood towards the heart. [from *ef-*, + Latin *ferre* = carry]

effervesce (ef-er-**vess**) *verb* to give off small bubbles of gas. **effervescent** *adjective*, **effervescence** *noun* [from Latin, = bubble over (compare *fervent*)]

effete (ĕ-**feet**) *adjective* having lost its vitality. **effeteness** *noun*

efficacious (ef-ĭ-**kay**-shŭs) *adjective* producing the desired result. **efficacy** (**ef**-ĭ-kă-see) *noun*

efficient (ĕ-**fish**-ĕnt) *adjective* acting effectively, producing results with little waste of effort. **efficiently** *adverb*, **efficiency** *noun* [from *ef-*, + Latin *-ficiens* = doing]

effigy (**ef**-ĭ-jee) *noun* a sculpture or model of a person.

effloresce (ef-lor-**ress**) *verb* 1 to burst into flower. 2 to turn to fine powder when exposed to air; (of salts) to come to the surface and crystallise. 3 (of a surface) to become covered with such salt particles. **efflorescence** *noun*, **efflorescent** *adjective*

effluence *noun* 1 a flowing out of light or electricity etc. 2 that which flows out.

effluent (**ef**-loo-ĕnt) *adjective* flowing out. – **effluent** *noun* something that flows out, especially sewage. [from *ef-*, + Latin *fluere* = to flow]

effort *noun* **1** the use of physical or mental energy to achieve something. **2** the energy exerted. **3** something produced by this.

effortless *adjective* done without effort. **effortlessly** *adverb*, **effortlessness** *noun*

effrontery (ĕ-**frunt**-ĕ-ree) *noun* shameless insolence.

effusion (ĕ-**few**-zhŏn) *noun* **1** a pouring forth. **2** an unrestrained outpouring of thought or feeling. [from *ef-*, + Latin *fusum* = poured]

effusive (ĕ-**few**-siv) *adjective* expressing emotions in an unrestrained way. **effusively** *adverb*, **effusiveness** *noun*

eft *noun* a newt.

EFTPOS (**eft**-pos) *abbreviation* electronic funds transfer at point of sale.

e.g. *abbreviation* = for example. [short for Latin *exempli gratia*]

egalitarian (ĕ-gal-ĭ-**tair**-ree-ăn) *adjective* holding the principle of equal rights for all persons. **–egalitarian** *noun* one who holds this principle. **egalitarianism** *noun* [from French *égal* = equal]

egestion (ee-**jes**-chŏn) *noun* the process of getting rid of waste products from the body.

egg[1] *noun* **1** (also **egg cell**) a reproductive cell produced by the female of birds, fish, reptiles, etc. **2** the hard-shelled egg of a domestic hen, used as food. ☐ **egg timer** a device for timing the cooking of a boiled egg.

egg[2] *verb* to urge (a person) to do something, *egging him on*.

eggcup *noun* a small cup for holding a boiled egg.

egghead *noun* (*informal*) an intellectual person.

eggplant *noun* **1** a plant with deep purple fruit used as a vegetable. **2** its fruit, also called *aubergine*.

eggshell *noun* the shell of an egg. **–eggshell** *adjective* **1** (of china) very fragile. **2** (of paint) with a slightly glossy finish.

ego (**ee**-goh *or* e-goh) *noun* (*plural* **egos**) **1** the self. **2** self-esteem, conceit. ☐ **ego trip** (*informal*) an activity undertaken with the sole purpose of self-indulgence. [Latin, = I]

egocentric (ee-goh-**sen**-trik *or* e-) *adjective* self-centred. **egocentricity** *noun*

egoism (ee-goh-izm *or* e-) *noun* **1** self-interest as the moral basis of behaviour. **2** = **egotism**.

egoist *noun*, **egoistic** *adjective*, **egoistically** *adverb*

Usage The meanings of *egoism* and *egotism* overlap, but in philosophy and psychology *egoism* is the term which is used to mean self-interest (often contrasted with *altruism*).

---

egotism (**ee**-gŏ-tizm *or* e-) *noun* the practice of talking too much about oneself, conceit; self-centredness. **egotist** *noun*, **egotistic** *adjective*, **egotistical** *adjective*, **egotistically** *adverb*

egregious (ĕ-**gree**-jŭs) *adjective* outstandingly bad, *egregious folly*.

egress (**ee**-gress) *noun* an exit. [from *e-*, + Latin *gressus* = going]

egret (**ee**-grĕt) *noun* a kind of heron with long feathers.

Egypt a republic in NE Africa. **Egyptian** *adjective* & *noun*

Egyptology *noun* the study of Egyptian antiquities. **Egyptologist** *noun*

eh (*pr.* ay) *interjection* (*informal*) an exclamation of enquiry or surprise.

Eid (*pr.* I'd) *noun* a Muslim festival held at the end of Ramadan. [Arabic, = festival; see **Bairam**, which means the same in Turkish]

eiderdown *noun* a quilt stuffed with soft material. [originally the soft down of the *eider*, a kind of Arctic duck]

Eiffel Tower an iron tower over 300 m high erected in Paris in 1887–9. [named after its French designer, Alexandre Gustave Eiffel (1832–1923)]

eigenfunction (I-gĕn-funk-shŏn) *noun* (in mathematics) that function under a given operation generates a multiple of itself.

eight *adjective* & *noun* **1** one more than seven (8, VIII). **2** an eight-oared rowing boat or its crew.

eighteen *adjective* & *noun* one more than seventeen (18, XVIII). **eighteenth** *adjective* & *noun*

eighth *adjective* & *noun* **1** next after seventh. **2** one of eight equal parts of a thing. **eighthly** *adverb*

eighty *adjective* & *noun* eight times ten (80, LXXX). **eighties** *plural noun* the numbers from 80 to 89, especially the years of a century or of a person's age. **eightieth** *adjective* & *noun*

Einstein (I'n-styn), Albert (1879–1955), German-born theoretical physicist, founder of the theory of relativity.

einsteinium (I'n-**sty**-nee-ŭm) *noun* an artificial radioactive metallic element of the actinide series (symbol Es).

Eire (**air**-rĕ) a former name of the Republic of Ireland, still often used to distinguish the country from Northern Ireland.

eisteddfod (I-ste*th*-vod or ĕ-**sted**-fŏd) *noun* (*plural* **eisteddfods** or **eisteddfodau**, *pr.* -dy) an annual gathering of poets and musicians for competitions. [Welsh]

either (**I**-*th*er or **ee**-*th*er) *adjective & pronoun* **1** one or the other of two, *either of you can go*. **2** each of two, *there are fields on either side of the river*. –**either** *adverb & conjunction* **1** as one alternative, *he is either mad or drunk*. **2** likewise, any more than the other, *the new lid doesn't fit, either*.

ejaculate (ĕ-**jak**-yŭ-layt) *verb* **1** to say suddenly and briefly. **2** to eject fluid (especially semen) from the body. **ejaculation** *noun*

eject *verb* **1** to thrust or send out forcefully, *the gun ejects spent cartridges*. **2** to expel, to compel to leave. □ **ejector seat** a seat that can eject the occupant out of an aircraft in an emergency, so as to descend by parachute. **ejection** *noun*, **ejectment** *noun*, **ejector** *noun* [from *e-*, + Latin *-jectum* = thrown]

eke (*pr.* eek) *verb* **eke out** to supplement, *eke out the meat with lots of vegetables*; to make (a living) laboriously, *eke out a living*.

elaborate (ĕ-**lab**-ŏ-răt) *adjective* with many parts or details, complicated, *an elaborate pattern*. –**elaborate** (ĕ-**lab**-ŏ-rayt) *verb* to work out or describe in detail. **elaborately** *adverb*, **elaboration** *noun* [from *e-*, + Latin *laborare* = to work]

El Alamein (el **al**-ă-mayn) the site of the decisive British victory of the North African campaign of 1940–43, 90 km west of Alexandria.

élan (ay-**lahn**) *noun* vivacity. [French]

eland (**ee**-lănd) *noun* a large African antelope with spirally twisted horns.

elapse *verb* (of time) to pass away. [from *e-*, + Latin *lapsum* = slipped]

elastic *adjective* **1** going back to its original length or shape after being stretched or squeezed. **2** adaptable, not rigid, *the rules are somewhat elastic*. –**elastic** *noun* cord or material made elastic by interweaving strands of rubber etc. **elastically** *adverb*, **elasticity** (ee-lass-**tiss**-ĭ-tee) *noun*

elasticated *adjective* made elastic by being interwoven with elastic thread.

elastomer (ĕ-**last**-ŏ-mer) *noun* a natural or synthetic rubber or rubber-like plastic. **elastomeric** *adjective*

elate *verb* to cause to feel very pleased or proud. **elation** *noun* [from *e-*, + Latin *latum* = carried]

elated *adjective* very happy and excited.

Elba a small island off the west coast of Italy, famous as the place of Napoleon's first exile 1814–15.

elbow *noun* **1** the joint between the forearm and upper arm; its outer part. **2** the part of a sleeve covering this. **3** a sharp bend in a pipe etc. –**elbow** *verb* to thrust with one's elbow. □ **elbow grease** vigorous polishing; hard work. **elbow room** plenty of room to work or move.

elder[1] *adjective* older, *elder sister*. –**elder** *noun* **1** an older person, *respect your elders*. **2** an official in certain Churches. **3** a person of recognised authority in an Aboriginal community. □ **elder statesman** an influential experienced person, especially a politician, of advanced years. [an old form of *older*]

elder[2] *noun* a tree or shrub with white flowers and dark berries. **elderberry** *noun* its berry.

elderly *adjective* rather old, past middle age.

eldest *adjective* oldest, first-born, *eldest son*. [an old form of *oldest*]

eldorado (el-dŏ-**rah**-doh) *noun* (*plural* **eldorados**) an imaginary land of riches. [from the name of a fictitious country or city abounding in gold, believed by the Spaniards and by Sir Walter Raleigh to exist upon the River Amazon]

elect *verb* **1** to choose by vote, *elect a chairman*. **2** to choose as a course, to decide, *he elected to become a lawyer*. –**elect** *adjective* chosen; *the president elect*, chosen but not yet in office. [from *e-*, + Latin *lectum* = chosen]

election *noun* **1** choosing or being chosen, especially by vote. **2** the process of electing representatives, especially Members of Parliament.

electioneer *verb* to busy oneself in an election campaign. **electioneering** *noun*

elective *adjective* **1** having the power to elect, *an elective assembly.* **2** chosen or filled by election, *an elective office.* **3** involving a choice, optional, *elective surgery; elective subjects.* –**elective** *noun* an elective course of study.

elector *noun* one who has the right to vote in an election. **electoral** *adjective*

electorate *noun* **1** the whole body of electors. **2** (*Austral.*) a district represented by a Member of Parliament elected by the people who live there.

Electra (ĕ-**lek**-tră) (*Gk. legend*) the daughter of Agamemnon and Clytemnestra, who urged her brother to kill their mother in revenge for the murder of their father.

electric *adjective* **1** of or producing electricity. **2** worked by electricity. **3** causing sudden excitement, *the news had an electric effect.* ▢ **electric chair** a chair in which criminals are executed by electrocution. **electric guitar** a guitar with a built-in microphone. **electric shock** the effect of a sudden discharge of electricity through the body of a person or animal, stimulating the nerves and contracting the muscles. **electric storm** a violent disturbance of the electrical condition of the atmosphere. [from Greek *elektron* = amber (which is easily given a charge of static electricity)]

electrical *adjective* **1** of or concerned with electricity, *electrical engineering.* **2** causing sudden excitement. **electrically** *adverb*

electrician (e-lek-**trish**-ăn) *noun* a person whose job is dealing with electricity and electrical equipment.

electricity *noun* **1** a form of energy occurring in certain particles (electrons and protons) and hence in larger bodies since they contain these. **2** a supply of electric current for lighting, heating, etc.

electrify *verb* (**electrified**, **electrifying**) **1** to charge with electricity. **2** to convert (a railway, farm, etc.) to the use of electric power. **3** to startle or excite suddenly. **electrification** *noun*

electro- *prefix* of or involving or caused by electricity.

electrocardiogram *noun* the pattern traced by an electrocardiograph.

electrocardiograph *noun* an instrument for detecting and recording the electric currents generated by heartbeats.

electrochemistry *noun* **1** the application of electricity to chemical processes. **2** the

scientific study of this. **electrochemical** *adjective*

electroconvulsive therapy *noun* treatment of mental illness by means of electric shocks that produce convulsions.

electrocute *verb* to kill by electricity. **electrocution** *noun*

electrode (ĕ-**lek**-trohd) *noun* a solid conductor through which electricity enters or leaves a vacuum tube etc. [from *electro-*, + Greek *hodos* = way]

electroencephalogram *noun* the pattern traced by an electroencephalograph.

electroencephalograph *noun* an instrument for detecting and recording the electric currents generated by activity of the brain.

electrolysis (ĕ-lek-**trol**-ĭ-sĭs) *noun* **1** chemical decomposition by electric current. **2** the breaking up of tumours, hair roots, etc. by electric current. **electrolytic** (ĕ-lek-trŏ-**lit**-ik) *adjective* [from *electro-*, + Greek *lusis* = loosening]

electrolyte (ĕ-**lek**-trŏ-lyt) *noun* a solution that conducts electric current, especially in an electric cell or battery.

electromagnet *noun* a magnet consisting of a metal core magnetised by a coil, carrying electric current, wound round it.

electromagnetic *adjective* having both electrical and magnetic properties. ▢ **electromagnetic radiation** emission of **electromagnetic waves** (e.g. radio waves, heat and light rays, X-rays) consisting of electric and magnetic fields that vary simultaneously. **electromagnetically** *adverb*

electromagnetism *noun* **1** magnetic forces produced by electricity. **2** the study of these.

electromotive *adjective* producing electric current.

electron (ĕ-**lek**-tron) *noun* an elementary particle, found in all atoms, that carries a charge of negative electricity and is the carrier of electric current in solids. ▢ **electron beam** a stream of electrons, as emitted from a cathode. **electron gun** a device for producing a narrow beam of electrons from a heated cathode. **electron microscope** a very high-powered microscope that uses beams of electrons instead of rays of light. [see *electric*]

electronic (e-lek-**tron**-ik) *adjective* **1** produced or worked by a flow of electrons in a vacuum, gas, or certain solids. **2** of or relating to electronics, *electronic engineering*. **electronics** *noun* **1** the development and application of electronic devices, for instance in transistors, computers, etc. **2** (as *plural noun*) electronic circuits. □ **electronic mail** *see* **email**. **electronically** *adverb*

electronvolt *noun* a unit of energy, the amount of energy gained by an electron when accelerated through a potential difference of one volt.

electroplate *verb* to coat with a thin layer of silver etc. by electrolysis. –**electroplate** *noun* objects plated in this way.

electroscope *noun* an instrument for detecting and measuring electricity, especially to indicate the ionisation of air by radioactivity.

electrostatic *adjective* of static electric charges. **electrostatics** *noun* the study of static electric charges.

electrotherapy *noun* the treatment of diseases etc. by the use of electricity.

electrovalent *adjective* (of an atomic bond) linked by electrostatic attraction between ions.

elegant *adjective* tasteful, refined, and dignified in appearance or style. **elegantly** *adverb*, **elegance** *noun*

elegiac (el-ĕ-**jy**-ăk) *adjective* used for elegies; mournful. **elegiacs** *plural noun* elegiac verses. □ **elegiac couplet** or **metre** a dactylic hexameter and pentameter.

elegy (**el**-ĕ-jee) *noun* a sorrowful or serious poem.

element *noun* **1** any of the parts that make up a whole. **2** any of the 100 or so substances composed of atoms with the same atomic number. **3** any of the four substances (earth, water, air, and fire) held in ancient and medieval philosophy to be basic. **4** an environment that is suitable or satisfying. **5** a trace, *there's an element of truth in the story*. **6** the wire that gives out heat in an electric heater, cooker, etc. **7** (in mathematics) a member of a set. **elements** *plural noun* **1** atmospheric agencies or forces, e.g. wind, rain, *exposed to the elements*. **2** the basic or elementary principles of a subject. **3** the bread and wine used in a Eucharist.

elementary *adjective* dealing with the simplest facts of a subject. □ **elementary particle** any of the subatomic particles that are not known to be composed of simpler particles. **elementarily** *adverb*, **elementariness** *noun*

elephant *noun* a very large land animal (a pachyderm) with a trunk and long curved ivory tusks. □ **the elephant in the room** a major problem or controversial issue which is obviously present but avoided as a subject for discussion because it is more comfortable to do so. [from Greek *elephas* = ivory]

elephantine (el-ĕ-**fan**-tyn) *adjective* **1** of or like elephants. **2** very large or clumsy.

elevate *verb* **1** to raise to a higher place or position, to lift up. **2** to raise to a higher moral or intellectual level. [from *e-*, + Latin *levare* = to lift]

elevation *noun* **1** elevating; being elevated. **2** the altitude of a place. **3** a piece of rising ground, a hill. **4** the angle that the direction of something (e.g. a gun) makes with the horizontal. **5** a plan or drawing showing one side of a structure, *a south elevation of the house*. □ **angle of elevation** the angle an ascending line makes with the horizontal.

elevator *noun* **1** something that hoists or raises things. **2** the movable part of a tailplane, used for changing an aircraft's attitude to its flight path. **3** a lift (= **lift** *noun* sense 3).

eleven *adjective* & *noun* **1** one more than ten (11, XI). **2** a team of eleven players at cricket etc.

eleventh *adjective* & *noun* **1** next after tenth. **2** one of eleven equal parts of a thing. □ **at the eleventh hour** at the latest possible time for doing something.

elf *noun* (*plural* **elves**) an imaginary small being with magic powers. **elfish** *adjective*

elfin *adjective* (of the face etc.) small and delicate.

Elgar, Sir Edward William (1857–1934), English composer, whose works include *The Enigma Variations*.

El Greco (el **grek**-oh) (1541–1614), Spanish painter of Greek origin (Domenikos Theotokopoulos). [Spanish, = the Greek]

elicit (ĕ-**lis**-ĭt) *verb* to draw out (information, a response, etc.).

elide *verb* to omit (a vowel or syllable), or be omitted, by elision.

eligible (**el**-ĭ-jĭ-bŭl) *adjective* **1** qualified to be chosen for a position or allowed a privilege etc. **2** regarded as suitable or desirable, especially for marriage. **eligibility** *noun*

Elijah (ĕ-**ly**-jă) a Hebrew prophet of the 9th century BC.

eliminate (ĕ-**lim**-ĭ-nayt) *verb* **1** to get rid of (something that is not wanted). **2** to exclude from a further stage of a competition etc. through defeat. **elimination** *noun*, **eliminator** *noun* [from Latin *e-* = out, + *limen* = entrance]

Eliot[1], George (pseudonym of Mary Ann Evans, 1819–80), English novelist, author of *Middlemarch* and *The Mill on the Floss*.

Eliot[2], T. S. (Thomas Stearns) (1888–1965), Anglo-American poet, critic, and dramatist, whose works include *The Waste Land* and *Murder in the Cathedral*.

Elisha (ĕ-**ly**-shă) a Hebrew prophet, disciple and successor of Elijah.

elision (ĕ-**li**-zhŏn) *noun* omission of part of a word in pronouncing it (e.g. *I'm* = I am).

elite (ĕ-**leet** *or* ay-**leet**) *noun* (also **élite**) **1** a group of people regarded as superior in some way and therefore favoured. **2** a size of letters in typewriting (12 characters per inch). [from Old French *élit* = chosen]

elitist (ĕ-**leet**-ĭst *or* ay-) *noun* (also **élitist**) one who advocates selecting and treating certain people as an elite. **elitism** *noun* (also **élitism**).

elixir (ĕ-**liks**-er) *noun* **1** a fragrant liquid used as a medicine or flavouring. **2** a remedy believed to cure all ills. [from Arabic *aliksir* = substance that would cure illness and change metals into gold]

Elizabeth the name of a queen of England and Ireland, reigning as Elizabeth I (1558–1603), and of a queen of the United Kingdom, Elizabeth II (from 1952), who is also head of the Commonwealth and head of state of some of its members, including Australia.

Elizabethan *adjective* of the time of Queen Elizabeth I's reign (1558–1603). –**Elizabethan** *noun* a person living at this time.

elk *noun* a large deer of northern Europe and Asia.

elkhorn *noun* a large Australian epiphytic fern, with fronds resembling the horns of an elk.

ellipse (ĕ-**lips**) *noun* a regular oval that can be divided into four identical quarters.

ellipsis (ĕ-**lip**-sĭs) *noun* (*plural* **ellipses**) the omission of words needed to complete a meaning or a grammatical construction.

elliptical (ĕ-**lip**-ti-kăl) *adjective* **1** of or shaped like an ellipse. **2** containing an ellipsis, having omissions. **elliptically** *adverb*

elm *noun* **1** a deciduous tree with rough serrated leaves. **2** its wood.

elocution (el-ŏ-**kew**-shŏn) *noun* a person's style of speaking; the art of speaking expressively. **elocutionist** *noun* [same origin as *eloquent*]

elongate (ee-long-gayt) *verb* to lengthen, to prolong. **elongation** *noun*

elope (ĕ-**lohp**) *verb* to run away secretly with a lover, especially in order to get married. **elopement** *noun*

eloquence (el-ŏ-kwĕns) *noun* fluent and powerful speaking.

eloquent (el-ŏ-kwĕnt) *adjective* speaking fluently and powerfully. **eloquently** *adverb* [from *e-*, + Latin *loqui* = speak]

El Salvador (el sal-vă-dor) a republic in Central America, on the Pacific coast.

else *adverb* **1** besides, other, *someone else*. **2** otherwise, if not, *run or else you'll be late*.

elsewhere *adverb* somewhere else.

elucidate (ĕ-**loo**-sĭ-dayt) *verb* to throw light on (a problem); to make clear. **elucidation** *noun*, **elucidatory** *adjective* [compare *lucid*]

elude (ĕ-**lood**) *verb* **1** to escape skilfully from, to avoid, *eluded his pursuers*. **2** to escape a person's understanding or memory etc., *the answer eludes me*. **elusion** *noun*

elusive (ĕ-**loo**-siv) *adjective* **1** eluding, escaping; difficult to find or catch. **2** difficult to remember or recall. **elusiveness** *noun*

Usage *Elusive* should not be confused with *illusive*, which means 'imagined, deceptive, unreal'.

---

elver *noun* a young eel.

elves *see* elf.

Elysium (ĕ-**liz**-ee-ŭm) *noun* **1** (*Gk. myth.*) the fields at the ends of the earth to which certain favoured heroes, exempted from death, were taken by the gods. **2** a place of ideal happiness. **Elysian** *adjective*

em- *prefix see* en-.

emaciated (ĕ-**may**-see-ayt-ĕd) *adjective* having become very thin from illness or starvation. **emaciation** *noun*

email (ee-mayl) (also **e-mail**) *noun* **1** (in full **electronic mail**) messages in electronic form sent from one computer system to one or more others connected via a network or telephone lines; the system of sending and receiving such messages. **2** a message sent or received by electronic mail. –**email** *verb* **1** to send email to (a person). **2** to send by email.

emanate (em-ă-nayt) *verb* to issue or originate from a source. **emanation** *noun*

emancipate (ĕ-**man**-sĭ-payt) *verb* to liberate, to set free from slavery or some form of restraint. **emancipation** *noun*, **emancipator** *noun*, **emancipatory** *adjective*

emasculate (ĕ-**mas**-kew-layt) *verb* 1 to castrate. 2 to deprive of force; *an emasculated law*, one made weak by alterations to it. **emasculation** *noun*, **emasculatory** *adjective*

embalm (em-**bahm**) *verb* to preserve (a corpse) from decay by using spices or chemicals. **embalmment** *noun*

embankment *noun* a long mound of earth or a stone structure to keep a river from spreading or to carry a road or railway.

embargo (em-**bar**-goh) *noun* (*plural* **embargoes**) an order forbidding commerce or other activity. [from Spanish *embargar* = restrain]

embark *verb* 1 to put or go on board a ship or aircraft at the start of a journey. 2 to begin an undertaking. **embarkation** *noun*

embarrass *verb* to make (a person) feel awkward or ashamed. **embarrassment** *noun*

embassy *noun* 1 an ambassador and his or her staff. 2 their official headquarters. 3 a deputation sent to a foreign government.

embattled *adjective* 1 prepared for battle, *embattled troops*. 2 fortified against attack.

embed *verb* (**embedded**, **embedding**) to fix firmly in a surrounding mass.

embellish (em-**bel**-ish) *verb* 1 to ornament. 2 to improve (a story etc.) by adding details that are entertaining but invented. **embellishment** *noun*

embers *plural noun* small pieces of live coal or wood in a dying fire.

embezzle *verb* to take fraudulently for one's own use money or property placed in one's care. **embezzlement** *noun*, **embezzler** *noun*

embitter *verb* to arouse bitter feelings in. **embitterment** *noun*

emblazon (em-**blay**-zŏn) *verb* to ornament with heraldic or other devices.

emblem *noun* a symbol, a device that represents something.

emblematic (em-blĕ-**mat**-ik) *adjective* serving as an emblem, symbolic.

embody *verb* (**embodied**, **embodying**) 1 to express (principles or ideas) in a visible form, *the house embodied her idea of a home*. 2 to incorporate, to include. **embodiment** *noun*

embolden *verb* to make bold, to encourage.

embolism (em-**bŏ**-lizm) *noun* an obstruction of an artery or vein by a clot of blood, air bubble, etc.

emboss *verb* to decorate with a raised design. **embossment** *noun*

embrace *verb* 1 to hold closely and affectionately in one's arms; (of two people) to do this to each other. 2 to accept eagerly, *embraced the opportunity*. 3 to adopt (a religion etc.). 4 to include. –**embrace** *noun* the act of embracing, a hug. [from *em-*, + Latin *brachium* = an arm]

embrasure (em-**bray**-*zh*er) *noun* 1 an opening in a wall for a door or window, with splayed sides. 2 a similar opening for a gun, widening towards the outside.

embrocation *noun* liquid for rubbing on the body to relieve aches or bruises.

embroider *verb* 1 to ornament with needlework. 2 to embellish (a story).

embroidery *noun* 1 embroidering. 2 embroidered material.

embroil *verb* to involve in an argument or quarrel etc. **embroilment** *noun*

embryo (**em**-bree-oh) *noun* (*plural* **embryos**) 1 an animal in the early stage of its development, before birth or emergence from an egg (used of a child in the first eight weeks of its development in the womb). 2 a rudimentary plant contained in a seed. 3 something in its very early stages. □ **in embryo** existing but undeveloped. [from *em-*, + Greek *bruii* = grow]

embryonic (em-bree-**on**-ik) *adjective* existing in embryo.

emend (ĕ-**mend**) *verb* to alter (something written) in order to remove errors. **emendation** (ee-men-**day**-shŏn) *noun*

emerald *noun* 1 a bright green precious stone. 2 its colour. □ **the Emerald Isle** Ireland.

emerge (ĕ-**merj**) *verb* 1 to come up or out into view. 2 (of facts or ideas) to be revealed by investigation, to become obvious. **emergence** *noun*, **emergent** *adjective*

emergency *noun* 1 a serious happening or situation needing prompt action. 2 a condition needing immediate treatment; a patient with this.

emeritus *adjective* retired and retaining a title as an honour, *emeritus professor*.

emery (**em**-ĕ-ree) *noun* a coarse abrasive used for polishing metal or wood etc.
□ **emery board** a small stiff strip of wood or cardboard coated with emery, for filing the nails. **emery paper** paper coated with emery.

emetic (ĕ-**met**-ik) *noun* a medicine used to cause vomiting.

EMF *abbreviation* electromotive force.

emigrant *noun* one who emigrates.

emigrate *verb* to leave one country and go to settle in another. **emigration** *noun* [from *e-* + *migrate*]

eminence (**em**-ĭ-nĕns) *noun* **1** the state of being famous or distinguished, *a professor of great eminence*. **2** a piece of rising ground. **3** a cardinal's title, *His Eminence*.

eminent (**em**-ĭ-nĕnt) *adjective* **1** famous, distinguished. **2** conspicuous, outstanding, *a man of eminent goodness*. **eminently** *adverb*

emir (em-**eer**) *noun* the title of various Muslim rulers. [from Arabic *amir* = ruler]

emirate (**em**-ĭ-răt) *noun* the territory of an emir.

emissary (**em**-ĭ-să-ree) *noun* a person sent to conduct negotiations. [from *e-*, + Latin *missum* = sent]

emit (ĕ-**mit**) *verb* (**emitted, emitting**) **1** to send out (light, heat, fumes, lava, etc.). **2** to utter, *she emitted a shriek*. **emission** *noun*, **emissive** *adjective* [from *e-*, + Latin *mittere* = send]

emitter *noun* **1** a person or thing that emits something. **2** the terminal of a transistor to which the input signal is normally supplied.

Emmanuel = **Immanuel**.

Emmy *noun* (also **Emmy award**) any of the statuettes awarded annually by the American Academy of Television Arts and Sciences to an outstanding television program or performer.

emo *noun* a style of rock music resembling punk but having more complex arrangements and lyrics that deal with more emotional subjects. [short for *emotional hardcore*]

emollient (ĕ-**mol**-ee-ĕnt) *adjective* softening or soothing the skin. –**emollient** *noun* an emollient substance. [from *e-*, + Latin *mollis* = soft]

emolument (ĕ-**mol**-yŭ-mĕnt) *noun* a fee received, a salary.

emoticon *noun* a representation using keyboard characters to convey emotion etc.

emotion *noun* an intense mental feeling, e.g. love or hate.

emotional *adjective* **1** of emotions. **2** showing emotion excessively. **emotionally** *adverb*, **emotionalism** *noun*

emotive (ĕ-**moh**-tiv) *adjective* arousing emotion.

empanel (em-**pan**-ĕl) *verb* (**empanelled, empanelling**) to list or select for service on a jury.

empathise (**em**-pă-thyz) *verb* (also **-ize**) to treat with empathy, to use empathy.

empathy (**em**-pă-thee) *noun* the power of identifying oneself mentally with (and so fully comprehending) a person or object of contemplation. **empathic** (em-**pa**-thik) *adjective* [from *em-*, + Greek *pathos* = feeling]

emperor *noun* the male ruler of an empire.
□ **emperor penguin** a penguin of the largest known species.

emphasis (**em**-fă-sĭs) *noun* (*plural* **emphases**) **1** special importance given to something, prominence, *the emphasis is on quality*. **2** vigour of expression, feeling, or action, *nodded his head with emphasis*. **3** the extra force used in speaking a particular syllable or word, or on a sound in music.

emphasise (**em**-fă-syz) *verb* (also **-ize**) to lay emphasis on.

emphatic (em-**fat**-ik) *adjective* using or showing emphasis, expressing oneself with emphasis. **emphatically** *adverb*

emphysema (em-fĭ-**see**-mă) *noun* a condition in which the air sacs of the lungs enlarge, causing breathlessness. [from Greek *emphusēma*]

empire *noun* **1** a group of countries ruled by a single supreme authority. **2** supreme power. **3** a large commercial organisation controlled by one person or group. □ **empire building** the process of deliberately acquiring extra territory or authority etc. **Empire style** a style of furniture or dress fashionable during the first (1804–14) or second (1852–70) French Empire.

empirical (em-**pi**-ri-kăl) *adjective* (of knowledge) based on observation or experiment, not on theory. **empirically** *adverb*

emplacement *noun* a place or platform for a gun or battery of guns.

employ *verb* **1** to give work to, to use the services of. **2** to make use of, *how do you* *employ your spare time? –***employ** *noun* in the **employ of** employed by.

employable *adjective* able to be employed.

employee (em-**ploi**-ee) *noun* a person who works for another in return for wages.

employer *noun* a person or firm that employs people.

employment *noun* 1 employing. 2 the state of being employed. 3 work done as an occupation or to earn a livelihood.

emporium (em-**por**-ree-ŭm) *noun* (*plural* **emporia** *or* **emporiums**) 1 a centre of commerce. 2 a large shop.

empower *verb* to give power or authority to, *police are empowered to arrest people*.

empress *noun* 1 the female ruler of an empire. 2 the wife or widow of an emperor.

empty *adjective* 1 containing nothing, *empty boxes*; *empty trucks*, not loaded. 2 without an occupant, *an empty chair*; *empty streets*, without people or traffic. 3 without effectiveness, *empty promises*. 4 lacking good sense or intelligence, *an empty head*. –**empty** *verb* (**emptied, emptying**) 1 to make or become empty. 2 to transfer (the contents of one thing) into another; to discharge itself or its contents. **empties** *plural noun* emptied boxes, bottles, or trucks etc. □ **empty- handed** *adjective* bringing or taking away nothing. **empty-headed** *adjective* lacking good sense or intelligence. **emptily** *adverb*, **emptiness** *noun*

emu (**ee**-mew) *noun* a large Australian flightless bird. □ **emu parade** (*Austral.*) a group of soldiers or children systematically picking up litter. **emu wren** a small Australian bird with long tail feathers like emu feathers. [from Portuguese *ema*]

emulate (**em**-yŭ-layt) *verb* to try to do as well as or better than; to imitate. **emulation** *noun*, **emulative** *adjective*, **emulator** *noun*

emulsify (ĕ-**mul**-sĭ-fy) *verb* (**emulsified, emulsifying**) to convert or be converted into an emulsion.

emulsion (ĕ-**mul**-shŏn) *noun* 1 a creamy liquid in which particles of oil or fat are evenly distributed. 2 a medicine or paint in this form. 3 the light-sensitive coating on photographic film, a mixture of silver compound in gelatine.

en- *prefix* (changing to **em-** before *b*, *m*, or *p*) in; into; on. [from Latin or Greek, = in]

enable *verb* 1 to give the means or authority to do something. 2 to make possible. 3 make (a device) operational; switch on.

enact *verb* 1 to decree, to make into a law. 2 to perform, to act (a play etc.).

enactment *noun* a law enacted.

enamel *noun* 1 a glasslike substance used for coating metal or pottery. 2 paint that dries hard and glossy. 3 the hard outer covering of teeth. 4 a painting done in enamel. –**enamel** *verb* (**enamelled, enamelling**) to coat or decorate with enamel.

enamoured (ĕ-**nam**-erd) *adjective* fond, *he was enamoured of the sound of his own voice*. [from *en-*, + French *amour* = love]

en bloc (on **blok**) *adverb* in a block, all at the same time. [French]

encamp *verb* to settle in a camp.

encampment *noun* a camp.

encapsulate *verb* 1 to enclose in or as if in a capsule. 2 to summarise. 3 to isolate. **encapsulation** *noun*

encase *verb* to enclose in a case.

encash *verb* to convert into cash. **encashment** *noun*

encephalitis (en-sef-ă-**ly**-tĭs) *noun* inflammation of the brain.

enchant *verb* 1 to put under a magic spell. 2 to fill with intense delight. **enchantment** *noun*, **enchanter** *noun*, **enchantress** *feminine noun*

encircle *verb* to surround. **encirclement** *noun*

enclave (**en**-klayv) *noun* a small territory belonging to one State but lying wholly within the boundaries of another.

enclitic (en-**klit**-ik) *adjective* (of a word) pronounced with so little emphasis that it forms part of the preceding word. –**enclitic** *noun* a word of this kind.

enclose *verb* 1 to put a wall or fence etc. round; to shut in on all sides. 2 to shut up in a receptacle; to put into an envelope along with a letter or into a parcel along with the contents.

enclosed *adjective* (of a religious community) living in isolation from the outside world.

enclosure *noun* 1 enclosing. 2 an enclosed area. 3 something enclosed with a letter etc.

encode *verb* to put into code; to put (data) into a coded form for processing by computer. **encoder** *noun*

encomium (en-**koh**-mee-ŭm) *noun* (*plural* encomiums) high praise given in a speech or writing.

encompass *verb* **1** to surround, to encircle. **2** to contain.

encore (**ong**-kor) *interjection* a call for repetition of a performance. –encore *noun* **1** this call. **2** the item performed in response to it. –encore *verb* to call for such a repetition of (an item); to call back (a performer) for this. [French, = again]

encounter *verb* **1** to meet, especially by chance or unexpectedly. **2** to find oneself faced with, *encounter difficulties*. **3** to meet in battle. –encounter *noun* **1** a sudden or unexpected meeting. **2** a battle.

encourage *verb* **1** to give hope or confidence to. **2** to urge, *encouraged him to try*. **3** to stimulate, to help to develop, *to encourage exports*. encouragement *noun*

encroach *verb* **1** to intrude upon someone's territory, rights, or time. **2** to advance beyond the original or proper limits, *the sea encroached gradually upon the land*. encroachment *noun*

encrust *verb* **1** to cover with a crust of hard material. **2** to ornament with a layer of jewels etc. encrustation *noun*

enculturation *noun* the gradual acquisition of the norms of a culture or group.

encumber *verb* to be a burden to, to hamper.

encumbrance *noun* something that encumbers.

encyclical (en-**sik**-lik-ăl) *noun* a letter written by the pope for wide circulation.

encyclopedia *noun* (also encyclopaedia) a book or set of books giving information on all branches of knowledge or of one subject, usually arranged alphabetically. [from Greek, = general education]

encyclopedic *adjective* (also encyclopaedic) giving or possessing information about many subjects or branches of one subject.

end *noun* **1** the extreme limit of something. **2** the part or surface forming this. **3** either half of a sports pitch or court, defended or occupied by one side or player. **4** the finish or conclusion of something, the latter or final part. **5** destruction, downfall, death. **6** a purpose or aim. –end *verb* **1** to bring to an end, to put an end to. **2** to come to an end; to reach a certain place or state eventually, *ended up laughing*. □ **end on** with the end facing one or adjoining the end of the next object. **end product** the final product of a manufacturing process. **keep one's end up** to do one's part in spite of difficulties. **make ends meet** to keep one's expenditure within one's income. **no end** (*informal*) to a great extent. **no end of** (*informal*) much or many of. **put an end to** to abolish, stop, or destroy.

endanger *verb* to cause danger to. □ **endangered species** a species of animal or plant that is in danger of becoming extinct.

endear *verb* to cause to be loved, *endeared herself to us all*.

endearing *adjective* inspiring affection.

endearment *noun* **1** a word or words expressing love. **2** liking, affection.

Endeavour the name of the ship captained by James Cook when he discovered the eastern coast of Australia in April 1770.

endeavour (en-**dev**-er) *verb* to attempt, to try. –endeavour *noun* an attempt.

endemic (en-**dem**-ik) *adjective* commonly found in a particular country, district, or group of people, *the disease is endemic in Africa*. [from *en-*, + Greek *demos* = people]

ending *noun* the final part.

endive (**en**-dyv) *noun* a curly-leaved plant used in salads.

endless *adjective* without end, never stopping, *endless patience*. □ **endless belt** one with the ends joined so that it forms a continuous strip for use in machinery etc.

endocrine (**end**-ŏ-kryn) *adjective* (of a gland) pouring its secretions straight into the blood, not through a duct.

endolymph (**end**-oh-limf) *noun* the fluid in the membranous labyrinth of the ear.

endometrium (end-oh-**meet**-ree-ŭm) *noun* the membrane lining the womb.

endoplasm *noun* the inner portion of the cytoplasm of a cell.

endorphin (en-**dor**-fĭn) *noun* any of a group of painkilling substances produced naturally within the brain and spinal cord.

endorse *verb* **1** to sign or add a comment on (a document); to sign the back of (a cheque) in order to obtain the money indicated. **2** to make an official entry on (a licence) about an offence by the holder. **3** to confirm (a statement); to declare one's approval of. endorsement *noun* [from Latin *in dorsum* = on the back]

endoskeleton *noun* an internal skeleton (like that of a vertebrate).

endosperm *noun* the food material enclosed with the embryo plant (which it nourishes) in many kinds of seed.

endothermic *adjective* (of a chemical reaction) involving absorption of heat.

endow *verb* 1 to provide with a permanent income, *endow a school*. 2 to provide with a power or ability or quality.

endowment *noun* 1 endowing. 2 an endowed income. 3 a natural ability.

endue *verb* to provide with a talent or quality etc., *experience endues us with patience*.

endurable *adjective* able to be endured.

endurance *noun* ability to withstand pain or hardship or prolonged use or strain.

endure *verb* 1 to experience pain or hardship or difficulties, to bear patiently. 2 to tolerate. 3 to remain in existence, to last.

endways *adverb* (also **endwise**) 1 with its end foremost. 2 end to end.

enema (**en**-ĕ-mă) *noun* 1 the insertion of liquid into the rectum through the anus by means of a syringe, for medical purposes. 2 this liquid or syringe.

enemy *noun* 1 one who is hostile towards another and seeks to harm the other. 2 a member of a hostile army or nation etc.; an opposing military force, ship, aircraft, etc.

energetic *adjective* full of energy, done with energy. **energetically** *adverb*

energise (**en**-er-jyz) *verb* (also **-ize**) 1 to give energy to. 2 to cause electricity to flow to.

energy *noun* 1 the capacity for vigorous activity. 2 the ability of matter or radiation to do work either because of its motion (*kinetic energy*), or because of its mass (released in nuclear fission etc.), or because of its electric charge etc. 3 fuel and other resources used for the operation of machinery etc., *the country's energy requirements*. [from *en-*, + Greek *ergon* = work]

enervate (**en**-er-vayt) *verb* to cause to lose vitality, *an enervating climate*.

enfeeble *verb* to make feeble.

enfold *verb* 1 to wrap up. 2 to clasp.

enforce *verb* to compel obedience to; to impose by force or compulsion, *the law was firmly enforced*. **enforcement** *noun*

enforceable *adjective* able to be enforced.

enfranchise *verb* 1 to give (a person) the right to vote in elections. 2 to free (a slave etc.). **enfranchisement** *noun*

engage *verb* 1 to take into one's employment. 2 to arrange beforehand to occupy (a seat etc.). 3 to promise, to pledge. 4 to occupy the attention of, *engaged her in conversation*. 5 to occupy oneself, *he engages in politics*. 6 to begin a battle against, *engaged the enemy troops*. 7 to interlock (parts of a gear) so as to transmit power; to become interlocked in this way.

engaged *adjective* 1 having promised to marry. 2 occupied or reserved by a person, occupied with business etc. 3 (of a telephone line) already in use.

engagement *noun* 1 engaging something; being engaged. 2 an appointment made with another person. 3 a promise to marry a specified person. 4 a battle.

engaging *adjective* attractive, charming.

Engels (**eng**-gĕlz), Friedrich (1820–95), German socialist, founder with Karl Marx of modern Communism.

engender (en-**jen**-der) *verb* to give rise to.

engine *noun* 1 a mechanical contrivance consisting of several parts working together, especially as a source of power. 2 the engine of a railway train. 3 a fire engine. [from Latin *ingenium* = clever invention (compare *ingenious*)]

engineer *noun* 1 a person who is skilled in a branch of engineering. 2 one who is in charge of machines and engines, e.g. on a ship. 3 one who plans or organises something. –**engineer** *verb* 1 to construct or control as an engineer. 2 (*informal*) to contrive or bring about, *he engineered a meeting between them*.

engineering *noun* the application of scientific knowledge to the control and use of power e.g. in the building of roads and bridges (*civil engineering*), machines (*mechanical engineering*), electrical apparatus (*electrical engineering*), etc.

England the country forming the southern part of Great Britain.

English *adjective* of England or its people or language. –**English** *noun* the English language, used in the UK, Australia, most Commonwealth and ex-Commonwealth countries, the USA, and often internationally. –**the English** English people. **Englishman**, **Englishwoman** *nouns*

English Channel the sea channel separating southern England from northern France.

engrave *verb* 1 to cut or carve (a design) into a hard surface; to ornament with a design in this way. 2 to fix deeply in the mind or memory. **engraver** *noun*

engraving *noun* a print made from an engraved metal plate.

engross (en-**grohs**) *verb* 1 to occupy fully by absorbing the attention. 2 to write out in large letters or in legal form. **engrossment** *noun*

engulf *verb* 1 to surround or cause to disappear by flowing round or over, to swamp. 2 to overwhelm.

enhance (en-**hahns** *or* en-**hans**) *verb* to increase the attractiveness or other qualities of. **enhancement** *noun*

enharmonic *adjective* (in music) of or having intervals smaller than a semitone. □ **enharmonic modulation** (in music) change of notation without change of pitch, e.g. from A♭ to G♯

enigma (ě-**nig**-mă) *noun* something very difficult to understand.

enigmatic (en-ig-**mat**-ik) *adjective* mysterious and puzzling. **enigmatically** *adverb*

enjoin *verb* 1 to order, to command. 2 to prohibit (from doing something) by an official injunction.

enjoy *verb* 1 to get pleasure from. 2 to have as an advantage or benefit, *to enjoy good health*. □ **enjoy oneself** to experience pleasure from what one is doing. **enjoyment** *noun*

enjoyable *adjective* giving enjoyment, pleasant. **enjoyably** *adverb*

enlarge *verb* 1 to make or become larger. 2 to reproduce (a photograph) on a larger scale. 3 to say more about something.

enlargement *noun* 1 enlarging; being enlarged. 2 something enlarged; a photograph printed larger than its negative.

enlarger *noun* an apparatus for making photographic enlargements.

enlighten *verb* to give knowledge to, to inform. **enlightenment** *noun*

enlightened *adjective* freed from ignorance or prejudice, *in these enlightened days*.

enlist *verb* 1 to take into or join the armed forces, *enlist as a soldier*. 2 to secure as a means of help or support, *enlisted their sympathy*. **enlistment** *noun*

enliven *verb* to make more lively. **enlivenment** *noun*

en masse (on **mass**) *adverb* all together. [French, = in a mass]

enmesh *verb* to entangle as if in a net.

enmity *noun* hostility between enemies.

ennoble *verb* 1 to make (a person) a noble. 2 to make (a person or thing) noble or more dignified. **ennoblement** *noun*

ennui (on-**wee**) *noun* boredom. [French]

enormity (ě-**norm**-ĭ-tee) *noun* 1 great wickedness, *the enormity of this crime*. 2 a serious crime, *these enormities*. 3 enormous size, magnitude, *the enormity of their task*.

Usage Many people regard this third use as incorrect, but it is now standard.

---

enormous *adjective* very large, huge. **enormously** *adverb*, **enormousness** *noun* [from *e-*, + Latin *norma* = standard]

enough *adjective*, *noun*, & *adverb* as much or as many as necessary.

en passant (on **pas**-ahn) *adverb* by the way. [French, = in passing]

enquire *verb* to ask. **enquirer** *noun*

Usage Although *enquire* and *inquire* may be used interchangeably, there is a tendency to use *enquire* as a formal word for 'ask' and *inquire* for 'make a formal investigation'. A similar distinction exists between *enquirer* and *inquirer*, and *enquiry* and *inquiry*.

---

enquiry *noun* (*plural* **enquiries**) 1 a question. 2 the act of asking or seeking information.

enrage *verb* to make furious.

enrapture *verb* to fill with intense delight.

enrich *verb* 1 to make richer. 2 to improve the quality of by adding things, *this food is enriched with vitamins*. **enrichment** *noun*

enrobe *verb* to put a robe on.

enrol *verb* (**enrolled**, **enrolling**) 1 to become a member of a society, institution, etc. 2 to admit as a member. **enrolment** *noun*

en route (on **root**) *adverb* on the way, *met him en route from Sydney to London*. [French]

ensconce (en-**skons**) *verb* to establish securely or comfortably.

ensemble (on-**sombl**) *noun* 1 a thing viewed as a whole. 2 a group of musicians who perform together; a passage of music for such a group. **3** a set of clothes worn together. [French]

enshrine *verb* **1** to enclose in a shrine. **2** to serve as a shrine for.

enshroud *verb* to cover completely.

ensign (**en**-syn) *noun* a military or naval flag; a special form of the national flag flown by ships. [the word is related to *insignia*]

enslave *verb* to make a slave of. **enslavement** *noun*

ensnare *verb* to catch as if in a snare.

ensue (ens-**yoo**) *verb* to happen afterwards or as a result, *a quarrel ensued*.

en suite (on **sweet**) (also **ensuite**) *adverb* forming a single unit. –**en suite** *noun* a bathroom attached to a bedroom. [French]

ensure *verb* to make safe or certain, to secure, *good food will ensure good health*.

Usage *Ensure* should not be confused with *insure* meaning 'to provide with financial insurance'.

ENT *abbreviation* ear, nose, and throat.

entablature (en-**tab**-lă-cher) *noun* the section including the architrave, frieze, and cornice of a building or structure, above the supporting columns.

entail (en-**tayl**) *verb* **1** to make necessary, to involve, *these plans entail great expense*. **2** to leave (land) to a line of heirs so that none of them can give it away or sell it. –**entail** *noun* the entailing of landed property; the property itself.

entangle *verb* **1** to tangle. **2** to entwine in something that it is difficult to escape from. **3** to involve in something complicated. **entanglement** *noun*

entente (on-**tont**) *noun* a friendly understanding between countries. [French]

enter *verb* **1** to go or come in or into. **2** to come on stage. **3** to penetrate, *the bullet entered his leg*. **4** to become a member of, *to enter the Navy*. **5** to put (a name, details, etc.) on a list or in a book. **6** to register as a competitor. **7** to record formally, to present for consideration, *entered a plea of not guilty*; *entered a protest*. ☐ **enter into** to engage in (a conversation); to subscribe to (an agreement); to form part of (one's plans etc.).

enteric (en-**te**-rik) *adjective* of the intestines. [from Greek *enteron* = intestine]

enteritis (en-tě-**ry**-tĭss) *noun* inflammation of the intestines.

enterprise *noun* **1** an undertaking, especially a bold or difficult one. **2** initiative. **3** business activity, *private enterprise*.

enterprising *adjective* full of initiative.

entertain *verb* **1** to amuse, to occupy agreeably. **2** to receive (a person) with hospitality, *they entertained me to lunch*. **3** to have in the mind, *entertain doubts*. **4** to consider favourably, *refused to entertain the idea*.

entertainer *noun* one who performs in entertainments, especially as an occupation.

entertainment *noun* **1** entertaining; being entertained. **2** amusement. **3** something performed before an audience to amuse or interest them.

enthalpy (**en**-thǎl-pee) *noun* the total amount of heat in a system.

enthral (en-**thrawl**) *verb* (**enthralled**, **enthralling**) to hold spellbound.

enthrone *verb* to place on a throne, especially with ceremony. **enthronement** *noun*

enthuse (en-**thewz**) *verb* **1** to show enthusiasm. **2** to fill with enthusiasm.

enthusiasm *noun* **1** a feeling of eager liking for or interest in something. **2** the object of this, *one of my enthusiasms*.

enthusiast *noun* one who is full of enthusiasm for something, *a sports enthusiast*.

enthusiastic *adjective* full of enthusiasm. **enthusiastically** *adverb*

entice *verb* to attract or persuade by offering something pleasant. **enticement** *noun*

entire *adjective* whole, complete. **entirely** *adverb*

entirety (en-**ty**-rětee) *noun* completeness, the total; *in its entirety*, in its complete form.

entitle *verb* **1** to give a title to (a book etc.). **2** to give a right, *the ticket entitles you to a seat*. **entitlement** *noun*

entity (**en**-tĭ-tee) *noun* something that exists as a separate thing.

entomb (en-**toom**) *verb* to place in a tomb, to bury. **entombment** *noun*

entomology (en-tǒ-**mol**-ǒjee) *noun* the scientific study of insects. **entomological** (en-tǒ-mǒ-**loj**-ikǎl) *adjective*, **entomologist** *noun* [from Greek *entomon* = insect, + -*logy*]

entourage (on-toor-**rah**z*h*) *noun* the people accompanying an important person. [from French *entourer* = to surround]

entrails (**en**-traylz) *plural noun* the intestines.

entrance[1] (**en**-trăns) *noun* 1 entering. 2 a door or passage by which one enters. 3 the right of admission; the fee charged for this. [from *enter*]

entrance[2] (en-**trahns** or en-**trans**) *verb* to fill with intense delight. **entrancement** *noun* [from *en-* + *trance*]

entrant *noun* one who enters, especially as a competitor.

entrap *verb* (**entrapped, entrapping**) to catch as if in a trap.

entreat *verb* to request earnestly or emotionally. **entreaty** *noun*

entrée (**on**-tray) *noun* 1 the right or privilege of admission. 2 a dish served before the main course of a meal.

entrench (en-**trench**) *verb* to establish firmly in a well-defended position; *entrenched attitude*, one that is not easily modified.

entrenchment *noun* 1 entrenching; being entrenched. 2 a trench made for defence.

entrepôt (**on**-trĕ-poh) *noun* a warehouse for temporary storage of goods in transit.

entrepreneur (on-trĕ-prĕ-**ner**) *noun* 1 a person who organises and manages a commercial undertaking, especially one involving commercial risk. 2 a contractor acting as intermediary. **entrepreneurial** *adjective*

entropy (**en**-trŏ-pee) *noun* a measure of the disorder of the molecules in substances etc. that are mixed or in contact with each other, indicating the amount of energy that (although it still exists) is not available for use because it has become more evenly distributed instead of being concentrated.

entrust *verb* to give as a responsibility, to place (a person or thing) in a person's care.

entry *noun* 1 entering. 2 a place of entrance. 3 an item entered in a list, diary, etc. 4 a person or thing entered in a race or competition; the number of entrants.

entwine *verb* to twine round, to interweave.

enumerate (ĕ-**new**-mĕ-rayt) *verb* to count, to mention (items) one by one. **enumeration** *noun*, **enumerator** *noun* [from *e-,* + Latin *numerare* = to number]

enunciate (ĕ-**nun**-see-ayt) *verb* 1 to pronounce (words). 2 to state clearly. **enunciation** *noun* [from *e-,* + Latin *nuntiare* = announce]

enuresis (en-yoo-**ree**-sĭs) *noun* involuntary passing of urine.

envelop (en-**vel**-ŏp) *verb* (**enveloped, enveloping**) to wrap up, to cover on all sides. **envelopment** *noun*

envelope (**en**-vĕ-lohp or **on**-) *noun* 1 a wrapper or covering, especially a folded and gummed cover for a letter. 2 the gas container of a balloon or airship.

enviable (**en**-vee-ăbŭl) *adjective* desirable enough to arouse envy. **enviably** *adverb*

envious *adjective* full of envy. **enviously** *adverb*

environment *noun* 1 the surroundings, conditions, and circumstances in which a person lives. 2 **the environment** the external conditions affecting the growth, development, and well-being of plants, animals, and humans, *a threat to the environment.* 3 (in computing) the overall structure within which a user, computer, or program operates. **environmental** *adjective*, **environmentally** *adverb*

environmentalist *noun* one who seeks to protect or improve the environment.

environs (en-**vyr**-ŏnz) *plural noun* the surrounding districts, especially round a town.

envisage (en-**viz**-ij) *verb* 1 to visualise, to imagine. 2 to foresee, *changes are envisaged.*

envoy (**en**-voi) *noun* 1 a messenger or representative. 2 a diplomatic minister ranking below an ambassador. [from French *envoyé* = sent]

envy *noun* 1 a feeling of discontent aroused by someone else's possession of things one would like to have oneself. 2 the object of this, *his car is the envy of his friends.* –**envy** *verb* (**envied, envying**) to feel envy of.

enzyme (**en**-zym) *noun* 1 a protein formed in living cells and assisting chemical processes (e.g. in digestion). 2 a similar substance produced synthetically for use in chemical processes, household detergents, etc.

Eocene (**ee**-oh-seen) *adjective* of the second epoch of the Tertiary period of geological time. –**Eocene** *noun* this epoch.

Eos (**ee**-oss) (*Gk. myth.*) the goddess of the dawn.

epaulette (ep-ă-let) *noun* an ornamental shoulder piece worn on uniforms.

ephemera (ĕ-**fem**-ĕ-ră) *plural noun* things of only short-lived usefulness.

ephemeral (ĕ-**fem**-ĕ-răl) *adjective* lasting only a very short time.

Ephesians (ĕ-**fee**-zhĕnz) the *Epistle to the Ephesians*, a book of the New Testament, an epistle to the Church at Ephesus on the coast of Asia Minor.

epi- *prefix* on; above; in addition. [from Greek *epi* = on]

epic *noun* 1 a long poem or other literary work telling of heroic deeds or history. 2 a book or film resembling this. 3 a subject fit to be told in an epic. –**epic** *adjective* of or like an epic, on a grand scale.

epicentre *noun* the point at which an earthquake reaches the earth's surface.

epicure (ep-ĭ-kewr) *noun* a person with refined tastes in food, literature, etc. **epicurism** *noun*

epicurean (ep-ĭ-kew-**ree**-ăn) *adjective* devoted to sensuous pleasure and luxury. –**epicurean** *noun* an epicurean person. [named after the Greek philosopher Epicurus (c. 300 BC), who sought freedom from anxiety and disturbance]

epidemic *noun* an outbreak of a disease etc. spreading rapidly through a community. [from *epi-*, + Greek *demos* = people]

epidermis (ep-ee-**der**-mĭs) *noun* the outer layer of the skin. **epidermal** *adjective* [from *epi-*, + Greek *derma* = skin]

epidiascope (ep-ee-**dy**-ă-skohp) *noun* a projector that can produce images of both opaque and transparent objects.

epidural (ep-ee-**dew**-răl) *adjective* (of an anaesthetic) injected round the nerves of the spinal cord and having the effect of anaesthetising the lower part of the body. –**epidural** *noun* an epidural injection.

epigeal (ep-ee-**jee**-ăl) *adjective* (of plant germination) in which the cotyledons appear above the ground. [from *epi-*, + Greek *ge* = earth]

epiglottis (ep-ee-**glot**-ĭss) *noun* the cartilage at the root of the tongue, that descends to cover the windpipe in swallowing. [from *epi-*, + Greek *glotta* = tongue]

epigram *noun* a short witty saying. **epigrammatic** *adjective* [from *epi-* + *-gram*]

epigraph *noun* an inscription. [from *epi-* + *-graph*]

epilepsy *noun* a disorder of the nervous system causing mild or severe convulsions, sometimes with loss of consciousness. **epileptic** *adjective* & *noun*

epilogue (ep-ĭ-log) *noun* a short concluding section in a literary work. [from *epi-*, + Greek *logos* = speech]

Epiphany (ĕ-**pif**-ănee) *noun* the Christian festival commemorating the showing of Christ to the Magi, celebrated on 6 January.

epiphyte (ep-ĭ-fyt) *noun* a plant growing on another but not parasitic. **epiphytic** (ep-ĭ-**fit**-ik) *adjective* [*epi-*, + Greek *phuton* = plant]

episcopal (ĕ-**pis**-kŏ-păl) *adjective* of a bishop or bishops; governed by bishops.

Episcopalian (ĕ-pis-kŏ-**pay**-lee-ăn) *adjective* of an episcopal Church. –**Episcopalian** *noun* a member of an episcopal Church.

episode *noun* 1 an incident or event forming one part of a sequence. 2 an incident in a story; one part of a serial.

Epistle (ĕ-**pis**-ŭl) *noun* any of the letters in the New Testament, written by the Apostles. –**epistle** *noun* (*humorous*) a letter.

epitaph (ep-ĭ-tahf) *noun* words inscribed on a tomb or describing a dead person. [from *epi-*, + Greek *taphos* = tomb]

epithelium (ep-ĭ-**theel**-ee-ŭm) *noun* (*plural* **epitheliums** or **epithelia**) the tissue forming the outer layer of the body and lining the alimentary canal and other hollow structures. [from *epi-*, + Greek *thēlē* = teat]

epithet (ep-ĭ-thet) *noun* a descriptive word or phrase, e.g. 'the Great' in *Alfred the Great*.

epitome (ĕ-**pit**-ŏ-mee) *noun* something that shows on a small scale the qualities of something much larger; a person who embodies a quality, *she is the epitome of kindness*.

epitomise (ĕ-**pit**-ŏ-myz) *verb* (also *-ize*) to be an epitome of.

EPNS *abbreviation* electroplated nickel silver.

epoch (ee-pok) *noun* 1 a particular period of history. 2 a division of a geological period. ☐ **epoch-making** *adjective* very important or remarkable, marking the beginning of a new epoch.

epode (ep-ohd) *noun* 1 a form of lyric poem with a long line followed by a shorter one. 2 the third of a group of three stanzas (*strophe*, *antistrophe*, *epode*) sung by the chorus in ancient Greek drama.

eponym (**ep**-ŏ-nim) *noun* **1** a person after whom a place, thing, etc. is named. **2** the name given, e.g. *spoonerism* after W.A. *Spooner*. **eponymous** (ĕ-**pon**-ĭ-mŭs) *adjective*

epoxy (ee-**pok**-see) *adjective* related to or derived from a compound with one oxygen atom and two carbon atoms bonded in a triangle. □ **epoxy resin** a synthetic thermosetting resin.

Epsom salts *plural noun* magnesium sulphate, used as a purgative.

equable (**ek**-wă-bŭl) *adjective* **1** even, unvarying; *an equable climate*, free from extremes of heat and cold. **2** even-tempered. **equably** *adverb*

equal *adjective* **1** the same in size, amount, value, etc. **2** having the same rights or status. –**equal** *noun* a person or thing that is equal to another. –**equal** *verb* (**equalled, equalling**) **1** to be equal to. **2** to produce or achieve something to match, *no one has equalled this score*. □ **be equal to** to have enough strength, courage, or ability etc. for. **equally** *adverb*

equalise *verb* (also **-ize**) **1** to make or become equal. **2** (in games) to equal an opponent's score. **equalisation** *noun*

equaliser *noun* (also **-izer**) **1** an equalising goal etc. **2** an electronic device or network for modifying frequency or phase response.

equalitarian (ee-kwol-ĭ-**tair**-ree-ăn) *adjective* = **egalitarian**.

equality *noun* being equal.

equanimity (ek-wă-**nim**-ĭ-tee) *noun* calmness of mind or temper. [from *equi-*, + Latin *animus* = mind]

equate (ĕ-**kwayt**) *verb* to consider to be equal or equivalent.

equation (ĕ-**kway**-zhŏn) *noun* **1** a mathematical statement that two expressions (connected by the sign =) are equal. **2** a formula indicating a chemical reaction by the use of symbols. **3** making equal.

equator (ĕ-**kway**-ter) *noun* an imaginary line round the earth at an equal distance from the North and South Poles.

equatorial (ek-wă-**tor**-ree-ăl) *adjective* of or near the equator.

Equatorial Guinea a republic of West Africa on the Gulf of Guinea.

equerry (**ek**-wĕ-ree) *noun* an officer of the British royal household, attending members of the royal family.

equestrian (ĕ-**kwest**-ree-ăn) *adjective* of horse-riding. –**equestrian** *noun* a person who is skilled at horse-riding. [from Latin *equus* = horse]

equi- *prefix* equal; equally. [from Latin *aequus* = equal]

equidistant (ee-kwee-**dis**-tănt) *adjective* at an equal distance.

equilateral (ee-kwĭ-**lat**-ĕ-răl) *adjective* having all sides equal. [from *equi-* + *lateral*]

equilibrium (ee-kwĭ-**lib**-ree-ŭm) *noun* (*plural* **equilibria**) a state of balance. [from *equi-*, + Latin *libra* = balance]

equine (**ek**-wyn) *adjective* of or like a horse. [from *equus* = horse]

equinox (**ek**-wĭ-noks *or* **eek**-) *noun* both times of year when day and night are of equal length (about 20 March and 22 September). **equinoctial** (ek-wĭ-**nok**-shăl) *adjective* [from *equi-*, + Latin *nox* = night]

equip *verb* (**equipped, equipping**) to supply with what is needed.

equipment *noun* **1** equipping. **2** the outfit, tools, and other things needed for a particular job or expedition etc.

equipoise (**ek**-wĭ-poiz) *noun* **1** equilibrium. **2** a counterbalance.

equitable (**ek**-wĭ-tă-bŭl) *adjective* fair and just. **equitably** *adverb*

equity (**ek**-wĭ-tee) *noun* fairness, impartiality. –**Equity** the actors' trade union. **equities** *plural noun* stocks and shares not bearing fixed interest.

equivalent *adjective* equal in value, importance, meaning, etc. –**equivalent** *noun* an equivalent thing, amount, or word. **equivalence** *noun* [from *equi-*, + Latin *valens* = worth]

equivocal (ĕ-**kwiv**-ŏ-kăl) *adjective* **1** able to be interpreted in two ways, ambiguous. **2** questionable, suspicious, *an equivocal character*. **equivocally** *adverb* [from *equi-*, + Latin *vocare* = to call]

equivocate (ĕ-**kwiv**-ŏ-kayt) *verb* to use ambiguous words in order to conceal the truth, to avoid committing oneself. **equivocation** *noun*

ER *abbreviation* Elizabetha Regina. [Latin, = Queen Elizabeth]

er *interjection* an expression of hesitation.

era (**eer**-ră) *noun* **1** a period of history; *the Christian era*, the period reckoned from the birth of Christ. **2** a major division of geological development.

eradicate (ĕ-**rad**-ĭ-kayt) *verb* to get rid of, to remove all traces of. **eradication** *noun*, **eradicator** *noun*, **eradicable** *adjective* [from Latin, = root out (*e-* = out, *radix* = a root)]

erase (ĕ-**rayz**) *verb* to rub or scrape out (marks, writing, etc.), to wipe out a recorded signal from (magnetic tape). [from *e-*, + Latin *rasum* = scraped]

eraser *noun* a thing that erases marks etc., a piece of rubber or other substance for rubbing out marks or writing.

erasure (ĕ-**ray**-zher) *noun* **1** erasing. **2** a word etc. that has been erased.

Erato (e-**rah**-toh) (*Gk. myth.*) the Muse of lyric poetry and hymns.

erbium (**er**-bee-ŭm) *noun* a soft silver-white metallic element of the lanthanide series (symbol Er).

ere (*pr.* air) *preposition* & *conjunction* (*old use*) before.

Erebus (e-rĕ-bŭs), **Mount** a volcano on Ross Island in Antarctica.

erect *adjective* **1** standing on end, upright, vertical. **2** (of a part of the body) enlarged and rigid from sexual excitement. **–erect** *verb* to set up, to build. **erector** *noun*

erectile (ĕ-**rek**-tyl) *adjective* (of parts of the body) able to become enlarged and rigid.

erection *noun* **1** erecting; being erected. **2** something erected, a building. **3** swelling and hardening (especially of the penis) in sexual excitement.

erg[1] *noun* a unit of work or energy.

erg[2] *noun* (*plural* **ergs** *or* **areg**) a large area of shifting sand dunes, as in the Sahara desert.

ergo *adverb* therefore.

ergonomics (ergŏ-**nom**-iks) *noun* study of work and its environment and conditions in order to achieve maximum efficiency. **ergonomic** *adjective*, **ergonomically** *adverb* [from Greek *ergon* = work, + *-nomia* = management]

Eriksson, Leif (c. 1000), Norwegian explorer, son of Erik the Red, who discovered land (variously identified as Labrador, Newfoundland, or New England) which he named Vinland.

Erik the Red 10th century, Norwegian explorer, who sailed from Iceland and explored Greenland, establishing a Norse settlement there.

Erin (e-rĭn) an ancient or poetic name for Ireland.

Eritrea (e-rĭ-**tray**-ă) an independent state in NE Africa, on the Red Sea, formerly a province of Ethiopia.

ERM *abbreviation* exchange-rate mechanism, a system for keeping the currencies of member countries fixed or 'pegged' and allowed to vary only slightly in relation to each other.

ermine *noun* **1** an animal of the weasel family, with brown fur that turns white in winter. **2** this white fur.

erode (ĕ-**rohd**) *verb* to wear away gradually, especially by rubbing or corroding. **erosion** (ĕ-**roh**-zhŏn) *noun*, **erosional** *adjective*, **erosive** *adjective* [from *e-*, + Latin *rodere* = gnaw]

Eros (**eer**-ross) (*Gk. myth.*) the god of love, Cupid.

erotic (ĕ-**rot**-ik) *adjective* of sexual love; arousing sexual desire. **erotically** *adverb*, **eroticism** *noun*

err (*pr.* er) *verb* (**erred**, **erring**) **1** to make a mistake, to be incorrect. **2** to sin. [from Latin *errare* = wander]

errand *noun* **1** a short journey on which a person goes or is sent to carry a message or deliver goods etc. **2** the purpose of a journey.

errant (e-rănt) *adjective* **1** erring, misbehaving. **2** (*literary* or *old use*) travelling in search of adventure, *a knight errant*. [same origin as *err*]

erratic (ĕ-**rat**-ik) *adjective* irregular or uneven in movement, quality, habit, etc.
☐ **erratic block** or **boulder** a large boulder brought from a distant place by the movement of a glacier. **erratically** *adverb*

erratum (e-**rah**-tŭm) *noun* (*plural* **errata**) an error in printing or writing, = corrigendum.

erroneous (ĕ-**roh**-nee-ŭs) *adjective* mistaken, incorrect. **erroneously** *adverb*

error *noun* **1** a mistake. **2** the condition of being wrong in opinion or conduct. **3** the amount of inaccuracy in a calculation or a measuring device, *an error of 2 per cent*.
☐ **in error** mistakenly, by mistake. [same origin as *err*]

ersatz *adjective* substitute, imitation.

Erse *noun* Irish Gaelic. – **Erse** *adjective* of or in Erse.

erstwhile *adjective* & *adverb* former, formerly.

erudite (**e-rŭ**-dyt) *adjective* having or showing great learning. **erudition** *noun*

erupt *verb* **1** to break out suddenly and violently. **2** (of a volcano) to shoot forth lava etc.; (of a geyser) to spurt water. **3** to form spots or patches on the skin. **4** (of a tooth) to break through the gum. **eruption** *noun* [from *e-*, + Latin *ruptum* = burst]

eruptive *adjective* **1** erupting; liable to erupt. **2** formed or characterised by eruptions.

erythrocyte (**e-reeth**-rŏ-syt) *noun* a red blood corpuscle. [from Greek *eruthros* = red, + *kutos* = vessel]

escalate (**ess-kă**-layt) *verb* to increase or cause to increase in intensity or extent. **escalation** *noun*

escalator *noun* a moving staircase consisting of a circulating belt forming steps.

escalope (**ess-kă**-lohp) *noun* a slice of boneless meat, especially veal.

escapade (ess-kă-**payd**) *noun* a piece of reckless or mischievous conduct.

escape *verb* **1** to get oneself free from confinement or control. **2** (of liquid or gas etc.) to get out of a container, to leak. **3** to succeed in avoiding (capture, punishment, etc.). **4** to be forgotten or unnoticed by; *his name escapes me*, I have forgotten it. **5** (of words, a sigh, etc.) to be uttered unintentionally. – **escape** *noun* **1** the act of escaping, the fact of having escaped. **2** a means of escaping. **3** a leakage of liquid or gas. **4** a temporary distraction or relief from reality or worry. **escaper** *noun*

escapee (ess-kă-**pee**) *noun* an escaper.

escapement *noun* mechanism regulating the movement of a watch or clock etc., a movable catch engaging the projections of a toothed wheel.

escapist *noun* one who likes to escape from the realities of life by absorbing the mind in entertainment or fantasy. **escapism** *noun*

escapology (ess-kă-**pol**-ŏ-jee) *noun* the methods and techniques of escaping from captivity or confinement. **escapologist** *noun*

escarpment *noun* a steep slope at the edge of a plateau.

eschatology (ess-kă-**tol**-ŏ-jee) *noun* the doctrines of the last things (death, judgment,

heaven, and hell). [from Greek *eschatos* = last, + *-logy*]

eschew (ĕss-**choo**) *verb* to avoid or abstain from (certain kinds of action or food etc.).

escort (**ess**-kort) *noun* **1** one or more persons or ships etc. accompanying a person or thing to give protection or as an honour. **2** a person accompanying a member of the opposite sex socially. – **escort** (ĕ-**skort**) *verb* to act as escort to.

escutcheon (ĕ-**skuch**-ŏn) *noun* a shield or emblem bearing a coat of arms.
☐ **a blot on one's escutcheon** a stain on one's reputation. [from Latin *scutum* = shield]

Esdras (**ez**-drăs) **1** either of two books of the Apocrypha. **2** (in the Vulgate) the books of Ezra and Nehemiah.

esker *noun* a long winding ridge of gravel deposited by a stream formed under a melting glacier. [from Irish *eiscir*]

Eskimo *noun* (*plural* **Eskimos** *or* **Eskimo**) **1** a member of an indigenous people inhabiting Canada, Alaska, Greenland, and eastern Siberia. **2** any of the languages of these peoples. [an Algonquian word, perhaps in the sense of 'people speaking a different language'; the folk etymology, 'eaters of raw flesh', is now discredited]

Usage The name *Inuit* is preferred by the people themselves, especially in Canada.

esky *noun* (*plural* **eskies**) (*trademark Austral.*) a portable insulated container for keeping food and drink cold.

esoteric (ess-ŏ-**te**-rik) *adjective* intended only for people with special knowledge or interest.

ESP *abbreviation* extrasensory perception.

espadrille (**ess**-pă-dril) *noun* a canvas shoe with a sole of plaited fibre.

espalier (ĕss-**pal**-ee-er) *noun* **1** a trellis or framework on which fruit trees or ornamental shrubs are trained. **2** a tree or shrub trained on this.

esparto (ĕss-**par**-toh) *noun* a kind of grass of Spain and North Africa, used in papermaking.

especial *adjective* **1** special, outstanding, *of especial interest*. **2** belonging chiefly to one person or thing, *for your especial benefit*.

especially *adverb* chiefly, more than in other cases.

Esperanto (ess-pĕ-**ran**-toh) *noun* an artificial language designed in 1887 for use by people of all nations.

espionage (**ess**-pee-ŏ-nah*zh*) *noun* spying or using spies to obtain secret information. [from French *espion* = spy]

esplanade (ess-plă-**nayd** *or* -**nahd**) *noun* a level area of ground where people may walk or ride for pleasure, especially by the sea.

espouse (ĕ-**spowz**) *verb* 1 to give support to (a cause). 2 to marry, to give (a woman) in marriage. **espousal** *noun*

espresso *noun* (*plural* espressos) 1 an apparatus for making coffee by forcing steam through powdered coffee beans. 2 coffee made in this way. [Italian, = pressed out]

esprit de corps (ess-pree dĕ **kor**) *noun* loyalty and devotion uniting the members of a group. [French, = spirit of the body]

espy *verb* (espied, espying) to catch sight of.

Esq. *abbreviation* Esquire; a courtesy title (in formal use) placed after a man's surname where no title is used before his name.

essay (**ess**-ay) *noun* 1 a short literary composition in prose. 2 an attempt. –essay (ess-**ay**) *verb* (essayed, essaying) to attempt.

essayist *noun* a writer of essays.

essence *noun* 1 all that makes a thing what it is, its nature. 2 an indispensable quality or element. 3 an extract of something, containing all its important qualities in concentrated form. 4 a liquid perfume. [from Latin *esse* = to be]

essential *adjective* 1 indispensable. 2 of or constituting a thing's essence; *its essential qualities*, those that make it what it is. **essentials** *plural noun* indispensable elements or things. **essentially** *adverb*

establish *verb* 1 to set up (a business or government etc.) on a permanent basis. 2 to settle (a person or oneself) in a place or position. 3 to cause people to accept (a custom or belief etc.). 4 to show to be true, to prove, *established his innocence*.

established *adjective* (of a Church or religion) that is made officially a country's national Church or religion.

establishment *noun* 1 establishing; being established. 2 an organised body of people maintained for a purpose, a household or staff of servants etc. 3 a business firm or public institution, its members or employees or premises. 4 a Church system established by law. □ **the Establishment** people who

are established in positions of power and authority, exercising influence in the background of public life or other activity and generally resisting changes.

estate *noun* 1 landed property. 2 a residential or industrial district planned as a unit. 3 all that a person owns, especially that left at his or her death. 4 (*old use*) condition, *the holy estate of matrimony*. □ **estate agent** one whose business is the selling or letting of houses and land.

esteem *verb* 1 to think highly of. 2 to consider or regard, *I should esteem it an honour*. –esteem *noun* favourable opinion, respect.

ester (**ess**-ter) *noun* a chemical compound formed when an acid and an alcohol interact in a certain way. **esterification** *noun*

Esther (**ess**-ter) 1 a beautiful Jewish woman who became the wife of the king of Persia (5th century BC). 2 the book of the Old Testament giving an account of this.

estimable (**ess**-tĭ-mă-bŭl) *adjective* worthy of esteem.

estimate (**ess**-tĭ-măt) *noun* 1 a judgment of a thing's approximate value or amount etc. 2 a contractor's statement of the sum which he estimates he will charge for performing specified work. 3 a judgment of character or qualities. –estimate (**ess**-tĭ-mayt) *verb* to form an estimate of. **estimation** *noun*, **estimator** *noun*

Estonia (ess-**toh**-neeă) a republic of NE Europe on the Gulf of Finland. **Estonian** *adjective* & *noun*

estrange *verb* to cause (people formerly friendly or loving) to become unfriendly or indifferent. **estrangement** *noun*

estuary (**ess**-tew-ă-ree) *noun* the mouth of a large river where its flow is affected by the ebb and flow of tides. **estuarine** *adjective* [from Latin *aestus* = tide]

et al. *abbreviation* = and others. [short for Latin *et alii*]

etc. *abbreviation* = et cetera, and other similar things, and the rest. **etceteras** *plural noun* the usual extras, sundries. [from Latin *et* = and, + *cetera* = the other things]

etch *verb* 1 to make (a pattern or picture) by engraving a metal plate with acids or corrosive substances, especially so that copies can be printed from this. 2 to impress deeply, *the scene is etched on my mind*. **etcher** *noun*

302

etching *noun* a copy printed from an etched plate.

eternal *adjective* **1** existing always without beginning or end. **2** unchanging, not affected by time. **3** (*informal*) ceaseless, too frequent, *these eternal arguments*. □ **the Eternal City** Rome. **eternally** *adverb*

eternity *noun* **1** infinite time, past or future. **2** the endless period of life after death. **3** (*informal*) a very long time.

ethane (**ee**-thayn) *noun* a carbon compound in the alkane series, found in natural gas.

ethanoic acid (eth-ă-**noh**-ik) *noun* acetic acid.

ethanol (**eth**-ă-nol) *noun* alcohol.

Ethelred (**eth**-ĕl-red) 'the Unready' (= rash, lacking good advice), king of England 978–1016.

ether (**ee**-ther) *noun* **1** a colourless liquid produced by the action of acids on alcohol, used as an anaesthetic and as a solvent. **2** the clear sky, the upper regions beyond the clouds. **3** a kind of substance formerly thought to fill all space and act as a medium for transmission of radio waves etc.

ethereal (ĕ-**theer**-ree-ăl) *adjective* **1** light and delicate, especially in appearance. **2** of heaven, heavenly. **ethereally** *adverb*

ethic (**eth**-ik) *adjective* of or involving morals. **–ethic** *noun* a moral principle or set of principles. [from Greek *ethos* = character]

ethical (**eth**-ikăl) *adjective* **1** of ethics. **2** morally correct, honourable. **ethically** *adverb*

ethics *noun* moral philosophy. **–ethics** *plural noun* moral principles, *medical ethics*.

Ethiopia a country of NE Africa. **Ethiopian** *adjective* & *noun*

ethnic *adjective* **1** (of a social group) having common national, racial, cultural, religious, or linguistic characteristics; especially (in Australia) designating a social group of migrants (or their descendants) whose original language is not English. **2** of or relating to ethnic groups, *ethnic broadcasting*; *ethnic dancing*. **3** denoting origin by birth or descent rather than nationality, *ethnic Turks*; *ethnic origins*. **–ethnic** *noun* (*Austral.* & *Amer.*) a member of an (especially minority) ethnic group. □ **ethnic cleansing** extermination or expulsion from a certain area of people of particular ethnic background. **ethnically** *adverb* [from Greek *ethnos* = nation]

ethnology (eth-**nol**-ŏ-jee) *noun* the scientific study of human races and their characteristics. **ethnological** (eth-nŏ-**loj**-i-kăl) *adjective* [from Greek *ethnos* = nation, + *-logy*]

ethology (ee-**thol**-ŏjee) *noun* the scientific study of character formation or of animal behaviour. **ethologist** *noun*

ethos (ee-thoss) *noun* the characteristic spirit and beliefs of a community, person, or literary work. [Greek, = character]

ethyl (**eth**-ĭl) *noun* a hydrocarbon group of atoms derived from ethane and present in **ethyl alcohol**, the alcohol found in wine, beer, whisky, etc.

ethylene (**eth**-ĭ-leen) *noun* a carbon compound in the alkene series, used in the manufacture of polythene etc.

etiolate (**ee**-tee-ŏ-layt) *verb* to make (a plant) pale through lack of light. **etiolation** *noun*

etiquette (et-ĭ-kĕt) *noun* the rules of correct behaviour in society or among the members of a profession.

Etna a volcano in Sicily.

Etruscan (ĕ-**trus**-kăn) *noun* **1** a native of ancient Etruria (modern Tuscany). **2** the language of the Etruscans.

étude (**ay**-tewd) *noun* a musical composition designed to develop a player's skill. [French, = a study]

etymology (et-ĭ-**mol**-ŏjee) *noun* **1** an account of the origin and development of a word. **2** the study of words and their origins. **etymological** (et-ĭ-mŏ-**loj**-ikăl) *adjective*, **etymologically** *adverb*, **etymologist** *noun* [from Greek *etumon* = original word, + *-logy*]

EU *abbreviation* European Union.

eu- (*pr.* yoo) *prefix* well. [from Greek]

eucalypt (**yoo**-kă-lipt) *noun* a eucalyptus tree.

eucalyptus (yoo-kă-**lip**-tŭs) *noun* (*plural* **eucalyptuses**) **1** any of a number of evergreen trees, mostly native to Australia and introduced elsewhere. **2** a strong-smelling oil obtained from eucalyptus leaves.

Eucharist (**yoo**-kă-rĭst) *noun* **1** the Christian sacrament in which bread and wine are consecrated and consumed. **2** the consecrated elements, especially the bread. **Eucharistic** *adjective* [from Greek, = thanksgiving]

euchred (**yoo**-kĕd) *adjective* (*Austral. informal*) defeated, exhausted. [from *euchre*, a card game, in which a player is *euchred* when prevented from making the tricks he or she has contracted to make]

Euclid (**yoo**-klĭd) (c. 300 BC), Greek mathematician, whose *Elements* was the standard work on geometry until the 19th century. Euclidean (yoo-**klid**-ee-ăn) *adjective*

eugenics (yoo-**jen**-iks) *noun* the science of the production of fine offspring by control of inherited qualities. eugenic *adjective*, eugenically *adverb*

Euler (**oi**-ler), Leonhard (1707–83), Swiss-born mathematician who made significant discoveries in most branches of mathematics.

Eulerian (oi-**leer**-ree-ăn) *adjective* (in graph theory) Eulerian network a network of edges and vertices in which there is a possible sequence (an Eulerian walk) in which every edge occurs once and only once.

eulogise (**yoo**-lŏ-jyz) *verb* (also -ize) to write or utter a eulogy of.

eulogistic (yoo-lŏ-**jist**-ik) *adjective* eulogising.

eulogy (**yoo**-lŏ-jee) *noun* a speech or piece of writing in praise of a person or thing. [from *eu-*, + Greek *-logia* = speaking]

Eumenides (yoo-**men**-ĭ-deez) (*Gk. myth.*) kindly powers sending fertility; a euphemistic name for the Furies.

eunuch (**yoo**-nŭk) *noun* a castrated man.

euphemism (**yoo**-fě-mizm) *noun* a mild or roundabout expression substituted for one considered improper or too harsh or blunt, *'pass away' is a euphemism for 'die'*. euphemistic (yoo-fě-**mist**-ik) *adjective*, euphemistically *adverb* [from *eu-*, + Greek *pheme* = speech]

euphonium (yoo-**foh**-nee-ŭm) *noun* a large brass wind instrument, a tenor tuba. [from *eu-*, + Greek *phone* = sound]

euphony (**yoo**-fŏnee) *noun* pleasantness of sounds, especially in words. euphonious (yoo-**foh**-nee-ŭs) *adjective*

euphoria (yoo-**for**-reeă) *noun* a feeling of general happiness. euphoric (yoo-**fo**-rik) *adjective* [from *eu-*, + Greek *phoros* = bearing]

Euphrates (yoo-**fray**-teez) a river of SW Asia, flowing from Turkey through Syria and Iraq to the Persian Gulf.

euploid (**yoo**-ploid) *adjective* having an equal number of all the chromosomes of the haploid set.

Eurasian (yoo-**ray**-zhăn) *adjective* 1 of Europe and Asia. 2 of mixed European and Asian parentage. –Eurasian *noun* a Eurasian person. [from *European* + *Asian*]

Eureka (yoo-**reek**-ă) □ Eureka flag a flag (borne by the miners at the Eureka Stockade) bearing a white cross on a blue background, with a white star at each end of the cross and one in the centre. Eureka stockade the scene of a clash at Ballarat in 1854 between gold diggers and police and the military.

eureka *interjection* I have found it, an exclamation of triumph at a discovery. [from Greek *heureka*, said to have been uttered by the Greek mathematician Archimedes (3rd century BC) on realising that the volume of an object can be calculated by the amount of water it displaces]

eurhythmics (yoo-**rith**-miks) *plural noun* (usually treated as *singular*) harmony of bodily movement, developed with music and dance into a system of education.

Euripides (yoo-**rip**-ĭ-deez) (5th century BC) Greek dramatist.

Euro- *prefix* Europe; European.

euro[1] *noun* the unit of money in the European Union.

euro[2] *noun* (*plural euros*) a kind of large kangaroo. [Adnyamathanha *yuru*]

Europa (yoo-**roh**-pă) (*Gk. myth.*) a woman who was wooed by Zeus in the form of a bull and carried off by him to Crete.

Europe a continent extending from Asia to the Atlantic Ocean and including the British Isles. European *adjective* & *noun*

European Union (abbreviation EU) an economic and political association of certain European countries with internal free trade and common external tariffs. Formerly known as the European Community (EC).

europium (yŭ-**roh**-pee-ŭm) *noun* a soft silver-white metallic element of the lanthanide series (symbol Eu).

Eurydice (yoo-**rid**-ĭ-see) (*Gk. myth.*) wife of Orpheus.

Eustachian tube (yoo-**stay**-shăn) *noun* the narrow passage from the pharynx to the cavity of the middle ear.

eustasy (**yoo**-stă-see) *noun* a uniform change of sea level throughout the world. eustatic (yoo-**stat**-ik) *adjective* [from *eu-*, + Greek *stasis* = standing]

euthanasia (yoo-thă-**nay**-zee-ă) *noun* the bringing about of an easy death for a person suffering from a painful incurable disease. [from *eu-*, + Greek *thanatos* = death]

eutrophic (yoo-**trof**-ik) *adjective* (of a lake) in which there are so many nutrients in the water that algae etc. grow excessively and the levels of water beneath them become starved of oxygen. [from *eu-*, + Greek *-trophia* = nourishment]

eV *abbreviation* electronvolt(s).

evacuate *verb* 1 to send (people) away from a place considered dangerous; to remove the occupants of (a place). 2 to empty (a vessel) of air etc. 3 to empty the contents of (the bowel or other organ). **evacuation** *noun* [from *e-*, + Latin *vacuus* = empty]

evacuee *noun* an evacuated person.

evade (ĕ-**vayd**) *verb* to avoid (a person or thing) by cleverness or trickery; *evade the question*, to avoid giving a direct answer. [from *e-*, + Latin *vadere* = go]

evaluate *verb* to find out or state the value of, to assess. **evaluation** *noun*

evanesce (ev-ă-**ness**) *verb* to fade from sight etc., to disappear. **evanescent** *adjective*, **evanescence** *noun*

evangelical (ee-van-**jel**-ikăl) *adjective* 1 according to the teaching of the gospel or the Christian religion. 2 of a Protestant group stressing the authority of Scripture, and believing that salvation is achieved by faith in the Atonement through Christ. –**Evangelical** *noun* a member of this group.

evangelise *verb* (also -**ize**) to preach or spread the gospel to, to win over to Christianity. **evangelisation** *noun* [from Greek, = announce good news (*eu* = well, *angelos* = messenger)]

evangelism (ĕ-**van**-jĕ-lizm) *noun* preaching or spreading of the gospel.

evangelist (ĕ-**van**-jĕ-lĭst) *noun* 1 any of the authors of the four Gospels (Matthew, Mark, Luke, John). 2 a person who preaches the gospel. **evangelistic** *adjective*

evaporate *verb* 1 to turn or be turned into vapour. 2 to lose or cause to lose moisture in this way. 3 to cease to exist, *their enthusiasm evaporated*. □ **evaporated milk** milk concentrated by partial evaporation and tinned. **evaporation** *noun* [from *e-* = out, + Latin *vapor* = steam]

evaporite *noun* a deposit of sodium chloride and other salts left when salt water evaporates.

evasion (ĕ-**vay**-zhŏn) *noun* 1 evading. 2 an evasive answer or excuse.

evasive (ĕ-**vay**-siv) *adjective* evading, not frank or straightforward. **evasively** *adverb*, **evasiveness** *noun*

Eve (in the Bible) the first woman.

eve *noun* 1 the evening or day before a festival, *Christmas Eve*. 2 the time just before an event, *on the eve of an election*. 3 (*old use*) evening.

even[1] *adjective* 1 level, free from irregularities, smooth. 2 uniform in quality. 3 (of temper) calm, not easily upset. 4 equally balanced or matched. 5 equal in number or amount. 6 (of a number) exactly divisible by two. 7 (of money or time or quantity) exact, not involving fractions, *an even dozen*. –**even** *verb* to make or become even. –**even** *adverb* 1 (used to emphasise a comparison) to a greater degree, *ran even faster*. 2 (used to suggest that something mentioned is unlikely or is an extreme case or should be compared with what might have happened etc.) *even if that is true*; *does he even suspect the danger?*; *even a child could understand that*; *didn't even try to avoid it* (let alone succeed).
□ **be** or **get even with** to have one's revenge on. **even chance** when success is as likely as failure. **even-handed** *adjective* impartial. **even money** or **evens** *plural noun* with equal stakes on both sides in a bet. **even now** in addition to previously; at this very moment. **even so** although that is the case. **evenly** *adverb*, **evenness** *noun*

even[2] *noun* (*poetic*) evening.

evening *noun* the part of the day between afternoon and bedtime. □ **evening dress** the kind of clothing usually worn for formal occasions in the evening; a woman's long formal dress. **evening star** a planet (especially Venus) when conspicuous in the west after sunset.

evensong *noun* a service of evening prayer, especially in the Anglican Church.

event *noun* 1 something that happens, especially something important. 2 the fact of a thing happening; *in the event of his death*, if he dies. 3 an item in a sports program. □ **at all events**, **in any event** in any case. **in the event** as things turned out. [from *e-*, + Latin *ventum* = come]

eventful *adjective* full of incidents.

eventide *noun* (*old use*) evening.

eventual *adjective* coming at last, ultimate, *his eventual success*. **eventually** *adverb*

eventuality (ĕ-ven-tew-**al**-ĭ-tee) *noun* a possible event.

eventuate *verb* to result, to be the outcome.

ever *adverb* 1 at all times, always, *ever hopeful*. 2 at any time, *the best thing I ever did*. 3 (used for emphasis) in any possible way, *why ever didn't you say so?* □ **Yours ever** see yours.

Everest, **Mount** the world's highest mountain (8848 m), in the Himalayas, named after Sir George Everest (1790–1866), surveyor-general of India.

evergreen *adjective* (of a tree or shrub) having green leaves throughout the year. –**evergreen** *noun* an evergreen tree or shrub.

everlasting *adjective* 1 lasting for ever. 2 lasting a very long time. 3 lasting too long, repeated too often, *his everlasting complaints*. 4 (of flowers) keeping shape and colour when dried. **everlastingly** *adverb*

evermore *adverb* for ever, always.

every *adjective* 1 each single one without exception, *enjoyed every minute*. 2 each in a series, *came every fourth day*. 3 all possible, *she shall be given every care*. □ **every one** each one. **every other day** or **week** etc., with one between each two selected. **every so often** at intervals, occasionally.

Usage *Every one* should be followed by a singular verb, *every one of them is* (not *are*) *guilty*.

everybody *pronoun* every person, all the people.

everyday *adjective* 1 worn or used on ordinary days. 2 usual, commonplace.

Everyman *noun* the ordinary or typical person, the 'man in the street'.

everyone *pronoun* everybody.

Usage Distinguish *everyone* meaning 'all the people, every person' (e.g. *Everyone likes to be appreciated*) from *every one* meaning 'each one', which is used of things as well as people (e.g. *The tree was full of pears but the birds ate every one*).

everything *pronoun* 1 all things, all. 2 the most important thing, *speed is everything*. □ **have everything** (*informal*) to possess every advantage or attraction.

everywhere *adverb* in every place.

evict (ĕ-**vikt**) *verb* to expel (a tenant) by legal process. **eviction** *noun* [from Latin *evictum* = expelled, defeated (also = convinced)]

evidence *noun* 1 anything that establishes a fact or gives reason for believing something. 2 statements made or objects produced in a lawcourt as proof or to support a case. –**evidence** *verb* to indicate, to be evidence of. □ **be in evidence** to be conspicuous.

evident *adjective* obvious to the eye or mind. **evidently** *adverb*

evidential (ev-ĭ-**den**-shăl) *adjective* of or based on or providing evidence.

evil *adjective* 1 morally bad, wicked. 2 harmful, intending to do harm. 3 very unpleasant or troublesome, *an evil temper*. –**evil** *noun* an evil thing, sin, harm. **evilly** *adverb*

evildoer *noun* one who does evil things.

evince (ĕ-**vins**) *verb* to indicate, to show that one has (a quality). [same origin as *evict*]

eviscerate (ĕ-**vis**-ĕ-rayt) *verb* 1 to take out the intestines of. 2 to empty (a thing) of its vital contents. **evisceration** *noun* [from *e-* + *viscera*]

evocative (ĕ-**vok**-ătiv) *adjective* tending to evoke.

evoke (ĕ-**vohk**) *verb* to call up or produce or inspire (memories, feelings, a response, etc.). **evocation** (ev-ŏ-**kay**-shŏn) *noun* [from *e-* = out, + Latin *vocare* = to call]

evolution (ee-vŏ-**loo**-shŏn) *noun* 1 the process by which something develops gradually into a different form. 2 the origination of living things by development from earlier forms. **evolutionary** *adverb*

evolve (ĕ-**volv**) *verb* 1 to develop or work out gradually, *evolve a plan*. 2 to develop or modify by evolution. **evolvement** *noun* [from *e-*, + Latin *volvere* = to roll]

ewe *noun* a female sheep. □ **ewe lamb** one's most cherished possession.

ewer (**yoo**-er) *noun* a wide-mouthed pitcher for holding water.

ex[1] *preposition* 1 (of goods) as sold from (a ship, factory, etc.); *ex-factory price*, the amount payable for goods at a factory etc., excluding the cost of delivery. 2 without, excluding; *ex dividend*, (of stocks or shares) not including the next dividend.

ex[2] *noun* (*informal*) a former husband or wife.

ex- *prefix* (changing to **ef-** before *f*; shortened to **e-** before many consonants). 1 out; away (as in *extract*). 2 up, upwards; thoroughly (as in *extol*). **3** formerly (as in *ex-president*). [from Latin *ex-* = out of]

exacerbate (egz-**ass**-er-bayt) *verb* **1** to make (pain, disease, anger, etc.) worse. **2** to irritate (a person). **exacerbation** *noun*

exact *adjective* **1** correct in every detail, free from error. **2** giving all details, *gave me exact instructions*. **3** capable of being precise, *the exact sciences*. **–exact** *verb* to insist on and obtain, *exacted payment* or *obedience*. **exaction** *noun*, **exactness** *noun* [from *ex-* = out, + Latin *actum* = performed]

exacting *adjective* making great demands, requiring or insisting on great effort, *an exacting task* or *an exacting teacher*.

exactitude *noun* exactness.

exactly *adverb* **1** in an exact manner. **2** (said in agreement) quite so, as you say.

exaggerate *verb* to make (a thing) seem larger or more than it really is. **exaggeration** *noun* [from *ex-* = upwards, + Latin *agger* = heap]

exalt (ĕg-**zawlt**) *verb* **1** to raise (a person) in rank, power, or dignity. **2** to praise highly. [from *ex-* = up, + Latin *altus* = high]

Usage *Exalt* is sometimes confused with *exult* which means 'to rejoice'.

exaltation *noun* **1** exalting; being exalted. **2** elation, spiritual delight.

exam *noun* (*informal*) an examination.

examination *noun* **1** examining; being examined or looked at. **2** the testing of knowledge or ability by oral or written questions or exercises. **3** a formal questioning of a witness or an accused person in a lawcourt.

examine *verb* **1** to look at in order to learn about or from; to look at closely. **2** to put questions or exercises etc. in order to test knowledge or ability. **3** to question formally in order to get information. **examiner** *noun*

examinee *noun* a person being tested in an examination.

example *noun* **1** a fact that illustrates a general rule; a thing that shows the quality or characteristics of others in the same group or of the same kind. **2** something (especially conduct) that is worthy of imitation. □ **for example** by way of illustrating a general rule. **make an example of** to punish as a

warning to others. **set an example** to behave in a way that is worthy of imitation.

exasperate *verb* to annoy greatly. **exasperation** *noun* [from *ex-* = thoroughly, + Latin *asper* = rough]

Excalibur (in legend) the name of King Arthur's magic sword.

ex cathedra (eks kăth-**ee**-drǎ) *adjective* & *adverb* with full authority (especially of a papal pronouncement). [Latin, = from the chair]

excavate *verb* **1** to make (a hole or channel) by digging; to dig out (soil). **2** to reveal or extract by digging. **excavation** *noun*, **excavator** *noun* [from *ex-* = out, + Latin *cavus* = hollow]

exceed *verb* **1** to be greater or more numerous than. **2** to go beyond the limit of, to do more than is warranted by, *exceeded his authority*. [from *ex-* = out, beyond, + Latin *cedere* = go]

exceedingly *adverb* very, extremely.

excel *verb* (**excelled**, **excelling**) **1** to be better than. **2** to be very good at something. □ **excel oneself** to do better than one has ever done before. [from *ex-*, + Latin *celsus* = lofty]

excellence *noun* very great merit or quality.

Excellency *noun* the title of high officials such as ambassadors and governors.

excellent *adjective* extremely good. **excellently** *adverb*

excelsior (ĕk-**sel**-see-or) *interjection* (as a motto etc.) higher. [Latin, = loftier]

except *preposition* not including, *they all left except me*. **–except** *verb* to exclude from a statement or calculation etc. [from *ex-* = out, + Latin *-ceptum* = taken]

excepting *preposition* except.

exception *noun* **1** excepting; being excepted. **2** a thing that does not follow the general rule. □ **take exception to** to object to. **the exception proves the rule** the excepting of some cases proves that the rule exists, or that it applies to all other cases. **with the exception of** except.

exceptionable *adjective* open to objection.

exceptional *adjective* **1** forming an exception, very unusual. **2** outstandingly good. **exceptionally** *adverb*

excerpt (**ek**-serpt) *noun* an extract from a book or film or piece of music etc. **–excerpt** (ek-**serpt**) *verb* to select excerpts from. **excerption** *noun*

excess *noun* **1** the exceeding of due limits. **2** the amount by which one number or quantity etc. exceeds another. **3** an agreed amount subtracted by an insurer from the total payment to be made to an insured person who makes a claim. ☐ **in excess of** more than.

excessive *adjective* greater than what is normal or necessary, too much. **excessively** *adverb*

exchange *verb* **1** to give or receive (one thing) in place of another. **2** to give to and receive from another person; *they exchanged glances*, looked at each other. – **exchange** *noun* **1** exchanging (goods, prisoners, words, blows, etc.). **2** the exchanging of money for its equivalent in another currency; the relation in value between the money of two or more countries. **3** a place where merchants or brokers etc. assemble to do business, *a stock exchange*. **4** the central telephone office of a district, where connections are made between lines concerned in calls.

exchangeable *adjective* able to be exchanged.

exchequer *noun* **1** a royal or national treasury. **2** a person's supply of money. [the word refers to the table, covered with a cloth divided into squares (a *chequered* pattern), on which the accounts of the Norman kings were kept by means of counters]

excise[1] (**ek**-syz) *noun* duty or tax levied on certain goods and licences etc. [from a Dutch word meaning 'tax']

excise[2] (ek-**syz**) *verb* to remove by cutting out or away. **excision** (ek-**si**-zhŏn) *noun* [from *ex-* = out, + Latin *caesum* = cut]

excitable *adjective* (of a person) easily excited. **excitability** *noun*

excite *verb* **1** to rouse the feelings of; to cause (a person) to feel strongly; to make eager. **2** to cause (a feeling or reaction), *it excited curiosity*. **3** to produce activity in (a nerve or organ of the body etc.). **4** to cause (a substance) to emit radiation; to put (an atom etc.) into a state of higher energy. [from *ex-* = out, + Latin *citare* = rouse]

excited *adjective* feeling or showing excitement. **excitedly** *adverb*

excitement *noun* **1** a state of great emotion, especially that caused by something pleasant. **2** something causing this.

exciting *adjective* causing great interest or eagerness. **excitingly** *adverb*

exclaim *verb* to cry out or utter suddenly from pain, pleasure, surprise, etc. [from *ex-* = out, + Latin *clamare* = to cry]

exclamation *noun* **1** exclaiming. **2** a word or words etc. exclaimed. ☐ **exclamation mark** the punctuation mark (!) placed after an exclamation.

exclamatory (ěks-**klam**-ǎ-tŏ-ree) *adjective* of, containing, or being an exclamation.

exclude *verb* **1** to keep out (a person or thing) from a place, group, or privilege etc. **2** to omit to ignore as irrelevant, *do not exclude this possibility*. **3** to make impossible, to prevent. **exclusion** *noun* [from *ex-* = out, + Latin *claudere* = to shut]

exclusive *adjective* **1** not admitting something else; *the schemes are mutually exclusive*, if you accept one you must reject the other. **2** (of groups or societies) admitting only certain carefully selected people to membership. **3** (of shops or their goods) high-class, catering only for the wealthy, expensive **4** (of terms etc.) excluding all but what is specified. **5** (of an article in a newspaper or goods in a shop) not published or obtainable elsewhere. **6** done or held etc. so as to exclude everything else, *his exclusive occupation*; *we have the exclusive rights*, not shared with others. – **exclusive** *adverb* not counting, *fifty members exclusive of partners*. **exclusively** *adverb*, **exclusiveness** *noun*, **exclusivity** *noun* [same origin as *exclude*]

excommunicate *verb* to cut off (a person) from participation in a Church, especially in its sacraments. **excommunication** *noun* [from Latin, = put out of the community]

excrement (**eks**-krě-měnt) *noun* faeces.

excrescence (eks-**kress**-ěns) *noun* **1** an outgrowth, especially an abnormal one, on an animal body or a plant. **2** an ugly or disfiguring addition, e.g. to a building. [from *ex-* = out, + Latin *crescens* = growing]

excreta (eks-**kree**-tǎ) *plural noun* waste matter expelled from the body, faeces and urine.

excrete (eks-**kreet**) *verb* to separate and expel (waste matter) from the body or tissues. **excretion** *noun*, **excretory** *adjective* [from *ex-* = out, + Latin *cretum* = separated]

excruciating (eks-**kroo**-shee-ayting) *adjective* **1** intensely painful. **2** (*informal*) very bad. [from *ex-* = thoroughly, + Latin *cruciatum* = tortured]

xculpate (**eks**-kul-payt) *verb* to free (a person) from blame, to clear of a charge of wrongdoing. **exculpation** *noun* [from *ex-* = away, + Latin *culpa* = blame]

xcursion *noun* **1** a short journey or ramble (returning afterwards to the starting point). **2** a pleasure trip made by a group. [from *ex-* = out, + Latin *cursus* = course]

xcursus (eks-**ker**-sŭs) *noun* (*plural* **excursuses**) a digression.

xcusable *adjective* able to be excused. **excusably** *adverb*

xcuse (ĕks-**kewz**) *verb* **1** to overlook or pardon (a slight offence or a person committing it) because of circumstances or some other reason. **2** (of a thing or circumstance) to justify a fault or error, *nothing can excuse such rudeness*. **3** to release from an obligation or duty; to grant exemption to. **–excuse** (ĕks-**kewss**) *noun* a reason put forward as a ground for excusing a fault etc. □ **excuse me** a polite apology for interrupting or disagreeing etc. **excuse oneself** to ask permission to leave; to apologise for leaving. [from *ex-* = away, + Latin *causa* = accusation]

xeat (**eks**-ee-at) *noun* leave of absence from school, college, etc. [Latin, = let him go out]

xecrable (**eks**-ĕ-krǎ-bŭl) *adjective* abominable. **execrably** *adverb*

xecrate (**eks**-ĕ-krayt) *verb* to detest greatly, to utter curses upon. **execration** *noun* [from *ex-*, + Latin *sacer* = holy]

xecutant (ĕg-**zek**-yŭ-tănt) *noun* a performer, especially of music.

xecute *verb* **1** to carry out (an order); to put (a plan etc.) into effect. **2** to perform (an action or manoeuvre). **3** to produce (a work of art). **4** to make legally valid e.g. by signing, *execute a will*. **5** to inflict capital punishment on. [from *ex-* = out, + Latin *sequi* = follow]

xecution *noun* **1** the carrying out or performance of something. **2** skill in playing music. **3** executing a condemned person.

xecutioner *noun* one who executes a condemned person.

xecutive (ĕg-**zek**-yŭ-tiv) *noun* a person or group that has administrative or managerial powers in a business or commercial organisation, or with authority to put the laws or agreements etc. of a government into effect. **–executive** *adjective* having the powers to execute plans or to put laws or agreements etc. into effect.

executor (ĕg-**zek**-yŭ-ter) *noun* a person appointed by a testator to carry out the terms of his or her will. **executrix** *feminine noun*

exegesis (eks-ĕ-**jee**-sĭs) *noun* an explanation of a text, especially of Scripture.

exemplary (ĕg-**zem**-plǎ-ree) *adjective* serving as an example; *exemplary conduct*, very good, an example to others.

exemplify (ĕg-**zem**-plĭ-fy) *verb* (**exemplified**, **exemplifying**) to serve as an example of. **exemplification** *noun*

exempt *adjective* not liable, free from an obligation or payment etc. that is required of others or in other cases. **–exempt** *verb* to make exempt. **exemption** *noun* [from *ex-* = out, + Latin *emptum* = taken]

exercise *noun* **1** the using or application of mental powers or of one's rights. **2** activity requiring physical exertion, done for the sake of health. **3** an activity or task designed for bodily or mental training; *military exercises*, a series of movements or operations designed for the training of troops. **4** an act of worship, *religious exercises*. **–exercise** *verb* **1** to use or employ (mental powers, rights, etc.). **2** to take or cause to take exercise; to train by means of exercises. **3** to perplex, to worry. □ **exercise book** a book for writing in, with a limp cover and ruled pages. [from Latin *exercere* = keep someone working]

exert *verb* to bring (a quality or influence etc.) into use, *exert all one's strength*. □ **exert oneself** to make an effort.

exertion *noun* **1** exerting; being exerted. **2** a great effort.

exeunt (**eks**-ee-ŭnt) *verb* (*stage direction*) they leave the stage. [Latin, = they go out]

exfoliate (eks-**foh**-lee-ayt) *verb* **1** (of tissue or mineral etc.) to come off in scales or layers. **2** (of a tree) to throw off layers of bark. **exfoliation** *noun* [from *ex-*, + Latin *folium* = leaf]

ex gratia (eks **gray**-shǎ) *adjective* done or given as a concession, without legal compulsion, *an ex gratia payment*. [Latin, = from favour]

exhale *verb* to breathe out. **exhalation** *noun* [from *ex-*, + Latin *halare* = breathe]

exhaust *verb* **1** to use up completely. **2** to make empty, to draw out the contents of, *exhaust a well*. **3** to tire out, *exhaust oneself*. **4** to find out or say all there is to say about (a subject); *exhaust the possibilities*, to try them all in turn. **–exhaust** *noun* **1** waste

gases or steam expelled from an engine etc.
2 the device through which they are sent out.
exhaustible *adjective* [from *ex-* = out, + Latin *haustum* = drained]

exhaustion (ĕg-**zaws**-chŏn) *noun*
1 exhausting something; being exhausted.
2 total loss of strength.

exhaustive *adjective* thorough, trying all possibilities, *we made an exhaustive search*. **exhaustively** *adverb*

exhibit (ĕg-**zib**-ĭt) *verb* to display, to present for the public to see. –**exhibit** *noun* a thing or collection of things exhibited. **exhibitor** *noun*

exhibition *noun* **1** exhibiting, being exhibited. **2** a display or show, *an exhibition of temper*. **3** a public display of works of art or industrial products etc. or of a skilled performance. **4** a minor scholarship.
☐ **make an exhibition of oneself** to behave so that one appears ridiculous.

exhibitionist *noun* a person who behaves in a way designed to attract attention to himself or herself. **exhibitionism** *noun*

exhilarate (ĕg-**zil**-ă-rayt) *verb* to make very happy or lively. **exhilaration** *noun* [from *ex-* = thoroughly, + Latin *hilaris* = cheerful (compare *hilarious*)]

exhort (ĕg-**zort**) *verb* to urge or advise earnestly. **exhortation** (eg-zor-**tay**-shŏn) *noun*, **exhortative** *adjective*, **exhortatory** *adjective* [from *ex-*, + Latin *hortari* = encourage]

exhume (eks-**hewm**) *verb* to dig up (something buried), e.g. for examination. **exhumation** (eks-hyoo-**may**-shŏn) *noun* [from *ex-* = out, + Latin *humare* = bury]

exigency (ĕg-**zij**-ĕn-see) *noun* **1** an urgent need, *the exigencies of the situation*. **2** an emergency, *in this exigency*.

exigent (**eks**-ĭ-jĕnt) *adjective* **1** urgent. **2** exacting, requiring much. **exigently** *adverb* [from Latin *exigere* = to exact]

exiguous (ĕg-**zig**-yoo-ŭs) *adjective* very small, scanty. **exiguousness** *noun*

exile *noun* **1** being sent away from one's country as a punishment. **2** long absence from one's country or home. **3** an exiled person. –**exile** *verb* to send (a person) into exile. ☐ **the Exile** the Captivity of the Jews in Babylon in the 6th century BC.

exist *verb* **1** to have a place as part of what is real, *do fairies exist?* **2** to have being under specified conditions, to occur or be found. **3** to

continue living, *we cannot exist without food*. [from *ex-*, + Latin *sistere* = stand]

existence *noun* **1** the state of existing, occurrence, presence. **2** continuance in life or being, *the struggle for existence*.

existent *adjective* existing, actual, current.

existential (eg-zĭs-**ten**-shăl) *adjective* **1** of existence. **2** of human experience as viewed by existentialism. **existentially** *adverb*

existentialism (eg-zĭs-**ten**-shă-lizm) *noun* a philosophical theory emphasising that people are responsible for their own actions and free to choose their development and destiny. **existentialist** *noun*

exit *verb* (*stage direction*) he or she leaves the stage. –**exit** *noun* **1** an actor's or performer's departure from the stage. **2** the act of going away or out, departure from a place or position etc. **3** a passage or door to go out by. –**exit** *verb* (**exited**, **exiting**) to make one's exit [Latin, = he or she goes out]

ex libris (eks **lib**-rĭs) *noun* an inscription indicating the owner of a book. [Latin, 'from the books of']

exocrine (**eks**-ŏ-kryn) *adjective* (of a gland) secreting through a duct.

exodus *noun* a departure of many people. –**Exodus** the second book of the Old Testament, telling of the exodus of the Jews from Egypt. [from Greek, = a way out (*ex* = out, *hodos* = way)]

ex officio (eks ŏ-**fish**-ee-oh) *adverb* because of his or her official position, *the director is a member of this committee ex officio*. –**ex-officio** *adjective* holding a position etc. ex officio, *an ex-officio member*. [Latin, = from office]

exonerate (ĕg-**zon**-ĕ-rayt) *verb* to free from blame, to declare (a person) to be blameless. **exoneration** *noun* [from *ex-* = out, + Latin *oneris* = of a burden]

exorbitant (ĕg-**zorb**-ĭ-tănt) *adjective* (of a price or demand) much too great. [from *ex-* = out, + Latin *orbita* = orbit]

exorcise (**eks**-or-syz) *verb* (also **-ize**) **1** to drive out (an evil spirit) by prayer. **2** to free (a person or place) of evil spirits. **exorcism** *noun*, **exorcist** *noun*

exoskeleton *noun* an external bony or leathery covering on an animal, e.g. the shell of a lobster.

exosphere *noun* the outermost region of the earth's atmosphere.

exothermic *adjective* (of a chemical reaction) giving off heat.

exotic (eg-**zot**-ik) *adjective* **1** (of plants, words, or fashions) introduced from abroad, not native. **2** striking and attractive through being colourful or unusual. **exotically** *adverb* [from Greek *exo* = outside]

expand *verb* **1** to make or become larger, to increase in bulk or importance. **2** to unfold or spread out. **3** to give a fuller account of, to write out in full (what is condensed or abbreviated). **4** to become genial, to throw off one's reserve. **expander** *noun* [from *ex-* = out, + Latin *pandere* = to spread]

expandable *adjective* able to be expanded.

expanse *noun* a wide area or extent of open land or space, etc.

expansion *noun* expanding, increase, extension.

expansionist *noun* a person who wishes a country or business to expand.

expansive *adjective* **1** able or tending to expand. **2** (of a person or manner) genial, communicating thoughts and feelings readily. **expansively** *adverb*, **expansiveness** *noun*

expatiate (ĕks-**pay**-shee-ayt) *verb* to speak or write about (a subject) at great length or in detail. **expatiation** *noun*, **expatiatory** *adjective*

expatriate (eks-**pat**-ree-ayt) *verb* to banish, to withdraw (oneself) from one's native country and live abroad. –**expatriate** (eks-**pat**-ree-ăt) *adjective* expatriated, living abroad; exiled. –**expatriate** (eks-**pat**-ree-ăt) *noun* an expatriate person. **expatriation** *noun* [from *ex-* = away, + Latin *patria* = native land]

expect *verb* **1** to think or believe that (a person or thing) will come or that (a thing) will happen. **2** to wish for and be confident that one will receive, to consider necessary, *he expects obedience*. **3** to think, to suppose. □ **be expecting** (*informal*) to be pregnant. [from *ex-* = out, + Latin *spectare* = to look]

expectant *adjective* filled with expectation. □ **expectant mother** a woman who is pregnant. **expectantly** *adverb*, **expectancy** *noun*

expectation *noun* **1** expecting, looking forward with hope or pleasure. **2** a thing that is expected to happen. **3** the probability that a thing will happen.

expectorant *noun* a medicine that causes a person to expectorate.

expectorate *verb* to cough and spit out phlegm from the throat or lungs, to spit. **expectoration** *noun* [from *ex-*, + Latin *pectoris* = of the chest]

expedient (ĕks-**pee**-dee-ĕnt) *adjective* **1** suitable for a particular purpose. **2** advantageous rather than right or just. –**expedient** *noun* a means of achieving something. **expediently** *adverb*, **expediency** *noun*

expedite (**eks**-pĕ-dyt) *verb* to help or hurry the progress of (business etc.), to perform (business) quickly.

expedition *noun* **1** a journey or voyage for a particular purpose. **2** the people or ships etc. making this. **3** promptness, speed.

expeditionary *adjective* of or used in an expedition, *an expeditionary force*.

expeditious (eks-pĕ-**dish**-ŭs) *adjective* acting or done speedily or efficiently. **expeditiously** *adverb*

expel *verb* (**expelled**, **expelling**) **1** to force or send or drive out. **2** to compel (a person) to leave a school or country etc. [from *ex-* = out, + Latin *pellere* = drive]

expend *verb* to spend (money, time, care, etc.), to use up.

expendable *adjective* **1** able to be expended. **2** not worth preserving, suitable for sacrificing in order to gain an objective.

expenditure *noun* **1** spending of money etc. **2** the amount expended.

expense *noun* **1** the cost or price of an activity. **2** a cause of spending money, *the car was a great expense*. **expenses** *plural noun* the amount spent in doing something; reimbursement for this. □ **at the expense of** so as to cause loss or damage to, *he succeeded but at the expense of his health*.

expensive *adjective* involving great expenditure, costing or charging more than the average. **expensively** *adverb*, **expensiveness** *noun*

experience *noun* **1** actual observation of facts or events; activity or practice in doing something. **2** skill or knowledge gained in this way. **3** an event or activity that gives one experience. –**experience** *verb* to observe or share in (an event etc.) personally, to be affected by (a feeling). [same origin as *experiment*]

experienced *adjective* having knowledge or skill gained from much experience.

experiential *adjective* involving or based on experience.

experiment *noun* a test or trial carried out to see how something works or find out what happens or to demonstrate a known fact. –**experiment** *verb* to conduct an experiment. **experimentation** *noun* [from Latin *experiri* = to test]

experimental *adjective* **1** of or used in or based on experiments. **2** still being tested. **experimentally** *adverb*, **experimentalism** *noun*

expert *noun* a person with great knowledge or skill in a particular thing. –**expert** *adjective* having great knowledge or skill.
□ **expert system** a computer program or set of programs designed to make the skills of experts available to others. **expertly** *adverb*

expertise (eks-per-**teez**) *noun* expert knowledge or skill.

expiate (**eks**-pee-ayt) *verb* to make amends for (wrongdoing). **expiation** *noun*, **expiatory** *adjective*

expire *verb* **1** to breathe out (air). **2** to breathe one's last, to die. **3** to come to the end of its period of validity, *this licence has expired*. **expiration** (eks-pĭ-**ray**-shŏn) *noun* [from *ex-*, + Latin *spirare* = breathe]

expiry *noun* the end of a period of validity, e.g. of a licence or contract.

explain *verb* **1** to make plain or clear, to show the meaning of. **2** to account for, *that explains his absence*. [from *ex-*, + Latin *planare* = make level or plain]

explanation *noun* **1** explaining. **2** a statement or fact that explains something.

explanatory (ĕks-**plan**-ă-tŏ-ree) *adjective* serving or intended to explain something.

expletive (ĕks-**plee**-tiv) *noun* a swear word or exclamation.

explicable (ĕks-**plik**-ăbŭl) *adjective* able to be explained.

explicit (ĕks-**pliss**-ĭt) *adjective* stating something in exact terms, not merely implying things. **explicitly** *adverb*, **explicitness** *noun* [from Latin, = unfolded]

explode *verb* **1** to expand suddenly with a loud noise because of the release of internal energy; to cause (a bomb etc.) to do this. **2** (of feelings) to burst out; (of a person) to show sudden violent emotion, *exploded with laughter*. **3** (of a population or a supply of goods etc.) to increase suddenly or rapidly. **4** to destroy (a theory) by showing it to be

false. □ **exploded diagram** one showing the parts of a structure in their relative positions but slightly separated from each other for greater clarity. [from *ex-* = out, + Latin *plaudere* = clap the hands (originally said of the audience clapping or hissing to drive a player off the stage)]

exploit (**eks**-ploit) *noun* a bold or notable deed. –**exploit** (ĕks-**ploit**) *verb* **1** to work or develop (mines and other natural resources). **2** to take full advantage of, to use (workers, resources, etc.) for one's own advantage. **exploitation** *noun*

exploratory (ĕks-**plo**-ră-tŏ-ree) *adjective* for the purpose of exploring.

explore *verb* **1** to travel into or through (a country etc.) in order to learn about it. **2** to examine by touch. **3** to examine or investigate (a problem, possibilities, etc.). **exploration** *noun* [from Latin, = search out]

explorer *noun* a person who explores unknown regions.

explosion *noun* **1** exploding; being exploded; a loud noise caused by this. **2** a sudden outburst of anger, laughter, etc. **3** a sudden great increase, *the population explosion*.

explosive *adjective* **1** able to explode, tending to explode. **2** likely to cause violent and dangerous reactions, dangerously tense, *an explosive situation*. –**explosive** *noun* an explosive substance. **explosively** *adverb*

exponent (ĕks-**poh**-nĕnt) *noun* **1** a person who sets out the facts or interprets something. **2** one who favours a particular theory or policy. **3** a raised figure or other symbol beside a number etc. (e.g. ^{3} in 2^3) indicating how many times the number is to be multiplied by itself.

exponential (eks-pŏ-**nen**-shăl) *adjective* (in mathematics) of or indicated by an exponent. □ **exponential curve** a curve representing an **exponential function**, in which a fixed quantity is multiplied by itself the number of times indicated by a variable exponent.

export (eks-**port** *or* **eks**-port) *verb* to send (goods etc.) to another country for sale. –**export** (**eks**-port) *noun* **1** exporting. **2** a thing exported. **exportation** *noun*, **exporter** *noun*, **exportable** *adjective* [from *ex-* = away, + Latin *portare* = carry]

expose *verb* **1** to leave (a person or thing) uncovered or unprotected, especially from the weather. **2** to subject to a risk etc. **3** to allow light to reach (photographic film or plate).

4 to make visible, to reveal. **5** to make known or reveal (a crime, fraud, impostor, etc.); to reveal the wrongdoings of (a person). [from *ex-* = out, + Latin *positum* = put]

exposition *noun* **1** expounding; an explanatory account of a plan or theory etc. **2** a large public exhibition. **3** (in music) the part of a movement in which themes are presented.

expostulate (ĕks-**poss**-tew-layt) *verb* to make a friendly protest, to reason or argue with a person. **expostulation** *noun*

exposure *noun* **1** exposing or being exposed to air, cold, or danger etc.; *died of exposure*, from the effects of being exposed to cold. **2** the exposing of photographic film or plate to the light; the length of time for which this is done. **3** a section of film exposed as a unit. **4** publicity. □ **exposure meter** a device measuring light and indicating the length of time needed for a photographic exposure.

expound *verb* to set forth or explain in detail.

express[1] *adjective* **1** definitely stated, not merely implied. **2** going or sent quickly; designed for high speed; (of a train or lift etc.) travelling rapidly to its destination with few or no intermediate stops. **3** (of a letter or parcel) delivered quickly by a special messenger or service. –**express** *adverb* at high speed, by express service. –**express** *noun* an express train. –**express** *verb* to send by express service.

express[2] *verb* **1** to make known (feelings or qualities). **2** to put (a thought etc.) into words. **3** to represent by means of symbols, e.g. in mathematics. **4** to press or squeeze out. □ **express oneself** to communicate one's thoughts or feelings.

expressible *adjective* able to be expressed.

expression *noun* **1** expressing, being expressed. **2** a word or phrase. **3** a look that expresses one's feelings. **4** speaking or playing music in a way that shows feeling for the meaning. **5** a collection of mathematical symbols expressing a quantity.

expressionism *noun* a style of painting, drama, or music seeking to express the artist's or writer's emotional experience rather than to represent the physical world realistically. **expressionist** *noun*

expressionless *adjective* without positive expression, not revealing one's thoughts or feelings, *an expressionless face*.

expressive *adjective* **1** serving to express, *a tone expressive of contempt*. **2** full of expression, *an expressive voice*. **expressively** *adverb*, **expressiveness** *noun*

expressly *adverb* **1** explicitly. **2** for a particular purpose.

expressway *noun* a multi-laned highway with separate carriageways for each direction and limited access, designed for high-speed traffic.

expulsion *noun* expelling; being expelled.

expulsive *adjective* expelling.

expunge (ĕks-**punj**) *verb* to wipe or rub out, to delete.

expurgate (**eks**-per-gayt) *verb* to remove objectionable matter from (a book etc.), to remove (such matter). **expurgation** *noun*, **expurgator** *noun*

exquisite (**eks**-kwiz-ĭt) *adjective* **1** having special beauty. **2** having excellent discrimination, *exquisite taste in dress*. **3** acute, keenly felt, *exquisite pain*. **exquisitely** *adverb* [from *ex-* = out, + Latin *quaesitum* = sought]

ex-service *adjective* formerly belonging to the armed services.

ex-serviceman, **ex-servicewoman** *nouns* a former member of the armed services.

extant (eks-**tant**) *adjective* still existing.

extempore (eks-**tem**-pŏ-ree) *adverb* & *adjective* (spoken or done) without preparation, impromptu. **extemporaneous** *adjective*

extemporise (eks-**tem**-peryz) *verb* (also -**ize**) to speak or produce extempore. **extemporisation** *noun* [from Latin *ex tempore* = impromptu (literally 'out of time')]

extend *verb* **1** to make longer in space or time. **2** to stretch out (a hand or foot or limb etc.). **3** to reach, to be continuous over an area or from one point to another, *our land extends to the river*. **4** to enlarge, to increase the scope of. **5** to offer or grant, *extend a welcome*. **6** (of a task) to stretch the ability of (a person) fully. □ **extended family** a family including all relatives living near. **extender** *noun* [from *ex-* = out, + Latin *tendere* = stretch]

extendible, **extensible**, **extensile** *adjectives* able to be extended.

extension *noun* **1** extending; being extended. **2** extent, range. **3** an addition or continuance; a section extended from the main part. **4** an additional period. **5** a subsidiary telephone distant from the main one; its number.

extensive *adjective* **1** large in area. **2** large in scope, wide-ranging. **extensively** *adverb*, **extensiveness** *noun*

extensor *noun* a muscle that extends or straightens out a part of the body.

extent *noun* **1** the space over which a thing extends. **2** the range or scope of something, *the full extent of his power*. **3** a large area, *an extent of marsh*.

extenuate (ĕks-**ten**-yoo-ayt) *verb* to make (a person's guilt or offence) seem less great by providing a partial excuse, *there were extenuating circumstances*. **extenuation** *noun*

exterior *adjective* on or coming from the outside. –**exterior** *noun* an exterior surface, part, or appearance. [Latin, = further out]

exterminate *verb* to get rid of by destroying all members or examples of (a race, disease, etc.). **extermination** *noun*, **exterminator** *noun* [from *ex-* = out, + Latin *terminus* = boundary]

external *adjective* **1** of or on the outside or visible part of something. **2** of or on the outside of the body, *for external use only*. **3** coming or obtained from an independent source, *external influences*. **4** belonging to the world outside a person or people, not in the mind. **externals** *plural noun* outward appearances. **externally** *adverb*

extinct *adjective* **1** no longer existing in living form, *extinct animals*. **2** (of a volcano) no longer active. **3** no longer burning. [same origin as *extinguish*]

extinction *noun* **1** extinguishing, being extinguished. **2** making or becoming extinct.

extinguish *verb* **1** to put out (a light, fire, or flame). **2** to end the existence of (hope, passion, etc.). [from Latin *extinguere* = quench]

extinguisher *noun* a device for discharging liquid chemicals or foam to extinguish a fire.

extirpate (**eks**-ter-payt) *verb* to root out and destroy completely. **extirpation** *noun*

extol (ĕks-**tohl**) *verb* (**extolled**, **extolling**) to praise enthusiastically.

extort *verb* to obtain by force, threats, or intimidation etc. **extortion** *noun* extorting (especially money). **extortioner** *noun* [from *ex-* = out, + Latin *tortum* = twisted]

extortionate (ĕks-**tor**-shŏ-năt) *adjective* excessively high in price, (of demands) excessive. **extortionately** *adverb*

extra *adjective* additional, more than is usual or expected. –**extra** *adverb* **1** more than usually, *extra strong*. **2** in addition, *postage extra*. –**extra** *noun* **1** an extra thing, something additional. **2** a thing for which an additional charge is made. **3** a run in cricket scored otherwise than from a hit by the bat. **4** a person engaged temporarily for a minor part or to form one of a crowd in a cinema film. [Latin, = outside]

extra- *prefix* outside; beyond (as in *extraterrestrial*). [from Latin, = outside]

extract (ĕks-**trakt**) *verb* **1** to take out by force or effort (something firmly fixed). **2** to obtain (money, information, etc.) from someone unwilling to give it. **3** to obtain (juice) by suction or pressure; to obtain (a substance) as an extract. **4** to obtain (information from a book etc.); to take or copy passages from (a book). **5** to derive (pleasure etc.). –**extract** (**eks**-trakt) *noun* **1** a substance separated from another by dissolving it or by other treatment. **2** a concentrated substance prepared from another. **3** a passage from a book, play, film, or music. **extractor** *noun* [from *ex-* = out, + Latin *tractum* = pulled]

extraction *noun* **1** extracting. **2** descent, lineage, *he is of Greek extraction*.

extractive *adjective* of or involving extraction; extracting minerals from the ground.

extraditable (eks-tră-**dy**-tă-bŭl) *adjective* liable to extradition; (of a crime) warranting extradition.

extradite (**eks**-tră-dyt) *verb* **1** to hand over (a person accused or convicted of a crime) to the country where the crime was committed. **2** to obtain (such a person) for trial or punishment. **extradition** (eks-tră-**dish**-ŏn) *noun* [from *ex-*, + Latin *traditum* = handed over]

extraneous (ĕks-**tray**-nee-ŭs) *adjective* **1** of external origin. **2** not belonging to the matter or subject in hand. **extraneously** *adverb*

extraordinary (ĕks-**traw**-dĭn-ree) *adjective* **1** very unusual or remarkable. **2** beyond what is usual or ordinary, *an extraordinary general meeting*. **extraordinarily** *adverb*

extrapolate (ĕks-**trap**-ŏ-layt) *verb* to make an estimate of (something unknown and outside the range of one's data) on the basis of available data. **extrapolation** *noun*

extrasensory *adjective* (of perception) achieved by some means other than the known senses.

extraterrestrial *adjective* of or from outside the earth or its atmosphere.

extravagant *adjective* **1** spending much more than is necessary. **2** (of prices) excessively high. **3** (of ideas, praise, or behaviour etc.) going beyond what is reasonable, not properly controlled. **extravagantly** *adverb*, **extravagance** *noun* [from *extra-*, + Latin *vagans* = wandering]

extravaganza (ěks-trav-ǎ-**gan**-ză) *noun* **1** a fanciful composition in music. **2** a lavish spectacular film or theatrical production.

extreme *adjective* **1** very great or intense, *extreme cold.* **2** at the end(s), furthest, outermost, *the extreme edge.* **3** going to great lengths in actions or views, not moderate. –**extreme** *noun* **1** either end of anything. **2** an extreme degree or act or condition. **extremely** *adverb* [from Latin, = furthest outside]

extremist *noun* a person who holds extreme views, especially in politics. **extremism** *noun*

extremity (ěks-**trem**-ĭ-tee) *noun* **1** an extreme point, the end of something. **2** an extreme degree of feeling or need or danger etc. **extremities** *plural noun* the hands and feet.

extricate (**eks**-trĭ-kayt) *verb* to disentangle or release from an entanglement or difficulty etc. **extricable** *adjective*, **extrication** *noun* [from *ex-*, + Latin *tricae* = entanglements]

extrovert (**eks**-trŏ-vert) *noun* a person more interested in the people and things around than in his or her own thoughts and feelings; a lively sociable person. **extroverted** *adjective* having these characteristics. [from *extro-* = outside, + Latin *vertere* = to turn]

extrude *verb* **1** to thrust or squeeze out. **2** to shape (metal or plastic etc.) by forcing through a die. **extrusion** *noun* [from *ex-*, + Latin *trudere* = to push]

extrusive *adjective* (of rock) produced by volcanic eruption (contrasted with *intrusive*).

exuberant (ěg-**zew**-bĕ-rănt) *adjective* **1** full of high spirits, very lively. **2** growing profusely, *plants with exuberant foliage.* **exuberantly** *adverb*, **exuberance** *noun*

exude (ěg-**zewd**) *verb* **1** to give off like sweat or a smell; (of liquid etc.) to ooze out in this way. **2** to show (pleasure, confidence, etc.) freely. **exudation** (eks-yoo-**day**-shŏn) *noun*

exult (ěg-**zult**) *verb* to rejoice greatly. **exultant** *adjective*, **exultation** *noun*

> Usage *Exult* is sometimes confused with *exalt* which means 'to raise in power or rank'.

eye *noun* **1** the organ of sight in man and animals. **2** the iris of this, *blue eyes.* **3** the region round it, *gave him a black eye.* **4** the power of seeing, observation, *sharp eyes.* **5** a thing like an eye; a spot on a peacock's tail; a leaf bud on a potato. **6** the hole in a needle, through which thread is passed. –**eye** *verb* (**eyed**, **eyeing**) to look at, to watch. ☐ **cast** or **run an eye over** to examine quickly. **eye of a storm** a relatively calm spot at the centre of a storm. **eye of the wind** the point from which the wind is blowing. **in the eyes of** in the opinion or judgment of. **keep an eye on** to watch carefully, to take care of. **make eyes at** to gaze at flirtatiously. **pick the eyes out of** to choose the best parts of. **see eye to eye** to be in full agreement with a person. **up to the eyes** deeply involved or occupied in something. **with an eye to** with the aim or intention of; with prudent attention to. **with one's eyes open** with full awareness.

eyeball *noun* the ball of the eye, within the lids. –**eyeball** *verb* (*informal*) to stare at.

eyebrow *noun* the fringe of hair growing on the ridge above the eye socket.

eyeful *noun* (*plural* **eyefuls**) **1** something thrown or blown into one's eye. **2** (*informal*) a thorough look, *having an eyeful.* **3** (*informal*) a remarkable or attractive sight.

eyeglass *noun* a lens for a defective eye.

eyelash *noun* one of the fringe of hairs on the edge of each eyelid.

eyeless *adjective* having no eyes.

eyelet *noun* **1** a small hole through which a rope or cord etc. is passed. **2** a metal ring strengthening this.

eyelid *noun* either of the two folds of skin that can be moved together to cover the eyeball.

eyeliner *noun* a cosmetic applied as a line round the eye.

eye-opener *noun* a fact or circumstance that brings enlightenment or great surprise.

eyepiece *noun* the lens or lenses to which the eye is applied at the end of a telescope or microscope etc.

315

eye-shade *noun* a device to protect eyes from strong light.

eyeshadow *noun* a cosmetic applied to the skin round the eyes.

eyesight *noun* **1** the ability to see. **2** range of vision, *within eyesight*.

eyesore *noun* a thing that is ugly to look at.

eyetooth *noun* (*plural* eyeteeth) a canine tooth in the upper jaw, under the eye.

eyewash *noun* **1** a lotion for the eye. **2** (*informal*) talk or behaviour intended to create a misleadingly good impression.

eyewitness *noun* a person who actually saw an accident or crime etc. take place.

Eyre, Edward John (1815–1901), English explorer, who made the first overland journey from Adelaide to King George Sound (WA). ☐ Lake Eyre a lake in SA, the largest Australian salt lake, 16 m below sea level.

eyrie (**eer**-ree) *noun* **1** the nest of an eagle or other bird of prey. **2** a house etc. perched high up.

Ezekiel (ĕ-**zee**-kee-ĕl) **1** a Hebrew prophet of the 6th century BC. **2** the book of the Old Testament containing his prophecies.

Ezra 1 a Jewish priest and scribe of the 5th or 4th century BC. **2** the book of the Old Testament dealing with the return of the Jews from Babylon under his leadership.

Ff

F *abbreviation* Fahrenheit.

Fabian (**fay**-bee-ăn) *noun* a member of the Fabian Society, an English socialist society founded in 1884, seeking social change through gradual reform. [named after the Roman general Fabius (c. 200 BC) whose strategy of caution and delay was successful against the Carthaginian invaders]

fable *noun* **1** a short (usually supernatural) story not based on fact, often with animals as characters and conveying a moral. **2** these stories or legends collectively. **3** an untrue account of something. [from Latin *fabula* = story]

fabled *adjective* told of in fables, legendary.

fabric *noun* **1** cloth, woven or knitted or felted material. **2** a plastic resembling this. **3** the frame or structure of something, the walls and floors and roof of a building.

fabricate *verb* **1** to construct, to manufacture. **2** to invent (a story); to forge (a document). **fabrication** *noun*, **fabricator** *noun*

fabulous *adjective* **1** told of in fables. **2** incredibly great, *fabulous wealth*. **3** (*informal*) wonderful, marvellous. **fabulously** *adverb*

façade (fă-**sahd**) *noun* (also **facade**) **1** the principal face or the front of a building. **2** an outward appearance, especially a deceptive one. [French (same origin as *face*)]

face *noun* **1** the front part of the head from forehead to chin. **2** the expression shown by its features, *a cheerful face*; *make* or *pull a face*, make a grimace. **3** the outward show or aspect of something. **4** the front or façade or right side of something; the dial-plate of a clock; the distinctive side of a playing card. **5** a coalface. **6** the striking-surface of a bat etc.; the working-surface of a tool. –**face** *verb* **1** to have or turn the face towards (a certain direction). **2** to be opposite to. **3** to meet confidently or defiantly; to accept and be prepared to deal with (unpleasant facts or problems). **4** to meet (an opponent) in a contest. **5** to present itself to, *the problem that faces us*. **6** to cover (a surface) with a layer of different material; to put a facing

on (a garment etc.). ☐ **face the music** to face unpleasant consequences bravely. **face up to** to face (a difficulty etc.) resolutely. **face value** the value printed or stamped on money; *take a thing at its face value*, assume that it is genuinely what it seems to be. **face washer** a facecloth. **have the face** to be impudent enough. **in the face of** despite. **lose face** to suffer loss of prestige through a humiliation. **save face** to avoid humiliation. **to a person's face** openly in his or her presence. [from Latin *facies* = appearance]

facebook *noun* (also **Facebook**) (*trademark*) a social networking site on the Internet. –**facebook** *verb* search for (someone) on the facebook site; post (something) on the facebook site.

facecloth *noun* a cloth for washing the face.

faceless *adjective* **1** without a face. **2** without identity. **3** purposely not identifiable.

facelift *noun* **1** cosmetic surgery to remove wrinkles etc. by tightening the skin of the face. **2** an alteration etc. that improves the appearance, e.g. of a building.

facet (**fas**-ĕt) *noun* **1** each of the many sides of a cut stone or jewel. **2** each aspect of a situation or problem.

facetious (fă-**see**-shŭs) *adjective* intended or intending to be amusing. **facetiously** *adverb*, **facetiousness** *noun*

facia (**fay**-shă) *noun* the instrument panel of a motor vehicle, the dashboard.

facial (**fay**-shăl) *adjective* of the face. –**facial** *noun* a beauty treatment for the face.

facile (**fa**-syl) *adjective* **1** easily done. **2** (of a person) able to do something easily, *a facile speaker*. **3** achieved easily but without attention to quality, superficial, *a facile solution*. [from Latin *facilis* = easy]

facilitate (fă-**sil**-ĭ-tayt) *verb* to make easy, to lessen the difficulty of. **facilitation** *noun*

facility (fă-**sil**-ĭ-tee) *noun* **1** the quality of being easy, absence of difficulty. **2** ease in doing something, *reads music with great facility*. **3** an opportunity or some equipment etc. that makes it easy to do something, *you shall have every facility*; *sports facilities*.

facing *noun* **1** an outer layer covering a surface. **2** a layer of material covering part of a garment etc. for contrast or to strengthen it.

facsimile (fak-**sim**-ĭ-lee) *noun* a reproduction of a document, book, or painting etc. [from Latin *fac* = make, + *simile* = a likeness]

fact *noun* **1** something known to have happened or to be true or to exist. **2** a thing asserted to be true as a basis for reasoning. □ **facts of life** (*informal*) knowledge of human sexual functions. [from Latin *factum* = thing done]

faction (**fak**-shŏn) *noun* a small united group within a larger one, especially in politics. **factional** *adjective*, **factionally** *adverb*

factitious (fak-**tish**-ŭs) *adjective* made for a special purpose, contrived.

factor *noun* **1** a circumstance or influence that contributes towards a result; *safety factor*, the margin of security against risks. **2** any of the numbers or mathematical expressions by which a larger number etc. can be divided exactly, *1, 2, 3, and 6 are factors of 6*. **3** a business agent.

factorial *noun* the product of a number and all those below it, *factorial four = 4 × 3 × 2 × 1*. (Symbol !). –**factorial** *adjective* of a factor or factorial.

factorise *verb* (also -ize) to find the factors of, to express in factors. **factorisation** *noun*

factory *noun* a building or buildings in which goods are manufactured. □ **factory farm** one organised on industrial lines. [from Latin *facere* = make or do]

factotum (fak-**toh**-tŭm) *noun* a servant or assistant doing all kinds of work. [from Latin *fac* = do, + *totum* = everything]

factual *adjective* based on or concerning facts. **factually** *adverb*

faculty (**fak**-ŭl-tee) *noun* **1** any of the powers of the body or mind, *the faculty of sight*. **2** a particular kind of ability, *a faculty for learning languages*. **3** a department teaching a particular subject in a university or college, *the Arts faculty*.

fad *noun* a person's particular like or dislike, a craze. **faddish** *adjective*, **faddist** *noun*

faddy *adjective* having petty likes and dislikes, e.g. about food. **faddiness** *noun*

fade *verb* **1** to lose or cause to lose colour, freshness, or vigour. **2** to disappear gradually, to become indistinct. **3** to cause (the sound or picture in broadcasting or cinema) to decrease or increase gradually. –**fade** *noun* an act or sound of fading. □ **fade-out** *noun* the fading out of something, especially a broadcast or cinema sound or picture.

faeces (**fee**-seez) *plural noun* waste matter discharged from the bowels. **faecal** (**fee**-kăl) *adjective*

Faeroe Islands (**fair**-roh) (also Faeroes) a group of islands in the North Atlantic between Iceland and Shetland, belonging to Denmark but partly independent. **Faeroese** *adjective & noun*

fag *verb* (fagged, fagging) to make tired, to exhaust. –**fag** *noun* **1** tiring work, drudgery, *what a fag!* **2** (*informal*) a cigarette. □ **fagged** or **fagged out** tired out.

faggot *noun* **1** a bundle of sticks or twigs bound together. **2** a ball of chopped seasoned liver, served baked.

faggoting *noun* embroidery in which threads are fastened together like faggots.

Fahrenheit (**fa**-rĕn-hyt) *adjective* of or using a temperature scale with the freezing point of water at 32° and the boiling point at 212°. [named after the German physicist G. Fahrenheit (died 1736)]

faience *noun* decorated and glazed earthenware and porcelain.

fail *verb* **1** to be unsuccessful in what is attempted. **2** to be or become insufficient; (of crops) to produce a very poor harvest. **3** to become weak or ineffective, to cease functioning, *the engine failed*. **4** to neglect or forget or be unable to do something, *he failed to appear*. **5** to disappoint the hopes of. **6** to become bankrupt. **7** to grade (a candidate) as not having passed an examination. –**fail** *noun* failure in an examination. □ **fail-safe** *adjective* (of equipment) reverting to a danger-free condition in the event of a breakdown or other failure. **without fail** for certain, whatever happens.

failing *noun* a weakness or fault. –**failing** *preposition* if (a thing) does not happen; if (a person) is not available.

failure *noun* **1** failing, non-performance of something, lack of success. **2** the ceasing of mechanism or power or a part of the body etc. to function, *heart failure*. **3** becoming bankrupt. **4** an unsuccessful person or thing or attempt.

fain *adverb* (old use) willingly.

faint *adjective* **1** not clearly perceived by the senses, indistinct; not intense in colour, sound, or smell. **2** weak, vague, *a faint hope*. **3** timid, feeble. **4** about to lose consciousness. **–faint** *verb* to lose consciousness temporarily through failure in the supply of blood to the brain. **–faint** *noun* an act or state of fainting. □ **faint-hearted** *adjective* timid. **faintly** *adverb*, **faintness** *noun*

fair¹ *noun* **1** a periodical gathering for the sale of goods, often with shows and entertainments, *the school's spring fair*. **2** an exhibition of commercial or industrial goods. **3** a gathering of amusements, sideshows, etc. for public entertainment. [from Latin *feriae* = holiday]

fair² *adjective* **1** (of the hair or skin) light in colour; (of a person) having fair hair. **2** (*old use*) beautiful. **3** (of weather) fine; (of winds) favourable. **4** just, unbiased, in accordance with the rules. **5** of moderate quality or amount. **–fair** *adverb* in a fair manner. □ **fair and square** straightforwardly, above board; exactly. **fair copy** a neat copy of a corrected document. **fair enough!** (*informal*) that is a reasonable or satisfactory proposition. **fair game** a legitimate target. **fair go** (*Austral.*), **fair play** equal opportunities and treatment for all. [from Old English *faeger*]

fairing *noun* a structure added to the exterior of a ship or aircraft etc. to streamline it.

Fair Isle one of the Shetland Islands, noted for its knitting designs in coloured wools.

fairly *adverb* **1** in a fair manner. **2** moderately, *fairly difficult*. **3** actually, *fairly jumped for joy*. □ **fairly and squarely** = fair and square.

fairway *noun* **1** a navigable channel. **2** part of a golf course between tee and green, kept free of rough grass.

fairy *noun* an imaginary small being supposed to have magical powers. □ **fairy floss** a fluffy mass of spun sugar. **fairy godmother** a benefactress who provides a sudden unexpected gift. **fairy lights** strings of small decorative coloured lights. **fairy penguin** a small blue-grey and white penguin. **fairy story**, **fairy tale** a tale about fairies or magic; an incredible story; a falsehood. [from an old word *fay*, from Latin *fata* = the Fates, three goddesses, who were believed to control people's lives]

fairyland *noun* **1** the world of fairies. **2** a very beautiful place.

fait accompli (fayt ah-**kom**-plee) *noun* a thing that is already done and not reversible. [French]

faith *noun* **1** reliance or trust in a person or thing. **2** belief in a religious doctrine. **3** a system of religious belief, *the Christian faith*. **4** a promise, loyalty, sincerity. □ **break faith** to break one's promise or loyalty. **faith cure** something that heals a person because he or she believes that it will do so. **faith healer** a person who practises **faith healing**, healing by prayer and religious faith, not by medical skill. **in good faith** with honest intention.

faithful *adjective* **1** loyal, trustworthy, conscientious. **2** true to the facts, accurate. **– the faithful** true believers (especially Muslims or Christians); loyal supporters. □ **Yours faithfully** *see* **yours**. **faithfully** *adverb*, **faithfulness** *noun*

faithless *adjective* **1** lacking religious faith. **2** false to promises, disloyal.

fake *noun* **1** something that looks genuine but is not, a forgery. **2** a person who tries to deceive others by pretending falsely to be something that he or she is not. **–fake** *adjective* faked, not genuine. **–fake** *verb* **1** to make (a thing) that looks genuine, in order to deceive people. **2** to pretend, *he faked illness*. **faker** *noun*

fakir (**fay**-keer) *noun* a Muslim or Hindu religious beggar regarded as a holy man. [Arabic, = a poor man]

Falangist (fă-**lan**-jĭst) *noun* **1** a member of a Christian political party in Lebanon. **2** a member of the Spanish Fascist and right-wing political party.

falcon (**fawl**-kŏn) *noun* a small long-winged hawk. **falconry** *noun* the breeding and training of hawks.

Falkland Islands (**fawlk**-lănd *or* **fawk**-) (also **Falklands**) a group of islands in the South Atlantic, a British dependency, captured by Argentina and recaptured by Britain in 1982. (The islands are known in Argentina as *Malvinas*.)

fall *verb* (**fell**, **fallen**, **falling**) **1** to come or go down freely, e.g. by force of weight or loss of balance or becoming detached. **2** to come as if by falling, *silence fell*. **3** to lose one's position or office, *fell from power*. **4** to hang down. **5** to decrease in amount, number, or intensity, *prices fell*; *her spirits fell*, she became depressed. **6** to slope downwards. **7** (of the face) to show dismay. **8** to cease to stand; *six wickets fell*, six batsmen were out. **9** to die in battle. **10** (of a fortress or city) to be captured. **11** to pass into a specified state, to become, *fall in love*; *fell asleep*. **12** to occur, to have as a date, *Easter fell early*. –**fall** *noun* **1** the act of falling. **2** giving way to temptation; **the Fall (of man)** Adam's sin and its results. **3** the amount by which something falls. **4** (*Amer.*) autumn. **falls** *plural noun* a waterfall. □ **fall back on** to retreat to; to turn to for help when something else has failed. **fall behind** to lag; to be in arrears. **fall down on** to fail in. **fall flat** to fail to produce a result. **fall for** (*informal*) to fall in love with; to be taken in by (a deception). **fall foul of** to collide with; to get into trouble with. **fall guy** (*informal*) an easy victim; a scapegoat. **fall in** to take one's place in military formation, to cause (troops) to do this; (of a building) to collapse inwards; to be deceived. **falling star** a meteor. **fall in with** to meet by chance; to agree to. **fall off** to decrease in size or number or quality. **fall out** to quarrel; to happen; to leave one's place in a military formation, to cause (troops) to do this. **fall over oneself** to be very awkward; to be very hasty or eager. **fall short** to be insufficient or inadequate. **fall short of** to fail to obtain or reach. **fall through** (of a plan) to fail, to come to nothing. **fall to** to begin working, fighting, or eating.

fallacious (fă-**lay**-shŭs) *adjective* containing a fallacy. **fallaciously** *adverb*, **fallaciousness** *noun*

fallacy (**fal**-ă-see) *noun* **1** a false or mistaken belief. **2** faulty reasoning. [from Latin *fallere* = deceive]

fallible (**fal**-ĭ-bŭl) *adjective* liable to make mistakes. **fallibility** (fal-ĭ-**bil**-ĭ-tee) *noun*

Fallopian tube (fă-**loh**-pee-ăn) *noun* either of two tubes carrying egg cells from the ovaries to the womb.

fallout *noun* **1** airborne radioactive debris from a nuclear explosion. **2** the adverse side effects of a situation.

fallow (**fal**-oh) *adjective* (of land) ploughed but left unplanted in order to restore its fertility.

fallow deer *noun* a kind of small deer, white-spotted in summer.

false *adjective* **1** wrong, incorrect. **2** deceitful, lying, unfaithful. **3** not genuine, sham, artificial, *false teeth*; *false economy*, one that does not result in a genuine saving. **4** improperly so called; *the false acacia*, not really an acacia tree. □ **false pretences** acts intended to deceive. **falsely** *adverb*, **falseness** *noun* [from Latin *falsum* = deceived]

falsehood *noun* **1** an untrue statement, a lie. **2** telling lies.

falsetto (fol-**set**-oh *or* fawl-) *noun* (*plural* **falsettos**) a high-pitched voice above one's natural range, especially when used by male singers. –**falsetto** *adverb* in a falsetto voice.

falsify *verb* (**falsified**, **falsifying**) **1** to alter (a document) fraudulently. **2** to misrepresent (facts). **falsification** *noun*

falsity *noun* **1** falseness. **2** a falsehood, an error.

falter *verb* **1** to go or function unsteadily. **2** to become weaker, to begin to give way, *his courage faltered*. **3** to speak or utter hesitatingly, to stammer. **falteringly** *adverb*

Falun Gong (**fal**-ŭn-gong) (a Taoist– Buddhist sect practising) a spiritual exercise and meditation regime with similarities to t'ai chi.

fame *noun* **1** the condition of being known to many people. **2** a good reputation.

famed *adjective* famous.

familiar *adjective* **1** well known, often seen or experienced, *a familiar sight*. **2** lacking formality, friendly and informal, *addressed him in familiar terms*. **3** too informal, assuming a greater degree of informality or friendship than is proper. **familiarly** *adverb*, **familiarity** *noun* [same origin as *family*]

familiarise *verb* (also **-ize**) **1** to make well acquainted (with a person or thing). **2** to make well known. **familiarisation** *noun*

family *noun* **1** parents and their children. **2** a person's children, *they have a large family*. **3** a set of relatives. **4** all the descendants of a common ancestor; their line of descent. **5** a group of things that are alike in some way. **6** a group of related plants or animals, *lions belong to the cat family*. □ **family circle** a group of close relatives. **Family Court of Australia** the court that administers family law, including divorce and custody matters. **family name** a surname. **family payment** a regular payment made by the government to families with an income below a certain level. **family planning** birth control. **family tree** a diagram showing how people in a family are related. [from Latin *familia* = household]

famine *noun* extreme scarcity (especially of food) in a region. [from Latin *fames* = hunger]

famished, **famishing** *adjectives* suffering from extreme hunger. [same origin as *famine*]

famous *adjective* **1** known to very many people. **2** (*informal*) excellent. **famously** *adverb*

fan[1] *noun* a device waved in the hand or operated mechanically to create a current of air. –**fan** *verb* (**fanned**, **fanning**) **1** to drive a current of air upon, with or as if with a fan. **2** to stimulate (flames etc.) in this way. **3** to spread from a central point, *troops fanned out*. □ **fan belt** a belt driving the fan that cools the radiator of a motor vehicle.

fan[2] *noun* an enthusiastic admirer or supporter. □ **fan club** an organised group of a person's admirers. **fan mail** letters from fans to the person they admire. [originally short for *fanatic*]

fanatic (fă-**nat**-ik) *noun* a person filled with excessive enthusiasm for something. **fanatical** *adjective*, **fanatically** *adverb*, **fanaticism** *noun*

fancier *noun* **1** a person with special knowledge of and love for something, *a cat fancier*. **2** one whose hobby is breeding animals or growing plants.

fanciful *adjective* **1** (of people) using the imagination freely, imagining things. **2** existing only in the imagination. **3** (of things) designed in a quaint or imaginative style. **fancifully** *adverb*

fancy *noun* **1** the power of imagining things, especially of an unreal or fantastic sort. **2** something imagined, an unfounded idea or belief. **3** an unreasoning desire for something. **4** a liking. –**fancy** *adjective* **1** ornamental, not plain, elaborate. **2** based on imagination not fact. –**fancy** *verb* (**fancied**, **fancying**) **1** to imagine. **2** to be inclined to believe or suppose. **3** (*informal*) to take a fancy to, to like. □ **fancy dress** a costume representing an animal, character of history or fiction, etc. **fancy-free** *adjective* without (especially emotional) commitments. **fancy oneself** (*informal*) to be conceited, to admire oneself. [originally a shortened spelling of *fantasy*]

fandango *noun* (*plural* **fandangoes**) **1** a lively Spanish dance for two people; music for this. **2** nonsense, tomfoolery. [Spanish]

fanfare *noun* a short showy or ceremonious sounding of trumpets.

fang *noun* **1** a long sharp tooth, especially of dogs and wolves. **2** a snake's tooth with which it injects venom.

fanlight *noun* a small (originally semicircular) window above a door or another window.

fantail *noun* a kind of pigeon or flycatcher with a fan-shaped tail.

fantasia (fan-**tay**-zee-ă) *noun* an imaginative musical or other composition.

fantasise (**fan**-tă-syz) *verb* (also **-ize**) to imagine in fantasy; to daydream.

fantastic *adjective* **1** absurdly fanciful. **2** designed in a very imaginative style. **3** (*informal*) very remarkable, excellent. **fantastically** *adverb*

fantasy *noun* **1** imagination, especially when producing very fanciful ideas. **2** a wild or fantastic product of the imagination, a daydream. **3** a fanciful design; a fantasia.

far *adverb* (**farther** *or* **further**, **farthest** *or* **furthest**) at, to, or by a great distance. –**far** *adjective* distant, remote. □ **a far cry from** greatly different from. **by far** by a great amount. **far and away** by far. **far and wide** over a large area. **Far East** China, Japan, and other countries of east and SE Asia, as perceived by Britain. **far-fetched** *adjective* (of an explanation etc.) strained, traced from something very remote and therefore unlikely. **far-out** *adjective* distant; (*informal*) unconventional, avant-garde; (*informal*) excellent. **far-reaching** *adjective* having a wide range, influence, or effect. **far-seeing** *adjective* showing great foresight.

farad (**fa**-răd) *noun* a unit of capacitance. [from *Faraday*]

Faraday (**fa**-ră-day), Michael (1791–1867), English physicist and chemist, discoverer of electromagnetic induction (the condition under which a permanent magnet can generate electricity).

faraday *noun* a unit of electrical charge used in the study of electrochemical reactions.

faraway *adjective* **1** remote. **2** (of a look) dreamy. **3** (of the voice) sounding as if from a distance.

farce *noun* **1** a light comedy. **2** this kind of drama. **3** absurd and useless proceedings, a pretence. **farcical** (**far**-sĭ-kăl) *adjective*, **farcically** *adverb*

fare *noun* **1** the price charged for a passenger to travel. **2** a passenger who pays a fare, especially for a hired vehicle. **3** food provided. –**fare** *verb* to have good or bad treatment, to progress, *how did they fare?*

farewell *interjection* goodbye. –**farewell** *noun* **1** leave-taking. **2** (*Austral.*) a function to mark a person's leaving a job or district.

–**farewell** verb (Austral.) to say goodbye to a person leaving.

farinaceous (fa-rĭ-**nay**-shŭs) adjective of or like starch or a starchy substance. [from Latin farina = flour]

farm noun 1 an area of land and its buildings, owned or rented by one management, used for raising crops or livestock. 2 a farmhouse. 3 a stretch of water used for raising fish etc. –**farm** verb 1 to grow crops or raise livestock. 2 to use (land) for this purpose. 3 to breed (fish etc.) commercially. ▢ **farm out** to send out or delegate (work) to be done by others.

farmer noun a person who owns or manages a farm.

farmhouse noun a dwelling attached to a farm.

farmyard noun the enclosed area round farm buildings.

farrago (fă-**rah**-goh) noun (plural farragos) a hotchpotch. [Latin, = mixed fodder]

Farrer, William James (1845–1906), wheat-breeder who developed 'Federation wheat'.

farrier (**fa**-ree-er) noun a smith who shoes horses. [from Latin ferrum = iron, an iron horseshoe]

farrow (**fa**-roh) verb (of a sow) to give birth to young pigs. –**farrow** noun 1 farrowing. 2 a litter of young pigs.

Farsi noun the Persian language.

farther adverb & adjective at or to a greater distance, more remote. **farthest** adverb & adjective at or to the greatest distance, most remote.

Usage These words are not commonly used except where the sense of 'distance' is involved, and even there many people prefer to use further and furthest.

farthing noun a former British coin worth one-quarter of a penny. [from Old English feorthing = one-fourth]

farthingale noun a hooped petticoat or padded roll of material formerly worn under a skirt (especially in the reign of Queen Elizabeth I) to make it stand out.

fasces (**fas**-eez) plural noun a bundle of rods with a projecting axe blade, carried before certain officials in ancient Rome as a symbol of authority.

fascia (**fay**-shă) noun 1 a long flat vertical surface of wood or stone, e.g. under eaves or a cornice. 2 = facia.

fascinate verb 1 to attract and hold the interest of; to charm greatly. 2 to deprive (a victim) of the power of escape by a fixed look, as a snake does. **fascination** noun, **fascinator** noun [from Latin, = cast a spell]

fascinating adjective having great attraction or charm.

fascinator noun a light, decorative woman's headpiece.

Fascism (**fash**-izm) noun a system of extreme right-wing dictatorial government. **Fascist** noun [from fasces, used as the emblem of the Italian Fascist party]

fashion noun 1 a manner or way of doing something, continue in this fashion. 2 the popular style of dress, customs, etc. at a given time; fashion shoes, shoes made with fashion (not function) in mind. –**fashion** verb to make into a particular form or shape. ▢ **after** or **in a fashion** to some extent but not very satisfactorily. **in fashion** fashionable. **out of fashion** no longer fashionable.

fashionable adjective 1 in or adopting a style that is currently popular. 2 frequented or used by stylish people, a fashionable hotel. **fashionably** adverb

fast[1] adjective 1 moving or done quickly. 2 producing or allowing quick movement, a fast road. 3 (of a clock etc.) showing a time ahead of the correct one. 4 (of a person) spending too much time and energy on pleasure, immoral. 5 (of photographic film) very sensitive to light; (of a lens) having a large aperture, allowing a short exposure to be used. 6 firmly fixed or attached. 7 (of colours or dyes) unlikely to fade or run. –**fast** adverb 1 quickly. 2 firmly, tightly, securely, stuck fast; fast asleep. ▢ **fast buck** (informal) money made quickly. **fast food** quickly-prepared food, especially that served or cooked in a restaurant. **fast-forward** verb to wind (a tape) at an accelerated speed. **fast reactor** a nuclear reactor using high-speed neutrons. **fast-talk** verb (informal) to persuade by eloquent or deceitful talk. **fast-track** verb to expedite. **fast worker** one who makes rapid progress, especially in furthering his or her own interests. **play fast and loose** to change one's attitude repeatedly, to ignore one's obligations.

fast[2] verb to go without food or without certain kinds of food, especially as a religious duty. –**fast** *noun* **1** fasting. **2** a day or season appointed for this.

fasten *verb* **1** to fix firmly, to tie or join together. **2** to fix (one's glance or attention) intently. **3** to become fastened, *the door fastens with a latch*. □ **fasten off** to tie or secure the end of a thread etc. **fasten on** to lay hold of; to single out for attack; to seize as a pretext.

fastener *noun* (also **fastening**) a device for fastening something.

fastidious (fas-**tid**-ee-ŭs) *adjective* **1** selecting carefully, choosing only what is good. **2** easily disgusted. **fastidiously** *adverb*, **fastidiousness** *noun*

fastness *noun* **1** the state of being fast or firm, *colour fastness*. **2** a stronghold.

fat *noun* **1** a whitish or yellowish substance, insoluble in water, found in animal bodies and certain seeds. **2** this substance prepared for use in cooking. –**fat** *adjective* (**fatter**, **fattest**) **1** containing much fat, covered with fat. **2** excessively plump. **3** (of an animal) made plump for slaughter. **4** thick, *a fat book*. **5** (*informal*) very little, not much, *a fat lot*; *fat chance*. **fatness** *noun*

fatal *adjective* **1** causing or ending in death. **2** causing disaster, *a fatal mistake*. **3** fateful, *the fatal day*. **fatally** *adverb*

fatalist *noun* a person who accepts and submits to what happens, regarding it as inevitable. **fatalism** *noun*, **fatalistic** *adjective*

fatality (fă-**tal**-ĭ-tee) *noun* death caused by accident or in war etc.; a victim of this.

fate *noun* **1** a power thought to control all events and impossible to resist. **2** a person's destiny. **Fates** *plural noun* (*Gk. myth.*) the three goddesses who presided over people's lives and deaths.

fated *adjective* destined by fate, doomed.

fateful *adjective* bringing or producing great and usually unpleasant events.

fathead *noun* (*informal*) a stupid person.

father *noun* **1** a male parent. **2** a male ancestor, *land of our fathers*. **3** the founder or originator of something. **4 the Father** God, the first person of the Trinity. **5** the title of certain priests, especially those belonging to religious orders. –**father** *verb* **1** to beget, to be the father of. **2** to found or originate (an idea or plan etc.). **3** to fix the paternity of (a child) on a certain person. □ **Father Christmas** = **Santa Claus**. **father figure** an older man who is respected and trusted by others like a father.

father-in-law *noun* (*plural* **fathers-in-law**) the father of one's wife or husband. **Father's Day** a tribute to fathers, in Australia the first Sunday in September. **fatherly** *adjective*, **fatherhood** *noun* [from Old English *faeder*]

fatherland *noun* one's native country.

fatherless *adjective* without a living father; without a known father.

fathom *noun* a measure of 6 feet (1.83 m), used in stating the depth of water. –**fathom** *verb* **1** to measure the depth of. **2** to get to the bottom of, to understand.

fathomless *adjective* too deep to fathom.

fatigue *noun* **1** tiredness resulting from hard work or exercise. **2** weakness in metals etc. caused by repeated stress. **3** any of the non-military duties of soldiers, e.g. cooking, cleaning. –**fatigue** *verb* to cause fatigue to. [from Latin *fatigare* = tire]

Fatima (died 632) the daughter of the Prophet Muhammad, and wife of the fourth caliph of the Muslim community, revered especially by Shi'ite Muslims.

fatstock *noun* livestock fattened for slaughter as food.

fatted *adjective* (of animals) fattened as food, *the fatted calf*.

fatten *verb* (**fattened**, **fattening**) to make or become fat.

fatty *adjective* like fat, containing fat. –**fatty** *noun* (*informal*) a fat person. □ **fatty acid** an organic acid of the kind that occurs in natural oils.

fatuous (**fat**-yoo-ŭs) *adjective* foolish, silly. **fatuously** *adverb*, **fatuousness** *noun*, **fatuity** (fă-**tew**-ĭ-tee) *noun*

fatwa (**fat**-wah) *noun* an authoritative ruling by an Islamic religious leader. [Arabic]

faucet (**faw**-sĕt) *noun* **1** a tap for a barrel. **2** (*Amer.*) any kind of tap.

fault *noun* **1** a defect or imperfection. **2** an offence, something wrongly done. **3** the responsibility for something wrong. **4** a break in the continuity of layers of rock, caused by movement of the earth's crust. **5** an incorrect serve in tennis etc. –**fault** *verb* **1** to find fault with, to declare to be faulty. **2** to make imperfect. □ **at fault** responsible for a mistake or shortcoming. **find fault with** to seek and find mistakes in, to complain about. [from Latin *fallere* = deceive]

faultless *adjective* without fault. **faultlessly** *adverb*, **faultlessness** *noun*

faulty *adjective* (**faultier**, **faultiest**) having a fault or faults, imperfect. **faultily** *adverb*, **faultiness** *noun*

faun (*pr.* fawn) *noun* (*Rom. myth.*) any of a class of gods of the woods and fields, with the legs and horns of a goat. [from the name of Faunus, an ancient Roman rural god (see *fauna*)]

fauna *noun* the animals of an area or period of time. [from the name of Fauna, an ancient Roman rural goddess, sister of Faunus (see *faun*)]

Faust (*pr.* fowst) a wandering astronomer and magician who lived in Germany c. 1488–1541, and was reputed to have sold his soul to the Devil.

fauvism (**foh**-vizm) *noun* a style of painting with vivid use of colour. **fauvist** *noun* [from French *fauve* = wild beast]

faux pas (foh **pah**) *noun* (*plural* **faux pas**, *pr.* foh **pahz**) an embarrassing blunder. [French, = false step]

favour *noun* **1** liking, goodwill, approval. **2** an act that is kindly or helpful beyond what is due or usual. **3** support or preference given to one person or group at the expense of another. **4** an ornament or badge etc. worn to show that one supports a certain political or other party. **–favour** *verb* **1** to regard or treat with favour. **2** to be in favour of. **3** to oblige, *favour us with a song*. **4** (of events or circumstances) to make possible or easy, to be advantageous to. **5** to resemble (one parent etc.), *the boy favours his father*. □ **be in** or **out of favour** to have or not have a person's goodwill. **in favour of** in support of, in sympathy with; to the advantage of; (of cheques) made out to (a person or his account).

favourable *adjective* **1** giving or showing approval. **2** pleasing, satisfactory, *made a favourable impression*. **3** helpful, advantageous, *favourable winds*. **favourably** *adverb*

favourite *adjective* liked or preferred above others. **–favourite** *noun* **1** a favoured person or thing. **2** a competitor generally expected to win.

favouritism *noun* unfair favouring of one person or group at the expense of another.

Fawkes, Guy (1570–1606), a conspirator in the Gunpowder Plot to blow up James I and his Parliament on 5 November 1605.

fawn¹ *noun* **1** a fallow deer in its first year. **2** light yellowish brown. **–fawn** *adjective* light yellowish-brown.

fawn² *verb* **1** (of a dog etc.) to try to win affection or attention by crouching close to a person and licking him or her. **2** to try to win favour by obsequious behaviour.

fax *noun* **1** the process of transmitting facsimiles of documents electronically. **2** a copy produced by this. **–fax** *verb* to transmit (a document) by this process. [from *facsimile*]

faze *verb* (*informal*) to disconcert, to daunt.

FBI *abbreviation* Federal Bureau of Investigation, a section of the Department of Justice in the USA, responsible for investigating violations of federal law and safeguarding national security.

fealty (**feel**-tee) *noun* loyalty, allegiance (originally the duty of a feudal tenant or vassal to his lord), *the oath of fealty*.

fear *noun* **1** an unpleasant emotion caused by the nearness of danger or expectation of pain etc. **2** the reverence or awe felt for God. **3** a danger, a likelihood. **–fear** *verb* **1** to feel fear of, to be afraid. **2** to reverence (God). **3** to have an uneasy feeling; to be politely regretful, *I fear there's none left*. □ **for fear of** because of the risk of. **without fear or favour** impartially.

fearful *adjective* **1** causing horror. **2** feeling fear. **3** (*informal*) very great, extremely bad. **fearfully** *adverb*

fearless *adjective* feeling no fear. **fearlessly** *adverb*, **fearlessness** *noun*

fearsome *adjective* frightening, alarming.

feasible (**fee**-zǐ-bŭl) *adjective* able to be done, possible. **feasibly** *adverb*, **feasibility** (fee-zǐ-**bil**-ĭ-tee) *noun*

Usage *Feasible* strictly means 'able to be done', as in *It is feasible to complete the extensions by Christmas*. It is sometimes used loosely to mean 'likely' or 'probable', as in *It's feasible that it will rain*, but this is not generally considered correct.

---

feast *noun* **1** a large elaborate meal. **2** a religious festival. **–feast** *verb* **1** to eat heartily. **2** to give a feast to. □ **feast one's eyes on** to gaze admiringly at. [from Latin *festus* = joyful]

feat *noun* a remarkable action or achievement.

feather *noun* **1** any of the structures that grow from a bird's skin and cover its body, consisting of a central shaft with a fringe of fine strands on each side. **2** long silky hair on a dog's or horse's legs. **–feather** *verb* **1** to cover or fit with feathers. **2** to turn (an oar) so that the blade passes through the air edgeways. **3** to make (propeller blades) rotate in such a way as to lessen the resistance of the air or water. □ **a feather in one's cap** an achievement one can be proud of. **feather bed** a mattress stuffed with feathers. **feather-brained** *adjective* empty-headed, silly. **feather one's nest** to enrich oneself when an opportunity occurs. **feather stitch** an ornamental stitch producing a feather-like pattern.

feathertail glider *noun* an Australian possum with a flat tail with very short fur and a fringe of stiff hairs like the barbs of a feather.

featherweight *noun* **1** a boxing weight between bantamweight and bantamweight, in amateur boxing 54–7 kg. **2** a very lightweight thing or person.

feathery *adjective* **1** light and soft like feathers. **2** covered with feathers.

feature *noun* **1** any of the named parts of the face (e.g. mouth, nose, eyes) that together make up its appearance. **2** a distinctive or noticeable quality of a thing. **3** a prominent article in a newspaper etc. **4** a long film forming the main item in a cinema program. **5** a broadcast based on one specific theme. –**feature** *verb* **1** to give special prominence to. **2** to be a feature of or in.

featureless *adjective* without distinctive features.

febrile (**fee**-bryl) *adjective* of or involving fever, feverish. **febrility** (fĕ-**bril**-ĭ-tee) *noun* [from Latin *febris*]

February *noun* the second month of the year. [named after *februa*, the ancient Roman feast of purification held in this month]

feckless *adjective* feeble and incompetent, irresponsible. **fecklessly** *adverb*, **fecklessness** *noun* [from Scottish *feck* = effect, + *-less* = without]

fecund (**feek**-ŭnd *or* **fek**-) *adjective* fertile. **fecundity** (fĕ-**kund**-ĭ-tee) *noun* [from Latin *fecundus*]

fed *see* **feed**. □ **fed up** (*informal*) discontented, displeased.

fedayeen (fe-dă-**yeen**) Arab guerrillas operating especially against Israel.

federal *adjective* **1** of a system of government in which several States unite under a central authority but remain independent in internal affairs. **2** belonging or relating to this group as a whole (not to its separate parts), *federal laws*; *federal election*. **3** of an association of

units that are largely independent. **federally** *adverb*, **federalism** *noun*, **federalist** *noun* [from Latin *foederis* = of a treaty]

federate *verb* **1** to unite on a federal basis. **2** to band together for a common object.

federation *noun* **1** federating. **2** a federated society or group of States. –**Federation** *noun* **1** the formation of the Commonwealth of Australia in 1901 by the uniting of the six Australian colonies. **2** a style of architecture current around 1901, with red brick, cream facings, turned veranda posts, and wooden fretted friezes. □ **Federation wheat** a drought-resistant wheat developed by William Farrer and named in 1901.

federative *adjective* federated, federal.

fee *noun* **1** a sum payable to an official or a professional person for advice or services. **2** a sum payable for membership of a society, entrance for an examination, transfer of a footballer, etc. **fees** *plural noun* charges for instruction at a school etc.

feeble *adjective* weak, without strength, force, or effectiveness. □ **feeble-minded** *adjective* mentally deficient or unintelligent. **feebly** *adverb*, **feebleness** *noun* [from Latin *flebilis* = wept over]

feed *verb* (**fed**, **feeding**) **1** to give food to; to put food into the mouth of. **2** to give as food to animals, *feed oats to horses*. **3** (of animals) to take food. **4** to serve as food for, to nourish. **5** to supply, to pass a supply of material to. **6** to send passes to (a player) in football etc. –**feed** *noun* **1** a meal (chiefly for animals or babies). **2** food for animals. **3** a pipe or channel etc. by which material is carried to a machine; the material itself. **4** a broadcast distributed by a satellite or network from a central source to a large number of radio or television stations. □ **feed shaft** the driving shaft that advances the cutting tool of a lathe.

feedback *noun* **1** return of part of the output of a system to its source, especially so as to modify the output. **2** the return of information about a product etc. to its supplier.

feeder *noun* **1** (of plants and animals) one that takes in food in a certain way, *a dainty feeder*. **2** a baby's feeding bottle. **3** a baby's bib. **4** a hopper or feeding apparatus in a machine. **5** a branch railway line, road, etc., linking outlying areas with a main system.

feel *verb* (**felt**, **feeling**) **1** to explore or perceive by touch. **2** to be conscious of, to be aware of being, *feel a pain*; *feel happy*. **3** to be affected by, *feels the cold badly*. **4** to give a certain sensation or impression, *the water feels warm*. **5** to have a vague conviction or impression of something. **6** to have as an opinion, to consider, *we felt it was necessary to do this*. –**feel** *noun* **1** the sense of touch. **2** the act of feeling. **3** the sensation produced by something touched. □ **feel for a person** to sympathise with him or her. **feel like** (*informal*) to be in the mood for. **feel one's way** to proceed carefully; to grope.

feeler *noun* **1** a long slender part or organ in certain animals, used for testing things by touch. **2** a cautious proposal or suggestion put forward to test people's reactions. □ **feeler gauge** a gauge with blades that can be inserted to measure gaps.

feeling *noun* **1** the power and capacity to feel, *had lost all feeling in his legs*. **2** mental or physical awareness, emotion. **3** an idea or belief not wholly based on reason, *had a feeling of safety*. **4** readiness to feel, sympathy, *showed no feeling for the sufferings of others*. **5** opinion, attitude, *the feeling of the meeting was against it*. **feelings** *plural noun* **1** the emotional side of a person's nature (contrasted with the intellect). **2** sympathies, opinions, *we have strong feelings on this matter*. □ **good feeling** friendliness.

feet *see* **foot**.

feign (*pr.* fayn) *verb* to pretend.

feint (*pr.* faynt) *noun* a slight attack or movement made in one place to divert attention from the main attack coming elsewhere. –**feint** *verb* to make a feint. –**feint** *adjective* (of ruled lines) faint.

feisty (**fy**-stee) *adjective* (**feistier**, **feistiest**) (*informal*) spirited, aggressive.

felafel (fĕ-**lahf**-ĕl) *noun* fried balls of mashed chick peas with spices. [Arabic *falăfil*]

feldspar *noun* any of a group of usually white or red rock-forming minerals that are aluminium silicates combined with various other metallic ions.

felicitate (fĕ-**liss**-ĭ-tayt) *verb* to congratulate. **felicitation** *noun*

felicitous (fĕ-**liss**-ĭ-tŭs) *adjective* (of words or remarks) well chosen, apt. **felicitously** *adverb*

felicity *noun* **1** being happy, great happiness. **2** a pleasing manner or style, *expressed himself with great felicity*.

feline (**fee**-lyn) *adjective* of cats, catlike. –**feline** *noun* an animal of the cat family. [from Latin *feles* = cat]

fell[1] *noun* a stretch of moorland or hilly land in north England.

fell[2] *adjective* (*poetical*) ruthless, cruel, destructive. □ **at one fell swoop** in a single deadly action.

fell[3] *verb* **1** to strike down by a blow. **2** to cut (a tree) down. **3** to stitch down (the edge of a seam) so that it lies flat.

fell[4] *noun* an animal's hide or skin with the hair.

fell[5] *see* **fall**.

fellmonger *noun* a dealer in sheepskins.

fellow *noun* **1** one who is associated with another, a comrade. **2** a thing of the same class or kind, the other of a pair. **3** a member of a learned society. **4** a member of the governing body of certain colleges. **5** (*informal*) a man or boy. **6** (*informal*) a boyfriend. □ **fellow feeling** sympathy with a person. **fellow-traveller** *noun* one who sympathises with the aims of the Communists or another political party but is not a member.

fellowship *noun* **1** friendly association with others, companionship. **2** a number of people associated together, a society; membership of this. **3** the position of a college fellow.

felon (**fel**-ŏn) *noun* a person who has committed a felony. [from Latin *fellonis* = of an evil person]

felony (**fel**-ŏ-nee) *noun* a crime regarded by the law as very serious. **felonious** (fĕ-**loh**-nee-ŭs) *adjective*

felspar *noun* = **feldspar**.

felt[1] *noun* a kind of cloth made by matting and pressing fibres. –**felt** *verb* **1** to make or become matted together like felt. **2** to cover with felt. □ **felt-tipped pen** (also **felt pen**) a pen with a writing point of felt or fibre.

felt[2] *see* **feel**.

female *adjective* **1** of the sex that can bear offspring or produce eggs. **2** (of plants) fruit-bearing, having a pistil and no stamens. **3** of a woman or women. **4** (of parts of machinery etc.) made hollow to receive a corresponding inserted part. –**female** *noun* a female person, animal, or plant.

feminine *adjective* **1** of, like, or suitable for women; having the qualities or appearance considered characteristic of a woman. **2** having the grammatical form suitable for the names of females or for words corresponding to these, *'lioness' is the feminine noun corresponding to 'lion'*. –**feminine** *noun*

(in grammar) a feminine word or gender.
femininity *noun* [from Latin *femina* = woman]

feminist *noun* a supporter of women's claims to be given rights equal to those of men.
feminism *noun*

femur (**fee**-mer) *noun* the thigh bone. **femoral** *adjective*

fen *noun* a low-lying marshy or flooded tract of land.

fence *noun* **1** a structure of rails, stakes, wire, etc., put round a field or garden to mark a boundary or keep animals from straying. **2** a raised structure for a horse to jump. **3** a person who knowingly buys and re-sells stolen goods. –**fence** *verb* **1** to surround with a fence. **2** to act as a fence for (stolen goods). **3** to engage in fencing. ☐ **sit on the fence** *see* sit. **fencer** *noun* [from *defence*]

fencing *noun* **1** fences; a length of fence. **2** the sport of fighting with foils or other kinds of sword.

fend *verb* **fend for** to provide a livelihood for; to look after. **fend off** to ward off. [from *defend*]

fender *noun* **1** a low frame bordering a fireplace to keep falling coals etc. from rolling into the room. **2** a pad or a bundle of rope hung over a vessel's side to prevent damage when it is alongside a wharf or another vessel.

feng shui (**fung**-shway) *noun* (originally in Chinese thought) a system of laws governing spatial arrangements. [from Chinese *feng* 'wind' + *shui* 'water']

Fenian (**fee**-nee-ăn) *noun* a member of an Irish organisation founded in about 1858 in the USA and Ireland for the overthrow of British rule in Ireland.

fennel *noun* a yellow-flowered plant with thick celery-like stalks used as a vegetable, and fragrant seeds used for flavouring.

fenugreek (**fen**-ŭ-greek) *noun* a leguminous plant with aromatic seeds used as flavouring.

feral (**fe**-răl) *adjective* **1** (of plants and animals) escaped and living wild. **2** brutal. **3** (*Austral. informal*) (of a person) dirty, unkempt; wild in behaviour. [Latin *ferus* = wild]

Ferdinand (1452–1516) king of Spain, who by succeeding to the thrones of Aragon and Castile effectively united Spain as one country.

ferment (fer-**ment**) *verb* **1** to undergo fermentation; to cause fermentation in. **2** to seethe with excitement or agitation.

–**ferment** (**fer**-ment) *noun* **1** fermentation. **2** something that causes this. **3** a state of seething excitement or agitation.

fermentation *noun* a chemical change caused by the action of an organic substance such as yeast, involving effervescence and the production of heat, e.g. when sugar is converted into alcohol.

Fermi (**fer**-mee), Enrico (1901–54), Italian-born American atomic physicist.

fermion *noun* any of several subatomic particles. [from *Fermi*]

fermium (**fer**-mee-ŭm) *noun* an artificial radioactive metallic element of the actinide series (symbol Fm). [from *Fermi*]

fern *noun* a kind of flowerless plant with feathery green leaves. **ferny** *adjective*

ferocious *adjective* fierce, savage. **ferociously** *adverb*, **ferocity** (fĕ-**ross**-ĭ-tee) *noun* [from Latin *ferox* = bold, fierce]

ferret *noun* a small animal of the weasel family kept for driving rabbits from burrows, killing rats, etc. –**ferret** *verb* (**ferreted**, **ferreting**) to search, to rummage. ☐ **ferret out** to discover by searching or rummaging. [from Latin *fur* = thief]

ferrety *adjective* (of the face) narrow and pointed like a ferret's.

ferric *adjective* of or containing iron. ☐ **ferric tape** one with a coating of ferric oxide. [from Latin *ferrum* = iron]

Ferris wheel *noun* a giant revolving vertical wheel with passenger cars on its outer edge. [named after its American inventor, G.W.G. Ferris (1859–96)]

ferrite *noun* any of a class of iron oxides, many of which have magnetic and insulating properties.

ferroconcrete *noun* reinforced concrete.

ferromagnetism *noun* the kind of magnetism found in substances such as iron, cobalt, nickel, and their alloys, with some ability to retain their magnetism after the magnetising field is removed. **ferromagnetic** *adjective*

ferrous (**fe**-rŭs) *adjective* containing iron, *ferrous and non-ferrous metals*. [from Latin *ferrum* = iron]

ferrule (**fe**-rool) *noun* a metal ring or cap strengthening the end of a stick or tube.

ferry *verb* (**ferried**, **ferrying**) **1** to convey (people or things) in a boat etc. across a stretch of water. **2** to transport from one place to another, especially as a regular service. **–ferry** *noun* **1** a boat etc. used for ferrying. **2** the place where it operates. **3** the service it provides. **ferryman** *noun*

fertile *adjective* **1** (of soil) rich in the materials needed to support vegetation. **2** (of plants) able to produce fruit; (of animals) able or likely to conceive or beget young. **3** (of seeds or eggs) capable of developing into a new plant or animal, fertilised. **4** (of the mind) able to produce ideas, inventive. **fertility** *noun*

fertilise *verb* (also **-ize**) **1** to make (soil etc.) fertile or productive. **2** to introduce pollen or sperm into (a plant or egg or female animal) so that it develops seed or young. **fertilisation** *noun*

fertiliser *noun* (also **-izer**) material (natural or artificial) added to soil to make it more fertile.

fervent (**fer**-věnt) *adjective* showing warmth of feeling. **fervently** *adverb*, **fervency** *noun* [from Latin *fervens* = boiling]

fervid *adjective* fervent. **fervidly** *adverb*

fervour *noun* warmth and intensity of feeling, zeal.

festal *adjective* of a festival.

fester *verb* **1** to make or become septic and filled with pus. **2** to cause continuing resentment.

festival *noun* **1** a day or time of religious or other celebration. **2** a series of performances of music, drama, films, etc., given periodically, *the Adelaide Festival*. [same origin as *feast*]

festive *adjective* of or suitable for a festival.

festivity *noun* a festive occasion or celebration.

festoon *noun* a chain of flowers, leaves, ribbons, etc., hung in a curve or loop as a decoration. **–festoon** *verb* to decorate with hanging ornaments.

feta (**fet**-ă) *noun* a soft white cheese made from ewe's milk or goat's milk. [from Greek *pheta*]

fetch *verb* **1** to go for and bring back. **2** to cause to come out, *fetched a sigh*. **3** (of goods) to sell for (a price), *your books won't fetch much*. **–fetch** *noun* a distance of water between two points. □ **fetch up** (*informal*) to arrive or end up somewhere.

fetching *adjective* attractive.

fête (*pr.* fayt) *noun* (also **fete**) **1** a festival. **2** an outdoor entertainment or sale, usually to raise funds for a cause or charity. **–fête** *verb* (**fêted**, **fêting**) to entertain (a person) in

celebration of some achievement etc. [same origin as *feast*]

fetid (**fet**-ĭd *or* **fee**-tĭd) *adjective* stinking. [from Latin *fetidus*]

fetish (**fet**-ish) *noun* **1** an object worshipped by primitive peoples who believe it to have magical powers or to be inhabited by a spirit. **2** anything to which foolishly excessive respect or attention is given. [from Portuguese *feitiço* = a charm]

fetlock *noun* the part of a horse's leg above and behind the hoof.

fetter *noun* a chain or shackle for a prisoner's ankles. **–fetter** *verb* **1** to put into fetters. **2** to impede or restrict.

fettle *noun* condition, trim, *in fine fettle*.

fettler *noun* a railway maintenance worker.

fettuccine (fet-ŭ-**chee**-nee) *noun* pasta in the form of ribbons. [Italian, = little ribbons]

feud (*pr.* fewd) *noun* lasting hostility between people or groups. **–feud** *verb* to carry on a feud.

feudal (**few**-dăl) *adjective* of or according to the **feudal system**, a method of holding land (during the Middle Ages in Europe) by giving one's services to the owner. **feudalism** *noun*, **feudalistic** *adjective*

fever *noun* **1** an abnormally high body temperature. **2** a disease characterised by this. **3** a state of nervous excitement or agitation.

fevered *adjective* affected with fever.

feverish *adjective* **1** having a fever; caused or accompanied by a fever. **2** restless with excitement or agitation. **feverishly** *adverb*, **feverishness** *noun*

few *adjective* & *noun* not many. □ **a few** some, not none. **a good few** or **quite a few** (*informal*) a fairly large number.

Usage See the note under **less**.

fey (*pr.* fay) *adjective* **1** clairvoyant. **2** having a strange other-worldly charm.

fez *noun* (*plural* **fezzes**) a high flat-topped red cap with a tassel, worn by Muslim men in certain countries. [named after Fez, a town in Morocco]

ff. *abbreviation* the following pages etc.

fiancé, **fiancée** (fee-**ahn**-say) *nouns* a man (*fiancé*) or woman (*fiancée*) to whom one is engaged to be married. [French, = betrothed]

fiasco (fee-**ass**-koh) *noun* (*plural* fiascos) a complete and ludicrous failure.

fiat (**fy**-at) *noun* an order or decree. [Latin, = let it be done]

fib *noun* an unimportant lie. –**fib** *verb* (fibbed, fibbing) to tell a fib. **fibber** *noun*

Fibonacci (fib-ŏ-**nah**-chee), Leonardo (c. 1200), Italian mathematician, after whom is named the **Fibonacci series** of numbers (1, 1, 2, 3, 5, 8, 13, etc.) in which each number after the first two is the sum of the two preceding numbers.

fibre *noun* **1** one of the thin strands of which animal and vegetable tissue or textile substances are made; a threadlike piece of glass. **2** a substance consisting of fibres; fibrous food material in plants, roughage. **3** strength of character, *moral fibre*. □ **fibre optics** the use of thin flexible fibres of glass or other transparent solids to transmit light signals.

fibreboard *noun* board made of compressed fibres.

fibreglass *noun* **1** textile fabric made from glass fibres. **2** plastic containing glass fibres.

fibrin (**fy**-brĭn) *noun* an insoluble protein formed in the process of blood-clotting from the soluble blood plasma protein **fibrinogen**.

fibro *noun* (also fibro-cement) (*Austral*.) a building material made from asbestos and cement.

fibroid (**fy**-broid) *adjective* consisting of fibrous tissue. –**fibroid** *noun* a benign fibroid tumour in the womb.

fibrositis (fy-brŏ-**sy**-tĭss) *noun* rheumatic pain in any tissue other than bones and joints.

fibrous (**fy**-brŭs) *adjective* like fibres; made of fibres.

fibula (**fib**-yŭ-lă) *noun* (*plural* fibulae) **1** the bone on the outer side of the lower part of the leg. **2** an ancient brooch or clasp.

fiche (*pr*. feesh) *noun* (*plural* fiche) a microfiche. [French, = slip of paper]

fickle *adjective* often changing, not constant or loyal. **fickleness** *noun*

fiction *noun* **1** a product of the imagination. **2** an invented story. **3** a class of literature consisting of books containing such stories. **fictional** *adjective*, **fictionally** *adverb* [from Latin *fictio* = pretending]

fictionalise *verb* (also -ize) to make into a fictional narrative. **fictionalisation** *noun*

fictitious (fik-**tish**-ŭs) *adjective* imagined, not real, not genuine. **fictitiously** *adverb*

FID *abbreviation* financial institutions duty.

Fid. Def. *abbreviation* Defender of the Faith (*see* defender). [short for Latin *Fidei Defensor*]

fiddle *noun* **1** (*informal*) a violin. **2** (*informal*) a piece of cheating, a swindle. –**fiddle** *verb* **1** (*informal*) to play the fiddle. **2** to fidget with something, to handle a thing aimlessly. **3** (*informal*) to cheat or swindle; to falsify (accounts etc.); to get by cheating. **fiddler** *noun*

fiddlesticks *interjection* nonsense.

fiddling *adjective* petty, trivial.

fiddly *adjective* (*informal*) small and awkward to use or do.

fidelity (fĭ-**del**-ĭ-tee) *noun* **1** faithfulness, loyalty. **2** accuracy, truthfulness. **3** the quality or precision of the reproduction of sound. [from Latin *fidelitas* = faithfulness]

fidget *verb* (fidgeted, fidgeting) **1** to make small restless movements. **2** to be uneasy, to make (a person) uneasy, to worry. –**fidget** *noun* a person who fidgets. **fidgets** *plural noun* fidgeting movements. **fidgety** *adjective* [from a dialect word *fidge* = twitch]

fie *interjection* (*old use*) for shame!

fief *noun* (*historical*) an estate held by a noble under feudalism.

field *noun* **1** a piece of open ground, especially one used for pasture or cultivation. **2** an area of land rich in some natural product, a coalfield, gasfield, or oilfield. **3** a battlefield. **4** a sportsground; the playing area marked out on this. **5** the space within which an electric, magnetic, or gravitational influence etc. can be felt; the force of that influence. **6** the area that can be seen or observed, *one's field of vision*. **7** the range of a subject or activity or interest, *an expert in the field of music*. **8** (in computers) one section of a record, representing a unit of information, *the firm's payroll record has one field for gross pay, one for deductions, and one for net pay*. **9** the scene or area of fieldwork, *field archaeology*. **10** all the competitors in an outdoor contest or sport; all except the one(s) specified; the fielding side in cricket. –**field** *verb* **1** to act as a fielder in cricket etc. **2** to stop and return (the ball) in cricket etc. **3** to put (a football or other team) into the field. **4** to deal successfully with (a series of questions). □ **field day** an exciting or productive time; a military exercise or review; a day spent in fieldwork. **field events** athletic sports other than races, e.g. jumping, shot-putting, etc. **field glasses** binoculars for outdoor use. **Field Marshal** an army officer of the highest rank. **field mouse** the type of mouse found in open country. **field sports** outdoor sports such as hunting, shooting, and fishing.

fielder *noun* a member of the side not batting in cricket etc.

fieldsman *noun* (*plural* **fieldsmen**) a fielder.

fieldwork *noun* practical work done outside libraries and laboratories, e.g. by surveyors, scientists, and social workers who visit people in their homes. **fieldworker** *noun*

fiend (*pr.* feend) *noun* **1** an evil spirit. **2** a very wicked or cruel person, one who causes mischief or annoyance. **3** a devotee or addict, *a fitness fiend.* **fiendish** *adjective*, **fiendishly** *adverb*

fierce *adjective* **1** violent in temper, manner, or action; not gentle. **2** eager, intense, *fierce loyalty.* **3** unpleasantly strong or extreme, *fierce heat.* **fiercely** *adverb*, **fierceness** *noun*

fiery *adjective* **1** consisting of fire, flaming. **2** looking like fire, bright red. **3** intensely hot, producing a burning sensation. **4** intense, passionate, *a fiery speech.* **5** easily roused to anger. **fierily** *adverb*, **fieriness** *noun*

fiesta (fee-**est**-ă) *noun* a religious festival in Spanish-speaking countries.

fife *noun* a kind of flute used with a drum in military music.

fifteen *adjective* & *noun* **1** one more than fourteen (15, XV). **2** a team of fifteen players, especially in Rugby Union football. **fifteenth** *adjective* & *noun*

fifth *adjective* & *noun* **1** next after fourth. **2** one of five equal parts of a thing. **3** a musical interval or chord spanning five alphabetical notes, e.g. C to G. □ **fifth column** an organised group working for the enemy within a country at war. (¶ General Mola, leading four columns of troops towards Madrid in the Spanish Civil War, declared that he had a fifth column inside the city.) **fifth columnist** a member of such a group. **fifthly** *adverb*

fifty *adjective* & *noun* five times ten (50, L). **fifties** *plural noun* the numbers from 50 to 59, especially the years of a century or of a person's age. □ **fifty-fifty** *adjective* & *adverb* (*informal*) shared or sharing equally between two; *a fifty-fifty chance,* an equal chance of

winning or losing, or of surviving etc. **fiftieth** *adjective* & *noun*

fig *noun* **1** a broad-leaved tree bearing a soft pear-shaped fruit. **2** this fruit. □ **fig leaf** a leaf of a fig tree, especially used for concealing the genitals.

fig. *abbreviation* figure.

fight *verb* (**fought, fighting**) **1** to struggle against (a person or country) in physical combat or in war. **2** to carry on (a battle). **3** to struggle or contend in any way; to strive to obtain or accomplish something. **4** to strive to overcome or destroy, *they fought the fire.* **5** to make one's way by fighting or effort. –**fight** *noun* **1** fighting, a battle. **2** a struggle or contest or conflict of any kind. **3** a boxing match.

fighter *noun* **1** a person who fights. **2** one who does not yield without a struggle. **3** a fast military aircraft designed for attacking other aircraft.

figment *noun* a thing that does not exist except in the imagination.

figurative (**fig**-yŭ-ră-tiv) *adjective* using or containing a figure of speech, metaphorical, not literal. **figuratively** *adverb*

figure *noun* **1** the written symbol of a number. **2** a diagram. **3** a decorative pattern; a pattern traced in dancing or skating. **4** a representation of a person or animal in drawing, painting, sculpture, etc. **5** a person as seen or studied, *saw a figure running along the beach*; *an important historical figure.* **6** external form or shape, bodily shape, *has a good figure.* **7** a geometrical shape enclosed by lines or surfaces. –**figure** *verb* **1** to represent in a diagram or picture. **2** to picture mentally, to imagine. **3** to form part of a plan etc.; to appear or be mentioned, *he figures in all books on the subject.* **4** (*informal*) to understand; to consider, to reckon; *that figures,* that is likely. **figures** *plural noun* arithmetic, *she is no good at figures.* □ **figure of speech** a word or phrase used for vivid or dramatic effect and not literally. **figure out** to work out by arithmetic; (*informal*) to interpret, to understand. [from Latin *figura* = shape]

figured *adjective* ornamented, decorated; *figured silk,* with designs woven into it. □ **figured bass** (in music) a bass part with numbers written below the notes to show which other notes should be played with them to complete the harmony.

figurehead *noun* **1** a carved image at the prow of a ship. **2** a person at the head of an organisation etc. but without real power.

figurine (**fig**-yŭ-reen) *noun* a statuette.

Fiji (**fee**-jee) a republic consisting of a large group of islands in the South Pacific east of Vanuatu. **Fijian** (fee-**jee**-ăn) *adjective* & *noun*

filament *noun* **1** a threadlike strand. **2** a fine wire in an electric lamp, giving off light when heated by the current. [same origin as *file*²]

filbert *noun* the nut of a cultivated hazel.

filch *verb* to pilfer, to steal (something of small value).

file¹ *noun* a steel tool with a roughened surface for shaping or smoothing things. –**file** *verb* to shape or smooth with a file.

file² *noun* **1** a holder or cover or box etc. for keeping papers together and in order for reference purposes. **2** its contents. **3** a collection of related data stored under one reference in a computer. **4** a line of people or things one behind the other; *in single file*, one at a time. –**file** *verb* **1** to place in a file. **2** to place on record, *file an application*. **3** (of a reporter) to send in (a story etc.). **4** to march in file, *they filed out*. [from Latin *filum* = thread (because a string or wire was put through papers to hold them in order]

filename *noun* an identifying name given to a computer file.

filial (**fil**-ee-ăl) *adjective* of or due from a son or daughter, *filial duty*. [from Latin *filius* = son, *filia* = daughter]

filibuster *noun* **1** a person who tries to delay or prevent the passage of a bill by making long speeches. **2** this action. –**filibuster** *verb* to delay things in this way.

filigree (**fil**-ĭ-gree) *noun* ornamental lacelike work in metal. **filigreed** *adjective*

filing cabinet *noun* a metal or wooden container with drawers for filing documents.

filings *plural noun* particles rubbed off by a file.

Filipino (filĭ-**pee**-noh) *noun* (*plural* **Filipinos**) a native of the Philippines. –**Filipino** *adjective* of the Philippines or Filipinos. **Filipina** *feminine noun*

fill *verb* **1** to make or become full; to occupy the whole of. **2** to block up (a hole or cavity). **3** to spread over or through, *smoke began to fill the room*. **4** to hold (a position); to appoint a person to (a vacant post). **5** to occupy (vacant time). –**fill** *noun* **1** enough to fill

something. **2** enough to satisfy a person's appetite or desire. □ **fill in** to complete by writing or drawing inside an outline; to complete (an unfinished document etc.); to act as a substitute; (*informal*) to inform (a person) more fully. **fill out** to enlarge; to become enlarged or plumper; to fill in (a document etc.). **fill the bill** to be suitable for what is required. **fill up** to fill completely; to fill the petrol tank of a car.

filler *noun* an object or material used to fill a cavity or to increase the bulk of something.

fillet *noun* **1** a piece of boneless meat from near the loins or ribs; a thick boneless piece of fish. **2** a strip of ribbon etc. worn round the head. **3** (in architecture) a narrow flat band between mouldings. –**fillet** *verb* (**filleted**, **filleting**) to remove the bones from (fish etc.).

filling *noun* **1** material used to fill a tooth cavity; the process of inserting this. **2** material put into a container, between layers of bread to form a sandwich, etc.

fillip *noun* **1** a quick smart blow or stroke given with a finger. **2** something that boosts or stimulates (trade etc.).

filly *noun* a young female horse.

film *noun* **1** a thin coating or covering layer. **2** a rolled strip or sheet coated with light-sensitive material used for taking photographs or making a motion picture; a single roll of this. **3** a motion picture. –**film** *verb* **1** to cover or become covered with a thin coating or covering layer. **2** to make a film of (a story etc.). **films** *plural noun* the cinema industry. □ **film star** a star actor or actress in films.

filmstrip *noun* a series of transparencies in a strip for projection.

filmy *adjective* (**filmier**, **filmiest**) thin and almost transparent. **filminess** *noun*

filter *noun* **1** a device or substance for holding back the impurities or solid particles in a liquid or gas passed through it. **2** a screen for preventing light of certain wavelengths from passing through. **3** a device for suppressing electrical or sound waves of frequencies other than the ones required. –**filter** *verb* **1** to pass or cause to pass through a filter; to remove (impurities etc.) in this way. **2** to come or make a way in or out gradually, *news filtered out; people filtered into the hall*. □ **filter bed** a tank or reservoir containing a layer of sand etc. for filtering large quantities of liquid. [from *felt*[1], originally used for making filters]

filth *noun* 1 disgusting dirt. 2 obscenity.

filthy *adjective* (**filthier**, **filthiest**)
1 disgustingly dirty. 2 obscene. –**filthy** *adverb* (*informal*) extremely, *filthy rich*. **filthily** *adverb*, **filthiness** *noun*

filtrate *noun* filtered liquid. –**filtrate** *verb* to filter. **filtration** *noun*

fin *noun* 1 a thin flat projection from the body of a fish etc., used by the animal for propelling and steering itself in the water. 2 an underwater swimmer's rubber flipper. 3 a small projection shaped like a fish's fin, e.g. to improve the stability of an aircraft or rocket.

final *adjective* 1 at the end, coming last. 2 putting an end to doubt or discussion or argument. –**final** *noun* 1 the last of a series of contests in sports or a competition. 2 the edition of a newspaper published latest in the day. **finals** *plural noun* the last set of examinations in a series. **finally** *adverb* [same origin as *finish*]

finale (fi-**nah**-lee) *noun* the final section of a musical composition or a drama.

finalise *verb* (also **-ize**) 1 to bring to an end. 2 to put into its final form. **finalisation** *noun*

finalist *noun* one who competes in the final.

finality (fy-**nal**-ĭ-tee) *noun* the quality of being final.

finance (fy-**nanss**) *noun* 1 the management of money. 2 money as support for an undertaking. –**finance** *verb* to provide the money for. **finances** *plural noun* the money resources of a country, company, or person. [from Old French *finer* = settle a debt]

financial (fy-**nan**-shăl) *adjective* 1 of finance. 2 (*Austral.*) financially solvent. 3 (of a club member etc.) with fees or dues fully paid. □ **financial year** a year as reckoned for accounts, tax, etc. (in Australia 1 July to 30 June). **financially** *adverb*

financier (fy-**nan**-see-er) *noun* a person who is engaged in financing businesses etc. on a large scale.

finch *noun* any of a number of related birds most of which have short stubby bills.

find *verb* (**found**, **finding**) 1 to discover by search, effort, or inquiry or by chance. 2 to become aware of, to discover (a fact). 3 to arrive at naturally, *water finds its own level*. 4 to succeed in obtaining, *can't find time*

to do it. 5 to supply, to provide, *who will find the money for the expedition?* 6 (of a jury etc.) to decide and declare, *found him innocent*. –**find** *noun* 1 the finding of something useful or pleasing. 2 a thing or person discovered, especially when valuable. □ **find favour** to be acceptable. **find one's feet** to become able to stand or walk; to develop one's ability to act independently. **find oneself** to discover one's natural powers or one's vocation. **find out** to get information about; to detect (a person) who has done wrong; to discover (a deception or fraud).

finder *noun* 1 one who finds something. 2 the viewfinder of a camera or a telescope.

findings *plural noun* the conclusions reached by means of an inquiry.

fine[1] *noun* a sum of money fixed as a penalty for an offence. –**fine** *verb* to punish by a fine. [from Latin *finis* = end (in the Middle Ages it referred to the sum paid to settle a lawsuit)]

fine[2] *adjective* 1 of high quality. 2 excellent, of great merit. 3 (of weather) bright and clear, free from rain and fog etc. 4 of slender thread or thickness; small-sized; consisting of small particles. 5 requiring very skilful workmanship. 6 difficult to perceive, *making fine distinctions*. 7 complimentary, especially in an insincere way, *said fine things about them*. 8 in good health, comfortable, *I'm fine, thank you*. –**fine** *adverb* 1 finely. 2 (*informal*) very well, *that will suit me fine*. –**fine** *verb* to make or become finer, thinner, or less coarse. □ **fine arts** those appealing to the sense of beauty, especially painting, sculpture, and architecture. **fine-drawn** *adjective* subtle; extremely thin. **fine-tooth comb** a comb with narrow close-set teeth; *go through something with a fine-tooth comb*, to examine it closely and thoroughly. **finely** *adverb*, **fineness** *noun* [same origin as *finish*]

finery[1] *noun* fine clothes or decorations.

finery[2] *noun* a hearth where pig iron is converted into wrought iron.

finesse (fi-**ness**) *noun* 1 delicate manipulation. 2 tact and cleverness. [French, = fineness]

fine-tune *verb* 1 to adjust very precisely. 2 to make delicate adjustments to (a plan etc.) in order to improve it.

finger *noun* 1 any of the five parts extending from each hand; any of these other than the thumb. 2 the part of a glove that fits over a finger. 3 a finger-like object. –**finger** *verb*

1 to touch or feel with the fingers. **2** to play (a musical instrument) with the fingers. □ **have a finger in the pie** to be actively involved in a project.

fingering *noun* **1** a method of using the fingers in playing a musical instrument or in typing. **2** an indication of this in a musical score, usually by numbers.

fingernail *noun* the nail on a finger.

fingerprint *noun* an impression of the ridges of the skin on the pad of a finger, especially as a means of identification.

fingerstall *noun* a sheath to cover an injured finger.

fingertip *noun* the tip of a finger. □ **have at one's fingertips** to be thoroughly familiar with (a thing).

finial *noun* an ornamental top to a gable, canopy, etc. [from *finis*]

finical *adjective* finicky.

finicking *adjective* & *noun* being finicky.

finicky *adjective* **1** excessively detailed, fiddly. **2** over-particular, fastidious.

finis (**fin**-ĭss) *noun* the end, especially of a book. [Latin, = end]

finish *verb* **1** to bring or come to an end, to complete. **2** to reach the end of a task or race etc. **3** to consume or get through all of, *finish the pie*. **4** to put the final touches to; to complete the manufacture of (woodwork, cloth, etc.) by surface treatment. – **finish** *noun* **1** the last stage of something. **2** the point at which a race etc. ends. **3** the state of being finished or perfect. **4** the method, texture, or material used for finishing woodwork etc. □ **finish off** to end; (*informal*) to kill. **finish with** to complete one's use of; to end one's association with. [from Latin *finis* = end]

finite (**fy**-nyt) *adjective* **1** limited, not infinite. **2** (of a set in mathematics) having a finite number of elements. □ **finite verb** one that agrees with its subject in person and number; *was*, *went*, and *says* are finite verbs, *going* and *to see* are not. [from Latin *finitum* = ended]

Finland a republic of NE Europe.

Finn *noun* a native of Finland.

Finnish *adjective* of the Finns or their language. – **Finnish** *noun* the language of the Finns.

fiord (*pr.* fyord) *noun* a long narrow inlet of the sea between high cliffs as in Norway and New Zealand. [Norwegian]

fipple *noun* a plug at the mouth-end of a wind instrument.

fiqh (feek) *noun* the theory or philosophy of Islamic law, based on the teachings of the Koran and the traditions of the Prophet.

fir *noun* **1** a kind of evergreen cone-bearing tree with needle-like leaves on its shoots. **2** its wood.

fire *noun* **1** combustion producing light and heat. **2** destructive burning, *insured against fire*. **3** burning fuel in a grate or furnace etc.; an electric or gas fire. **4** angry or excited feeling, enthusiasm. **5** the firing of guns, *hold your fire*. – **fire** *verb* **1** to send a bullet or shell from a gun etc.; to send out (a missile); to detonate. **2** to deliver or utter in rapid succession. **3** to dismiss (an employee) from a job. **4** to set fire to. **5** to catch fire; (of an internal-combustion engine) to undergo ignition. **6** to supply (a furnace etc.) with fuel. **7** to bake (pottery or bricks); to cure (tea or tobacco) by artificial heat. **8** to excite, to stimulate, *fired them with enthusiasm*. □ **fire alarm** a bell or other device giving warning of fire. **fire away** (*informal*) to begin, to go ahead. **fire brigade** an organised body of firefighters trained and employed to extinguish fires. **fire door** a fire-resistant door preventing the spread of fire. **fire drill** rehearsal of the procedure to be used in case of fire. **fire engine** a vehicle fitted with equipment used for fighting large fires. **fire escape** a special staircase or apparatus by which people may escape from a building etc. in case of fire. **fire irons** a poker, tongs, and shovel for tending a domestic fire. **fire station** the headquarters of a fire brigade. **fire-stick farming** (*Austral.*) a method of vegetation control by burning, especially as carried out by Aborigines. **fire trap** a building without sufficient exits in case of fire. **firer** *noun*

firearm *noun* a rifle, gun, pistol, or revolver.

firebrand *noun* a person who stirs up trouble.

firebreak *noun* an obstacle to the spread of fire in a forest etc.

firebug *noun* (*informal*) a person who deliberately sets fire to property.

firedamp *noun* the miners' name for methane, which is explosive when mixed in certain proportions with air.

firefly *noun* a kind of beetle that gives off a phosphorescent light.

firelighter *noun* a piece of flammable material to help start a fire in a grate.

fireman *noun* (*plural* **firemen**) **1** a member of a fire brigade. **2** one whose job is to tend a furnace etc.

fireplace *noun* **1** an open recess for a domestic fire, at the base of a chimney. **2** the surrounding structure. **3** a structure at a picnic area etc. in which a fire may be lit for cooking.

firepower *noun* the destructive capacity of guns etc.

fireproof *adjective* **1** that does not catch fire. **2** that does not break when heated, *fireproof dishes*.

fireside *noun* the part of a room near a fireplace, this as the centre of one's home.

firewall *noun* a part of a computer system or network that is designed to block unauthorised access while permitting outward communication.

firewood *noun* wood for use as fuel.

firework *noun* a device containing chemicals that burn or explode with spectacular effect, used at celebrations.

firing *see* **fire**. □ **firing line** the front line of a battle, from which troops fire at the enemy; a position at the forefront of an activity. **firing squad** a group ordered to fire a salute during a military funeral, or to shoot a condemned person.

firm¹ *noun* a partnership for carrying on a business; a commercial establishment.

firm² *adjective* **1** not yielding when pressed, hard, solid. **2** steady, not shaking. **3** securely fixed. **4** established, not easily changed or influenced; *a firm offer*, one that is not liable to be cancelled. –**firm** *adverb* firmly, *stand firm*. –**firm** *verb* to make or become firm or compact; to fix firmly.

firmament *noun* the sky with its clouds and stars.

firmware *noun* a kind of computer software programmed into a read-only memory.

first *adjective* coming before all others in time, order, or importance. –**first** *noun* **1** something that is first; the first day of a month; the first occurrence or achievement of something. **2** first-class honours in a university degree. **3** first gear. –**first** *adverb* **1** before all others. **2** before another event or time; *must finish this work first*, before doing something else. **3** for the first time, *when did you first see him?* □ **at first** at the beginning. **at first hand** obtained directly, from the original source. **first aid** treatment given to an injured person

before a doctor comes. **first base** the first of the bases that must be reached to score a run in baseball; *get to first base*, to achieve the first step towards an objective. **first blood** the first success in a contest. **first-born** *adjective* & *noun* eldest, the eldest child. **first class** a set of persons or things grouped together as better than others; the best accommodation in a boat or train or aircraft etc. **first-class** *adjective* of the best quality; very good; of or using the first class; (*adverb*) by the first class. **first cousin** *see* **cousin**. **first-day cover** an envelope with stamps postmarked on the first day of issue. **first-fruits** *plural noun* the first of a season's agricultural products, offered to God; the first results of work etc. **first gear** the lowest gear in a motor vehicle. **first name** a personal or Christian name. **first offender** a person with no previous conviction for an offence. **first officer** the mate on a merchant ship. **first past the post** a voting system in which voters each choose one candidate, and the one who receives the most votes is elected (though not necessarily having an absolute majority). **first person** *see* **person**. **first-rate** *adjective* & *adverb* of the best class, excellent; (*informal*) very well. **first thing** (*informal*) before anything else, *do it first thing*. **first violin** any of the group playing the leading part of two or more parts.

First Fleet a fleet of eleven ships that sailed from England carrying convicts, marines, and officials to establish a convict settlement in NSW. The fleet, under Captain Arthur Phillip, arrived at Sydney Cove on 26 January 1788.

firsthand *adjective* & *adverb* obtained directly from the original source.

firstly *adverb* first, as a first consideration.

firth *noun* an estuary or a narrow inlet of the sea in Scotland.

fiscal *adjective* of public revenue. [from Latin *fiscus* = treasury]

fish *noun* (*plural* usually **fish**) **1** a cold-blooded animal living wholly in water. **2** its flesh as food. **3** (*informal*) a person, *an odd fish*. –**fish** *verb* **1** to try to catch fish; *fish the river*, to catch fish from it. **2** to search for something in or under water or by reaching into something; (*informal*) to bring out or up in this way, *fished out his keys*. **3** to try to obtain by hinting or indirect questioning, *fishing for information*. □ **fish cake** a small cake of shredded fish and mashed potato. **fish finger** a small oblong piece of fish in batter or breadcrumbs. **fish kettle** an oval pan for boiling fish.

fisherman *noun* (*plural* **fishermen**)
1 a person who earns a living by fishing.
2 one who goes fishing as a sport.

fishery *noun* **1** a place where fish are caught or reared. **2** the industry of catching or breeding fish.

fishing *noun* trying to catch fish.
□ **fishing ground** an area used for fishing. **fishing rod** a long rod to which a line is attached, used for fishing. **fishing tackle** equipment used in fishing.

fishmeal *noun* ground dried fish used as a fertiliser.

fishmonger *noun* a shopkeeper who sells fish.

fishnet *adjective* (of fabric) made in a kind of open mesh.

fishy *adjective* (**fishier**, **fishiest**) **1** like fish, smelling or tasting of fish. **2** (*informal*) causing disbelief or suspicion. **fishiness** *noun*

fissile (**fi**-syl) *adjective* **1** tending to split. **2** capable of undergoing nuclear fission.

fission *noun* **1** splitting of the nucleus of certain atoms, with release of energy. **2** splitting or division of biological cells as a method of reproduction. [from Latin *fissum* = split]

fissionable *adjective* capable of undergoing nuclear fission.

fissure (**fish**-er) *noun* a cleft made by splitting or separation of parts.

fist *noun* **1** the hand when tightly closed, with the fingers bent into the palm. **2** (*informal*) handwriting.
□ **make a good** or **poor fist of** (*informal*) make a good (or bad) attempt at.

fisticuffs *noun* fighting with the fists.

fistula (**fiss**-tew-lă) *noun* **1** a long pipe-like ulcer. **2** an abnormal or surgically made passage in the body. **3** a natural pipe or spout in whales, insects, etc. **fistular** *adjective* [Latin, = a flute]

fit¹ *noun* **1** a brief spell of an illness or its symptoms, *a fit of coughing*. **2** a sudden violent seizure of epilepsy, apoplexy, etc., with convulsions or loss of consciousness. **3** an attack of strong feeling, *a fit of rage*. **4** a short period of a certain feeling or activity, an impulse, *a fit of energy*. □ **in fits and starts** in short bursts of activity, not steadily or regularly.

fit² *adjective* (**fitter**, **fittest**) **1** suitable or well adapted for something, good enough. **2** right and proper, fitting. **3** feeling in a suitable condition to do something. **4** in good athletic condition or health. –**fit** *verb* (**fitted**, **fitting**) **1** to be the right shape and size for something. **2** to put clothing on (a person) and adjust it to the right shape and size. **3** to put into place, *fit a lock on the door*. **4** to make or be suitable or competent, *his training fitted him for the position*. –**fit** *noun* the way a thing fits, *coat is a good fit*. □ **fit in** to make room or time etc. for; to be or cause to be harmonious or in a suitable relationship. **fit out** or **up** to supply or equip. **fitted sheet** a bed sheet edged with elastic to keep it secure on a mattress. **see** or **think fit** to decide or choose to do something, especially when this is unwise or without good reason. **fitly** *adverb*, **fitness** *noun*

fitful *adjective* occurring in short periods, not regularly or steadily. **fitfully** *adverb*

fitment *noun* a piece of fixed furniture.

fitter *noun* **1** a person who supervises the fitting of clothes etc. **2** a mechanic who fits together and adjusts the parts of machinery.

fitting *adjective* proper, suitable. –**fitting** *noun* the process of having a garment etc. fitted. **fittings** *plural noun* the fixtures and fitments of a building.

five *adjective* & *noun* one more than four (5, V). □ **five-star** *adjective* of the highest class.

fivefold *adjective* & *adverb* **1** five times as much or as many. **2** consisting of five parts.

fix *verb* **1** to fasten firmly. **2** to implant (facts or ideas) firmly in the mind or memory. **3** to direct (the eyes or attention) steadily. **4** to establish, to specify, *fixed a time for the meeting*. **5** to treat (a photographic image or a colour etc.) with a substance that prevents it from fading or changing colour. **6** to repair. **7** (*informal*) to deal with, to get even with. **8** (*informal*) to use bribery or deception or improper influence on, to arrange (the result of a race etc.) fraudulently. –**fix** *noun* **1** (*informal*) an awkward situation, *be in a fix*. **2** the finding of the position of a ship or aircraft etc. by taking bearings; the position found. **3** (*informal*) an addict's dose of a narcotic drug. □ **fixed assets** or **capital** machinery or property, or the capital invested in this, owned by a business company for carrying out manufacture etc. and not for resale. **fixed deposit** money deposited for a set period and at a fixed interest rate. **fixed star**

an ordinary star, one that (unlike the sun and planets) is so far from the earth that it seems to have no motion of its own. **fix on** to choose, to decide on. **fix up** to arrange; to organise; to provide for, *fixed him up for the night*.

fixation *noun* **1** fixing, being fixed. **2** an abnormal emotional attachment to a person or thing. **3** concentration on one idea, an obsession. **fixated** *adjective*

fixative *noun* **1** a substance for keeping things in position. **2** a substance for fixing colours etc., or for preventing perfumes from evaporating too quickly.

fixedly (**fiks**-ĕd-lee) *adverb* in a fixed way.

fixer *noun* **1** a person or thing that fixes something. **2** a substance for fixing photographic images.

fixity *noun* a fixed state, stability, permanence.

fixture *noun* **1** a thing that is fixed in position. **2** a person or thing that is firmly established and unlikely to leave. **3** a date appointed for a match or race etc.; the match or race itself.

fizz *verb* to make a hissing or spluttering sound as when gas escapes in bubbles from a liquid. −**fizz** *noun* **1** this sound. **2** a fizzy drink. **fizzy** *adjective*, **fizziness** *noun*

fizzer *noun* (*Austral. informal*) a failure or fiasco.

fizzle *verb* to make a feeble fizzing sound. □ **fizzle out** to end feebly or unsuccessfully.

fjord *noun* = **fiord**.

flab *noun* (*informal*) fat, flabbiness.

flabbergast *verb* to overwhelm with astonishment.

flabby *adjective* (**flabbier**, **flabbiest**) fat and limp, not firm. **flabbily** *adverb*, **flabbiness** *noun*

flaccid (**flak**-sĭd) *adjective* hanging loose or wrinkled, not firm. **flaccidly** *adverb*, **flaccidity** (flak-**sid**-ĭ-tee) *noun*

flag¹ *noun* **1** a piece of cloth attached by one edge to a staff or rope and used as the distinctive symbol of a country or as a signal. **2** an oblong device used as a signal that a taxi is for hire. **3** a small device of paper etc. resembling a flag. −**flag** *verb* (**flagged**, **flagging**) **1** to mark out with flags. **2** to signal with or as if with a flag; *flagged the vehicle down*, signalled to it to stop. □ **flag of convenience** a foreign flag of the nationality under which a ship is registered to evade taxation or regulations.

flag² *verb* (**flagged**, **flagging**) **1** to hang down limply, to droop. **2** to lose vigour. [from an old word *flag* = drooping]

flag³ *noun* a plant with bladed leaves, especially an iris.

flag⁴ *noun* a flagstone. −**flag** *verb* (**flagged**, **flagging**) to pave with flagstones. [from Old Norse *flaga* = slab of stone]

flagellate¹ (**flaj**-ĕ-layt) *verb* to whip. **flagellation** *noun*

flagellate² (**flaj**-ĕ-lăt) *adjective* (of protozoans) having whiplike projections. −**flagellate** *noun* a flagellate protozoan. [from Latin *flagellum* = a whip]

flageolet (flaj-ŏ-**let**) *noun* **1** a small pipe blown like a recorder. **2** an organ stop producing a similar quality of sound.

flagon *noun* **1** a large rounded bottle in which wine or cider etc. is sold, usually holding two litres. **2** a vessel with a handle, lip, and lid for serving wine at the table.

flagpole *noun* a flagstaff.

flagrant (**flay**-grănt) *adjective* (of an offence or error or an offender) very bad and obvious. **flagrantly** *adverb*, **flagrancy** *noun* [from Latin *flagrans* = blazing]

flagship *noun* **1** a ship that carries an admiral and flies his flag. **2** the principal vessel of a shipping line. **3** a firm's best or most important product.

flagstaff *noun* a pole on which a flag is hoisted.

flagstone *noun* a flat slab of rock used for paving. [from *flag⁴* + *stone*]

flail *noun* an old-fashioned tool for threshing grain, consisting of a strong stick hinged on a long handle. −**flail** *verb* **1** to beat with or as if with a flail. **2** to wave or swing about wildly. [from Latin *flagellum* = a whip]

flair *noun* a natural ability to do something well or to select and recognise what is good or useful etc. [French, = power to smell things]

flak *noun* **1** shells fired by anti-aircraft guns. **2** criticism; abuse. □ **flak jacket** a heavy protective jacket for soldiers etc, reinforced with metal. [short for German *Fliegerabwehrkanone* = anti-aircraft gun]

flake *noun* **1** a small light flat piece of snow. **2** a small thin leaflike piece of something. **3** dogfish or other shark sold as food. −**flake** *verb* **1** to come off in flakes. **2** to separate into flakes. □ **flake out** (*informal*) to collapse or fall asleep from exhaustion. **flaky** *adjective*

flambé (**flom**-bay) *adjective* (of food) covered with spirit and served alight. – **flambé** *verb* (**flambéed**, **flambéing**) to cover (food) with spirit and set alight. [French, = singed]

flamboyant *adjective* 1 coloured or decorated in a very showy way. 2 (of people) having a very showy appearance or manner. **flamboyantly** *adverb*, **flamboyance** *noun* [French, = blazing]

flame *noun* 1 a bright tongue-shaped portion of ignited gases burning visibly. 2 bright red. 3 passion, especially of love. – **flame** *verb* 1 to burn with flames, to send out flames. 2 to become bright red. 3 send an abusive message to a newsgroup etc. on the Internet. □ **flame gun** a device that projects a flame for destroying weeds etc. **flame-thrower** *noun* a weapon throwing a jet of flame.

flamenco (flă-**menk**-oh) *noun* (*plural* **flamencos**) a Spanish gypsy style of song or dance. [Spanish, = Flemish]

flaming *adjective* very hot or bright.

flamingo (flă-**ming**-goh) *noun* (*plural* **flamingoes**) a long-legged wading bird with a long neck and pinkish feathers.

flammable *adjective* able to be set on fire.

Usage See the note under **inflammable**.

flan *noun* an open pastry or sponge case filled with fruit or a savoury filling.

Flanders an area in the south-west of the Low Countries, now divided between Belgium, France, and Holland, the scene of much fighting in the First World War.

flange (*pr.* flanj) *noun* a projecting rim or edge.

flank *noun* 1 the fleshy part of each side of the body between the last rib and the hip. 2 the side of a building or mountain. 3 the right or left side of a body of troops etc. – **flank** *verb* to place or be situated at the side of.

flannel *noun* 1 a kind of loosely woven woollen fabric. 2 a cloth used for washing the face etc. 3 (*informal*) nonsense, flattery, bragging. – **flannel** *verb* (**flannelled**, **flannelling**) 1 to wash with a flannel. 2 (*informal*) to flatter. **flannels** *plural noun* trousers made of flannel or similar fabric.

flannelette *noun* cotton fabric made to look and feel like flannel.

flap *verb* (**flapped**, **flapping**) 1 to sway or be swayed up and down or from side to side, to wave about. 2 to give a light blow with something flat, *flapped at a fly*. 3 (*informal*) to be agitated or in a panic. – **flap** *noun* 1 the action or sound of flapping. 2 a light blow with something flat. 3 a broad piece hinged or attached at one side; a hinged or sliding section on an aircraft wing etc. used to control lift. 4 (*informal*) a state of agitation or fuss, *he is in a flap*.

flapjack *noun* a small thick pancake.

flare *verb* 1 to blaze with a sudden irregular flame. 2 to burst into sudden activity or anger, *tempers flared*. 3 to widen gradually outwards. – **flare** *noun* 1 a sudden outburst of flame. 2 a device producing a flaring light as a signal or for illumination. 3 a gradually widening shape. **flares** *plural noun* wide-bottomed trousers. □ **flare up** to burst into flame; to become suddenly angry.

flash *verb* 1 to give out a brief or intermittent bright light. 2 to come suddenly into view or into the mind, *the idea flashed upon me*. 3 to move rapidly, *the train flashed past*. 4 (of water) to rush along, to rise and flow. 5 to cause to shine briefly. 6 to signal with a light or lights. 7 to send (news etc.) by radio or telegraph. – **flash** *noun* 1 a sudden burst of flame or light. 2 a sudden showing of wit or feeling. 3 a very brief time, *in a flash*. 4 a rush of water. 5 a brief news item sent out by radio etc. 6 (in photography) flashlight. 7 a coloured patch of cloth as an emblem on a military uniform etc. – **flash** *adjective* (*informal*) flashy. □ **flash bulb** a bulb giving a bright light for flashlight photography. **flash drive** a data storage device containing flash memory. **flash flood** a sudden destructive flood. **flash in the pan** something that makes a promising start and then fails. (¶ Originally an explosion of gunpowder in the 'pan' of an old gun that failed to fire the charge in the barrel.) **flash memory** (in computing) a type of memory device that retains data in the absence of power.

flashback *noun* a scene in a story or film set in a time earlier than the main action.

flasher *noun* 1 (*informal*) a man who indecently exposes himself. 2 an automatic device for flashing a light intermittently.

flashing *noun* a strip of metal to prevent water entering at a joint in roofing etc.

flashlight *noun* 1 an electric torch. 2 a light giving an intense flash, used in photography.

flashpoint *noun* **1** the temperature at which vapour from oil etc. will ignite. **2** the point at which anger is ready to break out.

flashy *adjective* showy, gaudy. **flashily** *adverb*, **flashiness** *noun*

flask *noun* **1** a narrow-necked bottle. **2** a vacuum flask.

flat *adjective* (**flatter**, **flattest**) **1** horizontal, level. **2** spread out; lying at full length. **3** smooth and even; with a broad level surface and little depth, *a flat cap*. **4** (of a tyre) deflated because of a puncture etc. **5** absolute, unqualified, *a flat refusal*. **6** dull, monotonous. **7** (of drink) having lost its effervescence. **8** (of a battery etc.) unable to generate any more electric current. **9** (in music) below the correct pitch; *D flat* etc., a semitone lower than the corresponding note or key of natural pitch. – **flat** *adverb* **1** in a flat manner. **2** (*informal*) completely, *I am flat broke*. **3** (*informal*) exactly, *in ten seconds flat*. **4** below the correct pitch in music, *he was singing flat*. – **flat** *noun* **1** a flat thing or part, level ground. **2** a set of rooms on one floor, used as a residence. **3** (in music) a note that is a semitone lower than the corresponding one of natural pitch; the sign ♭ indicating this. □ **fall flat** to fail to win applause or appreciation. **flat feet** feet with less than the normal arch beneath. **flat out** at top speed; using all one's strength or resources. **flat race** a race over level ground, as distinct from a hurdle race or steeplechase. **flat rate** a rate that is the same in all cases, not proportional. **that's flat** (*informal*) that is definite. **flatly** *adverb*, **flatness** *noun*

flatfish *noun* a type of fish (e.g. sole) with both eyes on one side of a flattened body.

flatten *verb* to make or become flat.

flatter *verb* **1** to compliment (a person) excessively or insincerely, especially in order to win favour. **2** to gratify by honouring, *we were flattered to receive an invitation*. **3** to represent (a person or thing) favourably in a portrait etc. so that good looks are exaggerated. **flatterer** *noun* [from Old French *flater* = smooth down]

flattery *noun* **1** flattering. **2** excessive or insincere compliments.

flatulent (**flat**-yŭ-lĕnt) *adjective* causing or suffering from the formation of gas in the digestive tract. **flatulence** *noun*, **flatulency** *noun* [from Latin *flatus* = blowing]

flatworm *noun* a type of worm with a flattened body.

flaunt *verb* **1** to display proudly or ostentatiously. **2** (of a flag etc.) to wave proudly.

Usage *Flaunt* is sometimes confused with *flout*, meaning 'to disobey openly'.

flautist (**flaw**-tĭst) *noun* a flute player.

flavour *noun* **1** a distinctive taste. **2** a special quality or characteristic, *the story has a romantic flavour*. – **flavour** *verb* to give flavour to, to season.

flavouring *noun* a substance used to give flavour to food.

flaw *noun* an imperfection. – **flaw** *verb* to spoil with a flaw.

flawless *adjective* without a flaw, perfect. **flawlessly** *adverb*, **flawlessness** *noun*

flax *noun* **1** a blue-flowered plant cultivated for the textile fibre obtained from its stem and for its seeds (linseed). **2** its fibre.

flaxen *adjective* **1** made of flax. **2** pale yellow in colour like dressed flax, *flaxen hair*.

flay *verb* **1** to strip off the skin or hide of. **2** to criticise severely.

flea *noun* a small wingless jumping insect that feeds on human and animal blood. □ **flea bite** the bite of a flea; a trivial inconvenience or expense. **with a flea in one's ear** (*informal*) with a stinging rebuke.

fleck *noun* **1** a very small patch of colour. **2** a small particle, a speck. **flecked** *adjective* marked with specks.

fled *see* **flee**.

fledged *adjective* **1** (of young birds) with fully grown wing feathers, able to fly. **2** mature, trained and experienced, *a fully-fledged engineer*.

fledgeling *noun* a bird that is just fledged.

flee *verb* (**fled**, **fleeing**) **1** to run or hurry away. **2** to run away from, *fled the country*. **3** to pass away swiftly, to vanish, *all hope had fled*.

fleece *noun* **1** the woolly hair of a sheep or similar animal. **2** a soft fabric used for linings etc. – **fleece** *verb* **1** to defraud, to rob by trickery. **2** to remove the fleece from (a sheep). **fleecy** *adjective*

fleet¹ *noun* **1** the naval force of a country; a number of warships under one commander. **2** a number of ships or aircraft or buses etc. moving or working under one command or ownership. [from Old English *fleot* = ships]

fleet² *adjective* moving swiftly, nimble. **fleetly** *adverb*, **fleetness** *noun*

fleeting *adjective* passing quickly, brief, *a fleeting glimpse*.

Fleet Street London newspapers, the English national papers (most of which formerly had headquarters in Fleet Street, London).

Fleming¹ *noun* a native of Flanders.

Fleming², Sir Alexander (1881–1955), Scottish doctor and scientist, who in 1928 discovered the effect of penicillin on bacteria.

Flemish *adjective* of Flanders or its people or language. –**Flemish** *noun* the Flemish language.

flesh *noun* **1** the soft substance of an animal body, consisting of muscle and fat. **2** this tissue of animal bodies (excluding fish and sometimes fowl) as food. **3** the body as opposed to mind or soul. **4** the pulpy part of fruits and vegetables. □ **all flesh** (in the Bible) all living things; everyone. **flesh and blood** human nature, people with their emotions and weaknesses; *one's own flesh and blood*, relatives, descendants. **flesh wound** a wound that does not reach a bone or vital organ. **in the flesh** in bodily form, in person.

fleshy *adjective* **1** of or like flesh. **2** having much flesh, plump; (of plants or fruits etc.) pulpy. **fleshiness** *noun*

fleur-de-lis (fler-dĕ-**lee**) *noun* (*plural* **fleurs-de-lis**) a design of three petal-like parts used in heraldry. [French, = flower of lily]

flew *see* fly².

flex¹ *verb* to bend (a joint or limb); to move (a muscle) so that it bends a joint.

flex² *noun* flexible insulated wire used for carrying electric current to a lamp, iron, etc. [from Latin *flexum* = bent]

flexible *adjective* **1** able to bend easily without breaking. **2** adaptable, able to be changed to suit circumstances. **flexibly** *adverb*, **flexibility** *noun*

flexion *noun* bending, a bent state, especially of a joint or limb.

flexitime *noun* a system of flexible working hours.

flexor *noun* a muscle that bends a part of the body.

flick *noun* **1** a quick light blow or stroke, e.g. with a whip. **2** (*informal*) a cinema film; *the flicks*, a performance of films at a cinema. –**flick** *verb* to strike or remove with a quick light blow; to make a flicking movement.

□ **flick knife** a weapon with a blade that springs out when a button is pressed. **flick through** to turn over cards or pages etc. quickly.

flicker *verb* **1** to burn or shine unsteadily. **2** (of hope etc.) to occur briefly. **3** to quiver, to move quickly to and fro. –**flicker** *noun* a flickering movement or light; a brief occurrence of hope etc.

flier *noun* = flyer.

flight¹ *noun* **1** the process of flying; the movement or path of a thing through the air. **2** a journey made by air, transport in an aircraft making a particular journey. **3** a flock of birds or insects. **4** a number of aircraft regarded as a unit. **5** a series of stairs in a straight line or between two landings; a series of hurdles etc. in a race. **6** swift passage (of time). **7** an effort that is above the ordinary, *a flight of the imagination*. **8** the feathers etc. on a dart or arrow. □ **flight attendant** a passengers' attendant and waiter on an aircraft. **flight deck** the cockpit of a large aircraft. **flight recorder** an electronic device in an aircraft, recording information about its flight.

flight² *noun* fleeing, running or going away. □ **put to flight** to cause to flee. **take flight** or **take to flight** to flee.

flightless *adjective* (of birds, e.g. penguins) non-flying.

flighty *adjective* (**flightier**, **flightiest**) without a serious purpose or interest.

flimsy *adjective* (**flimsier**, **flimsiest**) **1** light and thin; of loose structure; fragile. **2** unconvincing, *a flimsy excuse*. **flimsily** *adverb*, **flimsiness** *noun*

flinch *verb* **1** to draw back in fear, to wince. **2** to shrink from one's duty etc.

Flinders, Matthew (1774–1814), English navigator who circumnavigated Van Diemen's Land (with George Bass) (1798–99), and the continent of Australia (1801–03). □ **Flinders Island** an island in Bass Strait.

fling *verb* (**flung**, **flinging**) **1** to throw violently, angrily, or hurriedly; *fling caution to the winds*, act rashly. **2** to put or send suddenly or forcefully, *flung him into prison*. **3** to rush, to go angrily or violently, *she flung out of the room*. –**fling** *noun* **1** the act or movement of flinging. **2** a kind of vigorous dance, *the Highland fling*. **3** a spell of indulgence in pleasure, *have a fling*.

flint *noun* **1** a very hard kind of stone that can produce sparks when struck against steel.

2 a piece of this. **3** a piece of hard alloy used to produce a spark.

flintlock *noun* an old type of gun fired by a spark from a flint.

flinty *adjective* (**flintier**, **flintiest**) like flint, very hard.

flip *verb* (**flipped**, **flipping**) **1** to flick. **2** to toss (a thing) with a sharp movement so that it turns over in the air. **3** (*informal*) to show great anger. – **flip** *noun* the action of flipping something. – **flip** *adjective* (*informal*) glib, flippant. □ **flip side** the reverse side of a gramophone record.

flippant *adjective* not showing proper seriousness. **flippantly** *adverb*, **flippancy** *noun*

flipper *noun* **1** a limb of certain sea animals (e.g. seals, turtles, penguins), used in swimming. **2** one of a pair of large flat rubber attachments worn on the feet for underwater swimming.

flirt *verb* **1** to pretend light-heartedly to court a person. **2** to toy, *flirted with the idea*; *flirting with death*, taking great risks. **3** to move (a thing) to and fro in short rapid jerks. – **flirt** *noun* a person who flirts. **flirtation** *noun*, **flirtatious** *adjective*

flit *verb* (**flitted**, **flitting**) **1** to fly or move lightly and quickly. **2** to decamp in a stealthy way. – **flit** *noun* a stealthy move of this kind.

flitch *noun* a side of bacon.

float *verb* **1** to rest or drift on the surface of a liquid without sinking; to be held up freely in air or gas. **2** to cause to do this. **3** to move lightly or casually. **4** to have or allow (currency) to have a variable rate of exchange. **5** to launch (a business company or a scheme), especially by getting financial support from the sale of shares. – **float** *noun* **1** a thing designed to float on liquid; a cork or quill used on a fishing line to show when the bait has been taken; any of the corks supporting the edge of a fishing net. **2** a floating device to control the flow of water, petrol, etc. **3** a structure to enable an aircraft to float on water. **4** a low cart; a platform on wheels carrying a display in a procession. **5** a horse float. **6** a sum of money made available for minor expenditures or for giving change. □ **floating rib** any of the ribs not joined to the breastbone.

floater *noun* **1** a person or thing that floats. **2** a person who frequently changes jobs. **3** (in South Australia) a meat pie (often with tomato sauce) served in thick pea soup.

floc *noun* a mass of fine particles looking like tufts of wool.

flocculent *adjective* like tufts of wool; in or showing tufts. **flocculence** *noun*

flock¹ *noun* **1** a number of sheep, goats, or birds kept together or feeding or travelling together. **2** a large number of people together. **3** a number of people in someone's charge; a Christian congregation. – **flock** *verb* to gather or go in a flock.

flock² *noun* **1** a tuft of wool or cotton etc. **2** wool or cotton waste used for stuffing mattresses etc., powdered wool or cloth.

floe *noun* a sheet of floating ice. [from Norwegian *flo* = layer]

flog *verb* (**flogged**, **flogging**) **1** to beat severely with a rod or whip, as a punishment. **2** (*informal*) to sell. **flogging** *noun*

flood *noun* **1** the coming of a great quantity of water over a place that is usually dry, the water itself; **the Flood** that of the time of Noah, described in Genesis. **2** a great outpouring or outburst, *a flood of abuse*. **3** the inflow of the tide. – **flood** *verb* **1** to cover or fill with a flood, to overflow. **2** (of a river etc.) to become flooded. **3** to come in great quantities, *letters flooded in*. **4** to overfill (a carburettor) with petrol. □ **be flooded out** to be forced to leave because of a flood. **flood plain** the flat area beside a river that becomes covered by water when the river floods. **flood tide** the rising tide.

floodgate *noun* a gate that can be opened or closed to control the flow of water, especially the lower gate of a lock.

floodlight *noun* a lamp used for producing a broad bright beam of light to light up a stage or building etc. – **floodlight** *verb* (**floodlit**, **floodlighting**) to illuminate with this.

floor *noun* **1** the lower surface of a room, the part on which one stands. **2** the bottom of the sea or of a cave etc. **3** (in legislative chambers) the place where members sit and speak. **4** a storey of a building, all the rooms having a continuous floor. – **floor** *verb* **1** to put a floor into (a building). **2** to knock down (a person) in a fight. **3** to baffle, to overwhelm (a person) with a problem or argument. □ **have the floor** to have the right to speak next in a debate.

floorboard *noun* one of the boards forming the floor of a room.

flooring *noun* boards etc. used as a floor.

floozie *noun* (also **floozy**) (*informal*) a woman, especially a promiscuous one.

flop *verb* (flopped, flopping) **1** to hang or sway heavily and loosely. **2** to fall or move or sit down clumsily. **3** (*informal*) to be a failure. – **flop** *noun* **1** a flopping movement or sound. **2** (*informal*) a failure. – **flop** *adverb* with a flop, *it fell flop on the floor*.

floppy *adjective* (floppier, floppiest) hanging heavily and loosely, not firm or rigid. □ **floppy disk** a flexible computer disk (usually enclosed in a square plastic case) for storing machine-readable data. **floppiness** *noun*

flora *noun* the plants of an area or period of time. [from the name of Flora, the ancient Roman goddess of flowers (Latin *flores* = flowers)]

floral *adjective* of flowers.

Florentine (**flo**-rĕn-tyn) *adjective* of Florence, a city of north Italy. – **Florentine** *noun* **1** a native of Florence. **2** a biscuit containing nuts and dried fruit on a chocolate base.

florescence (flŏ-**ress**-ĕns) *noun* the time or state of flowering or flourishing.

floret (**flo**-rĕt) *noun* **1** a small flower. **2** each of the small flowers that make up a composite flower such as a daisy.

Florey, Howard Walter, Baron (1898–1968), Australian pathologist who with Sir Ernst Chain developed penicillin for clinical use.

floribunda (flo-rĭ-**bun**-dă) *noun* a rose or other plant bearing dense clusters of flowers.

florid (**flo**-rĭd) *adjective* **1** elaborate and ornate. **2** (of the complexion) ruddy.

Florida (**flo**-rĭ-dă) a State forming a peninsula of the south-eastern USA.

florin (**flo**-rĭn) *noun* **1** a Dutch guilder. **2** a former coin worth two shillings.

florist (**flo**-rĭst) *noun* a person whose business is the selling or growing of flowers.

floss *noun* **1** a mass of silky fibres. **2** silk thread with little or no twist, used in embroidery. **3** (also **dental floss**) thread used for cleaning between teeth. – **floss** *verb* to clean (teeth) using dental floss. **flossy** *adjective*

flotation *noun* floating, especially the launching of a commercial venture.

flotilla (flŏ-**til**-ă) *noun* **1** a small fleet. **2** a fleet of boats or small ships. [Spanish, = little fleet]

flotsam *noun* wreckage found floating. □ **flotsam and jetsam** odds and ends.

flounce[1] *verb* to go in an impatient annoyed manner, *flounced out of the room*. – **flounce** *noun* a flouncing movement.

flounce[2] *noun* a deep frill of material sewn by its upper edge to a skirt etc.

flounced *adjective* trimmed with a flounce.

flounder[1] *noun* a small edible flatfish.

flounder[2] *verb* **1** to move clumsily and with difficulty as in mud. **2** to make mistakes or become confused when trying to do something.

flour *noun* fine meal or powder made from grain after the bran has been sifted out, used in cooking. – **flour** *verb* to cover or sprinkle with flour. **floury** *adjective* [old spelling of *flower*]

flourish *verb* **1** to thrive in growth or development. **2** to prosper, to be successful. **3** (of famous people) to be alive and working at a certain time. **4** to wave (a thing) dramatically. – **flourish** *noun* **1** a dramatic sweeping gesture. **2** a flowing ornamental curve in writing etc. **3** a fanfare. [from Latin *florere* = to flower]

flout *verb* to disobey openly and scornfully.

Usage *Flout* should not be confused with *flaunt* which means 'to display proudly'.

---

flow *verb* **1** to glide along as a stream, to move freely like a liquid or gas; to circulate. **2** to proceed steadily and continuously, *keep the traffic flowing*. **3** (of talk or literary style) to proceed smoothly and evenly. **4** to hang loosely; (of a line or curve) to be smoothly continuous. **5** to gush forth; (of the tide) to come in, to rise. **6** to come (from a source), to be the result. – **flow** *noun* **1** a flowing movement or mass. **2** the amount that flows. **3** an outpouring, a copious supply. **4** the inward movement of the tide towards the land, *ebb and flow*. □ **flow chart** a diagram showing the movement of things through a series of processes, e.g. in manufacturing; a diagram of a computer program or other structured process. **flow-on** (*Austral*.) a wage or salary increase granted as a consequence of one already made in a similar or related occupation.

flower *noun* **1** the part of a plant from which seed or fruit develops. **2** a blossom and its stem for use as a decoration etc., usually in groups. **3** a plant that is noted or cultivated for its fine flowers. **4** the best part of something. – **flower** *verb* **1** (of a plant) to produce flowers.

2 to cause or allow (a plant) to produce flowers. □ **in flower** with the flowers out. [compare *flora*]

flowered *adjective* ornamented with flowers.

flowerless *adjective* (of plants) non-flowering.

flowerpot *noun* a pot in which a plant may be grown.

flowery *adjective* **1** full of flowers. **2** (of language) full of ornamental phrases.

flown *see* fly².

flu *noun* (*informal*) influenza.

fluctuate *verb* (of levels, prices, etc.) to vary irregularly, to rise and fall. **fluctuation** *noun* [from Latin *fluctus* = a wave]

flue *noun* **1** a smoke duct in a chimney. **2** a channel for conveying heat.

fluent (**floo**-ĕnt) *adjective* **1** (of a person) able to speak smoothly and readily. **2** (of speech) coming smoothly and readily. **fluently** *adverb*, **fluency** *noun* [from Latin *fluens* = flowing]

fluff *noun* **1** a light soft downy substance. **2** (*informal*) a bungled attempt; a mistake in speaking. –**fluff** *verb* **1** to shake into a soft mass. **2** (*informal*) to bungle.

fluffy *adjective* (**fluffier, fluffiest**) having or covered with a soft mass of fur or fibres. **fluffiness** *noun*

fluid *noun* a substance that is able to flow freely as liquids and gases do. –**fluid** *adjective* **1** able to flow freely, not solid or rigid. **2** (of a situation) not stable. □ **fluid ounce** (*Brit.*) one-twentieth of a pint (approximately 28 ml); (*Amer.*) one-sixteenth of an American pint (approximately 30 ml). **fluidity** (floo-**id**-ĭ-tee) *noun* [from Latin *fluere* = to flow]

fluke¹ *noun* an accidental stroke of good luck.

fluke² *noun* **1** the broad triangular flat end of each arm of an anchor. **2** the barbed head of a harpoon etc. **3** one of the lobes of a whale's tail.

fluke³ *noun* **1** a kind of flatfish, especially the flounder. **2** a flatworm found as a parasite in sheep's liver.

flum *noun* (*Austral. informal*) a piece of luck.

flummery *noun* a sweet milk pudding.

flummox *verb* (*informal*) to baffle.

flung *see* fling.

flunk *verb* (*informal*) to fail, especially in an examination.

fluoresce (floo-ŏ-**ress**) *verb* to become fluorescent.

fluorescent (floo-ŏ-**ress**-ĕnt) *adjective* (of substances) taking in radiations and sending them out in the form of light; (of lamps) containing such a substance; (of a screen) coated with this. **fluorescence** *noun*

fluoridate (**floo**-ŏ-rĭ-dayt) *verb* to add traces of fluoride to drinking water to prevent or reduce tooth decay. **fluoridation** *noun*

fluoride *noun* a compound of fluorine and one other element.

fluorine (**floo**-ŏ-reen) *noun* a chemical element (symbol F), a pale yellow corrosive gas.

flurry *noun* **1** a short sudden rush of wind or rain or snow. **2** a commotion. **3** a state of nervous agitation. –**flurry** *verb* (**flurried, flurrying**) to fluster.

flush¹ *verb* **1** to become red in the face because of a rush of blood to the skin. **2** to cause (the face) to redden in this way. **3** to fill with pride, *flushed with success*. **4** to cleanse (a drain or toilet etc.) with a flow of water; to dispose of in this way. **5** (of water) to rush out in a flood. –**flush** *noun* **1** flushing of the face, a blush. **2** excitement caused by emotion, *the first flush of victory*. **3** a rush of water. **4** fresh growth of vegetation. –**flush** *adjective* **1** level, in the same plane, without projections. **2** (*informal*) well supplied with money.

flush² *verb* to cause (a bird) to fly up and away; to drive out.

fluster *verb* to make nervous and confused. –**fluster** *noun* a flustered state.

flute *noun* **1** a wind instrument consisting of a pipe with holes stopped by fingers or keys and a mouth-hole at the side or end. **2** an ornamental groove. –**flute** *verb* **1** to play on the flute. **2** to speak or utter in flutelike tones. **3** to make ornamental grooves in.

fluting *noun* ornamental grooves.

flutter *verb* **1** to move the wings hurriedly in flying or trying to fly. **2** to wave or flap quickly and irregularly; (of the heart) to beat feebly and irregularly. –**flutter** *noun* **1** a fluttering movement or beat. **2** a state of nervous excitement. **3** a stir, a sensation. **4** (*informal*) a slight gamble, *have a flutter*. **5** high-frequency variation in the pitch or loudness of reproduced sound.

fluvial (**floo**-vee-ăl) *adjective* of or found in rivers. [from Latin *fluvius* = river]

flux *noun* 1 a continuous succession of changes. 2 flowing, flowing out.

fly[1] *noun* 1 a two-winged insect. 2 a disease caused by one of various flies. 3 a natural or artificial fly used as bait in fishing. □ **fly-blown** *adjective* (of meat etc.) tainted by flies' eggs. **fly-fishing** *noun* fishing with flies as bait. **fly in the ointment** one small thing that spoils enjoyment. **no flies on** (*Austral. informal*) no lack of alertness in.

fly[2] *verb* (**flew**, **flown**, **flying**) 1 to move through the air by means of wings as a bird does. 2 to travel through the air or through space. 3 to travel in an aircraft. 4 to direct or control the flight of (an aircraft etc.); to transport in an aircraft. 5 to raise (a flag) so that it waves; (of a flag) to wave in the air. 6 to make (a kite) rise and stay aloft. 7 to go or move quickly, to rush along; (of time) to pass quickly. 8 to be scattered violently, *sparks flew in all directions.* 9 to become angry etc. quickly, *flew into a rage.* 10 to flee from, *must fly the country.* **–fly** *noun* 1 flying. 2 a flap of material on a garment to contain or cover a fastening, *trouser fly.* 3 a flap at the entrance of a tent. 4 a speed-regulating device in clockwork or machinery. □ **fly a kite** (*informal*) to do something in order to test public opinion. **fly at** to attack violently, either physically or with words. **fly-by-night** *adjective* (*informal*) unreliable, transient. **fly-half** *noun* a stand-off half in rugby football. **fly high** to behave very ambitiously. **fly in the face of** to disregard or disobey openly. **fly off the handle** (*informal*) to become uncontrollably angry. **fly-past** *noun* a ceremonial flight of aircraft past a person or place. **send flying** to knock (a person or thing) violently aside.

fly[3] *adjective* (*informal*) astute, knowing.

flycatcher *noun* a bird that catches insects in the air.

flyer *noun* (also **flier**) 1 a bird etc. that flies. 2 an animal or vehicle that moves very fast. 3 an airman or airwoman. 4 an airline passenger. 5 an information leaflet. 6 a high-flyer.

flying *adjective* able to fly. □ **flying buttress** a buttress that springs from a separate structure, usually forming an arch with the wall it supports. **flying colours** great credit gained in a test etc., *passed with flying colours.* **flying doctor** a doctor who visits patients (e.g. in the outback) by air (*see* **Australian Inland Mission**). **flying doe** a young female kangaroo. **flying fish** a tropical fish with winglike fins,

able to rise into the air. **flying fox** a fruit-eating bat; (*Austral.*) a carrier operated by a cable across a gorge or difficult terrain. **flying leap** a forward leap made while moving swiftly. **flying possum** or **phalanger** a tree-climbing gliding Australian marsupial (*see* **glider**). **flying saucer** an unidentified saucer-shaped object reported as seen in the sky (*see* **UFO**). **flying squad** a detachment of police etc. organised for rapid movement. **flying start** a vigorous start giving one an initial advantage. **flying visit** a brief or hasty visit.

Flying Dutchman a legendary spectral ship supposed to be seen in the region of the Cape of Good Hope, an omen of disaster.

flyleaf *noun* a blank leaf at the beginning or end of a book etc.

Flynn, John (1880–1951), Australian minister and missionary who in 1928 founded the Australian Inland Mission Aerial Medical Service (later known as the Royal Flying Doctor Service).

flyover *noun* a bridge that carries one road or railway over another.

flyscreen *noun* a frame fitted with fine mesh put over windows and doors to keep out flies.

flyweight *noun* a boxing weight below bantamweight, in amateur boxing 48–51 kg.

flywheel *noun* a heavy wheel revolving on a shaft to regulate machinery.

FM *abbreviation* frequency modulation.

foal *noun* the young of a horse or of a related animal. **–foal** *verb* to give birth to a foal. □ **in foal** (of a mare) pregnant.

foam *noun* 1 a collection of small bubbles formed in or on a liquid. 2 the froth of saliva or perspiration. 3 rubber or plastic in a light spongy form. **–foam** *verb* to form or send out foam. **foamy** *adjective*

fob[1] *noun* an ornament worn hanging from a watch chain etc.; a tab on a keyring.

fob[2] *verb* (**fobbed**, **fobbing**) **fob off** to palm (a thing) off; to get (a person) to accept something of little or no value instead of what he or she is seeking.

focaccia (fŏ-**kah**-chǎ) *noun* a type of Italian bread, often flavoured with herbs.

focal *adjective* of or at a focus.

fo'c's'le (**fohk**-sŭl) *noun* = **forecastle**.

focus (**foh**-kŭs) *noun* (*plural* **focuses** or **foci**, *pr*. **foh**-sy) 1 the point at which rays meet or from which they appear to proceed.

2 a fixed point used with a given directrix in the drawing of certain curves. **3** the point or distance at which an object is most clearly seen by the eye or through a lens. **4** an adjustment on a lens to produce a clear image at varying distances. **5** a centre of activity or interest etc. –**focus** *verb* (**focused**, **focusing**) **1** to adjust the focus of (a lens or the eye). **2** to bring into focus. **3** to concentrate or be concentrated or directed (on a centre etc.). [Latin, = hearth (the central point of a household)]

fodder *noun* dried food, hay, etc. for horses and farm animals.

foe *noun* an enemy.

foetid (**fee**-tĭd) *adjective* = **fetid**.

foetus (**fee**-tŭs) *noun* (*plural* **foetuses**) a developed embryo in the womb or egg; a human embryo more than eight weeks after conception. **foetal** *adjective*

fog *noun* **1** thick mist that is difficult to see through. **2** cloudiness on a photographic negative etc., obscuring the image. –**fog** *verb* (**fogged**, **fogging**) **1** to cover or become covered with fog or condensed vapour. **2** to cause cloudiness on (a negative etc.). **3** to bewilder, to perplex.

fogey *noun* = **fogy**.

foggy *adjective* (**foggier**, **foggiest**) **1** full of fog. **2** made opaque by condensed vapour etc., clouded. **3** obscure, vague, *only a foggy idea*. □ **not have the foggiest** (*informal*) to have no idea at all. **fogginess** *noun*

foghorn *noun* a sounding instrument for warning ships in fog.

fogy *noun* (*plural* **fogies**) a person with old-fashioned ideas, *an old fogy*.

föhn (*pr.* fern) *noun* a warm dry wind on the lee side of mountains, especially on the northern slopes of the Alps. [German from Latin *Favonius* = mild west wind]

foible (**foi**-bŭl) *noun* a harmless peculiarity in a person's character.

foil[1] *noun* **1** metal hammered or rolled into a thin sheet, *tin foil*. **2** a person or thing that contrasts strongly with another and therefore makes the other's qualities more obvious.

foil[2] *verb* to thwart, to frustrate.

foil[3] *noun* a long thin sword with a button on the point, used in fencing.

foist *verb* to cause a person to accept (something inferior or unwelcome or undeserved), *the job was foisted on us*.

[originally = dishonestly substitute a loaded dice]

fold[1] *verb* **1** to bend or turn (a flexible thing) so that one part lies on another; to close or flatten by pressing parts together. **2** to become folded; to be able to be folded. **3** to clasp (the arms etc.) about; to hold (a person or thing) close to one's breast. **4** to envelop. **5** to blend (an ingredient with others) by gently spooning one part over another. **6** to collapse, to cease to function, *the business had folded* or *folded up*. –**fold** *noun* **1** a folded part, a hollow between two thicknesses. **2** a line made by folding. **3** folding or curvature of strata in the earth's crust. **4** a hollow among hills or mountains. □ **fold mountains** mountains formed by folding of the earth's crust. **fold one's arms** to place them together or entwined across one's chest. **fold one's hands** to clasp or place them together.

fold[2] *noun* **1** an enclosure for sheep. **2** an established body of people with the same beliefs or aims; the members of a Church.

folder *noun* **1** a folding cover for loose papers. **2** a folded leaflet.

foliaceous (foh-lee-**ay**-shŭs) *adjective* of or like leaves.

foliage (**foh**-lee-ij) *noun* the leaves of a tree or plant. [from Latin *folium* = leaf]

foliate (**foh**-lee-ăt) *adjective* leaflike; having leaves or a specified number of leaflets. –**foliate** (**foh**-lee-ayt) *verb* to split or beat into thin layers. **foliation** *noun*

folic acid (**foh**-lik) *noun* a vitamin of the B group, deficiency of which causes anaemia.

folio (**foh**-lee-oh) *noun* (*plural* **folios**) **1** a large sheet of paper folded once, making two leaves of a book. **2** a book made of such sheets, the largest-sized volume. **3** the page-number of a printed book.

folk *noun* **1** people in general. **2** the people of a certain group or nation etc., *country folk*. **3** one's relatives. □ **folk dance**, **folk song**, etc., a dance, song, etc. in the traditional style of a country.

folklore *noun* the traditional beliefs and tales etc. of a community. **folklorist** *noun*

folksy *adjective* **1** simple in manner. **2** friendly, sociable.

follicle (**fol**-i-kŭl) *noun* **1** a very small sac or cavity in the body, especially one containing a hair root. **2** a group of cells surrounding an egg cell inside an ovary. [from Latin *folliculus* = a little bellows]

follow *verb* **1** to go or come after. **2** to go along (a path or road etc.). **3** to provide with a sequel or successor. **4** to take as a guide or leader or example; *follow the fashion*, conform to it. **5** to grasp the meaning of, to understand. **6** to take an interest in the progress of (events, a team, etc.). **7** to happen as a result, to result from. **8** to be necessarily true in consequence of something else. □ **follow on** (of a side in cricket) to have to bat again immediately after the first innings because of a low score. **follow-on** *noun* an instance of this. **follow suit** to play a card of the suit led; to follow a person's example. **follow through** to continue to a conclusion. **follow up** to add a further action or blow etc. to a previous one; to perform further work or investigation etc. upon. **follow-up** *noun*

follower *noun* **1** one who follows. **2** a person who believes in or supports a religion, teacher, or cause etc.

following *noun* a body of believers or supporters. –**following** *adjective* now to be mentioned, *answer the following questions*. –**following** *preposition* as a sequel to, after, *following the election, the share market was busy*.

folly *noun* **1** foolishness, a foolish act. **2** a costly ornamental building serving no practical purpose. [from French *folie* = madness]

foment (fŏ-**ment**) *verb* to arouse or stimulate (trouble, discontent, etc.). [from Latin *fomentum* = poultice]

fomentation (foh-men-**tay**-shŏn) *noun* **1** fomenting. **2** hot lotion applied to part of the body to relieve pain or inflammation.

fond *adjective* **1** affectionate, loving. **2** over-affectionate, doting. **3** (of hopes) cherished but unlikely to be fulfilled. □ **fond of** having a liking for, loving; much inclined to. **fondly** *adverb*, **fondness** *noun* [from *fon* = a fool]

fondant *noun* a soft sweet made of flavoured sugar. [French, = melting]

fondle *verb* to touch or stroke lovingly.

fondue (**fon**-doo) *noun* a dish of flavoured melted cheese. [French, = melted]

font¹ *noun* a basin or vessel (often of carved stone) in a church, to hold water for baptism. [from Latin *fontis* = of a fountain]

font² *noun* (also **fount**) (in printing) a set of type of one face and size.

food *noun* **1** any substance that can be taken into the body of an animal or plant to maintain its life and growth. **2** a solid substance of this kind, *food and drink*. □ **food chain** a series of plants and animals each of which serves as food for the next. **food poisoning** illness caused by bacteria or toxins in food. **food processor** an electrically driven device with blades for mixing, chopping, or slicing food. **food value** the nourishing power of a food. **food web** a number of connected food chains in an area.

foodstuff *noun* a substance used as food.

fool *noun* **1** a person who acts unwisely, one who lacks good sense or judgment. **2** a jester or clown in a household during the Middle Ages. **3** a creamy dessert of fruit purée mixed with cream or custard. –**fool** *verb* **1** to behave in a joking or teasing way. **2** to play about idly. **3** to trick or deceive (a person). □ **fool's paradise** happiness based on an illusion.

foolery *noun* foolish acts or behaviour.

foolhardy *adjective* bold but rash, delighting in taking unnecessary risks. **foolhardiness** *noun*

foolish *adjective* **1** lacking good sense or judgment. **2** (of actions) unwise. **3** ridiculous, *felt foolish*. **foolishly** *adverb*, **foolishness** *noun*

foolproof *adjective* **1** (of rules or instructions) plain and simple and unable to be misinterpreted. **2** (of machinery) very simple to operate.

foolscap *noun* a large size of writing paper. [so called from the use of a *fool's cap* (a jester's cap with bells) as a watermark]

foot *noun* (*plural* **feet**) **1** the end part of the leg below the ankle. **2** a similar part in animals, used in moving or to attach itself to things. **3** the lower end of a table or bed etc., the end opposite the head. **4** the part of a stocking covering the foot. **5** a person's step or tread or pace of movement, *fleet of foot*. **6** a lower usually projecting part of something (e.g. of a table leg); the part of a sewing machine that is lowered on to the material to hold it steady. **7** the lowest part of something that has height or length, the bottom of a hill, ladder, page, list, etc. **8** a measure of length, = 12 inches (30.48 cm). **9** a unit of rhythm in a line of poetry, usually containing a stressed syllable, e.g. each of the four divisions in

Jack/and Jill/went up/the hill. **–foot** *verb* to go on foot, to walk, *we shall have to foot it.* □ **feet of clay** a great weakness, in a person or thing that is honoured. **foot-and-mouth disease** a contagious disease of cattle etc. **foot the bill** to pay the bill. **have a foot in both camps** to be a member of each of two opposing factions. **have one foot in the grave** to be nearing death or very old. **on foot** walking not riding. **to one's feet** to a standing position. **under foot** on the ground, in a position to be trodden on. **under one's feet** in danger of being trodden on, in the way.

footage *noun* a length measured in feet, especially of exposed cinema or television film.

football *noun* 1 a large round or elliptical inflated leather ball. 2 a game played with this on a field, between two teams of players. □ **football pool** a form of gambling on the results of a number of football matches. **footballer** *noun*, **footballing** *noun*

footbridge *noun* a bridge for pedestrians, not for traffic.

footfall *noun* the sound of a footstep.

foothill *noun* one of the low hills near the bottom of a mountain or range.

foothold *noun* 1 a place just wide enough for a foot to be placed on when climbing etc. 2 a small but secure position gained in a business enterprise etc.

footing *noun* 1 a placing of the feet, a foothold; *lost his footing*, slipped. 2 a status, conditions, *they were on a friendly footing.*

footlights *plural noun* a row of lights along the front of a stage floor.

footling (**foot**-ling) *adjective* (*informal*) trivial.

footloose *adjective* independent, without responsibilities.

footman *noun* (*plural* **footmen**) a manservant (usually in livery) who admits visitors, etc.

footmark *noun* a footprint.

footnote *noun* a note printed at the bottom of a page.

footpath *noun* a path for pedestrians, a pavement.

footplate *noun* a platform for the driver etc. operating a locomotive.

footprint *noun* an impression left by a foot or shoe.

footslog *verb* (**footslogged**, **footslogging**) (*informal*) to walk, to march.

footsore *adjective* having feet that are sore from walking.

footstep *noun* a step taken in walking; the sound of this. □ **follow in someone's footsteps** to do as another person did before.

footstool *noun* a stool for resting the feet on when sitting.

footwear *noun* shoes and socks or stockings.

footwork *noun* the manner of moving or using the feet in dancing, boxing, football, etc.

footy *noun* (*Austral. informal*) football.

fop *noun* a dandy. **foppery** *noun*, **foppish** *adjective*

for *preposition* 1 in place of. 2 as the price or penalty of, *was fined for speeding*. 3 in defence or support or favour of. 4 with a view to, in order to find or obtain, *went for a walk*; *looking for a job*. 5 with regard to, in respect of, *ready for dinner*. 6 in the direction of, *set out for home*. 7 intended to be received by or belong to, *bought shoes for the children*. 8 so as to happen at a stated time, *an appointment for two o'clock*. 9 because of, on account of, *famous for its cheese*. 10 to the extent or duration of, *walked for two kilometres*; *it will last for years*. **–for** *conjunction* because, *they hesitated, for they were afraid*. □ **be for it** (*informal*) to be about to meet with punishment or trouble. **for ever** for all time, *promised to love each other for ever*; (*informal*) for a very long time. (Compare **forever**.)

for- *prefix* 1 away, off (as in *forgive*). 2 prohibiting (as in *forbid*). 3 abstaining or neglecting (as in *forgo, forsake*).

forage (*rhymes with* porridge) *noun* 1 food for horses and cattle. 2 foraging. **–forage** *verb* to go searching, to rummage. **forager** *noun*

foramen (fŏ-**ray**-men) *noun* (*plural* **foramina**) an opening or hole in a part of an animal or plant. [Latin, from *forare* = to bore a hole]

foray (**fo**-ray) *noun* a sudden attack or raid, especially to obtain something.

forbade *see* **forbid**.

forbear *verb* (**forbore**, **forborne**, **forbearing**) to refrain, to refrain from, *could not forbear criticising* or *from criticising*; *forbore to mention it.*

forbearance *noun* patience, tolerance.

forbearing *adjective & noun* being patient or tolerant.

forbid *verb* (**forbade** (*pr.* for-**bad**), **forbidden**, **forbidding**) **1** to order (a person) not to do something or not to enter, *forbid him to go*; *forbid him the court*. **2** to refuse to allow, *forbid the marriage*.

forbidding *adjective* looking unfriendly or uninviting, stern.

forbore, **forborne** *see* forbear.

force *noun* **1** strength, power, intense effort. **2** (in scientific use) a measurable influence tending to cause movement of a body; its intensity. **3** a body of troops or police. **4** a body of people organised or available for a purpose, *a labour force*. **5** compulsion. **6** effectiveness, legal validity, *the new rules come into force next week*. –**force** *verb* **1** to use force in order to get or do something, to compel, to oblige. **2** to exert force on, to break open by force, *forced the lock*. **3** to strain to the utmost, to strain too hard. **4** to impose, to inflict; *force a card on someone*, to make him or her select a particular one by trickery. **5** to cause or produce by effort, *forced a smile*. **6** to cause (plants etc.) to reach maturity earlier than is normal. □ **force a person's hand** to compel him or her to take action. **forced march** a lengthy march requiring special effort by troops etc. **force-land** *verb* to make a **forced landing**, an emergency landing of an aircraft. **force the issue** to make an immediate decision necessary. **force the pace** to adopt a high speed in a race etc. and so tire out others who are taking part. **in force** valid; in great strength or numbers.

force-feed *verb* (**force-fed**, **force-feeding**) to feed (a prisoner etc.) against his or her will.

forceful *adjective* powerful and vigorous, effective. **forcefully** *adverb*, **forcefulness** *noun*

forcemeat *noun* finely-chopped meat seasoned and used as stuffing.

forceps (**for**-seps) *noun* (*plural* **forceps**) pincers or tongs used by dentists, surgeons, etc.

forcible *adjective* done by force, forceful. **forcibly** *adverb*

Ford, Henry (1863–1947), American pioneer of mass production for motor vehicles.

ford *noun* a shallow place where a river may be crossed by wading or riding or driving through. –**ford** *verb* to cross in this way.

fordable *adjective* able to be forded.

fore *adjective* situated in front. –**fore** *adverb* in or at or towards the front. –**fore** *noun* the fore part. –**fore** *interjection* a cry to warn a person who may be hit by a golf ball that is about to be played. □ **fore-and-aft** *adjective* (of sails) set lengthwise on a ship or boat (as opposed to *square-rigged*).

fore- *prefix* before (as in *forecast*); in front (as in *foreleg*).

forearm[1] *noun* the arm from elbow to wrist or fingertips.

forearm[2] *verb* to arm or prepare in advance against possible danger etc.

forebears *plural noun* ancestors.

forebode *verb* to be an advance sign or token of (trouble).

foreboding *noun* a feeling that trouble is coming.

forecast *verb* (**forecast**, **forecasting**) to tell in advance (what is likely to happen). –**forecast** *noun* a statement that forecasts.

forecastle (**fohk**-sŭl) *noun* the forward part of certain ships, where formerly the crew had their accommodation.

foreclose *verb* **1** (of a firm etc. that has lent money on mortgage) to take possession of property when the loan is not duly repaid, *to foreclose a mortgage*. **2** to bar from a privilege. **foreclosure** *noun*

forecourt *noun* an enclosed space in front of a building, an outer court.

forefathers *plural noun* ancestors.

forefinger *noun* the finger next to the thumb.

forefoot *noun* (*plural* **forefeet**) an animal's front foot.

forefront *noun* the very front.

foregoing *adjective* preceding, previously mentioned.

foregone conclusion *noun* a result that can be foreseen easily and with certainty.

foreground *noun* **1** the part of a scene or picture that is nearest to an observer. **2** the most conspicuous position.

forehand *adjective* **1** (of a stroke in tennis etc.) played with the palm of the hand turned forwards. **2** on the side on which this is made. –**forehand** *noun* a forehand stroke. **forehanded** *adjective*

forehead (**fo**-rĕd *or* **for**-hed) *noun* the part of the face above the eyes.

foreign *adjective* **1** of or in or from another country, not of one's own country. **2** dealing with or involving other countries, *foreign affairs*. **3** not belonging naturally, *jealousy is foreign to her nature*. **4** coming from outside, *a foreign body in the eye*. □ **Foreign Legion** see **legion**. [from Latin *foris* = outside, abroad]

foreigner *noun* a person who was born in or comes from another country.

foreknowledge *noun* knowledge of something before it occurs.

foreland *noun* a cape or promontory.

foreleg *noun* an animal's front leg.

forelock *noun* a lock of hair just above the forehead.

foreman *noun* (*plural* **foremen**) **1** a worker supervising others. **2** the member of a jury acting as president and spokesperson.

Usage *Foreman* may be used of both men and women, and remains the usual name for a jury spokesperson. In sense 1, it is better replaced by *supervisor*.

---

foremost *adjective* **1** most advanced in position or rank. **2** most important. –**foremost** *adverb* in the foremost position etc.

forename *noun* a person's first name, a Christian name.

forenoon *noun* the day until noon, the morning.

forensic (fŏ-**ren**-sik) *adjective* **1** of or used in lawcourts. **2** of or involving **forensic medicine**, the medical knowledge needed in legal matters or police investigations (e.g. in a poisoning case). **forensically** *adverb*

foreordained *adjective* destined beforehand.

forepaw *noun* an animal's front paw.

forerunner *noun* a person or thing that comes in advance of another that it foreshadows.

foresee *verb* (**foresaw**, **foreseen**, **foreseeing**) to be aware of or realise (a thing) beforehand.

foreseeable *adjective* able to be foreseen; *the foreseeable future*, the period during which the course of events can be predicted.

foreshadow *verb* to be a sign of (something that is to come).

foreshore *noun* the shore between high-water mark and low-water mark, or between water and land that is cultivated or built on.

foreshorten *verb* to represent (an object, when drawing it) with shortening of certain lines to give an effect of distance; to cause such an effect in.

foresight *noun* **1** the ability to foresee and prepare for future needs. **2** the front sight of a gun.

foreskin *noun* the loose skin at the end of the penis.

forest *noun* trees and undergrowth covering a large area. **forested** *adjective*

forestall *verb* to prevent or foil (a person or his or her plans) by taking action first. [from Old English *foresteall* = ambush]

forester *noun* an officer in charge of a forest or of growing timber.

forestry *noun* the science or practice of planting and caring for forests.

foretaste *noun* an experience of something in advance of what is to come.

foretell *verb* (**foretold**, **foretelling**) to forecast, to prophesy.

forethought *noun* careful thought and planning for the future.

forever *adverb* continually, persistently, *the dog is forever barking*. (Compare **for ever**, see **for**.)

forewarn *verb* to warn beforehand.

foreword *noun* introductory remarks at the beginning of a book, usually written by someone other than the author.

forfeit (**for**-fĭt) *noun* something that has to be paid or given up as a penalty. –**forfeit** *adjective* paid or given up in this way. –**forfeit** *verb* to pay or give up as a forfeit. **forfeiture** *noun*

forgather *verb* to assemble.

forgave see **forgive**.

forge[1] *verb* to make one's way forward by effort, *forged ahead*.

forge[2] *noun* **1** a workshop with a fire and an anvil where metals are heated and shaped, especially one used by a smith for shoeing horses and working iron. **2** a furnace or hearth for melting or refining metal; the workshop containing it. –**forge** *verb* **1** to shape by heating in fire and hammering. **2** to make an imitation or copy of (a thing) in order to pass it off fraudulently as real. **forger** *noun*

forgery *noun* **1** forging, imitating fraudulently. **2** a fraudulent copy.

forget *verb* (**forgot**, **forgotten**, **forgetting**) **1** to lose remembrance of (a thing or duty etc.). **2** to put out of one's mind, to stop thinking about. □ **forget oneself** to behave without self-control or dignity.

forgetful *adjective* tending to forget things. **forgetfully** *adverb*, **forgetfulness** *noun*

forget-me-not *noun* a plant with small blue flowers.

forgive *verb* (**forgave, forgiven, forgiving**) to cease to feel angry or bitter towards (a person) or about (an offence). **forgiveness** *noun*

forgiving *adjective* willing to forgive.

forgo *verb* (**forwent, forgone, forgoing**) to give up, to go without.

forgot, forgotten *see* **forget**.

fork *noun* **1** a pronged instrument used in eating or cooking. **2** a pronged agricultural implement used for digging or lifting things. **3** a thing shaped like this. **4** a place where something separates into two or more parts; either of these parts. –**fork** *verb* **1** to lift or dig with a fork. **2** (of an object or road etc.) to form a fork by separating into two branches. **3** to follow one of these branches, *fork left*. □ **fork out** (*informal*) to hand over; to pay out money.

forklift *noun* (in full **forklift truck**) a truck with a forklike mechanical device for lifting and moving heavy objects.

forlorn *adjective* left alone and unhappy. □ **forlorn hope** the only faint hope left. **forlornly** *adverb*

form *noun* **1** the shape of something; its outward or visible appearance. **2** its structure, arrangement, or style. **3** a person or animal as it can be seen or touched. **4** the way in which a thing exists, *ice is a form of water*. **5** a class in a school. **6** a fixed or usual method of doing something, a formality; a set order of words in a ritual etc. **7** a document with blank spaces that are to be filled in with information. **8** (of a horse or athlete) condition of health and training; *is in good form*, performing well, (of a person) in good spirits. **9** a bench. **10** (*informal*) a criminal record. –**form** *verb* **1** to shape, to mould; to produce, to construct. **2** to bring into existence, to constitute, *form a committee*. **3** to be the material of. **4** to come into existence; to take shape, to become solid, *icicles formed*. **5** to develop in the mind, *formed a plan*; *formed a habit*, developed it. **6** to arrange in a certain formation.

formal *adjective* **1** conforming to accepted rules or customs; showing or requiring formality, *formal occasion*; *formal dress*. **2** outward, *only a formal resemblance*.

3 regular or geometrical in design, *formal gardens*. –**formal** *noun* an occasion on which formal or evening dress is worn, especially a secondary school dance. **formally** *adverb*

formaldehyde (for-**mal**-dĕ-hyd) *noun* a colourless gas used in solution as a preservative and disinfectant. [from *formic* (acid) + *aldehyde*]

formalin *noun* a solution of formaldehyde in water.

formalise *verb* (also **-ize**) to make formal or official. **formalisation** *noun*

formality (for-**mal**-ĭ-tee) *noun* **1** strict observance of rules and conventions. **2** a formal act, something required by law or custom.

format (**for**-mat) *noun* **1** the shape and size of a book etc. **2** a style of arrangement or procedure. **3** an arrangement of data etc. for processing or storage by computer. –**format** *verb* (**formatted, formatting**) to arrange in a format, especially for a computer.

formation *noun* **1** forming; being formed. **2** a thing formed. **3** a particular arrangement or order. [from Latin *formare* = to mould]

formative (**form**-ătiv) *adjective* forming something; *a child's formative years*, while its character is being formed.

former *adjective* **1** of an earlier period, *in former times*. **2** mentioned before another; *the former*, the one mentioned first of two.

Usage When referring to the first of three or more, *the first*, not *the former*, should be used.

---

formerly *adverb* in former times.

formica (for-**my**-kă) *noun* (*trademark*) a hard heat-resistant plastic used on surfaces.

formic acid *noun* a colourless acid contained in fluid emitted by ants. [from Latin *formica* = ant]

formidable (**for**-mĭ-dă-bŭl) *adjective* **1** inspiring fear or awe. **2** difficult to do or overcome. **formidably** *adverb* [from Latin *formido* = fear]

formless *adjective* without distinct or regular form.

formula *noun* (*plural* **formulas** *or in scientific usage* **formulae**, *pr.* **for**-mew-lee) **1** a set of chemical symbols showing the constituents of a substance. **2** a mathematical rule or statement expressed in algebraic symbols. **3** a fixed series of words, especially one

used on social or ceremonial occasions.
4 a form or set of words that embody an
agreement or enable it to be made. **5** a list of
ingredients. **6** the classification of a racing
car, especially by its engine capacity. [Latin,
= little form]

formulate *verb* to express in a formula; to
express clearly and exactly. **formulation** *noun*
[from *formula*]

fornicate (**for**-nĭ-kayt) *verb* (of people
not married to each other) to have sexual
intercourse voluntarily. **fornication** *noun* [from
Latin *fornicis* = of a brothel]

forsake *verb* (**forsook, forsaken, forsaking**)
1 to give up, to renounce, *forsaking their
former way of life.* **2** to withdraw one's help,
friendship, or companionship from, *he forsook
his wife and children.*

forswear *verb* (**forswore, forsworn,
forswearing**) to give up doing or using
something, to renounce.

fort *noun* a fortified building or position. [from
Latin *fortis* = strong]

forte¹ (**for**-tay) *noun* a person's strong point.
[from French *fort* = strong]

forte² (**for**-tay) *adverb* (in music) loudly.
[Italian]

forth *adverb* **1** out. **2** onwards, forwards, *from
this day forth*. □ **and so forth** and so on. **back
and forth** to and fro.

forthcoming *adjective* **1** about to come forth
or appear; *forthcoming events*, things about
to take place. **2** made available when needed,
money was not forthcoming. **3** (*informal*)
willing to give information.

forthright *adjective* frank, outspoken.

forthwith *adverb* immediately.

fortieth *see* **forty**.

fortification *noun* **1** fortifying. **2** a wall or
building constructed to defend a place.

fortify *verb* (**fortified, fortifying**) **1** to
strengthen (a place) against attack, especially
by constructing fortifications. **2** to strengthen
(a person) mentally or morally; to increase the
vigour of. **3** to increase the nutritive value of
(food, e.g. by adding vitamins); to strengthen
(wine, e.g. sherry) with alcohol. [same origin
as *fort*]

fortissimo *adverb* (in music) very loudly.

fortitude *noun* courage in bearing pain or
trouble. [from Latin *fortis* = strong]

Fort Knox an American military reservation
in Kentucky, site of the US Depository that
holds the bulk of the nation's gold bullion in
its vaults.

fortnight *noun* a period of two weeks. [from
an old word meaning 'fourteen nights']

fortnightly *adverb* & *adjective* happening or
appearing once a fortnight.

Fortran *noun* a high-level computer language
used in scientific work. [from the first letters
of *For*mula *Tran*slation]

fortress *noun* a fortified building or town.
[same origin as *fort*]

fortuitous (for-**tew**-ĭ-tŭs) *adjective*
happening by chance. **fortuitously** *adverb*,
fortuity *noun* [from Latin, = accidental]

Usage Distinguish *fortuitous* from *fortunate*.

---

fortunate *adjective* having, bringing, or
brought by good fortune. **fortunately** *adverb*

fortune *noun* **1** the events that chance brings
to a person or undertaking. **2** chance as a
power in the affairs of mankind. **3** a person's
destiny. **4** prosperity, success, *seek one's
fortune.* **5** a great amount of wealth, *left him a
fortune.* □ **fortune teller** a person who claims
to foretell future events in people's lives. **tell
fortunes** to be a fortune teller. [from Latin
fortuna = luck]

forty *adjective* & *noun* four times ten (40, XL).
forties *plural noun* the numbers, years, or
degrees of temperature from 40 to 49.
□ **forty winks** a nap. **fortieth** *adjective* & *noun*

forum *noun* (*plural* **forums** *or* **fora**) **1** the
public square or market place in an ancient
Roman city. **2** a place or meeting where a
public discussion is held. [Latin]

forward *adjective* **1** continuing in one's line
of motion; directed or moving towards the
front; situated in the front. **2** of or relating to
the future, *forward planning.* **3** having made
more than the normal progress. **4** too bold in
one's manner, presumptuous. **–forward** *noun*
an attacking player near the front in football
or hockey (= striker); this position. **–forward**
adverb forwards, in advance, ahead; towards
the future. **–forward** *verb* **1** to send on (a letter
etc.) to a new address. **2** to send or dispatch
(goods) to a customer. **3** to help to advance
(a person's interests). **forwardness** *noun*

forwards *adverb* **1** towards the front, onward
so as to make progress. **2** with the front
foremost.

forwent *see* forgo.

fosse *noun* a long ditch or trench, especially in fortification.

fossick *verb* (*Austral. informal*) to search for gold or other desirable things; to rummage.

fossil *noun* **1** the remains or impression of a prehistoric animal or plant once buried in earth and now hardened in rock. **2** a person who is out of date and unable to accept new ideas. □ **fossil fuel** coal etc. formed in the geological past, especially as distinguished from nuclear fuel.

fossilise *verb* (also -ize) to turn or be turned into a fossil. **fossilisation** *noun*

foster *verb* **1** to promote the growth or development of. **2** to take care of and bring up (a child that is not one's own). – **foster** *adjective* **1** related by fostering, *foster brother*; *foster parent*. **2** concerned with fostering, *foster care*. [from Old English *foster* = food]

Foucault (**foo**-koh), Jean Bernard Léon (1818–68), French physicist, inventor of the gyroscope, remembered for the huge pendulum whose swing demonstrated the rotation of the earth beneath it.

fought *see* fight.

foul *adjective* **1** causing disgust, having an offensive smell or taste. **2** morally offensive, evil. **3** (of language) disgusting, obscene. **4** (of weather) rough, stormy. **5** clogged, choked; (of a ship's bottom) overgrown with barnacles etc. **6** in collision; entangled. **7** unfair, against the rules of a game, *a foul stroke*. – **foul** *noun* a foul stroke or blow etc., breaking the rules of a game. – **foul** *verb* **1** to make or become foul. **2** to entangle or collide with, to obstruct. **3** to commit a foul against (a player) in a game. □ **foul-mouthed** *adjective* using foul language. **foul play** a foul in sport; a violent crime, especially murder. **foully** *adverb*

foulard (**foo**-lard) *noun* a kind of silky material used for ties etc. [French]

found¹ *see* find.

found² *verb* **1** to establish, to originate; to provide money for starting (an institution etc.). **2** to base or construct, *a novel founded on fact*. **founder** *noun* [from Latin *fundus* = bottom]

found³ *verb* **1** to melt and mould (metal); to fuse (materials for glass). **2** to make (an object) in this way. **founder** *noun*

foundation *noun* **1** the founding of an institution etc. **2** the institution itself; a fund of money established for a charitable purpose.

3 the solid ground or base from which a building is built up; (also **foundations**) the lowest part of a building, usually below ground level. **4** a cosmetic applied to the skin as the first layer of make-up. **5** the underlying principle or idea etc. on which something is based. **6** the material or part on which others are overlaid. □ **foundation stone** a stone laid ceremonially to celebrate the founding of a building.

founder¹,² *nouns see* found², found³.

founder³ *verb* **1** to stumble or fall. **2** (of a ship) to fill with water and sink. **3** to fail completely, *the plan foundered*. [same origin as *found²*]

foundling *noun* a deserted child of unknown parents.

foundry *noun* a factory or workshop where metal or glass is founded (*see* found³).

fount¹ *noun* **1** a source. **2** (*poetic*) a spring; a fountain.

fount² *noun see* font².

fountain *noun* **1** a spring of water, especially a jet of water made to spout artificially as an ornament. **2** a structure providing a supply of drinking water in a public place. □ **fountain pen** a pen that can be filled with ink.

four *adjective* & *noun* **1** one more than three (4, IV). **2** a four-oared boat or its crew. □ **four-poster** *noun* a bed with four posts to support a canopy. **four-square** *adjective* solidly based, steady; (*adverb*) squarely. **four-wheel drive** driving-power applied to all four wheels of a vehicle.

fourfold *adjective* & *adverb* **1** four times as much or as many. **2** consisting of four parts.

foursome *noun* **1** a company of four people. **2** a golf match between two pairs, with partners playing the same ball.

fourteen *adjective* & *noun* one more than thirteen (14, XIV). **fourteenth** *adjective* & *noun*

fourth *adjective* next after third. – **fourth** *noun* **1** something that is fourth. **2** one of four equal parts of a thing. **fourthly** *adverb*

fowl *noun* (*plural* fowls *or* fowl) **1** a kind of bird often kept at houses and farms to supply eggs and flesh for food. **2** the flesh of birds as food, *fish, flesh, and fowl*.

fox *noun* **1** a wild animal of the dog family with a pointed snout and reddish fur and a bushy tail. **2** its fur. **3** a crafty person. – **fox**

verb to deceive or puzzle by acting craftily. foxy *adjective*

foxglove *noun* a tall plant with purple or white flowers like the fingers of gloves.

foxhound *noun* a kind of hound bred and trained to hunt foxes.

foxie *noun* (*Austral. informal*) a fox terrier.

fox terrier *noun* a kind of short-haired terrier.

foxtrot *noun* a ballroom dance with slow and quick steps; music for this.

foyer (**foi**-er) *noun* the entrance hall of a theatre or cinema or of a hotel. [French, = hearth]

fracas (**frak**-ah) *noun* (*plural* fracas, *pr.* **frak**-ahz) a noisy quarrel or disturbance. [French]

fraction *noun* **1** a number that is not a whole number, e.g. $\frac{1}{3}$, 0.5. **2** a very small part or piece or amount. [same origin as *fracture*]

fractional *adjective* **1** of a fraction. **2** very small, *a fractional difference*.
□ **fractional distillation** separation of a mixture into its constituent parts by making use of the fact that they condense or vaporise at different temperatures. fractionally *adverb*

fractionate *verb* **1** to break up into parts. **2** to separate (a mixture) into its parts by fractional distillation. fractionation *noun*

fractious (**frak**-shŭs) *adjective* irritable, peevish. fractiously *adverb*, fractiousness *noun*

fracture *noun* breaking or breakage, especially of a bone. – **fracture** *verb* to cause a fracture in; to suffer a fracture. [from Latin *fractum* = broken]

fragile *adjective* **1** easily damaged or broken. **2** of delicate constitution, not strong. fragilely *adverb*, fragility (fră-**jil**-ĭ-tee) *noun*

fragment (**frag**-měnt) *noun* **1** a piece broken off something. **2** an isolated part. – **fragment** (frag-**ment**) *verb* to break or be broken into fragments. fragmentation *noun*

fragmentary (**frag**-měnt-ă-ree) *adjective* consisting of fragments.

fragrance *noun* **1** being fragrant. **2** something fragrant, perfume.

fragrant *adjective* having a pleasant smell.

frail *adjective* not strong, physically weak.

frailty *noun* **1** being frail, weakness. **2** moral weakness, liability to yield to temptation.

frame *noun* **1** a rigid structure forming a support for other parts of a building, vehicle, piece of furniture, etc. **2** an open case or a border in which a picture, door, pane of glass, etc. may be set. **3** the human or an animal body with reference to its size, *a small frame*. **4** a single exposure on a strip of cinema film. **5** (in computing) a graphic panel in a display window enclosing a self-contained section of data and permitting multiple, independent viewing. **6** a boxlike structure used for protecting plants from the cold. **7** a triangular structure for setting up balls in snooker etc.; a round of play using this. – **frame** *verb* **1** to put or form a frame round. **2** to construct. **3** to compose, to express in words, *frame a treaty* or *a question*. **4** (*informal*) to arrange false evidence against, so that an innocent person appears to be guilty. □ **frame of mind** a temporary state of mind. **frame of reference** a set of principles or standards by which ideas and behaviour etc. are evaluated. **frame-up** *noun* (*informal*) the arrangement of false evidence against an innocent person.

framework *noun* **1** the supporting frame of a building or other construction. **2** the structural basis of an organisation or a plan.

franc *noun* the unit of money in Switzerland and certain other countries.

France a republic in western Europe.

franchise (**fran**-chyz) *noun* **1** the right to vote at public elections. **2** authorisation to sell a company's goods or services in a particular area. – **franchise** *verb* to grant a franchise to.

Francis, St, of Assisi (1181/2–1226), Italian friar, founder of the Franciscan order, noted for his simple faith, deep humility, and love of nature.

Franciscan (fran-**sis**-kăn) *noun* a member of an order of friars (also called *Grey Friars*) founded by St Francis of Assisi, or of a corresponding order of nuns.

francium (**fran**-see-ŭm) *noun* a radioactive element of the alkali metal group (symbol Fr).

Franco- *prefix* French; *a Franco-German treaty*, between France and Germany.

frangipani (**fran**-jĭ-pan-ee) *noun* a small tree with fragrant white and yellow flowers.

Frank *noun* a member of a Germanic people that conquered Gaul in the 6th century, and from whom that country received the name of France. Frankish *adjective*

frank[1] *adjective* showing one's thoughts and feelings openly. frankly *adverb*, frankness *noun*

frank[2] *verb* to mark in a franking machine, a device that marks letters etc. passed through it and automatically counts up the total charge for these.

Frankenstein (**frank**-ĕn-styn) *noun* (more correctly Frankenstein's monster) a thing that becomes terrifying to its creator. [the name of a person in Mary Shelley's novel *Frankenstein* (1818), who constructed a human monster and endowed it with life]

frankfurt *noun* a smoked sausage, usually eaten hot. [from the name of Frankfurt in Germany, where it was originally made]

frankincense *noun* a kind of sweet-smelling gum burnt as incense.

Franklin¹, Benjamin (1706–90), American statesman, inventor, and scientist.

Franklin², Miles (Stella Maria(n) Sarah Miles) (1879–1954), Australian novelist, author of *My Brilliant Career*.

Franklin³ a river in SW Tasmania, listed as a World Heritage Area.

frantic *adjective* wildly excited or agitated by anxiety etc., frenzied. **frantically** *adverb* [from Greek *phrenetikos* = mad]

fraternal (fră-**ter**-năl) *adjective* of a brother or brothers. **fraternally** *adverb* [from Latin *frater* = brother]

fraternise (**frat**-er-nyz) *verb* (also -ize) to associate with others in a friendly way. **fraternisation** *noun*

fraternity (fră-**tern**-ĭ-tee) *noun* 1 being fraternal, brotherly feeling. 2 a religious brotherhood. 3 a group or company of people with common interests.

fratricide (**frat**-rĭ-syd) *noun* 1 the act of killing one's own brother or sister. 2 a person guilty of this. **fratricidal** *adjective*

Frau (*rhymes with* brow) *noun* (*plural* Frauen) the title of a German married woman, = Mrs.

fraud *noun* 1 criminal deception; a dishonest trick. 2 a person or thing that is not what it seems or pretends to be, an impostor.

fraudulent (**fraw**-dew-lĕnt) *adjective* acting with fraud; obtained by fraud. **fraudulently** *adverb*, **fraudulence** *noun*

fraught (*pr.* frawt) *adjective* filled, involving, *fraught with danger*. [from an old use, = loaded with freight]

Fräulein (**froi**-lyn) *noun* the title of a German unmarried woman, = Miss.

fray¹ *noun* a fight, a conflict, *ready for the fray*. [same origin as *affray*]

fray² *verb* (frayed, fraying) 1 to make worn so that there are loose threads, especially at the edge. 2 to strain or upset (nerves or temper). 3 to become frayed.

frazzle *noun* a completely exhausted state, *worn to a frazzle*.

freak *noun* 1 a person or thing that is abnormal in form. 2 something very unusual or irregular, *a freak storm*. 3 a person who dresses absurdly. 4 a person who is obsessed with what is specified, *a health freak*. –freak *verb* (*informal*) to become angry or scared; to scare or shock, *he freaked when he saw the damage*; *exams freak me out.* **freakish** *adjective*, **freaky** *adjective*

freckle *noun* a light brown spot on the skin. **freckled** *adjective* spotted with freckles.

Frederick¹ the name of three Holy Roman Emperors, including Frederick I 'Barbarossa' (= 'Redbeard', emperor 1152–90).

Frederick² the name of three kings of Prussia, including Frederick II 'the Great' (reigned 1740–86), the greatest soldier of his age.

free *adjective* (freer, freest) 1 (of a person) not a slave, not in the power of another or others; having social and political liberty. 2 (of a country or its citizens or institutions) not controlled by a foreign or despotic government; having representative government; having private rights that are respected. 3 not fixed or held down, able to move without hindrance. 4 unrestricted, not controlled by rules. 5 without, not subject to or affected by (an influence etc.), *free from blame*; *harbour is free of ice*. 6 without payment, costing nothing to the recipient. 7 (of place or time) not occupied, not being used; (of a person) without engagements or things to do. 8 coming or given or giving readily, *he is very free with his advice*. –free *verb* (freed, freeing) 1 to make free, to set at liberty. 2 to relieve, to rid or ease, *freed him from suspicion*. 3 to clear, to disengage or disentangle. □ for free (*informal*) provided without payment. **free and easy** informal. **free enterprise** the freedom of private business to operate without government control. **free fall** the unrestricted fall of a body towards earth under the force of gravity; the movement of a spacecraft in space without thrust from the engines. **free-for-all** *noun* a general fight in which anyone present can join; a discussion in which anyone present may join. **free hand** the right of taking what action one chooses. **free kick** a kick allowed to be taken in football without interference from opponents, as a minor penalty against them. **free port** one open to all traders alike, or free from duty on goods in transit. **free-range** *adjective* (of hens) allowed to range freely in search of food, not kept in a battery; (of eggs) from such hens. **free-selection** *noun* (*Austral. old use*) a scheme under which a block of Crown land could be selected and the freehold acquired on easy terms; the land so acquired. **free-select** *verb*, **free-selector** *noun* **free speech** the right to express opinions of any kind. **free-standing** *adjective* not supported by a framework. **free-to-air** (of a broadcast channel) able to be picked up by the general public without a special decoder; not cable or pay-television. **free trade** trade left to its natural course, without restrictions on imports etc. **free verse** (also **vers libre**) verse with no regular metrical pattern. **free vote** a parliamentary vote in which members are not subject to party discipline. **free will** the power of choosing one's own course of action. **free world** (*historical*) the non-Communist countries' name for themselves. **freely** *adverb*

freebie *noun* (*informal*) a thing given free of charge.

freedom *noun* **1** the condition of being free, independence. **2** frankness, outspokenness. **3** exemption from a defect or duty etc. **4** unrestricted use, *has the freedom of the library*. □ **freedom of the city** the full rights of citizenship, given to a person as an honour.

freehand *adjective* (of a drawing) done without ruler or compasses etc. –**freehand** *adverb* in a freehand manner.

freehold *noun* the holding of land or a house etc. in absolute ownership. **freeholder** *noun*

freelance *noun* a person who sells his or her services to various employers, not employed by one only. –**freelance** *verb* to work as a freelance.

freeloader *noun* (*informal*) a sponger.

freeman *noun* (*plural* **freemen**) **1** a free person, one who is not a slave or serf. **2** a holder of the freedom of a city.

Freemason *noun* a member of an international fraternity with elaborate secret rituals.

Freemasonry *noun* the system and institutions of Freemasons. –**freemasonry** *noun* sympathy and mutual help between people of similar interests.

freesia *noun* a fragrant flowering plant growing from a bulb.

freestyle *adjective* **1** (of swimming races) in which any style may be used, in practice usually the Australian crawl. **2** (of wrestling) with few restrictions on the holds permitted.

Freetown the capital of Sierra Leone.

freeway *noun* a multi-laned highway with separate carriageways for each direction and limited access, designed for fast motor traffic; an expressway.

freewheel *verb* **1** to ride a bicycle without pedalling. **2** to act without effort.

freewill *adjective* voluntary.

freeze *verb* (**froze, frozen, freezing**) **1** to be so cold that water turns to ice, *it was freezing in Berlin*. **2** to change or be changed from a liquid to a solid by extreme cold; to become full of ice or covered in ice. **3** to become very cold, or rigid from cold or fear etc.; to chill by cold or fear etc.; to keep very still, holding one's position. **4** to preserve (food) by refrigeration to below freezing point. **5** to make (credits or assets) unable to be realised. **6** to hold (prices, wages, etc.) at a fixed level. –**freeze** *noun* **1** a period of freezing weather. **2** the freezing of prices, wages, etc. □ **freeze-dry** *verb* to freeze and dry by evaporation of ice in a vacuum. **freeze up** to obstruct by the formation of ice. **freezing point** the temperature at which a liquid freezes. **freezing works** (*Austral.*) an abattoir freezing animal carcasses for export.

freezer *noun* a refrigerated container or compartment for preserving and storing perishable goods by freezing them and keeping them at a very low temperature.

freight (*pr.* frayt) *noun* **1** the transport of goods in containers or by water, air, or land. **2** the goods transported, cargo. **3** the charge for this. –**freight** *verb* to load (a ship) with cargo; to send or carry as cargo.

freighter (**frayt**-er) *noun* **1** a ship or aircraft carrying mainly freight. **2** a person or business receiving or forwarding freight.

Fremantle the port of Perth and chief port of WA, situated on the Swan River. **Fremantle doctor** a cool afternoon breeze.

French *adjective* of France or its people or language. –**French** *noun* the French language. □ **the French** French people. **French bean** a kidney bean or haricot bean used as a vegetable both as unripe pods and as ripe seeds. **French Canadian** a native of the

French-speaking area of Canada. **french chalk** finely powdered talc used as a lubricant etc. **French dressing** salad dressing of seasoned oil and vinegar. **French fries** fried oblong strips of potato. **French horn** a brass wind instrument with a long tube coiled in a circle. **French knitting** a form of circular knitting in which the yarn is looped over hooks on a hollow reel. Also called *tomboy stitch*. **French polish** shellac polish for wood; (*verb*) to polish with this. **French Revolution** the overthrow of the Bourbon monarchy in France, initiated in 1789. **French seam** a seam with the raw edges enclosed. **French stick** a long thin crusty loaf of white bread. **French window** a door with long glass panes on an outside wall, serving as both door and window. **take French leave** to absent oneself without permission. **Frenchman**, **Frenchwoman** *nouns*

frenzied *adjective* in a state of frenzy, wildly excited or agitated. **frenziedly** *adverb*

frenzy *noun* violent excitement or agitation. [same origin as *frantic*]

frequency *noun* **1** the state of being frequent, frequent occurrence. **2** the rate of the occurrence or repetition of something. **3** the number of cycles per second of a carrier wave; a band or group of similar frequencies, *audio frequency, radio frequency*. ☐ **frequency modulation** a modulation in which the frequency of the carrier wave is varied; used especially in broadcasting (abbreviation **FM**).

frequent (**free**-kwĕnt) *adjective* happening or appearing often. –**frequent** (frĕ-**kwent**) *verb* to go frequently to, to be often in (a place). **frequently** *adverb* [from Latin *frequens* = crowded]

frequentative (frĕ-**kwent**-ă-tiv) *adjective* (of a verb) expressing frequent repetition or intensity of an action (e.g. *chatter*). –**frequentative** *noun* a frequentative verb.

fresco (**fress**-koh) *noun* (*plural* **frescoes**) a picture painted on a wall or ceiling before the plaster is dry. [Italian, = fresh]

fresh *adjective* **1** newly made or produced or gathered etc., not stale. **2** newly arrived. **3** new or different, not previously known or used. **4** (of food) not preserved by salting, pickling, tinning, or freezing etc. **5** not salty, not bitter. **6** (of air or weather) cool, refreshing; (of wind) moderately strong. **7** bright and pure in colour, not dull or faded. **8** not weary, feeling vigorous. **9** (*informal*) presumptuous, forward. **freshly** *adverb*, **freshness** *noun*

freshen *verb* to make or become fresh.

freshwater *adjective* of fresh (not salty) water, not of the sea, *freshwater fish*.

fret[1] *verb* (**fretted**, **fretting**) **1** to make or become unhappy, to worry, to vex. **2** to wear away by gnawing or rubbing. –**fret** *noun* a state of unhappiness or worry, vexation.

fret[2] *noun* each of a series of raised bars or wires across the fingerboard of a guitar etc., against which the fingers stop the strings in playing. **fretted** *adjective* having frets.

fretful *adjective* constantly worrying or crying. **fretfully** *adverb*, **fretfulness** *noun*

fretsaw *noun* a very narrow saw fixed in a frame, for cutting patterns in thin wood.

fretwork *noun* carved work in decorative patterns, especially in wood cut with a fretsaw.

Freud (*pr*. froid), Sigmund (1856–1939), Austrian physician, the founder of psychoanalysis.

Freudian *adjective* of Sigmund Freud or his theories. **Freudian slip** an unintentional error that seems to reveal subconscious feelings.

Frey (*pr*. fray) (*Scand. myth*.) the god of fertility and dispenser of rain and sunshine.

Freya (**fray**-ă) (*Scand. myth*.) the goddess of love and of the night, sister of Frey.

friable (**fry**-ă-bŭl) *adjective* easily crumbled. **friability** *noun* [from Latin *friare* = to crumble]

friar *noun* a man who is a member of certain Christian religious orders (especially the Franciscans, Augustinians, Dominicans, and Carmelites). ☐ **friar's balsam** a kind of oil used as an inhalant. [from Latin *frater* = brother]

friary *noun* a monastery of friars.

fricassee (**frik**-ă-see) *noun* a dish of stewed or fried pieces of meat served in a thick sauce. [French]

friction *noun* **1** the rubbing of one thing against another. **2** the resistance of one surface to another that moves over it. **3** conflict between people with different ideas or personalities. **frictional** *adjective* [from Latin *frictum* = rubbed]

Friday *noun* the day of the week following Thursday. [from Old English *Frigedaeg* = day of Frigga]

fridge *noun* (*informal*) a refrigerator.

fried *see* **fry**[1].

friend *noun* **1** a person with whom one is on terms of mutual affection independently of sexual or family love. **2** a helpful thing or quality, *darkness was our friend*. **3** a helper or supporter; *Friends of the library*. **4 Friend** a member of the Society of Friends, a Quaker. **friendship** *noun*, **friendless** *adjective*

friendly *adjective* (**friendlier, friendliest**) **1** like a friend, kindly. **2** (of things) favourable, helpful. **3** helping, not harming, *environmentally friendly; user-friendly*. **–friendly** *noun* a friendly match. □ **friendly match** a match played for enjoyment and not in competition for a cup etc. **Friendly Society** a society for the mutual benefit of its members e.g. during illness or old age. **friendliness** *noun*

Friendly Islands Tonga.

Friesian (**free**-*zhǎn*) *noun* a breed of large black and white dairy cattle originally from Friesland, a province of the Netherlands; an animal of this breed.

frieze *noun* a band of sculpture or decoration round the top of a wall or building.

frigate (**frig**-*ǎt*) *noun* a small fast naval escort vessel or a small destroyer.

Frigga (*Scand. myth.*) wife of Odin and goddess of married love and the hearth.

fright *noun* **1** sudden great fear. **2** a ridiculous-looking person or thing.

frighten *verb* **1** to cause fright to. **2** to feel fright, *he doesn't frighten easily*. **3** to drive or compel by fright, *frightened them into concealing it*. □ **be frightened of** to be afraid of.

frightful *adjective* **1** causing horror. **2** ugly. **3** (*informal*) very great, extreme, extremely bad, *frightful weather*. **frightfully** *adverb*

frigid (**frij**-*ĭd*) *adjective* **1** intensely cold. **2** very cold and formal in manner. **3** (of a woman) unresponsive sexually. **frigidly** *adverb*, **frigidity** (frĭ-**jid**-ĭ-tee) *noun* [from Latin *frigidus* = cold]

frill *noun* **1** a gathered or pleated strip of trimming attached at one edge. **2** an unnecessary extra, *a simple funeral with no frills*. □ **frill-necked lizard** a large Australian lizard with an erectile membrane around the neck. **frilled** *adjective*, **frilly** *adjective*

fringe *noun* **1** an ornamental edging of hanging threads or cords etc. **2** something resembling this. **3** front hair cut short to hang over the forehead. **4** the edge of an area or a group etc. **–fringe** *verb* **1** to decorate with a fringe. **2** to form a fringe to. □ **fringe benefits** benefits that are provided for an employee or pensioner in addition to income.

frippery *noun* showy unnecessary finery or ornaments.

Frisian (**friz**-ee-ǎn) *adjective* of Friesland, a province of the Netherlands, or its people or language.

frisk *verb* **1** to leap or skip playfully. **2** to pass one's hands over (a person) in order to search for concealed weapons etc.

frisky *adjective* (**friskier, friskiest**) lively, playful. **friskiness** *noun*

frisson (**free**-sawn) *noun* an emotional thrill. [French, = a shiver]

fritillary (frĭ-**til**-ǎ-ree) *noun* **1** a plant with speckled bell-shaped flowers. **2** a kind of spotted butterfly.

fritter[1] *noun* a small flat fried cake of batter containing sliced fruit or meat etc. [from Latin *frictum* = fried]

fritter[2] *verb* to waste little by little, especially time or money, on trivial things. [from an old word *fritters* = fragments]

fritz *noun* (*South Australian*) a large bland sausage, sliced and eaten cold.

frivolous *adjective* lacking a serious purpose, pleasure-loving. **frivolously** *adverb*, **frivolity** *noun*

frizz *verb* to curl into a wiry mass. **–frizz** *noun* a frizzed condition; frizzed hair. **frizzy** *adjective*, **frizziness** *noun*

frizzle *verb* **1** to burn or cook with a sizzling noise. **2** to burn or shrivel by burning.

fro *adverb* **to and fro** *see* **to**.

frock *noun* **1** a woman's or girl's dress. **2** a monk's or priest's gown.

frog *noun* **1** a small cold-blooded jumping animal living both in water and on land. **2** a horny substance in the sole of a horse's foot. **3** a fastener consisting of a button and an ornamentally looped cord. □ **have a frog in one's throat** to be unable to speak except hoarsely.

frogman *noun* (*plural* **frogmen**) a swimmer equipped with a rubber suit, flippers etc., and an oxygen supply for swimming and working under water.

frogmarch *verb* to hustle (a person) forward forcibly with his or her arms held fast; to carry (a person) face downwards by means of four persons each holding a limb.

frogmouth *noun* a nocturnal bird with a large wide beak resembling a frog's mouth.

frolic *verb* (**frolicked**, **frolicking**) to play about in a lively cheerful way. **–frolic** *noun* lively cheerful playing or entertainment.

from *preposition* expressing separation or origin, **1** indicating the place, time, or limit that is the starting point, *travelled from Sydney*; *from ten o'clock*. **2** indicating source or origin, *water from the well*. **3** indicating separation, prevention, escape, etc., *released from prison*; *refrain from laughing*. **4** indicating difference or discrimination, *can't tell red from green*. **5** indicating cause, agent, or means, *died from starvation*. **6** indicating material used in a process, *wine is made from grapes*. □ **from day to day** daily, progressively. **from time to time** at intervals of time.

fromage frais (**from**-ah*zh* fray) *noun* a soft smooth low-fat cheese. [French, = fresh cheese]

frond *noun* a leaflike part of a fern or other flowerless plant or of a palm tree. [from Latin *frondis* = of a leaf]

front *noun* **1** the foremost or most important side or surface. **2** the part normally nearer or towards the spectator or line of motion, *the front of a bus*. **3** (also **front line**) the area where fighting is taking place in a war; the foremost line of an army etc. **4** an outward appearance or show; something serving as a cover for secret activities. **5** the forward edge of an advancing mass of cold or warm air. **6** the forward edge of a bushfire. **7** the part of the land facing the sea. **8** the part of a garment covering the front of the body. **9** the part of a theatre where the audience sits, facing the stage. **10** (in names) an organised political group, *the Patriotic Front*. **–front** *adjective* of the front; situated in front. **–front** *verb* **1** to face, to have the front towards, *fronting the sea* or *on the sea*. **2** (*informal*) to act as a front or cover. □ **front runner** the contestant who seems most likely to succeed. **front up** (*informal*) to show up, to appear. **in front** at the front of something; *in front of the children*, in their presence. [from Latin *frontis* = of the forehead]

frontage *noun* **1** the front of a building. **2** the land bordering its front. **3** the land bordering a river, lake, or the sea.

frontal *adjective* **1** of or on the front. **2** of or associated with a warm or cold front. **–frontal** *noun* a covering for the front of an altar.

frontbencher *noun* a Member of Parliament entitled to sit on the front benches in Parliament, which are reserved for ministers and shadow ministers.

frontier *noun* **1** the land border of a country. **2** the limit of attainment or knowledge achieved in a subject.

frontispiece (**frunt**-ĭss-peess) *noun* an illustration placed opposite the title page of a book.

frost *noun* **1** a weather condition with temperature below the freezing point of water. **2** a white powder-like coating of frozen vapour produced by this. **3** a chilling influence; great coolness of manner. **–frost** *verb* **1** to injure (a plant etc.) with frost. **2** to cover with frost or frosting. **3** to make (glass) opaque by roughening the surface.

frostbite *noun* injury to tissue of the body from freezing. **frostbitten** *adjective*

frosting *noun* sugar icing for cakes.

frosty *adjective* (**frostier**, **frostiest**) **1** cold with frost. **2** very cold and unfriendly in manner. **frostily** *adverb*, **frostiness** *noun*

froth *noun* foam. **–froth** *verb* to cause froth in, to foam. **frothy** *adjective*

frown *verb* to wrinkle one's brow in thought or disapproval. **–frown** *noun* a frowning movement or look. □ **frown at** or **on** to disapprove of.

frowsty *adjective* fusty, stuffy.

frozen *see* **freeze**.

fructose (**fruuk**-tohs) *noun* sugar of the kind found in fruit juice etc. [from Latin *fructus* = fruit]

frugal (**froo**-găl) *adjective* **1** careful and economical. **2** scanty, costing little, *a frugal meal*. **frugally** *adverb*, **frugality** *noun*

fruit *noun* **1** the seed-containing part of a plant. **2** this used as food. **3** any plant product used as food, *the fruits of the earth*. **4** the product or rewarding outcome of labour. **–fruit** *verb* **1** (of a plant) to produce fruit. **2** to cause or allow (a plant) to produce fruit. □ **fruit cake** a cake containing dried fruit. **fruit salad** various fruits cut up and mixed.

fruitcake *noun* (*informal*) a mad or eccentric person. [from *as nutty as a fruit cake*]

fruiterer *noun* a shopkeeper who deals in fruit.

fruitful *adjective* **1** producing much fruit. **2** producing good results. **fruitfully** *adverb*, **fruitfulness** *noun*

fruition (froo-**ish**-ŏn) *noun* the fulfilment of hopes; results attained by work. [from Latin *frui* = enjoy]

Usage This word does not mean 'fruiting' or 'becoming fruitful'.

fruitless *adjective* producing little or no result. **fruitlessly** *adverb*, **fruitlessness** *noun*

fruity *adjective* (**fruitier**, **fruitiest**) like fruit in smell or taste.

frump *noun* a dowdily-dressed woman. **frumpish** *adjective*

frustrate *verb* to prevent (a person) from achieving what he or she intends; to make (efforts) useless. **frustration** *noun* [from Latin *frustra* = in vain]

frustum *noun* (*plural* **frusta**) **1** the remainder of a cone or pyramid whose upper part has been cut off by a plane parallel to the base. **2** a part of a cone or pyramid cut off between two parallel planes. [Latin, = piece sawn off]

fry[1] *verb* (**fried**, **frying**) to cook or be cooked in boiling fat. – **fry** *noun* various internal parts of animals usually eaten fried, *lamb's fry*. □ **frying pan** a shallow pan used in frying.

fry[2] *plural noun* young or newly hatched fishes. **small fry** people of little importance; children.

fryer *noun* **1** a person who fries things. **2** a vessel for frying fish etc.

frypan *noun* a frying pan.

FTSE index (**fuut**-see) *abbreviation* a figure indicating the relative prices of shares on the London Stock Exchange. [acronym from *Financial Times Stock Exchange*]

fuchsia (**few**-shǎ) *noun* an ornamental shrub with red, purple, or white drooping flowers. [named after L. Fuchs, German botanist (1501–66)]

fuddle *verb* to stupefy, especially with alcoholic drink.

fuddy-duddy (*informal*) *adjective* out of date, unable to accept new ideas; quaintly fussy. – **fuddy-duddy** *noun* such a person.

fudge *noun* a soft sweet made of milk, sugar, and butter. – **fudge** *verb* to put together in a makeshift or dishonest way, to fake.

fuel *noun* **1** material for burning or lighting as a source of warmth, light, or energy, or used as a source of nuclear energy. **2** something that increases anger or other strong feelings. – **fuel** *verb* (**fuelled**, **fuelling**) to supply with fuel.

fug *noun* (*informal*) fustiness of air in a room. **fuggy** *adjective*, **fugginess** *noun*

fugitive (**few**-jĭ-tiv) *noun* a person who is fleeing or escaping from something. – **fugitive** *adjective* **1** fleeing, escaping. **2** transient. [from Latin *fugere* = flee]

fugue (*pr.* fewg) *noun* a musical composition in which one or more themes are introduced and used in complex patterns.

Fujiyama (foo-jee-**yah**-mǎ) a dormant or extinct volcano, Japan's highest peak.

Fulbright, (James) William (1905–95), American senator 1945–74, who in 1946 founded the international student exchange program named after him.

fulcrum (**ful**-krŭm) *noun* (*plural* **fulcra**) the point on which a lever turns.

fulfil *verb* (**fulfilled**, **fulfilling**) **1** to accomplish, to carry out (a task). **2** to do what is required by (a treaty etc.); to satisfy the requirements of. **3** to make (a prophecy) come true. □ **fulfil oneself** or **be fulfilled** (of person) to develop and use one's abilities etc. fully. **fulfilment** *noun*

full *adjective* **1** holding or having as much as the limits will allow. **2** having much or many, crowded, showing, *full of vitality*. **3** completely occupied with thinking, *full of himself*; *full of the news*, unable to keep from talking about it. **4** fed to satisfaction, *ate till he was full*. **5** copious, *give full details*. **6** complete, reaching the usual or specified extent or limit etc., *in full bloom*; *waited a full hour*. **7** plump, rounded, *a full figure*. **8** (of clothes) fitting loosely, made with much material hanging in folds. **9** (of tone) deep and mellow. – **full** *adverb* **1** completely. **2** exactly, *hit him full on the nose*. □ **full back** one of the defensive players near the goal in football, hockey, etc. **full-blooded** *adjective* vigorous, hearty; sensual. **full-blown** *adjective* fully developed. **full board** provision of bed and all meals at a hotel etc. **full face** with all the face towards the spectator. **full marks** the maximum marks possible in an examination etc. **full moon** the moon with its whole disc illuminated; the time when this occurs. **full-scale** *adjective* of the actual size, complete, not reduced. **full stop** the punctuation mark (.) used at the end of a sentence or abbreviation; *come to a full stop*, cease completely, be unable to proceed. **full time** the whole of a working day or week; the end of a football match etc. **full-time** *adjective* for or during the whole of the working day or week. **full-timer**

noun one employed to work a full working week. **full toss** (in cricket) a ball that pitches right up to the batsman. **in full** with nothing omitted; for the whole amount, *paid in full*. **to the full** thoroughly, completely.

fuller¹ *noun* a person who cleans and thickens freshly woven cloth with **fuller's earth**, a type of clay.

fuller² *noun* **1** a tool used by a smith to make a groove in a piece of iron etc. **2** this groove. **–fuller** *verb* to make a groove in (iron etc.) with a fuller.

fully *adverb* **1** completely, entirely. **2** no less than. □ **fully-fashioned** *adjective* shaped to fit the body.

fullness *noun* being full. □ **in the fullness of time** at the proper or destined time.

fulmar *noun* an Arctic seabird.

fulminate (**ful**-mĭ-nayt) *verb* to protest loudly and bitterly. **fulmination** *noun*, **fulminator** *noun* [from Latin *fulminare* = strike by lightning]

fulsome (**fuul**-sŏm) *adjective* praising something excessively and sickeningly.

Usage *Fulsome* should not be used to mean 'full' or 'copious' or 'plentiful'.

fumble *verb* **1** to touch or handle something awkwardly. **2** to grope about.

fume *noun* (usually **fumes**) strong-smelling smoke, gas, or vapour. **–fume** *verb* **1** to treat with chemical fumes, especially to darken wood, *fumed oak*. **2** to emit fumes. **3** to seethe with anger. [from Latin *fumus* = smoke]

fumigate (**few**-mĭ-gayt) *verb* to disinfect by means of fumes. **fumigation** *noun*

fun *noun* **1** light-hearted amusement. **2** a source of this. □ **fun run** an organised often non-competitive long-distance run. **make fun of** to cause people to laugh at (a person or thing).

Funafuti (foo-nă-**foo**-tee) the capital of Tuvalu.

Funchal (foon-**chal**) the capital of the Madeiras.

function *noun* **1** the special activity or purpose of a person or thing. **2** an important social or official ceremony. **3** any of the basic operations of a computer etc. **4** (in mathematics) a relationship between one element and another, or between several elements and one another. **–function** *verb*

to perform a function; to be in action. [from Latin *functum* = performed]

functional *adjective* **1** of a function or functions. **2** designed to perform a particular function without being decorative or luxurious. **functionally** *adverb*

functionalism *noun* belief in or stress on the practical application of a thing, especially in architecture and furniture design. **functionalist** *noun*

functionary *noun* an official.

fund *noun* **1** a stock of money, especially that available for a particular purpose. **2** an available stock or supply, *a fund of jokes*. **–fund** *verb* to provide with money.

fundamental *adverb* **1** of the basis or foundation of a subject etc., serving as a starting point. **2** very important, essential. **fundamentals** *plural noun* fundamental facts or principles. **fundamentally** *adverb* [from Latin *fundamentum* = foundation]

fundamentalism *noun* strict maintenance of the doctrines of any religion according to a strict, literal interpretation of scripture. **fundamentalist** *noun*

funeral *noun* **1** the ceremony of burying or cremating the dead. **2** a procession to this. **3** (*informal*) a person's unpleasant responsibility or concern, *that's your funeral*. [from Latin *funeris* = of a burial]

funerary (**few**-ně-ră-ree) *adjective* of or used for burial or a funeral.

funereal (few-**neer**-ree-ăl) *adjective* suitable for a funeral, dismal, dark. **funereally** *adverb*

funfair *noun* a fair consisting of amusements and sideshows.

fungal *adjective* of a fungus.

fungicide (**fung**-gĭ-syd) *noun* a fungus-destroying substance. **fungicidal** *adjective* [from *fungus*, + Latin *caedere* = kill]

fungoid (**fung**-goid) *adjective* like a fungus. **–fungoid** *noun* a fungoid plant.

fungous (**fung**-gŭs) *adjective* like a fungus.

fungus *noun* (*plural* **fungi**, *pr*. **fung**-gee *or* **fung**-gI, *or* **funguses**) any of those plants without leaves, flowers, or green colouring matter, growing on other plants or on decaying matter and including mushrooms, toadstools, and moulds.

funicular (fŭ-**nik**-yŭ-ler) *noun* a cable railway with ascending and descending cars counterbalancing each other. [from Latin *funis* = rope]

funk¹ *noun* (*informal*) **1** fear. **2** a coward. –**funk** *verb* (*informal*) to show fear; to fear and shirk.

funk² *noun* earthy, bluesy music with a heavy rhythmical beat. □ **funk art** an amusingly eccentric or unconventional art form.

funky *adjective* (*informal*) excellent, cool; offbeat.

funnel *noun* **1** a tube or pipe wide at the top and narrow at the bottom, for pouring liquids or powders etc. into small openings. **2** a metal chimney on a steam engine or steamship. –**funnel** *verb* (**funnelled**, **funnelling**) to move through a funnel or a narrowing space. [from Latin *fundere* = pour]

funnel-web *noun* a venomous spider of eastern Australia.

funny *adjective* (**funnier**, **funniest**) **1** causing amusement. **2** puzzling, hard to account for. **3** (*informal*) slightly unwell or insane. □ **funny bone** part of the elbow over which a very sensitive nerve passes. **funny business** trickery. **funnily** *adverb*

fur *noun* **1** the short fine soft hair covering the bodies of certain animals. **2** animal skin with the fur on it, especially when used for making or trimming clothes etc. **3** fabric imitating this. **4** a coat or cape etc. of real or imitation fur. **5** a coating formed on a sick or unhealthy person's tongue. **6** the coating formed by hard water on the inside of a kettle or pipes etc. –**fur** *verb* (**furred**, **furring**) to cover or become covered with fur.

furbelows *plural noun* showy trimmings.

furbish *verb* to polish, to clean or renovate.

furcate (**fer**-kayt) *adjective* forked, branched. –**furcate** *verb* to fork, to divide. **furcation** *noun* [from Latin *furca* = a fork]

Furies *plural noun* (*Gk. myth.*) snake-haired goddesses sent from the Underworld to punish crime.

furious *adjective* **1** full of anger. **2** violent, intense, *a furious pace*. **furiously** *adverb*

furl *verb* (**furled**, **furling**) to roll up and fasten (a sail, flag, or umbrella).

furlong *noun* one-eighth of a mile, 220 yards (approximately 201 metres).

furlough (**fer**-loh) *noun* leave of absence, especially military.

furnace *noun* **1** a closed fireplace for heating water to warm a building etc. by hot pipes. **2** an enclosed space for heating minerals or metals etc. or for making glass.

furnish *verb* **1** to equip (a room or house etc.) with furniture. **2** to provide or supply.

furnishings *plural noun* furniture and fitments, curtains, etc. in a room or house.

furniture *noun* **1** the movable articles (such as tables, chairs, beds, etc.) needed in a room or house etc. **2** accessories, e.g. the handles and lock on a door.

furore (**few**-ror *or* few-**ror**-ree) *noun* an uproar of enthusiastic admiration or fury. [from Latin *furor* = madness]

furphy *noun* (*Austral. informal*) a rumour, a false report.

furrier (**fu**-ree-er) *noun* a dealer in furs.

furrow *noun* **1** a long cut in the ground made by a plough or other implement. **2** a groove resembling this; a deep wrinkle in the skin. –**furrow** *verb* to make furrows in.

furry *adjective* **1** like fur. **2** covered with fur.

further *adverb* & *adjective* **1** more distant in space or time. **2** to a greater extent, more, additional, *shall enquire further*; *made further enquiries*. –**further** *verb* to help the progress of, *further someone's interests*. □ **further education** education beyond secondary school.

Usage See the note under **farther**.

furtherance *noun* the furthering of someone's interests etc.

furthermore *adverb* in addition, moreover.

furthermost *adjective* most distant.

furthest *adjective* most distant. –**furthest** *adverb* to or at the greatest distance.

Usage See the note under **farther**.

furtive *adjective* sly, stealthy. **furtively** *adverb*, **furtiveness** *noun* [from Latin *furtivus* = stolen]

fury *noun* **1** wild anger, rage. **2** violence of weather etc., *the storm's fury*. **3** a violently angry person, especially a woman. –**Fury** *noun* (*Gk. myth.*) each of the Furies (see entry). [from Latin *furia* = rage, an avenging spirit]

furze *noun* gorse.

fuse¹ *noun* (in an electric circuit) a short piece of wire designed to melt and break the circuit if the current exceeds a safe level. –**fuse** *verb* **1** to blend or amalgamate (metals, living bones, institutions, etc.) into a whole. **2** to fit (a circuit or appliance) with a fuse. **3** to cease or cause to cease functioning through the melting of a fuse. □ **fuse box** a small cupboard or box containing the fuses of an electrical system. [from Latin *fusum* = melted]

fuse² *noun* a length of easily burnt material for igniting a bomb or an explosive charge. –**fuse** *verb* to fit a fuse to. [from Latin *fusus* = a spindle]

fuselage (**few**-zĕ-lah*zh*) *noun* the body of an aeroplane.

fusible *adjective* able to be fused. **fusibility** *noun*

fusillade (few-zĭ-**layd**) *noun* **1** a simultaneous or continuous firing of guns. **2** a great outburst of questions, criticism, etc. [from French *fusil* = gun]

fusion (**few**-*zh*ŏn) *noun* **1** fusing, the blending or uniting of different things into a whole. **2** the union of atomic nuclei to form a heavier nucleus, usually with release of energy.

fuss *noun* **1** unnecessary excitement or activity. **2** a display of worry about something unimportant. **3** a vigorous protest or dispute. –**fuss** *verb* to make a fuss, to bother (a person) with unimportant matters or by fussing. □ **make a fuss of** to treat with a great display of attention or affection.

fusspot *noun* (*informal*) a person who fusses habitually.

fussy *adjective* (**fussier, fussiest**) **1** often fussing. **2** fastidious. **3** full of unnecessary detail or decoration. **fussily** *adverb*, **fussiness** *noun*

fustian *noun* a thick twilled cotton (usually dark) cloth.

fusty *adjective* **1** (of a room) stale-smelling, stuffy. **2** smelling of damp and mould. **3** old-fashioned in ideas etc. **fustiness** *noun*

futile (**few**-tyl) *adjective* producing no result, useless. **futility** (few-**til**-ĭ-tee) *noun* [from Latin *futilis* = leaking]

futon (**foo**-tonn) *noun* a light (originally Japanese) kind of mattress.

future *adjective* belonging or referring to the time coming after the present. –**future** *noun* **1** future time, events, or condition; *there's no future in it*, no prospect of success or advancement. **2** the future tense. **futures** *plural noun* goods or shares sold with an agreement to deliver them at a future date. □ **future life** existence after death. **future perfect** the tense of a verb that expresses a completed action in the future, e.g. *you will have finished it by Christmas*. **future tense** the tense of a verb that expresses future action, indicated in English by *shall* with 'I' and 'we' (*I shall return*) and *will* with other words (*they will return*). **in future** from this time onwards.

futuristic (few-tew-**rist**-ik) *adjective* looking suitable for the distant future, not traditional.

futurity (few-**tew**-rĭ-tee) *noun* future time.

fuzz *noun* **1** fluff, something fluffy or frizzy. **2** (*informal*) the police.

fuzzy *adjective* **1** like fuzz; covered with fuzz. **2** frizzy. **3** blurred, indistinct. **fuzzily** *adverb*, **fuzziness** *noun*

Gg

G *abbreviation* **1** giga-; gauss. **2** (of a film or video game) classified as 'for general audiences'.

g *abbreviation* **1** gram(s). **2** gravity; the acceleration due to this.

gab *noun* (*informal*) chatter. □ **have the gift of the gab** to be good at talking.

gabardine (**gab**-er-deen) *noun* a strong fabric woven in a twill pattern.

gabble *verb* to talk quickly and indistinctly. –**gabble** *noun* gabbled talk. **gabbler** *noun*

gabbro *noun* a dark volcanic rock.

gable *noun* the triangular upper part of an outside wall, between sloping roofs.

gabled *adjective* having a gable or gables.

Gabon (gă-**bon**) a republic on the west coast of Africa. **Gabonese** (gab-ŏ-**neez**) *adjective* & *noun* (*plural* **Gabonese**).

Gaborone (gab-ŏ-**roh**-nee) the capital of Botswana.

Gabriel (**gay**-bree-ĕl) **1** (in the Bible) the archangel who foretold the birth of Jesus to the Virgin Mary. **2** (in Islam) the archangel who revealed the Koran to the Prophet Muhammad.

gad *verb* (**gadded**, **gadding**) to be a gadabout.

gadabout *noun* a person who goes about constantly in search of pleasure.

gadfly *noun* a fly that bites horses and cattle.

gadget *noun* a small mechanical device or tool. **gadgetry** *noun* gadgets.

gadolinium (gad-ŏ-**lin**-ee-ŭm) *noun* a metallic element (symbol Gd) resembling steel in appearance. [named after J. Gadolin, Finnish mineralogist (died 1852)]

Gael (*pr.* gayl) *noun* a Scottish or Irish Celt.

Gaelic (**gay**-lik) *noun* **1** (also *pr.* **gal**-ik) the Celtic language of the Scots. **2** the Irish language. –**Gaelic** *adjective* of or in Gaelic.

gaff¹ *noun* a stick with an iron hook for landing large fish caught with rod and line. –**gaff** *verb* to seize with a gaff.

gaff² *noun* **blow the gaff** (*informal*) to reveal a plot or secret.

gaffe *noun* a blunder. [French]

gaffer *noun* (*informal*) the chief electrician in a film production unit. [contraction of *godfather*]

gag *noun* **1** something put into a person's mouth or tied across it to prevent him or her from speaking or crying out. **2** a device used by a dentist or surgeon for holding a patient's jaws open. **3** anything that prevents freedom of speech or of writing. **4** a joke or funny story, especially as part of a comedian's act. –**gag** *verb* (**gagged**, **gagging**) **1** to put a gag into or over the mouth of. **2** to prevent from having freedom of speech or of writing, *we cannot gag the press*. **3** to tell jokes or gags. **4** to retch or choke.

gaga (**gah**-gah) *adjective* (*informal*) **1** senile. **2** crazy.

gaggle *noun* **1** a flock of geese. **2** a disorderly group. –**gaggle** *verb* to cackle like geese.

gaiety *noun* **1** cheerfulness, a happy and light-hearted manner. **2** merrymaking.

gaily *adverb* **1** in a cheerful light-hearted manner. **2** in bright colours.

gain *verb* **1** to obtain, especially something desirable. **2** to make a profit. **3** to acquire gradually, to build up for oneself, *gained strength after illness*. **4** (of a clock etc.) to become ahead of the correct time. **5** to get nearer in racing or pursuit, *our horse was gaining on the favourite*. **6** to reach (a desired place), *gained the shore*. –**gain** *noun* **1** an increase in wealth or possessions. **2** an improvement, an increase in amount or power. □ **gain ground** to make progress. **gain time** to improve one's chances by arranging or accepting a delay. **gainer** *noun*

gainful *adjective* profitable. **gainfully** *adverb*

gainsay *verb* (**gainsaid**, **gainsaying**) (*formal*) to deny or contradict, *there is no gainsaying it*.

gait *noun* **1** a manner of walking or running. **2** any of the forward movements of a horse, such as trotting or cantering. [from a dialect word *gate* = going]

gaiter *noun* a covering of cloth or leather for the leg from knee to ankle, or for the ankle, or for part of a machine.

gala (**gah**-lă) *noun* a festive occasion, a fête.

galactic (gă-**lak**-tik) *adjective* **1** of a galaxy or galaxies. **2** of the Galaxy or Milky Way.

galah (gă-**lah**) *noun* **1** a rose-breasted Australian cockatoo with a grey back. **2** (*informal*) a fool or simpleton. [Yuwaalaraay (and other languages) *gilaa*]

Galahad (in legends of King Arthur) a knight of immaculate purity, destined to retrieve the Holy Grail.

galantine (**gal**-ăn-teen) *noun* white meat or fish boned, cooked, pressed, and set in aspic, served cold.

Galapagos Islands (gă-**lap**-ă-gŏs) a group of islands in the Pacific on the Equator, west of Ecuador (to which they belong).

Galatians (gă-**lay**-shănz) the *Epistle to the Galatians*, a book of the New Testament, an epistle of St Paul to the Church of Galatia in central Asia Minor.

galaxy (**gal**-ăk-see) *noun* **1** any of the large independent systems of stars existing in space. **2** a brilliant company of beautiful or famous people. **–the Galaxy 1** the galaxy containing the Earth. **2** the Milky Way.

gale *noun* **1** a very strong wind; *gale-force winds*, winds with a speed of 62–74 km/h. **2** a noisy outburst, *gales of laughter*.

galena (gă-**leen**-ă) *noun* the commonest kind of lead ore, lead sulphide.

Galilee the northern part of ancient Palestine west of the Jordan, now in Israel. □ **Sea of Galilee** (also called Lake Tiberias) an inland lake in northern Israel. **Galilean** *adjective* & *noun*

Galileo Galilei (gal-ĭ-**lay**-oh gal-ĭ-**lay**-ee) (1564–1642), Italian astronomer and physicist, one of the founders of modern science.

gall¹ (*pr.* gawl) *noun* **1** bile. **2** bitterness of feeling. **3** (*informal*) impudence. □ **gall bladder** a pear-shaped organ attached to the liver, storing and releasing bile.

gall² (*pr.* gawl) *noun* a sore spot on the skin of an animal, especially a horse, caused by rubbing. **–gall** *verb* to rub and make sore.

gall³ (*pr.* gawl) *noun* an abnormal growth produced by an insect, fungus, or bacterium on a plant, especially on an oak tree.

gallant (**gal**-ănt) *adjective* **1** brave, chivalrous. **2** fine, stately, *our gallant ship*. **gallantly** *adverb*, **gallantry** *noun*

galleon (**gal**-ee-ŏn) *noun* a large Spanish sailing ship used in the 15th–17th centuries.

gallery *noun* **1** a room or building for showing works of art. **2** a platform projecting from the inner wall of a church or hall. **3** the highest balcony in a theatre; the people occupying this. **4** the spectators at a golf match. **5** a raised covered platform or passage along the wall of a building. **6** a long room or passage, especially one used for a special purpose, *a shooting gallery*. □ **play to the gallery** to try to win favour by appealing to the taste of the general public.

galley *noun* (*plural* **galleys**) **1** a long low medieval ship propelled by sails and oars. **2** an ancient Greek or Roman warship propelled by oars. **3** the kitchen in a ship or aircraft.

Gallic (**gal**-ik) *adjective* **1** of ancient Gaul. **2** of France, typically French, *Gallic wit*.

galling (**gawl**-ing) *adjective* vexing, humiliating.

Gallipoli (gă-**lip**-ŏ-lee) a peninsula on the European side of the Dardanelles, the scene of heavy fighting in 1915–16 during the First World War.

gallium *noun* a soft bluish-white metallic element (symbol Ga) with many uses (e.g. as a semiconductor in electronic components).

gallivant *verb* (*informal*) to gad about.

gallon *noun* an imperial measure for liquids, = 4 quarts (4.546 litres).

gallop *noun* **1** a horse's fastest pace, with all four feet off the ground simultaneously in each stride. **2** a ride at this pace. **–gallop** *verb* (**galloped**, **galloping**) **1** to go at a gallop, to cause a horse to do this. **2** to go very fast, to rush; *galloping inflation*, getting worse rapidly.

gallows *noun* **1** a framework with a suspended noose for the hanging of criminals. **2** a structure on a farm consisting of two uprights and a crosspiece for skinning a carcass.

gallstone *noun* a small hard mass that sometimes forms in the gall bladder.

Gallup poll *noun* an estimate of public opinion, made by questioning a representative sample of people and used especially to forecast how people will vote in an election. [named after G.H. Gallup (1901–84), American statistician, who devised it]

galore *adverb* in plenty, *presents galore*.

galosh *noun* one of a pair of overshoes, usually rubber.

Galvani (gal-**vah**-nee), Luigi (1737–98), Italian anatomist, pioneer of research into the electrical properties of living things.

galvanic (gal-**van**-ik) *adjective* **1** producing an electric current by chemical action, *a galvanic cell*. **2** stimulating people into sudden activity. [named after *Galvani*]

galvanise *verb* (also **-ize**) **1** to stimulate into sudden activity. **2** to coat (iron) with zinc in order to protect it from rust, *galvanised iron*. **galvanisation** *noun* [same origin as *galvanic*]

galvanometer (gal-vă-**nom**-ĕ-ter) *noun* an instrument for measuring small electric currents.

galvo *noun* (*Austral. informal*) galvanised iron.

Gama (gah-mă), Vasco da (c. 1469–1524), Portuguese explorer, the first European to sail round the Cape of Good Hope.

Gambia (also **the Gambia**) a republic in West Africa. **Gambian** *adjective* & *noun*

gambit *noun* **1** an opening sequence of moves in chess in which a player deliberately sacrifices a pawn or piece in order to gain a favourable position. **2** an action or statement intended to secure some advantage.

gamble *verb* **1** to play games of chance for money. **2** to stake or risk money etc. in the hope of great gain; *gambled his fortune away*, lost it by gambling. **3** to stake one's hopes; *gambled on its being a fine day*. **–gamble** *noun* **1** gambling. **2** a risky attempt or undertaking. **gambler** *noun*

gambol *verb* (**gambolled, gambolling**) to jump or skip about in play. **–gambol** *noun* a gambolling movement.

game¹ *noun* **1** a form of play or sport, especially one with rules. **2** a single section forming a scoring unit in some games (e.g. in tennis or bridge). **3** a scheme or plan, a trick, *so that's her little game!* **4** wild animals or birds hunted for sport or food. **5** their flesh as food, *game pie*. **–game** *verb* to gamble for money stakes; *gaming rooms*, licensed for gambling. **–game** *adjective* **1** brave. **2** having spirit or energy, *are you game for a lark?* **games** *plural noun* athletics or sports; a sporting contest, *the Olympic Games*. □ **game point** the stage in a game when one side will win if it gains the next point; this point. **give the game away** to reveal a secret or scheme. **make game of** to make fun of, to ridicule. **the game is up** the secret

or deception is revealed. **gamely** *adverb*, **gameness** *noun*

game² *adjective* lame, *a game leg*.

gamelan (**gam**-ĕ-lan) *noun* **1** a SE Asian orchestra of percussion, string, and woodwind instruments. **2** a type of xylophone used in this. [Javanese]

gamesmanship *noun* the art of winning contests by upsetting the confidence of one's opponent.

gamete (**gam**-eet) *noun* a sexual cell that unites with another in reproduction, forming a zygote. **gametic** (gă-**met**-ik) *adjective* [from Greek *gamos* = marriage]

gamin (**gam**-ĭn) *noun* a street urchin; a child who looks or behaves like this. [French]

gamine (gam-**een**) *noun* **1** a girl gamin. **2** a small mischievous-looking young woman.

gamma *noun* the third letter of the Greek alphabet, = g. □ **gamma radiation** or **rays** X-rays of very short wavelength emitted by radioactive substances.

gammon *noun* **1** the bottom piece of a flitch of bacon, including a hind leg. **2** cured or smoked ham.

gammy *adjective* (*informal*) = **game²**.

gamut (**gam**-ŭt) *noun* **1** the whole range of musical notes used in medieval or modern music. **2** the whole series or range or scope of anything; *the whole gamut of emotion*, from greatest joy to deepest despair.

Ganay (gu-**ny**) *noun* **1** a member of an Aboriginal people of SE Victoria. **2** their language.

gander *noun* a male goose.

Gandhi (**gahn**-dee), Mohandas Karamchand, called 'Mahatma' (1869–1948), Indian statesman, who became the leader and symbol of the nationalist movement in opposition to British rule.

Ganesha (gă-**nay**-shă) an elephant-headed Hindu god, worshipped as the remover of obstacles and as patron of learning.

gang¹ *noun* **1** a number of workmen working together, *a road gang*. **2** a band of people going about together or working together, especially for some criminal purpose. **–gang** *verb* to combine in a gang; *they ganged up on him*, combined against him.

gang² *verb* (*Scottish*) to go.

Ganges (**gan**-jeez) a river in the north of India, held sacred by Hindus.

gang-gang *noun* a small grey cockatoo of SE Australia, the male of which has a red crest. [Wiradjuri, imitative]

gangling *adjective* tall, thin, and awkward-looking.

ganglion *noun* (*plural* ganglia) **1** a group of nerve cells from which nerve fibres radiate. **2** a cyst on a tendon sheath. **3** a centre of activity. ganglionic (gang-glee-**on**-ik) *adjective*

gangplank *noun* a movable plank used as a bridge for entering or leaving a boat.

gangrene *noun* death and decay of body tissue, usually caused by blockage of the blood supply to that part. gangrenous (**gang**-grĕ-nŭs) *adjective*

gangster *noun* a member of a gang of violent criminals.

gangue (*pr.* gang) *noun* valueless earth or other material in which ore is found.

gangway *noun* **1** a gap left for people to pass between rows of seats or through a crowd. **2** a passageway, especially on a ship. **3** a movable bridge from a ship to the land; the opening in a ship's side into which this fits.

ganja *noun* marijuana. [from Hindi *ganjha*]

gannet (**gan**-ĕt) *noun* a large seabird.

gantry *noun* a light bridge-like overhead framework for supporting a travelling crane, railway signals over tracks, etc.

Ganymede (**gan**-ee-meed) **1** (*Gk. myth.*) a Trojan youth who was so beautiful that he was carried off to be Zeus' cup-bearer. **2** the largest satellite of the planet Jupiter.

gaol see jail

gaoler see jailer

gap *noun* **1** a break or opening in something continuous such as a hedge or fence or wall, or between hills. **2** an unfilled space or interval. **3** something lacking, *a gap in one's education*. **4** a wide difference in ideas.

gape *verb* **1** to open the mouth wide. **2** to stare with open mouth, in surprise or wonder. **3** to open or be open wide, *a gaping chasm*. – gape *noun* an open-mouthed stare.

garage (**ga**-rah*zh*, **ga**-rahj, *or* gă-) *noun* **1** a building in which to keep a motor vehicle or vehicles. **2** an establishment where motor vehicles are repaired and serviced. **3** an establishment selling petrol and oil etc. – garage *verb* to put or keep in a garage. □ garage sale a sale (of household items) held usually in the garage of a private house.

garb *noun* clothing, especially of a distinctive kind, *clerical garb*. – garb *verb* to clothe.

garbage *noun* rubbish or refuse of all kinds, domestic waste.

garble *verb* to give a confused account of something, so that a message or story is distorted or misunderstood.

garbo *noun* (*Austral. informal*) a garbage collector.

garden *noun* a piece of cultivated ground, especially attached to a house. – garden *verb* to tend a garden. gardens *plural noun* ornamental public grounds. □ garden centre an establishment where plants and gardening tools etc. are sold. garden party a party held on a lawn or in a garden or park. lead up the garden path to entice, to mislead deliberately.

gardener *noun* a person who tends a garden, either as a job or as a hobby.

gardenia (gar-**deen**-ee-ă) *noun* **1** a tree or shrub with large fragrant white or yellow flowers. **2** its flower. [named after Dr A. Garden, Scottish naturalist (died 1791)]

garfish *noun* an edible fish with a spearlike lower jaw.

gargantuan (gar-**gan**-tew-ăn) *adjective* gigantic. [from the name of Gargantua, a giant in a story by Rabelais]

gargle *verb* to wash or rinse the inside of the throat with liquid held there by air breathed out from the lungs. – gargle *noun* a liquid used for this.

gargoyle *noun* a grotesque carved face or figure, especially as a gutter spout carrying water clear of a wall.

garish (**gair**-rish) *adjective* excessively bright, gaudy, over-decorated. garishly *adverb*

garland *noun* a wreath of flowers etc. worn or hung as a decoration. – garland *verb* to deck with a garland or garlands.

garlic *noun* **1** an onion-like plant. **2** its bulbous root that has a strong taste and smell, used for flavouring. garlicky *adjective*

garment *noun* an article of clothing.

garner *verb* to store up, to collect.

garnet *noun* a semi-precious stone of deep transparent red.

garnish *verb* to decorate (especially food for the table). – garnish *noun* something used for garnishing. garnishment *noun*

garret *noun* an attic, especially a poor one.

garrison *noun* **1** troops stationed in a town or fort to defend it; *a garrison town*, one that has a permanent garrison. **2** the building or fort they occupy. –**garrison** *verb* **1** to place a garrison in. **2** to occupy and defend, *troops garrisoned the town.*

garrotte (gă-**rot**) *noun* **1** a Spanish method of capital punishment by strangulation with a metal collar. **2** the apparatus used for this. **3** a cord or wire used to strangle a victim. –**garotte** *verb* to kill with a garrotte.

garrulous (**ga**-rŭ-lŭs) *adjective* talkative. **garrulously** *adverb*, **garrulousness** *noun*, **garrulity** (gă-**roo**-lĭ-tee) *noun*

garter *noun* a band especially of elastic worn round the leg to keep a stocking up. □ **garter stitch** rows of plain stitch in knitting.

garuda *noun* **1** (*Indian myth.*) a bird (half eagle, half man) ridden by the god Vishnu. **2** the national emblem of Indonesia.

gas *noun* (*plural* **gases**) **1** a substance with particles that can move freely, especially one that does not become liquid or solid at ordinary temperatures (other gases are usually called 'vapours'). **2** any of the gases or mixtures of gases used for lighting, heating, or cooking; *gas stove*, *gas fire*, etc., domestic appliances using gas as fuel. **3** poisonous gas used to disable an enemy in war; dangerous gas occurring naturally in a coal mine. **4** nitrous oxide or other gas used as an anaesthetic. **5** (*informal*) empty talk. **6** (*Amer. informal*, short for *gasoline*) petrol; *step on the gas*, press the accelerator pedal, hurry. –**gas** *verb* (**gassed**, **gassing**) **1** to expose to gas, to poison or overcome by gas. **2** (*informal*) to talk idly for a long time. □ **gas chamber** a room that can be filled with poisonous gas to kill animals or prisoners. **gas-fired** *adjective* heated by burning gas. **gas fitter** a mechanic who fits pipes etc. for gas heating or lighting. **gas mask** a protective device worn over the face to protect the wearer against poisonous gas.

gasbag *noun* (*informal*) a person who talks too much.

gaseous (**gas**-ee-ŭs) *adjective* of or like a gas.

gash *noun* a long deep slash or cut or wound. –**gash** *verb* to make a gash in.

gasket *noun* a flat sheet or ring of rubber or other soft material used for sealing a joint between metal surfaces to prevent gas or steam or liquid from entering or escaping.

gaslight *noun* light given by a jet of burning gas.

gasoline *noun* **1** a liquid distilled from petroleum, used for heating and lighting. **2** (*Amer.*) petrol.

gasometer (gas-**om**-ĕ-ter) *noun* a large round tank in which gas is stored and from which it is distributed through pipes.

gasp *verb* **1** to struggle for breath with the mouth open. **2** to draw in the breath sharply in astonishment etc. **3** to speak in a breathless way. –**gasp** *noun* a breath drawn in sharply. □ **be at one's last gasp** to be exhausted or at the point of death.

gassy *adjective* **1** of or like a gas. **2** using too many words.

gastric *adjective* of the stomach. □ **gastric flu** sickness and diarrhoea of unknown origin. [from Greek *gaster* = stomach]

gastritis (gas-**try**-tĭss) *noun* inflammation of the stomach.

gastroenteritis (gas-troh-en-tĕ-**ry**-tĭss) *noun* inflammation of the stomach and intestines.

gastronomy (gas-**tron**-ŏ-mee) *noun* the science of good eating and drinking. **gastronomic** (gas-trŏ-**nom**-ik) *adjective* [from Greek *gaster* = stomach, + *-nomia* = management]

gastropod (**gas**-trŏ-pod) *noun* a mollusc (such as a snail or limpet) that moves by means of a muscular 'foot' on its ventral surface and possesses two tentacles and eyes. [from Greek *gaster* = stomach, + *podos* = of the foot]

gasworks *noun* a place where gas for lighting and heating is manufactured.

gate *noun* **1** a movable barrier, usually on hinges, serving as a door in a wall or fence, or regulating the passage of water etc. **2** the opening it covers. **3** a means of entrance or exit. **4** an arrangement of slots controlling the movement of a gear lever in a motor vehicle. **5** an electrical device that controls the passage of electrical signals; (in computers) a circuit with one output that is activated only by a combination of input signals. **6** the number of spectators entering by payment to see a football match etc.; the amount of money taken.

gateau (**gat**-oh) *noun* (*plural* **gateaux**, *pr.* **gat**-ohz) a large rich cream cake. [from French *gâteau* = cake]

gatecrash *verb* to go to a private party etc. without being invited. **gatecrasher** *noun*

gatehouse *noun* a house built at the side of or over a large gate.

gatelegged *adjective* (of a table) having legs that can be moved out or in to support or lower drop leaves.

gateway *noun* 1 an opening or structure framing a gate. 2 any means of entrance or exit, *the gateway to success*.

gather *verb* 1 to bring or come together. 2 to collect, to obtain gradually. 3 to collect as harvest, to pluck. 4 to increase gradually, *gather speed*. 5 to understand or conclude, *I gather your proposal was accepted*. 6 to draw (parts) together; *his brow was gathered in thought*, was wrinkled. 7 to pull fabric into gathers; *a gathered skirt*, made with gathers at the waist. 8 (of a sore) to swell up and form pus. **gathers** *plural noun* a series of folds formed by drawing up fabric on a thread run through it like a drawstring.

gathering *noun* 1 an assembly of people. 2 an inflamed swelling with pus in it.

GATT *abbreviation* General Agreement on Tariffs and Trade, a treaty to which more than 80 countries are parties, to promote trade and economic development.

gauche (*pr.* **goh**sh) *adjective* lacking in ease and grace of manner, awkward and tactless. [French, = left-handed]

gaucherie (**goh**-shĕ-ree) *noun* gauche manners; a gauche action.

gaucho (**gow**-choh) *noun* (*plural* **gauchos**) a mounted herdsman in the South American pampas.

gaudy *adjective* (**gaudier, gaudiest**) showy or bright in a tasteless way. **gaudily** *adverb*, **gaudiness** *noun* [from Latin *gaudere* = rejoice]

gauge (*pr.* gayj) *noun* 1 a standard measure of contents, fineness of textiles, thickness of sheet metal, or diameter of bullets. 2 the distance between pairs of rails or between opposite wheels. 3 an instrument used for measuring, marked with regular divisions or units of measurement. 4 capacity, extent. 5 a means of estimating something. –**gauge** *verb* 1 to measure exactly. 2 to estimate, to form a judgment of.

Gauguin (**goh**-gan), Paul (1848–1903), French painter, who lived chiefly in the South Pacific islands from 1891.

Gaul an ancient region of Europe corresponding roughly to modern France and

Belgium. –**Gaul** *noun* a native or inhabitant of Gaul.

gaunt *adjective* 1 lean and haggard. 2 grim or desolate-looking. **gauntness** *noun*

gauntlet¹ *noun* 1 a glove with a wide cuff covering the wrist. 2 the cuff itself. 3 a glove with metal plates worn by soldiers in the Middle Ages. □ **throw down the gauntlet** to make a challenge to a fight. [from French *gant* = glove]

gauntlet² *noun* **run the gauntlet** to be exposed to continuous severe criticism or risk. [from a former military and naval punishment in which the victim was made to pass between two rows of men who struck him as he passed]

Gaurna (**gah**-nă) *noun see* Kaurna.

gauss (*rhymes with* house) *noun* (*plural* **gauss**) an electromagnetic unit of magnetic induction. [named after K. Gauss, German mathematician, physicist, and astronomer (1777–1855)]

Gautama (**gow**-tă-mă) the family name of the Buddha.

gauze *noun* 1 thin transparent woven material of silk or cotton etc. 2 fine wire mesh. **gauzy** *adjective* [from Gaza, a town in Israel]

gave *see* give.

gavel (**gav**-ĕl) *noun* a hammer used to call for attention or order at an auction or in a meeting or court.

gavotte (gă-**vot**) *noun* a lively old French dance; the music for it.

gawky *adjective* awkward and ungainly. **gawkiness** *noun*

gawp *verb* (*informal*) to stare stupidly.

gay *adjective* 1 (*informal*) homosexual; of homosexuals. 2 (*old use*) light-hearted and cheerful, happy and full of fun. 2 (*old use*) brightly coloured, dressed or decorated in bright colours. –**gay** *noun* (*informal*) a homosexual. **gayness** *noun*

Gaza Strip (**gah**-ză) a strip of coastal territory on the SE Mediterranean, including the town of Gaza, occupied by Israel in 1967 but becoming a self-governing enclave under the PLO–Israeli accord of 1994.

gaze *verb* to look long and steadily. –**gaze** *noun* a long steady look.

gazebo (gă-**zee**-boh) *noun* (*plural* **gazebos**) a structure, such as a raised turret or summer house, with a wide view.

gazelle *noun* a small graceful Asian or African antelope.

gazette *noun* the title of certain newspapers, or of official journals that contain public notices and lists of government appointments.

gazetteer (gaz-ĕ-**teer**) *noun* an index of place-names, names of rivers and mountains, etc.

gazillion *noun* (*informal*) a very large number or quantity.

gazump *verb* (*informal*) to disappoint (an intended purchaser) by raising the price after accepting his or her offer, especially for a house.

GB *abbreviation* **1** Great Britain. **2** (also **Gb**) gigabyte.

g'day *interjection* (*Austral. informal*) good-day.

GDP *abbreviation* gross domestic product.

gear *noun* **1** (often **gears**) a set of toothed wheels working together in a machine to transmit rotary motion, especially those connecting the engine of a motor vehicle to the road wheels. **2** a particular setting of these. **3** equipment, *hunting gear*. **4** (*informal*) clothes, *teenage gear*. **5** apparatus, appliances, *aircraft's landing gear*. –**gear** *verb* **1** to put machinery in gear. **2** to provide with or connect by gears. **3** to adjust or adapt; *a factory geared to the export trade*, organised for this specifically. □ **gear lever** a lever used to engage or change a gear. **in gear** with gear mechanism engaged. **out of gear** with it disengaged.

gearbox *noun* a set of gears with its casing; the case enclosing a gear mechanism.

gearing *noun* a set or arrangement of gears.

gecko (gek-oh) *noun* (*plural* **geckos**) a house lizard of warm climates, able to climb walls by the adhesive pads on its toes.

geebung (**jee**-bung) *noun* **1** any of several Australian shrubs or trees with an edible fruit. **2** this fruit. [Dharuk, probably *jibung*]

geek *noun* **1** (*Austral. informal*) a look. **2** (*informal*) a dull or socially inept person. **geeky** *adjective*

geese *see* **goose**.

gee-up *interjection* a command to a horse to move on or go faster.

geezer *noun* (*informal*) a person, an old man.

Geiger counter (**gy**-ger) *noun* a cylindrical device for detecting and measuring radioactivity. [named after H.J.W. Geiger (1882–1945), German nuclear physicist, who developed the first device of this kind]

geisha (**gay**-shǎ) *noun* a Japanese hostess trained to entertain men by dancing and singing.

gel (*pr.* jel) *noun* a jelly-like substance; *hair gel*, *shower gel*. –**gel** *verb* (**gelled**, **gelling**) to set as a gel.

gelatine *noun* a clear tasteless substance made by boiling the bones, skins, and connective tissue of animals, used in foods, medicine, and photographic film. [same origin as *jelly*]

gelatinise (jĕ-**lat**-ĭ-nyz) *verb* (also -**ize**) **1** to make or become gelatinous. **2** to coat or treat with gelatine. **gelatinisation** *noun*

gelatinous (jĕ-**lat**-ĭ-nǔs) *adjective* of or like gelatine, jelly-like.

gelato (jĕ-**lah**-toh) *noun* (*plural* **gelati**, *pr.* jĕ-**lah**-tee) a kind of ice cream having a soft smooth texture. [Italian]

geld *verb* to castrate, to spay.

gelding *noun* a gelded animal, especially a horse.

gelignite (**jel**-ig-nyt) *noun* an explosive containing nitroglycerine. [from *gelatine*, + Latin *ignis* = fire]

gem *noun* **1** (also **gemstone**) a precious stone, especially when cut and polished. **2** something valued because of its excellence or beauty.

Gemara (gĕ-**mah**-rǎ) *noun* a commentary on the Mishnah, written in Aramaic and forming the second part of the Talmud.

gemfish *noun* (*Austral.*) an edible sea fish, also called *hake*.

Gemini (**jem**-ĭ-ny) *noun* a sign of the zodiac, the Twins (Castor and Pollux), which the sun enters about 21 May. **Geminian** *adjective* & *noun*

gen (*pr.* jen) *noun* (*informal*) information. –**gen** *verb* (**genned**, **genning**) **gen up** (*informal*) to gain information; to give information to.

gender *noun* **1** the class in which a noun or pronoun is placed in grammatical grouping (in English, these are masculine, feminine, neuter, and common). **2** a person's sex. [from Latin *genus* = a kind]

gene (*pr.* jeen) *noun* each of the factors controlling heredity, carried by a chromosome. [from Greek -*genes* = born]

genealogy (jee-nee-**al**-ŏ-jee) *noun* **1** an account of descent from an ancestor given by listing the intermediate persons, a pedigree. **2** the science or study of family pedigrees. **genealogical** (jee-nee-ă-**loj**-i-kăl) *adjective*, **genealogist** *noun* [from Greek *genea* = race of people, + -*logy*]

genera *see* **genus**.

general *adjective* **1** of or affecting all or nearly all, not partial or local or particular. **2** involving various kinds, not specialised, *a general education*. **3** involving only main features, not detailed or specific, *spoke only in general terms*. **4** chief, head, *the general manager*; *the Attorney-General*. –**general** *noun* **1** an army officer ranking below a Field Marshal. **2** a lieutenant-general or major-general. **3** the chief of the Jesuits or other religious order. ☐ **general election** a state or federal election for representatives in Parliament for all seats. **general knowledge** knowledge of a wide variety of subjects. **general practitioner** a doctor who treats cases of all kinds. **general store** a shop, especially in a country town, that stocks a large range of goods. **in general** as a general rule, usually.

generalise *verb* (also -**ize**) **1** to draw a general conclusion from particular instances. **2** to speak in general terms, to use generalities. **3** to bring into general use. **generalisation** *noun*

generalissimo *noun* a commander of combined military, naval, and air forces, or of several armies.

generality (jen-ě-**ral**-ĭ-tee) *noun* **1** being general. **2** a general statement lacking precise details.

generally *adverb* **1** usually, as a general rule. **2** widely, for the most part, *the plan was generally welcomed*. **3** in a general sense, without regard to details, *speaking generally*.

generate *verb* to bring into existence, to produce.

generation *noun* **1** generating; being generated. **2** a single stage in descent or pedigree; *three generations*, children, parents, and grandparents; *first-generation Americans*, Americans whose parents were of some other nationality. **3** all persons born about the same time and therefore of the same age, *my generation*. **4** the average period (regarded as about 30 years) in which children grow up and take the former place of their parents. **5** (of machinery etc.) a set of models at one stage of development, *a new generation of computers*.

☐ **generation gap** lack of understanding between people of different generations.

generator *noun* **1** an apparatus for producing gases, steam, etc. **2** a machine for converting mechanical energy into electricity.

generic (jĕ-**ne**-rik) *adjective* of a whole genus or group. **generically** *adverb*

generous *adjective* **1** giving or ready to give freely, free from meanness or prejudice. **2** given freely, plentiful, *a generous gift*; *a generous portion*. **generously** *adverb*, **generosity** *noun*

genesis (**jen**-ĕ-sĭs) *noun* a beginning or origin. –**Genesis** the first book of the Old Testament, telling of the creation of the world. [Greek, = creation or origin]

genetic (jĕ-**net**-ik) *adjective* **1** of genes. **2** of genetics. **genetics** *noun* the scientific study of heredity. ☐ **genetic code** the storage system for genetic information in chromosomes. **genetic engineering** deliberate modification of hereditary features by treatment to transfer certain genes. **genetic fingerprinting** an analysis of body tissue or fluid to discover its cell structure, used for identifying a person involved in certain crimes or for proving a family relationship. **genetically** *adverb* [from *genesis*]

geneticist (jĕ-**net**-ĭ-sĭst) *noun* an expert in genetics.

Geneva (jĕ-**nee**-vă) a city in SW Switzerland, on the Lake of Geneva. ☐ **Geneva Conventions** a series of international agreements made at Geneva between 1864 and 1949 governing the status and treatment of hospitals, ambulances, wounded persons, prisoners of war, etc.

Genghis Khan (jeng-gĭs **kahn**) (1162– 1227), founder of the Mongol empire, which by the time of his death stretched from the Pacific to the Black Sea.

genial (**jee**-nee-ăl) *adjective* **1** kindly, pleasant, and cheerful. **2** mild, pleasantly warm, *a genial climate*. **genially** *adverb*, **geniality** (jee-nee-**al**-ĭ-tee) *noun*

genie (**jee**-nee) *noun* (in Arabian tales) a spirit or goblin with strange powers. [from Arabic *jinni*]

genital (**jen**-ĭ-t'l) *adjective* of animal reproduction or reproductive organs. **genitals** *plural noun* (also **genitalia**, *pr*. gen-ĭ-**tay**-lee-ă) *noun* the external sex organs of people and animals.

genitive (jen-ĭ-tiv) *noun* the grammatical case showing source or possession in certain languages, corresponding to the use of *of* or *from* in English.

genius *noun* (*plural* **geniuses**) **1** exceptionally great mental ability; any great natural ability. **2** a person possessing this. **3** a guardian spirit, *one's good* or *evil genius*. [Latin, = a spirit]

genocide (jen-ŏ-syd) *noun* deliberate extermination of a race of people. [from Greek *genos* = a race, + Latin *caedere* = kill]

genome (jee-nohm) *noun* the full set of an individual's chromosomes. [from *gene* + *chromosome*]

genotype (jen-ŏ-typ) *noun* the genetic constitution of an individual.

genre (*pr.* zhon-rĕ) *noun* a particular kind or style of art or literature (e.g. epic, romance, western). [French]

gent *noun* (*informal*) a man, a gentleman. –**the Gents** (*informal*) a men's public toilet.

genteel (jen-**teel**) *adjective* affectedly polite and refined. **genteelly** *adverb*

gentian (jen-**shăn**) *noun* an alpine plant usually with deep-blue bell-like flowers. **gentian violet** a dye used as an antiseptic.

gentile (jen-tyl) *noun* a person who is not Jewish. –**gentile** *adjective* of gentiles.

gentility (jen-**til**-ĭ-tee) *noun* good manners and elegance.

gentle *adjective* **1** mild, moderate, not rough or severe, *a gentle breeze*. **2** of good family, *is of gentle birth*. □ **the gentle sex** women. **gently** *adverb*, **gentleness** *noun*

gentlefolk *noun* people of good family.

gentleman *noun* (*plural* **gentlemen**) **1** a man of honourable and kindly behaviour. **2** a man of good social position. **3** (in polite use) a man. □ **gentleman-at-arms** *noun* a member of the sovereign's bodyguard. **gentleman's agreement** one that is regarded as binding in honour but not enforceable at law. **gentlemanly** *adjective*

gentrify *verb* (**gentrified**, **gentrifying**) to renovate or convert (housing etc.) so that it conforms to middle-class taste. **gentrification** *noun*

gentry *plural noun* **1** people next below the nobility in position and birth. **2** (*derogatory*) people, *these gentry*.

genuflect (jen-**yŭ**-flekt) *verb* to bend the knee and lower the body, especially in worship. **genuflexion** *noun*

genuine *adjective* really what it is said to be, *genuine pearls*; *with genuine pleasure*. **genuinely** *adverb*, **genuineness** *noun*

genus (jee-nŭs) *noun* (*plural* **genera**, *pr.* **jen**-ĕ-ră) **1** a group of animals or plants with common characteristics, usually containing several species. **2** (*informal*) a kind or sort. [Latin, = family or race]

geo- *prefix* earth. [from Greek *ge* = earth]

geode (jee-ohd) *noun* **1** a small cavity lined with crystals. **2** a rock containing this. [from Greek *geodes* = earthy]

geodesic (jee-oh-**dee**-sik) *adjective* (also **geodetic**, jee-oh-**det**-ik) of geodesy. □ **geodesic** (or **geodetic**) **dome** a dome built of short struts holding flat or triangular polygonal pieces, fitted together to form a rough hemisphere. **geodesic line** the shortest possible line between two points on a curved surface.

geodesy (jee-od-ĕ-see) *noun* the scientific study of the earth's shape and size. [from *geo-*, + Greek *-daisia* = division]

geographer *noun* an expert in geography.

geography *noun* **1** the scientific study of the earth's surface and its physical features, climate, products, and population. **2** the physical features and arrangement of a place. **geographic** *adjective*, **geographical** *adjective*, **geographically** *adverb* [from *geo-* + *-graphy*]

geologist *noun* an expert in geology.

geology (jee-ol-ŏ-jee) *noun* **1** the scientific study of the earth's crust and its strata. **2** the features and strata of the earth's crust. **geological** *adjective*, **geologically** *adverb* [from *geo-* + *-logy*]

geomagnetism (jee-oh-**mag**-nĕ-tizm) *noun* the scientific study of the earth's magnetic properties. **geomagnetic** *adjective*

geometry (jee-**om**-ĕ-tree) *noun* the branch of mathematics dealing with the properties and relations of lines, angles, surfaces, and solids. □ **geometric mean** *see* **mean**[3]. **geometric progression** a series of numbers (such as 1, 3, 9, 27) in which each term is the product of a constant figure and the previous term. **geometric** *adjective*, **geometrical** *adjective*, **geometrically** *adverb* [from *geo-*, + Greek *-metria* = measurement]

geomorphology (jee-oh-mor-**fol**-ŏ-jee) *noun* the scientific study of the physical features of the earth's (or other planet's) surface and their relation to its geological structures. [from *geo-*, + Greek *morphe* = a form, + *-logy*]

geophysics (jee-oh-**fiz**-iks) *noun* the study of the physical properties of the earth.

Geordie (**jor**-dee) *noun* a person from Tyneside in England.

George¹ the name of six kings of Great Britain and Ireland, who reigned as George I 1714–27, II 1727–60, III 1760–1820, IV 1820–30, V 1910–36, VI 1936–52.

George², St (date unknown) the patron saint of England.

George Town the capital of the Cayman Islands.

Georgetown the capital of Guyana.

georgette (jor-**jet**) *noun* a thin silky dress material.

Georgia¹ a State of the south-eastern USA. **Georgian¹** *adjective & noun*

Georgia² a republic to the east of the Black Sea, north of Turkey. **Georgian²** *adjective & noun*

Georgian³ (**jor**-jăn) *adjective* of the time of the Georges, kings of England, especially 1714–1830.

geosequestration *noun* the underground storage of carbon dioxide.

geosyncline (jee-oh-**sin**-klyn) *noun* a large trough or basin-shaped depression in the earth's crust, caused by subsidence.

geothermal (jee-oh-**ther**-măl) *adjective* of or using the heat produced in the earth's interior.

geotropism (jee-ŏ-**troh**-pizm) *noun* the way the growth of plants is affected by earth's gravity. **geotropic** (jee-ŏ-**trop**-ik) *adjective* [from *geo-*, + Greek *trope* = turning]

Geraldton wax *noun* a Western Australian shrub with large waxy white, pink, or purple flowers.

geranium *noun* a garden plant with red, pink, purple, or white flowers.

gerbil (**jer**-bĭl) *noun* a desert rodent with long hind legs.

geriatrics (je-ree-**at**-riks) *noun* the branch of medicine dealing with the diseases and care of old people. **geriatric** *adjective* [from Greek *geras* = old age, + *iatros* = doctor]

germ *noun* **1** a microorganism, especially one causing disease. **2** a portion of a living organism capable of becoming a new organism, the embryo of a seed, *wheat germ*.

3 a beginning or basis from which something may develop, *the germ of an idea*.

German *adjective* of Germany or its people or language. **– German** *noun* **1** a native of Germany. **2** the language of Germany. □ **German measles** a contagious disease like mild measles. **German shepherd** a dog of a large strong smooth-haired breed (also called *Alsatian*).

germane (jer-**mayn**) *adjective* relevant.

Germanic (jer-**man**-ik) *adjective* having German characteristics.

germanium (jer-**may**-nee-ŭm) *noun* a brittle greyish-white semi-metallic element (symbol Ge).

Germany a republic in Europe, divided from 1945 to 1990 into the Federal Republic of Germany (= West Germany) and the German Democratic Republic (= East Germany), united in October 1990.

germicide (**jerm**-ĭ-syd) *noun* a substance that kills germs or microorganisms. **germicidal** *adjective* [from *germ*, + Latin *caedere* = kill]

germinal *adjective* **1** of germs. **2** in the earliest stage of development. **3** productive of new ideas etc.

germinate *verb* **1** to begin to develop and grow, to put forth shoots. **2** to cause to do this. **germination** *noun*

gerontology (je-ron-**tol**-ŏ-jee) *noun* the scientific study of the process of ageing and of old people's special problems. [from Greek *gerontos* = of an old man, + *-logy*]

gerrymander (je-ree-**man**-der) *verb* to arrange the boundaries of electorates so as to give unfair advantages to one party or class in an election. [named after Governor Gerry of Massachusetts, who rearranged boundaries for this purpose in 1812]

Gershwin, George (1898–1937), American pianist and composer, whose works include *Rhapsody in Blue*, *An American in Paris*, and the folk opera *Porgy and Bess*.

gerund (**je**-rŭnd) *noun* a form of a verb (in English ending in *-ing*) that functions as a noun, e.g. *scolding* in *what is the use of my scolding him?*

gerundive (jĕ-**run**-div) *noun* a form of a Latin verb that functions as an adjective meaning 'that must or ought to be done etc.'

gesso (**jes**-oh) *noun* gypsum as used in painting or sculpture.

Gestapo (ges-**tah**-poh) *noun* the German secret police of the Nazi regime.

gestation (jes-**tay**-shŏn) *noun* **1** the process of carrying or being carried in the womb. **2** the time of this, from conception until birth. **3** private development of a plan etc.

gesticulate (jes-**tik**-yŭ-layt) *verb* to make expressive movements of the hands and arms. **gesticulation** *noun*

gesture (**jes**-cher) *noun* **1** an expressive movement of any part of the body. **2** something done to convey one's intentions or attitude, *a gesture of friendship*. –**gesture** *verb* to make a gesture.

get *verb* (**got**, **getting**) **1** to come into possession of, to obtain or receive. **2** to obtain radio transmissions from; to reach by telephone. **3** to fetch, *get your coat*. **4** to suffer (a punishment etc.); to contract (an illness). **5** to capture, to catch; *I'll get him for that*, catch and kill or injure him. **6** (*informal*) to understand, *I don't get your meaning*. **7** to prepare (a meal). **8** to bring or come into a certain condition, *get your hair cut*; *got wet*. **9** to move in a particular direction, to succeed in coming or going or bringing, *get off the grass*; *we got from Newcastle to here in an hour*. **10** to succeed in bringing or persuading, *got a message to her*; *got her to agree*. **11** (*informal*) annoy, *what gets me is the way he knows everything*. □ **get across** to communicate (an idea etc.). **get along** to get on. **get at** to reach; (*informal*) to mean, to imply; (*informal*) to imply a criticism of, *she keeps getting at the way I speak*; (*informal*) to tamper with, to bribe. **get away** to escape; *get away with something*, do it and yet escape blame or punishment or misfortune. **get by** (*informal*) to pass, to be accepted; to manage to survive. **get down** to swallow (a thing); to record in writing; (*informal*) to cause depression in (a person). **get down to** to begin working on. **get going** (*informal*) to begin moving or operating. **get in** to arrive. **get off** to begin a journey; to be acquitted; to escape with little or no punishment; to obtain an acquittal for, *a clever lawyer got him off*. **get off with** to become friendly with (a person), especially after attracting him or her deliberately. **get on** to manage; to make progress; to be on friendly or harmonious terms; to advance in age. **get on!** (*informal*) don't expect me to believe that. **get one's own back** (*informal*) to have one's revenge. **get out of** to avoid or get round. **get-out** *noun* a means of evading something. **get over** to

overcome (a difficulty); to recover from (an illness or shock etc.). **get round** to influence in one's favour, to coax; to evade a law or rule without actually breaking it. **get round to** to find time to deal with. **get through** to finish or use up; to pass an examination; to make contact by telephone. **get through to** (*informal*) to make (a person) understand. **get-together** *noun* (*informal*) a social gathering. **get up** to stand after sitting or kneeling etc., to get out of bed or from one's chair etc.; to prepare or organise; to acquire a knowledge of; to produce in a specified style; to dress in an outfit or costume. **get-up** *noun* (*informal*) an outfit or costume. **get up to** to become involved in (mischief etc.).

get-at-able *adjective* able to be reached.

getaway *noun* an escape, especially after committing a crime.

Gettysburg a small town in Pennsylvania, scene of a decisive battle of the American Civil War in July 1863, when the Confederate army was heavily defeated.

geyser *noun* **1** (*pr.* **gy**-zer) a natural spring sending up a column of hot water or steam at intervals. **2** (*pr.* **gee**-zer) a kind of water heater. [from the name of a hot spring in Iceland (*geysa* = gush)]

Ghana (**gah**-nă) a republic in West Africa. **Ghanaian** (gah-**nay**-ăn) *adjective* & *noun*

ghastly *adjective* **1** causing horror or fear, *a ghastly accident*. **2** (*informal*) very unpleasant, very bad, *a ghastly mistake*. **3** pale and ill-looking. **ghastliness** *noun* [related to *aghast* = horrified]

ghat (*pr.* gaht *or* gawt) *noun* (in India) **1** a flight of steps down to a river, a landing place. **2** a mountain pass. [Hindi]

ghee (*pr.* g'ee) *noun* Indian clarified butter made from the milk of a buffalo or cow. [Hindi]

gherkin (**ger**-kin) *noun* a small cucumber used for pickling.

ghetto (**get**-oh) *noun* (*plural* **ghettos**) a slum area occupied by a particular group, especially as a result of social or economic conditions. [from Italian *getto* = foundry (the first ghetto was in Venice, on the site of a foundry)]

ghost *noun* **1** a person's spirit appearing after his or her death. **2** something very slight; *he hasn't the ghost of a chance*, he has no chance at all. **3** a duplicated image in a defective telescope or a television picture. –**ghost** *verb* to write as a ghost writer. □ **ghost town** a town abandoned by all or most of its former inhabitants. **ghost writer** a person who writes a book, article, or speech for another to pass off as his or her own. **give up the ghost** to die. **ghostly** *adjective*, **ghostliness** *noun*

ghoul (*pr.* gool) *noun* **1** (in Muslim folklore) a spirit that robs graves and devours the corpses in them. **2** a person who enjoys gruesome things. **ghoulish** *adjective*, **ghoulishly** *adverb* [from Arabic *gul*]

GI[1] *noun* a private soldier in the US army. [short for *government* (or *general*) *issue*]

GI[2] *abbreviation* glycaemic index.

giant *noun* **1** an imaginary or mythical being of human form but superhuman size. **2** a person, animal, or plant that is much larger than the usual size. **3** a person of outstanding ability or influence. –**giant** *adjective* of a kind that is very large in size. **Giants** *plural noun* (*Gk. myth.*) a race of monstrous appearance and great strength who tried unsuccessfully to overthrow the Olympian gods. **giantess** *feminine noun*

gibber[1] (**jib**-er) *verb* to make unintelligible or meaningless sounds, especially when shocked or terrified.

gibber[2] (**gib**-er) *noun* (*Austral.*) a stone or rock. [Dharuk *giba* = stone]

gibberellin (jib-ĕ-**rel**-ĭn) *noun* any of a group of compounds that regulate the growth of plants.

gibberish (**jib**-ĕ-rish) *noun* unintelligible talk or sounds, nonsense.

gibbet (**jib**-ĕt) *noun* **1** a gallows. **2** an upright post with an arm from which an executed criminal was hung.

gibbon *noun* a long-armed ape of SE Asia.

gibbous (**jib**-ŭs) *adjective* **1** convex, protuberant, humped. **2** (of a moon or planet) having more than half (but less than the whole) of its disc illuminated.

gibe (*pr.* jyb) *verb* to jeer. –**gibe** *noun* a jeering remark.

giblets (**jib**-lĕts) *plural noun* the edible parts of the inside of a bird, taken out before it is cooked.

Gibraltar a fortified town and rocky headland at the southern tip of Spain on the Strait of Gibraltar that forms the outlet of the Mediterranean Sea to the Atlantic, a British naval and air base. **Gibraltarian** (jib-rawl-**tair**-ree-ăn) *adjective* & *noun*

Gibson Desert a desert lying west of central Australia. [named after Alfred Gibson who died there on Ernest Giles' 1874 expedition]

giddy *adjective* (**giddier**, **giddiest**) **1** having the feeling that everything is spinning round. **2** causing this feeling, *giddy heights*. **3** frivolous, flighty. **giddily** *adverb*, **giddiness** *noun*

gidgee[1] (**gij**-ee) *noun* **1** a small Australian acacia. **2** its close-grained dark red timber. [Yuwaalaraay *gijirr*]

gidgee[2] (**gij**-ee) *noun* an Aboriginal spear. [Nyungar *giji*]

gift *noun* **1** a thing given or received without payment. **2** a natural ability, *has a gift for languages*. **3** (*informal*) an easy task. –**gift** *verb* to give as a gift. □ **gift token** a voucher (given as a gift) for money to buy something. **look a gift horse in the mouth** to accept something ungratefully, examining it for faults.

gifted *adjective* having great natural ability.

gift-wrap *verb* (**gift-wrapped**, **gift-wrapping**) to wrap attractively as a gift.

gig[1] (g- *as in* get) *noun* a light two-wheeled horse-drawn carriage.

gig[2] (g- *as in* get) *noun* (*informal*) an engagement to play jazz etc., especially for a single performance.

gig[3] *abbreviation* gigabyte.

giga- (**gig**-ă *or* **gy**-gă) *prefix* one thousand million. [from Greek *gigas* = giant]

gigabyte *noun* one thousand megabytes.

gigantic *adjective* very large. **gigantically** *adverb*

giggle *verb* to laugh in a silly or nervous way. –**giggle** *noun* **1** this kind of laugh. **2** (*informal*) something amusing, a joke, *did it just for a giggle*.

GIGO *abbreviation* garbage in, garbage out (in computing, unreliable data will produce unreliable results).

gigolo (**jig**-ŏ-loh) *noun* (*plural* **gigolos**) a man who is paid by an older woman to be her escort or lover.

Gilbert, Sir William Schwenck (1836–1911), English comic dramatist who collaborated with the composer Sir Arthur Sullivan in writing fourteen comic operas.

gild *verb* (**gilded** *or* **gilt**, **gilding**) to cover with a thin layer of gold or gold paint. □ **gild the lily** to spoil something already beautiful by trying to improve it.

Giles, Ernest (1835–97), English explorer of central and Western Australia.

gilgai (**gil**-gy) *noun* (*Austral.*) a natural depression in undulating country in which rainwater collects. [Wiradjuri and Kamilaroi *gilgaay*]

gill (*pr.* jil) *noun* an imperial measure for liquids, = one quarter of a pint (142 ml).

gills (g- *as in* get) *plural noun* **1** the organ with which a fish breathes in water. **2** the vertical plates on the underside of a mushroom cap. □ **green about the gills** looking sickly.

gilt[1] *adjective* gilded, gold-coloured. –**gilt** *noun* a substance used for gilding. **gilts** *plural noun* gilt-edged securities. □ **gilt-edged** *adjective* (of investments) considered to be very safe.

gilt[2] *noun* a young sow.

gimbals (**jim**-bălz) *plural noun* a contrivance of rings and pivots for keeping instruments horizontal in a moving ship etc.

gimcrack (**jim**-krak) *adjective* showy, worthless, and flimsy, *gimcrack ornaments*.

gimlet (**gim**-lět) *noun* a small tool with a screw-like tip for boring holes.

gimmick (**gim**-ik) *noun* a trick, device, or mannerism used for attracting notice or publicity, or for making an entertainer etc. easily recognised and remembered. **gimmicky** *adjective*

gin[1] (*pr.* jin) *noun* **1** a trap or snare for catching animals. **2** a machine for separating raw cotton from its seeds. **3** a kind of crane and windlass.

gin[2] (*pr.* jin) *noun* a colourless alcoholic spirit flavoured with juniper berries. □ **gin rummy** a form of rummy for two players. [from the name of Geneva, a city in Switzerland]

gin[3] (*pr.* jin) *noun* (now *derogatory*) an Aboriginal woman. [from Dharuk *diyin* = woman, wife]

ginger *noun* **1** the hot-tasting root of a tropical plant. **2** this plant. **3** liveliness. **4** light reddish yellow. –**ginger** *verb* to make more lively, *ginger things up*. –**ginger** *adjective* ginger-coloured. □ **ginger ale, ginger beer** ginger-flavoured fizzy drinks. **ginger group** a group within a larger group, urging a more active or livelier policy. **ginger nut** a ginger-flavoured biscuit. **gingery** *adjective*

gingerbread *noun* a ginger-flavoured cake or biscuit.

gingerly *adverb* cautiously. –**gingerly** *adjective* cautious, *in a gingerly way*.

gingham (**ging**-ăm) *noun* a cotton fabric usually with a checked pattern. [from Dutch *gingang* from Malay *ginggang* = striped]

gingivitis (jin-jǐ-**vy**-tǐss) *noun* inflammation of the gums.

ginseng (**jin**-seng) *noun* **1** a plant found in eastern Asia and North America. **2** its root, used in medicine.

Giotto (**jot**-oh) (c. 1267–1337), Florentine painter.

gipsy *noun* = **gypsy**.

giraffe *noun* a long-necked African animal.

gird *verb* to encircle or attach with a belt or band, *he girded on his sword*. □ **gird up one's loins** to prepare for an effort.

girder *noun* a metal beam supporting part of a building or a bridge.

girdle[1] *noun* **1** a belt or cord worn round the waist. **2** an elastic corset. **3** a connected ring of bones in the body, *the pelvic girdle*. –**girdle** *verb* to surround.

girdle[2] *noun* a round iron plate for cooking things over heat (also called a *griddle*).

girl *noun* **1** a female child. **2** a young woman. **3** (*informal*) a woman of any age, a woman assistant or employee. **4** a man's girlfriend. **girlhood** *noun*

girlfriend *noun* a regular female companion or lover.

girlish *adjective* like a girl. **girlishly** *adverb*, **girlishness** *noun*

giro (**jy**-roh) *noun* a system of banking by which customers of participating financial institutions can make deposits, withdrawals, and transfers from their accounts at the Post Office.

girt *adjective* (*poetical*) girded.

girth *noun* **1** the distance round a thing. **2** a band passing under a horse's belly, holding the saddle in place.

gist (*pr.* jist) *noun* the essential points or general sense of anything.

Gita = **Bhagavadgita**.

give *verb* (**gave**, **given**, **giving**) **1** to cause another person to receive or have (especially something in one's possession or at one's disposal), to supply; *give me France for holidays*, I prefer it. **2** to deliver (a message). **3** (*informal*) to tell what one knows. **4** to utter, *gave a laugh*. **5** to pledge, *give one's word*. **6** to make over in exchange or payment. **7** to make or perform (an action or effort), to affect another person or thing with this, *gave him a scolding*; *gave the door a kick*; *I was given to understand*, was told. **8** to provide (a meal or party) as host. **9** to perform or present (a play etc.) in public. **10** to yield as a product or result. **11** to be the source of. **12** to permit a view of or access to, *the window gives on the street.* **13** to declare (judgment) authoritatively, *the umpire gave the batsman out.* **14** to be flexible, to yield when pressed or pulled. –give *noun* springiness, elasticity. ☐ give-and-take *noun* an exchange of talk and ideas; willingness on both sides to make concessions. give away to give as a present; to hand over (the bride) to the groom at a wedding; to reveal (a secret etc.) unintentionally; (*Austral.*) to give up, to abandon. give-away *noun* (*informal*) a thing given without charge; something that reveals a secret. give in to hand in (a document etc.); to acknowledge that one is defeated. give it to a person (*informal*) to reprimand or punish him or her; to award praise to him or her. give off to produce and emit, *petrol gives off fumes.* give or take (*informal*) add or subtract (an amount) in estimating. give out to distribute; to announce; to emit, *the chimney was giving out smoke*; to become exhausted or used up. give over to devote, *afternoons are given over to sport*; (*informal*) to cease doing something. give tongue to speak one's thoughts; (of hounds) to bark, especially on finding the scent. give up to cease (doing something); to part with; to surrender; to abandon hope; to declare a person to be incurable or a problem to be too difficult for oneself to solve; *he was given up for dead*, was assumed to be dead. give way to yield, to allow other traffic to go first; to collapse. giver *noun*

given *see* give. –given *adjective* **1** specified or stated, *all the people in a given area.* **2** having a certain tendency, *he is given to swearing.* ☐ given name a Christian name, a first name (given in addition to a family name).

gizmo *noun* (*informal*) a gadget.

gizzard *noun* a bird's second stomach, in which food is ground.

glacé (**gla**-say) *adjective* iced with sugar, preserved in sugar, *glacé fruits.* ☐ glacé icing icing made from icing sugar and water. [French, = iced]

glacial (**glay**-see-ăl) *adjective* **1** icy. **2** of or from glaciers or other ice, *glacial deposits.* glacially *adverb* [from Latin *glacies* = ice]

glaciated (**glays**-ee-ayt-ĕd) *adjective* covered with glaciers; affected by their action. glaciation *noun*

glacier (**glays**-ee-er) *noun* a river of ice moving very slowly.

glad *adjective* (**gladder**, **gladdest**) **1** pleased, expressing joy. **2** giving joy, *the glad news.* ☐ be glad of to be grateful for. gladly *adverb*, gladness *noun*

gladden *verb* to make glad.

glade *noun* an open space in a forest.

gladiator (**glad**-ee-ay-ter) *noun* a man trained to fight at public shows in ancient Rome. gladiatorial (glad-ee-ă-**tor**-ree-ăl) *adjective* [from Latin *gladius* = sword]

gladiolus *noun* (*plural* gladioli, *pr.* glad-ee-**oh**-ly) a garden plant with spikes of brightly-coloured flowers.

Gladstone bag *noun* a small case for clothes etc. hinged so that it opens into two approximately equal compartments. [named after W.E.Gladstone, British statesman (1809–98)]

glair *noun* white of egg; a thick substance made of or resembling this.

glamorise *verb* (also **-ize**) to make glamorous or romantic.

glamour *noun* **1** alluring beauty. **2** attractive and exciting qualities that arouse envy. glamorous *adjective*, glamorously *adverb* [from an old use of *grammar* = magic]

glance *verb* **1** to look briefly. **2** to strike at an angle and glide off an object, *a glancing blow*; *the ball glanced off his bat.* –glance *noun* **1** a brief look. **2** a stroke in cricket with the bat's face turned slantwise to the ball.

gland *noun* an organ that separates substances from the blood that are to be used by the body or expelled from it.

glanders *noun* a disease of horses etc.

glandular (**glan**-dew-ler) *adjective* of or like a gland. ☐ glandular fever a feverish illness in which certain glands are swollen.

glare *verb* **1** to shine with an unpleasant dazzling light. **2** to stare angrily or fiercely. –glare *noun* **1** a strong unpleasant light. **2** an angry or fierce stare.

glaring *adjective* **1** bright and dazzling. **2** very obvious, *a glaring error.* glaringly *adverb*

glass *noun* **1** a hard brittle substance (as used in windows), usually transparent. **2** an object made of this, e.g. a mirror. **3** a glass container for drinking from; its contents. **4** a barometer. –glass *verb* **1** to fit or enclose with glass. **2** (*informal*) to hit (someone) in the face with a beer glass etc. glasses *plural noun* spectacles; binoculars. □ **glass-blowing** *noun* shaping semi-molten glass by blowing air into it through a tube. **glass fibre** fabric woven from glass filaments; plastic reinforced with glass filaments.

glassful *noun* (*plural* **glassfuls**) the amount contained by a drinking glass.

glasshouse *noun* a greenhouse.

glasspaper *noun* paper coated with glass particles, used for smoothing wood etc.

glassy *adjective* **1** like glass in appearance. **2** with a dull expressionless stare, *glassy-eyed*. **glassily** *adverb*, **glassiness** *noun*

glaucoma (glaw-**koh**-mǎ) *noun* a condition caused by increased pressure of the fluid within the eyeball, causing weakening or loss of sight.

glaze *verb* **1** to fit or cover with glass. **2** to coat with a glossy surface. **3** to become glassy. –**glaze** *noun* a shiny surface or coating especially on pottery; the substance forming this. [from *glass*]

glazier (**glay**-zee-er) *noun* a person whose trade is to fit glass in windows etc.

gleam *noun* **1** a beam or ray of soft light, especially one that comes and goes. **2** a brief show of some quality, *a gleam of hope*. –**gleam** *verb* to send out gleams.

glean *verb* **1** to pick up grain left by harvesters. **2** to gather scraps of information. **gleanings** *plural noun* things gleaned. **gleaner** *noun*

glee *noun* **1** lively or triumphant joy. **2** a part-song, especially for male voices.

gleeful *adjective* full of glee. **gleefully** *adverb*

glen *noun* a narrow valley.

glib *adjective* ready with words but insincere or superficial. **glibly** *adverb*, **glibness** *noun* [from an old word *glibbery* = slippery]

glide *verb* **1** to move along smoothly. **2** to fly in a glider or in an aeroplane without engine power. –**glide** *noun* a gliding movement.

glider *noun* **1** a person or thing that glides. **2** a tree-dwelling Australian marsupial that glides through the air using flaps of skin between the fore and hind limbs as 'parachutes', *sugar glider*. **3** an aircraft without an engine.

gliding *noun* the sport of flying in gliders.

glimmer *noun* a faint gleam. –**glimmer** *verb* to gleam faintly.

glimpse *noun* a brief view. –**glimpse** *verb* to catch a glimpse of.

glint *noun* a very brief flash of light. –**glint** *verb* to send out a glint.

glissade (gli-**sayd**) *verb* **1** to glide or slide skilfully down a steep slope, especially in mountaineering. **2** to make a gliding step in dancing. –**glissade** *noun* a glissading movement or step.

glisten *verb* to shine like something wet or polished.

glitch *noun* (*informal*) a malfunction, a hitch.

glitter *verb* to sparkle. –**glitter** *noun* a sparkle.

glitz *noun* (*informal*) extravagant display; show-business glamour. **glitzy** *adjective*

gloaming *noun* the evening twilight.

gloat *verb* to be full of greedy or malicious delight.

global *adjective* **1** of the whole world, worldwide. **2** of or in the whole of a computer program or set of data. □ **global warming** an increase in the temperature of the earth's atmosphere, caused by the greenhouse effect. **globally** *adverb*

globe *noun* **1** an object shaped like a ball, especially one with the map of the earth on it. **2** the world, *travelled all over the globe*. **3** a hollow round glass object, such as a light bulb (*see* **light**[1]).

globular (**glob**-yŭ-ler) *adjective* shaped like a globe.

globule (**glob**-yool) *noun* a small rounded drop.

globulin (**glob**-yŭ-lĭn) *noun* a kind of protein found in animal and plant tissue.

glockenspiel (**glok**-ĕn-speel) *noun* a musical instrument consisting of tuned steel bars fixed in a frame and struck by two hammers, or with steel tubes or plates played from a keyboard. [German, = bell-play]

glomerulus (glom-e-**rŭ**-lŭs) *noun* (*plural* **glomeruli**) a cluster of small blood vessels (especially in the kidney) or nerve fibres. [Latin, = little ball]

gloom *noun* **1** semi-darkness. **2** a feeling of sadness and depression. –**gloom** *verb* to look sullen; to feel sad and depressed.

gloomy *adjective* (**gloomier**, **gloomiest**) **1** almost dark, unlighted. **2** depressed, sullen. **3** dismal, depressing. **gloomily** *adverb*, **gloominess** *noun*

glorify *verb* (**glorified**, **glorifying**) **1** to praise highly. **2** to worship. **3** to make something seem more splendid than it is, *the town's river is only a glorified creek*. glorification *noun*

glorious *adjective* **1** possessing or bringing glory. **2** splendid, *a glorious view*; *a glorious muddle*, very great. gloriously *adverb*

glory *noun* **1** fame and honour won by great deeds. **2** adoration and praise in worship, *glory to God*. **3** beauty, magnificence, *the glory of a sunset*. **4** a thing deserving praise and honour. –glory *verb* (gloried, glorying) to rejoice or pride oneself, *glorying in their success*. □ go to glory (*informal*) to be destroyed; to die.

gloss *noun* **1** the shine on a smooth surface. **2** an explanatory comment. –gloss *verb* to make glossy. □ gloss over to cover up (a mistake or fault). gloss paint a paint with a glossy finish.

glossary (glos-ă-ree) *noun* a list of technical or special words with their definitions. [from Greek *glossa* = tongue, language]

glossy *adjective* (glossier, glossiest) shiny; *glossy magazine*, one printed on glossy paper, with many illustrations. glossily *adverb*, glossiness *noun*

glottal *adjective* of the glottis. □ glottal stop a speech sound made by suddenly opening or shutting the glottis.

glottis *noun* the opening at the upper end of the windpipe between the vocal cords.

glove *noun* a covering for the hand, usually with separate divisions for each finger and the thumb. □ fit like a glove to fit exactly. glove puppet one fitting over the hand so that the fingers can move it.

glovebox *noun* a recess for small articles in the dashboard of a car.

gloved *adjective* wearing a glove or gloves.

glow *verb* **1** to send out light and heat without flame. **2** to have a warm or flushed look, colour, or feeling; *a glowing account*, very enthusiastic or favourable. –glow *noun* a glowing state, look, or feeling. □ glow-worm *noun* a kind of beetle that can give out a greenish light at its tail.

glower (*rhymes with* flower) *verb* to scowl, to stare angrily.

glucose (gloo-kohs) *noun* a form of sugar found in fruit juice. [same origin as *glycerine*]

glue *noun* a sticky substance used for joining things. –glue *verb* (glued, gluing) **1** to fasten with glue. **2** to attach or hold closely, *his ear was glued to the keyhole*. □ glue-sniffing *noun*

inhaling the fumes of plastic glue for their narcotic effects. glue-sniffer *noun*

glum *adjective* (glummer, glummest) sad and gloomy. glumly *adverb*, glumness *noun* [from dialect *glum* = to frown]

glut *verb* (glutted, glutting) **1** to supply with much more than is needed, *glut the market*. **2** to satisfy fully with food, *glut oneself* or *one's appetite*. –glut *noun* an excessive supply, *a glut of apples*. [same origin as *glutton*]

glutamate (gloo-tă-mayt) *noun* a substance used to bring out the flavour in food. [from *gluten*]

gluten (gloo-těn) *noun* a sticky protein substance that remains when starch is washed out of flour. [from Latin, = glue]

glutinous (gloo-tĭ-nŭs) *adjective* glue-like, sticky. [same origin as *gluten*]

glutton *noun* **1** a person who eats far too much. **2** a person with a great desire or capacity for something; *a glutton for punishment*, one who enjoys arduous tasks. **3** an animal of the weasel family. gluttonous *adjective*, gluttony *noun* [from Latin *gluttire* = to swallow]

glycaemic (gly-**see**-mik) *adjective* (also glycemic) of or relating to the presence of glucose in the bloodstream. □ glycaemic index a measure of how quickly a carbohydrate gets into a person's bloodstream as sugar (abbreviation GI).

glycerine (glis-ĕ-reen) *noun* a thick sweet colourless liquid used in ointments and medicines and in the manufacture of explosives. [from Greek *glukeros* = sweet]

glycerol (glis-ĕ-rol) *noun* (in chemistry) glycerine.

glycogen (gly-kŏ-jěn) a polysaccharide in animal tissues serving as a store of carbohydrates.

GM *abbreviation* **1** general manager. **2** genetically modified.

gm *abbreviation* gram(s).

GMO *abbreviation* genetically modified organism.

GMT *abbreviation* Greenwich Mean Time.

gnamma (nam-ă) *noun* (also namma, in full gnamma hole) a hole (commonly in granite) in which rainwater collects. [from Nyungar *ngama*]

gnarled (*pr.* narld) *adjective* (of a tree or hands) covered with knobbly lumps; twisted and misshapen.

gnash *verb* **1** to grind (one's teeth). **2** (of teeth) to strike together.

gnat *noun* a small biting fly.

gnaw *verb* (**gnawed**, **gnawed** *or* **gnawn**, **gnawing**) to bite persistently at something hard; *a gnawing pain*, hurting continuously.

gneiss (*pr.* nyss) *noun* a kind of coarse-grained metamorphic rock.

gnome *noun* **1** a kind of dwarf in fairy tales, living underground and guarding the treasures of the earth. **2** a model of such a dwarf as a garden ornament.

gnostic (**nos**-tik) *adjective* **1** of knowledge. **2** having special mystical knowledge.

GNP *abbreviation* gross national product.

gnu (*pr.* noo) *noun* an ox-like antelope.

go *verb* (**went**, **gone**, **going**) **1** to begin to move; to be moving; to pass from one point to another; *we must go at one o'clock*, must leave; *go shopping*, go out for this purpose. **2** to extend or lead from one place to another, *the road goes to Perth*. **3** to be in a specified state, *they went hungry*. **4** to be functioning, *that clock doesn't go*. **5** to make a specified movement or sound, *the gun went bang*; *the whistle has gone*, has sounded as a signal. **6** (of time) to pass; (of a distance) to be traversed or accomplished, *ten kilometres to go*. **7** to be allowable or acceptable, *anything goes*; *that goes without saying*, is too obvious to need to be mentioned. **8** to belong in some place or position, *plates go on the shelf*. **9** to be, on average, *it is cheap as things go nowadays*. **10** (of a story or tune etc.) to have a certain wording or content, *I forget how the chorus goes*. **11** to pass into a certain condition, *the fruit went bad*. **12** to make progress, to fare, *all went well*; *make the party go*, to make it lively and successful. **13** to be sold, *it's going cheap*. **14** (of money or supplies) to be spent or used up. **15** to be given up, dismissed, abolished, or lost, *some luxuries must go*; *my sight is going*, is becoming weaker. **16** to fail, to give way; to die. **17** to carry an action to a certain point; *will go to $50 for it*, will pay as much as that. **18** to be able to be put, *your clothes won't go in that suitcase*; *3 into 12 goes 4*, 3 is contained in 12 four times. **19** to be given or allotted, *his estate went to his nephew*. **20** to contribute, to serve, *it all goes to prove what I said*. **–go** *noun* (*plural* **goes**) **1** energy, *full of go*. **2** a turn or try, *have a go*. **3** a success, *make a go of it*. **–go** *adjective* (*informal*) functioning properly, *all systems are go*.

☐ **go about** to go to social functions; to tackle (a job etc.). **go ahead** to proceed immediately. **go-ahead** *noun* a signal to proceed immediately; (*adjective*) energetic, willing to try new methods. **go a long way** to go far; to last long or buy much; to have a great effect towards achieving something. **go along with** to agree with. **go back on one's word** to fail to keep a promise. **go-between** *noun* one who acts as a messenger or negotiator. **go by** to be guided or directed by. **go-by** *noun give a person the go-by*, to ignore him or her. **go down** (of a ship) to sink, (of the sun) to appear to descend towards the horizon, to set; to be written down; to be swallowed; to be received or accepted, *the suggestion went down very well*; (*informal*) to go to prison. **go down with** to become ill with (a disease). **go far** to achieve much; to contribute greatly towards something; *it doesn't go far*, does not last long or buy much. **go for** to like, to prefer, to choose; (*informal*) to attack. **go for it** (*informal*) go all out for success. **go-getter** *noun* (*informal*) one who is successful through being pushy or energetic. **go-go** *adjective* (*informal*) very active or energetic. **go in for** to compete in; to engage in (an activity). **go into** to become a member or occupant or patient in (an institution); to investigate (a problem). **go it!** (*informal*) an encouragement to act vigorously. **go it alone** to take action by oneself without assistance. **go off** to explode; to lose quality, to become stale; to fall asleep; to proceed, *the party went off well*; to dislike what one liked formerly, *I've gone off tea lately*. **go on** to continue; to talk lengthily; *to go on at someone*, (*informal*) to nag; *enough to be going on with*, enough for the moment. **go on!** (*informal*) do not expect me to believe that. **go out** to go to social functions; to be broadcast, *the program goes out live*; to be extinguished; to cease to be fashionable; *my heart went out to him*, I sympathised with him. **go out with** to have as a social companion of the opposite sex. **go round** to be enough for everyone. **go slow** to work at a deliberately slow pace as a form of industrial protest. **go-slow** *noun* a deliberately slow pace of this kind. **go to a person's head** (of alcohol) to make him or her slightly drunk; (of success etc.) to make him or her conceited. **go up** to rise in price; to explode; to burn rapidly. **go with** to match, to harmonise with. **go without** to put up with the lack of something. **on the go** in constant motion, active.

goad *noun* 1 a pointed stick for prodding cattle to move onwards. 2 something stimulating a person to activity. –**goad** *verb* to act as a stimulus to, *goaded her into answering back*.

goal *noun* 1 a structure or area into which players try to send a ball in certain games. 2 a point scored in this way. 3 an objective. □ **goal line** the end line of a football or hockey field. [from an old word *gol* = boundary]

goalie *noun* (*informal*) a goalkeeper.

goalkeeper *noun* a player whose chief task is to keep the ball out of the goal.

goalpost *noun* either of the pair of posts marking the limits of the goal.

goanna *noun* (*Austral.*) a large lizard. [from *iguana*]

goat *noun* 1 a small horned animal kept for its milk. 2 a related wild animal, *mountain goat*. □ **act the goat** (*informal*) to behave comically. **get someone's goat** (*informal*) to annoy him or her.

goatee (goh-**tee**) *noun* a short pointed beard.

goatherd *noun* a person who looks after a herd of goats.

gob *noun* (*informal*) the mouth.

gobble *verb* 1 to eat quickly and greedily. 2 to make a throaty sound like a turkeycock.

gobbledegook *noun* (*informal*) pompous language used by officials. [imitation of the sound a turkeycock makes]

Gobi Desert (**goh**-bee) a barren plateau of southern Mongolia and northern China.

goblet *noun* a drinking glass with a stem and a foot.

goblin *noun* a mischievous ugly elf.

go-cart *noun* 1 a simple four-wheeled structure for a child to play on (also called a *billycart*). 2 see **go-kart**.

god *noun* 1 **God** the creator and ruler of the universe in Christian, Jewish, and Muslim teaching. 2 a superhuman being regarded and worshipped as having power over nature and human affairs, *Mars was the Roman god of war*. 3 an image of a god, an idol. 4 a person or thing that is greatly admired or adored, *money is his god*. □ **the gods** (*informal*) the gallery of a theatre. **God-fearing** *adjective* sincerely religious. **God knows** this is something we cannot hope to know; I call God to witness.

godchild *noun* (*plural* **godchildren**) a child in relation to its godparent(s).

god-daughter *noun* a female godchild.

goddess *noun* a female god.

godet (**goh**-day *or* go-**det**) *noun* a triangular piece of material inserted in a skirt etc. to give fullness at the edge.

godfather *noun* 1 a male godparent. 2 the mastermind behind an illegal organisation.

godforsaken *adjective* wretched, dismal.

godhead *noun* divine nature. –**the Godhead** God.

Godiva (gŏ-**dy**-vă) the wife of an 11th-century earl of Mercia, who (according to a later legend) rode naked through Coventry as a condition of her husband's remitting some unpopular taxes.

godless *adjective* not having belief in God; wicked. **godlessly** *adverb*, **godlessness** *noun*

godlike *adjective* like God or a god.

godly *adjective* (**godlier**, **godliest**) sincerely religious. **godliness** *noun*

godmother *noun* a female godparent.

godown (**goh**-down) *noun* a warehouse in parts of Asia, especially in India.

godparent *noun* 1 a person who sponsors a child at baptism. 1 a person who undertakes to care for a child if orphaned.

godsend *noun* a piece of unexpected good fortune.

godson *noun* a male godchild.

Godspeed *noun* an expression of good wishes to a person starting a journey.

godwit *noun* a wading bird like a curlew but with a straight or slightly upward-curving bill.

goer *noun* a person or thing that goes; *car is a nice goer*, runs well; *churchgoer*, a person who goes to church regularly.

Goethe (**ger**-tě), Johann Wolfgang von (1749–1832), German writer, scholar, and statesman, whose works include *Faust*.

goffer (**goh**-fer) *verb* to crimp frills etc. with hot irons.

goggle *verb* to stare with wide-open eyes. □ **goggle-eyed** *adjective* with wide-open eyes.

goggles *plural noun* spectacles for protecting the eyes from wind, dust, or water etc.

going see **go**. –**going** *noun* 1 moving away, departing, *comings and goings*. 2 the state of the ground for walking or riding on, *rough going*. 3 rate of progress, *it was good going to get there by noon*. –**going** *adjective* 1 moving away, departing; *he has everything going for* *him*, all is operating in his favour. **2** existing, available, *there is cold beef going*. **3** current; *the going rate*, the current price. **4** active and prosperous, *a going concern*. ☐ **be going to do something** to be about to do it, to be likely to do it. **going-over** *noun* (*informal*) an inspection or overhaul; (*informal*) a thrashing. **goings-on** *plural noun* surprising behaviour or events.

goitre (**goi**-ter) *noun* an enlarged thyroid gland, often showing as a swelling in the neck.

go-kart *noun* (also **kart**) a kind of miniature racing car with a skeleton body.

gold *noun* **1** a chemical element (symbol Au), a yellow metal of very high value. **2** coins or other articles made of gold. **3** its colour. **4** the bullseye of an archery target; a shot that strikes this. **5** a gold medal (awarded as first prize). **6** something very good or precious. – **gold** *adjective* made of gold; coloured like gold. ☐ **gold dust** gold found naturally in fine particles. **gold-plated** *adjective* coated with gold. **gold reserve** gold held by a central bank to guarantee the value of a country's currency. **gold standard** a system by which the value of money is based on that of gold.

Gold Coast a coastal strip forming a city on the Queensland coast south of Brisbane, famous for its beaches including Surfers Paradise.

golden *adjective* **1** made of gold. **2** coloured like gold. **3** precious, excellent, *a golden opportunity*. ☐ **golden age** a time of great prosperity. **golden boy** or **girl** a popular or successful person. **Golden Fleece** (*Gk. legend*) the fleece of a winged golden ram, sought by Jason and the Argonauts. **golden handshake** a generous cash payment given by a firm to one of its executives as compensation for being dismissed or forced to retire. **golden jubilee** the 50th anniversary of an event. **golden mean** neither too much nor too little. **golden perch** an edible Australian freshwater fish, a callop. **golden rule** a basic principle of action. **golden syrup** a kind of pale treacle. **golden wedding** the 50th anniversary of a wedding.

Golden Gate a channel of water in California between San Francisco Bay and the Pacific, spanned by a suspension bridge.

Golden Mile an area south of Kalgoorlie, WA, very rich in gold.

goldfield *noun* an area where gold is found as a mineral.

goldfinch *noun* a songbird with a band of yellow across each wing.

goldfish *noun* (*plural* **goldfish**) a small reddish Chinese carp kept in a bowl or pond.

goldmine *noun* **1** a place where gold is mined. **2** a source of great wealth, *the shop was a little goldmine.*

goldrush *noun* a rush to a newly discovered goldfield.

goldsmith *noun* a person whose trade is making articles in gold.

golf *noun* a game in which a small hard ball is struck with clubs towards and into a series of holes. – **golf** *verb* to play golf. ☐ **golf ball** a ball used in golf; a spherical unit carrying the type in some electric typewriters. **golf club** a club used in golf; an association for playing golf; its premises. **golf course**, **golf links** an area of land on which golf is played. **golfer** *noun*

Golgotha (**gol**-gŏ-thǎ *or* gol-**goth**-ǎ) the Aramaic name of Calvary.

Goliath (gŏ-**ly**-ǎth) (in the Old Testament) a Philistine giant, traditionally slain by David with a stone from a sling.

golly *interjection* (*informal*) an exclamation of surprise.

gonad (**goh**-nad) *noun* an animal organ (such as a testis or ovary) producing gametes. [from Greek *gone* = seed]

gondola (**gon**-dŏ-lǎ) *noun* **1** a boat with high pointed ends, used on the canals in Venice. **2** a basket-like structure suspended beneath a balloon, for carrying passengers etc. [Italian]

gondolier (gon-dŏ-**leer**) *noun* a person who propels a gondola by means of a pole.

Gondwana (also **Gondwanaland**) a supercontinent believed to have existed in Palaeozoic times when Australia, Antarctica, South America, India, and Africa were joined.

gone *see* **go**. – **gone** *adjective* departed, past; *it's gone six o'clock*, later than this.

goner *noun* (*informal*) a person or thing that is dead, ruined, or doomed.

gonfalon (**gon**-fǎ-lŏn) *noun* a banner, often with streamers, hung from a crossbar.

gong *noun* **1** a round metal plate that resounds when struck, especially one used as a signal for meals. **2** a similar device operated electrically. **3** (*informal*) a medal.

gonorrhoea (gon-ŏ-**ree**-ǎ) *noun* a venereal disease causing a thick discharge from the sexual organs. [from Greek *gonos* = semen, + *rhoia* = a flow]

goo *noun* (*informal*) **1** sticky wet material. **2** sickly sentiment.

good *adjective* (**better**, **best**) **1** having the right or desirable properties, satisfactory, *good food*. **2** right, proper, expedient. **3** morally correct, virtuous, kindly. **4** (of a child) well-behaved. **5** gratifying, enjoyable, beneficial, *have a good time*; *good morning*, *good evening*, forms of greeting or farewell. **6** efficient, suitable, competent, *a good driver*; *good at chess*. **7** thorough, considerable, *a good beating*. **8** not less than, full, *walked a good ten kilometres*. **9** used in exclamations, *good God!* –**good** *noun* **1** that which is morally right; *up to no good*, doing something mischievous or criminal. **2** profit, benefit, *it will do him good*; *$5 to the good*, having made this profit. □ **the good** virtuous people. **as good as** practically, almost, *the war was as good as over*. **for good and all** permanently, finally. **good for** beneficial to; able to pay or undertake; *he is good for $100, for a 10-kilometre walk*; *good for you!*, well done! **good-for-nothing** *adjective* worthless; (*noun*) a worthless person. **Good Friday** the Friday before Easter, commemorating the Crucifixion. **good-looking** *adjective* having a pleasing appearance. **good-tempered** *adjective* having or showing good temper. **good will** an intention that good shall result; *good-will token*, a token of this (*see also* **goodwill**). **in good time** with no risk of being late; *all in good time*, in due course but without haste.

goodbye *interjection* & *noun* farewell, an expression used when parting or at the end of a telephone call. [short for *God be with you*]

goodish *adjective* **1** fairly good. **2** rather large or great, *it's a goodish way from the station*.

goodness *noun* **1** the quality of being good. **2** the good element of something; *the goodness is in the gravy*, this is the most nourishing part. **3** used instead of 'God' in exclamations, *goodness knows*; *for goodness' sake*; *thank goodness*. □ **have the goodness to** to be kind enough to (do something).

goods *plural noun* **1** movable property. **2** articles of trade, *leather goods*. **3** things to be carried by road and rail; *goods train*, a train carrying goods not passengers. □ **the goods** (*informal*) the genuine article, the real thing; *deliver the goods*, to produce what one has promised;

have the goods on a person, to have evidence of his or her guilt.

goodwill *noun* **1** a friendly feeling. **2** the established custom or popularity of a business, considered as an asset that can be sold.

goody *noun* (*informal*) **1** something good or attractive, especially to eat. **2** a person of good character, *the goodies and the baddies*. –**goody** *interjection* (*informal*) an exclamation of delight.

goody-goody *adjective* smugly virtuous. –**goody-goody** *noun* a goody-goody person.

gooey *adjective* (*informal*) **1** wet and sticky. **2** sickly and sentimental.

goof *noun* (*informal*) **1** a stupid person. **2** a mistake. –**goof** *verb* (*informal*) to bungle; to blunder.

goofy *adjective* (*informal*) stupid.

goog *noun* (*Austral*. *informal*) an egg.

googly *noun* a ball bowled in cricket so that it breaks in the opposite direction from what the batsman expected.

goon *noun* (*informal*) **1** a stupid person. **2** a hired ruffian.

goose *noun* (*plural* **geese**) **1** a web-footed bird larger than a duck. **2** its flesh as food. **3** (*informal*) a stupid person. □ **goose-flesh** or **goose pimples** *nouns* rough bristling skin caused by cold or fear. **goose-step** *noun* a way of marching without bending the knees.

gooseberry *noun* **1** a thorny shrub. **2** its edible berry. **3** a chaperone or an unwelcome companion to a pair of lovers, *to play gooseberry*.

gopher[1] *noun* **1** a burrowing rodent, native to N America. **2** a N American ground squirrel. **3** a tortoise of southern USA.

gopher[2] *noun* a tree, the wood of which was used to build Noah's ark. [Hebrew]

Gordian *adjective* **cut the Gordian knot** to solve a problem forcefully or by some unexpected means. [an intricate knot was tied by Gordius, king of ancient Phrygia; it was eventually cut, rather than untied, by Alexander the Great]

gore[1] *noun* thickened blood from a cut or wound. [from Old English *gor* = dirt]

gore[2] *noun* a triangular or tapering section of a skirt or a sail etc. **gored** *adjective* made with gores.

gore[3] *verb* to pierce with a horn or tusk.

gorge *noun* a narrow steep-sided valley. –gorge *verb* **1** to eat greedily; *gorge oneself*, stuff oneself with food. **2** to fill full, to choke up. □ **make a person's gorge rise** to sicken or disgust him or her. [French, = throat]

gorgeous *adjective* **1** richly coloured, magnificent. **2** (*informal*) very pleasant, beautiful. **gorgeously** *adverb*, **gorgeousness** *noun*

Gorgon *noun* (*Gk. myth.*) any of three snake-haired sisters whose looks turned to stone anyone who saw them. –gorgon *noun* a terrifying woman.

gorgonzola (gor-gŏn-**zoh**-lă) *noun* a rich strong blue-veined cheese from Gorgonzola in north Italy or elsewhere.

gorilla *noun* a large powerful African ape.

gormless *adjective* (*informal*) stupid.

gorse *noun* a wild evergreen shrub with yellow flowers and sharp thorns.

gory *adjective* **1** covered with blood. **2** involving bloodshed, *a gory battle*. **gorily** *adverb*, **goriness** *noun*

gosh *interjection* an exclamation of surprise.

goshawk (**goss**-hawk) *noun* a kind of large hawk with short wings.

gosling (**goz**-ling) *noun* a young goose.

gospel *noun* **1** the teachings of Christ recorded in the first four books of the New Testament; **Gospel** any of these books. **2** the Christian faith. **3** a thing one may safely believe, *you can take it as gospel*. **4** a set of principles that one believes in. □ **gospel music** evangelical singing in Black American style. [from Old English *god* = good, + *spel* = news]

gossamer *noun* **1** a fine filmy piece of cobweb made by small spiders. **2** any flimsy delicate material.

gossip *noun* **1** casual talk especially about other people's affairs. **2** a person who is fond of gossiping. –gossip *verb* to engage in or spread gossip. **gossipy** *adjective*

got *see* get. □ **have got** to possess, *she has got a car*. **have got to do it** must do it.

Goth *noun* a member of a Germanic tribe that invaded the Roman Empire from the east in the 3rd–5th centuries.

Gothic (**goth**-ik) *adjective* **1** of the Goths. **2** of the style of architecture common in western Europe in the 12th–16th centuries, with pointed arches and rich stone carving. –Gothic *noun* **1** this style. **2** (in printing) the heavy black type formerly used for printing German.

□ **Gothic novel** a kind of novel with sensational or horrifying events, popular in the 18th–19th centuries.

gotten an alternative form of **got**, used in the USA as a past participle as in *he has gotten him a job*. In Australian and British English it is mainly used in certain expressions such as *ill-gotten gains*.

gouache (goo-**ahsh**) *noun* **1** painting with opaque pigments ground in water and thickened with gum and honey. **2** these pigments.

gouda (**gow**-dă *or* **goo**-dă) *noun* a flat round Dutch cheese.

gouge (*pr.* gowj) *noun* a chisel with a concave blade, used for cutting grooves. –gouge *verb* **1** to cut out with a gouge. **2** to scoop or force out; *gouge out his eye*, force it out with one's thumb.

goulash (**goo**-lash) *noun* a stew of meat and vegetables, seasoned with paprika. [from Hungarian *gulyáshús* = herdsman's meat]

gourd (*pr.* goord) *noun* **1** the hard-skinned fleshy fruit of a climbing plant. **2** this plant. **3** a bowl or container made from the dried hollowed-out rind of this fruit.

gourmand (**goor**-mănd) *noun* a lover of food, a glutton.

Usage *Gourmand* is often applied to a person contemptuously, whereas *gourmet* is not.

---

gourmet (**goor**-may) *noun* a connoisseur of good food and drink. [French, = wine taster]

gout *noun* a disease causing inflammation of the joints, especially the toes, knees, and fingers. **gouty** *adjective*

Gove Peninsula a peninsula on the NE point of Arnhem Land, Northern Territory, which is an Aboriginal Reserve.

govern *verb* **1** to rule with authority; to conduct the affairs of a country or an organisation. **2** to keep under control, *to govern one's temper*. **3** to influence or direct, *be governed by the experts' advice*.

governance *noun* governing, control.

governess *noun* a woman employed to teach children in a private household.

government *noun* **1** governing, the system or method of governing. **2** the group or organisation governing a country. **3** the State as an agent; *a government grant*, given from State funds. **governmental** *adjective*

governor *noun* **1** a person who governs a province or colony. **2** the representative of the Crown in each of the Australian States. **3** the head of each State in the USA. **4** the head or a member of the governing body of an institution; *the governor of the prison*, the official in charge of it. **5** (*informal*) one's employer; one's father. **6** (*informal*) a form of address to a man regarded as being of superior status. **7** a mechanism that automatically controls speed or the intake of gas or water etc. in a machine. □ **governor-general** (*plural* **governor-generals** or **governors-general**) *noun* the representative of the Crown in Australia and other Commonwealth countries that recognise the Queen as head of State.

gown *noun* **1** a loose flowing garment, especially a woman's long dress. **2** a loose outer garment that is the official robe of members of a university, judges, etc. **3** a kind of overall, *a surgeon's gown*.

gowned *adjective* wearing a gown.

goy *noun* (*plural* **goyim** or **goys**) the Jewish name for a person who is not a Jew. [Hebrew, = people, nation]

Goya, Francisco José de (1746–1828), Spanish painter and etcher.

Goyder's Line a line dividing South Australia, north of which the annual rainfall is less than 355 mm, and conditions unsuitable for growing wheat. [named after G. W. Goyder (died 1898), Surveyor-General of SA]

GP *abbreviation* general practitioner.

GPO *abbreviation* General Post Office.

Graafian follicle *noun* a very small sac in the ovary of a mammal, in which egg cells (ova) develop and mature.

grab *verb* (**grabbed**, **grabbing**) **1** to grasp suddenly. **2** to take something greedily. **3** (*informal*) to make an impression on someone; *how does that music grab you?*, do you like it? –**grab** *noun* **1** a sudden clutch or attempt to seize. **2** a mechanical device for gripping things or lifting them. □ **grab bag** an assortment, a lucky dip, *a grab bag of election promises*. **up for grabs** (*informal*) available for anyone to take.

grace *noun* **1** the quality of being attractive, especially in movement, manner, or design. **2** elegance of manner; *he had the grace to apologise*, realised that this was right and proper, and did it. **3** favour, goodwill. **4** a delay or postponement granted as a favour, not as a right, *give him a week's grace*. **5** God's loving

mercy towards mankind. **6** a short prayer of thanks before or after a meal. **7** the title used in speaking of or to a duke, duchess, or archbishop, *his Grace, her Grace, their Graces*. –**grace** *verb* to confer honour or dignity on, to be an ornament to. □ **be in a person's good graces** to have his or her favour and approval. **days of grace** the time allowed by law or custom after the day on which a payment is officially due. **grace note** a music note that is not essential to the harmony but is added as an embellishment. **with good grace** or **with a good grace** as if willingly.

graceful *adjective* having or showing grace. **gracefully** *adverb*, **gracefulness** *noun*

graceless *adjective* **1** inelegant. **2** ungracious.

Graces *plural noun* (*Gk. myth.*) three beautiful goddesses, givers of beauty, charm, and skill.

gracious *adjective* **1** kind and pleasant in manner to inferiors. **2** of royal persons or their acts, *Her gracious Majesty the Queen*; *by gracious permission of His Royal Highness*. **3** showing divine grace, merciful. **4** showing qualities associated with good taste and breeding, *gracious living*. –**gracious** *interjection* an exclamation of surprise, *good gracious!* **graciously** *adverb*, **graciousness** *noun*

grad *noun* one-hundredth of a right angle.

gradation (grǎ-**day**-shŏn) *noun* a process of gradual change; a stage in such a process, *the gradations of colour between blue and green*.

grade *noun* **1** a step, stage, or degree in some rank, quality, or value, *Grade 1 potatoes*. **2** a class of people or things of the same rank or quality etc. **3** the mark given to a student for his or her standard of work. **4** gradient, slope. **5** a school class. –**grade** *verb* **1** to arrange in grades. **2** to give a grade to a student. **3** to adjust the gradient of a road. **4** to pass gradually into a grade or between grades. □ **make the grade** to reach the desired standard. [from Latin *gradus* = a step]

gradient (**gray**-dee-ĕnt) *noun* **1** the amount of slope in a road or railway or of a line or curve on a graph; *the road has a gradient of 1 in 10*, it rises 1 metre in every 10 metres of its length. **2** a sloping road or railway.

gradual *adjective* taking place by degrees, not sudden or steep. **gradually** *adverb*

graduate (**grad**-yoo-ăt) *noun* a person who holds a university degree. –**graduate** (**grad**-yoo-ayt) *verb* **1** to take a university degree. **2** to divide into graded sections. **3** to mark into regular divisions or units of measurement. **graduation** *noun*

Graeco-Roman (greek-oh-**roh**-măn) *adjective* of the ancient Greeks and Romans.

graffiti (gră-**fee**-tee) *plural noun* words or a drawing roughly scratched or scribbled on a wall. [Italian, = scratchings]

Usage *Graffiti* is by origin a plural noun and when treated as such takes a plural verb, e.g. *the graffiti are colourful*. The singular form is *graffito*. However, *graffiti* is often now used as a collective or mass noun, in which case it is followed by a singular verb, as in *Graffiti is art* or *That graffiti is offensive*.

---

graft¹ *noun* **1** a shoot from one tree fixed into a cut in another to form a new growth. **2** a piece of living tissue transplanted surgically to replace diseased or damaged tissue. **3** (*informal*) hard work. **–graft** *verb* **1** to put a graft in or on. **2** to join (a thing) inseparably to another. **3** (*informal*) to work hard.

graft² *noun* **1** obtaining some advantage in business or politics by bribery or unfair influence or other shady means. **2** a bribe or bribery used in this way. **3** the advantage gained by it.

Grail *noun* the Holy Grail, the cup or the platter used (according to legend) by Christ at the Last Supper, sought in prolonged quests by knights in medieval legends.

grain *noun* **1** a small hard seed of a food plant such as wheat or rice. **2** the gathered seeds of such plants. **3** the plants themselves. **4** a small hard particle, *a grain of sand*. **5** a unit of weight, about 65 milligrams. **6** the smallest possible amount, *he hasn't a grain of sense*. **7** the texture produced by the particles in flesh, stone, etc. or in photographic prints. **8** the pattern of lines made by fibres in wood or by layers in rock or coal etc.; the direction of threads in woven fabric. □ against the grain cutting or lying across a natural layer (in wood etc.); contrary to one's natural inclinations.

grainy *adjective* like grains in form, appearance, or texture. **graininess** *noun*

gram *noun* a unit of mass in the metric system, one thousandth part of a kilogram.

-gram *suffix* forming nouns meaning something written or drawn etc. (as in *diagram*). [from Greek *gramma* = thing written]

graminaceous (gram-ĭ-**nay**-shŭs) *adjective* of or like grass.

graminivorous (gram-ĭ-**niv**-ŏ-rŭs) *adjective* feeding on grass. [from Latin *graminis* = of grass, + *vorare* = devour]

gramma *noun* a variety of pumpkin.

grammar *noun* **1** the study of words and of the rules for their formation and their relationships to each other in sentences. **2** the rules themselves. **3** a book about these. **4** speech or writing judged as good or bad according to these rules, *his grammar is appalling*. □ grammar school (*Brit. historical*) a school with an academic curriculum including Latin and Greek; (*Austral.*) a (usually private) school modelled on this, but not necessarily teaching classics.

grammatical *adjective* in accordance with the rules of grammar. **grammatically** *adverb*

Grammy *noun* (*plural* Grammys or Grammies) each of a number of annual awards given by the American National Academy of Recording Arts and Sciences for achievement in the recording industry.

gramophone *noun* a record player. [altered from 'phonogram', from Greek *phone* = a sound, + *-gram*]

Grampians, the a range of low mountains in western Victoria. [named after the Scottish ranges]

grampus *noun* a large dolphin-like sea animal that blows loudly and heavily.

Gram stain *noun* (also Gram's stain) a method of differentiating bacteria by staining with a dye, then attempting to remove the dye with solvent, for purposes of identification. [named after H.C.J. *Gram*, Danish physician, died 1938]

gran *noun* (*informal*) grandmother.

granary *noun* a storehouse for grain.

grand *adjective* **1** splendid, magnificent. **2** of the highest rank, *the Grand Duke Alexis*. **3** dignified, imposing, *she puts on a grand manner*. **4** (*informal*) very enjoyable or satisfactory, *we had a grand time*. **5** including everything, final, *the grand total*. **–grand** *noun* **1** a grand piano. **2** (*informal*) a thousand dollars, *five grand*. □ grand opera opera in which everything is sung and there are no spoken parts. grand piano a large full-toned piano with horizontal strings. grand slam see slam. grandly *adverb*, grandness *noun*

Grand Canyon a long deep canyon formed by the Colorado River in Arizona, USA.

grandchild *noun* (*plural* grandchildren) the child of a person's son or daughter.

granddad *noun* (*informal*) **1** grandfather. **2** an elderly man.

granddaughter *noun* the daughter of a person's son or daughter.

grandee (gran-**dee**) *noun* a person of high rank.

grandeur (**grand**-yer) *noun* splendour, magnificence, grandness.

grandfather *noun* the father of a person's father or mother. □ **grandfather clock** a clock in a tall wooden case, worked by weights.

grandiose (**gran**-dee-ohss) *adjective* **1** imposing, planned on a large scale. **2** trying to be grand, pompous. **grandiosity** (gran-dee-**oss**-ĭ-tee) *noun*

grandma *noun* (*informal*) grandmother.

grand mal (gron **mal**) *noun* epilepsy with loss of consciousness. [French, = great sickness]

grandmother *noun* the mother of a person's father or mother.

grandpa *noun* (*informal*) grandfather.

grandparent *noun* a grandfather or grandmother.

Grand Prix (gron **pree**) *noun* any of various important motor or motorcycle racing contests, governed by international rules. [French, = great or chief prize]

grandson *noun* the son of a person's son or daughter.

grandstand *noun* the principal roofed building with rows of seats for spectators at a racetrack or sportsground.

grange *noun* (*Brit*.) a country house with farm buildings that belong to it.

granite *noun* a hard grey stone for building.

granny *noun* (*informal*) grandmother. □ **granny flat** a part of a house, or an adjacent building, made into self-contained accommodation for an elderly relative. **granny knot** a reef knot with the threads crossed the wrong way and therefore likely to slip.

Granny Smith *noun* a green-skinned Australian variety of apple. [named after Maria Ann ('Granny') Smith who first cultivated them in Sydney]

grant *verb* **1** to give or allow as a privilege; *grant a request*, permit what is requested. **2** to give formally, to transfer legally. **3** to admit or agree that something is true, *I grant that your offer is generous*. **–grant** *noun* something

granted, especially a sum of money; *research grant*, money given for research. □ **take for granted** to assume that (a thing) is true or sure to happen; to be so used to having (a thing) that one no longer appreciates it.

granular (**gran**-yŭ-ler) *adjective* like grains or granules. **granularity** *noun*

granulate (**gran**-yŭ-layt) *verb* **1** to form into grains or granules, *granulated sugar*. **2** to make rough and grainy on the surface. **granulation** *noun*

granule (**gran**-yool) *noun* a small grain.

grape *noun* a green or purple berry growing in clusters on vines, used for making wine.

grapefruit *noun* (*plural* grapefruit) a large round yellow citrus fruit with an acid juicy pulp.

grapevine *noun* **1** the kind of vine on which grapes grow. **2** a way by which news is passed on unofficially, *heard it on the grapevine*.

graph *noun* a diagram consisting of a line or lines showing the relationship between corresponding values of two quantities. **–graph** *verb* to draw a graph of. □ **graph paper** paper ruled into small squares, used for plotting graphs. [from Greek *-graphe* = writing]

-graph *suffix* forming nouns and verbs meaning something written or drawn etc. (as in *photograph*). [same origin as *graph*]

graphic (**graf**-ik) *adjective* **1** of drawing, painting, lettering, or engraving, *the graphic arts*; *a graphic artist*. **2** giving a vivid description, *a graphic account of the fight*. **graphics** *noun* **1** the use of diagrams in calculation or in design. **2** (as *plural*) lettering and drawings; computer graphics. □ **graphic equaliser** a device for varying the quality of an audio signal by controlling the strength of individual audio frequency bands independently of each other. **graphic novel** a novel published in comic-strip format.

graphical (**graf**-i-kăl) *adjective* **1** using diagrams or graphs. **2** = graphic (sense 1). □ **graphical user interface** a visual way of interacting with a computer using items such as windows, icons, and menus (abbreviation **GUI**).

graphically *adverb* in a graphic or graphical way.

graphite *noun* a soft black form of carbon used in lubrication, as a moderator in nuclear reactors, and in lead pencils.

graphology (gră-**fol**-ŏjee) *noun* the scientific study of handwriting, especially as a guide

to the writer's character. **graphologist** *noun*
[from *graph* + *-logy*]

-graphy *suffix* forming nouns that are
the names of descriptive sciences (as in
geography) or methods of writing or drawing
etc. (as in *photography*). [same origin as *graph*]

grapnel *noun* **1** a small anchor with three or
more flukes, used for boats and balloons. **2** a
hooked grappling instrument used in dragging
the bed of a lake or river.

grapple *verb* **1** to seize or hold firmly. **2** to
struggle at close quarters; *grapple with a*
problem, try to deal with it. □ **grappling iron**
a grapnel.

grasp *verb* **1** to seize and hold firmly,
especially with one's hands or arms. **2** to
understand, *he couldn't grasp what we meant.*
–**grasp** *noun* **1** a firm hold or grip; *within his*
grasp, close enough for him to grasp or obtain
it. **2** a mental hold, understanding, *a thorough*
grasp of his subject. □ **grasp at** to snatch
at. **grasp the nettle** to tackle a difficulty or
danger boldly.

grasping *adjective* greedy for money or
possessions.

grass *noun* **1** any of a group of common wild
low-growing plants with green blades and
stalks that are eaten by animals. **2** any species
of this plant (in botanical use including cereal
plants, reeds, and bamboos). **3** ground covered
with grass, lawn or pasture; *put animals out*
to grass, put them to graze. **4** (*informal*)
marijuana. **5** (*informal*) a person who grasses,
an act of grassing. –**grass** *verb* **1** to cover with
grass. **2** (*informal*) to turn informer.
□ **grass roots** the fundamental level or source;
ordinary people, the rank and file of a political
party or other group. **grass snake** a small
harmless snake. **grass tree** a small Australian
tree with a tall flowering spike and a crown of
grasslike leaves. **grass widow** a wife whose
husband is absent for some time.

grasshopper *noun* a jumping insect that
makes a shrill chirping noise.

grassland *noun* a wide area covered in grass
and with few trees.

grassy *adjective* like grass; covered with
grass.

grate¹ *noun* **1** a metal framework that keeps
fuel in a fireplace. **2** the recess where the fire
burns; the surrounding structure.

grate² *verb* **1** to shred into small pieces by
rubbing against a jagged surface. **2** to make
a harsh noise by rubbing, to sound harshly,

a grating laugh. **3** to have an unpleasant
irritating effect.

grateful *adjective* feeling or showing that
one values a kindness or benefit received.
gratefully *adverb* [from Latin *gratus* =
thankful, pleasing]

grater *noun* a device with a jagged surface for
grating food.

gratify *verb* (**gratified**, **gratifying**) to
give pleasure to, to satisfy (wishes etc.).
gratification *noun* [from Latin *gratus* =
pleasing]

grating *noun* a screen of spaced metal or
wooden bars placed across an opening.

gratis (**grah**-tĭss) *adverb* & *adjective* free of
charge. [Latin, = out of kindness]

gratitude *noun* being grateful.

gratuitous (grǎ-**tew**-ĭ-tǔs) *adjective* **1** given
or done without payment. **2** given or done
without good reason, *a gratuitous insult.*
gratuitously *adverb*

gratuity (grǎ-**tew**-ĭ-tee) *noun* money given in
recognition of services rendered, a tip.

gravamen (grǎ-**vay**-men) *noun* the essence
or most serious part of an accusation.

grave¹ *noun* **1** a hole dug in the ground to
bury a corpse. **2** the place where a corpse is
buried. **the grave** death, being dead. [from Old
English *graef* = hole dug out]

grave² *adjective* **1** serious, causing great
anxiety, *grave news.* **2** solemn, not smiling.
□ **grave accent** (*pr.* grahv), a backward-
sloping mark over a vowel, as in *à la carte.*
gravely *adverb* [from Latin *gravis* = heavy]

gravel *noun* coarse sand with small stones,
as used for roads and paths. –**gravel** *verb*
(**gravelled**, **gravelling**) to cover with gravel.

gravelly *adjective* **1** like gravel. **2** rough-
sounding, *a gravelly voice.*

graven *adjective* carved, *a graven image*;
graven on my memory, firmly fixed in it.

gravestone *noun* a stone monument over
a grave.

graveyard *noun* a burial ground.

gravitas *noun* dignity, seriousness, or solemnity
of manner. [from Latin *gravis* = serious]

gravitate *verb* to move or be attracted towards.

gravitation *noun* **1** gravitating. **2** the force of
gravity. **gravitational** *adjective*

gravity *noun* **1** seriousness, *the gravity of*
the situation. **2** solemnity. **3** the force that
attracts bodies towards the centre of the earth;

the intensity of this. □ **centre of gravity** the central point in an object about which its mass is evenly balanced. **gravity feed** a supply system in which a substance falls from a higher level to a lower one by force of gravity rather than by mechanical means. **specific gravity** *see* **specific**. [same origin as *grave*²]

gravy *noun* **1** juice that comes out of meat while it is cooking. **2** sauce made from this. □ **gravy train** (*informal*) a source of easy financial gain.

grayling *noun* a silver-grey freshwater fish.

graze¹ *verb* **1** to eat growing grass, *cattle grazing in the fields*. **2** to put (animals) into a field to eat the grass.

graze² *verb* **1** to touch or scrape lightly in passing. **2** to scrape the skin from. –**graze** *noun* a raw place where the skin has been scraped.

grazier (**gray**-zee-er) *noun* a large-scale sheep or cattle farmer.

grease *noun* **1** animal fat melted soft. **2** any thick semi-solid oily substance. –**grease** *verb* to put grease on or in. □ **grease a person's palm** (*informal*) to bribe him or her. **like greased lightning** (*informal*) very fast. **greaser** *noun*

greasepaint *noun* make-up used by actors and other performers.

greasy *adjective* (**greasier**, **greasiest**) **1** covered with grease. **2** containing much grease. **3** slippery, *the road was greasy after the storm*. **4** oily in manner. **greasily** *adverb*, **greasiness** *noun*

great *adjective* **1** much above average in size, amount, or intensity. **2** larger than others of similar kind, *the great grey kangaroo*. **3** of remarkable ability or character, important, *one of the great painters*; *Peter the Great*; *the great*, great people; *the greatest*, (*informal*) a very remarkable person or thing. **4** elaborate, intense, *told in great detail*. **5** doing something frequently or intensively or very well, *a great reader*. **6** (*informal*) very enjoyable or satisfactory, *we had a great time*. **7** of a family relationship that is one generation removed in ancestry or descent, as *great-grandfather*, *great-niece*; *great-great-grandfather*, *great-grandfather's father*. □ **great circle** a circle drawn on the surface of a sphere in such a way that its diameters pass through the centre of the sphere. **Great Dane** a dog of a very large powerful smooth-haired breed. **Great Exhibition** the first international exhibition of

the products of industry, held in the Crystal Palace in London in 1851. **Great Trek** the northward migration in 1835–7 of large numbers of Boers to the areas where they eventually founded the Transvaal Republic and the Orange Free State. **Great War** the First World War. **great white shark** the largest of the man-eating sharks. **greatness** *noun*

Great Australian Bight a wide bay on the south coast of Australia.

Great Barrier Reef the largest coral reef in the world, about 2000 km in length, roughly parallel to the NE coast of Australia.

Great Britain England, Wales, and Scotland considered as a unit.

greatcoat *noun* a heavy overcoat.

Great Dividing Range a long mountain range in eastern Australia, roughly parallel to the coast.

Great Lakes five large interconnected lakes (Superior, Michigan, Huron, Erie, Ontario) in North America.

greatly *adverb* by a considerable amount.

Great Plains a vast area of plains in Canada and the USA between the Rocky Mountains and the Mississippi River.

Great Rift Valley the extensive rift valley system running from the Jordan valley in Syria, along the Red Sea into Ethiopia, and southwards to Mozambique.

Great Sandy Desert a large tract of waterless country in north-central WA.

Great Victoria Desert a vast arid region of south-eastern Western Australia and western South Australia.

Great Wall of China a long defensive wall in northern China.

greave *noun* a piece of armour worn on the leg to protect the shin.

grebe (*pr.* greeb) *noun* a diving bird.

Grecian (**gree**-shăn) *adjective* Greek.

Greece a republic in SE Europe comprising a peninsula and numerous islands.

greed *noun* an excessive desire for food or wealth.

greedy *adjective* (**greedier**, **greediest**) **1** showing greed. **2** very eager or keen for something. **greedily** *adverb*, **greediness** *noun*

Greek *adjective* of Greece or its people or language. –**Greek** *noun* **1** a member of the people living in ancient or modern Greece. **2** their language. □ **Greek Church** the Greek

Orthodox Church (*see* orthodox). **it's Greek to me** I cannot understand its meaning.

green *adjective* **1** of the colour between blue and yellow, the colour of growing grass. **2** covered with grass or with growing leaves. **3** unripe, not seasoned; *wood is green*, not yet dry enough to burn well; *green bacon*, not smoked. **4** immature, inexperienced, easily deceived. **5** pale and sickly-looking; *green with envy*, very jealous. **6** supporting or concerned with the protection of the environment; *green products*, ones not harmful to the environment. **–green** *noun* **1** green colour. **2** a green substance or material; green clothes. **3** a green light. **4** a grassy area, *a bowling green*; *a putting green*; *an English village green*. **5** (also Green) a supporter of an environmentalist group, party, or cause. **Greens** *plural noun* (also **Green Party**) a political party concerned with conservation of the environment. **greens** *plural noun* green vegetables. □ **green ban** (*Austral.*) a prohibition, especially by a trade union, against a development considered likely to damage the environment. **green belt** an area of open land round a town, where the amount of building is restricted. **green-eyed monster** jealousy. **green fingers** skill in making plants grow. **green light** a signal to proceed on a road; (*informal*) permission to go ahead with a project. **Green Paper** a preliminary report of government proposals. **green room** a room used by actors etc. when not performing. **greenish** *adjective*, **greenly** *adverb*, **greenness** *noun*

greenback *noun* (*Amer.*) a US legal-tender note; the US dollar.

greenery *noun* green foliage or growing plants.

greenfly *noun* **1** one of the small green insects that suck juices from plants. **2** these insects collectively.

greengage *noun* a round plum with a greenish skin.

greengrocer *noun* **1** a shopkeeper selling vegetables and fruit. **2** a variety of cicada.

greengrocery *noun* a greengrocer's shop or goods.

greenhead *noun* an Australian ant with a powerful sting.

greenhorn *noun* an inexperienced person.

greenhouse *noun* a building with glass sides and roof, for rearing plants.

□ **greenhouse effect** the trapping of the sun's warmth in the earth's lower atmosphere, caused by high levels of carbon dioxide, methane, etc.

Greenland an island lying north-east of North America and mostly within the Arctic Circle, a part of Denmark but with control of its own internal affairs. **Greenlander** *noun*

Greenpeace an international organisation concerned with the conservation and protection of the environment.

greenstick fracture *noun* a kind of fracture, usually in children, in which the bone is partly broken and partly bent.

greenstone *noun* **1** a kind of green rock. **2** a variety of jade found in New Zealand.

Greenwich Mean Time (**gren**-ich) *noun* time on the line of longitude that passes through Greenwich in London, used as a basis for calculating time throughout the world.

greeny *adjective* rather green, *greeny-yellow*.

greet *verb* **1** to address (a person) on meeting or arrival. **2** to receive with a certain reaction, *the news was greeted with dismay*. **3** to present itself to one's sight or hearing, *the sight that greeted our eyes*.

greeting *noun* **1** words or gestures used to greet a person. **2** an expression of goodwill, *birthday greetings*.

gregarious (grĕ-**gair**-ee-ŭs) *adjective* **1** living in flocks or communities. **2** fond of company. **gregariously** *adverb*, **gregariousness** *noun* [from Latin *gregis* = of a flock]

Gregorian calendar (grĕ-**gor**-ree-ăn) the calendar introduced by Pope Gregory XIII in 1582, replacing the Julian calendar and still in general use.

Gregory, St, 'the Great' (c. 540–604), pope from 590, who sent St Augustine as head of a mission to convert England to the Christian faith.

gremlin *noun* (*informal*) a mischievous spirit said to cause mishaps to machinery.

grenache (**gren**-ash) *noun* a red wine grape variety.

Grenada (grĕ-**nay**-dă) an independent State in the West Indies, consisting of the island of Grenada and the southern Grenadines. **Grenadian** *adjective* & *noun*

grenade *noun* a small bomb thrown by hand or fired from a rifle.

Grenadine Islands (**gren**-ă-deen) (also Grenadines) a chain of small islands in the

West Indies, divided between St Vincent and Grenada.

Gretna Green a village just north of the Scottish/English border near Carlisle, formerly a popular place for runaway couples from England to be married according to Scots law.

grevillea (grĕ-**vil**-ee-ă) *noun* a genus of hardy evergreen Australian shrubs, many of which are popular garden plants. [named after C. F. Greville, botanist (died 1809)]

grew *see* grow.

Grey, Lady Jane (1537–54), queen of England for nine days, before being removed from the throne and beheaded in the Tower of London.

grey *adjective* 1 of the colour between black and white, coloured like ashes or lead; *he is going grey*, his hair is losing its colour; *a grey day*, without sun. 2 intermediate in character. –grey *noun* 1 grey colour. 2 a grey substance or material; grey clothes. 3 a grey horse. –grey *verb* to make or become grey. □ grey area that part of a matter where there are no exact rules about right and wrong etc. Grey Friars Franciscan friars, so called from their grey cloaks. grey-headed *adjective* with grey hair. grey matter the material of the brain and spinal cord; (*informal*) intelligence. grey nomad (*Austral. informal*) a retired person who travels extensively. grey nurse a variety of shark of south-eastern Australia. grey power influence, especially political, exerted by senior citizens. □ greyish *adjective*, greyness *noun*

greyhound *noun* a slender smooth-haired dog noted for its swiftness, used in coursing hares and in racing.

greylag *noun* the greylag goose, a grey wild European goose.

grid *noun* 1 a grating. 2 a network of squares on maps, numbered for reference. 3 any network of lines; an arrangement of electric-powered cables or gas-supply lines for distributing current or supplies over a large area. 4 a pattern of lines marking the starting places on a car-racing track. 5 a gridiron.

gridded *adjective* marked with a grid.

griddle *noun* = girdle².

gridiron (**grid**-I-ern) *noun* 1 a framework of metal bars for cooking on. 2 a field on which American football is played, with parallel lines marking the area of play; the game itself.

grief *noun* 1 deep sorrow. 2 something causing this. □ come to grief to meet with disaster, to fail, to fall.

grievance *noun* a real or imagined cause of complaint.

grieve *verb* 1 to cause grief to. 2 to feel grief.

grievous (**gree**-vŭs) *adjective* 1 causing grief. 2 serious; *grievous bodily harm*, serious injury. grievously *adverb*

Griffin, Walter Burley (1876–1937), American architect and landscape architect who won the competition for the design of Canberra.

griffin *noun* a creature in Greek mythology, with an eagle's head and wings on a lion's body.

griffon *noun* 1 one of a breed of terrier-like dogs with coarse hair. 2 a kind of vulture. 3 a griffin.

grill *noun* 1 a device on a cooker for radiating heat downwards. 2 meat, fish, or vegetables cooked under this or on a gridiron. 3 a gridiron for cooking on. 4 a metal grid, a grille. –grill *verb* 1 to cook with a grill or gridiron. 2 to be exposed to great heat. 3 to question closely and severely.

grille *noun* a grating, especially in a door or window.

grilse *noun* a young salmon returning from the sea to fresh water to spawn for the first time.

grim *adjective* (grimmer, grimmest) 1 stern or severe in appearance. 2 severe, unrelenting, merciless, *held on like grim death*. 3 without cheerfulness, unattractive, *a grim prospect*. grimly *adverb*, grimness *noun*

grimace (**grim**-ăs *or* grĭ-**mayss**) *noun* a contortion of the face expressing pain or disgust, or intended to cause amusement. –grimace *verb* to make a grimace.

grime *noun* dirt or soot ingrained in a surface or in the skin. –grime *verb* to blacken with grime. grimy *adjective*, griminess *noun*

Grimm, Jacob Ludwig Carl (1785–1863) and Wilhelm Carl (1786–1859), German linguistics scholars, remembered for their anthology of fairy tales.

grin *verb* (grinned, grinning) 1 to smile broadly, showing the teeth; *grin and bear it*, endure something without complaining. 2 to express by a grin, *he grinned his approval*. –grin *noun* a broad smile.

grind *verb* (ground, grinding) 1 to crush or be crushed into grains or powder. 2 to produce in this way. 3 to oppress or crush by cruelty. 4 to sharpen or smooth by friction. 5 to rub harshly together, *grind one's teeth*; *the bus ground to a halt*, stopped laboriously with a sound of grating. 6 to work something by turning a handle. **7** to study hard, *grinding away at his algebra.* **–grind** *noun* **1** the act of grinding. **2** hard monotonous work.

grinder *noun* **1** a person or thing that grinds. **2** a molar tooth.

grindstone *noun* a thick revolving disc used for sharpening or grinding things; *keep one's nose to the grindstone,* work hard without rest.

grip *verb* (**gripped, gripping**) **1** to take a firm hold of. **2** to hold a person's attention, *a gripping story.* **–grip** *noun* **1** a firm grasp or hold. **2** the power of gripping; a way of grasping or holding. **3** understanding, mental hold or control, *has a good grip of his subject.* **4** the part of a tool or machine etc. that grips things. **5** the part (of a weapon or device) designed to be held. **6** (*Amer.*) a suitcase or travelling bag. □ **come to grips with** to begin to cope with, to deal with (a problem) firmly. **get a grip on oneself** to regain one's self-control; to stop being slack. **lose one's grip** to become less competent than one was formerly.

gripe *verb* **1** to cause colic. **2** (*informal*) to grumble. **–gripe** *noun* **1** (*informal*) a grumble. **2** (often in *plural*) abdominal pain; colic.

grisly *adjective* causing fear, horror, or disgust, *all the grisly details.*

grist *noun* **1** grain to be ground or already ground. **2** malt crushed for brewing. □ **grist to the mill** a source of profit or advantage.

gristle *noun* tough flexible tissue of animal bodies, especially in meat. **gristly** *adjective*

grit *noun* **1** particles of stone or sand. **2** (also **gritstone**) a kind of sandstone with coarse angular grains, used for millstones. **3** courage and endurance. **–grit** *verb* (**gritted, gritting**) **1** to make a slightly grating sound. **2** to clench; *grit one's teeth,* to keep the jaws tightly together, especially when enduring pain or trouble. **gritty** *adjective,* **grittiness** *noun*

grizzle *verb* (*informal*) to whimper or whine, to complain. **–grizzle** *noun* a bout of grizzling. **grizzler** *noun*

grizzled *adjective* grey-haired or partly so.

grizzly *adjective* grey, grey-haired. **–grizzly** *noun* a **grizzly bear,** a large fierce grey bear of North America.

groan *verb* **1** to make a long deep sound expressing pain, grief, or disapproval. **2** to make a creaking noise resembling this. **–groan** *noun* the sound made in groaning.

groats *plural noun* crushed grain, especially oats.

grocer *noun* a shopkeeper who sells foods and household stores.

grocery *noun* a grocer's shop or goods. **groceries** *plural noun* goods sold by a grocer.

grog *noun* **1** a drink of spirits mixed with water. **2** (*Austral.*) any alcoholic drink.

groggy *adjective* weak and unsteady, especially after illness. **groggily** *adverb,* **grogginess** *noun*

groin *noun* **1** the groove where each thigh joins the trunk. **2** this area of the body, where the genitals are situated. **3** the curved edge where two vaults meet in a roof; an arch supporting a vault.

groined *adjective* built with groins.

grommet *noun* (also **grummet**) **1** a tube passed through the eardrum in surgery to make a communication with the middle ear. **2** an insulating washer placed round an electrical conductor to protect it as it passes through a hole in metal etc. **3** a ring of twisted rope used as a fastening, rowlock, etc.

groom *noun* **1** a person employed to look after horses. **2** a bridegroom. **–groom** *verb* **1** to clean and brush (an animal). **2** to make neat and trim. **3** to prepare (a person) for a career or position. **4** (of a paedophile) to prepare (a child) for a meeting, esp. via the Internet, with the intention of committing a sexual offence.

groomsman *noun* a man attending the bridegroom at a wedding.

Groote Eylandt an island off the east coast of Arnhem Land, NT.

groove *noun* **1** a long narrow channel in the surface of hard material. **2** a spiral cut on a gramophone disc for the needle or stylus. **3** a way of living that has become a habit, a rut. **–groove** *verb* to make a groove or grooves in.

groovy *adjective* (*informal*) excellent; fashionable.

grope *verb* **1** to feel about as one does in the dark, to seek by feeling. **2** to search mentally with some uncertainty, *groping for an answer.*

groper *noun* a large Australian and New Zealand sea fish. [Portuguese *garupa*]

Gropius (**groh**-pee-ŭs), Walter (1883–1969), German architect, designer, and teacher, founder and director of the Bauhaus.

grosgrain (**groh**-grayn) *noun* corded fabric of silky thread, used for ribbons etc.

gross (*pr.* grohss) *adjective* **1** thick, large-bodied; *a gross fellow*, repulsively fat; *gross vegetation*, growing thickly. **2** not refined, vulgar, *gross manners*. **3** glaringly obvious, outrageous, *gross negligence*. **4** total, whole, without deductions; *gross income*, income before tax etc. is deducted. **5** (*informal*) disgusting, repulsive. –**gross** *noun* (*plural* **gross**) twelve dozen (144) items; *ten gross*, 1440. –**gross** *verb* to produce or earn as total profit. □ **gross domestic product** the total value of goods produced and services provided in a country in one year (abbreviation **GDP**). **gross motor skills** the physical skills necessary for movements of the large muscles and joints of the body. **gross national product** the gross domestic product plus the total of net income from abroad (abbreviation **GNP**). **gross profit** the amount of profit before tax, expenses, etc. have been deducted. (Compare *net profit*.) **gross up** to work out (a gross amount) by taking the net amount and adding to it the total of tax etc. already paid or payable on this.

grotesque (groh-**tesk**) *adjective* very odd or unnatural, fantastically ugly or absurd. –**grotesque** *noun* a comically distorted figure; a design using fantastic human, animal, and plant forms. **grotesquely** *adverb*, **grotesqueness** *noun*

grotto (**grot**-oh) *noun* (*plural* **grottoes**) a picturesque cave.

grotty *adjective* (*informal*) unpleasant, dirty, or useless. [from *grotesque*]

grouch *verb* (*informal*) to grumble. –**grouch** *noun* (*informal*) **1** a grumble. **2** a grumbler. **grouchy** *adjective*

ground¹ *noun* **1** the solid surface of the earth, especially contrasted with the air surrounding it. **2** an area or position or distance on the earth's surface, *gain* or *lose ground*. **3** a foundation or reason for a theory or action, *there are no grounds for suspicion*. **4** soil, earth, *marshy ground*. **5** an area used for a particular purpose, *a football ground*. **6** the underlying part; a surface worked upon in embroidery or painting. –**ground** *verb* **1** to run aground. **2** to prevent (an aircraft or pilot) from flying. **3** to teach thoroughly, to give good basic training to. **4** to base, *it is grounded on fact*. □ **down to the ground** completely. **get off the ground** to rise in the air; to make a successful start. **ground floor** the floor at ground level in a building; *get in on the ground floor*, to be one of the first to

have the advantage of sharing in a promising enterprise. **ground plan** a plan of a building at ground level; an outline or general design of a scheme. **ground rule** a basic rule. **ground state** the lowest energy state of an atom etc.

ground² *see* **grind**. –**ground** *adjective* **ground glass** glass made non-transparent by grinding.

groundhog *noun* a North American marmot, a woodchuck.

grounding *noun* thorough teaching, basic training, *a good grounding in arithmetic*.

groundless *adjective* without basis, without good reason, *your fears are groundless*. **groundlessly** *adverb*

groundnut *noun* a peanut.

grounds *plural noun* **1** an area of enclosed land belonging to a large house or an institution. **2** solid particles that sink to the bottom of a liquid, *coffee grounds*.

groundsel *noun* a weed with small starry flowers.

groundsheet *noun* a waterproof sheet for spreading on the ground.

groundsman *noun* (*plural* **groundsmen**) (also **groundsperson**) a person employed to look after a sportsground or school grounds.

groundswell *noun* **1** heavy slow-moving waves caused by a distant or recent storm. **2** an increasingly forceful presence (especially of public opinion).

groundwork *noun* preliminary or basic work.

group *noun* **1** a number of persons or things gathered, placed, or classed together, or working together for some purpose. **2** a number of commercial companies under one owner. **3** an ensemble of musicians, *pop group*. **4** a combination of atoms that form a recognisable unit and are found in a number of compounds, *an alkyl group*. **5** a mathematical set, with an operation that combines any pair of its elements to yield a third, in which certain conditions are fulfilled. –**group** *verb* **1** to form or gather into a group or groups. **2** to place in a group; to organise into groups. □ **group captain** an officer in the air force. **group certificate** an employee's annual record of salary paid and tax deducted, for submission with a tax return. **group therapy** therapy in which patients with similar problems give each other psychological support.

groupware *noun* computer software facilitating collective working by a number of users.

grouse[1] *noun* (*plural* **grouse**) **1** a game bird with feathered feet. **2** its flesh as food.

grouse[2] *verb* (*informal*) to grumble. –**grouse** *noun* (*informal*) a grumble. **grouser** *noun*

grout *noun* a thin fluid mortar used to fill narrow cavities such as joints between stones or wall tiles. –**grout** *verb* to fill with grout.

grouter *noun* (*Austral. informal*) an unfair advantage; *come in on the grouter*, to start with an unfair advantage.

grove *noun* a group of trees, a small wood.

grovel *verb* (**grovelled**, **grovelling**) **1** to lie or crawl with the face downwards in a show of humility or fear. **2** to humble oneself.

grow *verb* (**grew**, **grown**, **growing**) **1** to increase in size or quantity; to become greater. **2** to develop; *the seeds are growing*, putting out shoots. **3** to be capable of developing as a plant, to flourish, *rice grows in warm climates*. **4** to become gradually, *he grew rich*. **5** to cause or allow to grow, to produce by cultivation, *grow a beard; grow roses*. □ **grow on** (of a custom or practice etc.) to become more acceptable to. **grow out of** (of a growing child) to become too large to wear (certain clothes); to become too mature for, *grew out of his childish habits*; to have as a source, to arise or develop from. **grow up** to develop, to become adult or mature. **growable** *adjective*

grower *noun* **1** a person who grows plants, fruit, or vegetables commercially. **2** a plant that grows in a certain way, *a rapid grower*.

growl *verb* **1** to make a low threatening sound. **2** to speak or say in a growling manner, to grumble. –**growl** *noun* **1** a growling sound. **2** a grumble. **growler** *noun*

grown *see* grow. –**grown** *adjective* **1** fully developed, adult, *a grown man*. **2** covered with a growth, *a wall grown over with ivy*. □ **grown-up** *adjective* adult; (*noun*) an adult person.

growth *noun* **1** the process of growing, development. **2** cultivation of produce. **3** something that grows or has grown, *a thick growth of weeds*. **4** an abnormal formation of tissue in the body, a tumour. □ **growth industry** one developing faster than most others. **growth ring** any of the concentric rings visible in a cut tree trunk that are formed by the annual increase in girth.

groyne *noun* a structure of wood, stone, or concrete projecting towards the sea, preventing sand and pebbles from being washed away by the current.

Grozny the capital of Chechnya.

grub *noun* **1** the thick-bodied wormlike larva of certain insects. **2** (*informal*) food. –**grub** *verb* (**grubbed**, **grubbing**) **1** to dig the surface of the soil. **2** to search laboriously, to rummage. □ **grub screw** a headless screw. **grub up** to clear away (roots) by digging; to dig up by the roots.

grubby *adjective* (**grubbier**, **grubbiest**) **1** infested with grubs. **2** dirty, unwashed. **grubbily** *adverb*, **grubbiness** *noun*

grudge *verb* to resent having to give or allow something; *I don't grudge him his success*, I admit that he deserves it. –**grudge** *noun* a feeling of resentment or ill will. **grudging** *adjective*, **grudgingly** *adverb*

gruel (**groo**-ĕl) *noun* a thin porridge made by boiling oatmeal in milk or water, especially for invalids.

gruelling (**groo**-ĕ-ling) *adjective* very tiring, exhausting.

gruesome (**groo**-sŏm) *adjective* filling one with horror or disgust, revolting, *the gruesome details of the murder*.

gruff *adjective* **1** (of the voice) low and harsh, hoarse. **2** having a gruff voice. **3** surly in manner. **gruffly** *adverb*, **gruffness** *noun*

grumble *verb* **1** to complain in a bad-tempered way. **2** to rumble, *thunder was grumbling in the distance*. –**grumble** *noun* **1** a complaint, especially a bad-tempered one. **2** a rumble. □ **grumbling appendix** (*informal*) one that causes pain from time to time without developing into appendicitis. **grumbler** *noun*

grummet *noun* = grommet.

grumpy *adjective* bad-tempered and gloomy. **grumpily** *adverb*, **grumpiness** *noun*

grunge *noun* **1** a style of rock music characterised by heavy guitar and low-fi production. **2** a fashion characterised by untidy loose-fitting clothes. **3** dirt, grime. **grungy** *adjective*

grunt *verb* **1** to make the gruff snorting sound characteristic of a pig. **2** to speak or utter with such a sound, *he grunted a reply*. **3** to grumble. –**grunt** *noun* a grunting sound.

gruyère (**groo**-yair) *noun* a kind of cheese with many holes.

gryphon (**grif**-ŏn) *noun* a griffin.

GST *abbreviation* goods and services tax.

G-suit *noun* a close-fitting inflatable suit worn by pilots and astronauts flying at high speed to prevent blood from draining away from the head and causing blackouts. [*G = gravity*]

GT *abbreviation* gran turismo (a kind of motor car). [Italian, = grand touring]

guano (**gwah**-noh) *noun* **1** dung of seabirds, used as manure. **2** an artificial manure, especially that made from fish.

guarantee *noun* **1** a formal promise to do what has been agreed, or that a thing is of specified quality and durability, with penalties for failure. **2** a formal promise given by one person to another that he or she will be responsible for something to be done, or for a debt to be paid, by a third person. **3** something offered or accepted as security. **4** a guarantor. –**guarantee** *verb* (**guaranteed**, **guaranteeing**) **1** to give or be a guarantee for; *guarantee his debts*, undertake to pay them if he does not. **2** to promise, to state with certainty.

guarantor *noun* a person who gives a guarantee.

guard *verb* **1** to watch over and protect, to keep safe. **2** to watch over and supervise or prevent from escaping. **3** to keep in check, to restrain; *guard your tongue*, do not be outspoken or indiscreet. **4** to take precautions, *guard against errors*. –**guard** *noun* **1** a state of watchfulness or alertness for possible danger. **2** a defensive attitude in boxing, fencing, cricket, etc. **3** a protector, a sentry. **4** a railway official in charge of a train. **5** a body of soldiers or others guarding a place or a person, serving as escort, or forming a separate part of an army. **6** a protecting part or device. □ **off one's guard** unprepared against attack or surprise. **on guard** acting as a protector or sentry; alert for possible danger etc. **on one's guard** alert for possible danger etc. **stand guard** to act as a protector or sentry.

guarded *adjective* cautious, discreet, *a guarded statement*.

guardian *noun* **1** one who guards or protects. **2** a person who undertakes legal responsibility for someone who is incapable of managing his or her own affairs, such as an orphaned child. □ **guardian angel** an angel thought of as watching over a person or place. **guardianship** *noun*

Guatemala (gwa-tě-**mah**-lă) **1** a republic in the north of Central America. **2** its capital city. **Guatemalan** *adjective* & *noun*

guava (**gwah**-vă) *noun* **1** a tropical American tree. **2** its edible orange-coloured acid fruit.

gudgeon[1] (**guj**-ŏn) *noun* a small freshwater fish used as bait.

gudgeon[2] (**guj**-ŏn) *noun* **1** a kind of pivot. **2** a socket for a rudder. **3** a metal pin or rod, *the gudgeon pin holds the piston and connecting rod together*.

Guernsey (**gern**-zee) the second largest of the Channel Islands. –**Guernsey** *noun* (*plural* **Guernseys**) a breed of dairy cattle originally from Guernsey.

guernsey *noun* (*Austral.*) a football jersey. □ **get a guernsey** (*informal*) to be selected for a team; to win recognition or approval.

guerrilla (gě-**ril**-ă) *noun* a person who takes part in **guerrilla warfare**, fighting or harassment by small groups acting independently. [Spanish, = little war]

guess *verb* **1** to form an opinion or make a statement or give an answer without calculating or measuring and without definite knowledge. **2** to think likely. **3** (*Amer.*) to suppose, *I guess we ought to be going*. –**guess** *noun* an opinion formed by guessing. □ **keep a person guessing** (*informal*) to keep him or her uncertain of one's feelings or future actions etc. **guesser** *noun*

guesstimate (**gess**-tĭ-mǎt) (also **guestimate**) *noun* (*informal*) an estimate based on guesswork and reasoning.

guesswork *noun* the process of guessing; an example of this.

guest *noun* **1** a person staying at another's house or visiting by invitation or being entertained to a meal. **2** a person lodging at a hotel. **3** a visiting performer taking part in an entertainment, *a guest artist*. □ **guest house** a superior boarding house.

guestbook *noun* **1** a book at a hotel, museum, etc., where visitors can record their personal details, comments, etc. **2** a facility on a website where visitors can record their comments.

guff *noun* (*informal*) empty talk, nonsense.

guffaw *noun* a coarse noisy laugh. –**guffaw** *verb* to give a guffaw.

GUI *abbreviation* graphical user interface.

guidance *noun* **1** guiding, being guided. **2** advising or advice on problems.

guide *noun* 1 a person who shows others the way. 2 one employed to point out interesting sights on a journey or visit. 3 an adviser; a person or thing that directs or influences one's behaviour. 4 a book of information about a place or a subject, *A Guide to Italy*. 5 a thing that marks a position, guides the eye, or steers moving parts. 6 Guide a member of a girls' organisation corresponding to the Scout Association. –**guide** *verb* to act as guide to. □ **guided missile** a missile that is under remote control or directed by equipment within itself. **guide dog** a dog trained to guide a blind person.

guidebook *noun* a book of information about a place, for travellers or visitors.

guideline *noun* a principle giving practical guidance.

guild *noun* (also **gild**) a society of people with similar interests and aims, any of the associations of craftsmen or merchants in the Middle Ages.

guilder (**gild**-er) *noun* a former unit of money in the Netherlands, a florin.

guildhall *noun* a hall built or used as a meeting place by a guild or corporation; a town hall.

guile (*rhymes with* mile) *noun* treacherous cunning, craftiness. **guileful** *adjective* full of guile. **guileless** *adjective* without guile. **guilelessly** *adverb*, **guilelessness** *noun*

guillotine (**gil**-ŏ-teen) *noun* 1 a machine with a heavy blade sliding down in grooves, used for beheading criminals in France. 2 a machine with a long blade or sharpened wheel for cutting paper or metal. 3 the fixing of times for taking votes on a bill in Parliament, in order to prevent it from being obstructed by an excessively long debate. –**guillotine** *verb* 1 to execute with a guillotine. 2 to cut with a guillotine. [named after Dr Guillotin, who suggested its use in France in 1789]

guilt *noun* 1 the fact of having committed some offence. 2 a feeling that one is to blame for something.

guiltless *adjective* without guilt, innocent.

guilty *adjective* (**guiltier**, **guiltiest**) 1 having done wrong. 2 feeling or showing guilt. **guiltily** *adverb*, **guiltiness** *noun*

Guinea a republic on the west coast of Africa. □ **Gulf of Guinea** a large inlet of the Atlantic Ocean south-east of Guinea.

guinea *noun* 1 (before decimal currency) the sum of 21 shillings ($2.10), used in stating professional fees or prizes. 2 a former British gold coin worth 21 shillings. □ **guinea fowl** a domestic fowl of the pheasant family, with grey feathers spotted with white. **guinea pig** a short-eared animal like a large rat, kept as a pet or for biological experiments; a person or thing used as a subject for experiment.

Guinea-Bissau (**bis**-ow) a republic on the west coast of Africa between Guinea and Senegal.

Guinevere (**gwin**-ĕ-veer) (in legends of King Arthur) the wife of King Arthur and mistress of Lancelot.

guise (*pr. as* guys) *noun* an outward manner or appearance put on in order to conceal the truth, a pretence, *they exploited him under the guise of friendship*.

guitar (gĭ-**tar**) *noun* a stringed musical instrument, played by plucking with the fingers or a plectrum; *electric guitar*, one with a built-in microphone.

guitarist *noun* a person who plays the guitar.

Gujarati (goo-jă-**rah**-tee) *noun* 1 a native of Gujarat (a State in western India). 2 a language descended from Sanskrit and spoken mainly in Gujarat.

gulf *noun* 1 an area of sea (larger than a bay) that is partly surrounded by land. 2 a deep hollow. 3 a wide difference in opinions or outlook. □ **the Gulf** the Persian Gulf.

Gulf of Carpentaria *see* Carpentaria.

Gulf Stream a warm ocean current flowing from the Gulf of Mexico to Europe.

Gulf War the war of 1991 in which an international coalition of forces, under the leadership of the US, defeated Iraqi forces occupying Kuwait.

gull *noun* a large seabird with long wings.

gullet *noun* the passage by which food goes from the mouth to the stomach, the throat.

gullible (**gul**-ĭ-bŭl) *adjective* easily deceived. **gullibility** (gul-ĭ-**bil**-ĭ-tee) *noun* [from an old word *gull* = a fool]

gully *noun* 1 (*Austral*.) a narrow valley or canyon. 2 a narrow channel cut by water or made for carrying rainwater away from a building. 3 (in cricket) a fielder between point and slips; this position.

gulp *verb* 1 to swallow (food or drink) hastily or greedily. 2 to suppress something by swallowing hard, *he gulped back his rage*. 3 to make a gulping movement, to choke or gasp, *gulping for breath.* **–gulp** *noun* **1** the act of gulping. **2** a large mouthful of liquid.

gum[1] *noun* the firm flesh in which the teeth are rooted. [from Old English *goma*]

gum[2] *noun* **1** a sticky substance exuded by some trees and shrubs, used for sticking things together. **2** chewing gum. **3** a gumdrop. **4** a gumtree. **–gum** *verb* (**gummed, gumming**) to smear or cover with gum; to stick together with gum. □ **gum arabic** gum exuded by some kinds of acacia. **gum up** (*informal*) to cause confusion or delay in, to spoil; *gum up the works*, to interfere with the smooth running of something. [from Latin *gummi*]

gumboil *noun* a small abscess on the gum.

gumboot *noun* a rubber boot, a wellington.

gumdrop *noun* a hard transparent sweet made of gelatine and gum arabic.

gummy *adjective* **1** sticky with gum. **2** showing the gums, toothless. **gumminess** *noun*

gumption (**gump**-shŏn) *noun* (*informal*) common sense and initiative.

gumtree *noun* a tree that exudes gum, a eucalyptus; *up a gumtree*, (*informal*) in great difficulties.

gun *noun* **1** any kind of firearm that sends shells or bullets from a metal tube. **2** a starting pistol. **3** a device that forces out a substance through a tube, *a grease gun*. **–gun** *verb* (**gunned, gunning**) **1** to shoot with a gun, *gunned him down*. **2** to accelerate (an engine) briskly. **–gun** *adjective* (*Austral*) (of a person) excellent or pre-eminent, *a gun shearer*. □ **be gunning for** to have as one's target for attack, to seek to destroy. **gun carriage** a wheeled structure on which a gun is mounted for transport. **gun cotton** an explosive made of acid-soaked cotton. **gun dog** a dog trained to retrieve game for shooters. **gun-runner** *noun* a person engaged in **gun-running**, extensive smuggling of guns and ammunition into a country.

gunboat *noun* a small armed vessel with heavy guns. □ **gunboat diplomacy** diplomacy backed by the threat of force.

gunfire *noun* the firing of guns.

gunge *noun* a sticky or messy mass of a substance.

gung-ho (gung-**hoh**) *adjective* enthusiastic, eager. [from Chinese *gonghe* work together]

gunk *noun* (*informal*) sticky or viscous material. [originally a detergent proprietary name]

gunman *noun* (*plural* **gunmen**) a man armed with a gun.

gunmetal *adjective* & *noun* dull bluish-grey, like the colour of metal formerly used for guns.

gunner *noun* **1** a soldier in an artillery unit, the official term for a private in such a unit. **2** a warrant officer in the navy, in charge of a battery of guns. **3** a member of an aircraft crew who operates a gun.

gunnery *noun* the construction and operating of large guns.

gunny *noun* coarse jute sacking.

gunpoint *noun* **at gunpoint** under threat of being shot by a gun held ready.

gunpowder *noun* an explosive of saltpetre, sulphur, and charcoal.

gunship *noun* **helicopter gunship** an armed helicopter.

gunshot *noun* **1** a shot fired from a gun. **2** the range of a gun, *within gunshot*.

gunsmith *noun* a person whose trade is making and repairing small firearms.

gunwale (**gun**-ăl) *noun* the upper edge of a small ship's or boat's side. [from *gun* + *wale* = a ridge (because it was formerly used to support guns)]

Gunwinygu (**guun**-win-goo) *noun* **1** a member of an Aboriginal people of Arnhem Land in the Northern Territory. **2** their language.

gunyah *noun* an Aboriginal temporary shelter. [from Dharuk *ganyi*]

guppy *noun* a small West Indian fish.

gurdwara (gerd-**wah**-ră) *noun* a Sikh temple. [from Sanskrit *guru* = teacher, + *dvara* = door]

gurgle *noun* a low bubbling sound. **–gurgle** *verb* to make this sound.

gurgler *noun* (*informal*) a plughole; a drain. □ **down the gurgler** down the drain; irretrievably lost.

Gurindji (**guur**-rin-jee) *noun* **1** a member of an Aboriginal people of the Victoria River area in the Northern Territory. **2** their language.

Gurkha (**ger**-kă) *noun* a member of a Hindu people in Nepal, forming regiments in the British army.

guru (**goo**-roo *or* **guu**-) *noun* (*plural* **gurus**) **1** a Hindu spiritual teacher or head of a religious sect. **2** an influential or revered teacher. [Sanskrit, = teacher]

gush *verb* **1** to flow or pour out suddenly or in great quantities. **2** to talk with extravagant enthusiasm or emotion, especially in an affected manner. **–gush** *noun* **1** a sudden or great outflow. **2** an outpouring of feeling, effusiveness.

gusher *noun* **1** an effusive person. **2** an oil well from which oil flows strongly without needing to be pumped.

gusset *noun* a triangular or diamond-shaped piece of cloth inserted in a garment to strengthen or enlarge it.

gust *noun* **1** a sudden rush of wind. **2** a burst of rain or smoke or sound. **–gust** *verb* to blow in gusts. **gusty** *adjective*, **gustily** *adverb*

gusto *noun* zest, great enjoyment in doing something.

gut *noun* **1** the lower part of the alimentary canal, the intestine. **2** a thread made from the intestines of animals, used surgically and for violin and racquet strings. **–gut** *adjective* **1** fundamental, basic, *a gut issue.* **2** instinctive, *a gut reaction.* **–gut** *verb* (**gutted**, **gutting**) **1** to remove the guts from (a fish). **2** to remove or destroy the internal fittings or parts of (a building), *the factory was gutted by fire.* **guts** *plural noun* **1** the internal organs of the abdomen. **2** the strength or vitality of something. **3** (*informal*) courage and determination. □ **hate a person's guts** (*informal*) to hate him or her intensely.

Gutenberg (**goo**-těn-berg), Johann (c. 1400–68), German printer, inventor of movable type.

gutless *adjective* (*informal*) lacking courage and determination.

gutser *noun* (*Austral. informal*) a bad fall, *he came a gutser.*

gutsy *adjective* (*informal*) **1** greedy. **2** courageous.

gutta-percha *noun* a tough rubber-like substance made from the juice of various Malayan trees.

gutter *noun* **1** a shallow trough under the eaves of a building, or a channel at the side of a street, for carrying off rainwater. **2** a slum environment. **–gutter** *verb* (of a candle) to burn unsteadily so that melted wax flows freely down the sides. [from Latin *gutta* = a drop]

guttering *noun* gutters; a length of gutter.

guttersnipe *noun* a dirty badly-dressed child who plays in slum streets.

guttural (**gut**-ŭ-răl) *adjective* throaty, harsh-sounding, *a guttural voice.* **gutturally** *adverb* [from Latin *guttur* = throat]

Guugu Yimidhirr (goo-goo **yim**-ĭ-deer) *noun* **1** a member of an Aboriginal people of the Cooktown region of northern Queensland. **2** their language.

guy¹ *noun* a rope or chain used to keep something steady or secured, *guy ropes.*

guy² *noun* **1** (*Brit.*) a figure in the form of a man dressed in old clothes, representing Guy Fawkes (*see* **Fawkes**) and burnt on 5 November. **2** (*informal*) a man. **3** (usually in *plural*) (*informal*) a person. **–guy** *verb* to ridicule, especially by comic imitation.

Guyana (gy-**an**-ă) a republic on the NE coast of South America. **Guyanese** (gy-ă-**neez**) *adjective* & *noun* (*plural* **Guyanese**).

Guyani (**guu**-yun-ee) *noun* **1** a member of an Aboriginal people of central South Australia. **2** their language, a dialect closely related to Adnyamathanha.

guzzle *verb* to eat or drink greedily. **guzzler** *noun*

gym (*pr.* jim) *noun* (*informal*) **1** a gymnasium. **2** gymnastics.

gymkhana (jim-**kah**-nă) *noun* a public display of athletics and sports competitions, especially horse-riding.

gymnasium *noun* a room fitted up for physical training and gymnastics. [from Greek *gumnos* = naked (because Greek men exercised naked)]

gymnast (**jim**-năst) *noun* an expert performer of gymnastics.

gymnastic *adjective* of gymnastics.

gymnastics *plural noun* exercises performed to develop the muscles or demonstrate agility; *mental gymnastics*, mental agility, elaborate reasoning. **–gymnastics** *noun* gymnastics as a subject of study or practice.

gymnosperm (**jim**-nŏ-sperm) *noun* a member of the group of plants (mainly trees) that have seeds not enclosed in an ovary. [from Greek *gumnos* = naked, + *sperma* = seed]

gynaecologist (gy-ně-**kol**-ŏ-jĭst) *noun* a specialist in gynaecology.

gynaecology (gy-ně-**kol**-ŏ-jee) *noun* the scientific study of the female reproductive system and its diseases. **gynaecological** *adjective* [from Greek *gune* = woman, + *-logy*]

gypsophila (jip-**sof**-ĭ-lă) *noun* a garden plant with many small white flowers.

gypsum (**jip**-sŭm) *noun* a chalk-like substance from which plaster of Paris is made, also used as a fertiliser.

gypsy *noun* a member of a travelling people in Europe. [from *Egyptian*, because gypsies were originally thought to have come from Egypt]

gyrate (jy-**rayt**) *verb* to move round in circles or spirals, to revolve. **gyration** (jy-**ray**-shŏn) *noun* [from Greek *guros* = a ring or circle]

gyratory (**jy**-ră-tŏ-ree) *adjective* gyrating, following a circular or spiral path.

gyro (**jy**-roh) *noun* (*plural* **gyros**) (*informal*) a gyroscope.

gyrocompass (**jy**-roh-kum-păs) *noun* a navigation compass using a gyroscope and so independent of the earth's rotation.

gyroscope (**jy**-rŏ-skohp) *noun* a device consisting of a heavy wheel which, when spinning fast, keeps the direction of its axis unchanged, used in navigation instruments in ships and in spacecraft etc. **gyroscopic** (jy-rŏ-**skop**-ik) *adjective* [same origin as *gyrate*]

Hh

ha *interjection* an exclamation of triumph or surprise.

ha. *abbreviation* hectare(s).

Habakkuk (**hab**-ă-kŭk *or* hă-**bak**-ŭk) **1** a Hebrew minor prophet probably of the 7th century BC. **2** the book of the Old Testament bearing his name.

habeas corpus (hay-bee-ăs **kor**-pŭs) *noun* an order requiring a person to be brought before a judge or into court, especially in order to investigate the right of the authorities to keep him or her imprisoned. [Latin, = you must have the body]

haberdasher *noun* a shopkeeper dealing in accessories for dress and in sewing goods.

haberdashery *noun* a haberdasher's goods.

habit *noun* **1** a settled way of behaving; something done frequently and almost without thinking; something that is hard to give up. **2** the long dress worn by a monk or nun. **3** a woman's riding dress.

habitable *adjective* suitable for living in.

habitat (**hab**-ĭ-tat) *noun* the natural environment of an animal or plant.

habitation *noun* **1** a place to live in. **2** inhabiting, being inhabited.

habitual *adjective* **1** done constantly, like or resulting from a habit. **2** regular, usual, *in his habitual place*. **3** doing something as a habit, *a habitual smoker*. **habitually** *adverb*

habituate *verb* to accustom. **habituation** *noun*

hachures (ha-**shoorz**) *plural noun* parallel lines used on maps to indicate the degree of slope in hills.

hack¹ *verb* **1** to cut or chop roughly. **2** to deal a rough blow or kick, *hacked at his shins*. **3** (*informal*) to gain unauthorised access to (computer files). **hacker** *noun*

hack² *noun* **1** a horse for ordinary riding; one that may be hired. **2** a person paid to do hard and uninteresting work, especially as a writer. **–hack** *verb* to ride on horseback at an ordinary pace, especially along roads.

hacking *adjective* (of a cough) short, dry, and frequent.

hackles *plural noun* the long feathers on the neck of a domestic cock and other birds. □ **with one's hackles up** (of a person) angry and ready to fight.

hackneyed (**hak**-need) *adjective* (of a saying) having lost its original impact through long overuse.

hacksaw *noun* a saw for cutting metal, with a short blade in a frame.

had *see* **have**.

haddock *noun* (*plural* **haddock**) a sea fish like cod but smaller, used for food.

Hades (**hay**-deez) *noun* **1** (*Gk. myth.*) the lord of the Underworld (which is known as 'the House of Hades'); the Underworld itself, the place where the spirits of the dead go. **2** hell.

Hadith (**had**-ith) *noun* a collection of sayings of the Prophet Muhammad and of traditions about him, now forming a supplement (the *Sunna*) to the Koran. [from Arabic *hadit* = tradition]

hadn't (*informal*) = had not.

Hadrian (**hay**-dree-ăn) Roman emperor 117–38. □ **Hadrian's Wall** a Roman defensive wall across northern England.

haematite (**hee**-mă-tyt) *noun* ferric oxide as ore. [from Greek *haima* = blood]

haematology (hee-mă-**tol**-ŏ-jee) *noun* the scientific study of blood and its diseases. [from Greek *haima* = blood, + -*logy*]

haemoglobin (hee-mŏ-**gloh**-bĭn) *noun* the red oxygen-carrying substance in the blood. [from Greek *haima* = blood]

haemophilia (hee-mŏ-**fil**-ee-ă) *noun* a tendency (usually inherited) to bleed severely from even slight injury, through failure of the blood to clot quickly. **haemophilic** *adjective* [from Greek *haima* = blood, + *philia* = loving]

haemophiliac (hee-mŏ-**fil**-ee-ak) *noun* a person suffering from haemophilia.

haemorrhage (**hem**-ŏ-rij) *noun* bleeding, especially when this is heavy. **–haemorrhage** *verb* to bleed heavily. [from Greek *haima* = blood, + *rhegnunai* = to burst]

haemorrhoids (**hem**-ŏ-roidz) *plural noun* varicose veins at or near the anus. [from Greek *haima* = blood, + *rhoia* = a flow]

hafnium (**haf**-nee-ŭm) *noun* a metallic element (symbol Hf) with a silver lustre, used in control rods of nuclear reactors.

haft *noun* the handle of a knife or dagger or cutting tool.

hag *noun* an ugly old woman.

Haggai (**hag**-I) 1 a Hebrew minor prophet of the 6th century BC. 2 a book of the Old Testament containing his prophecies.

haggard *adjective* looking worn from prolonged worry, illness, or exhaustion.

haggis *noun* a Scottish dish made from sheep's heart, lungs, and liver.

haggle *verb* to argue about price or terms when settling a bargain.

Hague (*pr.* hayg), **The**, the seat of government of the Netherlands.

ha-ha *noun* a sunk fence (*see* sunk).

hahnium (**hah**-nee-ŭm) *noun* the name formerly proposed by the American Chemical Society for the element now called dubnium, and by IUPAC for the element now called hassium.

haiku (**hy**-koo) *noun* a Japanese three-line poem of 17 syllables; an English imitation of this. [Japanese]

hail[1] *interjection* an exclamation of greeting. –hail *verb* to greet, to call to (a person or ship) in order to attract his or her attention. □ **hail from** to have come from. **Hail Mary** a prayer to the Virgin Mary beginning with these words.

hail[2] *noun* 1 pellets of frozen rain falling in a shower. 2 something coming in great numbers, *a hail of bullets*. –hail *verb* 1 to send down hail, *it is hailing*. 2 to come or send down like hail.

hailstone *noun* a pellet of hail.

hailstorm *noun* a storm of hail.

hair *noun* 1 each of the fine threadlike strands that grow from the skin of people and animals or on certain plants. 2 a mass of these, especially on the human head. □ **hair-raising** *adjective* terrifying, causing one's hair to stand on end in fear. **hair-splitting** *noun* splitting hairs (*see below*). **hair-trigger** *noun* a trigger that causes a gun to fire at the very slightest pressure. **split hairs** to make distinctions of meaning that are too small to be of any real importance.

hairbrush *noun* a brush for grooming the hair.

haircloth *noun* cloth woven from hair.

haircut *noun* 1 shortening the hair by cutting it. 2 the style in which it is cut.

hairdo *noun* (*plural* **hairdos**) 1 a hairstyle. 2 the process of arranging a person's hair.

hairdresser *noun* a person whose trade is to arrange and cut hair.

hairless *adjective* without hair, bald.

hairline *noun* 1 the edge of a person's hair round the face. 2 a very thin line.

hairpin *noun* a U-shaped pin for keeping the hair in place. □ **hairpin bend** a sharp U-shaped bend in a road.

hairspring *noun* a fine spring regulating the balance wheel in a watch.

hairstyle *noun* a particular way of arranging the hair.

hairy *adjective* (**hairier**, **hairiest**) 1 having much hair. 2 (*informal*) hair-raising; difficult. **hairiness** *noun*

Haiti (**hay**-tee) a republic in the West Indies. **Haitian** (**hay**-shǎn) *adjective* & *noun*

haj (**hahj**) *noun* (also **hajj**) the annual Muslim pilgrimage to Mecca. [Arabic *hajj*]

haji (**hahj**-ee) *noun* (also **hajji**) (*plural* **-is**) a Muslim who has made the pilgrimage to Mecca.

hake *noun* (*plural* **hake**) 1 an edible sea fish of the cod family. 2 = **gemfish**.

hakea (**hay**-kee-ǎ) *noun* an Australian tree or shrub with hard woody fruit.

halal (hah-**lahl**) *adjective* fulfilling all requirements of Islamic law, religiously acceptable according to Islamic law. –halal *noun* meat prepared in this way. [Arabic, = lawful]

halberd *noun* an ancient weapon that is a combined spear and battleaxe.

halcyon (**hal**-see-ǒn) *adjective* (of a period) happy and prosperous, *halcyon days*. [named after a bird formerly believed to have the power of calming wind and waves while it nested on the sea]

hale *adjective* strong, healthy, *hale and hearty*.

half *noun* (*plural* **halves**) 1 each of two equal or corresponding parts into which a thing is divided. 2 either of two equal periods of play in sports. 3 (*informal*) a half-back. –half *adjective* amounting to a half. –half *adverb* to the extent of a half, partly, half-cooked. □ **by half** excessively, *too clever by half*. **by halves** lacking thoroughness, *they never do things by halves*. **go halves** to share a thing equally. **half and half** being half of one thing and half of another. **half-back** *noun* a player between the forwards and the full backs in football and hockey; this position. **half-baked** *adjective* (*informal*) not competently planned; foolish. **half board** provision of bed, breakfast, and one main meal at a hotel etc. **half-breed** *noun* a person of mixed race. **half-brother** *noun* a brother related through one parent only. **half-caste** *noun* a person of mixed race. **half-hearted** *adjective* lacking in enthusiasm. **half-life** *noun* the time it takes the radioactivity of a substance to fall to half its original value. **half mast** a point about halfway up a mast, to which a flag is lowered as a mark of respect for a dead person. **half measures** a policy lacking thoroughness. **half nelson** a hold in wrestling, with an arm under the opponent's arm and behind his back. **half-past** *noun* half an hour after (any hour o'clock). **half-sister** *noun* a sister related through one parent only. **half-timbered** *adjective* (of a building) having a timber frame with the spaces filled in by brick or plaster. **half-time** *noun* the interval between the two halves of a game or contest. **half-tone** *noun* a black-and-white illustration in which light and dark shades are reproduced by means of small and large dots. **half-truth** *noun* a statement conveying only part of the truth. **half-volley** *noun* (in tennis) a return of the ball as soon as it has reached the ground; (in cricket) a ball so pitched that the batsman may hit it as it bounces; a hit of this kind.

halfpenny (**hayp**-nee) *noun* (*plural* **halfpennies** for separate coins, **halfpence** for a sum of money) a former coin worth half a penny.

halfway *adverb* at a point between and equally distant from two others. **–halfway** *adjective* situated halfway; *a halfway house*, a compromise.

halfwit *noun* (*informal*) an extremely foolish or stupid person. **half-witted** *adjective*

halibut *noun* (*plural* **halibut**) a large flatfish used for food.

halide *noun* a chemical compound of a halogen with another element or radical.

halite *noun* common rock salt, the natural form in which sodium chloride is found. [from Greek *hals* = salt]

halitosis (hal-ĭ-**toh**-sĭs) *noun* bad breath.

hall *noun* **1** a large room or a building for meetings, meals, concerts, etc. **2** (*Brit*.) a large country house, especially one with a landed estate. **3** a space or passage into which the front entrance of a house etc. opens. □ **hall of residence** a building for university students to live in.

hallelujah *interjection* & *noun* = **alleluia**.

Halley (**hal**-ee), Edmond (1656–1742), English astronomer. □ **Halley's comet** a bright comet that orbits the sun in about 76 years, whose reappearance in 1758 was predicted by Halley.

Usage The name of the comet is popularly mispronounced as (**hay**-lee).

halliard *noun* = **halyard**.

hallmark *noun* **1** a mark used to indicate the standard of gold, silver, and platinum on articles made of these. **2** a characteristic by which something is easily recognised. **hallmarked** *adjective* [originally a mark used at Goldsmiths' *Hall*, London]

hallo *interjection* & *noun* (*plural* **hallos**) = **hello**.

halloumi *noun* a firm white cheese made from goats' or ewes' milk.

hallow *verb* to make holy; to honour as holy.

Hallowe'en *noun* (also **Halloween**) 31 October, the eve of All Saints' Day.

hallucinate (hă-**loo**-sĭ-nayt) *verb* to experience hallucinations; to cause to do this.

hallucination (hă-loo-sĭ-**nay**-shŏn) *noun* **1** the illusion of seeing or hearing something when no such thing is present. **2** the thing seen or heard in this way. **hallucinatory** *adjective*

hallucinogen (hă-**loo**-sĭ-nŏ-jen) *noun* a substance etc. that causes hallucinations. **hallucinogenic** *adjective* [from *hallucinate*, + Greek *-genes* = born]

halo *noun* (*plural* **haloes**) **1** a disc or ring of light shown round the head of a sacred figure in paintings etc. **2** a disc of diffused light round a luminous body such as the sun or moon. **haloed** *adjective*

halogen (**hal**-ŏ-jĕn) *noun* any of the five chemically related elements: fluorine, chlorine, bromine, iodine, and astatine. [from Greek *halos* = of salt, + *-genes* = born]

halt *noun* **1** a temporary stop, an interruption of progress. **2** a stopping place on a railway line, used for local services only and without station buildings. **–halt** *verb* to come or bring to a halt.

halter *noun* **1** a length of rope or a leather strap put round a horse's head so that it may be led or fastened by this. **2** (also **halter-neck**) a strap passing round the back of the neck holding a dress or top up and leaving the back and shoulders bare; a garment held by this.

halva *noun* a confection of sesame flour and honey. [Yiddish from Turkish from Arabic *halwa*]

halve *verb* **1** to divide or share equally between two. **2** to reduce by half. **3** to draw (a hole or match in golf) with an opponent. **4** to fit (crossing timbers) together by cutting out half the thickness of each to make a **halving joint**.

halves *see* **half**.

halyard (**hal**-yerd) *noun* a rope or tackle for raising or lowering a sail, yard, or flag etc.

ham *noun* **1** the upper part of a pig's leg, dried and salted or smoked. **2** meat from this. **3** the back of the thigh and buttock. **4** (*informal*) a poor actor or performer. **5** (*informal*) the operator of an amateur radio station, *a radio ham*. **–ham** *verb* (**hammed**, **hamming**) (*informal*) to overact, to exaggerate one's actions deliberately, *hamming it up*. □ **ham-fisted**, **ham-handed** *adjectives* (*informal*) clumsy.

hamburger *noun* a flat round cake of minced beef served fried, often eaten in a bread roll. [short for *hamburger steak*; named after the city of Hamburg in Germany]

Hamilton the capital of Bermuda.

hamlet *noun* a small village.

hammada (ham-**ah**-dă) *noun* a bare rocky upland area of desert, blown clear of sand by the wind.

hammer *noun* **1** a tool with a heavy metal head used for breaking things, driving nails in, etc. **2** something shaped or used like this, e.g. an auctioneer's mallet, part of the firing device in a gun, the part of a piano mechanism that strikes the string. **3** a bone of the middle ear. **4** a metal ball of about 7 kg, attached to a wire for throwing as an athletic contest. **5** (*Austral. informal*) a person's back; *on one's hammer*, pursuing or criticising relentlessly (¶ originally rhyming slang, *hammer and tack*). **–hammer** *verb* **1** to hit or beat with a hammer, to strike loudly. **2** to force (information) into a person by repeating it continually. **3** to defeat utterly.

□ **come under the hammer** to be sold by auction. **hammer and tongs** fighting or arguing with great energy and noise. **hammer out** to devise (a plan) with great effort.

hammerbeam *noun* a beam that projects a short way into a hall etc. from the foot of one of the roof's principal rafters. **hammerbeam roof** a timber roof in which the rafters are supported by a series of brackets each resting on the one below.

hammerhead *noun* a kind of shark with a flattened head and eyes in lateral extensions of it.

hammock *noun* a hanging bed of canvas or rope network.

Hammurabi (ham-yoor-**rab**-ee) (died 1750 BC), a king of Babylonia, noted for the code of laws drawn up during his reign.

hamper¹ *noun* **1** a basketwork packing case. **2** a hamper or box of food as a present.

hamper² *verb* to prevent the free movement or activity of, to hinder.

hamster *noun* a small ratlike rodent with cheek pouches for carrying grain.

hamstring *noun* **1** any of the five tendons at the back of the human knee. **2** the great tendon at the back of an animal's hock. **–hamstring** *verb* (**hamstrung**, **hamstringing**) **1** to cripple by cutting the hamstring(s). **2** to cripple the activity or efficiency of.

hand *noun* **1** the end part of the arm below the wrist; *a hand of pork*, a part of the foreleg. **2** possession, control, care, *the child is in good hands*. **3** a part in an activity, *many people had a hand in it*. **4** active help, *give her a hand*. **5** a pledge of marriage, *asked for her hand*. **6** a manual worker in a factory or farm etc.; a member of a ship's crew. **7** skill or style of workmanship, a person with reference to skill, *has a light hand with pastry*; *an old hand at this*, an experienced person. **8** style of handwriting. **9** a pointer on a dial etc. **10** side or direction; the right or left side; each of two contrasted sides in an argument etc., *on the other hand*. **11** a unit of 4 inches (about 10 cm) used in measuring a horse's height. **12** the cards dealt to a player in a card game; one round of a card game. **13** (*informal*) applause, *got a big hand*. **14** done or operated or carried etc. by hand, *hand-stitched*; *handbrake*; *hand luggage*. **15** a bunch (of bananas). **–hand** *verb* to give or pass with one's hand(s) or otherwise.

☐ **at hand** close by; about to happen. **by hand** by a person (not a machine); delivered by a messenger, not through the post. **hand in glove with** working in close association with. **hand in hand** holding each other's hand; closely associated, linked together. **hand over** to put (a person or thing) into the custody or control of another person, to present. **hand over fist** (*informal*) with rapid progress, *making money hand over fist*. **hand-picked** *adjective* carefully chosen. **hands down** (of a victory won) easily, completely. **hands-on** *adjective* (of experience etc.) practical, working or operating a thing directly. **hands up!** an order to raise one's hand (e.g. in agreement) or both hands in surrender. **live from hand to mouth** to supply only one's immediate needs without provision for the future. **on hand** available. **on one's hands** resting on one as a responsibility. **out of hand** out of control; without delay or preparation, *rejected it out of hand*. **to hand** within reach; available.

handbag *noun* 1 a small bag for holding a purse and personal articles. 2 a travelling bag.

handbell *noun* a small bell rung by hand.

handbook *noun* a small book giving useful facts.

handcuff *noun* each of a pair of linked metal rings for securing a prisoner's wrists. –**handcuff** *verb* to put handcuffs on (a prisoner).

Handel, George Frederick (1685–1759), German-born composer, resident in England, whose works include *Messiah*.

handful *noun* (*plural* **handfuls**) 1 a quantity that fills the hand. 2 a small number of people or things. 3 (*informal*) a person who is difficult to control; a troublesome task.

handicap *noun* 1 a physical or mental disability. 2 a disadvantage imposed on a superior competitor in order to equalise chances; a race or contest in which this is imposed. 3 the number of strokes by which a golfer normally exceeds par for the course. 4 anything that lessens one's chance of success or makes progress difficult. –**handicap** *verb* (**handicapped**, **handicapping**) to impose or be a handicap on. **handicapper** *noun*

handicapped *adjective* suffering from a physical or mental disability.

handicraft *noun* work that needs both skill with the hands and artistic design, e.g. woodwork, needlework, pottery, etc.

handily *adverb* in a handy way.

handiwork *noun* 1 something done or made by the hands. 2 something done or made by a named person.

handkerchief *noun* (*plural* **handkerchiefs**) a small square of cloth, usually carried in a pocket, for wiping the nose etc. [from *hand* + *kerchief*]

handle *noun* 1 the part of a thing by which it is to be held, carried, or controlled. 2 a fact that may be taken advantage of, *gave a handle to his critics*. –**handle** *verb* 1 to touch, feel, or move with the hands. 2 to be able to be operated, *the car handles well*. 3 to manage, to deal with, *knows how to handle people*. 4 to deal in (goods). 5 to discuss or write about (a subject).

handlebar *noun* 1 the steering bar of a bicycle etc., with a handle at each end. 2 a thick curving moustache shaped like this.

handler *noun* a person who handles things; one in charge of a trained police dog.

handmade *adjective* made by hand.

handmaid *noun* (also **handmaiden**) (*old use*) a female servant.

handout *noun* 1 something distributed free of charge. 2 a prepared statement issued to the press etc.

handrail *noun* a narrow rail for people to hold as a support.

handshake *noun* grasping and shaking a person's hand with one's own as a greeting.

handsome *adjective* 1 good-looking. 2 generous, *a handsome present*. 3 (of a price or fortune etc.) very large. **handsomely** *adverb*, **handsomeness** *noun*

handspring *noun* a somersault in which a person lands first on the hands and then on the feet.

handstand *noun* balancing on one's hands with the feet in the air.

handwriting *noun* 1 writing done by hand with a pen or pencil. 2 a person's style of this.

handwritten *adjective* written by hand.

handy *adjective* (**handier**, **handiest**) 1 convenient to handle or use. 2 conveniently placed for being reached or used. 3 clever with one's hands. **handily** *adverb*, **handiness** *noun*

handyman *noun* (*plural* **handymen**) a person who is clever at doing household repairs etc. or who is employed to do odd jobs.

hang *verb* (**hung** (in senses 5 and 6 **hanged**), **hanging**) 1 to support or be supported

402

from above so that the lower end is free.
2 to cause (a door or gate) to rest on hinges so that it swings freely to and fro; to be placed in this way. **3** to stick (wallpaper) to a wall. **4** to decorate with drapery or hanging ornaments. **5** to execute or kill by suspending from a rope that tightens round the neck; to be executed in this way. **6** (*informal*) to damn, *I'm hanged if I know*. **7** to droop; *people hung over the gate*, leant over it. **8** to remain in the air, *smoke hung over the area*; *the threat is hanging over him*, remains as something unpleasant. **–hang** *noun* the way something hangs. □ **get the hang of** (*informal*) to get the knack of. **hang about** or **around** to loiter, not to disperse. **hang back** to show reluctance to take action or to advance. **hang fire** (of a gun) to be slow in going off; (of events) to be slow in developing. **hang on** to hold tightly; to depend on, *much hangs on this decision*; to attend closely to, *they hung on his words*; to remain in office, to stick to one's duty etc.; (*informal*) to wait for a short time. **hang out** (*informal*) to have one's home, to reside. **hang-out** *noun* (*informal*) a haunt, a place a person frequents. **hang together** (of people) to help or support one another; (of statements) to fit well together, to be consistent. **hang up** to end a telephone conversation by replacing the receiver; to cause delay or difficulty to. **hang-up** *noun* (*informal*) a difficulty; an inhibition.

hangar *noun* a shed for housing aircraft.

hangdog *adjective* shamefaced.

hanger *noun* **1** a person who hangs things. **2** a loop or hook by which something is hung. **3** a shaped piece of wood or plastic for hanging a garment on. □ **hanger-on** *noun* (*plural* **hangers-on**) a person who attaches himself or herself to another in the hope of personal gain.

hang-glider *noun* the frame used in **hang-gliding**, the sport of being suspended in an airborne frame controlled by one's own movements.

hangings *plural noun* draperies hung on walls.

hanging valley *noun* a valley that ends in a very steep descent to another valley, or to the sea.

hangman *noun* an executioner who hangs condemned persons.

hangnail *noun* torn skin at the root of a fingernail.

hangover *noun* **1** a severe headache or other unpleasant after-effects from drinking much alcohol. **2** something left from an earlier time.

Hang Seng index *noun* an index based on the average price of selected securities on the Hong Kong stock exchange.

hank *noun* a coil or length of wool or thread.

hanker *verb* to crave, to feel a longing.

hanky *noun* (*informal*) a handkerchief.

hanky-panky *noun* (*informal*) **1** trickery, dishonest dealing. **2** naughtiness.

Hannibal (**han**-ĭ-băl) (247–183/2 BC), Carthaginian general who led an army over the Alps to invade Italy.

Hanoi the capital of Vietnam.

Hanover 1 a city in northern Germany. **2** a former German State, whose ruler succeeded to the British throne in 1714 as George I. **3** the name of the British royal house from 1714 to the death of Queen Victoria in 1901. **Hanoverian** (han-ŏ-**veer**-ree-ăn) *adjective*

Hansard *noun* the official report of the debates and proceedings of Parliament. [named after the English printer whose firm originally compiled it]

Hanseatic League (han-see-**at**-ik) a medieval association of north German cities, formed in 1241 as a commercial alliance, that developed into an independent political power.

Hansen's disease *noun* leprosy. [named after the Norwegian physician G.H.A. Hansen (died 1912), who discovered the leprosy bacillus]

hansom *noun* (also **hansom cab**) (*old use*) a two-wheeled horse-drawn cab for two inside, with the driver seated behind.

Hanukka (**hah**-nŭ-kă) *noun* an eight-day Jewish festival of lights, beginning in December, commemorating the rededication of the Temple at Jerusalem in 165 BC. [Hebrew, = consecration]

Hanuman (hah-noo-**mahn**) (in Hinduism) a semi-divine monkey-like being with extraordinary powers, whose exploits are described in the Ramayana. **–hanuman** *noun* an Indian langur venerated by Hindus.

haphazard (hap-**haz**-erd) *adjective* done or chosen at random, without planning. **haphazardly** *adverb* [same origin as *happen*, + *hazard*]

hapless *adjective* unlucky. [same origin as *happen*, + *-less* = without]

haploid (**hap**-loid) *adjective* **1** (of a cell) having a single set of chromosomes not in pairs. **2** (of an organism) having haploid cells. –**haploid** *noun* a haploid cell or organism. [from Greek *haplous* = single]

happen *verb* **1** to occur (by chance or otherwise). **2** to have the (good or bad) fortune to do something. **3** to be the fate or experience of, *what happened to you?* □ **happen on** to find by chance. [from Old Norse *happ* = luck]

happening *noun* something that happens, an event.

happy *adjective* (**happier**, **happiest**) **1** feeling or showing pleasure or contentment. **2** fortunate. **3** (of words or behaviour) very suitable, pleasing. □ **happy event** the birth of a child. **happy-go-lucky** *adjective* taking events cheerfully as they happen. **happy hunting ground** a good place for finding things. **happy medium** something that achieves satisfactory avoidance of extremes. **happily** *adverb*, **happiness** *noun* [same origin as *happen*]

Hapsburg the name of an Austrian family to which belonged rulers of various countries of Europe from medieval times onwards.

hara-kiri (ha-ră-**ki**-ree) *noun* suicide involving disembowelment, formerly practised by Japanese army officers when in disgrace or under sentence of death. [from Japanese *hara* = belly, + *kiri* = cutting]

haram (hah-**rahm**) *noun* forbidden or proscribed by Islamic law.

harangue (hă-**rang**) *noun* a lengthy earnest speech. –**harangue** *verb* to make a harangue to.

Harare (hă-**rah**-ree) the capital of Zimbabwe.

harass (**ha**-răs *or* hă-**ras**) *verb* **1** to trouble and annoy continually. **2** to make repeated attacks on (an enemy). **harassment** (**ha**-răs-měnt *or* hă-**ras**-měnt) *noun* [from Old French *harer* = set the dog on someone]

harbinger (**har**-bĭn-jer) *noun* a person or thing whose presence announces the approach of another.

harbour *noun* a place of shelter for ships. –**harbour** *verb* **1** to give shelter to, to conceal (a criminal etc.). **2** to keep in one's mind, *harbour a grudge*.

hard *adjective* **1** firm, not yielding to pressure; not easily cut; *hard facts*, not disputable. **2** difficult to do or understand or answer. **3** causing unhappiness, difficult to bear.

4 severe, harsh, unsympathetic. **5** energetic, *a hard worker*. **6** (of weather) severe, frosty. **7** (of currency) not likely to drop suddenly in value. **8** (of drinks) strongly alcoholic; (of drugs) strong and likely to cause addiction. **9** (of water) containing mineral salts that prevent soap from lathering freely and cause a hard coating to form inside kettles, water tanks, etc. **10** (of colours or sounds) harsh to the eye or ear. **11** (of consonants) sounding sharp not soft, *the letter 'g' is hard in 'gun' and soft in 'gin'*. –**hard** *adverb* **1** with great effort, intensively, *worked hard*; *it's raining hard*. **2** with difficulty, *hard-earned money*. **3** so as to be hard, *hard-baked*. □ **hard and fast rules** rules that cannot be altered to fit special cases. **hard-boiled** *adjective* (of eggs) boiled until white and yolk have become solid; (of people) callous. **hard by** close by. **hard case** (*informal*) a highly stubborn person; (*Austral.*) a person who is amusingly unconventional. **hard cash** coins and banknotes, not a cheque or a promise to pay later. **hard copy** material produced in printed form by a computer or from a microfilm etc. and able to be read without a special device. **hard core** the stubborn unyielding nucleus of a group. **hard-core** *adjective* blatant, uncompromising; *hard-core pornography*, explicit, obscene. **hard court** a tennis court with a hard (not grass) surface. **hard disk** a rigid computer disk for storing large quantities of data (contrasting with a *floppy disk*). **hard drive** a disk drive used to read from and write to a hard disk. **hard-headed** *adjective* practical, not sentimental. **hard-hearted** *adjective* unsympathetic. **hard left**, **hard right** the stubbornly extremist section of a left- or right-wing group in politics. **hard line** unyielding adherence to a firm policy. **hard lines** worse luck than is deserved. **hard of hearing** slightly deaf. **hard up** (*informal*) short of money; *hard up for ideas*, short of these. **hard-wearing** *adjective* able to stand much wear. **hardness** *noun*

hardback *adjective* bound in stiff covers. –**hardback** *noun* a book bound in this way.

hardbitten *adjective* tough and realistic.

hardboard *noun* stiff board made of compressed wood pulp.

harden *verb* **1** to make or become hard or hardy. **2** to make or become unyielding. **hardener** *noun*

hardenbergia (har-děn-**ber**-jee-ă) *noun* an Australian climbing or trailing plant with masses of usually purple pea-flowers, also called *false sarsaparilla*.

hardihood *noun* boldness, daring.

hardly *adverb* **1** in a hard manner. **2** only with difficulty. **3** scarcely.

hardship *noun* severe discomfort or lack of the necessaries of life; a circumstance causing this.

hardware *noun* **1** tools and household implements etc. sold by a shop. **2** weapons, machinery. **3** the mechanical and electronic parts of a computer.

hardwood *noun* the hard heavy wood obtained from deciduous trees, e.g. oak and teak.

Hardy, Thomas (1840–1928), English novelist and poet, famous for his descriptions of English rural life.

hardy *adjective* (**hardier**, **hardiest**) **1** capable of enduring cold or difficult conditions. **2** (of plants) able to grow in the open air all the year round. **hardiness** *noun*

hare *noun* a field animal like a rabbit but larger. –**hare** *verb* to run rapidly. □ **hare-brained** *adjective* wild and foolish, rash.

Hare Krishna (**hah**-ree **krish**-nǎ) the title and mantra of a Hindu religious cult founded in the USA in 1966.

harelip *noun* a deformed lip (usually the upper lip) with a vertical slit in it like that of a hare.

Usage *Harelip* is often regarded as offensive, and *cleft lip* is the preferred term.

harem (hah-**reem** *or* **hair**-rěm) *noun* **1** the women of a Muslim household, living in a separate part of the house. **2** their apartments. [from Arabic *harim* = forbidden]

haricot bean (**ha**-rǐ-koh) *noun* a variety of French bean with white seeds; the dried seed of this bean.

hark *verb* listen. □ **hark back** to return to an earlier subject.

harlequin *adjective* in varied colours. [named after Harlequin, a former pantomime character usually dressed in a diamond-patterned costume]

harlot *noun* (*old use*) a prostitute. **harlotry** *noun*

harm *noun* damage, injury. –**harm** *verb* to cause harm to.

harmattan (har-mǎ-**tan**) *noun* a dry dusty wind that blows on the coast of West Africa from December to February.

harmful *adjective* causing harm. **harmfully** *adverb*

harmless *adjective* **1** unlikely to cause harm. **2** inoffensive. **harmlessly** *adverb*, **harmlessness** *noun*

harmonic *adjective* **1** of harmony in music. **2** (of tones) produced by vibration of a string etc. in any of certain fractions (half, third, quarter, fifth, etc.) of its length. **3** harmonious. –**harmonic** *noun* a harmonic tone or overtone. □ **harmonic minor scale** *see* **minor**. **harmonic progression** a series of quantities such as $\frac{1}{3}$, $\frac{1}{5}$, $\frac{1}{7}$, $\frac{1}{9}$.

harmonica *noun* a mouth organ.

harmonious *adjective* **1** forming a pleasing or consistent whole. **2** free from disagreement or ill feeling. **3** sweet-sounding, tuneful. **harmoniously** *adverb*

harmonise *verb* (*also* -**ize**) **1** to make or be harmonious. **2** to produce an agreeable artistic effect. **3** to add notes to (a melody) to form chords. **harmonisation** *noun*

harmonium *noun* a musical instrument with a keyboard, in which notes are produced by air pumped through brass reeds.

harmony *noun* **1** the state of being harmonious. **2** the combination of musical notes to produce chords. **3** a sweet or melodious sound.

harness *noun* **1** the straps and fittings by which a horse is controlled and fastened to the cart etc. that it pulls. **2** fastenings resembling this (e.g. for attaching a parachute to its wearer). –**harness** *verb* **1** to put a harness on (a horse); to attach by a harness. **2** to control and use (a river or other natural force) to produce electrical power etc.

Harold the name of two kings of England: Harold I (reigned 1035–40), Harold II (reigned 1066).

harp *noun* a musical instrument consisting of strings stretched on a roughly triangular frame, played by plucking with the fingers. –**harp** *verb* **harp on** to talk repeatedly and tiresomely about (a subject). **harpist** *noun*

harpoon *noun* a spearlike missile with a rope attached, for catching whales etc. –**harpoon** *verb* to spear with a harpoon.

harpsichord (**harp**-sǐ-kord) *noun* a keyboard instrument with the strings sounded by a

mechanism that plucks them. **harpsichordist**
noun [from *harp*, + Latin *chorda* = string]

harpy *noun* a grasping unscrupulous person.
[named after the Harpies, creatures in Greek
mythology with a woman's head and body and
a bird's wings and claws]

harridan (ha-rĭ-dăn) *noun* a bad-tempered
old woman.

harrier *noun* **1** a hound used for hunting hares.
2 a kind of falcon.

harrow *noun* a heavy frame with metal spikes
or discs for breaking up clods, covering seed,
etc. –**harrow** *verb* **1** to draw a harrow over
(land). **2** to distress greatly.

harry *verb* (**harried**, **harrying**) to harass.

harsh *adjective* **1** rough and disagreeable,
especially to the senses. **2** severe, cruel, *harsh
treatment*. **harshly** *adverb*, **harshness** *noun*

hart *noun* an adult male deer.

Hartog, Dirck (dates unknown), Dutch
mariner, the first European known to have
landed on the western coast of Australia
(in 1616).

harum-scarum *adjective* (*informal*) wild
and reckless.

Harvard the oldest American university,
founded in 1636 at Cambridge, Massachusetts.

harvest *verb* **1** the gathering of a crop
or crops; the season when this is done.
2 the season's yield of any natural product.
3 the product of any action. –**harvest** *verb*
to gather a crop, to reap. □ **harvest festival** a
festival of thanksgiving for the harvest, held
in church.

harvester *noun* **1** a reaper. **2** a reaping
machine.

Harvey, William (1578–1657), English
physician who discovered that blood circulates
in the veins and is not (as contemporary theory
held) absorbed as food.

has *see* **have**. □ **has-been** *noun* (*plural* **has-
beens**) (*informal*) a person or thing that is no
longer as famous or successful as formerly.

hash[1] *noun* **1** a dish of cooked or preserved
meat cut into small pieces and recooked.
2 a jumble, a mixture. –**hash** *verb* to
make (meat) into a hash. □ **make a hash of**
(*informal*) to make a mess of, to bungle. **settle
a person's hash** (*informal*) to deal with and
subdue him or her.

hash[2] *noun* (*informal*) hashish.

hashish *noun* the top leaves and tender parts
of hemp, dried for chewing or smoking as a
narcotic.

hasid *noun* (*plural* **hasidim**) a member of
a devout mystical Jewish sect. [Hebrew,
= pious]

hasn't (*informal*) = has not.

hasp *noun* a hinged metal strip with a slit in it
that fits over a U-shaped staple through which
a pin or padlock is then passed.

hassium (ha-see-ŭm) *noun* a very unstable
artificial element (symbol Hs). See also
hahnium.

hassle *noun* (*informal*) **1** a trouble or problem.
2 a quarrel or struggle. –**hassle** *verb* (*informal*)
to harass, to annoy.

hassock *noun* a thick firm cushion for
kneeling on in church.

hast (*old use*) the present tense of **have**, used
with *thou*.

haste *noun* urgency of movement or action,
hurry. □ **in haste** quickly, hurriedly. **make
haste** to act quickly.

hasten *verb* **1** to hurry. **2** to cause (a thing) to
be done earlier or to happen earlier.

Hastings a town on the SE coast of England,
scene of William the Conqueror's victory over
the Anglo-Saxon king Harold II in 1066.

hasty *adjective* (**hastier**, **hastiest**) **1** too
hurried. **2** said or made or done too quickly.
hastily *adverb*, **hastiness** *noun*

hat *noun* **1** a covering for the head, worn
especially outdoors. **2** this thought of as
symbolising a person's official position; *wear
two hats*, to have two official positions.
□ **hat trick** the taking of three wickets in
cricket by three successive balls from the same
bowler; the scoring of three goals or winning
of three victories by one person. **keep it under
your hat** keep it secret. **pass the hat round** to
collect contributions of money.

hatch[1] *noun* **1** an opening in a door or
floor or ceiling; an opening in a ship's
deck. **2** a movable cover over any of these.
3 an opening in a wall between two rooms.

hatch[2] *verb* **1** (of a young bird or fish etc.) to
emerge from an egg; (of an egg) to produce
a young animal. **2** to cause (eggs) to produce
young by incubating them. **3** to devise (a plot).
–**hatch** *noun* hatching; a brood hatched.

hatch[3] *verb* to mark with close parallel lines.
hatching *noun* these marks.

hatchback *noun* a car with a sloping back hinged at the top so that it can be opened; the back itself.

hatchery *noun* a place for hatching eggs, especially of fish, *a trout hatchery*.

hatchet *noun* a light short-handled axe. □ hatchet man (*informal*) a person hired to do unpleasant work, e.g. to dismiss workers, or to attack people.

hatchway *noun* a cover on a hatch in a ship's deck.

hate *noun* 1 hatred. 2 (*informal*) a hated person or thing. –hate *verb* 1 to feel hatred towards. 2 to dislike greatly. 3 (*informal*) to be reluctant, *I hate to interrupt you, but it's time to go.* hater *noun*

hateful *adjective* arousing hatred.

hath (*old use*) has.

hatless *adjective* not wearing a hat.

hatred *noun* violent dislike or enmity.

hatter *noun* a maker or seller of hats.

haughty (**haw**-tee) *adjective* (haughtier, haughtiest) proud of oneself and looking down on others. haughtily *adverb*, haughtiness *noun*

haul *verb* 1 to pull or drag forcibly. 2 to transport by a truck etc., to cart. 3 to turn a ship's course. –haul *noun* 1 hauling. 2 the amount gained as a result of effort, booty, *made a good haul*. 3 a distance to be traversed, *it's only a short haul from here*.

haulage *noun* transport of goods; the charge for this.

haulier (**hawl**-ee-er) *noun* a person or firm whose trade is transporting goods by road.

haunch *noun* 1 the fleshy part of the buttock and thigh. 2 the leg and loin of deer etc. as food.

haunt *verb* 1 (of ghosts) to be frequently in (a place) with manifestations of their presence and influence. 2 to be persistently in (a place). 3 to linger in the mind of, *the memory haunts me*. –haunt *noun* a place often visited by the person(s) named, *the café is a favourite haunt of students*.

haunted *adjective* frequented by a ghost or ghosts.

Hausa (**how**-să) *noun* (*plural* Hausa *or* Hausas) 1 a member of a people of the Sudan and northern Nigeria. 2 their language, which is widely used in West Africa.

haute couture (oht koo-**tewr**) *noun* high-class fashion, products of the leading fashion houses. [French]

haute cuisine (oht kwee-**zeen**) *noun* high-class cookery. [French]

Havana (hă-**van**-ă) the capital of Cuba.

have *verb* (had, having) 1 to be in possession of (a thing or quality); to possess in a certain relationship, *he has many enemies*. 2 to contain, *the house has six rooms*. 3 to experience, to undergo, *had a shock*. 4 to give birth to. 5 to put into a certain condition, *you had me worried*; *you have me there*, have me defeated or at a disadvantage. 6 (*informal*) to cheat or deceive, *we've been had*. 7 to engage in, to carry on, *had a talk with him*; *had breakfast*, ate it. 8 to allow, to tolerate, *won't have him bullied*. 9 to be under the obligation of, *we have to go now*. 10 to receive, to accept, *we had news of her*; *will you have a banana?* 11 to cause a thing to be done, *have one's hair cut*; *have three copies made*. –have *auxiliary verb*, used to form past tenses of verbs, *he has gone*; *we had expected it*. □ had better would find it wiser. have had it (*informal*) to have missed one's chance; to be near death, exhausted, no longer usable, etc. have it in for (*informal*) to show ill will towards (a person). have it out to settle a problem by frank discussion. have on (*informal*) to hoax. haves and have-nots people with and without wealth or privilege. have up to bring (a person) before a court of justice or an interviewer.

haven *noun* a refuge.

haven't (*informal*) = have not.

haver (**hay**-ver) *verb* to hesitate.

haversack *noun* a strong bag carried on the back or over the shoulder.

havoc (**hav**-ŏk) *noun* widespread destruction, great disorder. □ play havoc with to create havoc in.

Hawaii (hă-**wy**-ee) a State of the USA consisting of a group of islands in the Pacific. Hawaiian (hă-**wy**-ăn) *adjective* & *noun*

hawk[1] *noun* 1 a bird of prey with rounded wings shorter than a falcon's. 2 a person who favours an aggressive policy.

hawk[2] *verb* to clear the throat of phlegm noisily.

hawk[3] *verb* to carry (goods) about for sale.

hawker *noun* a person who hawks goods for a living.

Hawking, Stephen William (born 1942), British theoretical physicist who postulated the existence of black holes and multiple universes.

hawser (**haw**-zer) *noun* a heavy rope or cable for mooring or towing a ship.

hawthorn *noun* a thorny tree or shrub with small red berries.

hay *noun* grass mown and dried for fodder. □ **hay fever** catarrh caused by pollen or dust. **make hay while the sun shines** to seize opportunities for profit.

Haydn (**hy**-děn), Franz Joseph (1732–1809), Austrian-born composer.

haymaking *noun* mowing grass and spreading it to dry. **haymaker** *noun*

hayrick *noun* a haystack.

haystack *noun* a pile of hay firmly packed for storing, with a pointed or ridged top.

haywire *adjective* (*informal*) badly disorganised, out of control.

hazard (**haz**-ărd) *noun* 1 risk, danger, a source of this. 2 an obstacle (e.g. a bunker) on a golf course. – **hazard** *verb* to risk; *hazard a guess*, venture to make one.

hazardous *adjective* risky. **hazardously** *adverb*

haze *noun* 1 thin mist. 2 mental confusion or obscurity.

hazel *noun* 1 a bush with small edible nuts. 2 a light brownish colour.

hazelnut *noun* the fruit of the hazel.

hazy *adjective* (**hazier**, **haziest**) 1 misty. 2 vague, indistinct. 3 feeling confused or uncertain. **hazily** *adverb*, **haziness** *noun*

HB *abbreviation* (of a pencil lead) hard black.

H-bomb *noun* a hydrogen bomb.

HCF *abbreviation* highest common factor.

he *pronoun* 1 the male person or animal mentioned. 2 a person (male or female), *he who hesitates is lost.* – **he** *noun* a male animal; *a he-goat*, a male goat. □ **he-man** *noun* a well-built, muscular man.

head *noun* 1 the part of the body containing the eyes, nose, mouth, and brain. 2 the intellect, the imagination, the mind, *use your head.* 3 a mental ability or faculty, *has a good head for figures* or *heights.* 4 an image or picture of a person's head; the side of a coin on which the ruler's head appears; *heads* this side turned upwards after being tossed. 5 a person, an individual person or animal, *crowned heads*; *it costs $10 per head.* 6 a number of animals, *20 head of cattle.* 7 a thing like a head in form or position, e.g. the rounded end of a pin, the cutting or striking part of a tool etc., a rounded mass of leaves or petals etc. at the top of a stem, the flat surface of a drum or cask. 8 the top or upper end or front of something. 9 a body of water kept at a height (e.g. to work a watermill); a confined body of steam for exerting pressure. 10 (in place names) a promontory, *North Head.* 11 the chief person of a group or organisation etc.; a headmaster or headmistress. – **head** *verb* 1 to be at the head or top of. 2 to strike (a ball) with one's head in soccer. 3 to move in a certain direction, *we headed south*; *heading for disaster.* 4 to force to turn back or aside by getting in front of, *head him off.*
□ **come to a head** (of matters) to reach a crisis. **give a person his** or **her head** let a person move or act freely. **go to one's head** (of alcohol) to make one dizzy or slightly drunk; (of success) to make one conceited. **head-on** *adjective* & *adverb* with the head pointed directly towards something; colliding head to head. **head over heels** turning one's body upside-down in a circular movement; very much, *he is head over heels in love with her.* **in one's head** in one's mind, not written down. **keep one's head** to remain calm in a crisis. **lose one's head** to act foolishly. **make head or tail of** to be able to understand. **off one's head** crazy. **off the top of one's head** (*informal*) without careful consideration or investigation; impromptu. **over one's head** beyond one's understanding; (of another's promotion etc.) when one has a prior or stronger claim. **pull one's head in** (*Austral. informal*) to desist; to behave sensibly. **put heads together** to pool ideas. **turn a person's head** to make him or her vain.

headache *noun* 1 a continuous pain in the head. 2 (*informal*) a worrying problem.

headbanging *noun* (*informal*) violent shaking of the head to the rhythm of rock music. **headbanger** *noun*

headboard *noun* an upright panel along the head of a bed.

headdress *noun* an ornamental covering or band worn on the head.

header *noun* 1 a dive or plunge with head first. 2 a shot or pass made with the head in soccer. 3 a line or block of text at the top of each page of a document.

headgear *noun* a hat or headdress.

headhunting *noun* **1** (among certain peoples) the collecting of the heads of dead enemies as trophies. **2** the practice of approaching a specific person (usually employed elsewhere) to fill a particular position in an organisation. **headhunt** *verb*, **headhunter** *noun*

heading *noun* **1** a word or words put at the top of a section of printed or written matter as a title etc. **2** a horizontal passage in a mine.

headlamp *noun* a headlight.

headland *noun* a promontory.

headless *noun* having no head.

headlight *noun* **1** a powerful light mounted on the front of a motor vehicle or railway engine. **2** the beam from this.

headline *noun* a heading in a newspaper, especially the largest one at the top of the front page; *the news headlines*, a brief broadcast summary of news.

headlong *adverb* & *adjective* **1** falling or plunging with the head first. **2** in a hasty and rash way.

headman *noun* (*plural* **headmen**) the chief man of the tribe etc.

headmaster, **headmistress** *nouns* the principal teacher in a school, responsible for organising it.

headphones *plural noun* a pair of earphones fitting over the head, for listening to audio equipment etc.

headquarters *noun* or *plural noun* the place from which a military or other organisation is controlled.

headroom *noun* clearance above the head of a person or the top of a vehicle etc.

headscarf *noun* a scarf worn round the head.

headstone *noun* a stone set up at the head of a grave.

headstrong *adjective* self-willed and obstinate.

headward *adjective* & *adverb* towards the head. □ **headward erosion** the action of a stream that extends its valley upstream from its original source by erosion.

headwater *noun* (also **headwaters** *plural noun*) the stream(s) forming the sources of a river.

headway *noun* progress.

headwind *noun* a wind blowing from directly in front.

headword *noun* a word forming a heading, especially to an entry in a dictionary.

heady *adjective* **1** (of drinks) likely to intoxicate people. **2** (of success etc.) likely to cause conceit. **headily** *adverb*, **headiness** *noun*

heal *verb* **1** (of sore or wounded parts) to form healthy flesh again, to unite after being cut or broken. **2** to cause to do this. **3** to cure, *healing the sick*. **healer** *noun*

health *noun* **1** the state of being well and free from illness, *was restored to health*. **2** the condition of the body, *ill health*. □ **health centre** the headquarters of a group of local medical services. **health farm** an establishment where improved health is sought by dieting etc. **health foods** foods thought to have health-giving qualities; natural unprocessed foods.

healthful *adjective* producing good health, beneficial. **healthfully** *adverb*

healthy *adjective* (**healthier**, **healthiest**) **1** having or showing or producing good health. **2** beneficial. **3** (of things) functioning well. **healthily** *adverb*, **healthiness** *noun*

heap *noun* a number of things lying on one another; a mass of material so shaped. **–heap** *verb* **1** to pile or become piled in a heap. **2** to load with large quantities, to give large quantities of. **heaps** *plural noun* (*informal*) a great amount, plenty, *heaps of time*; *heaps better*.

hear *verb* (**heard**, **hearing**) **1** to perceive (sounds) with the ear. **2** to listen or pay attention to. **3** to listen to and try (a case) in a lawcourt. **4** to receive information or a message or letter etc. □ **have heard of** to be aware of the existence of; to have knowledge about. **hear! hear!** I agree. **not hear of** to refuse to allow, *won't hear of my paying for it*.

heard *see* **hear**.

hearer *noun* one who hears something, especially as a member of an audience.

hearing *noun* **1** the ability to hear; *within hearing distance*, near enough to be heard; *in my hearing*, in my presence, where I can hear. **2** an opportunity of being heard; trial of a case in a lawcourt (especially before a judge without a jury). □ **hearing aid** a small device that amplifies sound, worn by a partially deaf person.

hearsay *noun* things heard in rumours or gossip.

hearse (*pr.* herss) *noun* a vehicle for carrying the coffin at a funeral.

heart *noun* **1** the hollow muscular organ that keeps blood circulating in the body by contracting rhythmically. **2** the part of the body where this is, the bosom. **3** the centre of a person's emotions or affections or inmost thoughts, *knew it in her heart*. **4** the ability to feel emotion, *a tender heart*. **5** courage, *take heart*. **6** enthusiasm, *his heart isn't in it*. **7** a beloved person, *dear heart*. **8** the innermost part of a thing; the close compact head of a lettuce etc.; *the heart of the matter*, the vital part of it. **9** a symmetrical figure conventionally representing a heart. **10** a red figure shaped like this on playing cards; a playing card of the suit (hearts) marked with these. □ **after one's own heart** exactly to one's liking. **at heart** basically. **break a person's heart** *see* break. **by heart** memorised thoroughly. **change of heart** a change of feeling towards something. **have a heart!** (*informal*) be considerate or sympathetic. **have the heart to** to be hard-hearted enough to (do something). **heart attack** or **heart failure** sudden failure of the heart to function normally. **heart-rending** *adjective* very distressing. **heart-searching** *noun* examination by oneself of one's own feelings and motives. **heart-throb** *noun* (*informal*) a person with whom someone is infatuated. **heart-to-heart** *adjective* frank and personal, *a heart-to-heart talk*. **heart-warming** *adjective* causing people to rejoice. **have one's heart in the right place** to have kindly intentions. **have one's heart in one's mouth** to be violently alarmed. **to one's heart's content** as much as one wishes. **with all one's heart** sincerely, with the greatest goodwill.

heartache *noun* mental pain, deep sorrow.

heartbeat *noun* the pulsation of the heart.

heartbreak *noun* overwhelming unhappiness. **heartbreaking, heartbroken** *adjectives*

heartburn *noun* a burning sensation in the lower part of the chest resulting from indigestion.

hearten *verb* to make (a person) feel encouraged.

heartfelt *adjective* felt deeply or earnestly.

hearth (*pr.* harth) *noun* **1** the floor of a fireplace, the area in front of this. **2** the fireside as the symbol of domestic comfort, *hearth and home*. **3** the bottom part of a blast furnace; a fire for heating metal for forging etc.

heartily *adverb* **1** in a hearty way. **2** very, *heartily sick of it*.

heartland *noun* the central or most important part of an area etc.

heartless *adjective* not feeling pity or sympathy. **heartlessly** *adverb*, **heartlessness** *noun*

heartstrings *plural noun* one's deepest feelings of love or pity.

heartwood *noun* the dense inner part of a tree trunk, yielding the hardest timber.

hearty *adjective* (**heartier, heartiest**) **1** showing warmth of feeling, enthusiastic. **2** vigorous, strong, *hale and hearty*. **3** (of meals or appetites) large. –**hearty** *noun* a hearty person. **heartiness** *noun*

heat *noun* **1** a form of energy produced by the movement of molecules. **2** the sensation produced by this, hotness. **3** hot weather. **4** a condition of sexual excitement and readiness for mating in female animals, *be on heat*. **5** an intense feeling (especially of anger), tension; the most vigorous stage of a discussion; *take the heat out of a situation*, to reduce the anger or tension. **6** a preliminary or trial round in a race or contest. –**heat** *verb* to make or become hot or warm. □ **heat-seeking** *adjective* guided to its target by infrared radiation.

heated *adjective* (of a person or discussion) angry. **heatedly** *adverb*

heater *noun* a stove or other device supplying heat.

heath *noun* **1** (especially *Brit.*) an area of flat uncultivated land with low shrubs. **2** a small shrubby plant of the heather kind. **3** a small Australian shrub with white, pink, or red flowers.

heathen (**hee**-*thĕn*) *noun* a person who does not belong to a widely-held religion; a pagan. –**heathen** *adjective* of heathens. –**the heathen** heathen people.

heather *noun* an evergreen plant or shrub with small usually purple bell-shaped flowers, growing especially on moors and heaths.

Heath Robinson *noun* absurdly ingenious and impracticable in design or construction. [named after W. Heath Robinson, an English cartoonist (died 1944)]

heatwave *noun* a period of very hot weather.

heave *verb* (**heaved** (in sense 6 **hove**), **heaving**) **1** to lift or haul (something heavy) with great effort. **2** to utter with effort, *heaved a sigh*. **3** (*informal*) to throw, *heave a brick at him*. **4** to rise and fall regularly like waves at sea. **5** to pant; to retch. **6** (in nautical use) to come; *heave in sight*, come into view. **–heave** *noun* **1** the act of heaving. **2** a sideways shift of strata at a fault in the earth's crust.

heaven *noun* **1** the abode of God and of the righteous after death. **2 Heaven** God, Providence. **3** a place or state of supreme bliss; something delightful. **heavens** *interjection* an exclamation of surprise. **–the heavens** the sky as seen from the earth, in which the sun, moon, and stars appear. ☐ **heaven-sent** *adjective* providential, fortunate.

heavenly *adjective* **1** of heaven, divine. **2** of the heavens or sky; *heavenly bodies*, the sun and stars etc. **3** (*informal*) very pleasing.

Heaviside (**hev**-ee-syd), Oliver (1850–1925), English physicist noted for his discovery of the **Heaviside layer**, a layer of the ionosphere able to reflect long radio waves from one part of the earth to another.

heavy *adjective* (**heavier**, **heaviest**) **1** having great weight, difficult to lift, carry, or move. **2** of more than average weight, amount, or force, *heavy artillery*; *heavy rain*. **3** (of work) needing much physical effort. **4** severe, intense; *a heavy sleeper*, not easily woken. **5** dense, *a heavy mist*; *heavy bread*, doughy from not having risen. **6** (of ground) clinging, difficult to work or traverse. **7** (of food) stodgy and difficult to digest. **8** (of the sky) gloomy and full of clouds. **9** clumsy or ungraceful in appearance, effect, or movement. **10** unhappy, *with a heavy heart*. **11** dull and tedious; serious in tone; important, grave. **12** stern, severe. **–heavy** *noun* (*informal*) **1** a large violent person, a thug; a bodyguard. **2** an important or influential person in a school or business etc. **–heavy** *verb* (*informal*) to put pressure on (a person). ☐ **heavy-duty** *adjective* intended to withstand hard use. **heavy-handed** *adjective* clumsy; overbearing, oppressive; excessively liberal (with ingredients). **heavy industry** industry producing metal, machines, etc. **heavy metal** a type of loud rock music with a heavy beat. **heavy water** deuterium oxide, a substance with the same chemical properties as water but greater density. **make heavy weather of** to find (a thing) more difficult than it really is. **heavily** *adverb*, **heaviness** *noun*

heavyweight *noun* **1** a person of more than average weight. **2** the heaviest boxing weight, in amateur boxing over 81 kg. **3** a person

of great influence. **–heavyweight** *adjective* having great weight or influence.

Hebe (**hee**-bee) (*Gk. myth.*) the gods' cupbearer, daughter of Zeus and Hera.

Hebrew *noun* **1** a member of a Semitic people in ancient Palestine; an Israelite; a Jew. **2** their language; a modern form of this used in Israel. **–Hebrew** *adjective* **1** of the Hebrews. **2** of Hebrew. **Hebrews** the *Epistle to the Hebrews*, a book of the New Testament.

Hebrides (**heb**-rĭ-deez) two groups of islands off the north-west coast of Scotland. **Hebridean** (heb-rĭ-**dee**-ăn) *adjective* & *noun*

Hecate (**hek**-ă-tee) (*Gk. myth.*) a goddess associated with uncanny things, the ghost world, and witchcraft.

heck *noun* (*informal*, in oaths) hell.

heckle *verb* to interrupt and harass (a public speaker) with aggressive questions and abuse. **heckler** *noun*

HECS *abbreviation* Higher Education Contribution Scheme.

hectare (**hek**-tair) *noun* a unit of area, 10,000 sq. metres (100 ares or 2.471 acres). [from *hecto-*, + French *are*]

hectic *adjective* with feverish activity, *a hectic day*. **hectically** *adverb*

hecto- *prefix* one hundred (as in *hectogram* = 100 grams). [from Greek *hekaton* = a hundred]

Hector (*Gk. legend*) a Trojan prince, killed by Achilles at the siege of Troy.

hector *verb* to intimidate by bullying.

Hecuba (**hek**-yŭ-bă) (*Gk. legend*) wife of Priam king of Troy.

he'd (*informal*) = he had, he would.

hedge *noun* **1** a fence of closely-planted bushes or shrubs. **2** a means of protecting oneself against possible loss, *bought diamonds as a hedge against inflation*. **–hedge** *verb* **1** to surround or bound with a hedge. **2** to reduce the possible loss on (a bet etc.) by another speculation. **3** to avoid giving a direct answer or commitment. **hedger** *noun*

hedgehog *noun* a small insect-eating animal with a piglike snout and a back covered in stiff spines, able to roll itself up into a ball when attacked.

hedgerow *noun* a row of bushes etc. forming a hedge.

hedonist (**hee**-dŏ-nĭst *or* **hed**-) *noun* one who believes that pleasure is the chief good in life.

hedonism *noun*, **hedonistic** *adjective* [from Greek *hedone* = pleasure]

heebie-jeebies *plural noun* (*informal*) nervous anxiety or depression.

heed *verb* to pay attention to. **–heed** *noun* careful attention, *take heed*.

heedless *adjective* not taking heed. **heedlessly** *adverb*, **heedlessness** *noun*

hee-haw *noun* a donkey's bray.

heel[1] *noun* **1** the rounded back part of the human foot. **2** the part of a stocking etc. covering this. **3** a built-up part of a boot or shoe that supports a person's heel. **4** something like a heel in shape or position. **5** (*informal*) a dishonourable person. **–heel** *verb* **1** to repair the heels of (shoes etc.). **2** to pass the ball with the heel in rugby. ☐ **at** or **to heel** close behind; under control. **at** or **on the heels of** following closely after. **down at heel** (of a shoe) with the heel worn down by wear; (of a person) shabby. **take to one's heels** to run away. **well-heeled** *adjective* rich.

heel[2] *verb* to tilt (a ship) or become tilted to one side, *heeled over*.

heelball *noun* a mixture of hard wax and lampblack used by shoemakers for polishing; any similar mixture used in brass rubbing.

hefty *adjective* **1** (of a person) big and strong. **2** (of a thing) large and heavy, powerful; *a hefty sum*, a large sum. **heftily** *adverb*, **heftiness** *noun*

Hegel (**hay**-gĕl), Georg Wilhelm Friedrich (1770–1831), German idealist philosopher. **Hegelian** (hĕ-**gay**-lee-ăn) *adjective*

hegemony (hĕ-**gem**-ŏ-nee) *noun* leadership, especially by one country.

Hegira (**hej**-ĭ-ră) *noun* the flight of Muhammad from Mecca (AD 622), from which the Muslim era is reckoned. [from Arabic *hijra* = departure from a country]

Heidelberg School (**hy**-dĕl-berg) a late 19th-century Australian school of impressionist painters, amongst whom were Arthur Streeton, Charles Conder, Tom Roberts, and Frederick McCubbin. [the name comes from a suburb of Melbourne which inspired many of their paintings]

heifer (**hef**-er) *noun* a young cow, especially one that has not given birth to a calf.

heigh (*pr.* hay) *interjection* an exclamation of surprise or curiosity. **–heigh-ho** *interjection* an exclamation of boredom or disappointment.

height (*pr.* hite) *noun* **1** measurement from base to top; the measurement of a person etc. from head to foot as he or she stands. **2** the distance (of an object or position) above ground level or sea level. **3** a high place or area. **4** the highest degree of something.

heighten *verb* to make or become higher or more intense.

heinous (**hay**-nŭs *or* **hee**-) *adjective* very wicked.

heir (*pr.* air) *noun* a person who inherits property or rank etc. from its former owner. ☐ **heir apparent** the legal heir whose claim cannot be set aside by the birth of a person with a stronger claim to inherit. **heir presumptive** one whose claim may be set aside in this way.

heiress (**air**-ress) *noun* a female heir, especially to great wealth.

heirloom (**air**-loom) *noun* a possession that has been handed down in a family for several generations.

held *see* **hold**[1].

Helen (*Gk. legend*) wife of Menelaus king of Sparta, whose abduction by Paris led to the Trojan War.

helical (**hel**-i-kăl) *adjective* like a helix.

helicopter (**hel**-ee-kop-ter) *noun* a kind of aircraft with horizontal revolving blades or rotors. [from *helix* + Greek *pteron* = wing]

heliotrope (**hee**-lee-ŏ-trohp) *noun* **1** a plant with small sweet-smelling purple flowers. **2** a light purple colour. [from Greek *helios* = sun, + *trope* = turning (the plant turns its flowers to the sun)]

helipad (**hel**-ee-pad) *noun* a pad or landing ground for a helicopter.

heliport (**hel**-ee-port) *noun* a place equipped for helicopters to take off and land.

helium (**hee**-lee-ŭm) *noun* a chemical element (symbol He), a light colourless gas that does not burn, used in airships. [from Greek *helios* = sun]

helix (**hee**-liks) *noun* (*plural* **helices**, *pr.* **hee**-lĭ-seez) a spiral, especially a three-dimensional one, either like a corkscrew or flat like a watch spring. [Greek, = coil]

hell *noun* **1** the place of punishment for the wicked after death, the abode of devils. **2** a place or state of supreme misery, something extremely unpleasant. ☐ **hell-bent** *adjective* recklessly determined. **hell for leather** at full speed.

he'll (*informal*) = he will.

Hellas (**hel**-as) the ancient and modern Greek name for Greece.

hellebore (**hel**-ĕ-bor) *noun* a poisonous plant with white or greenish flowers.

Hellene (**hel**-een) *noun* a Greek. [from *Hellas*]

Hellenistic *adjective* of the Greek language and culture of the 4th–1st centuries BC.

Hellespont (**hel**-ĕss-pont) the ancient name for the Dardanelles.

hellfire *noun* the fire(s) of hell.

hellish *adjective* very unpleasant.

hello *interjection* & *noun* an exclamation used in greeting or to call attention or express surprise, or to answer a call on the telephone etc.

helm *noun* the tiller or wheel by which a ship's rudder is controlled. □ **at the helm** at the head of an organisation etc., in control.

helmet *noun* a protective head covering worn by a policeman, fireman, diver, cyclist, etc.

helmsman *noun* (*plural* **helmsmen**) a person who steers a ship by means of its helm.

helot (**hel**-ŏt) *noun* a serf in ancient Sparta.

help *verb* **1** to do part of another person's work for him or her. **2** to make it easier for (a person) to do something or for (a thing) to happen. **3** to do something for the benefit of (someone in need). **4** to prevent, to remedy, *it can't be helped*; *I couldn't help myself*, I was unable to avoid taking a certain action. –**help** *noun* **1** the action of helping or being helped. **2** a person or thing that helps. **3** a person employed to help with housework. □ **help a person to food** to serve him or her with it at a meal. **help oneself to** to serve oneself with (food) at a meal; to take without seeking assistance or permission. **help out** to give help (especially in a crisis). **helper** *noun*

helpful *adjective* giving help, useful. **helpfully** *adverb*, **helpfulness** *noun*

helping *noun* a portion of food given to one person at a meal.

helpless *adjective* **1** unable to manage without help, dependent on others. **2** incapable of action, indicating this, *helpless with laughter*; *gave him a helpless glance*. **helplessly** *adverb*, **helplessness** *noun*

helpmate *noun* a helper, a companion or partner who helps.

Helsinki (hel-**sink**-ee) the capital of Finland.

helter-skelter *adverb* in disorderly haste. –**helter-skelter** *noun* a tall spiral slide round a tower at a fair or showground etc.

helve *noun* the handle of a tool or weapon.

hem[1] *noun* the border of cloth where the edge is turned under and sewn or fixed down. –**hem** *verb* (**hemmed**, **hemming**) to turn and sew a hem on. □ **hem in** to surround and restrict the movement of, *enemy forces hemmed them in*. **hemmer** *noun*

hem[2] *interjection* = ahem.

Hemingway, Ernest Miller (1899–1961), American novelist and writer of short stories, whose works include *For Whom the Bell Tolls* and *A Farewell to Arms*.

hemisphere *noun* **1** half a sphere. **2** either of the halves into which the earth is divided either by the equator (the *Northern* and *Southern hemisphere*) or by a line passing through the poles (the *Eastern hemisphere*, including Europe, Asia, and Africa; *the Western hemisphere*, the Americas). [from Greek *hemi-* = half, + *sphere*]

hemispherical (hem-ĭss-**fe**-rĭ-kăl) *adjective* shaped like a hemisphere.

hemline *noun* the lower edge of a skirt or dress.

hemlock *noun* **1** a poisonous plant with small white flowers. **2** the poison made from it.

hemp *noun* **1** a plant from which coarse fibres are obtained for the manufacture of rope and cloth. **2** a narcotic drug made from this plant. **hempen** *adjective*

hemstitch *verb* to decorate with a kind of drawn-thread-work.

hen *noun* a female bird, especially of the common domestic fowl.

hence *adverb* **1** (*old use*) from here. **2** from this time, *five years hence*. **3** for this reason.

henceforth *adverb* (also **henceforward**) from this time on, in future.

henchman *noun* (*plural* **henchmen**) a trusty supporter.

Hendra Virus *noun* a virus carried by fruit bats, and potentially fatal to animals and humans. [first described in Hendra, a suburb of Brisbane, in 1994.]

Hengist the leader, along with his brother Horsa, of the Jutes who came to Britain in 449 and later set up a kingdom in Kent.

henna *noun* **1** a reddish-brown dye used especially on the hair. **2** the tropical plant from which this is obtained.

henpecked *adjective* (of a husband) nagged by a domineering wife.

Henry the name of eight kings of England, who reigned as Henry I 1100–35, Henry II 1154–89, Henry III 1216–72, Henry IV 1399–1413, Henry V 1413–22, Henry VI 1422–61, 1470–1, Henry VII 1485–1509, Henry VIII 1509–47.

henry *noun* (*plural* **henries**) a unit of inductance. [named after the American physicist J. Henry (died 1878)]

hepatic (hĕ-**pat**-ik) *adjective* of the liver. [from Greek *hepatos* = of the liver]

hepatitis (hep-ă-**ty**-tĭss) *noun* inflammation of the liver.

hepato- *prefix* relating to the liver. [Greek]

Hephaestus (hĕ-**fy**-stŭs) (*Gk. myth.*) the god of fire (especially the smithy fire), called Vulcan by the Romans.

hepta- *prefix* seven. [from Greek *hepta* = seven]

heptagon (**hep**-tă-gŏn) *noun* a geometric figure with seven sides. **heptagonal** (hep-**tag**-ŏ-năl) *adjective* seven-sided. [from *hepta-*, + Greek *gonia* = angle]

heptathlon (hep-**tath**-lon) *noun* an athletic contest in which each competitor takes part in the seven events it includes.

her *pronoun* **1** the objective case of *she*, *we saw her*. **2** (*informal*) = she, *it's her all right*. **–her** *adjective* **1** of or belonging to her, *her book*. **2** used in women's titles, *Her Majesty*.

Hera (**heer**-ră) (*Gk. myth.*) a goddess, sister and wife of Zeus and queen of the Olympian gods, identified by the Romans with Juno.

Heracles (**he**-ră-kleez) the Greek form of the name Hercules.

herald *noun* **1** an official in former times who made announcements and carried messages from a ruler. **2** a person or thing indicating the approach of something. **3** an official who records people's pedigrees and grants coats of arms. **–herald** *verb* to proclaim the approach of.

heraldic (hĕ-**ral**-dik) *adjective* of heralds or heraldry.

heraldry *noun* the study of coats of arms and the right to bear them.

herb *noun* a soft-stemmed plant that dies down to the ground after flowering; one with leaves or seeds etc. that are used as food or in medicine or for flavouring. **herby** *adjective* [from Latin *herba* = grass]

herbaceous (her-**bay**-shŭs) *adjective* of or like herbs. □ **herbaceous border** a garden border containing perennial flowering plants.

herbage *noun* grass and other field plants.

herbal *adjective* of herbs used in medicine or for flavouring. **–herbal** *noun* a book with descriptions of these.

herbalist *noun* a dealer in medicinal herbs.

herbicide *noun* a substance that is poisonous to plants, used to destroy unwanted vegetation. [from Latin *herba* = grass, + *caedere* = kill]

herbivore (**her**-bĭ-vor) *noun* a herbivorous animal.

herbivorous (her-**biv**-ŏ-rŭs) *adjective* feeding on plants. [from Latin *herba* = grass, + *vorare* = devour]

herculean (her-kew-**lee**-ăn) *adjective* **1** as strong as Hercules. **2** needing great strength or effort, *a herculean task*.

Hercules (**her**-kew-leez) (*Gk. myth.*) a hero, noted for his prodigious strength and courage. □ **Pillars of Hercules** the name given in ancient times to the two mountains at the eastern end of the Strait of Gibraltar.

herd *noun* **1** a number of cattle or other animals feeding or staying together. **2** a mob. **–herd** *verb* **1** to gather, stay, or drive as a group. **2** to tend (a herd of animals). □ **herd instinct** the instinct to think and behave like the majority of people.

herdsman *noun* (*plural* **herdsmen**) a person who tends a herd of animals.

here *adverb* **1** in or at or to this place. **2** at this point in a process or a series of events. **–here** *interjection* an exclamation calling attention to something or making a protest, or used as a reply (= I am here) in answer to a roll-call. □ **here and there** in or to various places. **here goes** I am about to begin. **here's to** I drink to the health of.

hereabouts *adverb* (also **hereabout**) somewhere near here.

hereafter *adverb* in future, from now on. **–hereafter** *noun* **the hereafter** the future, life after death.

hereby *adverb* by this means, by this act or decree etc.

hereditary (hĕ-**red**-ĭ-tă-ree) *adjective*
1 inherited, able to be passed or received from one generation to another. 2 holding a position by inheritance, *hereditary ruler*.

heredity (hĕ-**red**-ĭ-tee) *noun* inheritance of physical or mental characteristics from parents or ancestors. [from Latin *heredis* = of an heir]

Hereford *noun* a breed of red and white beef cattle; an animal of this breed.

herein *adverb* (*formal*) in this place, document, etc.

hereinafter *adverb* (*formal*) in a later part of this document etc.

hereof *adverb* (old use) of this.

heresy (**he**-rĕ-see) *noun* 1 an opinion that is contrary to the accepted beliefs of the Christian Church, or to those on any subject. 2 the holding of such an opinion.

heretic (**he**-rĕ-tik) *noun* a person who holds a heresy or is guilty of heresy. **heretical** (hĕ-**ret**-ĭ-kăl) *adjective*

herewith *adverb* with this, *enclosed herewith*.

heritable *adjective* able to be inherited.

heritage *noun* that which has been or may be inherited; circumstances or benefits passed down from previous generations.

hermaphrodite (her-**maf**-rŏ-dyt) *noun* a creature that has both male and female sexual organs in one individual. **hermaphroditic** (her-maf-rŏ-**dit**-ik) *adjective* [from *Hermes* + *Aphrodite*]

Hermes (**her**-meez) (*Gk. myth.*) the messenger of the gods, identified by the Romans with Mercury.

hermetic *adjective* with an airtight closure, *hermetic sealing*. **hermetically** *adverb*

hermit *noun* a person (especially a man in early Christian times) who has withdrawn from human society and lives in solitude. □ **hermit crab** a crab that uses a cast-off shell to protect its soft hinder parts. [from Greek *eremites* = of the desert]

Hermitage, **the** an art museum in St Petersburg, containing the collection begun by Catherine the Great.

hermitage *noun* 1 a hermit's dwelling place. 2 a red wine grape variety, usually called *shiraz*; a wine made from this (¶ named after the Hermitage region of France).

hernia *noun* an abnormal condition in which a part or organ of the body protrudes through a wall of the cavity (especially the abdomen) that normally contains it, a rupture.

hero *noun* (*plural* **heroes**) 1 a person admired for brave or noble deeds. 2 the chief male character in a story, play, or poem. □ **hero worship** excessive devotion to an admired person. **hero-worshipper** *noun*

Herod the name of four rulers in ancient Palestine, including Herod the Great, in whose reign Christ was born.

Herodotus (hĕ-**rod**-ŏ-tŭs) 5th century BC, Greek historian, the 'Father of History'.

heroic *adjective* having the characteristics of a hero, very brave. **heroics** *plural noun* overdramatic talk or behaviour. **heroically** *adverb*

heroin *noun* a powerful sedative drug prepared from morphine, used medically and by addicts.

heroine *noun* a female hero.

heroism *noun* heroic conduct or qualities.

heron *noun* a long-legged long-necked wading bird living in marshy places.

heronry *noun* a place where herons breed.

herpes (**her**-peez) *noun* a virus disease causing blisters on the skin. [from Greek *herpes* = shingles]

herpetology (her-pĕ-**tol**-ŏ-jee) *noun* the scientific study of reptiles. **herpetologist** *noun*

Herr (*pr.* hair) *noun* (*plural* **Herren**) the title of a German man, = Mr.

herring *noun* a North Atlantic fish much used for food; a similar Australian fish.

herringbone *noun* a zigzag pattern or arrangement; *herringbone tweed*, tweed woven in this pattern.

hers *possessive pronoun* of or belonging to her, *it is hers*; the thing(s) belonging to her, *hers are best*.

herself *pronoun* 1 the emphatic form of *she* and *her*, e.g. *she herself had said it*; *told me herself*. 2 the reflexive form of *her*, e.g. *she dressed herself*. □ **be herself** to behave in a normal manner without constraint; *she is not herself today*, is not in her normal good health or spirits. **by herself** without companions; without help.

Hertz (*pr.* herts), Heinrich Rudolf (1857–94), German physicist, a pioneer of radio communication.

hertz *noun* (*plural* hertz) a unit of frequency of electromagnetic waves, = one cycle per second. [named after H. R. *Hertz*]

Herzegovina (hert-sĕ-**gov**-ĭ-nă *or* hert-sĕ-gŏ-**vee**-nă) (also **Hercegovina**) a region in the Balkans forming the southern part of the country of Bosnia-Herzegovina.

he's (*informal*) = he is, he has.

Hesiod (**hee**-see-ŏd) (c. 700 BC) one of the oldest known Greek poets.

hesitant *adjective* hesitating. hesitantly *adverb*, hesitancy *noun*

hesitate *verb* **1** to be slow to speak, act, or move because one feels uncertain or reluctant, to pause in doubt. **2** to be reluctant, to scruple, *he wouldn't hesitate to break the rules if it suited him*. hesitation *noun* [from Latin *haesitare* = get stuck]

Hesperides (hess-**pe**-rĭ-deez) (*Gk. myth.*) **1** the daughters of Hesperus, guardians of a tree of golden apples. **2** the garden containing this tree, in the Isles of the Blessed at the western extremity of the world.

hessian *noun* strong coarse cloth made of hemp or jute, sackcloth.

het *adjective* het up (*informal*) excited, overwrought.

hetero- *prefix* other, different. [from Greek *heteros* = other]

heterodox (**het**-ĕ-rŏ-doks) *adjective* not orthodox. heterodoxy *noun* [from *hetero-*, + Greek *doxa* = opinion]

heterogeneous (het-ĕ-rŏ-**jee**-nee-ŭs) *adjective* made up of people or things that are unlike each other. heterogeneity (het-ĕ-rŏ-jĕ-**nee**-ĭ-tee) *noun* [from *hetero-*, + Greek *genos* = a kind]

heterosexual *adjective* feeling sexually attracted to people of the opposite sex. –heterosexual *noun* a heterosexual person. heterosexuality *noun*

heterotrophic (het-ĕ-rŏ-**troh**-fik) *adjective* (of organisms) deriving nourishment and carbon from organic substances. [from *hetero-*, + Greek *trophos* = feeder]

heterozygous (het-ĕ-rŏ-**zy**-gŭs) *adjective* having two different alleles, being formed from gametes carrying different alleles. [from *hetero-*, + *zygote*]

heuristic (hew-**riss**-tik) *adjective* **1** serving or helping to find out or discover something. **2** proceeding by trial and error. [from Greek *heuriskein* = to find]

hew *verb* (hewed, hewn, hewing) to chop or cut with an axe or sword etc.; to cut into shape. hewer *noun*

hewn *adjective* made or shaped by hewing.

hex *noun* a magic spell, a curse.

hexa- *prefix* six. [from Greek *hex* = six]

hexadecimal (heks-ă-**dess**-ĭ-măl) *adjective* based on 16, reckoning by sixteens. [from *hexa-* + *decimal*]

hexagon (**heks**-ă-gŏn) *noun* a geometric figure with six sides. hexagonal (heks-**ag**-ŏ-năl) *adjective* six-sided. [from *hexa-*, + Greek *gonia* = angle]

hexagram *noun* a six-pointed star formed by two intersecting triangles. [from *hexa-* + *-gram*]

hexahedron (heks-ă-**hee**-drŏn) *noun* a solid body with six faces. [from *hexa-*, + Greek *hedra* = base]

hexameter (heks-**am**-ĕ-ter) *noun* a line of six metrical feet. [from *hexa-*, + Greek *metron* = measure]

hey *interjection* an exclamation calling attention or expressing surprise or enquiry.

heyday *noun* the time of greatest success or prosperity, *it was in its heyday*.

Hezbollah (hez-bŏ-**lah**) *noun* an extreme Shi'ite Muslim group, active especially in Lebanon. [from Arabic, = party of God]

HF *abbreviation* high frequency.

hi *interjection* an exclamation expressing greeting or calling attention.

hiatus (hy-**ay**-tŭs) *noun* (*plural* hiatuses) a break or gap in a sequence or series. [Latin, = gaping]

hibernate (**hy**-ber-nayt) *verb* (of certain animals) to spend the winter in a state like deep sleep. hibernation *noun* [from Latin *hibernus* = of winter]

Hibernian (hy-**ber**-nee-ăn) *adjective* of Ireland. [from Latin *Hibernia* = Ireland]

hibiscus (hy-**biss**-kŭs) *noun* a cultivated shrub or tree with brightly coloured flowers.

hiccup (also **hiccough**) *noun* a sudden stopping of the breath with a gulp-like sound; hiccups an attack of hiccuping. –hiccup *verb* (hiccuped, hiccuping) to make a hiccup.

hickory *noun* **1** a North American tree related to the walnut. **2** its hard wood.

hid, hidden *see* hide².

hidalgo (hid-**al**-goh) *noun* (*plural* **hidalgos**) a member of the lower nobility in Spain. [from Spanish *hijo dalgo* = son of something]

hide¹ *noun* **1** an animal's skin (raw or dressed) as an article of commerce and manufacture. **2** (*informal*) the human skin. **3** (*informal*) impertinence, cheek, *he had the hide to say that.*

hide² *verb* (**hid**, **hidden**, **hiding**) **1** to put or keep out of sight, to prevent from being seen. **2** to keep secret. **3** to conceal oneself. **–hide** *noun* a place of concealment used when observing or hunting wild animals, *built a hide.* ☐ **hide-and-seek** *noun* a children's game in which some players conceal themselves and others try to find them.

hidebound *adjective* narrow-minded, refusing to abandon old customs and prejudices.

hideous *adjective* very ugly, revolting to the senses or the mind. **hideously** *adverb*, **hideousness** *noun*

hideout *noun* (*informal*) a hiding place.

hidey-hole *noun* (*informal*) a hiding place.

hiding¹ *noun* (*informal*) a thrashing.

hiding² *noun* the state of being or remaining hidden, *went into hiding.* ☐ **hiding place** a place where a person or thing is or could be hidden.

hierarchy (**hy**-ĕ-rark-ee) *noun* a system with grades of status or authority ranking one above another in a series. **hierarchical** *adjective* of or arranged in a hierarchy. [from Greek *hieros* = sacred, + *arkhein* = to rule]

hieroglyph (**hy**-ĕ-rŏ-glif) *noun* **1** one of the pictures or symbols used in ancient Egypt and elsewhere to represent sounds, words, or ideas. **2** a written symbol with a secret or cryptic meaning.

hieroglyphic (hy-ĕ-rŏ-**glif**-ik) *adjective* of or written in hieroglyphs. **hieroglyphics** *plural noun* hieroglyphs. [from Greek *hieros* = sacred, + *gluphe* = carving]

hi-fi *adjective* (*informal*) of high fidelity. **–hi-fi** *noun* (*informal*) hi-fi equipment.

higgledy-piggledy *adjective* & *adverb* completely mixed up, in utter disorder.

high *adjective* **1** extending far upwards, extending above the normal or average level. **2** situated far above the ground or above sea level. **3** measuring a specified distance from base to top. **4** ranking above others in importance or quality, *high priest.* **5** extreme,

intense, greater than what is normal or average, *high temperatures*; *high prices*; *a high opinion*, very favourable. **6** (of time) fully reached, *high noon*; *it's high time we left.* **7** noble, virtuous, *high ideals.* **8** (of a sound or voice) having rapid vibrations, not deep or low. **9** (of meat) beginning to go bad; (of game) hung until slightly decomposed and ready to cook. **10** (*informal*) intoxicated; under the influence of drugs. **–high** *noun* **1** a high, or the highest, level or figure, *exports reached a new high.* **2** an area of high barometric pressure. **3** (*informal*) a euphoric state, often drug-induced. **4** a high school. **–high** *adverb* **1** in or at or to a high level or position. **2** in or to a high degree; *play high*, play for high stakes; *feelings ran high*, were strong. ☐ **high altar** the chief altar of a church. **high and dry** aground; stranded, isolated. **high and low** everywhere, *hunted high and low.* **high and mighty** arrogant. **high chair** an infant's chair for use at meals. **High Church** that section of the Anglican Church that gives an important place to ritual and to the authority of bishops and priests. **high-class** *adjective* of high quality or social class. **high colour** a flushed complexion. **High Commission** an embassy from one Commonwealth country to another. **High Commissioner** the head of this. **High Court** (in full **High Court of Australia**) the supreme Federal Court in which constitutional questions are decided and which is the final court of appeal from State and Federal courts. **high explosive** explosive with a violently shattering effect. **high fidelity** reproduction of sound with little or no distortion. **high finance** dealing with large sums of money. **high-flown** (of language, etc.) extravagant, bombastic. **high-flyer** *noun* a person or thing with capacity for great achievements. **high frequency** (in radio) 3 to 30 megahertz. **high-handed** *adjective* using authority arrogantly. **high jump** an athletic competition of jumping over a high horizontal bar. **high-level** *adjective* (of negotiations) conducted by people of high rank; (of a computer language) designed for convenience in programming and requiring translation by an intermediate program before it can be understood by the computer; (of nuclear waste) highly radioactive and requiring long-term storage in isolation. **high life** or **living** a luxurious way of living. **high-minded** *adjective* having high moral principles. **high-pitched** *adjective* (of a voice or sound) high. **high-powered** *adjective* using great power or energy, forceful. **high priest** the chief priest. **high-profile** *adjective* involving much publicity. **high-rise** *adjective* (of a building) with many storeys. **high road** the main road. **high school** a secondary school. **high sea** or **seas** the open seas not under any country's jurisdiction. **high season** the period when a resort etc. regularly has most visitors. **high-speed** *adjective* operating at great speed. **high-spirited** *adjective* in high spirits, happy and lively. **high table** the chief table at a public dinner etc. **high tech** *noun* high technology. **high-tech** *adjective* employing, requiring, or involved in high technology. **high technology** advanced technology. **high tension** or **voltage** electrical potential large enough to injure or cause damage. **high tide** the tide at its highest level; the time when this occurs. **high treason** treason against one's country or ruler. **high water** high tide. **high-water mark** the level reached at high water; the highest point or value etc. recorded. **high wire** a high tightrope.

highbrow *adjective* very intellectual, cultured. –**highbrow** *noun* a highbrow person.

higher *adjective* & *adverb* more high; *higher animals* or *plants*, those that are highly developed and of complex structure. –**higher** *adverb* in or to a higher position etc.
☐ **higher education** education continuing beyond secondary schooling, e.g. at university.

highfalutin *adjective* (also **highfaluting**) (*informal*) pompous.

highland *adjective* of or in highlands. **highlands** *plural noun* mountainous country.

highlander *noun* a native or inhabitant of highlands.

highlight *noun* 1 a light or bright area in a painting etc. 2 the brightest or most outstanding feature of something, *the highlight of the tour*. –**highlight** *verb* 1 to draw special attention to, to emphasise. 2 to mark (written or printed words) with a bright colour.

highlighter *noun* a marker pen used to overlay colour on written or printed words in order to draw attention to them.

highly *adverb* 1 in a high degree, extremely, *highly amusing*; *highly commended*. 2 very favourably, *thinks highly of her*.
☐ **highly-strung** *adjective* (of a person) easily upset.

Highness *noun* the title used in speaking of or to a prince or princess, *His* or *Her* or *Your Highness*.

highway *noun* 1 a public road. 2 a main route by land, sea, or air.

highwayman *noun* (*plural* **highwaymen**) a man (usually on horseback) who robbed passing travellers in former times.

hijack *verb* to seize control of (a vehicle or aircraft in transit) in order to steal its goods or take its passengers hostage or force it to a new destination. –**hijack** *noun* a hijacking. **hijacker** *noun*

hike *noun* 1 a long walk, especially a cross-country walk taken for pleasure. 2 (*informal*) a hoist; an increase, *a price hike*. –**hike** *verb* 1 to go for a hike. 2 to walk laboriously. 3 (*informal*) to hoist; to increase. **hiker** *noun*

hilarious *adjective* 1 noisily merry. 2 extremely funny. **hilariously** *adverb*, **hilarity** (hĭ-**la**-rĭ-tee) *noun* [from Greek *hilaros* = cheerful]

hill *noun* 1 a natural elevation of the earth's surface not as high as a mountain. 2 a slope in a road etc. 3 a heap or mound.

Hillary, Sir Edmund (1919–2008), New Zealand mountaineer, who (with Tenzing Norgay) was the first to reach the summit of Mount Everest (1953).

hillbilly *noun* 1 folk music like that of the southern USA. 2 (*Amer. informal*) a person from a remote mountain area in a southern State of the USA.

hillock *noun* a small hill, a mound.

hillside *noun* the sloping side of a hill.

hilly *adjective* full of hills. **hilliness** *noun*

hilt *noun* the handle of a sword or dagger etc.
☐ **to the hilt** completely, *his guilt was proved up to the hilt*.

him *pronoun* 1 the objective case of **he**, *we saw him*. 2 (*informal*) = he, *it's him all right*.

Himalayas (him-ă-**lay**-ăz) a vast mountain system in Nepal and adjacent countries. **Himalayan** *adjective*

himself *pronoun* 1 the form of *him* used in reflexive constructions (e.g. *he cut himself*). 2 the form of *he* or *him* used for emphasis (e.g. *he himself had said it*; *told me himself*).
☐ **be himself** to behave in a normal manner without constraint; *he is not himself today*, is not in his normal good health or spirits. **by himself** without companions; without help.

Hinayana (hee-nă-**yah**-nă) *noun* a name given by followers of Mahayana Buddhism to the more orthodox schools of early Buddhism. [Sanskrit, = lesser vehicle]

418

hind¹ *noun* a female deer.

hind² *adjective* situated at the back, *hind legs*.

hinder¹ (**hin**-der) *verb* to keep (a person or thing) back by delaying progress.

hinder² (**hynd**-er) *adjective* hind, *the hinder part*.

Hindi (**hin**-dee) *noun* **1** one of the official languages of India, a form of Hindustani. **2** a group of spoken languages of northern India.

hindmost *adjective* furthest behind.

hindquarters *plural noun* the hind legs and parts adjoining these of a quadruped.

hindrance *noun* **1** something that hinders. **2** hindering, being hindered.

hindsight *noun* wisdom about an event after it has occurred.

Hindu *noun* a person whose religion is Hinduism. – **Hindu** *adjective* of the Hindus.

Hinduism (**hin**-doo-izm) *noun* a religion and philosophy of India, with a caste system and belief in reincarnation.

Hindustani (hin-dŭ-**stah**-nee) *noun* the language of much of northern India and (as colloquial Urdu) Pakistan.

hinge *noun* **1** a joint on which a lid, door, or gate etc. turns or swings. **2** a natural joint working similarly. **3** (in full **stamp hinge**) a small piece of gummed paper for fixing stamps in an album. – **hinge** *verb* **1** to attach or be attached by a hinge or hinges. **2** to depend, *everything hinges on this meeting*.

hint *noun* **1** a slight indication, a suggestion made indirectly. **2** a small piece of practical information, *household hints*. – **hint** *verb* to make a hint. □ **hint at** to refer indirectly to.

hinterland *noun* a district lying behind a coast etc. or served by a port or other centre.

hip¹ *noun* the projection formed by the pelvis and upper part of the thigh bone on each side of the body. **hips** *plural noun* the measurement round the body here. □ **hip bath** a small portable bath in which a person can sit immersed to the hips. **hip bone** the bone forming the hip. **hip pocket** a trouser pocket just behind the hip (where one's wallet may be carried); *feel it in the hip pocket*, to notice the cost of something. **hipped** *adjective*

hip² *noun* the fruit (red when ripe) of the wild rose.

hip³ *interjection* used in cheering, *hip, hip, hurray*.

hip⁴ *adjective* (*informal*) trendy, stylish.

hip hop *noun* a style of music featuring rap with electronic backing; the culture associated with this.

hippo *noun* (*plural* **hippos**) (*informal*) a hippopotamus.

Hippocratic (hip-ŏ-**krat**-ik) *adjective* of Hippocrates, a Greek physician of the 5th century BC. □ **Hippocratic oath** an oath (formerly taken by those beginning medical practice) to observe the code of professional behaviour.

hippodrome *noun* **1** (in names) a music hall or dance hall. **2** (in classical antiquity) a course for chariot races etc. [from Greek *hippos* = horse, + *dromos* = race, course]

hippopotamus *noun* (*plural* **hippopotamuses**) a large African river animal with tusks, short legs, and thick dark skin. [from Greek *hippos* = horse, + *potamos* = river]

hippy *noun* (*plural* **hippies**) (especially in the 1960s) a person rejecting conventional values, typically with long hair, beads, etc., sometimes using (or thought to be using) hallucinogenic drugs; in some cases withdrawing from conventional society and trying to live in universal peace.

hiragana (hi-ră-**gah**-nă) *noun* a form of Japanese syllabic writing.

hire *verb* to engage or grant the services of (a person) or the use of (a thing) temporarily, for payment. – **hire** *noun* hiring; payment for this. □ **hire purchase** a system by which a thing becomes the hirer's after a certain number of payments. **hirer** *noun*

hireling *noun* (usually *derogatory*) a person hired to work for another.

Hiroshima (hĭ-**rosh**-ĭ-mă *or* heer-rŏ-**shee**-mă) a Japanese city, target of the first atomic bomb (6 August 1945).

hirsute (**herss**-yoot) *adjective* hairy, shaggy.

his *adjective* & *possessive pronoun* **1** of or belonging to him; the thing(s) belonging to him. **2** used in men's titles, *His Majesty*.

Hispanic (hiss-**pan**-ik) *adjective* **1** of Spain; of Spain and Portugal. **2** of Spain and other Spanish-speaking countries. [from Latin *Hispania* = Spain]

Hispaniola (hiss-pan-ee-**oh**-lă) an island in the West Indies, divided into the Republic of Haiti (in the west) and the Dominican Republic (in the east).

hiss *noun* a sound like that of *s*. –**hiss** *verb*
1 to make this sound. 2 to express disapproval in this way.

histamine (**hist**-ă-mĭn) *noun* a chemical compound present in all body tissues, causing some allergic reactions.

histogram (**hist**-ŏ-gram) *noun* a diagram used in statistics, showing the frequency of a quantity's values by means of columns. [from Greek *histos* = mast, + -*gram*]

histology (hist-**ol**-ŏ-jee) *noun* the scientific study of organic tissues. **histological** *adjective* [from Greek *histos* = web, + -*logy*]

historian *noun* an expert in history; a writer of history.

historic (hiss-**to**-rik) *adjective* famous or important in history, *a historic figure*.

Usage Formerly the *h* was not pronounced and *an* was therefore used before it; this use is now old-fashioned.

---

historical *adjective* 1 belonging to or dealing with history or past events (as opposed to legend or prehistory). 2 concerned with history. **historically** *adverb*

historicity (hiss-tŏ-**riss**-ĭ-tee) *noun* the historical genuineness of an alleged event etc.

historiography (hiss-to-ree-**og**-ră-fee) *noun* the writing of history; the study of this. **historiographer** *noun*

history *noun* 1 a continuous methodical record of important or public events. 2 the study of past events, especially of human affairs. 3 past events; those connected with a person or thing. 4 an interesting or eventful past, *the house has a history*. □ **make history** to do something memorable; to be the first to do something. [from Greek *historia* = finding out, narrative]

histrionic (histree-**on**-ik) *adjective* 1 of acting. 2 dramatic or theatrical in manner. **histrionics** *plural noun* theatricals; dramatic behaviour intended to impress people. [from Latin *histrio* = actor]

hit *verb* (**hit**, **hitting**) 1 to strike with a blow or missile; to aim a blow etc.; to come against (a thing) with force; *it hits you in the eye*, is very obvious. 2 to propel (a ball etc.) with a bat or club; to score runs or points in this way. 3 to have an effect on (a person); to cause to suffer. 4 to get at, to come to (a thing aimed at), to find (what is sought). 5 to reach, *can't hit the high notes*; *hit a snag*, encountered a difficulty. –**hit** *noun* 1 a blow, a stroke.

2 a shot etc. that hits its target. 3 a success; *make a hit*, to win popularity. 4 (in computing) an instance of identifying an item of data that matches the requirements of a search; an instance of a website being accessed. □ **hit-and-run** *adjective* causing harm or damage and making off immediately. **hit back** to retaliate. **hit it off** to get on well (with a person). **hit list** (*informal*) a list of people to be killed or eliminated etc.; a list of things against which action is planned. **hit man** (*informal*) a hired assassin. **hit on** to discover suddenly or by chance. **hit-or-miss** *adjective* aimed or done carelessly.

hitch *verb* 1 to move (a thing) with a slight jerk. 2 to fasten or be fastened with a loop or hook etc.; *hitch one's wagon to a star*, to be very ambitious. 3 to hitchhike; to obtain (a lift) in this way. –**hitch** *noun* 1 a slight jerk. 2 a noose or knot of various kinds. 3 a temporary stoppage, a snag.

hitchhike *verb* to travel by seeking free rides in passing vehicles. **hitchhiker** *noun*

hi-tech *adjective* = high-tech.

hither *adverb* to or towards this place. □ **hither and thither** to and fro.

hitherto *adverb* until this time.

Hitler, Adolf (1889–1945), Austrian-born German dictator, leader of the National Socialist (Nazi) party, whose expansionist policy led to the Second World War.

Hittite *noun* a member of a powerful people in Asia Minor and Syria c.1900–700 BC.

HIV *abbreviation* human immunodeficiency virus, a virus which causes Aids.

hive *noun* 1 a box or other container for bees to live in. 2 the bees living in this. –**hive** *verb* to gather or live in a hive. □ **hive off** to swarm off separately like a group of bees; to assign (work) to a subsidiary department or company. **hive of industry** a place full of people working busily.

hives *plural noun* a skin eruption, especially nettle-rash.

h'm *interjection* = hum.

HMAS *abbreviation* Her (or His) Majesty's Australian Ship.

ho *interjection* an exclamation of triumph or scorn, or calling attention.

hoard *noun* a carefully saved and guarded store of money, food, or treasured objects. –**hoard** *verb* to save and store away. **hoarder** *noun*

hoarding *noun* a fence of light boarding, often used for displaying advertisements.

hoar frost *noun* frozen water vapour deposited on vegetation etc.

hoarse *adjective* 1 (of the voice) sounding rough, as if from a dry throat. 2 (of a person) having a hoarse voice. **hoarsely** *adverb*, **hoarseness** *noun*

hoary *adjective* 1 white or grey, *hoary hair*. 2 with hoary hair, aged. 3 (of a joke etc.) old.

hoax *verb* to deceive jokingly. **–hoax** *noun* a joking deception. **hoaxer** *noun*

hob *noun* 1 a flat metal shelf at the side of a fireplace, where a kettle or pan etc. can be heated. 2 a flat heating surface on a cooker.

Hobart the capital and port of Tasmania.

Hobbes, Thomas (1588–1679), English philosopher.

hobbit *noun* a member of an imaginary race of half-sized persons in stories by J.R.R. Tolkien.

hobble *verb* 1 to walk lamely. 2 to fasten the legs of (a horse etc.) so as to limit but not entirely prevent movement. **–hobble** *noun* 1 a hobbling walk. 2 a rope etc. for hobbling a horse.

hobby *noun* an occupation that a person carries on for pleasure, not as a main business.

hobby horse *noun* 1 a stick with a horse's head, used as a toy. 2 a topic that a person likes discussing.

hobgoblin *noun* a mischievous or evil spirit.

hobnail *noun* a heavy-headed nail for boot-soles. **hobnailed** *adjective* studded with these.

hobnob *verb* (**hobnobbed, hobnobbing**) to spend time together in a friendly way.

Hobson's choice *noun* a situation in which there is no alternative to the thing offered. [from the name of Thomas Hobson (17th century), who hired out horses and made people take the one nearest the stable door]

Ho Chi Minh (original name Nguyen That Thanh, 1890–1969), Vietnamese Communist statesman, who led his country in its struggle for independence.
□ **Ho Chi Minh City** official name (since 1975) for Saigon.

hock¹ *noun* the middle joint of an animal's hind leg.

hock² *noun* a dry white wine; originally a white wine from Hochheim in Germany.

hock³ *verb* (*informal*) to pawn. **–hock** *noun* **in hock** in pawn; in prison; in debt.

hockey *noun* 1 a game played on a field between two teams of players with curved sticks and a small hard ball. 2 ice hockey.

hocus-pocus *noun* trickery.

hod *noun* 1 a trough on a staff used by bricklayers for carrying mortar or bricks. 2 a cylindrical container for shovelling and holding coal.

hoe *noun* a tool with a blade on a long handle, used for loosening soil or scraping up weeds etc. **–hoe** *verb* (**hoed, hoeing**) to dig or scrape with a hoe.

hog *noun* 1 a castrated male pig reared for meat. 2 (*informal*) a greedy person. **–hog** *verb* (**hogged, hogging**) (*informal*) to take more than one's fair share of; to hoard selfishly. □ **go the whole hog** (*informal*) to do something thoroughly. **hog's back** a steep-sided ridge of a hill. **hoggish** *adjective*

hogmanay (**hog**-mă-nay) *noun* (*Scottish*) the last day of the year, 31 December.

hogshead *noun* 1 a large cask. 2 a liquid or dry measure for various commodities, usually about 236 litres (50 gallons).

hogwash *noun* (*informal*) nonsense, rubbish.

Hohenzollern (hoh-ĕn-**zol**-ern) the name of a German princely family from which came the kings of Prussia from 1701 to 1918 and German emperors from 1871 to 1918.

ho-ho *interjection* an exclamation of surprise, triumph, or mockery.

hoick *verb* (*informal*) to lift or bring out, especially with a jerk.

hoi polloi (hoi pŏ-**loi**) *noun* the common people, the masses. [Greek]

hoist *verb* to raise or haul up, to lift with ropes and pulleys etc. **–hoist** *noun* 1 an apparatus for hoisting things. 2 a pull or haul up, *give it a hoist*. 3 (*Austral*.) a rotary clothes line of adjustable height.

hoity-toity *adjective* haughty.

hokey-pokey *noun* (*informal*) deception, trickery.

hoki (**hok**-ee) *noun* an edible New Zealand fish. [Maori]

hold¹ *verb* (**held, holding**) 1 to take and keep in one's arms, hand(s), teeth, etc. 2 to keep in a particular position or condition; to grasp or keep so as to control; to detain in custody; *hold him to his promise*, insist that he keeps it.

3 to be able to contain, *jug holds a litre*.
4 to have in one's possession or as something one has gained, *he holds the record for the high jump*. **5** to support, to bear the weight of. **6** to remain in force; to remain unbroken under strain. **7** to keep possession of (a place or position etc.) against attack. **8** to keep (a person's attention) by being interesting. **9** to have the position of, to occupy (a job etc.). **10** to cause to take place, to conduct, *hold a meeting*. **11** to restrain, to cause to cease action or movement etc.; *hold your tongue*, stop talking. **12** to believe, to consider; to assert. –**hold** *noun* **1** the act or manner of holding something. **2** an opportunity or means of holding. **3** a means of exerting influence on a person. □ **get hold of** to acquire; to make contact with (a person). **hold back** to prevent (a person) from doing something; to hesitate; to refrain. **hold down** to be competent enough to keep (one's job). **hold forth** to speak lengthily. **hold it!** cease action etc. **hold off** to wait, not to begin, *the rain held off*. **hold on** to keep one's grasp of something; to refrain from ringing off (on the telephone); (*informal*) wait! **hold one's ground** or **hold one's own** to stand firm, to refuse to yield. **hold one's peace** or **hold one's tongue** to keep silent. **hold out** to offer (an inducement or hope); to last, *if supplies hold out*. **hold out for** to refuse to accept anything other than. **hold out on** (*informal*) to conceal something from; to refuse the requests etc. of. **hold over** to postpone. **hold something over** to threaten (a person) constantly with something. **hold the fort** to act as a temporary substitute; to cope in an emergency. **hold the line** to refrain from ringing off (on the telephone). **hold up** to hinder; to stop by the use of threats or force for the purpose of robbery. **hold-up** *noun* a stoppage or delay; robbery by armed robbers. **hold water** (of reasoning) to be sound. **hold with** (*informal*) to approve of. **no holds barred** all methods are permitted. **on hold** suspended; (of telephone call or caller) holding on. **take hold** to grasp; to become established. **holder** *noun*

hold² *noun* a cavity below a ship's deck, where cargo is stored.

holdall *noun* a portable case for carrying miscellaneous articles.

holding *noun* something held or owned; land held by an owner or tenant.
□ **holding company** one formed to hold the shares of other companies that it then controls.

hole *noun* **1** an empty place in a solid body or mass; a sunken place on a surface. **2** an animal's burrow. **3** a small or dark or wretched place. **4** (*informal*) an awkward situation. **5** a hollow or cavity into which a ball etc. must be sent in various games. **6** a section of a golf course between tee and hole; a point scored by a player who reaches the hole with the fewest strokes. **7** an opening through something. –**hole** *verb* **1** to make a hole or holes in; *the ship was holed*, its side was pierced. **2** to put into a hole.
□ **hole-and-corner** *adjective* underhand. **hole up** (*informal*) to hide oneself. **in holes** worn so much that holes have formed. **make a hole in** to use a large amount of.

holey *adjective* full of holes. □ **holey dollar** a coin made from a Spanish dollar with a circular piece (*a dump*) struck from the centre, used as currency in Australia between 1814 and 1828.

Holi (**hoh**-lee) *noun* a Hindu festival celebrated in February or March.

holiday *noun* **1** a day of festivity or recreation, when no work is done. **2** (also **holidays**) a period of this. –**holiday** *verb* (**holidayed, holidaying**) to spend a holiday. [from *holy* + *day* (because holidays were originally religious festivals)]

holidaymaker *noun* a person on holiday.

holiness *noun* being holy or sacred.
□ **His Holiness** the title of the pope.

holistic (hoh-**list**-ik) *adjective* (of medical treatment) treating the whole person, not just the symptoms. [from Greek *holos* = whole]

Holland the Netherlands.

holland *noun* a smooth hard-wearing linen fabric.

hollandaise sauce (**hol**-ăn-dayz) *noun* a creamy sauce containing butter, egg yolks, and vinegar.

holler *verb* (*Amer.*) to shout.

hollow *adjective* **1** having a hole inside, not solid. **2** sunken, *hollow cheeks*. **3** (of sound) echoing, as if from something hollow. **4** empty, worthless, *a hollow triumph*; *a hollow laugh*, cynical. –**hollow** *noun* a hollow or sunken place, a hole, a valley. –**hollow** *adverb* completely, *beat them hollow*. –**hollow** *verb* to make or become hollow, *hollow it out*. **hollowly** *adverb*

holly *noun* an evergreen shrub with prickly leaves and red berries.

hollyhock *noun* a plant with large showy flowers on a tall stem.

Hollywood a district of Los Angeles, centre of the American film-making industry.

Holmes, Sherlock, a private detective, the central figure in stories by Conan Doyle.

holmium (**hohl**-mee-ŭm) *noun* a silvery soft metallic element (symbol Ho).

holocaust (**hol**-ŏ-kawst) *noun* large-scale destruction, especially by fire. –**the Holocaust** the mass murder of Jews and other groups by Nazis in 1939–45. [from Greek *holos* = whole, + *kaustos* = burnt]

Holocene (**hol**-ŏ-seen) *adjective* of the second of the two epochs of the Quaternary period, lasting from about 10,000 years ago to the present day. –**Holocene** *noun* this epoch.

Holofernes (hol-ŏ-**fer**-neez) the Assyrian general of Nebuchadnezzar's forces, killed by Judith.

hologram (**hol**-ŏ-gram) *noun* an image produced (without using lenses) on photographic film in such a way that under suitable illumination a two- or three-dimensional representation of an object is seen. **holographic** *adjective*, **holography** *noun* [from Greek *holos* = whole, + -*gram*]

holster *noun* a leather case for a pistol or revolver, fixed to a belt or saddle or under the arm.

holy *adjective* (**holier**, **holiest**) **1** of God and therefore regarded with reverence, associated with God or religion, *the Holy Bible*. **2** consecrated, sacred, *holy water*. **3** devoted to the service of God, *a holy man*. □ **holier-than-thou** *adjective* self-righteous. **Holy Communion** *see* **Communion**. **Holy Father** a title of the pope. **Holy Ghost** the Holy Spirit. **holy of holies** a place or thing regarded as most sacred; the sacred inner chamber of a Jewish temple. **holy orders** *see* **order**. **Holy Spirit** the Third Person of the Trinity. **Holy Week** the week before Easter Sunday. **Holy Writ** the Bible.

Holy Land 1 the part of Palestine west of the Jordan, revered by Christians. **2** a region revered in a non-Christian religion.

Holy Roman Empire the European territories under a Frankish or German ruler who bore the title of Emperor from the coronation of Charlemagne (800) until abolished by Napoleon in 1806.

Holy See the papacy or papal court.

homage *noun* **1** things said as a mark of respect, *paid homage to his achievements*. **2** a formal expression of loyalty to a ruler etc.

home *noun* **1** the place where one lives, especially with one's family. **2** one's native land; the district where one was born or where one has lived for a long time or to which one feels attached. **3** a dwelling house, *Homes For Sale*. **4** an institution where those needing care may live, *an old people's home*. **5** the natural environment of an animal or plant. **6** the place to be reached by a runner in a race or in certain games. **7** a home match. –**home** *adjective* **1** of or connected with one's own home or country; done or produced there, *home garden*; *home market*. **2** played on one's own ground, *a home match*. –**home** *adverb* **1** to or at one's home, *go home*; *stay home*. **2** to the point aimed at, *the thrust went home*; *drive a nail home*, right in. –**home** *verb* **1** (of a trained pigeon) to fly home. **2** to be guided to a target; to make for a particular destination. □ **at home** in one's home; relaxed and at ease; familiar with a subject; available to callers. **bring home to** to cause to realise fully. **come home to** to become fully realised by. **home and dry** or **dried**, **home and hosed** having achieved one's aim. **home economics** the study of household management. **home from home** a place (other than home) where one feels comfortable and at home. **home-grown** *adjective* grown or produced at home. **home help** a person who helps with housework etc., especially in a service organised by a welfare agency. **home-made** *adjective* made at home. **home rule** government of a country by its own citizens. **home run** a hit in baseball that allows the batter to make a complete circuit of the bases. **home straight** or **stretch** the stretch of a racecourse between the last turn and the finishing line. **home truth** an unpleasant truth that a person is made to realise about himself or herself. **home unit** (also **unit**) (*Austral.*) a private residence that is one of several in a building.

homebody *noun* a person who likes to stay at home.

homecoming *noun* arrival at home.

homeland *noun* **1** one's native land. **2** any of the partially self-governing areas in South Africa formerly reserved under the apartheid system for Black South Africans (the official name for a Bantustan).

homeless *adjective* lacking a dwelling place. **homelessness** *noun*

homely *adjective* **1** simple and informal, not pretentious. **2** (of a person's appearance) plain, not beautiful. **3** comfortable, cosy. homeliness *noun*

homeopathic, homeostasis, etc. = homoeopathic, homoeostasis, etc.

homepage *noun* a person's or organisation's introductory document on the World Wide Web.

Homer (?c. 700 BC) Greek epic poet, traditionally the author of the *Iliad* and the *Odyssey*. Homeric (hoh-**me**rrik) *adjective*

homesick *adjective* feeling depressed through longing for one's home when one is away from it. homesickness *noun*

homespun *adjective* **1** made of yarn spun at home. **2** plain, simple. –homespun *noun* homespun fabric.

homestead (**hohm**-sted) *noun* **1** a farmhouse or similar building with the land and buildings round it. **2** (*Austral.*) the owner's residence on a sheep or cattle station.

homeward *adjective & adverb* going towards home. homewards *adverb* towards home.

homework *noun* **1** work that a pupil is required to do away from school. **2** (*informal*) preparatory work to be done before a discussion etc. takes place.

homey *adjective* like home, homely.

homicide (**hom**-ĭ-syd) *noun* **1** the killing of one person by another. **2** a person who kills another. homicidal *adjective* [from Latin *homo* = person, + *caedere* = kill]

homily *noun* a sermon, a moralising lecture.

homing *adjective* **1** (of a pigeon) trained to fly home, bred for long-distance racing. **2** (of a missile) having an inbuilt guidance system.

hominid (**hom**-ĭ-nid) *noun* a member of the zoological family that includes humans and their fossil ancestors. –hominid *adjective* of this family.

hominoid (**hom**-ĭ-noid) *noun* an animal resembling a human. –hominoid *adjective* like a human.

homo- *prefix* same. [from Greek *homos* = same]

homoeopathic (hohm-ee-ŏ-**path**-ik) *adjective* treating a disease by very small doses of drugs etc. that in a healthy person would produce symptoms like those of the disease itself. homoeopathy (hohm-ee-**op**-ă-thee) *noun* [from Greek *homoios* = alike, + *pathos* = suffering]

homoeostasis (hoh-mee-ŏ-**stay**-sĭss) *noun* **1** the tendency of the body to keep its own temperature, blood pressure, etc. at a constant level. **2** the tendency for plant and animal populations to remain constant in an area. [from Greek *homoios* = alike, + *stasis* = standing]

homogeneous (hohm-ŏ-**jee**-nee-ŭs *or* hom-) *adjective* of the same kind as the others; formed of parts that are all of the same kind. homogeneity (hohm-ŏ-jĕ-**nee**-ĭ-tee *or* hom-) *noun* [from *homo-*, + Greek *genos* = a kind]

homogenise (hŏ-**moj**-ĕ-nyz) *verb* (also -ize) to treat (milk) so that the particles of fat are broken down and the cream does not separate. homogenisation *noun*

homograph (**hom**-ŏ-grahf) *noun* a word that is spelt like another but has a different meaning or origin, e.g. *bat* (a flying animal) and *bat* (for striking a ball). [from *homo-* + *-graph*]

homoiotherm (hŏ-**moi**-ŏ-therm) *noun* a warm-blooded animal (contrasts with *poikilotherm*). homoiothermic *adjective* [from Greek *homoios* = alike, + *therme* = heat]

homologous (hŏ-**mol**-ŏ-gŭs) *adjective* having the same relation or relative position, corresponding. □ homologous chromosomes chromosomes that pair with each other in such a way that one member of each pair is carried by every gamete. homology *noun* [from *homo-*, + Greek *logos* = proportion]

homonym (**hom**-ŏ-nim) *noun* a word of the same spelling or sound as another but with a different meaning, e.g. *grate* (= fireplace), *grate* (= to rub), *great* (= large). [from *homo-*, + Greek *onoma* = name]

homophobia (hohm-ŏ-**foh**-bee-ă *or* hom-) a hatred or fear of homosexuals. homophobic *adjective* [from *homo-* + *phobia*]

homophone (**hom**-ŏ-fohn) *noun* a word with the same sound as another, e.g. *son, sun.* [from *homo-*, + Greek *phone* = sound]

homophonic (hom-ŏ-**fon**-ik) *adjective* (in music) in unison; with the accompanying parts moving in step with the melody.

Homo sapiens (hoh-moh **sap**-ee-enz) *noun* mankind regarded as a species. [Latin, = wise person]

homosexual (hoh-mŏ-**sek**-shoo-ăl *or* hom-ŏ-) *adjective* feeling sexually attracted only to people of the same sex. –homosexual *noun* a homosexual person. homosexuality *noun* [from *homo-* + *sexual*]

homozygous (hohm-ŏ-**zy**-gŭs *or* hom-) *adjective* having two genes that are the same allele, being formed from gametes carrying the same allele. [from *homo-* + *zygote*]

Hon. *abbreviation* **1** Honorary. **2** Honourable.

Honduras (hon-**dyoor**-răs) a republic in Central America. **Honduran** *adjective* & *noun*

hone (*rhymes with* stone) *noun* a fine-grained stone used for sharpening razors and tools. –**hone** *verb* **1** to sharpen on this. **2** to polish or refine (reasoning etc.).

honest *adjective* **1** truthful, trustworthy. **2** (of an act or feeling) showing such qualities, *an honest opinion*; *an honest piece of work*, done conscientiously. **3** (of gain etc.) got by fair means; *earn an honest living*, earn money fairly. □ **honest-to-goodness** *adjective* (*informal*) real, straightforward. [from Latin *honestus* = honourable]

honestly *adverb* **1** in an honest way. **2** really, *that's all I know, honestly*.

honesty *noun* **1** being honest. **2** a plant with seeds that form in round translucent pods.

honey *noun* (*plural* **honeys**) **1** a sweet sticky yellowish substance made by bees from nectar. **2** its colour. **3** sweetness, pleasantness; a sweet thing. **4** (*informal*) darling. □ **honey bee** the common bee that lives in a hive.

honeycomb *noun* **1** a bees' wax structure of six-sided cells for holding their honey and eggs. **2** a pattern or arrangement of six-sided sections. –**honeycomb** *verb* **1** to fill with holes or tunnels, *the rock was honeycombed with passages*. **2** to mark or sew in a honeycomb pattern.

honeydew *noun* **1** a cultivated variety of melon with pale skin and sweet green flesh. **2** a sweet sticky substance found on leaves and stems, excreted by aphids.

honeyeater *noun* a bird with a brush on the tongue for collecting nectar.

honeymoon *noun* **1** a holiday spent together by a newly-married couple. **2** an initial period of enthusiasm or goodwill. –**honeymoon** *verb* to spend a honeymoon.

honeysuckle *noun* a climbing shrub with fragrant yellow and pink flowers.

Hong Kong from 1 July 1997 a Special Administrative Region of China; formerly a British dependency, comprising Hong Kong Island, the Kowloon Peninsula, the New Territories and outlying islands.

Honiara (hon-ee-**ah**-ră) the capital of the Solomon Islands.

honk *noun* a loud harsh sound; the cry of the wild goose; the sound made by an old-style motor horn. –**honk** *verb* to make a honk, to sound (a horn).

honky-tonk *noun* a kind of ragtime music played on a piano, often with strings that give a tinny sound.

Honolulu the capital of Hawaii.

honorarium (on-ŏ-**rair**-ree-ŭm) *noun* (*plural* **honoraria** *or* **honorariums**) a voluntary payment made for services where no fee is legally required.

honorary *adjective* **1** given as an honour, *an honorary degree*. **2** (of an office or its holder) unpaid, *the honorary treasurer*.

honour *noun* **1** great respect, high public regard. **2** a mark of this; a privilege given or received; *passed with honours*, gained special distinction in an examination. **3** a source of this; a person or thing that brings honour. **4** good personal character; a reputation for honesty and loyalty etc. **5** a title of respect given to certain judges or people of importance, *your Honour*. –**honour** *verb* **1** to feel honour for. **2** to confer honour on. **3** to acknowledge and pay (a cheque etc. when it is due). **4** to observe the terms of (an agreement). □ **do the honours** to perform the usual civilities to guests or visitors etc. **honours degree** a university degree requiring a higher level of attainment than a pass degree. **honours list** a list of people awarded honours in recognition of their achievements. **in honour bound** or **on one's honour** under a moral obligation to do something. **on my honour** I swear it.

honourable *adjective* **1** deserving honour. **2** possessing or showing honour. –**Honourable** *adjective* the courtesy title given to certain high officials, judges, and members of parliament. **honourably** *adverb*

hood *noun* **1** a covering for the head and neck, either forming part of a garment or separate. **2** a loose hoodlike garment forming part of academic dress. **3** something resembling a hood in shape or use, e.g. a folding roof over a car, a canopy over a machine etc. **4** (*Amer.*) the bonnet of a car. **5** (*informal*) a hoodlum.

hooded *adjective* **1** having a hood. **2** (of animals) having a hoodlike part.

hoodlum *noun* a hooligan, a young thug.

hoodwink *verb* to deceive.

hoof *noun* (*plural* **hoofs** *or* **hooves**) the horny part of the foot of a horse and other animals. **–hoof** *verb* **hoof it** (*informal*) to go on foot. □ **on the hoof** (of livestock) alive, not slaughtered.

hook *noun* **1** a bent or curved piece of metal etc. for catching hold or for hanging things on. **2** something shaped like this; *the Hook of Holland*, a projecting point of land on the coast of Holland. **3** a curved cutting tool, *reaping hook*. **4** a hooked stroke in cricket or golf; (in boxing) a short swinging blow with the elbow bent. **–hook** *verb* **1** to grasp or catch with a hook; to fasten with a hook or hooks. **2** to propel (a ball) in a curving path; to pass (the ball) backward with the foot in rugby. **3** to make (a rug) by looping yarn through canvas with a hook. **4** (*informal*) to obtain, to steal. □ **be hooked on** (*informal*) to be addicted to or captivated by. **by hook or by crook** by some means no matter what happens. **hook and eye** a small metal hook and loop for fastening a dress etc. **hook, line, and sinker** entirely. **hook-up** *noun* (*informal*) interconnection of broadcasting transmissions. **off the hook** freed from a difficulty.

hookah (**huuk**-ă) *noun* an oriental tobacco pipe with a long tube passing through a glass container of water that cools the smoke as it is drawn through.

Hooke, Robert (1635–1703), English scientist and inventor. He formulated the law of elasticity (named **Hooke's Law**) that the strain in an elastic solid is proportional to the applied stress. Among his inventions were the balance-spring for watches, the wheel barometer, and the universal joint.

hooked *adjective* hook-shaped, *a hooked nose*.

hooker *noun* a player in the front row of the scrum in rugby, who tries to get the ball by hooking it.

hookey *noun* **play hookey** (*informal*) to play truant.

hookworm *noun* a worm (the male of which has hooklike spines) that can infest the intestines of humans and animals.

hooligan *noun* a young ruffian. **hooliganism** *noun*

hoon *noun* (*Austral. informal*) **1** a hooligan. **2** an exhibitionist. **3** a show-off, especially one who drives a car dangerously or at reckless speed.

hoop *noun* **1** a band of metal or wood etc. forming part of a framework. **2** this used as a child's toy for bowling along the ground, or for circus performers to jump through. **3** a small iron arch used in croquet. **4** (*Austral. informal*) a jockey. **–hoop** *verb* to bind or encircle with hoops. □ **be put** or **go through the hoops** to undergo a test or ordeal. **hoop pine** an Australian softwood timber tree.

hoopla *noun* **1** a game in which rings are thrown to encircle a prize. **2** (*informal*) commotion. **3** (*informal*) pretentious nonsense.

hoopoe (**hoo**-poo) *noun* a bird with a fanlike crest and striped wings and tail.

hooray *interjection* & *noun* **1** = **hurray**. **2** (*Austral. informal*) (also **hooroo**) goodbye.

hoot *noun* **1** the cry of an owl. **2** the sound made by a vehicle's horn or a steam whistle. **3** a cry expressing scorn or disapproval. **4** (*informal*) laughter; a cause of this. **–hoot** *verb* **1** to make a hoot or hoots. **2** to receive or drive away with scornful hoots. **3** to sound (a horn). □ **not care** or **give a hoot** or **two hoots** (*informal*) not to care at all.

hooter *noun* **1** a siren or steam whistle used as a signal. **2** a vehicle's horn.

hooves *see* **hoof**.

hop¹ *verb* **1** (of an animal) to spring from all feet at once, (of a person) to jump on one foot. **2** to cross by hopping. **3** (*informal*) to make a short quick trip. **–hop** *noun* **1** a hopping movement. **2** an informal dance. **3** a short flight or one stage in a long-distance flight. □ **hop in** or **out** (*informal*) to get into or out of a car. **hopping mad** (*informal*) very angry. **hop it** (*informal*) go away. **on the hop** (*informal*) bustling about; unprepared, *caught on the hop*.

hop² *noun* a climbing plant cultivated for its cones (*hops*), which are used for giving a bitter flavour to beer.

hope *noun* **1** a feeling of expectation and desire combined; a desire for certain events to happen. **2** a person, thing, or circumstance that gives cause for this. **3** what is hoped for. **–hope** *verb* to feel hope, to expect and desire, to feel fairly confident. □ **hoping against hope** hoping for something that is barely possible.

hopeful *adjective* **1** feeling hope. **2** causing hope, seeming likely to be favourable or successful. **–hopeful** *noun* a person who hopes or seems likely to succeed, *young hopefuls*.

hopefully *adverb* **1** in a hopeful way. **2** it is to be hoped, *hopefully, we shall be there by one o'clock*.

426

hopeless *adjective* **1** feeling no hope.
2 admitting no hope, *a hopeless case*.
3 inadequate, incompetent, *is hopeless at
tennis*. **hopelessly** *adverb*, **hopelessness** *noun*

hoplite (**hop**-lyt) *noun* a heavily-armed
infantry soldier in ancient Greece.

hopper¹ *noun* **1** one who hops; a hopping
insect. **2** a V-shaped container with an opening
at the base through which its contents can be
discharged into a machine etc.

hopper² *noun* a hop-picker.

hopsack *noun* a kind of coarsely-woven fabric.

hopscotch *noun* a children's game of
hopping and jumping over marked squares to
retrieve a stone tossed into these.

Horace (65–8 BC), Roman poet, whose works
include lyric verse and satires.

horde *noun* a large group or crowd.

horizon *noun* **1** the line at which earth and
sky appear to meet. **2** the limit of a person's
experience, knowledge, or interests.
□ **on the horizon** (of an event) imminent or
just becoming apparent. [from Greek *horizein*
= form a boundary]

horizontal *adjective* parallel to the horizon;
at the same level. **horizontally** *adverb*

hormone (**hor**-mohn) *noun* a substance
produced within the body of an animal or
plant (or made synthetically) and carried
by the blood or sap to an organ which it
stimulates. **hormonal** (hor-**moh**-năl) *adjective*

Hormuz (**hor**-muuz), **Strait of**, a strait
separating Iran from the Arabian peninsula,
through which sea traffic from the oil-rich
States of the Persian Gulf must pass.

horn *noun* **1** a hard pointed outgrowth on the
heads of certain animals. **2** the hard smooth
substance of which this consists. **3** a projection
resembling a horn. **4** any of various wind
instruments (originally made of horn, now
usually of brass) with a trumpet-shaped end;
the French horn (*see* **French**). **5** a device
for sounding a warning signal. **–horn** *verb*
1 to shorten or cut off the horns of (cattle).
2 to gore with the horns. □ **horn in** (*informal*)
to intrude, to interfere. **horn of plenty** *see*
cornucopia. **horn-rimmed** *adjective* (of
spectacles) with frames made of a material
like horn or tortoiseshell. **horned** *adjective*

hornbill *noun* a tropical bird with a hornlike
projection on its beak.

hornblende *noun* a black, green, or dark
brown mineral composed mainly of silicates
of calcium, magnesium, and iron.

hornet *noun* a large kind of wasp inflicting
a serious sting. □ **stir up a hornets' nest** to
provoke or cause trouble or opposition.

hornpipe *noun* a lively dance usually for one
person, traditionally associated with sailors.

horny *adjective* **1** of or like horn. **2** hardened
and calloused, *horny hands*.

horoscope *noun* **1** a forecast of a person's
future, based on an astrologer's diagram
showing the relative positions of the planets
and stars at a particular time. **2** this diagram.
[from Greek *hora* = hour (of birth), + *skopos*
= observer]

horrendous *adjective* (*informal*) horrifying.

horrible *adjective* **1** causing horror.
2 (*informal*) unpleasant. **horribly** *adverb*

horrid *adjective* horrible. **horridly** *adverb*

horrific *adjective* horrifying. **horrifically**
adverb

horrify *verb* (**horrified**, **horrifying**) to arouse
horror in, to shock.

horror *noun* **1** a feeling of loathing and
fear. **2** intense dislike or dismay. **3** a person
or thing causing horror. □ **horror film** one
full of violence presented sensationally for
entertainment. **horror-struck** or **horror-stricken**
adjectives horrified, shocked.

Horsa *see* **Hengist**.

hors-d'oeuvre (or-**dervr**) *noun* food served
as an appetiser at the start of a meal. [French,
= outside the work]

horse *noun* **1** a four-legged animal with a
flowing mane and tail, used for riding on or to
carry loads or pull carts etc. **2** an adult male
horse. **3** cavalry. **4** a frame on which something
is supported, *clothes horse*. **5** a vaulting horse
(*see* **vaulting**). **–horse** *verb* **horse around**
(*informal*) to indulge in horseplay.
□ **horse-drawn** *adjective* (of a vehicle) pulled
by a horse. **horse float** a closed vehicle for
transporting a horse. **horse latitudes** a belt
of calms between the trade winds and the
westerlies. **horse sense** (*informal*) plain
rough common sense. **horses for courses** the
matching of people with tasks. **straight from
the horse's mouth** (of information) from a
first-hand source.

horseback *noun* on horseback mounted on a horse.

horsebox *noun* a horse float.

horseflesh *noun* **1** the flesh of horses, as food. **2** horses, *a good judge of horseflesh*.

horsehair *noun* hair from a horse's mane or tail, used for padding furniture, making bows for stringed instruments, etc.

horseman *noun* a rider on horseback, especially a skilled one. **horsemanship** *noun*

horseplay *noun* boisterous play.

horsepower *noun* an imperial unit for measuring the power of an engine (550 foot-pounds per second, about 750 watts).

horseradish *noun* a plant with a hot-tasting root used to make a sauce.

horseshoe *noun* **1** a U-shaped strip of metal nailed to a horse's hoof. **2** anything shaped like this.

horsewhip *noun* a whip for horses. –horsewhip *verb* (**horsewhipped**, **horsewhipping**) to beat with a horsewhip.

horsewoman *noun* a woman rider on horseback, especially a skilled one.

horst *noun* a raised block of land between faults, formed either by uplift, or by the land on the other side of the faults sinking.

horsy *adjective* **1** of or like a horse. **2** interested in horses and horse racing; showing this in one's dress and conversation etc.

horticulture *noun* the art of garden cultivation. **horticultural** *adjective*, **horticulturist** *noun* [from Latin *hortus* = garden, + *culture*]

Horus (hor-rŭs) (*Egyptian myth.*) a god whose symbol was the hawk, protector of the monarchy.

Hosanna *interjection* & *noun* a cry of adoration to God and the Messiah.

hose *noun* **1** (also **hosepipe**) a flexible tube for conveying water. **2** hosiery. **3** (*old use*) breeches, *doublet and hose*. –hose *verb* to water or spray with a hose, *hose the car down*.

Hosea (hoh-**zee**-ă) **1** a Hebrew minor prophet of the 8th century BC. **2** a book of the Old Testament containing his prophecies.

hosier *noun* a dealer in stockings and socks.

hosiery *noun* (in shops) stockings and socks.

hospice (**hos**-pĭs) *noun* **1** a home for people who are ill, especially terminally, or who are destitute. **2** a lodging house for travellers, especially one kept by a religious order.

hospitable (hos-**pit**-ă-bŭl) *adjective* giving and liking to give hospitality. **hospitably** *adverb*

hospital *noun* an institution providing medical and surgical treatment for persons who are ill or injured. [from Latin *hospitium* = hospitality]

hospitalise (**hos**-pĭ-tă-lyz) *verb* (also **-ize**) to send or admit (a patient) to a hospital. **hospitalisation** *noun*

hospitality *noun* friendly and generous reception and entertainment of guests.

host¹ *noun* a large number of people or things. [same origin as *hostile*]

host² *noun* **1** a person who receives and entertains another as a guest. **2** an organism on which another organism lives as a parasite. –host *verb* to act as host to (a person) or at (an event). [same origin as *hospital*]

host³ *noun* the bread consecrated in the Eucharist. [from Latin *hostia* = sacrifice]

hostage *noun* a person held as security that the holder's demands will be satisfied.

hostel *noun* a lodging house for young travellers, students, or other special groups.

hostelry *noun* (*old use*) an inn.

hostess *noun* **1** a woman who receives and entertains a person as her guest. **2** (*informal*) (also **air hostess**) a female steward on an aircraft, a flight attendant.

Usage In sense 2 *flight attendant* is now the preferred name.

---

hostie *noun* (*Austral.informal*) an air hostess.

hostile *adjective* **1** of an enemy, *hostile aircraft*. **2** unfriendly, *a hostile glance*; *they are hostile towards reform*, are opposed to it. [from Latin *hostis* = an enemy]

hostility *noun* being hostile, enmity. **hostilities** *plural noun* acts of warfare.

hot *adjective* (**hotter**, **hottest**) **1** having great heat or high temperature; giving off heat; feeling heat. **2** producing a burning sensation to the taste. **3** eager, angry; excited, excitable, *in hot pursuit*; *a hot temper*; *he's hot on punctuality*, keen on it. **4** (of the scent in hunting) fresh and strong; (of news) fresh. **5** (*informal*, of a player) very skilful. **6** (of jazz etc.) strongly rhythmical and emotional. **7** (*informal*) radioactive. **8** (*informal*, of goods etc.) recently stolen. –hot *adverb* hotly, eagerly, angrily. –hot *verb* (**hotted**, **hotting**) (*informal*) to heat, to make or become hot; *things are hotting up*, becoming active or exciting. □ **hot air** (*informal*) empty or boastful talk. **hot-blooded** *adjective* excitable; passionate. **hot cross bun** a bun marked with a cross, traditionally eaten hot on Good Friday. **hot dog** a hot frankfurt in a roll of bread. **hot favourite** a competitor strongly fancied to win. **hot gospeller** (*informal*) an eager and enthusiastic preacher of the gospel. **hot potato** (*informal*) a situation etc. likely to cause trouble to the person handling it. **hot seat** (*informal*) the position of someone who has difficult responsibilities or is being subjected to searching questions. **hot stuff** (*informal*) a person of high spirit or skill or passions; something high-powered. **hot-tempered** *adjective* easily becoming very angry. **hot under the collar** angry, resentful, or embarrassed. **hot-water bottle** a small container to be filled with hot water for warmth in bed. **in hot water** (*informal*) in trouble or disgrace. **hotly** *adverb*, **hotness** *noun*

hotbed *noun* 1 a bed of earth heated by fermenting manure. 2 a place favourable to the growth of something evil.

hotchpotch *noun* a jumble.

hotel *noun* 1 an establishment providing meals and accommodation for payment. 2 (*Austral.*) a place licensed to sell alcoholic drinks to the public for consumption on the premises.

hotelier (hoh-**tel**-ee-er) *noun* a hotel-keeper.

hotfoot *adverb* in eager haste. –**hotfoot** *verb* **hotfoot it** to hurry eagerly.

hothead *noun* an impetuous person. **hotheaded** *adjective*

hothouse *noun* a heated building made of glass, for growing plants in a warm temperature.

hotline *noun* a telephone line exclusively for enquiries, assistance, information, etc.

hotplate *noun* a heated surface for cooking food or keeping it hot.

hotpot *noun* a stew containing meat and vegetables.

Hottentot *noun* 1 a member of a Black people of SW Africa. 2 their language.

Usage *Nama* is now the preferred name for this people and their language.

Houdini (hoo-**dee**-nee), Harry (real name Eric Weiss, 1874–1926), American escapologist.

hoummos *noun* = **hummus**.

hound *noun* 1 a dog used in hunting, a foxhound. 2 a contemptible man. –**hound** *verb* 1 to harass or pursue, *hounded him out of society*. 2 to urge, to incite, *hound them on*.

hour *noun* 1 a twenty-fourth part of a day and night, 60 minutes. 2 a time of day, a point of time, *always comes at the same hour; 17.00 hours*, this time on the 24-hour clock; *the bus leaves on the hour*, when the clock indicates a whole number of hours from midnight. 3 a short period of time; the time for action, *the hour has come*; the present time, *the question of the hour*. 4 (in the RC Church) prayers to be said at one of the seven times of day appointed for prayer, *a book of hours*. 5 a period for a specified activity, *the lunch hour*. **hours** *plural noun* a fixed period for daily work, *office hours are 9 to 5; after hours*.

hourglass *noun* a wasp-waisted glass container holding a quantity of fine sand that takes one hour to trickle from the upper to the lower section.

houri (**hoor**-ree) *noun* a young and beautiful woman of the Muslim paradise.

hourly *adjective* 1 done or occurring once an hour, *an hourly bus service*. 2 continual, frequent, *lives in hourly dread of discovery*. **hourly** *adverb* every hour.

house (*pr.* howss) *noun* 1 a building made for people (usually one family) to live in. 2 the people living in this, a household. 3 a building used for a particular purpose, *the opera house*. 4 a boarding-school residence; the pupils in this; a division of a day school for competitions etc. 5 a building used by an assembly, the assembly itself, *the Houses of Parliament*; *the House of Representatives*. 6 a business firm, *a banking house*. 7 the audience of a theatre; the theatre itself; a performance in this, *a full house; second house starts at 9 o'clock*. 8 a family or dynasty, *the House of Windsor*. 9 each of the twelve parts into which the heavens are divided in astrology. 10 a place of public refreshment; a restaurant, etc.; *a steak house*; *house wine*, selected by the management and sold at a special price. –**house** (*pr.* howz) *verb* 1 to provide accommodation for. 2 to store (goods etc.). 3 to encase (a part or fixture). □ **house arrest** detention in one's own house, not in prison. **House of Assembly** the lower house in the South Australian and Tasmanian State parliaments. **House of Commons** the assembly of elected representatives in the British Parliament. House of Lords the assembly of peers and bishops in the British Parliament. House of Representatives the lower house of the Australian Federal Parliament, of the US Congress, and of other national parliaments. house plant a plant for growing indoors. house-proud *adjective* giving great attention to the care and appearance of the home. house-to-house *adjective* calling at each house in turn. house-trained *adjective* (of animals) trained to be clean in the house; (*informal*) well-mannered. house-warming *noun* a party to celebrate the occupation of a new home. like a house on fire vigorously, excellently. on the house at the proprietor's expense.

houseboat *noun* a boat fitted up as a dwelling.

housebound *adjective* unable to leave one's house through illness etc.

housebreaker *noun* a burglar. housebreaking *noun*

housecoat *noun* a woman's long dresslike garment for informal wear in the house.

housecraft *noun* skill in household management.

housefly *noun* a common fly found in houses.

houseful *noun* all that a house can hold.

household *noun* all the occupants of a house living as a family. □ household word a familiar saying or name.

householder *noun* a person owning or renting a house.

housekeeper *noun* a person, especially a woman, employed to look after a household.

housekeeping *noun* 1 management of household affairs. 2 (*informal*) money to be used for this.

housemaid *noun* a woman servant in a house, especially one who cleans rooms.

housemaster, housemistress *nouns* a teacher in charge of a section of a boarding school.

housewife *noun* a woman managing a household. housewifely *adjective* [from the old meaning of *wife* = 'woman' (as in *fishwife*), not 'married woman']

housewifery (**howss**-wif-ree) *noun* household management.

housework *noun* the cleaning and cooking etc. done in housekeeping.

housing *noun* 1 accommodation. 2 a rigid casing enclosing machinery. 3 a shallow trench or groove cut in a piece of wood to receive an insertion. □ housing estate a number of houses in an area planned as a unit.

Houston (**hew**-stŏn) an inland port of Texas, an important centre for space research and manned space flight.

hove *see* heave.

hovel (**hov**-ĕl) *noun* a miserable dwelling.

Hovell, William Hilton, *see* Hume[2].

hover *verb* 1 (of a bird etc.) to remain in one place in the air. 2 to wait about, to linger, to wait close at hand.

hovercraft *noun* a vehicle that travels over land or water supported by air thrust downwards from its engines.

how *adverb* 1 by what means, in what way. 2 to what extent or amount etc. 3 in what condition. □ and how! (*informal*) very much so. how come? how did it come about that? why? how do you do? a formal greeting. how-d'ye-do *noun* (*informal*) an awkward state of affairs. how many what total. how much what amount, what price.

Howard, Catherine (died 1542), the fifth wife of Henry VIII.

howdah (**how**-dă) *noun* a seat, usually with a canopy, for riding on the back of an elephant or camel. [from Urdu from Arabic, = litter]

however *adverb* 1 in whatever way, to whatever extent, *will not succeed, however hard he tries*. 2 all the same, nevertheless, *later, however, he decided to go*.

howitzer *noun* a short gun firing shells, with a steep angle of fire.

howl *noun* 1 the long loud wailing cry of a dog etc. 2 a loud cry of amusement, pain, or scorn. 3 a similar noise made by a strong wind or in a loudspeaker. – howl *verb* 1 to make a howl. 2 to weep loudly. 3 to utter with a howl. □ howl down to prevent (a speaker) from being heard by howling scorn at him or her.

hoy *interjection* an exclamation used to call attention.

hoya *noun* a climbing shrub with pink, white, or yellow waxy flowers. [named after T. *Hoy*, English gardener (died 1821)]

hoyden *noun* a girl who behaves boisterously. hoydenish *adjective*

h.p. *abbreviation* (also hp) 1 hire purchase. 2 horsepower.

HQ *abbreviation* headquarters.

HTML *abbreviation* hypertext markup language.

HTTP *abbreviation* (also http) hypertext transfer (or transport) protocol.

hub *noun* 1 the central part of a wheel, from which spokes radiate. 2 a central point of activity, *the hub of the universe*.

Hubble, Edwin Powell (1889–1953), American astronomer, who demonstrated that the distance to a distant galaxy is directly proportional to its velocity of recession from the observer.
□ Hubble Space Telescope an orbiting astronomical observatory launched in 1990.

hubbub *noun* a loud confused noise of voices.

hubby *noun* (*informal*) a husband.

hubcap *noun* a round metal cover over the hub of a car wheel.

hubris (**hew**-brĭs) *noun* arrogant pride or presumption. hubristic *adjective* [Greek]

huckaback *noun* a strong linen or cotton fabric used for towels.

huckster *noun* 1 a hawker. 2 a mercenary person. –huckster *verb* to haggle.

huddle *verb* 1 to heap or crowd together into a small space. 2 to curl one's body closely, to nestle. –huddle *noun* a confused mass.
□ go into a huddle to gather together and hold a close or secret conference.

hue[1] *noun* a colour, a tint.

hue[2] *noun* hue and cry a general outcry of alarm, demand, or protest.

huff *noun* a fit of annoyance. –huff *verb* to blow. □ huffing and puffing blowing, blustering. in a huff annoyed and offended.

huffy, **huffish** *adjectives* in a huff.

hug *verb* (hugged, hugging) 1 to squeeze tightly in one's arms. 2 to keep close to, *the ship hugged the shore*. –hug *noun* a strong clasp with the arms.

huge *adjective* extremely large, enormous. hugely *adverb* very much. hugeness *noun*

hugger-mugger *adjective* & *adverb* 1 secretly, full of secrecy. 2 in disorder. –hugger-mugger *noun* 1 confusion. 2 secrecy.

Huguenot (**hew**-gĕ-noh) *noun* a member of the Calvinist French Protestants who were involved in almost continuous civil war with the Catholic majority during the 16th and 17th centuries.

hulk *noun* 1 the body of an old ship. 2 a large clumsy-looking person or thing.

hulking *adjective* (*informal*) bulky, clumsy.

hull *noun* 1 the framework of a ship or airship. 2 the cluster of leaves on a strawberry. 3 the pod of peas and beans. –hull *verb* to remove the hulls of (strawberries etc.).

hullabaloo *noun* an uproar.

hullo *interjection* & *noun* = hello.

hum[1] *verb* (hummed, humming) 1 to make a low steady continuous sound like that of a spinning object. 2 to utter a slight sound in hesitating. 3 to sing with closed lips. 4 (*informal*) to be in a state of activity, *things started humming; make things hum*. –hum *interjection* an exclamation of hesitation. –hum *noun* 1 a humming sound. 2 an exclamation of hesitation, *hums and haws*. □ hum and haw or ha to hesitate.

hum[2] (*Austral. informal*) *verb* to scrounge. –hum *noun* a scrounger.

human *adjective* 1 of or consisting of human beings (*see* man sense 1), *the human race*. 2 having the qualities that distinguish mankind, not divine or animal or mechanical; having mankind's better qualities (as kindness, pity, etc.). –human *noun* a human being.
□ human being any man or woman or child of the species *Homo sapiens*. human chain a line of people formed for passing things along. human interest something that appeals to personal emotions (in a newspaper story etc.). human rights those held to be claimable by any living person.

humane (hew-**mayn**) *adjective* kind-hearted, compassionate, merciful. humanely *adverb*

humanise *verb* (also -ize) 1 to make human, to give a human character to. 2 to make humane. humanisation *noun*

humanist (**hew**-mănĭst) *noun* a person who is concerned with the study of mankind and human affairs (as opposed to theological subjects), or who seeks to promote human welfare while not believing in a supernatural power or creator. humanism *noun* this study. humanistic *adjective*

humanitarian (hew-man-ĭ-**tair**-ree-ăn) *adjective* concerned with human welfare and the reduction of suffering. –humanitarian *noun* a humanitarian person. humanitarianism *noun*

humanity *noun* 1 the human race, people, *crimes against humanity*. 2 being human, human nature. 3 being humane, kind-heartedness. humanities *plural noun* arts subjects such as languages, literature, and history, as opposed to the sciences.

humanly *adverb* **1** in a human way.
2 by human means, with human limitations, *as accurate as is humanly possible*.

humanoid *adjective* having a human form or human characteristics. –**humanoid** *noun* a humanoid thing.

humble *adjective* **1** having or showing a modest estimate of one's own importance, not proud. **2** offered with such feelings, *humble apologies*. **3** of low social or political rank. **4** (of a thing) not large or showy or elaborate, *a humble cottage*. –**humble** *verb* to make humble, to lower the rank or self-importance of. ☐ **eat humble pie** to make a humble apology. (¶ From *umble pie*, that made with 'umbles', the edible offal of deer.) **humbly** *adverb*, **humbleness** *noun* [from Latin *humilis* = lowly]

humble-bee *noun* a bumble-bee.

humbug *noun* **1** misleading behaviour or talk that is intended to win support or sympathy. **2** a person who behaves or talks in this way. **3** a kind of hard boiled sweet usually flavoured with peppermint.

humdinger *noun* (*informal*) a remarkable person or thing.

humdrum *adjective* dull, commonplace, monotonous.

Hume[1], David (1711–76), Scottish philosopher and historian.

Hume[2], Hamilton (1795–1873), Australian explorer. In 1824, with William Hilton Hovell (1786–1875), he explored the country between Goulburn (NSW) and Port Phillip (Victoria), and discovered the Hume River (later named the Murray).

humerus (**hew**-mĕ-rŭs) *noun* the bone in the upper arm, from shoulder to elbow. **humeral** *adjective*

humid (**hew**-mĭd) *adjective* (of the air or climate) damp. **humidity** (hew-**mid**-ĭ-tee) *noun* dampness of the air.

humidifier (hew-**mid**-ĭ-fy-er) *noun* a device for keeping the air moist in a room or enclosed space.

humidify (hew-**mid**-ĭ-fy) *verb* (**humidified**, **humidifying**) to make humid.

humiliate *verb* to cause (a person) to feel disgraced. **humiliation** *noun*

humility *noun* a humble condition or attitude of mind.

hummingbird *noun* a small tropical bird that vibrates its wings rapidly, producing a humming sound.

hummock *noun* a hump in the ground.

hummus (**huu**-mŭs) *noun* (also **hoummos**) a dip made from ground chickpeas and sesame oil flavoured with lemon and garlic. [Turkish *humus*]

humoresque (hew-mŏ-**resk**) *noun* a light and lively musical composition.

humorist *noun* a writer or speaker who is noted for his or her humour.

humorous *adjective* full of humour. **humorously** *adverb*

humour *noun* **1** the quality of being amusing. **2** the ability to perceive and enjoy amusement, *sense of humour*. **3** a state of mind, *in a good humour*. **4** (*old use*) each of the four bodily fluids (blood, phlegm, choler, and melancholy) formerly believed to determine a person's physical and mental qualities. –**humour** *verb* to keep (a person) contented by giving way to his or her wishes. ☐ **aqueous humour** the transparent substance between the lens of the eye and the cornea. **vitreous humour** the transparent substance filling the eyeball.

hump *noun* **1** a rounded projecting part. **2** a deformity on a person's back, where there is abnormal curvature of the spine. **3 the hump** (*informal*) a fit of depression or annoyance. **4** a ridge across a road intended to cause vehicles to slow down. –**hump** *verb* **1** to form into a hump. **2** to hoist or shoulder (one's pack etc.). **humped** *adjective*

humpback *noun* **1** a hunchback. **2** a baleen whale with a dorsal fin forming a hump. ☐ **humpback bridge** a small steeply-arched bridge. **humpbacked** *adjective*

humph *interjection* & *noun* a sound expressing doubt or dissatisfaction.

humpy *noun* (*plural* **humpies**) (*Austral.*) **1** an Aboriginal hut. **2** a small hut or shanty. [from Yagara *numbi*]

humungous *adjective* (*informal*) very big.

humus (**hew**-mŭs) *noun* a rich dark organic material, formed by the decay of dead leaves and plants etc. and essential to the fertility of soil.

Hun *noun* **1** (*offensive*) a German. **2** a member of an Asiatic people who ravaged Europe in the 4th–5th centuries.

hunch *verb* to bend into a hump. **–hunch** *noun* **1** a hump; a hunk. **2** a feeling based on intuition.

hunchback *noun* **1** a person with a hump on his or her back. **2** this hump.

hundred *adjective* & *noun* **1** ten times ten (100, C), *five hundred* (¶ not *five hundreds*); *hundreds of people*, a large number. **2** a subdivision of a county. □ **hundred per cent** entirely, completely. **hundreds and thousands** tiny coloured sugar strands used for decorating cakes etc. **Hundred Years War** an intermittent conflict between France and England between the 1340s and 1450s. **hundredth** *adjective* & *noun*

hundredfold *adjective* & *adverb* one hundred times as much or as many.

hundredweight *noun* (*plural* **hundredweight**) an imperial measure of weight, 112 lb (about 50.8 kg). □ **metric hundredweight** 50 kg. **short hundredweight** (*Amer.*) 100 lb (about 45.4 kg).

hung *see* hang. □ **hung parliament** one that cannot reach decisions because there is no clear majority in voting.

Hungary a republic in central Europe. **Hungarian** (hung-**gair**-ree-ăn) *adjective* & *noun*

hunger *noun* **1** need for food, the uneasy sensation felt when one has not eaten for some time. **2** a strong desire for something. **–hunger** *verb* to feel hunger. □ **hunger strike** refusal of food, as a form of protest.

hungry *adjective* **1** feeling hunger. **2** eager, craving, *hungry for news*. **3** (*Austral. informal*) mean, stingy. **hungrily** *adverb*

hunk *noun* **1** a large piece cut off, *a hunk of bread*. **2** (*informal*) a large, strong, sexually attractive man.

hunt *verb* **1** to pursue (wild animals) for food or sport. **2** to pursue with hostility, to drive, *he was hunted away*. **3** to make a search, *hunted for it everywhere*; *hunt it out*, seek and find it. **4** to search (a district) for game. **5** to use (a horse or hounds) in hunting. **6** (of an engine) to run too fast and too slow alternately. **–hunt** *noun* **1** hunting. **2** an association of people hunting with a pack of hounds; the district where they hunt. □ **hunt down** to hunt (an animal etc.) until it is caught or killed; to hunt for and find. **hunt up** to search for and find.

Hunter a river of eastern NSW entering the sea at Newcastle. **Hunter Valley** an important coal-mining, wine-producing, and dairying region of NSW. [named after John Hunter (1737–1821), second-in-command of the First Fleet, and Governor of NSW (1794–99)]

hunter *noun* **1** one who hunts. **2** a horse used for hunting. **3** a watch with a hinged metal cover over the dial.

huntsman *noun* (*plural* **huntsmen**) **1** a hunter. **2** a large hairy Australian spider without a web.

Huon pine *noun* a large Tasmanian conifer.

hurdle *noun* **1** a portable rectangular frame with bars, used for a temporary fence. **2** an upright frame to be jumped over in a **hurdle race**. **3** an obstacle or difficulty. **hurdles** *plural noun* a hurdle race. **hurdler** *noun*

hurdy-gurdy *noun* **1** a stringed musical instrument played by turning a handle with the right hand and playing keys with the left. **2** (*informal*) a barrel organ.

hurl *verb* **1** to throw violently. **2** to utter vehemently, *hurl insults*. **–hurl** *noun* a violent throw.

hurley *noun* (also **hurling**) an Irish game resembling hockey, played with broad sticks.

hurly-burly *noun* a rough bustle of activity.

hurray *interjection* & *noun* (also **hurrah**) an exclamation of joy or approval.

hurricane (**hu**-rĭ-kăn) *noun* **1** a storm with violent wind, especially a West Indian cyclone. **2** a wind of 117 km/h or more. □ **hurricane lamp** a lamp with the flame protected from violent wind.

hurried *adjective* done with great haste. **hurriedly** *adverb*

hurry *noun* great haste; the need or desire for this. **–hurry** *verb* (**hurried, hurrying**) to move or do something with eager haste or too quickly; to cause to move etc. in this way. □ **hurry up** (*informal*) make haste. **in a hurry** hurrying; easily or willingly, *you won't beat that in a hurry*.

hurt *verb* (**hurt, hurting**) **1** to cause pain or damage or injury to. **2** to cause mental pain to, to distress. **3** to cause or feel pain, *my leg hurts*. **–hurt** *noun* an injury, harm.

hurtful *adjective* causing hurt. **hurtfully** *adverb*

hurtle *verb* to move or hurl rapidly.

husband *noun* a married man in relation to his wife. –**husband** *verb* to use economically, to try to save, *husband one's resources*. [from Old English *husbonda* = master of a house (*hus*)]

husbandry *noun* **1** farming. **2** management of resources. [from an old use of *husband* = person who manages things]

hush *verb* to make or become silent or quiet; *hush a thing up*, to prevent it from becoming generally known. –**hush** *noun* silence. □ **hush-hush** *adjective* (*informal*) kept very secret.

husk *noun* the dry outer covering of certain seeds and fruits. –**husk** *verb* to remove the husk(s) from.

husky[1] *adjective* (**huskier**, **huskiest**) **1** dry, like husks. **2** (of a person or voice) dry in the throat, hoarse. **3** big and strong, burly. **huskily** *adverb*, **huskiness** *noun*

husky[2] *noun* a dog of a powerful breed used in the Arctic for pulling sledges.

hussars (hŭ-**zarz**) *noun* any of several cavalry regiments.

hussy *noun* **1** a cheeky young woman. **2** an immoral woman.

hustings *noun* parliamentary election proceedings. [originally a temporary platform from which candidates for parliament could address the electors]

hustle *verb* **1** to jostle, to push roughly. **2** to hurry. **3** to bustle (a person); to make (a person) act quickly and without time to consider things, *hustled him into a decision*. –**hustle** *noun* hustling. **hustler** *noun*

hut *noun* **1** a small roughly-made house or shelter. **2** (*Austral.*) the employees' quarters on a sheep or cattle station.

hutch *noun* a boxlike pen for rabbits etc.

Hutu (**hoo**-too) *noun* (*plural* **Hutu** or **Hutus**) a member of a Bantu-speaking people forming the majority of the population of Rwanda and Burundi.

Huxley[1], Aldous Leonard (1894–1963), English novelist and essayist, grandson of T.H. Huxley. His works include *Brave New World* and *Eyeless in Gaza*.

Huxley[2], Thomas Henry (1825–95), English biologist and surgeon, a firm supporter of Darwin.

hyacinth *noun* **1** a plant with fragrant bell-shaped flowers, growing from a bulb. **2** purplish-blue.

hybrid *noun* **1** an animal or plant that is the offspring of two different species or varieties. **2** something made by combining two different elements. –**hybrid** *adjective* produced in this way, cross-bred. **hybridise** *verb*, **hybridisation** *noun*, **hybridism** *noun*

Hyde, Edward, *see* Jekyll.

hydra *noun* **1** a thing that is hard to get rid of. **2** a water snake. **3** a freshwater polyp with a tubular body and tentacles round the mouth. [named after the Hydra in Greek mythology, a water snake with many heads that grew again if cut off]

hydrangea (hy-**drayn**-jă) *noun* a shrub with white, pink, or blue flowers growing in clusters.

hydrant *noun* a pipe (especially in a street) with a nozzle to which a hose can be attached for drawing water from the main for fire-fighting etc.

hydrate *noun* a chemical compound of water with another compound or element. –**hydrate** *verb* to combine chemically with water; to cause to absorb water. **hydration** *noun*

hydraulic (hy-**drol**-ik) *adjective* **1** of water conveyed through pipes or channels. **2** operated by the movement of water or other fluid, *a hydraulic lift*. **3** concerned with the use of water in this way, *hydraulic engineer*. **4** hardening under water, *hydraulic cement*. **hydraulics** *noun* the science of the conveyance of liquids through pipes etc., especially as motive power. **hydraulically** *adverb* [from *hydro-*, + Greek *aulos* = pipe]

hydro *noun* (*plural* **hydros**) (*informal*) **1** a hydroelectric power plant. **2** a hotel etc. providing hydrotherapy.

hydro- *prefix* **1** water (as in *hydroelectric*). **2** (in chemical names) containing hydrogen (as in *hydrochloric*). [from Greek *hudor* = water]

hydrocarbon *noun* any of a class of compounds of hydrogen and carbon that are found in petrol, coal, and natural gas.

hydrocephalus (hy-drŏ-**sef**-ă-lŭs) *noun* a condition (especially of children) in which fluid accumulates on the brain. [from *hydro-*, + Greek *kephale* = head]

hydrochloric acid (hy-drŏ-**klo**-rik) *noun* a colourless corrosive acid containing hydrogen and chlorine.

hydrochloride *noun* a compound of an organic base with hydrochloric acid.

hydrocyanic acid *noun* prussic acid.

hydrodynamic *adjective* of the force exerted by a moving liquid, especially water. **hydrodynamics** *noun* the scientific study of this force.

hydroelectric *adjective* using water power to produce electricity. **hydroelectricity** *noun*

hydrofoil *noun* 1 a boat equipped with a structure designed to raise the hull out of the water when the boat is in motion, enabling it to travel fast and economically. 2 this structure.

hydrogen *noun* a chemical element (symbol H), a colourless odourless tasteless gas, the lightest element, combining with oxygen to form water. □ **hydrogen bomb** an immensely powerful bomb releasing energy by fusion of hydrogen nuclei. [from *hydro-*, + *-gen* = producing]

hydrogenate (hy-**droj**-ĕ-nayt) *verb* to charge with hydrogen; to cause to combine with hydrogen. **hydrogenation** *noun*

hydrogenous (hy-**droj**-ĕ-nŭs) *adjective* of or containing hydrogen.

hydrography (hy-**drog**-ră-fee) *noun* the scientific study of seas, lakes, rivers, etc. **hydrographer** *noun*, **hydrographic** *adjective* [from *hydro-* + *-graphy*]

hydrology (hy-**drol**-ŏ-jee) *noun* the scientific study of the properties of water, especially of its movement in relation to the land. **hydrological** *adjective* [from *hydro-* + *-logy*]

hydrolyse (**hy**-drŏ-lyz) *verb* to decompose by hydrolysis.

hydrolysis (hy-**drol**-ĭ-sĭs) *noun* decomposition of a substance by the chemical action of water. [from *hydro-*, + Greek *lusis* = loosening]

hydrometer (hy-**drom**-ĕ-ter) *noun* an instrument that measures the density of liquids.

hydrophilic (hy-drŏ-**fil**-ik) *adjective* having a tendency to combine with water; able to be wetted by water. [from *hydro-*, + Greek *philos* = loving]

hydrophobia (hy-drŏ-**foh**-bee-ă) *noun* 1 abnormal fear of water, especially as a symptom of rabies in humans. 2 rabies. **hydrophobic** *adjective* [from *hydro-* + *phobia*]

hydroplane *noun* a light fast motor boat designed to skim over the surface of water.

hydroponics (hy-drŏ-**pon**-iks) *noun* the art of growing plants without soil in sand etc.

containing water to which nutrients have been added. [from *hydro-*, + Greek *ponos* = labour]

hydrosphere *noun* the waters of the earth's surface. [from *hydro-* + *sphere*]

hydrostatic *adjective* of the pressure and other characteristics of water or other liquid at rest. **hydrostatics** *noun* the scientific study of these characteristics.

hydrotherapy *noun* the use of water (externally) in the treatment of disease and abnormal physical conditions.

hydrothermal *adjective* of hot water that occurs naturally underground. [from *hydro-*, + Greek *therme* = heat]

hydrotropic (hy-drŏ-**trop**-ik) *adjective* (of plant roots etc.) tending to turn towards or away from moisture. **hydrotropism** (hy-drŏ-**troh**-pizm) *noun* this tendency. [from *hydro-*, + Greek *trope* = turning]

hydrous (**hy**-drŭs) *adjective* (of substances) containing water.

hydroxide *noun* a compound of an element or radical with a hydroxyl.

hydroxyl (hy-**droks**-ĭl) *noun* a radical containing hydrogen and oxygen.

hyena *noun* a flesh-eating animal like a wolf, with a howl that sounds like wild laughter.

hygiene (**hy**-jeen) *noun* the practice of cleanliness in order to maintain health and prevent disease. [from Greek *hugieine* = of health]

hygienic (hy-**jeen**-ik) *adjective* 1 according to the principles of hygiene. 2 clean and free from disease-germs. **hygienically** *adverb*

hygienist (**hy**-jeen-ĭst) *noun* an expert in hygiene.

hygrometer (hy-**grom**-ĕ-ter) *noun* an instrument that measures humidity. [from Greek *hugros* = wet, + *metron* = measure]

hygroscopic (hy-grŏ-**skop**-ik) *adjective* (of a substance) having a tendency to absorb moisture from the air.

hymen *noun* a membrane partly closing the external opening of the vagina of a virgin girl or woman. [Greek *humen* = membrane]

hymenopterous (hy-mĕn-**op**-tĕ-rŭs) *adjective* of the kind of insects that includes ants, bees, and wasps, having four membranous wings. [from *hymen*, + Greek *pteron* = wing]

hymn *noun* a song of praise to God or a sacred being.

hymnal *noun* a book of hymns.

hyoscine (**hy**-ŏ-seen) *noun* a poisonous substance from which a sedative is made, found in plants of the nightshade family.

hype *noun* (*informal*) trickery; extravagant or misleading publicity. –**hype** *verb* **1** (*informal*) to deceive or publicise by this. **2** to overstimulate, *hyped up*.

hyper *adjective* (*informal*) hyperactive, energetic, highly-strung.

hyper- *prefix* over or above; excessive. [from Greek *huper* = over]

hyperactive *adjective* (of a person) abnormally and excessively active. **hyperactivity** *noun*

hyperbola (hy-**per**-bŏ-lă) *noun* the curve produced when a cone is cut by a plane that makes a larger angle with the base than the side of the cone does. **hyperbolic** (hy-per-**bol**-ik) *adjective* [same origin as *hyperbole*]

hyperbole (hy-**per**-bŏ-lee) *noun* an exaggerated statement that is not meant to be taken literally, e.g. *her feet were killing her*. **hyperbolical** (hy-per-**bol**-ik-ăl) *adjective* [from *hyper-*, + Greek *bole* = a throw]

hypercritical *adjective* excessively critical. **hypercritically** *adverb*

hypersensitive *adjective* excessively sensitive.

hypersonic *adjective* **1** of speeds more than about five times that of sound. **2** of sound frequencies above about 1000 megahertz. [from *hyper-* + *sonic*]

hypertension *noun* **1** abnormally high blood pressure. **2** great emotional tension.

hypertext *noun* (in computing) a software system allowing extensive cross-referencing between related sections of text and associated graphic material.
□ **hypertext markup language** a computer programming markup language used to prepare documents for display on the World Wide Web (abbreviation **HTML**). **hyptertext transfer** or **transport protocol** a method of transferring documents on the World Wide Web (abbreviation **HTTP**).

hyperventilation *noun* abnormally rapid breathing. **hyperventilate** *verb*

hypha *noun* (*plural* **hyphae**, *pr.* **hy**-fee) any of the microscopic threadlike strands that form the main part of mould and similar fungi. [from Greek *huphe* = web]

hyphen *noun* the sign (-) used to join two words together (e.g. *drip-dry*) or to divide a word into parts. –**hyphen** *verb* to hyphenate. [from Greek *huphen* = together]

hyphenate *verb* to join or divide with a hyphen. **hyphenation** *noun*

hypnosis (hip-**noh**-sĭs) *noun* **1** a state like sleep produced in a person who is then very susceptible to suggestion and acts only if told to do so. **2** production of this state. [from Greek *hupnos* = sleep]

hypnotherapy *noun* the treatment of disease etc. by hypnosis.

hypnotic (hip-**not**-ik) *adjective* **1** of or producing hypnosis or a similar condition. **2** (of a drug) producing sleep. –**hypnotic** *noun* a hypnotic drug. **hypnotically** *adverb*

hypnotise (hip-nŏ-tyz) *verb* (also **-ize**) **1** to produce hypnosis in (a person). **2** to fascinate, to dominate the mind or will of.

hypnotism (**hip**-nŏ-tizm) *noun* the production of hypnosis. **hypnotist** *noun*

hypo- *prefix* below; under. [from Greek *hupo* = under]

hypocaust (**hy**-pŏ-kawst) *noun* a system of underfloor heating by hot air, used in ancient Roman houses. [from *hypo-*, + Greek *kaustos* = burnt]

hypochondria (hy-pŏ-**kon**-dree-ă) *noun* a mental condition in which a person constantly imagines that he or she is ill. **hypochondriac** *noun* one who suffers from this.

hypocrisy (hip-**ok**-rĭ-see) *noun* falsely pretending to be virtuous, insincerity.

hypocrite (**hip**-ŏ-krit) *noun* a person who is guilty of hypocrisy. **hypocritical** (hip-ŏ-**krit**-ikăl) *adjective*, **hypocritically** *adverb* [from Greek, = acting a part]

hypodermic *adjective* injected beneath the skin; used for such injections. –**hypodermic** *noun* a **hypodermic syringe**, a syringe fitted with a hollow needle through which a liquid can be injected beneath the skin. **hypodermically** *adverb* [from *hypo-*, + Greek *derma* = skin]

hypogeal (hy-pŏ-**jee**-ăl) *adjective* (of plant germination) in which the cotyledons remain below the ground. [from *hypo-*, + Greek *ge* = earth]

hypotenuse (hy-**pot**-ĕ-newz) *noun* the side opposite the right angle in a right-angled triangle.

hypothalamus (hy-pŏ-**thal**-ă-mŭs) *noun*
(*plural* hypothalami, *pr*. -my) the part of the
brain that controls body temperature, thirst,
hunger, etc.

hypothermia *noun* the condition of having
an abnormally low body temperature. [from
hypo-, + Greek *therme* = heat]

hypothesis (hy-**poth**-ĕ-sĭs) *noun* (*plural*
hypotheses, *pr*. -seez) a supposition or
guess put forward to account for certain
facts and used as a basis for further
investigation by which it may be proved
or disproved.

hypothesise (hy-**poth**-ĕ-syz) *verb* (also
-ize) **1** to form a hypothesis. **2** to assume as a
hypothesis.

hypothetical (hy-pŏ-**thet**-ikăl) *adjective*
1 of or based on a hypothesis. **2** supposed
but not necessarily true. **hypothetically**
adverb

hyssop (**his**-ŏp) *noun* a small bushy aromatic
herb, formerly used medicinally.

hysterectomy (hiss-tĕ-**rek**-tŏ-mee) *noun*
surgical removal of the womb. [from Greek
hustera = womb, + -*ectomy* = cutting out]

hysteria (hiss-**teer**-ree-ă) *noun* wild
uncontrollable emotion or excitement. [from
Greek *hustera* = womb (once thought to be the
cause of hysterics)]

hysterical (hiss-**te**-ri-kăl) *adjective* caused
by hysteria; suffering from this; (of laughter)
uncontrollable. **hysterically** *adverb*

hysterics (hiss-**te**-riks) *plural noun* a
hysterical outburst.

Hz *abbreviation* hertz.

Ii

I *pronoun* the person who is speaking or writing and referring to himself or herself.

I. *abbreviation* island(s); isle(s).

iambic (I-**am**-bik) *adjective* of or using a metrical foot (the *iambus*) with one short or unstressed syllable followed by one long or stressed syllable. **iambics** *plural noun* lines of verse in iambic metre.

IB *abbreviation* International Baccalaureate (*see* baccalaureate).

Iberia (I-**beer**-ree-ă) the ancient name for the peninsula in SW Europe comprising Spain and Portugal. **Iberian** *adjective* & *noun*

ibex (**I**-beks) *noun* (*plural* ibexes *or* ibex) a mountain goat with long curving horns.

ibid. *abbreviation* in the same book or passage etc. [short for Latin *ibidem* = in the same place]

ibis (**I**-bĭs) *noun* a wading bird with a long curved bill, found in warm climates.

Iblis *noun* (in Islam) one of the names of the Devil.

Ibsen, Henrik (1828–1906), Norwegian dramatist.

ice *noun* **1** frozen water, a brittle transparent solid. **2** a portion of ice cream or water ice. **3** (*informal*) a form of methamphetamine which can be smoked. –**ice** *verb* **1** to become covered with ice, *the lake iced over*. **2** to cover or mix with ice; to make very cold, *iced tea*. **3** to decorate with icing. □ **Ice Age** a period when much of the northern hemisphere was covered with glaciers. **ice block** (*Austral.*) an edible concoction of frozen flavoured water on a stick. **ice cap** the permanent covering of ice in polar regions. **ice-cold** *adjective* as cold as ice. **ice cream** a sweet creamy frozen food. **ice field** a large expanse of floating ice. **ice hockey** a game resembling hockey, played on ice between teams of skaters with a flat disc (a *puck*) instead of a ball. **on ice** (*informal*) held in reserve, in a state of readiness; temporarily shelved.

iceberg *noun* a huge mass of ice floating in the sea with the greater part under water. □ **tip of the iceberg** a small evident part of something much larger that lies concealed.

Iceland an island republic in the North Atlantic. **Icelander** *noun*

Icelandic *adjective* of Iceland or its people or language. –**Icelandic** *noun* the language of Iceland.

ichneumon fly (ik-**new**-mŏn) *noun* a small insect that lays its eggs on or inside the larva of another insect.

ichthyosaurus (ik-thee-ŏ-**saw**-rŭs) *noun* (*plural* **ichthyosauruses**) an extinct sea animal with a long head, tapering body, four paddles, and a large tail. [from Greek *ichthus* = fish, + *sauros* = lizard]

icicle *noun* a pointed piece of ice hanging down, formed when dropping water freezes.

icing *noun* a mixture of sugar etc. used to decorate cakes and biscuits. □ **icing on the cake** an attractive but inessential addition or bonus. **icing sugar** powdered sugar used for making icing.

icon (**I**-kon) *noun* **1** an image or statue. **2** (in the Orthodox Church) a painting or mosaic of a sacred person, itself regarded as sacred. **3** (in computing) a symbol on a display screen representing a program, option, or window for selection. [from Greek *eikon* = image]

iconoclast (I-**kon**-ŏ-klast) *noun* a person who attacks cherished beliefs. **iconoclasm** *noun*, **iconoclastic** *adjective* [from Greek *eikon* = image, + *klastos* = broken]

iconography (I-kŏn-**og**-ră-fee) *noun* the illustration of a subject by drawings etc. [from Greek *eikon* = image, + *-graphy*]

icosahedron (I-koss-ă-**hee**-drŏn) *noun* a solid with twenty faces. [from Greek *eikosi* = twenty, + *hedra* = base]

icy *adjective* (**icier**, **iciest**) **1** very cold, as cold as ice, *icy winds*. **2** covered with ice, *icy roads*. **3** very cold and unfriendly in manner, *an icy voice*. **icily** *adverb*, **iciness** *noun*

ID *abbreviation* identification, identity.

I'd (*informal*) = I had, I would.

id *noun* a person's inherited psychological impulses considered as part of the unconscious.

Idaho (I-dă-hoh) a State of the north-western USA.

idea *noun* **1** a plan etc. formed in the mind by thinking. **2** a mental impression, *give him an idea of what is needed*. **3** an opinion. **4** a vague belief or fancy, a feeling that something is likely.

ideal *adjective* **1** satisfying one's idea of what is perfect, *ideal weather for swimming*. **2** existing only in an idea, visionary. –**ideal** *noun* a person or thing or idea that is regarded as perfect or as a standard for attainment or imitation. □ **ideal gas** an imaginary gas (used in calculations) whose behaviour conforms to the same simple law under all conditions. **ideally** *adverb*

idealise *verb* (also **-ize**) to regard or represent as perfect. **idealisation** *noun*

idealist (I-**dee**-ă-lĭst) *noun* a person who has high ideals and tries in an unrealistic way to achieve these. **idealism** *noun*, **idealistic** *adjective*

idée fixe (ee-day **feeks**) *noun* an idea that is dominant or keeps recurring. [French, = fixed idea]

identical *adjective* **1** the same, *this is the identical place we stayed in last year*. **2** similar in every detail, exactly alike, *no two people have identical fingerprints*. □ **identical twins** twins developed from a single fertilised ovum and therefore of the same sex and very similar in appearance. **identically** *adverb* [same origin as *identity*]

identify *verb* (**identified**, **identifying**) **1** to establish the identity of, to recognise as being a specified person or thing. **2** to consider to be identical, to equate, *one cannot identify wealth and happiness*. **3** to associate very closely in feeling or interest, *he has identified himself with the progress of the firm*. **4** to regard oneself as sharing the characteristics or fortunes of another person, *people like to identify with the characters in a film*. **identifiable** *adjective*, **identification** *noun*, **identifier** *noun*

Identikit *noun* (*trademark*) a set of pictures of features that can be put together to form a likeness (especially of a person who is sought by the police) based on descriptions given by witnesses.

identity *noun* **1** the state of being identical, absolute sameness. **2** the condition of being a specified person or thing; individuality, personality, *felt she'd lost her identity*.

3 identification or the result of it, *identity card*; *a case of mistaken identity*. **4** (*Austral. informal*) a well-known person.
□ **identity element** (in mathematics) the element in a group that when combined with any other element leaves that element unchanged, e.g. 1 is an identity element with respect to multiplication. **identity theft** the fraudulent practice of using another person's name and personal information in order to obtain credit, loans, etc. [from Latin *idem* = same]

ideogram (**id**-ee-ŏ-gram) *noun* a symbol indicating the idea (not the sounds forming the name) of a thing, e.g. numerals, Chinese characters, and symbols used in road signs. [from Greek *idea* = form, + *-gram*]

ideology (I-dee-**ol**-ŏjee) *noun* the ideas that form the basis of an economic or political theory etc., *in Marxist ideology*. **ideological** *adjective*, **ideologist** *noun* [from *idea* + *-logy*]

ides (*rhymes with* tides) *plural noun* the 15th day of March, May, July, and October, the 13th of other months, in the ancient Roman calendar.

idiocy *noun* **1** the state of being an idiot. **2** extreme stupidity. **3** stupid behaviour; a stupid action.

idiom (**id**-ee-ŏm) *noun* **1** a phrase that must be taken as a whole, usually having a meaning that is not clear from the meanings of the individual words, e.g. *foot the bill* and *a change of heart*. **2** the use of particular words or of words in an order that is regarded as standard, *the English idiom is 'wash up the dishes' but not 'wash up the baby'*. **3** the language used by a people or group, *in the scientific idiom*. **4** a characteristic style of expression in art or music etc. [from Greek *idios* = your own]

idiomatic (id-ee-ŏ-**mat**-ik) *adjective* **1** in accordance with idioms. **2** full of idioms. **idiomatically** *adverb*

idiosyncrasy (id-ee-ŏ-**sing**-kră-see) *noun* a person's own attitude of mind or way of behaving etc. that is unlike that of others. **idiosyncratic** (id-ee-oh-sing-**krat**-ik) *adjective* [from Greek *idios* = your own, + *sun* = with, + *krasis* = mixture]

idiot *noun* **1** a mentally deficient person who is permanently incapable of rational conduct. **2** (*informal*) a very stupid person. [from Greek *idiotes* = private citizen, uneducated person]

idiotic *adjective* very stupid. **idiotically** *adverb*

idle *adjective* **1** doing no work, not employed, not active or in use. **2** (of time) not spent in doing something. **3** avoiding work, lazy. **4** worthless, having no special purpose, *idle gossip*. –**idle** *verb* **1** to pass (time) without working, to be idle. **2** (of an engine) to run slowly in a neutral gear. **idleness** *noun*, **idler** *noun*, **idly** *adverb*

idol *noun* **1** an image of a god, used as an object of worship. **2** a person or thing that is the object of intense admiration or devotion. [from Greek *eidolon* = image]

idolatory (I-**dol**-ă-tree) *noun* **1** worship of idols. **2** excessive admiration or devotion. **idolater** *noun*, **idolatrous** *adjective* [from *idol*, + Greek *latreia* = worship]

idolise *verb* (also **-ize**) to feel excessive admiration or devotion to (a person or thing). **idolisation** *noun*

idyll (**id**-ĭl) *noun* **1** a short description (usually in verse) of a peaceful or romantic scene or incident, especially in country life. **2** a scene or incident of this kind.

idyllic (id-**il**-ik) *adjective* like an idyll, peaceful and happy. **idyllically** *adverb*

i.e. *abbreviation* = that is. [short for Latin *id est*]

IED *abbreviation* improvised explosive device.

if *conjunction* **1** on condition that, *he'll do it only if you pay him*. **2** in the event that, *if you are tired we will rest*. **3** supposing or granting that, *even if she said it she didn't mean it*. **4** even though, *I'll finish it, if it takes me all day*. **5** whenever, *if they asked for food, it was brought*. **6** whether, *see if you can turn the handle*. **7** (in exclamations of wish or surprise), *if only he would come!*; *well, if it isn't Simon!* –**if** *noun* a condition or supposition, *too many ifs about it*.

iffy *adjective* uncertain; doubtful.

igloo *noun* a dome-shaped Inuit hut built of blocks of hard snow. [from Inuit, = house]

Ignatius Loyola (ig-**nay**-shŭs loi-**oh**-lă), St 1491/5–1556, Spanish theologian, founder of the Jesuits.

igneous (**ig**-nee-ŭs) *adjective* **1** of fire, fiery. **2** (of rocks) formed when molten matter has solidified, either underground or after being expelled by a volcano. [from Latin *igneus* = fiery]

ignite (ig-**nyt**) *verb* **1** to set fire to. **2** to catch fire. [from Latin *ignis* = fire]

ignition (ig-**nish**-ŏn) *noun* **1** igniting; being ignited. **2** the mechanism providing the spark that ignites the fuel in an internal-combustion engine.

ignoble *adjective* not noble in character, aims, or purpose. **ignobly** *adverb*

ignominious (ig-nŏ-**min**-ee-ŭs) *adjective* bringing contempt or disgrace, humiliating. **ignominiously** *adverb*

ignominy (**ig**-nŏ-mĭ-nee) *noun* disgrace, humiliation.

ignoramus (ig-nŏ-**ray**-mŭs) *noun* (*plural* **ignoramuses**) an ignorant person. [Latin, = we do not know]

ignorant *adjective* **1** lacking knowledge, *ignorant of the facts*. **2** behaving rudely through lack of knowledge of good manners. **ignorantly** *adverb*, **ignorance** *noun*

ignore *verb* **1** to take no notice of, to disregard. **2** to refrain deliberately from acknowledging or greeting (a person). [from Latin *ignorare* = not to know]

iguana (ig-**wah**-nă) *noun* a large tree-climbing lizard of the West Indies and tropical America.

iguanodon (ig-**wah**-nŏ-don) *noun* a large dinosaur that fed on plants.

ikebana (ik-ĕ-**bah**-nă) *noun* the Japanese art of flower arrangement.

il- *prefix* see **in-**.

ileum (**il**-ee-ŭm) *noun* (*plural* **ilea**) the lowest part of the small intestine.

iliac (**il**-ee-ak) *adjective* of the flank or hip bone.

Iliad (**il**-ee-ăd) a Greek epic poem, traditionally ascribed to Homer, telling of the climax of the war at Troy (Ilium) between Greeks and Trojans.

ilium (**il**-ee-ŭm) *noun* the bone forming the upper part of the pelvis.

ilk *noun* of that ilk (*informal*) of that kind.

I'll (*informal*) = I shall, I will.

ill *adjective* **1** physically or mentally unwell. **2** (of health) unsound, not good. **3** harmful, *no ill effects*. **4** not favourable, *ill luck*. **5** hostile, unkind, *no ill feelings*; *ill humour*, bad temper. –**ill** *adverb* **1** badly, wrongly. **2** unfavourably. **3** imperfectly, scarcely, *ill provided for*; *can ill afford to do this*. –**ill** *noun* evil, harm, injury. □ **ill-advised** *adjective* unwise. **ill at ease** uncomfortable, embarrassed. **ill-bred** *adjective* having bad manners. **ill-fated** *adjective* unlucky. **ill-favoured** *adjective* unattractive. **ill-gotten** *adjective* gained by evil or unlawful means. **ill-mannered** *adjective* having bad manners. **ill-natured** *adjective* unkind.

ill-starred *adjective* unlucky. **ill-timed** *adjective* done or occurring at an unfortunate time. **ill-treat** *verb* to treat badly or cruelly. **ill-use** *verb* to ill-treat. **ill will** hostility, unkind feeling.

Illawarra (il-ă-**wo**-ră) a coastal district south of Sydney including the city of Wollongong.

illegal *adjective* against the law. **illegally** *adverb*, **illegality** (il-ĕ-**gal**-ĭ-tee) *noun*

illegible (i-**lej**-ĭ-bŭl) *adjective* not legible. **illegibly** *adverb*, **illegibility** *noun*

illegitimate (il-ĕ-**jit**-ĭ-măt) *adjective* **1** born of parents not married to each other. **2** contrary to law or to rules. **3** (of a conclusion in an argument etc.) not logical, wrongly inferred. **illegitimately** *adverb*, **illegitimacy** *noun*

illicit (i-**lis**-ĭt) *adjective* unlawful, not allowed. **illicitly** *adverb* [from *il-* = not, + Latin *licitus* = allowed]

Illinois (il-ĭ-**noi**) a State of the Middle West of the USA.

illiterate (i-**lit**-ĕ-răt) *adjective* unable to read and write, showing lack of education. **–illiterate** *noun* an illiterate person. **illiterately** *adverb*, **illiteracy** *noun*

illness *noun* **1** the state of being ill in body or mind. **2** a particular form of ill health.

illogical *adjective* not logical, contrary to logic. **illogically** *adverb*, **illogicality** *noun*

illuminate *verb* **1** to light up, to make bright. **2** to throw light on (a subject), to make understandable. **3** to decorate (a street or building etc.) with lights. **4** to decorate (a manuscript) with coloured designs. **illumination** *noun*, **illuminative** *adjective* [from *il-* = in, + Latin *lumen* = light]

illumine *verb* (*literary*) to light up.

illusion (i-**loo**-zhŏn) *noun* **1** something that a person wrongly supposes to exist. **2** a false belief about the nature of something. [from Latin *illudere* = to mock]

illusionist *noun* a person who produces illusions, a conjuror.

illusive (i-**loo**-siv) *adjective* illusory.

illusory (i-**loo**-zŏ-ree) *adjective* based on illusion, not real.

illustrate *verb* **1** to supply (a book or newspaper etc.) with drawings or pictures. **2** to make clear or explain by examples or pictures etc. **3** to serve as an example of. **illustrator** *noun*

illustration *noun* **1** illustrating. **2** a drawing or picture in a book etc. **3** an example used to explain something.

illustrative (**il**-ŭs-tră-tiv) *adjective* serving as an illustration or example. **illustratively** *adverb*

illustrious (i-**lus**-tree-ŭs) *adjective* famous and distinguished. **illustriousness** *noun*

illywhacker *noun* (*Austral. old use*) a confidence trickster.

ILO *abbreviation* International Labour Organisation.

I'm (*informal*) = I am.

im- *prefix* see **in-**.

image *noun* **1** a representation of the outward form of a person or thing, e.g. a statue (especially as an object of worship). **2** the optical appearance of something, produced in a mirror or through a lens etc. **3** something very like another in appearance, *he's the very image of his father*. **4** a mental picture. **5** a simile or metaphor. **6** the general impression of a person, firm, or product etc. as perceived by the public. **7** (in mathematics) a set formed by mapping.

imagery *noun* **1** the use of metaphorical language to produce pictures in the minds of readers or hearers. **2** images; statuary, carving.

imaginary *adjective* existing only in the imagination, not real. ☐ **imaginary number** (in mathematics) the square root of a negative number.

imagination *noun* imagining, the ability to imagine creatively or to use this ability to solve problems.

imaginative *adjective* having or showing imagination. **imaginatively** *adverb*

imagine *verb* **1** to form a mental image of, to picture in one's mind. **2** to think or believe; (*informal*) to suppose, *don't imagine you'll get away with it*. **3** to guess, *I can't imagine where it has gone*. **imaginable** *adjective*

imagism *noun* a 20th-century movement in poetry that avoided abstraction and sought clarity though precise images.

imago (i-**may**-goh) *noun* (*plural* **imagines**, *pr.* i-**may**-jĭ-neez) the fully developed stage of an insect's life, e.g. a butterfly.

imam (im-**ahm**) *noun* **1** the leader of prayers in a mosque. **2** the title of various Muslim religious leaders. [Arabic, = leader]

imbalance *noun* lack of balance, disproportion.

imbecile (**im**-bĭ-seel) *noun* **1** a mentally deficient person, an adult whose intelligence is equal to that of an average five-year-old child. **2** a stupid person. –**imbecile** *adjective* idiotic. **imbecility** (im-bĕ-**sil**-ĭ-tee) *noun*

imbibe (im-**byb**) *verb* **1** to drink. **2** to absorb (ideas etc.) into the mind. **3** to inhale (air).

imbroglio (im-**brohl**-yoh) *noun* (*plural* **imbroglios**) a confused situation, usually involving a disagreement. [Italian]

imbue (im-**bew**) *verb* **1** to fill (a person) with certain feelings, qualities, or opinions. **2** to saturate or dye (with a colour etc.).

IMF *abbreviation* International Monetary Fund.

imitable *adjective* able to be imitated.

imitate *verb* **1** to copy the behaviour of, to take as an example that should be followed. **2** to mimic playfully or for entertainment. **3** to make a copy of; to be like (something else). **imitator** *noun*

imitation *noun* **1** imitating. **2** something produced by this, a copy; *imitation leather*, a material made to look like leather. **3** the act of mimicking a person or thing for entertainment, *he does imitations*.

imitative (**im**-ĭ-tă-tiv) *adjective* imitating.

immaculate *adjective* **1** spotlessly clean. **2** free from moral blemish. **3** free from fault, right in every detail. ☐ **Immaculate Conception** the Roman Catholic doctrine that the Virgin Mary, from the moment of her conception by her mother, was and remained free from the taint of original sin. **immaculately** *adverb*, **immaculacy** *noun*

immanent (**im**-ă-nĕnt) *adjective* **1** (of qualities) inherent. **2** (of God) permanently pervading the universe. **immanence** *noun*

Usage Distinguish *immanent* from *imminent*.

Immanuel (i-**man**-yoo-ĕl) the name given to Christ as the deliverer of Judah prophesied by the prophet Isaiah.

immaterial *adjective* **1** having no physical substance, *as immaterial as a ghost*. **2** of no importance or relevance, *it is now immaterial whether he goes or stays*.

immature *adjective* not mature. **immaturity** *noun*

immeasurable *adjective* not measurable, immense. **immeasurably** *adverb*

immediate *adjective* **1** occurring or done at once, without delay. **2** nearest, next,

with nothing between, *the immediate neighbourhood*. **3** nearest in relation, *my immediate family*. **4** direct, without an intermediary. **immediately** *adverb* & *conjunction*, **immediacy** *noun*

immemorial *adjective* existing from before what can be remembered or found recorded, *from time immemorial*.

immense *adjective* exceedingly great. **immensity** *noun* [from *im-* = not, + Latin *mensum* = measured]

immensely *adverb* extremely.

immerse *verb* **1** to put completely into water or other liquid. **2** to absorb or involve deeply in thought or business etc. [from *im-* = in, + Latin *mersum* = dipped]

immersion *noun* **1** immersing; being immersed. **2** baptism by putting the whole body into water.

immigrant *adjective* **1** immigrating. **2** of immigrants. –**immigrant** *noun* a person who has immigrated; a descendant of recent immigrants.

immigrate *verb* to come into a foreign country as a permanent resident. **immigration** *noun* [from *im-* = in, + *migrate*]

imminent *adjective* (of events) about to occur, likely to occur at any moment. **imminence** *noun*

immiscible (i-**mis**-ĭ-bŭl) *adjective* not able to be mixed with another substance.

immobile *adjective* **1** immovable. **2** not moving. **immobility** *noun*

immobilise *verb* (also **-ize**) to make or keep immobile. **immobilisation** *noun*

immoderate *adjective* excessive, lacking moderation. **immoderately** *adverb*

immodest *adjective* **1** lacking in modesty, indecent. **2** conceited. **immodestly** *adverb*, **immodesty** *noun*

immolate (**im**-ŏ-layt) *verb* to sacrifice. **immolation** *noun*

immoral *adjective* not conforming to the accepted rules of morality, morally wrong (especially in sexual matters). **immorally** *adverb*, **immorality** (im-ŏ-**ral**-ĭ-tee) *noun*

immortal *adjective* **1** living for ever, not mortal. **2** famous for all time. –**immortal** *noun* an immortal being or person. **immortality** *noun*

immortalise *verb* (also **-ize**) to make immortal.

immovable *adjective* **1** unable to be moved. **2** unyielding, not changing in one's purpose; not moved emotionally. **3** (of property) consisting of land, houses, etc. **immovably** *adverb*, **immovability** *noun*

immune *adjective* having immunity; protected, exempt, *immune from* or *against* or *to infection*; *immune to criticism*. [from Latin *immunis* = exempt]

immunise *verb* (also **-ize**) to make immune, especially against infection. **immunisation** *noun*

immunity *noun* **1** the ability of an animal or plant to resist infection. **2** special exemption from a tax, duty, or penalty.

immuno- *prefix* of immunity to infection, *immunodeficiency*; *immunotherapy*.

immunology (im-yoo-**nol**-ŏjee) *noun* the scientific study of resistance to infection. **immunological** *adjective*, **immunologist** *noun*

immure (im-**yoor**) *verb* to imprison, to shut in. [from *im-* = in, + Latin *murus* = wall]

immutable (i-**mewt**-ă-bŭl) *adjective* unchangeable. **immutably** *adverb*, **immutability** *noun*

imp *noun* **1** a small devil. **2** a mischievous child.

impact (**im**-pakt) *noun* **1** a collision. **2** the force exerted when one body collides with another. **3** the force exerted by the influence of new ideas. **–impact** (im-**pakt**) *verb* **1** to pack, drive, or wedge firmly into something or together. **2** to have an effect, *these changes impact on everybody*. [from *im-* = in, + Latin *pactum* = driven]

impair *verb* to damage, to cause weakening of, *impair one's health*. **impairment** *noun* [from *im-* = in, + Latin *pejor* = worse]

impala (im-**pah**-lă) *noun* (*plural* impala) a small African antelope. [Zulu]

impale *verb* to fix or pierce by passing a sharp-pointed object into or through. [from *im-* = in, + Latin *palus* = a stake]

impalpable *adjective* **1** unable to be felt by touch, intangible. **2** not easily grasped by the mind. **impalpably** *adverb*, **impalpability** *noun*

impart *verb* **1** to give. **2** to reveal or make (information etc.) known. **impartation** *noun*

impartial (im-**par**-shăl) *adjective* not favouring one more than another. **impartially** *adverb*, **impartiality** (im-par-shee-**al**-ĭ-tee) *noun*

impassable *adjective* (of roads or barriers) impossible to travel on or over. **impassably** *adverb*, **impassability** *noun*

impasse (**im**-pahss) *noun* a deadlock. [French, = impassable place]

impassioned (im-**pash**-ŏnd) *adjective* full of deep feeling, *an impassioned appeal*.

impassive *adjective* not feeling or showing emotion. **impassively** *adverb*, **impassiveness** *noun*, **impassivity** *noun*

impasto *noun* the laying on of paint thickly so that it projects from the surface of the picture and gives a textured quality.

impatient *adjective* **1** unable to wait patiently. **2** showing lack of patience, irritated, *got an impatient reply*. **3** intolerant, *impatient of delay*. **impatiently** *adverb*, **impatience** *noun*

impeach *verb* **1** to accuse of treason or other serious crime against the State, and bring for trial. **2** to call into question, to disparage. **impeachment** *noun*

impeccable *adjective* faultless. **impeccably** *adverb*, **impeccability** *noun* [from *im-* = not, + Latin *peccare* = to sin]

impecunious (im-pĕ-**kew**-nee-ŭs) *adjective* having little or no money. **impecuniosity** *noun*

impedance (im-**pee**-dăns) *noun* **1** the total resistance of an electric circuit to the flow of alternating current. **2** a similar mechanical property.

Usage Distinguish *impedance* from *impediment*.

impede *verb* to hinder. [from Latin *impedire* = to shackle the feet (*im-* = in, + *pedis* = of a foot)]

impediment *noun* **1** a hindrance, an obstruction. **2** a defect that prevents something functioning properly; *a speech impediment*, a lisp or stammer. [same origin as *impede*]

impedimenta (im-ped-ĭ-**ment**-ă) *plural noun* encumbrances, baggage.

impel *verb* (impelled, impelling) **1** to urge or drive to do something, *curiosity impelled her to investigate*. **2** to send or drive forward, to propel. [from *im-* = towards, + Latin *pellere* = to drive]

impending *adjective* imminent. [from *im-* = in, + Latin *pendere* = hang]

impenetrable *adjective* unable to be penetrated. **impenetrably** *adverb*, **impenetrability** *noun*

impenitent *adjective* not penitent, not repentant. **impenitently** *adverb*, **impenitence** *noun*

imperative (im-**pe**-ră-tiv) *adjective* 1 expressing a command. 2 essential, obligatory, *it is imperative that tracks be made for firefighters.* –**imperative** *noun* 1 a command; a form of a verb used in making commands (e.g. *come in come here!*). 2 something essential or obligatory, *survival is the first imperative.* [from Latin *imperare* = to command]

imperceptible *adjective* not perceptible, very slight or gradual and therefore difficult to see. **imperceptibly** *adverb*

imperfect *adjective* 1 not perfect; incomplete. 2 of the tense of a verb used to denote action going on but not completed, especially in the past, e.g. *she was singing.* –**imperfect** *noun* the imperfect tense. **imperfectly** *adverb*

imperfection *noun* 1 being imperfect. 2 a mark or fault or characteristic that prevents a thing from being perfect.

imperial *adjective* 1 of an empire or an emperor or empress. 2 majestic. 3 (of a system of weights and measures) established by statute in the UK, used in Australia before the introduction of the metric system, and similarly being replaced in the UK. **imperially** *adverb* [from Latin *imperium* = supreme power]

imperialism *noun* belief in the desirability of acquiring colonies and dependencies. **imperialist** *noun*, **imperialistic** *adjective*

imperil *verb* (**imperilled**, **imperilling**) to endanger.

imperious (im-**peer**-ree-ŭs) *adjective* commanding, bossy. **imperiously** *adverb*, **imperiousness** *noun*

impermanent *adjective* not permanent. **impermanence** *noun*, **impermanency** *noun*

impermeable (im-**per**-mee-ă-bŭl) *adjective* not able to be penetrated, especially by liquid. **impermeability** *noun*

impersonal *adjective* 1 not influenced by personal feeling, showing no emotion. 2 not referring to any particular person. 3 having no existence as a person, *nature's impersonal forces.* 4 (of verbs) used with 'it' to make general statements such as 'it is raining' or 'it is hard to find one'. **impersonally** *adverb*, **impersonality** *noun*

impersonate *verb* 1 to play the part of. 2 to pretend to be (another person) for

entertainment or in fraud. **impersonation** *noun*, **impersonator** *noun*

impertinent *adjective* 1 insolent, not showing proper respect. 2 not pertinent, irrelevant. **impertinently** *adverb*, **impertinence** *noun*

imperturbable (im-per-**terb**-ăbŭl) *adjective* not excitable, calm. **imperturbably** *adverb*, **imperturbability** *noun*

impervious (im-**per**-vee-ŭs) *adjective* 1 not able to be penetrated, *impervious to water.* 2 not influenced, not responsive, *impervious to fear* or *argument.* [from *im-* = not, + Latin *per* = through, *via* = way]

impetigo (imp-ĕ-**ty**-goh) *noun* a contagious skin disease causing spots that form yellowish crusts.

impetuous (im-**pet**-yoo-ŭs) *adjective* 1 moving quickly or violently, *an impetuous dash.* 2 acting or done on impulse. **impetuously** *adverb*, **impetuosity** *noun*

impetus (**im**-pĕ-tŭs) *noun* (*plural* **impetuses**) 1 the force or energy with which a body moves. 2 a driving force, *the treaty gave an impetus to trade.* [Latin, = an attack]

impiety (im-**py**-ĕ-tee) *noun* lack of reverence.

impinge *verb* 1 to make an impact. 2 to encroach.

impious (**imp**-ee-ŭs) *adjective* not reverent, wicked. **impiously** *adverb*

impish *adjective* of or like an imp; mischievous. **impishly** *adverb*, **impishness** *noun*

implacable (im-**plak**-ăbŭl) *adjective* not able to be placated, relentless. **implacably** *adverb*, **implacability** *noun*

implant (im-**plahnt** *or* -**plant**) *verb* 1 to plant, to insert. 2 to insert or fix (ideas etc.) in the mind. 3 to insert (tissue or other substance) in a living thing. –**implant** (**im**-plahnt *or* -plant) *noun* a thing implanted, implanted tissue etc. **implantation** *noun*

implausible *adjective* not plausible. **implausibly** *adverb*, **implausibility** *noun*

implement (**im**-plĕ-mĕnt) *noun* a tool or instrument for working with. –**implement** (**im**-plĕ-ment) *verb* to put into effect, *we implemented the scheme.* **implementation** *noun*

implicate *verb* 1 to involve or show (a person) to be involved in a crime etc. 2 to lead to as a consequence or inference. [same origin as *implicit*]

444

implication *noun* 1 implicating; being implicated. 2 implying; being implied. 3 something that is implied.

implicit (im-**pliss**-ĭt) *adjective* 1 implied though not made explicit. 2 absolute, unquestioning, *implicit obedience*. **implicitly** *adverb* [from Latin, = folded in]

implode *verb* to burst or cause to burst inwards. **implosion** *noun*

implore *verb* to request earnestly, to entreat. **imploring** *adjective*, **imploringly** *adverb* [from *im-* = in, + Latin *plorare* = weep]

imply *verb* (**implied**, **implying**) 1 to suggest without stating directly, to hint. 2 to mean. 3 to involve the truth or existence of, *the beauty of the carving implies that they had skilled craftsmen*. [same origin as *implicit*]

Usage See usage note at **infer**.

---

impolite *adjective* not polite. **impolitely** *adverb*

impolitic (im-**pol**-ĭ-tik) *adjective* unwise, inexpedient.

imponderable (im-**pon**-dĕ-ră-bŭl) *adjective* 1 not able to be estimated. 2 weightless, very light. –**imponderable** *noun* any of the things such as emotions, qualities, etc., the effect of which is imponderable.

import (im-**port**) *verb* 1 to bring in from abroad or from an outside source. 2 to imply, to indicate. –**import** (**im**-port) *noun* 1 the importing of goods etc.; something imported. 2 meaning. 3 importance. **importation** *noun*, **importer** *noun* [from *im-* = in, + Latin *portare* = carry]

important *adjective* 1 having or able to have a great effect. 2 (of a person) having great authority or influence. 3 pompous, *he has an important manner*. **importantly** *adverb*, **importance** *noun*

importunate (im-**por**-tew-năt) *adjective* making persistent or pressing requests. **importunity** (im-per-**tewn**-ĭ-tee) *noun*

importune (im-per-**tewn**) *verb* to make insistent requests to.

impose *verb* 1 to put (a tax or obligation etc.), *imposed heavy duties on tobacco*. 2 to inflict, *imposed a great strain on our resources*. 3 to force to be accepted, *imposed his ideas on the group*. □ **impose on** to take unfair advantage of, *we don't want to impose on your hospitality*. [from *im-* = on, + Latin *positum* = placed]

imposing *adjective* impressive.

imposition *noun* 1 the act of imposing something. 2 something imposed, e.g. a tax or duty. 3 a burden imposed unfairly.

impossible *adjective* 1 not possible, unable to be done or to exist. 2 (*informal*) outrageous, unendurable, *an impossible person*. **impossibly** *adverb*, **impossibility** *noun*

impost (**im**-post) *noun* a tax or duty levied.

impostor *noun* a person who fraudulently pretends to be someone else.

imposture *noun* a fraudulent deception.

impotent (**im**-pŏ-tĕnt) *adjective* 1 powerless, unable to take action. 2 (of a man) unable to copulate or reach orgasm; unable to procreate. **impotently** *adverb*, **impotence** *noun*

impound *verb* 1 to take (another person's property) into a pound or into legal custody, to confiscate. 2 to shut up (animals etc.) in a pound.

impoverish *verb* 1 to cause to become poor. 2 to exhaust the natural strength or fertility of, *impoverished soil*. **impoverishment** *noun*

impracticable *adjective* incapable of being put into practice. **impracticably** *adverb*, **impracticability** *noun*

impractical *adjective* not practical, unwise. **impracticality** *noun*

imprecation (im-prĕ-**kay**-shŏn) *noun* a spoken curse.

imprecise *adjective* not precise. **imprecisely** *adverb*, **imprecision** *noun*

impregnable (im-**preg**-nă-bŭl) *adjective* safe against attack, *an impregnable fortress*. **impregnably** *adverb*, **impregnability** *noun*

impregnate (im-**preg**-nayt) *verb* 1 to introduce sperm or pollen into and fertilise (a female animal or plant); to make pregnant. 2 to penetrate all parts of (a substance), to fill or saturate, *the water was impregnated with salts*. **impregnation** *noun*

impresario (im-prĕ-**sah**-ree-oh) *noun* (*plural* **impresarios**) an organiser of public entertainment; the manager of an operatic or concert company etc. [Italian]

impress (im-**press**) *verb* 1 to make (a person) form a strong (usually favourable) opinion of something. 2 to fix firmly in the mind, *impressed on them the need for haste*. 3 to press a mark into, to stamp with a mark. –**impress** (**im**-press) *noun* an impressed mark.

impression *noun* **1** an effect produced on the mind. **2** an uncertain idea, belief, or memory. **3** an imitation of a person or sound, done for entertainment. **4** the impressing of a mark; an impressed mark. **5** a reprint of a book etc. made with few or no alterations to its contents. □ **be under the impression** to think (that something is a fact).

impressionable *adjective* easily influenced. **impressionably** *adverb*, **impressionability** *noun*

impressionism *noun* **1** a style of painting in the late 19th century giving the general impression of a subject, especially by using the effects of light, without elaborate detail. **2** a similar style in music or literature. **impressionist** *noun*, **impressionistic** *adjective*

impressive *adjective* making a strong impression, arousing admiration and approval. **impressively** *adverb*

imprimatur (im-prĭ-**may**-ter) *noun* authoritative permission or approval, especially from the Roman Catholic Church to print (a book etc.).

imprint (**im**-print) *noun* a mark made by pressing or stamping a surface. –**imprint** (im-**print**) *verb* **1** to impress or stamp a mark etc. on. **2** to establish firmly in the mind. **3** to make or become recognised by (a young bird or animal in the first hours of its life) as an object of trust.

imprison *verb* **1** to put into prison. **2** to keep in confinement. **imprisonment** *noun*

improbable *adjective* not likely to be true or to happen. **improbably** *adverb*, **improbability** *noun*

impromptu (im-**promp**-tew) *adverb* & *adjective* without preparation or rehearsal. –**impromptu** *noun* a musical composition that gives the impression of being composed impromptu. [from Latin *in promptu* = in readiness]

improper *adjective* **1** wrong, incorrect, *made improper use of the knife*. **2** not conforming to the rules of social or lawful conduct. **3** indecent. □ **improper fraction** one that is greater than unity, with the numerator greater than the denominator, e.g. $\frac{5}{3}$. **improperly** *adverb*

impropriety (im-prŏ-**pry**-ĕ-tee) *noun* being improper; an improper act or remark etc.

improve *verb* **1** to make or become better. **2** to make good or better use of, *improved the occasion*. □ **improved value** (of land) the value with the addition of improvements

(e.g. a house) **improve on** to produce something better than. **improvable** *adjective*

improvement *noun* **1** improving, being improved. **2** an addition or alteration that improves something or adds to its value.

improvident (im-**prov**-ĭ-dĕnt) *adjective* not providing for future needs, wasting one's resources. **improvidently** *adverb*, **improvidence** *noun*

improvise (**im**-prŏ-vyz) *verb* **1** to compose (a thing) impromptu. **2** to provide, in time of need, using whatever materials are at hand, *improvised a bed from cushions and rugs*. **improvisation** *noun*, **improviser** *noun*

imprudent (im-**proo**-dĕnt) *adjective* unwise, rash. **imprudently** *adverb*, **imprudence** *noun*

impudent (**im**-pew-dĕnt) *adjective* impertinent, cheeky. **impudently** *adverb*, **impudence** *noun*

impugn (im-**pewn**) *verb* to express doubts about the truth or honesty of, to try to discredit, *we do not impugn their motives*.

impulse *noun* **1** a push or thrust; impetus. **2** a stimulating force in a nerve, causing a muscle to react. **3** a sudden inclination to act, without thought for the consequences, *bought it on impulse*. [same origin as *impel*]

impulsion *noun* impelling, a push; impetus.

impulsive *adjective* **1** (of a person) habitually acting on impulse. **2** (of an action) done on impulse. **impulsively** *adverb*, **impulsiveness** *noun*

impunity (im-**pewn**-ĭ-tee) *noun* freedom from punishment or injury. [from *im-* = without, + Latin *poena* = penalty]

impure *adjective* not pure.

impurity *noun* **1** being impure. **2** a substance that makes another substance impure by being present in it.

imputation (im-pew-**tay**-shŏn) *noun* **1** imputing. **2** an accusation of wrongdoing. □ **imputation credit** an amount of paid company tax attributed to individual shareholders.

impute (im-**pewt**) *verb* to attribute, to ascribe.

in *preposition* expressing position or state: **1** of inclusion within the limits of space, time, circumstance, or surroundings etc. **2** of quantity or proportion, *they are packed in tens*. **3** of form or arrangement, *hanging in folds*. **4** of activity, occupation, or membership, *he is in the army*. **5** wearing as dress or colour etc., *went in jeans*. **6** of method

or means of expression, *spoke in French*.
7 with the instrument or means of, *written in ink*. **8** of identity, *found a friend in Mary*.
9 under the influence of, *spoke in anger*.
10 with respect to, *lacking in courage*. **11** as the content of, *there's not much in it*. **12** after the time of, *back in ten minutes*. **13** (of a female animal) pregnant with, *in calf*. **14** into. **15** towards, *ran in all directions*. –**in** *adverb* **1** expressing position bounded by certain limits, or motion to a point enclosed by these, *come in*. **2** at home, *will you be in?* **3** on or towards the inside, *with the fur side in*. **4** in fashion, season, or office; elected; in effective or favourable action, *my luck was in*; *the tide was in*, was high. **5** (in cricket and baseball) batting, *which side is in?* **6** having arrived or been gathered or received, *train is in*; *harvest is in*. –**in** *adjective* **1** internal; living etc. inside. **2** fashionable, *it's the in thing to do*.
□ **be in for** to be about to experience, *she is in for a surprise*; to be competing in. **be in on** (*informal*) to be aware of or sharing in (a secret or activity). **be in with** to be on good terms with. **in all** in total number. **ins and outs** the details of an activity or procedure. **in so far as** to the extent that, *he obeyed the rules only in so far as he agreed with them*.

in- *prefix* (changing to **il-** before *l*, **im-** before *b*, *m*, *p*, **ir-** before *r*) **1** in; into; on; towards (as in *include*, *invade*). [from Latin *in*] **2** not (as in *incorrect*, *indirect*). [compare the prefixes *an-*¹ and *un-*]

inability *noun* being unable.

in absentia (ab-**sent**-ee-ǎ) *adverb* in his or her or their absence. [Latin]

inaccessible *adjective* not accessible, unapproachable. **inaccessibly** *adverb*, **inaccessibility** *noun*

inaccurate *adjective* not accurate. **inaccurately** *adverb*, **inaccuracy** *noun*

inaction *noun* lack of action, doing nothing.

inactive *adjective* not active, showing no activity. **inactively** *adverb*, **inactivity** *noun*

inadequate *adjective* **1** not adequate, insufficient. **2** not sufficiently able or competent, *felt inadequate*. **inadequately** *adverb*, **inadequacy** *noun*

inadmissible *adjective* not allowable. **inadmissibly** *adverb*, **inadmissibility** *noun*

inadvertent (in-ǎd-**ver**-těnt) *adjective* unintentional. **inadvertently** *adverb*, **inadvertence** *noun*, **inadvertency** *noun*

inadvisable *adjective* not advisable. **inadvisably** *adverb*, **inadvisability** *noun*

inalienable (in-**ay**-lee-ě-nǎ-bǔl) *adjective* not able to be given away or taken away, *an inalienable right*. **inalienably** *adverb*, **inalienability** *noun*

inamorato (in-am-ǒ-**rah**-toh) *noun* a man with whom one is in love. **inamorata** *feminine noun* [Italian]

inane *adjective* silly, lacking sense. **inanely** *adverb*, **inanity** (in-**an**-ǐ-tee) *noun* [from Latin *inanis* = empty]

inanimate (in-**an**-ǐ-mǎt) *adjective* **1** (of rocks and other objects) lifeless; (of plants) lacking animal life. **2** showing no sign of life.

inapplicable (in-**ap**-lik-ǎ-bǔl) *adjective* not applicable.

inapprehensible (in-ap-rě-**hen**-sǐ-bǔl) *adjective* that cannot be grasped by the mind or perceived by the senses.

inappropriate (in-ǎ-**proh**-pree-ǎt) *adjective* unsuitable. **inappropriately** *adverb*, **inappropriateness** *noun*

inarticulate (in-ar-**tik**-yǔ-lǎt) *adjective* **1** not expressed in words, *an inarticulate cry*. **2** unable to speak distinctly, *was inarticulate with rage*. **3** unable to express one's ideas clearly. **inarticulately** *adverb*

inartistic *adjective* not artistic. **inartistically** *adverb*

inasmuch *adverb* **inasmuch as** since, because; (*old use*) in so far as.

inattention *noun* lack of attention, neglect.

inattentive *adjective* not attentive, not paying attention. **inattentively** *adverb*, **inattentiveness** *noun*

inaudible (in-**aw**-dǐ-bǔl) *adjective* not audible, unable to be heard. **inaudibly** *adverb*, **inaudibility** *noun*

inaugural (in-**awg**-yǔ-rǎl) *adjective* of or for an inauguration, *the inaugural ceremony*.

inaugurate (in-**awg**-yǔ-rayt) *verb* **1** to admit (a person) to office with a ceremony. **2** to enter ceremonially upon (an undertaking); to open (a building or exhibition etc.) formally. **3** to be the beginning of, to introduce. **inauguration** *noun*, **inaugurator** *noun*

inauspicious (in-aw-**spish**-ǔs) *adjective* not auspicious. **inauspiciously** *adverb*

inborn *adjective* existing in a person or animal from birth, natural, *an inborn ability*.

inbox *noun* (in computing) the window in which a user's received emails etc. are displayed.

inbred *adjective* **1** produced by inbreeding. **2** inborn.

inbreeding *noun* breeding from closely related individuals.

in-built *adjective* built-in.

Inc. *abbreviation* Incorporated.

Inca *noun* (*plural* Inca or Incas) a member of an American indigenous people in Peru etc. before the Spanish conquest.

incalculable *adjective* unable to be calculated. incalculably *adverb*, incalculability *noun*

incandescent (in-kan-**dess**-ĕnt) *adjective* glowing with heat, shining; *incandescent light*, light produced by a glowing white-hot filament. incandescence *noun* [from Latin, = becoming white]

incantation (in-kan-**tay**-shŏn) *noun* words or sounds to be uttered as a magic spell; the uttering of these. incantatory *adjective* [from *in-* = in, + Latin *cantare* = sing]

incapable *adjective* not capable. incapably *adverb*, incapability *noun*

incapacitate (in-kă-**pas**-ĭ-tayt) *verb* **1** to disable. **2** to make ineligible.

incapacity *noun* inability, lack of sufficient strength or power.

incarcerate (in-**kar**-sĕ-rayt) *verb* to imprison. incarceration *noun* [from *in-* = in, + Latin *carcer* = prison]

incarnate (in-**kar**-năt) *adjective* embodied in flesh, especially in human form, *a devil incarnate*. [from *in-* = in, + Latin *carnis* = of flesh]

incarnation (in-kar-**nay**-shŏn) *noun* embodiment, especially in human form. –the Incarnation the embodiment of God in human form as Christ.

incautious (in-**kaw**-shŭs) *adjective* not cautious, rash. incautiously *adverb*

incendiary (in-**send**-yă-ree) *adjective* **1** (of a bomb etc.) designed to cause a fire, containing chemicals that ignite. **2** of arson; guilty of arson. **3** tending to stir up strife, inflammatory. –incendiary *noun* **1** an incendiary bomb etc. **2** an arsonist. **3** a person who stirs up strife.

incense¹ (**in**-sens) *noun* **1** a substance that produces a sweet smell when burning.

2 its smoke, used especially in religious ceremonies.

incense² (in-**sens**) *verb* to make angry.

incentive (in-**sen**-tiv) *noun* something that rouses or encourages a person to some action or effort.

inception (in-**sep**-shŏn) *noun* the beginning of the existence of something.

incertitude *noun* uncertainty.

incessant (in-**sess**-ănt) *adjective* unceasing, continually repeated. incessantly *adverb*

incest (**in**-sest) *noun* sexual intercourse between people regarded as too closely related to marry each other.

incestuous (in-**sess**-tew-ŭs) *adjective* **1** involving incest. **2** guilty of incest.

inch *noun* **1** an imperial measure of length, one twelfth of a foot (= 2.54 cm). **2** a very small amount, *would not yield an inch*. –inch *verb* to move slowly and gradually, *they inched forward*. □ every inch entirely. within an inch of almost to the point of.

inchoate (in-**koh**-ayt) *adjective* just begun; not yet fully developed. inchoation *noun*

incidence (**in**-sĭ-dĕns) *noun* **1** the rate at which something occurs or affects people or things, the range of occurrence, *studied the incidence of the disease*. **2** the falling of something (e.g. a ray of light) on a surface. [from Latin *incidens* = happening]

incident *noun* **1** an event, especially a minor one. **2** a piece of hostile activity, *frontier incidents*. **3** a public disturbance or accident, *the protest march took place without incident*. **4** an event that attracts general attention. –incident *adjective* **1** liable to happen, accompanying something, *the risks incident to a pilot's career*. **2** (of rays of light etc.) falling on a surface, *incident light*.

incidental *adjective* **1** occurring as a minor accompaniment, *incidental expenses*. **2** liable to occur in consequence of or in connection with something, *the incidental hazards of exploration*. **3** casual, occurring by chance. □ incidental music music played as a background to the action of a film or play.

incidentally *adverb* **1** in an incidental way. **2** as an unconnected comment, by the way.

incinerate (in-**sin**-ĕ-rayt) *verb* to reduce to ashes, to destroy by fire. incineration *noun* [from *in-* = in, + Latin *cineris* = of ashes]

incinerator (in-**sin**-ĕ-ray-ter) *noun* a furnace or enclosed device for burning rubbish.

incipient (in-**sip**-ee-ěnt) *adjective* in its early stages, beginning, *incipient decay*.

incise (in-**syz**) *verb* to make a cut in (a surface); to engrave by cutting. [from *in-* = into, + Latin *caesum* = cut]

incision (in-**si**-zhŏn) *noun* 1 incising. 2 a cut, especially one made surgically into the body.

incisive (in-**sy**-siv) *adjective* clear and decisive, *made incisive comments*. **incisively** *adverb*, **incisiveness** *noun*

incisor (in-**sy**-zer) *noun* any of the sharp-edged front teeth in the upper and lower jaws.

incite (in-**syt**) *verb* to urge on to action, to stir up. **incitement** *noun* [from *in-* = towards, + Latin *citare* = rouse]

incivility *noun* lack of civility; an impolite act or remark.

inclement (in-**klem**-ěnt) *adjective* (of weather) cold, wet, or stormy. **inclemency** *noun*

inclination *noun* 1 a slope or slant; a leaning or bending movement. 2 a tendency. 3 a liking or preference.

incline (in-**klyn**) *verb* 1 to lean, to slope. 2 to bend (the head or body) forward. 3 to have or cause a certain tendency, to influence, *his manner inclines me to believe him.* –**incline** (**in**-klyn) *noun* a slope. □ **be inclined** to have a certain tendency or willingness, *the door is inclined to bang*; *I'm inclined to agree*. [from Latin *inclinare* = to bend]

include *verb* 1 to have or regard or treat as part of a whole. 2 to put into a certain category or list etc. **inclusion** *noun* [from Latin, = enclose]

inclusive *adjective* 1 including the limits mentioned and the part between, *pages 7 to 26 inclusive*. 2 including much or everything; *inclusive terms*, (at a hotel etc.) including all charges. **inclusively** *adverb*

incognito (in-kog-**nee**-toh) *adjective* & *adverb* with one's identity kept secret, *she was travelling incognito*. –**incognito** *noun* (*plural* **incognitos**) the identity assumed by one who is incognito. [Italian, = unknown]

incoherent (in-koh-**heer**-rěnt) *adjective* rambling in speech or in reasoning. **incoherently** *adverb*, **incoherence** *noun*

incombustible *adjective* not able to be burnt by fire.

income *noun* money received during a certain period (especially a year) as wages or salary, interest in investments, etc. □ **income tax** tax that must be paid on annual income.

incoming *adjective* 1 coming in, *the incoming tide*. 2 succeeding another person, *the incoming president*.

incommensurate *adjective* not commensurate; disproportionate.

incommode (in-kŏ-**mohd**) *verb* to inconvenience. **incommodious** *adjective*

incommunicable *adjective* unable to be communicated.

incommunicado (in-kŏ-mew-nǐ-**kah**-doh) *adjective* not allowed to communicate with others, *the prisoner was held incommunicado*.

incomparable (in-**komp**-ă-ră-bŭl) *adjective* without an equal, beyond comparison. **incomparably** *adverb*, **incomparability** *noun*

incompatible (in-kŏm-**pat**-ǐ-bŭl) *adjective* 1 not compatible. 2 inconsistent; *the two statements are incompatible*, cannot both be true. **incompatibly** *adverb*, **incompatibility** *noun*

incompetent (in-**kom**-pě-těnt) *adjective* not competent. **incompetently** *adverb*, **incompetence** *noun*

incomplete *adjective* not complete. **incompletely** *adverb*, **incompleteness** *noun*

incomprehensible (in-kom-prě-**hen**-sǐ-bŭl) *adjective* not able to be understood. **incomprehensibly** *adverb*, **incomprehensibility** *noun*

incomprehension (in-kom-prě-**hen**-shŏn) *noun* failure to understand.

inconceivable *adjective* 1 unable to be imagined. 2 (*informal*) impossible to believe, most unlikely. **inconceivably** *adverb*

inconclusive *adjective* (of evidence or an argument etc.) not fully convincing, not decisive. **inconclusively** *adverb*, **inconclusiveness** *noun*

incongruous (in-**kong**-groo-ŭs) *adjective* unsuitable, not harmonious. **incongruously** *adverb*, **incongruity** (in-kong-**groo**-ǐ-tee) *noun*

inconsequent (in-**kon**-sě-kwěnt) *adjective* not following logically, irrelevant. **inconsequently** *adverb*, **inconsequence** *noun*

inconsequential (in-kon-sě-**kwen**-shǎl) *adjective* not following logically, irrelevant; unimportant. **inconsequentially** *adverb*

inconsiderable *adjective* not worth considering, of small size or amount or value.

inconsiderate *adjective* not considerate towards other people. **inconsiderately** *adverb*, **inconsiderateness** *noun*

inconsistent *adjective* not consistent.
inconsistently *adverb*, inconsistency *noun*

inconsolable (in-kŏn-**soh**-lă-bŭl) *adjective*
not able to be consoled. inconsolably *adverb*,
inconsolability *noun*

inconspicuous *adjective* not conspicuous.
inconspicuously *adverb*, inconspicuousness
noun

incontestable (in-kŏn-**test**-ă-bŭl) *adjective*
indisputable. incontestably *adverb*

incontinent *adjective* unable to control
the excretion of one's urine and faeces.
incontinence *noun*

incontrovertible (in-kon-trŏ-**vert**-ĭ-bŭl)
adjective indisputable, undeniable.
incontrovertibly *adverb*, incontrovertibility
noun

inconvenience *noun* 1 being inconvenient.
2 a circumstance that is inconvenient.
–inconvenience *verb* to cause inconvenience
or slight difficulty to.

inconvenient *adjective* not convenient, not
suiting one's needs or requirements, slightly
troublesome. inconveniently *adverb*

incorporate (in-**kor**-pŏ-rayt) *verb*
1 to include as a part, *your suggestions will be
incorporated in the plan.* 2 to form into a legal
corporation. –incorporate (in-**kor**-pŏ-răt)
adjective incorporated. incorporation *noun*

incorrect *adjective* not correct. incorrectly
adverb, incorrectness *noun*

incorrigible (in-**ko**-rĭ-jĭ-bŭl) *adjective* (of a
person or faults etc.) not able to be reformed
or improved, *an incorrigible liar.* incorrigibly
adverb, incorrigibility *noun*

incorruptible (in-kŏ-**rupt**-ĭbŭl) *adjective*
1 not liable to decay. 2 not able to be corrupted
morally, e.g. by bribes. incorruptibility *noun*

increase (in-**kreess**) *verb* to make or become
greater in size, amount, or intensity. –increase
(**in**-kreess) *noun* 1 the process of increasing.
2 the amount by which something increases.
[from *in-* = in, + Latin *crescere* = grow]

increasingly *adverb* more and more.

incredible *adjective* 1 unbelievable.
2 (*informal*) hard to believe, very surprising.
incredibly *adverb*

incredulous (in-**kred**-yŭ-lŭs) *adjective*
unbelieving, showing disbelief. incredulously
adverb, incredulity (in-krĕ-**dew**-lĭ-tee) *noun*

increment (**in**-krĕ-mĕnt) *noun* an increase,
an added amount, *a salary with annual
increments of $1000.* incremental *adjective*

incriminate *verb* to indicate as involved in
wrongdoing, *his statement incriminated the
guard.* incrimination *noun*, incriminatory
adjective

incrustation *noun* 1 encrusting, being
encrusted. 2 a crust or deposit formed on a
surface.

incubate *verb* 1 to hatch (eggs) by the
warmth of a bird's body as it sits on them or
by artificial heat. 2 to cause (bacteria etc.) to
develop in suitable conditions. [from *in-* = on,
+ Latin *cubare* = to lie]

incubation *noun* incubating. □ incubation
period the time it takes for symptoms of a
disease to become apparent in an infected
person.

incubator *noun* 1 an apparatus for hatching
eggs or developing bacteria by artificial
warmth. 2 an apparatus in which babies
born prematurely can be kept in a constant
controlled heat and supplied with oxygen etc.

incubus (**ink**-yŭ-bŭs) *noun* (*plural* incubuses)
1 a burdensome person or thing. 2 an evil
spirit visiting a sleeping person. [from Latin
incubo = nightmare]

inculcate (**in**-kul-kayt) *verb* to implant (ideas
or habits) by persistent urging, *attempting to
inculcate obedience in the young.* inculcation
noun [from *in-* = on, + Latin *calcare* = to tread]

inculpate (**in**-kul-payt) *verb* to involve
in a charge of wrongdoing, to incriminate.
inculpation *noun*, inculpatory *adjective* [from
in- = in, + Latin *culpare* = to blame]

incumbency (in-**kum**-bĕn-see) *noun* the
position of an incumbent.

incumbent (in-**kum**-bĕnt) *adjective* forming
an obligation or duty, *it is incumbent on you to
warn people of the danger.* –incumbent *noun*
a person who holds a particular office or post.
[from *in-* = on, + Latin *-cumbens* = lying]

incur *verb* (incurred, incurring) to bring upon
oneself, *incurred great expense.* [from
in- = on, + Latin *currere* = to run]

incurable *adjective* unable to be cured.
–incurable *noun* a person with an incurable
disease. incurably *adverb*, incurability *noun*

incurious *adjective* feeling or showing no
curiosity about something. incuriously *adverb*

incursion *noun* a raid or brief invasion into
someone else's territory etc. [same origin as
incur]

indebted *adjective* owing money or gratitude.
indebtedness *noun*

indecent *adjective* **1** offending against recognised standards of decency. **2** unseemly, *with indecent haste*. □ **indecent assault** sexual assault not involving rape. **indecent exposure** exposing one's genitals in public. **indecently** *adverb*, **indecency** *noun*

indecipherable *adjective* unable to be deciphered.

indecision *noun* inability to make up one's mind, hesitation.

indecisive *adjective* not decisive. **indecisively** *adverb*, **indecisiveness** *noun*

indecorous (in-**dek**-ŏ-rŭs) *adjective* improper, not in good taste. **indecorously** *adverb*

indeed *adverb* **1** truly, really, *it was indeed remarkable*; *indeed?*, is that so? **2** used to intensify a meaning, *very nice indeed*. **3** admittedly, *it is, indeed, his first attempt*. **4** used to express surprise or contempt, *does she indeed!*

indefatigable (in-dĕ-**fat**-ig-ă-bŭl) *adjective* not becoming tired. **indefatigably** *adverb*

indefensible *adjective* unable to be defended, unable to be justified. **indefensibly** *adverb*, **indefensibility** *noun*

indefinable (in-dĕ-**fy**-nă-bŭl) *adjective* unable to be defined or described clearly. **indefinably** *adverb*

indefinite *adjective* not clearly defined or stated or decided, vague. □ **indefinite article** the word 'a' or 'an'.

indefinitely *adverb* **1** in an indefinite way. **2** for an unlimited period.

indelible *adjective* **1** (of a mark or stain or feeling) unable to be removed or washed away. **2** (of a pencil etc.) making an indelible mark. **indelibly** *adverb* [from *in-* = not, + Latin *delere* = destroy]

indelicate *adjective* **1** slightly indecent. **2** tactless. **indelicately** *adverb*, **indelicacy** *noun*

indemnify (in-**dem**-nĭ-fy) *verb* (**indemnified**, **indemnifying**) **1** to protect or insure (a person) against penalties incurred by his or her actions etc. **2** to compensate (a person) for injury suffered.

indemnity *noun* **1** protection or insurance against penalties incurred by one's actions. **2** compensation for damage done.

indent¹ (in-**dent**) *verb* **1** to make recesses or toothlike notches in; *an indented coastline*, one with deep recesses. **2** to start (a line of print or writing) further from the margin than the others, *indent the first line of each paragraph*. **3** to place an indent for goods or stores. **indentation** *noun*

indent² (**in**-dent) *noun* an official order for goods or stores.

indenture (in-**den**-cher) *noun* a written contract or agreement. **indentures** *plural noun* an agreement binding an apprentice to work for a master. –**indenture** *verb* to bind by indentures.

independence *noun* being independent. □ **Independence Day** an anniversary of the date on which a country achieved independence, e.g. in the US 4 July, Papua New Guinea 16 September.

independent *adjective* **1** not dependent on or controlled by another person or thing, *he is now independent of his parents*. **2** (of a school) private or non-government, supported largely by pupils' fees and endowments, and usually with some State aid. **3** not depending for its validity or operation on the thing(s) involved; *independent proof*, from another source. **4** self-governing. **5** having or providing a sufficient income to make it unnecessary for the possessor to earn a living, *he has independent means*. **6** not influenced by others in one's ideas or conduct. **7** unwilling to be under an obligation to others. –**Independent** *noun* a politician who is not committed to any political party. **independently** *adverb*

in-depth *adjective* thorough, very detailed.

indescribable *adjective* unable to be described, too great or beautiful or bad etc. to be described. **indescribably** *adverb*

indestructible *adjective* unable to be destroyed. **indestructibly** *adverb*, **indestructibility** *noun*

indeterminable *adjective* impossible to discover or decide. **indeterminably** *adverb*

indeterminate *adjective* not fixed in extent or character etc.; vague, left doubtful. **indeterminately** *adverb*

index *noun* (*plural* **indexes** *or* (in sense 2, and always in sense 3) **indices**) **1** a list of names, titles, subjects, etc., especially an alphabetical list indicating where in a book etc. each can be found. **2** a figure indicating the relative level of prices or wages compared with that at a previous date, *consumer price index*; *Dow-Jones index*. **3** the exponent of a number. –**index** *verb* **1** to make an index to (a book or collection of books etc.). **2** to enter in an index. **3** to adjust (wages, pensions, etc.)

according to changes in the cost of living based on the consumer price index.
□ **index finger** the forefinger. **indexation** *noun*, **indexer** *noun* [Latin, = pointer]

India a federal republic in southern Asia forming the greater part of the Indian subcontinent.

Indian *adjective* of India or Indians. –**Indian** *noun* **1** a native of India. **2** (in full **American Indian**) any of the indigenous inhabitants of the continent of America or their descendants. □ **Indian clubs** a pair of wooden or metal bottle-shaped clubs for swinging to exercise the arms. **Indian file** single file. **Indian ink** ink made with a black pigment (made originally in China and Japan). **Indian subcontinent** a large peninsula of Asia south of the Himalayas, divided between India, Pakistan, and Bangladesh. **Indian summer** a period of dry sunny weather in late autumn; a period of tranquil enjoyment late in life.

Usage The term 'Indian' to refer to the indigenous peoples of America is considered offensive by some. However, it is used by many indigenous peoples in the US and Canada as a term of pride and respect. The full form *American Indian* (and in Canada, *Canadian Indian*) are unambiguous alternatives.

Indiana (in-dee-**an**-ă) a State in the Middle West of the USA.

Indian Ocean the ocean to the south of India, extending from the east coast of Africa to the Malay Archipelago and Australia.

indiarubber *noun* a rubber for rubbing out pencil or ink marks.

indicate *verb* **1** to point out, to make known. **2** to be a sign of, to show the presence of. **3** to show the need of, to require. **4** to state briefly. **indication** *noun* [from *in-* = towards, + Latin *dicatum* = proclaimed]

indicative (in-**dik**-ă-tiv) *adjective* **1** giving an indication, *the style is indicative of the author's origin.* **2** (of a form of a verb) used in making a statement, not in a command or wish etc., e.g. *he said* or *he is coming.* –**indicative** *noun* this form of a verb.

indicator *noun* **1** a thing that indicates or points to something. **2** a meter or other device giving information about the functioning of a machine etc. **3** a device on a vehicle showing when the direction of travel is about to be altered. **4** a chemical compound (such as

litmus) that changes colour in the presence of a particular substance or condition.

indict (in-**dyt**) *verb* to make an indictment against (a person).

indictable (in-**dyt**-ă-bŭl) *adjective* (of an action) making the doer liable to be charged with a crime; (of a person) liable to this.

indictment (in-**dyt**-měnt) *noun* **1** a written statement of charges against an accused person. **2** an accusation, especially of serious wrongdoing.

Indies, the (*old use*) India and adjacent regions. □ **East Indies**, **West Indies** *see* separate entries.

indifferent *adjective* **1** feeling or showing no interest or sympathy, unconcerned. **2** neither good nor bad. **3** not of good quality or ability, *he is an indifferent footballer.* **indifferently** *adverb*, **indifference** *noun*

indigenous (in-**dij**-ĕ-nŭs) *adjective* **1** belonging to or descended from the earliest known inhabitants of a place. **2** (of plants or animals) native. [from Latin *indigena* = born in a country]

indigent (**in**-di-jĕnt) *adjective* needy, poverty-stricken. **indigence** *noun*

indigestible (in-di-**jest**-i-bŭl) *adjective* difficult or impossible to digest. **indigestibility** *noun*

indigestion (in-di-**jes**-chŏn) *noun* pain caused by difficulty in digesting food.

indignant *adjective* feeling or showing indignation. **indignantly** *adverb* [from Latin *indignari* = regard as unworthy]

indignation *noun* anger aroused by something thought to be unjust or wicked etc.

indignity *noun* **1** the quality of being humiliating. **2** treatment that makes a person feel undignified or humiliated.

indigo *noun* a deep blue dye or colour.

indirect *adjective* not direct. □ **indirect object** *see* **object**. **indirect question** or **speech** a speaker's words as reported by another person, involving changes of person and tense, and no quotation marks (e.g. *Paul said, "I am pleased"* becomes *Paul said that he was pleased*). **indirect taxes** those paid in the form of increased prices for goods etc., not on income or capital. **indirectly** *adverb*

indiscipline *noun* lack of discipline.

indiscreet *adjective* 1 not discreet, revealing secrets. 2 not cautious, unwise. **indiscreetly** *adverb*

indiscretion (in-dĭs-**kresh**-ŏn) *noun* 1 being indiscreet. 2 an indiscreet action or statement.

indiscriminate *adjective* showing no discrimination, doing or giving things without making a careful choice. **indiscriminately** *adverb*, **indiscrimination** *noun*

indispensable *adjective* not able to be dispensed with, essential. **indispensably** *adverb*, **indispensability** *noun*

indisposed *adjective* 1 slightly ill. 2 unwilling, *they seem indisposed to help us*.

indisposition *noun* 1 slight illness. 2 unwillingness.

indisputable (in-dĭs-**pewt**-ă-bŭl) *adjective* not able to be disputed, undeniable. **indisputably** *adverb*, **indisputability** *noun*

indissoluble (in-dĭ-**sol**-yŭ-bŭl) *adjective* firm and lasting, not able to be dissolved or destroyed. **indissolubly** *adverb*

indistinct *adjective* not distinct. **indistinctly** *adverb*, **indistinctness** *noun*

indistinguishable *adjective* not distinguishable. **indistinguishably** *adverb*

indite (in-**dyt**) *verb* to put into words, to compose and write (a letter etc.).

indium (**in**-dee-ŭm) *noun* a soft metallic element (symbol In), used in alloys and semiconductor devices.

individual *adjective* 1 single, separate, *each individual strand*. 2 of or for one person, *baked in individual portions*. 3 characteristic of one particular person or thing, *has a very individual style*. –**individual** *noun* 1 one person, plant, or animal considered separately. 2 (*informal*) a person, *a most unpleasant individual*. **individually** *adverb*, **individuality** (in-dĭ-vid-yoo-**al**-ĭ-tee) *noun*

individualist *noun* a person who is very independent in thought or action. **individualism** *noun*, **individualistic** *adjective*

indivisible (in-dĭ-**viz**-ĭ-bŭl) *adjective* not divisible. **indivisibly** *adverb*, **indivisibility** *noun*

Indo- *prefix* Indian (and).

Indo-China 1 the peninsula of SE Asia between India and China, containing Myanmar (Burma), Thailand, West Malaysia, Laos, Cambodia, and Vietnam. 2 (also **French Indo-China**) a former French dependency, the region that now consists of Laos, Cambodia, and Vietnam. **Indo-Chinese** *adjective* & *noun*

indoctrinate (in-**dok**-trĭ-nayt) *verb* to teach (a person) to accept a particular belief uncritically. **indoctrination** *noun* [from *in-* = in, + *doctrine*]

Indo-European *adjective* of the family of languages spoken over most of Europe and parts of Asia including north India. –**Indo-European** *noun* 1 this family of languages. 2 a speaker of any of these.

indolent (**in**-dŏ-lĕnt) *adjective* lazy. **indolently** *adverb*, **indolence** *noun*

indomitable (in-**dom**-ĭ-tă-bŭl) *adjective* having an unyielding spirit, stubbornly persistent when faced with difficulty or opposition. **indomitably** *adverb*, **indomitability** *noun* [from *in-* = not, + Latin *domitare* = to tame]

Indonesia (in-dŏ-**nee**-zhă) a republic in SE Asia consisting of a large group of islands including Java, Sumatra, Sulawesi, Bali, and Irian Jaya. **Indonesian** *adjective* & *noun*

indoor *adjective* situated, used, or done inside a building, *indoor games*; *an indoor aerial*.

indoors *adverb* inside a building.

Indra (in Hinduism) the most popular deity of the Rig-Veda, god of war and storms, warrior king of the heavens.

indubitable (in-**dew**-bĭ-tă-bŭl) *adjective* that cannot reasonably be doubted. **indubitably** *adverb* [from *in-* = not, + Latin *dubium* = doubt]

induce (in-**dewss**) *verb* 1 to persuade. 2 to produce or cause. 3 to bring on (labour in childbirth) by artificial means. [from *in-* = in, + Latin *ducere* = to lead]

inducement *noun* 1 inducing; being induced. 2 an attraction or incentive.

induct *verb* to install (a priest, school principal, etc.) formally into office. [same origin as *induce*]

inductance *noun* the property of producing an electric current by induction; the measure of this.

induction *noun* 1 inducting. 2 inducing. 3 logical reasoning that a general law exists because particular cases that seem to be examples of it exist. 4 production of an electric or magnetic state in an object by bringing an electrified or magnetic object close to but not touching it. 5 the drawing of a fuel mixture into the cylinder(s) of an internal-combustion

engine. 6 production of an electric current in a circuit by varying the magnetic field.
□ induction coil a device like a transformer, for generating an intermittent high voltage from a low voltage.

inductive *adjective* 1 of or using induction, *inductive reasoning*. 2 of electric or magnetic induction.

inductor *noun* a component in an electrical circuit having inductance.

indulge *verb* 1 to allow (a person) to have what he or she wishes. 2 to gratify (a wish). □ indulge in to allow oneself (something that gives pleasure), *he indulges in a catnap after lunch*.

indulgence *noun* 1 indulging. 2 being indulgent. 3 something allowed as a pleasure or privilege.

indulgent *adjective* indulging a person's wishes too freely; kind and lenient. indulgently *adverb*

Indus a river of southern Asia, flowing from Tibet through Kashmir and Pakistan to the Arabian Sea.

industrial *adjective* 1 of or engaged in industries, *industrial workers*. 2 for use in industries. 3 having many highly developed industries, *an industrial country*. □ industrial action a strike or other action taken by workers seeking improved pay or conditions. industrial park an area of land designated for businesses and light industry. industrial relations relations between management and workers. Industrial Revolution the change from a predominantly agricultural society to an industrial one, especially that which occurred in Britain in the late 18th and early 19th centuries. industrially *adverb*

industrialised *adjective* (also -ized) (of a country or area) made industrial. industrialisation *noun*

industrialist *noun* a person who owns or is engaged in managing an industrial business.

industrious *adjective* hard-working. industriously *adverb*, industriousness *noun*

industry *noun* 1 the manufacture or production of goods. 2 a particular branch of this; any business activity, *the tourist industry*. 3 the quality of being industrious. [from Latin *industria* = hard work]

inebriate (in-**ee**-bree-ăt) *adjective* drunken. –inebriate *noun* a drunken person; a drunkard.

inebriated (in-**ee**-bree-ayt-ĕd) *adjective* drunken. inebriation *noun*

inedible *adjective* not edible (because of its nature).

ineducable (in-**ed**-yŭ-kă-bŭl) *adjective* incapable of being educated.

ineffable (in-**ef**-ă-bŭl) *adjective* too great to be described, *ineffable joy*. ineffably *adverb* [from *in-* = not, + Latin *effari* = to utter]

ineffective *adjective* 1 not effective. 2 (of a person) inefficient. ineffectively *adverb*

ineffectual *adjective* not effectual. ineffectually *adverb*

inefficacious *adjective* (of a remedy etc.) not efficacious.

inefficient *adjective* not efficient. inefficiently *adverb*, inefficiency *noun*

inelastic *adjective* 1 not elastic; not adaptable. 2 (of a collision) involving a decrease in total kinetic energy.

inelegant *adjective* not elegant. inelegantly *adverb*, inelegance *noun*

ineligible *adjective* not eligible. ineligibility *noun*

ineluctable (in-ĕ-**luk**-tă-bŭl) *adjective* against which it is useless to struggle.

inept *adjective* unsuitable, absurd. ineptly *adverb*, ineptitude *noun* [from *in-* = not, + Latin *aptus* = suitable]

inequable (in-**ek**-wă-bŭl) *adjective* unfair.

inequality *noun* lack of equality in size, standard, or rank etc.; a mathematical statement that two expressions are unequal.

inequation *noun* (in mathematics) an inequality with one or more unknown variables.

inequitable (in-**ek**-wĭ-tă-bŭl) *adjective* unfair, unjust. inequitably *adverb*, inequity *noun*

ineradicable (in-ĕ-**rad**-ĭ-kă-bŭl) *adjective* unable to be rooted out. ineradicably *adverb*

inert *adjective* 1 (of matter) without power to move or act. 2 without active chemical or other properties, incapable of reacting, *an inert gas*. 3 not moving; slow to move or take action. inertly *adverb*, inertness *noun* [from Latin *iners* = idle]

inertia (in-**er**-shă) *noun* 1 inertness, slowness to take action. 2 the property of matter by which it remains in a state of rest or, if it is in motion, continues moving in a straight line, unless acted upon by an external force.

□ **inertia reel** a type of reel round which one end of a seat belt is wound so that the belt will tighten automatically over the wearer if it is pulled suddenly.

inescapable *adjective* unavoidable. **inescapably** *adverb*

inessential *adjective* not essential. –**inessential** *noun* an inessential thing.

inestimable (in-**est**-ĭ-mă-bŭl) *adjective* too great or intense or precious etc. to be estimated. **inestimably** *adverb*

inevitable (in-**ev**-ĭ-tă-bŭl) *adjective* **1** not able to be prevented, sure to happen or appear. **2** (*informal*) tiresomely familiar, *the tourist with his inevitable camera*. **inevitably** *adverb*, **inevitability** *noun* [from *in-* = not, + Latin *evitare* = avoid]

inexact *adjective* not exact. **inexactly** *adverb*, **inexactitude** *noun*

inexcusable *adjective* unable to be excused or justified. **inexcusably** *adverb*

inexhaustible *adjective* not able to be totally used up, available in unlimited quantity.

inexorable (in-**eks**-ŏ-ră-bŭl) *adjective* relentless, unable to be persuaded by request or entreaty. **inexorably** *adverb*

inexpedient *adjective* not expedient. **inexpediency** *noun*

inexpensive *adjective* not expensive, offering good value for the price. **inexpensively** *adverb*

inexperience *noun* lack of experience. **inexperienced** *adjective*

inexpert *adjective* not expert, unskilful. **inexpertly** *adverb*

inexplicable (in-ĕks-**plik**-ă-bŭl) *adjective* unable to be explained or accounted for. **inexplicably** *adverb*

inexpressible *adjective* unable to be expressed in words. **inexpressibly** *adverb*

in extremis (in eks-**tree**-mĭss) *adjective* **1** at the point of death. **2** in very great difficulties. [Latin, = in one's last moments]

inextricable (in-eks-**trik**-ă-bŭl) *adjective* **1** unable to be extricated. **2** unable to be disentangled or sorted out. **inextricably** *adverb*

infallible (in-**fal**-ĭ-bŭl) *adjective* **1** incapable of making a mistake or being wrong. **2** never failing, *an infallible remedy*. **infallibly** *adverb*, **infallibility** (in-fal-ĭ-**bil**-ĭ-tee) *noun*

infamous (**in**-fă-mŭs) *adjective* having or deserving a very bad reputation, detestable. **infamy** (**in**-fă-mee) *noun*

infancy *noun* **1** early childhood, babyhood. **2** an early stage of development.

infant *noun* a child during the earliest period of its life. [from Latin, = person unable to speak]

infanta (in-**fant**-ă) *noun* a daughter of the Spanish or (formerly) Portuguese king.

infanticide (in-**fant**-ĭ-syd) *noun* **1** the act of killing an infant soon after its birth. **2** a person who is guilty of this. [from *infant*, + Latin *caedere* = kill]

infantile (**in**-făn-tyl) *adjective* **1** of infants or infancy. **2** very childish. □ **infantile paralysis** poliomyelitis.

infantry *noun* troops who fight on foot. [from Italian *infante* = a youth]

infantryman *noun* (*plural* **infantrymen**) a member of an infantry regiment.

infatuated *adjective* temporarily filled with an intense unreasoning love for a person or thing. **infatuation** *noun* [from *in-* = in, + Latin *fatuus* = foolish]

infect *verb* **1** to affect or contaminate with a disease or with bacteria etc. that produce a diseased condition. **2** to inspire with a feeling. [from Latin *infectum* = tainted]

infection *noun* **1** infecting, being infected. **2** the spreading of disease, especially by air or water etc. **3** a disease that is spread in this way; a diseased condition.

infectious *adjective* **1** (of a disease) able to spread by air or water etc. **2** infecting with disease. **3** quickly spreading to others, *an infectious laugh*.

infer *verb* (**inferred**, **inferring**) to reach (an opinion) from facts or reasoning; to conclude. [from *in-*, + Latin *ferre* = bring]

Usage *Infer* differs from *imply*: if you imply something you suggest it or indicate it without necessarily stating it (e.g. *Her frown implied that she disapproved*). If you infer something you work it out from what has been said or done (e.g. *I inferred from her frown that she disapproved*).

inference (**in**-fĕ-rĕns) *noun* **1** inferring. **2** a thing inferred; a logical conclusion reached by reasoning. **inferential** (in-fĕ-**ren**-shăl) *adjective*

inferior *adjective* low or lower in rank, importance, quality, or ability. –**inferior** *noun* a person who is inferior to another, especially in rank. [Latin, = lower]

inferiority *noun* being inferior. □ **inferiority complex** a feeling of general inferiority, sometimes with aggressive behaviour in compensation; (*informal*) great lack of self-confidence.

infernal *adjective* **1** of hell, *the infernal regions*. **2** (*informal*) detestable, tiresome, *an infernal nuisance*. **infernally** *adverb*

inferno (in-**fer**-noh) *noun* (*plural* **infernos**) a raging fire; somewhere intensely hot; a place resembling hell. [Italian, = hell]

infertile *adjective* not fertile. **infertility** *noun*

infest *verb* (of pests or vermin etc.) to be numerous and troublesome in (a place). **infestation** *noun* [from Latin, = hostile]

infidel (**in**-fi-del) *noun* a person who does not believe in a religion. [from *in-* = not, + Latin *fidelis* = faithful]

infidelity *noun* unfaithfulness.

infighting *noun* **1** boxing with an opponent nearer than arm's length. **2** hidden conflict within an organisation.

infiltrate (**in**-fil-trayt) *verb* **1** to enter gradually and without being noticed, e.g. as settlers or spies. **2** to cause to do this. **3** to pass (fluid) by filtration. **infiltration** *noun*, **infiltrator** *noun*

infinite (**in**-fi-nit) *adjective* **1** having no limit, endless. **2** too great or too many to be measured or counted. **infinitely** *adverb*

infinitesimal (in-fin-i-**tess**-i-măl) *adjective* extremely small. **infinitesimally** *adverb*

infinitive (in-**fin**-i-tiv) *noun* a form of a verb that does not indicate a particular tense or number or person, in English used with or without *to*, e.g. *go* in 'let him go' or 'allow him to go'. [from *in-* = not, + Latin *finitivus* = definite]

infinity (in-**fin**-i-tee) *noun* an infinite number, extent, or time.

infirm *adjective* physically weak, especially from old age or illness; *infirm of purpose*, not resolute, hesitant.

infirmary *noun* **1** a hospital. **2** a room or rooms for sick people in a school or monastery etc.

infirmity *noun* **1** being infirm. **2** a particular physical weakness.

inflame *verb* **1** to provoke to strong feeling or emotion; to arouse anger in. **2** to cause inflammation in. **3** to aggravate.

inflammable *adjective* able to be set on fire.

Usage This word means the same as *flammable*; its opposite is *non-inflammable*.

---

inflammation *noun* redness and heat and pain produced in the body, especially as a reaction to injury or infection.

inflammatory (in-**flam**-ă-tŏ-ree) *adjective* **1** likely to arouse strong feeling or anger, *inflammatory remarks*. **2** causing or involving inflammation.

inflate *verb* **1** to fill or become filled with air or gas and swell up. **2** to puff up with pride etc. **3** to increase (a price etc.) artificially. **4** to resort to inflation of (currency). **inflatable** *adjective* [from *in-* = in, + Latin *flatum* = blown]

inflation *noun* **1** inflating; being inflated. **2** a general increase of prices and fall in the purchasing value of money.

inflationary *adjective* causing inflation.

inflect *verb* **1** to change the pitch of (the voice) in speaking. **2** to change the ending or form of (a word) to show its grammatical relation or number etc., e.g. *sing* changes to *sang* or *sung*; *child* changes to *children*. □ **point of inflection** the point at which a curve crosses its tangent. **inflection** *or* **inflexion** *nouns* [from *in-* = in, + Latin *flectere* = to bend]

inflexible *adjective* **1** not flexible, unable to be bent. **2** not able to be altered, *an inflexible rule*. **3** refusing to alter one's demands etc., unyielding. **inflexibly** *adverb*, **inflexibility** *noun*

inflict *verb* to cause (a blow or penalty etc.) to be suffered. **infliction** *noun*, **inflictor** *noun* [from *in-* = on, + Latin *flictum* = struck]

in-flight *adjective* occurring or provided during a flight.

inflorescence (in-flŏ-**ress**-ěns) *noun* **1** flowering. **2** the flower(s) of a plant; their arrangement on a stem etc.

inflow *noun* an inward flow; the amount that flows in, *a large inflow of cash*.

influence *noun* **1** the power to produce an effect, *the influence of the moon on the tides*. **2** the ability to affect someone's character or beliefs or actions. **3** a person or thing with this ability. – influence *verb* to exert influence on.

influential (in-floo-**en**-shăl) *adjective* having great influence. influentially *adverb*

influenza *noun* a virus disease causing fever, muscular pain, and catarrh.

influx *noun* an inflow, especially of people or things into a place.

info *noun* (*informal*) information.

inform *verb* **1** to give information to. **2** to reveal information to the police etc. about secret or criminal activities.

informal *adjective* not formal, without formality or ceremony. □ informal vote (*Austral.*) a vote or voting paper that is not valid. informally *adverb*, informality (in-for-**mal**-ĭ-tee) *noun*

Usage In this dictionary, words marked *informal* are used in everyday speech but should be avoided when writing or speaking formally.

informant *noun* a person who gives information.

information *noun* **1** facts told or heard or discovered. **2** facts fed into a computer etc. **3** the process of informing. □ information science or technology the study or use of processes (especially computers, microelectronics, and telecommunications) for storing, retrieving, and sending information.

informative *adjective* giving information.

informed *adjective* having good or sufficient knowledge of something, *an informed choice*.

informer *noun* a person who reveals information to the police etc. about secret or criminal activities.

infra *adverb* below or further on in a book etc. [Latin, = below]

infra- *prefix* below. [Latin]

infraction (in-**frak**-shŏn) *noun* infringement.

infrared *adjective* **1** (of radiation) having a wavelength that is slightly longer than that of visible light rays at the red end of the spectrum. **2** of or using this radiation.

infrastructure *noun* **1** the basic structural foundations of a society or enterprise. **2** roads, bridges, sewers, etc., regarded as a country's economic foundation.

infrequent *adjective* not frequent. infrequently *adverb*, infrequency *noun*

infringe *verb* **1** to break or act against (a rule or agreement etc.), to violate. **2** to encroach, *infringed upon his rights*. infringement *noun*

infuriate *verb* to enrage. infuriating *adjective*

infuse *verb* **1** to imbue, to instil, *infused them with courage*; *infused courage into them*. **2** to steep (tea or herbs etc.) in a liquid to extract the flavour; (of tea etc.) to undergo this process. infuser *noun* [from Latin *infusum* = poured in]

infusion *noun* **1** infusing, being infused. **2** a liquid made by infusing. **3** something added or introduced into a stock, *an infusion of new blood to improve the breed*.

ingenious *adjective* **1** clever at inventing new things or methods. **2** cleverly contrived, *an ingenious gadget*. ingeniously *adverb*, ingenuity (in-jĕ-**new**-ĭ-tee) *noun* [from Latin *ingenium* = genius]

ingenuous (in-**jen**-yoo-ŭs) *adjective* without artfulness, unsophisticated, *an ingenuous manner*. ingenuously *adverb*, ingenuousness *noun*

ingest (in-**jest**) *verb* to take in as food. ingestion *noun*

inglenook *noun* a nook forming a place for sitting beside a deeply recessed fireplace.

inglorious *adjective* **1** ignominious. **2** not bringing glory, obscure.

ingoing *adjective* going in.

ingot (**ing**-gŏt) *noun* a brick-shaped lump of cast metal, especially gold.

ingrained *adjective* **1** (of habits, feelings, or tendencies) firmly fixed. **2** (of dirt) marking a surface deeply.

ingratiate (in-**gray**-shee-ayt) *verb* ingratiate oneself to bring oneself into a person's favour, especially in order to gain an advantage. [from Latin *in gratiam* = into favour]

ingratitude *noun* lack of due gratitude.

ingredient *noun* any of the parts or elements in a mixture or combination. [from Latin *ingrediens* = going in]

ingress *noun* going in; the right to go in. [from *in-* = in, + Latin *gressus* = going]

ingrowing *adjective* growing abnormally into the flesh, *an ingrowing toenail*.

inguinal (**ing**-gwĭ-năl) *adjective* of the groin.

inhabit *verb* to live in (a place) as one's home or dwelling place. inhabitable *adjective*

inhabitant *noun* one who inhabits a place.

inhalant (in-**hay**-lănt) *noun* a medicinal substance to be inhaled.

inhale *verb* to breathe in, to draw into the lungs by breathing. **inhalation** (in-hă-**lay**-shŏn) *noun* [from *in-* = in, + Latin *halare* = breathe]

inhaler *noun* a device that produces or sends out a medicinal vapour to be inhaled.

inhere (in-**heer**) *verb* to be inherent.

inherent (in-**he**-rĕnt) *adjective* existing in something as a natural or permanent characteristic or quality. **inherently** *adverb*, **inherence** *noun* [from *in-* = in, + Latin *haerere* = to stick]

inherit *verb* 1 to receive (property or a title etc.) by legal right of succession or by a will etc. when its previous owner or holder has died. 2 to receive from a predecessor. 3 to receive (a characteristic) from one's parents or ancestors. **inheritor** *noun* [from *in-* = in, + Latin *heres* = heir]

inheritance *noun* 1 inheriting. 2 a thing that is inherited.

inhibit *verb* 1 to restrain, to prevent, *this substance inhibits the growth of mould.* 2 to hinder the impulses of (a person); to cause inhibitions in.

inhibition (in-hĭ-**bish**-ŏn) *noun* 1 inhibiting; being inhibited. 2 repression of or resistance to an instinct, impulse, or feeling.

inhospitable (in-hoss-**pit**-ă-bŭl) *adjective* 1 not hospitable. 2 (of a place or climate) giving no shelter or no favourable conditions.

in-house *adjective* done or existing within an institution or company, *an in-house movie.*

inhuman *adjective* brutal, lacking normal human qualities of kindness, pity, etc. **inhumanity** (in-hew-**man**-ĭ-tee) *noun*

inhumane (in-hew-**mayn**) *noun* not humane.

inimical (in-**im**-ikăl) *adjective* hostile, harmful. **inimically** *adverb* [from *in-* = not, + Latin *amicus* = friend]

inimitable (in-**im**-ĭ-tă-bŭl) *adjective* impossible to imitate. **inimitably** *adverb*

iniquitous (in-**ik**-wĭ-tŭs) *adjective* very unjust. [from *in-* = not, + *equity*]

iniquity (in-**ik**-wĭ-tee) *noun* 1 great injustice. 2 wickedness.

initial *adjective* of or belonging to the beginning, *the initial stages of the work.* –**initial** *noun* the first letter of a word or name; *a person's initials*, those of his or her names,

often used as a signature etc. –**initial** *verb* (**initialled**, **initialling**) to sign or mark with initials. **initially** *adverb* [from Latin *initium* = the beginning]

initiate (in-**ish**-ee-ayt) *verb* 1 to cause to begin, to start (a scheme) working, *he initiated certain reforms.* 2 to admit (a person) into membership of a society etc., often with special ceremonies. 3 to give (a person) basic instruction or information about something that is new to him or her. –**initiate** (in-**ish**-ee-ăt) *noun* an initiated person. **initiation** *noun*, **initiator** *noun*, **initiatory** *adjective*

initiative (in-**ish**-ee-ă-tiv) *noun* 1 the first step in a process. 2 the power or right to begin something. 3 the ability to initiate things, enterprise, *he lacks initiative.* □ **have the initiative** to be in a position to control the course of events, e.g. in a war. **on one's own initiative** without being prompted by others. **take the initiative** to be the first to take action.

inject *verb* 1 to force or drive (a liquid etc.) into something, especially by means of a syringe; to administer medicine etc. to (a person) in this way. 2 to introduce (a new element or quality), *inject some new ideas into the committee.* **injector** *noun* [from *in-* = in, + Latin *-jectum* = thrown]

injection *noun* 1 injecting; an instance of this. 2 a liquid etc. that is injected. □ **fuel injection** the spraying of liquid fuel into the cylinder(s) of an internal-combustion engine. **injection moulding** the process of moulding plastic material by injecting it, while it is hot, into a closed cooled mould.

injudicious (in-joo-**dish**-ŭs) *adjective* showing lack of good judgment, unwise. **injudiciously** *adverb*, **injudiciousness** *noun*

injunction *noun* an order or command, especially an order from a lawcourt stating that something must or must not be done.

injure *verb* 1 to cause injury to, to hurt. 2 to do wrong to.

injurious (in-**joo**-ree-ŭs) *adjective* causing or likely to cause injury.

injury *noun* 1 damage, harm. 2 a particular form of this, *a leg injury.* 3 a wrong or unjust act.

injustice *noun* 1 lack of justice. 2 an unjust action or treatment. □ **do a person an injustice** to make an unfair judgment about him or her.

ink *noun* 1 a coloured liquid or paste used in writing, printing, etc. 2 a black liquid squirted

by a cuttlefish or octopus for concealment.
3 a deep bluish-black colour. –ink *verb* to
mark or cover with ink, to apply ink to. –ink
adjective bluish-black.

Inkatha (in-**kah**-tǎ) a Zulu political
organisation in South Africa.

inkling *noun* a hint, a slight knowledge or
suspicion.

inky *adjective* **1** covered or stained with ink.
2 black like ink, *inky darkness*.

inlaid *see* inlay.

inland *adjective* & *adverb* in or towards the
interior of a country. –inland *noun* the parts of
a country remote from the sea or frontiers.

in-laws *plural noun* (*informal*) a person's
relatives by marriage.

inlay (in-**lay**) *verb* (inlaid, inlaying) to set
(pieces of wood or metal etc.) into a surface
so that they lie flush with it and form a
design. –inlay (**in**-lay) *noun* **1** inlaid material.
2 a design formed by this. **3** a dental filling
shaped to fit a tooth cavity.

inlet *noun* **1** a strip of water extending into the
land from a sea or lake, or between islands.
2 a way in, e.g. for water into a tank, *the inlet
pipe*.

inmate *noun* one of a number of inhabitants
of a hospital, prison, or other institution.

in memoriam (mĕ-**mor**-ree-ǎm) *noun* a
written article or notice in memory of a dead
person; an obituary. [Latin]

inmost *adjective* furthest inward.

inn *noun* a hotel, providing meals, liquor, and
accommodation.

innards *plural noun* (*informal*) **1** the stomach
and bowels, entrails. **2** any inner parts.

innate (in-**ayt**) *adjective* inborn. innately
adverb [from *in-* = in, + Latin *natus* = born]

inner *adjective* nearer to the centre or inside,
interior, internal. –inner *noun* the division
of a target next to the bullseye; a shot that
strikes this. □ inner tube a separate inflatable
tube inside the cover of a pneumatic tyre.

innermost *adjective* furthest inward.

innings *noun* (*plural* innings) **1** a batsman's
or side's turn at batting in cricket. **2** a period of
power or of opportunity to show one's ability.

innkeeper *noun* a person who keeps an inn.

innocent *adjective* **1** not guilty of a particular
crime etc. **2** free of all evil or wrongdoing, *as
innocent as a new-born babe*. **3** harmless, not
intended to be harmful, *innocent amusements*;

an innocent remark. **4** foolishly trustful.
–innocent *noun* a person (especially a child)
who is free of all evil or who is foolishly
trustful. innocently *adverb*, innocence *noun*
[from *in-* = not, + Latin *nocens* = doing harm]

innocuous (in-**ok**-yoo-ǔs) *adjective* harmless.
innocuously *adverb*, innocuousness *noun*,
innocuity *noun*

innovate *verb* to introduce a new process
or way of doing things. innovation *noun*,
innovator *noun*, innovatory *adjective* [from
in- = in, + Latin *novus* = new]

innuendo (in-yoo-**en**-doh) *noun* (*plural*
innuendoes) **1** an allusive or oblique remark
or hint, usually disparaging. **2** a remark with a
double meaning, usually suggestive.

innumerable *adjective* too many to be
counted. innumerably *adverb*

innumerate *adjective* not numerate.
innumeracy *noun*

inoculate *verb* to treat (a person or animal)
with vaccines or serums etc., especially as a
protection against a disease. inoculation *noun*

inoffensive *adjective* not offensive,
harmless.

inoperable (in-**op**-ĕ-rǎ-bǔl) *adjective* unable
to be cured by surgical operation.

inoperative *adjective* not functioning.

inopportune (in-**op**-er-tewn) *adjective*
coming or happening at an unsuitable time.
inopportunely *adverb*

inordinate (in-**or**-dǐ-nǎt) *adjective* excessive.
inordinately *adverb*

inorganic (in-or-**gan**-ik) *adjective* of mineral
origin, not organic. □ inorganic chemistry a
branch of chemistry dealing with inorganic
substances.

in-patient *noun* a patient who remains
resident in a hospital while undergoing
treatment.

input *noun* **1** what is put in. **2** the place
where energy or information etc. enters a
system. **3** the data, programs, etc. supplied to
a computer. –input *verb* (input *or* inputted,
inputting) to put in; to supply (data, programs,
etc.) to a computer.

inquest *noun* **1** a judicial investigation to
establish facts, especially about a death
that may not be the result of natural causes.
2 (*informal*) a detailed discussion of
something that is over, e.g. the playing of a
card game.

inquire *verb* to seek information, to make an inquiry. **inquirer** *noun* [from *in-* = into, + Latin *quaerere* = seek]

Usage See the note at **enquire**.

inquiry *noun* an investigation, especially an official one.

inquisition (in-kwĭ-**zish**-ŏn) *noun* a detailed questioning or investigation. **–the Inquisition** any of various tribunals of the Roman Catholic Church in the Middle Ages, especially the very severe one in Spain, to discover and punish heretics.

inquisitive *adjective* **1** eagerly seeking knowledge. **2** prying. **inquisitively** *adverb*

inquisitor (in-**kwiz**-ĭ-ter) *noun* a person who questions another searchingly.

inquisitorial (in-kwiz-ĭ-**tor**-ree-ăl) *adjective* of or like an inquisitor, prying.

inroad *noun* a sudden attack made into a country. □ **make inroads on** or **into** to use up large quantities of (resources etc.).

insalubrious (in-să-**loo**-bree-ŭs) *adjective* (of a place or climate) unhealthy.

insane *adjective* **1** not sane, mad. **2** extremely foolish. **insanely** *adverb*, **insanity** *noun*

insanitary *adjective* unclean and likely to be harmful to health.

insatiable (in-**say**-shă-bŭl) *adjective* unable to be satisfied, *an insatiable appetite*. **insatiably** *adverb*, **insatiability** *noun*

insatiate (in-**say**-shee-ăt) *adjective* never satisfied.

inscribe *verb* **1** to write or cut words etc. on (a surface), *inscribed their names on the stone*; *inscribed it with their names*. **2** to draw (one geometrical figure) within another so that certain points of their boundaries coincide. **3** to enter (a name) on a list or in a book. [from *in-* = on, + Latin *scribere* = write]

inscription *noun* **1** words or names inscribed on a monument, coin, or stone etc. **2** inscribing.

inscrutable (in-**skroot**-ă-bŭl) *adjective* baffling, impossible to understand or interpret. **inscrutably** *adverb*, **inscrutability** *noun*

insect *noun* a small animal with six legs, no backbone, and a body divided into three parts (head, thorax, abdomen).

insecticide *noun* a substance for killing insects. [from *insect*, + Latin *caedere* = kill]

insectivore (in-**sek**-tĭ-vor) *noun* an insectivorous animal or plant.

insectivorous (in-sek-**tiv**-ŏ-rŭs) *adjective* feeding on insects or other invertebrates. [from *insect*, + Latin *vorare* = devour]

insecure *adjective* not secure or safe. **insecurely** *adverb*, **insecurity** *noun*

inseminate (in-**sem**-ĭ-nayt) *verb* to insert semen into. **insemination** *noun*

insensible *adjective* **1** unconscious. **2** without feeling, unaware, *seemed insensible of his danger*. **3** callous. **4** (of changes) imperceptible. **insensibly** *adverb*, **insensibility** *noun*

insensitive *adjective* not sensitive. **insensitively** *adverb*, **insensitivity** *noun*

insentient (in-**sen**-shĕnt) *adjective* not sentient; inanimate.

inseparable *adjective* **1** unable to be separated. **2** liking to be constantly together. **inseparably** *adverb*, **inseparability** *noun*

insert (in-**sert**) *verb* to put (a thing) in or between or among. **–insert** (**in**-sert) *noun* a thing inserted. **insertion** *noun*

inset (in-**set**) *verb* (**inset** *or* **insetted**, **insetting**) to set or place in; to decorate with an inset, *the crown was inset with jewels*. **–inset** (**in**-set) *noun* something set into a larger thing.

inshore *adverb* & *adjective* near or nearer to the shore.

inside *noun* **1** the inner side, surface, or part. **2** (*informal*) (usually **insides**) the organs in the abdomen, the stomach and bowels. **–inside** *adjective* on or coming from the inside; *inside information*, information that is not available to outsiders; *an inside job*, a crime committed by someone living or working on the premises where it occurred. **–inside** *adverb* **1** on or in or to the inside. **2** (*informal*) in prison. **–inside** *preposition* on the inner side of, within; *inside an hour*, in less than an hour. □ **inside out** with the inner surface turned to face the outside; *turn a place inside out*, to search it thoroughly; *know a subject inside out*, to know it thoroughly.

insider *noun* **1** an accepted member of a certain group or profession. **2** a person privy to a secret.

insidious (in-**sid**-ee-ŭs) *adjective* spreading, developing, or acting inconspicuously but with harmful effect. **insidiously** *adverb*, **insidiousness** *noun*

insight *noun* **1** the ability to perceive and understand the true nature of something. **2** knowledge obtained by this.

insignia (in-**sig**-nee-ă) *plural noun* **1** the symbols of authority or office (e.g. the crown and sceptre of a king). **2** the identifying badge of a regiment etc.

insignificant *adjective* having little or no importance, value, or influence. insignificantly *adverb*, insignificance *noun*

insincere *adjective* not sincere. insincerely *adverb*, insincerity *noun*

insinuate (in-**sin**-yoo-ayt) *verb* **1** to hint artfully or unpleasantly. **2** to insert gradually or craftily, *insinuate oneself into a person's good graces*. insinuation *noun*

insipid (in-**sip**-ĭd) *adjective* **1** lacking in flavour. **2** lacking in interest or liveliness. insipidity (in-si-**pid**-ĭ-tee) *noun*

insist *verb* **1** to declare emphatically. **2** to demand emphatically, *I insist on your being there*. [from Latin *insistere* = stand firm]

insistent *adjective* **1** insisting, declaring or demanding emphatically. **2** forcing itself on one's attention, *the insistent throb of the engines*. insistently *adverb*, insistence *noun*

in situ (**sit**-yoo) *adverb* in its original place. [Latin]

insobriety (in-sŏ-**bry**-ĕ-tee) *noun* lack of sobriety, drunkenness.

insofar *adverb* in so far (*see* in).

insolation *noun* exposure to the sun's rays. [from *in-* = in, + Latin *sol* = sun]

insole *noun* **1** the inner sole of a boot or shoe. **2** a loose piece of material laid in the bottom of a shoe for warmth or comfort.

insolent (**in**-sŏ-lĕnt) *adjective* behaving insultingly, arrogant, contemptuous. insolently *adverb*, insolence *noun*

insoluble *adjective* **1** unable to be dissolved. **2** unable to be solved, *an insoluble problem*. insolubly *adverb*, insolubility *noun*

insolvent *adjective* unable to pay one's debts. insolvency *noun*

insomnia *noun* inability to sleep sufficiently. [from *in-* = without, + Latin *somnus* = sleep]

insomniac *noun* a person who suffers from insomnia.

insomuch *adverb* **1** to such an extent. **2** inasmuch.

insouciant (in-**soo**-see-ănt) *adjective* carefree, unconcerned. insouciance *noun* [from *in-* = not, + French *souciant* = caring]

inspect *verb* **1** to examine (a thing) carefully and critically, especially looking for flaws. **2** to examine officially; to visit in order to make sure that rules and standards are being observed. inspection *noun* [from *in-* = in, + Latin *specere* = to look]

inspector *noun* **1** a person whose job is to inspect things or supervise services etc. **2** a police officer above sergeant and below superintendent.

inspiration *noun* **1** inspiring. **2** an inspiring influence. **3** a sudden brilliant idea.

inspire *verb* **1** to stimulate (a person) to creative or other activity or to express certain ideas. **2** to fill with or instil a certain feeling, *he inspires confidence in us*. **3** to communicate ideas etc. by a divine agency, *the prophets were inspired by God*. [from *in-* = into, + Latin *spirare* = breathe]

inspiriting *adjective* encouraging.

instability *noun* lack of stability.

install *verb* **1** to place (a person) in office, especially with ceremonies. **2** to set (apparatus) in position and ready for use. **3** to settle in a place, *he was comfortably installed in an armchair*.

installation (in-stă-**lay**-shŏn) *noun* **1** installing; being installed. **2** apparatus etc. installed. **3** an art exhibit constructed on site.

instalment *noun* any of the parts in which something is presented or supplied, or a debt is paid, over a period of time.

instance *noun* a case or example of something. –instance *verb* to mention as an instance. □ in the first instance firstly.

instant *adjective* **1** occurring immediately, *there was instant relief*. **2** (of food) designed to be prepared quickly and easily. **3** (in commerce) of the current month, *the 4th instant*. –instant *noun* **1** an exact point of time; the present moment, *come here this instant!* **2** a very short space of time, a moment. [from Latin *instans* = urgent]

instantaneous (in-stăn-**tay**-nee-ŭs) *adjective* occurring or done instantly, *death was instantaneous*. instantaneously *adverb*

instantly *adverb* immediately.

instead *adverb* as an alternative or substitute.

instep *noun* **1** the upper surface of the foot between toes and ankle. **2** the part of a shoe etc. over or under this.

instigate *verb* to urge or incite; to bring about by persuasion, *instigated them to strike*; *instigated an inquiry*. instigation *noun*, instigator *noun*

instil *verb* (instilled, instilling) to implant (ideas etc.) into a person's mind gradually. instillation *noun*, instilment *noun* [from *in-* = in, + Latin *stilla* = a drop]

instinct *noun* **1** an inborn impulse or tendency to perform certain acts or behave in certain ways. **2** a natural ability, *has an instinct for finding a good place*.

instinctive *adjective* of, involving, or prompted by instinct. instinctively *adverb*

instinctual *adjective* instinctive.

institute *noun* **1** an establishment for further education. **2** a society or organisation for promotion of a scientific, educational, or social etc. activity. **3** the building used by an institute. –institute *verb* **1** to establish, to found. **2** to cause (an inquiry or a custom) to be started. [from *in-* = in, + Latin *statuere* = to set up]

institution *noun* **1** instituting; being instituted. **2** an institute, especially for a charitable or social activity. **3** an established law or custom or practice; (*informal*) a person who has become a familiar figure in some activity. institutional *adjective*

institutionalise *verb* (also -ize) **1** to make (a thing) institutional. **2** to place or keep (a person) in an institution that will provide the care needed; *become institutionalised*, to be so used to living in an institution that one cannot live independently. institutionalisation *noun*

instruct *verb* **1** to give (a person) instruction in a subject or skill. **2** to inform, *we are instructed by our agents that you owe us $50*. **3** to give instructions to. **4** to authorise (a solicitor or counsel) to act on one's behalf. instructor *noun* [same origin as *structure*]

instruction *noun* **1** a statement making known to a person what he or she is required to do; an order. **2** the process of teaching. **3** knowledge or teaching imparted. **4** an expression in a computer program defining and effecting an operation.

instructional *adjective* imparting knowledge.

instructive *adjective* giving or containing instruction, enlightening. instructively *adverb*

instrument *noun* **1** a tool or implement used for delicate or scientific work. **2** a measuring device giving information about the operation of an engine etc. or used in navigation. **3** a device designed for producing musical sounds. **4** a person used and controlled by another to perform an action, *was made the instrument of another's crime*. **5** a formal or legal document, *signed the instrument of abdication*.

instrumental *adjective* **1** serving as an instrument or means of doing something, *was instrumental in finding her a job*. **2** performed on musical instruments, *instrumental music*.

instrumentalist *noun* a musician who plays a musical instrument (as distinct from one who is a singer).

instrumentation *noun* **1** the arrangement or composition of music for instruments. **2** the provision or use of mechanical or scientific instruments.

insubordinate *adjective* disobedient, rebellious. insubordination *noun*

insubstantial *adjective* **1** not existing in reality, imaginary. **2** not made of a strong or solid substance; *insubstantial evidence*, weak, not well founded.

insufferable *adjective* **1** unbearable. **2** unbearably conceited or arrogant. insufferably *adverb*

insufficient *adjective* not sufficient; inadequate. insufficiently *adverb*, insufficiency *noun*

insufflate (**in**-sŭ-flayt) *verb* to blow or breathe (air, gas, powder, etc.) into a cavity of the body; to treat in this way. insufflation *noun*, insufflator *noun*

insular (**ins**-yŭ-ler) *adjective* **1** of or on an island. **2** of or like people who live on an island and are isolated from outside influences, narrow-minded, *insular prejudices*. insularity (ins-yŭ-**la**-rĭ-tee) *noun*

insulate (**ins**-yŭ-layt) *verb* **1** to cover or protect (a thing) with a substance or device that prevents the passage of electricity or sound or the loss of heat; *insulating tape*, tape that prevents the passage of electricity. **2** to isolate (a person or place) from influences that might affect it. insulation *noun*, insulator *noun* [from Latin *insula* = island]

insulin (**ins**-yŭ-lĭn) *noun* a hormone produced in the pancreas, controlling the absorption of sugar by the body.

insult (in-**sult**) *verb* to speak or act in a way that hurts the feelings or pride of (a person) and rouses his or her anger. –**insult** (**in**-sult) *noun* an insulting remark or action.

insuperable (in-**soop**-ĕ-rǎ-bŭl) *adjective* unable to be overcome, *an insuperable difficulty*.

insupportable *adjective* unbearable. **insupportably** *adverb*

insurable *adjective* able to be insured.

insurance *noun* **1** a contract undertaking to provide compensation for loss, damage, or injury etc., in return for a payment made in advance once or regularly. **2** the business of providing such contracts. **3** the amount payable to the company etc. providing the contract, a premium. **4** the amount payable by the company etc. in compensation. **5** anything done as a safeguard against loss or failure etc.

insure *verb* to protect by a contract of insurance; *the insured*, the person protected by this. **insurer** *noun*

Usage Distinguish *insure* from *ensure* meaning 'to make certain'.

insurgent (in-**ser**-jĕnt) *adjective* rebellious, rising in revolt. –**insurgent** *noun* a rebel. **insurgence** *noun*, **insurgency** *noun* [from *in-* = against, + Latin *surgere* = to rise]

insurmountable (in-ser-**mownt**-ǎ-bŭl) *adjective* unable to be surmounted or overcome.

insurrection (in-sŭ-**rek**-shŏn) *noun* rising in open resistance to established authority, rebellion. **insurrectionist** *noun*

insusceptible (in-sŭ-**sep**-tĭ-bŭl) *adjective* not susceptible.

intact *adjective* undamaged, complete. [from *in-* = not, + Latin *tactum* = touched]

intaglio (in-**tal**-yoh) *noun* (*plural* **intaglios**) **1** a kind of carving in which the design is sunk below the surface. **2** a gem carved in this way. [Italian]

intake *noun* **1** the process of taking something in, the place where liquid or air etc. is channelled into something. **2** the number or quantity of people or things etc. accepted or received, *a school's annual intake of pupils*.

intangible (in-**tan**-jĭ-bŭl) *adjective* **1** unable to be felt by touching. **2** unable to be grasped mentally. **intangibly** *adverb*

integer (**in**-tĕ-jer) *noun* a whole number, not a fraction. (¶ The set of integers includes positive and negative whole numbers and zero.) [Latin, = whole]

integral (**in**-tĕ-grǎl) *adjective* **1** (of a part) constituent, necessary to the completeness of a whole, *the cat is an integral part of their family*. **2** complete, forming a whole, *an integral design*. **3** of or denoted by an integer. □ **integral of a function** (in mathematics) another function that gives this function when differentiated; *definite integral*, a quantity found as the difference between the values of an integral for two specified values of its argument. **integrally** *adverb*

integrate (**in**-tĕ-grayt) *verb* **1** to combine or form (a part or parts) into a whole. **2** to bring or come into equal membership of a community. **3** (in mathematics) to find the integral of. □ **integrated circuit** a small piece of material replacing a conventional circuit of many components. **integration** *noun* [from Latin *integrare* = make whole]

integrity (in-**teg**-rĭ-tee) *noun* **1** honesty, incorruptibility. **2** wholeness, soundness.

integument (in-**teg**-yŭ-mĕnt) *noun* skin.

intellect (**in**-tĕ-lekt) *noun* the mind's power of reasoning and acquiring knowledge (contrasted with feeling and instinct).

intellectual (in-tĕ-**lek**-tew-ǎl) *adjective* **1** of the intellect. **2** needing use of the intellect, *an intellectual occupation*. **3** having a well-developed intellect and a taste for advanced knowledge. –**intellectual** *noun* an intellectual person. **intellectually** *adverb*

intelligence *noun* **1** mental ability, the power of learning and understanding. **2** information, news, especially that of military value. **3** the people engaged in collecting this. □ **intelligence quotient** (also **IQ**) a number that shows how a person's intelligence compares with that of an average normal person.

intelligent *adjective* **1** having great mental ability. **2** (of a device in a computer system) containing in itself a capacity to process information. □ **intelligent design** the theory that life, or the universe, cannot have arisen by chance or evolution, and was designed and created by an intelligent entity. **intelligently** *adverb*

intelligentsia (in-tel-ĭ-**jent**-see-ǎ) *noun* intellectual people regarded as a class.

intelligible (in-**tel**-ĭ-jĭbŭl) *adjective* able to be understood. **intelligibly** *adverb*, **intelligibility** *noun*

intemperate *adjective* 1 drinking alcohol excessively. 2 immoderate (in speech or conduct). **intemperately** *adverb*, **intemperance** *noun*

intend *verb* 1 to have in mind as what one wishes to do or achieve. 2 to plan that (a thing) shall be used or interpreted in a particular way. [from Latin *intendere* = to stretch, to aim]

intense *adjective* 1 strong in quality or degree, *intense heat*. 2 (of a person) emotional. **intensely** *adverb*

intensifier *noun* a word used to give force or emphasis, e.g. *really* in *he's really mad*.

intensify *verb* (**intensified**, **intensifying**) to make or become more intense. **intensification** *noun*

intensity *noun* 1 intenseness. 2 the amount of a quality, e.g. force or brightness.

intensive *adjective* employing much effort, concentrated. □ **intensive care** medical treatment with constant supervision of the patient. **intensively** *adverb*

intent *noun* intention, *with intent to kill*. –**intent** *adjective* 1 intending, having one's mind fixed on some purpose, *intent on killing*. 2 with one's attention concentrated, *an intent gaze*. □ **to all intents and purposes** practically, virtually. **intently** *adverb*, **intentness** *noun* [same origin as *intend*]

intention *noun* what one intends to do or achieve, one's purpose.

intentional *adjective* done on purpose, intended, not accidental. **intentionally** *adverb*

inter (in-**ter**) *verb* (**interred**, **interring**) to bury (a dead body) in the earth or in a tomb. [from *in-* = in, + Latin *terra* = earth]

inter- *prefix* between, among. [from Latin]

interact *verb* to have an effect upon each other. **interaction** *noun*

interactive *adjective* 1 interacting. 2 (in computers) allowing information to be transferred immediately both to and from a computer system and its user.

inter alia (**ay**-lee-ă) *adverb* among other things. [Latin]

interbreed *verb* (**interbred**, **interbreeding**) to breed with each other; to cross-breed.

intercalary (inter-**kal**-ă-ree) *adjective* (of a day or days or month) inserted to harmonise

the calendar year with the solar year; (of a year) having such addition(s).

intercede (inter-**seed**) *verb* to intervene on behalf of another person or as a peacemaker. [from *inter-*, + Latin *cedere* = go]

intercept (inter-**sept**) *verb* to stop or catch (a person or thing) between the starting point and the destination. –**intercept** (**in**-ter-sept) *noun* 1 a message or conversation that is picked up by intercepting a letter or a telephone or radio conversation. 2 the distance from the origin to either of the points at which a line cuts the axes of a graph. **interception** *noun*, **interceptor** *noun* [from *inter-*, + Latin *captum* = seized]

intercession (inter-**sesh**-ŏn) *noun* interceding, especially by prayer. **intercessor** *noun*

interchange (inter-**chaynj**) *verb* 1 to put (each of two things) into the other's place. 2 to make an exchange of, to give and receive (one thing for another). 3 to alternate. –**interchange** (**in**-ter-chaynj) *noun* 1 interchanging. 2 alternation. 3 a major junction of transport routes and systems (e.g. trains and buses), usually with parking facilities for private cars.

interchangeable *adjective* able to be interchanged. **interchangeability** *noun*

intercom (**in**-ter-kom) *noun* a system of communication by radio or telephone; the instrument used for this. [short for *intercommunication*]

interconnect *verb* to connect with each other. **interconnection** *noun*

intercontinental *adjective* connecting or carried on between two continents; (of missiles) able to be fired from one continent to another.

intercourse *noun* 1 any dealings or communication between people or countries. 2 sexual intercourse (*see* **sexual**), copulation.

interdenominational *adjective* of or involving more than one Christian denomination.

interdependent *adjective* dependent on each other. **interdependence** *noun*

interdict (inter-**dikt**) *verb* to prohibit or forbid authoritatively. –**interdict** (**in**-ter-dikt) *noun* an authoritative prohibition. **interdiction** *noun* [from *inter-*, + Latin *dictum* = said]

interdisciplinary *adjective* of or involving different branches of learning.

interest *noun* 1 a feeling of curiosity or concern about something. 2 the quality of arousing such a feeling, *the subject has no interest for me*. 3 a subject or hobby in which one is concerned, *music is one of his interests*. 4 an advantage, benefit, *she looks after her own interests*. 5 a legal right to a share in something; a financial stake in a business etc. 6 money paid for the use of money lent. –interest *verb* 1 to arouse the interest of. 2 to cause to take an interest in, *interested herself in welfare work*. [Latin, = it matters]

interested *adjective* 1 feeling or showing interest or curiosity. 2 having a private interest in something, *interested parties*.

interesting *adjective* arousing interest. interestingly *adverb*

interface *noun* 1 a surface forming a common boundary between two regions. 2 a place or piece of equipment where interaction occurs between two processes etc.; (in computers etc.) a program or device for connecting two pieces of equipment so that they can be operated jointly or for enabling a user to access a program. –interface *verb* to connect by means of an interface.

interfacing *noun* stiffish material placed between two layers of fabric in a garment etc.

interfere *verb* 1 to take a part in dealing with other people's affairs without right or invitation. 2 to obstruct wholly or partially. 3 (in physics) to produce interference.

interference *noun* 1 interfering. 2 the disturbance of received radio signals by unwanted signals. 3 the interaction of two or more waves, producing a new wave pattern.

interferon (inter-**feer**-ron) *noun* a protein substance that prevents the development of a virus in living cells.

interfuse *verb* 1 to intersperse. 2 to blend or fuse together. interfusion *noun*

interglacial *adjective* having a milder climate between glacial periods. –interglacial *noun* an interglacial period.

interim (**in**-tĕ-rĭm) *noun* an intervening period of time, *in the interim*. –interim *adjective* of or in such a period; *an interim report*, one made before the main report, showing what has happened so far. [Latin, = meanwhile]

interionic (in-ter-I-**on**-ik) *adjective* existing or occurring between ions, *interionic forces*.

interior *adjective* nearer to the centre, inner. –interior *noun* 1 an interior part or region; the central or inland part of a country. 2 the

inside of a building or room; *interior design* or *decoration*, decoration of this. [Latin, = further in]

interject *verb* to put in (a remark) when someone is speaking. [from *inter-*, + Latin *jactum* = thrown]

interjection *noun* 1 interjecting. 2 an interjected remark. 3 an exclamation such as *oh!* or *good heavens!*

interlace *verb* to weave or lace together.

interlard *verb* to insert contrasting remarks here and there in (a speech etc.), *interlarded his speech with quotations*.

interleave *verb* to insert leaves (usually blank) between the pages of (a book).

interline *verb* to put an extra layer of material between the fabric of (a garment) and its lining in order to give firmness or extra warmth. interlining *noun* this material.

interlinear *adjective* written or printed between the lines of a text.

interlock *verb* to fit into each other, especially so that parts engage. –interlock *noun* machine-knitted fabric with fine stitches.

interlocutor (inter-**lok**-yŭ-ter) *noun* a person who takes part in a conversation. [from *inter-*, + Latin *locutum* = spoken]

interloper *noun* an intruder, one who interferes in the affairs of others.

interlude *noun* 1 an interval between parts of a play etc. 2 something performed during this. 3 an intervening time or event etc. of a different kind from the main one. [from *inter-*, + Latin *ludus* = game]

intermarry *verb* (intermarried, intermarrying) 1 (of tribes, nations, or families etc.) to become connected by marriage. 2 to marry within one's own family. intermarriage *noun*

intermediary (inter-**meed**-yă-ree) *noun* a mediator, a go-between. –intermediary *adjective* 1 acting as an intermediary. 2 intermediate in position or form.

intermediate *adjective* coming between two things in time, place, or order.

interment (in-**ter**-mĕnt) *noun* burial.

Usage Distinguish *interment* from *internment*.

intermezzo (inter-**mets**-oh) *noun* (*plural* intermezzi) a short musical composition to be played between acts of a play etc. or between sections of a larger work, or independently. [Italian]

interminable (in-**ter**-mǐ-nǎ-bǔl) *adjective* endless; long and boring. interminably *adverb* [from *in-* = not, + *terminable*]

intermingle *verb* to mingle.

intermission *noun* an interval, a pause in work or action.

intermittent *adjective* occurring at intervals, not continuous, *intermittent rain*. intermittently *adverb* [from *inter-*, + Latin *mittere* = let go]

intermix *verb* to mix.

intermolecular *adjective* existing or occurring between molecules.

intern (in-**tern**) *verb* to compel (an enemy alien or prisoner of war etc.) to live in a special area or camp. – intern (**in**-tern) *noun* a resident junior doctor in a hospital.

internal *adjective* 1 of or in the inside of a thing. 2 of or in the interior of the body, *internal organs*. 3 of the domestic affairs of a country. 4 used or applying etc. within an organisation. 5 of the mind or soul. □ internal-combustion engine an engine that produces power by burning fuel inside the engine itself, not externally. internally *adverb*

internalise *verb* (also -ize) to learn or absorb into the mind as a fact, attitude, etc. internalisation *noun*

international *adjective* of or existing or agreed between two or more countries. □ International Court of Justice a judicial court of the United Nations that meets at The Hague. International Date Line *see* date[1]. International Monetary Fund an international organisation, with headquarters in Washington, DC, for promoting international trade and monetary cooperation and the stabilisation of exchange rates (abbreviation IMF). International System (of Units) a system of units based on the metre, kilogram, second, ampere, kelvin, candela, and mole (abbreviation SI). internationally *adverb*

internecine (inter-**nee**-syn) *adjective* destructive to each of the parties involved, *internecine war*. [from *inter-*, + Latin *necare* = kill]

internee (in-ter-**nee**) *noun* a person who is interned.

Internet *noun* an international information network linking computers, accessible to the public via modem links etc.

internment *noun* interning; being interned.

Usage Distinguish from *interment* meaning 'burial'.

interpersonal *adjective* between persons.

interplanetary *adjective* between planets.

interplay *noun* interaction.

Interpol *noun* International Criminal Police Commission, an organisation that coordinates investigations made by the police forces of member countries into crimes with an international basis.

interpolate (in-**ter**-pǒ-layt) *verb* 1 to interject. 2 to insert (new material) misleadingly into a book etc. 3 (in mathematics) to estimate and insert (a number or quantity etc.) between two others in a series. interpolation *noun*

interpose *verb* 1 to insert between; to interject. 2 to intervene. interposition *noun* [from *inter-*, + Latin *positum* = put]

interpret *verb* 1 to explain the meaning of. 2 to understand in a specified way. 3 to act as interpreter. interpretation *noun*

interpreter *noun* a person whose job is to translate a speech etc. into another language orally, in the presence of the speaker.

interpretive *adjective* interpreting.

interquartile *adjective* (of a range of values) between the upper and the lower quartiles.

interregnum (inter-**reg**-nǔm) *noun* 1 a period between the rule of two successive rulers. 2 an interval, a pause. [from *inter-*, + Latin *regnum* = reign]

interrelated *adjective* related to each other. interrelation *noun*

interrogate (in-**te**-rǒ-gayt) *verb* to question closely or formally. interrogation *noun*, interrogator *noun* [from *inter-*, + Latin *rogare* = ask]

interrogative (inter-**rog**-ǎ-tiv) *adjective* questioning, having the form of a question, *an interrogative tone*. □ interrogative pronoun *see* pronoun. interrogatively *adverb*

interrogatory (inter-**rog**-ǎ-tǒ-ree) *adjective* questioning.

interrupt *verb* 1 to break the continuity of. 2 to break the flow of a speech etc. by inserting a remark. 3 to obstruct (a view etc.). interruption *noun*, interrupter *noun* [from *inter-*, + Latin *ruptum* = broken]

intersect *verb* **1** to divide (a thing) by passing or lying across it. **2** (of lines or roads etc.) to cross each other. [from *inter-*, + Latin *sectum* = cut]

intersection *noun* **1** intersecting. **2** a place where lines or roads etc. intersect. **3** (in mathematics) the elements common to two or more sets.

intersperse *verb* to insert contrasting material here and there in (a thing). [from *inter-*, + Latin *sparsum* = scattered]

interstate *adjective & adverb* **1** existing or carried on between states. **2** to, in, from another state, *has gone interstate; went to school interstate; an interstate visitor*.

interstellar *adjective* between stars.

interstice (in-**ter**-stĭss) *noun* a small intervening space, a crevice. **interstitial** *adjective*

intertwine *verb* to twine together, to entwine.

interval *noun* **1** a time between two events or parts of an action. **2** a pause between two parts of a performance. **3** a space between two objects or points. **4** the difference in musical pitch between two notes. ▢ **at intervals** with some time or distance between, not continuous. [from Latin *intervallum* = space between ramparts]

intervene (inter-**veen**) *verb* **1** to occur in the time between events, *in the intervening years*. **2** to cause hindrance by occurring, *we should have finished harvesting but a storm intervened*. **3** to enter a discussion or dispute etc. in order to change its course or resolve it. **intervention** (inter-**ven**-shŏn) *noun* [from *inter-*, + Latin *venire* = come]

intervertebral *adjective* between the vertebrae.

interview *noun* a formal meeting or conversation with a person, held in order to assess his or her merits as a candidate etc. or to obtain comments and information. –**interview** *verb* to hold an interview with. **interviewer** *noun*

interviewee *noun* a person who is interviewed.

interweave *verb* (**interwove**, **interwoven**, **interweaving**) to weave (strands etc.) into one another; to become woven together.

intestate (in-**test**-ăt) *adjective* not having made a valid will before death occurs.

intestine (in-**test**-ĭn) *noun* the long tubular section of the alimentary canal, extending from the outlet of the stomach to the anus. ▢ **large intestine** the broader and shorter part of this, including the colon and rectum. **small intestine** the narrower and longer part. **intestinal** *adjective*

intimate[1] (**in**-tĭ-măt) *adjective* **1** having a close acquaintance or friendship with a person. **2** having a sexual relationship with a person. **3** private and personal. **4** (of knowledge) detailed and obtained by much study or experience. –**intimate** *noun* an intimate friend. **intimately** *adverb*, **intimacy** *noun*

intimate[2] (**in**-tĭ-mayt) *verb* to make known, especially by hinting. **intimation** *noun*

intimidate (in-**tim**-ĭ-dayt) *verb* to subdue or influence by frightening with threats or force. **intimidation** *noun* [from *in-* = in, + Latin *timidus* = timid]

intimism *noun* a style of painting in the 19th and early 20th centuries that concentrated on everyday life indoors as its subject matter. **intimist** *noun*

into *preposition* **1** to the inside of, to a point within, *went into the house; fell into the river; far into the night*. **2** to a particular state or condition or occupation, *got into trouble; grew into a butterfly; went into banking*. **3** actively interested and participating in, *he is into rock music*. **4** (in mathematics) indicating division; *4 into 20*, 20 divided by 4.

intolerable *adjective* unbearable. **intolerably** *adverb*

intolerant *adjective* not tolerant, unwilling to tolerate ideas or beliefs etc. that differ from one's own, *intolerant of opposition*. **intolerantly** *adverb*, **intolerance** *noun*

intonation (in-tŏ-**nay**-shŏn) *noun* **1** intoning. **2** the tone or pitch of the voice in speaking. **3** a slight accent, *a Welsh intonation*.

intone *verb* to recite in a chanting voice, especially on one note.

in toto *adverb* completely. [Latin]

intoxicant *adjective* causing intoxication. –**intoxicant** *noun* an intoxicating substance.

intoxicated *adjective* (of a person) drunk; stupefied by drugs; *intoxicated by success*, made greatly excited or reckless by it. **intoxication** *noun* [from *in-* = in, + Latin *toxicare* = to poison]

intra- *prefix* within. [from Latin]

intractable (in-**trakt**-ă-băl) *adjective* unmanageable, hard to deal with or control, *an intractable child*; *an intractable difficulty*. intractability *noun*

intramural *adjective* **1** situated or done within the walls of an institution etc. **2** forming part of ordinary university or college work.

intramuscular *adjective* into a muscle, *intramuscular injections*.

intransigent (in-**trans**-ĭ-jĕnt) *adjective* unwilling to compromise, stubborn. intransigence *noun*

intransitive (in-**trans**-ĭ-tiv) *adjective* (of a verb) used without being followed by a direct object, e.g. *hear* in *we can hear* (but not in *we can hear you*). intransitively *adverb*

intrauterine (in-tră-**yoo**-tĕ-ryn) *adjective* within the uterus.

intravenous (intră-**vee**-nŭs) *adjective* into a vein. intravenously *adverb*

intrepid (in-**trep**-ĭd) *adjective* fearless, brave. intrepidly *adverb*, intrepidity (in-trĕ-**pid**-ĭ-tee) *noun* [from *in-* = not, + Latin *trepidus* = alarmed]

intricate *adjective* very complicated. intricately *adverb*, intricacy (**in**-trĭ-kă-see) *noun* [from Latin *intricatum* = entangled]

intrigue (in-**treeg**) *verb* **1** to plot with someone in an underhand way, to use secret influence. **2** to rouse the interest or curiosity of, *the subject intrigues me*. –intrigue (also *pr*. **in**-treeg) *noun* **1** underhand plotting; an underhand plot. **2** (*old use*) a secret love affair. [from Latin *intricare* = to tangle]

intrinsic (in-**trin**-sik) *adjective* belonging to the basic nature of a person or thing; *the intrinsic value of a coin*, the value of the metal in it as opposed to its face value. intrinsically *adverb*

intro- *prefix* into; inwards. [from Latin]

introduce *verb* **1** to make (a person) known by name to others. **2** to announce (a speaker or broadcast program etc.) to listeners or viewers. **3** to bring (a bill) before Parliament. **4** to cause (a person) to become acquainted with a subject. **5** to bring (a custom or idea etc.) into use or into a system. [from *intro-*, + Latin *ducere* = to lead]

introduction *noun* **1** introducing; being introduced. **2** the formal presentation of one person to another. **3** a short explanatory section at the beginning of a book or speech etc. **4** an introductory treatise. **5** a short preliminary section leading up to the main part of a musical composition.

introductory *adjective* introducing a person or subject.

introit (**in**-troit) *noun* an introductory psalm, anthem, etc. in a church service.

introspection *noun* examination of one's own thoughts and feelings.

introspective *adjective* characterised by introspection. [from *intro-*, + Latin *specere* = to look]

introvert (**in**-trŏ-vert) *noun* a person who is concerned more with his or her own thoughts and feelings than with the people and things round him or her, a shy person. introverted *adjective* having these characteristics. introversion *noun* [from *intro-*, + Latin *vertere* = to turn]

intrude *verb* to come or join in without being invited or wanted. intrusion *noun* [from *in-* = in, + Latin *trudere* = to push]

intruder *noun* **1** a person who intrudes. **2** a burglar. **3** an enemy aircraft over one's territory.

intrusive *adjective* **1** intruding. **2** (of rock) that has been forced into cracks or cavities in the neighbouring rocks by pressure of the molten matter below the earth's crust.

intuition (in-tew-**ish**-ŏn) *noun* the power of knowing or understanding something immediately without reasoning or being taught. intuitional *adjective*

intuitive (in-**tew**-ĭ-tiv) *adjective* of or possessing or based on intuition. intuitively *adverb*

Inuit (**in**-yoo-it) *noun* (*plural* Inuit) **1** a member of any of several indigenous peoples of Canada, Alaska, and Greenland. **2** Inuktitut, the language of these peoples.

Inuk (**i**-nuuk) *noun* (*plural* Inuit) a member of any of the Inuit peoples. [Inuktitut *inuk* 'person']

Inuktitut (i-**nuuk**-tee-tuut) *noun* (*plural* Inuit) the language of the Inuit.

inundate (**in**-ŭn-dayt) *verb* **1** to flood, to cover with water. **2** to overwhelm as if with a flood. inundation *noun* [from *in-* = in, + Latin *unda* = a wave]

inure (in-**yoor**) *verb* **1** to accustom, especially to something unpleasant. **2** (in law) to take effect. inurement *noun*

in utero (**yoo**-tĕ-roh) *adverb* in the womb; before birth. [Latin]

in vacuo (**vak**-yoo-oh) *adverb* **1** in a vacuum. **2** in isolation, without reference to external circumstances etc. [Latin]

invade *verb* **1** to enter (territory) with armed forces in order to attack or damage or occupy it. **2** to crowd into. **3** to penetrate harmfully. **invader** *noun* [from *in-* = into, + Latin *vadere* = go]

invalid¹ (**in**-vă-lid) *noun* a person who is weakened by illness or injury, one who suffers from ill health for a long time. –**invalid** *verb* **1** to remove from active service because of ill health or injury, *he was invalided out of the army*. **2** to disable by illness.

invalid² (in-**val**-ĭd) *adjective* not valid.

invalidate (in-**val**-ĭ-dayt) *verb* to make ineffective or not valid as a piece of reasoning, law, etc. **invalidation** *noun*

invalidity (in-vă-**lid**-ĭ-tee) *noun* **1** lack of validity. **2** being an invalid.

invaluable *adjective* having a value that is too great to be measured. **invaluably** *adverb* [from *in-* = not, + *valuable*]

invariable (in-**vair**-ree-ă-bŭl) *adjective* not variable, always the same. **invariably** *adverb*

invariant *adjective* **1** invariable. **2** (of a point or line in a geometrical figure) remaining the same after a particular transformation. –**invariant** *noun* an invariant point or line. **invariance** *noun*

invasion *noun* invading, being invaded.

invasive (in-**vay**-siv) *adjective* invading; tending to spread, *an invasive plant*.

invective (in-**vek**-tiv) *noun* a violent attack in words, abusive language.

inveigh (in-**vay**) *verb* to attack violently or bitterly in words.

inveigle (in-**vay**-gŭl) *verb* to entice.

invent *verb* **1** to create by thought; to make or design (something that did not exist before). **2** to construct (a false or fictional story), *invented an excuse*. **inventor** *noun*

invention *noun* **1** inventing; being invented. **2** something invented.

inventive *adjective* able to invent things.

inventory (**in**-věn-tŏ-ree) *noun* a detailed list of goods or furniture etc. –**inventory** *verb* (**inventoried**, **inventorying**) to make an inventory of; to enter in an inventory.

inverse *adjective* reversed in position, order, or relation; *in inverse proportion*, with the first quantity increasing in proportion as the other decreases, or vice versa. –**inverse** *noun* **1** an inverse state. **2** a thing that is the exact opposite of another. **inversely** *adverb* [same origin as *invert*]

inversion *noun* **1** inverting; being inverted. **2** something that is inverted. **3** (in music) a form of a chord in which the root is not the lowest note.

inversive *adjective* inverting.

invert *verb* to turn (a thing) upside down; to reverse the position, order, or relationship etc. of. □ **inverted commas** quotation marks ' ' or " ". [from *in-* = in, + Latin *vertere* = to turn]

invertase *noun* an enzyme from yeast that catalyses the inversion of sucrose to produce **invert sugar**, a mixture of fructose and glucose.

invertebrate (in-**vert**-ĕ-brăt) *adjective* not having a backbone. –**invertebrate** *noun* an invertebrate animal.

invest *verb* **1** to use (money) to buy stocks, shares, or property etc. in order to earn interest or bring profit for the buyer. **2** to spend money, time, or effort on something that will be useful. **3** to confer a rank or office or power upon (a person). **4** to endow with a quality.

investigate *verb* **1** to make a careful study of (a thing) in order to discover the facts about it. **2** to make a search or systematic inquiry; to examine. **investigation** *noun*, **investigator** *noun*, **investigative** *adjective*

investigatory (in-**vest**-ĭ-gayt-ŏ-ree) *adjective* investigating.

investiture (in-**vest**-ĭ-cher) *noun* the process of investing a person with an honour, rank, or office etc.

investment *noun* **1** investing. **2** a sum of money invested. **3** something in which money, time, or effort is invested.

investor *noun* one who invests money.

inveterate (in-**vet**-ĕ-răt) *adjective* **1** habitual, *an inveterate smoker*. **2** firmly established, *inveterate prejudices*. **inveterately** *adverb*

invidious (in-**vid**-ee-ŭs) *adjective* likely to cause resentment because of real or imagined injustice. **invidiously** *adverb*, **invidiousness** *noun*

invigilate (in-**vij**-ĭ-layt) *verb* to supervise candidates at an examination. **invigilation** *noun*, **invigilator** *noun* [from *in-* = on, + Latin *vigilare* = keep watch]

invigorate (in-**vig**-ŏ-rayt) *verb* to fill with vigour, to give strength or courage to. [compare *vigour*]

invincible (in-**vin**-sĭbŭl) *adjective* unconquerable. **invincibly** *adverb*, **invincibility** *noun* [from *in*- = not, + Latin *vincere* = conquer]

inviolable (in-**vy**-ŏ-lă-bŭl) *adjective* not to be violated or profaned. **inviolably** *adverb*, **inviolability** *noun*

inviolate (in-**vy**-ŏ-lăt) *adjective* not violated or profaned.

invisible *adjective* not visible, unable to be seen. □ **invisible exports** or **imports** payment for services (such as insurance or shipping) made to or by another country. **invisible ink** colourless ink for writing words etc. that cannot be seen until the paper is heated or treated in some way. **invisibly** *adverb*, **invisibility** *noun*

invite (in-**vyt**) *verb* 1 to ask (a person) in a friendly way to come to one's house or to a gathering etc. 2 to ask (a person) formally to do something. 3 to ask for (comments, suggestions, etc.). 4 to act so as to be likely to cause (a thing) unintentionally, *you are inviting trouble*. 5 to attract, to tempt. –**invite** (**in**-vyt) *noun* (*informal*) an invitation. **invitation** *noun*

inviting *adjective* attracting one to do something, pleasant and tempting.

in vitro (vee-troh) *adverb & adjective* (of a biological process) taking place in a test tube or other laboratory equipment, *in vitro fertilisation*. [Latin]

invocation (in-vŏ-**kay**-shŏn) *noun* invoking, calling upon God in prayer.

invoice *noun* a list of goods sent or services performed, with prices and charges. –**invoice** *verb* 1 to make an invoice of (goods). 2 to send an invoice to (a person). [from French *envoyer* = send]

invoke (in-**vohk**) *verb* 1 to call upon (a deity) in prayer. 2 to call for the help or protection of, *invoked the law*. 3 to summon up (a spirit) with words. 4 to ask earnestly for (vengeance etc.). [from *in*- = in, + Latin *vocare* = to call]

involuntary *adjective* done without intention or without conscious effort of the will; *an involuntary movement* (e.g. jumping when startled). **involuntarily** *adverb*

involute (**in**-vŏ-loot) *adjective & noun* an **involute curve**, the path traced by a point on a piece of string as it unrolls from a plane curve.

involve *verb* 1 to contain within itself, to make necessary as a condition or result, *the plan involves much expense*. 2 to cause to share in an experience or effect; to include or affect in its operation, *the safety of the nation is involved*. 3 to bring (a person or thing) into difficulties, *it will involve us in much expense*. 4 to show (a person) to be concerned in a crime etc. **involvement** *noun* [from *in*- = in, + Latin *volvere* = to roll]

involved *adjective* 1 complicated. 2 concerned in something.

invulnerable (in-**vul**-nĕ-ră-bŭl) *adjective* not vulnerable; unable to be wounded or hurt. **invulnerability** *noun*

inward *adjective* 1 situated on the inside. 2 going towards the inside. 3 in the mind or spirit, *inward happiness*. –**inward** *adverb* inwards.

inwardly *adverb* 1 on the inside. 2 in the mind or spirit.

inwards *adverb* 1 towards the inside. 2 in the mind or spirit.

iodide (**I**-ŏ-dyd) *noun* a compound of iodine and one other element or radical.

iodine (**I**-ŏ-deen) *noun* a chemical element (symbol I), a substance found in sea water and certain seaweeds, used in solution as an antiseptic.

iodise (**I**-ŏ-dyz) *verb* (also **-ize**) to impregnate with iodine or a compound of it.

ion (**I**-ŏn) *noun* any of the electrically charged particles in certain substances.

Ionesco (yon-**esk**-oh), Eugène (1912–94), Romanian-born French dramatist, a leading exponent of the 'theatre of the absurd'.

Ionia (I-**oh**-nee-ă) the ancient Greek name for the central part of the west coast of Asia Minor. **Ionian** *adjective & noun*

Ionic (I-**on**-ik) *adjective* of the **Ionic order**, one of the five classical orders of architecture, characterised by columns with a scroll-like ornamentation at the top.

ionic (I-**on**-ik) *adjective* 1 of or using or containing ions. 2 (of an atomic bond) = **electrovalent**.

ionise (**I**-ŏ-nyz) *verb* (also **-ize**) to convert or be converted into ions. **ionisation** *noun*

ionosphere (I-**on**-ŏ-sfeer) *noun* an ionised region of the upper atmosphere, able to reflect radio waves for transmission to another part of the earth.

iota (I-**oh**-tă) *noun* **1** the Greek letter i. **2** the smallest possible amount, a jot, *it doesn't make an iota of difference*.

IOU *noun* a signed paper acknowledging that one owes a sum of money to the holder (= *I owe you*).

Iowa (I-ŏ-wă) a State in the Middle West of the USA.

ipecacuanha (i-pě-kak-yoo-**an**-ă) *noun* the dried root of a South American plant, used as an emetic or purgative.

Iphigenia (if-ĭ-jě-**ny**-ă) (*Gk. legend*) the daughter of Agamemnon, whom he offered as a sacrifice to the goddess Artemis, who saved her from death.

ipso facto (ip-soh **fak**-toh) *adverb* by that very fact or act. [Latin]

IQ *abbreviation* intelligence quotient.

ir- *prefix* see **in-**.

IRA *abbreviation* Irish Republican Army, an organisation seeking to achieve a united Ireland independent of Britain.

Iran (i-**rahn**) a republic in SW Asia on the eastern side of the Persian Gulf; formerly called Persia. **Iranian** (i-**ray**-nee-ăn) *adjective* & *noun*

Iraq (i-**rahk**) a republic in SW Asia lying between Iran and Saudi Arabia. **Iraqi** (i-**rah**-kee) *adjective* & *noun* (*plural* **Iraqis**).

irascible (i-**ras**-ĭ-bŭl) *adjective* irritable, hot-tempered. **irascibly** *adverb*, **irascibility** *noun*

irate (I-**rayt**) *adjective* angry, enraged. **irately** *adverb*

ire *noun* (*literary*) anger.

Ireland an island west of Great Britain, divided into Northern Ireland (which forms part of the UK) and the Republic of Ireland.

Irian Jaya (also called **West Papua**) a former name for the Indonesian province of Papua.

iridescent (i-rĭ-**dess**-ĕnt) *adjective* showing rainbow-like colours; showing a change of colour when its position is altered. **iridescence** *noun*

iridium (i-**rid**-ee-ŭm) *noun* a metallic element (symbol Ir) resembling polished steel.

Iris (*Gk. myth.*) the goddess of the rainbow.

iris *noun* **1** a plant with sword-shaped leaves and showy (often purple) flowers with large petals. **2** the flat circular coloured membrane in the eye, with a circular opening (the *pupil*) in the centre. **3** a diaphragm with a hole of adjustable size, especially for regulating the

amount of light admitted to a lens. [Greek, = rainbow]

Irish *adjective* of Ireland or its people or language. **–Irish** *noun* the Celtic language of Ireland. **–the Irish** Irish people. □ **Irish stew** a stew of mutton, potatoes, and onions. **Irishman, Irishwoman** *nouns*

irk *verb* to annoy, to be tiresome to.

irksome *adjective* tiresome.

iron *noun* **1** a metallic element (symbol Fe), a very common hard grey metal capable of being magnetised. **2** a tool made of this, *branding iron*. **3** a golf club with an iron or steel head. **4** an implement with a flat base that is heated for smoothing cloth or clothes etc. **5** a metal splint or support worn on the leg. **6** a preparation of iron as a tonic, *iron injections*. **7** something thought to be as unyielding as iron, *a will of iron*. **–iron** *adjective* **1** made of iron. **2** as strong or unyielding as iron, *an iron constitution*; *an iron will*. **–iron** *verb* to smooth (clothes etc.) with an iron; *iron out the difficulties*, deal with and remove them. **irons** *plural noun* fetters. □ **Iron Age** the period when weapons and tools were made of iron. **Iron Curtain** (*historical*) an invisible barrier of secrecy and restriction, preventing the free passage of people and information between the former USSR (and countries under its influence) and the Western world. **iron lung** a rigid case fitting over a patient's body, used for administering artificial respiration for a prolonged period by means of mechanical pumps. **iron man** or **woman** an endurance contest involving swimming, board-riding, running, et c.; a winner of this. **iron out** to remove (difficulties etc.). **iron rations** a small supply of tinned food etc. to be used only in an emergency. **many irons in the fire** many undertakings or resources.

ironbark *noun* an Australian eucalypt with a thick solid bark and hard dense timber.

ironic (I-**ron**-ik) *adjective* (also **ironical**) using or expressing irony. **ironically** *adverb*

ironing *noun* clothes etc. for ironing or just ironed. □ **ironing board** a narrow flat stand on which clothes etc. are ironed.

ironmonger (I-ern-mung-ger) *noun* a dealer in hardware (e.g. tools, household implements etc.). **ironmongery** *noun*

Ironsides *plural noun* Cromwell's cavalry troops during the English Civil War, so called from their hardiness in battle.

ironstone *noun* **1** hard iron ore. **2** a kind of hard white pottery.

ironwork *noun* articles such as gratings, rails, railings, etc. made of iron.

ironworks *noun* a place where iron is smelted or where heavy iron goods are made.

irony (**I**-rŏ-nee) *noun* **1** the expression of one's meaning by using words of the opposite meaning in order to make one's remarks forceful, e.g. *that will please him* (used of something that will not please him at all). **2** (of an occurrence) the quality of being so unexpected or ill-timed that it appears to be deliberately perverse.

irradiate (i-**ray**-dee-ayt) *verb* **1** to shine upon; to subject to radiation. **2** to subject (food) to radioactivity in order to preserve it and keep it fresh. **3** to throw light (on a subject). **irradiation** *noun*

irrational (i-**rash**-ŏ-năl) *adjective* **1** not rational, not guided by reasoning, illogical, *irrational fears* or *behaviour*. **2** not capable of reasoning. **3** (of numbers) that cannot be exactly expressed as a fraction, e.g. pi or the square root of 2. **irrationally** *adverb*, **irrationality** *noun*

irreconcilable *adjective* unable to be reconciled; opposed or incompatible. **irreconcilably** *adverb*

irrecoverable *adjective* unable to be recovered. **irrecoverably** *adverb*

irredeemable *adjective* unable to be redeemed; hopeless. **irredeemably** *adverb*

irreducible (i-rĕ-**dew**-sĭ-bŭl) *adjective* unable to be reduced, *an irreducible minimum*.

irrefutable (i-**ref**-yŭ-tă-bŭl) *adjective* unable to be refuted; undeniable. **irrefutably** *adverb*

irregular *adjective* **1** not regular, uneven, varying. **2** contrary to rules or to established custom. **3** (of troops) not belonging to the regular armed forces. **irregularly** *adverb*, **irregularity** *noun*

irrelevant (i-**rel**-ĕ-vănt) *adjective* not relevant. **irrelevantly** *adverb*, **irrelevance** *noun*

irreligious (i-rĕ-**lij**-ŭs) *adjective* not religious; irreverent.

irremediable (i-rĕ-**meed**-ee-ă-bŭl) *adjective* not able to be remedied. **irremediably** *adverb*

irremovable (i-rĕ-**moo**-vă-bŭl) *adjective* unable to be removed. **irremovably** *adverb*

irreparable (i-**rep**-ă-ră-bŭl) *adjective* unable to be repaired or made good, *irreparable damage* or *loss*. **irreparably** *adverb*

irreplaceable *adjective* unable to be replaced, being a loss that cannot be made good.

irrepressible (i-rĕ-**press**-ĭ-bŭl) *adjective* unable to be repressed or restrained.

irreproachable *adjective* blameless, faultless.

irresistible *adjective* too strong or convincing or delightful to be resisted. **irresistibly** *adverb*

irresolute (i-**rez**-ŏ-loot) *adjective* feeling or showing uncertainty, hesitating. **irresolutely** *adverb*, **irresolution** *noun*

irrespective *adjective* not taking something into account, *prizes are awarded to winners irrespective of nationality*.

irresponsible *adjective* not showing a proper sense of responsibility. **irresponsibly** *adverb*

irretrievable *adjective* unable to be retrieved or restored. **irretrievably** *adverb*

irreverent *adjective* not reverent, not respectful. **irreverently** *adverb*, **irreverence** *noun*

irreversible *adjective* not reversible, unable to be altered or revoked. **irreversibly** *adverb*

irrevocable (i-**rev**-ŏ-kă-bŭl) *adjective* unable to be revoked, final and unalterable. **irrevocably** *adverb*

irrigate *verb* **1** to supply (land or crops) with water by means of streams, channels, pipes, etc. **2** to wash (a wound) with a constant flow of liquid. **irrigation** *noun*, **irrigator** *noun*

irritable *adjective* **1** easily annoyed, bad-tempered. **2** (of an organ etc.) sensitive. **irritably** *adverb*, **irritability** *noun*

irritant *adjective* causing irritation. **– irritant** *noun* something that causes irritation.

irritate *verb* **1** to annoy, to rouse impatience or slight anger in (a person). **2** to cause itching. **3** to stimulate (an organ) to action. **irritation** *noun*

irrupt *verb* to enter forcibly or violently. **irruption** *noun* [from *ir-* = into, + Latin *ruptum* = burst]

is *see* be.

Isaiah (I-**zy**-ă) **1** a Hebrew major prophet of the 8th century BC. **2** a book of the Old Testament that bears his name.

ischium (**isk**-ee-ŭm) *noun* the curved bone forming the base of each half of the pelvis.

-ish *suffix* forming adjectives meaning of a certain nature (e.g. *impish*), somewhat (e.g. *shortish*), or approximate (e.g. *fiftyish*).

isinglass (**I**-zing-glahs) *noun* **1** a kind of gelatine obtained from fish. **2** mica.

Isis (**I**-sĭs) (*Egyptian myth*.) a nature-goddess, wife of Osiris and mother of Horus.

Islam (**iz**-lahm) *noun* **1** the Muslim religion, a monotheistic faith regarded as revealed through Muhammad as the Prophet of Allah. **2** the Muslim world. **Islamic** (iz-**lam**-ik) *adjective* [Arabic, = submission to God]

Islamabad (iz-**lahm**-ă-bad) the capital of Pakistan.

island (**I**-lănd) *noun* **1** a piece of land surrounded by water. **2** something resembling this because it is detached or isolated; *a traffic island*, a paved or raised area in the middle of a road, where people crossing may be safe from traffic.

islander (**I**-lăn-der) *noun* **1** an inhabitant of an island. **2 Islander** an indigenous inhabitant of the Torres Strait Islands; a person indigenous to a Pacific island.

isle (*rhymes with* mile) *noun* (*poetic* and in names) an island. [from Latin *insula* = island]

Isle of Man an island off the west coast of England, a British Crown possession with home rule.

islet (**I**-lĕt) *noun* a small island.
□ **islets of Langerhans** groups of pancreatic cells secreting insulin.

Ismaili (iz-**my**-lee) *noun* a member of any of various Shi'ite Muslim sects, of which the best known is that headed by the Aga Khan.

isn't (*informal*) = is not.

iso- *prefix* equal (as in *isobar*). [from Greek *isos* = equal]

isobar (**I**-sŏ-bar) *noun* a line, drawn on a map, connecting places that have the same atmospheric pressure. **isobaric** *adjective* [from *iso-*, + Greek *baros* = weight]

isocline (**I**-sŏ-klyn) *noun* a fold of land that has been compressed so much that its sides have become parallel. [from *iso-*, + Greek *klinein* = to slope]

isohyet (**I**-sŏ-hy-ĕt) *noun* a line, drawn on a map, connecting places that have the same amount of rain per year. [from *iso-*, + Greek *huetos* = rain]

isolate *verb* **1** to place apart or alone. **2** to separate (an infectious person) from others. **3** to separate (one substance etc.) from a compound. **isolation** *noun* [from Latin *insula* = island]

isolationism *noun* the policy of holding aloof from other countries or groups. **isolationist** *noun*

isomer (**I**-sŏ-mer) *noun* any of two or more substances whose molecules have the same atoms in different arrangements. **isomeric** (I-sŏ-**me**-rik) *adjective*, **isomerism** (I-**som**-ĕ-rizm) *noun* [from *iso-*, + Greek *meros* = a part]

isometric (I-sŏ-**met**-rik) *adjective* **1** (of muscle action) developing tension while the muscle is prevented from contracting. **2** (of a drawing or projection) drawing a three-dimensional object, without perspective, so that equal lengths along the three axes are drawn equal. **3** of equal measure. **4** (in geometry) preserving shapes and sizes. [from *iso-*, + Greek *metron* = measure]

isometry (I-**som**-ĕ-tree) *noun* an isometric transformation.

isomorph (**I**-sŏ-morf) *noun* a substance having the same form or composition as another. **isomorphic** *adjective*, **isomorphism** *noun* [from *iso-*, + Greek *morphe* = form]

isosceles (I-**sos**-ĕ-leez) *adjective* (of a triangle) having two sides equal. [from *iso-*, + Greek *skelos* = leg]

isostasy (I-**sos**-tă-see) *noun* the general state of equilibrium of the earth's crust. **isostatic** *adjective* [from *iso-*, + Greek *stasis* = standing]

isotherm (**I**-sŏ-therm) *noun* a line, drawn on a map, connecting places that have the same temperature. **isothermal** *adjective* [from *iso-*, + Greek *therme* = heat]

isotope (**I**-sŏ-tohp) *noun* one of two or more forms of a chemical element with different atomic weight and different nuclear properties but the same chemical properties. **isotopic** (I-sŏ-**top**-ik) *adjective* [from *iso-*, + Greek *topos* = place (i.e. in the periodic table of elements)]

isotropic (I-sŏ-**trop**-ik) *adjective* having the same physical properties in all directions. **isotropy** (I-**sot**-rŏ-pee) *noun*

Israel¹ the Hebrew nation or people (also called **children of Israel**) traditionally descended from Jacob. **Israelite** *adjective* & *noun*

Israel² a republic in the Middle East, at the eastern end of the Mediterranean Sea. **Israeli** (iz-**ray**-lee) *adjective & noun* (*plural* **Israelis**).

issue *noun* **1** an outgoing or outflow. **2** the issuing of things for use or for sale; the number or quantity issued. **3** one set of publications in a series issued regularly, *the May issue*. **4** a result, an outcome. **5** the point in question, an important topic for discussion; *make an issue of*, make a subject of contention. **6** offspring, *died without male issue*. –**issue** *verb* **1** to come or go or flow out. **2** to supply or distribute for use, *campers were issued with blankets*. **3** to put out for sale, to publish. **4** to send out, *issue orders*. **5** to result, to originate. □ **at issue** being discussed, disputed, or risked. **join** or **take issue** to proceed to argue.

Istanbul a port and the former capital of Turkey.

isthmus (**iss**-mŭs) *noun* (*plural* **isthmuses**) a narrow strip of land connecting two masses of land, *Isthmus of Panama*.

IT *abbreviation* information technology.

it *pronoun* **1** the thing mentioned or being discussed. **2** the person in question, *who is it?*; *it's me*. **3** used as the subject of a verb making a general statement about the weather (e.g. *it is raining*) or about circumstances etc. (e.g. *it is 2 kilometres to the station*), or as an indefinite object (*run for it!*). **4** used as the subject or object of a verb, with reference to a following clause or phrase, e.g. *it is seldom that he fails*; *I take it that you agree*. **5** exactly what is needed. **6** (in children's games) the player who has to catch others.

Usage See the note under **its**.

Italian *adjective* of Italy or its people or language. –**Italian** *noun* **1** a native of Italy. **2** the Italian language.

Italianate (i-**tal**-yă-nayt) *adjective* Italian in style or appearance.

italic (i-**tal**-ik) *adjective* **1** (of printed letters) sloping *like this*. **2** (of handwriting) compact and pointed like an early form of Italian handwriting. **italics** *plural noun* sloping printed letters *like these*.

italicise (i-**tal**-ĭ-syz) *verb* (also -**ize**) to put into italics.

Italy a republic in southern Europe comprising a boot-shaped peninsula and offshore islands of which the largest are Sicily and Sardinia.

itch *noun* **1** an itching feeling in the skin. **2** a restless desire or longing. –**itch** *verb* **1** to have or feel a tickling sensation in the skin, causing a desire to scratch the affected part. **2** to feel a restless desire or longing.
□ **have an itching palm** to be greedy for money.

itchy *adjective* having or causing an itch.
□ **have itchy feet** (*informal*) to be restless; to have an urge to travel. **itchiness** *noun*

item *noun* **1** a single thing in a list or among a number of things. **2** a single piece of news in a newspaper or bulletin. **3** (*informal*) a couple.

itemise *verb* (also -**ize**) to list, to state the individual items involved. **itemisation** *noun*

iterate (**it**-ĕ-rayt) *verb* **1** to repeat, to state repeatedly. **2** (in mathematics) to obtain a solution by repeating a process until a certain condition is satisfied. **iteration** *noun*, **iterative** *adjective* [from Latin *iterum* = again]

Ithaca (**ith**-ă-kă) an island off the western coast of Greece, legendary home of Odysseus.

itinerant (I-**tin**-ĕ-rănt) *adjective* travelling from place to place, *an itinerant preacher*. –**itinerant** *noun* an itinerant person; a tramp.

itinerary (I-**tin**-ĕ-ră-ree) *noun* a route, a list of places to be visited on a journey. [from Latin *itineris* = of a journey]

-itis *suffix* forming nouns meaning inflammation of (e.g. *appendicitis*). [Greek]

it'll (*informal*) = it will.

its *possessive pronoun* of or belonging to it.

it's (*informal*) = it is, it has, *it's very hot*; *it's broken all records*.

Usage *Its* and *it's* are often confused. The word *its* is the possessive form of *it*, and (like *hers*, *ours*, *theirs*, *yours*) has no apostrophe; correct usage is *the dog wagged its tail*, *the dog is hers*, *these are ours*. *It's* with the apostrophe is used where you can substitute *it is* or *it has*, e.g. *It's raining* (= 'It is raining'), *It's lost appeal* (= 'It has lost appeal').

itself *pronoun* the emphatic and reflexive form of *it*, *the food itself was good*; *the money doubled itself*.

IUD *abbreviation* intrauterine device, a coil or loop etc. placed inside the womb as a contraceptive.

IUPAC *abbreviation* International Union of Pure and Applied Chemistry.

IV *abbreviation* intravenous.

Ivan (**I**-văn) the name of several rulers of Russia, including Ivan III 'the Great' (reigned 1462–1505) and Ivan IV 'the Terrible' (reigned 1533–84).

I've (*informal*) = I have.

IVF *abbreviation* in vitro fertilisation.

ivory *noun* **1** the hard creamy-white substance forming the tusks of elephants etc.

2 an object made of this. **3** creamy-white colour. –**ivory** *adjective* creamy-white.
□ **ivory tower** a place or situation where people live secluded from the harsh realities of everyday life.

Ivory Coast a republic in West Africa.

ivy *noun* a climbing evergreen shrub with shiny often five-pointed leaves.

Jj

J *abbreviation* joule(s).

jab *verb* (**jabbed**, **jabbing**) to poke roughly, to thrust (a thing) into. –**jab** *noun* a rough blow or thrust, especially with something pointed.

jabber *verb* **1** to speak or say rapidly and unintelligibly. **2** to chatter continuously. –**jabber** *noun* jabbering talk or sound.

jabiru (**jab**-ŭ-**roo**) *noun* a large stork found in northern and eastern Australia, having greenish-black and white plumage and red legs.

jabot (*zh*ab-oh) *noun* ornamental frilling down the front of a shirt, blouse, or dress. [French]

jacaranda (jak-ă-**ran**-dă) *noun* a tropical American tree with blue or purple flowers.

jack *noun* **1** a portable device for raising heavy weights off the ground, especially one for raising the axle of a motor vehicle so that a wheel may be changed. **2** a ship's flag (smaller than an ensign) flown at the bow of a ship to show its nationality. **3** a playing card ranking below a queen in card games. **4** a small white ball aimed at in the game of bowls. **5** the male of various animals. **6** a device using a single plug to connect an electrical circuit. –**jack** *verb* to raise with a jack. –**jack** *adjective* (*Austral. informal*) **jack of** tired of, fed up with, *he got jack of waiting and took off.* □ **Jack Frost** frost personified. **jack in** (*informal*) to abandon (an attempt etc.). **jack-in-the-box** *noun* a toy figure that springs out of a box when the lid is lifted. **jack of all trades** one who can do many different kinds of work. **Jack tar** (*informal*) a sailor. **jack up** (*Austral. informal*) to refuse to cooperate.

jackal (**jak**-ăl) *noun* a wild flesh-eating animal of Africa and Asia, related to the dog, formerly supposed to hunt up the lion's prey for him.

jackanapes *noun* a pest or insolent fellow.

jackass *noun* **1** a male donkey. **2** a stupid or foolish person. **3** (in full **laughing jackass**) a kookaburra.

jackboot *noun* **1** a large boot reaching above the knee. **2** military oppression.

jackdaw *noun* a thievish small crow.

jackeroo *noun* a trainee on an Australian sheep or cattle station. –**jackeroo** *verb* (**jackerooed**, **jackerooing**) to work as a jackeroo.

jacket *noun* **1** a short coat, usually reaching to the hips. **2** an outer covering round a boiler etc. to lessen loss of heat. **3** a coloured paper wrapper in which a bound book is issued. **4** the skin of a potato baked without being peeled.

jackhammer *noun* a pneumatic hammer or drill.

jackknife *noun* **1** a large clasp-knife. **2** a dive in which the body is first bent double and then straightened. –**jackknife** *verb* (of an articulated vehicle) to fold one part against itself accidentally.

jackpot *noun* the accumulated stakes in various games, increasing in value until won. □ **hit the jackpot** to have sudden great success or good fortune.

Jack the Ripper a notorious murderer, never identified, held responsible for a series of murders of women in London in 1888–9.

jacky winter *noun* a small brown Australian flycatcher.

Jacob a Hebrew patriarch also called Israel (see entry).

Jacobean (jak-ŏ-**bee**-ăn) *adjective* of the reign of James I of England (1603–25). [from Latin *Jacobus* = James]

Jacobite (**jak**-ŏ-byt) *noun* a supporter of James II of England after his abdication (1688), or of the exiled Stuarts. [same origin as *Jacobean*]

jacquard (**jak**-ard) *noun* a fabric woven with an intricate figured pattern. [named after J. M. Jacquard, French inventor, died 1834]

jacuzzi (ja-**koo**-zee) *noun* (*trademark*) a large bath in which underwater jets of water are projected to massage the body.

jade[1] *noun* **1** a hard green, blue, or white stone from which ornaments are carved. **2** its green colour.

jade[2] *noun* **1** a poor worn-out horse. **2** a disreputable or bad-tempered woman.

jaded *adjective* **1** feeling or looking tired and bored. **2** (of the appetite) dulled, lacking zest for food.

Jaffa *noun* a large oval thick-skinned variety of orange, originally grown near the port of Jaffa in Israel.

Jagannatha (jag-ă-**nah**-thă) (in Hinduism) the form of Krishna worshipped in Puri, Orissa (*see* juggernaut).

jagged (**jag**-ĕd) *adjective* having an uneven edge or outline with sharp projections.

jaguar *noun* a large flesh-eating animal of the cat family, found in tropical America.

jail *noun* (also gaol) **1** a public prison. **2** confinement in this, *he was sentenced to three years' jail.* –**jail** *verb* (jailed, jailing) to put into jail. [from Latin *cavea*]

jailbreak *noun* (also gaolbreak) an escape from jail.

jailer *noun* (also gaoler) a person in charge of a jail or its prisoners.

Jain (*rhymes with* mine) *noun* a member of an Indian sect with doctrines like those of Buddhism. –**Jain** *adjective* of this sect. Jainism *noun*, Jainist *noun*

Jakarta (jă-**kar**-tă) (also Djakarta) the capital of Indonesia, situated in north-west Java.

jake *adjective* (*Austral. informal*) all right; fine, *she's jake.*

jalopy (jă-**lop**-ee) *noun* a battered old car.

jam¹ *verb* (jammed, jamming) **1** to squeeze or wedge into a space; to become wedged. **2** to make (part of a machine) immovable so that the machine will not work; to become unworkable in this way. **3** to crowd or block (an area) with people or things. **4** to thrust or apply forcibly, *jam the brakes on.* **5** to cause interference to (a radio transmission), making it unintelligible. –**jam** *noun* **1** a squeeze, crush, or stoppage caused by jamming. **2** a crowded mass making movement difficult, *traffic jam.* **3** (*informal*) a difficult situation, *I'm in a jam.* □ **jam-packed** *adjective* (*informal*) packed full and tightly. jam session improvised playing by a group of jazz musicians.

jam² *noun* **1** a sweet substance made by boiling fruit with sugar to a thick consistency. **2** (*informal*) something easy or pleasant. jammy *adjective*

Jamaica an island country in the Caribbean Sea. Jamaican *adjective* & *noun*

jamb (*pr.* jam) *noun* the vertical side post of a doorway or window frame. [from French *jambe* = leg]

jamboree (jam-bŏ-**ree**) *noun* **1** a large party, a celebration. **2** a large rally of Scouts.

James¹ the name of two kings of England and Scotland, James I (James VI of Scotland), king of Scotland 1567–1625 and England 1603–25, James II (James VII of Scotland), reigned 1685–8.

James², Henry (1843–1916), American novelist and critic, whose works include *Portrait of a Lady* and *The Ambassadors.*

James³, St, **1** 'the Great', an Apostle, martyred in AD 44; feast day, 25 July. **2** 'the Less', an Apostle; feast day, 1 May. **3** a person described as 'the Lord's brother', put to death in AD 62, to whom is ascribed the *Epistle of St James*, a book of the New Testament.

Jamestown the capital of St Helena.

jangle *noun* a harsh metallic sound. –**jangle** *verb* **1** to make or cause to make this sound. **2** to cause irritation to (nerves etc.) by discord.

janissary (**jan**-ŭ-să-ree) *noun* a Turkish soldier. [from Turkish *yeni* = new, + *çeri* = troops]

janitor (**jan**-ŭ-ter) *noun* the caretaker of a building. [from Latin *janua* = door]

January *noun* the first month of the year. [named after *Janus*]

Janus (**jay**-nŭs) (*Rom. myth.*) a god who was the guardian of doorways, gates, and beginnings, usually shown with two faces that look in opposite directions.

Japan an imperial monarchy in eastern Asia. Japanese *adjective* & *noun* (*plural* Japanese).

japan *noun* a kind of hard usually black varnish, especially a kind brought originally from Japan. –**japan** *verb* (japanned, japanning) to coat with japan.

japonica (jă-**pon**-ikă) *noun* an ornamental variety of quince, with red flowers. [Latin, = Japanese]

jar¹ *noun* **1** a cylindrical container made of glass or earthenware. **2** this with its contents; the amount it contains. [from Arabic *jarra* = pot]

jar² *verb* (jarred, jarring) **1** to make a sound that has a discordant or painful effect. **2** (of an action etc.) to be out of harmony, to have a harsh or disagreeable effect. **3** to cause an unpleasant jolt or a sudden shock. –**jar** *noun* a jarring movement or effect.

jardinière (*zh*ar-dǔn-**yair**) *noun* a large ornamental pot for holding indoor plants. [French]

jargon *noun* words or expressions developed for use within a particular group, hard for outsiders to understand and sounding ugly, *scientists' jargon*.

jarrah (**ja**-ră) *noun* a tall Western Australian eucalypt with hard, reddish-brown wood; the wood itself, native mahogany. [from Nyungar *jarrily*]

jasmine *noun* a shrub with fragrant yellow or white flowers.

Jason (*Gk. legend*) the leader of the Argonauts in quest of the Golden Fleece.

jasper *noun* an opaque variety of quartz, usually red, yellow, or brown.

jaundice (**jawn**-dǔs) *noun* a condition in which the skin becomes abnormally yellow as a result of excessive bile in the bloodstream. [from French *jaune* = yellow]

jaundiced *adjective* 1 discoloured by jaundice. 2 filled with resentment or jealousy.

jaunt *noun* a short trip, especially one taken for pleasure. –**jaunt** *verb* to take a jaunt.

jaunty *adjective* (**jauntier**, **jauntiest**) 1 cheerful and self-confident in manner. 2 (of clothes) stylish and cheerful. **jauntily** *adverb*, **jauntiness** *noun*

Java¹ (**jah**-vă) an island of Indonesia. **Javanese** *adjective & noun* (*plural* **Javanese**).

Java² *noun* (*trademark*) a general-purpose computer programming language designed to produce programs that will run on any computer system.

javelin (**jav**-ĕ-lĭn) *noun* a light spear thrown in sport or as a weapon.

jaw *noun* 1 either of the two bones that form the framework of the mouth and in which the teeth are set. 2 the lower of these; the part of the face covering it. 3 (*informal*) talkativeness; a lecture; a gossiping talk. –**jaw** *verb* (*informal*) to talk long and boringly; to gossip. **jaws** *plural noun* something resembling a pair of jaws, e.g. the gripping part of a tool.

jawbone *noun* either of the bones of the jaw.

jay *noun* a noisy chattering European bird of the crow family; any of various Australian birds resembling this, including the grey currawong.

jaywalk *verb* to walk carelessly on a road, without regard for traffic or signals. **jaywalker** *noun*

jazz *noun* 1 a type of music with strong rhythm and much syncopation, often improvised. 2 (*informal*) a matter; *and all that jazz*, and things of that sort. –**jazz** *verb* 1 to play or arrange as jazz. 2 to brighten, *jazz it up*.

jazzy *adjective* 1 of or like jazz. 2 flashy, showy, *a jazzy sports car*.

jealous (**jel**-ŭs) *adjective* 1 feeling or showing resentment towards a person whom one thinks of as a rival or as having advantages etc. 2 taking watchful care, *is very jealous of his own rights*. **jealously** *adverb*, **jealousy** *noun*

jeans *plural noun* casual trousers of denim or other cotton material. [from *jean* = twilled cotton cloth]

jeep *noun* (*trademark*) a small sturdy motor vehicle, especially in military use, with four-wheel drive. [from *G.P.*, short for 'general purposes']

jeer *verb* to laugh or shout at rudely and scornfully. –**jeer** *noun* a jeering remark or shout.

Jefferson, Thomas (1743–1826), 3rd President of the USA 1801–9, who drafted the Declaration of Independence (1775–6).

Jehovah (jĕ-**hoh**-vă) the traditional English form of one of the Hebrew names for God, now often written as *Yahweh*.

Jehovah's Witness *noun* a member of a fundamentalist Christian sect, denying many traditional Christian doctrines, and refusing military service and blood transfusion on religious grounds.

jejune (jĕ-**joon**) *adjective* 1 scanty, poor, (of land) barren. 2 unsatisfying to the mind. [from Latin *jejunus* = fasting]

Jekyll and Hyde *noun* a person in whom two personalities (one good, one evil) alternate. [named after the hero of a story (by R.L. Stevenson) who could transform himself from the respectable Dr Jekyll into the evil Mr Hyde by means of a potion that he drank]

jell *verb* (*informal*) 1 to set as jelly. 2 to take definite form, *our ideas began to jell*.

jellied *adjective* set in jelly, *jellied eels*.

jelly¹ *noun* 1 a soft solid food made of liquid set with gelatine, especially one prepared in a mould as a sweet dish. 2 a kind of jam made of strained fruit juice and sugar. 3 a substance of similar consistency, *petroleum jelly*. [from Latin *gelare* = freeze]

jelly² *noun* (*informal*) gelignite.

jellyfish *noun* (*plural* jellyfish) a sea animal with a jelly-like body and stinging tentacles.

jemmy *noun* a short crowbar used by burglars to force doors, windows, and drawers. –jemmy *verb* to force open with a jemmy.

Jenner, Edward (1749–1823), English physician, the pioneer of vaccination.

jenny *noun* a female donkey.

jeopardise (**jep**-er-dyz) *verb* (also -ize) to endanger.

jeopardy (**jep**-er-dee) *noun* danger.

jerboa (jer-**boh**-ă) *noun* a small desert rodent with long hind legs used for leaping.

jeremiad (je-rĕ-**my**-ăd) *noun* a long lamentation about one's troubles. [named after Jeremiah]

Jeremiah (je-rĕ-**my**-ah) **1** a Hebrew major prophet (c. 650–c. 585 BC). **2** the book of the Old Testament containing his prophecies. –Jeremiah *noun* a pessimistic person.

Jericho an ancient city north of the Dead Sea, on the West Bank.

jerk *noun* **1** a sudden sharp movement; an abrupt pull, push, or throw. **2** (*informal*) an annoying or stupid person. –jerk *verb* to pull, throw, or stop with a jerk; to move with a jerk or in short uneven movements.

jerkin *noun* a sleeveless jacket.

jerky *adjective* making abrupt starts and stops, not moving or acting smoothly. jerkily *adverb*, jerkiness *noun*

jeroboam (je-rŏ-**boh**-ăm) *noun* a wine bottle of four times the ordinary size. [named after a king of Israel (10th century BC)]

Jerome (jĕ-**rohm**), St (c. 342–420), scholar and monk, who translated the Bible from the original Hebrew and Greek into the language (Latin) of the people of his own time.

jerry *verb* (jerried, jerrying) (*Austral. informal*) to realise; to understand, *didn't jerry to it at first.*

jerry-built *adjective* built badly and with poor materials. jerry-builder *noun*

jerrycan *noun* a rectangular can for petrol or water, usually holding 5 gallons (22.7 litres).

Jersey the largest of the Channel Islands. –Jersey *noun* an animal of a breed of light brown dairy cattle, originally from Jersey.

jersey *noun* **1** plain machine-knitted fabric used for making clothes. **2** (*plural* jerseys) a close-fitting woollen pullover with sleeves.

Jerusalem the holy city of the Jews, sacred also to Christians and Muslims, the capital of Israel. □ Jerusalem artichoke a kind of sunflower with edible underground tubers; this tuber as a vegetable (¶ from Italian *girasole* = sunflower).

jest *noun* a joke. –jest *verb* to make jokes. □ in jest in fun, not seriously.

jester *noun* **1** a person who makes jokes. **2** a professional entertainer employed at a court in the Middle Ages.

Jesu (*old use*) = Jesus.

Jesuit (**jez**-yoo-ŭt) *noun* a member of the Society of Jesus, a Roman Catholic religious order.

Jesuitical (jez-yoo-**it**-ŭkăl) *adjective* **1** of or like Jesuits. **2** (*offensive*) using clever but false reasoning (such as the Jesuits were accused of by their enemies).

Jesus (also Jesus Christ) the central figure of the Christian religion, a Jew living in Palestine at the beginning of the 1st century AD, believed by Christians to be the Son of God.

jet[1] *noun* **1** a hard black mineral that can be polished, used as a gem. **2** its colour, deep glossy black. jet-black *adjective*

jet[2] *noun* **1** a stream of water, gas, flame, etc., shot out from a small opening. **2** a spout or opening from which this comes, a burner on a gas cooker. **3** a jet engine; a jet-propelled aircraft. –jet *verb* (jetted, jetting) **1** to spurt in jets. **2** (*informal*) to travel or convey by jet-propelled aircraft. □ jet engine an engine using jet propulsion. jet lag delayed physical effects of tiredness etc. felt after a long flight, especially owing to differences of local time. jet-propelled *adjective* propelled by jet engines. jet propulsion propulsion by engines that give forward thrust by sending out a high-speed jet of gases etc. at the back. jet set wealthy people who travel frequently by air, especially for pleasure. jet ski a jet-propelled vehicle like a motorcycle, for use on water. jet stream a jet from a jet engine; a strong wind blowing in a narrow range of altitudes in the upper atmosphere. [from French *jeter* = to throw]

jetsam *noun* goods thrown overboard from a ship in distress to lighten it, especially those that are washed ashore. [from *jettison*]

jettison *verb* **1** to throw (goods) overboard or (goods or fuel) from an aircraft, especially to lighten a ship or aircraft in distress. **2** to discard (what is unwanted). [same origin as *jet*[2]]

jetty *noun* a breakwater or landing stage. [from French *jetée* = thrown out (from the shore)]

Jew *noun* a person of Hebrew descent, or one whose religion is Judaism. □ **Jew's harp** a musical instrument consisting of a small U-shaped metal frame held in the teeth while a projecting metal strip is twanged with a finger. [from Hebrew, = of the tribe of Judah]

jewel *noun* **1** a precious stone. **2** an ornament for wearing, containing one or more precious stones. **3** a person or thing that is highly valued.

jewelled *adjective* ornamented or set with jewels.

jeweller *noun* a person who makes or deals in jewels or jewellery.

jewellery (**joo**-ĕl-ree) *noun* jewels or similar ornaments to be worn.

Jewess *noun* (*old use*, now considered *offensive*) a female Jew.

jewfish *noun* any of several large Australian fish, used as food, including mulloway, catfish, and a perchlike fish.

Jewish *adjective* of Jews or Judaism.

Jewry *noun* the Jewish people.

Jezebel (**jez**-ĕ-bĕl) 9th century BC the pagan wife of Ahab king of Israel. –**Jezebel** *noun* a shameless or immoral woman.

jib[1] *noun* **1** a triangular sail stretching forward from the mast. **2** the projecting arm of a crane. □ **the cut of his jib** his general appearance or manner.

jib[2] *verb* (**jibbed, jibbing**) **1** to refuse to proceed in some action. **2** (of a horse) to stop suddenly and refuse to go forwards. □ **jib at** to show unwillingness and dislike for (a course of action).

jibbah *noun* a long cloth coat worn by Muslim men in some countries. [from Egyptian Arabic]

jiffy *noun* (*informal*) a moment, *in a jiffy*.

jig *noun* **1** a lively jumping dance; the music for this. **2** a device that holds a piece of work and guides the tools working on it. **3** a template. –**jig** *verb* (**jigged, jigging**) to move up and down rapidly and jerkily.

jiggered *adjective* **I'll be jiggered** (*informal*) an exclamation of astonishment.

jiggery-pokery *noun* (*informal*) trickery, underhand dealing.

jiggle *verb* to rock or jerk lightly.

jigsaw *noun* **1** a mechanically operated saw with a small stiff blade that moves to and fro. **2** a **jigsaw puzzle**, a picture pasted on board and cut with a jigsaw into irregular pieces that are then shuffled and reassembled as a pastime.

jihad (jŭ-**hahd**) *noun* (in Islam) **1** a war or struggle against unbelievers. **2** (**greater jihad**) the spiritual struggle within oneself against sin. [Arabic]

jilt *verb* to drop or abandon (a person) after having courted or promised to marry him or her.

Jindiworobak (jin-dee-**wo**-rŏ-bak) *noun* a member of a literary group formed in 1938 to promote Australian values in art and literature. [Wuywurung]

jingle *verb* to make or cause to make a metallic ringing or clinking sound like that of small bells or of keys struck together. –**jingle** *noun* **1** a jingling sound. **2** verse or words with simple catchy rhymes or repetitive sounds.

jingoism (**jing**-goh-izm) *noun* an aggressive attitude combining excessive patriotism and contempt for other countries. **jingoist** *noun*, **jingoistic** *adjective*

jink *verb* to dodge by turning suddenly and sharply. –**jink** *noun* an act of jinking. □ **high jinks** noisy merrymaking, boisterous fun.

jinn, jinnee *nouns* (*plural* **jinn**) (*Islamic myth.*) any of the supernatural beings able to appear in human and animal form and to help or hinder human beings. [from Arabic *jinni; jinn* is the plural in Arabic]

jinx *noun* (*informal*) a person or thing that is thought to bring bad luck.

jitter *verb* (*informal*) to feel nervous, to behave nervously. **jitters** *plural noun* (*informal*) nervousness.

jittery *adjective* (*informal*) nervy. **jitteriness** *noun*

jive *noun* fast lively jazz music; dancing to this. –**jive** *verb* to dance to such music.

Jnr. *abbreviation* Junior.

Joachim (**joh**-ă-kim), St, the husband of St Anne and father of the Virgin Mary.

Joan of Arc, St (1412–31), French national heroine, who led French forces against the English in the Hundred Years War, and relieved Orleans. After being captured she was tried and burnt at the stake as a heretic. Feast day, 30 May.

Job (*pr.* johb)**1** a good Hebrew man who endured his troubles with patience and ultimately remained convinced of the goodness of God. **2** a book of the Old Testament giving an account of this. □ **Job's comforter** a person who aggravates the distress of the person he or she is supposed to be comforting, like those who counselled Job.

job[1] *noun* **1** a piece of work to be done. **2** a paid position of employment, *got a job at the factory*. **3** something one has to do, a responsibility, *it's your job to lock the gates*. **4** something completed, a product of work, *a neat little job*. **5** (*informal*) a crime, especially a robbery. **6** (*informal*) a difficult task, *you'll have a job to move it*. □ **a bad job** a difficult state of affairs, *make the best of a bad job*. **a good job** a satisfactory or fortunate state of affairs, *it's a good job the police came when they did*. **job lot** a collection of miscellaneous articles bought together. **just the job** (*informal*) exactly what is wanted.

job[2] *verb* (*Austral. informal*) to hit.

jobber *noun* **1** a person who does piece-work. **2** a principal or wholesaler dealing on the Stock Exchange.

jobbery *noun* corrupt dealing.

jobbing *adjective* doing single specific pieces of work for payment, *a jobbing gardener*.

jobless *adjective* unemployed, out of work.

jockey *noun* (*plural* **jockeys**) a person who rides horses in horse races, especially a professional rider. –**jockey** *verb* (**jockeyed**, **jockeying**) to manoeuvre in order to gain an advantage, *jockeying for position*; *jockeyed him into doing it*, forced him by skilful or unfair methods.

jockstrap *noun* a support for the male genitals, worn especially for sport.

jocose (jŏ-**kohss**) *adjective* joking. **jocosely** *adverb* [from Latin *jocus* = a joke]

jocular (**jok**-yŭ-ler) *adjective* joking, avoiding seriousness. **jocularly** *adverb*, **jocularity** (jok-yŭ-**la**-rŭ-tee) *noun*

jocund (**jok**-ŭnd) *adjective* merry, cheerful.

jodhpurs (**jod**-perz) *plural noun* riding-breeches reaching to the ankle, fitting closely below the knee and loosely above it. [named after Jodhpur in India]

Joel (*pr.* **joh**-ĕl) **1** a Hebrew minor prophet of the 5th or possibly 9th century BC. **2** a book of the Old Testament containing his prophecies.

joey *noun* a young kangaroo, wallaby, or possum.

jog *verb* (**jogged**, **jogging**) **1** to give a slight knock or push to; to shake with a push or jerk. **2** to rouse or stimulate, *jogged his memory*. **3** to move up and down with an unsteady movement. **4** (of a horse) to move at a jogtrot. **5** to run at a leisurely pace with short strides, as a form of exercise. –**jog** *noun* **1** a slight shake or push, a nudge. **2** a slow walk or trot. □ **jog on** or **along** to proceed slowly or laboriously. **jogger** *noun*

joggle *verb* to shake slightly; to move by slight jerks. –**joggle** *noun* a joggling movement, a slight shake.

jogtrot *noun* a slow regular trot.

John[1] king of England 1199–1216.

John[2], St **1** an Apostle, credited with the authorship of the fourth Gospel, Revelation, and three epistles of the New Testament. Feast days, 27 December and 6 May. **2** the fourth Gospel. **3** any of the three epistles attributed to St John.

john dory *noun* (*plural* **dory** or **dories**) an edible sea fish.

johnny *noun* (*informal*) a fellow. □ **johnny-come-lately** *noun* a newcomer, an upstart.

John of the Cross, St (1542–91), Spanish mystic and poet. Feast day, 14 December.

Johnson, Samuel (1709–84), English poet, critic, and lexicographer, whose famous *Dictionary* was published in 1755.

John the Baptist, St, a preacher who was the cousin of Jesus Christ, whom he baptised. Feast days, 24 June and 29 August.

joie de vivre (*zh*wah dĕ **veevr**) *noun* a feeling of great enjoyment of life. [French, = joy of living]

join *verb* **1** to put together; to fasten, unite, or connect. **2** to come together, to become united with; *the Darling joins the Murray near Wentworth*, meets and flows into it. **3** to take part with others in doing something, *joined in the chorus*. **4** to come into the company of, *join us for lunch*. **5** to become a member of, *joined the Navy*. **6** to take or resume one's place in, *joined his ship*. –**join** *noun* a point, line, or surface where things join. □ **join battle** to begin fighting. **join forces** to combine efforts. **join hands** to clasp each other's hands. **join up** to enlist in the armed forces.

joiner *noun* a person who makes furniture, house fittings, and other woodwork that is lighter than a carpenter's products.

joinery *noun* the work of a joiner.

joint *adjective* **1** shared, held, or done by two or more people together, *a joint account*. **2** sharing in an activity etc., *joint authors*. –**joint** *noun* **1** a place where two things are joined. **2** a structure in an animal body by which bones are fitted together. **3** a place or device at which two parts of a structure are joined. **4** any of the parts into which a butcher divides a carcass; this cooked and served. **5** a crack or fissure in a mass of rock. **6** (*informal*) a meeting place for drinking etc. **7** (*informal*) a marijuana cigarette. –**joint** *verb* **1** to connect by a joint or joints. **2** to fill up masonry joints with mortar etc., to point. **3** to divide (a carcass) into joints; *joint a chicken*, divide it into pieces by cutting through each joint. **4** (of rocks) to form cracks or fissures. □ **joint-stock company** a business company with capital contributed and held jointly by a number of people. **out of joint** dislocated; in disorder.

jointly *adverb* so as to be shared or done by two or more people together.

joist *noun* any of the parallel beams, extending from wall to wall, on which floorboards or ceiling laths are fixed.

jojoba (hŏ-**hoh**-bă) *noun* a plant with seeds yielding an oily extract used in cosmetics etc.

joke *noun* **1** something said or done to cause laughter. **2** a ridiculous person, thing, or circumstance. –**joke** *verb* to make jokes. **jokingly** *adverb*

joker *noun* **1** a person who jokes. **2** (*informal*) a fellow. **3** an extra playing card used in certain card games as the highest trump.

jokey *adjective* joking, not serious.

jollification *noun* merrymaking, festivity.

jollify *verb* (**jollified**, **jollifying**) to be or cause to be jolly.

jollity *noun* being jolly, merriment, merrymaking.

jolly *adverb* (**jollier**, **jolliest**) **1** full of high spirits, cheerful, merry. **2** cheerful because slightly drunk. **3** very pleasant, delightful. –**jolly** *adverb* (*informal*) very, *jolly good*. –**jolly** *verb* (**jollied**, **jollying**) (*informal*) to keep (a person) in a good humour, especially in order to win cooperation, *jolly him along*.

jolly boat *noun* a ship's boat, smaller than a cutter, built with overlapping planks.

Jolly Roger *noun* a black flag, usually with a white skull and crossbones, traditionally associated with pirates.

jolt *verb* **1** to shake or dislodge with a jerk. **2** to move along jerkily, as on a rough road. **3** to give a mental shock to. –**jolt** *noun* **1** a jolting movement or effect. **2** a surprise or shock.

Jonah (**joh**-nă) **1** a Hebrew minor prophet who tried to escape God's call, went to sea, was swallowed by a large fish, and later vomited out on to dry land, and finally obeyed God. **2** a book of the Old Testament giving an account of this. –**Jonah** *noun* a person who is believed to bring bad luck.

Jonathan *noun* a red-skinned eating apple.

jonquil (**jon**-kwil) *noun* a kind of narcissus with clusters of fragrant flowers.

Jordan 1 a river rising in Syria and Lebanon and flowing south through the Sea of Galilee to the Dead Sea. **2** the Hashemite Kingdom of Jordan, a country in the Middle East, bordering on the east of Israel. **Jordanian** (jor-**day**-nee-ăn) *adjective* & *noun*

Joseph, St, a carpenter of Nazareth, husband of the Virgin Mary to whom he was betrothed at the time of the Annunciation. Feast day, 19 March.

josh *verb* (*informal*) to hoax, to tease in a good-natured way.

Joshua 1 the Israelite leader who succeeded Moses and led his people into the Promised Land. **2** the sixth book of the Old Testament, telling of the conquest of Canaan by the Israelites.

joss *noun* a Chinese idol. □ **joss house** a temple. **joss stick** a thin stick that burns to give off a smell of incense.

jostle *verb* to push roughly, especially when in a crowd.

jot *noun* a very small amount, *not one jot or tittle*. –**jot** *verb* (**jotted**, **jotting**) to write briefly or hastily, *jot it down*.

jotter *noun* a notepad or notebook.

jottings *plural noun* jotted notes.

joule (*pr*. jool) *noun* a unit of work or energy. [named after the English physicist J. P. Joule (1818–89)]

journal (**jer**-năl) *noun* **1** a daily record of news, events, or business transactions. **2** a newspaper or periodical. [from Latin, = by day]

journalese (jer-nă-**leez**) *noun* a style of language used in inferior newspaper writing, full of hackneyed or artificially elaborate phrases.

journalist (**jer**-nă-lŭst) *noun* a person who writes for newspapers or magazines or prepares news to be broadcast on radio or television etc. journalism *noun*, journalistic *adjective*

journey *noun* (*plural* journeys) **1** a continued course of going or travelling. **2** the distance travelled or the time required for this, *a day's* or *four days' journey*. –journey *verb* (journeyed, journeying) to make a journey. [from French, = a day's travel (*jour* = day)]

journeyman *noun* (*plural* journeymen) **1** a qualified mechanic or artisan who works for another. **2** a reliable but not outstanding worker.

joust (*pr.* jowst) *verb* to fight on horseback with lances.

Jove Jupiter, the king of the gods in Roman mythology. by Jove! an exclamation of surprise. Jovian *adjective*

jovial (**joh**-vee-ăl) *adjective* full of cheerful good humour. jovially *adverb*, joviality (joh-vee-**al**-ŭ-tee) *noun*

jowl (*rhymes with* howl) *noun* **1** the jaw or cheek. **2** an animal's dewlap; similar loose skin on a person's throat.

joy *noun* **1** a deep emotion of pleasure, gladness. **2** a thing that causes this. □ no joy (*informal*) no satisfaction or success.

Joyce, James Augustine Aloysius (1882–1941), Irish novelist, author of *Ulysses* and *Finnegans Wake*.

joyful *adjective* full of joy. joyfully *adverb*, joyfulness *noun*

joyless *adjective* without joy.

joyous *adjective* joyful. joyously *adverb*

joyride *noun* a car ride taken for pleasure, usually without the owner's permission. joyrider *noun*, joyriding *noun*

joystick *noun* **1** the control lever of an aircraft. **2** a device for moving a cursor on a display screen.

JP *abbreviation* Justice of the Peace.

JPEG (**jay**-peg) *noun* (in computing) a format for compressing images. [acronym of *J*oint *P*hotographic *E*xperts *G*roup]

Jr. *abbreviation* Junior.

jubilant *adjective* showing joy, rejoicing. [from Latin *jubilans* = shouting for joy]

jubilation *noun* rejoicing.

jubilee *noun* **1** a special anniversary, *silver* (25th), *golden* (50th), or *diamond* (60th) *jubilee*. **2** a time of rejoicing.

Judaea (joo-**dee**-ă) an ancient name for the southern district of Palestine, west of the Jordan. Judaean *adjective*

Judaic (joo-**day**-ik) *adjective* of or characteristic of the Jews or Judaism.

Judaism (**joo**-day-izm) *noun* the religion of the Jewish people, with belief in one God and based on the teachings of the Old Testament and the Talmud. [same origin as *Jew*]

Judas (also Judas Iscariot) the disciple who betrayed Christ. –Judas *noun* a betrayer or traitor.

judder *verb* to shake noisily or violently. –judder *noun* a juddering movement or effect.

Jude, St, an Apostle (martyred in Persia with St Simon) to whom the last epistle in the New Testament is ascribed. Feast day (with St Simon), 28 October.

judge *noun* **1** a public officer appointed to hear and try cases in a lawcourt. **2** a person appointed to decide who has won a contest. **3** a person who is able to give an authoritative opinion on the merits of something. **4** (in ancient Israel) any of the warrior leaders in the period between Joshua and the kings. –judge *verb* **1** to try (a case) in a lawcourt. **2** to act as judge of (a contest). **3** to form and give an opinion about. **4** to estimate, *judged the distance accurately*. [from Latin *judex* = judge]

judgment *noun* (also judgement) **1** judging, being judged. **2** the decision of a judge etc. in a lawcourt, *the judgment was in his favour*. **3** ability to judge wisely, good sense, *he lacks judgment*. **4** misfortune considered or jokingly said to be a punishment sent by God, *it's a judgment on you!* **5** an opinion, *in the judgment of most people*. □ Judgment Day or Day of Judgment (in Judaism, Christianity, and Islam) the day of the Last Judgment, when God will judge all mankind.

judgmental (juj-**men**-t'l) *adjective* (also judgemental) **1** involving judgment. **2** inclined to make moral judgments.

Judges the seventh book of the Old Testament, describing the gradual conquest of Canaan under various leaders (called *judges*).

judicature (**joo**-dŭ-kă-choor) *noun* **1** the administration of justice. **2** a body of judges.

judicial (joo-**dish**-ăl) *adjective* **1** of lawcourts or the administration of justice. **2** of a judge or judgment. **3** able to judge things wisely. **judicially** *adverb* [from Latin *judicis* = of a judge]

judiciary (joo-**dish**-ă-ree) *noun* the whole body of judges in a country.

judicious (joo-**dish**-ŭs) *adjective* judging wisely, showing good sense. **judiciously** *adverb*

Judith a book of the Apocrypha recounting the story of Judith, a rich Israelite widow, who saved her people from Nebuchadnezzar's army by captivating his general, Holofernes, and cutting off his head while he slept.

judo *noun* a Japanese system of unarmed combat. [from Japanese *ju* = gentle, + *do* = way]

judoka (*pr*. **joo**-doh-kǎ) *noun* (*plural* **judoka**) (also **judoist**) a student of or expert in judo.

jug *noun* **1** a vessel for holding and pouring liquids, with a handle and a shaped lip. **2** (*informal*) prison. –**jug** *verb* (**jugged**, **jugging**) **1** to cook (hare or rabbit) by stewing it (formerly in a jug or jar). **2** (*informal*) to put into prison. **jugful** *noun* (*plural* **jugfuls**).

juggernaut *noun* **1** a large overwhelmingly powerful object or institution etc. **2** a very large heavy transport vehicle. [Juggernaut (also Jagannatha) is a title of a Hindu god whose image was dragged in procession on a huge wheeled vehicle; some devotees are said to have thrown themselves under its wheels]

juggle *verb* **1** to toss and catch a number of objects skilfully for entertainment, keeping one or more in the air at one time. **2** to manipulate skilfully when handling several objects. **3** to rearrange (facts or figures) in order to achieve something or to deceive people.

juggler *noun* one who juggles, an entertainer who performs juggling tricks.

jugular (**jug**-yŭ-ler) *noun* a **jugular vein**, either of the two great veins of the neck carrying blood from the head.

juice *noun* **1** the liquid content of fruits, vegetables, or meat. **2** liquid secreted by an organ of the body, *the digestive juices*. **3** (*informal*) petrol or electricity. –**juice** *verb* to extract juice from.

juicy *adjective* (**juicier**, **juiciest**) **1** full of juice. **2** (*informal*) interesting, especially because of its scandalous nature, *juicy stories*. **juicily** *adverb*, **juiciness** *noun*

ju-jitsu (joo-**jit**-soo) *noun* a Japanese method of self-defence using throws, punches, etc., and seeking to use the opponent's strength and weight to his disadvantage. [from Japanese *ju* = gentle, + *jutsu* = skill]

ju-ju (**joo**-joo) *noun* **1** an object venerated in West Africa as a charm or fetish. **2** the magic attributed to this.

jujube *noun* a jelly-like sweet.

jukebox *noun* a machine that automatically plays a selected record when a coin is inserted.

Julian calendar the calendar introduced by Julius Caesar, replaced by the Gregorian calendar.

julienne (joo-lee-**en**) *noun* **1** vegetables or other food cut into thin strips. **2** a clear broth containing thin strips of vegetables. –**julienne** *adjective* cut into thin strips.

Julius Caesar (100–44 BC), Roman general, statesman, and historian, who completed the conquest of Gaul and established himself in supreme authority in Rome.

July *noun* the seventh month of the year. [named after Julius Caesar, who was born in this month]

jumble *verb* to mix in a confused way. –**jumble** *noun* articles jumbled together, a muddle. □ **jumble sale** a sale of miscellaneous second-hand goods to raise money for a charity.

jumbo *noun* (*plural* **jumbos**) **1** something very large of its kind. **2** a **jumbo jet**, a very large jet aircraft able to carry several hundred passengers.

jumbuck *noun* (*Austral. informal*) a sheep.

jump *verb* **1** to move up off the ground etc. by bending and then extending the legs or (of fish) by a movement of the tail. **2** to move suddenly with a jump or bound; to rise suddenly from a seat etc.; *jump in*, to get quickly into a car etc. **3** to pass over by jumping; to use (a horse) for jumping. **4** to pass over (a thing) to a point beyond; to skip (part of a book etc.) in reading or studying. **5** to give a sudden movement from shock or excitement. **6** to rise suddenly in amount or in price or value. **7** to leave (rails or a track) accidentally. **8** to pounce on, to attack suddenly. –**jump** *noun* **1** a jumping movement. **2** a sudden movement caused by shock etc. **3** a sudden rise in amount or price or value. **4** a sudden change to a different condition or set of circumstances; a gap in a series etc. **5** an obstacle to be jumped over.

□ **have the jump on** (*informal*) to have an advantage over. **jump at** to accept eagerly. **jump bail** to fail to come for trial when summoned after being released on bail. **jumped-up** *adjective* having risen suddenly from a low position or status. **jumping-off place** a starting point. **jump jet** a jet aircraft that can take off directly upwards. **jump lead** = jumper lead. **jump ship** (of a sailor) to desert one's ship. **jump the gun** to start or act before the permitted time. **jump the queue** to obtain something without waiting for one's proper turn. **jump to conclusions** to reach them too hastily. **jump to it** to make an energetic start.

jumper¹ *noun* **1** a person or animal that jumps, *is a good jumper*. **2** a short wire used to make or break an electrical circuit. □ **jumper lead** a cable for conveying current from one battery to another.

jumper² *noun* **1** a knitted garment for the upper part of the body. **2** a loose outer jacket worn by sailors. **3** a pinafore dress.

jumpsuit *noun* a one-piece garment for the whole body, like that worn by paratroopers.

jumpy *adjective* nervous.

junction *noun* **1** a place where things join. **2** a place where roads or railway lines etc. meet and unite.

juncture (**junk**-cher) *noun* a point of time; a critical convergence of events.

June *noun* the sixth month of the year. [named after Juno]

Jung (*pr.* yuung), Carl Gustav (1875–1961), Swiss psychologist, who originated the concepts of two types of personality (introvert and extrovert) and of the existence of a 'collective unconscious' derived from ancestral experiences. **Jungian** *adjective* & *noun*

jungle *noun* **1** land overgrown with tangled vegetation, especially in the tropics. **2** a wild tangled mass. **3** a scene of bewildering complexity or confusion, or of ruthless struggle, *the blackboard jungle* (in schools), *concrete jungle* (in cities). **jungly** *adjective* [from Hindi *jangal* = forest]

junior *adjective* **1** younger in age; *Tom Brown junior*, the younger person of that name. **2** lower in rank or authority. **3** for younger children, *junior school*. –**junior** *noun* **1** a junior person; *he is my junior*, is younger than I am. **2** a person employed to work in a junior capacity, *the office junior*. **3** a member of a junior school. **4** (*Amer. informal*) the son in a family. [Latin, = younger]

juniper (**joo**-nŭ-per) *noun* an evergreen shrub with prickly leaves and dark purplish berries.

junk¹ *noun* **1** discarded material, rubbish. **2** (*informal*) anything regarded as useless or of little value, *all that junk in the boot of the car*. □ **junk food** food that is not regarded as nutritious. **junk mail** unsolicited advertising or promotional material delivered to letter boxes. **junk shop** a shop selling miscellaneous cheap second-hand goods.

junk² *noun* a kind of flat-bottomed ship with sails, used in the China Seas.

junket *noun* **1** a sweet custard-like food made of milk curdled with rennet and flavoured. **2** a feast, merrymaking. **3** an official's tour at public expense. –**junket** *verb* (**junketed**, **junketing**) to feast, to make merry. [from Old French *jonquette* = a rush basket (used to carry junket)]

junkie *noun* (*informal*) a drug addict. [from a slang meaning of *junk*, = a drug]

Juno (**jew**-noh) (*Rom. myth.*) a great goddess of the Roman State, identified with Hera.

Junoesque (jew-noh-**esk**) *adjective* resembling the goddess Juno in stately beauty.

junta *noun* a group of people who combine to rule a country, especially having seized power after a revolution. [Spanish]

Jupiter (**jew**-pŭ-ter) **1** (*Rom. myth.*) the chief of the gods, identified with Zeus. **2** the largest planet of the solar system.

Jura (**joor**-rǎ) a system of mountains on the border of France and Switzerland.

Jurassic (jŭ-**rass**-ik) *adjective* of the second period of the Mesozoic era. –**Jurassic** *noun* this period.

jurisdiction (joor-ŭss-**dik**-shŏn) *noun* **1** authority to interpret and apply the law. **2** official power exercised within a particular sphere of activity. **3** the extent or territory over which legal or other power extends. [from Latin *juris* = of the law, + *dictum* = said]

jurisprudence (joor-ŭss-**proo**-děns) *noun* the study of law or of a particular part of law, *medical jurisprudence*. **jurisprudential** *adjective* [from Latin *juris* = of law, + *prudentia* = knowledge]

jurist (**joor**-rŭst) *noun* a person who is skilled in the law. **juristic** *adjective*, **juristical** *adjective*, **juristically** *adverb*

juror (**joor**-rer) *noun* **1** a member of a jury. **2** a person taking an oath.

jury *noun* 1 a body of people sworn to give a verdict on a case presented to them in a court of law. 2 a body of people appointed to select the winner(s) in a competition. □ **jury box** an enclosure for the jury in a lawcourt. [from Latin *jurare* = take an oath]

jury-rigged *adjective* set up as a makeshift.

just *adjective* 1 giving proper consideration to the claims of everyone concerned. 2 deserved, right in amount etc., *a just reward*. 3 well grounded in fact. –**just** *adverb* 1 exactly, *just at that spot*. 2 barely, no more than, by only a short distance, *I just managed it; just below the knee*. 3 at this moment or only a little time ago, *he has just gone*. 4 (*informal*) simply, merely, *we are just good friends*. 5 quite, *not just yet*. 6 (*informal*) positively, really, *it's just splendid*. □ **just about** (*informal*) almost exactly or completely. **just in case** as a precaution. **just now** at this moment; a little time ago. **just so** exactly arranged, *she likes everything just so*; it is exactly as you say. **justly** *adverb*, **justness** *noun* [from Latin *justus* = rightful]

justice *noun* 1 just treatment, fairness. 2 legal proceedings, *a court of justice*. 3 a judge or magistrate; the title of a judge, *Mr Justice White*. □ **do justice to** to show (a thing) to advantage; to show appreciation of. **Justice of the Peace** a person authorised to witness oaths, statutory declarations, etc.

justiciary (jus-**tish**-ă-ree) *noun* one who administers justice.

justifiable *adjective* able to be justified. **justifiably** *adverb*

justify *verb* (justified, justifying) 1 to show (a person, statement, or act etc.) to be right or just or reasonable. 2 to be a good or sufficient reason for, *increased production justifies an increase in wages*. 3 to adjust (a line of type in printing) so that it fills a space neatly. **justification** *noun*

Justinian (jus-**tin**-ee-ăn) 483–565, Roman emperor from 527, noted for his codification of the law.

jut *verb* (jutted, jutting) to project, *it juts out*.

Jute *noun* a member of a Low German tribe that invaded and settled in southern England in the 5th century.

jute *noun* fibre from the bark of certain tropical plants, used for making sacks etc.

Jutland a peninsula that forms the continental part of Denmark.

Juvenal (**joo**-vě-năl) (c. 60–c. 130), Roman satirist, who attacked the vice and folly of Roman society.

juvenile (**joo**-vě-nyl) *adjective* 1 youthful, childish. 2 for young people. –**juvenile** *noun* a young person. □ **juvenile delinquent** a young offender against the law, below the age when he or she may be held legally responsible for his or her actions. **juvenile delinquency**. [from Latin *juvenis* = young person]

juxtapose (juks-tă-**pohz**) *verb* to put (things) side by side. **juxtaposition** *noun* [from Latin *juxta* = next, + *positum* = put]

Kk

K *abbreviation* **1** kelvin(s). **2** one thousand. **3** (in computing) a unit of 1024 (often taken as 1000) bytes.

k *abbreviation* (*informal*) kilometre, *we did 600 ks a day.*

K2 the second-highest peak in the world, in the western Himalayas.

Kaaba (**kah**-ă-bă) *noun* a shrine at Mecca containing a sacred black stone.

kabbalah (kă-**bă**-lă) *noun* (also **cabbala**) **1** the Jewish mystical tradition. **2** any esoteric doctrine or occult lore.

kabuki (kă-**boo**-kee) *noun* a form of classical Japanese theatre. [from Japanese *ka* = song, + *bu* = dance, + *ki* = art]

Kabul (**kah**-buul) the capital of Afghanistan.

kadaitcha (kă-**dy**-chă) *noun* (also **kurdaitcha**) **1** an Aboriginal mission of vengeance (against an Aborigine who has been judged guilty of a serious offence against customary Law); the ritual accompanying this. **2** (in full **kadaitcha man**) an Aborigine empowered by the elders to perform the killing. [probably from Aranda *gwerdaje*]

Kaddish (**kad**-ish) *noun* a Jewish prayer of sanctification recited in the synagogue service and as a doxology. [from Aramaic *kaddis* = holy]

Kaffir *noun* (*historical*) a member or language of a Bantu people of South Africa. [from Arabic *kafir* = infidel]

Kafka, Franz (1883–1924), Czech novelist who wrote in German about the conflicts between individuals and the State.

kaiser (**ky**-zer) *noun* the title of the German and Austrian emperors until 1918.

Kakadu (kak-ă-**doo**) a national park in Arnhem Land in the Northern Territory, noted for its wetlands, native flora and fauna, and rock paintings.

Kalahari Desert (kal-ă-**hah**-ree) a high barren plateau in southern Africa, mainly in Botswana.

kale *noun* a kind of cabbage with curly leaves that do not form a compact head.

kaleidoscope (kă-**ly**-dŏ-skohp) *noun* a toy consisting of a tube containing small brightly coloured fragments of glass etc. and mirrors that reflect these to form changing patterns. **kaleidoscopic** (kă-ly-dŏ-**skop**-ik) *adjective* [from Greek *kalos* = beautiful, + *eidos* = form, + *skopein* = look at]

Kali (**kah**-lee) (in Hinduism) the most terrifying goddess, wife of Siva, often identified with Durga, and usually portrayed as black, naked, old, and hideous, with a protruding bloodstained tongue.

Kalimantan (kal-ĭ-**man**-tan) a region of Indonesia, comprising the southern part of Borneo.

kalpa (**kal**-pă) *noun* (in Hinduism and Buddhism) the period between the beginning and the end of the world, considered as one day of Brahma (4320 million human years). [Sanskrit]

Kama (**kah**-mă) (in Hinduism) the god of sexual love, usually portrayed as a beautiful youth with a bow of sugar cane, a bowstring of bees, and arrows of flowers. [Sanskrit]

Kama Sutra (**soo**-tră) an ancient Sanskrit treatise on the art of love and sexual technique.

kame *noun* a short irregular ridge of sand and gravel deposited by a stream running under a glacier. [a Scottish form of *comb*]

kameez (kă-**meez**) *noun* a tunic worn by both sexes in some countries of southern Asia.

kamikaze (kam-ĭ-**kah**-zee) *noun* (in the Second World War) **1** a Japanese aircraft laden with explosives and suicidally crashed on a target by its pilot. **2** the pilot of this. [from Japanese *kami* = divinity, + *kaze* = wind]

Kamilaroi (**kam**-ĭ-lă-roi) *noun* **1** a member of an Aboriginal people of east-central NSW and southern Queensland. **2** their language.

Kampala (kam-**pah**-lă) the capital of Uganda.

kampong *noun* a Malayan enclosure or village.

Kampuchea (kam-poo-**chee**-ă) a former name of Cambodia. **Kampuchean** *adjective* & *noun*

Kanaka (kă-**nak**-ă) *noun* a Pacific Islander, especially (formerly) one kidnapped and forced to serve as a labourer in the sugar and cotton industries of Queensland.

Kanchenjunga (kan-chen-**juung**-gă) the third-highest peak in the world, situated east of Mount Everest in the Himalayas.

Kandinsky, Wassily (1866–1944), Russian painter and theorist, usually considered the originator of abstract painting.

kangaroo *noun* an Australian marsupial with short forelimbs, a large thick tail, and long strong hind legs enabling it to jump along. –kangaroo *verb* (**kangarooed**, **kangarooing**) (*Austral.*) **1** to hunt kangaroos. **2** (of a car) to move along in a series of jerks.
□ **kangaroo bar** (*Austral.*) = **bullbar**. **kangaroo court** a court formed illegally by a group of people (e.g. prisoners or strikers) to settle disputes among themselves. **kangaroo mouse** a hopping mouse. **kangaroo paw** a Western Australian plant with woolly flowers shaped like a kangaroo's paw, the floral emblem of WA. **kangaroo rat** a rat kangaroo (*see* **rat**). **kangaroo thorn** a prickly acacia, often planted as a hedge. [from Guugu Yimidhirr *gungurru* = a large black or grey kangaroo]

Kangaroo Island a large island off the coast of South Australia.

kangha (**kang**-gă) *noun* a comb worn in the hair by Sikhs. [Punjabi]

kanji (**kun**-jee) *noun* Japanese writing using Chinese characters.

Kansas a State in the Middle West of the USA.

Kant (*pr.* kahnt), Immanuel (1724–1804), German philosopher.

kaolin (**kay**-ŏ-lǐn) *noun* a fine white clay used in making porcelain and in medicine. [from Chinese *gaoling*, the name of a mountain]

kapok (**kay**-pok) *noun* a substance resembling cotton wool, used for padding things. [from Malay *kapoq*]

kaput (kă-**puut**) *adjective* (*informal*) ruined, destroyed, dead; out of order. [from German *kaputt*]

kara *noun* a steel bracelet worn by Sikhs. [Punjabi]

Karachi (kă-**rah**-chee) a seaport and former capital of Pakistan.

karah parshad *noun* sanctified food of sugar, butter, and flour distributed at Sikh ceremonies. [Punjabi]

karaoke (ka-ree-**oh**-kee) *noun* a form of entertainment in which a person sings along to a backing track. [Japanese]

karate (kă-**rah**-tee) *noun* a Japanese system of unarmed combat in which the hands and feet are used as weapons. [from Japanese *kara* = empty, + *te* = hand]

karma *noun* **1** (in Buddhism and Hinduism) the sum of a person's actions in one of his or her successive existences, thought to decide his or her fate for the next. **2** (*informal*) the sum of good or bad luck, viewed as resulting from one's actions; destiny. **3** (*informal*) a person's spiritual or emotional state. [Sanskrit, = action, fate]

Karnak a village in Egypt, site of the northern complex of buildings of ancient Thebes.

Karoo (kă-**roo**) *noun* (also **Karroo**) a high plateau in southern Africa, waterless in the dry season. [from Hottentot *karo* = dry]

karri (**ka**-ree) *noun* a tall Western Australian eucalypt with a straight smooth trunk; the hard red wood of this tree. [from Nyungar]

karst *noun* a limestone region with underground streams and many cavities. [from the name of Karst, a limestone region in Yugoslavia]

kart *noun* (also **go-kart**) a kind of miniature racing car with a skeleton body. **karting** *noun* the sport of racing in this.

kasbah (**kaz**-bah) *noun* the citadel of an Arab city in North Africa, or the old crowded part near this. [from Arabic *kasba* = citadel]

Kashmir a former State on the northern border of India, since 1947 disputed between India and Pakistan.

katakana (kah-tă-**kah**-nă) *noun* a set of 46 Japanese characters that convert foreign words into a legible form for the Japanese.

Kata Tjuta (kah-tă-**joo**-tă) a group of giant monoliths of red rock in central Australia, part of the Uluru-Kata Tjuta National Park. Formerly called the *Olgas*.

Kathmandu (kat-man-**doo**) the capital of Nepal.

kauri (**kowr**-ee) *noun* a coniferous tree of New Zealand, yielding **kauri gum**. [Maori]

Kaurna (**gah**-nă) (also **Gaurna**) *noun* **1** a member of an Aboriginal people of south-eastern South Australia, including what is now Adelaide. **2** their language.

kayak (**ky**-ak) *noun* **1** an Inuit canoe with a sealskin covering closed round the waist of the occupant. **2** a small covered canoe resembling this. [Inuit]

Kazakhstan (ka-zăk-**stahn**) a republic of central Asia to the west of China and to the south of Russia. **Kazakh** *adjective* & *noun*

KBE *abbreviation* Knight Commander of the Order of the British Empire.

kc/s *abbreviation* kilocycles per second.

Keats, John (1795–1821), English poet, a principal figure of the Romantic movement.

kebab (kĕ-**bab**) *noun* small pieces of meat, vegetables, etc. cooked on a skewer.

kedgeree (**kej**-ĕ-ree) *noun* a dish of rice, fish, and hard-boiled eggs. [from Hindi *khichri*, a dish of rice, split peas or lentils, and onions]

keel *noun* **1** the timber or steel structure along the base of a ship, on which the ship's framework is built up. **2** a structure resembling this. – **keel** *verb* to become tilted; to overturn, to collapse, *keeled over*. □ **on an even keel** steady.

keelhaul *verb* (*historical*) to drag (a person) through the water under the keel of a ship as a punishment.

Keeling Islands = Cocos Islands.

keen[1] *adjective* **1** sharp, having a sharp edge or point. **2** (of sound or light) acute, penetrating. **3** piercingly cold, *keen wind*. **4** (of prices) low because of competition. **5** intense, *keen interest*. **6** showing or feeling intense interest or desire, *a keen swimmer; is keen to go*. **7** perceiving things very distinctly, *keen sight*. □ **keen on** (*informal*) much attracted to. **keenly** *adverb*, **keenness** *noun*

keen[2] *noun* an Irish funeral song accompanied by wailing. – **keen** *verb* to utter the keen; to utter in a wailing tone.

keep *verb* (**kept**, **keeping**) **1** to remain or cause to remain in a specified state, position, or condition. **2** to prevent or hold back from doing something, to detain, *what kept you?* **3** to put aside for a future time. **4** to pay proper respect to; *keep a promise*, not break it. **5** to celebrate (a feast or ceremony). **6** to guard or protect, to keep safe; *keep goal* or *wicket*, be goalkeeper or wicketkeeper. **7** to continue to have, to have and not give away, *keep the change*. **8** to provide with the necessities of life. **9** to own and look after (animals) for one's use or enjoyment, *keep chickens*. **10** to manage, *keep a shop*. **11** to have (a commodity) regularly in stock or for sale. **12** to make entries in (a diary or accounts etc.); to record in this way. **13** to continue doing something,

to do frequently or repeatedly, *the strap keeps breaking*. **14** to continue in a specified direction, *keep straight on*. **15** (of food) to remain in good condition; *the work* or *news will keep*, can be put aside until later. – **keep** *noun* **1** provision of the necessities of life, the food required for this, *she earns her keep*. **2** the central tower or other strongly fortified structure in a castle. □ **for keeps** (*informal*) permanently. **keep a secret** not tell it to others. **keep down** to keep low in amount or number, *it keeps the weeds down*; to eat and not vomit (food). **keep fit** to be and remain healthy. **keep house** to look after a house or a household. **keep on** to continue doing something; to nag, *she keeps on at me*. **keep one's hair** or **shirt on** (*informal*) to remain calm. **keep one's head above water** to keep out of debt. **keep the peace** to obey the laws and refrain from causing trouble. **keep to oneself** to keep (a thing) secret; to avoid meeting people, *keeps himself to himself*. **keep under** to repress. **keep up** to progress at the same pace as others; to prevent from sinking or getting low; to continue to observe, *keep up old customs*; to continue, *kept up the attack all day*; to maintain in proper condition, *the cost of keeping up a large house*. **keep up with the Joneses** to strive to remain on terms of obvious social equality with one's neighbours.

keeper *noun* **1** a person who keeps or looks after something; the custodian of a museum or forest etc. **2** a wicketkeeper or goalkeeper. **3** a plain ring worn to preserve the hole in a pierced ear; a sleeper.

keeping *noun* **1** custody, charge, *in safe keeping*. **2** harmony, conformity, *a style that is in keeping with his dignity*.

keepsake *noun* a thing that is kept in memory of the giver.

keffiyeh (kef-**ee**-ay) *noun* a kerchief worn as a headdress by Arab men in some countries. [Arabic]

keg *noun* a small barrel; a barrel of beer.

Kelly, Ned (Edward) (1855–80), an Australian bushranger who was outlawed in Victoria in 1878 and sentenced to death in 1880, but became a folk hero.

kelp *noun* a large brown seaweed.

kelpie *noun* an Australian breed of short-haired sheepdog.

Kelvin, William Thomson, 1st Baron (1824–1907), British physicist, noted for his work in thermodynamics and the introduction of an absolute temperature scale.

kelvin *noun* a degree (equivalent to the Celsius degree) of the Kelvin scale of temperature (with zero at absolute zero, −273.15°C). [named after Lord Kelvin]

ken *noun* the range of sight or knowledge, *beyond my ken.* –**ken** *verb* (*Scottish*) to know.

Kennedy, John Fitzgerald (1917–63), 35th President of the USA (1961–3), assassinated at Dallas, Texas.

kennel *noun* a shelter for a dog. –**kennel** *verb* (**kennelled**, **kennelling**) to put into a kennel. **kennels** *plural noun* a boarding or breeding establishment for dogs.

Kentucky a State of the central south-eastern USA.

Kenya (**ken**-yǎ *or* **keen**-yǎ) a republic in east Africa. **Kenyan** *adjective* & *noun*

Kepler, Johannes (1571–1630), German astronomer and mathematician, whose laws recognised the elliptical orbits of the planets round the sun.

kept *see* keep.

keratin (**ke**-rǎ-tǐn) *noun* a strong protein substance forming the basis of horns, claws, nails, feathers, hair, etc. [from Greek *keratos* = of horn]

kerb *noun* a concrete edging to a pavement, street, etc.

kerchief *noun* **1** a square scarf worn on the head. **2** a handkerchief.

kerfuffle *noun* (*informal*) fuss, commotion.

kernel *noun* **1** the softer (usually edible) part inside the shell of a nut or fruit stone. **2** the part of a grain or seed within the husk. **3** the central or important part of a subject, plan, or problem etc.

kerosene (**ke**-rǒ-seen) *noun* a fuel oil distilled from petroleum etc., paraffin oil.

kerygma (kě-**rig**-mǎ) *noun* the Christian gospel as proclaimed in the early Church.

kesh *noun* the uncut hair of Sikhs. [Punjabi]

kestrel *noun* a kind of small falcon.

ketch *noun* a small sailing boat with two masts.

ketchup *noun* a thick sauce made from tomatoes and vinegar etc., used as a seasoning.

ketone (**kee**-tohn) *noun* any of a class of organic compounds including acetone.

kettle *noun* a container with a spout and handle, for boiling water in. □ **a pretty kettle of fish** an awkward state of affairs. **kettle hole** a deep bowl-shaped depression in the ground formed where a large detached piece of glacier ice had become embedded in the boulder clay and then melted.

kettledrum *noun* a percussion instrument consisting of a large hemispherical bowl over which a piece of skin, parchment, or plastic is stretched.

key¹ *noun* **1** a small piece of metal shaped so that it will move the bolt of a lock and so lock or unlock something. **2** a similar instrument for grasping and turning something, e.g. for winding a clock or tightening a spring etc. **3** each of a set of levers or buttons to be pressed by the fingers in playing a musical instrument or operating a computer terminal, typewriter, etc. **4** something that provides access or control or insight, *the key to the mystery*; *a key industry*, one that is important to other industries and to a country's economy. **5** a set of answers to problems; a word or set of symbols for interpreting a code etc., or for extracting items of data from a computer. **6** a system of related notes in music, based on a particular note, *the key of C major*. **7** the general tone or degree of intensity of something; *all in the same key*, monotonous in character. **8** roughness of surface helping plaster or paint to adhere to it. **9** a piece of wood or metal etc. inserted between others to hold them secure. **10** a device for making or breaking an electric circuit, e.g. in telegraphy or to operate the ignition in a motor vehicle. **11** the winged fruit of certain trees, e.g. sycamore. –**key** *verb* (**keyed**, **keying**) **1** to roughen (a surface) so that plaster or paint will adhere well. **2** to link closely with something else, *the factory is keyed to the export trade*. **3** to enter (data) into a computer system etc. by using a keyboard, *key it in*. □ **keyed up** stimulated, nervously tense. **key signature** the sharps or flats after the clef in a musical score, showing its key.

key² *noun* a reef, a low island, *Florida Keys*.

keyboard *noun* **1** the set of keys on a piano, computer, typewriter, etc. **2** an electronic musical instrument with keys arranged as on a piano. –**keyboard** *verb* to key (data) into a computer system etc.

keyhole *noun* the hole by which a key is put into a lock. □ **keyhole surgery** surgery carried out through a very small incision.

Keynes (*pr.* kaynz), John Maynard, 1st Baron (1883–1946), English economist, advocate of the planned economy with positive intervention by the State. **Keynesian** *adjective*

keynote *noun* **1** the note on which a key in music is based. **2** the prevailing tone or idea of a speech, conference, etc.

keypad *noun* a small keyboard or set of buttons for operating a telephone, electronic device, etc.

keyring *noun* a ring on which keys are threaded.

keystone *noun* **1** the central wedge-shaped stone at the summit of an arch, locking the others in position. **2** the central principle of a system, policy, etc.

keyword *noun* **1** the key to a code etc. **2** a significant word, especially used in indexing and information retrieval.

kg *abbreviation* kilogram(s).

KGB *abbreviation* the secret police of the former USSR.

khaki (**kah**-kee) *adjective* & *noun* dull brownish-yellow, the colour used for military uniforms. [from Urdu, = dust-coloured]

Khalsa *noun* the body of fully initiated Sikhs formed in 1699 by the tenth and last Guru (Gobind Singh), the brotherhood of the pure. [from Persian *khalisa* = pure]

khan (*pr.* kahn) *noun* the title of rulers and officials in Central Asia.

Khartoum (kar-**toom**) the capital of Sudan.

Khedive (kĕ-**deev**) *noun* the title of the viceroy of Egypt under Turkish rule.

Khmer (*pr.* kmair) *noun* **1** a native or inhabitant of the ancient kingdom of Khmer in SE Asia or of the Khmer Republic (the official name in 1970–5 of what is now Cambodia). **2** their language, the official language of Cambodia. □ **Khmer Rouge** (*pr.* roo*zh*) the Communist guerrilla organisation in the wars there in the 1960s and 1970s, holding power 1975–9.

Khufu (**koo**-foo) (also known as **Cheops**) (c. 2551–2528 BC), an ancient Egyptian pharaoh, who commissioned the building of the great pyramid at Giza.

Khyber Pass (**ky**-ber) the major mountain pass on the border between northern Pakistan and Afghanistan.

kHz *abbreviation* kilohertz.

kibble *verb* to grind coarsely.

kibbutz (kib-**uuts**) *noun* (*plural* **kibbutzim**, *pr.* kib-uuts-**eem**) a communal settlement in Israel. [from Hebrew *kibbus* = a gathering]

kibbutznik (kib-**uuts**-nik) *noun* a member of a kibbutz.

kiblah *noun* the direction of the Kaaba in Mecca, towards which Muslims turn in prayer. [Arabic]

kick *verb* **1** to strike, thrust, or propel with the foot. **2** (in football) to score by kicking the ball into goal. **3** (of a gun) to recoil when fired. –**kick** *noun* **1** an act of kicking; a blow from being kicked. **2** (*informal*) a thrill, a pleasurable effect, *get a kick out of it*; *did it for kicks*. **3** (*informal*) an interest or activity, *the health food kick*. **4** the recoil of a gun when it is fired. □ **alive and kicking** (*informal*) fully active. **kick about** or **around** to treat roughly or inconsiderately; to go idly from place to place; to be unused or unwanted. **kick off** to start a football game by kicking the ball; (*informal*) to begin proceedings. **kick-off** *noun* kicking off in football. **kick one's heels** to be kept waiting. **kick out** (*informal*) to drive out forcibly; to dismiss. **kick over the traces** *see* **trace²**. **kick the bucket** (*informal*) to die. **kick the habit** (*informal*) to give it up. **kick up** (*informal*) to create (a fuss or noise). **kicker** *noun*

kickback *noun* **1** a recoil. **2** (*informal*) payment for help in making a profit etc.

kick-start *verb* **1** to start (the engine of a motorcycle etc.) by pushing down a lever with one's foot. **2** to start or restart (a process etc.) by providing some initial impetus. **kick-starter** *noun*

kid *noun* **1** a young goat. **2** leather made from its skin. **3** (*informal*) a child. –**kid** *verb* (**kidded**, **kidding**) **1** to give birth to a young goat. **2** (*informal*) to deceive (especially for fun), to tease. □ **handle** or **treat with kid gloves** to treat tactfully.

kidnap *verb* (**kidnapped**, **kidnapping**) to carry off (a person) by force or fraud in order to obtain a ransom. **kidnapper** *noun*

kidney *noun* (*plural* **kidneys**) **1** either of a pair of glandular organs that remove waste products from the blood and secrete urine. **2** this as food. □ **kidney bean** a red-skinned kidney-shaped bean. **kidney dish** a kidney-shaped dish, oval and indented at one side. **kidney machine** an apparatus that performs the functions of a kidney.

Kiel Canal (*pr.* keel) a canal connecting the North Sea with the Baltic.

Kierkegaard (**keer**-kĕ-gard), Søren (1813–55), Danish philosopher and theologian.

Kiev (**kee**-eff) the capital of the Ukraine.

Kigali (ki-**gah**-lee) the capital of Rwanda.

kikuyu (ky-**koo**-yoo) *noun* a perennial grass, used for lawns.

Kilimanjaro (kil-ĭ-măn-**jah**-roh) an extinct volcano in Tanzania, with twin peaks, one of which is the highest mountain in Africa (5895m).

kill *verb* **1** to cause the death of (a person or animal); to destroy the vitality of (a plant etc.). **2** to put an end to (a feeling etc.). **3** to switch off (a light, engine, etc.). **4** to make (a colour, flavour, sound, etc.) ineffective. **5** to spend (time) unprofitably while waiting for something. **6** (*informal*) to cause severe pain to, *my feet are killing me*. **7** (*informal*) to overwhelm with amusement etc. –**kill** *noun* **1** the act of killing. **2** the animal(s) killed by a hunter. □ **kill off** to get rid of by killing. **kill two birds with one stone** to achieve two purposes with one action.

killer *noun* **1** a person, animal, or thing that kills. **2** (*informal*) an impressive or formidable thing; a hilarious joke. □ **killer whale** a black and white whale with a prominent dorsal fin.

killick *noun* a heavy stone used by small boats as an anchor; a small anchor.

killjoy *noun* a person who spoils the enjoyment of others.

kiln *noun* an oven for hardening or drying things such as pottery, bricks, or hops, or for burning lime. [from Latin *culina* = kitchen]

kilo (**kee**-loh) *noun* (*plural* **kilos**) a kilogram.

kilo- (kil-ŏ) *prefix* one thousand. [from Greek *khilioi* = thousand]

kilobyte *noun* (in computing) 1024 bytes as a measure of memory size etc.

kilocycle *noun* a kilohertz.

kilogram *noun* the basic unit of mass in the International System of Units (2.205 lb). □ **kilogram force** (*plural* **kilograms force**) a unit of force, that force which acting on a mass of 1 kilogram gives it an acceleration equal to that resulting from gravity at the earth's surface.

kilohertz *noun* a unit of frequency of electromagnetic waves, = 1000 cycles per second.

kilojoule *noun* 1000 joules, especially used in measuring the energy value of foods.

kilolitre *noun* 1000 litres (220 imperial gallons).

kilometre (**kil**-ŏ-mee-ter *or* kĭ-**lom**-ĕ-ter) *noun* a distance of 1000 metres (0.62 miles).

kiloton (**kil**-ŏ-tun) *noun* (also **kilotonne**) a unit of explosive force equal to 1000 tons (or tonnes) of TNT.

kilovolt *noun* 1000 volts.

kilowatt *noun* the power of 1000 watts. □ **kilowatt-hour** *noun* an amount of energy equal to one kilowatt operating for one hour.

kilt *noun* a knee-length pleated skirtlike garment of tartan wool, worn as part of a Scottish Highland man's dress or by women and children. –**kilt** *verb* **1** to tuck up (skirts) round the body. **2** to arrange in vertical pleats.

kilter *noun* good working order, *out of kilter*.

Kimberley, **the** the NW corner of Australia bounded in the south by the Fitzroy River and in the east by the Ord River.

kimono (kim-**oh**-noh) *noun* (*plural* **kimonos**) **1** a long loose Japanese robe with wide sleeves, worn with a sash. **2** a dressing gown resembling this.

kin *noun* a person's relative(s).

kina (**kee**-nă) *noun* the unit of money in Papua New Guinea.

kind[1] *noun* a class of similar things or animals, a type. □ **a kind of** something that belongs (approximately) to the class named. **in kind** (of payment) in goods or natural produce, not in money; *repaid his insolence in kind*, by being insulting in return. **kind of** (*informal*) slightly, *I felt kind of sorry for him*. **of a kind** similar.

Usage Correct usage is *this kind of thing* or *these kinds of things*, not 'these kind of things'.

kind[2] *adjective* gentle and considerate in one's manner or conduct towards others. **kind-hearted** *adjective*, **kindness** *noun*

kindergarten *noun* a school or class for young children at the beginning of their education. [from German *kinder* = children, + *garten* = garden]

kindle *verb* **1** to set on fire; to cause (a fire) to begin burning. **2** to arouse or stimulate, *kindled our hopes*. **3** to become kindled.

kindling *noun* small pieces of wood for lighting fires.

kindly *adjective* (kindlier, kindliest) kind in character, manner, or appearance. –kindly *adverb* **1** in a kind way. **2** please, *kindly shut the door*. □ **not take kindly to** to be displeased by. kindliness *noun*

kindred (**kin**-drĕd) *noun* a person's relative(s). –kindred *adjective* **1** related. **2** of a similar kind, *chemistry and kindred subjects*. □ **a kindred spirit** a person whose tastes are similar to one's own.

kine *plural noun* (*old use*) cows, cattle.

kinematic (kin-ĕ-**mat**-ik) *adjective* of motion considered abstractly without reference to force or mass. kinematics *noun* the science of pure motion.

kinesis (kĭ-**nee**-sĭs *or* ky-) *noun* movement of an organism in no particular direction in response to an external stimulus such as light (contrasted with *taxis*, directed movement in response to a stimulus).

kinetic (kĭ-**net**-ik *or* ky-) *adjective* of or produced by movement; characterised by movement. kinetics *noun* **1** the science of the relations between the motions of objects and the forces acting upon them. **2** the study of the mechanisms and rates of chemical reactions or other processes. □ **kinetic art** art that depends for its effect on the movement of some of its parts, e.g. in air currents. kinetic energy *see* energy. kinetic poetry poetry that depends for its effect on the layout of the words on the page. [from Greek *kinetikos* = moving]

King, Martin Luther (1929–68), Black Baptist minister and American civil rights leader.

king *noun* **1** a man who is the supreme ruler of an independent country by right of succession to the throne. **2** a person or thing regarded as supreme in some way; *king of beasts*, the lion. **3** a large species of animal, *king penguin*. **4** the piece in chess that has to be protected from checkmate. **5** a piece in draughts that has been crowned on reaching the opponent's end of the board. **6** a playing card bearing a picture of a king and ranking next above queen. Kings either of two books of the Old Testament recording Jewish history of the 10th–6th centuries BC. □ **king-size** or **king-sized** *adjectives* extra large. kingly *adjective*

kingdom *noun* **1** a country ruled by a king or queen. **2** the spiritual reign of God; *thy Kingdom come*, may the rule of God be established. **3** a division of the natural world, *the animal* or *vegetable kingdom*. □ **kingdom come** the next world; *till kingdom come*, for an unending period.

kingfish *noun* any of various large edible fish including the trevally, yellowtail, and mulloway.

kingfisher *noun* a small bird with bright bluish plumage that dives to catch fish.

king-hit *noun* (*Austral. informal*) a knock-out blow.

King Island an island in Bass Strait to the NW of Tasmania.

kingpin *noun* **1** a vertical bolt used as a pivot. **2** an indispensable person or thing.

kingship *noun* being a king; a king's position or reign.

Kingston the capital of Jamaica.

Kingstown the capital of St Vincent.

kink *noun* **1** a short twist in a wire, rope, or hair etc. **2** a mental or moral peculiarity. –kink *verb* to form or cause to form kinks.

kinky *adjective* (kinkier, kinkiest) **1** full of kinks. **2** (*informal*) bizarre, eccentric.

kinsfolk *plural noun* a person's relatives. kinsman, kinswoman *nouns*

Kinshasa (kin-**shah**-să) the capital of the Democratic Republic of Congo.

kinship *noun* the relationship of kin.

kiosk (**kee**-osk) *noun* **1** a small light open structure where newspapers or refreshments are sold. **2** (*Austral.*) a building in which refreshments are served in a park, zoo, etc. [from Persian, = pavilion]

kip *noun* (*informal*) **1** a place to sleep. **2** a sleep. –kip *verb* (kipped, kipping) (*informal*) to sleep.

kipper *noun* a kippered herring. –kipper *verb* to cure (fish) by splitting, cleaning, and drying it in the open air or in smoke.

kipsy *noun* (also kipsie) (*Austral. informal*) a house, home, lean-to, or shelter.

Kirghizia *see* Kyrgyzstan.

Kiribati (ki-rĭ-**bas**) a republic consisting of a group of islands in the Pacific north-east of Australia. –Kiribati *adjective* of Kiribati or its inhabitants.

kirk *noun* (*Scottish*) a church.

kirpan *noun* a Sikh sword. [Punjabi]

kirtle *noun* (*old use*) **1** a woman's gown or outer petticoat. **2** a man's tunic or coat.

Kirundi (ki-**ruun**-dee) *noun* a Bantu language, the official language of Burundi.

Kishinev (ki-shi-**nyof**) (also Chisinau) the capital of Moldova.

kismet (**kiz**-met) *noun* destiny, fate. [Turkish]

kiss *noun* a touch or caress given with the lips. –**kiss** *verb* **1** to touch with the lips in affection or as a greeting or in reverence. **2** to greet each other in this way. **3** to touch gently. □ **kiss of death** an apparently friendly act causing ruin. **kiss of life** mouth-to-mouth resuscitation.

Kiswahili (kis-wah-**hee**-lee) *noun* the Swahili language.

kit *noun* **1** the clothing and personal equipment of a soldier etc. or a traveller. **2** the equipment needed for a particular activity or situation, *a first-aid kit*. **3** a set of parts sold together to be assembled, *in kit form*. –**kit** *verb* (**kitted**, **kitting**) to equip with kit, *kit a person out* or *up*.

kitbag *noun* a bag for holding a soldier's or traveller's kit.

kitchen *noun* a room in which meals are prepared. □ **kitchen-sink school** a school of artists or dramatists whose subjects were domestic scenes, often drab or sordid. **kitchen tea** (*Austral.*) a party, given for a bride-to-be, to which guests bring gifts of kitchen articles.

kitchenette *noun* a small room or an alcove used as a kitchen.

kite *noun* **1** a large bird of prey of the hawk family. **2** a toy consisting of a light framework to be flown in a strong wind on the end of a long string. □ **fly a kite** to make an experiment in order to gauge people's opinion.

kith *noun* **kith and kin** kinsfolk; friends and relations.

kitsch (*pr.* kich) *noun* pretentiousness and lack of good taste in art; art of this type. –**kitsch** *adjective* tasteless, garish, or sentimental. [German]

kitten *noun* the young of a cat or of a hare or rabbit or ferret. –**kitten** *verb* to give birth to kittens. □ **have kittens** (*informal*) to be very agitated or nervous. **kittenish** *adjective*

kitty *noun* **1** the pool of stakes to be played for in some card games. **2** a fund of money for communal use.

kiwi (**kee**-wee) *noun* a New Zealand bird that does not fly, with a long bill, rudimentary wings, and no tail. –**Kiwi** *noun* (*plural* **Kiwis**) (*informal*) a New Zealander. □ **kiwi fruit** a green-fleshed small oval fruit with brown hairy skin, also called *Chinese gooseberry*.

kJ *abbreviation* kilojoule(s).

kl *abbreviation* kilolitre(s).

Klee, Paul (1879–1940), Swiss painter, a modernist with a highly individual style.

kleptomania (klep-tŏ-**may**-nee-ă) *noun* an uncontrollable tendency to steal things, with no desire to use or profit by them. **kleptomaniac** *noun* a person with this tendency. [from Greek *kleptes* = thief, + *mania*]

Klondike a river and district in Yukon, Canada, where gold was discovered in 1896.

km *abbreviation* kilometre(s); *km/h*, kilometres per hour.

knack *noun* **1** the ability to do something skilfully. **2** a habit, *it has a knack of going wrong*.

knacker *noun* a person who buys and slaughters useless horses, selling the meat and hides.

knackered *adjective* (*informal*) exhausted, worn out; not working.

knapsack *noun* a bag worn strapped on the back for carrying necessaries, used by soldiers on a march or by hikers.

knapweed *noun* a common weed like a thistle but without prickles.

knave *noun* **1** (*old use*) a rogue. **2** the jack in playing cards. **knavish** *adjective*, **knavery** *noun*

knead *verb* **1** to work (moist flour or clay) into dough by pressing and stretching it with the hands. **2** to make (bread etc.) in this way. **3** to massage with kneading movements.

knee *noun* **1** the joint between the thigh and the lower part of the human leg; the corresponding joint in animals; *fall on* or *to one's knees*, to kneel. **2** the part of a garment covering this. **3** the upper surface of the thigh of a sitting person, *sit on my knee*. **4** something shaped like a bent knee. –**knee** *verb* **1** to touch or strike with the knee. **2** to cause trousers etc. to bulge at the knee; (of trousers etc.) to bulge at the knee. □ **knee breeches** breeches reaching to or just below the knee. **knee-deep** *adjective* of or in sufficient depth to cover a person up to the knees; *knee-deep in work*, deeply occupied. **knee-jerk** *noun* an involuntary jerk of the leg when a tendon below the knee is struck; *knee-jerk reaction*, an automatic reaction.

kneecap *noun* **1** the small bone covering the front of the knee joint. **2** a protective covering for the knee.

kneecapping *noun* shooting in the legs to lame a person as a punishment.

kneel *verb* (**knelt, kneeling**) to take or be in a position where the body is supported on the knees with the lower leg bent back, especially in prayer or reverence.

kneeler *noun* a hassock or cushion for kneeling on, especially in church.

knell *noun* the sound of a bell tolled solemnly after a death or at a funeral.

knelt *see* kneel.

Knesset (**knes**-ĕt) *noun* the parliament of the State of Israel.

knew *see* know.

Kngwarreye (nǎ-**wah**-ray), Emily Kame (c. 1910–96), Australian Aboriginal artist.

knickerbockers *plural noun* loose-fitting breeches gathered in at the knee.

knickers *plural noun* a woman's or girl's undergarment covering the lower part of the body and having separate legs or leg-holes.

knick-knack *noun* a small ornamental article.

knife *noun* (*plural* **knives**) **1** a cutting instrument or weapon consisting of a sharp blade with a handle. **2** the cutting blade of a machine. **–knife** *verb* to cut or stab with a knife. □ **have got one's knife into a person** to be persistently malicious or vindictive towards him or her. **knife-pleats** *plural noun* narrow flat pleats. **on a knife-edge** in a situation involving extreme tension or anxiety about the outcome. **war to the knife** relentless enmity.

knight *noun* **1** a man awarded a non-hereditary title (*Sir*) by a sovereign. **2** (*old use*) a man raised to an honourable military rank by a king etc. **3** a chess piece, usually with the form of a horse's head. **–knight** *verb* to confer a knighthood on. □ **knight of the road** (*old use*) a bushranger; a swagman. **Knights Hospitallers** a military religious order founded in the 11th century. **Knights Templars** a military order founded in 1118 to protect pilgrims from bandits in the Holy Land. **knightly** *adverb*

knighthood *noun* the rank of knight.

knit *verb* (**knitted** *or* **knit, knitting**) **1** to make (a garment or fabric etc.) from yarn formed into interlocking loops either by long needles held in the hands or on a machine. **2** to form (yarn) into fabric etc. in this way. **3** to make a plain (not purl) stitch in knitting. **4** to unite or grow together, *the broken bones had knit well*; *a well-knit frame*, compact bodily structure.

–knit *noun* a garment or fabric made by knitting. □ **knit one's brow** to frown. **knitter** *noun*

knitting *noun* work in the process of being knitted. □ **knitting needle** each of the long needles used for knitting by hand.

knitwear *noun* knitted garments.

knob *noun* **1** a rounded projecting part, especially one forming the handle of a door or drawer, or a control on a machine etc. **2** a small lump of butter, coal, etc. □ **with knobs on** (*informal*) that and more. **knobby** *adjective*

knobbly *adjective* with many small projecting lumps.

knock *verb* **1** to strike with an audible sharp blow. **2** to make a noise by striking something, e.g. at a door to summon a person or gain admittance. **3** (of an engine) to make a thumping or rattling noise while running, to pink. **4** to drive or make by knocking, *knock a nail in*; *knocked a hole in it*. **5** (*informal*) to say critical or insulting things about. **–knock** *noun* **1** an act or sound of knocking. **2** a sharp blow. **3** (in an engine) knocking, pinking. □ **knock about** to treat roughly; to wander casually. **knock back** (*informal*) to swallow (food or drink); (*Austral. informal*) to refuse, to rebuff. **knock-back** *noun* (*Austral. informal*) a refusal, a rebuff. **knock down** to dispose of (an article) at auction. **knock-down** *adjective* (of prices) very low. **knock-kneed** *adjective* having **knock knees**, an abnormal inward curving of the legs at the knees. **knock off** (*informal*) to cease work; to complete (work) quickly; to deduct (an amount) from a price; (*informal*) to steal; (*informal*) to kill. **knock-on effect** an alteration that causes similar alterations elsewhere. **knock out** to make unconscious by hitting on the head; to disable (a boxer) in this way so that he is unable to rise or continue in a specified time; to defeat in a knockout competition; to exhaust or disable. **knock spots off** (*informal*) to be easily superior to. **knock up** to rouse by knocking at the door; to make or arrange hastily; to score (runs) at cricket; to make exhausted or ill. **knock-up** *noun* a practice or casual game at tennis etc.

knockabout *adjective* rough, boisterous. **–knockabout** *noun* (*Austral.*) a handyman on a farm or station.

knocker *noun* **1** a person who knocks. **2** a hinged metal flap for rapping against a door to summon a person. □ **on the knocker** (*Austral. informal*) promptly.

knockout *adjective* **1** that knocks a boxer etc. out; *knockout drops*, liquid added to a drink to cause unconsciousness when swallowed. **2** (of a competition) in which the loser of each successive round is eliminated. **–knockout** *noun* **1** a blow that knocks a boxer out. **2** a knockout competition. **3** (*informal*) an outstanding or irresistible person or thing.

knoll (*pr.* nohl *or* nol) *noun* a hillock, a mound.

Knossos (**knos**-ŏs) the principal city of Crete in Minoan times, containing the remains of the Palace of Minos.

knot *noun* **1** an intertwining of one or more pieces of thread or rope etc. to fasten them together; *a knot of ribbon*, a piece tied and used as an ornament. **2** a tangle. **3** a hard mass in something, especially on a tree trunk where a branch joins it. **4** a round cross-grained spot in timber where a branch joined; *knot-hole*, a hole formed where this has fallen out. **5** a cluster of people or things. **6** a unit of speed used by ships at sea and by aircraft, = one nautical mile per hour (1.85 km/h). **–knot** *verb* (**knotted, knotting**) **1** to tie or fasten with a knot. **2** to entangle. □ **at a rate of knots** (*informal*) very rapidly. **tie in knots** (*informal*) to make (a person) baffled or confused.

knotgrass *noun* a common weed with nodes in its stems and small pale pink flowers.

knotty *adjective* **1** full of knots. **2** puzzling, full of problems or difficulties.

know *verb* (**knew, known, knowing**) **1** to have in one's mind or memory as a result of experience, learning, or information. **2** to feel certain, *I know I left it here!* **3** to recognise (a person); to have had social contact with; to be familiar with (a place). **4** to recognise with certainty, *knows a bargain when she sees one*. **5** to understand and be able to use (a subject, language, or skill), *she knows how to please people*; *knows better than to do that*, is too wise or well-mannered to do it. □ **in the know** (*informal*) having inside information. **know-all** *noun* a person who behaves as if he or she knows everything. **know-how** *noun* practical knowledge or skill in a particular activity. **knowable** *adjective*

knowing *adjective* showing knowledge or awareness, showing that one has inside information. **knowingly** *adverb*

knowledge *noun* **1** knowing. **2** all that a person knows. **3** all that is known, an organised body of information.

knowledgeable *adjective* well-informed.

known *see* **know**.

Knox (*pr.* noks), John (c. 1505–72), Scottish Protestant reformer.

knuckle *noun* **1** a finger-joint. **2** the knee-joint of an animal, or the part joining the leg to the foot, especially as a joint of meat. **–knuckle** *verb* to strike or press or rub with the knuckles. □ **knuckle down** to begin to work earnestly. **knuckle under** to yield, to submit.

knuckleduster *noun* a metal device worn over the knuckles to protect them and increase the injury done by a blow.

knurl (*pr.* nerl) *noun* a small projecting ridge etc. **knurled** *adjective* having raised ridges or small knobs round the rim to provide grip.

KO *abbreviation* knockout. **KO'd** knocked out.

koala (koh-**ah**-lă) *noun* an Australian tree-dwelling marsupial with thick grey fur and large ears, feeding on the leaves of certain eucalypts. [from Dharuk *gula*]

Koch (*pr.* kok), Robert (1843–1910), German bacteriologist who identified the organisms causing anthrax, tuberculosis, and cholera.

kohl *noun* a black powder used as eye make-up. [from Arabic *kuhl*]

kohlrabi (kohl-**rah**-bee) *noun* a cabbage with an edible turnip-shaped stem. [German]

koine (**koy**-nee) *noun* a common language shared by various peoples, a lingua franca. [Greek, = common]

Kokoda Track (popularly known as the **Kokoda Trail**) a 240 km track between Port Moresby and Kokoda village, where in 1942 Australian and Papuan soldiers successfully resisted the southward advance of the Japanese army.

kookaburra *noun* an Australian kingfisher with a cry resembling laughter. Formerly called the *laughing jackass*. [Wiradjuri *gugubarra*]

Koori (**koor**-ree) *noun* an Aboriginal person from SE Australia. [Awabakal *gurri*]

Usage see **aborigine**.

koppie *noun* (also **kopje**) (in South Africa) a small hill. [Afrikaans]

koradji (kŏ-**raj**-ee) *noun* an Aborigine with recognised skills in traditional medicine. [Dharuk *garraaji* = doctor]

Koran (kor-**rahn**) *noun* (also Qur'an) the Islamic sacred book, believed to be the word of God as dictated to Muhammad, written in Arabic. [from Arabic *kur'an* = reading]

Korea (kŏ-**ree**-ă) a peninsula of eastern Asia between the Sea of Japan and the Yellow Sea, formerly one country, now divided between the Republic of Korea (= South Korea) and the Democratic People's Republic of Korea (= North Korea).

Korean *adjective* of Korea or its people or language. –**Korean** *noun* 1 a person from North or South Korea. 2 the language of Korea. □ Korean War a war between North and South Korea from 1950–3, the South Koreans being supported by United Nations forces.

Kosciuszko (koz-ee-**os**-koh) Australia's highest mountain (2228 m), situated in the Snowy Mountains, NSW. [named by the explorer P. E. Strzelecki in 1840 after the Polish patriot Thaddeus Kosciuszko (1746–1817)]

kosher (**koh**-sher) *adjective* 1 (of food etc.) conforming to the requirements of Jewish dietary laws. 2 (*informal*) genuine, correct, legitimate. –**kosher** *noun* 1 kosher food. 2 a shop selling this. [from Hebrew *kasher* = proper]

kowhai (**koh**-I) *noun* a New Zealand tree or shrub with golden flowers. [Maori]

kowtow *verb* to behave with exaggerated respect towards a person. [the *kowtow* (Chinese *ketou*) was a former Chinese custom of touching the ground with one's forehead as a sign of worship or submission]

kraal (*pr.* krahl) *noun* (in South Africa) 1 a village of huts enclosed by a fence. 2 an enclosure for cattle or sheep. [Afrikaans]

Krakatoa (krak-ă-**toh**-ă) a small volcanic island between Java and Sumatra, scene of a great eruption in 1883.

kremlin *noun* a citadel within a Russian town. □ the Kremlin that of Moscow; the Russian government. [from Russian *kreml'*]

krill *noun* the mass of tiny crustaceans that forms the principal food of certain whales. [from Norwegian, = tiny fish]

kris (*pr.* krees) *noun* a Malay dagger with a wavy blade.

Krishna (in Hinduism) one of the most popular gods, the eighth and most important avatar of Vishnu.

krona *noun* the unit of money in Sweden (*plural* kronor) and Iceland (*plural* kronur).

krone *noun* (*plural* kroner) the unit of money in Denmark and Norway.

krypton (**krip**-ton) *noun* a chemical element (symbol Kr), a colourless odourless gas used in various types of lamps and bulbs.

Kshatriya (**kshah**-tree-ă) *noun* a member of the second of the four great Hindu classes, the warrior or baronial class. [from Sanskrit *kshatra* = rule]

Kuala Lumpur (kwah-lă **luum**-poor) the capital of Malaysia.

Kublai Khan (koo-blă **kahn**) (1216–94), Mongol emperor of China from 1259, grandson of Genghis Khan.

kudos (**kew**-doss) *noun* (*informal*) honour and glory. [from Greek]

kudu (**koo**-doo) *noun* a large African antelope with white stripes and spiral horns.

Kufic (**kew**-fik) *noun* an early form of the Arabic alphabet, found especially in inscriptions. [from the name of Cufa, a city in Iraq]

Ku Klux Klan an American secret society hostile to Blacks, originally formed in the southern States after the Civil War.

kumkum (**kuum**-kuum) *noun* 1 a red powder used by Hindu women to make a small spot on the forehead. 2 this spot. [Hindi]

kumquat *noun* = cumquat.

kung fu (kuung **foo**) *noun* a Chinese form of unarmed combat, similar to karate. [from Chinese *gong* = merit, + *fu* = master]

Kuomintang (**kwoh**-min-tang) *noun* a nationalist party founded in China in 1912, eventually defeated by the Communist Party in 1949 and subsequently forming the central administration of Taiwan.

Kurd *noun* a member of a pastoral people living in Kurdistan. Kurdish *adjective* & *noun*

Kurdistan a mountainous region including parts of Turkey, Iraq, Iran, Syria, Armenia, and Azerbaijan, inhabited by the Kurds.

kurrajong (**ku**-ră-jong) *noun* an Australian evergreen tree with cream bell-flowers that are reddish brown inside. [from Dharuk *garrajung* = fishing line (made from the fibre of this tree)]

Kuurn Kopan Noot (**kuurn** kuup-
ahn **nuut**) *noun* **1** a member of an
Aboriginal people of SW Victoria. **2** their
language.

Kuwait (koo-**wayt**) **1** a monarchy bordering
on the Persian Gulf. **2** its capital city. **Kuwaiti**
adjective & *noun*

kV *abbreviation* kilovolt(s).

kW *abbreviation* kilowatt(s).

kwashiorkor (kwo-shee-**or**-kor) *noun* a
tropical disease especially of children, caused
by protein deficiency. [the name given to the
disease in Ghana]

kWh *abbreviation* kilowatt-hour(s).

kylie *noun* (*Austral.*) a boomerang. [Nyungar
garli]

Kyrgyzstan (keer-gĭ-**stahn**) (also **Kirghizia**)
a republic to the west of China and to the
south of Kazakhstan. **Kyrgyz** *adjective* & *noun*

Ll

L *abbreviation* learner driver.

l *abbreviation* litre(s).

laager (**lah**-ger) *noun* (in southern Africa) an encampment formed by tying wagons together in a circle. [Afrikaans]

lab *noun* (*informal*) a laboratory.

label *noun* **1** a slip of paper, cloth, or metal etc. fixed on or beside an object and showing its nature, owner, name, destination, or other information about it. **2** a descriptive word or phrase classifying people etc. –**label** *verb* (**labelled**, **labelling**) **1** to attach a label to. **2** to describe or classify, *he was labelled as a troublemaker*.

labia (**lay**-bee-ă) *plural noun* the lips of the female genitals; *labia majora*, the fleshy outer folds; *labia minora*, the inner folds.

labial (**lay**-bee-ăl) *adjective* of the lips. [from Latin *labia* = lips]

labiate (**lay**-bee-ăt) *adjective* of the family of plants that have flowers with the corolla or the calyx divided into two parts resembling lips. –**labiate** *noun* a labiate plant.

Labor *noun* (in full **Australian Labor Party**) a political party originally formed to represent the interests of working people.

laboratory (lă-**bo**-ră-tŏ-ree) *noun* a room or building equipped for scientific experiments or research etc. [same origin as *labour*]

laborious *adjective* **1** needing much effort or perseverance. **2** showing signs of great effort, not spontaneous. **3** hard-working. **laboriously** *adverb*

labour *noun* **1** physical or mental work, exertion. **2** a task; *a labour of Hercules*, a herculean task. **3** the pains or contractions of the womb at childbirth. **4** workers, working people distinguished from management or considered as a political force. –**labour** *verb* **1** to exert oneself, to work hard. **2** to have to make a great effort, to operate or progress only with difficulty, *the engine was labouring*. **3** to treat at great length or in excessive detail, *I will not labour the point*. □ **labour camp** a penal settlement with forced labour by prisoners. **Labour Day** a day celebrated in honour of workers, in many countries 1 May; (in Australia) a public holiday (varying in date from state to state) celebrating the introduction of the eight-hour working day. **labour-intensive** *adjective* (of an industry) needing to employ many people. **Labour Party** a political party in the UK and some other countries, representing the interests of workers (*see also* **Labor**). **labour-saving** *adjective* designed to reduce the amount of work or effort needed. [from Latin *labor* = toil]

laboured *adjective* showing signs of great effort, not spontaneous.

labourer *noun* a person employed to do unskilled manual work or to assist a skilled worker.

Labrador (**lab**-ră-dor) an area in NE Canada, united with Newfoundland to form a province. –**labrador** *noun* a retriever dog of a breed with a smooth black or golden coat.

labrum (**lay**-brŭm) *noun* (*plural* **labra**) **1** the upper part of the mouth of an insect, crustacean, etc. **2** the outer edge of various kinds of shell. [Latin, = lip]

laburnum *noun* an ornamental tree with hanging clusters of yellow flowers.

labyrinth (**lab**-ĭ-rinth) *noun* **1** a complicated network of paths through which it is difficult to find one's way. **2** the complex cavity of the inner ear. **labyrinthine** *adjective*

lace *noun* **1** fabric or trimming made in an ornamental openwork design. **2** a cord or narrow leather strip threaded through holes or hooks for pulling opposite edges together and securing them. –**lace** *verb* **1** to fasten with a lace or laces. **2** to pass (a cord) through; to interwine. **3** to flavour or fortify (a drink) with a dash of spirits.

lacerate (**las**-ĕ-rayt) *verb* **1** to injure (flesh) by tearing. **2** to wound (feelings). **laceration** *noun*

Lachlan a river in NSW, a tributary of the Murrumbidgee. [named after Lachlan Macquarie (1762–1824)]

lachrymal (**lak**-rĭ-măl) *adjective* of tears, secreting tears, *lachrymal ducts*. [from Latin *lacrima* = a tear]

lachrymose (**lak**-rĭ-mohs) *adjective* tearful.

lack *noun* the state or fact of not having something. –lack *verb* to be without or not have (a thing) when it is needed; *they lack for nothing*, have plenty of everything.

lackadaisical (lak-ă-**day**-zikăl) *adjective* lacking vigour or determination.

lackey *noun* (*plural* lackeys) 1 a footman, a servant. 2 a person's servile follower.

lacklustre *adjective* 1 lacking in vitality, force, or conviction. 2 (of the eye etc.) not bright.

laconic (lă-**kon**-ik) *adjective* using few words, terse. laconically *adverb*

lacquer (**lak**-er) *noun* a hard glossy varnish. –lacquer *verb* to coat with lacquer.

lacrosse (lă-**kross**) *noun* a game played between two teams on a field with a goal at each end, with players using a netted crook (a crosse) to catch, carry, or throw the ball. [from French *la crosse* = the crook]

lactate (lak-**tayt**) *verb* to secrete milk in the breasts or udder. lactation *noun*

lacteal *adjective* of milk.

lactic *adjective* of milk. □ lactic acid the acid found in sour milk. [from Latin *lactis* = of milk]

lactose *noun* a sugar present in milk.

lacuna (lă-**kew**-nă) *noun* (*plural* lacunae, *pr.* lă-**kew**-nee) a gap, a section missing. [Latin, = a pool]

lacy *adjective* like lace.

lad *noun* 1 a boy or youth. 2 (*informal*) a fellow, a man.

ladder *noun* 1 a set of crossbars (*rungs*) between two uprights of wood etc., used as a means of climbing up or down something. 2 a vertical strip of unravelled stitching in a stocking etc. resembling a ladder. 3 a means or series of stages by which a person may advance in his or her career etc., *the political ladder*. –ladder *verb* to cause a ladder in (a stocking etc.); to develop a ladder.

laden *adjective* loaded with a cargo or burden.

la-di-da *adjective* (*informal*) having an affected manner or pronunciation.

lading (**lay**-ding) *noun* cargo; *bill of lading* (*see* bill¹).

ladle *noun* a utensil with a deep bowl and a long handle, for transferring liquids. –ladle *verb* to transfer with a ladle.

lady *noun* 1 a woman of good social position; a woman of polite and kindly behaviour. 2 (in

polite use) a woman. 3 (*old use*) a wife, *the colonel's lady*. 4 Lady a title used by peeresses, female relatives of peers, wives and widows of knights, etc. 5 a woman with authority over a household etc., *the lady of the house*. 6 a woman to whom a man is chivalrously devoted. □ the Ladies a women's public toilet. Lady Chapel a chapel within a large church, dedicated to the Virgin Mary.
Lady Day the Feast of the Annunciation, 25 March. lady-in-waiting *noun* a lady attending a queen or princess. Our Lady the Virgin Mary. [from Old English *hlæfdige* = a person who makes the bread (compare *lord*)]

ladybird *noun* a small flying beetle, usually reddish-brown with black spots.

ladylike *adjective* polite and suitable for a lady.

ladyship *noun* a title used in speaking to or about a woman of the rank of Lady, *your ladyship*.

lag¹ *verb* (lagged, lagging) to go too slow, to fail to keep up with others. –lag *noun* lagging; a delay. lagger *noun*

lag² *verb* (lagged, lagging) to encase (pipes or a boiler etc.) in a layer of insulating material to prevent loss of heat.

lag³ *noun* (*Austral. historical*) a convict, *old lags*.

lager (**lah**-ger) *noun* a kind of light beer. [from German *lager* = a store]

laggard *noun* a person who lags behind.

lagging *noun* material used to lag pipes etc.

lagoon *noun* 1 a saltwater lake separated from the sea by a sandbank or coral reef etc. 2 a small freshwater lake near a larger lake or river. [from Latin *lacuna* = pool]

laid *see* lay³. □ laid-back *adjective* (*informal*) relaxed.

lain *see* lie².

lair¹ *noun* 1 a sheltered place where a wild animal regularly sleeps or rests. 2 a person's hiding place.

lair² *noun* (*Austral. informal*) a youth or man who dresses flashily and shows off; a larrikin. –lair *verb* lair up to dress or behave as a lair.

laird *noun* (*Scottish*) a landowner.

lairy *adjective* (*Austral. informal*) flashy; vulgar.

laissez-faire (lay-say-**fair**) *noun* a policy of non-interference. [French, = allow to do]

laity (**lay**-ĭ-tee) *noun* lay people as distinct from the clergy, *the laity*.

lake *noun* a large body of water entirely surrounded by land.

aksa (**luk**-să) *noun* an Asian dish of rice noodles served in a spicy sauce or curry.

Lakshmi (**luk**-shmee) (in Hinduism) the goddess of prosperity, consort of Vishnu. She assumes different forms in order to accompany her husband in his different incarnations.

Lalor (**law**-lă), Peter (1827–89), Australian politician, leader of the Eureka rebellion in 1854.

lam *verb* (**lammed**, **lamming**) (*informal*) to hit hard, to thrash; *lammed into him*, attacked him physically or verbally.

lama (**lah**-mă) *noun* a priest of the form of Buddhism found in Tibet and Mongolia. [from Tibetan *blama* = superior]

lamaism (**lah**-mă-izm) *noun* Tibetan Buddhism.

Lamarck (la-**mahk**), Jean Baptiste de (1744–1829), French botanist and zoologist who (among others) anticipated Darwin's theory of organic evolution, and who espoused the theory of inheritance of acquired characteristics. **Lamarckism** *noun*

lamasery (lă-**mah**-sě-ree) *noun* a monastery of lamas.

lamb *noun* **1** a young sheep. **2** its flesh as food. **3** (*informal*) a gentle or endearing person. –**lamb** *verb* **1** to give birth to a lamb. **2** to tend lambing ewes. ☐ **Lamb of God** Christ (compared to the lamb sacrificed by Jews at the Passover). **lamb's fry** lamb's liver as food.

lambaste (lam-**bayst**) *verb* (*informal*) to beat or reprimand severely.

lambent *adjective* **1** (of a flame or light) playing about a surface. **2** (of eyes) softly radiant. **3** (of wit) lightly brilliant. [from Latin *lambens* = licking]

lambskin *noun* the skin of a lamb, either with its wool on (used in making clothing etc.) or as leather.

lambswool *noun* soft fine wool from a young sheep.

lame *adjective* **1** unable to walk normally because of an injury or defect, especially in a foot or leg. **2** (of an excuse or argument) weak, unconvincing. –**lame** *verb* to make lame. ☐ **lame duck** a person or firm etc. that is in difficulties and unable to manage without help. **lamely** *adverb*, **lameness** *noun*

lamé (**lah**-may) *noun* a fabric in which gold or silver thread is interwoven.

lamellibranch (lă-**mel**-ee-brank) *noun* a bivalve mollusc of the class including oysters. [from Latin *lamella* = little plate, + Greek *branchia* = gills]

lament *noun* **1** a passionate expression of grief. **2** a song or poem expressing grief. –**lament** *verb* to feel or express grief or regret. [from Latin *lamentari* = weep]

lamentable (**lam**-ĕn-tă-bŭl) *adjective* regrettable, deplorable. **lamentably** *adverb*

lamentation (lam-ĕn-**tay**-shŏn) *noun* **1** lamenting. **2** a lament, an expression of grief. **Lamentations** a book of the Old Testament telling of the desolation after the destruction of Jerusalem and the Temple in 586 BC.

lamented *adjective* mourned for.

lamina (**lam**-ĭ-nă) *noun* (*plural* **laminae**) **1** a thin plate, scale, or layer of rock or tissue. **2** the broad blade-like part of a leaf. [Latin, = layer, plate]

laminate (**lam**-ĭ-năt) *noun* a laminated material.

laminated *adjective* made of layers joined one upon the other, *laminated glass*. [from Latin *lamina* = layer]

laminex *noun* (*trademark*) a hard, durable plastic laminate used as a surfacing material for tables, cupboards, etc.

lamington *noun* (*Austral.*) a cube of sponge cake dipped in chocolate icing and covered with desiccated coconut. [named after Baron Lamington, Governor of Queensland 1895–1901]

lamp *noun* **1** a device for giving light, either by the use of electricity or gas or by burning oil or spirit. **2** a glass container enclosing a filament that is made to glow by electricity. **3** an electrical device producing radiation, *an infrared lamp*.

lampoon (lam-**poon**) *noun* a piece of writing that attacks a person by ridiculing him or her. –**lampoon** *verb* to ridicule in a lampoon.

lamprey *noun* (*plural* **lampreys**) a small eel-like water animal with a round mouth used as a sucker for attaching itself to things.

lampshade *noun* a shade placed over a lamp to soften or screen its light.

LAN *abbreviation* local area network.

Lancaster the name of the English royal house that ruled England from 1399 (Henry IV) until the death of Henry VI (1471).

Lancastrian *adjective* **1** of Lancashire, an English county. **2** of the Lancaster family or of the Red Rose party supporting it in the Wars of the Roses. – **Lancastrian** *noun* a Lancastrian person.

lance *noun* **1** a weapon consisting of a long wooden shaft with a pointed metal head, used by mounted knights or cavalry in the Middle Ages. **2** a device resembling this, used for spearing fish etc. – **lance** *verb* **1** to pierce with a lance. **2** to prick or cut open with a surgical lancet. □ **lance corporal** a non-commissioned army officer ranking below a corporal.

Lancelot (**lan**-sĕ-lot *or* **lahn**-) (in legends of King Arthur) the most famous of Arthur's knights, lover of Queen Guinevere.

lancer *noun* a soldier of a certain cavalry regiment formerly armed with lances.

lancet *noun* **1** a pointed two-edged knife used by surgeons. **2** a tall narrow pointed arch or window.

land *noun* **1** the solid part of the earth's surface, the part not covered by water or sea. **2** the ground or soil as used for farming etc. **3** an expanse of country, *forest land*. **4** a country, State, or nation, *the land of our fathers*; *in the land of the living*, alive. **5** property consisting of land. – **land** *verb* **1** to arrive or put on land from a ship. **2** to bring (an aircraft or its passengers etc.) down to the ground or other surface; to come down in this way. **3** to alight after a jump or fall. **4** to bring (a fish) to land; to win (a prize) or obtain (an appointment etc.), *landed an excellent job*. **5** to arrive or cause to arrive at a certain place, stage, or position, *landed up in gaol*; *landed us all in a mess*. **6** to strike with a blow, *landed him one in the eye*. **7** to present with a problem etc., *landed us with the job of sorting it out*. □ **land agent** (*Austral.*) an estate agent. **land crab** a small freshwater Australian crayfish. **land rights** the rights of the original inhabitants of a country to possess ancestral land, especially sacred tribal grounds.

landau (**lan**-daw) *noun* a kind of four-wheeled horse-drawn carriage.

landed *adjective* **1** owning land, *landed gentry*. **2** consisting of land, *landed estates*.

landfall *noun* approach to land after a journey by sea or air.

landfill *noun* **1** waste material etc. used to reclaim land. **2** this process of waste disposal.

landform *noun* a natural feature of the earth's surface.

landing *noun* **1** the process of coming or bringing something to land or of alighting after a jump etc. **2** a place where people and goods may be landed from a boat etc. **3** a level area at the top of a flight of stairs or between such flights. □ **landing craft** naval craft designed for putting ashore troops and equipment. **landing gear** the undercarriage of an aircraft. **landing stage** a platform for landing from a boat. **landing strip** an airstrip.

landlady *noun* **1** a woman who owns and lets land or a house or rooms etc. to a tenant. **2** a woman who keeps a boarding house etc.

landlocked *adjective* almost or entirely surrounded by land.

landlord *noun* **1** a person who owns and lets land or a house or room etc. to a tenant. **2** one who keeps a boarding house etc.

landlubber *noun* a person who is not used to the sea or sailing.

landmark *noun* **1** a conspicuous and easily recognised feature of a landscape. **2** an event that marks a stage or change in the history of something.

landmine *noun* an explosive mine laid in or on the ground.

landowner *noun* a person who owns land.

landscape *noun* **1** the scenery of a land area. **2** a picture of this. – **landscape** *verb* to lay out (an area) attractively, with natural features.

landslide *noun* **1** the sliding down of a mass of land on a slope or mountain. **2** an overwhelming majority of votes for one side in an election.

landsman *noun* (*plural* **landsmen**) a person who is not a sailor.

landward *adjective* & *adverb* towards the land. **landwards** *adverb*

lane *noun* **1** a narrow road, track, or passage. **2** a strip of road for a single line of traffic; a strip of track or water for a runner, rower, or swimmer in a race. **3** a route prescribed for or regularly followed by ships or aircraft, *shipping lanes*.

langar *noun* (in Sikhism) **1** the gurdwara dining hall. **2** the food served there. [from Persian]

language *noun* **1** words and their use. **2** a system of words of a particular community, country, or countries. **3** a system of signs or symbols used for conveying information. **4** a system of words, phrases, and symbols by means of which a computer can be programmed. **5** a particular style of wording. **6** the vocabulary of a particular group of people, *medical language*. □ **language laboratory** a room equipped with recording devices etc. for learning a language by repeated practice. [from Latin *lingua* = tongue]

languid (**lang**-gwĭd) *adjective* lacking vigour or vitality. **languidly** *adverb*

languish (**lang**-gwish) *verb* **1** to lose or lack vitality. **2** to live under miserable conditions, to be neglected. **3** to pine.

languishing *adjective* putting on a languid look in an attempt to win sympathy or affection.

languor (**lang**-ger) *noun* **1** tiredness, listlessness. **2** a languishing expression. **3** oppressive stillness of the air. **languorous** *adjective*

langur (**lang**-ger) *noun* a long-tailed Asian monkey.

lank *adjective* **1** tall and lean. **2** (of grass) long and limp; (of hair) straight and limp.

lanky *adjective* (**lankier**, **lankiest**) ungracefully lean and long or tall. **lankiness** *noun*

lanolin (**lan**-ŏ-lĭn) *noun* fat extracted from sheep's wool and used as a basis for ointments.

lantana (lan-**tah**-nǎ) *noun* an ornamental plant that has become a weed in parts of eastern Australia.

lantern *noun* **1** a transparent case for holding a light and shielding it against wind etc. outdoors. **2** a projection with windows on each side, on top of a dome or room. □ **lantern-jawed** *adjective* having long thin jaws so that the face has a hollow look.

lanthanide (**lan**-thǎ-nyd) *noun* any of the series of fifteen metallic elements from lanthanum to lutetium in the periodic table.

lanthanum (**lan**-thǎ-nǔm) *noun* a silvery-white metallic element (symbol La).

lanyard *noun* **1** a short rope or line used on a ship to fasten something or secure it. **2** a cord worn round the neck or on the shoulder, to which a knife or whistle etc. may be attached.

Laos (*rhymes with* mouse) a small landlocked republic in SE Asia. **Laotian** (lah-**oh**-shǎn) *adjective* & *noun*

Lao-tzu (low-**tsoo**) **1** the legendary founder of Taoism and traditional author of its most sacred scripture. **2** this scripture.

lap¹ *noun* **1** the flat area formed by the upper part of the thighs of a seated person. **2** the part of a dress etc. covering this. □ **in a person's**

lap as his or her responsibility; *in the lap of the gods*, for fate to decide. **in the lap of luxury** in great luxury.

lap² *noun* **1** an overlapping part; the amount of overlap. **2** a single circuit of something, e.g. of a racecourse. **3** one section of a journey, *the last lap*. –**lap** *verb* (**lapped**, **lapping**) **1** to fold or wrap round. **2** to overlap. **3** to be one or more laps ahead of (another competitor) in a race. □ **lap of honour** a ceremonial circuit of a racetrack or sports field etc. by the winner(s).

lap³ *verb* (**lapped**, **lapping**) **1** to take up (liquid) by movements of the tongue, as a cat does. **2** to flow with ripples making a gentle splashing sound, *waves lapped the shore* or *against the shore*. □ **lap up** to consume avidly.

La Paz the administrative capital of Bolivia.

lapdog *noun* a small pampered dog.

lapel (lǎ-**pel**) *noun* a flap at the edge of each front of a coat etc., folded back to lie against its outer surface. **lapelled** *adjective* having lapels. [from *lap*²]

lapidary (**lap**-ĭ-dǎ-ree) *adjective* of stones, engraved on stone. [from Latin *lapis* = a stone]

lapis lazuli (lap-ĭss **laz**-yǔ-lee) *noun* a bright blue semi-precious stone.

Lapland a region at the north of Scandinavia, mostly within the Arctic Circle. **Laplander** *noun*

laplap *noun* (in Papua New Guinea and South Pacific countries) a cloth worn round the waist forming a loose skirt.

Lapp *noun* **1** a Laplander. **2** the language of Lapland. **Lappish** *adjective*

lapse *noun* **1** a slight error, especially one caused by forgetfulness, weakness, or inattention. **2** backsliding, a decline into an inferior state. **3** the passage of a period of time. **4** the termination of a privilege or legal right through disuse. –**lapse** *verb* **1** to fail to maintain one's position or standard. **2** (of rights and privileges) to be lost or no longer valid because not used, claimed, or renewed. [from Latin *lapsum* = slipped]

laptop *noun* a portable computer.

larboard *noun* (*old use*) = **port**³.

larceny (**lar**-sě-nee) *noun* theft of personal goods. **larcenous** *adjective*

larch *noun* a tall cone-bearing deciduous tree of the pine family.

lard *noun* a white greasy substance prepared from pig fat and used in cooking. –**lard** *verb* **1** to place strips of fat bacon in or on (meat) before cooking, in order to prevent it from becoming dry while roasting. **2** to embellish (talk or writing) with foreign or technical terms. **lardy** *adjective*

larder *noun* a room or cupboard for storing food.

Lardil (**lar**-dil *or* ler-) *noun* **1** a member of an Aboriginal people living on Mornington Island in the Gulf of Carpentaria. **2** their language.

large *adjective* **1** of considerable size or extent. **2** of the larger kind, *the large intestine*. –**large** *adverb* in a large way, on a large scale, *bulk* or *loom large*. ☐ **at large** free to roam about, not in confinement; in a general way, at random; as a whole, in general, *is popular with the country at large*. **large-scale** *adjective* drawn to a large scale so that many details can be shown, *a large-scale map*; extensive, involving large quantities etc., *large-scale operations*. **largeness** *noun*

largely *adverb* to a great extent, *his success was largely due to luck*.

largesse (lar-**zhess**) *noun* money or gifts generously given.

largish *adjective* fairly large.

largo *adverb* (in music) in a slow tempo and dignified style. –**largo** *noun* (*plural* **largos**) a passage or movement to be played in this way. [Italian]

lariat (**la**-ree-ăt) *noun* a lasso, a rope used to catch or tether a horse etc.

lark¹ *noun* any of several small sandy-brown birds, especially the skylark. **rise with the lark** to get up early.

lark² *noun* (*informal*) **1** a playful adventurous action. **2** an amusing incident. –**lark** *verb* (*informal*) to play light-heartedly, *to lark about*.

larkspur *noun* a plant with spur-shaped blue or pink flowers.

larrikin *noun* (*Austral.*) **1** a person who acts with apparent disregard for social or political conventions; a troublemaker. **2** (*historical*) a hooligan.

larva *noun* (*plural* **larvae**, *pr.* **lar**-vee) an insect or other animal in the first stage of its life after coming out of the egg. **larval** *adjective* [from Latin, = ghost, mask]

laryngitis (la-rĭn-**jy**-tĭss) *noun* inflammation of the larynx.

larynx (**la**-rinks) *noun* the part of the throat containing the vocal cords. **laryngeal** *adjective*

lasagne (lah-**san**-yĕ) *noun* **1** pasta formed into sheets. **2** a baked dish of this pasta layered with a sauce of meat or vegetables, béchamel sauce, and cheese. [Italian, plural of *lasagna*]

Lascar (**lask**-er) *noun* a sailor from the countries south-east of India.

lascivious (lă-**siv**-ee-ŭs) *adjective* lustful. **lasciviously** *adverb*, **lasciviousness** *noun*

laser (**lay**-zer) *noun* a device that generates an intense and highly concentrated beam of light or other electromagnetic radiation. [from the initials of 'light amplification (by) stimulated emission (of) radiation']

lash *verb* **1** to move in a whip-like movement, *lashed its tail*. **2** to strike with a whip; to beat or strike violently, *rain lashed against the panes*. **3** to attack violently in words. **4** to fasten or secure with cord etc., *lashed them together*. –**lash** *noun* **1** a stroke with a whip etc. **2** the flexible part of a whip. **3** an eyelash. ☐ **lash out** to attack with blows or words; to spend lavishly.

lashings *plural noun* (*informal*) a lot, *lashings of cream*.

lass *noun* a girl, a young woman.

Lassa fever *noun* a serious disease of tropical Africa, caused by a virus. [named after Lassa in Nigeria]

Lasseter's Reef a reported but undiscovered reef of gold in central Australia.

lassitude *noun* tiredness, listlessness.

lasso (la-**soo**) *noun* (*plural* **lassoes**) a rope with a running noose, used for catching cattle. –**lasso** *verb* (**lassoed**, **lassoing**) to catch with a lasso. [from Spanish *lazo* = lace]

last¹ *adjective* & *adverb* **1** after all others in position or time, coming at the end. **2** latest, most recent, most recently; *last night*, in the night that has just passed. **3** remaining as the only one(s) left, *our last hope*. **4** least likely or suitable, *she is the last person I'd have chosen*. –**last** *noun* **1** a person or thing that is last. **2** the last performance of certain actions, *breathe one's last*. **3** the last mention or sight of something, *shall never hear the last of it*. ☐ **at last** or **at long last** in the end, after much delay. **last-ditch** *adjective* final, desperate, *a last-ditch attempt*. **last-minute** *adjective* at the latest possible time when an event etc. can be altered or influenced. **last post** a military bugle call sounded at sunset, also at military funerals etc. **last rites** sacred rites for a person about to die. **last straw** a slight addition to one's difficulties that makes them unbearable.

Last Supper the meal eaten by Christ and his disciples on the eve of the Crucifixion. **last trump** a trumpet call to wake the dead on Judgment Day. **last word** the final statement in a dispute; a definitive statement; the latest fashion. **on one's** or **its last legs** near death or the end of usefulness.

last² *verb* **1** to continue for a period of time, to endure, *the rain lasted all day*. **2** to be sufficient for one's needs, *enough food to last us for three days*. □ **last out** to be strong enough or sufficient to last.

last³ *noun* a block of wood or metal shaped like a foot, used in making and repairing shoes.

lasting *adjective* able to last for a long time.

lastly *adverb* in the last place, finally.

latch *noun* **1** a small bar fastening a door or gate, lifted from its catch by a lever. **2** a spring-lock that catches when the door is closed. **–latch** *verb* to fasten or be fastened with a latch. □ **latch on to** (*informal*) to cling to; to get possession of; to take in as an idea. **on the latch** fastened by a latch but not locked.

latchkey *noun* the key of an outer door; *latchkey child*, one who is alone at home after school until a parent returns from work.

late *adjective* & *adverb* **1** after the proper or usual time. **2** flowering or ripening late in the season. **3** far on in the day or night or a period of time or a series etc., *in the late 1920s*. **4** of recent date or time, *the latest news*. **5** no longer alive; no longer holding a certain position, *the late president*. □ **of late** lately. **lateness** *noun*

lately *adverb* in recent times, not long ago.

latent (**lay**-těnt) *adjective* existing but not yet active or developed or visible. □ **latent heat** the heat required to turn a solid into a liquid or vapour, or a liquid into a vapour, without change of temperature. **latency** *noun*

lateral (**lat**-ě-răl) *adjective* of, at, or towards the side(s). □ **lateral line** a line of pores opening into sensory organs along each side of the body of many fishes and amphibians. **lateral thinking** a method of solving problems without using conventional logic. **laterally** *adverb* [from Latin *lateris* = of a side]

latex (**lay**-teks) *noun* **1** a milky fluid exuded from the cut surfaces of certain plants, e.g. the rubber plant. **2** a synthetic product resembling this, used in paints and adhesives. [Latin, = liquid]

lath (*pr*. lath) *noun* (*plural* **laths**) a narrow thin strip of wood, used in trellises or as a support for plaster etc.

lathe (*pr*. layth) *noun* a machine for holding and turning pieces of wood or metal etc. against a tool that will cut them to shape.

lather *noun* **1** a froth produced by soap or detergent mixed with water. **2** frothy sweat, especially on horses. **3** a state of agitation. **–lather** *verb* **1** to cover with lather. **2** to form a lather.

Latin *noun* the language of the ancient Romans. **–Latin** *adjective* **1** of or in Latin. **2** of the countries or peoples (e.g. France, Spain, Portugal, Italy) using languages developed from Latin. □ **Latin America** the parts of Central and South America where Spanish or Portuguese is the main language. **Latin-American** *adjective* & *noun*

latitude *noun* **1** the distance of a place from the equator, measured in degrees. **2** a region, especially with reference to temperature; *high latitudes*, regions near the North or South Pole; *low latitudes*, near the equator. **3** freedom from restrictions on actions or opinions. [from Latin, = breadth]

latrine (lă-**treen**) *noun* a toilet in a camp or barracks etc., a trench or pit for human excreta where there are no sewers.

latter *adjective* **1** mentioned after another; *the latter*, the one mentioned second of two things. **2** nearer to the end, *the latter half of the year*. □ **latter-day** *adjective* modern, recent. **Latter-day Saints** Mormons' name for themselves.

Usage When referring to the last of three or more, *the last*, not *the latter*, should be used.

latterly *adverb* of late, nowadays.

lattice (**lat**-ĭss) *noun* **1** a framework of crossed laths or bars with spaces between, used as a screen or fence etc. **2** a structure resembling this. □ **lattice energy** the energy required to separate the ions of a crystal to an infinite distance from one another. **lattice window** one made with a lattice or with small panes set in strips of lead.

Latvia a republic of NE Europe on the shore of the Baltic Sea. **Latvian** *adjective* & *noun*

laud *verb* (*formal*) to praise. [from Latin *laudare* = to praise]

laudable (**law**-dă-bŭl) *adjective* praiseworthy.

laudanum (**lawd**-nŭm) *noun* opium prepared for use as a sedative.

laudatory (**law**-dă-tŏ-ree) *adjective* expressing praise.

Usage Distinguish *laudable* and *laudatory*.

---

laugh *verb* **1** to make the sounds and movements of the face and body that express lively amusement or amused scorn. **2** to have these emotions. **3** to utter or treat with a laugh; *laughed it off*. –**laugh** *noun* **1** an act, sound, or manner of laughing. **2** (*informal*) an amusing incident. □ **laughing gas** nitrous oxide, which can cause involuntary laughter in a person who inhales it. **laughing jackass** the kookaburra. **laughing stock** a person or thing that is ridiculed. **laugh on the other side of one's face** to change from amusement to dismay. **laugh out of court** to make fun of (a thing) so that no one gives it serious consideration.

laughable *adjective* causing people to laugh, ridiculous.

laughter *noun* the act, sound, or manner of laughing.

launch[1] *verb* **1** to send forth by hurling or thrusting, to send on its course, *launch a rocket*. **2** to cause (a ship) to move or slide from land into the water. **3** to start; to initiate, *launch an attack* or *a business; launch a book*, to introduce it publicly. **4** to enter boldly or freely into a course of action. –**launch** *noun* the process of launching a ship or spacecraft. □ **launching pad** or **launch pad** a concrete platform from which spacecraft are launched. **launch out** to spend money freely; to start on an ambitious enterprise.

launch[2] *noun* **1** a large motor boat. **2** a warship's largest boat.

launder *verb* **1** to wash and iron (clothes etc.). **2** to be washable. **3** to transfer (funds etc.) so as to make their source seem legitimate.

laundromat *noun* (also **launderette**) an establishment fitted with washing machines and dryers to be used by customers for a fee.

laundry *noun* **1** a room where clothes etc. are washed. **2** a business establishment that launders things for customers. **3** a batch of clothes etc. for laundering or newly laundered.

laureate (**lo**-ree-ăt) *adjective* wreathed with laurel as an honour. □ **Poet Laureate** the poet appointed to write poems for British State occasions. [from *laurel*]

laurel (*rhymes with* quarrel) *noun* **1** an evergreen shrub with smooth glossy leaves. **2** (also **laurels**) a wreath of laurel leaves as an emblem of victory or poetic merit. □ **look to one's laurels** to beware of losing one's position of superiority. **rest on one's laurels** to cease to strive for further successes.

lava (**lah**-vă) *noun* flowing molten rock discharged from a volcano; the solid substance formed when this cools.

lavatory *noun* **1** a toilet. **2** a room, building, or compartment with a toilet in it. [from Latin *lavare* = to wash]

lavender *noun* **1** a shrub with fragrant purple flowers that are dried and used to scent linen etc. **2** light purple.

lavish (**lav**-ish) *adjective* **1** giving or producing something in large quantities. **2** plentiful, *a lavish display*. –**lavish** *verb* to bestow lavishly. **lavishly** *adverb*, **lavishness** *noun* [from Old French *lavasse* = downpour of rain]

Lavoisier (lah-**vwah**-zee-ay), Antoine Laurent (1743–94), French scientist, regarded as the father of modern chemistry.

law *noun* **1** a rule established among a community by authority or custom. **2** a body of such rules. **3** their controlling influence, their operation as providing a remedy against wrongs, *law and order*. **4** the subject or study of such rules. **5** (*informal*) the police. **6** something that must be obeyed, *his word was law*. **7** a factual statement of what always happens in certain circumstances, e.g. of regular natural occurrences, *the laws of nature; the law of gravity*. □ **go to law** to ask a lawcourt to decide about a problem or claim. **law-abiding** *adjective* obeying the law. **a law unto oneself** or **itself** a person or thing that does not behave in the customary fashion. **take the law into one's own hands** to right a wrong oneself without legal sanction.

lawbreaker *noun* a person who breaks the law.

lawcourt *noun* a room or building in which legal cases are heard and judged.

lawful *adjective* permitted or recognised by law, *lawful business*. **lawfully** *adverb*

lawless *adjective* **1** (of a country) where laws do not exist or are not applied. **2** disregarding the law, uncontrolled, *lawless brigands*. **lawlessly** *adverb*, **lawlessness** *noun*

lawn[1] *noun* fine woven cotton or synthetic material.

lawn² *noun* an area of closely-cut grass in a garden or park, or used for a game, *croquet lawn*. ☐ lawn tennis *see* tennis.

lawnmower *noun* a machine for cutting the grass of lawns.

Lawrence, D.H. (David Herbert) (1885–1930), English novelist, poet, critic, and painter.

lawrencium (lă-**ren**-see-ŭm) *noun* an artificial radioactive metallic element of the actinide series (symbol Lr).

Lawson¹, Henry Archibald (1867–1922), Australian writer of poetry and short stories dealing with bush life.

Lawson², William (1774–1850), English-born Australian explorer who, with Gregory Blaxland and W. C. Wentworth, crossed the Blue Mountains in 1813.

lawsuit *noun* the process of bringing a problem or claim etc. before a court of law for settlement.

lawyer (**loi**-er) *noun* a person who is trained and qualified in legal matters.

lax *adjective* slack, not strict or severe, *discipline was lax*. **laxly** *adverb*, **laxity** *noun* [from Latin, *laxus* = loose]

laxative (**laks**-ă-tiv) *noun* a medicine that stimulates the bowels to empty. **–laxative** *adjective* having this effect.

lay¹ *noun* (*old use*) a poem meant to be sung, a ballad. [from Old French *lai*]

lay² *adjective* **1** not ordained into the clergy, *lay preacher*. **2** not professionally qualified, especially in law or medicine. [from Greek *laos* = people]

lay³ *verb* (**laid**, **laying**) **1** to place or put on a surface or in a certain position, *laid the vase on the table*. **2** to place or arrange in a horizontal position, to put in place, *lay a carpet*; *lay the table*, arrange things on a table for a meal; *lay the fire*, put fuel etc. ready for lighting. **3** to place or assign, *lay emphasis on neatness*; *laid the blame on her*. **4** to formulate, to establish, *we laid our plans*. **5** to cause to subside, *laid the dust*; *laid the ghost*, made it cease being troublesome. **6** to present or put forward for consideration, *laid claim to it*. **7** (of a hen bird) to produce (an egg or eggs) from the body. **8** to stake as a wager, to bet. **–lay** *noun* the way in which something lies. ☐ in lay (of hens) laying eggs regularly. lay about one to hit out on all sides. lay bare to expose, to reveal. lay claim to to claim as one's right. lay down to put on the ground etc.; to give up (office); to establish

as a rule or instruction; to store (wine) in a cellar for future use. lay down the law to talk authoritatively or as if sure of being right. lay hold of to grasp. lay in to provide oneself with a stock of. lay into (*informal*) to thrash; to reprimand harshly. lay it on the line (*informal*) to offer without reserve; to speak frankly. lay low to overthrow; to humble; to incapacitate by illness. lay off to discharge (workers) temporarily owing to shortage of work; (*informal*) to cease, especially from causing trouble or annoyance. lay-off *noun* a temporary discharge. lay on to inflict blows forcefully; to provide. lay open to break the skin of (part of the body); to expose to criticism. lay out to arrange according to a plan; to prepare (a body) for burial; to spend (money) for a purpose; to knock unconscious; *laid himself out to help us*, made every effort. lay to rest to bury in a grave. lay up to store or save; to cause to be confined to bed or unfit for work etc. lay waste to destroy the crops and buildings etc. of (a district). [from Old English *lecgan*]

Usage See note at lie².

lay⁴ *past tense* of lie².

layabout *noun* a loafer, a person who lazily avoids working for a living.

lay-by *noun* (*plural* lay-bys) **1** (*Austral.*) a system of reserving an article in a shop by paying a deposit and instalments. **2** (especially *Brit.*) an area beside a road, canal, or railway, where vehicles may stop without obstructing the flow of traffic. **–lay-by** *verb* (*Austral.*) to purchase using lay-by.

layer *noun* **1** a thickness of material (often one of several) laid over a surface. **2** a person etc. that lays something. **3** a shoot fastened down for propagation by layering. **–layer** *verb* **1** to arrange in layers. **2** to propagate by fastening down a shoot to take root while still attached to the parent plant.

layette *noun* the clothes and bedding etc. prepared for a new-born baby.

lay figure *noun* a jointed wooden figure of the human body, used by artists for arranging drapery on etc. [from an old Dutch word *led* = joint]

layman, **laywoman** *nouns* (*plural* laymen, laywomen) a layperson.

layout *noun* an arrangement of parts etc. according to a plan.

layperson *noun* (*plural* **laypeople**) **1** a non-ordained member of a Church. **2** a person lacking professional or specialised knowledge in a particular subject. [from *lay²*]

laze *verb* to spend time idly or in idle relaxation. **–laze** *noun* an act or period of lazing.

lazy *adjective* (**lazier**, **laziest**) **1** unwilling to work; doing little work. **2** showing or characterised by lack of energy, *a lazy yawn*. □ **lazy Susan** a revolving food stand for a table. **lazily** *adverb*, **laziness** *noun*

lazybones *noun* (*informal*) a lazy person.

lb. *abbreviation* = pound(s) weight. [short for Latin *libra*]

l.b.w. *abbreviation* leg before wicket.

LCD *abbreviation* **1** lowest common denominator. **2** liquid crystal display.

LCM *abbreviation* lowest common multiple.

lea *noun* (*poetic*) a meadow.

leach *verb* to make (liquid) percolate through soil or ore etc.; to remove (soluble matter) in this way, *leach it out*.

lead¹ (*pr.* leed) *verb* (**led**, **leading**) **1** to cause to go with oneself; to guide, especially by going in front or by holding the hand or an attached rein etc. **2** to influence the actions or opinions of, *what led you to believe this?* **3** to be a route or means of access, *the door leads into a passage*. **4** to have as its result, *this led to confusion*. **5** to live or pass (one's life), *was leading a double life*. **6** to be in first place or position in, to be ahead, *lead the world in electronics*. **7** to be the leader or head of, to control. **8** to make one's start; (in boxing) to make one's first punch in a series. **9** (in card games) to play as one's first card; to be the first player. **–lead** *noun* **1** guidance given by going in front, an example. **2** a clue, *it gives us a lead*. **3** a leading place, leadership, *take the lead*; the amount by which one competitor is in front, *a lead of 5 points*. **4** an electrical conductor (usually a wire) conveying current from a source to a place of use. **5** a strap or cord etc. for leading or restraining a dog or other animal. **6** the act or right of playing one's card first in a card game; the card played. **7** the chief part in a play or other performance, one who takes this part, *play the lead*; *the lead singer*. □ **lead by the nose** to control the actions of (a person) completely. **lead on** to entice into going further than was intended; to mislead. **lead screw** a screw that moves the carriage of a lathe. **lead someone a dance** to

cause a person much trouble, especially by making him or her search. **lead up the garden path** to mislead. **lead up to** to serve as an introduction to or preparation for; to direct the conversation towards.

lead² (*pr.* led) *noun* **1** one of the elements (symbol Pb), a heavy metal of dull greyish colour. **2** a thin stick of graphite forming the writing substance in a pencil. **3** a lump of lead used in taking soundings in water. **leads** *plural noun* strips of lead used to cover a roof; a piece of roof covered with these. □ **lead pencil** a pencil of graphite enclosed in wood. **swing the lead** (*informal*) to pretend to be ill in order to avoid work.

leaded (**led**-ĕd) *adjective* covered or framed with lead; mixed with lead.

leaden (**led**-ĕn) *adjective* **1** made of lead. **2** heavy, slow as if weighted with lead. **3** lead-coloured, dark grey, *leaden skies*.

leader *noun* **1** a person or thing that leads. **2** one who has the principal part in something; the head of a group etc.; (in an orchestra) the principal first-violin player. **3** one whose example is followed, *a leader of fashion*. **4** a leading article in a newspaper.

leadership *noun* **1** being a leader. **2** ability to be a leader. **3** the leaders of a group.

leading¹ (**leed**-ing) *see* **lead¹**. □ **leading article** a long article in a newspaper, giving editorial opinions. **leading lady** or **man** one taking the chief part in a play etc. **leading light** a prominent member of a group. **leading question** one that is worded so that it prompts a person to give the desired answer (¶ not the same as a *searching question*).

leading² (**led**-ing) *noun* a covering or framework of lead (metal).

leadlight (**led**-lyt) *noun* a window constructed of various pieces of usually coloured or stained glass fixed in strips of lead.

leaf *noun* (*plural* **leaves**) **1** a flat structure (usually green) growing from the stem or branch of a plant or directly from the root. **2** the state of having leaves out, *tree is in leaf*. **3** a single thickness of the paper forming the pages of a book. **4** a very thin sheet of metal, *gold leaf*. **5** a hinged flap of a table; an extra section inserted to extend a table. □ **leaf mould** soil or compost consisting chiefly of decayed leaves. **leaf through** to turn over the leaves of a book. **take a leaf out of someone's book** to follow that person's example.

leafless *adjective* having no leaves.

leaflet *noun* **1** a small leaf or leaflike part of a plant. **2** a printed sheet of paper (sometimes folded but not stitched) giving information, especially for distribution free of charge.

leafy *adjective* **1** covered in leaves; full of trees etc., *leafy suburbs*. **2** consisting chiefly of leaves, *leafy vegetables*.

league¹ *noun* **1** a group of people or countries who combine formally for a particular purpose. **2** a group of sports clubs that compete against each other for a championship. **3** a class of contestants, *he is out of his league*. –**league** *verb* to form a league. □ **in league with** allied with; conspiring with. **league table** a table of contestants etc. in order of merit.

league² *noun* (*old use*) a measure of distance, usually about 3 miles (or 5 km).

League of Nations an association of countries with the aim of achieving international peace, security, and cooperation, established in 1919 and superseded by the United Nations.

leak *noun* **1** a hole or crack etc. through which liquid or gas may accidentally get in or out. **2** the liquid or gas passing through this. **3** such an escape of liquid or gas. **4** a similar escape of an electric charge; the charge itself. **5** a disclosure of secret information. –**leak** *verb* **1** (of liquid or gas etc.) to escape through an opening. **2** (of a container) to allow such an escape, to let out (liquid or gas). **3** to disclose, *leaked the news to a reporter.* □ **leak out** (of a secret) to become known despite efforts to keep it secret. **leaky** *adjective*

leakage *noun* **1** leaking. **2** a thing or amount that has leaked out.

lean¹ *adjective* **1** (of a person or animal) without much flesh. **2** (of meat) containing little or no fat. **3** scanty, *a lean harvest*. –**lean** *noun* the lean part of meat. □ **lean years** years of scarcity. **leanness** *noun*

lean² *verb* (**leaned** *or* **leant**, **leaning**) **1** to put or be in a sloping position. **2** to rest against or on something for support. **3** to rely or depend for help. □ **lean on** (*informal*) to seek to influence by intimidation. **lean-to** *noun* a building with its roof resting against the side of a larger building.

Leander (*Gk. legend*) a man who swam the Hellespont every night to his lover the priestess Hero until he was drowned in a storm.

leaning *noun* a tendency or partiality.

leap *verb* (**leaped** *or* **leapt**, **leaping**) to jump vigorously. –**leap** *noun* a vigorous jump. □ **by leaps and bounds** with very rapid progress. **leap year** a year with an extra day (29 February), occurring every four years.

leap-frog *noun* a game in which each player in turn takes a running vault with parted legs over another who is bending down. –**leap-frog** *verb* (**leap-frogged**, **leap-frogging**) **1** to perform this vault. **2** to overtake alternately.

learn *verb* (**learned** (*pr.* lernt *or* lernd) *or* **learnt**, **learning**) **1** to gain knowledge of or skill in (a subject etc.) by study or experience or by being taught; *learn it by heart*, memorise it thoroughly so that one can repeat it. **2** to become aware by information or from observation.

learned (**lern**-ĕd) *adjective* **1** having much knowledge acquired by study, *learned men*. **2** of or for learned people, *a learned society*. **learnedly** *adverb*

learner *noun* a person who is learning a subject or skill.

learning *noun* knowledge obtained by study.

lease *noun* a contract by which the owner of land or a building etc. allows another person to use it for a specified time, usually in return for payment. –**lease** *verb* **1** to grant the use of (a property) by lease. **2** to obtain or hold (a property) by lease. □ **a new lease of life** a chance to continue living or to live more happily because of recovery from illness or anxiety, or (of things) to continue in use after repair.

leasehold *noun* the holding of land or a house or flat etc. by means of a lease. **leaseholder** *noun*

leash *noun* a strap etc. for leading or restraining a dog; a lead. –**leash** *verb* to hold on a leash.

least *adjective* **1** smallest in amount or degree. **2** lowest in rank or importance. –**least** *noun* the least amount or degree. –**least** *adverb* in the least degree. □ **at least** not less than what is stated; anyway. **to say the least of it** putting the case moderately.

leather *noun* **1** material made from animal skins by tanning or a similar process. **2** the leather part(s) of something. **3** a piece of leather for polishing with.

leatherback *noun* the largest existing turtle, having a leathery shell.

leatherhead *noun* an Australian bird (a honeyeater) with a leathery featherless head.

leatherjacket *noun* a tough-skinned sea fish.

leatherwood *noun* a Tasmanian tree with highly scented flowers from which bees make a distinctive honey.

leathery *adjective* as tough as leather.

leave[1] *verb* (**left**, **leaving**) **1** to go away from; to go away finally or permanently. **2** to cease to belong to (a group) or live at (a place); to cease working for an employer. **3** to cause or allow to remain, *left the door open*; to depart without taking, *left my umbrella on the bus*; *he leaves a wife and two children*, is survived by these. **4** to give as a legacy. **5** to allow to stay or proceed without interference, *left him to get on with it*; *leave the dog alone*. **6** to refrain from consuming or dealing with, *left all the fat*; *let's leave the washing-up*. **7** to entrust or commit to another person, *I'll leave it to you*. **8** to deposit for collection or transmission, *leave your coat in the hall*; *leave a message*. **9** to abandon, to desert, *was left in the lurch*. □ **leave off** to cease; to cease to wear. **leave out** to omit, not to include.

leave[2] *noun* **1** permission. **2** official permission to be absent from duty; the period for which this lasts. □ **leave-taking** *noun* taking one's leave. **on leave** absent with official permission. **take leave of one's senses** to go mad. **take one's leave** to say farewell and go away.

leaven (**lev**-ĕn) *noun* **1** a substance (e.g. yeast) that produces fermentation in dough. **2** a quality or influence that lightens or enlivens something. –**leaven** *verb* **1** to add leaven to. **2** to modify by an addition; to enliven.

leavings *plural noun* what is left.

Lebanon (**leb**-ă-non) a republic at the eastern end of the Mediterranean Sea. **Lebanese** *adjective* & *noun* (*plural* **Lebanese**).

lecher *noun* a lecherous man.

lecherous *adjective* having an excessive sexual desire, lustful. **lechery** *noun*

lectern *noun* a stand with a sloping top to hold a Bible (from which the lesson is read) in church, or a lecturer's notes etc.

lecture *noun* **1** a speech giving information about a subject to an audience or class. **2** a long serious speech, especially one giving reproof or warning. –**lecture** *verb* **1** to give a lecture or series of lectures. **2** to talk to (a person) seriously or reprovingly. **lecturer** *noun* [from Latin *lectum* = read]

LED *abbreviation* light-emitting diode, a semiconductor diode which glows when a voltage is applied.

led *see* **lead**[1].

Leda (**lee**-dă) (*Gk. myth.*) queen of Sparta, loved by Zeus who visited and wooed her in the form of a swan.

ledge *noun* a narrow horizontal projection, a narrow shelf.

ledger *noun* a tall narrow book used by a business firm as an account book or to record trading transactions.

lee *noun* shelter, the sheltered side or part of something.

leech *noun* **1** a small blood-sucking worm usually living in water. **2** a person who drains the resources of another.

leek *noun* a plant related to the onion but with broader leaves and a cylindrical white bulb.

leer *verb* to look slyly or maliciously or lustfully. –**leer** *noun* a leering look.

leery *adjective* (*informal*) wary, suspicious.

lees *plural noun* sediment in wine etc.

leeward (**lee**-werd; *in nautical use* **loo**-erd) *adjective* situated on the side turned away from the wind. –**leeward** *noun* the leeward side or region.

Leeward Islands (**lee**-werd) a group of islands in the West Indies, of which the largest are Guadeloupe, Antigua, St Kitts, and Montserrat.

leeway *noun* **1** a ship's sideways drift from its course. **2** a degree of freedom of action, *these instructions give us plenty of leeway*.

left[1] *see* **leave**[1]. □ **left luggage** luggage deposited temporarily at a railway station etc.

left[2] *adjective* & *adverb* on or towards the left-hand side. –**left** *noun* **1** the left-hand side or region. **2** the left hand; a blow with this. **3** (in marching) the left foot. **4** (often **Left**) the left wing of a political party or other group. □ **have two left feet** to be clumsy. **left field** a surprising or unconventional position or style. **left hand** the hand that in most people is less used, on the same side of the body as the heart. **left-hand** *adjective* of or towards this side of a person or the corresponding side of a thing. **left-handed** *adjective* using the left hand usually, by preference; (of a blow or tool) made with or operated by the left hand; (of a screw) to be tightened by turning towards the left; (of a compliment) ambiguous in meaning. **left-hander** *noun* a left-handed person or blow.

left wing the radical, progressive, or socialist section of society, a political party, etc. (¶ The term originated with the National Assembly in France (1789–91), where the nobles sat on the president's right hand and the commons on the left.) **left-winger** *noun* [from an old word = 'weak']

leftist *noun* a supporter of socialism; one who belongs to the left of a socialist group. **–leftist** *adjective* of the left wing in politics etc. **leftism** *noun*

leftovers *plural noun* things remaining when the rest is finished, especially food not finished at a meal.

leg *noun* **1** each of the projecting parts of an animal's body, on which it stands or moves. **2** this as food. **3** either of the two lower limbs of the human body; an artificial replacement of this. **4** the part of a garment covering this. **5** each of the projecting supports beneath a chair or other piece of furniture. **6** any branch of a forked object. **7** a section of a journey. **8** each of a pair of matches between the same opponents. **9** the side of a cricket field behind the batsman as he or she faces the bowler; *long leg*, *short leg*, *square leg*, fielders at various positions there. □ **give a leg up** to help to mount a horse etc., or to get over an obstacle or difficulty. **has not a leg to stand on** has no facts or sound reasons to support this argument. **leg before wicket** (of a batsman in cricket) out because of illegally obstructing the ball with any part of the body other than the hand. **leg it** (*informal*) to walk or run rapidly; to go on foot. **leg-pull** *noun* (*informal*) a hoax. **leg-room** *noun* space for the legs of a seated person. **leg warmer** each of a pair of usually knitted garments covering the leg from ankle to thigh.

legacy (**leg**-ă-see) *noun* **1** money or an article left to someone in a will. **2** something received from a predecessor or because of earlier events etc., *a legacy of distrust*.

legal *adjective* **1** of or based on law; *my legal adviser*, a solicitor etc. **2** in accordance with the law; authorised or required by law. □ **legal aid** payment from public funds towards the cost of legal advice or proceedings. **legally** *adverb*, **legality** (lĕ-**gal**-ĭ-tee) *noun* [from Latin *legis* = of a law]

legalise *verb* (also **-ize**) to make legal. **legalisation** *noun*

legate (**leg**-ăt) *noun* an envoy, especially one representing the Pope.

legatee (leg-ă-**tee**) *noun* a person who receives a legacy.

legation (lĕ-**gay**-shŏn) *noun* **1** a diplomatic minister and staff. **2** his or her official residence.

legato (lĕ-**gah**-toh) *adverb* (in music) in a smooth even manner. [Italian]

legend (**lej**-ĕnd) *noun* **1** a story (which may or may not be true) handed down from the past. **2** such stories collectively. **3** an inscription on a coin or medal. **4** a caption. **5** an explanation on a map etc. of the symbols used. [from Latin *legenda* = things to be read]

legendary (**lej**-ĕn-dă-ree) *adjective* **1** of or based on legends; described in a legend. **2** (*informal*) famous, often talked about.

legerdemain (**lej**-er-dĕ-mayn) *noun* sleight of hand, conjuring tricks. [from French, = light of hand]

leger line (**lej**-er) *noun* a short line added in a musical score for notes above or below the range of the staff.

leggings *plural noun* **1** close-fitting stretch trousers worn by women or children. **2** protective outer coverings for each leg from knee to ankle.

leggy *adjective* having noticeably long legs.

legible (**lej**-ĭ-bŭl) *adjective* (of print or handwriting) clear enough to be deciphered, readable. **legibly** *adverb*, **legibility** *noun* [from Latin *legere* = to read]

legion (**lee**-jŏn) *noun* **1** a division of the ancient Roman army. **2** a vast group, a multitude, *such stories are legion*. □ **American Legion** an American association of ex-servicemen and women. **Foreign Legion** a body of foreign volunteers in an army, especially the French army. **legionary** *adjective* & *noun*

legionnaire (lee-jŏ-**nair**) *noun* a member of a legion. □ **legionnaires' disease** a form of bacterial pneumonia first identified in an outbreak at a meeting of the American Legion in 1976.

legislate (**lej**-ĭss-layt) *verb* to make laws. [from Latin *legis* = of a law, + *latio* = proposing]

legislation (lej-ĭss-**lay**-shŏn) *noun* **1** legislating. **2** the laws themselves.

legislative (**lej**-ĭss-lă-tiv) *adjective* making laws. □ **Legislative Assembly** the sole house of parliament in Queensland, the Northern Territory, and the Australian Capital Territory, and the lower house of the New South Wales,

Victorian, and Western Australian Parliaments. **Legislative Council** the upper house of the Parliaments of all Australian States except Queensland.

legislator (lej-ĭss-lay-ter) *noun* a member of a legislative assembly.

legislature (lej-ĭss-lă-cher) *noun* a country's legislative assembly.

legitimate (lĕ-jit-ĭ-măt) *adjective* **1** in accordance with the law or rules. **2** logical, justifiable, *a legitimate reason for absence*. **3** (of a child) born of parents who are married to each other. **legitimately** *adverb*, **legitimacy** *noun*

legitimise (lĕ-jit-ĭ-myz) *verb* (also **-ize**) to make legitimate.

legless *adjective* **1** without legs. **2** (*informal*) drunk.

legume (**leg**-yoom) *noun* **1** a leguminous plant. **2** a fruit or pod of this, especially when edible.

leguminous (lĕ-**gew**-mĭ-nŭs) *adjective* of the family of plants that bear their seeds in pods, e.g. peas and beans.

lei (*pr.* lay) *noun* (in Polynesian countries) a garland of flowers worn round the neck. [Hawaiian]

Leibniz (**lyb**-nits), Gottfried Wilhelm (1646–1716), German philosopher and mathematician.

Leichhardt (**lyk**-hart), Friedrich Wilhelm Ludwig (1813–48), German-born explorer who disappeared during his attempt to cross the Australian continent from east to west in 1848.

leisure (le*zh*-er) *noun* time that is free from work, time in which one can do as one chooses. ☐ **at leisure** not occupied; in an unhurried way. **at one's leisure** when one has time.

leisured *adjective* having plenty of leisure.

leisurely (le*zh*-er-lee) *adjective* & *adverb* without hurry. **leisureliness** *noun*

leitmotiv (**lyt**-moh-teef) *noun* (also **leitmotif**) a theme associated with a particular person or idea etc. throughout a musical composition. [German]

lemming *noun* a small mouselike rodent of Arctic regions, one species of which migrates in large numbers and is said to run into the sea and drown.

lemon *noun* **1** an oval fruit with acid juice. **2** the tree that bears it. **3** its pale yellow colour. **4** (*informal*) something disappointing or unsuccessful. ☐ **lemon curd** or **cheese** a thick

conserve made with lemons, butter, eggs, and sugar. **lemony** *adjective*

lemonade *noun* a drink made from lemon juice; an artificial substitute for this.

lemur (**lee**-mer) *noun* a monkey-like animal of Madagascar.

lend *verb* (**lent**, **lending**) **1** to give or allow the use of (a thing) temporarily on the understanding that it or its equivalent will be returned. **2** to provide (money) temporarily in return for payment of interest. **3** to contribute as a temporary help or effect etc., *lend dignity to the occasion*. ☐ **lend a hand** to help. **lend an ear** to listen. **lend itself to** to be suitable for. **lender** *noun*

Lend-Lease *noun* an arrangement made in 1941 whereby the USA supplied equipment to Britain and her allies, originally as a loan in return for the use of British-owned military bases.

length *noun* **1** measurement or extent from end to end, especially along a thing's greatest dimension. **2** the amount of time occupied by something, *the length of our holiday*. **3** the distance a thing extends used as a unit of measurement; the length of a horse or boat etc. as a measure of the lead in a race. **4** the degree of thoroughness in an action, *went to great lengths*. **5** a piece of cloth or other material from a larger piece, *a length of wire*. ☐ **at length** after a long time; taking a long time; in detail.

lengthen *verb* to make or become longer.

lengthways *adverb* in the direction of the length of something. **lengthwise** *adverb* & *adjective*

lengthy *adjective* very long; long and boring. **lengthily** *adverb*, **lengthiness** *noun*

lenient (**lee**-nee-ĕnt) *adjective* merciful, not severe (especially in awarding punishment), mild. **leniently** *adverb*, **lenience** *noun* [from Latin *lenis* = gentle]

Lenin (real name Vladimir Ilyich Ulyanov, 1870–1924), Russian revolutionary statesman, Premier and virtual dictator of the Communist State that he established after the fall of the Tsar.

Leningrad the name by which St Petersburg was known from 1924–91.

lens *noun* (*plural* **lenses**) **1** a piece of glass or glasslike substance with one or both sides curved, for use in optical instruments. **2** a combination of lenses used in photography etc. **3** the transparent part of the eye, behind the pupil.

Lent *noun* the period from Ash Wednesday to Easter Eve, of which the 40 weekdays are observed as a time of fasting and penitence. **Lenten** *adjective*

lent *see* lend.

lentil *noun* **1** a kind of bean plant. **2** its edible seed.

lento *adverb* (in music) slowly. [Italian]

Leo (**lee**-oh) *noun* a sign of the zodiac, the Lion, which the sun enters about 21 July. **Leonian** *adjective* & *noun*

Leonardo da Vinci (lee-ŏ-**nar**-doh dah **vin**-chee) (1452–1519), Italian painter and designer, a man of versatile talents. His most famous paintings include the *Mona Lisa* and the *Last Supper* fresco.

leonine (**lee**-ŏ-nyn) *adjective* of or like a lion.

leopard (**lep**-erd) *noun* a large African and South Asian flesh-eating animal of the cat family (also called a *panther*), having a yellowish coat with dark spots or a black coat. **leopardess** *feminine noun*

leotard (**lee**-ŏ-tard) *noun* a close-fitting one-piece garment worn by gymnasts, dancers, etc.

leper *noun* a person with leprosy.

lepidopterous (lep-ĭ-**dop**-tĕ-rŭs) *adjective* of the group of insects that includes moths and butterflies. [from Greek *lepidos* = of a scale, + *pteron* = wing]

leprechaun (**lep**-rĕ-kawn) *noun* (in Irish folklore) an elf resembling a little old man. [from Irish, = a small body]

leprosy *noun* an infectious disease affecting skin and nerves, resulting in mutilations and deformities. Also called *Hansen's disease*. **leprous** *adjective*

lerp *noun* a sweet waxy secretion of **lerp insect** larvae on the leaves of certain eucalypts. [from Wemba-wemba]

lesbian *noun* a homosexual woman. –**lesbian** *adjective* of lesbians; of homosexuality in women. **lesbianism** *noun* [named after Lesbos, because the ancient Greek poetess Sappho, who wrote love poems to women, lived there]

Lesbos (**lez**-boss) the largest of the Greek islands, off the western coast of Turkey.

lèse-majesté (layz-**ma**-*zh*ess-tay) *noun* **1** an insult to a sovereign or ruler. **2** (*humorous*) presumptuous behaviour. [French]

lesion (**lee**-*zh*ŏn) *noun* a harmful change in the tissue of an organ of the body, caused by injury or disease. [from Latin *laesio* = injury]

Lesotho (lĕ-**soo**-too) an independent kingdom surrounded by the Republic of South Africa.

less *adjective* **1** not so much of, a smaller quantity of, *eat less meat*. **2** smaller in amount or degree etc., *of less importance*. –**less** *adverb* to a smaller extent. –**less** *noun* a smaller amount or quantity etc., *will not take less*. –**less** *preposition* minus, deducting, *a year less three days*; *was paid $400, less tax*.

> **Usage** The word *less* is used of things that are measured by amount (e.g. in *eat less butter*; *use less fuel*). Its use of things measured by number is regarded as incorrect (e.g. in *we need less workers*; correct usage is *fewer workers*).

lessee (less-**ee**) *noun* a person who holds a property by lease.

lessen *verb* to make or become less.

lesser *adjective* not so great as the other.

lesson *noun* **1** a thing to be learnt by a pupil. **2** an amount of teaching given at one time; *give lessons in a subject*, give systematic instruction in it. **3** an example or experience by which one can learn, *let this be a lesson to you!* **4** a passage from the Bible read aloud during a church service.

lessor (less-**or**) *noun* a person who lets a property on lease.

lest *conjunction* **1** in order that not, to avoid the risk that, *lest we forget*. **2** that, *were afraid lest we should be late*.

let¹ *noun* **1** stoppage, *without let or hindrance*. **2** (in tennis etc.) an obstruction of the ball in certain ways, requiring the ball to be served again.

let² *verb* (**let**, **letting**) **1** to allow to, not to prevent or forbid, *let me see it*. **2** to cause to, *let us know what happens*. **3** to cause to come, go, or pass, *let the cat in*; *let the rope down*; *a piece was let into it*, was inserted, especially into the surface. **4** to allow the use of (rooms or land) for payment; *house to let*, available in this way. **5** used as an auxiliary verb in requests or commands (*let's try*; *let there be light*), assumptions (*let x equal 5*), and challenges (*let him do his worst*). –**let** *noun* the letting of property etc., *a long let*. □ **let alone** to refrain from interfering with or doing; apart from, far less or more, *we can't afford one, let alone three*; *I'm too tired to walk, let alone run*. **let be** to refrain from interfering with or doing. **let down** to let out air from (a balloon or tyre etc.); to fail to support or satisfy, to disappoint; to lengthen (a garment) by adjusting the hem; *let one's hair down*, to abandon conventional restraint in one's behaviour. **let-down** *noun* a disappointment. **let fly** to shoot or send out violently; to hurl strong abuse. **let go** to set at liberty; to stop holding; to cease discussion of, to ignore; *let oneself go*, to behave in an unrestrained way, to cease to take trouble. **let in for** to involve in (loss or difficulty). **let loose** to release. **let off** to fire (a gun); to cause (a bomb) to explode; to ignite (a firework); to excuse from doing (duties etc.); to give little or no punishment to. **let off steam** to allow it to escape; to do something that relieves one's pent-up energy or feelings. **let on** (*informal*) to reveal a secret. **let out** to release from restraint or obligation; to make (a garment) looser by adjusting the seams; to let (rooms etc.) to tenants. **let-out** *noun* a way of escaping an obligation. **let up** (*informal*) to become less intense; to relax one's efforts. **let-up** *noun* a reduction in intensity; relaxation of effort.

-let *suffix* small; young.

lethal (lee-thǎl) *adjective* causing or able to cause death. **lethally** *adverb*

lethargy (leth-er-jee) *noun* extreme lack of energy or vitality. **lethargic** (lěth-**ar**-jik) *adjective*, **lethargically** *adverb*

Lethe (lee-thee) (*Gk. myth.*) one of the rivers of the Underworld, whose water when drunk made the souls of the dead forget their life on earth.

Leto (lee-toh) (*Gk. myth.*) the mother (by Zeus) of Artemis and Apollo.

let's (*informal*) = let us.

letter *noun* 1 a symbol representing a sound used in speech. 2 a written message addressed to one or more persons, usually sent by post. −**letter** *verb* to inscribe letters on; to draw or inscribe letters. □ **letter of credit** a letter from a bank authorising the bearer to draw money from another bank. **letter of the law** its exact requirements (as opposed to its spirit or true purpose). **to the letter** paying strict attention to every detail. [from Latin *littera* = letter of the alphabet]

letterbox *noun* 1 a box into which letters are delivered. 2 a box where letters may be posted for delivery, a postbox. −**letterbox** *verb* make unsolicited deliveries of advertising material etc. to a letterbox.

letterhead *noun* a printed heading on stationery; stationery with this.

letterpress *noun* the printed words in an illustrated book.

lettuce *noun* a garden plant with broad crisp leaves used in salads.

leucocyte (lew-kŏ-syt) *noun* a white blood cell. [from Greek *leukos* = white, + *kutos* = vessel]

leucoplast *noun* colourless organelle found in plant cells, used for the storage of starch or oil.

leukaemia (lew-**kee**-mee-ǎ) *noun* a disease in which the white blood cells multiply uncontrollably in the body tissues and usually in the blood. [from Greek *leukos* = white, + *haima* = blood]

Levant (lě-**vant**) *noun* the countries and islands in the eastern part of the Mediterranean Sea. **Levantine** (lev-ǎn-tyn) *adjective & noun*

levee (lev-ee) *noun* an embankment built up naturally along a river, or made artificially as a protection against floods.

level *noun* 1 an imaginary line or plane joining points of equal height. 2 a measured height or value etc., position on a scale, *the level of alcohol in the blood*. 3 relative position in rank or class or authority, *decisions at Cabinet level*. 4 a more or less flat surface or layer or area. 5 an instrument for testing a horizontal line. −**level** *adjective* 1 horizontal. 2 (of ground) flat, without hills or hollows. 3 on a level with; at the same height, rank, or position on a scale. 4 steady, uniform, (of a voice) not changing in tone. −**level** *verb* (**levelled**, **levelling**) 1 to make or become level, even, or uniform; *level up* or *down*, to bring up or down to a standard; *level out*, to become level. 2 to knock down (buildings) to the ground. 3 to aim (a gun or missile). 4 to direct (an accusation or criticism) at a person.
□ **do one's level best** (*informal*) to make all possible efforts. **level crossing** a place where a road and a railway (or two railways) cross each other at the same level. **level-headed** *adjective* mentally well-balanced, sensible. **on the level** (*informal*) with no dishonesty or deception. **leveller** *noun* [from Latin *libella* = a small balance]

lever (lee-ver) *noun* 1 a bar or other device pivoted on a fixed point (the *fulcrum*) in order to lift something or force something open. 2 a projecting handle used in the same way to operate or control machinery etc. −**lever** *verb* to use a lever; to lift or move by means of this. [from Latin *levare* = raise]

leverage *noun* **1** the action or power of a lever. **2** power, influence.

leveret (**lev**-ĕ-rĕt) *noun* a young hare.

leviathan (lĕ-**vy**-ă-thăn) *noun* something of enormous size and power. [named after a sea monster in the Bible]

levitate *verb* to rise or cause to rise and float in the air in defiance of gravity. **levitation** *noun*

Leviticus (lĕ-**vit**-i-kŭs) the third book of the Old Testament, containing details of laws and ritual.

levity (**lev**-ĭ-tee) *noun* a humorous attitude, especially towards matters that should be treated with respect. [from Latin *levis* = lightweight]

levy *verb* (**levied, levying**) **1** to impose or collect (a payment etc.) by authority or by force. **2** to enrol (troops etc.). **–levy** *noun* **1** levying. **2** the payment etc. levied.

lewd *adjective* **1** indecent, treating sexual matters in a vulgar way. **2** lascivious. **lewdly** *adverb*, **lewdness** *noun*

Lewis, Clive Staples (1898–1963), English literary scholar, whose writings include Christian and moral themes, science fiction, and children's stories, including the 'Narnia' chronicles.

lexical *adjective* **1** of the words of a language. **2** of a lexicon or dictionary.

lexicography (lek-sĭ-**kog**-ră-fee) *noun* the process of compiling a dictionary. **lexicographer** *noun*, **lexicographical** *adjective* [from Greek *lexis* = word, + *-graphy*]

lexicon *noun* **1** a dictionary of certain languages, especially Greek and Hebrew. **2** the vocabulary of a person, language, area of knowledge, etc.

ley (*pr.* lay) *noun* (*plural* **leys**) land that is temporarily sown with grass.

Leyden jar (**lay**-dĕn) *noun* a kind of electrical condenser with a glass jar as a dielectric between sheets of tin foil, invented in 1745 at Leyden (now Leiden) in Holland.

LF *abbreviation* low frequency.

Lhasa (**lah**-să) the capital of Tibet.

liability *noun* **1** being liable. **2** (*informal*) a handicap, a disadvantage. **liabilities** *plural noun* debts, obligations.

liable (**ly**-ă-bŭl) *adjective* **1** held responsible by law; legally obliged to pay a tax or penalty etc. **2** exposed or open (to something undesirable), *he is liable to migraines*. **3** apt or likely (to do something), *the bridge is liable to collapse*.

Usage The use of *liable* in sense 3, though common, is considered incorrect by some people.

---

liaise (lee-**ayz**) *verb* (*informal*) to act as a liaison or go-between.

liaison (lee-**ay**-zŏn) *noun* **1** communication and cooperation between units of an organisation. **2** a person who acts as a link or go-between. **3** pronouncing a normally silent consonant at the end of a word when the next word begins with a vowel sound. [from French *lier* = bind]

liana (lee-**ah**-nă) *noun* a climbing and twining plant of tropical forests.

liar *noun* a person who tells lies.

lib *noun* (*informal*) liberation, *women's lib*.

Lib. *abbreviation* Liberal.

libel (**ly**-bĕl) *noun* **1** a published false statement that damages a person's reputation. **2** the act of publishing it, *was charged with libel*. **3** (*informal*) a statement or anything that brings discredit on a person or thing, *the portrait is a libel on him*. **–libel** *verb* (**libelled, libelling**) to utter or publish a libel against. **libellous** *adjective* [from Latin *libellus* = little book]

liberal *adjective* **1** giving generously. **2** ample, given in large amounts. **3** not strict or literal, *a liberal interpretation of the rules*. **4** (of education) broadening the mind in a general way, not only training it in technical subjects. **5** tolerant, open-minded, especially in religion and politics. **6** Liberal of the Liberal Party. **–Liberal** *noun* a member of the Liberal Party, an Australian political party favouring private enterprise (and opposed to socialism). □ **Liberal Democrat** a member of the Liberal Democratic Party in the UK. **Liberalism** *noun*, **liberally** *adverb*, **liberality** (lib-ĕ-**ral**-ĭ-tee) *noun* [from Latin *liber* = free]

liberalise *verb* (also **-ize**) to make less strict. **liberalisation** *noun*

liberate *verb* to set free, especially from control by an authority that is considered to be oppressive. **liberation** *noun*, **liberator** *noun* [same origin as *liberty*]

Liberia (ly-**beer**-ree-ă) a republic on the coast of West Africa. **Liberian** *adjective* & *noun*

libertarian (lib-er-**tair**-ree-ăn) *noun* a person who favours absolute liberty of thought and action.

libertine (**lib**-er-teen) *noun* a person who lives an irresponsible and immoral life.

liberty *noun* **1** freedom from captivity, slavery, imprisonment, or despotic control by others. **2** the right or power to do as one chooses. **3** a right or privilege granted by authority. **4** the setting aside of convention, improper familiarity; *take the liberty of doing* or *to do something*, venture to do it. □ **at liberty** (of a person) not imprisoned, free; allowed, *you are at liberty to leave*; not occupied or engaged. **Liberty Hall** a place where one may do as one likes. **Statue of Liberty** a statue on an island at the entrance to New York harbour, a symbol of welcome to immigrants. **take liberties** to behave too familiarly towards a person; to interpret facts etc. too freely. [from Latin *liber* = free]

libidinous (lǐ-**bid**-ǐ-nǔs) *adjective* lustful.

libido (lǐ-**bee**-doh) *noun* (*plural* **libidos**) emotional energy or urge, especially that associated with sexual desire. **libidinal** *adjective* [Latin, = lust]

Libra (**lib**-rǎ) *noun* a sign of the zodiac, the Scales, which the sun enters about 22 September. **Libran** *adjective* & *noun*

librarian *noun* a person in charge of or assisting in a library. **librarianship** *noun*

library (**ly**-brǎ-ree) *noun* **1** a collection of books for reading or borrowing. **2** a room or building where these are kept. **3** a similar collection of recordings, films, computer routines, etc. **4** a series of books issued in similar bindings as a set. [from Latin *libri* = books]

libretto (lǐ-**bret**-oh) *noun* (*plural* **librettos** *or* **libretti**) the words of an opera or other long musical work. **librettist** *noun* [Italian, = little book]

Libreville (**leeb**-rě-vil) the capital of Gabon.

Libya a republic in North Africa, bordering on the Mediterranean Sea. **Libyan** *adjective* & *noun*

lice *see* **louse**.

licence *noun* (*Amer.* **license**) **1** a permit from the government or other authority to own or do something or to carry on a certain trade. **2** permission. **3** disregard of rules or customs etc., lack of due restraint in behaviour. **4** a writer's or artist's exaggeration, or disregard of rules etc., for the sake of effect, *poetic licence*. [from Latin *licere* = be allowed]

license *verb* to grant a licence to or for, to authorise; *licensed restaurant*, authorised to sell alcoholic drinks.

licensee *noun* a person who holds a licence, especially to sell alcoholic drinks.

licentiate (ly-**sen**-shee-ǎt) *noun* one who holds a certificate showing that he or she is competent to practise a certain profession.

licentious (ly-**sen**-shǔs) *adjective* disregarding the rules of conduct, especially in sexual matters. **licentiousness** *noun*

lichee *noun* = **lychee**.

lichen (**ly**-kěn) *noun* a dry-looking plant that grows on rocks, tree trunks, etc., usually green or yellow or grey.

lich-gate *noun* (also **lych-gate**) a roofed gateway to a churchyard.

lick *verb* **1** to pass the tongue over; to take up or make clean by doing this. **2** (of waves or flames) to move like a tongue, to touch lightly. **3** (*informal*) to defeat; to thrash. –**lick** *noun* **1** an act of licking with the tongue. **2** a blow with a stick etc. **3** a slight application (of paint etc.). **4** (*informal*) a fast pace, *going at quite a lick*. □ **lick into shape** to make presentable or efficient. **lick one's wounds** to remain in retirement trying to recover after a defeat.

licking *noun* (*informal*) **1** a defeat. **2** a thrashing.

lid *noun* **1** a hinged or removable cover for a box or pot etc. **2** an eyelid. □ **put the lid on** (*informal*) to be the culmination of; to put a stop to. **lidded** *adjective*

lie¹ *noun* **1** an intentionally false statement, *tell a lie*. **2** a thing that deceives. –**lie** *verb* (**lied**, **lying**) **1** to tell a lie or lies; *lied his way out of the trouble*, got himself out of it by lying. **2** to be deceptive. □ **give the lie to** to show that something is untrue. **lie detector** an instrument that can detect changes in the pulse rate or respiration etc. brought on by the tension caused by telling lies.

lie² *verb* (**lay**, **lain**, **lying**) **1** to have or put one's body in a flat or resting position on a more or less horizontal surface. **2** (of a thing) to be at rest on a surface. **3** to be or be kept or remain in a specified state, *the road lies open*; *machinery lay idle*; *lie in ambush*. **4** to be situated, *the island lies near the coast*. **5** to exist or be found, *the remedy lies in education*. **6** (in Law) to be admissible or able to be upheld, *an action* or *appeal will not lie*. –**lie** *noun* the way or position in which something lies.

☐ **lie down** to have a brief rest in or on a bed etc. **lie-down** *noun* such a rest. **lie down under** to accept (an insult etc.) without protest. **lie in** (*informal*) to lie idly in bed late in the morning. **lie-in** *noun* such lying. **lie in state** (of a dead eminent person) to be laid in a public place of honour before burial or cremation. **lie low** to conceal oneself or one's intentions. **take it lying down** to accept an insult etc. without protest.

Usage *Lie* is often confused with the verb *lay*. The difference is that *lay* always has an object, while *lie* does not. This can be remembered simply by the phrases *you lay something* but *you lie somewhere*. Correct uses of *lie* are: *she lies down, she is lying down, she lay down, she has lain down*. Correct uses of *lay* are: *she lays the baby in her cot, she is laying the baby in her cot, she laid the baby in her cot, she has laid the baby in her cot*.

Liechtenstein (**lik**-těn-styn) a small independent principality between Austria and Switzerland. **Liechtensteiner** *noun*

lied (*pr.* leed) *noun* (*plural* **lieder**) a German song, especially of the Romantic period, and usually for solo voice and piano.

lief (*pr.* leef) *adverb* (*old use*) gladly, willingly, *I had* or *would as lief stay as go*.

liege (*pr.* leej) *noun* (also **liege lord**) one's feudal superior; one's king.

lien (*pr.* leen) *noun* (in law) the right to hold another person's property until a debt on it is paid.

lieu (*pr.* lew) *noun* **in lieu** instead, in place, *accepted a cheque in lieu of cash*. [French, = place]

lieutenant (lef-**ten**-ănt) *noun* **1** an army officer next below a captain. **2** a navy officer next below a lieutenant commander. **3** an officer ranking just below one specified, *lieutenant colonel, lieutenant commander*. **4** a deputy, a chief assistant, a substitute. [from French *lieu* = place, + *tenant* = holding]

life *noun* (*plural* **lives**) **1** being alive, the ability to function and grow that distinguishes animals and plants (before their death) from rocks and synthetic substances. **2** living things, *plant life; is there life on Mars?* **3** a living form or model, *portrait is drawn from life*. **4** liveliness, interest, *full of life*. **5** the period for which a person or organism is or has been or will be alive; *life imprisonment* or *a life sentence*, a sentence of imprisonment

for the rest of one's life. **6** (*informal*) a life sentence. **7** a person's or people's activities or fortunes or manner of existence, *in private life; school life*. **8** the business, pleasures, and social activities of the world, *we do see life!* **9** a biography. **10** a period during which something exists or continues to function, *the battery has a life of two years*.
☐ **for one's life** or **for dear life** in order to escape death or as if to do this. **life cycle** the series of forms into which a living thing changes until the first form appears again. **life expectancy** the average length of time that a person of a specified age may be expected to live. **life jacket** a jacket of buoyant or inflatable material to support a person's body in the water. **life sciences** biology and related subjects. **life-size, life-sized** *adjectives* of the same size as the person or thing represented. **life-support** *adjective* (of equipment) providing and maintaining suitable conditions for life in unnatural circumstances, e.g. severe illness, space travel, etc. **not on your life** (*informal*) most certainly not. **this life** life on earth (as opposed to an existence after death). **to the life** exactly like the original.

lifebelt *noun* a belt of buoyant or inflatable material to support a person's body in the water.

lifeblood *noun* **1** a person's or animal's blood, necessary to life. **2** an influence that gives vitality to something.

lifeboat *noun* **1** a small boat carried on a ship for use if the ship has to be abandoned at sea. **2** a boat specially constructed for going to the help of people in danger at sea along a coast.

lifebuoy *noun* a device to keep a person afloat.

lifeguard *noun* an expert swimmer employed to rescue swimmers who are in danger of drowning.

lifeless *adjective* **1** without life, dead or never having had life. **2** unconscious. **3** lacking vitality. **lifelessly** *adverb*, **lifelessness** *noun*

lifelike *adjective* exactly like a real person or thing.

lifeline *noun* **1** a rope etc. used in rescuing people, e.g. one attached to a lifebelt. **2** a diver's signalling line. **3** a sole means of communication or transport or help. **4** a thing which provides a means of escape from a difficult situation.

lifelong *adjective* continued all one's life.

lifesaver *noun* **1** (*Austral.*) an expert swimmer who supervises surfing beaches etc. especially to rescue swimmers from drowning. **2** a person or thing that is of great help; a boon.

lifestyle *noun* a person's way of life.

lifetime *noun* the duration of a person's life or of a thing's existence; *the chance of a lifetime*, the best chance one will ever get.

lift *verb* **1** to raise to a higher level or position; *lift one's eyes*, look up. **2** to take up from the ground or from its resting place. **3** to dig up (e.g. potatoes etc. at harvest or plants for storing). **4** (*informal*) to steal; to copy. **5** to go up, to rise; (of fog etc.) to disperse. **6** to remove or abolish (restrictions). –**lift** *noun* **1** lifting; being lifted. **2** a ride as a passenger without payment. **3** an apparatus for transporting people or goods from one floor of a building to another. **4** a ski lift or chairlift. **5** the upward pressure that air exerts on an aircraft in flight. **6** a feeling of elation, *the praise gave me a lift*. □ **lift-off** *noun* the vertical take-off of a rocket or spacecraft. **lift-out** *noun* a loose or detachable section of a magazine, newspaper, etc.

ligament *noun* the tough flexible tissue that holds bones together or keeps organs in place in the body. [from Latin *ligare* = bind]

ligature (**lig**-ă-cher) *noun* **1** a thing used in tying, especially in surgical operations. **2** a tie in music. **3** joined printed letters such as œ. –**ligature** *verb* to tie with a ligature. [from Latin *ligare* = bind]

light¹ *noun* **1** the agent that stimulates the sense of sight, a kind of radiation. **2** the presence, amount, or effect of this. **3** a source of light, e.g. a lamp, *leave the light on*. **4** a flame or spark; something used to produce this. **5** brightness; the bright parts of a picture etc. **6** enlightenment; *light dawned on him*, he began to understand. **7** the aspect of something, the way it appears to the mind, *sees the matter in a different light*. **8** a window or opening to admit light. –**light** *adjective* **1** full of light, not in darkness. **2** pale, *light blue*. –**light** *verb* (**lit**, **lighted** (¶ see note at end of entry) **1** to set burning; to begin to burn. **2** to cause to give out light. **3** to provide with light; to guide with a light. **4** to brighten. **lights** *plural noun* **1** traffic lights (*see* **traffic**). **2** a person's mental attitude, *did his best according to his lights*. □ **bring or come to light** to reveal or be revealed, to make or become known. **in the light of** taking into account. **light bulb** or **globe** a glass globe containing an inert gas and a metal filament, providing light when an electric current is

passed through it. **light meter** an exposure meter. **light pen** a pen-like photoelectric device for communicating with a computer by movement, e.g. when passed over a bar code (*see* **bar¹**). **light up** to put lights on at dusk; to make or become bright with light, colour, or animation; to begin to smoke a pipe or cigarette. **light year** the distance light travels in one year (about 6 million million miles or 9.5 million million kilometres).

Usage Preferred use is *he lit the lamps*, *the lamps were lit* (rather than *lighted* in either phrase), but *holding a lighted torch* (not *a lit torch*).

---

light² *adjective* **1** having little weight, not heavy; easy to lift, carry, or move. **2** of less than average weight, amount, or force. **3** (of work) needing little physical effort. **4** not intense; *a light sleeper*, one easily woken. **5** not dense, *light mist*. **6** (of food) easy to digest. **7** moving easily and quickly. **8** cheerful, free from worry, *with a light heart*. **9** not profound or serious, intended as entertainment, *light music*. –**light** *adverb* lightly, with little load, *we travel light*. □ **light-fingered** *adjective* apt to steal. **light-headed** *adjective* feeling slightly faint, dizzy; delirious. **light-hearted** *adjective* cheerful, without cares; too casual, not treating a thing seriously. **light industry** industry producing small or light articles. **make light of** to treat as unimportant, *he made light of his injuries*. **lightly** *adverb*, **lightness** *noun*

light³ *verb* (**lit** *or* **lighted** (¶ preferred use is **lit**), **lighting**) to find accidentally, *we lit on this book*.

lighten¹ *verb* **1** to shed light on. **2** to make or become brighter. **3** to produce lightning.

lighten² *verb* **1** to make or become lighter in weight. **2** to relieve or be relieved of care or worry. **3** to reduce (a penalty).

lighter¹ *noun* a device for lighting cigarettes.

lighter² *noun* a flat-bottomed boat used for loading and unloading ships that are not brought to a wharf or into a harbour, and for transporting goods in a harbour.

lighthouse *noun* a tower or other structure containing a beacon light to warn or guide ships.

lighting *noun* equipment for providing light to a room or building or street etc.; the light itself.

lightning *noun* a flash of bright light produced by natural electricity, between clouds or a cloud and the ground. –**lightning** *adjective* very quick, *with lightning speed*; *a lightning strike*, a labour strike begun without warning. ☐ **lightning conductor** a metal rod or wire fixed to an exposed part of a building etc., to divert lightning into the earth.

lights *plural noun* the lungs of sheep, pigs, etc., used as food for animals.

lightship *noun* a moored or anchored ship with a beacon light, serving the same purpose as a lighthouse.

lightsome *adjective* **1** agile. **2** merry.

lightweight *noun* **1** a person of less than average weight. **2** a boxing weight between welterweight and featherweight, in amateur boxing 57–60 kg. **3** a person of little influence. –**lightweight** *adjective* not having great weight or influence.

ligneous (**lig**-nee-ŭs) *adjective* **1** like wood. **2** (of plants) woody. [from Latin *lignum* = wood]

lignin (**lig**-nĭn) *noun* the material that stiffens the cell walls of woody tissue in plants.

lignite (**lig**-nyt) *noun* a brown coal of woody texture.

lignum (**lig**-nŭm) *noun* any of several Australian plants that form dense thickets. ☐ **lignum vitae** (**vee**-ty) a tall rainforest tree producing a durable timber.

like¹ *adjective* **1** having some or all the qualities or appearance etc. of, similar; *what is he like?*, what sort of person is he? **2** characteristic of, *it was like him to do that*. **3** in a suitable state or the right mood for something, *it looks like rain*; *we felt like a walk*. **4** such as, for example, *in subjects like music*. –**like** *preposition* in the manner of, to the same degree as, *he swims like a fish*. –**like** *conjunction* (*informal*) **1** in the same manner as, to the same degree as, *do it like I do*. **2** as if, *she doesn't act like she belongs here*. –**like** *adverb* (*informal*) likely, *as like as not they'll refuse*. –**like** *noun* one that is like another, a similar thing, *shall not see his like again*; *the likes of you*, people like you. ☐ **and the like** and similar things. **like-minded** *adjective* having similar tastes or opinions.

like² *verb* **1** to find pleasant or satisfactory. **2** to wish for, *should like to think it over*. **likes** *plural noun* the things one likes or prefers.

likeable *adjective* pleasant, easy for a person to like.

likelihood *noun* being likely, probability.

likely *adjective* (**likelier**, **likeliest**) **1** such as may reasonably be expected to occur or be true etc., *he is likely to be late*. **2** seeming to be suitable, *the likeliest place*. **3** showing promise of being successful, *a likely lad*. –**likely** *adverb* probably, *you are quite* or *very* or *most* or *more likely right*. **likeliness** *noun*

liken *verb* to point out the resemblance of (one thing to another), *he likened the heart to a pump*.

likeness *noun* **1** being like, a resemblance. **2** a copy, portrait, or picture.

likewise *adverb* **1** moreover, also. **2** similarly, *do likewise*.

liking *noun* **1** what one likes, one's taste, *is it to your liking?* **2** one's feeling that one likes something, *a liking for it*.

lilac *noun* **1** a shrub with fragrant purplish or white flowers. **2** pale purple. –**lilac** *adjective* of lilac colour.

lilliputian (lilĭ-**pew**-shăn) *adjective* very small. –**lilliputian** *noun* a very small person or thing. [named after the inhabitants of Lilliput, a country in Swift's *Gulliver's Travels*, who were only six inches (15 cm) tall]

lilly-pilly *noun* **1** a small eastern Australian tree with dark green leaves and purplish to white edible berries. **2** the fruit of this tree.

Lilongwe (lee-**long**-way) the capital of Malawi.

lilt *noun* a light pleasant rhythm; a song or tune having this.

lilting *adjective* having a light pleasant rhythm.

lily *noun* **1** a plant growing from a bulb, with large white or coloured flowers. **2** a plant of this family. ☐ **lily-livered** *adjective* cowardly. **lily of the valley** a spring flower with small fragrant white bell-shaped flowers. **lily-white** *adjective* as white as a lily.

Lima (**lee**-mǎ) the capital of Peru.

lima bean *noun* a bean plant with large flat white edible seeds; the seed of this plant.

limb *noun* **1** a projecting part of an animal body, used in movement or in grasping things. **2** a main branch of a tree. **3** an arm of a cross. **4** a mischievous child. ☐ **out on a limb** isolated, stranded; at a disadvantage because separated from others.

limber *adjective* flexible, supple, lithe. –**limber** *verb* to make limber. ☐ **limber up** to exercise in preparation for athletic activity.

Limbo (formerly in some Christian beliefs) the supposed abode of souls not admitted to heaven (e.g. because they were not baptised) but not condemned to punishment. **–limbo** *noun* (*plural* **limbos**) an intermediate state or condition (e.g. of a plan not yet accepted but not rejected), a condition of being neglected and forgotten.

limbo *noun* (*plural* **limbos**) a West Indian dance in which the dancer bends back and passes repeatedly under a gradually lowered horizontal bar.

lime¹ *noun* a white substance (calcium oxide) used in making cement and mortar and as a fertiliser. **–lime** *verb* to treat with lime.

lime² *noun* **1** a round yellowish-green fruit like a lemon but smaller and more acid. **2** (also **lime-green**) its colour.

lime³ *noun* (in full **lime tree**) a tree with smooth heart-shaped leaves and fragrant yellow flowers, a linden.

limelight *noun* great publicity. [named after the brilliant light, obtained by heating lime, formerly used to illuminate the stages of theatres]

limerick *noun* a type of humorous poem with five lines. [named after *Limerick*, a town in Ireland]

limestone *noun* a kind of rock from which lime is obtained by heating.

limey *noun* (*plural* **limeys**) (*informal*) a British person. [named after *lime juice*, which was formerly issued to British sailors as a drink to prevent scurvy]

limit *noun* **1** the point, line, or level beyond which something does not continue. **2** the greatest amount allowed, *the speed limit*. **3** (*informal*) something that is as much as or more than one can tolerate, *she really is the limit!* **4** (in mathematics) a quantity that a function or the sum of a series can be made to approach as closely as desired. **–limit** *verb* to serve as a limit to; to set a limit to, to keep within limits. [from Latin *limes* = boundary]

limitation *noun* **1** limiting; being limited. **2** a lack of ability; *knows his limitations*, knows what he cannot achieve.

limited *adjective* **1** confined within limits. **2** few, scanty. ☐ **limited liability company** (also **limited company**) a business company whose members are liable only to a limited degree for its debts.

limo *noun* (*plural* **limos**) (*informal*) a limousine.

limousine (lim-ŏ-**zeen**) *noun* a large luxurious car.

limp¹ *verb* to walk or proceed lamely. **–limp** *noun* a limping walk.

limp² *adjective* **1** not stiff or firm. **2** lacking strength or energy, wilting. **limply** *adverb*, **limpness** *noun*

limpet *noun* a small shellfish that sticks tightly to rocks.

limpid *adjective* (of liquids etc.) clear, transparent. **limpidity** *noun*

linchpin *noun* **1** a pin passed through the end of an axle to keep the wheel in position. **2** a person or thing that is vital to an organisation or plan etc.

Lincoln, Abraham (1809–65), 16th President of the USA (1860–5), noted for his policy of emancipation of slaves.

linctus *noun* a soothing syrupy cough mixture. [from Latin *linctum* = licked]

linden *noun* a lime tree.

Lindisfarne (**lin**-dĭs-farn) a small island (also called Holy Island) off the coast of Northumberland, from the 7th century a missionary centre of the Celtic Church.

line¹ *noun* **1** a straight or curved continuous extent of length without breadth. **2** a long narrow mark on a surface. **3** something resembling this, a band of colour, a wrinkle or crease in the skin; **the Line** the equator. **4** an outline, the shape to which something is designed; *a proposal along these lines*, with these general features. **5** a limit, a boundary. **6** each of a set of military fieldworks or boundaries of an encampment. **7** a row of people or things; a row of words on a page or in a poem; *an actor's lines*, the words of his part in a play. **8** a brief letter, *drop me a line*. **9** a series of ships, buses, or aircraft etc. regularly travelling between certain places; the company running these. **10** a connected series; several generations of a family, *a line of kings*. **11** a direction, course, or track, *line of march*. **12** a single pair of rails in a railway; a branch of a railway system, *the main line north*. **13** a course of procedure, thought, or conduct, *in the line of duty*; *don't take that line with me*. **14** a department of activity; a type of business; *not my line*, not among my interests or skills. **15** a piece of cord used for a particular purpose, *fishing with rod and line*. **16** a wire or cable used to connect electricity or telephones; connection by this, *the line is bad*. **–line** *verb* **1** to mark with lines. **2** to arrange in a line, *line them up*. ☐ **come** or **bring into line** to become or cause to become a straight line or row; to conform or cause to conform with others. **get a line on** (*informal*) to discover information about. **in line for** likely to get (e.g. promotion). **in line with** in accordance with. **line-ball** *noun* a ball striking the boundary line in tennis; (*Austral.*) a borderline case, an indecisive event. **line drawing** a drawing done with pen or pencil or a pointed instrument, chiefly in lines and solid masses. **line graph** a graph in which the points are joined with straight lines. **line of force** (in a field of force) a line whose direction at any point is the direction of the magnetic field or electric field there. **line-out** *noun* parallel lines of opposing forwards formed in rugby when the ball is thrown in. **line segment** a part of a straight line, usually denoted by the pair of letters used to identify its end-points. **line-up** a line of people formed for inspection etc. [from Latin *linea* = linen thread]

line² *verb* **1** to cover the inside surface of (a thing) with a layer of different material. **2** to be the lining of. □ **line one's pockets** or **purse** to make a lot of money, especially by underhand or dishonest methods. [from *linen* (used for linings)]

lineage (**lin**-ee-ij) *noun* ancestry, the line of descendants of an ancestor.

lineal (**lin**-ee-ăl) *adjective* of or in a line, especially as a descendant. **lineally** *adverb*

lineaments (**lin**-ee-ă-měnts) *plural noun* the features of a face.

linear (**lin**-ee-er) *adjective* **1** of a line; of length. **2** arranged in a line. **3** (of an equation, function, etc.) in which only the first power of any variable occurs. **linearity** *noun*

linen *noun* **1** cloth made of flax. **2** shirts and household articles (sheets, tablecloths, etc.) that were formerly made of this. [from Latin *linum* = flax]

liner¹ *noun* a large ship or aircraft travelling on a regular route.

liner² *noun* a removable lining, *bin liners*; *nappy liners*.

linesman *noun* (*plural* **linesmen**) **1** an official assisting the referee in certain games, especially in deciding whether or where a ball crosses a line. **2** a person employed to test the safety of railway lines, or to keep electrical or telephone wires in repair.

ling¹ *noun* a kind of heather.

ling² *noun* **1** a sea fish of northern Europe, used (usually salted) as food. **2** an edible sea fish of southern waters, also called *beardie*.

linger *verb* **1** to stay a long time, especially as if reluctant to leave. **2** to dawdle. **3** to remain alive although becoming weaker.

lingerie (**lan**-*zh*ĕ-ree) *noun* women's underwear and nightclothes. [from French *linge* = linen]

lingo *noun* (*plural* **lingoes**) (*informal*) a foreign language; jargon.

lingua franca (ling-gwă **frank**-ă) *noun* a language used between the people of an area where several languages are spoken. [from Italian, = Frankish tongue]

linguist (**ling**-gwĭst) *noun* a person skilled in languages or linguistics. [from Latin *lingua* = language]

linguistic (ling-**gwist**-ik) *adjective* of language or linguistics. **linguistics** *noun* the scientific study of languages and their structure.

liniment *noun* a liquid for rubbing on the skin to relieve soreness.

lining *noun* **1** a layer of material used to line something; the material itself. **2** the tissue covering the inner surface of an organ of the body.

link *noun* **1** one ring or loop of a chain. **2** a cuff link. **3** a connecting part; a person who is a connection between others. – **link** *verb* to make or be a connection between; *link hands*, to clasp each other's hand.

linkage *noun* linking; a link; a system of links.

links *noun* or *plural noun* a golf course.

Linnaeus (lin-**ee**-ŭs), Carolus (Carl Linné, 1707–78), Swedish naturalist, who established the system of classifying plants by giving them a Latin name in two parts (the *genus* or group name, and *species* identifying the individual plant).

linnet (**lin**-ĕt) *noun* **1** a kind of finch. **2** (*Austral.*) a yellow-throated honeyeater.

lino (**ly**-noh) *noun* linoleum.

linocut *noun* a design cut in relief on a layer of thick linoleum; a print made from this.

linoleum (lĭ-**noh**-lee-ŭm) *noun* a kind of floor covering made by pressing a thick coating of powdered cork and linseed oil etc. on to a canvas backing. [from Latin *linum* = flax, + *oleum* = oil]

linseed *noun* the seed of flax, pressed to form **linseed oil**, an oil used in paint and varnish. [from Latin *linum* = flax, + *seed*]

lint *noun* **1** a soft material used for dressing wounds, consisting of linen with one side scraped so that it is fluffy. **2** fluff.

lintel *noun* a horizontal piece of timber or stone etc. over a door or other opening.

lion *noun* a large powerful flesh-eating animal of the cat family. □ **the lion's share** the largest or best part of something that is divided. (¶ In the fable the lion demanded most (or, in one version, all) of the prey in return for his help in the kill.) **lioness** *feminine noun*

lionise *verb* (also **-ize**) to treat (a person) as a celebrity.

lip *noun* **1** either of the fleshy edges of the mouth-opening; a similar edge. **2** (*informal*) impudence. **3** the edge of a cup or other hollow container or of an opening. **4** a projecting part of such an edge shaped for pouring. □ **lip-read** *verb* to understand what a person is saying by watching the movements of his or her lips, not by hearing. **pay lip-service to** to state that one approves of something but fail to support it by actions. **lipped** *adjective*

lipase (**lip**-ayz) *noun* an enzyme able to break down fats.

lipectomy *noun* (*plural* **lipectomies**) a surgical procedure to remove unwanted body fat.

lipid *noun* any of a group of compounds that are esters of fatty acids or fat-like substances and are found in living tissues. [from Greek *lipos* = fat]

lipoma (li-**poh**-mă) *noun* (*plural* **lipomas** or **lipomata**) a benign tumour of fatty tissue.

liposuction *noun* a technique in cosmetic surgery for removing excess fat from under the skin by suction.

lipping *noun* a treatment applied to the edges of prefabricated boards to screen the core material.

lipstick *noun* **1** a stick of cosmetic for colouring the lips. **2** this cosmetic.

liquefy *verb* (**liquefied**, **liquefying**) to make or become liquid. **liquefaction** *noun*

liqueur (lik-**yoor**) *noun* a strong sweet alcoholic spirit with fragrant flavouring. [French, = liquor]

liquid *noun* a substance like water or oil that flows freely but is not a gas. **–liquid** *adjective* **1** in the form of a liquid. **2** having the clearness of water. **3** (of sounds) flowing clearly and pleasantly. **4** (of assets) easily converted into cash. □ **liquid crystal display** a form of visual display in electronic devices, in which

the reflectivity of a matrix of liquid crystals changes as a signal is applied (abbreviation **LCD**). [from Latin *liquidus* = flowing]

liquidambar *noun* a tree yielding a resinous gum.

liquidate *verb* **1** to pay or settle (a debt). **2** to close down (a business) and divide its assets between its creditors. **3** to get rid of, especially by killing. □ **go into liquidation** (of a business) to be closed down and its assets divided, especially in bankruptcy. **liquidation** *noun*, **liquidator** *noun*

liquidise *verb* (also **-ize**) to cause to become liquid; to crush into a liquid pulp.

liquidiser *noun* (also **-izer**) a device for liquidising fruit and vegetables.

liquidity (li-**kwid**-ĭ-tee) *noun* **1** being liquid. **2** the availability of liquid assets. □ **liquidity ratio** the ratio between the current liabilities of an organisation and the funds that might easily be made available to meet them.

liquor (**lik**-er) *noun* **1** alcoholic drink. **2** juice produced in cooking, liquid in which food has been boiled.

liquorice (**lik**-ŏ-rish) *noun* (also **licorice**) **1** a black substance used in medicine and as a sweet. **2** the plant from whose root it is obtained. [from Greek *glukus* = sweet, + *rhiza* = root]

lira (**leer**-ră) *noun* (*plural* **lire**) the unit of money in Turkey and formerly in Italy.

Lisbon the capital of Portugal.

lisle (*rhymes with* mile) *noun* a fine smooth cotton thread used especially for stockings. [from the name of Lille in France, where it was originally made]

lisp *noun* a speech defect in which s is pronounced like th (as in *thin*) and z like *th* (as in *they*). **–lisp** *verb* to speak or utter with a lisp.

lissom (**liss**-ŏm) *adjective* lithe, agile.

list[1] *noun* a series of names, items, figures, etc. written or printed. **–list** *verb* to make a list of; to enter (a name etc.) in a list. □ **enter the lists** to make or accept a challenge, especially in a controversy. [from Old English *liste* = border]

list[2] *verb* (of a ship) to lean over to one side. **–list** *noun* a listing position, a tilt.

listen *verb* **1** to make an effort to hear something; to wait alertly in order to hear a sound. **2** to hear something by doing this, to pay attention. **3** to allow oneself to be persuaded by a suggestion or request. □ **listen in** to overhear a conversation, especially by telephone; to listen to a radio broadcast.

listener *noun* **1** a person who listens; *a good listener*, one who can be relied on to listen attentively or sympathetically. **2** a person listening to a radio broadcast.

Lister, Joseph, 1st Baron (1827–1912), English surgeon, inventor of antiseptic techniques in surgery.

listeria *noun* a bacterium (active in certain foods) which can cause disease in people and animals. [named after Baron Lister]

listeriosis *noun* a disease caused by infection by listeria.

listless *adjective* without energy or vitality, showing no enthusiasm. **listlessly** *adverb*, **listlessness** *noun* [from an old word *list* = desire, + *-less*]

Liszt (*pr.* list), Franz (Ferenc) (1811–86), Hungarian composer and noted pianist.

lit *see* light¹, light³.

litany *noun* **1** a form of prayer consisting of a series of supplications to God, recited by a priest and with set responses by the congregation. **2** a long monotonous recital, *a litany of complaints*.

literacy (**lit**-ĕ-răsee) *noun* the ability to read and write.

literal *adjective* **1** taking words in their primary or basic sense, without allowing for metaphorical or figurative use of language, e.g. the phrase *upset the apple cart* has the literal meaning 'to knock over a cart loaded with apples', but it is usually used metaphorically to mean 'to spoil a careful plan or arrangement'. **2** (of a translation etc.) keeping exactly to the original words. **3** (of a person) tending to interpret things in a literal way, unimaginative. **literally** *adverb*, **literalness** *noun* [same origin as *letter*]

literary (**lit**-ĕ-ră-ree) *adjective* of or concerned with literature.

literate (**lit**-ĕ-răt) *adjective* able to read and write. **–literate** *noun* a literate person. [same origin as *letter*]

literature *noun* **1** writings that are valued for their beauty of form, especially novels and poetry and plays etc. as contrasted with technical books and journalism. **2** the writings of a country or a period or on a particular

subject. **3** (*informal*) printed pamphlets, brochures, or leaflets etc. [same origin as *letter*]

lithe (*pr.* lythe) *adjective* flexible, supple, agile.

lithium (**lith**-ee-ŭm) *noun* a metallic element (symbol Li), with numerous commercial uses in alloys, lubricating greases, chemical reagents, etc.

lithograph *noun* a picture etc. printed by lithography. [from Greek *lithos* = stone, + *-graph*]

lithography (lith-**og**-răfee) *noun* a process of printing from a smooth surface (e.g. a metal plate) treated so that ink will adhere to the design to be printed and not to the rest of the surface. **lithographic** *adjective*

lithology (lith-**ol**-ŏ-jee) *noun* the scientific study of the nature and composition of stones and rocks. **lithological** *adjective* [from Greek *lithos* = stone, + *-logy*]

lithosphere (**lith**-ŏ-sfeer) *noun* the solid crust of the earth (contrasted with the hydrosphere and the atmosphere). [from Greek *lithos* = stone, + *sphere*]

Lithuania (lith-yoo-**ay**-nee-ă) a republic of NE Europe, between Latvia and Poland. **Lithuanian** *adjective* & *noun*

litigant (**lit**-ĭ-gănt) *noun* a person who is involved in a lawsuit, one who goes to law. [from Latin *litigare* = start a lawsuit]

litigation (lit-ĭ-**gay**-shŏn) *noun* a lawsuit; the process of going to law.

litmus *noun* a blue colouring matter that is turned red by acids and can be restored to blue by alkalis. □ **litmus paper** paper stained with this, used to tell whether a solution is acid or alkaline. **litmus test** (*informal*) a real or indicative test.

litotes (ly-**toh**-teez) *noun* an ironic understatement, e.g. *I shan't be sorry* = I shall be glad.

litre (**lee**-ter) *noun* a metric unit of capacity equal to 1000 cubic centimetres (about $1\frac{3}{4}$ pints), used for measuring liquids.

litter *noun* **1** odds and ends of rubbish left lying about. **2** the young animals brought forth at a birth. **3** a means of transport consisting of a couch in a frame carried on the shoulders of bearers. **4** straw etc. put down as bedding for animals. **5** granulated absorbent material for use by pets, especially cats, as an indoor toilet. **–litter** *verb* **1** to make untidy by scattering odds and ends; to scatter as litter. **2** to give birth to (a litter of young).

litterbug *noun* a person who carelessly drops litter in a street etc.

little *adjective* **1** small in size, amount, or intensity etc., not great or big or much; unimportant. **2** smaller than others of the same kind, *little finger*. **3** working on only a small scale, *a little shopkeeper*. **4** young, younger, *our little boy; his little sister*. –**little** *noun* only a small amount, some but not much; a short time or distance. –**little** *adverb* **1** to a small extent only, *little-known authors*. **2** not at all, *he little knows*. □ **little by little** gradually, by a small amount at a time. **the little people** the fairies.

littoral *adjective* of or on the shore. –**littoral** *noun* a region lying along the shore. [from Latin *litoris* = of the shore]

liturgy (**lit**-er-jee) *noun* a fixed form of public worship used in churches. **liturgical** (lit-**er**-jĭ-kăl) *adjective*, **liturgically** *adverb*

live¹ (*rhymes with* hive) *adjective* **1** alive. **2** actual, not pretended, *a real live burglar*. **3** glowing, burning, *a live coal*. **4** (of a shell or match) not yet exploded or used. **5** (of a wire or cable etc.) charged with or carrying electricity. **6** of interest or importance at the present time, *noise pollution is a live issue*. **7** (of a broadcast) transmitted while actually happening or being performed, not recorded or edited. □ **a live wire** a highly energetic forceful person.

live² (*rhymes with* give) *verb* **1** to have life, to be or remain alive; (of things without life) to remain in existence. **2** to be kept alive, *living on fruit*. **3** to get a livelihood, *they lived on* or *off her earnings; live by one's wits*, to get money or food etc. by ingenious or dishonest methods. **4** to have one's dwelling place, *they lived in tents*. **5** to conduct one's life in a certain way, *lived like a hermit; lived a peaceful life; live a lie*, express it by one's life. □ **lived-in** *adjective* inhabited, (of a room) used frequently. **live down** to live in such a way that (a past guilt or scandal etc.) becomes forgotten. **live in** or **out** (of an employee) to live on or off the premises. **live it up** to live in a lively extravagant way. **live up to** to live or behave in accordance with, *did not live up to his principles*; to fulfil, *lived up to her expectations*.

liveable (**liv**-ă-bŭl) *adjective* suitable for living; *felt that life wasn't liveable*, was unbearable; *liveable in*, (of a house etc.) suitable for living in; *liveable with*, easy to live with.

livelihood (**lyv**-lee-huud) *noun* a means of living; a way in which a person earns a living.

livelong (**liv**-long) *adjective* **the livelong day** the whole length of the day.

lively *adverb* (**livelier**, **liveliest**) full of life or energy, vigorous and cheerful, full of action. □ **look lively** to move more quickly or energetically. **liveliness** *noun*

liven *verb* to make or become lively, *liven it up; things livened up*.

liver *noun* **1** a large organ in the abdomen, secreting bile. **2** the liver of certain animals, used as food. **3** dark reddish brown.

liveried *adjective* wearing a livery.

liverish *adjective* **1** suffering from a disorder of the liver. **2** irritable, glum.

liverwort (**liv**-er-wert) *noun* any of a group of small creeping plants growing in damp places, of which some kinds have liver-shaped leaves and some resemble mosses.

livery *noun* **1** a distinctive uniform worn by a servant etc. **2** the distinctive colours used for a company's vehicles, products, etc. □ **livery stables** stables where horses are kept for their owner in return for a fee, or where horses may be hired.

lives *see* **life**.

livestock *noun* animals kept for use or profit, e.g. cattle or sheep etc. on a farm.

livid *adjective* **1** of the colour of lead, bluish-grey. **2** (*informal*) furiously angry.

living *adjective* **1** alive; *the living*, people who are now alive. **2** (of a likeness) exact, true to life, *she is the living image of her mother*. **3** (of rock) not detached from the earth; (of water) always flowing. –**living** *noun* **1** being alive. **2** a means of earning or providing enough food etc. to sustain life. **3** a manner of life, *their standard of living*. **4** a position held by a member of the clergy and providing him or her with an income and/or property. □ **living room** a room for general use during the day. **living wage** a wage on which it is possible to live. **within living memory** within the memory of people who are still alive.

Livy (59 BC–AD 17), Roman historian.

lizard *noun* a reptile with a rough or scaly hide, four legs, and a long tail.

Ljubljana (loo-blee-**ah**-nă) the capital of Slovenia.

llama (**lah**-mă) *noun* a South American animal related to the camel but with no hump.

lm *abbreviation* lumen.

lo *interjection* (*old use*) see.

load *noun* **1** something carried. **2** the quantity that can be carried, e.g. on a cart. **3** material (such as stones, sand, etc.) carried along by a stream or glaciers. **4** a unit of weight or measure for certain substances. **5** the amount of electric current supplied by a dynamo or generating station. **6** a burden of responsibility, worry, or grief. – **load** *verb* **1** to put a load in or on; to fill with goods or cargo etc.; to receive a load. **2** to fill heavily. **3** to weight with something heavy; to give a bias to a dice etc. **4** to put ammunition into (a gun) or film into (a camera) ready for use. **5** to put (a program or data etc.) into a computer. **loads** *plural noun* (*informal*) plenty, *loads of time*. □ **get a load of this** (*informal*) take notice. **load line** a ship's Plimsoll line. **load-shedding** *noun* cutting off of the supply of electric current on certain lines when the demand is greater than the supply available. **loader** *noun*

loaded *adjective* (*informal*) **1** very rich. **2** drunk or under the influence of drugs. □ **loaded question** one that is worded so as to trap a person into saying something damaging.

loading *noun* (*Austral.*) a payment in addition to wages for skill, productivity, etc.

loadstone *noun* = lodestone.

loaf¹ *noun* (*plural* **loaves**) **1** a mass of bread shaped in one piece. **2** an oblong-shaped cake or other food, *date loaf, meat loaf*. **3** (*informal*) the head, *use your loaf!* [from Old English *hlaf*]

loaf² *verb* to spend time idly, to stand or saunter about. **loafer** *noun*

loam *noun* rich soil containing clay, sand, and decayed vegetable matter. **loamy** *adjective*

loan *noun* **1** something lent, especially a sum of money. **2** lending, being lent; *on loan*, lent; *have the loan of*, borrow. – **loan** *verb* to lend.

Usage Many people regard the use of *loan* as a verb as incorrect.

loath (*rhymes with* both) *adjective* unwilling, *was loath to depart*. **nothing loath** quite willing.

loathe (*rhymes with* clothe) *verb* to feel great hatred and disgust for. **loathing** *noun* this feeling.

loathsome *adjective* arousing loathing, repulsive.

loaves *see* loaf¹.

lob *verb* (**lobbed**, **lobbing**) to send or strike (a ball) slowly or in a high arc in cricket or tennis etc. – **lob** *noun* a lobbed ball in tennis etc.; a slow underarm delivery in cricket.

lobar (loh-ber) *adjective* of a lobe, especially of the lung, *lobar pneumonia*.

lobby *noun* **1** a porch or entrance hall; an anteroom. **2** (in a parliament house) a large hall open to the public and used for interviews with MPs etc. **3** either of two corridors to which MPs retire when a vote is taken in the House, *division lobby*. **4** a body of people lobbying an MP etc. or seeking to influence legislation, *the anti-abortion lobby*. – **lobby** *verb* (**lobbied**, **lobbying**) to seek to persuade (an MP or other person) to support one's cause, by personal interview or correspondence.

lobe *noun* a rounded flattish part or projection (especially of an organ of the body); the lower soft part of the ear. **lobed** *adjective*

lobelia (lŏ-bee-lee-ă) *noun* a low-growing garden plant with blue, red, white, or purple flowers, used especially for edging.

lobster *noun* **1** a large marine shellfish with eight legs and two long claws that turns scarlet after being boiled. **2** its flesh as food. □ **lobster pot** a basket for trapping lobsters.

lobworm *noun* a large earthworm used as fishing bait.

local *adjective* **1** belonging to a particular place or a small area. **2** affecting a particular place, not general, *a local anaesthetic*. – **local** *noun* an inhabitant of a particular district. □ **local area network** a communication network linking a number of computers in close proximity (abbreviation LAN). **local colour** details characteristic of the scene in which a novel etc. is set, added to make it seem more real. **local government** the system of administration of a city, town, shire, municipality, etc. by the elected representatives of people who live there. **locally** *adverb* [from Latin *locus* = place]

locale (loh-kahl) *noun* the scene or locality of operations or events.

localise *verb* (also **-ize**) to make local, not general, to confine within a particular area, *a localised infection*.

locality (loh-kal-ĭ-tee) *noun* a thing's position, the site or neighbourhood of something.

locate *verb* **1** to discover the place where (a thing) is, *locate the electrical fault*. **2** to assign to or establish in a particular location; *be located*, be situated.

location *noun* **1** the place where something is situated. **2** finding a thing's location; being found. **3** a natural (as opposed to studio-based) setting for a film or broadcast, *filmed on location*.

locative (**lok**-ă-tiv) *noun* & *adjective* the **locative case**, the grammatical case expressing place or position.

loch (*pr.* lok) *noun* (*Scottish*) a lake or an arm of the sea.

loci *see* **locus**.

lock¹ *noun* **1** a device for fastening a door or lid etc. into position when it is closed, with a bolt that needs a key or other device to work it; *under lock and key*, locked up. **2** a wrestling-hold that keeps an opponent's arm or leg etc. from moving. **3** a player in the second row of the scrum in rugby. **4** a mechanism for exploding the charge in a gun. **5** a section of a canal or river where the water level changes, fitted with gates and sluices so that water can be let in or out to raise or lower boats from one level to another. **6** a decompression chamber. **7** the interlocking of parts. **8** the turning of a vehicle's front wheels by use of the steering wheel; the maximum extent of this. –**lock** *verb* **1** to fasten or be able to be fastened with a lock. **2** to shut into a place that is fastened by a lock. **3** to store away securely or inaccessibly, *his capital is locked up in land*. **4** to bring or come into a rigidly fixed position, to jam. **5** to go or convey (a boat) through a lock. □ **lock out** to shut out by locking a door. **lock-out** *noun* an employer's procedure of refusing to allow workers to enter their place of work until certain conditions are agreed to. **lock, stock, and barrel** completely, including everything. **lock-up** *adjective* able to be locked up; (*noun*) premises that can be locked up; a room or building where prisoners can be detained temporarily. **lockable** *adjective*

lock² *noun* a portion of hair that hangs together. **locks** *plural noun* the hair of the head.

Locke, John (1632–1704), English philosopher, who argued that the only source of knowledge is sensory experience.

locker *noun* a small cupboard or compartment, usually lockable, especially for an individual's use in a public place.

locket *noun* a small ornamental case holding a portrait or lock of hair etc., worn on a chain round the neck.

lockjaw *noun* a form of tetanus in which the jaws become rigidly closed.

locksmith *noun* a maker and mender of locks.

loco¹ *noun* (*plural* **locos**) (*informal*) a locomotive.

loco² *adjective* (*informal*) crazy. [Spanish, = insane]

locomotion *noun* moving, the ability to move from place to place.

locomotive *noun* an engine for drawing a train along rails. –**locomotive** *adjective* of locomotion, *locomotive power*. [from Latin *locus* = place, + *motivus* = moving]

locum (**loh**-kŭm) *noun* a deputy acting for a doctor or member of the clergy. [short for Latin *locum tenens* = person holding the place]

locus (**loh**-kŭs) *noun* (*plural* **loci**, *pr.* **loh**-sy) **1** the exact place of something. **2** the line or curve etc. formed by all the points satisfying certain conditions or by movement of a point or line etc. [Latin, = place]

locust (**loh**-kŭst) *noun* **1** a kind of grasshopper that migrates in swarms and eats all the vegetation of a district. **2** (*informal*) a cicada.

locution (lŏ-**kew**-shŏn) *noun* **1** a word, phrase, or idiom. **2** a style of speech. [from Latin *locutum* = spoken]

lode *noun* a vein of metal ore.

lodestar *noun* a star used as a guide in navigation, especially the pole star.

lodestone *noun* **1** a magnetic oxide of iron. **2** a piece of this used as a magnet.

lodge *noun* **1** a cabin or hut; a holiday house, *a ski lodge*. **2** a small house on a property, occupied by a caretaker or other employee. **3 The Lodge** the Prime Minister's official residence in Canberra. **4** the members or meeting place of a branch of a society such as the Freemasons. –**lodge** *verb* **1** to provide with sleeping quarters or temporary accommodation. **2** to live as a lodger. **3** to deposit; to be or become embedded, *the bullet lodged in his brain*. **4** to present formally for attention, *lodged a complaint*.

lodger *noun* a person living in another's house and paying for this accommodation.

lodging *noun* a place where one lodges. **lodgings** *plural noun* a room or rooms (not in a hotel) rented for living in.

loess (**loh**-ĕss) *noun* a layer of fine light-coloured dust, found in large areas of Asia, Europe, and America and very fertile when irrigated, thought to have been deposited by winds during the Ice Age. [German]

lo-fi *adjective* (also **low-fi**) **1** of or employing sound reproduction of a lower quality than hi-fi. **2** (of popular music) recorded and produced with basic equipment and thus having a raw and unsophisticated sound.

loft *noun* **1** a space under the roof of a house. **2** a space under the roof of a stable or barn, used for storing hay etc. **3** a gallery or upper level in a church or hall, *the organ loft*. **4** a backward slope in the face of a golf club. **5** a lofted stroke. **–loft** *verb* to send (a ball) in a high arc.

lofty *adjective* (**loftier**, **loftiest**) **1** (of things) very tall, towering. **2** (of thoughts or aims etc.) noble. **3** haughty, *a lofty manner*. **loftily** *adverb*, **loftiness** *noun*

log¹ *noun* **1** a length of tree trunk that has fallen or been cut down. **2** a short piece of this, especially as firewood. **3** a device for gauging a ship's speed. **4** a detailed record of a ship's voyage or an aircraft's flight; any similar record. **–log** *verb* (**logged**, **logging**) **1** to enter (facts) in a logbook. **2** to achieve (a certain speed, distance, or number of hours worked etc.) as recorded in a logbook or similar record, *the pilot had logged 200 hours on jets*. ☐ **log cabin** a hut built of logs. **log on** or **off** (also **log in** or **out**) to open or close one's access to a computer system.

log² *noun* a logarithm, *log tables*.

loganberry *noun* a large dark red cultivated fruit resembling a blackberry.

logarithm (**log**-ă-ri*th*'m) *noun* one of a series of numbers set out in tables which make it possible to work out problems by adding and subtracting numbers instead of multiplying and dividing. **logarithmic** *adjective* [from Greek *logos* = reckoning, + *arithmos* = number]

logbook *noun* a book containing a detailed record of a voyage, car trips, things done, etc.

logger *noun* a person whose job is to cut down forest trees for timber.

loggerheads *plural noun* **at loggerheads** disagreeing, arguing, or quarrelling.

loggia (**loj**-ă) *noun* an open-sided gallery or arcade, especially one looking on an open court or forming part of a house and facing a garden. [Italian, = lodge]

logging *noun* cutting down forest trees for timber.

logic (**loj**-ik) *noun* **1** the science of reasoning. **2** a particular system or method of reasoning. **3** a chain of reasoning regarded as good or bad. **4** the ability to reason correctly. **5** the principles used in designing a computer or any of its units; the circuit(s) involved in this. **logician** *noun* [from Greek *logos* = word, reason]

logical (**loj**-ikăl) *adjective* **1** of or according to logic, correctly reasoned. **2** (of an action etc.) in accordance with what seems reasonable or natural. **3** capable of reasoning correctly. **logically** *adverb*, **logicality** (loj-ĭ-**kal**-ĭ-tee) *noun*

Logie *noun* an Australian award for excellence in television acting or directing. [named after John Logie Baird, Scottish inventor of television (1888–1946)]

logistics (lŏ-**jist**-iks) *plural noun* the organisation of supplies and services etc. **logistic** *adjective*

logo (**loh**-goh) *noun* (*plural* **logos**) a printed symbol used by an organisation as its emblem. [abbreviation of *logotype*, from Greek *logos* = word, + *type*]

-logy *suffix* forming nouns meaning a subject of study (e.g. *biology*). [from Greek *-logia* = study]

loin *noun* **1** the side and back of the body between the ribs and the hip bone. **2** a joint of meat that includes the vertebrae of this part.

loincloth *noun* a piece of cloth worn round the body at the hips, especially as the only garment.

Loire (*pr.* lwahr) France's longest river, flowing into the Atlantic Ocean at St Nazaire.

loiter *verb* to linger or stand about idly; to proceed slowly with frequent stops. **loiterer** *noun*

Loki (**loh**-kee) (*Scand. myth.*) a spirit of evil and mischief who contrived the death of Balder.

LOL *abbreviation* (especially in electronic communications) laughing out loud.

loll *verb* **1** to lean lazily against something; to stand or sit or rest lazily. **2** to hang loosely, *the dog's tongue was lolling out*.

lollipop *noun* a large round usually flat boiled sweet on a small stick.

lollop *verb* (**lolloped**, **lolloping**) (*informal*) to flop about, to move in clumsy bounds.

lolly *noun* **1** (*Austral.*) a sweet. **2** (*informal*) money. ☐ **do one's lolly** (*informal*) to lose one's temper. **lolly water** (*Austral. informal*) soft drink.

Lomé (loh-**may**) the capital of Togo.

London the capital of England and of the United Kingdom. **Londoner** *noun*

Londonderry a city and county of Northern Ireland.

lone *adjective* solitary, without companions, *a lone horseman.* □ **lone pair** a pair of electrons in the outer shell of an atom that are not involved in bonding.

lonely *adjective* **1** solitary, without companions. **2** sad because one lacks friends or companions. **3** (of places) far from inhabited places, remote, not often frequented, *a lonely road.* **loneliness** *noun* [from *lone*]

loner *noun* one who prefers not to associate with others.

lonesome *adjective* lonely; causing loneliness.

long[1] *adjective* **1** having great length in space or time. **2** having a certain length or duration, *two metres* or *two hours long*. **3** seeming to be longer than it really is, *ten long years*. **4** lasting, going far into the past or future, *a long memory*; *take the long view*, consider the later effects. **5** (*informal*) having much of a certain quality, *he's not long on tact.* **6** of elongated shape. **7** (of vowel sounds) having a pronunciation that is considered to last longer than that of a corresponding 'short' vowel (the *a* in *cane* is long, in *can* it is short). **–long** *adverb* **1** for a long time, by a long time; *I shan't be long*, shall not take a long time. **2** throughout a specified time, *all day long*; *I am no longer a child*, am not now or henceforth. □ **as** or **so long as** provided that, on condition that. **in the long run** in the end, over a long period. **the long and the short of it** all that need be said; the general effect or result. **long-distance** *adjective* travelling or operating between distant places. **long division** the process of dividing one number by another with all calculations written down. **long drink** one that is large in quantity or fills a tall glass. **long face** a dismal expression. **long in the tooth** rather old. **long johns** (*informal*) underpants with long legs. **long jump** an athletic competition of jumping as far as possible along the ground in one leap. **long-life** *adjective* remaining usable or serviceable for a long time. **long-lived** *adjective* having a long life; lasting for a long time. **long odds** very uneven odds in betting. **long off, long on** (in cricket) a fielder far behind the bowler on the off (or on) side; this position. **long-playing** *adjective* (of a record) playing for about 10 to 30 minutes on each side (abbreviation **LP**).

long-range *adjective* having a long range; relating to a period far into the future. **long shot** a wild guess or venture. **long-sighted** *adjective* able to see clearly only what is at a distance. **long-standing** *adjective* having existed for a long time, *a long-standing grievance*. **long-suffering** *adjective* bearing provocation patiently. **long suit** many playing cards of one suit in a hand; a thing at which one excels, *modesty is not his long suit.* **long-term** *adjective* of or for a long period. **long ton** *see* **ton**. **long wave** a radio wave of frequency less than 300 kHz. **long weekend** a weekend extended by a third day, especially a public holiday. **long-winded** *adjective* talking or writing at tedious length.

long[2] *verb* to feel a longing.

longboat *noun* the largest boat carried by a sailing ship.

longbow *noun* a large bow drawn by hand and shooting a feathered arrow.

longevity (lon-**jev**-ĭ-tee) *noun* long life. [from Latin *longus* = long, + *aevum* = age]

longhand *noun* ordinary writing, contrasted with shorthand or typing or printing.

longhorn *noun* an animal of a breed of cattle with long horns.

longing *noun* an intense persistent wish.

Long Island an island of New York State.

longitude (**long**-gĭ-tewd) *noun* the distance east or west (measured in degrees) from the meridian of Greenwich in England.

longitudinal (long-gĭ-**tew**-dĭ-năl) *adjective* **1** of longitude. **2** of or in length, measured lengthwise. **longitudinally** *adverb*

longshore *adjective* found on the shore; employed along the shore, especially near a port. □ **longshore drift** the movement of sand, shingle, etc., along a coast by the action of waves, tides, and currents.

longshoreman *noun* (*plural* **longshoremen**) a person employed in loading and unloading ships from the shore.

Long Tan the site of an important battle fought between Australian forces and the Vietcong in 1966.

longways, longwise *adverbs* lengthways.

loo *noun* (*informal*) a toilet.

loofah (**loo**-fă) *noun* the dried pod of a kind of gourd, used as a rough sponge. [from Arabic *lufa*]

look *verb* 1 to use or direct one's eyes in order to see or search or examine something. 2 to direct one's eyes or one's attention. 3 (of things) to face in a certain direction. 4 to have a certain appearance, to seem to be, *the fruit looks ripe*; *made him look a fool*. –**look** *noun* 1 the act of looking, a gaze or glance. 2 an inspection or search, *have a look for it*. 3 appearance, *is blessed with good looks*; *the 60s look*; *I don't like the look of this*, find it alarming. □ **look after** to take care of; to attend to. **look-alike** *noun* a person or thing closely resembling another. **look down on** or **look down one's nose at** to regard with contempt. **look forward to** to be waiting eagerly (or sometimes with anxiety etc.) for an expected thing or event. **look in** to make a short visit. **look-in** *noun* a chance of participation or success, *didn't get a look-in*. **look into** to investigate. **look on** to be a spectator. **look out** to be vigilant. **look sharp** to make haste. **look to** to rely on; to consider carefully. **look up** to search for information about, *look up words in a dictionary*; to improve in prospects, *things are looking up*; to go to visit, *look us up*. **look up to** to admire and respect as superior.

looker-on *noun* (*plural* **lookers-on**) a spectator.

looking glass *noun* a glass mirror.

lookout *noun* 1 looking out, a watch. 2 a person who keeps watch. 3 a place from which observation is kept. 4 a prospect of luck, *it's a poor lookout for us*. 5 a person's own concern, *that's his lookout*.

loom[1] *noun* an apparatus for weaving cloth.

loom[2] *verb* to come into view suddenly; to appear close at hand or with threatening aspect.

loony *noun* (*informal*) a lunatic. –**loony** *adjective* (*informal*) crazy. [short for *lunatic*]

loop *noun* 1 the shape produced by a curve that crosses itself. 2 any path or pattern shaped roughly like this. 3 (in graph theory) a line joining a vertex to itself. 4 a length of cord or wire etc. that crosses itself and is fastened at the crossing. 5 a complete circuit for electrical current. 6 a set of computer instructions that is carried out repeatedly until some specified condition is satisfied. 7 a curved piece of metal serving as a handle. 8 a strip of fabric etc. attached to a garment or object so that it can be hung on a peg. –**loop** *verb* 1 to form into a loop or loops. 2 to fasten or join with a loop or loops. 3 to enclose in a loop. □ **loop the**

loop (of an aircraft) to fly in a vertical circle, turning upside down between climb and dive.

loophole *noun* 1 a way of evading a rule or contract etc., especially through an omission or inexact wording in its provisions. 2 a narrow opening in the wall of a fort etc., for shooting or looking through or to admit light or air.

loose *adjective* 1 freed from bonds or restraint; (of an animal) not tethered or shut in; *a loose ball*, (in football etc.) not in any player's possession. 2 detached or detachable from its place, not rigidly fixed. 3 not fastened together; not held or packed or contained in something. 4 not organised strictly, *a loose confederation*. 5 slack, relaxed, not tense or tight. 6 not compact; not dense in texture, arranged at wide intervals, *a loose weave*. 7 inexact, vague, careless. 8 slack in moral principles or conduct. –**loose** *adverb* loosely, *loose-fitting*. –**loose** *verb* 1 to release. 2 to untie or loosen. 3 to fire a gun or missile, *loosed off a round of ammunition*. □ **at a loose end** unoccupied. **loose box** a stall in which a horse can move about. **loose-leaf** *adjective* (of a notebook etc.) with each leaf separate and removable. **loosely** *adverb*, **looseness** *noun*

loosen *verb* to make or become loose or looser. □ **loosen a person's tongue** to make him or her talk freely. **loosen up** to relax; to limber up.

loot *noun* goods taken from an enemy or by theft. –**loot** *verb* to plunder; to take as loot; to steal from or rob shops or houses left unprotected after a violent event. **looter** *noun*

lop *verb* (**lopped**, **lopping**) to cut away branches or twigs of; to cut off.

lope *verb* to run with a long bounding stride. –**lope** *noun* a long bounding stride.

lop-eared *adjective* having drooping ears.

lopsided *adjective* with one side lower, smaller, or heavier than the other.

loquacious (lŏ-**kway**-shŭs) *adjective* talkative. **loquaciously** *adverb*, **loquacity** (lŏ-**kwass**-ĭ-tee) *noun* [from Latin *loqui* = speak]

lord *noun* 1 a master, ruler, or sovereign; **the Lord** God or Christ. 2 a nobleman. 3 (*Brit*.) the title or form of address to certain peers or high officials. –**lord** *verb* to domineer, *lording it over the whole club*. □ **Lord Mayor** the mayor of certain large cities. **the Lord's Prayer** the prayer taught by Christ to his disciples, beginning 'Our Father'. **Lord's Supper** the

Eucharist. [from Old English *hlaford* = person who keeps the bread (compare *lady*)]

Lord Howe Island an island 700 km northeast of Sydney.

lordly *adjective* **1** haughty, imperious. **2** suitable for a lord, *a lordly mansion*.

lordship *noun* a title used in speaking to or about a man of the rank of 'Lord', *your lordship*.

lore *noun* a body of traditions and knowledge on a subject or possessed by a class of people, *bird lore*; *gypsy lore*.

Lorelei (**lor**-rĕ-ly) a rock or cliff on the Rhine with a remarkable echo, in German legend the home of a siren of the same name whose song lured boatmen to destruction.

lorgnette (lorn-**yet**) *noun* a pair of eyeglasses or opera glasses on a long handle.

lorikeet *noun* a small brightly coloured Australian parrot.

lorry *noun* a truck.

lory *noun* a brightly coloured parrot feeding on pollen and nectar.

Los Angeles (loss **an**-jĕ-leez) a city on the coast of California, the second largest in the USA.

lose *verb* (**lost**, **losing**) **1** to be deprived of (e.g. by death or accident). **2** to cease to have or maintain, *lose confidence*; *lose one's balance*. **3** to become unable to find, to miss from amongst one's possessions. **4** to fail to keep (a thing etc.) in sight or to follow (a piece of reasoning) mentally; *lose one's way*, to fail to find the right path etc. **5** to fail to obtain or catch, *lost the contract*. **6** to get rid of, *lose weight*; *managed to lose our pursuers*. **7** to suffer defeat. **8** to waste time or an opportunity, *lost twenty minutes through bursting a tyre*. **9** to suffer loss, to be worse off, *we lost on the deal*. **10** (of a clock) to become slow; *it loses two minutes a day*, becomes this amount behind the correct time. □ **lose ground** to be forced to retreat or give way. **lose one's heart** to fall in love. **lose one's life** to be killed. **lose out** (*informal*) to be unsuccessful; not to get a full chance or advantage. **losing battle** one in which defeat seems certain. **loser** *noun*

loss *noun* **1** losing; being lost. **2** a person or thing lost. **3** money lost in a business transaction; the excess of outlay over returns. **4** a disadvantage or suffering caused by losing something. □ **be at a loss** to be puzzled, to be unable to know what to do or say. **loss-leader**

noun a popular article sold at a loss to attract customers who will then buy other articles.

lost *see* **lose**. –**lost** *adjective* **1** strayed or separated from its owner, *a lost dog*. **2** engrossed, *lost in thought*. □ **be lost on** to fail to influence or draw the attention of, *our hints were lost on him*. **get lost!** (*informal*) cease being annoying. **lost cause** an undertaking that can no longer be successful.

lot¹ *noun* **1** one of a set of objects used in making a selection by methods depending on chance, *cast* or *draw lots for it*. **2** this method of selecting; the choice resulting from it, *was chosen by lot*; *the lot fell on me*. **3** a person's share, what falls to him or her by lot or chance; a person's fate or appointed task etc. **4** a piece of land; (*Amer.*) an area for a particular purpose, *a parking lot*. **5** an article or set of articles put up for sale at an auction etc. □ **bad lot** a person of bad character. **cast** or **throw in one's lot with** to decide to join and share the fortunes of. [from Old English *hlot* = share]

lot² *noun* **1** a number of people or things of the same kind; *the lot*, the total quantity. **2** (*informal*) a large number or amount, *has a lot of friends*; *there's lots of time*, plenty. **3** much, *feeling a lot better*.

LOTE (*rhymes with* boat) *noun* languages other than English.

loth (*pr.* lohth) = **loath**.

Lothario (lŏ-**thair**-ree-oh) *noun* (*plural* **Lotharios**) a libertine. [named after a character in Rowe's play *The Fair Penitent* (1703)]

lotion *noun* a medicinal or cosmetic liquid applied to the skin.

lottery *noun* **1** a system of raising money by selling numbered tickets and distributing prizes to the holders of numbers drawn at random. **2** something where the outcome is governed by luck.

lotto *noun* a game resembling bingo but with numbers drawn instead of called.

lotus (**loh**-tŭs) *noun* (*plural* **lotuses**) **1** a kind of tropical water lily. **2** a mythical fruit represented as inducing a state of lazy and luxurious dreaminess. □ **lotus position** a cross-legged position adopted for meditating.

loud *adjective* **1** easily heard, producing much noise. **2** (of colours etc.) unpleasantly bright, gaudy. –**loud** *adverb* loudly. □ **loud hailer** an electronic device that amplifies the sound of a voice which can then be heard at a distance. **out loud** aloud. **loudly** *adverb*, **loudness** *noun*

loudspeaker *noun* an apparatus that converts electrical impulses into audible sound.

Louis (**loo**-ee) the name of 18 kings of France, including Louis XIV (reigned 1643–1715), known as the Sun King.

Louisiana (loo-eez-ee-**an**-ă) a State of the south-western USA.

lounge *verb* to loll, to sit or stand about idly. –**lounge** *noun* **1** a **lounge room**, a sitting room in a house. **2** a waiting room at an airport etc., with seats for waiting passengers. **3** a public room (in a hotel) for sitting in. **4** a sofa. ☐ **lounge suit** a man's ordinary suit for day wear. **lounger** *noun*

lour (*rhymes with* sour) *verb* **1** to frown or scowl. **2** (of clouds or the sky etc.) to look dark and threatening.

Lourdes (*pr*. loord) a town in SW France where in 1858 a peasant girl, Bernadette Soubirous, claimed to have had visions of the Virgin Mary. It is now a major centre of pilgrimage.

louse *noun* **1** (*plural* **lice**) a small insect that lives as a parasite on animals or plants. **2** (*plural* **louses**) (*informal*) a contemptible person.

lousy *adjective* **1** infested with lice. **2** (*informal*) disgusting; very bad or ill.

lout *noun* an ill-mannered or badly-behaved youth. **loutish** *adjective*

Louvre (*pr*. loovr) the national museum and art gallery of France, in Paris.

louvre (**loo**-ver) *nouns* one of a set of overlapping slats arranged to admit air but exclude light or rain. [from Old French *lovier* = skylight]

louvred (**loo**-verd) *adjective* fitted with louvres.

lovable *adjective* easy to love.

lovage (**luv**-ij) *noun* a herb with leaves that are used for flavouring soups and in salads.

love *noun* **1** warm liking or affection for a person, affectionate devotion. **2** sexual affection or passion. **3** God's benevolence towards mankind. **4** strong liking for a thing, *love of music*. **5** affectionate greetings, *send one's love*. **6** a loved person, a sweetheart; (*informal*) a form of address. **7** (in games) no score, nil; *love all*, neither side has yet scored; *a love game*, in which the loser has not scored at all. –**love** *verb* **1** to feel love for. **2** to like greatly, to take pleasure in having or doing something. ☐ **for love** because of affection; without receiving payment; *cannot get it for love or money*, by any means. **in love** feeling

love (especially sexual love) for another person. **love affair** a romantic or sexual relationship between two people who are in love; a strong feeling of fondness (for a thing), *a love affair with Vienna*. **love child** a child of unmarried parents. **love-hate relationship** an intense emotional response involving both love and hate.

lovebird *noun* a kind of parakeet that seems to show great affection for its mate; a budgerigar.

loveless *adjective* without love.

lovelorn *adjective* pining with love; forsaken by one's lover.

lovely *adjective* (**lovelier, loveliest**) **1** beautiful, attractive. **2** (*informal*) delightful, *having a lovely time*. **loveliness** *noun*

lover *noun* **1** a person who is in love with another. **2** a person with whom another is having sexual relations. **3** one who likes or enjoys something, *lovers of music*.

lovesick *adjective* languishing because of love.

loving *adjective* feeling or showing love. **lovingly** *adverb*

low¹ *adjective* **1** not high or tall, not extending far upwards. **2** (of ground) not far above sea level, low in relation to surrounding land. **3** ranking below others in importance or quality. **4** ignoble, vulgar, *low cunning*; *keeps low company*. **5** less than what is normal in amount or intensity etc., *low prices*; *a low opinion*, unfavourable. **6** (of a sound or voice) deep not shrill, having slow vibrations. **7** not loud, *spoke in a low voice*. **8** lacking in vigour, depressed. –**low** *noun* **1** a low level or figure, *share prices reached a new low*. **2** an area of low barometric pressure. –**low** *adverb* **1** in or at or to a low level or position. **2** in or to a low degree. **3** in a low tone, (of sound) at a low pitch. ☐ **Low Church** that section of the Anglican Church that gives only a low place to ritual and the authority of bishops and priests. **low-class** *adjective* of low quality or social class. **Low Countries** the Netherlands, Belgium, and Luxembourg. **low-down** *adjective* dishonourable; (*noun*) (*informal*) the true facts, inside information. **low frequency** (in radio) 30 to 300 kilohertz. **low-key** *adjective* restrained, not intense or emotional. **low-level** *adjective* (of a computer language) close in form to machine code; (of nuclear waste) having a small degree of radioactivity. **low-pitched** *adjective* (of a voice or sound) low. **low profile** avoidance of attention or publicity. **low season** the period when a resort etc. has relatively few visitors. **Low Sunday** the Sunday after Easter. **low tide** the tide at its lowest level; the time when this occurs. **low water** low tide.

low² *noun* the deep sound made by cattle, a moo. –**low** *verb* to make this sound.

lowan *noun* (*Austral*.) a mallee fowl. [Wemba-wemba]

lowbrow *adjective* not intellectual or cultured. –**lowbrow** *noun* a lowbrow person.

lower¹ *adjective* **1** less high in place or position. **2** situated on less high land or to the south; *Lower Egypt*, the part nearest to the Nile delta. **3** ranking below others; *the lower animals* or *plants*, those of relatively simple structure, not highly developed; *lower classes*, people of the lowest social rank. **4** (of a geological or archaeological period) earlier in its occurrence. (¶ See the note at **upper**.) –**lower** *adverb* in or to a lower position etc. –**lower** *verb* **1** to let or haul down. **2** to make or become lower; to reduce in amount or quantity etc.; *lower one's eyes*, to direct one's gaze downwards. □ **lower case** letters that are not capitals. **Lower Chamber** or **House** the larger and usually elected body in a two-house legislature; (in the Federal Parliament) the House of Representatives; (in the State Parliaments of New South Wales, Victoria, and Western Australia) the Legislative Assembly, and (in those of South Australia and Tasmania) the House of Assembly.

lower² *verb* = **lour**.

lowest *adjective* least high in position or status. □ **lowest common denominator** the lowest common multiple of the denominators of several fractions (abbreviation **LCD**). **lowest common multiple** the lowest quantity that is a multiple of two or more given numbers (abbreviation **LCM**).

lowland *noun* low-lying land. –**lowland** *adjective* of or in lowland. **lowlander** *noun*

lowly *adjective* (**lowlier**, **lowliest**) of humble rank or condition. **lowliness** *noun*

loyal *adjective* steadfast in one's allegiance to a person or cause or to one's country or sovereign. **loyally** *adverb*, **loyalty** *noun*

loyalist *noun* a person who is loyal, especially to the established government during a revolt. –**Loyalist** *noun* a supporter of the union between Northern Ireland and Great Britain. **loyalism** *noun*

lozenge *noun* **1** a four-sided diamond-shaped figure. **2** a small sweet or tablet to be dissolved in the mouth.

LP *abbreviation* a long-playing record.

LPG *abbreviation* liquefied petroleum gas.

L-plate *noun* a sign bearing the letter 'L', fixed to a motor vehicle being driven by a learner.

LSD *noun* a powerful drug that produces hallucinations (= lysergic acid diethylamide).

Lt. *abbreviation* **1** lieutenant. **2** light.

Ltd. *abbreviation* Limited (= 'limited (liability) company').

Luanda (loo-**an**-dă) the capital of Angola.

lubra (**loo**-bră) *noun* (now considered *offensive*) an Aboriginal woman. [Aboriginal]

lubricant (**loo**-bri-kănt) *noun* a lubricating substance.

lubricate (**loo**-bri-kayt) *verb* to oil or grease (machinery etc.) so that it moves easily. **lubrication** *noun*, **lubricator** *noun* [from Latin *lubricus* = slippery]

lucerne (**loo**-sern) *noun* a cloverlike plant used for fodder.

lucid (**loo**-sĭd) *adjective* **1** clearly expressed, easy to understand. **2** sane; *lucid intervals*, periods of sanity between periods of insanity. **lucidly** *adverb*, **lucidity** (loo-**sid**-ĭ-tee) *noun* [from Latin *lucidus* = bright]

Lucifer (**loo**-sĭ-fer) **1** Satan, the Devil. **2** (*poetic*) the planet Venus when it appears in the sky before sunrise, the morning star.

luck *noun* **1** chance thought of as a force that brings either good or bad fortune. **2** the events etc. (either favourable or unfavourable to one's interests) that it brings. **3** good fortune, *it will bring you luck*. □ **in luck** having good fortune. **out of luck** not in luck.

luckless *adjective* unlucky.

lucky *adjective* (**luckier**, **luckiest**) having or bringing or resulting from good luck. □ **the Lucky Country** a (chiefly ironic) name for Australia (¶ from the title of a book by Donald Horne). **lucky dip** a receptacle containing different articles from which people may draw one at random, with a chance of getting something of good value. **luckily** *adverb*

lucrative (**loo**-kră-tiv) *adjective* profitable, producing much money. **lucrativeness** *noun*

lucre (**loo**-ker) *noun* (*derogatory*) money; money-making as a motive for action.

☐ **filthy lucre** (*humorous*) money. [from Latin *lucrum* = profit]

Lucretius (loo-**kree**-shŭs) (c. 94 BC–c. 55 BC), Roman poet and philosopher.

Lucullan (loo-**kul**-ăn) *adjective* (of a feast etc.) very sumptuous or luxurious. [named after the Roman general Lucullus (1st century BC), famous for his lavish banquets]

Luddite (**lud**-dyt) *noun* 1 a member of the bands of English workers (1811–16) who destroyed newly introduced machinery that they thought would cause unemployment. 2 a person who similarly opposes the introduction of new technology or methods. [probably named after Ned *Lud*, a person who destroyed some machinery in about 1779]

luderick (**loo**-dĕ-rik) *noun* a dark-coloured Australian sea and estuarine fish, also called *blackfish*. [Ganay *luderag*]

ludicrous (**loo**-dĭ-krŭs) *adjective* absurd, ridiculous, laughable. **ludicrously** *adverb*

ludo *noun* a simple game played with dice and counters on a special board. [Latin, = I play]

luff *verb* to bring a ship's head nearer to the direction from which the wind is blowing.

Luftwaffe (**luuft**-vah-fĕ) the German air force before and during the Second World War. [German, = air weapon]

lug¹ *verb* (**lugged**, **lugging**) to drag or carry with great effort.

lug² *noun* an ear-like part or projection on an object, by which it may be carried or fixed in place etc.

luge (*pr.* loozh) *noun* a short raised toboggan. [Swiss French]

luggage *noun* suitcases and bags etc. containing a person's belongings taken on a journey.

lugger *noun* a small ship with four-cornered sails.

lugubrious (lŭ-**goo**-bree-ŭs) *adjective* dismal, mournful. **lugubriously** *adverb* [from Latin *lugubris* = mourning]

lugworm *noun* a large marine worm used as bait.

Luke, St, 1 an evangelist, traditionally the author of the third Gospel and the Acts of the Apostles. Feast day, 18 October. 2 the third Gospel.

lukewarm *adjective* 1 only slightly warm. 2 not enthusiastic, *got a lukewarm reception*. [from *luke* = tepid, + *warm*]

lull *verb* 1 to soothe or send to sleep. 2 to calm (suspicions etc.). 3 (of a storm or noise) to lessen, to become quiet. –**lull** *noun* a temporary period of quiet or inactivity.

lullaby *noun* a soothing song sung to put a child to sleep.

lumbago (lum-**bay**-goh) *noun* rheumatic pain in the muscles of the loins. [from Latin *lumbus* = loin]

lumbar *adjective* of or in the loins.

lumber *noun* 1 unwanted or disused articles of furniture etc.; any useless material. 2 partly prepared timber. –**lumber** *verb* 1 to encumber. 2 to fill up (space) inconveniently. 3 to move in a heavy clumsy way.

lumberjack *noun* (especially *N. Amer.*) one whose trade is the cutting, conveying, or preparing of forest timber, a logger.

lumberjacket *noun* a hip-length jacket fastening up to the neck.

lumen (**loo**-men) *noun* a unit of flux of light.

luminary (**loo**-mĭ-nă-ree) *noun* 1 a natural light-giving body, especially the sun or moon. 2 an eminent or influential person.

luminescent (loo-mĭ-**ness**-ĕnt) *adjective* emitting light without being hot. **luminescence** *noun* [from Latin *lumen* = light]

luminous (**loo**-mĭ-nŭs) *adjective* emitting light, glowing in the dark. **luminosity** (loo-mĭ-**noss**-ĭ-tee) *noun* [from Latin *lumen* = light]

lump¹ *noun* 1 a hard or compact mass, usually one without a regular shape. 2 a protuberance or swelling. 3 a heavy dull or stupid person. 4 (*informal*) a great quantity, a lot. –**lump** *verb* to put or consider together, to treat as alike, *lump them together*. ☐ **lump in the throat** a feeling of pressure there caused by emotion. **lump sum** a single payment covering a number of items or paid all at once, not in instalments.

lump² *verb* **lump it** (*informal*) to put up with something one dislikes.

lumpish *adjective* heavy and dull or stupid.

lumpy *adjective* (**lumpier**, **lumpiest**) full of lumps; covered in lumps. **lumpiness** *noun*

lunacy *noun* 1 insanity. 2 great folly. [from *lunatic*]

lunar *adjective* of the moon. **lunar month** the interval between new moons (about $29\frac{1}{2}$ days); four weeks. [from Latin *luna* = moon]

lunatic *noun* an insane person; one who is extremely foolish or reckless. –**lunatic** *adjective* insane, extremely foolish or reckless.

☐ **lunatic asylum** (*old use*) a mental home or mental hospital. **lunatic fringe** a few eccentric or fanatical members of a political or other group. [from Latin *luna* = moon (because formerly people were thought to be affected by changes of the moon)]

lunch *noun* a meal taken in the middle of the day. –**lunch** *verb* **1** to eat lunch. **2** to entertain to lunch.

luncheon *noun* (*formal*) lunch.

lung *noun* either of the two breathing-organs, in the chest of humans and most vertebrates, that draw in air and bring it into contact with the blood. ☐ **lung-power** *noun* the power of one's voice.

lunge *noun* **1** a sudden forward movement of the body towards something; a thrust. **2** a long rope on which a horse is held by its trainer while it is made to canter in a circle. –**lunge** *verb* (**lunged, lunging**) **1** to make a lunge. **2** to exercise (a horse) on a lunge.

lungfish *noun* a freshwater fish having both lungs and gills.

lupin *noun* a garden plant with tall tapering spikes of flowers, bearing seeds in pods.

lupine (**loo**-pyn) *adjective* of or like wolves.

lurch[1] *noun* **leave in the lurch** to abandon (a person etc.) so that he or she is left in an awkward situation.

lurch[2] *noun* an unsteady swaying movement to one side. –**lurch** *verb* to make such a movement, to stagger.

lurcher *noun* a dog of a breed that is a cross between a collie and a greyhound, often used by poachers for retrieving game.

lure (*pr.* loor *or* lyoor) *noun* **1** something that attracts, entices, or allures. **2** its power of attracting. **3** a bait or decoy for wild animals, a device used to attract and recall a trained hawk. –**lure** *verb* to entice, to attract by the promise of pleasure or gain.

lurex *noun* (*trademark*) **1** a type of yarn containing glittering metallic threads. **2** fabric made from this.

lurid (**loo**-rĭd) *adjective* **1** in glaring colours or combinations of colour. **2** sensationally and shockingly vivid, *the lurid details*. **luridly** *adverb*, **luridness** *noun*

lurk *verb* **1** to lie hidden while waiting to attack. **2** to wait near a place furtively or unobtrusively. **3** to be latent or lingering, *a lurking sympathy for the rebels*. –**lurk** *noun* (*Austral. informal*) a dodge or scheme.

Lusaka (loo-**sah**-kă) the capital of Zambia.

luscious (**lush**-ŭs) *adjective* **1** richly sweet in taste or smell. **2** voluptuously attractive. **lusciously** *adverb*, **lusciousness** *noun*

lush *adjective* **1** (of grass etc.) growing thickly and strongly. **2** luxurious, *lush furnishings*. **lushly** *adverb*, **lushness** *noun*

Lusitania a British liner that was sunk by a German submarine in the Atlantic in 1915.

lust *noun* **1** intense sexual desire. **2** any intense desire for something, *lust for power*. –**lust** *verb* to feel lust. **lustful** *adjective*, **lustfully** *adverb*

lustre (**lus**-ter) *noun* **1** the soft brightness of a smooth or shining surface. **2** glory, distinction, *add lustre to the assembly*. **3** a kind of metallic glaze on pottery and porcelain. **lustrous** *adjective* [from Latin *lustrare* = illuminate]

lusty *adjective* (**lustier, lustiest**) strong and vigorous, full of vitality. **lustily** *adverb*, **lustiness** *noun*

lute (*pr.* loot) *noun* a stringed musical instrument with a pear-shaped body, played by plucking, popular in the 14th–17th centuries. **lutenist** *noun*

lutein *noun* a yellow pigment found in egg yolk.

lutetium (loo-**tee**-shee-ŭm) *noun* a rare silver-white metallic element of the lanthanide series (symbol Lu).

Luther (**loo**-ther), Martin (1483–1546), German theologian, founder of the Protestant Reformation in Germany. **Lutheran** *adjective* & *noun*, **Lutheranism** *noun*

lux *noun* a unit of illumination. [Latin, = light]

Luxembourg 1 a grand duchy lying between France and Germany. **2** its capital city. **Luxembourger** *noun*

Luxor a city of Egypt, site of the southern complex of monuments of ancient Thebes.

luxuriant *adjective* growing profusely. **luxuriance** *noun*

Usage *Luxuriant* is used to describe plants, hair, beards, etc. which are growing well or thickly. *Luxurious* things are comfortable and often costly, e.g. *a luxurious hotel*.

---

luxuriate *verb* to feel great enjoyment, to enjoy as luxury, *luxuriating in the warm sun*.

luxurious *adjective* supplied with luxuries, very comfortable. **luxuriously** *adverb*, **luxuriousness** *noun*

Usage See usage note under luxuriant.

luxury *noun* **1** surroundings and food, dress, etc. that are choice and costly. **2** luxuriousness; self-indulgence. **3** something costly that is enjoyable but not essential. [from Latin *luxus* = plenty]

lychee (**ly**-chee) *noun* **1** a fruit consisting of a sweetish white pulp in a thin brown shell. **2** the tree (originally from China) that bears this.

lych-gate *noun* = lich-gate.

lycra *noun* (*trademark*) a kind of fabric containing elasticated threads, used especially for swimsuits, leotards, etc.

lye *noun* **1** water made alkaline with wood ashes. **2** any alkaline solution for washing things.

lying *see* lie¹, lie².

lymph (*pr.* limf) *noun* **1** a colourless fluid from tissues or organs of the body, containing white blood cells. **2** the fluid used in vaccination against smallpox. □ lymph gland or node any of the small glands in the lymphatic system (a network of vessels carrying lymph) that protect against infection. lymphatic (lim-**fat**-ik) *adjective* [from Latin *lympha* = water]

lymphocyte (**limf**-ŏ-syt) *noun* a kind of leucocyte present in lymph nodes and in the spleen. [from *lymph*, + Greek *kutos* = vessel]

lynch (*pr.* linch) *verb* (of a mob) to execute or punish violently, without a lawful trial. [named after William Lynch, an American judge who allowed this kind of punishment in about 1780]

lynx (*pr.* links) *noun* (*plural* lynxes) a wild animal of the cat family with spotted fur, noted for its keen sight. □ lynx-eyed *adjective* keen-sighted.

lyre *noun* an ancient musical instrument with strings fixed in a U-shaped frame.

lyrebird *noun* an Australian bird, the male of which can spread its tail in the shape of a lyre.

lyric (**li**-rik) *adjective* of poetry that expresses the poet's thoughts and feelings. –lyric *noun* **1** a lyric poem. **2** the words of a song. [from *lyre*]

lyrical (**li**-ri-kăl) *adjective* **1** = lyric, using language suitable for this. **2** songlike. **3** (*informal*) expressing oneself enthusiastically, *wax lyrical*. lyrically *adverb*

lyricist (**li**-rĭ-sĭst) *noun* a writer of lyrics.

lysin (**ly**-sĭn) *noun* a substance that is able to cause disintegration of living cells or bacteria. [from Greek *lusis* = loosening]

Mm

M *abbreviation* **1** mega-. **2** (as a film or video game classification) Mature; not recommended for persons under 15 years of age.

m *abbreviation* **1** metre(s). **2** mile(s). **3** million(s).

m- *prefix* denoting commercial activity conducted via mobile phones.

MA *abbreviation* **1** Master of Arts. **2** (as a film or video game classification) Mature Accompanied; restricted to persons 15 years of age and over.

ma *noun* (*informal*) mother.

ma'am (*pr.* mahm *or* mam) *noun* madam (used especially in addressing a royal lady).

Mabo (**mah**-boh), Koiki (Eddie) Mabo (1939–92), an Australian Mer (Murray) Islander, a member of the Aboriginal Arts Board of the Australia Council. His name was given to the benchmark judgment of the High Court of Australia in 1992 recognising continuous possession of their lands by the Torres Strait Mer (Murray) Islanders before these lands were annexed by Queensland (*see also* native title).

macabre (mă-**kahbr**) *adjective* gruesome, suggesting death.

macadam (mă-**kad**-ăm) *noun* layers of broken stone used in road-making, each layer being rolled hard before the next is put down. macadamise *verb* (also -ize). [named after a Scottish engineer, J. McAdam (died 1836)]

macadamia (mak-ă-**day**-mee-ă) *noun* an Australian rainforest tree cultivated for its large edible nut; this nut.

macaque (mă-**kahk**) *noun* a monkey of India and SE Asia, including the Barbary ape and the rhesus monkey.

macaroni *noun* pasta formed into long tubes.

macaroon *noun* a small flat sweet cake or biscuit made with sugar, egg white, and ground almonds or coconut.

Macarthur a pioneering Australian pastoralist family. Elizabeth (?1767–1850) and John (1766–1834) were instrumental in establishing the fine-wool industry with a Spanish merino breeding program.

macaw (mă-**kaw**) *noun* a brightly coloured American parrot with a long tail.

Macbeth (c. 1005–57), King of Scotland 1040–57.

Maccabees (**mak**-ă-beez) a family of Jewish patriots who led opposition to Syrian oppression from 168 BC. **2** four books of Jewish history, of which the first two are in the Apocrypha. Maccabean *adjective*

McCarthyism *noun* the policy of hunting out suspected Communists and removing them, especially from public office. [named after the American senator J. R. McCarthy (died 1957)]

macchiato (mak-ee-**ah**-toh) *noun* a black coffee with a small amount of milk or cream.

McCubbin, Frederick (1855–1917), Australian landscape painter and member of the Heidelberg School.

MacDonnell Ranges a series of ranges in the south-central region of the Northern Territory, the highest peak being Mount Zeil (1519 m).

mace[1] *noun* a ceremonial staff carried or placed before an official, especially that symbolising the Speaker's authority in the House of Representatives.

mace[2] *noun* a spice made from the dried outer covering of nutmeg.

Macedonia (mas-ĕ-**doh**-nee-ă) **1** (also Macedon) an ancient country, lying at the northern end of the Greek peninsula. **2** a region in the NE of modern Greece. **3** a landlocked republic in the Balkans. Macedonian *adjective* & *noun*

mach (*pr.* mahk) *noun* mach number the ratio of the speed of a body to the speed of sound in the same medium; a body travelling at *mach one* is travelling at the speed of sound, *mach two* is twice this. [named after the Austrian physicist Ernst Mach (1838–1916)]

machete (mă-**shet**-ee) *noun* a broad heavy knife used especially in Central America and the West Indies as a tool and weapon.

machiavellian (makee-ă-**vel**-ee-ăn) *adjective* elaborately cunning or deceitful. [named after Niccolo dei Machiavelli (1469–1527), an Italian statesman who advised the use of any means, however unscrupulous, that would strengthen the State]

machinations (mash-ĭ-**nay**-shŏnz) *plural noun* clever scheming, things done by this.

machine *noun* 1 an apparatus for applying mechanical power, having several parts each with a definite function. 2 something operated by such apparatus, e.g. a bicycle or aircraft. 3 a complex controlling system of an organisation, *the publicity machine*. –machine *verb* to make, produce, or work on (a thing) with a machine; to stitch with a sewing machine. ☐ machine gun an automatic gun giving continuous fire. machine language a language (*see* language sense 4) to which a particular computer can respond directly without further translation. machine-readable *adjective* in a form that a computer can respond to. machine tool a mechanically operated tool. [from Greek *mekhane* = device]

machinery *noun* 1 machines. 2 a mechanism. 3 an organised system for doing something.

machinist *noun* a person who makes or works machinery; one who operates machine tools.

machismo (mă-**chiz**-moh) *noun* virility or manly courage; a show of this. [same origin as *macho*]

macho (**mach**-oh) *adjective* exhibiting machismo; aggressively masculine. [Spanish, = male]

mackerel *noun* (*plural* mackerel) an edible seafish. ☐ mackerel sky rows of small white fleecy clouds.

McKillop, St Mary (Mary of the Cross) (1842–1909), Australian nun who founded the Sisters of St Joseph of the Sacred Heart, and worked for the education of poor children.

McKinley, Mount the highest mountain in North America, in Alaska (6194 m).

mackintosh *noun* 1 waterproof material of rubber and cloth. 2 a raincoat. [named after the Scottish inventor of a waterproof material, C. Macintosh (died 1843)]

Macquarie, Lachlan (1762–1824), Scottish Governor of NSW, 1810–21.
☐ Macquarie Island an island about 1400 km south-east of Tasmania, containing a scientific base and a sanctuary for the island's rare

flora and fauna, including the endemic royal penguin. Macquarie perch an edible Australian freshwater fish.

macramé (mă-**krah**-may) *noun* 1 a fringe or trimming of knotted thread or cord. 2 the art of making this. [from Turkish *makrama* = bedspread]

macro *noun* (in computing) a set of instructions grouped together as a single instruction.

macro- *prefix* 1 long. 2 large, large-scale. [from Greek *makros* = long, large]

macrobiotic *adjective* relating to or following a diet intended to prolong life, comprising pure vegetable foods, brown rice, etc.

macrocosm (**mak**-rŏ-kozm) *noun* 1 the universe. 2 any great whole. [from Greek *makros* = long, + *cosmos*]

macroeconomics *noun* the study of the economy as a whole (compare *microeconomics*). macroeconomic *adjective*

macromolecule *noun* a molecule containing a very large number of atoms.

macroscopic (makrŏ-**skop**-ik) *adjective* 1 visible to the naked eye. 2 regarded in terms of large units. macroscopically *adverb* [from Greek *makros* = long, + *skopein* = look at]

mad *adjective* (madder, maddest) 1 having a disordered mind, not sane. 2 extremely foolish, *a mad scheme*. 3 wildly enthusiastic, *is mad about sport*. 4 (*informal*) very annoyed. 5 frenzied, *a mad scramble*. 6 wildly light-hearted. ☐ like mad (*informal*) with great haste, energy, or enthusiasm. mad cow disease *see* BSE. madly *adverb*, madness *noun*

Madagascar an island republic off the SE coast of Africa.

madam *noun* 1 a word used in speaking politely to a woman, or prefixed to the name of her office in formal address, *Madam Chairman*. 2 a conceited or presumptuous young woman. [from French *ma dame* = my lady]

Madame (mă-**dahm**) *noun* (*plural* Mesdames, *pr.* may-**dahm**) the title of a French-speaking woman, = Mrs or madam.

madcap *noun* a wildly impulsive person. –madcap *adjective* wildly impulsive.

madden *verb* to make mad or angry, to irritate.

madder *noun* **1** a plant with yellowish flowers. **2** a red dye got from its root or made synthetically.

made *see* **make**.

Madeira (mă-**dee**-ră) the largest of a group of islands (**the Madeiras**) in the Atlantic Ocean off NW Africa, which are in Portuguese possession but partly autonomous. –**Madeira** *noun* a fortified white wine produced in Madeira. ☐ **Madeira cake** a rich plain sponge cake.

Mademoiselle (mad-mwă-**zel**) *noun* (*plural* **Mesdemoiselles**, *pr.* mayd-mwă-**zel**) the title of a French-speaking girl or unmarried woman, = Miss or madam.

madhouse *noun* (*informal*) **1** a mental home or mental hospital. **2** a scene of confused uproar.

madman *noun* (*informal*) a man who is mentally ill.

madonna *noun* a picture or statue of the Virgin Mary. ☐ **madonna lily** a tall lily with white flowers. [from Old Italian *ma donna* = my lady]

Madras (mă-**dras**) a seaport on the east coast of India, now Chennai.

madras *noun* a light cotton fabric often with coloured stripes.

madrasa (mă-**dra**-să) *noun* (also **madrasah**, or **medrese**) a college for Islamic instruction. [from Arabic *darasa* = to study]

Madrid the capital of Spain.

madrigal (**mad**-rĭ-găl) *noun* **1** a part-song for voices, usually without instrumental accompaniment. **2** a short love poem.

madwoman *noun* (*informal*) a woman who is mentally ill.

maelstrom (**mayl**-strŏm) *noun* **1** a great whirlpool. **2** a confused state. [from Dutch *malen* = whirl, + *stroom* = stream]

maestro (**my**-stroh) *noun* (*plural* **maestros**) **1** a great musical composer, teacher, or conductor. **2** a master of any art. [Italian, = master]

Mafia (**mah**-fee-ă) *noun* an organised group of criminals originating in Sicily, now especially in Italy and the USA. –**mafia** *noun* a network of persons regarded as exerting hidden influence. [Sicilian dialect, = bragging]

magazine *noun* **1** a paper-covered illustrated periodical publication containing articles or stories etc. by a number of writers. **2** a store for arms and ammunition, or for explosives.

3 a chamber for holding cartridges to be fed into the breech of a gun. **4** a similar device in a camera or slide projector. [from Arabic *makhazin* = storehouses]

Magellan (mă-**gel**-ăn), Ferdinand (c. 1480–1521), Portuguese explorer, who reached South America and rounded the continent through the strait that now bears his name.

magenta (mă-**jen**-tă) *noun* & *adjective* bright purplish red.

maggot *noun* a larva, especially of a fly.

maggoty *adjective* **1** infested with maggots. **2** (*Austral. informal*) angry; bad-tempered.

Magi (**mayj**-I) *plural noun* the 'wise men' from the East who brought offerings to the infant Christ at Bethlehem.

magic *noun* **1** the supposed art of controlling events or effects etc. by supernatural power. **2** superstitious practices based on belief in this. **3** a mysterious and enchanting quality, *the magic of a spring day*. –**magic** *adjective* of magic; used in producing magic, *magic words*. ☐ **magic carpet** a mythical carpet able to transport a person on it to any place. **magic lantern** a simple form of projector using glass slides. **magical** *adjective*, **magically** *adverb*

magician (mă-**jish**-ăn) *noun* **1** a person who is skilled in magic. **2** a conjuror.

magisterial (ma-jĭs-**teer**-ree-ăl) *adjective* **1** of a magistrate. **2** having or showing authority, imperious. **magisterially** *adverb*

magistracy (**maj**-ĭ-stră-see) *noun* **1** the office of magistrate. **2** magistrates collectively.

magistrate *noun* an official with authority to administer the law, hear and judge minor cases, and hold preliminary hearings. [from Latin *magister* = master]

magma *noun* a fluid or semi-fluid material under the earth's crust, from which igneous rock is formed by cooling.

Magna Carta (**kar**-tă) the charter establishing people's rights concerning personal and political liberty, obtained by the English from King John in 1215.

magnanimous (mag-**nan**-ĭ-mŭs) *adjective* noble and generous in one's conduct, not petty. **magnanimously** *adverb*, **magnanimity** (mag-nă-**nim**-ĭ-tee) *noun* [from Latin *magnus* = great, + *animus* = mind]

magnate (**mag**-nayt) *noun* a wealthy and influential person, especially in business. [from Latin *magnus* = great]

magnesia (mag-**nee**-zhă) *noun* a white powder that is a compound of magnesium, used as an antacid and mild laxative.

magnesium (mag-**nee**-zee-ŭm) *noun* a chemical element (symbol Mg), a silvery-white metal that burns with an intensely bright flame.

magnet *noun* **1** a piece of iron or steel etc. that can attract iron and that points north and south when suspended. **2** a person or thing that exerts a powerful attraction.

magnetic *adverb* **1** having the properties of a magnet. **2** produced or acting by magnetism. **3** having the power to attract people, *a magnetic personality.* □ **magnetic compass** one using a magnetic needle that points north and south. **magnetic pole** either of the two points, in the region of the geographical North and South Poles, indicated by the needle of a magnetic compass. **magnetic tape** a strip of plastic coated or impregnated with magnetic particles for use in the recording and reproduction of audio or video signals or other data. **magnetically** *adverb*

magnetise *verb* (also **-ize**) **1** to give magnetic properties to. **2** to attract as a magnet does. **3** to exert attraction on (a person or people). **magnetisation** *noun*

magnetism *noun* **1** the properties and effects of magnetic substances. **2** the scientific study of these. **3** great charm and attraction, *personal magnetism.*

magneto (mag-**nee**-toh) *noun* (*plural* **magnetos**) a small electric generator using permanent magnets, especially one used to produce electricity for the spark in the ignition system of an engine. [from *magnet*]

Magnificat *noun* a canticle beginning 'My soul doth magnify the Lord', the words of the Virgin Mary at the Annunciation (Luke 1:46–55).

magnification *noun* **1** magnifying. **2** the amount by which a lens etc. magnifies things.

magnificent *adjective* **1** splendid in appearance etc. **2** excellent in quality. **magnificently** *adverb*, **magnificence** *noun* [same origin as *magnify*]

magnify *verb* (**magnified**, **magnifying**) **1** to make (an object) appear larger than it really is, as a lens or microscope does. **2** to exaggerate. **3** (*old use*) to praise, *My soul doth magnify the Lord.* □ **magnifying glass** a lens (often mounted in a frame) that magnifies

things. **magnifier** *noun* [from Latin *magnus* = great, + *facere* = make]

magnitude *noun* **1** largeness, size. **2** importance. **3** the degree of brightness of a star. □ **of the first magnitude** very important. [from Latin *magnus* = great]

magnolia (mag-**noh**-lee-ă) *noun* a shrub or tree with dark green leaves and large waxlike flowers.

magnum *noun* a wine bottle of twice the standard size (1.5 litres). [Latin, = large thing]

magnum opus *noun* a great work of art, literature, etc.; the greatest work of an artist, writer, etc. [Latin]

magpie *noun* **1** a black and white Australian bird with a melodious song. **2** (in the northern hemisphere) a noisy black and white crow. **3** a chatterer. **4** a person who collects objects at random. □ **magpie lark** a black and white Australian bird that builds a mud nest and has a loud piping call.

Magritte (mah-**greet**), René (1898–1967), Belgian surrealist painter.

Magyar (**mag**-yar) *noun* **1** a member of a people originally from western Siberia, now predominant in Hungary. **2** their language, Hungarian. –**Magyar** *adjective* of the Magyars. □ **magyar sleeve** a plain sleeve cut in one piece with the body of a garment.

Mahabharata (mah-hă-**bah**-rătă) one of the two great Sanskrit epics of the Hindus (the other is the Ramayana), dating in its present form from c. AD 400.

maharaja (mah-hă-**rah**-jă) *noun* the former title of certain Indian princes. [Hindi, = great rajah]

maharanee (mah-hă-**rah**-nee) *noun* the former title of a maharaja's wife or widow. [Hindi, = great ranee]

maharishi (mah-hă-**rish**-ee) *noun* a Hindu man of great wisdom. [Hindi, = great sage]

mahatma (mă-**hat**-mă) *noun* (in India etc.) a title of respect for a person regarded with reverence. [from Sanskrit, = great soul]

Mahayana *noun* a form of Buddhism practised especially in China, Tibet, Japan, and Korea, typically concerned with personal spiritual practice and the ideal of the bodhisattva. [Sanskrit, = greater vehicle]

Mahdi (**mah**-dee) *noun* **1** the title of a spiritual and temporal leader expected by Muslims. **2** a claimant of this title, especially a former leader of insurrection in the Sudan. [from Arabic *mahdiy* = he who is guided right]

mah-jong *noun* a Chinese game for four people, played with pieces called tiles.

Mahler, Gustav (1860–1911), Austrian composer and conductor; he wrote nine symphonies and several collections of songs.

mahogany (mǎ-**hog**-ǎnee) *noun* 1 a very hard reddish-brown wood much used for furniture. 2 the tropical tree that produces this. 3 its colour.

mahout (mǎ-**howt**) *noun* (in India etc.) an elephant driver. [Hindi]

maid *noun* 1 (*old use*) a maiden, a girl. 2 a female servant doing indoor work.

maiden *noun* (*old use*) a girl or young unmarried woman; a virgin. –**maiden** *adjective* 1 unmarried, *maiden aunt*. 2 (of a horse) not yet having won a prize. 3 first, *a maiden speech*; *maiden voyage*.
□ **maiden name** a woman's family name before she marries. **maiden over** an over in cricket in which no runs are scored. **maidenly** *adjective*, **maidenhood** *noun*

maidenhair *noun* a fern with fine hairlike stalks and delicate foliage.

maidenhead *noun* 1 virginity. 2 the hymen.

maidservant *noun* a female servant.

mail[1] *noun* 1 the official conveyance of letters, parcels, etc.; the postal service. 2 the letters, parcels, etc. conveyed. 3 a single delivery or collection of these. 4 messages distributed by a computer system; email. –**mail** *verb* to send by post or by email. □ **mailing list** a list of people to whom advertising matter etc. is to be posted. **mail order** an order for goods to be sent by post.

mail[2] *noun* body armour made of metal rings or chains.

mailbag *noun* a large bag for carrying mail.

mailbox *noun* a box into which letters are posted or delivered; a letterbox.

mailman *noun* a person who delivers the mail; a postman.

maim *verb* to wound or injure so that some part of the body is useless.

main *adjective* principal, most important; greatest in size or extent. –**main** *noun* 1 the main pipe, channel, or cable in a public system for conveying water, gas, or (usually **mains**) electricity. 2 (*old use*) the mainland; the high seas. □ **have an eye to the main chance** to be considering one's own interests.

in the main for the most part, on the whole. **Spanish Main** part of the NE coast of South America.

Maine a State of the north-eastern USA.

mainframe *noun* 1 the central processing unit of a computer. 2 a large computer system.

mainland *noun* a country or continent without its adjacent islands.

mainly *adverb* for the most part, chiefly.

mainmast *noun* the principal mast of a sailing ship.

mainspring *noun* 1 the principal spring of a watch or clock etc. 2 the chief force motivating the actions of a person or group.

mainstay *noun* 1 the strong cable that secures the mainmast. 2 the chief support.

mainstream *noun* the dominant trend of opinion or style etc.

maintain *verb* 1 to cause to continue, to keep in existence. 2 to keep in repair, *the house is well maintained*. 3 to support, to provide for, to bear the expenses of, *maintaining his son at university*. 4 to assert as true.

maintenance *noun* 1 maintaining; being maintained. 2 keeping equipment etc. in repair. 3 provision of the means to support life; an allowance of money for this, especially paid for a spouse or children after separation or divorce.

maisonette (may-zǒ-**net**) *noun* 1 a semi-detached house. 2 a flat.

maize *noun* 1 a tall cereal plant bearing grain on large cobs. 2 its grain. 3 the yellow colour of maize cobs.

majestic *adjective* stately and dignified, imposing. **majestically** *adverb*

majesty *noun* 1 impressive stateliness. 2 sovereign power. 3 the title used in speaking of or to a sovereign or a sovereign's wife or widow, *His* or *Her* or *Your Majesty*.

major *adjective* 1 greater, very important, *major roads*. 2 (of a surgical operation) serious or life-threatening. 3 (in music) of or based on a scale which has a semitone next above the third and seventh notes and a whole tone elsewhere. –**major** *noun* 1 an army officer below lieutenant colonel and above captain. 2 an officer in charge of a section of band instruments, *drum major*. 3 a student's main subject or course. 4 (in Australian Rules) a goal, scoring six points. –**major** *verb* to specialise (in a certain subject) at college or university. □ **major general** an army officer

540

next below lieutenant general. [Latin, = larger, greater]

Majorca (mă-**yor**-kă) a Mediterranean island off the east coast of Spain.

major-domo (may-jer-**doh**-moh) *noun* (*plural* **major-domos**) the head steward of a great household.

majority *noun* **1** the greatest part of a group or class. **2** the number by which votes for one party etc. exceed those for the next or for all combined. **3** (in law) full age, *attained his majority*. □ **majority verdict** a verdict supported by more than half of a jury but not unanimous.

makarrata (mak-ă-**rah**-tă) *noun* an Aboriginal ceremonial ritual symbolising the restoration of peace after a dispute; an agreement. [from Yolngu *makarrata*]

make *verb* (**made**, **making**) **1** to construct, create, or prepare from parts or from other substances. **2** to draw up as a legal document or contract, *make a will*. **3** to establish (laws or rules or structures). **4** to arrange ready for use, *make the beds*. **5** to cause to exist, to produce, *make difficulties*; *make peace*. **6** to result in, to amount to, *two and two make four*. **7** to cause to be or become, *it made me happy*. **8** to frame in the mind, *made a decision*. **9** to succeed in arriving at or achieving a position, *we made Canberra by midnight*; *she finally made the team*. **10** (*informal*) to catch (a train etc.). **11** to form, to serve for, *this makes pleasant reading*; to turn out to be, *she made a good teacher*. **12** to gain or acquire, *make a profit*; *make friends*, to become friends. **13** to consider to be, *what do you make the time?*; *see what you can make of her letter*, how to interpret it. **14** to cause or compel, *make him repeat it*. **15** to perform (an action etc.), *make an attempt*; *make war*. **16** to ensure the success of, *wine can make the meal*; *this made my day*. **17** to act as if intending to do something, *he made to go*. –**make** *noun* **1** making; the way a thing is made. **2** the origin of manufacture, *a Japanese make of car*. □ **be made for** to be ideally suited to. **be the making of** to be the main factor in the success of. **have it made** (*informal*) to be sure of success. **have the makings of** to have the essential qualities for becoming, *he had the makings of a good manager*. **a made man** one who has attained success in his life or career. **make believe** to pretend. **make-believe** *adjective* pretended; (*noun*) pretence. **make do** to manage with

something that is not really adequate or satisfactory. **make for** to proceed towards, to try to reach; to tend to bring about, *it makes for domestic harmony*. **make good** to become successful or prosperous; *make good the loss*, pay compensation; *make good the damage*, repair it; *made good his escape*, succeeded in escaping. **make it** to achieve what one wanted, to be successful. **make it up** to become reconciled after a quarrel. **make it up to someone** to compensate him or her. **make love** to have sexual intercourse; (*old use*) to try to win the affection of, to embrace and kiss in courtship. **make money** to make a large profit. **make much** or **little of** to treat as important or unimportant. **make off** to go away hastily. **make off with** to carry away, to steal. **make out** to write out (a list etc.); to manage to see or read, *made out a shadowy figure*; to understand the nature of, *I can't make him out*; to assert or claim or pretend to be, *made him out to be a fool*; (*informal*) to fare, *how did you make out?* **make over** to transfer the ownership of; to convert for a new purpose. **make room** to clear a space for something by moving another person or thing. **make shift** = make do. **make time** to contrive to find time to do something. **make up** to form or constitute; to put together, to prepare (medicine etc.); to invent (a story etc.); to compensate (for a loss or mistake); to complete (an amount) by supplying what is lacking; to apply cosmetics to; *make up one's mind*, to decide. **make-up** *noun* cosmetics applied to the skin, especially of the face; the way something is made up, its composition or constituent parts; a person's character and temperament. **make up to a person** to curry favour with him or her. **on the make** (*informal*) intent on gain.

makeover *noun* a complete transformation or remodelling.

maker *noun* one who makes something. **our Maker** God.

makeshift *noun* a temporary or improvised substitute. –**makeshift** *adjective* serving as this.

makeweight *noun* **1** a small quantity added to make up the full weight. **2** anything added to make up for a deficiency.

mal- *prefix* bad; badly (as in *malnourished*). [from Latin *male* = bad]

Malabo (mă-**lah**-boh) the capital of Equatorial Guinea.

Malacca (mă-**lak**-ă) *noun* a brown cane made
from the stem of a kind of palm tree. [named
after Malacca in Malaysia]

Malachi (**mal**-ă-ky) **1** a Hebrew prophet
of the 5th century BC. **2** the book of the Old
Testament containing his prophecies.

malachite (**mal**-ă-kyt) *noun* a green mineral
that can be polished.

maladjusted *adjective* (of a person) not
well adjusted to his or her own circumstances.
maladjustment *noun*

maladministration *noun* bad or improper
management of business or public affairs.

maladroit (**mal**-ă-droit) *adjective* bungling.

malady (**mal**-ă-dee) *noun* an illness, a disease.
[from French *malade* = ill]

Malagasy (mală-**gas**-ee) *adjective* of
Madagascar. –**Malagasy** *noun* **1** a native
or inhabitant of Madagascar. **2** the official
language of Madagascar.

malaise (mal-**ayz**) *noun* a feeling of illness or
mental uneasiness. [from French, = bad ease]

malapropism (**mal**-ă-prop-izm) *noun* a
comical confusion of words, e.g. *the very
pineapple of politeness* (for *the very pinnacle
of politeness*). [named after Mrs Malaprop in
Sheridan's play *The Rivals* (1775)]

malapropos (mal-aprŏ-**poh**) *adverb*
& *adjective* inopportunely said, done, or
happening.

malaria (mă-**lair**-ree-ă) *noun* a disease
causing fever that recurs at intervals,
transmitted by mosquitoes. **malarial** *adjective*
[from Italian *mala aria* = bad air, which was
once thought to cause the disease]

Malawi (mă-**lah**-wee) a republic in south
central Africa. **Malawian** *adjective* & *noun*

Malay (mă-**lay**) *adjective* of a people living
in Malaysia and Indonesia. –**Malay** *noun*
1 a member of this people. **2** their language.

Malaya a group of States forming part of
Malaysia. **Malayan** *adjective* & *noun*

Malay Archipelago a large group of
islands, including Sumatra, Java, Borneo, the
Philippines, and New Guinea, lying SE of the
continent of Asia and north of Australia.

Malaysia (mă-**lay**-*zh*ă) a parliamentary
monarchy in SE Asia, a federation of states
and territories of the Malay peninsula south of
Thailand, and Sabah and Sarawak. **Malaysian**
adjective & *noun*

malcontent (**mal**-kŏn-tent) *noun* a person
who is discontented and inclined to rebel.

Maldives (**mawl**-divz) a republic consisting
of a group of islands south-west of India.
Maldivian (mawl-**div**-ee-ăn) *adjective* & *noun*

Male (**mah**-lay) the capital of the Maldives.

male *adjective* **1** of the sex that can beget
offspring by fertilising egg cells produced
by the female. **2** (of plants) having flowers
that contain pollen-bearing organs and not
seeds. **3** of a man or men, *male voice choir*.
4 (of parts of machinery etc.) designed to enter
or fill a corresponding hollow part. –**male**
noun a male person, animal, or plant.

malediction (mal-ě-**dik**-shŏn) *noun* a curse.
[from Latin *male* = evilly, + *diction*]

maledictory (mal-ě-**dik**-tŏ-ree) *adjective*
expressing a curse.

malefactor (**mal**-ě-fak-ter) *noun* a
wrongdoer. **malefaction** (mal-ě-**fak**-shŏn)
noun [from Latin *male* = evilly, + *factor* =
doer]

malevolent (mă-**lev**-ŏ-lĕnt) *adjective*
wishing harm to others. **malevolently** *adverb*,
malevolence *noun* [from Latin *male* = evilly,
+ *volens* = wishing]

malformation *noun* faulty formation.

malformed *adjective* faultily formed.

malfunction *noun* faulty functioning.
–**malfunction** *verb* to function faultily.

Mali (**mah**-lee) an inland republic in
West Africa. **Malian** *adjective* & *noun*

malice *noun* a desire to harm others or to
tease. [from Latin *malus* = evil]

malicious (mă-**lish**-ŭs) *adjective* feeling,
showing, or caused by malice. **maliciously**
adverb

malign (mă-**lyn**) *adjective* **1** harmful, *a malign
influence*. **2** showing malice. –**malign** *verb*
to say unpleasant and untrue things about,
maligning an innocent person. **malignity**
(mă-**lig**-nĭ-tee) *noun* [same origin as *malice*]

malignant (mă-**lig**-nănt) *adjective* **1** (of a
tumour) growing uncontrollably (the opposite
is *benign*). **2** feeling or showing great ill will.
malignantly *adverb*, **malignancy** *noun*

malinger (mă-**ling**-ger) *verb* to pretend to be
ill in order to avoid work. **malingerer** *noun*

mall (*pr.* mawl *or* mal) *noun* **1** a sheltered walk
or promenade. **2** an enclosed shopping centre
or a shopping area where traffic is excluded,
Rundle Mall; *Pitt Street Mall*.

mallard (**mal**-erd) *noun* (*plural* mallard) a kind of wild duck, the male of which has a glossy green head.

malleable (**mal**-ee-ă-bŭl) *adjective* **1** able to be hammered or pressed into shape. **2** easy to influence, adaptable. **malleability** *noun* [from Latin *malleare* = to hammer]

mallee (**mal**-ee) *noun* (*Austral*.) **1** any of many usually small eucalypts flourishing in semi-arid areas. **2** scrub formed by these; an area where this scrub is the main vegetation, *mallee country*; *grew up out in the mallee*. ☐ **mallee fowl** a large mound-building bird; a lowan. [probably Wemba-wemba *mali*]

mallet *noun* **1** a hammer, usually of wood. **2** a similarly shaped instrument with a long handle, for striking the ball in croquet or polo. [from Latin *malleus* = a hammer]

mallow *noun* a plant with hairy stems and leaves, bearing purple, pink, or white flowers.

malmsey (**mahm**-zee) *noun* a kind of strong sweet wine. [from the name of Monemvasia in Greece]

malnutrition *noun* insufficient nutrition.

malodorous (mal-**oh**-dŏ-rŭs) *adjective* stinking.

Malpighian layer (mal-**pig**-ee-ăn) *noun* the layer of the epidermis that is next to the dermis and in which cell division takes place.

malpractice *noun* **1** wrongdoing. **2** improper or negligent professional treatment, especially by a doctor.

malt *noun* **1** grain (usually barley) that has been allowed to sprout and is then dried, used for brewing or distilling or vinegar-making. **2** (*informal*) malt whisky, malt liquor. – **malt** *verb* to make or be made into malt. ☐ **malted milk** a drink made from dried milk and malt. **malt whisky** whisky made entirely from malted barley.

Malta an island republic in the Mediterranean Sea. ☐ **Maltese cross** a cross with four equal arms broadening outwards, often indented at the ends. **Maltese** *adjective* & *noun* (*plural* **Maltese**).

Malthus, Thomas Robert (1766–1834), English clergyman and economist who taught that the increase of population would inevitably outstrip food supplies. **Malthusian** *adjective*, **Malthusianism** *noun*

maltose *noun* a sugar formed from starch by the action of saliva or malt.

maltreat *verb* to ill-treat. **maltreatment** *noun*

Malvinas (mal-**vee**-năs) the name by which the Falkland Islands are known in Argentina.

mama (mă-**mah**) *noun* (*old use*) mother.

mammal *noun* a member of the class of animals that suckle their young. **mammalian** (mă-**may**-lee-ăn) *adjective* [from Latin *mamma* = breast]

mammary (**mam**-ă-ree) *adjective* of the breasts. **mammary gland** a milk-secreting gland.

mammogram *noun* an X-ray image of the breast(s).

Mammon *noun* wealth personified, regarded as an evil influence.

mammoth *noun* a large extinct elephant with a hairy coat and curved tusks. – **mammoth** *adjective* huge. [from Russian]

man *noun* (*plural* **men**) **1** a human being, a creature distinguished from other animals by superior mental development, power of articulate speech, and upright posture. **2** mankind. **3** an adult male person. **4** an individual male person considered as an expert or one's assistant or opponent etc., *if you want a good teacher, he's your man*. **5** a person of unspecified sex, an individual person, *every man for himself*. **6** a manly person; *is he man enough to do it?*, is he brave enough? **7** a male servant, employee, or worker. **8** an ordinary soldier etc., not an officer. **9** each of the set of small objects moved on a board in playing board games such as chess and draughts. – **man** *verb* (**manned**, **manning**) to supply with people for service or to operate something, *man the pumps*. ☐ **be one's own man** to be independent. **man about town** a man who spends much of his time in sophisticated social amusements. **man-hour** *noun* the amount of work that one person can do in an hour, considered as a unit. **man in the street** an ordinary person, not an expert. **man-made** *adjective* made by man, not by nature, synthetic. **man of the world** *see* **world**. **man-sized** *adjective* of the size of a man; adequate for a man. **man to man** with frankness. **to a man** all without exception. [from Old English *mann*]

mana (**mah**-nă) *noun* inborn authority, charisma.

manacle (**man**-ă-kŭl) *noun* each of a pair of fetters for the hands. – **manacle** *verb* to fetter with manacles. [from Latin *manus* = hand]

manage *verb* **1** to have under effective control. **2** to be the manager of (a business etc.). **3** to operate (a tool or machinery) effectively. **4** to succeed in doing or producing something (often with inadequate means), to be able to cope, *managed without help*. **5** to contrive to persuade (a person) to do what one wants, by use of tact or flattery or other means. □ **managing director** a person having executive control or authority. **manageable** *adjective* [from Latin *manus* = hand]

management *noun* **1** managing; being managed. **2** the process of managing a business; people engaged in this.

manager *noun* **1** a person who is in charge of the affairs of a business etc. **2** one who deals with the business affairs of a sports team or entertainer etc. **3** one who manages affairs in a certain way, *she is a good manager*. **managerial** (mană-**jeer**-ree-ăl) *adjective*

manageress *noun* a woman manager of a business etc.

Managua (mă-**nag**-wă) the capital of Nicaragua.

Manama (man-**ah**-mă) the capital of Bahrain.

manchester *noun* (*Austral.*) household linen. [from *Manchester* in England]

Manchu (man-**choo**) *noun* **1** a member of a Tartar people who conquered China and founded the last imperial dynasty (1644–1912). **2** their language, now spoken in part of NE China.

Manchuria (man-**choo**-ree-ă) a region forming the NE portion of China.

mandala (**man**-dă-lă) *noun* a symbolic pattern used in Hindu and Buddhist art and meditation. [Sanskrit, = a disc]

mandarin (**man**-dă-rĭn) *noun* **1** a high-ranking influential official. **2** a kind of small flattened-orange usually with a loose skin. –**Mandarin** *noun* the language formerly used by officials and educated persons in China; any of the varieties of this spoken as a common language in China, especially the northern variety.

mandatary (**man**-dă-tă-ree) *noun* a person or state holding a mandate.

mandate *noun* **1** authority to perform a certain task or apply certain policies. **2** (*historical*) a commission from the League of Nations to a member state to administer a territory. –**mandate** *verb* **1** to give authority to (a delegate). **2** to commit (a territory to

be governed) to a mandatary. [from Latin *mandatum* = commanded]

mandatory (**man**-dă-tŏ-ree) *adjective* obligatory, compulsory. **mandatorily** *adverb*

Mandela (man-**del**-ă), Nelson Rolihlahla (born 1918), South African statesman, civil rights leader, leader of the African National Congress, President of South Africa 1994–99.

mandible (**man**-dĭ-bŭl) *adjective* **1** a jaw, especially the lower one. **2** either of the parts of a bird's beak. **3** the corresponding part in insects etc.

mandir *noun* a Hindu temple.

mandolin (**man**-dŏ-lin) *noun* a musical instrument of the lute family, played with a plectrum.

mandrake *noun* a poisonous plant with white or purple flowers and large yellow fruit.

mandrel *noun* **1** (in a lathe) the shaft to which work is fixed while being turned etc. **2** a cylindrical rod round which metal or other material is forged or shaped.

mandrill *noun* a large baboon of West Africa.

mane *noun* **1** the long hair on a horse's or lion's neck. **2** a person's long hair.

Manet (**man**-ay), Édouard (1832–83), French painter who greatly influenced the impressionists. His works include *The Picnic* (*Le Déjeuner sur l'herbe*) and *A Bar at the Folies-Bergère*.

manful *adjective* brave, resolute. **manfully** *adverb*

manga *noun* Japanese cartoons, comic books, and animated films, often intended for a mature audience.

manganese (**mang**-gă-neez) *noun* a chemical element (symbol Mn), a hard brittle grey metal; its black oxide.

manganin (**mang**-gă-nin) *noun* a copper alloy containing manganese and nickel, used for making electrical resistors.

mange (*pr.* maynj) *noun* a skin disease affecting hairy animals, caused by a parasite.

manger *noun* a long open trough or box in a stable etc. for horses or cattle to eat from.

mangle¹ *noun* a wringer. –**mangle** *verb* to press (clothes etc.) in a mangle.

mangle² *verb* to damage by cutting or crushing roughly, to mutilate.

mango *noun* (*plural* **mangoes**) **1** a tropical fruit with yellowish flesh. **2** the tree that bears it.

mangrove *noun* a tropical tree or shrub growing in shore-mud and swamps, with many tangled roots above ground.

mangy (**mayn**-jee) *adjective* (**mangier**, **mangiest**) **1** having mange. **2** squalid, shabby.

manhandle *verb* **1** to move (a thing) by human effort alone. **2** to treat roughly.

Manhattan an island at the mouth of the Hudson River, now a borough of the city of New York, with financial, commercial, and cultural establishments.

Manhattan Project the code name for an American project set up in 1942 to develop an atomic bomb.

manhole *noun* an opening (usually with a cover) in a floor, ceiling, footpath, etc. for a person to gain access.

manhood *noun* **1** the state of being a man; *reach manhood*, become an adult male person. **2** manly qualities, courage. **3** the men of a country.

manhunt *noun* an organised search for a person, especially a criminal.

mania (**may**-nee-ă) *noun* **1** mental illness marked by periods of great excitement and violence. **2** extreme enthusiasm for something. [Greek, = madness]

maniac (**may**-nee-ak) *noun* a person affected with mania.

maniacal (mă-**ny**-ă-kăl) *adjective* of or like a mania or a maniac. **maniacally** *adverb*

manic (**man**-ik) *adjective* of or affected with mania. □ **manic-depressive** *adjective* of a mental disorder with alternating bouts of excitement and depression; (*noun*) a person suffering from this disorder.

manicure *noun* cosmetic care and treatment of the hands and fingernails. –**manicure** *verb* to apply such treatment to. **manicurist** *noun* [from Latin *manus* = hand, + *cura* = care]

manifest *adjective* clear and unmistakable. –**manifest** *verb* to show (a thing) clearly, to give signs of, *the crowd manifested its approval by cheering*. –**manifest** *noun* a list of cargo or passengers carried by a ship or aircraft etc. **manifestly** *adverb*, **manifestation** *noun*

manifesto *noun* (*plural* **manifestos**) a public declaration of principles and policy.

manifold *adjective* of many kinds, very varied. –**manifold** *noun* a pipe or chamber (in a mechanism) with several openings that connect with other parts. [from *many* + *fold*¹]

manikin *noun* **1** a little man, a dwarf. **2** an artist's lay figure; an anatomical model of the body.

Manila (mă-**nil**-ă) the capital of the Philippines.

manila (mă-**nil**-ă) *noun* a kind of brown paper used for wrapping and for envelopes.

manioc (**man**-ee-ok) *noun* **1** cassava. **2** flour made from this.

manipulable *adjective* able to be manipulated.

manipulate *verb* **1** to handle, manage, or use (a thing) skilfully. **2** to arrange or influence cleverly or craftily; *manipulate figures*, alter or adjust them to suit one's purposes. **manipulation** *noun*, **manipulator** *noun* [from Latin *manus* = hand]

mankind *noun* human beings in general, the human race.

manly *adjective* having the qualities expected of a man (e.g. strength and courage), suitable for a man. **manliness** *noun*

Mann, Thomas (1875–1955), German novelist and essayist.

manna *noun* **1** (in the Bible) a substance miraculously supplied as food to the Israelites in the wilderness after the exodus from Egypt. **2** something unexpected and delightful. **3** an edible white sweet substance exuded by many eucalypts. □ **manna gum** a eucalypt yielding manna.

manned *see* **man**. –**manned** *adjective* (of a spacecraft etc.) containing a human crew.

mannequin (**man**-ĕ-kĭn *or* -kwĭn) *noun* **1** a dressmaker's or window dummy. **2** a fashion model.

manner *noun* **1** the way a thing is done or happens. **2** a person's bearing or way of behaving towards others. **3** kind, sort; *all manner of things*, every kind of thing. **manners** *plural noun* social behaviour, *good manners*; polite social behaviour, *has no manners*. □ **in a manner of speaking** as one might say (used to qualify or weaken what one says).

mannered *adjective* **1** having manners of a certain kind, *well-mannered*. **2** full of mannerisms, *a mannered style*.

mannerism *noun* **1** a distinctive personal habit or way of doing something. **2** a style of European art in the 16th century, involving contorted figures. **mannerist** *noun*

mannerly *adjective* polite.

mannish *adjective* having masculine characteristics, suitable for a man.

manoeuvre (mă-**noo**-ver) *noun* **1** a planned and controlled movement of a vehicle or a body of troops etc. **2** a skilful or crafty proceeding, a trick, *the manoeuvres of politicians to achieve their purposes*. –**manoeuvre** *verb* **1** to move a thing's position or course etc. carefully, *manoeuvred the car into the garage*. **2** to perform manoeuvres. **3** to guide skilfully or craftily, *manoeuvred the conversation towards money*. **manoeuvres** *plural noun* large-scale exercises of troops or ships, *on manoeuvres*. [from Latin, = work by hand (*manus* = hand, *operari* = to work)]

man-of-war *noun* (*plural* **men-of-war**) an armed ship of a country's navy.

manometer (mă-**nom**-ĕ-ter) *noun* a pressure gauge for gases and liquids. [from Greek *manos* = thin, + *meter*]

manor *noun* a large country house (**manor house**) or the landed estate belonging to it; a medieval estate in which a feudal lord had legal rights over the land and tenants. **manorial** (man-**or**-ree-ăl) *adjective*

manpower *noun* **1** power supplied by human physical effort. **2** the number of people working on a particular task or available for work or service.

mansard (**man**-sard) *noun* a type of roof that has a steep lower part and a less steep upper part on all four sides of a building. [named after F. Mansard, French architect]

manse *noun* a church minister's house.

manservant *noun* (*plural* **menservants**) a male servant.

mansion (**man**-shŏn) *noun* a large grand house.

manslaughter *noun* the act of killing a person unlawfully but not intentionally, or by negligence.

mantel *noun* a mantelpiece.

mantelpiece *noun* **1** a structure of wood or marble etc. above and around a fireplace. **2** (also **mantelshelf**) a shelf above a fireplace.

mantilla (man-**til**-ă) *noun* a lace veil worn by Spanish women over the hair and shoulders.

mantis *noun* (in full **praying mantis**) an insect resembling a grasshopper. [Greek *mantis* = prophet]

mantissa *noun* the part of a logarithm after the decimal point (contrasted with the *characteristic*). [Latin, = makeweight]

mantle *noun* **1** a loose sleeveless cloak. **2** something likened to this, a covering, *a mantle of secrecy*. **3** a fragile gauzy cover fixed round the flame of a gas lamp, producing a strong light when heated. **4** the region of very dense rock between the earth's crust and its core. –**mantle** *verb* to envelop or cover as if with a mantle.

mantra *noun* a word or words repeated to aid concentration in Hindu or Buddhist meditation, yoga, etc. [Sanskrit, = instrument of thought]

mantrap *noun* a trap for catching trespassers or poachers etc.

Manu (**mun**-oo) (*Hindu myth.*) the first man, survivor of the great flood, and father of the human race.

manual *adjective* **1** of the hands. **2** done or operated by the hand(s), *manual labour*; *manual gear-change*, operated by the driver, not automatically. –**manual** *noun* **1** a handbook. **2** an organ keyboard played with the hands, not the feet. **manually** *adverb* [from Latin *manus* = hand]

manufacture *verb* **1** to make or produce (goods) on a large scale by machinery. **2** to invent, *manufactured an excuse*. –**manufacture** *noun* the process of manufacturing. **manufacturer** *noun* [from Latin *manu* = by hand, + *facere* = make]

manumit (man-yŭ-**mit**) *verb* (**manumitted**, **manumitting**) to set (a slave) free. **manumission** *noun* [from Latin *manu* = by hand, + *mittere* = send]

manure *noun* any substance (e.g. dung or compost or artificial material) used as a fertiliser. –**manure** *verb* to apply manure to.

manuscript (**man**-yŭ-skript) *noun* **1** something written by hand, not typed or printed. **2** an author's work as written or typed, not a printed book. [from Latin *manu* = by hand, + *scriptum* = written]

Manx *adjective* of the Isle of Man. –**Manx** *noun* the Celtic language of the Manx people. ☐ **Manx cat** a tailless variety of domestic cat.

many *adjective* (**more**, **most**) great in number, numerous; *many a time*, many times. –**many** *noun* many people or things, *many were found*.

Maoism (**mow**-izm; *first part rhymes with* cow) *noun* the doctrines of Mao Tse-tung. **Maoist** *noun*

Maori (**mow**-ree; *first part rhymes with* cow) *noun* **1** (*plural* **Maoris**) a member of the indigenous people of New Zealand. **2** their language. □ **Maori Wars** the wars fought intermittently in 1845–8 and 1860–72 between Maoris and the New Zealand government over the sale of Maori lands.

Mao Tse-tung (mowtsee-**tuung**) (also **Mao Zedong**, 1893–1976), Chinese Communist statesman, founder of the People's Republic of China in 1949, President until 1959, Chairman of the Communist Party until his death.

map *noun* a representation (usually on a plane surface) of the earth's surface or a part of it, or of the sky showing the positions of the stars etc. **–map** *verb* (**mapped, mapping**) **1** to make a map of. **2** to plan in detail, *map out your time*. **3** (in mathematics) to associate each element of (a set) with an element of another set.

maple *noun* a kind of tree with broad leaves, grown for ornament or for its wood. □ **maple leaf** a leaf of the maple, the emblem of Canada.

mapping *noun* **1** the making of a map. **2** (in mathematics) a relationship, a function (= **function** sense 4).

Maputo (mă-**poo**-toh) the capital of Mozambique.

Maquis (mah-**kee**) *noun* (*plural* **Maquis**) **1** the French resistance movement during the German occupation (1940–45). **2** a member of this.

mar *verb* (**marred, marring**) to damage, to spoil.

marabou (**ma**-ră-boo) *noun* **1** a large African stork. **2** its down used as a trimming.

maracas (mă-**rak**-ăz) *plural noun* a pair of club-like gourds containing beans, beads, etc., shaken as a musical instrument.

Maralinga a site, about 850 km north-west of Adelaide at the northern edge of the Nullarbor Plain, used in 1956–7 for British nuclear tests.

marasmus (mă-**raz**-mŭs) *noun* progressive wasting away of the body, especially in children. **marasmic** *adjective*

marathon *noun* **1** a long-distance running race, usually of 42.195 km (26 miles 385 yards). **2** any very long race or other test of endurance. [named after Marathon in Greece, where an invading Persian army was defeated in 490 BC; a man who fought at the battle ran to Athens, announced the victory, and died]

marauding (mă-**raw**-ding) *adjective* going about in search of plunder or prey. **marauder**

noun one who does this. [from French *maraud* = rogue]

marble *noun* **1** a kind of limestone that can be polished, used in sculpture and building. **2** a piece of sculpture in marble, *the Elgin Marbles*. **3** a small ball made of glass or clay etc. used in games played by children. **–marble** *adjective* like marble, hard and smooth and white or mottled. □ **lose one's marbles** (*informal*) to lose one's mental faculties.

marbled *adjective* having a veined or mottled appearance; (of meat) with alternating layers of lean and fat.

marcasite (**mark**-ă-syt) *noun* crystallised iron pyrites; a piece of this used as an ornament.

March *noun* the third month of the year. [named after Mars, Roman god of war]

march *verb* **1** to walk in a military manner with regular paces, to walk in an organised column. **2** to walk purposefully, *marched up to the boss*. **3** to cause to march or walk, *marched them up the hill*; *he was marched off*. **4** to progress steadily, *time marches on*. **–march** *noun* **1** marching; the distance covered by marching troops etc.; *a protest march*, a demonstration taking the form of a parade. **2** progress, *the march of events*. **3** music suitable for marching to. □ **get one's marching orders** to be told to go, to be dismissed. **march past** a ceremonial march past a saluting point. **on the march** marching, advancing. **marcher** *noun* [from Latin *marcus* = hammer]

marches *plural noun* border regions.

marchioness (**mar**-shŏ-ness) *noun* **1** the wife or widow of a marquess. **2** a woman holding the rank of marquess in her own right.

Marconi (mar-**koh**-nee), Guglielmo (1874–1937), Italian electrical engineer, a pioneer of radio communication.

Marco Polo (c. 1254–c. 1324), Venetian traveller, famous for his account of his travels in China and central Asia and his return via Sumatra, India, and Persia.

Marcus Aurelius *see* **Aurelius**.

Mardi Gras (mar-dee-**grah**) **1** Shrove Tuesday in some Catholic countries; celebrations held on this day. **2** (*Austral.*) a carnival or fair at any time.

mare *noun* the female of a horse or related animal. □ **mare's nest** a discovery that is thought to be interesting but turns out to be false or worthless.

margarine (mar-jă-**reen**) *noun* a substance used like butter, made from animal or vegetable fats.

margin *noun* **1** an edge or border of a surface. **2** a blank space round printed or written matter on a page. **3** an amount over and above the essential minimum, *was defeated by a narrow margin*; *margin of safety*. **4** (in commerce) the difference between cost price and selling price, *profit margins*.

marginal *adjective* **1** written in a margin, *marginal notes*. **2** of or at an edge. **3** very slight in amount, *its usefulness is marginal*; *marginal seat* or *electorate*, one where an MP has only a small majority and may easily be defeated at the next election. ☐ **marginal cost** the cost of producing one extra unit above a set number. **marginally** *adverb*

marginalise *verb* (also **-ize**) to treat (a person, a social group, an issue, etc.) as insignificant or less important. **marginalisation** *noun*

marguerite (marg-ĕ-**reet**) *noun* a large daisy-like flower.

Marie Antoinette (**mah**-ree ahn-twah-**net**) (1755–93), queen of France (as the wife of Louis XVI), executed during the French Revolution.

marigold *noun* a garden plant with golden or bright yellow flowers.

marijuana (ma-rĭ-**wah**-nă) *noun* the dried leaves, stems, and flowering tops of the hemp plant, used as a hallucinogenic drug.

marimba (mă-**rim**-bă) *noun* **1** a xylophone of Africa and Central America. **2** a modern orchestral instrument evolved from this.

marina (mă-**ree**-nă) *noun* a harbour for yachts and pleasure boats. [same origin as *marine*]

marinade (ma-rĭ-**nayd**) *noun* a seasoned flavoured liquid in which meat or fish is soaked before being cooked. –**marinade** *verb* (also **marinate**) to steep in a marinade.

marine (mă-**reen**) *adjective* **1** of or living in the sea, *marine animals*. **2** of shipping, nautical, *marine insurance*. **3** for use at sea. –**marine** *noun* **1** a country's shipping, *the mercantile marine*. **2** a member of a body of troops trained to serve on land or sea. [from Latin *mare* = sea]

Mariner (**ma**-rĭ-ner) *noun* a series of US planetary probes (1962–77), of which 11 and 12 were renamed Voyager 1 and 2.

mariner (**ma**-rĭ-ner) *noun* a sailor, a seaman.

marionette (ma-ree-ŏ-**net**) *noun* a puppet worked by strings.

marital (**ma**-rĭ-tăl) *adjective* of marriage, of or between husband and wife. **maritally** *adverb* [from Latin *maritus* = husband]

maritime (**ma**-rĭ-tym) *adjective* **1** living or situated or found near the sea, *maritime provinces*. **2** of seafaring or shipping, *maritime law*. [same origin as *marine*]

marjoram (**mar**-jŏ-răm) *noun* a herb with fragrant leaves, used in cooking.

Mark, St, **1** an Apostle, traditional author of the second Gospel. Feast day, 25 April. **2** the second Gospel.

mark¹ *noun* **1** a line or area that differs in appearance from the rest of a surface, especially one that spoils it. **2** a distinguishing feature or characteristic. **3** something that indicates the presence of a quality or feeling, *as a mark of respect*. **4** a symbol placed on a thing to indicate its origin, ownership, or quality; *Mark One* or *Two*, the first or second design of a machine or piece of equipment etc. **5** a written or printed symbol, *punctuation marks*. **6** a lasting impression, *poverty had left its mark*. **7** a unit awarded for the merit or quality of a piece of work or a performance, *got high marks*. **8** a target, a standard to be aimed at; *not feeling up to the mark*, not feeling well. **9** a line or object serving to indicate position. **10** (in Australian Rules) the catching before it reaches the ground of a ball kicked at least 15 metres. –**mark** *verb* **1** to make a mark on. **2** to distinguish with a mark, to characterise. **3** to assign marks of merit to. **4** to notice, to watch carefully, *mark my words!* **5** to keep close to (an opposing player in sport) so as to prevent his or her getting the ball. **6** (in Australian Rules) to take the ball in a fair catch. ☐ **make one's mark** to make a significant achievement, to become famous. **mark down** to notice and remember the place etc. of; to reduce the price of. **mark time** to move the feet rhythmically as if in marching but without advancing; to occupy time in routine work without making progress. **mark up** to increase the price of.

mark² *noun* (in full **Deutschmark**) the former unit of money in Germany.

Mark Antony *see* Antony.

markdown *noun* a reduction in price.

marked *adjective* clearly noticeable, *a marked improvement*. ☐ **a marked man** one who is singled out, e.g. as an object of vengeance. markedly (**mark**-ĕd-lee) *adverb*

marker *noun* **1** a person or tool that marks; one who records the score in games etc. **2** a broad felt-tipped pen. **3** something that serves to mark a position.

market *noun* **1** a gathering for the sale of goods or livestock. **2** a space or building used for this. **3** the conditions or opportunity for buying or selling, *found a ready market*. **4** a place where goods may be sold, *foreign markets*; a particular class of buyers, *the teenage market*. **5** the stock market. –**market** *verb* to offer for sale; to promote the sale of (products) by advertising etc.
□ **be in the market for** to wish to buy or obtain. **market forces** the influences of business, supply and demand, etc. on prices, wages, jobs, etc. without interference or control from government. **market garden** a small farm where vegetables and fruit are grown for market. **market place** an open space where a market is held in a town; the commercial world. **market price** the current price; the going rate. **market research** study of consumers' needs and preferences. **market value** the amount for which something can be sold, its current value. **on the market** offered for sale. [from Latin *merx* = merchandise]

marketable *adjective* able or fit to be sold.

marking *noun* **1** a mark or marks. **2** the colouring of an animal's skin, feathers, or fur.

markka (**mark**-ă) *noun* the unit of money in Finland.

marksman *noun* (*plural* marksmen) a person who is a skilled shot. **marksmanship** *noun*

markup *noun* the amount added to the cost price of goods to cover overheads and profit.
□ **markup language** a computer programming language used to manipulate text, data, etc., through a series of tags assigned to the various structural elements of the text or data.

marl *noun* a soil consisting of clay and lime, a valuable fertiliser. **marly** *adjective*

marlin *noun* (*plural* marlin *or* marlins) a long-nosed sea fish.

marlinspike *noun* a pointed tool used to separate strands of rope or wire.

Marlowe, Christopher (1564–93), English dramatist and poet; his best-known plays are *Edward II* and *Dr Faustus*.

marmalade *noun* a kind of jam made from citrus fruit, especially oranges.

marmoset (**mar**-mŏ-zet) *noun* a small bushy-tailed monkey of tropical America.

marmot (**mar**-mŏt) *noun* a small burrowing animal of the squirrel family.

Maronite (**ma**-rŏ-nyt) *noun* a member of a Christian sect of Syrian origin, living chiefly in Lebanon.

maroon[1] (mă-**rohn** *or* -**roon**) *noun* **1** a brownish-red colour. **2** a kind of firework that explodes with a sound like a cannon, used as a warning signal. –**maroon** *adjective* brownish-red.

maroon[2] (mă-**roon**) *verb* to abandon or isolate (a person), e.g. on an island or in a deserted place.

marque (*pr.* mark) *noun* a make of motor car, as opposed to a specific model. [French, = *mark*[1]]

marquee (mar-**kee**) *noun* a large tent used for a party or an exhibition etc.

marquess (**mar**-kwĕs) *noun* a British nobleman ranking between a duke and an earl.

marquetry (**mar**-kĕ-tree) *noun* inlaid work in wood or ivory etc.

marquis (**mar**-kwĭs) *noun* a foreign nobleman ranking between a duke and a count.

marquise (mar-**keez**) *noun* **1** the wife or widow of a marquis. **2** a woman holding the rank of marquis in her own right.

marram (**ma**-răm) *noun* a shore grass that binds sand.

marriage *noun* **1** the state in which a man and a woman are formally and legally united. **2** the act or ceremony of being married. **3** a close union. □ **marriage celebrant** *see* celebrant.

marriageable *adjective* old enough or fit for marriage.

marron (**ma**-rŏn) (*plural* marron *or* marrons) a large freshwater crayfish of WA. [Nyungar *marran*]

marron glacé (ma-ron **gla**-say) *noun* a chestnut preserved in sugar as a sweet. [French, = iced chestnut]

marrow *noun* **1** the soft fatty substance in the cavities of bones; *felt chilled to the marrow*, right through. **2** the large fruit of a plant of the gourd family, used as a vegetable.

marrowbone *noun* a bone containing edible marrow.

marry *verb* (married, marrying) **1** to unite or give or take in marriage. **2** to take a husband or wife in marriage, *she never married*.

3 to unite, to put (things) together as a pair. [from Latin *maritus* = husband]

Mars 1 (*Rom. myth.*) the god of war, identified with Ares. 2 one of the planets, with a characteristic red colour.

Marsala (mah-**sah**-lă) *noun* a dark sweet fortified wine of a kind originally made in Sicily.

Marseillaise (mar-sě-**layz**) *noun* the national anthem of France.

marsh *noun* low-lying watery ground. □ marsh gas methane. marshy *adjective*

marshal *noun* 1 an officer of high or the highest rank, *Air Marshal*; *Field Marshal*. 2 an official with responsibility for arranging public events or ceremonies. 3 an official at a race. –marshal *verb* (marshalled, marshalling) 1 to arrange in proper order. 2 to cause to assemble. 3 to usher. □ marshalling yard a railway yard in which goods trains etc. are assembled for dispatch.

Marshall, George C(atlett) (1880–1959), American general and statesman who initiated a program of economic aid to European countries after the Second World War.

Marshall Islands a republic consisting of a group of islands in the NW Pacific, north of Kiribati and Nauru.

marshmallow *noun* a soft sweet made from sugar, egg white, and gelatine.

marsupial (mar-**soo**-pee-ăl *or* -**syoo**-) *noun* an animal such as the kangaroo, the female of which has a pouch in which its young are carried until they are fully developed. □ marsupial mole a small blind, burrowing marsupial of arid Australia. marsupial mouse any of many small carnivorous marsupials, a popular name for the dunnart, mulgara, and others. marsupial rat a small carnivorous marsupial of arid central Australia. [from Greek *marsupion* = pouch]

mart *noun* 1 a market. 2 (in combined forms) a shop, *a hardware mart*; *a piano mart*.

marten *noun* a weasel-like animal with thick soft fur.

Martial (**mar**-shăl) (c. 40–c. 104), Roman writer of epigrams.

martial (**mar**-shăl) *adjective* of war, warlike, *martial music*. □ martial arts fighting sports such as judo and karate. martial law military rule imposed on a country temporarily in an emergency, suspending ordinary law. [from Latin, = of Mars, the Roman god of war]

Martian (**mar**-shăn) *adjective* of the planet Mars. –Martian *noun* (in science fiction etc.) an inhabitant of Mars.

Martin, St (died 397), a patron saint of France. Feast day, 11 November.

martin *noun* 1 a bird of the swallow family. 2 a swallow-like migratory bird.

martinet (mar-tǐ-**net**) *noun* a person who demands strict obedience.

martingale *noun* a strap or set of straps fastened at one end to the noseband and at the other end to the girth, to prevent a horse from rearing etc.

Martuthunira (**mar**-too-*th*oo-ni-ru) *noun* 1 a member of an Aboriginal people of NW Western Australia. 2 their language.

martyr *noun* 1 a person who suffers death rather than give up the Christian faith. 2 one who undergoes death or great suffering in support of a belief, cause, or principle. 3 one who suffers greatly; *is a martyr to rheumatism*, suffers constantly from this. –martyr *verb* to put to death or torment as a martyr. martyrdom *noun* [from Greek, = witness]

marvel *noun* a wonderful thing. –marvel *verb* (marvelled, marvelling) to be filled with wonder.

Marvell, Andrew (1621–78), English poet and satirist.

marvellous *adjective* astonishing, excellent. marvellously *adverb*

Marx, Karl Heinrich (1818–83), German political philosopher and economist, founder of modern communism with Friedrich Engels.

Marxism *noun* the political and economic theory of Karl Marx, on which Communism is based. Marxist *adjective* & *noun*

Mary[1] (in the Bible) 1 the Blessed Virgin Mary, mother of Jesus Christ. 2 Mary Magdalene (= of Magdala in Galilee), a follower of Christ. Feast day, 22 July.

Mary[2] the name of two queens of England, Mary I (reigned 1553–8), Mary II (reigned, with William III, 1689–94).

Mary Celeste (sě-**lest**) an American brig that set sail from New York for Genoa and was found in good order but abandoned in the North Atlantic in December 1872.

Maryland a State on the Atlantic coast of the USA.

Mary, Queen of Scots (1542–87), queen of Scotland 1542–67, beheaded after the discovery of a Catholic plot against Elizabeth I of England.

marzipan (**mar**-zee-pan) *noun* a paste of ground almonds and sugar, made into small cakes or sweets or used to coat large cakes.

Masada (mă-**sah**-dă) a fortress on a steep hill west of the Dead Sea, the last Jewish stronghold during the revolt against Roman rule, where in AD 73 the defenders committed mass suicide rather than surrender.

Masai (**mah**-sy *or* ma-**sy**) *noun* (*plural* Masai) **1** a member of a pastoral people of Kenya and Tanzania. **2** their language.

mascara *noun* a cosmetic for darkening the eyelashes. [from Italian, = mask]

mascarpone (mas-kă-**poh**-nee) *noun* a soft Italian cream cheese.

mascot *noun* **1** a person or thing believed to bring good luck to its owner. **2** a figurine mounted on the bonnet of a car etc.

masculine *adjective* **1** of, like, or suitable for men; having the qualities or appearance considered characteristic of a man. **2** having the grammatical form suitable for the names of males or for words corresponding to these, *'hero' is a masculine noun, 'heroine' is the corresponding feminine noun.* –**masculine** *noun* (in grammar) a masculine word or gender. **masculinity** *noun*

maser (**may**-zer) *noun* a device for amplifying microwaves. [from the initial letters of 'microwave amplification by the stimulated emission of radiation']

Maseru (ma-**sair**-roo) the capital of Lesotho.

mash *noun* **1** grain or bran etc. cooked in water to form a soft mixture, used as animal food. **2** (*informal*) mashed potatoes. **3** a soft pulp. –**mash** *verb* to beat or crush into a soft mixture.

mask *noun* **1** a covering worn over the face (or part of it) as a disguise or for protection. **2** a carved or moulded replica of a face. **3** a respirator worn over the face to filter air for breathing or to supply gas for inhaling. **4** the face or head of a fox. **5** a screen used in photography to exclude part of the image. –**mask** *verb* **1** to cover with a mask. **2** to disguise, screen, or conceal.

masochist (**mas**-ŏ-kĭst) *noun* **1** a person who derives sexual excitement and satisfaction from his or her own pain or humiliation. **2** one who enjoys what seems to be painful or tiresome. **masochism** *noun*, **masochistic** *adjective*

Mason *noun* a Freemason. **Masonic** (mă-**sonn**-ik) *adjective*, **Masonry** *noun*

mason *noun* a person who builds or works with stone.

masonry *noun* mason's work; stonework.

masquerade (mas-kě-**rayd** *or* mahs-) *noun* a false show or pretence. –**masquerade** *verb* to pretend to be what one is not, *masqueraded as a policeman.* [from Spanish *máscara* = mask]

mass[1] *noun* **1** a coherent unit of matter with no specific shape. **2** a large quantity or heap, an unbroken extent; *the garden was a mass of flowers*, was full of flowers. **3** (in technical usage) the quantity of matter a body contains (called *weight* in non-technical usage). –**mass** *verb* to gather or assemble into a mass.
□ **the mass** the majority. **the masses** the common people. **mass media** *see* media. **mass meeting** one attended by a large number of people. **mass noun** a noun that is not normally countable and not used with the indefinite article, e.g. *butter*. **mass number** the total number of protons and neutrons in a nucleus. **mass-produce** *verb* to manufacture large numbers of identical articles by standardised processes. **mass production** manufacturing in this way.

mass[2] *noun* (especially in the Catholic Church) **1** a celebration of the Eucharist. **2** the form of service used in this; a musical setting of certain parts of the text.

Massachusetts a State of the north-eastern USA.

massacre (**mass**-ă-ker) *noun* slaughter of a large number of people or animals. –**massacre** *verb* to slaughter in large numbers.

massage (**mas**-ahzh) *noun* rubbing and kneading the body to lessen pain or stiffness. –**massage** *verb* to treat in this way.

masseur (ma-**ser**) *noun* a person who practises massage professionally. **masseuse** (ma-**serz**) *feminine noun*

massif (**ma**-seef) *noun* mountain heights forming a compact group. [French, = massive]

massive *adjective* **1** large and heavy or solid. **2** unusually large. **3** substantial, *a massive improvement.* **massively** *adverb*, **massiveness** *noun*

mast[1] *noun* **1** a long upright pole that supports a ship's sails. **2** a tall pole from which a flag is flown. **3** a tall steel structure for the aerials of a radio or television transmitter.

☐ **before the mast** serving as an ordinary seaman (quartered in the forecastle). **masted** *adjective*

mast[2] *noun* the fruit of the beech, oak, etc., used as food for pigs.

mastectomy (mas-**tek**-tŏ-mee) *noun* surgical removal of a breast.

master *noun* 1 a man who has control of people or things. 2 the captain of a merchant ship. 3 the male head of a household. 4 the male owner of a dog etc. 5 an employer, *masters and men*. 6 a male teacher, a schoolmaster. 7 Master the holder of a university degree as *Master of Arts* etc. 8 a respected teacher. 9 a person with very great skill, a great artist. 10 a chess player of proven ability at international level. 11 a document, film, or record etc. from which a series of copies is made. 12 Master a title prefixed to the name of a boy who is not old enough to be called *Mr.* –**master** *verb* 1 to overcome, to bring under control. 2 to acquire knowledge or skill in. ☐ **master file** (in computing) a permanent file containing current information that is updated periodically. **master key** a key that opens a number of locks, each also opened by a separate key. **Master of Ceremonies** a person in charge of a social or other occasion, who introduces the events or performers. **master stroke** an outstandingly skilful act of policy etc. **master switch** a switch controlling the supply of electricity etc. to an entire system. [from Latin *magister* = master]

masterful *adjective* 1 domineering. 2 very skilful. **masterfully** *adverb*

masterly *adjective* worthy of a master, very skilful.

mastermind *noun* 1 a person with outstanding mental ability. 2 the person directing an enterprise. –**mastermind** *verb* to plan and direct (a project or campaign).

masterpiece *noun* 1 an outstanding piece of workmanship. 2 a person's best piece of work.

mastery *noun* 1 complete control, supremacy. 2 thorough knowledge or skill, *his mastery of Arabic*.

masthead *noun* 1 the highest part of a ship's mast. 2 the title details of a newspaper at the head of its front or editorial page.

mastic *noun* 1 a gum or resin exuded from certain trees. 2 a type of cement.

masticate *verb* to chew (food). **mastication** *noun* [from Greek *mastichan* = gnash the teeth]

mastiff *noun* a large strong dog with drooping ears.

mastodon (**mast**-ŏ-don) *noun* a large extinct animal resembling the elephant.

mastoid *noun* part of a bone behind the ear. [from Greek *mastoeides* = breast-shaped]

masturbate *verb* to stimulate the genitals with the hand. **masturbation** *noun*

mat *noun* 1 a piece of material used as a floor covering, a doormat. 2 a small pad or piece of material placed under an ornament or vase etc. or under a hot dish, to protect the surface on which it stands. 3 a thick pad for landing on in gymnastics etc. –**mat** *verb* (**matted**, **matting**) to make or become entangled to form a thick mass, *matted hair*. ☐ **on the mat** (*informal*) being reprimanded.

Matabele (mat-ă-**bee**-lee) *noun* (*plural* **Matabele**) a member of a Bantu-speaking people of Zimbabwe.

matador (**mat**-ă-dor) *noun* a performer whose task is to fight and kill the bull in a bullfight. [from Spanish *matar* = kill]

Mata Hari (mah-tă **hah**-ree) (real name: Margaretha Geertruida Zelle) (1876–1917), Dutch dancer, courtesan, and secret agent, who worked for both the French and the German intelligence services before being executed by the French as a spy.

match[1] *noun* a short piece of wood or pasteboard with a head made of material that bursts into flame when rubbed on a rough or specially prepared surface.

match[2] *noun* 1 a contest in a game or sport. 2 a person or animal with abilities equalling those of one met in contest, *meet one's match*; *you are no match for him*, not strong enough or skilled enough to defeat him. 3 a person or thing exactly like or corresponding to another. 4 a marriage; *they made a match of it*, married. 5 a person considered as a partner for marriage, especially with regard to rank or fortune. –**match** *verb* 1 to place in competition, *the teams were matched with* or *against each other*. 2 to equal in ability or skill etc. 3 to be alike or correspond in colour, quality, quantity, etc. 4 to find something similar to, *I want to match this wool*. 5 to put or bring together as corresponding, *matching overseas students with host families*.

☐ **match point** the stage in a match when one side will win if it gains the next point; this point.

matchboard *noun* board with a tongue cut along one edge and a groove along another, so as to fit with similar boards.

matchbox *noun* a box for holding matches (*match*[1]).

matchless *adjective* unequalled.

matchmaker *noun* a person who is fond of scheming to bring about marriages. matchmaking *adjective* & *noun*

matchstick *noun* the stem of a match.

matchwood *noun* 1 wood that splinters easily. 2 wood reduced to splinters.

mate[1] *noun* 1 a friend or companion; a fellow worker. 2 an informal form of address, especially to another man. 3 each of a mated pair of birds or animals. 4 each of a pair (of things), e.g. socks, shoes, *can't find the mate to this shoe*. 5 (*informal*) a partner in marriage. 6 a fellow member or sharer, *teammate*; *room-mate*. 7 an officer on a merchant ship ranking next below the master. 8 a worker's assistant, *plumber's mate*. –mate *verb* 1 to put or come together as a pair or as corresponding. 2 to put (two birds or animals) together so that they can breed; to come together in order to breed.

mate[2] *noun* a situation in chess in which the capture of a king cannot be prevented. –mate *verb* to put into this situation.

mater (**may**-ter) *noun* (*old use*) mother. [Latin]

material *noun* 1 the substance or things from which something is or can be made or with which something is done, *clay is used as material for bricks*; *writing materials*; *select those regarded as officer material*, those with qualities that make them suitable to become officers. 2 cloth, fabric. 3 facts, information, or events etc. to be used in composing something, *gathering material for a book on poverty*. –material *adjective* 1 of matter; consisting of matter; of the physical (as opposed to spiritual) world, *material things*; *had no thought of material gain*. 2 of bodily comfort, *our material well-being*. 3 important, significant, relevant, *at the material time*; *is this material to the issue?* [from Latin *materia* = matter]

materialise *verb* (also -ize) 1 to appear or become visible, *the ghost didn't materialise.* 2 to become a fact, to happen, *if the threatened strike materialises.* materialisation *noun*

materialism *noun* 1 excessive concern with material possessions rather than spiritual or intellectual values. 2 belief that only the material world exists. materialist *noun*, materialistic *adjective*

materially *adverb* substantially, considerably.

maternal (mă-**ter**-năl) *adjective* 1 of a mother, of motherhood. 2 motherly. 3 related through one's mother; *maternal uncle*, one's mother's brother. maternally *adverb* [from Latin *mater* = mother]

maternity (mă-**ter**-nĭ-tee) *noun* 1 motherhood. 2 of or suitable or caring for women in pregnancy or childbirth, *maternity dress*; *maternity hospital.*

mateship *noun* 1 the bond between partners or friends. 2 comradeship as an ideal.

matey *adjective* sociable, friendly. –matey *noun* (*informal*, as a form of address) mate. matily *adverb*, matiness *noun*

mathematician *noun* a person who is skilled in mathematics.

mathematics *noun* the science of number, quantity, and space. –mathematics *plural noun* the use of mathematics in calculation, *his mathematics are weak*. mathematical *adjective*, mathematically *adverb*

maths *noun* (*informal*) mathematics.

matilda *noun* (*Austral.*) a swag. ☐ **waltzing matilda** carrying one's swag (*see also* Waltzing Matilda).

matinée (**mat**-ĭ-nay) *noun* an afternoon performance at a theatre or cinema. ☐ **matinée coat** or **jacket** a baby's short coat.

matins *noun* 1 the first of the daily services of prayer in the Roman Catholic Church, originally said or sung at midnight or daybreak. 2 morning prayer, especially in the Anglican Church. [from Latin *matutinus* = of morning]

Matisse (ma-**teess**), Henri Émile Benoit (1869–1954), French painter and sculptor, known for his use of strong, clear colours.

matriarch (**may**-tree-ark) *noun* a woman who is head of a family or tribe. matriarchal (may-tree-**ark**-ăl) *adjective* [from Latin *mater* = mother, + Greek *arkhein* = to rule]

matriarchy (**may**-tree-ark-ee) *noun* 1 a social organisation in which the mother is head of the family and descent is through the female line. 2 a society in which women have most of the authority.

matricide (**may**-trĭ-syd) *noun* **1** the act of killing one's mother. **2** a person who is guilty of this. **matricidal** *adjective* [from Latin *mater* = mother, + *caedere* = kill]

matriculate (mă-**trik**-yŭ-layt) *verb* to admit or be admitted to membership of a university. **matriculation** *noun*

matrimony (**mat**-rĭ-mŏnee) *noun* marriage. **matrimonial** (mat-rĭ-**moh**-nee-ăl) *adjective*

matrix (**may**-triks) *noun* (*plural* **matrices**) **1** a mould in which something is cast or shaped. **2** a place in which a thing is developed. **3** an array of mathematical quantities etc. in rows and columns; *column matrix*, one that contains only one column of quantities; *row matrix*, with only one row. **4** (in computers) an interconnected array of circuit elements that resembles a lattice or grid.

matron *noun* **1** a married woman, especially one who is dignified and middle-aged or elderly. **2** a woman nurse and housekeeper at a school etc. **3** (*old use*) the senior nursing officer in a hospital or other institution, now usually called *Director* or *Superintendent of Nursing*. □ **matron of honour** a married woman as the chief attendant of the bride at a wedding.

matronly *adjective* like or suitable for a dignified married woman.

matt *adjective* (of a colour or surface etc.) having a dull finish, not shiny.

matter *noun* **1** that which occupies space in the visible world, as opposed to spirit or mind or qualities etc. **2** a particular substance or material, *colouring matter*. **3** a discharge from the body; pus. **4** material for thought or expression; the content of a book or speech as distinct from its form, *subject matter*. **5** things of a specified kind, *reading matter*. **6** a situation or business being considered, *it's a serious matter*; *a matter for complaint*. **7** a quantity, *for a matter of 40 years*. –**matter** *verb* to be of importance, *it doesn't matter*. □ **the matter** the thing that is amiss, the trouble or difficulty, *what's the matter?* **for that matter** as far as that is concerned. **a matter of course** an event etc. that follows naturally or is to be expected. **a matter of fact** something that is a fact not an opinion etc. **matter-of-fact** *adjective* strictly factual and not imaginative or emotional, down-to-earth. **no matter** it is of no importance. [same origin as *material*]

Matterhorn an Alpine peak on the Swiss-Italian border rising to 4477 m.

Matthew, St **1** an Apostle, to whom the first Gospel is ascribed. Feast day, 21 September. **2** the first Gospel.

matting *noun* mats; material for making these.

mattock *noun* an agricultural tool with the blade set at right angles to the handle, used for loosening soil and digging out roots.

mattress *noun* a fabric case filled with soft, firm, or springy material, or a similar case filled with air or water, used on or as a bed.

maturation (mat-yŭ-**ray**-shŏn) *noun* the process of maturing, ripening.

mature *adjective* **1** having reached full growth or development. **2** having or showing fully developed mental powers, capable of reasoning and acting sensibly. **3** ripe, seasoned; (of wine) having reached a good stage of development. **4** (of a bill of exchange etc.) due for payment. –**mature** *verb* to make or become mature. **maturely** *adverb*, **maturity** *noun* [from Latin *maturus* = ripe]

matutinal (mă-**tew**-tĭ-năl) *adjective* of or occurring in the morning.

maudlin *adjective* sentimental in a silly or tearful way, especially from drunkenness.

maul *verb* to treat roughly, to injure by rough handling or clawing.

maulana (mow-**lah**-nă) *noun* a Muslim man revered for his religious learning or piety.

maulstick *noun* a stick used to support the hand in painting.

maunder *verb* to talk in a rambling way.

Maundy *noun* the ceremony of washing people's feet on **Maundy Thursday**, the Thursday before Easter, celebrated in commemoration of the Last Supper and Christ's washing of the Apostles' feet.

Mauritania (mo-rĭ-**tay**-nee-ă) a republic in NW Africa. **Mauritanian** *adjective* & *noun*

Mauritius (mă-**rish**-ŭs) an island republic in the Indian Ocean east of Madagascar. **Mauritian** *adjective* & *noun*

mausoleum (maw-sŏ-**lee**-ŭm) *noun* a magnificent tomb. [named after that erected at Halicarnassus in Asia Minor for King Mausolus in the 4th century BC]

mauve (*rhymes with* cove) *adjective* & *noun* pale purple.

maverick (**mav**-ĕ-rik) *noun* **1** an unbranded calf or other young animal. **2** an unorthodox or independent-minded person, one who dissents from the ideas and beliefs of a group to which he or she belongs.

maw *noun* the jaws, mouth, or stomach of a voracious animal.

mawkish *adjective* sentimental in a sickly way.

Mawson, Sir Douglas (1882–1958), English-born Australian scientist and Antarctic explorer. **–Mawson** an Australian research base in Antarctica.

maxilla *noun* (*plural* **maxillae**) **1** a jaw, especially the upper one. **2** a corresponding part in insects etc.

maxim *noun* a general truth or rule of conduct, e.g. 'waste not, want not'.

maximal *adjective* greatest possible.
maximally *adverb*

maximise *verb* (also **-ize**) to increase to a maximum. **maximisation** *noun*

maximum *noun* (*plural* **maxima**) the greatest or greatest possible number, amount, or intensity etc. **–maximum** *adjective* greatest, greatest possible. [Latin, = greatest thing]

May *noun* the fifth month of the year.
□ **May Day** 1 May, kept as a festival with dancing or as an international holiday in honour of workers. [named after Maia, Roman goddess]

may *auxiliary verb* (see also **might²**) expressing possibility (*it may be true*), or permission (*you may go*), or wish (*long may she reign*), or uncertainty (*whoever it may be*).

Maya (**mah**-yă) *noun* **1** a member of an indigenous people living in Mexico until the 15th century. **2** their language. **Mayan** *adjective*

maya (**mah**-yă) *noun* **1** (in Hinduism) illusion, magic. **2** (in Hindu and Buddhist philosophy) the power by which the universe becomes manifest; the material world, regarded as illusory. [Sanskrit]

maybe *adverb* perhaps, possibly.

mayday *noun* an international radio signal of distress. [representing the pronunciation of French *m'aidez* = help me]

Mayflower the ship in which, in 1620, the Pilgrim Fathers sailed from Plymouth to establish the first colony in New England on the coast of North America.

mayhem *noun* violent or damaging action.

mayn't (*informal*) = may not.

mayonnaise (may-ŏ-**nayz**) *noun* a creamy sauce made with egg yolks, oil, and vinegar.

mayor *noun* the head of the council of a municipality, district, town etc. **mayoral** (**mair**-răl) *adjective*

mayoress *noun* **1** a mayor's wife, or other lady performing her ceremonial duties. **2** (*old use*) a woman mayor.

maypole *noun* a tall pole, with ribbons attached to its top, for dancing round on May Day.

Mazdaism (**maz**-dă-izm) *noun* Zoroastrianism, worship of Ahura Mazda.

maze *noun* **1** a complicated network of paths, a labyrinth. **2** a network of paths and hedges designed as a puzzle in which to try to find one's way. **3** a state of bewilderment.

mazurka (mă-**zerk**-ă) *noun* a lively Polish dance in triple time; music for this.

MB *abbreviation* **1** Bachelor of Medicine. **2** (also **Mb**) megabyte(s).

MBA *abbreviation* Master of Business Administration.

Mbabane (mbah-**bah**-nee) the capital of Swaziland.

MBE *abbreviation* Member of the Order of the British Empire.

Mbps *abbreviation* megabits per second.

MC *abbreviation* **1** Master of Ceremonies. **2** Military Cross.

MCC *abbreviation* Marylebone Cricket Club in London, until 1969 the governing body that made the rules of cricket.

Mc/s *abbreviation* megacycle(s) per second (= megahertz).

MD *abbreviation* Doctor of Medicine.

me *pronoun* **1** the objective case of *I*. **2** (*informal*) = I, *it's me*.

mea culpa *interjection* acknowledgment of guilt or error.

mead *noun* an alcoholic drink of fermented honey and water.

meadow *noun* a field of grass, especially one used for hay.

meagre (**mee**-ger) *adjective* scanty in amount.

meal¹ *noun* **1** an occasion when food is eaten. **2** the food itself. □ **make a meal of** to make (a task) seem unnecessarily laborious. **meals on wheels** a service that delivers hot meals by car to elderly or infirm persons. **meal ticket** a person or thing that provides one with food.

meal² *noun* **1** coarsely-ground grain or pulse. **2** any powdery substance made by grinding, *almond meal*.

mealtime *noun* the usual time for a meal.

mealy *adjective* **1** like or containing meal, dry and powdery. **2** mealy-mouthed. □ **mealy-mouthed** *adjective* trying excessively to avoid offending people.

mean¹ *verb* (**meant**, **meaning**) **1** to have as one's purpose or intention. **2** to design or destine for a purpose. **3** to intend to convey (a sense) or to indicate or refer to (a thing). **4** (of words) to have as an equivalent in the same or another language, *'maybe' means 'perhaps'*. **5** to entail, to involve, *it means catching the early train*. **6** to be likely or certain to result in, *this means war*. **7** to be of a specified importance, *the honour means a lot to me*. □ **mean business** (*informal*) to be ready to take action, not merely talk. **mean it** not to be joking or exaggerating; really to intend to do what is said.

mean² *adjective* **1** not generous, miserly. **2** poor in quality or appearance; low in rank; *he is no mean cricketer*, he is a very good one. **3** unkind, spiteful; vicious, nasty. **4** (*informal*) formidable, skilful, *a mean fighter*. **meanly** *adverb*, **meanness** *noun*

mean³ *adjective* (of a point or quantity) equally far from two extremes, average. –**mean** *noun* **1** a middle point, condition, or course etc. **2** (also **arithmetic mean**) the value arrived at by adding several quantities together and dividing the total by the number of quantities; the average. □ **geometric mean** the value arrived at by multiplying two quantities together and finding the square root of their product, or by multiplying three quantities and finding the cube root, and so on.

meander (mee-**an**-der) *verb* **1** (of a stream) to follow a winding course, flowing slowly and gently. **2** to wander in a leisurely way. –**meander** *noun* a winding course. [named after the Maeander, a river in Turkey]

meaning *noun* what is meant. –**meaning** *adjective* full of meaning, expressive, *gave him a meaning look*. □ **with meaning** in a way that is full of meaning, significantly.

meaningful *adjective* full of meaning, significant. **meaningfully** *adverb*

meaningless *adjective* with no meaning. **meaninglessly** *adverb*

means *noun* that by which a result is brought about; *transported the students by means of buses*, by using buses. –**means** *plural noun* resources; money or other wealth considered as a means of supporting oneself, *has private means*. □ **by all means** certainly. **by no means** not nearly, *it is by no means certain*. **means test** an official investigation to establish a person's neediness before financial help is given from public funds. **means-test** *verb* to subject to or base on a means test. [from *mean³*]

meant *see* **mean¹**.

meantime *adverb* meanwhile. –**meantime** *noun* the intervening period, *in the meantime*. [from *mean³* + *time*]

meanwhile *adverb* **1** in the intervening period of time. **2** at the same time, while something else takes place. [from *mean³* + *while*]

measles *noun* an infectious disease producing small red spots on the whole body.

measly *adjective* **1** affected with measles. **2** (*informal*) meagre.

measurable *adjective* able to be measured.

measure *noun* **1** the size or quantity of something, found by measuring. **2** extent, amount, *he is in some measure responsible*; *had a measure of success*. **3** a unit, standard, or system used in measuring, *the metre is a measure of length*. **4** a device used in measuring, e.g. a container of standard size or a marked rod or tape. **5** the rhythm or metre of poetry; the time of a piece of music; a bar of music. **6** suitable action taken for a particular purpose; a law or proposed law, *measures to stop tax evasion*. **7** a layer of rock or mineral. –**measure** *verb* **1** to find the size, quantity, or extent of something by comparing it with a fixed unit or with an object of known size. **2** to be of a certain size, *it measures two metres by four*. **3** to mark or deal out a measured quantity, *measured out their rations*. **4** to estimate (a quality etc.) by comparing it with some standard. □ **beyond measure** very much, very great, *kindness beyond measure*. **for good measure** in addition to what was needed; as a finishing touch. **made to measure** made in accordance with measurements taken. **measure one's length** to fall flat on the ground. **measure up to** to reach the standard required by.

measured *adjective* **1** rhythmical, regular in movement, *measured tread*. **2** carefully considered, *in measured language*.

measurement *noun* 1 measuring. 2 size etc. found by measuring and expressed in units.

meat *noun* 1 animal flesh as food (usually excluding fish and poultry). 2 informative matter; the chief part, *the meat of the report*. □ **meat ant** a mound-building Australian ant with a red head and purplish body, and a painful bite. **meat pie** stewed meat in a small pastry case. **meatless** *adjective*

meaty *adjective* (**meatier**, **meatiest**) 1 like meat. 2 full of meat, fleshy. 3 full of informative matter, *a meaty book*.

Mecca 1 a city in Saudi Arabia, the birthplace of Muhammad and chief place of Muslim pilgrimage. 2 a place that people with certain interests are eager to visit.

mechanic *noun* a person skilled in using or repairing machines or tools.

mechanical *adjective* 1 of machines or mechanism. 2 worked or produced by machinery. 3 (of a person or action) like a machine, as if acting or done without conscious thought. 4 (of work) needing little or no thought. 5 of or belonging to the science of mechanics. □ **mechanical engineer** a person qualified in the design and construction of machines. **mechanically** *adverb* [from Greek *mekhane* = machine]

mechanics *noun* 1 the scientific study of motion and force. 2 the science of machinery. –**mechanics** *plural noun* the processes by which something is done or functions.

mechanise (**mek**-ă-nyz) *verb* (also **-ize**) 1 to equip with machines, to use machines in or for. 2 to give a mechanical character to. **mechanisation** *noun*

mechanism *noun* 1 the way a machine works. 2 the structure of parts of a machine. 3 the process by which something is done, *the mechanism of government*.

medal *noun* a small flat piece of metal, often shaped like a coin, bearing a design and commemorating an event or given as an award for an achievement. –**medal** *verb* (*informal*) (in a sporting contest) win a medal.

medallion (mě-**dal**-yŏn) *noun* 1 a large medal. 2 a large circular ornamental design, e.g. on a carpet.

medallist *noun* one who wins a medal as a prize, *gold medallist*.

meddle *verb* 1 to interfere in people's affairs. 2 to tinker. **meddler** *noun*

meddlesome *adjective* often meddling.

Mede *noun* an inhabitant of ancient Persia (Media). □ **the law of the Medes and Persians** an unchanging law.

Medea (mě-**dee**-ă) (*Gk. legend*) a sorceress and princess of Colchis, who helped Jason to obtain the Golden Fleece.

media (**meed**-ee-ă) *plural noun* see **medium**. □ **the media** newspapers and broadcasting etc., by which information is conveyed to the general public.

Usage This word is the plural of *medium* and should have a plural verb, e.g. *the media are* (not *is*) *influential*. When referring to one of these services use *medium*, e.g. *television is a powerful medium*.

---

mediaeval *adjective* = **medieval**.

medial (**mee**-dee-ăl) *adjective* situated in the middle, intermediate between two extremes. **medially** *adverb* [from Latin *medius* = middle]

median (**mee**-dee-ăn) *adjective* situated in or passing through the middle. –**median** *noun* 1 a median point or line etc. 2 a straight line from any vertex of a triangle to the middle of the opposite side. 3 the value of the middle item in a list of statistics arranged in order of size. □ **median strip** a usually raised strip in the middle of a road separating opposing lanes of traffic.

mediant (**mee**-dee-ănt) *noun* (in music) the third note of a diatonic scale.

mediate (**mee**-dee-ayt) *verb* 1 to act as negotiator or peacemaker between the opposing sides in a dispute. 2 to bring about (a settlement) in this way. **mediation** *noun*, **mediator** *noun* [from Latin *medius* = middle]

medical *adjective* of or involving the science of medicine; of this as distinct from surgery; *medical examination*, physical examination by a doctor to determine a person's state of health. –**medical** *noun* (*informal*) a medical examination. □ **medical certificate** a certificate giving the results of a medical examination, stating whether a person is fit for work etc. **medical practitioner** a physician or surgeon. **medically** *adverb* [from Latin *medicus* = doctor]

medicament (mě-**dik**-ă-měnt) *noun* any medicine or ointment etc.

Medicare *noun* (in Australia) the Federal system of universal basic health insurance, partly financed by a levy on taxable incomes.

medicate *verb* to treat or impregnate with a medicinal substance, *medicated gauze*. **medication** *noun*

Medici (med-ĭ-chee) the name of an Italian family prominent especially in Florence and Tuscany in the 15th–17th centuries.

medicinal (mĕ-**diss**-ĭ-năl) *adjective* of medicine; having healing properties. **medicinally** *adverb*

medicine (med-ĭ-sĭn) *noun* **1** the scientific study of the prevention and cure of diseases and disorders of the body. **2** this as distinct from surgery. **3** a substance used to treat a disease etc., especially one taken by mouth. ☐ **medicine man** a person believed to have powers of healing; a witchdoctor. **take one's medicine** to submit to punishment for one's wrongdoing.

medico *noun* (*informal*) a doctor or medical student.

medieval (med-ee-**ee**-văl) *adjective* of the Middle Ages. [from Latin *medius* = middle, + *aevum* = age]

Medina (mĕ-**deen**-ă) a city in Saudi Arabia, the second holiest city of Islam (after Mecca), containing Muhammad's tomb and the site of the first Islamic mosque.

mediocre (meed-ee-**oh**-ker) *adjective* **1** of medium quality, neither good nor bad. **2** second-rate. **mediocrity** (meed-ee-**ok**-rĭ-tee) *noun*

meditate *verb* **1** to think deeply and quietly. **2** to plan in one's mind. **meditation** *noun*

meditative (med-ĭ-tă-tiv) *adjective* meditating; accompanied by meditation. **meditatively** *adverb*

Mediterranean *adjective* of or characteristic of the Mediterranean Sea or the regions bordering on it. – **Mediterranean** *noun* the **Mediterranean Sea**, a sea lying between Europe and North Africa. ☐ **Mediterranean climate** a climate with hot dry summers and warm wet winters. [from Latin, = sea in the middle of the earth (*media* = middle, + *terra* = land)]

medium *noun* (*plural* **media**, in sense 7 **mediums**) **1** a middle quality or degree of intensiveness etc.; *the happy medium*, avoidance of extremes which are unpleasant. **2** a substance or surroundings in which something exists or moves or is transmitted, *air is the medium through which sound travels*. **3** an environment. **4** a liquid (e.g. oil or water) in which pigments are mixed for use in painting. **5** an agency or means by which something is done, *the use of television as a medium for advertising*. (¶ See the entry for **media**.) **6** the material or form used by an artist or composer, *sculpture is his medium*. **7** (*plural* **mediums**) a person who claims to be able to communicate with the spirits of the dead. – **medium** *adjective* intermediate between two extremes or amounts, average, moderate. ☐ **medium wave** a radio wave having a wavelength between 300 kHz and 3 MHz. [Latin, = middle thing]

medlar *noun* **1** a fruit like a small brown apple that is not edible until it begins to decay. **2** the tree that bears it.

medley *noun* (*plural* **medleys**) **1** an assortment of things. **2** music combining passages from different sources.

medulla (mĕ-**dul**-ă) *noun* **1** the marrow within a bone; the substance of the spinal cord. **2** the hindmost section of the brain (not including the cerebellum). **3** the central part of certain organs, e.g. that of the kidney. **4** the soft internal tissue of plants. **medullary** *adjective* [Latin, = pith, marrow]

Medusa (mĕ-**dew**-să) (*Gk. myth.*) one of the Gorgons, beheaded by Perseus.

meek *adjective* quiet and obedient, making no protest. **meekly** *adverb*, **meekness** *noun*

meerkat *noun* a small African mongoose.

meerschaum (**meer**-shăm) *noun* a tobacco pipe with a bowl made from a white clay-like substance that darkens in use. [German, = sea-foam]

meet¹ *verb* (**met**, **meeting**) **1** to come face to face with, to come together (e.g. socially or for discussion). **2** to come into contact, to touch. **3** to go to a place to be present at the arrival of, *I will meet your train*. **4** to make the acquaintance of, to be introduced. **5** to come together as opponents in a contest or battle. **6** to find oneself faced (with a thing); to experience or receive, *met with difficulties*; *met his death*. **7** to deal with (a problem); to satisfy (a demand etc.); to pay (the cost or what is owing). – **meet** *noun* a meeting of athletes etc. for a competition or of people and hounds for a hunt. ☐ **meet a person halfway** to respond readily to a person's advances; to make a compromise. **meet the eye** or **ear** to be visible or audible; *there's more in it than meets the eye*, there are hidden qualities or complications; *meet a person's eye*, to look directly at the eyes of a person who is looking at one's own. **meet up with** (*informal*) to meet (a person).

meet² *adjective* (*old use*) suitable, proper.

meeting *noun* **1** coming together. **2** an assembly of people for discussion etc. or (of Quakers) for worship. **3** a race meeting.

meg *noun* a megabyte.

mega- (**meg**-ă) *prefix* **1** large (as in *mega-bucks*, *megastore*). **2** one million (as in *megavolts*, *megawatts*). [from Greek *megas* = great]

megabit *noun* (in computing) a unit of data size or network speed, equal to one million or (strictly) 1,048,576 bits (per second).

megabyte *noun* (in computing) a measure of storage capacity, = 1,048,576 (i.e. 2^{20}) bytes.

megacycle *noun* **1** one million cycles as a unit of wave frequency. **2** (*informal*) megahertz.

megadeath *noun* the death of one million people (regarded as a unit in estimating the possible casualties in nuclear war).

megahertz *noun* a unit of frequency of electromagnetic waves, = one million cycles per second.

megajoule (**meg**-ă-jool) *noun* one million joules.

megalith (**meg**-ă-lith) *noun* a huge stone used in the building of prehistoric monuments. **megalithic** (megă-**lith**-ik) *adjective* using such stones. [from *mega-*, + Greek *lithos* = stone]

megalomania (meg-ă-lŏ-**may**-nee-ă) *noun* **1** a form of madness in which a person has exaggerated ideas of his or her own importance etc. **2** an obsessive desire to do things on a grand scale. **megalomaniac** *noun* & *adjective* [from *mega-* + *mania*]

megalopolis (meg-ă-**lop**-ŏ-lĭs) *noun* (*plural* **megalopolises**) an extremely large city. [from Greek *mega-*, + *polis* = city]

megaphone *noun* a funnel-shaped device used for directing and amplifying a speaker's voice so that it can be heard at a distance. [from *mega-*, + Greek *phone* = voice]

megastar *noun* (*informal*) a very famous entertainer.

megaton (**meg**-ă-tun) *noun* (also **megatonne**) a unit of explosive power equal to that of one million tons (or tonnes) of TNT.

megavolt *noun* a unit of electromotive force equal to one million volts.

megawatt *noun* a unit of electrical power equal to one million watts.

megohm *noun* a unit of electrical resistance equal to one million ohms.

meiosis (my-**oh**-sĭs) *noun* the process of division of the nuclei of cells in which gametes are formed each containing half the normal number of chromosomes. [Greek, = lessening]

meitnerium (myt-**neer**-ee-ŭm) *noun* a very unstable artificial element (symbol Mt).

Mekong (mee-**kong**) the major river of SE Asia, flowing from Tibet along the Burma–Laos and Thailand–Laos borders and across Cambodia and Vietnam to the South China Sea.

melaleuca (mel-ă-**loo**-kă) *noun* a tree or shrub with profuse ball or bottlebrush flowers of white, yellow, purple, or red.

melamine (**mel**-ă-meen) *noun* a resilient kind of plastic.

melancholia (mel-ăn-**koh**-lee-ă) *noun* mental depression. **melancholic** (mel-ăn-**kol**-ik) *adjective*

melancholy (**mel**-ăn-kŏ-lee) *noun* **1** mental depression; thoughtful sadness. **2** an atmosphere of gloom. **–melancholy** *adjective* sad, gloomy, depressing. [from Greek *melas* = black, + *khole* = bile]

Melanesia (mel-ă-**nee**-zhă) a group of islands in the SW Pacific, containing the Bismarck Archipelago, the Solomon Islands, Santa Cruz, Vanuatu, New Caledonia, Fiji, and the intervening islands. **Melanesian** *adjective* & *noun* [from Greek *melas* = black, + *nesos* = island]

melanin (**mel**-ă-nin) *noun* a dark pigment found in skin and hair. [from Greek *melas* = black]

melanoma (mel-ă-**noh**-mă) *noun* a malignant skin tumour.

Melba, Dame Nellie (real name Helen Porter Mitchell, 1861–1931), Australian operatic soprano. ☐ **do a Melba** return from retirement; make several farewell appearances. **Melba toast** very thin crisp toast. **peach Melba** a dessert of vanilla ice cream and peaches topped with a sauce of puréed raspberries.

Melbourne (**mel**-bŭn) the capital of Victoria and the second largest city in Australia. ☐ **Melbourne Cup** a horse race of 3200 m run on the first Tuesday in November at Flemington racecourse in Melbourne.

Melburnian (mel-**ber**-nee-ăn) *adjective* & *noun*

mêlée (**mel**-ay) *noun* 1 a confused fight. 2 a muddle.

mellifluous (mě-**lif**-loo-ŭs) *adjective* sweet-sounding. [from Latin *mel* = honey, + *fluere* = to flow]

mellow *adjective* 1 sweet and rich in flavour. 2 (of sound or colour) soft and rich, free from harshness or sharp contrast. 3 made kindly and sympathetic by age or experience. 4 genial, jovial. –**mellow** *verb* to make or become mellow. **mellowly** *adverb*, **mellowness** *noun*

melodeon *noun* (also **melodion**) a small organ or harmonium.

melodic (mě-**lod**-ik) *adjective* of melody. □ **melodic minor scale** *see* **minor**.

melodious (mě-**loh**-dee-ŭs) *adjective* full of melody. **melodiously** *adverb*

melodrama (**mel**-ŏ-drah-mă) *noun* 1 a play full of suspense in a sensational and emotional style. 2 plays of this kind. 3 a situation in real life resembling this. **melodramatic** (mel-ŏ-dră-**mat**-ik) *adjective*, **melodramatically** *adverb* [from Greek *melos* = music, + *drama*]

melody *noun* 1 sweet music, tunefulness. 2 a song or tune, *old Irish melodies*. 3 the main part in a piece of harmonised music. [from Greek *melos* = music, + *oide* = song]

melon *noun* a large sweet fleshy fruit with a thick skin, e.g. *rockmelon*, *watermelon*. □ **melon hole** (*Austral.*) a gilgai.

Melpomene (mel-**pom**-ě-nee) (*Gk.* & *Rom. myth.*) the Muse of tragedy.

melt *verb* 1 to make into or become liquid by heat. 2 (of food) to be softened or dissolved easily, *it melts in the mouth*. 3 to make or become gentler through pity or love. 4 to dwindle or fade away; to pass slowly into something else, *one shade of colour melted into another*. □ **melting point** the temperature at which a solid melts. **melting pot** a place or situation where things are being mixed or reconstructed, *all our ideas must go back into the melting pot*. **melt water** water resulting from the melting of snow and ice, especially in a glacier.

meltdown *noun* the melting of (and consequent damage to) a structure, e.g. the overheated core of a nuclear reactor.

melton *noun* a heavy woollen cloth with close-cut nap, used for overcoats. [from the name of Melton Mowbray in England]

Melville, Herman (1819–91), American novelist and poet, author of *Moby Dick*.

Melville Island an island north of Darwin. Together with Bathurst Island it is the homeland of the Tiwi people who regained ownership of it in 1978.

member *noun* 1 a person or thing that belongs to a particular group of society. 2 **Member** (in full **Member of Parliament**) a person formally elected to take part in the proceedings of a parliament. 3 a part of a complex structure. 4 a part of the body. [from Latin *membrum* = limb]

membership *noun* 1 being a member. 2 the total number of members.

membrane (**mem**-brayn) *noun* thin flexible skinlike tissue, especially that covering or lining organs or other structures in animals and plants. **membranous** (**mem**-bră-nŭs) *adjective*

memento (mě-**ment**-oh) *noun* (*plural* **mementoes**) a souvenir. [Latin, = remember]

memo (**mem**-oh) *noun* (*plural* **memos**) (*informal*) a memorandum.

memoir (**mem**-wahr) *noun* a written account of events that one has lived through or of the life or character of a person whom one knew, *write one's memoirs*.

memorable (**mem**-ŏ-răbŭl) *adjective* worth remembering; easy to remember. **memorably** *adverb*, **memorability** *noun*

memorandum (mem-ŏ-**ran**-dŭm) *noun* (*plural* **memoranda**) 1 a note or record of events written as a reminder, for future use. 2 an informal written communication from one person to another in an organisation. [from Latin, = thing to be remembered]

memorial *noun* an object, institution, or custom established in memory of an event or person. –**memorial** *adjective* serving as a memorial.

memorise *verb* (also **-ize**) to learn (a thing) so as to know it from memory.

memory *noun* 1 the ability to keep things in one's mind or to recall them at will. 2 remembering; a thing remembered, *memories of childhood*. 3 the length of time over which people's memory extends, *within living memory*. 4 the part of a computer in which data or instructions can be stored for retrieval; the storage capacity of a computer. □ **from memory** recalled into one's mind without the aid of notes etc. **in memory of** in honour of a person or thing that is

remembered with respect. **memory stick**
(*trademark*) = **flash drive**. [from Latin *memor*
= remembering]

men *see* man.

menace *noun* 1 something that seems likely
to bring harm or danger; a threatening quality.
2 an annoying or troublesome person or thing.
–**menace** *verb* to threaten with harm or danger.
menacingly *adverb*

menagerie (mĕ-**naj**-ĕ-ree) *noun* a collection
of wild or strange animals in captivity, for
exhibition.

Menander (mĕ-**nan**-der) late 4th century BC,
Greek dramatist, the leading writer of comedy
in the Hellenistic period.

menarche (**men**-ar-kee) *noun* the onset of
first menstruation.

mend *verb* 1 to make whole (something that
is damaged), to repair. 2 to make or become
better; *mend one's manners*, improve them;
mend matters, to set right or improve the state
of affairs. –**mend** *noun* a repaired place.
☐ **on the mend** improving in health or
condition. **mender** *noun*

mendacious (men-**day**-shŭs) *adjective*
untruthful, telling lies. **mendaciously** *adverb*,
mendacity (men-**dass**-ĭ-tee) *noun* [from Latin
mendax = lying]

Mendel (**men**-dĕl), Gregor Johan (1822–84),
Moravian monk, founder of the science of
genetics.

Mendeleev (men-del-**ay**-ef), Dmitri
Ivanovich (1834–1907), Russian chemist, who
developed the periodic table of elements (*see*
periodic).

mendelevium (men-dĕ-**lee**-vee-ŭm) *noun*
an artificial radioactive metallic element of the
actinide series (symbol Md).

Mendelssohn (**men**-dĕl-sŏn), (Jakob
Ludwig) Felix (1809–47), German composer.

mendicant (**men**-dĭ-kănt) *adjective* begging;
mendicant friars, friars who depend on alms
for a living. –**mendicant** *noun* a beggar; a
mendicant friar. [from Latin *mendicans* =
begging]

menfolk *plural noun* men in general; the men
of one's family.

menhir (**men**-heer) *noun* a tall upright stone
set up in prehistoric times. [from Breton *men*
= stone, + *hir* = long]

menial (**meen**-ee-ăl) *adjective* lowly,
degrading, *menial tasks*. –**menial** *noun* a

servant, a person who does humble tasks.
menially *adverb*

meninges (mĕ-**nin**-jeez) *plural noun* the
membranes that enclose the brain and spinal
cord.

meningitis (men-ĭn-**jy**-tĭss) *noun*
inflammation of the meninges.

meniscus (mĕ-**nis**-kŭs) *noun* (*plural* **menisci**)
1 the curved upper surface of liquid in a tube,
caused by surface tension. 2 a lens that is
convex on one side and concave on the other.
[from Greek *meniskos* = crescent]

menopause (**men**-ŏ-pawz) *noun* the time
of life during which a woman finally ceases
to menstruate. **menopausal** *adjective* [from
Greek *menos* = of a month, + *pause*]

menorah (mĕ-**nor**-ră) *noun* 1 a holy seven-
branched candelabrum used in the Temple
in ancient Jerusalem. 2 a candelabrum with
any number of branches used in modern
synagogues and Jewish houses. [Hebrew, =
candlestick]

Mensa an organisation admitting as members
people who pass an intelligence test showing
that they have a high IQ.

menses *plural noun* the blood etc. discharged
in menstruation. [Latin, = months]

menstrual (**men**-stroo-ăl) *adjective* of or in
menstruation.

menstruate (**men**-stroo-ayt) *verb* to
experience the discharge of blood from the
womb that normally occurs in women between
puberty and middle age at approximately
monthly intervals. **menstruation** *noun* [from
Latin *menstruus* = monthly]

mensuration (men-shŭ-**ray**-shŏn) *noun*
measuring; the mathematical rules for finding
lengths, areas, and volumes. [from Latin
mensura = measure]

mental *adjective* 1 of the mind; existing in
or performed by the mind; *mental arithmetic*,
calculations done without the aid of written
figures. 2 (*informal*) suffering from a
disorder of the mind, mad.☐ **mental age**
the level of a person's mental development
expressed as the age at which this level is
reached by an average person. **mental block**
an inability to remember something due to
subconscious factors. **mental deficiency** lack
of normal intelligence through imperfect
mental development. **mental hospital** an
establishment for the care of patients suffering
from mental illness. **mentally** *adverb* [from
Latin *mentis* = of the mind]

mentality (men-**tal**-ĭ-tee) *noun* a person's mental ability or characteristic attitude of mind.

menthol *noun* a solid white substance obtained from peppermint oil or made synthetically, used as a flavouring and to relieve pain. [from Latin *mentha* = mint]

mentholated *adjective* impregnated with menthol.

mention *verb* to speak or write about briefly; to refer to by name; *was mentioned in dispatches*, mentioned by name for bravery. –**mention** *noun* mentioning; being mentioned. □ **don't mention it** a polite reply to thanks or to an apology. **not to mention** and as another important thing.

mentor (**men**-tor) *noun* a trusted adviser. [from Mentor in Greek legend, who advised Odysseus' son]

menu (**men**-yoo) *noun* **1** a list of dishes to be served or available in a restaurant etc. **2** a list of options, displayed on a screen, from which a user selects what he or she requires a computer to do.

meow *noun* & *verb* = **mew**[1].

Mephistopheles (mef-ĭs-**tof**-ĕ-leez) (in the legend of Faust) the demon to whom Faust sold his soul.

Mer (*pr.* mair) *see* **Murray Island**.

mercantile (**mer**-kăn-tyl) *adjective* trading; of trade or merchants. □ **mercantile marine** the merchant navy.

Mercator (mer-**kay**-ter), Gerard Kremer (1512–94), Flemish geographer, inventor of a system of map projection.

mercenary (**mer**-sĕ-nă-ree) *adjective* **1** working merely for money or other reward, grasping. **2** (of professional soldiers) hired to serve a foreign country. –**mercenary** *noun* a professional soldier serving a foreign country. **mercenarily** *adverb*, **mercenariness** *noun*

mercer *noun* a dealer in textile fabrics. **mercery** *noun*

mercerised *adjective* (also **-ized**) (of cotton fabric or thread) treated with a substance that gives greater strength and a slight gloss.

merchandise *noun* goods or commodities bought and sold, goods for sale. –**merchandise** *verb* **1** to buy and sell, to trade. **2** to promote sales of (goods etc.).

merchant *noun* **1** a wholesale trader. **2** a retail trader. **3** (*informal*) a person who is fond of a certain activity, *speed merchants*. □ **merchant**

bank a bank dealing in commercial loans and the financing of businesses. **merchant navy** shipping employed in commerce. **merchant ship** a ship carrying merchandise.

merchantable *adjective* saleable, marketable.

merchantman *noun* (*plural* **merchantmen**) a merchant ship.

merciful *adjective* **1** showing mercy. **2** giving relief from pain or suffering, *a merciful death*. **mercifully** *adverb*

merciless *adjective* showing no mercy. **mercilessly** *adverb*

mercurial (mer-**kew**-ree-ăl) *adjective* **1** of or caused by mercury, *mercurial poisoning*. **2** having a lively temperament. **3** liable to sudden changes of mood.

Mercury 1 (*Rom. myth.*) the messenger of the gods, identified with Hermes. **2** the planet nearest the sun, in the solar system.

mercury *noun* a chemical element (symbol Hg), a heavy silvery normally liquid metal, used in thermometers and barometers etc. **mercuric** (mer-**kew**-rik) *adjective*, **mercurous** *adjective* [from the name of the planet Mercury]

mercy *noun* **1** refraining from inflicting punishment or pain on an offender or enemy etc. who is in one's power. **2** a disposition to behave in this way, *a tyrant without mercy*. **3** a merciful act; a thing to be thankful for, *it's a mercy no one was killed*. –**mercy** *interjection* an exclamation of surprise or fear, *mercy on us!* □ **at the mercy of** wholly in the power of; liable to danger or harm from. **mercy killing** euthanasia.

mere[1] *adjective* nothing more or better than what is specified; *mere words*, words alone, without deeds; *it's no mere theory*, is not only a theory. **merely** *adverb*

mere[2] *noun* (*poetic*) a lake.

merest *adjective* very small or insignificant, *the merest trace of colour*.

meretricious (me-rĕ-**trish**-ŭs) *adjective* showily attractive but cheap or insincere. [from Latin *meretrix* = prostitute]

merge *verb* **1** to unite or combine into a whole, *the two companies merged* or *were merged*. **2** to pass slowly into something else, to blend or become blended. [from Latin *mergere* = dip]

merger *noun* the combining of two commercial companies etc. into one.

meridian (mĕ-**rid**-ee-ăn) *noun* any of the great semicircles on the globe, passing through a given place and the North and South Poles; *the meridian of Greenwich*, the meridian shown on maps as 0° longitude.

meringue (mĕ-**rang**) *noun* 1 a mixture of sugar and white of egg baked crisp. 2 a small cake of this.

merino (mĕ-**ree**-noh) *noun* (*plural* **merinos**) 1 a kind of sheep with fine soft wool. 2 a kind of fine soft woollen yarn or fabric.

meristem (**me**-rĭ-stem) *noun* the growing tissue of plants, consisting of small cells. [from Greek *meristos* = divisible]

merit *noun* 1 the quality of deserving to be praised, excellence. 2 a feature or quality that deserves praise; *judge it on its merits*, according to its own qualities. –**merit** *verb* (**merited**, **meriting**) to deserve. [from Latin *meritum* = deserved]

meritocracy (me-rĭ-**tok**-ră-see) *noun* 1 government or control by people of high ability, selected by some form of competition. 2 these people. [from *merit* + *-cracy*]

meritorious (me-rĭ-**tor**-ree-ŭs) *adjective* having merit, deserving praise. **meritoriously** *adverb*, **meritoriousness** *noun*

Merlin (in legends of King Arthur) a magician who aided King Arthur.

merlin *noun* a kind of small falcon.

mermaid *noun* an imaginary sea creature, a woman with a fish's tail in place of legs. **merman** *noun* (*plural* **mermen**) a similar male creature. [from *mere*² (old word, = sea), + *maid*, *man*]

merry *adjective* (**merrier**, **merriest**) 1 cheerful and lively, joyous. 2 (*informal*) cheerful because slightly drunk. □ **make merry** to hold lively festivities. **merrily** *adverb*, **merriment** *noun*

merry-go-round *noun* 1 a machine with a revolving platform fitted with wooden horses or cars etc. for riding on. 2 a busy cycle of activities.

merrymaking *noun* lively festivities.

mesa (**may**-să) *noun* a flat-topped hill or rocky plateau with almost vertical sides. [Spanish, = table]

mescaline (**mesk**-ă-leen) *noun* a drug that produces hallucinations, made from the dried button-shaped tops of a Mexican cactus.

mesclun *noun* a Provençal green salad made from a mixture of edible leaves and flowers.

Mesdames *see* Madame.

Mesdemoiselles *see* Mademoiselle.

mesh *noun* 1 one of the spaces between threads in a net, sieve, or wire screen etc. 2 network fabric. –**mesh** *verb* (of a toothed wheel etc.) to engage with another or others.

mesmerise *verb* (also **-ize**) to hypnotise, to dominate the attention or will of.

mesmerism *noun* hypnosis. **mesmeric** (mez-**me**-rik) *adjective*

mesolithic (mess-ŏ-**lith**-ik) *adjective* of the middle part of the Stone Age, between the palaeolithic and the neolithic. –**mesolithic** *noun* this period. [from Greek *mesos* = middle, + *lithos* = stone]

meson (**mee**-zon) *noun* an unstable elementary particle intermediate in mass between a proton and an electron.

Mesopotamia (mess-ŏ-pŏ-**tay**-mee-ă) a region of SW Asia between the rivers Tigris and Euphrates, now within Iraq. [from Greek *mesos* = middle, + *potamos* = river]

mesosphere (**mess**-ŏ-sfeer) *noun* the region of the earth's atmosphere from the top of the stratosphere to an altitude of about 80 km. [from Greek *mesos* = middle, + *sphere*]

Mesozoic (mess-ŏ-**zoh**-ik) *adjective* of the geological era lasting from about 248 to 65 million years ago. –**Mesozoic** *noun* this era.

mess *noun* 1 a dirty or untidy condition; an untidy collection of things; something spilt. 2 a difficult or confused situation, trouble. 3 any disagreeable substance or concoction; a domestic animal's excreta. 4 (*informal*) a person who looks untidy or dirty or slovenly. 5 (in the armed forces) a group who take meals together; the place where such meals are eaten. –**mess** *verb* 1 to make untidy or dirty. 2 to muddle or bungle (business etc.), *messed it up*. 3 to potter, *mess about* or *around*. 4 to meddle or tinker. 5 to take one's meals with a military or other group, *they mess together*. □ **make a mess of** to bungle.

message *noun* 1 a spoken, written, recorded, or electronic communication. 2 the inspired moral or social teaching of a prophet or writer etc., *a film with a message*. –**message** *verb* to send a message to, especially by electronic means. □ **get the message** (*informal*) to understand what is meant or implied.

messenger *noun* the bearer of a message.

Messiah (mĕ-**sy**-ă) *noun* 1 the expected deliverer and ruler of the Jewish people, whose coming was prophesied in the Old Testament. **2** Jesus Christ, regarded by Christians as this. **Messianic** *adjective* [from Hebrew, = the anointed one]

Messieurs *see* **Monsieur**.

messmate *noun* (*Austral.*) any of various rough-barked eucalypts.

Messrs (**mess**-erz) *abbreviation* plural of Mr.

messy *adjective* (**messier**, **messiest**) **1** untidy or dirty, slovenly. **2** causing a mess, *a messy task*. **3** complicated and difficult to deal with. **messily** *adverb*, **messiness** *noun*

met *see* **meet**¹.

metabolise (mĕ-**tab**-ŏ-lyz) *verb* (also **-ize**) to process (food) in metabolism.

metabolism (mĕ-**tab**-ŏ-lizm) *noun* the process by which food is built up into living material or used to supply energy in a living organism. ☐ **basal metabolism** the metabolism that occurs in an organism when it is completely at rest. **metabolic** (met-ă-**bol**-ik) *adjective* [from Greek *metabole* = change]

metacarpus (met-ă-**kar**-pŭs) *noun* the part of the hand between the wrist and the fingers; the set of bones in this. **metacarpal** *adjective*

metal *noun* any of a class of mineral substances such as gold, silver, copper, iron, uranium, etc., or an alloy of any of these. **–metal** *adjective* made of metal. **–metal** *verb* (**metalled**, **metalling**) **1** to cover or fit with metal. **2** to make or mend (a road) with road metal.

metallic (mĕ-**tal**-ik) *adjective* **1** of or like metal. **2** (of sound) like metals struck together, sharp and ringing. **metallically** *adverb*

metalliferous (met-ă-**lif**-ĕ-rŭs) *adjective* (of rocks etc.) containing metal.

metallurgy (**met**-ă-ler-jee *or* mĕ-**tal**-er-jee) *noun* **1** the scientific study of the properties of metals and alloys. **2** the art of working metals or of extracting them from their ores. **metallurgical** (met-ă-**ler**-ji-kăl) *adjective*, **metallurgist** *noun* [from *metal*, + Greek *-ourgia* = working]

metalwork *noun* **1** shaping objects from metal. **2** a shaped metal object.

metamorphic (met-ă-**mor**-fik) *adjective* (of rock) having had its structure or other properties changed by natural agencies (such as heat and pressure), as in the transformation of limestone into marble. [from Greek *meta-* = change, + *morphe* = form]

metamorphose (met-ă-**mor**-fohz) *verb* to change or be changed in form or character.

metamorphosis (met-ă-**mor**-fŏ-sĭs) *noun* (*plural* **metamorphoses**) a change of form or character. [same origin as *metamorphic*]

metaphor (**met**-ă-for) *noun* the application of a word or phrase to something that it does not apply to normally, in order to indicate a comparison with the literal usage, e.g. the *evening of one's life*, *food for thought*, *cut off one's nose to spite one's face*. (Compare *simile*, in which the word 'like' or 'as' is used, e.g. *as hungry as an ox*.) ☐ **mixed metaphor** an unsuitable combination of metaphors, e.g. *a virgin land, pregnant with possibilities*. **metaphorical** (met-ă-**fo**-ri-kăl) *adjective*, **metaphorically** *adverb* [from Greek *metapherein* = to transfer]

metaphysics (met-ă-**fiz**-iks) *noun* **1** a branch of philosophy that deals with the nature of existence and of truth and knowledge. **2** (*loosely*) abstract or subtle thought; mere theory. **metaphysical** *adjective*

metatarsus (met-ă-**tar**-sŭs) *noun* the part of the foot between the ankle and the toes; the set of bones in this. **metatarsal** *adjective*

mete (*pr.* meet) *verb* **mete out** to give as what is due, *mete out punishment to wrongdoers*.

meteor (**meet**-ee-er *or* **meet**-ee-or) *noun* a bright moving body seen in the sky, formed by a small mass of matter from outer space that becomes luminous from compression of air as it enters the earth's atmosphere. [from Greek *meteoros* = high in the air]

meteoric (meet-ee-**o**-rik) *adjective* **1** of meteors. **2** like a meteor in brilliance or sudden appearance, *a meteoric career*.

meteorite (**meet**-ee-ŏ-ryt) *noun* a fallen meteor, a fragment of rock or metal reaching the earth's surface from outer space.

meteoroid (**meet**-ee-ŏ-roid) *noun* a body moving through space, of the same nature as those which become visible as meteors when they enter the earth's atmosphere.

meteorology (meet-ee-ŏ-**rol**-ŏ-jee) *noun* the scientific study of atmospheric conditions, especially in order to forecast weather. **meteorological** (meet-ee-ŏ-rŏ-**loj**-ikăl) *adjective*, **meteorologist** *noun* [from Greek *meteoros* = high in the air, + *-logy*]

meter¹ *noun* a device designed to measure and indicate the quantity of a substance supplied, or the distance travelled and fare payable, or the time that has elapsed, etc. **–meter** *verb* (**metered**, **metering**) to measure by meter. [from *mete*]

meter² *noun* (*Amer.*) = **metre**.

methadone *noun* a strong narcotic drug used to relieve pain, and as a substitute for morphine or heroin.

methamphetamine *noun* an amphetamine derivative used as stimulant.

methane (**mee**-thayn) *noun* a colourless inflammable gas that occurs in coal mines and marshy areas.

methanol (**meth**-ă-nol) *noun* the simplest alcohol, whose molecules contain the methyl group of atoms, used to make methylated spirit.

methinks *verb* (*old use*) I think.

method *noun* 1 a procedure or way of doing something. 2 orderliness, *he's a man of method*. [from Greek *methodos* = pursuit of knowledge]

methodical (mě-**thod**-i-kăl) *adjective* orderly, systematic. **methodically** *adverb*

Methodist *noun* a member of a Protestant religious denomination originating in the 18th century and based on the teachings of John and Charles Wesley and their followers. **Methodism** *noun*

methodology (meth-ŏ-**dol**-ŏ-jee) *noun* 1 the science of method and procedure. 2 the methods used in a particular activity.

methought *verb* (*old use*) I thought.

Methuselah (mě-**thoo**-zě-lă) a Hebrew patriarch, grandfather of Noah, said to have lived for 969 years. –**methuselah** *noun* a wine bottle of about eight times the standard size.

methyl (**meth**-ĭl) *noun* a chemical unit present in methane and in many organic compounds. ☐ **methyl orange** a colouring matter that becomes red when added in stronger acids and yellow in weaker ones, used to distinguish between them.

methylated spirit(s) *noun* a form of alcohol (made unpleasant for drinking) used as a solvent and for heating.

meticulous (mě-**tik**-yŭ-lŭs) *adjective* giving or showing great attention to detail, very careful and exact. **meticulously** *adverb*, **meticulousness** *noun*

métier (**may**-tee-ay) *noun* one's trade, profession, or field of activity; what one does best. [French]

metonymy (mě-**ton**-ĭ-mee) *noun* substitution of the word for an attribute for that of the thing meant, e.g. *respect for the cloth* instead of *respect for the clergy*. [from Greek *meta-* = change, + *onoma* = name]

metre *noun* 1 a unit of length in the metric system (about 39.4 inches). 2 rhythm in poetry; a particular form of this. [from Greek *metron* = measure]

metric *adjective* 1 of or using the metric system. 2 of poetic metre. ☐ **metric system** a decimal system of weights and measures, using the metre, litre, and gram as units. **metric ton** a tonne (1000 kilograms). **metrically** *adverb*

metrical *adjective* of or composed in rhythmic metre, not prose, *metrical psalms*.

metricate *verb* to change or adapt to the metric system of measurement. **metrication** *noun*

Metro *noun* (*informal*) the underground railway in Paris.

metronome (**met**-rŏ-nohm) *noun* a device that sounds a click at a set number of times per minute, used to indicate tempo for a person practising music. [from Greek *metron* = measure, + *nomos* = law]

metropolis (mě-**trop**-ŏ-lĭs) *noun* the chief city of a country or region. [from Greek *meter* = mother, + *polis* = city]

metropolitan (met-rŏ-**pol**-ĭ-tăn) *adjective* of a metropolis.

mettle *noun* courage or strength of character. ☐ **on one's mettle** determined to show one's courage or ability.

mettlesome *adjective* spirited, courageous.

mettwurst (**met**-voorst *or* -werst) *noun* a seasoned, dried, and smoked sausage of lean beef and salt pork. [from German *mett* = meat, pork, + *wurst* = sausage]

mew¹ *noun* the characteristic cry of a cat. –**mew** *verb* to make this sound.

mew² *noun* a gull.

mews *noun* a set of what were formerly stables, now rebuilt or converted into houses etc. [first used of royal stables in London, built on the site of hawks' cages (called *mews*)]

Mexico a federal republic in Central America. ☐ **Mexican wave** a wave-like movement produced when successive sections of a seated crowd of spectators stand, raise their arms, and sit down again. (¶ First observed at World Cup football matches in Mexico City in 1986.)

Mexico City the capital of Mexico. **Mexican** *adjective* & *noun*

mezzanine (**mets**-ă-neen) *noun* an extra storey between ground floor and first floor, often in the form of a wide balcony. [from Italian *mezzano* = middle]

mezzo (**met**-soh) *adverb* (in music) moderately; *mezzo forte*, moderately loudly. □ **mezzo-soprano** *noun* a voice between soprano and contralto; a singer with this voice; a part written for it. [Italian, = half]

mezzotint (**met**-soh-tint) *noun* **1** a method of engraving in which the plate is roughened to give areas of shadow and smoothed to give areas of light. **2** a print produced by this. [from *mezzo* + *tint*]

mg *abbreviation* milligram(s).

MHA *abbreviation* Member of the House of Assembly.

MHR *abbreviation* Member of the House of Representatives.

MHz *abbreviation* megahertz.

mia-mia (**my**-ă-my-ă) *noun* an Aboriginal hut. [Nyungar *maya* or *maya-maya*]

miaow *noun* & *verb* = **mew**[1].

miasma (mee-**az**-mă or my-) *noun* unpleasant or unwholesome air. [Greek, = pollution]

mica (**my**-kă) *noun* a mineral substance used as an electrical insulator.

Micah (**my**-kă) **1** a Hebrew minor prophet. **2** a book of the Old Testament bearing his name.

mice *see* **mouse**.

Michael, St, one of the archangels. Feast day, 29 September (Michaelmas Day).

Michaelmas (**mik**-ĕl-măs) *noun* a Christian festival in honour of St Michael (29 September).

Michelangelo (my-kĕl-**an**-jĕ-loh) (Michelangelo Buonarroti) (1475–1564), Italian sculptor, painter, architect, and poet, whose works include the decoration of the ceiling of the Sistine chapel.

Michigan (**mish**-ĭ-găn) a State of the northern USA. □ **Lake Michigan** one of the five Great Lakes of North America.

mickery *noun* a depression in sandy soil where water collects, especially in a dry river bed. [Wangganguru *migiri*]

mickey[1] *noun* a bull calf, usually unbranded.

mickey[2] *noun* **take the mickey (out of)** (*informal*) to tease or ridicule.

micro *noun* (*plural* **micros**) (*informal*) a microcomputer or microprocessor.

micro- *prefix* **1** very small. **2** one-millionth of a unit (as in *microgram*). [from Greek *mikros* = small]

microammeter (my-kroh-**am**-ee-ter) *noun* an instrument that measures electric current in millionths of an ampere.

microbe *noun* a microorganism, especially one that causes disease or fermentation. [from *micro-*, + Greek *bios* = life]

microbiology *noun* the scientific study of microorganisms. **microbiologist** *noun*

microchip *noun* a very small piece of silicon or similar material made so as to work like a complex wired electric circuit.

microcircuit *noun* an integrated circuit or other small electrical circuit.

microclimate *noun* the climate of a particular small area.

micrococcus *noun* (*plural* **micrococci**) a very small oval or spherical bacterium. [from *micro-*, + Latin *coccus* = berry]

microcomputer *noun* a very small computer.

microcosm (**my**-krŏ-kozm) *noun* a world in miniature; something regarded as resembling something else on a very small scale. [from Greek *mikros kosmos* = little world]

microdot *noun* a photograph of a document etc. reduced to the size of a dot.

microeconomics *noun* the branch of economics dealing with individual commodities, producers, etc. (compare *macroeconomics*). **microeconomic** *adjective*

microelectronics *noun* the design, manufacture, and use of microchips and microcircuits. **microelectronic** *adjective*

microfiche (**my**-krŏ-feesh) *noun* (*plural* **microfiche**) a sheet of microfilm in a form suitable for filing like an index card.

microfilm *noun* a length of film on which written or printed material is photographed in greatly reduced size. –**microfilm** *verb* to photograph on this.

microhabitat *noun* a limited area of one kind of habitat, differing from the areas round it.

microlight *noun* a kind of motorised hang-glider.

micrometer (my-**krom**-ĕ-ter) *noun* an instrument for measuring small lengths or angles.

micron (**my**-kron) *noun* one-millionth of a metre.

Micronesia (my-krŏ-**nee**-*zh*ă) **1** part of the western Pacific Ocean including the Mariana, Caroline, and Marshall Islands, Nauru, and Kiribati. **2** a federation of States comprising the 600 islands of the Caroline Islands in the western Pacific Ocean east of the Philippines. [from *micro-*, + *nesos* = island]

microorganism *noun* an organism that cannot be seen by the naked eye, e.g. a bacterium or virus.

microphone *noun* an instrument for picking up sound waves for recording, amplifying, or broadcasting. [from *micro-*, + Greek *phone* = sound]

microprocessor *noun* an integrated circuit containing all the functions of a computer's central processing unit.

micropyle (**my**-kroh-pyl) *noun* an opening in a female cell of a plant or animal, through which a fertilising cell may enter. [from *micro-*, + Greek *pule* = gate]

microscope *noun* an instrument with lenses that magnify objects or details too small to be seen by the naked eye. [from *micro-*, + Greek *skopein* = look at]

microscopic *adjective* **1** of the microscope. **2** too small to be visible without the aid of a microscope. **3** extremely small. **microscopically** *adverb*

microscopy (my-**kros**-kŏ-pee) *noun* use of the microscope.

microsecond *noun* one-millionth of a second.

microsurgery *noun* intricate surgery using a microscope to see the tissue and instruments involved.

microswitch *noun* a switch that can be operated rapidly by a small movement.

microwave *noun* **1** an electromagnetic wave of length between about 30 cm and 1 mm. **2** a **microwave oven**, an oven using such waves to heat food very quickly. –**microwave** *verb* to cook (food) in a microwave oven.

mid *adjective* in the middle of, middle, *in mid-air*; *to mid-August*. □ **mid-life** *noun* middle age. **mid-off**, **mid-on** *nouns* a fielder in cricket near the bowler on the off (or on) side; this position.

Midas (**my**-dăs) *noun* **the Midas touch** the ability to make money in all one's activities. [named after a legendary king in Asia Minor, whose touch turned all things to gold]

midday *noun* the middle of the day, noon.

midden *noun* a heap of dung; a rubbish heap.

middle *adjective* **1** at an equal distance from extremes or outer limits. **2** occurring halfway between beginning and end. **3** intermediate in rank or quality; moderate in size etc., *a man of middle height*. –**middle** *noun* **1** a middle point, position, time, area, or quality etc. **2** the waist. **3** the form of a Greek verb used when the subject of the verb is acting upon himself or herself.
□ **in the middle of** during or halfway through (an activity etc.). **middle age** the period between youth and old age. **middle-aged** *adjective* of middle age. **Middle Ages** about AD 1000–1400. **middle C** the note C that occurs near the middle of the piano keyboard. **middle class** the class of society between the upper and working classes, including business and professional people. **Middle East** an area of SW Asia and northern Africa, the area covered by countries from Egypt to Iran inclusive. **middle-of-the-road** *adjective* favouring a moderate policy, avoiding extremes. **middle school** the middle grades especially of independent schools, the upper primary and lower secondary years. **middle-sized** *adjective* of medium size.

middlebrow (*informal*) *adjective* having or appealing to only moderately intellectual tastes. –**middlebrow** *noun* a middlebrow person.

middleman *noun* (*plural* **middlemen**) **1** any of the traders handling a commodity between producer and consumer. **2** an intermediary.

middleweight *noun* a boxing weight between light heavyweight and welterweight, in amateur boxing 71–75 kg.

middling *adjective* moderately good. –**middling** *adverb* moderately.

middy *noun* (*Austral.*) a medium-sized measure of beer; the glass containing this.

midfield *noun* the central part of a sports field away from the goals.

midge *noun* a small biting gnatlike insect.

midget *noun* an extremely small person or thing. –**midget** *adjective* extremely small.

MIDI *noun* (also **midi**) an interface allowing electronic musical instruments and computers to be connected. [acronym from *musical instrument digital interface*]

midnight *noun* twelve o'clock at night; the time near this. □ **midnight sun** the sun visible at midnight in polar regions during the summer.

Midrash an ancient Jewish commentary on part of the Hebrew scriptures.

midrib *noun* the principal rib of a leaf.

midriff *noun* the front part of the body or of a garment just above the waist.

midshipman *noun* (*plural* **midshipmen**) the rank of a naval cadet training to be an officer.

midst *noun* the middle part.
□ **in the midst of** among, surrounded by.

midstream *noun* the middle of a stream or river. □ **in midstream** in the middle of an action etc.

midsummer *noun* the middle of summer.

midway *adverb* halfway between places.

Midwest *noun* the region of the USA including the northern states from Ohio west to the Rocky Mountains.

midwicket *noun* a position in cricket on the leg side opposite the middle of the pitch.

midwife *noun* (*plural* **midwives**) a person trained to assist women in childbirth.

midwifery (mid-**wif**-ĕ-ree) *noun* the work of a midwife.

midwinter *noun* the middle of the winter.

mien (*pr.* meen) *noun* a person's manner or bearing.

miffed *adjective* (*informal*) offended, put out.

might[1] *noun* great strength or power, *with all one's might*. □ **with might and main** with all one's power and energy.

might[2] *auxiliary verb* used as the past tense of **may**[1] or to express possibility, *we told her she might go*; *it might be true*; *you might call at the bakery*, I should like you to do so; *you might have offered*, ought to have offered.
□ **might-have-been** *noun* an event or person that might have developed but did not.

mightn't (*informal*) = might not.

mighty *adjective* (**mightier**, **mightiest**)
1 having or showing great strength or power. **2** very great in size. –**mighty** *adverb* (*informal*) very. **mightily** *adverb*, **mightiness** *noun*

mignonette (min-yŏ-**net**) *noun* **1** an annual plant with fragrant greyish-green leaves. **2** a kind of small lettuce.

migraine (**my**-grayn *or* **mee**-) *noun* a severe form of headache often accompanied by nausea and disturbance of vision.

migrant (**my**-grănt) *adjective* migrating.
–**migrant** *noun* **1** a migrant person, especially an immigrant. **2** a migratory animal.

Usage An *emigrant* leaves a country; an *immigrant* arrives in a country.

migrate (my-**grayt**) *verb* **1** to leave one place and settle in another. **2** (of animals) to go periodically from one place to another, living in each place for part of a year. **migration** *noun* [from Latin *migrare* = migrate]

migratory (my-**gray**-tŏ-ree *or* **my**-gră-tŏ-ree) *adjective* of or involving migration; migrating.

mihrab (**mee**-rahb) *noun* a niche or slab in a mosque, showing the direction of Mecca. [Arabic, = praying-place]

mikado (mǐ-**kah**-doh) *noun* (*plural* **mikados**) an emperor of Japan.

mike *noun* (*informal*) a microphone.

mil *noun* one-thousandth of an inch, used especially in measuring the diameter of wire.

milch *adjective* giving milk. □ **milch cow** a cow kept for its milk rather than for beef; a person or organisation from whom money is easily obtained.

mild *adjective* **1** moderate in intensity, character, or effect; not severe or harsh or drastic. **2** (of a person) gentle in manner. **3** not strongly flavoured, not sharp or strong in taste. □ **mild steel** steel that is strong and tough but not readily tempered. **mildly** *adverb*, **mildness** *noun*

mildew *noun* a minute fungus that forms a white coating on things exposed to damp.

mildewed *adjective* coated with mildew.

mile *noun* **1** an imperial measure of length, 1760 yards (about 1.609 kilometres); **nautical mile** a unit used in navigation, 2025 yards (1.852 kilometres). **2** (*informal*) a great distance or amount, *miles too big*. [from Latin *mille* = thousand (paces)]

mileage *noun* **1** distance measured in miles or (loosely) kilometres. **2** the distance a vehicle travels per unit of fuel. **3** (*informal*) continuing benefit, *got a lot of mileage out of her injury*.

milestone *noun* **1** a stone set up beside a road to show the distance in miles to a given point. **2** a significant event or stage in life or history.

milieu (**meel**-yer) *noun* (*plural* **milieux**, *pr.* **meel**-yer) environment, surroundings. [French]

militant *adjective* prepared to take aggressive action in support of a cause. – **militant** *noun* a militant person. **militancy** *noun*

militarise *verb* (also -**ize**) **1** to make military or warlike. **2** to equip with military resources. **3** to imbue with militarism.

militarism (**mil**-ĭ-tă-rizm) *noun* reliance on military strength and methods. **militarist** *noun*

militaristic *adjective* warlike.

military *adjective* of soldiers or the army or all armed forces, *military service*; *the military*, armed forces as distinct from police or civilians. [from Latin *miles* = soldier]

militate (**mil**-ĭ-tayt) *verb* to serve as a strong influence, *several factors militated against the success of our plan*.

Usage *Militate* is sometimes confused with *mitigate* which means 'to make less severe or intense'.

militia (mĭ-**lish**-ă) *noun* a military force, especially one consisting of civilians trained as soldiers and available to supplement the regular army in an emergency. [same origin as *military*]

milk *noun* **1** a white fluid secreted by female mammals as food for their young. **2** the milk of cows, used as food by human beings. **3** a milk-like liquid, e.g. that in a coconut. – **milk** *verb* **1** to draw milk from (a cow or goat etc.). **2** to extract juice from (a tree etc.). **3** to exploit or get money undeservedly from, *milking the company*. □ **in milk** (of cows) secreting milk. **milk bar** a shop selling milk, snack food, magazines, etc. **milk chocolate** chocolate made with milk. **milk powder** dehydrated milk. **milk shake** a drink made of milk, ice cream, and flavouring, mixed or shaken until frothy. **milk tooth** any of the first (temporary) teeth in young mammals.

milker *noun* **1** an animal, especially a cow, that gives milk. **2** a person who milks an animal; a milking machine.

milkman *noun* (*plural* **milkmen**) a person who delivers milk to customers' houses.

milko *noun* (*Austral. informal*) a milkman.

milksop *noun* a weak or timid boy or man.

milky *adjective* (**milkier**, **milkiest**) **1** of or like milk. **2** made with milk; containing much milk. **3** (of a gem or liquid) cloudy, not clear. □ **Milky Way** the broad faintly luminous band of stars encircling the sky, the Galaxy. **milkiness** *noun*

Mill, John Stuart (1806–73), English philosopher and economist.

mill *noun* **1** machinery for grinding corn; a building fitted with this. **2** any machine for grinding or crushing a solid substance into powder or pulp, *coffee mill*. **3** a machine or a building fitted with machinery for processing material of certain kinds, *cotton mill*; *paper mill*; *sawmill*. – **mill** *verb* **1** to grind or crush in a mill. **2** to produce in a mill. **3** to produce regular markings on the edge of (a coin), *silver coins with a milled edge*. **4** to cut or shape (metal) with a rotating tool. **5** (of people or animals) to move round and round in a confused mass. □ **go** or **put through the mill** to undergo or subject to training, experience, or suffering. **mill race** a current of water that works a mill wheel. **mill wheel** the wheel that drives a watermill.

millennium (mĭ-**len**-ee-ŭm) *noun* (*plural* **millenniums** *or* **millennia**) **1** a period of 1000 years. **2** the thousand-year reign of Christ on earth prophesied in the Bible. **3** a period of great happiness and prosperity for everyone. [from Latin *mille* = thousand, + *annus* = year]

millepede *noun* = **millipede**.

Miller, Arthur (1915–2005), American playwright whose works include *Death of a Salesman* and *The Crucible*.

miller *noun* a person who owns or runs a mill, especially a flour mill.

millet *noun* **1** a kind of cereal plant producing a large crop of small seeds. **2** its seeds, used as food.

millpond *noun* a pool of water retained by a dam for use in a watermill; *sea was like a millpond*, very calm.

milli- *prefix* **1** thousand. **2** one-thousandth. [from Latin *mille* = thousand]

milliard *noun* one thousand million.

millibar *noun* one-thousandth of a bar as a unit of pressure in meteorology.

milligram *noun* one-thousandth of a gram.

millilitre *noun* one-thousandth of a litre.

millimetre *noun* one-thousandth of a metre.

milliner *noun* a person who makes or sells women's hats.

millinery *noun* 1 a milliner's work. 2 women's hats sold in a shop.

million *adjective & noun* 1 one thousand thousand (1,000,000), *a few million* (¶ not *a few millions*). 2 a million dollars. 3 an enormous number. **millionth** *adjective & noun*

millionaire *noun* a person who has a million dollars, pounds, etc., one who is extremely wealthy.

millipede (**mil**-ĭ-peed) *noun* (also **millepede**) a small crawling creature like a centipede but usually with two pairs of legs on each segment of its body. [from Latin *mille* = thousand, + *pedes* = feet]

millisecond *noun* one-thousandth of a second.

millstone *noun* 1 each of a pair of circular stones between which corn is ground. 2 a great burden that impedes progress, *a millstone round one's neck*.

millwright *noun* a person who designs or erects mills.

milt *noun* the roe of a male fish, fish sperm discharged into the water over the eggs laid by the female.

Milton, John (1608–74), English poet, best known for his epic poem *Paradise Lost*.

mimbar *noun* the set of steps used as a pulpit in a mosque. (The imam preaches from the second step.) [from Arabic *minbar*]

mime *noun* acting with gestures and without words; a performance using this. –**mime** *verb* to act with mime.

mimic *verb* (**mimicked**, **mimicking**) 1 to copy the appearance or ways of (a person etc.) playfully or for entertainment. 2 to pretend to be, (of things) to resemble closely. –**mimic** *noun* a person who is clever at mimicking others, especially for entertainment. **mimicry** *noun*

mimosa (mim-**oh**-ză) *noun* any of several usually tropical trees or shrubs, especially the kind with clusters of small ball-shaped fragrant flowers.

mina *noun* = **myna**.

minaret (min-ă-**ret**) *noun* a tall slender tower on or beside a mosque, with a balcony from which a muezzin calls Muslims to prayer. [from Arabic *manara* = lighthouse]

minatory (**min**-ă-tŏ-ree) *adjective* threatening. [from Latin *minari* = threaten]

mince *verb* 1 to cut into small pieces in a machine with revolving blades. 2 to walk or speak in an affected way, trying to appear refined. –**mince** *noun* 1 minced meat. 2 mincemeat. □ **mince pie** a pie containing mincemeat. **not to mince matters** or **one's words** to speak bluntly.

mincemeat *noun* a mixture of currants, raisins, sugar, apples, candied peel, etc., used in pies. □ **make mincemeat of** to defeat utterly; to destroy utterly in argument.

mincer *noun* a machine with revolving blades for mincing food.

mind *noun* 1 the ability to be aware of things and to think and reason, originating in the brain. 2 a person's thoughts and attention, *keep your mind on the job*. 3 remembrance, *keep it in mind*. 4 opinion, *change one's mind*; *to my mind he's a genius*. 5 a way of thinking and feeling, *state of mind*. 6 sanity, normal mental faculties; *in one's right mind*, sane; *out of one's mind*, insane or extremely agitated. –**mind** *verb* 1 to take care of, to attend to, *minding the baby* or *the shop*. 2 to feel annoyance or discomfort at, to object to, *she doesn't mind the cold*; *I wouldn't mind a cup of tea*, would like one. 3 to bear in mind, to give heed to or concern oneself about, *never mind the expense*; *mind you*, please take note. 4 to remember and take care, *mind you lock the door*. 5 to be careful about, *mind the step*; *mind how you carry that tray*. □ **have a good** or **half a mind to** to feel tempted or inclined to. **have a mind of one's own** to be capable of forming opinions independently of others. **in two minds** undecided. **mind-bending** *adjective* (*informal*) strongly influencing the mind. **mind-blowing** *adjective* (*informal*) unbelievable, amazing; (of drugs) causing hallucinations. **mind-boggling** *adjective* (*informal*) unbelievable, amazing. **mind one's Ps and Qs** to be careful in one's speech or behaviour. **mind-reader** *noun* a thought-reader. **mind's eye** the faculty of imagination. **on one's mind** constantly in one's thoughts, causing worry.

minded *adjective* 1 having a mind of a certain kind, *independent-minded*. 2 having certain interests, *politically minded*; *football-minded*. 3 inclined or disposed to do something, *could do it if he were so minded*.

minder *noun* one whose job is to attend to or take care of a person or thing.

mindful *adjective* taking thought or care of something, *mindful of his public image*.

mindless *adjective* without a mind, without intelligence. **mindlessly** *adverb*

mindset *noun* an attitude or frame of mind.

mine¹ *adjective* & *possessive pronoun* of or belonging to me; the thing(s) belonging to me.

mine² *noun* 1 an excavation in the earth for extracting metal or coal etc. 2 an abundant source of something, *a mine of information*. 3 a receptacle filled with explosive, placed in or on the ground or in water ready to explode when something strikes it or passes near it. –**mine** *verb* 1 to dig for minerals; to extract (metal or coal etc.) in this way. 2 to lay explosive mines in (an area). 3 to search (books etc.) for information, *mine the archive*. ☐ **mine detector** an instrument for detecting the presence of explosive mines.

minefield *noun* 1 an area where explosive mines have been laid. 2 (*informal*) a subject or situation full of difficulties and dangers.

minelayer *noun* a ship or aircraft for laying explosive mines.

miner¹ *noun* a person who works in a mine.

miner² *noun* an Australian yellow-billed honeyeater, *noisy miner; bell miner*, the bellbird.

Usage The *myna* is an unrelated bird; see entry for **myna**.

---

mineral *noun* 1 an inorganic substance that occurs naturally in the earth. 2 an ore or other substance obtained by mining. –**mineral** *adjective* of or containing minerals. ☐ **mineral water** water containing dissolved mineral salts or gases, found in nature or artificially produced.

mineralogy (min-ĕ-**ral**-ŏ-jee) *noun* the scientific study of minerals. **mineralogical** *adjective*, **mineralogist** *noun* [from *mineral* + *-logy*]

Minerva (*Rom. myth.*) the goddess of wisdom and learning, identified with Athene.

minestrone (min-ĕ-**stroh**-nee) *noun* an Italian soup containing chopped vegetables and pasta.

minesweeper *noun* a ship for clearing away explosive mines laid in the sea.

Ming *noun* porcelain belonging to the time of the Ming dynasty in China (1368–1644).

mingle *verb* 1 to mix, to blend. 2 to go about among people, *mingled with the crowd*.

mingy *adjective* (*informal*) mean, stingy.

mini- *prefix* miniature. [short for *miniature*]

miniature (**min**-ĭ-cher) *adjective* very small; made or represented on a small scale. –**miniature** *noun* 1 a very small and detailed portrait. 2 a small-scale copy or model of something. ☐ **in miniature** on a very small scale.

miniaturise *verb* (also **-ize**) to produce in a very small version. **miniaturisation** *noun*

miniaturist *noun* a person who paints miniatures.

minibus *noun* a small bus.

minim *noun* 1 a note in music, lasting half as long as a semibreve. 2 one-sixtieth of a fluid drachm, about one drop.

minimal *adjective* very small, the least possible. **minimally** *adverb*

minimalism *noun* the use of simple or basic forms in design, art, etc.; including only the minimum. **minimalist** *adjective* & *noun*

minimise *verb* (also **-ize**) 1 to reduce to a minimum. 2 to estimate at the smallest possible amount; to represent at less than the true value or importance.

minimum *noun* (*plural* **minima**) the lowest or the lowest possible number, amount, or intensity etc. [Latin, = least thing]

mining *noun* 1 the process of extracting minerals etc. from the earth. 2 the process of laying explosive mines.

minion (**min**-yŏn) *noun* (*derogatory*) a subordinate assistant.

miniskirt *noun* a very short skirt.

minister *noun* 1 a person at the head of a government department. 2 a diplomatic representative usually ranking below ambassador. 3 a member of the clergy, especially in a Protestant church. –**minister** *verb* to attend to people's needs, *the nurses ministered to the wounded*. **ministerial** (min-ĭs-**teer**-ree-ăl) *adjective* [Latin, = servant]

ministry *noun* 1 a government department headed by a minister. 2 a period of government under one leader; his or her body of ministers. 3 the profession, functions, or period of tenure of a religious minister.

mink *noun* 1 a small stoatlike animal of the weasel family. 2 its highly valued fur. 3 a coat made of this.

minkey *noun* a modified form of hockey for younger players.

Minnesota (min-ĕ-**soh**-tă) a State of the north central USA.

minnow (**min**-oh) *noun* a small freshwater fish of the carp family.

Minoan (min-**oh**-ăn) *adjective* of the Bronze Age civilisation of Crete (about 3000–1000 BC). – **Minoan** *noun* a person of this civilisation. [named after *Minos* king of Crete]

minor *adjective* 1 lesser, less important, *minor roads*; *a minor operation*, a surgical operation that does not involve danger to the patient's life. 2 (in music) of or based on a scale which has the third and sixth notes a semitone lower than in the major scale, tending to create a melancholy effect. – **minor** *noun* 1 a person under full legal age. 2 (in Australian Rules) a behind. □ **minor planet** an asteroid. [Latin, = smaller, lesser]

Minorca a Mediterranean island off the east coast of Spain.

minority *noun* 1 the smallest part of a group or class. 2 a small group differing from others. 3 (in law) the state of being under full age, *during his minority*.

Minotaur (**my**-nŏ-tor) (*Gk. myth.*) the creature, half man and half bull, kept in the labyrinth in Crete and finally slain by Theseus. [from *Minoan*, + Greek *tauros*- = bull]

Minsk the capital of Belarus.

minster *noun* 1 a large or important church. 2 the church of a monastery.

minstrel *noun* a travelling singer and musician in the Middle Ages.

mint¹ *noun* 1 a place authorised to make a country's coins. 2 a vast amount, *the new car cost a mint*. – **mint** *verb* 1 to make (coins) by stamping metal. 2 to invent or coin (a word etc.). □ **in mint condition** fresh and unsoiled as if newly from the mint. [from Latin *moneta* = coins; a mint]

mint² *noun* 1 a plant with fragrant leaves that are used for flavouring sauces and drinks etc. 2 peppermint; a sweet flavoured with this. **minty** *adjective* [from Latin *mentha* = mint]

minuet (min-yoo-**et**) *noun* a slow stately dance in triple time; music suitable for this.

minus (**my**-nŭs) *preposition* 1 reduced by the subtraction of, *seven minus three equals four* (7 − 3 = 4). 2 (*informal*) without, deprived of, *returned minus his shoes*. – **minus** *adjective* less than zero (= negative), less than the amount or number indicated, *a minus quantity*; *temperatures of minus ten degrees*, ten degrees below zero; *A minus*, a grade slightly below A (written as A−). – **minus** *noun* 1 the sign −. 2 a disadvantage, *tell me the pluses and minuses*. [Latin, = less]

minuscule (**min**-ŭs-kewl) *adjective* extremely small.

minute¹ (**min**-ŭt) *noun* 1 one-sixtieth of an hour. 2 a very short time, a moment. 3 an exact point of time. 4 one-sixtieth of a degree used in measuring angles. 5 a memorandum. – **minute** *verb* to make a note of; to record in the minutes of an assembly's proceedings. **minutes** *plural noun* an official record of the proceedings of an assembly or committee etc. made during a meeting.

minute² (my-**newt**) *adjective* 1 extremely small. 2 very detailed and precise, *a minute examination*. **minutely** *adverb* [from Latin *minutus* = little]

minutiae (min-**yoo**-shee-ee) *plural noun* very small details.

minx *noun* a cheeky or mischievous girl.

Miocene (**my**-ŏ-seen) *adjective* of the fourth epoch of the Tertiary period. – **Miocene** *noun* this epoch.

miracle *noun* 1 a remarkable and welcome event that seems impossible to explain by means of the known laws of nature and which is therefore attributed to a supernatural agency. 2 a remarkable example or specimen, *it's a miracle of ingenuity*. □ **miracle play** a medieval religious play. [from Latin *mirari* = to wonder]

miraculous *adjective* of or like a miracle, wonderful. **miraculously** *adverb*

mirage (mĭ-**rah**z*h*) *noun* an optical illusion caused by atmospheric conditions, especially making sheets of water seem to appear in a desert or on a hot road. [from French *se mirer* = be reflected]

mire *noun* 1 swampy ground, bog. 2 mud or sticky dirt. – **mire** *verb* 1 to plunge in mire. 2 to involve in difficulties. 3 to spatter with mire, to soil. **miry** *adjective*

mirrnyong *noun* (also **mirnyong**) (*Austral.*) an archaeologically significant mound of ashes, shells, and other debris.

mirror *noun* a piece of glass backed with amalgam so that reflections can be seen in it. – **mirror** *verb* to reflect in or as if in a mirror. □ **mirror image** a reflection or copy in which the right and left sides of the original are reversed. [from Latin *mirare* = look at]

mirth *noun* merriment, laughter. **mirthful** *adjective*, **mirthless** *adjective*

mis- *prefix* badly, wrongly.

misadventure *noun* a piece of bad luck; *death by misadventure*, (in law) death caused unintentionally by a deliberate act but with no crime involved.

misalliance *noun* an unsuitable alliance; marriage with a person of lower social status.

misanthropist (mis-**an**-thrŏ-pĭst) *noun* (also **misanthrope**, **mis**-ăn-throhp) a person who hates mankind or avoids people in general.

misanthropy (mis-**an**-thrŏ-pee) *noun* dislike of people in general. **misanthropic** (mis-an-**throp**-ik) *adjective* [from Greek *misos* = hatred, + *anthropos* = human being]

misapprehend (mis-ap-rĕ-**hend**) *verb* to misunderstand. **misapprehension** *noun*

misappropriate (mis-ă-**proh**-pree-ayt) *verb* to take dishonestly, especially for one's own use. **misappropriation** *noun*

misbegotten *adjective* contemptible.

misbehave *verb* to behave badly. **misbehaviour** *noun*

miscalculate *verb* to calculate incorrectly. **miscalculation** *noun*

miscall *verb* to give a wrong or inappropriate name to.

miscarriage (mis-**ka**-rij) *noun* **1** abortion occurring without being induced. **2** a mistake or failure to achieve the correct result, *a miscarriage of justice*. **3** the failure (of a letter etc.) to reach its destination.

miscarry *verb* (**miscarried**, **miscarrying**) **1** (of a pregnant woman) to have a miscarriage. **2** (of a scheme etc.) to go wrong, to fail. **3** (of a letter etc.) to fail to reach its destination.

miscast *verb* (**miscast**, **miscasting**) to cast (an actor) in an unsuitable role.

miscellaneous (mis-ĕ-**lay**-nee-ŭs) *adjective* **1** of various kinds, *miscellaneous items*. **2** of mixed composition or character, *a miscellaneous collection*. [from Latin *miscellus* = mixed]

miscellany (mĭ-**sel**-ă-nee) *noun* a collection of various items.

mischance *noun* misfortune.

mischief *noun* **1** conduct (especially of children) that is annoying or does slight damage but is not malicious. **2** a tendency to tease or cause annoyance playfully, *full of mischief*. **3** harm or damage, *did a lot of mischief*. □ **make mischief** to cause discord or ill feeling. **mischief-maker** *noun* a person who does this.

mischievous (**mis**-chĭ-vŭs) *adjective* (of a person) full of mischief; (of an action) brought about by mischief. **mischievously** *adverb*

miscible (**mis**-ĭ-bŭl) *adjective* able to be mixed. **miscibility** *noun* [from Latin *miscere* = mix]

misconceive (mis-kŏn-**seev**) *verb* to misunderstand, to interpret incorrectly.

misconception (mis-kŏn-**sep**-shŏn) *noun* a wrong interpretation.

misconduct (mis-**kon**-dukt) *noun* **1** bad behaviour. **2** adultery. **3** mismanagement.

misconstrue (mis-kŏn-**stroo**) *verb* to misinterpret. **misconstruction** *noun* misinterpretation.

miscount *verb* to count incorrectly. **–miscount** *noun* an incorrect count.

miscreant (**mis**-kree-ănt) *noun* a wrongdoer, a villain.

misdeed *noun* a wrong or improper act, a crime.

misdemeanour (mis-dĕ-**meen**-er) *noun* a misdeed, wrongdoing.

misdirect *verb* to direct incorrectly. **misdirection** *noun*

mise en scène (meez on **sayn**) *noun* **1** the scenery, properties, and positions of actors on the stage for an acted play. **2** the surroundings of an event. [French]

miser *noun* a person who hoards money and spends as little as possible. **miserly** *adjective*, **miserliness** *noun* [same origin as *misery*]

miserable *adjective* **1** full of misery, feeling very unhappy or uneasy or uncomfortable. **2** surly and discontented, disagreeable. **3** unpleasant, *miserable weather*. **4** wretchedly poor in quality or surroundings etc., *a miserable attempt*; *miserable slums*. **miserably** *adverb*

misère (mi-**zair**) *noun* (in cards) a declaration undertaking to win no tricks. [French, = poverty]

miserere (mi-zĕ-**rair**-ree) *noun* a cry for mercy.

misery *noun* **1** a feeling of great unhappiness or discomfort. **2** something causing this. **3** (*informal*) a discontented or disagreeable person. [from Latin *miser* = wretched]

misfire *verb* **1** (of a gun) to fail to go off correctly. **2** (of an engine etc.) to fail to start, to fail to function correctly. **3** to fail to have the intended effect, *the joke misfired.* –**misfire** *noun* a failure of this kind.

misfit *noun* **1** a person who is not well suited to his or her work or environment. **2** a garment etc. that does not fit. **3** (in full **misfit river**) a river which is smaller than expected from the size of its valley.

misfortune *noun* bad luck; an unfortunate event.

misgiving *noun* a feeling of doubt or slight fear or mistrust.

misgovernment *noun* bad government.

misguided *adjective* mistaken in one's opinions or actions; ill-judged. **misguidedly** *adverb*

mishandle *verb* to deal with (a thing) badly or inefficiently.

mishap (**mis**-hap) *noun* an unlucky accident.

mishear *verb* (**misheard, mishearing**) to hear incorrectly.

mishit *verb* (**mishit, mishitting**) to hit (a ball) faultily or badly. –**mishit** *noun* a faulty or bad hit.

mishmash *noun* a confused mixture.

Mishnah *noun* the collection of decisions on Jewish legal and ritual observance that form the main text of the Talmud.

misinform *verb* to give wrong information to.

misinterpret *verb* to interpret incorrectly. **misinterpretation** *noun*

misjudge *verb* to form a wrong opinion of; to estimate incorrectly. **misjudgment** (also **misjudgement**) *noun*

mislay *verb* (**mislaid, mislaying**) to put (a thing) in a place and be unable to remember where it is, to lose temporarily.

mislead *verb* (**misled, misleading**) to lead astray; to cause (a person) to gain a wrong impression of something.

mismanage *verb* to manage (affairs) badly or wrongly. **mismanagement** *noun*

mismatch *verb* to match unsuitably or incorrectly. –**mismatch** *noun* a bad match.

misname *verb* to miscall.

misnomer (mis-**noh**-mer) *noun* a name or description that is wrongly applied to something. [from *mis-*, + Latin *nomen* = name]

misogynist (mis-**oj**-ĭ-nĭst) *noun* a person who hates women. **misogyny** *noun* [from Greek *misos* = hatred, + *gune* = woman]

misplace *verb* **1** to put (a thing) in the wrong place. **2** to place (one's confidence etc.) unwisely. **3** to use (words or action) in an unsuitable situation, *misplaced humour.* **misplacement** *noun*

misprint *noun* an error in printing.

mispronounce *verb* to pronounce incorrectly. **mispronunciation** *noun*

misquote *verb* to quote incorrectly. **misquotation** *noun*

misread *verb* (**misread** (*pr.* mis-**red**), **misreading**) to read or interpret incorrectly.

misrepresent *verb* to represent in a false or misleading way. **misrepresentation** *noun*

misrule *noun* bad government.

miss[1] *verb* **1** to fail to hit, reach, or catch (an object). **2** to fail to see, hear, or understand etc., *we missed the turn-off; missed that remark.* **3** to fail to catch (a train etc.) or keep (an appointment) or meet (a person); to fail to seize (an opportunity). **4** to omit, to lack. **5** to notice the absence or loss of. **6** to feel regret at the absence or loss of; *old Smith won't be missed*, no one will feel regret at his absence or death. **7** to avoid, *go this way and you'll miss the traffic.* **8** (of an engine etc.) to misfire. –**miss** *noun* failure to hit or attain what is aimed at. □ **give a thing a miss** to avoid it, to leave it alone. **miss out** to omit. **miss out on** to fail to get benefit or enjoyment from. **miss the boat** or **the bus** (*informal*) to lose an opportunity. [from Old English *missan*]

miss[2] *noun* **1** a girl or unmarried woman. **2 Miss** a title used of or to a girl or unmarried woman, *Miss Smith.* [short for *mistress*]

missal *noun* a book containing the prayers used in the Mass in the Roman Catholic Church. [from Latin *missa* = mass (*mass*[2])]

misshapen *adjective* badly shaped, distorted.

missile *noun* an object or weapon suitable for throwing, projecting, or directing at a target. [from Latin *missum* = sent]

missing *adjective* **1** lost, not in its place, *two pages are missing.* **2** not present, *he's always missing when there's work to be done.* **3** absent from home and with one's whereabouts unknown, *she's listed as a missing person.* **4** (of a soldier etc.) neither present after a battle nor known to have been killed.

□ **missing link** a thing lacking to complete a series; a hypothetical intermediate type, especially between humans and apes.

mission *noun* 1 a task or goal assigned to a person or a group; a journey undertaken as part of this, *a fact-finding mission*. 2 a person's vocation, *his mission in life*. 3 a group of people sent, especially to a foreign country, to conduct negotiations or to spread a religious faith. 4 a missionary post or organisation. 5 (especially *old use*) an Aboriginal settlement administered by a religious community etc. 6 a series of religious services etc. for spreading the Christian faith, *a beach mission*. [from Latin *missio* = a sending]

missionary *noun* a person who is sent to spread the Christian faith amongst a community.

missis *noun* (also **missus**) (*informal*) 1 wife, *how's the missis?* 2 a form of address to a woman, used without her name.

Mississippi 1 the greatest river of North America, flowing south from Minnesota to the Gulf of Mexico. 2 a State of the south-eastern USA.

missive *noun* a written message, a letter. [same origin as *missile*]

Missouri 1 a major river of the USA, flowing from the Rocky Mountains to join the Mississippi near St Louis. 2 a State of the central USA.

misspell *verb* (**misspelt** *or* **misspelled**, **misspelling**) to spell incorrectly.

misspend *verb* (**misspent**, **misspending**) to spend badly or unwisely.

mist *noun* 1 water vapour near the ground in drops smaller than raindrops, clouding the atmosphere less thickly than fog does. 2 condensed vapour clouding a window etc. 3 something resembling mist in its form or effect. – **mist** *verb* to cover or become covered with mist, *my glasses misted over*.

mistakable *adjective* able to be mistaken for another person or thing.

mistake *noun* an incorrect idea or opinion; something done incorrectly; *by mistake*, as the result of carelessness or forgetfulness etc. – **mistake** *verb* (**mistook**, **mistaken**, **mistaking**) 1 to misunderstand the meaning or intention of. 2 to choose or identify wrongly, *mistake one's vocation*; *she is often mistaken for her sister*.

mistaken *adjective* 1 wrong in one's opinion, *you are mistaken*. 2 applied unwisely, *mistaken kindness*. **mistakenly** *adverb*

mister *noun* (*informal*) a form of address to a man, used without his name.

mistime *verb* to say or do (a thing) at a wrong time.

mistletoe *noun* a plant with white berries that grows as a parasite on trees.

mistook *see* **mistake**.

mistral (**mis**-trăl *or* mis-**trahl**) *noun* a cold north or north-west wind in southern France.

mistreat *verb* to treat badly. **mistreatment** *noun*

mistress *noun* 1 a woman who is in a position of authority or control. 2 the female head of a household. 3 the female owner of a dog or other animal. 4 a female teacher. 5 a man's female lover with whom he has a continuing illicit sexual relationship.

mistrial *noun* a trial invalidated by an error in procedure etc.

mistrust *verb* to feel no trust in. – **mistrust** *noun* lack of trust. **mistrustful** *adjective*, **mistrustfully** *adverb*

misty *adjective* (**mistier**, **mistiest**) 1 full of mist. 2 indistinct in form or idea etc. **mistily** *adverb*, **mistiness** *noun*

misunderstand *verb* (**misunderstood**, **misunderstanding**) to form an incorrect interpretation or opinion of.

misuse (mis-**yooz**) *verb* 1 to use wrongly or incorrectly. 2 to treat badly. – **misuse** (mis-**yooss**) *noun* wrong or incorrect use.

Mitchell, Sir Thomas Livingstone (1792–1855), Scottish-born Australian surveyor and explorer who led four expeditions in eastern Australia in the 1830s.
□ **Mitchell grass** a hardy tussocky grass of arid Australia providing valuable fodder.

mite *noun* 1 a very small spider-like animal found in food, *cheese mites*. 2 a very small contribution, *offered a mite of comfort*. 3 a very small creature; a small child.

Mithras (**mith**-ras) (*Persian myth.*) the god of light, also worshipped in the ancient Roman world. **Mithraic** *adjective*, **Mithraism** *noun*

mitigate (**mit**-ĭ-gayt) *verb* to make less intense or serious or severe; *mitigating circumstances*, facts that partially excuse wrongdoing. **mitigation** *noun* [from Latin *mitigare* = make mild]

mitochondrion (my-toh-**kon**-dree-ŏn) *noun* (*plural* mitochondria) an organelle present in most living cells, containing enzymes. [from Greek *mitos* = thread, + *khondrion* = granule]

mitosis (my-**toh**-sĭs) *noun* the process of division of a cell or its nucleus, in which each chromosome splits lengthways into two identical sets, one for each of the two new cells. mitotic *adjective* [from Greek *mitos* = thread]

mitre (**my**-ter) *noun* 1 the tall headdress worn by bishops and abbots as a symbol of office. 2 a joint or join of two pieces of wood or cloth etc. with their ends evenly tapered so that together they form a right angle. –mitre *verb* (mitred, mitring) 1 to join in this way, *mitred corners*. 2 to bestow a mitre on.

mitt *noun* 1 a mitten. 2 a fielder's glove in softball or baseball. 3 (*informal*) a hand or fist.

mitten *noun* a kind of glove that has no partition between the fingers.

mix *verb* 1 to put different things together so that the substances etc. are no longer distinct; to make or prepare (a thing) by doing this. 2 to be capable of being blended, *oil will not mix with water*. 3 to combine, to be able to be combined, *mix business with pleasure*; *drinking and driving don't mix*. 4 (of a person) to be sociable or harmonious. –mix *noun* 1 a mixture. 2 a mixture prepared commercially from suitable ingredients for making something, *cake mix*; *concrete mix*. ☐ mix it (*informal*) to start fighting. mix up to mix thoroughly; to confuse (things) in one's mind; to make (a person) feel confused; *be mixed up in a crime* etc., to be involved in it. mix-up *noun*

mixed *adjective* 1 composed of various qualities or elements. 2 containing people from various races or social classes. 3 for people of both sexes, *a mixed party*. ☐ mixed bag an assortment of different things or people. mixed blessing a thing that has advantages and also disadvantages. mixed doubles a doubles game in tennis with a man and woman as partners on each side. mixed economy an economy in which some businesses etc. are run by the State, others by private enterprise. mixed farming with both crops and livestock. mixed feelings a mixture of pleasure and dismay at the same event. mixed marriage a marriage between people of different race or religion. mixed number a number made up of a whole number and a fraction. mixed-up *adjective* (*informal*)

mentally or emotionally confused; not well-adjusted socially.

mixer *noun* 1 a device that mixes or blends things, *food mixers*. 2 a person who gets on in a certain way with others, *a good mixer*. 3 a drink to be mixed with another (stronger) drink.

mixture *noun* 1 mixing; being mixed. 2 something made by mixing, a combination of things, ingredients, or qualities etc.

mizen *noun* (also mizzen) (in full mizen-sail) the lowest sail, set lengthways, on a mizen-mast. ☐ mizen-mast *noun* the mast that is next aft of the mainmast.

ml *abbreviation* millilitre(s).

MLA *abbreviation* Member of the Legislative Assembly.

MLC *abbreviation* Member of the Legislative Council.

Mlle(s) *abbreviations* Mademoiselle, Mesdemoiselles.

mm *abbreviation* millimetre(s).

Mme(s) *abbreviation* Madame, Mesdames.

MMR *abbreviation* measles, mumps, and rubella (a vaccination given to children).

MMS *abbreviation* Multimedia Messaging Service, a system that allows mobile phones to send and receive colour pictures and sound clips as well as text messages.

mnemonic (nĕ-**mon**-ik) *noun* a verse or other aid to help one remember facts. [from Greek *mnemonikos* = for the memory]

mo *noun* (*informal*) 1 a moment, *half a mo*. 2 a moustache.

moa *noun* an extinct flightless New Zealand bird resembling the ostrich.

moan *noun* 1 a low mournful inarticulate sound, usually indicating pain or suffering. 2 a grumble. –moan *verb* 1 to utter a moan; to say with a moan. 2 (of wind etc.) to make a sound like a moan. 3 to grumble.

moat *noun* a deep wide ditch surrounding a castle or house etc., usually filled with water.

mob *noun* 1 a large disorderly crowd of people, a rabble. 2 the common people. 3 a gang; a group of people with common interests, *They're a Weird Mob*. 4 (*Austral.*) a flock or herd. 5 (*Austral.*) a large number of things of any kind. 6 (in Aboriginal English) one's own particular people. –mob *verb* (mobbed, mobbing) to crowd round in great numbers either to attack or to admire.

□ **mob rule** rule imposed and enforced by the mob. [from Latin *mobile vulgus* = excitable crowd]

mob cap *noun* a large round cap worn indoors by women in the 18th and early 19th centuries.

mobile (**moh**-byl) *adjective* **1** movable, not fixed; able to move or be moved easily and quickly. **2** (of the features of the face) readily changing expression. **3** (of a person) able to change social status. –**mobile** *noun* **1** a structure of metal, plastic, or cardboard etc. that may be hung so that its parts move freely in currents of air. **2** (*informal*) a mobile phone. □ **mobile home** a large caravan permanently parked and used as a residence. **mobile phone** a portable telephone without physical connection to a network. **mobility** (moh-**bil**-ĭ-tee) *noun* [from Latin *movere* = to move]

mobilise (**moh**-bĭ-lyz) *verb* (also **-ize**) **1** to assemble (troops) for service; to prepare for war or other emergency. **2** to assemble for a particular purpose, *they mobilised support from all parties*. **mobilisation** *noun*

mobster *noun* (*informal*) a gangster.

moccasin (**mok**-ă-sĭn) *noun* a kind of soft leather shoe, as originally worn by some indigenous North American peoples.

mocha (**mok**-ă) *noun* a kind of coffee; flavouring made with this. [named after Mocha on the Red Sea, from where the coffee first came]

mock *verb* **1** to make fun of by imitating, to mimic. **2** to scoff or jeer; to defy contemptuously. –**mock** *adjective* sham, imitation, *mock cream*; *a mock battle*. □ **mock orange** a shrub with strongly scented white flowers. **mock turtle soup** soup made from calf's head or other meat, to resemble turtle soup. **mock-up** *noun* a model of something, to be used for testing or study.

mockery *noun* **1** ridicule, contempt. **2** a ridiculous or unsatisfactory imitation, a travesty. **3** a ridiculously futile action etc.

mockingbird *noun* a bird that mimics the notes of other birds.

mod *adjective* (*informal*) modern; stylish. □ **mod cons** (*informal*) modern conveniences.

modal (**moh**-dăl) *adjective* of a mode or modes. □ **modal verb** an auxiliary verb (e.g. *would*) used to indicate the mood of another verb.

mode *noun* **1** the way in which a thing is done. **2** the current fashion. **3** (in music) each of a number of traditional scale systems. **4** (in statistics) the value that occurs most frequently in a given set of data.

model *noun* **1** a three-dimensional reproduction of something, usually on a smaller scale. **2** a simplified description of a system, situation, or process, often in mathematical terms. **3** a design or style of structure, e.g. of a car, *this year's model*. **4** a garment by a well-known designer; a copy of this. **5** a person or thing regarded as excellent of its kind and worthy of imitation. **6** a person employed to pose for an artist. **7** a person employed to display clothes in a shop etc. by wearing them. –**model** *adjective* excellent of its kind, exemplary. –**model** *verb* (**modelled**, **modelling**) **1** to make a model of (a thing) in clay or wax etc.; to shape (clay etc.) into a model. **2** to design or plan (a thing) in accordance with a model, *the new method is modelled on the old one*. **3** to work as an artist's model or as a fashion model; to display (clothes) in this way. **4** to make a model of (a system etc.; *see* **model** *noun* sense 2) in order to make calculations or investigations about it.

modem (**moh**-děm) *noun* a device linking a computer system and a telephone line so that data can be transmitted and received. [short for *mo*dulator-*dem*odulator]

moderate (**mod**-ĕ-răt) *adjective* **1** medium in amount, intensity, or quality etc. **2** keeping or kept within reasonable limits, not extreme or excessive; *a moderate climate*, mild, not intensely hot or intensely cold. **3** not holding extremist views. –**moderate** (**mod**-ĕ-răt) *noun* a person with moderate views in politics etc. –**moderate** (**mod**-ĕ-rayt) *verb* **1** to make or become moderate or less intense etc. **2** to act as moderator of or to. □ **in moderation** in moderate amounts. **moderately** *adverb*, **moderation** *noun*

moderator *noun* **1** an arbitrator, a mediator. **2** a Presbyterian minister or Uniting Church member presiding over a church court or synod. **3** a substance used in nuclear reactors to slow down neutrons.

modern *adjective* **1** of the present or recent times, *modern history*. **2** in current fashion, not antiquated. **3** (of artistic or literary forms) new and experimental, not following traditional styles. –**modern** *noun* a person of modern times or with modern tastes or style. **modernity** (mŏ-**dern**-ĭ-tee) *noun*

modernise *verb* (also **-ize**) to make modern, to adapt to modern ideas or tastes etc. **modernisation** *noun*

modernism *noun* modern views or methods, especially the rejection of realism and traditionalism in the art and literature of the first half of the 20th century.

modernist *noun* one who favours modernism. **modernistic** *adjective*

modest *adjective* **1** not vain, not boasting about one's merits or achievements. **2** rather shy, not putting oneself forward. **3** moderate in size or amount etc.; not showy or splendid in appearance. **4** (of a woman) showing regard for conventional decencies in dress or behaviour. **modestly** *adverb*, **modesty** *noun* [from Latin, = keeping the proper measure]

modicum (**mod**-ĭ-kŭm) *noun* a small amount.

modify *verb* (**modified**, **modifying**) **1** to make less severe or harsh or violent. **2** to make partial changes in, *some sections of the text have been modified*. **3** (in grammar) to qualify by describing, *adjectives modify nouns*. **modification** *noun*

modish (**moh**-dish) *adjective* fashionable. **modishly** *adverb*, **modishness** *noun*

modular *adjective* consisting of independent units.

modulate *verb* **1** to adjust or regulate; to moderate. **2** to vary the tone or pitch of (one's voice). **3** to pass from one key to another in music. **4** to alter the amplitude, frequency, or phase of (a carrier wave) so as to convey a particular signal. **modulation** *noun*

module (**mod**-yool) *noun* **1** a unit or standard used in measuring. **2** a standardised part or an independent unit in furniture, buildings, an electronic system, or a spacecraft etc. **3** a unit of training or education.

modulo *preposition* when all quantities are expressed as their remainders when divided by (a specified number, the **modulus**), *4 is the same as 9 modulo 5*.
☐ **modulo arithmetic** a form of arithmetic done with a limited set of consecutive numbers beginning with 0.

modulus *noun* (*plural* **moduli**) **1** the magnitude of a real or complex number without regard to its sign. **2** a constant factor or ratio, e.g. *Young's modulus*. **3** a number used as a devisor for considering numbers in sets giving the same remainder when divided by it.

modus operandi (moh-dŭs op-ĕ-**ran**-dee) *noun* the way a person or thing works. [Latin]

modus vivendi (moh-dŭs viv-**en**-dee) *noun* **1** a way of living or coping. **2** an arrangement that enables parties who are in dispute to carry on instead of having their activities paralysed until the dispute has been settled. [Latin, = way of living]

Mogadishu (mog-ă-**dish**-oo) the capital of Somalia.

moggie *noun* (*informal*) a cat.

Mogul (**moh**-gŭl) *noun* **1** a member of a Mongolian dynasty in India in the 16th–19th centuries. **2** mogul (*informal*) an important or influential person. –**Mogul** *adjective* of the Moguls.

mohair *noun* **1** the fine silky hair of the angora goat, or a mixture of it with wool or cotton. **2** yarn or fabric made from this. [from Arabic, = special]

Mohammed = **Muhammad**.

Mohammedan *adjective* & *noun* = Muslim.

Usage The term *Mohammedan* (or *Muhammadan*) is not used by Muslims, and is often regarded as offensive.

Mohawk (**moh**-hawk) *noun* **1** a member of an indigenous North American people. **2** their language. **3** a hairstyle in which the sides of the head are shaved and the remaining strip of hair is worn stiffly erect and often brightly coloured.

Mohican (moh-**hee**-kăn) *noun* **1** a member of an indigenous North American people. **2** a Mohawk hairstyle.

Moho *noun* (also **Mohorovičić discontinuity**) the boundary surface between the earth's crust and its mantle. [named after A. Mohorovičić, Croatian seismologist (died 1936)]

Mohs' scale (*pr.* mohz) *noun* a scale of hardness used for classifying minerals. [named after Friedrich Mohs (1773–1839), German mineralogist who devised it]

moiré (**mwah**-ray) *noun* a fabric that looks like watered silk.

moist *adjective* slightly wet, damp. **moistness** *noun*

moisten (**moi**-sĕn) *verb* to make or become moist.

moisture *noun* water or other liquid diffused through a substance or present in the air as vapour or condensed on a surface.

moisturise *verb* (also **-ize**) to make (the skin) less dry by use of certain cosmetics. **moisturiser** *noun*

Mojave Desert (mow-**hah**-vee) (also Mohave) a desert in southern California, USA.

moke noun (*informal*) a donkey or inferior horse.

moksha noun (in Hinduism) liberation from the chain of births impelled by the law of karma; the bliss attained by this. [from Sanskrit *moksa*]

molar[1] (**moh**-ler) noun any of the teeth at the back of the jaw that have broad tops and are used for grinding food in chewing. – **molar** adjective of these teeth. [from Latin *mola* = millstone]

molar[2] (**moh**-ler) adjective of moles (mole[4]). ☐ **molar solution** a solution containing one mole of the dissolved substance per cubic decimetre. **molarity** (moh-**la**-rĭ-tee) noun

molasses (mŏ-**las**-ĕz) noun **1** uncrystallised syrup drained from raw sugar. **2** (*Amer.*) treacle.

Moldavia (mol-**day**-vee-ă) a former principality on the Danube. **Moldavian** adjective & noun

Moldova (mol-**doh**-vă) (also Moldavia) a republic in south-eastern Europe bounded by Romania and Ukraine. **Moldovan** or **Moldavian** adjective & noun

mole[1] noun a small permanent dark spot on the human skin.

mole[2] noun a structure built out into the sea as a breakwater or causeway.

mole[3] noun **1** a small burrowing animal with dark velvety fur and very small eyes. **2** a person working within an organisation who secretly passes confidential information to another organisation or country.

mole[4] noun the quantity of a substance of which the mass in grams is the same number as its relative molecular mass.

molecule (**mol**-ĕ-kewl) noun **1** the smallest unit (usually consisting of a group of atoms) into which a substance can be divided while still retaining the substance's chemical qualities. **2** a small particle. ☐ **molecular weight = relative molecular mass**. **molecular** (mŏ-**lek**-yŭ-ler) adjective [from Latin, = little mass]

molehill noun a small mound of earth thrown up by a burrowing mole. ☐ **make a mountain out of a molehill** to behave as if a small difficulty were a very great one.

moleskin noun strong cotton cloth, the surface of which has been shaved before

dyeing. – **moleskins** *plural noun* trousers made of moleskin.

molest (mŏ-**lest**) verb **1** to annoy or pester (a person) in a hostile way or in a way that causes injury. **2** to attack or interfere with (a person), especially sexually. **molestation** noun, **molester** noun [from Latin *molestus* = troublesome]

Molière (**mol**-ee-air) (real name Jean-Baptiste Poquelin, 1622–73), French comic dramatist.

mollify verb (**mollified, mollifying**) to soothe the anger of. **mollification** noun [from Latin, = soften]

mollusc (**mol**-ŭsk) noun any of a group of animals which have soft bodies and hard shells (e.g. snails, oysters, mussels) or no shell (e.g. slugs, octopuses). [from Latin *mollis* = soft]

mollycoddle verb to coddle excessively, to pamper.

mollydooker noun (*Austral. informal*) (also mollydook) a left-handed person.

moloch (**moh**-lok) noun a slow-moving Australian desert lizard of grotesque appearance.

Molotov cocktail noun a kind of improvised incendiary bomb thrown by hand. [named after the Russian statesman V. M. Molotov (1890–1986)]

molten adjective melted, made liquid by very great heat.

Molucca Islands (mŏ-**luk**-ă) (also Moluccas) a group of islands in Indonesia. **Moluccan** adjective & noun

molybdenum (mŏ-**lib**-dĕ-nŭm) noun a metallic element (symbol Mo), used as a strengthening agent in steels and other alloys.

moment noun **1** a very brief portion of time. **2** an exact point of time; *he'll be here any moment*, at any time now, very soon. **3** importance, *these are matters of great moment*. ☐ **at the moment** now. **for the moment** for now, temporarily. **in a moment** instantly; very soon. **the man of the moment** the one who is important or the centre of attention now. **moment of truth** a time of test or crisis (¶ from a Spanish phrase referring to the final sword-thrust in a bullfight).

momentary (**moh**-mĕn-tă-ree) adjective lasting only a moment. **momentarily** adverb

momentous (mŏ-**ment**-ŭs) adjective of great importance.

momentum (mŏ-**ment**-ŭm) noun **1** the quantity of motion of a moving body, the product of its mass and velocity. **2** impetus gained by movement, *the sledge gathered momentum as it ran downhill.* **3** strength or continuity derived from an initial effort, *the campaign is gaining momentum.* [Latin, = movement]

Monaco (mon-ă-koh) **1** a principality on the French Riviera. **2** its capital city. **Monacan** *adjective & noun*

Mona Lisa (moh-nă **lee**-ză) a painting (now in the Louvre) by Leonardo da Vinci, of a woman with an enigmatic smile. Also known as *La Gioconda.*

monarch (**mon**-erk *or* -ark) *noun* **1** a ruler with the title of king, queen, emperor, or empress. **2** a large orange and black butterfly. **monarchic** (mŏ-**nark**-ik), **monarchical** *adjectives* [from Greek *monos* = alone, + *arkhein* = to rule]

monarchist (**mon**-er-kĭst) *noun* a person who favours government by a monarch or who supports a monarch against opponents of this system. **monarchism** *noun*

monarchy (**mon**-er-kee) *noun* **1** a form of government in which a monarch is the supreme ruler. **2** a country with this form of government.

monastery (**mon**-ă-stě-ree) *noun* a building in which monks live as a secluded community under religious vows. [from Greek *monazein* = live alone]

monastic (mŏ-**nast**-ik) *adjective* of monks or monasteries. **monastically** *adverb*

monasticism (mŏ-**nast**-ĭ-sizm) *noun* the way of life practised by monks.

monaural (mon-**or**-răl) *adjective* monophonic. [from *mono-*, + Latin *auris* = ear]

Monday *noun* the day of the week following Sunday. [from Old English *monandaeg* = day of the moon]

Monet (**mon**-ay), Claude Oscar (1840–1926), French Impressionist painter.

monetarism (**mun**-ě-tă-rizm) *noun* the theory that governments can control inflation by controlling the money supply. **monetarist** *noun*

monetary (**mun**-ě-tă-ree) *adjective* **1** of a country's currency, *our monetary system.* **2** of or involving money, *its monetary value.* **monetarily** *adverb*

money *noun* **1** coin, portable pieces of stamped metal in use as a medium of

exchange. **2** coins and banknotes. **3** (*plural* **moneys** *or* **monies**) any form of currency. **4** an amount of money, wealth; *there's money in it,* much profit can be made from it. □ **in the money** (*informal*) winning money prizes; having plenty of money. **make money** to make a profit; to become rich by doing this. **money-back** *adjective* (of a guarantee) promising to return a customer's money if he or she is not satisfied. **money box** a closed box into which savings or contributions are dropped through a slit. **money for jam** or **for old rope** (*informal*) profit for little or no trouble. **money-grubber** *noun* (*informal*) one who is greedily intent on making money. **money market** trade in short term stocks, loans, etc. **money order** a printed order for the payment of money, issued by and payable at a post office. **money-spinner** *noun* something that brings in much profit. [same origin as *mint*[1]]

moneyed (**mun**-eed) *adjective* wealthy.

moneylender *noun* a person who lends money in return for payment of interest.

-monger *suffix* **1** a dealer or trader, *ironmonger; fellmonger.* **2** (usually *derogatory*) a person who promotes, encourages, or spreads something, *warmonger; scandalmonger.*

Mongol (mong-gŏl) *adjective* Mongolian. –**Mongol** *noun* a Mongolian person.

Mongolia (mong-**goh**-leeă) a republic north of China, formerly extending to eastern Europe. **Mongolian** *adjective & noun*

mongolism (mong-gŏ-lizm) *noun* Down syndrome.

Usage The term *Down syndrome* is now preferred.

Mongoloid (mong-gŏ-loid) *adjective* resembling the Mongols in racial characteristics, having yellowish skin, a broad flat face, and straight black hair. –**Mongoloid** *noun* a Mongoloid person.

mongoose (**mon**-gooss) *noun* (*plural* **mongooses**) a stoat-like tropical animal that can attack and kill venomous snakes.

mongrel (**mung**-grěl) *noun* **1** a dog of no definable type or breed. **2** an animal of mixed breed. –**mongrel** *adjective* of mixed origin or character. [from *mingle*]

moniker (**mon**-ĭ-ker) *noun* (*informal*) a person's name or nickname.

monitor *noun* **1** a device used for observing or testing the operation of something. **2** a television screen used to check or select transmissions. **3** a visual display unit, a computer screen. **4** a person who listens to and reports on foreign broadcasts etc. **5** a pupil who is given special duties in a school. **6** a large lizard. **–monitor** *verb* to keep watch over; to record or test or control the working of. [from Latin *monere* = warn]

monk *noun* a member of a community of men living apart from the world under the rules of a religious order. [same origin as *mono-*]

monkey *noun* (*plural* **monkeys**) **1** an animal of a group closely related to man, especially one of the small long-tailed species. **2** a mischievous person. **–monkey** *verb* (**monkeyed**, **monkeying**) to play about mischievously; *don't monkey with the switch*, do not tamper with it.
□ **monkey business** (*informal*) mischief; underhand dealings. **monkey tricks** (*informal*) mischief. **monkey wrench** a wrench with an adjustable jaw.

monkish *adjective* of or like a monk.

monkshood *noun* a poisonous plant with blue hood-shaped flowers.

mono *adjective* monophonic. **–mono** *noun* (*plural* **monos**) monophonic sound or recording.

mono- *prefix* one; single. [from Greek *monos* = alone]

monochrome (**mon**-ŏ-krohm) *adjective* done in only one colour or in black and white. **monochromatic** (mon-ŏ-krŏ-**mat**-ik) *adjective* [from *mono-*, + Greek *khroma* = colour]

monocle (**mon**-ŏ-kŭl) *noun* an eyeglass for one eye only. [from *mono-*, + Latin *oculus* = eye]

monocotyledon (mon-ŏ-kot-ĭ-**lee**-dŏn) *noun* a flowering plant that has a single cotyledon. **monocotyledonous** *adjective*

monocular (mŏ-**nok**-yŭ-ler) *adjective* with one eye; using or intended for use with one eye. **–monocular** *noun* a monocular optical device. [same origin as *monocle*]

monogamy (mŏ-**nog**-ă-mee) *noun* the system of being married to only one person at a time. **monogamous** *adjective* [from *mono-*, + Greek *gamos* = marriage]

monogram (**mon**-ŏ-gram) *noun* two or more letters (especially a person's initials) combined in one design. [from *mono-* + *-gram*]

monogrammed *adjective* marked with a monogram.

monograph (**mon**-ŏ-grahf) *noun* a scholarly treatise on a single subject or on some aspect of a subject. [from *mono-* + *-graph*]

monohybrid *noun* a hybrid produced from parents which differ from each other in only one inherited characteristic.

monolith (**mon**-ŏ-lith) *noun* a large single upright block of stone. [from *mono-*, + Greek *lithos* = stone]

monolithic (mon-ŏ-**lith**-ik) *adjective* **1** consisting of one or more monoliths. **2** like a monolith in being single and massive, *a monolithic organisation*.

monologue (**mon**-ŏ-log) *noun* a long speech by one performer or by one person in a group. [from *mono-*, + Greek *logos* = word]

monomania (mon-ŏ-**may**-nee-ă) *noun* an obsession with one idea or interest. **monomaniac** *noun* a person with such an obsession.

monomer *noun* **1** a unit in a polymer molecule. **2** a compound with molecules that can unite to form a polymer. **monomeric** *adjective* [from *mono-*, + Greek *meros* = a part]

monophonic (mon-ŏ-**fon**-ik) *adjective* (of sound reproduction) using only one transmission channel. [from *mono-*, + Greek *phone* = sound]

monoplane *noun* a type of aeroplane with only one set of wings.

monopolise *verb* (also **-ize**) to take exclusive control or use of; *monopolise the conversation*, give others no chance to join in. **monopolisation** *noun*

monopolist (mŏ-**nop**-ŏ-list) *noun* one who has a monopoly. **monopolistic** *adjective*

monopoly (mŏ-**nop**-ŏ-lee) *noun* **1** exclusive possession of the sale of some commodity or service. **2** sole possession or control of anything. **–Monopoly** *noun* (*trademark*) a board game in which squares represent town properties which players 'buy' with imitation money. [from *mono-*, + Greek *polein* = sell]

monorail *noun* a railway in which the track consists of a single rail.

monosaccharide *noun* any sugar that cannot be broken down by hydrolysis into simpler sugars.

monosyllable (**mon**-ŏ-sil-ă-bŭl) *noun* a word of one syllable. **monosyllabic** (mon-ŏ-sĭ-**lab**-ik) *adjective*

monotheism (**mon**-ŏ-th'ee-izm) *noun* the doctrine that there is only one God. **monotheist** *noun*, **monotheistic** *adjective* [from *mono-*, + Greek *theos* = god]

monotone (**mon**-ŏ-tohn) *noun* a level unchanging sound or tone of voice in speaking or singing.

monotonous (mŏ-**not**-ŏ-nŭs) *adjective* lacking in variety or variation; tiring or boring because of this. **monotonously** *adverb*

monotony (mŏ-**not**-ŏ-nee) *noun* a monotonous condition.

monotreme (**mon**-ŏ-treem) *noun* an egg-laying Australasian mammal (either the platypus or the echidna). [from *mono-*, + Greek *trema* = hole]

monovalent (mon-ŏ-**vay**-lĕnt) *adjective* univalent.

monoxide (mŏ-**nok**-syd) *noun* an oxide with one atom of oxygen.

Monroe (mun-**roh**), James (1758–1831), 5th President of the USA, who formulated the **Monroe Doctrine** that opposed interference of European countries in the affairs of the Americas.

Monrovia (mon-**roh**-vee-ă) the capital of Liberia.

Monseigneur (mawn-sen-**yer**) *noun* the title of an eminent Frenchman.

Monsieur (mŏs-**yer**) *noun* (*plural* **Messieurs**, *pr.* mes-**yer**) the title of a Frenchman, = Mr or sir.

Monsignor (mon-**seen**-yor) *noun* the title of certain Roman Catholic priests and officials.

monsoon *noun* **1** a seasonal wind blowing in South Asia. **2** the rainy season accompanying the south-west monsoon. [from Arabic *mausim* = fixed season]

monster *noun* **1** a large ugly or frightening creature. **2** an animal or plant that is very abnormal in form. **3** anything of huge size. **4** an extremely cruel or wicked person. –**monster** *adjective* huge. [from Latin *monstrum* = marvel]

monstrance (**mon**-străns) *noun* (in the RC Church) a framed open or transparent holder in which the consecrated bread of the Eucharist is exposed for veneration. [from Latin *monstrare* = to show]

monstrosity (mon-**stros**-ĭ-tee) *noun* a monstrous thing.

monstrous (**mon**-strŭs) *adjective* **1** like a monster, huge. **2** outrageous, very wrong or absurd. **monstrously** *adverb*

montage (mon-**tah**z*h*) *noun* **1** the process of making a composite picture or piece of music etc. by putting together pieces from other pictures, designs, or compositions. **2** a picture etc. produced in this way. **3** the combination of short disconnected shots in cinematography to compress background information or provide atmosphere etc.

Montaigne (mon-**tayn**), Michel Eyquem de (1533–92), French essayist.

Montana (mon-**tan**-ă) a State of the north-western USA.

Mont Blanc (mon-**blon**) a peak in the Alps on the French-Italian border, the highest mountain in western Europe (4807 m).

montbretia (mon-**bree**-shă) *noun* a plant of the iris family with small bright orange-coloured flowers on long stems.

Monte Carlo one of the three communes of Monaco, famous as a gambling resort and as the terminus of a car rally.

Montenegro (mon-tĕ-**neg**-roh) a republic in SE Europe on the eastern side of the Adriatic Sea, formerly part of Yugoslavia. **Montenegrin** *adjective* & *noun*

Montessori (mon-tĕ-**sor**-ree), Maria (1870–1952), Italian educationist, who devised a system for training young children.

Monteverdi (mon-tĕ-**vair**-dee), Claudio (1567–1643), Italian Renaissance composer of sacred and secular music.

Montevideo (mon-tĕ-vĭ-**day**-oh) the capital of Uruguay.

Montezuma (mon-tĕ-**zoom**-ă) (1466–1520), the last ruler of the Aztec empire in Mexico, defeated by the Spaniards under Cortés.

month *noun* **1** any of the twelve portions into which a year is divided. **2** the period between the same dates in successive months. [related to *moon* (because time was measured by changes in the moon's appearance)]

monthly *adjective* happening, published, or payable etc. once a month. –**monthly** *adverb* once a month. –**monthly** *noun* a monthly magazine etc.

monument *noun* **1** anything (especially a structure) designed or serving to celebrate or commemorate a person or event etc.

2 a structure that is preserved because of its historical importance.

monumental *adjective* 1 of or serving as a monument, *monumental brasses in the church*. 2 (of a literary work) massive and of permanent importance. 3 extremely great, *a monumental achievement*.
☐ **monumental mason** a maker of tombstones etc.

moo *noun* the low deep sound made by a cow. –**moo** *verb* to make this sound.

mooch *verb* (*informal*) to walk slowly and aimlessly.

mood *noun* 1 a temporary state of mind or spirits. 2 the feeling or tone conveyed by a literary or artistic work, *the visual mood of a film*. 3 a fit of bad temper or depression, *he's in one of his moods*. 4 a grammatical form of a verb that shows whether it is a statement (e.g. *he stopped*) or a command (e.g. *stop!*) etc.
☐ **in the mood** in a willing state of mind.

moody *adjective* gloomy, sullen; liable to become like this. **moodily** *adverb*, **moodiness** *noun*

moon *noun* 1 the natural satellite of the earth, made visible by light that it reflects from the sun. 2 this when it is visible, *there's no moon tonight*. 3 a natural satellite of any planet. 4 something regarded as unlikely to be attained, *promised us the moon*, made very extravagant promises. –**moon** *verb* to move or look or pass time dreamily or listlessly.
☐ **many moons ago** a long time ago. **over the moon** (*informal*) overjoyed.

moonbeam *noun* a ray of moonlight.

Moonie *noun* (*informal, offensive*) a member of the Unification Church. [from the name of its founder, Sun Myung Moon]

moonless *adjective* without a moon.

moonlight *noun* light from the moon. –**moonlight** *verb* (*informal*) to have two paid jobs, one during the day and the other in the evening.

moonlit *adjective* lit by the moon.

moonrise *noun* the rising of the moon; the time of this.

moonshine *noun* foolish ideas.

moonstone *noun* a semi-precious stone, a form of feldspar with a pearly appearance.

moonstruck *adjective* crazy.

moony *adjective* listless, dreamy. **moonily** *adverb*

Moor *noun* a member of a Muslim people of NW Africa. **Moorish** *adjective*

moor[1] *noun* (*Brit.*) a stretch of open uncultivated land with low shrubs (e.g. heather).

moor[2] *verb* to secure (a boat or other floating thing) to a fixed object by means of cable(s).

moorhen *noun* a small waterbird.

moorings *plural noun* 1 cables etc. by which something is moored. 2 a place where a boat is moored.

moose *noun* (*plural moose*) a large animal of North America closely related to or the same as the European elk.

moot *adjective* debatable, undecided, *that's a moot point*. –**moot** *verb* to raise (a question) for discussion.

mop *noun* 1 a bundle of yarn or soft material fastened at the end of a stick, used for cleaning floors. 2 a small device of similar shape for various purposes, *dish-mop*. 3 a thick mass of hair. –**mop** *verb* (**mopped**, **mopping**) to clean or wipe with a mop etc.; to wipe away.
☐ **mop up** to wipe up with a mop etc.; to finish off a task; to clear (an area) of the remnants of enemy troops etc. after a victory.

mope *verb* to be in low spirits and listless.

moped (**moh**-ped) *noun* a motorised bicycle. [from *motor* + *pedal*]

mopoke (**moh**-pohk) *noun* an Australian and New Zealand owl, a boobook.

moraine (mŏ-**rayn**) *noun* a mass of debris carried down and deposited by a glacier.

moral *adjective* 1 of or concerned with the goodness and badness of human character or with the principles of what is right and wrong in conduct, *moral philosophy*. 2 virtuous. 3 capable of understanding and living by the rules of morality. 4 based on people's sense of what is right or just, not on legal rights and obligations, *we had a moral obligation to help*. 5 psychological, mental, not physical or concrete, *moral courage*; *moral support*, encouragement and approval. –**moral** *noun* 1 a moral lesson or principle. 2 a moral certainty. **morals** *plural noun* a person's moral habits, especially sexual conduct.
☐ **moral certainty** a probability so great that no reasonable doubt is possible. **moral hazard** (in economics) lack of incentive to guard against risk where one is protected from its consequences, e.g. by insurance. **morally** *adverb* [from Latin *mores* = customs]

morale (mŏ-**rahl**) *noun* the state of a person's or group's spirits and confidence.

moralise *verb* (also **-ize**) to talk or write about the principles of right and wrong and conduct etc.

moralist *noun* a person who expresses or teaches moral principles. **moralistic** *adjective*

morality (mŏ-**ral**-ĭ-tee) *noun* **1** moral principles or rules. **2** a particular system of morals, *commercial morality*. **3** being moral, conforming to moral principles; goodness or rightness. □ **morality play** a drama popular in the 16th century illustrating a moral lesson with characters that represent virtues and vices.

morass (mŏ-**rass**) *noun* **1** a marsh, a bog. **2** an entanglement, something that confuses or impedes people.

moratorium (mo-rǎ-**tor**-ree-ŭm) *noun* (*plural* **moratoriums**) **1** legal authorisation to debtors to postpone payment. **2** a temporary ban or suspension on some activity, *asked for a moratorium on strikes*. [from Latin *morari* = to delay]

Moravia a region of the Czech Republic, bordering on Slovakia.
□ **Moravian Church** a Protestant sect with the Bible as the only source of faith. **Moravian** *adjective* & *noun*

morbid *adjective* **1** (of the mind or ideas) unwholesome, preoccupied with gloomy or unpleasant things. **2** caused by or indicating disease, unhealthy, *a morbid growth*. **morbidly** *adverb*, **morbidness** *noun*, **morbidity** (mor-**bid**-ĭ-tee) *noun* [from Latin *morbus* = disease]

mordant (**mor**-dǎnt) *adjective* **1** characterised by a biting sarcasm. **2** corrosive. **–mordant** *noun* **1** a chemical substance used to fix dyes on fabric. **2** a corrosive liquid used to etch lines on a printing plate. [from French, = biting]

mordent *noun* the alternation of a written note in music with the note immediately below it.

More, Sir Thomas (1478–1535), English statesman and writer, author of *Utopia*, Lord Chancellor of England 1529–32, Roman Catholic saint. Feast day, 22 June.

more *adjective* greater in quantity or intensity etc. **–more** *noun* a greater quantity or number. **–more** *adverb* **1** in a greater degree. **2** again, *once more*. □ **more or less** in a greater or less degree; approximately.

moreish *adjective* (*informal*) (of food) so tasty that it causes a desire for more.

morello (mŏ-**rel**-oh) *noun* (*plural* **morellos**) a bitter kind of dark cherry.

moreover *adverb* besides, in addition to what has already been said.

mores (**mor**-rayz) *plural noun* the customs or conventions of a community.

Moreton Bay the bay on which Brisbane stands. □ **Moreton Bay bug** an edible marine crustacean of northern Australia. **Moreton Bay fig** a massive fig tree with large buttresses, glossy leaves, and edible fruits.

morganatic (mor-gǎ-**nat**-ik) *adjective* (of a marriage) between a man of high rank and a woman of low rank who retains her former status, their children having no claim to the father's possessions or title. **morganatically** *adverb*

morgue (*pr*. morg) *noun* a mortuary. [French; originally the name of a Paris mortuary]

moribund (**mo**-rĭ-bund) *adjective* in a dying state.

Mormon (**mor**-mŏn) *noun* a member of a religious organisation (the Church of Jesus Christ of Latter-day Saints) founded in the USA in 1830.

morn *noun* (*poetic*) morning.

mornay *noun* a cheese-flavoured white sauce, *tuna mornay*.

morning *noun* **1** the early part of the day, ending at noon or at the midday meal. **2** sunrise, dawn, *when morning broke*. □ **morning dress** formal dress for a man consisting of a tailcoat, striped trousers, and top hat. **morning star** a bright star or planet (especially Venus) seen in the east before sunrise.

Mornington Island a large island in the Gulf of Carpentaria, home to the Lardil Aboriginal people.

Morocco a kingdom in North Africa. **Moroccan** *adjective* & *noun*

morocco *noun* a fine flexible leather made (originally in Morocco) from goatskins, or an imitation of this.

moron (**mor**-ron) *noun* **1** an adult with intelligence equal to that of an average child of 8–12 years. **2** (*informal*) a very stupid person. **moronic** (mŏ- **ron**-ik) *adjective* [from Greek *moros* = foolish]

Moroni (mŏ-**roh**-nee) the capital of Comoros.

morose (mŏ-**rohss**) *adjective* sullen, gloomy, and unsociable. **morosely** *adverb*, **moroseness** *noun*

morph *verb* change smoothly and gradually from one image to another using computer animation techniques. **–morph** *noun* an image processed in this way. [shortened from *metamophosis*]

Morpheus (**mor**-fee-ŭs) (*Rom. myth.*) the god of dreams.

morphia (**mor**-fee-ă) *noun* morphine. [named after Morpheus]

morphine (**mor**-feen) *noun* a drug made from opium, used for relieving pain.

morphology (mor-**fol**-ŏ-jee) *noun* the study of the forms of things, especially of animals and plants and of words and their structure. **morphological** *adjective*

morris dance *noun* a traditional English folk dance performed by groups of people in costumes with ribbons and bells. [originally 'Moorish dance']

morrow *noun* (*poetic*) the following day.

Morse *noun* the **Morse code** (used in signalling), in which letters of the alphabet are represented by various combinations of short and long sounds or flashes of light (dots and dashes). [named after its inventor S. F. B. Morse (1791–1872), American pioneer of the use of the electric telegraph]

morsel *noun* a small quantity; a small amount or piece of food. [from Latin *morsus* = bite]

mortal *adjective* **1** subject to death. **2** causing death, fatal, *a mortal wound*. **3** deadly, lasting until death, *mortal enemies*; *in mortal combat*. **4** intense, *in mortal fear*. **5** (*informal*) without exception, *sold every mortal thing*. **–mortal** *noun* a person who is subject to death, a human being. □ **mortal sin** (in RC teaching) sin that causes death of the soul or that prevents salvation. **mortally** *adverb* [from Latin *mortis* = of death]

mortality (mor-**tal**-ĭ-tee) *noun* **1** being mortal, subject to death. **2** loss of life on a large scale. □ **mortality rate** the death rate.

mortar *noun* **1** a mixture of lime or cement with sand and water, for joining bricks or stones. **2** a vessel of hard material in which substances are pounded with a pestle. **3** a short cannon for firing shells at a high angle. **–mortar** *verb* **1** to plaster or join (bricks etc.) with mortar. **2** to attack with mortars.

mortarboard *noun* a cap with a stiff square top worn as part of academic dress.

mortgage (**mor**-gij) *verb* to give someone a claim on (property) as security for payment of a debt or loan. **–mortgage** *noun* **1** mortgaging. **2** an agreement giving a claim of this kind. **3** the amount of money borrowed or lent against the security of a property in this way.

mortician (mor-**tish**-ăn) *noun* (*Amer.*) an undertaker. [same origin as *mortal*]

mortify *verb* (**mortified**, **mortifying**) **1** to humiliate greatly. **2** to subdue by discipline or self-denial. **3** (of flesh) to become gangrenous. **mortification** *noun*

mortise (**mor**-tĭss) *noun* (also **mortice**) a hole in one part of a wooden structure into which the end of another part is inserted so that the two are held together. **–mortise** *verb* to cut a mortise in; to join with a mortise. □ **mortise lock** a lock that is set into (not on) the framework of a door.

mortuary (**mor**-chă-ree) *noun* a place where dead bodies may be kept temporarily. [from Latin *mortuus* = dead]

morwong *noun* (also **mowie**) an edible sea fish of southern Australia and New Zealand.

Mosaic (mŏ-**zay**-ik) *adjective* of Moses or his teaching, *Mosaic Law*.

mosaic (mŏ-**zay**-ik) *noun* a pattern or picture made by placing together small pieces of glass or stone etc. of different colours.

Moscow (**moss**-koh) the capital of the Russian Federation.

moselle (moh-**zel**) *noun* a light medium-dry white wine from the Moselle valley in Germany; (loosely) a similar Australian wine.

Moses Hebrew patriarch who led the Jews from bondage in Egypt towards the Promised Land, and gave them the Ten Commandments.

mosey *verb* (*informal*) to go in a leisurely or aimless way.

mosh *verb* (*informal*) to dance to rock music in a violent manner involving colliding with others and headbanging. □ **mosh pit** an area where moshing occurs, especially in front of the stage at a rock concert.

Moslem *adjective* & *noun* = **Muslim**.

mosque (*pr.* mosk) *noun* a Muslim place of worship.

mosquito (mŏs-**kee**-toh) *noun* (*plural* **mosquitoes**) a kind of gnat, the female of which bites and sucks blood from people and animals. [Spanish, = little fly]

moss *noun* a small flowerless plant that forms a dense growth on moist surfaces or in bogs. □ **moss stitch** a pattern formed of alternating plain and purl stitches in knitting.

Mossad (mo-**sad**) the Israeli secret service. [Hebrew, = agency]

mossie (**moz**-ee) *noun* (*Austral. informal*) a mosquito.

mossy *adjective* (**mossier**, **mossiest**) like moss; covered in moss.

most *adjective* greatest in quantity or intensity etc. **–most** *noun* the greatest quantity or number. **–most** *adverb* **1** in the greatest degree. **2** very, *a most amusing book*. □ **at most** or **at the most** not more than. **for the most part** in most cases, in most of its extent. **make the most of** to use to the best advantage; to represent at its best or at its worst.

mostly *adverb* for the most part.

mote *noun* a particle of dust.

motel (moh-**tel**) *noun* a roadside hotel providing accommodation in self-contained units for motorists. [from *motor + hotel*]

motet (moh-**tet**) *noun* a short usually unaccompanied sacred choral work.

moth *noun* **1** an insect resembling a butterfly but usually flying at night. **2** a small similar insect that lays its eggs in cloth or fur fabrics on which its larvae feed. □ **moth-eaten** *adjective* damaged by moth larvae; antiquated, decrepit.

mothball *noun* a small ball of naphthalene etc. placed in stored clothes to keep away moths. □ **in mothballs** stored out of use for a considerable time.

mother *noun* **1** a female parent. **2** a quality or condition that gives rise to another, *necessity is the mother of invention*. **3** a woman who is head of a female religious community, *Mother Superior*. **–mother** *verb* to look after in a motherly way. □ **mother country** a country in relation to its colonies. **mother-in-law** *noun* (*plural* **mothers-in-law**) the mother of one's wife or husband. **mother-of-pearl** *noun* a pearly substance lining the shells of oysters and mussels etc. **Mother's Day** a day to honour mothers, in Australia the second Sunday in May. **mother tongue** one's native language. **motherhood** *noun* [from Old English *modor*]

motherboard *noun* a printed circuit board containing the principal components of a computer or other electronic device, to which other boards may be connected.

mothercraft *noun* skill in looking after children as a mother.

motherland *noun* one's native country.

motherless *adjective* without a living mother.

motherly *adjective* like a mother, showing a mother's kindliness and tenderness. **motherliness** *noun*

mothproof *adjective* (of clothes) treated so as to repel moths. **–mothproof** *verb* to treat (clothes) in this way.

motif (moh-**teef**) *noun* **1** a recurring design or feature in a literary or artistic work. **2** a short melody or theme that recurs and is developed in a piece of music. **3** an ornament sewn on a dress etc.

motile *adjective* capable of moving. **motility** *noun*

motion *noun* **1** moving, change of position. **2** manner of movement. **3** change of posture; a particular movement, a gesture. **4** a formal proposal that is to be discussed and voted on at a meeting. **5** emptying of the bowels; faeces. **–motion** *verb* to make a gesture directing (a person) to do something, *motioned him to sit beside her*. □ **go through the motions** to do something in a perfunctory or insincere manner. **in motion** moving, not at rest. **motion picture** a story or record of events recorded on film for showing to an audience in a cinema or elsewhere. [from Latin *motio* = movement]

motionless *adjective* not moving.

motivated *adjective* having a definite and positive desire to do things.

motivate *verb* **1** to give a motive or incentive to, to be the motive of. **2** to stimulate the interest of, to inspire. **motivation** *noun*

motive *noun* that which induces a person to act in a certain way. **–motive** *adjective* producing movement or action; *motive power*, that which drives machinery etc. [from Latin *motivus* = moving]

motley *adjective* **1** multicoloured. **2** made up of various sorts, *a motley group*. **–motley** *noun* (*old use*) a jester's particoloured dress.

motocross *noun* a motorcycle race over rough ground (also called a *scramble*).

motor *noun* **1** a machine that supplies motive power for a vehicle or boat etc. or for another device with moving parts; an internal-combustion engine. **2** a motor car. **–motor** *adjective* **1** giving or producing motion;

motor nerves, those that carry impulses from the brain etc. to the muscles. **2** driven by a motor, *motor boat*; *motor mower*. **3** of or for motor vehicles, *the motor show*. **–motor** *verb* to go or convey in a motor car.
☐ **motor car** a short-bodied motor vehicle that can carry a driver and usually passengers. **motor vehicle** a vehicle with a motor engine, for use on ordinary roads. [from Latin *motor* = mover]

motorbike *noun* a motorcycle.

motorcade *noun* a procession or parade of motor vehicles. [from *motor* + *cavalcade*]

motorcycle *noun* a two-wheeled motor-driven road vehicle that cannot be driven by pedals. **motorcyclist** *noun*

motorised *adjective* (also **-ized**) **1** equipped with a motor. **2** (of troops etc.) equipped with motor vehicles.

motorist *noun* the driver of a motor car.

motorway *noun* (*Brit.*) an expressway.

motte *noun* a mound forming the site of an ancient castle or camp etc.

mottled *adjective* marked or patterned with irregular patches of colour. [from *motley*]

motto *noun* (*plural* **mottoes**) **1** a short sentence or phrase adopted as a rule of conduct or as expressing the aims and ideals of a family or country or institution etc. **2** a sentence inscribed on an object. **3** a maxim or riddle etc. in a paper cracker. [Italian, = word]

mould¹ *noun* **1** a hollow container into which a soft or liquid substance is poured to set or cool into a desired shape. **2** a pudding etc. made in a mould. **–mould** *verb* **1** to cause to have a certain shape; to produce by shaping. **2** to guide or control the development of, *mould his character*. **moulder** *noun*

mould² *noun* a fine furry growth of very small fungi, forming on things that lie in moist warm air.

mould³ *noun* soft fine loose earth that is rich in organic matter, *leaf mould*.

moulder *verb* to decay into dust, to rot away.

moulding *noun* a moulded object, especially an ornamental strip of plaster or wood etc. decorating or outlining something.

mouldy *adjective* (**mouldier**, **mouldiest**) **1** covered with mould. **2** stale, smelling of mould. **3** (*informal*) dull, worthless. **mouldiness** *noun*

moult (*pr.* mohlt) *verb* (of a bird, animal, or insect) to shed feathers, hair, or skin etc. before a new growth. **–moult** *noun* the process of moulting.

mound *noun* **1** a mass of piled-up earth or stones; a small hill. **2** a heap or pile. **–mound** *verb* to heap up in a mound or mounds.

mount¹ *noun* (*old use*, except before a name) a mountain or hill, *Mount Kosciuszko*; *Mount Everest*. [from Latin *mons* = mountain]

mount² *verb* **1** to ascend, to go upwards; to rise to a higher level. **2** to get or put on to a horse etc. for riding; to provide with a horse for riding. **3** to increase in amount, total, or intensity, *the death toll mounted*. **4** to put into place on a support; to fix in position for use or display or study. **5** to take action to effect (something); *mount an offensive*, to arrange and begin it. **6** to place on guard, *mount sentries round the palace*. **–mount** *noun* **1** a horse for riding. **2** something on which a thing is mounted for support or display etc.

mountain *noun* **1** a mass of land that rises to a great height, a very high hill. **2** a large heap or pile; a huge quantity. **3** a large surplus stock, *grain mountain*.
☐ **mountain ash** the rowan tree; any of many eucalypts growing in cool, damp mountain gullies. **mountain bike** a sturdy bicycle with thick tyres and many gears for riding over rough ground. **mountain devil** a moloch.

mountaineer *noun* a person who is skilled in mountain climbing. **mountaineering** *noun* the sport of climbing mountains.

mountainous *adjective* **1** full of mountains, *mountainous country*. **2** huge.

mountebank (**mountt**-ĕ-bank) *noun* a swindler or charlatan.

mounted *adjective* serving on horseback, *mounted police*.

Mountie *noun* (*informal*) a member of the Royal Canadian Mounted Police.

mourn *verb* to feel or express sorrow for a person who has died or regret for a thing that is lost or past.

mourner *noun* one who mourns; one who attends a funeral.

mournful *adjective* sorrowful, showing grief. **mournfully** *adverb*, **mournfulness** *noun*

mourning *noun* black or dark clothes worn as a conventional sign of bereavement.

mouse *noun* (*plural* **mice**) **1** a small rodent with a long thin tail. **2** a shy or timid person.

587

3 (*plural* **mouses**) a small hand-held device with buttons for controlling a cursor on a computer screen. **–mouse** *verb* to hunt or catch mice. ☐ **mouse-coloured** *adjective* dull greyish-brown.

mousetrap *noun* a trap for catching mice.

moussaka (moo-**sah**-kǎ) *noun* a Greek dish consisting of layers of minced meat and eggplant, usually with cheese sauce.

mousse (*pr.* mooss) *noun* **1** a dessert of cream or a similar substance flavoured with fruit or chocolate. **2** meat or fish purée mixed with cream etc. and shaped in a mould. **3** a frothy creamy substance, e.g. one used for styling hair. [French, = froth]

moustache (mǔs-**tahsh**) *noun* hair growing visibly on a person's upper lip.

mousy *adjective* **1** mouse-coloured. **2** quiet and shy or timid.

mouth (*pr.* mowth) *noun* **1** the opening through which food is taken into an animal's body. **2** (*informal*) talkativeness; impudence. **3** the opening of a bag, cave, cannon, trumpet, etc. **4** the place where a river enters the sea. **–mouth** (*pr.* mow*th*) *verb* **1** to form (words) with the lips without speaking them aloud. **2** to utter insincerely or without understanding, *mouthing platitudes*. **3** to declaim words pompously or with exaggerated distinctness. ☐ **mouth off** (*informal*) to speak wildly or thoughtlessly; to boast. **mouth organ** a small rectangular wind instrument played by passing it along the lips while blowing or sucking air. **mouth-to-mouth** *adjective* (of resuscitation) in which a person breathes into a subject's lungs through the mouth. **mouth-watering** *adjective* (of food) looking or smelling delicious, appetising.

mouthful *noun* **1** an amount that fills the mouth. **2** a small quantity of food etc. **3** a lengthy word or phrase; one that is difficult to utter.

mouthguard *noun* a device to protect teeth, worn in the mouth by players of contact sports.

mouthpiece *noun* **1** the part of a device or musical instrument etc. that is placed between or near the lips. **2** a person who speaks on behalf of another or others.

mouthwash *noun* a liquid for cleansing the mouth.

movable *adjective* able to be moved; *a movable feast*, one that changes its date each year (e.g. Easter). **movables** *plural noun*

furniture and other possessions that can be moved, not fixtures.

move *verb* **1** to change or cause to change in position, place, or posture. **2** to be or cause to be in motion. **3** to change one's place of residence. **4** to cause (bowels) to empty; to be emptied thus. **5** to make progress, *the work moves slowly*. **6** to make a move in a board game. **7** to provoke a reaction or emotion in, *moved her to laughter; felt very moved*, very affected with emotion. **8** to prompt or incline, to motivate, *what moved them to invite us?; he works as the spirit moves him*, only when he chooses. **9** to put forward formally for discussion and decision at a meeting. **10** to initiate some action, *unless the employers move quickly, there will be a strike*. **11** to live or be active in a particular group, *she moves in the best circles*. **–move** *noun* **1** the act or process of moving. **2** the moving of a piece in a board game; a player's turn to do this. **3** a calculated action done to achieve some purpose, *a move towards settling the dispute*. ☐ **get a move on** (*informal*) to hurry. **move in** to take possession of a new dwelling etc. **move over** or **up** to alter position in order to make room for another. **on the move** moving from one place to another; progressing. **mover** *noun* [from Latin *movere* = to move]

movement *noun* **1** moving; being moved. **2** action, activity, *watch every movement*. **3** the moving parts in a mechanism, especially of a clock or watch. **4** a series of combined actions by a group to achieve some purpose, the group itself, *the anti-nuclear movement*. **5** a trend, *the movement towards more casual styles in fashion*. **6** one of the principal divisions in a long musical work.

movie *noun* (*informal*) a film for viewing in a cinema or on video, DVD, etc. [short for *moving picture*]

moving *adjective* affecting the emotions, *a very moving story*. ☐ **moving picture** a motion picture. **moving staircase** an escalator.

mow *verb* (**mowed, mown, mowing**) to cut down (grass or grain etc.), to cut the grass etc. from, *mow the lawn*. **mow down** to kill or destroy at random or in great numbers.

mower *noun* a person or machine that mows.

Mozambique (moh-zam-**beek**) a republic in East Africa. **Mozambican** *noun*

Mozart (**moh**-tsart), Wolfgang Amadeus (1756–91), Austrian composer whose works include symphonies, concertos, and operas.

mozzarella (mot-să-**rel**-ă) *noun* a soft Italian curd cheese.

MP *abbreviation* (*plural* MPs) Member of Parliament.

MP3 *abbreviation* a means of compressing a sound sequence into a very small file, used as a way of downloading files from the Internet.

MPEG (**em**-peg) *abbreviation* an international standard for encoding and compressing video images. [acronym from *Motion Pictures Experts Group*]

Mr *noun* (*plural* Messrs) the title prefixed to a man's name or to the name of his office, *Mr Jones*; *Mr Speaker*. [short for *mister*]

Mrs *noun* (*plural* Mrs) the title prefixed to a married woman's name. [short for *mistress*]

MS *abbreviation* 1 (*plural* MSS) manuscript. 2 multiple sclerosis.

Ms (*pr.* mĭz *or* miz) *noun* the title prefixed to a woman's name that avoids indicating marital status. [from *Mrs* and *Miss*]

Mt *abbreviation* Mount.

much *adjective* existing in great quantity. –**much** *noun* a great quantity. –**much** *adverb* 1 in a great degree, *much to my surprise*. 2 approximately, *much the same*. □ **much of a muchness** very alike, very nearly the same.

muck *noun* 1 farmyard manure. 2 (*informal*) dirt, filth. 3 (*informal*) untidy things, a mess. –**muck** *verb* to make dirty, to mess. □ **muck about** or **around** (*informal*) to fool or mess about. **muck in** (*informal*) to share tasks or expenses equally. **muck out** to remove muck from, *mucking out the stables*. **muck up** (*informal*) to spoil; to misbehave. **muck-up** *noun* (*informal*) a mess or muddle.

muckraking *noun* (*informal*) seeking out and exposing scandal. **muckraker** *noun*

mucky *adjective* covered with muck, dirty.

mucous (**mew**-kŭs) *adjective* of or like mucus; covered with mucus; *mucous membrane*, the moist skin lining the nose, mouth, throat, etc.

mucus (**mew**-kŭs) *noun* the moist sticky substance that lubricates and forms a protective covering on the inner surface of hollow organs of the body.

mud *noun* wet soft earth. □ **his name is mud** (*informal*) he is in disgrace. **mud map** a map drawn with a stick in the dirt. **mud-slinging** *noun* (*informal*) speaking evil of someone, trying to damage someone's reputation.

mudbrick *noun* a brick made from baked mud.

mudcrab *noun* a large edible Australian crab found on muddy shores.

muddle *verb* 1 to bring into a state of confusion and disorder. 2 to confuse (a person) mentally. 3 to confuse or mistake (one thing for another). –**muddle** *noun* a muddled condition, disorder. □ **muddle-headed** *adjective* liable to muddle things, mentally confused. **muddle on** or **along** to work in a haphazard way. **muddle through** to succeed in the end in spite of one's inefficiency. **muddler** *noun*

muddy *adjective* (**muddier**, **muddiest**) 1 like mud; full of mud. 2 (of colour) not clear or pure. –**muddy** *verb* (**muddied**, **muddying**) to make muddy. **muddiness** *noun*

mudflat *noun* a stretch of muddy land left uncovered at low tide.

mudguard *noun* a curved cover above the wheel of a cycle etc. to protect the rider from the mud it throws up.

mudlark *noun* 1 (*Austral.*) a magpie lark. 2 a child who plays in mud. 3 a horse that races well on a wet and heavy track.

mudskipper *noun* any of several small fish that are able to move about on mudflats.

muesli (**mewz**-lee) *noun* a food of mixed cereals, dried fruit, nuts, etc.

muezzin (moo-**ez**-ĭn) *noun* a man who proclaims the hours of prayer for Muslims, usually from a minaret.

muff¹ *noun* a short tubelike covering of fur etc. into which both hands are thrust from opposite ends to keep them warm.

muff² *verb* (*informal*) to bungle or blunder.

muffin *noun* 1 a large cupcake, often with fruit or savoury ingredients added to the mixture. 2 a light flat round cake made from yeast dough, eaten toasted and buttered.

muffle *verb* 1 to wrap or cover for warmth or protection. 2 to wrap up or pad in order to deaden its sound. 3 to deaden, to make less loud or less distinct. [from *muff¹*]

muffler *noun* 1 something used to muffle sound, especially the silencer fitted to a car's exhaust pipe. 2 a scarf worn round the neck for warmth.

mufti¹ *noun* plain clothes worn by one who also wears uniform, *in mufti*.

mufti² *noun* a Muslim legal expert empowered to give rulings on religious matters.

mug¹ *noun* **1** a large drinking vessel (usually with a handle) for use without a saucer. **2** its contents. **3** (*informal*) the face or mouth. **4** (*informal*) a person who is easily deceived. –**mug** *verb* (**mugged**, **mugging**) to rob (a person) with violence, especially in a public place. □ **a mug's game** (*informal*) an activity that is unlikely to bring profit or reward. **mugger** *noun*

mug² *verb* **mug up** (*informal*) to learn (a subject) by studying hard, *mugged it up*.

muggins *noun* (*informal*) a person who is easily deceived or victimised.

muggy *adjective* (**muggier**, **muggiest**) oppressively damp and warm, *a muggy day*; *muggy weather*. **mugginess** *noun*

Muhammad (mŭ-**ham**-ăd) (also **Mohammed**) (c. 570–632), the founder of the Islamic faith and community.

mujahedin (muu-jah-hĭ-**deen**) *plural noun* (also **mujahidin**) guerrilla fighters in Islamic countries, especially those who are fighting against non-Muslim forces. [Arabic, = one who fights a war]

Mulba (**mul**-bă) *noun* an Aboriginal person from the Pilbara region of Western Australia.

―――――――――――――――――

Usage see aborigine.

―――――――――――――――――

mulberry *noun* **1** a purple or white fruit rather like a blackberry. **2** the tree that bears it. **3** dull purplish red.

mulch *noun* a mixture of wet straw, grass, leaves, etc., spread on the ground to protect plants or retain moisture. –**mulch** *verb* to cover with a mulch.

mulct *verb* to take away money from (a person), e.g. by a fine or taxation, or by dubious means.

mule¹ *noun* **1** an animal that is the offspring of a horse and a donkey, known for its stubbornness. **2** (*informal*) a stupid or obstinate person. **3** (*informal*) a courier for illegal drugs.

mule² *noun* a backless slipper.

mulesing *noun* the practice of cutting away the loose folds of skin in the crutch area of a sheep in order to reduce the risk of blowfly strike. [named after J. H. W. Mules, Australian sheep-raiser (died 1946) who introduced the practice]

muleteer (mew-lĕ-**teer**) *noun* a mule driver.

mulga (**mul**-gă) *noun* **1** any of several acacias of dry inland Australia; the wood of these trees. **2 the mulga** the bush; remote, sparsely populated country. □ **mulga Bill** a bush simpleton. [Kamilaroi, Yuwaalaraay, and other languages *malga*]

mulgara (**mul**-gă-ră) *noun* a small carnivorous marsupial of inland arid Australia, popularly called a marsupial mouse.

mulish (**mewl**-ish) *adjective* stubborn. **mulishly** *adverb*, **mulishness** *noun*

mull¹ *verb* to heat (wine or beer etc.) with sugar and spices, as a drink.

mull² *verb* **mull over** to think over, to ponder.

mullah (**mul**-ă) *noun* a Muslim who has studied Islamic theology and sacred law.

mullenise *verb* (also **-ize**) (*Austral. historical*) to clear and prepare (scrub-covered land) for cultivation by using a heavy roller to break down the mallee. [from Charles *Mullens*, a South Australian farmer]

mullet (**mul**-ĕt) *noun* an edible sea fish, *red mullet*; *grey mullet*.

mulligatawny (mul-ĭ-gă-**taw**-nee) *noun* a highly seasoned soup flavoured like curry. [from Tamil *milagutannir* = pepper-water]

mullion (**mul**-yŏn) *noun* an upright strip between the panes of a tall window.

mullock (**mul**-ŏk) *noun* (*Austral*.) **1** refuse left after mining. **2** rubbish, nonsense. □ **poke mullock at** (*informal*) to ridicule.

mulloway *noun* a large edible Australian sea and estuarine fish. Also known as *butterfish*, *jewfish*, or *kingfish*. [Yaralde *malowe*]

mullygrubber *noun* (in cricket) a ball delivered so that it does not bounce after it hits the ground but rolls along instead.

multi- *prefix* many. [from Latin *multus* = many]

multicellular *adjective* consisting of many cells.

multicoloured *adjective* with many colours.

multicultural *adjective* composed of various cultural and ethnic groups, *a multicultural society*. **multiculturalism** *noun*

multifarious (mul-tĭ-**fair**-ree-ŭs) *adjective* very varied, of many kinds, *his multifarious duties*. **multifariously** *adverb*

multilateral (mul-tee-**lat**-ĕ-răl) *adjective* (of an agreement etc.) involving three or more parties. **multilaterally** *adverb*

multimedia *noun* (especially in computing) the combined use of text, sound, graphics, video, and animation. **–multimedia** *adjective* (of art, education, etc.) using more than one medium of expression, communication, etc.

multimillionaire *noun* a person with a fortune of several million dollars etc.

multinational *adjective* (of a business company) operating in several countries. **–multinational** *noun* a multinational company.

multiplayer *adjective* denoting a computer game etc. for or involving more than one player.

multiple *adjective* having several or many parts, elements, or components. **–multiple** *noun* a quantity that contains another (a *factor*) a number of times without remainder, *30 is a multiple of 10*. □ **multiple sclerosis** a chronic progressive disease in which patches of tissue harden in the brain or spinal cord, causing partial or complete paralysis.

multiplex *adjective* having many parts or forms; consisting of many elements.

multiplicand *noun* the quantity that is to be multiplied by the multiplier.

multiplication *noun* multiplying, being multiplied. □ **multiplication sign** the sign × (as in 2 × 3) indicating that one quantity is to be multiplied by another. **multiplication tables** a series of lists showing the results when a number is multiplied by each number (especially 1 to 12) in turn.

multiplicity (mul-tĭ-**plis**-ĭ-tee) *noun* a great variety.

multiplier *noun* **1** the number by which a quantity is multiplied. **2** a device for increasing a small electric current so that it can be used or measured more easily.

multiply *verb* (**multiplied, multiplying**) **1** (in mathematics) to take a specified quantity a specified number of times and find the quantity produced, *multiply 6 by 4 and get 24*. **2** to make or become many; *rabbits multiply rapidly*, they increase in number by breeding.

multiracial (mul-tee-**ray**-shăl) *adjective* composed of people of many races.

multi-storey *adjective* having several storeys.

multitasking *noun* (in computers) the performance of a number of different tasks simultaneously.

multitude *noun* a great number of things or people.

multitudinous (mul-tĭ-**tewd**-ĭ-nŭs) *adjective* very numerous.

mum[1] *adjective* (*informal*) silent, *keep mum*. **mum's the word** say nothing about this.

mum[2] *noun* (*informal*) mother.

Mumbai (muum-**by**) the official name (since 1995) for Bombay.

mumble *verb* to speak or utter indistinctly. **–mumble** *noun* indistinct speech. **mumbler** *noun*

mumbo-jumbo *noun* **1** meaningless ritual. **2** words or actions that are deliberately obscure in order to mystify or confuse people.

mummer *noun* an actor in a traditional mime.

mummify *verb* (**mummified, mummifying**) to preserve (a corpse) by embalming it as in ancient Egypt.

mummy[1] *noun* (*informal*) mother.

mummy[2] *noun* **1** the body of a person or animal embalmed for burial so as to preserve it, especially in ancient Egypt. **2** a dried-up body preserved from decay by an accident of nature.

mumps *noun* a viral disease that causes painful swellings in the neck.

munch *verb* to chew steadily and vigorously.

mundane (mun-**dayn**) *adjective* **1** dull, routine. **2** worldly, not spiritual. [from Latin *mundus* = world]

mung *noun* (in full **mung bean**) a plant producing small beans that can be cooked or sprouted to produce bean sprouts.

Munich (**mew**-nik) a city in southern Germany, capital of Bavaria. □ **Munich Pact** an agreement between Britain, France, Germany, and Italy, signed at Munich in 1938, ceding part of Czechoslovakia to Germany. It is remembered as an act of appeasement.

municipal (mew-**nis**-ĭ-păl) *adjective* of a municipality or its self-government.

municipality (mew-nis-ĭ-**pal**-ĭ-tee) *noun* a district with its own local government.

munificent (mew-**nif**-ĭ-sĕnt) *adjective* splendidly generous. **munificently** *adverb*, **munificence** *noun* [from Latin *munus* = gift]

munitions (mew-**nish**-ŏnz) *plural noun* military weapons, ammunition, equipment, etc. [from Latin *munitum* = fortified]

muntry *noun* (*plural* **muntries**) an Australian low shrub bearing edible fruit; the fruit itself, also called *native apple*. [Yaralde probably *mandharri*]

munyeroo (mun-yĕ-**roo**) *noun* an Australian succulent plant with edible seeds and leaves. [Diyari *manyurra*]

muon (**mew**-on) *noun* an unstable elementary particle like an electron, but with a much greater mass.

mural (**mew**-răl) *adjective* of or on a wall. –mural *noun* a wall-painting, a fresco. [from Latin *murus* = wall]

murder *noun* 1 the intentional and unlawful killing of one person by another. 2 (*informal*) something very difficult or unpleasant or painful. –murder *verb* 1 to kill (a person) unlawfully and intentionally. 2 (*informal*) to ruin by bad performance or pronunciation etc. murderer *noun*, murderess *feminine noun*

murderous *adjective* 1 involving murder; capable of or intent on murder. 2 very angry, suggesting murder, *a murderous look*.

murk *noun* darkness, poor visibility.

murky *adjective* (murkier, murkiest) 1 dark, gloomy. 2 (of liquid) muddy, full of sediment. 3 secretly scandalous, *his murky past*. murkily *adverb*, murkiness *noun*

murmur *noun* 1 a low continuous sound. 2 a low abnormal sound made by the heart. 3 softly spoken words. 4 a subdued expression of feeling, *murmurs of discontent*. –murmur *verb* to make a murmur; to speak or utter in a low voice.

Murphy's law *noun* a humorous expression of the apparent perverseness of things (roughly, 'anything that can go wrong will go wrong').

Murray Australia's principal river, flowing from the Snowy Mountains westward to the Southern Ocean. □ Murray cod a large edible groper-like freshwater fish. Murray grey an Australian breed of grey beef cattle; an animal of this breed.

Murray Island an island (also called Mer) in Torres Strait, traditional homeland of the Meriam people (*see* Mabo).

Murri *noun* an Aboriginal person from south and central Queensland. [Kamilaroi *mari*]

Usage see aborigine.

Murrumbidgee a river rising in the Snowy Mountains and flowing west to become a tributary of the Murray.

Mururoa (moo-rŭ-**roh**-ă) an atoll in the southern Pacific, site of French testing of nuclear devices.

Muscat (**mus**-kat) the capital of Oman.

muscat (**mus**-kăt) *noun* a kind of grape; a sweet fortified wine made from muscat grapes.

muscle *noun* 1 a band or bundle of fibrous tissue able to contract and relax and so produce movement in an animal body. 2 a part of the body made chiefly of such tissue. 3 muscular power. 4 strength, *trade unions with plenty of muscle*. –muscle *verb* muscle in (*informal*) to force one's way.

Muscovite (**mus**-kŏ-vyt) *adjective* of Moscow. –Muscovite *noun* a native or inhabitant of Moscow.

muscular *adjective* 1 of or affecting the muscles. 2 having well-developed muscles. muscularity (mus-kew-**la**-rĭ-tee) *noun*

Muse *noun* (*Gk. & Rom. myth.*) each of the nine sister goddesses presiding over branches of learning and the arts.

muse *verb* to ponder; to say meditatively.

museum *noun* a building or room in which objects of historical, scientific, or other interest are stored and exhibited. [from Greek, = place of the Muses (goddesses of the arts and sciences)]

mush *noun* 1 soft pulp. 2 feeble sentimentality. mushy *adjective*

mushroom *noun* 1 an edible fungus with a stem and domed cap, noted for its rapid growth. 2 pale yellowish brown. –mushroom *verb* 1 to spring up rapidly in large numbers, *video shops mushroomed across the country*. 2 to rise and spread in the shape of a mushroom. 3 to gather mushrooms.

music *noun* 1 the art of arranging the sounds of voice(s) or instrument(s) or both in a pleasing sequence or combination. 2 the sound(s) or composition(s) produced; a written or printed score for this. 3 any pleasant sound or series of sounds, e.g. birdsong. □ music hall a hall or theatre used for variety entertainment; the entertainment itself. [from Greek, = of the Muses (see *museum*)]

musical *adjective* 1 of music; *musical instruments*, devices producing music by means of tuned strings or membranes or air in pipes, or electronically. 2 fond of or skilled in music. 3 accompanied by music; set to music. –musical *noun* a play or film in which songs and dancing alternate with the dialogue.

☐ **musical box** a box with a mechanical device that produces music by means of a toothed cylinder that strikes a comb-like metal plate. **musical chairs** a game in which players walk round chairs (one fewer than the number of players) till the music stops, when the one who finds no chair is eliminated and a chair is removed before the next round. **musically** *adverb*

musician *noun* a person who plays or composes music; one whose profession is music. **musicianship** *noun*

musicology *noun* the study of the history and forms of music. **musicologist** *noun*

musk *noun* 1 a substance secreted by the male musk deer or certain other animals, or produced artificially, used as the basis of perfumes. 2 a plant with a musky smell. ☐ **musk deer** a small Asian deer without antlers. **musk rose** a rambling rose with a musky fragrance.

musket *noun* a long-barrelled gun formerly used by infantry, now replaced by the rifle.

musketeer *noun* a soldier armed with a musket.

muskrat *noun* 1 a large rat-like water animal of North America. 2 its fur (also called *musquash*).

musky *adjective* smelling like musk.

Muslim *noun* one who believes in the Islamic faith. – **Muslim** *adjective* of Muslims or their faith.

muslin *noun* a kind of thin cotton cloth.

muso (**mew**-zoh) *noun* (*plural* **musos**) (*informal*) a musician, especially a professional.

musquash (**mus**-kwosh) *noun see* **muskrat**.

mussel *noun* a kind of bivalve mollusc, the marine variety of which is edible.

must¹ *auxiliary verb*, used to express necessity or obligation (*you must go*), certainty (*night must fall*), or insistence (*I must repeat, all precautions were taken*). – **must** *noun* (*informal*) a thing that should not be overlooked or missed, *this job is a must*.

must² *noun* grape juice etc. undergoing fermentation; new wine.

mustang (**mus**-tang) *noun* a wild horse of Mexico and California.

mustard *noun* 1 a plant with yellow flowers and with black or white sharp-tasting seeds in long pods. 2 these seeds ground and made

into paste as a condiment. 3 darkish yellow colour. – **mustard** *adjective* darkish yellow. ☐ **mustard gas** a kind of poison gas that burns the skin.

muster *verb* 1 to assemble; to cause to assemble; (*Austral.*) to round up livestock. 2 to summon, *muster* or *muster up one's strength*. – **muster** *noun* an assembly or gathering of people or things. ☐ **pass muster** to be accepted as adequate.

mustn't (*informal*) = must not.

musty *adjective* (**mustier**, **mustiest**) 1 stale, smelling or tasting mouldy. 2 antiquated. **mustily** *adverb*, **mustiness** *noun*

mutable (**mew**-tă-bŭl) *adjective* liable to change, fickle. **mutability** *noun* [from Latin *mutare* = to change]

mutagen (**mew**-tă-jĕn) *noun* something causing genetic mutation, e.g. radiation. **mutagenic** *adjective*

mutant (**mew**-tănt) *noun* a living thing that differs basically from its parents as a result of genetic change. – **mutant** *adjective* differing in this way.

mutate (mew-**tayt**) *verb* to undergo or cause to undergo mutation.

mutation *noun* 1 a change or alteration in form. 2 a mutant.

mutatis mutandis (mew-tah-tiss mew-**tan**-diss) *adverb* when the necessary alteration of details has been made (in comparing things). [Latin]

mute *adjective* 1 silent, refraining from speaking. 2 not having the power of speech, dumb. 3 not expressed in words, *in mute adoration*. 4 (of a letter) not pronounced, *the k in 'knight' is mute*. 5 (of colour) subdued. – **mute** *noun* 1 a dumb person. 2 a device fitted to a musical instrument to deaden its sound. – **mute** *verb* 1 to deaden or muffle the sound of. 2 to make less intense. **mutely** *adverb*, **muteness** *noun*

mutilate *verb* to injure or disfigure by cutting off a part. **mutilation** *noun*, **mutilator** *noun*

mutineer (mew-tĭ-**neer**) *noun* one who mutinies.

mutinous (**mew**-tĭ-nŭs) *adjective* rebellious, ready to mutiny. **mutinously** *adverb*

mutiny (**mew**-tĭ-nee) *noun* open rebellion against authority, especially by members of the armed forces against their officers. – **mutiny** *verb* (**mutinied**, **mutinying**) to engage in mutiny.

mutt *noun* (*informal*) **1** a stupid person. **2** a dog.

mutter *verb* **1** to speak or utter in a low unclear tone. **2** to utter subdued grumbles. – **mutter** *noun* muttering; muttered words.

mutton *noun* the flesh of sheep as food.

muttonbird *noun* any of various seabirds, including the short-tailed shearwater which breeds in SE Australia, especially on Bass Strait islands.

mutual (**mew**-chew-ăl) *adjective* **1** (of a feeling or action) felt or done by each towards or to the other, *mutual affection*; *mutual aid*. **2** having the same specified relationship to each other, *mutual enemies*. **3** (*informal*) common to two or more people, *our mutual friend*. **mutually** *adverb*

Usage Some people object to the use in sense 3, although it is often found; the alternative word 'common' could be taken to mean 'ill-bred'.

muzak (**mew**-zak) *noun* (*trademark*) piped music, recorded light music as a background.

muzzle *noun* **1** the projecting nose and jaws of certain animals (e.g. dogs). **2** the open end of a firearm. **3** a strap or wire etc. put over an animal's head to prevent it from biting or feeding. – **muzzle** *verb* **1** to put a muzzle on (an animal). **2** to silence, to prevent (a person or newspaper etc.) from expressing opinions freely.

muzzy *adjective* dazed, feeling stupefied. **muzzily** *adverb*, **muzziness** *noun*

MW *abbreviation* **1** megawatt(s). **2** medium wave.

my *adjective* **1** of or belonging to me. **2** used in forms of address (*my lord*, *my dear*), or exclamations of surprise etc. (*my God!*).

myalgia (my-**al**-jă) *noun* a pain in a muscle or group of muscles.

myall (**my**-ăl) *noun* **1** an Australian acacia with silvery foliage and hard scented wood. **2** an Aborigine living in a traditional manner (as distinct from one living among whites). – **myall** *adjective* **1** (of an Aborigine) living in a traditional manner. **2** (of an animal or plant) wild. [Dharuk *mayal* or *miyal* = a stranger, an Aborigine from another tribe]

Myanmar (mee-an-**mah**) the official name (since 1989) of Burma.

mycelium (my-**see**-lee-ŭm) *noun* (*plural* **mycelia**) the mass of very fine white threadlike

strands of a fungus that divide and multiply. [from Greek *mukes* = mushroom]

Mycenaean (my-sĕ-**nee**-ăn) *adjective* of a Bronze Age civilisation of Greece (c. 1500–1100 BC), remains of which were found at Mycenae in the Peloponnese and elsewhere.

mycology (my-**kol**-ŏ-jee) *noun* the study of fungi. **mycologist** *noun*

myna (**my**-nă) *noun* (also **mina**) a noisy bird of the starling family, introduced into Australia from Asia.

myopia (my-**oh**-pee-ă) *noun* short-sightedness.

myopic (my-**op**-ik) *adjective* short-sighted. **myopically** *adverb* [from Greek *muo* = shut, + *ops* = eye]

myriad (**mi**-ree-ăd) *noun* a vast number. [from Greek *murioi* = 10,000]

myriapod (**mi**-ree-ă-pod) *noun* a small crawling creature with very many legs, e.g. centipedes and millipedes. [from *myriad*, + Greek *podos* = of the foot]

myrmidon (**mer**-mid-ŏn) *noun* a henchman.

myrrh (*rhymes with* fur) *noun* a kind of gum resin used in perfumes and medicine and incense.

myrtle (**mer**-t'l) *noun* an evergreen shrub with dark leaves and scented white flowers.

myself *pronoun* corresponding to *I* and *me*, used in the same ways as **himself**.

mysterious *adjective* full of mystery, puzzling or obscure. **mysteriously** *adverb*

mystery *noun* **1** a matter that remains unexplained or secret. **2** the quality of being unexplained or obscure, *its origins are shrouded in mystery*. **3** the practice of making a secret of things. **4** a religious truth that is beyond human powers to understand. **5** a story or play that deals with a puzzling crime. ☐ **mystery play** a kind of medieval religious drama.

mystic (**mis**-tik) *adjective* **1** of hidden or symbolic meaning, especially in religion, *mystic ceremonies*. **2** inspiring a sense of mystery and awe. – **mystic** *noun* a person who seeks to obtain union with God by spiritual contemplation and self-surrender.

mystical (**mis**-tik-ăl) *adjective* **1** of mystics or mysticism. **2** having spiritual meaning, value, or symbolism. **mystically** *adverb*

mysticism (**mis**-tĭ-sizm) *noun* **1** mystical quality. **2** being a mystic.

mystify *verb* (**mystified**, **mystifying**)
   1 to cause (a person) to feel puzzled.
   2 to wrap in mystery. **mystification** *noun*

mystique (mis-**teek**) *noun* an aura of mystery
   or mystical power.

myth (*pr*. mith) *noun* 1 a traditional story
   containing ideas or beliefs about ancient
   times or about natural events (such as the
   four seasons). 2 such stories collectively, *in
   myth and legend*. 3 an imaginary person or
   thing. 4 an idea that forms part of the beliefs
   of a group or class but is not founded on fact.
   [from Greek *muthos* = story]

mythical (**mith**-i-kăl) *adjective* 1 of myths,
   existing in myths. 2 imaginary, fancied.

mythology (mith-**ol**-ŏjee) *noun* 1 a body of
   myths, *Greek mythology*. 2 study of myths.
   mythological *adjective*, **mythologist** *noun*
   [from *myth* + -*logy*]

myxomatosis (mik-sŏ-mă-**toh**-sĭs) *noun* a
   fatal viral disease of rabbits.

Nn

N *abbreviation* (also **N.**) north, northern.

naan (*pr.* nahn) *noun* a type of traditional Indian and Pakistani bread, leavened with yeast.

nab *verb* (**nabbed, nabbing**) (*informal*)
1 to catch (a wrongdoer) in the act, to arrest.
2 to seize, to grab.

nabob (**nay**-bob) *noun* **1** a Muslim official under the Mogul empire. **2** a wealthy person.

nacre (**nay**-ker) *noun* **1** mother-of-pearl. **2** the shellfish from which this is obtained. **nacreous** (**nay**-kree-ŭs) *adjective*

nadir (**nay**-deer) *noun* the lowest point; the time of deepest depression. [from Arabic *nazir* = opposite (i.e. to the zenith)]

naevus (**nee**-vŭs) *noun* (*plural* **naevi**, *pr.* **nee**-vy) **1** a birthmark consisting of a red patch on the skin. **2** = **mole¹**.

nag¹ *verb* (**nagged, nagging**) **1** to make scolding remarks to, to find fault continually. **2** (of pain or worry) to be felt persistently.

nag² *noun* (*informal*) a horse.

Nagasaki (nag-ă-**sah**-kee) Japanese city, target of the second atomic bomb attack (9 August 1945); *see also* **Hiroshima**.

Nahum (**nay**-hŭm) **1** a Hebrew minor prophet. **2** a book of the Old Testament containing his prophecies.

naiad (**ny**-ad) *noun* a water nymph.

nail *noun* **1** the layer of horny substance over the outer tip of a finger or toe. **2** a claw or talon. **3** a small metal spike driven in with a hammer to hold things together or as a peg or protection or ornament. **–nail** *verb* **1** to fasten with a nail or nails. **2** to catch or arrest, *nailed the intruder*. **3** to keep (a person, attention, etc.) fixed. □ **hit the nail on the head** to guess right; to state the truth exactly. **nail down** to pin down (*see* **pin**). **nail polish** or **varnish** a substance for giving a shiny tint to the nails. **on the nail** (especially of payment) without delay.

nainsook (**nayn**-suuk) *noun* a fine soft cotton fabric. [Hindi]

Nairobi (ny-**roh**-bee) the capital of Kenya.

naive (ny-**eev**) *adjective* (also **naïve**)
1 showing a lack of experience or of informed judgment. **2** (of artists or their work) without using formal training. **naively** *adverb*, **naivety** (ny-**eev**-tee) *noun*

naked *adjective* **1** without clothes on, nude. **2** without the usual coverings, protection, or ornamentation etc.; *a naked sword*, without its sheath. **3** undisguised, *the naked truth*.
□ **naked eye** the eye unassisted by a telescope or microscope etc. **nakedly** *adverb*, **nakedness** *noun*

naltrexone *noun* a synthetic drug, similar to morphine, which blocks opiate receptors in the nervous system.

Nama *noun* (*plural* **Nama** *or* **Namas**)
1 a member of a people of S Africa and Namibia. **2** their language.

> Usage *Hottentot* is sometimes used as the name for this people and their language, but *Nama* is preferred.

namaste (**nah**-mă-stay) *noun* the traditional Indian greeting with the hands held together as if in prayer.

Namatjira, Albert (1902–59), Aboriginal Australian landscape artist.

namby-pamby *adjective* lacking positive character, feeble, not manly. **–namby-pamby** *noun* a person of this kind.

name *noun* **1** a word or words by which a person, animal, place, or thing is known or indicated. **2** a reputation, *it has got a bad name*; *made a name for himself*, became famous. **3** a famous person, *the film has some big names in it*. **–name** *verb* **1** to give a name to. **2** to state the name(s) of. **3** to nominate or appoint to an office etc. **4** to mention or specify; *name the day*, to arrange a date, especially of a woman fixing the date for her wedding. □ **call a person names** to speak abusively to or about him or her. **have to one's name** to possess. **in name only** so called but not so in reality. **in the name of** invoking or calling to witness, by authority of, under the pretence of. **nameable** *adjective*

nameless *adjective* **1** having no name or no known name. **2** not mentioned by name, anonymous, *others who shall be nameless*. **3** too bad to be named, *nameless horrors*.

namely *adverb* that is to say, specifically.

namesake *noun* a person or thing with the same name as another.

Namibia (nă-**mib**-ee-ă) a republic in SW Africa. **Namibian** *adjective* & *noun*

namma *noun* = **gnamma**.

nan *noun* (*informal*) nanny.

Nanak, Guru (1469–1539), founder of Sikhism.

Nandi (in Hinduism) the bull of Siva, which is his vehicle and symbolises fertility.

nankeen (nan-**keen**) *noun* a kind of cotton cloth, originally made in Nanking in China from naturally yellow cotton.

nanna = **nan**.

nanny *noun* **1** a child's nurse. **2** (*informal*) grandmother. **3** (in full **nanny goat**) a female goat.

nannygai (**nan**-ee-gy) *noun* an edible Australian sea fish, also called *redfish*.

nano- *prefix* **1** one thousand-millionth part, *nanometre, nanosecond*. **2** extremely small. [from Greek *nanos* = dwarf]

nanobot *noun* a very small self-propelled machine, especially one that has some degree of autonomy and can reproduce.

nanotechnology *noun* chemical and biological engineering that involves the manipulation of molecules.

nap[1] *noun* a short sleep or doze, especially during the day. –**nap** *verb* (**napped**, **napping**) to have a nap. □ **catch a person napping** to catch a person off guard. **napper** *noun*

nap[2] *noun* short raised fibres on the surface of cloth (especially velvet) or leather.

napalm (**nay**-pahm) *noun* a jelly-like petrol substance used in incendiary bombs.

nape *noun* the back part of the neck.

napery *noun* household linen, especially table linen.

naphtha (**naf**-thă) *noun* an inflammable oil obtained from coal or petroleum.

naphthalene (**naf**-thă-leen) *noun* a strong-smelling white substance obtained from coal tar, used in dyes and mothballs.

Napier (**nay**-pee-er), John (1550–1617), Scottish inventor of logarithms.

napkin *noun* **1** a square piece of cloth or paper used at meals to protect one's clothes or for wiping one's lips or fingers. **2** a baby's nappy. **3** a sanitary pad (*see* **sanitary**).

Napoleon the name of three rulers of France, including Napoleon I, emperor 1804–15. **Napoleonic** *adjective*

nappa (**nap**-ă) *noun* leather made by a special process from the skin of sheep or goats.

nappy *noun* a piece of towelling or other absorbent material wrapped around a baby's bottom to absorb or retain urine and faeces.

narcissism (**nar**-sĭ-sizm) *noun* abnormal self-love or self-admiration. **narcissistic** (nar-sĭ-**sis**-tik) *adjective* [from Narcissus, the name of a youth in Greek mythology who fell in love with his own reflection in water]

narcissus (nar-**sis**-ŭs) *noun* (*plural* **narcissi**) any of a group of flowers including jonquils and daffodils, especially the kind with heavily-scented single white flowers.

narcosis (nar-**koh**-sĭs) *noun* a state of sleep or drowsiness, especially one produced by drugs.

narcotic (nar-**kot**-ik) *adjective* (of a substance) inducing sleep, drowsiness, stupor, or insensibility. –**narcotic** *noun* a narcotic drug.

nardoo *noun* an Australian clover-like fern growing near water, the spores of which may be ground and used as food. [from *ngardu*, which occurs in many Aboriginal languages]

nark *noun* (*informal*) **1** a police spy or informer. **2** (*Austral.*) a nagging or whingeing person. –**nark** *verb* (*informal*) to annoy.

narrate (nă-**rayt**) *verb* to tell (a story); to give an account of; to utter or write a narrative. **narration** *noun*, **narrator** *noun*

narrative (**na**-ră-tiv) *noun* a spoken or written account of something. –**narrative** *adjective* in the form of narrative.

narrow *adjective* **1** of small width in proportion to length. **2** having or allowing little space, *within narrow bounds*. **3** with little scope or variety, small, *a narrow circle of friends*. **4** with little margin, *a narrow escape*; *a narrow majority*. **5** narrow-minded. –**narrow** *verb* to make or become narrower. **narrows** *plural noun* the narrow part of a strait, river, etc. □ **narrow-minded** *adjective* rigid in one's views and sympathies, not tolerant. **narrowly** *adverb*, **narrowness** *noun*

narwhal (**nar**-wăl) *noun* an Arctic animal related to the whale, the male of which has a long tusk with a spiral groove.

NASA (**nas**-ă) *abbreviation* (also Nasa) National Aeronautics and Space Administration, a body responsible for organising US space research.

nasal (**nay**-zăl) *adjective* **1** of the nose. **2** (of a voice or speech) sounding as if the breath came out through the nose. **nasally** *adverb* [from Latin *nasus* = nose]

nascent (**nas**-ĕnt *or* **nay**-) *adjective* beginning to be or develop. **nascency** *noun*

NASDAQ (**naz**-dak) *abbreviation* (in the US) National Association for Securities Dealers Automated Quotations, a computerised system for trading in securities.

nashi *noun* an apple-like pear. [Japanese]

Nassau (**nass**-aw) the capital of the Bahamas.

nasturtium (nă-**ster**-shŭm) *noun* a trailing garden plant with bright orange, yellow, or red flowers and round flat leaves.

nasty *adjective* **1** unpleasant. **2** unkind, spiteful. **3** difficult to deal with, *a nasty problem*. –**nasty** *noun* an unpleasant person or thing. **nastily** *adverb*, **nastiness** *noun*

Natal (nă-**tahl**) (also KwaZulu Natal) the eastern coastal province of South Africa.

natal (**nay**-t'l) *adjective* of or from one's birth. [from Latin *natus* = born]

nation *noun* a large community of people of mainly common descent, language, history, etc., usually inhabiting a particular territory and under one government. [from Latin *natio* = birth; race]

national *adjective* of a nation, common to a whole nation. –**national** *noun* a citizen or subject of a particular country.
□ **national anthem** a song of loyalty or patriotism adopted by a country. **national debt** the total amount owed by the government of a country to those who have lent money to it. **national football** Australian Rules football. **national park** an area of natural beauty protected by the government for the use and enjoyment of the people. **National Party** an Australian political party formed to represent rural interests, formerly the Country Party. **national service** a period of compulsory service in a country's armed forces. **National Trust** a trust for the preservation of places of historic interest or natural beauty. **nationally** *adverb*

nationalise *verb* (also **-ize**) to convert (industries etc.) from private to government ownership. **nationalisation** *noun*

nationalism *noun* **1** patriotic feeling or principles or efforts. **2** a movement favouring independence for a country that is controlled by or forms part of another. **nationalist** *noun*, **nationalistic** *adjective*

nationality *noun* the condition of belonging to a particular nation.

nationwide *adjective* extending over the whole of a nation.

native *adjective* **1** belonging to a person or thing by nature, inborn, natural. **2** (of a person) belonging to a particular place by birth; (of a thing) belonging to a person because of his or her place of birth, *one's native land* or *language*. **3** grown, produced, or originating in a specified place. **4** of the natives of a place. –**native** *noun* **1** a person who was born in a specified place, *a native of Canada*. **2** a local inhabitant of a place. **3** (often *offensive*) an indigenous (especially non-European) inhabitant of a country, e.g. an Aborigine, as regarded by colonial settlers. **4** (*historical*) a white person born in Australia, as opposed to an immigrant Australian. **5** an animal or plant grown or originating in a specified place.
□ **native bear** a koala. **native cat** a quoll. **native companion** a brolga. **native title** the right of the Aboriginal and Islander people of Australia to own their traditional land, a right which the High Court of Australia recognised in 1992 (*see also* Mabo). [from Latin *nativus* = born]

nativity *noun* a person's birth with regard to its place or circumstances, especially *the Nativity*, that of Christ. –**Nativity** *noun* a picture of a scene with Christ as a newborn infant.

NATO (**nay**-toh) *abbreviation* (also Nato) North Atlantic Treaty Organisation, an association of European and North American States formed in 1949 for the purposes of collective security.

natter *verb* (*informal*) to chat. –**natter** *noun* (*informal*) a chat.

natterjack *noun* a kind of small toad with a yellow stripe down its back, that runs instead of hopping.

natty *adjective* (**nattier**, **nattiest**) neat and trim, dapper. **nattily** *adverb*

natural *adjective* **1** of, existing in, or produced by nature; *a country's natural*

resources, its mineral deposits, forests, etc.
2 in accordance with the course of nature,
normal, *a natural death*. **3** (of a person)
having certain inborn qualities or abilities, *a
natural leader*. **4** not looking artificial; not
affected in manner etc. **5** not surprising, to be
expected. **6** (in music, of a note) neither sharp
nor flat, *B natural*. **–natural** *noun* **1** a person
or thing that seems to be naturally suited for
something. **2** (in music) a natural note; the
sign for this (♮). **3** a pale fawn colour.
□ **natural childbirth** a system of childbirth
in which the mother has been taught to
relax and so needs little or no anaesthetic.
natural gas gas found in the earth's crust, not
manufactured. **natural history** the study of
animal and vegetable life. **natural number**
a whole number greater than 0. **natural
selection** survival of the organisms that are
best adapted to their environment while
the less well adapted ones die out. **natural
wastage** *see* **wastage**. **naturally** *adverb*,
naturalness *noun*

naturalise *verb* (also **-ize**) **1** to admit (a
person of foreign birth) to full citizenship of a
country. **2** to adopt (a foreign word or custom)
into the language or customs of a country.
3 to introduce and acclimatise (an animal or
plant) into a country where it is not native.
4 to cause to appear natural; *daffodil bulbs
suitable for naturalising*, suitable for planting
so that they appear to be growing wild.
naturalisation *noun*

naturalism *noun* realism in art and literature;
drawing or painting or representing things as
they are in nature. **naturalistic** *adjective*

naturalist *noun* an expert in natural history.

nature *noun* **1** the world with all its features
and living things; the physical power that
produces these; **Nature** this power personified.
2 a kind, sort, or class, *things of this nature*;
the request was in the nature of a command.
3 the complex of qualities and characteristics
innate in a person or animal. **4** a thing's
essential qualities, its characteristics.
□ **nature strip** (*Austral.*) a piece of land
planted with grass or shrubs between a
fence or footpath and roadway, or between
carriageways. **nature study** the practical study
of plant and animal life. **nature trail** a path
through the countryside where interesting
natural objects can be seen. [from Latin
natus = born]

naturist *noun* a nudist. **naturism** *noun*

naturopathy (nach-ŭ-**rop**-ǎ-thee) *noun*
the treatment of illness etc. without drugs,
usually involving diet, exercise, massage, etc.
naturopath *noun*, **naturopathic** *adjective*

naught *noun* (*old use*) nothing, = **nought**.

naughty *adjective* (**naughtier**, **naughtiest**)
1 behaving badly, disobedient. **2** improper,
shocking or amusing people by mild
indecency. **naughtily** *adverb*, **naughtiness**
noun [from *naught*]

Nauru (now-**roo**) an island republic in the SW
Pacific. **Nauruan** *adjective* & *noun*

nausea (**naw**-zee-ǎ) *noun* a feeling of sickness
or disgust. [originally 'seasickness', from
Greek *naus* = ship]

nauseate (**naw**-zee-ayt) *verb* to affect with
nausea.

nauseous (**naw**-zee-ŭs) *adjective* causing or
feeling nausea; disgusting.

nautical *adjective* of sailors or seamanship.
nautical mile *see* **mile**. [from Greek *nautes* =
sailor]

nautiloid (**naw**-tĭ-loid) *noun* any of a group
of molluscs of which all but the nautilus are
found only as fossils.

nautilus (**naw**-tĭ-lŭs) *noun* (*plural* **nautiluses**)
a mollusc with a spiral shell divided into
compartments.

Navajo (**nav**-ǎ-hoh) *noun* **1** a member of an
indigenous American people of New Mexico
and Arizona. **2** their language.

naval *adjective* of a navy, or warships; *a naval
power*, a country with a strong navy.

nave *noun* the body of a church apart from the
chancel, aisles, and transepts.

navel (**nay**-věl) *noun* **1** the small hollow in the
centre of the abdomen where the umbilical
cord was attached. **2** the central point of
something. □ **navel orange** a large orange
with a navel-like formation at the top.

navigable (**nav**-ig-ǎ-bŭl) *adjective* **1** (of
rivers or seas) suitable for ships to sail in.
2 (of a ship etc.) able to be steered and sailed.
navigability *noun*

navigate *verb* **1** to sail in or through (a sea
or river etc.). **2** to direct the course of (a ship,
aircraft, or vehicle etc.). **3** move around a
website, the Internet, etc. **navigation** *noun*,
navigator *noun* [from Latin *navis* = ship, +
agere = to drive]

navvy *noun* a labourer employed in making
roads, railways, canals, etc. where digging is

necessary. [short for 'navigator', = person who constructs a 'navigation' (= canal)]

navy *noun* **1** a country's warships. **2** the officers and personnel of these. **3** (in full **navy blue**) very dark blue like that used in naval uniform. **–navy** *adjective* navy blue. [from Latin *navis* = ship]

nawab (nă-**wahb**) *noun* **1** the title of a distinguished Muslim in Pakistan. **2** (*old use*) the title of a governor or nobleman in India.

nay *adverb* (*old use*) no.

Nazareth a town of Galilee in Israel, where Christ spent his youth.

Nazi (**nah**-tsee) *noun* (*plural* **Nazis**) a member of the National Socialist party in Germany, brought to power by Hitler. **–Nazi** *adjective* of the Nazis. **Nazism** *noun* [short for *national* as pronounced in German]

NB *abbreviation* note well. [from Latin *nota bene*]

NCO *abbreviation* non-commissioned officer.

N'Djamena (njă-**may**-nă) the capital of Chad.

NE *abbreviation* north-east, north-eastern.

Neanderthal (nee-**an**-der-tahl) *adjective* of **Neanderthal man**, an extinct type of mankind living in the Old Stone Age in Europe.

neap *noun* **neap tide** the tide when there is the least rise and fall of water, halfway between spring tides.

Neapolitan (nee-ă-**pol**-ĭ-tăn) *adjective* of Naples, a city in southern Italy. □ **Neapolitan ice cream** ice cream made in layers of different colours and flavours, popularly chocolate, strawberry, and vanilla.

near *adverb* **1** at, to, or within a short distance or interval. **2** nearly, *as near as I can guess*. **–near** *preposition* near to. **–near** *adjective* **1** with only a short distance or interval between, *in the near future*. **2** closely related. **3** (of a part of a vehicle, horse, or road) on the left side, *the near-side front wheel*; *near hind leg*. **4** with little margin, *a near escape*. **–near** *verb* to draw near. **near miss** something that missed its objective only narrowly; not a direct hit but near enough to do damage. **near-sighted** *adjective* short-sighted. **near thing** something achieved or missed by only a narrow margin; a narrow escape. **nearness** *noun*

nearby *adjective* near in position, *a nearby house*. **–nearby** *adverb* (also **near by**) not far off, *they live nearby*.

nearly *adverb* **1** closely; *we are nearly related*, are closely related. **2** almost. □ **not nearly** nothing like, far from, *not nearly enough*.

neat *adjective* **1** simple and clean and orderly in appearance. **2** done or doing things in a precise and skilful way. **3** undiluted, *neat whisky*. **4** (*informal*, as a general term of approval) excellent; useful; pleasing. **neatly** *adverb*, **neatness** *noun*

neaten *verb* to make or become neat.

Nebraska (nĕ-**bras**-kă) a State of the central USA.

Nebuchadnezzar (neb-yŭ-kăd-**nez**-er) king of Babylon 605–562 BC, who captured and destroyed Jerusalem in 586 BC.

nebula (**neb**-yŭ-lă) *noun* (*plural* **nebulae**, *pr.* **neb**-yŭ-lee) a bright or dark patch in the sky caused by a distant galaxy or a cloud of dust or gas. **nebular** *adjective* [Latin, = mist]

nebuliser (**neb**-yŭ-ly-zer) *noun* (also **-izer**) a device for producing a fine spray of liquid.

nebulous (**neb**-yŭ-lŭs) *adjective* indistinct, having no definite form, *nebulous ideas*.

necessarily *adverb* as a necessary result, inevitably.

necessary *adjective* **1** essential in order to achieve something. **2** unavoidable, happening or existing by necessity, *the necessary consequence*. **– the necessary** (*informal*) money or action needed for a purpose, *do* or *provide the necessary*. **necessaries** *plural noun* things without which life cannot be maintained or is exceedingly harsh.

necessitate (nĕ-**sess**-ĭ-tayt) *verb* to make necessary, to involve as a condition or accompaniment or result.

necessitous (nĕ-**sess**-ĭ-tŭs) *adjective* needy.

necessity (nĕ-**sess**-ĭ-tee) *noun* **1** the state or fact of being necessary, *the necessity of adequate food*. **2** a necessary thing. **3** the compelling power of circumstances. **4** a state of need or great poverty or hardship.

neck *noun* **1** the narrow part of the body connecting the head to the shoulders. **2** the part of a garment round this. **3** the length of a horse's head and neck as a measure of its lead in a race. **4** the flesh of an animal's neck as food. **5** the narrow part of anything (especially of a bottle or cavity); a narrow connecting part or channel. □ **get it in the neck** (*informal*) to suffer a reprimand or a severe blow. **neck and neck** running level in a race. **risk** or **save one's**

neck to risk or save one's own life. **up to one's neck in** (*informal*) very deeply involved in.

neckband *noun* a strip of material round the neck of a garment.

neckerchief *noun* a square of cloth worn round the neck.

necklace *noun* an ornament of precious stones or metal or beads etc. worn round the neck.

neckline *noun* the outline formed by the edge of a garment at or below the neck.

necktie *noun* a strip of folded material worn round the neck, passing under the collar and knotted in front.

necromancy (**nek**-rŏ-man-see) *noun* **1** the art of predicting events by allegedly communicating with the dead. **2** witchcraft. **necromancer** *noun* [from Greek *nekros* = corpse, + *manteia* = divination]

necropolis (ně-**krop**-ŏ-lĭs) *noun* a cemetery, especially an ancient one. [from Greek *nekros* = corpse, + *polis* = city]

nectar *noun* **1** (*Gk. myth.*) the drink of the gods. **2** any delicious drink. **3** a sweet fluid produced by plants and collected by bees for making honey.

nectarine (**nek**-tă-rǐn) *noun* a kind of peach that has a thin smooth skin and firm flesh.

nectary (**nek**-tă-ree) *noun* the nectar-secreting part of a plant or flower.

née (*pr.* nay) *adjective* born (used in giving a married woman's maiden name, *Mrs Jane Smith, née Jones*). [French]

need *noun* **1** circumstances in which a thing or course of action is required, *there is no need to worry*. **2** a situation of great difficulty or misfortune, *a friend in need*. **3** lack of necessaries, poverty. **4** a requirement, a thing necessary for life, *my needs are few*. –**need** *verb* **1** to be in need of, to require. **2** to be under a necessity or obligation, *need you ask?* ☐ **if need be** if necessary.

needful *adjective* necessary.

needle *noun* **1** a small thin piece of polished steel with a point at one end and a hole for thread at the other, used in sewing. **2** something resembling this in shape or use, e.g. one of the long thin leaves of pine trees, a sharp pointed rock, an obelisk (*Cleopatra's Needle*), the sharp hollow end of a hypodermic syringe, a record stylus. **3** a long thin piece of smooth metal or plastic etc. with one or both ends pointed, used in knitting by hand. **4** the pointer of a compass or gauge. –**needle** *verb* (*informal*) to annoy or provoke.

needlecraft *noun* skill in needlework.

needlepoint *noun* a kind of fine embroidery on canvas.

needless *adjective* not needed, unnecessary, **needlessly** *adverb*

needlework *noun* sewing or embroidery.

needn't (*informal*) = need not.

needs *adverb* of necessity; *must needs do it*, foolishly insists on doing it, cannot help doing it; *needs must do it*, must do it.

needy *adjective* (**needier**, **neediest**) lacking the necessaries of life, extremely poor. **neediness** *noun*

ne'er *adverb* (*poetic*) never. ☐ **ne'er-do-well** *noun* a good-for-nothing person.

nefarious (ně-**fair**-ree-ŭs) *adjective* wicked. **nefariously** *adverb* [from Latin *nefas* = wrong]

negate (ně-**gayt**) *verb* to nullify, to disprove. **negation** *noun* [from Latin *negare* = deny]

negative *adjective* **1** expressing or implying denial, refusal, or prohibition; *a negative reply*, saying 'no'. **2** not positive, lacking positive qualities or characteristics; *the result of the test was negative*, indicated that a specific substance etc. was not present. **3** (of a quantity) less than zero, minus. **4** containing or producing the kind of electric charge carried by electrons; *negative terminal of a battery*, the one through which current enters from an external circuit. **5** (of a photograph) having the lights and shades of the actual object or scene reversed, or its colours represented by complementary ones. –**negative** *noun* **1** a negative statement or reply or word; *the answer is in the negative*, is 'no'. **2** a negative quality or quantity. **3** a negative photograph, from which positive pictures can be obtained. –**negative** *verb* **1** to veto. **2** to contradict (a statement). **3** to neutralise (an effect). ☐ **negative pole** the south-seeking pole of a magnet. **negative sign** the sign (−). **negatively** *adverb*, **negativity** *noun*

neglect *verb* **1** to pay no attention or not enough attention to. **2** to fail to take proper care of. **3** to omit to do something, e.g. through carelessness or forgetfulness. –**neglect** *noun* neglecting, being neglected. **neglectful** *adjective*

negligée (**neg**-lĭ-*zh*ay) *noun* (also **néglige**) a woman's light flimsy ornamental dressing gown.

negligence (**neg**-lĭ-jĕns) *noun* lack of proper care or attention, carelessness. **negligent** *adjective*, **negligently** *adverb*

negligible (**neg**-lĭ-jĭ-bŭl) *adjective* very small in amount etc. and not worth taking into account. **negligibly** *adverb*

negotiable (nĕ-**goh**-shǎ-bŭl) *adjective* 1 able to be modified after discussion, *the salary is negotiable*. 2 (of a cheque etc.) able to be converted into cash or transferred to another person.

negotiate (nĕ-**goh**-shee-ayt) *verb* 1 to try to reach an agreement or arrangement by discussion; to arrange in this way, *negotiated a treaty*. 2 to get or give money in exchange for (a cheque or bonds etc.). 3 to get over or through (an obstacle or difficulty) successfully. **negotiation** *noun*, **negotiator** *noun* [from Latin *negotium* = business]

Negro *noun* (*plural* **Negroes**) a member of a black-skinned race that originated in Africa. **Negress** *feminine noun* [from Latin *niger* = black]

Usage The terms *Negro* and *Negress* are now often considered offensive, and *Black* is usually preferred.

Negroid *adjective* having the physical characteristics that are typical of Black people of African ethnic origin, with black skin, tightly curled hair, and a flattish nose. **–Negroid** *noun* a Negroid person.

Nehemiah (nee-ĕ-**my**-ǎ) 1 a Jewish leader of the 5th century BC. 2 a book of the Old Testament telling of his reforms.

neigh (*pr.* nay) *noun* the long high-pitched cry of a horse. **–neigh** *verb* to make this cry.

neighbour *noun* 1 a person who lives near or next to another. 2 a fellow human being. 3 a person or thing situated near or next to another. [from Old English *neahgebur* = near dweller]

neighbourhood *noun* 1 a district. 2 the people living in it. □ **in the neighbourhood of** somewhere near, approximately. **neighbourhood watch** systematic vigilance by citizens in order to combat crime in their neighbourhood.

neighbouring *adjective* living or situated near by.

neighbourly *adjective* like a good neighbour, kind and friendly. **neighbourliness** *noun*

Neilson, John Shaw (1872–1942), Australian lyric poet.

neither (**ny**-ther or **nee**-ther) *adjective* & *pronoun* not either, *neither of them likes it*. **–neither** *adverb* & *conjunction* 1 not either, *she neither knew nor cared*. 2 also not, *you don't know and neither do I*. □ **be neither here nor there** to be of no importance or relevance.

Usage Note that the pronoun *neither* is followed by a singular verb.

Nelson, Horatio, Viscount Nelson, Duke of Bronté (1758–1805), British admiral killed at Trafalgar.

nelson *noun* a kind of hold in wrestling.

nematode (**nem**-ǎ-tohd) *noun* a kind of slender worm, a roundworm. [from Greek *nematos* = of a thread]

nem. con. *abbreviation* unanimously. [short for Latin *nemine contradicente* = with nobody disagreeing]

nemesis (**nem**-ĕ-sĭs) *noun* the infliction of deserved and unavoidable punishment. [named after Nemesis, goddess of retribution in Greek mythology]

neo- *prefix* new, recent, a new form of. [from Greek *neos* = new]

neoclassical *adjective* (also **neoclassic**) of or in a style of art, literature, or music that is based on or influenced by classical style. **neoclassicism** *noun*

neodymium (nee-oh-**dim**-ee-ŭm) *noun* a silver-white metallic element of the lanthanide series (symbol Nd).

neo-impressionist *noun* any of a group of painters whose style was similar to that of the impressionists but with greater detail. **neo-impressionism** *noun*

neolithic (nee-ŏ-**lith**-ik) *adjective* of the later part of the Stone Age. **–neolithic** *noun* this period. [from *neo-*, + Greek *lithos* = stone]

neologism (nee-**ol**-ŏ-jizm) *noun* a newly coined word. [from *neo-*, + Greek *logos* = word]

neon (**nee**-on) *noun* a chemical element (symbol Ne), a kind of gas that glows orange-red when electricity is passed through it.

neophyte (**nee**-ŏ-fyt) *noun* 1 a new convert. 2 (in the Catholic Church) a novice of a religious order. **3** a beginner. [from *neo-*, + Greek *phuton* = plant]

Neoplatonism (nee-oh-**play**-tŏ-nizm) *noun* a philosophy dating from the 3rd century, in which Platonic ideas are combined with oriental mysticism. **Neoplatonist** *noun*

neoprene (**nee**-ŏ-preen) *noun* a tough synthetic rubber-like substance.

Nepal (nĕ-**pawl**) a kingdom north-east of India. **Nepalese** (nep-ă-**leez**) *adjective* & *noun* (*plural* **Nepalese**).

Nepali (nĕ-**pawl**-ee) *noun* the language of Nepal.

nephew (**nef**-yoo) *noun* the son of one's brother or sister, or of one's brother-in-law or sister-in-law. [from Latin *nepos*]

nephritis (nĕ-**fry**-tĭss) *noun* inflammation of kidneys. [from Greek *nephros* = kidney]

nepotism (**nep**-ŏ-tizm) *noun* favouritism shown to relatives in appointing them to jobs. [from Latin *nepos* = nephew]

Neptune 1 (*Rom. myth.*) the god of water, identified with the sea god Poseidon. **2** the third largest of the planets.

neptunium (nep-**choo**-nee-ŭm) *noun* a radioactive metallic element of the actinide series, occurring only in trace amounts in nature (symbol Np).

nerd *noun* (*informal*) a foolish, uninteresting, or socially awkward person. **nerdy** *adjective*

Nero (AD 15–68), Roman emperor 54–68.

nerve *noun* **1** any of the fibres or bundles of fibres carrying impulses of sensation or of movement between the brain or spinal cord and all parts of the body. **2** courage, coolness in danger, *lose one's nerve*. **3** (*informal*) impudent boldness, *had the nerve to ask for more*. **–nerve** *verb* to give strength, vigour, or courage to; *nerve oneself*, to brace oneself to face danger or suffering. **nerves** *plural noun* nervousness; a condition in which a person suffers from mental stress and easily becomes anxious or upset. ☐ **get on a person's nerves** to be irritating to him or her. **nerve centre** a centre of control from which instructions are sent out. **nerve gas** a poison gas that affects the nervous system. **nerve-racking** *adjective* inflicting great strain on the nerves. [from Latin *nervus* = sinew]

nerveless *adjective* incapable of effort or movement, *the knife fell from his nerveless fingers*.

nervous *adjective* **1** of the nerves or nervous system, *a nervous disorder*. **2** excitable, easily agitated; timid. **3** uneasy, *a nervous laugh*. ☐ **nervous breakdown** loss of mental and emotional stability. **nervous system** the system of nerves throughout the body. **nervously** *adverb*, **nervousness** *noun*

nervy *adjective* (**nervier**, **nerviest**) nervous, easily agitated, uneasy. **nerviness** *noun*

ness *noun* a headland, *Loch Ness*.

nest *noun* **1** a structure or place in which a bird lays its eggs and shelters its young. **2** a place where certain creatures (e.g. mice, wasps) live, or produce and keep their young. **3** a snug or secluded shelter or retreat. **4** a set of similar articles designed to fit inside each other in a series, *a nest of tables*. **–nest** *verb* **1** to make or have a nest. **2** (of objects) to fit together or inside one another. **3** (in computing) to make (a set of procedures, commands, etc.) operate within each other in a program. ☐ **nest egg** a sum of money saved for future use.

nestle *verb* **1** to curl up or press oneself comfortably into a soft place. **2** to lie half-hidden or sheltered.

nestling *noun* a bird too young to leave the nest.

net¹ *noun* **1** openwork material of thread, cord, or wire etc. woven or joined at intervals. **2** a piece of this used for a particular purpose, e.g. covering or protecting something, catching fish, dividing a tennis court, surrounding a goal. **3** Net = the Internet. **–net** *verb* (**netted**, **netting**) **1** to make by forming threads into a net; to make netting. **2** to place nets in; to cover or confine with or as if with a net. **3** to catch in or as if in a net. **4** to hit (a ball) into the net of a goal.

net² *adjective* (also **nett**) **1** remaining when nothing more is to be taken away; *net profit*, profit after tax, expenses, etc. have been deducted from the gross profit; *net weight*, weight of contents only, excluding wrappings. **2** (of an effect etc.) positive, excluding unimportant effects or those that cancel each other out, *the net result*. **–net** *verb* (**netted**, **netting**) to obtain or yield as net profit.

netball *noun* a game between two teams of seven players in which goals are scored by throwing a ball through a net hanging from a ring on a high post.

nether (**neth**-er) *adjective* lower, *the nether regions*. **nethermost** *adjective*

Netherlands, the a kingdom in Europe, also called *Holland*. **Netherlander** *noun*

netting *noun* fabric of netted thread, cord, or wire etc.

nettle *noun* 1 a common wild plant with hairs on its leaves that sting and redden the skin when they are touched. 2 a plant resembling this. –**nettle** *verb* to irritate, to provoke.
□ **nettle-rash** *noun* an eruption on the skin with red patches like those made by nettle stings.

network *noun* 1 an arrangement or pattern with intersecting lines, *a network of railways*. 2 a chain of interconnected people, operations, computers, or broadcasting stations, *a spy network*. 3 (in graph theory) an arrangement of points with lines connecting them. –**network** *verb* 1 establish a network. 2 link (machines) to operate interactively. 3 (often as **networking** *noun*) interact with others to exchange information and develop useful contacts.

neural (**new**-răl) *adjective* of nerves.
□ **neural arch** each of the bony arches of the vertebrae, making up the **neural canal** in which the spinal cord is contained. [from Greek *neuron* = nerve]

neuralgia (new-**ral**-jă) *noun* sharp intermittent pain along the course of a nerve, especially in the head or face. **neuralgic** *adjective* [from Greek *neuron* = nerve, + *algos* = pain]

neuritis (new-**ry**-tĭss) *noun* inflammation of a nerve or nerves.

neurology (new-**rol**-ŏ-jee) *noun* the scientific study of nerve systems and their diseases. **neurological** *adjective*, **neurologist** *noun* [from Greek *neuron* = nerve, + *-logy*]

neuron (**new**-ron) *noun* (also **neurone**, *pr.* **new**-rohn) a nerve cell and its appendages. [Greek, = nerve]

neurosis (new-**roh**-sĭs) *noun* (*plural* **neuroses**) a mental disorder producing depression or abnormal behaviour, sometimes with physical symptoms but with no evidence of disease.

neurosurgery *noun* surgery performed on the nervous system. **neurosurgeon** *noun*

neurotic (new-**rot**-ik) *adjective* 1 of or caused by a neurosis. 2 (of a person) subject to abnormal anxieties or obsessive behaviour. **neurotically** *adverb*

neurotransmitter *noun* a chemical substance released from a nerve fibre that effects the transfer of an impulse to another nerve or muscle.

neuter (**new**-ter) *adjective* 1 (of a noun) neither masculine nor feminine. 2 (of plants) without male or female parts. 3 (of insects) sexually undeveloped, sterile. –**neuter** *noun* 1 a neuter word. 2 a neuter plant or insect. 3 a castrated animal. –**neuter** *verb* to castrate or spay. [Latin, = neither]

neutral *adjective* 1 not supporting or assisting either side in a dispute or conflict. 2 belonging to a country or person etc. that is neutral, *neutral ships*. 3 having no positive or distinctive characteristics; not definitely one thing or the other. 4 (of colours) not strong or positive; grey or fawn. 5 (of a substance) neither acid nor alkaline. 6 neither positive nor negative. –**neutral** *noun* 1 a neutral person or country; one who is a subject of a neutral country. 2 grey or fawn colour. 3 neutral gear.
□ **neutral gear** a position of a gear mechanism in which the engine is disconnected from driven parts. **neutrally** *adverb*, **neutrality** (new-**tral**-ĭ-tee) *noun* [from Latin *neuter* = neither]

neutralise *verb* (also **-ize**) to make ineffective by an opposite force or effect. **neutralisation** *noun*

neutrino (new-**tree**-noh) *noun* (*plural* **neutrinos**) an elementary particle with zero electric charge and probably zero mass. [Italian; same origin as *neutral*]

neutron (**new**-tron) *noun* a particle of about the same mass as a proton but with no electric charge, present in the nuclei of all atoms except those of ordinary hydrogen.
□ **neutron bomb** a nuclear bomb that kills people by intense radiation but does little damage to buildings etc. **neutron number** the number of neutrons in the nucleus of an atom. [from *neutral*]

Nevada (ně-**vah**-dă) a State of the western USA.

névé (**nev**-ay) *noun* packed snow turning to ice at the head of a glacier.

never *adverb* 1 at no time, on no occasion; *never-ending*, *never-failing*, not ending or failing ever. 2 not at all, *never fear*. 3 (*informal*) surely not, *you never left the key in the lock!* 4 not, *never a care*. –**never** *interjection* (*informal*) surely not.
□ **never mind** do not be troubled; do not trouble about, *never mind the cost*. **the never-never** *noun* (*informal*) hire purchase; (*Austral.*) the remote outback. **well I never!**

an exclamation of surprise. [from *ne* = not, + *ever*]

nevermore *adjective* at no future time.

nevertheless *adverb* & *conjunction* in spite of this.

new *adjective* **1** not existing before; recently made, invented, discovered, or experienced. **2** unfamiliar, unaccustomed, *it was new to me*; *I am new to the job*. **3** recently changed or renewed, different, *the new boss*. –**new** *adverb* newly, recently, just, *new-born*; *new-laid*. □ **New Australian** (*old use*) a post-war immigrant to Australia, especially one whose first language was not English. **new chum** (*Austral.*) a newcomer, a novice. **New Commonwealth** *see* **commonwealth. new moon** the moon when it is seen in the evening as a crescent; (on calendars) the precise moment when the moon is in conjunction with the sun and is invisible. **New Testament** *see* **testament. New World** the Americas. **new year** the first few days of January. **New Year's Day** 1 January. **New Year's Eve** 31 December. **newish** *adjective*, **newness** *noun*

New Age a movement characterised by alternative approaches to traditional Western culture, especially in the areas of religion, medicine, the environment, etc.

New Britain the largest island of the Bismarck Archipelago to the north-east of New Guinea, administratively part of Papua New Guinea.

New Caledonia an island in the SW Pacific, in French possession.

newcomer *noun* a person who has arrived recently.

newel (**new**-ĕl) *noun* **1** a post that supports the handrail of a stair at the top or bottom of a staircase. **2** the central pillar of a winding stair.

New England 1 an extensive tableland district of NE New South Wales, including the towns of Tamworth, Glen Innes, and Armidale. **2** a district of north-eastern USA.

newfangled *adjective* (*derogatory*) objectionably new in method or style. [from *new*, + *fang* = seize]

Newfoundland (**new**-fŭnd-lănd) a large island at the mouth of the St Lawrence, united with Labrador as a province of Canada. –**Newfoundland** *noun* a dog of a large breed with a thick dark coat. **Newfoundlander** *noun*

New Guinea a large island to the north of Australia, divided between the independent state of Papua New Guinea in the east and Papua (part of Indonesia) in the west.

New Hampshire a State of the north-eastern USA.

New Holland a former name for Australia, originally given to the western part of the continent in the 17th century.

New Ireland an island to the north of New Britain in the Bismarck Archipelago, administratively part of Papua New Guinea.

New Jersey a State of the USA, bordering on the Atlantic.

newly *adverb* recently, freshly. □ **newly-wed** *adjective* recently married; (*noun*) a recently-married person.

New Mexico a State of the south-western USA.

news *noun* **1** information about recent events. **2** a broadcast report of this. **3** newsworthy information, *when a man bites a dog, that's news*. □ **news-stand** *noun* a stall where newspapers are sold.

newsagent *noun* a shopkeeper who sells newspapers and usually stationery. **newsagency** *noun*

newscast *noun* a broadcast news report. **newscaster** *noun*

newsflash *noun* a single item of important news, broadcast urgently and often interrupting other programs.

newsletter *noun* an informal printed report giving information that is of interest to members of a club etc.

New South Wales a State in SE Australia. □ **New South Welshman** a native or resident of New South Wales.

newspaper *noun* **1** a printed publication, usually issued daily or weekly, containing news reports, advertisements, articles on various subjects, etc. **2** the sheets of paper forming this, *wrapped in newspaper*.

Newspeak *noun* ambiguous euphemistic language used especially in political propaganda. [the name of an artificial official language in George Orwell's *Nineteen Eighty-Four*]

newsprint *noun* the type of paper on which a newspaper is printed.

newsreel *noun* a cinema film showing current items of news.

newsworthy *adjective* important or interesting enough to be mentioned as news.

newsy *adjective* (*informal*) full of news.

newt *noun* a small lizard-like creature that can live in water or on land.

Newton, Sir Isaac (1642–1727), English mathematician and physicist, who made important discoveries about light, gravity, and motion. **Newtonian** *adjective*

newton *noun* a unit of force. [named after Sir Isaac Newton]

New York 1 the most populous city of the USA, at the mouth of the Hudson River. **2** a State of the USA, bordering on the Atlantic. **New Yorker** *noun*

New Zealand a country in the South Pacific east of Australia, consisting of two major islands (North and South Islands) and several smaller ones. **New Zealander** *noun*

next *adjective* **1** lying, living, or being nearest to something. **2** coming nearest in order, time, or sequence; soonest come to. **–next** *adverb* in the next place or degree; on the next occasion. **–next** *noun* the next person or thing. □ **next-best** *adjective* second-best. **next door** in the next house or room. **next-door** *adjective* living or situated next door, *my next-door neighbour*. **next door to** not far from, almost, *it's next door to impossible*. **next of kin** one's closest relative. **next to** almost, *it is next to impossible*. **next world** life after death.

nexus *noun* (*plural* **nexuses**) a connected group or series.

Ngaanyatjara (**ngah**-nyah-jah-ru) *noun* **1** a member of an Aboriginal people of the desert region of WA. **2** their language, a dialect of the Western Desert language.

Ngarigo (**ngah**-rig-oh) *noun* **1** a member of an Aboriginal people who lived in SE New South Wales and NE Victoria. **2** their language.

niacin (**ny**-ă-sĭn) *see* **nicotinic acid**.

Niagara a river forming the US-Canada border between Lakes Erie and Ontario, famous for its spectacular waterfalls.

Niamey (**nyah**-may) the capital of Niger.

nib *noun* the point of a pen.

nibble *verb* **1** to take small quick or gentle bites. **2** to eat in small amounts, *no nibbling between meals*. **3** to show interest in (an offer etc.) but without being definite. **–nibble** *noun* **1** a small quick bite. **2** a very small amount of food. **nibbler** *noun*

Nibelungenlied (**nee**-bĕ-luung-ĕn-leed) a 13th-century Germanic poem telling of the life and death of Siegfried, a prince of the Netherlands.

nibs *noun* **his nibs** (*informal*) a humorous title used in referring to an important or self-important person.

Nicaragua (nik-ă-**rag**-yoo-ă) a republic in Central America. **Nicaraguan** *adjective* & *noun*

nice *adjective* **1** pleasant, satisfactory. **2** (of a person) kind, good-natured. **3** (*ironically*) difficult, bad, *this is a nice mess*. **4** needing precision and care, involving fine distinctions, *it's a nice point*. **5** fastidious. **nicely** *adverb*, **niceness** *noun* [the word originally meant 'stupid', from Latin *nescius* = ignorant]

Nicene Creed (**ny**-seen) a formal statement of Christian belief based on that adopted at the Council of Nicaea (325).

nicety (**ny**-sĕ-tee) *noun* **1** precision. **2** a subtle-distinction or detail. □ **to a nicety** exactly.

niche (*pr*. nich *or* neesh) *noun* **1** a shallow recess, especially in a wall. **2** a position in life or employment to which the holder is well suited, *has found his niche*. [from Latin *nidus* = nest]

Nicholas¹ the name of two emperors of Russia. Nicholas II was forced to abdicate after the Russian Revolution (1917) and was murdered along with his family by the Bolsheviks a year later.

Nicholas², St (4th century), bishop of Myra in Lycia, patron saint of children, sailors, and Russia. Feast day, 6 December.

nick *noun* **1** a small cut or notch. **2** (*informal*) a police station; a prison. **–nick** *verb* **1** to make a nick in. **2** (*informal*) to steal. **3** (*informal*) to catch or arrest (a criminal). **4** (*Austral. informal*) to go quickly or briefly, *nick into town*; *nick off*, leave. □ **in good nick** (*informal*) in good condition. **in the nick of time** only just in time.

nickel *noun* **1** a chemical element (symbol Ni), a hard silvery-white metal much used in alloys. **2** (*Amer.*) a 5-cent piece. □ **nickel silver** an alloy of nickel, zinc, and copper. **nickel steel** a type of stainless steel with chromium and nickel.

nickname *noun* a name given humorously to a person instead of or as well as the real name. **–nickname** *verb* to give a nickname to.

[originally a *nekename*, from *an eke-name* (*eke* = additional, + *name*)]

Nicosia (nik-ŏ-**see**-ă) the capital of Cyprus.

nicotine (**nik**-ŏ-teen) *noun* a poisonous substance found in tobacco. [from the name of J. Nicot, who introduced tobacco in France in 1560]

nicotinic acid *noun* a vitamin of the B group, a deficiency of which causes pellagra. Also called *niacin*.

nictitate *verb* to blink or wink. □ nictitating membrane the third or inner eyelid of birds, fishes, and some other animals. nictitation *noun* [from Latin *nictare* = blink]

niece *noun* the daughter of one's brother or sister, or of one's brother-in-law or sister-in-law.

Nietzsche (**nee**-chě), Friedrich Wilhelm (1844–1900), German philosopher of Polish descent, who is known for formulating the idea of the 'superman'.

nifty *adjective* (*informal*) **1** smart, stylish. **2** excellent, clever.

Niger 1 (**ny**-jer) a river of West Africa, flowing into the Gulf of Guinea. **2** (nee-**zhair**) a landlocked republic of West Africa, north of Nigeria.

Nigeria a federal republic on the coast of West Africa. Nigerian *adjective* & *noun*

niggard *noun* a stingy person.

niggardly (**nig**-erd-lee) *adjective* stingy.

nigger *noun* (*offensive*) a Black or dark-skinned person. □ nigger in the woodpile a hidden cause of trouble or inconvenience.

niggle *verb* **1** to fuss over details, to find fault in a petty way. **2** to nag. –niggle *noun* a trifling complaint or criticism; a worry or annoyance. niggling *adjective*

nigh (*rhymes with* by) *adverb* & *preposition* near.

night *noun* **1** the dark hours between sunset and sunrise. **2** nightfall. **3** a specified or appointed night; an evening on which a performance or other activity occurs, *the first night of the play*. □ night-long *adjective* & *adverb* throughout the night. night-night (*informal*) good night. night safe a receptacle provided at a bank so that money etc. can be deposited when the bank is closed. night school classes provided in the evening for people who are at work during the day. night shift a shift of workers employed during the night. night-time *noun* night.

nightcap *noun* **1** a soft cap for wearing in bed. **2** an alcoholic or hot drink taken at bedtime.

nightclub *noun* a club that is open at night, providing food, drink, and entertainment.

nightdress *noun* a woman's or child's loose garment for wearing in bed.

nightfall *noun* the coming of darkness at the end of the day.

nightgown *noun* a nightdress or nightshirt.

nightie *noun* (*informal*) a nightdress.

Nightingale, Florence (1820–1910), British nurse and medical reformer who became famous during the Crimean War, where she became known as the 'Lady of the Lamp'.

nightingale *noun* a small reddish-brown thrush, the male of which sings melodiously both by night and in the day.

nightjar *noun* a night-flying bird with a harsh cry.

nightly *adjective* **1** happening, done, or existing etc. in the night. **2** happening every night. –nightly *adverb* every night.

nightmare *noun* **1** a bad dream. **2** (*informal*) a terrifying or very unpleasant experience. nightmarish *adjective*

nightshade *noun* any of several wild plants with poisonous berries.

nightshirt *noun* a long shirt for wearing in bed.

nightwatchman *noun* **1** a person employed to keep watch at night in a building that is closed. **2** (in cricket) an inferior batsman sent in near the close of a day's play.

nihilism (**ny**-ĭ-lizm) *noun* **1** rejection of all religious and moral principles. **2** the theory that nothing has real existence. nihilist *noun*, nihilistic *adjective* [same origin as *nil*]

Nikkei index *noun* an index of shares traded on the Tokyo Stock Exchange.

nil *noun* nothing. [from Latin *nihil* = nothing]

Nile a river flowing from east central Africa through Egypt to the Mediterranean Sea.

nimble *adjective* **1** able to move quickly, agile. **2** (of the mind or wits) able to think quickly. nimbly *adverb*, nimbleness *noun*

nimbostratus (nim-boh-**strah**-tŭs) *noun* a low dark grey cloud, from which rain or snow often falls.

nimbus *noun* (*plural* nimbi *or* nimbuses) **1** the halo of a saint etc. **2** a rain cloud. [Latin, = cloud, aureole]

nincompoop *noun* a foolish person.

nine *adjective* & *noun* one more than eight (9, IX). □ **dressed up to the nines** dressed very elaborately. **nine days' wonder** something that attracts much attention at first but is soon forgotten.

9/11 *see* **September 11**.

ninepins *noun* the game of skittles played with nine objects to be knocked down by rolling a ball. **ninepin** *noun* any of these objects.

nineteen *adjective* & *noun* one more than eighteen (19, XIX). □ **talk nineteen to the dozen** to talk incessantly. **nineteenth** *adjective* & *noun*

ninety *adjective* & *noun* nine times ten (90, XC). **nineties** *plural noun* the numbers from 90 to 99, especially the years of a century or of a person's life. **ninetieth** *adjective* & *noun*

Nineveh (**nin**-ĕ-vĕ) the capital of Assyria from c. 700 BC to 612 BC

ninny *noun* a foolish person.

ninth *adjective* & *noun* **1** next after eighth. **2** one of nine equal parts of a thing. **ninthly** *adverb*

niobium (ny-**oh**-bee-ŭm) *noun* a silver-grey metallic element, used in superconducting alloys (symbol Cs).

nip¹ *verb* (**nipped**, **nipping**) **1** to pinch or squeeze sharply; to bite quickly with the front teeth. **2** to break off by doing this, *nip off the sideshoots*. **3** to pain or harm with biting cold, *a nipping wind*. **4** (*informal*) to go quickly, *nip out*. –**nip** *noun* **1** a sharp pinch, squeeze, or bite. **2** biting coldness, *a nip in the air*. □ **nip in the bud** to destroy at an early stage of development.

nip² *noun* a small drink of spirits.

nipper *noun* **1** (*informal*) a young boy or girl. **2** the great claw of a lobster or similar animal. **3** (*Austral.*) a burrowing shellfish used as bait. **nippers** *plural noun* pincers or forceps for gripping things or cutting things off.

nipple *noun* **1** a small projection in the centre of a male or female mammal's breasts, containing (in females) the outlets of the milk-secreting organs. **2** the teat of a feeding bottle. **3** a nipple-like projection.

Nipponese (nip-ŏ-**neez**) *adjective* & *noun* (*plural* **Nipponese**) Japanese.

nippy *adjective* (*informal*) **1** nimble, quick. **2** bitingly cold. **nippiness** *noun*

nirvana (ner-**vah**-nă) *noun* (in Buddhist and Hindu teaching) the state of perfect bliss attained when the soul is freed from all suffering and absorbed into the supreme spirit. [Sanskrit]

nisi *adjective* see **decree nisi**.

Nissen hut *noun* a tunnel-shaped hut of corrugated iron with a cement floor.

nit *noun* **1** the egg of a louse or other parasite; the insect laying this. **2** (*informal*) a stupid or foolish person. □ **nit-picking** *noun* fault-finding in a petty way.

nitrate (**ny**-trayt) *noun* **1** a salt or ester of nitric acid. **2** potassium or sodium nitrate used as a fertiliser.

nitric (**ny**-trik) *adjective* of or containing nitrogen. □ **nitric acid** a colourless caustic highly corrosive acid.

nitrify *verb* **1** to impregnate with nitrogen. **2** to convert into nitrites or nitrates. **nitrification** *noun*

nitrite *noun* any salt or ester of nitrous acid.

nitrogen (**ny**-trŏ-jĕn) *noun* a chemical element (symbol N), a colourless odourless gas forming about four-fifths of the atmosphere. □ **nitrogen cycle** the series of processes by which nitrogen from the air is converted into compounds that are deposited in the soil, from which they are assimilated by plants that are eaten by animals, and returned to the atmosphere when these organic substances decay. **nitrogenous** (ny-**troj**-ĕ-nŭs) *adjective*

nitroglycerine (ny-trŏ-**gliss**-ĕ-reen) *noun* a powerful explosive made by adding glycerine to a mixture of nitric and sulphuric acids.

nitrous (**ny**-trŭs) *adjective* of or containing nitrogen. □ **nitrous oxide** a colourless gas used as an anaesthetic, laughing gas.

nitty-gritty *noun* (*informal*) the basic facts or realities of a matter.

nitwit *noun* (*informal*) a stupid or foolish person.

Niue (**new**-ay) an island in the South Pacific east of Tonga, the largest coral island in the world.

nix *noun* (*informal*) nothing.

No. *abbreviation* (also **no.**) number. [from Latin *numero* = by number]

no *adjective* **1** not any. **2** not a, quite other than, *she is no fool*. –**no** *adverb* **1** used as a denial or refusal of something. **2** not at all, *no better than before*. –**no** *noun* (*plural*

noes) a negative reply or vote; a person voting against something. ☐ **no-ball** *noun* an unlawfully delivered ball in cricket etc.; (*verb*) to declare (a bowler) to have bowled this. **no fear** (*informal*) it is not likely; certainly not. **no go** the task is impossible, the situation is hopeless. **no-go area** an area to which entry is forbidden to certain people or groups. **no-hoper** (*informal*) an incompetent person, a failure. **no man's land** an area not firmly assigned to any one owner; a space between the fronts of two opposing armies in war. **no-no** *noun* (*informal*) a thing that is not acceptable or possible. **no one** no person, nobody. **no way** (*informal*) that is impossible. **no-win** *adjective* (of a situation) in which success is impossible.

Noah a Hebrew patriarch, said to have made the ark which saved his family and specimens of every animal from the flood sent by God to destroy the world.

nob *noun* (*informal*) **1** the head. **2** a person of wealth or high social position.

nobble *verb* (*informal*) **1** to tamper with (a racehorse) to prevent its winning. **2** to get hold of or influence by underhand means. **3** to catch (a criminal).

nobelium (noh-**bee**-lee-ŭm) *noun* an artificial radioactive metallic element of the actinide series (symbol No).

Nobel prize (noh-**bel**) any of the prizes awarded annually for outstanding achievements in the sciences, literature, economics, and the promotion of world peace, from the bequest of Alfred Nobel (1833–96), the Swedish inventor of dynamite.

nobility (noh-**bil**-ĭ-tee) *noun* nobleness of mind, character, or rank. **– the nobility** people of aristocratic birth or rank, titled people.

noble *adjective* **1** belonging to the aristocracy by birth or rank. **2** possessing excellent qualities, especially character; free from pettiness or meanness. **3** imposing in appearance, *a noble edifice*. **–noble** *noun* a nobleman or noblewoman. ☐ **noble gas** any of a group of gases that seldom or never combine with other elements to form compounds. **nobly** *adverb*, **nobleness** *noun*

nobleman, **noblewoman** *nouns* a member of the nobility.

noblesse oblige (noh-bless ŏ-**blee***zh*) noble people must behave nobly, privilege entails responsibility. [French]

nobody *pronoun* no person. **–nobody** *noun* a person of no importance or authority, *he's nobody* or *a nobody*. ☐ **like nobody's business** (*informal*) very much, intensively.

nocturnal (nok-**ter**-năl) *adjective* **1** of or in the night. **2** active in the night, *nocturnal animals*. **nocturnally** *adverb* [from Latin *noctis* = of night]

nocturne (**nok**-tern) *noun* a dreamy piece of music.

nod *verb* (**nodded**, **nodding**) **1** to move the head down and up again quickly as a sign of agreement or casual greeting; to indicate (agreement etc.) in this way. **2** to let the head fall forward in drowsiness; to be drowsy. **3** (of plumes or flowers etc.) to bend downwards and sway. **–nod** *noun* a nodding movement in agreement or greeting; *give* or *get the nod*, to give or get agreement or a signal to proceed. ☐ **a nodding acquaintance** a slight acquaintance with a person or subject. **land of Nod** sleep. **nod off** to fall asleep.

node (*rhymes with* load) *noun* **1** a knoblike swelling. **2** the point on the stem of a plant where a leaf or bud grows out. **3** a point at which a curve crosses itself. **4** a point in a vibrating string etc. where it is not moving.

nodule (**nod**-yool) *noun* a small rounded lump, a small node. **nodular** *adjective*

Noel (noh-**el**) *noun* (in carols) Christmas.

noggin *noun* **1** a small mug. **2** a small measure of alcohol, usually $\frac{1}{4}$ pint (about 140 ml). **3** (*informal*) the head.

nogging *noun* **1** brickwork in a wooden frame. **2** a short horizontal piece of wood used to strengthen an upright in a partition wall.

Noh (*pr.* noh) *noun* a form of traditional Japanese drama.

noise *noun* **1** a sound, especially one that is loud, harsh, or confused or undesired. **2** (in electronics) disturbances or fluctuations that interfere with the sound or picture or data being processed. **–noise** *verb* to make public; *noised it abroad*, made it generally known.

noiseless *adjective* without a sound. **noiselessly** *adverb*

noisome (**noi**-sŏm) *adjective* (*literary*) harmful; evil-smelling; objectionable. [from *annoy*]

noisy *adjective* (**noisier**, **noisiest**) making much noise. **noisily** *adverb*, **noisiness** *noun*

Nolan, Sir Sidney Robert (1917–92), Australian artist, whose paintings depict scenes from Australian life and history.

nomad (noh-mad) *noun* **1** a member of a tribe that roams from place to place seeking pasture for its animals. **2** a wanderer. **nomadism** *noun*, **nomadic** (nŏ-**mad**-ik) *adjective*

nom de plume (nom dě **ploom**) *noun* (*plural* **noms de plume**, *pr.* the same) a writer's pseudonym. [French, = pen name]

nomenclature (nŏ-**men**-klă-cher) *noun* a system of names, e.g. those used in a particular science.

nominal (**nom**-ĭ-năl) *adjective* **1** in name only, *nominal ruler of that country*. **2** (of an amount or sum of money) very small but charged or paid as a token that payment is required, *a nominal fee*. □ **nominal value** the face value of a coin etc. **nominally** *adverb* [from Latin *nomen* = name]

nominate (**nom**-ĭ-nayt) *verb* **1** to name as candidate for or future holder of an office. **2** to appoint as a place or date for a meeting etc. **nomination** *noun*, **nominator** *noun* [from Latin *nominare* = to name]

nominative (**nom**-ĭ-nă-tiv) *noun* the form of a noun used when it is the subject of a verb.

nominee (nom-ĭ-**nee**) *noun* a person who is nominated by another.

non- *prefix* not. [from Latin *non* = not]

Usage The number of words which can be formed with the prefix *non-* is almost unlimited, and many of those whose meaning is obvious are not listed below.

nonagenarian (non-ă-jě-**nair**-ree-ăn *or* noh-nă-) *noun* a person who is in his or her nineties. [from Latin *nonageni* = ninety each]

nonagon *noun* a plane figure with nine sides and angles.

non-aligned (non-ă-**lynd**) *adjective* not in alliance with any bloc. **non-alignment** *noun*

nonce *noun* □ **for the nonce** for the time being. **nonce word** a word coined for one occasion only.

nonchalant (**non**-shă-lănt) *adjective* not feeling or showing anxiety or excitement, calm and casual. **nonchalantly** *adverb*, **nonchalance** *noun* [from French *non* = not, + *chaloir* = be concerned]

non-combatant (non-**com**-bă-tănt) *noun* **1** a member of an army etc. whose duties do not involve fighting, e.g. a doctor or chaplain. **2** a civilian during a war.

non-commissioned *adjective* not holding a commission, *non-commissioned officers*.

non-committal (non-kŏ-**mi**-t'l) *adjective* not committing oneself, not showing what one thinks or which side one supports.

non compos mentis *adjective* insane. [Latin = not in control of one's mind]

non-conductor *noun* a substance that does not conduct heat or electricity.

nonconformist *noun* a person who does not conform to established principles. –**Nonconformist** *noun* a member of certain Protestant sects that do not conform to the teaching or practices of the Anglican Church or other established Churches.

non-contributory *adjective* not involving payment of contributions, *a non-contributory pension scheme*.

non-cooperation *noun* failure or refusal to cooperate, especially as a protest.

nondescript (**non**-dě-skript) *adjective* lacking in distinctive characteristics and therefore not easy to classify. –**nondescript** *noun* a nondescript person or thing.

non-drinker *noun* a person who does not drink alcohol.

none *pronoun* **1** not any. **2** no person(s), no one, *none can tell*. –**none** *adverb* by no amount, not at all, *is none the worse for it*. □ **none other** no other person. **none the less** = nonetheless. **none too** not very, not at all, *he's none too pleased*.

Usage In sense 1, *none* may be followed by either a singular or a plural verb. The singular construction is preferred (*none of the candidates has failed*), but the plural is very common (*none of them have failed*).

nonentity (non-**en**-tǐ-tee) *noun* a person or thing of no importance. [from *non-* + *entity*]

nones (*pr.* nohnz) *plural noun* the ninth day (counting inclusively) before the ides in the ancient Roman calendar, i.e. the 7th day of March, May, July, and October, and the 5th of the other months.

nonetheless *adverb* (also **none the less**) nevertheless.

non-event *noun* an event that was expected or intended to be important but proves to be disappointing.

non-existent *adjective* not existing.

non-ferrous *adjective* (of a metal) not iron or steel.

non-fiction *noun* a class of literature that includes books in all subjects other than fiction.

non-flammable *adjective* unable to be set on fire.

Usage See the note under inflammable.

---

nong *noun* (also **ning-nong**) (*Austral. informal*) a foolish or stupid person.

non-inflammable *adjective* unable to be set on fire.

non-intervention *noun* the policy of not interfering in other people's disputes.

non-iron *adjective* (of fabric) not needing to be ironed.

nonpareil (**non**-pă-rel) *noun* an unrivalled person or thing. [French, = not equal]

non-party *adjective* not belonging to or supported by a political party.

nonplus (non-**plus**) *verb* (**nonplussed**, **nonplussing**) to perplex completely. [from Latin *non plus* = not further]

non-proliferation *noun* the prevention of an increase in something, especially possession of nuclear weapons.

non-resident *adjective* 1 not living on the premises, *a non-resident caretaker*. 2 (of a job) not requiring the holder to live in. –**non-resident** *noun* a person not staying at a hotel etc., *open to non-residents*.

nonsense *noun* 1 words put together in a way that does not make sense. 2 absurd or foolish talk or ideas or behaviour. [from *non-* + *sense*]

nonsensical (non-**sen**-sĭ-kăl) *adjective* not making sense, absurd, foolish. **nonsensically** *adverb*

non sequitur (non **sek**-wĭ-ter) *noun* a conclusion that does not follow from the evidence given. [Latin, = it does not follow]

non-smoker *noun* a person who does not smoke. **non-smoking** *adjective*

non-starter *noun* 1 a horse that is entered for a race but does not run in it. 2 (*informal*) a person or an idea etc. that is not worth considering for a particular purpose.

non-stick *adjective* coated with a substance that food will not stick to during cooking.

non-stop *adjective* 1 (of a train or plane etc.) not stopping at intermediate places. 2 not ceasing, *non-stop chatter*. –**non-stop** *adverb* without stopping or pausing.

non-voting *adjective* (of shares) not entitling the holder to a vote.

noodle *noun* 1 a foolish person. 2 (*informal*) the head.

noodles *plural noun* pasta in narrow strips, used in soups etc.

nook *noun* a secluded place or corner, a recess.

noon *noun* twelve o'clock in the day, midday.

noonday *noun*, **noontide** *nouns* midday.

Noonuccal, Oodgeroo (formerly Kath Walker, 1920–93), Aboriginal Australian poet and activist for Aboriginal rights.

noose *noun* a loop of rope etc. with a knot that tightens when pulled.

nor *conjunction* and not.

Nordic *adjective* 1 of or relating to a physical type found especially in Scandinavia, tall and blond with blue eyes. 2 of Scandinavia or Finland. 3 (of skiing) involving cross-country work and jumping.

Norfolk Island (**nor**-fŏk) a small Pacific island about 1670 km NE of Sydney, administered by Australia. The island was used as a penal settlement for convicts (1788–1814 and 1825–56). ☐ **Norfolk Island pine** a tall coniferous tree.

norm *noun* 1 a standard or pattern or type considered to be representative of a group. 2 a standard amount of work etc. to be done or produced.

normal *adjective* 1 conforming to what is standard or usual. 2 free from mental or emotional disorders. 3 (of a line) at right angles, perpendicular. –**normal** *noun* 1 the normal value or standard etc. 2 a line at right angles. ☐ **normal distribution** a function that represents the distribution of many random variables as a symmetrical bell-shaped graph. **normalcy** *noun*, **normally** *adverb*, **normality** *noun*

normalise *verb* (also **-ize**) to make or become normal. **normalisation** *noun*

Norman *adjective* of the Normans. –**Norman** *noun* a member of the people of Normandy in northern France. ☐ **Norman Conquest** *see* **conquest**.

Normandy a region of NW France bordering on the English Channel.

normative (**norm**-ă-tiv) *adjective* of or establishing a norm.

Norse *adjective* of ancient Norway or Scandinavia. **–Norse** *noun* the Norwegian language or the Scandinavian group of languages. [from Dutch *noord* = north]

Norseman *noun* (*plural* **Norsemen**) a Viking.

north *noun* **1** the point or direction to the left of a person facing east. **2** the northern part of something. **–north** *adjective* & *adverb* towards or in the north; *a north wind*, blowing from the north. ☐ **North Pole** the northernmost point of the earth. **north pole** (of a magnet) the pole that is attracted to the north. **North Star** the pole star.

North America the northern half of the American land mass (*see* **America**).

northbound *adjective* travelling or leading northwards.

North Carolina (ka-rŏ-**ly**-nă) a State of the USA on the Atlantic coast.

North Dakota (dă-**koh**-tă) a State of the north central USA.

north-east *noun* the point or direction midway between north and east. **north-easterly** *adjective* & *noun*, **north-eastern** *adjective*

northeaster *noun* a north-east wind.

northerly *adjective* in or towards the north; *a northerly wind*, blowing from the north (approximately). **–northerly** *noun* a northerly wind.

northern *adjective* of or in the north. ☐ **Northern hemisphere** the half of the earth north of the equator. **northern lights** the aurora borealis.

northerner *noun* a native or inhabitant of the north.

Northern Ireland a unit of the UK comprising the six north-eastern districts (and former counties) of the island of Ireland.

northernmost *adjective* furthest north.

Northern Territory a self-governing territory in central northern Australia.

northing *noun* **1** a distance travelled or measured northward. **2** a northerly direction.

North Korea *see* **Korea**.

North Sea that part of the Atlantic Ocean between the mainland of Europe and the east coast of Britain.

northward *adjective* & *adverb* towards the north. **northwards** *adverb*

north-west *noun* the point or direction midway between north and west. **north-westerly** *adjective* & *noun*, **north-western** *adjective*

northwester *noun* a north-west wind.

North West Shelf an area of continental shelf off the north-west coast of Australia containing a huge natural gas field.

Norway a kingdom in northern Europe.

Norwegian *adjective* of Norway or its people or language. **–Norwegian** *noun* **1** a native or inhabitant of Norway. **2** the language of Norway.

Nos. *abbreviation* (also **nos.**) numbers.

nose *noun* **1** the organ at the front of the head in humans and animals, containing the nostrils and used for breathing and smelling. **2** a sense of smell. **3** the ability to detect things of a particular kind, *has a nose for scandal*. **4** the open end of a tube or piping etc. **5** the front end or projecting front part of something. **–nose** *verb* **1** to detect or search by using one's sense of smell. **2** to pry or search, *nosing around*. **3** to smell at; to rub with the nose; to push the nose against or into. **4** to push one's way cautiously ahead, *the car nosed past the obstruction*. ☐ **get up a person's nose** (*informal*) to annoy a person. **on the nose** (*Austral. informal*) smelling offensive; (of behaviour etc.) unacceptable. **pay through the nose** to pay an unfairly high price. **put a person's nose out of joint** to disconcert, frustrate, or make (a person) envious. **rub a person's nose in it** to remind him or her humiliatingly of an error. **turn up one's nose at** to reject or ignore contemptuously. **under one's nose** where one can or should see it clearly. **with one's nose in the air** haughtily.

nosebag *noun* a bag containing fodder, for hanging on a horse's head.

nosebleed *noun* bleeding from the nose.

nosedive *noun* **1** an aeroplane's steep downward plunge with the nose first. **2** any sudden drop or plunge. **–nosedive** *verb* to make such a dive or fall.

nosegay *noun* a small bunch of flowers. [from *nose* + *gay* = ornament]

nosh *noun* (*informal*) food. **–nosh** *verb* (*informal*) to eat. ☐ **nosh-up** *noun* (*informal*) a meal. [Yiddish]

nostalgia (nos-**tal**-jă) *noun* sentimental memory of or longing for things of the past.

[from Greek *nostos* = return home, + *algos* = pain (= homesickness)]

nostalgic (nos-**tal**-jik) *adjective* feeling or producing nostalgia. nostalgically *adverb*

Nostradamus (nos-tră-**dah**-mŭs), Michel de Notredame (1503–66), Provençal astrologer famous for his prophecies.

nostril *noun* either of the two openings in the nose through which air is admitted.

nostrum (**nos**-trŭm) *noun* a quack remedy.

nosy *adjective* inquisitive. □ Nosy Parker an inquisitive person. nosily *adverb*, nosiness *noun*

not *adverb* expressing a negative, denial, or refusal. not at all a polite reply to thanks.

notable *adjective* worthy of notice, remarkable, eminent. –notable *noun* an eminent person.

notably *adverb* remarkably; especially.

notary (**noh**-tă-ree) *noun* (in full notary public, *plural* notaries public) a person officially authorised to witness the signing of documents and to perform other formal transactions. notarial *adjective*

notation *noun* a system of signs or symbols representing numbers, quantities, musical notes, etc.

notch *noun* 1 a V-shaped cut or indentation. 2 each of the levels in a graded system, *everyone moved up a notch*. –notch *verb* 1 to make a notch or notches in. 2 to score, *notched up another win*.

note *noun* 1 a brief record of something, written down to aid the memory. 2 a short or informal letter; a memorandum; a formal diplomatic communication. 3 a short comment on or explanation of a word or passage in a book etc. 4 a written or printed promise to pay money; a banknote, *$5 notes*. 5 a tone of definite pitch made by a voice, instrument, or engine etc. 6 a written sign representing the pitch and duration of a musical sound. 7 any of the keys on a piano etc. 8 a significant sound or indication of feelings etc., *a note of optimism*. 9 eminence, distinction, *a family of note*. 10 notice, attention; *take note of what he says*, pay attention to it. –note *verb* 1 to notice, to pay attention to. 2 to write down, *noted it down*. [from Latin *nota* = a mark]

notebook *noun* 1 a book with blank pages on which to write memoranda. 2 a small portable computer.

notecase *noun* a wallet for holding bank notes.

noted *adjective* famous, well-known.

notelets *plural noun* a set of pieces of small folded ornamental notepaper.

notepaper *noun* paper for writing letters on.

noteworthy *adjective* worthy of notice, remarkable.

nothing *noun* 1 no thing, not anything. 2 no amount, nought. 3 non-existence; what does not exist. 4 a person or thing of no importance. –nothing *adverb* not at all, in no way, *it's nothing like as good*. □ for nothing without payment, free; without a reward or result. nothing doing (*informal*) a statement of refusal or failure.

notice *noun* 1 news or information of what has happened or is about to happen; *at short notice*, with little time for preparation. 2 a formal announcement that one is to end an agreement or leave a job at a specified time, *gave him a month's notice*. 3 written or printed information or instructions displayed publicly. 4 attention, observation, *it escaped my notice*. 5 an account or review in a newspaper. –notice *verb* 1 to perceive, to become aware of; to take notice of. 2 to remark upon, to speak of. □ take notice to show signs of interest; *take no notice of it*, ignore it, take no action about it. [from Latin *notus* = known]

noticeable *adjective* easily seen or noticed. noticeably *adverb*

noticeboard *noun* a board on which notices may be displayed.

notifiable *adjective* that must be notified; *notifiable diseases*, those that must be reported to the public health authorities.

notify *verb* (notified, notifying) 1 to inform. 2 to report, to make (a thing) known. notification *noun*

notion *noun* 1 an idea or opinion, especially one that is vague or probably incorrect. 2 an understanding or intention, *has no notion of discipline*. notions *plural noun* small items used in sewing (e.g. thread, buttons), haberdashery.

notional (**noh**-shŏ-năl) *adjective* hypothetical; assumed to be correct or valid for a particular purpose, *an estimate based on notional figures*. notionally *adverb*

notochord (noh-tŏ-kord) *noun* a rudimentary spinal cord or spinal column. [from Greek *noton* = back, + *chord²*]

notorious (nŏ-**tor**-ree-ŭs) *adjective* well-known, especially in an unfavourable way. **notoriously** *adverb*, **notoriety** (noh-tŏ-**ry**-ĕ-tee) *noun* [from Latin *notus* = known]

notwithstanding *preposition* in spite of. −**notwithstanding** *adverb* nevertheless.

Nouakchott (**nwak**-shot) the capital of Mauritania.

nougat (**noo**-gah) *noun* a chewy sweet made of nuts, sugar or honey, and egg white. [French]

nought (*pr*. nawt) *noun* **1** the figure 0. **2** nothing.

noughties *plural noun* (*informal*) the decade from 2000 to 2009.

Noumea (noo-**mee**-ă) the capital of New Caledonia.

noun *noun* a word or phrase used as the name of a person, place, or thing. □ **common nouns** words such as *man*, *dog*, *table*, and *sport*, which are used of whole classes of people or things. **proper nouns** words such as *John* and *Smith* and *Brisbane* which name a particular person or thing. [from Latin *nomen* = name]

nourish (**nu**-rish) *verb* **1** to keep (a person, animal, or plant) alive and healthy by means of food. **2** to foster or cherish (a feeling etc.). **nourishment** *noun* [from Latin *nutrire*]

nous (*rhymes with* house) *noun* (*informal*) common sense. [Greek, = the mind]

nouveau riche (noo-voh **reesh**) *noun* (*plural* **nouveaux riches**, *pr*. same) a person who has acquired wealth only recently, especially one who makes a display of it. [French, = new rich]

nouvelle cuisine (noo-vel kwi-**zeen**) *noun* a style of cooking that avoids traditional rich sauces and emphasises fresh ingredients and attractive presentation. [French, = new cookery]

nova (**noh**-vă) *noun* (*plural* **novae**) a star that suddenly becomes much brighter for a short time. [Latin, = new]

novel *noun* a book-length story. −**novel** *adjective* of a new kind, *a novel experience*. [from Latin *novus* = new]

novelette *noun* a short novel.

novelist *noun* a writer of novels.

novella *noun* (*plural* **novellas**) a short novel or narrative story. [Italian]

novelty *noun* **1** the quality of being novel. **2** a novel thing or occurrence. **3** a small unusual object, especially one suitable for giving as a present. [same origin as *novel*]

November *noun* the eleventh month of the year. [from Latin *novem* = nine, because it was the ninth month in the ancient Roman calendar]

novice (**nov**-ĭss) *noun* **1** a person who is inexperienced in the work etc. that he or she is doing, a beginner. **2** one who has been accepted into a religious order but has not yet taken the final vows.

noviciate (nŏ-**vish**-ee-ăt) *noun* the period of being a novice in a religious order.

now *adverb* **1** at the time when or of which one is writing or speaking. **2** by this time. **3** immediately, *must go now*. **4** (with no reference to time, giving an explanation or comfort etc.) I beg or wonder or warn you or am telling you, *now why didn't I think of that?* −**now** *conjunction* as a consequence of the fact, simultaneously with it, *now that you have come, we'll start*; *I do remember, now you mention it*. −**now** *noun* the present time, *they ought to be here by now*. □ **for now** until a later time, *goodbye for now*. **now and again** or **now and then** occasionally.

nowadays *adverb* at the present time (contrasted with years ago).

nowhere *adverb* not anywhere. −**nowhere** *pronoun* no place. □ **in the middle of nowhere** (*informal*) in a remote place.

nowise *adverb* in no way, not at all.

nowt *noun* (*informal* or *dialect*) nothing.

noxious (**nok**-shŭs) *adjective* unpleasant and harmful. [from Latin *noxius* = harmful]

nozzle *noun* the vent or spout of a hose etc. through which a stream of liquid or air is directed. [= little nose]

NSW *abbreviation* New South Wales.

NT *abbreviation* Northern Territory.

nth *adjective* **to the nth degree** to the utmost.

nuance (**new**-ahns) *noun* a subtle difference in meaning, a shade of meaning.

nub *noun* **1** a small knob or lump. **2** the central point or core of a matter or problem.

nubbly *adjective* full of small lumps.

Nubia (**new**-bee-ă) a region of southern Egypt and northern Sudan. **Nubian** *adjective* & *noun*

nubile (**new**-byl) *adjective* marriageable, physically attractive, *nubile young women*. [from Latin *nubere* = become the wife of]

nuclear *adjective* **1** of a nucleus. **2** of or using nuclear energy, *nuclear weapons*; *nuclear power*. ☐ **nuclear energy** energy that is released or absorbed during reactions taking place in the nuclei of atoms. **nuclear family** a father, mother, and their child or children. **nuclear physics** the branch of physics dealing with atomic nuclei and their reactions. **nuclear power** power generated by a nuclear reactor; a country that has nuclear weapons. **nuclear reactor** *see* **reactor**.

nucleate (**new**-klee-ayt) *verb* **1** to form into a nucleus. **2** to form a nucleus. **nucleated** *adjective*

nucleic acid (new-**klee**-ik) *noun* an acid of either of the two types (DNA and RNA) present in all living cells.

nucleon *noun* a proton or neutron. ☐ **nucleon number** the total number of protons and neutrons in a nucleus.

nucleonics (new-klee-**on**-iks) *noun* the branch of science and engineering that deals with the practical uses of nuclear energy. **nucleonic** *adjective*

nucleus (**new**-klee-ŭs) *noun* (*plural* **nuclei**, *pr.* **new**-klee-I) **1** the central part or thing round which others are collected. **2** something established that will receive additions, *this collection of books will form the nucleus of a new library*. **3** the central positively charged portion of an atom. **4** the central part of a seed or of a plant or animal cell. [Latin, = kernel]

nude *adjective* not clothed, naked. –**nude** *noun* a nude human figure in a painting etc. ☐ **in the nude** not clothed, naked. **nudity** *noun*

nudge *verb* **1** to poke (a person) gently with the elbow in order to draw his or her attention quietly. **2** to push slightly or gradually. –**nudge** *noun* this movement.

nudist (**newd**-ĭst) *noun* a person who believes that going unclothed is good for the health. **nudism** *noun*

nugatory (**new**-gă-tŏ-ree) *adjective* **1** futile, trivial. **2** inoperative, not valid.

nugget (**nug**-ĕt) *noun* **1** a rough lump of gold or platinum as found in the earth. **2** something small and valuable, *nuggets of information*.

nuggety *adjective* (*Austral.*) (of a person) thickset, stocky, sturdy.

nuisance *noun* a source of annoyance, an annoying person or thing.

nuke *noun* (*informal*) a nuclear bomb, weapon, etc.

Nuku'alofa (noo-koo-ă-**loh**-fă) the capital of Tonga.

null *adjective* **1** having no legal force, *declared the agreement null and void*. **2** (in mathematics) empty; having no elements, *null set*. **3** (of a matrix) all the elements of which are zeros. ☐ **null hypothesis** (in statistics) the hypothesis that differences in the data are due to chance fluctuation and not to the effect etc. that is being considered. **nullity** *noun* [from Latin *nullus* = none]

nulla-nulla *noun* a hardwood club, used traditionally by Aborigines for fighting and hunting. [Dharuk *ngala ngala*]

Nullarbor Plain a vast arid limestone plateau lying north of the Great Australian Bight. [Latin *nulla arbor* = not a tree]

nullify *verb* (**nullified**, **nullifying**) **1** to make (a thing) null. **2** to cancel or neutralise the effect of. **nullification** *noun*

numb *adjective* deprived of the power to feel or move, *numb with cold* or *shock*. –**numb** *verb* to make numb. **numbly** *adverb*, **numbness** *noun*

numbat *noun* the banded anteater, a small rare marsupial, now found only in SW Western Australia. [Nyungar *numbad*]

number *noun* **1** a symbol or word indicating how many, a numeral. **2** a numeral identifying a person or thing (e.g. a telephone or a house in a street) by its position in a series. **3** a single issue of a magazine. **4** a song or piece of music, etc., especially as an item in a theatrical performance. **5** (*informal*) a person or an object (such as a garment or car) considered as an item. **6** a total of people or things; *a number of*, some; *numbers of*, very many. **7** the category 'singular' or 'plural' in grammar. **8 Numbers** the fourth book of the Old Testament, telling of the wanderings of the Israelites in the desert. –**number** *verb* **1** to count, to find out how many. **2** to amount to. **3** to assign a number to (each in a series); to distinguish or identify by its position in a series. **4** to include or regard as, *I number him among my friends*. ☐ **his days are numbered** he has not long to live or to remain in his present position. **number one** (*informal*) oneself, *take care of number one*. **number plate** a plate on a motor vehicle showing its registration number.

numberless *adjective* innumerable.

numerable *adjective* able to be counted.

numeracy *noun* basic mathematical competence. (Compare *literacy*.)

numeral (**new**-mĕ-răl) *noun* a symbol that represents a certain number, a figure. [from Latin *numerus* = number]

numerate (**new**-mĕ-răt) *adjective* having basic mathematical competence.

numeration (new-mĕ-**ray**-shŏn) *noun* numbering.

numerator (**new**-mĕ-ray-ter) *noun* the number written above the line in a vulgar fraction, showing how many of the parts indicated by the denominator are to be taken (e.g. 2 in $\frac{2}{3}$).

numerical (new-**me**-rĭ-kăl) *adjective* of a number or series of numbers, *placed in numerical order*. **numerically** *adverb*

numerous (**new**-mĕ-rŭs) *adjective* many; consisting of many items. [from Latin *numerus* = number]

numinous (**new**-mĭ-nŭs) *adjective* 1 indicating the presence of a divinity. 2 spiritual; awe-inspiring. [from Latin *numen* = a presiding deity]

numismatics (new-miz-**mat**-iks) *noun* the scientific study of coins and similar objects (e.g. medals). **numismatist** *noun* [from Greek *nomisma* = coin]

numskull *noun* (also **numbskull**) a stupid person.

nun *noun* a member of a community of women living apart from the world under the rules of a religious order. [from Latin *nonna* = nun]

nuncio (**nun**-shee-oh) *noun* (*plural* **nuncios**) a diplomatic representative of the pope, accredited to a civil government. [Italian]

Nunga (**nung**-gă) *noun* an Aboriginal person from southern South Australia.

Usage see **aborigine**.

---

nunnery *noun* a convent for nuns.

nuptial (**nup**-shăl) *adjective* of marriage; of a wedding ceremony. **nuptials** *plural noun* a wedding.

nurse *noun* 1 a person trained to care for sick, injured, or infirm people. 2 a woman employed to take charge of young children. –**nurse** *verb* 1 to work as a nurse; to look after in this way. 2 to feed or be fed at the breast

or udder. 3 to hold carefully. 4 to give special care to, *nursed her new seedlings*. 5 to harbour or nurture (a grudge etc.). □ **nursing home** a privately run hospital or home for sick or elderly people. [same origin as *nourish*]

nursemaid *noun* a young woman employed to take charge of young children.

nursery *noun* 1 a room or place set apart for young children. 2 a place where young children are looked after while parents are working etc. 3 a place where young plants are reared for transplantation and usually for sale. □ **nursery rhyme** a simple traditional song or story in rhyme for children. **nursery slopes** easy slopes suitable for beginners at a skiing resort.

nurseryman *noun* (*plural* **nurserymen**) an owner of or worker in a plant nursery.

nursling *noun* (also **nurseling**) a baby or young animal that is being suckled.

nurture (**ner**-cher) *verb* 1 to nourish and rear. 2 to bring up, *a delicately nurtured girl*. –**nurture** *noun* nurturing; nourishment.

nut *noun* 1 fruit consisting of a hard shell round an edible kernel. 2 this kernel. 3 (*informal*) the head. 4 (*informal*) an insane or eccentric person. 5 a small piece of metal with a hole in its centre, designed for use with a bolt; *the nuts and bolts of something*, practical details. 6 a small lump of a solid substance, e.g. coal or butter.

nutcrackers *plural noun* a pair of pincers for cracking nuts.

nuthatch *noun* a small climbing bird that feeds on nuts and insects, a sittella.

nutmeg *noun* the hard fragrant seed of a tropical tree, ground or grated as spice.

nutrient (**new**-tree-ĕnt) *adjective* nourishing. –**nutrient** *noun* a nourishing substance. [from Latin *nutrire* = nourish]

nutriment (**new**-trĭ-mĕnt) *noun* nourishing food.

nutrition (new-**trish**-ŏn) *noun* nourishment. **nutritional** *adjective*, **nutritionally** *adverb*

nutritious (new-**trish**-ŭs) *adjective* nourishing, efficient as food. **nutritiousness** *noun*

nutritive (**new**-trĭ-tiv) *adjective* nourishing. –**nutritive** *noun* a nourishing substance.

nuts *adjective* (*informal*) crazy.

nutshell *noun* the hard outer shell of a nut. □ **in a nutshell** expressed in the briefest possible way.

nutty *adjective* **1** full of nuts. **2** tasting like nuts. **3** (*informal*) crazy. **nuttiness** *noun*

Nuuk the capital of Greenland, formerly known as Godthaab.

nuzzle *verb* to press or rub gently with the nose.

NW *abbreviation* north-west, north-western.

nylon *noun* **1** a synthetic fibre of great lightness and strength. **2** fabric made from this.

nymph (*pr*. nimf) *noun* **1** (in mythology) a semi-divine maiden living in the sea or woods etc. **2** a young insect that resembles its parents in form.

nymphomania (nim-fŏ-**may**-nee-ă) *noun* excessive sexual desire in a woman. **nymphomaniac** *noun* & *adjective*

Nyoongah (**n'yuung**-ah) *noun* an Aboriginal person from the region around Perth in Western Australia.

Usage see aborigine.

Nyungar (**n'yuung**-ah) *noun* **1** a member of an Aboriginal people of south-western WA. **2** their language.

NZ *abbreviation* New Zealand.

Oo

O *interjection* = **oh**.

O' *preposition* of, *six o'clock*.

oaf *noun* (*plural* **oafs**) an awkward lout; a stupid person. **oafish** *adjective*

oak *noun* **1** a deciduous forest tree with irregularly-shaped leaves, bearing acorns. **2** its wood.

oaken *adjective* made of oak.

oakum *noun* loose fibre obtained by picking old rope to pieces.

OAM *abbreviation* Medal of the Order of Australia.

oar *noun* **1** a pole with a flat blade at one end, used to propel a boat by its leverage against water. **2** a rower. □ **put one's oar in** to interfere.

oarsman, **oarswoman** *nouns* a rower.

oarsmanship *noun* skill in rowing.

oasis (oh-**ay**-sĭs) *noun* (*plural* **oases**, *pr.* oh-**ay**-seez) **1** a fertile spot in a desert, with a spring or well of water. **2** an area or period of calm.

oast *noun* a kiln for drying hops. □ **oast house** a building containing this.

oath *noun* **1** a solemn undertaking or declaration, appealing to God or a revered object as witness. **2** casual use of the name of God etc. in anger or to give emphasis. □ **on** or **under oath** having made a solemn oath.

oatmeal *noun* **1** meal prepared from oats, used to make porridge etc. **2** greyish-fawn colour.

oats *plural noun* **1** a hardy cereal plant grown in cool climates for food. **2** its grain. □ **sow one's wild oats** to lead a wild life while young.

OAU *abbreviation* Organisation of African Unity.

ob- *prefix* (changing to **oc-** before *c*, **of-** before *f*, **op-** before *p*) **1** to; towards (as in *observe*). **2** against (as in *opponent*). **3** in the way; blocking (as in *obstruct*). [from Latin *ob* = towards, against]

Obadiah (oh-bǎ-**dy**-ǎ) **1** a Hebrew minor prophet. **2** a book of the Old Testament, bearing his name.

obbligato (ob-lĭ-**gah**-toh) *noun* (*plural* **obbligatos**) an important accompanying part in a musical composition. [Italian]

obdurate *adjective* (**ob**-dew-rǎt) *adjective* stubborn and unyielding. **obduracy** *noun*

OBE *abbreviation* Officer of the Order of the British Empire.

obeah (**oh**-bee-ǎ) *noun* (also **obi**) a kind of African sorcery practised in the West Indies.

obedient *adjective* doing what one is told to do, willing to obey. **obediently** *adverb*, **obedience** *noun*

obeisance (ŏ-**bay**-sǎns) *noun* a deep bow or curtsy. **obeisant** *adjective*

obelisk (**ob**-ĕ-lisk) *noun* a tall pillar set up as a monument. [from Greek, = little rod]

obese (oh-**beess**) *adjective* very fat. **obesity** (ŏ-**bee**-sĭ-tee) *noun* [from Latin *obesus* = having over-eaten]

obey *verb* (**obeyed**, **obeying**) to do what is commanded by (a person, law, or instinct etc.); to be obedient.

obfuscate (**ob**-fŭs-kayt) *verb* **1** to make (a subject) obscure. **2** to bewilder. **obfuscation** *noun*

obituary (ŏ-**bit**-yǎ-ree) *noun* a notice of a person's death, especially in a newspaper, often with a short account of his or her life and achievements.

object (**ob**-jekt) *noun* **1** something solid that can be seen or touched. **2** a person or thing to which some action or feeling is directed, *an object of pity*. **3** a purpose, an intention. **4** (in grammar) a noun or its equivalent acted upon by a transitive verb or by a preposition ('him' is the object in *the dog bit him* and *against him*). –**object** (ŏb-**jekt**) *verb* to say that one is not in favour of something, to protest. □ **direct object** the noun or its equivalent directly affected by the action of a transitive verb (see sense 4); **indirect object** the noun or its equivalent indirectly affected; in *send him a letter*, 'the letter' is the direct object and 'him' (= to him) is the indirect object. **no object** not forming an important or limiting factor; *expense no object*, the cost will not be grudged. **object lesson** a striking practical illustration of some principle. **objector** *noun* [from *ob-* = in the way, + Latin *-jectum* = thrown]

objection *noun* **1** a feeling of disapproval or opposition; a statement of this. **2** a reason for objecting; a drawback in a plan etc.

objectionable *adjective* causing objections or disapproval, unpleasant. **objectionably** *adverb*

objective (ŏb-**jek**-tiv) *adjective* **1** having real existence outside a person's mind, not subjective. **2** not influenced by personal feelings or opinions, *an objective account of the problem*. **3** (in grammar) of the objective case. **–objective** *noun* something one is trying to achieve or to reach or capture. □ **objective case** the form of a word used when it is the object of a verb or preposition. **objectively** *adverb*

objet d'art (ob-*zh*ay **dar**) *noun* (*plural* **objets d'art**, *pr.* same) a small artistic object. [French, = object of art]

oblate (**ob**-layt) *adjective* (of a spheroid) flattened at the poles.

oblation (ŏb-**lay**-shŏn) *noun* an offering to a divine being.

obligation *noun* **1** being obliged to do something. **2** what one must do in order to comply with an agreement or law etc., one's duty. □ **under an obligation** owing gratitude to another person for some service or benefit.

obligatory (ŏ-**blig**-ă-tŏ-ree) *adjective* required by law, rule, or custom; compulsory, not optional.

oblige *verb* **1** to compel by law, agreement, custom, or necessity. **2** to help or gratify by performing a small service, *oblige me with a loan*. □ **be obliged to a person** to be indebted to him or her for some service. [from *ob-* = to, + Latin *ligare* = bind]

obliging *adjective* courteous and helpful. **obligingly** *adverb*

oblique (ŏ-**bleek**) *adjective* **1** slanting. **2** expressed indirectly, not going straight to the point, *an oblique reply*. □ **oblique angle** an acute or obtuse angle. **obliquely** *adverb*

obliterate (ŏ-**blit**-ĕ-rayt) *verb* to blot out, to destroy leaving no clear traces. **obliteration** *noun* [from Latin, = erase (*ob* = over, *littera* = letter)]

oblivion (ŏ-**bliv**-ee-ŏn) *noun* **1** the state of being forgotten. **2** the state of being oblivious.

oblivious (ŏ-**bliv**-ee-ŭs) *adjective* unaware or unconscious of something, *oblivious of* or *to her surroundings*.

oblong *noun* a rectangular shape with one pair of sides longer than the other. **–oblong** *adjective* having this shape.

obnoxious (ŏb-**nok**-shŭs) *adjective* very unpleasant, objectionable. **obnoxiously** *adverb*

oboe (**oh**-boh) *noun* a woodwind instrument of treble pitch. **oboist** *noun* [from French *haut* = high, + *bois* = wood]

obscene (ŏb-**seen**) *adjective* indecent in a repulsive or very offensive way. **obscenely** *adverb*

obscenity (ŏb-**sen**-ĭ-tee) *noun* **1** being obscene. **2** an obscene action or word etc.

obscure *adjective* **1** dark, indistinct. **2** remote from people's observation. **3** not famous, *an obscure poet*. **4** not easily understood, not clearly expressed. **–obscure** *verb* to make obscure, to conceal from view. **obscurely** *adverb*, **obscurity** *noun*

obsequies (**ob**-sĕ-kweez) *plural noun* funeral rites.

obsequious (ŏb-**see**-kwee-ŭs) *adjective* excessively or sickeningly respectful. **obsequiously** *adverb*, **obsequiousness** *noun*

observable *adjective* able to be observed.

observance *noun* the keeping of a law, rule, or custom etc.; the keeping or celebrating of a religious festival or of a holiday.

observant *adjective* quick at noticing things. **observantly** *adverb*

observation *noun* **1** observing; being observed. **2** a comment or remark.

observatory (ŏb-**zerv**-ă-tŏ-ree) *noun* a building designed and equipped for scientific observation of the stars, weather, etc.

observe *verb* **1** to see and notice; to watch carefully. **2** to pay attention to (rules etc.). **3** to keep or celebrate (a religious festival or holiday). **4** to remark. **observer** *noun* [from *ob-* = towards, + Latin *servare* = to watch]

obsess (ŏb-**sess**) *verb* to occupy the thoughts of (a person) continually.

obsession (ŏb-**sesh**-ŏn) *noun* **1** obsessing; being obsessed. **2** a persistent idea that dominates a person's thoughts. **obsessional** *adjective*

obsessive *adjective* of or causing or showing obsession. **obsessively** *adverb*

obsidian (ŏb-**sid**-ee-ăn) *noun* a dark glassy kind of hardened lava or volcanic rock.

obsolescent (ob-sŏ-**less**-ĕnt) *adjective* becoming obsolete, going out of use or out of fashion. **obsolescence** *noun*

obsolete (**ob**-sŏ-leet) *adjective* no longer used, antiquated. [from Latin *obsoletus* = worn out]

obstacle *noun* a thing that obstructs progress. □ **obstacle race** a race in which artificial or natural obstacles have to be passed. [from *ob-* = in the way, + Latin *stare* = to stand]

obstetrician (ob-stĕ-**trish**-ăn) *noun* a specialist in obstetrics.

obstetrics (ŏb-**stet**-riks) *noun* the branch of medicine and surgery that deals with childbirth. **obstetric** *adjective*, **obstetrical** *adjective* [from Latin, = of a midwife]

obstinate *adjective* **1** keeping firmly to one's opinion or to one's chosen course of action, not easily persuaded. **2** not easily overcome. **obstinately** *adverb*, **obstinacy** *noun*

obstreperous (ŏb-**strep**-ĕ-rŭs) *adjective* noisy, unruly. **obstreperously** *adverb*

obstruct *verb* **1** to prevent or hinder movement along (a path etc.) by means of an object or objects placed in it, *obstructing the highway*. **2** to prevent or hinder the movement, progress, or activities of, *obstructing the public*.

obstruction *noun* **1** obstructing; being obstructed. **2** a thing that obstructs.

obstructive *adjective* causing or intended to cause obstruction.

obtain *verb* **1** to get, to come into possession of (a thing) by effort or as a gift. **2** to be established or in use as a rule or custom, *this custom still obtains in some countries*. **obtainable** *adjective* [from *ob-* = to, + Latin *tenere* = hold]

obtrude (ŏb-**trood**) *verb* to force (oneself or one's ideas) on others. **obtrusion** *noun* [from *ob-*, + Latin *trudere* = to push]

obtrusive (ŏb-**troo**-siv) *adjective* obtruding oneself; unpleasantly noticeable. **obtrusively** *adverb*

obtuse (ŏb-**tewss**) *adjective* **1** of blunt shape, not sharp or pointed. **2** stupid, slow at understanding. □ **obtuse angle** an angle of more than 90° but less than 180°. **obtusely**

adverb, **obtuseness** *noun* [from *ob-* = towards, + Latin *tusum* = blunted]

obverse (**ob**-verss) *noun* the side of a coin or medal etc. that bears the head or the principal design. [from *ob-* = towards, + Latin *versum* = turned]

obviate (**ob**-vee-ayt) *verb* to make unnecessary, *the bypass obviates the need to drive through the town*.

obvious *adjective* easy to see or recognise or to understand. **obviously** *adverb* [from Latin *ob viam* = in the way]

oc- *prefix* see **ob-**.

occasion *noun* **1** the time at which a particular event takes place. **2** a special event, *this is quite an occasion*. **3** a suitable time for doing something, an opportunity. **4** a need, a reason, or cause, *had no occasion to speak French*. –**occasion** *verb* to cause. □ **on occasion** when need arises, occasionally.

occasional *adjective* **1** happening from time to time but not regularly or frequently, *occasional showers*. **2** used or meant for a special event, *occasional verses*. **occasionally** *adverb*

Occident (**ok**-sĭ-dĕnt) *noun* the West as opposed to the Orient. [from Latin, = sunset]

occidental (ok-sĭ-**den**-t'l) *adjective* western. –**Occidental** *noun* a native of the western world.

occiput (**ok**-sĭ-pŭt) *noun* the back of the head. **occipital** (ok-**sip**-ĭ-t'l) *adjective* [from *oc-*, + Latin *caput* = head]

occlude *verb* to stop up, to obstruct. □ **occluded front** the atmospheric condition that occurs when a cold front overtakes a mass of warm air, and warm air is driven upwards, producing a long period of steady rain. **occlusion** *noun*

occult (ŏ-**kult**) *adjective* secret, hidden except from those with more than ordinary or natural knowledge. [from Latin *occultum* = hidden]

occupant *noun* a person occupying a place, dwelling, or position. **occupancy** *noun*

occupation *noun* **1** occupying; being occupied. **2** taking or holding possession by force, especially of a defeated country or district. **3** an activity that keeps a person busy; one's employment.

occupational *adjective* of or caused by one's □ occupation, *an occupational disease*. **occupational therapy** mental or physical activities designed to aid recovery from certain illnesses.

occupy *verb* (occupied, occupying) **1** to dwell in, to inhabit. **2** to take possession of and establish one's troops in (a country or strategic position etc.) in war. **3** to place oneself in (a building etc.) as a political or other demonstration. **4** to take up or fill (space or a position). **5** to hold as one's official position, *he occupies the post of manager*. **6** to keep (a person or his or her time) filled with activity. **occupier** *noun*

occur *verb* (occurred, occurring) **1** to come into being as an event or process. **2** to be found to exist in some place or conditions, *these plants occur in marshy areas*. □ **occur to** to come into the mind of.

occurrence (ŏ-**ku**-rĕns) *noun* **1** occurring. **2** an incident or event.

ocean *noun* **1** the seas surrounding the continents of the earth, especially one of the very large named areas of this, *the Atlantic, Pacific, Indian, Arctic, and Southern Oceans*. **2** an immense expanse or amount. □ **ocean-going** *adjective* (of ships) made for crossing the sea, not for coastal or river journeys. [from Oceanus, the river that the ancient Greeks thought surrounded the world]

Oceania (oh-shee-**ah**-nee-ă) the islands of the Pacific Ocean and adjacent seas. **Oceanian** *adjective* & *noun*

oceanic (oh-shee-**an**-ik) *adjective* of the ocean.

oceanography (oh-shă-**nog**-ră-fee) *noun* the scientific study of the ocean. **oceanographer** *noun* [from ocean + -graphy]

ocelot (**o**-sĕ-lot) *noun* **1** a leopard-like cat of Central and South America. **2** its fur.

ochre (**oh**-ker) *noun* **1** a yellow, red, or brownish mineral consisting of clay and iron oxide, used as a pigment. **2** pale brownish yellow.

ocker *noun* a rough and uncultivated Australian male (especially as a stereotype). **–ocker** *adjective* characteristic of an ocker; distinctively Australian.

o'clock *adverb* **1** = of the clock (used in specifying the hour), *six o'clock*. **2** according to a method for indicating relative position by imagining a clock dial with the observer at the centre, 'twelve o'clock' being directly ahead or above, *enemy aircraft are approaching at two o'clock*. [short for *of the clock*]

octa- *prefix* (also octo-) eight. [from Greek *okto* = eight]

octagon (**ok**-tă-gŏn) *noun* a geometric figure with eight sides. **octagonal** (ok-**tag**-ŏ-năl) *adjective* having eight sides. [from *octa-*, + Greek *gonia* = angle]

octahedron (ok-tă-**hee**-drŏn) *noun* a solid geometric shape with eight faces.

octane (**ok**-tayn) *noun* a hydrocarbon compound occurring in petrol.

octave (**ok**-tăv) *noun* **1** a series of eight consecutive notes on a scale, between and including the upper and lower note; the interval between the upper and lower note; each of these two notes; these two notes played together. **2** a verse of eight lines, especially the first eight lines of a sonnet. [from Latin *octavus* = eighth]

octet (ok-**tet**) *noun* **1** a group of eight instruments or voices; a musical composition for these. **2** the first eight lines of a sonnet. [from *octo-*]

octo- *prefix* see octa-.

October *noun* the tenth month of the year. [from Latin *octo* = eight, because it was the eighth month in the ancient Roman calendar]

octogenarian (ok-toh-jĕ-**nair**-ree-ăn) *noun* a person who is in his or her eighties. [from Latin *octogeni* = 80 each]

octopus *noun* (*plural* octopuses) a sea animal with a soft body and eight long tentacles. [from *octo-*, + Greek *pous* = foot]

ocular (**ok**-yŭ-ler) *adjective* of, for, or by the eyes; visual. [from Latin *oculus* = eye]

oculist (**ok**-yŭ-lĭst) *noun* a specialist in the treatment of diseases and defects of the eyes.

odd *adjective* **1** unusual, strange, eccentric, *an odd sort of person*. **2** not regular or habitual or fixed, *does odd jobs*; *at odd moments*. **3** (of a number) not even, not exactly divisible by 2; designated by such a number. **4** being the remaining one of a set or series of which the other member(s) are lacking, *found an odd glove*; *several odd volumes*; *you're wearing odd socks*, two that do not form a pair. **5** exceeding a round number or amount, *keep the odd money*; *forty odd*, between 40 and 50. □ **odd man out** a person or thing differing in some way from others of a group. **oddly** *adverb*, **oddness** *noun*

oddity *noun* **1** strangeness. **2** an unusual person, thing, or event.

oddment *noun* something left over, an isolated article.

odds *plural noun* **1** the probability that a certain thing will happen; this expressed as a ratio, *the odds are 5 to 1 against throwing a six*. **2** the ratio between amounts staked by parties to a bet, *gave odds of 3 to 1*. □ **at odds with** in disagreement or conflict with. **it makes no odds** it makes no difference; *it's no odds to him*, does not concern him. **odds and ends** oddments. **odds-on** *adjective* with success more likely than failure; with betting odds in favour of its success.

ode *noun* a poem expressing noble feelings, often addressed to a person or celebrating an event. [from Greek *oide* = song]

Odin (**oh**-din) (*Scand. myth.*) the supreme god and creator.

odious (**oh**-dee-ŭs) *adjective* hateful, detestable. **odiously** *adverb*, **odiousness** *noun*

odium (**oh**-dee-ŭm) *noun* widespread hatred or disgust felt towards a person or actions. [Latin, = hatred]

odometer (oh-**dom**-ĕ-ter) *noun* an instrument for measuring the distance travelled by a wheeled vehicle. [from Greek *hodos* = way, + *meter*]

odour (**oh**-der) *noun* a smell. **odorous** *adjective* [Latin *odor* = smell]

odourless *adjective* without odour.

Odysseus (ŏ-**dis**-ee-ŭs) (*Gk. legend*) king of Ithaca (called Ulysses by the Romans) who took ten years to return to Ithaca after the Trojan Wars while his wife Penelope waited.

odyssey (**od**-ĭ-see) *noun* (*plural* **odysseys**) a long adventurous journey. [named after the *Odyssey*, a Greek epic poem telling of the wanderings of Odysseus]

OECD *abbreviation* Organisation for Economic Cooperation and Development.

oedema (ĕ-**dee**-mă) *noun* excess of fluid in body tissues, causing swelling. Also called *dropsy*.

Oedipus (**ee**-dĭ-pŭs) (*Gk. legend*) son of Laius, king of Thebes, and his wife Jocasta. Unaware of his own identity, he killed his father and married his mother. □ **Oedipus complex** sexual feeling towards one's parent of the opposite sex.

oenology (ee-**nol**-ŏ-jee) *noun* the study of wines. **oenologist** *noun* [from Greek *oinos* = wine, + *-logy*]

o'er *preposition & adverb* (*poetic*) over.

oesophagus (ĕ-**sof**-ă-gŭs) *noun* the canal from the mouth to the stomach, the gullet.

oestrogen (**ees**-trŏ-jĕn) *noun* a hormone capable of developing and maintaining female bodily characteristics.

of *preposition* **1** indicating relationships. belonging to; originating from. **2** concerning, *told us of his travels*. **3** composed or made from, *built of brick*. **4** with reference or regard to, *never heard of it*. **5** for, involving, directed towards, *love of one's country*. **6** so as to bring separation or relief from, *cured him of smoking*. **7** during, *he comes of an evening*. □ **of itself** by itself or in itself.

of- *prefix* see **ob-**.

off *adverb* **1** away, at or to a distance, *rode off*; *is 5 kilometres* or *3 years off*. **2** out of position, not touching or attached, separate, *take the lid off*. **3** disconnected, not functioning, no longer obtainable, cancelled, *turn the gas off*; *the wedding is off*; *take the day off*, away from work. **4** to the end, completely, so as to be clear, *finish off*; *sell them off*. **5** situated as regards money or supplies, *how are you off for cash?* **6** (in a theatre) behind or at the side(s) of the stage, *noises off*. **7** (of food) beginning to decay. –**off** *preposition* **1** from, away from, not on, *fell off a ladder*; *off duty*. **2** abstaining from, not attracted to for the time being, *is off his food* or *off smoking*; *off form* or *off his game*, not performing as well as usual. **3** leading from, not far from, *in a street off the Mall*. **4** deducted from, *$5 off the price*. **5** at sea a short distance from, *sank $5 off Cape Horn*. –**off** *adjective* **1** (of a part of a vehicle, horse, or road) on the right-hand side, *the off front wheel*. **2** in or from or towards the side of a cricket field towards which the batsman's feet are pointed when receiving the ball. –**off** *noun* **1** the off side in cricket. **2** the start of a race etc., *ready for the off*. □ **off chance** a slight possibility. **off colour** not in the best of health. **off day** a day when a person is not at his or her best. **off-key** *adjective* out of tune. **off-peak** *adjective* in or used at a time that is less popular or less busy, *off-peak electricity*. **off-putting** *adjective* (*informal*) repellent, disconcerting. **off-season** *noun* the time when business etc. is fairly slack. **off-stage** *adjective & adverb* not on the stage, not visible to the audience. **off white** white with a grey or yellowish tinge.

offal *noun* the edible parts (e.g. heart, kidneys, liver, head) that are considered less valuable than the flesh when an animal carcass is cut up for food.

offbeat *adjective* unconventional, unusual.

offcut *noun* a remnant of timber etc.

offence *noun* **1** breaking of the law, an illegal act. **2** a feeling of annoyance or resentment, *give* or *take offence*.

offend *verb* **1** to cause offence or displeasure to. **2** to do wrong, *offend against the law*. **offender** *noun*

offensive *adjective* **1** causing offence, insulting, *offensive remarks*. **2** disgusting, repulsive, *an offensive smell*. **3** used in attacking, aggressive, *offensive weapons*. –**offensive** *noun* an aggressive action or campaign; *take the offensive*, to begin hostilities. **offensively** *adverb*, **offensiveness** *noun*

offer *verb* (**offered, offering**) **1** to present (a thing) so that it may be accepted or rejected, or considered. **2** to state what one is willing to do, pay, or give. **3** to show for sale. **4** to provide, to give opportunity, *the job offers prospects of promotion.* –**offer** *noun* **1** an expression of willingness to give, do, or pay something. **2** an amount offered, *offers above $500*. □ **on offer** for sale at a certain price or at a reduced price. [from *of-* = to, + Latin *ferre* = bring]

offering *noun* a gift or contribution etc. that is offered.

offertory *noun* **1** the act of offering bread and wine for consecration at the Eucharist. **2** money collected in a religious service.

offhand *adjective* **1** without previous thought or preparation. **2** (of behaviour etc.) casual or curt and unceremonious. –**offhand** *adverb* in an offhand way. **offhanded** *adjective*, **offhandedly** *adverb*

office *noun* **1** a room or building used as a place of business, especially for clerical and similar work or for a special department, *the enquiry office*. **2** the staff working there. **3** the premises, staff, or authority of certain government departments, *the Tax Office*. **4** a position of authority or trust, the holding of an official position, *seek office; be in office,* hold such a position. **5** an authorised form of Christian worship, *the Office for the Dead*. **6** a piece of kindness or a service, *through the good offices of his friends; the last offices,* ceremonial rites for the dead.

□ **office block** a large building designed to contain business offices. **office hours** the hours during which a business is open.

officer *noun* **1** a person holding a position of authority or trust, an official, *customs officers*. **2** a person who holds authority in any of the armed services or on a passenger ship. **3** a policeman or policewoman.

official *adjective* **1** of an office or position of authority, *in his official capacity*. **2** suitable for or characteristic of officials and bureaucracy, *official red tape*. **3** properly authorised, *the news is official*. –**official** *noun* a person holding office. **officially** *adverb*

officialdom *noun* officials collectively.

officiate (ŏ-**fish**-ee-ayt) *verb* to act in an official capacity, to be in charge.

officious (ŏ-**fish**-ŭs) *adjective* asserting one's authority, bossy. **officiously** *adverb*

offing *noun* **in the offing** in view, not far away in distance or future time.

offline *adjective* & *adverb* not controlled by or connected to a computer; unavailable on or not connected to the Internet.

offload *verb* to unload.

offset *verb* (**offset, offsetting**) to counterbalance or compensate for. –**offset** *noun* **1** an offshoot. **2** a method of printing in which the ink is transferred to a rubber surface and from this to paper.

offshoot *noun* **1** a side shoot. **2** a subsidiary product.

offshore *adjective* & *adverb* **1** (of wind) blowing from the land towards the sea. **2** at sea some distance from the shore. **3** (of goods, funds, etc.) made or registered overseas, *offshore investments; printed offshore*.

offside *adjective* & *adverb* **1** (of a player in soccer etc.) in a position where he or she may not legally play the ball. **2** opposed; not supportive.

offsider *noun* (*Austral.*) a partner or assistant.

offspring *noun* (*plural* **offspring**) **1** the child or children of a particular person or persons. **2** the young of an animal.

oft *adverb* (*old use*) often.

often *adverb* **1** frequently, many times, at short intervals. **2** in many instances.

ogee (**oh**-jee) *noun* the line of a double continuous curve, as in S.

ogive (**oh**-jyv) *noun* **1** a diagonal groin or rib of a vault. **2** a pointed arch. **3** (in statistics) a cumulative frequency graph.

ogle (oh-gŭl) *verb* to eye flirtatiously.

ogre *noun* **1** a cruel or man-eating giant in fairy tales and legends. **2** a terrifying person. **ogress** *feminine noun*

oh *interjection* **1** an exclamation of surprise, delight, desire, or pain. **2** used for emphasis, *oh yes I will!*

Ohio (oh-**hy**-oh) a State of the north-eastern USA.

ohm (*rhymes with* Rome) *noun* a unit of electrical resistance. [named after the German physicist G. S. Ohm (1787–1854)]

ohmmeter (**ohm**-mee-ter) *noun* a device for measuring electrical resistance in ohms.

Ohm's Law *noun* the law that current is directly proportional to voltage and inversely proportional to resistance.

oil *noun* **1** a thick slippery liquid that will not dissolve in water. **2** petroleum. **3** a form of petroleum used as fuel, *oil-heater*. **4** oil paint. **5** (*informal*) an oil painting. –**oil** *verb* to apply oil to, to lubricate or treat with oil; *oiled silk*, silk made waterproof by being treated with oil. **oils** *plural noun* oil paints; oilskins. □ **oil colour** oil paint. **oil-fired** *adjective* using oil as fuel. **oil paint** paint made by mixing powdered pigment in oil. **oil painting** a picture painted in oil colours; *she is no oil painting*, is ugly. **oil tanker** a ship with tanks for transporting oil in bulk. [from Latin *oleum* = olive oil]

oilcake *noun* cattle food made from linseed or similar seeds after the oil has been pressed out.

oilcan *noun* a can with a long nozzle through which oil flows, used for oiling machinery.

oilcloth *noun* strong fabric treated with oil and used to cover tables etc.

oilfield *noun* an area where oil is found in the ground or beneath the sea.

oilskin *noun* cloth waterproofed by treatment with oil. **oilskins** *plural noun* waterproof clothing made of this.

oily *adjective* (**oilier**, **oiliest**) **1** of or like oil; covered in oil; containing much oil. **2** unpleasantly smooth in manner; trying to win favour by flattery. **oiliness** *noun*

ointment *noun* a thick slippery paste rubbed on the skin to heal roughness or injuries or inflammation etc.

OK *adverb* & *adjective* (*informal*) all right, satisfactory. –**OK** *noun* (*informal*) approval, agreement to a plan etc. –**OK** *verb* (*informal*) to give one's approval or agreement to. [perhaps from the initials of *oll* (or *orl*) *korrect*, a humorous spelling of *all correct*, first used in the USA in 1839]

okapi (ŏ-**kah**-pee) *noun* (*plural* **okapis**) an animal of Central Africa, like a giraffe but with a shorter neck and a striped body.

okay *adverb*, *adjective*, *noun*, & *verb* (*informal*) = **OK**.

Oklahoma a State of the south central USA.

okra (**oh**-kră *or* ok-ră) *noun* a tropical plant with seed pods that are used as a vegetable.

old *adjective* **1** having lived or existed for a long time. **2** made long ago; used, established, or known for a long time. **3** shabby from age or wear. **4** of a particular age, *ten years old*, *a ten-year-old*. **5** not recent or modern, *in the old days*. **6** former, original, *in its old place*; *old boy* or *old girl*, a former pupil of a school. **7** skilled through long experience, *an old hand at negotiating*. **8** (*informal*) used for emphasis in friendly or casual mention, *good old Bob*; *any old time*. □ **the old** old people. **of old** of or in former times; *we know him of old*, since long ago. **old age** the period of a person's life from about 65 or 70 onwards. **Old Bailey** the Central Criminal Court in London. **old boy network** discrimination in employment, especially favouring former fellow students of private schools. **old country** a native country. **old-fashioned** *adjective* in a fashion that is no longer in style; having the ways or tastes current in former times. **old gold** dull gold colour. **old hand** an experienced person. **old hat** (*informal*) tediously familiar or outdated. **old maid** an elderly spinster. **old-maidish** *adjective* fussy and prim. **old man** (*informal*) one's employer, manager, husband, or father. **old man kangaroo** a fully grown male kangaroo. **old man saltbush** a drought-resistant fodder shrub of the Australian interior. **old man's beard** a kind of clematis with masses of grey fluffy hairs round the seeds. **old master** a great painter of former times (especially the 13th–17th centuries in Europe); a painting by such a painter. **Old Nick** the Devil. **old school tie** group loyalty amongst ex-students especially of private schools. **Old Testament** *see* **testament**. **old-time** *adjective* belonging to former times. **old-timer** *noun* a person with long experience or standing. **old wives' tale** an old but foolish belief. **old woman** a fussy or timid man; (*informal*) one's wife or mother. **Old World** Europe, Asia, and Africa, as distinct from the Americas. **oldish** *adjective*, **oldness** *noun*

olden *adjective* (*old use*) of old; old.

oldie *noun* (*informal*) an old person or thing.

oleaginous (o-lee-**aj**-ĭ-nŭs *or* oh-) *adjective* like oil. [from Latin *oleum* = oil]

oleander (o-lee-**an**-der *or* oh-) *noun* a poisonous evergreen shrub with red, white, yellow, or pink flowers.

olfactory (ol-**fak**-tŏ-ree) *adjective* concerned with smelling, *olfactory organs*.

Olgas, the *see* Kata Tjuta.

oligarch (**ol**-ĭ-gark) *noun* a member of an oligarchy.

oligarchy (**ol**-ĭ-gar-kee) *noun* **1** a form of government in which power is in the hands of a few people. **2** these people. **3** a country governed in this way. [from Greek *oligoi* = few, + *arkhein* = to rule]

Oligocene (**ol**-ĭ-gŏ-seen) *adjective* of the third epoch of the Tertiary period. **–Oligocene** *noun* this period.

Oliphant, Sir Mark (Marcus) Laurence Elwin (1901–2000), Australian nuclear physicist, Governor of SA 1971–76.

olive *noun* **1** a small oval fruit with a hard stone and bitter pulp from which an oil (*olive oil*) is obtained. **2** the evergreen tree that bears it. **3** a greenish colour. **–olive** *adjective* greenish like an unripe olive; (of the complexion) yellowish-brown. ☐ **olive branch** something done or offered to show one's desire to make peace.

Olympiad (ŏ-**limp**-ee-ad) *noun* **1** a period of four years between celebrations of the Olympic Games, used by the ancient Greeks in dating events. **2** a celebration of the modern Olympic Games. **3** a regular contest, especially an international one, *Maths Olympiad*.

Olympian (ŏ-**limp**-ee-ăn) *adjective* **1** of Olympus, celestial. **2** (of manners etc.) majestic and imposing. **3** Olympic.

Olympic (ŏ-**limp**-ik) *adjective* of the **Olympic Games**, athletic and other contests held every 4th year at Olympia in Greece in ancient times and revived since 1896 as international competitions, held each time in a different part of the world. **Olympics** *plural noun* the Olympic Games.

Olympus (ŏ-**limp**-ŭs) a mountain in NE Greece, the home of the major gods in Greek mythology.

om *noun* (in Buddhism and Hinduism etc.) a mystic syllable considered the most sacred mantra.

Oman (oh-**mahn**) a sultanate in Arabia. **Omani** (oh-**mah**-nee) *adjective* & *noun* (*plural* **Omanis**).

Omar Khayyám (**oh**-mar ky-**ahm**) (died 1123), Persian poet, mathematician, and astronomer, author of the *Rubaiyat*.

omasum (ŏ-**may**-sŭm) *noun* the third stomach of a ruminant animal.

ombudsman (**om**-buudz-măn) *noun* (*plural* **ombudsmen**) an official appointed to investigate individuals' complaints against public authorities. [Swedish, = legal representative]

omega (**oh**-mĕ-gă) *noun* the last letter of the Greek alphabet, = o. ☐ **omega-3 fatty acid** an unsaturated fatty acid of a kind occurring chiefly in fish oils. [from Greek *o mega* = great O]

omelette (**om**-lĕt) *noun* a dish made of beaten eggs cooked in a frying pan, often served folded round a savoury or sweet filling.

omen (**oh**-men) *noun* an event regarded as a prophetic sign.

ominous (**om**-ĭ-nŭs) *adjective* **1** looking or seeming as if trouble is at hand, *an ominous silence*. **2** giving or being an omen, predictive. **ominously** *adverb* [from *omen*]

omission *noun* **1** omitting; being omitted. **2** something that has been omitted or not done.

omit *verb* (**omitted**, **omitting**) **1** to leave out, not to insert or include. **2** to leave not done, to neglect or fail to do.

omni- *prefix* all. [from Latin *omnis* = all]

omnibus *noun* **1** (*formal*) a bus. **2** a volume containing a number of books or stories previously published separately. **–omnibus** *adjective* comprising several items. [Latin, = for everybody]

omnipotent (om-**nip**-ŏ-tĕnt) *adjective* having unlimited power or very great power. **omnipotence** *noun* [from *omni-* + *potent*]

omnipresent *adjective* present everywhere.

omniscient (om-**nis**-ee-ĕnt) *adjective* knowing everything, having very extensive knowledge. **omniscience** (om-**nis**-ee-ĕns) *noun* [from *omni-*, + Latin *sciens* = knowing]

omnivore (**om**-niv-or) *noun* an omnivorous animal.

omnivorous (om-**niv**-ŏ-rŭs) *adjective* 1 feeding on both plants and animal flesh. 2 (*humorous*) reading whatever comes one's way. [from *omni-*, + Latin *vorare* = devour]

on *preposition* 1 supported by, attached to, covering, *sat on the floor*; *lives on her pension*; *got any money on you?*, are you carrying any with you? 2 using as a basis, ground, or reason etc., *was arrested on suspicion*; *profits on sales*. 3 close to, *they live on the coast*; in the direction of, *the army advanced on Paris*; *on form* or *on his game*, performing at his usual high standard. 4 (of time) exactly at, during, *on the next day*. 5 in a certain manner or state, *on the cheap*; *on one's best behaviour*. 6 concerning, engaged with, so as to affect, *a book on grammar*; *on holiday*; *is on the pill*, taking it; *the drinks are on me*, at my expense. 7 broadcast or played by means of, *heard it on the radio*; *played a piece on the viola*. 8 added to, *5 cents on the price of petrol*. **–on** *adverb* 1 so as to be supported by or attached to or covering something, *put the lid on*. 2 further forward, towards something, *move on*; *from that day on*; *broadside on*, with that part forward. 3 with continued movement or action, *slept on*. 4 in operation or activity; (of a play etc.) being performed or broadcast; (of an actor etc.) performing on the stage; (of gas, water, or electric current) running, available, activated; (of an event) due to take place, not cancelled; (of an employee) on duty. **–on** *adjective* in, from, or towards the part of a cricket field on the batsman's side and in front of the wicket. **–on** *noun* the on side in cricket. □ **be on** (*informal*) to be willing to participate in something; to be practicable or acceptable, *this plan just isn't on*; *you're on!*, (*informal*) I accept your proposition or wager. **be** or **keep on at** (*informal*) to nag. **be on to a thing** to notice it or realise its importance. **on and off** from time to time, not continually. **on and on** continuing, continually. **on high** in or to heaven or a high place. **on to** to a position on (*see* **onto**).

onager (**on**-ă-ger) *noun* a wild ass.

once *adverb*, *conjunction*, & *noun* 1 on one occasion only; one time or occurrence, *once is enough*. 2 at all, ever, as soon as, *once I can get this job done*. 3 formerly, *people who once lived here*. □ **once and for all** in a final manner, conclusively. **once in a while** from time to time, not often. **once more** an additional time. **once-over** *noun* (*informal*) a

rapid inspection, *give it the once-over*. **once upon a time** at some vague time in the past.

oncology (ong-**kol**-ŏ-jee) *noun* the scientific study of tumours. **oncologist** *noun* [from Greek *ogkos* = mass, + *-logy*]

oncoming *adjective* approaching.

one *adjective* single, individual; forming a unity. **–one** *noun* 1 the smallest whole number (1, I). 2 a single thing or person. **–one** *pronoun* 1 a person, *loved ones*. 2 any person; the speaker or writer as representing people in general, *one simply doesn't do that*. □ **one another** each other. **one day** at some unspecified date. **one-liner** (*informal*) a joke or witty remark in the form of a single brief sentence. **one-man** *adjective* done or managed by one person. **one-off** *adjective* made as single article only, not repeated, *a one-off job*. **one-sided** *adjective* (of opinions or judgments) unfair, prejudiced. **one-time** *adjective* former. **one-track mind** a mind that can think of only one topic. **one-upmanship** *noun* the art of maintaining a psychological advantage over others. **one-way street** a street in which traffic may move in one direction only. **one-way ticket** a single ticket, not a return.

O'Neill, Eugene Gladstone (1888–1953), American playwright whose works include *The Iceman Cometh* and *Long Day's Journey into Night*.

onerous (**oh**-nĕ-rŭs) *adjective* burdensome. [from Latin *onus* = burden]

oneself *pronoun* corresponding to **one** (*pronoun*, sense 2), used in the same ways as **himself**.

ongoing *adjective* continuing to exist or progress.

onion *noun* a vegetable with an edible rounded bulb that has a strong smell and strong flavour. □ **know one's onions** (*informal*) to know one's subject or one's job thoroughly. **oniony** *adjective*

online *adjective* & *adverb* controlled by or connected to a computer; available on or performed using the Internet or other network.

onlooker *noun* a spectator.

only *adjective* 1 being the one specimen or all the specimens of a class, sole. 2 most or best worth considering, *gliding is the only sport*. **–only** *adverb* 1 without anything or anyone else; and that is all. 2 no longer ago than, *saw her only yesterday*. **–only** *conjunction* but then, *he makes good resolutions, only he never* keeps them. □ **only too** extremely, *we'll be only too pleased.*

o.n.o. *abbreviation* or nearest offer.

onomatopoeia (on-ŏ-mat-ŏ-**pee**-ă) *noun* the formation of words that imitate or suggest what they stand for, e.g. *sizzle*, *plop*, *clink*. **onomatopoeic** *adjective* [from Greek, = word-making]

onrush *noun* an onward rush.

onset *noun* **1** a beginning, *the onset of winter.* **2** an attack or assault.

onshore *adjective* **1** on the shore; on land. **2** (of wind) blowing from the sea towards the land.

onside *adjective* & *adverb* not offside.

onslaught (**on**-slawt) *noun* a fierce attack.

onto *preposition* to a position on.

Usage Many people prefer not to use *onto*, and write *on to* in all cases. Note that *onto* cannot be used where *on* is an adverb, e.g. *we walked on to the river* (= continued walking until we reached it).

---

ontology (on-**tol**-ŏ-jee) *noun* a branch of philosophy dealing with the nature of being. **ontological** *adjective* [from Greek *ontos* = of a being, + -*logy*]

onus (**oh**-nŭs) *noun* the duty or responsibility of doing something; *the onus of proof rests with you*, you must prove what you say. [Latin, = burden]

onward *adverb* & *adjective* with an advancing motion, further on. **onwards** *adverb*

onyx (**on**-iks) *noun* a stone like marble with different colours in layers.

Oodgeroo *see* **Noonuccal**, Oodgeroo.

oodles *noun* (*informal*) a great quantity.

ooh *interjection* an exclamation of surprise, pleasure, or pain.

oops *interjection* an exclamation on falling, slipping, or making an obvious mistake etc.

ooze *verb* **1** (of liquid) to trickle or flow out slowly. **2** (of a substance or wound etc.) to exude a liquid; to allow to trickle out slowly. **3** to show (a feeling) freely, *ooze confidence*. –**ooze** *noun* mud at the bottom of a river or sea.

op *abbreviation* **1** operation. **2** opportunity, *op shop.*

op- *prefix see* **ob-**.

opacity (ŏ-**pas**-ĭ-tee) *noun* being opaque.

opal *noun* an iridescent quartz-like stone often used as a gem.

opalescent (oh-pă-**less**-ĕnt) *adjective* iridescent like an opal. **opalescence** *noun*

opaque (oh-**payk**) *adjective* **1** not transparent, not allowing light to pass through. **2** (of a statement etc.) not clear.

op art *noun* art in a style that gives an illusion of movement. [the word *op* is short for *optical*]

OPEC (**oh**-pek) *abbreviation* Organisation of Petroleum Exporting Countries.

open *adjective* **1** not closed or blocked up; not sealed or locked. **2** not covered or concealed; not restricted; *an open championship*, for which anyone may enter. **3** admitting visitors or customers. **4** spread out, unfolded. **5** with wide spaces between solid parts, *open texture*. **6** frank, communicative; undisguised, public, *with open hostility*. **7** not yet settled or decided. **8** available, *three courses are open to us*. **9** willing to receive, *we are open to offers*. **10** (of a cheque) not crossed. –**open** *noun* an open championship or competition. –**open** *verb* **1** to make or become open or more open. **2** to begin or establish, to make a start, *open a business* or *a debate*; *to open fire*, to begin firing. **3** to declare ceremonially to be open to the public. □ **the open** open space; open country; open air; *into the open*, into public view. **in the open air** not inside a house or building. **open-air** *adjective* taking place in the open air. **open-and-shut** *adjective* (*informal*) perfectly straightforward. **open-cut** *adjective* (of a mine or mining) with layers of earth removed from the surface and worked from above, not from shafts. **open day** a day when the public may visit a place that is not normally open to them. **open-ended** *adjective* with no fixed limit, *an open-ended contract*. **open-handed** *adjective* generous in giving. **open-heart surgery** surgery with the heart exposed and with blood circulating temporarily through a bypass. **open house** hospitality to all comers. **open letter** a letter of comment or protest addressed to a person by name but printed in a newspaper. **open mind** a mind that is unprejudiced or undecided. **open-plan** *adjective* without partition walls or fences. **open prison** a prison with few physical restraints on the prisoners. **open question** a matter on which no final verdict has yet been made or on which none is possible. **open sandwich** a slice of bread covered with a layer of meat or cheese etc. **open secret** one known to so many people that it is no longer a secret. **open set** (in mathematics) a set that is not closed (i.e. does not include all its own boundaries). **open-source** denoting software for which the original source code is made freely available. **open verdict** a verdict that does not specify whether a crime is involved in the case of a person's death. **openness** *noun*

opener *noun* **1** a person or thing that opens something. **2** a device for opening tins or bottles.

opening *noun* **1** a space or gap; a place where something opens. **2** the beginning of something. **3** an opportunity.

openly *adverb* without concealment, publicly, frankly.

openwork *noun* a pattern with spaces between threads or strips of metal etc.

opera *noun* **1** a play in which the words are sung to a musical accompaniment. **2** dramatic works of this kind. –**opera** *plural noun* see **opus**. □ **opera glasses** small binoculars for use at the opera or theatre.

operable *adjective* **1** able to be operated. **2** able to be treated by a surgical operation.

operate *verb* **1** to be in action; to produce an effect, *the new tax operates to our advantage*. **2** to control the functioning of, *he operates the lift*. **3** to perform a surgical or other operation. □ **operating system** software that is used to control a computer and to allow applications or programs to be run (abbreviation **OS**). **operating theatre** a room for surgical operations. [from Latin *operari* = to work]

operatic *adjective* of or like opera.

operation *noun* **1** operating; being operated. **2** the way a thing works. **3** a piece of work, something to be done, *begin operations*. **4** a mathematical process performed on one or more elements, e.g. multiplication. **5** strategic military activities in war or during manoeuvres. **6** an act performed by a surgeon, on any part of the body, to take away or deal with a diseased, injured, or deformed part.

operational *adjective* **1** of, engaged in, or used in operations. **2** able to function, *is the system operational yet?*

operative *adjective* **1** having an effect, working or functioning. **2** of surgical operations. –**operative** *noun* a worker, especially in a factory.

operator *noun* **1** a person who operates a machine; one who engages in business or runs

a business etc. **2** one who makes connections of lines at a telephone exchange.

operculum (ŏ-**per**-kew-lŭm) *noun* (*plural* **opercula**) **1** a movable flap or plate etc. covering a fish's gills or the opening of a mollusc's shell. **2** a similar structure in plants.

operetta *noun* a short or light opera.

ophthalmic (off-**thal**-mik) *adjective* of or for the eyes. [from Greek *ophthalmos* = eye]

ophthalmology (off-thal-**mol**-ŏ-jee) *noun* the scientific study of the eye and its diseases. **ophthalmologist** *noun* [from *ophthalmic* + *-logy*]

opiate (**oh**-pee-ăt) *noun* **1** a sedative drug containing opium. **2** a thing that soothes the feelings or dulls activity.

opine (oh-**pyn**) *verb* to express or hold as one's opinion.

opinion *noun* **1** a belief or judgment that is held firmly but without actual proof of its truth; a view held as probable. **2** what one thinks on a particular point. **3** a judgment or comment(s) given by an expert who is consulted. □ **opinion poll** an estimate of public opinion made by questioning a representative sample of people. [from Latin *opinari* = believe]

opinionated *adjective* having strong opinions and holding them obstinately.

opium *noun* a drug made from the juice of certain poppies, smoked or chewed as a stimulant or narcotic, and used in medicine as a sedative.

opossum (ŏ-**poss**-ŭm) *noun* **1** a small furry American marsupial that lives in trees. **2** (*Austral. old use*) a possum.

Oppenheimer (**op**-ĕn-hy-mĕ), Julius Robert (1904–67), American theoretical physicist who led the team that designed and built the first atomic bomb during the Second World War.

opponent *noun* a person or group opposing another in a contest or war. [from Latin *opponere* = to set against]

opportune (**op**-er-tewn) *adjective* **1** (of time) suitable or favourable for a purpose. **2** done or occurring at a favourable time. **opportunely** *adverb* [from *op-*, + Latin *portus* = harbour (originally used of wind blowing a ship towards a harbour)]

opportunist (**op**-er-tewn-ĭst) *noun* one who grasps opportunities, often in an unprincipled way. **opportunism** *noun*

opportunity *noun* a time or set of circumstances that are suitable for a particular purpose. □ **opportunity cost** the price that must be paid for choosing one alternative rather than another, e.g. the loss of arable land to provide space for new housing. **opportunity shop** (*Austral.*) a shop run by a charity selling donated second-hand clothing and other goods.

oppose *verb* **1** to show resistance to, to argue or fight against. **2** to place opposite; to place or be in opposition to. **3** to represent (things) as contrasting. □ **as opposed to** in contrast with.

opposite *adjective* **1** having a position on the other or further side, facing. **2** of a contrary kind, as different as possible from; *the opposite sex*, men in relation to women or vice versa; *they travelled in opposite directions*, moving away from or towards each other. –**opposite** *noun* an opposite thing or person. –**opposite** *adverb* & *preposition* in an opposite place, position, or direction to (a person or thing).
□ **one's opposite number** a person holding a similar position to oneself in another group or organisation. [from Latin *oppositum* = placed against]

opposition *noun* **1** resistance, being hostile or in conflict or disagreement. **2** the people who oppose a proposal etc.; one's competitors or rivals. **3** placing or being placed opposite; contrast. –**the Opposition** the chief parliamentary party opposed to the one that is in office.

oppress *verb* **1** to govern harshly, to treat with continual cruelty or injustice. **2** to weigh down with cares or unhappiness. **oppression** *noun*, **oppressor** *noun* [from *op-* = against, + *press*]

oppressive *adjective* **1** oppressing. **2** difficult to endure. **3** (of weather) sultry and tiring. **oppressively** *adverb*, **oppressiveness** *noun*

opprobrious (ŏ-**proh**-bree-ŭs) *adjective* (of words etc.) showing scorn or reproach, abusive.

opprobrium (ŏ-**proh**-bree-ŭm) *noun* great disgrace brought by shameful conduct.

op shop (*Austral.*) = **opportunity shop**.

opt *verb* to make a choice. □ **opt out** to choose not to participate. [from Latin *optare* = wish for]

optative (op-**tay**-tiv) *adjective* of the form of a verb used in Greek in expressing a wish. –**optative** *noun* this form.

optic *adjective* of the eye or the sense of sight. **optics** *noun* the scientific study of sight and of light as its medium. [from Greek *optos* = seen]

optical *adjective* **1** of the sense of sight. **2** aiding sight; *optical instruments*, telescopes etc. □ **optical fibre** thin glass fibre used in fibre optics. **optical illusion** a mental misinterpretation of something seen, caused by its deceptive appearance. **optically** *adverb*

optician (op-**tish**-ăn) *noun* a maker or seller of spectacles and other optical equipment.

optimal *adjective* optimum.

optimise *verb* (also **-ize**) to make as effective or favourable as possible. **optimisation** *noun*

optimism *noun* a tendency to take a hopeful view of things, or to expect that results will be good. **optimist** *noun* [from Latin *optimus* = best]

optimistic *adjective* showing optimism, hopeful. **optimistically** *adverb*

optimum *adjective* best, most favourable. –**optimum** *noun* the best or most favourable conditions or amount etc. [Latin, = best thing]

option *noun* **1** freedom to choose, *had no option but to go*. **2** a thing that is or may be chosen, *none of the options is satisfactory*. **3** the right to buy or sell something at a certain price within a limited time, *we have 10 days' option on the house*. □ **keep one's options open** to avoid committing oneself, so that one still has a choice. [same origin as *opt*]

optional *adjective* not compulsory. **optionally** *adverb*

optometrist (op-**tom**-ĕ-trĭst) *noun* (*Austral.* & *Amer.*) a person who tests eyesight and supplies lenses to correct defects of vision. **optometry** *noun*

opulent (op-yŭ-lĕnt) *adjective* **1** wealthy, rich. **2** abundant, luxuriant. **opulently** *adverb*, **opulence** *noun* [from Latin *opes* = wealth]

opus (oh-pŭs) *noun* (*plural* **opera**) a musical composition numbered as one of a composer's works (usually in order of publication), *Beethoven opus 15*. [Latin, = work]

or *conjunction* **1** as an alternative, *are you coming or going?* **2** also known as, *hydrophobia or rabies*.

oracle *noun* **1** a place where the ancient Greeks consulted one of their gods for advice or prophecy. **2** the reply given. **3** a person or thing regarded as able to give wise guidance. **oracular** (ŏ-**rak**-yŭ-ler) *adjective* [from Latin *orare* = speak]

oracy (o-ră-see) *noun* the ability to express oneself well in speaking.

oral (o-răl) *adjective* **1** spoken not written, *oral evidence*. **2** of the mouth; done or taken by mouth. **–oral** *noun* (*informal*) a spoken (not written) examination. **orally** *adverb* [from Latin *oris* = of the mouth]

orange *noun* **1** a round juicy citrus fruit with reddish-yellow peel. **2** reddish yellow. **–orange** *adjective* orange-coloured. □ **orange stick** a small thin stick (originally of wood from an orange tree) for manicuring the nails.

Orangeman *noun* (*plural* **Orangemen**) a member of a political society formed in 1795 to support Protestantism in Ireland. [named after William of Orange (William III)]

Orange River the longest river in South Africa, flowing generally westward across almost the whole continent into the Atlantic.

orang-utan (ŏ-rang-oo-**tang**) *noun* a large long-armed ape of Borneo and Sumatra. [from Malay, = wild man]

oration (ŏ-**ray**-shŏn) *noun* a long speech, especially of a ceremonial kind. [from Latin *orare* = speak]

orator *noun* a person who makes public speeches; one who is good at public speaking.

oratorical (o-ră-**to**-ri-kăl) *adjective* of or like oratory.

oratorio (o-ră-**tor**-ree-oh) *noun* (*plural* **oratorios**) a musical composition for solo voices, chorus, and orchestra, usually with a biblical theme.

oratory (o-ră-tŏ-ree) *noun* **1** the art of public speaking. **2** eloquent speech. **3** a small chapel or place for private worship.

orb *noun* **1** a sphere or globe. **2** an ornamental globe surmounted by a cross, forming part of the royal regalia.

orbit *noun* **1** the curved path of a planet, satellite, or spacecraft etc. round another body; *in orbit*, moving in an orbit. **2** the path of an electron round the nucleus of an atom. **3** a sphere of influence. **–orbit** *verb* to move in an orbit; to travel in an orbit round (a body). **orbiter** *noun* [from Latin *orbis* = circle]

orbital (or-bĭ-tăl) *adjective* of an orbit, *orbital velocity*. **orbitally** *adverb*

orchard *noun* **1** a piece of land planted with fruit trees. **2** these trees. [from Latin *hortus* = garden, + *yard*]

orchestra *noun* **1** a large body of people playing various musical instruments, including stringed and wind instruments. **2** (in full **orchestra pit**) the part of a theatre where these sit, in front of the stalls and lower than the stage. **orchestral** (or-**kess**-trăl) *adjective* [Greek, = space where the chorus danced during a play]

orchestrate (or-kĕs-trayt) *verb* **1** to compose or arrange (music) for performance by an orchestra. **2** to coordinate (things) deliberately, *an orchestrated series of protests*. **orchestration** *noun*

orchid (or-kĭd) *noun* **1** a plant with beautiful long-lasting irregularly-shaped flowers. **2** its flower.

orchidectomy *noun* surgical removal of one or both testicles.

orchis (or-kĭs) *noun* an orchid, especially a wild one.

Ord a river in the far north of WA, dammed in 1972 for irrigation, creating Lake Argyle, the largest artificial lake in Australia.

ordain *verb* **1** to appoint ceremonially to perform spiritual functions in the Christian Church. **2** (of God or fate) to destine, *providence ordained that they should meet*. **3** to appoint or decree authoritatively.

ordeal (or-**deel**) *noun* a difficult experience that tests a person's character or power of endurance.

order *noun* **1** the way in which things are placed in relation to one another. **2** a proper or customary sequence. **3** a condition in which every part or unit is in its right place or in a normal or efficient state, *in good working order*; *out of order*. **4** the condition brought about by good and firm government and obedience to the laws, *law and order*. **5** a system of rules or procedure. **6** a command, an instruction given with authority. **7** a request to supply goods; the goods themselves. **8** a written direction (especially to a bank or post office) to pay money, or giving authority to do something, *a money order*. **9** a rank or class in society, *the lower orders*. **10** a kind, sort, or quality, *showed courage of the highest order*. **11** a monastic organisation or institution, *the Franciscan Order*. **12** a Masonic or similar fraternity. **13** a company of people distinguished by a particular honour, *the Order of Australia*. **14** a style of ancient Greek or Roman architecture distinguished by the type of column used. **15** a group of plants or animals classified as similar in many ways. **–order** *verb* **1** to put in order, to arrange methodically. **2** to issue a command to, to command that (something shall be done). **3** to give an order for (goods etc.); to tell a waiter to serve (certain food). □ **orders** *plural noun* or **holy orders** the status of an ordained person, *in holy orders*; *take holy orders*, to be ordained. **in order to** or **that** with the intention that, with the purpose of. **on order** (of goods) ordered but not yet received. **order about** to keep on giving commands to. **Order of Australia** an Australian four-tiered system of honours: **OAM** Medal of the Order of Australia; **AM** Member of the Order of Australia; **AO** Officer of the Order of Australia; **AC** Companion of the Order of Australia (the highest honour). **order paper** a written or printed program of business for a committee or parliament etc. for one day.

ordered *adjective* arranged in order. □ **ordered pair** a set of two numbers or mathematical symbols etc. in which it makes a difference which is placed first, e.g. a pair of Cartesian coordinates.

orderly *adjective* **1** well arranged, in good order, tidy. **2** methodical, *an orderly mind*. **3** obedient to discipline, well behaved, *an orderly crowd*. **–orderly** *noun* **1** a soldier in attendance on an officer to assist him or take messages etc. **2** an attendant in a hospital. □ **orderly officer** the officer on duty for a particular day. **orderliness** *noun*

ordinal *noun* any of the **ordinal numbers**, the numbers defining a thing's position in a series, e.g. *first, fifth, twentieth*. (Compare *cardinal numbers*.) [same origin as *ordinary*]

ordinance *noun* a rule made by authority, a decree.

ordinand (**or**-dĭ-nand) *noun* a candidate for ordination.

ordinary *adjective* usual, customary, not exceptional. □ **in the ordinary way** if the circumstances were not exceptional. **ordinary shares** *see* **preference shares**. **out of the ordinary** unusual. **ordinarily** *adverb* [from Latin *ordinis* = of a row or an order]

ordinate (**or**-dĭ-năt) *noun* (in mathematics) the second member of an ordered pair, measured parallel to the y-axis. (Compare *abscissa*.)

ordination *noun* ordaining or being ordained as a member of the clergy.

ordnance *noun* military supplies and materials; the government service dealing with these.

Ordovician (or-dŏ-**vish**-ee-ăn) *adjective* of the second period of the Palaeozoic era. **–Ordovician** *noun* this period.

ore *noun* solid rock or mineral, found in the earth's crust, from which metal or other useful or valuable substances can be extracted, *iron ore*.

oregano (o-rĕ-**gah**-noh) *noun* a variety of wild marjoram used as a seasoning.

Oregon (**o**-rĕ-gon) a State of the USA on the Pacific coast.

Orestes (o-**rest**-eez) (*Gk. legend*) son of Agamemnon and Clytemnestra. He killed his mother and her lover Aegisthus to avenge their murder of Agamemnon.

organ *noun* **1** a musical instrument consisting of pipes that sound notes when air is forced through them, played by keys pressed with the fingers and pedals pressed with the feet. **2** a distinct part of an animal or plant body, adapted for a particular function, *digestive organs*; *organs of speech*. **3** a medium of communication (e.g. a newspaper) giving the views of a particular group. □ **organ of Corti** the structure in a mammal's ear by which sound is directly perceived. [from Greek *organon* = tool]

organdie (**or**-găn-dee) *noun* a fine translucent usually stiffened cotton fabric.

organelle *noun* a structure within a cell.

organic (or-**gan**-ik) *adjective* **1** of or affecting an organ or organs of the body, *organic diseases*. **2** of or formed from living things, *organic matter*. **3** (of food etc.) produced without the use of artificial fertilisers or pesticides. **4** organised or arranged as a system of related parts, *the business forms an organic whole*. □ **organic chemistry** chemistry of carbon compounds, which are present in all living matter and in substances derived from it. **organically** *adverb*

organisation *noun* (also **-ization**) **1** organising; being organised. **2** an organised body of people; an organised system. **organisational** *adjective*

organise *verb* (also **-ize**) **1** to arrange in an orderly or systematic way. **2** to make arrangements for, *organise a party*. **3** to form (people) into an association for a common purpose. **4** to make organic, to make into living tissue. organiser noun [same origin as organ]

organism noun a living being, an individual animal or plant.

organist noun one who plays the organ.

organza (or-**gan**-ză) noun thin stiff transparent dress fabric of silk or synthetic fibre.

orgasm (or-gazm) noun the climax of sexual excitement. orgasmic (or-**gaz**-mik) adjective

orgy noun 1 a wild drunken party or revelry. 2 great indulgence in one or more activities, an orgy of spending.

oriel window (o-ree-ĕl or or-) noun a kind of projecting window in an upper storey.

Orient (o-ree-ĕnt or or-) noun the East, countries east of the Mediterranean, especially East Asia. [from Latin, = sunrise]

orient verb 1 to place or determine the position of (a thing) with regard to the points of the compass; orient a map, place it so that its bearings correspond to one's own. 2 to face or direct (towards a certain direction). □ orient oneself to get one's bearings; to become accustomed to a new situation.

oriental (o-ree-**en**-t'l or or-) adjective of the Orient, of the eastern or Asian world or its civilisation. –Oriental noun a native of the Orient.

orientate (o-ree-ĕn-tayt or or-) verb to orient.

orientation (o-ree-ĕn-**tay**-shŏn or or-) noun 1 orienting; being oriented. 2 position relative to surroundings. 3 an introduction to a subject or situation.

orienteering (o-ree-ĕn-**teer**-ring or or-) noun the sport of finding one's way on foot across rough country by map and compass.

orifice (o-rĭ-fĭss) noun the opening of a cavity. [from Latin oris = of the mouth]

origami (o-rĭ-**gah**-mee) noun the Japanese art of folding paper into attractive shapes. [from Japanese ori = fold, + kami = paper]

origin noun 1 the point, source, or cause from which a thing begins its existence. 2 a person's ancestry or parentage, a man of humble origin. 3 (in mathematics) the point from which coordinates are measured. [from Latin origo = source]

original adverb 1 existing from the first, earliest. 2 being a thing from which a copy or translation has been made. 3 first-hand, not imitative, new in character or design.

4 thinking or acting for oneself, inventive, creative, an original mind. –original noun the first form of something, the thing from which another is copied. □ original sin the condition of wickedness thought to be common to all mankind since Adam's sin. originally adverb, originality noun

originate verb 1 to give origin to, to cause to begin. 2 to have origin, to begin. origination noun, originator noun

oriole (or-ree-ohl) noun a kind of bird of which the male has black and yellow plumage.

Orion (ŏ-**ry**-ŏn) 1 (Gk. legend) a giant and hunter, said to have been turned into a constellation on his death. 2 a constellation containing many bright stars including Orion's belt, three stars in a short line.

ormolu (or-mŏ-loo) noun 1 gilded bronze or a gold-coloured alloy of copper, used in decorating furniture. 2 articles made of or decorated with this. [from French or moulu = powdered gold]

ornament noun 1 a decorative object or detail. 2 decoration, adornment, for use, not for ornament. 3 a person or thing that adds distinction, an ornament to his profession. –ornament verb to decorate, to be an ornament to. ornamentation noun [from Latin ornare = adorn]

ornamental adjective serving as an ornament.

ornate (or-**nayt**) adjective elaborately ornamented. [from Latin ornatum = adorned]

ornithology (or-nĭ-**thol**-ŏ-jee) noun the scientific study of birds. ornithological adjective, ornithologist noun [from Greek ornithos = of a bird, + -logy]

orography (o-**rog**-ră-fee) noun the scientific study of the formation and features of mountains. □ orographic rain rain in mountainous areas caused by moist air being forced to rise and therefore cool. orographic adjective [from Greek oros = mountain, + -graphy]

orphan noun a child whose parents are dead. –orphan verb to make (a child) an orphan.

orphanage noun an institution where orphans are housed and cared for.

Orphism (or-fizm) noun 1 an ancient Greek mystic religion associated with the legendary musician Orpheus. 2 an artistic movement in the early 20th century using the techniques of cubism but with a less austere style. Orphic adjective

orris (o-rĭss) *noun* a kind of iris that has a fragrant root (orris root) that is dried for use in perfumery and medicine.

ortho- *prefix* right; straight; correct. [from Greek *orthos* = straight]

orthoclase *noun* a common kind of feldspar consisting mainly of potassium aluminium silicate, found in granite.

orthodontics (or-thŏ-**don**-tiks) *noun* correction of irregularities in the teeth and jaws. orthodontist *noun* a specialist in orthodontics. orthodontic *adjective* [from *ortho-*, + Greek *odontos* = of a tooth]

orthodox *adjective* of or holding correct, conventional, or currently accepted beliefs, especially in religion; *orthodox Jews*, those who follow traditional observances strictly. □ Orthodox Church the Eastern or Greek Church (recognising the Patriarch of Constantinople as its head), and the national Churches of Russia, Romania, etc., in communion with it. orthodoxy *noun* [from *ortho-*, + Greek *doxa* = opinion]

orthogonal (or-**thog**-ŏ-năl) *adjective* right-angled.

orthographic (or-thŏ-**graf**-ik) *adjective* orthographic projection a way of drawing a three-dimensional object without showing perspective.

orthography (or-**thog**-ră-fee) *noun* spelling, especially with reference to its correctness. [from *ortho-* + *-graphy*]

orthopaedics (or-thŏ-**pee**-diks) *noun* the branch of surgery dealing with the correction of deformities in bones or muscles. orthopaedic *adjective* [from *ortho-*, + Greek *paideia* = rearing of children (because the treatment was originally of children)]

orthoptics (or-**thop**-tiks) *noun* remedial treatment of the eye muscles. orthoptic *adjective*, orthoptist *noun* [from *ortho-* + *optic*]

orthotics *noun* the branch of medicine concerned with the provision and use of artificial supports or braces.

Orwell, George (pseudonym of Eric Arthur Blair, 1903–50), English novelist and essayist, best known for his satires *Animal Farm* and *Nineteen Eighty-Four* against totalitarian government.

oryx *noun* a large African antelope with straight horns.

OS *abbreviation* operating system.

Oscar *noun* any of the statuettes awarded by the Academy of Motion Picture Arts and Sciences (in Hollywood, USA) for excellence in the acting or directing of films.

oscillate (**oss**-ĭ-layt) *verb* 1 to move to and fro like a pendulum. 2 to vary between extremes of opinion or condition etc. 3 (of an electric current) to reverse its direction with high frequency. oscillation *noun*, oscillator *noun*

oscilloscope (ŏ-**sil**-ŏ-skohp) *noun* a device for showing oscillations as a display on the screen of a cathode ray tube.

osier (**oh**-zee-er) *noun* 1 a kind of willow with flexible twigs used in basketwork. 2 a twig from this.

Osiris (ŏ-**sy**-rĭs) (*Egyptian myth.*) a god said to have died and been restored to a new life as ruler of the afterlife.

Oslo (**oz**-loh) the capital of Norway.

osmium (**oz**-mee-ŭm) *noun* a hard and dense silver-white metallic element (symbol Os).

osmoregulation *noun* regulation of the diffusion of fluids, especially in the body of a living organism.

osmosis (oz-**moh**-sĭs) *noun* diffusion of fluid through a porous partition into another fluid. osmotic (oz-**mot**-ik) *adjective* [from Greek *osmos* = a push]

osprey (**oss**-pray) *noun* (*plural* ospreys) a large bird preying on fish in inland waters.

ossicle *noun* a small bone or piece of bonelike substance in the skeleton of an animal. [from Latin *ossiculum* = little bone]

ossify *verb* (ossified, ossifying) to change into bone; to make or become hard like bone. ossification *noun* [from Latin *os* = bone]

ostensible (oss-**ten**-sĭ-bŭl) *adjective* pretended, put forward as a reason etc. to conceal the real one. ostensibly *adverb* [from Latin *ostendere* = to show]

ostensive (oss-**ten**-siv) *adjective* showing something directly.

ostentation *noun* a showy display intended to impress people. ostentatious (oss-ten-**tay**-shŭs) *adjective*, ostentatiously *adverb*

osteopath (**oss**-tee-ŏ-path) *noun* a practitioner who treats certain diseases and abnormalities by manipulating bones and muscles. osteopathy (oss-tee-**op**-ă-thee) *noun* this treatment. osteopathic (oss-tee-ŏ-**path**-ik) *adjective* [from Greek *osteon* = bone, + *-patheia* = suffering]

osteoporosis (os-tee-oh-pŏ-**roh**-sĭs) *noun* a condition in which the bones become brittle, often caused by hormonal changes or calcium deficiency.

ostler (**oss**-ler) *noun* a person in charge of stabling horses at an inn.

ostracise (**oss**-tră-syz) *verb* (also **-ize**) to refuse to associate with, to cast out from a group or from society. **ostracism** *noun* [from Greek *ostrakon* = piece of pottery (because people voted that a person should be banished by writing his name on this)]

ostrich *noun* **1** a swift-running African bird that cannot fly, said to bury its head in the sand when pursued, in the belief that it then cannot be seen. **2** a person who refuses to face an awkward truth.

other *adjective* **1** alternative, additional, being the remaining one or ones of a set of two or more, *has no other income*; *try the other shoe*; *my other friends*. **2** not the same, *wouldn't want her to be other than she is*. **–other** *noun* & *pronoun* the other person or thing, *where are the others?* **–other** *adverb* otherwise. □ **the other day** or **week** etc., a few days or weeks etc. ago.

otherwise *adverb* **1** in a different way, *could not have done otherwise*. **2** in other respects, *is otherwise correct*. **3** if circumstances were different; or else, *write it down, otherwise you'll forget*. **–otherwise** *adjective* in a different state, not as supposed, *the truth is quite otherwise*.

otiose (**oh**-tee-ohs) *adjective* serving no practical purpose.

Ottawa the capital of Canada.

otter *noun* a fish-eating water animal with webbed feet, a flat tail, and thick brown fur.

Ottoman *adjective* of the Turkish dynasty founded by Osman or Othman (1259–1326), his branch of the Turks, or the empire ruled by his descendants (late 13th–early 20th century). **–Ottoman** *noun* an Ottoman person.

ottoman *noun* **1** a long cushioned seat without back or arms. **2** a storage box with a padded top.

Ouagadougou (wah-gă-**doo**-goo) the capital of Burkina.

oubliette (oo-blee-et) *noun* a secret dungeon to which entrance is through a trapdoor. [from French *oublier* = forget]

ouch *interjection* an exclamation of sudden pain or annoyance.

ought *auxiliary verb* expressing duty, rightness, advisability, or strong probability. **oughtn't** (*informal*) = ought not.

Ouija (**wee**-jă) *noun* (*trademark*) (also **Ouija board**) a board marked with the alphabet, used in seances.

ounce *noun* **1** a unit of weight equal to one-sixteenth of a pound (about 28 grams). **2** a very small quantity. □ **fluid ounce** *see* **fluid**.

our *adjective* of or belonging to us.

ours *possessive pronoun*, belonging to us; the thing(s) belonging to us.

Usage It is incorrect to write *our's* (see the note under **its**).

ourselves *pronoun* corresponding to *we* and *us*, used in the same ways as **himself**.

oust (*pr.* ow- *as in* cow) *verb* to drive out, to eject from office or a position or employment etc.

out *adverb* **1** away from or not in a place; not in its normal or usual state; not at home; *the tide is out*, is low. **2** not in effective or favourable action; no longer in fashion or in office; (in cricket etc.) having had one's innings ended; (of workers) on strike; (of a light or fire etc.) no longer burning. **3** in error, *the estimate was 10% out*. **4** no longer visible, *paint it out*. **5** not possible, *swimming is out until the weather warms up*. **6** unconscious. **7** into the open; into existence or hearing or view etc., published, visible, revealed, *the sun is out*; *the secret is out*; *her new book is out*; *the flowers are out*, opened, no longer in bud; *the best game out*, the best one known to exist. **8** to or at an end, completely, *tired out*; *sold out*. **9** in finished form, *type it out*. **10** (in radio conversations) transmission ends. **–out** *preposition* (*informal*) out of. **–out** *noun* a way of escape. **–out** *interjection* get out. **–out** *verb* to come or go out, *the truth will out*. □ **be out to** to be acting with the intention of, *is out to cause trouble*. **out-and-out** *adjective* thorough, extreme. **out of** from within or among; beyond the range of; so as to be without a supply of; (of an animal) born of. **out of date** no longer fashionable or current or valid, *this passport is out of date*. **out-of-date** *adjective* out of date, *an out-of-date passport*. **out of doors** in the open air. **out of the way** no longer an obstacle; remote; unusual. **out of this world** incredibly good. **out with it** say what you are thinking.

out- *prefix* **1** out of, away from, outward (as in *outcast*). **2** external, separate (as in *outhouse*). **3** more than, so as to exceed (as in *outbid*, *outgrow*, *out-talk*).

outback *noun* (*Austral.*) remote inland districts.

outbid *verb* (outbid, outbidding) to bid higher than (another person).

outboard *adjective* (of a motor) attached to the outside of the stern of a boat.

outbreak *noun* a breaking out of anger, war, fire, a disease etc.

outbuilding *noun* an outhouse.

outburst *noun* a bursting out of steam or anger or laughter etc.

outcast *noun* a person who has been driven out of a group or rejected by society.

outclass *verb* to surpass greatly.

outcome *noun* the result or effect of an event etc.

outcrop *noun* **1** part of an underlying layer of rock that projects on the surface of the ground. **2** a breaking out.

outcry *noun* **1** a loud cry. **2** a strong protest.

outdated *adjective* out of date.

outdistance *verb* to get far ahead of (a person) in a race etc.

outdo *verb* (outdid, outdone, outdoing) to do better than (another person etc.).

outdoor *adjective* **1** of or for use in the open air. **2** enjoying open-air activities, *she's an outdoor type*.

outdoors *adverb* in or into the open air. **outdoors** *noun* the open air.

outer *adjective* further from the centre or from the inside, exterior, external. –**outer** *noun* **1** the division of a target further from the bullseye; a shot that strikes this. **2** (*Austral.*) an unsheltered spectator area at a racecourse or sports ground. □ **on the outer** (*Austral. informal*) excluded. **outer space** the universe beyond the earth's atmosphere.

outermost *adjective* furthest outward, most remote.

outface *verb* to disconcert (a person) by one's defiant or confident manner.

outfall *noun* an outlet where water falls or flows out.

outfield *noun* the outer part of a cricket, baseball, or softball field.

outfit *noun* **1** complete equipment or a set of things for a purpose. **2** a set of clothes to be worn together. **3** (*informal*) an organisation, a group of people regarded as a unit.

outfitter *noun* a supplier of equipment or of men's clothing.

outflank *verb* to get round the flank of (an enemy).

outflow *noun* an outward flow; the amount that flows out.

outgoing *adjective* **1** going out. **2** sociable and friendly. **outgoings** *plural noun* expenditure.

outgrow *verb* (outgrew, outgrown, outgrowing) **1** to grow faster than. **2** to grow out of (clothes or habits).

outgrowth *noun* **1** something that grows out of another thing. **2** a natural development, an effect.

outhouse *noun* a building (e.g. a shed or barn etc.) belonging to but separate from a house.

outing *noun* a pleasure trip.

outlandish *adjective* looking or sounding strange or foreign. **outlandishness** *noun*

outlast *verb* to last longer than.

outlaw *noun* (in the Middle Ages) a person who was punished by being placed outside the protection of the law. –**outlaw** *verb* **1** to make (a person) an outlaw. **2** to declare to be illegal.

outlay *noun* what is spent on something.

outlet *noun* **1** a way out for water or steam etc. **2** a means or occasion for giving vent to one's feelings or energies. **3** a market for goods; a shop, *a fast-food outlet*.

outlier *noun* a younger rock formation exposed in older rocks.

outline *noun* **1** a line or lines showing the shape or boundary of something. **2** a statement or summary of the chief facts about something. **3** a symbol in shorthand. –**outline** *verb* to draw or describe in outline; to mark the outline of. □ **in outline** giving only an outline.

outlook *noun* **1** a view on which one looks out, *a pleasant outlook over the park*. **2** a person's mental attitude or way of looking at something. **3** future prospects.

outlive *verb* to live longer than.

outlying *adjective* situated far from a centre, remote.

outmanoeuvre *verb* to outdo in manoeuvring.

outmoded *adjective* no longer fashionable or acceptable.

outnumber *verb* to exceed in number.

outpace *verb* to go faster than.

outpatient *noun* a person who visits a hospital for treatment but does not remain resident there.

outport *noun* a port that serves a nearby major port, often being in a better position for receiving large ships.

outpost *noun* 1 a detachment of troops stationed at a distance from the main army. 2 any distant branch or settlement.

output *noun* 1 the product of a process; the amount produced. 2 the electrical power etc. delivered by an apparatus. 3 the printout or results supplied by a computer. 4 the place where energy or information leaves a system. – **output** *verb* (**output** or **outputted**, **outputting**) (of a computer) to supply (results).

outrage *noun* 1 an act that shocks public opinion. 2 violation of rights, *safe from outrage*. – **outrage** *verb* to commit an outrage against; to shock and anger greatly.

outrageous *adjective* greatly exceeding what is moderate or reasonable, shocking. **outrageously** *adverb*

outrank *verb* to be of higher rank than.

outré (**oo**-tray) *adjective* eccentric; unseemly. [French, = exaggerated]

outreach *verb* to reach further than; to surpass. – **outreach** *noun* an organisation's involvement with the wider community.

outrider *noun* a mounted attendant or a motorcyclist riding as guard with a carriage or procession.

outrigger *noun* 1 a beam, spar, or structure projecting from the side of a ship for various purposes. 2 a strip of wood fixed parallel to a canoe by struts projecting from it, to give stability. 3 a boat with either of these.

outright *adverb* 1 completely, entirely, not gradually; *bought the house outright*, by a single payment. 2 openly, frankly, *told him outright*. – **outright** *adjective* thorough, complete, *an outright fraud*.

outrun *verb* (**outran**, **outrun**, **outrunning**) 1 to run faster or further than. 2 to go beyond (a specified point or limit).

outsell *verb* (**outsold**, **outselling**) to sell or be sold in greater quantities than.

outset *noun* the beginning, *from the outset of his career*.

outshine *verb* (**outshone**, **outshining**) to surpass in splendour or excellence.

outside *noun* the outer side, surface, or part. – **outside** *adjective* 1 of or coming from the outside; *outside interests*, interests other than work. 2 (of a player in football etc.) positioned nearest to the edge of the field, *outside left*. 3 greatest possible, *the outside price*. – **outside** *adverb* on or at or to the outside. – **outside** *preposition* on the outer side of; at or to the outside of; other than, *has no interests outside his work*. □ **at the outside** (of amounts) at most. **outside broadcast** one that is not made from a studio.

outsider *noun* 1 a non-member of a certain group or profession etc. 2 a horse or person thought to have no chance in the race or competition entered.

outsize *adjective* much larger than average.

outskirts *plural noun* the outer districts or outlying parts, especially of a town.

outsource *verb* to contract (work) out.

outspoken *adjective* speaking or spoken without reserve, very frank.

outspread *adjective* spread out.

outstanding *adjective* 1 conspicuous. 2 exceptionally good. 3 not yet paid or settled, *some of his debts are still outstanding*. **outstandingly** *adverb*

outstation *noun* (*Austral.*) 1 a sheep or cattle station at some distance from the head station. 2 an Aboriginal community at some distance from the centre on which it depends for services and supplies.

outstay *verb* to stay longer than.

outstretched *adjective* stretched out.

outstrip *verb* (**outstripped**, **outstripping**) 1 to outrun. 2 to surpass.

outvote *verb* to defeat by a majority of votes.

outward *adjective* 1 situated on the outside. 2 going towards the outside. 3 in one's expression or actions etc. as distinct from in one's mind or spirit. – **outward** *adverb* outwards.

outwardly *adverb* on the outside.

outwards *adverb* towards the outside.

outwash *noun* a deposit of silt, sand, and gravel washed out from a glacier by melt water.

outweigh *verb* to be greater in weight, importance, or significance than.

outwit *verb* (outwitted, outwitting) to get the better of (a person) by one's cleverness or craftiness.

outwork *noun* an advanced or detached part of a fortification.

outworker *noun* an employee working from home instead of at the factory, office, etc.

outworn *adjective* worn out, damaged by wear.

ouzo (**oo**-zoh) *noun* A Greek aniseed-flavoured alcoholic drink.

ova *see* ovum.

oval *noun* 1 a rounded symmetrical shape longer than it is broad. 2 a sports ground (not necessarily oval-shaped). –oval *adjective* having this shape. [from Latin *ovum* = egg]

ovary (**oh**-vă-ree) *noun* 1 either of the two organs in which egg cells are produced in female animals. 2 part of the pistil in a plant, from which fruit is formed. ovarian (ŏ-**vair**-ree-ăn) *adjective* [from Latin *ovum* = egg]

ovation (ŏ-**vay**-shŏn) *noun* enthusiastic applause. [from Latin *ovare* = rejoice]

oven *noun* an enclosed chamber in which things are cooked or heated.

ovenproof *adjective* (of dishes etc.) able to be used in an oven.

ovenware *noun* dishes for cooking and serving food.

over *adjective* 1 with movement outwards and downwards from the brink or from an upright position. 2 with movement from one side to the other or so that a different side is showing. 3 across a street or other space or distance, *she is over here from New Zealand*. 4 so as to cover or touch a whole surface, *brush it over*. 5 with transference or change from one hand or one side or one owner etc. to another, *went over to the enemy*; *hand it over*. 6 (in radio conversation) it is your turn to transmit. 7 besides, in addition or excess. 8 with repetition, *ten times over*. 9 thoroughly, with detailed consideration, *think it over*. 10 at an end, *the battle is over*. –over *noun* a series of 6 balls bowled in cricket. –over *preposition* 1 in or to a position higher than. 2 above and across, so as to clear. 3 throughout the length or extent of, during, *over the years*; *stayed over the weekend*. 4 so as to visit or examine all parts, *saw over the house*; *went over the plan again*. 5 transmitted by, *heard it over the radio*.

6 while engaged with, *we can talk over dinner*. 7 concerning, *quarrelling over money*. 8 more than, *over $50*. 9 in superiority or preference to, *the Coalition's victory over Labor*. 10 (in mathematics) divided by. 11 recovered from (an illness etc.). ☐ over and above besides. over and over so that the same point comes uppermost repeatedly; repeated many times.

over- *prefix* 1 above (as in *overlay*). 2 too much, excessively (as in *over-anxiety*, *over-anxious*).

overact *verb* to act one's part in an exaggerated manner.

overall *noun* a garment worn to protect other clothing, which it covers. –overall *adjective* 1 including everything, total. 2 taking all aspects into account. –overall *adverb* in all parts, taken as a whole. overalls *plural noun* a one-piece garment covering body and legs, worn as protective clothing.

overarm *adjective* & *adverb* 1 (in cricket etc.) bowling or bowled with the hand brought forward and down from above shoulder level. 2 (in swimming) with the arm lifted out of the water and stretched forward beyond the head.

overawe *verb* to inspire with deep respect.

overbalance *verb* to lose balance and fall over; to cause to do this.

overbear *verb* (overbore, overborne, overbearing) 1 to bear down by weight or force. 2 to repress by power or authority.

overbearing *adjective* domineering.

overblown *adjective* (of a flower etc.) too fully open, past its prime.

overboard *adverb* from within a ship into the water.

overbook *verb* to book too many passengers or visitors for (an aircraft flight or a hotel etc.).

overburden *verb* to burden excessively.

overcast *adjective* (of the sky) covered with cloud. –overcast *verb* (overcast, overcasting) to stitch over (an edge) to prevent it from fraying.

overcharge *verb* 1 to charge too high a price. 2 to fill too full.

overcoat *noun* a warm outdoor coat.

overcome *verb* (overcame, overcome, overcoming) 1 to win a victory over, to succeed in subduing. 2 to be victorious. 3 to make helpless, to deprive of proper control of oneself, *they were overcome by gas fumes* or *by grief*. 4 to find a way of dealing with (a problem etc.).

overcrowd *verb* to crowd too many people into (a place or vehicle etc.).

overdo *verb* (**overdid, overdone, overdoing**) **1** to do (a thing) excessively. **2** to cook (food) too long. □ **overdo it** or **things** to work too hard; to exaggerate.

overdose *noun* too large a dose of a drug etc. –**overdose** *verb* to take an overdose.

overdraft *noun* overdrawing of a bank account; the amount by which an account is overdrawn.

overdraw *verb* (**overdrew, overdrawn, overdrawing**) to draw more from (a bank account) than the amount credited; *be overdrawn*, to have done this.

overdrive *noun* a mechanism providing an extra gear above the normal top gear in a vehicle.

overdue *adjective* not paid or arrived etc. by the due or expected time.

overeat *verb* (**overate, overeaten, overeating**) to eat too much.

overestimate *verb* to form too high an estimate of.

overexpose *verb* to expose for too long. **overexposure** *noun*

overfeed *verb* (**overfed, overfeeding**) to feed too much.

overfill *verb* to fill too full or to overflowing.

overfish *verb* to catch so many fish from (a certain area) that next season's supply is reduced.

overflow *verb* **1** to flow over (the edge, limits, or banks etc.). **2** (of a crowd) to spread beyond the limits of (a room etc.). –**overflow** *noun* **1** what overflows. **2** an outlet for excess liquid.

overfly *verb* (**overflew, overflown, overflying**) to fly over or beyond (a place or territory).

overfull *adjective* overfilled, too full.

overgrown *adjective* **1** having grown too large. **2** covered with weeds etc. **overgrowth** *noun*

overhang *verb* (**overhung, overhanging**) to jut out over. –**overhang** *noun* an overhanging part.

overhaul *verb* **1** to examine and make any necessary repairs or changes. **2** to overtake. –**overhaul** *noun* an examination and repair etc.

overhead *adverb* & *adjective* above the level of one's head, in the sky. **overheads**

plural noun the expenses involved in running a business (e.g. rent, heating, cleaning) that are not directly related to a particular product or department etc. □ **overhead projector** a projector that gives an image on a vertical screen behind the operator's head.

overhear *verb* (**overheard, overhearing**) to hear accidentally or without the speaker's knowledge or intention.

overheat *verb* to make or become too hot or too intensive.

overjoyed *adjective* filled with very great joy.

overkill *noun* **1** a surplus of capacity for destruction above what is needed to defeat or destroy an enemy. **2** excess; excessive behaviour.

overland *adverb* & *adjective* by land, not by sea. –**overland** *verb* (*Austral.*) to drive (stock) a long distance over land. **overlander** *noun*

overlap *verb* (**overlapped, overlapping**) **1** to extend beyond the edge of (a thing) and partly cover it. **2** to coincide partially, *our holidays overlap*. –**overlap** *noun* overlapping; an overlapping part or amount.

overlay[1] (oh-ver-**lay**) *verb* (**overlaid, overlaying**) **1** to cover with a surface layer. **2** to lie on top of. –**overlay** (**oh**-ver-lay) *noun* a thing laid over another.

overlay[2] *past tense* of **overlie**.

overleaf *adverb* on the other side of a leaf of a book etc.

overlie *verb* (**overlay, overlain, overlaying**) to lie on top of; to smother by doing this.

overload *verb* to put too great a load on or into. –**overload** *noun* a load that is too great.

overlock *verb* to stitch over (an edge) to prevent fraying. **overlocker** *noun* a sewing machine which overlocks.

overlook *verb* **1** to have a view of or over (a place) from above. **2** to oversee. **3** to fail to observe or consider. **4** to take no notice of, to allow (an offence) to go unpunished.

overlord *noun* a supreme lord.

overly *adverb* excessively.

overman *verb* (**overmanned, overmanning**) to provide with too many people as workers or crew etc.; to overstaff.

overmuch *adverb* too much.

overnight *adverb* **1** during the night. **2** for a night, *stayed overnight*. **3** immediately, *things improved overnight*. –**overnight** *adjective*

1 of, for, or during a night, *an overnight stop in Tokyo*. **2** immediate, *an overnight success*.

overpass *noun* a road that crosses another by means of a bridge.

overpay *verb* (**overpaid, overpaying**) to pay too highly.

overplay *verb* to give too much importance to. □ **overplay one's hand** to take unjustified risks by overestimating one's strength.

overpower *verb* to overcome by greater strength or numbers.

overpowering *adjective* (of heat or feelings) extremely intense.

overrate *verb* to value or assess too highly.

overreach *verb* **overreach oneself** to fail through being too ambitious.

over-react *verb* to respond more strongly than is justified.

override *verb* (**overrode, overridden, overriding**) **1** to set aside (an order) by having, or behaving as if one had, superior authority. **2** to prevail over, *considerations of safety override all others*. **3** to intervene and cancel the operation of (an automatic mechanism).

overripe *adjective* too ripe.

overrule *verb* to set aside (a decision etc.) by using one's authority.

overrun *verb* (**overran, overrun, overrunning**) **1** to spread over and occupy or injure, *the place is overrun with mice*. **2** to exceed (a limit or time allowed etc.).

overseas *adverb* & *adjective* across or beyond the sea, abroad.

oversee *verb* (**oversaw, overseen, overseeing**) to supervise (work or workers).

overseer *noun* **1** a person who supervises others, especially workers. **2** a person who manages a rural property.

oversew *verb* (**oversewed, oversewn, oversewing**) to sew together (two edges) so that each stitch lies over the edges.

overshadow *verb* **1** to cast a shadow over. **2** to make (a person or thing) seem unimportant in comparison.

overshoe *noun* a shoe worn over an ordinary one as a protection against wet etc.

overshoot *verb* (**overshot, overshooting**) to pass beyond (a target or limit etc.), *the plane overshot the runway when landing*.

overshot *adjective* (of a waterwheel) turned by water falling on it from above.

oversight *noun* **1** supervision. **2** an unintentional omission or mistake.

oversimplify *verb* (**oversimplified, oversimplifying**) to misrepresent (a problem etc.) by stating it in terms that are too simple.

oversized *adjective* of more than the usual size.

oversleep *verb* (**overslept, oversleeping**) to sleep longer than intended.

overspend *verb* (**overspent, overspending**) to spend too much.

overspill *noun* **1** what spills over or overflows. **2** the surplus population of a town etc. who seek accommodation in other districts.

overstaff *verb* to provide with more than the necessary number of staff.

overstate *verb* to exaggerate. **overstatement** *noun*

overstay *verb* to stay longer than; *overstay one's welcome*, to stay so long that one is no longer welcome.

overstep *verb* (**overstepped, overstepping**) to go beyond (a limit).

overstock *verb* **1** to stock with more animals than one's land can feed. **2** to stock with too many items.

overstrung *adjective* (of a piano) with strings in sets crossing each other obliquely.

oversubscribed *adjective* with applications for (an issue of shares etc.) in excess of the number offered.

overt (oh-**vert**) *adjective* done or shown openly, *overt hostility*. **overtly** *adverb*

overtake *verb* (**overtook, overtaken, overtaking**) **1** to come abreast with or level with. **2** to pass (a moving person or vehicle) by faster movement. **3** to exceed (a compared value or amount).

overtax *verb* **1** to tax too heavily. **2** to put too heavy a burden or strain on.

overthrow *verb* (**overthrew, overthrown, overthrowing**) to cause the downfall of, *overthrew the government*. –**overthrow** *noun* **1** downfall, defeat. **2** a fielder's throwing of a ball beyond an intended point.

overtime *adverb* in addition to regular working hours. –**overtime** *noun* **1** time worked in this way. **2** payment for this.

overtone *noun* **1** an additional quality or implication, *overtones of malice in his* *comments*. **2** (in music) any of the tones above the lowest in a harmonic series.

overtook *see* overtake.

overture *noun* **1** an orchestral composition forming a prelude to an opera or ballet etc. **2** a composition resembling this. **overtures** *plural noun* a friendly approach showing willingness to begin negotiations; a formal proposal or offer.

overturn *verb* to turn over; to cause to turn over.

overuse (oh-ver-**yooz**) *verb* to use excessively. –**overuse** (oh-ver-**yoos**) *noun* excessive use.

overview *noun* a general survey.

overweening *adjective* arrogant, presumptuous.

overweight *adjective* weighing more than is normal or required or permissible.

overwhelm *verb* **1** to bury or drown beneath a huge mass. **2** to overcome completely, especially by force of numbers. **3** to make helpless with emotion.

overwhelming *adjective* irresistible through force of numbers or amount or influence etc.

overwind *verb* (**overwound**, **overwinding**) to wind (a watch etc.) beyond the proper stopping point.

overwork *verb* **1** to work or cause to work so hard that one becomes exhausted. **2** to make excessive use of, *an overworked phrase*. –**overwork** *noun* excessive work causing exhaustion.

overwrite *verb* **1** to write on top of (other writing). **2** (in computing) to destroy (data) in (a file etc.) by replacing with new data.

overwrought (oh-ver-**rawt**) *adjective* in a state of nervous agitation.

Ovid (**ov**-ĭd) (43 BC–c. AD 17), Roman poet in the age of Augustus.

oviduct (**oh**-vĭ-dukt) *noun* a canal through which ova pass from the ovary, especially in egg-laying creatures. [from *ovum* + *duct*]

oviparous (oh-**vip**-ă-rŭs) *adjective* producing young from eggs that are expelled from the body and then hatched (in contrast to *viviparous*). [from *ovum*, + Latin *-parus* = bearing]

ovipositor (oh-vĭ-**poz**-ĭ-ter) *noun* a pointed tube-shaped organ through which a female insect deposits its eggs. [from *ovum*, + Latin *positum* = placed]

ovoid (**oh**-void) *adjective* egg-shaped. –**ovoid** *noun* an ovoid shape or mass. [from *ovum*]

ovulate (**ov**-yŭ-layt) *verb* to produce or discharge an ovum from an ovary. **ovulation** *noun* [from Latin *ovum* = egg]

ovule (**oh**-vewl) *noun* **1** a small part in a plant's ovary that develops into a seed when fertilised. **2** an unfertilised ovum.

ovum (**oh**-vŭm) *noun* (*plural* **ova**) a female egg cell capable of developing into a new individual when fertilised by male sperm. [Latin, = egg]

owe *verb* **1** to be under an obligation to pay or repay (money etc.) in return for what one has received, to be in debt. **2** to have a duty to render, *owe allegiance to one's country*. **3** to feel (gratitude etc.) towards another in return for a service. **4** to have (a thing) as a result of the work or action of another person or cause, *we owe this discovery to Newton*.

Owen, Wilfrid (1893–1918), English poet of the First World War.

owing *adjective* owed and not yet paid. ☐ **owing to** caused by; because of.

owl *noun* a bird of prey with a large head, large eyes, and a hooked beak, usually flying at night. **owlish** *adjective*

owlet *noun* a small or young owl.

own *adjective* belonging to oneself or itself. –**own** *verb* **1** to have as one's property, to possess. **2** to acknowledge that one is the author or possessor or father etc. of. **3** to confess, *she owns to having said it*. ☐ **come into one's own** to receive one's due, to achieve recognition. **get one's own back** (*informal*) to have one's revenge. **hold one's own** to succeed in holding one's position; not to lose strength. **of one's own** belonging to oneself exclusively. **on one's own** alone; independently. **own to** to confess to. **own up** (*informal*) to confess, to admit that one is guilty.

owner *noun* one who owns something as his or her property. **ownership** *noun*

ox *noun* (*plural* **oxen**) **1** an animal of the kind kept as domestic cattle or related to these. **2** a fully grown bullock, used as a draught animal or as food.

oxalic acid *noun* a very poisonous acid found in sorrel and rhubarb leaves.

oxbow (bow *rhymes with* go) *noun* **1** a horseshoe bend in a river. **2** (in full **oxbow lake**) a curved lake formed from a horseshoe

bend in a river where the main stream has cut
across the narrow end and no longer flows
around the loop of the bend. [from *oxbow* =
the U-shaped collar on the yoke of oxen]

oxen *see* ox.

Oxford a city in England, seat of a major
university.

oxidant *noun* an oxidising agent.

oxidation *noun* the process of combining or
causing to combine with oxygen.

oxide *noun* a compound of oxygen and one
other element.

oxidise *verb* (also -ize) **1** to combine or cause
to combine with oxygen. **2** to coat with an
oxide. **3** to make or become rusty. oxidation
noun

Oxley, John Joseph William Molesworth
(c. 1785–1828), English-born Australian
explorer, surveyor, and pioneer settler in the
Bowral area.

oxtail *noun* the tail of an ox, used to make
soup or stew.

oxyacetylene (ok-see-ǎ-**set**-ǐ-leen) *adjective*
using a mixture of oxygen and acetylene,
especially in the cutting and welding of
metals.

oxygen *noun* a chemical element (symbol O),
a colourless odourless tasteless gas existing
in air and combining with hydrogen to form
water.

oxygenate *verb* to supply, treat, or mix with
oxygen. oxygenation *noun*

oxyhaemoglobin (ok-see-heem-ŏ-**gloh**-
bǐn) *noun* a bright red compound of oxygen
and haemoglobin present in oxygenated blood.

oxymoron (ok-see-**mor**-ron) *noun* putting
together words which seem to contradict one
another, e.g. *bitter-sweet*.

oxytocin (ok-see-**toh**-sǐn) *noun* a hormone
controlling contractions of the womb.

oyez (oh-**yez**) *interjection* a cry uttered
(usually three times) by a public crier or court
officer to call for attention.

oyster *noun* a kind of shellfish used as food,
some types of which produce pearls inside
their shells. ☐ oyster bed a part of the seabed
where oysters breed or are bred.

oystercatcher *noun* a wading sea bird which
feeds on shellfish.

Oz *noun* (*informal*) **1** Australia. **2** an Australian.
–Oz *adjective* (*informal*) Australian.

oz *abbreviation* ounce(s).

ozone (**oh**-zohn) *noun* a form of oxygen with
a sharp smell, formed by electrical discharges
through oxygen or through the interaction of
oxygen and ultraviolet light. ☐ ozone layer
a layer in the stratosphere where ozone is
generated, serving to protect the earth from
harmful ultraviolet rays from the sun. [from
Greek *ozein* = to smell]

Pp

P *abbreviation* **1** (on road signs) parking. **2** (of a first driver's licence) provisional or (in some states) probationary, *P-plates*.

p (also **p.**) *abbreviation* **1** page.

pa *noun* (*informal*) **1** father. [short for *papa*]

pace¹ *noun* **1** a single step made in walking or running. **2** the distance passed in this. **3** a style of walking or running (especially of horses). **4** speed in walking or running. **5** the rate of progress in some activity. **–pace** *verb* **1** to walk with a slow or regular pace. **2** to walk to and fro across (a room etc.). **3** to measure by pacing, *pace it out*. **4** to set the pace for (a runner etc.). □ **keep pace** to advance at an equal rate. **put a person through his paces** to test his ability. **set the pace** to set the speed, especially by leading. **pacer** *noun*

pace² (**pah**-chay *or* **pay**-see) *preposition* although (a named person) may not agree. [Latin, = with the permission of]

pacemaker *noun* **1** a runner etc. who sets the pace for another. **2** an electrical device placed on the heart to stimulate contractions.

pachyderm (**pak**-ĭ-derm) *noun* a thick-skinned animal, especially an elephant or rhinoceros. **pachydermatous** *adjective* [from Greek *pakhus* = thick, + *derma* = skin]

Pacific *adjective* of the Pacific Ocean. **–Pacific** *noun* the Pacific Ocean, the world's largest ocean, lying between Asia and Australia in the west and the Americas in the east.

pacific (pă-**sif**-ik) *adjective* peaceful; making or loving peace. **pacifically** *adverb* [from Latin *pacis* = of peace]

pacifist (**pas**-ĭ-fĭst) *noun* a person who totally opposes war, believing that disputes should be settled by peaceful means. **pacifism** *noun*

pacify (**pas**-ĭ-fy) *verb* (**pacified**, **pacifying**) **1** to calm and quieten. **2** to establish peace in. **pacification** *noun* [from Latin *pacis* = of peace]

pack¹ *noun* **1** a collection of things wrapped or tied together for carrying. **2** a set of things packed for selling. **3** a backpack or rucksack. **4** a complete set of playing cards (usually 52). **5** a group of hounds or wolves etc. **6** a gang of people; an organised group of Cub Scouts or Brownies; a rugby team's forwards. **7** a large amount or collection, *a pack of lies*. **–pack** *verb* **1** to put (things) into a container for transport or storing or for marketing; to fill with things in this way. **2** to be able to be packed, *this dress packs easily*. **3** to cram, press, or crowd together into, to fill (a space) in this way; *the hall was packed out*, was very crowded. **4** to cover or protect (a thing) with something pressed tightly on, in, or round it. □ **go to the pack** (*Austral. informal*) to deteriorate. **pack ice** large crowded floating pieces of ice in the sea. **pack it in** (*informal*) to cease doing something. **pack off** to send (a person) away. **pack up** to put one's things together in readiness for departing or ceasing work; (*informal*, of machinery etc.) to break down. **send packing** to dismiss abruptly. **packer** *noun*

pack² *verb* to select (a jury etc.) fraudulently so that their decisions will be in one's favour.

package *noun* **1** a parcel. **2** a box etc. in which goods are packed. **3** a set of items that go together; a package deal. **4** (in computing) a set of applications or software providing a range of functions. **–package** *verb* to put together in a package. □ **package deal** a number of proposals or items offered or accepted as a whole. **package holiday** or **tour** one with travel, accommodation, etc. at an inclusive price.

packaging *noun* wrapping(s) or container(s) for goods.

packet *noun* **1** a small package. **2** (*informal*) a considerable sum of money, *won a packet*. **3** a mailboat.

packhorse *noun* a horse for carrying loads.

pact *noun* an agreement, a treaty.

pad¹ *noun* **1** a flat cushion; a piece of soft material used to protect against jarring or to add bulk or to hold or absorb fluid etc., or used for rubbing. **2** a padded protection for the leg and ankle in certain games. **3** a set of sheets of writing paper or drawing paper fastened together at one edge. **4** the soft fleshy underpart at the end of a finger, or of the foot of certain animals. **5** a flat surface from which spacecraft are launched or where helicopters take off and land. **6** (*Austral.*) a path made by animals. **7** (*informal*) a lodging. **–pad** *verb* (**padded**, **padding**) **1** to put a pad or pads on or into. **2** to stuff. **3** to fill (a book or speech etc.) with unnecessary material in order to lengthen it. □ **padded cell** a room with padded walls in a mental hospital etc.

pad² *verb* (**padded**, **padding**) to walk, especially with a soft dull steady sound of steps.

padding *noun* material used to pad things.

paddle¹ *noun* **1** a short oar with a broad blade, used without a rowlock. **2** an instrument shaped like this. **3** one of the boards on a paddle wheel. **–paddle** *verb* **1** to propel by using a paddle or paddles. **2** to row gently. □ **paddle one's own canoe** to be independent. **paddle wheel** a wheel with boards round its rim that drive a **paddle boat** or **paddle steamer. paddler** *noun*

paddle² *verb* to walk with bare feet in shallow water for pleasure; to dabble (the feet or hands) gently in water. **–paddle** *noun* a spell of paddling.

paddock *noun* **1** (*Austral.*) an enclosed piece of land, usually part of a rural property. **2** (*Brit.*) a small field where horses are kept. **3** an enclosure at a racecourse where horses or racing cars are brought together before a race.

Paddy *noun* (*informal*) a nickname for an Irishman.

paddy¹ *noun* (*informal*) a rage, a temper.

paddy² *noun* **1** a field where rice is grown. **2** rice that is still growing or in the husk.

paddymelon *noun* (also **pademelon**) any of several small wallabies, especially of eastern Australia. [probably from Dharuk *badimaliyan*]

padlock *noun* a detachable lock with a U-shaped bar or a chain etc. that fastens through the loop of a staple or ring. **–padlock** *verb* to fasten with a padlock.

padre (**pah**-dray) *noun* a chaplain in the armed forces. [Italian, = father]

paean (**pee**-ăn) *noun* a song of praise or triumph. [from Greek, = hymn]

paediatrician (peed-ee-ă-**trish**-ăn) *noun* a specialist in paediatrics.

paediatrics (peed-ee-**at**-triks) *noun* the branch of medicine dealing with children and their diseases. **paediatric** *adjective* [from Greek *paidos* = of a child, + *iatros* = doctor]

paedophilia (pee-dŏ-**fil**-ee-ă *or* ped-ŏ-) *noun* sexual attraction felt by an adult towards a child. **paedophile** *noun* a person displaying paedophilia.

paella (py-**el**-ă) *noun* a Spanish dish of rice, chicken, seafood, etc. cooked and served in a large shallow pan.

pagan (**pay**-găn) *adjective* **1** heathen. **2** holding the belief that deity exists in natural forces; nature-worshipping, especially in contrast to believing in Christianity, Judaism, etc. **–pagan** *noun* a pagan person. **paganism** *noun* [same origin as *peasant*]

Paganini (pag-ă-**nee**-nee), Niccolò (1782–1840), Italian violinist and composer.

page¹ *noun* **1** a leaf in a book or newspaper etc. **2** one side of this. **3** (in computing) a section of stored data, especially that which can be displayed on a screen at one time. **4** (on the World Wide Web) a file referenced by one URL. [from Latin *pagina* = page]

page² *noun* a boy or man usually in uniform employed to go on errands or act as door attendant etc; a boy attendant of a person of rank or a bride. **–page** *verb* to summon (a person) by making an announcement, sending a messenger, or by means of a pager. [from Greek *paidion* = small boy]

pageant (**paj**-ĕnt) *noun* a public show consisting of a procession of people in costume and displays on floats, or an outdoor performance of a historical play. **pageantry** *noun*

pageboy *noun* **1** = page². **2** a woman's hairstyle with the hair rolled under at the ends.

pager *noun* a radio device with a bleeper, used to contact the wearer.

paginate *verb* to number the pages of (a book etc.). **pagination** *noun*

pagoda (pă-**goh**-dă) *noun* a Hindu temple shaped like a pyramid, or a Buddhist tower with several storeys.

paid *see* pay. **–paid** *adjective* receiving money in exchange for goods or services, *a paid assistant*; *paid holidays*, during which normal wages continue to be paid. □ **paid-up** *adjective* having paid one's subscription, *a paid-up member*. **put paid to** (*informal*) to put an end to the hopes, prospects, or activities of.

pail *noun* a bucket.

pain *noun* **1** an unpleasant feeling caused by injury or disease of the body. **2** mental suffering. **3** punishment, or the threat of this, *on* or *under pain of death*. **4** (also **pain in the neck**) (*informal*) an annoying person or thing. **–pain** *verb* to cause pain to. **pains** *plural noun* careful effort, trouble taken, *take pains with the work*. [from Latin *poena* = punishment]

pained *adjective* distressed and annoyed, *a pained look*.

painful *adjective* **1** causing pain. **2** (of a part of the body) suffering pain. **3** causing trouble or difficulty, laborious. **painfully** *adverb*, **painfulness** *noun*

painkiller *noun* a medicine etc. that lessens pain.

painless *adjective* not causing pain. **painlessly** *adverb*, **painlessness** *noun*

painstaking *adjective* careful, using or done with great care and effort.

paint *noun* colouring matter for applying in liquid form to a surface. **–paint** *verb* **1** to coat or decorate with paint. **2** to make a picture or portray by using paint(s). **3** to describe vividly; *he's not so black as he is painted*, not as bad as he is said to be. **4** to apply (liquid or cosmetic) to the skin; *paint one's face*, to use or apply make-up. **paints** *plural noun* a collection of tubes or cakes of paint. □ **painted lady** an orange butterfly with black and white spots.

paintbox *noun* a box holding dry paints for use by an artist.

paintbrush *noun* a brush for applying paint.

painter¹ *noun* a person who paints as an artist or as a decorator.

painter² *noun* a rope attached to the bow of a boat for tying it up. [from Old French *penteur* = rope]

painting *noun* a painted picture.

paintwork *noun* **1** a painted surface. **2** the work of painting.

pair *noun* **1** a set of two things or people, a couple. **2** an article consisting of two joined corresponding parts, *a pair of scissors*. **3** an engaged or married couple. **4** two mated animals. **5** the other member of a pair, *can't find a pair to this sock*. **6** either or both of two MPs of opposite parties who are absent from a division by mutual arrangement. **–pair** *verb* **1** to arrange or be arranged in couples. **2** (of animals) to mate. **3** to partner (a person) with a member of the opposite sex. **4** to make a pair in Parliament. □ **pair off** to form into pairs. [from Latin *paria* = equal things]

Paisley *adjective* having a pattern of tapering petal-shaped figures with much detail. [named after Paisley in Scotland]

Pakistan (pak-ĭ-**stahn** *or* pah-kĭ-) a republic in southern Asia. **Pakistani** *adjective* & *noun* (*plural* **Pakistanis**).

pal *noun* (*informal*) a friend. **–pal** *verb* (**palled**, **palling**) **pal up** (*informal*) to become friends. [from a gypsy word *pal* = brother]

palace *noun* **1** the official residence of a sovereign, president, archbishop, or bishop. **2** a splendid mansion. [from Palatium, the name of a hill on which the house of the emperor Augustus stood in ancient Rome]

Palaeocene (**pal**-ee-ŏ-seen) *adjective* of the earliest epoch of the Tertiary period. **–Palaeocene** *noun* this epoch.

palaeography (pal-ee-**og**-ră-fee) *noun* the study of ancient writing and documents. **palaeographer** *noun*, **palaeographic** *adjective* [from Greek *palaios* = old, + *-graphy*]

palaeolithic (pal-ee-ŏ-**lith**-ik) *adjective* of the early part of the Stone Age. **–palaeolithic** *noun* this period. [from Greek *palaios* = old, + *lithos* = stone]

palaeontology (pal-ee-on-**tol**-ŏ-jee) *noun* the scientific study of life in the geological past. **palaeontologist** *noun* [from Greek *palaios* = old, + *ontology*]

Palaeozoic (pal-ee-ŏ-**zoh**-ik) *adjective* of the geological era between the Precambrian and Mesozoic, lasting from about 590 to 248 million years ago. **–Palaeozoic** *noun* this era. [from Greek *palaios* = old, + *zoion* = animal]

palanquin (pal-ăn-**keen**) *noun* a covered litter for one person, used in India.

palatable (**pal**-ă-tă-bŭl) *adjective* pleasant to the taste or to the mind.

palate (**pal**-ăt) *noun* **1** the roof of the mouth. **2** the sense of taste. **palatal** *adjective*

palatial (pă-**lay**-shăl) *adjective* like a palace, spacious and splendid. **palatially** *adverb*

palaver (pă-**lah**-ver) *noun* **1** tedious fuss and bother; a prolonged business. **2** profuse or idle talk; cajolery. **3** (*historical*) a parley, especially between Africans and traders. [from Portuguese *palavra* = word]

pale¹ *adjective* **1** (of a person's face) having little colour, lighter than normal. **2** (of colour or light) faint, not bright or vivid. **–pale** *verb* to turn pale. **palely** *adverb*, **paleness** *noun* [from Latin *pallidus* = pallid]

pale² *noun* **1** a stake forming part of a fence. **2** a boundary. □ **beyond the pale** outside the bounds of acceptable behaviour. [from Latin *palus* = pointed stick set in the ground]

Palestine a territory in the Middle East on the eastern coast of the Mediterranean Sea. An agreement between Israel and the PLO in 1993 has given some autonomy to Palestine. □ **Palestine Liberation Organisation** *see* PLO. **Palestinian** *adjective* & *noun*

palette (**pal**-ĕt) *noun* a thin board with a thumb hole, on which an artist mixes colours when painting. □ **palette knife** an artist's knife for mixing or spreading paint; a knife with a long blunt round-ended flexible blade for spreading or smoothing soft substances in cookery etc.

palfrey (**pawl**-free) *noun* (*old use*) a horse for ordinary riding especially for ladies.

Pali (**pah**-lee) *noun* a language closely related to Sanskrit in which many sacred Buddhist texts are written.

palimpsest (**pal**-ĭmp-sest) *noun* **1** writing material or a manuscript on which the original writing has been removed to make room for other writing. **2** a monumental brass turned and re-engraved on the reverse side.

palindrome (**pal**-ĭn-drohm) *noun* a word or phrase that reads the same backwards as forwards, e.g. *Glenelg*, *nurses run*. [from Greek *palindromos* = running back again]

paling *noun* **1** fencing made of wooden posts or railings. **2** one of its uprights.

palisade (pal-ĭ-**sayd**) *noun* a fence of pointed stakes. □ **palisade cells** or **layer** a layer of long cells that are parallel to each other and often at right angles to the surface of the structure (especially a leaf) of which they form part. [same origin as *pale²*]

palish *adjective* rather pale.

pall¹ (*pr.* pawl) *noun* **1** a cloth spread over a coffin. **2** something forming a dark heavy covering, *a pall of smoke*. [from Latin *pallium* = cloak]

pall² (*pr.* pawl) *verb* to become uninteresting or boring. [from *appal*]

Palladian (pă-**lay**-dee-ăn) *adjective* of or in the neoclassical style of Palladio.

Palladio (pă-**lah**-dee-oh), Andrea (1508–80), Italian architect.

palladium (pă-**lay**-dee-ŭm) *noun* a rare silver-white metallic element resembling platinum (symbol Pd).

pallbearer *noun* a person helping to carry the coffin or walking beside it at a funeral.

pallet¹ *noun* **1** a mattress stuffed with straw. **2** a hard narrow bed, a makeshift bed.

pallet² *noun* a large tray or platform for carrying goods that are being lifted or in storage, especially one that can be raised by a forklift truck.

palliasse (**pal**-ee-ass) *noun* a straw mattress.

palliate (**pal**-ee-ayt) *verb* to make less intense or less severe. **palliation** *noun* [same origin as *pall¹*]

palliative (**pal**-ee-ă-tiv) *adjective* reducing the bad effects of something. –**palliative** *noun* something that does this. □ **palliative care** care of the terminally ill.

pallid (**pal**-ĭd) *adjective* pale, especially from illness.

pallor (**pal**-er) *noun* paleness.

pally *adjective* (*informal*) friendly.

palm *noun* **1** the inner surface of the hand between the wrist and the fingers. **2** the part of a glove that covers this. **3** a palm tree. **4** an imaginary award for success, *carried off the palm*. –**palm** *verb* to conceal in one's hand. □ **palm off** to get (a thing) accepted fraudulently. **Palm Sunday** the Sunday before Easter, commemorating Christ's triumphal entry into Jerusalem when the people strewed leaves in his path. **palm tree** a kind of tree growing in warm or tropical climates, with no branches and with large leaves growing in a mass at the top.

palmate (**pal**-mayt) *adjective* shaped like a hand with the fingers spread out.

palmetto (pal-**met**-oh) *noun* (*plural* **palmettos**) a kind of small palm tree with fan-shaped leaves.

palmist *noun* a person who is skilled in palmistry.

palmistry (**pahm**-ĭ-stree) *noun* the supposed art of telling a person's future or interpreting character by examining the lines or creases etc. in the palm of his or her hand.

palmy (**pahm**-ee) *adjective* **1** full of palms. **2** flourishing, *in their former palmy days*.

palomino (pal-ŏ-**mee**-noh) *noun* (*plural* **palominos**) a golden or cream-coloured horse with a light-coloured mane and tail.

palp *noun* an organ at or near the mouth of certain insects and crustaceans, used for feeling and tasting things.

palpable (**pal**-pă-bŭl) *adjective* **1** able to be touched or felt. **2** easily perceived, obvious. **palpably** *adverb*, **palpability** *noun* [from Latin *palpare* = touch]

palpate (pal-**payt**) *verb* to examine by feeling with the hands, especially as part of a medical examination. **palpation** *noun*

palpitate (**pal**-pĭ-tayt) *verb* **1** to pulsate, to throb rapidly. **2** (of a person) to quiver with fear or excitement. **palpitation** *noun*

palsied (**pawl**-zeed) *adjective* affected with palsy.

palsy (**pawl**-zee) *noun* paralysis, especially with involuntary tremors.

paltry (**pawl**-tree) *adjective* (**paltrier, paltriest**) worthless, trivial, contemptible.

pampas (**pam**-păs) *noun* vast grassy plains in South America. □ **pampas grass** a kind of tall ornamental grass with feathery plumes.

pamper *verb* to treat very indulgently; to spoil (a person) with luxury.

pamphlet (**pam**-flět) *noun* a leaflet or paper-covered booklet containing information.

Pan (*Gk. myth.*) the god of flocks and herds, half man and half goat, believed to be able to cause sudden fear ('panic'). □ **Pan flute** *see* **panpipes.**

pan¹ *noun* **1** a metal or earthenware vessel with a flat base and often without a lid, used for cooking and other domestic purposes. **2** its contents. **3** any similar vessel. **4** the bowl of a pair of scales. **5** a toilet bowl. **6** a depression in the ground, *claypan*; *salt pan*. –**pan** *verb* (**panned, panning**) **1** to wash (gravel) in a pan in search of gold. **2** (*informal*) to criticise severely. □ **pan out** (of circumstances or events) to turn out in a specified way.

pan² *verb* (**panned, panning**) **1** to turn (a camera) horizontally to give a panoramic effect or follow a moving object. **2** (of a camera) to turn in this way.

pan- *prefix* **1** all (as in *panorama*). **2** of the whole of a continent or racial group etc. (as in *pan-African*). [from Greek *pan* = all]

panacea (pan-ă-**see**-ă) *noun* a remedy for all kinds of diseases or troubles. [from *pan-*, + Greek *akos* = remedy]

panache (pă-**nash**) *noun* a confident stylish manner.

Panama (**pan**-ă-mah) a Central American republic. □ **Panama Canal** a canal across the isthmus of Panama, connecting the Atlantic and Pacific Oceans. **Panama City** the capital of Panama. **Panamanian** (pan-ă-**may**-nee-ăn) *adjective* & *noun*

panama (pan-ă-**mah**) *noun* a hat of fine pliant strawlike material. [from *Panama*]

pancake *noun* **1** a thin round cake of batter fried on both sides, sometimes rolled up with filling. **2** make-up in the form of a flat cake. □ **Pancake Day** Shrove Tuesday (the day before Ash Wednesday), on which pancakes are traditionally eaten. **pancake landing** a landing in which an aircraft descends vertically in a level position. [from *pan*¹ + *cake*]

panchromatic (pan-krŏ-**mat**-ik) *adjective* sensitive to all colours of the visible spectrum. [from *pan-*, + Greek *khroma* = colour]

pancreas (**pang**-kree-ăs) *noun* a gland near the stomach discharging a digestive secretion into the duodenum and insulin into the blood. **pancreatic** (pang-kree-**at**-ik) *adjective* [from *pan-*, + Greek *kreas* = flesh]

panda *noun* **1** (also **giant panda**) a large rare bearlike black and white animal living in the mountains of south-west China. **2** (also **red panda**) a raccoon-like animal of India.

pandemic (pan-**dem**-ik) *adjective* (of a disease) occurring over a whole country or the whole world. [from *pan-*, + Greek *demos* = people]

pandemonium (pan-dĕ-**moh**-nee-ŭm) *noun* uproar. [from *pan-* + *demon*]

pander *verb* **pander to** to gratify (weakness or vulgar tastes), *pandering to the public interest in scandal.*

Pandora (*Gk. myth.*) the first woman, who opened a store-jar that let loose all kinds of misfortunes upon mankind. □ **Pandora's box** a thing that once activated will generate many unmanageable problems.

pane *noun* a single sheet of glass in a window or door.

panegyric (pan-ĕ-**ji**-rik) *noun* a speech or piece of writing praising a person or thing.

panel *noun* **1** a distinct usually rectangular section of a surface. **2** a strip of board or other material forming a separate section of a wall, door, or cabinet etc.; a section of the metal bodywork of a vehicle. **3** a strip of material set lengthwise in or on a garment. **4** a group of people assembled to discuss or decide something. **5** a list of jurors; a jury. –**panel** *verb* (**panelled, panelling**) to cover or decorate with panels. □ **panel van** (*Austral.*) a vehicle like a station wagon but with a single row of seats and usually closed sides.

panelling *noun* **1** a series of panels in a wall. **2** wood used for making panels.

panellist *noun* a member of a panel.

pang *noun* a sudden sharp feeling of pain or a painful emotion, *pangs of jealousy*.

panic *noun* sudden terror, wild infectious fear. –**panic** *verb* (**panicked, panicking**) to affect or be affected with panic. ☐ **panic stations** positions taken up in an emergency. **panic-stricken** *adjective* affected with panic. **panicky** *adjective* [from Greek *panikos*, from *Pan*, the name of the god]

panicle *noun* a loose branching cluster of flowers.

Pankhurst, Mrs Emmeline (1858–1928), British suffragette leader.

pannier *noun* **1** a large basket, especially one of a pair carried on either side of a pack animal. **2** a bag or container carried similarly on a motorcycle or bicycle. [from Latin *panarium* = bread basket]

pannikin *noun* a small metal cup. ☐ **pannikin boss** a person with minor authority.

panoply (**pan**-ŏ-plee) *noun* a splendid array. [from *pan-*, + Greek *hopla* = weapons]

panorama *noun* **1** a view of a wide area; a picture or photograph of this. **2** a view of a constantly changing scene or series of events. **panoramic** (pan-ŏ-**ram**-ik) *adjective* [from *pan-*, + Greek *horama* = view]

panpipes *plural noun* (also **Pan flute**) a musical instrument made of a series of short pipes of different lengths fixed together. [named after the Greek god Pan]

pansy *noun* a garden plant of the violet family, with broad flat rounded richly-coloured petals. [from French *pensée* = thought]

pant[1] *verb* **1** to breathe with short quick breaths. **2** to utter breathlessly. **3** to be extremely eager. –**pant** *noun* a panting breath.

pant[2] *see* **pants**.

pantaloons *plural noun* baggy trousers gathered at the ankles.

pantechnicon (pan-**tek**-nik-ŏn) *noun* (*Brit.*) a kind of large van for moving furniture etc.

pantheism (**pan**-thee-izm) *noun* the belief that God is everything and everything is God. **pantheist** *noun*, **pantheistic** *adjective*

pantheon (**pan**-thee-ŏn) *noun* **1** a temple dedicated to all the gods. **2** the gods of a people collectively. [from *pan-*, + Greek *theos* = god]

panther *noun* **1** a leopard. **2** (*Amer.*) a puma.

panties *plural noun* (*informal*) underpants for women or children.

pantihose *noun* (also **pantyhose**) a woman's skintight garment covering the feet, legs, and lower part of the body.

pantile (**pan**-tyl) *noun* a curved roof tile. [from *pan*[1] + *tile*]

pantomime *noun* **1** a type of drama based on a fairy tale, usually produced at Christmas. **2** expressive movements of the face and body used to convey a story or meaning. –**pantomime** *verb* to express a story or meaning by such movements. [from *pan-* + *mime* (because in its most ancient form an actor mimed the different parts)]

pantry *noun* **1** a room or cupboard for storing food. **2** a room in which china, glasses, cutlery, etc. are kept. [from Latin *panis* = bread]

pants *plural noun* **1** underpants. **2** trousers or slacks. ☐ **pants suit** a woman's suit of jacket and trousers. [short for *pantaloons*]

panzer (**pants**-er) *adjective* (of German troops) armoured, *panzer divisions*.

pap *noun* **1** soft or semi-liquid food suitable for infants or invalids. **2** mash, pulp.

papa *noun* (*old use*, children's word) father.

papacy (**pay**-pă-see) *noun* the position or authority of the pope; the system of Church government by popes. [from Latin *papa* = pope]

papal (**pay**-păl) *adjective* of the pope or the papacy.

paparazzo (pap-ă-**raht**-soh) *noun* (*plural* **paparazzi**) a freelance photographer who pursues celebrities to photograph them.

papaya *noun* = **pawpaw**.

paper *noun* **1** a substance manufactured in thin sheets from wood fibre, rags, etc., used for writing or printing or drawing on or for wrapping things. **2** a newspaper. **3** wallpaper. **4** a set of examination questions, *the history paper*. **5** a document. **6** an essay or dissertation, especially one read to a learned society. –**paper** *verb* to cover (walls etc.) with wallpaper. ☐ **on paper** in writing; in theory, when judged from written or printed evidence, *the scheme looks good on paper*. **paper clip** a piece of bent wire or plastic for holding sheets of paper together. **paper money** banknotes and money orders etc. as distinct from coin. **paper over the cracks** to seek to conceal flaws or disagreement. **paper tiger** a person or thing that has a threatening appearance but can do no harm. [from *papyrus*]

paperback *adjective* bound in a flexible paper binding, not in a stiff cover. –**paperback** *noun* a book bound in this way.

paperbark *noun* any of several Australian trees with papery bark.

paperknife *noun* a blunt knife for slitting open uncut pages or sealed envelopes etc.

paperweight *noun* a heavy object placed on loose papers to keep them in place.

paperwork *noun* routine clerical work and record-keeping.

papier mâché (pap-ee-yay **ma**-shay) *noun* moulded paper pulp used for making boxes, trays, or ornaments etc. [French, = chewed paper]

papilla (pă-**pil**-ă) *noun* (*plural* **papillae**, *pr*. pă-**pil**-ee) a small projection on a part of an animal or plant (e.g. one of those forming the surface of the tongue). **papillary** *adjective* [Latin, = nipple]

papist (**pay**-pĭst) *noun* (*derogatory*) a Roman Catholic.

papoose (pă-**poos**) *noun* an indigenous North American baby or young child. [Algonquian]

pappadam (**pup**-ă-dum) *noun* a thin crisp bread made of lentil flour, eaten with curry. [Tamil]

paprika (**pap**-rik-ă *or* pă-**pree**-kă) *noun* red pepper; a ground condiment made from this. [Hungarian]

pap smear *noun* a test carried out on a smear taken from the cervix, used to detect cancer. [named after G.N. *Papanicolaou*, the American scientist who invented this procedure]

Papua (**pah**-poo-ă) a province of Indonesia comprising the western half of the island of New Guinea and adjacent smaller islands.

Papua New Guinea an independent country in the Pacific off the NE coast of Australia, comprising the eastern half of the island of New Guinea and adjacent smaller islands.

papyrus (pă-**py**-rŭs) *noun* 1 a reed-like water plant with thick fibrous stems from which a kind of paper was made by the ancient Egyptians. 2 this paper. 3 (*plural* **papyri**) a manuscript written on this.

par *noun* 1 an average or normal amount, condition, or degree etc., *was feeling below par*. 2 the face value of stocks and shares etc.; *at par*, at face value. 3 (in golf) the number of strokes that a first-class player should normally require for a hole or course. □ **on a par with** on an equal footing with. [from Latin *par* = equal]

para-¹ *prefix* 1 beside (as in *parallel*). 2 beyond (as in *paradox*). [from Greek *para* = beside or past]

para-² *prefix* protecting (as in *parasol*). [from Italian *para* = defend]

parable *noun* a story told to illustrate a moral or spiritual truth. [from Greek *parabole* = comparison (same origin as *parabola*)]

parabola (pă-**rab**-ŏ-lă) *noun* a curve like the path of an object thrown into the air and falling back to earth. [from *para-¹* = beside, + Greek *bole* = a throw]

parabolic (pa-ră-**bol**-ik) *adjective* 1 of or expressed in a parable. 2 of or like a parabola.

paracetamol (pa-ră-**see**-tă-mol) *noun* a medicinal drug used to relieve pain and reduce fever; a tablet of this.

parachute *noun* a rectangular or umbrella-shaped device used to slow the descent of a person or heavy object falling from a great height, especially from a moving aircraft; *parachute troops*, troops trained to descend by parachute. –**parachute** *verb* to descend by parachute; to drop (supplies etc.) by parachute. **parachutist** *noun* [from *para-²* + *chute* = a fall]

parade *noun* 1 a formal assembly of troops for inspection or roll-call etc. 2 (in full **parade ground**) a place where this is regularly held. 3 a procession of people or things, especially in a display or exhibition. 4 an ostentatious display, *makes a parade of his virtues*. 5 a public square, promenade, or street. –**parade** *verb* 1 to assemble for parade. 2 to march in procession or ceremonially. 3 to make a display of. □ **on parade** taking part in a parade.

paradigm (**pa**-ră-dym) *noun* something serving as an example or model of how things should be done. **paradigmatic** (pa-ră-dig-**mat**-ik) *adjective* [from *para-¹*, + Greek *deiknunai* = to show]

paradise *noun* 1 heaven. 2 Eden. [from ancient Persian, = a park or garden]

paradox (**pa**-ră-doks) *noun* a statement etc. that seems to contradict itself or to conflict with common sense but which contains a truth (e.g. 'more haste, less speed'). **paradoxical** (pa-ră-**doks**-i-kăl) *adjective*, **paradoxically** *adverb* [from *para-*[1], + *doxa* = opinion]

paraffin *noun* an oil obtained from petroleum or shale, used as a fuel. □ **liquid paraffin** a tasteless form of this used as a mild laxative. **paraffin wax** paraffin in solid form.

paragon (**pa**-ră-gŏn) *noun* a model of excellence, an apparently perfect specimen.

paragraph *noun* one or more sentences on a single theme, forming a distinct section of a piece of writing and beginning on a new (often indented) line. – **paragraph** *verb* to arrange in paragraphs. [from *para-*[1] + *-graph*]

Paraguay (**pa**-ră-gwy) an inland republic in South America. **Paraguayan** (pa-ră-**gwy**-ăn) *adjective* & *noun*

parakeet (**pa**-ră-keet) *noun* a kind of small parrot, often with a long tail.

parallax (**pa**-ră-laks) *noun* an apparent difference in the position or direction of an object when it is viewed from different points. **parallactic** (pa-ră-**lak**-tik) *adjective*

parallel *adjective* 1 (of lines or planes) continuously at the same distance from each other. 2 having this relationship, *the road runs parallel to* (or *with*) *the railway*. 3 similar, having features that correspond, *parallel situations*. 4 (of processes) occurring or performed simultaneously. – **parallel** *noun* 1 an imaginary line on the earth's surface or a corresponding line on a map parallel to and passing through all points equidistant from the equator. 2 a person or situation etc. that is parallel to another, *drew a parallel between the two situations*. – **parallel** *verb* (**paralleled**, **paralleling**) 1 to be parallel to. 2 to find or mention something parallel or corresponding; to compare. □ **parallel imports** goods imported by unlicensed distributors for sale at less than the manufacturer's official retail price. **parallelism** *noun* [from *para-*[1], + Greek *allelos* = each other]

parallelepiped (pa-ră-lel-ĕ-**py**-ped) *noun* a solid body of which each face is a parallelogram.

parallelogram (pa-ră-**lel**-ŏ-gram) *noun* a plane four-sided figure with its opposite sides parallel to each other. [from *parallel* + *-gram*]

Paralympian *noun* a competitor in the Paralympics.

Paralympics *plural noun* an international athletic competition, modelled on the Olympic Games, for disabled athletes. **Paralympic** *adjective*

paralyse *verb* 1 to affect with paralysis, to make unable to act or move normally. 2 to bring to a standstill.

paralysis *noun* 1 loss of the power of movement, caused by disease or injury to nerves. 2 inability to move normally. [from Greek *para* = on one side, + *lusis* = loosening]

paralytic (pa-ră-**lit**-ik) *adjective* 1 affected with paralysis. 2 (*informal*) very drunk. – **paralytic** *noun* a person affected with paralysis.

Paramaribo (pa-ră-**ma**-rĭ-boh) the capital of Suriname.

paramecium (pa-ră-**mee**-see-ŭm) *noun* a very small one-celled organism that is roughly oval in shape and fringed with cilia.

paramedic *noun* a member of the paramedical services, especially a member of an ambulance crew with advanced medical training.

paramedical *adjective* supplementing and supporting medical work.

parameter (pă-**ram**-ĕ-ter) *noun* 1 (in mathematics) a quantity that is constant in the case considered but varies in different cases. 2 a variable quantity or quality that restricts or gives a particular form to the thing it characterises. 3 a specification that is used in a computer program or routine and that can be given a different value whenever this is repeated. 4 a limit or boundary. [from *para-*[1] = beside, + Greek *metron* = measure]

Usage The use of *parameter* in sense 4, though common, is unacceptable to some people.

---

paramilitary *adjective* organised like a military force but not part of the armed services. – **paramilitary** *noun* a member of a paramilitary organisation. [from *para-*[1] = beside, + *military*]

paramount *adjective* chief in importance, supreme.

paramour (**pa**-ră-moor) *noun* a married person's illicit lover. [from French *par amour* = by love]

parang (**pah**-rang) *noun* a heavy Malayan sheath knife.

paranoia (pa-ră-**noi**-ă) *noun* **1** a mental disorder in which a person has delusions, e.g. of grandeur or persecution. **2** an abnormal tendency to suspect and mistrust others. [Greek, = distraction]

paranoiac (pa-ră-**noi**-ak) *adjective* of, like, or suffering from paranoia. –**paranoiac** *noun* a person suffering from paranoia.

paranoid (**pa**-ră-noid) *adjective* & *noun* = paranoiac.

paranormal *adjective* (of occurrences or powers) presumed to operate outside normal laws; supernatural.

parapet (**pa**-ră-pĕt) *noun* a low protective wall along the edge of a balcony, roof, or bridge etc.

paraphernalia (pa-ră-fer-**nay**-lee-ă) *noun* numerous small pieces of equipment etc. [from Greek, = personal articles that a woman could keep after her marriage as opposed to her dowry which went to her husband (Greek *para* = beside, + *pherne* = dowry)]

paraphrase (**pa**-ră-frayz) *verb* to express the meaning of (a passage) in other words. –**paraphrase** *noun* rewording in this way; a reworded passage. [from *para-*¹ + *phrase*]

paraplegia (pa-ră-**plee**-jee-ă) *noun* paralysis of the legs and part or all of the trunk. **paraplegic** *adjective* & *noun* [from *para-*¹, + Greek *plexis* = a stroke]

parapsychology (pa-ră-sy-**kol**-ŏ-jee) *noun* the scientific study of mental perceptions (e.g. those occurring in clairvoyance and telepathy) that seem to be outside normal mental abilities.

parasite *noun* **1** an animal or plant that lives on or in another from which it draws its nourishment. **2** a person who lives off another or others and gives no useful return. **parasitic** (pa-ră-**sit**-ik) *adjective*, **parasitically** *adverb* [from Greek *parasitos* = guest at a meal]

parasol *noun* a light umbrella used to give shade from the sun. [from *para-*², + Italian *sole* = sun]

paratrooper *noun* a member of the paratroops.

paratroops *plural noun* parachute troops. [from *parachute* + *troops*]

parboil *verb* to boil (food) until it is partly cooked.

parcel *noun* **1** a thing or things wrapped up for carrying or for sending by post. **2** a piece of land. –**parcel** *verb* (**parcelled, parcelling**) **1** to

wrap up as a parcel. **2** to divide into portions, *parcelled it out*. [same origin as *particle*]

parch *verb* to make hot and dry or thirsty.

parchment *noun* **1** a heavy paper-like material made from animal skins; a manuscript written on this. **2** a kind of paper resembling this. [from the city of Pergamum, now in Turkey, where parchment was made in ancient times]

pardalote (**par**-dă-loht) *noun* any of several small colourful spotted Australian birds.

pardon *noun* **1** forgiveness. **2** cancellation of the punishment incurred through a crime or conviction, *a free pardon*. **3** kind indulgence, e.g. for a discourtesy or for failing to hear or understand, *I beg your pardon*. –**pardon** *verb* (**pardoned, pardoning**) to forgive; to overlook (a slight discourtesy etc.) kindly.

pardonable *adjective* able to be pardoned. **pardonably** *adverb*

pare (*pr.* pair) *verb* **1** to trim by cutting away the edges of; to peel. **2** to reduce little by little, *pared down their expenses*. [from Latin *parare* = prepare]

parenchyma (pă-**reng**-kĭ-mă) *noun* **1** the tissue of an organ or gland of the body, as distinguished from flesh or connective tissue. **2** the soft and succulent material found in the softer parts of leaves, pulp of fruits, bark and pith of stems, etc.

parent *noun* **1** a person who has given birth to, fathered, or adopted a child; a father or mother. **2** an ancestor. **3** an animal or plant from which others are derived. **4** a source from which other things are derived, *the parent company*. –**parent** *verb* to be a parent (of). **parenthood** *noun* [from Latin *parens* = producing offspring]

parentage (**pair**-rĕn-tij) *noun* descent from parents, ancestry.

parental (pă-**ren**-t'l) *adjective* of parents.

parenthesis (pă-**ren**-thĕ-sĭs) *noun* (*plural* **parentheses**) **1** an additional word, phrase, or sentence inserted in a passage that is grammatically complete without it, and usually marked off by brackets, dashes, or commas. **2** either of the pair of round brackets (like these) used for this. ☐ **in parenthesis** between brackets as a parenthesis; as an aside or digression in a speech etc. [Greek, = putting in besides]

parenthetic (pa-rĕn-**thet**-ik) *adjective* **1** of or as a parenthesis. **2** interposed as an aside or digression. parenthetical *adjective*, parenthetically *adverb*

par excellence (par **eks**-el-ahns) *adverb* more than all others, in the highest degree. [French, = because of special excellence]

parfait (**par**-fay) *noun* **1** a rich iced dessert made of eggs and cream. **2** layers of ice cream and fruit etc. served in a tall glass.

pariah (pă-**ry**-ă) *noun* an outcast.

parietal bone (pă-**ry**-ĕ-tăl) *noun* either of a pair of bones forming part of the sides and top of the skull.

parings (**pair**-ringz) *plural noun* pieces pared off.

Paris[1] the capital of France. Parisian (pă-**riz**-ee-ăn) *adjective & noun*

Paris[2] (*Gk. legend*) a Trojan prince, whose abduction of Helen from her husband Menelaus, king of Sparta, provoked the Trojan War.

parish *noun* **1** an area having its own church or churches and clergy. **2** the people of a parish. [from Greek, = neighbourhood (Greek *para* = beside, *oikein* = dwell)]

parishioner (pă-**rish**-ŏ-ner) *noun* a member of a parish church.

parity (**pa**-rĭ-tee) *noun* **1** equality, equal status or pay etc. **2** being valued at par.

park *noun* **1** a public garden or recreation ground in a town. **2** a large area of land kept in its natural state for the public benefit, *a national park*. **3** a large protected area where wild animals are kept in captivity, *a wildlife park*. **4** a parking area for vehicles. **5** an area of land designated for industry, business, etc., *technology park*. – park *verb* **1** to place and leave (a vehicle) temporarily. **2** (*informal*) to deposit temporarily; *park oneself*, to sit down. □ parking ticket a notice of a fine imposed for parking a vehicle illegally.

parka *noun* **1** a hooded skin jacket worn by Inuits. **2** a windproof or waterproof jacket similar to this.

parker *noun* (*informal*) a car's parking light.

Parkes, Sir Henry (1815–96), English-born Australian politician, five times Premier of NSW, a supporter of Federation and free trade.

Parkinson's disease *noun* a disease of the nervous system causing tremor and weakness of the muscles. [named after the English surgeon J. Parkinson, who described it in 1817]

parkland *noun* open grassland with clumps of trees etc.

parlance (**par**-lăns) *noun* a way of speaking, especially in regard to choice of words. [same origin as *parley*]

parley *noun* (*plural* parleys) a discussion, especially between enemies or opponents to settle points in dispute. – parley *verb* (parleyed, parleying) to hold a parley. [from French *parler* = speak]

parliament (**par**-lă-měnt) *noun* an assembly that makes the laws of a country or state. [same origin as *parley*]

parliamentarian (par-lă-men-**tair**-ree-ăn) *noun* a member of a parliament.

parliamentary (par-lă-**ment**-ă-ree) *adjective* of parliament; *parliamentary language*, polite, as required in parliamentary debates. □ parliamentary privilege freedom of speech granted to MPs during a meeting of parliament with consequent immunity from prosecution in a civil case.

parlour *noun* **1** (*old use*) the sitting room of a family in a private house. **2** a room in a mansion or convent etc. where people may receive visitors and converse privately. **3** a shop providing specified services, goods, etc., *beauty parlour*. □ parlour game an indoor game. [from French *parler* = speak]

parlous (**par**-lŭs) *adjective* (*formal*) perilous, hard to deal with.

parmesan (**par**-mě-zăn) *noun* a kind of hard cheese made originally at Parma in Italy, usually grated before use.

Parnassus a mountain of central Greece, in antiquity sacred to the Muses. Parnassian *adjective*

parochial (pă-**roh**-kee-ăl) *adjective* **1** of a church parish. **2** merely local; showing interest in a limited area only. parochialism *noun*

parody (**pa**-rŏ-dee) *noun* **1** a comic imitation of a well-known literary work or style etc. **2** a grotesque imitation, a travesty. – parody *verb* (parodied, parodying) to mimic humorously, to compose a parody of. parodist *noun* a writer of parodies. [from *para*-[1] = beside, + Greek *oide* = song]

parole (pă-**rohl**) *noun* **1** temporary or permanent release of a prisoner before his or her sentence has expired, on the promise of good behaviour. **2** such a promise. – parole *verb* to release on parole. [French, = word of honour]

paroxysm (**pa**-rŏk-sizm) *noun* a spasm, a sudden attack or outburst of pain, rage, or laughter etc.

parquet (**par**-kay) *noun* flooring of wooden blocks arranged in a pattern. **parquetry** *noun*

parrot *noun* **1** a tropical bird with a short hooked bill and often with brightly coloured plumage. **2** a person who repeats another's words or imitates his actions unintelligently.

parry *verb* (**parried**, **parrying**) **1** to ward off (an opponent's weapon or blow) by using one's own weapon etc. to block the thrust. **2** to evade (an awkward question) skilfully. –**parry** *noun* parrying.

parse (*pr.* parz) *verb* to identify the grammatical form and function of (a word or words in a sentence). [from Latin *pars* = part (of speech)]

parsec (**par**-sek) *noun* a unit of distance used in astronomy, about $3\frac{1}{4}$ light years. [from *parallax* + *second*]

Parsee (par-**see**) *noun* a person who believes in Zoroastrianism, especially one living in India.

parsimonious (par-sĭ-**moh**-nee-ŭs) *adjective* stingy, very sparing in the use of resources. **parsimoniously** *adverb*, **parsimony** (**par**-sĭ-mŏ-nee) *noun*

parsley *noun* a garden plant with crinkled green leaves used for flavouring and garnishing food.

parsnip *noun* **1** a plant with a large yellowish tapering root. **2** this root used as a vegetable.

parson *noun* a member of the clergy, especially a rector or vicar. □ **parson's nose** the rump of a cooked fowl.

parsonage *noun* a parson's house.

part *noun* **1** some but not all of a thing or number of things. **2** a division of a book or broadcast serial etc., especially as much as is issued at one time. **3** a region. **4** an integral element, *she is part of the family.* **5** a distinct portion of a human or animal body or of a plant. **6** a component of a machine or structure. **7** each of several equal portions of a whole; *a fourth part*, a quarter; *three parts*, three-quarters. **8** a portion allotted; a share of work etc. **9** the character assigned to an actor in a play etc.; the words spoken by this character; a copy of these. **10** the melody or other line of music assigned to a particular voice or instrument. **11** a side in an agreement or in a dispute; *for* or *on my part*, as far as I am concerned. –**part** *adverb* in part, partly.

–**part** *verb* **1** to separate or divide; to cause to do this; *part one's hair*, to make a parting. **2** to leave one another's company. □ **in good part** good-humouredly, without taking offence. **in part** partly. **part and parcel of** an essential part of. **part company** to go different ways after being together; to cease to associate. **part of speech** one of the classes into which words are divided in grammar (noun, adjective, pronoun, verb, adverb, preposition, conjunction, interjection). **part-song** *noun* a song with three or more voice parts, often without accompaniment. **part time** less than full time. **part-time** *adjective* for or during only part of the working day or week. **part-timer** *noun* one employed in part-time work. **part with** to give up possession of, to hand over.

partake *verb* (**partook**, **partaken**, **partaking**) **1** to participate. **2** to take a part or portion, especially of food. **partaker** *noun*

parthenogenesis (par-thĕ-nŏ-**jen**-ĕ-sĭs) *noun* reproduction from gametes without fertilisation. **parthenogenetic** (par-thĕ-nŏ-jĕ-**net**-ik) *adjective* [from Greek *parthenos* = virgin, + *genesis*]

Parthenon (**par**-thĕ-non) the temple of Athene Parthenos (= the maiden) built on the Acropolis at Athens in 447–432 BC.

Parthian (**par**-thee-ăn) *adjective* of the ancient kingdom of Parthia, SE of the Caspian Sea, or its people. –**Parthian** *noun* a native of Parthia. □ **Parthian shot** a sharp remark made by a person on leaving. (¶ The horsemen of Parthia were renowned for turning to shoot their arrows at the enemy while retreating.)

partial (**par**-shăl) *adjective* **1** in part but not complete or total, *a partial eclipse*. **2** biased, unfair. □ **be partial to** to have a strong liking for. **partially** *adverb*

partiality (par-shee-**al**-ĭ-tee) *noun* **1** bias, favouritism. **2** a strong liking.

participate (par-**tiss**-ĭ-payt) *verb* to have a share, to take part in something. **participant** *noun*, **participation** *noun* [from Latin *pars* = part, + *capere* = take]

participle (**par**-tĭ-si-pŭl) *noun* a word formed from a verb (e.g. *going*, *gone*; *sleeping*, *slept*) and used in compound verbs (*she is going* or *has gone*) or as an adjective (*sleeping dogs*). □ **past participle** usually ends in -*ed*, e.g. *washed*, *jumped*, with some common exceptions, e.g. *eaten*, *slept*. **present participle** ends in -*ing*, e.g. *washing*, *eating*, *sleeping*. **participial** (par-tĭ-**sip**-ee-ăl) *adjective*

particle *noun* **1** a very small portion of matter. **2** the smallest possible amount, *he hasn't a particle of sense*. **3** a minor part of speech or a common prefix or suffix, e.g. *non-*, *un-*, *-ness*. [from Latin, = little part]

particoloured *adjective* coloured partly in one colour and partly in another or others.

particular *adjective* **1** relating to one person or thing as distinct from others, individual, *this particular tax is no worse than others*. **2** special, exceptional, *took particular trouble*. **3** selecting carefully, insisting on certain standards, *is very particular about what he eats*. – **particular** *noun* a detail, a piece of information. □ **in particular** particularly, especially, *we liked this one in particular*; specifically, *did nothing in particular*. **particularly** *adverb*, **particularity** (pă-tik-yŭ-**la**-rĭ-tee) *noun* [same origin as *particle*]

particularise *verb* (also -**ize**) to specify, to name specially or one by one. **particularisation** *noun*

parting *noun* **1** leave-taking. **2** a line where hair is combed away in different directions. □ **parting shot** = Parthian shot.

partisan (par-tĭ-**zan**) *noun* **1** a strong and often uncritical supporter of a person, group, or cause. **2** a guerrilla. **partisanship** *noun*

partition (par-**tish**-ŏn) *noun* **1** division into parts. **2** a part formed in this way. **3** a structure that divides a room or space, a thin wall. – **partition** *verb* **1** to divide into parts; to share out in this way. **2** to divide (a room etc.) by means of a partition.

partly *adverb* to some extent but not completely or wholly.

partner *noun* **1** one who shares with another or others in some activity, especially in a business firm where he or she shares risks and profits. **2** either of two people dancing together or playing on the same side in a game. **3** either member of a married or unmarried couple. – **partner** *verb* to be the partner of; to put together as partners. **partnership** *noun*

partook see **partake**.

partridge *noun* **1** a game bird with brown feathers and a plump body. **2** its flesh as food.

parturition (par-tew-**rish**-ŏn) *noun* the process of giving birth to young, childbirth.

party *noun* **1** a social gathering, usually of invited guests. **2** a number of people traveling or working together as a unit, *a search party*. **3** a group of people united in support of a cause or policy etc., especially a political group organised on a national basis to put forward its policies and candidates for office. **4** the person(s) forming one side in an agreement or dispute. **5** a person who participates in, knows of, or supports an action or plan etc., *refused to be a party to the conspiracy*. – **party** *verb* (**partied**, **partying**) to attend a party. □ **party line** a shared telephone line; the set policy of a political party. [from *part*]

Parvati (**par**-vă-tee) (in Hinduism) a benevolent goddess, wife of Siva, mother of Skanda and Ganesha, identified in her malevolent aspect with Durga and Kali.

Pascal (pas-**kahl**) *noun* a computer language, used especially in training. [named after Blaise Pascal (1623–62), French mathematician, physicist, and religious philosopher]

pascal (**pas**-kăl) *noun* a unit of pressure. [named after Blaise Pascal]

paschal (**pas**-kăl) *adjective* **1** of the Jewish Passover; *the paschal lamb*, one sacrificed at Passover. **2** of Easter.

pash (*Austral. informal*) *noun* **1** a passionate kiss. **2** an infatuation. – **pash** *verb* to kiss passionately.

pashmina *noun* a shawl made from goat's wool.

Pashto (**pu**'sh-toh) *noun* the Iranian language of the Pathans.

paspalum (pas-**pay**-lŭm) *noun* a robust grass of non-arid regions.

pass[1] *verb* (**passed**, **passing**) **1** to go, proceed, or move onward or past something. **2** to cause to move across, over, or past. **3** to go from one person to another, to be transferred, *his title passed to his eldest son*. **4** to hand or transfer; (in ball games) to send the ball to another player of one's own side. **5** to discharge from the body as or with excreta. **6** to change from one state or condition into another. **7** to come to an end. **8** to happen, to be done or said, *we heard what passed between them*. **9** to occupy (time). **10** to circulate, to be accepted or currently known in a certain way. **11** to be tolerated or allowed. **12** to examine and declare satisfactory; to approve (a law etc.), especially by vote. **13** to achieve the required standard in performing (a test); to be accepted as satisfactory. **14** to go beyond. **15** to utter; to pronounce as a decision, *passed some remarks*; *pass judgment*. **16** (in a card game or a quiz) to refuse one's turn. – **pass** *noun* **1** passing, especially of an examination or at

cards. **2** a movement made with the hand(s)
or something held. **3** a permit to go into or out
of a place or to be absent from one's quarters.
4 transference of the ball to another player
of one's own side in ball games. **5** a critical
state of affairs, *things have come to a pretty
pass*. **6** (*informal*) a gesture, action, or remark
intended to lead to seduction. □ **pass away**
to cease; to die. **pass off** to cease gradually;
(of an event) to take place and be completed,
the meeting passed off smoothly; to offer or
dispose of (a thing) under false pretences,
passed it off as his own; to evade or dismiss
(an awkward remark etc.) lightly. **pass on** to
die. **pass out** (*informal*) to faint. **pass over** to
disregard; to ignore the claims of (a person)
to promotion etc. **pass the buck** *see* buck ².
pass up (*informal*) to refuse to accept (an
opportunity etc.). **pass water** to urinate. [from
Latin *passus* = pace]

pass² *noun* a gap in a mountain range, allowing
access to the other side.

passable *adjective* **1** able to be passed.
2 satisfactory, fairly good but not outstanding.
passably *adverb*

passage *noun* **1** the process of passing. **2** the
right to pass through, right of conveyance
as a passenger by sea or air, *book your
passage*. **3** a journey by sea or air. **4** a way
through, especially with walls on either side.
5 a tubelike structure through which air or
secretions etc. pass in the body; (*informal*)
back passage, the rectum. **6** a particular
section of a literary or musical work.
□ **passage of arms** a fight; a dispute.

passageway *noun* a passage giving a way
through.

passbook *noun* a book recording a
customer's deposits and withdrawals from a
bank or building society account.

passé (pah-**say**) *adjective* no longer
fashionable; past its prime. [French]

passenger *noun* **1** a person (other than the
driver, pilot, or members of the crew etc.)
travelling in a vehicle or ship or aircraft.
2 a member of a team or crew who does no
effective work.

passer-by *noun* (*plural* **passers-by**) a person
who happens to be going past a thing.

passim (**pas**-im) *adverb* throughout or at
many points in a book or article etc. [Latin, =
everywhere]

passing *adjective* not lasting long, casual,
a passing glance. –**passing** *noun* the end of

something, a death. □ **passing note** (in music)
a note that does not belong to the harmony but
is put in to make a smooth transition.

passion *noun* **1** strong emotion. **2** an outburst
of anger. **3** sexual love. **4** great enthusiasm
for something, the object of this, *chess is his
passion*. –**Passion** *noun* **1** the sufferings of
Christ on the cross. **2** the account of this in the
Gospels. **3** a musical setting for this account.
□ **passion flower** a climbing plant with
flowers thought to resemble the crown of
thorns and symbolise the Passion of Christ.
Passion Sunday the fifth Sunday in Lent.
[from Latin *passio* = suffering]

passionfruit *noun* the edible fruit of some
kinds of passion flower.

passionate *adjective* **1** full of passion,
showing or moved by strong emotion. **2** (of
emotion) intense. **passionately** *adverb*

passive *adjective* **1** acted upon and not active.
2 not resisting, submissive. **3** lacking initiative
or forceful qualities. **4** (of substances) inert,
not active. –**passive** *noun* the form of a verb
used when the subject of the sentence receives
the action, e.g. *was seen* in *he was seen there*.
□ **passive resistance** resistance by refusal
to cooperate. **passive smoking** the process
of breathing in smoke from cigarettes etc.
smoked by others, considered as a health risk.
passively *adverb*, **passiveness** *noun*, **passivity**
(pă-**siv**-ĭ-tee) *noun*

passkey *noun* **1** a key to a door or gate. **2** a
master key.

Passover *noun* **1** a Jewish festival
commemorating the liberation of the Israelites
from slavery in Egypt. **2** the paschal lamb.
[from *pass over*, because God spared the Jews
from the fate that affected the Egyptians]

passport *noun* **1** an official document issued
by a government identifying the holder as one
of its citizens and entitling him or her to travel
abroad under its protection. **2** a thing that
enables one to obtain something, *such ability
is a passport to success*. [from *pass*¹ + *port*¹]

password *noun* a secret word, phrase, or
set of characters, used as a code to gain
admission, access to a computer system, etc.

past *adjective* belonging or referring to the
time before the present; (of time) gone by.
–**past** *noun* **1** time that is gone by, *in the past*.
2 past events. **3** a person's past life or career,
especially one that is discreditable, *a man
with a past*. **4** the past tense. –**past** *preposition*
1 beyond in time or place, *hurried past me*.

2 beyond the limits, power, range, or stage of, *past belief*; *she's past caring what happens.* **–past** *adverb* beyond in time or place, up to and further, *drove past.* □ **past it** (*informal*) too old. **past master** a thorough master in or of a subject, an expert. **past tense** any of the tenses of a verb that express past action (e.g. *he came*, *he had come*). **not put it past a person** (*informal*) regard a person as morally capable of doing it.

pasta (**pas**-tă *or* **pahs**-) *noun* a type of dough made into various shapes (e.g. macaroni, spaghetti), used fresh or dried. [Italian, = paste]

paste *noun* **1** a moist fairly stiff mixture, especially of a powdery substance and a liquid. **2** an adhesive. **3** an easily spread preparation of ground meat, fish, nuts, etc., *fish paste*; *peanut paste.* **4** a hard glasslike substance used in making imitation gems. **–paste** *verb* **1** to fasten with paste. **2** to coat with paste. **3** (*informal*) to beat or thrash.

pasteboard *noun* a kind of thin board made of layers of paper or wood fibres pasted together.

pastel (**pas**-t'l) *noun* **1** a chalk-like crayon. **2** a drawing made with this. **3** a light delicate shade of colour.

pastern (**pas**-tern) the part of a horse's foot between fetlock and hoof.

Pasteur (pas-**ter**), Louis (1822–95), French chemist and bacteriologist.

pasteurise (**pahs**-chĕ-ryz) *verb* (also **-ize**) to sterilise (milk etc.) partially by heating and then chilling it. **pasteurisation** *noun* [named after Louis Pasteur]

pastiche (pas-**teesh**) *noun* a musical or other composition made up of selections from various sources.

pastille (**pas**-teel *or* **pas**-t'l) *noun* a small flavoured sweet for sucking, a lozenge.

pastime *noun* something done to pass time pleasantly, a recreation.

pastor (**pah**-ster) *noun* a member of the clergy in charge of a church or congregation; a person exercising spiritual guidance. [Latin, = shepherd]

pastoral (**pahs**-tŏ-răl) *adjective* **1** of shepherds or country life, *a pastoral scene.* **2** of stock raising; (of land) used for raising stock, *pastoral districts.* **3** of a pastor; concerned with spiritual guidance. **4** concerned with the general welfare of members of a group, school, etc.

pastoralist *noun* (*Austral.*) a sheep farmer or cattle farmer.

pastry *noun* **1** dough made of flour, fat, and water, used for covering pies or holding a filling. **2** food made with this. **3** a cake in which pastry is used. [from *paste*]

pasturage (**pahs**-chŭ-rij) *noun* **1** land for pasture. **2** the right to graze animals on this.

pasture *noun* **1** land covered with grass and similar plants suitable for grazing animals. **2** grass etc. on such land. **–pasture** *verb* **1** to put (animals) to graze in a pasture. **2** (of animals) to graze. [same origin as *pastor*]

pasty¹ (**pas**-tee *or* **pahs**-) *noun* pastry with a filling of meat, vegetables, or fruit etc., baked without a dish.

pasty² (**pay**-stee) *adjective* **1** of or like paste. **2** unhealthily pale, *pasty-faced.*

pat *verb* (**patted**, **patting**) **1** to tap gently with the open hand or with something flat. **2** to flatten or shape by doing this. **–pat** *noun* **1** a patting movement. **2** the sound of this. **3** a small mass of butter or other soft substance. **–pat** *adverb* & *adjective* known and ready for any occasion, *had his answer pat.* □ **a pat on the back** congratulations.

Patagonia the southernmost region of South America, chiefly a dry barren plateau in southern Argentina and Chile. **Patagonian** *adjective* & *noun*

patch *noun* **1** a piece of material or metal etc. put over a hole to mend it. **2** a piece of plaster or a pad placed over a wound etc., or a shield over the eye, to protect it. **3** a large or irregular area on a surface, differing in colour or texture etc. from the rest. **4** a piece of ground, especially for growing vegetables, *cabbage patch.* **5** a small area of anything, *patches of fog.* **6** a short period, *went through a bad patch last summer.* **7** (in computing) a small piece of code inserted to correct or enhance a program. **–patch** *verb* **1** to put a patch or patches on. **2** to serve as a patch for. **3** to piece (things) together. □ **not a patch on** (*informal*) not nearly as good as. **patch pocket** a pocket made by sewing a piece of cloth on the surface of a garment. **patch up** to repair with patches; to put together hastily or as a makeshift; to settle (a quarrel etc.).

patchwork *noun* **1** a kind of needlework in which assorted small pieces of cloth are joined edge to edge, often in a pattern. **2** anything made of assorted pieces.

patchy *adjective* (**patchier, patchiest**)
1 having patches, existing in patches, *patchy rain*. **2** uneven in quality. **patchily** *adverb*, **patchiness** *noun*

pate (*pr.* payt) *noun* (*old use*) the head.

pâté (**pa**-tay) *noun* paste of meat, fish, etc., *liver pâté*. [French]

patella (pă-**tel**-ă) *noun* the kneecap.

paten (**pat**-ĕn) *noun* a metal plate on which bread is placed at the Eucharist.

patent (**pay**-tĕnt) *noun* **1** letters patent; the right granted by these. **2** an invention or process protected in this way. **–patent** *adjective* **1** obvious, unconcealed, *his patent dislike of the plan*. **2** protected by a patent, *patent medicines*. **–patent** *verb* to obtain or hold a patent for. □ **letters patent** an official document conferring a right or title, especially one giving the holder the sole right to make, use, or sell an invention. **patent leather** leather with a glossy varnished surface. **patently** *adverb*

patentee (pay-tĕn-**tee**) *noun* one who holds a patent.

pater (**pay**-ter) *noun* (*old use*) father. [Latin]

paternal (pă-**ter**-năl) *adjective* **1** of a father; of fatherhood. **2** fatherly. **3** related through one's father; *paternal grandmother*, one's father's mother. **paternally** *adverb* [from Latin *pater* = father]

paternalism (pă-**ter**-nă-lizm) *noun* the policy of governing or controlling people in a paternal way, providing for their needs but giving them no responsibility. **paternalistic** *adjective*

paternity (pă-**ter**-nĭ-tee) *noun* **1** fatherhood, being a father. **2** descent from a father. [from Latin *pater* = father]

paternoster (pat-er-**noss**-ter) *noun* the Lord's Prayer, especially in Latin.

Paterson, Andrew Barton ('Banjo') (1864–1941), Australian writer of bush ballads, author of 'The Man from Snowy River', 'Clancy of the Overflow', and 'Waltzing Matilda'.

Paterson's curse *noun* a kind of bugloss, an introduced weed in Australia, but valued in some areas by apiarists and as drought fodder. Also called *Salvation Jane*.

path *noun* **1** a way by which people pass on foot, a track. **2** a line along which a person or thing moves. **3** a course of action. **4** (in graph theory) a sequence through a network of edges and vertices in which no vertex appears more than once.

Pathan (pă-**tahn**) *noun* a member of a people living in parts of Afghanistan and Pakistan.

pathetic (pă-**thet**-ik) *adjective* **1** arousing pity or sadness. **2** miserably inadequate. **pathetically** *adverb* [same origin as *pathos*]

pathfinder *noun* an explorer.

pathogen *noun* an agent causing disease. **pathogenic** *adjective*

pathological (pa-thŏ-**loj**-i-kăl) *adjective* **1** of pathology. **2** of or caused by a physical or mental disorder, *a pathological liar*. **pathologically** *adverb*

pathologist (pă-**thol**-ŏ-jĭst) *noun* an expert in pathology.

pathology (pă-**thol**-ŏ-jee) *noun* **1** the scientific study of diseases of the body. **2** abnormal changes in body tissue, caused by disease. [from Greek *pathos* = suffering, + *-logy*]

pathos (**pay**-thoss) *noun* a quality that arouses pity or sadness. [Greek, = feeling or suffering]

pathway *noun* a footway or track.

patience *noun* **1** calm endurance of hardship or annoyance or inconvenience or delay etc. **2** perseverance. **3** a card game (usually for one player) in which cards have to be brought into a particular arrangement.

patient *adjective* having or showing patience. **–patient** *noun* a person receiving treatment (or registered to receive any necessary treatment) by a doctor or dentist etc. **patiently** *adverb* [from Latin *patiens* = suffering]

patina (**pat**-ĭ-nă) *noun* **1** a green incrustation on the surface of old bronze. **2** a gloss on the surface of wooden furniture etc., produced by age.

patio (**pat**-ee-oh *or* **pay**-shee-oh) *noun* (*plural* **patios**) **1** a paved area beside a house, used for outdoor meals or relaxation. **2** an inner courtyard, open to the sky, in a Spanish or Spanish-American house. [Spanish]

patois (**pat**-wah) *noun* a dialect. [French, = rough speech]

patriarch (**pay**-tree-ark *or* **pat**-ree-ark) *noun* **1** the male head of a family or tribe; **the Patriarchs** the men named in the book of Genesis as the ancestors of mankind or of the tribes of Israel. **2** a bishop of high rank in certain Churches. **3** a venerable old man. **patriarchal** *adjective* [from Greek *patria* = family, + *arkhein* = to rule]

patrician (pǎ-**trish**-ǎn) *noun* a member of the aristocracy, especially in ancient Rome. –**patrician** *adjective* aristocratic. [from Latin, = having a noble father]

patricide (**pat**-rǐ-syd) *noun* **1** the crime of killing one's own father. **2** a person who is guilty of this. [from Latin *pater* = father, + *caedere* = kill]

Patrick, St (5th century), missionary and patron saint of Ireland. Feast day, 17 March.

patrimony (**pat**-rǐ-mǒ-nee) *noun* **1** property inherited from one's father or ancestors, a heritage. **2** a church's endowed income or property. [from Latin *patris* = of a father]

patriot (**pay**-tree-ǒt *or* **pat**-ree-ǒt) *noun* a person who loves his or her country and loyally supports it. [from Greek *patris* = fatherland]

patriotic (pat-ree-**ot**-ik *or* pay-tree-**ot**-ik) *adjective* loyally supporting one's country. **patriotically** *adverb*, **patriotism** *noun*

patrol *verb* (**patrolled**, **patrolling**) to walk or travel regularly through (an area or building) in order to see that all is secure and orderly. –**patrol** *noun* **1** patrolling, *on patrol*. **2** the person(s), ship(s), or aircraft whose job is to patrol an area. **3** a unit of usually 6 members of a Scout troop or Guide company. [from French *patouiller* = paddle in mud]

patron (**pay**-trǒn) *noun* **1** a person who gives encouragement or financial or other support to an activity or cause etc. **2** a regular customer of a shop or restaurant etc. □ **patron saint** a saint regarded as giving special protection to a person, place, or activity. **patroness** *feminine noun* [from Latin *patronus* = protector]

patronage (**pat**-rǒ-nij) *noun* **1** support given by a patron. **2** a customer's support of a shop, business, or service. **3** the control of appointments to office, privileges, etc. **4** patronising behaviour.

patronise (**pat**-rǒ-nyz) *verb* (also -**ize**) **1** to act as a patron towards, to support or encourage. **2** to be a regular customer at (a shop etc.). **3** to treat in a condescending way.

patronising *adjective* (also -**izing**) condescending. **patronisingly** *adverb*

patronymic (pat-rǒ-**nim**-ik) *noun* a person's name that is taken from the name of the father or a male ancestor. [from Greek *patros* = of a father, + *onoma* = name]

patter¹ *verb* **1** to make a series of light quick taps. **2** to run with short quick steps. –**patter** *noun* a series of light quick tapping sounds.

patter² *noun* rapid and often glib or deceptive speech, e.g. that used by a conjuror or salesperson etc.

pattern *noun* **1** an arrangement of lines, shapes, or colours; a decorative design. **2** a model, design, or instructions according to which something is to be made; a mould for casting. **3** a sample of cloth or other material. **4** an excellent example, a model. **5** the regular form or order in which a series of actions or qualities etc. occur, *behaviour patterns*. –**pattern** *verb* **1** to model according to a pattern. **2** to decorate with a pattern.

patty *noun* **1** a small pie or pasty. **2** a small flat cake of minced meat, fish, etc. □ **patty cake** a small cake, a cupcake. **patty pan** or **tin** a baking tin with cup-shaped hollows for cooking little pies, cupcakes, etc.

paucity (**paw**-sǐ-tee) *noun* smallness of supply or quantity. [from Latin *pauci* = few]

Paul, St (original name Saul, 1st century AD), the first great Christian missionary, whose journeys are described in the Acts of the Apostles, Feast day, 29 June.

paunch *noun* **1** the belly. **2** a protruding abdomen.

pauper *noun* a very poor person. [Latin, = poor]

pauperise *verb* (also -**ize**) to make into a pauper, to impoverish greatly. **pauperisation** *noun*

pause *noun* a temporary stop in action or speech. –**pause** *verb* to make a pause. □ **give pause to** to cause (a person) to hesitate. [from Greek *pauein* = to stop]

pavane (pǎ-**vahn**) *noun* a kind of stately dance; the music for this.

pave *verb* to cover (a road or path etc.) with stones or concrete etc. to make a hard surface. □ **pave the way** to prepare the way for changes etc. [from Latin *pavire* = ram down]

pavement *noun* a paved surface; a paved path for pedestrians at the side of a road.

pavilion *noun* **1** a light building or other structure used as a shelter, e.g. in a park. **2** a building used for exhibitions at a show or fair. **3** a building at a sports ground for use by players and spectators.

Pavlov (**pav**-lof), Ivan Petrovich (1849–1936), Russian physiologist, noted for his study of conditioned reflexes in dogs. **Pavlovian** *adjective*

Pavlova (pav-**loh**-vă), Anna (1881–1931), Russian ballerina, best known for the solo dance *The Dying Swan*.

pavlova *noun* an open meringue case filled with cream and fruit. [originally *Austral.*, this dessert was named after Anna Pavlova who visited Australia in 1926 and 1929]

paw *noun* **1** the foot of an animal that has claws. **2** (*informal*) a person's hand. –**paw** *verb* **1** to strike with a paw. **2** to scrape (the ground) with a hoof. **3** (*informal*) to touch awkwardly or rudely with the hands.

pawky *adjective* (**pawkier**, **pawkiest**) drily humorous. **pawkily** *adverb*, **pawkiness** *noun*

pawl *noun* a lever with a catch that engages with the notches of a ratchet.

pawn[1] *noun* **1** a chess piece of the smallest size and value. **2** a person whose actions are controlled by others. [from Latin *pedo* = foot soldier]

pawn[2] *verb* to deposit (a thing) with a pawnbroker as security for money borrowed. –**pawn** *noun* something deposited as a pledge. □ **in pawn** deposited as a pawn. **pawn ticket** a receipt for a thing deposited with a pawnbroker. [from Old French *pan* = pledge]

pawnbroker *noun* a person licensed to lend money on the security of personal property deposited with him or her.

pawnshop *noun* a pawnbroker's place of business.

pawpaw (**paw**-paw) *noun* **1** an orange melon-shaped tropical fruit. **2** the palmlike tree bearing this.

pay *verb* (**paid**, **paying**) **1** to give (money) in return for goods or services. **2** to give what is owed; to hand over the amount of (wages, a debt, ransom, etc.); to undergo (a penalty). **3** to bear the cost of something. **4** to be profitable or worth while. **5** to bestow, render, or express, *pay attention*; *paid them a visit*; *paid them a compliment*. **6** to let out (a rope) by slackening it. –**pay** *noun* **1** payment. **2** wages. □ **in the pay of** employed by. **pay-as-you-earn** *noun* a method of collecting income tax by deducting it at source from wages or interest etc. **pay back** to return (money); to take revenge on (a person). **pay for** to suffer or be punished because of (a mistake etc.). **pay its way** to make enough profit to cover expenses. **pay off** to pay in full and be free from (a debt) or discharge (an employee); (*informal*) to yield good results, *the risk paid off*; *pay off old scores*, to get even with a person for

past wrongdoing. **pay-off** *noun* (*informal*) payment; reward or retribution; a climax, especially of a joke or story. **pay one's way** not to get into debt. **pay out** to punish or take revenge on (a person); to tease or ridicule. **pay television** a cable television service for which viewers pay a subscription fee. **pay up** to pay in full; to pay what is demanded. **payer** *noun* [from Latin *pacare* = appease]

payable *adjective* which must or may be paid.

PAYE *abbreviation* pay-as-you-earn.

payee (pay-**ee**) *noun* a person to whom money is paid or is to be paid.

payload *noun* **1** the part of an aircraft's load from which revenue is derived (e.g. passengers or cargo). **2** the total weight of bombs or instruments carried by an aircraft or rocket etc.

paymaster *noun* an official who pays troops or workers etc.

payment *noun* **1** paying. **2** money given in return for goods or services. **3** reward, compensation.

payola (pay-**oh**-lă) *noun* a bribe offered to promote a commercial product.

payroll *noun* a list of a firm's employees receiving regular pay. □ **payroll tax** a tax paid by employers, based on the wages and salaries paid out.

PC *abbreviation* **1** police constable. **2** personal computer. **3** politically correct; political correctness.

p.c. *abbreviation* per cent.

PDA *noun* a small portable computer used to store information such as addresses and telephone numbers, and for simple word processing etc. [abbreviation of *personal digital assistant*]

PDF *abbreviation* (in computing) a file format for capturing and sending electronic documents in exactly the intended format. [acronym from *Portable Document Format*]

PE *abbreviation* physical education.

pea *noun* **1** a climbing plant bearing seeds in pods. **2** the seed of certain varieties of this, used as a vegetable. □ **pea green** bright green. **pea-shooter** *noun* a toy tube from which peas or pellets are shot by blowing.

peace *noun* **1** a state of freedom from war; cessation of war. **2** a treaty ending a war, *signed the peace*. **3** freedom from civil disorder, *a breach of the peace*. **4** quiet, calm;

peace of mind, freedom from anxiety. **5** a state of harmony between people, absence of strife. □ **peace-offering** *noun* something offered to show that one is willing to make peace. [from Latin *pax* = peace]

peaceable *adjective* **1** not quarrelsome, desiring to be at peace with others. **2** peaceful, without strife. **peaceably** *adverb*

peaceful *adjective* **1** characterised by peace. **2** belonging to a state of peace not of war. **peacefully** *adverb*, **peacefulness** *noun*

peacemaker *noun* a person who brings about peace.

peach *noun* **1** a round juicy fruit with downy yellowish or reddish skin and a rough stone. **2** the tree that bears this. **3** (*informal*) a person or thing that is greatly admired; an attractive young woman. **4** yellowish-pink colour. **–peach** *adjective* yellowish-pink. □ **peach Melba** a dish of ice cream and peaches with raspberry syrup. **peachy** *adjective*

peacock *noun* a male bird with long tail-feathers that can be spread upright like a fan. **–peacock** *verb* to show one's pride ostentatiously. □ **peacock blue** brilliant blue like the feathers on a peacock's neck.

peahen *noun* the female of a peacock.

peak¹ *noun* **1** a pointed top, especially of a mountain. **2** the mountain itself. **3** any shape, edge, or part that tapers to form a point. **4** a projecting part of the edge of a cap. **5** the point of highest value, achievement, or intensity, etc.; *peak hours*, the hours when traffic is heaviest. **–peak** *verb* to reach its peak in value or intensity etc.

peak² *verb* to waste away, *peak and pine*.

peaked¹ *adjective* having a peak.

peaked², **peaky** *adjectives* having a drawn and sickly appearance. **peakiness** *noun*

peal *noun* **1** the loud ringing of a bell or set of bells. **2** a set of bells with different notes. **3** a loud burst of thunder or laughter. **–peal** *verb* to sound or cause to sound in a peal.

peanut *noun* **1** a plant bearing pods that ripen underground, containing two edible seeds. **2** this seed. **peanuts** *plural noun* (*informal*) a trivial or contemptibly small amount, especially of money. □ **peanut butter** or **paste** a paste of ground roasted peanuts.

pear *noun* **1** a rounded fleshy fruit that tapers towards the stalk. **2** the tree that bears this. **go pear-shaped** (*informal*) go wrong; become

disordered. **pear-shaped** having hips and thighs that are disproportionately wide in relation to the upper part of the body.

pearl *noun* **1** a round usually white mass of a lustrous substance formed inside the shells of certain oysters, valued as a gem. **2** an imitation of this. **3** something resembling it in shape. **4** something valued because of its excellence or beauty. **–pearl** *adjective* (of a light bulb) made of opaque glass. □ **cast pearls before swine** to offer a good thing to someone who is incapable of appreciating it. **pearl barley** barley grains ground small. **pearl button** a button made of real or imitation mother-of-pearl.

Pearl Harbor an American naval base on the island of Oahu, Hawaii, attacked by the Japanese on 7 December 1941.

pearly *adjective* **1** like pearls. **2** containing pearls; decorated with pearls. □ **Pearly Gates** (*humorous*) the gates of heaven.

peasant (**pez**-ănt) *noun* **1** (in some countries) a farm labourer or small farmer. **2** (*derogatory*) an ill-mannered person. □ **Peasants' Revolt** a rising of English peasants in 1381 in protest against social injustices. **peasantry** *noun* peasants. [from Latin *paganus* = villager]

pease pudding *noun* a pudding of peas and eggs etc., boiled in a cloth.

peat *noun* vegetable matter decomposed by the action of water in bogs etc. and partly carbonised, used in horticulture or cut in pieces as fuel. **peaty** *adjective*

pebble *noun* **1** a small stone worn round and smooth by the action of water. **2** a kind of rock crystal used for spectacle lenses; a lens of this. **pebbly** *adjective*

pecan (**pee**-kăn) *noun* **1** a pinkish-brown nut with an edible kernel. **2** a hickory producing this.

peccadillo (pek-ă-**dil**-oh) *noun* (*plural* **peccadilloes**) a trivial offence. [Spanish, = little sin]

peck¹ *verb* **1** to strike or nip or pick up with the beak. **2** to make (a hole) with the beak. **3** to kiss lightly and hastily. **–peck** *noun* **1** a stroke or nip made with the beak. **2** a light hasty kiss. □ **pecking order** a series of ranks of status or authority in which people dominate those below themselves and are dominated by those above (as observed among domestic fowls).

peck² *noun* an imperial measure of capacity for dry goods, = 2 gallons (9.09 litres).

pecker *noun* a bird that pecks. □ **keep your pecker up** (*informal*) stay cheerful.

peckish *adjective* (*informal*) hungry.

pectin *noun* a gelatinous substance found in ripe fruits etc., causing jams to set.

pectoral (**pek**-tŏ-răl) *adjective* **1** of, in, or on the chest or breast, *pectoral muscles*. **2** worn on the breast, *a pectoral cross*. [from Latin *pectoris* = of the breast]

peculate (**pek**-yŭ-layt) *verb* to embezzle (money). **peculation** *noun*, **peculator** *noun* [same origin as *peculiar*]

peculiar *adjective* **1** strange, eccentric. **2** belonging exclusively to a particular person, place, or thing, *customs peculiar to the 18th century*. **3** particular, special, *a point of peculiar interest*. [from Latin *peculium* = private property]

peculiarity *noun* **1** being peculiar. **2** a characteristic. **3** something unusual, an eccentricity.

peculiarly *adverb* **1** in a peculiar way. **2** especially, *peculiarly annoying*.

pecuniary (pĕ-**kewn**-yă-ree) *adjective* of or in money, *pecuniary aid*. [from Latin *pecunia* = money (from *pecu* = cattle, because in early times wealth consisted in cattle and sheep)]

pedagogue (**ped**-ă-gog) *noun* **1** (*old use*) a schoolteacher. **2** (*derogatory*) a person who teaches in a pedantic way. [from Greek, = slave who led a boy to school]

pedagogy *noun* the science of teaching. **pedagogics** *noun*

pedal *noun* a lever operated by the foot in a motor vehicle or cycle or other machine, or in certain musical instruments. –**pedal** *verb* (**pedalled, pedalling**) **1** to work the pedal(s) of. **2** to move or operate by means of pedals; to ride a bicycle. [from Latin *pedis* = of a foot]

pedalo (**ped**-ă-loh) *noun* (*plural* **pedalos**) a pleasure boat operated by pedals.

pedant (**ped**-ănt) *noun* a person who parades his or her learning or who insists unimaginatively on strict observance of formal rules and details in the presentation of knowledge. **pedantry** *noun*, **pedantic** (pĕ-**dan**-tik) *adjective*, **pedantically** *adverb* [same origin as *pedagogue*]

Pedder, Lake a former lake in SW Tasmania, now flooded and serving as a reservoir for the Gordon River hydroelectric power scheme.

peddle *verb* **1** to sell (goods) as a pedlar. **2** to sell (drugs) illegally. **3** to promote (ideas etc.). [from *pedlar*]

peddler *noun* a person who sells drugs illegally.

pederast (**ped**-ĕ-rast) *noun* (also **paederast**) a man who commits homosexual acts with a boy. **pederasty** *noun* [from Greek *paidos* = of a boy, + *erastes* = lover]

pedestal *noun* **1** a base supporting a column, pillar, or statue etc. **2** the column supporting a washbasin. □ **put a person on a pedestal** to admire or respect him or her greatly. [from Italian *piede* = foot, + *stall*[1]]

pedestrian *noun* a person who is walking, especially in a street. –**pedestrian** *adjective* **1** of walking; of or for pedestrians. **2** unimaginative, dull. □ **pedestrian crossing** a street crossing where pedestrians have priority over traffic. [from Latin *pedis* = of a foot]

pedicel (**ped**-ĭ-sĕl) *noun* a small stalklike structure in a plant or animal.

pedicure (**ped**-ĭ-kewr) *noun* care or treatment of the feet and toenails.

pedigree *noun* a line or list of ancestors, especially of a distinguished kind. –**pedigree** *adjective* (of animals) having a recorded line of descent that shows pure breeding.

pediment (**ped**-ĭ-mĕnt) *noun* **1** a triangular part crowning the front of a building. **2** a broad sloping rock surface at the foot of a steep mountain slope in desert regions.

pedlar *noun* a person who goes from house to house selling small articles.

pedometer (pĕ-**dom**-ĕ-ter) *noun* a device that calculates the distance a person walks by counting the number of steps taken. [from Latin *pedis* = of a foot, + *meter*]

peduncle (pĕ-**dung**-kĕl) *noun* the stalk of a flower, fruit, or cluster.

peek *verb* to peep or glance. –**peek** *noun* a peep or glance.

peel[1] *noun* the skin of certain fruits and vegetables; the outer coating of prawns etc. –**peel** *verb* **1** to remove the peel of. **2** to strip away, to pull off (a skin or covering). **3** to be able to be peeled. **4** to come off in strips or layers; to lose skin or bark etc. in this way. □ **peel off** to veer away from a formation of which one formed part. **peeler** *noun*

peel[2] *noun* a small square tower built as a fortification in the 16th century near the border between England and Scotland.

peelings *plural noun* strips of skin peeled from potatoes etc.

peep¹ *verb* **1** to look through a narrow opening. **2** to look quickly or surreptitiously or from a concealed place. **3** to come briefly or partially into view, to show slightly. **–peep** *noun* a brief or surreptitious look.
□ **peeping Tom** a furtive voyeur.

peep² *noun* a weak high chirping sound like that made by young birds. **–peep** *verb* to make this sound.

peephole *noun* a small hole to peep through.

peer¹ *verb* **1** to look searchingly or with difficulty. **2** to peep out. [from *appear*]

peer² *noun* **1** one who is the equal of another in rank, merit, quality, or age etc. **2** a member of the peerage in Britain, a duke, marquis, earl, viscount, or baron. □ **peer group** a group of people who are associated and are of the same age, status, or social background. **peer-to-peer** denoting a network in which each computer can act as a server for the others. [from Latin *par* = equal]

peerage *noun* **1** peers, the nobility. **2** the rank of peer or peeress.

peeress *noun* a female peer; a peer's wife.

peerless *adjective* without equal; superb.

peeve *verb* (*informal*) **1** to annoy. **2** to grumble. **–peeve** *noun* (*informal*) **1** a cause of annoyance. **2** a mood of vexation.

peeved *adjective* (*informal*) annoyed.

peevish *adjective* irritable. **peevishly** *adverb*, **peevishness** *noun*

peewee *noun* (also **peewit**) **1** (in Australia) a magpie lark. **2** (in the UK) a kind of plover named from its cry.

peg *noun* **1** a wooden or metal pin or bolt for fastening things together, hanging things on, holding a tent rope taut, or marking a position; *a peg on which to hang a sermon* etc., a suitable theme or pretext for it. **2** a clothes-peg. **3** a wooden pin for adjusting the strings of a violin etc. **4** a drink or measure of spirits. **–peg** *verb* (**pegged**, **pegging**) **1** to fix or mark by means of a peg or pegs. **2** to keep (wages or prices) at a fixed amount. □ **off the peg** (of clothes) ready-made. **peg away** to work diligently, to be persistent in doing something. **peg out** (*informal*) to die. **take a person down a peg** to reduce a person's pride, to humble him or her.

Pegasus (**peg**-ă-sŭs) **1** (*Gk. myth.*) an immortal winged horse. **2** a northern constellation.

pejorative (pĕ-**jo**-ră-tiv) *adjective* disparaging, derogatory. **pejoratively** *adverb* [from Latin *pejor* = worse]

Peking (pee-**king**) *see* **Beijing**.

Pekingese *noun* (*plural* **Pekingese**) a dog of a breed with short legs, flat face, and long silky hair.

pelagic (pĕ-**laj**-ik) *adjective* (of fish etc.) living near the surface of the open sea. [from Greek *pelagos* = sea]

pelargonium (pel-ă-**goh**-nee-ŭm) *noun* a plant with showy flowers and fragrant leaves (the cultivated variety is usually called *geranium*).

pelican *noun* a large waterbird of warm regions, with a pouch in its long bill for storing fish.

pelisse (pel-**eess**) *noun* **1** a woman's long cloak-like garment with armholes or sleeves. **2** a fur-lined cloak, especially as part of a hussar's uniform.

pellagra (pĕ-**lag**-ră) *noun* a disease due to a deficiency of niacin, causing cracking of the skin, often ending in insanity.

pellet *noun* **1** a small rounded closely-packed mass of a soft substance. **2** a slug of small shot.

pellicle *noun* a thin skin or membrane.

pell-mell *adverb* & *adjective* in a hurrying disorderly manner, headlong.

pellucid (pĕ-**loo**-sĭd) *adjective* very clear.

pelmet (**pel**-mĕt) *noun* a valance or ornamental strip above a window etc., especially to conceal a curtain rod.

Peloponnese (**pel**-ŏ-pŏ-neess) the mountainous southern peninsula of Greece. **Peloponnesian** (pel-ŏ-pŏ-**nee**-shăn) *adjective*

pelt¹ *noun* an animal skin, especially with the fur or hair still on it.

pelt² *verb* **1** to throw missiles at. **2** (of rain etc.) to come down fast. **3** to run fast. □ **at full pelt** as fast as possible.

pelvis *noun* the basin-shaped framework of bones at the lower end of the body. **pelvic** *adjective*

pen¹ *noun* a small fenced enclosure, especially for cattle, sheep, poultry, etc. **–pen** *verb* (**penned**, **penning**) to shut in or as if in a pen.

pen² *noun* a device with a metal point for writing with ink. **–pen** *verb* (**penned**, **penning**) to write (a letter etc.). □ **pen name** an author's pseudonym. **pen-pushing** *noun* (*informal*) clerical work. [from Latin *penna* = feather (because a pen was originally a sharpened quill)]

pen³ *noun* a female swan.

penal (**pee**-năl) *adjective* of or involving punishment, especially according to law; *a penal offence*, one for which the law imposes a punishment. □ **penal colony** (*historical*) a colony to which convicts were transported. [from Latin *poena* = punishment]

penalise *verb* (also **-ize**) **1** to inflict a penalty on. **2** to place at a serious disadvantage. **penalisation** *noun*

penalty *noun* **1** a punishment for breaking a law or rule or contract. **2** a disadvantage or hardship brought on by some action or quality, *the penalties of fame*. **3** a disadvantage to which a sports player or team must submit for breaking a rule. **4** a handicap imposed on a player or team that has won a previous contest. □ **penalty rates** (*Austral.*) increased rates of pay for employees working overtime or on public holidays.

penance (**pen**-ăns) *noun* **1** an act performed as an expression of penitence. **2** (in the RC and Orthodox Church) a sacrament including confession, absolution, and an act of penitence imposed by the priest. □ **do penance** to perform an act of this kind.

pence *see* **penny**.

penchant (**pon**-shon *or* **pen**-shănt) *noun* a liking or inclination, *he has a penchant for old films*. [French]

pencil *noun* **1** an instrument for drawing or writing, consisting of a thin stick of graphite or coloured chalk etc. enclosed in a cylinder of wood or fixed in a metal case. **2** something used or shaped like this. **–pencil** *verb* (**pencilled**, **pencilling**) to write or draw or mark with a pencil. □ **pencil pine** a narrow conifer.

pendant *noun* a hanging ornament, especially one attached to a chain worn round the neck. [from Latin *pendens* = hanging]

pendent *adjective* hanging.

pending *adjective* **1** waiting to be decided or settled. **2** about to come into existence, *patent pending*. **–pending** *preposition* **1** during, *pending these negotiations*. **2** until, *pending his return*. [same origin as *pendant*]

pendulous (**pen**-dew-lŭs) *adjective* hanging downwards, hanging so as to swing freely.

pendulum (**pen**-dew-lŭm) *noun* **1** a weight hung from a cord so that it can swing freely. **2** a rod with a weighted end that regulates the movement of a clock etc. □ **swing of the pendulum** the tendency for public opinion to favour an opposite policy or political party etc. after a time.

Penelope (pĕ-**nel**-ŏ-pee) (*Gk. legend*) the wife of Odysseus, who remained faithful to him during his long years of absence after the fall of Troy.

peneplain (**peen**-ĕ-playn) *noun* a region that has almost become a plain through erosion.

penetrable (**pen**-ĕ-tră-bŭl) *adjective* able to be penetrated. **penetrability** *noun*

penetrate *verb* **1** to make a way into or through, to pierce. **2** to enter and permeate. **3** to see into or through, *our eyes could not penetrate the darkness*. **4** to discover or understand, *penetrated their secrets*. **5** to be absorbed by the mind, *my hint didn't penetrate*. **penetration** *noun*, **penetrator** *noun* [from Latin *penitus* = inside]

penetrating *adjective* **1** having or showing great insight. **2** (of a voice or sound) loud and carrying, piercing.

penetrative (**pen**-ĕ-tră-tiv) *adjective* able to penetrate, penetrating.

penfriend *noun* a friend with whom a person corresponds without meeting.

penguin *noun* a flightless black and white seabird of the southern hemisphere, especially Antarctic and subantarctic regions, with wings developed into scaly flippers used for swimming.

penicillin (pen-ĭ-**sil**-ĭn) *noun* an antibiotic of the kind obtained from mould fungi. [from the Latin name of the mould used]

peninsula (pĕ-**nins**-yŭ-lă) *noun* a piece of land that is almost surrounded by water or projecting far into the sea. **peninsular** *adjective* [from Latin *paene* = almost, + *insula* = island]

penis (**pee**-nĭs) *noun* the organ by which a male animal copulates and (in mammals) urinates. [Latin, = tail]

penitent *adjective* feeling or showing regret that one has done wrong. **–penitent** *noun* a penitent person. **penitently** *adverb*, **penitence** *noun*

penitential (pen-ĭ-**ten**-shăl) *adjective* of penitence or penance.

penitentiary (pen-ĭ-**ten**-shă-ree) *noun* (*Amer.*) a federal or State prison.

penknife *noun* a small folding knife, usually carried in a person's pocket. [originally used for sharpening quill pens]

pennant (**pen**-ănt) *noun* **1** a long tapering flag flown on a ship. **2** a flag awarded for success in sports etc.

penniless *adjective* having no money, very poor, destitute.

pennon *noun* **1** a long narrow triangular or swallow-tailed flag. **2** a long pointed streamer on a ship. **3** a flag.

Pennsylvania a State of the north-eastern USA. **Pennsylvanian** *adjective* & *noun*

penny *noun* (*plural* **pennies** for separate coins, **pence** for a sum of money) **1** a former Australian bronze coin worth $\frac{1}{12}$ of a shilling (approximately 1 cent). **2** a British coin worth $\frac{1}{100}$ of £1. **3** a very small sum of money, *it won't cost you a penny*. □ **penny black** the first adhesive postage stamp (invented in the UK in 1840), printed in black. **penny farthing** an old type of bicycle with a very large front wheel and a small rear one. **penny-pinching** *adjective* niggardly; (*noun*) niggardliness. **spend a penny** (*informal*) to use a toilet.

penology (pee-**nol**-ŏ-jee) *noun* the scientific study of crime, its punishment, and prison management. **penological** *adjective* [from Latin *poena* = punishment, + *-logy*]

pension (**pen**-shŏn) *noun* a periodic payment made by a government to people who are above a certain age or widowed or to certain disabled people, or by an employer to a retired employee. –**pension** *verb* **1** to pay a pension to. **2** to dismiss or allow to retire with a pension, *pensioned him off*. [from Latin *pensio* = payment]

pensionable *adjective* **1** entitled to receive a pension. **2** (of a job) entitling a person to receive a pension.

pensioner *noun* a person who receives a retirement or other pension.

pensive *adjective* deep in thought; thoughtful and gloomy. **pensively** *adverb*, **pensiveness** *noun* [from Latin *pensare* = consider]

pent *adjective* shut in a confined space, *pent in* or *up*. □ **pent-up** *adjective* shut in; kept from being expressed, *pent-up anger*. [from *pen*¹]

penta- *prefix* five. [from Greek *pente* = five]

pentagon (**pen**-tă-gŏn) *noun* a geometric figure with five sides. –**the Pentagon** a five-sided building near Washington, headquarters of the US Department of Defence and of the leaders of the armed forces; the department itself. [from *penta-*, + Greek *gonia* = angle]

pentagonal (pen-**tag**-ŏ-năl) *adjective* five-sided.

pentagram (**pen**-tă-gram) *noun* a five-pointed star. [from *penta-* + *-gram*]

pentameter (pen-**tam**-ĕ-ter) *noun* a line of verse with five metrical feet. [from *penta-*, + Greek *metron* = measure]

Pentateuch (**pen**-tă-tewk) *noun* the first five books of the Old Testament. [from *penta-*, + Greek *teukhos* = book]

pentathlon (pen-**tath**-lŏn) *noun* an athletic contest in which each competitor takes part in the five events it includes. [from *penta-*, + Greek *athlon* = contest]

pentatonic (pen-tă-**tonn**-ik) *adjective* of the **pentatonic scale** in music, a scale consisting of five notes. [from *penta-* + *tonic*]

Pentecost (**pen**-tĕ-kost) *noun* **1** the Jewish harvest festival, fifty days after the second day of the Passover. **2** the seventh Sunday after Easter, Whit Sunday. [from Greek, = fiftieth day]

Pentecostal (pen-tĕ-**kos**-t'l) *adjective* of or designating Christian sects that emphasise the gifts of the Holy Spirit, and who are often fundamentalist in outlook, and express religious feelings by clapping, shouting, dancing, etc.

penthouse *noun* a flat or dwelling on the roof or top floor of a tall building.

penultimate (pĕ-**nul**-tĭ-măt) *adjective* last but one. [from Latin *paene* = almost, + *ultimate*]

penumbra (pĕ-**num**-bră) *noun* (*plural* **penumbrae**) a region of partial shadow surrounding the complete shadow (the *umbra*) of an opaque body, where some light, but not the full amount, reaches a surface. **penumbral** *adjective* [from Latin *paene* = almost, + *umbra* = shade]

penurious (pĕ-**new**-ree-ŭs) *adjective* **1** poverty-stricken. **2** stingy. [from Latin *penuria* = poverty]

penury (**pen**-yŭ-ree) *noun* extreme poverty.

peony (**pee**-ŏ-nee) *noun* a garden plant with large round red, pink, or white flowers.

people *plural noun* **1** human beings in general. **2** the persons belonging to a place or forming a group or social class; the subjects or citizens of a State. **3 the people** ordinary persons, those not having high rank or office etc. **4** a person's parents or other relatives. –**people** *noun* the persons composing a community, tribe, race, or nation, *the English-speaking peoples*. –**people** *verb* to fill (a place) with people, to populate. [from Latin *populus* = people]

pep *noun* (*informal*) vigour, energy. –**pep** *verb* (**pepped, pepping**) (*informal*) to fill with vigour, to enliven, *pep it up*. ☐ **pep pill** a pill containing a stimulant drug. **pep talk** a talk urging the hearer(s) to great effort or courage. [from *pepper*]

peplum *noun* a short flounce from the waist of a garment.

pepper *noun* **1** a hot-tasting powder made from the dried berries of certain plants, used to season food. **2** a kind of capsicum grown as a vegetable. –**pepper** *verb* **1** to sprinkle with pepper. **2** to pelt with small missiles. **3** to sprinkle here and there. ☐ **pepper-and-salt** *adjective* woven with light and dark threads producing an effect of small dots. **pepper mill** a mill for grinding peppercorns by hand. **pepper tree** an introduced South American tree with small red aromatic fruit.

peppercorn *noun* the dried black berry from which pepper is made. ☐ **peppercorn rent** a very low rent, virtually nothing.

peppermint *noun* **1** a kind of mint grown for its strong fragrant oil, used in medicine and in sweets etc. **2** the oil itself. **3** a sweet flavoured with this.

peppery *adjective* **1** like pepper, containing much pepper. **2** hot-tempered.

pepsin *noun* an enzyme contained in gastric juice, helping to digest food. [from Greek *pepsis* = digestion]

peptic *adjective* of digestion. ☐ **peptic ulcer** an ulcer in the stomach or duodenum.

peptide *noun* a compound consisting of a chain of amino acids, chemically linked.

per *preposition* **1** for each, *$2 per metre*. **2** in accordance with, *as per instructions*; *as per usual*, (*informal*) as usual. **3** by means of, *per post*. ☐ **per annum** for each year. **per capita** for each person. **per cent** in or for every hundred, *three per cent* (3%). [from Latin, = through; *cent* from Latin *centum* = hundred]

per- *prefix* **1** through (as in *perforate*). **2** *thoroughly* (as in *perturb*). **3** away entirely; towards badness (as in *pervert*). [from Latin *per* = through]

perambulate (pĕ-**ram**-bew-layt) *verb* **1** to walk through, over, or round (an area), to travel through and inspect. **2** to walk about. **perambulation** *noun* [from *per-*, + Latin *ambulare* = to walk]

perambulator *noun* a child's pram.

perceive *verb* to become aware of, to see or notice. [from Latin *percipere* = seize, understand]

percentage (per-**sen**-tij) *noun* **1** the rate or proportion per cent (*see* **per**). **2** a proportion or part.

percentile (per-**sen**-tyl) *noun* **1** any of the points at which a range of statistical data is divided to make 100 equal groups. **2** any of these groups.

perceptible *adjective* able to be perceived. **perceptibly** *adverb*, **perceptibility** *noun*

perception *noun* perceiving; ability to perceive.

perceptive *adjective* having or showing insight and sensitive understanding. **perceptively** *adverb*, **perceptiveness** *noun*

perceptual *adjective* of or involving perception.

perch¹ *noun* **1** a bird's resting place (e.g. a branch); a bar or rod provided for this purpose. **2** a high place or narrow ledge etc. on which a person sits or positions himself or herself. –**perch** *verb* to rest or place on or as if on a perch. [from Latin *pertica* = pole]

perch² *noun* (*plural* **perch**) **1** an introduced freshwater fish with spiny fins, redfin. **2** any of various Australian sea or freshwater fishes.

perchance *adverb* (*old use*) perhaps.

percipient (per-**sip**-ee-ĕnt) *adjective* perceiving; perceptive. **percipience** *noun*

percolate (**per**-kŏ-layt) *verb* **1** to filter or cause to filter, especially through small holes. **2** to prepare (coffee) in a percolator. **percolation** *noun* [from *per-*, + Latin *colum* = strainer]

percolator *noun* a pot in which coffee is prepared and served, in which boiling water is made to circulate through ground coffee held in a perforated drum.

percussion (per-**kush**-ŏn) *noun* **1** the striking of one object against another. **2** percussion instruments in an orchestra. ☐ **percussion**

cap a small metal or paper device containing explosive powder that explodes when it is struck, used as a detonator or in a toy pistol.

percussion instrument a musical instrument (e.g. drum, cymbals) played by striking. percussionist noun, percussive adjective [from Latin percussum = hit]

perdition (per-**dish**-ŏn) noun eternal damnation. [from Latin perditum = destroyed]

peregrination (pe-rĕ-grĭ-**nay**-shŏn) noun travelling; a journey. [from Latin per = through, + ager = field]

peregrine (**pe**-rĕ-grin) noun (in full peregrine falcon) a falcon that can be trained to hunt and catch small animals and birds.

peremptory (pĕ-**remp**-tŏ-ree) adjective imperious, insisting on obedience. peremptorily adverb, peremptoriness noun

perennial (pĕ-**ren**-yăl) adjective 1 lasting a long time or for ever; constantly recurring, a perennial problem. 2 (of a plant) living for several years. – perennial noun a perennial plant. perennially adverb [from per-, + Latin annus = year]

perentie (pĕ-**ren**-tee) noun the largest Australian lizard, a giant monitor lizard of desert country. [Diyari pirrinthi]

perestroika (pe-rĕ-**stroi**-kă) noun restructuring, especially of the Russian economy after 1985. [Russian]

perfect (**per**-fekt) adjective 1 complete, having all its essential qualities. 2 faultless, excellent. 3 exact, precise, a perfect circle. 4 entire, total, a perfect stranger. – perfect (**per**-fekt) noun the perfect tense. – perfect (per-**fekt**) verb to make perfect. □ perfect interval (in music) a fourth or fifth interval in its usual form, or an octave. perfect number a number equal to the sum of its factors, e.g. 6 = 1 + 2 + 3. perfect tense the tense of a verb that expresses a completed past action, indicated in English by have or has (e.g. he has returned). [from Latin perfectum- = completed]

perfection noun 1 making or being perfect. 2 a person or thing considered perfect. □ to perfection perfectly.

perfectionist noun a person who is satisfied with nothing less than what he or she thinks is perfect. perfectionism noun

perfectly adverb 1 in a perfect way. 2 completely, quite, perfectly satisfied.

perfidious (per-**fid**-ee-ŭs) adjective treacherous, disloyal. perfidiously adverb,

perfidy (**per**-fĭ-dee) noun [from per- = becoming bad, + Latin fides = faith]

perforate verb 1 to make a hole or holes through; to pierce with a row or rows of tiny holes so that part(s) can be torn off easily. 2 to penetrate. perforation noun [from per-, + Latin forare = bore through]

perforce adverb by force of circumstances, necessarily.

perform verb 1 to carry into effect, to accomplish, to do. 2 to go through (a particular proceeding), to execute, performed the ceremony. 3 to function. 4 to act in a play etc.; to play an instrument or sing or do tricks before an audience. □ performing art any of the arts that involve public performance, e.g. dance, drama, music. performer noun

performance noun 1 the process or manner of performing. 2 a notable action or achievement. 3 the performing of a play or other entertainment. 4 (informal) a fuss; a scene. □ performance art a form of visual art in which the activity of the artist takes a central part.

perfume noun 1 a sweet smell. 2 a fragrant liquid for giving a pleasant smell, especially to the body. – perfume verb to give a sweet smell to; to apply perfume to. [from per- + fume (originally used of smoke from burning substances)]

perfumery (per-**few**-mĕ-ree) noun perfumes; the preparation of these.

perfunctory (per-**funk**-tŏ-ree) adjective 1 done as a duty or routine but without much care or interest. 2 (of a person) acting in this way. perfunctorily adverb, perfunctoriness noun

pergola (**per**-gŏ-lă or per-**goh**-lă) noun 1 (Austral.) a horizontal wooden framework with vertical supports, attached to a house and usually with climbing plants trained over it. 2 an arbour or covered walk formed of climbing plants trained over trelliswork.

perhaps adverb it may be, possibly.

peri- prefix around (as in perimeter). [from Greek peri = around]

perianth (**pe**-ree-anth) noun the outer part of a flower. [from peri-, + Greek anthos = flower]

pericardium noun the membranous sac enclosing the heart. [from peri-, + Greek kardia = heart]

pericarp (**pe**-ree-karp) *noun* a seed vessel such as a pea pod. [from *peri-*, + Greek *karpos* = fruit]

Pericles (**pe**-rĭ-kleez) (c. 495–429 BC), Athenian statesman and general.

periglacial *adjective* (of a landscape) influenced by glaciation in its formation.

perihelion (pe-ree-**hee**-lee-ŏn) *noun* (*plural* perihelia) the point in a planet's or comet's orbit when it is closest to the sun (contrasts with *aphelion*).

peril *noun* serious danger. [from Latin *periculum* = danger]

perilous *adjective* full of risk, dangerous. **perilously** *adverb*

perilymph *noun* the fluid between the membranous labyrinth and the bony labyrinth of the ear.

perimeter (pĕ-**rim**-ĕ-ter) *noun* 1 the outer edge or boundary of a closed geometric figure or of an area. 2 the length of this. [from *peri-*, + Greek *metron* = measure]

period *noun* 1 a length or portion of time. 2 a time with particular characteristics, *the colonial period*. 3 the time allocated for a lesson in school. 4 an occurrence of menstruation. 5 a complete sentence. 6 a full stop in punctuation. –**period** *adjective* (of furniture, dress, or architecture) belonging to a past age.

periodic *adjective* occurring or appearing at intervals. □ **periodic table** a table of the elements in order of their atomic numbers, in which chemically related elements tend to appear in the same column or row.

periodical *adjective* periodic. –**periodical** *noun* a magazine etc. published at regular intervals. **periodically** *adverb*

periodicity (peer-ree-ŏ-**diss**-ĭ-tee) *noun* being periodic, the tendency to recur at intervals.

periodontics (pe-ree-oh-**don**-tiks) *noun* the branch of dentistry concerned with the structures surrounding and supporting the teeth.

peripatetic (pe-rĭ-pă-**tet**-ik) *adjective* going from place to place. [from *peri-*, + Greek *patein* = to walk]

peripheral (pĕ-**rif**-ĕ-răl) *adjective* 1 of or on the periphery. 2 of minor but not central importance to something. –**peripheral** *noun* any input, output, or storage device that can be controlled by the central processing unit of a computer.

periphery (pĕ-**rif**-ĕ-ree) *noun* 1 the boundary of a surface or area; the region immediately inside or beyond this. 2 the fringes of a subject etc. [from Greek, = circumference]

periphrasis (pĕ-**rif**-ră-sĭs) *noun* (*plural* periphrases) a roundabout phrase or way of speaking, a circumlocution. [from *peri-*, + Greek *phrasis* = speech]

periscope *noun* an apparatus with a tube and mirror(s) by which a person in a trench or submerged submarine etc. can see things that are otherwise out of sight. [from *peri-*, + Greek *skopein* = look at]

perish *verb* 1 to suffer destruction; to become extinct; to die a violent or untimely death. 2 to rot, to lose or cause (rubber or other fabric) to lose its normal qualities. 3 to distress or wither by cold or exposure.

perishable *adjective* liable to decay or go bad in a short time. **perishables** *plural noun* perishable foods.

perishing *adjective* (*informal*) very cold.

peristalsis (pe-rĭ-**stal**-sĭs) *noun* the automatic muscular movements by which the digestive tract moves its contents along. **peristaltic** *adjective*

peritoneum (pe-rĭ-tŏ-**nee**-ŭm) *noun* the membrane lining the abdomen.

peritonitis (pe-rĭ-tŏ-**ny**-tĭss) *noun* inflammation of the peritoneum.

periwig *noun* (*old use*) a wig.

periwinkle[1] *noun* an evergreen trailing plant with blue or white flowers.

periwinkle[2] *noun* a winkle.

perjure (**per**-jer) *verb* **perjure oneself** to give false evidence wilfully while on oath.

perjured *adjective* 1 involving perjury, *perjured evidence*. 2 guilty of perjury.

perjury (**per**-jŭ-ree) *noun* the deliberate giving of false evidence while on oath; the evidence itself. **perjurious** (per-**joor**-ree-ŭs) *adjective* [from Latin *perjurare* = break an oath]

perk[1] *verb* to raise (the head etc.) briskly or jauntily. □ **perk up** to regain or cause to regain courage, confidence, or vitality; to smarten up. [from *perch*[1]]

perk[2] *noun* (*informal*) a perquisite.

perky *adjective* (perkier, perkiest) lively and cheerful. **perkily** *adverb*, **perkiness** *noun*

perm *noun* a method of setting the hair in waves or curls and then treating it with chemicals so that the style lasts for several months. –**perm** *verb* to give a perm to.

permaculture *noun* a system of agriculture intended to be self-sustaining.

permafrost *noun* the permanently frozen subsoil in polar regions. [from *permanent* + *frost*]

permanency *noun* 1 permanence. 2 a permanent thing or arrangement.

permanent *adjective* lasting or meant to last indefinitely. □ **permanent tooth** a tooth replacing a milk tooth in a mammal, and capable of lasting all or most of the mammal's life. **permanent wave** a perm. **permanently** *adverb*, **permanence** *noun* [from *per-*, + Latin *manens* = remaining]

permanganate (per-**mang**-gă-nayt) *noun* a salt of an acid containing manganese.

permeable (**per**-mee-ă-bŭl) *adjective* able to be permeated by fluids etc. **permeability** *noun*

permeate (**per**-mee-ayt) *verb* to pass or flow or spread into every part of. **permeation** *noun* [from *per-*, + Latin *meare* = to pass]

Permian (**per**-mee-ăn) *adjective* of the final period of the Palaeozoic era. –**Permian** *noun* this period.

permissible *adjective* such as may be permitted, allowable. **permissibly** *adverb*

permission *noun* consent or authorisation to do something.

permissive *adjective* 1 giving permission. 2 tolerant, allowing much freedom in social conduct and sexual matters. **permissively** *adverb*, **permissiveness** *noun*

permit (per-**mit**) *verb* (**permitted**, **permitting**) 1 to give permission or consent to; to authorise. 2 to give opportunity, to make possible, *weather permitting*. –**permit** (**per**-mĭt) *noun* a written order giving permission, especially for entry into a place. [from *per-*, + Latin *mittere* = send]

permutation (per-mew-**tay**-shŏn) *noun* 1 variation of the order of a set of things. 2 any one of these arrangements. 3 a selection of specified items from a larger group, to be arranged in a number of combinations. [from *per-*, + Latin *mutare* = to change]

permute (per-**mewt**) *verb* to vary the order or arrangement of.

pernicious (per-**nish**-ŭs) *adjective* having a very harmful effect.

pernickety *adjective* (*informal*) fastidious, scrupulous.

peroration (pe-rŏ-**ray**-shŏn) *noun* the rhetorical ending of a speech.

peroxide *noun* a compound containing the maximum proportion of oxygen, especially **hydrogen peroxide** which is used as an antiseptic or to bleach hair. –**peroxide** *verb* to bleach with hydrogen peroxide.

perpendicular *adjective* 1 at a right angle (90°) to another line or surface. 2 upright, at right angles to the horizontal. 3 (of a cliff etc.) having a vertical face. 4 **Perpendicular** of the style of English Gothic architecture in the 14th–15th centuries, with vertical tracery in large windows. –**perpendicular** *noun* a perpendicular line or direction. **perpendicularly** *adverb*, **perpendicularity** *noun* [from Latin, = plumb line]

perpetrate (**per**-pĕ-trayt) *verb* to commit (a crime or error); to be guilty of (a blunder etc.). **perpetration** *noun*, **perpetrator** *noun*

perpetual *adjective* 1 lasting for a long time, not ceasing. 2 (*informal*) frequent, often repeated, *this perpetual quarrelling*. **perpetually** *adverb* [from Latin, = uninterrupted]

perpetuate *verb* to preserve from being forgotten or from going out of use. **perpetuation** *noun*

perpetuity (per-pĕ-**tew**-ĭ-tee) *noun* the state or quality of being perpetual. □ **in perpetuity** for ever.

perplex *verb* 1 to bewilder, to puzzle. 2 to make more complicated. [from *per-*, + Latin *plexum* = twisted together]

perplexedly (per-**pleks**-ĕd-lee) *adverb* in a perplexed way.

perplexity *noun* bewilderment.

per pro. *abbreviation* through the agency of (indicating that a person is signing on behalf of another). [from Latin *per procurationem*]

perquisite (**per**-kwĭ-zĭt) *noun* a profit, allowance, or privilege etc. given or looked upon as one's right in addition to wages or salary, a perk.

perry *noun* a drink like cider, made from the fermented juice of pears.

per se *adverb* by or in itself; intrinsically. [Latin]

persecute *verb* 1 to subject to constant hostility or cruel treatment, especially because of religious or political beliefs. 2 to harass. □ **persecution complex** or **mania** an irrational obsessive fear that others are scheming against one. **persecution** *noun*, **persecutor** *noun* [from Latin *persecutum* = pursued]

Persephone (per-**sef**-ŏ-nee) (*Gk. myth.*) the daughter of the corn goddess Demeter, carried off by Pluto and made queen of the Underworld, but allowed to return to earth for part of each year.

Perseus (**per**-see-ŭs) (*Gk. myth.*) the son of Zeus and Danaë, who cut off the head of the gorgon Medusa and rescued Andromeda.

persevere *verb* to continue steadfastly, especially in something that is difficult or tedious. **perseverance** *noun* [from *per-*, + Latin *severus* = strict]

Persia the former name of Iran.

Persian *adjective* of Persia or its people or language. –**Persian** *noun* **1** a native or inhabitant of Persia. **2** the language of Persia (*Farsi*). □ **Persian cat** a cat of a breed with long silky fur. **Persian lamb** the silky tightly-curled fur of lambs of a kind of Asian sheep.

Persian Gulf an arm of the Arabian Sea, between the Arabian peninsula and mainland Asia.

persiflage (**per**-sĭ-flahzh) *noun* banter.

persimmon (**per**-sĭ-mŏn) *noun* **1** the edible orange plumlike fruit of an American or East Asian tree. **2** this tree.

persist *verb* **1** to continue firmly or obstinately, *she persists in breaking the rules*. **2** to continue to exist, *the custom persists in some areas*. **persistent** *adjective*, **persistently** *adverb*, **persistence** *noun*, **persistency** *noun* [from *per-*, + Latin *sistere* = to stand]

person *noun* **1** an individual human being; his or her living body. **2** any of the three modes of being of the Godhead; *the three Persons of the Trinity*, the Father (*First Person*), the Son (*Second Person*), the Holy Spirit (*Third Person*). **3** (in grammar) any of the three classes of personal pronouns and verb forms, referring to the person speaking (*first person*, = I, me, we, us), or spoken to (*second person*, = thou, thee, you), or spoken of (*third person*, = he, him, she, her, it, they, them). □ **in person** physically present. [from *persona*]

persona (per-**soh**-nă) *noun* (*plural* **personae**) = personality (sense 1). [Latin, = mask used by an actor]

personable (**per**-sŏn-ă-bŭl) *adjective* good-looking.

personage (**per**-sŏn-ij) *noun* a person, especially one of importance or distinction.

persona grata (per-soh-nă **grah**-tă) *noun* (*plural* **personae gratae**) a person who is acceptable, especially a diplomat acceptable to a foreign government. [Latin]

personal *adjective* **1** one's own or a particular person's own, *will give it my personal attention*. **2** of one's own or another's private life, *a personal matter*. **3** designed for use by one person, *a personal stereo*; *a personal computer*. **4** making remarks about a person's appearance or private affairs, especially in a critical or hostile way, *don't let us become personal*. **5** done or made etc. in person, *several personal appearances*. **6** of the body and clothing, *personal hygiene*. **7** existing as a person, *a personal God*. □ **personal pronoun** *see* **pronoun**.

personalise *verb* (also **-ize**) **1** to make personal, especially by marking as one's own property. **2** to personify.

personality *noun* **1** a person's own distinctive character. **2** a person with distinctive qualities, especially pleasing ones. **3** a celebrity. **personalities** *plural noun* personal remarks of a critical or hostile kind.

personally *adverb* **1** in person, not through an agent, *showed us round personally*. **2** as a person, in a personal capacity, *we don't know him personally*. **3** in a personal manner, *don't take it personally*. **4** as regards oneself, *personally, I like it*.

persona non grata (per-soh-nă non **grah**-tă) *noun* (*plural* **personae non gratae**) an unacceptable or unwelcome person. [Latin]

personify (per-**sonn**-ĭ-fy) *verb* (**personified**, **personifying**) **1** to represent (an idea) in human form or (a thing) as having human characteristics, *Justice is personified as a blindfolded woman holding a pair of scales*. **2** to embody in one's life or behaviour, *he was vanity personified*. **personification** *noun*

personnel (per-sŏ-**nel**) *noun* **1** the body of people employed in any work, staff. **2** the department (in a business firm etc.) dealing with employees and their welfare. [French, = personal]

perspective *noun* **1** the art of drawing solid objects on a flat surface so as to give the right impression of their relative position, size, solidity, etc. **2** the apparent relationship between visible objects as to position, distance, etc. **3** a view of a visible scene or of facts and events. **4** a mental picture of the relative importance of things.

☐ **in perspective** drawn according to the rules of perspective; with its relative importance understood. [from Latin *perspectum* = looked through]

perspex *noun* (*trademark*) a tough unsplinterable transparent plastic material.

perspicacious (per-spĭ-**kay**-shŭs) *adjective* having or showing great insight. **perspicaciously** *adverb*, **perspicacity** *noun*

perspicuity (per-spĭ-**kew**-ĭ-tee) *noun* clearness of statement or explanation.

perspicuous (per-**spik**-yoo-ŭs) *adjective* expressed or expressing things clearly. **perspicuously** *adverb*

perspire *verb* to sweat. **perspiration** *noun* [from *per-*, + Latin *spirare* = breathe]

persuade *verb* to cause (a person) to believe or do something by reasoning with him or her. **persuadable** *adjective*, **persuasible** *adjective* [from *per-*, + Latin *suadere* = induce]

persuasion *noun* 1 persuading, being persuaded. 2 persuasiveness. 3 belief, especially religious belief, *people of the same persuasion*.

persuasive *adjective* able or trying to persuade. **persuasively** *adverb*, **persuasiveness** *noun*

pert *adjective* 1 cheeky. 2 lively, jaunty. **pertly** *adverb*, **pertness** *noun*

pertain (per-**tayn**) *verb* 1 to be relevant, *evidence pertaining to the case*. 2 to belong as part, *the church and lands pertaining to it*. [from Latin *pertinere* = belong]

Perth the capital city of WA, situated on the banks of the Swan River.

pertinacious (per-tĭ-**nay**-shŭs) *adjective* holding firmly to an opinion or course of action, persistent and determined. **pertinaciously** *adverb*, **pertinacity** (per-tĭ-**nass**-ĭ-tee) *noun* [from *per-* + *tenacious*]

pertinent *adjective* pertaining, relevant. **pertinently** *adverb*, **pertinence** *noun*, **pertinency** *noun*

perturb *verb* to disturb greatly, to make anxious or uneasy. **perturbation** *noun* [from *per-*, + Latin *turbare* = disturb]

Peru a republic in South America on the Pacific coast. **Peruvian** (pě-**roo**-vee-ăn) *adjective* & *noun*

peruse (pě-**rooz**) *verb* to read (a document etc.) carefully. **perusal** (pě-**roo**-zăl) *noun* [from *per-* + *use*]

pervade *verb* to spread or be present throughout, to permeate. **pervasion** *noun* [from *per-*, + Latin *vadere* = go]

pervasive (per-**vay**-siv) *adjective* pervading; able to pervade. **pervasiveness** *noun*

perverse (per-**verss**) *adjective* 1 obstinately doing something different from what is reasonable or required, intractable. 2 indicating or characterised by a tendency of this kind, *a perverse satisfaction*. **perversely** *adverb*, **perverseness** *noun*, **perversity** *noun* [same origin as *pervert*]

perversion *noun* 1 perverting; being perverted. 2 a perverted form of something.

pervert (per-**vert**) *verb* 1 to turn (a thing) from its proper course or use, *pervert the course of justice*. 2 to lead astray from right behaviour or beliefs, to corrupt. **–pervert** (**per**-vert) *noun* a perverted person. [from *per-*, + Latin *vertere* = to turn]

pervious (**per**-vee-ŭs) *adjective* 1 permeable, allowing something to pass through. 2 accessible, receptive, *pervious to new ideas*. [from *per-*, + Latin *via* = way]

peseta (pě-**say**-tă) *noun* the former unit of money in Spain.

peso (**pay**-soh) *noun* (*plural* **pesos**) the unit of money in several Latin-American countries, and in the Philippines.

pessimism *noun* a tendency to take a gloomy view of things or to expect that results will be bad. **pessimist** *noun* [from Latin *pessimus* = worst]

pessimistic *adjective* showing pessimism. **pessimistically** *adverb*

pest *noun* 1 a troublesome or annoying person or thing. 2 an insect or animal that is destructive to cultivated plants or to stored food etc. [from Latin *pestis* = plague]

pester *verb* to make persistent requests; to annoy with frequent requests or questions.

pesticide *noun* a substance for destroying harmful insects etc. [from *pest*, + Latin *caedere* = kill]

pestiferous (pes-**tif**-ě-rŭs) *adjective* troublesome. [from *pest*, + Latin *ferre* = carry]

pestilence *noun* a deadly epidemic disease. [same origin as *pest*]

pestilential (pes-tĭ-**len**-shăl) *adjective* troublesome, pernicious.

pestle *noun* a club-shaped instrument for pounding substances in a mortar.

pesto *noun* an Italian sauce of crushed basil, parmesan, olive oil, pine nuts, and garlic, used on pasta etc.

PET *abbreviation* polyethylene terephthalate.

pet¹ *noun* **1** an animal that is tamed and treated with affection, kept for companionship or amusement. **2** a darling or favourite, *teacher's pet*. –**pet** *adjective* **1** kept or treated as a pet, *pet lamb*. **2** favourite; *pet aversion*, something one particularly dislikes. –**pet** *verb* (**petted**, **petting**) **1** to treat with affection. **2** to fondle. □ **pet name** a name (other than the real name) used affectionately.

pet² *noun* a fit of ill temper.

petal *noun* any of the coloured outer parts of a flower head.

petard (pě-**tard**) *noun* (*old use*) a kind of small bombshell. □ **hoist with one's own petard** injured by one's own devices against others.

Peter, St (died c. AD 67) an Apostle, traditionally connected with Rome, to whom two of the epistles in the New Testament are ascribed. Feast day, 29 June.

Peter I 'the Great' (1672–1725), emperor of Russia 1682–1725.

peter *verb* **peter out** to diminish gradually and cease to exist.

Peter Pan the hero of J. M. Barrie's play of the same name (1904), a boy who never grew up.

petersham *noun* strong corded ribbon used to strengthen waistbands etc.

petiole (**pet**-ee-ohl) *noun* a slender stalk joining a leaf to a stem.

petit (pě-**tee**) *adjective* **petit bourgeois** (*pr.* **boor**-zhwah) a member of the lower middle classes. **petit four** (*plural* **petits fours**) a small fancy cake or other sweet delicacy, usually served with coffee at the end of a meal. **petit mal** a mild form of epilepsy without loss of consciousness. **petit point** (*pr.* pwan) embroidery on canvas using small stitches. [French, = small]

petite (pě-**teet**) *adjective* (of a woman) of small dainty build. [French, = small]

petition *noun* **1** an earnest request. **2** a formal document appealing to an authority for a right or benefit etc., especially one signed by a large number of people. **3** a formal application made to a court of law for a writ or order etc. –**petition** *verb* to make or address a petition to. **petitioner** *noun* [from Latin *petere* = seek]

Petrarch (**pet**-rark), Francesco Petrarca (1304–74), Italian lyric poet and scholar. □ **Petrarchan sonnet** a sonnet of the form used by Petrarch, having an octave (8 lines) followed by a sestet (6 lines).

petrel *noun* a kind of seabird that flies far from land.

Petri dish (**pet**-ree *or* **pee**-tree) *noun* a shallow covered dish used for growing bacteria. [named after J.R. Petri, German bacteriologist (died 1921)]

petrify *verb* (**petrified**, **petrifying**) **1** to change or cause to change into a stony mass. **2** to paralyse or stun with astonishment or fear etc. **petrification** *noun* [from Greek *petra* = rock]

petrochemical *noun* a chemical substance obtained from petroleum or natural gas.

petrodollar *noun* a dollar earned by a country that exports petroleum (= oil).

petrol *noun* an inflammable liquid made from petroleum, used as fuel in internal-combustion engines.

petroleum (pě-**troh**-lee-ŭm) *noun* a mineral oil found underground, refined for use as fuel (e.g. petrol, paraffin) or for use in dry-cleaning etc. □ **petroleum jelly** a greasy translucent substance obtained from petroleum, used as a lubricant etc. [from Greek *petra* = rock, + *oleum* = oil]

petticoat *noun* a woman's or girl's dress-length undergarment worn hanging from the shoulders or waist beneath a dress or skirt. [from *petty* = little, + *coat*]

pettifogging *adjective* trivial, paying too much attention to unimportant details.

petting *noun* **1** affectionate treatment. **2** erotic fondling.

petty *adjective* (**pettier**, **pettiest**) **1** unimportant, trivial, *petty details*. **2** minor, on a small scale, *petty theft*; *petty sessions*. **3** small-minded, *petty spite*. □ **petty cash** a small amount of money kept by an office etc. for or from small payments. **petty officer** an NCO in the navy. **pettily** *adverb*, **pettiness** *noun* [from French *petit* = small]

petulant (**pet**-yŭ-lǎnt) *adjective* peevish. **petulantly** *adverb*, **petulance** *noun*

petunia *noun* a garden plant with funnel-shaped flowers in bright colours.

pew *noun* **1** one of the long benchlike seats with a back and sides, usually fixed in rows, for the congregation in a church. **2** (*informal*) a seat, *take a pew*.

pewter *noun* 1 a grey alloy of tin with lead or other metal, used for making mugs and dishes etc. 2 articles made of this. 3 the colour of pewter. –**pewter** *adjective* made of pewter; coloured like pewter.

PG *abbreviation* (as a film or video game classification) parental guidance recommended.

pH (pee-**aych**) *noun* a measure of the acidity or alkalinity of a solution.

phaeton (**fay**-tŏn) *noun* an old type of open horse-drawn carriage with four wheels.

phagocyte (**fag**-ŏ-syt) *noun* a leucocyte or other cell that can absorb foreign matter (e.g. bacteria) in the body. [from Greek *phagein* = eat, + *kutos* = vessel]

phalanger (fă-**lan**-jer) *noun* any of several Australian tree-dwelling marsupials, including cuscuses and brush-tailed possums, with thick fur and webbed hind feet.

phalanx *noun* a number of people forming a compact mass or banded together for a common purpose. [Greek]

phallic (**fal**-ik) *adjective* of or resembling a model of the penis in erection, symbolising generative power in nature. [from Greek *phallos* = penis]

phantasm (**fan**-tazm) *noun* a phantom. **phantasmal** *adjective*

phantasmagoria (fan-taz-mă-**gor**-ree-ă) *noun* a shifting scene of real or imagined figures.

phantom *noun* 1 a ghost, an apparition. 2 something without reality, as seen in a dream or vision. [from Greek, = something made visible]

pharaoh (**fair**-roh) *noun* the title of the king of ancient Egypt. [from ancient Egyptian *pr-ʿo* = great house]

Pharisee *noun* 1 a member of an ancient Jewish sect represented in the New Testament as making a show of sanctity and piety. 2 a hypocritical self-righteous person. **pharisaical** (fa-rĭ-**say**-i-kăl) *adjective*

pharmaceutical (farm-ă-**sew**-ti-kăl) *adjective* of or engaged in pharmacy, of medicinal drugs, *a pharmaceutical chemist*.

pharmaceutics (farm-ă-**sew**-tiks) *noun* = pharmacy (sense 1).

pharmacist (**farm**-ă-sĭst) *noun* a person who is skilled in pharmacy; a pharmaceutical chemist.

pharmacology (farm-ă-**kol**-ŏ-jee) *noun* the scientific study of medicinal drugs and their effects on the body. **pharmacological** *adjective*, **pharmacologist** *noun* [from Greek *pharmakon* = drug, + *-logy*]

pharmacopoeia (farm-ă-kŏ-**pee**-ă) *noun* 1 a book containing a list of medicinal drugs with directions for their use. 2 a stock of medicinal drugs.

pharmacy (**farm**-ă-see) *noun* 1 the preparation and dispensing of medicinal drugs. 2 a shop where these are sold, a dispensary. [from Greek *pharmakon* = drug]

Pharos (**fair**-ros) a large lighthouse, one of the Seven Wonders of the World, erected c. 280 BC on the island of Pharos off the coast of Egypt and destroyed in 1375.

pharyngitis (fa-rĭn-**jy**-tĭss) *noun* inflammation of the pharynx.

pharynx (**fa**-rinks) *noun* the cavity at the back of the nose and throat.

phase *noun* 1 a stage of change or development or of a recurring sequence of changes. 2 any of the forms in which the moon or a planet appears as part or all of its disc is seen illuminated (new moon, first quarter, full moon, last quarter). 3 the stage that a regularly varying quantity (e.g. an alternating electric current) has reached in relation to zero or another chosen value. –**phase** *verb* to carry out (a program etc.) in stages. □ **phase in** or **out** to bring gradually into or out of use.

PhD *abbreviation* Doctor of Philosophy.

pheasant (**fez**-ănt) *noun* 1 a long-tailed game bird with bright feathers. 2 its flesh as food.

phenobarbitone (feen-ŏ-**bar**-bĕ-tohn) *noun* a medicinal drug used to calm the nerves and induce sleep.

phenol (**fee**-nol) *noun* a white crystalline solid used as an antiseptic and disinfectant.

phenome *noun* 1 the phenotypic counterpart or expression of a genome. 2 the complete set of phenotypic characteristics of an organism. **phenomic** *adjective*

phenomenal *adjective* extraordinary, remarkable. **phenomenally** *adverb*

phenomenon (fĕ-**nom**-ĕ-nŏn) *noun* (*plural* **phenomena**) 1 a fact or occurrence or change perceived by any of the senses or by the mind, *snow is a rare phenomenon in Adelaide*. 2 a remarkable person or thing, a wonder. [Greek, = visible thing]

671

Usage Note that *phenomena* is a plural; it is
incorrect to speak of *this phenomena* or of
phenomenas.

phenomics *plural noun* the branch of science
concerned with the phenomic characteristics
of organisms.

phenotype (**fee**-nŏ-typ) *noun* an individual's
visible set of characteristics, determined by
the genotype and the environment. phenotypic
adjective

pheromone (**fe**-rŏ-mohn) *noun* a substance,
secreted by an animal, that is detected by
others of the same species and produces a
response in them. [from Greek *pherein* =
convey, + *hormone*]

phew *interjection* an exclamation of wonder,
surprise, impatience, or discomfort etc.

phial (**fy**-ăl) *noun* a small glass bottle,
especially for perfume or liquid medicine.

phil- *prefix* see philo-.

philander (fĭ-**lan**-der) *verb* (of a man) to flirt.
philanderer *noun*

philanthropic (fil-ăn-**throp**-ik) *adjective*
1 benevolent. 2 concerned with human
welfare and the reduction of suffering.
philanthropically *adverb*

philanthropist (fĭ-**lan**-thrŏ-pĭst) *noun* a
philanthropic person.

philanthropy (fĭ-**lan**-thrŏ-pee) *noun* love of
mankind, benevolence; philanthropic acts and
principles. [from *phil-*, + Greek *anthropos* =
human being]

philately (fĭ-**lat**-ĕ-lee) *noun* stamp-collecting.
philatelist *noun*, philatelic (fil-ă-**tel**-ik)
adjective [from *phil-*, + Greek *ateleia* = not
needing to pay (because postage has been paid
for by buying a stamp)]

Philemon (fĭ-**lee**-mŏn) the *Epistle to
Philemon*, a book of the New Testament, an
epistle of St Paul to a wealthy Christian of
Phrygia in Asia Minor.

philharmonic (fil-ar-**mon**-ik) *adjective* (in
names of symphony orchestras and music
societies) devoted to music.

Philip, St, 1 an Apostle, commemorated
with St James the Less on 1 May. 2 'the
Evangelist', one of seven deacons appointed
by the early Church at Jerusalem.

Philippians (fĭ-**lip**-ee-ănz) the *Epistle to the
Philippians*, a book of the New Testament, an
epistle of St Paul to the Church at Philippi in
Macedonia.

philippic (fĭ-**lip**-ik) *noun* a bitter verbal
attack. [originally applied to the speeches of
Demosthenes against Philip II of Macedon]

Philippines, the a republic in SE Asia
consisting of a chain of islands of the Malay
Archipelago, the chief of which are Luzon
and Mindanao. Philippine *adjective* of the
Philippines, Filipino.

Philistine (**fil**-ĭ-styn) *noun* a member of
a people in ancient Palestine who were
enemies of the Israelites. –philistine *noun*
an uncultured person, one whose interests
are material and commonplace. –philistine
adjective having or showing uncultured tastes.

Phillip, Arthur (1738–1814), commander of
the First Fleet and first Governor of NSW.

Phillips *adjective* (*trademark*) (of a screw)
with a cross-shaped slot in the head; (of a
screwdriver) with a corresponding point.

philo- *prefix* (becoming phil- before vowels
and *h*) fond of; lover of (as in *philosophy*).
[from Greek *philein* = to love]

philology (fĭ-**lol**-ŏ-jee) *noun* the scientific
study of languages and their development.
philological *adjective*, philologist *noun* [from
philo-, + Greek *logos* = word]

philosopher *noun* 1 an expert in philosophy
or in one of its branches. 2 one who expounds
a particular philosophical system. 3 one who
speaks or behaves philosophically.

philosophical *adjective* 1 of philosophy.
2 calmly reasonable, bearing unavoidable
misfortune unemotionally. philosophically
adverb

philosophise *verb* (also -ize) to reason like a
philosopher; to moralise.

philosophy *noun* 1 the search, by logical
reasoning, for understanding of the basic
truths and principles of the universe, life,
and morals, and of human perception and
understanding of these. 2 a system of ideas
concerning this or a particular subject; a
system of principles for the conduct of life.
3 advanced learning in general, *Doctor of
Philosophy*. 4 calm endurance of misfortune
etc. [from *philo-*, + Greek *sophia* = wisdom]

philtre (**fil**-ter) *noun* a supposedly magic potion.

phishing *noun* illegally acquiring a person's
bank account details etc. via a bogus email etc.

phlegm (*pr.* flem) *noun* **1** thick mucus in the throat and bronchial passages, ejected by coughing. **2** (*old use*) one of the four humours.

phlegmatic (fleg-**mat**-ik) *adjective* **1** not easily excited or agitated. **2** sluggish, apathetic. **phlegmatically** *adverb*

phloem (**floh**-ĕm) *noun* the tissue in plant stems that carries the food materials made by photosynthesis to all parts of the plant.

phlox (*pr.* floks) *noun* a plant with a cluster of reddish, purple, or white flowers at the end of each stem.

Phnom Penh (nom **pen**) the capital of Cambodia.

phobia (**foh**-bee-ă) *noun* a lasting abnormal fear or great dislike of something. [from Greek *phobos* = fear]

Phoenician (fŏ-**nee**-shăn) *noun* a member of an ancient Semitic people of the eastern Mediterranean. –**Phoenician** *adjective* of the Phoenicians.

phoenix (**fee**-niks) *noun* a mythical bird of the Arabian desert, said to live for hundreds of years and then burn itself on a funeral pile, rising from its ashes young again to live for another cycle.

phone *noun* (*informal*) a telephone. –**phone** *verb* (*informal*) to telephone. □ **on the phone** using the telephone; having an instrument connected to a telephone system. **over the phone** by use of the telephone. [short for *telephone*]

phonecard *noun* a card containing prepaid units for use in a public telephone.

phoneme (**foh**-neem) *noun* a unit of significant sound in a language (e.g. the sound of *c* in *cat*, which differs from the *b* in *bat* and distinguishes the two words). **phonemic** (foh-**neem**-ik) *adjective*

phonetic (fŏ-**net**-ik) *adjective* **1** representing each speech sound by a particular symbol that is always used for that sound; *the phonetic alphabet*, a set of symbols used in this way. **2** (of spelling) corresponding to pronunciation. **3** of phonetics. **phonetics** *plural noun* speech sounds; (*noun*) the study of these. **phonetically** *adverb* [from Greek *phonein* = speak]

phoney *adjective* (**phonier**, **phoniest**) (*informal*) sham, not genuine; insincere. –**phoney** *noun* (*informal*) a phoney person or thing.

phonograph (**fohn**-ŏ-grahf) *noun* (*Amer.*) a record player. [from Greek *phone* = sound, + *-graph*]

phonology (fŏ-**nol**-ŏ-jee) *noun* the study of the sounds in a language. [from Greek *phone* = sound, + *-logy*]

phosphate (**foss**-fayt) *noun* a salt or ester of phosphoric acid; an artificial fertiliser composed of or containing this.

phosphor (**foss**-fer) *noun* a synthetic fluorescent or phosphorescent substance.

phosphoresce (foss-fŏ-**ress**) *verb* to be phosphorescent.

phosphorescent (foss-fŏ-**ress**-ĕnt) *adjective* luminous, glowing with a faint light without burning or perceptible heat. **phosphorescence** *noun*

phosphoric (foss-**fo**-rik) *adjective* of or containing phosphorus.

phosphorous *adjective* **1** containing or relating to phosphorus. **2** phosphorescent.

Usage The correct spelling for the noun denoting the chemical element is *phosphorus*, while the correct spelling for the adjective meaning 'relating to or containing phosphorus' is *phosphorous*.

---

phosphorus (**foss**-fŏ-rŭs) *noun* a chemical element (symbol P) existing in several forms; a yellowish waxy form of it that appears luminous in the dark. [from Greek *phos* = light, + *-phoros* = bringing]

photo *noun* (*plural* **photos**) a photograph. □ **photo finish** a very close finish of a race, photographed to enable the judge to decide the winner.

photo- *prefix* light (as in *photograph*). [from Greek *photos* = of light]

photocopier *noun* a machine for photocopying documents etc.

photocopy *noun* a copy (of a document etc.) made by photographing the original. –**photocopy** *verb* (**photocopied**, **photocopying**) to make a photocopy of.

photodiode (foh-toh-**dy**-ohd) *noun* a diode that allows current to flow when light falls on it.

photoelectric *adjective* of or using the electrical effects of light. □ **photoelectric cell** an electronic device which emits an electric current when light falls on it, used e.g. to measure light for photography, to count

673

objects passing it, or to cause a door to open when someone approaches it. **photoelectricity** *noun*

photoemission *noun* the emission of electrons from a surface as a result of light falling on it.

photofit *noun* a likeness of a person (especially one who is sought by the police) that is put together by assembling photographs of separate features.

photogenic (foh-tŏ-**jen**-ik) *adjective* being a good subject for photography, coming out well in photographs.

photograph (**foh**-tŏ-grahf *or* -graf) *noun* a picture formed by means of the chemical action of light or other radiation on a sensitive surface; a still picture made with a camera. –**photograph** *verb* **1** to take a photograph of. **2** to come out in a certain way when photographed, *it photographs badly.* [from *photo-* + *-graph*]

photographer (fŏ-**tog**-ră-fer) *noun* a person who takes photographs.

photographic (foh-tŏ-**graf**-ik) *adjective* **1** of or used in or produced by photography. **2** (of the memory) recalling accurately what was seen, as if by a process of photography. **photographically** *adverb*

photography (fŏ-**tog**-ră-fee) *noun* the taking and processing of photographs.

photon (**foh**-tonn) *noun* an indivisible unit of electromagnetic radiation, with energy proportional to the frequency of radiation.

photosensitive *adjective* reacting to light.

photoshop *verb* (**photoshopped**, **photoshopping**) to edit or alter (an image) digitally using computer software. [from *Adobe Photoshop*, the proprietary name of such a software package]

photosynthesis (foh-toh-**sin**-thě-sĭs) *noun* the process by which green plants use sunlight to convert carbon dioxide (taken from the air) and water into complex substances. [from *photo-* + *synthesis*]

phototransistor *noun* a transistor that responds to light falling on it by generating and amplifying an electric current.

phototropic (foh-tŏ-**trop**-ik) *adjective* (of the movement or growth of a plant) responding to the direction from which light falls upon it. **phototropism** (foh-tŏ-**troh**-pizm) *noun* [from *photo-,* + Greek *trope* = turning]

phrase *noun* **1** a group of words forming a unit, especially as an idiom or a striking or clever way of saying something. **2** a group of words (usually without a finite verb) forming a unit within a sentence or clause, e.g. *in the garden.* **3** the way something is worded, *we didn't like his choice of phrase.* **4** a short distinct passage forming a unit in a melody. –**phrase** *verb* **1** to express in words. **2** to divide (music) into phrases. □ **phrase book** a book listing common phrases and their equivalents in a foreign language, for use by travellers. [from Greek *phrazein* = declare]

phraseology (fray-zee-**ol**-ŏ-jee) *noun* wording, the way something is worded. [from *phrase* + *-logy*]

phut *noun* a sound like air etc. escaping in a short burst. □ **go phut** to burst or explode with this sound; (*informal*) to come to nothing.

phylactery (fĭ-**lak**-tĕ-ree) *noun* **1** a small leather box containing Hebrew texts, worn by Jews at weekday morning prayer. **2** a protective charm. [from Greek *phulassein* = protect]

phylum (**fy**-lŭm) *noun* (*plural phyla*) any of the larger groups into which plants and animals are divided, containing species with the same general form. [from Greek *phulon* = race]

physic (**fiz**-ik) *noun* (*old use*) medicine.

physical *adjective* **1** of the body, *physical fitness*; *a physical examination.* **2** of matter or the laws of nature (as opposed to moral, spiritual, or imaginary things), *the physical world*; *a physical map*, one showing mountains and rivers and other natural features. **3** of physics. –**physical** *noun* (*informal*) a physical examination. □ **physical chemistry** a branch of chemistry in which physics is used to study substances and their reactions. **physical education** instruction in physical exercise and sports (abbreviation **PE**). **physical geography** a branch of geography dealing with the natural features of the earth's surface (e.g. mountains, lakes, rivers). **physically** *adverb* [same origin as *physics*]

physician (fĭ-**zish**-ăn) *noun* a doctor, especially one who practises medicine (as distinct from surgery) or is a specialist in this (as distinct from a general practitioner).

physicist (**fiz**-ĭ-sĭst) *noun* an expert in physics.

physics (**fiz**-iks) *noun* **1** the scientific study of the properties and interactions of matter and energy. **2** these properties etc. [from Greek *phusikos* = natural]

physiognomy (fiz-ee-**on**-ŏ-mee) *noun* the features of a person's face. [from Greek *phusis* = nature, + *gnomon* = indicator]

physiology (fiz-ee-**ol**-ŏ-jee) *noun* **1** the scientific study of the bodily functions of living organisms and their parts. **2** these functions. **physiological** (fiz-ee-ŏ-**loj**-i-kăl) *adjective*, **physiologist** *noun* [from Greek *phusis* = nature, + *-logy*]

physiotherapy (fiz-ee-oh-th'**e**-ră-pee) *noun* treatment of a disease, injury, deformity, or weakness by massaging, exercises, heat, etc. **physiotherapist** *noun* [from Greek *phusis* = nature, + *therapy*]

physique (fi-**zeek**) *noun* a person's physical build and muscular development. [French]

phytoplankton (fy-tŏ-**plank**-tŏn) *noun* plankton consisting of tiny plants. [from Greek *phuton* = plant, + *plankton*]

pi (*rhymes with* my) *noun* a letter of the Greek alphabet (π = p) used as a symbol for the ratio of the circumference of a circle to its diameter (approximately 3.14159).

pianism *noun* the art or technique of piano playing.

pianissimo *adverb* (in music) very softly. [Italian]

pianist *noun* a person who plays the piano.

piano¹ (pee-**an**-oh) *noun* (*plural* **pianos**) a musical instrument in which metal strings are struck by hammers operated by pressing the keys of a keyboard. □ **piano accordion** an accordion in which the melody is played on a small piano-like keyboard. [short for *pianoforte*]

piano² (pee-**ah**-noh) *adverb* (in music) softly.

pianoforte (pee-ah-noh-**for**-tee) *noun* a piano. [from Italian *piano* = soft, + *forte* = loud (because it can produce soft notes and loud notes)]

pianola (pee-ă-**noh**-lă) *noun* (*trademark*) a player-piano (*see* **player**).

piastre (pee-**ast**-er) *noun* a small coin of various Middle Eastern countries.

piazza (pee-**ats**-ă) *noun* a public square in an Italian town.

pica (**py**-kă) *noun* **1** a size of letters in typewriting (10 per inch). **2** a unit of length for measuring printing-type, about 4.2 mm.

picador (**pik**-ă-dor) *noun* a mounted man with a lance in bullfighting.

picaresque (pik-ă-**resk**) *adjective* (of a style of fiction) dealing with the adventures of rogues.

Picasso, Pablo (1881–1973), Spanish painter, who lived in France, a founder of cubism.

piccalilli *noun* pickle of chopped vegetables, mustard, and hot spices.

piccaninny *noun* (often *offensive*) a Black child.

piccolo *noun* (*plural* **piccolos**) a small flute sounding an octave higher than the ordinary one. [Italian, = small]

pick¹ *verb* **1** to use a pointed instrument or the fingers or beak etc. in order to make a hole in or remove bits from (a thing); *pick at one's food*, to eat it in small bits or without appetite. **2** to detach (a flower or fruit) from the plant bearing it. **3** to select carefully; *pick a winner*, choose a person or thing that will later prove to be successful. –**pick** *noun* **1** picking. **2** selection; *have first pick*, the right to choose first. **3** the best part; *pick of the bunch*, the best of the lot. □ **pick a lock** to use a piece of wire or a pointed tool to open it without a key. **pick a person's brains** to extract ideas or information from him or her for one's own use. **pick a person's pocket** to steal its contents while he or she is wearing the garment. **pick a quarrel** to provoke one deliberately. **pick holes in** to find fault with. **pick off** to pluck off; to select and shoot or destroy one by one as opportunity arises. **pick on** to single out, especially as a target for nagging or harassment. **pick out** to take from among a number of things; to recognise; to distinguish from surrounding objects or areas; to play (a tune) by searching for the right notes. **pick over** to select the best of. **pick up** to lift or take up; to call for and take with one, to take aboard (passengers or freight etc.); (of police etc.) to catch, to find and take into custody; to get or acquire by chance or casually; to meet casually and become acquainted with; to succeed in seeing or hearing by means of apparatus; to recover health, to show an improvement; to recover speed; *pick up speed*, accelerate. **picker** *noun*

pick² *noun* **1** a pickaxe. **2** a plectrum.

pick-a-back *adverb* = piggyback.

pickaxe *noun* a tool consisting of a curved iron bar with one or both ends pointed, mounted at right angles to its handle, used for breaking hard ground or stones etc.

picket *noun* **1** one or more persons stationed by strikers outside their place of work to dissuade others from entering. **2** an outpost of troops; a party of sentries. **3** a pointed stake set into the ground, e.g. as part of a fence. –**picket** *verb* (**picketed, picketing**) **1** to station or act as a picket during a strike. **2** to post as a military picket. **3** to secure or enclose with a stake or stakes. [from French *piquet* = pointed post]

pickings *plural noun* **1** scraps of good food etc. remaining, gleanings. **2** odd gains or perquisites; profits from pilfering.

pickle *noun* **1** food (especially a vegetable) preserved in vinegar or brine. **2** vinegar or brine used for this. **3** (*informal*) a plight, a mess. –**pickle** *verb* to preserve in pickle.

pickled *adjective* (*informal*) drunk.

pickpocket *noun* a thief who picks people's pockets.

pickup *noun* **1** a small van with low sides. **2** a device producing an electric signal in response to change; a device on a musical instrument which converts sound vibrations into electrical signals for amplification.

picnic *noun* **1** an informal meal taken in the open air for pleasure; an excursion for this. **2** (*informal*) something very agreeable or easily done. **3** (*Austral. informal*) a difficult or awkward task or situation. –**picnic** *verb* (**picnicked, picnicking**) to take part in a picnic. **picnicker** *noun*

pico- (**pee**-koh) *prefix* one million millionth of a unit, *picometre*. [from Spanish *pico* = beak, little bit]

picot (**pee**-koh) *noun* one of a series of small loops of twisted thread forming an ornamental edging.

picric acid *noun* a yellow substance used in dyeing and in explosives.

Pict *noun* a member of an ancient people of northern Britain. **Pictish** *adjective*

pictogram, pictograph *nouns* **1** a pictorial symbol used as a form of writing. **2** a chart using pictures to represent statistical information. **pictographic** *adjective* [from Latin *pictum* = painted, + *-gram*, *-graph*]

pictorial *adjective* **1** of or expressed in a picture or pictures. **2** illustrated by pictures. **3** picturesque. –**pictorial** *noun* a newspaper or magazine in which pictures are the main feature. **pictorially** *adverb*

picture *noun* **1** a representation of a person or people or object(s) etc. made by painting, drawing, or photography, especially as a work of art. **2** a portrait. **3** something that looks beautiful, *the garden is a picture*. **4** a scene, the total impression produced on one's sight or mind. **5** a perfect example, *she is a picture of health*. **6** a cinema film; *go to the pictures*, go to the cinema. **7** the image on a television screen. –**picture** *verb* **1** to represent in a picture. **2** to describe vividly. **3** to form a mental picture of, *picture to yourself a deserted beach.* □ **in the picture** fully informed. **picture window** a large window facing an attractive view. [from Latin *pictum* = painted]

picturesque (pik-chŭ-**resk**) *adjective* **1** forming a striking and pleasant scene. **2** (of words or a description) very expressive, vivid. **picturesquely** *adverb*, **picturesqueness** *noun*

piddling *adjective* (*informal*) trivial, unimportant.

pidgin (**pij**-ĭn) *noun* a simplified form of English or another language, containing elements of the local language(s) and used for communication (e.g. in parts of Papua New Guinea) between people speaking different languages, *pidgin English*. [from the Chinese pronunciation of *business* (because it was used by traders)]

pie *noun* a baked dish of meat, fish, or fruit etc. enclosed in or covered with pastry or other crust. □ **pie chart** a diagram representing quantities as sectors of a circle. **pie in the sky** a prospect (considered unrealistic) of future happiness.

piebald *adjective* (of a horse etc.) with irregular patches of white and black or other dark colour. [from *pie* = magpie, + *bald*]

piece *noun* **1** one of the distinct portions of which a thing is composed or into which it is divided or broken. **2** one of a set of things, *three-piece suite*. **3** something regarded as a unit, *a fine piece of work*. **4** a musical, literary, or artistic composition. **5** a coin, *ten-cent piece*. **6** one of the set of small objects moved on a board in playing board games; a chessman (strictly, other than a pawn). **7** a fixed unit of work, *payment by the piece*; *piece-rates*, payment according to this (not by the hour). –**piece** *verb* to make by joining or adding pieces together. □ **go to pieces** (of a person) to lose one's strength or ability etc., to collapse. **in one piece** not broken. **of a piece** of the same kind, consistent. **a piece of one's**

mind a reproach or scolding giving one's frank criticisms. **say one's piece** to make a prepared statement; to give one's opinion.

pièce de résistance (pee-ess dĕ ray-**zee**-stahns) *noun* **1** the principal dish at a meal. **2** the most important or remarkable item. [French]

piecemeal *adjective* & *adverb* done piece by piece, part at a time.

piecework *noun* work paid for by the amount produced.

pied (*rhymes with* tide) *adjective* particoloured, piebald, *pied currawong*. □ **Pied Piper** (in German legend) a piper who rid the town of Hamelin of its rats by luring them away with his music and, when refused the promised fee, lured away all the children.

piedmont (**peed**-mont) *noun* a region at the foot of mountains.

pier (*pr.* peer) *noun* **1** a structure built out into the sea to serve as a breakwater, landing stage, or promenade. **2** each of the pillars or similar structures supporting an arch or bridge. **3** solid masonry between windows etc.

pierce *verb* **1** to go into or through like a sharp-pointed instrument; to make a hole in (a thing) in this way. **2** to force one's way into or through.

piercing *adjective* **1** (of cold or wind etc.) penetrating sharply. **2** (of a voice or sound) shrilly audible.

piety (**py**-ĕ-tee) *noun* piousness. [from Latin *pietas* = dutiful behaviour]

piffle *noun* (*informal*) nonsense, worthless talk.

piffling *adjective* (*informal*) trivial, worthless.

pig *noun* **1** a domestic or wild animal with short legs, cloven hooves, and a broad blunt snout. **2** (*informal*) a greedy, dirty, or unpleasant person; a difficult or unpleasant thing. **3** an oblong mass of metal from a smelting furnace; pig iron. – **pig** *verb* (**pigged**, **pigging**) **pig it** to live in dirty conditions or in a disorderly way. □ **buy a pig in a poke** to buy a thing without seeing it or knowing whether it will be satisfactory. **pig-headed** *adjective* obstinate, stubborn. **pig iron** crude iron from a smelting furnace.

pigeon *noun* **1** a bird of the dove family. **2** (*informal*) a person's business or responsibility, *that's your pigeon* (¶ from a Chinese pronunciation of the word *business*).

□ **pigeon-chested** *adjective* (of a person) having a deformed chest in which the breastbone forms a protruding curve. **pigeon-toed** *adjective* having the toes turned inwards. [from Old French *pijon* = young bird]

pigeonhole *noun* **1** a small recess for a pigeon to nest in. **2** one of a set of small compartments in a desk or cabinet, used for holding papers or letters etc. – **pigeonhole** *verb* **1** to put away for future consideration or indefinitely. **2** to classify mentally as belonging to a particular group or kind.

piggery *noun* **1** a pig-breeding establishment. **2** a pigsty.

piggy *adjective* like a pig; *piggy eyes*, small eyes like those of a pig. □ **piggy bank** a money box made in the shape of a hollow pig.

piggyback *noun* a ride on a person's shoulders and back or on the top of a larger object. – **piggyback** *adverb* carried in this way. – **piggyback** *adjective* mounted on the back of another object, *a piggyback plug*. [from *pick-a-back*]

piglet *noun* a young pig.

pigment *noun* colouring matter. – **pigment** *verb* to colour (skin or other tissue) with natural pigment. **pigmentation** *noun* [from Latin *pingere* = to paint]

pigskin *noun* leather made from the skin of a pig.

pigsty *noun* **1** a partly-covered pen for pigs. **2** a very dirty or untidy place.

pigtail *noun* either of a pair of bunches of hair at each side of the head.

pike[1] *noun* **1** a long wooden shaft with a pointed metal head. **2** (*plural* **pike**) a large voracious northern-hemisphere freshwater fish with a long narrow snout; any of several similar Australian sea fishes.

pike[2] *verb* (*Austral. informal*) **pike out on** to go back on (one's word, an arrangement, etc.).

piked *adjective* (of a position in acrobatics etc.) with the legs straight and forming an angle with the body at the hips, *piked somersault*.

pikelet *noun* a small thick pancake, also called a *drop scone*.

pikestaff *noun* the wooden shaft of a pike. □ **plain as a pikestaff** quite plain or obvious. [from *packstaff*, a pedlar's smooth staff]

pilaff (pĭ-**laf**) *noun* (also **pilau**) a dish of rice with meat or fish, spices, etc.

pilaster (pĭ-**last**-er) *noun* a rectangular column, especially an ornamental one that projects from a wall into which it is set.

Pilate, Pontius (1st century AD), the Roman governor of Judaea who presided at the trial of Jesus Christ.

Pilates *noun* a system of exercises using special apparatus, designed to improve physical strength, flexibility, and posture, and enhance mental awareness. [named after Joseph Pilates (died 1967), German physical fitness specialist who devised the system]

Pilbara (**pil**-bă-ră) a vast region in NW Western Australia, associated especially with mining.

pilchard *noun* a small sea fish related to the herring.

pile¹ *noun* a heavy beam of metal, concrete, or timber driven vertically into the ground as a foundation or support for a building or bridge. [from Latin *pilum* = spear]

pile² *noun* **1** a number of things lying one upon another. **2** a funeral pyre. **3** (*informal*) a large quantity, *a pile of work*. **4** (*informal*) a large quantity of money, *made a pile*. **5** a lofty building or complex of buildings. –**pile** *verb* **1** to heap, stack, or load. **2** to crowd, *they all piled into one car*. □ **pile it on** (*informal*) to exaggerate. **pile up** to accumulate; (*informal*) to run (a ship) on the rocks or aground; to cause (a vehicle) to crash. **pile-up** *noun* (*informal*) a collision of several motor vehicles. [from Latin *pila* = pillar]

pile³ *noun* cut or uncut loops on the surface of a fabric. [from Latin *pila* = pillar]

piles *plural noun* haemorrhoids.

pilfer *verb* to steal small items or in small quantities. **pilferer** *noun*, **pilferage** *noun*

pilgrim *noun* a person who travels to a sacred or revered place as an act of religious devotion. □ **Pilgrim Fathers** the English Puritans who founded the colony of Plymouth, Massachusetts, in 1620.

pilgrimage *noun* a pilgrim's journey; a journey made to a place as a mark of respect (e.g. to a person's birthplace).

pill¹ *noun* a small ball or flat round piece of medicinal substance for swallowing whole. □ **bitter pill** a humiliation. **the pill** (*informal*) a contraceptive pill; *on the pill*, taking this regularly. [from Latin *pila* = ball]

pill² *verb* (of fabric) to form tiny balls of fibre on the surface.

pillage *verb* to plunder. –**pillage** *noun* plunder. **pillager** *noun*

pillar *noun* **1** a vertical structure used as a support or ornament. **2** something resembling this in shape, *a pillar of rock*. **3** a person regarded as one of the chief supporters of something, *a pillar of the community*. □ **from pillar to post** from one place or situation to another. **pillar box** (*old use* & *Brit.*) a postbox shaped like a pillar and painted red. **Pillars of Hercules** *see* **Hercules**. [from Latin *pila* = pillar]

pillbox *noun* **1** a small round box for holding pills. **2** a hat shaped like this. **3** a small concrete shelter for a gun emplacement.

pillion *noun* a saddle for a passenger seated behind the driver of a motorcycle. □ **ride pillion** to ride on this as a passenger.

pillory *noun* a wooden framework with holes for the head and hands, into which offenders were formerly locked for exposure to public ridicule. –**pillory** *verb* (**pilloried**, **pillorying**) **1** to put into the pillory as a punishment. **2** to hold up to public ridicule or scorn.

pillow *noun* a cushion used (especially in bed) for supporting the head. –**pillow** *verb* to rest or prop up on or as if on a pillow.

pillowcase, **pillowslip** *nouns* a cloth cover into which a pillow is placed for use.

pilot *noun* **1** a person who operates the flying controls of an aircraft. **2** a person qualified to take charge of ships entering or leaving a harbour or travelling through certain waters. **3** a guide. –**pilot** *verb* (**piloted**, **piloting**) **1** to act as pilot of. **2** to guide. –**pilot** *adjective* experimental, testing (on a small scale) how a scheme etc. will work, *a pilot project*. □ **pilot light** a small jet of gas kept alight and lighting a larger burner when this is turned on; an electric indicator light.

pilotage *noun* piloting; the charge for this.

pimento (pĭ-**ment**-oh) *noun* (*plural* **pimentos**) **1** allspice; the West Indian tree yielding this. **2** (also **pimiento**) a sweet red capsicum.

pimp *noun* **1** a man who lives off the earnings of a prostitute or brothel. **2** (*Austral. informal*) an informer. –**pimp** *verb* **1** to act as a pimp. **2** (*Austral. informal*) to inform authorities, to tell tales.

pimpernel (**pim**-per-nel) *noun* a wild plant with small scarlet, blue, or white flowers that close in cloudy or wet weather.

pimple *noun* a small hard inflamed spot on the skin. **pimply** *adjective*

PIN *abbreviation* personal identification number, a number allocated by a bank etc. to a customer, e.g. for use with a card to obtain cash from an automatic teller machine.

pin *noun* 1 a short thin stiff piece of metal with a sharp point and a round broadened head, used for fastening fabrics or papers etc. together or (with an ornamental head) as a decoration, *drawing pin, hairpin, safety pin*. 2 a peg of wood or metal used for various purposes. 3 a stick with a flag on it, placed in a hole on a golf course to mark its position. 4 a bottle-shaped wooden object used in tenpin bowling and similar games. 5 a rolling pin. –**pin** *verb* (**pinned, pinning**) 1 to fasten with a pin or pins. 2 to transfix with a weapon or arrow etc. and hold fast; to restrict and make unable to move, *he was pinned under the wreckage*. 3 to attach or fix; *we pinned our hopes on you*, counted on you to succeed; *pinned the blame on her*, made her the scapegoat. **pins** *plural noun* (*informal*) legs, *quick on his pins*. □ **pin down** to establish clearly; to make (a person) agree to keep to a promise or arrangement etc. or declare his or her intentions definitely. **pins and needles** a tingling sensation; *on pins and needles*, in a state of anxiety or suspense. **pin-stripe** *noun* a very narrow stripe on cloth; cloth with parallel stripes of this kind. **pin-striped** *adjective* having pin-stripes. **pin-tuck** *noun* a very narrow ornamental tuck. **pin-tucked** *adjective* ornamented with pin-tucks. **pin-up** *noun* (*informal*) a picture of an attractive or famous person, for pinning on a wall; the subject of this.

pinafore *noun* an apron. □ **pinafore dress** a dress without collar or sleeves, worn over a blouse or jumper. [from *pin* + *afore* = before]

pinball *noun* a game played on a sloping board on which a ball is projected so that it strikes pins or targets or falls into a pocket.

pince-nez (**panss**-nay) *noun* (*plural* **pince-nez**) a pair of glasses with a spring that clips on the nose and no side pieces. [French, = pinch-nose]

pincers *plural noun* 1 a tool for gripping and pulling things, consisting of a pair of pivoted jaws with handles that are pressed together to close them. 2 the claw-like parts of a lobster etc. □ **pincer movement** an attack in which forces converge from each side on an enemy position.

pinch *verb* 1 to squeeze tightly or painfully between two surfaces, especially between finger and thumb; *look pinched with cold*, have a drawn appearance from feeling unpleasantly cold. 2 to stint, to be niggardly, *pinching and scrimping*. 3 (*informal*) to steal. 4 (*informal*) to arrest. –**pinch** *noun* 1 pinching, squeezing. 2 stress or pressure of circumstances, *began to feel the pinch*. 3 as much as can be held between the tips of the thumb and forefinger. □ **at a pinch** in time of difficulty or necessity.

pincushion *noun* a small pad into which pins are stuck to keep them ready for use.

pine¹ *noun* 1 an evergreen coniferous tree with needle-shaped leaves growing in clusters. 2 its wood.

pine² *verb* 1 to waste away through grief or yearning. 2 to feel an intense longing.

pineapple *noun* 1 a large juicy tropical fruit with a tough prickly segmented skin. 2 the plant that bears it.

Pine Gap a classified Australian and US joint defence space-research facility near Alice Springs.

ping *noun* a short sharp ringing sound. –**ping** *verb* 1 to make or cause to make this sound. 2 (*Austral.*) (of a vehicle engine) emit a series of high-pitched explosive sounds caused by faulty combustion. **pinger** *noun*

ping-pong *noun* table tennis.

pinion¹ (**pin**-yŏn) *noun* a bird's wing, especially the outer segment. –**pinion** *verb* 1 to clip the wings of (a bird) to prevent it from flying. 2 to restrain (a person) by holding or binding his or her arms or legs.

pinion² (**pin**-yŏn) *noun* a small cogwheel that engages with a larger one or with a rack.

pink¹ *noun* 1 pale red colour. 2 a garden plant with fragrant white, pink, or variegated flowers. 3 the best or most perfect condition, *the pink of perfection*. –**pink** *adjective* 1 of pale red colour. 2 (*informal*) mildly socialist. □ **in the pink** (*informal*) in very good health. **pinkness** *noun*

pink² *verb* 1 to pierce slightly. 2 to cut a zigzag edge on. □ **pinking shears** dressmaker's scissors with serrated blades for cutting a zigzag edge.

pinnacle *noun* 1 a pointed ornament on a roof. 2 a peak. 3 the highest point.

pinnate *adjective* (of a compound leaf) having leaflets on either side of the stem.

Pinocchio a puppet whose nose grows longer when he tells a lie, the subject of a book of the same name by Carlo Collodi, real name Carlo Lorenzini (1826–90).

pinpoint *adjective* showing or needing care and precision, *with pinpoint accuracy*. –**pinpoint** *verb* to locate or identify precisely.

pinprick *noun* a small annoyance.

pint *noun* a measure for liquids, $\frac{1}{8}$ of a gallon (568 cc). □ **pint-sized** *adjective* (*informal*) very small.

Pinter (**pin**-ter), Harold (1930–2008), English playwright, whose works include *The Caretaker*, *The Homecoming*, and *No Man's Land*.

Pintupi (**pin**-tŭ-pee) *noun* **1** a member of an Aboriginal people of the Gibson Desert region of WA. **2** their language, a dialect of the Western Desert language.

pioneer (py-ŏ-**neer**) *noun* a person who is one of the first to enter or settle a new region or to investigate a new subject or method etc. –**pioneer** *verb* to be a pioneer; to take part in (a course of action etc.) that leads the way for others to follow. [from French *pionnier* = foot soldier]

pious *adjective* **1** devout in religion. **2** ostentatiously virtuous. **piously** *adverb*, **piousness** *noun* [from Latin *pius* = dutiful]

pip[1] *noun* one of the small seeds of an apple, pear, orange, etc.

pip[2] *noun* **1** a spot on a domino, dice, or playing card. **2** a star (indicating rank) on the shoulder of an army officer's uniform.

pip[3] *verb* (**pipped**, **pipping**) (*informal*) **1** to hit with a shot. **2** to defeat. □ **pip at the post** to defeat at the last moment.

pip[4] *noun* a disease of poultry and other birds. □ **the pip** (*informal*) a feeling of disgust, depression, or bad temper.

pip[5] *noun* a short high-pitched sound.

pipe *noun* **1** a tube through which something can flow. **2** a wind instrument consisting of a single tube; each of the tubes by which sound is produced in an organ; **the pipes** bagpipes. **3** a boatswain's whistle; its sounding. **4** a narrow tube with a bowl at one end in which tobacco burns for smoking; the quantity of tobacco held by this. –**pipe** *verb* **1** to convey (water etc.) through pipes. **2** to transmit (music or a broadcast program etc.) by wire or cable. **3** to play (music) on a pipe; to lead, bring, or summon by sounding a pipe etc. **4** to utter in a

shrill voice. **5** to ornament (a dress etc.) with piping. **6** to force (icing or cream etc.) through an aperture to make ornamental shapes. □ **pipe down** (*informal*) to cease talking; to become less noisy or less insistent. **pipe dream** an impractical hope or scheme. **pipe up** to begin to play a pipe or to sing or speak.

pipeline *noun* **1** a pipe for conveying petroleum etc. to a distance. **2** a channel of supply or information. □ **in the pipeline** on the way; in the process of being prepared.

piper *noun* a person who plays on a pipe or bagpipes.

pipette (pi-**pet**) *noun* a slender tube, usually filled by suction, used in a laboratory for transferring or measuring small quantities of liquids.

pipi (**pip**-ee) *noun* a bivalve mollusc, often used as bait. [Maori]

piping *noun* **1** pipes; a length of pipe. **2** a pipelike fold (often enclosing a cord) ornamenting edges or seams of clothing or upholstery. **3** an ornamental line of icing etc. piped on food. □ **piping hot** (of water or food) very hot. **piping shrike** a magpie, the South Australian faunal emblem.

pipit *noun* a kind of small bird resembling a lark.

pipsqueak *noun* (*informal*) a small or unimportant but self-assertive fellow.

piquant (**pee**-kănt) *adjective* **1** pleasantly sharp in its taste or smell. **2** pleasantly stimulating or exciting to the mind. **piquantly** *adverb*, **piquancy** *noun* [same origin as *pique*]

pique (*pr.* peek) *verb* **1** to hurt the pride or self-respect of. **2** to stimulate, *their curiosity was piqued*. –**pique** *noun* a feeling of hurt pride. [from French *piquer* = to prick]

piqué (**pee**-kay) *noun* a firm fabric especially of cotton, woven with a ribbed or honeycomb effect.

piranha (pĭ-**rahn**-ă) *noun* a fierce tropical American freshwater fish. [Portuguese]

pirate *noun* **1** a person on a ship who unlawfully attacks and robs another ship at sea, or who makes a plundering raid on the shore. **2** the ship used for this. **3** one who infringes another's copyright or business rights, or who broadcasts without authorisation, *a pirate radio station*. –**pirate** *verb* to reproduce (a book etc.) or trade (goods) without due authorisation. **piratical** *adjective*, **piracy** (**py**-ră-see) *noun* [from Greek *peiraein* = to attack]

pirouette (pi-roo-**et**) *noun* a spinning movement of the body while balanced on the point of the toe or the ball of the foot. –**pirouette** *verb* to perform a pirouette. [French, = spinning top]

Pisa (**pee**-ză) a city in northern Italy, noted for its 'Leaning Tower', the campanile of its cathedral (12th century).

Pisces (**py**-seez) *noun* a sign of the zodiac, the Fishes, which the sun enters about 20 February. **Piscean** *adjective* & *noun*

Pissarro (pee-**sar**-roh), Camille (1830–1903), French impressionist painter.

pistachio (pis-**tah**-shee-oh) *noun* (*plural* **pistachios**) a kind of nut with an edible green kernel.

piste (*pr.* peest) *noun* a ski run of compacted snow.

pistil *noun* the seed-producing part of a flower, comprising ovary, style, and stigma.

pistol *noun* a small gun held in one hand.

piston *noun* **1** a sliding disc or cylinder fitting closely inside a tube in which it moves up and down as part of an engine or pump. **2** the sliding valve in a trumpet or other brass wind instrument.

pit *noun* **1** a hole in the ground, especially one from which material is dug out, *chalk pit*. **2** a coal mine. **3** a depression in the skin or in any surface. **4** seats on the ground floor of a theatre behind the stalls. **5** a sunken area in a workshop floor, giving access to the underside of motor vehicles. **6** a place (at a racecourse) at which racing cars are serviced and refuelled during a race. –**pit** *verb* (**pitted**, **pitting**) **1** to make pits or depressions in, to become marked with hollows, *pitted with craters*. **2** to remove stones from (cherries, olives, etc.). **3** to match or set in competition, *he was pitted against a strong fighter.* □ **the pits** (*informal*) the worst or most despicable person, place, or thing. **pit bull terrier** a variety of bull terrier dog, noted for its ferocity. **pit-head** *noun* the top of a coal mine shaft; the area surrounding this. [from Latin *puteus* = a well]

pit-a-pat *noun* a quick tapping sound. –**pit-a-pat** *adverb* with this sound.

Pitcairn Islands a British dependency comprising a group of islands in the South Pacific, north-east of New Zealand, settled in 1790 by mutineers from HMS *Bounty*.

pitch¹ *noun* a dark resinous tarry substance that sets hard, used for caulking seams of ships etc. –**pitch** *verb* to coat with pitch.

□ **pitch-black, pitch-dark** *adjectives* quite black, with no light at all.

pitch² *verb* **1** to throw or fling. **2** to erect and fix (a tent or camp). **3** to set at a particular degree, slope, or level, *pitched their hopes high.* **4** to fall heavily. **5** (in cricket) to cause the ball to strike the ground near the wicket in bowling; (of a bowled ball) to strike the ground. **6** (in baseball and softball) to throw (the ball) to the batter. **7** (of a ship or vehicle) to plunge forward and backward alternately. **8** to tell (a yarn or excuse etc.). –**pitch** *noun* **1** the act or process of pitching. **2** the steepness of a slope. **3** the intensity of a quality etc. **4** the degree of highness or lowness of a musical note or a voice. **5** a place at which a street performer or trader etc. is stationed. **6** a playing field for football, hockey, etc., the area between and near the wickets in cricket. **7** a salesman's persuasive talk. □ **pitched battle** a battle fought by troops in prepared positions, not a skirmish. **pitch in** (*informal*) to begin to work vigorously; to join in; to contribute (money etc.). **pitch into** (*informal*) to attack or reprimand vigorously.

pitchblende *noun* a mineral ore (uranium oxide) that yields radium.

pitcher¹ *noun* the baseball or softball player who delivers the ball to the batter.

pitcher² *noun* a large (usually earthenware) jug or two-handled vessel for holding and pouring liquids; *little pitchers have long ears*, children are apt to overhear things.

pitchfork *noun* a long-handled fork with two prongs, used for pitching hay. –**pitchfork** *verb* **1** to lift or move (a thing) with a pitchfork. **2** to thrust (a person) forcibly into a position or office etc.

piteous *adjective* deserving or arousing pity. **piteously** *adverb*

pitfall *noun* an unsuspected danger or difficulty.

pith *noun* **1** the spongy tissue in the stems of certain plants or lining the rind of oranges etc. **2** the essential part, *the pith of the argument*.

pithy *adjective* (**pithier**, **pithiest**) **1** like pith; containing much pith. **2** brief and full of meaning, *pithy comments*.

pitiable *adjective* deserving or arousing pity or contempt. **pitiably** *adverb*

pitiful *adjective* pitiable. **pitifully** *adverb*

pitiless *adjective* showing no pity. **pitilessly** *adverb*

Pitjantjatjara (**pich**-ăn-jă-jah-ră *or* **pich**-ăn-jah-ră) *noun* **1** a member of an Aboriginal people of northern SA. **2** their language, a dialect of the Western Desert language.

piton (**pee**-tonn) *noun* a spike or peg with a hole through which a rope can be passed, driven into a rock or crack as a support in rock-climbing.

pitot tube (**pee**-toh) *noun* an open-ended tube bent at right angles, used in instruments that measure wind speed, the rate of flow of liquids, etc. [named after the French scientist Henri Pitot (1695–1771)]

pitta *noun* a kind of flat bread with a hollow inside, originally from Greece and the Middle East.

pittance *noun* a very small allowance of money. [same origin as *pity* and *piety* (the word *pittance* originally meant 'pious gift')]

Pitta-pitta *noun* **1** a member of an Aboriginal people of central Queensland. **2** their language.

pitted *see* pit.

pitter-patter *noun* a light tapping sound.

pituitary (pǐ-**tew**-ǐ-tă-ree) *noun* the **pituitary gland**, a small ductless gland at the base of the brain, with important influence on growth and bodily functions.

pituri (**pich**-ŭ-ree) *noun* a shrub found in central Australia, whose leaves were traditionally chewed as a narcotic. [Yandruwandha *bijirri*]

pity *noun* **1** a feeling of sorrow for another person's suffering. **2** a cause for regret, *what a pity*. –**pity** *verb* (**pitied**, **pitying**) to feel pity for. □ **take pity on** to feel concern for and therefore help (a person who is in need or difficulty). [same origin as *piety*]

pivot *noun* **1** a central point or shaft etc. on which something turns or swings. **2** a pivoting movement. –**pivot** *verb* (**pivoted**, **pivoting**) to turn or place to turn on a pivot.

pivotal *adjective* of a pivot.

pixel *noun* any of the minute illuminated areas making up an image on a display screen. **pixelate** *verb*

pixie *noun* a small supernatural being in fairy tales. □ **pixie hood** a woman's or child's hood with a pointed crown.

Pizarro (pǐ-**zah**-roh), Francisco (c. 1478–1541), Spanish conqueror of the Inca empire in Peru.

pizazz (pǐ-**zaz**) *noun* (*informal*) zest, liveliness.

pizza (**peets**-ă) *noun* an Italian dish consisting of a layer of dough baked with a savoury topping. [Italian, = pie]

pizzicato (pits-i-**kah**-toh) *adverb* plucking the string of a musical instrument which is normally played with a bow. [Italian]

placard *noun* a poster or other notice for displaying.

placate (plă-**kayt**) *verb* to pacify, to conciliate. **placatory** *adjective*

place *noun* **1** a particular part of space or of an area on a surface. **2** a particular town, district, building, etc., *one of the places we visited*. **3** (in names) a short street; a square or the buildings round it. **4** a passage or part in a book etc.; the part one has reached in reading, *lose one's place*. **5** a proper position for a thing; a position in a series; one's rank or position in a community; a duty appropriate to this. **6** a position of employment. **7** a space or seat or accommodation for a person, *keep me a place on the train*. **8** one's home or dwelling, *let's go to your place*. **9** (in racing) a position among placed competitors, especially second or third. **10** a step in the progression of an argument or statement, *in the first place, the dates are wrong*. **11** the position of a figure after a decimal point etc., *correct to 3 decimal places*. –**place** *verb* **1** to put into a particular place, rank, position, or order etc.; to find a place for. **2** to locate, to identify in relation to circumstances etc., *I know his face but can't place him*. **3** to put or give, *placed an order with the firm*. □ **be placed** (in a race) to be among the first three. **in place of** instead of. **out of place** in the wrong position or environment; unsuitable. **place setting** a set of dishes or cutlery for one person at table. **place value** the value assigned to each position of a figure in a number (e.g. in 3237, the first 3 has a value of 3000, the second of 30). [from Greek *plateia* = broad way]

placebo (plă-**see**-boh) *noun* (*plural* **placebos**) a harmless substance given as if it were medicine, to humour a patient or as a dummy pill etc. in a controlled experiment. [Latin, = I shall please]

placement *noun* placing.

placenta (plă-**sent**-ă) *noun* an organ that develops in the womb during pregnancy and supplies the developing foetus with nourishment. **placental** *adjective*

placid *adjective* calm and peaceful, not easily made anxious or upset. **placidly** *adverb*,

placidity (plă-**sid**-ĭ-tee) *noun* [from Latin *placidus* = gentle]

placket *noun* an opening or slit in a garment (e.g. above the cuff or below the neckline) to make it easier to get on and off; a flap of fabric under such an opening.

plagiarise (**play**-jă-ryz) *verb* (also **-ize**) to take and use (another person's ideas or writings or inventions) as one's own. **plagiarism** *noun* [from Latin *plagiarius* = kidnapper]

plague (*pr.* playg) *noun* **1** a deadly contagious disease, especially the bubonic plague in London in 1665. **2** an infestation of a pest, *a plague of locusts*. **3** (*informal*) a nuisance. **–plague** *verb* to annoy, to pester.

plaice *noun* (*plural* **plaice**) an edible European and American flatfish.

plaid (*pr.* plad *or* playd) *noun* tartan cloth.

plain *adjective* **1** unmistakable, easy to see or hear or understand. **2** not elaborate or intricate, not luxurious, *plain cooking*; *plain water*, without flavouring etc.; *plain chocolate*, dark chocolate without milk. **3** straightforward, candid, *some plain speaking*. **4** ordinary; homely in manner, without affectation. **5** lacking beauty. **–plain** *adverb* plainly, simply, *it's plain stupid*. **–plain** *noun* **1** a large area of level country. **2** the ordinary stitch in knitting, producing a smooth surface towards the knitter. □ **plain clothes** civilian clothes as distinct from uniform or official dress. **plain flour** flour that does not contain a raising agent. **plain sailing** a course of action that is free from difficulties. **plain-spoken** *adjective* frank. **plainly** *adverb*, **plainness** *noun* [from Latin *planus* = flat]

plainsong *noun* (also **plainchant**) a medieval type of church music for voices singing in unison, without regular rhythm.

plaintiff *noun* the party that brings an action in a court of law (opposed to the *defendant*). [from Latin *planctus* = complaint]

plaintive *adjective* sounding sad. **plaintively** *adverb*, **plaintiveness** *noun* [same origin as *plaintiff*]

plait (*pr.* plat) *verb* to weave or twist (three or more strands) into one rope-like length. **–plait** *noun* something plaited. [from Latin *plicatum* = folded]

plan *noun* **1** a drawing showing the relative position and size of parts of a building etc. **2** a map of a town or district. **3** a method or way of proceeding thought out in advance; *it all* *went according to plan*, happened as planned. **–plan** *verb* (**planned**, **planning**) **1** to make a plan or design of. **2** to arrange a method etc. for, to make plans. **planner** *noun*

planar (**play**-ner) *adjective* **1** of or in the form of a plane (**plane²** senses 1 and 2). **2** (of a network in graph theory) that can be represented in a plane, with its vertices as separate points and no edges meeting except at their end points.

planarian (plă-**nair**-ree-ăn) *noun* a kind of flatworm usually living in fresh water.

Planck, Max Karl Ernst Ludwig (1858–1947), German theoretical physicist, the originator of the quantum theory.

plane¹ *noun* a tall spreading tree with broad leaves.

plane² *noun* **1** a flat or level surface. **2** an imaginary surface of this kind. **3** a level of thought, existence, or development, *he thinks on a different plane*. **4** an aeroplane. **–plane** *adjective* lying in a plane, level, *a plane figure* or *surface*. [same origin as *plain*]

plane³ *noun* **1** a tool with a blade projecting from the base, used for smoothing the surface of wood by paring shavings from it. **2** a similar tool for smoothing metal. **–plane** *verb* to smooth or pare with a plane.

planet *noun* any of the heavenly bodies moving round a star, especially those orbiting the sun. **planetary** *adjective* [from Greek *planetes* = wanderer (because it was not a 'fixed star')]

planetarium (plan-ĕ-**tair**-ree-ŭm) *noun* a room with a domed ceiling on which lights are projected to show the appearance of the stars and planets in the sky at any chosen place or time.

plangent (**plan**-jĕnt) *adjective* (of sounds) **1** resonant, reverberating. **2** loud and mournful. **plangency** *noun* [from Latin *plangens* = lamenting]

plank *noun* **1** a long flat piece of timber several inches thick. **2** one of the basic principles of a political platform.

planking *noun* a structure or floor of planks.

plankton *noun* the forms of organic life (chiefly microscopic) that drift or float in the sea or in fresh water. **planktonic** *adjective* [from Greek, = wandering]

planned *see* plan.

planning *noun* making plans, especially with reference to the controlled design of buildings and development of land.

plant *noun* **1** a living organism that makes its own food from inorganic substances and has neither the power of movement nor special organs of sensation and digestion. **2** a small plant (distinguished from a tree or shrub). **3** a factory or its machinery and equipment. **4** (*Austral.*) the portable equipment and stock of a drover or stockman. **5** (*informal*) something deliberately placed for discovery by others, especially so as to incriminate a person. **–plant** *verb* **1** to place in the ground or in soil for growing; to put plants or seeds into (ground or soil) for growing. **2** to fix or set or place in position. **3** to station (a person) as a lookout or spy. **4** to conceal (stolen or incriminating articles) in a place where they will be discovered and mislead the discoverer. [from Latin *planta* = a shoot]

Plantagenet (plan-**taj**-ĕ-nĕt) *noun* any of the kings of England from Henry II to Richard III (1154–1485).

plantain¹ (**plan**-tĭn) *noun* a common wild plant with flat leaves spread close to the ground, bearing seeds that are used as food for birds.

plantain² (**plan**-tĭn) *noun* a tropical tree and fruit resembling the banana.

plantation *noun* **1** a number of cultivated plants or trees; the area of land on which they grow. **2** an estate on which cotton, tobacco, or tea etc. is cultivated.

planter *noun* **1** a person who owns or manages a plantation. **2** a container for decorative plants.

plaque (*pr.* plahk *or* plak) *noun* **1** a flat inscribed plate of metal, stone, or porcelain, especially fixed on a wall as an ornament or memorial. **2** a substance that forms on teeth, where bacteria can live.

plasma (**plaz**-mă) *noun* **1** the colourless fluid part of blood, in which the corpuscles are suspended. **2** a kind of gas containing positively and negatively charged particles in approximately equal numbers.

plasmolysis (plaz-**mol**-ĭ-sĭs) *noun* contraction of the protoplasm of a plant cell when it is immersed in a solution that is more concentrated than the fluid in the cell. [from *plasma*, + Greek *lusis* = loosening]

plaster *noun* **1** a soft mixture of lime, sand, and water etc. used for coating walls and

ceilings. **2** plaster of Paris; a cast made of this fitted round a broken limb etc. **3** sticking plaster; a piece of this. **–plaster** *verb* **1** to cover (a wall etc.) with plaster or a similar substance. **2** to coat or daub; to cover thickly. **3** to make smooth with a fixative etc., *his hair was plastered down*. □ **plaster cast** a cast of a statue etc. made in plaster; plaster moulded round a part of the body to keep it rigid. **plaster of Paris** white paste made from gypsum, used for making moulds or casts. **plasterer** *noun*

plasterboard *noun* board with a core of plaster, used for making partitions etc.

plastic (**plass**-tik) *noun* a synthetic resinous substance that can be given any permanent shape, e.g. by moulding it under pressure while heated. **–plastic** *adjective* **1** made of plastic, *plastic bag*. **2** able to be shaped or moulded, *clay is a plastic substance*. **3** giving form to clay or wax etc.; *the plastic arts*, those concerned with sculpture, ceramics, etc. □ **plastic money** (*informal*) a credit or debit card, which can be used instead of cash. **plastic surgeon** a specialist in **plastic surgery**, the repairing or replacing of injured or defective external tissue. **plasticity** (plas-**tiss**-ĭ-tee) *noun*

plasticine *noun* (*trademark*) a plastic substance used for modelling things.

plasticise (**plas**-tĭ-syz) *verb* (also **-ize**) to make or become plastic. **plasticiser** *noun*

plate *noun* **1** an almost flat usually circular utensil from which food is eaten or served; its contents; *guests were asked to bring a plate*, bring a contribution of food (to a party etc.). **2** a similar shallow vessel for the collection of money in church. **3** dishes and other domestic utensils made of gold, silver, or other metal. **4** plated metal; objects made of this. **5** a silver or gold cup as a prize for a horse race etc.; the race itself. **6** a flat thin sheet of metal, glass, or other rigid material. **7** this coated with material sensitive to light or other radiation, for use in photography etc. **8** a flat piece of metal on which something is engraved or bearing a name or registration number etc. **9** an illustration on special paper in a book. **10** a thin flat structure or formation in a plant or animal body. **11** any of the very large nearly rigid sheets of rock that make up the earth's surface. **12** a piece of plastic material moulded to the shape of the gums or roof of the mouth for holding artificial teeth; (*informal*) a denture. **13** a flat piece of whitened rubber marking the station of the batter (*home plate*) or pitcher in baseball or softball. –**plate** *verb* **1** to cover with plates of metal. **2** to coat (metal) with a thin layer of silver, gold, or tin. **2** to serve or arrange on a plate. □ **on a plate** (*informal*) available without the recipient having to make an effort. **plate glass** glass of fine quality for shop windows etc. **plateful** *noun* (*plural* **platefuls**).

plateau (**plat**-oh) *noun* (*plural* **plateaux**, *pr.* **plat**-oh) **1** an area of fairly level high ground. **2** a state in which there is little variation following an increase. [from French *plat* = flat]

platelet *noun* a small colourless disc found in the blood and involved in clotting.

platform *noun* **1** a level surface raised above the surrounding ground or floor, especially one from which a speaker addresses an audience. **2** a raised area along the side of the line at a railway station, where passengers wait for, board, or alight from trains. **3** a floor area at the entrance to a bus or tram. **4** the declared policy or program of a political party. **5** a thick sole of a shoe; a shoe with such a sole.

Plath, Sylvia (1932–63), American poet and novelist.

platinum *noun* a chemical element (symbol Pt), a silver-white metal that does not tarnish. □ **platinum blonde** a woman with very light blonde hair. [from Spanish *plata* = silver]

platitude (**plat**-ĭ-tewd) *noun* a commonplace remark, especially one uttered solemnly as if it were new. **platitudinous** *adjective*

Plato (**play**-toh) (429–347 BC), Greek philosopher, a disciple of Socrates.

Platonic (plă-**tonn**-ik) *adjective* of Plato or his doctrines. –**platonic** *adjective* **1** (of love or friendship) intimate and affectionate but not sexual. **2** confined to words or theory, not leading to actions.

platoon *noun* a subdivision of a military company.

platter *noun* a large flat dish or plate for serving food.

platypus (**plat**-ĭ-puus) *noun* (*plural* **platypuses**) an Australian animal (a monotreme) with a ducklike bill, webbed feet, and a flat tail, that lays eggs but suckles its young. [from Greek *platus* = broad, + *pous* = foot]

plaudits (**plaw**-dĭts) *plural noun* a round of applause; emphatic approval. [same origin as *applaud*]

plausible (**plaw**-zĭ-bŭl) *adjective* **1** (of a statement) seeming to be reasonable or probable but not proved. **2** (of a person) persuasive but deceptive. **plausibly** *adverb*, **plausibility** *noun*

play *verb* **1** to occupy oneself in a game or other recreational activity. **2** to take part in (a game), *play netball*. **3** to compete against (a player or team) in a game. **4** to occupy (a specified position) in a game. **5** to move (a piece), put (a card) on the table, or strike (a ball etc.) in a game. **6** to act in a drama etc.; to act the part of. **7** to perform (a part in a process). **8** to perform on (a musical instrument); to perform (a piece of music). **9** to cause (a disc or tape etc.) to produce sound. **10** to move lightly or irregularly; to allow (light or water) to fall on something; (of a fountain or hose) to discharge water. **11** to allow (a hooked fish) to exhaust itself by its pulling against the line. –**play** *noun* **1** playing; *a play on words*, a pun. **2** activity, operation, *other influences came into play*. **3** a literary work written for performance on the stage, a similar work for broadcasting. **4** free movement, *bolts should have a centimetre of play*. □ **in** or **out of play** (of a ball) being used, or temporarily out of use according to the rules, in a game. **play-acting** *noun* playing a part in a play; pretending. **play along** to pretend to cooperate. **play at** to perform in a trivial or half-hearted way. **play back** to play (what has recently been recorded) on a tape recorder etc. **play-back** *noun* playing back sound; a device for doing this. **play ball** (*informal*) to cooperate. **play by ear** to perform (music) without having seen a written score; to proceed in (a matter) step by step going by one's instinct or by results. **play down** to minimise the importance of. **played out** exhausted of energy. **play into someone's hands** to do something that unwittingly gives that person an advantage. **play lunch** (*Austral. informal*) a snack eaten by schoolchildren at the mid-morning break; the break itself. **play off** to play an extra match to decide a drawn position; *play off one person against another*, to oppose one person against another in order to serve one's own interests. **play-off** *noun* a match played to decide a draw or tie. **play on** to affect and make use of (a person's sympathy etc.). **play the game** to keep the rules; to behave honourably. **play the market** to speculate in stocks etc. **play up** to put all one's energy into a game; (*informal*) to be mischievous and unruly, to annoy by doing this. **play up to** to try to win the favour of or encourage (a person) by flattery etc. **play with** to toy with. **play with fire** to treat frivolously something that could prove dangerous.

playa (**ply**-ă) *noun* **1** a flat area of clay or silt etc. at the bottom of a sunken area in a desert, where rainwater collects to form a temporary lake. **2** this lake. [Spanish, = a beach]

playboy *noun* a pleasure-loving usually rich man.

player *noun* **1** a person who takes part in a game. **2** a performer on a musical instrument. **3** an actor. **4** a piece of equipment for playing compact discs, records, tapes, videos, etc. □ **player-piano** *noun* a piano fitted with an apparatus that enables it to play automatically with the turning of a perforated paper roll.

playfellow *noun* a playmate.

playful *adjective* **1** full of fun. **2** in a mood for play, not serious. **playfully** *adverb*, **playfulness** *noun*

playground *noun* **1** a piece of ground for children to play on. **2** a favourite place for recreation.

playing card *noun* each of a pack or set of 52 rectangular cards used to play a variety of games, marked on one side to show one of 13 ranks in one of 4 suits.

playmate *noun* a child's companion in play.

playpen *noun* a portable enclosure for a young child to play in.

plaything *noun* **1** a toy. **2** a person treated as a thing to play with.

playtime *noun* time assigned for children to play.

playwright *noun* a person who writes plays, a dramatist. [from *play*, + *wright* = maker]

plaza (**plah**-ză) *noun* **1** a public square in a town. **2** (used in names) a set of shops. [Spanish, = place]

plea *noun* **1** a formal statement (especially of 'guilty' or 'not guilty') made by or on behalf of a person charged in a lawsuit. **2** an appeal or entreaty, *a plea for mercy.* **3** an excuse, *on the plea of ill health.* □ **plea bargaining** an arrangement between prosecutor and defendant whereby the defendant pleads guilty to a lesser charge in the expectation of leniency. [same origin as *please*]

plead *verb* (**pleaded, pleading**) **1** to put forward as a plea in a lawcourt. **2** to address a lawcourt as an advocate; to put forward (a case) in court. **3** to make an appeal or entreaty.

4 to put forward as an excuse, *pleaded a previous engagement.* □ **plead with** to entreat.

pleasant *adjective* **1** pleasing, giving pleasure to the mind or feelings or senses. **2** having an agreeable manner. **pleasantly** *adverb*, **pleasantness** *noun*

pleasantry *noun* a humorous remark.

please *verb* **1** to give pleasure to, to make (a person etc.) feel satisfied or glad. **2** to be so kind as to, *please ring the bell.* **3** to think fit; to have the desire, *take what you please.* – **please** *adverb* a polite phrase of request.
□ **if you please** (*formal*) please; an ironical phrase, pointing out unreasonableness, *and so, if you please, we're to get nothing!* **please oneself** to do as one chooses. [from Latin *placere* = satisfy]

pleased *adjective* feeling or showing pleasure or satisfaction.

pleasurable *adjective* causing pleasure. **pleasurably** *adverb*

pleasure *noun* **1** a feeling of satisfaction or joy, enjoyment. **2** a source of pleasure. **3** choice, desire, *at your pleasure.* – **pleasure** *adjective* done or used for pleasure, *a pleasure trip.*

pleat *noun* a flat fold made by doubling cloth on itself. – **pleat** *verb* to make a pleat or pleats in. [from *plait*]

plebeian (plĕ-**bee**-ăn) *adjective* **1** of the lower social classes. **2** uncultured, vulgar. – **plebeian** *noun* a member of the lower classes, especially in ancient Rome. [from Latin *plebs* = the common people]

plebiscite (**pleb**-ĭ-syt) *noun* a referendum. [from Latin *plebs* = the common people, + *scitum* = a decree]

plebs *plural noun* plebeians.

plectrum *noun* (*plural* **plectra**) a small piece of metal or bone or ivory or plastic for plucking or strumming the strings of a musical instrument.

pled *see* **plead**.

pledge *noun* **1** a thing deposited as security for payment of a debt or fulfilment of a contract etc., and liable to be forfeited in case of failure. **2** a token of something, *as a pledge of his devotion.* **3** a toast drunk to someone's health. **4** a solemn promise, *under pledge of secrecy.* – **pledge** *verb* **1** to deposit (an article) as a pledge. **2** to promise solemnly. **3** to drink to the health of.

Pleiades (ply-ă-deez) *plural noun* the 'Seven Sisters', a group of seven stars in the constellation Taurus.

Pleistocene (ply-stŏ-seen) *adjective* of the first of the two epochs of the Quaternary period. –**Pleistocene** *noun* this epoch.

plenary (pleen-ă-ree) *adjective* attended by all members, *a plenary session of the assembly*. [from Latin *plenus* = full]

plenipotentiary (plen-ĭ-pŏ-**ten**-shă-ree) *noun* an envoy with full powers to take action or make decisions etc. on behalf of the government he or she represents. –**plenipotentiary** *adjective* having these powers. [from Latin *plenus* = full, + *potentia* = power]

plenteous (**plen**-tee-ŭs) *adjective* (*literary*) plentiful. **plenteously** *adverb*

plentiful *adjective* in large quantities or numbers, abundant. **plentifully** *adverb*

plenty *noun* quite enough, as much as one could need or desire. –**plenty** *adverb* (*informal*) quite, fully, *it's plenty big enough*. [from Latin *plenus* = full]

pleonasm (**plee**-ŏ-nazm) *noun* an expression in which a word is redundant, as in 'a dead corpse'.

plethora (**pleth**-ŏ-ră) *noun* an over-abundance. [from Greek *plethein* = be full]

pleural (**ploor**-răl) *adjective* of the two membranes (*pleurae*) that line the chest and surround the lungs.

pleurisy (**ploor**-rĭ-see) *noun* inflammation of the membrane (*pleura*) lining the chest and surrounding the lungs. [from Greek *pleura* = ribs]

pliable *adjective* 1 bending easily, flexible. 2 easily influenced. **pliably** *adverb*, **pliability** *noun* [from French *plier* = to bend]

pliant (**ply**-ănt) *adjective* pliable. **pliantly** *adverb*, **pliancy** *noun*

pliers *plural noun* pincers having jaws with flat surfaces that can be brought together for gripping small objects or wire etc.

plight[1] *noun* a serious and difficult situation.

plight[2] *verb* (*old use*) to pledge; *plight one's troth*, to promise to marry.

Plimsoll line *noun* (also **Plimsoll mark**) a mark on a ship's side showing how far it may legally go down in the water when loaded. [named after the English politician Samuel Plimsoll]

plinth *noun* a block or slab forming the base of a column or a support for a vase etc.

Pliny 'the Elder' (Gaius Plinius Secundus) (23–79), Roman statesman, author of the encyclopedic *Natural History*.

Pliocene (ply-ŏ-seen) *adjective* of the final epoch of the Tertiary period. –**Pliocene** *noun* this epoch.

plissé (**plee**-say) *noun* fabric that has been treated to give it a crinkled appearance. [French, = pleated]

PLO *abbreviation* Palestine Liberation Organisation, a political and military organisation campaigning for the rights of Palestinian Arabs in the Middle East.

plod *verb* (**plodded, plodding**) 1 to walk doggedly or laboriously, to trudge. 2 to work at a slow but steady rate. –**plod** *noun* plodding. **plodder** *noun*

plonk[1] *verb* to throw or place or drop down heavily.

plonk[2] *noun* (*informal*) cheap or inferior wine.

plop *noun* a sound like that of something dropping into water without a splash.

plot *noun* 1 a small piece of land, *vegetable plot*. 2 the story in a play, novel, or film. 3 a conspiracy, a secret plan. –**plot** *verb* (**plotted, plotting**) 1 to make a plan or map of. 2 to mark on a chart or diagram. 3 to plan secretly, to contrive a secret plan. **plotter** *noun*

plough (*rhymes with* cow) *noun* 1 an implement for cutting furrows in soil and turning it up, drawn by a tractor or horse(s). 2 an implement resembling a plough, *snow plough*. 3 **the Plough** a constellation also called the Great Bear. –**plough** *verb* 1 to turn up (earth) or cast out (roots etc.) with a plough; to cut (a furrow). 2 to make one's way or advance laboriously, *ploughed through the mud* or *through a book*. 3 to advance violently, *the truck ploughed into the barrier as it crashed*. □ **plough back** to turn (growing grass etc.) into the soil to enrich it; to reinvest (profits) in the business that produced them.

ploughshare *noun* the cutting blade of a plough.

plover (**pluv**-er) *noun* a kind of wading bird. [from Latin *pluvia* = rain]

ploy *noun* (*informal*) a cunning manoeuvre to gain an advantage.

pluck *verb* 1 to pick (a flower or fruit); to pull out (a hair or feather etc.). 2 to strip (a bird) of its feathers. 3 to pull at or twitch. 4 to sound (the string of a musical instrument) by pulling and then releasing it with the finger(s) or a plectrum. **–pluck** *noun* **1** plucking, a pull. **2** courage, spirit. ☐ **pluck up courage** to summon up one's courage.

plucky *adjective* (**pluckier**, **pluckiest**) showing pluck, brave. **pluckily** *adverb*

plug *noun* **1** something fitting into and stopping or filling a hole or cavity. **2** a device with metal pins that fit into a socket to make an electrical connection. **3** (*informal*) a spark plug. **4** (*informal*) a piece of favourable publicity for a commercial product. **5** a cake of tobacco; a piece of this cut off for chewing. **–plug** *verb* (**plugged**, **plugging**) **1** to put a plug into, to stop with a plug. **2** (*informal*) to shoot or strike (a person etc.). **3** (*informal*) to mention favourably; to seek to popularise (a song, product, policy, etc.) by constant commendation. ☐ **plug away** to work diligently or persistently. **plug in** to connect electrically by inserting a plug into a socket.

plum *noun* **1** a fleshy fruit with sweet pulp and a flattish pointed stone. **2** the tree that bears it. **3** (*old use*) a dried grape or raisin used in cooking; *plum cake* or *pudding*, one containing such fruit. **4** reddish-purple colour. **5** a good thing; the best of a collection, something considered good and desirable, *a plum job*.

plumage (**ploo**-mij) *noun* a bird's feathers. [same origin as *plume*]

plumb¹ (*pr.* plum) *noun* a piece of lead tied to the end of a cord, used for finding the depth of water or testing whether a wall etc. is vertical. **–plumb** *adverb* **1** exactly, *plumb in the middle*. **2** (*Amer. informal*) completely, *plumb crazy*. **–plumb** *verb* **1** to measure or test with a plumb line. **2** to reach, *plumbed the depths of misery*. **3** to get to the bottom of (a matter). ☐ **out of plumb** not vertical. **plumb line** a cord with a plumb attached. [from Latin *plumbum* = lead (the metal)]

plumb² (*pr.* plum) *verb* **1** to work as a plumber. **2** to provide with a plumbing system; to fit (a thing) as part of this.

plumber (**plum**-er) *noun* a person whose job is to fit and repair plumbing.

plumbing (**plum**-ing) *noun* **1** a system of water pipes, cisterns, and drainage pipes etc. in a building. **2** the work of a plumber.

plume (*pr.* ploom) *noun* **1** a feather, especially a large one used for ornament. **2** an ornament of feathers or similar material. **3** something

resembling this, *a plume of smoke*. **–plume** *verb* to preen, *the bird plumed itself* or *its feathers*. ☐ **plume oneself** to pride oneself. [from Latin *pluma* = feather]

plumed (*pr.* ploomd) *adjective* ornamented with plumes.

plummet *noun* **1** a plumb or plumb line. **2** a weight attached to a fishing line to keep a float upright. **–plummet** *verb* (**plummeted**, **plummeting**) to fall or plunge steeply.

plummy *adjective* **1** full of plums. **2** (of the voice) sounding affectedly full and rich in tone.

plump¹ *adjective* having a full rounded shape. **–plump** *verb* to make or become plump. **plumpness** *noun*

plump² *verb* to drop or plunge abruptly, *plumped down*. **–plump** *adverb* with a sudden or heavy fall. ☐ **plump for** to choose or vote for wholeheartedly, to decide on.

plumule (**ploom**-yool) *noun* **1** the rudimentary stem of an embryo plant. **2** a little feather of down. [from Latin *plumula* = little feather]

plunder *verb* to rob (a place or person) forcibly or systematically, to steal or embezzle. **–plunder** *noun* **1** the taking of goods or money etc. in this way. **2** the goods etc. acquired. **plunderer** *noun*

plunge *verb* **1** to thrust or go forcefully into something. **2** to descend suddenly. **3** to jump or dive into water. **4** to enter or cause to enter a condition or set of circumstances, *plunged the world into war*. **5** (of a horse) to start forward violently; (of a ship) to thrust its bows down into the water, to pitch. **6** to gamble heavily; to run deeply into debt. **–plunge** *noun* plunging, a dive. ☐ **take the plunge** to take a bold decisive step.

plunger *noun* **1** the part of a mechanism that works with a plunging or thrusting movement. **2** a rubber cup on a handle for removing blockages by alternate thrusting and suction.

pluperfect (ploo-**per**-fekt) *adjective* of the tense of a verb used to denote an action completed before some past point of time, e.g. *we had arrived*.

plural (**ploor**-răl) *noun* the form of a noun or verb used with reference to more than one person or thing, *the plural of 'child' is 'children'*. **–plural** *adjective* **1** of this form. **2** of more than one. **plurality** *noun* [from Latin *pluris* = of more]

pluralism *noun* a form of society with many minority groups and cultures; multiculturalism. **pluralist** *noun*, **pluralistic** *adjective*

plus *preposition* **1** with the addition of. **2** (*informal*) with, having gained, possessing, *returned home plus a wife.* **–plus** *adjective* **1** more than the amount indicated; *beta plus*, a grade slightly above beta (written as B +). **2** above zero, *temperature between minus ten and plus ten degrees.* **–plus** *noun* **1** the sign (+). **2** an advantage. □ **plus fours** knickerbockers worn especially by golfers. [Latin, = more]

plush *noun* a kind of cloth with long soft nap, used in furnishings. **–plush** *adjective* **1** made of plush. **2** plushy. [from Latin *pilus* = hair]

plushy *adjective* luxurious. **plushiness** *noun*

Plutarch (**ploo**-tark) (Lucius Mestrius Plutarchus) (c. 46–c.120), Greek Platonist philosopher and biographer.

Pluto (**ploo**-toh) **1** (*Gk. myth.*) a title of Hades, lord of the Underworld. **2** the ninth planet, for most of its orbit the outermost planet, of the solar system (technically now regarded as a dwarf planet).

plutocrat (**ploo**-tŏ-krat) *noun* a person who is powerful because of his or her wealth. **plutocracy** (ploo-**tok**-rǎ-see) *noun*, **plutocratic** *adjective* [from Greek *ploutos* = wealth, + *-kratia* = power]

plutonic *adjective* (of igneous rocks) formed by crystallisation of molten material at a great depth underground.

plutonium (ploo-**toh**-nee-ŭm) *noun* a chemical element (symbol Pu), a radioactive substance used in nuclear weapons and reactors. [named after the planet Pluto]

ply¹ *noun* **1** a thickness or layer of wood or cloth etc. **2** a strand in yarn, *3-ply wool*. **3** plywood. [same origin as *pliable*]

ply² *verb* (**plied**, **plying**) **1** to use or wield (a tool or weapon). **2** to work at, *ply one's trade*. **3** to work steadily. **4** to keep offering or supplying, *plied her with food* or *with questions*. **5** to go to and fro regularly, *the boat plies between the two ports*. **6** (of a taxi driver etc.) to move or wait about looking for custom, *ply for hire*. [from *apply*]

Plymouth Brethren a Calvinistic religious body formed about 1830 at Plymouth in England.

plywood *noun* strong thin board made by gluing layers with the grain crosswise.

PM *abbreviation* Prime Minister.

p.m. *abbreviation* after noon. [short for Latin *post meridiem*]

PMS *abbreviation* premenstrual syndrome.

PMT *abbreviation* premenstrual tension.

pneumatic (new-**mat**-ik) *adjective* filled with or operated by compressed air, *pneumatic drills*. **pneumatically** *adverb* [from Greek *pneuma* = wind]

pneumonia (new-**moh**-nee-ǎ) *noun* inflammation of one or both lungs. [from Greek *pneumon* = lung]

PNG *abbreviation* Papua New Guinea.

PO *abbreviation* Post Office.

poach¹ *verb* **1** to cook (an egg removed from its shell) in simmering water. **2** to cook (fish or fruit etc.) by simmering it in a small amount of liquid.

poach² *verb* **1** to take (game or fish) illegally from private land or water. **2** to trespass or encroach on something that properly belongs to another person. **poacher** *noun* [same origin as *pouch*]

pock *noun* **1** one of the spots that erupt on the skin in smallpox or chickenpox. **2** a scar left by this. □ **pock-marked** *adjective* marked by scars or pits.

pocket *noun* **1** a small baglike part sewn into or on a garment, for holding money or small articles. **2** one's resources of money; *beyond my pocket*, more than I can afford. **3** a pouchlike compartment in a suitcase or on a car door etc. **4** any of the pouches at the corners or sides of a billiard table, into which balls are driven. **5** an isolated group or area, *small pockets of resistance*. **–pocket** *adjective* **1** of a size or shape suitable for carrying in a pocket, *pocket calculators*. **2** smaller than the usual size, *a pocket dictionary*. **–pocket** *verb* **1** to put into one's pocket. **2** to take for oneself (dishonestly or otherwise). **3** to send (a ball) into a pocket on a billiard table. **4** to suppress or hide (one's feelings), *pocketing his pride*. □ **in pocket** having gained in a transaction. **out of pocket** having lost in a transaction. **out-of-pocket expenses** cash expenses incurred while doing something. **pocket knife** a knife with folding blade(s), for carrying in the pocket. **pocket money** money for small expenses; money allowed regularly to children. [from Old French *pochet* = little pouch]

pocketbook *noun* **1** a notebook. **2** a small booklike case for holding money or papers.

pocketful *noun* (*plural* **pocketfuls**) the amount that a pocket will hold.

pod[1] *noun* a long seed vessel like that of a pea or bean. **–pod** *verb* (**podded**, **podding**) **1** to bear or form pods. **2** to remove (peas etc.) from their pods.

pod[2] *noun* a school of marine animals, e.g. whales.

podcast *noun* a digital recording of a radio broadcast or similar program, made available on the Internet for downloading to a computer or personal audio player etc. **–podcast** *verb* to transmit (a program) in this way. [from *iPod*, proprietary name for a brand of personal audio player]

poddy *noun* (*Austral*.) a hand-fed calf.

Podgorica (pod-go-**ree**-să) the capital of Montenegro.

podgy *adjective* short and fat.

podiatry (pŏ-**dy**-ă-tree) *noun* the treatment of ailments of the feet. Formerly called *chiropody*. **podiatrist** *noun* [from Greek *podos* = foot, + *iatros* = physician]

podium (**poh**-dee-ŭm) *noun* (*plural* **podia**) a pedestal or platform. [from Greek *podion* = little foot]

podzol *noun* an infertile soil found in regions with a cold climate, in which minerals (such as iron and aluminium oxides) have been washed from the surface layers into lower layers. [from Russian *pod* = under, + *zola* = ashes]

podzolise *verb* (also **-ize**) to convert or be converted into podzol.

Poe, Edgar Allan (1809–49), American short-story writer, poet, and critic, best known for his macabre tales of the supernatural.

poem *noun* a literary composition in verse, especially one expressing deep feeling or noble thought in an imaginative way. [from Greek *poiema* = thing made]

poet *noun* a writer of poems. □ **Poet Laureate** *see* **laureate**. **poetess** *feminine noun* (*old-fashioned* or *contemptuous*).

poetic *adjective* of or like poetry; of poets. □ **poetic justice** suitable and well-deserved punishment or reward.

poetical *adjective* poetic, written in verse, *poetical works*. **poetically** *adverb*

poetry *noun* **1** poems; a poet's art or work. **2** a quality that pleases the mind as poetry does, *the poetry of motion*.

pogrom (**pog**-rŏm) *noun* an organised massacre, especially that of Jews in eastern Europe in 1905–6. [Russian, = destruction]

poignant (**poin**-yănt) *adjective* arousing sympathy; deeply moving to the feelings; keenly felt, *poignant grief*. **poignantly** *adverb*, **poignancy** *noun* [from French, = pricking]

poikilotherm (**poi**-kil-ŏ-therm) *noun* a cold-blooded animal (contrasts with *homoiotherm*). **poikilothermic** *adjective* [from Greek *poikilos* = changeable, + *therme* = heat]

poinsettia (poin-**set**-ee-ă) *noun* a plant with large usually scarlet petal-like bracts.

point *noun* **1** the tapered or sharp end of something, the tip. **2** a projection, a promontory of land. **3** (in geometry) that which has position but not magnitude, e.g. the intersection of two lines. **4** a dot used as a punctuation mark etc.; a decimal point. **5** a particular place or spot; an exact moment; a stage or degree of progress, increase, or temperature etc. **6** each of the directions marked on the compass; a corresponding direction towards the horizon. **7** a unit of measurement, value, or scoring. **8** a separate item of detail, *we differ on several points*. **9** a distinctive feature or characteristic; *it has its points*, has certain useful features. **10** the essential thing, the thing under discussion, *come to the point*. **11** the important feature of a story, joke, or remark. **12** effectiveness, purpose, value, *there's no point in wasting time*. **13** a fielder in cricket near the batsman on the off side; this position. **14** an electrical socket, *power points*. **15** each of the tapering movable rails by which a train is directed from one line to another. **16** each of a set of electrical contacts in the distributor of a motor vehicle. **–point** *verb* **1** to direct or aim, *pointed a gun at her*. **2** to be directed or aimed. **3** to direct attention; to indicate; *it all points to a conspiracy*, is evidence of one. **4** to sharpen. **5** to fill in the joints of (brickwork etc.) with mortar or cement. □ **a case in point** one that is relevant to what has just been said. **make a point of** to treat as important, to do something with ostentatious care. **on the point of** on the very verge of (an action). **point duty** (of a police officer) being stationed at a particular point to regulate traffic. **point of no return** the point in a long-distance journey at which one must continue onward because supplies are insufficient to enable one to return to the starting point; the point after which one cannot withdraw from an action. **point of view** a way of looking at a matter. **point out** to indicate, to draw attention to. **point up** to emphasise. **to the point** relevant; relevantly. [from Latin *punctum* = pricked]

point-blank *adjective* **1** (of a shot) aimed or fired at very close range. **2** (of a remark) direct, straightforward, *a point-blank refusal*. **–point-blank** *adverb* in a point-blank manner, *refused point-blank*.

pointed *adjective* **1** tapering or sharpened to a point. **2** (of a remark or manner) clearly aimed at a particular person or thing; emphasised. **pointedly** *adverb*

pointer *noun* **1** a thing that points to something; a mark or rod that points to figures etc. on a dial or scale. **2** a rod used to point to things on a blackboard etc. **3** a symbol on a computer screen used to point to things, positioned by moving a mouse or similar device. **4** (*informal*) a hint or indication. **5** a dog of a breed that on scenting game stands rigidly with muzzle pointing towards it.

pointillism (**pwan**-tĭ-lizm) *noun* a technique of painting, used especially by the neo-impressionists, in which the paint is applied in tiny spots of various colours that are blended by the eye of the spectator. **pointillist** *noun*

pointless *adjective* **1** without a point. **2** having no purpose or meaning. **pointlessly** *adverb*

poise *verb* **1** to balance or be balanced. **2** to hold suspended or supported. **–poise** *noun* **1** balance, the way something is poised. **2** a dignified and self-assured manner.

poised *adjective* (of a person) having poise, dignified and self-assured.

poison *noun* **1** a substance that can destroy the life or harm the health of a living animal or plant. **2** a harmful influence. **–poison** *verb* **1** to give poison to; to kill with poison. **2** to put poison on or in. **3** to corrupt, to fill with prejudice, *poisoned their minds*. □ **poison pen** a person who writes malicious or libellous anonymous letters. **poisoner** *noun* [same origin as *potion*]

poisonous *adjective* **1** containing or having the effect of poison. **2** likely to corrupt people, *a poisonous influence*.

poke *verb* **1** to thrust with the end of a finger or a stick etc. **2** to thrust or be thrust forward; to protrude. **3** to produce by poking, *poked a hole in it*. **4** to search, to pry, *poking about in the cupboard*. **–poke** *noun* a poking movement, a thrust or nudge. □ **poke fun at** to ridicule.

poke one's nose into something to pry or intrude.

poker¹ *noun* a stiff metal rod for poking a fire.

poker² *noun* a card game in which players bet. □ **poker face** a face that does not reveal thoughts or feelings. **poker machine** a coin-operated gambling machine operated by pulling down a lever or pressing a button.

pokie *noun* (*informal*) poker machine, *play the pokies*.

poky *adjective* (**pokier**, **pokiest**) small and cramped, *poky little rooms*. **pokiness** *noun* [from *poke*]

Poland a republic in central Europe.

polar *adjective* **1** of or near the North Pole or South Pole. **2** of one of the poles of a magnet. **3** directly opposite in character or tendency. □ **polar bear** a white bear living in Arctic regions. **polar coordinate** a coordinate that uses a distance and an angle to fix a position.

polarise *verb* (also **-ize**) **1** to confine similar vibrations of (light waves etc.) to a single direction or plane. **2** to give polarity to. **3** to set or become set at opposite extremes of opinion, *public opinion had polarised*. **polarisation** *noun*

polarity (poh-**la**-rĭ-tee) *noun* **1** the possessing of negative and positive poles. **2** the electrical condition of a body (positive or negative).

polaroid *noun* (*trademark*) **1** a material that polarises the light passing through it, used in spectacle lenses etc. to protect the eyes from glare. **2** a kind of camera that develops and prints a photograph instantly when an exposure is made.

polder *noun* an area reclaimed from the sea or a river, especially in the Netherlands.

Pole *noun* a Polish person.

pole¹ *noun* a long slender rounded piece of wood or metal, especially one used as part of a supporting structure or in propelling a barge etc. **–pole** *verb* to push along by using a pole. □ **pole jump** or **vault** a vault over a high crossbar with the help of a pole held in the hands. **pole position** the most favourable position on the starting grid in a motor race, in the front row and on the inside of the first bend (also *poll position*). [same origin as *pale²*]

pole² *noun* **1** either extremity of the earth's or other body's axis; either of two points in the sky about which the stars appear to rotate, the North Pole or South Pole. **2** each of the two points in a magnet which attract or repel magnetic bodies. **3** the positive or negative terminal of an electric cell or battery. **4** each of two opposed principles. □ **be poles apart** to differ greatly. **pole star** a star in the Little Bear, near the North Pole in the sky. [from Greek *polos* = axis]

poleaxe *noun* **1** a battleaxe with a long handle. **2** a butcher's implement for slaughtering cattle. –**poleaxe** *verb* to strike down with or as if with a poleaxe.

polecat *noun* **1** a small dark brown animal of the weasel family with an unpleasant smell. **2** (*Amer.*) a skunk.

polemic (pŏ-**lem**-ik) *noun* a verbal attack on a belief or opinion. –**polemic** *adjective* (also **polemical**) **1** controversial. **2** argumentative. [from Greek *polemos* = war]

polenta (pŏ-**len**-tă) *noun* cooked cornmeal.

police *noun* **1** a civil force responsible for the keeping of public order; its members. **2** a force responsible for enforcing the regulations of an organisation etc., *military police*. –**police** *verb* **1** to keep order in (a place) by means of police, to provide with police. **2** to administer, to control. □ **police officer** a policeman or policewoman. **police state** a country (usually a totalitarian State) in which political police supervise and control citizens' activities. **police station** the office of a local police force.

policeman *noun* (*plural* **policemen**) a man who is a member of a police force.

policewoman *noun* (*plural* **policewomen**) a woman member of a police force.

policy[1] *noun* the course or general plan of action adopted by a government, party, or person. [same origin as *political*]

policy[2] *noun* a contract of insurance; the document containing this. [from Greek, = evidence]

polio (**poh**-lee-oh) *noun* poliomyelitis.

poliomyelitis (poh-lee-oh-my-ě-**ly**-tĭss) *noun* an infectious disease caused by a virus, producing temporary or permanent paralysis.

Polish *adjective* of Poland or its people or language. –**Polish** *noun* the language of Poland.

polish *verb* **1** to make or become smooth and glossy by rubbing. **2** to make better by correcting or putting finishing touches. –**polish** *noun* **1** smoothness and glossiness. **2** the process of polishing. **3** a substance for polishing a surface. **4** a high degree of

elegance. □ **polish off** to finish off. **polisher** *noun*

polished *adjective* elegant, refined, perfected, *polished manners*; *a polished performance*.

polite *adjective* **1** having good manners, socially correct. **2** refined, *polite society*. **politely** *adverb*, **politeness** *noun* [from Latin *politus* = polished]

politic *adjective* showing good judgment, prudent. □ **the body politic** the State or a similar organised system.

political *adjective* **1** of or engaged in politics. **2** of the way a country is governed, *its political system*. □ **political asylum** refuge in foreign territory for refugees from political persecution. **political correctness** the avoidance of language or action which insults, excludes, or marginalises a person or group, e.g. women, racial and cultural minorities, etc (abbreviation **PC**). **political prisoner** a person imprisoned for a political offence. **politically** *adverb* [from Greek *politeia* = government]

politician *noun* a person who is engaged in politics, an MP.

politics *noun* **1** the science and art of governing a country. **2** political affairs or life. **3** manoeuvring for power etc. within a group, *office politics*. –**politics** *plural noun* political principles or affairs or tactics.

polka *noun* a lively dance for couples, of Bohemian origin. □ **polka dots** round dots evenly spaced to form a pattern on fabric.

poll (*rhymes with* hole) *noun* **1** voting at an election; the counting of votes; the number of votes recorded, *a heavy poll*. **2** the place where voting is held. **3** an estimate of public opinion made by questioning a representative sample of people. **4** (*old use*) the head. –**poll** *verb* **1** to vote at an election. **2** (of a candidate) to receive as votes. **3** to cut off the horns of (cattle) or the top of (a tree etc.). □ **polling booth**, **polling station** a place where votes are recorded. **poll position** = **pole position**. **poll tax** a tax on each (or on each adult) person.

pollard (**pol**-erd) *noun* **1** a tree that is polled so as to produce a close head of young branches. **2** an animal that has cast or lost its horns; an ox or sheep or goat of a hornless breed. –**pollard** *verb* to make (a tree) into a pollard. [from *poll* = head]

pollen *noun* a fine powdery substance produced by the anthers of flowers, containing the fertilising element. □ **pollen count** an index of the amount of pollen in the air, published as a warning to those who are allergic to it. [Latin, = fine flour]

pollinate *verb* to shed pollen on; to fertilise with pollen. **pollination** *noun*, **pollinator** *noun*

Pollock, Jackson (1912–56), American abstract expressionist painter, whose painting *Blue Poles* is in the Australian National Gallery.

pollutant *noun* a substance causing pollution.

pollute *verb* 1 to make dirty or impure, especially by adding harmful or offensive substances. 2 to corrupt, *polluting the mind*. **pollution** *noun*

Pollux 1 (*Gk. myth.*) the immortal twin brother of Castor (who was mortal), sons of Zeus and Leda. 2 a bright star in the constellation Gemini.

polo *noun* a game like hockey, played by teams on horseback with long-handled mallets. **polo neck** a high round turned-over collar.

polonaise (pol-ŏ-**nayz**) *noun* a stately dance of Polish origin; music for this or in this style.

polonium (pŏ-**loh**-nee-ŭm) *noun* a radioactive metallic element (symbol Po).

poltergeist (**pol**-ter-gyst) *noun* a ghost or spirit that throws things about noisily. [from German *poltern* = make a disturbance, + *geist* = ghost]

poltroon (pol-**troon**) *noun* (*old use*) a coward.

poly- *prefix* 1 many (as in *polyhedron*). 2 (in names of plastics) polymerised. [from Greek *polus* = much]

polyamide *noun* a natural or synthetic fibre (such as silk or nylon) composed of polymers of the same amide group.

polyandry (**pol**-ee-an-dree) *noun* the system of having more than one husband at a time. **polyandrous** *adjective* [from *poly-*, + Greek *andros* = of a man]

polyanthus *noun* a flower cultivated from hybridised primulas. [from *poly-*, + Greek *anthos* = flower]

polychrome (**pol**-ee-krohm) *adjective* painted, printed, or decorated in many colours. [from *poly-*, + Greek *khroma* = colour]

polyester *noun* a polymerised substance, especially as a synthetic resin or fibre.

polyethylene (pol-ee-**eth**-ĭ-leen) *noun* = polythene. □ **polyethylene terephthalate** a plastic polymer used in fabrics and packaging.

polygamy (pŏ-**lig**-ă-mee) *noun* the system of having more than one wife (or husband) at a time. **polygamous** *adjective*, **polygamist** *noun* [from *poly-*, + Greek *gamos* = marriage]

polyglot (**pol**-ee-glot) *adjective* knowing, using, or written in several languages. – **polyglot** *noun* a person who knows several languages. [from *poly-*, + Greek *glotta* = language]

polygon (**pol**-ee-gon) *noun* a geometric figure with many (usually five or more) sides. **polygonal** (pŏ-**lig**-ŏ-năl) *adjective* [from *poly-*, + Greek *gonia* = corner]

polygyny (pŏ-**lij**-ĭ-nee) *noun* the system of having more than one wife at a time. **polygynous** *adjective* [from *poly-*, + Greek *gune* = woman]

polyhedron (pol-ee-**hee**-drŏn) *noun* a solid figure with many (usually seven or more) faces. **polyhedral** *adjective* [from *poly-*, + Greek *hedra* = base]

polymer (**pol**-ĭ-mer) *noun* a compound whose molecule is formed from a large number of simple molecules combined. [from *poly-*, + Greek *meros* = part]

polymerise (**pol**-ĭ-mĕ-ryz) *verb* (also **-ize**) to combine or become combined into a polymer. **polymerisation** *noun*

Polynesia (pol-ĭ-**nee**-zhă) the islands of a large area in the Pacific Ocean, including New Zealand, Hawaii, Samoa, and Tahiti. **Polynesian** *adjective* & *noun* [from *poly-*, + Greek *nesos* = island]

polynomial (pol-ĭ-**noh**-mee-ăl) *noun* an algebraic expression that is the sum of terms containing different powers of the same variable. – **polynomial** *adjective* of a polynomial.

polyp (**pol**-ĭp) *noun* 1 a simple organism with a tube-shaped body, e.g. one of the organisms of which coral is composed. 2 an abnormal growth projecting from a mucous membrane, e.g. in the nose.

polyphonic (pol-ĭ-**fon**-ik) *adjective* (of music) written in counterpoint. **polyphony** *noun* [from *poly-*, + Greek *phone* = sound]

polyploid *adjective* 1 (of a cell) having more than two sets of chromosomes. 2 (of an organism) having polyploid cells. – **polyploid** *noun* a polyploid cell or organism. **polyploidy** *noun* [from *poly-*, made to look like *haploid* and *diploid*]

polysaccharide *noun* a carbohydrate that can be broken down into two or more simple sugars.

polystyrene (pol-ee-**sty**-reen) *noun* a kind of plastic, a polymer of styrene, used in insulation and packaging.

polysyllabic (pol-ee-sĭ-**lab**-ik) *adjective* having many syllables, *polysyllabic words*.

polytheism (**pol**-ee-thee-izm) *noun* belief in or worship of more than one god. **polytheist** *noun*, **polytheistic** *adjective* [from *poly-*, + Greek *theos* = god]

polythene *noun* a kind of tough light plastic material, used in packaging and insulating materials.

polytonal *adjective* (of music) using more than one key.

polyunsaturated *adjective* of a kind of fat or oil that (unlike animal and dairy fats) is not associated with the formation of cholesterol in the blood.

polyurethane (pol-ee-**yoor**-rĕ-thayn) *noun* a kind of synthetic resin or plastic, used in adhesives, paints, etc.

polyvinyl (pol-ee-**vy**-nĭl) *adjective* made from polymerised vinyl. □ **polyvinyl acetate** a soft plastic polymer used in paints and adhesives. **polyvinyl chloride** a plastic used for insulation of electrical wiring etc. and as fabric for furnishings etc.

pom *noun* (*Austral. informal*) a pommy.

pomander (pŏ-**man**-der) *noun* a ball of mixed sweet-smelling substances or a round container for this, used to perfume cupboards etc.

pomegranate (**pom**-ĕ-gran-ăt) *noun* **1** a tropical fruit with tough rind and reddish pulp enclosing many seeds. **2** the tree that produces it. [from Latin *pomum* = apple, + *granatum* = having many seeds]

pommel *noun* **1** a knob on the handle of a sword. **2** an upward projection at the front of a saddle. **–pommel** *verb* (**pommelled**, **pommelling**) to pummel. □ **pommel horse** a vaulting horse fitted with two curved handgrips. [from Latin *pomum* = apple]

pommy *noun* (*Austral. informal*) a British (especially English) person. **–pommy** *adjective* British; English.

pomp *noun* stately and splendid ceremonial. [from Greek, = procession]

Pompeii (pom-**pay**-ee) an ancient town southeast of Naples, buried in volcanic ash from the eruption of Vesuvius in AD 69.

pom-pom¹ *noun* an automatic quick-firing gun.

pom-pom² *noun* = **pompon**.

pompon *noun* **1** a decorative tuft or ball. **2** a type of dahlia or other flower with small tightly-clustered petals.

pompous *adjective* full of ostentatious dignity and self-importance. **pompously** *adverb*, **pomposity** *noun* [from *pomp*]

poncho *noun* (*plural* **ponchos**) **1** a blanket-like piece of cloth with a slit in the centre for the head, worn as a cloak. **2** a garment shaped like this. [South American Spanish]

pond *noun* a small area of still water.

ponder *verb* **1** to be deep in thought. **2** to think something over thoroughly. [from Latin *ponderare* = weigh]

ponderous *adjective* **1** heavy, unwieldy. **2** laborious in style. **ponderously** *adverb* [from Latin *ponderis* = of weight]

pong *noun* (*informal*) a stink. **–pong** *verb* (*informal*) to stink.

poniard (**pon**-yerd) *noun* (*old use*) a dagger.

pontiff *noun* (in full **supreme** or **sovereign pontiff**) the Pope. [from Latin *pontifex* = chief priest]

pontifical (pon-**tif**-ĭ-kăl) *adjective* **1** of a pontiff. **2** pompously dogmatic. **pontifically** *adverb*

pontificate (pon-**tif**-ĭ-kayt) *verb* to speak in a pontifical way. **–pontificate** (pon-**tif**-ĭ-kăt) *noun* the office of bishop or pope. **pontificator** *noun*

pontoon¹ *noun* **1** a kind of flat-bottomed boat. **2** each of a number of boats or hollow metal cylinders etc. used to support a temporary bridge (**pontoon bridge**). [from Latin *pontis* = of a bridge]

pontoon² *noun* **1** a card game in which players try to acquire cards with face value totalling 21. **2** a score of 21 from two cards in this game. [from French *vingt-et-un* = 21]

pony *noun* a horse of any small breed.

ponytail *noun* long hair drawn back and tied at the back of the head so that it hangs down.

Ponzi scheme *noun* a form of fraud in which belief in the success of a non-existent enterprise is fostered by the payment of quick returns to the first investors from money invested by later investors. [named after Charles Ponzi (1882–1949), who carried out such a fraud (1919–1920)]

poo *noun* (*informal*) faeces. **–poo** *verb* (*informal*) (**pooed**, **pooing**) to defecate.

poodle *noun* a dog with thick curly hair often clipped or shaved in a pattern.

pooh *interjection* an exclamation of impatience or contempt. ☐ **pooh-pooh** *verb* to dismiss (an idea etc.) scornfully.

pool¹ *noun* **1** a small area of still water, especially one that is naturally formed. **2** a shallow patch of water or other liquid lying on a surface, a puddle. **3** a swimming pool. **4** a deep place in a river.

pool² *noun* **1** a common fund, e.g. that containing the total stakes in a gambling venture. **2** a common supply of vehicles, commodities, or services etc. for sharing between a number of people. **3** a game resembling snooker. **–pool** *verb* to put into a common fund or supply, for sharing.

poop *noun* **1** the stern of a ship. **2** a raised deck at the stern.

pooped *adjective* (*informal*) exhausted; tired out.

poor *adjective* **1** having little money or means. **2** deficient in something, *poor in minerals*. **3** scanty, inadequate, less good than is usual or expected, *a poor crop*; *he is a poor driver*; *poor soil*, not fertile. **4** lacking in spirit, despicable. **5** deserving pity or sympathy, unfortunate, *poor fellow!* ☐ **the poor** poor people. **poor-spirited** *adjective* timid. **poorness** *noun*

poorly *adverb* in a poor way, badly. **–poorly** *adjective* unwell, *feeling poorly*.

pop¹ *noun* **1** a small sharp explosive sound. **2** a fizzy drink. **–pop** *verb* (**popped**, **popping**) **1** to make or cause or cause to make a pop. **2** to put quickly or suddenly, *pop it in the oven*. **3** to come or go quickly or suddenly or unexpectedly, *popped out for coffee*. **4** (*informal*) to take (a drug). ☐ **pop-eyed** *adjective* with bulging eyes.

pop² *noun* (*informal*) father.

pop³ *adjective* in a popular modern style. **–pop** *noun* pop music, *top of the pops*; *pop group*, one performing pop music. ☐ **pop art** art that uses themes drawn from popular culture. **pop music** modern popular music (e.g. rock music) appealing particularly to younger people. [short for *popular*]

popcorn *noun* kernels of corn heated so that they burst to form fluffy balls.

Pope, Alexander (1688–1744), English poet.

pope *noun* (as title **Pope**) the bishop of Rome, head of the Roman Catholic Church. [from Greek *papas* = father]

popery *noun* (*derogatory*) the papal system; the Roman Catholic religion.

popgun *noun* a child's toy gun that shoots a cork etc. with a popping sound.

popinjay *noun* a fop; a conceited person.

popish *adjective* (*derogatory*) of Roman Catholicism or the papal system.

poplar *noun* a kind of tall slender tree, often with leaves that quiver easily.

poplin *noun* a plain woven fabric usually of cotton.

popper *noun* (*informal*) a press stud.

poppet *noun* (*informal*) a small or dainty person; a darling.

popping crease *noun* a line marking the limit of the batsman's position in cricket.

poppy *noun* a plant with showy flowers and milky juice.

poppycock *noun* (*informal*) nonsense.

populace (**pop**-yŭ-lăs) *noun* the general public.

popular *adjective* **1** liked or enjoyed by many people. **2** of or for the general public. **3** (of a belief etc.) held by many people, *popular superstitions*. ☐ **popular front** a political party representing left-wing groups. **popularly** *adverb*, **popularity** *noun* [from Latin *populus* = people]

popularise *verb* (also **-ize**) **1** to make generally liked. **2** to make generally known; to present (a subject etc.) for non-specialists. **popularisation** *noun*

populate *verb* to supply with a population; to form the population of.

population *noun* the inhabitants of a place, district, or country; the total number of these.

populous *adjective* thickly populated.

porcelain (**por**-sĕ-lĭn) *noun* **1** the finest kind of china. **2** objects made of this.

porch *noun* a roofed shelter forming the approach to the entrance of a building. [from Latin *porticus* (compare *portico*)]

porcupine *noun* a rodent with a body and tail covered with protective spines. [from Latin *porcus* = pig, + *spine*]

pore¹ *noun* one of the tiny openings on an animal's skin or on a leaf, through which moisture may be emitted (e.g. as sweat) or taken in. [from Greek *poros* = passage]

pore² *verb* pore over to study (a thing) with close attention. [related to *peer¹*]

pork *noun* the (especially unsalted) flesh of a pig, used as food. [from Latin *porcus* = pig]

porker *noun* a pig raised for food; a young fattened pig.

porn *noun* (*informal*) pornography.

pornography *noun* writings, pictures, or films etc. that are intended to stimulate erotic feelings by description or portrayal of sexual activity. pornographic *adjective* [from Greek *porne* = prostitute, + *-graphy*]

porous (**por**-rŭs) *adjective* **1** containing pores. **2** able to be permeated by fluid or air. porosity (pŏ-**ross**-ĭ-tee) *noun* [same origin as *pore¹*]

porphyry (**por**-fĭ-ree) *noun* a kind of rock containing crystals of minerals. [from Greek, = purple stone]

porpoise (**por**-pŭs) *noun* a sea animal resembling a dolphin or small whale, with a blunt rounded snout. [from Latin *porcus* = pig, + *piscis* = fish]

porridge *noun* a food made by boiling oatmeal or other meal or cereal to a thick paste in water or milk.

porringer *noun* a small basin-shaped dish from which porridge is eaten, especially by children.

port¹ *noun* **1** a harbour. **2** a town with a harbour, especially one where goods are imported or exported by ship. [from Latin *portus* = harbour]

port² *noun* **1** an opening in a ship's side for entrance, loading, etc. **2** a porthole. **3** a place where signals enter or leave a data-transmission system or computer.

port³ *noun* the left-hand side (when facing forward) of a ship or aircraft (contrasts with *starboard*). –port *verb* to turn this way, *port your helm.*

port⁴ *noun* a sweet usually dark red fortified wine. □ port-wine stain a deep red naevus, typically on the face. [from the city of Oporto in Portugal]

port⁵ *noun* (*Austral.*) a suitcase, school bag, travelling bag, etc. [from *portmanteau*]

portable *adjective* **1** able to be carried or shifted, *portable CD player*; *portable classrooms.* **2** able to be transferred, *a portable pension.* –portable *noun* a portable version of a thing, e.g. classroom. portability *noun* [from Latin *portare* = carry]

portal *noun* a doorway or gateway, especially an imposing one. [from Latin *porta* = gate]

Port Arthur an inlet in SE Tasmania and the site of a penal settlement from 1830 to 1877.

Port-au-Prince (port-oh-**prins**) the capital of Haiti.

portcullis *noun* a strong heavy vertical grating that can be lowered in grooves to block the gateway to a castle etc. [from French, = sliding door (*porte* = door)]

portend (por-**tend**) *verb* to foreshadow. [from Latin *pro-* = forwards, + *tendere* = stretch]

portent (**por**-tent) *noun* an omen, a significant sign of something to come.

portentous (por-**ten**-tŭs) *adjective* ominous, being a sign of some extraordinary (usually calamitous) event.

porter¹ *noun* a gatekeeper or doorkeeper of a large building. [from Latin *porta* = gate]

porter² *noun* **1** a person employed to carry luggage or other goods. **2** a kind of dark beer. [from Latin *portare* = carry]

portfolio *noun* (*plural* portfolios) **1** a case for holding loose sheets of paper or drawings etc. **2** a set of investments held by one investor. **3** the position of a minister of State; the department(s) for which he or she is responsible. [from Italian *portare* = carry, + *foglio* = sheet of paper]

porthole *noun* a window-like structure in the side of a ship or aircraft.

portico (**port**-ĭ-koh) *noun* (*plural* porticoes) a structure consisting of a roof supported on columns, usually forming a porch to a building. [from Latin *porticus* = porch]

portion *noun* **1** a part or share of something. **2** the amount of food allotted to one person. **3** one's destiny or lot. –portion *verb* to divide into portions, to distribute in portions, *portion it out.*

Port Jackson the port of Sydney, NSW. □ Port Jackson fig an evergreen tree with inedible fruits. Port Jackson shark a small harmless shark of southern Australia.

Portland cement *noun* cement made from chalk and clay.

Port Louis (**loo**-ee) the capital of Mauritius.

portly *adjective* (portlier, portliest) stout and dignified. portliness *noun*

portmanteau (port-**man**-toh) *noun* a trunk for clothes etc. that opens into two equal parts. ☐ **portmanteau word** an invented word combining the sounds and meanings of two others, e.g. *motel*, *smog*. [from French *porter* = carry, + *manteau* = coat]

Port Moresby (**morz**-bee) the capital of Papua New Guinea.

Port of Spain the capital of Trinidad and Tobago.

Porto Novo (**noh**-voh) seaport and capital of Benin.

Port Phillip (*historical*) the name given to that part of the Colony of New South Wales which in 1851 became the Colony of Victoria. ☐ **Port Phillip Bay** the large inlet on the south coast of Victoria, near which the city of Melbourne now stands.

portrait *noun* 1 a picture, drawing, or photograph of a person or animal. 2 a description in words. **portraitist** *noun*

portray (por-**tray**) *verb* 1 to make a picture of. 2 to describe in words or represent in a play etc. **portrayal** *noun*

Portugal a republic in SW Europe.

Portuguese *adjective* of Portugal or its people or language. –**Portuguese** *noun* 1 (*plural* **Portuguese**) a native of Portugal. 2 the language of Portugal. ☐ **Portuguese man-of-war** a sea animal with stinging tentacles; a bluebottle.

pose *verb* 1 to put into or take a desired position for a portrait or photograph etc. 2 to take a particular attitude for effect. 3 to pretend to be, *posed as an expert*. 4 to put forward, to present, *pose a question* or *a problem*. –**pose** *noun* 1 an attitude in which a person etc. is posed. 2 an affectation, a pretence.

Poseidon (pŏ-**sy**-dŏn) (*Gk. myth.*) the god of earthquakes and the sea.

poser *noun* a puzzling question or problem.

poseur (poh-**zer**) *noun* a person who poses for effect or behaves affectedly.

posh *adjective* (*informal*) very smart, luxurious.

posit (**poz**-ĭt) *verb* to assume as a fact, to postulate.

position *noun* 1 the place occupied by a person or thing. 2 the proper place for something, *in* or *out of position*. 3 an advantageous location, *manoeuvring for position*. 4 the way in which a thing or its parts are placed or arranged. 5 a situation in relation to other people or things, *this puts me in a difficult position*. 6 a point of view, *what is their position on university fees?* 7 rank or status, high social standing. 8 paid employment, a job. –**position** *verb* to place in a certain position. [from Latin *positum* = placed]

positive *adjective* 1 stated formally or explicitly, *positive rules*. 2 definite, leaving no room for doubt, *we have positive proof*. 3 holding an opinion confidently. 4 (*informal*) clear, out-and-out, *it's a positive miracle*. 5 constructive and helpful, *made some positive suggestions*. 6 having specific or definite qualities or characteristics; *the result of the test was positive*, indicated that a specific substance etc. was present. 7 (of a quantity) greater than zero. 8 containing or producing the kind of electrical charge produced by rubbing glass with silk; *positive terminal of a battery*, the one through which electric current leaves the battery. 9 (of a photograph) having the lights and shades or colours as in the actual object or scene photographed, not as in a negative. 10 (of an adjective or adverb) in the primary form (e.g. *big*) as distinct from the comparative (*bigger*) or superlative (*biggest*). –**positive** *noun* a positive quality, quantity, photograph, etc. ☐ **positive pole** the north-seeking pole of a magnet. **positive sign** the sign +. **positively** *adverb*, **positiveness** *noun*

positron (**poz**-ĭ-tron) *noun* an elementary particle with the mass of an electron and a charge the same as an electron's but positive. [from *positive*]

posse (**poss**-ee) *noun* a group of law-enforcers; a strong force or company. [same origin as *possible*]

possess *verb* 1 to hold belonging to oneself, to have or own. 2 to occupy or dominate the mind of, *be possessed by a devil* or *with an idea*. **possessor** *noun*

possession *noun* 1 possessing; being possessed. 2 a thing possessed. ☐ **take possession of** to become the owner or possessor of.

possessive *adjective* 1 showing a desire to possess or to retain what one possesses. 2 of or indicating possession; *the possessive form of a word*, e.g. *John's, the baker's*. ☐ **possessive pronoun** *see* **pronoun**. **possessively** *adverb*, **possessiveness** *noun*

possibility *noun* 1 the fact or condition of being possible. 2 something that may exist or happen. 3 a capability of being used or of producing good results, *the plan has possibilities*.

possible *adjective* capable of existing or happening or of being done or used etc. –**possible** *noun* a candidate who may be successful, one who may become a member of a team. [from Latin *posse* = be able]

possibly *adverb* 1 in accordance with possibility, *can't possibly do it*. 2 perhaps, for all one knows to the contrary.

possie (**poz**-ee) *noun* (*Austral. informal*) a position.

possum *noun* 1 an Australian long-tailed furry marsupial that lives in trees, formerly called *opossum*. 2 (*informal*) an American opossum. ☐ **play possum** to pretend to be unaware of something (⁋ from the possum's habit of feigning death when in danger).

post[1] *noun* 1 a piece of timber or metal set upright in the ground etc. to support something or to mark a position. 2 the starting post or winning post in a race; *left at the post*, outdistanced from the start; *beaten at the post*, defeated at the last moment. –**post** *verb* 1 to announce by putting up a notice or placard etc.; *post no bills*, a warning that notices must not be pasted up. 2 make (information) available on the Internet; send a message to an Internet bulletin board or newsgroup. [from Latin *postis* = post]

post[2] *noun* 1 the place where a soldier is on watch, a place of duty, *the sentries are at their posts*. 2 a place occupied by soldiers, especially a frontier fort; the soldiers there. 3 a place occupied for purposes of trade, especially in a region that is not yet fully settled, *trading posts*. 4 a position of paid employment, *got a post with an insurance firm*. –**post** *verb* 1 to place or station, *we posted sentries*. 2 to appoint to a post or command. ☐ **last post** *see* **last**[1].

post[3] *noun* 1 the official conveyance of letters etc. 2 the letters etc. conveyed. 3 a single collection or delivery of these. –**post** *verb* 1 to put (a letter etc.) into a post office or postbox for transmission. 2 to enter in an official ledger. ☐ **keep a person posted** to keep him or her informed. **Post Office** the organisation responsible for postal services (in Australia called *Australia Post*). **post office** a building or room where postal business is carried on. **post office box** a numbered box at a post office to which mail is delivered. [same origin as *position*]

post- *prefix* after (as in *post-war*). [Latin]

postage *noun* the charge for sending something by post. ☐ **postage stamp** a small adhesive stamp for sticking on things to be posted, showing the amount paid.

postal *adjective* 1 of the post. 2 by post, *postal vote*.

postbox *noun* a public box into which letters are inserted for transmission.

postcard *noun* a card for sending messages by post without an envelope, usually having a picture on one side and space on the other side for the message and the address.

post-chaise (**pohst**-shayz) *noun* (*old use*) a carriage that could be hired from one stage to another, or that was drawn by horses hired in this way.

postcode *noun* a group of figures or letters and figures included in a postal address to assist sorting.

postdate *verb* to put a date on (a document or cheque etc.) that is later than the actual one.

poster *noun* a large sheet of paper announcing or advertising something, for display in a public place. [from *post*[1]]

poste restante (pohst ress-**tahnt**) *noun* a department in a post office where letters are kept until called for. [French, = letters remaining]

posterior *adjective* situated behind or at the back. –**posterior** *noun* the buttocks. [Latin, = further back]

posterity (poss-**te**-ri-tee) *noun* 1 future generations. 2 a person's descendants.

postern (**poss**-tern) *noun* a small entrance at the back or side of a fortress etc.

postgraduate *adjective* (of studies) carried on after taking a first degree. –**postgraduate** *noun* a student engaged on such studies.

post-haste *adverb* with great speed or haste. [from *post*[3] + *haste*]

posthumous (**poss**-tew-mŭs) *adjective* 1 (of a child) born after its father's death. 2 coming or happening after a person's death, *a posthumous award*; *a posthumous novel*, published after the author's death. **posthumously** *adverb* [from Latin *postumus* = last]

post-impressionist *noun* a painter using a style that was a reaction against impressionism. **post-impressionism** *noun*

postman *noun* (*plural* **postmen**) a person who delivers or collects letters etc.

postmark *noun* an official mark stamped on something sent by post, giving the place and date of marking. –**postmark** *verb* to mark with a postmark.

postmaster, **postmistress** *nouns* an official in charge of certain post offices.

post-mortem *adverb & adjective* after death. –**post-mortem** *noun* **1** an examination made after death to determine its cause. **2** (*informal*) a detailed discussion of something that is over. [Latin, = after death]

post-natal *adjective* existing or occurring immediately after birth or childbirth. [from *post-*, + Latin *natus* = born]

postpone *verb* to keep (an event) from occurring until a later time, *postpone the meeting*. **postponement** *noun* [from *post-*, + Latin *ponere* = to place]

postscript *noun* a paragraph added at the end of something (especially in a letter, after the signature). [from *post-*, + Latin *scriptum* = written]

postulant (*poss*-tew-lănt) *noun* a candidate for admission to a religious order.

postulate (*poss*-tew-layt) *verb* to assume (a thing) to be true, especially as a basis for reasoning. –**postulate** (*poss*-tew-lăt) *noun* something postulated. **postulation** *noun* [from Latin *postulare* = to claim]

posture (*poss*-cher) *noun* an attitude of the body, the way a person etc. stands, sits, or walks. [same origin as *position*]

postwar *adjective* existing or occurring after a war.

posy *noun* a small bunch of flowers.

pot[1] *noun* **1** a rounded vessel of earthenware, metal, or glass etc. used for holding liquids or solids, or for cooking in. **2** the contents of a pot. **3** (*informal*) a prize in an athletic contest, especially a silver cup. **4** (*informal*) a large amount, *pots of money*. –**pot** *verb* (**potted**, **potting**) **1** to plant in a pot. **2** to pocket (a ball) in billiards etc. **3** (*informal*) to abridge, *a potted edition*. **4** to shoot; to kill by a pot-shot. □ **go to pot** (*informal*) to deteriorate, to become ruined. **pot belly** a protuberant belly; a person with this. **pot luck** whatever is available for a meal etc., *take pot luck with us*. **pot plant** a plant grown in a flowerpot. **pot roast** a piece of meat cooked slowly in a covered dish. **pot-roast** *verb* to cook in this way. **pot-shot** *noun* a shot aimed casually.

pot[2] *noun* (*informal*) marijuana.

potable (*poh*-tă-bŭl) *adjective* drinkable. [from Latin *potare* = to drink]

potash *noun* any of various salts of potassium, especially potassium carbonate. [from *pot*[1] + *ash*[2] (because it was first obtained from vegetable ashes washed in a pot)]

potassium (pŏ-*tas*-ee-ŭm) *noun* a soft silvery-white metallic element (symbol K) that is essential to life. [from *potash*]

potato *noun* (*plural* **potatoes**) **1** a plant with starchy tubers that are used as food. **2** one of these tubers. [from South American *batata* (potatoes were first brought to Europe from South America)]

potent (*poh*-těnt) *adjective* having great natural power or influence, able to have a strong effect, *potent drugs*. **potency** *noun* [from Latin *potens* = able]

potentate (*poh*-těn-tayt) *noun* a monarch or ruler. [from *potent*]

potential (pŏ-*ten*-shăl) *adjective* capable of coming into being or of being developed or used etc., *a potential source of energy*. –**potential** *noun* **1** an ability, a capacity, or resources etc. available for development or use. **2** the quantity determining the energy of mass in a gravitational field or of charge in an electric field. □ **potential difference** the difference of electric potential between two points, measured in volts. **potentially** *adverb*, **potentiality** *noun* [from Latin *potentia* = power]

potentiometer (pŏ-ten-shee-*om*-ě-ter) *noun* an instrument for measuring or adjusting electrical potential.

pothole *noun* **1** a deep cylindrical hole formed in rock (e.g. in limestone) by the action of water, an underground cave. **2** a hole in the surface of a road. –**pothole** *verb* to explore underground potholes. **potholer** *noun*

potion (*poh*-shŏn) *noun* a liquid for drinking as a medicine or drug etc. [from Latin *potus* = having drunk something]

potometer (poh-*tom*-ě-ter) *noun* a device for measuring the rate at which a plant takes up water. [from Greek *poton* = drink, + *meter*]

potoroo (pot-ŏ-*roo*) *noun* a small long-nosed Australian marsupial, also called *rat kangaroo*. [probably from Dharuk *badaru*]

pot-pourri (poh-*poor*-ree) *noun* **1** a scented mixture of dried petals and spices. **2** a literary or musical medley. [French, = rotten pot]

potsherd (**pot**-sherd) *noun* a broken piece of earthenware, especially in archaeology.

pottage *noun* (*old use*) a soup; a stew.

potter¹ *noun* a person who makes earthenware dishes or ornaments etc.

potter² *verb* to work on trivial tasks in a leisurely relaxed way. **potterer** *noun*

pottery *noun* 1 vessels and other objects made of baked clay. 2 a potter's work or workshop.

potty¹ *adjective* (**pottier**, **pottiest**) (*informal*) 1 trivial, insignificant. 2 crazy.

potty² *noun* (*informal*) a child's chamber pot.

pouch *noun* a small bag or baglike formation. –**pouch** *verb* 1 to put into a pouch; to pocket. 2 to make (part of a dress) hang like a pouch. [from French *poche* = bag or pocket]

pouffe (*pr*. poof) *noun* a padded stool or footrest. [French]

poulterer *noun* a dealer in poultry and game.

poultice (**pohl**-tïss) *noun* a soft heated mass applied to an inflamed or sore area of skin. –**poultice** *verb* to apply a poultice to.

poultry (**pohl**-tree) *noun* domestic fowls, ducks, geese, turkeys, etc., especially as a source of food.

pounce *verb* to spring or swoop down on and grasp, e.g. as prey; *pounce on a mistake*, to spot it quickly. –**pounce** *noun* a pouncing movement.

Pound, Ezra Weston Loomis (1885–1972), American poet and critic.

pound¹ *noun* 1 an imperial measure of weight, 16 oz. avoirdupois (0.4536 kg) or 12 oz. troy (0.3732 kg). 2 the unit of money of Britain and certain other countries.

pound² *noun* 1 a place where stray animals, or motor vehicles left in unauthorised places, are taken and kept until claimed. 2 a natural basin surrounded by rocky terrain, *Wilpena Pound*.

pound³ *verb* 1 to crush or beat with heavy repeated strokes. 2 to deliver heavy blows or repeated gunfire etc. 3 to make one's way heavily, *pounding along*. 4 (of the heart) to beat heavily, to thump.

pour *verb* 1 to flow or cause to flow in a stream or shower. 2 to pour tea etc. into cups; to serve by pouring. 3 to rain heavily. 4 to come or go or send out in large amounts or numbers, *refugees poured out of the country*; *letters poured in*. 5 to send (words or music etc.) out freely, *he poured out his story*. **pourer** *noun*

pout *verb* to push out one's lips, (of lips) to be pushed out, especially as a sign of annoyance or sulking. –**pout** *noun* a pouting expression.

pouter *noun* a kind of pigeon that can inflate its crop greatly.

poverty *noun* 1 being poor, great lack of money or resources; *monks who were vowed to poverty*, who renounced the right to individual ownership of property. 2 scarcity, lack. 3 inferiority, poorness. □ **poverty line** the minimum income level needed to obtain the necessities of life. **poverty-stricken** *adjective* affected by poverty. **poverty trap** the condition of being so dependent on State benefits that an increase in one's income means that one loses some of these and is no better off.

POW *abbreviation* prisoner of war.

powder *noun* 1 a mass of fine dry particles. 2 a medicine or cosmetic in this form. 3 gunpowder. –**powder** *verb* 1 to apply powder to; to cover with powder. 2 to reduce to powder. □ **powder blue** pale blue. **powder puff** a soft or fluffy pad for applying powder to the skin. **powder room** a ladies' toilet in a shop etc. [from Latin *pulveris* = of dust]

powdered *adjective* made into powder.

powdery *adjective* like powder. **powderiness** *noun*

power *noun* 1 the ability to do something. 2 vigour, energy, strength. 3 a property, *great heating power*. 4 control, influence, *the party in power*. 5 authority, *their powers are defined by law*. 6 an influential person, country, or organisation etc. 7 (*informal*) a large amount, *did me a power of good*. 8 (in mathematics) the product of a number multiplied by itself a given number of times, *the third power of 2 = 2 × 2 × 2 = 8*. 9 mechanical or electrical energy as opposed to hand labour; *power tools*, tools using such energy. 10 the electricity supply, *a power failure*. 11 capacity for exerting mechanical force, horsepower. 12 the magnifying capacity of a lens. –**power** *verb* 1 to equip with mechanical or electrical power. 2 (*informal*) to travel with great speed or strength. □ **power point** a socket on a wall etc. where electrical appliances can be connected to the mains. **power politics** political action based on threats to use force. **power station** a building where electrical power is generated for distribution.

powerful *adjective* having great power, strength, or influence. **powerfully** *adverb*

powerless *adjective* without power to take action, wholly unable.

powwow *noun* a meeting for discussion.

pp. *abbreviation* pages.

p.p. *abbreviation* (also **pp**) per pro.

P-plate *noun* a sign bearing the letter 'P', fixed to a motor vehicle being driven by a person with a provisional or (in some States) probationary licence. **P-plater** *noun*

PPS *abbreviation* post-postscript, = an additional postscript.

PR *abbreviation* **1** public relations. **2** proportional representation.

practicable *adjective* able to be done. **practicability** *noun*

practical *adjective* **1** involving activity as distinct from study or theory, *has had practical experience.* **2** suitable for use, *an ingenious but not very practical invention.* **3** (of people) clever at doing and making things, *a practical handyman.* **4** virtual, *he has practical control of the firm.* **–practical** *noun* a practical examination; practical study. □ **practical joke** a humorous trick played on a person by a **practical joker. practicality** (prak-tĭ-**kal**-ĭ-tee) *noun* [from Greek *prattein* = do]

practically *adverb* **1** in a practical way. **2** virtually, almost.

practice *noun* **1** action as opposed to theory, *it works well in practice.* **2** a habitual action, custom, *it is our practice to supply good material.* **3** repeated exercise to improve one's skill, a spell of this, *target practice.* **4** professional work, the business carried on by a doctor, lawyer, etc.; the patients or clients regularly consulting these, *a large practice.* □ **out of practice** no longer possessing a former skill.

practise *verb* (*Amer.* **practice**) **1** to do something repeatedly in order to become skilful. **2** to carry out in action, to do something habitually, *practise what you preach.* **3** to do something actively, *a practising Catholic.* **4** (of a doctor or lawyer etc.) to be actively engaged in professional work. [same origin as *practical*]

practised *adjective* experienced, expert.

practitioner (prak-**tish**-ŏ-ner) *noun* a professional or practical worker, especially in medicine.

Prado (**prah**-doh) the Spanish national art gallery, in Madrid.

pragmatic (prag-**mat**-ik) *adjective* treating things from a practical point of view, *a pragmatic approach to the problem.* **pragmatically** *adverb* [from Greek *pragma* = deed]

pragmatism (**prag**-mă-tizm) *noun* treating things in a pragmatic way. **pragmatist** *noun*

Prague (*pr.* prahg) the capital of the Czech Republic.

Praia (**pry**-ă) the capital of Cape Verde Islands.

prairie *noun* a large treeless tract of grassland, especially in North America. [from Latin *pratum* = meadow]

praise *verb* **1** to express approval or admiration of. **2** to honour (God) in words. **–praise** *noun* praising, approval expressed in words. [from Latin *pretium* = value]

praiseworthy *adjective* deserving praise.

praline (**prah**-leen *or* **pray**-leen) *noun* a sweet made by browning nuts in boiling sugar.

pram *noun* a four-wheeled carriage for a baby, pushed by a person walking. [short for *perambulator*]

prana (**prah**-nă) *noun* (in Hinduism) breath as the life-giving force. [Sanskrit]

prance *verb* to move springily in eagerness.

prang *verb* (*informal*) to crash an aircraft or vehicle; to damage by impact. **–prang** *noun* (*informal*) a crash; damage by impact.

prank *noun* mischief, a practical joke.

praseodymium (pray-zee-oh-**dim**-ee-ŭm) *noun* a soft silver-white metallic element of the lanthanide series (symbol Pr).

prattle *verb* to chatter in a childish way. **–prattle** *noun* childish chatter.

prawn *noun* a smallish edible marine shellfish which turns pink when cooked. □ **come the raw prawn** (*Austral. informal*) to try to deceive (a person), *don't come the raw prawn with me.*

pray *verb* **1** to say prayers. **2** to entreat. **3** = please, *pray be seated.*

prayer *noun* **1** a solemn request or thanksgiving to God or to an object of worship. **2** a set form of words used in this, *the Lord's Prayer.* **3** a religious service, *morning prayer.* **4** the act of praying. **5** entreaty to a person. □ **prayer book** a book of set prayers. **prayer mat** a small carpet on which Muslims kneel to pray. **prayer wheel** a revolving cylindrical box inscribed with or containing prayers, used especially by the Buddhists of Tibet.

pre- *prefix* before, beforehand. [from Latin *prae* = before]

preach *verb* **1** to deliver (a sermon or religious address); to speak in public in support of a religion; *preach the gospel*, make it known by preaching. **2** to advocate, to urge people to a certain quality, practice, or action, *they preached economy*. **3** to give moral advice in an obtrusive way. **preacher** *noun*

preamble (pree-**am**-bŭl) *noun* a preliminary statement; the introductory part of a document or law etc. [from *pre-*, + Latin *ambulare* = go]

prearrange *verb* to arrange beforehand. **prearrangement** *noun*

Precambrian (pree-**kam**-bree-ăn) *adjective* of the earliest geological era, preceding the Cambrian period and Palaeozoic era. –**Precambrian** *noun* this era.

precarious (prĕ-**kair**-ree-ŭs) *adjective* unsafe, not secure. **precariously** *adverb* [from Latin *precarius* = uncertain]

precast *adjective* (of concrete) cast in blocks before use.

precaution *noun* something done in advance to avoid a risk; *take precautions*, do things as a precaution. **precautionary** *adjective* [from *pre-* + *caution*]

precede (prĕ-**seed**) *verb* to come or go or place before in time or order etc. [from *pre-*, + Latin *cedere* = go]

precedence (**press**-ĕ-dĕnss *or* **pree**-sĕ-dĕnss) *noun* priority in time or order. □ **take precedence** to have priority.

precedent (**pree**-sĕ-dĕnt *or* **press**-ĕ-dĕnt) *noun* a previous case that is taken as an example to be followed.

precentor (prĕ-**sent**-er) *noun* a person who leads the singing or (in a synagogue) the prayers of a congregation.

precept (**pree**-sept) *noun* a command, a rule of conduct.

preceptor (prĕ-**sept**-er) *noun* a teacher, an instructor.

precinct (**pree**-sinkt) *noun* **1** an enclosed area around a building; a specially defined area, *a shopping precinct*. **2** (*Amer.*) a subdivision of a county, city, etc. for election and police purposes. **precincts** *plural noun* the area surrounding a place, *searched the precincts of the hotel*. [from *pre-*, + Latin *cinctum* = surrounded]

precious *adjective* **1** of great value or worth. **2** beloved. **3** affectedly refined. **4** (*informal,* used ironically) considerable, *did him a precious lot of good*. –**precious** *adverb* (*informal-*) very, *there's precious little left*. □ **precious metals** gold, silver, and platinum. **precious stone** a piece of mineral having great value, especially as used in jewellery. **preciously** *adverb*, **preciousness** *noun* [from Latin *pretium* = value]

precipice (**press**-ĭ-pĭss) *noun* a very steep or vertical face of a cliff or rock etc. [from Latin *praeceps* = headlong]

precipitate (prĕ-**sip**-ĭ-tayt) *verb* **1** to throw down headlong. **2** to send rapidly into a certain state or condition, *precipitated the country into war*. **3** to cause to happen suddenly or soon, *this action precipitated a crisis*. **4** to cause (a substance) to be deposited in solid form from a solution in which it is present. **5** to condense (vapour) into drops which fall as rain or dew etc. –**precipitate** (prĕ-**sip**-ĭ-tăt) *noun* a substance precipitated from a solution; moisture condensed from vapour and deposited (e.g. rain, dew). –**precipitate** (prĕ-**sip**-ĭ-tăt) *adjective* **1** headlong, violently hurried, *a precipitate departure*. **2** (of a person or action) hasty, rash. **precipitately** *adverb* [from Latin *praeceps* = headlong]

precipitation *noun* **1** rain, dew, or snow; the amount of this. **2** precipitating or being precipitated.

precipitous (prĕ-**sip**-ĭ-tŭs) *adjective* like a precipice, steep. **precipitously** *adverb*

précis (**pray**-see) *noun* (also **precis**) (*plural* **précis**, *pr*. **pray**-seez) a summary. –**précis** *verb* (**précised**, **précising**) to make a précis of. [French, = precise]

precise *adjective* **1** exact, correctly and clearly stated. **2** taking care to be exact. [from Latin *praecisum* = cut short]

precisely *adverb* **1** in a precise manner, exactly. **2** (said in agreement) quite so, as you say.

precision (prĕ-**sizh**-ŏn) *noun* accuracy; *precision tools*, tools designed for very accurate work.

preclude (pree-**klood**) *verb* to exclude the possibility of, to prevent. [from *pre-*, + Latin *claudere* = to shut]

precocious (prĕ-**koh**-shŭs) *adjective* **1** (of a child) having developed certain abilities earlier than is usual. **2** (of abilities or knowledge) showing such development. **precociously** *adverb*, **precocity** (prĕ-**koss**-ĭ-tee) *noun* [from Latin *praecox* = ripe very early]

preconceived *adjective* (of an idea or opinion) formed beforehand, formed before full knowledge or evidence is available.

preconception *noun* a preconceived idea.

precondition *noun* a condition that must be fulfilled before something else can happen.

precursor (pree-**ker**-ser) *noun* **1** a person or thing that precedes another, a forerunner. **2** a thing that precedes a later and more developed form, *rocket bombs were the precursors of space probes*.

predator (**pred**-ă-ter) *noun* a predatory animal. [from Latin, = plunderer]

predatory (**pred**-ă-tŏ-ree) *adjective* **1** (of animals) preying upon others. **2** plundering or exploiting others.

predecease (pree-dĕ-**seess**) *verb* to die earlier than (another person).

predecessor (**pree**-dĕ-sess-er) *noun* **1** the former holder of an office or position. **2** an ancestor. **3** a thing to which another has succeeded. [from *pre*-, + Latin *decessor* = person departed]

predestination *noun* **1** the doctrine that God has foreordained all that happens, or that certain souls are destined for salvation and eternal life and others are not. **2** destiny, fate.

predestine *verb* to destine beforehand, to appoint as if by fate.

predetermine *verb* to determine in advance, to predestine. **predetermination** *noun*

predicament (prĕ-**dik**-ă-mĕnt) *noun* a difficult or unpleasant situation.

predicate (**pred**-ĭ-kăt) *noun* the part of a sentence that says something about the subject, e.g. 'is short' in *life is short*. [from Latin *praedicare* = proclaim]

predicative (prĕ-**dik**-ă-tiv) *adjective* forming part of the whole of the predicate, e.g. 'old' in *the dog is old* (but not in *the old dog*). Compare *attributive*. **predicatively** *adverb*

predict *verb* to forecast, to prophesy. **prediction** *noun*, **predictor** *noun* [from *pre*-, + Latin *dictum* = said]

predictable *adjective* able to be predicted. **predictably** *adverb*, **predictability** *noun*

predilection (pree-dĭ-**lek**-shŏn) *noun* a special liking, a preference. [from *pre*-, + Latin *dilectum* = selected]

predispose *verb* **1** to influence in advance; *we are predisposed in his favour*, inclined to favour him. **2** to render liable, e.g. to a disease.

predisposition *noun* a state of mind or body that renders a person liable to act or behave in a certain way or to be subject to certain diseases.

predominant *adjective* predominating. **predominantly** *adverb*, **predominance** *noun*

predominate *verb* **1** to be greater than others in number or intensity etc., to be the main element. **2** to have or exert control.

pre-eminent *adjective* excelling others, outstanding. **pre-eminently** *adverb*, **pre-eminence** *noun*

pre-empt *verb* to take possession of (a thing) before anyone else can do so; to forestall. **pre-emption** *noun*

pre-emptive *adjective* pre-empting; *a pre-emptive attack*, one intended to disable an enemy and prevent him or her from attacking.

preen *verb* (of a bird) to smooth (its feathers) with its beak. □ **preen oneself** to groom oneself; to congratulate oneself, to show self-satisfaction.

prefab *noun* (*informal*) a prefabricated building.

prefabricate *verb* to manufacture in sections that are ready for assembly on a site. **prefabrication** *noun*

preface (**pref**-ăs) *noun* an introductory statement at the beginning of a book or speech. –**preface** *verb* **1** to provide or introduce with a preface. **2** to lead up to (an event), *the music that prefaced the ceremony*.

prefatory (**pref**-ă-tŏ-ree) *adjective* serving as a preface, preliminary, *prefatory remarks*.

prefect *noun* **1** a senior pupil in a school, authorised to maintain discipline. **2** the chief administrative official of a district in France, Japan, and other countries. **3** any of various senior officials in ancient Rome. **4** a senior teacher in some schools, with administrative duties. [from Latin *praefectus* = overseer]

prefer *verb* (**preferred**, **preferring**) **1** to choose as more desirable, to like better. **2** to put forward (an accusation etc.) for consideration by an authority, *they preferred charges of forgery against him*. **3** to promote (a person). [from Latin *prae* = before, + *ferre* = carry]

preferable (**pref**-ĕ-ră-bŭl) *adjective* more desirable. **preferably** *adverb*

preference (**pref**-ĕ-rĕns) *noun* **1** preferring; being preferred. **2** a thing preferred. **3** a prior right to something. **4** the favouring of one person etc. before another. –**preference** *verb*

(*Austral.*) to direct preferences to (a candidate or party). □ **in preference to** as a thing etc. preferred over (another). **preference shares** or **stock** that on which dividend is paid before profits are distributed to holders of ordinary shares etc.

preferential (pref-ĕ-**ren**-shǎl) *adjective* giving or receiving preference, *preferential treatment*. □ **preferential voting** a voting system in which voters number candidates in order of preference, and where these preferences are taken into account if there is no candidate with an absolute majority on first preferences. **preferentially** *adverb*

preferment *noun* promotion.

prefigure *verb* to represent or imagine beforehand.

prefix *noun* (*plural* **prefixes**) **1** a word or syllable (e.g. *co-*, *ex-*, *non-*, *out-*, *pre-*) placed in front of a word to add to or change its meaning. **2** a title (e.g. *Mr*) placed before a name. –**prefix** *verb* **1** to put as a prefix. **2** to put as an introduction.

pregnant *adjective* **1** (of a woman or female animal) having a child or young developing in the womb. **2** full of meaning, significant, *there was a pregnant pause*. **3** full, *the situation was pregnant with danger*. **pregnancy** *noun* [from *pre-*, + Latin *gnasci* = be born]

prehensile (pree-**hen**-syl) *adjective* (of an animal's limb or tail etc.) able to grasp things. [from Latin *prehendere* = seize]

prehistoric *adjective* **1** of the ancient period before written records of events were made. **2** (*informal*) completely out of date.

prehistory *noun* **1** prehistoric events or times. **2** the study of these.

prejudge *verb* to form a judgment on (a person or action etc.) before a proper inquiry is held or before full information is available.

prejudice *noun* **1** an unreasoning opinion or like or dislike of something; *racial prejudice*, prejudice against people of other races. **2** harm to someone's rights etc. –**prejudice** *verb* **1** to cause (a person) to have a prejudice. **2** to cause harm to, *it may prejudice our rights*. □ **without prejudice** (of an offer made for the purpose of settling a dispute) which must not be interpreted as an admission of liability, or used in evidence. [from Latin *prae* = before, + *judicium* = judgment]

prejudiced *adjective* having a prejudice.

prejudicial (prej-ŭ-**dish**-ǎl) *adjective* harmful to someone's rights or claims etc.

prelate (**prel**-ǎt) *noun* a high-ranking member of the clergy, e.g. a bishop.

preliminary *adjective* coming before a main action or event etc. and preparing for it. –**preliminary** *noun* a preliminary action, event, or examination etc. [from *pre-*, + Latin *limen* = threshold]

prelude (**prel**-yood) *noun* **1** an action or event that precedes another and leads up to it. **2** the introductory part of a poem etc. **3** (in music) an introductory movement preceding a fugue or forming the first piece of a suite; a short piece of music of similar type. [from *pre-*, + Latin *ludere* = to play]

premarital (pree-**ma**-rĭ-tǎl) *adjective* of the time before marriage.

premature (**prem**-ǎ-tewr) *adjective* occurring or done before the usual or proper time, too early; *premature baby*, one born at least three weeks before the expected time. **prematurely** *adverb*

premeditated (pree-**med**-ĭ-tayt-ĕd) *adjective* planned beforehand, *a premeditated crime*. **premeditation** *noun*

premenstrual (pree-**men**-stroo-ǎl) *adjective* of the time immediately before each menstruation, *premenstrual tension*.

premier (**prem**-ee-er) *adjective* first in importance, order, or time. –**premier** *noun* **1 Premier** the head of the government of an Australian State. **2** (in Britain etc.) a prime minister. **premiers** *plural noun* a sporting team that wins a premiership. [French, = first]

première (**prem**-yair) *noun* the first public performance or showing of a play or film. –**première** *verb* to give a première of. [French, = first]

premiership *noun* an organised competition among sporting clubs; the winning of this.

premise (**prem**-ĭss) *noun* (also **premiss**) a statement on which reasoning is based.

premises (**prem**-ĭ-sĕz) *plural noun* a house or other building with its grounds and outbuildings etc.; *on the premises*, in the buildings or grounds concerned.

premiss (**prem**-ĭss) *noun* = **premise**.

premium (**pree**-mee-ŭm) *noun* **1** an amount or instalment to be paid for an insurance policy. **2** an addition to ordinary wages or charges etc., a bonus. **3** a fee for instruction, especially that paid by an apprentice. □ **at a premium** above the nominal or usual price; highly valued or esteemed. **put a**

premium on to attach especial value to; to provide an incentive for (a certain action etc.). [from Latin *praemium* = reward]

premolar (pree-**moh**-ler) *noun* a tooth between the canines and the molars.

premonition (prem-ŏ-**nish**-ŏn) *noun* a feeling that something (bad) is going to happen. [from *pre-*, + Latin *monere* = warn]

preoccupation *noun* 1 the state of being preoccupied. 2 a thing that fills one's thoughts.

preoccupied *adjective* having one's thoughts deeply engaged in something; inattentive in manner because of this.

preordain *verb* to ordain or determine beforehand.

prep *noun* 1 school work that a student is required to do outside lessons. 2 a school period during which this is done. 3 a first class at some primary or junior schools. □ prep school a preparatory school. [short for *preparation*]

pre-package *verb* (also pre-pack) to pack (goods) ready for sale before distributing them.

preparation *noun* 1 preparing; being prepared. 2 a thing done to make ready for something; *make preparations for*, prepare for. 3 = prep. 4 a substance or mixture prepared for use, e.g. as food or medicine, *a preparation of bismuth*.

preparatory (prě-**pa**-ră-tŏ-ree) *adjective* preparing for something, *preparatory training*. –preparatory *adverb* in a preparatory way. □ preparatory school a school where pupils are prepared for a higher school or (in the US) for college or university.

prepare *verb* 1 to make or get ready. 2 to make (food or other substances) ready for use. □ be prepared to to be ready and willing to (do something). [from *pre-*, + Latin *parare* = make ready]

preparedness (prě-**pair**-rěd-něss) *noun* readiness.

prepay *verb* (prepaid, prepaying) to pay (a charge) beforehand; to pay the postage of (a letter etc.) beforehand, e.g. by buying and affixing a stamp. prepayment *noun*

preponderant (prě-**pond**-ě-rănt) *adjective* preponderating. preponderantly *adverb*, preponderance *noun*

preponderate (prě-**pond**-ě-rayt) *verb* to be greater than others in number or intensity etc. [from Latin *praeponderare* = outweigh]

preposition *noun* a word used with a noun or pronoun to show place, position, time, or means, e.g. *at home*, *in the hall*, *on Sunday*, *by train*. prepositional *adjective* [from *pre-*, + Latin *positum* = placed]

prepossessing *adjective* attractive, making a good impression, *not very prepossessing*.

preposterous (prě-**poss**-tě-rŭs) *adjective* utterly absurd, outrageous. preposterously *adverb* [from Latin, = back to front (from *prae* = before, + *posterus* = behind)]

Pre-Raphaelite (pree-**raf**-ě-lyt) *noun* any of a group of 19th-century artists who aimed at producing work in the style of the Italian artists of before the time of Raphael.

prerequisite (pree-**rek**-wĭ-zĭt) *adjective* required as a condition or in preparation for something else. –prerequisite *noun* a prerequisite thing.

prerogative (prě-**rog**-ă-tiv) *noun* a right or privilege belonging to a particular person or group. [from Latin, = people voting first]

presage (**pres**-ij) *noun* 1 an omen. 2 a presentiment. –presage (prě-**sayj**) *verb* 1 to foreshadow, to be an advance sign of. 2 to predict.

presbyter (**prez**-bĭ-ter) *noun* (in some Churches) an elder.

Presbyterian (prez-bĭ-**teer**-ree-ăn) *adjective* of a Presbyterian Church, a Protestant church governed by elders who are all of equal rank. –Presbyterian *noun* a member of the Presbyterian Church. Presbyterianism *noun* [from Greek *presbuteros* = elder]

presbytery (**prez**-bĭ-tě-ree) *noun* 1 a council of presbyters, or of ministers, elders, and other Church members representing the parishes in a district; the district represented by this body. 2 the eastern part of a chancel. 3 the house of a Roman Catholic priest.

preschool *adjective* of the time before a child is old enough to attend school. –preschool *noun* a kindergarten.

prescribe *verb* 1 to advise the use of (a medicine etc.). 2 to lay down as a course or rule to be followed. [from *pre-*, + Latin *scribere* = write]

Usage *Prescribe* should not be confused with *proscribe* which means 'to forbid'.

prescript (**pree**-skript) *noun* a law, rule, or command.

prescription *noun* **1** a doctor's written instruction for the composition and use of a medicine. **2** the medicine prescribed in this way. **3** prescribing.

prescriptive *adjective* **1** laying down rules. **2** (of grammatical rules etc.) prescribing what should be used, not descriptive. **3** prescribed by custom.

preselection *noun* the selection of a candidate for a forthcoming election by members of a political party.

presence *noun* **1** being present in a place, *your presence is required*. **2** a person's bearing, impressiveness of bearing, *has a fine presence*. **3** a person or thing that is or seems to be present in a place, *felt a presence in the room*. □ **presence of mind** ability to act quickly and in a practical way in an emergency.

present¹ (**prez**-ĕnt) *adjective* **1** being in the place in question, *no one else was present*. **2** being dealt with or discussed, *in the present case*. **3** existing or occurring now, *the present Prime Minister*. –**present** *noun* **1** present time, the time now passing. **2** the present tense. □ **at present** now. **for the present** for now, temporarily. **present-day** *adjective* of present times, modern. **present tense** the tense of the verb that expresses action now going on or habitually performed (e.g. *they are playing, we go to school five days a week*). [from Latin *praesens* = being at hand]

present² (**prez**-ĕnt) *noun* something given or received as a gift.

present³ (prĕ-**zent**) *verb* **1** to give as a gift or award, to offer for acceptance; *the cheque has not been presented*, has not been handed in for payment. **2** to introduce (a person) to another or others. **3** to bring (a play or new product etc.) to the public. **4** to show, to reveal, *presented a brave front to the world*. **5** to level or aim (a weapon). □ **present arms** to hold a rifle etc. vertically in front of the body as a salute. **present oneself** to appear or attend, e.g. for an examination. **presenter** *noun*

presentable *adjective* fit to be presented to someone, of good appearance.

presentation *noun* **1** presenting; being presented. **2** something that is presented.

presentiment (prĕ-**zent**-ĭ-mĕnt) *noun* a feeling of something that is about to happen, a foreboding.

presently *adverb* **1** soon, after a short time. **2** now.

preservation *noun* preserving; being preserved.

preservative *adjective* preserving things. –**preservative** *noun* a substance that preserves perishable foods.

preserve *verb* **1** to keep safe; to keep in an unchanged condition. **2** to keep from decay; to treat (food, e.g. fruit or meat) so that it can be kept for future use. **3** to keep (game, or a river etc.) undisturbed, for private use. –**preserve** *noun* **1** (also **preserves**) preserved fruit; jam. **2** an area where game or fish are preserved. **3** activities or interests etc. regarded as belonging to a particular person. **preserver** *noun* [from *pre-*, + Latin *servare* = keep]

pre-set *verb* (**pre-set**, **pre-setting**) to set beforehand.

preside *verb* to be president or chairperson; to have the position of authority or control. [from Latin *prae* = in front, + *-sidere* = sit]

president *noun* **1** a person who is the head of a club, society, or council etc. **2** the head of a republic. **3** the person presiding over the Australian Senate. **presidency** *noun*, **presidential** *adjective* [from *preside*]

press¹ *verb* **1** to apply weight or force steadily to (a thing). **2** to squeeze juice etc. from. **3** to make by pressing. **4** to flatten or smooth; to iron (clothes etc.). **5** to exert pressure on (an enemy etc.); to oppress. **6** to urge or entreat, to demand insistently, *press for a 35-hour week*. **7** to force the acceptance of, *they pressed sweets upon us*. **8** to insist upon, *don't press that point*. **9** to throng closely. **10** to push one's way. –**press** *noun* **1** pressing, *give it a press*. **2** crowding, a throng of people. **3** hurry, pressure of affairs, *the press of modern life*. **4** an instrument or machinery for compressing, flattening, or shaping something. **5** a printing press; a printing or publishing firm. **6** newspapers and periodicals, the people involved in writing or producing these, *a press photographer*. **7** a large shelved cupboard for linen etc. □ **be pressed for** to have barely enough of, *we are pressed for time*. **press conference** an interview given to journalists by a person who wishes to make an announcement or answer questions. **press cutting** a cutting from a newspaper. **press release** a statement issued to newspapers. **press stud** a small fastener for clothes etc., with two parts that engage when pressed together. **press-up** *noun* a push-up. [from Latin *pressum* = squeezed]

press² *verb* (*old use*) to force to serve in the army or navy. □ **press gang** *noun* a group who coerce people into doing something; (*verb*) to force into joining or doing something. **press into service** to bring into use as a makeshift.

pressing *adjective* **1** urgent, *a pressing need*. **2** urging something strongly, *a pressing invitation*. **–pressing** *noun* a thing made by pressing, a record, CD, or series of these made at one time.

pressure *noun* **1** the exertion of continuous force upon something. **2** the force exerted, that of the atmosphere, *pressure is high in eastern areas*. **3** a compelling or oppressive influence, *is under pressure to vote against it*; *the pressures of business life*. **–pressure** *verb* to try to compel (a person) into some action. □ **pressure cooker** a pan in which things can be cooked quickly by steam under high pressure. **pressure group** an organised group seeking to influence policy by concerted action and intensive propaganda.

pressurise *verb* (also **-ize**) **1** to keep (a closed compartment, e.g. an aircraft cabin) at a constant atmospheric pressure. **2** to pressure (a person etc.). □ **pressurised water reactor** a nuclear reactor in which the coolant is water at high pressure. **pressurisation** *noun*

prestige (press-**teezh**) *noun* respect for a person resulting from his or her good reputation, past achievements, etc. [from Latin, = an illusion]

prestigious (press-**tij**-ŭs) *adjective* having or bringing prestige.

presto *adverb* (especially in music) quickly.

prestressed *adjective* (of concrete) strengthened by means of stretched wires within it.

presumably *adverb* as it may be presumed.

presume *verb* **1** to take for granted; to suppose to be true. **2** to take the liberty of doing something, to venture, *may we presume to advise you?* **3** to be presumptuous. □ **presume on** to make unscrupulous use of, to take unwarranted liberties because of, *they are presuming on her good nature*.

presumption *noun* **1** presuming a thing to be true; something presumed. **2** presumptuous behaviour.

presumptive *adjective* giving grounds for presumption. □ **heir presumptive** *see* **heir**.

presumptuous (prĕ-**zump**-tew-ŭs) *adjective* behaving with impudent boldness; acting

without authority. **presumptuously** *adverb*, **presumptuousness** *noun*

presuppose *verb* **1** to take for granted. **2** to require as a prior condition, *effects presuppose causes*. **presupposition** *noun*

pre-tax *adjective* before tax has been deducted.

pretence *noun* **1** pretending, make-believe. **2** claim, e.g. to merit or knowledge. **3** pretentiousness.

pretend *verb* **1** to create a false appearance of something, either in play or so as to deceive others. **2** to claim falsely that one has or is something. **3** to lay claim, *he pretended to the title*; *pretended to exact knowledge*, claimed to have this. **pretendedly** *adverb* [from Latin *prae* = in front, + *tendere* = to offer]

pretender *noun* **1** a person who pretends. **2** a person who claims a throne or title etc.

pretension *noun* **1** the assertion of a claim to something. **2** pretentiousness.

pretentious (prĕ-**ten**-shŭs) *adjective* showy; pompous. **pretentiously** *adverb*, **pretentiousness** *noun*

preterite (**pret**-ĕ-rĭt) *noun* a tense of a verb that expresses a past action or state.

preternatural (pree-ter-**nach**-ŭ-răl) *adjective* outside the ordinary course of nature, unusual. **preternaturally** *adverb* [from Latin *praeter* = beyond, + *natural*]

pretext (**pree**-tekst) *noun* a reason put forward to conceal one's true reason. [from Latin *praetextus* = an outward display]

Pretoria (prĕ-**tor**-ree-ă) the capital of Transvaal and administrative capital of South Africa.

prettify *verb* (**prettified, prettifying**) to make (a thing) look superficially pretty or pleasing.

pretty *adjective* (**prettier, prettiest**) **1** attractive in a delicate way. **2** considerable; *cost me a pretty penny*, a lot of money. **–pretty** *adverb* fairly, moderately, *pretty good*. □ **pretty much** or **nearly** or **well** almost. **pretty-pretty** *adjective* with the prettiness overdone. **prettily** *adverb*, **prettiness** *noun*

pretzel (**pret**-zĕl) *noun* a crisp knot-shaped biscuit flavoured with salt. [German]

prevail *verb* **1** to be victorious, to gain the mastery. **2** to be more usual or frequent than others, to exist or occur generally, *the prevailing wind*. □ **prevail on** to persuade. [from *pre-*, + Latin *valere* = have power]

prevalent (**prev**-ă-lĕnt) *adjective* existing or occurring generally, widespread. **prevalently** *adverb*, **prevalence** *noun* [same origin as *prevail*]

prevaricate (prě-**va**-rĭ-kayt) *verb* to speak evasively or misleadingly. **prevarication** *noun*, **prevaricator** *noun* [from Latin, = walk crookedly]

prevent *verb* 1 to keep (a thing) from happening, to make impossible. 2 to keep (a person) from doing something. **preventable** *adjective*, **prevention** *noun* [from *pre-*, + Latin *ventum* = come]

preventative *adjective* & *noun* = preventive.

preventive *adjective* preventing something. –**preventive** *noun* a thing that prevents something. □ **preventive medicine** the branch of medicine concerned with the prevention of disease.

preview *noun* an advance showing or viewing of a film or play etc. before it is shown to the general public.

previous *adjective* 1 coming before in time or order. 2 done or acting prematurely. **previously** *adverb* [from *pre-*, + Latin *via* = way]

pre-war *adjective* existing or occurring before a certain war, especially before that of 1914–18 or 1939–45.

prey (*pr.* pray) *noun* 1 an animal that is hunted or killed by another for food. 2 a person or thing that falls victim to an enemy or fear or disease etc. –**prey** *verb* (**preyed**, **preying**) **prey on** to seek or take as prey; to have a harmful influence on, *the problem preyed on his mind.* □ **bird** or **beast of prey** one that kills and eats other birds or animals. [from Latin *praeda* = booty]

Priam (**pry**-am) (*Gk. legend*) the king of Troy at the time of the Trojan War.

price *noun* 1 the amount of money for which a thing is bought or sold. 2 the odds in betting. 3 what must be given or done etc. in order to achieve something, *peace at any price.* –**price** *verb* to fix or find or estimate the price of. □ **at a price** at a high cost. **price oneself out of the market** to charge such a high price for one's goods or services that no one will buy them. **price tag** a label on an item showing its price; the cost of an undertaking etc. **price war** competitive price cutting amongst traders.

priceless *adjective* 1 invaluable. 2 (*informal*) very amusing or absurd.

pricey *adjective* (*informal*) expensive.

prick *verb* 1 to pierce slightly, to make a tiny hole in. 2 to goad by causing mental awareness, *my conscience is pricking me.* 3 to feel a pricking sensation. 4 to mark (a pattern etc.) with pricks or dots. –**prick** *noun* pricking; a mark or puncture made by this. □ **prick out** to plant out (seedlings) in small holes pricked in soil. **prick up one's ears** (of a dog) to raise the ears erect when on the alert; (of a person) to become suddenly attentive. **pricker** *noun*

prickle *noun* 1 a small thorn. 2 one of the hard pointed spines on an echidna etc. 3 a pricking sensation. –**prickle** *verb* to feel or cause a sensation of pricking.

prickly *adjective* 1 having prickles. 2 (of a person) irritable, touchy. □ **prickly pear** a kind of cactus with pear-shaped edible fruit; its fruit. **prickliness** *noun*

pride *noun* 1 a feeling of pleasure or satisfaction in one's actions, qualities, or possessions etc. 2 a person or thing that is a source of pride. 3 a proper sense of what is fitting for one's position or character, self-respect. 4 an unduly high opinion of one's own qualities or merits. 5 a company (of lions). –**pride** *verb* **pride oneself on** to be proud of. □ **pride of place** the most prominent position.

priest *noun* 1 an ordained minister of the Catholic or Orthodox Church, or of the Anglican Church (ranking above deacon and below bishop). 2 a person who is appointed to perform religious rites in a non-Christian religion. **priesthood** *noun*

priestess *noun* a female priest of a non-Christian religion.

Priestley, Joseph (1733–1804), English chemist, noted for his work on gases and for the discovery of what is now called oxygen.

priestly *adjective* of, like, or suitable for a priest.

prig *noun* a self-righteous person, one who displays or demands exaggerated correctness, especially in behaviour. **priggery** *noun*, **priggish** *adjective*, **priggishness** *noun*

prim *adjective* (**primmer**, **primmest**) stiffly formal and precise in manner or appearance or behaviour, disliking what is rough or improper. **primly** *adverb*, **primness** *noun*

prima (**pree**-mă) *adjective* **prima ballerina** the chief female dancer in a ballet. **prima donna** the chief female singer in an opera; a temperamentally self-important person. [Italian, = first]

primacy (**pry**-mă-see) *noun* pre-eminence.

prima facie (pry-mă **fay**-see) *adverb* at first sight; from a first impression, *seems prima facie to be guilty*. – prima facie *adjective* (of evidence) based on the first impression, *can see a prima facie reason for it*. [Latin]

primal (**pry**-măl) *adjective* 1 primitive, primeval. 2 chief, fundamental.

primary *adjective* 1 earliest in time or order, first in a series, *the primary meaning of a word*. 2 of the first importance, chief. □ primary colours those colours from which all others can be made by mixing, (of paint) red, yellow, and blue, (of light) red, green, and violet. primary education or school that in which the rudiments of knowledge are taught. primary industry agriculture, forestry, fishing, etc., as distinct from manufacturing industry. primary producer a worker in primary industry. primarily (**pry**-mă-rĭ-lee) *adverb* [same origin as *prime*[1]]

primate (**pry**-mayt) *noun* 1 a member of the highly developed order of animals that includes man, apes, and monkeys. 2 an archbishop.

prime[1] *adjective* 1 chief, most important, *the prime cause*. 2 first-rate, excellent, *prime beef*. 3 fundamental. – prime *noun* the state of greatest perfection, the best part, *in the prime of life*. □ prime factor a factor that is a prime number, *the prime factors of 12 are 3, 2, and 2*. prime minister the chief minister in a government, e.g. in the Australian Federal Government. prime mover an initial natural or mechanical source of motive power, e.g. the motor of a semitrailer; the author of a fruitful idea. prime number a number (e.g. 2, 3, 5, 7, 11) that can be divided exactly only by itself and unity. [from Latin *primus* = first]

prime[2] *verb* 1 to prepare (a thing) for use or action; *prime a pump*, cause liquid to flow into it to start it working. 2 to prepare (a surface) for painting by coating it with a substance that prevents the first coat of paint from being absorbed. 3 to equip (a person) with information. 4 to give (a person) plenty of food or drink in preparation for something.

primer[1] (**pry**-mer) *noun* a substance used to prime a surface for painting.

primer[2] (**pry**-mer) *noun* an elementary textbook.

primeval (pry-**mee**-văl) *adjective* of the earliest times of the world, ancient. primevally

adverb [from Latin *primus* = first, + *aevum* = age]

primitive *adjective* 1 of or at an early stage of civilisation, *primitive man*. 2 simple or crude, using unsophisticated techniques, *primitive tools*. primitively *adverb*

primogeniture (pry-mŏ-**jen**-ĭ-cher) *noun* 1 the fact of being a first-born child. 2 the system by which an eldest son inherits all his parents' property. [from Latin *primo* = first, + *genitus* = born]

primordial (pry-**mor**-dee-ăl) *adjective* primeval. primordially *adverb*

primrose *noun* 1 a European plant bearing pale yellow flowers in spring. 2 pale yellow. [from Latin *prima rosa* = first rose]

primula *noun* a perennial plant (of a kind including the primrose and polyanthus) with clusters of flowers in various colours.

prince *noun* 1 a male member of a royal family; (in Britain) a son or grandson of the sovereign. 2 a ruler, especially of a small State, *Prince Rainier of Monaco*. 3 a nobleman of various countries. □ prince consort a title conferred on the husband (who is himself a prince) of a reigning queen. Prince Charming a fairy tale prince and hero. [from Latin *princeps* = chieftain]

princeling *noun* a young or petty prince.

princely *adjective* 1 of a prince; worthy of a prince. 2 splendid, generous.

princess *noun* 1 the wife of a prince. 2 a female member of a royal family; (in Britain) a daughter or granddaughter of the sovereign.

principal *adjective* first in rank or importance, chief. – principal *noun* 1 the person with highest authority in an organisation etc.; the head of certain schools or colleges. 2 a person who takes a leading part in an activity or in a play etc. 3 a person for whom another acts as agent, *I must consult my principal*. 4 a capital sum as distinguished from the interest or income on it. [same origin as *prince*]

Usage Distinguish *principal* from *principle*, which is used of 'a rule or general law of conduct'.

---

principality (prin-sĭ-**pal**-ĭ-tee) *noun* a country ruled by a prince.

principally *adverb* for the most part, chiefly.

principle *noun* 1 a basic truth or a general law or doctrine that is used as a basis of reasoning or a guide to action or behaviour. **2** a personal code of right conduct, *a man of principle*; *has no principles*. **3** a general or scientific law shown in the way something works or used as the basis for the construction of a machine etc. □ **in principle** as regards the main elements but not necessarily the details. **on principle** because of the principles of conduct one accepts, *we refused on principle*. [from Latin *principium* = source]

print *verb* **1** to press (a mark or design etc.) on a surface; to impress or stamp (a surface or fabric etc.) in this way. **2** to produce (lettering on a book or newspaper etc.) by applying inked type to paper; to publish in this way. **3** to write with letters like those used in printing books etc. **4** to produce a positive picture from (a photographic negative or transparency) by transmission of light. –**print** *noun* **1** a mark or indentation left where something has pressed on a surface. **2** printed lettering or writing, words in printed form. **3** a printed picture or design. **4** printed fabric. □ **in print** available from a publisher, not out of print. **out of print** with all its printed copies sold. **printed circuit** an electric circuit with thin strips of conducting material on a flat insulating sheet (instead of wires). **printing press** a machine for printing. **print media** newspapers, journals, magazines.

printer *noun* **1** a person whose job or business is the printing of books, newspapers, etc. **2** a machine that prints.

printout *noun* material produced in printed form from a computer or teleprinter.

prior[1] *adjective* earlier, coming before another or others in time, order, or importance. –**prior** *adverb* **prior to** before, *prior to 1700*.

prior[2] *noun* the monk who is head of a religious house or order or (in an abbey) ranks next below an abbot. **prioress** *feminine noun* [Latin, = former, more important]

priority *noun* **1** being earlier or more important; precedence in rank etc., the right to be first. **2** something that is (or that a person considers to be) more important than other items or consideration. [from *prior*]

priory *noun* a monastery governed by a prior; a nunnery governed by a prioress.

prise *verb* to force out or open by leverage.

prism *noun* **1** a solid geometric shape with ends that are similar, equal, and parallel. **2** a transparent body of this form, usually

triangular and made of glass, that breaks up light into the colours of the rainbow.

prismatic (priz-**mat**-ik) *adjective* **1** of or like a prism. **2** (of colours) formed or distributed as if by a prism, rainbow-like. **prismatically** *adverb*

prison *noun* **1** a building used to confine people who are convicted or (in certain cases) accused of crimes. **2** any place of custody or confinement. **3** imprisonment as a punishment. □ **prison camp** a camp serving as a prison for prisoners of war etc.

prisoner *noun* **1** a person kept in prison. **2** a person who is in custody and on trial for a criminal offence. **3** a captive. **4** a person or thing kept in confinement or held in another's grasp etc. □ **prisoner of conscience** a person imprisoned for his or her political or religious views. **prisoner of war** an enemy captured in a war.

prissy *adjective* prim. **prissily** *adverb*, **prissiness** *noun*

pristine (**pris**-teen) *adjective* in its original and unspoilt condition. [from Latin *pristinus* = former]

privacy (**pry**-vă-see *or* **priv**-ă-see) *noun* being private, seclusion.

private *adjective* **1** of or belonging to a particular person or persons, not public, *private property*. **2** not holding public office, *speaking as a private citizen*; *in private life*, as a private person, not as an official or public performer etc. **3** not to be made known publicly, confidential. **4** (of a place) secluded. **5** (of education or medical treatment) conducted outside the publicly funded system, at the individual's expense, *private schools*; *private patients*. –**private** *noun* a soldier of the lowest rank. □ **in private** in the presence only of the person(s) directly concerned, not in public. **private enterprise** management of business by private individuals or companies (contrasted with State ownership or control); an individual's initiative. **private eye** (*informal*) a private detective. **private means** an income available from investments etc., not as an earned wage or salary. **private member** an MP not holding a government appointment. **private parts** the genitals. **private school** a school supported mainly by pupils' fees. Also called an *independent school*. **private sector** all the businesses etc. that are run by private enterprise, not by the State. **private soldier** an ordinary soldier, other than officers. **privately** *adverb*

privation (pry-**vay**-shŏn) *noun* loss or lack of something, especially of the necessaries of life. [from Latin *privatus* = deprived]

privatise (**pry**-vă-tyz) *verb* (also **-ize**) to transfer (a business etc.) from State to private ownership. **privatisation** *noun*

privet (**priv**-ĕt) *noun* a bushy evergreen European shrub used for hedges, and now a serious pest in the Australian bush.

privilege *noun* a special right, advantage, or immunity granted to a person or group, *parliamentary privilege* (see **parliamentary**). [from Latin *privus* = of an individual, + *legis* = of law]

privileged *adjective* having a privilege or privileges.

privy *adjective* (*old use*) hidden, secret. **–privy** *noun* (*old use* & *Amer.*) a toilet. □ **be privy to** to share in the secret of (a person's plans etc.). **Privy Council** (in Britain) a body of people advising the sovereign on matters of State, formerly hearing appeals against judgments of the Australian High Court and state Supreme Courts. **privily** *adverb* [from Latin, = private]

prize[1] *noun* **1** an award given as a symbol of victory or superiority. **2** something striven for or worth striving for. **3** something that can be won in a lottery etc. **–prize** *adjective* winning or likely to win a prize; excellent of its kind. **–prize** *verb* to value highly. [from *price*]

prize[2] *noun* a ship or property captured at sea during a war.

prize[3] *verb* = prise.

prizefighter *noun* a professional boxer.

pro[1] *noun* (*plural* **pros**) (*informal*) a professional.

pro[2] *adjective* & *preposition* (of an argument or reason) for, in favour (of). **–pro** *noun* (*plural* **pros**) a reason for or in favour. □ **pros and cons** reasons for and against something. [from Latin *pro* = for, + *contra* = against]

pro- *prefix* **1** favouring or supporting (as in *pro-life*). **2** deputising or substituted for (as in *pronoun*). **3** onwards, forwards (as in *proceed*). [from Latin *pro* = for; in front of]

proactive *adjective* (of a person, policy, etc.) taking the initiative.

probability *noun* **1** being probable. **2** something that is probable; the most probable event. **3** a ratio expressing the chances that a certain event will occur.

probable *adjective* likely to happen or be true. **–probable** *noun* a candidate likely to

be successful; a person who will probably become a member of a team. **probably** *adverb* [same origin as *prove*]

probate (**proh**-bayt) *noun* **1** the official process of proving that a will is valid. **2** a copy of a will with a certificate that it is valid, handed to executors. [from Latin *probatum* = tested, proved]

probation *noun* **1** the testing of a person's behaviour or abilities etc. **2** a system whereby certain offenders are supervised by an official (**probation officer**) as an alternative to imprisonment. [same origin as *prove*]

probationary *adjective* of or in the nature of probation. □ **probationary licence** a licence issued to a driver after incurring a certain number of demerit points; (in some states) a licence issued to a newly qualified driver (also called a *provisional licence*).

probationer *noun* a person who is undergoing a probationary period of testing, e.g. a hospital nurse at an early stage of training.

probe *noun* **1** a device for exploring an otherwise inaccessible place or object etc.; a blunt-ended surgical instrument for exploring a wound; *space probe*, an unmanned exploratory spacecraft transmitting information about its environment etc. **2** a penetrating investigation. **–probe** *verb* **1** to explore with a probe. **2** to penetrate with something sharp. **3** to make a penetrating investigation of. [from Latin *probare* = to test]

probity (**proh**-bĭ-tee) *noun* honesty, integrity. [from Latin *probus* = good]

problem *noun* **1** something difficult to deal with or understand. **2** something difficult that has to be accomplished, answered, or dealt with. [from Greek, = an exercise]

problematic *adjective* (also **problematical**) difficult to deal with or understand. **problematically** *adverb*

proboscis (prŏ-**boss**-ĭss) *noun* (*plural* **probosces**) **1** a long flexible snout, an elephant's trunk. **2** an elongated mouthpart in certain insects, used for sucking things. [from Greek *pro* = in front, + *boskein* = feed]

procedure *noun* a series of actions done or appointed to be done in order to accomplish something; a way of conducting business. **procedural** *adjective*

proceed (prŏ-**seed**) *verb* **1** to go forward or onward, to make one's way. **2** to continue, to carry on an activity, *please proceed with* *your work.* **3** to start a lawsuit, *he proceeded against the newspaper for libel.* **4** to come forth, to originate, *the evils that proceed from war.* [from *pro-*, + Latin *cedere* = go]

proceedings *plural noun* **1** a lawsuit, *start proceedings for divorce.* **2** what takes place at a formal meeting of a society etc. **3** a published report of a discussion or conference etc.

proceeds (**proh**-seedz) *plural noun* the amount of money produced by a sale etc.

process¹ (**proh**-sess) *noun* **1** a series of actions or operations used in making, manufacturing, or achieving something. **2** a series of changes, a natural operation, *the digestive process.* **3** a course of events or time. **4** a lawsuit; a summons or writ. **5** a natural projection on the body or on a plant. **– process** *verb* **1** to put through a manufacturing or other process or course of treatment; *your application is being processed*, is being dealt with; *processed cheese*, treated to avoid further ripening or deterioration. **2** to perform operations on (data). [same origin as *proceed*]

process² (prŏ-**sess**) *verb* to go in procession. [from *procession*]

procession *noun* a number of people or vehicles or boats etc. going along in an orderly line. **processional** *adjective*

processor *noun* a machine that processes things, e.g. *central processor*, *food processor*.

pro-choice *adjective* favouring the right of a woman to choose to have an abortion.

proclaim *verb* **1** to announce officially or publicly, to declare. **2** to make known unmistakably as being, *his accent proclaimed him a Scot.* **proclamation** *noun*

proclivity (prŏ-**kliv**-ĭ-tee) *noun* a tendency.

proconsul (proh-**kon**-s'l) *noun* the governor of an ancient Roman province.

procrastinate (prŏ-**kras**-tĭ-nayt) *verb* to postpone action, to be dilatory. **procrastination** *noun*, **procrastinator** *noun* [from *pro-*, + Latin *crastinus* = of tomorrow]

procreate (proh-kree-**ayt**) *verb* to bring (a living thing) into existence by the natural process of reproduction, to generate. **procreation** *noun*, **procreative** *adjective*

Procrustean (prŏ-**krust**-ee-ăn) *adjective* seeking to enforce conformity with a theory etc. by violent methods (e.g. by omitting all that contradicts it). [named after Procrustes, a

robber in Greek legend, who fitted victims to his bed by stretching them or lopping bits off]

proctor *noun* an officer at certain universities with disciplinary functions.

procumbent *adjective* lying on the face; prostrate.

procure *verb* to obtain by care or effort, to acquire. **procurable** *adjective*, **procuration** *noun*, **procurement** *noun* [from *pro-*, + Latin *curare* = look after]

prod *verb* (**prodded**, **prodding**) **1** to poke. **2** to urge or stimulate into action. **– prod** *noun* **1** a poke. **2** a stimulus to action. **3** a pointed instrument for prodding things.

prodigal *adjective* **1** recklessly wasteful or extravagant. **2** lavish. **– prodigal** *noun* a recklessly extravagant person. **prodigally** *adverb*, **prodigality** (prod-ĭ-**gal**-ĭ-tee) *noun* [from Latin *prodigus* = generous]

prodigious (prŏ-**dij**-us) *adjective* **1** marvellous, amazing. **2** enormous. **prodigiously** *adverb*

prodigy (**prod**-ĭ-jee) *noun* **1** a person with exceptional qualities or abilities; a child with abilities very much beyond those appropriate to his or her age. **2** a marvellous thing, a wonderful example of something. [from Latin *prodigium* = good omen]

produce (prŏ-**dewss**) *verb* **1** to bring forward for inspection, consideration, or use. **2** to bring (a play or performance etc.) before the public. **3** to bring into existence; to cause (a reaction or sensation etc.); to bear or yield (offspring or products). **4** to manufacture. **5** to extend (a straight line). **– produce** (**prod**-yewss) *noun* **1** an amount or thing produced. **2** agricultural and natural products, *dairy produce.* [from *pro-*, + Latin *ducere* = to lead]

producer *noun* **1** a person producing articles or agricultural products etc. (contrasted with a *consumer*). **2** one who directs the acting of a play. **3** one who is responsible for control of expenditure, schedule, and quality in the production of a film or a broadcast program.

product *noun* **1** something produced by a natural process or by agriculture or manufacture or as a result. **2** (in mathematics) the result obtained by multiplying two quantities together.

production *noun* **1** producing; being produced; *go into production*, begin being manufactured. **2** a thing produced, especially a play or film. **3** the amount produced.

□ **production line** a sequence of machines and workers through which things move to undergo successive stages of production.

productive *adjective* tending or able to produce things, especially in large quantities. **productively** *adverb*, **productiveness** *noun*

productivity *noun* productiveness; efficiency in industrial production.

profane (prŏ-**fayn**) *adjective* **1** secular, not sacred, *sacred and profane music*. **2** irreverent, blasphemous. –**profane** *verb* to treat (a thing) with irreverence or lack of due respect. **profanely** *adverb*, **profanity** (prŏ-**fan**-ĭ-tee) *noun*, **profanation** *noun* [from Latin *profanus* = outside the temple]

profess *verb* **1** to state that one has (a quality or feeling etc.), to pretend, *she professed ignorance* or *to be ignorant of this law*. **2** to affirm one's faith in (a religion).

professed *adjective* **1** avowed, openly acknowledged by oneself, *a professed Christian*. **2** falsely claiming to be something, *a professed friend*. **3** having taken the vows of a religious order, *a professed nun*. **professedly** (prŏ-**fess**-ĕd-lee) *adverb*

profession *noun* **1** an occupation, especially one that involves knowledge and training in a branch of advanced learning, *the dental profession*. **2** the people engaged in an occupation of this kind. **3** a declaration or avowal, *made professions of loyalty*.

professional *adjective* **1** of or belonging to a profession or its members. **2** having or showing the skill of a professional. **3** doing a certain kind of work as a full-time occupation or to make a living or (of sportsmen, contrasted with *amateur*) for payment. –**professional** *noun* **1** a person working or performing for payment. **2** someone highly skilled. **professionally** *adverb*

professionalism *noun* the qualities or skills of a profession or professionals.

professor *noun* **1** a university teacher of the highest rank. **2** (in the USA) a university lecturer. **professorship** *noun*, **professorial** (prof-ĕ-**sor**-ree-ăl) *adjective*

proffer (**prof**-er) *verb* to offer. [from *pro-* + *offer*]

proficient (prŏ-**fish**-ĕnt) *adjective* doing something correctly and competently through training or practice, skilled. **proficiently** *adverb*, **proficiency** *noun* [from Latin *proficiens* = making progress]

profile (**proh**-fyl) *noun* **1** a side view, especially of the human face. **2** a drawing or other representation of this. **3** a short account of a person's character or career. **4** an outline. **5** a vertical cross-section of a structure. **6** a chart or graphic representation of statistical data. –**profile** *verb* to represent in profile; to give a profile of. □ **keep a low profile** to avoid attention.

profit *noun* **1** an advantage or benefit obtained from doing something. **2** money gained in a business transaction, the excess of returns over outlay. –**profit** *verb* (**profited**, **profiting**) **1** to bring advantage to. **2** to obtain an advantage or benefit. □ **profit-sharing** *noun* allowing a company's employees to share directly in its profits.

profitable *adjective* bringing profit or benefits. **profitably** *adverb*, **profitability** *noun*

profiteer *noun* a person who makes excessive profits, especially by taking advantage of times of difficulty or scarcity (e.g. in war).

profiteering *noun* being a profiteer.

profiterole (prŏ-**fit**-ĕ-rohl) *noun* a small hollow cake of choux pastry with sweet or savoury filling.

profligate (**prof**-lĭ-găt) *adjective* **1** recklessly wasteful or extravagant. **2** dissolute. –**profligate** *noun* a profligate person. **profligacy** *noun*

pro forma *adverb* as a matter of form or politeness. –**pro forma** *adjective* **1** done or produced as a matter of form. **2** denoting a standard document or form. **3** (of a financial statement) showing potential or expected income, costs, assets, or liabilities. –**pro forma** *noun* a standard document or form. [Latin]

profound *adjective* **1** deep, intense, *takes a profound interest in it*. **2** having or showing great knowledge of or insight into a subject. **3** requiring much study or thought. **profoundly** *adverb*, **profundity** *noun* [from Latin *profundus* = deep]

profuse (prŏ-**fewss**) *adjective* **1** lavish, extravagant, *profuse gratitude*. **2** plentiful, *a profuse variety*. **profusely** *adverb*, **profuseness** *noun* [from *pro-*, + Latin *fusum* = poured]

profusion (prŏ-**few**-zhŏn) *noun* abundance, a plentiful supply, *a profusion of roses*.

progenitor (prŏ-**jen**-ĭ-ter) *noun* an ancestor.

progeny (**proj**-ĕ-nee) *noun* offspring, descendants.

progesterone (prŏ-**jest**-ĕ-rohn) *noun* a hormone that prevents ovulation and prepares the uterus for pregnancy.

prognosis (prog-**noh**-sĭs) *noun* (*plural* **prognoses**) a forecast or advance indication, especially of the course of a disease. [from Greek *pro* = before, + *gnosis* = knowing]

prognostic (prog-**nost**-ik) *noun* **1** a prediction. **2** an advance indication. –**prognostic** *adjective* making or giving this.

prognosticate (prog-**nost**-ĭ-kayt) *verb* **1** to predict. **2** to be an advance indication of. **prognostication** *noun*, **prognosticator** *noun*

program *noun* (also **programme**, except in computing contexts) **1** a plan of intended procedure. **2** a descriptive notice or list of an organised series of events (e.g. of a concert or a course of study). **3** these events. **4** a radio or television broadcast. **5** a series of coded instructions for a computer or other machine. –**program** *verb* (**programmed**, **programming**; *Amer.* **programed**, **programing**) **1** to make a program or definite plan of. **2** to instruct (a computer etc.) by means of a program. [from Greek *programma* = public notice]

programmable *adjective* able to be programmed.

progress (**proh**-gress) *noun* **1** forward or onward movement. **2** an advance or development, especially to a better state. –**progress** (prŏ-**gress**) *verb* **1** to move forward or onward. **2** to advance or develop, especially to a better state. □ **in progress** taking place, in the course of occurring. **progression** *noun* [from *pro-*, + Latin *gressus* = going]

progressive *adjective* **1** making continuous forward movement. **2** proceeding steadily or in regular degrees, *a progressive improvement*. **3** (of a card game or dance etc.) with a periodic change of partners. **4** (of a disease) gradually increasing in its effect. **5** advancing in social conditions or efficiency etc., *a progressive nation* or *company*. **6** favouring rapid progress or reform, *a progressive party* or *policy*. –**progressive** *noun* one who favours a progressive policy. **progressively** *adverb*, **progressiveness** *noun*

prohibit *verb* (**prohibited**, **prohibiting**) to forbid. **prohibition** *noun*, **prohibitor** *noun* [from Latin, = keep off]

prohibitive *adjective* preventing or intended to prevent the use or abuse or purchase of something, *prohibitive taxes*; *prohibitive prices*, very high prices. **prohibitively** *adverb*

project (prŏ-**jekt**) *verb* **1** to extend outward from a surface, *a projecting balcony*. **2** to cast or throw outward. **3** to cause (a picture or shadow) to fall on a surface. **4** to imagine (a thing or oneself) in another situation or another person's feelings or a future time. **5** to plan (a scheme or course of action). **6** to represent (a solid thing) systematically on a plane surface, as maps of the earth are made. –**project** (**proh**-jekt *or* **proj**-ekt) *noun* **1** a plan or scheme; a planned undertaking. **2** a task set as an educational exercise, requiring students to do their own research and present the results. [from *pro-*, + Latin *-jectum* = thrown]

projectile (prŏ-**jek**-tyl) *noun* a missile (e.g. a bullet, arrow, or rocket) that can be projected forcefully.

projection *noun* **1** projecting; being projected. **2** something that projects from a surface. **3** a thing that is projected. **4** a representation of the surface of the earth on a plane surface. **5** an estimate of future situations or trends etc. based on a study of present ones.

projectionist *noun* a person whose job is to operate a projector.

projector *noun* an apparatus for projecting photographs or a cinema film or graphic material etc. on to a screen.

prolactin *noun* a hormone secreted by the pituitary gland that stimulates milk production after childbirth.

prolapse (prŏ-**laps**) *verb* (of an organ of the body) to slip forward or down out of its place. –**prolapse** (**proh**-laps) *noun* the prolapsing of an organ of the body. [from *pro-* = forward, + Latin *lapsum* = fallen]

proleg (**proh**-leg) *noun* any of the fleshy limbs growing from the abdomen of a caterpillar or other larva.

proletarian (proh-lĕ-**tair**-ree-ăn) *adjective* of the proletariat. –**proletarian** *noun* a member of the proletariat. –

proletariat (proh-lĕ-**tair**-ree-ăt) *noun* the working class (contrasted with the bourgeoisie).

pro-life *adjective* opposed to legalised abortion and euthanasia.

proliferate (prŏ-**lif**-ĕ-rayt) *verb* to produce new growth or offspring rapidly, to multiply. **proliferation** *noun* [from Latin *proles* = offspring, + *ferre* = to bear]

prolific (prŏ-**lif**-ik) *adjective* producing much fruit or many flowers or offspring; *a*

prolific writer, one who writes many works.
prolifically *adverb*

prolix (**proh**-liks) *adjective* lengthy, tediously wordy. **prolixity** (prŏ-**liks**-ĭ-tee) *noun* [from Latin *prolixus* = poured forth]

prologue (**proh**-log) *noun* **1** an introduction to a poem or play etc. **2** an act or event serving as an introduction to something. [from Greek *pro-* = before, + *logos* = speech]

prolong (prŏ-**long**) *verb* to lengthen (a thing) in extent or duration. **prolongation** (proh-long-**gay**-shŏn) *noun*

prolonged *adjective* continuing for a long time.

prom *noun* **1** a promenade concert. **2** (*Amer.*) a formal dance, especially one held at the end of high school or college.

promenade (prom-ĕ-**nahd**) *noun* **1** a leisurely walk in a public place. **2** a paved public walk (especially along a sea front), an esplanade. **– promenade** *verb* to go or take for a promenade, to parade. ☐ **promenade concert** one at which part of the audience is not seated and can move about. [from French *se promener* = to walk]

Prometheus (prŏ-**mee**-thee-ŭs) (*Gk. myth.*) a Titan, who stole fire from the gods and was punished by being chained to a rock where an eagle fed on his liver.

promethium (prŏ-**mee**-thee-ŭm) *noun* a radioactive metallic element of the lanthanide series (symbol Pm).

prominent *adjective* **1** jutting out, projecting. **2** conspicuous. **3** important, well-known, *prominent citizens*. **prominently** *adverb*, **prominence** *noun*

promiscuous (prŏ-**miss**-kew-ŭs) *adjective* **1** indiscriminate. **2** having sexual relations with many people. **promiscuously** *adverb*, **promiscuity** (prom-ĭss-**kew**-ĭ-tee) *noun*

promise *noun* **1** a declaration that one will give or do or not do a certain thing. **2** an indication of something that may be expected to come or occur. **3** an indication of future success or good results, *his work shows promise*. **– promise** *verb* **1** to make a promise to, to declare that one will give or do or not do something. **2** to make (a thing) seem likely; *it promises well*, seems likely to give good results. ☐ **Promised Land** Canaan, which was promised by God to Abraham and his descendants; any place of expected happiness.

promising *adjective* likely to turn out well or produce good results. **promisingly** *adverb*

promissory (**prom**-ĭ-sŏ-ree) *adjective* conveying a promise. ☐ **promissory note** a signed promise to pay a sum of money.

promontory (**prom**-ŏn-tŏ-ree) *noun* high land jutting out into the sea or a lake.

promote *verb* **1** to raise (a person) to a higher rank or office. **2** to initiate or help the progress of, *promote friendship between nations*. **3** to publicise (a product) in order to sell it. **promoter** *noun* [from *pro-*, + Latin *motum* = moved]

promotion *noun* promoting; being promoted. **promotional** *adjective*

prompt *adjective* **1** made, done, or doing something without delay. **2** punctual. **– prompt** *adverb* punctually. **– prompt** *verb* **1** to incite or stimulate (a person) to action. **2** to cause (a feeling, thought, or action). **3** to assist by supplying (an actor or speaker) with words that should or could come next. **– prompt** *noun* an act of prompting; something said to prompt an actor or speaker. ☐ **prompt side** the side of a stage (usually to the actors' left) where the prompter is placed. **promptly** *adverb*, **promptness** *noun*, **promptitude** *noun* [from Latin *promptum* = produced]

prompter *noun* a person (placed out of sight of the audience) who prompts actors on the stage.

promulgate (**prom**-ŭl-gayt) *verb* to make known to the public, to proclaim. **promulgation** *noun*, **promulgator** *noun*

prone *adjective* **1** lying face downwards (contrasted with *supine*). **2** likely to do or suffer something, *prone to jealousy*; *accident-prone*. **proneness** *noun*

prong *noun* each of the projecting pointed parts of a fork.

pronged *adjective* having a certain number or kind of prongs; *a three-pronged attack*, in three areas.

pronoun (**proh**-nown) *noun* a word used as a substitute for a noun; *demonstrative pronouns*, this, that, these, those; *interrogative pronouns*, who? what? which? etc.; *personal pronouns*, I, me, we, us, thou, thee, you, ye, he, him, she, her, it, they, them; *possessive pronouns*, my, mine, your, yours, her, hers, etc.; *reflexive pronouns*, myself, oneself, etc.; *relative pronouns*, who, what, which, that.

pronounce *verb* **1** to utter (a speech sound) distinctly or correctly or in a certain way, *can't pronounce the letter r*. **2** to declare formally, *I now pronounce you man and wife*. **3** to declare as one's opinion, *the wine was pronounced excellent*. [from *pro-*, + Latin *nuntiare* = announce]

pronounced *adjective* definite, noticeable, *she walks with a pronounced limp*.

pronouncement *noun* a declaration.

pronto *adverb* (*informal*) immediately. [Spanish; same origin as *prompt*]

pronunciation (prŏ-**nun**-see-ay-shŏn) *noun* 1 the way a word is pronounced. 2 the way a person pronounces words.

proof *noun* 1 a fact or thing that shows or helps to show that something is true or exists. 2 a demonstration of the truth of something, *in proof of my statement*. 3 the process of testing whether something is true or good or valid, *put it to the proof*. 4 a standard of strength for distilled alcoholic liquors, *80% proof*. 5 a trial impression of printed matter, produced so that corrections can be made. 6 a trial print of a photograph. –**proof** *adjective* able to resist or withstand penetration or damage, *waterproof*. –**proof** *verb* 1 to make a proof of (printed matter etc.). 2 to make (a fabric) proof against something, especially water or bullets.

proofread *verb* to read and correct (printer's proofs, a draft document, etc.). **proofreader** *noun*

prop[1] *noun* 1 a support used to keep something from falling or sagging. 2 a person or thing depended on for support or help. –**prop** *verb* (**propped**, **propping**) to support with or as if with a prop, to keep from falling or failing, *prop it up*.

prop[2] *noun* (*informal*) a stage property.

prop[3] (*Austral.*) *verb* (of a horse) to stop suddenly when going at speed. –**prop** *noun* such a stop.

propaganda *noun* publicity intended to spread ideas or information that will persuade or convince people.

propagandist *noun* a person who puts forward propaganda.

propagate *verb* 1 to breed or reproduce from parent stock, *propagate these plants from seeds or cuttings*. 2 to spread (news or ideas etc.). 3 to transmit, *the vibrations are propagated through the rock*. **propagation** *noun*, **propagator** *noun*

propane (**proh**-payn) *noun* a hydrocarbon found in petroleum and used as a fuel.

propel *verb* (**propelled**, **propelling**) to drive or push forward, to give an onward movement

to. **propellent** *adjective* [from *pro-*, + Latin *pellere* = to drive]

propellant *noun* a propelling agent, e.g. an explosive that propels a bullet from a firearm, fuel that provides thrust for a rocket, compressed gas that forces out the contents of an aerosol container.

propeller *noun* a revolving device with blades for propelling a ship or aircraft to which it is fitted.

propensity (prŏ-**pen**-sĭ-tee) *noun* a tendency or inclination, *a propensity to laziness*.

proper *adjective* 1 suitable, appropriate, *not a proper time for singing*. 2 correct, according to rules, *the proper way to hold the bat*. 3 according to social conventions, respectable. 4 strictly so called, *we drove from the suburbs to the city proper*. 5 (*informal*) thorough, complete, *he made a proper fool of himself*. ☐ **proper fraction** one that is less than unity, with the numerator less than the denominator, e.g. $\frac{3}{4}$. **proper name** or **noun** the name of an individual person or thing, e.g. *Jane*, *Perth*. **properly** *adverb* [from Latin *proprius* = your own]

property *noun* 1 a thing or things owned. 2 real estate, someone's land, *their property borders on ours*. 3 a movable object (other than furniture or scenery) used on stage during a performance of a play etc. 4 a quality or characteristic, *it has the property of dissolving grease*. [same origin as *proper*]

prophecy (**prof**-ĕ-see) *noun* 1 the power of prophesying, *the gift of prophecy*. 2 a statement that tells what will happen.

prophesy (**prof**-ĕ-sy) *verb* (**prophesied**, **prophesying**) to declare beforehand (what will happen), to preach or give instruction in religion as if by divine inspiration. [from Greek *pro* = before, + *phanai* = speak]

prophet *noun* 1 a person who foretells the future. 2 a religious teacher inspired by God. ☐ **the Prophet** Muhammad. **prophetess** *feminine noun*

prophetic *adjective* (also **prophetical**) 1 prophesying the future. 2 of a prophet or prophets. **prophetically** *adverb*

prophylactic (prof-ĭ-**lak**-tik) *adjective* tending to prevent a disease or misfortune. –**prophylactic** *noun* 1 a preventive medicine or action. 2 a condom. **prophylactically** *adverb* [from Greek *prophulaxis* = guarding]

propinquity (prŏ-**ping**-kwĭ-tee) *noun* nearness.

propitiate (prŏ-**pish**-ee-ayt) *verb* to win the favour or forgiveness of, to placate. propitiation *noun*, propitiatory *adjective*

propitious (prŏ-**pish**-ŭs) *adjective* favourable, giving a good omen or a suitable opportunity. propitiously *adverb*

proponent (prŏ-**poh**-nĕnt) *noun* the person who puts forward a theory or proposal etc. [from *pro*-, + Latin *ponere* = to place]

proportion *noun* 1 a fraction or share of a whole. 2 a ratio, *the proportion of men to women.* 3 the correct relation in size, amount, or degree between one thing and another or between parts of a thing. –proportion *verb* to give correct proportions to; to make (one thing) proportionate to another. proportions *plural noun* size, dimensions, *a ship of majestic proportions.* [from *pro*- + *portion*]

proportional *adjective* in correct proportion, corresponding in size or amount or degree. ☐ proportional representation an electoral system in which each party has a number of seats in proportion to the number of votes for its candidates. proportionally *adverb*

proportionate *adjective* in proportion, corresponding, *the cost is proportionate to the quality.* proportionately *adverb*

proposal *noun* 1 the proposing of something. 2 the thing proposed. 3 a request that a person should agree to be married to the person asking.

propose *verb* 1 to put forward for consideration; *propose a toast,* ask people formally to drink a toast. 2 to have and declare as one's plan or intention, *we propose to wait.* 3 to nominate as a candidate. 4 to make a proposal of marriage. proposer *noun* [from *pro*-, + Latin *positum* = put]

proposition *noun* 1 a statement, an assertion. 2 a proposal; a scheme proposed. 3 (*informal*) a problem or undertaking, something to be dealt with, *not a paying proposition.* –proposition *verb* (*informal*) to put a proposal to (a person).

propound *verb* to put forward for consideration. propounder *noun* [same origin as *proponent*]

proprietary (prŏ-**pry**-ĕ-tă-ree) *adjective* 1 manufactured and sold by one particular firm, usually under a patent, *proprietary medicines.* 2 of an owner or ownership. ☐ proprietary company (*Austral.*) a private company whose membership is limited by law and which has no public share issue.

proprietary name or **term** the name of a product etc. registered by its owner as a trademark and not usable by another without permission. [same origin as *property*]

proprietor (prŏ-**pry**-ĕ-ter) *noun* the owner of a business. proprietress *feminine noun*

proprietorial (prŏ-pry-ĕ-**tor**-ree-ăl) *adjective* of or indicating ownership.

propriety (prŏ-**pry**-ĕ-tee) *noun* 1 being proper or suitable. 2 correctness of behaviour or morals; *the proprieties,* the requirements of correct behaviour in society.

proprioceptor (prop-ree-oh-**sep**-ter) *noun* a sensory nerve ending that reacts to stimuli from within the organism. [from Latin *proprius* = one's own, + *receptor*]

propulsion *noun* the process of propelling or being propelled.

pro rata (proh **rah**-tă) *adjective* proportional, *if costs increase, there will be a pro rata increase in prices.* –pro rata *adverb* proportionally. *prices will increase pro rata.* [Latin, = according to the rate]

prorogue (prŏ-**rohg**) *verb* 1 to discontinue the meetings of (a parliament etc.) without dissolving it. 2 (of a parliament etc.) to have its meetings discontinued in this way. prorogation (proh-rŏ-**gay**-shŏn) *noun* [from Latin *prorogare* = prolong]

prosaic (prŏ-**zay**-ik) *adjective* lacking poetic beauty or fantasy, unimaginative, plain and ordinary. prosaically *adverb* [from *prose*]

proscenium (prŏ-**seen**-ee-ŭm) *noun* the part of a theatre stage in front of the curtain, with its enclosing arch (the proscenium arch). [from Greek *pro* = before, + *skene* = stage]

proscribe *verb* 1 to forbid by law. 2 to denounce as dangerous etc. proscription *noun*, proscriptive *adjective* [from Latin *proscribere* = to outlaw]

Usage *Proscribe* is sometimes confused with *prescribe*. A doctor *prescribes* medicine to make you better, whereas the use of heroin is *proscribed*.

prose *noun* written or spoken language not in verse form.

prosecute *verb* 1 to take legal proceedings against (a person etc.) for a crime. 2 to carry on or conduct, *prosecuting their trade.* prosecutor *noun* [from Latin *prosecutus* = pursued]

prosecution *noun* 1 prosecuting; being prosecuted. 2 the party prosecuting another for a crime.

proselyte (**pross**-ĕ-lyt) *noun* a convert to a religion or opinion etc., especially to the Jewish faith.

proselytise (**pross**-ĕ-ly-tyz) *verb* (also -ize) to try to convert people to one's beliefs or opinions.

Proserpine (prŏ-**ser**-pĭ-nee) (*Rom. myth.*) the Roman name for Persephone.

prosody (**pross**-ŏ-dee) *noun* the study of verse forms and poetic metres.

prospect (**pross**-pekt) *noun* 1 an extensive view of a landscape etc.; a mental view of matters. 2 an expectation, a possibility, *prospects of success*. 3 a chance of success or advancement, *a job with prospects*. 4 a possible customer or client etc.; a competitor likely to be successful. –**prospect** (prŏ-**spekt**) *verb* to explore in search of something, *prospecting for gold*. **prospector** *noun* [from Latin *pro* = forward, + *specere* = to look]

prospective (prŏ-**spek**-tiv) *adjective* expected to be or to occur, future, possible, *prospective customers*.

prospectus (prŏ-**spek**-tŭs) *noun* a printed document describing and advertising the chief features of a school or business enterprise.

prosper *verb* to be successful, to thrive.

prosperous *adjective* financially successful. **prosperously** *adverb*, **prosperity** *noun*

prostate (**pross**-tayt) *noun* the **prostate gland**, a gland round the neck of the bladder in males. **prostatic** (prŏ-**stat**-ik) *adjective*

prosthesis (pross-**thee**-sĭs) *noun* (*plural* **prostheses**) an artificial limb or other part. **prosthetic** *adjective*

prostitute *noun* a person, typically a woman, who engages in sexual activity for payment. –**prostitute** *verb* 1 to make a prostitute of, *prostitute oneself*. 2 to put to an unworthy use, *prostituting their artistic abilities*. **prostitution** *noun* [from Latin, = for sale]

prostrate (**pross**-trayt) *adjective* 1 face downwards. 2 lying horizontally. 3 overcome, exhausted, *prostrate with grief*. –**prostrate** (pross-**trayt**) *verb* to cause to be prostrate; *prostrate oneself*, to cast oneself face downward on the ground in humility or adoration. **prostration** *noun* [from Latin *prostratum* = laid flat]

prosy (**proh**-zee) *adjective* prosaic, dull. **prosily** *adverb*, **prosiness** *noun*

protactinium (proh-tak-**tin**-ee-ŭm) *noun* a radioactive metallic element of the actinide series (symbol Pa).

protagonist (proh-**tag**-ŏ-nĭst) *noun* 1 the chief person in a drama. 2 one of the chief contenders in a contest. 3 an advocate or champion of a cause etc. [from *proto-*, + Greek *agonistes* = actor]

Usage The use in sense 3 is considered incorrect by some people.

---

protasis (**prot**-ă-sĭs) *noun* (*plural* **protases**) the clause that contains 'if' or 'whether' etc. in a sentence expressing a condition, e.g. 'if you move' in *if you move I shall fire*. [Greek, = proposition]

protea (**proh**-tee-ă) *noun* a South African shrub with many species, having spectacular flower heads.

protean (**proh**-tee-ăn *or* proh-**tee**-ăn) *adjective* variable, versatile; taking many forms. [from *Proteus*]

protease (**proh**-tee-ayz) *noun* any of a number of enzymes that break down proteins.

protect *verb* to keep from harm or injury. **protection** *noun* [from *pro-*, + Latin *tectum* = covered]

protectionism *noun* the policy of protecting home industries from foreign competition, e.g. by controlling imports. **protectionist** *noun*

protective *adjective* protecting, giving protection. **protectively** *adverb*

protector *noun* a person or thing that protects something.

protectorate *noun* a weak or underdeveloped country that is under the official protection and partial control of a stronger one.

protégé (**prot**-ĕ-zhay) *noun* someone helped by a person taking an interest in his or her welfare or career. **protégée** (**prot**-ĕ-zhay) *noun* a female protégé. [French, = protected]

protein (**proh**-teen) *noun* an organic compound containing nitrogen, occurring in plant and animal tissue and forming an essential part of the food of animals.

pro tem *adverb* & *adjective* (*informal*) for the time being. [short for Latin *pro tempore*]

718

protest (**proh**-test) *noun* a statement or action showing one's disapproval of something.
–**protest** (prŏ-**test**) *verb* **1** to express one's disapproval of something, *protested against funding cuts.* **2** to declare firmly or solemnly, *protesting their innocence.* □ **under protest** unwillingly and after making protests.
protester *noun* [from *pro*-, + Latin *testari* = say on oath]

Protestant (**prot**-ĕ-stănt) *noun* a member of any of the Christian bodies that separated from the Church of Rome in the Reformation, or of their later branches. **Protestantism** *noun* [because in the 16th century many people protested (= declared firmly) their opposition to the Catholic Church]

protestation (prot-ĕ-**stay**-shŏn) *noun* a firm declaration, *protestations of loyalty.*

Proteus (**proh**-tee-ŭs) (*Gk. myth.*) a sea god with the power of assuming different shapes.

proto- *prefix* first. [from Greek *protos* = first or earliest]

protocol (**proh**-tŏ-kol) *noun* **1** etiquette with regard to people's rank or status. **2** the first or original draft of an agreement (especially between States), signed by those making it, in preparation for a treaty. **3** (in computing etc.) a set of rules governing communication or the transmission of information.

proton (**proh**-ton) *noun* a particle of matter with a positive electric charge. □ **proton number** the number of protons in a nucleus.

protoplasm (**proh**-tŏ-plazm) *noun* the contents of a living cell, consisting of a nucleus enclosed in cytoplasm. **protoplasmic** *adjective* [from *proto*- + *plasma*]

prototype (**proh**-tŏ-typ) *noun* a first or original example of something from which others have been or will be developed, a trial model (e.g. of an aircraft). [from *proto*- + *type*]

protozoon (proh-tŏ-**zoh**-ŏn) *noun* (*plural* **protozoa**) a minute usually microscopic animal. **protozoan** *adjective* & *noun* [from *proto*-, + Greek *zoion* = animal]

protract (prŏ-**trakt**) *verb* to prolong in duration. **protraction** *noun* [from *pro*-, + Latin *tractum* = drawn out]

protractor *noun* an instrument for measuring angles, usually a semicircle marked off in degrees.

protrude *verb* to project from a surface. **protrusion** *noun*, **protrusive** *adjective* [from *pro*-, + Latin *trudere* = to push]

protuberance *noun* a protuberant part.

protuberant (prŏ-**tew**-bĕ-rănt) *adjective* bulging outwards from a surface. [from *pro*-, + Latin *tuber* = a swelling]

proud *adjective* **1** feeling or showing justifiable pride. **2** marked by such feeling, *a proud day for us.* **3** full of self-respect and independence, *too proud to ask for help.* **4** having an unduly high opinion of one's own qualities or merits. **5** slightly projecting; (of flesh) overgrown round a healing wound.
–**proud** *adverb* (*informal*) proudly; *they did us proud,* treated us lavishly or with great honour. **proudly** *adverb* [from Old French *prud* = brave]

Proust (*pr.* proost), Marcel (1871–1922), French novelist, essayist, and critic.

provable *adjective* able to be proved.

prove *verb* **1** to give or be proof of. **2** to establish the validity of (a will). **3** to be found to be, *it proved to be a good thing.* **4** (of dough) to rise because of the action of yeast, before being baked. □ **prove oneself** to show that one has the required character or abilities. [from Latin *probare* = to test]

proven (**proo**-vĕn) *adjective* proved, *a person of proven ability.*

provenance (**prov**-ĕ-năns) *noun* a place of origin. [from *pro*-, + Latin *venire* = come]

Provence (prov-**ahns**) a district of SE France containing the French Riviera. **Provençal** (prov-ahn-**sahl**) *adjective* & *noun*

provender (**prov**-ĕn-der) *noun* **1** fodder. **2** (*humorous*) food.

proverb *noun* a short well-known saying stating a general truth, e.g. *many hands make light work.* **Proverbs** *noun* a book of the Old Testament, containing proverbs ascribed to Solomon. [from *pro*-, + Latin *verbum* = word]

proverbial (prŏ-**verb**-ee-ăl) *adjective* **1** of or like a proverb; mentioned in a proverb. **2** well-known, notorious, *his meanness is proverbial.* **proverbially** *adverb*

provide *verb* **1** to cause (a person) to have possession or use of something; to supply. **2** to give or supply the necessities of life, *has to provide for his family.* **3** to make suitable preparation for something, *try to provide against emergencies.* **provider** *noun* [from Latin *providere* = foresee]

provided *conjunction* on the condition, *we will come provided that our expenses are paid.*

providence *noun* 1 being provident. 2 God's or nature's care and protection. 3 Providence God.

provident *adjective* showing wise forethought for future needs or events, thrifty. [same origin as *provide*]

providential (prov-ĭ-**den**-shǎl) *adjective* happening very luckily. providentially *adverb*

providing *conjunction* = provided.

province *noun* 1 one of the principal administrative divisions in certain countries. 2 a sphere of knowledge, learning, responsibility, or concern, *estimates of expenditure are the treasurer's province.* □ the provinces the whole of a country outside its capital city.

provincial (prŏ-**vin**-shǎl) *adjective* 1 of a province or provinces, *provincial government.* 2 having only limited interests and narrow-minded views, *provincial attitudes.* –provincial *noun* a native or inhabitant of a province or of the provinces. provincialism *noun*

provision *noun* 1 providing; preparation of resources etc. for future needs, *made provision for their old age.* 2 a statement or clause in a treaty or contract etc. stipulating something, *under the provisions of his will.* –provision *verb* to supply with provisions of food etc. provisions *plural noun* a supply of food and drink.

provisional *adjective* arranged or agreed upon temporarily but possibly to be altered later. □ provisional licence a driver's licence issued to a newly qualified driver, which imposes certain restrictions. (In some states called a *probationary licence.*) provisionally *adverb*

proviso (prŏ-**vy**-zoh) *noun* (*plural* provisos) something that is insisted upon as a condition of an agreement.

provisory (prŏ-**vy**-zŏ-ree) *adjective* conditional.

provocation *noun* 1 provoking; being provoked. 2 something that provokes anger or retaliation.

provocative (prŏ-**vok**-ǎ-tiv) *adjective* 1 arousing or likely to arouse anger, interest, or sexual desire. 2 deliberately annoying. provocatively *adverb*

provoke *verb* 1 to make angry. 2 to rouse or incite (a person) to action. 3 to produce as a reaction or effect. [from *pro-*, + Latin *vocare* = summon]

provoking *adjective* annoying.

provost (**prov**-ŏst) *noun* 1 the head of certain colleges, schools, etc. 2 the head of the chapter in certain cathedrals.

prow (*rhymes with* cow) *noun* the projecting front part of a ship or boat.

prowess (-ow- *as in* cow) *noun* great ability or daring.

prowl *verb* 1 to go about stealthily in search of prey or plunder or to catch others unawares. 2 to pace or wander restlessly. –prowl *noun* prowling, *on the prowl.* prowler *noun*

proximate (**proks**-ĭ-mǎt) *adjective* nearest, next before or after.

proximity (proks-**im**-ĭ-tee) *noun* 1 nearness in space or time. 2 neighbourhood, *in the proximity of the school.* [from Latin *proximus* = nearest]

proxy *noun* a person authorised to represent or act for another, the use of such a person, *voted by proxy.*

prude (*pr.* prood) *noun* a person of extreme or exaggerated propriety concerning behaviour or speech; one who is easily shocked by sexual matters. prudery *noun*

prudent *adjective* showing carefulness and foresight, avoiding rashness. prudently *adverb*, prudence *noun* [same origin as *provide*]

prudential (proo-**den**-shǎl) *adjective* showing or involving prudence. prudentially *adverb*

prudish (**proo**-dish) *adjective* like a prude, showing prudery. prudishly *adverb*, prudishness *noun*

prune¹ *noun* a dried plum.

prune² *verb* 1 to trim by cutting away dead or overgrown branches or shoots. 2 to improve by removing unnecessary parts. 3 to reduce, *costs must be pruned.*

Prussian *adjective* of Prussia, a former country of north Europe. –Prussian *noun* a Prussian person. □ Prussian blue a deep blue colour.

prussic acid *noun* a highly poisonous acid, hydrocyanic acid.

pry *verb* (**pried**, **prying**) to inquire or investigate or peer impertinently (and often furtively).

PS *abbreviation* postscript.

psalm (*pr.* sahm) *noun* a sacred song, especially one of those in the Book of Psalms in the Old Testament. [from Greek, = song sung to the harp]

psalmist (**sahm**-ĭst) *noun* a writer of psalms.

psalter (**sawl**-ter) *noun* a copy of the Book of Psalms.

pseudo (s'**yoo**-doh) *adjective* false, insincere.

pseudo- *prefix* false. [Greek, = false]

pseudonym (s'**yoo**-dŏ-nim) *noun* a false name used by an author. [from *pseudo*, + Greek *onoma* = name]

pseudopodium (s'yoo-dŏ-**poh**-dee-ŭm) *noun* (*plural* **pseudopodia**) a temporary protrusion of cell tissue used for movement, feeding, etc., by some protozoa and other animals. [from *pseudo-*, + Greek *podos* = of a foot]

psoriasis (sŏ-**ry**-ă-sĭs) *noun* a skin disease causing red scaly patches.

psst *interjection* an exclamation to attract someone's attention furtively.

psych (*pr.* syk) *verb* (*informal*) **1** to work out the intentions of (a person) or the solution of (a problem) by use of psychology. **2** to intimidate (a person) by making him or her feel uneasy. □ **psych up** (*informal*) to make (oneself or another person) ready emotionally.

psyche (**sy**-kee) *noun* **1** the human soul or spirit. **2** the human mind. [Greek]

psychedelic (sy-kĕ-**del**-ik) *adjective* **1** of or producing hallucinations and similar experiences full of vivid or luminous colours. **2** (of colours, patterns, etc.) vivid, colourful, often abstract. [from *psyche*, + Greek *delos* = clear]

psychiatrist (sy-**ky**-ă-trĭst) *noun* a specialist in psychiatry. [from *psycho-*, + Greek *iatreia* = healing]

psychiatry (sy-**ky**-ă-tree) *noun* the study and treatment of mental disease. **psychiatric** (sy-kee-**at**-rik) *adjective*

psychic (**sy**-kik) *adjective* **1** of the soul or mind. **2** concerned with processes that seem to be outside physical or natural laws, having or involving extrasensory perception or occult powers. **psychically** *adverb* [same origin as *psycho-*]

psychical (**sy**-kik-ăl) *adjective* psychic, *psychical research*. **psychically** *adverb*

psycho- *prefix* of the mind. [from *psyche*]

psychoanalyse *verb* to treat (a person) by psychoanalysis.

psychoanalysis *noun* a method of examining or treating mental conditions that involves bringing to light certain things in a person's unconscious mind that may be influencing behaviour and mental state. **psychoanalytic** *adjective*, **psychoanalytical** *adjective*

psychoanalyst *noun* a specialist in psychoanalysis.

psychological *adjective* **1** of or affecting the mind and its workings. **2** of psychology. □ **psychological warfare** actions or propaganda etc. designed to weaken an enemy's morale. **psychologically** *adverb*

psychologist *noun* a specialist or expert in psychology.

psychology *noun* **1** the study of the mind (as deduced from behaviour) and how it works. **2** mental characteristics. [from *psycho-* + *-logy*]

psychopath (**sy**-kŏ-path) *noun* a person suffering from a severe mental disorder, especially with aggressive antisocial behaviour. **psychopathic** (sy-kŏ-**pa**-thik) *adjective*

psychosis (sy-**koh**-sĭs) *noun* (*plural* **psychoses**) a severe mental disorder involving a person's whole personality.

psychosomatic (sy-kŏ-sŏ-**mat**-ik) *adjective* of or involving both the mind and the body; *psychosomatic illness*, one that is caused or aggravated by mental stress. **psychosomatically** *adverb* [from *psycho-*, + Greek *somatos* = of the body]

psychotherapy (sy-kŏ-th'**e**-ră-pee) *noun* the treatment of mental disorders by the use of psychological methods. **psychotherapist** *noun*

psychotic (sy-**kot**-ik) *adjective* of or suffering from a psychosis. –**psychotic** *noun* a person suffering from a psychosis.

PT *abbreviation* physical training.

pt. *abbreviation* pint.

pterodactyl (te-rŏ-**dak**-til) *noun* a kind of extinct reptile with wings. [from Greek *pteron* = wing, + *daktulos* = finger]

PTO *abbreviation* please turn over.

Ptolemy (2nd century), Greek astronomer and geographer, who worked in Alexandria, and developed the theory that the earth was the stationary centre of the universe. **Ptolemaic** *adjective*

Pty *abbreviation* Proprietary.

pub *noun* (*informal*) a place licensed to sell alcoholic drinks to the general public for consumption on the premises, often providing meals and accommodation to travellers. [short for *public house*]

puberty (**pew**-ber-tee) *noun* the stage at which a person's reproductive organs are in the process of becoming mature and he or she becomes capable of producing offspring. **pubertal** *adjective*

pubescence (pew-**bess**-ĕns) *noun* **1** the beginning of puberty. **2** a soft down on plants, insects, etc. **pubescent** *adjective*

pubic (**pew**-bik) *adjective* of the lower part of the abdomen, at the front of the pelvis, *pubic hair*.

public *adjective* of, for, or known to people in general, not private. –**public** *noun* members of the community in general or a particular section of this, *the Australian public*.
☐ **in public** openly, not in private. **public address system** a system of loudspeakers etc. to make speech or music audible over a wide area. **public company** a business company whose shares may be bought and sold on the open market. **public prosecutor** a law officer conducting prosecutions on behalf of the State or in the public interest. **public relations** the promotion of goodwill between an organisation etc. and the general public. **public school** (in Australia, Scotland, USA, etc.) a school funded and managed by the State (also called a *government school*); (in England and Wales) a secondary school (usually a boarding school) for fee-paying pupils. **public sector** all the businesses etc. that are owned or controlled by the State, not by private enterprise. **public servant** (*Austral*.) an employee of the **public service**, all government departments, apart from the armed services. **public spirit** readiness to do things for the benefit of people in general. **public-spirited** *adjective* showing public spirit. [from Latin *publicus* = of the people]

publican *noun* **1** a hotel-keeper. **2** (in the Bible) a tax collector.

publication *noun* **1** publishing; being published. **2** something published, e.g. a book or newspaper.

publicise *verb* (also **-ize**) to bring to the attention of the public, to advertise.

publicist *noun* a person who draws public attention to a person or thing.

publicity *noun* **1** public attention directed upon a person or thing. **2** the process of drawing public attention to a person or thing; the spoken, written, or other material by which this is done.

publicly *adverb* in public, openly.

publish *verb* **1** to issue copies of (a book etc.) to the public. **2** to make generally known. **3** to announce formally, *publish the banns of marriage*. [from *public*]

publisher *noun* a person or firm that issues copies of a book or newspaper etc. to the public (distinguished from a *printer* who prints books etc. but does not issue them).

Puccini (puu-**chee**-nee), Giacomo (1858–1924), Italian composer, best known for his operas *Tosca* and *La Bohème*.

puce (*pr.* pewss) *adjective* & *noun* brownish-purple. [French, = flea-colour]

puck *noun* the hard rubber disc used in ice hockey.

pucker *verb* to come together in small wrinkles or bulges; to cause to do this. –**pucker** *noun* a wrinkle or bulge made in this way.

puckish *adjective* impish.

pudding *noun* **1** a sweet or savoury dish, especially one containing flour, suet, etc., cooked by baking, boiling, or steaming, *Christmas pudding*; *steak and kidney pudding*. **2** a cold light or creamy dessert. **3** a kind of sausage, *black pudding* (see **black**). **4** (*informal*) a fat and rather stupid person.

puddle *noun* a small pool of rainwater on a road or other liquid on a surface. –**puddle** *verb* **1** to stir (molten iron) so as to expel carbon and produce wrought iron. **2** to work into a wet mixture.

pudenda (pew-**den**-dă) *plural noun* the genitals, especially of a woman. **pudendal** *adjective* [from Latin *pudere* = be ashamed]

pudgy *adjective* (**pudgier**, **pudgiest**) podgy.

Pueblo (**pweb**-loh) *noun* (*plural* **Pueblos**) a member of certain indigenous American peoples living in pueblo settlements. –**pueblo** *noun* (*plural* **pueblos**) a town or village in Spain, Central America, or the SW USA, especially a Pueblo settlement.

puerile (**pyoor**-ryl) *adjective* showing immaturity, suitable only for children, *asking puerile questions*. **puerility** (pyoor-**ril**-ĭ-tee) *noun* [from Latin *puer* = boy]

puerperal (pew-**er**-pĕ-răl) *adjective* of or associated with childbirth, *puerperal fever*.

Puerto Rico (pwer-toh **ree**-koh) an island in the West Indies. **Puerto Rican** *adjective* & *noun*

puff *noun* 1 a short light blowing of breath or wind etc.; smoke or vapour sent out by this. 2 a powder puff. 3 a cake of puff pastry or choux pastry filled with cream etc., *cream puffs*. 4 a piece of extravagant praise in a review or advertisement for a book or play etc. –**puff** *verb* 1 to send out a puff or puffs; to blow (smoke etc.) in puffs; to smoke (a pipe etc.) in puffs. 2 to breathe hard, to pant. 3 to make or become inflated, to swell. 4 to advertise with extravagant praise.
□ **puff adder** a large poisonous African viper that inflates the upper part of its body when excited. **puff pastry** very light flaky pastry. **puff sleeve** or **puffed sleeve** a sleeve that is very full at the shoulder.

puffball *noun* a fungus with a ball-shaped spore case that bursts open when ripe.

puffin *noun* a seabird with a short striped bill.

puffy *adjective* (**puffier**, **puffiest**) puffed out, swollen. **puffiness** *noun*

pug *noun* a dog of a dwarf breed resembling the bulldog. □ **pug-nosed** *adjective* having a short flattish nose.

pugilist (**pew**-jĭ-lĭst) *noun* a professional boxer. **pugilism** *noun*, **pugilistic** *adjective*

pugnacious (pug-**nay**-shŭs) *adjective* eager to fight, aggressive. **pugnaciously** *adverb*, **pugnacity** (pug-**nas**-ĭ-tee) *noun* [from Latin *pugnare* = to fight]

puissance (**pwee**-săns) *noun* (in showjumping) a test of a horse's ability to jump high obstacles.

puja (**poo**-jă) *noun* a Hindu act of worship, often involving an offering of flowers.

puke *verb* (*informal*) to vomit.

pukka (**puk**-ă) *adjective* (*informal*) real, genuine.

Pulitzer (**puul**-ĭt-ser), Joseph (1847–1911), American newspaper owner and editor.
□ **Pulitzer Prize** any of a group of money prizes established under his will and offered annually to American citizens for work in music, journalism, American history, and literature.

pull *verb* 1 to exert force upon (a thing) so as to move it towards oneself or towards the source of the force; *pull a muscle*, damage it by abnormal strain; *pull a gun*, draw it and prepare to use it; *pull a horse*, to check it so as to lose a race. 2 to remove by pulling, *pull the cork*. 3 to propel (a boat) by pulling on its oars. 4 (in cricket) to strike the ball to the leg side; (in golf) to hit the ball widely to the left. 5 to exert a pulling or driving force, *the engine is pulling well*. 6 to attract, *attractions that pull the crowds*. –**pull** *noun* 1 the act of pulling; the force exerted by this. 2 a means of exerting influence. 3 a deep draught of a drink; a draw at a pipe etc. 4 a prolonged effort in walking etc., *the long pull up the hill*.
□ **pull a fast one** (*informal*) to act unfairly in order to gain an advantage. **pull a person's leg** to deceive a person playfully. **pull back** to retreat or withdraw; to cause to do this. **pull down** to demolish; to cause general weakness or ill health in, *his illness pulled him down*. **pull in** to obtain as wages or profit; (of a train) to enter and stop at a station; (of a vehicle) to move to the side of the road or off the road; (*informal*) to take into custody. **pull off** to succeed in achieving or winning something. **pull oneself together** to regain one's self-control. **pull one's punches** to avoid using one's full force. **pull one's weight** to do one's fair share of work. **pull out** to withdraw or cause to withdraw; (of a train) to move out of a station; (of a vehicle) to move away from the side of a road, or from behind another vehicle to overtake it. **pull rank** to make unfair use of one's senior rank in demanding obedience or a privilege. **pull round** to recover or cause to recover from illness. **pull strings** to use one's influence, often secretly. **pull through** to come or bring successfully through an illness or difficulty. **pull together** to cooperate. **pull up** to stop or cause (a person or vehicle etc.) to stop; to reprimand.

pullet *noun* a young domestic hen from the time of beginning to lay until the first moult.

pulley *noun* (*plural* **pulleys**) a wheel over which a rope, chain, or belt passes, used in lifting things or to drive or be driven by an endless belt.

pullover *noun* a knitted garment (with no fastenings) for the upper part of the body, put on over the head.

pulmonary (**pul**-mŏ-nă-ree) *adjective* of or affecting the lungs. [from Latin *pulmo* = lung]

pulp *noun* 1 the soft moist part of fruit. 2 the soft tissue inside a tooth. 3 any soft moist mass of material, especially of wood fibre as used for making paper. –**pulp** *verb* to reduce to pulp; to become pulpy. □ **pulp fiction** cheap popular books etc. (originally printed on rough paper).

pulpit *noun* a raised enclosed platform (as in a church or chapel), used in preaching or conducting a religious service.

pulpy *adjective* like pulp; containing much pulp. **pulpiness** *noun*

pulsar *noun* a source (in space) of radio signals that pulsate in a rapid regular rhythm.

pulsate (pul-**sayt**) *verb* to expand and contract rhythmically; to vibrate, to quiver. **pulsation** *noun*, **pulsator** *noun*

pulse¹ *noun* 1 the rhythmical throbbing of the arteries as blood is propelled along them; this as felt in the wrists or temples etc. 2 any steady throb. 3 a single beat or throb. –**pulse** *verb* to pulsate. [from Latin *pulsum* = driven, beaten]

pulse² *noun* the edible seed of peas, beans, lentils, etc.

pulverise *verb* (also -**ize**) 1 to crush into powder. 2 to become powder. 3 to defeat thoroughly. **pulverisation** *noun* [from Latin *pulveris* = of dust]

puma (**pew**-mă) *noun* a large brown American animal of the cat family.

pumice (**pum**-ĭss) *noun* a light porous kind of lava used for rubbing stains from the skin or as powder for polishing things.
□ **pumice stone** pumice; a piece of this.

pummel *verb* (**pummelled**, **pummelling**) to strike repeatedly, especially with the fist(s).

pump¹ *noun* 1 a machine or device for forcing liquid, air, or gas into or out of something. 2 a fire engine with pumping apparatus. 3 a machine for raising water for domestic use. –**pump** *verb* 1 to raise, move, or inflate by means of a pump. 2 to use a pump. 3 to empty by using a pump, *pump the ship dry*. 4 to move vigorously up and down like a pump handle. 5 to pour or cause to pour forth as if by pumping. 6 to question (a person) persistently to obtain information.

pump² *noun* a light shoe worn for dancing etc.

pumpernickel *noun* German wholemeal rye bread.

pumpkin *noun* the large round orange-coloured fruit of a trailing plant, used as a vegetable or as a filling for pies.

pun *noun* a humorous use of a word to suggest another that sounds the same; a play on words, e.g. 'the sole has no feet and therefore no sole,

poor soul'. –**pun** *verb* (**punned**, **punning**) to make a pun or puns.

punch¹ *verb* 1 to strike with the fist. 2 (*Amer.*) to herd, *cattle-punching*. –**punch** *noun* 1 a blow with the fist. 2 (*informal*) vigour, effective force, *a speech with plenty of punch in it*. □ **punch-drunk** *adjective* stupefied from or as if from being punched.

punch² *noun* a device for making holes in metal or leather, or for stamping a design on material. –**punch** *verb* to perforate with a punch; to make (a hole etc.) with a punch. [same origin as *puncture*]

punch³ *noun* a drink made of wine, spirits, or cold tea mixed with fruit juices, soft drinks, etc.

punchline *noun* words that give the climax of a joke or story.

punchy *adjective* having vigour, forceful.

punctilious (punk-**til**-ee-ŭs) *adjective* very careful to carry out duties or details of ceremony etc. correctly, conscientious. **punctiliously** *adverb*, **punctiliousness** *noun* [from Latin *punctillum* = little point]

punctual *adjective* arriving or doing things at the appointed time, neither early nor late. **punctually** *adverb*, **punctuality** *noun*

punctuate *verb* 1 to insert punctuation marks in. 2 to interrupt at intervals, *his speech was punctuated with cheers*. [from Latin *punctum* = a point]

punctuation *noun* punctuating; the marks used for this. □ **punctuation mark** any of the marks (e.g. full stop, comma, question mark) used in written or printed material to separate sentences etc. and to make the meaning clear.

puncture *noun* a small hole made by something sharp, especially one made accidentally in a pneumatic tyre. –**puncture** *verb* 1 to make a puncture in; to suffer a puncture. 2 to reduce the pride or confidence of, *punctured his conceit*. [from Latin *punctum* = pricked]

pundit *noun* a person who is an authority on a subject. [from Hindi *pandit* = learned (person)]

pungent (**pun**-jĕnt) *adjective* 1 having a strong sharp taste or smell. 2 (of remarks) penetrating, biting. 3 mentally stimulating. **pungently** *adverb*, **pungency** *noun* [from Latin *pungens* = pricking]

Punic Wars three wars between Rome and Carthage in the 3rd and 2nd centuries BC.

punish *verb* **1** to cause (an offender) to suffer for his or her offence. **2** to inflict a punishment for, *vandalism should be severely punished.* **3** to treat roughly, to test severely, *the race was run at a punishing pace.* [from Latin *poena* = penalty]

punishable *adjective* liable to be punished, especially by law, *punishable offences.*

punishment *noun* **1** punishing; being punished. **2** that which an offender is made to suffer because of his or her wrongdoing.

punitive (**pew**-nĭ-tiv) *adjective* inflicting or intended to inflict punishment.

Punjab (**pun**-jahb) a State of NW India. **Punjabi** *adjective* & *noun*

punk *noun* **1** (in full **punk rock**) a deliberately outrageous style of rock music. **2** (in full **punk rocker**) a devotee of punk rock. **3** (*informal*) a young hooligan, a lout. –**punk** *adjective* **1** of punk rock or its devotees. **2** (*informal*) worthless.

punnet (**pun**-ĕt) *noun* a small container for seedlings or soft fruit, especially berries.

punt[1] *noun* a flat-bottomed boat propelled by thrusting a pole against the bottom of a river. –**punt** *verb* **1** to propel (a punt) with a pole in this way. **2** to carry or travel in a punt. **punter** *noun*

punt[2] *verb* to kick (a football) after it has dropped from the hands and before it touches the ground. –**punt** *noun* a kick of this kind. **punter** *noun*

punt[3] *verb* **1** to lay a stake against the bank in certain card games. **2** (*informal*) to bet on a horse etc.; to speculate in shares. –**punt** *noun* a bet. **punter** *noun*

puny (**pew**-nee) *adjective* (**punier**, **puniest**) undersized; feeble.

pup *noun* **1** a young dog; *in pup*, (of a bitch) pregnant. **2** a young wolf, rat, or seal. –**pup** *verb* (**pupped**, **pupping**) to give birth to a pup or pups. ☐ **sell someone a pup** to swindle a person by pretending that the thing sold is more valuable than it really is.

pupa (**pew**-pă) *noun* (*plural* **pupae**, *pr.* **pew**-pee) a chrysalis. **pupal** *adjective*

pupate (pew-**payt**) *verb* to become a pupa. **pupation** *noun*

pupil *noun* **1** a person who is taught by another. **2** an opening in the centre of the iris of the eye, through which light passes to the retina. [from Latin *pupilla* = little girl or doll

(the use in sense 2 refers to the tiny images of people and things that can be seen in the eye)]

puppet *noun* **1** a kind of doll that can be made to move by various means as an entertainment. **2** a person or group whose actions are entirely controlled by another.

puppeteer *noun* a person who works puppets.

puppetry *noun* manipulation of puppets.

puppy *noun* a young dog. ☐ **puppy fat** temporary fatness of a child or adolescent.

purblind (**per**-blynd) *adjective* **1** partially blind, dim-sighted. **2** stupid, dim-witted.

Purcell (**per**-sĕl), Henry (1659–95), the first English opera composer.

purchase *verb* to buy. –**purchase** *noun* **1** buying. **2** something bought. **3** a firm hold to pull or raise something or prevent it from slipping, leverage. **purchaser** *noun*

purdah (**per**-dă) *noun* the system in some Muslim or Hindu communities of keeping women from the sight of men or strangers. [Urdu, = veil]

pure *adjective* **1** not mixed with any other substance, free from impurities. **2** mere, nothing but, *pure nonsense.* **3** free from evil or sin. **4** chaste. **5** dealing with theory only, not with practical applications, *pure mathematics.* **pureness** *noun*

purée (**pew**-ray) *noun* pulped fruit or vegetables etc. –**purée** *verb* (**puréed**, **puréeing**) to make into purée. [French, = squeezed]

purely *adverb* **1** in a pure way. **2** entirely, only, *he acquired books purely for show.*

purgative (**per**-gă-tiv) *noun* a strong laxative.

purgatory (**per**-gă-tŏ-ree) *noun* **1** (in RC and Orthodox belief) a place or condition in which souls undergo purification by temporary punishment. **2** a place or condition of suffering. **purgatorial** (per-gă-**tor**-ree-ăl) *adjective* [same origin as *purge*]

purge (*pr.* perj) *verb* **1** to cause emptying of the bowels of (a person) by means of a purgative. **2** to rid of people or things considered undesirable or harmful. **3** to atone for (an offence, especially contempt of court). –**purge** *noun* **1** purging, ridding of undesirable things etc. **2** a purgative. [from Latin *purgare* = make pure]

purify *verb* (**purified**, **purifying**) to make pure, to cleanse from impurities. **purifier** *noun*, **purification** *noun*, **purificatory** *adjective*

Purim (puu-**reem**) *noun* a Jewish festival commemorating the defeat of Haman's plot to massacre the Jews.

purist *noun* a stickler for correctness, especially in language. **purism** *noun*

Puritan *noun* a member of the party of English Protestants in the 16th and 17th centuries who wanted simpler forms of church ceremony and strictness and gravity in behaviour. **–puritan** *noun* a person who is extremely strict in morals and who looks upon some kinds of fun and pleasure as sinful. **puritanical** (pew-rĭ-**tan**-i-kăl) *adjective* [from Latin *puritas* = purity]

purity *noun* pureness.

purl[1] *noun* a knitting stitch that produces a ridge towards the knitter. **–purl** *verb* to make this stitch. [from Scottish *pirl* = twist]

purl[2] *verb* (of a stream) to flow with a swirling motion and babbling sound.

purler *noun* (*informal*) a headlong fall.

purlieu (**perl**-yoo) *noun* one's usual haunts. **purlieus** *plural noun* the outskirts of a place.

purloin (per-**loin**) *verb* (*formal* or *humorous use*) to steal.

purple *noun* a colour obtained by mixing red and blue. **–purple** *adjective* of this colour. **–purple** *verb* to become purple. □ **purple passage** a very ornate passage in a literary work.

purport (**per**-port) *noun* the meaning or intention of something said or written. **–purport** (per-**port**) *verb* to pretend, to be intended to seem, *the letter purports to come from you*. **purportedly** *adverb*

purpose *noun* 1 an intended result, something for which effort is being made, *this will serve our purpose*. 2 intention to act, determination. **–purpose** *verb* to intend. □ **on purpose** by intention in order to do something, not by chance. **purpose-built** *adjective* built for a particular purpose. **to no purpose** with no result. [same origin as *propose*]

purposeful *adjective* having or showing a particular purpose, with determination. **purposefully** *adverb*, **purposefulness** *noun*

purposeless *adjective* without a purpose.

purposely *adverb* on purpose.

purr *verb* 1 (of a cat etc.) to make the low vibrant sound that a cat makes when pleased. 2 (of machinery etc.) to make a similar sound. **–purr** *verb* a purring sound.

purse *noun* 1 a small pouch of leather etc. for carrying money. 2 (*Amer.*) a handbag. 3 money, funds. 4 a sum of money as a present or prize. **–purse** *verb* to pucker, *pursing her lips*. □ **hold the purse strings** to have control of expenditure. [from Latin *bursa* = a bag]

purser *noun* a ship's officer in charge of accounts, especially on a passenger ship. [from *purse*]

pursuance *noun* performance or carrying out of something, *in pursuance of my duties*.

pursuant *adverb* **pursuant to** in accordance with.

pursue *verb* 1 to chase in order to catch or kill. 2 to afflict continually, *was pursued by misfortunes*. 3 to continue, to proceed along, *we pursued our course*. 4 to engage in, *pursuing her hobby*. **pursuer** *noun*

pursuit *noun* 1 pursuing, *in pursuit of the fox*. 2 an activity, something at which one works or gives one's time.

purvey (per-**vay**) *verb* (**purveyed**, **purveying**) to supply (articles of food) as a trader. **purveyor** *noun* [same origin as *provide*]

pus *noun* thick yellowish matter produced by inflamed or infected tissue.

push *verb* 1 to exert force upon (a thing) so as to move it away from oneself or from the source of the force; *push one's way*, go forward by pushing. 2 to thrust or cause to thrust outwards. 3 to extend by effort, *the frontier was pushed further west*. 4 to make a vigorous effort in order to succeed or to surpass others. 5 to press (a person) to do something, to put a strain on the abilities or tolerance of, *don't push him for payment*. 6 to urge the use or adoption of (goods or ideas etc.), e.g. by advertisement; *push drugs*, sell them illegally. **–push** *noun* 1 the act of pushing, the force exerted by this. 2 a vigorous effort; a military attack made in order to advance. 3 enterprise, self-assertion, determination to get on. 4 (*Austral.*) a gang. □ **at a push** in time of difficulty or necessity. **give** or **get the push** (*informal*) to dismiss or be dismissed (from one's job etc.). **push around** to treat contemptuously and unfairly; to bully. **push off** (*informal*) to go away. **push one's luck** (*informal*) to take undue risks. **push-start** *verb* to start (a motor vehicle) by pushing it along to turn the engine; (*noun*) a start made in this way. **push-up** *noun* an exercise in which a person lies face downwards and presses down on the hands so that the shoulders and trunk are raised.

pushbike *noun* a bicycle.

pushbutton *noun* a button to be pushed to operate an electrical device. –**pushbutton** *adjective* operated in this way.

pushchair *noun* a folding chair on wheels, in which a child can be pushed along.

pusher *noun* **1** a seller of illegal drugs. **2** (*Austral.*) a pushchair, a stroller.

pushful *adjective* pushy.

pushing *adjective* (of a person) **1** pushy. **2** (*informal*) having nearly reached a (specified age), *pushing forty*.

pushover *noun* (*informal*) **1** something that is easily done. **2** a person who is easily convinced or charmed etc.

Pushkin, Alexander Sergeevich (1799–1837), the first national poet of Russia.

pushy *adjective* self-assertive, determined to get on. **pushiness** *noun*

pusillanimous (pew-sĭ-**lan**-ĭ-mŭs) *adjective* timid, cowardly. [from Latin *pusillus* = small, + *animus* = mind]

puss *noun* a cat.

pussy *noun* (*informal*) a cat.
□ **pussy willow** a willow with furry catkins.

pussyfoot *verb* (*informal*) **1** to move stealthily. **2** to act cautiously, to avoid committing oneself.

pustule (**pus**-tewl) *noun* a pimple or blister, especially one containing pus. **pustular** *adjective*

put *verb* (**put, putting**) **1** to move (a thing) to a specified place; to cause to occupy a certain place or position; to send. **2** to cause to be in a certain state or relationship, *put the machine out of action*; *put her at her ease*. **3** to subject, *put it to the test*. **4** to estimate, *I put the cost at $400*. **5** to express or state, *put it tactfully*. **6** to impose as a tax etc. **7** to stake (money) in a bet. **8** to place as an investment, *put his money into land*. **9** to lay (blame) on. **10** (of ships) to proceed, *put into harbour*. **11** to hurl (a shot or weight) as an athletic sport. –**put** *noun* a throw of the shot or weight. □ **be hard put** to have difficulty in doing or providing something. **put across** to communicate (an idea etc.). **put away** (*informal*) to put into prison or a mental institution; to consume (food or drink). **put back** to return to its former place; to change (a planned event) to a later time. **put by** to save for future use. **put down** to suppress by force or authority; to snub; to have (an animal) destroyed; to enter (a person's name) as one

who will subscribe; to reckon or consider, *put him down as a fool*; to attribute, *put it down to nervousness*. **put-down** *noun* (*informal*) a snub. **put in** to make (an appearance); to enter (a claim); to spend (time) working. **put in for** to apply for. **put it on** (*informal*) to pretend an emotion. **put off** to postpone; to postpone an engagement with (a person); to make excuses and try to avoid; to dissuade, to repel, *the smell puts me off*. **put on** to stage (a play etc.); to increase, *putting on weight*; to cause to operate, *put the radio on*. **put one over a person** (*informal*) to make him or her believe something false. **put one's foot down** to insist on something firmly; to accelerate a motor vehicle. **put one's foot in it** to make a blunder. **put out** to disconcert, annoy, or inconvenience (a person); to extinguish (a light or fire); to dislocate (a joint). **put over** = put across. **put the clock back** to go back to a past age or an out-of-date practice. **put through** to complete (a business transaction) successfully; to connect by telephone; to cause to undergo, *put it through severe tests*. **put two and two together** to draw a conclusion from the facts one knows. **put up** to construct or build; to raise the price of; to provide or contribute, *the firm will put up the money*; to offer for sale; to display (a notice); to present as an idea or proposal; to give or receive accommodation; to attempt or offer, *they put up no resistance*. **put-up** *adjective* concocted fraudulently, *a put-up job*. **put up to** to persuade (a person) into, *who put him up to it?* **put up with** to endure, to tolerate.

putative (**pew**-tă-tiv) *adjective* reputed, supposed, *his putative father*.

putrefy (**pew**-trĕ-fy) *verb* (**putrefied, putrefying**) to rot, to decay or cause to decay. **putrefaction** (pew-trĕ-**fak**-shŏn) *noun* [from Latin *puter* = rotten]

putrescent (pew-**tress**-ĕnt) *adjective* decaying, rotting. **putrescence** *noun*

putrid (**pew**-trĭd) *adjective* **1** decomposed, rotting. **2** foul-smelling. **3** (*informal*) very distasteful or unpleasant.

putsch (*pr.* puuch) *noun* an attempt at political revolution; a violent uprising.

putt (*rhymes with* cut) *verb* to strike (a golf ball) lightly to make it roll along the ground. –**putt** *noun* a stroke of this kind.
□ **putting green** (in golf) a smooth area of grass round a hole.

puttee *noun* a strip of cloth wound spirally round the leg from ankle to knee for support or protection. [from Hindi *patti* = bandage]

putter *noun* a golf club used in putting.

putty *noun* a soft paste that sets hard, used for fixing glass in window frames, filling up holes, etc.

puzzle *noun* 1 a question that is difficult to answer; a problem. 2 a problem or toy designed to test one's knowledge, ingenuity, or patience. –**puzzle** *verb* to cause (a person etc.) to be uncertain about what a thing is or what to do because of its complex or difficult nature; to make hard thought necessary, *a puzzling problem*. □ **puzzle out** to solve or understand by patient thought or ingenuity. **puzzlement** *noun*

puzzler *noun* a puzzling problem.

PVC *abbreviation* polyvinyl chloride.

Pygmalion (pig-**may**-lee-ŏn) (*Gk. legend*) a king of Cyprus who made an ivory statue of a beautiful woman and loved it so deeply that at his request Aphrodite gave it life.

pygmy (**pig**-mee) *noun* 1 a person or thing of unusually small size. 2 a member of a dwarf Black people of equatorial Africa. –**pygmy** *adjective* very small.

pyjamas *plural noun* a suit of loose trousers and jacket or top for sleeping in. [from Urdu *pay jama* = leg-clothes]

pylon *noun* 1 a tall structure used as a support (especially for electricity cables) or as a boundary. 2 a monumental gateway, as at the entrance to an Egyptian temple. 3 a structure marking a path for aircraft. [from Greek *pule* = gate]

Pyongyang the capital of North Korea.

pyramid *noun* a structure with a flat (usually square) base and with sloping sides that meet at the top, especially one built by the ancient Egyptians as a tomb or by the Aztecs and Mayas as a platform for a temple.
□ **pyramid selling** a method of selling goods in which agency rights are sold to an increasing number of distributors at successively lower levels, with only those at the bottom of the

pyramid actually selling any goods. **pyramidal** (pi-**ram**-i-dăl) *adjective*

pyre (*rhymes with* fire) *noun* a pile of wood etc. for burning a corpse as part of a funeral rite. [from Greek *pur* = fire]

Pyrenees a range of mountains between France and Spain. **Pyrenean** *adjective*

pyrethrum (py-**reeth**-rŭm) *noun* 1 a kind of chrysanthemum with finely divided leaves. 2 an insecticide made from its dried flowers.

pyretic (py-**ret**-ik) *adjective* of or producing fever.

pyrex *noun* (*trademark*) a hard heat-resistant glass.

pyrites (py-**ry**-teez) *noun* a mineral that is a sulphide of iron (*iron pyrites*) or copper and iron (*copper pyrites*).

pyroclastic *adjective* (of rock) formed from fragments resulting from a volcanic eruption. [from Greek *pur* = fire, + *klastos* = broken]

pyromania (py-rŏ-**may**-nee-ă) *noun* an uncontrollable impulse to set things on fire. **pyromaniac** *noun* a person with such an impulse. [from Greek *pur* = fire, + *mania*]

pyrotechnic (py-rŏ-**tek**-nik) *adjective* of or like fireworks. **pyrotechnics** *plural noun* 1 the art of making fireworks. 2 a firework display. 3 any loud or brilliant display. [from Greek *pur* = fire, + *tekhne* = art]

Pyrrhic victory (**pi**-rik) *noun* a victory gained at too great a cost, like that of Pyrrhus (king of Epirus) over the Romans in 279 BC.

Pythagoras (py-**thag**-ŏ-răs) late 6th century BC, Greek philosopher and mathematician. □ **Pythagoras' theorem** the mathematical theorem that the square on the hypotenuse of a right-angled triangle is equal to the sum of the squares on the other two sides. **Pythagorean** *adjective & noun*

python (**py**-thŏn) *noun* a large snake that squeezes its prey so as to suffocate it.

pyx (*pr.* piks) *noun* a vessel in which bread consecrated for Holy Communion is kept.

Qq

Qantas (**kwon**-tăs) an Australian airline founded in 1920. [from the initials of Queensland and Northern Territory Aerial Services]

Qatar (ka-**tar**) a sheikhdom on the west coast of the Persian Gulf. **Qatari** *adjective & noun* (*plural* **Qataris**).

QC *abbreviation* Queen's Counsel.

QED *abbreviation* quod erat demonstrandum. [Latin, = which was the thing that had to be proved]

qibla *noun* = **kiblah**.

Qld. *abbreviation* Queensland.

qua (*pr*. kway) *conjunction* in the capacity or character of, *putting his duty qua citizen above other loyalties*. [Latin]

quack¹ *noun* the harsh cry of a duck. –**quack** *verb* to utter this sound. [imitation of the sound]

quack² *noun* **1** a person who falsely claims to have medical skill or to have remedies that will cure diseases etc. **2** (*informal*) any doctor. [from Dutch *quacken* = to boast]

quad¹ (*pr*. kwod) *noun* **1** a quadrangle. **2** each of a set of quadruplets.

quad² *adjective & noun* quadraphonic.

quadrangle (**kwod**-rang-gŭl) *noun* a four-sided court bordered by large buildings. [from *quadri-* + *angle¹*]

quadrant (**kwod**-rănt) *noun* **1** a quarter of a circle or of its circumference. **2** an instrument with an arc of 90° marked off in degrees, for measuring angles.

quadraphonic (kwod-ră-**fon**-ik) *adjective* (of sound reproduction) using four transmission channels. [from *quadri-*, + Greek *phone* = sound]

quadrat (**kwod**-răt) *noun* a small area of land taken as a sample for an ecological study.

quadratic (kwod-**rat**-ik) *adjective* **quadratic equation** an equation involving the square (and no higher power) of one or more of the unknown quantities or variables. **quadratics** *plural noun* such equations.

quadri- *prefix* four. [from Latin *quattuor* = four]

quadriceps (**kwod**-rĭ-seps) *noun* the four-headed muscle at the front of the thigh.

quadrilateral (kwod-rĭ-**lat**-ĕ-răl) *noun* a geometric figure with four sides. –**quadrilateral** *adjective* having four sides. [from *quadri-* + *lateral*]

quadrille (kwod-**ril**) *noun* a square dance for four couples; the music for this.

quadriplegia (kwod-rĭ-**plee**-jee-ă) *noun* paralysis of both arms and both legs. **quadriplegic** *adjective & noun* [from *quadri-* + Greek *plexis* = a stroke]

quadruped (**kwod**-rŭ-ped) *noun* a four-footed animal. [from *quadri-*, + Latin *pedis* = of a foot]

quadruple *adjective* **1** consisting of four parts; involving four people or groups, *a quadruple alliance*. **2** four times as much as, *we shall need quadruple that number of lights*. –**quadruple** *verb* to multiply or become multiplied by four; *costs had quadrupled*, had increased to four times the original amount. **quadruply** *adverb* [from *quadri-*]

quadruplet (kwod-**roo**-plĕt) *noun* each of four children born at one birth.

quadruplicate (kwod-**roo**-plĭ-kăt) *noun* **in quadruplicate** as four identical examples or copies.

quaestor (**kwee**-ster) *noun* a magistrate in ancient Rome who acted as the State treasurer etc.

quaff (*pr*. kwof) *verb* to drink (a thing) in long draughts.

quagmire (**kwog**-myr *or* **kwag**-myr) *noun* a bog or marsh.

quail¹ *noun* (*plural* **quail** *or* **quails**) a bird related to the partridge, used as food.

quail² *verb* to flinch, to show fear.

quaint *adjective* odd in a pleasing way, attractive through being unusual or old-fashioned. **quaintly** *adverb*, **quaintness** *noun*

quake *verb* to shake or tremble from unsteadiness; to shake with fear. –**quake** *noun* **1** a quaking movement. **2** (*informal*) an earthquake.

Quaker *noun* a member of the Society of Friends (*see* society). Quakerism *noun*

qualification *noun* **1** qualifying; being qualified. **2** a thing that qualifies a person to do something or to have a certain right etc. **3** something that limits or restricts a meaning, *this statement needs certain qualifications*. qualificatory *adjective*

qualify *verb* (qualified, qualifying) **1** to make or become competent, eligible, or legally entitled to do something. **2** to make (a statement etc.) less general or extreme, to limit its meaning, *'in all cases' needs to be qualified as 'in all known cases'; we gave it only qualified approval*, not complete approval. **3** to describe, to attribute some quality to, *they qualified him as ambitious*; *adjectives qualify nouns*. qualifier *noun*

qualitative (kwol-ĭ-tă-tiv) *adjective* of or concerned with the presence but not the quantity of a substance, *qualitative analysis*.

quality *noun* **1** a degree or level of excellence, *goods of high quality*. **2** general excellence, *it has quality*. **3** a characteristic, something that is special in a person or thing, *she has the quality of inspiring confidence*. [from Latin *qualis* = of what kind]

qualm (*pr.* kwahm) *noun* **1** a misgiving, a pang of conscience. **2** a sudden feeling of sickness or faintness.

quandary (kwon-dă-ree) *noun* a state of perplexity; a difficult situation.

quandong (kwon-dong) *noun* an Australian shrub or tree, especially one with red fruit containing an edible kernel. Also known as *native peach*. [Wiradjuri *guwandhaang*]

quango (kwang-goh) *noun* (*plural* quangos) an administrative body with financial support from and senior appointments made by the government but not controlled by it. [from the initials of *quasi-autonomous non-governmental organisation*]

quantify (kwon-tĭ-fy) *verb* (quantified, quantifying) to express as a quantity. quantifiable *adjective*, quantification *noun*

quantitative (kwon-tĭ-tă-tiv) *adjective* of or concerned with quantity, *quantitative analysis*.

quantity *noun* **1** an amount or number of things; a specified or considerable amount or number; *it is found in quantity* or *in quantities*, in large amounts. **2** ability to be measured through having size, weight, amount, or number. **3** a thing that has this ability; a

figure or symbol representing it. [from Latin *quantus* = how much]

quantum (kwon-tŭm) *noun* (*plural* quanta) **1** a minimum amount of a physical quantity (such as energy) that can exist in a given situation. **2** the amount required, desired, or allowed. □ quantum leap a sudden great advance. quantum theory a theory of physics based on the assumption that energy exists in indivisible units.

quarantine (kwo-răn-teen) *noun* **1** isolation imposed on people or animals who may have been exposed to an infectious or contagious disease that they could spread to others. **2** the period of this isolation. –quarantine *verb* to put into quarantine. [from Italian *quaranta* = forty (the original period of isolation was 40 days)]

quark *noun* any of a group of hypothetical components of elementary particles.

quarrel¹ *noun* **1** a violent disagreement; breaking of friendly relations. **2** a cause for complaint against a person or his or her actions, *we have no quarrel with him*. –quarrel *verb* (quarrelled, quarrelling) **1** to engage in a quarrel; to break off friendly relations. **2** to disagree or complain, *we are not quarrelling with this decision*. [from Latin *querela* = complaint]

quarrel² *noun* an arrow shot from a crossbow.

quarrelsome *adjective* liable to quarrel with people. quarrelsomeness *noun*

quarry¹ *noun* **1** an intended prey or victim being hunted. **2** something that is sought or pursued.

quarry² *noun* an open excavation from which stone or sand or clay etc. is obtained. –quarry *verb* (quarried, quarrying) **1** to obtain (stone etc.) from a quarry. **2** to search laboriously in order to extract information etc. □ quarry tile an unglazed floor tile.

quart *noun* a measure of capacity for liquids, 2 pints or a quarter of a gallon (a British quart = 1.136 litres).

quarter *noun* **1** each of the four equal parts into which a thing is divided. **2** a quarter of a US or Canadian dollar, 25 cents. **3** a fourth part of a year. **4** a fourth part of a lunar month. **5** a point of time 15 minutes before or after every hour. **6** a direction or point of the compass; a district; a division of a town. **7** a person or group, especially regarded as a possible source of help or information etc., *got no sympathy from that quarter*.

8 mercy towards an enemy or opponent, *gave no quarter*. **9** (in certain games) each of the four equal periods into which a match is divided. **–quarter** *verb* **1** to divide into quarters. **2** to place (a symbol) in one of the divisions of a shield or coat of arms. **3** to put (soldiers etc.) into lodgings. **4** (of a dog etc.) to search (ground) in every direction. **quarters** *plural noun* lodgings, accommodation. □ **quarter-final** *noun* one of the matches or rounds preceding a semifinal. **quarter-light** *noun* a small triangular window in a car. [from Latin *quartus* = fourth]

quarterdeck *noun* the part of the upper deck of a ship nearest the stern, usually reserved for the ship's officers.

quarterly *adjective* & *adverb* produced or occurring once in every quarter of the year. **–quarterly** *noun* a quarterly periodical.

quartermaster *noun* **1** (in the army) a regimental officer in charge of stores and assigning quarters etc. **2** a naval petty officer in charge of steering and signals etc.

quartet *noun* **1** a group of four instruments or voices; a musical composition for these. **2** a set of four.

quartile (**kwor**-tyl) *noun* **1** any of three points at which a range of statistical data is divided to make four groups of equal size. **2** any of these groups.

quarto *noun* the size of a book or page or sheet of paper given by folding a sheet of standard size twice to form four leaves.

quartz (*pr.* kwortz) *noun* a hard mineral occurring in various forms. □ **quartz clock** or **watch** one operated by electric vibrations of a quartz crystal. **quartz lamp** a quartz tube with mercury vapour as a light source.

quasar (**kway**-zar) *noun* a starlike object that is the source of intense electromagnetic radiation. [from *quasi-* + *stellar*]

quash *verb* **1** to annul, to reject (by legal authority) as not valid, *quashed the conviction*. **2** to suppress or crush (a rebellion etc.).

quasi- (**kway**-zy or **kwah**-zee) *prefix* seeming to be something but not really so, *a quasi-scientific explanation*. [from Latin *quasi* = as if]

quatercentenary (kwat-er-sen-**teen**-ă-ree) *noun* a 400th anniversary. [from Latin *quater* = four times, + *centenary*]

Quaternary (kwă-**ter**-nă-ree) *adjective* of the geological period of the Cenozoic era following the Tertiary and including present times. **–Quaternary** *noun* this period.

quatrain (**kwot**-rayn) *noun* a stanza of four lines. [from French *quatre* = four]

quatrefoil (**kat**-rĕ-foil) *noun* **1** a leaf or flower with four lobes. **2** an ornament shaped like this.

quattrocento (kwah-troh-**chen**-toh) *noun* Italian art of the 15th century.

quaver *verb* **1** to tremble, to vibrate. **2** to speak in a trembling voice. **–quaver** *noun* **1** a quavering sound. **2** a note in music, lasting half as long as a crotchet.

quay (*pr.* kee) *noun* a landing place, usually built of stone or iron, alongside which ships can be tied up for loading and unloading.

queasy *adjective* (**queasier**, **queasiest**) **1** feeling slightly sick. **2** having a digestion that is easily upset. **3** (of food) causing a feeling of sickness. **4** squeamish. **queasiness** *noun*

Quebec 1 a province of eastern Canada. **2** its capital.

queen *noun* **1** a woman who is the supreme ruler of an independent country by right of succession to the throne. **2** a king's wife. **3** a woman or place or thing regarded as supreme in some way. **4** a playing card bearing a picture of a queen. **5** (*informal*, *offensive*) a male homosexual. **6** a piece in chess. **7** a perfect fertile female of a bee or ant or similar insect. **–queen** *verb* to convert (a pawn in chess) to a queen when it reaches the opponent's end of the board; to be converted in this way. □ **Queen-Anne** *adjective* in the style of English furniture and architecture popular in the early 18th century, characterised by careful proportions, lack of ornament, and the curved cabriole leg. **queen mother** a dowager queen who is the mother of a reigning king or queen. **Queen's Counsel** counsel to the Crown, taking precedence over other barristers. **queen-size** *adjective* extra large, but smaller than king-size, *a queen-size bed*.

queenly *adjective* like a queen in appearance or manner. **queenliness** *noun*

Queensland a State comprising the NE part of Australia. □ **Queensland blue** a variety of pumpkin having a deep blue-grey skin. **Queensland nut** = **macadamia**.

queer *adjective* **1** strange, odd, eccentric. **2** causing one to feel suspicious, of questionable character. **3** slightly ill or faint, *feel queer*. **4** (*informal*, *offensive*) homosexual. **–queer** *verb* to spoil. □ **in Queer Street** (*informal*) in difficulties, in debt or trouble. **queer a person's pitch** (*informal*) to spoil his or her chances beforehand. **queerly** *adverb*, **queerness** *noun*

quell *verb* to suppress, to reduce to submission, *quelled the rebellion*.

quench *verb* **1** to extinguish (a fire or flame). **2** to satisfy (one's thirst) by drinking. **3** to cool (a heated thing) by water.

quern *noun* a hand mill for grinding corn or pepper.

querulous (kwe-rŭ-lŭs) *adjective* complaining peevishly. **querulously** *adverb* [same origin as *quarrel*]

query *noun* **1** a question. **2** a question mark. –**query** *verb* (**queried**, **querying**) to ask a question or express doubt about. [from Latin *quaere* = ask!]

quesadilla *noun* a heated cheese-filled tortilla.

quest *noun* the act of seeking something, a search.

question *noun* **1** a sentence requesting information or an answer. **2** something being discussed or for discussion; a problem requiring solution. **3** the raising of doubt, *whether we shall win is open to question*. –**question** *verb* **1** to ask questions of (a person). **2** to express doubt about. ☐ **in question** being referred to or discussed; being disputed, *his honesty is not in question*. **it is a question of** this is what is required or involved; *it is only a question of time*, it will happen sooner or later. **no question of** no possibility of. **out of the question** completely impracticable. **question mark** the punctuation mark (?) placed after a question. **question time** a period in Parliament when MPs may question ministers. **questioner** *noun* [from Latin *quaesitum* = sought for]

questionable *adjective* open to doubt or suspicion; not certainly true or advisable or honest. **questionably** *adverb*

questionnaire (kwes-chŏ-**nair** *or* kes-) *noun* a list of questions seeking information about people's opinions or customs etc., especially for use in a survey.

queue (*pr.* kew) *noun* a line or series of people awaiting their turn for something. –**queue** *verb* (**queued**, **queuing**) to wait in a queue. [from Latin *cauda* = tail]

quibble *noun* a petty objection. –**quibble** *verb* to make petty objections. **quibbler** *noun*

quiche (*pr.* keesh) *noun* an open tart, usually with a savoury filling. [French]

quick *adjective* **1** taking only a short time to do something or to be done. **2** able to notice

or learn or think quickly. **3** (of temper) easily roused. **4** (*old use*) alive, *the quick and the dead*. –**quick** *noun* the sensitive flesh below the nails; *be cut to the quick*, to have one's feelings deeply hurt. –**quick** *adverb* quickly, *quick-drying*. ☐ **quick-witted** *adjective* quick at understanding a situation or making jokes. **quickly** *adverb*, **quickness** *noun*

quicken *verb* **1** to make or become quicker. **2** to stimulate, to make or become livelier, *our interest quickened*. **3** to reach a stage in pregnancy (**the quickening**) when the foetus makes movements that can be felt by the mother.

quicklime *noun* = **lime¹**.

quicksand *noun* an area of loose wet deep sand into which heavy objects will sink.

quicksilver *noun* mercury.

quickstep *noun* a ballroom dance with quick steps; music for this.

quid¹ *noun* (*plural* **quid**) (*informal*) (in Britain, and formerly in Australia) one pound, £1. ☐ **make a quick quid** (*informal*) to earn money easily, often by dubious means. **not the full quid** (*Austral. informal*) mentally deficient.

quid² *noun* a lump of tobacco for chewing.

quid pro quo *noun* a thing given in return for something else. [Latin, = something for something]

quiescent (kwee-**ess**-ĕnt) *adjective* inactive, quiet. **quiescence** *noun* [from Latin *quiescens* = becoming quiet]

quiet *adjective* **1** with little or no sound, not loud or noisy. **2** with little or no movement. **3** free from disturbance or vigorous activity, peaceful. **4** silent, *be quiet!* **5** unobtrusive, done in a restrained manner, *had a quiet laugh about it*. **6** (of colours or dress etc.) subdued, not showy. –**quiet** *noun* quietness. –**quiet** *verb* to make or become quiet, to calm. ☐ **on the quiet** unobtrusively; secretly. **quietly** *adverb*, **quietness** *noun* [from Latin *quietus* = calm]

quieten *verb* to make or become quiet.

quietude (**kwy**-ĕ-tewd) *noun* quietness.

quiff *noun* an upright tuft of hair above the forehead.

quill *noun* **1** one of the large feathers on a bird's wing or tail. **2** an old type of pen made from this. **3** each of an echidna's or porcupine's spines. **4** the hollow stem of a feather.

quilt *noun* a padded bed cover. –**quilt** *verb* to line with padding and fix with cross lines or other patterns of stitching.

quin *noun* each of a set of quintuplets.

quince *noun* **1** a hard yellowish pear-shaped fruit for cooking. **2** the tree bearing it. □ **get on one's quince** (*Austral. informal*) to annoy, to exasperate.

quinine (kwĭ-**neen**) *noun* a bitter-tasting medicinal drug used to treat malaria and in tonics.

quinquereme (**kwing**-kwĕ-reem) *noun* an ancient Roman galley.

quinsy (**kwin**-zee) *noun* a severe inflammation of the throat, often with an abscess on one of the tonsils.

quintessence (kwin-**tess**-ĕns) *noun* **1** an essence of a substance. **2** the essence or essential part of a theory or speech or condition etc. **3** a perfect example of a quality.

quintet *noun* **1** a group of five instruments or voices; a musical composition for these. **2** a set of five. [from Latin *quintus* = fifth]

quintuple (**kwin**-tew-pŭl) *adjective* **1** consisting of five parts; involving five people or groups. **2** five times as much. –**quintuple** *verb* to multiply or become multiplied by five.

quintuplet (kwin-**tew**-plĕt) *noun* each of five children born at one birth. [from Latin *quintus* = fifth]

quip *noun* a witty or sarcastic remark. –**quip** *verb* (**quipped, quipping**) to utter as a quip.

quire *noun* **1** 25 (formerly 24) sheets of writing paper. **2** each of the folded sheets that are sewn together in bookbinding.

quirk *noun* **1** a peculiarity of a person's behaviour. **2** a trick of fate.

quisling (**kwiz**-ling) *noun* a traitor, especially one who collaborates with an enemy occupying his or her country. [named after V. Quisling, a pro-Nazi Norwegian leader in the Second World War]

quit *verb* (**quitted, quitting**) **1** to go away from, to leave; *gave the tenant notice to quit*, gave him or her notice to leave the premises. **2** to give up or abandon (a task etc.). **3** (*informal*) to cease, *quit grumbling*. –**quit** *adjective* rid, *glad to be quit of the trouble*.

quitch *noun* a kind of grass with long creeping roots, couch grass.

quite *adverb* **1** completely, entirely, *quite finished*. **2** to some extent, somewhat, *quite a long time*. **3** really, actually, *it's quite a change*. **4** (as an answer) I agree, *quite* or *quite so*.

□ **quite a few** a considerable number. **quite something** a remarkable thing.

Quito (**kee**-toh) the capital of Ecuador.

quits *adjective* even with, on even terms as a result of retaliation or repayment.

quitter *noun* (*informal*) a person who gives up too easily.

quiver[1] *noun* a case for holding arrows.

quiver[2] *verb* to shake or vibrate with a slight rapid motion. –**quiver** *noun* a quivering movement or sound.

qui vive (kee **veev**) *noun* **on the qui vive** on the alert, watchful. [French, = (long) live who?, used as a sentry's challenge]

quixotic (kwik-**sot**-ik) *adjective* chivalrous and unselfish to an extravagant or impractical extent. **quixotically** *adverb* [named after Don Quixote, hero of a Spanish story]

quiz *noun* (*plural* **quizzes**) a series of questions testing general knowledge, especially as a form of entertainment. –**quiz** *verb* (**quizzed, quizzing**) **1** to examine by questioning. **2** (*old use*) to stare at curiously.

quizmaster *noun* the person who puts the questions to people taking part in a quiz game or similar entertainment.

quizzical (**kwiz**-i-kăl) *adjective* **1** done in a questioning way. **2** gently amused. **quizzically** *adverb* [from *quiz*]

quoit (*pr.* koit *or* kwoit) *noun* a ring of metal or rubber or rope thrown to encircle a peg in the game of **quoits**.

quokka (**kwok**-ă) *noun* a small Western Australian greyish-brown short-tailed wallaby. [Nyungar probably *gwaga*]

quoll (*pr.* kwol) *noun* an Australian long-tailed spotted carnivorous marsupial, also called a *native cat*. [from Guugu Yimidhirr *dhigul*]

quorum (**kwor**-ŭm) *noun* the minimum number of people that must be present at a meeting before its proceedings are to be regarded as valid. **quorate** *adjective* [Latin, = of which people]

quota *noun* **1** a fixed share that must be done, contributed, or received. **2** the maximum number or amount of people or things that may be admitted e.g. to a country or institution or allowed as exports. [from Latin *quot* = how many]

quotable *adjective* worth quoting.

quotation *noun* **1** quoting; being quoted. **2** a passage quoted. **3** an amount stated as

the current price of stocks or commodities.
4 a contractor's statement of the sum for
which he or she is willing to perform specified
work. □ **quotation marks** punctuation marks
(either single ' ' or double " ") enclosing
words quoted or put by way of apology round
a slang or similar word.

quote *verb* **1** to repeat or write out words from
a book or speech, *quote the Bible* or *from the
Bible*. **2** to mention in support of a statement,
can you quote a recent example? **3** to state
the price of (goods or services); to give a
quotation or estimate. **4** (in dictation etc.)

begin the quotation, open the inverted commas
(*see* unquote). –quote *noun* (*informal*)
1 a passage quoted. **2** a price quoted.

quoth (*rhymes with* both) *verb* (*old use*) said.

quotient (**kwoh**-shĕnt) *noun* the result
obtained when one amount is divided by
another (e.g. 3 in '12 ÷ 4 = 3'). [from Latin,
= how many times]

Qur'an *noun* Arabic spelling of Koran. [Arabic]

q.v. *abbreviation* which see (used as an
indication that the reader should look at the
reference given). [short for Latin *quod vide*]

Rr

R *abbreviation* (also **R.**) **1** (in names) River. **2** Regina, *Elizabeth R.* **3** Rex, *George R.* **4** (as a film classification) restricted to viewers 18 years and over. **5** registered as a trademark.

Ra (*pr.* rah) (*Egyptian myth.*) the sun god.

RAAF *abbreviation* Royal Australian Air Force.

Rabat (ră-**bat**) the capital of Morocco.

rabbet *noun* a step-shaped channel cut along the edge of a piece of wood etc. to receive another piece or the glass of a window etc. –**rabbet** *verb* (**rabbeted**, **rabbeting**) **1** to join or fix with a rabbet. **2** to cut a rabbet in.

rabbi (**rab**-I) *noun* (*plural* **rabbis**) the religious leader of a Jewish congregation. [Hebrew, = my master]

rabbinical (ră-**bin**-i-kăl) *adjective* of rabbis or Jewish doctrines or law.

rabbit *noun* **1** a burrowing animal with long ears and a short furry tail. **2** (*informal*) a person who is a poor performer at a game. –**rabbit** *verb* (**rabbited**, **rabbiting**) **1** to hunt rabbits. **2** to talk lengthily or in a rambling way. **rabbity** *adjective*

rabble *noun* **1** a disorderly crowd, a mob. **2 the rabble** the common people, the lowest social classes.

Rabelais (**rab**-ĕ-lay), François (c. 1494–1553), French writer of robust satire.

rabid (**rab**-ĭd) *adjective* **1** furious, fanatical, *rabid hate*; *a rabid Socialist*. **2** affected with rabies. **rabidly** *adverb*, **rabidity** (ră-**bid**-ĭ-tee) *noun* [from Latin *rabidus* = raving]

rabies (**ray**-beez) *noun* a contagious fatal virus disease affecting dogs and similar animals, transmitted to humans usually by the bite of an infected animal and causing madness; hydrophobia.

raccoon *noun* (also **racoon**) a North American animal with a bushy tail, sharp snout, and greyish-brown fur.

race¹ *noun* **1** a contest of speed in reaching a certain point or in doing or achieving something; *a race against time*, an effort to get something done before a certain time. **2** a strong fast current of water. **3** a channel for the balls in a ball bearing. **4** (*Austral.*) a fenced passageway for drafting sheep or cattle. –**race** *verb* **1** to compete in a race; to have a race with. **2** to engage in horse racing, *a racing man*. **3** to move or cause to move or operate at full speed, *raced his engine*. **races** *plural noun* a series of races for horses or dogs at fixed times on a regular course.
☐ **not in the race** (*Austral. informal*) having no chance. **race meeting** a series of horse races in one place. **racer** *noun*

race² *noun* **1** each of the major divisions of humankind, having distinct physical characteristics. **2** a number of people related by common descent. **3** a genus, species, breed, or variety of animals or plants; *the race* or *the human race*, humankind.
☐ **race relations** relations between members of different races in the same country.

racecourse *noun* a place where horse races are run.

racehorse *noun* a horse bred or kept for racing.

raceme (ră-**seem**) *noun* flowers evenly spaced along a central stem, with the ones at the base opening first (as in lupins, hyacinths, etc.). [from Latin *racemus* = grape bunch]

racetrack *noun* a track for horse or vehicle races.

rachel (ră-**shel**) *noun* a pale fawn colour used in cosmetics. –**rachel** *adjective* of this colour.

Rachmaninov (rak-**man**-ĭ-noff), Sergei Vasilyevich (1873–1943), Russian composer and pianist.

racial (**ray**-shăl) *adjective* of or based on race. **racially** *adverb*

racialism *noun* racism. **racialist** *noun*

Racine (ra-**seen**), Jean (1639–99), French dramatist.

racism (**ray**-sizm) *noun* **1** belief in the superiority of a particular race; prejudice based on this. **2** antagonism towards people of other races. **3** the theory that human abilities etc. are determined by race. **racist** *noun*

rack¹ *noun* **1** a framework, usually with bars or pegs, for holding things or for hanging things on. **2** a bar or rail with teeth or cogs into which those of a wheel or gear etc. fit. **3** an

instrument of torture on which people were tied and stretched. **–rack** *verb* to inflict great torment on, *was racked with pain*.
☐ **rack off** (*Austral. informal*) to go away; (as an exclamation) get lost! **rack one's brains** to think hard about a problem. **rack railway** a railway having a cogged rail with which a cogged wheel on the train engages for driving the train up a steep slope.

rack² *noun* destruction, *go to rack and ruin*.

rack³ *noun* a joint of lamb etc. including the front ribs.

racket¹ *noun see* **racquet**.

racket² *noun* **1** a din, a noisy fuss. **2** a business or other activity in which dishonest methods are used. **3** (*informal*) a line of business; a dodge. **–racket** *verb* to move about noisily, to engage in wild social activities, *racketing about*.

racketeer *noun* a person who runs or works in a racket or dishonest business. **racketeering** *noun*

rackety *adjective* noisy.

raconteur (rak-on-**ter**) *noun* a person who tells anecdotes. **raconteuse** *feminine noun* [French]

racoon *noun see* **raccoon**.

racquet *noun* (also **racket**) a stringed bat used in tennis and similar games. **racquets** *plural noun* a ball game for two or four people played with racquets in a four-walled court. [from Arabic *rahat* = palm of the hand]

racy *adjective* (**racier, raciest**) spirited and vigorous in style. **racily** *adverb*, **raciness** *noun*

radar *noun* **1** a system for detecting the presence, position, or movement etc. of objects by sending out short radio waves that they reflect. **2** apparatus used for this.
☐ **radar trap** an arrangement using radar to detect vehicles travelling faster than the speed limit. [from the initial letters of *radio detection and ranging*]

raddled *adjective* worn out.

radial (**ray**-dee-ăl) *adjective* of rays or radii; having spokes or lines or other features radiating from a central point. **–radial** *noun* **1** a radial-ply tyre. **2** a radial part.
☐ **radial-ply** *adjective* (of a tyre) having fabric layers with cords lying radial to the hub of the wheel (not crossing each other). **radially** *adverb*

radian (**ray**-dee-ăn) *noun* a unit of plane angle; the angle at the centre of a circle

formed by the radii of an arc equal in length to the radius.

radiant *adjective* **1** giving out rays of light. **2** looking very bright and happy. **3** transmitting heat by radiation; (of heat) transmitted in this way. **radiantly** *adverb*, **radiance** *noun*, **radiancy** *noun*

radiate *verb* **1** to spread outwards (especially in lines or rays) from a central point; to cause to do this. **2** to send out (light or heat etc.) in rays; to be sent out as radiation. **3** to give forth a feeling of, *she radiated confidence*. [from Latin *radius* = ray]

radiation *noun* **1** radiating; being radiated. **2** the sending out of the rays and atomic particles characteristic of radioactive substances; these rays and particles.

radiator *noun* **1** a device that radiates heat, either a portable electrical or oil-filled heater, or a fixed metal case through which steam or hot water circulates. **2** an engine-cooling apparatus in a motor vehicle or an aircraft.

radical *adjective* **1** going to the root or foundation of something, fundamental. **2** drastic, thorough, *radical changes* or *reforms*. **3** desiring radical reforms; holding extremist views. **–radical** *noun* **1** a person desiring radical reforms or holding extremist views. **2** a group of atoms forming part of a compound and remaining unaltered during its ordinary chemical changes. **3** the root of a word. **4** a mathematical quantity forming or expressed as the root of another. **radically** *adverb*, **radicalism** *noun* [from Latin *radicis* = of a root]

radicle *noun* an embryo root (e.g. of a pea or bean). [from Latin, = little root]

radio *noun* (*plural* **radios**) **1** the process of sending and receiving messages etc. by invisible electromagnetic radiation. **2** an apparatus for sending or receiving messages etc. in this way; a transmitter or receiver. **3** sound broadcasting; a sound-broadcasting station, *Radio Australia*. **–radio** *adjective* **1** of or using radio. **2** of or involving stars etc. from which radio waves are received or reflected, *radio astronomy*. **–radio** *verb* (**radioed**, **radioing**) to send, signal, or communicate with by radio. ☐ **radio frequency** a band of electromagnetic wave frequencies used in telecommunications, ranging from 10^4 to 10^{11} or 10^{12} Hz. **radio star** a small celestial object emitting strong radio waves. **radio telescope** an instrument used to detect radio emissions from the sky, whether from natural celestial objects or from artificial satellites. [from Latin *radius* = ray]

radio- *prefix* **1** of rays or radiation. **2** of radio.

radioactive *adjective* of or showing radioactivity.

radioactivity *noun* the property of having atoms that break up spontaneously and send out radiation capable of penetrating opaque bodies and producing electrical and chemical effects.

radiocarbon *noun* a radioactive form of carbon that is present in organic materials and is used in carbon dating (*see* carbon).

radiographer *noun* a person who is skilled in radiography.

radiography (ray-dee-**og**-ră-fee) *noun* the production of X-ray photographs. [from *radio-* + *-graphy*]

radioisotope *noun* a radioactive isotope that decays spontaneously.

radiology (ray-dee-**ol**-ŏ-jee) *noun* the scientific study of X-rays and similar radiation. **radiologist** *noun* [from *radio-* + *-logy*]

radiotherapy *noun* treatment of disease etc. by X-rays or similar forms of radiation.

radish *noun* **1** a plant with a crisp hot-tasting root that is eaten raw. **2** its root. [from Latin *radix* = root]

radium *noun* a radioactive metallic element (symbol Ra), obtained from pitchblende. [from Latin *radius* = ray]

radius *noun* (*plural* radii, *pr.* **ray**-dee-I) **1** a straight line extending from the centre of a circle or sphere to its circumference. **2** the length of this line; the distance from a centre, *within a radius of 2 kilometres*. **3** the thicker of the two long bones in the forearm; the corresponding bone in animals. [from Latin *radius* = a spoke or ray]

radix *noun* (*plural* radices) a number used as the basis of a numeration scale.

radon (**ray**-don) *noun* a chemical element, a radioactive gas (symbol Rn).

Rafferty's rules *noun* (*Austral. informal*) no rules at all.

raffia *noun* soft fibre from the leaves of a kind of palm tree, used for tying up plants and for making mats etc.

raffish *adjective* looking vulgarly flashy, disreputable, or rakish. **raffishness** *noun*

raffle *noun* a lottery with an object as the prize, especially as a method of raising money for a charity. **–raffle** *verb* to offer (a thing) as the prize in a raffle.

raft *noun* a flat floating structure made of timber or other materials, used especially as a substitute for a boat.

rafter *noun* one of the sloping beams forming the framework of a roof.

rag¹ *noun* **1** a torn, frayed, or worn piece of woven material. **2** rags used as material for stuffing things or making paper etc. **3** (*derogatory*) a newspaper, *the local rag*. **rags** *plural noun* old and torn clothes. □ **rag-and-bone man** an itinerant dealer in old clothes and discarded articles.

rag² *verb* (ragged, ragging) (*informal*) to tease, to play practical jokes on (a person). **–rag** *noun* (*informal*) a practical joke, a piece of fun.

rag³ *noun* a piece of ragtime.

raga (**rah**-gă) *noun* (in Indian music) **1** notes used as a basis for improvisation. **2** a piece of music using a particular raga. [Sanskrit, = colour; musical tone]

ragamuffin *noun* a person in ragged dirty clothes.

ragbag *noun* **1** a bag in which scraps of fabric etc. are kept for use. **2** a miscellaneous collection.

rage *noun* **1** violent anger; a fit of this. **2** a craze; *be all the rage*, to be temporarily very popular or fashionable. **3** (*Austral. informal*) a lively party. **–rage** *verb* **1** to show violent anger. **2** (of a storm or battle etc.) to be violent, to continue furiously. **3** (*Austral. informal*) to have a good time.

ragged (**rag**-ĕd) *adjective* **1** torn, frayed. **2** wearing torn clothes. **3** jagged; uneven. **4** faulty, lacking finish, smoothness, or uniformity, *a ragged performance*. **raggedly** *adverb*, **raggedness** *noun*

raglan *noun* a type of sleeve that continues to the neck and is joined to the body of the garment by sloping seams. [named after Lord Raglan, British military commander (died 1855)]

ragout (ră-**goo**) *noun* a stew of meat and vegetables. [French]

ragtag and bobtail *noun* (*derogatory*) riff-raff, disreputable people.

ragtime *noun* a form of jazz music.

raid *noun* 1 a sudden attack and withdrawal made by a military party or by ships or aircraft. 2 an attack made in order to steal. 3 a surprise visit by police etc. to arrest suspected people or seize illicit goods. –**raid** *verb* to make a raid on (a place etc.). **raider** *noun*

rail[1] *noun* 1 a horizontal or sloping bar forming part of a fence or the top of banisters or a protection against contact or falling over etc., or for hanging things on. 2 any of the lines of metal bars on which trains or trams run. 3 railways as a means of transport, *send it by rail*. –**rail** *verb* to fit or protect with a rail, *rail it off*. □ **go off the rails** (*informal*) to become disorganised or out of control or crazy.

rail[2] *noun* a kind of small wading bird.

rail[3] *verb* to complain or protest or reproach strongly, *railing at him*.

railing *noun* a fence of rails supported on upright metal bars.

raillery *noun* good-humoured joking or teasing.

railroad *noun* (*Amer.*) a railway. –**railroad** *verb* to rush or force into hasty action, *railroaded him into accepting*.

railway *noun* 1 a set of rails on which trains run. 2 a system of transport using these; the organisation and people required for its working. 3 a track on which equipment with wheels is run.

raiment *noun* (*old use*) clothing.

rain *noun* 1 condensed moisture of the atmosphere falling in separate drops. 2 a fall or spell of this; *the rains*, the rainy season in tropical countries. 3 a shower of things. –**rain** *verb* to send down rain; to fall as or like rain. □ **be rained off** (of an event) to be prevented by rain from taking place. **rain bird** a bird whose cry is said to foretell rain. **rain check** a ticket for later use if rain postpones a sporting fixture; a voucher (issued to a shopper) promising that an out-of-stock item advertised in a sale will be made available later at the sale price. **rain shadow** a region in the lee of mountains where the rainfall is low because it is sheltered from the prevailing winds.

rainbow *noun* an arch of colours formed in rain or spray by the sun's rays. □ **rainbow trout** a large North American trout, introduced into rivers in Australia.

Rainbow Serpent (also **Rainbow Snake**) (in Aboriginal lore) a spirit associated with water, medicine, and fertility.

raincoat *noun* a waterproof or water-resistant coat.

raindrop *noun* a single drop of rain.

rainfall *noun* the total amount of rain falling within a given area in a given time.

rainforest *noun* thick forest in tropical areas where there is heavy rainfall.

rainwash *noun* the process by which sand or gravel etc. is washed away from its original position by rainwater; this material.

rainwater *noun* water that has fallen as rain, not obtained from wells etc.

rainy *adjective* (**rainier**, **rainiest**) in or on which much rain falls. □ **save for a rainy day** to save money etc. for a time when one may need it.

raise *verb* 1 to bring to or towards a higher or upright position; to lift up. 2 to increase the amount or level of, *raise prices*. 3 to cause, to rouse, *raise doubts*; *raise a laugh*, cause people to laugh; *raise from the dead*, restore to life. 4 to breed or grow, *raise sheep* or *corn*. 5 to bring up, to rear, *raise a family*. 6 to collect, to manage to obtain, *raise an army*; *raise a loan*. 7 to put forward, *raise objections*. 8 to cause to come or appear, *raise the ghost*. –**raise** *noun* an increase in wages or salary. □ **raise Cain** or **raise the roof** (*informal*) to make an uproar; to show great anger. **raise one's glass to** to drink a toast to. **raise the alarm** to give a warning of imminent danger. **raise the siege** to end it by withdrawing the besieging forces or compelling them to withdraw. **raising agent** a substance (e.g. yeast or baking powder) that makes bread or cake etc. swell and become light in texture.

raisin *noun* a partially dried grape.

raison d'être (ray-zawn **detr**) *noun* the reason for or purpose of a thing's existence. [French]

raj (*pr.* rahj) *noun* the period of British rule in India. [Hindi, = reign]

rajah (**rah**-jă) *noun* (in former times) an Indian king or prince. [Hindi]

rake[1] *noun* 1 a tool with prongs used for drawing together hay or fallen leaves etc. or for smoothing loose soil or gravel. 2 an implement resembling this, used e.g. by a croupier for drawing in money at a gaming table. –**rake** *verb* 1 to gather or smooth with a rake. 2 to search, *have been raking among old papers*. 3 to direct gunfire along (a line) from end to end; to direct one's eyes or a camera in this way. □ **rake-off** *noun* (*informal*) a commission or share of profits. **rake up** to revive the memory of (a quarrel or other unpleasant incident).

rake² *noun* a backward slope (e.g. of a ship's mast or funnel, or of a driver's seat). –**rake** *verb* to set at a sloping angle.

rake³ *noun* a man who lives an irresponsible and immoral life.

rakish *adjective* like a rake (*rake³*), jaunty. **rakishly** *adverb*, **rakishness** *noun*

Raleigh (**ral**-ee), Sir Walter (c. 1552–1618), Elizabethan explorer.

rally¹ *verb* (**rallied, rallying**) **1** to bring or come together for a united effort. **2** to reassemble for another effort after defeat. **3** to rouse or revive, *rally one's courage*. **4** to recover one's strength after illness. **5** (of share prices etc.) to increase after falling. –**rally** *noun* **1** an act of rallying; a recovery of energy or spirits etc. **2** (in tennis etc.) a series of strokes before a point is scored. **3** a mass meeting of people with a common interest. **4** a driving competition for cars or motorcycles over public roads.

rally² *verb* (**rallied, rallying**) to tease, to ridicule in a good-humoured way.

RAM *abbreviation* (in computing) random-access memory; a temporary working memory that can be read from and written to.

ram *noun* **1** an uncastrated male sheep. **2** a battering-ram or similar device. **3** a striking or plunging device in various machines. –**ram** *verb* (**rammed, ramming**) **1** to force or drive into place by pressure. **2** to strike and push heavily; to crash against. **rammer** *noun*

Rama the hero of the Ramayana, the seventh incarnation of Vishnu, and the Hindu model of the ideal man.

Ramadan (**ram**-ă-dan) *noun* the ninth month of the Muslim year, when Muslims fast between sunrise and sunset.

Ramayana (rah-**my**-ă-nă) *noun* one of the two great Sanskrit epics of the Hindus (the other is the Mahabharata), composed (c. 300 BC), which tells how Rama rescued his wife Sita from Ravana, the ten-headed demon king of Sri Lanka.

ramble *verb* **1** to walk for pleasure. **2** to talk or write disconnectedly, to wander from the subject. –**ramble** *noun* a walk taken for pleasure, with or without a definite route.

rambler *noun* **1** a person who rambles; one who goes for a ramble. **2** a climbing rose.

rambling *adjective* **1** wandering. **2** speaking or spoken or written disconnectedly, wandering from one subject to another. **3** (of a plant) straggling, climbing. **4** (of a house, street, or town etc.) extending in various directions irregularly.

ramekin (**ram**-ĕ-kin) *noun* **1** a small mould for baking and serving an individual portion of food. **2** something baked and served in this, *cheese ramekins*.

Rameses (**ram**-seez) the name of 11 Egyptian pharaohs, of whom the most famous are **Rameses II** 'the Great' (1290–1224 BC) and **Rameses III** (1194–1163 BC).

ramification *noun* **1** an arrangement of branching parts. **2** a part of a complex structure, something arising from it. **3** a consequence. [from Latin *ramus* = branch]

ramify *verb* (**ramified, ramifying**) to form or cause to form into branching parts.

ramjet *noun* a type of jet engine in which air is drawn in and compressed by motion through the air.

ramp¹ *noun* **1** a slope joining two levels of floor, ground etc. **2** a movable set of stairs put beside an aircraft so that people may enter or leave. **3** (*Austral.*) a cattle grid.

ramp² *noun* (*informal*) a swindle or racket, especially one that involves charging excessively high prices.

rampage (ram-**payj**) *verb* to behave violently, to race about wildly or destructively. –**rampage** (**ram**-payj) *noun* violent behaviour. □ **on the rampage** rampaging.

rampant *adjective* **1** (in heraldry, of a lion etc.) standing on one hind leg with the opposite foreleg raised, *a lion rampant*. **2** unrestrained, flourishing excessively, *disease was rampant in the poorer districts*. [from *ramp¹*]

rampart *noun* a broad bank of earth built as a fortification, usually topped with a parapet and wide enough for troops etc. to walk on.

ramrod *noun* an iron rod formerly used for ramming a charge into muzzle-loading guns. □ **like a ramrod** stiff and straight.

ramshackle *adjective* tumbledown, rickety.

RAN *abbreviation* Royal Australian Navy.

ran *see* **run**.

ranch *noun* **1** a cattle-breeding establishment, especially in North America. **2** a farm where certain other animals are bred, *a mink ranch*. –**ranch** *verb* to farm on a ranch. **rancher** *noun*

rancid (**ran**-sĭd) *adjective* smelling or tasting unpleasant like stale fat.

rancour (**rank**-er) *noun* bitter feeling or ill will. **rancorous** *adjective*, **rancorously** *adverb*

rand *noun* the unit of money in South Africa and Namibia.

random *adjective* 1 made, done, etc., without method or conscious choice, *a random choice*. 2 (*informal*) strange, inexplicable, unexpected. –**random** *noun* a person who is at a place by chance; a person who is not a member of a particular group; an outsider. ☐ **at random** without a particular aim or purpose or principle. **random access** *see* **access**.

randy *adjective* (**randier**, **randiest**) lustful, eager for sexual gratification. **randiness** *noun*

ranee (**rah**-nee) *noun* a rajah's wife or widow. [Hindi]

rang *see* **ring²**.

range *noun* 1 a line or tier or series of things, *a range of mountains*. 2 an extent, the limits between which something operates or varies. 3 (in mathematics) the subset of a codomain which is actually used. 4 the distance over which one can see or hear, or to which a sound, signal, or missile can travel; the distance that a ship or aircraft etc. can travel without refuelling. 5 the distance to a thing being aimed at or looked at, *at close range*. 6 a large open stretch of grazing or hunting ground. 7 a place with targets for shooting-practice. 8 a fireplace with ovens etc. for cooking in; an electric or gas stove. –**range** *verb* 1 to arrange in a row or ranks or in a specified way. 2 to extend, to reach. 3 to vary between limits. 4 to wander or go about a place.

rangefinder *noun* a device for calculating the distance of an object to be shot at or photographed.

ranger *noun* 1 a keeper of a park or forest. 2 a member of a body of mounted troops policing a thinly populated area. –**Ranger** *noun* a senior Guide.

ranging-rod *noun* a rod used in surveying for setting a straight line.

Rangoon (rang-**goon**) (from 1989 officially called **Yangon**) the capital of Burma (Myanmar).

rangy (**rayn**-jee) *adjective* tall and thin.

rank¹ *noun* 1 a line of people or things; *the ranks*, ordinary soldiers (not officers).

2 a place where taxis stand to await hire. 3 a place in a scale of quality or value etc.; a position or grade, *ministers of Cabinet rank*. 4 high social position, *people of rank*. –**rank** *verb* 1 to arrange in a rank. 2 to assign a rank to. 3 to have a certain rank or place, *he ranks among the great statesmen*. ☐ **close ranks** to maintain solidarity. **the rank and file** the ordinary undistinguished people of an organisation.

rank² *adjective* 1 growing too thickly and coarsely. 2 (of land) full of weeds. 3 foul-smelling. 4 unmistakably bad, out-and-out, *rank poison*; *rank injustice*. **rankly** *adverb*, **rankness** *noun*

rankle *verb* to cause lasting and bitter annoyance or resentment.

ransack *verb* 1 to search thoroughly or roughly. 2 to rob or pillage (a place).

ransom *noun* the release of a captive in return for money or other payment demanded by the captors; the payment itself. –**ransom** *verb* 1 to obtain the release of (a captive) in return for payment. 2 to hold (a captive) to ransom. ☐ **hold to ransom** to hold (a captive) and demand ransom for his or her release; to demand concessions from (a person etc.) by threatening some damaging action. [same origin as *redeem*]

rant *verb* to make a speech loudly and violently and theatrically.

rap¹ *noun* 1 a quick sharp blow. 2 a knock, a tapping sound. 3 (*informal*) blame, punishment, *take the rap*. 4 (*informal*) a chat. 5 a rhyming monologue recited rhythmically to **rap music**, a style of popular music with a pronounced beat. –**rap** *verb* (**rapped**, **rapping**) 1 to strike quickly and sharply. 2 to make a knocking or tapping sound. 3 to reprimand. 4 to perform rap music; to talk in the style of rap. ☐ **rap out** to say suddenly or sharply.

rap² *noun* **not care** or **give a rap** not care at all.

rap³ (*informal*) *noun* praise, commendation. –**rap** *verb* to praise.

rapacious (ră-**pay**-shŭs) *adjective* greedy and grasping (especially for money), plundering and robbing others. **rapaciously** *adverb*, **rapacity** (ră-**pas**-ĭ-tee) *noun* [from Latin *rapax* = grasping]

rape¹ *noun* the act or crime of having sexual intercourse with a person without her or his consent. –**rape** *verb* to commit rape on (a person). [from Latin *rapere* = seize]

rape² *noun* a plant grown as food for sheep and for its seed from which oil is obtained.

Raphael¹ (**raf**-ay-ĕl) one of the archangels.

Raphael², Raffaello Sanzio (1483–1520), Italian Renaissance painter and architect.

rapid *adjective* **1** quick, swift. **2** (of a slope) descending steeply. **rapids** *plural noun* a swift current in a river, caused by a steep downward slope in the river bed. **rapidly** *adverb*, **rapidity** (ră-**pid**-ĭ-tee) *noun*

rapier (**ray**-pee-er) *noun* a thin light double-edged sword, used for thrusting.

rapine (**ra**-pyn) *noun* plundering.

rapist (**ray**-pĭst) *noun* a person who commits rape.

rapport (ra-**por**) *noun* a harmonious and understanding relationship between people.

rapscallion *noun* a rascal.

rapt *adjective* very intent and absorbed, enraptured. **raptly** *adverb* [from Latin *raptum* = seized]

rapture *noun* intense delight.
□ **in raptures** feeling or expressing rapture. **rapturous** *adjective*, **rapturously** *adverb*

rare¹ *adjective* **1** seldom found or occurring, very uncommon. **2** (*informal*) exceptionally good, *had a rare time*. **3** of low density, thin, *the rare atmosphere in the Himalayas*.
□ **rare earth** any of a group of metallic elements with similar chemical properties. **rarely** *adverb*, **rareness** *noun*

rare² *adjective* (of meat) cooked so that the inside is still red.

rarebit *noun* Welsh rarebit *see* Welsh.

rarefied (**rair**-rĕ-fyd) *adjective* **1** (of air etc.) less dense than is normal, thin, like that on high mountains. **2** (of an idea etc.) very subtle.

raring (**rair**-ring) *adjective* (*informal*) enthusiastic, *raring to go*.

rarity (**rair**-rĭ-tee) *noun* **1** rareness. **2** something uncommon; a thing valued because it is rare.

rascal *noun* **1** a dishonest person. **2** a mischievous person. **rascally** *adjective*

rash¹ *noun* an eruption of spots or patches on the skin.

rash² *adjective* acting or done without due consideration of the possible consequences or risks. **rashly** *adverb*, **rashness** *noun*

rasher *noun* a slice of bacon or ham.

rasp *noun* **1** a coarse file with raised sharp points on its surface. **2** a rough grating sound. **–rasp** *verb* **1** to scrape with a rasp. **2** to make a rough grating sound, *a rasping voice*. **3** to utter gratingly, *he rasped out orders*. **4** to have a grating effect upon (a person's feelings).

raspberry *noun* **1** an edible sweet red conical berry. **2** the bush that bears it. **3** (*informal*) a vulgar sound or expression of disapproval or rejection. □ **raspberry jam tree** a Western Australian acacia with wood that smells like raspberry jam.

Rasputin (ras-**pew**-tĭn), Grigori Efimovich (1871–1916), Russian religious fanatic, who exerted great influence over the Tsar and his family during the First World War.

Rasta *noun* a Rastafarian.

Rastafarian (ras-tă-**fair**-ree-ăn) *noun* a member of a Jamaican sect regarding Blacks as a people chosen by God for salvation, the former Emperor Haile Selassie of Ethiopia as the Messiah, and their true homeland as Africa. **–Rastafarian** *adjective* of Rastafarians. [from *Ras Tafari* (*ras* = chief), the name by which Haile Selassie was known]

rat *noun* **1** a rodent resembling a mouse but larger. **2** a scoundrel, a treacherous person. **–rat** *verb* (**ratted**, **ratting**) to withdraw treacherously from an undertaking, to break a promise, *he ratted on us*. □ **rat kangaroo** a small ratlike marsupial, e.g. bettong or potoroo. **rat race** a fiercely competitive struggle to maintain one's position in work or life.

ratafia (rat-ă-**fee**-ă) *noun* a liqueur or biscuit flavoured with fruit kernels.

ratatouille (ra-tă-**too**-ee) *noun* a vegetable dish of zucchini, eggplant, tomatoes, onions, and peppers, fried and stewed in oil. [French]

ratbag *noun* (*informal*) **1** an unpleasant or obnoxious person. **2** an eccentric or unconventional person.

ratchet (**rach**-ĕt) *noun* **1** a series of notches on a bar or wheel in which a catch engages to prevent backward movement. **2** the bar or wheel bearing these.

rate¹ *noun* **1** a standard of reckoning, obtained by expressing the quantity or amount of one thing with respect to another, *walked at a rate of 7 kilometres per hour*. **2** a measure of value or charge or cost, *postal rates*. **3** speed, *drove at a great rate*. **4** a local government tax assessed on the value of land and buildings; *the rates*, the amount payable. **–rate** *verb*

1 to estimate the worth or value of. **2** to assign a value to. **3** to consider, to regard as, *we rate him among our benefactors*. **4** to rank or be regarded in a certain way, *he rates as a benefactor*. **5** to deserve, *that joke didn't rate a laugh*. **6** to levy rates on (property); to value (property) for the purpose of assessing rates. □ **at any rate** in any possible way, no matter what happens; at least. **at this** or **that rate** (*informal*) if this is true or a typical specimen; if things continue as now. [from Latin *ratum* = reckoned]

rate² *verb* to reprimand angrily.

rateable *adjective* liable to rates (*see* rate¹ *noun* sense 4).□ **rateable value** the value at which a house etc. is assessed for rates.

ratepayer *noun* a person liable to pay rates (*see* rate¹ *noun* sense 4).

rather *adverb* **1** slightly, more so than not, *rather dark*. **2** more exactly, *he is lazy rather than incompetent*. **3** more willingly, by preference, *would rather not go*. **4** (*informal*) emphatically yes, *do you like it? Rather!* □ **had rather** would rather.

ratify *verb* (ratified, ratifying) to confirm or assent formally and make (an agreement etc.) officially valid. **ratification** *noun*

rating *noun* **1** the classification assigned to a person or thing in respect of quality, popularity, etc. **2** the amount payable as a local rate. **3** a non-commissioned sailor.

ratio (**ray**-shee-oh) *noun* (*plural* ratios) the relationship between two amounts reckoned as the number of times one contains the other. [from Latin, = reckoning]

ratiocinate (rat-ee-**oss**-ĭ-nayt) *verb* to reason, especially in a formal way. **ratiocination** *noun*

ration *noun* a fixed quantity (especially of food) allowed to one person. – **ration** *verb* to limit (food etc.) to a fixed ration; to allow (a person) only a certain amount. [same origin as *ratio*]

rational *adjective* **1** able to reason. **2** sane. **3** based on reasoning, using reason or logic and rejecting explanations that involve the supernatural etc.□ **rational number** one which is able to be expressed as a ratio of whole numbers. (¶The set of rational numbers comprises fractions and integers.) **rationally** *adverb*, **rationality** (rash-ŏ-**nal**-ĭ-tee) *noun*

rationale (rash-ŏ-**nahl**) *noun* a fundamental reason, the logical basis of something.

rationalise *verb* (also -ize) **1** to make logical and consistent, *tried to rationalise English*

spelling. **2** to invent a rational explanation of, *tried to rationalise their fears*. **3** to make (a process or an industry) more efficient by reorganising so as to eliminate waste of labour, time, or materials. **rationalisation** *noun*

rationalism *noun* **1** the use of rational explanations of the supernatural etc. **2** the policy of making industry etc. more efficient by eliminating wastage, *economic rationalism*. **rationalist** *noun*

rattan (ră-**tan**) *noun* a climbing palm with long thin jointed pliable stems, used for furniture-making.

rattle *verb* **1** to make or cause to make a rapid series of short sharp hard sounds; to cause such sounds by shaking something. **2** to move or travel with a rattling noise. **3** to utter rapidly, *rattled off the oath*. **4** (*informal*) to agitate or fluster, to make nervous. – **rattle** *noun* **1** a rattling sound. **2** a device or toy for making a rattling sound. **3** noise, an uproar.

rattlesnake *noun* a poisonous American snake with a rattling structure in its tail.

rattletrap *noun* a rickety old vehicle etc.

rattling *adjective* **1** that rattles. **2** vigorous, brisk, *a rattling pace*. – **rattling** *adverb* (*informal*) very, *a rattling good story*.

ratty *adjective* (rattier, rattiest) (*informal*) angry, irritable.

raucous (**raw**-kŭs) *adjective* loud and harsh-sounding. **raucously** *adverb*, **raucousness** *noun*

ravage *verb* to do great damage to, to devastate. **ravages** *plural noun* damage, devastation.

rave *verb* **1** to talk wildly or furiously; to talk nonsensically in delirium; *raving mad*, completely mad. **2** (of the wind or sea) to howl, to roar. **3** to speak with rapturous admiration. – **rave** *noun* **1** (*informal*) a very enthusiastic review of a book or play etc. **2** an all-night dance party with techno music, often associated with designer drugs. □ **rave on** (*informal*) to talk tediously and at length.

ravel *verb* (ravelled, ravelling) to tangle; to become tangled. – **ravel** *noun* a tangle.

raven *noun* a large bird with glossy black feathers and a hoarse cry. – **raven** *adjective* (especially of hair) glossy black.

ravening (**rav**-ĕ-ning) *adjective* hungrily seeking prey.

ravenous (**rav**-ĕ-nŭs) *adjective* very hungry. **ravenously** *adverb*

ravine (ră-**veen**) *noun* a deep narrow gorge or cleft between mountains.

ravioli (rav-ee-**oh**-lee) *plural noun* small pasta cases stuffed with meat, cheese, etc. [Italian]

ravish *verb* 1 to rape. 2 to fill with delight, to enrapture. **ravishment** *noun*

ravishing *adjective* very beautiful, filling people with delight.

raw *adjective* 1 not cooked. 2 in its natural state, not yet or not fully processed or manufactured, *raw hides*. 3 (of alcohol) undiluted. 4 crude in artistic quality, lacking finish. 5 inexperienced, untrained, fresh to something, *raw recruits*. 6 stripped of skin and with the underlying flesh exposed; sensitive because of this. 7 (of an edge of cloth) not a selvage and not hemmed. 8 (of weather) damp and chilly. –**raw** *noun* a raw and sensitive patch on the skin; *touched him on the raw*, wounded his feelings on something about which he was sensitive. □ **in the raw** naked; in a raw state; crude, without a softening or refining influence, *life in the raw*. **raw-boned** *adjective* gaunt. **a raw deal** unfair treatment. **raw material** any material or product that is processed to make another; that from which something is made; people who are to be trained. **rawness** *noun*

rawhide *noun* untanned leather.

Rawlplug *noun* (*trademark*) a thin cylindrical plug for holding a screw or nail in masonry.

ray¹ *noun* 1 a single line or narrow beam of light or other radiation. 2 a trace of something good, *a ray of hope*. 3 one of a set of radiating lines, parts, or things. [from Latin *radius* = ray]

ray² *noun* any of several large sea fish related to the shark and used as food, especially the skate.

rayon *noun* a synthetic fibre or fabric made from cellulose.

raze *verb* to destroy completely, to tear down to the ground. [from Latin *rasum* = scraped]

razoo (rah-**zoo**) *noun* (*Austral. informal*) an imaginary coin of trivial value; *haven't got a brass razoo*, have no money at all; *not worth a brass razoo*, worth nothing.

razor *noun* an instrument with a sharp blade or cutters, used in cutting hair especially from the skin. □ **razor grinder** an Australian flycatcher with a grinding or rasping call. [from *raze*]

razorback *noun* 1 an animal with a sharp ridged back. 2 (*Austral.*) a steep-sided ridge.

razzamatazz *noun* (*informal*) showy publicity or display.

razzle-dazzle *noun* (*informal*) 1 excitement, bustle. 2 extravagant publicity.

RC *abbreviation* Roman Catholic.

Rd *abbreviation* road.

re (*pr.* ree) *preposition* in the matter of, about, concerning.

re- *prefix* 1 again (as in *redecorate*, *revisit*). 2 back again, with return to a previous state (as in *re-enter*, *reopen*). [Latin]

reach *verb* 1 to stretch out or extend. 2 to go as far as, to arrive at. 3 to stretch out one's hand in order to touch, grasp, or take something, *reached for his gun*. 4 to establish communication with, *you can reach me by phone*. 5 to achieve, to attain, *reached a speed of 100 km/h; reached a conclusion*. 6 to sail with the wind blowing at right angles to the ship's course. –**reach** *noun* 1 an act of reaching. 2 the distance over which a person or thing can reach; the extent covered by one's mental powers or abilities. 3 a continuous extent of a river between two bends or of a canal between two locks.

reachable *adjective* able to be reached.

react *verb* to cause or undergo a reaction.

reaction *noun* 1 a response to a stimulus or act or situation etc. 2 a chemical change produced by two or more substances acting upon each other. 3 the occurrence of one condition after a period of the opposite, e.g. of depression after excitement.

reactionary *adjective* opposed to (especially political) change or reform; conservative. –**reactionary** *noun* a person who favours reactionary policies.

reactivate *verb* to restore to a state of activity. **reactivation** *noun*

reactive *adjective* 1 showing reaction. 2 reacting rather than taking the initiative. 3 susceptible to chemical reaction.

reactor *noun* (also **nuclear reactor**) an apparatus for the controlled production of nuclear energy.

read (*pr.* reed) *verb* (**read** (*pr.* red), **reading**) 1 to be able to understand the meaning of (written or printed words or symbols). 2 to speak (written or printed words etc.) aloud, *read to the children; read them a story*. 3 to study or discover by reading, *we read about the accident*. 4 to carry out a course of study; *he is reading Law*, is studying Law.

5 to interpret mentally, to find implications, *don't read too much into it*. **6** to have a certain wording, *the sign reads 'Keep Left'*. **7** to copy, search, extract, or transfer (computerised data); to do this in or on (any storage device or medium). **8** (of a measuring instrument) to indicate or register, *the thermometer reads 20°*. –**read** *noun* (*informal*) **1** a session of reading, *had a nice quiet read*. **2** a thing in regard to its readability, *an interesting read*. ☐ **read a person's hand** to interpret the markings on it as a fortune-teller does. **read between the lines** to discover a hidden or implicit meaning in something. **read-only** *adjective* (of a computer memory) with contents that can be copied, searched, extracted, or transferred but not changed. **read-out** *noun* the output or display of data from a computer etc. **read up** to make a special study of (a subject) by reading. **well read** (of a person) having knowledge of a subject or good general acquaintance with literature through reading.

readable *adjective* **1** pleasant and interesting to read. **2** legible. **readability** *noun*

readdress *verb* to alter the address on (a letter etc.).

reader *noun* **1** a person who reads. **2** a book containing passages for practice in reading. **3** a university teacher of rank next below professor. **4** a machine producing an image that can be read from microfilm etc.

readership *noun* the readers of a newspaper etc.; the number of these.

readily *adverb* **1** without reluctance, willingly. **2** without difficulty.

readiness *noun* being ready.

reading *noun* **1** the act of one who reads. **2** being read; the way something is read; an occasion when something is read. **3** books etc. intended to be read. **4** the amount that is indicated or registered by a measuring instrument.

readjust *verb* **1** to adjust (a thing) again. **2** to adapt oneself again. **readjustment** *noun*

ready *adjective* (**readier**, **readiest**) **1** in a fit state for immediate action or use. **2** willing, *always ready to help a friend*. **3** about or inclined to do something, *looked ready to collapse*. **4** quick, *a ready wit*. **5** easily available, *found a ready market*. –**ready** *adverb* beforehand, *ready cooked*. ☐ **at the ready** ready for action. **ready-made** *adjective* (of clothes) made for selling in standard shapes and sizes, not to individual customers' orders; (of opinions or excuses etc.) of a standard type, not original. **ready money** actual coin or notes; payment on the spot, not credit. **ready reckoner** a collection of answers to the kind of calculations commonly needed in business etc.

reafforest *verb* (also **reforest**) to replant (former forest land) with trees. **reafforestation** *noun*

reagent (ree-**ay**-jĕnt) *noun* a substance used to produce a chemical reaction.

real *adjective* **1** existing as a thing or occurring as a fact, not imaginary. **2** genuine, natural, not imitation, *real pearls*. **3** true, complete, worthy of the name, *there's no real cure*. **4** (of income or value etc.) with regard to its purchasing power. **5** consisting of immovable property such as land or houses, *real property*, *real estate*. –**real** *adverb* (*informal*) really, very. ☐ **real number** any rational or irrational number. **real-time** *adjective* (of a computer system) able to receive continually changing data from outside sources, process these data rapidly, and supply results that can influence their sources.

realign *verb* **1** to align again. **2** to regroup in politics etc. **realignment** *noun*

realise *verb* (also **-ize**) **1** to be fully aware of, to accept as a fact, *realised his mistake*. **2** to convert (a hope or plan) into a fact, *our hopes were realised*. **3** to convert (securities or property) into money by selling. **4** to obtain or bring in as profit; (of goods) to fetch as a price. **realisation** *noun*

realism *noun* **1** (in art and literature) being true to nature, representing things as they are in reality. **2** the attitude of a realist.

realist *noun* a person who faces facts, one whose ideas and practices are based on facts not on ideals or illusions.

realistic *adjective* **1** true to nature, closely resembling what is imitated or portrayed. **2** facing facts, based on facts not on ideals or illusions. **3** (of wages or prices) high enough to pay the worker or seller adequately. **realistically** *adverb*

reality *noun* **1** the quality of being real; resemblance to an original. **2** all that is real, the real world as distinct from imagination or fantasy, *lost touch with reality*. **3** something that exists or that is real, *the realities of the situation*. ☐ **reality television** television programming that follows real people in their everyday lives or in an artificial situation.

really *adverb* **1** in fact. **2** positively, indeed, *a really nice girl*. **3** an expression of interest, surprise, or mild protest.

realm (*pr.* relm) *noun* **1** a kingdom. **2** a field of activity or interest, *the realms of science*.

ream *noun* a quantity of paper (about 500 sheets) of the same size. **reams** *plural noun* a great quantity of written matter.

reap *verb* **1** to cut (grain or a similar crop) as a harvest. **2** to receive as the consequence of actions. **reaper** *noun*

reappear *verb* to appear again. **reappearance** *noun*

reappraisal (ree-ă-**pray**-zăl) *noun* a new appraisal.

rear¹ *noun* the back part of something. **– rear** *adjective* situated at or in the rear.
☐ **bring up the rear** *see* **bring**. **rear admiral** a naval officer ranking below vice admiral.

rear² *verb* **1** to bring up and educate (children); to breed and look after (animals); to cultivate (crops). **2** to build or set up (a monument etc.). **3** (of a horse etc.) to raise itself on its hind legs. **4** (of a structure) to extend to a great height.

rearguard *noun* a body of troops whose job is to protect the rear of the main force.

rearm *verb* to arm again. **rearmament** *noun*

rearmost *adjective* furthest back.

rearrange *verb* to arrange in a different way or order. **rearrangement** *noun*

rearward *adjective* & *adverb* towards the rear. **rearwards** *adverb*

reason *noun* **1** a motive, cause, or justification of something; a fact put forward as this. **2** the ability to think and understand and draw conclusions. **3** sanity, *lost his reason*. **4** good sense or judgment; what is right, practical, or possible. **– reason** *verb* **1** to use one's ability to think and draw conclusions, to state as a step in this. **2** to try to persuade someone by giving reasons.

Usage *The reason (why) … is …* should be followed by *that*, not *because*. Correct usage is *The reason why I am late is that my car wouldn't start* (not 'the reason is because my car wouldn't start').

---

reasonable *adjective* **1** ready to use or listen to reason, sensible, *a reasonable person*. **2** in accordance with reason, not absurd, logical. **3** moderate, not expensive or extortionate, *reasonable prices*. **reasonably** *adverb*, **reasonableness** *noun*

reassemble *verb* to assemble again.

reassure (ree-ă-**shoor**) *verb* to restore confidence to, to remove the fears or doubts of. **reassurance** *noun*

Réaumur scale (ray-oh-**mewr**) *noun* a scale of temperature with 80 divisions between 0° (the melting point of ice) and 80° (the boiling point of water). [named after the French scientist R.A.F. de Réaumur (1683–1757)]

rebate¹ (**ree**-bayt) *noun* a reduction in the amount to be paid, a partial refund. [from *re-* + *abate*]

rebate² (**ree**-bayt) *noun* = **rabbet**.

rebel (**reb**-ĕl) *noun* a person who rebels. **– rebel** (rĕ-**bel**) *verb* (**rebelled, rebelling**) **1** to refuse to continue allegiance to an established government; to take up arms against it. **2** to resist authority or control; to refuse to obey, to protest strongly. [from *re-* + Latin *bellare* = to fight]

rebellion *noun* open resistance to authority, especially organised armed resistance to an established government.

rebellious *adjective* rebelling, insubordinate. **rebelliously** *adverb*, **rebelliousness** *noun*

rebirth *noun* a return to life or activity, a revival.

rebound (rĕ-**bownd**) *verb* **1** to spring back after an impact. **2** to have an adverse effect upon the originator. **– rebound** (**ree**-bownd) *noun* an act or instance of rebounding.
☐ **on the rebound** (of a hit or catch) made to a ball that is rebounding; (of an action etc.) done while still reacting to depression or disappointment.

rebuff *noun* an unkind or contemptuous refusal, a snub. **– rebuff** *verb* to give a rebuff to.

rebuild *verb* (**rebuilt, rebuilding**) to build again after destruction or demolition.

rebuke *verb* to reprove sharply or severely. **– rebuke** *noun* a sharp or severe reproof.

rebus (**ree**-bŭs) *noun* (*plural* **rebuses**) a representation of a name or word by means of a picture or pictures suggesting its syllables.

rebut (rĕ-**but**) *verb* (**rebutted, rebutting**) to refute or disprove (evidence or an accusation). **rebuttal** *noun* [from *re-* + *butt*⁴]

recalcitrant (rĕ-**kal**-sĭ-trănt) *adjective* disobedient, resisting authority or discipline.

recalcitrance *noun* [from Latin, = kicking back]

recall *verb* **1** to summon (a person) to return from a place. **2** to bring back into the mind, to remember or cause to remember. **3** to withdraw (a faulty product etc.) from sale or request its return. –**recall** *noun* recalling, being recalled.

recant (rĕ-**kant**) *verb* to withdraw one's former statement or belief etc. formally, rejecting it as wrong or heretical. **recantation** *noun* [from *re-*, + Latin *cantare* = sing]

recap (**ree**-kap) *verb* (**recapped, recapping**) (*informal*) to recapitulate. –**recap** *noun* (*informal*) a recapitulation.

recapitulate (ree-kă-**pit**-yŭ-layt) *verb* to state again the main points of what has been said or discussed. **recapitulation** *noun* [from *re-*, + Latin *capitulum* = chapter]

recapture *verb* **1** to capture (a person or thing that has escaped or been lost to an enemy). **2** to succeed in experiencing (a former state or emotion) again. –**recapture** *noun* recapturing.

recast *verb* (**recast, recasting**) to cast again, to put into a different form.

recce (**rek**-ee) *noun* (*informal*) a reconnaissance.

recede *verb* **1** to go or shrink back from a certain point, to seem to go away from the observer, *the floods receded; the shore receded as we sailed away*. **2** to slope backwards, *a receding forehead*. [from *re-*, + Latin *cedere* = go]

receipt (rĕ-**seet**) *noun* **1** receiving, being received, *on receipt of your letter*. **2** a written acknowledgement that something has been received or that money has been paid. **3** (*old use*) a recipe. –**receipt** *verb* to mark (a bill) as having been paid.

receive *verb* **1** to acquire, accept, or take in (something offered, sent, or given). **2** to experience, to be treated with, *it received close attention*. **3** to take the force, weight, or impact of. **4** to serve as a receptacle for. **5** to allow to enter as a member or guest. **6** to greet on arrival. [from *re-* = back again, + Latin *capere* = take]

receiver *noun* **1** a person or thing that receives something. **2** one who accepts stolen goods while knowing them to be stolen. **3** an official appointed by a court to administer the property of a bankrupt person or company, or property subject to litigation. **4** a radio or television apparatus that receives broadcast signals and converts them into sound or a picture. **5** the part of a telephone that receives the incoming sound and is held to the ear.

receivership *noun* **1** the office of receiver. **2** the state of being dealt with by a receiver, *in receivership*.

receiving *noun* the crime of accepting stolen goods while knowing them to be stolen.

recent *adjective* not long past, happening or begun in a time shortly before the present. **recently** *adverb*

receptacle *noun* something for holding or containing what is put into it.

reception *noun* **1** receiving; being received. **2** the way something is received, *the speech got a cool reception*. **3** an assembly held to receive guests, *a wedding reception*. **4** a place where hotel guests or a firm's clients are received on arrival. **5** the receiving of broadcast signals, the efficiency of this, *reception was poor*. **6** a first class at school.

receptionist *noun* a person employed to receive and direct callers or clients or patients.

receptive *adjective* able or quick or willing to receive knowledge, ideas, or suggestions etc. **receptiveness** *noun*, **receptivity** *noun*

receptor *noun* an organ of the body that is able to respond to a stimulus (such as light or pressure) and transmit a signal through a sensory nerve.

recess (rĕ-**sess** *or* **ree**-sess) *noun* **1** a part or space set back from the line of a wall etc.; a small hollow place inside something. **2** temporary cessation from business, a time of this, *while parliament is in recess*. **3** the mid-morning break between classes at school; a snack eaten during this break. –**recess** *verb* to make a recess in or of (a wall etc.); to set back. [same origin as *recede*]

recession *noun* **1** receding from a point or level. **2** a temporary decline in economic activity or prosperity.

recessional *noun* a hymn sung while clergy and choir withdraw after a church service.

recessive *adjective* **1** tending to recede. **2** (of inherited characteristics) remaining latent when a dominant characteristic is present.

recharge *verb* to charge (a battery or gun etc.) again. **rechargeable** *adjective*

recherché (rĕ-**shair**-shay) *adjective* **1** devised or selected with care. **2** far-fetched. [French]

recidivist (rĕ-**sid**-ĭ-vĭst) *noun* a person who constantly commits crimes and seems unable to be cured of criminal tendencies, a persistent offender. **recidivism** *noun* [from *re-*, + Latin *cadere* = to fall]

recipe *noun* **1** directions for preparing a dish etc. in cookery. **2** a way of achieving something, *a recipe for success*. [Latin, = take!]

recipient (rĕ-**sip**-ee-ĕnt) *noun* a person who receives something.

reciprocal (rĕ-**sip**-rŏ-kăl) *adjective* **1** given or received in return, *reciprocal help*. **2** given or felt by each towards the other, mutual, *reciprocal affection*. **3** corresponding but the other way round, *I thought he was a shop assistant, while he made the reciprocal mistake and thought that I was*. –**reciprocal** *noun* a mathematical expression so related to another that their product is unity (e.g. $\frac{2}{3}$ *is the reciprocal of* $\frac{3}{2}$). **reciprocally** *adverb* [from Latin, = moving backwards and forwards]

reciprocate (rĕ-**sip**-rŏ-kayt) *verb* **1** to give and receive; to make a return for something done, given, or felt. **2** (of a machine part) to move backward and forward alternately. **reciprocation** *noun*

reciprocity (ress-ĭ-**pross**-ĭ-tee) *noun* a reciprocal condition or action; the giving of privileges in return for similar privileges.

recital *noun* **1** reciting. **2** a long account of a series of events. **3** a musical entertainment given by one performer or group.

recitation *noun* **1** reciting. **2** a thing recited.

recitative (ress-ĭ-tă-**teev**) *noun* a narrative or conversational part of an opera or oratorio, sung in a rhythm imitating that of ordinary speech.

recite *verb* **1** to repeat (a passage) aloud from memory, especially before an audience. **2** to state (facts) in order. [from Latin, = read aloud]

reckless *adjective* wildly impulsive, rash. **recklessly** *adverb*, **recklessness** *noun* [from *reck* = heed, + *-less* = without]

reckon *verb* **1** to count up. **2** to include in a total or as a member of a particular class. **3** to have as one's opinion, to feel confident, *I reckon we shall win*. **4** to rely or base one's plans, *we reckoned on your support*.
□ **day of reckoning** the time when one must atone for one's actions or be punished. **reckon with** to take into account; *a person or thing to be reckoned with*, one that must be considered as important.

reckoner *noun* an aid to reckoning, a ready reckoner (*see* **ready**).

reclaim *verb* **1** to take action so as to recover possession of. **2** to make (flooded or waste land) usable, e.g. by draining or irrigating it. **reclamation** (rek-lă-**may**-shŏn) *noun*

recline *verb* to have or put one's body in a more or less horizontal or leaning position. [from *re-*, + Latin *-clinare* = to lean]

recluse (rĕ-**klooss**) *noun* a person who lives alone and avoids mixing with people. **reclusive** *adjective* [from *re-* = away, + Latin *clausum* = shut]

recognisable *adjective* (also **-izable**) able to be recognised. **recognisably** *adverb*

recognisance (rĕ-**kog**-nĭ-zăns) *noun* (also **-izance**) a pledge made to a lawcourt or magistrate that a person will observe some condition (e.g. keep the peace) or appear when summoned; a sum of money pledged as surety for this.

recognise *verb* (also **-ize**) **1** to know again, to identify from one's previous knowledge or experience. **2** to realise or admit the nature of, *recognised the hopelessness of the situation*. **3** to acknowledge or accept formally as genuine or valid, *France has recognised the island's new government*. **4** to show appreciation of (ability or service etc.) by giving an honour or reward. **5** (of a chairman in a formal debate) to allow (a particular person) the right to speak next. [from *re-*, + Latin *cognoscere* = know]

recognition *noun* recognising; being recognised; *a presentation in recognition of his services*, as a token of appreciation.

recoil *verb* **1** to move or spring back suddenly, to rebound. **2** to draw oneself back in fear or disgust. **3** to have an adverse effect upon the originator. –**recoil** *noun* the act or sensation of recoiling.

recollect *verb* to remember. **recollection** *noun*

recommence (ree-kŏ-**menss**) *verb* to begin again. **recommencement** *noun*

recommend *verb* **1** to advise (a course of action or a treatment etc.). **2** to praise as worthy of employment, favour, or trial etc. **3** (of qualities or conduct) to make acceptable or desirable, *this plan has much to recommend it*. **recommendation** *noun*

recompense (**rek**-ŏm-penss) *verb* to repay or reward, to compensate. –**recompense** *noun* payment or reward etc. in return for something.

reconcilable *adjective* able to be reconciled.

reconcile (**rek**-ŏn-syl) *verb* 1 to restore friendship between (people) after an estrangement or quarrel. 2 to induce (a person or oneself) to accept an unwelcome fact or situation, *this reconciled him to living far from home*. 3 to bring (facts or statements etc.) into harmony or compatibility when they appear to conflict. [from *re-* + *conciliate*]

reconciliation *noun* 1 the action or an act of reconciling. 2 (*Austral.*) unity between indigenous and non-indigenous Australians.

recondite (**rek**-ŏn-dyt) *adjective* (of a subject) obscure; (of an author) writing about an obscure subject. [from *re-*, + Latin *conditum* = hidden]

recondition *verb* to overhaul and make any necessary repairs to.

reconnaissance (rĕ-**kon**-ă-săns) *noun* an exploration or examination of an area in order to obtain information about it (especially for military purposes); a preliminary survey. [French, = recognition]

reconnoitre (rek-ŏ-**noi**-ter) *verb* to make a reconnaissance of (an area); to make a preliminary survey.

reconsider *verb* to consider again, especially with the possibility of changing one's former decision. **reconsideration** *noun*

reconstitute *verb* to reconstruct; to reorganise. **reconstitution** *noun*

reconstituted *adjective* (of food) dried and later restored to its original form, usually by adding water.

reconstruct *verb* 1 to construct or build again. 2 to create or enact (past events) again, e.g. in investigating the circumstances of a crime. **reconstruction** *noun*

record (**rek**-ord) *noun* 1 information preserved in a permanent form, especially in writing. 2 a document etc. bearing this. 3 a disc bearing recorded sound. 4 facts known about a person's past, *has a good record of service*; *have a record* or *a police record*, to have past convictions which are on record. 5 the best performance or most remarkable event etc. of its kind that is known; *hold the record*, to be the one who achieved this. **–record** (**rek**-ord) *adjective* best, highest, or most extreme hitherto recorded, *a record crop*. **–record** (rĕ-**kord**) *verb* 1 to set down in writing or other permanent form. 2 to preserve (sound or visual scenes) on a disc or magnetic tape etc. for later reproduction. 3 (of a measuring-instrument)

to register. □ **for the record** so that facts may be recorded. **off the record** stated unofficially or not for publication. **on record** preserved in written records. **record-breaking** *adjective* surpassing all previous records. **record player** an apparatus for reproducing sound from discs on which it is recorded.

recorder *noun* 1 a person or thing that records something. 2 a kind of flute held forward and downwards from the mouth as it is played.

recording *noun* 1 a process by which audio or video signals are recorded for later reproduction. 2 the disc or tape etc. produced. 3 the recorded material.

recount (rĕ-**kownt**) *verb* to narrate, to tell in detail, *recounted his adventures*. [from Old French *reconter* = tell]

re-count (**ree**-kownt) *verb* to count again. **–re-count** *noun* a second counting, especially of election votes to check the totals.

recoup (rĕ-**koop**) *verb* 1 to recover what one has lost or its equivalent, *recoup oneself* or *recoup one's losses*. 2 to reimburse or compensate, *recoup him for his losses*.

recourse (rĕ-**korss**) *noun* a source of help. **have recourse to** to turn to (a person or thing) for help.

recover *verb* 1 to regain possession, use, or control of. 2 to obtain as compensation, *sought to recover damages from the company*. 3 to return to a normal condition after illness or unconsciousness. □ **recover oneself** to regain consciousness or calmness, or one's balance. **recovery** *noun*

recoverable *adjective* able to be recovered.

re-create *verb* to create again.

recreation (rek-ree-**ay**-shŏn) *noun* 1 the process or means of refreshing or entertaining oneself. 2 a pleasurable activity. **recreational** *adjective* [from *re-* + *creation*]

recriminate *verb* to make recriminations.

recrimination *noun* an angry retort or accusation made in retaliation. [from *re-*, + Latin *criminare* = accuse]

recrudesce (rek-roo-**dess**) *verb* (of a disease or sore or discontent) to break out again. **recrudescent** *adjective*, **recrudescence** *noun* [from *re-*, + Latin *crudescere* = to become raw]

recruit *noun* 1 a person who has just joined the armed forces and is not yet trained. 2 a new member of a society or other group. **–recruit** *verb* 1 to form (an army or other group) by enlisting recruits. **2** to enlist (a person) as a recruit. **3** to refresh, *recruit one's strength*. **recruitment** *noun*

rectal *adjective* of the rectum.

rectangle *noun* a four-sided geometric figure with four right angles, especially one with adjacent sides unequal in length. [from Latin *rectus* = straight or right, + *angle*]

rectangular *adjective* shaped like a rectangle.

rectifiable *adjective* able to be rectified.

rectifier *noun* a device that converts alternating current to direct current.

rectify *verb* (**rectified**, **rectifying**) **1** to put right, to correct, *rectify the error*. **2** to purify or refine, especially by distillation. **3** to convert (alternating current) to direct current. **rectification** *noun* [from Latin *rectus* = right]

rectilinear (rek-tĭ-**lin**-ee-er) *adjective* bounded by straight lines, *a rectilinear figure*. [from Latin *rectus* = straight, + *linear*]

rectitude *noun* moral goodness; correctness of behaviour or procedure. [from Latin *rectus* = right]

rector *noun* **1** (in the Anglican Church) a member of the clergy in charge of a parish. **2** (in the Catholic Church) the priest in charge of a church or religious institution. **3** the head of certain universities, colleges, and schools. [Latin, = ruler]

rectory *noun* the house of a rector.

rectum *noun* the last section of the large intestine, between colon and anus. [Latin, = straight (intestine)]

recumbent *adjective* lying down, reclining. [from *re-*, + Latin *cumbens* = lying]

recuperate (rĕ-**koo**-pĕ-rayt) *verb* **1** to recover, to regain (one's health or strength) after illness or exhaustion. **2** to recover (losses). **recuperation** *noun*, **recuperative** *adjective*

recur *verb* (**recurred**, **recurring**) to happen again, to keep occurring. ☐ **recurring decimal** a decimal fraction in which the same figures are repeated indefinitely, e.g. 2.666 … or 4.014014 … [from *re-*, + Latin *currere* = to run]

recurrent (rĕ-**ku**-rĕnt) *adjective* recurring, *a recurrent problem*. **recurrence** *noun*

recurve (ree-**kerv**) *verb* to bend or be bent backwards, *a flower with recurved petals*.

recusant (**rek**-yŭ-zănt) *noun* a person who refuses to submit to authority or to comply with a regulation. [from Latin *recusare* = to refuse]

recycle *verb* to convert (waste material) into a form in which it can be reused. **recyclable** *adjective*

red *adjective* (**redder**, **reddest**) **1** of the colour of blood or a colour approaching this. **2** (of the face) flushed with anger or shame, (of the eyes) bloodshot or reddened when weeping. **3** (*informal*) Communist, favouring Communism. **4** anarchist. – **red** *noun* **1** red colour. **2** a red substance or material; red clothes. **3** a red light. **4** the debit side of an account. **5** a Communist. **6** an anarchist. ☐ **in the red** having a debit balance, in debt. **red blood cell** or **corpuscle** one that contains haemoglobin and carries oxygen and carbon dioxide to and from the tissues, an erythrocyte. **red-blooded** *adjective* full of vigour. **red carpet** privileged treatment given to an important visitor. **Red Centre** central Australia. **red-handed** *adjective* in the act of crime, *was caught red-handed*. **red herring** a smoked herring; a misleading clue; something that draws attention away from the matter under consideration. **red-hot** *adjective* so hot that it glows red; highly excited or angry; (of news) fresh, completely new. **Red Indian** (*offensive*) an indigenous North American person. **red lead** red oxide of lead, used as a pigment. **red-letter day** a day that is memorable because of some joyful occurrence. **red light** a signal to stop on a road or railway; a warning or refusal. **red shift** the displacement of the spectrum to longer wavelengths in the light coming from receding galaxies. **red tape** use of too many rules and forms in official business. **reddish** *adjective*, **redly** *adverb*, **redness** *noun*

redback *noun* a venomous Australian spider with a red stripe on the female.

redbreast *noun* a robin.

Red Crescent the equivalent of the Red Cross in Muslim countries.

Red Cross an international organisation for the treatment of the sick and wounded in war and for helping those affected by large-scale natural disasters.

redcurrant *noun* a small round edible red berry; the bush bearing it.

redden *verb* to make or become red.

redecorate *verb* to decorate freshly. **redecoration** *noun*

redeem *verb* 1 to buy back, to recover (a thing) by payment or by doing something. 2 to clear (a debt etc.) by paying it off, *redeem the mortgage*. 3 to convert (tokens etc.) into goods or cash. 4 to obtain the freedom of (a person) by payment. 5 to save from damnation or from the consequences of sin. 6 to make up for faults or deficiencies, *it has one redeeming feature*. □ **redeem oneself** to make up for one's former fault. [from *re-*, + Latin *emere* = buy]

redeemable *adjective* able to be redeemed.

redeemer *noun* one who redeems something. –**the Redeemer** Christ as the redeemer of mankind.

redemption *noun* redeeming; being redeemed.

redeploy *verb* to send (troops or workers etc.) to a new place or task. **redeployment** *noun*

redevelop *verb* (**redeveloped**, **redeveloping**) to develop (especially land) afresh. **redevelopment** *noun*

redfin *noun* (*Austral.*) an introduced edible freshwater fish, the European perch.

redfish *noun* any of several Australian fish, especially the nannygai.

Red Guard any of various radical groups and their members, especially (i) an organised detachment of workers during the Russian Bolshevik revolution of 1917, (ii) a youth movement during the Cultural Revolution in China, 1966–76.

redhead *noun* a person with reddish hair.

rediffusion *noun* relaying of broadcast programs from a central receiver.

redirect *verb* to direct or send to another place, to readdress. **redirection** *noun*

redo (ree-**doo**) *verb* (**redid**, **redone**, **redoing**) 1 to do again. 2 to redecorate.

redolent (**red**-ŏ-lĕnt) *adjective* 1 smelling strongly, *redolent of onions* (¶ not *redolent of the smell of onions*). 2 full of memories, *a town redolent of age and romance*. **redolence** *noun* [from *re-*, + Latin *olens* = smelling]

redouble *verb* 1 to double again. 2 to make or become more intense, *redoubled their efforts*.

redoubt (rĕ-**dowt**) *noun* an outwork or fieldwork with no defences flanking it. [from Latin *reductum* = withdrawn]

redoubtable *adjective* formidable, especially as an opponent. [from French *redouter* = to fear]

redound *verb* to come back as an advantage or disadvantage, to accrue, *this will redound to our credit*. [from Latin *redundare* = to overflow]

redox (**ree**-doks) *noun* a chemical reaction in which one substance is oxidised and another reduced. –**redox** *adjective* of or involving this reaction.

redress (rĕ-**dress**) *verb* to set right, to rectify, *redress the balance*. –**redress** *noun* reparation, amends for a wrong done, *has no chance of redress for this damage*.

Red Sea a long narrow landlocked sea between North Africa and the Arabian Peninsula.

reduce *verb* 1 to make or become less. 2 to make lower in rank or status. 3 to slim. 4 to subdue; to bring by force or necessity into a specified state or condition, *was reduced to despair* or *to borrowing*. 5 to convert into a simpler or more general form, *reduce the fraction to its lowest terms*; *the problem may be reduced to two main elements*. 6 to remove oxygen from a compound, or add hydrogen or electrons to it. 7 to boil off excess liquid from (a sauce etc.) to concentrate it. 8 to restore (a fractured or dislocated bone) to its proper position. □ **reduced circumstances** poverty after a period of prosperity. **reducer** *noun*, **reducible** *adjective* [from *re-*, + Latin *ducere* = bring]

reduction *noun* 1 reducing; being reduced. 2 the amount by which something is reduced, especially in price.

redundant *adjective* 1 superfluous. 2 (of workers) no longer needed for any available job and therefore liable to dismissal. 3 (of apparatus etc.) being a duplicate in case of failure of the corresponding part or unit. **redundancy** *noun* [same origin as *redound*]

reduplicate *verb* to double (a letter or syllable), e.g. *bye-bye*, *goody-goody*.

redwood *noun* 1 a very tall evergreen coniferous tree of California. 2 its reddish wood.

re-echo *verb* (**re-echoed**, **re-echoing**) to echo; to echo repeatedly, to resound.

reed *noun* 1 a water or marsh plant with tall straight hollow stems. 2 its stem. 3 a vibrating part that produces the sound in certain wind instruments.

reedy *adjective* 1 full of reeds. 2 like a reed in slenderness or (of grass) thickness. 3 (of the voice) having the thin high tone of a reed instrument. reediness *noun*

reef[1] *noun* 1 a ridge of rock or shingle or sand that reaches to or close to the surface of water. 2 a lode of ore; the bedrock surrounding this.

reef[2] *noun* each of several strips at the top or bottom of a sail that can be drawn in so as to reduce the area of sail exposed to the wind. –reef *verb* to shorten (a sail) by drawing in a reef or reefs. □ reef knot a symmetrical double knot that is very secure.

reefer *noun* a thick double-breasted jacket.

reek *noun* a foul or stale smell. –reek *verb* to smell strongly or unpleasantly.

reel *noun* 1 a cylinder or similar device on which something is wound. 2 this and what is wound on it; the amount held by a reel. 3 a lively folk or Scottish dance; music for this. –reel *verb* 1 to wind on or off a reel. 2 to pull (a thing) in by using a reel. 3 to stagger; to have a violent swinging or spinning motion. □ reel off to rattle off (a story etc.).

re-elect *verb* to elect again. re-election *noun*

re-enter *verb* to enter again. re-entry *noun*

re-entrant *adjective* (of an angle) pointing inwards, reflex.

re-establish *verb* to establish again. re-establishment *noun*

reeve *noun* (*Brit. old use*) the chief magistrate of a town or district.

re-examine *verb* to examine again. re-examination *noun*

refectory (rĕ-**fek**-tŏ-ree) *noun* the dining room of a monastery, college, or similar establishment. [from Latin *refectum* = refreshed]

refer *verb* (referred, referring) 1 to make an allusion, to direct people's attention by words, *I wasn't referring to you.* 2 to send on or direct (a person) to some authority, specialist, or source of information. 3 to turn to (a thing) for information, *we referred to the list of rules.* 4 to ascribe. [from *re-* = back, + Latin *ferre* = bring]

referable (rĕ-**fer**-rĕ-bŭl) *adjective* able to be referred.

referee *noun* 1 an umpire in various sports. 2 a person to whom disputes are referred for decision, an arbitrator. 3 a person willing to testify to the character or ability of someone applying for a job. –referee *verb* (refereed, refereeing) to act as referee in (a game etc.).

reference *noun* 1 the act of referring. 2 something that can be referred to as an authority or standard. 3 a statement referring to or mentioning something, *made no reference to recent events.* 4 a direction to a book or page or file etc. where information can be found; the book or passage etc. cited in this way. 5 a testimonial. 6 a person willing to testify to someone's character, ability, or financial circumstances. □ in or with reference to in connection with, about. reference book a book providing information for reference but not designed to be read straight through. reference library one containing books that can be consulted but not taken away. terms of reference the scope of an inquiry etc.

referendum *noun* (*plural* referendums or referenda) the referring of a question to the people of a country etc. for direct decision by a general vote; a vote taken in this way. [Latin, = referring]

referral (rĕ-**fer**-răl) *noun* referring; being referred.

refill (ree-**fil**) *verb* to fill again. –refill (**ree**-fil) *noun* 1 a second or later filling. 2 the material used for this; a thing that replaces something used up.

refine *verb* 1 to remove impurities or defects from. 2 to make elegant or cultured.

refinement *noun* 1 refining; being refined. 2 elegance of behaviour or manners etc. 3 an improvement added to something. 4 a piece of subtle reasoning, a fine distinction.

refiner *noun* one whose business is to refine crude oil, metal, or sugar etc.

refinery *noun* a factory where crude substances are refined.

refit (ree-**fit**) *verb* (refitted, refitting) to renew or repair the fittings of. –refit (**ree**-fit) *noun* refitting. refitment *noun*

reflate *verb* to cause reflation of (a financial system).

reflation *noun* the process of restoring a financial system to its previous condition when deflation has been carried out too fast or too far. reflationary *adjective*

reflect *verb* 1 to throw back (light, heat, or sound). 2 to be thrown back in this way. 3 (of a mirror etc.) to show an image of. 4 to correspond to (a thing) because of its influence, *improved methods of agriculture were reflected in larger crops.* 5 to bring (credit or discredit). 6 to bring discredit,

this failure reflects upon the whole industry.
7 to think deeply, to consider; to remind
oneself of past events. [from *re-*, + Latin
flectere = to bend]

reflection *noun* **1** reflecting; being reflected.
2 reflected light or heat etc.; a reflected image.
3 discredit; a thing that brings this. **4** deep
thought; an idea or statement produced by this.

reflective *adjective* **1** reflecting. **2** thoughtful,
in a reflective mood.

reflector *noun* **1** a thing that reflects light or
heat or images. **2** a red disc or fitment on the
back of a vehicle, making it visible in the dark
by reflecting the lights of vehicles behind it.

reflex (**ree**-fleks) *noun* **1** a reflex action.
2 reflected light; a reflected image.
☐ **reflex action** an involuntary or instinctive
movement in response to a stimulus. **reflex
angle** an angle of more than 180°. **reflex
camera** one in which the image given by the
lens is reflected by an angled mirror to the
viewfinder. [from *reflect*]

reflexive *adjective* (of a word or form)
referring back to the subject of the verb, in
which the action of the verb is performed on
its subject, e.g. *he washed himself.* –**reflexive**
noun a reflexive word or form.
☐ **reflexive pronoun** any of the pronouns
myself, himself, itself, themselves, etc.

reflexology *noun* the practice of massaging
points on the feet, hands, and head to relieve
tension and treat illness. **reflexologist** *noun*

refloat *verb* to set (a stranded ship) afloat
again.

reflux *noun* a backward flow.

reforest = **reafforest.**

reform *verb* to make or become better by
removal or abandonment of imperfections
or faults. –**reform** *noun* **1** reforming; being
reformed. **2** a change to improve something.
☐ **Reformed Church** one that accepted the
principles of the Reformation, especially
the Calvinist Church. **Reform Judaism** a
liberalised form of Judaism. **reformer** *noun*

re-form *verb* to form again.

reformation (ref-er-**may**-shŏn) *noun*
reforming; being reformed; a great change for
the better in public affairs. **the Reformation**
the 16th-century movement for reform of
certain practices and doctrines of the Church
of Rome, resulting in the establishment of
Reformed or Protestant Churches.

reformatory (rĕ-**form**-ă-tŏ-ree) *noun* an
institution where young offenders against the
law are sent to be reformed.

refract (rĕ-**frakt**) *verb* to bend (a ray of light)
at the point where it enters water or glass etc.
obliquely. **refraction** *noun*, **refractor** *noun*,
refractive *adjective* [from *re-*, + Latin *fractum*
= broken]

refractory *adjective* **1** resisting control or
discipline, stubborn, *a refractory child.* **2** (of
a disease etc.) not yielding to treatment. **3** (of
a substance) resistant to heat; hard to fuse or
work.

refrain[1] **1** the lines of a song that are repeated
at the end of each verse. **2** the main part of a
song, after the verse. **3** the music for either
of these.

refrain[2] *verb* to keep oneself from doing
something, *please refrain from talking.*

refresh *verb* to restore the strength and vigour
of (a person etc.) by food, drink, or rest.
☐ **refresh a person's memory** to stimulate
a person's memory by reminding him or
her. **refresher course** a course of instruction
enabling a qualified person to keep abreast of
recent developments in the subject. **refresher**
noun

refreshing *adjective* **1** restoring strength and
vigour. **2** welcome and interesting because of
its novelty.

refreshment *noun* **1** refreshing; being
refreshed. **2** something that refreshes,
especially food and drink. **refreshments** *plural
noun* food and drink that do not constitute a
meal.

refrigerant *noun* a substance used for
cooling things or for keeping things cold.

refrigerate *verb* to make extremely cold,
especially in order to preserve and store food.
refrigeration *noun* [from *re-*, + Latin *frigus*
= cold]

refrigerator *noun* a cabinet or room in which
food is stored at a very low temperature.

refuel *verb* (**refuelled, refuelling**) to replenish
the fuel supply of (especially a ship or
aircraft).

refuge *noun* shelter from pursuit, danger,
or trouble; a place giving this; *took refuge
in silence,* became silent in order to avoid
difficulty. [from *re-*, + Latin *fugere* = flee]

refugee *noun* a person who has left home
and seeks refuge elsewhere e.g. from war or
persecution or some natural disaster.

refund (rĕ-**fund**) *verb* to pay back (money received, or expenses that a person has incurred). –**refund** (**ree**-fund) *noun* money refunded, repayment.

refurbish *verb* to make clean or bright again; to redecorate.

refusal *noun* refusing; being refused. ☐ **first refusal** the right to accept or refuse something before the choice is offered to others.

refuse¹ (rĕ-**fewz**) *verb* **1** to say or show that one is unwilling to accept or give or do something, *refused to go*; *refused him permission to go*; *refused my request*; *car refused to start*, would not start. **2** (of a horse) to be unwilling to jump (a fence).

refuse² (**ref**-yooss) *noun* what is rejected as worthless, waste material.

refute *verb* to prove that (a statement or opinion or person) is wrong. **refutable** *adjective*, **refutation** (ref-yŭ-**tay**-shŏn) *noun*

Usage *Refute* is sometimes used to mean 'to deny', but this use is generally considered incorrect. If you *deny* something, you say that it is not true. If you *refute* it, you prove that it is not true.

reg *noun* a flat area of desert covered with gravel or boulders, a stony desert.

regain *verb* **1** to obtain possession, use, or control of (a thing) again after losing it. **2** to reach again, *regained the shore*.

regal (**ree**-găl) *adjective* like or fit for a king or queen. **regally** *adverb*, **regality** (rĕ-**gal**-ĭ-tee) *noun* [from Latin *regis* = of a king]

regale (rĕ-**gayl**) *verb* to feed or entertain well, *regaled themselves on caviar*; *regaled them with stories of the campaign*.

regalia (rĕ-**gay**-lee-ă) *plural noun* **1** the emblems of royalty used at coronations, *the regalia include crown, sceptre, and orb*. **2** the emblems or costumes of an order (e.g. the Order of Australia) or of a certain rank or office.

regard *verb* **1** to look steadily at. **2** to consider to be, *we regard the matter as serious*. **3** to concern or have a connection with, *he is innocent as regards the first charge*. –**regard** *noun* **1** a steady gaze. **2** heed, consideration, *acted without regard to the safety of others*. **3** respect, *we have a great regard for him as our chairman*. **regards** *plural noun* kindly greetings conveyed in a message, *give him my regards*. ☐ **as regards** or **in regard to** or **with regard to** regarding, concerning, in respect of.

regardful *adjective* mindful.

regarding *preposition* concerning, with reference to, *laws regarding picketing*.

regardless *adverb* heedlessly, paying no attention to something, *regardless of expense*.

regatta *noun* a number of boat or yacht races organised as a sporting event. [from Italian]

regency *noun* **1** being a regent; a regent's period of office. **2** a group of people acting as regent. –**the Regency** the period 1810–20 in England, when George, Prince of Wales, acted as regent.

regenerate (rĕ-**jen**-ĕ-rayt) *verb* **1** to give new life or vigour to. **2** to reform spiritually or morally. –**regenerate** (rĕ-**jen**-ĕ-răt) *adjective* spiritually born again, reformed. **regeneration** *noun*

regent *noun* a person appointed to rule a country while the monarch is too young or unable to rule, or is absent. –**regent** *adjective* acting as regent, *Prince Regent*. [from Latin *regens* = ruling]

reggae (**reg**-ay) *noun* a West Indian style of music with a strongly accented subsidiary beat.

regicide (**rej**-ĭ-syd) *noun* **1** the killing of a king. **2** a person involved in this. [from Latin *regis* = of a king, + *caedere* = kill]

regime (ray-**zheem**) *noun* **1** a method or system of government or administration. **2** a particular government. **3** a regimen.

regimen (**rej**-ĭ-mĕn) *noun* a prescribed course of exercise, way of life, and diet.

regiment *noun* **1** a permanent unit of an army, usually divided into companies or troops or battalions. **2** an operational unit of artillery, tanks, armoured cars, etc. **3** a large array or number of things. –**regiment** *verb* to organise (people or work or data etc.) rigidly into groups or into a pattern. **regimentation** *noun*

regimental *adjective* of an army regiment. **regimentals** *plural noun* the uniform of an army regiment.

Regina (rĕ-**jy**-nă) *noun* a reigning queen, *Elizabeth Regina*. [Latin, = queen]

region *noun* **1** a continuous part of a surface or space or body, with more or less definite boundaries or with certain characteristics. **2** an administrative division of a country. ☐ **in the region of** approximately. **regional** *adjective*, **regionally** *adverb*

register *noun* **1** an official list of names or items or attendances etc. **2** the book or other document(s) in which this is kept. **3** a mechanical device for indicating or recording speed, force, numbers, etc. automatically, *cash register*. **4** exact correspondence of position; *out of register*, not corresponding exactly. **5** the range of a human voice or of a musical instrument. **6** the kinds of words (e.g. informal, formal, literary) and the manner of speaking or writing that vary according to the situation and the relationship of the people involved. –**register** *verb* **1** to enter or cause to be entered in a register. **2** to set down formally in writing; to present for consideration. **3** to notice and remember. **4** (of an instrument) to indicate or record something automatically. **5** to make an impression on a person's mind, *his name did not register with me*. **6** to express (an emotion) on one's face or by gesture. ☐ **registered post** a postal service with special precautions for safety and compensation in case of loss.

registrar (rej-ĭ-**strar**) *noun* **1** an official with responsibility for keeping written records or registers. **2** the chief administrative officer in a university, college, or school. **3** a doctor undergoing hospital training to be a specialist.

registration *noun* registering; being registered. ☐ **registration number** a combination of letters and figures identifying a motor vehicle.

registry *noun* **1** registration. **2** a place where written records or registers are kept. ☐ **registry office** a place where civil marriages are performed and where records of births, deaths, and marriages are made.

regnant *adjective* reigning. [from Latin *regnare* = to reign]

regress (rĕ-**gress**) *verb* to go back to an earlier or more primitive form or state. –**regress** (**ree**-gress) *noun* regressing. **regression** *noun*, **regressive** *adjective* [from *re-*, + Latin *gressus* = gone]

regret *noun* a feeling of sorrow for the loss of a person or thing, or of annoyance or disappointment or repentance; *send one's regrets*, to send polite expressions of regret or apology. –**regret** *verb* (**regretted**, **regretting**) to feel regret about.

regretful *adjective* feeling regret. **regretfully** *adverb*

regrettable *adjective* that is to be regretted, *a regrettable incident*. **regrettably** *adverb*

regroup *verb* to form into new groups.

regular *adjective* **1** acting or recurring or done in a uniform manner, or constantly at a fixed time or interval, *regular customers*; *his pulse is regular*; *keep regular hours*, to get up and go to bed at about the same times always. **2** conforming to a principle or to a standard of procedure. **3** even, symmetrical; *a regular pentagon*, with sides of equal length. **4** usual, normal, habitual, *has no regular occupation*; *regular fries*, a normal or standard serve (not a large one). **5** belonging to the permanent armed forces of a country, *regular soldiers*; *the regular navy*. **6** (of a verb or noun etc.) having inflections that are of a normal type. **7** (*informal*) complete, out-and-out, *it's a regular mess*. –**regular** *noun* **1** a member of the permanent armed forces of a country. **2** (*informal*) a regular customer or client etc. **regularly** *adverb*, **regularity** *noun* [from Latin *regula* = a rule]

regularise *verb* (also **-ize**) **1** to make regular. **2** to make lawful or correct, *regularise the position* or *situation*. **regularisation** *noun*

regulate *verb* **1** to control or direct by means of rules and restrictions. **2** to adjust or control (a thing) so that it works correctly or according to one's requirements. **regulator** *noun*

regulation *noun* **1** regulating; being regulated. **2** a rule or restriction. –**regulation** *adjective* as required by regulations. [same origin as *regular*]

regurgitate (rĕ-**gerj**-ĭ-tayt) *verb* **1** to bring (swallowed food) up again to the mouth. **2** to cast or pour out again. **regurgitation** *noun*

rehabilitate *verb* **1** to restore (a person) to a normal life by training, after a period of illness or imprisonment. **2** to reinstate. **3** to restore (a building etc.) to a good condition or for a new purpose. **rehabilitation** *noun*

rehash (ree-**hash**) *verb* to put (old material) into a new form with no great change or improvement. –**rehash** (**ree**-hash) *noun* **1** rehashing. **2** something made of rehashed material.

rehearsal *noun* **1** rehearsing. **2** a practice or trial performance.

rehearse *verb* **1** to practise before performing in public. **2** to train (a person) by doing this. **3** to say over, to give an account of, *rehearsing his grievances*.

reheat *verb* to heat again.

rehouse (ree-**howz**) *verb* to provide with new accommodation.

Reich (*rhymes with* like) *noun* the former German State, most often used to refer to the Third Reich, the Nazi regime from 1933 to 1945.

reign (*pr.* rayn) *noun* **1** a sovereign's rule; the period of this. **2** the controlling or dominating effect of a person or thing, *a reign of terror*. –**reign** *verb* **1** to rule as king or queen. **2** to be supreme, to dominate; *silence reigned*, there was silence; *the reigning champion*, the one who is champion at present.
☐ **Reign of Terror** *see* terror. [from Latin *regnum* = royal authority]

reimburse *verb* to repay, to refund. **reimbursement** *noun*

rein *noun* (also **reins**) a long narrow strap fastened to the bit of a bridle and used to guide or check a horse being ridden or driven; a similar device to restrain a toddler etc. –**rein** *verb* to check or control with reins; *rein in*, to pull in or restrain with (or as with) reins.
☐ **give free rein to** to allow freedom to, *give one's imagination free rein*. **keep a tight rein on** to allow little freedom to. [same origin as *retain*]

reincarnate (ree-in-**kar**-nayt) *verb* to bring back (a soul after death) into another body. –**reincarnate** (ree-in-**kar**-năt) *adjective* reincarnated. **reincarnation** *noun*

reindeer *noun* (*plural* reindeer) a kind of deer with large antlers, living in Arctic regions.

reinforce *verb* to strengthen or support by additional persons or material or an added quantity. ☐ **reinforced concrete** concrete with metal bars or wire embedded in it to increase its strength.

reinforcement *noun* **1** reinforcing; being reinforced. **2** a thing that reinforces. **reinforcements** *plural noun* additional persons or ships etc. sent to reinforce armed forces.

reinstate *verb* to restore to a previous position. **reinstatement** *noun*

reissue *verb* to issue (a thing) again. –**reissue** *noun* something reissued.

reiterate (ree-**it**-ě-rayt) *verb* to say or do again or repeatedly. **reiteration** *noun* [from *re-*, + Latin *iterum* = again]

reject (rě-**jekt**) *verb* **1** to refuse to accept; to put aside or send back as not to be chosen, used, or done etc. **2** to react against, *the body may reject the transplanted tissue*. **3** to fail to give due affection to, *the child was rejected by both his parents*. –**reject** (**ree**-jekt) *noun* a person or thing that is rejected, especially as being below standard. **rejection** *noun* [from *re-* = away, + Latin *-jectum* = thrown]

rejig *verb* (**rejigged**, **rejigging**) **1** to re-equip (a factory etc.) for a new type of work. **2** (*informal*) to rearrange.

rejoice *verb* to feel or show great joy.

rejoin[1] (ree-**join**) *verb* to join again.

rejoin[2] (rě-**join**) *verb* to say in answer; to retort.

rejoinder *noun* something said in answer or retort.

rejuvenate (rě-**joo**-vě-nayt) *verb* to restore youthful appearance or vigour to. **rejuvenation** *noun* [from *re-*, + Latin *juvenis* = young]

relapse *verb* to fall back into a previous condition, or into a worse state after improvement. –**relapse** *noun* relapsing, especially after partial recovery from illness. [from *re-*, + Latin *lapsum* = slipped]

relate *verb* **1** to narrate; to tell in detail. **2** to bring into relation. ☐ **relate to** to establish a relation between, *trying to relate these effects to a possible cause*; to have reference to or a connection with, *he notices only what relates to himself*; to establish a sympathetic or successful relationship with (a person or thing), *learning to relate to children*.

related *adjective* having a common descent or origin.

relation *noun* **1** the way in which one thing is related to another; a similarity or correspondence or contrast between people or things or events. **2** being related. **3** a person who is a relative. **4** narrating, being narrated. **relations** *plural noun* **1** dealings with others, *the country's foreign relations*. **2** sexual intercourse, *had relations with him*. **relationship** *noun*

relative *adjective* **1** considered in relation or proportion to something else, *the relative merits of the two plans*; *lived in relative comfort*. **2** having a connection with, *facts relative to the matter in hand*. **3** (in grammar) referring or attached to an earlier noun, clause, or sentence; *relative pronoun*, e.g. 'who' in 'the man who came to dinner'. –**relative** *noun* a person who is related to another by parentage or descent or marriage.
☐ **relative atomic mass** the ratio of the average mass of one atom of an element to one-twelfth of the mass of an atom of carbon-12. Also

called *atomic weight*. relative density the ratio of the density of a substance to the density of a standard (usually water or air). relative molecular mass the ratio of the average mass of one molecule of an element or compound to one-twelfth of the mass of an atom of carbon-12. Also called *molecular weight*. relatively *adverb*, relativeness *noun*

relativity *noun* 1 relativeness. 2 Einstein's theory of the universe, showing that all motion is relative and treating time as a fourth dimension related to space.

relax *verb* 1 to become or cause to become less tight or tense. 2 to make or become less strict, *relax the rules*. 3 to make or become less anxious or formal; to cease work or effort and indulge in recreation. relaxation *noun* [from *re-* = back, + Latin *laxus* = loose]

relay (**ree**-lay) *noun* 1 a fresh set of people or animals taking the place of others who have completed a spell of work, *operating in relays*. 2 a fresh supply of material to be used or worked on. 3 a relay race. 4 a relayed message or transmission. 5 an electronic device that receives and passes on a signal, often strengthening it. –relay (ree-**lay**) *verb* (relayed, relaying) to receive and pass on or retransmit (a message or broadcast etc.). ☐ relay race a race between teams in which each person in turn covers a part of the total distance.

re-lay *verb* (re-laid, re-laying) to lay again.

release *verb* 1 to set free. 2 to remove from a fixed position; to allow to fall or fly etc., *released an arrow*. 3 to issue (a film) for general exhibition; to make (information or a recording etc.) available to the public. –release *noun* 1 releasing; being released; *a happy release*, death as a merciful release from suffering. 2 a handle or catch etc. that unfastens a device or machine-part. 3 information or a film or recording etc. released to the public, *a press release*.

relegate (**rel**-ĕ-gayt) *verb* 1 to send or consign to a less important place or condition. 2 to transfer (a sports team) to a lower division of a league etc. relegation *noun* [from *re-* = back, + Latin *legatum* = sent]

relent *verb* to become less stern, to abandon one's harsh intentions and be more lenient. [from *re-* = back, + Latin *lentus* = flexible]

relentless *adjective* 1 not relenting. 2 unceasing in its severity, *relentless pressure*. relentlessly *adverb*, relentlessness *noun*

relevant (**rel**-ĕ-vănt) *adjective* related to the matter in hand. relevance *noun*

reliable *adjective* 1 able to be relied on. 2 consistently good in quality or performance. reliably *adverb*, reliability *noun*

reliance *noun* 1 relying. 2 trust or confidence felt about something. reliant *adjective*

relic (**rel**-ik) *noun* 1 something that survives from an earlier age. 2 a surviving trace of a custom or practice. 3 part of a holy person's body or belongings kept after his or her death as an object of reverence. relics *plural noun* remnants, residue. [same origin as *relinquish*]

relief *noun* 1 ease given by reduction or removal of pain or anxiety or a burden etc. 2 something that relaxes tension or breaks up monotony, *a humorous scene serving as comic relief*. 3 assistance given to people in special need, *a relief fund for the earthquake victims*. 4 a person taking over another's turn of duty; a replacement, *a relief teacher*. 5 the raising of the siege of a besieged town, *the relief of Sarajevo*. 6 a method of carving or moulding in which the design projects from the surface. 7 a piece of carving etc. done in this way. 8 a similar effect achieved by the use of colour or shading. ☐ relief map a map showing hills and valleys either by shading or by their being moulded in relief. [from *re-*, + Latin *levis* = light]

relieve *verb* 1 to give relief to; to bring or be a relief to. 2 to introduce variation into, to make less monotonous. 3 to take a thing from (a person), *the thief had relieved him of his watch*. 4 to raise the siege of (a town). 5 to release (a person) from a duty or task by taking his or her place or providing a substitute. ☐ relieve one's feelings to use strong language or vigorous behaviour when annoyed. relieve oneself to urinate or defecate.

religion *noun* 1 belief in the existence of a superhuman controlling power, especially of God or gods, usually expressed in worship. 2 a particular system of faith and worship, *the Christian religion*. 3 something compared to religious faith as a controlling influence on a person's life, *football is his religion*. 4 life under monastic vows. [from Latin *religio* = reverence]

religious *adjective* 1 of religion, *a religious service*. 2 believing firmly in a religion and paying great attention to its practices. 3 of a monastic order; *a religious house*, a monastery or convent. 4 very conscientious, *with*

religious attention to detail. – religious *noun*
(*plural* religious) a person bound by monastic
vows. religiously *adverb*

relinquish *verb* 1 to give up or cease from
(a plan, habit, or belief etc.). 2 to surrender
possession of. 3 to cease to hold, *relinquished
the reins.* relinquishment *noun* [from *re-*
= behind, + Latin *linquere* = to leave]

reliquary (**rel**-ĭ-kwă-ree) *noun* a receptacle
for a relic or relics of a holy person.

relish *noun* 1 great enjoyment of food or other
things. 2 an appetising flavour or attractive
quality. 3 a strong-tasting substance or food
eaten with plainer food to add flavour. – relish
verb to enjoy greatly.

relive *verb* to live (an experience etc.) over
again, especially in the imagination.

reload *verb* to load again.

relocate (ree-loh-**kayt**) *verb* to move (a
person or thing) to a different place. relocation
noun

reluctant *adjective* unwilling, grudging one's
consent. reluctantly *adverb*, reluctance *noun*
[from Latin, = struggling against something]

rely *verb* (relied, relying) rely on to trust
confidently, to depend on for help etc.

remain *verb* 1 to be there after other parts
have been removed or used or dealt with.
2 to be in the same place or condition during
further time, to continue to be, *remained
in Adelaide; remained faithful.* [from *re-*
= behind, + Latin *manere* = stay]

remainder *noun* 1 the remaining people
or things or part. 2 the quantity left after
subtraction or division. – remainder *verb*
to dispose of unsold copies of (a book) at a
reduced price.

remains *plural noun* 1 what remains after
other parts or things have been removed or
used. 2 ancient buildings or objects that have
survived when others are destroyed, relics.
3 a dead body, *his mortal remains.*

remake *verb* (remade, remaking) to make
again. – remake *noun* something remade.

remand *verb* to send back (a prisoner) into
custody while further evidence is sought.
– remand *noun* remanding, being remanded.
□ on remand held in custody after being
remanded. remand centre a place where
young offenders are sent temporarily. [from
re-, + Latin *mandare* = entrust]

remark *noun* a written or spoken comment,
anything that is said. – remark *verb* 1 to make
a remark, to say. 2 to notice.

remarkable *adjective* worth noticing,
exceptional, unusual. remarkably *adverb*

remarry *verb* (remarried, remarrying) to
marry again. remarriage *noun*

Rembrandt (**rem**-brănt) (1606–69), Dutch
painter.

remediable (rĕ-**meed**-ee-ă-bŭl) *adjective*
able to be remedied.

remedial (rĕ-**meed**-ee-ăl) *adjective* providing
a remedy for a disease or deficiency.

remedy *noun* something that cures or relieves
a disease or that puts a matter right. – remedy
verb (remedied, remedying) to be a remedy
for, to put right. [from *re-*, + Latin *mederi*
= heal]

remember *verb* 1 to keep in one's mind.
2 to recall knowledge or experience to one's
mind; to be able to do this. 3 to make a present
to, *remembered me in his will.* 4 to mention
as sending greetings, *remember me to your
mother.* □ remember oneself to remember
one's intentions or to behave with suitable
dignity after a lapse. [from *re-*, + Latin *memor*
= mindful]

remembrance 1 remembering; being
remembered; memory. 2 something that
reminds people, a memento or memorial.
□ Remembrance Day 11 November, the
anniversary of the armistice that in 1918
ended the First World War, when those killed
in the two World Wars and in later wars are
remembered.

remind *verb* to cause to remember or think of
something.

reminder *noun* a thing that reminds someone;
a letter sent to remind someone.

reminisce (rem-ĭ-**niss**) *verb* to think or talk
about past events and experiences.

reminiscence (rem-ĭ-**niss**-ĕns) *noun*
1 thinking or talking about past events.
2 a spoken or written account of what one
remembers, *wrote his reminiscences.* 3 a thing
that is reminiscent of something else.

reminiscent (rem-ĭ-**niss**-ĕnt) *adjective*
1 inclined to reminisce, *in reminiscent mood.*
2 having characteristics that recall something
to one's mind, *his style is reminiscent of
Picasso's.* reminiscently *adverb*

remiss (rĕ-**miss**) *adjective* negligent, *you have
been remiss in your duties* or *very remiss.*

remission *noun* **1** God's pardon or forgiveness of sins. **2** the remitting of a debt or penalty; the shortening of a convict's prison sentence on account of his or her good behaviour. **3** reduction of the force or intensity of something, *slight remission of the pain*.

remit *verb* (remitted, remitting) **1** to cancel (a debt); to refrain from inflicting (a punishment). **2** to make or become less intense, *we must not remit our efforts*. **3** to send (money etc.) to a person or place, *please remit the interest to my home address*. **4** to send (a matter for decision) to some authority. **5** to postpone. **6** (of God) to forgive (sins). [from *re-* = back, + Latin *mittere* = send]

remittance *noun* **1** the sending of money to a person. **2** the money sent.

remnant *noun* **1** a small remaining quantity, part, or number of people or things. **2** a surviving trace of something. **3** a small piece of cloth left when the rest of the roll has been used or sold. [compare *remain*]

remodel *verb* (remodelled, remodelling) to model again or differently; to reconstruct or reorganise.

remonstrance (rĕ-**mon**-străns) *noun* remonstrating, a protest.

remonstrate (**rem**-ŏn-strayt) *verb* to make a protest, *remonstrated with him about his behaviour*. [from *re-* = against, + Latin *monstrare* = to show]

remorse *noun* deep regret for one's wrongdoing. remorseful *adjective*, remorsefully *adverb* [from *re-* = back, + Latin *morsum* = bitten]

remorseless *adverb* relentless. remorselessly *adverb*

remote *adjective* **1** far apart; far away in place or time, *the remote past*. **2** far from civilisation, *a remote village*. **3** not close in relationship or connection, *a remote ancestor*; *remote causes*. **4** slight, *I haven't the remotest idea*. ☐ remote control control of apparatus etc. from a distance, usually by means of electricity or radio; the controlling device. remotely *adverb*, remoteness *noun* [from Latin *remotum* = removed]

remount *verb* to mount again.

removal *noun* **1** removing; being removed. **2** transfer of furniture etc. to a different house.

removalist *noun* (*Austral.*) a person or firm that moves household or office furniture.

remove *verb* **1** to take off or away from the place occupied. **2** to take off (clothing). **3** to dismiss from office. **4** to get rid of, *this removes the last of my doubts*. –remove *noun* a stage or degree, a degree of difference, *this is several removes from the truth*. removable *adjective*, remover *noun*

removed *adjective* distant, remote, *a dialect not far removed from Cockney*; *a cousin once removed*, a cousin's child or parent, *twice removed*, a cousin's grandchild or grandparent.

remunerate (rĕ-**mewn**-ĕ-rayt) *verb* to pay or reward (a person) for services rendered. remuneration *noun* [from *re-*, + Latin *muneris* = of a gift]

remunerative (rĕ-**mewn**-ĕ-ră-tiv) *adjective* giving good remuneration, profitable.

Remus (**ree**-mŭs) (*Rom. legend*) the twin brother of Romulus.

Renaissance (rĕ-**nay**-săns) *noun* the revival of art and literature in Europe (influenced by classical forms) in the 14th–16th centuries; the period of this. –renaissance *noun* any similar revival. [French, = rebirth]

renal (**ree**-năl) *adjective* of the kidneys.

rename *verb* to give a fresh name to.

rend *verb* (rent, rending) to tear.

render *verb* **1** to give, especially in return or exchange or as something due, *a reward for services rendered*. **2** to present or send in; *account rendered*, a bill previously sent in and not yet paid. **3** to cause to become, *rendered him helpless*. **4** to give a performance of (a play or character). **5** to translate, *rendered into English*. **6** to melt down (fat). **7** to cover (stone or brick) with a first coat of plaster. **8** (in computing) to process (an image etc.) in order to make it appear solid and three-dimensional. [from Latin *reddere* = give back]

rendezvous (**ron**-day-voo) *noun* (*plural* rendezvous, *pr.* **ron**-day-vooz) **1** a pre-arranged meeting. **2** a pre-arranged or regular meeting place. –rendezvous *verb* (rendezvoused, rendezvousing) to meet at a rendezvous. [from French *rendez-vous* = present yourself]

rendition (ren-**dish**-ŏn) *noun* the way a dramatic role or musical piece etc. is rendered or performed. [same origin as *render*]

renegade (**ren**-ĕ-gayd) *noun* someone who deserts from a group, cause, or faith etc. [from *re-* = back, + Latin *negare* = deny]

renege (rĕ-**neg**) *verb* **1** (in card games) to fail to follow suit when able to do so. **2** to go back on one's word. □ **renege on** to fail to keep (a promise etc.); to disappoint (a person).

renew *verb* **1** to restore to its original state. **2** to replace with a fresh supply, *the tyres need renewing*. **3** to get or make or give again, *renewed their acquaintance* or *requests*. **4** to arrange for a continuation or continued validity of, *renew one's licence* or *subscription*. **renewable** *adjective*, **renewal** *noun*

rennet (**ren**-ĕt) *noun* a substance used to curdle milk in making cheese or junket.

rennin *noun* the enzyme in rennet that causes milk to curdle.

Renoir, Pierre Auguste (1841–1919), French impressionist painter.

renounce *verb* **1** to give up (a claim or right etc.) formally, *renounced his title*. **2** to reject, to refuse to abide by (an agreement etc.). **renouncement** *noun* [from *re-* = back, + Latin *nuntiare* = announce]

renovate (**ren**-ŏ-vayt) *verb* to repair, to renew. **renovation** *noun*, **renovator** *noun* [from *re-*, + Latin *novus* = new]

renown (*rhymes with* down) *noun* fame.

renowned *adjective* famous, celebrated.

rent¹ *see* rend. – **rent** *noun* a torn place in a garment etc., a split.

rent² *noun* payment made periodically for the use of land or accommodation, or for a service or equipment such as a telephone. – **rent** *verb* **1** to pay rent for temporary use of. **2** to allow to be used in return for payment of rent.

rentable *adjective* able to be rented.

rental *noun* **1** the amount paid or received as rent. **2** renting.

renumber *verb* to change the numbering of.

renunciation (rĕ-nun-see-**ay**-shŏn) *noun* renouncing, giving something up.

reopen *verb* to open again.

reorder *verb* **1** to order again; to order further supplies of. **2** to put into a different sequence.

reorganise *verb* (also -**ize**) to organise in a new way. **reorganisation** *noun*

rep¹ *noun* textile fabric with a corded effect, used for curtains and upholstery.

rep² *noun* (*informal*) a business firm's travelling representative.

rep³ *noun* (*informal*) repertory, *a rep theatre* or *company*.

repaint *verb* to paint again or differently.

repair¹ *verb* **1** to put into good or sound condition after damage or the effects of wear and tear. **2** to put right, to make amends for; *repaired the omission*, did what had been omitted. – **repair** *noun* **1** the act or process of repairing something. **2** condition as regards being repaired, *keep it in good repair*. **repairer** *noun* [from *re-*, + Latin *parare* = make ready]

repair² *verb* to go, *repaired to the lounge*. [same origin as *repatriate*]

repairable *adjective* able to be repaired.

reparable (**rep**-ă-ră-bŭl) *adjective* (of a loss etc.) able to be made good.

reparation (rep-ă-**ray**-shŏn) *noun* making amends. **reparations** *plural noun* compensation for war damage, demanded by the victor from a defeated enemy.

repartee (rep-ar-**tee**) *noun* a witty reply; ability to make witty replies.

repast (rĕ-**pahst**) *noun* (*formal*) a meal.

repatriate (ree-**pat**-ree-ayt) *verb* to send or bring back (a person) to his or her own country. **repatriation** *noun* [from *re-*, + Latin *patria* = native country]

repay *verb* (**repaid**, **repaying**) **1** to pay back (money). **2** to do or make or give in return. **repayment** *noun*

repayable *adjective* able or needing to be repaid.

repeal *verb* to withdraw (a law) officially. – **repeal** *noun* the repealing of a law.

repeat *verb* **1** to say, do, or occur again. **2** to say aloud (something heard or learnt by heart), *repeat the oath after me*. **3** to tell to another person (something told to oneself). **4** (of food) to produce a taste in one's mouth intermittently for some time after being eaten. **5** to supply a further consignment of. – **repeat** *noun* **1** repeating. **2** something that is repeated; a repeated broadcast. **3** (in music) a passage intended to be repeated; a mark indicating this. □ **repeat itself** to recur in the same form. **repeat oneself** to say or do the same thing again. [from *re-*, + Latin *petere* = seek]

repeatable *adjective* able to be repeated; suitable for being repeated.

repeatedly *adverb* again and again.

repeater *noun* a device that repeats a signal.

repêchage (**rep**-ĕ-char*zh*) *noun* (also **repechage**) (in rowing etc.) an extra contest in which the runners-up in the eliminating heats compete for a place in the final. [French]

repel *verb* (**repelled**, **repelling**) **1** to drive away, *repelled the attackers*. **2** to refuse to accept, *repelled all offers of help*. **3** to be impossible for (a substance) to penetrate, *the surface repels moisture*. **4** to push away from itself by an unseen force (the opposite of *attract*), *one north magnetic pole repels another*. **5** to be repulsive or distasteful to. [from *re-*, + Latin *pellere* = to drive]

repellent *adjective* **1** repelling, arousing distaste. **2** not penetrable by a specified substance, *the fabric is water-repellent*. –**repellent** *noun* a substance that repels something, *insect repellents*.

repent *verb* to feel regret about (what one has done or failed to do). **repentance** *noun*, **repentant** *adjective* [from *re-* + *penitent*]

repercussion (ree-per-**kush**-ŏn) *noun* **1** the recoil of something after impact. **2** an echo. **3** an indirect effect or reaction.

repertoire (**rep**-er-twar) *noun* a stock of songs, plays, or acts etc. that a person or company knows and is prepared to perform.

repertory (**rep**-er-tŏ-ree) *noun* **1** a repertoire. **2** theatrical performance of various plays for short periods by one company.
□ **repertory company or theatre** one giving such performances.

repetition *noun* repeating, being repeated; an instance of this.

repetitious (rep-ĕ-**tish**-ŭs) *adjective* repetitive.

repetitive (rĕ-**pet**-ĭ-tiv) *adjective* characterised by repetition. **repetitively** *adverb*

repine (rĕ-**pyn**) *verb* to fret, to be discontented. [from *re-* + *pine*²]

replace *verb* **1** to put back in place. **2** to take the place of. **3** to find or provide a substitute for. **replacement** *noun*

replaceable *adjective* able to be replaced.

replant *verb* to plant again or differently.

replay (ree-**play**) *verb* to play (a match or recording etc.) again. –**replay** (**ree**-play) *noun* the replaying of a match or of a recorded incident in a game etc.

replenish *verb* to fill (a thing) again; to renew (a supply etc.). **replenishment** *noun* [from *re-*, + Latin *plenus* = full]

replete (rĕ-**pleet**) *adjective* **1** well stocked or supplied. **2** full, gorged. **repletion** *noun* [from *re-*, + Latin *-pletum* = filled]

replica (**rep**-lik-ă) *noun* an exact copy or reproduction of something.

replicate *verb* **1** to make a replica of. **2** to repeat (an experiment etc.). **replication** *noun*

reply *verb* (**replied**, **replying**) to make an answer; to say in answer. –**reply** *noun* **1** replying. **2** what is replied, an answer.

report *verb* **1** to give an account of (something seen, done, or studied); to tell as news; *report progress*, to state what has been done so far. **2** to write or give a description of (an event etc.) for publication or broadcasting. **3** to make a formal accusation about (an offence or offender). **4** to present oneself as having arrived or returned. **5** to be responsible to a certain person as one's superior or supervisor. –**report** *noun* **1** a spoken or written account of something seen, done, or studied. **2** a description for publication or broadcasting. **3** a periodical statement about a student's or employee's work and conduct. **4** rumour, a piece of gossip. **5** an explosive sound like that made by a gun. [from *re-* = back, + Latin *portare* = carry]

reportage (rep-or-**tahz**h) *noun* the reporting of news for the press etc.; a typical style of doing this.

reportedly *adverb* according to reports.

reporter *noun* a person employed to report news etc. for publication or broadcasting.

repose¹ *noun* **1** rest, sleep. **2** a peaceful state or effect, tranquillity. –**repose** *verb* to rest, to lie.

repose² *verb* to place (trust etc.).

repository *noun* **1** a place where things are stored. **2** a person, book, etc. regarded as a store of information etc.

repossess *verb* to regain possession of (goods on which credit payments have not been kept up). **repossession** *noun*

repoussé (rĕ-**poo**-say) *adjective* (of metalwork) chased or embossed by hammering from the reverse side. [from *re-*, + French *pousser* = to push]

repp *noun* = rep¹.

reprehend (rep-rĕ-**hend**) *verb* to rebuke. [from *re-*, + Latin *prehendere* = to grasp]

reprehensible (rep-rĕ-**hen**-sĭ-bŭl) *adjective* deserving rebuke. **reprehensibly** *adverb*

represent *verb* **1** to show (a person, thing, or scene) in a picture or play etc. **2** to describe or declare to be, *representing himself as an expert*. **3** to state in polite protest or remonstrance, *we must represent* to them the risks involved. **4** to symbolise, *in Roman numerals C represents* 100. **5** to be an example or embodiment of, *the election results represent the views of the electorate.* **6** to act as a deputy or agent for; to speak for. representation *noun*

representative *adjective* **1** typical of a group or class. **2** containing examples of a number of types, *a representative selection.* **3** consisting of elected representatives; based on representation by these, *representative government.* –representative *noun* **1** a sample or specimen of something. **2** a person's or company's agent. **3** a person chosen to represent another or others, or to take part in a legislative assembly on their behalf.
☐ House of Representatives the lower house of the Australian Federal Parliament, of the US Congress, and of other national parliaments.

repress *verb* to keep down, to suppress; to keep (emotions etc.) from finding an outlet. repression *noun*

repressed *adjective* suffering from repression of the emotions.

repressive *adjective* serving or intended to repress a person or thing. repressively *adverb*

reprieve (rĕ-**preev**) *noun* **1** postponement or cancellation of a punishment, especially of the death sentence. **2** temporary relief from danger; postponement of trouble. –reprieve *verb* to give a reprieve to.

reprimand (**rep**-rĭ-mahnd) *noun* a rebuke, especially a formal or official one. –reprimand *verb* to give a reprimand to.

reprint (ree-**print**) *verb* to print again in the same or a new form. –reprint (**ree**-print) *noun* the reprinting of a book; a book reprinted.

reprisal (rĕ-**pry**-zăl) *noun* an act of retaliation; *take reprisals,* retaliate.

reproach *verb* to express disapproval to (a person) for a fault or offence. –reproach *noun* **1** reproaching; an instance of this. **2** a thing that brings disgrace or discredit.
☐ above or beyond reproach deserving no blame, perfect. reproachful *adjective,* reproachfully *adverb*

reprobate (**rep**-rŏ-bayt) *noun* an immoral or unprincipled person.

reprobation (rep-rŏ-**bay**-shŏn) *noun* strong condemnation.

reproduce *verb* **1** to produce a copy of (a picture etc.). **2** to cause to be seen or heard again or to occur again. **3** to have a specified

quality when reproduced, *some colours don't reproduce well.* **4** to produce further members of the same species by natural means; to produce (offspring).

reproducible *adjective* able to be reproduced.

reproduction *noun* **1** reproducing; being reproduced. **2** a copy of a painting etc.
☐ reproduction furniture furniture made in imitation of an earlier style.

reproductive *adjective* of or belonging to reproduction, *the reproductive system.*

reprographic (ree-prŏ-**graf**-ik) *adjective* of or involving the copying of documents etc. by photography, xerography, etc. [from *reproduce* + *-graph*]

reproof *noun* an expression of condemnation for a fault or offence.

reprove *verb* to give a reproof to.

reptile *noun* a member of the class of cold-blooded animals with a backbone and relatively short legs or no legs at all, e.g. snakes, lizards, crocodiles, tortoises. reptilian (rep-**til**-ee-ăn) *adjective & noun* [from Latin *reptilis* = crawling]

republic *noun* a country in which the supreme power is held by the people or their elected representatives, or by an elected or nominated president. [from Latin *res publica* = public affairs]

republican *adjective* of, like, or advocating a republic. –republican *noun* a person advocating republican government. –Republican *noun* a member of the Republican Party, one of the two main political parties in the USA.

repudiate (rĕ-**pew**-dee-ayt) *verb* to reject or disown utterly, to deny, *repudiate the accusation; repudiate the agreement,* to refuse to abide by it. repudiation *noun,* repudiator *noun*

repugnant (rĕ-**pug**-nănt) *adjective* distasteful, objectionable. repugnance *noun* [from *re-* = against, + Latin *pugnans* = fighting]

repulse *verb* **1** to drive back (an attacking force). **2** to reject (an offer or help etc.) firmly, to rebuff. [same origin as *repel*]

repulsion *noun* **1** repelling; being repelled. **2** a feeling of strong distaste, revulsion.

repulsive *adjective* **1** arousing disgust. **2** repelling things, *a repulsive force.* repulsively *adverb,* repulsiveness *noun*

reputable (rep-yŭ-tă-bŭl) *adjective* having a good reputation, respected. **reputably** *adverb*

reputation *noun* **1** what is generally said or believed about a person or thing. **2** public recognition for one's abilities or achievements, *built up a reputation*. [from Latin *reputare* = consider]

repute (rĕ-**pewt**) *noun* reputation, *I know him by repute*.

reputed (rĕ-**pewt**-ĕd) *adjective* said or thought to be; *his reputed father*, the man thought to be his father. **reputedly** *adverb*

request *noun* asking or being asked for a thing or to do something; a thing asked for; *a request show*, one consisting of items asked for by the public. **–request** *verb* to make a request for. ☐ **by** or **on request** in response to a request. [same origin as *require*]

requiem (rek-wee-ĕm) *noun* a special Mass for the repose of the soul(s) of the dead; a musical setting for this. [Latin, = rest]

require *verb* **1** to need, to depend on for success or fulfilment etc., *cars require regular servicing*. **2** to order or oblige, *customers are required to present their bags for checking*. **3** to wish to have, *will you require tea?* [from *re-*, + Latin *quarere* = seek]

requirement *noun* a thing required; a need.

requisite (rek-wĭ-zĭt) *adjective* required by circumstances, necessary to success. **–requisite** *noun* a thing needed for some purpose.

requisition *noun* an official order laying claim to the use of property or materials; a formal written demand for something that is needed. **–requisition** *verb* to demand or order by a requisition.

requite (rĕ-**kwyt**) *verb* **1** to make a return for (a service) or to (a person). **2** to avenge (a wrong or injury etc.). **requital** *noun*

reredos (reer-doss) *noun* an ornamental screen covering the wall above the back of an altar. [from Old French *arere* = behind, + *dos* = back]

re-route (ree-**root**) *verb* to send or carry by a different route.

rerun *verb* (**reran**, **rerunning**) to run again. **–rerun** *noun* **1** an act of rerunning. **2** a repeat of a film etc.

resale *noun* sale to another person of something one has bought.

rescind (rĕ-**sind**) *verb* to repeal or cancel (a law or rule etc.). **rescission** *noun* [from *re-*, + Latin *scindere* = to cut]

rescue *verb* to save or bring away from attack or capture or danger etc. **–rescue** *noun* rescuing, being rescued. **rescuer** *noun*

research (rĕ-**serch** *or* ree-serch) *noun* careful study and investigation, especially in order to discover new facts or information. **–research** *verb* to do research into, *the subject has been fully researched*. **researcher** *noun*

resell *verb* (**resold**, **reselling**) to sell (what one has bought) to another person.

resemble *verb* to be like (another person or thing). **resemblance** *noun* [from *re-*, + Latin *similis* = like]

resent (rĕ-**zent**) *verb* to feel displeased and indignant about, to feel insulted by (something said or done). **resentment** *noun* [from *re-* = against, + Latin *sentire* = feel]

resentful *adjective* feeling resentment. **resentfully** *adverb*

reservation *noun* **1** reserving; being reserved. **2** a reserved seat or accommodation etc., a record of this, *our hotel reservations*. **3** a limitation on one's agreement or acceptance of an idea etc., *we accept the plan in principle but have certain reservations*; *without reservation*, completely, wholeheartedly. **4** an area of land reserved for occupation by peoples indigenous to the US.

reserve *verb* **1** to put aside or keep back for a later occasion or for special use. **2** to retain, *the company reserves the right to offer a substitute*. **3** to order or set aside (seats or accommodation etc.) for a particular person to use at a future date. **4** to postpone, *reserve judgment*. **–reserve** *noun* **1** something reserved for future use; an extra amount or stock kept available for use when needed. **2** (also **reserves**) forces outside the regular armed services and liable to be called out in an emergency; a member of these. **3** an extra player chosen in case a substitute should be needed in a team. **4** an area of land set aside for some special purpose or for the exclusive use of certain people, *a nature reserve*; *an Aboriginal reserve*. **5** a limitation on one's agreement or acceptance of an idea etc. **6** a reserve price. **7** a tendency to avoid showing one's feelings and to lack cordiality towards other people. ☐ **in reserve** in a state of being unused but available. **reserve bank** a country's central bank administering government monetary policy, *the Reserve*

Bank of Australia. **reserve price** the lowest price that will be accepted for something sold by public auction or from an exhibition. [from *re-* = back, + Latin *servare* = keep]

reserved *adjective* (of a person) reticent; showing reserve of manner.

reservist *noun* a member of a country's reserve forces.

reservoir (**rez**-er-vwar) *noun* **1** a natural or artificial lake that is a source or store of water. **2** a container for a supply of fuel or other liquid. **3** a supply or collection of information etc.

reshuffle *verb* **1** to shuffle (cards) again. **2** to interchange the posts or responsibilities of (a group of people). –**reshuffle** *noun* reshuffling, *a Cabinet reshuffle*.

reside *verb* **1** to have one's home (in a certain place), to dwell permanently. **2** to be present or vested in a person, *supreme authority resides in the President*. [from *re-*, + Latin *-sidere* = sit]

residence *noun* **1** a place where one resides. **2** a house, *desirable residence for sale*. **3** residing; *take up one's residence*, to begin to dwell. ☐ **in residence** living in a specified place for the performance of one's work or duties.

resident *adjective* residing, in residence. –**resident** *noun* **1** a permanent inhabitant of a place, not a visitor. **2** (at a hotel) a person staying overnight. **3** a junior doctor working under supervision in a hospital. [from *re-*, + Latin *-sidens* = sitting]

residential (rez-ĭ-**den**-shăl) *adjective* **1** containing or suitable for private houses, *a residential area*. **2** connected with or based on residence, *residential qualifications for voters*.

residual (rĕ-**zid**-yoo-ăl) *adjective* left over as a residue. **residually** *adverb*

residuary (rĕ-**zid**-yoo-ă-ree) *adjective* **1** residual. **2** of the residue of an estate; *residuary legatee*, the one who inherits the remainder of an estate after specific items have been allotted to others.

residue (**rez**-ĭ-dew) *noun* the remainder, what is left over.

residuum (rĕ-**zid**-yoo-ŭm) *noun* (*plural* **residua**) a residue, especially after combustion or evaporation.

resign *verb* to give up or surrender (one's job, property, or claim etc.). ☐ **resign oneself to**

to be ready to accept and endure, to accept as inevitable. [from Latin *resignare* = unseal]

resignation *noun* **1** resigning. **2** a document or statement conveying that one wishes to resign. **3** a resigned attitude or expression.

resigned *adjective* having or showing patient acceptance of an unwelcome task or situation. ☐ **be resigned to** to resign oneself to. **resignedly** (rĕ-**zyn**-ĕd-lee) *adverb*

resilient (rĕ-**zil**-ee-ĕnt) *adjective* **1** springing back to its original form after being bent or stretched, springy. **2** (of a person) readily recovering from shock or depression etc. **resiliently** *adverb*, **resilience** *noun* [from *re-* = back, + Latin *-siliens* = jumping]

resin (**rez**-ĭn) *noun* **1** a sticky substance that oozes from pine trees and many other plants, used in making varnish etc. **2** a similar substance made synthetically, used as a plastic or in making plastics. **resinous** *adjective*

resist *verb* **1** to oppose, to use force in order to prevent something from happening or being successful. **2** to regard (a plan or idea) unfavourably. **3** to be undamaged or unaffected by, to prevent from penetrating, *pans that resist heat*. **4** to refrain from accepting or yielding to, *can't resist chocolates* or *temptation*. [from *re-* = against, + Latin *sistere* = stand firmly]

resistance *noun* **1** resisting; the power to resist something. **2** an influence that hinders or stops something. **3** the property of resisting the passage of heat or electricity; the measure of this. **4** (also **Resistance**) a secret organisation resisting the authorities, especially within a conquered or enemy-occupied country. ☐ **the line of least resistance** the easiest method or course.

resistant *adjective* offering resistance, capable of resisting, *heat-resistant plastics*.

resistive *adjective* **1** resistant. **2** having electrical resistance.

resistivity (rez-iss-**tiv**-ĭ-tee) *noun* the power of a specified material to resist the passage of electric current.

resistor *noun* a device having resistance to the passage of electric current.

resit *verb* (**resat**, **resitting**) to sit (an examination) again after a previous failure.

reskill *verb* to teach or equip with new skills.

resolute (**rez**-ŏ-loot) *adjective* showing great determination. **resolutely** *adverb*, **resoluteness** *noun* [same origin as *resolve*]

resolution *noun* **1** the quality of being resolute, great determination. **2** a mental pledge, something one intends to do, *New Year resolutions*. **3** a formal statement of opinion agreed on by a committee or assembly. **4** the solving of a problem or question. **5** the process of separating something or being separated into constituent parts.

resolve *verb* **1** to decide firmly. **2** (of a committee or assembly) to pass a resolution. **3** to solve or settle (a problem or doubts etc.). **4** (in music) to convert or be converted into concord. **5** to separate into constituent parts; *the resolving power of a lens*, its ability to magnify things distinctly. **–resolve** *noun* **1** something one has decided to do, a resolution, *and she kept her resolve*. **2** great determination. [from *re-*, + Latin *solvere* = loosen]

resolved *adjective* (of a person) resolute.

resonant (**rez**-ŏ-nănt) *adjective* resounding, echoing. **resonance** *noun* [from *re-*, + Latin *sonans* = sounding]

resonate (**rez**-ŏ-nayt) *verb* to produce or show resonance, to resound. **resonator** *noun*

resort (rĕ-**zort**) *verb* **1** to turn for help; to adopt as an expedient, *resorted to violence*. **2** to go, especially as a frequent or customary practice, *police watched the bars to which he was known to resort*. **–resort** *noun* **1** an expedient, resorting to this, *compulsion is our only resort*; *without resort to violence*. **2** a place resorted to, a popular holiday place. ☐ **as a last resort** when everything else has failed.

resound (rĕ-**zownd**) *verb* **1** (of a voice or sound etc.) to fill a place with sound; to produce echoes. **2** (of a place) to be filled with sound; to echo.

resounding *adjective* (of an event etc.) notable, *a resounding victory*. **resoundingly** *adverb*

resource *noun* **1** something to which one can turn for help or support or to achieve one's purpose. **2** a means of relaxation or amusement. **3** ingenuity, quick wit. **resources** *plural noun* **1** available assets, *we pooled our resources*. **2** a source of wealth to a country, *natural resources such as minerals*.

resourceful *adjective* clever at finding ways of doing things. **resourcefully** *adverb*, **resourcefulness** *noun*

respect *noun* **1** admiration felt towards a person or thing that has good qualities or achievements; politeness arising from this. **2** attention, consideration, *showing respect for people's feelings*. **3** relation, reference, *this is true with respect to English but not to French*. **4** a particular detail or aspect, *in this one respect*. **–respect** *verb* to feel or show respect for. **respects** *plural noun* polite greetings; *pay one's respects*, make a polite visit; *pay one's last respects*, by attending a person's funeral or a lying in state. **respecter** *noun* [from *re-* = back, + Latin *specere* = to look]

respectable *adjective* **1** of moderately good social standing; honest and decent; proper in appearance or behaviour. **2** of a moderately good standard or size etc., not bringing disgrace or embarrassment, *a respectable score*. **respectably** *adverb*, **respectability** *noun*

respectful *adjective* showing respect. **respectfully** *adverb*, **respectfulness** *noun*

respecting *preposition* concerning, with respect to.

respective *adjective* belonging to each as an individual, *were given places according to their respective ranks*.

respectively *adverb* for each separately in the order mentioned.

respiration *noun* **1** breathing. **2** a plant's absorption of oxygen and emission of carbon dioxide.

respirator *noun* **1** a device worn over the nose and mouth to filter or purify the air before it is inhaled. **2** an apparatus for giving artificial respiration.

respiratory (rĕ-**spi**-ră-tŏ-ree *or* **ress**-pră-tree) *adjective* of or involving respiration.

respire *verb* to breathe; (of plants) to perform the process of respiration. [from *re-*, + Latin *spirare* = breathe]

respite (**ress**-pyt) *noun* **1** an interval of rest or relief. **2** delay permitted before an obligation must be fulfilled or a penalty suffered.

resplendent *adjective* brilliant with colour or decorations. **resplendently** *adverb* [from *re-*, + Latin *splendens* = glittering]

respond *verb* to make an answer. **respond to** to act or behave in answer to or because of, *the vehicle responds to its controls*; *the disease did not respond to treatment*, was not cured or relieved by it; *she responds to kindness*, behaves better if treated kindly. [from *re-*, + Latin *spondere* = promise]

respondent *noun* 1 one who responds, e.g. to a questionnaire. 2 the defendant in a lawsuit, especially in a divorce case.

response *noun* 1 an answer. 2 any part of the liturgy said or sung in answer to the priest. 3 an act, feeling, or movement produced by a stimulus or by another's action.

responsibility *noun* 1 being responsible. 2 something for which one is responsible.

responsible *adjective* 1 legally or morally obliged to take care of something or to carry out a duty; liable to be blamed for loss or failure etc. 2 having to account for one's actions, *you will be responsible to the president himself.* 3 capable of rational conduct, *a responsible person.* 5 involving important duties, *a responsible position.* 6 being the cause of something, *the plague was responsible for many deaths.* **responsibly** *adverb*

responsive *adjective* responding warmly and favourably to an influence. **responsiveness** *noun*

respray *verb* to spray again. **–respray** *noun* the act or process of respraying.

rest¹ *verb* 1 to be still, to cease from movement, action, or working, especially in order to regain one's vigour. 2 to cause or allow to do this, *sit down and rest your feet.* 3 (of a matter under discussion) to be left without further investigation. 4 to place or be placed for support, *rested the parcel on the table.* 5 to rely, *the case rests on evidence of identification.* 6 (of a look) to alight, to be directed, *his gaze rested on his son.* **–rest** *noun* 1 inactivity or sleep as a way of regaining one's vigour; a period of this. 2 a prop or support for an object. 3 an interval of silence between notes in music; a sign indicating this. □ **at rest** not moving; free from trouble or anxiety. **come to rest** to cease movement. **rest home** a place where old or frail people are cared for. **rest room** a toilet in a public building. [from Old English *raest* = bed]

rest² *verb* to remain in a specified state, *rest assured, it will be a success.* **–rest** *noun* the rest the remaining part; the others. □ **rest with** to be left in the hands or charge of, *it rests with you to suggest terms.* [from Latin *restare* = stay behind]

restaurant (**res**-tă-ront) *noun* a place where meals can be bought and eaten.

restaurateur (res-tă-ră-**ter**) *noun* a person who owns and manages a restaurant.

rested *adjective* refreshed by resting.

restful *adjective* giving rest or a feeling of rest. **restfully** *adverb*, **restfulness** *noun*

restitution *noun* 1 restoration of a thing to its proper owner or its original state. 2 reparation for injury or damage. [from *re-*, + Latin *statutum* = established]

restive *adjective* restless, resisting control because made impatient by delay or restraint. **restively** *adverb*, **restiveness** *noun*

restless *adjective* 1 unable to rest or to be still. 2 without rest or sleep, *a restless night.* **restlessly** *adverb*, **restlessness** *noun*

restock *verb* to renew one's stock.

restoration *noun* 1 restoring; being restored. 2 a model, drawing, or reconstruction of a supposed original form of an extinct animal, ruined building, etc. □ **the Restoration** the re-establishment of the monarchy in Britain in 1660 when Charles II became king.

restorative (rĕ-**sto**-ră-tiv) *adjective* tending to restore health or strength. **–restorative** *noun* a restorative food or medicine or treatment.

restore *verb* 1 to bring back to its original state, e.g. by repairing or rebuilding. 2 to bring back to good health or vigour. 3 to put back in its former position, to reinstate. **restorer** *noun*

restrain *verb* to hold back (a person or thing) from movement or action; to keep under control.

restrained *adjective* showing restraint.

restraint *noun* 1 restraining; being restrained. 2 something that restrains, a limiting influence. 3 avoidance of exaggeration in literary or artistic work.

restrict *verb* to put a limit on; to subject to limitations. **restriction** *noun*

restrictive *adjective* restricting. □ **restrictive practices** an industrial agreement that limits competition or output.

restructure *verb* to give a new structure to.

result *noun* 1 that which is produced by an activity or operation, an effect. 2 a statement of the score or marks or the name of the winner in a sporting event, competition, or examination. 3 an answer or formula etc. obtained by calculation. **–result** *verb* 1 to occur as a result, *the troubles that resulted from the merger.* 2 to have a specified result, *the match resulted in a draw.* □ **get results** to achieve a significant and satisfactory result.

resultant *adjective* occurring as a result, *the resultant profit.* **–resultant** *noun* a vector

765

whose effect is equal to the combined effects of two or more given vectors.

resume *verb* **1** to get or take or occupy again; *resume one's seat*, to sit down again. **2** to begin again; to begin to speak or work or use again. **resumption** *noun* [from *re-*, + Latin *sumere* = take up]

résumé (*rez*-yoom-ay) *noun* **1** a summary. **2** a curriculum vitae. [French, = summed up]

resurgence (rĕ-*ser*-jĕns) *noun* a rise or revival after defeat, destruction, or disappearance etc. **resurgent** *adjective* [from *re-*, + Latin *surgens* = rising]

resurrect *verb* to bring back to life or into use, *resurrect an old custom*.

resurrection *noun* **1** rising from the dead; **the Resurrection** that of Christ. **2** revival after disuse. [same origin as *resurgence*]

resuscitate (rĕ-*sus*-ĭ-tayt) *verb* **1** to bring or come back from unconsciousness. **2** to revive (a custom or institution etc.). **resuscitation** *noun*

retail *noun* the selling of goods to the general public (not for resale). **–retail** *adjective* & *adverb* in the retail trade. **–retail** *verb* **1** to sell or be sold in the retail trade. **2** to recount, to relate details of. **retailer** *noun*

retain *verb* **1** to keep in one's possession or use. **2** to continue to have, not to lose, *the fire had retained its heat*. **3** to keep in one's memory, *she retained a clear impression of the building*. **4** to hold in place; *a retaining wall*, one supporting and confining a mass of earth or water. **5** to book the services of (a barrister). [from *re-*, + Latin *tenere* = to hold]

retainer *noun* **1** a fee paid to retain certain services. **2** (*old use*) an attendant of a person of rank. □ **old retainer** (*humorous use*) a faithful old servant.

retake *verb* (**retook**, **retaken**, **retaking**) to take again.

retaliate (rĕ-*tal*-ee-ayt) *verb* to repay an injury or insult etc. with a similar one; to make a counter-attack. **retaliation** *noun*, **retaliatory** (rĕ-*tal*-yă-tŏ-ree) *adjective* [from *re-*, + Latin *talis* = the same kind]

retard (rĕ-*tard*) *verb* to cause delay to, to slow the progress of. **retardation** *noun* [from *re-*, + Latin *tardus* = slow]

retarded *adjective* backward in mental or physical development.

retch (*rhymes with* fetch) *verb* to strain one's throat as if vomiting.

retell *verb* (**retold**, **retelling**) to tell (a story etc.) again.

retention *noun* retaining.

retentive *adjective* able to retain things, *a retentive memory*. **retentiveness** *noun*

rethink *verb* (**rethought**, **rethinking**) to think about again; to plan again and differently.

reticent (*ret*-ĭ-sĕnt) *adjective* not revealing one's thoughts and feelings readily, discreet. **reticently** *adverb*, **reticence** *noun*

reticulated (rĕ-*tik*-yŭ-layt-ĕd) *adjective* divided into a network or into small squares with intersecting lines. **reticulation** *noun*

reticulum (rĕ-*tik*-yŭ-lŭm) *noun* (*plural* **reticula**) a ruminant's second stomach. [Latin, = a small net]

retina (*ret*-ĭ-nă) *noun* (*plural* **retinas**) a layer of membrane at the back of the eyeball, sensitive to light.

retinol (*ret*-ĭ-nol) *noun* either of two forms of vitamin A.

retinue (*ret*-ĭ-new) *noun* a number of attendants accompanying an important person.

retire *verb* **1** to give up one's regular work because of advancing age; to cause (an employee) to do this. **2** to withdraw, to retreat. **3** to go to bed or to one's private room. **retirement** *noun* [from French *retirer* = draw back]

retired *adjective* **1** who has retired. **2** withdrawn from society or from observation, secluded.

retiree *noun* a retired person.

retiring *adjective* shy, avoiding society.

retort¹ *verb* to make a quick or witty or angry reply. **–retort** *noun* retorting; a reply of this kind. [from *re-*, + Latin *tortum* = twisted]

retort² *noun* **1** a vessel (usually of glass) with a long downward-bent neck, used in distilling liquids. **2** a receptacle used in making gas or steel.

retouch *verb* to improve or alter (a picture or photograph) by making minor alterations or removing flaws etc.

retrace *verb* to trace back to the source or beginning; *retrace one's steps*, go back the way one came. **retraceable** *adjective*

retract *verb* **1** to pull (a thing) back or in, *the snail retracts its horns*. **2** to withdraw (a statement); to refuse to keep to (an agreement). **retractable** *adjective*, **retraction**

noun, **retractor** noun [from *re-*, + Latin *tractum* = pulled]

retractile (rĕ-**trak**-tyl) *adjective* (of a part of the body) retractable.

retrain *verb* to train again or for something different.

retread (ree-**tred**) *verb* to put a fresh tread on (a tyre) by moulding rubber to a used foundation. – **retread** (**ree**-tred) *noun* a retreaded tyre.

retreat *verb* to withdraw after being defeated or when faced with danger or difficulty; to go away to a place of shelter. – **retreat** *noun* **1** retreating; the military signal for this. **2** a military bugle call at sunset. **3** withdrawal into privacy or seclusion; a place for this. **4** a period of withdrawal from worldly activities for prayer and meditation. [same origin as *retract*]

retrench *verb* **1** to reduce the amount of, *retrench one's operations*. **2** to reduce one's expenditure or operations, *we shall have to retrench*. **3** (especially *Austral.*) to make (an employee) redundant; to sack in order to reduce costs. **retrenchment** *noun*

retrial *noun* the trying of a lawsuit again.

retribution (ret-rĭ-**bew**-shŏn) *noun* a deserved punishment. [from *re-*, + Latin *tributum* = assigned]

retributive (rĕ-**trib**-yŭ-tiv) *adjective* happening or inflicted as retribution.

retrievable *adjective* able to be retrieved.

retrieval *noun* retrieving; being retrieved.

retrieve *verb* **1** to regain possession of. **2** to find again or extract (stored information etc.). **3** (of a dog) to find and bring in (killed or wounded game). **4** to rescue, to restore to a flourishing state, *retrieve one's fortunes*. **5** to set right (a loss or error or a bad situation). – **retrieve** *noun* possibility of recovery, *beyond retrieve*. [from Old French *retrover* = find again]

retriever *noun* a dog of a breed that is often trained to retrieve game.

retro- *prefix* back; backwards (as in *retrograde*). [from Latin *retro* = backwards]

retroactive *adjective* effective as from a past date. **retroactively** *adverb*

retrograde *adjective* **1** going backwards, *retrograde motion*. **2** reverting to a less good condition.

retrogress (ret-rŏ-**gress**) *verb* to move backwards; to deteriorate. **retrogression**

noun, **retrogressive** *adjective* [from *retro-* + *progress*]

retro-rocket *noun* an auxiliary rocket discharging its exhaust in the opposite direction to the main rockets, used for slowing a spacecraft.

retrospect *noun* a survey of past time or events. ☐ **in retrospect** when one looks back on a past event or situation. [from *retro-* + *prospect*]

retrospection *noun* looking back, especially on the past.

retrospective *adjective* **1** looking back on the past. **2** applying to the past as well as the future, *the law could not be made retrospective*. – **retrospective** *noun* an exhibition, recital, etc. showing an artist's development over a lifetime. **retrospectively** *adverb*

retroverted (**ret**-roh-ver-tĕd) *adjective* turned backwards. **retroversion** *noun* [from *retro-*, + Latin *vertere* = to turn]

retrovirus (**ret**-roh-vy-rŭs) *noun* any of a group of RNA viruses (including HIV) which insert a DNA copy of their genome into the host cell in order to replicate.

retry *verb* (**retried**, **retrying**) to try (a lawsuit or a defendant) again.

return *verb* **1** to come or go back. **2** to bring, give, put, or send back. **3** to yield (a profit). **4** to say in reply. **5** to state or describe officially, especially in answer to a formal demand for information. **6** (of an electorate) to elect as an MP, government, etc. – **return** *noun* **1** coming or going back. **2** bringing, giving, putting, or sending back. **3** the proceeds or profits of a transaction, *brings a good return on one's investment*. **4** a return ticket. **5** a return match or game. **6** a formal report, e.g. of a set of transactions, *income tax return*. ☐ **returned serviceman** or **servicewoman** one who has served in a war overseas. **returning officer** the official conducting an election in an electorate and announcing the result. **return match** or **game** a second match or game between the same opponents. **return ticket** a ticket for a journey to a place and back to one's starting point. **returnable** *adjective*

reunify *verb* to reunite. **reunification** *noun*

reunion *noun* **1** reuniting; being reunited. **2** a social gathering of people who were formerly associated.

reunite *verb* to unite again after separation.

reusable *adjective* able to be reused.

reuse (ree-**yooz**) *verb* to use again. – **reuse** (ree-**yooss**) *noun* using or being used again.

Reuters (**roi**-terz) an international news agency owned and directed by various newspaper associations of Britain and the Commonwealth, established by Baron von Reuter (1816–99).

rev *noun* a revolution of an engine. – **rev** *verb* (**revved, revving**) **1** (of an engine) to revolve. **2** to cause (an engine) to run quickly, especially when starting.

Rev. *abbreviation* Reverend, *the Rev. John Smith* or *the Rev. J. Smith* or *the Rev. Mr Smith*.

revalue *verb* **1** to re-assess the value of. **2** to give a new (higher) value to (a currency). **revaluation** *noun*

revamp *verb* to renovate; to give a new appearance to.

Revd *abbreviation* Reverend.

reveal *verb* to make known; to uncover and allow to be seen. [from Latin *revelare* = unveil]

reveille (rĕ-**val**-ee) *noun* a military waking-signal sounded on a bugle or drums. [from French *réveillez* = wake up!]

revel *verb* (**revelled, revelling**) **1** to take great delight, *some people revel in gossip*. **2** to hold revels. **revels** *plural noun* lively festivities or merrymaking. **reveller** *noun*

revelation *noun* **1** revealing, making known something that was secret or hidden. **2** something revealed, especially something surprising. – **Revelation** the last book of the New Testament (*see* **Apocalypse**).

revelry *noun* revelling; revels.

revenge *noun* **1** punishment or injury inflicted in return for what one has suffered. **2** a desire to inflict this. **3** opportunity to defeat in a return game an opponent who won the first game. – **revenge** *verb* to avenge; *be revenged* or *revenge oneself*, to get satisfaction by inflicting vengeance. **revengeful** *adjective*

revenue (**rev**-ĕ-new) *noun* **1** income, especially of a large amount. **2** a country's annual income from taxes, duties, etc., used for paying public expenses. [French, = returned]

reverberate (rĕ-**verb**-ĕ-rayt) *verb* to echo, to resound. **reverberant** *adjective*, **reverberation** *noun*, **reverberative** *adjective* [from *re*-, + Latin *verberare* = to lash]

revere (rĕ-**veer**) *verb* to feel deep respect or religious veneration for.

reverence *noun* a feeling of awe and respect or veneration. – **reverence** *verb* to feel or show reverence towards.

reverend *adjective* **1** deserving to be treated with respect. **2 the Reverend** the title of a member of the clergy. – **reverend** *noun* (*informal*) a member of the clergy.
☐ **Reverend Mother** the Mother Superior of a convent. [from Latin, = person to be revered]

reverent *adjective* feeling or showing reverence. **reverently** *adverb* [from Latin, = revering]

Usage Distinguish *reverent* from *reverend*. *Reverent* means 'showing respect', while *reverend* means 'deserving respect'.

reverie (**rev**-ĕ-ree) *noun* a daydream, a state of daydreaming.

revers (rĕ-**veer**) *noun* (*plural* revers, *pr.* rĕ-**veerz**) a turned-back front edge of the neck of a jacket or bodice. [French, = reverse]

reversal *noun* reversing; being reversed.

reverse *adjective* facing or moving in the opposite direction; opposite in character or order; upside-down. – **reverse** *verb* **1** to turn the other way round or up, or inside out. **2** to convert to the opposite kind or effect, *reversed the tendency*; *reverse the charges*, make the recipient (not the caller) pay for a telephone call. **3** to annul (a decree or decision etc.). **4** to move in the opposite direction; (of a vehicle) to travel backwards. **5** to make (an engine or machine) work in the opposite direction; to cause (a vehicle) to travel backwards. – **reverse** *noun* **1** the reverse side or effect. **2** the opposite of the usual manner, *the name was printed in reverse*. **3** a piece of misfortune, *they suffered several reverses*. **4** reverse gear.
☐ **reverse gear** a gear used to make a vehicle etc. travel backwards. **reversely** *adverb* [same origin as *revert*]

reversible *adjective* able to be reversed; (of a garment) able to be worn with either side turned outwards.

reversion *noun* **1** reverting. **2** the legal right to possess something when its present holder relinquishes it; the returning of a right or property in this way. **reversionary** *adjective*

Usage Note that *reversion* does not mean *reversal*.

revert *verb* **1** to return to a former condition or habit. **2** to return to a subject in talk or thought. **3** (of property etc.) to return or pass to another owner by reversion. [from *re-* = back, + Latin *vertere* = to turn]

review *noun* **1** a general survey of past events or of a subject. **2** a re-examination or reconsideration; *the salary scale is under review*, is being reconsidered. **3** a ceremonial inspection of troops or a fleet etc. **4** a published report assessing the merits of a book or play etc. –**review** *verb* **1** to survey. **2** to re-examine or reconsider. **3** to inspect (troops or a fleet etc.) ceremonially. **4** to write a review of (a book or play etc.). **reviewer** *noun*

Usage Distinguish *review* from *revue*, meaning 'a type of entertainment'.

---

revile *verb* to criticise angrily in abusive language. **revilement** *noun*

revise *verb* **1** to re-examine and alter or correct. **2** to go over (work already learnt) in preparation for an examination. [from *re-*, + Latin *visere* = examine]

revision *noun* **1** revising; being revised. **2** a revised version or form.

revisit *verb* to pay another visit to.

revival *noun* **1** reviving; being revived. **2** something brought back into use or fashion. **3** a reawakening of interest in religion; a special effort with meetings etc. to promote this.

revivalist *noun* a person who organises or conducts meetings to promote a religious revival. **revivalism** *noun*

revive *verb* **1** to come or bring back to life, consciousness, or strength. **2** to come or bring back into use, activity, or fashion etc. **reviver** *noun* [from *re-*, + Latin *vivere* = to live]

revocable (**rev**-ŏ-kă-bŭl) *adjective* able to be revoked.

revoke (rĕ-**vohk**) *verb* **1** to withdraw or cancel (a decree or licence etc.). **2** (in cards) to renege. [from *re-*, + Latin *vocare* = to call]

revolt *verb* **1** to take part in a rebellion. **2** to be in a mood of protest or defiance. **3** to feel strong disgust. **4** to cause a feeling of strong disgust in (a person). –**revolt** *noun* **1** an act or state of rebelling or defying authority. **2** a sense of disgust. [same origin as *revolve*]

revolting *adjective* causing disgust.

revolution *noun* **1** substitution of a new system of government, especially by force. **2** any complete change of method or conditions etc., *a revolution in the treatment of burns*. **3** revolving, rotation; a single complete orbit or movement of this kind. [same origin as *revolve*]

revolutionary *adjective* **1** of political revolution. **2** involving a great change, *revolutionary new ideas*. –**revolutionary** *noun* a person who begins or supports a political revolution.

revolutionise *verb* (also **-ize**) to alter (a thing) completely, *this will revolutionise our lives*.

revolve *verb* **1** to turn or cause to turn round, to rotate. **2** to move in a circular orbit. **3** to turn over (a problem etc.) in one's mind. [from *re-*, + Latin *volvere* = to roll]

revolver *noun* a pistol with a revolving magazine, usually holding six cartridges.

revue *noun* an entertainment consisting of a series of items such as sketches and songs. [French]

revulsion *noun* **1** a feeling of strong disgust. **2** a sudden violent change of feeling, *a revulsion of public feeling in favour of the accused woman*.

reward *noun* **1** something given or received in return for what is done or for a service or merit. **2** a sum of money offered for the detection of a criminal or return of lost property etc. –**reward** *verb* to give a reward to.

rewarding *adjective* (of an occupation) well worth doing.

rewind *verb* (**rewound**, **rewinding**) to wind (a film or tape etc.) back to or towards the beginning. –**rewind** *noun* rewinding.

rewire *verb* to renew the electrical wiring of.

reword *verb* to change the wording of.

rewrite *verb* (**rewrote**, **rewritten**, **rewriting**) to write (a thing) again in a different form or style.

Rex *noun* a reigning king. [Latin, = king]

Reykjavik (**rayk**-yă-vik) the capital of Iceland.

Rh *abbreviation* Rhesus.

rhapsodise *verb* (also **-ize**) to talk or write about something in an ecstatic way.

rhapsody *noun* **1** an ecstatic written or spoken statement. **2** a romantic musical composition in an irregular form. [from Greek *rhapsoidos* = one who stitches songs together]

rhenium (**ree**-nee-ŭm) *noun* a rare silver-white metallic element (symbol Re).

rheostat (**ree**-ŏ-stat) *noun* an instrument used to control the current in an electrical circuit by varying the amount of resistance in it. [from Greek *rheos* = a stream, + *statos* = stationary]

rhesus (**ree**-sŭs) *noun* a small monkey common in northern India, used in biological experiments. □ **rhesus factor** a substance present in the blood of most people and some animals, causing a blood disorder in a newborn baby whose blood is **rhesus positive** (= containing this substance) while its mother's blood is **rhesus negative** (= not containing it).

rhetoric (**ret**-ŏ-rik) *noun* 1 the art of using words impressively, especially in public speaking. 2 language used for its impressive sound; affected or exaggerated expressions. [from Greek *rhetor* = orator]

rhetorical (rĕ-**to**-ri-kăl) *adjective* expressed in a way that is designed to be impressive. □ **rhetorical question** something phrased as a question only for dramatic effect and not to seek an answer, e.g. *who cares?* (= nobody cares). **rhetorically** *adverb*

rheumatic (roo-**mat**-ik) *adjective* of or affected with rheumatism. □ **rheumatic fever** a serious form of rheumatism with fever, chiefly in children.

rheumatism (**room**-ă-tizm) *noun* any of several diseases causing pain in the joints, muscles, or fibrous tissue, especially a form of arthritis.

rheumatoid *adjective* of rheumatism. □ **rheumatoid arthritis** a disease causing inflammation and stiffening of the joints.

Rhine a river of western Europe, flowing from the Alps through Germany and the Netherlands to the North Sea.

rhinestone *noun* an imitation diamond.

rhino *noun* (*plural* **rhino** or **rhinos**) (*informal*) a rhinoceros.

rhinoceros *noun* (*plural* **rhinoceroses**) a large thick-skinned animal (pachyderm) of Africa and south Asia, with a horn or two horns on its nose. [from Greek *rhinos* = of the nose, + *keras* = horn]

rhizome (**ry**-zohm) *noun* a rootlike stem growing along or under the ground and sending out both roots and shoots.

Rhode Island a State of the north-eastern USA.

Rhodes[1] a Greek island in the Aegean Sea, off the coast of Turkey.

Rhodes[2], Cecil John (1853–1902), British statesman in South Africa, who was instrumental in the development of Rhodesia. □ **Rhodes Scholarship** a scholarship tenable at Oxford University by students from certain overseas countries.

Rhodesia (roh-**dee**-shă) 1 the former name of a large area of central-southern Africa, divided into Northern Rhodesia (now Zambia) and Southern Rhodesia (now Zimbabwe). 2 the name adopted by Southern Rhodesia after Northern Rhodesia became the independent republic of Zambia in 1963. **Rhodesian** *adjective* & *noun*

rhodium (**roh**-dee-ŭm) *noun* a hard silver-white metallic element (symbol Rh).

rhododendron (roh-dŏ-**den**-drŏn) *noun* an evergreen shrub with large clusters of trumpet-shaped flowers. [from Greek *rhodon* = rose, + *dendron* = tree]

rhomboid (**rom**-boid) *adjective* like a rhombus. –**rhomboid** *noun* a quadrilateral of which only the opposite sides and angles are equal.

rhombus (**rom**-bŭs) *noun* a geometric figure shaped like the diamond on playing cards, a parallelogram with all sides equal.

Rhône a river rising in the Alps and flowing through France to the Mediterranean Sea.

rhubarb *noun* a garden plant with fleshy reddish leaf-stalks that are used like fruit.

rhyme *noun* 1 identity of sound between words or syllables or the endings of lines of verse (e.g. *line/mine/pine*, *visit/is it*). 2 a poem with rhymes. 3 a word providing a rhyme to another. –**rhyme** *verb* to form a rhyme; to have rhymes. □ **without rhyme or reason** with no sensible or logical reason.

rhythm (**rith**-ĕm) *noun* 1 the pattern produced by emphasis and duration of notes in music or by long and short or stressed syllables in words. 2 a movement with a regular succession of strong and weak elements, *the rhythm of the heart beating*. 3 a constantly recurring sequence of events. **rhythmic** *adjective*, **rhythmical** *adjective*, **rhythmically** *adverb*

ria (**ree**-ă) *noun* a long narrow inlet of the sea formed where part of a river valley has become submerged.

rib *noun* **1** each of the curved bones round the chest. **2** a cut of meat from this part of an animal. **3** a curved structural part resembling a rib, e.g. a raised moulding on a ceiling. **4** each of the hinged rods forming the framework of an umbrella. **5** a vein in a leaf or an insect's wing. **6** a raised pattern of lines in knitting. –rib *verb* (**ribbed, ribbing**) **1** to support (a structure) with ribs. **2** to knit in rib. **3** (*informal*) to tease.

ribald (**rib**-ăld) *adjective* humorous in a cheerful but vulgar or disrespectful way. **ribaldry** *noun*

riband (**rib**-ănd) *noun* a ribbon.

ribbed *adjective* **1** with raised ridges. **2** knitted in rib.

ribbon *noun* **1** a narrow band of fine ornamental material used for decoration or for tying something. **2** a ribbon of special colour or pattern worn to indicate the award of a medal or order etc. **3** a long narrow strip of material, e.g. an inked strip used in a typewriter; *in ribbons* or *torn to ribbons*, torn into ragged strips. □ **ribbon development** the building of houses along a main road, extending outwards from a town.

ribcage *noun* the framework of ribs round the chest.

riboflavin *noun* a vitamin of the B group, found in liver, milk, and eggs.

ribonucleic acid *see* RNA.

rice *noun* **1** a kind of grass grown in marshes in hot countries, producing seeds that are used as food. **2** these seeds. □ **rice paper** paper made from the pith of an oriental tree, used for painting and in cookery.

rich *adjective* **1** having much wealth. **2** having a large supply of something, *the country is rich in natural resources*. **3** splendid, made of costly materials, elaborate, *rich furnishings*. **4** producing or produced abundantly, *rich soil*; *a rich harvest*. **5** (of food) containing a large proportion of fat, butter, eggs, or spices etc. **6** (of a mixture in an internal-combustion engine) containing more than the normal proportion of fuel. **7** (of colour, sound, or smell) pleasantly deep or strong. **8** highly amusing. **richness** *noun*

Richard the name of three kings of England, who reigned as Richard I 1189–99, Richard II 1377–99, Richard III 1483–5.

Richardson, Henry Handel (Ethel Florence Lindesay Robertson, née Richardson) (1870–1946), Australian novelist, author of *The Getting of Wisdom* and *The Fortunes of Richard Mahony*.

Richelieu (**reesh**-lee-er), Armand Jean du Plessis (1585–1642), French cardinal and statesman.

riches *plural noun* a great quantity of money, property, or valuable possessions.

richly *adjective* **1** in a rich way. **2** thoroughly, *the book richly deserves its success*.

Richter scale (**rik**-ter) *noun* a scale for measuring the magnitude of earthquakes. [named after the American seismologist C.F. Richter (1900–85)]

rick¹ *noun* a built stack of hay etc.

rick² *noun* a slight sprain or strain. –**rick** *verb* to sprain or strain slightly.

rickets *noun* a children's disease caused by deficiency of vitamin D, resulting in softening and deformity of the bones.

rickety *adjective* shaky, insecure. **ricketiness** *noun*

rickrack *noun* = ricrac.

rickshaw *noun* a light two-wheeled hooded vehicle, drawn by one or more people. [from Japanese *jin-riki-sha* = person-power-vehicle]

ricochet (**rik**-ŏ-shay) *verb* (**ricocheted** (*pr.* **rik**-ŏ-shayd), **ricocheting** (*pr.* **rik**-ŏ-shay-ing) to rebound from a surface as a missile does when it strikes with a glancing blow. –**ricochet** *noun* a rebound of this kind; a hit made by it.

ricotta (ri-**kot**-ă) *noun* a soft Italian cheese.

ricrac *noun* a zigzag braid trimming.

rid *verb* (**rid, ridding**) to free from something unpleasant or unwanted, *rid the house of mice*; *was glad to be rid of him*. □ **get rid of** to cause to go away; (*informal*) to succeed in selling.

riddance *noun* ridding. □ **good riddance** a welcome freedom from a person or thing one is rid of.

ridden *see* ride. –**ridden** *adjective* full of or dominated by, *ant-ridden cupboards*; *guilt-ridden*.

riddle¹ *noun* **1** a question or statement designed to test ingenuity or give amusement in finding its answer or meaning. **2** something puzzling or mysterious.

riddle² *noun* a coarse sieve for gravel or cinders etc. –**riddle** *verb* **1** to pass (gravel etc.) through a riddle, *riddle the ashes*. **2** to pierce with many holes, *riddled the car with bullets*. **3** to permeate thoroughly, *be riddled with disease*.

ride *verb* (**rode**, **ridden**, **riding**) **1** to sit on and be carried by (a horse etc.). **2** to go on horseback or on a bicycle, train, or other conveyance. **3** to sit on and manage a horse. **4** to be supported on, to float or seem to float, *the ship rode the waves* or *at anchor*; *the moon was riding high*. **5** to yield to (a blow) so as to reduce its impact. –**ride** *noun* **1** a spell of riding. **2** a journey in a vehicle. **3** the feel of a ride, *the car gives a smooth ride*. **4** a device such as a merry-go-round or roller coaster ridden at an amusement park, showground, etc. □ **let it ride** to take no further action. **ride high** to be successful. **ride out the storm** to survive a storm or difficulty successfully. **ride up** (of a garment) to work upwards when worn. **take for a ride** (*informal*) to deceive or swindle.

rider *noun* **1** a person who rides a horse or bicycle etc. **2** an additional clause supplementing a statement etc.; an expression of opinion added to a verdict.

riderless *adjective* without a rider.

ridge *noun* **1** a narrow raised strip, a line where two upward-sloping surfaces meet. **2** an elongated region of high barometric pressure.

ridged *adjective* formed into ridges.

ridgy-didge *adjective* (*Austral. informal*) all right, genuine.

ridicule *noun* the process of making a person or thing appear ridiculous. –**ridicule** *verb* to subject to ridicule, to make fun of. [from Latin *ridere* = to laugh]

ridiculous *adjective* **1** deserving to be laughed at, especially in a scornful way. **2** not worth serious consideration, preposterous. **ridiculously** *adverb*

riding *noun* an electoral division of a shire.

Riesling (**reez**-ling) *noun* a kind of grape; a dry white wine made from this.

rife *adjective* **1** occurring frequently, widespread, *crime was rife in the city*. **2** well provided, full, *the country was rife with rumours of war*.

riffle *verb* to turn (pages) in quick succession, to leaf through quickly.

riff-raff *noun* the rabble; disreputable people.

rifle *noun* a gun with a long barrel cut with spiral grooves to make the bullet spin and so travel more accurately when fired. –**rifle** *verb* **1** to search and rob, *rifled the safe*. **2** to cut spiral grooves in (a gun barrel).

rift *noun* **1** a cleft in earth or rock. **2** a crack or split in an object; a break in cloud. **3** a breach in friendly relations between people or in the unity of a group. □ **rift valley** a steep-sided valley formed by subsidence of the earth's crust.

rig[1] *verb* (**rigged**, **rigging**) **1** to provide with clothes or equipment, *rigged them out*. **2** to fit (a ship) with spars, ropes, sails, etc. **3** to set up (a structure) quickly or with makeshift materials. –**rig** *noun* **1** the way a ship's masts and sails etc. are arranged. **2** equipment for a special purpose, e.g. for drilling an oil well, *a test rig*; *an oil rig*. **3** a large truck; a semitrailer. **4** (*informal*) an outfit of clothes, *in full rig*. □ **rig-out** *noun* (*informal*) an outfit of clothes.

rig[2] *verb* (**rigged**, **rigging**) to manage or control fraudulently, *the election was rigged*.

Riga (**ree**-gă) capital and chief port of Latvia.

rigger *noun* a worker on an oil rig.

rigging *noun* the ropes etc. used to support masts and set or work the sails on a ship.

right *adjective* **1** (of conduct or actions etc.) morally good, in accordance with justice. **2** proper, correct, true, *the right answer*; *right side*, (of fabric) the side meant to show. **3** in a good or normal condition, *all's right with the world*; *in his right mind*, sane. **4** (*informal*) real, properly so called, *made a right mess of it*. **5** of the right-hand side. –**right** *noun* **1** what is just, a fair claim or treatment; something one is entitled to. **2** the right-hand part or region. **3** the right hand; a blow with this. **4** (in marching) the right foot. **5** (often **Right**) the right wing of a political party or other group. –**right** *verb* **1** to restore to a proper or correct or upright position, *managed to right the boat*. **2** to set right, to make amends or take vengeance for, *to right the wrong*. **3** to correct, *the fault will right itself*. –**right** *adverb* **1** on or towards the right-hand side, *turn right*. **2** straight, *go right on*. **3** (*informal*) immediately, *I'll be right back*. **4** all the way, completely, *went right round it*. **5** exactly, *right in the middle*. **6** very, fully, *to be right glad*. **7** rightly, *you did right to come*. **8** all right, that is correct, I agree. □ **by right** or **rights** if right were done. **in the right** having justice or truth on one's side. **on the right side of** in the favour of or liked by (a person); *on the right side of forty*, not yet 40 years old. **right angle** an angle of 90°; *at right angles*, placed at or turning through a right angle. **right-angled** *adjective* having a right angle.

right away immediately. right hand the hand that in most people is used more than the left, on the side opposite the left hand. right-hand *adjective* of or towards, this side of a person or the corresponding side of a thing; *a person's right-hand man*, indispensable or chief assistant. right-handed *adjective* using the right hand usually, by preference; (of a blow or tool) made with or operated by the right hand; (of a screw) to be tightened by turning towards the right. right-hander *noun* a right-handed person or blow. right-minded *adjective* having proper or honest principles. right of way the right to pass over another's land, a path that is subject to such a right; the right to proceed, while another vehicle must wait. right oh! (*informal*) an expression of agreement. Right Reverend the title of an Anglican bishop. right wing those who support more conservative or traditional policies than others in their group (¶ See note at *left wing* left²). right-winger *noun*. she'll be right (*Austral. informal*) all will be well. she's right (*Austral. informal*) all is in order. too right (*informal*) an expression of agreement.

righteous *adjective* 1 doing what is morally right, making a show of this. 2 morally justifiable, *full of righteous indignation*. righteously *adverb*, righteousness *noun*

rightful *adjective* in accordance with what is just or proper or legal. rightfully *adverb*

rightist *noun* a member of the right wing of a political party. – rightist *adjective* of the right wing in politics etc. rightism *noun*

rightly *adverb* justly, correctly, properly, justifiably.

rightness *noun* being just, correct, proper, or justifiable.

rigid *adjective* 1 stiff, not bending or yielding. 2 strict, inflexible, *rigid rules*. rigidly *adverb*, rigidity (rǐ-**jid**-ǐ-tee) *noun*

rigmarole (**rig**-mǎ-rohl) *noun* 1 a long rambling statement. 2 a complicated formal procedure.

rigor mortis (**rig**-er **mor**-tǐss) *noun* stiffening of the body after death. [Latin]

rigorous (**rig**-ŏ-rǔs) *adjective* 1 strict, severe, *rigorous discipline*. 2 strictly accurate or detailed, *a rigorous search*. 3 harsh, unpleasant, *a rigorous climate*. rigorously *adverb*

rigour (**rig**-er) *noun* 1 severity, strictness. 2 harshness of weather or conditions, *the rigours of famine*.

Rig Veda *noun* the oldest of the Vedas, composed in the second millennium BC. [Sanskrit]

rile (*rhymes with* mile) *verb* (*informal*) to annoy, to irritate.

rill *noun* a small stream.

rim *noun* 1 the edge or border of something more or less circular. 2 the outer edge of a wheel, on which a tyre is fitted.

rime *noun* frost. rimed *adjective* coated with frost.

rimless *adjective* (of spectacles) made without frames.

rimmed *adjective* edged, bordered, *red-rimmed eyes*.

rind (*rhymes with* mind) *noun* a tough outer layer or skin on fruit, cheese, bacon, etc.

ring¹ *noun* 1 the outline of a circle. 2 something shaped like this, a circular band. 3 a small circular band of precious metal worn on the finger. 4 a circular or other enclosure for a circus or sports event or cattle show etc.; a square area in which a boxing match or wrestling match is held. 5 a combination of people acting together for control of operations or policy etc., *a drug ring* – ring *verb* 1 to enclose with a ring, to encircle. 2 to put a ring on (a bird etc.) to identify it. 3 (*Austral.*) to outdo (one's fellow shearers) by shearing the most sheep in a given period, *ring the shed*. ☐ ring finger the third finger, especially of the left hand, on which a wedding ring is worn. ring-pull *noun* a ring on a can for pulling to break its seal. ring road a bypass encircling a town. run or make rings around to do things much better than (another person).

ring² *verb* (rang, rung, ringing) 1 to give out a loud clear resonant sound, like that of a bell when struck. 2 to cause (a bell) to do this. 3 to sound a bell as a summons; to signal by ringing, *bells rang out the old year*. 4 to be filled with sound, *the stadium rang with cheers*. 5 (of ears) to be filled with a ringing or humming sound. 6 to telephone. – ring *noun* 1 the act of ringing a bell. 2 a ringing sound or tone. 3 a tone or feeling of a particular kind; *it has the ring of truth*, sounds true. 4 (*informal*) a telephone call. ☐ ring a bell (*informal*) to arouse a vague memory, to sound faintly familiar. ring off to end a telephone call by replacing the receiver. ring the changes to vary things. ring the curtain up or down to signal that the curtain on a theatre stage should be raised or lowered; to mark the beginning or end of an enterprise etc. **ring up** to make a telephone call to (a person etc.); to record (an amount) on a cash register.

ringbark *verb* to kill (a tree) by cutting a ring of bark from around the trunk.

ringbinder *noun* a loose-leaf binder with ring-shaped clasps that can be opened to pass through holes in the paper.

ringer *noun* 1 a person who rings bells. 2 (*informal*) a person's double; *be a ringer for* or *a dead ringer for*, to look exactly like (a person). 3 (*Austral. informal*) the fastest shearer in a shed; a person who excels (at any activity etc.); the best of anything. 4 (*Austral.*) a station hand or stockman.

ring-in *noun* (*Austral. informal*) 1 a fraudulent substitution; the thing substituted. 2 an outsider; the odd one out in a group or set.

ringleader *noun* a person who leads others in mischief or wrongdoing or in opposition to authority.

ringlet *noun* a long tubular curl.

ringmaster *noun* the person in charge of a circus performance.

ringside *noun* the area immediately beside a boxing ring.

ringtail *noun* (in full **ringtail possum**) any of several Australian possums with a long prehensile tail that curls at the end.

ringworm *noun* a skin disease producing round scaly patches on the skin, caused by a fungus.

rink *noun see* **skating rink**.

rinse *verb* 1 to wash lightly with water. 2 to wash out soap or impurities from. – **rinse** *noun* 1 rinsing. 2 a solution washed through hair to tint or condition it.

Rio de Janeiro (jă-**neer**-roh) the chief port and former capital of Brazil.

Rio Grande (*pr.* grand) a North American river flowing from Colorado south-east to the Gulf of Mexico.

riot *noun* 1 a wild disturbance by a crowd of people. 2 a profuse display of something, *a riot of colour*. 3 (*informal*) a very amusing thing or person. – **riot** *verb* to take part in a riot or in disorderly revelry.

☐ **read the riot act** to insist that noise or disobedience etc. must cease. **run riot** to behave in an unruly way; (of plants) to grow or spread in an uncontrolled way. **rioter** *noun*

riotous *adjective* 1 disorderly, unruly. 2 boisterous, unrestrained. **riotously** *adverb*

RIP *abbreviation* rest in peace. [short for Latin *requiescat* (or *requiescant*) *in pace*]

rip *verb* (**ripped**, **ripping**) 1 to tear apart, to remove by pulling roughly. 2 to become torn. 3 to rush along. 4 to use a program to copy (sound or video data on a CD or DVD) to a computer's hard drive. – **rip** *noun* 1 ripping; a torn place. 2 a stretch of rough water where currents meet. ☐ **let rip** (*informal*) to refrain from checking the speed of (a thing) or from interfering; to speak or utter violently. **rip off** (*informal*) to defraud; to steal. **rip-off** *noun* (*informal*) something fraudulent; a theft. **rip-roaring** *adjective* wildly noisy. **ripper** *noun*

ripcord *noun* a cord for pulling to release a parachute from its pack.

ripe *adjective* 1 (of fruit or grain etc.) ready to be gathered and used. 2 matured and ready to be eaten or drunk, *ripe cheese*. 3 (of a person's age) advanced, *lived to a ripe old age*. 4 ready, prepared or able to undergo something, *the time is ripe for revolution*. **ripely** *adverb*, **ripeness** *noun*

ripen *verb* to make or become ripe.

riposte (rĭ-**posst**) *noun* a quick counterstroke; a quick retort. – **riposte** *verb* to deliver a riposte.

ripple *noun* 1 a small wave or series of waves. 2 something resembling this in appearance or movement. 3 a gentle sound that rises and falls, *a ripple of laughter*. – **ripple** *verb* to form or cause ripples. ☐ **ripple tank** a tray of liquid fitted with a device for making ripples, used for studying the action of waves.

ripsaw *noun* a saw for sawing wood along the grain.

Rip van Winkle a character in a story (by Washington Irving) who slept for 20 years and awoke to find the world completely changed.

rise *verb* (**rose**, **risen**, **rising**) 1 to come or go upwards; to grow or extend upwards. 2 to get up from lying, sitting, or kneeling; to get out of bed. 3 (of a meeting) to cease to sit for business. 4 to become upright or erect. 5 to come to life again after death, *Christ is risen*. 6 to rebel, *rise in revolt*. 7 (of the wind) to begin to blow or to blow more strongly. 8 (of the sun etc.) to become visible above the horizon. 9 to increase in amount, number, or intensity, *prices are rising*; *her spirits rose*, she began to feel more cheerful. 10 to achieve a higher position or status, *rose to the rank of* *colonel*; *rise to the occasion*, to prove oneself able to deal with an unexpected situation. **11** (of bread or cake etc.) to swell by the action of yeast or other raising agent. **12** to have its origin, to begin or begin to flow, *the river rises in the Great Dividing Range*. –**rise** *noun* **1** rising, an upward movement. **2** an upward slope; a small hill. **3** an increase in amount, number, or intensity; an increase in wages. **4** an upward movement in rank or status. ☐ **get** or **take a rise out of** to draw (a person) into a display of annoyance or into making a retort. **give rise to** to cause. **rising five** etc. (of a child) nearing the age of five. **rising generation** young people, those who are growing up.

riser *noun* **1** a person or thing that rises, *an early riser*. **2** a vertical piece between treads of a staircase.

rising *noun* a revolt.

risk *noun* **1** the possibility of meeting danger or suffering harm or loss; exposure to this. **2** a person or thing insured or similarly representing a source of risk, *not a good risk*. –**risk** *verb* to expose to the chance of injury or loss; to accept the risk of.

risky *adjective* (**riskier**, **riskiest**) full of risk. **riskily** *adverb*, **riskiness** *noun*

Risorgimento (rĭ-sorj-ĭ-**ment**-oh) *noun* a movement in the 19th century to unite Italy.

risotto (rĭ-**zot**-oh) *noun* (*plural* **risottos**) an Italian dish of rice cooked in stock with meat or fish, vegetables, cheese, etc.

risqué (**ris**-kay) *adjective* (of a story) slightly indecent. [French]

rissole *noun* a small ball or cake of minced meat or fish mixed with potato or breadcrumbs etc. and usually fried.

rite *noun* a religious or other solemn ritual. ☐ **rites of passage** ceremonies (religious or non-religious) at birth, puberty, mating, and death.

ritual *noun* **1** the series of actions used in a religious or other ceremony; a particular form of this. **2** a procedure regularly followed. –**ritual** *adjective* of or done as a ritual. **ritually** *adverb*, **ritualistic** *adjective*

rival *noun* **1** a person or thing competing with another. **2** a person or thing that can equal another in quality. –**rival** *adjective* being a rival or rivals. –**rival** *verb* (**rivalled**, **rivalling**) to be comparable to, to seem or be as good as. **rivalry** *noun* [from Latin *rivalis* = person using the same stream (*rivus* = stream)]

riven (**riv**-ĕn) *adjective* split, torn violently.

river *noun* **1** a large natural stream of water flowing in a channel. **2** a great flow, *rivers of blood*. [from Latin *ripa* = bank]

Riverina a rich agricultural region of southern NSW between the Lachlan and Murray Rivers, with the Murrumbidgee flowing through it.

Riverland a South Australian region in the Murray Valley, producing fruit and wine.

riverside *noun* the land along a river bank.

rivet (**riv**-ĕt) *noun* a nail or bolt for holding two pieces of metal together, its headless end being beaten or pressed down to form a head when it is in place. –**rivet** *verb* (**riveted**, **riveting**) **1** to fasten with a rivet. **2** to flatten (the end of a bolt) when it is in place. **3** to fix, to make immovable, *she stood riveted to the spot*. **4** to attract and hold the attention of. **riveter** *noun*

Riviera (riv-ee-**air**-ră), **the** the region along the Mediterranean coast of SE France, Monaco, and NW Italy, famous for its natural beauty and containing many holiday resorts. –**riviera** *noun* a region thought to resemble this.

rivulet (**riv**-yŭ-lĕt) *noun* a small stream.

Riyadh (ree-**ad**) the capital of Saudi Arabia.

RMB *abbreviation* roadside mailbox.

RNA *abbreviation* ribonucleic acid, a nucleic acid in living cells, involved in protein synthesis.

roach *noun* (*plural* **roach**) a small European freshwater fish related to the carp, introduced into Australian rivers.

road *noun* **1** a way by which people, animals, or vehicles may pass between places, especially one with a prepared surface. **2** a way of reaching or achieving something, *the road to success*; *you're in the road*, in the way, as an obstruction. ☐ **on the road** travelling, especially as a sales representative, performer, or swagman. **road hog** a reckless or inconsiderate driver. **road metal** broken stone for making the foundation of a road or railway. **road sense** ability to behave safely on roads, especially in traffic. **road test** a test of a vehicle by using it on a road. **road-test** *verb* to test in this way. **road toll** the number of people killed in motor vehicle accidents. **road train** (*Austral*.) a truck pulling one or more long trailers.

roadblock *noun* a barricade set up by the police or army to stop traffic for inspection or search etc.

roadhouse *noun* a petrol station with restaurant on a main road in a country area.

roadside *noun* the border of a road.

Road Town the capital of the British Virgin Islands.

roadway *noun* a road; the part of this intended for vehicles.

roadworks *plural noun* construction or repair of roads.

roadworthy *adjective* (of a vehicle) fit to be used on a road. **roadworthiness** *noun*

roam *verb* to wander. –**roam** *noun* a wander.

roaming *noun* the use or ability to use a mobile phone etc. on a different network, overseas, etc.

roan *adjective* (of an animal) having a coat that is thickly sprinkled with white or grey hairs. –**roan** *noun* a roan horse or other animal.

roar *noun* 1 a long deep loud sound, like that made by a lion. 2 loud laughter. –**roar** *verb* 1 to give a roar. 2 to express in this way, *the crowd roared its approval*. 3 to be full of din. **roarer** *noun*

roaring *adjective* 1 noisy. 2 briskly active, *did a roaring trade*. –**roaring** *adverb* noisily. □ **roaring forties** stormy ocean tracts between latitudes 40° and 50° S; the prevailing westerly winds of this region.

roast *verb* 1 to cook (meat etc.) in an oven or by exposure to heat. 2 to expose to great heat. 3 to undergo roasting. 4 to criticise severely. –**roast** *adjective* roasted, *roast beef*. –**roast** *noun* roast meat; a joint of meat for roasting.

roasting *adjective* very hot.

rob *verb* (**robbed**, **robbing**) 1 to steal from; to commit robbery. 2 to deprive of what is due or normal, *robbing us of our sleep*. □ **rob Peter to pay Paul** to pay one debt by borrowing what one needs and so incurring another. **robber** *noun*, **robbery** *noun* [from Old French *robe* = booty]

robe *noun* a long loose garment, especially a ceremonial one or one worn as an indication of rank etc. –**robe** *verb* to dress in a robe.

Roberts, Tom (1856–1931), English-born Australian artist, one of the founders of the Heidelberg school.

Robespierre (**rohbs**-pee-air), Maximilien de (1758–94), French revolutionary leader.

robin *noun* (also **robin redbreast**) 1 a small brown red-breasted European bird. 2 any of many Australian birds with a similar appearance.

Robin Hood a semi-legendary English medieval outlaw, said to have robbed the rich and helped the poor.

Robinson Crusoe the hero of a novel by Defoe, who survives a shipwreck and lives on a desert island.

robot (**roh**-bot) *noun* 1 (in science fiction) a machine that resembles and can act like a person. 2 a piece of apparatus operated by remote control. 3 a person who seems to act like a machine. [from Czech *robota* = compulsory labour]

robotic (rŏ-**bot**-ik) *adjective* of or using robots. **robotics** *plural noun* use of robots in manufacturing.

robust (rŏ-**bust**) *adjective* strong, vigorous. **robustly** *adverb*, **robustness** *noun* [from Latin *robur* = strength]

roc *noun* a gigantic bird of Eastern legend.

rock¹ *noun* 1 the hard part of the earth's crust, underlying the soil. 2 a mass of this; a large stone or boulder. □ **on the rocks** (*informal*) (of a business, marriage, etc.) in difficulties, about to collapse; (of a drink) served neat with ice cubes. **rock-bottom** *adjective* (*informal*, of prices etc.) very low. **rock cake** a small fruit cake with a flat base and a rugged surface. **rock garden** an artificial mound or bank with plants growing between large stones or rocks. **rock lobster** (*Austral.*) a marine crayfish. **rock salt** common salt (sodium chloride) as it is found in the earth. **rock wallaby** a small bushy-tailed wallaby living in rocky country.

rock² *verb* 1 to move or be moved gently to and fro while supported on something. 2 to shake violently. 3 to disturb greatly by shock, *the scandal rocked the country*. –**rock** *noun* 1 rocking; a rocking movement. 2 a kind of loud modern music with a heavy beat. □ **rock and roll** (also **rock 'n' roll**) a kind of popular music dating from the 1950s with a strong beat and elements of blues. **rock the boat** (*informal*) to do something that upsets the plans or progress of one's group.

rocker *noun* 1 a thing that rocks something or is rocked. 2 each of the curved bars on which a rocking chair etc. is mounted. 3 a rocking chair. 4 a switch that pivots between the 'on' and 'off' positions. 5 a devotee of rock music. □ **off one's rocker** (*informal*) crazy.

rockery *noun* a rock garden.

rocket¹ *noun* 1 a firework or similar device that rises into the air when ignited and then explodes. 2 a structure that flies by expelling gases that are the products of combustion, used to propel a warhead or a spacecraft; a bomb or shell propelled by this. 3 (*informal*) a reprimand. –**rocket** *verb* (**rocketed**, **rocketing**) to move rapidly upwards or away.

rocket² *noun* a plant whose leaves are used in salads.

rocking chair *noun* a chair mounted on rockers or with springs so that it can be rocked by the sitter.

rocking horse *noun* a wooden horse mounted on rockers or springs so that it can be rocked by a child sitting on it.

rockmelon *noun* a small round melon with orange flesh, also called *cantaloupe*.

rocky¹ *adjective* (**rockier**, **rockiest**) 1 of or like rock. 2 full of rocks.

rocky² *adjective* (**rockier**, **rockiest**) unsteady. **rockily** *adverb*, **rockiness** *noun*

Rocky Mountains (also **Rockies**) the great mountain system running north-south in western North America.

rococo (rŏ-**koh**-koh) *noun* an ornate style of decoration common in Europe in the 18th century. –**rococo** *adjective* of or in this style.

rod *noun* 1 a slender straight round stick or metal bar. 2 a cane or birch used for flogging people. 3 a fishing rod; an angler with the right to use this on a specified stretch of water. 4 a rod-shaped structure in the retina, not sensitive to coloured light.

rode *see* **ride**.

rodent *noun* an animal (e.g. rat, mouse, squirrel) with strong front teeth used for gnawing things. [from Latin *rodens* = gnawing]

rodeo (roh-**day**-oh) *noun* (*plural* **rodeos**) 1 a round-up of cattle on a ranch, for branding etc. 2 an exhibition of cowboys' skill in handling animals. 3 an exhibition of motorcycle riding.

Rodin (roh-**dan**), Auguste (1840–1917), French sculptor.

rodomontade (rod-ŏ-mon-**tayd**) *noun* boastful talk or behaviour.

roe¹ *noun* a mass of eggs in a female fish's ovary (*hard roe*); a male fish's milt (*soft roe*).

roe² *noun* (*plural* **roe** *or* **roes**) a kind of small deer.

roebuck *noun* a male roe-deer.

roentgenium *noun* an artificial radioactive element (symbol Rg).

rogaine (**roh**-gayn) *noun* (*Austral.*) a marathon orienteering event usually taking 24 hours to complete. **rogainer** *noun*, **rogaining** *noun*

rogations *plural noun* a special litany for use on **Rogation Days**, the three days before Ascension Day. [from Latin *rogare* = ask]

roger *interjection* (in signalling) your message has been received and understood.

rogue *noun* 1 a dishonest or unprincipled person. 2 a mischievous person. 3 a wild animal driven away from the herd or living apart from it, *rogue elephant*.
☐ **rogues' gallery** a collection of photographs of criminals. **roguery** *noun*

roguish *adjective* mischievous, affectedly playful. **roguishly** *adverb*, **roguishness** *noun*

Rohypnol *noun* (*trademark*) a powerful sedative drug.

roister *verb* to make merry noisily. **roisterer** *noun*

role *noun* 1 an actor's part. 2 a person's or thing's character or expected function.
☐ **role model** a person looked to by others as an example in a particular role. **role-playing** *noun* an exercise in which people act a part in an improvised drama.

roll *verb* 1 to move or cause to move along in contact with a surface, either on wheels or by turning over and over. 2 to turn on an axis or over and over; to cause to revolve. 3 to form into a cylindrical or spherical shape; *rolled into one*, combined in one person or thing. 4 to wind into or as a covering. 5 to flatten by means of a roller, *roll out the pastry*. 6 to rock from side to side, e.g. in walking. 7 to move or pass steadily, *the years rolled on*. 8 to undulate, *rolling hills*. 9 to make a long continuous vibrating sound, *the thunder rolled*. –**roll** *noun* 1 a cylinder formed by turning flexible material over and over upon itself without creasing it. 2 something having this shape, an undulation, *rolls of fat*. 3 a small individual portion of bread baked in a rounded shape; this split and containing filling. 4 an official list or register, *an electoral roll*. 5 a rolling movement. 6 a long steady vibrating sound. ☐ **be rolling in** to have a large supply of. **roll-call** *noun* the calling of a list of names, to check that all are present. **rolled gold** a thin coating of gold applied to another metal. **rolled oats** husked and crushed oats. **roll in** to arrive in great numbers or quantities; (*informal*) to arrive casually. **rolling mill** a machine or factory for rolling metal into various shapes. **rolling pin** a cylindrical device rolled over dough to flatten it. **rolling stock** railway engines and carriages and wagons etc. **rolling stone** a person who does not settle and live or work in one place. **rolling strike** industrial action in the form of a series of strikes, each for a limited period. **roll-neck** *adjective* (of a sweater) having a high turned-over neck. **roll of honour** a list of people whose achievements are honoured. **roll-on** *adjective* (of a cosmetic) applied by means of a ball that rotates in the neck of a container. **roll-top desk** a desk with a flexible cover that slides in curved grooves. **roll up** (*informal*) to arrive casually; to appear on the scene. [from Latin *rotula* = little wheel]

roller *noun* 1 a cylinder used for flattening or spreading things, or on which something is wound. 2 a long swelling wave.
□ **roller coaster** a railway at an amusement park or showground etc., with a series of alternate steep ascents and descents. **roller skate** a boot or a frame for a boot with four small wheels attached for gliding over a hard surface. **roller skating** skating on roller skates.

rollerblade *noun* (*trademark*) a roller skate with four wheels one behind the other. –**rollerblade** *verb* to skate using such boots.

rollicking *adjective* full of boisterous high spirits. [from *romp* + *frolic*]

roly-poly *noun* 1 a pudding consisting of suet pastry spread with jam, rolled up, and boiled. 2 a bushy Australian plant that breaks free and is rolled about by the wind. –**roly-poly** *adjective* plump, podgy.

ROM *abbreviation* (in computing) read-only memory (*see* **read**).

Roman *adjective* 1 of ancient or modern Rome. 2 of the ancient Roman republic or empire. 3 of the Christian Church of Rome, Roman Catholic. –**Roman** *noun* 1 a member of the ancient Roman republic or empire. 2 a native or inhabitant of Rome. 3 a Roman Catholic. **Romans** the *Epistle to the Romans*, an epistle of St Paul to the Church at Rome. –**roman** *noun* plain upright type (not italic), like that used for the definitions in this dictionary. □ **Roman Catholic** of the Church that acknowledges the pope as its head; a

member of this Church. **Roman Catholicism** the faith of the Roman Catholic Church. **Roman nose** a nose with a high bridge. **Roman numerals** letters representing numbers (I = 1, V = 5, X = 10, L = 50, C = 100, D = 500, M = 1000).

romance (rŏ-**manss**) *noun* 1 an imaginative story, literature of this kind, *medieval romances*. 2 a romantic situation, event, or atmosphere. 3 a love story; a love affair resembling this. 4 a picturesque exaggeration or falsehood. –**romance** *verb* to exaggerate or distort the truth in an imaginative way.
□ **Romance languages** the group of European languages descended from Latin (French, Italian, Spanish, etc.).

Romanesque (roh-mă-**nesk**) *noun* a style of art and architecture in Europe from about 1050 to 1200, with massive vaulting and round arches. –**Romanesque** *adjective* of this style.

Romania (also **Rumania**) a republic in eastern Europe. **Romanian** *adjective* & *noun*

Romanov (roh-mă-nof) the name of a dynasty that ruled in Russia from 1613 to 1917.

romantic *adjective* 1 appealing to the emotions by its imaginative, heroic, or picturesque quality. 2 involving a love affair. 3 enjoying romantic situations. 4 (also **Romantic**; of music or literature) richly imaginative, not conforming to classical conventions. –**romantic** *noun* a person who enjoys romantic situations etc. **romantically** *adverb*

Romany (**rom**-ă-nee) *noun* 1 a gypsy. 2 the language of gypsies. –**Romany** *adjective* of Romanies or their language. [from a Romany word *rom* = man]

romp *verb* 1 to play about together in a lively way, as children do. 2 (*informal*) to get along easily; *romped home*, came in as an easy winner. –**romp** *noun* a spell of romping.

rompers *plural noun* a young child's one-piece garment.

Romulus (*Rom. legend*) the founder of Rome, who with his twin brother Remus was suckled by a she-wolf after being abandoned.

rondeau (**ron**-doh) *noun* a short poem with only two rhymes throughout and the opening words used twice as a refrain.

rondo *noun* (*plural* **rondos**) a piece of music with a theme that recurs several times.

ronin (**roh**-nĭn) *noun* (*plural* **ronin** or **ronins**) (in feudal Japan) a wandering samurai who had no lord or master.

roo *noun* (*Austral.*) a kangaroo. □ **roo bar** a bull bar (*see* **bull**).

rood *noun* **1** a crucifix, especially one raised on the middle of the rood screen. **2** (*old use*) a quarter of an acre. □ **Holy Rood** (*old use*) the Cross of Jesus Christ. **rood screen** a carved wooden or stone screen separating the nave from the chancel in a church.

roof *noun* (*plural* **roofs**) **1** a structure covering the top of a house or building. **2** the top of a car or tent etc.; *roof of the mouth*, a structure forming the upper part of the mouth cavity. **–roof** *verb* to cover with a roof; to be the roof of. □ **have a roof over one's head** to have somewhere to live. **hit** or **raise the roof** (*informal*) to become very angry. **roof rack** a framework to carry luggage etc. on the roof of a car.

roofing *noun* material used for a roof.

rook¹ *noun* a black crow that nests in colonies. **–rook** *verb* to swindle, to charge (a person) an extortionate price. [from Old English *hroc*]

rook² *noun* a chess piece with a top shaped like battlements. [from Arabic *rukk*]

rookery *noun* **1** a colony of rooks; a place where these nest. **2** a colony or breeding place of penguins or seals.

rookie *noun* (*informal*) a new recruit; a novice.

room *noun* **1** space that is or could be occupied by something; *make room for*, to clear a space or position etc. for a person or thing. **2** a part of a building enclosed by walls or partitions; the people present in this. **3** opportunity or scope or ability to allow something, *no room for dispute*. **rooms** *plural noun* a set of rooms occupied by a person or family.

roomful *noun* the amount that a room will hold.

roomy *adjective* (**roomier**, **roomiest**) having plenty of room to contain things.

roost *noun* a place where birds perch or where they settle for sleep. **–roost** *verb* (of birds) to perch; to settle for sleep. □ **come home to roost** (of an action) to react unfavourably on the doer.

rooster *noun* a male domestic fowl.

root¹ *noun* **1** the part of a plant that attaches it to the earth and absorbs water and nourishment from the soil; *a person's roots*, a place emotionally regarded as an ancestral home. **2** the part attaching root to its support, a rhizome. **3** a small plant with root attached, for transplanting. **4** an edible root, a plant with this (e.g. carrot, turnip), *root crops*. **5** the part of a bodily organ or structure that is embedded in tissue, *the root of a tooth*. **6** a source or basis, *the root of all evil*; *get to the root of the matter*, discover its source and tackle it there. **7** a number in relation to a given number which it produces when multiplied by itself once (= *square root*) or a specified number of times, *2 is the cube root of 8* ($2 \times 2 \times 2 = 8$). **–root** *verb* **1** to take root; to cause to do this. **2** to cause to stand fixed and unmoving, *was rooted to the spot by fear*. **3** to establish deeply and firmly, *the feeling is deeply rooted*. □ **root-mean-square** *noun* the square root of the arithmetic mean (see **mean³**) of the squares of a set of numbers. **root out** or **up** to drag or dig up by the roots; to get rid of. **take root** to send down roots; (of an idea etc.) to become established.

root² *verb* **1** (of an animal) to turn up ground with its snout or beak in search of food. **2** to rummage; to find or extract by doing this, *root out some facts and figures*. □ **root for** (*Amer. informal*) to support actively.

rootless *adjective* **1** having no root or roots. **2** (of a person) having no roots in a community.

rootstock *noun* **1** a rhizome. **2** a plant into which a graft is inserted.

rope *noun* **1** strong thick cord; a length of this. **2** a quantity of similar things strung together, *a rope of pearls*. **–rope** *verb* **1** to fasten, secure, or catch with rope. **2** to fence off with rope(s). □ **give a person enough rope** to allow freedom of action in the hope that he or she will bring about his or her own downfall. **rope a person in** to persuade him or her to take part in an activity. **rope ladder** a ladder made of two long ropes connected by short crosspieces. **the ropes** the procedure for doing something, *know or learn the ropes*.

ropeable *adjective* (*Austral. informal*) (also **ropable**) angry.

ropy *adjective* (**ropier**, **ropiest**) **1** (of a substance) forming long sticky threads. **2** (*informal*) poor in quality. **ropiness** *noun*

Roquefort (**rok**-for) *noun* (*trademark*) a kind of blue cheese, made from ewes' milk.

rorqual (**ror**-kwăl) *noun* a whale with a dorsal fin.

rort *noun* (*Austral. informal*) **1** a dishonest trick or scheme. **2** a wild party. –**rort** *verb* (*Austral. informal*) **1** to engage in dishonest practice. **2** to manipulate (a system, ballot, etc.) fraudulently. **rorter** *noun*

rosary *noun* **1** a set series of prayers used in the Roman Catholic Church; a book containing this. **2** a string of 55 or 165 beads for keeping count of this. **3** a similar bead-string used in other religions.

rose[1] *noun* **1** a bush or shrub bearing ornamental usually fragrant flowers. **2** its flower. **3** a deep pink colour; *see things through rose-coloured spectacles*, to take an unduly cheerful view of things. **4** the perforated sprinkling-nozzle of a watering can, hose, or shower-head. –**rose** *adjective* deep pink. □ **rose water** a fragrant liquid perfumed with roses. **rose window** a circular window in a church, with a pattern of tracery. **Wars of the Roses** *see* war.

rose[2] *see* rise.

rosé (**roh**-zay) *noun* a light pink wine. [French, = pink]

roseate (**roh**-zee-ăt) *adjective* deep pink, rosy.

Roseau (**roh-zoh**) the capital of Dominica.

rosella[1] (roh-**zel**-ă) *noun* **1** a brightly coloured Australian parakeet. **2** a sheep which is losing its wool and is therefore easy to shear.

rosella[2] *noun* an Australian shrub with fruit used for jam.

rosemary (**rohz**-mă-ree) *noun* an evergreen shrub with fragrant leaves that are used for flavouring food.

rosery *noun* a rose garden.

Rosetta stone a basalt stone (now in the British Museum) found in Egypt in 1799, dating from (c. 200 BC), with parallel inscriptions in hieroglyphs, demotic Egyptian, and Greek, providing the key to the decipherment of ancient Egyptian texts.

rosette *noun* **1** a rose-shaped badge or ornament made of ribbon etc. **2** a rose-shaped carving. [French, = little rose]

rosewood *noun* any of several fragrant close-grained woods used for making furniture.

rosin (**roz**-ĭn) *noun* a kind of resin.

Ross, Sir James Clark (1800–62), English polar explorer, after whom the Ross Sea, Ross Barrier, and Ross Island in the Antarctic are named.

Rossini (rŏ-**seen**-ee), Gioacchino Antonio (1792–1868), Italian composer of operas.

Ross River virus *noun* a virus carried by mosquitoes causing a rash, and joint and muscle pain. [from the name of a Queensland river]

roster (**ros**-ter) *noun* a list showing people's turns of duty etc. –**roster** *verb* to place on a roster.

rostrum (**ros**-trŭm) *noun* (*plural* **rostra** *or* **rostrums**) a platform for one person, especially for public speaking.

rosy *adjective* (**rosier**, **rosiest**) **1** rose-coloured, deep pink. **2** promising, hopeful, *a rosy future*. **rosily** *adverb*, **rosiness** *noun*

rot *verb* (**rotted**, **rotting**) **1** (of animal or vegetable matter) to lose its original form by chemical action caused by bacteria or fungi etc. **2** to perish or become weak through lack of use or activity. –**rot** *noun* **1** rotting; rottenness. **2** (*informal*) nonsense, an absurd statement or argument. **3** a series of failures, *a rot set in*.

rota (**roh**-tă) *noun* a list of duties to be done or people to do them in rotation. [Latin, = wheel]

Rotarian (roh-**tair**-ree-ăn) *noun* a member of a Rotary Club.

rotary *adjective* rotating; acting by rotating, *a rotary hoe*. □ **Rotary Club** a local branch of an international association (**Rotary International**) formed by business and professional people for the purpose of rendering service to the community.

rotate *verb* **1** to revolve; to cause to revolve. **2** to arrange or deal with in a recurrent series. **3** to take turns, to be used in turn, *the crews rotate every three weeks*. □ **rotation of crops** the practice of growing a different crop each year on a plot of land in a regular order, to avoid exhausting the soil. **rotation** *noun*, **rotator** *noun* [same origin as *rota*]

rotational *adjective* of or using rotation.

rotatory (**roh**-tă-tŏ-ree) *adjective* rotating.

rote *noun* **by rote** by memory without thought of the meaning, *knew it only by rote*; by a fixed procedure, *working by rote*.

rotisserie (rŏ-**tiss**-ĕ-ree) *noun* a revolving spit for roasting meat.

rotor *noun* **1** a rotating part of a machine. **2** a horizontally-rotating vane of a helicopter.

rotten *adjective* **1** rotting; rotted; breaking easily or falling to pieces from age or use.

2 morally corrupt. **3** (*informal*) contemptible, worthless. **4** (*informal*) unpleasant, *rotten weather*. ☐ **rotten borough** (in the 19th century) an English borough that was still represented by an MP although the population had become severely reduced in number. **rottenly** *adverb*, **rottenness** *noun*

rotter *noun* (*informal*) a contemptible person.

Rottnest Island a small island off the Western Australian coast near Perth. [from Dutch *Rottenest* = rat nest, so called because of the population of quokkas which were originally thought to be a kind of rat]

Rottweiler (**rot**-vy-ler) *noun* a dog of a large black German breed.

rotund (rŏ-**tund**) *adjective* rounded, plump. **rotundity** *noun* [from Latin, = round]

rotunda (rŏ-**tun**-dă) *noun* a circular domed building or hall.

rouble (**roo**-bŭl) *noun* the unit of money in Russia.

roué (**roo**-ay) *noun* a dissolute elderly man.

rouge (*pr.* roo*zh*) *noun* **1** a reddish cosmetic for colouring the cheeks, blusher. **2** a fine red powder used for polishing metal. **– rouge** *verb* to colour with rouge. [French, = red]

rough *adjective* **1** having an uneven or irregular surface, coarse in texture, not level or smooth. **2** not gentle or restrained or careful, violent; *rough weather*, stormy; *rough luck*, hard luck. **3** lacking finish or delicacy, not perfected or detailed; *a rough estimate*, approximate. **– rough** *adverb* roughly; in rough conditions; *sleeping rough*, not in a proper bed etc., especially out of doors. **– rough** *noun* **1** something rough; rough ground. **2** hardship, *take the rough with the smooth*. **3** an unfinished state. **4** a rough drawing or design etc. **5** a ruffian or hooligan. **– rough** *verb* **1** to make rough. **2** to shape or plan or sketch roughly, *roughed out a scheme*. ☐ **rough-and-ready** *adjective* full of rough vigour and not refined; rough or crude but effective; without elaborate equipment etc. **rough-and-tumble** *noun* a haphazard fight or struggle. **rough diamond** a diamond not yet cut; a person of good nature but lacking polished manners. **rough house** (*informal*) a disturbance with violent behaviour or fighting. **rough it** to do without ordinary comforts. **rough justice** treatment that is approximately fair. **rough up** (*informal*) to treat (a person) violently. **roughly** *adverb*, **roughness** *noun*

roughage *noun* indigestible material in plants that are used as food (e.g. bran, green vegetables, and certain fruits), which stimulates the action of the intestines.

roughcast *noun* plaster of lime and gravel, used for covering the outsides of buildings. **– roughcast** *verb* (**roughcast**, **roughcasting**) to coat with this.

roughen *verb* to make or become rough.

roughneck *noun* (*informal*) a rough or rowdy person.

roughshod *adjective* (of a horse) having shoes with the nail heads left projecting to prevent slipping. ☐ **ride roughshod over** to treat inconsiderately or arrogantly.

roughy *noun* (*Austral.*) **1** = **tommy rough**. **2** a small reef-dwelling fish.

roulette (roo-**let**) *noun* a gambling game in which a small ball falls at random into one of the compartments on a revolving disc. [French, = little wheel]

round *adjective* **1** having a curved shape or outline; shaped like a circle, sphere, or cylinder. **2** full, complete, *a round dozen*. **– round** *noun* **1** a round object. **2** a circular or recurring course or series; *the daily round*, ordinary occupations of the day; *a round of drinks*, one for each person in a group. **3** a route on which things are to be inspected or delivered, *a doctor's rounds*; *a round of golf*, playing all holes on a course once. **4** a musical composition for two or more voices in which each sings the same melody but starts at a different time. **5** a single shot or volley of shots from one or more firearms; ammunition for this. **6** one stage in a competition or struggle; one section of a boxing match. **– round** *preposition* **1** so as to circle or enclose. **2** at points on or near the circumference of, *sat round the table*; *talked round the subject*, did not tackle it directly. **3** having as its axis or central point, *the earth moves round the sun*. **4** visiting in a series or all over, to all points of interest in, *went round the cafés*; *were shown round the museum*. **5** on or to the further side of, *the shop round the corner*. **– round** *adverb* **1** in a circle or curve; by a circuitous route. **2** so as to face in a different direction, *turn the chair round*. **3** round a place or group; in every direction. **4** to a person's house etc., *I'll be round in an hour*. **5** into consciousness after unconsciousness, *he isn't round yet*. **– round** *verb* **1** to make or become round. **2** to make into a round figure or number;

round it up, increase it in order to do this (e.g. make $1.90 into $2.00); *round it down*, decrease it similarly. **3** to travel round, *the car rounded the corner*. ☐ **in the round** (of sculpture) with all sides shown, not attached to a background; (of a theatre) with seats on all sides of the stage. **round about** near by; approximately. **round dance** one in which dancers form a ring. **round figure** or **number** one without odd units. **round off** to bring (a thing) into a complete state. **round on** to make an attack or retort in retaliation, especially unexpectedly. **round robin** a statement signed by a number of people (often with signatures in a circle to conceal who signed first); a tournament in which each competitor plays every other. **Round Table** that at which King Arthur and his knights sat so that none might have precedence. **round table conference** an assembly for discussion. **round the clock** continuously throughout day and night. **round trip** a trip to one or more places and back again. **round up** to gather (animals, people, or things) into one place. **round-up** *noun* a rounding up; a summary.

roundabout *noun* **1** a merry-go-round; *lose on the swings what you gain on the roundabouts*, break even. **2** a road junction with a circular structure round which traffic has to pass in the same direction. –**roundabout** *adjective* indirect, not using the shortest or most direct route or phrasing etc., *heard the news in a roundabout way*.

roundel *noun* a circular identifying mark on an aircraft etc.

rounder *noun* the unit of scoring in rounders.

rounders *noun* a team game played with bat and ball, in which players have to hit the ball and run round a circuit of bases.

Roundhead *noun* a supporter of the Parliament party in the English Civil War. [so called because they wore their hair cut short at a time when long hair was in fashion for men]

roundly *adverb* **1** thoroughly, severely, *was roundly scolded*. **2** in a rounded shape.

roundsman *noun* (*plural* **roundsmen**) (*Austral.*) a journalist covering a specific subject, *the paper's political roundsman*.

roundworm *noun* a worm with a rounded body.

rouse¹ (*pr.* rowz) *verb* **1** to cause (a person) to wake. **2** to cause to become active or excited. **3** (of a person etc.) to wake.

rouse² (*pr.* rows) *verb* (*Austral.*) to scold, *she roused on me when I broke the glass*.

rouseabout (**rows**-ă-bowt) *noun* (*Austral.*) an unskilled worker, especially on a farm or in a shearing shed.

rousing *adjective* vigorous, stirring.

Rousseau¹ (roo-**soh**), Henri Julien (1844–1910), French painter.

Rousseau² (roo-**soh**), Jean-Jacques (1712–78), Swiss-born French philosopher.

roustabout *noun* a rouseabout.

rout¹ *noun* utter defeat; a disorderly retreat of defeated troops. –**rout** *verb* to defeat completely; to put to flight.

rout² *verb* **1** to fetch or force out, *routed him out of bed*. **2** to rummage.

route (*pr.* root) *noun* the course or way taken to get from starting point to destination. –**route** *verb* (**routed**, **routeing**) to send by a certain route.

router (*rhymes with* outer) *noun* a tool for cutting grooves and shaping mouldings etc. in wood.

routine (roo-**teen**) *noun* **1** a standard course or procedure; a series of acts performed regularly in the same way. **2** a set sequence of movements in a dance or other performance. **3** a sequence of instructions to a computer. –**routine** *adjective* in accordance with routine. **routinely** *adverb*

roux (*pr.* roo) *noun* a mixture of heated fat and flour used as a basis for a sauce. [French, = browned (flour)]

rove *verb* to roam. ☐ **roving commission** authority to travel as may be necessary in connection with one's inquiries or other work. **roving eye** a tendency to flirt with many people.

rover *noun* **1** a wanderer. **2** (in Australian Rules) a small agile member of a ruck.

row¹ (*rhymes with* go) *noun* **1** a number of people or things in a line. **2** a line of seats across a theatre etc.

row² (*rhymes with* go) *verb* **1** to propel (a boat) by using oars. **2** to carry in a boat that one rows. –**row** *noun* a spell of rowing; an excursion in a rowing boat. ☐ **rowing boat** a boat for rowing. **rower** *noun*

row³ (*rhymes with* cow) *noun* (*informal*) **1** a loud noise. **2** a quarrel, a heated argument. **3** the process or condition of being reprimanded, *we got into a row for being late*.

–**row** verb (*informal*) **1** to quarrel or argue heatedly. **2** to reprimand.

rowan (**roh**-ăn) *noun* a tree that bears hanging clusters of scarlet berries, the mountain ash.

rowboat *noun* a rowing boat.

rowdy (*rhymes with* cloudy) *adjective* (**rowdier**, **rowdiest**) noisy and disorderly. –**rowdy** *noun* a rowdy person. **rowdily** *adverb*, **rowdiness** *noun*, **rowdyism** *noun*

rowlock (**rol**-ŏk) *noun* a device on the side of a boat serving as a fulcrum for an oar and keeping it in place.

royal *adjective* **1** of, suitable for, or worthy of a king or queen. **2** belonging to the family of a king or queen; in the service or under the patronage of royalty. **3** splendid, first-rate; of exceptional size etc. –**royal** *noun* (*informal*) a member of a royal family. □ **royal blue** deep vivid blue. **Royal Commission** a body of people appointed by the representative of the Crown at the request of the Government to investigate and report on something. **royal icing** hard icing for cakes, made with icing sugar and egg white. **royal jelly** a substance secreted by worker bees and fed to future queen bees. **royally** *adverb* [from Latin *regalis* = regal]

Royal Academy of Arts an institution established in 1768 to foster the arts of painting, sculpture, and architecture in Britain.

royalist *noun* a person who favours monarchy. –**Royalist** *noun* a supporter of the monarchy in the English Civil War.

Royal Society the oldest and most prestigious society in Britain, founded in 1662; any of the similar bodies formed in each Australian state.

royalty *noun* **1** being royal. **2** a royal person or persons, *in the presence of royalty*. **3** payment to an author etc. for each copy of the book sold or for each public performance of his or her work; payment to a patentee for the use of the patent. **4** payment by a mining or oil company to the owner of the land used.

r.p.m. *abbreviation* revolutions per minute.

RSI *abbreviation* repetitive strain injury, caused by prolonged use of certain muscles.

RSL *abbreviation* Returned and Services League of Australia, an organisation providing assistance to returned Australian servicemen and servicewomen and their families.

RSPCA *abbreviation* Royal Society for the Prevention of Cruelty to Animals.

RSVP *abbreviation* (in an invitation) please reply. [short for French, *répondez s'il vous plait*]

Rt. *abbreviation* Right; *Rt. Honourable*, Right Honourable; *Rt. Rev.*, Right Reverend.

rub *verb* (**rubbed**, **rubbing**) **1** to press something against (a surface) and slide it to and fro; to apply in this way. **2** to polish or clean by rubbing; to make or become dry, smooth, or sore etc. in this way; *rub brasses*, to take an impression of brass memorial tablets by rubbing coloured wax or chalk etc. over paper laid upon them. –**rub** *noun* **1** the act or process of rubbing. **2** a difficulty or impediment, *there's the rub*. □ **rub along** (*informal*) to manage to get on without undue difficulty. **rub down** to dry, smooth, or reduce the level of (a thing) by rubbing. **rub it in** to emphasise or remind a person constantly of an unpleasant fact. **rub off** to be removed or transferred by or as if by rubbing. **rub out** to remove (marks etc.) by using a rubber; (*informal*) to murder. **rub shoulders with** to associate with (certain people). **rub up the wrong way** to irritate or repel (a person) by one's actions.

rubber¹ *noun* **1** a tough elastic substance made from the coagulated juice of certain tropical plants or synthetically. **2** a piece of this or other substance for rubbing out pencil or ink marks, an eraser. **3** a person who rubs something; a device for rubbing things. □ **rubber stamp** a device for imprinting a mark on to a surface; one who mechanically gives approval to the actions of another person or group. **rubber-stamp** *verb* to approve automatically without due consideration.

rubber² *noun* a match of three successive games at bridge or whist etc.

rubberise *verb* (also **-ize**) to treat or coat with rubber.

rubbery *adjective* like rubber.

rubbing *noun* a reproduction or impression made of a memorial brass or other relief design by placing paper over it and rubbing with pigment.

rubbish *noun* **1** waste or worthless material. **2** nonsense. –**rubbish** *verb* to criticise severely, to disparage. **rubbishy** *adjective*

rubble *noun* waste or rough fragments of stone or brick etc.

rubella *noun* German measles.

Rubens (**roo**-běnz), Sir Peter Paul (1577–1640), Flemish painter.

Rubicon (**roo**-bǐ-kǒn) *noun* **cross the Rubicon** to take a decisive step that commits one to an enterprise. (¶ The river Rubicon, in NE Italy, was the ancient boundary between Gaul and Italy; by crossing it into Italy Julius Caesar committed himself to war against the Senate and Pompey.)

rubicund (**roo**-bǐ-kŭnd) *adjective* (of the complexion) red, ruddy. [same origin as *ruby*]

rubidium (roo-**bid**-ee-ŭm) *noun* a rare soft silver reactive metallic element of the alkali metal group (symbol Rb).

rubric (**roo**-brik) *noun* words put as a heading or a note of explanation or a direction of how something must be done.

ruby *noun* **1** a red gem. **2** deep red colour. –**ruby** *adjective* deep red. □ **ruby wedding** the 40th anniversary of a wedding. [from Latin *rubeus* = red]

ruche (*pr.* roosh) *noun* a gathered trimming. –**ruche** *verb* to gather (fabric) ornamentally.

ruck[1] *verb* to crease, to wrinkle. –**ruck** *noun* a crease or wrinkle.

ruck[2] *noun* **1** an undistinguished crowd of people or things. **2** (in Australian Rules) a group of three players who follow the play without fixed positions. **3** (in rugby) a loose scrum with the ball on the ground.

rucksack *noun* a backpack. [from German *rücken* = back, + *sack*[1]]

ructions *plural noun* (*informal*) protests and noisy argument.

rudder *noun* a vertical piece of metal or wood hinged to the stern of a boat or rear of an aeroplane and used for steering.

ruddy *adjective* (**ruddier**, **ruddiest**) **1** reddish; (of a person's face) having a fresh healthy reddish colour. **2** (*informal*) bloody. **ruddily** *adverb*, **ruddiness** *noun*

rude *adjective* **1** impolite, showing no respect or consideration. **2** primitive, roughly made, *rude stone implements*. **3** vigorous, hearty, *rude health*. **4** violent, startling, *a rude awakening*. **rudely** *adverb*, **rudeness** *noun* [from Latin *rudis* = raw, wild]

rudiment (**roo**-dǐ-měnt) *noun* a part or organ that is incompletely developed. **rudiments** *plural noun* basic or elementary principles, *learning the rudiments of chemistry*. **rudimentary** (roo-dǐ-**ment**-ǎ-ree) *adjective*

rue[1] *noun* a shrub with bitter leaves formerly used in medicine.

rue[2] *verb* (**rued**, **ruing**) to repent or regret; *he'll live to rue it*, will some day regret it.

rueful *adjective* showing or feeling good-humoured regret. **ruefully** *adverb*

ruff[1] *noun* **1** a deep starched pleated frill worn around the neck in the 16th century. **2** a projecting or coloured ring of feathers or fur round the neck of a bird or animal. **3** a wading bird.

ruff[2] *verb* to trump in card games. –**ruff** *noun* an act of trumping.

ruffian *noun* a violent lawless person.

ruffle *verb* **1** to disturb the smoothness or evenness of. **2** to upset the calmness or even temper of (a person). **3** to become ruffled. –**ruffle** *noun* a gathered ornamental frill.

rug *noun* **1** a thick floor mat. **2** a piece of thick warm fabric used as a blanket or coverlet.

rugby *noun* the game of **rugby football**, a kind of football played with an oval ball that may be kicked or carried.
□ **rugby league** a form of the game with teams of 13. **rugby union** a form of the game with teams of 15. [named after Rugby School in England, where it was first played]

rugged *adjective* **1** having an uneven surface or an irregular outline, craggy. **2** rough but kindly and honest, *a rugged individualist*. **ruggedly** *adverb*, **ruggedness** *noun*

rugger *noun* (*informal*) rugby football.

rugose (**roo**-gohs) *adjective* wrinkled or ridged.

ruin *noun* **1** severe damage or destruction. **2** complete loss of one's fortune, resources, or prospects. **3** the remains of something decayed or destroyed, *the house was a ruin*; *the ruins of Pompeii*. **4** a cause of ruin. –**ruin** *verb* to damage (a thing) so severely that it is useless; to bring into a ruined condition. **ruination** *noun* [from Latin *ruere* = to fall]

ruinous *adjective* **1** bringing or likely to bring ruin. **2** in ruins, ruined, *the house is in a ruinous condition*. **ruinously** *adverb*

rule *noun* **1** a statement of what can, must, or should be done in a certain set of circumstances or in playing a game. **2** the customary or normal state of things or course of action, *overseas holidays became the rule*. **3** exercise of authority, control, governing, *countries that were under French rule*. **4** a straight often jointed measuring device used by carpenters etc. –**rule** *verb* **1** to have authoritative control over people or a country, to govern. **2** to keep (a person or feeling etc.) under control, to dominate. **3** to give a decision as judge or other authority, *the chairman ruled that the question was out of order*. **4** to draw (a line) using a ruler or other straight edge; to mark parallel lines on (writing paper etc.). ☐ **as a rule** usually, more often than not. **rule of thumb** a rough practical method of procedure. **rule out** to exclude as irrelevant or ineligible. **rule the roost** to be the dominant person. [from Latin *regula* = a rule]

ruler *noun* **1** a person who rules by authority. **2** a straight strip of wood or metal etc. used for measuring or for drawing straight lines.

ruling *noun* an authoritative decision.

rum[1] *noun* alcoholic spirit distilled from sugarcane residues or molasses.

rum[2] *adjective* (*informal*) strange, odd, *he's a rum'un*.

Rumania = Romania.

rumba *noun* a ballroom dance of Cuban origin; music for this.

rumble[1] *verb* **1** to make a deep heavy continuous sound, like thunder. **2** to utter in a deep voice. –**rumble** *noun* a rumbling sound.

rumble[2] *verb* (*informal*) to detect the true character of, to see through (a deception).

rumbustious *adjective* (*informal*) boisterous, uproarious.

ruminant (**roo**-mĭ-nănt) *noun* an animal that chews the cud. –**ruminant** *adjective* ruminating.

ruminate (**roo**-mĭ-nayt) *verb* **1** to chew the cud. **2** to meditate, to ponder. **rumination** *noun*, **ruminative** *adjective*

rummage *verb* to make a search by turning things over or disarranging them. –**rummage** *noun* a search of this kind. ☐ **rummage sale** a jumble sale.

rummy *noun* a card game in which players try to form sets or sequences of cards.

rumour *noun* information spread by word of mouth but not certainly true. –**rumour** *verb* be **rumoured** to be spread as a rumour. [from Latin *rumor* = noise]

rump *noun* **1** the buttocks; the corresponding part of a bird. **2** a cut of meat from an animal's hindquarters.

rumple *verb* to make or become crumpled; to make (something smooth) untidy.

rumpus *noun* (*informal*) an uproar, an angry dispute. ☐ **rumpus room** a room in a house for games and play.

run *verb* (**ran**, **run**, **running**) **1** to move with quick steps, never having both or all feet on the ground at once. **2** to go or travel smoothly or swiftly; (of salmon) to go up river in large numbers from the sea; *run free*, (of a sailing ship) be travelling with the wind blowing from astern. **3** to compete in a race or contest; to seek election, *ran for President*. **4** to spread rapidly or beyond the intended limit, *the dye has run*. **5** to flow or cause to flow, to exude liquid, *run some water into it*; *smoke makes my eyes run*; *run dry*, to become dry; *feeling ran high*, became intense. **6** to function, to be in action, *left the engine running*; (of a computer program) to operate. **7** (of a film or magnetic tape etc.) to pass between spools so as to show, play, or perform its contents. **8** to travel or convey from point to point, *the bus runs every hour*; *we'll run you home*; *run the blockade*, to continue to pass through it; *run contraband goods*, smuggle them in. **9** to extend, *a fence runs round the property*; *the money won't run to it*, will not be enough. **10** to be current, operative, or valid, *the lease runs for 20 years*; *musical ability runs in the family*. **11** to pass or cause to pass (into a specified condition), *supplies are running low*; *run a temperature*, to be feverish. **12** to cause to run, go, extend, or function; to cause (a computer program) to operate. **13** to manage, to organise, *who runs the country?* **14** to own and use (a vehicle etc.). **15** (of a newspaper) to print as an item. **16** to sew (fabric) loosely or quickly. –**run** *noun* **1** an act or spell or course of running. **2** a point scored in cricket, baseball, or softball. **3** a ladder in a stocking or knitted fabric. **4** a continuous stretch, sequence, or spell. **5** a general demand for goods etc., *there has been a run on frozen turkeys*; *a run on the bank*, a sudden withdrawal of deposits by many customers. **6** a large number of salmon going up river from the sea. **7** a general type or class of things. **8** an enclosure where domestic animals can range. **9** (*Austral.*) a sheep or cattle station. **10** a track for some purpose, *a ski run*. **11** permission to make unrestricted use of something, *he has the run of the house*. **12** a short trip or excursion, *a run in the car*. ☐ **on the run** fleeing from pursuit or capture. **run across** to happen to meet or find. **run after** to seek the company or attentions of. **run away** to leave quickly or secretly. **run**

away with to elope with (a person); to win (a prize etc.) easily; to accept (an idea) too hastily; to require (much money) in expense. **run down** to stop because not rewound; to reduce the numbers of; to knock down with a moving vehicle or ship; to discover after searching; to speak of in a slighting way; *be run down*, to be weak or exhausted. **run-down** *noun* a detailed analysis. **run for it** to try to escape by running. **run in** (*informal*) to arrest and take into custody; to run (a new engine) carefully into good working order. **run into** to collide with; to happen to meet. **run off** to run away; to produce (copies) on a machine. **run-of-the-mill** *adjective* ordinary, not special. **run out** (of time or a stock of something) to become used up, (of a person) to have used up one's stock; to escape from a container; to put down the wicket of (a running batsman). **run over** to knock down or crush with a vehicle; to study or repeat quickly. **run risks** to take risks. **run through** to examine or repeat etc. quickly; to use up quickly or recklessly. **run-through** *noun* the process of running through something. **run up** to raise (a flag) on a mast; to allow (a bill) to mount; to add up (a column of figures); to make quickly by sewing, *run up some curtains*. **run-up** *noun* the period leading to an event.

runabout *noun* a small car, boat, or aircraft.

runaway *noun* a person who has run away. –**runaway** *adjective* 1 having run away or become out of control. 2 won easily, *a runaway victory*.

rune (*pr.* roon) *noun* any of the letters in an alphabet used by early Germanic peoples. **runic** *adjective* [from Old Norse *rún* = magic sign]

rung¹ *noun* one of the crosspieces of a ladder etc.

rung² *see* ring².

runner *noun* 1 a person or animal that runs; one taking part in a race. 2 a messenger. 3 a creeping stem that issues from the main stem and takes root. 4 a groove, rod, or roller for a thing to move on; each of the long strips on which a sledge etc. slides. 5 a long narrow strip of carpet, or of ornamental cloth for a table etc. □ **runner bean** a kind of climbing bean. **runner-up** *noun* a person or team finishing second in a competition.

running *see* run. –**running** *adjective* 1 performed while running, *a running jump* or *kick*. 2 following each other without interval, *for four days running*. 3 continuous, *a running*

battle; *running commentary*, one on an event as it happens. □ **in** or **out of the running** with a good chance or with no chance of winning. **make the running** to set the pace. **running stitch** a line of evenly spaced stitches made by a straight thread passing in and out of the material.

runny *adjective* 1 semi-liquid. 2 tending to flow or to exude fluid.

runt *noun* an undersized person or animal; *the runt of a litter*, the smallest animal in a litter.

runway *noun* a prepared surface on an airfield, on which aircraft take off and land.

rupee (roo-**pee**) *noun* the unit of money in India, Pakistan, Sri Lanka, and certain other countries. [from Urdu *rupiyah*]

rupiah (roo-**pee**-ă) *noun* the unit of money in Indonesia.

rupture *noun* 1 breaking; a breach. 2 an abdominal hernia. –**rupture** *verb* 1 to burst or break (tissue etc.); to become burst or broken. 2 to affect with a hernia. [from Latin *ruptum* = broken]

rural *adjective* of, in, or like the countryside. [from Latin *ruris* = of the country]

ruse (*pr.* rooz) *noun* a deception or trick.

rush¹ *noun* a marsh plant with a slender pithy stem used for making mats, chair seats, baskets, etc.

rush² *verb* 1 to go or come or convey with great speed. 2 to act hastily; to force into hasty action; *rush one's fences*, to act with undue haste. 3 to attack or capture with a sudden assault. –**rush** *noun* 1 rushing; an instance of this. 2 a period of great activity. 3 a sudden great demand for goods etc. 4 a sudden migration of people to a gold discovery. –**rush** *adjective* done with haste or with minimum delay, *a rush job*. **rushes** *plural noun* (*informal*) the first prints of a cinema film before it is cut and edited. □ **rush hour** the time each day when traffic is busiest.

rusk *noun* a kind of biscuit, especially one used for feeding babies.

Russell, Bertrand Arthur William (1873–1970), British philosopher, mathematician, and reformer.

russet *adjective* soft reddish-brown. –**russet** *noun* russet colour. [from Latin *russus* = red]

Russia (also **Russian Federation**) a country in eastern Europe and northern Asia, the largest state in the world.

Russian *adjective* of Russia or its people or language. **–Russian** *noun* **1** a native or inhabitant of Russia. **2** the language of Russia. □ **Russian roulette** an act of bravado in which a person holds to his or her head a revolver of which one (unknown) chamber contains a bullet, and pulls the trigger. **Russian salad** salad of diced vegetables in mayonnaise.

Russo- *prefix* Russian and, *Russo-Japanese*.

rust *noun* **1** a reddish-brown or yellowish-brown coating formed on iron or other metal by the effect of moisture, and gradually corroding it. **2** a reddish-brown colour. **3** a plant disease with rust-coloured spots; the fungus causing this. **–rust** *verb* **1** to affect or be affected with rust. **2** to lose quality or efficiency by lack of use. **rustless** *adjective*, **rustproof** *adjective*

rustic *adjective* **1** having the qualities ascribed to rural people or peasants, simple and unsophisticated, or rough and unrefined. **2** made of rough timber or untrimmed branches, *rustic seat* or *bridge*. **–rustic** *noun* a country person, a peasant.

rusticate *verb* **1** to settle in the country and live a rural life. **2** to mark (masonry) with sunk joints or a roughened surface. **rustication** *noun* [from *rustic*]

rustle *verb* **1** to make a sound like that of paper being crumpled; to cause to do this. **2** to steal (horses or cattle), *cattle rustling*. **–rustle** *noun* a rustling sound. □ **rustle up** (*informal*) to prepare or produce, *try and rustle up a meal*. **rustler** *noun*

rusty *adjective* (**rustier**, **rustiest**) **1** affected with rust. **2** rust-coloured. **3** having lost quality or efficiency by lack of use. **rustiness** *noun*

rut[1] *noun* **1** a deep track made by wheels in soft ground. **2** a habitual usually dull course of life, *getting into a rut*.

rut[2] *noun* the periodic sexual excitement of a male deer, goat, or ram etc. **–rut** *verb* (**rutted**, **rutting**) to be affected with this.

Ruth a book of the Old Testament telling the story of Ruth, the great-grandmother of David.

ruthenium (roo-**thee**-nee-ŭm) *noun* a hard silver-white metallic element (symbol Ru).

Rutherford, Sir Ernest, 1st Baron (1871–1937), British physicist, born in New Zealand, widely regarded as the founder of nuclear physics.

rutherfordium (ru-thĕ-**for**-dee-ŭm) *noun* a very unstable artificial element (symbol Rf).

ruthless *adjective* having no pity or compassion. **ruthlessly** *adverb*, **ruthlessness** *noun* [from *ruth* = pity]

rutile (**roo**-tyl) *noun* an ore of titanium.

rutted *adjective* marked with ruts.

Rwanda (roo-**an**-dă) a republic in East Africa. **Rwandan** *adjective* & *noun*

rye *noun* **1** a kind of cereal used for making flour or as food for cattle. **2** a kind of whisky made from rye.

Ss

S *abbreviation* (also **S.**) **1** Saint. **2** south; southern. **3** siemens.

SA *abbreviation* South Australia.

Sabah (**sab**-ah) a State of Malaysia made up of North Borneo and some islands.

sabbath *noun* a day of rest and religious observance kept by most Christians on Sunday, Jews and Seventh-Day Adventists on Saturday, and Muslims on Friday. [from Hebrew, = rest]

sabbatical (să-**bat**-ikăl) *adjective* **1** of or like the sabbath. **2** of or occurring every seventh day or year. □ **sabbatical leave** leave granted to a university teacher for travel and research.

Sabin (**say**-bĭn), Albert Bruce (1906–93), American microbiologist, who developed an oral vaccine, named after him, against poliomyelitis.

sable *noun* **1** a small weasel-like animal of Arctic and adjacent regions, valued for its dark brown fur. **2** its fur. –**sable** *adjective* black, gloomy.

sabot (**sab**-oh) *noun* a shoe hollowed out from one piece of wood, or with a wooden sole.

sabotage (**sab**-ŏ-tah*zh*) *noun* wilful damaging of machinery or materials, or disruption of work, by dissatisfied workers or hostile agents. –**sabotage** *verb* **1** to commit sabotage on. **2** to destroy or render useless, *sabotaged my plans*.

saboteur (sab-ŏ-**ter**) *noun* a person who commits sabotage.

sabre (**say**-ber) *noun* **1** a cavalry sword with a curved blade. **2** a light fencing sword with a tapering blade. □ **sabre rattling** bellicose threats.

sac *noun* a baglike part in an animal or plant.

saccharin (**sak**-ă-rĭn) *noun* a very sweet substance used as a substitute for sugar. [from Latin *saccharum* = sugar]

saccharine (**sak**-ă-reen) *adjective* intensely and unpleasantly sweet.

sachet (**sash**-ay) *noun* **1** a small bag filled with a sweet-smelling substance for laying among clothes etc. to scent them. **2** a sealed plastic or paper pack containing a single portion of a substance. [French, = little sack]

sack¹ *noun* **1** a large bag of strong coarse fabric for storing and carrying goods. **2** this with its contents; the amount it contains. **3 the sack** (*informal*) dismissal from one's employment or position, *got the sack*. –**sack** *verb* **1** to put into a sack or sacks. **2** (*informal*) to dismiss from a job. □ **sack race** a race in which each competitor is in a sack up to the waist or neck and moves by shuffling or jumping along. **sackful** *noun* (*plural* **sackfuls**).

sack² *verb* to plunder (a captured town etc.) in a violent destructive way. –**sack** *noun* the act or process of sacking a place.

sackbut *noun* an early form of trombone.

sackcloth *noun* coarse fabric for making sacks; *sackcloth and ashes*, a symbol of regret and repentance. (¶ From the ancient custom of wearing sackcloth and sprinkling ashes on one's head in penitence or mourning.)

sacking *noun* material for making sacks.

sacral (**say**-krăl) *adjective* **1** of the sacrum. **2** of or for sacred rites.

sacrament *noun* **1** any of the symbolic Christian religious ceremonies, especially baptism and the Eucharist. **2** the consecrated elements in the Eucharist, especially the bread. **sacramental** *adjective* [same origin as *sacred*]

sacred *adjective* **1** associated with or dedicated to God or a god; regarded with reverence because of this. **2** dedicated to some person or purpose, *sacred to the memory of those who fell in battle*. **3** connected with religion, not secular, *sacred music*. **4** sacrosanct. □ **sacred cow** an idea or institution which its supporters will not allow to be criticised. (¶ The phrase refers to Hindu respect for the cow as a sacred animal.) **sacred site** a place with spiritual significance for Aboriginal people. [from Latin *sacer* = holy]

sacrifice *noun* **1** the slaughter of a victim or the presenting of a gift or doing of an act in order to win the favour of a god. **2** the giving up of a valued thing for the sake of another that is more important or more worthy. **3** the thing offered or given up. **4** the sale of something at much less than its real value. **–sacrifice** *verb* **1** to offer or give up as a sacrifice. **2** to give up (a thing) in order to achieve something else, *Don't sacrifice accuracy for speed*. **3** to sell at much less than its real value. **sacrificial** (sak-rĭ-**fish**-ăl) *adjective* [from Latin, = make a thing sacred]

sacrilege (**sak**-rĭ-lij) *noun* disrespect or damage to something regarded as sacred. **sacrilegious** (sak-rĭ-**lij**-ŭs) *adjective* [from Latin *sacer* = sacred, + *legere* = take away]

sacristan (**sak**-rĭ-stăn) *noun* the person in charge of the contents of a church, especially the sacred vessels, linen etc. used in worship.

sacristy (**sak**-rĭ-stee) *noun* the place in a church where sacred vessels etc. are kept.

sacrosanct (**sak**-rŏ-sankt) *adjective* reverenced or respected and therefore secure from violation or damage. [from Latin *sacro* = by a sacred rite, + *sanctus* = holy]

sacrum (**say**-krŭm) *noun* the triangular bone that forms the back of the pelvis.

sad *adjective* (**sadder**, **saddest**) **1** showing or causing sorrow, unhappy. **2** regrettable. **3** (of cake or pastry etc.) dense from not having risen. **sadly** *adverb*, **sadness** *noun*

sadden *verb* to make sad.

saddle *noun* **1** a seat for a rider, placed on a horse or other animal or forming part of a bicycle etc. **2** a saddle-shaped thing, a ridge of high land between two peaks. **3** a joint of meat consisting of the two loins. **–saddle** *verb* **1** to put a saddle on (an animal). **2** to burden (a person) with a task. □ **in the saddle** on horseback; in a controlling position. **saddle stitching** a long running stitch made with thick thread, used decoratively.

saddlebag *noun* a strong bag fixed behind a saddle or as one of a pair slung over a horse etc.

saddler *noun* one who makes or deals in saddles and harness.

saddlery *noun* a saddler's goods or business.

Sadducee (**sad**-yŭ-see) *noun* a member of a Jewish sect at the time of Christ.

sadhu (**sah**-doo) *noun* a Hindu or Jain ascetic and religious mendicant. [Sanskrit, = holy man]

sadism (**say**-dizm) *noun* enjoyment of inflicting or watching cruelty; this as a form of sexual perversion. **sadist** *noun*, **sadistic** (să-**dis**-tik) *adjective*, **sadistically** *adverb* [named

after a French novelist, the Marquis de Sade, noted for his descriptions of sadism]

safari (să-**fah**-ree) *noun* **1** a hunting or exploratory expedition, especially in East Africa. **2** a similar expedition organised as a holiday tour. □ **safari park** a park where exotic wild animals are kept in the open for visitors to see. **safari suit** a lightweight short-sleeved suit. [from Arabic *safara* = to travel]

safe *adjective* **1** free from risk or danger, not dangerous. **2** providing security or protection. **–safe** *adverb* safely; *play safe*, not take risks. **–safe** *noun* **1** a strong locked cupboard or cabinet for valuables. **2** a ventilated cabinet for storing food. □ **on the safe side** allowing a margin of security against risks. **safe conduct** the right to pass through a district on a particular occasion without risk of arrest or harm (e.g. in time of war); a document guaranteeing this. **safe deposit** a building containing safes and strongrooms for hire separately. **safe period** (in birth control) the time in a woman's menstrual cycle when sexual intercourse is least likely to result in conception. **safe sex** sexual activity with precautions (especially the use of condoms) against disease (especially AIDS). **safely** *adverb*, **safeness** *noun* [from Latin *salvus* = uninjured]

safeguard *noun* a means of protection. **–safeguard** *verb* to protect.

safety *noun* being safe, freedom from risk or danger. □ **safety catch** a device that prevents a mechanism from being operated accidentally or dangerously; a locking device on a gun trigger. **safety curtain** a fireproof curtain that can be lowered to cut off a theatre stage from the auditorium. **safety house** a refuge for children escaping from harassment, needing adult help, etc. **safety lamp** a miner's lamp with the flame protected so that it will not ignite firedamp. **safety net** a net placed to catch an acrobat etc. in case he or she falls from a height. **safety pin** a brooch-like pin with a rounded guard to hold the point. **safety ramp** a steep sidetrack as an emergency stop from a dangerous road. **safety razor** a razor with a guard to prevent the blade from cutting the skin deeply. **safety valve** a valve that opens automatically to relieve excessive pressure in a steam boiler; an outlet for releasing feelings of anger or excitement etc. harmlessly.

safflower *noun* a European plant like a thistle, a source of a red dye and a cooking oil.

saffron *noun* 1 the orange-coloured stigmas of a kind of crocus, used for colouring and flavouring food. 2 the colour of these. □ **saffron thistle** an introduced noxious weed.

sag *verb* (**sagged, sagging**) 1 to sink or curve down in the middle under weight or pressure. 2 to hang loosely and unevenly, to droop. –**sag** *noun* sagging.

saga (**sah**-gǎ) *noun* 1 a medieval Icelandic or Norwegian heroic family tale. 2 a linked series of novels or histories. 3 a long story with many episodes.

sagacious (sǎ-**gay**-shǔs) *adjective* showing wisdom in one's understanding and judgment of things. **sagaciously** *adverb*, **sagacity** (sǎ-**gas**-ǐ-tee) *noun* [from Latin *sagax* = wise]

sage[1] a herb with fragrant greyish-green leaves used to flavour food.

sage[2] *adjective* profoundly wise; having wisdom gained from experience. –**sage** *noun* a profoundly wise man. **sagely** *adverb*

Sagittarius (saj-ǐ-**tair**-ree-ǔs) a sign of the zodiac, the Archer, that the sun enters about 22 November. **Sagittarian** *adjective* & *noun*

sago *noun* a starchy food in the form of hard white grains, used in puddings, obtained from the pith of a kind of palm tree (the **sago palm**).

Sahara a great desert of North Africa extending from the Atlantic to the Red Sea.

Sahel (sǎ-**hel**) the belt of dry savannah south of the Sahara in West Africa.

sahib (**sah**-ib) *noun* a former title of address to European men in India. [from Arabic, = friend or lord]

said *see* say.

sail *noun* 1 a piece of canvas or other fabric spread on rigging to catch the wind and drive a ship or boat along. 2 these sails collectively. 3 a journey by ship or boat. 4 something resembling a sail in function, *the sails of a windmill*. –**sail** *verb* 1 to travel on water by use of sails or engine power. 2 to start on a voyage, *we sail next week*. 3 to travel on or over (water) in a ship or boat, *sailed the seas*. 4 to control the navigation of (a ship); to set (a toy boat) afloat. 5 to move swiftly and smoothly; to walk in a stately manner.

sailboard *noun* a kind of surfboard to which a sail is fixed.

sailcloth *noun* 1 canvas for sails. 2 a strong canvas-like dress material.

sailing ship *noun* a ship driven by sails.

sailor *noun* 1 a member of a ship's crew; a member of a country's navy, especially one below the rank of officer. 2 a traveller considered as liable or not liable to seasickness, *a bad* or *good sailor*. □ **sailor hat** a straw hat with a flat top and straight brim.

sailplane *noun* a glider designed for soaring.

saint *noun* 1 a holy person, one declared (in the RC or Orthodox Church) to have won a high place in heaven and to be worthy of veneration. 2 the title of such a person or of one receiving veneration, or used in the name of a church not called after a saint (e.g. *St Saviour's*, *St Cross*). 3 any of the souls of the dead in paradise. 4 a member of the Christian Church or (in certain religious bodies) of one's own branch of it. 5 a very good, patient, or unselfish person. **sainthood** *noun* [from Latin *sanctus* = holy]

St Bernard a very large dog of a breed originally kept by monks in the Alps to rescue travellers (*see* **Bernard**).

Saint Elmo's fire *noun* see **corposant**.

St George's the capital of Grenada.

St Helena (hě-**lee**-nǎ) a solitary island in the South Atlantic, a British dependency, famous as the place of Napoleon's exile (1815–21) and death.

St John Ambulance an organisation providing first aid, nursing, ambulance, and welfare services.

St John's the capital of Antigua and Barbuda.

St Kitts and Nevis (**nee**-vǐs) a State consisting of two adjoining islands in the West Indies.

St Lawrence a river of North America flowing from Lake Ontario to the Atlantic Ocean.

St Lucia (**loo**-shǎ) an island State of the West Indies.

saintly *adjective* (**saintlier, saintliest**) like a saint, very virtuous. **saintliness** *noun*

St Paul's Cathedral a cathedral in London, built between 1675 and 1711 by Sir Christopher Wren.

St Peter's Basilica the Roman Catholic basilica in the Vatican City, Rome.

St Petersburg a port on an inlet of the Gulf of Finland and the second largest city in Russia, called Petrograd from (1914–24) and Leningrad from 1924–91.

St Vincent an island State of the West Indies consisting of the island of St Vincent and some of the Grenadines.

St Vincent de Paul Society an international Catholic lay charitable organisation for helping the poor and needy, established in Australia in 1854. (*See also* Vincent de Paul, St.)

sake¹ *noun* for the sake of in order to please or honour (a person) or get or keep (a thing).

sake² (**sah**-kee) *noun* Japanese rice wine.

Sakti (**suk**-tee) (in Hinduism) the female principle of divine energy, especially when personified as the supreme deity.

salaam (să-**lahm**) *noun* **1** a common greeting in many Arabic-speaking and Muslim countries. **2** an obeisance, with or without the salutation, consisting of a low bow of the head and body with the right palm on the forehead. –salaam *verb* to make a salaam to. [from Arabic *salam* = peace]

salacious (să-**lay**-shŭs) *adjective* lewd, erotic. salaciously *adverb*, salaciousness *noun*, salacity (să-**lass**-ĭ-tee) *noun*

salad *noun* a cold dish consisting of one or more vegetables (usually raw), often chopped or sliced and seasoned. □ salad days the time when one was youthful and inexperienced.

Saladin (1137–93), sultan of Egypt, who successfully invaded the Holy Land and recaptured Jerusalem from the Crusaders.

salamander (**sal**-ă-mand-er) *noun* **1** a lizard-like animal related to the newts. **2** (in mythology) a lizard-like animal living in fire.

salami (să-**lah**-mee) *noun* a strongly flavoured originally Italian sausage.

sal ammoniac (sal ă-**moh**-nee-ak) *noun* ammonium chloride.

salaried *adjective* receiving a salary.

salary *noun* a fixed payment made by an employer at regular intervals to a person doing other than manual or mechanical work, usually calculated on an annual or quarterly or monthly basis. [from Latin *salarium* = salt money, money given to Roman soldiers to buy salt]

sale *noun* **1** selling; being sold. **2** an instance of this, the amount sold, *made a sale*; *our sales were enormous*. **3** an event at which goods are sold, especially by public auction or for charity. **4** disposal of a shop's stock at reduced prices, e.g. at the end of a season. □ for or on sale offered for purchase. sales talk persuasive talk designed to make people buy goods or accept an idea.

saleable *adjective* fit for sale, likely to find a purchaser.

saleroom *noun* a room where goods are displayed for sale or in which auctions are held.

salesman *noun* (*plural* salesmen) a man employed to sell goods.

salesmanship *noun* skill in selling.

salesperson *noun* a salesman or saleswoman.

saleswoman *noun* (*plural* saleswomen) a woman employed to sell goods.

saleyard *noun* a place where livestock are sold.

salient (**say**-lee-ĕnt) *adjective* projecting, prominent, most noticeable, *the salient features of the plan*. –salient *noun* a projecting part, especially of a battle-line. [from Latin *saliens* = leaping]

saline (**say**-lyn) *adjective* salty, containing salt or salts. salinity (să-**lin**-ĭ tee) *noun*

Salinger (**sal**-ĭn-jer), Jerome David (1919–2010), American novelist, whose best-known work is the novel *The Catcher in the Rye*.

saliva (să-**ly**-vă) *noun* the colourless liquid discharged into the mouth by various glands, assisting in chewing and digestion.

salivary (să-**ly**-vă-ree) *adjective* of or producing saliva, *salivary glands*.

salivate (**sal**-ĭ-vayt) *verb* to produce saliva. salivation *noun*

Salk, Jonas Edward (1914–95), American microbiologist, who developed the first effective vaccine, named after him, against poliomyelitis.

sallow¹ *adjective* (of a person's skin or complexion) yellowish. sallowness *noun*

sallow² *noun* a willow tree, especially of a low-growing or shrubby kind.

sally¹ *noun* **1** a sudden rush forward in attack, a sortie. **2** an excursion. **3** a lively or witty remark. –sally *verb* (sallied, sallying) sally out or forth to make a sally (in attack) or an excursion. [same origin as *salient*]

sally² *noun* a eucalypt or acacia resembling a willow.

salmon *noun* **1** (*plural* salmon) a large introduced fish with pinkish flesh, much valued for food and sport. **2** a similar native

fish. **3** salmon-pink. ☐ **salmon-pink** *adjective*
& *noun* orange-pink like the flesh of salmon.

salmonella *noun* a bacterium that causes
food poisoning and various diseases. [from the
name of D. E. Salmon, American veterinary
surgeon]

Salome (să-**loh**-mee) the stepdaughter of
Herod Antipas (son of Herod the Great) and
daughter of Herodias. She danced before her
father and (at her mother's instigation) asked
for John the Baptist to be beheaded.

salon (**sal**-on) *noun* **1** an elegant room in a
continental great house, for receiving
guests. **2** a room or establishment where a
hairdresser, beauty specialist, or couturier etc.
receives clients.

saloon *noun* **1** a public room for a specified
purpose, *billiard saloon*. **2** a public room on a
ship. **3** (in full **saloon bar**) a more comfortable
bar in a hotel. **4** (in full **saloon car**) a car for
a driver and passengers, with a closed body
and a boot.

salsa *noun* **1** a savoury sauce or dip.
2 contemporary dance music of Caribbean
origin, incorporating elements of jazz and rock
music. [Spanish, = sauce]

salsify (**sal**-sĭ-fee) *noun* a plant with a long
fleshy root cooked as a vegetable.

salt *noun* **1** sodium chloride, a substance
obtained from mines or by evaporation of sea
water, used to flavour and preserve food. **2** a
chemical compound formed from the reaction
of a base with an acid. **3** a salt cellar. –**salt**
adjective tasting of salt; impregnated with or
preserved in salt. –**salt** *verb* **1** to season with
salt. **2** to preserve in salt. **3** to put aside for the
future, *salt it away*. **4** to make (a mine) appear
rich by fraudulently inserting precious metal
into it before it is viewed. **salts** *plural noun* a
substance resembling salt in form, especially a
laxative. ☐ **old salt** an experienced sailor. **salt
cellar** a dish or perforated pot holding salt for
use at meals. **salt lick** a place where animals
go to lick rock or earth impregnated with salt.
salt marsh a marsh that is flooded by the sea
at high tide. **salt of the earth** people with a
wholesome influence upon society. **salt pan**
a natural or artificial hollow by the sea where
salt is obtained from sea water by evaporation;
a dried-up salt lake. **take it with a grain** or
pinch of salt not believe it wholly. **worth
one's salt** competent, deserving one's position.

saltbush *noun* any of various Australian
shrubs or herbs growing in dry saline soil.

saltdamp *noun* (in South Australia) saline
rising damp.

salting *noun* a marsh that is covered by the
sea when the tide rises.

saltire (**sal**-tyr) *noun* a St Andrew's cross
X, dividing a shield into four compartments.

saltpetre (solt-**peet**-er) *noun* a salty white
powder (potassium nitrate) used in making
gunpowder.

salty *adjective* (**saltier**, **saltiest**) containing or
tasting of salt. **saltiness** *noun*

salubrious (să-**loo**-bree-ŭs) *adjective* health-
giving. **salubrity** *noun* [from Latin *salus* =
health]

salutary (**sal**-yŭ-tă-ree) *adjective* producing
a beneficial or wholesome effect [from Latin
salus = health]

salutation (sal-yŭ-**tay**-shŏn) *noun* a word or
words or gesture of greeting; an expression
of respect.

salute *noun* **1** a formal military movement or
position of the body, or a discharge of guns or
use of flags, as a sign of respect. **2** a gesture
of respect, greeting, or polite recognition. **3** an
expression of respect or admiration. –**salute**
verb **1** to perform a formal military salute; to
greet with this. **2** to greet with a polite gesture.
3 to express respect or admiration for. [from
Latin *salus* = health]

Salvador *see* **El Salvador**. **Salvadorean**
(sal-vă-**dor**-ree-ăn) *adjective* & *noun*

salvage *noun* **1** rescue of a wrecked or
damaged ship or its cargo; rescue of property
from fire or other disaster. **2** the goods or
property saved. **3** the saving and use of waste
paper, scrap metal, etc. **4** the items saved.
–**salvage** *verb* to save from loss or for use as
salvage. [from Latin *salvare* = save]

salvation *noun* **1** saving of the soul from sin
and its consequences; the state of being saved.
2 preservation from loss or calamity; a thing
that preserves from these, *the loan was our
salvation*.

Salvation Army an international Christian
organisation founded on military lines to do
charitable work and spread Christianity.

Salvation Jane (*South Australian*) =
Paterson's curse.

salve[1] *noun* **1** a soothing ointment.
2 something that soothes a conscience or
wounded feelings. –**salve** *verb* to soothe
(conscience etc.).

salve² *verb* to save from a wreck or fire. **salvor** *noun*

salver *noun* a tray (usually of metal) on which letters, cards, or refreshments are placed for handing to people.

salvo *noun* (*plural* **salvoes**) **1** the firing of a number of guns simultaneously, especially as a salute. **2** a volley of applause.

sal volatile (sal vŏ-**lat**-ĭ-lee) *noun* a flavoured solution of ammonium carbonate, used for drinking as a remedy for faintness.

samadhi (să-**mah**-dee) *noun* (in Buddhism and Hinduism) a state of intense concentration achieved through meditation, considered in yogic practice to be the final stage at which union with the divine is reached. [Sanskrit]

Samaritan *noun* **good Samaritan** someone who readily gives help to a person in distress who has no claim on him or her. [from the parable of the Good Samaritan in the Bible]

samarium (să-**mair**-ee-ŭm) *noun* a hard silver-white metallic element of the lanthanide series (symbol Sm).

Sama Veda *noun* one of the four Vedas, a collection of melodies and liturgical chants, with much of its material drawn from the Rig Veda. [Sanskrit]

samba *noun* a ballroom dance of Brazilian origin; the music for this. [Portuguese]

same *adjective* **1** identical, one, *they belong to the same family*; *Sri Lanka and Ceylon are the same country*. **2** being of one kind, *they went out together wearing the same dress*. **3** not changed or changing or different, *the same old story*. **4** corresponding in essentials, *she comes the same day every week*. **5** previously mentioned. **–same** *pronoun* the same person or thing, *same for me, please*; *would do the same again*. **–same** *adverb* similarly, in the same manner, *we still feel the same about it*. □ **same here** (*informal*) the same applies to me; I agree. **sameness** *noun*

Usage The use of *same* as a pronoun to refer to a thing or person just mentioned, as in *I've finished your book and am returning same*, has a legal or commercial flavour. In general use it is best avoided.

Samoa (să-**moh**-ă) a group of islands in the Pacific Ocean, of which the eastern part (**American Samoa**) is a territory of the USA, and the western part (**Samoa**, formerly called

Western Samoa) is an independent country. **Samoan** *adjective* & *noun*

samosa (să-**moh**-să) *noun* an Indian triangular pastry fried in ghee or oil, with meat or spiced vegetable filling. [Hindustani]

samovar (**sam**-ŏ-var) *noun* a metal urn with an interior heating-tube to keep water at boiling point for making tea, used in Russia and elsewhere. [Russian, = self-boiler]

Samoyed (**sam**-oid) *noun* a dog of a white Arctic breed. [Russian]

sampan *noun* a small flat-bottomed boat used along coasts and rivers of China. [from Chinese *sanpan* (from *san* = three, *pan* = boards)]

samphire (**sam**-fyr) *noun* a plant with fragrant fleshy leaves, growing on cliffs.

sample *noun* **1** a small separated part showing the quality of the whole, a specimen. **2** part of an audio recording. **–sample** *verb* **1** to test by taking a sample or getting an experience of. **2** use (part of an audio recording etc.) in a new recording. □ **sample bag** (*Austral.*) a show bag.

sampler *noun* **1** a thing that takes samples. **2** a piece of embroidery worked in various stitches to display skill in needlework. **3** a collection of representative items; *a record sampler*, one having individual tracks from various other records.

samsara (sam-**sah**-ră) *noun* (in Buddhism, Hinduism, and Jainism) the soul's passage through a series of lives. [Sanskrit, = a wandering through]

Samson probably 11th century BC, an Israelite leader famous for his strength, betrayed by Delilah to the Philistines.

Samuel 1 a Hebrew prophet of the 11th century BC. **2** either of two historical books of the Old Testament.

samurai (**sam**-yŭ-ry) *noun* (*plural* **samurai**) **1** a Japanese army officer. **2** a member of the former military caste in Japan.

Sana'a (**sah**-nă) the capital of Yemen.

sanatorium *noun* (*plural* **sanatoriums**) an establishment for treating chronic diseases (e.g. tuberculosis) or convalescents. [from Latin *sanare* = heal]

sanctify *verb* (**sanctified**, **sanctifying**) to make holy or sacred. **sanctification** *noun* [from Latin *sanctus* = holy]

sanctimonious (sank-tĭ-**moh**-nee-ŭs) *adjective* making a show of righteousness or piety. **sanctimoniously** *adverb*, **sanctimoniousness** *noun*

sanction *noun* **1** permission or approval for an action or behaviour etc. **2** action taken by a country to penalise and coerce a country or organisation that is considered to have violated a law or code of practice or basic human rights. **–sanction** *verb* to give sanction, a penalty or reward to (a law). [from Latin *sancire* = make holy]

sanctity *noun* sacredness, holiness.

sanctuary *noun* **1** a sacred place. **2** the holiest part of a temple; the part of a chancel containing the altar. **3** an area where birds or wild animals are protected and encouraged to breed. **4** refuge, a place of refuge, *seek sanctuary*. [from Latin *sanctus* = holy]

sanctum *noun* **1** a holy place. **2** a person's private room. [Latin, = holy thing]

sand *noun* **1** very fine loose fragments resulting from the wearing down of rock, found in deserts, seashores, river beds, etc.; *the sands are running out*, the time allowed is nearly at an end (¶ from the use of sand in an hourglass). **2** an expanse of sand; a sandbank. **3** light brown colour like that of sand. **–sand** *verb* **1** to sprinkle or cover with sand. **2** to smooth or polish with sand or sandpaper. □ **sand dune** loose sand formed into a mound by wind.

sandal *noun* a light shoe consisting of a sole with straps or thongs over the foot.

sandalwood *noun* a kind of scented wood from a tropical tree, important in early European trade in the Pacific.

sandbag *noun* a bag filled with sand, used to protect a wall or building (e.g. in war, or as a defence against rising flood water), or as a ruffian's weapon. **–sandbag** *verb* (**sandbagged**, **sandbagging**) **1** to protect with sandbags. **2** to hit with a sandbag.

sandbank *noun* a deposit of sand under water, causing a river etc. to be shallow at that point.

sandblast *verb* to clean with a jet of sand driven by compressed air or steam.

sandcastle *noun* a castle-shaped structure made of sand at the beach or in a sandpit.

sander *noun* a device for sanding things.

sandgroper *noun* (*informal*) a native or resident of Western Australia.

sandhill *noun* = sand dune.

sandhopper *noun* a little crustacean found in numbers on beaches.

Sandinista (san-di-**neest**-ă) *noun* a member of a revolutionary guerrilla organisation in Nicaragua, in power (1979–90). [named after A.C. Sandino (1893–1934), Nicaraguan nationalist leader]

sandman *noun* an imaginary visitor causing sleepiness in children towards bedtime.

sandpaper *noun* paper with a coating of sand or other abrasive substance, used for smoothing or polishing surfaces. **–sandpaper** *verb* to smooth or polish with sandpaper.

sandpiper *noun* any of several birds with long pointed bills, living in open wet sandy places.

sandpit *noun* a hollow partly filled with sand for children to play in.

sandshoe *noun* a canvas shoe with rubber sole used primarily for sport (formerly, for wearing on the sand).

sandstone *noun* a sedimentary rock formed of compressed sand.

sandstorm *noun* a desert storm of wind with clouds of sand.

sandwich *noun* **1** two or more slices of bread with a layer of filling between. **2** something resembling this in arrangement. **–sandwich** *verb* to insert (a thing) between two others. □ **sandwich course** a course of training with alternating periods of instruction and practical work. [invented by the Earl of Sandwich (1718–92) so that he could eat while gambling]

sandy *adjective* (**sandier**, **sandiest**) **1** like sand; covered with sand. **2** (of hair) yellowish-red; (of a person) having hair of this colour. □ **sandy blight** acute conjunctivitis affecting people in arid parts of Australia. **sandiness** *noun*

sane *adjective* **1** having a sound mind, not mad. **2** showing good judgment, sensible and practical. **sanely** *adverb* [from Latin *sanus* = healthy]

sang *see* sing.

sangat *noun* a congregation or assembly of Sikhs. [Punjabi]

sanger (*rhymes with* hanger) *noun* (*Austral. informal*) a sandwich.

sangfroid (sahn-**frwah**) *noun* calmness in danger or difficulty. [French, = cold blood]

sangha (**sang**-gă) *noun* the Buddhist monastic order, including monks, nuns, and novices.

sanguinary (**sang**-gwĭ-nǎ-ree) *adjective*
1 full of bloodshed. **2** bloodthirsty. [from Latin
sanguis = blood]

sanguine (**sang**-gwĭn) *adjective* hopeful,
optimistic.

Sanhedrin (san-**hee**-drĭn *or* **san**-ĭ-drĭn) *noun*
the supreme Jewish council and court of
justice at Jerusalem in New Testament times.

sanitary (**san**-ĭ-tree) *noun* **1** of hygiene;
hygienic. **2** of sanitation. □ **sanitary pad**
or **towel** an absorbent pad worn during
menstruation. [from Latin *sanus* = healthy]

sanitation *noun* arrangements to protect
public health, especially by drainage and the
efficient disposal of sewage.

sanitise *verb* (also **-ize**) to make hygienic.

sanity *noun* the state or condition of being
sane.

San José (**hoh**-zay) the capital of Costa Rica.

San Juan (*pr.* hwahn) the capital of Puerto
Rico.

sank *see* **sink**.

San Marino (mǎ-**ree**-noh) **1** a small
independent republic in NE Italy. **2** the capital
of this republic.

San Salvador the capital of El Salvador.

sanserif (san-**se**-rĭf) *adjective* without serifs.
–sanserif *noun* a form of typeface without
serifs (like the headwords in this dictionary).

Sanskrit *noun* the ancient language of the
Hindus in India, one of the oldest known Indo-
European languages.

Santa Claus a person said to bring children
presents on the night before Christmas. [from
the Dutch name *Sante Klaas* = St Nicholas]

Santiago (san-tee-**ah**-goh) the capital of
Chile.

Santo Domingo (dŏ-**ming**-goh) the capital
of the Dominican Republic.

São Tomé (sow to-**may**) the capital of
São Tomé and Príncipe (*pr.* **prin**-sĭ-pee), a
republic consisting of two islands and several
islets off the west coast of Africa.

sap[1] *noun* **1** the vital liquid that circulates in
plants, carrying food to all parts. **2** (*informal*)
a foolish person. **–sap** *verb* (**sapped**, **sapping**)
to exhaust (strength etc.) gradually.

sap[2] *noun* a trench or tunnel made in order to
get closer to an enemy.

sapient (**say**-pee-ĕnt) *adjective* (*literary*)
wise. [from Latin *sapiens* = wise]

sapling *noun* a young tree. [from *sap*[1]]

saponify (sǎ-**pon**-ĭ-fy) *verb* (**saponified**,
saponifying) to make (fat or oil) or become
made into soap by combining with an alkali.
saponification *noun* [from Latin *sapo* = soap]

sapper *noun* a soldier (especially a private) of
the engineer corps.

sapphire *noun* **1** a transparent blue precious
stone. **2** its colour. **–sapphire** *adjective* bright
blue.

Sappho (**saf**-oh) early 7th century BC, Greek
poet from the island of Lesbos.

saprophyte (**sap**-rŏ-fyt) *noun* a fungus or
similar plant living on dead organic matter.
saprophytic (sap-rŏ-**fit**-ik) *adjective* [from
Greek *sapros* = putrid, + *phuton* = plant]

sapwood *noun* the soft outer layers of
recently formed wood in a tree, between the
heartwood and the bark.

saraband (**sa**-rǎ-band) *noun* a slow Spanish
dance; the music for this.

Saracen (**sa**-rǎ-sĕn) *noun* an Arab or Muslim
of the time of the Crusades.

Sarajevo (sa-rǎ-**yay**-voh) the capital of
Bosnia-Herzegovina.

Sarawak (sǎ-**rah**-wak) a State of Malaysia on
the NW coast of Borneo.

sarcasm (**sar**-kazm) *noun* **1** an ironical remark
or taunt. **2** the use of such taunts.

sarcastic (sar-**kas**-tik) *adjective* using or
showing sarcasm. **sarcastically** *adverb* [from
Greek *sarkazein* = tear the flesh]

sarcoma (sar-**koh**-mǎ) *noun* a malignant
tumour on connective tissue.

sarcophagus (sar-**kof**-ǎ-gǔs) *noun* (*plural*
sarcophagi) a stone coffin, often decorated
with carvings. [from Greek *sarkos* = of flesh,
+ *-phagos* = eating]

sardine *noun* a young pilchard or similar
small fish, often tinned as food tightly packed
in oil.

Sardinia a large island in the Mediterranean
Sea, west of Italy, an administrative region of
Italy. **Sardinian** *adjective* & *noun*

sardonic (sar-**don**-ik) *adjective* humorous in a
grim or sarcastic way. **sardonically** *adverb*

sargasso (sar-**gas**-oh) *noun* (*plural*
sargassos) a kind of seaweed with berry-like
air vessels, found floating in masses.

Sargasso Sea (sar-**gas**-oh) a region of the
western Atlantic Ocean, so called from the
masses of sargasso found in it.

sarge *noun* (*informal*) sergeant.

sari (**sah**-ree) *noun* (*plural* **saris**) a length of cotton or silk cloth draped round the body, worn as the main garment chiefly by women of the Indian subcontinent. [Hindi]

sarod (să-**rohd**) *noun* a lute used in classical N Indian music.

sarong (să-**rong**) *noun* a SE Asian skirtlike garment worn by both sexes, consisting of a strip of cloth worn tucked around the waist or under the armpits.

SARS (sarz) *noun* severe acute respiratory syndrome, a contagious viral disease.

sarsaparilla (sars-pă-**ril**-ă) *noun* 1 a plant whose roots are used as a flavouring and formerly as a tonic. 2 a native plant with strongly flavoured leaves, used as tea. 3 *see* **hardenbergia**.

sarsen (**sar**-sĕn) *noun* a large sandstone boulder carried by ice during a glacial period.

sarsenet (**sar**-snĕt) *noun* a soft silk fabric used mainly for linings.

sartorial (sar-**tor**-ree-ăl) *adjective* of tailoring, of men's clothing, *sartorial elegance*. [from Latin *sartor* = tailor]

Sartre (*pr.* sartr), Jean-Paul (1905–80), French existentialist philosopher, novelist, and dramatist.

sash[1] *noun* a long strip of cloth worn round the waist or over one shoulder and across the body for ornament or as part of a uniform. [from Arabic *shash* = turban]

sash[2] *noun* either of a pair of frames holding the glass panes of a window and sliding up and down in grooves. □ **sash cord** strong cord used for attaching a weight to each end of a sash so that it can be balanced at any height. [from French *châssis* = frame]

sashimi *noun* a Japanese dish of garnished raw fish in thin slices.

Sassoon (să-**soon**), Siegfried Louvain (1886–1967), English writer and poet of the First World War.

sat *see* sit.

Satan the Devil.

Satanic (să-**tan**-ik) *adjective* of Satan. –**satanic** *adjective* devilish, hellish.

Satanism *noun* worship of Satan, using distorted forms of Christian worship. **Satanist** *noun*

satay (**sah**-tay) *noun* a Malaysian and Indonesian dish consisting of small pieces of meat grilled on a skewer, and usually served with a spicy sauce.

satchel *noun* a small bag for carrying light articles (especially school books), hung over the shoulder or carried on the back. [from Latin *saccellus* = little sack]

sate (*pr.* sayt) *verb* to satiate.

sateen (să-**teen**) *noun* a closely-woven cotton fabric resembling satin.

satellite *noun* 1 a heavenly body revolving round a planet; an artificial body placed in orbit to revolve similarly. 2 a person's follower or hanger-on. 3 a country that is subservient to another and follows its lead. □ **satellite dish** a concave dish-shaped aerial for receiving broadcasting signals transmitted by satellite. **satellite town** a smaller town dependent on a larger one near it. [from Latin *satelles* = guard]

Sati (**sut**-ee) (in Hinduism) the wife of Siva, reborn as Parvati. According to some accounts she died by throwing herself into a sacred fire.

satiable (**say**-shă-bul) *adjective* able to be satiated.

satiate (**say**-shee-ayt) *verb* to satisfy fully, to glut or cloy with an excess of something. **satiation** *noun* [from Latin *satis* = enough (compare *satisfaction*)]

satiety (să-**ty**-ĕ-tee) *noun* the condition or feeling of being satiated.

satin *noun* a silky material woven in such a way that it is glossy on one side only. –**satin** *adjective* smooth as satin. □ **satin bowerbird** (also **satin bird**) a bird of eastern Australia having glossy black plumage with a blue sheen. **satiny** *adjective*

satinette (sat-ĭ-**net**) *noun* a fabric resembling satin.

satinwood *noun* 1 the smooth hard wood of various tropical trees, used for making furniture. 2 a tree yielding this.

satire *noun* 1 the use of ridicule, irony, or sarcasm in speech or writing. 2 a novel, play, or film etc. that ridicules people's hypocrisy or foolishness in this way, often by parody.

satirical (să-**ti**-ri-kăl) *adjective* using satire, criticising in a humorous or sarcastic way. **satirically** *adverb*

satirise (**sat**-ĭ-ryz) *verb* (also -**ize**) to attack with satire, to describe satirically.

satirist (**sat**-ĭ-rĭst) *noun* a person who writes satires or uses satire.

satisfaction *noun* **1** satisfying; being satisfied. **2** something that satisfies a desire or gratifies a feeling. **3** compensation for injury or loss, *demand satisfaction*. [from Latin *satis* = enough, + *facere* = make]

satisfactory *adjective* satisfying expectations or needs, adequate. **satisfactorily** *adverb*

satisfy *verb* (**satisfied, satisfying**) **1** to give (a person) what he or she wants or demands or needs, to make pleased or contented; *be satisfied with something* or *to do something*, to demand no more than this, to consider that this is enough. **2** to put an end to (a demand or craving) by giving what is required, *satisfy one's hunger*. **3** to provide with sufficient proof, to convince; *the police are satisfied that his death was accidental*, they feel certain of this. **4** to pay (a creditor). [same origin as *satisfaction*]

satrap *noun* the governor of a province in the ancient Persian empire.

satsuma (sat-**soo**-mă) *noun* **1** a kind of purple plum with purple flesh. **2** a kind of mandarin orange originally grown in Japan. [named after Satsuma, a province of Japan]

saturate *verb* **1** to make thoroughly wet, to soak. **2** to cause to absorb or accept as much as possible; *the market for used cars is saturated*, can take no more. **3** to cause (a substance) to combine with or absorb the greatest possible amount of another substance. □ **saturation point** the stage of being fully saturated. **saturation** *noun*

Saturday *noun* the day of the week following Friday. [named after Saturn]

Saturn 1 (*Rom. myth.*) a god of agriculture. **2** a large planet of the solar system, with 'rings' composed of small icy particles.

saturnalia (sat-er-**nay**-lee-ă) *noun* wild revelry. [from Latin *Saturnalia*, an ancient Roman festival of Saturn, celebrated in December]

saturnine (**sat**-er-nyn) *adjective* (of a person or looks) having a gloomy forbidding appearance.

satyr (**sat**-er) *noun* **1** (*Gk. & Rom. myth.*) any of a class of woodland gods in human form but having a goat's ears, tail, and legs. **2** a grossly lustful man.

sauce *noun* **1** a liquid or semi-liquid preparation served with food to add flavour or richness. **2** (*informal*) impudence.

saucepan *noun* a cooking vessel, usually round and with a long handle at the side, used for cooking on top of a stove.

saucer *noun* **1** a small shallow curved dish on which a cup stands. **2** something shaped like this.

saucy *adjective* (**saucier, sauciest**) **1** impudent. **2** jaunty. **saucily** *adverb*, **sauciness** *noun*

Saudi (*rhymes with* cloudy) *noun* (*plural* **Saudis**) a native or inhabitant of Saudi Arabia.

Saudi Arabia a kingdom in the Middle East, occupying most of the Arabian peninsula, named after its first king, Ibn Saud (died 1953). **Saudi Arabian** *adjective* & *noun*

sauerkraut (**sowr**-krowt) *noun* a German dish of chopped pickled cabbage.

Saul 11th century BC, the first king of Israel.

sauna (**saw**-nă) *noun* a Finnish-style steam bath; a building or room for this. [Finnish]

saunter *verb* to walk in a leisurely way. –**saunter** *noun* a leisurely walk or walking-pace.

saurian (**sor**-ree-ăn) *adjective* of or like a lizard. –**saurian** *noun* an animal of the lizard family. [from Greek *sauros* = lizard]

sausage *noun* minced seasoned meat enclosed in a cylindrical case made from animal entrails or synthetic material. □ **sausage meat** meat prepared for this or as a stuffing etc. **sausage roll** sausage meat enclosed in a pastry roll.

sauté (**soh**-tay) *adjective* fried quickly in a small amount of fat, *sauté potatoes*. –**sauté** *verb* (**sautéd** or **sautéed, sautéing**) to cook in this way. [from French *sauter* = to jump]

Sauternes (soh-**tern**) *noun* a sweet white wine. [from Sauternes in France]

Sauvignon (**soh**-veen-yon) *noun* **1** (in full **Sauvignon blanc**) a white grape and the white wine made from it. **2** *see* **Cabernet Sauvignon**.

savage *adjective* **1** in a primitive or uncivilised state, *savage tribes*. **2** wild and fierce, *savage animals*. **3** cruel and hostile, *savage criticism*. **4** (*informal*) very angry. –**savage** *noun* a member of a savage tribe. –**savage** *verb* to attack savagely, to maul. **savagely** *adverb*, **savageness** *noun*, **savagery** *noun* [from Latin *silvaticus* = of the woods, wild]

savannah (să-**van**-ă) *noun* a grassy plain in hot regions, with few or no trees.

savant (**sav**-ănt) *noun* a learned person.

save *verb* **1** to rescue, to keep from danger, harm, or capture. **2** to free from the power of sin or its spiritual consequences. **3** to avoid wasting, *save fuel*. **4** to keep for future use or enjoyment; to put aside (money) for future use. **5** to make unnecessary, *did it to save a journey* or *to save you a journey*. **6** (in sports) to prevent an opponent from scoring. –**save** *noun* the act of saving in sports. –**save** *preposition* except, *in all cases save one*. □ **save one's breath** to keep silent because it would be useless to speak. **saver** *noun* [from Latin *salvus* = safe]

saveloy (**sav**-ĕ-loi) *noun* a kind of pork sausage.

saving *noun* the act of rescuing or keeping from danger etc. –**saving** *adjective* that saves. –**saving** *preposition* except. **savings** *plural noun* money put aside for future use. □ **saving grace** a good quality that redeems a person or thing whose other qualities are not good.

saviour *noun* a person who rescues or delivers people from harm or danger. □ **the** or **our Saviour** Christ as the saviour of humankind.

savoir faire (sav-wahr **fair**) *noun* knowledge of how to behave in any situation that may arise, social tact. [French, = knowing how to do]

savory *noun* a low-growing herb with a spicy smell and flavour, used in cooking.

savour *noun* **1** the taste or smell of something. **2** the power to arouse enjoyment, *felt that life had lost its savour*. –**savour** *verb* **1** to have a certain taste or smell. **2** to taste or smell (a thing) with enjoyment. **3** to give a certain impression, *the reply savours of impertinence*. [from Latin *sapor* = flavour]

savoury *adjective* **1** having an appetising taste or smell. **2** having a salt or piquant and not sweet flavour. –**savoury** *noun* a savoury snack, especially served as an appetiser. **savouriness** *noun*

savoy (să-**voi**) *noun* a hardy cabbage with wrinkled leaves. [from *Savoy*, a region in SE France]

savvy *noun* (*informal*) common sense, understanding. –**savvy** *verb* (*informal*) to understand.

saw¹ *noun* a tool with a zigzag edge for cutting wood etc. –**saw** *verb* (**sawed**, **sawn**, **sawing**) **1** to cut with a saw. **2** to make a to-and-fro movement like that of sawing, *sawed away at her viola*.

saw² *noun* an old saying, a maxim.

saw³ *see* **see¹**.

sawdust *noun* powdery fragments of wood produced when timber is sawn.

sawfish *noun* a large sea fish having a blade-like snout with jagged edges that it uses as a weapon.

sawfly *noun* an insect that is destructive to plants, which it pierces with a jagged organ in order to lay its eggs.

sawmill *noun* a mill with power-operated saws where timber is cut into planks etc.

sawn *see* **saw¹**. □ **sawn-off** *adjective* (of a gun) with part of the barrel removed by sawing, so that it can be handled more easily.

sawyer *noun* a person who saws timber, especially for a living.

sax *noun* (*informal*) a saxophone.

saxe *noun* (also **saxe-blue**) light blue with a greyish tinge.

saxifrage (**saks**-ĭ-frij) *noun* a plant growing on rocky or sandy ground, with clusters of small white, yellow, or red flowers.

Saxon *noun* **1** a member of a Germanic people who occupied parts of England in the 5th–6th centuries. **2** their language. –**Saxon** *adjective* of the Saxons or their language.

Saxony a large region and former Kingdom of Germany.

saxophone *noun* a brass wind instrument with a reed in the mouthpiece, and with keys like those of a clarinet. [from the name of A. Sax, its Belgian inventor]

saxophonist (saks-**off**-ŏ-nĭst) *noun* a person who plays the saxophone.

say *verb* (**said**, **saying**) **1** to utter or recite in a speaking voice. **2** to state, to express in words; to have a specified wording, *the notice says 'keep out'*. **3** to give as an argument or excuse, *there's much to be said on both sides*. **4** to give as one's opinion or decision, *it's hard to say which of them is taller*. **5** to suppose as a possibility; to take (a specified amount) as being near enough, *let's allow, say, an hour for the meeting*. –**say** *noun* a share in a decision, *has no say in the matter*. –**say** *interjection* (*informal*) = I say. □ **have one's say** to say all one wishes to say. **I'll say** (*informal*) indeed. **I say** an expression of surprise or admiration, or calling attention or opening a conversation. **say-so** *noun* the power to decide something; a command; a mere assertion without proof.

saying *noun* a well-known phrase or proverb or other statement.

SBS *abbreviation* Special Broadcasting Service.

scab *noun* **1** a crust forming over a wound or sore as it heals. **2** a skin disease or plant disease that causes scablike roughness. **3** (*informal, derogatory*) a blackleg. –**scab** *verb* (**scabbed, scabbing**) **1** to form a scab; to heal by doing this. **2** (*informal, derogatory*) to act as a blackleg. **scabby** *adjective*

scabbard *noun* the sheath of a sword or dagger or bayonet.

scabies (**skay**-beez) *noun* a contagious skin disease causing itching.

scabious (**skay**-bee-ŭs) *noun* a wild or cultivated annual herbaceous plant with thickly-clustered blue, pink, or white flowers.

scaffold *noun* **1** a wooden platform for the execution of criminals; **the scaffold** death by execution. **2** scaffolding. –**scaffold** *verb* to fit scaffolding to (a building).

scaffolding *noun* **1** a temporary structure of poles or tubes and planks providing workers with platforms to stand on while building or repairing a house etc. **2** the poles etc. from which this is made.

scalable *adjective* able to be scaled.

scalar (**skay**-ler) *adjective* (in mathematics) having magnitude but not direction. –**scalar** *noun* a scalar quantity (e.g. speed). [same origin as *scale³*]

scald *verb* **1** to injure with hot liquid or steam. **2** to heat (milk) to near boiling point. **3** to cleanse (pans etc.) with boiling water. –**scald** *noun* an injury to the skin by scalding.

scale¹ *noun* **1** each of the thin overlapping plates of horny membrane or hard substance that protect the skin of many fishes and reptiles. **2** something resembling this (e.g. on a plant); a flake of skin. **3** an incrustation inside a boiler or kettle etc. in which hard water is regularly used; a similar incrustation on teeth. –**scale** *verb* **1** to remove scales or scale from. **2** to come off in scales or flakes.
□ **the scales fell from their eyes** they were no longer deceived. [from Old French *escale* = flake, from an Old Germanic word *skalo*]

scale² *noun* the pan of a balance. **scales** *plural noun* an instrument for weighing things.
□ **tip** or **turn the scale(s)** to be the decisive factor in a situation. **turn the scales at** to weigh, *turned the scales at 65 kilos*. [from Old Norse *skál* = bowl, from *skalo* (see *scale¹*)]

scale³ *noun* **1** an ordered series of units, degrees, or qualities etc. for purposes of measurement or classification. **2** an arrangement of notes in a system of music, ascending or descending by fixed intervals. **3** the ratio of the actual measurements of something and those of a drawing or map or model of it, a line with marks showing this, *the scale is 1 centimetre to the kilometre*; *a scale model*, one with measurements in uniform proportion to those of the original. **4** the relative size or extent of something, *war on a grand scale*. –**scale** *verb* **1** to climb, *scaled the cliff*. **2** to represent in measurements or extent in proportion to the size of the original.
□ **scale up** or **down** to make larger or smaller in proportion. [from Latin *scala* = ladder]

scalene (**skay**-leen) *adjective* (of a triangle etc.) having unequal sides. [from Greek *skalenos* = unequal]

scallop (**skol**-ŏp) *noun* **1** a shellfish with two hinged fan-shaped shells. **2** either shell of this, used as a container in which food is cooked and served. **3** each of a series of semicircular curves used as an ornamental edging. –**scallop** *verb* (**scalloped, scalloping**) **1** to cook in a scallop shell. **2** to ornament with scallops. **scalloping** *noun*

scallywag *noun* a rascal.

scalp *noun* **1** the skin of the head excluding the face. **2** this with the hair, formerly cut or torn away as a trophy from an enemy's head. –**scalp** *verb* to take the scalp of.

scalpel (**skal**-pĕl) *noun* a surgeon's or artist's small light straight knife.

scaly *adjective* (**scalier, scaliest**) covered in scales or scale (**scale¹**).

scam *noun* (*informal*) a trick or swindle, a racket.

scamp *noun* a rascal. –**scamp** *verb* to do (work) hastily and inadequately.

scamper *verb* to run hastily; to run about playfully as a child does. –**scamper** *noun* a scampering run.

scampi (**skamp**-ee) *plural noun* large prawns; these as food. [Italian]

scan *verb* (**scanned, scanning**) **1** to look at all parts of (a thing) intently. **2** to glance at quickly and not thoroughly. **3** to sweep a radar or electronic beam over (an area) in search of something. **4** to resolve (a picture) into elements of light and shade for television transmission. **5** to analyse the rhythm of (a line of verse). **6** (of verse) to be correct in rhythm. –**scan** *noun* scanning.

scandal *noun* **1** something shameful or disgraceful. **2** gossip about other people's faults and wrongdoing. [from Greek, = stumbling-block]

scandalise *verb* (also **-ize**) to shock by something shameful or disgraceful.

scandalmonger *noun* a person who invents or spreads scandal.

scandalous *adjective* **1** shameful, disgraceful. **2** containing scandal, *scandalous reports*. **scandalously** *adverb*

Scandinavia Norway, Sweden, and Denmark (sometimes also Finland, Iceland, and the Faeroe Islands) considered as a unit. **Scandinavian** *adjective & noun*

scandium (**skan**-dee-ŭm) *noun* a soft silver-white metallic element (symbol Sc).

scanner *noun* a device for scanning or systematically examining all parts of something (*see* **scan** *verb* sense 3).

scansion (**skan**-shŏn) *noun* the scanning of lines of verse; the way verse scans.

scant *adjective* scanty, insufficient, *was treated with scant courtesy*.

scanty *adjective* (**scantier, scantiest**) **1** of small amount or extent, *scanty vegetation*. **2** barely enough. **scantily** *adverb*, **scantiness** *noun*

scapegoat *noun* a person who is made to bear blame or punishment that should rightly fall on others. [named after the goat which, in ancient Jewish religious custom, was allowed to escape into the wilderness after the high priest had symbolically laid the sins of the people upon it]

scapula (**skap**-yŭ-lă) *noun* (*plural* **scapulae**, *pr.* **skap**-yŭ-lee) the shoulder blade.

scar[1] *noun* **1** a mark left where a wound or injury or sore has healed, or on a plant from which a leaf has fallen. **2** a mark left by damage. **3** a lasting effect produced by grief etc. –**scar** *verb* (**scarred, scarring**) to mark with a scar; to form a scar or scars.

scar[2] *noun* a steep craggy part of a mountainside or cliff.

scarab (**ska**-răb) *noun* **1** a kind of beetle. **2** the sacred dung beetle of ancient Egypt. **3** a carving of a beetle, engraved with symbols on the flat side, used in ancient Egypt as a charm.

scarce *adjective* not enough to supply a demand or need, rare. □ **make oneself scarce**

(*informal*) to go away, especially so as to keep out of the way.

scarcely *adverb* **1** only just, almost not, *she is scarcely 17 years old*; *I scarcely know him*. **2** not, surely not, *you can scarcely expect me to believe that*.

scarcity *noun* being scarce; a shortage.

scare *verb* to frighten or become frightened suddenly. –**scare** *noun* a sudden fright; alarm caused by a rumour, *a bomb scare*.

scarecrow *noun* **1** an object resembling a human figure dressed in old clothes, set up in a field to scare birds away from crops. **2** a badly-dressed or grotesque person.

scaremonger *noun* a person who raises unnecessary or excessive alarm. **scaremongering** *noun*

scarf[1] *noun* (*plural* **scarves**) a piece of material worn round the neck, over the shoulders, or round the head, for warmth or ornament.

scarf[2] *noun* a joint made by thinning the ends of two pieces of timber etc., so that they overlap without an increase of thickness, and fastening them with bolts etc. –**scarf** *verb* to join in this way.

scarify *verb* (**scarified, scarifying**) **1** to loosen the surface of (soil etc.). **2** to make slight cuts in (skin or tissue) surgically.

scarlatina (skar-lă-**tee**-nă) *noun* scarlet fever.

scarlet *adjective* of brilliant red colour. –**scarlet** *noun* **1** scarlet colour. **2** a scarlet substance or material; scarlet clothes. □ **scarlet fever** an infectious fever caused by bacteria, producing a scarlet rash.

scarp *noun* a steep slope on a hillside.

scarper *verb* (*informal*) to run away.

scary *adjective* (**scarier, scariest**) **1** frightening. **2** easily frightened.

scat[1] *interjection* go!

scat[2] *noun* jazz singing that imitates musical instruments.

scathing (**skay**-*th*'ing) *adjective* **1** (of criticism) very severe. **2** making very severe criticisms.

scatter *verb* **1** to throw or put here and there, to cover in this way, *scatter gravel on the road* or *scatter the road with gravel*; *there were some scattered settlements*, situated far apart. **2** to go or send in different directions. –**scatter** *noun* scattering; the extent over which something is scattered. □ **scatter diagram** a graph in which the values of two variables are plotted along two axes, the pattern of the resulting points revealing any relationship present.

scatterbrain *noun* a person who is unable to concentrate or do things in a systematic way. **scatterbrained** *adjective*

scatty *adjective* (**scattier**, **scattiest**) (*informal*) scatterbrained, crazy. **scattily** *adverb*, **scattiness** *noun*

scavenge *verb* **1** (of an animal) to search for decaying flesh as food. **2** to search for usable objects or material among rubbish or discarded things. **scavenger** *noun*

scenario (sĕ-**nah**-ree-oh) *noun* (*plural* **scenarios**) **1** the outline or script of a film, with details of the scenes. **2** a detailed summary of the action of a play, with notes on scenery and special effects. **3** an imagined sequence of events. [Italian]

Usage Note that *scenario* does not mean 'scene' or 'situation'.

---

scene *noun* **1** the place of an actual or fictional event; *the scene of the crime*, where it happened. **2** a piece of continuous action in a play or film; a subdivision of an act. **3** an incident thought of as resembling this. **4** a dramatic outburst of temper or emotion, a stormy interview, *made a scene*. **5** stage scenery. **6** a landscape or view as seen by a spectator, *the rural scene before us*. **7** (*informal*) an area of action, a way of life, *the political scene*; *not my scene*, not what I like or want to take part in. □ **be on the scene** to be present. **scene shifter** a person who moves the scenery on a theatre stage. [from Greek *skene* = stage]

scenery *noun* **1** the general appearance of a landscape. **2** picturesque features of a landscape. **3** structures used on a theatre stage to represent features in the scene of the action.

scenic (**see**-nik) *adjective* having fine natural scenery, *the scenic road along the coast*. **scenically** *adverb*

scent *noun* **1** the characteristic pleasant smell of something. **2** a sweet-smelling liquid made from essence of flowers or aromatic chemicals. **3** the trail left by an animal and perceptible to hounds' sense of smell, indications that can be followed similarly, *followed* or *lost the scent*; *on the scent of talent*. **4** an animal's sense of smell, *dogs hunt by scent*. –**scent** *verb* **1** to discover by sense of smell, *the dog scented a rat*. **2** to begin to suspect the presence or

existence of, *she scented trouble*. **3** to put scent on (a thing); to make fragrant. **scented** *adjective* [from Latin *sentire* = perceive]

sceptic (**skep**-tik) *noun* a sceptical person; one who doubts the truth of religious doctrines.

sceptical (**skep**-ti-kăl) *adjective* inclined to disbelieve things, doubting or questioning the truth of claims or statements etc. **sceptically** *adverb* [from Greek *skeptikos* = thoughtful]

scepticism (**skep**-tĭ-sizm) *noun* a sceptical attitude of mind.

sceptre (**sep**-ter) *noun* a staff carried by a king or queen as a symbol of sovereignty.

schadenfreude *noun* the enjoyment of another's misfortune. [German, from *Schaden* 'harm' + *Freude* 'joy']

schedule (**shed**-yool) *noun* a program or timetable of planned events or of work. –**schedule** *verb* to include in a schedule, to appoint for a certain time, *the train is scheduled to stop at Maitland*. □ **on schedule** punctual according to the timetable. [from Latin *scedula* = little piece of paper]

schematic (skee-**mat**-ik) *adjective* in the form of a diagram or chart. **schematically** *adverb*

schematise (**skee**-mă-tyz) *verb* (also **-ize**) to put into schematic form; to formulate in regular order. **schematisation** *noun*

scheme (*pr.* skeem) *noun* **1** a plan of work or action. **2** a secret or underhand plan, *a scheme to defraud people*. **3** an orderly planned arrangement, *a colour scheme*. –**scheme** *verb* to make plans; to plan in a secret or underhand way. **schemer** *noun* [from Greek *skhema* = form]

scherzo (**skairts**-oh) *noun* (*plural* **scherzos**) a lively vigorous musical composition or independent section of a longer work. [Italian, = joke]

Schiller (**shil**-er), Johann Christoph Friedrich von (1759–1805), German dramatist and poet.

schism (*pr.* sizm) *noun* division into opposing groups because of a difference in belief or opinion, especially in a religious body. [from Greek *skhisma* = a split]

Usage In addition to the pronunciation given, this word is sometimes pronounced *shizm* or *skizm*.

---

schismatic (siz-**mat**-ik) *adjective* of schism. –schismatic *noun* a person who takes part in a schism. schismatically *adverb*

schist (*pr.* shist) *noun* a kind of metamorphic rock formed in layers.

schizo (**skits**-oh) *adjective* & *noun* (*plural* schizos) (*informal*) = schizophrenic.

schizoid (**skits**-oid) *adjective* resembling or suffering from schizophrenia. –schizoid *noun* a schizoid person.

schizophrenia (skits-ŏ-**freen**-ee-ă) *noun* a mental disorder in which a person becomes unable to act or think in a rational way, often with delusions and withdrawal from social relationships. [from Greek *skhizein* = to split, + *phren* = mind]

schizophrenic (skits-ŏ-**fren**-ik) *adjective* of or suffering from schizophrenia. –schizophrenic *noun* a schizophrenic person.

schmaltz (*pr.* shmawlts) *noun* sugary sentimentality, especially in music or literature. schmaltzy *adjective* [from German, = lard]

schmick *adjective* (also smick) (*Austral. informal*) stylish, excellent.

schnapps (*pr.* shnaps) *noun* a kind of strong gin.

schnitzel (**shnits**-ĕl) *noun* a fried veal cutlet. [German, = slice]

Schoenberg (**shern**-berg), Arnold Franz Walter (1874–1951), Austrian composer.

scholar *noun* 1 a person with great learning in a particular subject. 2 a person who is skilled in academic work. 3 a person who holds a scholarship. scholarly *adjective* [same origin as *school*[1]]

scholarship *noun* 1 a grant of money towards education, usually gained by means of a competitive examination. 2 great learning in a particular subject. 3 the methods and achievements characteristic of scholars and academic work.

scholastic (skŏ-**last**-ik) *adjective* of schools or education, academic. scholastically *adverb*

school[1] *noun* 1 an institution for educating or giving instruction, especially for children. 2 its buildings. 3 its pupils. 4 the time during which teaching is done there, *school ends at 4.30 p.m.* 5 the process of being educated in a school, *always hated school.* 6 the department of one branch of study in a university, *the history school.* 7 experience that gives discipline or instruction, *learned his tactics*

in a hard school. 8 a group or succession of philosophers, artists, etc. following the same teachings or principles. 9 a group of gamblers or drinkers. –school *verb* to train or discipline. □ of the old school according to old standards, *a gentleman of the old school.* school leaver a person who has just left school for good. school of thought a particular way of looking at a problem; those who hold this. [from Greek *skhole* = leisure, lecture place]

school[2] *noun* a shoal, e.g. of fish or whales. [from Old English *scolu* = troop]

schoolboy *noun* a boy at school.

schoolchild *noun* (*plural* schoolchildren) a child at school.

schoolgirl *noun* a girl at school.

schoolie (*Austral. informal*) *noun* a secondary school student, especially one who has just finished year 12.

schooling *noun* education, training, especially in a school.

schoolmaster *noun* a male schoolteacher.

schoolmistress *noun* a female schoolteacher.

schoolteacher *noun* a teacher in a school.

schooner (**skoo**-ner) *noun* 1 a kind of sailing ship with two or more masts. 2 a large beer glass or its contents.

Schopenhauer (**shoh**-pĕn-howr), Arthur (1788–1860), German philosopher.

Schrödinger (**shrer**-ding-er), Erwin (1887–1961), Austrian physicist who advanced the theoretical study of atoms and particles.

Schubert (**shoo**-bert), Franz (1797–1828), Austrian composer.

Schumann (**shoo**-măn), Robert Alexander (1810–56), German composer.

sciatic (sy-**at**-ik) *adjective* of the hip or the sciatic nerve, the largest nerve in the human body, running from pelvis to thigh.

sciatica (sy-**at**-ikă) *noun* neuralgia of the hip and thigh, pain in the sciatic nerve.

science *noun* 1 a branch of knowledge requiring systematic study and method, especially one of those dealing with substances, animal and vegetable life, and natural laws; *natural sciences*, e.g. biology, geology, and the physical sciences; *physical sciences*, e.g. physics, chemistry. 2 an expert's skilful technique, *with skill and science.* □ science fiction stories based on imaginary future scientific discoveries or changes of the environment or space travel and life on other planets. [from Latin *scientia* = knowledge]

scientific *adjective* **1** of or used in a science, *scientific apparatus*. **2** of scientists. **3** using careful and systematic study, observations, and tests of conclusions etc. □ **scientific notation** (in calculators) writing large numbers as a power of 10 multiplied by a number less than 10. **scientifically** *adverb*

scientist *noun* an expert in one or more of the natural or physical sciences.

Scientology *noun* (*trademark*) a religious system based on self-knowledge and spiritual fulfilment through courses of study and training. **Scientologist** *noun*

sci-fi (**sy**-fy) *noun* (*informal*) science fiction.

scimitar (**sim**-ĭ-ter) *noun* a short curved Oriental sword.

scintilla (sin-**til**-ă) *noun* a trace, *not a scintilla of evidence*.

scintillate (**sin**-tĭ-layt) *verb* **1** to sparkle, to give off sparks. **2** to be brilliant, *a scintillating discussion*. **scintillation** *noun* [from Latin *scintilla* = spark]

scion (**sy**-ŏn) *noun* a descendant of a family, especially a noble one. [from Old French *cion* = a twig]

scissors *plural noun* a cutting instrument made of two blades with handles for the thumb and finger(s) of one hand, pivoted so that the cutting edges can be closed on what is to be cut. [from Latin *scissum* = cut]

sclera (**skleer**-ră) *noun* = sclerotic.

sclerosis (sklě-**roh**-sĭs) *noun* a diseased condition in which soft tissue (e.g. of arteries) hardens. [from Greek *sklerosis* = hardening]

sclerotic (sklě-**rot**-ik) *adjective* of or having sclerosis. –**sclerotic** *noun* the tough outer coating in the eye round the iris; the white of the eye.

scoff[1] *verb* to jeer, to speak contemptuously. **scoffer** *noun*

scoff[2] *verb* (*informal*) to eat (food) quickly or greedily.

scold *verb* to rebuke (especially a child). –**scold** *noun* (*old use*) a nagging woman.

scoliosis (skol-ee-**oh**-sĭs) *noun* a lateral curvature of the spine. [from Greek *skolios* = bent]

sconce *noun* an ornamental bracket fixed to a wall for holding a candle or electric light.

scone (*pr*. skon) *noun* a soft flat cake of flour, fat, and milk, baked quickly.

scoop *noun* **1** a deep shovel-like tool for taking up and moving grain, sugar, coal, etc. **2** a ladle, a device with a small round bowl and a handle used for serving ice cream etc. **3** a scooping movement. **4** a piece of news discovered and published by one newspaper in advance of its rivals. –**scoop** *verb* **1** to lift or hollow with or as if with a scoop. **2** to forestall (a rival newspaper) with a news scoop.

scoot *verb* to run or dart; to go away hastily.

scooter *noun* **1** a child's toy vehicle with a footboard on wheels and a long steering-handle. **2** a kind of lightweight motorcycle with a protective shield extending from below the handlebars to where the rider's feet rest.

scope *noun* **1** the range of something, *the subject is outside the scope of this inquiry*. **2** opportunity, outlet, *a kind of work that gives scope for her abilities*. [from Greek *skopos* = target]

scorch *verb* **1** to burn or become burnt on the surface; to make or become discoloured in this way. **2** (*informal*) to drive or ride at a very high speed. –**scorch** *noun* a mark made by scorching.

scorcher *noun* (*informal*) a very hot day.

scorching *adjective* (*informal*) extremely hot.

score *noun* **1** the number of points made by each player or side in a game, or gained in a competition etc. **2** a record of this, a reckoning. **3** a reason or motive, *was rejected on the score of being old-fashioned*; *on that score*, so far as that matter is concerned. **4** a set of twenty; *scores of things*, very many. **5** a line or mark cut into something. **6** a copy of a musical composition showing the notes on sets of staves. **7** the music for an opera or musical comedy etc. **8** a record of money owing. –**score** *verb* **1** to gain (a point or points) in a game etc.; to make a score. **2** to keep a record of the score. **3** to be worth as points in a game, *a goal scores 6 points*. **4** to achieve, *scored a great success*. **5** to have an advantage, *he scores by knowing the language well*. **6** to make a clever retort that puts an opponent at a disadvantage. **7** to cut a line or mark(s) into (a thing). **8** to write out as a musical score; to arrange (a piece of music) for instruments. □ **know the score** (*informal*) to know the essential facts. **score off** (*informal*) to defeat in argument or repartee. **score out** or **through** to cancel by drawing a line through (words etc.). **scorer** *noun*

scoreboard *noun* a board where the score is displayed.

scorn *noun* strong contempt; *laughed it to scorn*, ridiculed it. –scorn *verb* 1 to feel or show strong contempt for. 2 to reject or refuse scornfully, *would scorn to ask for favours*.

scornful *adjective* feeling or showing scorn. scornfully *adverb*, scornfulness *noun*

Scorpio *noun* a sign of the zodiac, the Scorpion, which the sun enters about 23 October. Scorpian *adjective* & *noun*

scorpion *noun* a small animal of the spider group with lobster-like claws and a sting in its long jointed tail.

Scot *noun* a native of Scotland.

Scotch *adjective* of Scotland or Scottish people or their form of English. –Scotch *noun* 1 the Scottish dialect. 2 Scotch whisky, the kind distilled in Scotland especially from malted barley. □ Scotch broth soup or stew containing pearl barley and vegetables. Scotch terrier a small terrier with rough hair and short legs.

Usage Modern Scots prefer to use the words *Scots* and *Scottish*, not *Scotch*, except when the word is applied to whisky or in the compounds listed above.

scotch *verb* to put an end to, *scotched the rumour*.

scot-free *adjective* 1 unharmed; not punished. 2 free of charge. [from *scot* = tax, + *free*]

Scotland the country forming the northern part of Great Britain. □ Scotland Yard the headquarters of the London Metropolitan Police; its Criminal Investigation Department.

Scots *adjective* Scottish. –Scots *noun* the Scottish dialect. Scotsman, Scotswoman *nouns*

Scott, Robert Falcon (1868–1912), English explorer of the Antarctic, who died on the return journey from the South Pole.

Scottish *adjective* of Scotland or its people or their form of the English language.

scoundrel *noun* a dishonest or unprincipled person. scoundrelly *adverb*

scour¹ *verb* 1 to cleanse or brighten by rubbing. 2 to clear out (a channel or pipe etc.) by the force of water flowing through or over it. 3 to purge drastically. –scour *noun* scouring, the action of water on a channel etc., *the scour of the tide*. scourer *noun*

scour² *verb* to travel over (an area) in search of something, to search thoroughly.

scourge (*pr.* skerj) *noun* 1 a whip for flogging people. 2 a person or thing regarded as a great affliction. –scourge *verb* 1 to flog with a whip. 2 to afflict greatly.

scout¹ *noun* 1 a person sent out to gather information, e.g. about an enemy's movements or strength. 2 a ship or aircraft designed for reconnoitering. 3 Scout a member of the Scout Association, a youth organisation (originally for boys) intended to develop character by outdoor activities. –scout *verb* to act as scout; to make a search.

scout² *verb* to reject (an idea) scornfully.

scowl *noun* a sullen or angry frown. –scowl *verb* to make a scowl.

scrabble *verb* 1 to make a scratching movement or sound with the hands or feet. 2 to grope busily or struggle to find or obtain something.

scrag *noun* the bony part of an animal's carcass as food; neck of mutton or the less meaty end (scrag-end) of this. –scrag *verb* (scragged, scragging) (*informal*) to seize roughly by the neck; to handle roughly.

scraggy *adjective* (scraggier, scraggiest) lean and bony. scraggily *adverb*, scragginess *noun*

scram *verb* (*informal*) to go away. [from *scramble*]

scramble *verb* 1 to move as best one can over rough ground; to move hastily and awkwardly. 2 to struggle eagerly to do or obtain something. 3 (of aircraft or their crew) to hurry and take off quickly, e.g. in order to attack an invading enemy. 4 to mix together indiscriminately. 5 to cook (egg) by mixing its contents and heating the mixture in a pan until it thickens. 6 to make (a telephone conversation etc.) unintelligible except to a person with a special receiver, by altering the frequencies on which it is transmitted. –scramble *noun* 1 a climb or walk over rough ground. 2 an eager struggle to do or obtain something. 3 a motorcycle race over rough ground.

scrambler *noun* an electronic device for scrambling a transmitted telephone conversation or unscrambling it at the receiving end.

scrap¹ *noun* 1 a small detached piece of something, a fragment; a remnant. 2 rubbish, waste material; discarded metal suitable for being reprocessed. –scrap *verb* (scrapped, scrapping) to discard as useless. □ **scrap heap** a heap of waste material. **scrap merchant** a dealer in scrap.

scrap² *noun* (*informal*) a fight or quarrel. –scrap *verb* (**scrapped, scrapping**) (*informal*) to fight; to quarrel.

scrapbook *noun* a book with blank pages for drawing and sticking cuttings in.

scrape *verb* **1** to make (a thing) clean, smooth, or level by passing the hard edge of something across it. **2** to pass (an edge) across in this way. **3** to remove by doing this, *scrape mud off shoes*. **4** to excavate by scraping, *scrape a hole*. **5** to damage by scraping. **6** to make the sound of scraping. **7** to pass along or through something with difficulty, with or without touching it. **8** to obtain or amass with difficulty or by careful saving, *scrape a living*; *scrape something together* or *up*. **9** to be very economical. –scrape *noun* **1** a scraping movement or sound. **2** a scraped mark or injury. **3** a thinly applied layer of butter etc. on bread. **4** an awkward situation resulting from an escapade. □ **scrape acquaintance** to contrive to become acquainted (with a person). **scrape the barrel** to be driven to using one's last and inferior resources because the better ones are finished. **scrape through** to get through a testing situation or pass (an examination etc.) by only a small margin.

scraper *noun* a device used for scraping things.

scrappy *adjective* made up of scraps or odds and ends or disconnected elements. **scrappily** *adverb*, **scrappiness** *noun*

scrapyard *noun* a place where scrap is collected.

scratch *verb* **1** to make a shallow mark or wound on (a surface) with something sharp. **2** to form by scratching. **3** to scrape with the fingernails in order to relieve itching; *scratch my back and I'll scratch yours*, promote my interests and I will promote yours. **4** to make a thin scraping sound. **5** to obtain with difficulty, *scratch a living*. **6** to cancel by drawing a line through, *scratch it out*. **7** to withdraw from a race or competition, *was obliged to scratch*; *scratched his horse*. –scratch *noun* **1** a mark or wound made by scratching. **2** a spell of scratching. **3** a line from which competitors start in a race when they receive no handicap; *a scratch player*, one who receives no handicap in a game. –scratch *adjective* collected from whatever is available, *a scratch team*. □ **start from scratch** to begin at the

very beginning; to begin with no advantage or preparation. **up to scratch** up to the required standard. **scratchy** *adjective*, **scratchily** *adverb*, **scratchiness** *noun*

scrawl *noun* bad handwriting; something written in this. –scrawl *verb* to write in a scrawl.

scrawny *adjective* scraggy.

scream *verb* **1** to make a long piercing cry of pain, terror, annoyance, or excitement. **2** to utter in a screaming tone. **3** (of the wind or a machine etc.) to make a loud piercing sound. **4** to laugh uncontrollably. –scream *noun* **1** a screaming cry or sound. **2** (*informal*) an extremely amusing person or thing.

scree *noun* a mass of loose stones on a mountainside, sliding when trodden on.

screech *noun* a harsh high-pitched scream or sound. –screech *verb* to make a screech; to utter with a screech.

screed *noun* **1** a tiresomely long list or letter or other document. **2** a strip of plaster, wood, or other material fixed to a wall or floor etc. as a guide to the correct thickness of a coat of plaster or concrete to be laid. **3** a finishing layer of mortar, cement, etc. spread over a floor. –screed *verb* to level by means of a screed; to apply (material) as a screed.

screen *noun* **1** an upright structure used to conceal, protect, or divide something. **2** anything serving a similar purpose, *under the screen of night*. **3** a windscreen. **4** a blank surface on which pictures, cinema films, etc. are projected. **5** the surface of a television set or visual display unit on which the images appear. **6** a large sieve or riddle, especially one used for sorting grain or coal etc. into sizes. –screen *verb* **1** to shelter, conceal, or protect. **2** to protect (a person) from discovery or deserved blame by diverting suspicion from him or her. **3** to show (images or a cinema film etc.) on a screen; to broadcast (a television program). **4** to pass (grain or coal etc.) through a screen. **5** to examine systematically in order to discover something, e.g. a person's suitability for a post where national security is involved, or the presence or absence of a substance or disease. □ **screen door** a door fitted with a flyscreen. **screen printing** a process like stencilling with ink or dye forced through a prepared sheet of fine fabric. **screen saver** a computer program which, after a set time, replaces an unchanging screen display with a moving image to prevent damage.

screen test a test of a person's suitability for taking part in a film.

screenplay *noun* the script of a film.

screw *noun* 1 a metal pin with a spiral ridge (the *thread*) round its length, used for holding things together by being twisted in under pressure, or secured by a nut. 2 a thing turned like a screw and used for tightening something or exerting pressure. 3 a propeller, especially of a ship or motor boat. 4 the act of screwing. 5 (*informal*) a prison officer. –**screw** *verb* 1 to fasten or tighten with a screw or screws; to fasten by twisting like a screw; *her head is screwed on the right way*, she has sound common sense. 2 to turn (a screw); to twist or become twisted. 3 to oppress; to extort, *screwed a promise out of her*. □ **have a screw loose** (*informal*) to be slightly mad. **put the screws on** (*informal*) to put pressure on, e.g. to intimidate or extort money. **screw cap, screw top** a cap that screws on to the opening of a container. **screw-top** *adjective* **screw up** to contract (one's eyes); to twist (one's face) out of the natural expression, e.g. in disgust; to summon up (one's courage); (*informal*) to bungle, to mismanage.

screwball *adjective & noun* (*informal*) crazy, a crazy person.

screwdriver *noun* a tool with a narrow end for turning screws that have a matching slotted head.

screwy *adjective* (**screwier**, **screwiest**) (*informal*) 1 crazy, eccentric. 2 absurd.

scribble *verb* 1 to write hurriedly or carelessly. 2 to make meaningless marks. –**scribble** *noun* something scribbled; hurried or careless writing; scribbled meaningless marks. **scribbler** *noun* [same origin as *scribe*]

scribe *noun* 1 a person who (before the invention of printing) made copies of writings. 2 (in New Testament times) a professional religious scholar. **scribal** *adjective* [from Latin *scribere* = write]

scrim *noun* a loosely-woven cotton fabric.

scrimmage *noun* a confused struggle; a skirmish.

scrimp *verb* to skimp.

scrimshank *verb* (*informal*) to shirk work.

scrip *noun* an extra share or shares (in a business company) issued instead of a dividend, *a scrip issue*. [short for *subscription receipt*]

script *noun* 1 handwriting. 2 a style of printed or typewritten characters resembling this. 3 the text of a play, film, or broadcast talk etc. 4 a candidate's written answer-paper in an examination. –**script** *verb* to write a script for (a film etc.). [from Latin *scriptum* = written]

scripture *noun* any sacred writings. –**Scripture** or **the Scriptures** the sacred writings of the Christians (the Old and New Testaments) or the Jews (the Old Testament). **scriptural** *adjective* [same origin as *script*]

scrofula (**skrof**-yŭ-lă) *noun* a disease causing glandular swellings. **scrofulous** *adjective*

scroll *noun* 1 a roll of paper or parchment. 2 an ornamental design resembling a scroll or in spiral form. –**scroll** *verb* to move (a display on a computer screen) up or down.

Scrooge *noun* a miser. [named after a character in Dickens's novel *A Christmas Carol*]

scrotum (**skroh**-tŭm) *noun* the pouch of skin that encloses the testicles in most mammals, behind the penis. **scrotal** *adjective*

scrounge *verb* (*informal*) 1 to cadge. 2 to collect by foraging. **scrounger** *noun*

scrub¹ *noun* vegetation consisting of stunted trees or shrubs; land covered with this. **scrubby** *adjective*

scrub² *verb* (**scrubbed**, **scrubbing**) 1 to rub hard with something coarse or bristly; to clean in this way with a wet brush. 2 (*informal*) to cancel, to scrap, *we'll have to scrub our plans*. –**scrub** *noun* scrubbing, being scrubbed, *give it a scrub*. □ **scrub up** (of a surgeon etc.) to clean the hands and arms by scrubbing, before an operation.

scrubber *noun* a beast that has been bred in or has escaped into the wild.

scruff *noun* the back of the neck as used to grasp, lift, or drag a person or animal.

scruffy *adjective* (**scruffier**, **scruffiest**) shabby and untidy. **scruffily** *adverb*, **scruffiness** *noun*

scrum *noun* 1 a scrummage. 2 a milling crowd; a confused struggle. □ **scrum-half** *noun* a half-back who puts the ball into the scrum.

scrummage *noun* (in rugby football) the grouping of the forwards of each side with arms interlocked and heads down to push against each other and try to heel back the ball thrown on the ground between them.

scrumptious *adjective* (*informal*) delicious, delightful.

scrunch *verb* to crunch, crush, or crumple.

scruple *noun* a feeling of doubt or hesitation about doing or allowing an action, produced by one's conscience or principles. –scruple *verb* to hesitate because of scruples.

scrupulous (**skroop**-yŭ-lŭs) *adjective* 1 very conscientious even in small matters; painstakingly careful and thorough. 2 strictly honest or honourable. scrupulously *adverb*, scrupulousness *noun*

scrutineer *noun* a person who scrutinises ballot papers.

scrutinise *verb* (also -ize) to look at or examine carefully.

scrutiny *noun* a careful look or examination of something.

scuba *noun* a portable underwater breathing apparatus. [from the initials of *self-contained underwater breathing apparatus*]

scud *verb* (scudded, scudding) to move along straight, fast, and smoothly, *clouds were scudding across the sky*. –scud *noun* clouds or spray driven by the wind; a short shower of driving rain.

scuff *verb* 1 to scrape or drag (one's feet) in walking. 2 to mark or wear away by doing this. 3 to scrape (a thing) with one's foot or feet. –scuff *noun* a mark made by scuffing.

scuffle *noun* a confused struggle or fight at close quarters. –scuffle *verb* to take part in a scuffle.

scull *noun* 1 each of a pair of small oars used by a single rower. 2 an oar that rests on the stern of a boat, worked with a screw-like movement. –scull *verb* to row with sculls.

scullery *noun* a room where dishes etc. are washed up.

scullion *noun* (*old use*) a cook's boy assistant; one who washes dishes.

sculpt *verb* (*informal*) to sculpture.

sculptor *noun* a person who makes sculptures. sculptress *feminine noun*

sculptural *adjective* of sculpture.

sculpture *noun* 1 the art of carving in wood or stone or producing shapes in cast metal. 2 a work made in this way. –sculpture *verb* to represent in sculpture; to decorate with sculptures; to be a sculptor. [from Latin *sculpere* = carve]

scum *noun* 1 impurities that rise to the surface of a liquid; a film of material floating on the surface of a stretch of water. 2 people regarded as the most worthless part of the population. –scum *verb* (scummed, scumming) 1 to

remove the scum from. 2 to form a scum. scummy *adjective*

scungy *adjective* (*informal*) disagreeable, squalid.

scupper *noun* an opening in a ship's side to carry off water from the deck. –scupper *verb* 1 to sink (a ship) deliberately. 2 (*informal*) to wreck.

scurf *noun* 1 flakes of dry skin, especially from the scalp. 2 any dry scaly matter on a surface. scurfy *adjective*

scurrilous (**sku**-rĭ-lŭs) *adjective* 1 abusive and insulting. 2 coarsely humorous. scurrilously *adverb*, scurrility (sku-**ril**-ĭ-tee) *noun*

scurry *verb* (scurried, scurrying) to run or move hurriedly, especially with quick short steps; to hurry. –scurry *noun* 1 scurrying, a rush. 2 a flurry of rain or snow.

scurvy *noun* a disease caused by lack of vitamin C in the diet. –scurvy *adjective* paltry; dishonourable, contemptible. scurvily *adverb*, scurviness *noun*

scut *noun* a short tail, especially that of a hare, rabbit, or deer.

scuttle[1] *noun* 1 a bucket or portable boxlike container for holding a supply of coal in a room. 2 the part of a car body between the windscreen and the bonnet. [from Latin *scutella* = dish]

scuttle[2] *noun* a small opening with a lid, on a ship's deck or side or in a roof or wall. –scuttle *verb* to let water into (a ship) in order to sink it. [from Spanish *escotar* = to cut out]

scuttle[3] *verb* to scurry; to hurry away. –scuttle *noun* a scuttling run; a hasty departure. [from *scud*]

Scylla (**sil**-ă) (*Gk. myth.*) a female sea monster who devoured men from ships when they tried to navigate the narrow channel between her cave and the whirlpool Charybdis.

scythe (*pr.* syth) *noun* an implement with a slightly curved blade on a long wooden pole with two handles, used for cutting long grass or grain. –scythe *verb* to cut with a scythe.

SD card *noun* a memory card with flash memory for use in digital cameras, mobile phones, etc. [from the initials *secure digital*]

SE *abbreviation* south-east; south-eastern.

se- *prefix* 1 apart; aside (as in *secluded*). 2 without (as in *secure*). [Latin]

sea *noun* 1 the expanse of salt water that covers most of the earth's surface and surrounds the continents. **2** any part of this as opposed to dry land or fresh water; a named section of it partly enclosed by land, *the Mediterranean Sea*. **3** a large inland lake of either salt or fresh water, *the Sea of Galilee*. **4** the waves of the sea; the movement or state of these; *a heavy sea*, with great waves. **5** a vast expanse of something, *a sea of faces*. □ **at sea** in a ship on the sea; perplexed, not knowing how to proceed. **by sea** carried or conveyed in a ship. **on the sea** in a ship on the sea; situated on a coast. **sea anchor** a bag dragged in the water to slow the drifting of a vessel. **sea anemone** a tube-shaped sea animal with petal-like tentacles round its mouth. **sea change** a notable or unexpected transformation; (*Austral.*) a significant change in lifestyle, especially by moving from the city to a seaside town. **sea cucumber** a sea animal with a long thin body. **sea fish** a fish living in the sea, not a freshwater fish. **sea green** bluish-green. **sea-green** *adjective* **sea horse** a small fish with a horselike head at right angles to its body, and a tail that can be wrapped round a support. **sea lane** a lane for ships (*see* **lane**, sense 3). **sea legs** ability to walk steadily on the deck of a moving ship, *hasn't got his sea legs yet*. **sea level** the level corresponding to that of the surface of the sea halfway between high and low water. **sea lion** a kind of large seal of the Pacific Ocean. **sea mew** a gull. **sea salt** salt obtained from sea water by evaporation. **sea serpent** a huge serpentine monster reported as seen in the sea. **sea urchin** a sea animal with a round shell covered in sharp spikes.

seabird *noun* a bird that frequents the sea or land near the sea.

seaboard *noun* the coast or its outline.

seaborgium (see-**bor**-gee-ŭm) *noun* a very unstable artificial element (symbol Sg).

seafarer *noun* a seafaring person.

seafaring *adjective* & *noun* working or travelling on the sea, especially as one's regular occupation.

seafood *noun* fish or shellfish from the sea eaten as food.

seafront *noun* the part of a town facing the sea.

seagoing *adjective* **1** (of ships) ocean-going. **2** (of people) seafaring.

seagull *noun* a gull.

seal¹ *noun* an amphibious sea animal with short limbs that serve chiefly for swimming, and thick fur or bristles.

seal² *noun* **1** a gem or piece of metal etc. with an engraved design that is pressed on wax or other soft material to leave an impression. **2** this impression or a piece of wax bearing it, attached to a document as a guarantee of authenticity, or to an envelope or box or room etc. to show that (while the seal is unbroken) the contents have not been tampered with since it was affixed. **3** a mark, event, or action etc. serving to confirm or guarantee something, *gave it their seal of approval*. **4** a small decorative paper sticker resembling a postage stamp. **5** a substance or fitting used to close an opening etc. and prevent air or liquid etc. from passing through it. –**seal** *verb* **1** to affix a seal to. **2** to stamp or certify as authentic in this way. **3** to close securely so as to prevent penetration; to coat or surface with a protective substance or sealant; *a sealed road*, a road covered with bitumen. **4** to stick down (an envelope etc.); *it's a sealed book to me*, it is a subject of which I have no understanding. **5** to settle or decide, *his fate was sealed*. □ **seal off** to prevent access to (an area).

sealant *noun* a substance used for coating a surface to make it watertight.

sealer *noun* a ship or hunter that hunts seals.

sealing wax *noun* a substance that is soft when heated but hardens when cooled, used for sealing letters etc.

sealskin *noun* the skin or prepared fur of a seal used as a clothing material.

seam *noun* **1** the line or groove where two edges join, especially of cloth or leather etc. or wood. **2** a surface line such as a wrinkle or scar. **3** a layer of coal etc. in the ground. –**seam** *verb* **1** to join by means of a seam. **2** to mark with a wrinkle or scar etc. □ **seam bowler** a bowler in cricket who makes the ball bounce off its seam.

seaman *noun* (*plural* **seamen**) **1** a sailor, especially one below the rank of officer. **2** a person who is skilled in seafaring.

seamanship *noun* skill in seafaring.

seamstress (**seem**-strĕs) *noun* a woman whose job is sewing things.

seamy *adjective* (**seamier**, **seamiest**) showing seams. □ **seamy side** the less presentable or less attractive aspect of life.

seance (**say**-ahns) *noun* a spiritualist meeting. [French, = sitting]

seaplane *noun* an aeroplane, especially one with floats, designed to alight on and take off from a stretch of water.

seaport *noun* a port on the coast.

sear *verb* to scorch or burn the surface of; *a searing pain*, a burning pain.

search *verb* **1** to look or go over (a place etc.) in order to find something. **2** to examine the clothes and body of (a person) to see if something is concealed there. **3** to examine thoroughly, *search your conscience.* –**search** *noun* the act or process of searching. □ **search engine** a computer program that searches for items on the Internet etc. **searching question** one that probes deeply. **search party** a group of people organised to look for a lost person or thing. **search warrant** a warrant allowing officials to enter the premises of a person thought to be concealing stolen property etc. **searcher** *noun*

searching *adjective* (of an examination) thorough.

searchlight *noun* **1** an outdoor electric lamp with a reflector producing a powerful beam that can be turned in any direction, used e.g. for discovering hostile aircraft. **2** its beam.

seascape *noun* a picture or view of the sea.

seashell *noun* the shell of any mollusc living in salt water.

seashore *noun* land close to the sea.

seasick *adjective* made sick or queasy by the motion of a ship. **seasickness** *noun*

season *noun* **1** a section of the year with distinct characteristics of temperature and rainfall. **2** the time of year when something is common or plentiful, or when an activity takes place, *the cricket season.* **3** an indefinite period. –**season** *verb* **1** to give extra flavour to (food) by adding salt or pepper or other sharp-tasting substances. **2** to bring into a fit condition for use by drying or treating or allowing to mature; to become seasoned in this way. **3** to make (people) competent by training and experience, *seasoned soldiers.* □ **in season** (of food) available plentifully and in good condition for eating; (of an animal) on heat; (of advice) given when likely to be heeded. **out of season** (of food) not in season. **season ticket** a ticket that allows a person to travel between certain destinations, or to attend performances etc., for a specified period.

seasonable *adjective* **1** suitable for the season, *hot weather is seasonable in summer.* **2** timely, opportune. **seasonably** *adverb*

seasonal *adjective* of a season or seasons, varying according to these, *the seasonal migration of geese; fruit-picking is seasonal work.*

Usage Note the difference between *seasonal* and *seasonable.*

seasoning *noun* a substance used to season food.

seat *noun* **1** a thing made or used for sitting on. **2** a place where one sits; a place for one person to sit in a theatre or vehicle etc. **3** the right to sit as a member of a council or committee or parliament etc.; such a member's electorate. **4** the horizontal part of a chair etc. on which a sitter's body rests. **5** the part supporting another part in a machine. **6** the buttocks; the part of a skirt or trousers covering these. **7** the place where something is based or located, *the seat of government.* **8** (*Brit.*) a country mansion. **9** the manner in which a person sits on a horse etc. –**seat** *verb* **1** to cause to sit; *seat oneself* or *be seated*, to sit down. **2** to provide sitting accommodation for, *the hall seats 500.* **3** to put a seat on (a chair). **4** to put (machinery) on its support. □ **seat belt** a strap securing a person to a seat in a vehicle or aircraft, for safety.

seated *adjective* **1** sitting. **2** (of garments) having the seat worn out or misshapen from sitting.

seaward *adjective* & *adverb* towards the sea. **seawards** *adverb*

seaweed *noun* any of various plants that grow in the sea or on rocks washed by the sea.

seaworthy *adjective* (of a ship) in a fit state for a sea voyage.

sebaceous (sĕ-**bay**-shŭs) *adjective* secreting an oily or greasy substance, *sebaceous glands.* [from Latin *sebum* = grease]

sec *abbreviation* secant.

secant (see-kănt) *noun* a straight line that cuts a curve, especially a circle, at two points. □ **secant of an angle** the ratio of the length of the hypotenuse to the length of the side adjacent to that angle in a right-angled triangle. [from Latin *secans* = cutting]

secateurs (sek-ă-**terz** *or* **sek**-ă-terz) *plural noun* clippers used with one hand for pruning plants. [from Latin *secare* = to cut]

secede (sĕ-**seed**) *verb* to withdraw oneself from membership of an organisation. [from *se-* = aside, + Latin *cedere* = go]

secession (sĕ-**sesh**-ŏn) *noun* seceding.

seclude *verb* to keep (a person) apart from others.

secluded *adjective* (of a place) screened or sheltered from view. [from *se-* = aside, + Latin *claudere* = to shut]

seclusion (sĕ-**kloo**-*zh*ŏn) *noun* secluding; being secluded, privacy.

second¹ (**sek**-ŏnd) *adjective* **1** next after first. **2** another after the first, *a second chance.* **3** of a secondary kind, subordinate, inferior, *second quality; the second eleven.* **–second** *noun* **1** something that is second; the second day of a month. **2** second-class honours in a university degree. **3** second gear. **4** an attendant of a person taking part in a duel or boxing match. **5** a sixtieth part of a minute of time or angular measurement. **6** (*informal*) a short time, *wait a second.* **–second** *adverb* in second place, rank, or position. **–second** *verb* **1** to assist. **2** to state formally that one supports a motion that has been put forward by another person, in order to show that the proposer is not isolated or as a means of bringing it to be voted on. **seconds** *plural noun* **1** goods rated second-class in quality, having some flaws. **2** a second helping of food. **3** a second course at a meal. □ **second-best** *adjective* of second or inferior quality; *come off second-best*, to be the loser in a contest or dispute. **second childhood** childishness caused by mental weakness in old age. **second class** a group of persons or things, or a standard of accommodation, achievement, etc., less good than first class (but better than third). **second-class** *adjective* of second or lesser quality; of or using less good accommodation etc. than first class; (*adverb*) in or by second-class accommodation etc., *we travelled second-class.* **second cousin** *see* cousin. **second fiddle** a subsidiary or secondary role, *had to play second fiddle to his brother.* **second gear** the second lowest gear in a vehicle. **at second hand** obtained indirectly, not from the original source. **second-hand** *adjective* & *adverb* (also **secondhand**) bought after use by a previous owner; dealing in used goods, *a second-hand shop*; at second hand, obtained or experienced in this way. **second in command** the person next in rank to the commanding or chief officer or official. **second lieutenant** an army officer immediately below lieutenant. **second**

name a surname. **second nature** a habit or characteristic that has become automatic, *secrecy is second nature to him.* **second officer** the assistant mate on a merchant ship. **second person** *see* person. **second-rate** *adjective* not of the best quality, rated second-class. **second sight** the supposed power to foresee future events. **second teeth** adults' permanent teeth, appearing after the milk teeth have fallen out. **second thoughts** a change of mind after reconsideration. **second wind** recovery of one's ease of breathing during exercise, after having become out of breath. **seconder** *noun* [from Latin *secundus* = next]

second² (sĕ-**kond**) *verb* to transfer (an officer or official) temporarily to another appointment or department. **secondment** *noun*

secondary *adjective* **1** coming after what is primary. **2** of lesser importance or rank etc. than the first. **3** derived from what is primary or original, *secondary sources.* □ **secondary colours** colours obtained by mixing two primary colours. **secondary education** or **school** that for people who have received primary education but have not yet proceeded to a university or occupation. **secondarily** *adverb*

secondly *adverb* second, as a second consideration.

secrecy *noun* **1** being kept secret. **2** keeping things secret, *was pledged to secrecy.*

secret *adjective* **1** kept or intended to be kept from the knowledge or view of others, to be known only by specified people. **2** working or operating secretly. **–secret** *noun* **1** something kept or intended to be kept secret. **2** a mystery, a thing no one properly understands, *the secrets of nature.* **3** a method (not known to everyone) for attaining something, *the secret of good health.* □ **in secret** secretly. **in** or **in on the secret** among those who know something kept secret from most people. **secret agent** a spy acting for a country. **secret ballot** one in which individual voters' choices are not made public. **secret police** a police force operating in secret for political purposes. **secret service** a government department responsible for conducting espionage. **secret society** a society whose members are sworn to secrecy about it. **secretly** *adverb* [from Latin *secretum* = set apart]

secretarial (sek-rĕ-**tair**-ree-ăl) *adjective* of or involving the work of a secretary.

secretariat (sek-rĕ-**tair**-ree-ăt) *noun* an administrative office or department; its members or premises.

secretary (sek-rĕ-tă-ree) *noun* 1 a person employed to help deal with correspondence, typing, filing, and similar routine work. 2 an official in charge of the correspondence and records of an organisation. 3 the head of a public service department. □ secretary bird a long-legged African bird with a crest likened to quill pens placed behind a writer's ear. secretary-general *noun* the principal administrator of a large organisation. Secretary of State (in the US) the chief government official responsible for foreign affairs.

secrete (sĕ-**kreet**) *verb* 1 to put (an object) into a place of concealment. 2 to form and send out (a substance) into the body, either for excretion (*kidneys secrete urine*) or for use within the body (*the liver secretes bile*). secretor *noun*, secretory *adjective* [from *secret*]

secretion (sĕ-**kree**-shŏn) *noun* 1 secreting; being secreted. 2 a substance secreted by an organ or cell of the body.

secretive (**seek**-rĕ-tiv) *adjective* making a secret of things unnecessarily, uncommunicative. secretively *adverb*, secretiveness *noun*

sect *noun* a group of people with religious or other beliefs that differ from those more generally accepted.

sectarian (sek-**tair**-ree-ăn) *adjective* 1 of or belonging to a sect or sects. 2 narrow-mindedly putting the beliefs or interests of one's sect before more general interests.

section *noun* 1 a distinct part or portion of something. 2 a cross-section. 3 the process of cutting or separating something surgically. 4 (*Austral.*) a fare stage on a bus or tram route. 5 (*Amer. & Austral. old use*) an area of surveyed land. –section *verb* to divide into sections. [from Latin *sectum* = cut]

sectional *adjective* 1 of a section or sections. 2 of one section of a group or community as distinct from others or from the whole. 3 made in sections, *sectional fishing rod*.

sector *noun* 1 any of the parts into which a battle area is divided for the purpose of controlling operations. 2 a similar division of an activity, *the private sector of industry*. 3 a section of a circular area between two lines drawn from its centre to its circumference.

4 (in computing) a subdivision of a track on a magnetic disk.

secular (**sek**-yŭ-ler) *adjective* 1 concerned with worldly affairs rather than spiritual ones. 2 not involving or belonging to religion, *secular music*; *secular clergy*, clergy who are not members of a monastic community. secularity (sek-yŭ-**la**-rĭ-tee) *noun*

secure *adjective* safe (especially against attack); certain not to slip or fail, reliable. –secure *verb* 1 to make secure. 2 to fasten securely. 3 to obtain. 4 to guarantee by pledging something as security, *the loan is secured on the property*. securely *adverb* [from Latin, = free from worry (*se-* = apart, *cura* = care)]

security *noun* 1 a state or feeling of being secure; something that gives this. 2 the safety of a country or organisation against espionage, theft, or other danger. 3 a thing that serves as a guarantee or pledge, *offered the deeds of his house as security for the loan*. 4 a certificate showing ownership of financial stocks, bonds, or shares. □ security blanket a blanket or piece of material carried by a child; anything giving a sense of security. Security Council a principal council of the United Nations seeking to maintain peace and security.

sedan (sĕ-**dan**) *noun* 1 (in full sedan chair) an enclosed chair for one person (used in the 17th–18th centuries), mounted on two poles and carried by two bearers. 2 a car with a closed body, seating at least four people.

sedate (sĕ-**dayt**) *adjective* calm and dignified, not lively. –sedate *verb* to treat (a person) with sedatives. sedately *adverb*, sedateness *noun*, sedation *noun* [from Latin *sedatum* = made calm]

sedative (**sed**-ă-tiv) *adjective* having a calming or soothing effect. –sedative *noun* a sedative medicine or influence.

sedentary (**sed**-ĕn-tă-ree) *adjective* 1 spending much time seated, *sedentary workers*. 2 requiring much sitting, *sedentary work*. [from Latin *sedens* = sitting]

sedge *noun* a grasslike plant growing in marshes or near water; a bed of this.

sediment *noun* 1 very fine particles of solid matter suspended in a liquid or settling to the bottom of it. 2 solid matter (e.g. sand, gravel) that is carried by water or wind and settles on the surface of land. [from Latin *sedere* = sit]

sedimentary (sed-ĭ-**ment**-ă-ree) *adjective* of or like sediment; *sedimentary rocks*, those formed from sediment carried by water or wind.

sedimentation *noun* the depositing of a sediment.

sedition (sĕ-**dish**-ŏn) *noun* words or actions that make people rebel against the authority of the State. **seditious** (sĕ-**dish**-ŭs) *adjective*

seduce (sĕ-**dewss**) *verb* **1** to persuade (especially into wrongdoing) by offering temptations, *was seduced into betraying his country*. **2** to tempt (a person) immorally into sexual intercourse. **seducer** *noun* [from *se-* = aside, + Latin *ducere* = to lead]

seduction *noun* **1** seducing; being seduced. **2** a tempting and attractive feature, *the seductions of country life*.

seductive *adjective* tending to seduce, alluring. **seductively** *adverb*, **seductiveness** *noun*

sedulous (**sed**-yŭ-lŭs) *adjective* diligent and persevering. **sedulously** *adverb*, **sedulousness** *noun*

see¹ *verb* (**saw**, **seen**, **seeing**) **1** to perceive with the eyes; to have or use the power of doing this. **2** to perceive with the mind, to understand, *I can't see why not*; *see?*, do you understand? **3** to have a certain opinion about; *as I see it*, in my opinion. **4** to consider, to take time to do this, *must see what can be done*; *let me see, how can we fix it?* **5** to watch, to be a spectator of, *went to see a film*. **6** to look at for information, *see page 310*. **7** to meet, to be near and recognise, *saw her in church*. **8** to discover, *see who is at the door*. **9** to experience, to undergo, *saw service during the war*; *won't see 50 again*, is over this age. **10** to grant or obtain an interview with, to consult, *the manager will see you now*; *must see the doctor about my wrist*. **11** to escort, to conduct, *see her to the door*. **12** to make sure, *see that this letter goes today*. □ **see about** to attend to. **see off** to accompany to the point of departure for a journey and take leave of (a person) when he or she sets out; to chase away (an intruder). **see red** to be suddenly filled with fury. **see stars** to see dancing lights before one's eyes as the result of a blow on the head. **see the back of** to be rid of. **see the light** to understand after failing to do so, to realise one's mistakes. **see things** to have hallucinations. **see through** to understand the true nature of, not be deceived by; *see a thing through*, not abandon it before it is completed. **see-through** *adjective* transparent. **see to** to attend to.

see² *noun* the position or district of a bishop or archbishop. [from Latin *sedes* = seat]

seed *noun* (*plural* **seeds** *or* **seed**) **1** a fertilised ovule of a plant, capable of developing into a plant like its parent. **2** seeds as collected for sowing, *to be kept for seed*. **3** semen; milt. **4** (*old use*) offspring, descendants, *Abraham and his seed*. **5** something from which a tendency or feeling etc. can develop, *sowing the seeds of doubt in their minds*. **6** (*informal*) a seeded player. –**seed** *verb* **1** to plant seeds in; to sprinkle with seeds. **2** to place particles in (a cloud) to cause condensation and produce rain. **3** to remove seeds from (fruit). **4** to name (a strong player) as not to be matched against another named in this way in the early rounds of a knockout tournament, so as to increase the interest of later rounds. □ **go** or **run to seed** to cease flowering as seed develops; to become shabby and careless of appearance; to deteriorate in ability or efficiency. **seed potato** a potato kept for seed.

seedless *adjective* not containing seeds.

seedling *noun* a very young plant growing from a seed.

seedpearl *noun* a very small pearl.

seedy *adjective* (**seedier**, **seediest**) **1** full of seeds. **2** (*informal*) looking shabby and disreputable. **3** (*informal*) feeling slightly ill. **seedily** *adverb*, **seediness** *noun*

seeing *see* see¹. □ **seeing that** in view of the fact that, because.

seek *verb* (**sought**, **seeking**) to make a search or inquiry for; to try to find, obtain, or do. □ **seek out** to seek specially, to make a special effort to meet and address (a person).

seem *verb* to appear to be or to exist or to be true.

seeming *adjective* having an appearance of being something but not necessarily being this in fact. **seemingly** *adverb*

seemly *adjective* proper, suitable, in accordance with accepted standards of good taste. **seemliness** *noun*

seen *see* see¹.

seep *verb* to ooze slowly out or through.

seepage (**seep**-ij) *noun* seeping; the amount that seeps out.

seer *noun* **1** a prophet, a person who sees visions. **2** one who sees. [from *see¹*]

seersucker *noun* fabric woven with a puckered surface. [from Persian, = milk and sugar, or a striped garment]

see-saw *noun* **1** a children's amusement consisting of a long board balanced on a central support so that when a person sits on each end the two can make one end go up and the other down alternately. **2** an up-and-down change that is constantly repeated. –**see-saw** *verb* to ride on a see-saw; to make this movement.

seethe *verb* **1** to bubble or surge as in boiling. **2** to be very agitated or excited.

segment (**seg**-měnt) *noun* a part cut off or separable or marked off as though separable from the other parts of a thing. □ **segment of a circle** the part enclosed between an arc and the chord joining the ends of the arc. **segmental** (seg-**men**-tăl) *adjective*

segmented (seg-**ment**-ĕd) *adjective* divided into segments. **segmentation** *noun*

segregate (**seg**-rĕ-gayt) *verb* **1** to put apart from the rest, to isolate. **2** to separate (people) according to their race or sex. **segregation** *noun* [from *se-* = apart, + Latin *gregatum* = herded]

segregationist *noun* a person who is in favour of racial segregation.

seigneur (sayn-**yer**) *noun* a feudal lord. **seigneurial** *adjective* [same origin as *senior*]

Seine (*pr.* sayn) a river of northern France, flowing through Paris to the English Channel.

seine (*pr.* sayn) *noun* a large fishing net that hangs vertically with floats at the top and weights at the bottom, the ends being drawn together to enclose fish as it is hauled ashore.

seismic (**syz**-mik) *adjective* **1** of an earthquake or earthquakes. **2** of or using vibrations of the earth that are produced artificially by explosions. **seismically** *adverb*

seismogram (**syz**-mŏ-gram) *noun* the record given by a seismograph. [from Greek *seismos* = earthquake, + *-gram*]

seismograph (**syz**-mŏ-grahf) *noun* an instrument for detecting, recording, and measuring earthquakes. [from Greek *seismos* = earthquake, + *-graph*]

seismography (syz-**mog**-ră-fee) *noun* the study or recording of natural or artificially produced seismic effects. **seismographer** *noun*, **seismographic** *adjective*

seismology (syz-**mol**-ŏ-jee) *noun* seismography. **seismological** *adjective*, **seismologist** *noun* [from Greek *seismos* = earthquake, + *-logy*]

seismometer (syz-**mom**-ĕ-ter) *noun* a seismograph. [from Greek *seismos* = earthquake, + *meter*]

seize *verb* **1** to take hold of (a thing) forcibly, suddenly, or eagerly. **2** to take possession of (a thing) forcibly or by legal right, *seize smuggled goods*. **3** to have a sudden overwhelming effect on, *panic seized us*. **4** to seize up. □ **seize on** to make use of (an excuse etc.) eagerly. **seize up** (of a moving part or the machine containing it) to become stuck or jam because of friction or undue heat.

seizure (**see**-zher) *noun* **1** seizing; being seized. **2** a sudden attack of epilepsy or apoplexy etc., a stroke.

seldom *adverb* rarely, not often.

select *verb* to pick out as best or most suitable. –**select** *adjective* **1** chosen for excellence. **2** (of a society) exclusive, admitting only certain people as members. □ **select committee** a small committee appointed to make a special investigation. [from *se-* = apart, + Latin *legere* = pick]

selection *noun* **1** selecting, being selected. **2** the people or things selected. **3** a collection of things from which a choice can be made. **4** (*Austral.*) = **free-selection**. **5** (*Austral.*) a small farm or rural property.

selective *adjective* **1** choosing; involving choice. **2** chosen or choosing carefully. **selectively** *adverb*, **selectivity** *noun*

selector *noun* **1** a person who selects, especially one choosing the members of a sports team. **2** a device in a machine etc. that selects the appropriate gear, circuit, etc. **3** (*Austral.*) a free-selector; a farmer owning a small property.

Selene (sĕ-**lee**-nee) (*Gk. myth.*) the goddess of the moon.

selenium (sĕ-**leen**-ee-ŭm) *noun* a chemical element (symbol Se) that is a semiconductor and has various applications in electronics. [from Greek *selene* = moon]

self *noun* (*plural* **selves**) **1** a person as an individual, *one's own self*. **2** a person's special nature; *she is her old self again*, has regained her former personality. **3** one's own interests, advantage, or pleasure, *always puts self first*. **4** (*humorous* or in commerce) myself, herself, himself, etc., *I have got tickets for self and friend*; *the cheque is payable to self.* –**self** *adjective* of the same colour or material as that used for the whole, *a dress with self belt.*

self- *prefix* of, to, or done by oneself or itself.

self-addressed *adjective* (of an envelope for containing a reply) addressed to oneself.

self-assertive *adjective* asserting oneself confidently. self-assertion *noun*

self-assured *adjective* self-confident. self-assurance *noun*

self-catering *adjective* catering for oneself, especially while on holiday.

self-centred *adjective* thinking chiefly of oneself or one's own affairs, selfish.

self-command *noun* self-control.

self-confessed *adjective* openly admitting oneself to be, *a self-confessed coward*.

self-confident *adjective* having confidence in one's own abilities. self-confidence *noun*

self-conscious *adjective* embarrassed or unnatural in manner from knowing that one is being observed by others. self-consciousness *noun*

self-contained *adjective* 1 complete in itself; (of accommodation) having all the necessary facilities and not sharing these. 2 (of a person) able to do without the company of others.

self-control *noun* ability to control one's behaviour and not act emotionally. self-controlled *adjective*

self-defeating *adjective* (of a course of action etc.) frustrating the purpose for which it was intended.

self-defence *noun* defence of oneself, or of one's rights or good reputation etc., against attack.

self-denial *noun* deliberately going without the things one would like to have.

self-destruct *verb* to destroy itself.

self-determination *noun* 1 determination of one's own fate or course of action, free will. 2 a nation's determination of its own form of government or its allegiance.

self-effacing *adjective* keeping oneself in the background. self-effacement *noun*

self-employed *adjective* working independently and not for an employer.

self-esteem *noun* one's good opinion of oneself.

self-evident *adjective* clear without proof or explanation or further evidence.

self-explanatory *adjective* so easy to understand that it needs no further explanation.

self-governing *adjective* (of a country) governing itself. self-government *noun*

self-help *noun* use of one's own powers to achieve things, without dependence on aid from others.

self-important *adjective* having a high opinion of one's own importance, pompous. self-importance *noun*

self-indulgent *adjective* greatly indulging one's own desires for comfort and pleasure. self-indulgence *noun*

self-interest *noun* one's own personal advantage.

selfish *adjective* acting or done according to one's own interests and needs without regard for those of others, keeping good things for oneself and not sharing. selfishly *adverb*, selfishness *noun*

selfless *adjective* unselfish. selflessly *adverb*, selflessness *noun*

self-loading *adjective* (of a firearm) reloading itself after being fired, automatic.

self-made *adjective* having risen from poverty or obscurity and achieved success by one's own efforts, *a self-made man*.

self-pity *noun* feeling sorry for oneself.

self-portrait *noun* a portrait of himself or herself by an artist; an account of himself or herself by a writer.

self-possessed *adjective* calm and dignified. self-possession *noun*

self-preservation *noun* protection of oneself from harm or injury; the instinct to ensure one's own survival.

self-raising *adjective* (of flour) containing a raising agent and for use without additional baking powder.

self-regard *noun* regard for oneself.

self-reliant *adjective* independent, relying on one's own abilities and resources. self-reliance *noun*

self-respect *noun* proper regard for oneself and one's own dignity and principles etc.

self-righteous *adjective* smugly sure of one's own righteousness.

self-sacrifice *noun* sacrifice of one's own interests and desires so that others may benefit. self-sacrificing *adjective*

selfsame *adjective* the very same, *died in the selfsame house where he was born*.

self-satisfied *adjective* pleased with oneself and one's own achievements, conceited. **self-satisfaction** *noun*

self-seeking *adjective* & *noun* seeking to promote one's own interests rather than those of others.

self-service *adjective* (of a restaurant, shop, or service station) at which customers help themselves and pay a cashier for what they have taken.

self-sown *adjective* grown from seed that has dropped naturally from the plant.

self-styled *adjective* using a name or description one has adopted without right, *a self-styled scholar*.

self-sufficient *adjective* able to provide what one needs without outside help.

self-supporting *adjective* able to support oneself or itself without help.

self-taught *adjective* having taught oneself without formal teaching from another person.

self-willed *adjective* obstinately doing what one wishes, stubborn.

self-winding *adjective* (of a watch or clock) having a mechanism that winds it automatically.

sell *verb* (sold, selling) **1** to transfer the ownership of (goods etc.) in exchange for money. **2** to keep a stock of (goods) for sale, to be a dealer in, *do you sell chocolates?* **3** to promote sales of, *the author's name alone will sell many copies*. **4** (of goods) to find buyers, *the book is selling well*. **5** to be on sale at a certain price, *it sells for $1.50*. **6** to persuade a person into accepting (a thing) by convincing him or her of its merits, *tried to sell him the idea of merging the two departments*. –**sell** *noun* **1** the manner of selling something; *hard sell*, aggressive selling. **2** (*informal*) a deception, a disappointment. □ **sell down the river** to betray; to defraud. **sell off** to dispose of by selling, especially at a reduced price. **sell-off** *noun* disposal of assets, especially by governments. **sell out** to dispose of (all one's stock etc.) by selling; to betray. **sell-out** *noun* the selling of all tickets for a show etc., a great commercial success; a betrayal. **sell up** to sell one's house or business etc.

seller *noun* **1** a person who sells something. **2** a thing that sells well or badly, *those sandals were good sellers*. □ **seller's market** a state of affairs when goods are scarce and prices are high.

selvedge *noun* (also **selvage**) **1** an edge of cloth so woven that it does not unravel. **2** a tape-like border along the edge of cloth, intended to be removed or hidden. [from *self* + *edge*]

selves *see* self.

semantic (sĕ-**man**-tik) *adjective* of meaning in language, of semantics. **semantics** *noun* **1** the branch of linguistics concerned with meanings. **2** meaning, connotation. [from Greek *sema* = sign]

semaphore (**sem**-ă-for) *noun* **1** a system of signalling by holding the arms in certain positions to indicate letters of the alphabet. **2** a device with mechanically moved arms, used for signalling on railways. –**semaphore** *verb* to signal by semaphore. [from Greek *sema* = sign, + *phoros* = carrying]

semblance (**sem**-blăns) *noun* **1** an outward appearance (either real or pretended), a show, *spoke with a semblance of friendship*. **2** a resemblance or likeness to something.

semen (**see**-mĕn) *noun* the whitish sperm-bearing fluid produced by male animals. [Latin, = seed]

semester (sĕ-**mess**-ter) *noun* a half-year course or term in a university or college. [from Latin *semestris* = six-monthly]

semi *noun* (*plural* semis) (*informal*) **1** a semifinal. **2** a semitrailer. **3** a semi-detached house.

semi- *prefix* half; partly. [Latin, = half]

semibreve (**sem**-ee-breev) *noun* the longest note in common use in music, lasting as long as two minims.

semicircle *noun* half of a circle; something arranged in this shape. □ **semicircular canals** the three tubular channels in the inner part of the ear that are filled with fluid and help to maintain balance. **semicircular** *adjective*

semicolon (sem-ee-**koh**-lŏn) *noun* the punctuation mark (;) used to separate parts of a sentence where there is a more distinct break than that represented by a comma.

semiconductor *noun* a substance that (in certain conditions) conducts electricity but not as well as most metals do. **semiconducting** *adjective*

semi-detached *adjective* (of a house) being one of a pair of houses that have one wall in common with each other but are detached from other houses.

semifinal *noun* the match or round preceding the final. **semifinalist** *noun* one who takes part in this.

semi-fitted *adjective* (of a garment) shaped to the body but not closely fitted.

semillon (**sem**-ee-yon) *noun* a variety of white grape; a wine made from this.

seminal (**semĭ**-năl) *adjective* **1** of seed or semen. **2** giving rise to new developments, *seminal ideas*.

seminar (**sem**-ĭ-nar) *noun* a small class for advanced discussion and research.

seminary (**sem**-ĭ-nă-ree) *noun* a training college for priests or rabbis. **seminarist** *noun*

semi-permeable *adjective* (of a membrane etc.) allowing small molecules to pass through it but not large ones.

semiprecious *adjective* (of a gem) less valuable than those called precious.

semiquaver *noun* a note in music, lasting as long as half a quaver.

semi-skilled *adjective* having or requiring some training but less than that needed for skilled work.

Semite (**see**-myt) *noun* a member of the group of races that includes the Jews and Arabs and formerly the Phoenicians and Assyrians.

Semitic (sĕ-**mit**-ik) *adjective* of the Semites or their languages.

semitone *noun* the smallest interval used in European music, half of a tone.

semitrailer *noun* an articulated vehicle consisting of a prime mover and a detachable trailer.

semolina *noun* hard round grains left when wheat has been ground and sifted, used to make puddings and pasta. [from Italian *semola* = bran]

sempstress *noun* = seamstress.

senate (**sen**-ăt) *noun* **1** Senate the upper house of the parliamentary assemblies of Australia, the USA, France, and certain other countries. **2** the governing council in ancient Rome. **3** the governing body of certain universities. [from Latin *senatus* = council of elders]

senator (**sen**-ă-ter) *noun* a member of a senate. **senatorial** (sen-ă-**tor**-ree-ăl) *adjective*

send *verb* (**sent**, **sending**) **1** to order, cause, or enable to go to a certain destination; to have (a thing) conveyed. **2** to send a message or letter, *she sent to say she was coming*. **3** to cause to move or go; *sent him flying*, knocked him

headlong; *sent his temperature up*; *the sermon sent us to sleep*. **4** to cause to become, *sent him mad*. □ **send away for** to order (goods etc.) by post. **send for** to order (a person) to come to one's presence; to order (a thing) to be brought or delivered from elsewhere. **send-off** *noun* a friendly demonstration at a person's departure. **send up** (*informal*) to make fun of (a thing) by imitating it. **send-up** *noun* (*informal*) a humorous imitation. **send word** to send information. **sender** *noun*

Seneca (**sen**-ĕ-kă) (died AD 65), Roman writer and statesman, a Stoic philosopher.

Senegal (sen-ĕ-**gawl**) a republic in West Africa. **Senegalese** (sen-ĕ-gă-**leez**) *adjective* & *noun* (*plural* **Senegalese**).

seneschal (**sen**-ĕ-shăl) *noun* the steward of a medieval great house.

senile (**see**-nyl) *adjective* suffering from bodily or mental weakness because of old age; (of illness etc.) characteristic of elderly people. **senility** (sĕ-**nil**-ĭ-tee) *noun* [from Latin *senilis* = old]

senior *adjective* **1** older in age; *Tom Brown senior*, the older person of that name. **2** higher in rank or authority. **3** for older children, *senior school*. –**senior** *noun* **1** a senior person, *seniors are entitled to concessions*; *he is my senior*, is older than I am. **2** a member of a senior school. □ **senior citizen** an older person. **seniority** *noun* [Latin, = older]

senna *noun* the dried pods or leaves of a tropical tree, used as a laxative.

señor (sen-**yor**) *noun* (*plural* **señores**) the title of a Spanish-speaking man, = Mr or sir.

señora (sen-**yor**-ră) *noun* the title of a Spanish-speaking woman, = Mrs or madam.

señorita (sen-yor-**ree**-tă) *noun* the title of a Spanish-speaking girl or unmarried woman, = Miss.

sensation *noun* **1** an awareness or feeling produced by stimulation of a sense organ or of the mind. **2** ability to feel such stimulation, *loss of sensation in the fingers*. **3** a condition of eager interest, excitement, or admiration aroused in a number of people; a person or thing arousing this. [same origin as *sense*]

sensational *adjective* **1** producing eager interest or excitement or admiration in many people. **2** (*informal*) extraordinary. **sensationally** *adverb*

sensationalism *noun* use of subject matter, words, or style etc. in order to produce excessive emotional excitement in people. **sensationalist** *noun*

sense *noun* 1 any of the special powers by which a living thing becomes aware of things; *the five senses*, the faculties of sight, hearing, smell, taste, and touch, by which the external world is perceived; *sixth sense* (*see* sixth). 2 ability to perceive or feel or be conscious of a thing, awareness or recognition of something, *has no sense of shame*; *sense of humour*, ability to appreciate humour. 3 the power of making a good judgment about something, practical wisdom, *had the sense to get out of the way*. 4 the way in which a word or phrase or passage etc. is to be understood, its meaning or one of its meanings. 5 possession of a meaning or of reasonableness. –**sense** *verb* 1 to perceive by one of the senses. 2 to become aware of (a thing) by getting a mental impression, *sensed that he was unwelcome*. 3 (of a machine) to detect. **senses** *plural noun* sanity; *in one's senses*, sane; *he has taken leave of his senses*, has gone mad. □ **come to one's senses** to regain consciousness; to become sensible after behaving stupidly. **make sense** to have a meaning; to be a sensible and practicable idea. **make sense of** to find a meaning in. **sense organ** any of the organs (e.g. the eye or ear) by which the body becomes aware of stimuli from the external world. [from Latin *sensus* = faculty of feeling]

senseless *adjective* 1 not showing good sense, foolish. 2 unconscious. **senselessness** *noun*

sensibility *noun* the ability to feel things mentally, sensitiveness; delicacy of feeling.

Usage This word does not mean 'possession of good sense'.

sensible *adjective* 1 having or showing good sense. 2 aware, *we are sensible of the honour you have done us*. 3 (of clothing) practical rather than fashionable, *sensible shoes*. **sensibly** *adverb*

sensitise *verb* (also **-ize**) to make sensitive or abnormally sensitive. **sensitisation** *noun*

sensitive *adjective* 1 affected by something, responsive to stimuli, *plants are sensitive to light*. 2 receiving impressions quickly and easily, *sensitive fingers*. 3 alert and considerate about other people's feelings. 4 easily hurt or offended. 5 (of an instrument etc.) readily responding to or recording slight changes of

condition. 6 (of a subject) requiring tactful treatment. **sensitively** *adverb*, **sensitivity** *noun*

sensor *noun* a device (e.g. a photoelectric cell) that reacts to a certain stimulus.

sensory (sen-sŏ-ree) *adjective* of the senses, receiving or transmitting sensations, *sensory nerves*.

sensual (sens-yoo-ăl) *adjective* 1 physical, gratifying to the body, *sensual pleasures*. 2 indulging oneself with physical pleasures, showing that one does this, *a sensual face*. **sensually** *adverb*, **sensuality** (sens-yoo-**al**-ĭ-tee) *noun*

sensuous (sens-yoo-ŭs) *adjective* affecting or appealing to the senses, especially by beauty or delicacy. **sensuously** *adverb*

Usage *Sensuous* does not have the implication of undesirable behaviour that *sensual* can have.

sent *see* send.

sentence *noun* 1 a set of words containing a verb (either expressed or understood), that is complete in itself as an expression of thought, and conveying a statement, question, exclamation, or command. 2 the punishment awarded by a lawcourt to a person convicted in a criminal trial; declaration of this. –**sentence** *verb* to pass sentence upon (a person); to condemn (to punishment). [from Latin *sententia* = opinion]

sententious (sen-**ten**-shŭs) *adjective* putting on an air of wisdom; dull and moralising. **sententiously** *adverb*, **sententiousness** *noun*

sentient (sen-shĕnt) *adjective* capable of perceiving and feeling things, *sentient beings*. [from Latin *sentiens* = feeling]

sentiment *noun* 1 a mental attitude produced by one's feeling about something, an opinion. 2 emotion as opposed to reason, sentimentality. [from Latin *sentire* = feel]

sentimental *adjective* 1 showing or influenced by romantic or nostalgic feeling. 2 characterised by emotions as opposed to reason. **sentimentally** *adverb*, **sentimentality** (sen-tĭ-men-**tal**-ĭ-tee) *noun*

sentinel *noun* a sentry.

sentry *noun* a soldier posted to keep watch and guard something. □ **sentry box** a wooden structure large enough to shelter a standing sentry.

Seoul (*pr.* sohl) the capital of South Korea.

sepal (**sep**-ăl) *noun* one of the leaflike parts forming the calyx of a flower.

separable (**sep**-ă-ră-bŭl) *adjective* able to be separated. **separably** *adverb*, **separability** *noun*

separate (**sep**-ă-răt) *adjective* forming a unit by itself, not joined or united with others. –**separate** (**sep**-ă-rayt) *verb* **1** to divide, to make separate; to keep apart; *separate the cream*, extract it from the milk. **2** to be between, *Torres Strait separates Papua New Guinea from Australia*. **3** to become separate; to go different ways; to withdraw oneself from a union; to cease to live together as a married couple. **separates** *plural noun* individual items of outer clothing for wearing together in various combinations. **separately** *adverb* [from *se-* = apart, + Latin *parare* = make ready]

separation *noun* **1** separating; being separated. **2** a legal arrangement by which a married couple live apart but without ending the marriage.

separatist (**sep**-ă-ră-tĭst) *noun* a person who favours separation from a larger unit, e.g. so as to achieve political independence. **separatism** *noun*

separator *noun* a machine that separates things (e.g. cream from milk).

Sephardi (sě-**far**-dee) *noun* (*plural* **Sephardim**) a Jew of Spanish or Portuguese descent, as distinct from an Ashkenazi. **Sephardic** *adjective*

sepia (**seep**-eeă) *noun* **1** brown colouring matter originally made from the black fluid of the cuttlefish, used in inks and water colours. **2** rich reddish-brown colour. –**sepia** *adjective* of sepia colour. [from Greek, = cuttlefish]

sepsis *noun* a septic condition.

September *noun* the ninth month of the year. [from Latin *septem* = seven, because it was the seventh month of the ancient Roman calendar]

September 11 11 September 2001, the date of the terrorist attacks on the World Trade Center in New York and the Pentagon in Washington.

septet *noun* a group of seven instruments or voices; a musical composition for these. [from Latin *septem* = seven]

septic *adjective* infected with harmful microorganisms that cause pus to form. □ **septic tank** a tank into which sewage is conveyed and in which it remains until the activity of bacteria makes it liquid enough

to drain away. [from Greek *septikos* = made rotten]

septicaemia (sep-tĭ-**seem**-ee-ă) *noun* blood poisoning. [from *septic*, + Greek *haima* = blood]

septuagenarian (sep-tew-ă-jě-**nair**-ree-ăn) *noun* a person in his or her seventies. [from Latin *septuageni* = 70 each]

Septuagint (**sep**-tew-ă-jĭnt) *noun* the Greek version of the Old Testament. [from Latin *septuaginta* = 70]

septum *noun* (*plural* **septa**) a partition between two cavities, e.g. that in the nose between the nostrils. [from Latin *saeptum* = enclosed]

sepulchral (sě-**pul**-krăl) *adjective* **1** of a tomb, *sepulchral monument*. **2** looking or sounding dismal, funereal; *a sepulchral voice*, deep and hollow-sounding.

sepulchre (**sep**-ŭl-ker) *noun* a tomb. [from Latin *sepultum* = buried]

sequel *noun* **1** what follows or arises out of an earlier event. **2** a novel or film etc. that continues the story of an earlier one.

sequence *noun* **1** the following of one thing after another in an orderly or continuous way. **2** a series without gaps, a set of things that belong next to each other in a particular order; *in sequence*, in this order; *out of sequence*, not in it. **3** a section dealing with one scene or topic in a cinema film. –**sequence** *verb* to arrange in sequence. [from Latin *sequens* = following]

sequential (sě-**kwen**-shăl) *adjective* **1** forming a sequence, following in succession. **2** occurring as a result. **sequentially** *adverb*

sequester (sě-**kwes**-ter) *verb* **1** to seclude. **2** to confiscate.

sequestrate (sě-**kwes**-trayt) *verb* to confiscate. **sequestration** *noun*, **sequestrator** *noun*

sequin (**see**-kwĭn) *noun* a circular spangle ornamenting clothing or other material. **sequinned** *adjective*

sequoia (sě-**kwoi**-ă) *noun* a coniferous tree of California, growing to a great height.

seraglio (sě-**rahl**-yoh) *noun* (*plural* **seraglios**) the harem of a Muslim palace.

seraph *noun* (*plural* **seraphim** or **seraphs**) a member of the highest order of angels in ancient Christian belief.

seraphic (sě-**raf**-ik) *adjective* like a seraph, angelic. **seraphically** *adverb*

Serb *noun* a Serbian. –**Serb** *adjective* Serbian.

Serbia a country in SE Europe, formerly part of Yugoslavia. **Serbian** *adjective* & *noun*

Serbo-Croat (ser-boh-**kroh**-at) *noun* the language of the Serbs and Croats, combining Serbian and Croatian elements.

serenade *noun* a song or tune played by a lover to his lady, or suitable for this. –**serenade** *verb* to sing or play a serenade to.

serendipity (se-rĕn-**dip**-ĭ-tee) *noun* the making of pleasant discoveries by accident; the knack of doing this. **serendipitous** *adjective*

serene *adjective* 1 calm and cheerful. 2 the title used in speaking of or to members of certain European royal families, *His* or *Her* or *Your Serene Highness*. **serenely** *adverb*, **serenity** (sĕ-**ren**-ĭ-tee) *noun*

serf *noun* 1 a farm labourer who was forced to work for his landowner in the Middle Ages. 2 an oppressed labourer. **serfdom** *noun* [same origin as *servant*]

serge *noun* a strong twilled worsted fabric used for making clothes.

sergeant *noun* 1 a non-commissioned army officer ranking above corporal. 2 a police officer ranking just below inspector. □ **sergeant major** a warrant officer assisting the adjutant of a regiment or battalion.

serial *noun* a story presented in a series of instalments. –**serial** *adjective* of or forming a series. □ **serial composition** serialism. **serial number** a number that identifies one item in a series of things. **serially** *adverb*

serialise *verb* (also -**ize**) to produce as a serial. **serialisation** *noun*

serialism *noun* a technique of musical composition using the twelve notes of the chromatic scale arranged in a fixed order.

seriatim (se-ree-**ay**-tĭm) *adverb* point by point, taking one subject etc. after another in an orderly sequence.

series *noun* (*plural* **series**) 1 a number of things of the same kind, or related to each other in a similar way, occurring or arranged or produced in order. 2 a set of stamps or coins etc. issued at one time or in one reign. [Latin, = row or chain]

serif (**se**-rĭf) *noun* a slight projection finishing off the stroke of a printed letter (as in T, contrasted with sanserif T).

serio-comic *adjective* partly serious and partly comic.

serious *adjective* 1 solemn and thoughtful, not smiling. 2 sincere, in earnest, not casual or light-hearted, *made a serious attempt*. 3 important, *this is a serious decision*. 4 causing great concern, not slight, *serious illness*. **seriously** *adverb*, **seriousness** *noun*

serjeant-at-arms *noun* an official of Parliament, or of a court or city, with ceremonial duties.

sermon *noun* 1 a talk on a religious or moral subject, especially one delivered by a member of the clergy during a religious service. 2 a long moralising talk.

sermonise *verb* (also -**ize**) to give a long moralising talk.

serpent *noun* a snake, especially a large one. [from Latin *serpens* = creeping]

serpentine *adjective* twisting and curving like a snake, *a serpentine road*.

serrated (sĕ-**ray**-tĕd) *adjective* having a series of small projections like the teeth of a saw. **serration** *noun* [from Latin *serratum* = sawn]

serried (*rhymes with* buried) *adjective* (of rows of people or things) arranged in a close series.

serum (**seer**-rŭm) *noun* (*plural* **sera** *or* **serums**) 1 the thin yellowish fluid that remains from blood when the rest has clotted. 2 this taken from an immunised animal and used for inoculations. 3 any watery fluid from animal tissue (e.g. in a blister). [Latin, = whey]

servant *noun* 1 a person employed to do domestic work in a household or as a personal attendant on a master or mistress. 2 an employee considered as performing services for his employer, *a faithful servant of the company*. 3 a devoted follower, *servant of Christ*. [from Latin *servus* = slave]

serve *verb* 1 to perform services for (a person or community etc.), to work for, *served his country*; *served the national interest*, helped it. 2 to be employed or performing a spell of duty, to be a member of the armed forces, *served in the Navy*. 3 to be suitable for, to do what is required, *it will serve our purpose*; *it will serve*. 4 to provide a facility for, *the area is served by a number of buses*. 5 to spend time in, to undergo, *serve an apprenticeship*; *served a prison sentence*. 6 to set out or present (food etc.) for others to consume; to attend to (customers in a shop). 7 (of a quantity of food) to be enough for, *this recipe* *serves six persons*. **8** to set the ball in play in tennis etc. **9** to assist the priest officiating in a religious service. **10** to deliver (a legal writ etc.) to the person named, *served him with the writ* or *served the writ on him*. **11** to treat in a certain way, *she was most unjustly served*. **–serve** *noun* **1** a serving. **2** a service in tennis etc.; a person's turn for this; the ball served. **3** (*Austral. informal*) harsh criticism, a reprimand, *give someone a serve*. □ **it serves him** or **her right** an expression of satisfaction at seeing a person get something unpleasant that he or she deserved.

server *noun* **1** a person who serves or attends to the requirements of another. **2** (in tennis etc.) the player who serves the ball. **3** (in computing) a program which manages shared access to a centralised resource or service in a network; a device on which such a program is run.

servery *noun* a room or counter from which meals etc. are served.

service *noun* **1** being a servant, a servant's status, *be in service; go into service*. **2** the occupation or process of working for an employer or of assisting another person or persons. **3** a department of people employed by the government or by a public organisation; *the Public Service* (*see* **public**). **4** a system or arrangement that performs work for customers or supplies public needs, *laundry services are available*; *the bus service*; *essential services*, public supply of water, electricity, etc. **5** a branch of the armed forces; *the services*, the navy, army, and air force. **6** use, assistance; a helpful or beneficial act, *did me a service*; *be of service*, to be useful, to help. **7** a meeting of a congregation for worship of God; a religious ceremony. **8** the serving of a legal writ. **9** the serving of food or goods; provision of help for customers or clients, *quick service*. **10** a set of dishes, plates, etc. for serving a meal, *a dinner service*. **11** the act or manner or turn of serving in tennis etc.; the game in which one serves, *lost his service*. **12** maintenance and repair of a car or of machinery or appliances at intervals. **–service** *verb* **1** to maintain or repair (a piece of machinery etc.). **2** to supply with service(s). **3** to pay the interest on, *the amount needed to service this loan*. □ **service industry** an industry providing services (e.g. gas, electricity) not goods. **service station** a place where petrol etc. is sold to motorists.

serviceable *adjective* **1** usable. **2** suitable for ordinary use or wear, hard-wearing. **serviceably** *adverb*, **serviceability** *noun*

serviceman *noun* a man who is a member of the armed services.

servicewoman *noun* a woman who is a member of the armed services.

serviette *noun* a table napkin.

servile (**ser**-vyl) *adjective* **1** suitable for a servant, menial, *servile tasks*. **2** excessively submissive, lacking independence, *servile flattery* or *imitation*. **servilely** *adverb*, **servility** (ser-**vil**-ĭ-tee) *noun* [same origin as *servant*]

serving *noun* a helping.

servitor (**ser**-vĭ-ter) *noun* (*old use*) a servant, an attendant.

servitude *noun* the condition of being forced to work for others and having no freedom.

servo *noun* (*plural* **servos**) a mechanism, motor, or other device using a small input of mechanical power to activate large brakes, valves, etc.

sesame (**sess**-ă-mee) *noun* **1** a plant of tropical Asia with seeds that are used as food or as a source of oil. **2** its seeds. □ **Open Sesame** a special way of obtaining access to something that is usually inaccessible. (¶These words were used, in one of the Arabian Nights stories, to cause a door to open.)

sesquicentenary *noun* a 150th anniversary. [from Latin *semi*, + *que* = and, + *centenary*]

session *noun* **1** a meeting or series of meetings for discussing or deciding something; the period during which these are regularly held. **2** a period spent continuously in an activity, *a recording session*. **3** (in certain educational institutions) the part of the year, or a division of it, in which teaching takes place. □ **in session** assembled for business. [from Latin *sessio* = setting]

sestet *noun* the last six lines of a sonnet, resolving the theme of the octave.

Set (*Egyptian myth.*) an evil god who murdered Osiris.

set *verb* (**set**, **setting**) **1** to put or place; to cause to stand in position. **2** to put in contact with; *set fire to*, to cause to burn. **3** to fix in position; to adjust the hands of (a clock) or the mechanism of (a trap etc.); *set the table*, lay it for a meal. **4** to represent as happening in a certain place, or at a certain time, *the story is set in Egypt in 2000 BC*. **5** to provide a tune for, *set it to music*. **6** to make or become hard, firm, or established, *the jelly set*; *they are set against change*, have this as a permanent attitude; *the blossom fell before it* (or *the fruit*)

had set, before fruit had developed from it.
7 to fix, decide, or appoint, *set a date for the
wedding*. **8** to arrange and protect (a broken
bone) so that it will heal. **9** to fix (hair) while
it is damp so that it will dry in the desired
style. **10** to place (a jewel) in a surrounding
framework; to decorate with jewels, *the
bracelet is set with emeralds*. **11** to establish,
set a new record for the high jump. **12** to
offer or assign as something to be done, *set
them a task*. **13** to put into a specified state,
set them free; *set it swinging*. **14** to have a
certain movement, *the current sets strongly
eastwards*. **15** to be brought towards or below
the horizon by the earth's movement, *the sun
sets*. **16** (in certain dances) to face another
dancer and make certain steps, *set to your
partners*. –**set** *noun* **1** a number of people or
things that are grouped together as similar or
forming a unit. **2** a group of games forming
a unit or part of a match in tennis etc. **3** (in
mathematics) a collection of things having
a common property. **4** a radio or television
receiver. **5** the way something sets or is set or
placed or arranged, *the set of his shoulders*.
6 the process or style of setting hair. **7** the
scenery in use for a play or film; the stage etc.
where this is being performed, *be on the set
by 7 a.m.* **8** a slip or shoot for planting, *onion
sets*. **9** (*Austral. informal*) a grudge, *have a
set on someone*. ☐ **be set on** to be determined
about. **set about** to begin (a task); to attack
with blows or words. **set back** to halt or slow
the progress of; to cause a change for the
worse; (*informal*) to cost, *it set me back $50*.
set eyes on to catch sight of. **set forth** to set
out. **set in** to become established, *depression
had set in*. **set off** to begin a journey; to cause
to begin, *set off a chain reaction*; to ignite or
cause to explode; to improve the appearance
of (a thing) by providing a contrast. **set
one's hand to** to begin (a task); to sign (a
document). **set one's teeth** to clench them.
set out to declare or make known, *set out the
terms of the agreement*; to begin a journey;
set out to do something, to make a start with
the intention of doing it. **set piece** a formal
or elaborate arrangement, especially in art or
literature. **set sail** to hoist sail(s); to begin a
voyage. **set square** a right-angled triangular
plate for drawing lines in a certain relation
to each other. **set theory** the study of sets in
mathematics, without regard to the nature of
their individual constituents. **set to** to begin
doing something vigorously; to begin fighting
or arguing. **set-to** *noun* a fight; an argument.
set up to place in view; to arrange; to begin or

create (a business etc.); to establish in some
capacity; to begin making (a loud sound); to
cause; to supply adequately, *I'm set up with
reading matter for the journey*; (*informal*) to
lead on in order to fool, cheat, or incriminate
(a person); *set up house*, to establish a
household. **set-up** *noun* the structure of an
organisation; (*informal*) a trick or conspiracy,
a frame-up.

setback *noun* something that sets back
progress.

settee *noun* a long seat with a back and
usually with arms, for two or more people.

setter *noun* **1** a person or thing that sets
something. **2** a dog of a long-haired breed that
is trained to stand rigid when it scents game.

setting *noun* **1** the way or place in which
something is set. **2** music for the words of a
song etc. **3** a set of cutlery or crockery for one
person.

settle[1] *verb* **1** to place (a thing etc.) so that
it stays in position. **2** to establish or become
established more or less permanently. **3** to
make one's home, to occupy as settlers, *settled
in Canada*; *colonists settled the coast*. **4** to
sink or come to rest, to cause to do this, to
become compact in this way, *dust settled on
the shelves*; *let the earth settle after digging*.
5 to arrange as desired; to end or arrange
conclusively; to deal with, *settled the dispute*.
6 to make or become calm or orderly; to stop
being restless; *she can't settle to work*, she is
too restless to concentrate steadily. **7** to pay (a
debt, bill, or claim etc.). **8** to bestow legally,
settled all his property on his wife.
☐ **settle down** to become settled after
wandering, movement, restlessness, or
disturbance etc. **settle a person's hash** *see*
hash. **settle up** to pay what is owing.

settle[2] *noun* a wooden seat for two or more
people, with a high back and arms and often a
boxlike compartment from seat to floor.

settlement *noun* **1** settling; being settled.
2 a business or financial arrangement. **3** an
amount or property settled legally on a person.
4 a place occupied by settlers or colonists etc.

settler *noun* a person who goes to live
permanently in a previously unoccupied land,
a colonist.

seven *adjective* & *noun* one more than six
(7, VII). ☐ **seven deadly sins** *see* **deadly**.
seven seas all the oceans of the world; the
Arctic, Antarctic, North and South Atlantic,
North and South Pacific, and Indian Oceans.

Seven Sisters the Pleiades. **Seven Wonders of the World** the seven most spectacular man-made structures of the ancient world, traditionally the pyramids of Egypt, the Hanging Gardens of Babylon, the Mausoleum of Halicarnassus, the temple of Diana (Artemis) at Ephesus, the Colossus of Rhodes, the statue of Zeus at Olympia in Greece, the Pharos of Alexandria. **Seven Years War** a war (1756–63) that ranged Britain, Prussia, and Hanover against Austria, France, Russia, Saxony, Sweden, and Spain.

sevenfold *adjective* & *adverb* **1** seven times as much or as many. **2** consisting of seven parts.

seventeen *adjective* & *noun* one more than sixteen (17, XVII). **seventeenth** *adjective* & *noun*

seventh *adjective* & *noun* **1** next after sixth. **2** each of seven equal parts of a thing. ▢ **Seventh-Day Adventist** a member of a strict Protestant denomination who originally expected the second coming of Christ in 1844 and still preach that his return is imminent, and observe Saturday as the sabbath. **seventh heaven** a state of intense delight. **seventhly** *adverb*

seventy *adjective* & *noun* seven times ten (70, LXX). **seventies** *plural noun* the numbers from 70 to 79, especially the years of a century or of a life. **seventieth** *adjective*

sever (**sev**-er) *verb* (**severed**, **severing**) to cut or break off from a whole, to separate; *sever a contract*, to end it.

several *adjective* **1** a few, more than two but not many. **2** separate, individual, *we all went our several ways*. –**several** *pronoun* several people or things.

severally *adverb* separately.

severance (**sev**-ĕ-răns) *noun* severing; being severed. ▢ **severance pay** an amount of money paid to an employee on termination of his or her contract.

severe (sĕ-**veer**) *adjective* **1** strict, without sympathy, imposing harsh rules on others. **2** intense, forceful, *severe gales*. **3** making great demands on endurance or energy or ability etc., *the pace was severe*. **4** plain and without decoration, *a severe style of dress*. **severely** *adverb*, **severity** (sĕ-**ve**-rĭ-tee) *noun*

Seville (sĕ-**vil** *or* sev-**il**) *noun* a **Seville orange**, a bitter orange used for making marmalade. [named after Seville in Spain]

sew *verb* (**sewed**, **sewn** *or* **sewed**, **sewing**) **1** to fasten by passing thread again and again through material, using a threaded needle or an awl etc. or a sewing machine. **2** to make, attach, or fasten by sewing. **3** to work with needle and thread or with a sewing machine.

sewage *noun* liquid waste matter drained away from houses, towns, factories, etc. for disposal. ▢ **sewage farm** a farm on which a town's sewage is treated and used as manure. **sewage works** a place where sewage is purified so that it can safely be discharged into a river etc.

sewer[1] (**soh**-er) *noun* a person or thing that sews.

sewer[2] (*rhymes with* fewer) *noun* a pipe connecting drains for carrying away sewage. –**sewer** *verb* to provide or drain with sewers.

sewerage *noun* **1** a system of sewers; drainage by this. **2** sewage.

sewing *noun* work to be sewn. ▢ **sewing machine** a machine for sewing or stitching things.

sewn *see* sew.

sex *noun* **1** either of the two main groups (*male* and *female*) into which living things are placed according to their reproductive functions; the fact of belonging to one of these. **2** sexual feelings or impulses; mutual attraction between members of the two sexes. **3** sexual intercourse, *have sex with someone*. –**sex** *verb* to judge the sex of, *to sex chickens*. ▢ **sex act** sexual intercourse. **sex appeal** sexual attractiveness. **sex chromosome** a chromosome concerned in determining which sex an organism is to be. **sexer** *noun* [from Latin *secus* = division]

Usage For sense 1, some people prefer to use the word *gender*.

sexagenarian (seks-ă-jĕ-**nair**-ree-ăn) *noun* a person in his or her sixties. [from Latin *sexageni* = 60 each]

sexist *adjective* **1** discriminating in favour of members of one sex. **2** assuming that a person's abilities and social functions are predetermined by his or her sex. –**sexist** *noun* a person who does this. **sexism** *noun*

sexless *adjective* **1** lacking sex, neuter. **2** not involving sexual feelings. **sexlessly** *adverb*

sextant *noun* an instrument used in navigating and surveying, for finding one's position by measuring the altitude of the sun etc.

[from Latin *sextus* = sixth (because early sextants contained 60°, one-sixth of a circle)]

sextet *noun* a group of six instruments or voices; a musical composition for these. [from Latin *sextus* = sixth]

sexton *noun* an official whose job is to take care of a church and churchyard.

sextuple (**seks**-tew-pŭl) *adjective* sixfold.

sextuplet (**seks**-tup-lĕt) *noun* each of six children born at one birth. [from Latin *sextus* = sixth]

sexual *adjective* 1 of sex or the sexes or the relationship or feelings etc. between them. 2 (of reproduction) occurring by fusion of male and female cells. □ sexual intercourse copulation (especially of man and woman), insertion of the penis into the vagina. sexually *adverb*

sexuality (seks-yoo-**al**-ĭ-tee) *noun* 1 the fact of belonging to one of the sexes. 2 sexual characteristics or impulses.

sexy *adjective* (sexier, sexiest) sexually attractive or stimulating. sexiness *noun*

Seychelles (say-**shelz**) a republic consisting of a group of islands in the Indian Ocean. Seychellois (say-shel-**wah**) *adjective & noun*

sh *interjection* hush.

shabby *adjective* (shabbier, shabbiest) 1 worn and threadbare, not kept in good condition; (of a person) poorly dressed. 2 unfair, dishonourable, *a shabby trick*. shabbily *adverb*, shabbiness *noun*

shack *noun* a roughly-built hut or shed. □ shack up (*informal*) to live together as if married.

shackle *noun* one of a pair of iron rings joined by a chain, for fastening a prisoner's wrists or ankles. –shackle *verb* 1 to put shackles on. 2 to impede or restrict, *shackled by tradition*.

Shackleton, Sir Ernest Henry (1874–1922), Irish-born explorer of the Antarctic.

shade *noun* 1 comparative darkness or coolness found where something blocks rays of light or heat. 2 shelter from the sun's light and heat; a place sheltered from these. 3 the darker part of a picture. 4 a colour; a degree or depth of colour, *in shades of blue*. 5 a different variety, *all shades of opinion*. 6 a small amount, *she's a shade better today*. 7 a ghost. 8 a screen used to block or moderate light or heat; a translucent cover for a lamp to soften or screen its light; an eye-shade. –shade *verb* 1 to block the rays of. 2 to give shade to;

to make dark. 3 to darken (parts of a drawing etc.) so as to give effects of light and shade or gradations of colour. 4 to pass gradually into another colour or variety, *the blue here shades into green; where socialism shaded into communism*. shades *plural noun* 1 the darkness of night or evening. 2 reminders of some person or thing, *shades of the 1930s*.

shadow *noun* 1 shade. 2 a patch of this with the shape of the body that is blocking the rays. 3 a person's inseparable attendant or companion. 4 a slight trace, *no shadow of doubt*. 5 a shaded part of a picture. 6 gloom, *the news cast a shadow over the proceedings*. 7 something weak or unsubstantial, a ghost, *worn to a shadow*. –shadow *verb* 1 to cast shadow over. 2 to follow and watch secretly. 3 to observe (a person) closely at work, for educational purposes. □ shadow-boxing *noun* boxing against an imaginary opponent as a form of training. Shadow Cabinet members of the Opposition party who comment on matters for which Cabinet ministers hold responsibility. shadower *noun*

shadowy *adjective* 1 like a shadow. 2 full of shadows.

shady *adjective* (shadier, shadiest) 1 giving shade. 2 situated in the shade, *a shady corner*. 3 disreputable, not completely honest, *shady dealings*. shadily *adverb*, shadiness *noun*

shaft *noun* 1 a spear or arrow or similar device; its long slender stem. 2 a remark aimed or striking like an arrow, *shafts of wit*. 3 a ray (of light); a bolt (of lightning). 4 any long narrow straight part of something, e.g. of a supporting column or a golf club. 5 a large axle. 6 each of a pair of long bars between which a horse is harnessed to draw a vehicle. 7 a vertical or sloping passage or opening giving access to a mine or giving an outlet for air or smoke etc.

shag *noun* 1 a rough mass of hair or fibre. 2 a strong coarse kind of tobacco. 3 a kind of cormorant.

shaggy *adjective* (shaggier, shaggiest) 1 having long rough hair or fibre. 2 rough, thick, and untidy, *shaggy hair*. □ shaggy-dog story a lengthy anecdote with a peculiar twist of humour at the end. shaggily *adverb*, shagginess *noun*

shah *noun* the former ruler of Iran. [Persian, = king]

shahid (shă-**heed**) *noun* a Muslim martyr. [Arabic]

Shaitan (shay-**tahn**) *noun* (also Shaytan) (in Muslim countries) the Devil or an evil spirit.

shake *verb* (shook, shaken, shaking)
1 to move quickly and often jerkily up and down or to and fro. **2** to dislodge by doing this, *shook sand off her towel*. **3** to make uneasy; to shock or disturb; to upset the calmness of. **4** to make less firm. **5** (of a voice) to tremble, to become weak or faltering. –shake *noun* **1** shaking; being shaken. **2** a shaking movement. **3** a jolt or shock. **4** a milk shake. **5** a moment, *shall be there in two shakes*. □ no great shakes (*informal*) not very good. shake down to become harmoniously adjusted to new conditions etc., to settle down. shake hands to clasp right hands in greeting or parting or in agreement. shake up to mix by shaking; to restore to shape by shaking; to rouse from sluggishness or a set habit. shake-up *noun* an upheaval; a reorganisation.

shakedown *noun* **1** a process of adjustment. **2** an improvised bed.

shaker *noun* **1** a person or thing that shakes. **2** a container in which ingredients for cocktails etc. are mixed by being shaken. **3** Shaker a member of an American religious sect, leading a celibate and simple life.

Shakespeare, William (1564–1616), England's most famous dramatist, born at Stratford-upon-Avon. Shakespearean (also Shakespearian) *adjective*

Shakti = Sakti.

shaky *adjective* (shakier, shakiest) **1** shaking, unsteady, trembling. **2** unreliable, wavering. shakily *adverb*, shakiness *noun*

shale *noun* stone that splits easily into fine pieces, rather like slate.

shall *auxiliary verb* (shalt is used with *thou*)
1 used with first person pronouns (*I* and *we*) to express future statements and questions (but *will* is used with second and third persons *you, he, she, it,* and *they*), *if we pick the fruit we shall die* (but *they will die*); *shall I make some coffee?* **2** used with second and third person subjects in promises or statements of intention or obligation, *with labour you shall earn your food*; *the last shall be first*; *thou shalt not kill*. **3** sometimes *shall* is used in questions with words other than *I* or *we* because *will* would sound like a request, e.g. *shall you take the children?* (but it is more likely that an Australian would say *Are you going to take the children?*).

Usage If you want to be strictly correct, keep to the above rules; but nowadays many people use *will* after *I* and *we* as a simple future (especially in informal speech and writing), and it is not usually regarded as wrong.

shallot (shă-**lot**) *noun* **1** an onion-like plant that forms clusters of bulbs as it grows. **2** (loosely) a spring onion.

shallow *adjective* **1** not deep, *a shallow stream*. **2** not thinking or thought out deeply, not capable of deep feelings. –shallow *noun* a shallow place. –shallow *verb* to make or become shallow. shallowly *adverb*, shallowness *noun*

shalt (*old use* or *religious use*) the present tense of shall, used with *thou*.

shalwar (**shul**-var) *noun* loose trousers worn by both sexes in some countries of southern Asia.

sham *noun* **1** a pretence, a thing or feeling that is not genuine. **2** a person who shams. –sham *adjective* pretended, not genuine. –sham *verb* (shammed, shamming) to pretend or pretend to be, *to sham illness*; *sham dead*. shammer *noun*

shaman (**shah**-măn) *noun* a witchdoctor or priest claiming direct access to, and influence in, the spiritual world, with power to guide souls, cure illnesses, etc. shamanism *noun*

shamble *verb* to walk or run in an awkward or lazy way. –shamble *noun* a shambling movement.

shambles *noun* a scene or condition of great bloodshed or disorder. [the word originally meant 'slaughterhouse']

shambolic (sham-**bol**-ik) *adjective* (*informal*) chaotic, very disorganised.

shame *noun* **1** a painful mental feeling aroused by a sense of having done something wrong or dishonourable or improper or ridiculous. **2** ability to feel this, *he has no shame*. **3** a person or thing that causes shame. **4** something regrettable, a pity, *it's a shame you can't come*. –shame *verb* to bring shame on, to make ashamed; to compel by arousing feelings of shame, *they were shamed into contributing more*.

shamefaced *adjective* looking ashamed.

shameful *adjective* causing shame, disgraceful. shamefully *adverb*

shameless *adjective* having or showing no feeling of shame, impudent. shamelessly *adverb*

shammy *noun* (*informal*) chamois leather.

shampoo *noun* **1** a liquid used to lather and wash the hair. **2** a liquid or chemical for cleaning the surface of a carpet or upholstery, or for washing a car. **3** shampooing, *booked a shampoo and set.* –**shampoo** *verb* to wash or clean with a shampoo. [from Hindi]

shamrock *noun* a clover-like plant with three leaves on each stem, the national emblem of Ireland.

shandy *noun* a mixed drink of beer with lemonade or ginger beer.

shanghai (shang-**hy**) *verb* (shanghaied, shanghaiing) **1** to take (a person) by force or trickery and compel him or her to do something. **2** (*Austral.*) to shoot with a catapult. –**shanghai** *noun* (*Austral.*) a catapult. [named after Shanghai, a seaport in China]

shank *noun* **1** the leg, *long shanks*. **2** the leg from knee to ankle; the corresponding part of an animal's leg (especially as a cut of meat). **3** a long narrow part of something, a shaft. □ **Shanks's mare** or **pony** one's own legs as a means of conveyance.

shan't = shall not.

shantung *noun* a kind of soft Chinese silk; fabric resembling this.

shanty¹ *noun* a shack. □ **shanty town** a settlement consisting of shanties.

shanty² *noun* a sailors' traditional song. [from French *chantez* = sing!]

shape *noun* **1** an area or form with a definite outline; the appearance produced by this. **2** the form or condition in which something appears, *a monster in human shape*. **3** the proper form or condition of something, *get it into shape*. **4** a pattern or mould. –**shape** *verb* **1** to give a certain shape to. **2** to develop into a certain shape or condition; *it is shaping well* or *shaping up well*, looks promising. **3** to adapt or modify (one's plans or ideas etc.). **shaper** *noun*

shapeless *adjective* **1** having no definite shape. **2** not shapely. **shapelessly** *adverb*

shapely *adjective* (shapelier, shapeliest) having a pleasing shape, well formed or proportioned. **shapeliness** *noun*

shard *noun* a broken piece of pottery or glass etc.

share¹ *noun* **1** a part given to an individual out of a larger amount which is being divided or of a burden or achievement; the part one is entitled to have or do. **2** any of the equal parts forming a business company's capital and entitling the holder to a proportion of the profits. –**share** *verb* **1** to give portions of (a thing) to two or more people, *share it out*. **2** to give away part of, *would share his last crust*. **3** to have a share of; to use, possess, endure, or benefit from (a thing) jointly with others, *share a room*; *we share the credit*. □ **go shares** to share things equally. **sharer** *noun*

share² *noun* a ploughshare.

sharefarmer *noun* (*Austral.*) a tenant farmer who receives a share of the profits from the owner. **sharefarm** *noun* & *verb*

shareholder *noun* a person who owns a share or shares in a business company.

shareware *noun* computer software available free of charge for sharing with other computer users.

sharia (sha-**ree**-ă) *noun* (also **shariah**) Islamic canonical law based on the teaching of the Koran and the traditions of the Prophet. [from Arabic]

shark *noun* **1** a large usually voracious sea fish with a triangular fin on its back. **2** a person who ruthlessly extorts money from another or others, a swindler.

sharp *adjective* **1** having a fine edge or point that is capable of cutting or piercing, not blunt. **2** narrowing to a point or edge, *a sharp ridge*. **3** steep, angular, not gradual, *a sharp slope*; *a sharp turn*. **4** well-defined, distinct, *in sharp focus*. **5** intense, forceful; loud and shrill; (of temper) irritable; *she has a sharp tongue*, often speaks harshly and angrily. **6** (of tastes and smells) producing a smarting sensation. **7** quick to see or hear or notice things, intelligent. **8** quick to seize an advantage; *be too sharp for him*, to outwit him. **9** unscrupulous. **10** vigorous, brisk, *a sharp walk*. **11** (in music) above the correct pitch; *C sharp, F sharp*, etc., a semitone higher than the corresponding note or key of natural pitch. –**sharp** *adverb* **1** punctually, *at six o'clock sharp*. **2** suddenly, *stopped sharp*. **3** at a sharp angle, *turn sharp right at the junction*. **4** above the correct pitch in music, *was singing sharp*. –**sharp** *noun* **1** (in music) a note that is a semitone higher than the corresponding one of natural pitch; the sign # indicating this. **2** (*informal*) a swindler. **3** a medium-length, round-eyed fine needle for hand sewing. □ **sharp-eyed** *adjective* quick at noticing things. **sharp practice** business dealings that are dishonest or barely honest. **sharply** *adverb*, **sharpness** *noun*

sharpen *verb* to make or become sharp.
sharpener *noun*

sharper *noun* a swindler, especially at cards.

sharpish *adjective* rather sharp. –sharpish
adverb (*informal*) quickly, briskly.

sharpshooter *noun* a skilled marksman.

Shastra (**shahs**-tră) *noun* any of the sacred
writings of the Hindus.

shatter *verb* 1 to break or become broken
violently into small pieces. 2 to destroy utterly,
shattered our hopes. 3 to disturb or upset the
calmness of, *we were shattered by the news*.

shave *verb* 1 to scrape (growing hair) off the
skin with a razor; to scrape (the skin) to do
this; to remove hair from the chin etc. 2 to cut
or scrape thin slices from the surface of (wood
etc.). 3 to graze gently in passing. 4 to reduce
or remove, *shave production costs*; *shave ten
per cent off our estimates*. –shave *noun* the
shaving of hair from the face, *needs a shave*.
□ **close shave** (*informal*) a narrow escape from
injury or risk or failure.

shaven *adjective* shaved.

shaver *noun* 1 a person or thing that shaves.
2 an electric razor. 3 (*informal*) a youngster.

shavings *plural noun* thin strips of wood etc.
shaved off the surface of a piece.

Shaw, George Bernard (1856–1950), Irish
playwright, critic, and political writer.

shawl *noun* a large piece of fabric worn round
the shoulders or head, or wrapped round a
baby, as a covering.

she *pronoun* 1 the female person or animal
mentioned; a thing (e.g. a vehicle, ship, or
aircraft) personified as female. 2 (*Austral.
informal*) it; the state of affairs; *she'll be right*;
she's jake, everything's all right. –she *noun* a
female animal; *she-bear*, a female bear.

sheaf *noun* (*plural* sheaves) 1 a bundle of
stalks of corn etc. tied together after reaping.
2 a bundle of arrows, papers, or other things
laid lengthwise together.

shear *verb* (sheared, shorn *or* sheared,
shearing) 1 to cut or trim with shears or other
sharp device; to remove (a sheep's wool) in
this way. 2 to strip bare, to deprive, *shorn
of his glory*. 3 to break or distort, or become
broken or distorted. –shear *noun* 1 a type of
fracture or distortion produced by pressure,
in which each successive layer (e.g. of a mass
of rock) slides over the next. 2 transformation
of a geometrical figure or solid in which one
line or plane remains fixed and those parallel

to it move sideways (so that, for example,
E becomes *E*). shearer *noun*

shears *plural noun* a clipping or cutting
instrument working like scissors but much
larger and usually operated with both hands.

shearwater *noun* a seabird with long wings,
skimming close to the water as it flies.

sheath *noun* (*plural* sheaths, *pr.* sheeths *or*
shee*thz*) 1 a close-fitting covering; a cover
for a blade or tool. 2 a condom. 3 a woman's
close-fitting dress. □ **sheath knife** a dagger-
like knife carried in a sheath.

sheathe (*pr.* shee*th*) *verb* 1 to put into a
sheath. 2 to encase in a covering.

sheaves *see* sheaf.

shed¹ *noun* a one-storeyed building for storage
or shelter, or for use as a workshop or place
for shearing, milking, etc.

shed² *verb* (shed, shedding) 1 to lose (a thing)
by a natural falling off, *trees shed their leaves*.
2 to take off, *shed one's clothes*. 3 to allow to
pour forth, *shed tears*; *shed one's blood*, to be
wounded or killed for one's country etc. 4 to
send forth, *shed warmth*. □ **shed light on** to
help to explain.

she'd (*informal*) = she had, she would.

sheen *noun* gloss, lustre. sheeny *adjective*

sheep *noun* (*plural* sheep) a grass-eating
animal with a thick fleecy coat, kept in
flocks for its fleece and for its flesh as meat;
as well be hanged for a sheep as a lamb,
commit a big crime rather than a small one
if the punishment is the same. □ **like sheep**
(of people) easily led or influenced. **separate
the sheep from the goats** to separate the
good from the wicked. **sheep dip** a liquid for
cleansing sheep of vermin or preserving their
wool. **sheep run** (*Austral.*) a tract of land for
grazing sheep. **sheep station** (*Austral.*) a large
property for raising sheep.

sheepdog *noun* a dog trained to guard and
herd sheep; *Old English sheepdog*, a dog of a
large shaggy-coated breed.

sheepfold *noun* an enclosure for sheep.

sheepish *adjective* bashful, embarrassed
through shame. sheepishly *adverb*,
sheepishness *noun*

sheepshank *noun* a knot used to shorten a
rope without cutting it.

sheepskin *noun* 1 a garment or rug made of
sheep's skin with the fleece on. 2 leather made
from sheep's skin.

sheer¹ *adjective* **1** pure, not mixed or qualified, *sheer luck*. **2** (of a rock or fall etc.) having a vertical or almost vertical surface, with no slope. **3** (of fabric) very thin, transparent. –**sheer** *adverb* directly, straight up or down, *the cliff rises sheer from the sea*.

sheer² *verb* to swerve from a course. □ **sheer off** to go away; to leave (a person or topic that one dislikes or wishes to avoid).

sheet¹ *noun* **1** a large rectangular piece of cotton or other fabric, used in pairs as inner bedclothes between which a person sleeps. **2** a large thin piece of any material (e.g. paper, glass, metal). **3** a piece of paper for writing or printing on; a complete and uncut piece (of the size in which it is made). **4** a wide expanse of water, ice, or flame, etc. –**sheet** *verb* **1** to provide or cover with sheets. **2** to form into sheets. **3** (of rain etc.) to fall in sheets. □ **sheet lightning** lightning that looks like a sheet of light across the sky.

sheet² *noun* a rope or chain attached to the lower corner of a sail, to secure or adjust it. □ **sheet anchor** a thing on which one depends for security or stability.

sheeting *noun* material for making sheets.

shehadeh (shě-**hah**-dě) *noun* the Muslim profession of faith ('there is no god but Allah, and Muhammad is the prophet of Allah'). [Arabic]

sheikh (*pr.* shayk *or* sheek) *noun* the leader of an Arab tribe or village. **sheikhdom** *noun* the territory of a sheikh. [Arabic, = old man]

sheila *noun* (*Austral. informal*) a girl or woman.

shekel (**shek**-ěl) *noun* the unit of money in Israel. **shekels** *plural noun* (*informal*) money, riches.

sheldrake *noun* (*plural* **shelduck**) a wild duck with bright plumage, living on coasts.

shelduck *noun* a female sheldrake. –**shelduck** *plural noun* (*see* **sheldrake**).

shelf *noun* (*plural* **shelves**) **1** a flat rectangular piece of wood or metal or glass etc. fastened horizontally to a wall or in a cupboard or bookcase for things to be placed on. **2** something resembling this, a ledge or steplike projection. □ **on the shelf** (of a person) made to be inactive as no longer of use; (of an unmarried woman) past the age when she is regarded as likely to be sought in marriage. **shelf life** the time for which a stored thing remains usable.

shell *noun* **1** the hard outer covering of eggs, nut kernels, and of animals such as snails, crabs, and tortoises. **2** the walls of an unfinished or burnt-out building or ship. **3** any structure that forms a firm framework or covering. **4** the metal framework of the body of a vehicle. **5** a light boat for rowing races. **6** a metal case filled with explosive, to be fired from a large gun. **7** a group of electrons in an atom, with almost equal energy. –**shell** *verb* **1** to remove the shell of, *shell peas*. **2** to fire explosive shells at. □ **come out of one's shell** to become more sociable and less shy. **shell out** (*informal*) to pay out (money, or a required amount). **shell-pink** *adjective* & *noun* delicate pale pink. **shell shock** nervous breakdown resulting from exposure to battle conditions. [from Old English *sciell* that has the same origin as *scale¹* and *scale²*]

she'll (*informal*) = she will.

shellac (shě-**lak**) *noun* thin flakes of a resinous substance used in making varnish. –**shellac** *verb* (**shellacked**, **shellacking**) to varnish with shellac.

Shelley¹, Mary Wollstonecraft (1797–1851), English novelist, author of *Frankenstein*.

Shelley², Percy Bysshe (1792–1822), English Romantic poet.

shellfish *noun* a water animal that has a shell, including molluscs such as oysters and mussels, and crustaceans such as lobsters and prawns.

shelter *noun* **1** something that serves as a shield or barrier against attack, danger, heat, wind, etc. **2** a structure built to keep rain etc. off people, *a bus shelter*; *a shelter-shed*. **3** refuge, a shielded condition, *seek shelter from the rain*. **4** a place giving refuge, e.g. to homeless people. –**shelter** *verb* **1** to provide with shelter. **2** to protect from blame, trouble, or competition. **3** to find or take shelter. □ **sheltered workshop** a place offering employment for people with disabilities.

shelve *verb* **1** to arrange on a shelf or shelves. **2** to fit (a wall or cupboard etc.) with shelves. **3** to put aside for later consideration; to reject (a plan etc.) temporarily or permanently. **4** to slope, *the sea floor shelves here*.

shelves *see* **shelf**.

shelving *noun* shelves; material for making these.

shemozzle *noun* (*informal*) a rumpus, a brawl.

shenanigans (shĕ-**nan**-ĭ-gănz) *plural noun* (*informal*) **1** high-spirited behaviour. **2** trickery.

sheoak *noun* (*Austral.*) a casuarina.

shepherd *noun* a man who tends a flock of sheep while they are at pasture. **–shepherd** *verb* to guide or direct (people). □ **shepherd's pie** a pie of minced meat topped with mashed potato. **shepherdess** *feminine noun* [from *sheep + herd*]

Sheraton (**she**-ră-tŏn) *noun* a late 18th-century style of English furniture, named after its designer Thomas Sheraton (died 1806).

sherbet *noun* **1** a cooling Oriental drink of weak sweet fruit juice. **2** a fizzy sweet drink or the powder from which this is made. **3** a flavoured water ice. [from Arabic *sharba* = a drink]

sheriff *noun* **1** (in Australia) an administrative officer of the Supreme Court. **2** (in the USA) the chief law-enforcing officer of a county. **3** (in the UK) (also **High Sheriff**) the chief executive officer of the Crown in a county. [from *shire + reeve* = officer]

Sherpa *noun* a member of a Himalayan people living on the borders of Nepal and Tibet.

sherry *noun* a strong white wine (either sweet or dry), originally from southern Spain. [from *Jerez* in Spain]

she's (*informal*) = she is, she has.

Shetland *adjective* of Shetland or the Shetland Islands. □ **Shetland Islands** (also **Shetlands**) a group of about 100 Scottish islands north-east of Scotland. **Shetland pony** a pony of a very small rough-coated breed. **Shetlander** *noun*

Shia *noun* **1** one of the two main branches of Islam, followed by about a tenth of Muslims, especially in Iran, which rejects the first three Sunni caliphs and regards Ali, the fourth caliph, as Muhammad's first true successor. **2** an adherent of this branch of Islam.

shibboleth (**shib**-ŏ-leth) *noun* an old slogan or principle that is still considered essential by some members of a party, *outworn shibboleths*. [from the story in the Bible, in which 'shibboleth' was a kind of password]

shield *noun* **1** a piece of armour carried on the arm to protect the body against missiles or thrusts. **2** a drawing or model of a triangular shield used for displaying a coat of arms; a trophy in the form of this. **3** an object, structure, or layer of material that protects something. **4** a mass of ancient rock under a land area. **–shield** *verb* to protect or screen; to protect from discovery.

shift *verb* **1** to change or move from one position to another. **2** to change form or character. **3** to transfer (blame or responsibility etc.). **4** (*informal*) to move quickly. **5** to manage to do something. **–shift** *noun* **1** a change of place, form, or character etc. **2** a set of workers who start work as another set finishes, the time for which they work, *the night shift*. **3** a piece of evasion. **4** a scheme for achieving something. **5** a woman's straight-cut dress. □ **make shift** *see* make. **shift for oneself** to manage without help. **shift one's ground** to change the basis of one's argument. **shifter** *noun*

shifter *noun* (*Austral.*) a shifting spanner.

shifting *see* shift. □ **shifting cultivation** a primitive form of agriculture, especially in the tropics, in which land is cultivated until it is exhausted, then deserted for another area. **shifting spanner** an adjustable spanner.

shiftless *adjective* lazy and inefficient, lacking resourcefulness. **shiftlessly** *adverb*, **shiftlessness** *noun*

shifty *adjective* (**shiftier**, **shiftiest**) evasive, not straightforward in manner or character; untrustworthy. **shiftily** *adverb*, **shiftiness** *noun*

Shi'ite (**shee**-I't) *noun* (also **Shiite**) an adherent of the Shia branch of Islam. **–Shi'ite** *adjective* of or relating to Shia.

shilling *noun* **1** a monetary unit in Kenya, Uganda, and Tanzania. **2** a former Australian and British coin worth 12 pence.

shilly-shally *verb* (**shilly-shallied**, **shilly-shallying**) to be unable to make up one's mind firmly. [from *shall I? shall I?*]

shim *noun* a thin wedge or slip of material used in machinery to make parts fit together.

shimmer *verb* to shine with a soft light that appears to quiver. **–shimmer** *noun* a shimmering effect.

shimmy *noun* a dance involving shaking of the whole body.

shin *noun* **1** the front of the leg below the knee. **2** the lower part of the foreleg in cattle, especially as a cut of beef. **–shin** *verb* (**shinned**, **shinning**) to climb by using arms and legs (not on a ladder).

shindig *noun* (*informal*) **1** a festive gathering, especially a boisterous one. **2** a shindy.

shindy *noun* (*informal*) a din; a brawl.

shine *verb* (**shone** (in sense 5 **shined**), **shining**)
1 to give out or reflect light, to be bright, to glow. **2** (of the sun etc.) to be visible and not obscured by clouds. **3** to excel in some way, *does not shine in maths; shining example*, an excellent one. **4** to direct the light of, *shine the torch on it*. **5** (*informal*) to polish. –**shine** *noun* **1** brightness. **2** a high polish.

shiner *noun* (*informal*) a black eye.

shingle¹ *noun* **1** a rectangular slip of wood used as a roof tile. **2** shingled hair; shingling the hair. –**shingle** *verb* **1** to roof with shingles. **2** to cut (a person's hair) in a short tapering style at the back, with all ends exposed.

shingle² *noun* small rounded pebbles; a stretch of these on a shore.

shingles *noun* a painful viral disease, with blisters forming along the path of a nerve or nerves.

Shinto *noun* (also **Shintoism**) a Japanese religion revering ancestors and nature spirits. [from Chinese *shen dao* = way of the gods]

shinty *noun* a game like hockey or hurling.

shiny *adjective* (**shinier**, **shiniest**) shining, rubbed until glossy. **shininess** *noun*

ship *noun* a large seagoing vessel. –**ship** *verb* (**shipped**, **shipping**) **1** to put or take on board a ship for conveyance to a destination. **2** to transport. □ **ship one's oars** to take them from the rowlocks and lay them in the boat. **take ship** to go on board a ship for a journey.

shipboard *noun* **on shipboard** on board a ship.

shipbuilding *noun* the business of constructing ships. **shipbuilder** *noun*

shipmate *noun* a person travelling or working on the same ship as another.

shipment *noun* **1** the putting of goods on a ship. **2** the amount shipped, a consignment.

shipper *noun* a person or firm whose business is transporting goods by ship.

shipping *noun* **1** ships, especially those of a country or port. **2** transporting goods by ship.

shipshape *adverb* & *adjective* in good order, tidy.

shipwreck *noun* the destruction of a ship by storm or striking a rock etc.

shipwrecked *adjective* having suffered a shipwreck.

shipwright *noun* a shipbuilder.

shipyard *noun* a shipbuilding establishment.

shiralee *noun* (*Austral. old use*) an itinerant's swag.

shiraz *noun* a variety of grape making a red table wine.

shire *noun* **1** (in some Australian states) a rural district with its own elected council. **2** (in the UK) a county.

shirk *verb* to avoid (a duty or work etc.) selfishly or unfairly. **shirker** *noun*

shirr *verb* to gather (cloth) with parallel elastic threads run through it. **shirring** *noun*

shirt *noun* an outer garment for the upper body made of cotton, etc., usually having a collar and sleeves and buttons down the front. □ **in one's shirtsleeves** with no jacket over one's shirt. **keep one's shirt on** (*informal*) to keep one's temper. **put one's shirt on** (*informal*) to bet all one has on (a horse etc.).

shirting *noun* material for making shirts.

shirty *adjective* (**shirtier**, **shirtiest**) (*informal*) annoyed, angry. **shirtily** *adverb*, **shirtiness** *noun*

shish kebab (shish kĕ-**bab**) *noun* pieces of meat and vegetable grilled on skewers. [from Turkish]

Shiva (**shee**-vă) = **Siva**.

shiver¹ *verb* to tremble slightly, especially with cold or fear. –**shiver** *noun* a shivering movement; *it gives me the shivers*, makes me shiver with fear or horror. **shivery** *adjective*

shiver² *verb* to shatter. **shivers** *plural noun* shattered fragments.

SHM *abbreviation* simple harmonic motion.

shoal¹ *noun* a great number of fish swimming together. –**shoal** *verb* to form shoals.

shoal² *noun* a shallow place; an underwater sandbank. –**shoal** *verb* to become shallow. **shoals** *plural noun* hidden dangers or difficulties.

shock¹ *noun* **1** the effect of a violent impact or shake. **2** a violent shake of the earth's crust in an earthquake. **3** a sudden violent effect upon a person's mind or emotions (e.g. by news of a disaster). **4** an acute state of weakness caused by physical injury or pain or by mental shock. **5** an electric shock (*see* electric). –**shock** *verb* **1** to affect with great indignation, horror, or disgust; to seem highly improper, scandalous, or outrageous to (a person). **2** to give an electric shock to. **3** to cause an acute state of weakness in (a person or animal). □ **shock absorber** a device for absorbing vibration in a vehicle. **shock tactics** sudden violent action taken to achieve one's purpose. **shock troops** troops specially trained for violent assaults. **shock wave** a sharp wave of increased atmospheric pressure, caused by an explosion or by a body moving faster than sound.

shock² *noun* a bushy untidy mass of hair.

shocker *noun* (*informal*) a shocking person or thing; a very bad specimen.

shocking *adjective* **1** causing great shock, indignation, or disgust, scandalous. **2** (*informal*) very bad, *shocking weather*. **shockingly** *adverb*

shod *see* shoe. **–shod** *adjective* having shoes of a specified kind, *sensibly shod*.

shoddy *adjective* (**shoddier**, **shoddiest**) of poor quality or workmanship. **shoddily** *adverb*, **shoddiness** *noun*

shoe *noun* **1** an outer covering for a person's foot, with a fairly stiff sole. **2** a horseshoe. **3** an object like a shoe in appearance or use. **4** the part of a brake that presses against the wheel or its drum in a vehicle. **–shoe** *verb* (**shod**, **shoeing**) to fit with a shoe or shoes. □ **be in a person's shoes** to be in his or her situation or plight. **shoe tree** a shaped block for keeping a shoe in shape.

shoehorn *noun* a curved piece of metal or other stiff material for easing one's heel into the back of a shoe.

shoelace *noun* a cord for fastening together the edges of a shoe's uppers.

shoemaker *noun* a person whose trade is making or mending boots and shoes.

shoestring *noun* a shoelace. □ **on a shoestring** (*informal*) with only a small amount of money, e.g. in running a business.

shogun (**shoh**-gŭn) *noun* the hereditary commander of the army in feudal Japan.

shone *see* shine.

shonky *adjective* (*Austral. informal*) unreliable, dishonest.

shoo *interjection* a sound uttered to frighten animals away. **–shoo** *verb* (**shooed**, **shooing**) to drive away by this.

shook *see* shake. □ **shook on** (*Austral. informal*) keen on. **shook up** (*informal*) upset.

shoot *verb* (**shot**, **shooting**) **1** to fire (a gun or other weapon, or a missile); to use a gun etc., *he can't shoot straight*. **2** to kill or wound with a missile from a gun etc. **3** to hunt with a gun for sport. **4** to send out swiftly or violently, *he shot the rubbish into the bin*. **5** to move swiftly, *the car shot past me*. **6** (of a plant)

to put forth buds or shoots. **7** to slide (the bolt of a door) into or out of its fastening. **8** to have one's boat move swiftly under (a bridge) or over (rapids etc.). **9** to take a shot at goal. **10** to photograph or film. **–shoot** *noun* **1** a young branch of new growth of a plant. **2** an expedition for shooting game; land where this is held. □ **have shot one's bolt** to have made one's last possible effort. **shoot a line** (*informal*) to try to impress or convince someone by boastful talk. **shoot down** to cause (a flying aircraft) to fall to the ground by shooting; to argue effectively against (a person, an argument, etc.). **shoot one's mouth off** (*informal*) to talk too freely. **shoot-out** *noun* (*informal*) a decisive gun battle. **shoot through** (*Austral. informal*) to depart quickly, to escape. **shoot up** to rise suddenly; (of a person) to grow rapidly; (*informal*) to inject (a drug). **shooter** *noun*

shooting *noun* an act or instance of shooting. **–shooting** *adjective* moving quickly, *a shooting pain*. □ **shooting gallery** a place for shooting at targets with rifles etc. **shooting star** a small meteor appearing like a star, moving rapidly, and then disappearing. **shooting stick** a walking stick with a small folding seat at the handle end. **the whole shooting match** (*informal*) everything.

shop *noun* **1** a building or room where goods or services are on sale to the public. **2** a workshop. **3** one's own work or profession as a subject of conversation, *she is always talking shop*. **–shop** *verb* (**shopped**, **shopping**) **1** to go to a shop or shops to buy things. **2** (*informal*) to inform against (a person), especially to the police. □ **all over the shop** (*informal*) in great disorder, scattered everywhere. **shop around** to look for the best bargain. **shop floor** workers as distinct from management or senior officials of a trade union. **shop-soiled** *adjective* soiled or faded from being on display in a shop. **shop steward** an elected representative of workers in a factory etc. **shopper** *noun*

shopkeeper *noun* a person who owns or manages a shop.

shoplifter *noun* a person who steals goods that are on display in a shop, after entering as a customer. **shoplifting** *noun*

shopping *noun* **1** buying goods in shops. **2** the goods bought. □ **shopping centre** an area where shops are concentrated. **shopping mall** *see* mall.

shore¹ *noun* the land along the edge of the sea or of a large body of water.

shore² *verb* to prop or support with a length of timber set at a slant. – **shore** *noun* a support of this kind.

shoreline *noun* the line of a shore.

shoreward *adjective* & *adverb* towards the shore. **shorewards** *adverb*

shoring *noun* the shores (*shore² noun*) that support something; material for these.

shorn *see* **shear**.

short *adjective* 1 measuring little from end to end in space or time. 2 seeming to be shorter than it really is, *for one short hour*. 3 not lasting, not going far into the past or future, *a short memory*. 4 insufficient, having an insufficient supply, *water is short; we are short of water; short-staffed*. 5 (*informal*) having little of a certain quality, *he's short on tact*. 6 concise, brief. 7 curt. 8 (of vowel sounds) relatively brief or light (*see* **long**, sense 7). 9 (of an alcoholic drink) small and concentrated, made with spirits. 10 (of temper) easily lost. 11 (of pastry) rich and crumbly through containing much fat. – **short** *adverb* suddenly, abruptly, *stopped short*. – **short** *noun* (*informal*) 1 a short circuit. 2 a short film. – **short** *verb* (*informal*) to short-circuit. □ **for short** as an abbreviation, *Samantha is called Sam for short*. **in short supply** scarce. **make short work of** to deal with (a thing) rapidly. **short-change** *verb* to rob by giving insufficient change; to cheat (a person). **short circuit** a connection (usually a fault) in an electrical circuit in which current flows by a shorter route than the normal one. **short-circuit** *verb* to cause a short circuit in; to bypass. **short cut** a route or method that is quicker than the usual one. **short division** the process of dividing one number by another without writing down one's calculations. **short for** an abbreviation of, *'Tony' is short for 'Antony'*. **short-handed** *adjective* having an insufficient number of workers or helpers. **short-lived** *adjective* having a short life; not lasting long. **short odds** nearly even odds in betting. **short of** without going the length of, *will do anything for her short of having her to stay*. **short selling** selling stocks or other securities or commodities in advance of acquiring them, and relying on the price falling so that a profit can be made. **short shrift** curt treatment. **short-sighted** *adjective* able to see clearly only what is close; lacking foresight. **short-tempered** *adjective* easily becoming angry. **short-term**

adjective of or for a short period. **short ton** *see* **ton**. **short wave** a radio wave of about 10 to 100 metres wavelength. **shortish** *adjective*, **shortness** *noun*

shortage *noun* a lack of something that is needed, insufficiency.

shortbread *noun* a rich sweet biscuit.

shortcake *noun* shortbread.

shortcoming *noun* failure to reach a required standard; a fault.

shorten *verb* to make or become shorter.

shortening *noun* fat used to make pastry etc. rich and crumbly.

shortfall *noun* a deficit.

shorthand *noun* a method of writing very rapidly, using quickly-made symbols.

shorthorn *noun* one of a breed of cattle with short horns.

shortlist *noun* a list of selected candidates from whom the final choice will be made. – **shortlist** *verb* to put on a shortlist.

shortly *adverb* 1 in a short time, not long, soon, *coming shortly; shortly afterwards*. 2 in a few words. 3 curtly.

shorts *plural noun* trousers that do not reach to the knee.

Shostakovich (shost-ă-**koh**-vich), Dmitri (1906–75), Russian composer.

shot *see* **shoot**. – **shot** *adjective* (of fabric) woven or dyed so that different colours show at different angles. – **shot** *noun* 1 the firing of a gun etc.; the sound of this. 2 a person with regard to skill in shooting, *he's a good shot*. 3 (*plural* **shot**) a single missile for a cannon or gun, a non-explosive projectile. 4 lead pellets for firing from small guns. 5 a heavy ball thrown as a sport. 6 the launching of a rocket or spacecraft. 7 a stroke in tennis, cricket, or billiards etc. 8 an attempt to hit something or reach a target. 9 an attempt to do something, *have a shot at this crossword*. 10 an injection. 11 (*informal*) a dram of spirits. 12 a photograph; the scene photographed; a single continuous photographed scene in a cinema film. □ **like a shot** without hesitation, willingly. **shot in the arm** a stimulus, an encouragement. **shot in the dark** a mere guess. **shot put** a sporting event based on throwing a heavy ball.

shotgun *noun* a gun for firing small shot at close range.

shott *noun* a shallow brackish or salt lake or marsh, usually dry in summer, in parts of North Africa.

should *auxiliary verb*, used to express **1** duty or obligation, *you should have told me*. **2** an expected future event, *they should be here by ten*. **3** a possible event, *if you should happen to see him*. **4** with *I* and *we* to form a polite statement or a conditional clause, *I should like to come*; *if their forecast had been right, they would have won and we should have lost*; *I should say it's about right*.

Usage *Would* is now commonly used in place of *should* in sense 4.

---

shoulder *noun* **1** the part of the body at which an arm, foreleg, or wing is attached; the part of the human body between this and the neck. **2** the part of a garment covering a shoulder. **3** the upper foreleg and adjacent parts of an animal as a cut of meat. **4** a projection compared to the human shoulder, *the shoulder of a bottle*. **5** a strip of land next to a road. –**shoulder** *verb* **1** to push with one's shoulder. **2** to take (a burden) upon one's shoulders. **3** to take (blame or responsibility) upon oneself. □ **put one's shoulder to the wheel** to make an effort. **shoulder arms** to hold a rifle with the barrel against one's shoulder. **shoulder bag** a handbag hung on a strap over the shoulder. **shoulder blade** either of the two large flat bones at the top of the back.

shouldn't (*informal*) = should not.

shout *noun* **1** a loud cry or utterance of words calling attention or expressing joy, excitement, or disapproval. **2** (*Austral. informal*) a person's turn to buy a round of drinks. –**shout** *verb* **1** to utter a shout; to utter or call loudly. **2** (*Austral. informal*) to buy a round of drinks; to provide (a drink, meal, etc.); to treat (a person) to a drink, meal, etc. □ **shout down** to silence (a person) by shouting.

shove (*pr.* shuv) *noun* a rough push. –**shove** *verb* **1** to push roughly. **2** (*informal*) to put, *shove it in the drawer*.

shovel *noun* **1** a tool for scooping up earth or snow etc., usually shaped like a spade with the edges turned up. **2** a large mechanically-operated device used for the same purpose. –**shovel** *verb* (**shovelled, shovelling**) **1** to shift or clear with or as if with a shovel. **2** to scoop or thrust roughly, *shovelling food into his mouth*.

shoveller *noun* a duck with a broad shovel-like beak.

show *verb* (**showed, shown, showing**) **1** to allow or cause to be seen; to offer for inspection or viewing. **2** to demonstrate; to point out; to prove; to cause (a person) to understand, *show us how it works; showed them the door*, dismissed them. **3** to conduct, *show them in* or *out*. **4** to present an image of, *this picture shows the hotel*. **5** to exhibit in a show. **6** to treat in a certain way, *showed us much kindness*. **7** to be able to be seen, *the label is showing*. **8** (*informal*) to prove one's ability or worth to, *we'll show them!* **9** (*informal*) to appear, to come when expected. –**show** *noun* **1** showing; being shown. **2** a display; a public exhibition for competition, entertainment, or advertisement etc., a fair or pageant, *motor show; Royal Easter Show*. **3** a play, especially a musical; a television program; any public entertainment or performance. **4** (*informal*) any business or undertaking, *he runs the whole show*. **5** an outward appearance, an insincere display, *under a show of friendship*. **6** a pompous display. □ **give the show away** to reveal things that were intended to be secret. **no show** (*Austral. informal*) no chance. **show bag** (*Austral.*) a bag of goods, especially advertisers' samples, formerly given free, at an agricultural or annual show, also called a *sample bag*. **show business** the entertainment or theatrical profession. **show off** to display well, proudly, or ostentatiously; to try to impress people; to have a tantrum. **show-off** *noun* a person who tries to impress others. **show of hands** raising of hands to vote for or against something. **show oneself** to be seen in public. **show one's face** to let oneself be seen. **show up** to make or be clearly visible; to reveal (a fault or inferiority etc.); (*informal*) to appear, to come when expected.

showbiz *noun* (*informal*) = **show business**.

showcase *noun* a glass-covered case in which things are exhibited.

showdown *noun* **1** a final test. **2** disclosure of intentions or conditions etc.

shower *noun* **1** a brief fall of rain or snow etc., or of bullets, dust, stones, etc. **2** a sudden influx of letters or gifts etc. **3** a cubicle or bath in which one stands under a spray of water; the apparatus used for this; the act of bathing in a shower. **4** a party for giving gifts, especially to a prospective bride, *bridal shower*. –**shower** *verb* **1** to pour down or come in a shower.

2 to send or give (many letters or gifts etc.) to. **3** to wash oneself in a shower.

showerproof *adjective* (of fabric) able to keep out slight rain.

showery *adjective* (of weather) with many showers.

showground *noun* an open outdoor space where a show or fair is held.

showing *noun* the evidence or quality that a person shows, *on today's showing, he will fail.*

showjumping *noun* the sport of riding horses to jump over obstacles, in competition.

showman *noun* (*plural* showmen) **1** an organiser of circuses or similar entertainments. **2** a person who is good at showmanship.

showmanship *noun* skill in presenting an entertainment or goods or one's abilities to the best advantage.

shown *see* show.

showpiece *noun* an excellent specimen used for exhibition.

showplace *noun* a house or place that tourists etc. go to see.

showroom *noun* a room in which goods are displayed for inspection.

showy *adjective* (showier, showiest) **1** making a good display. **2** brilliant, gaudy. showily *adverb*, showiness *noun*

shrank *see* shrink.

shrapnel *noun* **1** an artillery shell containing bullets or pieces of metal which it scatters as it explodes. **2** the pieces it scatters. [named after H. Shrapnel, the British officer who invented it in about 1806]

shred *noun* **1** a small piece torn or cut from something. **2** a small amount, *not a shred of evidence*. –shred *verb* (shredded, shredding) to tear or cut into shreds. shredder *noun*

shrew *noun* **1** a small mouselike animal. **2** a sharp-tempered scolding woman.

shrewd *adjective* having or showing sound judgment and common sense; clever. shrewdly *adverb*, shrewdness *noun*

shrewish *adjective* sharp-tempered and scolding.

shriek *noun* a shrill cry or scream. –shriek *verb* to make a shriek; to utter with a shriek.

shrift *noun* (*old use*) confession and absolution. □ short shrift *see* short.

shrike *noun* a bird with a strong hooked beak that impales its prey (small birds and insects) on thorns. *See also* piping shrike.

shrill *adjective* piercing and high-pitched in sound. –shrill *verb* to sound or utter shrilly. shrilly *adverb*, shrillness *noun*

shrimp *noun* **1** a small shellfish often used as food, pink when boiled. **2** (*informal*) a very small person.

shrine *noun* an altar, chapel, or other place that is hallowed because of its special associations.

shrink *verb* (shrank, shrunk, shrinking) **1** to make or become smaller, especially by the action of moisture, heat, or cold, *it shrank; it has shrunk*. **2** to draw back so as to avoid something, to withdraw; to be unwilling to do something (e.g. because of shame or dislike). –shrink *noun* (*informal*) a psychiatrist or psychotherapist. □ shrink fit an extremely tight fit formed by shrinking one metal part round another. shrink-wrap *verb* to wrap (an article) in material that shrinks tightly round it.

shrinkage *noun* **1** the process of shrinking; the amount by which something has shrunk. **2** (in commerce) loss by theft or wastage etc.

shrivel *verb* (shrivelled, shrivelling) **1** to shrink and wrinkle from great heat or cold or lack of moisture. **2** to cause to shrivel.

shroud *noun* **1** a sheet in which a dead body is wrapped for burial; a garment for the dead. **2** something that conceals, *wrapped in a shroud of secrecy*. **3** one of a set of ropes supporting the mast of a ship. –shroud *verb* **1** to wrap in a shroud. **2** to protect or conceal in wrappings. **3** to conceal, *his past life is shrouded in mystery*.

Shrove Tuesday the day before Ash Wednesday.

shrub *noun* a woody plant smaller than a tree and usually divided into separate stems from near the ground. shrubby *adjective*

shrubbery *noun* an area planted with shrubs.

shrug *verb* (shrugged, shrugging) to raise (the shoulders) as a gesture of indifference, doubt, or helplessness. –shrug *noun* this movement. □ shrug off to dismiss (a thing) as unimportant.

shrunk *see* shrink.

shrunken *adjective* having shrunk.

shudder *verb* **1** to shiver violently with horror, fear, or cold. **2** to make a strong shaking movement. –shudder *noun* a shuddering movement.

shuffle *verb* **1** to walk without lifting the feet clear of the ground; to move (one's feet) in this way. **2** to slide (cards) over one another so as to change their order. **3** to rearrange, to jumble. **4** to keep shifting one's position. **5** to get rid of (a burden etc.) shiftily, *shuffled off the responsibility on to others*; *shuffled out of it*. –**shuffle** *noun* **1** a shuffling movement or walk. **2** shuffling of cards etc. **3** a rearrangement, *the latest Cabinet shuffle*. **shuffler** *noun*

shun *verb* (**shunned, shunning**) to avoid, to keep away from.

shunt *verb* **1** to move (a train) on to a sidetrack. **2** to divert into an alternative course. **3** to divert (a decision etc.) on to another person. –**shunt** *noun* shunting; being shunted. **shunter** *noun*

shush *interjection* & *verb* (*informal*) = hush.

shut *verb* (**shut, shutting**) **1** to move (a door, lid, window, etc.) into position so that it blocks an opening. **2** to move or be moved into such a position, *the lid shuts automatically*. **3** to prevent access to (a place or receptacle etc.) by shutting a door etc.; *shut one's eyes* or *ears* or *mind to a thing*, to refuse to take notice of it or hear it. **4** to bring or fold the parts of (a thing) together, *shut the book*. **5** to keep in or out by shutting a door etc., *shut out the noise*. **6** to trap (a finger or dress etc.) by shutting something on it. □ **shut down** to cease working or business, either for the day or permanently; to cause to do this. **shut-eye** *noun* (*informal*) sleep. **shut off** to stop the flow of (water or gas etc.) by shutting a valve. **shut up** to shut securely; to shut all the doors and windows of (a house); to put away in a box etc.; (*informal*) to stop talking or making a noise, to cause to do this, to silence; *shut up shop*, = shut down.

shutdown *noun* **1** a closure of a factory or system. **2** a turning off of a computer or computer system.

shutter *noun* **1** a panel or screen that can be closed over a window. **2** a device that opens and closes the aperture of a camera lens to allow light to fall on the film. [from *shut*]

shuttered *adjective* **1** fitted with shutters. **2** with the shutters closed.

shuttle *noun* **1** a holder carrying the weft-thread to and fro across the loom in weaving; a similar thread-carrying device used in tatting, knotting, etc. **2** a bobbin carrying the lower thread in a sewing machine. **3** a vehicle used in a shuttle service. **4** a shuttlecock. **5** a space shuttle. –**shuttle** *verb* to move or travel or send to and fro. □ **shuttle diplomacy** diplomacy that involves travelling between the countries involved in a dispute. **shuttle service** a transport service in which a vehicle goes to and fro over a relatively short distance.

shuttlecock *noun* **1** a small rounded piece of cork with a ring of feathers, or of other material made in this shape, struck to and fro in badminton. **2** something that is passed repeatedly to and fro.

shy¹ *adjective* (**shyer, shyest**) **1** (of a person) timid and lacking self-confidence in the presence of others, avoiding company, reserved. **2** (of behaviour) showing shyness, *a shy smile*. **3** (of an animal) timid and avoiding observation. –**shy** *verb* (**shied, shying**) to jump or move suddenly in alarm. **shyly** *adverb*, **shyness** *noun*

shy² *verb* (**shied, shying**) to fling or throw (a stone etc.). –**shy** *noun* a throw.

shyster *noun* (*informal*) a rogue.

SI *abbreviation* Système International d'Unités. [French, = International System of Units]

Siamese *adjective* of Siam (now called Thailand) or its people or language. –**Siamese** *noun* (*plural* **Siamese**) **1** a native of Siam. **2** the language of Siam. **3** a Siamese cat. □ **Siamese cat** a cat of a breed that has short pale fur with darker face, ears, tail, and feet. **Siamese twins** twins whose bodies are joined in some way at birth.

Sibelius (sĭ-**bay**-lee-ŭs), Jean (1865–1957), Finnish composer whose music reflects his deep feeling for his native country.

Siberia a region of Russia in northern Asia, noted for its harsh winters. **Siberian** *adjective*

sibilant *adjective* having a hissing sound. –**sibilant** *noun* one of the speech sounds that sound like hissing, e.g. *s*, *sh*. **sibilance** *noun* [from Latin *sibilans* = hissing]

sibling *noun* a child in relation to another or others of the same parent, a brother or sister.

sibyl (**sib**-ĭl) *noun* (in ancient times) a woman acting as the reputed mouthpiece of a god, uttering prophecies and oracles. □ **Sibylline Books** a collection of prophecies in Greek hexameter verses, ascribed to the sibyls, consulted by magistrates of ancient Rome in times of national crises.

sic (*pr.* sik) *adverb* used or spelt in that way. [Latin, = thus]

Usage This word is placed in brackets after a word that seems odd or is wrongly spelt, to show that one is quoting it exactly as it was given.

Sicily a large island in the Mediterranean Sea, off the 'toe' of Italy. **Sicilian** *adjective* & *noun*

sick *adjective* **1** physically or mentally unwell. **2** likely to vomit, *feel sick*. **3** distressed, disgusted, *sick at heart*; *their ignorance makes me sick*. **4** bored with something through having already had or done too much of it, *I'm sick of cricket*. **5** finding amusement in misfortune or in morbid subjects, *sick jokes*. –**sick** *verb* (*informal*) to vomit, *sicked it up*. –**sick** *noun* (*informal*) vomit. □ **be sick** to vomit. **sick leave** leave of absence because of illness. **sick list** a list of people who are ill, especially in a regiment; *on the sick list*, ill. **sick pay** pay given to an employee who is absent through illness.

sickbay *noun* a room or rooms for sick people in a ship or boarding school etc.

sickbed *noun* the bed of a sick person.

sicken *verb* **1** to begin to be ill; *be sickening for a disease*, showing the first signs of it. **2** to make or become distressed or disgusted.

sickening *adjective* annoying; disgusting.

sickie *noun* (*Austral. informal*) a day's sick leave, often with insufficient medical reason.

sickle *noun* **1** a tool with a curved blade and a short handle, used for cutting corn etc. **2** something shaped like this, e.g. the crescent moon.

sickly *adjective* (**sicklier**, **sickliest**) **1** often ill, *a sickly child*. **2** unhealthy-looking. **3** causing ill health, *a sickly climate*. **4** causing sickness or distaste, *a sickly smell*; *sickly sentimentality*. **5** weak, *a sickly smile*.

sickness *noun* **1** illness. **2** a disease. **3** vomiting.

sickroom *noun* a room occupied by a sick person, or kept ready for this.

siddha *noun* (in Hinduism) an ascetic who has achieved enlightenment. [Sanskrit]

siddhi *noun* (in Hinduism) **1** complete understanding, enlightenment. **2** a supernatural power possessed by a siddha. [Sanskrit]

side *noun* **1** any of the more or less flat inner or outer surfaces of an object, especially as distinct from the top and bottom, front and back, or ends. **2** either surface of a flat object (e.g. a piece of paper). **3** any of the bounding lines of a plane figure such as a triangle or square. **4** either of the two halves into which an object or body can be divided by a line down its centre. **5** the part near the edge and away from the centre of something; *take* or *put*

on one side, aside. **6** a slope of a hill or ridge. **7** the region next to a person or thing, *he stood at my side*. **8** one aspect or view of something, *study all sides of the problem*; *she is on the fat side*, rather fat. **9** one of two opposing groups or teams etc. **10** the line of descent through father or mother, *his mother's side of the family*. **11** (*informal*) swank, *she puts on side*. –**side** *adjective* at or on the side, *side door*. –**side** *verb* to take the side of a person in a dispute, *he sided with his son*. □ **on the side** as a sideline; as a surreptitious or illicit activity. **side by side** standing close together. **side drum** a small double-headed drum. **side effect** a secondary (usually less desirable) effect. **side issue** an issue that is not the main one. **side road** a road leading off a main road; a minor road. **side saddle** a saddle for a woman rider to sit on with both legs on the same side of the horse, not astride. **side street** a street lying aside from main ones. **side table** a table at the side of a room or apart from the main table. **side view** a view of something sideways. **side whiskers** whiskers on the cheek.

sideboard *noun* a table or flat-topped piece of dining room furniture with drawers and cupboards for china etc. **sideboards** *plural noun* (*informal*) side-whiskers.

sideburns *plural noun* short side-whiskers.

sidecar *noun* a small vehicle attached to the side of a motorcycle, to seat a passenger.

sidekick *noun* (*informal*) a close associate; a subordinate; an offsider.

sidelight *noun* **1** light from one side (not front or back). **2** minor or casual light shed on a subject etc. **3** each of a pair of small lights at the front of a vehicle. **4** a light at either side of a ship under way.

sideline *noun* **1** something done in addition to one's main work or activity. **2** a line bounding the side of a hockey pitch, tennis court, etc. **sidelines** *plural noun* the space just outside the sidelines where spectators sit or stand. □ **on the sidelines** away from the main action.

sidelong *adverb* & *adjective* to one side, sideways, *a sidelong glance*.

sidereal (sy-**deer**-ree-ăl) *adjective* of or measured by the stars. [from Latin *sideris* = of a star]

sideshow *noun* a small show forming part of a large one (e.g. at a fair).

sidesman *noun* (*plural* **sidesmen**) one who acts as an usher etc. at a church service.

sidestep *verb* **1** to avoid by stepping sideways. **2** to evade (a question or responsibility etc.).

sidestroke *noun* **1** a stroke towards or from a side. **2** a swimming stroke in which the swimmer lies on his or her side.

sidetrack *noun* a railway siding. **–sidetrack** *verb* to divert from the main course or issue.

sidewalk *noun* (*Amer.*) a pavement at the side of a road.

sideways *adverb* & *adjective* **1** to or from one side (not forwards or back). **2** with one side facing forward, *sat sideways*.

siding *noun* a short track by the side of a railway, used for shunting.

sidle (*rhymes with* bridle) *verb* to advance in a timid, furtive, or cringing manner; to edge. [from *sidelong*]

SIDS *abbreviation* sudden infant death syndrome.

siege *noun* the surrounding and blockading of a town or fortified place, in order to capture it, or of a house etc. that is occupied by persons using force or threats. ☐ **lay siege to** to begin besieging. **raise the siege** *see* **raise**.

siemens (**see**-měnz) *noun* the unit of electrical conductance, the reciprocal of the ohm. [named after Ernst Werner von Siemens (1816–92), German electrical engineer]

sienna (see-**en**-ă) *noun* a kind of clay used as colouring matter. ☐ **burnt sienna** reddish-brown. **raw sienna** brownish-yellow. [from Siena, a town in Italy]

sierra (see-**e**-ră) *noun* a long chain of mountains with sharp slopes and an irregular outline, in Spain or Spanish America. [from Latin *serra* = a saw]

Sierra Leone (see-**e**-ră lee-**ohn**) a republic on the coast of West Africa. **Sierra Leonean** *adjective* & *noun*

siesta (see-**est**-ă) *noun* an afternoon nap or rest, especially in hot countries. [Spanish, from Latin *sexta* = sixth (hour)]

sieve (*pr.* siv) *noun* a utensil consisting of a frame with wire mesh or gauze, used for sorting solid or coarse matter (which is retained in it) from liquid or fine matter (which passes through), or for reducing a soft mixture squeezed through it to a uniform pulp. **–sieve** *verb* to put through a sieve.

sift *verb* **1** to sieve. **2** to sprinkle lightly from a perforated container. **3** to examine carefully and select or analyse. **4** (of snow or light) to fall as if from a sieve. **sifter** *noun*

sigh *noun* a long deep breath given out audibly, expressing sadness, tiredness, relief, etc. **–sigh** *verb* **1** to give a sigh; to express with a sigh. **2** (of wind etc.) to make a similar sound. **3** to yearn.

sight *noun* **1** the faculty of seeing, ability to see. **2** seeing, being seen, *lost sight of it*. **3** the range over which a person can see or an object can be seen, *within sight of the castle*. **4** a thing seen or visible or worth seeing, a display, *their roses are a wonderful sight this year*. **5** something regarded as unsightly or looking ridiculous, *she looks a sight in those clothes*. **6** (*informal*) a great quantity, *a darned sight better*. **7** a device looked through to help aim or observe with a gun or telescope etc.; aim or observation using this; *set one's sights on*, aim at. **–sight** *verb* **1** to get a sight of, to observe the presence of, *we sighted land*. **2** to aim or observe by using the sight in a gun or telescope etc. ☐ **at** or **on sight** as soon as a person or thing has been seen, *shoot on sight*; *she plays music at sight*, without preliminary practice or study of the score. **in sight** visible; clearly near at hand, *victory was in sight*. **lower one's sights** to adopt a less ambitious policy. **sight-reading** *noun* playing or singing music at sight. **sight screen** a large movable white structure placed in line with the wicket to help the batsman see the ball in cricket. **sight unseen** without previous inspection.

sighted *adjective* having sight, not blind.

sightless *adjective* blind.

sightly *adjective* attractive to look at. **sightliness** *noun*

sightseeing *noun* visiting places of interest in a town etc. **sightseer** *noun*

sign *noun* **1** something perceived that suggests the existence of a fact or quality or condition, either past, present, or future, *it shows signs of decay* or *of being a success*. **2** a mark or device with a special meaning, a symbol. **3** a signboard or other visual object used similarly; the device on this; a notice. **4** an action or gesture conveying information or a command etc. **5** any of the twelve divisions of the zodiac (*see* **zodiac**); a symbol representing one of these. **–sign** *verb* **1** to make a sign, *signed to me to come*. **2** to write (one's name) on a document etc. to guarantee that it is genuine or has one's authority or consent, or to acknowledge receipt of something, *signed his name*; *signed the letter*; *sign here*.

3 to convey by signing a document, *signed away her right to the house*. **4** to engage or be engaged as an employee by signing a contract of employment. **5** to use sign language. □ sign language a series of gestures used by deaf or dumb people for communication. sign off (in broadcasting) to announce the end of one's program or transmission. sign on or up to sign a contract of employment; to register oneself (e.g. for a course). [from Latin *signum* = a mark]

signal *noun* **1** a sign or gesture giving information or a command; a message made up of such signs. **2** an act or event that immediately produces a general reaction, *his arrival was the signal for an outburst of cheering*. **3** an object placed to give notice or warning, *traffic signals*; *railway signals*. **4** a sequence of electrical impulses or radio waves transmitted or received. –signal *verb* (signalled, signalling) to make a signal or signals; to direct, communicate with, or announce in this way. –signal *adjective* remarkably good or bad, *a signal success*. □ signal box a small railway building with signalling apparatus. signaller *noun*, signally *adverb* [same origin as *sign*]

signalise *verb* (also -ize) to make noteworthy.

signatory (sig-nă-tŏ-ree) *noun* any of the parties who sign a treaty or other agreement.

signature *noun* **1** a person's name or initials written by himself or herself in signing something. **2** a key signature (*see* key) or time signature (*see* time) in music. □ signature tune a special tune used to announce a particular program or performer. [same origin as *sign*]

signboard *noun* a board bearing the name or symbol of a shop or hotel etc. and displayed in front of it.

signet (sig-nĕt) *noun* a person's seal used with or instead of a signature. □ signet ring a ring with an engraved design, formerly used as a seal. [same origin as *sign*]

significance *noun* **1** what is meant by something, *what is the significance of this symbol?* **2** being significant, importance, *the event is of no significance*.

significant *adjective* **1** having a meaning. **2** full of meaning, *a significant glance*. **3** important, noteworthy, *significant developments*. significantly *adverb*

signification *noun* meaning.

signify *verb* (signified, signifying) **1** to be a sign or symbol of. **2** to have as a meaning. **3** to make known, *signified her approval*. **4** to be of importance, to matter, *it doesn't signify*. [from Latin *signum* = sign]

signor (seen-yor) *noun* the title of an Italian man, = Mr or sir.

signora (seen-yor-ră) *noun* the title of an Italian woman, = Mrs or madam.

signorina (seen-yor-ree-nă) *noun* the title of an Italian unmarried woman or girl, = Miss or madam.

signpost *noun* a post at a road junction etc. with arms showing the names of places along each of the roads to which these point. –signpost *verb* to provide with a post or posts of this kind.

Sihanouk *see* Norodom Sihanouk.

Sikh (*pr.* seek) *noun* a member of a monotheistic Indian religion, founded in the Punjab, combining elements of Hinduism and Islam. Sikhism *noun* [Hindi, = disciple]

silage (sy-lij) *noun* green fodder stored and fermented in a silo.

silence *noun* **1** absence of sound. **2** avoidance or absence of speaking or of making a sound. **3** the fact of not mentioning something or of refusing to betray a secret. –silence *verb* to make silent. □ in silence without speaking or making a sound. [from Latin *silere* = to be silent]

silencer *noun* a device for reducing the sound made by a gun or a vehicle's exhaust etc.

silent *adjective* **1** not speaking, not making or accompanied by a sound. **2** saying little. □ silent cop (*Austral. informal*) a small raised concrete dome in the centre of a street to control traffic. silent majority people of moderate opinions who rarely make themselves heard. silently *adverb*

silhouette (sil-oo-et) *noun* **1** a dark shadow or outline seen against a light background. **2** a profile portrait in solid black. –silhouette *verb* to show as a silhouette, *she was silhouetted against the screen*. [named after a French author, E. de Silhouette (died 1767)]

silica (sil-ĭ-kă) *noun* a compound of silicon occurring as quartz or flint and in sandstone and other rocks. siliceous (sĭ-lish-ŭs) *adjective* [from Latin *silicis* = of flint]

silicate (sil-ĭ-kayt) *noun* any of the insoluble compounds of silica.

silicon (**sil**-ĭ-kŏn) *noun* a chemical element (symbol Si), found widely in the earth's crust in its compound forms. □ **silicon chip** a microchip made of silicon.

silicone (**sil**-ĭ-kohn) *noun* any of the organic compounds of silicon, widely used in paints, varnish, and lubricants.

Silicon Valley the Santa Clara valley SE of San Francisco, USA, where many microelectronic firms are established.

silicosis (sil-ĭ-**koh**-sĭs) *noun* an abnormal condition of the lungs caused by inhaling dust that contains silica.

silk *noun* 1 the fine strong soft fibre produced by a silkworm in making its cocoon, or by certain other insects or spiders. 2 thread or cloth made from it; fabric resembling this. 3 clothing made from silk. 4 (*informal*) a Queen's Counsel, entitled to wear a silk gown. 5 fine soft strands like threads of silk. □ **take silk** to become a Queen's Counsel.

silken *adjective* like silk.

silkworm *noun* a caterpillar (of a kind of moth) that feeds on mulberry leaves and spins its cocoon of silk.

silky *adjective* (**silkier**, **silkiest**) as soft, fine, or smooth as silk. □ **silky oak** a tall Australian tree, the largest of the grevillea species, with fern-like foliage and orange flowers. **silkily** *adverb*, **silkiness** *noun*

sill *noun* a strip of stone, wood, or metal at the base of a window or door.

silly *adjective* (**sillier**, **silliest**) 1 lacking good sense, foolish, unwise. 2 feeble-minded. 3 (of a fielder's position in cricket) close to the batsman, *silly mid-on*. –**silly** *noun* (*informal*) a foolish person. □ **silly billy** (*informal*) a foolish person. **silliness** *noun* [the word originally meant 'feeble' (from an older word *seely* = happy or fortunate)]

silo (**sy**-loh) *noun* (*plural* **silos**) 1 a pit or airtight structure in which green crops are pressed and undergo fermentation for use as fodder. 2 a pit or tower for storing grain or cement or radioactive waste. 3 an underground place where a missile is kept ready for firing.

silt *noun* sediment deposited by water in a channel or harbour etc. –**silt** *verb* to block or clog or become blocked with silt, *the harbour is or has silted up*.

Silurian (sy-**lew**-ree-ăn) *adjective* of the geological period following the Ordovician, during which the first land plants appeared. –**Silurian** *noun* this period.

silvan *adjective* 1 of the woods. 2 having woods, rural. [from Latin *silva* = a wood]

silver *noun* 1 a chemical element (symbol Ag), a shiny white precious metal. 2 coins made of this or of an alloy resembling it. 3 silver dishes or ornaments; household cutlery of any metal. 4 a silver medal (awarded as second prize). 5 the colour of silver. –**silver** *adjective* made of silver; coloured like silver. –**silver** *verb* 1 to coat or plate with silver. 2 to give a silvery appearance to; to become silvery; (of hair) to turn grey or white. □ **born with a silver spoon in one's mouth** destined to be wealthy. **silver birch** a birch tree with silver-coloured bark. **silver fox** a fox with black fur tipped with white; its fur. **silver gilt** gilded silver; imitation gilding of yellow lacquer over silver leaf. **silver jubilee** a 25th anniversary. **silver lining** a consolation or hopeful prospect in the midst of misfortune. **silver paper** tin foil. **silver-plated** *adjective* coated with silver. **silver wedding** the 25th anniversary of a wedding.

silverbeet *noun* (*Austral.*) a plant with large green leaves and fleshy stalks, used as a vegetable.

silverfish *noun* 1 a silver-coloured fish. 2 a small silvery wingless insect found in books and damp places.

silverside *noun* a joint of beef cut from the haunch, below topside.

silversmith *noun* a person whose trade is making articles in silver.

silvertail *noun* (*Austral. informal*) a socially prominent person.

silverware *noun* articles made of silver.

silvery *adjective* 1 like silver in colour or appearance. 2 having a clear gentle ringing sound.

SIM *noun* (also **SIM card**) a smart card in a mobile phone, carrying an identification number unique to the owner, storing personal data, and preventing operation if removed. [acronym from *s*ubscriber *i*dentification *m*odule]

simian (**sim**-ee-ăn) *adjective* monkey-like. [from Latin *simia* = monkey]

similar *adjective* 1 like, alike, resembling something but not the same. 2 of the same kind, nature, or amount. 3 (of geometrical figures) the same in shape but not in size. **similarly** *adverb*, **similarity** (sim-ĭ-**la**-rĭ-tee) *noun* [from Latin *similis* = like]

simile (**sim**-ĭ-lee) *noun* a figure of speech in which one thing is compared to another, e.g. *he's as fit as a fiddle*; *went through it like a hot knife through butter*. [from Latin *similis* = like]

similitude (sĭ-**mil**-ĭ-tewd) *noun* similarity.

simmer *verb* **1** to keep (a pan or its contents) almost at boiling point; to be kept like this; to boil very gently. **2** to be in a state of excitement, anger, or laughter which is only just kept under control. □ **simmer down** to become less excited or agitated.

Simon, St 1st century, an Apostle. Feast day (with St Jude), 28 October.

simony (**sy**-mŏ-nee) *noun* the buying or selling of ecclesiastical positions.

simoom (sĭ-**moom**) *noun* a hot dry dust-laden desert wind. [from Arabic *samma* = to poison]

simper *verb* to smile in an affected way. –**simper** *noun* an affected smile.

simple *adjective* **1** of one element or kind, not compound or complex. **2** not complicated or elaborate; not showy or luxurious. **3** foolish; inexperienced. **4** feeble-minded. **5** of humble rank, *simple ordinary people*. □ **simple harmonic motion** a regular oscillating motion such as that of a weight bouncing from a spring or a string vibrating on a musical instrument. **simple interest** interest paid only on the original capital, not on the interest added to it. **simple time** (in music) rhythm with two, three, or four crotchets or quavers in each bar.

simpleton *noun* a foolish or easily-deceived person; a halfwit.

simplicity *noun* being simple.

simplify *verb* (simplified, simplifying) to make simple, to make easy to do or understand. **simplification** *noun*

simplistic *adjective* over-simplifying.

simply *adverb* **1** in a simple manner. **2** absolutely, without doubt. **3** merely.

Simpson Desert an area of sandhills and spinifex in central Australia. [named after A. A. Simpson, President of the Royal Geographical Society]

simulate *verb* **1** to reproduce the conditions of (a situation), e.g. by means of a model, for study, testing, or training etc. **2** to pretend to have or feel, *they simulated indignation*. **3** to imitate the form or condition of. **simulation** *noun*, **simulator** *noun* [from Latin *similis* = like]

simulated *adjective* (of furs or pearls etc.) manufactured to look like natural products.

simulcast *noun* a simultaneous broadcast of a program on television and radio. –**simulcast** *verb* to broadcast in this way.

simultaneous (sim-ŭl-**tay**-nee-ŭs) *adjective* occurring or operating at the same time. □ **simultaneous equations** equations involving two or more variables that have the same value in each equation. **simultaneously** *adverb*, **simultaneity** (sim-ŭl-tă-**nee**-ĭ-tee) *noun*

sin¹ *noun* **1** the breaking of a religious or moral law; an act which does this. **2** a serious fault or offence. **3** (*informal*) something contrary to common sense, *it's a sin to stay indoors on this fine day*. –**sin** *verb* (sinned, sinning) to commit a sin.

sin² *abbreviation* sine.

Sinai (**sy**-ny *or* **sy**-nee-I) a peninsula, mostly desert, at the north end of the Red Sea, now part of Egypt.

since *preposition* in the period after (a certain event or past time). –**since** *adverb* **1** between a certain event or past time and now, *she married and we haven't seen her since*. **2** ago, before now, *it happened long since*. –**since** *conjunction* **1** in the time after. **2** for the reason that, because, *since we have no money, we can't buy it*.

sincere *adjective* free from pretence or deceit in feeling, manner, or actions. □ **Yours sincerely** *see* **yours**. **sincerely** *adverb*, **sincerity** (sin-**se**-rĭ-tee) *noun* [from Latin *sincerus* = pure]

sine (*rhymes with* mine) *noun* (in a right-angled triangle) the ratio of the length of a side opposite one of the acute angles to the length of the hypotenuse.

sinecure (**sin**-ĕ-kewr *or* **sy**-) *noun* an official position that gives the holder profit or honour with no work attached. [from Latin *sine cura* = without care]

sine die (sy-nee **dy**-ee) *adverb* indefinitely, with no appointed date, *the business was adjourned sine die*. [Latin, = without a day]

sine qua non (sy-nee kway **non** *or* see-nay kwah **nohn**) *noun* an indispensable condition or qualification. [Latin, = without which not]

sinew (**sin**-yoo) *noun* **1** tough fibrous tissue uniting muscle to bone. **2** a tendon. **sinews** *plural noun* muscles; strength. **sinewy** *adjective* like sinew; muscular.

sinful *adjective* full of sin, wicked. **sinfully** *adverb*, **sinfulness** *noun*

sing *verb* (**sang**, **sung**, **singing**) **1** to make musical sounds with the voice, especially in a set tune. **2** to perform (a song). **3** to make a humming, buzzing, or whistling sound, *the kettle sings*. **4** (*informal*) to turn informer. □ **sing a person's praises** to praise him or her greatly. **sing out** to call out loudly.

Singapore 1 a republic in SE Asia consisting of the island of Singapore and over fifty smaller islands, situated south of the Malay peninsula. **2** a city and port, the capital of this country. **Singaporean** (sing-ă-**por**-ree-ăn) *adjective & noun*

singe (*pr.* sinj) *verb* (**singed**, **singeing**) to burn slightly; to burn the ends or edges of. – **singe** *noun* a slight burn.

singer *noun* a person who sings, especially as a professional.

Singhalese = **Sinhalese**.

single *adjective* **1** one only, not double or multiple. **2** designed for one person or thing, *single beds*. **3** taken separately, *every single thing*. **4** unmarried. **5** (of a ticket) valid for an outward journey only, not to return. **6** (of a flower) having only one circle of petals. – **single** *noun* **1** one person or thing, a single one. **2** a room etc. for one person. **3** a single ticket. **4** a pop record with one piece of music on each side. **5** a hit for one run in cricket. **6** an unmarried or unattached person. – **single** *verb* to choose or distinguish from others, *singled him out*. **singles** *noun* a game with one player on each side. □ **single-breasted** *adjective* (of a coat) fastening but not overlapping widely across the breast. **single combat** a duel. **single-decker** *noun* a train carriage or a bus with only one deck. **single figures** any number from 1 to 9 inclusive. **single file** *see* **file²**. **single-handed** *adjective* without help from others. **single-minded** *adjective* with one's mind set on a single purpose. **single parent** a person bringing up children without a partner. **single-pole switch** a switch that opens or closes one electrical circuit at a time. **singly** *adverb*

singlet *noun* an undergarment covering the trunk, also called a *vest*.

singleton (**sing**-gĕl-tŏn) *noun* a single person or thing.

singsong *adjective* with a monotonous rise and fall of the voice in speaking. – **singsong** *noun* **1** a singsong manner of speaking. **2** an informal singing of well-known songs by a group of people.

singular *noun* the form of a noun or verb used with reference to one person or thing, *the singular is 'man', the plural is 'men'*. – **singular** *adjective* **1** of this form. **2** uncommon, extraordinary, *spoke with singular shrewdness*. **singularly** *adverb*, **singularity** (sing-gew-**la**-ri-tee) *noun*

Sinhalese (sin-hă-**leez**) *adjective* of the majority people of Sri Lanka or their language. – **Sinhalese** *noun* (*plural* **Sinhalese**) **1** a Sinhalese person. **2** the Sinhalese language.

sinister *adjective* **1** suggestive of evil. **2** involving wickedness, criminal, *sinister motives*. [from Latin, = on the left (which was thought to be unlucky)]

sink *verb* (**sank**, **sunk**, **sinking**) **1** to fall slowly downwards, to come gradually to a lower level or pitch. **2** to become wholly or partly submerged in water etc.; (of a ship) to go to the bottom of the sea. **3** to pass into a less active condition, *she sank into sleep*. **4** to lose value or strength etc. gradually. **5** to cause or allow to sink; *must sink our differences*, disregard them. **6** to dig (a well) or bore (a shaft). **7** to engrave (a die). **8** to send (a ball) into a pocket or hole in billiards, golf, etc. **9** to invest (money). – **sink** *noun* **1** a fixed basin with a drainage pipe and usually with a water supply, in a kitchen etc. **2** a cesspool; *a sink of iniquity*, a place where evil people or practices tend to collect. □ **sink-hole** *noun* a pool or marsh into which a stream's water flows and disappears by evaporating or by percolating into the underlying soil. **sink in** to penetrate; to become understood. **sinking feeling** a feeling caused by hunger or fear. **sinking fund** a fund set aside for the purpose of wiping out a country's or business company's debt gradually, or for some other purpose.

sinker *noun* a weight used to sink a fishing line or a line used in taking soundings.

sinless *adjective* free from sin.

sinner *noun* a person who sins.

Sinn Fein (shin-**fayn**) a nationalist political party in Ireland. [Irish, = we ourselves]

Sino- (**sy**-noh-) *prefix* Chinese; Chinese and, *Sino-Japanese*, *Sino-Tibetan*.

sinter *verb* to form or cause (a powdery substance) to form into a solid mass by heating. – **sinter** *noun* a solid mass formed in this way.

sinuous (**sin**-yoo-ŭs) *adjective* with many curves, undulating. **sinuously** *adverb* [same origin as *sinus*]

sinus (**sy**-nŭs) *noun* (*plural* sinuses) a cavity in bone or tissue, especially that in the skull connecting with the nostrils. [Latin, = curve]

sinusitis (sy-nŭ-**sy**-tĭss) *noun* inflammation of a sinus.

Sioux (*pr.* soo) *noun* (*plural* Sioux) a member of a group of indigenous peoples of North America, especially of the Great Plains.

sip *verb* (sipped, sipping) to take a sip; to drink in small mouthfuls. –**sip** *noun* 1 the act of sipping. 2 a small mouthful of liquid.

siphon (**sy**-fŏn) *noun* 1 a pipe or tube in the form of an upside-down U, used for forcing liquid to flow from one container to another by utilising atmospheric pressure. 2 a bottle from which aerated water is forced out through a tube by pressure of gas. 3 the sucking-tube of some insects or small animals. –**siphon** *verb* 1 to flow or draw out through a siphon. 2 to take from a source, *we siphoned off funds for this purpose*. [Greek, = pipe]

sir *noun* a polite form of address to a man. –**Sir** *noun* a title prefixed to the name of a knight or baronet, *Sir Henry Parkes*. [from *sire*]

sire *noun* 1 (*old use*) a father or male ancestor. 2 (*old use*) a title of respect, used to a king. 3 the male parent of an animal. –**sire** *verb* (of an animal) to be the sire of, to beget. [same origin as *senior*]

siren *noun* 1 a device that makes a loud prolonged sound as a signal. 2 a dangerously fascinating woman. [named after the Sirens in Greek legend, women who lived on an island and by their singing lured seafarers to destruction on the rocks surrounding it]

Sirius (**si**-ree-ŭs) the Dog Star, the brightest of the fixed stars, apparently following on the heels of the hunter Orion.

sirloin *noun* the upper (best) part of loin of beef. [from *sur-* = over, + *loin*]

sirocco (sĭ-**rok**-oh) *noun* (*plural* siroccos) a hot wind that reaches Italy from Africa. [from Arabic *shark* = east wind]

sisal (**sy**-săl) *noun* 1 rope-fibre made from the leaves of a tropical plant. 2 the plant itself.

sissy *noun* an effeminate boy or man; a cowardly person. [from *sis* = sister]

sister *noun* 1 a daughter of the same parents as another person. 2 a fellow woman; one who is a fellow member of a group or sect. 3 a nun; Sister the title of a nun. 4 a female hospital nurse in authority over others. □ **sister city** a city twinned with another. **sister-in-law**

noun (*plural* sisters-in-law) the sister of one's husband or wife; the wife of one's brother. **sister ship** a ship built in the same design as another. **sisterly** *adjective*

sisterhood *noun* 1 the relationship of sisters. 2 an order of nuns; a society of women doing religious or charitable work.

Sistine Chapel (**sis**-teen) a chapel in the Vatican, built by Sixtus IV (Pope 1471–84), containing Michelangelo's painted ceiling and his fresco of the Last Judgment.

Sisyphus (**sis**-ĭ-fŭs) (*Gk. myth.*) a king of Corinth whose punishment in Hades for his misdeeds was to roll a large stone up a hill from which it continually rolled back.

sit *verb* (sat, sitting) 1 to take or be in a position in which the body rests more or less upright on the buttocks, *we were sitting gossiping*; *sit one's horse*, to sit or keep one's seat on it. 2 to cause to sit, to place in a sitting position, *sat him down*. 3 to pose for a portrait. 4 (of birds) to perch; (of certain animals) to rest with legs bent and body along the ground. 5 (of birds) to remain on the nest to hatch eggs. 6 to be situated, to lie. 7 to be a candidate for, *sit an examination*; *sit for a scholarship*. 8 to occupy a seat as a member of a committee etc. 9 (of Parliament or a lawcourt or committee) to be in session. 10 (of clothes) to fit in a certain way, *the coat sits badly on the shoulders*. □ **sit at a person's feet** to be his or her pupil or disciple. **sit back** to relax one's efforts. **sit down** to take a seat after standing. **sit-down** *adjective* (of a meal) taken seated. **sit-in** *noun* occupation of a building etc. as a form of protest. **sit in judgment** to make judgments about other people. **sit on the fence** to avoid taking sides in a dispute. **sit out** to take no part in (a dance etc.); to stay till the end of, *had to sit the concert out*. **sit tight** (*informal*) to remain firmly where one is; to take no action and not yield. **sit up** to rise to a sitting posture from lying down; to sit upright and not slouch; to remain out of bed, *sat up late*; *make a person sit up*, to cause a person surprise or alarm; to arouse his or her interest.

sitar (**sit**-ar *or* sĭ-**tar**) *noun* an Indian stringed musical instrument, played by plucking. [Hindi, = three-stringed]

sitcom *noun* (*informal*) a situation comedy.

site *noun* 1 the ground on which a town or building stood or stands or is to stand. 2 the place where some activity or event takes place or took place, *camping site*; *the site of the battle*. 3 a website. –**site** *verb* to locate, to provide with a site. [from Latin *situs* = position]

sittella (sĭ-**tel**-ă) *noun* a small Australian tree-running bird, a nuthatch.

sitter *noun* 1 a person who is seated. 2 one who is sitting for a portrait. 3 a babysitter. 4 a sitting hen. 5 (*informal*) an easy catch or shot; something easy to do.

sitting *see* sit. –sitting *adjective* (of an animal) not running; (of a game bird) not flying, *shot a sitting pheasant*. –sitting *noun* 1 the time during which a person or assembly etc. sits continuously, *an all-night sitting of Parliament; lunch is served in two sittings*. 2 a clutch of eggs. □ **sitting duck** or **target** a person or thing that is a helpless victim of attack. **sitting room** a room used for sitting in, not a bedroom. **sitting tenant** one already in occupation of rented accommodation etc.

situate *verb* to place or put in a certain position. □ **be situated** to be in a certain position or circumstances.

situation *noun* 1 a place (with its surroundings) that is occupied by something. 2 a set of circumstances. 3 a position of employment. □ **save the situation** to prevent a disaster. **situation comedy** a comedy in which humour derives from characters' misunderstandings and embarrassments. [same origin as *site*]

Usage *Situation* is often used unnecessarily. Note the gain in clarity if you omit the word *situation* where it occurs in the sentence, *A strike situation by workers in a factory situation may lead to a crisis situation*.

Siva (**see**-vă *or* **shee**-vă) (in Hinduism) a deity associated with the powers of reproduction and dissolution, regarded by some as the supreme being and by others as a member of the triad with Brahma and Vishnu.

six *noun* 1 one more than five (6, VI). 2 (also **sixer**) a hit in cricket scoring six runs by clearing the boundary without first touching the ground. –six *adjective* that amount to six.

sixfold *adjective & adverb* 1 six times as much or as many. 2 consisting of six parts.

sixpence *noun* (*old use*) the sum of 6d. (= 5 cents); a coin worth this.

sixpenny *adjective* costing sixpence.

sixteen *adjective & noun* one more than fifteen (16, XVI). **sixteenth** *adjective & noun*

sixth *adjective & noun* 1 next after fifth. 2 one of six equal parts of a thing. 3 a musical interval or chord spanning six alphabetical notes, e.g. C to A. □ **sixth sense** a supposed extra power of perception other than the five physical ones; intuition. **sixthly** *adverb*

sixty *adjective & noun* six times ten (60, LX). **sixties** *plural noun* the numbers from 60 to 69, especially the years of a century or of a person's life. **sixtieth** *adjective & noun*

size¹ *noun* 1 the measurements or extent of something. 2 any of the series of standard measurements in which things of the same kind are made and sold. –size *verb* to group or sort according to size. □ **size up** to estimate the size of; (*informal*) to form a judgment of (a person or situation etc.). **the size of it** (*informal*) the way it is, the facts about it.

size² *noun* a gluey solution used to glaze paper or stiffen textiles etc. –size *verb* to treat with size.

sizeable *adjective* of large or fairly large size.

sizzle *verb* 1 to make a hissing sound like that of frying. 2 (*informal*) to be very hot; to be angry or resentful.

SJ *abbreviation* Society of Jesus.

Skanda (in Hinduism) the war god, first son of Siva and Parvati and brother of Ganesha.

skate¹ *noun* (*plural* **skate**) a large flatfish used as food.

skate² *noun* 1 one of a pair of blades attached to the soles of boots or shoes so that the wearer can glide over ice; a boot or shoe with such a blade attached. 2 = roller skate. –skate *verb* to move on skates; to perform (a specified figure) in this way. □ **get one's skates on** (*informal*) to make haste. **skate over a subject** to make only a passing reference to it. **skater** *noun*

skateboard *noun* a small board with wheels like those of roller skates, for riding on (as a sport) while standing. **skateboarding** *noun*, **skateboarder** *noun*

skating rink *noun* a stretch of natural or artificial ice used for skating; a smooth floor used for roller skating.

skedaddle *verb* (*informal*) to go away quickly.

skeg *noun* 1 a short fin under a surfboard. 2 (*Austral. informal*) a skeghead.

skeghead *noun* (*Austral. informal*) a surfer.

skein (*pr.* skayn) *noun* 1 a loosely-coiled bundle of yarn or thread. 2 a number of wild geese etc. in flight.

skeletal (**skel**-ĕ-t'l *or* skĕ-**lee**-t'l) *adjective* of or like a skeleton.

skeleton *noun* 1 the supporting structure of an animal body, consisting of bones. 2 the shell or other hard structure covering or supporting an invertebrate animal. 3 a very lean person or animal. 4 any supporting structure or framework, e.g. of a building. 5 an outline of a literary work etc. □ **skeleton in the cupboard** a discreditable secret. **skeleton key** a key made so as to fit many locks. **skeleton staff** the minimum needed to do the essential things in work that normally requires more staff. [from Greek *skeletos* = dried-up]

skerrick *noun* (*Austral. informal*) the slightest amount, *not a skerrick left*.

sketch *noun* 1 a rough drawing or painting. 2 a brief account of something. 3 a short usually comic play. –**sketch** *verb* to make a sketch or sketches; to make a sketch of. □ **sketch map** a roughly drawn map. **sketcher** *noun* [from Greek *skhedios* = impromptu]

sketchbook *noun* a pad of drawing paper for sketching on.

sketchy *adjective* (**sketchier**, **sketchiest**) rough and not detailed or careful or substantial. **sketchily** *adverb*, **sketchiness** *noun*

skew *adjective* slanting, askew. –**skew** *verb* to make skew, to turn or twist round. □ **on the skew** askew.

skewbald *adjective* (of an animal) with irregular patches of white and another colour (strictly, not including black; *see* **piebald**).

skewer *noun* a pin thrust through meat etc. to hold it compactly together while it is cooked. –**skewer** *verb* to pierce or hold in place with a skewer or other pointed object.

ski (*pr.* skee) *noun* (*plural* **skis**) one of a pair of long narrow strips of wood etc. fixed under the feet for travelling over snow. –**ski** *verb* (**ski'd**, **skiing**) to travel on skis. □ **ski lift** a device for carrying skiers up a slope, usually on seats slung from an overhead cable. **ski run** a slope suitable for skiing down as a sport. **skier** *noun* [Norwegian]

skid *verb* (**skidded**, **skidding**) (of a vehicle or its wheels) to slide on slippery ground. –**skid** *noun* 1 a skidding movement. 2 a log or plank etc. used to make a track over which heavy objects may be dragged or rolled. 3 a runner on a helicopter, for use when landing. 4 a

wedge or a wooden or metal shoe that acts as a braking device on the wheel of a cart. □ **put the skids under** (*informal*) to cause to hurry; to hasten the downfall of. **skid-pan** *noun* a surface specially prepared to cause skids, used for practice in controlling skidding vehicles. **skid row** a slum area where vagrants live.

skiff *noun* a small light boat for rowing or sculling.

skilful *adjective* having or showing great skill. **skilfully** *adverb*

skill *noun* ability to do something well.

skilled *adjective* 1 skilful. 2 (of work) needing great skill; (of a worker) highly trained or experienced in such work.

skillet *noun* a frying pan.

skillion *noun* (*Austral.*) a lean-to attached to a dwelling.

skim *verb* (**skimmed**, **skimming**) 1 to take (floating matter) from the surface of a liquid; to clear (a liquid) in this way. 2 to move lightly and quickly over a surface; to glide through air. 3 to read quickly, noting only the chief points, *skim through a newspaper* or *skim it*. 4 to steal or embezzle (money) in small amounts over a period of time. □ **skim milk** milk from which the cream has been removed.

skimming *noun* the fraudulent copying of credit or debit card details with a card swipe or other device.

skimp *verb* to supply or use rather less than what is needed, to scrimp.

skimpy *adjective* (**skimpier**, **skimpiest**) scanty, especially through being skimped. **skimpily** *adverb*, **skimpiness** *noun*

skin *noun* 1 the flexible continuous covering of the human or other animal body. 2 an animal's skin removed from its body, with or without the hair still attached. 3 material made from this. 4 a vessel for water or wine, made from an animal's whole skin. 5 a person's complexion. 6 an outer layer or covering. 7 the skin-like film that forms on the surface of certain liquids. –**skin** *verb* (**skinned**, **skinning**) 1 to strip or scrape the skin from. 2 to cover or become covered with new skin, *the wound had skinned over*. □ **by the skin of one's teeth** only just, barely. **get under a person's skin** (*informal*) to interest or annoy him or her greatly. **save one's skin** to avoid injury or loss. **skin-deep** *adjective* superficial. **skin diver** one who engages in **skin diving**, the sport of swimming deep under water with flippers and breathing apparatus.

skinflint *noun* a miserly person.

skinhead *noun* a youth with close-cropped hair, often perceived as aggressive, violent, and racist.

skink *noun* a small smooth-bodied lizard.

skinny *adjective* (**skinnier**, **skinniest**) **1** (of a person or animal) very thin. **2** miserly.

skint *adjective* (*informal*) having no money left.

skintight *adjective* (of clothing) very close-fitting.

skip¹ *verb* (**skipped**, **skipping**) **1** to move along lightly, especially by taking two steps with each foot in turn. **2** to jump with a skipping rope. **3** to pass quickly from one subject or point to another. **4** to omit in reading or dealing with a thing. **5** (*informal*) to go away hastily or secretly. –**skip** *noun* a skipping movement.

skip² *noun* **1** a cage or bucket in which people or materials are raised and lowered in mines and quarries. **2** a large container for holding and carrying away builders' rubbish etc.

skipjack *noun* an edible Australian fish, trevally.

skipper¹ *noun* **1** one who skips. **2** a small dark thick-bodied butterfly.

skipper² *noun* a captain. –**skipper** *verb* to captain.

skipping rope *noun* a length of rope, usually with a handle at each end, turned over the head and under the feet as a person jumps.

skirl *noun* the shrill sound characteristic of bagpipes. –**skirl** *verb* to make this sound.

skirmish *noun* a minor fight or conflict. –**skirmish** *verb* to take part in a skirmish.

skirt *noun* **1** a woman's garment hanging from the waist; this part of a garment. **2** the flap of a saddle. **3** the hanging part round the base of a hovercraft. **4** a cut of beef from the lower flank. –**skirt** *verb* **1** to go or be situated along the edge of. **2** to avoid dealing directly with (a question or controversial topic etc.).

skirting *noun* (also **skirting board**) a narrow board round the wall of a room, close to the floor.

skit *noun* a short play or piece of writing that is a humorous imitation of a serious one; a piece of humorous mimicry.

skite (*Austral. informal*) *verb* to boast. –**skite** *noun* **1** a boaster. **2** boasting.

skittish *adjective* frisky. **skittishly** *adverb*, **skittishness** *noun*

skittle *noun* one of the wooden pins set up to be bowled down with a ball or disc in the game of **skittles**. –**skittle** *verb* to knock down like skittles; to defeat.

skive *verb* (*informal*) to dodge a duty. □ **skive off** (*informal*) to go away in order to dodge a duty. **skiver** *noun*

skivvy *noun* (*Austral.*) a thin high-necked long-sleeved garment.

Skopje (**skop**-yay) the capital of the Republic of Macedonia.

skua (**skew**-ă) *noun* a seabird like a large gull.

skulduggery *noun* (*informal*) trickery.

skulk *verb* to loiter or move or conceal oneself stealthily.

skull *noun* **1** the bony framework of the head; the part of this protecting the brain. **2** a representation of this. □ **skull and cross bones** a picture of a skull with two thigh bones crossed below it as an emblem of death or piracy, or used as a warning symbol.

skullcap *noun* a small close-fitting cap with no peak, worn on top of the head.

skunk *noun* **1** a black bushy-tailed American animal about the size of a cat, able to spray an evil-smelling liquid from glands near its tail. **2** (*informal*) a term of contempt for a person.

sky *noun* **1** the region of the clouds or upper air. **2** climate or weather shown by this, *heavy skies*. –**sky** *verb* (**skied**, **skying**) to hit (a ball) to a great height. □ **sky-blue** *adjective* & *noun* bright clear blue. **sky-high** *adjective* & *adverb* very high. **sky marshal** a plain-clothes armed guard on an aeroplane employed to counter hijacking etc.

skydiver *noun* one who engages in the sport of **skydiving**, jumping from an aircraft and not opening the parachute until the last safe moment.

Skye the largest island of the Inner Hebrides in NW Scotland.

skylark *noun* a lark that soars while singing. –**skylark** *verb* to play about light-heartedly.

skylight *noun* a window set in the line of a roof or ceiling.

skyline *noun* the outline of hills, buildings, etc. seen against the sky.

skyrocket *noun* a rocket that rises high into the air before exploding. –**skyrocket** *verb* to rise sharply.

skyscape *noun* a picture or view of the sky.

skyscraper *noun* a very tall building with many storeys.

skyward *adjective* & *adverb* towards the sky. **skywards** *adverb*

slab *noun* a flat broad fairly thick piece of something solid.

slack[1] *adjective* 1 loose, not tight or tense. 2 slow, sluggish; negligent. 3 (of trade or business) with little happening, not busy. –**slack** *noun* the slack part of a rope etc., *haul in the slack*. –**slack** *verb* 1 to slacken. 2 to be idle or lazy about work. **slacker** *noun*, **slackly** *adverb*, **slackness** *noun*

slack[2] *noun* coal dust or very small pieces of coal left when coal is screened.

slacken *verb* to make or become slack.

slacks *plural noun* trousers for informal or sports wear.

slag *noun* solid non-metallic waste matter left when metal has been separated from ore by smelting. □ **slag heap** a mound of waste matter from a mine etc.

slain *see* slay.

slake *verb* 1 to satisfy or make less strong, *slake one's thirst*. 2 to combine (lime) chemically with water.

slalom (**slah**-lŏm *or* **slay**-lŏm) *noun* 1 a ski race down a zigzag course. 2 an obstacle race in canoes, cars, etc., or on skateboards, skates, water-skis, etc. [Norwegian]

slam *verb* (**slammed**, **slamming**) 1 to shut forcefully with a loud noise. 2 to put, knock, or hit forcefully. 3 (*informal*) to criticise severely. –**slam** *noun* 1 a slamming noise. 2 the winning of 12 or 13 tricks in the game of bridge. □ **grand slam** the winning of all 13 tricks in the game of bridge; the winning of all of a group of championships in tennis or golf etc. **slam dunk** a basketball shot in which the player jumps and pushes the ball into the basket forcibly; (*verb*) to perform this shot.

slander *noun* 1 a false statement uttered maliciously that damages a person's reputation. 2 the crime of uttering this. –**slander** *verb* to utter a slander about. **slanderous** *adjective*, **slanderously** *adverb*

slang *noun* words, phrases, or particular meanings of these, that are used very informally for vividness or novelty or to avoid being conventional. –**slang** *verb* to use abusive language to. **slangy** *adjective*

slant *verb* 1 to slope. 2 to present (news etc.) from a particular point of view. –**slant** *noun* 1 a slope. 2 the way something is presented, an attitude or bias.

slantwise *adverb* in a slanting position.

slap *verb* (**slapped**, **slapping**) 1 to strike with the open hand or with something flat. 2 to lay forcefully, *slapped the money on the counter*. 3 to place hastily or carelessly, *slapped paint on the walls*. –**slap** *noun* a blow with the open hand or with something flat. –**slap** *adverb* with a slap, directly, *ran slap into him*. □ **slap-happy** *adjective* (*informal*) cheerfully casual or irresponsible. **slap-up** *adjective* (*informal*) first-class, *a slap-up meal*.

slapdash *adjective* hasty and careless. –**slapdash** *adverb* in a slapdash way.

slapstick *noun* comedy with boisterous activities.

slash *verb* 1 to make a sweeping stroke or strokes with a sword, knife, or whip etc.; to strike or cut in this way. 2 to reduce drastically. 3 to criticise vigorously. –**slash** *noun* 1 a slashing cut; a wound made by this. 2 an oblique stroke.

slat *noun* one of the thin narrow strips of wood, metal, or plastic arranged so as to overlap and form a screen, e.g. in a Venetian blind.

slate *noun* 1 a kind of metamorphic rock that is easily split into flat smooth plates. 2 a piece of this used as roofing-material or (formerly) for writing on. –**slate** *verb* 1 to cover or roof with slates. 2 (*informal*) to criticise severely, to scold. □ **a clean slate** a record of good conduct with nothing discreditable; *wipe the slate clean*, to forgive and forget past offences. **on the slate** (*informal*) recorded as a debt, on credit. **slate-blue** *adjective* & *noun* greyish-blue. **slate-grey** *adjective* & *noun* bluish-grey. **slaty** *adjective*

slather *noun* **open slather** (*Austral. informal*) freedom to operate without restraint; a free-for-all.

slattern *noun* a slovenly woman. **slatternly** *adjective*

slaughter *noun* 1 the killing of animals for food. 2 the ruthless killing of a great number of people or animals, a massacre. –**slaughter** *verb* 1 to kill (animals) for food. 2 to kill ruthlessly or in great numbers. 3 (*informal*) to defeat utterly. **slaughterer** *noun*

slaughterhouse *noun* a place where animals are killed for food.

Slav *noun* a member of any of the peoples of eastern and central Europe who speak a Slavonic language.

slave *noun* **1** a person who is the property of another and obliged to work for him or her. **2** one who is dominated by another person or by an influence, *a slave to housework*. **3** a person compelled to work very hard for someone else, a drudge. **4** a mechanism controlled by another mechanism and repeating its actions. –**slave** *verb* to work very hard. □ **slave-driver** *noun* a person who makes others work very hard. **slave labour** forced labour. **slave trade** the procuring, transporting, and selling of slaves.

slaver[1] *noun* a ship or person engaged in the slave trade.

slaver[2] (**slav**-er) *verb* to have saliva flowing from the mouth. –**slaver** *noun* this saliva.

slavery *noun* **1** the condition of a slave. **2** the existence of slaves, *to abolish slavery*. **3** very hard work, drudgery.

slavish *adjective* **1** like a slave, excessively submissive. **2** showing no independence or originality. **slavishly** *adverb*, **slavishness** *noun*

Slavonic (slă-**von**-ik) *adjective* of the group of languages including Russian and Polish.

slay *verb* (**slew**, **slain**, **slaying**) to kill.

sleaze *noun* (*informal*) sleaziness; a sleazy person. [backformation from *sleazy*]

sleazy *adjective* (**sleazier**, **sleaziest**) (*informal*) sordid, corrupt, immoral. **sleaziness** *noun*

sled *noun* a sledge.

sledge *noun* a narrow cart with runners instead of wheels, used for travelling on snow or bare ground or in sport for travelling downhill at speed. **sledging** *noun* this sport.

sledgehammer *noun* a large heavy hammer swung with both hands, like an axe.

sleek *adjective* **1** smooth and glossy, *sleek hair*. **2** looking well-fed and thriving. –**sleek** *verb* to make sleek by smoothing. **sleekly** *adverb*, **sleekness** *noun*

sleep *noun* **1** the natural recurring condition of rest in animals, in which there is unconsciousness with the nervous system inactive and muscles relaxed. **2** a spell of this, *a long sleep*. **3** the inert condition of hibernating animals. –**sleep** *verb* (**slept**, **sleeping**) **1** to be in a state of sleep. **2** to spend (time) in sleeping. **3** to stay for a night's sleep. **4** to provide with sleeping accommodation, *the cottage sleeps four*. □ **sleep in** to sleep late.

sleep on it to delay deciding about something until the next day.

sleeper *noun* **1** one who sleeps. **2** each of the beams on which the rails of a railway etc. rest. **3** a sleeping car; a berth in this. **4** a ring worn in a pierced ear to keep the hole from closing.

sleeping *see* sleep. □ **sleeping bag** a padded bag for sleeping in, especially while camping. **sleeping car** a railway carriage fitted with berths or beds for passengers. **sleeping partner** a partner in a business firm who does not take part in its actual work. **sleeping sickness** a disease with symptoms that include extreme sleepiness, spread by the bite of the tsetse fly.

sleepless *adjective* unable to sleep, insomniac; without sleep. **sleeplessly** *adverb*, **sleeplessness** *noun*

sleepout *noun* (*Austral.*) a verandah, porch, or outbuilding providing sleeping accommodation.

sleepwalker *noun* a person who walks about while asleep, a somnambulist. **sleepwalk** *verb*

sleepy *adjective* (**sleepier**, **sleepiest**) **1** feeling or showing a desire to sleep. **2** inactive, without stir or bustle, *a sleepy little town*. **sleepily** *adverb*, **sleepiness** *noun*

sleepyhead *noun* a sleepy person.

sleet *noun* snow and rain falling at the same time; hail or snow that melts while falling. –**sleet** *verb* send down sleet, *it is sleeting*. **sleety** *adjective*

sleeve *noun* **1** the part of a garment covering the arm or part of it. **2** a tube enclosing a rod or another tube. **3** a windsock; a drogue towed by an aircraft. **4** the cover of a gramophone record. □ **up one's sleeve** concealed but available for use, in reserve; *laugh up one's sleeve*, to laugh secretly or be secretly pleased with oneself. **sleeved** *adjective*

sleeveless *adjective* without sleeves.

sleigh (*pr.* slay) *noun* a sledge, especially one used as a passenger vehicle drawn by horses.

sleight (*rhymes with* bite) *noun* **sleight of hand** great skill in using the hands to perform conjuring tricks etc. [from Norse *slaegth* = slyness]

slender *adjective* **1** slim and graceful. **2** small in amount, scanty, *slender means*. **slenderness** *noun*

slept *see* sleep.

Slessor, Kenneth Adolf (1901–71), Australian poet and journalist.

sleuth (*pr.* slooth) *noun* a detective. –**sleuth** *verb* to search for information as a detective does.

slew[1] *verb* to turn or swing round.

slew[2] *see* slay.

slice *noun* 1 a thing broad piece (or a wedge) cut from something. 2 a portion or share. 3 an implement with a thin broad blade for lifting or serving fish etc. 4 a slicing stroke in golf. –**slice** *verb* 1 to cut into slices. 2 to cut from a larger piece. 3 to cut cleanly or easily. 4 to strike (a ball, in golf) so that it spins away from the direction intended. **slicer** *noun*

slick *adjective* 1 done or doing things smoothly and cleverly but perhaps with some trickery. 2 smooth in manner or speech. 3 smooth and slippery. –**slick** *noun* a slippery place; a thick patch of oil floating on the sea. –**slick** *verb* to make sleek.

slicker *noun see* city slicker.

slide *verb* (slid, sliding) 1 to move or cause to move along a smooth surface without lifting or rolling. 2 to glide more or less erect over ice or another smooth surface without skates. 3 to move or cause to move quietly or unobtrusively, *slid a coin into his hand.* 4 to pass gradually into a condition or habit. –**slide** *noun* 1 the act of sliding. 2 a smooth surface for sliding on. 3 a chute for goods etc. or for children to play on. 4 a sliding part of a machine or instrument. 5 a small glass plate on which things are placed for examination under a microscope. 6 a mounted picture or transparency for showing on a blank surface by means of a projector. 7 a hairslide. □ **let things slide** to fail to give them proper attention, to make no effort to control them. **slide rule** a ruler with a sliding central strip, marked with logarithmic scales and used for making calculations rapidly. **sliding scale** a scale of fees, taxes, or wages etc. that varies in accordance with the variation of some standard.

slight *adjective* 1 not much, not great; not thorough; *paid not the slightest attention,* paid none at all. 2 slender, not heavily built. –**slight** *verb* to treat or speak of (a person etc.) as not worth one's attention; to insult by lack of respect or courtesy. –**slight** *noun* an insult given in this way. **slightly** *adverb*, **slightness** *noun*

slim *adjective* (slimmer, slimmest) 1 of small girth or thickness, not heavily built. 2 small, insufficient, *only a slim chance of success.* –**slim** *verb* (slimmed, slimming) 1 to make

oneself slimmer by dieting, exercise, etc. 2 to reduce in numbers or scale, *slim down the workforce.* **slimly** *adverb*, **slimness** *noun*, **slimmer** *noun*

slime *noun* an unpleasant slippery thick liquid substance.

slimline *adjective* of slender design.

slimy *adjective* (slimier, slimiest) 1 like slime; covered or smeared with slime. 2 disgustingly dishonest, meek, or flattering. **slimily** *adverb*, **sliminess** *noun*

sling *noun* 1 a belt, strap, or chain etc. looped round an object to support or lift it. 2 a bandage looped round the neck to form a support for an injured arm. 3 a looped strap used to throw a stone or other missile. 4 (*Austral.*) a bribe. –**sling** *verb* (slung, slinging) 1 to suspend or lift with a sling. 2 to hurl (a stone) with a sling. 3 (*informal*) to throw. □ **sling-back** *adjective* (of a shoe) with a strap round the back of the foot. **sling mud at** *see* mud. **sling off at** (*Austral. informal*) to mock, to ridicule. **sling one's hook** (*informal*) to run away.

slingshot *noun* a catapult.

slink *verb* (slunk, slinking) to move in a stealthy, guilty, or shamefaced way.

slinky *adjective* 1 moving in a slinking way. 2 smooth and sinuous. 3 (of clothes) close-fitting and flowing. **slinkily** *adverb*

slip[1] *verb* (slipped, slipping) 1 to slide accidentally, to lose one's balance in this way. 2 to go or put or be put with a smooth movement. 3 to escape hold or capture by being slippery or not grasped firmly. 4 to make one's way quietly or unobserved. 5 to detach or release; *slip a stitch,* (in knitting) to transfer it to the other needle without looping the yarn through it. 6 to escape, to become detached from, *the ship slipped her moorings*; *it slipped my memory.* –**slip** *noun* 1 the act of slipping. 2 an accidental or casual mistake. 3 a loose covering or garment; a petticoat; a pillowcase. 4 a slipway. 5 a fielder in cricket stationed on the off side just behind the wicket; this position; *the slips,* this part of the field. □ **give a person the slip** to escape from a person or avoid him or her skilfully. **let slip** to release accidentally or deliberately; to miss (an opportunity); to reveal news etc. unintentionally or thoughtlessly. **slip knot** a knot that can slide easily along the rope etc. on which it is tied, or one that can be undone by pulling. **slip of the pen** or **tongue** a small mistake in which one thing is written or said accidentally instead of another. **slip-on** *adjective* (of clothes) easily slipped on, usually without fastenings. **slipped disc** *see* **disc** sense 3. **slip rail** (*Austral.*) a fence rail which can be slipped out to make an opening. **slip road** a road for entering or leaving a freeway etc. **slip stitch** a loose hemming stitch not visible externally; a slipped stitch in knitting. **slip-stitch** *verb* to sew with a slip stitch. **slip up** (*informal*) to make an accidental or casual mistake. **slip-up** *noun*

slip² *noun* 1 a small piece of paper, especially for writing on. 2 a cutting taken from a plant for grafting or planting. □ **a slip of a girl** a small slim girl.

slip³ *noun* a thin liquid containing fine clay, used for coating pottery.

slipper *noun* a light loose comfortable shoe for indoor wear.

slippery *adjective* 1 smooth and difficult to hold; causing slipping by its wetness or smoothness. 2 (of a person) not to be trusted to keep an agreement etc., *a slippery customer*. □ **slippery dip** (*Austral.*) a slide for children to play on. **slipperiness** *noun*

slippy *adjective* (*informal*) slippery. □ **look slippy** (*informal*) to make haste.

slipshod *adjective* not doing things carefully; not done or arranged carefully.

slipstream *noun* a current of air driven backward as something is propelled forward.

slipway *noun* a sloping structure used as a landing stage or on which ships are built or repaired.

slit *noun* a narrow straight cut or opening. –**slit** *verb* (**slit, slitting**) 1 to cut a slit in. 2 to cut into strips.

slither *verb* (*informal*) to slide unsteadily, to move with an irregular slipping movement.

slithery *adjective* (*informal*) causing slithering; liable to slither.

sliver (**sliv**-er) *noun* a thin strip cut or split from wood or glass etc.

slob *noun* (*informal, derogatory*) a lazy, untidy, or fat person.

slobber *verb* to slaver or dribble; *slobber over a person*, to behave with repulsively excessive affection to him or her.

sloe (*rhymes with* go) *noun* blackthorn; its small bluish-black plum-like fruit.

slog *verb* (**slogged, slogging**) 1 to hit hard. 2 to work or walk hard and steadily. –**slog** *noun*

1 a hard hit. 2 a spell of hard steady work or walking. **slogger** *noun*

slogan *noun* a word or phrase adopted as a motto; a short catchy phrase used in advertising.

sloop *noun* a kind of ship with one mast.

slop *verb* (**slopped, slopping**) 1 to spill over or cause to spill; to splash liquid on. 2 to plod clumsily, especially through mud or puddles etc. –**slop** *noun* 1 weak unappetising drink or liquid food. 2 a quantity of slopped liquid. 3 swill fed to pigs. **slops** *plural noun* household liquid refuse. □ **slop about** to move about in a slovenly manner.

slope *verb* 1 to lie or turn at an angle from the horizontal or vertical. 2 to place in this position. –**slope** *noun* 1 a sloping surface or direction; a stretch of rising or falling ground. 2 the amount by which something slopes. □ **slope off** (*informal*) to go away.

sloppy *adjective* (**sloppier, sloppiest**) 1 having a liquid consistency that splashes easily; excessively liquid. 2 slipshod. 3 weakly sentimental. □ **sloppy joe** a loose sweater. **sloppily** *adverb*, **sloppiness** *noun*

slosh *verb* (*informal*) 1 to pour (liquid) clumsily. 2 to splash; to move with a splashing sound. 3 to hit, *sloshed him on the chin*. –**slosh** *noun* (*informal*) 1 a splashing sound. 2 a blow.

slot *noun* 1 a narrow opening through which something is to be put. 2 a groove, channel, or slit into which something fits. 3 a position in a series or scheme; *the program has its regular slot*, its regular time for transmission. –**slot** *verb* (**slotted, slotting**) 1 to make a slot or slots in. 2 to put into a slot. □ **slot machine** a machine operated by a coin put in a slot, e.g. to dispense small articles.

sloth (*rhymes with* both) *noun* 1 laziness. 2 an animal of tropical America that lives in trees and is capable of only very slow movement.

slothful *adjective* lazy. **slothfully** *adverb*

slouch *verb* to stand or sit or move in a lazy awkward way, not with an upright posture. –**slouch** *noun* a slouching movement or posture. □ **slouch hat** a hat with a wide flexible brim, especially, with left brim turned up, associated with the Australian army. **sloucher** *noun*

slough¹ (*rhymes with* cow) *noun* a swamp or marshy place.

slough² (*pr.* sluf) *verb* to shed, *a snake sloughs its skin periodically*. –**slough** *noun* a snake's cast skin; dead tissue that drops away.

Slovak Republic (**sloh**-vak) (also **Slovakia**) a country in central Europe, formerly part of Czechoslovakia. **Slovak** *adjective & noun*

sloven (**sluv**-ĕn) *noun* a slovenly person.

Slovenia (slŏ-**vee**-nee-ă) a republic in central Europe, lying to the south of Austria. **Slovene**, **Slovenian** *adjectives & nouns*

slovenly (**sluv**-ĕn-lee) *adjective* careless and untidy in appearance; not methodical in work. **slovenliness** *noun*

slow *adjective* **1** not quick or fast; acting or moving or done without haste or rapidity. **2** (of a clock) showing a time earlier than the correct one. **3** mentally dull, stupid. **4** lacking liveliness, sluggish, *business is slow today*. **5** (of photographic film) not very sensitive to light, (of a lens) having only a small aperture, needing a long exposure. **6** tending to cause slowness. –**slow** *adverb* slowly, *go slow*. –**slow** *verb* to reduce the speed of, to go more slowly, *slow down* or *up*. □ **slow motion** (of a cinema film) making movements appear to be performed much more slowly than in real life. **slowly** *adverb*, **slowness** *noun*

Usage *Slow* occurs as an adverb in combinations such as *slow-acting* and *slow-moving*, and in the expressions *go slow* and *go-slow* (see **go**). *Slowly* should be used in other adverbial contexts such as *She walks too slowly* and *He drives as slowly as possible*.

slowcoach *noun* a person who is slow in actions or work.

slub *noun* a thick lump in yarn or thread.

sludge *noun* thick greasy mud; something resembling it.

slug[1] *noun* **1** a small slimy animal like a snail without a shell. **2** a roundish lump of metal; a bullet of irregular shape; a pellet for firing from an airgun.

slug[2] *verb* (**slugged**, **slugging**) to strike with a hard heavy blow. –**slug** *noun* a blow of this kind.

sluggard *noun* a slow or lazy person.

sluggish *adjective* slow-moving, not alert or lively. **sluggishly** *adverb*, **sluggishness** *noun*

sluice (*pr.* slooss) *noun* **1** a sliding gate for controlling the volume or flow of water in a stream etc. **2** the water controlled by this. **3** a channel carrying off water. **4** a place where objects are rinsed. **5** the act of rinsing. –**sluice** *verb* **1** to let out (water) by means of a sluice. **2** to flood, scour, or rinse with a flow of water.

slum *noun* a dirty overcrowded district inhabited by very poor people. –**slum** *verb* **slum it** (*informal*) to put up with less comfortable conditions than usual.

slumber *noun* sleep. –**slumber** *verb* to sleep. **slumberer** *noun*

slump *noun* a sudden or great fall in prices or values or in the demand for goods etc. –**slump** *verb* **1** to undergo a slump. **2** to sit or flop down heavily and slackly.

slung *see* **sling**.

slunk *see* **slink**.

slur *verb* (**slurred**, **slurring**) **1** to write or pronounce indistinctly with each letter or sound running into the next. **2** to mark (notes) with a slur in music; to perform in the way indicated by this. **3** to pass lightly over (a fact etc.), *slurred it over*. **4** to speak ill of. –**slur** *noun* **1** a slurred letter or sound. **2** a curved line placed over notes in music to show that they are to be sung to one syllable or played smoothly without a break. **3** discredit, *a slur on his reputation*.

slurp *verb* to make a noisy sucking sound in eating or drinking. –**slurp** *noun* this sound.

slurry (*rhymes with* hurry) *noun* thin mud; thin liquid cement.

slush *noun* **1** partly melted snow on the ground. **2** silly sentimental talk or writing. □ **slush fund** a fund of money for illegal purposes such as bribery.

slushy *adjective* **1** like slush. **2** sentimental. –**slushy** *noun* (*Austral.*) a cook's assistant.

slut *noun* (*derogatory*) a slovenly or promiscuous woman. **sluttish** *adjective*

sly *adjective* (**slyer**, **slyest**) **1** done or doing things in an unpleasantly cunning and secret way. **2** mischievous and knowing, *with a sly smile*. □ **on the sly** slyly, secretly. **slyly** *adverb*, **slyness** *noun*

smack[1] *noun* **1** a slap. **2** a hard hit. **3** a loud kiss. –**smack** *verb* to slap, to hit hard; *smack one's lips*, to close and then part them noisily in enjoyment. –**smack** *adverb* (*informal*) with a smack, directly, *went smack through the window*.

smack[2] *noun* a slight flavour or trace of something. –**smack** *verb* to have a slight flavour or trace of something, *his manner smacks of conceit*.

smack[3] *noun* a boat with a single mast used for coasting or fishing.

smack⁴ *noun* (*informal*) a hard drug, especially heroin, sold or used illegally.

small *adjective* **1** not large or big. **2** not great in size, importance, or number etc. **3** of the smaller kind, *the small intestine*. **4** doing things on a small scale, *a small farmer*. **5** petty. **–small** *noun* the most slender part of something; *small of the back*, the part at the back of the waist. **–small** *adverb* in a small size or way; into small pieces, *chop it small*. □ **look or** or **feel small** to be humiliated. **small change** coins as opposed to notes. **small fry** *see* **fry²**. **small hours** the hours soon after midnight. **small-minded** *adjective* narrow or selfish in outlook. **small print** matter printed in small type, limitations (in a contract etc.) stated inconspicuously in this way. **small-scale** *adjective* drawn to a small scale so few details are shown; not extensive, involving only small quantities etc. **small talk** social conversation on unimportant subjects. **small-time** *adjective* of an unimportant level, *small-time crooks*. **smallness** *noun*

smallgoods *plural noun* (*Austral.*) cooked meats and meat products.

smallholding *noun* a piece of agricultural land smaller than a farm.

smallpox *noun* a contagious disease (now eliminated) caused by a virus, with pustules that often left disfiguring scars.

smarmy *adjective* (*informal*) trying to win favour by flattery or excessive politeness, fulsome. **smarmily** *adverb*, **smarminess** *noun*

smart *adjective* **1** forceful, brisk, *a smart pace*. **2** clever, ingenious. **3** neat and elegant. **4** (of a device) capable of some independent and seemingly intelligent action. **–smart** *verb* to feel a stinging pain (bodily or mental). **–smart** *noun* a stinging pain. □ **smart alec** (*informal*) a know-all. **smartly** *adverb*, **smartness** *noun*

smarten *verb* to make or become smarter.

smash *verb* **1** to break or become broken suddenly and noisily into pieces. **2** to strike or move with great force. **3** to strike (a ball) forcefully downwards in tennis etc. **4** to crash (a vehicle); to have a crash. **5** to overthrow or destroy, *police smashed the drug ring*. **6** to ruin or become ruined financially. **–smash** *noun* **1** the act or sound of smashing. **2** a collision. **3** a disaster; financial ruin. **smash-and-grab raid** a robbery done by smashing a shop window and grabbing goods. **smash hit** (*informal*) an extremely successful thing.

smattering *noun* a slight superficial knowledge of a language or subject.

smear *verb* **1** to spread with a greasy, sticky, or dirty substance. **2** to try to damage the reputation of. **–smear** *noun* **1** something smeared on a surface; a mark made by this. **2** a specimen of material smeared on a microscope slide for examination. **3** an attempt to damage a reputation, *a smear campaign*.

smeary *adjective* **1** smeared. **2** tending to smear things.

smell *noun* **1** the faculty of perceiving things by their action on the sense organs of the nose. **2** the quality that is perceived in this way. **3** an unpleasant quality of this kind. **4** an act of smelling something. **–smell** *verb* (**smelt**, **smelling**) **1** to perceive the smell of; to detect or test by one's sense of smell. **2** to give off a smell. **3** to give off an unpleasant smell.

smelling salts *plural noun* (chiefly *historical*) a solid preparation of ammonia used for smelling as a stimulant to relieve faintness.

smelly *adjective* (**smellier**, **smelliest**) having a strong or unpleasant smell.

smelt¹ *see* **smell**.

smelt² *verb* to heat and melt (ore) so as to obtain the metal it contains; to obtain (metal) in this way.

smelt³ *noun* a small fish related to salmon.

smidgen *noun* a very small amount.

smile *noun* a facial expression indicating pleasure or amusement, with the lips stretched and turning upwards at their ends. **–smile** *verb* **1** to give a smile; to express by smiling, *smiled her thanks*. **2** to look bright or favourable; *fortune smiled on us*, favoured us. **smiler** *noun*

smirch *verb* **1** to smear or soil. **2** to bring discredit upon (a reputation). **–smirch** *noun* a smear, discredit.

smirk *noun* a self-satisfied smile. **–smirk** *verb* to give a smirk.

smite *verb* (**smote**, **smitten**, **smiting**) **1** to hit hard. **2** to have a sudden effect on, *his conscience smote him*.

Smith¹, Adam (1723–90), Scottish philosopher and economist.

Smith², Joseph (1805–44), American founder of the Mormon sect.

smith *noun* **1** a person who makes things in metal. **2** a blacksmith.

smithereens *plural noun* small fragments.

Smith Family an Australian voluntary welfare organisation established in 1922.

smithy *noun* a blacksmith's workshop.

smitten *see* smite. □ **smitten with** affected by (a disease, desire, etc.).

smock *noun* an overall shaped like a long loose shirt. –**smock** *verb* to ornament with smocking.

smocking *noun* a decoration of close gathers stitched into a honeycomb pattern.

smog *noun* fog polluted by smoke. [from *smoke* + *fog*]

smoke *noun* 1 the visible vapour given off by a burning substance. 2 an act or spell of smoking tobacco, *wanted a smoke*. 3 (*informal*) a cigarette or cigar. –**smoke** *verb* 1 to give out smoke or steam or other visible vapour. 2 (of a fireplace) to send smoke into a room instead of up the chimney. 3 to darken with smoke, *smoked glass*. 4 to preserve by treating with smoke, *smoked salmon*. 5 to draw into the mouth the smoke from a cigarette, cigar, or pipe; to use (a cigarette etc.) in this way; to do this as a habit. □ **big smoke** *see* big. **smoke bomb** a bomb that gives out dense smoke when it explodes. **smoke out** to drive out by means of smoke.

smokeless *adjective* 1 free from smoke. 2 producing little or no smoke, *smokeless fuel*.

smoker *noun* a person who smokes tobacco as a habit.

smokescreen *noun* a mass of smoke used to conceal the movement of troops or ships; something intended to conceal or disguise one's activities.

smoking ceremony (*Austral.*) *noun* (in Aboriginal culture) a ceremony in which smoke is used for ritual purposes, especially after a death.

smoking gun *noun* a piece of incontrovertible incriminating evidence.

smoko *noun* (*Austral. informal*) a break from work (originally time to have a cigarette etc.).

smoky *adjective* 1 giving off much smoke. 2 covered or filled with smoke. 3 greyish.

smolt *noun* a young salmon at the stage when it is covered with silvery scales and migrates to the sea for the first time.

smoodge *verb* (*Austral.*) 1 to behave amorously. 2 to toady.

smooth *adjective* 1 having an even surface with no projections, free from roughness. 2 not harsh in sound or taste. 3 moving evenly

without jolts or bumping. 4 pleasantly polite but perhaps insincere. –**smooth** *adverb* smoothly, *the course of true love never did run smooth*. –**smooth** *verb* 1 to make or become smooth. 2 to remove problems or dangers from, *smooth a person's path*. –**smooth** *noun* a smoothing touch or stroke. □ **smooth-tongued** *adjective* pleasantly polite or convincing but insincere. **smoothly** *adverb*, **smoothness** *noun*

smorgasbord (**smor**-găs-bord) *noun* 1 a buffet meal with a variety of dishes to choose from. 2 a medley; a variety. [Swedish]

smote *see* smite.

smother *verb* 1 to suffocate or stifle; to be suffocated. 2 to put out or keep down (a fire) by heaping ash on it. 3 to cover thickly. 4 to restrain or suppress, *she smothered a smile*.

smoulder *verb* 1 to burn slowly with smoke but no flame. 2 to burn inwardly with concealed anger or jealousy etc. 3 (of feelings) to exist in a suppressed state, *discontent smouldered*.

SMS *abbreviation* Short Message (or Messaging) Service, a system that enables mobile phone users to send and receive text messages. –**SMS** *noun* a text message that is sent or received using SMS. –**SMS** *verb* (**SMSs, SMSed, SMSing**) to send someone a text message using SMS.

SMTP *abbreviation* Simple Mail Transfer (or Transport) Protocol, a standard for the transmission of email on a computer network.

smudge *noun* a dirty or blurred mark. –**smudge** *verb* 1 to make a smudge on or with. 2 to become smudged or blurred. **smudgy** *adjective*

smug *adjective* (**smugger, smuggest**) self-satisfied. **smugly** *adverb*, **smugness** *noun*

smuggle *verb* 1 to convey secretly. 2 to bring (goods) into or out of a country illegally, especially without paying customs duties. **smuggler** *noun*

smut *noun* 1 a small flake of soot; a small black mark made by this or otherwise. 2 indecent talk, pictures, or stories.

smutty *adjective* 1 marked with smuts. 2 (of talk or pictures or stories) indecent.

snack *noun* 1 a small or casual or hurried meal. 2 (*Austral. informal*) an easy task. □ **snack bar** a place where snacks are sold.

snaffle *noun* a horse's bit without a curb. –**snaffle** *verb* 1 to put a snaffle on. 2 (*informal*) to seize, to acquire, *snaffle up a bargain*.

snag *noun* **1** a jagged projection. **2** a tear or caught thread in fabric that has caught on a snag. **3** an unexpected difficulty. **–snag** *verb* (**snagged**, **snagging**) to catch or tear or be caught on a snag. **snaggy** *adjective*

snail *noun* a soft-bodied animal with a shell that can enclose its whole body. □ **snail mail** (*informal*) ordinary mail as opposed to email. **snail's pace** a very slow pace.

snake *noun* **1** a reptile with a long narrow body and no legs. **2** a treacherous person. □ **snake charmer** an entertainer who seems to make snakes move to music. [from Old English *snaca*]

snakeskin *noun* leather made from snakes' skins.

snaky *adjective* **1** of or like a snake. **2** winding, sinuous. **3** (*Austral. informal*) angry, irritable.

snap *verb* (**snapped**, **snapping**) **1** to make or cause to make a sharp cracking sound. **2** to break suddenly or with a cracking sound, *the rope snapped*. **3** to bite or try to bite with a snatching movement. **4** to take or accept eagerly, *snapping up bargains*. **5** to speak with sudden irritation. **6** to move smartly, *snapped to attention*. **7** to take a snapshot of. **–snap** *noun* **1** the act or sound of snapping. **2** a fastener that closes with a snap. **3** a small crisp brittle biscuit, *ginger snaps*. **4** a sudden brief spell of cold weather. **5** a snapshot. **6** Snap a card game in which players call 'Snap' when two similar cards are exposed. **–snap** *adverb* with a snapping sound. **–snap** *adjective* sudden, done or arranged at short notice, *a snap election*. □ **snap-freeze** *verb* to freeze (food) rapidly for storing, so that it keeps its natural qualities. **snap one's fingers** to make a cracking noise by flipping the thumb against a finger, usually in order to draw attention. **snap one's fingers at** to defy; to regard with contempt. **snap out of it** (*informal*) to make oneself recover quickly from an illness or mood etc. **snap up** to take or accept eagerly.

snapdragon *noun* a garden plant with flowers that have a mouth-like opening, also called *antirrhinum*.

snapper *noun* **1** a person or thing that snaps. **2** any of several sea fish used as food.

snappish *adjective* bad-tempered and inclined to snap at people. **snappishly** *adverb*

snappy *adjective* (**snappier**, **snappiest**) (*informal*) **1** brisk, vigorous. **2** neat and elegant. **3** snappish. □ **make it snappy** (*informal*) be quick about it. **snappily** *adverb*

snapshot *noun* **1** a photograph taken informally or casually. **2** a brief look or summary.

snare *noun* **1** a trap for catching birds or animals, usually with a noose. **2** something liable to entangle a person or expose him or her to danger or failure etc. **3** each of the strings of gut or coiled metal stretched across a side drum to produce a rattling effect. **4** a snare drum. **–snare** *verb* to trap in a snare. □ **snare drum** a drum with snares.

snarl[1] *verb* **1** to growl angrily with the teeth bared. **2** to speak or utter in a bad-tempered way. **–snarl** *noun* the act or sound of snarling.

snarl[2] *verb* to tangle; to become entangled. **–snarl** *noun* a tangle. □ **snarl up** to make or become jammed or tangled, *traffic was snarled up*. **snarl-up** *noun*

snatch *verb* **1** to seize quickly or eagerly. **2** to take quickly or when a chance occurs, *snatched a few hours' sleep*. **–snatch** *noun* **1** the act of snatching. **2** a short or brief part, *snatches of song*; *she works in snatches*, in short spells.

snazzy *adjective* (*informal*) smart, stylish. **snazzily** *adverb*, **snazziness** *noun*

sneak *verb* **1** to go or convey furtively. **2** (*informal*) to steal furtively. **3** (*informal*) to tell tales. **–sneak** *noun* (*informal*) a tell-tale. **–sneak** *adjective* acting or done without warning, *sneak raider*. **sneaky** *adjective*

sneakers *plural noun* soft-soled canvas etc. shoes.

sneaking *adjective* persistent but not openly acknowledged, *a sneaking affection*.

sneer *noun* a scornful expression or remark. **–sneer** *verb* to show contempt by a sneer.

sneeze *noun* a sudden audible involuntary expulsion of air through the nose and mouth, to expel an irritant substance from the nostrils. **–sneeze** *verb* to give a sneeze. □ **not to be sneezed at** (*informal*) not to be despised, worth having.

snick *noun* **1** a small cut or notch. **2** a light glancing stroke in cricket. **–snick** *verb* **1** to cut a snick in. **2** to hit with a light glancing stroke.

snicker *verb* to snigger. **–snicker** *noun* a snigger.

snide *adjective* (*informal*) **1** (of coins etc.) counterfeit. **2** sneering in a sly way, *a snide remark*.

sniff *verb* **1** to draw up air audibly through the nose. **2** to draw in through the nose as one breathes; to try the smell of. **–sniff** *noun* the act or sound of sniffing. □ **sniff at** (*informal*) to show contempt for. **sniffer dog** a dog trained to scent the presence of drugs or explosives. **sniffer** *noun*

sniffle *verb* to sniff slightly or repeatedly. **–sniffle** *noun* the act or sound of sniffling.

sniffy *adjective* (*informal*) disdainful, contemptuous. **sniffily** *adverb*

snigger *noun* a sly giggle. **–snigger** *verb* to give a snigger.

snip *verb* (**snipped, snipping**) to cut with scissors or shears in small quick strokes. **–snip** *noun* **1** the act or sound of snipping. **2** a piece snipped off. **3** (*informal*) a bargain; a certainty; something very easy to do. **snips** *plural noun* a small pair of shears for cutting metal.

snipe *noun* (*plural* **snipe**) a wading bird with a long straight bill, frequenting marshes. **–snipe** *verb* **1** to fire shots from a hiding place. **2** to make sly critical remarks attacking a person or thing. **sniper** *noun*

snippet *noun* **1** a small piece cut off. **2** a fragment of information or news; a brief extract. [from *snip*]

snitch *verb* (*informal*) to steal.

snivel *verb* (**snivelled, snivelling**) **1** to run at the nose; to sniffle. **2** to cry or complain in a miserable whining way.

snob *noun* a person who has an exaggerated respect for social position or wealth or for certain attainments or tastes, and who despises people whom he or she considers inferior. **snobbery** *noun*

snobbish *adjective* of or like a snob. **snobbishly** *adverb*, **snobbishness** *noun*

snogging *noun* (*informal*) kissing and caressing.

snood *noun* a loose baglike ornamental hairnet worn at the back of the head.

snook¹ *noun* (*informal*) a contemptuous gesture with thumb to nose and fingers spread out. □ **cock a snook** to make this gesture; to show cheeky contempt.

snook² *noun* a barracuda.

snooker *noun* **1** a game played on a billiard table with 15 red and 6 other coloured balls. **2** a position in snooker where a direct shot would lose points. **–snooker** *verb* **1** to subject to a snooker. **2** (*informal*) to thwart, to defeat.

snoop *verb* (*informal*) to pry inquisitively. **–snoop** *noun* the act of snooping. **snooper** *noun*, **snoopy** *adjective*

snooty *adjective* (**snootier, snootiest**) (*informal*) haughty and contemptuous. **snootily** *adverb*

snooze *noun* a nap. **–snooze** *verb* to take a snooze.

snore *noun* a snorting or grunting sound made during sleep. **–snore** *verb* to make such sounds. **snorer** *noun*

snorkel *noun* **1** a breathing tube to enable a person to swim under water. **2** a device by which a submerged submarine can take in and expel air. **snorkelling** *noun* swimming with the aid of a snorkel.

snort *noun* a rough sound made by forcing breath suddenly through the nose, usually expressing annoyance or disgust. **–snort** *verb* **1** to utter a snort. **2** to inhale (a usually illegal drug, especially cocaine) through the nose.

snot *noun* (*informal*) mucous discharge from the nose. **snotty** *adjective*

snout *noun* **1** an animal's long projecting nose or nose and jaws. **2** the projecting front part of something.

snow *noun* **1** crystals of ice that form from atmospheric vapour and fall to earth in light white flakes. **2** a fall or layer of snow. **3** something resembling snow. **–snow** *verb* **1** to send down snow, *it is snowing*. **2** to scatter or fall like snow. □ **snowed under** covered with snow; overwhelmed with a mass of letters or work etc. **snow goose** a white Arctic goose. **snow pea** a variety of pea eaten whole (including the pod), also called *mangetout*. **snow-white** *adjective* & *noun* pure white.

snowball *noun* snow pressed into a small compact mass for throwing in play. **–snowball** *verb* **1** to throw snowballs at; to play in this way. **2** to grow quickly in size or intensity, as a snowball does when rolled in more snow.

snowbound *adjective* **1** prevented by snow from going out or travelling. **2** blocked by snow.

snowdrop *noun* a small flower growing from a bulb, with hanging white flowers blooming in early spring.

snowfall *noun* a fall of snow; the amount that falls.

snowflake *noun* a flake of snow.

snowline *noun* the level above which an area is covered permanently with snow.

snowman *noun* (*plural* **snowmen**) a figure made in snow roughly in the shape of a person.

snowplough *noun* a device for clearing a road or railway track by pushing snow aside.

snowstorm *noun* a storm in which snow falls.

Snowy Mountains an alpine skiing area in south-eastern NSW. It is the site of a major hydroelectric scheme.

snub¹ *verb* (**snubbed**, **snubbing**) to reject or humiliate (a person) by treating him or her scornfully or in an unfriendly way. –**snub** *noun* treatment of this kind.

snub² *adjective* (of the nose) short and stumpy. **snub-nosed** *adjective*

snuff¹ *noun* powdered tobacco for sniffing into the nostrils.

snuff² *verb* to put out (a candle) by covering or pinching the flame. □ **snuff it** (*informal*) to die. **snuffer** *noun*

snuffle *verb* to sniff in a noisy way, to breathe noisily through a partly blocked nose. –**snuffle** *noun* a snuffling sound. **snuffly** *adjective*

snug *adjective* (**snugger**, **snuggest**) cosy; (of a garment) close-fitting. **snugly** *adverb*

snuggery *noun* a snug and private place; a den.

snuggle *verb* to nestle, to cuddle.

so *adverb* & *conjunction* **1** to the extent or in the manner or with the result indicated, *it was so dark that we could not see*. **2** very, *we are so pleased to see you*. **3** for that reason, *and so they ran away*. **4** also, *if you go, so shall I*. –**so** *pronoun* that, the same thing, *do you think so?*; *and so say all of us*. □ **and so on** and others of the same kind. **or so** or about that number or amount, *two hundred or so*. **so as to** in order to. **so-called** *adjective* called by that name or description but perhaps not deserving it. **so long!** (*informal*) goodbye till we meet again. **so many** nothing but, *went down like so many skittles*. **so much** nothing but, *the findings were so much rubbish*; *so much for that idea*, no more need be said of it. **so-so** *adjective* & *adverb* (*informal*) only moderately good or well. **so that** in order that; with the result that. **so what?** that fact has no importance.

soak *verb* **1** to place or lie in a liquid so as to become thoroughly wet. **2** (of liquid) to penetrate gradually; (of rain etc.) to drench. **3** to absorb, *soak it up with a sponge*; *soak up knowledge*. **4** (*informal*) to extract much money from (a person) by charging or taxing him or her very heavily. –**soak** *noun* **1** the act or process of soaking. **2** a hollow in the ground where water collects.

so-and-so *noun* (*plural* **so-and-so's**) **1** a person or thing that need not be named. **2** (*informal*, to avoid using a vulgar word) an unpleasant or objectionable person.

soap *noun* **1** a substance used for washing and cleaning things, made of fat or oil combined with an alkali. **2** (*informal*) a soap opera. –**soap** *verb* to apply soap to. □ **soap opera** (*informal*) a broadcast serial with a domestic setting. (¶ A type of broadcast originally sponsored by soap manufacturers in the USA.)

soapsuds *plural noun* froth of soapy water.

soapy *adjective* **1** like soap. **2** covered or impregnated with soap. **3** (*informal*) trying to win favour by flattery or excessive politeness. **soapiness** *noun*

soar *verb* **1** to rise high in flight. **2** to rise very high, *prices soared*.

sob *noun* an uneven drawing of breath in weeping or when out of breath. –**sob** *verb* (**sobbed**, **sobbing**) to weep or breathe or utter with sobs. □ **sob story** (*informal*) a narrative meant to arouse sympathy.

sober *adjective* **1** not intoxicated. **2** serious and self-controlled, not frivolous. **3** (of colour) not bright or conspicuous. –**sober** *verb* to make or become sober, *sober up* or *down*. **soberly** *adverb*

sobriety (sŏ-**bry**-ĕ-tee) *noun* being sober.

sobriquet (**soh**-brĭ-kay) *noun* a nickname. [French]

soccer *noun* a form of football played with a spherical ball that may not be handled during play except by the goalkeeper. [short for *Association football*]

sociable (**soh**-shă-bŭl) *adjective* fond of company; characterised by friendly companionship. **sociably** *adverb*, **sociability** *noun*

social *adjective* **1** living in an organised community, not solitary. **2** of society or its organisation; of the mutual relationships of people or classes living in an organised community, *social problems*. **3** of or designed for companionship and sociability, *a social club*. **4** sociable. –**social** *noun* a social gathering. □ **social climber** a person seeking to gain a higher rank in society. **social cost** the consequences for society as a whole that result from a particular policy etc. **social democracy** a political system favouring a mixed economy and democratic social change. **social engineering** the process of reorganising society. **social science** the scientific study of human society and social relationships. **social security** government assistance for those who are unemployed, ill, disabled, etc. **social welfare** services provided by the government, including education, health, and housing. **social worker** a person trained to help people with social problems. **socially** *adverb* [from Latin *socius* = companion]

socialise *verb* (also **-ize**) **1** to organise in a socialistic manner. **2** to behave sociably, to take part in social activities. **socialisation** *noun*

socialism *noun* **1** a political and economic theory advocating that land, transport, natural resources, and the chief industries should be owned and managed by the State. **2** a policy or practice based on this. **socialist** *noun*, **socialistic** *adjective*

socialite (**soh**-shă-lyt) *noun* a person who is prominent in fashionable society.

society *noun* **1** an organised community; the system of living in this. **2** people of the higher social classes. **3** company, companionship, *always enjoy his society*; *he is at his best in society*. **4** a group of people organised for some common purpose. □ **Society of Friends** a Christian movement (also called *Quakers*) with no written creed or ordained ministers, whose central belief is the 'Inner Light' or Christ's direct working in the soul. **Society of Jesus** Jesuits. [same origin as *social*]

Society Islands a group of islands (including Tahiti) in French Polynesia.

sociology (soh-see-**ol**-ŏ-jee) *noun* the scientific study of human society and its development and institutions, or of social problems. **sociological** *adjective*, **sociologist** *noun* [from *socio-* = of society, + *-logy*]

sock[1] *noun* a short stocking not reaching the knee. □ **pull one's socks up** (*informal*) to make an effort to do better. **put a sock in it** (*informal*) be quiet.

sock[2] *verb* (*informal*) to hit forcefully. –**sock** *noun* (*informal*) a forceful blow.

socket *noun* **1** a hollow into which something fits, *a tooth socket*. **2** a device for receiving an electric plug or bulb in order to make a connection.

sockeye *noun* a kind of salmon.

Socrates (**sok**-ră-teez) (469–399 BC), Athenian philosopher, who taught Plato.

sod *noun* turf; a piece of this.

soda *noun* **1** a compound of sodium in common use, especially sodium carbonate (*washing soda*), bicarbonate (*baking soda*), or hydroxide (*caustic soda*). **2** soda water, *whisky and soda*. □ **soda bread** bread made with baking soda (not yeast). **soda fountain** an apparatus in which soda water is stored under pressure, ready to be drawn out. **soda water** water made fizzy by being charged with carbon dioxide under pressure.

sodden *adjective* made very wet.

sodium (**soh**-dee-ŭm) *noun* a chemical element (symbol Na), a soft silver-white metal. **sodium lamp** a lamp using an electrical discharge in sodium vapour and giving a yellow light, often used in street lighting.

Sodom a town of ancient Palestine, said to have been destroyed (along with Gomorrah) by fire from heaven for the wickedness of its inhabitants.

sofa *noun* a long upholstered seat with a back and raised ends or arms.

soffit *noun* the undersurface of an arch or architrave. [same origin as *suffix*]

Sofia (**soh**-fee-ă) the capital of Bulgaria.

soft *adjective* **1** not hard or firm. **2** smooth, not rough or stiff. **3** not loud. **4** gentle, soothing; *a soft answer*, a good-tempered one. **5** not physically robust, feeble. **6** easily influenced, tender-hearted. **7** (*informal*) easy, comfortable, *a soft job*; *soft living*. **8** (of currency) likely to drop suddenly in value. **9** (of drinks) non-alcoholic. **10** (of drugs) mild; not likely to cause addiction. **11** (of water) free from mineral salts that prevent soap from lathering. **12** (of colour or light) not bright or dazzling; (of an outline) not sharp. **13** (of consonants) not hard (*see* **hard**, sense 11). –**soft** *adverb* softly; *fall soft*, on a soft surface. □ **soft-boiled** *adjective* (of eggs) boiled but without allowing yolk and white to become set. **soft fruit** small stoneless fruits such as strawberries and currants. **soft furnishings** curtains and rugs etc. **soft-hearted** *adjective* compassionate. **soft option** the easier alternative. **soft-pedal** *verb* (*informal*) to refrain from emphasising. **soft soap** semi-liquid soap; (*informal*) persuasive talk; flattery. **soft spot** a feeling of affection towards a person or thing. **soft touch** (*informal*) a gullible person, especially over money. **softly** *adverb*, **softness** *noun*

softball *noun* a modified form of baseball; the ball used in this, larger than a baseball.

soften *verb* to make or become soft or softer. □ **soften up** to make weaker by attacking repeatedly; to make less able to resist (salesmanship etc.) by making preliminary approaches. **softener** *noun*

softie *noun* (*informal*) a person who is physically weak or not hardy, or who is soft-hearted.

software *noun* computer programs or the disks or tapes containing these, or other interchangeable material for performing operations (as distinct from *hardware*).

softwood *noun* wood from coniferous trees, easily sawn.

soggy *adjective* 1 sodden. 2 moist and heavy in texture. **soggily** *adverb*, **sogginess** *noun*

soigné (**swahn**-yay) *adjective* (of a woman, **soignée**) well-groomed and sophisticated. [French, = taken care of]

soil¹ *noun* 1 the loose upper layer of earth in which plants grow. 2 ground as territory, *on native soil*.

soil² *verb* to make or become dirty.

soirée (**swah**-ray) *noun* a social gathering in the evening, e.g. for music. [French, = evening]

sojourn (**soh**-jern *or* **soj**-ern) *noun* a temporary stay. –**sojourn** *verb* to stay at a place temporarily.

solace (**sol**-ăs) *noun* comfort in distress; something that gives this. –**solace** *verb* to give solace to. [from Latin *solari* = to console]

solar (**soh**-ler) *adjective* 1 of or derived from the sun, *solar energy*. 2 reckoned by the sun, *solar time*. □ **solar battery** or **cell** a device converting solar radiation into electricity. **solar heating** heating derived from solar energy. **solar plexus** the network of nerves at the pit of the stomach; this area. **solar system** the sun with the heavenly bodies that revolve round it. [from Latin *sol* = sun]

solarium (sŏ-**lair**-ree-ŭm) *noun* (*plural* **solaria**) a room or balcony, often enclosed with glass, where sunlight can be enjoyed for medical purposes or for pleasure.

sold *see* **sell**. □ **sold on** (*informal*) enthusiastic about.

solder (**sol**-der *or* **sohl**-der) *noun* a soft alloy used to cement metal parts together. –**solder** *verb* to join with solder. □ **soldering iron** a tool used hot for applying solder. [from Latin *solidare* = make firm or solid]

soldier *noun* a member of an army, especially a private or NCO. –**soldier** *verb* to serve as a soldier. □ **soldier of fortune** an adventurous person ready to serve any country or person

that will hire him. **soldier on** (*informal*) to persevere doggedly. **soldier settler** (*Austral. old use*) an ex-serviceman who acquired land under a **soldier settlement** scheme.

soldierly *adjective* like a soldier.

soldiery *noun* soldiers collectively or as a class.

sole¹ *noun* 1 the undersurface of a foot. 2 the part of a shoe or stocking etc. that covers this (often excluding the heel). –**sole** *verb* to put a sole on (a shoe).

sole² *noun* a kind of flatfish used as food.

sole³ *adjective* 1 one and only, *our sole objection is this*. 2 belonging exclusively to one person or group, *we have the sole right to sell these cars*. **solely** *adverb* [from Latin *solus* = alone]

solecism (**sol**-ě-sizm) *noun* a mistake in the use of language; an offence against good manners or etiquette. [from Greek *soloikos* = speaking incorrectly]

solemn *adjective* 1 not smiling or cheerful. 2 dignified and impressive, *a solemn occasion*. 3 formal; accompanied by a religious or other ceremony. **solemnly** *adverb*, **solemnity** (sŏ-**lem**-nĭ-tee) *noun*

solemnise (**sol**-ěm-nyz) *verb* (also -**ize**) 1 to celebrate (a festival etc.). 2 to perform (a marriage ceremony) with formal rites. **solemnisation** *noun*

solenoid (**sol**-ě-noid) *noun* a coil of wire that becomes magnetic when an electrical current is passed through it.

sol-fa (**sol**-fah) *see* **tonic sol-fa**.

solicit (sŏ-**liss**-ĭt) *verb* to seek to obtain, to ask earnestly, *solicit votes* or *for votes*. **solicitation** *noun*

solicitor *noun* a lawyer who advises clients on legal matters and prepares legal documents for them but who does not represent them as an advocate except in certain lower courts.

solicitous (sŏ-**liss**-ĭ-tŭs) *adjective* anxious and concerned about a person's welfare or comfort. **solicitously** *adverb* [from Latin *sollicitus* = worrying]

solicitude (sŏ-**liss**-ĭ-tewd) *noun* solicitous concern.

solid *adjective* 1 keeping its shape, firm; not liquid or gas. 2 not hollow. 3 of the same substance throughout, *solid silver*. 4 continuous, without a break, *for two solid hours*. 5 strongly constructed, not flimsy. 6 having three dimensions; concerned with solids, *solid geometry*. **7** sound and reliable, *there are solid arguments against it*. **8** unanimous, *the miners are solid on this issue*. –**solid** *noun* **1** a solid substance or body or food. **2** a body or shape with three dimensions. ☐ **solid state** a state of matter in which the constituent atoms or molecules occupy fixed positions with respect to each other and cannot move freely (other states are the liquid, gas, and plasma states). **solid-state** *adjective* using transistors (which make use of the electronic properties of solids) instead of valves. **solidly** *adverb*, **solidity** (sŏ-**lid**-ĭ-tee) *noun*

Solidarity an independent trade union movement in Poland.

solidarity *noun* unity resulting from common interests, feelings, or sympathies.

solidify (sŏ-**lid**-ĭ-fy) *verb* (**solidified**, **solidifying**) to make or become solid.

solifluction *noun* gradual movement of waterlogged soil etc. down a slope. [from Latin *solum* = soil, + *fluctio* = flowing]

soliloquise (sŏ-**lil**-ŏ-kwyz) *verb* (also **-ize**) to utter a soliloquy.

soliloquy (sŏ-**lil**-ŏ-kwee) *noun* a speech in which a person expresses his or her thoughts aloud without addressing anyone. [from Latin *solus* = alone, + *loqui* = speak]

solipsism *noun* (in philosophy) the view that the self is all that exists or can be known. **solipsist** *noun*, **solipsistic** *adjective*

solitaire (sol-ĭ-**tair**) *noun* **1** a diamond or other gem set by itself. **2** a game for one person, in which marbles are removed from their places on a special board after jumping others over them. **3** a card game for one person.

solitary *adjective* **1** alone, without companions. **2** single, *a solitary example*. **3** not frequented, lonely, *a solitary valley*. –**solitary** *noun* **1** a recluse. **2** (*informal*) solitary confinement. ☐ **solitary confinement** isolation in a separate cell as a punishment. **solitarily** *adverb* [from Latin *solus* = alone]

solitude *noun* being solitary.

solo *noun* (*plural* **solos**) **1** a musical composition or passage for a single voice or instrument. **2** a pilot's flight in an aircraft without an instructor or companion. **3** solo whist. –**solo** *adjective* & *adverb* unaccompanied, alone, *for solo flute*; *flying solo*. ☐ **solo whist** a card game like whist

in which one player may oppose the others. [Italian, = alone]

soloist *noun* a person who performs a solo.

Solomon king of Israel (c. 970–930 BC), son of David, famous for his wisdom and magnificence. ☐ **Song of Solomon** (also called the *Song of Songs* or *Canticles*) a book of the Old Testament, an anthology of love poems ascribed to Solomon. **Wisdom of Solomon** a book of the Apocrypha containing a meditation on wisdom.

Solomon Islands (also **Solomons**) a country consisting of a group of islands in the South Pacific.

Solon (**soh**-lon) early 6th century BC, Athenian statesman and poet.

solstice (**sol**-stĭs) *noun* either of the times in the year when the sun is furthest from the equator; the point reached by the sun at these times; *winter solstice*, about 21 June; *summer solstice*, about 22 December. [from Latin *sol* = sun, + *sistere* = stand still]

soluble (**sol**-yŭ-bŭl) *adjective* **1** able to be dissolved in liquid. **2** able to be solved. **solubly** *adverb*, **solubility** (sol-yŭ-**bil**-ĭ-tee) *noun* [same origin as *solve*]

solute (**sol**-yoot) *noun* a substance that is dissolved in another substance.

solution *noun* **1** a liquid in which something is dissolved. **2** dissolving or being dissolved into liquid form. **3** the process of solving a problem etc.; the answer found. ☐ **solution set** (in mathematics) all the correct solutions to a problem. [same origin as *solve*]

solvable *adjective* able to be solved.

solve *verb* to find the answer to (a problem or puzzle) or the way out of (a difficulty). **solver** *noun* [from Latin *solvere* = unfasten]

solvent *adjective* **1** having enough money to pay one's debts and liabilities. **2** able to dissolve another substance. –**solvent** *noun* a liquid used for dissolving something. **solvency** *noun*

Solzhenitsyn (sol-*zh*ĕ-**nit**-sĭn), Alexander (1918–2008), Russian novelist, imprisoned and later deported to the West (1974) for his criticisms of the Soviet regime.

Somalia (sŏ-**mah**-lee-ă) a republic in north-east Africa. **Somali** *adjective* & *noun* (*plural* **Somalis**).

somatic (sŏ-**mat**-ik) *adjective* of the body. [from Greek *soma* = body]

sombre (**som**-ber) *adjective* dark, gloomy, dismal. **sombrely** *adverb* [from Latin *sub* = under, + *umbra* = shade]

sombrero (som-**brair**-roh) *noun* (*plural* **sombreros**) a felt or straw hat with a very wide brim, worn especially in Latin-American countries. [from Spanish *sombra* = shade (same origin as *sombre*)]

some *adjective & pronoun* **1** an unspecified quantity, *buy some apples*; *some few*, some but not many. **2** an amount that is less than the whole, *some of them were late*. **3** an unspecified person or thing, *some fool locked the door*. **4** a considerable quantity, *that was some years ago*. **5** approximately, *waited some 20 minutes*. **6** (*informal*) remarkable, *that was some storm!* □ **some time** at some point in time.

Usage *Some time* is written as two words when it means 'at some unspecified time'. *Sometime* as a single word means 'former' or 'formerly'. *Sometimes* means 'at some times'.

somebody *noun & pronoun* **1** an unspecified person. **2** a person of importance.

somehow *adverb* **1** in some unspecified or unexplained manner, *I never liked her, somehow*. **2** by one means or another, *must get it finished somehow*.

someone *noun & pronoun* somebody.

someplace *adverb* (*Amer.*) somewhere.

somersault (**sum**-er-solt) *noun* **1** an acrobatic movement in which a person rolls head over heels on the ground or in the air. **2** a complete about-turn, *the government has done a somersault on promised tax cuts*. –**somersault** *verb* to perform a somersault. [from Latin *supra* = above, + *saltus* = a leap]

something *noun & pronoun* **1** an unspecified thing; *see something of a person*, meet him or her occasionally or for a short time; *he is something of an expert*, to some extent. **2** an important or praiseworthy thing. □ **something like** approximately, *it cost something like $10*; rather like, *it's something like a rabbit*.

sometime *adjective* former, *her sometime friend*. –**sometime** *adverb* formerly.

Usage See the note on *some time* (see entry for **some**).

sometimes *adverb* at some times but not all the time.

somewhat *adverb* to some extent, *it is somewhat difficult*.

somewhere *adverb* at, in, or to an unspecified place or position. □ **get somewhere** (*informal*) to achieve some success.

Somme a river of NE France, flowing into the English Channel, the scene of heavy fighting during the First World War.

somnambulist (som-**nam**-bew-list) *noun* a sleepwalker. **somnambulism** *noun* [from Latin *somnus* = sleep, + *ambulare* = to walk]

somnolent (**som**-nŏ-lĕnt) *adjective* sleepy; asleep. **somnolence** *noun* [from Latin *somnus* = sleep]

son *noun* **1** a male child in relation to his parents. **2** a male descendant. **3** a form of address to a boy or young man. □ **son-in-law** *noun* (*plural* **sons-in-law**) a daughter's husband.

sonar (**soh**-ner) *noun* a device for detecting objects under water by reflection of sound waves. [from *sound navigation and ranging*]

sonata (sŏ-**nah**-tă) *noun* a musical composition for one instrument or two, usually with three or four movements. □ **sonata form** a musical form with a central development, often used in sonatas and symphonies. [from Italian *sonare* = to sound]

sonatina (sonn-ă-**tee**-nă) *noun* a simple or short sonata.

song *noun* **1** singing. **2** a musical composition for singing. □ **go for a song** to be sold very cheaply. **make a song and dance** (*informal*) to make a great fuss. **Song of Songs** the Song of Solomon (*see* **Solomon**). **Song of the Three Holy Children** a book of the Apocrypha.

songbird *noun* a bird with a musical cry.

songster *noun* **1** a singer. **2** a songbird. **songstress** *feminine noun*

sonic *adjective* of or involving sound waves. □ **sonic boom** a loud noise heard when the shock wave caused by an aircraft travelling at supersonic speed reaches the hearer. [from Latin *sonus* = sound]

sonnet *noun* a poem of 14 lines with lengths and rhymes in accordance with any of several patterns.

sonny *noun* (*informal*) a form of address to a boy or young man.

sonorous (**sonn**-ŏ-rŭs) *adjective* resonant, giving a deep powerful sound. [from Latin *sonor* = sound]

sook (*rhymes with* book) *noun* (*Austral. informal*) a cry-baby, a timid person.

sool (*rhymes with* tool) *verb* (*Austral. informal*) to urge a dog to attack, to harass.

soon *adverb* 1 in a short time, not long after the present or a specified time. 2 early, quickly, *spoke too soon*. □ **as soon** as readily, as willingly. **as soon as** at the moment that, as early as; as readily or willingly as. **sooner or later** at some time, eventually.

soot *noun* the black powdery substance that rises in the smoke of coal or wood etc.

sooth *noun* (*old use*) truth.

soothe *verb* to calm, to ease (pain etc.). **soothing** *adjective*

soothsayer *noun* a person who foretells the future. [from *sooth + say*]

sooty *adjective* (**sootier, sootiest**) 1 full of soot; covered with soot. 2 like soot, black.

sop *noun* 1 a piece of bread dipped in liquid before being eaten or cooked. 2 a concession that is made in order to pacify or bribe a troublesome person. **–sop** *verb* (**sopped, sopping**) 1 to dip (a thing) in liquid. 2 to soak up (liquid) with something absorbent.

sophism (**sof**-izm) *noun* a piece of sophistry.

sophist (**sof**-ĭst) *noun* a person who uses sophistry. [named after the Sophists, Greek philosophers of the 5th century BC, who taught rhetoric and skilled reasoning]

sophisticated (sŏ-**fist**-ĭ-kay-tĕd) *adjective* 1 characteristic of fashionable life and its ways; experienced in this and lacking natural simplicity. 2 complicated, elaborate, *sophisticated electronic devices*. **sophistication** *noun*

sophistry (**sof**-ĭst-ree) *noun* clever and subtle but perhaps misleading reasoning. [from Greek *sophos* = wise]

Sophocles (**sof**-ŏ-kleez) (c. 496–406 BC), Greek dramatist.

soporific (sop-ŏ-**rif**-ik) *adjective* tending to cause sleep. **–soporific** *noun* a medicinal substance that causes sleep. [from Latin *sopor* = sleep, + *facere* = make]

sopping *adjective* very wet, drenched.

soppy *adjective* (**soppier, soppiest**) (*informal*) sentimental in a sickly way; silly; infatuated. **soppily** *adverb*, **soppiness** *noun*

soprano (sŏ-**prah**-noh) *noun* (*plural* **sopranos**) 1 the highest female or boy's singing voice. 2 a singer with such a voice; a part written for it. [from Italian *sopra* = above]

sorbet (**sor**-bay) *noun* a frozen concoction of fruit, fruit juice, or liqueur, syrup, and egg whites. [same origin as *sherbet*]

sorcerer *noun* a magician, especially one supposedly aided by evil spirits. **sorceress** *feminine noun*

sorcery *noun* a sorcerer's art or practices.

sordid *adjective* 1 dirty, squalid. 2 (of motives or actions) lacking dignity, not honourable, mercenary. **sordidly** *adverb*, **sordidness** *noun*

sore *adjective* 1 causing pain from injury or disease. 2 suffering pain, *felt sore all over*. 3 causing mental pain or annoyance, *a sore subject*. 4 (*old use*) serious, *in sore need*. 5 distressed, vexed. **–sore** *noun* 1 a sore place, especially where the skin is raw. 2 a source of distress or annoyance. **soreness** *noun*

sorely *adverb* seriously, very, *I was sorely tempted*.

sorghum (**sor**-gŭm) *noun* a kind of tropical cereal grass.

sorrel[1] (*rhymes with* coral) *noun* a herb with sharp-tasting leaves used in salads.

sorrel[2] (*rhymes with* coral) *adjective* & *noun* light reddish-brown; a horse of this colour.

sorrow *noun* 1 mental suffering caused by loss or disappointment etc. 2 something that causes this. **–sorrow** *verb* to feel sorrow, to grieve.

sorrowful *adjective* feeling or showing sorrow. **sorrowfully** *adverb*

sorry *adjective* 1 feeling pity, regret, or sympathy; *sorry!*, I am sorry, I beg your pardon. 2 wretched, *in a sorry plight*.

sort *noun* 1 a particular kind or variety, *this sort of thing*; *these sorts of things*. 2 (*informal*) a person with regard to character, *quite a good sort*. **–sort** *verb* to arrange according to sort or size or destination etc. □ **of a sort** or **of sorts** not fully deserving the name given. **out of sorts** slightly unwell or depressed. **sort of** (*informal*) somewhat, rather, *I sort of expected it*. **sort out** to disentangle; to select from others; (*informal*) to deal with or punish. **sorter** *noun*

sortie (**sor**-tee) *noun* 1 an attack by troops coming out from a besieged place. 2 a flight of an aircraft on a military operation. [from French *sortir* = go out]

SOS *noun* (*plural* SOSs) **1** an international coded signal of extreme distress. **2** an urgent appeal for help or response.

sot *noun* a drunkard. **sottish** *adjective*

sotto voce (sot-oh **voh**-chay) *adverb* in an undertone. [Italian]

sou (*pr.* soo) *noun* **1** a former French coin of low value. **2** (*informal*) a very small amount of money.

soubrette (soo-**bret**) *noun* **1** a pert maidservant or similar character in comedy. **2** an actress taking this part.

soubriquet (soo-brǐ-kay) *noun* = sobriquet.

soufflé (**soo**-flay) *noun* a light spongy dish made with beaten egg white. [from French *souffler* = to blow]

sough (*pr.* suf *or* sow) *verb* to make a moaning or whispering sound as the wind does in trees. – **sough** *noun* this sound.

sought *see* seek. □ **sought-after** *adjective* much in demand; generally desired.

soul *noun* **1** the spiritual or immortal element in a person. **2** a person's mental, moral, or emotional nature, *his whole soul revolted from it*; *cannot call his soul his own*, is completely under the control of another person. **3** a personification or pattern; *she is the soul of honour*, incapable of dishonourable conduct. **4** a person, *there's not a soul about*. **5** Black American culture and racial identity. **6** soul music. □ **soul-destroying** *adjective* deadeningly monotonous or depressing. **soul mates** people ideally suited to each other. **soul music** a kind of music with rhythm and blues, gospel and rock elements. **soul-searching** *noun* examination of one's conscience.

soulful *adjective* **1** having or showing deep feeling. **2** emotional. **soulfully** *adverb*

soulless *adjective* **1** lacking sensitivity or noble qualities. **2** dull, uninteresting.

sound¹ *noun* **1** vibrations that travel through the air and are detectable (at certain frequencies) by the ear. **2** the sensation produced by these vibrations; a particular kind of it, *the sound of music*. **3** a sound made in speech. **4** sound reproduced in a film etc. **5** the mental impression produced by a statement or description etc., *we don't like the sound of the new scheme*. – **sound** *verb* **1** to produce or cause to produce sound, *sound the trumpet*. **2** to utter, to pronounce, *the 'h' in 'hour' is not sounded*. **3** to give an impression when heard, *it sounds like a magpie*; *the news sounds good*, seems to be good. **4** to give an audible signal

for, *sound the retreat*. **5** to test by noting the sound produced, *the doctor sounds a patient's lungs with a stethoscope*. □ **sound barrier** the high resistance of air to objects moving at speeds near that of sound. **sound broadcasting** radio as opposed to television. **sound effects** sounds (other than speech or music) made artificially for use in a play or film etc. **sound off** (*informal*) to express one's opinions loudly and freely. **sound out** to question cautiously. **sound system** equipment for the high-fidelity recording and reproduction of sound. **sounder** *noun* [from Latin *sonus* = a sound]

sound² *adjective* **1** healthy, not diseased or damaged. **2** correct, logical, well-founded, *sound reasoning*. **3** financially secure, *a sound investment*. **4** thorough, *a sound thrashing*; *sound sleep*, deep and unbroken. – **sound** *adverb* soundly, *the baby is sound asleep*. **soundly** *adverb*, **soundness** *noun* [from Old English *gesund* = healthy]

sound³ *verb* **1** to test the depth or quality of the bottom of (the sea or a river etc.), especially by a weighted line (**sounding line**); to measure depth etc. in this way. **2** to examine with a probe. – **sound** *noun* a surgeon's probe. **sounder** *noun* [from Latin *sub* = under, + *unda* = wave]

sound⁴ *noun* a strait (of water); an inlet, *Milford Sound*. [from Old English *sund* = swimming or sea]

sounding *noun* measurement of the depth of water (*see* sound³).

soundproof *adjective* not able to be penetrated by sound. – **soundproof** *verb* to make soundproof.

soundtrack *noun* **1** a strip on cinema film for recording sound. **2** the sound itself.

soup *noun* liquid food made of stock from stewed meat, fish, or vegetables etc. – **soup** *verb* **soup up** (*informal*) to increase the power of (an engine); to enliven. □ **in the soup** (*informal*) in difficulties or trouble. **soup kitchen** a place where soup and other food is supplied free to the needy in times of distress. **soupy** *adjective*

soupçon (**soop**-sawn) *noun* a very small quantity, a trace, *add a soupçon of garlic*. [French, = suspicion]

sour *adjective* **1** tasting sharp like unripe fruit. **2** not fresh, tasting or smelling sharp or unpleasant from fermentation or staleness. **3** (of soil) excessively acid, deficient in lime. **4** bad-tempered, disagreeable in manner, *gave* *me a sour look.* **–sour** *verb* to make or become sour, *was soured by misfortune.* □ **sour cream** cream deliberately fermented by the action of bacteria. **sour grapes** said when a person pretends to despise something he or she cannot have. (¶ From the fable of the fox who wanted some grapes but found that they were out of reach and so pretended that they were sour and undesirable anyway.) **sourly** *adverb*, **sourness** *noun*

source *noun* **1** the place from which something comes or is obtained. **2** the starting point of a river. **3** a person or book etc. supplying information. **–source** *verb* to obtain, *we've managed to source the necessary spare parts.* □ **at source** at the point of origin. **source code** a text listing of commands to be compiled or assembled into an executable computer program.

sourpuss *noun* (*informal*) a sour-tempered person.

soursob *noun* a yellow-flowered introduced garden weed, especially common in SA and Victoria.

souse (*rhymes with* house) *verb* **1** to steep in pickle, *soused herrings*. **2** to plunge or soak in liquid; to drench, to throw (liquid) over a thing.

south *noun* **1** the point or direction opposite north. **2** the southern part of something. **–south** *adjective* & *adverb* towards or in the south; *a south wind*, blowing from the south. □ **South Pole** the southernmost pole of the earth. **south pole** (of a magnet) the pole that is attracted to the south.

South Africa a republic occupying the southernmost part of the continent of Africa. **South African** *adjective* & *noun*

South America the southern half of the American land mass (*see* America).

South Australia a State comprising the central southern part of Australia.

South Carolina (ka-rŏ-**ly**-nǎ) a State of the USA on the Atlantic coast.

South Dakota (dǎ-**koh**-tǎ) a State in the north central USA.

south-east *noun* the point or direction midway between south and east. **south-easterly** *adjective* & *noun*, **south-eastern** *adjective*

southeaster *noun* a south-east wind.

southerly *adjective* in or towards the south; *a southerly wind*, blowing from the south

(approximately). **–southerly** *noun* a southerly wind.

southern *adjective* of or in the south. □ **southern lights** the aurora australis.

Southern Cross **1** a constellation in the southern sky. **2** the Eureka flag. **3** the name of the aeroplane in which Charles Kingford Smith made the first Pacific crossing by air in 1928.

southerner *noun* a native or inhabitant of the south.

southernmost *adjective* furthest south.

Southern Ocean the body of water surrounding the continent of Antarctica.

southing *noun* **1** a distance travelled or measured southward. **2** a southerly direction.

South Korea see Korea.

southpaw *noun* a left-handed person, especially in sports.

South Sea (*old use*) the South Pacific Ocean.

southward *adjective* towards the south. **southwards** *adverb*

south-west *noun* the point or direction midway between south and west. **south-westerly** *adjective* & *noun*, **south-western** *adjective*

southwester *noun* a south-west wind.

souvenir (soo-vě-**neer**) *noun* something bought or given or kept as a reminder of an incident or a place visited. [from French *se souvenir* = remember]

sou'wester *noun* a waterproof hat, usually of oilskin, with a broad flap at the back.

sovereign (**sov**-rěn) *noun* **1** a king or queen who is the supreme ruler of a country. **2** a former British gold coin, nominally worth £1. **–sovereign** *adjective* **1** supreme, *sovereign power*. **2** possessing sovereign power, independent, *sovereign states*. **3** very effective, *a sovereign remedy*. **sovereignty** *noun* [from Latin *super* = over]

soviet (**soh**-vee-ět *or* **sov**-ee-ět) *noun* an elected council in the former USSR. **–Soviet** *adjective* of the former Soviet Union. □ **Supreme Soviet** the governing council of the former USSR or of any of its constituent republics. [from Russian *sovet* = council]

Soviet Union the former Union of Soviet Socialist Republics.

sow[1] (*rhymes with* go) *verb* (**sowed**, **sown** *or* **sowed**, **sowing**) **1** to plant or scatter (seed) for growth; to plant seed in (a field etc.).

2 to implant or spread (feelings or ideas), *they sowed hatred amongst the people*. **sower** *noun*

sow² (*rhymes with* cow) *noun* a fully-grown female pig.

Soweto (sŏ-**wet**-oh) a group of townships near Johannesburg in South Africa.

soy *noun* (also **soya**) **1** (in full **soy bean** or **soya bean**) a kind of bean (originally from SE Asia) from which an edible oil and flour are obtained. **2** (in full **soy sauce** or **soya sauce**) a sauce made by fermenting soy beans in brine, used widely in Asian cooking. □ **soy milk** a beverage of soaked and ground soy beans with water, often used as a milk substitute.

Soyuz (**soi**-uuz) any of a series of manned spacecraft launched by the former USSR, used especially in missions that involve docking. [Russian, = union]

sozzled *adjective* (*informal*) very drunk.

spa (*pr.* spah) *noun* a curative mineral spring; a place with such a spring. [from *Spa*, a town in Belgium with a mineral spring]

space *noun* **1** the boundless expanse in which all objects exist and move. **2** a portion of this, an area or volume for a particular purpose, *the box takes too much space*; *parking spaces.* **3** an interval between points or objects, an empty area, *separated by a space of 3 metres*; *there's a space for your signature.* **4** the area of paper used in writing or printing something, *would take too much space to explain in detail.* **5** a large area, *the wide open spaces.* **6** outer space (*see* **outer**). **7** an interval of time, *within the space of an hour.* **–space** *verb* to arrange with spaces between, *space them 15 cm apart.* □ **space blanket** a light metal-coated plastic sheet designed to retain heat. **spaced out** (*informal*) euphoric or disorientated, especially from taking drugs. **space heater** a self-contained device for heating the room etc. in which it is placed. **space probe** an unmanned rocket with instruments to detect conditions in outer space. **space shuttle** a spacecraft for repeated use e.g. between earth and a space station. **space station** an artificial satellite used as a base for operations in space. **space-time continuum** fusion of the concepts of space and time, with time as a fourth dimension. [from Latin *spatium* = a space]

spacecraft *noun* (*plural* **spacecraft**) a vehicle for travelling in outer space.

spaceman, **spacewoman** *nouns* a person who travels in outer space.

spaceship *noun* a spacecraft.

spacesuit *noun* a sealed pressurised suit allowing the wearer to leave a spacecraft and move about independently in outer space.

spacious (**spay**-shŭs) *adjective* providing much space, roomy. **spaciousness** *noun*

spade¹ *noun* **1** a tool for digging ground, with a broad metal blade and a wooden handle. **2** a tool of similar shape for other purposes. □ **call a spade a spade** to call a thing by its proper name; to speak plainly or bluntly. **spadeful** *noun* (*plural* **spadefuls**). [from Old English *spadu*]

spade² *noun* a playing card of the suit (**spades**) marked with black figures shaped like an inverted heart with a short stem. [from Italian *spada* = sword]

spadework *noun* hard work done in preparation for something.

spaghetti (spă-**get**-ee) *noun* pasta made in solid sticks, between macaroni and vermicelli in thickness. [from Italian, = little strings]

Spain a country in SW Europe.

spam *noun* junk email.

span¹ *noun* **1** the extent from end to end or across. **2** the distance (reckoned as 9 inches or 23 cm) between the tips of a person's thumb and little finger when these are stretched apart. **3** the distance or part between the uprights supporting an arch or bridge. **4** length in time from beginning to end, *the span of life.* **–span** *verb* (**spanned**, **spanning**) **1** to extend across, to bridge. **2** to stretch one's hand across in one span, *span an octave on the piano.*

span² *see* **spick**.

spandrel *noun* the space between the curve of an arch and the surrounding rectangular moulding or framework, or between the curves of adjoining arches and the moulding above.

spangle *noun* a small thin piece of glittering material, especially one of many ornamenting a dress etc. **–spangle** *verb* to cover with spangles or sparkling objects.

Spaniard *noun* a native of Spain.

spaniel *noun* a kind of dog with long drooping ears and a silky coat. [from French, = Spanish dog]

Spanish *adjective* of Spain or its people or language. **–Spanish** *noun* the language of Spain.

spank *verb* to slap on the buttocks.

spanking *adjective* (*informal*) brisk, lively, *a spanking pace.*

spanner *noun* a tool for gripping and turning the nut on a bolt etc. □ **a spanner in the works** (*informal*) a drawback or impediment.

spar[1] *noun* a strong pole used for a mast, yard, or boom on a ship.

spar[2] *noun* any of several kinds of non-metallic mineral that split easily.

spar[3] *verb* (**sparred**, **sparring**) **1** to box, especially for practice. **2** to quarrel or argue. □ **sparring partner** a boxer employed to give another boxer practice; a person with whom one enjoys frequent arguments.

spare *verb* **1** to be merciful towards, to refrain from hurting or harming; *spare me this ordeal*, do not inflict it on me; *if I am spared*, if I live so long. **2** to use with great restraint; *does not spare himself*, works very hard. **3** to part with, *we can't spare him until next week*; to afford to give, *can you spare me a moment?*; *enough and to spare*, more than is needed. –**spare** *adjective* **1** additional to what is usually needed or used, in reserve for use when needed, *a spare wheel*; *spare time*, time not needed for work or other purposes. **2** thin; lean. **3** small in quantity, *on a spare diet*. –**spare** *noun* a spare part or thing kept in reserve for use when needed. □ **spare rib** a cut of pork from the lower ribs. **spare tyre** an extra tyre carried for emergencies; (*informal*) a roll of fat round the waist. **sparely** *adverb*, **spareness** *noun*

sparing (**spair**-ring) *adjective* economical, not generous or wasteful. **sparingly** *adverb*

spark *noun* **1** a fiery particle, e.g. one thrown off by a burning substance or caused by friction. **2** a flash of light produced by an electrical discharge. **3** a particle of a quality or of energy or genius, *he hasn't a spark of generosity in him*. **4** a lively young fellow. –**spark** *verb* to give off a spark or sparks. □ **spark off** to trigger off. **spark plug** a device producing an electrical spark to fire the mixture in an internal-combustion engine.

sparkle *verb* **1** to shine brightly with flashes of light. **2** to show brilliant wit or liveliness. –**sparkle** *noun* a sparkling light or brightness. □ **sparkling wine** wine that is effervescent.

sparkler *noun* **1** a sparking firework. **2** (*informal*) a diamond.

sparrow *noun* a small brownish-grey bird.

sparrowhawk *noun* a small hawk that preys on small birds.

sparse *adjective* thinly scattered, not dense. **sparsely** *adverb*, **sparsity** *noun*, **sparseness** *noun* [from Latin *sparsum* = scattered]

Sparta a city in the southern Peloponnese in Greece, whose citizens in ancient times were renowned for hardiness. **Spartan** *adjective* & *noun*

spartan *adjective* (of conditions) simple and sometimes harsh, without comfort or luxuries. (¶ See **Sparta**.)

spasm *noun* **1** a strong involuntary contraction of a muscle. **2** a sudden brief spell of activity or emotion, *a spasm of coughing*.

spasmodic (spaz-**mod**-ik) *adjective* **1** occurring at irregular intervals. **2** of or like a spasm; characterised by spasms. **spasmodically** *adverb*

spastic *adjective* physically disabled because of a condition (especially cerebral palsy) in which there are faulty links between the brain and the motor nerves, causing jerky or involuntary movements through difficulty in controlling the muscles. –**spastic** *noun* a person suffering from this condition. **spasticity** (spas-**tiss**-ĭ-tee) *noun*

spat[1] *see* **spit**[1].

spat[2] *noun* a short gaiter covering the instep and ankle.

spate (*pr.* spayt) *noun* a sudden flood or rush, *a spate of orders*. □ **in spate** (of a river) flowing strongly at an abnormally high level.

spathe (*pr.* spay*th*) *noun* a large petal-like part of a flower, surrounding a central spike.

spatial (**spay**-shăl) *adjective* of or relating to space; existing in space. **spatially** *adverb* [same origin as *space*]

spätlese (**shpet**-layz-ĕ) *noun* a white wine made from grapes picked late in the season, and therefore sweeter. [German, = late picking]

spatter *verb* **1** to scatter or fall in small drops. **2** to splash with drops, *spattered her dress with mud*. –**spatter** *noun* a splash or splashes; the sound of spattering.

spatula (**spat**-yǔ-lă) *noun* a tool with a broad blunt flexible blade, used for spreading, scraping, mixing, etc.

spatulate (**spat**-yǔ-lăt) *adjective* shaped like a spatula, with a broad rounded end.

spawn *noun* **1** the eggs of fish or frogs or shellfish. **2** (*derogatory*) offspring. **3** the threadlike matter from which fungi grow, *mushroom spawn*. –**spawn** *verb* **1** to deposit spawn; to produce from spawn. **2** to generate, especially in large numbers, *the reports spawned by that committee*.

spay *verb* to sterilise (a female animal) by removing the ovaries.

speak *verb* (**spoke**, **spoken**, **speaking**) **1** to utter words in an ordinary voice (not singing); to hold a conversation; to make a speech, *he spoke for an hour*. **2** to utter (words); to express or make known, *she spoke the truth*. **3** to use or be able to use (a specified language) in speaking, *we speak French*. **4** to make a polite or friendly remark, *she always speaks when we meet*. **5** to be evidence of something, *the facts speak for themselves*, need no supporting evidence. □ **be on speaking terms** to be on friendly terms with each other. **not** or **nothing to speak of** very little, only very slightly. **so to speak** if I may express it this way. **speak for oneself** to give one's own opinion. **speak one's mind** to give one's opinion frankly. **speak out** to speak loudly or freely; to speak one's mind. **speak up** to speak more loudly; to speak out.

speaker *noun* **1** a person who speaks; one who makes a speech. **2** a loudspeaker. **–the Speaker** the presiding officer in a legislative assembly, e.g. the House of Representatives.

spear *noun* **1** a weapon for hurling, with a long shaft and a pointed tip. **2** a pointed stem, e.g. of asparagus. **–spear** *verb* to pierce with or as if with a spear.

spearhead *noun* the foremost part of an attacking or advancing force. **–spearhead** *verb* to be the spearhead of.

spearmint *noun* a common garden mint used in cookery and to flavour chewing gum.

spec *noun* **on spec** (*informal*) as a speculation, without being certain of achieving what one wants.

special *adjective* **1** of a particular kind, for a particular purpose, not general, *a special key*; *special training*. **2** exceptional in amount, quality, or intensity, *take special care of it*. **3** in which a person specialises, *medieval history is his special subject*. **–special** *noun* **1** a special thing; a special bus or edition etc. **2** an item being sold at a reduced price. □ **Special Broadcasting Service** a multicultural radio and television service providing international news and foreign language films and drama. **special education** education of children with special needs or learning difficulties. **specially** *adverb*

specialise *verb* (also **-ize**) **1** to study a subject etc. with special intensity; to become a specialist. **2** to have a product etc. to which one devotes special attention, *the shop specialises in bicycles*. **3** to adapt for a particular purpose, *specialised organs such as the ear*. **specialisation** *noun*

specialist *noun* a person who is an expert in a special branch of a subject, especially of medicine.

speciality (spesh-ee-**al**-ĭ-tee) (also **specialty**, *pr*. **spesh**-ăl-tee) *noun* a special quality, characteristic, or product; an activity in which a person specialises.

species (**spee**-sheez) *noun* (*plural* **species**) **1** a group of animals or plants within a genus, differing only in minor details from the others. **2** a kind or sort. [Latin, = appearance]

specific (spĕ-**sif**-ik) *adjective* **1** particular, clearly distinguished from others, *the money was given for a specific purpose*. **2** expressing oneself in exact terms, not vague, *please be specific about your requirements*. **–specific** *noun* a specific aspect or influence; a remedy for a specific disease or condition. □ **specific gravity** the ratio between the weight of a substance and that of the same volume of a standard substance (usually water for liquids and solids, air for gases). **specific heat capacity** the amount of heat needed to raise the temperature of the unit mass of a substance by a given amount (usually 1 degree). **specifically** *adverb*

specification *noun* **1** specifying; being specified. **2** the details describing something to be done or made.

specify *verb* (**specified**, **specifying**) to mention (details, ingredients, etc.) clearly and definitely; to include in a list of specifications.

specimen *noun* **1** a part or individual taken as an example of a whole or of a class, especially for investigation or scientific examination. **2** a quantity of a person's urine etc. taken for testing. **3** (*informal*) a person of a special sort, *he seems a peculiar specimen*.

specious (**spee**-shŭs) *adjective* seeming good or sound at first sight but lacking real merit, *specious reasoning*. **speciously** *adverb* [from Latin *speciosus* = attractive]

speck *noun* a small spot or particle.

speckle *noun* a small spot, a speck, especially as a natural marking.

speckled *adjective* marked with speckles.

specs *plural noun* (*informal*) spectacles.

spectacle *noun* **1** a striking or impressive sight, *a magnificent spectacle.* **2** a lavish public show or pageant. **3** a ridiculous sight, *made a spectacle of himself.* spectacles *plural noun* a pair of lenses set in a frame, worn before the eyes to assist sight or for protection from sunlight or dust etc. spectacled *adjective* [from Latin *spectare* = look at]

spectacular *adjective* striking, impressive, amazing. –spectacular *noun* **1** a spectacular performance. **2** a lavishly-produced film etc. spectacularly *adverb*

spectator *noun* a person who watches a show, game, or incident etc. □ spectator sports sports that attract many spectators.

spectra *see* spectrum.

spectral *adjective* **1** of or like a spectre. **2** of the spectrum. spectrally *adverb*

spectre (**spek**-ter) *noun* **1** a ghost. **2** a haunting fear of future trouble, *the spectre of defeat loomed over them.* [same origin as *spectrum*]

spectrometer (spek-**trom**-ĕ-ter) *noun* a spectroscope that can be used for measuring spectra. [from *spectrum* + *meter*]

spectroscope (**spek**-trŏ-skohp) *noun* an instrument for producing and examining spectra. [from *spectrum* + Greek *skopein* = look at]

spectroscopy (spek-**tros**-kŏ-pee) *noun* the examination and investigation of spectra.

spectrum *noun* (*plural* spectra) **1** the bands of colour as seen in a rainbow, forming a series according to their wavelengths. **2** a similar series of bands of sound. **3** an entire range of related qualities or ideas etc., *the whole spectrum of science.* [Latin, = image]

speculate *verb* **1** to form opinions about something without having definite knowledge or evidence. **2** to buy or sell goods or stocks and shares etc. in the hope of making a profit but with risk of loss; to do this rashly. speculation *noun*, speculator *noun* [from Latin *speculari* = spy out]

speculative (**spek**-yŭ-lă-tiv) *adjective* **1** of or based on speculation, *speculative reasoning.* **2** involving financial speculation and risk of loss. speculatively *adverb*

sped *see* speed.

speech *noun* **1** the act, power, or manner of speaking. **2** words spoken; a spoken communication to an audience. **3** language

or dialect. □ speech therapy treatment to improve defective speech.

speechless *adjective* silent; unable to speak because of great emotion. speechlessly *adverb*

speed *noun* **1** the rate in time at which something moves or operates. **2** rapidity of movement. **3** the sensitivity of photographic film to light, the power of a lens to admit light. **4** (*informal*) an amphetamine drug. –speed *verb* (speed (in sense 3 speeded), speeding) **1** to move or pass quickly, *the years sped by.* **2** to send quickly, *to speed you on your way.* **3** to travel at an illegal or dangerous speed. □ at speed rapidly. speed up to move or work at greater speed; to cause to do this.

speedboat *noun* a fast motor boat.

speedo *noun* (*plural* speedos) (*informal*) a speedometer.

speedometer (spee-**dom**-ĕ-ter) *noun* a device in a motor vehicle, showing its speed. [from *speed* + *meter*]

speedway *noun* **1** a track or arena for motor vehicle racing, especially for motorcycles. **2** (*Amer.*) a road or track reserved for fast traffic.

speedwell *noun* a wild plant with small blue flowers.

speedy *adjective* **1** moving quickly. **2** done or coming without delay. speedily *adverb*

speleology (speel-ee-**ol**-ŏ-jee) *noun* the exploration and scientific study of caves. speleological *adjective*, speleologist *noun* [from Greek *spelaion* = cave, + *-logy*]

spell[1] *noun* **1** words supposed to have magic power. **2** the state of being influenced by this, *laid them under a spell.* **3** fascination, attraction, *the spell of eastern countries.*

spell[2] *verb* (spelt, spelling) **1** to write or name in their correct sequence the letters that form (a word or words). **2** (of letters) to form as a word, *c a t spells 'cat'.* **3** to have as a necessary result, *these changes spell ruin to the farmer.* □ spell out to spell aloud; to make out (words) laboriously letter by letter; to state explicitly, to explain in detail. speller *noun*

spell[3] *noun* **1** a period of time. **2** a period of a certain type of weather, *during the cold spell.* **3** a period of a certain activity, *did a spell of driving.* **4** (*Austral.*) a period of rest from work.

spellbound *adjective* with the attention held as if by a spell, entranced.

spellchecker *noun* a computer program for checking the spelling of words in a file of text against the words in a stored dictionary. **spellcheck** *verb* & *noun*

spelling bee *noun* a competition in spelling.

spelt¹ *see* spell².

spelt² *noun* a kind of wheat.

spencer *noun* a woman's undergarment like a thin jumper, worn for warmth.

spend *verb* (**spent**, **spending**) **1** to pay out (money) in buying something. **2** to use for a certain purpose, to use up, *don't spend too much time on it.* **3** to pass, *spent a holiday in Fiji.* **spender** *noun*

spendthrift *noun* a person who spends money extravagantly and wastefully.

Spenser, Edmund (c. 1552–99), English poet, author of *The Faerie Queene.*

spent *see* spend. –**spent** *adjective* used up, having lost its force or strength.

sperm *noun* **1** (*plural* **sperms** *or* **sperm**) a spermatozoon. **2** semen. □ **sperm whale** a large whale from which a waxy oil can be obtained. [from Greek *sperma* = seed]

spermatic *adjective* of sperm; *spermatic cord*, that supporting the testicle within the scrotum.

spermatozoon (sper-mă-tŏ-**zoh**-ŏn) *noun* (*plural* **spermatozoa**) a male reproductive cell in semen, capable of fertilising an ovum. [from *sperm*, + Greek *zoion* = animal]

spermicide (**sperm**-ĭ-syd) *noun* a substance that kills sperm. **spermicidal** *adjective* [from *sperm*, + Latin *caedere* = kill]

spew *verb* **1** to vomit. **2** to cast out in a stream.

sphagnum (**sfag**-nŭm) *noun* a kind of moss that grows on bogs.

sphere (*pr.* sfeer) *noun* **1** a perfectly round solid geometric figure. **2** something shaped like this. **3** a field of action or influence or existence, a person's place in society, *it took him out of his sphere.* [from Greek *sphaira* = ball]

spherical (**sfe**-ri-kăl) *adjective* shaped like a sphere. **spherically** *adverb*, **sphericity** *noun*

spheroid (**sfeer**-roid) *noun* a sphere-like but not perfectly spherical solid. **spheroidal** *adjective*

sphincter (**sfink**-ter) *noun* a ring of muscle surrounding an opening in the body and able to close it by contracting. [from Greek *sphingein* = bind tight]

sphinx *noun* **1 the Sphinx** (*Gk. myth.*) a winged monster at Thebes that killed all who could not answer the riddle it put to them. **2** any of the ancient stone statues in Egypt with a recumbent lion's body and a human or animal's head, especially the large one near the pyramids at Giza. **3** a statue resembling these. **4** a person who does not reveal his or her thoughts and feelings.

spice *noun* **1** a substance (obtained from plants) with a strong taste or smell, used for flavouring food. **2** such substances collectively, *the spice market.* **3** a thing that adds zest or excitement, *variety is the spice of life.* –**spice** *verb* to flavour with spice.

Spice Islands a former name for the Molucca Islands.

spick and span *adjective* neat and clean; new-looking.

spicy *adjective* (**spicier**, **spiciest**) **1** like spice; flavoured with spice. **2** (of stories) slightly scandalous or improper. **spicily** *adverb*, **spiciness** *noun*

spider *noun* **1** an animal (not an insect) with a segmented body and eight jointed legs, spinning webs to trap insects that are its prey. **2** (*Austral.*) a soft drink with a scoop of ice cream in it.

spidery *adjective* **1** having thin angular lines like a spider's legs. **2** like a cobweb. **3** full of spiders.

spied *see* spy.

spiel (*pr.* speel) *noun* (*informal*) a glib or lengthy speech, usually intended to persuade. [German, = game]

spigot (**spig**-ŏt) *noun* a peg or plug used to stop the vent of a cask or to control the flow of a tap.

spike *noun* **1** a sharp projecting point; a pointed piece of metal. **2** an ear of corn. **3** a long cluster of flowers with short stalks (or no stalks) on a central stem. –**spike** *verb* **1** to put spikes on, *spiked running shoes.* **2** to pierce or fasten with a spike. **3** (*informal*) to add alcohol or a drug to (a drink), especially without the drinker's knowledge. **spikes** *plural noun* running shoes with spikes in the soles. **spiky** *adjective*

spikenard (**spyk**-nard) *noun* **1** a tall sweet-smelling plant. **2** a fragrant ointment formerly made from this.

spill¹ *noun* a thin strip of wood or of twisted paper used to transfer flame, e.g. for lighting a pipe.

spill² *verb* (**spilt, spilling**) **1** to cause or allow (a liquid etc.) to run over the edge of its container. **2** (of liquid etc.) to become spilt. **3** (*informal*) to make known, *spilt the news*. **–spill** *noun* **1** spilling; being spilt. **2** a fall. □ **spill blood** to shed blood in killing or wounding. **spill over** to overflow from something that is full. **spill the beans** (*informal*) to let out information indiscreetly.

spillage *noun* **1** spilling; **2** the amount spilt.

spin *verb* (**spun, spinning**) **1** to turn or cause to turn rapidly on its axis; *spin a coin*, toss it; *my head is spinning*, I feel dizzy. **2** to draw out and twist (raw cotton or wool etc.) into threads; to make (yarn) in this way. **3** (of a spider or silkworm) to make from a fine threadlike material emitted from the body, *spinning its web*. **–spin** *noun* **1** a spinning movement. **2** a short drive in a vehicle. **3** the presentation of information in a particular way; a slant, especially a favourable one. □ **spin a yarn** to tell an invented story, especially in order to deceive someone. **spin bowler** a bowler who gives the ball a spinning movement so that it changes direction after bouncing. **spin doctor** (*informal*) a political spokesperson employed to give a favourable interpretation of events to the media. **spin-dry** *verb* to remove excess moisture centrifugally from washed articles by spinning them in a machine with a rapidly rotating drum. **spin-dryer** or **spin-drier** *noun* **spin-off** *noun* a benefit or product produced incidentally from a larger process or while developing this. **spin out** to cause to last a long time.

spina bifida (spy-nă **bif**-ĭ-dă) *noun* an abnormal congenital condition in which certain bones of the spine are not properly developed and allow the meninges or spinal cord to protrude. [Latin, = cleft spine]

spinach *noun* **1** a vegetable with dark green leaves. **2** (*Austral.*) silverbeet.

spinal *adjective* of the spine. □ **spinal column** the spine. **spinal cord** the rope-like mass of nerve fibres enclosed within the spinal column.

spindle *noun* **1** a slender rod on which thread is twisted or wound in spinning. **2** a pin or axis that revolves or on which something revolves.

spindly *adjective* long or tall and thin.

spindrift *noun* spray blown along the surface of the sea.

spine *noun* **1** the backbone. **2** any of the sharp needle-like projections on certain plants

(e.g. cacti) and animals (e.g. hedgehogs). **3** the part of a book where the pages are hinged; this section of the jacket or cover. □ **spine-chiller** *noun* a spine-chilling book or film etc. **spine-chilling** *adjective* causing a thrill of terror.

spineless *adjective* **1** having no backbone. **2** lacking determination or strength of character. **spinelessness** *noun*

spinet (**spin**-ĕt) *noun* a kind of small harpsichord with one string to each note.

spinifex *noun* a coarse tussocky grass with spiny leaves found in inland Australia. [from Latin, = spine-maker]

spinnaker (**spin**-ă-ker) *noun* a large triangular extra sail on a racing yacht.

spinner *noun* **1** a person or thing that spins. **2** a spin bowler. **3** (in fishing) revolving bait.

spinney *noun* (*plural* **spinneys**) (*Brit.*) a small wood; a thicket.

spinning *see* spin. □ **spinning jenny** an early spinning machine operating several spindles at a time. **spinning wheel** a household device for spinning fibre into yarn, with a spindle driven by a wheel.

Spinoza (spin-**oh**-ză), Baruch de (1632–77), Dutch philosopher.

spinster *noun* an unmarried woman. [the original meaning was 'one who spins']

spiny *adjective* full of spines, prickly.

spiracle (**spy**-ră-kŭl) *noun* **1** any of the external openings through which an insect breathes. **2** the blowhole of a whale etc. [from Latin *spirare* = breathe]

spiral *adjective* advancing or ascending in a continuous curve (either two-dimensional or three-dimensional) that winds round a central point or axis. **–spiral** *noun* **1** a spiral line; a thing of spiral form. **2** a continuous increase or decrease in two or more quantities alternately because of their dependence on each other, *the spiral of rising wages and prices*. **–spiral** *verb* (**spiralled, spiralling**) to move in a spiral course. **spirally** *adverb*

spire *noun* a pointed structure in the form of a tall cone or pyramid, especially on a church tower.

spirit *noun* **1** a person's mind, feelings, or animating principle as distinct from the body, *we shall be with you in spirit*. **2** soul. **3** a disembodied soul, a ghost. **4** life and consciousness not associated with a body, *God is pure spirit*. **5** a person's nature. **6** a person with specified mental or moral

qualities, *a few brave spirits went swimming*.
7 the characteristic quality or mood of
something, *the spirit of the times*; *the spirit
of the law*, its real purpose as distinct from a
strict interpretation of its words. **8** liveliness,
readiness to assert oneself, *answered with
spirit*. **9** a distilled extract; purified alcohol.
–**spirit** *verb* to carry off swiftly and secretly,
spirited him away. **spirits** *plural noun* **1** a
person's feeling of cheerfulness or depression.
2 strong distilled alcoholic drink, e.g. whisky
or gin. □ **the Spirit** the Holy Spirit (*see* holy).
spirit lamp a lamp that burns methylated
spirit or a similar fluid. **spirit level** a glass
tube nearly filled with liquid and containing
an air bubble, used to test whether something
is horizontal by means of the position of this
bubble. [from Latin *spiritus* = breath]

spirited *adjective* **1** full of spirit, lively; ready
to assert oneself. **2** having mental spirit or
spirits of a specified kind, *a poor-spirited
creature*. **spiritedly** *adverb*

spiritless *adjective* not spirited.

spiritual *adjective* **1** of the human spirit or
soul, not physical or worldly. **2** of the Church
or religion. –**spiritual** *noun* a religious folk
song originally of American Blacks. **spiritually**
adverb, **spirituality** *noun*

spiritualism *noun* the belief that spirits of
the dead can and do communicate with the
living; practices based on this. **spiritualist**
noun, **spiritualistic** *adjective*

spirituous *adjective* containing much
alcohol; *spirituous liquors*, those that are
distilled and not only fermented.

spirogyra (spy-rŏ-**jy**-ră) *noun* a simple
freshwater plant that has spiral bands of
chlorophyll. [from Greek *speira* = coil, + *gura*
= round]

spit¹ *verb* (**spat** or **spit**, **spitting**) **1** to eject
from the mouth; to eject saliva. **2** to make a
noise like spitting as a cat does when angry or
hostile; (of a person) to show anger, *spitting
with fury*. **3** to utter violently, *he spat curses at
me*. **4** to fall lightly, *it's spitting with rain*. –**spit**
noun **1** spittle. **2** the act of spitting. **3** an exact
likeness, *he's the dead spit of his father*.
□ **spit and polish** cleaning and polishing of
equipment etc., especially by soldiers. **spitting
image** an exact likeness.

spit² *noun* **1** a long thin metal spike thrust
through meat to hold it while it is roasted. **2** a
long narrow strip of land projecting into the
sea. –**spit** *verb* (**spitted**, **spitting**) to pierce
with or as if with a spit.

spit³ *noun* a spade's depth of earth.

spite *noun* a malicious desire to hurt, annoy,
or humiliate another person. –**spite** *verb* to
hurt or annoy etc. from spite. □ **in spite of** not
being prevented by, *we enjoyed ourselves in
spite of the weather*.

spiteful *adjective* full of spite; showing
or caused by spite. **spitefully** *adverb*,
spitefulness *noun*

spitfire *noun* a fiery-tempered person.

spittle *noun* saliva, especially that ejected
from the mouth.

spittoon *noun* a receptacle for spitting into.

splash *verb* **1** to cause (liquid) to fly about in
drops; to wet with such drops. **2** (of liquid) to
be splashed. **3** to move or fall with splashing,
we splashed through the puddles. **4** to decorate
with irregular patches of colour etc. **5** to
display in large print, *the news was splashed
across the front page*. **6** to spend (money)
freely and ostentatiously. –**splash** *noun*
1 splashing; a sound or mark made by this.
2 a quantity of liquid splashed. **3** (*informal*)
a small quantity of soda water or other liquid
in a drink. **4** a patch of colour or light. **5** a
striking or ostentatious display or effect.
splashy *adjective*

splashdown *noun* the alighting of a
spacecraft on the sea.

splatter *verb* to splash noisily. –**splatter** *noun*
a noisy splashing sound.

splay *verb* to spread apart; to slant (the sides
of an opening) so that the inside is wider than
the outside or vice versa; *he splayed his feet*,
placed them with the toes turned outwards not
forwards. –**splay** *adjective* splayed.

spleen *noun* **1** an organ of the body situated
at the left of the stomach and involved in
maintaining the proper condition of the blood.
2 bad temper, peevishness.

splendid *adjective* **1** magnificent,
displaying splendour. **2** excellent, *a splendid
achievement*. **splendidly** *adverb* [from Latin
splendidus = shining]

splendiferous *adjective* (*informal*) splendid.

splendour *noun* brilliance; magnificent
display or appearance, grandeur.

splenetic (splĕ-**net**-ik) *adjective* peevish.
[from *spleen*]

splice *verb* **1** to join (two ends of rope) by
untwisting and interweaving the strands of
each. **2** to join (pieces of film, magnetic
tape, timber, etc.) by overlapping the ends.

–splice *noun* a join made by splicing.
□ get spliced (*informal*) to get married.

splint *noun* a strip of rigid material bound
to an injured part of the body to prevent
movement, e.g. while a broken bone heals.
–splint *verb* to secure with a splint.

splinter *noun* a thin sharp piece of wood
or stone etc. broken off from a larger piece.
–splinter *verb* to break or become broken into
splinters. □ splinter group a small group that
has broken away from a larger one, e.g. in a
political party. splintery *adjective*

split *verb* (split, splitting) 1 to break or become
broken into parts, especially lengthwise or
along the grain of wood etc. 2 to divide into
parts; to divide and share. 3 to come apart,
to tear, *this coat has split at the seams.* 4 to
divide or become divided into disagreeing or
hostile groups. 5 (*informal*) to reveal a secret;
split on a person, to inform on him or her.
–split *noun* 1 splitting; being split. 2 the place
where something has split or torn. 3 something
split or divided. 4 a sweet dish of split fruit
with cream or ice cream etc., *banana split.*
splits *noun* an acrobatic position in which the
legs are stretched in opposite directions and
at right angles to the trunk. □ split hairs *see*
hair. split infinitive an infinitive with a word
or words placed between *to* and the verb, e.g.
to thoroughly understand (¶ see note below).
split-level *adjective* (of a building) having
adjoining rooms at a level midway between
successive storeys in other parts. split one's
sides to laugh very heartily. split personality
(*informal*) schizophrenia. split second a
very brief moment. split-second *adjective*
extremely rapid; accurate to a very small
fraction of time, *split-second timing.* split
shift a shift in which there are two or more
periods of duty. split the difference to decide
on an amount halfway between two proposed
amounts. split up to split, to separate.

Usage Split infinitives are common in informal
speech, but many people consider them
incorrect. Often they can be avoided by simply
reordering the verb and adverb, e.g. by saying *to
understand thoroughly* rather than *to thoroughly
understand.* Note, however, that changing the
word order can sometimes create a clumsy or
ambiguous sentence, which is less desirable than
a split infinitive.

---

splitting *adjective* (of a headache) very
severe, feeling as if it will split one's head.

splodge *noun* & *verb* = splotch.

splosh *verb* (*informal*) to splash. –splosh *noun*
(*informal*) a splash.

splotch *noun* a splash or blotch on material
etc. –splotch *verb* to mark with splotches.

splurge *noun* an ostentatious display,
especially of wealth. –splurge *verb* to make a
splurge, to spend money freely.

splutter *verb* 1 to make a rapid series of
spitting sounds. 2 to speak or utter rapidly or
indistinctly (e.g. in rage). –splutter *noun* a
spluttering sound.

spoil *verb* (spoilt *or* spoiled, spoiling) 1 to
damage, to make useless or unsatisfactory. 2 to
become unfit for use. 3 to harm the character
of (a person) by lack of discipline or excessive
generosity or pampering. –spoil *noun* 1 earth
etc. brought up during excavation or dredging.
2 = spoils. spoils *plural noun* 1 plunder;
benefits gained by a victor. 2 profitable
advantages of an official position.
□ be spoiling for to desire eagerly, *he is
spoiling for a fight.* [from Latin *spolium* =
plunder]

spoiler *noun* a device on an aircraft to slow
it down by interrupting the airflow; a similar
device on a vehicle to prevent it from being
lifted off the road when travelling very fast.

spoilsport *noun* a person who spoils the
enjoyment of others.

spoke[1] *noun* each of the bars or wire rods that
connect the centre or hub of a wheel to its rim.
□ put a spoke in a person's wheel to thwart
his or her intentions.

spoke[2], **spoken** *see* speak.

spokeshave *noun* a tool for planing
something curved.

spokesman, spokeswoman *nouns* a
person who speaks on behalf of a group.

spokesperson *noun* a spokesman or
spokeswoman.

spoliation (spoh-lee-**ay**-shŏn) *noun* pillaging.

spondee *noun* a metrical foot with two long
or stressed syllables, as in the phrase *no hope.*

sponge *noun* 1 a kind of water animal with
a porous structure. 2 the skeleton of this, or a
substance of similar texture, used for washing,
cleaning, or padding. 3 a thing of light open
texture; something absorbent. 4 sponge cake.
5 sponging; a wash with a sponge. 6 a sponger.
–sponge *verb* 1 to wipe or wash with a
sponge. 2 to live off the generosity of others,
to cadge, *to sponge on people.* □ sponge bag
a waterproof bag for toilet articles. sponge

cake a cake with a light, open texture. sponge pudding a pudding like a sponge cake. sponge rubber rubber made with many small spaces like a sponge. throw up the sponge see throw.

sponger noun a person who sponges on others.

spongy adjective (spongier, spongiest) like a sponge in texture, soft and springy.

sponsor noun 1 a person who assumes responsibility for an immigrant, trainee, etc. 2 a godparent. 3 a person who puts forward a proposal, e.g. for a new law. 4 a person or firm that provides funds for a broadcast or for a musical, artistic, or sporting event. 5 a person who subscribes to charity in return for a specified activity by another person. –sponsor verb to act as sponsor for. sponsorship noun [from Latin sponsum = promised]

spontaneous (spon-**tay**-nee-ŭs) adjective resulting from natural impulse, not caused or suggested from outside, not forced.
□ spontaneous combustion the bursting into flame of a substance (e.g. a mass of oily rags) because of heat produced by its own rapid oxidation and not by flame etc. from an external source. spontaneously adverb, spontaneity (spon-tă-**nee**-ĭ-tee) noun [from Latin sponte = of your own accord]

spoof noun (informal) a hoax; a humorous imitation.

spook noun (informal) a ghost.

spooky adjective (informal) ghostly, eerie. spookiness noun

spool noun a reel on which something is wound, e.g. yarn, photographic film, or magnetic tape. –spool verb 1 to wind or become wound on a spool. 2 (in computing) send (data for printing or peripheral processing) to an intermediate store.

spoon noun 1 a utensil consisting of an oval or round bowl and a handle, used for conveying food to the mouth or for stirring or measuring things. 2 the amount it contains. –spoon verb 1 to take or lift with a spoon. 2 to hit (a ball) feebly upwards. 3 (informal, old use) to behave amorously. spoonful noun (plural spoonfuls).

spoonbill noun a wading bird with a very broad flat tip to its bill.

spoonerism noun interchange of the initial sounds of two words, usually as a slip of the tongue, e.g. he's a boiled sprat (= spoiled brat). [named after the Rev. W. A. Spooner

(1844–1930), said to have made such errors in speaking]

spoonfeed verb (spoonfed, spoonfeeding) 1 to feed with liquid food from a spoon. 2 to give excessive help to (a person etc.) so that the recipient does not need to make any effort.

spoor noun the track or scent left by an animal.

sporadic (spŏ-**rad**-ik) adjective occurring here and there, scattered. sporadically adverb [from Greek sporas = scattered]

sporangium (spŏ-**ran**-jee-ŭm) noun (plural sporangia) the receptacle in which spores are formed in some plants. [from Greek spora = spore, + angeion = vessel]

spore noun one of the tiny reproductive cells of plants such as fungi and ferns. [from Greek spora = seed]

sporran (spo-răn) noun a pouch worn hanging in front of the kilt as part of Highland dress.

sport noun 1 an athletic (especially outdoor) activity. 2 any game or pastime; an outdoor pastime such as hunting or fishing. 3 such activities or pastimes collectively, the world of sport. 4 amusement, fun, we said it in sport. 5 (informal) a sportsmanlike person. 6 an animal or plant that is strikingly different from its parent(s). 7 (Austral.) a familiar form of address, especially between males. –sport verb 1 to play, to amuse oneself. 2 to wear or display, she sported a diamond ring. sports plural noun athletic activities; a meeting for competition in these, the school sports.
□ sports car an open low-built fast car. sports coat or jacket a man's jacket for informal wear (not part of a suit).

sporting adjective 1 interested in sport, concerned with sport, a sporting man. 2 sportsmanlike. □ a sporting chance a reasonable chance of success.

sportive adjective playful. sportively adverb

sportsground noun a piece of land for sports, usually with an area for spectators.

sportsman noun 1 a person who takes part in sports. 2 a person who behaves fairly and generously. sportswoman feminine noun, sportsmanlike adjective, sportsmanship noun

sporty adjective (informal) 1 fond of sport. 2 dashing. sportily adverb, sportiness noun

spot noun 1 a roundish area different in colour from the rest of a surface. 2 a roundish mark or stain. 3 a pimple. 4 a particular place or locality. 5 (informal) a small amount of something, *a spot of leave*. **6** a drop, *a few spots of rain*. **7** a spotlight. **–spot** *verb* (**spotted, spotting**) **1** to mark with a spot or spots. **2** (*informal*) to catch sight of; to detect or recognise, *spotted him at once as an American*. **3** to watch for and take note of, *train-spotting*. **4** (of a bushfire) ignite ahead of the main front when burning embers, leaves, etc., are carried forward by the wind. □ **in a spot** (*informal*) in difficulties. **on the spot** without delay or change of place; at the scene of action; (of a person) alert, equal to dealing with a situation; *put him on the spot*, to put him in a difficult position, to compel him to take action or justify himself. **spot check** a check made suddenly on something chosen at random. **spot-on** *adverb* (*informal*) precisely. **spot welding** welding of small areas that are in contact. **spotter** *noun*

spotless *adjective* free from stain or blemish, perfectly clean. **spotlessly** *adverb*

spotlight *noun* a beam of light directed on a small area, a lamp giving this. **–spotlight** *verb* (**spotlighted, spotlighting**) **1** to direct a spotlight on. **2** to draw attention to, to make conspicuous.

spotty *adjective* (**spottier, spottiest**) marked with spots. **spottiness** *noun*

spouse *noun* a person's husband or wife. **spousal** *adjective* [from Latin *sponsus* = betrothed]

spout *noun* **1** a projecting tube through which liquid is poured or conveyed. **2** a jet of liquid. **–spout** *verb* **1** to come or send out forcefully as a jet of liquid. **2** to utter or speak lengthily. □ **up the spout** (*informal*) broken or ruined, in a hopeless condition; pregnant.

sprain *verb* to injure (a joint or its muscles or ligaments) by wrenching it violently. **–sprain** *noun* an injury caused in this way.

sprang *see* **spring.**

sprat *noun* a small herring-like fish.

sprawl *verb* **1** to sit, lie, or fall with the arms and legs spread out loosely. **2** to spread out in an irregular or straggling way. **–sprawl** *noun* a sprawling attitude, movement, or arrangement, *urban sprawl.*

spray[1] *noun* **1** a single shoot or branch with its leaves, twigs, and flowers. **2** a bunch of cut flowers etc. arranged decoratively. **3** an ornament in similar form.

spray[2] *noun* **1** water or other liquid dispersed in very small drops. **2** a liquid preparation for spraying. **3** a device for spraying liquid.

–spray *verb* to send out (liquid) or be sent out in very small drops; to wet with liquid in this way. □ **spray gun** a gunlike device for spraying liquid. **spray-paint** *verb* to paint (a surface) by means of a spray. **sprayer** *noun*

spread *verb* (**spread, spreading**) **1** to open out, to unroll or unfold, *the peacock spreads its tail*; *spread the map out*. **2** to become longer or wider, *the stain began to spread*. **3** to cover the surface of, to apply as a layer, *spread the bread with jam*; *spread the paint evenly*. **4** to be able to be spread, *it spreads like butter*. **5** to make or become more widely known, felt, or suffered, *spread the news*; *panic spread*. **6** to distribute or become distributed, *settlers spread inland*. **7** to distribute over a period, *spread the payments over 12 months*. **–spread** *noun* **1** spreading; being spread. **2** the extent, expanse, or breadth of something. **3** expansion; *middle-aged spread*, increased bodily girth in middle age. **4** a bedspread. **5** (*informal*) a lavish meal. **6** the range of something. **7** a sweet or savoury paste for spreading on bread. □ **spread eagle** the figure of an eagle with legs and wings extended, as an emblem. **spread oneself** to talk or write lengthily; to spend or provide things lavishly.

spreadeagle *verb* **1** to place (a person) with arms and legs spread out. **2** to defeat utterly.

spreadsheet *noun* a computer program that allows tabulated numerical data (e.g. accounts) to be manipulated and retrieved.

spree *noun* (*informal*) a lively outing, some fun; *a shopping* or *spending spree*, an outing or period in which one shops or spends freely.

sprig[1] *noun* **1** a small branch, a shoot. **2** an ornament or decoration in this form.

sprig[2] *noun* a small tapering headless tack.

sprightly *adjective* (**sprightlier, sprightliest**) lively, full of energy. **sprightliness** *noun*

spring *verb* (**sprang, sprung, springing**) **1** to jump; to move rapidly or suddenly, especially in a single movement. **2** to grow or issue, to arise, *weeds sprang up*; *their discontent springs from distrust of their leaders*. **3** to become warped or split. **4** to rouse (game) from an earth or covert; *spring a prisoner from gaol*, to contrive an escape. **5** to cause to operate suddenly, *sprang the trap*. **6** to produce or develop suddenly or unexpectedly, *sprang a surprise on us*. **–spring** *noun* **1** the act of springing, a jump. **2** a device (usually of bent or coiled metal) that reverts to its original position after being compressed or tightened or stretched, used to drive clockwork or (in groups) to make a seat etc. more comfortable. **3** elasticity. **4** a place where water or oil comes up naturally from the ground; the flow of this. **5** the season in which vegetation begins to appear, from September to November in the southern hemisphere. □ **spring a leak** to develop a leak. **spring balance** a device that measures weight by the tension of a spring. **spring-clean** verb to clean one's home thoroughly, especially in spring. **spring onion** a young onion eaten raw in salad. **spring roll** a snack consisting of vegetables wrapped in a pancake and fried as a roll. **spring tide** the tide when there is the largest rise and fall of water, occurring shortly after the new and full moon.

springboard noun a flexible board for giving impetus to a person who jumps on it, used in gymnastics and in diving.

springbok noun a South African gazelle that can spring high into the air.

springtime noun the season of spring.

springy adjective (**springier**, **springiest**) able to spring back easily after being squeezed or stretched. **springiness** noun

sprinkle verb to scatter or fall in small drops or particles; to scatter small drops etc. on (a surface). –**sprinkle** noun a sprinkling.

sprinkler noun a device for sprinkling water.

sprinkling noun **1** something sprinkled. **2** a few here and there.

sprint verb to run at full speed, especially over a short distance. –**sprint** noun a run of this kind; a similar spell of maximum effort in swimming, cycling, etc. **sprinter** noun

sprite noun an elf, fairy, or goblin.

sprocket noun each of a series of teeth on a wheel, engaging with links on a chain.

sprout verb **1** to begin to grow or appear; to put forth shoots. **2** to cause to spring up as a growth, has sprouted horns. –**sprout** noun **1** the shoot of a plant. **2** a Brussels sprout (see **Brussels**). **3** a bean sprout.

spruce[1] adjective neat and trim in appearance, smart. –**spruce** verb to smarten, spruce oneself up. **sprucely** adverb, **spruceness** noun

spruce[2] noun a kind of fir with dense foliage; its wood.

spruik (pr. sprook) verb (Austral.) to hold forth in public, especially to advertise a show or sideshow. **spruiker** noun

sprung see spring. –**sprung** adjective fitted with springs, a sprung seat.

spry adjective (**spryer**, **spryest**) active, nimble, lively. **spryly** adverb, **spryness** noun

spud noun (informal) a potato.

spume noun froth, foam.

spun see spin. □ **spun silk** yarn or fabric made from waste silk. **spun sugar** a fluffy mass made from boiled sugar drawn into long threads.

spunk noun **1** (informal) courage. **2** (Austral. informal) a (sexually) attractive man.

spunky adjective (**spunkier**, **spunkiest**) **1** (informal) spirited, brave. **2** (Austral. informal) (sexually) attractive.

spur noun **1** a device with a projecting point or toothed wheel, worn on a rider's heel for urging on a horse. **2** a stimulus or incentive. **3** something shaped like a spur; a hard projection on a cock's leg; a slender hollow projection on a flower. **4** a ridge projecting from a mountain. **5** a branch road or railway. –**spur** verb (**spurred**, **spurring**) **1** to urge (one's horse) on by pricking it with spurs. **2** to urge on, to incite, he spurred the men to greater effort. **3** to stimulate, it spurred their interest. □ **on the spur of the moment** on an impulse, without previous planning. **win one's spurs** to prove one's ability, to win distinction.

spurious (**spewr**-ree-ŭs) adjective not genuine or authentic. **spuriously** adverb, **spuriousness** noun

spurn verb to reject scornfully.

spurred adjective having spurs, fitted with spurs.

spurt verb **1** to gush, to send out (a liquid) suddenly. **2** to increase one's speed suddenly. –**spurt** noun **1** a sudden gush. **2** a short burst of activity; a sudden increase in speed.

sputnik (**spuut**-nik) noun a Russian artificial satellite orbiting the earth. [Russian, = fellow-traveller]

sputter verb to splutter; to make a series of quick explosive sounds, sausages sputtered in the pan. –**sputter** noun a sputtering sound.

sputum (**spew**-tŭm) noun spittle, matter that is spat out.

spy noun a person who secretly watches or gathers information about the activities of others and reports the result; one employed by a government to do this in another country. –**spy** verb (**spied**, **spying**) **1** to see, to catch sight of. **2** to be a spy, to keep watch secretly, he was spying on them; spy out the land, investigate its features etc. secretly. **3** to pry.

spyglass *noun* a small telescope.

spyhole *noun* a peephole.

sq. *abbreviation* square.

squab (*pr.* skwob) *noun* **1** a young pigeon. **2** a stuffed seat or cushion, especially as part (usually the back) of a car seat.

squabble *verb* to quarrel in a petty or noisy way. –**squabble** *noun* a quarrel of this kind.

squad *noun* a small group of people working or being trained together.

squadron *noun* **1** a unit of an air force. **2** a division of a cavalry unit or armoured formation, consisting of two troops. **3** a detachment of warships.

squalid *adjective* **1** dirty and unpleasant, especially because of neglect or poverty. **2** morally degrading. **squalidly** *adverb*, **squalor** *noun* [from Latin *squalidus* = rough, dirty]

squall *noun* **1** a harsh cry or scream, especially of a baby. **2** a sudden storm of wind, especially with rain, snow, or sleet. –**squall** *verb* to utter a squall. **squally** *adjective*

squander *verb* to spend wastefully.

square *noun* **1** a geometric figure with four equal sides and four right angles. **2** an area or object shaped like this. **3** a four-sided area surrounded by buildings. **4** an L-shaped or T-shaped instrument for obtaining or testing right angles. **5** the product obtained when a number is multiplied by itself, *9 is the square of 3* ($9 = 3 \times 3$). **6** (*informal*) a person considered old-fashioned or conventional. –**square** *adjective* **1** of square shape. **2** right-angled, *the desk has square corners*. **3** of or using units that express the measure of an area; *one square metre*, a unit equal to the area of a square with sides one metre long. **4** properly arranged, tidy, *get things square*. **5** (also **all square**) equal, with no balance of advantage or debt etc. on either side. **6** straightforward, uncompromising, *we got a square refusal*. **7** fair, honest, *a square deal*. **8** (*informal*) old-fashioned, conventional. –**square** *adverb* squarely, directly, *hit him square on the jaw*. –**square** *verb* **1** to make right-angled, *square the corners*. **2** to mark with squares, *squared paper*. **3** to place evenly or squarely, *he squared his shoulders*. **4** to multiply (a number) by itself; *3 squared is 9* ($3^2 = 9$), $3 \times 3 = 9$. **5** to settle or pay, *that squares the account*. **6** (*informal*) to secure the cooperation of (a person) by payment or bribery. **7** to be or make consistent, *his story*

doesn't square with yours; *try and square the two stories*. □ **back to square one** back to the starting point in an enterprise etc., with no progress made. **on the square** (*informal*) honest; honestly. **square dance** a dance in which four couples face inwards from four sides. **square leg** a fielder in cricket on the batsman's leg side and nearly in line with the wicket; this position. **square meal** a large satisfying meal. **square peg in a round hole** a person who is not fitted for his or her job. **square-rigged** *adjective* with the principal sails at right angles to the length of the ship. **square root** a number of which the given number is the square (see *noun* sense 5), *3 is the square root of 9*. **square up to** to assume a boxer's fighting attitude; to face and tackle (a difficulty) resolutely. **square wave** a waveform in which the variable takes each of two constant values in turn, jumping instantaneously from one to the other. **squarely** *adverb*, **squareness** *noun* [from Latin *quadra* = a square]

squash[1] *verb* **1** to crush, to squeeze or become squeezed flat or into pulp. **2** to pack tightly, to crowd, to squeeze into a small space. **3** to suppress, *squashed the rebellion*. **4** to silence with a crushing reply. –**squash** *noun* **1** a crowd of people squashed together. **2** the sound of something being squashed. **3** a crushed mass. **4** a drink made from crushed fruit. **5** a game played with racquets and a small ball in a closed court. **squashy** *adjective*

squash[2] *noun* a kind of gourd used as a vegetable; the plant that bears it.

squat *verb* (**squatted**, **squatting**) **1** to sit on one's heels or crouch with knees drawn up closely. **2** (of an animal) to crouch close to the ground. **3** (*informal*) to sit. **4** to be a squatter, to occupy as a squatter. –**squat** *noun* **1** a squatting posture. **2** occupying a place as a squatter; the place itself. –**squat** *adjective* short and thick, dumpy.

squatter *noun* **1** one who sits in a squatting posture. **2** a person who settles on unoccupied land in order to acquire a legal right to it. **3** a person who takes temporary possession of unoccupied buildings for living in, without authority. **4** (*Austral.*) a grazier.

squaw *noun* (*offensive*) an indigenous North American woman or wife.

squawk *noun* a loud harsh cry. –**squawk** *verb* **1** to utter a squawk. **2** (*informal*) to complain.

squeak *noun* a short high-pitched cry or sound. –**squeak** *verb* **1** to utter or make a squeak. **2** (*informal*) to become an informer. □ **a narrow squeak** (*informal*) a narrow escape from danger or failure. **squeaker** *noun*

squeaky *adjective* (**squeakier, squeakiest**) making a squeaking sound. **squeakily** *adverb*, **squeakiness** *noun*

squeal *noun* a long shrill cry or sound. –**squeal** *verb* **1** to make this cry or sound. **2** (*informal*) to protest sharply. **3** (*informal*) to become an informer. **squealer** *noun*

squeamish *adjective* **1** easily sickened or disgusted or shocked. **2** excessively scrupulous about principles. **squeamishly** *adverb*, **squeamishness** *noun*

squeegee (skwee-**jee**) *noun* a tool with a rubber blade or roller on a handle, used for sweeping or squeezing away water or moisture.

squeeze *verb* **1** to exert pressure on from opposite or all sides. **2** to treat in this way so as to extract moisture or juice; to extract (moisture etc.) by squeezing. **3** to force into or through, to force one's way, to crowd, *we squeezed six people into the car; she squeezed through the gap*. **4** to produce by pressure or effort. **5** to obtain by compulsion or strong urging, *squeeze a promise from them*. **6** to extort money etc. from; to harass in this way, *heavy taxation is squeezing small firms*. –**squeeze** *noun* **1** squeezing; being squeezed. **2** an affectionate clasp or hug. **3** a small amount of liquid produced by squeezing, *a squeeze of lemon juice*. **4** a crowd or crush, the pressure of this, *we all got in, but it was a tight squeeze*. **5** hardship or difficulty caused by shortage of money or time etc. **6** restrictions on borrowing etc. during a financial crisis.

squeezer *noun* a device for squeezing juice from fruit by pressure.

squelch *verb* to make a sound like someone treading in thick mud. –**squelch** *noun* this sound.

squib *noun* a small firework that makes a hissing sound and then explodes. □ **damp squib** something intended to impress people but failing to do so.

squid *noun* a sea creature related to the cuttlefish, with ten arms round the mouth.

squidgy *adjective* (*informal*) squashy, *a squidgy ball*.

squiggle *noun* a short curly line, especially in handwriting. **squiggly** *adverb*

squint *verb* **1** to have an eye that is turned abnormally from the line of gaze of the other, to be cross-eyed. **2** to look at (a thing) with the eyes turned sideways or half shut, or through a narrow opening. –**squint** *noun* **1** a squinting position of the eyeballs. **2** a stealthy or sideways glance. **3** (*informal*) a look, *have a squint at this*. –**squint** *adjective* (*informal*) askew.

squire *noun* **1** (in Britain) a country gentleman, especially the chief landowner in a district. **2** (as an informal form of address) sir.

squirearchy *noun* landowners collectively, especially as having political or social influence. [from *squire* + *hierarchy*]

squirm *verb* **1** to wriggle or writhe. **2** to feel embarrassment or uneasiness. –**squirm** *noun* a squirming movement.

squirrel *noun* **1** a small tree-climbing animal with a bushy tail and red or grey fur. **2** its fur.

squirt *verb* to send out (liquid) or be sent out from or as if from a syringe; to wet in this way. –**squirt** *noun* **1** a syringe. **2** a jet of liquid. **3** (*informal*) a small or unimportant but self-assertive person.

squish *noun* a slight squelch. **squishy** *adjective*

squiz *noun* (*Austral. informal*) a look.

Sri Lanka a republic consisting of a large island (formerly called Ceylon) south of India. **Sri Lankan** *adjective* & *noun*

SS *abbreviation* **1** saints. **2** steamship. **3** the Nazi special police force (German *Schutzstaffel*).

St *abbreviation* **1** Saint. **2** Street.

stab *verb* (**stabbed, stabbing**) **1** to pierce or wound with a pointed tool or weapon. **2** to aim a blow with or as if with a pointed weapon. **3** to cause a sensation of being stabbed, *a stabbing pain*. –**stab** *noun* **1** the act of stabbing; a blow, thrust, or wound made by stabbing. **2** a sensation of being stabbed, *she felt a stab of fear*. **3** (*informal*) an attempt, *have a stab at it*. □ **a stab in the back** a treacherous attack.

stabilise (**stay**-bǐ-lyz) *verb* (also **-ize**) to make or become stable. **stabilisation** *noun*

stabiliser *noun* (also **-izer**) **1** a device to prevent a ship from rolling or to aid in keeping a child's bicycle upright. **2** an arrangement for stabilising an amount, effect, etc.

stability (stǎ-**bil**-ǐ-tee) *noun* being stable.

stable[1] *adjective* firmly fixed or established; not readily changing or fluctuating; not easily destroyed or decomposed. **stably** *adverb* [from Latin *stabilis* = standing firm]

stable² *noun* **1** a building in which horses are kept. **2** an establishment for training racehorses; the horses from a particular establishment. **3** racing cars, products, or people originating from or working for the same establishment. **–stable** *verb* to put or keep in a stable.

staccato (stă-**kah**-toh) *adjective* & *adverb* (especially in music) in a sharp disconnected manner, not running on smoothly. [Italian, = detached]

stack *noun* **1** an orderly pile or heap. **2** a haystack. **3** (*informal*) a large quantity, *have stacks* or *a whole stack of work to get through*. **4** a number of aircraft stacked for landing. **5** a number of chimneys standing together; an isolated tall factory chimney; a chimney or funnel for smoke on a steamer etc. **6** a part of a library where books are compactly stored. **7** an isolated pillar of rock just off a coast where there are cliffs. **8** (*informal*) a crash in a motor vehicle etc. **–stack** *verb* **1** to pile in a stack or stacks. **2** to arrange (cards) secretly for cheating; *the cards were stacked against him*, circumstances put him at a disadvantage. **3** to instruct (aircraft) to fly round the same point at different altitudes while waiting to land. **4** (*informal*) to crash (a motor vehicle etc).

stadium *noun* a sportsground surrounded by tiers of seats for spectators.

staff *noun* **1** a stick or pole used as a weapon or support or measuring stick, or as a symbol of authority. **2** a body of officers assisting a commanding officer and concerned with an army, regiment, or fleet etc. as a whole. **3** a group of assistants by whom a business is carried on; those responsible to a manager or person of authority. **4** people in authority within an organisation (as distinct from pupils etc.), or those doing administrative work as distinct from manual work. **5** (*plural* **staves**) one of the sets of five horizontal lines on which music is written. **–staff** *verb* to provide with a staff of employees or assistants. □ **staff officer** a member of a military staff (see sense 2).

stag *noun* a fully-grown male deer. □ **stag beetle** a beetle with branched projecting mouthparts that resemble a stag's antlers. **stag party** a party of or for men only.

stage *noun* **1** a platform on which plays etc. are performed before an audience. **2** theatrical work, the profession of actors and

actresses. **3** a raised floor or platform, e.g. on scaffolding. **4** a point or period in the course or development of something, *the talks have reached a critical stage*. **5** a stopping place on a route; the distance between two of these; *we travelled by easy stages*, a short distance at a time. **6** a section of a space rocket with a separate engine, jettisoned when its fuel is exhausted. **–stage** *verb* **1** to present (a play etc.) on the stage. **2** to arrange and carry out, *decided to stage a sit-in*. □ **go on the stage** to become an actor or actress. **stage fright** nervousness on facing an audience. **stage-manage** *verb* to organise things as or like a stage manager. **stage manager** the person responsible for the scenery and other practical arrangements in the production of a play. **stage-struck** *adjective* having an obsessive desire to become an actor or actress. **stage whisper** a whisper that is meant to be overheard.

stagecoach *noun* a horse-drawn coach that formerly ran regularly between two places.

stagecraft *noun* skill in writing or staging plays.

stager *noun* **old stager** an experienced person.

stagflation *noun* a state of inflation without a corresponding increase in demand and employment.

stagger *verb* **1** to move or go unsteadily, as if about to fall. **2** to shock deeply, to cause astonishment, worry, or confusion to, *we were staggered by the news*. **3** to place in a zigzag or alternating arrangement. **4** to arrange (people's holidays or hours of work etc.) so that their times do not coincide exactly. **–stagger** *noun* an unsteady staggering movement.

staging *noun* scaffolding; a platform or support, especially a temporary one. □ **staging post** a regular stopping place on a long route.

staggering *adjective* bewildering, astonishing, *the total cost is staggering*. □ **staggering bob** (*Austral.*) a newly born calf.

stagnant *adjective* **1** (of water) not flowing, still and stale. **2** showing no activity, *business was stagnant*. **stagnancy** *noun*

stagnate (stag-**nayt**) *verb* **1** to be stagnant. **2** (of a person) to become dull through inactivity and lack of variety or opportunity. **stagnation** *noun* [from Latin *stagnum* = a pool]

stagy (**stay**-jee) *adjective* theatrical in style or manner.

staid (*pr.* stayd) *adjective* steady and serious in manner, tastes, etc., sedate.

stain *verb* **1** to discolour or become discoloured by a substance. **2** to blemish, *it stained his good reputation.* **3** to colour with a pigment that penetrates. –**stain** *noun* **1** a mark caused by staining. **2** a blemish, *without a stain on his character.* **3** a liquid used for staining things. □ **stained glass** glass coloured with transparent colouring.

stainless *adjective* free from stains or blemishes. □ **stainless steel** steel containing chromium and not liable to rust or tarnish under ordinary conditions.

stair *noun* each of a set of fixed steps. **stairs** *plural noun* a set of these.

staircase *noun* a flight of stairs (often with banisters) and its supporting structure.

stairway *noun* a staircase.

stairwell *noun* the shaft in which a staircase is built.

stake *noun* **1** a stick or post sharpened at one end for driving into the ground as a support or marker etc. **2** the post to which a person was bound for execution by being burnt alive; *the stake*, this method of execution. **3** money etc. wagered on the result of a race or other event. **4** something invested in an enterprise and giving a share or interest in it. –**stake** *verb* **1** to fasten or support with stakes. **2** to mark (an area) with stakes. **3** to wager or risk (money etc.) on an event. **stakes** *plural noun* (in horse races) money offered as a prize; the race itself. □ **at stake** being risked, depending on the outcome of an event. **stake a claim** to claim or obtain a right to something. **stake out** to place under surveillance.

stalactite (**stal**-ăk-tyt) *noun* a deposit of calcium carbonate hanging like an icicle from the roof of a cave etc. [from Greek *stalaktos* = dripping]

stalagmite (**stal**-ăg-myt) *noun* a deposit like a stalactite but standing like a pillar on the floor of a cave etc. [from Greek *stalagma* = a drop]

stale *adjective* **1** lacking freshness; dry, musty, or unpleasant because not fresh. **2** uninteresting because not new or because heard often before, *stale news* or *jokes.* **3** having one's ability to perform spoilt by too much practice. –**stale** *verb* to make or become stale. **stalely** *adverb*, **staleness** *noun*

stalemate *noun* **1** a drawn position in chess, in which a player can make no move without

putting the king in check. **2** a deadlock, a drawn contest. –**stalemate** *verb* to bring to a position of stalemate or deadlock.

Stalin, Joseph (real name Dzhugashvili, 1879–1953), Soviet statesman, General Secretary of the Communist Party of the USSR 1922–53.

stalk[1] *noun* **1** the main stem of a plant. **2** a stem attaching a leaf, flower, or fruit to another stem or to a twig. **3** a similar support of a part or organ in animals or of a device.

stalk[2] *verb* **1** to walk in a stately or imposing manner. **2** to track or pursue (game etc.) stealthily. □ **stalking horse** a person or thing used to conceal one's real intentions. **stalker** *noun*

stall[1] *noun* **1** a stable or cow house; a compartment for one animal in this. **2** a compartment for one person. **3** a seat with its back and sides more or less enclosed, in a church etc. **4** each of the set of seats (*the stalls*) in the part of a theatre nearest to the stage. **5** a stand from which things are sold. **6** stalling of an engine or aircraft. –**stall** *verb* **1** to place or keep (an animal) in a stall, especially for fattening. **2** (of an engine) to stop suddenly because of an overload or insufficient fuel. **3** (of an aircraft) to begin to drop because the speed is too low for the plane to answer to its controls. **4** to cause (an engine or aircraft) to stall.

stall[2] *verb* to use delaying tactics in order to gain time; to stave off (a person or request) in this way. [from *stall* = pickpocket's helper]

stallion (**stal**-yŏn) *noun* an uncastrated male horse, especially one kept for breeding.

stalwart (**stawl**-wert) *adjective* **1** sturdy. **2** strong and faithful, *stalwart supporters.* –**stalwart** *noun* a stalwart person.

stamen (**stay**-měn) *noun* the male fertilising organ of flowering plants, bearing pollen.

stamina (**stam**-ĭ-nă) *noun* staying power, ability to withstand prolonged physical or mental strain.

stammer *verb* to speak or utter with involuntary pauses or rapid repetitions of the same syllable. –**stammer** *noun* stammering speech; a tendency to stammer. **stammerer** *noun*

stamp *verb* **1** to bring one's foot down heavily on the ground, *stamped hard* or *stamped his foot.* **2** to walk with loud heavy steps. **3** to strike or press with a device that leaves a mark or pattern etc.; to cut or shape in this way. **4** to fix a postage or other stamp to. **5** to give a certain character to, *this achievement stamps him as a genius*. –**stamp** *noun* **1** the act or sound of stamping. **2** an instrument for stamping a pattern or mark; the mark itself. **3** a piece of paper bearing an official design, for affixing to an envelope or document to indicate that postage or duty or other fee has been paid. **4** a distinguishing mark, a clear indication, *the story bears the stamp of truth*. ☐ **stamp collecting** the collecting of postage stamps as objects of interest or value, also called *philately*. **stamp duty** a tax imposed on certain kinds of legal documents. **stamping ground** (*informal*) a person's or animal's usual haunt or place of action. **stamp on** to crush by stamping; to quell. **stamp out** to extinguish by stamping, *stamped out the fire*; to suppress (a rebellion etc.) by force.

stampede *noun* **1** a sudden rush of a herd of frightened animals. **2** a rush of people under a sudden common impulse. –**stampede** *verb* to take part or cause to take part in a stampede; to cause to act hurriedly.

stance (*pr.* stanss *or* stahnss) *noun* the position in which a person or animal stands; a player's attitude for making a stroke, e.g. in golf.

stanch *verb* to restrain the flow of (blood etc.) or from (a wound).

stanchion (**stan**-shŏn) *noun* an upright bar or post forming a support.

stand *verb* (**stood**, **standing**) **1** to have, take, or keep a stationary upright position, *we were standing talking about the weather*. **2** to be situated. **3** to place, to set upright, *stand the vase on the table*. **4** to remain firm or valid or in a specified condition, *the offer still stands*; *the thermometer stood at 40°*. **5** to remain stationary or unused. **6** to offer oneself for election, *she stood for Parliament*. **7** to undergo, *he stood trial for murder*. **8** to steer a specified course in sailing. **9** to put up with, to endure, *I can't stand that noise*. **10** to provide at one's own expense, *stood him a drink*. –**stand** *noun* **1** a stationary condition. **2** a position taken up, *took his stand near the door*. **3** resistance to attack, the period of this, *made a stand*. **4** a halt to give a performance, *the band did a one-night stand*. **5** a rack or pedestal etc. on which something may be placed, *umbrella stand*. **6** a raised structure with seats at a sportsground etc. **7** a table, booth, or other (often temporary) structure where things are exhibited or sold.

8 a standing place for vehicles, *taxi stand*. **9** a witness box; *take the stand*, to give evidence. ☐ **as it stands** in the present state of affairs; in its present condition, unaltered. **it stands to reason** it is obvious or logical. **stand a chance** to have a chance of success. **stand alone** to be unequalled. **stand-alone** *adjective* (of a computer) operating independently of a network or other system. **stand by** to look on without interfering; to support or side with (a person) in a difficulty or dispute; to stand ready for action; to keep to (a promise or agreement). **stand-by** *adjective* ready for use or action as a substitute etc.; (*noun*) a person or thing available as a substitute or in an emergency. **stand down** to suspend (a person's) employment; to withdraw (e.g. from a competition). **stand for** to represent, '*US*' *stands for* '*United States*'; (*informal*) to tolerate. **stand in** to deputise. **stand-in** *noun* a person who deputises for another, especially for an actor. **stand off** to remain at a distance; to lay off (employees) temporarily. **stand-off** *adjective* (of a missile) launched by an aircraft but having a long range and its own guidance system. **stand-offish** *adjective* aloof in manner. **stand on** to insist on formal observance of, *stand on ceremony*. **stand on end** (of hair) to become erect from fear or horror. **stand on one's own feet** to be independent. **stand one's ground** not to yield. **stand out** to be conspicuous; to persist in opposition or in one's demands, *they stood out for a ten per cent rise*. **stand over** to supervise (a person or thing) closely; to be postponed. **stand to** to stand ready for action. **stand up** to come to or place in a standing position; to be valid, *that argument won't stand up*; *stand a person up*, fail to keep an appointment with him or her. **stand-up** *adjective* (of a collar) upright, not turned down; (of a fight) vigorous, actual; (of a meal) eaten while standing. **stand up for** to defend or support (a person or opinion). **stand up to** to resist courageously; to remain durable in (hard use or wear).

standard *noun* **1** a thing, quality, or specification by which something may be tested or measured. **2** the required level of quality. **3** the average quality, *the standard of her work is high*. **4** a specified level of proficiency. **5** a distinctive flag. **6** an upright support. **7** a shrub that has been grafted on an upright stem, *standard roses*. –**standard** *adjective* **1** serving as or conforming to a standard, *standard measures of length*. **2** of average or usual quality, not of special design etc., *the standard model of this car*. **3** of recognised merit or authority, *the standard book on spiders*. **4** widely used and regarded as the usual form, *standard English*. ☐ **standard deviation** a statistical quantity used for measuring how data deviate from their mean value. **standard gauge** the standard distance (1435 mm) between the rails of railway lines. **standard lamp** a household lamp set on a tall pillar on a base. **standard of living** the level of material comfort enjoyed by a person or group.

standardise *verb* (also **-ize**) to cause to conform to a standard. **standardisation** *noun*

standing *adjective* **1** upright. **2** (of a jump) performed without a run. **3** permanent, remaining effective or valid, *a standing invitation*. **–standing** *noun* **1** status, *people of high standing*. **2** past duration, *a friendship of long standing*.

standover *adjective* (*Austral.*) threatening, intimidating, *standover tactics*.

standpipe *noun* a vertical pipe for fluid to rise in, e.g. to provide a water supply outside or at a distance from buildings.

standpoint *noun* a point of view.

standstill *noun* a stoppage, inability to proceed.

stank *see* stink.

Stanley the capital of the Falkland Islands.

stanza *noun* a verse of poetry.

staphylococcus *noun* (*plural* staphylococci, *pr.* staf-ĭ-lŏ-**kok**-I) a kind of microorganism that causes pus to form. [from Greek *staphule* = bunch of grapes, + *kokkos* = berry]

staple[1] *noun* **1** a U-shaped piece of metal or wire for holding something in place. **2** a piece of metal or wire driven into papers etc. and clenched to fasten them. **–staple** *verb* to secure with a staple or staples. **stapler** *noun*

staple[2] *adjective* principal, standard, *rice is their staple food*. **–staple** *noun* a staple food or product etc.

star *noun* **1** a celestial body appearing as a point of light in the night sky. **2** (in astronomy) any large light-emitting gaseous ball, such as the sun. **3** a celestial body regarded as influencing a person's fortunes, *thank your lucky stars*. **4** a figure, object, or ornament with rays or radiating points; an asterisk; a star-shaped mark indicating a category of excellence. **5** a brilliant person; a famous actor, actress, or other performer. **–star** *verb* (starred, starring) **1** to put an asterisk or star

symbol beside (a name or item in a list etc.). **2** to present or perform as a star actor. ☐ **Star of David** the six pointed star used as a Jewish and Israeli symbol. **Stars and Stripes** the national flag of the USA. **Star-Spangled Banner** the national anthem of the USA. **star turn** the principal item in an entertainment. **Star Wars** the popular name for the US Strategic Defense Initiative (*see* strategic).

starboard *noun* the right-hand side (when facing forward) of a ship or aircraft. **–starboard** *verb* to turn this way.

starch *noun* **1** a white carbohydrate that is an important element in human food. **2** a preparation of this or other substances for stiffening fabrics. **3** stiffness of manner. **–starch** *verb* to stiffen with starch.

starchy *adjective* (starchier, starchiest) **1** of or like starch. **2** containing much starch. **3** stiff and formal in manner. **starchiness** *noun*

stardom *noun* being a star actor or performer.

stare *verb* **1** to gaze fixedly with the eyes wide open, especially in astonishment. **2** (of the eyes) to be wide open with fixed gaze. **–stare** *noun* a staring gaze.

starfish *noun* a star-shaped sea creature.

starfruit *noun* a star-shaped tropical fruit.

stargazing *noun* (*humorous*) **1** studying the stars as an astronomer or astrologer. **2** daydreaming.

stark *adjective* **1** stiff in death. **2** desolate, cheerless, *stark prison conditions*. **3** sharply evident, *in stark contrast*. **4** downright, complete, *stark madness*. **5** completely naked. **–stark** *adverb* completely, wholly, *stark raving mad*. **starkly** *adverb*, **starkness** *noun*

starlight *noun* light from the stars.

starling *noun* a noisy bird with glossy blackish speckled feathers, that forms large flocks.

starlit *adjective* lit by starlight.

starry *adjective* (starrier, starriest) **1** set with stars. **2** shining like stars. ☐ **starry-eyed** *adjective* romantically enthusiastic; enthusiastic but impractical.

start *verb* **1** to begin or cause to begin a process or course of action; (of an engine) to begin running. **2** to cause or enable to begin, to establish or found. **3** to begin a journey. **4** to make a sudden movement from pain or surprise etc. **5** to spring suddenly, *started from his seat*. **6** (of timber) to spring from its proper position. **7** to rouse (game etc.) from its lair or covert. **–start** *noun* **1** the beginning of a journey, activity, or race; the place where a race starts. **2** an opportunity for or assistance in starting. **3** an advantage gained or allowed in starting; the amount of this, *had 10 seconds* or *10 metres start.* **4** a sudden movement of surprise or pain etc. □ **start up** to start; to set in motion; to start an activity etc.

starter *noun* **1** a person or thing that starts something. **2** one who gives the signal for a race to start. **3** a horse or competitor at the start of a race, *list of probable starters.* **4** the first course of a meal. □ **for starters** (*informal*) to start with.

startle *verb* to cause to make a sudden movement from surprise or alarm; to take by surprise.

startling *adjective* surprising, astonishing.

starve *verb* **1** to die or suffer acutely from lack of food; to cause to do this. **2** to suffer or cause to suffer for lack of something needed, *was starved of affection.* **3** (*informal*) to feel very hungry. **4** to force by starvation, *starved them into surrender.* □ **starvation diet** not enough food to support life adequately. **starvation** *noun*

stash *verb* (*informal*) to stow.

state *noun* **1** the quality of a person's or thing's characteristics or circumstances. **2** an excited or agitated condition of mind, *she got into a state.* **3** a grand imposing style, *arrived in state.* **4** (often **State**) an organised community under one government (*the State of Israel*) or forming part of a federal republic (*the United States of America*) or a federal union (*the Australian States*). **5** civil government, *matters of state.* **–state** *adjective* **1** of, for, or concerned with the State; *state schools*, those run by public authorities. **2** involving ceremony, used or done on ceremonial occasions, *a state funeral.* **–state** *verb* **1** to express in spoken or written words. **2** to fix or specify, *must be inspected at stated intervals.* □ **lie in state** *see* lie². **state of play** the current situation. **state of the art** the current stage of (especially technological) development. **state-of-the-art** *adjective*. **the States** the USA.

stateless *adjective* (of a person) not a citizen or subject of any country.

stately *adjective* (**statelier**, **stateliest**) dignified, imposing, grand. **stateliness** *noun*

statement *noun* **1** stating. **2** something stated. **3** a formal account of facts; a written report of a financial account.

stateroom *noun* **1** a state apartment. **2** a passenger's private compartment on a ship.

statesman, **stateswoman** *nouns* a person who is skilled or prominent in the management of State affairs. **statesmanship** *noun*

static *adjective* **1** (of force) acting by weight without motion (as opposed to *dynamic*). **2** not moving, stationary. **3** not changing. **–static** *noun* **1** atmospherics. **2** = **static electricity**, electricity present in a body and not flowing as current. **statics** *noun* a branch of physics that deals with bodies at rest or forces in equilibrium. [from Greek *statikos* = standing]

station *noun* **1** a place where a person or thing stands or is stationed. **2** an establishment or building where a public service is based or which is equipped for certain activities, *the fire station; a quarantine station.* **3** a broadcasting establishment with its own frequency. **4** a stopping place on a railway with buildings for passengers or goods or both. **5** position in life, status, *she had ideas above her station.* **6** (*Austral.*) a large sheep or cattle farm. **–station** *verb* to put at or in a certain place for a purpose. □ **Stations of the Cross** a series of locations on the traditional route in Jerusalem from Pilate's house to Calvary, followed by pilgrims; a series of 14 images or pictures representing events in Christ's Passion before which prayers are said in certain Churches. **station wagon** (*Austral.*) a car with a rear door and no boot, with luggage space behind the back seat (which can be folded down to create more luggage space). [from Latin *statio* = a standing]

stationary *adjective* **1** not moving; not movable. **2** not changing in condition or quantity etc.

stationer *noun* one who sells writing materials (paper, pens, ink etc.).

stationery *noun* writing paper, envelopes, and other articles sold by a stationer.

stationmaster, **stationmistress** *nouns* an official in charge of a railway station.

statistic (stă-**tist**-ik) *noun* an item of information expressed in numbers.

statistician (stat-ĭss-**tish**-ăn) *noun* an expert in statistics.

statistics (stă-**tist**-iks) *noun* the science of collecting, classifying, and interpreting information based on the numbers of things. **statistical** *adjective*, **statistically** *adverb*

statuary (**stat**-yoo-ă-ree) *noun* statues.

statue *noun* a sculptured, cast, or moulded figure of a person or animal, usually of life size or larger.

statuesque (stat-yoo-**esk**) *adjective* like a statue in size or dignity or stillness.

statuette (stat-yoo-**et**) *noun* a small statue.

stature (**stat**-yer) *noun* 1 the natural height of the body. 2 greatness gained by ability or achievement.

status (**stay**-tŭs) *noun* (*plural* statuses) 1 a person's position or rank in relation to others; a person's or thing's legal position. 2 high rank or prestige. □ status symbol a possession or activity etc. regarded as evidence of a person's high status. [from Latin *status* = a standing]

status quo (stay-tŭs **kwoh**) *noun* the state of affairs as it is or as it was before a recent change, *restore the status quo*. [Latin, = the state in which]

statute (**stat**-yoot) *noun* 1 a law passed by Parliament or a similar body. 2 one of the rules of an institution. [from Latin *statutum* = set up]

statutory (**stat**-yŭ-tŏ-ree) *adjective* fixed or done or required by statute. statutorily *adverb*

staunch *adjective* firm in attitude, opinion, or loyalty. staunchly *adverb*

stave *noun* 1 one of the curved strips of wood forming the side of a cask or tub. 2 a staff in music (*see* staff sense 5). –stave *verb* (**stove** or **staved**, **staving**) to dent or break a hole, *stove* or *staved it in*. □ stave off (**staved**, **staving**) to ward off permanently or temporarily, *we staved off disaster*.

stay[1] *noun* 1 a rope or wire supporting or bracing a mast, spar, pole, etc. 2 any prop or support.

stay[2] *verb* 1 to continue to be in the same place or state, *stay here*; *stay awake*; *stay away from the meeting*, not go to it. 2 to remain or dwell temporarily, especially as a guest or visitor. 3 to satisfy temporarily, *we stayed our hunger with a sandwich*. 4 to postpone, *stay judgment*. 5 to pause in movement, action, or speech. 6 to show endurance, e.g. in a race or task; *stay the course*, be able to reach the end of the race etc. –stay *noun* 1 a period of temporary dwelling or visiting, *had a short stay in Canberra*. 2 a postponement, e.g. of carrying out a judgment, *was granted a stay of execution*.
□ stay-at-home *adjective* remaining at home habitually; (*noun*) *a person who does this*. staying power endurance. stay put to remain where it is placed; to remain where one is.

stay-stitch *verb* to make a line of stitches close to a curved or bias-cut edge to prevent it from stretching when worked on.

stayer *noun* a person with great staying power.

stays *plural noun* (*old use*) a corset.

STD *abbreviation* 1 subscriber trunk dialling. 2 sexually transmitted disease.

stead (*pr*. sted) *noun* in a person's or things stead instead of this person or thing. stand a person in good stead to be of great advantage or service to him or her.

steadfast (**sted**-fahst) *adjective* firm and not changing or yielding, *a steadfast refusal*. steadfastly *adverb*, steadfastness *noun*

steady *adjective* (**steadier**, **steadiest**) 1 firmly supported or balanced, not shaking or rocking or tottering. 2 done, operating, or happening in a uniform and regular manner, *a steady pace*. 3 behaving in a serious and dependable manner, not frivolous or excitable. –steady *noun* (*informal*) a regular boyfriend or girlfriend. –steady *adverb* steadily. –steady *verb* (**steadied**, **steadying**) to make or become steady. □ go steady (*informal*) to go about regularly with a member of the opposite sex though not yet engaged to be married to him or her. steady on! slow!; stop! steady state perfect equilibrium without beginning or end. steadily *adverb*, steadiness *noun*

steak *noun* 1 a thick slice of meat (especially beef) or fish, cut for grilling or frying etc. 2 beef from the front of an animal, cut for stewing or braising.

steal *verb* (**stole**, **stolen**, **stealing**) 1 to take another person's property without right or permission, to take dishonestly. 2 to obtain by surprise or a trick or surreptitiously, *stole a kiss*; *stole a look at her*. 3 to move secretly or without being noticed, *stole out of the room*. –steal *noun* (*informal*) an easy task; a good bargain. □ steal a march on to gain an advantage over (a person) secretly or slyly or by acting in advance of him or her. steal the show to outshine other performers unexpectedly.

stealth (*pr*. stelth) *noun* stealthiness.

stealthy (**stel**-thee) *adjective* (**stealthier**, **stealthiest**) acting or done in a quiet or secret way so as to avoid being noticed. stealthily *adverb*, stealthiness *noun*

steam *noun* 1 the gas into which water is changed by boiling, used as motive power. 2 the mist that forms when steam condenses in the air. 3 energy or power; *run out of steam*, to become exhausted before something is finished. –**steam** *verb* **1** to give out steam or vapour. **2** to cook or treat by steam. **3** to move by the power of steam, *the ship steamed down the river.* □ **steamed up** (*informal*) excited or angry. **steam engine** an engine or locomotive driven by steam. **steam iron** an electric iron that can emit jets of steam from its flat surface. **steam up** to cover or become covered with condensed steam. **steamy** *adjective*

steamboat *noun* a steam-driven boat, especially a paddle-wheel craft used widely on rivers in the 19th century.

steamer *noun* **1** a steam-driven ship. **2** a container in which things are cooked or treated by steam.

steamroller *noun* a heavy slow-moving engine with a large roller, used in road-making. –**steamroller** *verb* to crush or defeat or force through by weighty influence.

steamship *noun* a steam-driven ship.

stearate (**steer**-rayt) *noun* a salt or ester of stearic acid.

stearic acid (stee-**a**-rik) *noun* a white fatty acid obtained from animal or vegetable fats. [from Greek *stear* = tallow]

steed *noun* (*poetical*) a horse.

steel *noun* **1** a very strong alloy of iron and carbon much used for making vehicles, tools, weapons etc.; *nerves of steel*, very strong nerves. **2** a tapered usually roughened steel rod for sharpening knives. –**steel** *verb* to make hard or resolute, *steel oneself* or *steel one's heart.* □ **steel band** a band of musicians with instruments usually made from oil drums. **steel wool** fine shavings of steel massed together for use as an abrasive. **worthy of one's steel** worthy as one's opponent in a fight (¶ *steel* = sword).

steely *adjective* (**steelier**, **steeliest**) like steel in colour or hardness.

steelyard *noun* a weighing apparatus with a graduated arm along which a weight slides.

steep¹ *verb* **1** to soak or be soaked in liquid. **2** to permeate thoroughly, *the story is steeped in mystery.*

steep² *adjective* **1** sloping sharply not gradually. **2** (*informal*, of a price) unreasonably high. **steeply** *adverb*, **steepness** *noun*

steepen *verb* to make or become steeper.

steeple *noun* a tall tower with a spire on top, rising above the roof of a church.

steeplechase *noun* **1** a horse race across country or on a course with hedges and ditches to jump. **2** a cross-country race for runners. **3** a long-distance hurdle race. **steeplechaser** *noun* [so called because the race originally had a distant steeple in view as its goal]

steeplejack *noun* a man who climbs tall chimneys or steeples to do repairs.

steer¹ *verb* **1** to direct the course of. **2** to guide (a vehicle or boat etc.) by its mechanism. **3** to be able to be steered, *the car steers well.* □ **steer clear of** to take care to avoid. **steerer** *noun*

steer² *noun* a young male of domestic cattle, castrated and raised for beef.

steerage *noun* **1** steering. **2** (*old use*) the cheapest section of accommodation for passengers in a ship, situated below decks.

steering *noun* the mechanism by which a vehicle or boat etc. is steered. □ **steering committee** a committee deciding the order of business, the general course of operations, etc. **steering wheel** a wheel for controlling the steering mechanism.

steersman *noun* (*plural* **steersmen**) a person who steers a ship.

stegosaurus (steg-ŏ-**sor**-rŭs) *noun* a plant-eating dinosaur with two rows of bony plates along its back. [from Greek *stege* = covering, + *sauros* = lizard]

stellar *adjective* of a star or stars. [from Latin *stella* = star]

stem¹ *noun* **1** the main central part (usually above the ground) of a tree, shrub, or plant. **2** a slender part supporting a fruit, flower, or leaf. **3** any slender upright part, e.g. that of a wineglass between bowl and foot. **4** the main part of a noun or verb, from which other parts or words are made e.g. by altering the endings. **5** the curved timber or metal piece at the fore end of a ship; a ship's bows. –**stem** *verb* (**stemmed**, **stemming**) to remove the stems from. □ **stem cell** an undifferentiated cell from which specialised cells develop. **stem from** to arise from, to have as its source.

stem² *verb* (**stemmed**, **stemming**) to restrain the flow of, to dam up.

stench *noun* a foul smell.

stencil *noun* **1** a sheet of metal or card etc. with a design cut out, which can be painted or inked over to produce a corresponding design on the surface below. **2** a waxed sheet from which a stencil is made by a typewriter. **3** the decoration or lettering etc. produced by a stencil. –**stencil** *verb* (**stencilled**, **stencilling**) to produce or ornament by means of a stencil.

stenographer (stĕ-**nog**-ră-fer) *noun* a person who can write shorthand; one employed to do this.

stenography (stĕ-**nog**-ră-fee) *noun* shorthand. [from Greek *stenos* = narrow, + -*graphy*]

stentorian (sten-**tor**-ree-ăn) *adjective* (of a voice) extremely loud. [from the name of Stentor, a herald in ancient Greek legend]

step *verb* (**stepped**, **stepping**) **1** to lift and set down the foot or alternate feet as in walking. **2** to move a short distance in this way, *step aside*; *step into a job*, to acquire it without effort. –**step** *noun* **1** a complete movement of one foot and leg in stepping. **2** the distance covered by this. **3** a short distance, *it's only a step to the shops*. **4** a series of steps forming a particular pattern in dancing. **5** the sound of a step; a manner of stepping as seen or heard, *I recognised your step*. **6** a rhythm of stepping, as in marching. **7** each of a series of things done in some process or course of action. **8** a level surface for placing the foot on in climbing up or down. **9** a stage in a scale of promotion or precedence. **steps** *plural noun* a stepladder. □ **in step** stepping in time with other people in marching or dancing; conforming to what others are doing. **out of step** not in step. **step by step** one out at a time; proceeding steadily from one stage to the next. **step in** to intervene. **step on it** (*informal*) to hurry. **step out** to walk briskly, to stride; to take part in lively social activities. **step up** to increase, *step up the voltage*. **watch your step** be careful.

step- *prefix* related by remarriage of one parent. □ **stepchild** (*plural* **stepchildren**), **stepdaughter**, **stepson** *nouns* the child of one's wife or husband, by an earlier marriage. **stepbrother**, **stepsister** *nouns* the child of one's stepfather or stepmother. **stepfather**, **stepmother**, **step-parent** *nouns* the husband or wife of one's parent, by a later marriage.

Stephen¹ king of England 1135–54.

Stephen², St (died c. AD 35), the first Christian martyr. Feast day, (in the Western Church) 26 December, (in the Eastern Church) 27 December.

stepladder *noun* a short ladder with flat steps (not rungs) and a framework that supports it.

steppe (*pr.* step) *noun* a level grassy plain with few trees, especially in SE Europe and Siberia.

stepping stone *noun* **1** a raised stone providing a place to step on in crossing a stream etc. **2** a means or stage of progress towards achieving something.

stereo (**ste**-ree-oh *or* **steer**-ree-oh) *noun* (*plural* **stereos**) **1** stereophonic sound or recording. **2** a stereophonic sound system, CD player, radio, tape recorder, etc.

stereophonic (ste-ree-ŏ-**fon**-ik *or* steer-) *adjective* (of sound reproduction) using two transmission channels in order to give the effect of naturally-distributed sound. **stereophonically** *adverb*, **stereophony** (-**off**-ŏnee) *noun* [from Greek *stereos* = solid, + *phone* = sound]

stereoscope (**ste**-ree-ŏ-skohp *or* **steer**-) *noun* a device for giving a stereoscopic effect.

stereoscopic (ste-ree-ŏ-**skop**-ik *or* steer-) *adjective* giving a three-dimensional effect, e.g. in photographs. **stereoscopically** *adverb* [from Greek *stereos* = solid, + *skopein* = look at]

stereotype (**ste**-ree-ŏ-typ *or* **steer**-) *noun* **1** an idea or character etc. that is standardised in a conventional form without individuality; a preconceived and over-simplified idea of the characteristics which typify a person, situation, etc. **2** a printing-plate cast from a mould. –**stereotype** *verb* to standardise as a stereotype; *stereotyped phrases*, standardised and hackneyed phrases. [from Greek *stereos* = solid, + *type* (= fixed type formerly used in printing)]

sterile (**ste**-ryl) *adjective* **1** barren. **2** free from living microorganisms. **3** unproductive, *a sterile discussion*. **sterility** (stĕ-**ril**-ĭ-tee) *noun*

sterilise (**ste**-rĭ-lyz) *verb* (also -**ize**) **1** to make sterile or free from microorganisms. **2** to make unable to produce offspring, especially by removal or obstruction of reproductive organs. **sterilisation** *noun*

sterling *noun* British money. –**sterling** *adjective* **1** (of precious metal) genuine, of standard purity. **2** excellent, of solid worth, *her sterling qualities*.

stern¹ *adjective* strict and severe, not lenient or cheerful or kindly. **sternly** *adverb*, **sternness** *noun*

stern² *noun* the rear end of a boat or ship.

sternum *noun* the breastbone. **sternal** *adjective*

steroid (**ste**-roid *or* **steer**-) *noun* any of a group of organic compounds that includes certain hormones and other bodily secretions.

stertorous (**ster**-tŏ-rŭs) *adjective* making a snoring or rasping sound. **stertorously** *adverb* [from Latin *stertere* = to snore]

stet *verb* (placed beside a word that has been crossed out by mistake) let it stand as written or printed. [Latin, = let it stand]

stethoscope (**steth**-ŏ-skohp) *noun* an instrument for listening to sounds within the body, e.g. breathing and heartbeats. [from Greek *stethos* = breast, + *skopein* = look at]

stetson *noun* a slouch hat with a very wide brim and a high crown.

stevedore (**stee**-vě-dor) *noun* a man employed in loading and unloading ships.

Stevenson, Robert Louis (1850–94), Scottish-born novelist, poet, and essayist, author of *Kidnapped* and *Treasure Island*.

stew *verb* **1** to cook or be cooked by simmering for a long time in a closed vessel. **2** (*informal*) to study hard, *stewing over his books*. −**stew** *noun* a dish (especially of meat) made by stewing. □ **in a stew** (*informal*) in a state of great anxiety or agitation. **stew in one's own juice** to be obliged to suffer the consequence of one's own actions.

steward *noun* **1** a passengers' attendant and waiter on a ship, aircraft, or train. **2** a person employed to manage another's property. **3** one whose job is to arrange for the supply of food to a college or club etc. **4** any of the officials managing a race meeting or show etc.

stewardess *noun* a female steward, especially on a ship or aircraft.

stick¹ *noun* **1** a short relatively slender piece of wood for use as a support or weapon or as firewood; *only a few sticks of furniture*, items of furniture. **2** a walking stick. **3** the implement used to propel the ball in hockey, polo, etc. **4** punishment by caning or beating. **5** a slender more or less cylindrical piece of a substance, e.g. chalk, rhubarb, dynamite. **6** a number of bombs released in succession to fall in a row. **7** (*informal*) a person (as specified), *not a bad old stick*. □ **stick insect** an insect with a twiglike body. **the sticks** (*Austral. informal*) a remote rural area; the outback.

stick² *verb* (**stuck**, **sticking**) **1** to thrust (a thing or its point) into something, to stab. **2** to fix by means of a pointed object. **3** (*informal*) to put, *stick the parcel on the table*. **4** to fix or be fixed by glue or suction etc. or as if by

these. **5** to fix or be fixed in one place and unable to move, *the boat stuck on a sandbank*. **6** (*informal*) to remain in the same place, *they stuck indoors all day*. **7** (*informal*, of an accusation) to be established as valid, *we couldn't make the charges stick*. **8** (*informal*) to endure, to tolerate. **9** (*informal*) to impose a difficult or unpleasant task upon, *we were stuck with the job of clearing up*. □ **stick at it** (*informal*) to continue one's efforts. **stick in one's throat** to be against one's principles. **stick-in-the-mud** *noun* a person who will not adopt new ideas etc. **stick it out** to endure to the end in spite of difficulty or unpleasantness. **stick one's neck out** to expose oneself deliberately to danger or argument. **stick out** to stand above the surrounding surface; to be conspicuous. **stick out for** to persist in demanding. **stick to** to remain faithful to (a friend or promise etc.); to abide by and not alter, *he stuck to his story*; *stick to it*, = stick at it; *stick to one's guns*, hold one's position against attack or argument. **stick up** (*informal*) to rob by threatening with a gun. **stick-up** *noun* (*informal*) a robbery of this kind. **stick up for** (*informal*) = stand up for. **stick with** to remain with or faithful to.

sticker *noun* **1** an adhesive label or sign. **2** a person who persists in his or her efforts.

sticking plaster *noun* a strip of fabric with an adhesive on one side, used for covering small cuts.

sticking point *noun* the point at which a thing stops and holds fast; a stumbling block.

stickjaw *noun* (*informal*) hard toffee or a similar sweet.

stickleback *noun* a small fish with sharp spines on its back.

stickler *noun* a person who insists on something, *a stickler for punctuality*.

sticky *adjective* (**stickier**, **stickiest**) **1** sticking or tending to stick to what is touched. **2** (of weather) hot and humid, causing perspiration. **3** (*informal*) difficult, awkward, *a sticky problem*. **4** (*informal*) very unpleasant, *he'll come to a sticky end*. □ **sticky tape** an adhesive usually transparent cellulose or plastic tape. **sticky wicket** a pitch that is still damp after rain and is difficult for batsmen; (*informal*) difficult circumstances. **stickily** *adverb*, **stickiness** *noun*

stickybeak (*Austral. informal*) *noun* an inquisitive person. −**stickybeak** *verb* to snoop, to pry.

stiff *adjective* 1 not bending or moving or changing its shape easily. 2 not fluid, thick and hard to stir, *a stiff dough*. 3 difficult, *a stiff examination*. 4 formal in manner, not pleasantly sociable or friendly. 5 (of a price or penalty) high, severe. 6 (of a breeze) blowing briskly. 7 (of a drink or dose) strong. 8 (*informal*) to an extreme degree, *bored stiff*. –**stiff** *noun* (*informal*) a corpse. □ **stiff-necked** *adjective* obstinate; haughty. **stiff upper lip** fortitude in enduring grief etc. **stiffly** *adverb*, **stiffness** *noun*

stiffen *verb* to make or become stiff. **stiffener** *noun*

stifle *verb* 1 to suffocate, to feel or cause to feel unable to breathe for lack of air. 2 to restrain or suppress, *stifled a yawn*. **stifling** *adjective*

stigma *noun* (*plural* **stigmas**) 1 a mark of shame, a stain on a person's good reputation. 2 the part of a pistil that receives the pollen in pollination. [Greek, = mark]

stigmata (**stig**-mă-tă) *plural noun* marks corresponding to those left on Christ's body by the nails and spear at his Crucifixion.

stigmatise (**stig**-mă-tyz) *verb* (also -**ize**) to brand as something disgraceful, *he was stigmatised as a coward*.

stile[1] *noun* an arrangement of steps or bars for people to climb in order to get over a fence etc. but preventing the passage of animals.

stile[2] *noun* a vertical piece in the frame of a panelled door or a sash window etc.

stiletto *noun* (*plural* **stilettos**) 1 a dagger with a narrow blade. 2 a pointed device for making eyelets etc. □ **stiletto heel** a high pointed heel on a shoe. [Italian, = little dagger]

still[1] *adjective* 1 without moving, without or almost without motion or sound. 2 (of drinks) not sparkling or fizzy. –**still** *noun* 1 silence and calm, *in the still of the night*. 2 a photograph as distinct from a motion picture; a single photograph taken from a cinema film. –**still** *verb* to make or become still, *to still the waves*. –**still** *adverb* 1 without or almost without moving. 2 then or now or for the future as before, *the Pyramids are still standing*. 3 nevertheless. 4 in a greater amount or degree, *that would be still better or better still*. □ **still birth** a birth in which the child is born dead. **still life** a painting of lifeless things such as cut flowers or fruit. **stillness** *noun*

still[2] *noun* a distilling apparatus, especially for making spirits.

stillborn *adjective* 1 born dead. 2 (of an idea or plan) not developing.

stilt *noun* 1 either of a pair of poles with a rest for the foot some way up it, enabling the user to walk with feet at a distance above the ground. 2 each of a set of piles or posts supporting a building etc. 3 a long-legged wading bird.

stilted *adjective* stiffly or artificially formal, *written in stilted language*.

Stilton *noun* a rich blue-veined cheese.

stimulant *adjective* stimulating. –**stimulant** *noun* a stimulant drug or drink; a stimulating event etc.

stimulate *verb* 1 to make more vigorous or active. 2 to apply a stimulus to. **stimulation** *noun*, **stimulator** *noun*

stimulative (**stim**-yŭ-lă-tiv) *adjective* stimulating.

stimulus *noun* (*plural* **stimuli**, *pr.* **stim**-yŭ-ly) something that rouses a person or thing to activity or energy or that produces a reaction in an organ or tissue of the body. [Latin, = goad]

sting *noun* 1 a sharp-pointed part or organ of an insect etc., used for wounding and often injecting poison. 2 a stiff sharp-pointed hair on certain plants, causing inflammation if touched. 3 infliction of a wound by a sting; the wound itself. 4 any sharp bodily or mental pain, a wounding effect, *the sting of remorse*. –**sting** *verb* (**stung**, **stinging**) 1 to wound or affect with a sting; to be able to do this. 2 to feel or cause to feel sharp bodily or mental pain. 3 to stimulate sharply as if by a sting, *I was stung into answering rudely*. 4 (*informal*) to cheat (a person) by overcharging; to extort money from. □ **stinging nettle** a nettle that stings.

stingray *noun* a fish with a flattened diamond-shaped body and a long poisonous serrated spine at the base of its tail.

stingy (**stin**-jee) *adjective* (**stingier**, **stingiest**) spending or giving or given grudgingly or in small amounts. **stingily** *adverb*, **stinginess** *noun*

stink *noun* 1 an offensive smell. 2 (*informal*) an offensive fuss, *kicked up a stink about it*. –**stink** *verb* (**stank** or **stunk**, **stunk**, **stinking**) 1 to give off an offensive smell. 2 to seem very unpleasant or unsavoury or dishonest, *the whole business stinks*.

stinker *noun* **1** a person or thing that stinks. **2** (*informal*) something offensive or severe or difficult to do.

stinking *adjective* **1** that stinks. **2** (*informal*) very unpleasant. **–stinking** *adverb* (*informal*) extremely, *stinking rich*.

stint *verb* to restrict to a small allowance, to be niggardly, *don't stint on food*. **–stint** *noun* **1** a limitation of supply or effort, *gave help without stint*. **2** a fixed or allotted amount of work, *did her stint of tidying*.

stipend (**sty**-pěnd) *noun* a salary, the official income of a member of the clergy. [from Latin *stips* = wages, + *pendere* = to pay]

stipendiary (sty-**pend**-yǎ-ree) *adjective* receiving a stipend. □ **stipendiary magistrate** a paid professional magistrate.

stipple *verb* **1** to paint, draw, or engrave in small dots (not in lines or strokes). **2** to roughen the surface of (cement etc.).

stipulate *verb* to demand or insist upon as part of an agreement. **stipulation** *noun*

stir[1] *verb* (**stirred, stirring**) **1** to move or cause to move, *not a leaf stirred*; *wind stirred the sand*. **2** to mix or move (a substance) by moving a spoon etc. round and round in it. **3** to arouse or excite or stimulate, *the story stirred their interest*. **–stir** *noun* **1** the act or process of stirring, *give the soup a stir*. **2** a commotion or disturbance, excitement, *the news caused a stir*.

stir[2] *noun* (*informal*) prison.

stirring *adjective* exciting, stimulating.

stirrup *noun* **1** a metal or leather support for a rider's foot, hanging from the saddle. **2** a bone in the middle ear. □ **stirrup pants** trousers with stirrup-like loops for the feet, designed to keep the fabric taut. **stirrup pump** a small portable pump with a stirrup-shaped footrest, used for extinguishing small fires.

stitch *noun* **1** a single movement of a threaded needle in and out of fabric in sewing or tissue in surgery. **2** a single complete movement of a needle or hook in knitting or crochet. **3** the loop of thread made in this way. **4** a particular method of arranging the thread, *cross stitch*; *purl stitch*. **5** the least bit of clothing, *without a stitch on*. **6** a sudden sharp pain in the muscles at the side of the body. **–stitch** *verb* to sew, to join or close with stitches. □ **in stitches** (*informal*) laughing uncontrollably.

stoat *noun* the ermine, especially when its fur is brown.

stobie pole *noun* (in South Australia) a pole of steel and concrete carrying electricity cables. [named after J.C. Stobie 1895–1953, South Australian designer]

stock *noun* **1** an amount of something available for use, *a stock of jokes*. **2** the total of goods kept by a trader or shopkeeper. **3** livestock. **4** a line of ancestry, *a woman of Irish stock*. **5** money lent to a government in return for fixed interest. **6** the capital of a business company; a portion of this held by an investor (differing from *shares* in that it is not issued in fixed amounts). **7** a person's standing in the opinion of others; *his stock is high*, he is well thought of. **8** liquid made by stewing bones, meat, fish, or vegetables, used as a basis for making soup, sauce, etc. **9** a garden plant with fragrant single or double flowers. **10** the lower and thicker part of a tree trunk. **11** a growing plant into which a graft is inserted. **12** a part serving as the base, holder, or handle for the working parts of an implement or machine; *the stock of a rifle*, the wooden or metal part to which the barrel is attached. **13** a cravat worn by a horse-rider. **14** a piece of black or purple fabric worn over the shirt front by a member of the clergy. **–stock** *adjective* **1** kept in stock and regularly available, *one of our stock items*. **2** commonly used, *a stock argument*. **–stock** *verb* **1** to keep (goods) in stock. **2** to provide with goods, livestock, or a supply of something, *stocked his farm with Jersey cows*; *a well-stocked library*. □ **in stock** available in a shop etc. without needing to be obtained specially. **out of stock** sold out. **stock car** an ordinary car strengthened for use in racing where deliberate bumping is allowed. **Stock Exchange** a place where stocks and shares are publicly bought and sold; an association of dealers conducting such business according to fixed rules. **stock-in-trade** *noun* all the stock and other requisites for carrying on a trade or business. **stock market** the Stock Exchange; transactions there. **stock-still** *adjective* motionless. **stock up** to assemble a stock of goods etc.

stockade *noun* a protective fence of upright stakes.

stockbreeder *noun* a farmer who raises livestock. **stockbreeding** *noun*

stockbroker *noun* = broker (sense 2). **stockbroking** *noun*

stockholder *noun* a person who holds financial stock or shares.

Stockholm the capital of Sweden.

stockinet *noun* fine stretchable machine-knitted fabric used for underwear etc.

stocking *noun* a close-fitting covering for the foot and part or all of the leg. □ **stocking stitch** alternate rows of plain and purl in knitting, giving a plain smooth surface on one side.

stockist *noun* a business firm that stocks certain goods for sale.

stockman *noun* (*plural* **stockmen**) (*Austral.*) a man in charge of livestock.

stockpile *noun* an accumulated stock of goods or materials etc. kept in reserve. –**stockpile** *verb* to accumulate a stockpile of.

stockpot *noun* a large cooking pot in which stock is made and kept.

stockroom *noun* a room where goods kept in stock are stored.

stocks *plural noun* **1** a wooden framework with holes for the legs of a seated person, used like the pillory. **2** a framework on which a ship rests during construction. □ **on the stocks** being constructed or repaired.

stocktaking *noun* **1** making an inventory of the stock in a shop etc. **2** a review of one's position and resources.

stocky *adjective* (**stockier**, **stockiest**) short and solidly built. **stockily** *adverb*, **stockiness** *noun*

stockyard *noun* an enclosure with pens etc. for the sorting or temporary keeping of livestock.

stodge *noun* (*informal*) stodgy food.

stodgy *adjective* (**stodgier**, **stodgiest**) **1** (of food) heavy and filling, indigestible. **2** (of a book etc.) written in a heavy uninteresting way. **3** (of a person) uninteresting, not lively. **stodgily** *adverb*, **stodginess** *noun*

stoic (**stoh**-ik) *noun* a stoical person. [named after the Stoics, Greek and Roman philosophers of the 3rd century BC onwards, who taught that goodness is based on knowledge and that the truly wise man is indifferent to changes of fortune]

stoical (**stoh**-ikăl) *adjective* calm and not excitable, bearing difficulties or discomfort without complaining. **stoically** *adverb*

stoicism (**stoh**-ĭ-sizm) *noun* being stoical.

stoke *verb* to tend and put fuel on (a furnace or fire etc.). □ **stoke up** to stoke and add fuel to; (*informal*) to eat large quantities of food.

stokehold *noun* a compartment in which a steamship's fires are tended.

stoker *noun* **1** a person who stokes a furnace etc., especially on a ship. **2** a mechanical device for doing this.

STOL *abbreviation* short take-off and landing, a system in which an aircraft needs only a short run for taking off and landing.

stole[1] *noun* **1** a clerical vestment consisting of a long strip of silk or other material worn round the neck with the ends hanging down in front. **2** a woman's wide scarf-like garment worn round the shoulders.

stole[2], **stolen** *see* **steal**.

stolid *adjective* not feeling or showing emotion, not excitable. **stolidly** *adverb*, **stolidity** (stŏ-**lid**-ĭ-tee) *noun*

stoma (**stoh**-mă) *noun* (*plural* **stomata**) **1** a small mouthlike opening. **2** one of the tiny openings in the outer surface of a leaf or stem. [Greek, = mouth]

stomach *noun* **1** the internal organ in which the first part of digestion occurs. **2** the abdomen. **3** appetite for food. **4** appetite or spirit for danger or an undertaking etc., *had no stomach for the fight*. –**stomach** *verb* to endure or tolerate, *can't stomach all that violence*. □ **stomach ache** pain in the belly or bowels. **stomach pump** a syringe for emptying the stomach or forcing liquid into it.

stomp *verb* to tread heavily.

stone *noun* **1** a piece of rock, usually detached from the earth's crust and of fairly small size. **2** stones or rock as a substance or material, e.g. for building. **3** a piece of stone shaped for a particular purpose, e.g. a tombstone or millstone. **4** a precious stone (*see* **precious**). **5** a small piece of hard substance formed in the bladder, kidney, or gall bladder. **6** the hard case round the kernel of certain fruits. **7** (*plural* **stone**) a unit of weight, = 14 lb (6.35 kg). –**stone** *adjective* made of stone, *stone floors*. –**stone** *verb* **1** to pelt with stones. **2** to remove the stones from (fruit). □ **leave no stone unturned** to try every possible means. **Stone Age** the very early period of civilisation when weapons and tools were made of stone not metal. **stone fruit** a fruit (e.g. plum, peach, cherry) containing a single stone. **stone's throw** a short distance.

stone- *prefix* completely, *stone-cold*, *stone-deaf*.

stoned *adjective* (*informal*) very drunk or under the influence of drugs.

stonefish *noun* a venomous tropical fish found on coral reefs.

Stonehenge a megalithic monument in southern England, dating from the Bronze Age.

stoneless *adjective* without stones.

stonemason *noun* a person who cuts and dresses stone or builds in stone.

stonewall *verb* to obstruct by stonewalling.

stonewalling *noun* **1** batting in cricket without attempting to score runs. **2** obstructing a discussion etc. by non-committal replies.

stonework *noun* stone(s) forming a building or other structure.

stonker *verb* (*Austral. informal*) to tire out; to defeat, to thwart.

stony *adjective* **1** full of stones. **2** hard as stone, unfeeling. **3** not responsive, *a stony gaze*. ☐ **stony-broke** *adjective* (*informal*) = **broke**. **stonily** *adverb*

stood *see* **stand**.

stooge *noun* (*informal*) **1** a comedian's assistant, used as a target for jokes. **2** a subordinate who does routine work. **3** a person whose actions are entirely controlled by another. **–stooge** *verb* (*informal*) **1** to act as a stooge. **2** to wander about aimlessly.

stool *noun* **1** a movable seat without arms or a back. **2** a footstool. **3** the base of a plant from which new stems or foliage shoot up. ☐ **stool pigeon** a person acting as a decoy, especially to trap a criminal.

stools *plural noun* faeces.

stoop *verb* **1** to bend forwards and down. **2** to condescend, to lower oneself morally, *he wouldn't stoop to cheating*. **–stoop** *noun* a posture of the body with shoulders bent forwards, *he walks with a stoop*.

stop *verb* (**stopped**, **stopping**) **1** to put an end to (movement, progress, operation, etc.), to cause to halt or pause. **2** to refrain from continuing; to cease motion or working. **3** (*informal*) to stay, *we stopped to tea*. **4** to keep back, to refuse to give or allow, *they stopped her wages*; *stop a cheque*, order the bank not to honour it when it is presented for payment. **5** to close by plugging or obstructing, to fill a cavity in (a tooth). **6** to press down a string or block a hole in a musical instrument in order to obtain the desired pitch. **–stop** *noun* **1** stopping; being stopped, a pause or check, *ran without a stop*; *put a stop to it*, cause it to cease. **2** a place where a train or bus etc. stops regularly. **3** a punctuation mark, especially a full stop. **4** an obstruction or device that stops or regulates movement or operation. **5** a row of organ pipes providing tones of one quality; the knob or lever controlling these; *pull out all the stops*, make all possible efforts. **6** any of the standard sizes of aperture in an adjustable lens. ☐ **double stopping** the simultaneous playing of notes on adjacent strings of a violin etc. **stop at nothing** to be completely ruthless or unscrupulous. **stop down** to reduce the aperture of a lens in photography. **stop-go** *noun* alternate stopping and progressing. **stop light** a red light in traffic signals; one of a pair of red lights on the rear of a motor vehicle, showing when brakes are applied. **stop off** or **over** to break one's journey. **stop press** late news inserted in a newspaper after printing has begun.

stopcock *noun* a valve in a pipe to regulate the flow of liquid or gas; the handle etc. on the outside of the pipe by which it is adjusted.

stopgap *noun* a temporary substitute.

stopover *noun* a break in one's journey, especially for a night.

stoppage *noun* **1** stopping; being stopped. **2** an obstruction.

Stoppard, Tom (born 1937), Czech-born British playwright, whose works include *Rosencrantz and Guildenstern are Dead*.

stopper *noun* a plug for closing a bottle etc. **–stopper** *verb* to close with a stopper. ☐ **put a stopper on** to cause to cease.

stopwatch *noun* a watch with a mechanism for starting and stopping it at will, used in timing races etc.

storage *noun* **1** storing of goods etc. or of information. **2** space available for this. **3** the charge for it. ☐ **storage battery** an apparatus for storing electrical energy, consisting of a group of rechargeable electric cells.

store *noun* **1** a stock or supply of something available for use. **2** a large shop selling goods of many kinds. **3** a storehouse, a warehouse where things are stored. **4** a device in a computer or calculator for storing and retrieving information. **–store** *verb* **1** to collect and keep for future use. **2** to put into a store. **3** to put (furniture etc.) into a warehouse for temporary keeping. **4** to stock with something useful, *a mind well stored with information*. ☐ **in store** being stored; kept available for use; destined to happen, imminent, *there's a surprise in store for you*. **set store by** to value greatly. **store cattle** cattle kept for breeding or for future fattening.

storehouse *noun* a building where things are stored; *a storehouse of information*, a book etc. containing much information.

storekeeper *noun* 1 a shopkeeper. 2 a person in charge of a store or stores.

storeroom *noun* a room used for storing things.

storey *noun* (*plural* **storeys**) one horizontal section of a building, all the rooms at the same level. **storeyed** *adjective*

stork *noun* a large long-legged wading bird with a long straight bill, sometimes nesting on buildings and humorously pretended to be the bringer of babies.

storm *noun* 1 a violent disturbance of the atmosphere with strong winds and usually rain, thunder, etc. 2 a violent shower of missiles or blows. 3 a great outbreak of applause, anger, or criticism etc. 4 a violent military attack on a place. –**storm** *verb* 1 (of wind or rain) to rage, to be violent. 2 to move or behave violently or very angrily, to rage, *stormed out of the room*; *stormed at us for being late*. 3 to attack or capture by storm, *they stormed the citadel*. □ **storm in a teacup** great agitation over a trivial matter. **storm petrel** a kind of petrel said to be active before storms. **storm troops** troops trained for assault; the Nazi political militia. **take by storm** to capture by a violent attack; to captivate rapidly.

stormy *adjective* (**stormier**, **stormiest**) 1 full of storms, affected by storms, *a stormy night*; *stormy coasts*. 2 (of wind etc.) violent as in a storm. 3 full of violent anger or outbursts, *a stormy interview*. □ **stormy petrel** a storm petrel (*see* **storm**); a person whose presence seems to foretell or attract trouble. **stormily** *adverb*, **storminess** *noun*

story[1] *noun* 1 an account of an incident or of a series of incidents, either true or invented. 2 (also **storyline**) the plot of a novel or play etc. 3 a report of an item of news; material for this. 4 (*informal*) a lie. [same origin as *history*]

story[2] *noun* = **storey**.

storyteller *noun* 1 a person who narrates stories. 2 (*informal*) a liar.

stoup (*pr.* stoop) *noun* a stone basin for holy water, especially in the wall of a church.

stoush (*Austral. informal*) *verb* to thrash, to punch. –**stoush** *noun* a fight; fighting.

stout *adjective* 1 of considerable thickness or strength, *a stout stick*. 2 (of a person) solidly built and rather fat. 3 brave and resolute, *a stout heart*. –**stout** *noun* a strong dark beer brewed with roasted malt or barley. **stoutly** *adverb*, **stoutness** *noun*

stove[1] *noun* a closed apparatus burning fuel or electricity for heating or cooking.

stove[2] *see* **stave**.

stow *verb* to place in a receptacle for storage. □ **stow away** to put away in storage or in reserve; to conceal oneself as a stowaway. [from *bestow*]

stowage *noun* 1 stowing; being stowed. 2 space available for this. 3 the charge for it.

stowaway *noun* a person who conceals himself or herself on a ship or aircraft etc. so as to travel without charge or unseen.

straddle *verb* 1 to sit or stand across (a thing) with the legs or supports wide apart. 2 to stand with the legs wide apart. 3 to drop shells or bombs short of and beyond (a certain point).

Stradivarius (strad-ĭ-**vair**-ree-ŭs) *noun* a violin or other stringed instrument made by Antonio Stradivari (c. 1644–1737), Italian violin-maker, or his followers.

strafe (*pr.* strahf *or* strayf) *verb* to bombard, to harass with gunfire.

straggle *verb* 1 to grow or spread in an irregular or untidy manner, not remaining compact. 2 to go or wander separately not in a group; to drop behind others. **straggler** *noun*

straggly *adjective* straggling.

straight *adjective* 1 extending or moving continuously in one direction, not curved or bent. 2 correctly arranged, in proper order, tidy. 3 in unbroken succession, *ten straight wins*. 4 candid, not evasive; honest. 5 not modified or elaborate; without additions. 6 conventional; heterosexual. –**straight** *adverb* 1 in a straight line; *he shoots straight*, with good aim. 2 direct, without delay, *went straight home*. 3 straightforwardly, *told him straight*. –**straight** *noun* the straight part of something, e.g. the last section of a racecourse. □ **go straight** to live an honest life after being a criminal. **straight angle** an angle of 180°. **straight away** without delay. **straight-edge** *noun* a bar with one edge accurately straight, used for testing straightness. **straight face** one without a smile even though amused. **straight fight** a contest between only two candidates. **straight off** (*informal*) without hesitation or deliberation etc., *I can't tell you straight off*. **straightness** *noun*

straighten *verb* to make or become straight.

straightforward *adjective* **1** honest, frank. **2** (of a task etc.) without complications. **straightforwardly** *adverb*, **straightforwardness** *noun*

strain¹ *verb* **1** to stretch tightly, to make taut. **2** to injure or weaken by excessive stretching or by over-exertion, *strain one's heart*. **3** to make an intense effort; *strain one's ears*, try hard to hear. **4** to apply (a meaning or rule etc.) beyond its true application. **5** to pass through a sieve or similar device in order to separate solids from the liquid containing them; (of liquid) to filter. **–strain** *noun* **1** straining; being strained; the force exerted. **2** an injury caused by straining a muscle etc. **3** a severe demand on one's mental or physical strength or on one's resources; exhaustion caused by this. **4** a passage from a tune. **5** the tone or style of something written or spoken, *continued in a more cheerful strain*.

strain² *noun* **1** a line of descent of animals, plants, or microorganisms; a variety or breed of these, *a new strain of flu virus*. **2** a slight or inherited tendency in a character, *there's a strain of insanity in the family*.

strained *adjective* (of behaviour or manner) produced by effort, not arising from genuine feeling; *strained relations*, unpleasant tension between people.

strainer *noun* **1** a device for keeping something taut. **2** a utensil for straining liquids.

strait *adjective* (*old use*) narrow, restricted. **–strait** *noun* a narrow stretch of water connecting two seas, *Bass Strait*. **straits** *plural noun* a strait; a difficult state of affairs, *in dire straits*.

straitened *adjective* made narrow, not spacious enough. □ **straitened circumstances** barely sufficient money to live on. [from *strait*]

straitjacket *noun* a strong jacket-like garment put round a violent person to restrain his or her arms.

strait-laced *adjective* very prim and proper.

strake *noun* a continuous line of planking or metal plates from stem to stern of a ship.

strand¹ *noun* **1** one of the threads or wires etc. twisted together to form a rope, yarn, or cable. **2** a single thread or strip of fibre. **3** a lock of hair.

strand² *noun* a shore. **–strand** *verb* to run or cause to run aground.

stranded *adjective* left in difficulties, e.g. without funds or means of transport.

strange *adjective* **1** not familiar or well known; not one's own, alien. **2** unusual, surprising, *it's strange that you haven't heard*. **3** fresh, unaccustomed, *she is strange to the work*. **strangely** *adverb*, **strangeness** *noun*

stranger *noun* **1** a person in a place or company etc. to which he or she does not belong; a person one does not know. **2** one who is unaccustomed to a certain feeling, experience, or task, *a stranger to poverty*.

strangle *verb* **1** to kill or be killed by squeezing the throat. **2** to restrict or prevent the proper growth, operation, or utterance of. **strangler** *noun* [from Greek *strangale* = a halter]

stranglehold *noun* a strangling grip.

strangulate *verb* to compress (a vein, intestine etc.) so that nothing can pass through it.

strangulation *noun* **1** strangling; being strangled. **2** strangulating; being strangulated.

strap *noun* **1** a strip of leather or other flexible material, often with a buckle, for holding things together or in place. **2** a shoulder strap. **3** a loop for grasping to steady oneself in a moving vehicle. **–strap** *verb* (**strapped**, **strapping**) **1** to secure with a strap or straps. **2** to bind (an injury), *strap it up*. **3** to beat with a strap.

strapless *adjective* without shoulder straps.

strapping *adjective* tall and healthy-looking. **–strapping** *noun* **1** straps; material for making these. **2** sticking plaster etc. used for binding wounds or injuries.

strata *see* stratum. □ **strata title** registered ownership of a certain amount of space (rather than ground area) in a multi-storey building, a block of home units, etc.

stratagem (**strat**-ă-jĕm) *noun* a cunning method of achieving something; a piece of trickery.

strategic *adjective* (also **strategical**, stră-**tee**-jik-ăl) **1** of strategy. **2** giving an advantage, *a strategic position*. □ **Strategic Defense Initiative** a proposed US system (popularly known as 'Star Wars') in which enemy weapons would be destroyed in space by lasers, missiles, etc. launched or directed from orbiting military satellites. **strategic materials**

those essential for war. **strategic weapons** missiles etc. that can reach an enemy's home territory (as distinct from *tactical weapons* which are for use in a battle or at close quarters). **strategically** *adverb*

strategist (strat-ĕ-jĭst) *noun* an expert in strategy.

strategy (strat-ĕ-jee) *noun* **1** the planning and directing of the whole operation of a campaign or war. **2** a plan or policy to achieve something, *our economic strategy*. [from Greek *strategos* = a general]

strathspey (strath-**spay**) *noun* a kind of Scottish dance; music for this.

stratified *adjective* arranged in strata. **stratification** *noun*

stratocumulus (strah-toh-**kewm**-yŭ-lŭs) *noun* dark masses of low cloud, frequently merging to cover the whole sky.

stratosphere (strat-ŏ-sfeer) *noun* a layer of the earth's atmosphere between about 10 and 60 km above the earth's surface. [from *stratum* + *sphere*]

stratum (strah-tŭm) *noun* (*plural* strata) **1** one of a series of layers, especially of rock in the earth's crust. **2** a social level or class, *the various strata of society*. [Latin, = thing spread]

Usage The word *strata* is the plural of *stratum*; it is incorrect to speak of *a strata* or *this strata*, or of *stratas*.

---

stratus (strah-tŭs) *noun* (*plural* strati) a continuous horizontal sheet of cloud. [Latin, = spread]

Strauss[1] (*rhymes with* house), Johann (II) (1825–99), Austrian composer (son of Johann I (1804–49), composer of dance music), famous for his waltzes.

Strauss[2] (*rhymes with* house), Richard (1864–1949), German composer and conductor, whose best-known works include tone poems, songs, and the opera *Der Rosenkavalier*.

Stravinsky (strǎ-**vin**-skee), Igor (1882–1971), Russian-born composer, best known for the ballets *Petrushka*, *The Firebird*, and *The Rite of Spring*.

straw *noun* **1** dry cut stalks of grain used as material for bedding, fodder, thatching, etc. **2** a single stalk or piece of this. **3** a narrow straw-like tube of paper or plastic etc. for sucking up liquid in drinking. □ **a straw in the wind** a slight indication of how things may

develop. **straw poll** or **vote** an unofficial poll as a test of general feeling.

strawberry *noun* a soft juicy edible red fruit with yellow seeds on the surface; the plant that bears it. □ **strawberry mark** a reddish birthmark.

stray *verb* **1** to leave one's group or proper place with no settled destination or purpose, to roam. **2** to go aside from a direct course; to depart from a subject. –**stray** *adjective* **1** having strayed. **2** isolated, occurring here and there not as one of a group, *a stray bullet*. –**stray** *noun* a person or domestic animal that has strayed; a stray thing.

streak *noun* **1** a thin line or band of a different colour or substance from its surroundings; *a streak of lightning*, a flash. **2** an element in a person's character, *has a jealous streak*. **3** a spell or series, *had a long winning streak*. –**streak** *verb* **1** to mark with streaks. **2** to move very rapidly. **3** to run naked through a public place as a humourous or defiant act. **streaker** *noun*

streaky *adjective* full of streaks; (of bacon etc.) with alternate layers or streaks of fat and lean. **streakily** *adverb*, **streakiness** *noun*

stream *noun* **1** a body of water flowing in its bed, a river, especially a small one. **2** a flow of any liquid or of a mass of things or people. **3** (in certain schools) a section into which children with the same level of ability are placed. **4** the current or direction of something flowing or moving, *against the stream*. –**stream** *verb* **1** to flow or move as a stream. **2** to emit a stream of, to run with liquid, *the wound streamed blood*; *with streaming eyes*. **3** to float or wave at full length. **4** to arrange (schoolchildren) in streams. □ **on stream** in active operation or production. **stream of consciousness** a continuous inner flow of thoughts and awareness of surroundings, especially as captured in literature.

streamer *noun* **1** a long narrow flag. **2** a long narrow ribbon or strip of paper attached at one or both ends.

streaming *noun* (in computing) a method of relaying data over a network as a steady continuous stream.

streamline *verb* **1** to give a streamlined form to. **2** to make more efficient by simplifying, removing superfluities, etc.

streamlined *adjective* having a smooth even shape that offers the least resistance to movement through air or water.

street *noun* a public road in a town or city with houses aligned on one or both sides. ☐ **streets ahead of** (*informal*) much superior to. **up one's street** (*informal*) within one's field of knowledge or interests. [from Latin *strata via* = paved way]

streetcar *noun* (*Amer.*) a tram.

Streeton, Sir Arthur Ernest (1867–1943), Australian painter, member of the Heidelberg School.

streetwise *adjective* familiar with the ways of modern urban life.

strength *noun* **1** the quality of being strong; the intensity of this. **2** a source of strength; the particular respect in which a person or thing is strong, *his strength is in his mathematical ability*. **3** the number of people present or available, the full complement, *the department is below strength*. ☐ **in strength** in large numbers, *supporters were present in strength*. **on the strength of** on the basis of, using (a fact etc.) as one's support.

strengthen *verb* to make or become stronger.

strenuous *adjective* **1** energetic, making great efforts. **2** requiring great effort, *a strenuous task*. **strenuously** *adverb*, **strenuousness** *noun*

streptococcus *noun* (*plural* **streptococci**, *pr.* strep-tŏ-**kok**-I) any of a group of bacteria that cause serious infections. **streptococcal** *adjective* [from Greek *streptos* = twisted, + *kokkos* = berry]

streptomycin (strep-tŏ-**my**-sin) *noun* a kind of antibiotic drug. [from Greek *streptos* = twisted, + *mukes* = fungus]

stress *noun* **1** a force acting on or within a thing and tending to distort it, e.g. by pressing, pulling, or twisting it. **2** difficult circumstances, mental or physical distress caused by these. **3** = emphasis (*see* **emphasis** senses 1 and 3). –**stress** *verb* **1** to lay emphasis on. **2** to cause stress to. [from *distress*]

stressful *adjective* causing stress.

stretch *verb* **1** to pull out tightly or into a greater length, extent, or size. **2** to be able to be stretched without breaking; to tend to become stretched, *knitted fabrics stretch*. **3** to be continuous from a point or between points. **4** to thrust out one's limbs and tighten the muscles after being relaxed. **5** to make great demands on the abilities of (a person). **6** to strain to the utmost or beyond a reasonable limit; *stretch the truth*, to exaggerate or lie. –**stretch** *noun* **1** stretching; being stretched. **2** the ability to be stretched, *this elastic has* lost its stretch. **3** a continuous expanse or tract; a continuous period of time. **4** (*informal*) a period of service or imprisonment. –**stretch** *adjective* able to be stretched, *stretch fabrics*. ☐ **at full stretch** without interruption. **at full stretch** or **fully stretched** working to the utmost of one's powers. **stretch a point** to agree to something beyond the limit of what is normally allowed. **stretch one's legs** to go walking as a relief from sitting or lying.

stretcher *noun* **1** a framework of poles, canvas, etc. for carrying a sick or injured person in a lying position. **2** (*Austral.*) a collapsible single bed. **3** any of various devices for stretching things or holding things taut or braced. **4** a board against which a rower braces his or her feet.

strew *verb* (**strewed**, **strewn** *or* **strewed**, **strewing**) to scatter over a surface; to cover with scattered things.

striated (stry-**ay**-tĕd) *adjective* marked with striations.

striation (stry-**ay**-shŏn) *noun* any of a series of ridges, furrows, or linear marks.

stricken *adjective* affected or overcome by an illness, shock, or grief, *stricken with flu*; *grief-stricken*.

strict *adjective* **1** precisely limited or defined, without exception or deviation. **2** requiring or giving complete obedience or exact performance, not lenient or indulgent. **strictly** *adverb*, **strictness** *noun*

stricture *noun* **1** severe criticism or condemnation. **2** abnormal constriction of a tubelike part of the body.

stride *verb* (**strode**, **stridden**, **striding**) **1** to walk with long steps. **2** to stand astride. –**stride** *noun* **1** a single long step, the length of this. **2** a person's manner of striding. **3** progress, *has made great strides towards independence*. ☐ **get into one's stride** to settle into a fast and steady pace of work. **take it in one's stride** to do it without needing a special effort.

strident (stry-dĕnt) *adjective* loud and harsh. **stridently** *adverb*, **stridency** *noun* [from Latin *stridens* = creaking]

strife *noun* **1** quarrelling, conflict. **2** (*Austral. informal*) trouble of any kind.

strike *verb* (**struck**, **striking**) **1** to bring or come into sudden hard contact with; to inflict (a blow); to knock with a blow or stroke. **2** to attack suddenly; (of a disease) to afflict. **3** (of lightning) to descend upon and blast. **4** to produce (sparks or a sound etc.) by striking something; to produce (a musical note) by pressing a key; to make (a coin or medal) by stamping metal etc.; *strike a match*, ignite it by friction; *strike a bargain*, make one. **5** to bring into a specified state by or as if by striking, *he was struck blind*. **6** to indicate (the hour) or be indicated by a sound, *clock struck two; two o'clock struck*. **7** (of plant cuttings) to put down roots. **8** to reach (gold or mineral oil etc.) by digging or drilling. **9** to occur to the mind of, to produce a mental impression on, *an idea struck me*; *she strikes me as being efficient*. **10** to lower or take down (a flag or tent etc.). **11** to stop work in protest about a grievance. **12** to penetrate or cause to penetrate; to fill with sudden fear etc. **13** to proceed in a certain direction, *strike north-west through the forest*. **14** to arrive at (an average or balance) by balancing or equalising the items. **15** to assume (an attitude) suddenly and dramatically. **–strike** *noun* **1** an act or instance of striking. **2** an attack. **3** a workers' refusal to work, in protest about a grievance. **4** a sudden discovery of gold or oil etc. □ **on strike** (of workers) striking. **strike off** to cross off; to remove (a person) from a professional register because of misconduct. **strike out** to cross out. **strike pay** an allowance made by a trade union to members on strike. **strike up** to begin playing or singing; to start (a friendship etc.) rapidly or casually.

strikebreaker *noun* a person who works while fellow employees are on strike or who is employed in place of strikers.

striker *noun* **1** a person or thing that strikes. **2** a worker who is on strike. **3** a hockey or soccer player whose main function is to try to score goals.

striking *adjective* sure to be noticed, attractive and impressive. **strikingly** *adverb*

Strine *noun* a humorous respelling of relaxed Australian English speech, e.g. *egg nishner* for *air conditioner*. [= *Australian* in Strine]

string *noun* **1** narrow cord. **2** a length of this or some other material used to fasten or lace or pull something, or interwoven in a frame to form the head of a racquet. **3** a piece of catgut or cord or wire stretched and caused to vibrate so as to produce tones in a musical instrument. **4** a strip of tough fibre on a bean etc. **5** a set of objects strung together or of people or events coming after one another. **6** the racehorses trained at one stable. **7** something ranked as one's first or second etc. resource; *have two*

strings to one's bow, not be obliged to rely on only one resource. **8** a condition that is insisted upon, *the offer has no strings attached*. **–string** *verb* (**strung**, **stringing**) **1** to fit or fasten with string(s). **2** to thread (beads etc.) on a string. **3** to trim the tough fibre from (beans). **strings** *plural noun* stringed instruments; their players. □ **pull strings** *see* pull. **string along** (*informal*) to deceive. **string along with** (*informal*) to accompany. **string bag** a shopping bag made of net. **string course** a projecting horizontal line of bricks etc. round a building. **string out** to spread out in a line; to cause to last a long time. **string quartet** a quartet for stringed instruments. **string theory** a cosmological theory based on the existence of threadlike concentrations of energy within the structure of space-time. **string up** to kill by hanging.

stringed *adjective* (of musical instruments) having strings that are played by being touched, or with a bow or a plectrum.

stringent (**strin**-jĕnt) *adjective* **1** (of a rule) strict. **2** (of financial conditions) tight. **stringently** *adverb*, **stringency** *noun*

stringy *adjective* **1** like string. **2** (of beans etc.) having a strip of tough fibre.

stringybark *noun* an Australian eucalypt with tough fibrous bark.

strip¹ *verb* (**stripped**, **stripping**) **1** to take off (clothes or coverings or parts etc.); *strip a machine down*, take it apart to inspect or adjust it. **2** to undress oneself. **3** to deprive, e.g. of property or titles. **4** to tear away; *stripped the gearwheel*, tore off its cogs.

strip² *noun* a long narrow piece or area. □ **strip light** a tubular fluorescent lamp. **tear a strip off a person** (*informal*) to rebuke him or her angrily.

stripe *noun* **1** a long narrow band on a surface, differing in colour or texture from its surroundings. **2** a chevron on a sleeve, indicating the wearer's rank.

striped *adjective* marked with stripes.

stripling *noun* a youth.

stripper *noun* **1** a person or thing that strips something. **2** a device or solvent for removing paint etc. **3** a machine used to harvest grain.

stripy *adjective* (*informal*) striped.

strive *verb* (**strove**, **striven**, **striving**) **1** to make great efforts. **2** to carry on a conflict.

strobe *noun* (*informal*) a stroboscope.

stroboscope (**stroh**-bŏ-skohp) *noun* an apparatus for producing a rapidly flashing light. **stroboscopic** (-**skop**-ik) *adjective* [from Greek *strobos* = whirling, + *skopein* = look at]

strode *see* stride.

stroke[1] *noun* **1** the act or process of striking something. **2** a sudden inability to feel and move, caused by blockage or rupture of an artery in the brain; apoplexy. **3** a single movement or action or effort, a successful or skilful effort, *he hasn't done a stroke of work*; *a stroke of genius*; *a stroke of luck*, a sudden fortunate occurrence. **4** each of a series of repeated movements; a particular sequence of these (e.g. in swimming). **5** one hit at the ball in various games; (in golf) this used as a unit of scoring. **6** the oarsman nearest the stern of a racing boat, setting the time of the stroke. **7** a mark made by a movement of a pen or paintbrush etc. **8** the sound made by a clock striking; *on the stroke of ten*, exactly at ten o'clock. –**stroke** *verb* to act as stroke to (a boat or crew).

stroke[2] *verb* to pass the hand gently along the surface of. –**stroke** *noun* an act or spell of stroking.

stroll *verb* to walk in a leisurely way. –**stroll** *noun* a leisurely walk.

stroller *noun* a folding chair on wheels, in which a child can be pushed along.

strong *adjective* **1** having power of resistance to being broken, damaged, or captured etc. **2** capable of exerting great power, physically powerful; powerful through numbers, resources, or quality; *a strong candidate*, one likely to win; *strong acids*, those with a powerful chemical effect. **3** concentrated, having a large proportion of a flavouring or colouring element; (of a drink) containing much alcohol. **4** having a considerable effect on one of the senses, *a strong smell*. **5** having a specified number of members, *an army 5000 strong*. **6** (of verbs) changing the vowel in the past tense (as *ring/rang, strike/struck*), not adding a suffix (as *float/floated*). –**strong** *adverb* strongly, vigorously, *going strong*. □ **strong-arm tactics** use of force or sheer strength. **strong language** forcible language, oaths or swearing. **strong-minded** *adjective* having a determined mind. **strong point** a thing at which one excels; a specially fortified position in a system of defences. **strong suit** a suit (in a hand of cards) in which one can take tricks; a thing at which one excels. **strongly** *adverb*

strongbox *noun* a strongly-made small chest for valuables.

stronghold *noun* **1** a fortified place. **2** a centre of support for a cause etc.

strongroom *noun* a room designed for storage and protection of valuables against fire or theft.

strontium (**stron**-tee-ŭm) *noun* a chemical element (symbol Sr), a soft silver-white metal, having a radioactive isotope that concentrates in bones when taken into an animal's body.

strop *noun* a strip of leather on which a razor is sharpened; an implement or machine serving the same purpose. –**strop** *verb* (**stropped**, **stropping**) to sharpen on or with a strop.

stroppy *adjective* (*informal*) bad-tempered, awkward to deal with.

strove *see* strive.

struck *see* strike. □ **struck on** (*informal*) impressed with, liking.

structural *adjective* **1** of a structure or framework. **2** used in the construction of buildings etc., *structural steel*. **structurally** *adverb*

structure *noun* **1** the way in which something is constructed or organised. **2** a supporting framework or the essential parts of a thing. **3** a constructed thing; a complex whole; a building. [from Latin *structura* = thing built]

strudel (**stroo**-dĕl) *noun* thin pastry filled and baked, *cherry strudel*.

struggle *verb* **1** to move one's limbs or body in a vigorous effort to get free. **2** to make a vigorous effort under difficulties; to make one's way or a living etc. with difficulty. **3** to try to overcome an opponent or problem etc. –**struggle** *noun* a spell of struggling; a vigorous effort; a hard contest.

strum *verb* (**strummed**, **strumming**) **1** play (a guitar or similar instrument) by sweeping the thumb or a plectrum up or down the strings. **2** play casually or unskilfully on a stringed instrument. –**strum** *noun* the sound made by strumming.

strumpet *noun* (*old use*) a prostitute.

strung *see* string. □ **strung up** mentally tense or excited.

strut *noun* **1** a bar of wood or metal inserted into a framework to strengthen and brace it. **2** a strutting walk. –**strut** *verb* (**strutted**, **strutting**) to walk in a pompous self-satisfied way.

'struth *interjection* (*informal*) an exclamation of surprise. [short for *God's truth*]

strychnine (**strik**-neen) *noun* a bitter highly poisonous substance, used in very small doses as a stimulant.

Strzelecki (strez-**lek**-ee), Sir Paul Edmund de (1797–1873), Polish-born explorer and scientist who climbed and named Mount Kosciuszko, and explored much of Tasmania.

Stuart¹ the name of the royal house of Scotland from the accession (1371) of Robert II, and of Britain from the accession of James VI of Scotland to the English throne as James I (1603) until the death of Queen Anne (1714).

Stuart², John McDouall (1815–66), Scottish immigrant explorer who crossed Australia from south to north and back, opening up country that became the route of the Overland Telegraph Line.

stub *noun* **1** a short stump. **2** the counterfoil of a cheque or receipt or ticket etc. **–stub** *verb* (**stubbed, stubbing**) to strike against a hard object, *stub one's toe*; *stub out a cigarette*, extinguish it by pressing it against something hard.

stubble *noun* **1** the lower ends of the stalks of cereal plants left in the ground after the harvest is cut. **2** a short stiff growth of hair or beard, especially that growing after shaving. **stubbly** *adjective*

stubborn *adjective* obstinate, not docile, not easy to control or deal with. **stubbornly** *adverb*, **stubbornness** *noun*

stubby *adjective* short and thick. **–stubby** *noun* a short squat beer bottle, usually of 375 ml capacity.

stucco *noun* plaster or cement used for coating surfaces of walls or moulding to form architectural decorations. **stuccoed** *adjective* [Italian]

stuck *see* stick². **–stuck** *adjective* **1** unable to move or make progress, *I'm stuck!* **2** (of an animal) that has been stabbed or had its throat cut. □ **get stuck into** (*informal*) to begin working seriously at (a job etc.). **stuck-up** *adjective* (*informal*) conceited; snobbish. **stuck with** (*informal*) unable to get rid of.

stud¹ *noun* **1** a short large-headed nail; a rivet; a small knob projecting from a surface. **2** a device like a button on a shank, used e.g. to fasten a detachable shirt collar. **–stud** *verb* (**studded, studding**) to decorate with studs or precious stones set into a surface; to strengthen with studs.

stud² *noun* **1** a number of horses kept for breeding. **2** the place where these are kept. **3** (*informal*) a sexually attractive man. □ **at stud** (of a male horse) available for breeding on payment of a fee. **stud book** a book containing the pedigrees of horses.

student *noun* a person who is studying, especially at a school, college, or place of higher or further education. [from Latin *studens* = studying]

studied *adjective* carefully and intentionally contrived, *she answered with studied indifference*.

studio *noun* (*plural* studios) **1** the workroom of a painter, sculptor, photographer, etc. **2** a room or premises where cinema films are made. **3** a room from which radio or television programs are regularly broadcast or in which recordings are made. [same origin as *study*]

studious *adjective* **1** involving study; habitually spending much time in studying. **2** deliberate, painstaking, *studious politeness*. **studiously** *adverb*, **studiousness** *noun*

study *noun* **1** the process of studying; the pursuit of some branch of knowledge. **2** its subject; a thing that is investigated; *his face was a study*, he looked astounded. **3** a work presenting the result of investigations into a particular subject, *the book is a study of Australian-English pronunciation*. **4** a musical composition designed to develop a player's skill. **5** a preliminary drawing, *a study of a head*. **6** a room used by a person for work that involves studying. **–study** *verb* (**studied, studying**) **1** to give one's attention to acquiring knowledge of (a subject). **2** to examine attentively, *we studied the map*. **3** to give care and consideration to, *she studies the convenience of others*. [from Latin *studium* = zeal]

stuff *noun* **1** material. **2** unnamed things, belongings, subject matter, activities, etc., *leave your stuff in the hall*; *he knows his stuff*, is an expert in his subject or trade; *that's the stuff!*, that is good or what is required. **3** valueless matter, trash, *stuff and nonsense!* **–stuff** *verb* **1** to pack or cram; to fill tightly; to stop up. **2** to fill the empty skin etc. of (a bird or animal) with material to restore its original shape, e.g. for exhibition in a museum. **3** to fill with padding. **4** to fill with savoury stuffing. **5** to fill (a person or oneself) with food; to eat greedily. □ **stuffed shirt** (*informal*) a pompous person. **stuff up** (*informal*) to mismanage, to bungle. **stuff-up** *noun* (*informal*) a bungle, a mess.

stuffing *noun* **1** padding used to stuff cushions etc. **2** a savoury mixture put as a filling into poultry, rolled meat, vegetables, etc. before cooking. □ **knock the stuffing out of** (*informal*) to make feeble or weak; to defeat utterly.

stuffy *adjective* (**stuffier**, **stuffiest**) **1** lacking fresh air or sufficient ventilation. **2** dull, uninteresting. **3** (of the nose) blocked with secretions so that breathing is difficult. **4** (*informal*) old-fashioned and narrow-minded. **stuffily** *adverb*, **stuffiness** *noun*

stultify *verb* (**stultified**, **stultifying**) to impair or make ineffective, *their uncooperative approach has stultified the discussions*. **stultification** *noun* [from Latin *stultus* = foolish]

stumble *verb* **1** to strike one's foot on something and lose one's balance. **2** to walk with frequent stumbles. **3** to make a blunder or frequent blunders in speaking or playing music etc., *stumbled through the recitation*. –**stumble** *noun* an act of stumbling. □ **stumble across** or **on** to discover accidentally. **stumbling block** an obstacle, something that causes difficulty or hesitation.

stump *noun* **1** the base of a tree remaining in the ground when the rest has fallen or been cut down. **2** a corresponding remnant of a broken tooth or an amputated limb or of something worn down. **3** one of the three uprights of a wicket in cricket. **4** (in Queensland especially) one of the piles on which a house is built. –**stump** *verb* **1** to walk stiffly or noisily. **2** (of a wicketkeeper) to put out (a batsman) by dislodging the bails while the batsman is out of the crease. **3** (*informal*) to be too difficult for, to baffle, *the question stumped him*. □ **stump-jump plough** (*Austral.*) a plough designed to cultivate land where stumps are left in the ground. **stump up** (*informal*) to produce (an amount of money), to pay what is required.

stumpy *adjective* (**stumpier**, **stumpiest**) short and thick. **stumpiness** *noun*

stun *verb* (**stunned**, **stunning**) **1** to knock senseless. **2** to daze or shock by the impact of strong emotion.

stung *see* **sting**.

stunk *see* **stink**.

stunning *adjective* (*informal*) extremely attractive. **stunningly** *adverb*

stunt¹ *verb* to hinder the growth or development of.

stunt² *noun* (*informal*) something unusual or difficult done as a performance or to attract attention, *a publicity stunt*. □ **stunt flying** aerobatics. **stunt man** a man employed to take an actor's place in performing difficult stunts.

stupa (**stew**-pă) *noun* a round usually domed Buddhist monument, usually containing a sacred relic. [Sanskrit]

stupefy *verb* (**stupefied**, **stupefying**) **1** to dull the wits or senses of. **2** to stun with astonishment. **stupefaction** *noun* [from Latin *stupere* = be amazed]

stupendous (stew-**pend**-ŭs) *adjective* amazing, exceedingly great. **stupendously** *adverb*

stupid *adjective* **1** not intelligent or clever, slow at learning or understanding things. **2** in a state of stupor, *he was knocked stupid*. **stupidly** *adverb*, **stupidity** *noun* [from Latin *stupidus* = dazed]

stupor (**stew**-per) *noun* a dazed or almost unconscious condition brought on by shock, drugs, drink, etc. [same origin as *stupefy*]

sturdy *adjective* strongly built, hardy, vigorous. **sturdily** *adverb*, **sturdiness** *noun*

sturgeon *noun* (*plural* **sturgeon**) a large sharklike fish with flesh that is valued as food and roe that is made into caviar.

Sturt, Charles (1795–1869), English explorer of Australia who established the system of the west-flowing rivers. □ **Sturt's desert pea** a leguminous plant with a bright red flower, South Australia's floral emblem. **Sturt's desert rose** a shrub with a large mauve flower, the floral emblem of the Northern Territory.

stutter *verb* to stammer, especially by repeating the first consonants of words. –**stutter** *noun* stuttering speech; a tendency to stutter.

sty¹ *noun* a pigsty.

sty² *noun* (also **stye**) an inflamed swelling on the edge of the eyelid.

Stygian (**stij**-ee-ăn) *adjective* of or like the Styx or Hades; gloomy, murky.

style *noun* **1** the manner of writing, speaking, or doing something (contrasted with the subject matter or the thing done). **2** shape or design, *a new style of coat*. **3** elegance, distinction. **4** a narrow extension of the ovary in a plant, supporting the stigma. –**style** *verb* to design, shape, or arrange, especially in a fashionable style. □ **in style** elegantly, luxuriously. [same origin as *stylus*]

stylised *adjective* (also **-ized**) made to conform to a conventional style.

stylish *adjective* in fashionable style, elegant. **stylishly** *adverb*, **stylishness** *noun*

stylist *noun* **1** a person who achieves or aims at a good style in what he or she does. **2** a person who styles things.

stylistic *adjective* of literary or artistic style. **stylistically** *adverb*

stylus *noun* (*plural* **styli** or **styluses**) a needle-like device (usually a polished jewel) used to cut grooves in records or to follow such grooves in reproducing sound from records. [from Latin *stilus* = pointed writing instrument]

styptic (**stip**-tik) *adjective* checking the flow of blood by causing blood vessels to contract. [from Greek *stupho* = to contract]

styrene *noun* a liquid hydrocarbon used in plastics.

Styx (*pr.* stiks) (*Gk. myth.*) one of the rivers of the Underworld, over which Charon ferried the souls of the dead.

suasion (**sway**-zhŏn) *noun* persuasion. □ **moral suasion** a strong recommendation that is not an order.

suave (*pr.* swahv) *adjective* smooth-mannered. **suavely** *adverb*, **suavity** *noun* [from Latin *suavis* = agreeable]

sub *noun* (*informal*) **1** a submarine. **2** a subscription. **3** a substitute.

sub- *prefix* (often changing to **suc-**, **suf-**, **sum-**, **sup-**, **sur-**, **sus-** before certain consonants) **1** under (as in *substructure*). **2** subordinate, secondary (as in *subsection*). [from Latin *sub* = under]

subaltern (**sub**-ăl-tern) *noun* an officer below the rank of captain, especially a second lieutenant.

subantarctic *adjective* of regions bordering on the Antarctic Circle.

subaqua *adjective* (of sport etc.) taking place under water.

subarctic *adjective* of regions bordering on the Arctic Circle.

subatomic *adjective* (of a particle of matter) occurring in an atom; smaller than an atom.

subcommittee *noun* a committee formed for a special purpose from some members of the main committee.

subconscious *adjective* of our own mental activities of which we are not fully aware. **–subconscious** *noun* the part of the mind in which these activities take place. **subconsciously** *adverb*

subcontinent *noun* a large land mass that forms part of a continent.

subcontract (sub-kŏn-**trakt**) *verb* to give or accept a contract to carry out all or part of another contract. **subcontractor** *noun*

subculture *noun* a social culture within a larger culture.

subcutaneous (sub-kew-**tay**-nee-ŭs) *adjective* under the skin. [from *sub-*, + Latin *cutis* = skin]

subdivide *verb* to divide into smaller parts after a first division. **subdivision** *noun*

subdominant *noun* (in music) the fourth note of a major or minor scale.

subduction *noun* the process by which the edge of one plate of the earth's crust passes under the edge of another where they collide. [from *sub-*, + Latin *ductum* = conveyed]

subdue *verb* **1** to overcome, to bring under control. **2** to make quieter or less intense; *subdued lighting*, not strong or intense.

subeditor *noun* **1** an assistant editor. **2** a person who prepares material for printing in a book or newspaper etc.

subheading *noun* a subordinate heading.

subhuman *adjective* less than human; not fully human.

subject (**sub**-jekt) *adjective* **1** not politically independent, *subject peoples*. **2** owing obedience to, under the authority of, *we are all subject to the laws of the land*. **–subject** (**sub**-jekt) *noun* **1** a person subject to a particular political rule, any member of a State except the supreme ruler. **2** the person or thing that is being discussed, described, represented, or studied. **3** the word or words in a sentence that name who or what does the action or undergoes what is stated by the verb, e.g. *'the book'* in *the book fell off the table*. **4** each of the principal themes in a sonata etc. **–subject** (sŭb-**jekt**) *verb* **1** to bring (a country) under one's control. **2** to cause to undergo or experience, *subjecting the metal to severe tests*. □ **subject matter** the matter treated in a book or speech etc. **subject to** liable to, *she is subject to migraines*; depending upon as a condition, *subject to your approval*; *subject to contract*, provided that a contract is made.

subjection *noun* [from *sub-*, + Latin *-jectum* = thrown]

subjective (sŭb-**jek**-tiv) *adjective* **1** existing in a person's mind and not produced by things outside it, not objective. **2** depending on personal taste or views etc. **subjectively** *adverb*

subjoin *verb* to add at the end.

sub judice (sub **joo**-dĭ-see) *adjective* under judicial consideration, not yet decided (and therefore not to be commented upon). [Latin, = under a judge]

subjugate (**sub**-jŭ-gayt) *verb* to subdue or bring (a country etc.) into subjection. subjugation *noun* [from Latin *sub* = under, + *jugum* = a yoke]

subjunctive *adjective* of the form of a verb used in expressing what is imagined or wished or possible, e.g. *'were'* in *if I were you*. –subjunctive *noun* a subjunctive form. [from *sub-*, + Latin *junctum* = joined]

sublet *verb* (**sublet, subletting**) to let (accommodation etc. that one holds by lease) to a subtenant.

sublimate (**sub**-lĭ-mayt) *verb* **1** to divert the energy of (an emotion or impulse arising from a primitive instinct) into a culturally higher activity. **2** to sublime (a substance); to purify. **sublimation** *noun*

sublime *adjective* **1** of the most exalted, noble, or impressive kind. **2** extreme, lofty, like that of a person who does not fear the consequences, *with sublime indifference*. –sublime *verb* **1** to convert (a solid substance) into a vapour by heat (and usually allow it to solidify again). **2** to undergo this process. **3** to purify; to make sublime. **sublimely** *adverb*, **sublimity** (sŭ-**blim**-ĭ-tee) *noun*

subliminal (sub-**lim**-ĭ-năl) *adjective* below the threshold of consciousness. [from *sub-*, Latin *limen* = threshold]

sub-machine gun *noun* a lightweight machine gun held in the hands for firing.

submarine *adjective* under the surface of the sea, *submarine cables*. –submarine *noun* a ship that can operate under water.

submediant (sub-**mee**-dee-ănt) *noun* (in music) the sixth note of a major or minor scale.

submerge *verb* **1** to place below water or other liquid, to flood. **2** (of a submarine) to dive, to go below the surface. **submergence**

noun, **submersion** *noun* [from *sub-*, + Latin *mergere* = dip]

submersible *noun* a ship or other craft that can operate under water.

submicroscopic *adjective* too small to be seen by an ordinary microscope.

submission *noun* **1** submitting; being submitted. **2** something submitted; a theory etc. submitted by counsel to a judge or jury. **3** being submissive, obedience.

submissive *adjective* submitting to power or authority, willing to obey. **submissively** *adverb*, **submissiveness** *noun*

submit *verb* (**submitted, submitting**) **1** to yield (oneself) to the authority or control of another, to surrender. **2** to subject (a person or thing) to a process. **3** to present for consideration or decision. [from *sub-*, + Latin *mittere* = send]

subnormal *adjective* **1** less than normal. **2** below the normal standard of intelligence.

subordinate (sŭ-**bor**-dĭ-năt) *adjective* **1** of lesser importance or rank. **2** working under the control or authority of another person. –subordinate (sŭ-**bor**-dĭ-năt) *noun* a person in a subordinate position. –subordinate (sŭ-**bor**-dĭ-nayt) *verb* to make subordinate, to treat as of lesser importance than something else. **subordination** *noun* [from *sub-*, + Latin *ordinare* = arrange]

suborn (sŭ-**born**) *verb* to induce (a person) by bribery or other means to commit perjury or some other unlawful act. **subornation** *noun*

subplot *noun* a subordinate plot in a play.

subpoena (sŭ-**pee**-nă) *noun* a writ commanding a person to appear in a lawcourt. –subpoena *verb* (**subpoenaed, subpoenaing**) to summon with a subpoena. [from Latin *sub poena* = under a penalty (because there is a punishment for not obeying)]

sub rosa *adjective* & *adverb* in confidence, in secrecy. [Latin, = under the rose, which was an emblem of secrecy]

subroutine *noun* a self-contained section of a computer program.

subscribe *verb* **1** to contribute (a sum of money); *subscribe to a periodical*, pay in advance for a series of issues. **2** to sign, *subscribe one's name*; *subscribe a document*. **3** to express one's agreement, *we cannot subscribe to this theory*. [from *sub-*, + Latin *scribere* = write]

subscriber *noun* **1** a person who subscribes. **2** one who rents a telephone. □ **subscriber trunk dialling** a system of dialling numbers in trunk calls instead of asking an operator to obtain these.

subscript *adjective* written or printed below the level of a letter etc. (e.g. 2 in H_2O).

subscription *noun* **1** subscribing. **2** money subscribed. **3** a fee for membership of a society etc.

subsection *noun* a division of a section.

subsequent *adjective* **1** following in time or order or succession, coming after. **2** (of a stream) flowing in the direction in which the land slopes after its surface has been eroded (contrasted with *consequent* = flowing in the original direction). **subsequently** *adverb* [from *sub-*, + Latin *sequens* = following]

subservient *adjective* **1** subordinate. **2** servile, obsequious. **subservience** *noun* [from *sub-*, + Latin *serviens* = serving]

subset *noun* (in mathematics) a set contained within a larger one.

subside *verb* **1** to sink to a lower or to the normal level. **2** (of land) to sink, e.g. because of mining operations underneath. **3** to become less active or intense, *the excitement subsided*. **4** (of a person) to sink into a chair etc. **subsidence** (sŭb-**sy**-dĕns *or* **sub**-sĭ-dĕns) *noun* [from *sub-*, + Latin *sidere* = settle]

subsidiary *adjective* **1** of secondary importance. **2** (of a business company) controlled by another. **–subsidiary** *noun* a subsidiary thing. [same origin as *subsidy*]

subsidise *verb* (also **-ize**) to pay a subsidy to or for; to support by subsidies.

subsidy *noun* a grant of money paid to an industry or other cause needing help, or to keep down the price at which commodities etc. are sold to the public. [from Latin *subsidium* = assistance]

subsist *verb* to exist or continue to exist; to keep oneself alive, *they managed to subsist on a diet of vegetables*. [from Latin *subsistere* = stand firm]

subsistence *noun* subsisting; a means of doing this. □ **subsistence farming** farming in which almost all the crops etc. are consumed by the farmer's household. **subsistence level** merely enough to supply the bare necessities of life.

subsoil *noun* soil lying immediately beneath the surface layer.

subsonic *adjective* (of speed) less than the speed of sound; (of aircraft) flying at subsonic speeds, not supersonic. **subsonically** *adverb*

substance *noun* **1** matter with more or less uniform properties; a particular kind of this. **2** the essence of something spoken or written, *we agree with the substance of this argument*. **3** reality, solidity. **4** (*old use*) wealth and possessions, *waste one's substance*. **5** an intoxicating or narcotic chemical or drug, *substance abuse*. [from Latin *substantia* = essence]

substandard *adjective* below the usual or required standard.

substantial *adjective* **1** of solid material or structure. **2** of considerable amount, intensity, or validity, *a substantial fee*; *substantial reasons*. **3** possessing much property or wealth, *substantial farmers*. **4** in essentials, virtual, *we are in substantial agreement*. **substantially** *adverb*

substantiate (sŭb-**stan**-shee-ayt) *verb* to support (a statement or claim etc.) with evidence, to prove. **substantiation** *noun*

substantive (**sub**-stăn-tiv) *adjective* (also sŭb-**stan**-tiv) (of military rank) permanent, not temporary. **–substantive** *noun* a noun.

substation *noun* a subordinate station, e.g. for the distribution of electric current.

substitute *noun* a person or thing that acts or serves in place of another. **–substitute** *verb* **1** to put or use as a substitute. **2** (*informal*) to serve as a substitute. **substitution** *noun* [from *sub-*, + Latin *statuere* = to set up]

substratum (sub-**strah**-tŭm) *noun* (*plural* **substrata**) an underlying layer or substance.

substructure *noun* an underlying or supporting structure.

subsume *verb* to bring or include under a particular rule or classification etc. [from *sub-*, + Latin *sumere* = take up]

subtenant *noun* a person who rents accommodation etc. from one who holds it by lease not freehold. **subtenancy** *noun*

subtend *verb* (of a line or arc) to form (an angle) at a point where lines drawn from each end of it meet. [from *sub-*, + Latin *tendere* = to stretch]

subterfuge (**sub**-ter-fewj) *noun* a trick or excuse used in order to avoid blame or defeat, trickery.

subterranean (sub-tĕ-**rayn**-ee-ăn) *adjective* underground. [from *sub-*, + Latin *terra* = ground]

subtext *noun* an underlying theme or message in writing or speech.

subtitle *noun* 1 a subordinate title. 2 a caption on a cinema film, showing the dialogue etc. of a silent film or translating that of a foreign one. –**subtitle** *verb* to provide with a subtitle.

subtle (**sut**'l) *adjective* 1 slight and difficult to detect or analyse. 2 making or able to make fine distinctions, having acute perception, *a subtle mind*. 3 ingenious, crafty. **subtly** *adverb*, **subtlety** (**sut**'l-tee) *noun*

subtotal *noun* the total of part of a group of figures.

subtract *verb* to deduct, to remove (a part, quantity, or number) from a greater one. **subtraction** *noun* [from *sub-*, + Latin *tractum* = pulled]

subtropical *adjective* of regions bordering on the tropics.

suburb *noun* a residential district lying outside the central part of a town. **suburban** *adjective* [from *sub-*, + Latin *urbs* = city]

subvention (sŭb-**ven**-shŏn) *noun* a subsidy. [from Latin *subvenire* = assist]

subversion *noun* subverting.

subversive *adjective* tending to subvert.

subvert (sŭb-**vert**) *verb* to overthrow the authority of (a religion or government etc.) by weakening people's trust or belief. [from *sub-*, + Latin *vertere* = to turn]

subway *noun* an underground passage, e.g. for pedestrians to cross below a road or for a railway.

subwoofer *noun* a loudspeaker component designed to reproduce very low bass frequencies.

subzero *adjective* (of temperatures) below zero.

suc- *prefix* see **sub-**.

succeed *verb* 1 to be successful. 2 to come next to in time or order, to follow, to take the place previously filled by. [from *suc-*, + Latin *cedere* = go]

success *noun* 1 a favourable outcome; doing what was desired or attempted; the attainment of wealth, fame, or position. 2 a person or thing that is successful.

successful *adjective* having success. **successfully** *adverb*

succession *noun* 1 following in order; a series of people or things following each other. 2 succeeding to the throne or to an inheritance or position; the right of doing this; the sequence of people with this right. 3 the sequence of plant and animal communities that replace one another in an area. □ **in succession** one after another.

successive *adjective* following one after another, in an unbroken series. **successively** *adverb*

successor *noun* a person or thing that succeeds another.

succinct (sŭk-**sinkt**) *adjective* concise, expressed briefly and clearly. **succinctly** *adverb*, **succinctness** *noun* [from Latin *succinctum* = tucked up]

Succoth (**suk**-ŏth) *noun* the Jewish festival of thanksgiving (the Feast of Tabernacles), commemorating the time when they sheltered in the wilderness. [from Hebrew]

succour (**suk**-er) *noun* (*literary*) help given in time of need. –**succour** *verb* (*literary*) to give such help. [from Latin *succurrere* = run to a person's aid]

succulent (**suk**-yŭ-lĕnt) *adjective* 1 juicy. 2 (of plants) having thick fleshy leaves or stems. –**succulent** *noun* a succulent plant.

succumb (sŭ-**kum**) *verb* to give way to something overpowering. [from *suc-*, + Latin *cumbere* = to lie]

such *adjective* 1 of the same kind or degree, *people such as these*. 2 of the kind or degree described, *there's no such person*. 3 so great or intense, *it gave her such a fright*. –**such** *pronoun* that, the action or thing referred to, *such being the case, we can do nothing*. □ **as such** as what has been specified, in itself, *interested in getting a good photo, not the bridge as such*. **such-and-such** *adjective* particular but not now specified, *says he will arrive at such-and-such a time but is always late*.

suchlike *adjective* (*informal*) of the same kind.

suck *verb* 1 to draw (liquid or air etc.) into the mouth by using the lip muscles; to draw liquid etc. from (a thing) in this way. 2 to squeeze in the mouth by using the tongue, *sucking a toffee*. 3 to draw in, *plants suck moisture from the soil*; *the canoe was sucked into the whirlpool*. 4 (*informal*) to be very bad, disgusting, etc., *uniform sucks*. –**suck** *noun* the act or process of sucking. □ **suck in** to absorb;

(*informal*) to involve (a person); (*informal*) to deceive, *sucked in by their sweet talk*. suck up to (*informal*) to toady to.

sucker *noun* 1 a person or thing that sucks. 2 an organ of certain animals, or a device of rubber etc., that can adhere to a surface by suction. 3 a shoot coming up from the roots or underground stem of a tree or shrub. 4 (*informal*) a person who is easily deceived.

sucking *adjective* (of a child or animal) not yet weaned.

suckle *verb* 1 to feed (young) at the breast or udder. 2 (of young) to take milk in this way.

suckling *noun* a child or animal that is not yet weaned.

Sucre (**soo**-kray) the legal capital and seat of the judiciary of Bolivia.

sucrose (**soo**-krohz) *noun* sugar obtained from plants such as sugar cane or sugar beet. [from French *sucre* = sugar]

suction *noun* 1 sucking. 2 production of a partial or complete vacuum so that external atmospheric pressure forces fluid or other substance into the vacant space or causes adhesion of surfaces, *vacuum cleaners work by suction*.

Sudan (soo-**dahn**) a republic in north-east Africa. Sudanese (soo-dă-**neez**) *adjective* & *noun* (*plural* Sudanese).

sudden *adjective* happening or done quickly, unexpectedly, or without warning. □ all of a sudden suddenly. sudden death (*informal*) decision of a drawn or tied contest by the result of the next game or point. sudden infant death syndrome the unexplained death of a baby in its sleep (abbreviation SIDS). suddenly *adverb*, suddenness *noun*

sudoku *noun* a number puzzle in which players insert numbers into a grid consisting of nine squares subdivided into a further nine squares. [from Japanese *su* number + *doku* place]

Sudra (**soo**-dră) *noun* a member of the lowest of the four great Hindu classes, the worker class. [Sanskrit]

suds *plural noun* soapsuds. sudsy *adjective*

sue *verb* (sued, suing) 1 to begin legal proceedings against. 2 to make an application, *sue for peace*.

suede (*pr.* swayd) *noun* 1 leather with the flesh side rubbed so that it has a velvety nap. 2 (also suede cloth) a woven fabric

resembling suede. [from *Suède*, the French name for Sweden, where it was first made]

suet *noun* hard fat from round the kidneys of cattle and sheep, used in cooking.

Suez an isthmus connecting Egypt to the Sinai peninsula, site of the Suez Canal, a canal connecting the Mediterranean with the Red Sea.

suf- *prefix* see sub-.

suffer *verb* 1 to undergo or be subjected to (pain, loss, grief, damage, etc.). 2 to feel pain or grief; to be subjected to damage or a disadvantage. 3 to permit. 4 to tolerate. sufferer *noun*, suffering *noun* [from *suf-*, + Latin *ferre* = to bear]

sufferance *noun* on or under sufferance tolerated but only grudgingly or because there is no positive objection.

suffice (sŭ-**fys**) *verb* to be enough; to meet the needs of.

sufficient *adjective* enough. sufficiently *adverb*, sufficiency *noun*

suffix *noun* (*plural* suffixes) a letter or combination of letters added at the end of a word to make another word (e.g. *y* added to *rust* to make *rusty*) or as an inflexion (e.g. *ing* added to *suck* to make *sucking*). [from *suf-* + *fix*]

suffocate *verb* 1 to kill by stopping the breathing. 2 to cause discomfort to (a person) by making breathing difficult. 3 to be suffocated. suffocation *noun* [from *suf-*, + Latin *fauces* = throat]

suffrage (**suf**-rij) *noun* the right to vote in political elections. [from Latin, = vote]

suffragette (suf-ră-**jet**) *noun* a woman who, in the early 20th century, agitated for women to have the suffrage.

suffragist *noun* a person who favours giving the suffrage to more people or groups (e.g. women or young people).

suffuse (sŭ-**fewz**) *verb* (of colour or moisture) to spread throughout or over. suffusion *noun* [from *suf-*, + Latin *fusum* = poured]

Sufi (**soo**-fee) *noun* a Muslim ascetic and mystic. Sufic *adjective*, Sufism *noun*

sugar *noun* a sweet crystalline substance obtained from the juices of various plants. –sugar *verb* to sweeten with sugar; to coat with sugar. □ sugar bag (*Austral.*) wild honey. sugar beet the kind of beet from which sugar is extracted. sugar cane a tropical grass with tall jointed stems from which sugar is obtained. sugar loaf a solid cone-shaped mass of sugar, as sold in former times. sugar soap an abrasive compound for cleaning or removing paint. [from Arabic *sukkar*]

sugary *adjective* 1 containing or resembling sugar. 2 sweet, excessively sweet in style or manner. sugariness *noun*

suggest *verb* 1 to cause (an idea or possibility) to be present in the mind. 2 to propose (a plan or theory) for acceptance or rejection.

suggestible *adjective* 1 easily influenced by people's suggestions. 2 that may be suggested. suggestibility *noun*

suggestion *noun* 1 suggesting; being suggested. 2 something suggested. 3 a slight trace, *a suggestion of a French accent*.

suggestive *adjective* 1 conveying a suggestion. 2 tending to convey an indecent or improper meaning. suggestively *adverb*, suggestiveness *noun*

suicidal *adjective* 1 of suicide. 2 (of a person) liable to commit suicide. 3 destructive to one's own interests. suicidally *adverb*

suicide *noun* 1 the intentional killing of oneself; an instance of this. 2 a person who commits suicide. 3 an act that is destructive to one's own interests; *political suicide*, ruination of one's own or one's party's political prospects. –suicide *verb* to commit suicide. □ commit suicide to kill oneself intentionally. [from Latin *sui* = of yourself, + *caedere* = kill]

suit *noun* 1 a set of clothing to be worn together, especially a jacket and trousers or skirt. 2 clothing for use in a particular activity, *a bathing suit*. 3 a set of armour. 4 any of the four sets (spades, hearts, diamonds, clubs) into which a pack of cards is divided. 5 a lawsuit. 6 (*formal*) a request or appeal; *press one's suit*, to request persistently. –suit *verb* 1 to satisfy, to meet the demands or needs of. 2 to be convenient or right for. 3 to give a pleasing appearance or effect upon, *red doesn't suit her*. 4 to adapt, to make suitable, *suit your style to your audience*.

suitable *adjective* right for the purpose or occasion. suitably *adverb*, suitability *noun*

suitcase *noun* a rectangular case for carrying clothes, usually with a hinged lid and a handle.

suite *noun* 1 a set of rooms or furniture. 2 a set of attendants, a retinue. 3 a set of musical pieces or extracts.

suiting *noun* material for making suits.

suitor *noun* 1 a man who is courting a woman. 2 a person bringing a lawsuit. [from Latin *secutor* = follower]

Sukhumi (sü-**koo**-mee) the capital of Abkhazia.

Sulawesi (suul-ă-**way**-see) a large island of Indonesia, east of Borneo, formerly called Celebes.

sulcus *noun* (*plural* sulci, *pr.* **sul**-sy) a groove or furrow. [Latin]

sulfa, sulfur, etc. *see* sulpha, sulphur, etc..

sulk *verb* to be sulky. sulks *plural noun* a fit of sulkiness.

sulky *adjective* (sulkier, sulkiest) sullen, silent or aloof because of resentment or bad temper. sulkily *adverb*, sulkiness *noun*

sullen *adjective* 1 gloomy and unresponsive from resentment or bad temper. 2 dark and dismal, *sullen skies*. sullenly *adverb*, sullenness *noun*

Sullivan, Sir Arthur (1842–1900), English composer, noted for the comic operas produced with W. S. Gilbert.

sully *verb* (sullied, sullying) to stain or blemish, to spoil the purity or splendour of, *sullied his reputation*.

sulpha *adjective* sulphonamide, *sulpha drugs*.

sulphate *noun* a salt of sulphuric acid.

sulphonamide (sul-**fon**-ă-myd) *noun* any of a group of chemical compounds with antibacterial properties.

sulphur *noun* (also sulfur) a chemical element (symbol S), a pale yellow substance that burns with a blue flame and a stifling smell, used in industry and medicine. □ sulphur dioxide a colourless pungent toxic gas, used as a food preservative.

Usage In general use the standard Australian spelling is *sulphur* and the standard US spelling is *sulfur*. In science, however, *sulfur* is now the standard form in all related words in the field in Australian and US contexts.

---

sulphuretted *adjective* containing sulphur in combination with another substance.

sulphuric (sul-**few**-rik) *adjective* containing a proportion of sulphur. □ sulphuric acid a strong corrosive acid.

sulphurous (**sul**-few-rŭs) *adjective* 1 of or like sulphur. 2 containing a proportion of sulphur.

sultan *noun* the ruler of certain Muslim countries. [from Arabic, = ruler]

sultana *noun* **1** a seedless raisin; *sultana grape*, the small yellow grape from which it is produced. **2** the wife, mother, sister, or daughter of a sultan.

sultanate *noun* the territory of a sultan.

sultry *adjective* (**sultrier, sultriest**) **1** hot and humid. **2** (of a woman) passionate and sensual. **sultriness** *noun*

sum *noun* **1** a total. **2** a particular amount of money, *for the sum of $50*. **3** a problem in arithmetic, *good at sums*. –**sum** *verb* (**summed, summing**) to find the sum of. □ **in sum** briefly, in summary. **sum total** a total. **sum up** to give the total of; to summarise; (of a judge) to summarise the evidence or argument; to form an opinion of, *sum a person up*. [from Latin *summa* = main thing]

sum- *prefix* see **sub-**.

Sumatra (sŭ-**mah**-trǎ) a large island of Indonesia, separated from the Malay Peninsula by the Strait of Malacca.

Sumerian (soo-**meer**-ree-ǎn) *noun* a member of an ancient people of southern Mesopotamia (Sumer) in the 4th millennium BC.

summarise *verb* (also **-ize**) to make or be a summary of. **summariser** *noun*

summary *noun* a statement giving the main points of something briefly. –**summary** *adjective* **1** brief, giving the main points only, *a summary account*. **2** done or given without delay or attention to detail or formal procedure, *summary dismissal*. **summarily** *adverb* [same origin as *sum*]

summation (sum-**ay**-shŏn) *noun* finding of a total or sum; summing up.

summer *noun* the warmest season of the year, from December to February in the southern hemisphere. □ **summer house** a light building in a garden or park, providing shade in summer.

summertime *noun* the season of summer.

summery *adjective* like summer; suitable for summer.

summit *noun* **1** the highest point of something; the top of a mountain. **2** a **summit conference**, a meeting between heads of two or more governments. [from Latin *summus* = highest]

summon *verb* **1** to send for (a person); to order to appear in a lawcourt. **2** to call

together, to order to assemble, *summon a meeting*. **3** to gather together (one's strength or courage) in order to do something. **4** to call upon (a person etc.) to do something, *summon the fort to surrender*. [from *sum-*, + Latin *monere* = warn]

summons *noun* **1** a command to do something or appear somewhere. **2** an order to appear in a lawcourt; a document containing this. –**summons** *verb* to serve with a summons.

sumo (**soo**-moh) *noun* a kind of Japanese wrestling.

sump *noun* **1** an inner casing holding lubricating oil in a petrol engine. **2** a hole or low area into which waste liquid drains.

sumptuous *adjective* splendid and costly-looking. **sumptuously** *adverb*, **sumptuousness** *noun* [from Latin *sumptus* = cost]

sun *noun* **1** the star round which the earth travels and from which it receives light and warmth. **2** this light or warmth, *let the sun in*. **3** any fixed star with or without planets. –**sun** *verb* (**sunned, sunning**) to expose to the sun; *sun oneself*, to bask in sunshine. □ **sun god** the sun worshipped as a god. **Sun King** Louis XIV of France. **sun-up** *noun* sunrise.

sunbathe *verb* to expose one's body to the sun.

sunbeam *noun* a ray of sun.

sunblock *noun* = sunscreen.

sunburn *noun* reddening or inflammation of the skin caused by exposure to sun. **sunburnt** *adjective*

sundae (**sun**-day) *noun* a dish of ice cream and fruit, nuts, syrup, etc.

Sunday *noun* **1** the first day of the week, observed by Christians as a day of rest and worship. **2** a newspaper published on Sundays. □ **Sunday school** a school for religious instruction of children, held on Sundays. [from Old English *sunnandaeg* = day of the sun]

sunder *verb* to break or tear apart, to sever.

sundew *noun* a small bog plant with hairs secreting moisture that traps insects.

sundial *noun* a device that shows the time by means of the shadow of a rod or plate on a scaled dial.

sundown *noun* sunset.

sundowner *noun* (*Austral.*) a swagman arriving at sundown, too late to work for his meal.

sundry *adjective* various, several. sundries *plural noun* various small items not named individually. □ all and sundry everyone.

sunfish *noun* a large ocean fish with an almost spherical body.

sunflower *noun* a tall garden plant bearing large flowers with golden petals round a dark centre, producing seeds that yield an edible oil.

sung *see* sing.

sunglasses *plural noun* spectacles with tinted lenses to protect the eyes from sunlight or glare.

sunhat *noun* a hat worn to protect the head from sun.

sunk *see* sink. – sunk, sunken *adjectives* lying below the level of the surrounding area. □ sunk fence a ditch strengthened by a wall, forming a boundary without interrupting the view.

sunlamp *noun* a lamp producing ultraviolet rays, with effects like those of the sun.

sunless *adjective* without sunshine.

sunlight *noun* light from the sun.

sunlit *adjective* lit by sunlight.

Sunna *noun* a traditional portion of Islamic law based on Muhammad's words or acts, accepted (together with the Koran) as authoritative by Muslims.

Sunni *noun* 1 one of the two main branches of Islam, commonly described as orthodox, and differing from the Shia in its understanding of the Sunna and in its rejection of Ali as Muhammad's first successor. 2 an adherent of this branch of Islam. – Sunni *adjective* (also Sunnite) of or relating to Sunni. [Arabic]

sunny *adjective* (sunnier, sunniest) 1 bright with sunlight, full of sunshine. 2 (of a person or mood) cheerful. □ the sunny side the more cheerful aspect of circumstances. sunnily *adverb*

sunrise *noun* the rising of the sun; the time of this. □ sunrise industry a new and expanding industry.

sunroof *noun* a panel in the roof of a car, opened to admit fresh air and sunlight.

sunscreen *noun* a cream or lotion used to protect the skin from the sun's harmful ultraviolet rays.

sunset *noun* 1 the setting of the sun; the time of this. 2 the western sky full of colour at sunset.

sunshade *noun* 1 a parasol. 2 an awning.

sunshine *noun* direct sunlight uninterrupted by cloud.

Sunshine Coast a strip of the Queensland coast approximately 100 km north of Brisbane.

sunspot *noun* 1 one of the dark patches sometimes observed on the sun's surface. 2 (*informal*) a place with a sunny climate. 3 an area of skin damage caused by exposure to the sun.

sunstroke *noun* illness caused by too much exposure to sun.

suntan *noun* the brownish colouring of skin caused by exposure to the sun. – suntan *verb* to colour the skin with a suntan.

sup *verb* (supped, supping) 1 to take (liquid) by sips or spoonfuls. 2 to eat supper. – sup *noun* a mouthful of liquid, *neither bite nor sup*.

sup- *prefix* see sub-.

super *noun* (*informal*) 1 high-octane petrol. 2 superannuation. 3 superphosphate. 4 a superintendent. 5 a supernumerary actor. – super *adjective* (*informal*) excellent, superb.

super- *prefix* 1 over, beyond (as in *superimpose*, *superhuman*). 2 of greater size etc. (as in *supermarket*). 3 extremely (as in *superabundant*). 4 beyond (as in *supernatural*). [from Latin *super* = over]

superabundant *adjective* very abundant, more than enough. superabundance *noun*

superannuant *noun* (*Austral.*) a recipient of a superannuation pension.

superannuate *verb* 1 to discharge (an employee) into retirement with a pension. 2 to discard as too old for use.

superannuation *noun* 1 superannuating. 2 a pension granted to an employee on retirement; payment(s) contributed towards this during employment. [from *super-*, + Latin *annus* = a year]

superb *adjective* of the most impressive or splendid kind, excellent. superbly *adverb* [from Latin *superbus* = proud]

supercharge *verb* to increase the power of (an engine) by using a device that supplies air or fuel at above the normal pressure. supercharger *noun*

supercilious (soo-per-**sil**-ee-ŭs) *adjective* with an air of superiority, haughty and scornful. **superciliously** *adverb*, **superciliousness** *noun* [from Latin *supercilium* = eyebrow]

superconductivity *noun* the property of certain metals, at temperatures near absolute zero, of having no electrical resistance, so that once a current is started it flows without a voltage to keep it going. **superconductive** *adjective*, **superconductor** *noun*

supercontinent *noun* a large land mass thought to have divided to form the present continents.

supercool *verb* to cool (a liquid) below its freezing point without its becoming solid or crystalline.

superego (soo-per-**ee**-goh) *noun* a person's ideals for himself or herself, acting like a conscience in directing his or her behaviour.

supererogation (soo-per-e-rŏ-**gay**-shŏn) *noun* the doing of more than is required by duty, *works of supererogation*. [from *super-*, + Latin *erogare* = pay out]

superficial *adjective* 1 of or on the surface, not deep or penetrating, *a superficial wound*; *superficial knowledge*, not thorough or penetrating. 2 (of a person) having no depth of character or feeling. **superficially** *adverb*, **superficiality** (soo-per-fish-ee-**al**-ĭ-tee) *noun* [from *super-*, + Latin *facies* = face]

superfine *adjective* 1 of extra quality. 2 extra fine.

superfluity (soo-per-**floo**-ĭ-tee) *noun* a superfluous amount.

superfluous (soo-**per**-floo-ŭs) *adjective* more than is required. **superfluously** *adverb* [from *super-*, + Latin *fluere* = flow]

superheat *verb* to heat (liquid) above its boiling point without allowing it to vaporise; to heat (vapour) above boiling point.

superhuman *adjective* 1 beyond ordinary human capacity or power. 2 higher than humanity, divine.

superimpose *verb* to lay or place (a thing) on top of something else. **superimposition** *noun*

superintend *verb* to supervise. **superintendence** *noun*

superintendent *noun* 1 a person who superintends. 2 a senior police officer.

superior *adjective* 1 higher in position or rank. 2 better or greater in some way; of high or higher quality. 3 showing that one feels oneself to be better or wiser etc. than others, conceited, supercilious. 4 not influenced by, not giving way to, *she is superior to flattery*. –**superior** *noun* 1 a person or thing of higher rank, ability, or quality. 2 the head of a monastery or other religious community. **superiority** *noun* [Latin, = higher]

superlative (soo-**per**-lă-tiv) *adjective* 1 of the highest degree or quality, *a man of superlative wisdom*. 2 of a grammatical form that expresses the highest or a very high degree of quality, e.g. *dearest, shyest, best*. –**superlative** *noun* a superlative form of a word. **superlatively** *adverb* [from Latin *superlatum* = carried above]

superman *noun* (*plural* **supermen**) a man of superhuman powers.

supermarket *noun* a large self-service shop selling groceries and household goods.

supernatural *adjective* of or caused by power above the forces of nature. **supernaturally** *adverb*

supernova *noun* (*plural* **supernovae**) a star that suddenly increases very greatly in brightness because of an explosion disrupting its structure.

supernumerary (soo-per-**new**-mĕ-ră-ree) *adjective* in excess of the normal number, extra. –**supernumerary** *noun* a supernumerary person or thing.

superphosphate *noun* a fertiliser containing soluble phosphates.

superpose *verb* to place (a geometrical figure) upon another so that their outlines coincide. **superposition** *noun* [from *super-*, + Latin *positum* = placed]

superpower *noun* one of the most powerful nations of the world.

superscribe *verb* to write (a word or words) at the top of or outside a document etc. [from *super-*, + Latin *scribere* = write]

superscript *adjective* written or printed just above and to the right of a word, figure, or symbol (e.g. 2 in $3^2 = 9$).

superscription *noun* a word or words written at the top or on the outside.

supersede (soo-per-**seed**) *verb* 1 to take the place of, *cars have superseded horse-drawn carriages*. 2 to put or use in place of (another person or thing). [from *super-*, + Latin *sedere* = sit]

supersonic *adjective* of or having a speed greater than that of sound.

superstar *noun* a great star in entertainment etc.

superstition *noun* **1** belief that events can be influenced by certain acts or circumstances that have no demonstrable connection with them; an idea or practice based on this. **2** a belief that is held by a number of people but without foundation.

superstitious *adjective* based on or influenced by superstition. **superstitiously** *adverb*, **superstitiousness** *noun*

superstore *noun* a large supermarket.

superstructure *noun* a structure that rests upon something else; a building as distinct from its foundations.

supertanker *noun* a very large tanker.

supertonic *noun* (in music) the second note of a major or minor scale.

supervene (soo-per-**veen**) *verb* to occur as an interruption or a change from some condition or process. **supervention** (soo-per-**ven**-shŏn) *noun* [from *super-*, + Latin *venire* = come]

supervise *verb* to direct and inspect (work or workers or the operation of an organisation). **supervision** *noun*, **supervisor** *noun*, **supervisory** *adjective* [from *super-*, + Latin *visum* = seen]

supine (**soo**-pyn) *adjective* **1** lying face upwards (contrasted with *prone*). **2** not inclined to take action, indolent. –**supine** *noun* a verbal noun in Latin with only two cases, an accusative ending in *-um* and an ablative ending in *-u*. **supinely** *adverb*

supper *noun* an evening meal or snack, the last meal of the day.

supplant *verb* to oust and take the place of.

supple *adjective* bending easily, flexible, not stiff. **supplely** *adverb*, **suppleness** *noun*

supplejack *noun* a climbing or twining shrub.

supplement (**sup**-lĕ-mĕnt) *noun* **1** a thing added as an extra or to make up for a deficiency. **2** a part added to a book etc. to give further information or to treat a particular subject; a set of special pages issued with a newspaper. –**supplement** (**sup**-lĕ-ment) *verb* to provide or be a supplement to.
□ **supplement of an angle** another angle that when added to the first makes 180° (compare *complement*). **supplemental** *adjective*, **supplementation** *noun* [same origin as *supply*]

supplementary *adjective* serving as a supplement. –**supplementary** *noun* (*informal*) a supplementary examination.
□ **supplementary angles** angles which add up to 180°.

suppliant (**sup**-lee-ănt) *noun* a person asking humbly for something.

supplicate *verb* to ask humbly for, to beseech. **supplication** *noun* [from Latin, = kneel]

supplier *noun* one who supplies something.

supply *verb* (**supplied**, **supplying**) **1** to give or provide with (something needed or useful); to make available for use. **2** to make up for, to satisfy, *supply a need*. –**supply** *noun* **1** providing of what is needed. **2** a stock or store; an amount of something provided or available, *the water supply; an inexhaustible supply of fish*. [from *sup-*, + Latin *-plere* = fill]

support *verb* **1** to keep from falling or sinking, to hold in position, to bear the weight of. **2** to give strength to, to enable to last or continue, *too little food to support life*. **3** to supply with necessaries, *he has a family to support*. **4** to assist by one's approval or presence or by subscription to funds; to be a fan of (a particular sports team); *support a resolution*, speak or vote in favour of it. **5** to take a secondary part, *the play has a strong supporting cast*. **6** to corroborate, to bring facts to confirm (a statement etc.). **7** to endure or tolerate, *we cannot support such insolence*. –**support** *noun* **1** supporting, being supported, *we need your support*. **2** a person or thing that supports. **supporter** *noun* [from *sup-*, + Latin *portare* = carry]

supportive *adjective* providing support and encouragement.

suppose *verb* **1** to be inclined to think, to accept as true or probable, *I don't suppose they will come*. **2** to assume as true for the purpose of argument, *suppose the world were flat*. **3** to consider as a proposal, *suppose we try another*. **4** to require as a condition, to presuppose, *that supposes a mechanism without flaws*. □ **be supposed to** to be expected or intended to; to have as a duty.

supposed *adjective* believed to exist or to have a certain character or identity, *his supposed brother*.

supposedly (sŭ-**poh**-zĕd-lee) *adverb* according to supposition.

supposition *noun* supposing, what is supposed, *the article is based on supposition not on fact*.

supposititious (sup-ŏ-**zish**-ŭs) *adjective* hypothetical, based on supposition.

suppository (sŭ-**poz**-ĭ-tŏ-ree) *noun* a medical preparation designed to be inserted in the rectum or vagina to dissolve.

suppress *verb* 1 to put an end to the activity or existence of, especially by force or authority, *suppress the rebellion*. 2 to keep from being known or seen, *suppress the truth*. **suppression** *noun*

suppressible *adjective* able to be suppressed.

suppressor *noun* a person or thing that suppresses; a device to suppress electrical interference.

suppurate (**sup**-yŭ-rayt) *verb* to form pus, to fester. **suppuration** *noun*

supra (**soo**-prǎ) *adverb* above or further back in the book etc. [Latin, = above]

supra- *prefix* above, over.

supranational *adjective* transcending national limits.

supremacy (soo-**prem**-ǎ-see) *noun* being supreme; the position of supreme authority or power.

supreme *adjective* 1 highest in authority or rank, *the supreme commander*. 2 highest in importance or intensity or quality, most outstanding, *supreme courage*; *the supreme sacrifice*, involving one's death (e.g. in war). 3 (of food) served in a rich cream sauce, *chicken supreme*. □ **Supreme Court** the highest court of law in an Australian State. **supremely** *adverb* [from Latin *supremus* = highest]

supremo *noun* (*plural* **supremos**) a supreme leader or ruler.

sur-¹ *prefix* see **sub-**.

sur-² *prefix* = super- (as in *surcharge*).

sura (**soor**-rǎ) *noun* a chapter or section of the Koran. [Arabic]

surcharge *noun* 1 payment demanded in addition to the usual charge. 2 an additional or excessive load. 3 a mark printed over a postage stamp, changing its value. –**surcharge** *verb* 1 to make a surcharge on; to charge extra. 2 to overload. 3 to print a surcharge on (a stamp).

surd *noun* a mathematical quantity (especially a root) that cannot be expressed in finite terms of whole numbers or quantities.

sure *adjective* 1 having or seeming to have sufficient reason for one's beliefs, free from doubts; *be sure of a person*, able to rely on him or her. 2 certain to do something or to happen, *the book is sure to be a success*. 3 undoubtedly true, *one thing is sure*. 4 reliable, secure, unfailing, *there's only one sure way*; *be sure to write*, do not fail to write. –**sure** *adverb* (*informal*) certainly, *it sure was cold*. □ **as sure as** as certainly as. **for sure** for certain. **make sure** to act so as to be certain; to ensure. **sure enough** certainly, in fact. **sure-fire** *adjective* (*informal*) certain to succeed. **sure-footed** *adjective* never slipping or stumbling. **to be sure** it is admitted, certainly, *she's not perfect, to be sure*. **sureness** *noun*

surely *adverb* 1 in a sure manner, without doubt; securely. 2 used for emphasis, *surely you won't desert us?* 3 (as an answer) certainly, *'Will you help?' 'Surely.'*

surety (**shoor**-rĕ-tee) *noun* 1 a guarantee. 2 a person who makes himself or herself responsible for another person's payment of a debt or performance of an undertaking.

surf *noun* 1 the swell of the sea breaking on the shore or reefs; the foam produced by this. 2 a swim in the surf, especially with the intention of riding waves; the riding of a wave. –**surf** *verb* 1 to ride the waves either on a surfboard, or by streamlining one's body and letting it be carried by the waves. 2 to explore the Internet by moving from site to site in search of information. **surfing** *noun*

surface *noun* 1 the outside of an object. 2 any of the sides of an object. 3 the uppermost area, the top of a table or desk etc., *a working surface*. 4 the top of a body of water. 5 the outward appearance of something; the qualities etc. perceived by casual observation (as distinct from deeper or hidden ones). –**surface** *adjective* of or on the surface only; of the surface of the earth or sea (as distinct from in the air or underground, or under water). –**surface** *verb* 1 to put a specified surface on. 2 to come or bring to the surface. 3 (*informal*) to wake after sleep or unconsciousness. □ **surface mail** mail carried by sea not by air. **surface tension** tension of the surface-film of a liquid, tending to make its surface area as small as possible.

surfboard *noun* a long narrow board used in surfing. **surfboarding** *noun*

surfeit (**ser**-fĭt) *noun* too much of something (especially food and drink); a feeling of discomfort arising from this. –**surfeit** *verb* to cause to take too much of something, to satiate, to cloy.

surfer *noun* (also **surfie**) a person who goes surfing.

Surfers Paradise a tourist resort on the Gold Coast, Queensland.

surge *verb* to move forward in or like waves; to increase in volume or intensity. –**surge** *noun* a wave; a surging movement or increase, an onrush. [from Latin *surgere* = rise]

surgeon *noun* a medical practitioner who performs surgical operations.

surgery *noun* 1 the treatment of injuries and disorders and disease by cutting or manipulation of the affected parts. 2 the place where a doctor or dentist etc. gives advice and treatment to patients. 3 the hours during which a doctor etc. is available to patients at a surgery. [from Greek, = handiwork]

surgical *adjective* of surgery or surgeons; used in surgery. □ **surgical spirit** methylated spirits used in surgery for cleansing etc. **surgically** *adverb*

Suriname (soo-rĭ-**nam**) (also **Surinam**) a republic on the north coast of South America. **Surinamer** *noun*, **Surinamese** *adjective* & *noun* (*plural* **Surinamese**).

surly *adjective* (**surlier**, **surliest**) bad-tempered and unfriendly. **surlily** *adverb*, **surliness** *noun*

surmise (ser-**myz**) *noun* a conjecture. –**surmise** *verb* to conjecture.

surmount *verb* to overcome (a difficulty); to get over (an obstacle). □ **be surmounted by** to have on or over the top, *the spire is surmounted by a weathervane.*

surmountable *adjective* able to be overcome.

surname *noun* the name held by all members of a family, as distinct from a first or Christian name. –**surname** *verb* to give as a surname.

surpass *verb* to do or be better than, to excel.

surpassing *adjective* greatly excelling or exceeding others. **surpassingly** *adverb*

surplice (ser-plĭs) *noun* a loose white vestment with full sleeves, worn over the cassock by clergy and choir at a religious service.

surplus (ser-plŭs) *noun* an amount left over after what is required has been used, especially an excess of public revenue over expenditure during a financial year.

surprise *noun* 1 the emotion aroused by something sudden or unexpected. 2 an event or thing that arouses this emotion. 3 the process of catching a person etc. unprepared; *a surprise attack* or *visit*, one made unexpectedly. –**surprise** *verb* 1 to cause to feel surprise. 2 to come upon or attack suddenly and without warning; to capture in this way. 3 to startle (a person) into action by catching him or her unprepared. 4 to discover (a secret etc.) by unexpected action.

surprised *adjective* experiencing surprise. □ **be surprised at** to be scandalised or shocked by, *we are surprised at your behaviour*.

surprising *adjective* causing surprise. **surprisingly** *adverb*

surrealism (sŭ-**ree**-ă-lizm) *noun* a 20th-century movement in art and literature that seeks to express what is in the unconscious mind by depicting objects and events as seen in dreams etc. **surrealist** *noun*, **surrealistic** *adjective* [from *sur-²* + *real*]

surrender *verb* 1 to hand over, to give into another person's power or control, especially on demand or under compulsion. 2 to give oneself up, to accept an enemy's demand for submission; *surrender to one's bail*, to appear duly in a lawcourt after being released on bail. 3 to give way to an emotion, *surrendered herself to grief*. 4 to give up one's rights under (an insurance policy) in return for a smaller sum payable immediately. –**surrender** *noun* surrendering; being surrendered. [from *sur-²* + *render*]

surreptitious (su-rĕp-**tish**-ŭs) *adjective* acting or done stealthily. **surreptitiously** *adverb* [from Latin, = seized secretly]

surrogate (**su**-rŏ-găt) *noun* a deputy. □ **surrogate mother** a woman who bears a child on behalf of another. **surrogacy** *noun*

surround *verb* 1 to come or lie or be all round. 2 to place all round; to encircle with enemy forces. –**surround** *noun* a border or edging; a floor covering between carpet and walls. □ **be surrounded by** or **with** to have on all sides.

surroundings *plural noun* the things or conditions around and liable to affect a person or place.

surtax *noun* an additional tax, especially on income over a certain amount.

surtitle *noun* a caption projected on to a screen above the stage, translating opera text as it is being sung.

surveillance (ser-**vay**-lăns) *noun* supervision or close observation, especially of a suspected person.

survey (ser-**vay**) *verb* **1** to look at and take a general view of. **2** to make or present a survey of, *the report surveys progress made in the past year*. **3** to examine the condition of (a building etc.). **4** to measure and map out the size, shape, position, and elevation etc. of (an area of the earth's surface). –**survey** (**ser**-vay) *noun* **1** a general look at something. **2** a general examination of a situation or subject; an account of this. **3** the surveying of land etc.; a map or plan produced by this. [from *sur-²*, + Latin *videre* = see]

surveyor *noun* a person whose job is to survey land or buildings.

survival *noun* **1** surviving. **2** something that has survived from an earlier time.

survive *verb* **1** to continue to live or exist. **2** to live or exist longer than; to remain alive or in existence after, *few flowers survived the frost*. [from *sur-²*, + Latin *vivere* = to live]

survivor *noun* one who survives; one who survives another.

sus = suss.

sus- *prefix* see sub-.

Susanna a book of the Apocrypha telling of the false accusation of adultery brought against Susanna by two elders.

susceptible (sŭ-**sep**-tĭ-bŭl) *adjective* **1** liable to be affected by something; *susceptible to colds*, catching colds easily. **2** impressionable, falling in love easily. **3** able to undergo something; *susceptible of proof*, able to be proved. **susceptibly** *adverb* [from Latin *susceptum* = caught up]

susceptibility *noun* being susceptible. **susceptibilities** *plural noun* a person's feelings that may be hurt or offended.

susceptive (sŭ-**sep**-tiv) *adjective* susceptible.

suspect (sŭ-**spekt**) *verb* **1** to have an impression of the existence or presence of, *we suspected a trap*. **2** to have suspicions or doubts about, to mistrust, *we suspect their motives*. **3** to feel that (a person) is guilty but have little or no proof. –**suspect** (**sus**-pekt) *noun* a person who is suspected of a crime etc. –**suspect** (**sus**-pekt) *adjective* suspected, open to suspicion.

suspend *verb* **1** to hang up. **2** to keep from falling or sinking in air or liquid etc., *particles are suspended in the fluid*. **3** to postpone,

suspend judgment. **4** to put a temporary stop to. **5** to deprive temporarily of a position or a right. □ **suspended sentence** sentence of imprisonment that is not enforced subject to good behaviour. **suspend payment** (of a business company) to cease paying any of its debts when it recognises that it is insolvent and unable to pay them all. [from *sus-*, + Latin *pendere* = hang]

suspender *noun* an attachment to hold up a sock or stocking by its top. □ **suspender belt** a woman's undergarment with suspenders for holding up stockings.

suspense *noun* a state or feeling of anxious uncertainty while awaiting news or an event etc.

suspension *noun* **1** suspending; being suspended. **2** the means by which a vehicle is supported on its axles. **3** a substance consisting of a fluid in which particles are suspended. □ **suspension bridge** a bridge suspended from cables that pass over supporting towers near each end.

suspicion *noun* **1** suspecting; being suspected. **2** a partial or unconfirmed belief. **3** a slight trace.

suspicious *adjective* feeling or causing suspicion. **suspiciously** *adverb*

suss *adjective* (*informal*) suspect, suspicious. –**suss** *verb* (**sussed**, **sussing**) (*informal*) **suss out** to investigate or reconnoitre; to work out. –**suss** *noun* (*informal*) **1** a suspect. **2** a suspicion.

sustain *verb* **1** to support. **2** to keep alive; *sustaining food*, food that keeps up one's strength. **3** to keep (a sound or effort etc.) going continuously. **4** to undergo, to suffer, *sustained a defeat*. **5** to endure without giving way, *sustained the attack*. **6** to confirm or uphold the validity of, *the objection was sustained*. **sustainable** *adjective* [from *sus-*, + Latin *tenere* = hold]

sustenance (**sus**-tě-năns) *noun* **1** the process of sustaining life by food. **2** the food itself, nourishment.

Sutherland, Dame Joan (born 1926), Australian operatic soprano.

Sutra (**soo**-tră) *noun* **1** a short saying or a collection of these in Hindu literature. **2** the narrative part of Buddhist literature. **3** Jainist scripture. [Sanskrit, = thread]

suttee (su-**tee**) *noun* **1** the act or custom (now illegal) of a Hindu widow sacrificing herself on her husband's funeral pyre. **2** a Hindu

908

widow who did this. [from Sanskrit *sati* = good wife]

suture (**soo**-cher) *noun* surgical stitching of a wound; a stitch or thread etc. used in this. –**suture** *verb* to stitch (a wound). [from Latin *sutura* = sewing]

Suva (**soo**-vă) the capital of Fiji.

suzerain (**soo**-ză-rayn) *noun* **1** a country or ruler that has some authority over another country that is self-governing in its internal affairs. **2** an overlord in feudal times. **suzerainty** *noun*

svelte (*pr.* svelt) *adjective* (of a person) slender and graceful.

SW *abbreviation* south-west; south-western.

swab (*pr.* swob) *noun* **1** a mop or absorbent pad for cleansing, drying, or absorbing things. **2** a specimen of a secretion taken with this. –**swab** *verb* (**swabbed**, **swabbing**) to cleanse or wipe with a swab.

swaddle *verb* to swathe in wraps or clothes or warm garments. **swaddling-clothes** *plural noun* strips of cloth formerly wrapped round a newborn baby to restrain its movements.

swag *noun* **1** loot. **2** a carved ornamental festoon of flowers and fruit, hung by its ends. **3** (*Austral.*) a bundle of personal belongings carried by a tramp etc. **4** (*Austral.*) a large quantity, *received a swag of mail*.

swage *noun* **1** a die or stamp for shaping wrought iron. **2** a tool for bending metal etc. –**swage** *verb* to shape with a swage.

swagger *verb* to walk or behave in a self-important manner, to strut. –**swagger** *noun* a swaggering walk or way of behaving. –**swagger** *adjective* (*informal*) smart, fashionable.

swagman *noun* (*plural* **swagmen**) (*Austral.*) a tramp.

Swahili (swah-**hee**-lee) *noun* **1** a Bantu people of Zanzibar and the adjacent coasts. **2** their language, a Bantu language widely used in East Africa.

swain *noun* **1** (*old use*) a country youth. **2** (*poetic*) a young lover or suitor.

swallow[1] *verb* **1** to cause or allow (food etc.) to go down one's throat; to work the muscles of the throat as when doing this. **2** to take in so as to engulf or absorb, *she was swallowed up in the crowd*. **3** to accept; *swallow a story*, believe it too easily; *swallow an insult*, accept it meekly. **4** to repress (a sound or emotion etc.), *swallowed a sob*. –**swallow** *noun* the act

of swallowing; the amount swallowed in one movement. □ **swallow-hole** *noun* an opening, especially in limestone areas, where a stream disappears into the ground.

swallow[2] *noun* a small migratory insect-eating bird with a forked tail. □ **swallow-dive** *noun* a dive with arms outspread at the start.

swam *see* **swim**.

swami (**swah**-mee) *noun* a Hindu religious teacher or holy man. [Hindi]

swamp *noun* a marsh. –**swamp** *verb* **1** to flood; to drench or submerge in water. **2** to overwhelm with a great mass or number of things. **swampy** *adjective*

Swan a river in the south-west corner of WA, the site of Perth and Fremantle.

swan *noun* a large waterbird with a long slender-neck, traditionally white, but including the black swan of WA. –**swan** *verb* (**swanned**, **swanning**) (*informal*) to go in a leisurely majestic way like a swan, *swanning around*.

swank *noun* (*informal*) **1** boastful behaviour, ostentation. **2** a person who behaves in this way. –**swank** *verb* (*informal*) to behave with swank. **swanky** *adjective*

swannery *noun* a place where swans are kept.

swansdown *noun* a swan's fine soft down, used for trimmings.

swansong *noun* a person's last performance, achievement, or composition. [from the old belief that a swan sang sweetly when about to die]

swap *verb* (**swapping**, **swapped**) to exchange. –**swap** *noun* **1** an exchange. **2** a thing suitable for swapping.

sward *noun* an expanse of short grass.

swarf (*pr.* sworf) *noun* chips or filings of wood, metal, etc. [from Old Norse *svarf* = filedust]

swarm[1] *noun* **1** a large number of insects, birds, small animals, or people flying or moving about in a cluster. **2** a cluster of bees leaving the hive with a queen bee to establish a new home. –**swarm** *verb* **1** to move in a swarm, to come together in large numbers. **2** (of bees) to cluster in a swarm. **3** (of a place) to be crowded or overrun, *swarming with tourists*.

swarm[2] *verb* **swarm up** to climb by gripping with the hands or arms and legs.

swarthy (**swor**-*th*ee) *adjective* (**swarthier**, **swarthiest**) having a dark complexion.

swashbuckling *adjective* swaggering aggressively. **swashbuckler** *noun*

swastika (**swos**-tik-ă) *noun* a symbol formed by a cross with the ends bent at right angles, formerly used as a Nazi emblem.

swat *verb* (**swatted**, **swatting**) to hit hard with something flat; to crush (a fly etc.) in this way. **swatter** *noun*

swath (*pr.* swawth) *noun* (*plural* **swaths**, *pr.* swaw*thz*) **1** the space that a scythe or mower cuts in one sweep or passage. **2** a line of grass or wheat etc. lying after being cut. **3** a broad strip.

swathe (*pr.* sway*th*) *verb* to wrap in layers of bandage or wrappings or warm garments.

SWAT team *noun* **1** (in the US) a group of elite police marksmen who specialise in high-risk tasks such as hostage rescue. **2** any group of specialists brought in to solve a difficult or urgent problem. [acronym from *Special Weapons and Tactics*]

sway *verb* **1** to swing or cause to swing gently; to lean from side to side or to one side. **2** to influence the opinions, sympathy, or actions of, *his speech swayed many voters*. **3** to waver in one's opinion or attitude. – **sway** *noun* **1** a swaying movement. **2** influence, power, *hold sway*.

Swaziland (**swah**-zee-land) a kingdom in SE Africa. **Swazi** *adjective* & *noun* (*plural* **Swazis**).

swear *verb* (**swore**, **sworn**, **swearing**) **1** to state or promise on oath, *swear it* or *swear to it*. **2** (*informal*) to state emphatically, *swore he hadn't touched it*. **3** to cause to take an oath, *swore him to secrecy*; *the jury had been sworn*. **4** to use curses or profane language in anger or surprise etc. □ **swear by** (*informal*) to have great confidence in. **swear in** to admit (a person) to office etc. by causing him or her to take an oath. **swear off** to swear to abstain from. **swear word** a profane word used in anger etc. **swearer** *noun*

sweat *noun* **1** moisture that is given off by the body through the pores of the skin. **2** a state of sweating or being covered by sweat. **3** (*informal*) a state of great anxiety. **4** (*informal*) a laborious task. **5** moisture forming in drops on a surface, e.g. by condensation. – **sweat** *verb* **1** to give out sweat; to cause to do this. **2** to be in a state of great anxiety. **3** to work long and hard. □ **sweat blood** to work very hard at something; to be in a state of great anxiety.

sweated labour labour of workers who have to endure long hours, low wages, and poor conditions.

sweatband *noun* a band of absorbent material for absorbing or wiping away sweat.

sweater *noun* a jumper or pullover.

sweatshirt *noun* a sleeved cotton sweater.

sweatshop *noun* a place where sweated labour is used.

sweaty *adjective* damp with sweat.

Swede *noun* a native of Sweden.

swede *noun* a large yellow variety of turnip.

Sweden a kingdom in northern Europe.

Swedish *adjective* of Sweden or its people or language. – **Swedish** *noun* the language of Sweden.

sweep *verb* (**swept**, **sweeping**) **1** to clear away with or as if with a broom or brush. **2** to clean or clear (a surface or area) by doing this. **3** to move or remove by pushing, *the floods swept away fences*. **4** to go smoothly and swiftly or majestically, *she swept out of the room*. **5** to extend in a continuous line or slope, *the mountains sweep down to the sea*. **6** to pass quickly over or along, *winds sweep the hillside*; *a new fashion is sweeping the country*. **7** to touch lightly. **8** to make (a bow or curtsy) with a smooth movement. – **sweep** *noun* **1** a sweeping movement. **2** a sweeping line or slope. **3** the act of sweeping with a broom etc., *give it a good sweep*. **4** a chimney sweep. **5** a sweepstake. □ **make a clean sweep** to get rid of everything or of all staff etc.; to win all the prizes. **sweep all before one** to be very successful.

sweeper *noun* **1** a person who sweeps a place. **2** a device or machine that sweeps carpets, streets, etc. **3** a person employed to sweep up wool in a shearing shed. **4** a soccer or hockey player positioned just in front of the goalkeeper to tackle attacking players.

sweeping *adjective* **1** of great scope, comprehensive, *sweeping changes*. **2** (of a statement) making no exceptions or limitations, *sweeping generalisations*. **sweepings** *plural noun* dust or scraps etc. collected by sweeping.

sweepstake *noun* **1** a form of gambling on horse races etc. in which the money staked is divided among those who have drawn numbered tickets for the winners. **2** a race etc. with betting of this kind.

sweet *adjective* 1 tasting as if containing sugar, not bitter. 2 fragrant. 3 melodious. 4 fresh, (of food) not stale, (of water) not salt. 5 pleasant, gratifying, (*informal*) pretty or charming. 6 having a pleasant nature, lovable. –**sweet** *noun* 1 a small shaped piece of sweet substance, usually made with sugar or chocolate and flavoured or with filling. 2 a sweet dish forming one course of a meal. 3 a beloved person. □ **sweet and sour** cooked in sauce containing sugar and either vinegar or lemon. **sweet corn** a kind of maize with sweet grains. **sweet pea** a climbing garden plant with fragrant flowers in many colours. **sweet potato** a tropical climbing plant with sweet tuberous roots used for food. **sweet-talk** *verb* (*informal*) to persuade by flattery. **sweet tooth** a liking for sweet things. **sweet william** a garden plant with clustered fragrant-flowers. **sweetly** *adverb*, **sweetness** *noun*

sweetbread *noun* an animal's thymus gland or pancreas used as food.

sweeten *verb* to make or become sweet or sweeter.

sweetener *noun* 1 a substance used to sweeten food or drink. 2 (*informal*) a bribe.

sweetheart *noun* a person's beloved, one of a pair of people in love with each other.

sweetmeat *noun* a sweet; a very small fancy cake.

swell *verb* (**swelled**, **swollen** *or* **swelled**, **swelling**) 1 to make or become larger because of pressure from within; to curve outwards. 2 to make or become larger in amount, volume, numbers, or intensity. –**swell** *noun* 1 the act or state of swelling. 2 the heaving of the sea with waves that do not break. 3 a gradual increase of loudness in music; a mechanism in an organ for obtaining this. 4 (*informal*) a person of high social position. –**swell** *adjective* (*informal*) smart; excellent. □ **swelled** *or* **swollen head** (*informal*) conceit.

swelling *noun* an abnormally swollen place on the body.

swelter *verb* to be uncomfortably hot, to suffer from the heat.

swept *see* **sweep**. □ **swept-wing** *adjective* (of aircraft) with wings slanting backwards from the direction of flight.

swerve *verb* to turn or cause to turn aside from a straight course. –**swerve** *noun* a swerving movement or direction.

Swift, Jonathan (1667–1745), Anglo-Irish poet and satirist, whose greatest work was *Gulliver's Travels*.

swift *adjective* quick, rapid. –**swift** *noun* a swiftly-flying insect-eating bird with long narrow wings. **swiftly** *adverb*, **swiftness** *noun*

swiftie *noun* (*Austral. informal*) a deceptive trick, *pull a swiftie*.

swig *verb* (**swigged**, **swigging**) (*informal*) to take a drink or drinks of, *swigging beer*. –**swig** *noun* (*informal*) a drink or swallow.

swill *verb* 1 to pour water over or through, to wash or rinse. 2 (of water) to pour. 3 to drink in large quantities. –**swill** *noun* 1 a rinse, *give it a swill*. 2 a sloppy mixture of waste food fed to pigs.

swim *verb* (**swam**, **swum**, **swimming**) 1 to propel the body through water by movements of the limbs, fins, or tail etc. 2 to cross by swimming. 3 to cause to swim, *swim your horse across the stream*. 4 to float. 5 to be covered or flooded with liquid, *eyes swimming in tears*. 6 to seem to be whirling or waving, to have a dizzy sensation, *everything swam before her eyes*; *my head is swimming*. –**swim** *noun* 1 a period of swimming. 2 a deep pool frequented by fish in a river. 3 the main current of affairs. □ **in the swim** active in or knowing what is going on. **swimming costume** a garment worn for swimming. **swimming pool** an artificial pool for swimming in.

swimmer *noun* a person who swims. **swimmers** *noun* (*Austral*.) a swimsuit.

swimmingly *adverb* with easy unobstructed progress.

swimsuit *noun* a garment worn for swimming.

swindle *verb* to cheat (a person) in a business transaction; to obtain by fraud. –**swindle** *noun* a piece of swindling; a fraudulent person or thing. **swindler** *noun*

swine *plural noun* pigs. –**swine** *noun* (*plural* **swine**) (*informal*) a hated person or thing.

swineherd *noun* (*old use*) a person taking care of a number of pigs.

swing *verb* (**swung**, **swinging**) 1 to move to and fro while hanging or supported; to cause to do this. 2 to hang by its ends, *swung a hammock between the two trees*. 3 to turn (a wheel etc.) smoothly; to turn to one side or in a curve, *the car swung into the drive*. 4 to walk or run with an easy rhythmical movement. 5 to lift with a swinging movement. 6 to change from one opinion or mood etc. to another.

7 to influence (voting etc.) decisively. **8** (*informal*) to be executed by hanging. **9** to play (music) with a swing rhythm. **–swing** *noun* **1** a swinging movement, action, or rhythm. **2** a seat slung by ropes or chains for swinging in; a swingboat; a spell of swinging in this. **3** the extent to which a thing swings; the amount by which votes, opinions, or points scored etc. change from one side to the other. **4** a kind of jazz with the time of the melody varied while the accompaniment is in strict time. □ **in full swing** with activity at its greatest. **swing bridge** a bridge that can be swung aside to allow ships to pass. **swing door** a door that opens in either direction and closes itself when released. **swing the lead** *see* **lead²**. **swing-wing** *noun* an aircraft wing that can be moved to slant backwards. **swinger** *noun*

swingboat *noun* a boat-shaped swing at fairs.

swingeing (**swinj**-ing) *adjective* **1** (of a blow) forcible. **2** huge in amount, number, or scope, *a swingeing increase in taxation*.

swinging voter *noun* a voter not permanently supporting a particular political party.

swinish *adjective* like a swine, beastly.

swipe *verb* (*informal*) **1** to hit with a swinging blow. **2** to steal, especially by snatching. **3** to pass (a card with a magnetic strip) across an electronic device which reads the information encoded on it. **–swipe** *noun* (*informal*) a swinging blow.

swirl *verb* to move, flow, or carry along with a whirling movement. **–swirl** *noun* a swirling movement.

swish *verb* to strike or move or cause to move with a hissing sound. **–swish** *noun* a swishing sound. **–swish** *adjective* (*informal*) smart, fashionable.

Swiss *adjective* of Switzerland or its people. **–Swiss** *noun* (*plural* **Swiss**) a native of Switzerland. □ **Swiss roll** a thin flat sponge cake spread with jam etc. and rolled up.

switch *noun* **1** a device that is operated to complete or break open an electric circuit. **2** a device at the junction of railway tracks for diverting trains from one track to another. **3** a flexible shoot cut from a tree; a tapering rod or whip resembling this. **4** a tress of real or false hair tied at one end. **5** a shift or change in opinion, methods, or policy etc. **–switch** *verb* **1** to turn (an electrical or other appliance) on or off by means of a switch. **2** to transfer (a train) to another track. **3** to divert (thoughts or talk) to another subject. **4** to change or exchange (positions, methods, or policy etc.). **5** to whip with a switch.

switchback *noun* **1** a railway at an amusement park etc. with a series of alternate steep descents and ascents, a roller coaster. **2** a road with alternate ascents and descents.

switchboard *noun* a panel with a set of switches for making telephone connections or operating electric circuits.

Swithin, St (died 862), bishop of Winchester. Feast day, 15 July.

Switzerland a federal republic in central Europe.

swivel *noun* a link or pivot between two parts enabling one of them to revolve without turning the other. **–swivel** *verb* (**swivelled**, **swivelling**) to turn on or as if on a swivel.

swizz *noun* (also **swizzle**) (*informal*) a swindle, a disappointment.

swollen *see* **swell**.

swoon *verb* to faint. **–swoon** *noun* a faint.

swoop *verb* to come down with a rushing movement like a bird upon its prey; to make a sudden attack. **–swoop** *noun* a swooping movement or attack. □ **at one fell swoop** *see* **fell²**.

swop *verb* (**swopped**, **swopping**) & *noun* = **swap**.

sword (*pr.* sord) *noun* a weapon with a long blade and a hilt. □ **sword dance** a dance in which swords are brandished or in which performers step about swords placed on the ground.

swordfish *noun* a sea fish with a long swordlike upper jaw.

swordsman *noun* (*plural* **swordsmen**) a person of good or specified skill with a sword. **swordsmanship** *noun*

swordstick *noun* a hollow walking stick containing a blade that can be used as a sword.

swore, **sworn** *see* **swear**. **–sworn** *adjective* open and determined in devotion or enmity, *sworn friends; sworn enemies*.

swot *verb* (**swotted**, **swotting**) (*informal*) to study hard. **–swot** *noun* (*informal*) **1** hard study. **2** a person who studies hard. [a dialect word for *sweat*]

swum *see* **swim**.

swung *see* **swing**.

sybarite (**sib**-ă-ryt) *noun* a person who is excessively fond of comfort and luxury. **sybaritic** (sib-ă-**rit**-ik) *adjective*

sycamore (**sik**-ă-mor) *noun* a large tree of the maple family.

sycophant (**sik**-ŏ-fant) *noun* a person who tries to win people's favour by flattering them. **sycophancy** *noun*, **sycophantic** (sik-ŏ-**fan**-tik) *adjective*, **sycophantically** *adverb*

Sydney the largest Australian city and the capital of NSW. Situated on the shores of Port Jackson, it was the site of the first white settlement of Australia in 1788.

Sydneysider *noun* a native or resident of Sydney.

syl- *prefix see* **syn-**.

syllabic (sĭ-**lab**-ik) *adjective* of or in syllables. **syllabically** *adverb*

syllable (**sil**-ă-bŭl) *noun* one of the units of sound into which a word can be divided, *there are two syllables in 'unit', three in 'divided', and one in 'can'*. □ **in words of one syllable** put very simply or bluntly. [from *syl-*, + Greek *lambanein* = take]

syllabus (**sil**-ă-bŭs) *noun* (*plural* **syllabuses**) an outline of the subjects that are included in a course of study.

syllogism (**sil**-ŏ-jizm) *noun* a form of reasoning in which a conclusion is reached from two statements, as in *'All men must die; I am a man; therefore I must die'*. [from *syl-*, + Greek *logos* = reason]

sylph (*pr.* silf) *noun* a slender girl or woman.

sym- *prefix see* **syn-**.

symbiosis (sim-bee-**oh**-sĭs) *noun* **1** an association of two different organisms living attached to each other or one within the other, usually to the advantage of both. **2** a similar relationship between people or groups. **symbiotic** (sim-bee-**ot**-ik) *adjective* [from *sym-*, + Greek *bios* = life]

symbol *noun* **1** a thing regarded as suggesting something or embodying certain characteristics, *the cross is the symbol of Christianity; the lion is the symbol of courage*. **2** a mark or sign with a special meaning, such as mathematical signs (e.g. + and – for addition and subtraction), punctuation marks, written or printed forms of notes in music. [from Greek *sumbolon* = token]

symbolic *adjective* (also **symbolical**) of, using, or used as a symbol. **symbolically** *adverb*

symbolise *verb* (also **-ize**) **1** to be a symbol of. **2** to represent by means of a symbol. **symbolisation** *noun*

symbolism *noun* use of symbols to express things. **symbolist** *noun*

symmetrical (sĭ-**met**-rik-ăl) *adjective* able to be divided into parts that are the same in size and shape and similar in position on either side of a dividing line (**line symmetry**) or a central point (**radial** or **rotational symmetry**). **symmetrically** *adverb* [from *sym-* + *metrical*]

symmetry (**sim**-ĕ-tree) *noun* **1** being symmetrical. **2** pleasing proportion between parts of a whole.

sympathetic *adjective* **1** feeling, expressing, or resulting from sympathy. **2** likeable, *he's not a sympathetic character*. **3** showing approval or support, *he is sympathetic to our plan*. □ **sympathetic nervous system** the parts of the autonomic nervous system that mobilise bodily energies for dealing with stress or emergency. **sympathetically** *adverb*

sympathise *verb* (also **-ize**) to feel or express sympathy. **sympathiser** *noun*

sympathy *noun* **1** sharing or the ability to share another person's emotions or sensations. **2** a feeling of pity or tenderness towards one suffering pain, grief, or trouble. **3** liking for each other produced in people who have similar opinions or tastes. □ **be in sympathy with** to be in agreement with; to feel approval of (an opinion or desire). [from *sym-*, + Greek *pathos* = feeling]

symphonic (sim-**fon**-ik) *adjective* of or like a symphony. □ **symphonic poem** an orchestral piece, usually descriptive or rhapsodic. **symphonically** *adverb*

symphony (**sim**-fŏ-nee) *noun* a long elaborate musical composition (usually in several movements) for a full orchestra. □ **symphony orchestra** a large orchestra playing symphonies etc. [from *sym-*, + Greek *phone* = sound]

symposium (sim-**poh**-zee-ŭm) *noun* (*plural* **symposia**) a meeting for discussion of a particular subject.

symptom *noun* a sign of the existence of a condition, especially a perceptible change from what is normal in the body or its functioning, indicating disease or injury.

symptomatic (simp-tŏ-**mat**-ik) *adjective* serving as a symptom.

syn- *prefix* (changing to **syl-** or **sym-** before certain consonants) **1** with, together (as in *synchronise*). 2 alike (as in *synonym*). [from Greek *sun* = with]

synagogue (**sin**-ă-gog) *noun* a building for public Jewish worship. [from Greek, = assembly]

synapse (**sy**-naps) *noun* a gap between two nerve cells, across which impulses pass by diffusion of a neurotransmitter.

sync (*pr.* sink) *noun* (also **synch**) (*informal*) synchronisation, *out of sync*.

synchromesh (**sing**-krŏ-mesh) *noun* a device that makes parts of a gear revolve at the same speed while they are being brought into contact. [shortened from *synchronised mesh*]

synchronic (sing-**kron**-ik) *adjective* concerned with a subject as it exists at a particular time, not with its historical antecedents. **synchronically** *adverb*

synchronise (**sing**-krŏ-nyz) *verb* (also **-ize**) 1 to occur or exist at the same time. 2 to operate at the same rate and simultaneously. 3 to cause to occur or operate at the same time; to cause (watches etc.) to show the same time. **synchronisation** *noun*, **synchroniser** *noun* [from *syn-*, + Greek *khronos* = time]

synchronism (**sing**-krŏ-nizm) *noun* 1 being or treated as synchronous or synchronic. 2 synchronising.

synchronous (**sing**-krŏ-nŭs) *adjective* 1 existing or occurring at the same time. 2 operating at the same rate and simultaneously.

syncline *noun* a trough-shaped fold in rock strata (contrasting with *anticline*).

syncopate (**sing**-kŏ-payt) *verb* to change the beats or accents in (a passage of music) by putting a strong stress instead of a weak one (and vice versa). **syncopation** *noun*

syncretism (**sing**-krĕ-tizm) *noun* the combining of different beliefs or principles, especially in an attempt to reconcile them.

syndicate (**sin**-dĭ-kăt) *noun* an association of people or firms combining to carry out a business or commercial undertaking. –**syndicate** (**sin**-dĭ-kayt) *verb* 1 to combine into a syndicate. 2 to publish through an association that acquires stories, articles, cartoons, etc. for simultaneous publication in numerous newspapers and periodicals. **syndication** *noun*

syndrome (**sin**-drohm) *noun* 1 a set of signs and symptoms that together indicate the presence of a disease or abnormal condition.

2 a combination of opinions, behaviour, etc. that are characteristic of a particular condition.

synergy (**sin**-er-jee) *noun* the combined effect of two or more agents, especially when greater than the sum of their separate effects. [from *syn-*, + Greek *ergon* = work]

synod (**sin**-ŏd) *noun* a council attended by clergy and (in some Churches) lay people to discuss church matters. [from Greek, = meeting]

synonym (**sin**-ŏ-nim) *noun* a word or phrase with a meaning similar to that of another in the same language. **synonymous** (sĭ-**non**-ĭ-mŭs) *adjective* [from *syn-*, + Greek *onoma* = name]

synopsis (sĭ-**nop**-sĭs) *noun* (*plural* **synopses**) a summary; a brief general survey. [from *syn-*, + Greek *opsis* = seeing]

synoptic (sĭ-**nop**-tik) *adjective* 1 of or forming a synopsis. 2 of the **Synoptic Gospels**, those of Matthew, Mark, and Luke that have many similarities.

synovia (sy-**noh**-vee-ă) *noun* a thick sticky fluid lubricating joints etc. in the body. □ **synovial membrane** a membrane round a joint or tendon, secreting synovial fluid. **synovial** *adjective*

syntax (**sin**-taks) *noun* the way in which words are arranged to form phrases and sentences. **syntactic** (sin-**tak**-tik) *adjective*, **syntactically** *adverb* [from *syn-*, + Greek *taxis* = arrangement]

synthesis (**sin**-thĕ-sĭs) *noun* (*plural* **syntheses**) 1 the combining of separate parts or elements to form a complex whole. 2 the combining of substances to form a compound; artificial production of a substance that occurs naturally in plants or animals. [from *syn-*, + Greek *thesis* = placing]

synthesise (**sin**-thĕ-syz) *verb* (also **-ize**) to make by synthesis.

synthesiser *noun* (also **-izer**) an electronic device for combining sounds so as to reproduce the musical tones of conventional instruments or produce a variety of artificial ones.

synthetic *adjective* 1 made by synthesis; manufactured as opposed to produced naturally, *synthetic rubber*. 2 artificial, affected, insincere. –**synthetic** *noun* a synthetic substance or fabric (e.g. nylon). **synthetically** *adverb*

syphilis (**sif**-ĭ-lĭs) *noun* a venereal disease transmitted by contact or contracted by an unborn child from its mother's blood.

syphon *noun* & *verb* = siphon.

Syria a republic in the Middle East. Syrian *adjective* & *noun*

syringe (sĭ-**rinj**) *noun* 1 a device for drawing in liquid and forcing it out again in a fine stream. 2 a hypodermic syringe (*see* hypodermic). –syringe *verb* to wash out or spray with a syringe.

syrinx (**si**-rinks) *noun* the part of a bird's throat where its song is produced.

syrup *noun* a thick sweet liquid; water in which sugar is dissolved. syrupy *adjective* [from Arabic *sharab* = a drink]

system *noun* 1 a set of connected things or parts that form a whole or work together, *a railway system*; *the nervous system* (see nervous); *the solar system* (see solar). 2 an animal body as a whole, *too much alcohol poisons the system*. 3 a set of rules, principles, or practices forming a particular philosophy or form of government etc. 4 a method of classification or notation or measurement etc., *the metric system*. 5 orderliness, being systematic, *she works without system*.

□ **get a thing out of one's system** to be rid of its effects. systems analysis analysis of an operation in order to decide how a computer may be used to perform it. systems analyst an expert in systems analysis. [from Greek, = setting up]

systematic *adjective* methodical, according to a plan and not casually or at random. systematically *adverb*

systematise (**sis**-tĕ-mă-tyz) *verb* (also -ize) to arrange according to a system. systematisation *noun*

systemic (sis-**tem**-ik) *adjective* 1 of or affecting the body as a whole. 2 (of a fungicide etc.) entering a plant by way of the roots or shoots and passing into the tissues. systemically *adverb*

systemise *verb* (also -ize) to systematise. systemisation *noun*

systole (**sis**-tŏ-lee) *noun* the rhythmical contraction of chambers of the heart, alternating with diastole to form the pulse. systolic (sis-**tol**-ik) *adjective*

Tt

T *abbreviation* tesla.

ta *interjection* (*informal*) thank you.

TAB *abbreviation* Totalisator Agency Board, the government board that controls off-course betting; a branch of this.

tab¹ *noun* a small projecting flap or strip, especially one by which something can be grasped, hung, fastened, or identified. –**tab** *verb* (**tabbed**, **tabbing**) to provide with tabs. □ **keep a tab** or **tabs on** (*informal*) to keep account of, to keep under observation. **pick up the tab** (*informal*) to pay the bill.

tab² *noun see* **tabulator**.

tabard (**tab**-ard) *noun* **1** a short tunic-like garment open at the sides, worn by a herald, emblazoned with the arms of the sovereign. **2** a woman's garment shaped like this.

tabby *noun* a **tabby cat**, a cat with grey or brownish fur and dark stripes.

tabernacle *noun* **1** (in the Bible) the portable shrine used by the Israelites during their wanderings in the wilderness. **2** (in the RC Church) a receptacle containing consecrated elements of the Eucharist. **3** a meeting place for worship used by some Nonconformist groups.

tabla *noun* a pair of small Indian drums played with the hands, often to accompany the sitar.

table *noun* **1** a piece of furniture consisting of a flat top supported on one or more legs. **2** food provided at table; *she keeps a good table*, provides good meals. **3** the flat part of a machine tool on which material is put to be worked. **4** a list of facts or figures systematically arranged, especially in columns; *learn one's tables*, to learn the multiplication tables etc. in mathematics. –**table** *verb* to submit (a motion or report in Parliament etc.) for discussion. □ **at table** while taking a meal at a table. **on the table** offered for consideration or discussion. **table linen** tablecloths, napkins, etc. **table manners** ability to behave properly while eating at the table. **table mat** a mat for protecting the surface of a table from hot dishes etc. **table tennis** a game played with bats and a light hollow ball on a table with a net across it. **turn the tables** *see* **turn**. [from Latin *tabula* = plank]

tableau (**tab**-loh) *noun* (*plural* **tableaux**, *pr.* **tab**-lohz) **1** a silent and motionless group of people etc. arranged to represent a scene. **2** a dramatic or picturesque scene. [French, = little table]

tablecloth *noun* a cloth for covering a table, especially at meals.

table d'hôte (tahbl **doht**) *noun* a meal consisting of a set menu at a fixed price, especially in a hotel. [French, = host's table]

tableland *noun* a plateau of land.

tablespoon *noun* **1** a large spoon for serving food at the table. **2** the amount held by this (20 ml). **tablespoonful** *noun* (*plural* **tablespoonfuls**).

tablet *noun* **1** a slab or panel bearing an inscription or picture, especially one fixed to a wall as a memorial. **2** a small flattish piece of a solid substance (e.g. soap). **3** a small measured amount of a drug compressed into a solid form.

tabloid *noun* a newspaper (usually popular in style) with pages that are half the size of those of larger newspapers.

taboo *noun* a ban or prohibition on something that is regarded by religion or custom as not to be done, touched, spoken, or used etc. –**taboo** *adjective* prohibited by a taboo, *taboo words*.

tabor (**tay**-ber) *noun* a small drum formerly used to accompany a pipe.

tabular (**tab**-yŭ-ler) *adjective* arranged or displayed in a table or list.

tabulate (**tab**-yŭ-layt) *verb* to arrange (facts or figures) in the form of a table or list. **tabulation** *noun*

tabulator *noun* **1** a person or thing that tabulates facts or figures. **2** (also **tab**) a device on a typewriter or keyboard for advancing to a series of set positions, e.g. when setting information out in columns.

tachograph (**tak**-ŏ-grahf) *noun* a device that automatically records the speed and travel time of a motor vehicle in which it is fitted. [from Greek *tachos* = speed, + *-graph*]

tachometer (tă-**kom**-ĕ-ter) *noun* an instrument for measuring the speed of a vehicle etc. or of the rotation of its engine. [from Greek *tachos* = speed, + *meter*]

tacit (**tas**-ĭt) *adjective* implied or understood without being put into words. **tacitly** *adverb* [from Latin *tacitus* = not speaking]

taciturn (**tas**-ĭ-tern) *adjective* habitually saying very little, uncommunicative. **taciturnity** (tas-ĭ-**tern**-ĭ-tee) *noun*

Tacitus (**tas**-ĭ-tŭs) (born c. AD 56), Roman historian of the early Roman empire.

tack¹ *noun* 1 a small nail with a broad head. 2 a long stitch used to hold fabric in position lightly or temporarily, or (*tailor's tacks*) to mark the place for a tuck etc. 3 the direction of a ship's course as determined by the position of its sails; a temporary oblique course to take advantage of a wind; *port tack*, with the wind on the port side. 4 a course of action or policy, *he's on the wrong tack*. – **tack** *verb* 1 to nail with a tack or tacks. 2 to stitch with tacks. 3 to add as an extra thing, *a service charge was tacked on to the bill.* 4 to sail a zigzag course in order to take advantage of a wind; to make a tack or tacks.

tack² *noun* riding saddles, bridles, etc. [from *tackle* = equipment]

tackle *noun* 1 a set of ropes and pulleys for lifting weights or working a ship's sails. 2 equipment for a task or sport, *fishing tackle*. 3 the act of tackling in football. – **tackle** *verb* 1 to grapple with, to try to deal with or overcome (an awkward thing or an opponent or problem); *tackle a person about something*, to initiate a discussion about an awkward matter. 2 (in hockey, football, etc.) to intercept or seize and stop (an opponent running with the ball). **tackler** *noun*

tacky *adjective* 1 (of paint or varnish etc.) slightly sticky, not quite dry. 2 (*informal*) cheaply made; in poor taste. **tackiness** *noun*

taco *noun* (*plural tacos*) a Mexican dish of a folded tortilla filled with meat etc.

tact *noun* skill in avoiding offence or in winning goodwill by saying or doing the right thing. [from Latin *tactus* = sense of touch]

tactful *adjective* having or showing tact. **tactfully** *adverb*

tactic *noun* a piece of tactics.

tactical *adjective* 1 of tactics. 2 (of bombing etc.) done in immediate support of armed forces (distinguished from *strategic*). 3 planning or planned skilfully. □ **tactical weapons** *see* **strategic weapons**. **tactically** *adverb*

tactician (tak-**tish**-ăn) *noun* an expert in tactics.

tactics *noun* the art of placing or manoeuvring forces skilfully in a battle (distinguished from *strategy*). – **tactics** *plural noun* manoeuvring; procedure adopted in order to achieve something. [from Greek *taktika* = things arranged]

tactile (**tak**-tyl) *adjective* of or using the sense of touch, *tactile organs*. **tactility** *noun* [from Latin *tactum* = touched]

tactless *adjective* lacking in tact. **tactlessly** *adverb*, **tactlessness** *noun*

tad *noun* (*informal*) a small amount or degree, *a tad cheaper*.

tadpole *noun* the larva of a frog or toad etc. at the stage when it lives in water and has gills and a tail. [from old words *tad* = toad, + *poll* = head]

tae kwon do (tay kwon **doh**) *noun* a modern Korean system of unarmed combat. [Korean = art of hand and foot fighting]

TAFE (*pr*. tayf) *abbreviation* Technical and Further Education, a system of mainly vocational education and training; an institution providing this.

taffeta *noun* a shiny silklike dress fabric.

taffrail (**taf**-rayl) *noun* a rail round the stern of a vessel.

tag¹ *noun* 1 a metal or plastic point at the end of a shoelace etc. 2 a label tied or stuck into something to identify it or show its price etc. 3 an identifying mark made by a graffiti artist. 4 any loose or ragged end or projection. 5 a stock phrase or much-used quotation. 6 (in computing) a label assigned to an item of data. – **tag** *verb* (**tagged**, **tagging**) 1 to label with a tag. 2 to attach, to add as an extra thing, *a postscript was tagged on to her letter*. 3 (*informal*) to follow, to trail behind. □ **tag along** (*informal*) to go along with another or others.

tag² *noun* a children's game in which one chases the rest until he or she touches another.

Tagalog (tă-**gah**-log) *noun* 1 a member of the principal people of the Philippines. 2 their language.

tagboard *noun* a board on which electronic components can be mounted for experiments.

tagliatelle (tahl-yah-**tel**-ee) *noun* pasta in ribbon-shaped strips.

Tahiti (tah-**hee**-tee) one of the Society Islands of French Polynesia in the South Pacific, administered by France. **Tahitian** (tah-**hee**-shăn) *adjective* & *noun*

t'ai chi (ty **chee**) *noun* (in full **t'ai chi ch'uan**) a Chinese martial art and system of exercises with slow controlled movements.

taiga (**ty**-gă) *noun* the coniferous forest lying between tundra and steppe, especially in Siberia. [Russian]

tail *noun* **1** the hindmost part of an animal, especially when extending beyond the rest of the body; *with his tail between his legs*, (of an animal or person) looking defeated or dejected. **2** something resembling this in its shape or position; the rear part; an inferior part; a part that hangs down or behind. **3** (*informal*) a person following or shadowing another. **–tail** *verb* **1** to remove the stalks of, *top and tail the beans*. **2** (*informal*) to follow closely, to shadow. **3** (*Austral.*) to follow, herd, and tend (livestock). ☐ **on a person's tail** following closely. **tail away** = tail off (*see below*). **tail end** the hindmost or very last part. **tail lamp** or **light** a light at the back of a vehicle, train, or bicycle. **tail off** to become fewer, smaller, or slighter; to fall behind in a straggling line; (of remarks etc.) to end inconclusively. **tail wind** a following wind. **turn tail** *see* turn.

tailcoat *noun* a man's coat with a long divided flap at the back, worn as part of formal evening or morning dress.

tailgate *noun* a downward-hinged or removable flap at the back of a cart or truck; a rear door in a motor vehicle. **–tailgate** *verb* (*informal*) to follow the vehicle in front very closely.

tailless *adjective* having no tail.

tailor *noun* a maker of (usually men's) clothes, especially to order. **–tailor** *verb* **1** to make (clothes) as a tailor; to make in a simple smoothly-fitting design. **2** to make or adapt for a special purpose, *the new factory is tailored to our needs*. ☐ **tailor-made** *adjective* made by a tailor; perfectly suited for the purpose.

tailplane *noun* the horizontal surface of the tail of an aeroplane.

tails *plural noun* **1** a tailcoat; evening dress with this. **2** the reverse of a coin, turned upwards after being tossed.

tailspin *noun* an aircraft's spiral dive with the tail making wider circles than the front.

tailstock *noun* an adjustable part of a lathe, with a fixed spindle to support one end of the workpiece.

taint *noun* a trace of some bad quality, decay, or infection. **–taint** *verb* to affect with a taint; *tainted meat*, slightly decayed.

taipan (**ty**-pan) *noun* a long venomous snake of northern Australia and New Guinea. [Wik-Mungkan *dhayban*]

Taipei (ty-**pay**) the capital of Taiwan.

Taiwan (ty-**wahn**) an island republic off the south-east coast of China, regarded by China as one of its provinces. **Taiwanese** *adjective* & *noun*

Tajikistan (tah-jee-ki-**stahn**) a mountainous republic in central Asia (formerly part of the USSR), lying to the north of Afghanistan and to the west of China. **Tajik** *adjective* & *noun*

Taj Mahal (tahj mă-**hahl**) a mausoleum at Agra in northern India, completed c. 1648 by the Mogul emperor Shah Jahan in memory of his favourite wife.

take *verb* (**took**, **taken**, **taking**) **1** to get into one's hands by effort. **2** to get possession of, to capture, to win, *took many prisoners*; *took first prize*. **3** to be successful or effective, *the inoculation did not take*. **4** to remove from its place, *someone has taken my bicycle*. **5** to subtract. **6** to make use of, to indulge in, *take this opportunity*; *take a holiday*; *take the first turning on the left*, go into it. **7** to occupy (a position), especially as one's right; *take a chair*, sit down on one; *take the chair*, act as chairperson. **8** to obtain after fulfilling necessary conditions, *take a degree*; to obtain the use of by payment, *take lodgings*. **9** to use as a means of transport, *take the train*. **10** to consume, *we'll take tea now*. **11** to require, *it takes a strong man to lift that*; *do you take sugar?*, do you use it in tea etc. **12** to cause to come or go with one; to carry or remove, *take the letters to the post*. **13** to be affected by; to catch, *the sticks took fire*. **14** to experience or exert (a feeling or effort), *took pity on him*; *take care*. **15** to find out and record, *take his name*; *we'll take your measurements*. **16** to interpret in a certain way, *we take it that you are satisfied*; *I take your point*, accept that it is valid. **17** to adopt a specified attitude towards, *take things coolly*; *take it well*, not be upset or resentful. **18** to accept, to endure, *take risks*; *he can't take a joke*, resents being laughed at. **19** to perform, to deal with, to move round or over, *take a decision*; *took the corner too fast*; *take an examination*, sit for it; *take a subject at school*, to study or teach it. **20** to make by photography; to photograph (a person or thing). **–take** *noun* **1** the amount of game or fish etc. taken or caught. **2** a scene or sequence of actions photographed at one time, without interruption, in making a cinema film. **3** (*informal*) a swindle. □ **be taken by** or **with** to find attractive. **be taken ill** to become ill. **take after** to resemble (a parent etc.). **take away** to remove or carry away; to subtract. **take-away** *adjective* (of food) bought at a restaurant for eating elsewhere; (*noun*) a restaurant selling this. **take back** to withdraw (a statement); to carry (a person) back in thought to a past time. **take down** to write down (spoken words); to humiliate; to remove (a building or structure) by taking it to pieces. **take-home pay** the amount remaining after tax etc. has been deducted from wages. **take in** to accept into one's house etc.; to include; to make (a garment etc.) smaller; to understand; to deceive or cheat (a person); (*informal*) to visit (a place) en route. **take it into one's head** to decide suddenly. **take it out of** to exhaust the strength of. **take it out on** to work off one's frustration by attacking or maltreating (a person etc.). **take it upon oneself** to undertake, to assume a responsibility. **take life** to kill. **take off** to take (clothing etc.) from the body; to mimic humorously; to leave the ground and become airborne; *take oneself off*, depart; *I take off my hat to him*, applaud him as admirable. **take-off** *noun* a piece of humorous mimicry; the process of taking off in flying. **take on** to acquire; to undertake (work or responsibility); to engage (an employee); to agree to play against (a person in a game). **take out** to escort on an outing; to obtain or get (an insurance policy etc.) issued; *take him out of himself*, make him forget his troubles. **take over** to take control of (a business etc.). **take part** to share in an activity. **take sides** to support one side or another. **take stock** to make an inventory of the stock in a shop etc.; to examine one's position and resources. **take to** to adopt as a habit or custom or course; to go to as a refuge; to develop a liking or ability for; (*informal*) to attack. **take up** to take as a hobby or business; to make a protégé of (a person); to occupy (time or space); to begin (residence etc.); to resume at the point where something was left; to challenge or correct (a speaker); to investigate (a matter) further; to shorten (a garment); to accept (an offer etc.); *take him up on his offer*, accept it. **take up with** to begin to associate with.

takeover *noun* assumption of control (especially of a business).

taker *noun* a person who takes something (especially a bet), *there were no takers*.

taking *adjective* attractive, captivating.
takings *plural noun* money taken in business, receipts.

talc *noun* **1** a form of magnesium silicate that is powdered for use as a lubricant. **2** talcum powder.

talcum *noun* = talc (sense 1). □ **talcum powder** talc powdered and usually perfumed, applied to the skin to make it feel smooth and dry.

tale *noun* **1** a narrative or story. **2** a report spread by gossip.

talebearer *noun* a person who tells tales (*see* tell).

talent *noun* **1** special or very great ability; people who have this. **2** a unit of money used in certain ancient countries. [from Greek *talanton* = sum of money]

talented *adjective* having talent.

Taliban (**tal**-ĭ-ban) a fundamentalist Muslim movement that took control of much of Afghanistan in 1995, and later established an Islamic state. The Taliban was overthrown by US-led forces in 2001 following the events of September 11.

talisman (**tal**-ĭz-măn) *noun* (*plural* talismans) an object supposed to bring good luck. **talismanic** *adjective* [from Greek *telesma* = consecrated object]

talk *verb* **1** to convey or exchange ideas by spoken words. **2** to have the power of speech, *a child learning to talk*. **3** to express, utter, or discuss in words, *you are talking nonsense*; *talk scandal*. **4** to use (a particular language), *talk French*. **5** to affect or influence by talking, *talked him into going to Antarctica*. **6** to give away information, *we have ways of making you talk*. –**talk** *noun* **1** talking, conversation, discussion. **2** a style of speech, *baby talk*. **3** an informal lecture. **4** rumour, gossip, its theme, *there is talk of a general election*; *it's the talk of the town*. **5** talking or promises etc. without action or results. □ **talk down to** to silence (a person) by talking loudly or persistently; to bring (a pilot or aircraft) to a landing by radio instructions from the ground. **talk down to** to speak to in condescendingly simple language. **talk over** to discuss. **talk show** an interview program on radio or television, a chat show. **talk through one's hat** to talk nonsense. **talk to** (*informal*) to reprove; *gave him a talking-to*, a reproof. **talker** *noun*

talkative *adjective* talking very much.

talkback *noun* a radio program in which listeners telephone the studio and participate.

tall *adjective* **1** of more than average height. **2** having a certain height, *170 cm tall.* □ **tall order** (*informal*) a difficult task. **tall poppy** (*Austral.*) a conspicuously successful person, especially if exciting envy. **tall story** one that is difficult to believe (and probably untrue). **tallish** *adjective*, **tallness** *noun*

tallboy *noun* a tall chest of drawers.

Tallinn city and port, capital of Estonia.

tallow *noun* animal fat used to make candles, soap, lubricants, etc.

tally *noun* **1** the reckoning of a debt or score. **2** a total score or amount. –**tally** *verb* (**tallied, tallying**) to correspond, *see that the goods tally with what we ordered*; *the two witnesses' stories tallied.*

tally-ho *interjection* a hunter's cry to the hounds on sighting the fox.

Talmud (**tal**-muud) *noun* a collection of ancient writings on Jewish civil and ceremonial law and tradition.

talon (**tal**-ŏn) *noun* a claw, especially of a bird of prey.

tamarillo (tam-ă-**ril**-oh) *noun* the egg-shaped red fruit of a South American shrub, also called *tree tomato*.

tamarind (**tam**-ă-rind) *noun* **1** a tropical tree bearing fruit with acid pulp. **2** its fruit. [from Arabic *tamr-hindi* = Indian date]

tamarisk (**tam**-ă-risk) *noun* an evergreen shrub with feathery branches and spikes of pink or white flowers.

tambour (**tam**-boor) *noun* **1** a drum. **2** a circular frame for holding fabric taut while it is being embroidered.

tambourine (tam-bŏ-**reen**) *noun* a percussion instrument consisting of a small hoop with parchment stretched over one side, and jingling metal discs in slots round the hoop.

tame *adjective* **1** (of animals) gentle and not afraid of human beings, not wild or fierce. **2** docile. **3** not exciting or interesting. –**tame** *verb* to make tame or manageable. **tameable** *adjective*, **tamely** *adverb*, **tameness** *noun*, **tamer** *noun*

Tamil (**tam**-ĭl) *noun* **1** a member of a people of southern India and Sri Lanka. **2** their language. □ **Tamil Tigers** a Tamil military and guerrilla organisation in Sri Lanka seeking independence for their community especially in the north of the island.

tammar *noun* a small greyish-brown wallaby of southern and south-western Australia and adjacent islands. [Nyungar *damar*]

tam-o'-shanter *noun* a beret with a soft full top. [named after Tam o'Shanter, hero of a poem by the Scottish poet Robert Burns]

tamp *verb* to pack or ram down tightly.

tamper *verb* **tamper with** to meddle or interfere with, to alter without authority, *he tampered with the switches*; to influence illegally, to bribe, *tamper with a jury.*

tampon *noun* a plug of absorbent material inserted into the body to stop a wound or absorb natural secretions, especially menstrual blood.

tan¹ *verb* (**tanned, tanning**) **1** to convert (animal hide) into leather by treating it with tannic acid or mineral salts etc. **2** to make or become brown by exposure to sun. **3** (*informal*) to thrash. –**tan** *noun* **1** yellowish brown. **2** brown colour in skin exposed to sun. **3** tree bark used in tanning hides. –**tan** *adjective* yellowish-brown.

tan² *abbreviation* tangent.

tandem *noun* **1** a bicycle with seats and pedals for two or more people one behind another. **2** an arrangement of people or things one behind another. –**tandem** *adverb* one behind another. □ **in tandem** arranged in this way. [Latin, = at length]

tandoori *noun* food cooked over charcoal in a clay oven (**tandoor**).

T'ang the name of a dynasty which ruled in China from 618 to c. 906.

tang *noun* **1** a strong flavour or smell. **2** a projection on the blade of a knife or chisel etc. by which it is held firm in its handle.

Tanganyika *see* Tanzania.

tangelo (**tan**-jě-loh) *noun* a hybrid of a tangerine and a grapefruit; the tree bearing this fruit. [from *tangerine*, + *pomelo* = grapefruit]

tangent (**tan**-jěnt) *noun* a straight line that touches the outside of a curve but does not intersect it. □ **go off at a tangent** to diverge suddenly from a line of thought etc. or from the matter in hand. **tangent of an angle** the ratio of the sides (other than the hypotenuse) opposite and adjacent to an angle in a right-angled triangle. [from Latin *tangens* = touching]

tangential (tan-**jen**-shǎl) *adjective* **1** of or along a tangent. **2** divergent. **3** peripheral.

tangerine (tan-jĕ-**reen**) *noun* **1** a kind of small flattened orange. **2** its deep orange-yellow colour. [named after *Tangier*]

tangible (**tan**-jĭ-bŭl) *adjective* **1** able to be perceived by touch. **2** clear and definite, real, *tangible advantages*. **tangibly** *adverb*, **tangibility** *noun* [from Latin *tangere* = to touch]

Tangier (tan-**jeer**) a seaport of Morocco, almost opposite Gibraltar.

tangle *verb* **1** to twist or become twisted into a confused mass. **2** to entangle. **3** to become involved in conflict with. –**tangle** *noun* a tangled mass or condition.

tango[1] *noun* (*plural tangos*) a ballroom dance with gliding steps; music for this. –**tango** *verb* to dance the tango.

tango[2] *noun* tangerine colour.

tangram *noun* a Chinese puzzle consisting of a square cut into seven pieces to be combined into various figures.

tangy (**tang**-ee) *adjective* (**tangier**, **tangiest**) having a strong flavour or smell.

tank *noun* **1** a large container for holding liquid or gas. **2** (*Austral.*) a reservoir or dam. **3** a heavily armoured tracked fighting vehicle carrying guns. □ **tank top** a sleeveless close-fitting round-necked upper garment.

tankard *noun* a large one-handled drinking vessel, usually of silver or pewter and often with a lid.

tanker *noun* a ship, aircraft, or vehicle for carrying oil or other liquid in bulk.

tanner *noun* a person who tans hides into leather.

tannery *noun* a place where hides are tanned into leather.

tannic *adjective* of tannin. □ **tannic acid** tannin.

tannin *noun* **1** any of several compounds obtained from various tree barks and oak galls, used chiefly in tanning and dyeing. **2** a compound obtained from grape skins, seeds, and stalks, giving an astringency to some red wines. **3** a compound found in tea leaves which can make the tea taste astringent.

tantalise *verb* (also -**ize**) to tease or torment by the sight of something that is desired but kept out of reach or withheld. [from the name of Tantalus]

tantalum (**tan**-tă-lŭm) *noun* a hard white metallic element, symbol Ta.

Tantalus (**tan**-tă-lŭs) (*Gk. myth.*) a king punished for his sins by being condemned to stand in Hades surrounded by water and fruit that receded when he tried to reach them.

tantamount (**tant**-ă-mownt) *adjective* equivalent, *his request was tantamount to a command*. [from Italian *tanto montare* = amount to so much]

tantra *noun* each of a class of Hindu, Buddhist, or Jain sacred texts that deal with mystical and magical practices. **tantric** *adjective* [Sanskrit]

tantrum *noun* an outburst of bad temper, especially in a child.

Tanzania (tan-ză-**nee**-ă) a republic in East Africa, consisting of a mainland area (the former republic of Tanganyika) and the islands of Zanzibar and Pemba. **Tanzanian** *adjective* & *noun*

Taoism (**tow**-izm) *noun* one of the two major Chinese religious and philosophical systems (the other is Confucianism), whose central concept and goal is the Tao, the code of behaviour in harmony with the natural order. **Taoist** *noun*

tap[1] *noun* **1** a device for drawing liquid from a cask or for allowing liquid or gas to come from a pipe in a controllable flow. **2** a device for cutting a screw-thread inside a cavity. **3** a connection for tapping a telephone. –**tap** *verb* (**tapped**, **tapping**) **1** to fit a tap into (a cask) in order to draw out its contents. **2** to draw off (liquid) by means of a tap or through an incision. **3** to extract or obtain supplies or information from. **4** to cut a screw-thread inside (a cavity). **5** to make a connection in (a circuit etc.) so as to divert electricity or fit a listening device for overhearing telephone communications. □ **on tap** (of liquid or gas) ready to be drawn off by a tap; (*informal*) available. **tap root** the chief root of a plant, growing straight downwards.

tap[2] *verb* (**tapped**, **tapping**) **1** to strike with a quick light blow, to knock gently on (a door etc.). **2** to strike (an object) lightly against something. –**tap** *noun* **1** a quick light blow, the sound of this. **2** tap-dancing. □ **tap dance** a dance in which an elaborate rhythm is tapped with the feet; (*verb*) to perform a tap dance.

tape *noun* **1** a narrow strip of woven cotton etc. used for tying, fastening, or labelling things; a piece of this stretched across a racetrack at the finishing line. **2** a narrow continuous strip of paper or other flexible material; adhesive tape; insulating tape; magnetic tape. **3** a tape measure. **4** a tape recording. –**tape** *verb* **1** to tie, fasten, or seal with tape. **2** to record on magnetic tape. □ **have a person** or **thing taped** (*informal*) to understand fully; to have an organised method of dealing with it. **tape deck** a machine for playing and recording audiotapes. **tape measure** a strip of tape or flexible metal marked in centimetres or inches etc. for measuring length. **tape-record** *verb* to record on a tape recorder. **tape recorder** an apparatus for recording and reproducing sounds or computer data on magnetic tape. **tape recording** a recording made on magnetic tape.

taper *noun* a slender candle, burnt to give a light or to light other candles etc. **–taper** *verb* to make or become gradually narrower. □ **taper off** to make or become less in amount etc. or cease gradually.

tapestry (tap-ĕs-tree) *noun* a piece of strong material with a pictorial or ornamental design woven into it or embroidered on it, used for hanging on walls or as an upholstery fabric. [from French *tapis* = carpet]

tapeworm *noun* a tapelike worm that can live as a parasite in the intestines of man and other animals.

tapioca (tap-ee-**oh**-kă) *noun* a starchy substance in hard white grains obtained from cassava and used for making puddings.

tapir (tay-per) *noun* a piglike animal with a long flexible snout.

tappet *noun* a projection in a piece of machinery that causes a certain movement by tapping against something, used e.g. to open and close a valve.

tar[1] *noun* **1** a thick dark inflammable liquid obtained by distilling wood, coal, or peat etc. **2** a similar substance formed by burning tobacco. **–tar** *verb* (**tarred, tarring**) to coat with tar. □ **be tarred with the same brush** to have the same faults as someone else.

tar[2] *noun* (*informal*) a sailor.

Tara (**tah**-ră) a hill in Ireland, site in early times of the residence of high kings of Ireland.

taradiddle *noun* (*informal*) a petty lie; nonsense.

taramasalata (ta-ră-mă-să-**lah**-tă) *noun* pâté made from the roe of mullet or cod.

tarantella (ta-răn-**tel**-ă) *noun* a rapid whirling southern Italian dance; the music for this.

tarantula (tă-**ran**-tew-lă) *noun* **1** (*Austral.*) a huntsman spider. **2** a large black spider of southern Europe. **3** a large hairy tropical spider.

Tarawa (**ta**-ră-wă) the capital of Kiribati.

tarboosh (tar-**boosh**) *noun* a cap like a fez.

tardy *adjective* (**tardier, tardiest**) **1** slow to act or move or happen. **2** behind time. **tardily** *adverb*, **tardiness** *noun* [from Latin *tardus* = slow]

tare[1] (*pr.* tair) *noun* a kind of vetch, especially as a weed in grain fields.

tare[2] (*pr.* tair) *noun* an allowance made to the purchaser for the weight of the container in which goods are packed, or for the vehicle transporting them, in instances where the goods are weighed together with their container or vehicle.

target *noun* **1** the object or mark that a person tries to hit in shooting etc.; a disc painted with concentric circles for this purpose in archery. **2** a person or thing against which criticism or scorn etc. is directed. **3** an objective, a minimum result aimed at, *export targets*. **–target** *verb* (**targeted, targeting**) **1** to aim (a weapon etc.) at a target. **2** to plan or schedule (a thing) so as to attain an objective.

targum *noun* an Aramaic version of the Hebrew scriptures, with interpretations.

tariff *noun* **1** a list of fixed charges, especially for rooms and meals etc. at a hotel. **2** duty to be paid on imports or exports.

tarmac *noun* (*trademark*) tarmacadam. **–tarmac** *noun* an area surfaced with tarmacadam, especially on an airfield. **–tarmac** *verb* (**tarmacked, tarmacking**) to surface with tarmacadam.

tarmacadam *noun* road materials of stone or slag bound with tar.

tarn *noun* a small mountain lake.

tarnish *verb* **1** to lose or cause (metal) to lose its lustre by exposure to air or damp. **2** to stain or blemish (a reputation etc.). **–tarnish** *noun* loss of lustre; a stain or blemish.

taro (**ta**-roh) *noun* (*plural taros*) a tropical plant with edible tuberous roots.

tarot (**ta**-roh) *noun* a game played with a pack of 78 special cards that are also used for fortune telling.

tarpaulin (tar-**paw**-lin) *noun* **1** canvas made waterproof, especially by being tarred. **2** a sheet of this used as a covering. [from *tar*[1] + *pall*[1]]

tarragon (**ta**-ră-gŏn) *noun* a plant with leaves that are used for flavouring salads, vinegar, etc.

tarry[1] (**tah**-ree) *adjective* of or like tar.

tarry[2] (**ta**-ree) *verb* (**tarried, tarrying**) (*old use*) to delay in coming or going.

tarsal *adjective* of the tarsus. **–tarsal** *noun* one of the tarsal bones.

tarsus *noun* the seven small bones that make up the ankle.

tart¹ *adjective* **1** sharp-tasting, acid. **2** sharp in manner, biting, *a tart reply*. **tartly** *adverb*, **tartness** *noun*

tart² *noun* **1** a pie containing fruit or sweet filling. **2** a piece of pastry with jam etc. on top. **3** (*informal*) a prostitute; a promiscuous woman. – **tart** *verb* **tart up** (*informal*) to dress or decorate gaudily or with cheap smartness; to smarten up.

tartan *noun* **1** the distinctive pattern of a Scottish Highland clan, with coloured stripes crossing at right angles. **2** a similar pattern. **3** fabric woven in such a pattern.

Tartar *noun* **1** a member of a group of Central Asian peoples including Mongols and Turks. **2 tartar** a person who is violent-tempered or difficult to deal with.

tartar *noun* **1** a hard chalky deposit that forms on the teeth. **2** a reddish deposit that forms on the side of a cask in which wine is fermented. □ **cream of tartar** *see* **cream**. [origin unknown]

tartare sauce (**tar**-tair) *noun* (also **tartar sauce**) a sauce of mayonnaise containing chopped gherkins, capers, etc.

tartaric (tar-**ta**-rik) *adjective* of or derived from tartar, *tartaric acid*.

tartlet *noun* a small pastry tart.

tarwhine (**tar**-wyn) *noun* (*Austral*.) an edible silvery sea fish. [probably Dharuk *darra-wayin*]

Tarzan the hero of novels by the American author Edgar Rice Burroughs (1875–1950) and subsequent films and television series. He is a man of powerful physique reared by apes in the jungle.

Tas. *abbreviation* Tasmania.

taser *noun* a weapon firing barbs that cause temporary paralysis.

Tashkent (tash-**kent**) the capital of Uzbekistan.

task *noun* a piece of work to be done. – **task** *verb* to make great demands upon (a person's powers). □ **take a person to task** to rebuke him or her. **task force** a group and resources specially organised for a particular task.

taskmaster *noun* a person considered with regard to the way in which he or she imposes tasks, *a hard taskmaster*.

Tasman, Abel Janszoon (1603–59), Dutch explorer, after whom Tasmania (which he named Van Diemen's Land) and the Tasman Sea are named.

Tasmania (taz-**mayn**-ee-ă) an island State of the Commonwealth of Australia lying off the south-east coast of Australia.

Tasmanian *adjective* of or relating to Tasmania. – **Tasmanian** *noun* a native or inhabitant of Tasmania. □ **Tasmanian devil** a small black bearlike carnivorous marsupial, found only in Tasmania. **Tasmanian tiger** an extinct carnivorous marsupial with brown-striped sandy fur. Also called *thylacine*.

Tasman Sea the sea (part of the South Pacific) between Australia and New Zealand.

tassel *noun* **1** a bunch of threads tied at one end and hanging loosely, used as an ornament. **2** the tassel-like head of certain plants (e.g. maize). **tasselled** *adjective*

Tassie (**taz**-ee) (*informal*) *noun* **1** Tasmania. **2** a Tasmanian. – **Tassie** *adjective* Tasmanian.

taste *noun* **1** the sensation caused in the tongue by things placed upon it. **2** the faculty of perceiving this sensation. **3** a small quantity of food or drink taken as a sample; a slight experience of something, *a taste of fame*. **4** a liking. **5** ability to perceive and enjoy what is beautiful or harmonious or to know what is fitting for an occasion etc.; choice made according to this; *the remark was in bad taste*, was unsuitable or offensive. – **taste** *verb* **1** to discover or test the flavour of (a thing) by taking it into the mouth. **2** to be able to perceive flavours. **3** to have a certain flavour, *it tastes sour*. **4** to experience, *taste the joys of freedom*. □ **taste bud** one of the small projections on the tongue by which flavours are perceived. **taster** *noun*

tasteful *adjective* showing good taste. **tastefully** *adverb*, **tastefulness** *noun*

tasteless *adjective* **1** having no flavour. **2** showing poor taste, *tasteless decorations*. **tastelessly** *adverb*, **tastelessness** *noun*

tasty *adjective* (**tastier**, **tastiest**) having a strong flavour; appetising. **tastily** *adverb*, **tastiness** *noun*

Taswegian *adjective* & *noun* (*humorous*) = Tasmanian.

tat *adjective* (**tatted**, **tatting**) to do tatting; to make by tatting.

ta-ta *interjection* (*informal*) goodbye.

tattered *adjective* ragged, torn into tatters.

tatters *plural noun* rags, irregularly torn pieces.

tatting *noun* **1** a kind of lace made by hand with a small shuttle. **2** the process of making this.

tattle *verb* to chatter or gossip idly; to reveal information in this way. – **tattle** *noun* idle chatter or gossip.

tattoo¹ *noun* **1** an evening drum or bugle signal calling soldiers back to their quarters. **2** an elaboration of this with music and marching, as an entertainment, *Edinburgh tattoo*. **3** a drumming or tapping sound. [from Dutch *taptoe* = close the tap (of the cask)]

tattoo² *verb* to mark (skin) with indelible patterns by puncturing it and inserting a dye; to make (a pattern) in this way. – **tattoo** *noun* a tattooed pattern. [Tahitian]

tatty *adjective* (**tattier**, **tattiest**) (*informal*) **1** ragged; shabby and untidy. **2** tawdry, fussily ornate. **tattily** *adverb*, **tattiness** *noun*

taught *see* **teach**.

taunt *verb* to jeer at, to try to provoke with scornful remarks or criticism. – **taunt** *noun* a taunting remark. [from French *tant pour tant* = tit for tat]

taupe (tohp *or* tawp) *noun* grey with a tinge of another colour, usually brown.

Taurus (**taw**-rŭs) *noun* a sign of the zodiac, the Bull, which the sun enters about 21 April. **Taurean** *adjective* & *noun*

taut *adverb* stretched firmly, not slack. **tautly** *adverb*

tauten *verb* to make or become taut.

tautology (taw-**tol**-ŏ-jee) *noun* saying of the same thing over again in different words, especially using a word or phrase of the same grammatical construction, as in 'free, gratis, and for nothing'. **tautological** (taw-tŏ-**loj**-ikăl) *adjective*, **tautologous** (taw-**tol**-ŏ-gŭs) *adjective* [from Greek *tauto* = the same, + *logos* = word]

tavern *noun* a place licensed to sell alcoholic drinks for consumption on the premises. [from Latin *taberna* = hut]

taw *noun* **1** a favourite marble. **2** the line from which a game of marbles starts. **taws** *plural noun* the game of marbles. □ **back to taws** (*informal*) back to the beginning.

tawdry (**taw**-dree) *adjective* (**tawdrier**, **tawdriest**) showy or gaudy but without real value. **tawdrily** *adverb*, **tawdriness** *noun* [from *St Audrey's lace* (cheap finery formerly sold at St Audrey's fair at Ely in England)]

tawny *adjective* brownish-yellow or brownish-orange.

tax *noun* **1** a sum of money to be paid by people or business firms to a government, to be used for public purposes. **2** something that makes a heavy demand, *a tax on one's strength*. – **tax** *verb* **1** to impose a tax on; to require (a person) to pay tax. **2** to make heavy demands on. **3** to accuse in a challenging or reproving way, *taxed him with having left the door unlocked*. □ **tax-free** *adjective* exempt from taxes. **tax haven** a country where income tax etc. is low. **tax return** an official declaration of income which is used to assess the tax payable. [from Latin *taxare* = calculate]

taxable *adjective* able or liable to be taxed.

taxation *noun* the imposition or payment of tax.

taxi *noun* (*plural* **taxis**) (also **taxicab**) a car that plies for hire, usually with a meter to record the fare payable. – **taxi** *verb* (**taxied**, **taxiing**) **1** to go or convey in a taxi. **2** (of aircraft) to move along ground or water under its own power, especially before or after flying. [short for *taxi-meter cab*]

taxidermy (**tak**-see-derm-ee) *noun* the art of preparing and mounting the skins of animals in lifelike form. **taxidermist** *noun* [from Greek *taxis* = arrangement, + *derma* = skin]

taxman *noun* (*plural* **taxmen**) a collector of taxes; the taxation office personified.

taxonomy (taks-**on**-ŏ-mee) *noun* the scientific process of classifying living things.

taxpayer *noun* a person who pays tax (especially income tax).

TB *abbreviation* (*informal*) tuberculosis.

Tbilisi (t'bi-**lee**-see) the capital of the republic of Georgia.

T-bone *noun* a piece of loin steak containing a T-shaped bone.

Tchaikovsky (chy-**kof**-skee), Pyotr (1840–93), Russian composer.

tea *noun* **1** (in full **tea plant**) an evergreen shrub grown in Sri Lanka, China, etc.; its dried leaves. **2** the hot drink that is made by steeping these in boiling water. **3** a drink made by steeping the leaves of other plants in water, *camomile tea*; *peppermint tea*. **4** the main evening meal. **5** a light meal in the morning or afternoon at which tea is served. □ **tea bag** a small porous bag holding about a teaspoonful of tea for infusion. **tea break** an interruption of work allowed for drinking tea etc. **tea chest** a light cubical chest lined with thin sheets of lead or tin, in which tea is exported. **tea cosy** a cover placed over a teapot to keep the tea hot. **tea leaf** a leaf of tea, especially after infusion.

tea party a party at which tea is served. **tea room** a small restaurant where tea and other refreshments are served. **tea rose** a scented rose introduced from China with the tea ships. **tea set** a set of cups and plates etc. for serving tea. **tea towel** a towel for drying washed crockery etc. **tea tree** any of various aromatic Australian shrubs of the myrtle family, including some whose leaves have been used as a substitute for tea. [from Chinese *t'e*]

teacake *noun* a kind of bun usually served toasted and buttered.

teach *verb* (**taught**, **teaching**) **1** to impart information or skill to (a person) or about (a subject etc.). **2** to do this for a living. **3** to put forward as a fact or principle, *Christ taught forgiveness*, *taught that we must forgive our enemies*. **4** to cause to adopt (a practice etc.) by example or experience; (*informal*) to deter by punishment etc., *that will teach you not to meddle*.

teachable *adjective* **1** able to learn by being taught. **2** (of a subject) able to be taught.

teacher *noun* a person who teaches others, especially in a school.

teaching *noun* what is taught, *the teachings of the Church*.

teacup *noun* a cup from which tea or other hot liquids are drunk.

teak *noun* **1** the strong heavy wood of a tall evergreen Asian tree, used for making furniture and in shipbuilding. **2** the tree itself. **3** an Australian tree yielding a similar wood.

teal *noun* (*plural* **teal**) a small freshwater duck.

team *noun* **1** a set of players forming one side in certain games and sports. **2** a set of people working together. **3** two or more animals harnessed together to draw a vehicle or farm implement. –**team** *verb* to combine into a team or set or for a common purpose. ☐ **team spirit** willingness to act for the good of one's group rather than oneself.

teamwork *noun* organised cooperation.

teapot *noun* a pot with a handle, lid, and spout, in which tea is made and from which it is poured.

tear¹ (*pr.* tair) *verb* (**tore**, **torn**, **tearing**) **1** to pull forcibly apart or away or to pieces. **2** to make (a hole or a split) in this way. **3** to become torn, to be able to be torn, *paper tears easily*. **4** to subject (a person etc.) to conflicting desires or demands, *torn between love and duty*. **5** to run, walk, or travel hurriedly. –**tear** *noun* a hole or split caused

by tearing. ☐ **tear apart** to divide totally; to distress greatly; to destroy; to search (a place) exhaustively; to criticise severely. **tear one's hair** to pull it in anger, perplexity, or despair.

tear² (*pr.* teer) *noun* a drop of the salty water that appears in or flows from the eye as the result of grief or other emotion, or irritation by fumes etc. ☐ **in tears** shedding tears. **tear gas** a gas that causes severe irritation of the eyes.

tearaway *noun* an impetuous hooligan.

teardrop *noun* a single tear.

tearful *adjective* shedding or ready to shed tears, sad. **tearfully** *adverb*

tearing (**tair**-ring) *adjective* violent, overwhelming, *in a tearing hurry*.

tease *verb* **1** to try to provoke in a playful or unkind way by jokes or questions or petty annoyances. **2** to pick (wool etc.) into separate strands. **3** to brush up the nap on (cloth). –**tease** *noun* a person who is fond of teasing others.

teasel (**tee**-zĕl) *noun* **1** a plant with bristly heads formerly used to brush up nap on cloth. **2** a device used for this purpose. [from *tease* sense 2]

teaser *noun* (*informal*) a problem that is difficult to solve.

teaspoon *noun* **1** a small spoon for stirring tea. **2** the amount held by this (5 ml). **teaspoonful** *noun* (*plural* **teaspoonfuls**).

teat *noun* **1** a nipple on an animal's milk-secreting organ. **2** a device of rubber etc. on a feeding bottle, through which the contents are sucked.

technetium (tek-**nee**-shee-ŭm) *noun* a radioactive metallic element, the first to be artificially created (in 1937) (symbol Tc).

technical *adjective* **1** of the mechanical arts and applied sciences, *a technical education* or *college*. **2** of a particular subject or craft etc. or its techniques, *the technical terms of chemistry*; *technical skill*. **3** (of a book etc.) requiring specialised knowledge, using technical terms. **4** in a strict legal sense, *technical assault*. **5** of a mechanical nature, *technical troubles*. **technically** *adverb* [from Greek *tekhnikos* = skilful]

technicality (tek-nĭ-**kal**-ĭ-tee) *noun* **1** being technical. **2** a technical word, phrase, or point, *he was acquitted on a technicality*.

technician (tek-**nish**-ăn) *noun* **1** an expert in the techniques of a particular subject or craft. **2** a skilled mechanic.

Technicolor *noun* **1** (*trademark*) a process of producing cinema films in colour. **2** technicolour vivid or artificially brilliant colour.

technique (tek-**neek**) *noun* the method of doing or performing something (especially in an art or science); skill in this.

techno *noun* a style of popular music using electronic equipment and synthesised repetitive sounds.

technologist *noun* an expert in technology.

technology *noun* **1** the scientific study of mechanical arts and applied sciences (e.g. engineering). **2** these subjects, their practical application in industry etc. **technological** *adjective*, **technologically** *adverb* [from Greek *tekhne* = skill, + *-logy*]

tectonics (tek-**tonn**-iks) *noun* the scientific study of the earth's structural features as a whole. [from Greek *tekton* = carpenter]

teddy bear *noun* a soft furry toy bear. [named after US President Theodore ('Teddy') Roosevelt in about 1906]

Te Deum (tee **dee**-ŭm) *noun* a Latin canticle beginning 'Te Deum laudamus' (= we praise thee O God).

tedious (**tee**-dee-ŭs) *adjective* tiresome because of its length or slowness or dullness, boring. **tediously** *adverb*, **tediousness** *noun* [from Latin *taedium* = tiresomeness]

tedium (**tee**-dee-ŭm) *noun* tediousness.

tee *noun* **1** the letter T. **2** the cleared space from which a player strikes the ball in golf at the beginning of play for each hole. **3** a small pile of sand or piece of wood etc. on which the ball is placed for being struck. **4** the mark aimed at in quoits, bowls, and curling. –**tee** *verb* (**teed**, **teeing**) to place (a ball) on a tee in golf. ☐ **tee off** to play the ball from the tee. **tee up** (*informal*) to arrange.

teeball *noun* a game like softball, in which the ball is hit from a tee instead of being pitched.

teem[1] *verb* **1** to be full of, *the river was teeming with fish*. **2** to be present in large numbers, *fish teem in that river*.

teem[2] *verb* (of water or rain etc.) to flow in large quantities, to pour.

teenage *adjective* of teenagers.

teenaged *adjective* in one's teens.

teenager *noun* a person in his or her teens.

teens *plural noun* the years of a person's age or degrees of temperature from 13 to 19.

teeny *adjective* (**teenier**, **teeniest**) (*informal*) tiny.

teenybopper *noun* (*informal*) a young teenager (usually a girl) who follows the latest fashions in clothes, music, etc.

teeshirt *noun* = T-shirt.

teeter *verb* to stand or move unsteadily.

teeth *see* tooth.

teethe *verb* (of a baby) to have its first teeth beginning to grow through the gums. ☐ **teething troubles** problems arising in the early stages of an enterprise.

teetotal *adjective* abstaining completely from alcoholic drinks. **teetotaller** *noun*

teflon *noun* (*trademark*) a material used to coat the inside of pots and pans to prevent food from sticking.

Tegucigalpa (tay-goo-sĭ-**gal**-pă) the capital of Honduras.

Tehran (tay-**rahn**) the capital of Iran.

tele- *prefix* far; at a distance (as in *telescope*). [from Greek *tele* = far off]

telecast *noun* a television broadcast. –**telecast** *verb* to transmit by television.

telecommunications *plural noun* the means of communication over long distances, as by cable, satellite, telegraph, telephone, radio, or television.

teleconference *noun* a conference linking participants in different locations by telecommunication devices. **teleconferencing** *noun*

telegram *noun* a message sent by telegraph. [from *tele-* + *-gram*]

telegraph *noun* a system or apparatus for sending messages to a distance, especially by transmission of electrical impulses along wires. –**telegraph** *verb* to send (a message) or communicate with (a person) by telegraph. ☐ **telegraph pole** a pole supporting overhead wires for use in telegraphy etc. [from *tele-* + *-graph*]

telegraphist (tĕ-**leg**-ră-fĭst) *noun* a person whose job is to send and receive messages by telegraph.

telegraphy (tĕ-**leg**-ră-fee) *noun* the process of communication by telegraph. **telegraphic** (tel-ĕ-**graf**-ik) *adjective*

Telemann (**tel**-ĕ-mahn), Georg Philipp (1681–1767), German composer.

telemarketing *noun* the marketing of goods or services by unsolicited telephone calls. **telemarketer** *noun*

teleology (tee-lee-**ol**-ŏ-jee) *noun* the doctrine that there is evidence of design or purpose in nature. **teleological** (tee-lee-ŏ-**loj**-i-kăl) *adjective* [from Greek *telos* = end, + *-logy*]

telepathic (tel-ĕ-**path**-ik) *adjective* of or using telepathy; able to communicate by telepathy.

telepathy (tĕ-**lep**-ă-thee) *noun* communication from one mind to another without the use of speech, writing, or gestures etc. [from *tele-*, + Greek *pathos* = feeling]

telephone *noun* 1 a system of transmitting sound (especially speech) to a distance by wire, cord, or radio. 2 an instrument used in this, with a receiver and mouthpiece and a bell to indicate an incoming call. –**telephone** *verb* to send (a message) or speak to (a person) by telephone. ☐ **telephone directory** or **book** a book listing the names and numbers of people who have a telephone. **telephone number** a number assigned to a particular instrument and used in making connections to it. **telephonic** (tel-ĕ-**fon**-ik) *adjective*, **telephonically** *adverb* [from *tele-*, + Greek *phone* = voice]

telephonist (tĕ-**lef**-ŏ-nĭst) *noun* an operator in a telephone exchange or at a switchboard.

telephony (tĕ-**lef**-ŏ-nee) *noun* the process of transmitting sound by telephone.

telephoto lens *noun* a lens producing a large image of a distant object that is photographed.

teleprinter *noun* a device for transmitting, receiving, and printing telegraph messages.

telescope *noun* an optical instrument using lenses or mirrors or both to make distant objects appear larger when viewed through it. –**telescope** *verb* 1 to make or become shorter by sliding overlapping sections one inside another. 2 to compress or become compressed forcibly. 3 to condense so as to occupy less space or time. ☐ **radio telescope** an apparatus for collecting radio waves emitted by celestial objects and recording their intensity etc. [from *tele-*, + Greek *skopein* = look at]

telescopic *adjective* 1 of a telescope; magnifying like a telescope. 2 visible only through a telescope, *telescopic stars*. 3 capable of being telescoped, *telescopic umbrella*. **telescopically** *adverb*

teletext *noun* a system in which information can be selected and produced on the screen of a suitably modified television set.

telethon *noun* a very long television program, especially to raise money for charity. [*tele-* + *-thon* as in *marathon*]

televise *verb* to transmit by television.

television *noun* 1 a system for reproducing on a screen visual images transmitted (usually with sound) by radio signals or cable. 2 (also **television set**) an apparatus with a screen for receiving pictures transmitted in this way. 3 televised programs; television as a medium of communication. [from *tele-* + *vision*]

telex *noun* 1 a system of telegraphy in which printed messages are transmitted and received by teleprinters installed in the senders' and receivers' offices, using public transmission lines. 2 a message sent or received by telex. –**telex** *verb* to send (a message) or communicate with (a person) by telex.

Tell, William, a legendary hero (traditionally placed in the 14th century) of the liberation of Switzerland, who was required to hit with an arrow an apple placed on the head of his son.

tell *verb* (**told**, **telling**) 1 to make known, especially in spoken or written words. 2 to give information to. 3 to utter, *tell the truth*. 4 to reveal a secret, *promise you won't tell*. 5 to decide or determine, *how do you tell which button to press?* 6 to distinguish, *I can't tell him from his brother*. 7 to produce a noticeable effect, *the strain began to tell on him*. 8 to count; *tell one's beads*, to say prayers while counting beads on a rosary. 9 to direct or order, *tell them to wait*. ☐ **tell fortunes** *see* **fortune**. **tell off** (*informal*) to reprimand or scold. **tell on** (*informal*) to reveal the activities of (a person) by telling others. **tell tales** to report what is meant to be secret. **tell the time** to read the time from a clock.

teller *noun* 1 a person who tells or gives an account of something. 2 a person employed to receive and pay out money in a bank. 3 a person appointed to count votes.

telling *adjective* having a noticeable effect, striking, *a telling argument*.

telltale *noun* 1 a person who tells tales. 2 a mechanical device that serves as an indicator. –**telltale** *adjective* revealing or indicating something, *a telltale blush*.

telluric *adjective* 1 of the earth. 2 of the soil.

tellurium *noun* an element (symbol Te) chemically related to sulphur and selenium, used in semiconductors.

telly *noun* (*informal*) television; a television set.

temerity (tĕ-**me**-rĭ-tee) *noun* audacity, rashness.

temper *noun* 1 the state of the mind as regards calmness or anger, *in a good temper*. 2 a fit of anger, *in a temper*. 3 calmness under provocation, *keep* or *lose one's temper*. 4 a tendency to have fits of anger, *have a temper*. 5 the condition of a tempered metal as regards hardness and elasticity. –**temper** *verb* 1 to bring (metal) or be brought to the required degree of hardness and elasticity by heating and then cooling. 2 to bring (clay etc.) to the required consistency by moistening and mixing. 3 to moderate or soften the effects of; *temper justice with mercy*, be merciful in awarding punishment. [from Latin *temperare* = mix]

tempera *noun* a method of painting with powdered colours mixed with egg or size, used in Europe chiefly in the 12th–15th centuries.

temperament *noun* a person's nature as it controls the way he or she behaves, feels, and thinks, *a nervous temperament*.

temperamental *adjective* 1 of or in a person's temperament. 2 not having a calm temperament, having fits of excitable or moody behaviour. **temperamentally** *adverb*

temperance *noun* 1 self-restraint in one's behaviour or in eating and drinking. 2 total abstinence from alcoholic drinks.

temperate *adjective* 1 self-restrained in one's behaviour, moderate. 2 (of climate) having a mild temperature without extremes of heat and cold. **temperately** *adverb*

temperature *noun* 1 the intensity of heat or cold in a body or room or country etc. 2 a measure of this shown by a thermometer. 3 an abnormally high temperature of the body, *have a temperature*.

tempest *noun* a violent storm. [from Latin *tempestas* = weather]

tempestuous (tem-**pest**-yoo-ŭs) *adjective* stormy, full of commotion.

Templar *noun* a member of the Knights Templars (*see* knight).

template *noun* 1 a pattern or gauge, usually of thin board or metal, used as a guide for cutting metal, stone, or wood etc. or pieces of fabric, or for shaping plaster or concrete etc.

2 a timber or metal plate used to distribute weight in a wall or under a beam. 3 something that serves as a model or example.

temple¹ *noun* a building dedicated to the presence or service of a god or gods. [from Latin *templum* = consecrated place]

temple² *noun* the flat part at each side of the head between forehead and ear. [from Latin *tempora* = sides of the head]

tempo *noun* (*plural* tempos *or* tempi) 1 the time, speed, or rhythm of a piece of music, *in waltz tempo*. 2 the pace of any movement or activity. [Italian, from Latin *tempus* = time]

temporal (**tem**-pŏ-răl) *adjective* 1 secular, of worldly affairs as opposed to spiritual. 2 of or denoting time. 3 of the temple(s) of the head.

temporary (**tem**-pŏ-ră-ree) *adjective* lasting or meant to last for a limited time only, not permanent. –**temporary** *noun* a person employed temporarily. **temporarily** *adverb* [from Latin *temporis* = of a time]

temporise *verb* (also -ize) to compromise temporarily, or avoid giving a definite answer or decision, in order to gain time. **temporisation** *noun*, **temporiser** *noun*

tempt *verb* 1 to persuade or try to persuade (especially into doing something wrong or unwise) by the prospect of pleasure or advantage. 2 to arouse a desire in, to attract; *I'm tempted to question this*, feel inclined to do so. 3 to risk provoking (fate or Providence) by deliberate rashness. **tempter** *noun*, **temptress** *feminine noun* [from Latin *temptare* = to test]

temptation *noun* 1 tempting; being tempted. 2 something that tempts or attracts.

tempting *adjective* attractive, inviting, *a tempting offer*.

tempura (tem-**poo**-ră) *noun* a Japanese dish of seafood or vegetables fried in batter.

ten *adjective* & *noun* one more than nine (10, X).

tenable (**ten**-ă-bŭl) *adjective* 1 able to be defended against attack or objection, *a tenable position* or *theory*. 2 (of an office) able to be held for a certain time or by a certain class of person etc. **tenability** *noun* [from Latin *tenere* = to hold]

tenacious (tĕ-**nay**-shŭs) *adjective* 1 holding or clinging firmly to something (e.g. rights or principles). 2 (of memory) retentive. 3 sticking firmly together or to an object or surface. **tenaciously** *adverb*, **tenacity** (tĕ-**nass**-ĭ-tee) *noun*

tenancy *noun* **1** the use of land or buildings as a tenant. **2** the period of this.

tenant *noun* **1** a person who rents land or buildings from a landlord. **2** (in law) an occupant or owner of land or a building. –**tenant** *verb* to occupy as a tenant. [from Latin *tenens* = holding]

tend¹ *verb* to take care of or look after (a person or thing). [from *attend*]

tend² *verb* **1** to be likely to behave in a certain way or to have a certain characteristic. **2** to have a certain influence, *recent laws tend to increase customers' rights*. **3** to take a certain direction, *the track tends upwards*. [from Latin *tendere* = to stretch]

tendency *noun* **1** the way a person or thing tends to be or behave, *a tendency to fat* or *towards fatness*; *homicidal tendencies*. **2** the direction in which something moves or changes, a trend, *an upward tendency*.

tendentious (ten-**den**-shŭs) *adjective* (of a speech or piece of writing etc.) aimed at helping a cause, not impartial.

tender¹ *adjective* **1** not tough or hard, easy to chew, *tender meat*. **2** easily damaged, delicate, *tender plants*; *of tender age*, young and vulnerable. **3** sensitive, painful when touched. **4** easily moved to pity or sympathy, *a tender heart*. **5** loving, gentle. **tenderly** *adverb*, **tenderness** *noun* [from Latin *tener* = soft]

tender² *verb* **1** to offer formally, *tender one's resignation*. **2** to make a tender (for goods or work). –**tender** *noun* a formal offer to supply goods or carry out work at a stated price; *put work out to tender*, ask for such offers. □ **legal tender** currency that must, by law, be accepted in payment.

tender³ *noun* **1** a person who tends or looks after something. **2** a vessel or vehicle travelling to and from a larger one to convey stores or passengers etc. **3** a truck attached to a steam locomotive, carrying fuel and water etc. [from *tend¹*]

tenderfoot *noun* a newcomer who is unused to hardships; an inexperienced person.

tenderise *verb* (also -**ize**) to make more tender. **tenderiser** *noun*

tenderloin *noun* the middle part of pork loin.

tendon *noun* a strong band or cord of tissue connecting a muscle to some other part.

tendril *noun* **1** a threadlike part by which a climbing plant clings to a support. **2** a slender curl of hair etc.

tenement (**ten**-ĕ-mĕnt) *noun* **1** (in law) land or other permanent property held by a tenant, *lands and tenements*. **2** a flat or room rented for living in. **3** a large block of flats.

Tenerife (ten-ĕ-**reef**) a volcanic island that is the largest of the Canary Islands.

tenet (**ten**-ĕt) *noun* a firm belief, principle, or doctrine of a person or group. [Latin, = he or she holds]

tenfold *adjective* & *adverb* ten times as much or as many.

Tennessee (ten-ĕ-**see**) a State of the central south-eastern USA.

tennis *noun* **1** (also **lawn tennis**) a game in which two or four players strike a soft ball with racquets over a net stretched across an open court. **2** (also **real tennis**) a similar older game, played with a hard ball in a walled court. [from French *tenez* = receive! (called by the person serving)]

Tennyson, Alfred, 1st Baron (1809–92), English poet.

tenon (**ten**-ŏn) *noun* a projection shaped to fit into a mortise.

tenor (**ten**-er) *noun* **1** the general routine or course of something, *disrupting the even tenor of his life*. **2** the general meaning or drift, *the tenor of his lecture*. **3** the highest ordinary adult male singing voice; a singer with this; a part written for it. **4** a musical instrument with approximately the range of a tenor voice, *tenor saxophone*.

tenpin bowling *noun* an indoor game in which players try to knock down with a ball ten pins or skittles at the end of an alley.

tense¹ *noun* any of the forms of a verb that indicate the time of action etc. as past, present, or future, *'came' is the past tense of 'come'*. [from Latin *tempus* = time]

tense² *adjective* **1** stretched tightly. **2** with muscles tight in attentiveness for what may happen. **3** unable to relax, edgy. **4** causing tenseness, *a tense moment*. –**tense** *verb* to make or become tense. **tensely** *adverb*, **tenseness** *noun* [from Latin *tensum* = stretched]

tensile (**ten**-syl) *adjective* **1** of tension; *tensile strength*, resistance to breaking under tension. **2** capable of being stretched. **tensility** (ten-**sil**-ĭ-tee) *noun*

tension *noun* **1** stretching; being stretched. **2** tenseness, the condition when feelings are tense. **3** the effect produced by forces pulling against each other. **4** electromotive force, voltage, *high-tension cables*. **5** the degree of tightness of stitches in sewing or knitting; (in knitting) the number of stitches and rows to a unit of measurement (e.g. 20 stitches to 10 cm).

tent *noun* a portable shelter or dwelling made of canvas etc. [same origin as *tense²*]

tentacle *noun* a slender flexible part extending from the body of certain animals (e.g. snails, octopuses), used for feeling or grasping things or moving. **tentacled** *adjective*

tentative (**tent**-ă-tiv) *adjective* hesitant, not definite, done as a trial, *a tentative suggestion*. **tentatively** *adverb* [same origin as *tempt*]

tenter *noun* a machine for stretching cloth to dry during manufacture.

tenterhook *noun* each of the hooks that hold cloth stretched for drying during its manufacture. □ **on tenterhooks** in a state of suspense or strain because of uncertainty.

tenth *adjective & noun* **1** next after ninth. **2** one of ten equal parts of a thing. **tenthly** *adverb*

tenuous (**ten**-yoo-ŭs) *adjective* **1** very thin in form or consistency, *tenuous threads*. **2** having little substance or validity, very slight, *tenuous- distinctions*. **tenuously** *adverb*, **tenuousness** *noun*, **tenuity** (tĕ-**new**-ĭ-tee) *noun* [from Latin *tenuis* = thin]

tenure (**ten**-yer) *noun* the holding of office or of land or other permanent property or accommodation etc.; the period or manner of this, *freehold tenure*; *she was granted security of tenure for six months*.

tepee (**tee**-pee) *noun* a conical tent, as formerly used by some North American indigenous peoples.

tepid *adjective* slightly warm, lukewarm. **tepidly** *adverb*, **tepidity** (tĕ-**pid**-ĭ-tee) *noun*

terabyte *noun* (in computing) a unit of information equal to one million million or (strictly) 2^{40} bytes.

teraglin (tĕ-**rag**-lĭn) *noun* (also **trag**) an edible sea fish.

terbium (**ter**-bee-ŭm) *noun* a silver-white metallic element of the lanthanide series (symbol Tb).

tercentenary (ter-sen-**teen**-ă-ree) *noun* a 300th anniversary. [from Latin *ter* = three times, + *centenary*]

term *noun* **1** the time for which something lasts, a fixed or limited time, *during his term of office*; *a term of imprisonment*. **2** completion

of this, *a pregnancy approaching term*. **3** one of the periods, each lasting for a number of weeks, during which instruction is given in a school, college, or university or in which a lawcourt holds sessions, alternating with holidays or vacations. **4** each of the quantities or expressions in a mathematical series or ratio etc. **5** a word or phrase considered as the name or symbol of something, *'the nick' is a slang term for 'prison'*. –**term** *verb* to call by a certain term or expression, *this music is termed plainsong*. **terms** *plural noun* **1** language or the manner of its use, *we protested in strong terms*. **2** stipulations made, conditions offered or accepted, *peace terms*. **3** payment offered or asked, *a loan on easy terms*. **4** a relation between people, *on friendly terms*. □ **come to terms** to reach an agreement; to reconcile oneself to a difficulty etc., *came to terms with his handicap*. **terms of reference** the defined scope of an inquiry or other activity. [from Latin *terminus* = boundary]

termagant (**ter**-mă-gănt) *noun* a shrewish bullying woman.

terminable *adjective* able to be terminated.

terminal *adjective* **1** of, forming, or situated at the end or boundary of something. **2** forming or undergoing the last stage of a fatal disease, *terminal cancer*. **3** of or done each term, *terminal examinations*. –**terminal** *noun* **1** a terminating point or part. **2** a terminus for trains or long-distance buses; a building (where air passengers arrive and depart. **3** a point of connection in an electric circuit or device. **4** an apparatus for transmitting messages to and from a computer or communications system etc. □ **terminal velocity** the maximum speed reached by a falling body when the frictional resistance of the air etc. through which it is falling matches the gravitational pull. **terminally** *adverb*

terminate *verb* to end. □ **terminating decimals** decimals that do not recur but come to an end, e.g. $0.5 (= \frac{1}{2})$ or $0.25 (= \frac{1}{4})$. **termination** *noun*, **terminator** *noun* [same origin as *terminus*]

terminology *noun* **1** the technical terms of a particular subject. **2** the proper use of words as names or symbols. **terminological** *adjective* [from *term* + -*logy*]

terminus *noun* (*plural* **termini**, *pr.* **ter**-min-I) the end of something; the last station at the end of a railway or bus route. [Latin, = the end]

termite *noun* a small insect that is very destructive to timber, especially in tropical areas (popularly called *white ant*, but not of the ant family).

tern *noun* a seabird with long pointed wings and a forked tail.

ternary *adjective* composed of three parts. [from Latin *terni* = three each]

Terpsichore (terp-**sik**-ŏ-ree) (*Gk. & Rom. myth.*) the Muse of lyric poetry and dance.

Terra Australis Incognita 'unknown southern land', the name given by early European cartographers etc. to a landmass presumed to exist south of the known world. [Latin]

terrace *noun* **1** a raised level place; one of a series of these into which a hillside is shaped for cultivation. **2** a flight of wide shallow steps, e.g. for spectators at a sportsground. **3** a paved area beside a house. **4** a row of houses joined to each other by party walls. **5** a street, especially with buildings on only one side. –terrace *verb* to form into a terrace or terraces. □ terrace house one house in a terrace. [from Latin *terra* = earth]

terracotta *noun* **1** a kind of brownish-red unglazed pottery. **2** its colour. [Italian, = baked earth]

terra firma *noun* dry land; the ground. [Latin]

terrain (tě-**rayn**) *noun* a stretch of land with regard to its natural features. [from Latin *terra* = earth]

terra nullius *noun* land assumed to belong to no one and so to be available to be taken over (*see also* native title). [Latin]

terrapin (**te**-ră-pin) *noun* an edible North American freshwater tortoise.

terrarium (tě-**rair**-ree-ŭm) *noun* (*plural* terrariums) **1** a place for keeping small land animals. **2** a sealed transparent globe etc. containing growing plants. [from Latin *terra* = earth, + *aquarium*]

terrazzo (tě-**raht**-soh) *noun* (*plural* terrazzos) a flooring material of stone chips set in concrete and given a smooth surface.

terrestrial (tě-**rest**-ree-ăl) *adjective* **1** of the earth. **2** of or living on land. [from Latin *terra* = earth]

terrible *adjective* **1** appalling, distressing. **2** extreme, hard to bear, *the heat was terrible*. **3** (*informal*) very bad, *I'm terrible at tennis*. **terribly** *adverb* [from Latin *terrere* = frighten]

terrier *noun* a kind of small hardy active dog.

terrific *adjective* (*informal*) **1** of great size or intensity, *a terrific sum of money*. **2** excellent, *you did a terrific job*. **terrifically** *adverb*

terrify *verb* (terrified, terrifying) to fill with terror.

terrine (tě-**reen**) *noun* **1** a coarse-textured pâté. **2** an earthenware dish holding this.

territorial *adjective* **1** of a territory, *territorial rights*. **2** tending to defend a territory, *a territorial animal*. □ territorial waters the sea within a certain distance of a country's coast and subject to its control. **territorially** *adverb*

Territorian *noun* (*Austral.*) a person native to or resident in the Northern Territory.

territory *noun* **1** land under the control of a ruler, State, or city etc. **2** Territory an organised division of a country, especially one not yet admitted to the full rights of a State, *the Australian Capital Territory*; *the Northern Territory*. **3** an area for which a person has responsibility. **4** a sphere of action or thought, a province. **5** an area claimed or dominated by one person, group, or animal and defended against others. □ the Territory (*Austral.*) the Northern Territory. [from Latin *terra* = earth]

terror *noun* **1** extreme fear. **2** a terrifying person or thing. **3** (*informal*) a formidable person; a troublesome person or thing. □ the Terror or Reign of Terror the period of the French Revolution during 1793–4 when Robespierre and his supporters ruthlessly executed opponents to their regime. **terror-stricken** *adjective* stricken with terror. [from Latin *terrere* = frighten]

terrorise *verb* (also -ize) to fill with terror; to coerce by terrorism. **terrorisation** *noun*

terrorism *noun* use of violence and intimidation, especially for political purposes. **terrorist** *noun*

terry *noun* (also terry towelling) a cotton fabric used for towels etc., with raised loops left uncut.

terse *adjective* concise; curt. **tersely** *adverb*, **terseness** *noun* [from Latin *tersum* = polished]

tertiary (**ter**-shă-ree) *adjective* **1** coming after secondary, of the third rank or stage etc. **2** (of education) above secondary level. **3** Tertiary of the first geological period of the Cenozoic era, during which mammals (but not humans) appeared. –Tertiary *noun* the Tertiary period. [from Latin *tertius* = third]

terylene *noun* (*trademark*) a kind of synthetic textile fibre.

tesla *noun* a unit of magnetic induction, = 10,000 gauss. [named after N. Tesla, Croatian-born American scientist (1856–1943)]

tessellated (**tess**-ě-lay-těd) *adjective* (of a pavement) made from small flat pieces of stone in various colours arranged in a pattern.

test *noun* 1 a critical examination or evaluation of the qualities or abilities etc. of a person or thing. 2 a means or procedure for making this. 3 a minor examination (especially in a school). 4 a test match. –**test** *verb* to subject to a test. □ **put to the test** to cause to undergo a test. **stand the test** to undergo it successfully. **test case** a lawsuit providing a decision that is taken as applying to similar cases in the future. **test match** a cricket or rugby match between teams of certain countries, usually one of a series in a tour. **test tube** a tube of thin glass with one end closed, used in laboratories. **test-tube baby** (*informal*) one conceived outside a mother's body (by *in vitro* fertilisation) and then implanted in her uterus. **tester** *noun*

testa *noun* (*plural* testae) the outer protective covering of a seed.

testament *noun* 1 (usually **last will and testament**) a will. 2 (*informal*) a written statement of one's beliefs. 3 a covenant. □ **Old Testament** the books of the Bible telling of the history of the Jews and their beliefs. **New Testament** the books of the Bible telling of the life and teaching of Christ and his earliest followers. [from Latin *testis* = witness]

testamentary *adjective* of or given in a person's will.

testate (**tes**-tayt) *adjective* having left a valid will at death.

testator (tes-**tay**-ter) *noun* a person who has made a will. **testatrix** *noun* a woman testator.

testes *see* testis.

testicle *noun* a male reproductive organ in which sperm-bearing fluid is produced, (in man) each of the two enclosed in the scrotum.

testify *verb* (testified, testifying) 1 to bear witness to (a fact etc.); to give evidence. 2 to be evidence of. [from Latin *testis* = witness]

testimonial *noun* 1 a formal statement testifying to a person's character, abilities, or qualifications. 2 something given to a person to show appreciation of his or her services or achievements.

testimony *noun* 1 a declaration or statement (especially one made under oath). 2 evidence in support of something.

testis *noun* (*plural* testes, *pr.* **tes**-teez) a testicle.

testosterone (tess-**toss**-tě-rohn) *noun* a male sex hormone.

testy *adjective* easily annoyed, irritable. **testily** *adverb*, **testiness** *noun*

tetanus (tet-ă-nŭs) *noun* a disease in which the muscles contract and stiffen (as in lockjaw), caused by bacteria that enter the body. [from Greek *tetanos* = a spasm]

tetchy *adjective* peevish, irritable. **tetchily** *adverb*

tête-à-tête (tayt-ah-**tayt**) *noun* a private conversation, especially between two people. –**tête-à-tête** *adverb* & *adjective* together in private. [French, = head to head]

tether *noun* a rope or chain by which an animal is fastened while grazing. –**tether** *verb* to fasten (an animal) with a tether. □ **at the end of one's tether** having reached the limit of one's endurance.

tetra- *prefix* four. [Greek, = four]

tetrachloride *noun* a compound of an element or radical with four atoms of chlorine.

tetrahedron (tet-ră-**hee**-drŏn) *noun* a solid with four faces, a pyramid with three triangular faces and a triangular base. [from *tetra-*, + Greek *hedra* = base]

tetrarch *noun* (*Roman history*) a governor of a fourth part of a country or province.

Tetun (**tet**-uun) *noun* (also **Tetum**) one of the official languages of East Timor. Several varieties of Tetun exist and are spoken on Timor.

Teutonic (tew-**tonn**-ik) *adjective* 1 of the Germanic peoples (Teutons) or their languages. 2 German.

tex *noun* a unit of weight used to express the fineness of fibres and yarns. [short for *textile*]

Texas a State of the southern USA. **Texan** *adjective* & *noun*

text *noun* 1 the wording of something written or printed. 2 the main body of a book or page etc. as distinct from illustrations or notes. 3 a sentence from Scripture used as the subject of a sermon or discussion. 4 a book or play etc. prescribed for study. 5 data in textual form, especially as stored, processed, or displayed in a word processor etc. –**text** *verb* send a text message to. □ **text editor** (in computing) a system or program allowing the user to enter and edit text. **text message** electronic communication sent and received via a mobile phone. [from Latin *textus* = literary style]

textbook *noun* a book of information for use in studying a subject.

textile *noun* a woven or machine-knitted fabric. –textile *adjective* of textiles. [from Latin *textum* = woven]

textual *adjective* of or in a text. textually *adverb*

texture *noun* the way a fabric or other substance feels to the touch; its thickness, firmness, or solidity.

textured *adjective* 1 having a certain texture, *coarse-textured*. 2 (of yarn or fabric) crimped, curled, or looped.

Thackeray, William Makepeace (1811–63), English satirical novelist, best known for *Vanity Fair*.

Thai (*pr.* ty) *adjective* of Thailand or its people or language. –Thai *noun* 1 a native or inhabitant of Thailand. 2 the language of Thailand.

Thailand (**ty**-land) a kingdom in SE Asia (formerly known as Siam).

Thalia (thă-**ly**-ă) (*Gk. & Rom. myth.*) the Muse of comedy.

thalidomide (thă-**lid**-ŏ-myd) *noun* a sedative drug found (in 1961) to have caused malformation of the limbs of babies whose mothers took it during pregnancy. [from its chemical name]

thallium (**thal**-ee-ŭm) *noun* a chemical element (symbol Tl), a soft white poisonous metallic substance.

Thames (*pr.* temz) a river of southern England, flowing through London to the North Sea.

than *conjunction* used to introduce the second element in a comparison, *his brother is taller than he is* or *taller than him*.

Usage These forms are preferred to *taller than he*.

thane *noun* (*historical*) 1 (in Anglo-Saxon England) a man who held land from the king or other superior in return for performing military service. 2 a man who held land from the Scottish king, a Scottish nobleman or chief of a clan.

thank *verb* to express gratitude to; *he has only himself to thank*, it is his own fault. thanks *plural noun* expressions of gratitude; (*informal*) thank you. □ thanks to on account of, as the result of. thank you a polite expression of thanks.

thankful *adjective* feeling or expressing gratitude.

thankfully *adverb* 1 in a thankful way. 2 we are thankful, *thankfully, it has stopped raining*.

Usage The second use is similar to that of *hopefully* which many people regard as unacceptable.

thankless *adjective* not likely to win thanks, *a thankless task*.

thanksgiving *noun* an expression of gratitude, especially to God. –Thanksgiving *noun* (also Thanksgiving Day) a holiday for giving thanks to God, in the USA on the fourth Thursday in November, in Canada on the second Monday in October.

that *adjective & pronoun* (*plural those*) the, the person or thing referred to or pointed to or understood; the further or less obvious one of two. –that *adverb* so, to such an extent, *I'll go that far*. –that *relative pronoun* used instead of *which, who,* or *whom* to introduce a clause that is essential in order to define or identify something, *the house that Jack built*; *the man that she married*. –that *conjunction* introducing a dependent clause, *we hope that all will go well.* □ that's that that is settled or finished.

thatch *noun* 1 a roof covering of straw, reeds, or palm leaves. 2 (*informal*) a thick growth of hair on the head. –thatch *verb* to roof or cover with thatch; to make (a roof) of thatch. thatcher *noun*

thaw *verb* 1 to pass into a liquid or unfrozen state after being frozen. 2 to become warm enough to melt ice etc. or to lose numbness. 3 to become less cool or less formal in manner. 4 to cause to thaw. –thaw *noun* thawing; weather that thaws ice etc.

the *adjective* (called the *definite article*) 1 applied to a noun standing for a specific person or a thing (*the Premier*; *the man in grey*), or representative of all of a kind (*diseases of the eye*; *the rich*), or an occupation or pursuit etc. (*too fond of the bottle*). 2 (*pr. thee*) used to emphasise excellence or importance; *he's the Sir Lawrence*, the one who is so famous. 3 (*informal*) my, our, your, etc., *the wife*. 4 (of prices) per, *cherries at $10 the kilo*. –the *adverb* in that degree, by that amount, *all the better*; *the more the merrier*.

theatre *noun* 1 a building or outdoor structure for the performance of plays and similar entertainments. 2 a room or hall for lectures etc. with seats in tiers. 3 an operating theatre. 4 a scene of important events, *Kuwait was* *the theatre of war*. **5** the writing, acting, and producing of plays. [from Greek *theatron* = place for seeing things]

theatrical *adjective* **1** of or for the theatre. **2** (of behaviour) exaggerated and designed to make a showy effect. **theatricals** *plural noun* theatrical performances, *amateur theatricals*; theatrical behaviour. **theatrically** *adverb*, **theatricality** *noun*

Thebes (*pr.* theebz) **1** an ancient city of Upper Egypt that was the capital c. 1550–1290 BC, rich in monuments on both banks of the Nile. **2** a city of Greece, north-west of Athens, leader of the whole of Greece for a short period in the 4th century BC. **Theban** *adjective* & *noun*

theca (**th'ee**-kă) *noun* (*plural* **thecae**, *pr.* **th'ee**-see) **1** a case or sheath enclosing some organ or part of an animal's body. **2** a part of a plant serving as a receptacle.

thee *pronoun* the objective case of **thou**.

theft *noun* stealing.

their *adjective* of or belonging to them. **theirs** *possessive pronoun*, of or belonging to them, the thing(s) belonging to them.

Usage It is incorrect to write *their's* (see the note under **its**).

---

theism (**th'ee**-izm) *noun* belief in the existence of gods or a god, especially a God supernaturally revealed to man and maintaining a personal relation to his creatures. **theist** *noun*, **theistic** *adjective* [from Greek *theos* = a god]

them *pronoun* **1** the objective case of **they**, *we saw them*. **2** (*informal*) = they, *it's them all right*.

thematic (th'ee-**mat**-ik) *adjective* of or according to a theme or themes. **thematically** *adverb*

theme (*pr.* theem) *noun* **1** the subject about which a person speaks, writes, or thinks. **2** a melody that is repeated or on which variations are constructed. □ **theme park** an amusement park in which all the activities etc. are related to a particular subject.

themselves *pronoun* corresponding to *they* and *them*, used in the same ways as **himself**.

then *adverb* **1** at that time. **2** next, after that; and also. **3** in that case, therefore, *if that's yours, then this must be mine*. – **then** *adjective* of that time, *the then President*. – **then** *noun* that time, *from then on*.

thence *adverb* from that place or source.

thenceforth, **thenceforward** *adverbs* from then on.

theocracy (th'ee-**ok**-ră-see) *noun* **1** government by God or a god directly or through priests. **2** a country governed in this way. [from Greek *theos* = a god, + -*cracy*]

theodolite (th'ee-**od**-ŏ-lyt) *noun* a surveying instrument with a rotating telescope used for measuring horizontal and vertical angles.

theologian (th'ee-ŏ-**loh**-jăn) *noun* an expert in theology.

theology (th'ee-**ol**-ŏ-jee) *noun* the study of religion; a system of religion. **theological** *adjective*, **theologically** *adverb* [from Greek *theos* = a god, + -*logy*]

theorem *noun* **1** a mathematical statement to be proved by a chain of reasoning. **2** a rule in algebra etc., especially one expressed as a formula. [from Greek *theorema* = theory]

theoretical *adjective* based on theory not on practice or experience. **theoretically** *adverb*

theorise *verb* (also -**ize**) to form a theory or theories.

theory *noun* **1** a set of ideas formulated (by reasoning from known facts) to explain something, *Darwin's theory of evolution*. **2** an opinion or supposition. **3** ideas or suppositions in general (contrasted with *practice*). **4** a statement of the principles on which a subject is based, *theory of music*.

theosophy (th'ee-**oss**-ŏ-fee) *noun* any of several systems of philosophy that aim at a direct knowledge of God by means of spiritual ecstasy and contemplation. **theosophical** *adjective*, **theosophist** *noun* [from Greek *theos* = a god, + *sophia* = wisdom]

therapeutic (th'e-ră-**pew**-tik) *adjective* of the relief or healing of disease etc., curative. **therapeutics** *noun* medical treatment of disease. **therapeutically** *adverb*

therapist *noun* a specialist in a certain kind of therapy.

therapy *noun* **1** any treatment designed to relieve or cure a disease or disability etc. **2** a particular type of treatment, e.g. physiotherapy, psychotherapy. [from Greek *therapeia* = healing]

Theravada (th'e-ră-**vah**-dă) *noun* a form of Buddhism practised in Sri Lanka and parts of SE Asia, considered more conservative than Mahayana Buddhism.

there *adverb* **1** in, at, or to that place. **2** at that point in a process or series of events. **3** in that matter, *I can't agree with you there*. **4** used for emphasis in calling attention, *hey, you there!* **5** used to introduce a sentence where the verb comes before its subject, *there was plenty to eat*. –**there** *noun* that place, *we live near there*. –**there** *interjection* an exclamation of satisfaction or dismay (*there! what did I tell you!*) or used to soothe a child etc. (*there, there!*).

thereabouts *adverb* **1** somewhere near there. **2** somewhere near that number or quantity or time etc.

thereafter *adverb* after that.

thereby *adverb* by that means; *thereby hangs a tale*, there is something that could be told about that.

therefore *adverb* for that reason.

therein *adverb* (*formal*) in that place; in that respect.

thereof *adverb* (*formal*) of that, of it.

thereto *adverb* (*formal*) to that, to it.

thereupon *adverb* in consequence of that; immediately after that.

therm *noun* a unit of heat, used especially in measuring a gas supply (= 100,000 British thermal units or 1.055×10^8 joules). [from Greek *therme* = heat]

thermal *adjective* **1** of heat; using or operated by heat. **2** warm or hot, *thermal springs*. –**thermal** *noun* a rising current of hot air. □ **thermal unit** a unit for measuring heat.

thermionic valve (ther-mee-**on**-ik) *noun* a vacuum tube in which a flow of electrons is emitted by heated electrodes, used in radio etc. [from *thermo-* + *ion*]

thermistor (ther-**mist**-er) *noun* an electrical resistor whose resistance decreases as its temperature increases, used e.g. for measuring and controlling the passage of electric current. [from *thermal resistor*]

thermo- *prefix* heat. [from Greek]

thermocouple *noun* a device for measuring temperatures by means of the thermoelectric voltage developing between two pieces of wire of different metals joined to each other at each end.

thermodynamics *noun* a branch of physics dealing with the relation between heat and other forms of energy. **thermodynamic** *adjective*

thermoelectric *adjective* producing electricity by difference of temperature.

thermometer *noun* an instrument for measuring temperature, especially a graduated glass tube containing mercury or alcohol that expands when heated. [from *thermo-* + *meter*]

thermonuclear *adjective* of nuclear reactions that occur only at very high temperatures. □ **thermonuclear bomb** a bomb that uses such reactions.

thermopile *noun* a set of connected thermocouples, especially for measuring small quantities of radiant heat.

thermoplastic *adjective* becoming soft and plastic when heated and hardening when cooled. –**thermoplastic** *noun* a thermoplastic substance.

thermos *noun* (*trademark*) a kind of vacuum flask.

thermosetting *adjective* (of plastics) setting permanently when heated.

thermosphere *noun* the region of the atmosphere beyond the mesosphere.

thermostat *noun* a device that automatically regulates temperature by cutting off and restoring the supply of heat to a piece of equipment or a room etc. **thermostatic** *adjective*, **thermostatically** *adverb* [from *thermo-*, + Greek *statos* = standing]

thesaurus (thĕ-**saw**-rŭs) *noun* (*plural* thesauri, *pr.* thĕ-**saw**-ry, or **thesauruses**) **1** a book containing sets of words arranged in groups of similar meaning or related concepts. **2** a dictionary or encyclopedia, *A Thesaurus of the Arts*. [from Greek, = treasury]

these *see* this.

Theseus (**th'ee**-see-ŭs) (*Gk. legend*) the national hero of Athens, whose exploits include the slaying of the Minotaur in Crete.

thesis (**th'ee**-sĭs) *noun* (*plural* theses, *pr.* -seez) **1** a statement or theory put forward and supported by arguments. **2** a lengthy written essay submitted by a candidate for a university degree. [from Greek, = placing]

Thespian (**thess**-pee-ăn) *adjective* of tragedy or the drama. –**Thespian** *noun* an actor or actress. [named after Thespis, Greek tragic dramatist of the 6th century BC]

Thessalonian (thess-ă-**loh**-nee-ăn) *adjective* of ancient Thessalonia (modern Salonika), a city in NE Greece. –**Thessalonian** *noun* a native of Thessalonia. **Thessalonians** the *Epistle to the Thessalonians*, either of two books of the New Testament, letters of St Paul to the Church at Thessalonia.

Thessaloniki (thess-ă-lŏ-**nee**-kee) (also Salonica) a major port in NE Greece and the second largest city in Greece, the capital of the present-day Greek region of Macedonia.

they *pronoun* **1** the people or things mentioned. **2** people in general, *they say the play is a success.* **3** those in authority, *they are putting a tax on margarine.* **4** used informally instead of 'he or she', *I am never angry with anyone unless they deserve it.*

Usage The use of *they* in sense 4 as a singular pronoun, though common, is considered incorrect by some people.

---

they'd (*informal*) = they had; they would. they'll (*informal*) = they will. they're (*informal*) = they are. they've (*informal*) = they have.

thiamine (**th'y**-ă-mĭn) *noun* vitamin B₁, found in unrefined cereals, beans, and liver.

thick *adjective* **1** of great or specified distance between opposite surfaces. **2** (of a line etc.) broad not fine. **3** made of thick material, *a thick coat.* **4** having units that are crowded or numerous, dense, *a thick forest*; *thick fog*; *thick darkness*, difficult to see through. **5** densely covered or filled, *the cat's dish was thick with ants.* **6** (of a liquid or paste) relatively stiff in consistency, not flowing easily; *thick soup*, thickened. **7** (of the voice) not sounding clear. **8** (of an accent) very noticeable, *a thick brogue.* **9** (*informal*) stupid. **10** (*informal*) on terms of close association or friendliness, *her parents are very thick with mine.* –thick *adverb* thickly, *blows came thick and fast.* –thick *noun* the busiest part of a crowd, fight, or activity, *in the thick of it.* □ thick head stupidity; a feeling of muzziness. thick-skinned *adjective* not very sensitive to criticism or snubs. through thick and thin in spite of all the difficulties. thickish *adjective*, thickly *adverb*

thicken *verb* to make or become thicker or of a stiffer consistency; *the plot thickens*, becomes more complicated. thickener *noun*

thicket *noun* a number of shrubs and small trees etc. growing close together.

thickhead *noun* (*informal*) a stupid person. thickheaded *adjective*

thickness *noun* **1** the quality of being thick; the extent to which something is thick. **2** a

layer, *use three thicknesses of paper.* **3** the part between opposite surfaces, *steps cut in the thickness of the wall.*

thickset *adjective* **1** with parts set or growing close together, *a thickset hedge.* **2** having a stocky or burly body.

thief *noun* (*plural* thieves) one who steals, especially stealthily and without violence. thievish *adjective*, thievery *noun*

thieve *verb* to be a thief; to steal.

thigh *noun* the part of the human leg between hip and knee; the corresponding part in other animals.

thimble *noun* a small metal or plastic cap worn on the end of the finger to protect it and push the needle in sewing.

thimbleful *noun* (*plural* thimblefuls) a very small quantity of liquid to drink.

Thimphu (**tim**-poo) the capital of Bhutan.

thin *adjective* (thinner, thinnest) **1** of small thickness or diameter. **2** (of a line etc.) narrow, not broad. **3** made of thin material, *a thin dress.* **4** lean, not plump. **5** not dense; not plentiful. **6** having units that are not crowded or numerous. **7** (of a liquid or paste) flowing easily, not thick. **8** lacking strength or substance or an important ingredient, feeble, *a thin excuse.* –thin *adverb* thinly, *cut the bread thin.* –thin *verb* (thinned, thinning) to make or become thinner. □ have a thin time (*informal*) to have an uncomfortable or wretched time. thin end of the wedge a change that will open the way to further similar ones. thin out to make or become fewer or less crowded; *thin out seedlings*, remove a few to improve the growth of the rest. thin-skinned *adjective* over-sensitive to criticism or snubs. thinly *adverb*, thinness *noun*, thinnish *adjective*

thine *adjective* & *possessive pronoun* (*old use*) of or belonging to thee; the thing(s) belonging to thee.

thing *noun* **1** whatever is or may be an object of perception or knowledge or thought. **2** an unnamed object or item, *there are 6 things on my list.* **3** an inanimate object as distinct from a living creature. **4** (in pity or contempt) a creature, *poor thing!* **5** an act, fact, idea, or task etc., *a difficult thing to do*; *she takes things too seriously.* **6** a specimen or type of something, *the latest thing in hats.* □ do one's own thing (*informal*) to follow one's own interests or urges. have a thing about (*informal*) to have an obsession or prejudice about. **make a thing of it** to get excited about it; to insist that it is important. **the thing** what is conventionally proper or is fashionable; what is important or suitable, *that bowl is just the thing for roses*.

things *plural noun* **1** personal belongings, clothing, *pack your things*. **2** implements or utensils, *my painting things*. **3** circumstances or conditions, *things began to improve*.

thingumajig *noun* (also **thingummy**, **thingumabob**, *or* **thingy**) (*informal*) a thing or person whose name one cannot remember.

think *verb* (**thought**, **thinking**) **1** to exercise the mind in an active way, to form connected ideas. **2** to have as an idea or opinion, *we think we shall win*. **3** to form as an intention or plan, *can't think what to do next*; *she's thinking of emigrating*; *I couldn't think of doing that*, I regard that course as unacceptable. **4** to take into consideration, *think how nice it would be*. **5** to call to mind, to remember, *can't think where I put it*. **6** to be of the opinion, to judge, *it is thought to be a fake*. **–think** *noun* (*informal*) an act of thinking, *must have a think about that*. ☐ **think aloud** to utter one's thoughts as they occur. **think better of it** to change one's mind after reconsideration. **think nothing of** to consider unremarkable. **think over** to reach a decision about by thinking. **think tank** an organisation providing advice and ideas, especially on national and commercial problems. **think twice** to consider very carefully before doing something. **think up** (*informal*) to invent or produce by thought.

thinker *noun* a person who thinks deeply or in a specified way, *an original thinker*.

thinking *adjective* using thought or rational judgment about things, *any thinking person*.

thinner *noun* a substance for thinning paint.

third *adjective* next after second. **–third** *noun* **1** something that is third. **2** third-class honours in a university degree. **3** third gear. **4** one of three equal parts of a thing. ☐ **third age** a period of active retirement; old age, *University of the Third Age*. **third degree** long and severe questioning by police to get information or a confession. **third-degree burn** a burn of the most severe kind, affecting lower layers of tissue. **third party** another person etc. besides the two principal ones involved. **third-party insurance** that in which the insurer gives protection to the insured against liability for damage or injury to any other person. **third person** *see* **person**. **third-rate** *adjective*

very inferior in quality. **Third Reich** the Nazi regime in Germany, 1933–45. **Third World** the developing countries of Asia, Africa, and Latin America. **thirdly** *adverb*

thirst *noun* **1** the feeling caused by a desire or need to drink. **2** a strong desire, *a thirst for adventure*. **–thirst** *verb* to feel a thirst.

thirsty *adjective* **1** feeling thirst. **2** (of land) in need of water. **3** (*informal*) causing thirst, *thirsty work*. **thirstily** *adverb*

thirteen *adjective* & *noun* one more than twelve (13, XIII). **thirteenth** *adjective* & *noun*

thirty *adjective* & *noun* three times ten (30, XXX). **thirties** *plural noun* the numbers from 30 to 39, especially the years of a century or of a person's life, or degrees of temperature. ☐ **Thirty-nine Articles** the set of statements adopted by the Church of England in 1571 as a definition of the doctrines it upheld. **Thirty Years War** the religious wars of 1618–48, fought chiefly on German soil. **thirtieth** *adjective* & *noun*

this *adjective* & *pronoun* (*plural* **these**) **1** the person or thing close at hand or touched, or just mentioned or about to be mentioned; the nearer or more obvious one of two. **2** the present day or time, *she ought to have been here by this*. **–this** *adverb* (*informal*) to such an extent, *we're surprised he got this far*. ☐ **this and that** various things.

thistle *noun* a prickly plant with purple, white, or yellow flowers.

thistledown *noun* the very light fluff on thistle seeds by which they are carried by the wind.

thither *adverb* (*old use*) to or towards that place.

Thomas[1], Rover (1926–98), Australian Aboriginal artist.

Thomas[2], St (1st century AD), an Apostle, who refused to believe that Christ had risen from the dead unless he could see and touch his wounds. Feast day, 21 December. ☐ **doubting Thomas** a sceptical person.

Thomas Aquinas *see* **Aquinas**.

thong *noun* **1** a narrow strip of hide or leather used as a fastening or lash etc. **2** (*Austral.*) a light backless sandal with a thong between the big toe and the other toes.

Thor (*Scand. myth.*) the god of thunder and the weather. Thursday is named after him.

thorax (**thor**-raks) *noun* the part of the body between the head or neck and the abdomen.

thoracic (thŏ-**rass**-ik) *adjective* [Greek, = breast-plate]

thorium (**thor**-ree-ŭm) *noun* a radioactive metallic element (symbol Th).

thorn *noun* 1 a sharp pointed projection on a plant. 2 a thorny tree or shrub. □ **a thorn in one's flesh** a constant source of annoyance.

thornless *adjective* having no thorns.

thornproof *adjective* unable to be penetrated by thorns.

thorny *adjective* (**thornier**, **thorniest**) 1 having many thorns. 2 like a thorn. 3 troublesome, difficult to deal with, *a thorny problem*.

thorough *adjective* complete in every way; not merely superficial, doing things or done with great attention to detail. **thoroughly** *adverb*, **thoroughness** *noun*

thoroughbred *adjective* (especially of a horse) bred of pure or pedigree stock. –**thoroughbred** *noun* a thoroughbred animal.

thoroughfare *noun* a public way open at both ends. □ **no thoroughfare** (as a notice) this road is private or is obstructed.

thoroughgoing *adjective* thorough.

those *see* **that**.

Thoth (*Egyptian myth.*) a moon god, the god of wisdom, justice, and writing, patron of the sciences, and messenger of the sun god Ra.

thou *pronoun* (*old use*, in speaking to one person) you.

though *conjunction* in spite of the fact that, even supposing, *it's true, though hard to believe*. –**though** *adverb* (*informal*) however, *she's right, though*.

thought¹ *noun* 1 the process or power of thinking. 2 a way of thinking that is characteristic of a particular class, nation, or period, *in modern thought*. 3 meditation, *deep in thought*. 4 an idea or chain of reasoning produced by thinking. 5 an intention, *we had no thought of giving offence*. 6 consideration, *after serious thought*. □ **thought-provoking** *adjective* giving rise to serious thought.

thought² *see* **think**.

thoughtful *adjective* 1 thinking deeply; often absorbed in thought. 2 (of a book, writer, or remark etc.) showing signs of careful thought. 3 showing thought for the needs of others, considerate. **thoughtfully** *adverb*, **thoughtfulness** *noun*

thoughtless *adjective* 1 not alert to possible effects or consequences. 2 inconsiderate. **thoughtlessly** *adverb*, **thoughtlessness** *noun*

thousand *adjective* & *noun* ten hundred (1000, M), *a few thousand* (not *a few thousands*). **thousandth** *adjective* & *noun*

thousandfold *adjective* & *adverb* one thousand times as much or as many.

thrall (*pr.* thrawl) *noun* **in thrall** in bondage or slavery.

thrash *verb* 1 to beat with a stick or whip. 2 to defeat thoroughly in a contest. 3 to thresh. 4 to hit with repeated blows like a flail; to make violent movements. □ **thrash out** to discuss thoroughly.

thread *noun* 1 a thin length of any substance. 2 a length of spun cotton or wool etc. used in making cloth or in sewing or knitting. 3 something compared to this; *lose the thread of an argument*, lose the chain of thought connecting it; *pick up the threads*, proceed with something after an interruption. 4 the spiral ridge of a screw. –**thread** *verb* 1 to pass a thread through the eye of (a needle). 2 to pass (a strip of film etc.) through or round something into the proper position for use. 3 to put (beads) on a thread. 4 to cut a thread on (a screw). □ **thread one's way** to make one's way through a crowd or streets etc. **threader** *noun*

threadbare *adjective* 1 (of cloth) with the nap worn off and threads visible. 2 (of a person) wearing threadbare or shabby clothes.

threadworm *noun* a small threadlike worm, especially one sometimes found in the rectum of children.

threat *noun* 1 an expression of one's intention to punish or hurt or harm a person or thing. 2 an indication of something undesirable, *there's a threat of rain*. 3 a person or thing regarded as liable to bring danger or catastrophe, *machinery was seen as a threat to people's jobs*.

threaten *verb* 1 to make a threat or threats against (a person etc.); to try to influence by threats. 2 to be a warning of, *the clouds threatened rain*. 3 to seem likely to be or do something undesirable, *the scheme threatens to be expensive*. 4 to be a threat to, *the dangers that threaten us*.

three *adjective* & *noun* one more than two (3, III). □ **three-cornered** *adjective* triangular; (of a contest) between three parties. **three-dimensional** *adjective* having three dimensions (length, breadth, depth). **three-handed** *adjective* (of a card game) played by three people. **three-legged** *adjective* having three legs; *three-legged race*, a race between pairs of runners with the right leg of one tied to the left leg of the other. **three-piece** *noun* a three-piece suit of clothes or suite of furniture. **three-ply** *adjective* made of three strands or layers. **three-quarter** *adjective* consisting of three-quarters of a whole; (*noun*) a player with a position just behind the half-backs in rugby football. **three-quarters** *noun* three parts out of four; (*adverb*) to this extent. **the three Rs** reading, (w)riting, and (a)rithmetic, as the basis of elementary education. **three-wheeler** *noun* a vehicle with three wheels; a tricycle.

threefold *adjective* & *adverb* **1** three times as much or as many. **2** consisting of three parts.

threesome *noun* three people together, a trio.

thresh *verb* **1** to beat out or separate (grain) from husks of corn. **2** to make violent movements, *threshing about*.

threshold *noun* **1** a piece of wood or stone forming the bottom of a doorway. **2** the entrance of a house etc. **3** the point of entry or beginning of something, *on the threshold of a new era*. **4** the lowest limit at which a stimulus becomes perceptible. **5** the highest limit at which pain etc. is bearable.

threw *see* **throw**.

thrice *adverb* (*old use*) three times.

thrift *noun* economical management of money or resources. [same origin as *thrive*]

thriftless *adjective* not thrifty, wasteful.

thrifty *adjective* (**thriftier, thriftiest**) practising thrift, economical. **thriftily** *adverb*

thrill *noun* a nervous tremor caused by emotion or sensation, a wave of feeling or excitement. **–thrill** *verb* to feel or cause to feel a thrill.

thriller *noun* an exciting story, play, or film, especially one involving crime.

thrive *verb* (**throve** *or* **thrived, thrived** *or* **thriven, thriving**) **1** to grow or develop well and vigorously. **2** to prosper, to be successful, *a thriving industry*. [from Old Norse *thrífask* = prosper]

throat *noun* **1** the front of the neck. **2** the passage in the neck through which food passes to the oesophagus and air passes to the lungs. **3** a narrow passage or funnel.

throaty *adjective* **1** uttered deep in the throat. **2** hoarse. **throatily** *adverb*, **throatiness** *noun*

throb *verb* (**throbbed, throbbing**) **1** (of the heart or pulse etc.) to beat with more than usual force or rapidity. **2** to vibrate or sound with a persistent rhythm; *a throbbing wound*, giving pain in a steady rhythm. **–throb** *noun* throbbing.

throes *plural noun* severe pangs of pain. □ **in the throes of** (*informal*) struggling with the task of, *in the throes of revising for exams*.

thrombosis (throm-**boh**-sĭs) *noun* (*plural* **thromboses**) formation of a clot of blood in a blood vessel or organ of the body. [from Greek *thrombos* = lump]

throne *noun* **1** the special chair or seat used by a king, queen, or bishop etc. on ceremonial occasions. **2** sovereign power, *came to the throne*. **–throne** *verb* to enthrone. [from Greek *thronos* = high seat]

throng *noun* a crowded mass of people. **–throng** *verb* **1** to come or go or press in a throng. **2** to fill (a place) with a throng.

throttle *noun* a valve controlling the flow of fuel or steam etc. to an engine; the lever or pedal operating this. **–throttle** *verb* to strangle.

through *preposition* **1** from end to end or side to side of; entering at one side and coming out at the other. **2** between or among, *tramping through long grass*. **3** from beginning to end of; so as to have finished or completed; *he is through his exam*, has passed it. **4** (*Amer.*) up to and including, *Monday through Friday*. **5** by reason of, by the agency or means or fault of, *lost it through carelessness*. **–through** *adverb* **1** through something. **2** with a connection made to a desired telephone etc., *you're through*. **3** finished, *wait till I'm through with these papers*. **4** having no further dealings, *I'm through with him!* **–through** *adjective* going through something; (of traffic) passing through a place without stopping; (of travel or passengers etc.) going to the end of a journey without a change of line or vehicle etc. □ **through and through** through again and again; thoroughly, completely.

throughout *preposition* & *adverb* right through, from beginning to end of (a place, course, or period).

throughput *noun* the amount of material processed.

throve *see* **thrive**.

throw *verb* (**threw, thrown, throwing**) **1** to send with some force through the air or in a certain direction; *throw a shadow*, cause there to be one. **2** to use as a missile, *throw stones*.

939

3 to hurl to the ground, *the horse threw its rider*. **4** (*informal*) to disconcert, *the question threw me*. **5** to put (clothes etc.) on or off hastily or casually. **6** to cause (dice) to fall to the table; to obtain (a number) by this. **7** to shape (rounded pottery) on a potter's wheel. **8** to turn, direct, or move (a part of the body) quickly, *threw his head back*. **9** to cause to be in a certain state, *they were thrown out of work*; *thrown into confusion*. **10** to move (a switch or lever) so as to operate it. **11** to have (a fit or tantrum). **12** to give (a party). –**throw** *noun* **1** the act of throwing. **2** the distance something is or may be thrown. □ **throw away** to part with as useless or unwanted; to fail to make use of, *throw away an opportunity*. **throw-away** *adjective* to be thrown away after one use. **throw in** to include (a thing) with what one is selling, without additional charge; to put in (a remark) casually or as an addition; to resign from (a job). **throw-in** *noun* the throwing in of a ball at football after it has gone out of play over the touchline. **throw in the towel** = throw up the sponge (*see below*). **throw off** to manage to get rid of or become free from, *throw off a cold* or *one's pursuers*; to compose easily as if without effort, *threw off a few lines of verse*. **throw oneself into** to engage vigorously in. **throw oneself on** to entrust oneself entirely to (a person's mercy etc.). **throw out** to throw away; to put out suddenly or forcibly; to expel (a troublemaker etc.); to reject (a proposed plan etc.). **throw over** to desert or abandon. **throw the book at** (*informal*) to make all possible charges against (a person). **throw together** to bring (people) casually into association. **throw up** to raise quickly or suddenly; to bring to notice, *his researches threw up some interesting facts*; to resign from, *throw up one's job*; to vomit. **throw up** or **in the sponge** to admit defeat or failure and abandon a contest or effort. (⁋ From the practice of admitting defeat in a boxing match by throwing into the air the sponge used between rounds.) **thrower** *noun*

throwback *noun* an animal etc. showing characteristics of an ancestor that is earlier than its parents.

thrum *verb* (**thrummed**, **thrumming**) to strum; to sound monotonously. –**thrum** *noun* a thrumming sound.

thrush[1] *noun* any of several songbirds, especially one with a brownish back and speckled breast.

thrush[2] *noun* **1** an infection in which a minute fungus produces white patches in the mouth

and throat, especially in children. **2** a similar infection of the vagina.

thrust *verb* (**thrust**, **thrusting**) **1** to push forcibly. **2** to make a forward stroke with a sword etc. **3** to put forcibly into a position or condition, to force the acceptance of, *some have greatness thrust upon them*. –**thrust** *noun* **1** a thrusting movement or force. **2** a hostile remark aimed at a person. **3** the drift or gist of an argument or remark. **thruster** *noun*

Thucydides (thew-**sid**-ĭ-deez) (c. 455– c. 400 BC), Greek historian from Athens.

thud *noun* a low dull sound like that of a blow or something that does not resound. –**thud** *verb* (**thudded**, **thudding**) to make a thud; to fall with a thud.

thug *noun* a vicious or brutal ruffian. **thuggery** *noun* [the *Thugs* were members of an organisation of robbers and assassins in India, suppressed in the 1830s]

thulium (**thoo**-lee-ŭm) *noun* a soft silver-white metallic element of the lanthanide series (symbol Tm).

thumb *noun* **1** the short thick finger set apart from the other four. **2** the part of a glove covering this. –**thumb** *verb* to wear or soil, or turn pages etc., with the thumbs; *a well-thumbed book*, one that shows signs of much use. □ **be all thumbs** to be very clumsy at handling things. **thumb a lift** to obtain a lift by signalling with one's thumb, to hitchhike. **thumb drive** a flash drive. **thumb one's nose** to cock a snook (*see* snook). **thumbs down** a gesture of rejection. **thumb-stall** *noun* a sheath to cover an injured thumb. **thumbs up** a gesture or exclamation of satisfaction. **under a person's thumb** completely under his or her influence.

thumbnail *noun* the nail on a thumb; *thumbnail sketch*, a brief description of something.

thumbscrew *noun* **1** a former instrument of torture for crushing the thumb. **2** a screw with a flattened head for the thumb to turn.

thump *verb* to beat, strike, or knock heavily (especially with the fist); to thud. –**thump** *noun* a heavy blow; the sound made by this.

thumping *adjective* (*informal*) very big, *a thumping lie*.

thunder *noun* **1** the loud noise accompanying lightning. **2** any similar noise, *thunders of applause*. –**thunder** *verb* **1** to sound with thunder, *it thundered*. **2** to make a noise like thunder, to sound loudly, *the train thundered* *past*. **3** to utter loudly; to make a forceful attack in words, *reformers thundered against gambling*. ☐ **steal a person's thunder** to use a person's ideas or words etc. before he or she is able to do so. (¶ From the remark of a dramatist (c. 1710) when the stage thunder intended for his play was taken and used for another.) **thundery** *adjective*, **thunderer** *noun*

thunderbolt *noun* **1** an imaginary destructive missile thought of as sent to earth with a lightning flash. **2** a very startling and formidable event or statement.

thundering *adjective* (*informal*) very big, *a thundering nuisance*.

thunderous *adjective* like thunder.

thunderstorm *noun* a storm accompanied by thunder.

thunderstruck *adjective* amazed.

Thursday *noun* the day of the week following Wednesday. [from Old English *thuresdaeg* = day of thunder, named after Thor]

Thursday Island an island in Torres Strait about 35 km north-west of Cape York; the commercial and administrative centre of the Torres Strait Islands.

thus *adverb* **1** in this way, like this, *hold the wheel thus*. **2** as a result of this, *he was the eldest son and thus heir to the title*. **3** to this extent, *thus far*.

thwack *verb* to strike with a heavy blow. – **thwack** *noun* a heavy blow; the sound of this.

thwart *verb* to prevent (a person) from doing what he or she intends; to prevent (a plan etc.) from being accomplished. – **thwart** *noun* a rower's bench across a boat.

thy *adjective* (*old use*) of or belonging to thee.

thylacine (**th'y**-lă-seen) *see* Tasmanian tiger.

thyme (*pr. a*stime) *noun* any of several herbs with fragrant leaves. [from Greek *thumon*]

thymus *noun* a gland near the base of the neck (in humans, it becomes much smaller at the end of childhood).

thyristor (th'y-**rist**-er) *noun* a switch in the form of a semiconductor device in which a small electric current is used to start the flow of a large current. [from Greek *thura* = gate, + *transistor*]

thyroid *noun* the thyroid gland, a large ductless gland at the front of the neck, secreting a hormone which regulates the body's growth and development. [from Greek *thureos* = shield]

thyself *pronoun* corresponding to *thee* and *thou*, used in the same ways as himself.

tiara (tee-**ah**-ră) *noun* **1** a woman's ornamental crescent-shaped headdress, worn on ceremonial occasions. **2** the pope's diadem, pointed at the top and surrounded by three crowns.

Tiber (**ty**-ber) a westward-flowing river of central Italy, on which Rome stands.

Tiberius (ty-**beer**-ree-ŭs), Roman emperor AD 14–37.

Tibet (tĭ-**bet**) a former country north of India; a self-governing region of China since 1965. Tibetan *adjective* & *noun*

tibia *noun* the inner of the two bones extending from the knee to the ankle; the shin-bone.

tic *noun* an involuntary spasmodic twitching of the muscles, especially of the face. [French]

tick[1] *noun* **1** a regularly repeated clicking sound, especially that of a watch or clock. **2** (*informal*) a moment. **3** a mark (often ✓) placed against an item in a list or a school exercise etc. to show that it has been checked or is correct. – **tick** *verb* **1** (of a clock etc.) to make a series of ticks. **2** to put a tick beside (an item). ☐ **tick off** to mark with a tick; (*informal*) to reprimand. **tick over** (of an engine) to idle; (of activities) to continue in a routine way. **tick-tock** *noun* the ticking of a large clock. **what makes a person tick** what makes a person behave as he or she does.

tick[2] *noun* any of several blood-sucking mites or parasitic insects.

tick[3] *noun* the case of a mattress or pillow or bolster, holding the filling.

ticker *noun* (*informal*) **1** a watch. **2** a teleprinter. **3** the heart. ☐ **ticker tape** *noun* paper tape from a teleprinter etc; this or similar material thrown from a window etc. to honour a famous or significant person or group of people.

ticket *noun* **1** a written or printed piece of card or paper that entitles the holder to a certain right (e.g. to travel by train or bus etc. or to a seat in a cinema) or serves as a receipt. **2** a certificate of qualification as a ship's master or pilot etc. **3** a document certifying membership of a trade union. **4** a label attached to a thing and giving its price or other particulars. **5** an official notification of a traffic offence, *parking ticket*. **6** a list of the candidates put forward by one party in an election. – **ticket** *verb* (ticketed, ticketing) to put a ticket on (an article for sale etc.). ☐ **have tickets on oneself**

941

(*Austral. informal*) to be conceited. **the ticket** (*informal*) the correct or desirable thing, *that's just the ticket*. **ticket-of-leave** *noun* (*Austral. historical*) a permit allowing a convict specified privileges, especially leave.

ticking *noun* strong fabric for making ticks for mattresses or pillows etc.

tickle *verb* 1 to touch or stroke lightly so as to cause a slight tingling sensation, usually with involuntary movement and laughter. 2 to feel this sensation, *my foot tickles*. 3 to amuse, to please (a person's vanity or sense of humour etc.). – **tickle** *noun* the act or sensation of tickling.

ticklish *adjective* 1 sensitive to tickling. 2 (of a problem) requiring careful handling. **ticklishness** *noun*

tidal *adjective* of or affected by a tide or tides. □ **tidal wave** a great ocean wave, e.g. one caused by an earthquake; a great wave of enthusiasm or indignation etc. **tidally** *adverb*

tiddler *noun* (*informal*) 1 a small fish. 2 an unusually small thing.

tiddly[1] *adjective* (*informal*) very small.

tiddly[2] *adjective* (*informal*) slightly drunk.

tiddlywink *noun* one of the small counters flicked into a cup in the game of **tiddlywinks**.

tide *noun* 1 the regular rise and fall in the level of the sea, caused by the attraction of the moon and the sun. 2 water as moved by this. 3 a trend of opinion, fortune, or events, *the rising tide of discontent*. 4 (*old use*) a season, *Yuletide*. – **tide** *verb* to float with the tide. □ **tide a person over** to help him or her through a difficult period by providing what is needed.

tideless *adjective* without tides.

tidings *plural noun* news.

tidy *adjective* (**tidier**, **tidiest**) 1 neat and orderly in arrangement or in one's ways. 2 (*informal*) fairly large, considerable, *left a tidy fortune when he died*. – **tidy** *noun* a receptacle for odds and ends. – **tidy** *verb* (**tidied**, **tidying**) to make tidy. **tidily** *adverb*, **tidiness** *noun*

tie *verb* (**tied**, **tying**) 1 to attach, fasten, or bind with a cord or something similar. 2 to arrange (string or ribbon or a necktie etc.) to form a knot or bow; to form (a knot or bow) in this way. 3 to unite (notes in music) with a tie. 4 to make the same score as another competitor, *they tied for second place*. 5 to restrict or limit to certain conditions or to an occupation or place etc. – **tie** *noun* 1 a cord etc. used for

fastening or by which something is tied. 2 a necktie. 3 something that unites things or people, a bond. 4 something that restricts a person's freedom of action. 5 a curved line (in a musical score) over two notes of the same pitch, indicating that the second is not sounded separately. 6 equality of score between two or more competitors. 7 a sports match between two of a set of competing teams or players. □ **fit to be tied** (*informal*) very angry. **tie beam** a horizontal beam connecting rafters. **tie-dyeing** *noun* a method of producing dyed patterns by tying parts of a fabric so that they are protected from the dye. **tie in** to link or (of information or facts) to agree or be connected with something else. **tie up** to fasten with a cord etc.; to invest or reserve (capital etc.) so that it is not readily available for use; to make restrictive conditions about (a bequest etc.); to occupy (a person) so that he or she has no time for other things. **tie-up** *noun* a connection, a link.

tiebreak *noun* (also **tiebreaker**) a means of deciding a winner from competitors who have tied.

tiepin *noun* an ornamental pin for holding a necktie in place.

tier (*pr.* teer) *noun* 1 any of a series of rows, ranks, or units of a structure placed one above the other. 2 (often **tiers**) (in Tasmania and *old use* in SA) a forested mountain range.

tiered (*pr.* teerd) *adjective* arranged in tiers.

Tierra del Fuego (tee-e-ră del **fway**-goh) an archipelago off the southern tip of South America, divided between Chile and Argentina.

tiff *noun* a petty quarrel.

tiffin *noun* (in India, Sri Lanka, etc.) a light meal, especially at midday.

tiger *noun* a large Asian animal of the cat family, with yellowish and black stripes. □ **tiger cat** any of several animals resembling the tiger (e.g. the ocelot); the largest of the Australian marsupial cats. **tiger lily** a tall garden lily with dark-spotted orange flowers. **tiger moth** a moth with wings that are streaked like a tiger's skin. **tiger prawn** a very large prawn with dark vertical stripes. **tiger shark** a voracious striped or spotted shark. **tiger snake** a highly venomous Australian snake.

tight *adjective* 1 fixed or fastened or drawn together firmly and hard to move or undo. 2 fitting closely, made so that a specified thing cannot penetrate, *a tight joint*; *watertight*; *tight controls*, strictly imposed. 3 with things or people arranged closely together, *a tight little group*; *a tight schedule*, leaving no time to spare. **4** tense, stretched so as to leave no slack. **5** (*informal*) drunk. **6** (of money or materials) not easily obtainable; (of the money market) in which money and credit are severely restricted. **7** stingy, *tight with his money*. **–tight** *adverb* tightly, *hold tight*. □ **in a tight corner** or **spot** in a difficult situation. **tight-fisted** *adjective* stingy. **tight-lipped** *adjective* keeping the lips compressed firmly together to restrain one's emotion or comments; grim-looking. **tightly** *adverb*, **tightness** *noun*

tighten *verb* to make or become tighter. □ **tighten one's belt** to content oneself with less food etc. when supplies are scarce.

tightrope *noun* a rope stretched tightly high above the ground, on which acrobats perform.

tights *plural noun* a close-fitting garment covering the feet, legs, and lower part of the body, worn by women, and by acrobats, dancers, etc.

tigress *noun* a female tiger.

Tigris (**ty**-grĭs) a river of SW Asia, flowing from Turkey through Iraq east of the Euphrates, which it joins.

tilde (**til**-dĕ) *noun* the mark ~ put over a letter (e.g. Spanish n when this is pronounced as in *señor*).

tile *noun* **1** a thin slab of baked clay or other materials used in rows for covering roofs, walls, or floors; *carpet tiles*, carpet made in small squares for laying in rows. **2** any of the small flat pieces used in mah-jong. **–tile** *verb* to cover with tiles.

tiling *noun* a surface made of tiles.

till¹ *verb* to prepare and use (land) for growing crops. [from Old English *tilian* = try]

till² *preposition* & *conjunction* = until. [from Old English *til* = to]

Usage See the note at **until**.

---

till³ a receptacle for money in a shop or bank etc., especially with a mechanism for recording transactions, a cash register. [origin unknown]

tiller *noun* a horizontal bar by which the rudder of a small boat is turned in steering.

tilt *verb* **1** to move or cause to move into a sloping position. **2** to run or thrust with a lance in jousting. **–tilt** *noun* tilting; a sloping position. □ **at full tilt** at full speed; with full force. **tilt at windmills** to battle with enemies who are only imaginary. (¶ From the story of Don Quixote who attacked windmills, thinking they were giants.)

timber *noun* **1** wood prepared for use in building or carpentry. **2** trees suitable for this. **3** a piece of wood or a wooden beam used in constructing a house or ship.

timbered *adjective* **1** (of a building) constructed of timber or with a timber framework. **2** (of land) wooded.

timberline *see* **tree line**.

timbre (*pr.* tambr) *noun* the characteristic quality of the sound produced by a particular voice or instrument. [French]

timbrel *noun* (*old use*) a tambourine.

Timbuktu **1** a town in Mali in West Africa. **2** a very remote place.

time *noun* **1** all the years of the past, present, and future. **2** the passing of these taken as a whole, *time will show who is right*. **3** a portion of time associated with certain events, conditions, or experiences, *in Victorian times*; *in times of hardship*; *have a good time*, enjoy oneself. **4** a portion of time between two points; the point or period allotted, available, or suitable for something, *the time it takes to do this*; *now is the time to buy*; *lunch time*. **5** the point of time when something must occur or end. **6** an occasion or instance, *the first time we saw him*; *I told you three times*; *four times three*, three taken four times. **7** a point of time stated in hours and minutes of the day, *the time is exactly two o'clock*. **8** any of the standard systems by which time is reckoned, *Eastern Standard Time*. **9** measured time spent in work etc., *works part time*. **10** tempo in music, rhythm depending on the number and accentuation of beats in a bar. **–time** *verb* **1** to choose the time or moment for, to arrange the time of. **2** to measure the time taken by (a race or runner or a process etc.). **times** *plural noun* contemporary circumstances and customs, *times are bad*; *a sign of the times*. □ **at the same time** in spite of this, however. **do time** (*informal*) to serve a prison sentence. **for the time being** until some other arrangement is made. **from time to time** at intervals. **have no time for** to be unable or unwilling to spend time on; to despise. **in no time** in an instant, very rapidly. **in time** not late; eventually, sooner or later. **on time** punctually. **time and a half** payment at one and a half times the usual rate, especially for working overtime. **time-and-motion** *adjective* concerned with measuring the efficiency of industrial or other operations. **time bomb** a bomb that can be set to explode after a certain interval. **time-consuming** *adjective* occupying much time. **time exposure** a photographic exposure in which the shutter is left open for more than a second or two and not operated at an automatically-controlled speed. **time-honoured** *adjective* honoured because of long tradition or custom. **time lag** an interval of time between two connected events. **the time of one's life** a period of exceptional enjoyment. **time-sharing** *noun* the automatic sharing of a computer system to serve two or more users concurrently. **time signature** a sign in a piece of music following the key signature, expressed as a fraction with the numerator showing the number of beats in a bar and the denominator the length of the note, e.g. $\frac{3}{4}$ indicates the rhythm of three quarter notes (crotchets) to a bar. **time zone** a region (between two lines of longitude) where a common standard time is used.

timekeeper *noun* **1** a person who records time, especially in a game. **2** a person in respect of punctuality; a watch or clock in respect of its accuracy of operation, *a good timekeeper*.

timeless *adjective* **1** not to be thought of as having duration. **2** not affected by the passage of time.

timely *adjective* occurring at just the right time, *a timely warning*. **timeliness** *noun*

timepiece *noun* a clock or watch.

timer *noun* a person who times something; a timing device.

timetable *noun* a list showing the time at which certain events will take place, e.g. the series of lessons in school or the arrival and departure of public transport vehicles.

timid *adjective* easily alarmed, not bold, shy. **timidly** *adverb*, **timidity** (tǐ-**mid**-ǐ-tee) *noun* [from Latin *timidus* = nervous]

timing *noun* the way something is timed.

Timor (**tee**-mor) an island in the southern Malay Archipelago, divided between the independent state of East Timor and West Timor (part of Indonesia). □ **Timor Sea** the part of the Indian Ocean between Timor and NW Australia. **Timorese** *adjective* & *noun*

timorous (**tim**-ŏ-rŭs) *adjective* timid. **timorously** *adverb*, **timorousness** *noun* [from Latin *timor* = fear]

Timothy, St (1st century AD), a convert and colleague of St Paul, to whom two of the epistles in the New Testament are addressed.

timpani (**timp**-ă-nee) *plural noun* kettledrums. [Italian]

timpanist *noun* a person who plays the timpani in an orchestra.

tin *noun* **1** a chemical element (symbol Sn), a silvery-white metal. **2** iron or steel sheets coated with tin. **3** a box or other container made of tin plate, one in which food is sealed for preservation. –**tin** *verb* (**tinned**, **tinning**) **1** to coat with tin. **2** to seal in a tin for preservation. □ **tin can** a tin for preserving food. **tin foil** a thin sheet of tin, aluminium, or tin alloy, used for wrapping and packing things. **tin god** a person who is unjustifiably given great veneration. **Tin Pan Alley** the world of composers and publishers of popular music. (¶ Originally the name given to a district in New York where many songwriters and music publishers were based.) **tin plate** sheet iron or steel coated thinly with tin. **tin-plated** *adjective* coated with tin.

tincture *noun* **1** a solution consisting of a medicinal substance dissolved in alcohol, *tincture of quinine*. **2** a slight tinge or trace of some element or quality. –**tincture** *verb* to tinge. [same origin as *tint*]

tinder *noun* any dry substance that catches fire easily.

tinderbox *noun* **1** a metal box formerly used in kindling a fire, containing dry material that caught fire from a spark produced by flint and steel. **2** a thing that is readily ignited.

tine *noun* any of the points or prongs of a fork, comb, or antler.

tinea (**tin**-ee-ă) *noun* a fungal disease of the skin, e.g. athlete's foot.

ting *noun* a sharp ringing sound. –**ting** *verb* to make a ting.

tinge (*pr.* tinj) *verb* (**tinged**, **tingeing**) **1** to colour slightly, *tinged with pink*. **2** to give a slight trace of some element or quality to, *their admiration was tinged with envy*. –**tinge** *noun* a slight colouring or trace. [same origin as *tint*]

tingle *verb* to have a slight pricking or stinging sensation. –**tingle** *noun* this sensation.

tinker *noun* **1** a travelling mender of pots and pans. **2** a spell of tinkering, *have a tinker at it*.

–**tinker** *verb* to work at something casually, trying to repair or improve it.

tinkle *noun* a series of short light ringing sounds. –**tinkle** *verb* to make or cause to make a tinkle.

tinny *adjective* 1 of or like tin; (of metal objects) not looking strong or solid. 2 having a metallic taste or a thin metallic sound.

tinpot *adjective* worthless.

tinsel *noun* a glittering metallic substance used in strips or threads to give an inexpensive sparkling effect. **tinselled** *adjective*

tint *noun* 1 a variety of a particular colour. 2 a slight trace of a different colour, *red with a bluish tint*. –**tint** *verb* to apply or give a tint to, to colour slightly. [from Latin *tinctum* = stained]

tintinnabulation *noun* a ringing or tinkling of bells.

Tintoretto, Jacopo Robusti (1518–94), Venetian painter.

tiny *adjective* (**tinier**, **tiniest**) very small.

tip[1] *noun* 1 the very end of a thing, especially of something small or tapering. 2 a small part or piece fitted to the end of something, *cigarettes with filter tips*. –**tip** *verb* (**tipped**, **tipping**) to provide with a tip, *filter-tipped*. □ **on the tip of one's tongue** just about to be spoken or remembered.

tip[2] *verb* (**tipped**, **tipping**) 1 to tilt or topple; to cause to do this. 2 to discharge (the contents of a truck or jug etc.) by doing this. 3 to strike or touch lightly. 4 to name as a likely winner of a contest etc. 5 to make a small present of money to (a person), especially in acknowledgement of his or her services. –**tip** *noun* 1 a small money present. 2 private or special information (e.g. about horse races or the stock market) likely to profit the receiver if he or she acts upon it. 3 a small but useful piece of advice on how to do something. 4 a slight tilt or push. 5 a place where rubbish etc. is tipped. 6 (*informal*) a very untidy place. □ **tip off** to give an advance warning or hint or inside information to (a person). **tip-off** *noun* advance or inside information etc. **tip the balance** or **scale** to be just enough to cause one scale-pan to go lower than the other; to be the deciding factor for or against something. **tipper** *noun*

tippet *noun* a small cape or collar of fur etc. with ends hanging down in front.

tipple *verb* to drink (wine or spirits etc.); to be in the habit of drinking. –**tipple** *noun* (*informal*) alcoholic or other drink.

tipster *noun* a person who gives tips about horse races etc.

tipsy *adjective* slightly drunk; showing or caused by slight intoxication, *a tipsy lurch*. **tipsily** *adverb*, **tipsiness** *noun* [from *tip*[2]]

tiptoe *verb* (**tiptoed**, **tiptoeing**) to walk very quietly or carefully, with heels not touching the ground. □ **on tiptoe** walking or standing in this way.

tiptop *adjective* (*informal*) excellent, very best, *tiptop quality*. [from *tip*[1]]

tirade (ty-**rayd**) *noun* a long angry or violent piece of criticism or denunciation.

Tiranë (tee-**rah**-nă) the capital of Albania.

tire[1] *verb* to make or become tired.

tire[2] *noun* (*Amer.*) a tyre.

tired *adjective* feeling that one would like to sleep or rest. □ **tired of** having had enough of (a thing or activity) and feeling impatient or bored.

tireless *adjective* not tiring easily, having inexhaustible energy. **tirelessly** *adverb*

tiresome *adjective* annoying.

tiro (**ty**-roh) *noun* (*plural* **tiros**) (also **tyro**) a beginner, a novice. [Latin, = recruit]

tissue (**tish**-oo) *noun* 1 the substance forming an animal or plant body; a particular kind of this, *muscular tissue*. 2 tissue paper. 3 a disposable piece of soft absorbent paper used as a handkerchief etc. 4 fine gauzy fabric. 5 something thought of as an interwoven series, *a tissue of lies*. □ **tissue paper** very thin soft paper used for wrapping and packing things.

tit[1] *noun* any of several small birds, often with a dark top to the head.

tit[2] *noun* **tit for tat** an equivalent given in retaliation for an injury etc.

Titan (**ty**-tăn) *noun* 1 (*Gk. myth.*) any of the older gods who preceded the Olympians. 2 a person of great size, strength, or importance.

Titanic (ty-**tan**-ik) a British passenger liner that struck an iceberg in the Atlantic on her maiden voyage in 1912 and sank with the loss of 1490 lives.

titanic (ty-**tan**-ik) *adjective* gigantic, immense. [from *Titan*]

titanium (ty-**tay**-nee-ŭm) *noun* a grey metallic element (symbol Ti), used in alloys for parts of aircraft, space vehicles, etc. [same origin as *titanic*]

titbit *noun* a choice bit of something, e.g. of food or of gossip or information.

tithe (*pr.* ty*th*) *noun* **1** one tenth of the annual produce of agriculture etc., formerly paid as tax to support clergy and church. **2** a tenth part. – **tithe** *verb* **1** to pay tithes. **2** to subject to tithes. [from Old English *teotha* = tenth]

Titian (**tish**-ăn) (Tiziano Vecellio, c. 1488–1576) Italian painter. – **Titian** *adjective* bright golden auburn, red (as a colour of hair, favoured by Titian in his pictures).

Titicaca (tit-ĭ-**kah**-kă), **Lake** a lake in the Andes, between Peru and Bolivia, the highest large lake in the world.

titillate (**tit**-ĭ-layt) *verb* to excite or stimulate pleasantly. **titillation** *noun*

titivate (**tit**-ĭ-vayt) *verb* (*informal*) to smarten up; to put the finishing touches to. **titivation** *noun*

title *noun* **1** the name of a book, poem, or picture etc. **2** a word used to show a person's rank or office (e.g. *king*, *mayor*, *captain*) or used in speaking of or to him or her (e.g. *Lord*, *Mrs*, *Doctor*). **3** the legal right to ownership of property; a document conferring this. **4** a championship in sport, *the world heavyweight title*. – **title** *verb* to give a title to (a book etc.). ◻ **title deed** a legal document proving a person's title to a property. **title page** a page at the beginning of a book giving the title, author's name, and other particulars. **title role** the part in a play etc. from which the title is taken, e.g. the part of Hamlet in the play of that name. [from Latin *titulus* = title]

titled *adjective* having a title of nobility, *titled ladies*.

titmouse *noun* (*plural* **titmice**) a tit (= *tit*[1]).

titrate (ty-**trayt**) *verb* to calculate the amount of a constituent in (a substance) by using a standard reagent. **titration** *noun*

titre (**ty**-ter) *noun* the strength of a solution or the quantity of a constituent discovered by titration.

titter *noun* a high-pitched giggle. – **titter** *verb* to give a titter.

tittle-tattle *verb* & *noun* = tattle.

titular (**tit**-yŭ-ler) *adjective* **1** of or belonging to a title. **2** having the title of ruler etc. but without real authority, *the titular head of the State*.

Titus[1] (**ty**-tŭs), Roman emperor 79–81.

Titus[2] (**ty**-tŭs), St (1st century AD), a convert and helper of St Paul, to whom an epistle of the New Testament is addressed.

Tiwi (**tee**-wee) *noun* **1** a member of an Aboriginal people living on Melville and Bathurst Islands. **2** their language.

tizzy *noun* (*informal*) a state of nervous agitation or confusion, *in a tizzy*. – **tizzy** *verb* (**tizzied**, **tizzying**) (*Austral.*) to titivate, to adorn, *she tizzied herself up for the formal*.

tjukurpa (chŭ-**ker**-pă) *noun* (*Austral.*) = **Dreamtime**.

T-junction *noun* a junction where one road or pipe etc. meets another but does not cross it, forming the shape of a T.

TLC *abbreviation* (*informal*) tender loving care.

TNT *abbreviation* trinitrotoluene, a powerful explosive.

to *preposition* **1** in the direction of, so as to approach or reach or be in (a place, position, or state etc.), *walked to the station*; *rose to power*; *was sent to prison*; *back to back*. **2** as far as, not falling short of, *patriotic to the core*; *from noon to 2 o'clock*; *goods to the value of $10*; *cooked to perfection*. **3** as compared with, in respect of, *won by 3 goals to 2*; *made to measure*; *his remarks were not to the point*. **4** for (a person or thing) to hold, possess, or be affected etc. by, *give it to me*; *spoke to her*; *kind to animals*; *accustomed to it*; *drank a toast to the bride*. – **to** (with a verb) **1** forming an infinitive, or expressing purpose or consequence etc., *he wants to go*; *does it to annoy*. **2** used alone when the verb is understood, *meant to call but forgot to*. – **to** *adverb* **1** in or into the normal or required position; to a closed or almost closed position, *push the door to*. **2** into a state of consciousness, *when she came to*. **3** into a state of activity, *set to*. ◻ **to and fro** backwards and forwards. **toing and froing** going to and fro.

toad *noun* **1** a froglike animal living chiefly on land. **2** a disliked person. ◻ **toad-in-the-hole** *noun* sausages baked in batter.

toadstool *noun* a fungus (especially a poisonous one) with a round top and a slender stalk.

toady *noun* a person who flatters and behaves obsequiously to another in the hope of gain or advantage for himself or herself. – **toady** *verb* (**toadied**, **toadying**) to behave as a toady.

toast *noun* **1** a slice of toasted bread. **2** the person or thing in whose honour a company is requested to drink; the call to drink or an

instance of drinking in this way. **–toast** *verb*
1 to brown the surface of (bread etc.) by
placing before a fire or other source of heat.
2 to warm (one's feet etc.) in this way. **3** to
honour or pledge good wishes to by drinking.
[from Latin *tostum* = dried up]

toaster *noun* an electrical device for toasting
bread.

toastmaster, toastmistress *nouns* a
person who announces the toasts at a public
dinner, reception, etc.

tobacco *noun* **1** a plant grown for its leaves
that are used for smoking or for making
snuff. **2** its leaves, especially as prepared for
smoking.

tobacconist *noun* a shopkeeper who sells
cigarettes, cigars, and tobacco.

Tobago (tŏ-**bay**-goh) an island in the West
Indies, forming part of the country of **Trinidad
and Tobago**. **Tobagan** *adjective* & *noun*,
Tobagonian (toh-bă-**goh**-nee-ăn) *adjective*
& *noun*

-to-be *suffix* soon to become, *the bride-to-be*.

Tobit (**toh**-bĭt) a book of the Apocrypha, a
romance of the Jewish captivity.

toboggan *noun* a long light narrow sledge
curved upwards at the front, used for sliding
downhill. **tobogganing** *noun* the sport of
riding on a toboggan.

Tobruk (tŏ-**bruuk**) a port on the
Mediterranean coast of Libya, the scene of
heavy fighting during the Second World War.

toby jug *noun* a mug or jug in the form of an
old man with a three-cornered hat.

toccata (tŏ-**kah**-tă) *noun* a musical
composition for a piano or organ etc., in a free
style with rapid running passages. [Italian,
= touched]

tocsin *noun* an alarm bell or signal.

today *noun* this present day or age. **–today**
adverb **1** on this present day. **2** at the present
time.

toddle *verb* **1** (of a young child) to walk with
short unsteady steps. **2** (*informal*) to walk.

toddler *noun* a child who has only recently
learnt to walk.

Todd River a river in the Northern Territory
flowing only after heavy rains. It is the scene
of an annual regatta, a race for bottomless
canoes propelled by runners in the dry bed
of the Todd at Alice Springs. [named after
Sir Charles Todd (1826–1910), English
astronomer, meteorologist, and electrical

engineer, who conceived and supervised the
building of the overland telegraph between
Adelaide and Darwin (completed in 1872).]

toddy *noun* a sweetened drink of spirits and
hot water.

to-do *noun* a fuss or commotion.

toe *noun* **1** one of the divisions (five in
humans) of the front part of the foot. **2** the part
of a shoe or stocking that covers the toes. **3** the
lower end or tip of a tool etc. **–toe** *verb* (**toed,
toeing**) **1** to touch or reach with the toes.
2 to put a toe on or repair the toe of (a shoe
or stocking). □ **be on one's toes** to be alert
or eager. **toe the line** to conform (especially
under compulsion) to the requirements of
one's group or party.

toehold *noun* a slight foothold.

toenail *noun* the nail on a toe.

toey *adjective* (*Austral. informal*) restless,
anxious, touchy.

toff *noun* (*informal, derogatory*) a
distinguished or well-dressed person. **toffy**
adjective

toffee *noun* a sweet made with heated butter
and sugar etc. □ **toffee apple** a toffee-coated
apple on a stick. **toffee-nosed** *adjective*
(*informal*) snobbish, pretentious.

tofu (**toh**-foo) *noun* a mild-flavoured curd
made from mashed soya beans.

tog *verb* (**togged, togging**) (*informal*) **tog up**
or **out** to dress. **togs** *plural noun* (*informal*)
clothes; (*Austral.*) a swimming costume.

toga (**toh**-gă) *noun* a loose flowing outer
garment worn by men in ancient Rome.

together *adverb* **1** in or into company or
conjunction, towards each other, so as to
unite. **2** one with another, *compare them
together*. **3** simultaneously, *both together
exclaimed*. **4** in an unbroken succession, *he is
away for weeks together*. **–together** *adjective*
(*informal*) (of a person) well organised, stable.
□ **together with** as well as, and also. [from *to*
+ *gather*]

togetherness *noun* being together; feeling
or belonging together.

toggle *noun* **1** a fastening device consisting
of a short piece of wood or metal etc. secured
by its centre and passed through a loop or hole
etc. **2** a device or computing command that
reverses the state of a system. □ **toggle switch**
a switch operated by a projecting lever.

Togo (**toh**-goh) a republic in West Africa.
Togolese *adjective* & *noun* (*plural* **Togolese**).

toil *verb* 1 to work long or laboriously. 2 to move laboriously, *we toiled up the hill*. –toil *noun* hard or laborious work. ▢ **toil-worn** *adjective* worn by toil; showing marks of this. **toiler** *noun*

toilet *noun* 1 a large receptacle (usually a fixture) for urine and faeces, usually flushed by running water. 2 a room, building, or compartment containing this. 3 the process of dressing and grooming oneself. ▢ **toilet paper** paper for use in a toilet. **toilet soap** soap for washing oneself.

toiletries *plural noun* (in shops) articles or preparations used in washing and grooming oneself.

toils *plural noun* a snare.

toilsome *adjective* involving toil.

tokay (toh-**kay**) *noun* a sweet Hungarian wine; a similar wine produced elsewhere.

token *noun* 1 a sign, symbol, or evidence of something, *a token of our esteem*. 2 a keepsake or memorial of friendship etc. 3 a voucher or coupon that can be exchanged for goods, *book token*. 4 a device like a coin bought for use with machines etc. –**token** *adjective* serving as a token or pledge but often on a small scale, *token resistance*. ▢ **by the same token** similarly; moreover.

tokenism *noun* making only a token effort or granting only small concessions, especially to minority or suppressed groups.

Tok Pisin (tok **pis**-in) a Melanesian English-based pidgin spoken in Papua New Guinea.

Tokyo (**toh**-kee-oh) the capital of Japan.

told *see* tell. ▢ **all told** counting everything or everyone, *we were 16 all told*.

tolerable *adjective* 1 able to be tolerated, endurable. 2 fairly good, passable. **tolerably** *adverb*, **tolerableness** *noun*

tolerance *noun* 1 willingness or ability to tolerate a person or thing. 2 the permitted variation in the measurement or weight etc. of an object.

tolerant *adjective* having or showing tolerance. **tolerantly** *adverb*

tolerate *verb* 1 to permit without protest or interference. 2 to bear (pain etc.); to be able to take (a medicine) or undergo (radiation etc.) without harm. **toleration** *noun* [from Latin *tolerare* = endure]

Tolkien (**tol**-keen), John Ronald Reuel (1892–1973), British writer and philologist, famous for his fantasies *The Hobbit* and *The Lord of the Rings*.

toll¹ (*rhymes with* hole) *noun* 1 a fee paid for the use of a public road or bridge etc. or for service rendered. 2 the loss or damage caused by a disaster or incurred in achieving something; *the death toll in the earthquake*, the number of deaths it caused. ▢ **take its toll** to be accompanied by loss or injury etc. **toll booth** (also **tollbooth**) a booth on a road or roadside from which tolls are collected. **toll gate** a gate across a road to prevent anyone passing until the toll has been paid. [from Greek *telos* = tax]

toll² (*rhymes with* hole) *verb* 1 to ring (a bell) with slow strokes, especially for a death or funeral. 2 (of a bell) to sound in this way; to indicate by tolling. –**toll** *noun* the stroke of a tolling bell.

tollway *noun* an expressway for which users pay a fee.

Tolpuddle martyrs six farm labourers of the village of Tolpuddle in England, sentenced to transportation in 1834 for trying to form a union to obtain an increase in wages.

Tolstoy, Count Leo Nikolaevich (1828–1910), Russian writer, best known for his epic novels *War and Peace* and *Anna Karenina*.

tom *noun* (in full **tom-cat**) a male cat. ▢ **Tom, Dick, and Harry** (*usually derogatory*) ordinary people, people taken at random. [short for Thomas, a man's name]

tomahawk *noun* 1 a light axe, especially one formerly used as a tool or weapon by some North American indigenous peoples. 2 (*Austral.*) a hatchet. [from an Algonquian language]

tomato *noun* (*plural* **tomatoes**) 1 a glossy red or yellow fruit eaten as a vegetable. 2 the plant bearing this.

tomb (*pr.* toom) *noun* 1 a grave or other place of burial. 2 a vault or stone monument in which one or more people are buried.

tombolo (tom-**boh**-loh) *noun* (*plural* **tombolos**) a sand or gravel bar connecting an island to the mainland or another island, especially on the coast of Italy. [Italian, = sand dune]

tomboy *noun* an energetic girl who enjoys activities traditionally or stereotypically associated with boys. ▢ **tomboy stitch** *see* **French knitting**.

tombstone *noun* a memorial stone set up over a grave.

tome (*rhymes with* home) *noun* a book or volume, especially a large heavy one.

tomfool *adjective* extremely foolish. –tomfool *noun* an extremely foolish person. tomfoolery *noun*

tommygun *noun* a sub-machine gun. [from the name of its American inventor, J.T. Thompson (died 1940)]

tommyrot *noun* (*informal*) nonsense, an absurd statement or argument.

tommy rough *noun* (also tommy ruff) a small edible sea fish of southern Australian waters.

tomography (tŏ-**mog**-ră-fee) *noun* a method of radiography displaying details in a selected plane within the body.

tomorrow *noun* 1 the day after today. 2 the near future. –tomorrow *adverb* on the day after today; at some future date.

Tom Thumb *noun* 1 the tiny hero of a nursery tale. 2 a very small person. 3 a dwarf variety of certain plants.

tomtit *noun* tit (*tit*¹), especially a blue tit.

tom-tom *noun* 1 an African or Asian drum beaten with the hands. 2 a deep-toned drum used in jazz bands.

ton (*pr.* tun) *noun* 1 a measure of weight, either a long ton (2240 lb. or 1016.05 kg) or a short ton (2000 lb. or 907.19 kg). 2 a measure of capacity for various materials. 3 a unit of volume in shipping. 4 (*informal*) a large amount, *tons of money*. 5 (*informal*) a speed of 100 km/h or m.p.h.; a score of 100. □ metric ton a tonne.

tonal (**toh**-năl) *adjective* 1 of a tone or tones. 2 of tonality. tonally *adverb*

tonality (tŏ-**nal**-ĭ-tee) *noun* 1 the character of a melody, depending on the scale or key in which it is composed. 2 the colour scheme of a picture.

tone *noun* 1 a musical or vocal sound, especially with reference to its pitch, quality, and strength. 2 the manner of expression in speaking or writing, *an apologetic tone*. 3 any one of the five intervals between one note and the next which, together with two semitones, make up an octave. 4 proper firmness of the organs and tissues of the body, *muscle tone*. 5 a tint or shade of a colour; the general effect of colour or of light and shade in a picture. 6 the general spirit or character prevailing, *set the tone with a dignified speech*. –tone *verb* 1 to give a particular tone of sound or colour to. 2 to

harmonise in colour, *the curtains tone* or *tone in with the wallpaper*. 3 to give proper firmness to (muscles, organs, or skin etc.). □ tone-deaf *adjective* unable to perceive accurately differences of musical pitch. tone down to make or become softer in tone of sound or colour; to make (a statement) less strong or harsh. tone poem an orchestral composition illustrating a poetic idea. tone up to make or become brighter or more vigorous or intense. toner *noun* [from Greek *tonos* = tension]

toneless *adjective* without positive tone, not expressive. tonelessly *adverb*

Tonga a kingdom consisting of a group of islands in the Pacific, also called the Friendly Islands. Tongan *adjective* & *noun*

tongs *plural noun* an instrument with two arms joined at one end, used for grasping and holding things.

tongue *noun* 1 the fleshy muscular organ in the mouth, used in tasting, licking, swallowing, and (in humans) speaking. 2 the tongue of an ox etc. as food. 3 the ability to speak or manner of speaking, *a persuasive tongue*; *have lost one's tongue*, be too bashful or surprised to speak. 4 a language, *his native tongue is German*; *the gift of tongues*, the power to speak in unknown languages (as given to Christ's followers, recorded in Acts 2). 5 a projecting strip or flap. 6 a tapering jet of flame. –tongue *verb* to start or stop a note or produce staccato or other effects in (a wind instrument) by use of the tongue. □ tongue-lashing *noun* a severe rebuke. tongue-tied *adjective* silent because of shyness or embarrassment; unable to speak normally because the ligament connecting the tongue to the base of the mouth is abnormally short. tongue-twister *noun* a sequence of words that is difficult to pronounce quickly and correctly, e.g. *she sells seashells*. with one's tongue hanging out thirsty; eagerly expectant. with one's tongue in one's cheek speaking with sly sarcasm.

tongued *adjective* 1 having a tongue. 2 having a specified manner of speaking, *sharp-tongued*.

tonguing *noun* use of the tongue in playing a wind instrument (see tongue *verb*).

tonic *noun* 1 a medicine with an invigorating effect, taken after illness or weakness. 2 anything that restores people's energy or good spirits. 3 a keynote in music. 4 tonic water. –tonic *adjective* having the effect of a tonic, toning up the muscles etc. □ tonic sol-fa the system of syllables *doh, ray, me, fah, soh, la, te* used (especially in teaching singing) to represent the notes of the musical scale. **tonic water** mineral water, especially if slightly flavoured with quinine.

tonight *noun* **1** the present evening or night. **2** the evening or night of today. –**tonight** *adverb* on the present evening or night or that of today.

tonnage (**tun**-ij) *noun* **1** the carrying capacity of a ship or ships, expressed in tons. **2** the charge per ton for carrying cargo or freight.

tonne (*pr.* tonn *or* tun) *noun* (also **metric ton**) a measure of weight, 1,000 kg.

tonsil *noun* either of two small organs at the sides of the throat near the root of the tongue. **tonsillar** *adjective*

tonsillitis *noun* inflammation of the tonsils.

tonsure (**ton**-sher) *noun* **1** shaving the top or all of the head of a person entering certain priesthoods or monastic orders. **2** the part of the head shaven in this way. **tonsured** *adjective* [from Latin *tonsor* = barber]

too *adverb* **1** to a greater extent than is desirable. **2** (*informal*) very, *he's not too well today*. **3** also, *take the others too.* ▢ **too bad** (*informal*) regrettable, a pity.

took *see* **take**.

tool *noun* **1** a thing (usually something held in the hand) for working upon something. **2** a simple machine, e.g. a lathe. **3** anything used in an occupation or pursuit, *a dictionary is a useful tool*. **4** a person used as a mere instrument by another. –**tool** *verb* **1** to shape or ornament by using a tool. **2** to provide oneself or equip (a factory etc.) with necessary tools, *tool up*. **3** (*informal*) to drive or ride in a casual or leisurely way, *tooling along*.

toolache (too-**lay**-chee) *noun* a large wallaby of SE South Australia and western Victoria, now extinct. [Yaralde, probably *dulaj*]

toolbar *noun* (in computing) a strip of icons used to perform certain functions.

toolmaker *noun* a person who makes precision tools.

toot[1] (*rhymes with* boot) *noun* a short sound produced by a horn or whistle etc. –**toot** *verb* to make or cause to make a toot.

toot[2] (*rhymes with* foot) *noun* (*Austral. informal*) a toilet.

tooth *noun* (*plural* **teeth**) **1** each of the hard white bony structures rooted in the gums, used for biting and chewing. **2** a similar structure

in the mouth or alimentary canal of certain invertebrate animals. **3** a toothlike part or projection, e.g. on a gear, saw, comb, or rake. **4** a liking for a particular type of food, *he has a sweet tooth.* ▢ **fight tooth and nail** to fight very fiercely. **in the teeth of** in spite of; in opposition to; directly against (the wind). **put teeth into** to make (a law or regulation) able to be applied effectively.

toothache *noun* an ache in a tooth or teeth.

toothbrush *noun* a brush for cleaning the teeth. ▢ **toothbrush moustache** a short straight bristly one.

toothcomb *noun* a comb with fine close-set teeth (¶ properly a *fine-tooth comb*, taken as a *fine toothcomb*).

toothed *adjective* **1** having teeth. **2** having teeth of a certain kind, *sharp-toothed*.

toothless *adjective* having no teeth.

toothpaste *noun* paste for cleaning the teeth.

toothpick *noun* a small pointed piece of wood etc. for removing bits of food from between the teeth.

toothy *adjective* having many or large teeth.

tootle *verb* **1** to toot gently or repeatedly. **2** (*informal*) to go in a casual or leisurely way, *tootle around*.

top[1] *noun* **1** the highest point or part of something; the upper surface. **2** the highest rank or degree, the highest or most honourable position, *he is at the top of his profession*. **3** the utmost degree of intensity, *shouted at the top of his voice*. **4** a thing forming the upper part of something, the creamy part of milk; a garment covering the upper part of the body. **5** the covering or stopper of a bottle or tube. **6** top gear. –**top** *adjective* highest in position, rank, place, or degree, *at top speed*; *top prices*. –**top** *verb* (**topped**, **topping**) **1** to provide or be a top for. **2** to reach the top of. **3** to be higher than, to surpass; *top the list*, to be at the top of it. **4** to add as a final thing or finishing touch. **5** to remove the top of (a plant or fruit). ▢ **on top** above; in a superior position; in addition. **on top of** in addition to; having mastered (a thing) thoroughly; *be on top of the world*, very happy. **top drawer** the highest social position, *out of the top drawer*. **top-dress** *verb* to apply manure etc. on the top of soil without ploughing it in. **top dressing** this process; the substance used. **Top End** the northern part of the Northern Territory. **Top Ender** a native or resident of the Top End. **top-flight** *adjective* of the highest rank; most successful. **top gear** the highest gear, allowing parts to revolve fast. **top hat** a man's tall stiff black or grey hat worn with formal dress. **top-heavy** *adjective* overweighted at the top and therefore in danger of falling over. **top-notch** *adjective* (*informal*) first-rate. **top-ranking** *adjective* of the highest rank. **top secret** of the highest category of secrecy. **top up** to fill up (a half-empty container).

top² *noun* a toy that spins on its point when set in motion by hand or by a string or spring etc. □ **sleep like a top** to sleep soundly.

topaz (**toh**-paz) *noun* a semi-precious stone of various colours, especially yellow.

topcoat *noun* **1** an overcoat. **2** an outer coat of paint etc.

toper (**toh**-per) *noun* a habitual drunkard.

topiary (**toh**-pee-er-ee) *noun* the art of clipping shrubs etc. into ornamental shapes.

topic *noun* the subject of a discussion or written work. [from Greek *topos* = place]

topical *adjective* having reference to current events. **topically** *adverb*, **topicality** (top-ĭ-**kal**-ĭ-tee) *noun*

topknot *noun* a tuft or crest or knot of ribbon etc. on top of the head.

topless *adjective* **1** without a top. **2** (of clothes) having no upper part; (of a person) wearing such clothes.

topmost *adjective* highest.

topography (tŏ-**pog**-ră-fee) *noun* the features of a place or district, the position of its rivers, mountains, roads, buildings, etc. **topographical** (top-ŏ-**graf**-i-kăl) *adjective* [from Greek *topos* = place, + *-graphy*]

topology (tŏ-**pol**-ŏ-jee) *noun* the branch of mathematics dealing with geometrical properties that are unaffected by certain changes in the shape or size of the figures and surfaces concerned. **topological** *adjective* [from Greek *topos* = place, + *-logy*]

topple *verb* **1** to fall headlong or as if top-heavy, to totter and fall. **2** to cause to do this. **3** to overthrow, to cause to fall from authority, *the crisis toppled the government*. [from *top¹*]

topside *noun* **1** a joint of beef cut from the upper part of the haunch. **2** the side of a ship above the waterline.

topsoil *noun* the top layer of soil as distinct from the subsoil.

topsy-turvy *adverb* & *adjective* **1** in or into a state of great disorder. **2** upside down.

toque (*rhymes with* coke) *noun* a woman's close-fitting brimless hat with a high crown.

tor *noun* a hill or rocky peak.

Torah (**tor**-ră) *noun* **1** the revealed will of God, especially the laws given to Moses. **2** the Pentateuch; a scroll containing this.

torch *noun* **1** a small hand-held electric lamp powered by a battery or electric power cell, contained in a case. **2** a burning stick of resinous wood, or of combustible material fixed on a stick and ignited, used as a light for carrying in the hand.

torchlight *noun* the light of a torch or torches; *a torchlight procession*, one in which burning torches are used.

tore *see* tear¹.

toreador (**to**-ree-ă-dor) *noun* a bullfighter, especially on horseback. [from Spanish *toro* = bull]

torment (**tor**-ment) *noun* **1** severe physical or mental suffering. **2** something causing this. **–torment** (tor-**ment**) *verb* **1** to subject to torment. **2** to tease or try to provoke by annoyances etc. **tormentor** *noun* [from Latin *tortum* = twisted]

torn *see* tear¹.

tornado (tor-**nay**-doh) *noun* (*plural* **tornadoes**) **1** a violent and destructive whirlwind advancing in a narrow path. **2** a loud outburst, *a tornado of applause*. [from Spanish, = thunderstorm]

torpedo *noun* (*plural* **torpedoes**) a cigar-shaped explosive underwater missile, launched against a ship from a submarine or surface ship or from an aircraft. **–torpedo** *verb* **1** to destroy or attack with a torpedo. **2** to ruin or wreck (a policy or conference etc.) suddenly. [Latin, = large sea fish that can give an electric shock which causes numbness]

torpid *adjective* sluggish and inactive. **torpidly** *adverb*, **torpidity** (tor-**pid**-ĭ-tee) *noun* [from Latin *torpidus* = numb]

torpor (**tor**-per) *noun* a torpid condition.

torque (*pr.* tork) *noun* a force causing rotation in a mechanism. □ **torque converter** a device to transmit the correct torque from engine to axle in a motor vehicle. [from Latin *torquere* = to twist]

Torrens system *noun* (also **Torrens title**) a system of government registration of land ownership used in Australia and some other countries. [named after Sir Robert Richard Torrens (1814–84), who introduced the legislation in the South Australian parliament in 1857]

torrent *noun* **1** a rushing stream of water or lava. **2** a downpour of rain. **3** a violent flow, *a torrent of words*.

torrential (to-**ren**-shăl) *adjective* like a torrent.

Torres Strait (**to**-rĕz) a stretch of water between Cape York Peninsula, Queensland, and the southern coast of Papua New Guinea. □ **Torres Strait Islander** an inhabitant of the Torres Strait Islands. **Torres Strait Islands** a group of more than 70 islands in the Torres Strait, inhabited by people Melanesian in origin, an Australian possession. [named after Luis Vaez de Torres, who discovered the Strait in 1606]

torrid (*rhymes with* horrid) *adjective* **1** (of climate or land) very hot and dry. **2** intense, passionate. □ **torrid zone** the tropics. [from Latin *torridus* = parched]

torsion (**tor**-shŏn) *noun* **1** twisting, especially of one end of a thing while the other is held fixed. **2** the state of being spirally twisted. [same origin as *torture*]

torso (**tor**-soh) *noun* (*plural* **torsos**) **1** the trunk of the human body. **2** a statue lacking head and limbs. [Italian, = stump]

tort *noun* (in Law) any private or civil wrong (other than breach of contract) for which the wronged person may claim damages. [same origin as *torture*]

torte (**tor**-tĕ) *noun* a kind of rich layer cake. [German]

tortellini (tor-tĕ-**lee**-nee) *plural noun* small pasta cases stuffed with meat, cheese, etc., rolled and shaped into rings. [Italian]

tortilla (tor-**tee**-yă) *noun* a thin flat maize cake eaten hot. [Spanish]

tortoise (**tor**-tŭs) *noun* a slow-moving four-footed reptile with its body enclosed in a hard shell, living on land or in fresh water.

tortoiseshell (**tor**-tŭs-shel) *noun* **1** the semi-transparent mottled yellowish-brown shell of certain turtles, used for making combs etc. **2** a cat or butterfly with mottled colouring resembling this. – **tortoiseshell** *adjective* having such colouring.

tortuous (**tor**-tew-ŭs) *adjective* **1** full of twists and turns. **2** (of policy etc.) devious, not straightforward. **tortuously** *adverb*, **tortuosity** (tor-tew-**os**-ĭ-tee) *noun* [from Latin *tortum* = twisted]

torture *noun* **1** the infliction of severe pain as a punishment or means of coercion. **2** a method of torturing. **3** severe physical or mental pain. – **torture** *verb* **1** to inflict torture upon; to subject to great pain or anxiety. **2** to force out of its natural position or shape. **torturer** *noun* [from Latin *tortum* = twisted]

Tory *noun* **1** (*informal*) a member of the British Conservative Party. **2** (*historical*) a member of the political party in England in the 17th–19th centuries, opposed to the Whigs, which gave rise to the Conservative Party. **3** a derogatory name for a political conservative. – **Tory** *adjective* (*informal*) Conservative or conservative.

tosh *noun* (*informal*) nonsense.

toss *verb* **1** to throw lightly or carelessly or easily; *toss one's head*, to throw it back in contempt or impatience. **2** to send (a coin) spinning in the air to decide something according to the way it lies after falling. **3** to throw or roll about from side to side restlessly or with an uneven motion. **4** to coat (food) by gently shaking it in flour etc. – **toss** *noun* **1** a tossing action or movement. **2** the result obtained by tossing a coin. □ **toss in** (*informal*) to give up (a job etc.). **toss off** to drink rapidly; to finish or compose rapidly or without much thought of effort. **toss up** to toss a coin. **toss-up** *noun* the tossing of a coin; an even chance.

tot[1] *noun* **1** a small child. **2** (*informal*) a small quantity of alcoholic drink, especially spirits.

tot[2] *verb* (**totted**, **totting**) **tot up** (*informal*) to add up, *tot this up*; *it tots up to $20*. [short for *total*]

total *adjective* **1** including everything or everyone, comprising the whole, *the total number of persons*; *a total eclipse*, in which the whole disc of the moon etc. is obscured. **2** utter, complete, *in total darkness*. – **total** *noun* the total number or amount, a count of all the items. – **total** *verb* (**totalled**, **totalling**) **1** to reckon the total of. **2** to amount to. **totally** *adverb* [from Latin *totum* = the whole]

totalisator *noun* (also **-izator**) a device automatically registering the number and amount of bets staked, with a view to dividing the total amount among those betting on the winner.

totalise *verb* (also **-ize**) to find the total of.

totalitarian (toh-tal-ĭ-**tair**-ree-ăn) *adjective* of a form of government in which no rival parties or loyalties are permitted, usually demanding total submission of the individual to the requirements of the State.

totality (toh-**tal**-ĭ-tee) *noun* **1** the quality of being total. **2** a total number or amount.

tote¹ (*informal*) a totalisator.

tote² *verb* (*informal*) to carry.
□ **tote bag** a large bag for shopping etc.

totem (**toh**-tĕm) *noun* **1** a natural object, especially an animal, adopted as the emblem of a clan or family, especially among indigenous peoples. **2** an image of this.
□ **totem pole** a pole carved or painted with a series of totems.

t'other (*informal*) = the other.

totter *verb* **1** to walk unsteadily. **2** to rock or shake as if about to collapse. **–totter** *noun* an unsteady or shaky walk or movement. **tottery** *adjective*

toucan (**too**-kan) *noun* a tropical American bird with an immense beak.

touch *verb* **1** to be or come together so that there is no space between; to meet (another object) in this way. **2** to put one's hand etc. on (a thing) lightly. **3** to press or strike lightly. **4** to move or meddle with, to harm. **5** to have to do with in the slightest degree, to attempt, *the firm doesn't touch business of that kind*. **6** to eat or drink even a little of, *she hasn't touched her breakfast*. **7** to reach, *the scales touched 80 kg*. **8** to equal in excellence, *no other cloth can touch it for quality*. **9** to affect slightly. **10** to rouse sympathy or other emotion in. **11** (*informal*) to persuade to give money as a loan or gift, *touched him for $10*. **–touch** *noun* **1** the act or fact of touching. **2** the faculty of perceiving things or their qualities through touching them. **3** small things done in producing a piece of work, *put the finishing touches*. **4** a performer's way of touching the keys or strings of a musical instrument etc. **5** a manner or style of workmanship, a person's special skill, *he hasn't lost his touch*. **6** a relationship of communication or knowledge, *we've lost touch with her*. **7** a slight trace, *a touch of sarcasm in his voice*; *a touch of flu*. **8** the part of a football field outside the touchlines. **9** (*informal*) the act of obtaining money from a person; *a soft touch*, a person who readily gives money when asked.
□ **in touch with** in communication with; having interest in or information about. **out of touch** no longer in touch with a person or subject etc. **touch-and-go** *adjective* uncertain as regards result. **touch bottom** to reach the worst point of misfortune etc. **touch down**

(in rugby football) to touch the ball on the ground behind either goal line; (of an aircraft) to land. **touch off** to cause to explode; to cause to start, *his arrest touched off a riot*. **touch on** to deal with or mention (a subject) briefly. **touch-typing** *noun* typewriting without looking at the keys. **touch up** to improve (a thing) by making small alterations or additions. **touch wood** to touch something made of wood in superstitious or humorous hope that this will avert bad luck.

touchable *adjective* able to be touched.

touchdown *noun* the act of touching down.

touché (**too**-shay) *interjection* an acknowledgement that one's opponent has made a hit in fencing or a valid accusation or criticism in a discussion. [French, = touched]

touched *adjective* **1** caused to feel warm sympathy or gratitude. **2** slightly mad.

touching *adjective* rousing kindly feelings or sympathy or pity. **–touching** *preposition* concerning. **touchingly** *adverb*

touchline *noun* the side limit of a football field.

touchpaper *noun* paper impregnated with a substance that will make it burn slowly for igniting fireworks etc.

touchstone *noun* a standard or criterion by which something is judged. [formerly, a kind of stone against which gold and silver were rubbed to test their purity]

touchy *adjective* (**touchier, touchiest**) easily offended. **touchily** *adverb*, **touchiness** *noun*

tough *adjective* **1** difficult to break or cut or chew. **2** able to endure hardship, not easily hurt, damaged, or injured. **3** unyielding, stubborn, resolute; *get tough with him*, to adopt a firm attitude in dealing with him. **4** difficult, *a tough job*. **5** (*informal*, of luck etc.) hard, unpleasant. **–tough** *noun* a rough and violent person, *young toughs*. **–tough** *interjection* (*informal*) bad luck.
□ **tough-minded** *adjective* realistic and not sentimental. **toughly** *adverb*, **toughness** *noun*

toughen *verb* to make or become tough.

Toulouse-Lautrec (too-looz loh-**trek**), Henri de (1864–1901), French painter, best known for his brightly-coloured posters and scenes of Parisian nightlife.

toupee (**too**-pay) *noun* a wig; an artificial patch of hair worn to cover a bald spot. [from French *toupet* = hair-tuft]

tour *noun* a journey through a country, town, or building etc. visiting various places or things of interest, playing matches, or giving performances. **–tour** *verb* to make a tour of. □ **on tour** touring. [same origin as *turn*]

tour de force (toor dĕ **forss**) *noun* (*plural* **tours de force**, *pr.* same) an outstandingly skilful performance or achievement. [French]

tourism *noun* **1** visiting places as a tourist. **2** the business of providing accommodation and services etc. for tourists.

tourist *noun* a person who is making a tour. □ **tourist class** a class of passenger accommodation in a ship or aircraft etc., lower than first class.

touristy *adjective* designed to attract tourists.

tourmaline (**toor**-mă-leen) *noun* a mineral of various colours, possessing unusual electric properties and used as a gem.

tournament (**toor**-nă-mĕnt) *noun* a contest of skill between a number of competitors, involving a series of matches.

tournedos (**toor**-nĕ-doh) *noun* (*plural* **tournedos**) a small piece of fillet of beef cooked with a strip of fat wrapped round it.

tourniquet (**toor**-nĭ-kay) *noun* a device or a strip of material drawn tightly round a limb to stop the flow of blood from an artery by compressing it.

tousle (**tow**-zĕl) *verb* to make (hair etc.) untidy by ruffling it.

tout (*rhymes with* scout) *verb* **1** to try busily to obtain orders for one's goods or services, *touting for custom.* **2** to pester people to buy, *touting information.* **–tout** *noun* a person who touts things; a tipster touting information about racehorses etc.

tow¹ (*rhymes with* go) *noun* short coarse fibres of flax or hemp, used for making yarn etc. □ **tow-coloured** *adjective* (of hair) very light in colour. **tow-headed** *adjective* having tow-coloured hair.

tow² (*rhymes with* go) *verb* to pull along behind one. **–tow** *noun* towing, being towed. □ **in tow** being towed; (*informal*) following behind, under one's charge, *he arrived with his family in tow.* **on tow** being towed. **tow bar** a bar fitted to a car for towing a caravan etc.

toward *preposition* = towards.

towards *preposition* **1** in the direction of, *walked* or *faced towards the sea.* **2** in relation to, regarding, *the way he behaved towards his children.* **3** for the purpose of achieving or promoting, *efforts towards peace.* **4** as a contribution to, *put the money towards a new*

bicycle. **5** near, approaching, *towards four o'clock.*

towel *noun* a piece of absorbent cloth or paper for drying oneself or wiping things dry. **–towel** *verb* (**towelled**, **towelling**) **1** to wipe or dry with a towel. **2** (*informal*) to thrash or beat.

towelling *noun* fabric for making towels.

tower *noun* a tall usually square or circular structure, either standing alone (e.g. as a fort) or forming part of a church or castle or other large building. **–tower** *verb* to be of great height; to be taller or more eminent that others, *he towered above everyone.* □ **tower block** a very tall block of flats or offices. **tower of strength** a person who gives strong and reliable support.

towering *adjective* **1** very tall, lofty. **2** (of rage etc.) extreme, intense.

town *noun* **1** a collection of dwellings and other buildings, larger than a township or village, especially one not created a city. **2** any densely populated area, as opposed to the country. **3** the inhabitants of a town. **4** the central business and shopping area of a neighbourhood, *prefers shopping in town to shopping in the suburbs.* □ **go to town** (*informal*) to do something lavishly or with great enthusiasm. **on the town** (*informal*) enjoying the entertainments of town. **town clerk** an official responsible for the administration of a local government area. **town crier** (*historical*) an official who makes public announcements in the streets. **town hall** a building containing local government offices and usually a hall for public events. **town house** a terrace house or a house in a compact planned group in a town; a residence in town especially of a person with a house in the country. **town planning** preparation of plans for the regulated growth and improvement of towns. [from Old English *tun* = enclosure]

townscape *noun* **1** a picture of a town. **2** the general appearance of a town.

township *noun* **1** (in Australia) a small town. **2** (*historical*) (in South Africa) an urban area set aside for Black occupation.

townspeople *noun* the people of a town.

toxaemia (tok-**see**-mee-ă) *noun* **1** blood poisoning. **2** a condition in pregnancy in which blood pressure is abnormally high.

toxic *adjective* **1** of or caused by poison. **2** poisonous. **toxicity** (tok-**siss**-ĭ-tee) *noun* [from Greek, = poison for arrows (*toxa* = arrows)]

toxicology *noun* the scientific study of poisons. **toxicological** *adjective*, **toxicologist** *noun* [from *toxic* + *-logy*]

toxin *noun* a poisonous substance of animal or vegetable origin, especially one formed in the body by microorganisms. [from *toxic*]

toxophilite (tok-**soff**-ĭ-lyt) *noun* a lover of archery.

toxophily (tok-**soff**-ĭ-lee) *noun* archery. [from Greek *toxa* = arrows, + *philia* = loving]

toy *noun* 1 a thing to play with, especially for a child. 2 a thing intended for amusement rather than for serious use. –**toy** *adjective* 1 serving as a toy. 2 (of a dog) of a diminutive breed or variety, kept as a pet. –**toy** *verb* **toy with** to handle or finger idly; to deal with or consider without seriousness, *toyed with the idea of going to Hawaii*.

trace¹ *noun* 1 a track or mark left behind. 2 a visible or other sign of what has existed or happened. 3 a very small quantity, *contains traces of soda*. –**trace** *verb* 1 to follow or discover by observing marks, tracks, pieces of evidence, etc. 2 to mark out, to sketch the outline of, to form (letters etc.) laboriously, *traced his signature shakily*; *the policy he traced out was never followed*. 3 to copy (a map or drawing etc.) on transparent paper placed over it or by using carbon paper below. □ **trace element** a substance occurring or required, especially in soil, only in minute amounts. **traceable** *adjective*

trace² *noun* each of the two side straps, chains, or ropes by which a horse draws a vehicle. □ **kick over the traces** (of a person) to become insubordinate or reckless.

tracer *noun* 1 a person or thing that traces. 2 a bullet that leaves a trail of coloured light, smoke, etc. by which its course can be observed. 3 a radioactive substance that can be traced in its course through the human body or a series of reactions etc. by the radiation it produces.

tracery *noun* 1 an openwork pattern in stone (e.g. in a church window). 2 a decorative pattern of lines resembling this. [from *trace*¹]

trachea (tră-**kee**-ă) *noun* the windpipe.

tracheole (**trak**-ee-ohl) *noun* a tiny branch of a trachea in an arthropod.

trachoma (tră-**koh**-mă) *noun* a contagious disease of the eye causing grainy inflammation of the inner surface of the eyelids and leading eventually to blindness.

tracing *noun* a copy of a map or drawing etc. made by tracing it. □ **tracing paper** transparent paper for making tracings.

track *noun* 1 a mark or series of marks left by a moving person, animal, or thing. 2 a course taken. 3 a course of action or procedure; *you're on the right track*, following the right line of procedure or inquiry etc. 4 a path or rough road, especially one made by people or animals or carts etc. passing. 5 a prepared course for racing etc. 6 a section of a record, tape, or compact disc, etc. containing one song, section of music, etc. 7 (in a computer etc.) the path along which information is recorded on a tape or disk. 8 a continuous line of railway; *single track*, only one pair of rails. 9 a continuous band round the wheels of a tank or tractor etc. –**track** *verb* 1 to follow the track of; to find or observe by doing this. 2 (of a stylus) to follow a groove. 3 (of a cine-camera) to move along a set path while taking a picture. □ **in one's tracks** (*informal*) where one stands; instantly. **keep** or **lose track of** to keep or fail to keep oneself informed about. **make tracks** (*informal*) to go away. **make tracks for** (*informal*) to go to or towards. **track events** (in sports) races as distinct from field events (*see* field). **track record** a person's past achievements.

tracker *noun* a person or thing that tracks. □ **tracker dog** a police dog tracking by scent.

tracksuit *noun* a warm loose-fitting suit worn for exercising etc.

tract¹ *noun* 1 a large stretch of land. 2 a system of connected parts in an animal body along which something passes, *the digestive tract*.

tract² *noun* a pamphlet containing a short essay, especially on a religious subject.

tractable *adjective* easy to manage or deal with, docile. **tractability** *noun*

traction *noun* 1 pulling or drawing a load along a surface. 2 a continuous pull on a limb etc. in medical treatment. □ **traction engine** a steam or diesel engine for drawing a heavy load along a road or across a field etc. [from Latin *tractum* = pulled]

tractor *noun* 1 a powerful motor vehicle for pulling farm machinery or other heavy equipment. 2 a device supplying traction. [same origin as *traction*]

trad *adjective* (*informal*) traditional.

trade *noun* 1 exchange of goods for money or other goods. 2 business of a particular kind, *the tourist trade*. 3 business carried on to earn one's living or for profit (distinguished from a *profession*), a skilled handicraft, *he's a butcher by trade*; *learn a trade*. **4** the people engaged in a particular trade, *we sell cars to the trade, not to private buyers*. **5** a trade wind. **–trade** *verb* **1** to engage in trade, to buy and sell. **2** to exchange (goods etc.) in trading. □ **trade deficit** or **gap** the difference in value or amount between a country's exports and its imports. **trade in** to give (a used article) as partial payment for another article. **trade-in** *noun* an article given in this way. **trade name** a name given by a manufacturer to a proprietary article or material; the name by which a thing is known in the trade; the name under which a person or firm trades. **trade-off** *noun* a balancing factor; an exchange as a compromise. **trade on** to make great use of for one's own advantage, *trading on his brother's reputation*. **trade secret** a technique used in the trade but kept from being generally known. **trade union** (*plural* **trade unions**) an organised association of employees engaged in a particular type of work, formed to protect and promote their common interests. **trade unionist** a member of a trade union. **trade wind** one of the winds blowing continually towards the equator over most of the tropics, from the north-east in the northern hemisphere and south-east in the southern hemisphere.

trademark (also **trade mark**) *noun* a manufacturer's or trader's registered emblem or name etc. used to identify goods. **–trademark** *verb* provide with a trademark.

trader *noun* **1** a person engaged in trading; a shopkeeper or supplier. **2** a merchant ship.

tradesman, **tradeswoman** *nouns* (*plural* **tradesmen**, **tradeswomen**) = **tradesperson**.

tradesperson *noun* a person engaged in or skilled in a trade.

tradie *noun* (*Austral. informal*) a tradesperson.

trading *noun* buying and selling.

tradition *noun* **1** the handing down of beliefs or customs from one generation to another, especially without writing. **2** a belief or custom handed down in this way; a long-established custom or method of procedure. [from Latin *traditum* = handed on]

traditional *adjective* **1** of, based on, or obtained by tradition. **2** (of jazz) in the style of the early 20th century. □ **traditional owner** an Aborigine who is a member of a local descent group having certain rights in a tract of land. **traditionally** *adverb*

traditionalist *noun* a person who follows or upholds traditional beliefs etc.

traduce (tră-**dewss**) *verb* to misrepresent in an unfavourable way. **traducement** *noun*

Trafalgar (tră-**fal**-ger) a cape on the south coast of Spain, near which the British fleet under Nelson won a great victory over the fleets of France and Spain in 1805.

traffic *noun* **1** vehicles, ships, or aircraft moving along a route. **2** trading, especially when illegal or morally wrong, *drug traffic*. **–traffic** *verb* (**trafficked**, **trafficking**) to trade. □ **traffic lights** an automatic signal controlling traffic at junctions etc. by means of coloured lights. **trafficker** *noun*

tragedian (tră-**jee**-dee-ăn) *noun* **1** a writer of tragedies. **2** an actor in tragedy.

tragedienne (tră-jee-dee-**en**) *noun* an actress in tragedy.

tragedy *noun* **1** a serious play with unhappy events or a sad ending. **2** the branch of drama that consists of such plays. **3** an event that causes great sadness, a calamity. [from Greek *tragos* = goat, + *oide* = song]

tragic *adjective* **1** of or in the style of tragedy, *he was a great tragic actor*. **2** sorrowful. **3** causing great sadness, calamitous. **–tragic** *noun* (*informal*) a person devoted to a specified activity, interest, etc., *a cricket tragic*. □ **tragic irony** a device, originally in Greek tragedy, by which words carry a tragic, especially prophetic, meaning to the audience, unknown to the character speaking.

tragical *adjective* **1** sorrowful. **2** causing great sadness. **tragically** *adverb*

tragicomedy (traj-ee-**kom**-ĕ-dee) *noun* a play with both tragic and comic elements.

trail *verb* **1** to drag or be dragged along behind, especially on the ground. **2** to hang or float loosely; (of a plant) to grow lengthily downwards or along the ground. **3** to move wearily; to lag or straggle. **4** to be losing in a game or other contest; to be losing to (a specified team etc.). **5** to diminish, to become fainter, *her voice trailed away*. **6** to follow the trail of, to track. **–trail** *noun* **1** something that trails or hangs trailing. **2** a line of people or things following behind something. **3** a mark left where something has passed, a trace, *vandals left a trail of wreckage*; *a snail's slimy trail*. **4** a track or scent followed in hunting. **5** a beaten path, especially through a wild region. [from Latin *tragula* = net for dragging a river]

trailblazer *noun* **1** a person who marks a new track through wild country. **2** a pioneer of a new idea or project etc.

trailer *noun* **1** a vehicle designed to be hauled by another. **2** a short extract from a film, shown in advance to advertise it. **3** a person or thing that trails.

train *noun* **1** a railway engine with a series of linked carriages or trucks. **2** a number of people or animals moving in a line, *a camel train*. **3** a body of followers, a retinue. **4** a sequence of things, *a train of events*; *a train of thought*; *certain consequences followed in its train*, after it, as a result. **5** a set of parts in machinery, actuating one another in a series. **6** part of a long dress or robe that trails on the ground behind the wearer. **7** a line of combustible material placed to lead fire to an explosive. –**train** *verb* **1** to bring to a desired standard of efficiency, condition, or behaviour etc. by instruction and practice. **2** to undergo such a process, *she trained as a secretary*. **3** to make or become physically fit for a sport by exercise and diet. **4** to teach and accustom (a person or animal) to do something. **5** to aim (a gun or camera etc.), *trained his camera on the cat*. **6** to cause (a plant) to grow in the required direction. □ **in train** in preparation, *put matters in train for the election*. **in training** undergoing training for a sport; physically fit as a result of this. **out of training** not fit in this way. **trainable** *adjective* [same origin as *traction*]

trainee *noun* a person being trained for an occupation etc.

trainer *noun* **1** a person who trains; one who trains people or animals. **2** a rubber-soled running shoe.

traipse *verb* (*informal*) to trudge.

trait (*pr.* tray *or* trayt) *noun* a characteristic. [from French]

traitor *noun* a person who behaves disloyally; one who betrays his or her country. **traitorous** *adjective* [same origin as *tradition*]

trajectory (tră-**jek**-tŏ-ree) *noun* the path of a bullet or rocket etc. or of a body moving under certain forces. [from *trans*-, + Latin *jactum* = thrown]

tram *noun* a public passenger vehicle running on rails laid in the road.

tramlines *plural noun* **1** rails for a tram. **2** (*informal*) the pair of parallel lines at each side of a doubles court in tennis etc.

trammel *noun* a kind of dragnet for catching fish. –**trammel** *verb* (**trammelled**, **trammelling**) to hamper. **trammels** *plural noun* things that hamper one's activities.

tramp *verb* **1** to walk with heavy steps. **2** to travel on foot across (an area), *tramping the hills*. **3** to trample, *tramp it down*. –**tramp** *noun* **1** the sound of heavy footsteps. **2** a long walk, *went for a tramp*. **3** a person who goes from place to place as a vagrant. **4** a cargo boat that does not travel on a regular route.

trample *verb* to tread repeatedly with heavy or crushing steps; to crush or harm in this way.

trampoline (**tram**-pŏ-leen) *noun* a sheet of strong canvas attached by springs to a horizontal frame, used for jumping on in acrobatic leaps. [from Italian *trampoli* = stilts]

tramway *noun* the rails for a tram.

trance *noun* **1** a state like sleep, e.g. that induced by hypnosis. **2** a dreamy state in which a person is absorbed with his or her own thoughts. [same origin as *transit*]

tranquil *adjective* calm and undisturbed, not agitated. **tranquilly** *adverb*, **tranquillity** *noun*

tranquillise *verb* (also **-ize**) to make tranquil, to calm.

tranquilliser *noun* (also **-izer**) a drug used to relieve anxiety and make a person feel calm.

trans- *prefix* across; through; beyond. [from Latin *trans* = across]

transact *verb* to perform or carry out (business). **transactor** *noun*

transaction *noun* **1** transacting. **2** business transacted. **transactions** *plural noun* a record of its proceedings published by a learned society. **transactional** *adjective*

transatlantic *adjective* **1** on or from the other side of the Atlantic. **2** crossing the Atlantic, *a transatlantic flight*.

transceiver (tran-**seev**-er) *noun* a combined radio transmitter and receiver. [from *transmitter* + *receiver*]

transcend (tran-**send**) *verb* **1** to go or be beyond the range of (human experience, belief, or powers of description etc.). **2** to surpass. [from *trans*-, + Latin *scandere* = climb]

transcendent (tran-**sen**-děnt) *adjective* going beyond the limits of ordinary experience, surpassing. **transcendently** *adverb*, **transcendence** *noun*, **transcendency** *noun*

transcendental (tran-sen-**den**-t'l) *adjective* **1** transcendent. **2** abstract; obscure; visionary. □ **Transcendental Meditation** a technique of meditation and relaxation based on yoga. **transcendentally** *adverb*

transcontinental *adjective* extending or travelling across a continent.

transcribe *verb* 1 to copy in writing; to write out (shorthand etc.) in ordinary characters. 2 to record (sound) for later reproduction or broadcasting. 3 to arrange (music) for a different instrument etc. transcriber *noun*, transcription *noun* [from *trans-*, + Latin *scribere* = write]

transcript *noun* a written or recorded copy.

transducer *noun* a device that converts waves etc. from one system and conveys related waves to another (e.g. a radio receiver, which receives electromagnetic waves and sends out sound waves). [from *trans-*, + Latin *ducere* = to lead]

transect *noun* (in ecology) a line or belt of vegetation marked out for study. [from *trans-*, + Latin *sectum* = cut]

transept (**tran**-sept) *noun* the part that is at right angles to the nave in a cross-shaped church; either arm of this, *the north and south transepts*. [from *trans-*, + Latin *septum* = partition]

transexual *noun see* transsexual.

transfer (trans-**fer**) *verb* (**transferred**, **transferring**) 1 to convey, move, or hand over (a thing) from one place or person or group etc. to another. 2 to convey (a drawing or pattern etc.) from one surface to another. 3 to change from one station, route, or conveyance to another during a journey. 4 to change to another group or occupation etc., *she has transferred to the new shop*. –transfer (**trans**-fer) *noun* 1 transferring, being transferred. 2 a document that transfers property or a right from one person to another. 3 a design that is or can be transferred from one surface to another; paper bearing such a design. [from *trans-*, + Latin *ferre* = carry]

transferable (trans-**fer**-ră-bŭl) *adjective* able to be transferred. transferability *noun*

transference (**trans**-fě-rĕns) *noun* transferring; being transferred.

transferral (trans-**fer**-răl) *noun* transferring; being transferred.

transfiguration *noun* 1 a change of form or appearance. 2 the Transfiguration the Christian festival (6 August) commemorating Christ's transfiguration on the mountain.

transfigure *verb* to make a great change in the appearance of, especially to something nobler or more beautiful, *her face was transfigured by happiness*.

transfix *verb* 1 to pierce with or impale on something sharp. 2 to make (a person) motionless with fear or astonishment etc.

transform *verb* 1 to make a great change in the appearance or character of, *the caterpillar is transformed into a butterfly*. 2 to change the voltage of (electric current). 3 to become transformed. 4 (in mathematics) to change a set of values to a new set of values according to some rule. transformation *noun*, transformational *adjective*

transformer *noun* an apparatus for reducing or increasing the voltage of alternating current.

transfuse *verb* to give a transfusion of (a fluid) to (a person or animal).

transfusion *noun* an injection of blood or other fluid into a blood vessel of a person or animal. [from *trans-*, + Latin *fusum* = poured]

transgenic *adjective* (of an organism) having genetic material artificially introduced from another species.

transgress *verb* 1 to break (a rule or law etc.); to go beyond (a limitation). 2 (*old use*) to sin. transgression *noun*, transgressor *noun* [from *trans-*, + Latin *gressus* = gone]

transhumance (tranz-**hew**-măns) *noun* the moving of livestock from one pasture to another at the beginning or end of a season.

transient (**tran**-zee-ĕnt) *adjective* passing away quickly, not lasting or permanent. –transient *noun* a temporary visitor or worker etc. transience *noun* [from *trans-*, + Latin *iens* = going]

transistor *noun* 1 a semiconductor device with three electrodes, used in electronic amplification and control circuits. 2 a transistor radio, a portable radio set equipped with transistors. [from *trans*fer + re*sistor*]

transistorise *verb* (also -ize) to equip with transistors.

transit *noun* 1 the process of going, conveying, or being conveyed across, over, or through, *the goods were delayed in transit*. 2 the apparent passage of a heavenly body across the disc of the sun or a planet or across the meridian of a place, *to observe the transit of Venus*. –transit *verb* (**transited**, **transiting**) to make a transit across. □ transit camp a camp for temporary accommodation of soldiers or refugees etc. transit lounge an airport lounge for passengers waiting between flights. transit visa a visa allowing the holder to pass through a country but not to stay there. [from *trans-*, + Latin *itum* = gone]

transition (tran-**si**-*zhŏn*) *noun* the process of changing from one state or style etc. to another, *the transition from childhood to adult life*. transitional *adjective*, transitionally *adverb*

transitive *adjective* (of a verb) used with a direct object either expressed or understood, e.g. *pick peas* or *pick till you are tired* (but not in *he picked at the hole to make it bigger*). transitively *adverb*

transitory *adjective* existing for a time but not lasting. transitorily *adverb*, transitoriness *noun*

translate *verb* 1 to express in another language or in simpler words, or in code for use in a computer. 2 to be able to be translated, *the poems don't translate well*. 3 to interpret, *we translated his silence as disapproval*. 4 to move or change, especially from one person, place, or condition, to another. 5 (in the Bible) to convey to heaven without death. translatable *adjective*, translation *noun*, translator *noun* [from *trans-*, + Latin *latum* = carried]

transliterate *verb* to represent (letters or words) in the letters of a different alphabet. transliteration *noun* [from *trans-*, + Latin *littera* = letter]

translocation *noun* the movement of substances from one part of a plant to another.

translucent (tranz-**loo**-sĕnt) *adjective* allowing light to pass through but not transparent. translucence *noun*, translucency *noun* [from *trans-*, + Latin *lucens* = shining]

transmigration *noun* migration.
□ **transmigration of the soul** the passing of a person's soul into another body after death.

transmissible *adjective* able to be transmitted.

transmission *noun* 1 transmitting; being transmitted. 2 a broadcast. 3 the gear by which power is transmitted from engine to axle in a motor vehicle.

transmit *verb* (transmitted, transmitting) 1 to send or pass on from one person, place, or thing to another, *transmit the message*; *the disease is transmitted by mosquitoes*. 2 to allow to pass through or along, to be a medium for, *iron transmits heat*. 3 to send out (a signal or program etc.) by telegraph wire or radio waves. [from *trans-*, + Latin *mittere* = send]

transmittable *adjective* able to be transmitted.

transmitter *noun* a person or thing that transmits; a device or equipment for transmitting electric or radio signals.

transmogrify *verb* (transmogrified, transmogrifying) (*humorous*) to transform, especially in a magical or surprising way. transmogrification *noun*

transmute *verb* to cause (a thing) to change in form, nature, or substance. transmutation *noun* [from *trans-*, + Latin *mutare* = to change]

transoceanic *adjective* 1 on or from the other side of the ocean. 2 crossing the ocean.

transom *noun* 1 a horizontal bar of wood or stone across the top of a door or window. 2 a window above the transom of a door or larger window.

transparency (trans-**pair**-rĕn-see) *noun* 1 being transparent. 2 a photographic slide, especially on film as distinct from glass.

transparent (trans-**pair**-rĕnt) *adjective* 1 allowing light to pass through so that objects behind can be seen clearly. 2 easily understood; (of an excuse or motive etc.) of such a kind that the truth behind it is easily perceived. 3 clear and unmistakable, *a man of transparent honesty*. transparently *adverb* [from *trans-*, + Latin *parens* = appearing]

transpire *verb* 1 (of information etc.) to leak out, to become known, *no details of the contract were allowed to transpire*. 2 (*informal*) to happen, *we'll see what transpires*. 3 (of plants) to give off watery vapour from the surface of leaves etc. transpiration *noun* [from *trans-*, + Latin *spirare* = breathe]

Usage The use in sense 2 is considered incorrect by some people.

---

transplant (trans-**plant** *or* -**plahnt**) *verb* 1 to remove and replant or establish elsewhere. 2 to transfer (living tissue or an organ) from one part of the body or one person or animal to another. 3 to be able to be transplanted. –**transplant** (**trans**-plant *or* -plahnt) *noun* 1 transplanting of tissue or an organ. 2 something transplanted. transplantation *noun*

transport (trans-**port**) *verb* 1 to convey from one place to another. 2 (*old use*) to deport (a criminal) to a penal settlement. 3 to carry away by strong emotion, *she was transported with joy*. –**transport** (**trans**-port) *noun* 1 the act or process of transporting something. 2 means of conveyance, *have you got transport?* **3** a ship or aircraft for carrying troops or supplies. **4** the condition of being carried away by strong emotion, *in transports of rage.* **transportation** *noun* [from *trans-*, + Latin *portare* = carry]

transportable *adjective* able to be transported. –**transportable** *noun* a building that is transportable.

transporter *noun* a vehicle used to transport other vehicles, heavy machinery, etc.

transpose *verb* **1** to cause (two or more things) to change places, to change the position of (a thing) in a series. **2** to put (a piece of music) into a different key. –**transpose** *noun* **transpose of a matrix** the matrix that results from interchanging the rows and columns of a given matrix. **transposition** *noun* [from *trans-*, + Latin *positum* = placed]

transsexual *noun* **1** a person who has the physical characteristics of one sex but psychologically feels himself or herself to be of the opposite sex. **2** a person whose sex has been changed by surgery.

transship *verb* (**transshipped**, **transshipping**) to transfer (cargo) from one ship or conveyance to another. **transshipment** *noun*

transubstantiation *noun* the doctrine that the bread and wine in the Eucharist are converted by consecration into the body and blood of Christ, though their appearance remains the same. [from *trans-*, + *substance*]

transuranic (tranz-yoo-**ran**-ik) *adjective* belonging to a group of radioactive elements whose atoms are heavier than those of uranium.

Transvaal (tranz-**vahl**) a province of the Republic of South Africa, lying north of the Orange Free State and separated from it by the River Vaal.

transverse *adjective* lying or acting in a crosswise direction. **transversely** *adverb* [from *trans-*, + Latin *versum* = turned]

transvestism *noun* dressing in the clothing of the opposite sex; cross-dressing. **transvestite** *noun* a person who indulges in this. [from *trans-*, + Latin *vestire* = clothe]

Transylvania (tran-sil-**vay**-nee-ă) a large tableland region in Romania, associated with the legend of Dracula.

trap *noun* **1** a device for catching and holding animals. **2** an arrangement for capturing or detecting a person unawares or for making a person betray himself or herself; anything

deceptive. **3** a golf bunker. **4** a device for sending something into the air to be shot at. **5** a compartment from which a greyhound is released at the start of a race. **6** a device for preventing the passage of water or steam or silt etc.; a U-shaped or S-shaped section of a pipe that holds liquid and so prevents foul gases from coming up from a drain. **7** a two-wheeled carriage drawn by a horse. **8** a trapdoor. –**trap** *verb* (**trapped**, **trapping**) to catch or hold in a trap.

trapdoor *noun* a door in a floor, ceiling, or roof. □ **trapdoor spider** a large spider that digs a burrow, covering it with a hinged flap like a trapdoor.

trapeze *noun* a horizontal bar hung by ropes as a swing for acrobatics.

trapezium (tră-**pee**-zee-ŭm) *noun* **1** a quadrilateral in which two opposite sides are parallel and the other two are not. **2** (*Amer.*) a trapezoid (sense 1). [from Greek *trapeza* = table]

trapezoid (**trap**-ĕ-zoid) *noun* **1** a quadrilateral in which no sides are parallel. **2** (*Amer.*) a trapezium (sense 1). **trapezoidal** (trap-ĕ-**zoi**-dăl) *adjective*

trapper *noun* a person who traps animals, especially for furs.

trappings *plural noun* **1** ornamental accessories or adjuncts, *he had all the trappings of high office but very little power.* **2** the harness of a horse, especially when ornamental.

Trappist *noun* a member of a Cistercian order founded at La Trappe in France, noted for silence and other austerities.

traps[1] *plural noun* percussion instruments in a jazz band.

traps[2] *plural noun* (*informal*) personal belongings, baggage.

trash *noun* **1** worthless stuff, rubbish. **2** worthless people. –**trash** *verb* (*informal*) to wreck. **trashy** *adjective*

trauma (**traw**-mă) *noun* **1** a wound or injury. **2** emotional shock producing a lasting effect upon a person. **traumatise** (also -**ize**) *verb* [Greek, = a wound]

traumatic (traw-**mat**-ik) *adjective* **1** of or causing trauma. **2** (*informal*, of an experience) distressing.

travail (**trav**-ayl) *noun* **1** (*literary*) painful or laborious effort. **2** (*old use*) the pains of childbirth. **–travail** *verb* (*literary*) to make a painful or laborious effort.

travel *verb* (**travelled, travelling**) **1** to go from one place or point to another, to make a journey. **2** to journey along or through; to cover (a distance) in travelling. **3** to go from place to place as a salesperson, *he travels in carpets.* **–travel** *noun* **1** travelling, especially in foreign countries. **2** the range, rate, or method of movement of a machine part. □ **travel agency** or **agent** one making arrangements for travellers. **travelling crane** a crane travelling along an overhead support. **travel sickness** a feeling of nausea caused by motion when travelling. [the original meaning was *travail*]

travelled *adjective* experienced in travelling.

traveller *noun* **1** a person who travels or is travelling. **2** a travelling salesperson. **3** a gypsy; a swagman; an itinerant worker. □ **traveller's cheque** a cheque for a fixed amount, sold by a bank etc. and usually able to be cashed in various countries. **traveller's joy** wild clematis.

travelogue (**trav**-ĕ-log) *noun* a film or illustrated lecture about travel. [from *travel* + Greek *logos* = word]

traverse (**trav**-ers) *noun* **1** a thing (especially part of a structure) that lies across another. **2** a zigzag course or road; each leg of this. **3** a lateral movement across something. **4** a steep slope that has to be crossed from side to side in mountaineering. **–traverse** (tră-**vers** or **trav**-ers) *verb* to travel across; to lie or extend across. **traversal** *noun* [same origin as *transverse*]

travesty (**trav**-ĕ-stee) *noun* an absurd or inferior imitation, *his trial was a travesty of justice.* **–travesty** *verb* (**travestied, travestying**) to make or be a travesty of. [from French *travesti* = having changed clothes]

trawl *noun* a large wide-mouthed fishing net dragged along the bottom of the sea etc. by a boat. **–trawl** *verb* **1** to fish with a trawl or seine. **2** to catch by trawling.

trawler *noun* a boat used in trawling.

tray *noun* **1** a flat utensil, usually with a raised edge, on which small articles are placed for display or carrying. **2** a shallow open container for papers or small articles, sometimes forming a compartment in a trunk, cabinet, etc. **3** (*Austral.*) the flat open part of a truck on which goods are carried.

treacherous *adjective* **1** behaving with or showing treachery. **2** not to be relied on, deceptive, not giving a firm support, *the roads were icy and treacherous.* **treacherously** *adverb*, **treacherousness** *noun*

treachery *noun* betrayal of a person or cause; an act of disloyalty.

treacle *noun* a thick sticky dark liquid produced when sugar is refined.

treacly *adjective* **1** like treacle. **2** excessively sweet or sentimental.

tread *verb* (**trod, trodden, treading**) **1** to set one's foot down; to walk or step; (of a foot) to be set down. **2** to walk on; to press or crush with the feet; to make (a path or trail or mark etc.) by walking. **3** (of a male bird) to copulate with (a female bird). **–tread** *noun* **1** the manner or sound of walking, *a heavy tread.* **2** the top surface of a stair. **3** the part of a wheel or tyre etc. that touches the ground. □ **tread on a person's toes** (*informal*) to offend or vex him or her. **tread the boards** to be an actor. **tread water** to keep oneself upright in water by making treading movements with the legs.

treadle (**tred**'l) *noun* a lever worked by the foot to drive a wheel, e.g. in a sewing machine. **–treadle** *verb* to work a treadle.

treadmill *noun* **1** a wide mill wheel turned by the weight of people treading on steps fixed round its edge, formerly worked by prisoners as a punishment. **2** tiring monotonous routine work.

treason *noun* treachery towards one's country or its ruler (e.g. by plotting the sovereign's death or engaging in war against him or her). **treasonous** *adjective* [from Latin *traditum* = handed over, betrayed; compare *tradition*]

treasonable *adjective* involving the crime of treason. **treasonably** *adverb*

treasure *noun* **1** precious metals or gems; a hoard of these, *buried treasure.* **2** a highly valued object, *art treasures.* **3** a beloved or highly valued person. **–treasure** *verb* to value highly, to keep or store as precious, *a treasured possession; treasure it up.* □ **treasure hunt** a search for treasure; a game in which players try to find a hidden object. **treasure trove** gold or silver coins or plate or bullion found hidden and of unknown ownership; something very useful or desirable that a person finds. [from Greek *thesauros* = treasury]

treasurer *noun* a person in charge of the funds of an institution or club etc. □ **the Treasurer** the minister responsible for the Treasury.

treasury *noun* a place in which treasure is stored; something regarded as containing things of great value or interest, *the book is a treasury of useful information*. □ **the Treasury** the department managing the public revenue of a country. **treasury bill** any of the bills of exchange issued by the government in return for sums of money lent by bankers, brokers, etc.

treat *verb* 1 to act or behave towards or deal with (a person or thing) in a certain way, *treated him roughly*; *treat it as a joke*. 2 to present or deal with (a subject), *recent events are treated in detail*. 3 to give medical or surgical treatment to, *treated him for sunstroke*; *how would you treat a sprained ankle?* 4 to subject (a substance or thing) to a chemical or other process. 5 to supply (a person) with food or entertainment etc. at one's own expense in order to give pleasure; to buy, give, or allow to have as a treat, *treated myself to a taxi*. 6 to negotiate terms, *treating with their enemies to secure a ceasefire*. –**treat** *noun* 1 something that gives great pleasure, especially something not always available or that comes unexpectedly. 2 an entertainment etc. designed to do this. 3 the treating of others to something at one's own expense; *it's my treat*, I will pay. [from Latin *tractare* = to handle]

treatise (**tree**-tĭss) *noun* a written work dealing systematically with one subject. [same origin as *treat*]

treatment *noun* 1 the process or manner of dealing with a person or thing. 2 something done in order to relieve or cure an illness or abnormality etc.

treaty *noun* 1 a formal agreement between two or more countries. 2 a formal agreement between people, especially for the purchase of property at a price agreed between buyer and seller (not by auction). [same origin as *treat*]

treble *adjective* 1 three times as much or as many. 2 (of a voice etc.) high-pitched, soprano. –**treble** *noun* 1 a treble quantity or thing. 2 a hit in the narrow ring between the two middle circles of a dartboard, scoring treble. 3 a high-pitched or soprano voice etc.; a person with this. 4 (in sound recording and reproduction) the upper range of audible frequencies. –**treble** *verb* to make or become three times as much or as many, *costs had trebled*. **trebly** *adverb* [same origin as *triple*]

tree *noun* 1 a perennial plant with a single stem or trunk that is usually without branches for some distance above the ground. 2 a Christmas tree. 3 a framework of wood for various purposes; *shoe-tree*, see **shoe**. 4 a family tree (*see* **family**). –**tree** *verb* to force (a person or animal) to take refuge up a tree. □ **tree change** (*Austral. informal*) a significant change in lifestyle, especially by moving from the city to a country town. **tree diagram** a diagram which has branches like a tree, used for classifying information. **tree house** a structure built in a tree, for children to play in. **tree line** the level of land above which no trees grow. **tree surgeon** a person who treats decayed trees in order to preserve them. **up a tree** (*informal*) in great difficulties.

treecreeper *noun* a small bird that creeps up tree trunks feeding on insects in the bark.

treeless *adjective* without trees.

treetop *noun* the topmost branches of a tree.

trefoil (**tref**-oil) *noun* 1 a plant with three leaflets, e.g. clover. 2 an ornament or design shaped like this. [from Latin *tres* = three, + *folium* = leaf]

trek *noun* a long arduous journey. –**trek** *verb* (**trekked**, **trekking**) to make a trek. [from Dutch *trekken* = pull]

trellis *noun* a light framework of crossing wooden or metal bars, used to support climbing plants.

tremble *verb* 1 to shake involuntarily from fear or cold etc., to quiver. 2 to be in a state of great anxiety or agitation, *I tremble to think what has become of him*. –**tremble** *noun* a trembling or quivering movement, a tremor.

trembler *noun* a spring that makes an electrical contact when shaken.

trembly *adjective* (*informal*) trembling.

tremendous *adjective* 1 immense. 2 (*informal*) excellent, *gave a tremendous performance*. **tremendously** *adverb*, **tremendousness** *noun* [from Latin, = causing people to tremble]

tremolo (**trem**-ŏ-loh) *noun* (*plural* **tremolos**) 1 a trembling or vibrating effect in music. 2 a device in an organ or an electric guitar used to produce tremolo. [Italian]

tremor (**trem**-er) *noun* 1 a slight shaking or trembling movement, a vibration; *an earth tremor*, a slight earthquake. 2 a thrill of fear or other emotion.

tremulous (**trem**-yŭ-lŭs) *adjective*
1 trembling from nervousness or weakness.
2 easily made to quiver. **tremulously** *adverb*
[from Latin *tremulus* = trembling]

trench *noun* a long narrow hole cut in the
ground, e.g. for drainage or to give troops
shelter from enemy fire. **–trench** *verb* to dig
trenches in (ground). □ **trench coat** a belted
coat or raincoat with pockets and flaps like
those of a military uniform coat.

trenchant (**tren**-chănt) *adjective* (of
comments or policies etc.) penetrating, strong
and effective, *made some trenchant criticisms*
or *reforms*. **trenchantly** *adverb*, **trenchancy**
noun

trencherman *noun* (*plural* **trenchermen**)
a person with regard to the amount he or she
usually eats; *a good trencherman*, one who
eats heartily. [from *trencher* = platter]

trend *noun* the general direction that
something takes, a continuing tendency, *the
trend of prices is upwards*.

trendsetter *noun* a person who leads the
way in fashion etc.

trendy *adjective* (**trendier**, **trendiest**)
(*informal*) up to date, following the latest trends
of fashion. **–trendy** *noun* (*informal*) a trendy
person. **trendily** *adverb*, **trendiness** *noun*

trepan (trĕ-**pan**) *noun* & *verb* (**trepanned**,
trepanning) = trephine.

trephine (trĕ-**feen**) *noun* a surgeon's
cylindrical saw for removing a section of the
skull. **–trephine** *verb* to cut with a trephine.

trepidation (trep-ĭ-**day**-shŏn) *noun* a state
of fear and anxiety, nervous agitation. [from
Latin *trepidare* = be afraid]

trespass *verb* **1** to enter a person's land or
property unlawfully. **2** to intrude or make use
of unreasonably, *trespass on someone's time*
or *hospitality*. **3** (*old use*) to sin or do wrong,
*as we forgive them that trespass against
us*. **–trespass** *noun* **1** the act of trespassing.
2 (*old use*) sin, wrongdoing, *forgive us our
trespasses*. **trespasser** *noun* [from Old French
trespasser = pass over (same origin as *trans-
+ pass*[1])]

tress *noun* a lock of hair. **tresses** *plural noun*
the hair of the head.

trestle *noun* **1** each of a pair or set of supports
on which a board is rested to form a table.
2 an open braced framework for supporting
a bridge. □ **trestle table** a table supported by
trestles.

trevally (trĕ-**val**-ee) *noun* (*plural* **trevally** or
trevallies) any of several Australian sea fish.

trews *plural noun* close-fitting usually tartan
trousers.

tri- *prefix* three, three times, triple. [from Latin
tres or Greek *treis* = three]

triable *adjective* able to be tried.

triacetate (try-**ass**-ĕ-tayt) *noun* **cellulose
triacetate** a form of cellulose acetate having
a very large molecule built up of units each
containing three acetate groups, used for
making synthetic fibres.

triad (**try**-ad) *noun* **1** a group or set of three.
2 a Chinese secret organisation.

trial *noun* **1** an examination in a lawcourt by
a judge in order to decide upon the guilt or
innocence of an accused person. **2** the process
of testing qualities or performance by use
and experience. **3** a sports match to test the
ability of players who may be selected for an
important team. **4** a test of individual ability
on a motorcycle over rough ground or on
a road. **5** a person or thing that tries one's
patience or endurance; a hardship. □ **on trial**
undergoing a trial; on approval. **trial and
error** the process of succeeding in an attempt
by trying repeatedly and learning from one's
failures. **trial balance** a comparison of the total
of debits and of credits in a ledger etc. to make
sure that they are the same, showing that the
procedure of double entry is being followed
correctly. [from *try*]

triamble *noun* a South Australian variety of
pumpkin with three lobes.

triangle *noun* **1** a geometric figure with three
sides and three angles. **2** something shaped
like this; a percussion instrument consisting of
a steel rod bent into this shape and struck with
another steel rod. [from *tri-* + *angle*[1]]

triangular *adjective* **1** shaped like a triangle.
2 involving three people, *a triangular contest*.

triangulate *verb* **1** to divide into triangles.
2 to measure or map out (an area) in surveying
by means of calculations based on a network
of triangles measured from a baseline.
triangulation *noun*

triantelope (try-**an**-tĕ-lohp) *noun* (*Austral*.)
a huntsman spider. [from *tarantula*]

Triassic (try-**as**-ik) *adjective* of the earliest
period of the Mesozoic era. **–Triassic** *noun* this
period.

triathlon (try-**ath**-lon) *noun* an athletic
contest in which competitors take part in

three events (usually swimming, cycling, and running). triathlete *noun*

tribal *adjective* of a tribe or tribes.

tribe *noun* **1** a group of families or communities, linked by social, religious, or blood ties, and usually having a common culture and dialect and a recognised leader. **2** a set or class of people, a flock, *he despises the whole tribe of politicians*.

tribesman *noun* a member of a racial tribe. tribeswoman *noun*

tribulation (trib-yŭ-**lay**-shŏn) *noun* great affliction; a cause of this.

tribunal (try-**bew**-năl) *noun* a board of officials appointed to make a judgment or act as arbitrators on a particular problem or on problems of a certain kind.

tribune (**trib**-yoon) *noun* **1** (in ancient Rome) an official chosen by the people to protect their liberties; an officer in periodic command of a legion. **2** a leader of the people. **3** a dais, a rostrum.

tributary *noun* a river or stream that flows into a larger one or a lake. –tributary *adjective* flowing in this way.

tribute *noun* **1** something said, done, or given as a mark of respect or admiration etc. **2** an indication of the effectiveness of, *his recovery is a tribute to the doctor's skill*. **3** payment that one country or ruler was formerly obliged to pay to a more powerful one. □ **pay tribute to** to express respect or admiration for. [from Latin *tributum* = assigned]

trice *noun* **in a trice** in an instant.

triceps (**try**-seps) *noun* the large muscle at the back of the upper arm, which straightens the elbow. [Latin, = three-headed (because its end is attached at three points)]

triceratops *noun* (try-**se**-ră-tops) a three-horned dinosaur with a bony frill round the neck.

trichloromethane (try-klor-roh-**mee**-thayn) *noun* chloroform.

trick *noun* **1** something done in order to deceive or outwit someone. **2** a deception or illusion, *a trick of the light*. **3** a particular technique, the exact or best way of doing something. **4** a feat of skill done for entertainment, *conjuring tricks*. **5** a mannerism, *he has a trick of repeating himself*. **6** a mischievous, foolish, or discreditable act; a practical joke. **7** the cards played in one round of a card game; the round itself; a point gained

as a result of this. **8** a person's turn of duty at the helm of a ship, usually for two hours. –trick *verb* **1** to deceive or persuade by a trick, to mislead. **2** to deck or decorate, *trick it out* or *up*. □ **do the trick** (*informal*) to achieve what is required. **trick or treat** a phrase said by children who call at houses at Hallowe'en seeking to be given sweets etc. and threatening to do mischief if these are not provided.

trickery *noun* use of tricks, deception.

trickle *verb* **1** to flow or cause to flow in a thin stream. **2** to come or go slowly or gradually, *people trickled into the hall*. –trickle *noun* a trickling flow, a small amount coming or going slowly, *a trickle of information*.

trickster *noun* a person who tricks or cheats people.

tricksy *adjective* full of tricks, playful.

tricky *adjective* (trickier, trickiest) **1** crafty, deceitful. **2** requiring skilful handling, *a tricky task*. trickily *adverb*, trickiness *noun*

tricolour (**trik**-ŏ-ler) *noun* a flag with three colours in stripes, especially those of France and Ireland. [from *tri- + colour*]

tricot (**tree**-koh) *noun* fine knitted fabric. [French, = knitting]

tricuspid (try-**kus**-pĭd) *adjective* having three points, *a tricuspid valve*.

tricycle *noun* a three-wheeled pedal-driven vehicle.

trident (**try**-dĕnt) *noun* a three-pronged spear, carried by Neptune and Britannia as a symbol of power over the sea. [from *tri-*, + Latin *dens* = tooth]

tried *see* try.

triennial (try-**en**-ee-ăl) *adjective* **1** lasting for three years. **2** happening every third year. triennially *adverb* [from *tri-*, + Latin *annus* = year]

trier *noun* **1** a person who tries hard, one who always does his or her best. **2** a tester.

trifle *noun* **1** something of only slight value or importance. **2** a very small amount, especially of money, *it cost a mere trifle*; *he seems a trifle angry*, slightly angry. **3** a dessert made of sponge cake soaked in wine or sherry, layered with fruit, custard, and cream. –trifle *verb* to behave or talk frivolously. □ **trifle with** to toy with; to treat casually or without due seriousness. trifler *noun*

trifling *adjective* trivial.

trig *noun* (*informal*) trigonometry. □ **trig point** a reference point on high ground, used in surveying.

trigger *noun* a lever or catch for releasing a spring, especially so as to fire a gun. –**trigger** *verb* to trigger off. □ **trigger-happy** *adjective* apt to shoot on slight provocation. **trigger off** to set in action, to be the immediate cause of.

trigonometry (trig-ŏ-**nom**-ĕ-tree) *noun* the branch of mathematics dealing with the relationship of sides and angles of triangles etc. **trigonometric** *adjective*, **trigonometrical** *adjective*, **trigonometrically** *adverb* [from Greek *trigonon* = triangle, + *-metria* = measurement]

trike *noun* (*informal*) a tricycle.

trilateral (try-**lat**-ĕ-răl) *adjective* having three sides or three participants. [from *tri-* + *lateral*]

trilby *noun* a man's soft felt hat with a lengthwise dent in the crown and a narrow brim.

trilingual (try-**ling**-gwăl) *adjective* speaking or using three languages. [from *tri-*, + Latin *lingua* = language]

trill *noun* **1** a vibrating sound made by the voice or in birdsong. **2** quick alternation of two notes in music that are a tone or semitone apart. –**trill** *verb* to sound or sing with a trill.

trillion *noun* **1** a million million. **2** (now less often) a million million million. [from *tri-* + *million*]

trilobite (**try**-lŏ-byt) *noun* a sea creature of Palaeozoic times, an invertebrate with a segmented body and jointed limbs. [from *tri-*, + Greek *lobos* = lobe]

trilogy (**tril**-ŏ-jee) *noun* a group of three related books, films, operas, etc. [from *tri-*, + Greek *-logia* = writings]

trim *adjective* (**trimmer**, **trimmest**) neat and orderly; having a smooth outline or compact structure. –**trim** *verb* (**trimmed**, **trimming**) **1** to make neat or smooth by cutting away irregular parts. **2** to remove or reduce by cutting. **3** to ornament. **4** to make (a boat or aircraft) evenly balanced by arranging the position of its cargo or passengers or ballast. **5** to arrange (sails) to suit the wind. **6** (*informal*) to cheat out of money; to get the better of (a person) in a bargain etc. –**trim** *noun* **1** condition as regards readiness or fitness, *in good trim*. **2** the trimming on a dress or furniture etc.; the colour or type of upholstery and other fittings in a car. **3** the trimming of hair etc. **4** the balance or the even horizontal position of a

boat in the water or an aircraft in the air. **trimly** *adverb*, **trimness** *noun*, **trimmer** *noun*

trimaran (**try**-mă-ran) *noun* a vessel like a catamaran, with three hulls side by side. [from *tri-* + *catamaran*]

trimester (try-**mess**-ter) *noun* a period of three months, especially as part of a pregnancy.

trimming *noun* something added as an ornament or decoration on a dress or furniture etc. **trimmings** *plural noun* pieces cut off when something is trimmed; the usual accompaniments of something, extras, *roast turkey and all the trimmings*.

Trinidad an island in the West Indies, forming part of the republic of **Trinidad and Tobago**. **Trinidadian** (trin-ĭ-**day**-dee-ăn) *adjective* & *noun*

trinity *noun* **1** being three. **2** a group of three. □ **the Trinity** the three persons of the Godhead (Father, Son, Holy Spirit) as constituting one God. **Trinity Sunday** the Sunday after Whit Sunday, celebrated in honour of the Holy Trinity.

trinket *noun* a small fancy article or piece of jewellery.

trinomial (try-**noh**-mee-ăl) *noun* an algebraic expression consisting of three terms joined by + or –. [from *tri-* + *binomial*]

trio (**tree**-oh) *noun* (*plural* **trios**) **1** a group or set of three. **2** a group of three singers or players; a musical composition for these. [from Latin *tres* = three]

triode (**try**-ohd) *noun* **1** a thermionic valve with three electrodes. **2** a semiconductor rectifier with three terminals. [from *tri-* + *electrode*]

trip *verb* (**tripped**, **tripping**) **1** to walk, run, or dance with quick light steps; (of rhythm) to run lightly. **2** to take a trip to a place. **3** (*informal*) to have a long visionary experience caused by a drug. **4** to stumble, to catch one's foot on something and fall; to cause to do this. **5** to make a slip or blunder; to cause to do this. **6** to release (a switch or catch) so as to operate a mechanism. –**trip** *noun* **1** a journey or excursion, especially for pleasure. **2** (*informal*) a long visionary experience caused by a drug. **3** a stumble. **4** a device for tripping a mechanism. □ **trip up** to stumble or cause to stumble; to make a slip or blunder; to cause (a person) to do this so as to detect him or her in an error or inconsistency.

tripartite (try-**par**-tyt) *adjective* consisting of three parts.

tripe *noun* **1** the stomach of an ox etc. as food. **2** (*informal*) nonsense; something worthless.

Tripitaka (trip-ee-**tah**-kǎ) *noun* the sacred canon of Theravada Buddhism.

triple *adjective* **1** consisting of three parts; involving three people or groups. **2** three times as much or as many. – **triple** *verb* to make or become three times as much or as many. □ **triple crown** the pope's tiara (*see* tiara). **triple jump** an athletic contest comprising a hop, a step, and a long jump. **triple time** (in music) rhythm with three beats to the bar. **triply** *adverb* [from Latin *triplus* = three times as much]

triplet *noun* **1** one of three children or animals born at one birth. **2** a set of three things. [from *triple*]

triplex *adjective* triple, threefold.

triplicate (**trip**-lǐ-kǎt) *noun* one of three things that are exactly alike. – **triplicate** *adjective* threefold; being a triplicate. □ **in triplicate** as three identical copies. [from Latin *triplex* = triple]

tripod (**try**-pod) *noun* a three-legged stand for a camera or surveying instrument etc. [from *tri-*, + Greek *podos* = of a foot]

Tripoli the capital of Libya.

tripper *noun* a person who goes on a pleasure trip.

triptych (**trip**-tik) *noun* a picture or carving on three panels fixed or hinged side by side, especially as an altarpiece. [from *tri-* + *diptych*]

tripwire *noun* a wire stretched close to the ground, activating a trap or warning device etc. when disturbed.

trireme (**try**-reem) *noun* an ancient Greek or Roman warship with three banks of oars. [from *tri-*, + Latin *remus* = oar]

trisect (try-**sekt**) *verb* to divide into three equal parts. **trisection** *noun* [from *tri-*, + Latin *sectum* = cut]

trite (*rhymes with* kite) *adjective* (of a phrase or opinion) commonplace, hackneyed. [from Latin *tritum* = worn by use]

Triton (**try**-tǒn) (*Gk. myth.*) **1** the son of Poseidon. **2** a member of the minor sea gods, usually represented as a man with a fish's tail carrying a trident and a shell trumpet.

triumph *noun* **1** the fact of being successful or victorious; joy at this. **2** a great success or

achievement. – **triumph** *verb* to be successful or victorious; to rejoice at one's success etc. □ **triumph over** to overcome.

triumphal *adjective* of or celebrating a triumph. □ **triumphal arch** one built to commemorate a victory.

triumphant *adjective* **1** victorious, successful. **2** rejoicing at success etc. **triumphantly** *adverb*

triumvirate (try-**um**-vǐ-rǎt) *noun* a ruling group of three persons. [from Latin *trium virorum* = of three men]

trivet (**triv**-ět) *noun* an iron stand, especially a tripod, for a kettle or pot etc. placed over a fire. □ **as right as a trivet** (*informal*) in good condition or health or circumstances. [from Latin, = three-footed (compare *tripod*)]

trivia *plural noun* trivial things.

trivial *adjective* of only small value or importance. **trivially** *adverb*, **triviality** (triv-ee-**al**-ǐ-tee) *noun* [from Latin, = commonplace]

trochee (**troh**-kee) *noun* a metrical foot consisting of one long or stressed syllable followed by one short or unstressed syllable. **trochaic** (trǒ-**kay**-ik) *adjective*

trod, trodden *see* tread.

troglodyte (**trog**-lǒ-dyt) *noun* **1** a cave dweller, especially in ancient times. **2** a hermit. **3** (*derogatory*) a person who is regarded as being deliberately ignorant or old-fashioned. [from Greek *trogle* = hole]

Troilus (in medieval legend) the forsaken lover of Cressida.

Trojan *adjective* of Troy or its people. – **Trojan** *noun* a native or inhabitant of Troy. □ **Trojan horse** (*Gk. legend*) the hollow wooden horse used by the Greeks (who concealed warriors inside it) to enter Troy. **Trojan War** (*Gk. legend*) the ten-year siege of Troy by the Greeks, ending in its capture after the trick of the wooden horse. **work like a Trojan** to work with great energy and endurance.

troll[1] (*rhymes with* hole *or* doll) *verb* **1** to sing in a carefree jovial way. **2** to fish by drawing bait along in the water.

troll[2] (*rhymes with* hole *or* doll) *noun* (*Scand. myth*) a member of a race of supernatural beings formerly thought of as giants but now as friendly but mischievous dwarfs.

trolley *noun* (*plural* trolleys) **1** a table, basket, stand, or platform on wheels or castors for transporting food, luggage, shopping, etc.

2 a low truck running on rails. □ **trolley bus** a bus powered by electricity from an overhead wire to which it is linked by a pole and contact-wheel.

trollop *noun* a disreputable woman; a prostitute.

trombone *noun* **1** a large brass wind instrument with a sliding tube. **2** a large green or yellow variety of pumpkin, bulbous at one end. [from Italian *tromba* = trumpet]

trompe-l'œil (tromp-**ler**-ee) *noun* a painting etc. designed to make the spectator think that the objects represented are real. [French, = deceives the eye]

troop *noun* **1** a company of people or animals, especially when moving. **2** a cavalry unit commanded by a captain; a unit of artillery. **3** a unit of three or more Scout patrols. **–troop** *verb* to assemble or go as a troop or in great numbers. **troops** *plural noun* soldiers, armed forces. □ **trooping the colour** the ceremony of carrying the regimental flag along ranks of soldiers.

trooper *noun* **1** a soldier in a cavalry or armoured unit. **2** (*historical*) a mounted police officer in Australia. □ **swear like a trooper** to swear forcibly.

trophic *adjective* of nutrition. □ **trophic level** each of the levels into which a set of organisms in an ecosystem is grouped according to what they feed on. [from Greek *trophe* = nourishment]

trophy *noun* **1** something taken in war or hunting etc. as a souvenir of success. **2** an object awarded as a prize or token of victory.

tropic *noun* a line of latitude 23° 27′ north of the equator (**tropic of Cancer**) or the same latitude south of it (**tropic of Capricorn**). **tropics** *plural noun* the region between these, with a hot climate. [from Greek *trope* = turning (because the sun seems to turn back when it reaches these points)]

tropical *adjective* of or found in or like the tropics.

tropism (**troh**-pizm) *noun* the turning or movement of an organism in response to an external stimulus, e.g. that of plant leaves etc. in response to light.

troposphere (**trop**-ŏ-sfeer) *noun* the layer of atmospheric air extending about 6–10 kilometres upwards from the earth's surface. [from Greek *tropos* = turning, + *sphere*]

troppo *adjective* (*Austral. informal*) mentally disturbed, allegedly from spending too much time in the tropics; mad, crazy, *gone troppo*.

trot *noun* **1** the running action of a horse etc. with legs moving as in a walk. **2** a slowish run. **3** (*Austral. informal*) an uninterrupted sequence; a run of luck, *having a bad trot*. **–trot** *verb* (**trotted, trotting**) **1** to go or cause to go at a trot. **2** (*informal*) to walk or go, *trot round to the deli*. **trots** *plural noun* (*Austral. informal*) trotting races; a meeting for these. □ **on the trot** (*informal*) continually busy, *kept him on the trot*; in succession, *for five weeks on the trot*. **trot out** (*informal*) to produce, to bring out for inspection or approval etc., *trotted out the same old excuse*. **trotting race** a horse race in which the horses pull small vehicles.

Trotsky, Leon (originally Lev Davidovich Bronstein, 1879–1940), Russian leader and revolutionary urging worldwide socialist revolution.

Trotskyist *noun* a supporter of Trotsky; a radical left-wing Communist. **Trotskyism** *noun*, **Trotskyite** *noun*

trotter *noun* **1** a horse of a special breed trained for trotting races. **2** an animal's foot as food, *pigs' trotters*.

troubadour (**troo**-bă-door) *noun* a lyric poet in southern France etc. in the 11th–13th centuries, singing mainly of chivalry and courtly love.

trouble *noun* **1** difficulty, inconvenience; distress, vexation; misfortune. **2** a cause of any of these. **3** conflict, public unrest; **the Troubles** rebellions and unrest in Ireland in 1919–23 and in Northern Ireland from 1968. **4** unpleasantness involving punishment or rebuke. **5** faulty functioning of a mechanism or of the body or mind, *engine trouble*; *stomach trouble*. **–trouble** *verb* **1** to cause trouble, distress, pain, or inconvenience to. **2** to be disturbed or worried, to be subjected to inconvenience or unpleasant exertion, *don't trouble about it*. □ **in trouble** involved in something liable to bring punishment or rebuke. **make trouble** to stir up disagreement, disturbance, or unpleasantness. **take trouble** to use much care and effort in doing something; *take the trouble to do something*, exert oneself to do it. **trouble spot** a place where trouble frequently occurs. [same origin as *turbid*]

troublemaker *noun* a person who habitually stirs up trouble.

troubleshoot *verb* **1** to analyse and solve serious problems for a company or other organisation. **2** to trace and correct faults in a mechanical or electronic system. **troubleshooter** *noun*

troublesome *adjective* giving trouble; causing annoyance.

trough (*pr.* trof) *noun* **1** a long narrow open receptacle, especially for holding water or food for animals. **2** a channel for conveying liquid. **3** a depression between two waves or ridges. **4** an elongated region of low atmospheric pressure.

trounce *verb* **1** to thrash. **2** to defeat heavily.

troupe (*pr.* troop) *noun* a company of actors or acrobats etc.

Usage *Troupe* and *troop* have a common French origin, but they are now separate words with separate uses.

---

trouper (**troop**-er) *noun* **1** a member of a theatrical troupe. **2** a staunch colleague, *a good trouper*.

trousers *plural noun* a two-legged outer garment reaching from the waist usually to the ankles.

trousseau (**troo**-soh) *noun* a bride's collection of clothing etc. to begin married life. [from French, = bundle]

trout *noun* (*plural* **trout**) any of several chiefly freshwater fish valued as food and game.

trowel *noun* **1** a small tool with a flat blade for spreading mortar etc. **2** a small garden tool with a curved blade for lifting plants or scooping things. [from Latin *trulla* = scoop]

Troy (*Gk. legend*) a city in Asia Minor, besieged in ancient times for ten years by Greek forces in their attempt to recover Helen, wife of Menelaus, who had been abducted by the Trojan prince Paris.

troy weight *noun* a system of weights used for precious metals and gems, in which 1 pound = 12 ounces or 5760 grains. [said to be from a weight used at Troyes in France]

truant *noun* **1** a child who stays away from school without leave. **2** a person who absents himself or herself from work or duty. **–truant** *verb* to play truant. □ **play truant** to stay away as a truant. **truancy** *noun* [the word originally meant 'idle rogue', from a Celtic word related to Welsh *truan* = miserable]

truce *noun* an agreement to cease hostilities temporarily.

truck[1] *noun* **1** a large strong motor vehicle for transporting goods etc.; a lorry. **2** an open container on wheels for transporting goods; an open railway wagon. [from *truckle*]

truck[2] *noun* dealings. □ **have no truck with** to have no dealings with.

truckie *noun* (also **trucker**) (*Austral. informal*) the driver of a truck.

truckle *verb* to submit obsequiously, *refusing to truckle to bullies*. □ **truckle bed** = trundle bed.

truculent (**truk**-yŭ-lĕnt) *adjective* defiant and aggressive. **truculently** *adverb*, **truculence** *noun*

trudge *verb* to walk laboriously. **–trudge** *noun* a trudging walk.

true *adjective* **1** in accordance with fact. **2** in accordance with correct principles or an accepted standard, rightly so called, genuine and not false, *he was the true heir; the true north*, north according to the earth's axis, not the magnetic north. **3** exact, accurate; (of the voice etc.) in good tune. **4** accurately placed or balanced or shaped. **5** loyal, faithful. **–true** *adverb* truly, accurately. □ **true blue** completely true to one's principles, firmly loyal; (*Austral.*) genuine, Australian. **trueness** *noun*

truffle *noun* **1** a rich-flavoured fungus that grows underground and is valued as a delicacy. **2** a soft sweet made of a chocolate mixture.

trug *noun* a shallow usually wooden basket used by gardeners.

Truganini (truug-ă-**nee**-nee) (c. 1812–76), a Tasmanian Aborigine, daughter of Mangana, chief of the Bruny Island people, once believed to be the last Tasmanian Aborigine.

truism (**troo**-izm) *noun* **1** a statement that is obviously true, especially one that is hackneyed, e.g. *nothing lasts for ever*. **2** a statement that merely repeats an idea already implied in one of its words, e.g. *there's no need to be unnecessarily careful*.

truly *adverb* **1** truthfully. **2** sincerely, genuinely, *we are truly grateful*. **3** faithfully, loyally. □ **Yours truly** *see* yours.

trump[1] *noun* (*old use*) the sound of a trumpet.

trump[2] *noun* **1** a playing card of a suit temporarily ranking above others. **2** (*informal*) a person who behaves in a helpful or useful way. **–trump** *verb* to take (a card or trick) with a trump; to play a trump. □ **trump card** a card of the trump suit; a valuable resource, a means of getting what one wants. **trump up** to invent (an excuse or accusation etc.) fraudulently. **turn up trumps** (*informal*) to turn out successfully; to behave with great kindness or generosity. [from *triumph*]

trumpery *adjective* showy but worthless. –**trumpery** *noun* worthless finery; rubbish. [from French *tromper* = deceive]

trumpet *noun* **1** a metal wind instrument with a bright ringing tone, consisting of a narrow straight or curved tube flared at the end. **2** something shaped like this. –**trumpet** *verb* (**trumpeted**, **trumpeting**) **1** to blow a trumpet; to proclaim by or as if by the sound of a trumpet. **2** (of an elephant) to make a loud resounding sound with its trunk.

trumpeter *noun* **1** a person who plays or sounds a trumpet. **2** an edible Australian fish, said to make a trumpeting sound when removed from the water.

truncate (trung-**kayt**) *verb* to shorten by cutting off the top or end. **truncation** *noun*

truncheon (**trun**-chŏn) *noun* a short thick stick carried as a weapon, especially by police. [from Latin *truncus* = tree trunk]

trundle *verb* to roll along, to move along heavily on a wheel or wheels. □ **trundle bed** a low bed on wheels so that it can be pushed under another.

trunk *noun* **1** the main stem of a tree. **2** the body apart from head and limbs. **3** a large box with a hinged lid for transporting or storing-clothes etc. **4** the long flexible nose of an elephant. **trunks** *plural noun* shorts worn by men or boys for swimming, boxing etc. □ **trunk call** a long-distance telephone call. **trunk line** a main line or route of a railway, telephone system, etc. **trunk road** an important main road.

truss *noun* **1** a bundle of hay or straw. **2** a compact cluster of flowers or fruit. **3** a framework of beams or bars supporting a roof or bridge etc. **4** a padded belt or other device worn to support a hernia. –**truss** *verb* **1** to tie or bind securely, *truss him up*; *truss a chicken*, fasten its legs and wings securely before cooking. **2** to support (a roof or bridge etc.) with trusses.

trust *noun* **1** firm belief in the reliability, truth, or strength etc. of a person or thing. **2** confident expectation. **3** responsibility arising from trust placed in the person given authority, *a position of trust*. **4** property legally entrusted to a person with instructions to use it for another's benefit or for a specified purpose. **5** an organisation founded to promote or preserve something, *the National Trust*. **6** an association of business firms, formed to reduce or defeat competition; *anti-trust legislation*, laws to combat this. –**trust** *verb* **1** to have or place trust in, to entrust. **2** to treat as reliable. **3** to hope earnestly, *I trust he is not hurt*. □ **in trust** held as a trust (see sense 4). **on trust** accepted without investigation, *don't take the statement on trust*; on credit, *they bought goods on trust*. **trust to** to place reliance on, *trusting to luck*. [from Old Norse *traustr* = strong]

trustee *noun* **1** a person who holds and administers property in trust for another. **2** a member of a group of people managing the business affairs of an institution.

trustful *adjective* full of trust, not feeling or showing suspicion. **trustfully** *adverb*, **trustfulness** *noun*

trusting *adjective* having trust, trustful.

trustworthy *adjective* worthy of trust, reliable. **trustworthiness** *noun*

trusty *adjective* (*old use*) trustworthy, *his trusty sword*. –**trusty** *noun* a prisoner who is given special privileges or responsibilities.

truth *noun* **1** the quality of being true. **2** something that is true. □ **truth table** a list indicating the truth or falsehood of various combinations of statements.

truthful *adjective* **1** habitually telling the truth. **2** true, *a truthful account of what happened*. **truthfully** *adverb*, **truthfulness** *noun*

try *verb* (**tried**, **trying**) **1** to attempt, to make an effort to do something, *try to remember* (see note below). **2** to test, to use or do or test the possibilities of something in order to discover whether it is satisfactory or useful for a purpose, *try your strength*; *try soap and water*; *try shaking it*. **3** to try to open (a door or window) in order to discover whether it is locked. **4** to be a strain on, *small print tries the eyes*. **5** to examine and decide (a case or issue) in a lawcourt; to hold a trial of (a person), *he was tried for murder*. –**try** *noun* **1** an attempt. **2** a touchdown by a player in rugby football, scoring points and entitling the scoring side to a kick at goal. □ **try it on** (*informal*) to do something experimentally in order to discover whether it will be tolerated. **try-on** *noun* (*informal*) an experimental action of this kind. **try on** to put (a garment etc.) on to see whether it fits and looks well. **try one's hand** to attempt something for the first time. **try one's luck** to attempt something to see if one can be successful. **try out** to test by use. **try-out** *noun* a test of this kind. **try-square** *noun* a carpenter's square usually with one wooden and one metal limb. [the original meaning was 'to separate or distinguish things']

Usage *Try and* followed by a verb (e.g. *try and remember* or *don't try and be clever*) is common in informal speech, but in formal writing it is better to use *try to*, as in *try to remember* and *don't try to be clever*.

---

trying *adjective* putting a strain on one's temper or patience, annoying.

trypsin (**trip**-sĭn) *noun* the chief digestive enzyme in the fluid secreted by the pancreas.

tryst (*pr.* trist) *noun* (*old use*) a meeting, especially of lovers.

tsar (*pr.* zar) *noun* the title of the former emperor of Russia. [Russian, from Latin *Caesar*]

tsetse fly (**tset**-see *or* **tet**-see) *noun* a tropical African fly that carries and transmits disease (especially sleeping sickness) by its bite.

T-shirt *noun* a short-sleeved shirt having the shape of a T when spread out flat.

T-square *noun* a T-shaped instrument for measuring or obtaining right angles.

tsunami (tsoo-**nah**-mee) *noun* **1** a series of long high sea waves caused by earth movement. **2** an exceptionally large tidal wave. [Japanese]

tuan (**tew**-ăn) *noun* **1** a largely tree-dwelling brush-tailed carnivorous Australian marsupial. **2** a flying possum. [Wathawarung *duwan*]

tuart (**tew**-art) *noun* a Western Australian eucalypt; its hard yellowish wood. [Nyungar, probably *duward*]

tub *noun* **1** an open flat-bottomed usually round container used for washing or for holding liquids or soil for plants etc. **2** (*informal*) a bath.

tuba (**tew**-bă) *noun* a large low-pitched brass wind instrument. [Latin, = trumpet]

tubal *adjective* of a tube or tubes.

tubby *adjective* (**tubbier**, **tubbiest**) short and fat. **tubbiness** *noun* [from *tub*]

tube *noun* **1** a long hollow cylinder, especially for holding or conveying liquids etc. **2** a hollow cylindrical organ in the body, *Fallopian tubes*. **3** a cylinder of flexible

material with a screw cap, holding pastes etc. ready for use. **4** a cathode ray tube in a television set. **5** (*Austral. informal*) a can of beer. **6** (in full **inner tube**) the inflatable part of a pneumatic tyre.

tuber *noun* a short thick rounded root (e.g. of a dahlia) or underground stem (e.g. of a potato), producing buds from which new plants will grow. **tuberous** *adjective* [Latin, = a swelling]

tubercle (**tew**-ber-kŭl) *noun* a small rounded projection or swelling.

tubercular (tew-**ber**-kew-ler) *adjective* of or affected with tuberculosis.

tuberculosis (tew-ber-kew-**loh**-sĭs) *noun* **1** an infectious wasting disease affecting various parts of the body, in which tubercles appear on body tissue. **2** tuberculosis of the lungs. [from Latin *tuberculum* = little swelling]

tuberose (**tew**-bĕ-rohz) *noun* a tropical plant with fragrant white funnel-shaped flowers.

tubing *noun* tubes; a length of tube.

tubular *adjective* tube-shaped; (of furniture) made of tube-shaped pieces.

tubule (**tew**-bewl) *noun* a small tube or tube-shaped part.

tuck *noun* a flat fold stitched in a garment etc. to make it smaller or as an ornament. **–tuck** *verb* **1** to put a tuck or tucks in (a garment etc.). **2** to turn (ends or edges etc.) or fold (a part) in, into, or under something so as to be concealed or held in place. **3** to cover snugly and compactly, *tucked him up in bed*. **4** to put away compactly, *tucked it in a drawer*. □ **tuck in** (*informal*) to eat food heartily. **tuck-in** *noun* (*informal*) a large meal. **tuck into** (*informal*) to eat (food) heartily. **tuck shop** a school shop selling lunches and snack food, a canteen.

Tucker, Albert (1914–99), Australian painter, pioneer of expressionism and surrealist painting in Australia.

tucker *noun* (*Austral. informal*) food. □ **tucker bag** or **box** a container for food.

Tudor *noun* a member of the royal family of England from Henry VII to Elizabeth I. **–Tudor** *adjective* of the Tudors; of or imitating the style of houses etc. of that period.

Tuesday *noun* the day of the week following Monday. [from Old English *Tiwesdaeg*, named after *Tyr*, the Norse god of war]

tufa (**tew**-fă) *noun* **1** porous rock formed round springs of mineral water. **2** tuff.

tuff *noun* rock formed from volcanic ashes.

tuft *noun* a bunch of threads, grass, feathers, or hair etc. held or growing together at the base. –**tuft** *verb* to make depressions in (a mattress or cushion) by stitching tightly through it at a number of points, so as to hold the stuffing in place.

tufted *adjective* having a tuft or tufts; (of a bird) having a tuft of projecting feathers on its head.

tug *verb* (**tugged, tugging**) **1** to pull vigorously or with great effort. **2** to tow by means of a tug. –**tug** *noun* **1** a vigorous pull. **2** (also **tugboat**) a small powerful boat for towing others. □ **tug of war** a contest in which two teams hold a rope at opposite ends and pull until one hauls the other over a central point.

tuition (tew-**ish**-ŏn) *noun* the process of teaching, instruction. [from Latin *tuitio* = looking after something]

tulip *noun* a garden plant growing from a bulb, with a large cup-shaped flower on a tall stem. [from old Turkish *tuliband* = turban (because the flowers are this shape)]

tulle (*pr.* tewl) *noun* a kind of fine silky net used for veils and dresses.

tumble *verb* **1** to fall helplessly or headlong; to cause to do this (e.g. by pushing). **2** to fall in value or amount. **3** to roll over and over in a disorderly way. **4** to move or rush in a hasty careless way, *tumbled into bed.* **5** to throw or push carelessly in a confused mass. **6** to rumple or disarrange. **7** to perform a somersault or other acrobatic feat. –**tumble** *noun* **1** a tumbling fall. **2** an untidy state, *things were all in a tumble.* **3** a somersault or other acrobatic feat. □ **tumble-dryer** *noun* a machine for drying washing in a heated drum that rotates. **tumble to** (*informal*) to realise or grasp (the meaning of something).

tumbledown *adjective* falling or fallen into ruin, dilapidated.

tumbler *noun* **1** a drinking glass with no handle or foot. **2** a pivoted piece in a lock that holds the bolt until lifted by a key. **3** any of several kinds of pivoted or swivelling parts in a mechanism. □ **tumbler-dryer** *noun* a tumble-dryer.

tumbleweed *noun* a plant forming a globular bush that breaks off in late summer and is rolled about by the wind.

tumbrel *noun* (also **tumbril**) (*old use*) an open cart, especially the kind used to carry condemned people to the guillotine during the French Revolution.

tumescent (tew-**mess**-ĕnt) *adjective* swelling. **tumescence** *noun* [from Latin *tumere* = to swell]

tumid (**tew**-mĭd) *adjective* swollen, inflated.

tummy *noun* (*informal*) the stomach.

tumour (**tew**-mer) *noun* an abnormal mass of new tissue growing on or in the body.

tumult (**tew**-mult) *noun* **1** an uproar. **2** a state of confusion and agitation, *her mind was in a tumult.*

tumultuous (tew-**mul**-tew-ŭs) *adjective* making a tumult. **tumultuously** *adverb*

tumulus (**tewm**-yŭ-lŭs) *noun* (*plural* **tumuli**) an ancient burial mound.

tun *noun* a large cask for wine or beer etc.

tuna (**tew**-nă) *noun* (*plural* **tuna**) **1** a large edible sea fish, also called *tunny*. **2** its flesh as food.

tundra *noun* the vast level treeless Arctic regions where the subsoil is frozen.

tune *noun* a melody, especially a well-marked one. –**tune** *verb* **1** to put (a musical instrument) in tune. **2** to tune in (a radio receiver etc.). **3** to adjust (an engine) to run smoothly. □ **in tune** playing or singing at the correct musical pitch; *in tune with one's surroundings*, in harmonious adjustment to them. **out of tune** not in tune. **to the tune of** to the considerable sum or amount of, *received compensation to the tune of $5000.* **tune in** to set a radio receiver to the right wavelength to receive a certain transmitted signal. **tune up** (of an orchestra) to bring instruments to the correct or uniform pitch. **tuner** *noun*, **tunable** *adjective*

tuneful *adjective* melodious, having a pleasing tune. **tunefully** *adverb*, **tunefulness** *noun*

tuneless *adjective* not melodious, without a tune. **tunelessly** *adverb*

tungsten (**tung**-stĕn) *noun* a chemical element (symbol W), a heavy grey metallic substance used for the filaments of electric lamps and in making a kind of steel. [from Swedish *tung* = heavy, + *sten* = stone]

tunic *noun* **1** a close-fitting jacket worn as part of a uniform. **2** a loose usually sleeveless garment worn over a shirt etc., reaching to the knees or above. **3** a hip-length garment worn over trousers or skirt.

tunicate (**tew**-ni-kayt) *noun* a small sea creature with a hard outer skin.

tuning fork *noun* a steel device like a two-pronged fork, which produces a note of fixed pitch (usually middle C) when struck.

Tunis (**tew**-nǐs) the capital of Tunisia.

Tunisia (tew-**niz**-ee-ǎ) a republic in North Africa. **Tunisian** *adjective & noun*

tunnel *noun* an underground passage; a passage for a road or railway through a hill or under a river etc.; a passage made by a burrowing animal. –**tunnel** *verb* (**tunnelled**, **tunnelling**) to dig a tunnel; to make a tunnel through.

tunny *noun* tuna.

tupong (**too**-pong) *noun* (also **toopong**) a small, chiefly sea fish of SE Australia (known in SA as *congolli*). [Kuurn Kopan Noot *dubong*]

tuppence *noun* = twopence.

tuppenny *adjective* = twopenny.

turban *noun* **1** a man's headdress of a scarf wound round a cap, worn especially by Muslims and Sikhs. **2** a woman's hat resembling this. [from old Turkish *tuliband* (compare *tulip*)]

turbid *adjective* **1** (of liquids) muddy, not clear. **2** confused, disordered, *a turbid imagination*. **turbidly** *adverb*, **turbidity** (ter-**bid**-ĭ-tee) *noun* [from Latin *turba* = crowd, disturbance]

turbine (**ter**-byn) *noun* a machine or motor driven by a wheel that is turned by a flow of water or gas, *gas turbines*. [from Latin *turbinis* = of a whirlwind]

turbo *noun* (*plural* **turbos**) **1** a turbocharger. **2** a motor vehicle fitted with this.

turbo- *prefix* turbine.

turbocharger *noun* a supercharger driven by a turbine that is powered by the engine's exhausts.

turbofan *noun* **1** a fan connected to or driven by a turbine. **2** a jet engine equipped with this for additional thrust.

turbojet *noun* **1** a turbine engine that delivers its power in the form of a jet of hot gases. **2** an aircraft driven by this instead of by propellers.

turboprop *noun* **1** a jet engine in which a turbine is used as a turbojet and also to drive a propeller. **2** an aircraft driven by this.

turbot *noun* a large flat European sea fish valued as food.

turbulent (**ter**-bew-lěnt) *adjective* **1** in a state of commotion or unrest; (of air or water) moving violently and unevenly. **2** unruly. **turbulently** *adverb*, **turbulence** *noun* [same origin as *turbid*]

tureen (tew-**reen**) *noun* a deep covered dish from which soup is served at the table.

turf *noun* (*plural* **turfs** or **turves**) **1** short grass and the surface layer of earth bound together by its roots. **2** a piece of this cut from the ground. **3** a slab of peat for fuel. –**turf** *verb* to lay (ground) with turf. □ **the turf** the racecourse; horse racing. **turf out** (*informal*) to throw out.

turgid (**ter**-jǐd) *adjective* **1** swollen or distended and not flexible. **2** (of language or style) pompous, not flowing easily. **turgidly** *adverb*, **turgidity** (ter-**jid**-ĭ-tee) *noun* [from Latin *turgere* = to swell]

turgor (**terg**-er) *noun* the normal rigid condition of the cells of plants, caused by the pressure of the water taken up from the soil etc.

Turing, Alan Mathison (1912–54), British mathematician who (in 1936) showed the potential of a machine (the future computer) to process a problem by following a sequence of rules.

Turk *noun* a native or inhabitant of Turkey.

Turkey a republic in SW Asia and SE Europe.

turkey *noun* (*plural* **turkeys**) **1** a large bird reared for its flesh. **2** its flesh as food. □ **talk turkey** (*informal*) to talk in a frank and businesslike way. [the name was originally used of a kind of fowl imported through Turkey in the 16th century]

turkeycock *noun* a male turkey.

Turkish *adjective* of Turkey or its people or language. –**Turkish** *noun* the language of Turkey. □ **Turkish bath** exposure of the whole body to hot air or steam to induce sweating, followed by washing. **Turkish delight** a sweet consisting of lumps of flavoured gelatine coated in powdered sugar.

Turkmenistan (terk-men-ĭ-**stahn**) a republic of western central Asia, north of Iran and east of the Caspian Sea. **Turkmen** *adjective & noun*

turmeric (**ter**-mě-rik) *noun* **1** a tropical Asian plant of the ginger family. **2** its powdered root used as a spice (especially in curries), or as a yellow dye.

turmoil (**ter**-moil) *noun* a state of great disturbance or confusion.

turn *verb* **1** to move or cause to move round a point or axis; *turn somersaults*, perform them by turning one's body. **2** to change or cause to change in position so that a different side becomes uppermost or nearest to a certain point. **3** to give a new direction to, to take a new direction, to aim or become aimed in a certain way, *the river turns north at this point*. **4** to go or move or travel round, to go to the other side of; *turn the enemy's flank*, pass round it so as to attack from the side or rear. **5** to pass (a certain hour or age), *it's turned midnight*. **6** to cause to go, to send or put, *turn the horse into the field*. **7** to change or become changed in nature, form, or appearance etc., *the caterpillar turned into a chrysalis*. **8** to make or become sour, *the milk has turned*. **9** to make or become nauseated, *it turns my stomach*. **10** to shape in a lathe. **11** to give an elegant form to. –**turn** *noun* **1** turning; being turned; a turning movement. **2** a change of direction or condition etc.; the point at which this occurs. **3** an angle; a bend or corner in a road. **4** character or tendency, *he's of a mechanical turn of mind*. **5** service of a specified kind, *did me a good turn*; *it served its turn*, served a useful purpose. **6** an opportunity or obligation etc. that comes to each of a number of people or things in succession, *wait your turn*. **7** a short performance in an entertainment. **8** (*informal*) an attack of illness; a momentary nervous shock. □ **at every turn** in every place; continually. **in turn** in succession; *in one's turn*, when one's turn comes. **not turn a hair** to show no agitation. **out of turn** before or after one's turn; *speak out of turn*, to speak in an indiscreet or presumptuous way. **to a turn** so as to be cooked perfectly. **turn down** to fold down; to reduce the volume or flow of (sound, gas, or heat etc.) by turning a knob or tap; to reject. **turn-down** *adjective* (of a collar) folding downwards. **turn in** to hand in; to deliver as a score etc.; (*informal*) to go to bed; (*informal*) to abandon as a plan or work. **turn off** to enter a side road; to stop the flow or operation of by turning a tap or switch; (*informal*) to cause to lose interest. **turn of speed** ability to go fast. **turn on** to start the flow or operation of by turning a tap or switch; (of events etc.) to depend on; (*informal*) to excite (a person); (*informal*) to intoxicate (with drugs). **turn one's back on** to abandon. **turn out** to expel; to turn off (an electric light etc.); to equip or dress, *well turned out*; to produce by work; to empty and search or clean, *turn out your cupboards*; (*informal*) to

come out, to attend a meeting etc.; to call (a military guard) from the guardroom; to prove to be, to be eventually, *we'll see how things turn out*. **turn-out** *noun* the process of turning out a room etc.; the number of people who come to a public or social function; something arrayed, an outfit; an area at the side of a road for a car to pull over to let others pass. **turn over** to hand over; to transfer; to consider carefully, *turn it over in your mind*. **turn over a new leaf** to abandon one's previous bad ways. **turn round** to unload and reload (a ship etc.) so that it is ready to leave again. **turn tail** to run away. **turn the corner** to pass a critical point safely, e.g. in an illness. **turn the tables** to reverse a situation and put oneself in a superior position. **turn to** to set about one's work. **turn turtle** to capsize. **turn up** to discover or reveal; to be found; to make one's appearance; to happen or present itself; to increase the volume or flow of (sound, gas, or heat etc.) by turning a knob or tap. **turn-up** *noun* a turned-up part, especially at the lower end of trouser legs; (*informal*) an unexpected event, *a turn-up for the books*. [from Greek *tornos* = lathe]

turnaround *noun* **1** the process of unloading and reloading a ship etc.; the progress through a system; the time taken for this. **2** a complete and abrupt change of fortune, attitude, etc.

turncoat *noun* a person who changes his or her principles.

Turner, Joseph Mallord William (1775–1851), English landscape painter.

turner *noun* a person who works with a lathe.

turnery *noun* **1** work on a lathe. **2** its products.

turning *noun* a place where one road meets another, forming a corner. □ **turning point** a point at which a decisive change takes place; the peak or nadir of a curve in a graph.

turnip *noun* **1** a plant with a round white root used as a vegetable and for feeding cattle etc. **2** its root.

turnkey *noun* (*old use*) a gaoler.

turnover *noun* **1** turning over. **2** a small pasty in which a piece of pastry is folded over so as to enclose filling. **3** the amount of money turned over in a business. **4** the rate at which goods are sold. **5** the rate at which workers leave and are replaced, *a rapid turnover of staff*.

turnpike *noun* (*old use* & *Amer.*) a toll gate; a road with toll gates.

turnstile *noun* a device for admitting people to a building etc. one at a time, with barriers (often of horizontal bars) that revolve round a central post as each person passes through.

turntable *noun* a circular revolving platform or support, e.g. for the record in a record player.

turpentine (**ter**-pĕn-tyn) *noun* an oil distilled from the resin of certain trees, used for thinning paint and as a solvent.

turpitude (**ter**-pĭ-tewd) *noun* wickedness. [from Latin *turpis* = shameful]

turps *noun* (*informal*) turpentine.

turquoise (**ter**-kwoiz) *noun* 1 a greenish-blue semi-precious stone. 2 a greenish-blue colour. –**turquoise** *adjective* of this colour. [French, = Turkish stone]

turret *noun* 1 a small tower-like projection on a building or defensive wall. 2 a low usually revolving structure protecting a gun and gunners in a ship, aircraft, fort, or tank. 3 a rotating holder for various dies and cutting tools in a lathe or drill etc. **turreted** *adjective* [from French *tour* = tower]

turtle *noun* 1 a sea creature resembling a tortoise, with flippers used in swimming. 2 its flesh, used for making soup. □ **turn turtle** *see* **turn**. **turtle dove** a wild dove noted for its soft cooing.

turtleneck *noun* a high round close-fitting neck on a knitted garment.

Tuscany a region of west central Italy. **Tuscan** *adjective* & *noun*

tusk *noun* one of the pair of long pointed teeth that project outside the mouth in the elephant, walrus, etc.

tussle *noun* a struggle, a conflict. –**tussle** *verb* to take part in a tussle.

tussock *noun* a tuft or clump of grass.

tussore (**tuss**-or) *noun* a strong but coarse silk.

Tutankhamun (too-tǎn-kah-**moon** *or* too-tǎn-**kah**-mǔn) (c. 1370–1352 BC), a boy Egyptian pharaoh whose tomb was found virtually intact in 1922.

tutelage (**tew**-tĕ-lij) *noun* 1 guardianship. 2 instruction.

tutor *noun* 1 a private teacher. 2 a university teacher directing the studies of undergraduates. 3 an instruction book, *a guitar tutor*. –**tutor** *verb* to act as tutor to, to teach. [Latin, = guardian]

tutorial (tew-**tor**-ree-ǎl) *adjective* of or as a tutor. –**tutorial** *noun* a period of tuition given by a university or college tutor.

Tutsi (**tuut**-see) *noun* (*plural* **Tutsi** *or* **Tutsis**) a member of a Bantu-speaking people forming a minority of the population of Rwanda and Burundi but who formerly dominated the Hutu majority.

tutti-frutti (too-tee-**froo**-tee) *noun* ice cream containing or flavoured with mixed fruits. [Italian, = all fruits]

tut-tut *interjection* an exclamation of impatience, annoyance, or rebuke.

tutu (**too**-too) *noun* a ballet dancer's short skirt made of layers of stiffened frills. [French]

Tuvalu (too-**vah**-loo) an independent country of the Commonwealth consisting of a group of nine islands in the western Pacific (formerly the Ellice Islands). **Tuvaluan** *adjective* & *noun*

tuxedo (tuk-**see**-doh) *noun* (*plural* **tuxedos** *or* **tuxedoes**) a dinner jacket; a suit including this.

TV *abbreviation* television.

twaddle *noun* nonsense.

Twain, Mark (pseudonym of Samuel Langhorne Clemens, 1835–1910), American writer, author of *The Adventures of Tom Sawyer* and *The Adventures of Huckleberry Finn*.

twain *adjective* & *noun* (*old use*) two.

twang *noun* 1 a sharp ringing sound like that made by a tense wire when plucked. 2 a nasal intonation in speech. –**twang** *verb* to make or cause to make a twang; to play (a guitar etc.) by plucking the strings.

tweak *verb* to pinch and twist sharply; to pull with a sharp jerk. –**tweak** *noun* a sharp pinch, twist, or pull.

twee *adjective* affectedly dainty or quaint.

tweed *noun* a twilled usually woollen material, often woven of mixed colours. **tweeds** *plural noun* clothes made of tweed. **tweedy** *adjective* [originally a mistake; the Scottish word *tweel* (= twill) was wrongly read as *tweed* by being confused with the River Tweed]

tweet *noun* 1 the chirp of a small bird. 2 a posting on the twitter social networking site. –**tweet** *verb* 1 to make a tweet. 2 to send a message to.

tweeter *noun* a small loudspeaker for reproducing high-frequency signals.

tweezers *plural noun* small pincers for picking up or pulling very small things.

twelfth *adjective* & *noun* 1 next after eleventh. 2 any of twelve equal parts of a thing. □ **twelfth man** a reserve member of a cricket team. **Twelfth Night** 5 January, the Eve of Epiphany. **twelfthly** *adverb*

twelve *adjective* & *noun* one more than eleven (12, XII). □ **twelve-note** *adjective* (of music) using the twelve chromatic notes of the octave arranged in a chosen order without a conventional key.

twenty *adjective* & *noun* twice ten (20, XX). **twenties** *plural noun* the numbers or years or degrees of temperature from 20 to 29. □ **twenty-two** *noun* a line across the ground 22 metres from either goal in hockey and rugby football; the space enclosed by this. **twentieth** *adjective* & *noun*

24-7 *adverb* (also **24/7**) (*informal*) twenty-four hours a day, seven days a week; all the time.

twerp *noun* (*informal*) a stupid or objectionable person.

twice *adverb* **1** two times, on two occasions. **2** in a double amount or degree, *twice as strong*.

twiddle *verb* to twirl or handle aimlessly; to twist (a thing) quickly to and fro. **–twiddle** *noun* **1** a slight twirl. **2** a twirled mark or sign. □ **twiddle one's thumbs** to twist them round each other idly for lack of occupation. **twiddly** *adjective* [from *twirl* and *fiddle*]

twig[1] *noun* a small shoot issuing from a branch or stem.

twig[2] *verb* (**twigged, twigging**) (*informal*) to realise or grasp (the meaning of something).

twilight *noun* light from the sky when the sun is below the horizon (especially after sunset); the period of this. □ **twilight of the gods** (*Scand. myth.*) the destruction of the gods and of the world in conflict with the powers of evil. **twilight zone** an area or concept that is undefined or intermediate.

twill *noun* textile fabric woven so that parallel diagonal lines are produced. **twilled** *adjective* woven in this way.

twin *noun* **1** either of two children or animals born at one birth. **2** either of two people or things that are exactly alike. **–twin** *adjective* being a twin or twins, *twin sisters*. **–twin** *verb* (**twinned, twinning**) to combine as a pair. □ **twin beds** a pair of single beds. **twin-engined** *adjective* having two engines. **twin set** a woman's matching jumper and cardigan. **twin towns** two towns (usually in different countries) that establish special cultural and social links. [from Old English *twinn* = double]

twine *noun* strong thread or string made of two or more strands twisted together. **–twine** *verb* to twist, to wind or coil.

twinge (*pr.* twinj) *noun* a slight or brief pang.

twinkle *verb* **1** to shine with a light that flickers rapidly, to sparkle. **2** (of the eyes) to be bright or sparkling with amusement. **3** (of the feet in dancing etc.) to move with short rapid movements. **–twinkle** *noun* a twinkling light or look or movement. □ **in the twinkling of an eye** in an instant.

twirl *verb* to twist lightly or rapidly. **–twirl** *noun* **1** a twirling movement. **2** a twirled mark or sign. **twirly** *adjective*

twist *verb* **1** to wind (strands etc.) round each other so as to form a single cord, to interweave. **2** to make by doing this. **3** to pass or coil round something. **4** to give a spiral form to, e.g. by turning the ends in opposite directions. **5** to take a spiral or winding form or course, to turn or bend round. **6** to rotate or revolve; to cause to do this. **7** to wrench out of its normal shape; *a twisted mind*, one that works in a perverted way. **8** to distort the meaning of, *tried to twist his words into an admission of guilt*. **9** (*informal*) to swindle. **–twist** *noun* **1** twisting; being twisted. **2** something formed by twisting, a turn in a twisting course. **3** a dance with vigorous twisting of the body. **4** a peculiar tendency of mind or character. **5** (*informal*) a swindle. □ **round the twist** (*informal*) crazy. **twist a person's arm** (*informal*) to coerce him or her. **twisty** *adjective*, **twister** *noun*

twister *noun* (*Amer.*) a tornado.

twit[1] *verb* (**twitted, twitting**) to taunt.

twit[2] *noun* (*informal*) a foolish or insignificant person.

twitch *verb* **1** to pull with a light jerk. **2** to quiver or contract spasmodically. **–twitch** *noun* a twitching movement.

twitchy *adjective* (*informal*) nervous. **twitchiness** *noun*

twitter *verb* **1** to make a series of light chirping sounds. **2** to talk rapidly in an anxious or nervous way. **–twitter** *noun* **1** twittering. **2** (*trademark*) a social networking site on the Internet.

two *adjective* & *noun* one more than one (2, II). □ **be in two minds** to be undecided. **in two** in or into two pieces. **two-dimensional** *adjective* having two dimensions (length, breadth). **two-edged** *adjective* having two cutting edges; cutting both ways (*see* **cut**). **two-faced** *adjective* insincere, deceitful. **two-piece** *noun* a suit of clothes or a woman's swimsuit consisting of two separate parts.

two-ply *adjective* made of two strands or layers. **two-stroke** *adjective* (of an engine) having its power cycle completed in one up-and-down movement of the piston. **two-time** *verb* (*informal*) to be unfaithful to; to double-cross. **two-way** *adjective* involving two ways or participants; *two-way radio*, a radio capable of transmitting and receiving signals; *two-way switch*, a switch that allows electric current to be turned on or off from either of two points; *two-way traffic*, lanes of traffic travelling in opposite directions.

two bob *noun* (*Austral. informal*, *old use*) two shillings. □ **have two bob each way** to be non-committal; to hedge one's bets. **mad as a two-bob watch** crazy.

twofold *adjective* & *adverb* **1** twice as much or as many. **2** consisting of two parts.

twopence (**tup**-ĕns) *noun* (*old use*) the sum of two pence; *don't care twopence*, care hardly at all.

twopenny (**tup**-ĕ-nee) *adjective* (*old use*) costing or worth twopence. □ **twopenny-halfpenny** *adjective* insignificant, almost worthless.

twosome *noun* two people together, a couple or pair.

tycoon *noun* a wealthy and influential businessman or industrialist, a magnate. [from Japanese *taikun* = great prince]

tying *see* tie.

type *noun* **1** a class of people or things that have characteristics in common, a kind. **2** a typical example or instance. **3** (*informal*) a person of specified character, *brainy types*. **4** a letter or figure etc. used in printing; a set, supply, kind, or size of these, *printed in large type*. –**type** *verb* **1** to classify according to type. **2** to write with a typewriter or computer by pressing the keys. [from Greek *tupos* = impression]

typecast *verb* (**typecast**, **typecasting**) to cast (an actor or actress) in the kind of part which seems to suit him or her best.

typeface *noun* a set of printing types in one design.

typescript *noun* a typewritten document.

typesetter *noun* **1** a person who sets type for printing. **2** a machine for doing this. **typesetting** *noun*

typewriter *noun* a machine for producing characters similar to those of print by pressing keys which cause raised metal letters etc. to strike the paper, usually through an inked ribbon. [the word *typewriter* at first meant the person using the machine, as well as the machine itself]

typewritten *adjective* written with a typewriter.

typhoid fever *noun* a serious infectious feverish disease that attacks the intestines, caused by bacteria taken into the body in food or drink. [from *typhus*]

typhoon (ty-**foon**) *noun* a violent hurricane in the western Pacific or East Asian seas. [from Chinese *tai fung* = great wind]

typhus *noun* an infectious disease with fever, great weakness, and purple spots on the body. [from Greek *tuphos* = vapour]

typical *adjective* **1** having the distinctive qualities of a particular type of person or thing, serving as a representative specimen, *a typical dentist*. **2** characteristic, *he answered with typical curtness*. **typically** *adverb* [same origin as *type*]

typify (**tip**-ĭ-fy) *verb* (**typified**, **typifying**) to be a representative specimen of.

typist *noun* a person who types, especially one employed to do so.

typography (ty-**pog**-ră-fee) *noun* **1** the art or practice of printing. **2** the style or appearance of printed matter. **typographical** (ty-pŏ-**graf**-i-kăl) *adjective* [from *type* + *-graphy*]

tyrannical (tĭ-**ran**-i-kăl) *adjective* as or like a tyrant, obtaining obedience from everyone by force or threats. **tyrannically** *adverb*

tyrannise (**ti**-ră-nyz) *verb* (also **-ize**) to rule as or like a tyrant.

tyrannosaur (tĭ-**ran**-ŏ-sor) *noun* a very large dinosaur (also called *Tyrannosaurus rex*) that walked on its hind legs. [from Greek *turannos* = tyrant, + *sauros* = lizard]

tyrannous (**ti**-ră-nŭs) *adjective* tyrannical.

tyranny (**ti**-ră-nee) *noun* **1** government by a tyrannical ruler. **2** oppressive or tyrannical use of power.

tyrant (**ty**-rănt) *noun* a ruler or other person who uses power in a harsh or oppressive way, one who insists on absolute obedience. [from Greek *turannos* = ruler with full power]

tyre *noun* (*Amer.* tire) a covering fitted round the rim of a wheel to absorb shocks, usually of reinforced rubber filled with air or covering a pneumatic inner tube.

tyro *noun* = tiro.

Uu

UAI *abbreviation* (*Austral.*) Universities Admission Index.

uber- *prefix* denoting an outstanding or an extreme example of a particular person or thing.

ubiquitous (yoo-**bik**-wĭ-tŭs) *adjective* being everywhere at the same time. **ubiquity** *noun* [from Latin *ubique* = everywhere]

U-boat *noun* a German submarine, especially in the war of (1939–45). [short for German *Unterseeboot* = undersea boat]

udder *noun* a baglike milk-secreting organ of a cow or ewe or goat etc., with two or more teats.

UFO (also *ufo*) *abbreviation* & *noun* (*plural* **UFOS**) unidentified flying object, a term often applied to supposed vehicles ('flying saucers') piloted by beings from outer space.

Uganda (yoo-**gan**-dă) a landlocked republic in East Africa. **Ugandan** *adjective* & *noun*

ugh (*pr.* uh) *interjection* an exclamation of disgust or horror.

ugh boot *noun* (also **ugg**) (*trademark*) a fleecy-lined boot with untanned upper.

ugli (**ug**-lee) *noun* (*plural* **uglis**) a citrus fruit that is a hybrid of grapefruit and tangerine. [from *ugly*]

ugly *adjective* (**uglier**, **ugliest**) **1** unpleasant to look at or to hear. **2** unpleasant in any way; hostile and threatening, *the crowd was in an ugly mood*. □ **ugly customer** an unpleasantly formidable person. **ugly duckling** a person who at first seems unpromising but later becomes much admired or very able (¶ like the cygnet in the brood of ducks in Hans Andersen's story). **ugliness** *noun* [from Old Norse *uggligr* = frightening]

UHF *abbreviation* ultra-high frequency.

UHT *abbreviation* ultra heat treated (of milk, for long keeping).

UK *abbreviation* United Kingdom.

Ukraine (yoo-**krayn**) a republic in eastern Europe to the north of the Black Sea, formerly a republic of the USSR. **Ukrainian** *adjective* & *noun*

ukulele (yoo-kŭ-**lay**-lee) *noun* a small four-stringed guitar.

Ulan Bator (oo-lahn **bah**-tor) the capital of Mongolia.

ulcer *noun* an open sore on the surface of the body or one of its organs. **ulcerous** *adjective*

ulcerate *verb* to cause an ulcer in or on; to become affected with an ulcer. **ulceration** *noun*

ulema (**uu**-lĕ-mă) *noun* **1** a body of Muslim scholars of sacred law and theology. **2** a member of this. [Arabic]

ulna (**ul**-nă) *noun* the thinner of the two long bones in the forearm; the corresponding bone in an animal. **ulnar** *adjective*

Ulster 1 a former province of Ireland comprising the present Northern Ireland and the counties of Cavan, Donegal, and Monaghan (which are now in the Republic of Ireland). **2** (used loosely) = Northern Ireland. □ **Ulster Unionist, Ulster Democratic Unionist** a member of one or other of the political parties in Northern Ireland seeking to maintain the union of Northern Ireland with Britain.

ulterior *adjective* beyond what is obvious or admitted, *ulterior motives*. [Latin, = further (compare *ultra-*)]

ultimate *adjective* **1** last, final; *the ultimate deterrent*, threatened use of nuclear weapons. **2** basic, fundamental, *the ultimate cause*. **ultimately** *adverb* [from Latin *ultimus* = last]

ultimatum (ul-tĭ-**may**-tŭm) *noun* (*plural* **ultimatums**) a final demand or statement of terms, rejection of which may lead to ending of friendly relations or a declaration of war. [same origin as *ultimate*]

ultra- *prefix* beyond, extremely, excessively, *ultra-conservative*, *ultra-modern*. [from Latin *ultra* = beyond]

ultra-high *adjective* (of frequency) in the range of 300 to 3000 MHz.

ultramarine (ultră-mă-**reen**) *adjective* & *noun* bright deep blue.

ultramicroscope *noun* a kind of optical microscope used to detect particles smaller than a wavelength of light.

ultrasonic (ultră-**sonn**-ik) *adjective* (of sound waves) with a pitch that is above the upper limit of normal human hearing. **ultrasonics** *noun* the science and application of ultrasonic waves.

ultrasound *noun* ultrasonic waves, used in medical diagnosis and treatment.

ultraviolet *adjective* **1** (of radiation) having a wavelength that is slightly shorter than that of visible light rays at the violet end of the spectrum. **2** of or using this radiation.

Uluru (oo-lŭ-**roo**) a red sandstone rock mass, the largest monolith in the world and an Aboriginal sacred site, in the south-west of the Northern Territory. Formerly called *Ayers Rock*.

Ulysses the Roman name for Odysseus. ☐ **Ulysses butterfly** a large swallowtail butterfly with brilliant blue wings.

umbel (**um**-bĕl) *noun* a flower cluster like that of parsley, in which the flowers are on stalks of nearly equal length springing from the same point on the main stem. [from Latin *umbella* = sunshade]

umbelliferous (um-bĕ-**lif**-ĕ-rŭs) *adjective* bearing umbels. [from *umbel*, + Latin *ferre* = to bear]

umber *noun* a natural colouring matter like ochre but darker and browner. ☐ **burnt umber** reddish-brown.

umbilical (um-**bil**-i-kăl) *adjective* of the navel. ☐ **umbilical cord** the flexible tubular structure of tissue connecting the placenta to the navel of the foetus and carrying nourishment to the foetus while it is in the womb; an essential connecting-line.

umbra *noun* (*plural* **umbrae**, *pr.* **um**-bree, *or* **umbras**) the dark central part of the shadow cast by the earth or the moon in an eclipse, or of a sunspot. [Latin, = shade]

umbrage (**um**-brij) *noun* a feeling of being offended. ☐ **take umbrage** to take offence. [from Latin *umbra* = shadow]

umbrella *noun* **1** a portable protection against rain, consisting of a circular piece of fabric mounted on a foldable frame of spokes attached to a central stick that serves as a handle. **2** any kind of general protecting force or influence. [from Italian *ombrella* = a little shade]

umlaut (**uum**-lowt) *noun* **1** a vowel change in related words (e.g. *man/men*, or in German *Mann/Männer*). **2** the mark used over a vowel in German etc. to indicate this change, as with

ä, ö, and ü. [from German *um* = about, + *laut* = sound]

umma (**uum**-ă) *noun* the Islamic community.

umpire *noun* a person appointed to see that the rules of a game or contest are observed and to settle disputes (e.g. in a game of cricket or baseball), or to give a decision on any disputed question. –**umpire** *verb* to act as umpire in (a game).

umpteen *adjective* (*informal*) very many. **umpteenth** *adjective*

UN *abbreviation* United Nations.

'un *pronoun* (*informal*) one, *a good 'un.*

un- *prefix* **1** not (as in *uncertain*, *uncertainty*). **2** reversing the action indicated by the simple verb (as in *unlock* = release from being locked).

Usage The number of words with this prefix is almost unlimited, and many of those whose meaning is obvious are not listed below.

---

unaccompanied *adjective* **1** not accompanied. **2** without musical accompaniment.

unaccountable *adjective* **1** unable to be explained or accounted for. **2** not accountable for one's actions etc. **unaccountably** *adverb*

unadulterated *adjective* pure.

Unaipon (oo-**ny**-pon), David (1873–1967), Aboriginal Australian writer, inventor, and preacher. ☐ **David Unaipon Award** an award for Aboriginal and Torres Strait Islander writers, instituted in 1988.

unalloyed (un-ă-**loid**) *adjective* not alloyed, pure, *unalloyed joy.*

unanimous (yoo-**nan**-ĭ-mŭs) *adjective* all agreeing in an opinion or decision; (of an opinion or decision etc.) held or given by everyone. **unanimously** *adverb*, **unanimity** (yoo-nă-**nim**-ĭ-tee) *noun* [from Latin *unus* = one, + *animus* = mind]

unanswerable *adjective* unable to be answered or refuted by a good argument to the contrary. **unanswerably** *adverb*

unarmed *adjective* not armed, without weapons.

unashamed *adjective* feeling no guilt. **unashamedly** (un-ă-**shaym**-ĕd-lee) *adverb*

unasked *adjective* not asked, without being requested.

unassailable *adjective* unable to be attacked or queried. **unassailably** *adverb*

unassuming *adjective* not arrogant, unpretentious.

unattached *adjective* **1** not attached to another thing, person, or organisation. **2** not engaged or married.

unattended *adjective* (of a vehicle etc.) having no person in charge of it.

unavailing *adjective* ineffectual; achieving nothing.

unaware *adjective* not aware.

unawares *adverb* unexpectedly; without noticing.

unbacked *adjective* **1** having no back or no backing. **2** (in betting) having no backers.

unbalanced *adjective* **1** not balanced. **2** mentally unsound.

unbar *verb* (**unbarred**, **unbarring**) to remove the bar from (a gate etc.) so as to allow it to be opened.

unbearable *adjective* not bearable, unable to be endured. **unbearably** *adverb*

unbeatable *adjective* impossible to defeat or surpass.

unbeaten *adjective* not defeated; (of a record etc.) not surpassed.

unbecoming *adjective* **1** not suited to the wearer, *an unbecoming hat*. **2** not suitable, *behaviour unbecoming to a gentleman*.

unbeknown *adjective* (*informal*) unknown; *they did it unbeknown to us*, without our being aware of it.

unbelief *noun* incredulity, disbelief.

unbelievable *adjective* not believable. **unbelievably** *adverb*

unbeliever *noun* a person who does not believe, especially one not believing in Christianity or Islam. **unbelieving** *adjective*

unbend *verb* (**unbent**, **unbending**) **1** to change or become changed from a bent position. **2** to become relaxed or affable.

unbending *adjective* inflexible, refusing to alter one's demands.

unbiased *adjective* not biased.

unbidden *adjective* not commanded or invited.

unblock *verb* to remove an obstruction from.

unbolt *verb* to release (a door etc.) by drawing back the bolt(s).

unborn *adjective* not yet born.

unbosom *verb* **unbosom oneself** to reveal one's thoughts or feelings.

unbounded *adjective* boundless, without limits.

unbridled *adjective* unrestrained, *unbridled insolence*.

unbuckle *verb* to release the buckle(s) of (a strap, shoe, etc.).

unburden *verb* to remove a burden from. ☐ **unburden oneself** to tell what one knows.

uncalled-for *adjective* offered or intruded impertinently or unjustifiably.

uncanny *adjective* **1** strange and rather frightening. **2** extraordinary, beyond what is normal, *they predicted the results with uncanny accuracy*. **uncannily** *adverb*, **uncanniness** *noun*

uncared-for *adjective* neglected.

unceasing *adjective* not ceasing; continuous. **unceasingly** *adverb*

unceremonious *adjective* without proper formality or dignity. **unceremoniously** *adverb*

uncertain *adjective* **1** not known certainly. **2** not knowing certainly. **3** not to be depended on, *his aim is uncertain*. **4** changeable, *an uncertain temper*. ☐ **in no uncertain terms** clearly and forcefully. **uncertainly** *adverb*, **uncertainty** *noun*

unchangeable *adjective* unable to be changed.

uncharitable *adjective* making severe judgments about people or acts.

unchristian *adjective* contrary to Christian principles, uncharitable.

uncial (**un**-see-ăl) *adjective* of or written in a script with rounded letters that are not joined together, found in manuscripts of the 4th–8th centuries and partly resembling modern capital letters. –**uncial** *noun* an uncial letter, style, or manuscript. [from Latin *uncia* = inch]

uncle *noun* **1** a brother or brother-in-law of one's father or mother. **2** (*informal*) an unrelated male friend of a child's parents. ☐ **Uncle Sam** (*informal*) the people of the USA. [from Latin *avunculus* = uncle]

unclothe *verb* **1** to remove the clothes from. **2** to uncover. **unclothed** *adjective*

uncoil *verb* to unwind from being coiled.

uncommon *adjective* not common, unusual.

uncommunicative *adjective* not inclined to give information or an opinion etc., silent.

uncompromising (un-**kom**-prŏ-my-zing) *adjective* not allowing or seeking compromise, inflexible.

unconcern *noun* lack of concern, indifference.

unconcerned *adjective* not feeling or showing concern, free from anxiety. **unconcernedly** *adverb*

unconditional *adjective* not subject to conditions or limitations, *unconditional surrender*. **unconditionally** *adverb*

unconscionable (un-**kon**-shŏ-nǎ-bŭl) *adjective* **1** unscrupulous. **2** contrary to what one's conscience feels is right, outrageous. **unconscionably** *adverb*

unconscious *adjective* **1** not conscious, not aware. **2** done or spoken etc. without conscious intention, *unconscious humour*. –**unconscious** *noun* the unconscious mind, that part of the mind whose content is not normally accessible to consciousness but which is found to affect behaviour. **unconsciously** *adverb*, **unconsciousness** *noun*

unconstitutional *adjective* not in accordance with the constitution of a country etc. **unconstitutionally** *adverb*

uncooperative *adjective* not cooperative.

uncoordinated *adjective* not coordinated.

uncouple (un-**kup**-ŭl) *verb* to disconnect (railway carriages etc.) from being connected by a coupling.

uncouth (un-**kooth**) *adjective* awkward or clumsy in manner, boorish. [from *un-*, + Old English *cuth* = known]

uncover *verb* **1** to remove the covering from. **2** to reveal or expose, *their deceit was uncovered*.

uncrowned *adjective* not crowned. □ **uncrowned king** or **queen** a person who is acknowledged as pre-eminent in a specified group or subject etc.

unction (**unk**-shŏn) *noun* **1** anointing with oil, especially as a religious rite for consecration or healing. **2** pretended earnestness; excessive politeness. [from Latin *unctum* = oiled]

unctuous (**unk**-tew-ŭs) *adjective* having an oily manner, smugly earnest or virtuous. **unctuously** *adverb*, **unctuousness** *noun* [same origin as *unction* and *unguent*]

uncut *adjective* not cut; (of a gem) not shaped by cutting; (of fabric) with the loops of the pile not cut.

undeceive *verb* to disillusion (a person).

undecided *adjective* **1** not yet settled or certain, *the point is still undecided*. **2** not yet having made up one's mind.

undemonstrative *adjective* not expressing one's feelings openly.

undeniable *adjective* impossible to deny, undoubtedly true. **undeniably** *adverb*

under *preposition* **1** in or to a position lower than, below. **2** less than, *it took us just under an hour*. **3** inferior to, of lower rank than, *no one under a bishop*. **4** governed or controlled by, *the country prospered under his rule*. **5** undergoing, *the road is under repair*. **6** subject to an obligation imposed by, *he is under contract to our firm*. **7** in accordance with, *it is permissible under our agreement*. **8** designated or indicated by, *writes under an assumed name*. **9** in the category of, *file it under 'Estimates'*. **10** (of land) planted with, *50 hectares under wheat*. **11** propelled by, *under sail*; *under one's own steam*, moving without external aid. **12** attested by, *under my hand* (= signature) *and seal*. –**under** *adverb* **1** in or to a lower position or subordinate condition. **2** in or into a state of unconsciousness. **3** below a certain quantity, rank, or age etc., *children of five and under*. –**under** *adjective* lower, situated underneath, *the under layers*. □ **under age** not old enough, especially for some legal right; not yet of adult status. **under the sun** anywhere in the world, existing. **under way** moving on water; in progress.

under- *prefix* **1** below, beneath (as in *underseal*). **2** lower, subordinate (as in *undermanager*). **3** insufficient, incompletely (as in *undercooked*).

underachieve *verb* to do less well than was expected, especially in schoolwork. **underachiever** *noun*

underarm *adjective* & *adverb* **1** in the armpit. **2** (in cricket etc.) bowling or bowled with the hand brought forward and upwards and not raised above shoulder level. **3** (in tennis) with the racquet moved similarly.

underbelly *noun* the undersurface of an animal etc., especially as being vulnerable to attack.

underbid *verb* (**underbid**, **underbidding**) **1** to make a lower bid than (another person). **2** to bid less than is justified in the game of bridge.

undercarriage *noun* an aircraft's landing wheels and their supports.

undercharge *verb* to charge too low a price.

underclass *noun* a subordinate social class; the lowest social group in a community, consisting of its least privileged members (e.g. the poor and the unemployed).

undercliff *noun* a terrace or lower cliff formed by a landslide.

underclothes *plural noun* underwear.

underclothing *noun* underclothes.

undercoat *noun* **1** a layer of paint under a finishing coat; the paint used for this. **2** (in animals) a coat of hair under another.

undercover *adjective* **1** doing things secretly, done secretly. **2** engaged in spying by working among those to be spied on, *undercover agents*.

undercroft *noun* a crypt.

undercurrent *noun* **1** a current that is below a surface or below another current. **2** an underlying feeling, influence, or trend.

undercut *verb* (undercut, undercutting) **1** to cut away the part below. **2** to sell or work for a lower price than (another person). –**undercut** *noun* **1** the underside of sirloin. **2** a hairstyle in which the hair on the lower part of the head is cut very short, while the rest is left long.

underdeveloped *adjective* not fully developed; (of a film) not developed enough to give a satisfactory image; (of a country) not having reached its potential level in economic development.

underdog *noun* a person or country etc. in an inferior or subordinate position.

underdone *adjective* not thoroughly done; (of meat) not completely cooked throughout.

underemployed *adjective* not fully employed.

underestimate *verb* to make too low an estimate of. –**underestimate** *noun* an estimate that is too low. **underestimation** *noun*

underexpose *verb* to expose for too short a time. **underexposure** *noun*

underfed *adjective* not sufficiently fed.

underfelt *noun* felt for laying under a carpet.

underfloor *adjective* situated beneath the floor.

underfoot *adverb* on the ground, under one's feet.

undergarment *noun* a piece of underwear.

undergo *verb* (underwent, undergone, undergoing) to experience, to endure, to be subjected to, *the new aircraft underwent intensive trials*.

undergraduate *noun* a member of a university who has not yet taken a degree.

underground (un-der-**grownd**) *adverb* **1** under the surface of the ground. **2** in secret; into secrecy or hiding. –**underground** (**un**-der-grownd) *adjective* **1** under the surface of the ground. **2** secret, of a secret political organisation or one for resisting enemy forces controlling a country. –**underground** (**un**-der-grownd) *noun* **1** an underground railway. **2** an underground organisation. –**underground** (**un**-der-grownd) *verb* to lay (cables etc.) underground.

undergrowth *noun* shrubs and bushes etc. growing closely, especially when beneath trees.

underhand (**un**-der-hand) *adjective* **1** done or doing things in a sly or secret way. **2** (in cricket etc.) underarm. –**underhand** (un-der-**hand**) *adverb* in an underhand manner. **underhanded** *adjective*

underlay[1] (un-der-**lay**) *verb* (underlaid, underlaying) to lay something under (a thing) as a support or in order to raise it. –**underlay** (**un**-der-lay) *noun* a layer of material (e.g. felt, rubber, etc.) laid under another as a protection or support.

underlay[2] (un-der-**lay**) *past* of underlie.

underlie *verb* (underlay, underlain, underlying) **1** to lie or exist beneath. **2** to be the basis of (a theory etc.), to be the facts that account for, *the underlying reasons for her behaviour*.

underline *verb* **1** to draw a line under. **2** to emphasise.

underling *noun* a subordinate.

undermentioned *adjective* mentioned below.

undermine *verb* **1** to make a mine or tunnel beneath, especially one causing weakness at the base. **2** to weaken gradually, *his health or confidence was undermined*.

undermost *adjective* & *adverb* furthest underneath.

underneath *preposition* beneath, below; on the inside of (a thing). –**underneath** *adverb* at, in, or to a position underneath something.

underpaid *adjective* paid too little.

underpants *plural noun* an undergarment covering the lower part of the body from the waist or hips to the top of the thighs, and having separate leg-holes.

underpart *noun* the part underneath.

underpass *noun* a road that passes under another; a crossing of this kind.

underpay *verb* (**underpaid**, **underpaying**) to pay too little to (a person) or in discharge of (a debt).

underpin *verb* (**underpinned**, **underpinning**) to support, to strengthen from beneath.

underprivileged *adjective* less privileged than others, not enjoying the normal standard of living or rights in a community.

underrate *verb* to have too low an opinion of.

underscore *verb* to underline.

undersea *adjective* below the surface of the sea.

undersell *verb* (**undersold**, **underselling**) to sell at a lower price than (another person).

undershoot *verb* (**undershot**, **undershooting**) (of an aircraft) to land short of, *the plane undershot the runway*.

undershot *adjective* (of a waterwheel) turned by water flowing under it.

underside *noun* the side or surface underneath.

undersigned *adjective* who has or have signed at the bottom of this document, *we, the undersigned*.

undersized *adjective* of less than the usual size.

underskirt *noun* a skirt for wearing beneath another, a petticoat.

underslung *adjective* **1** supported from above. **2** (of a vehicle chassis) hanging lower than the axles.

underspend *verb* (**underspent**, **underspending**) to spend too little.

understaffed *adjective* having less than the necessary number of staff.

understand *verb* (**understood**, **understanding**) **1** to perceive the meaning, importance, or nature of; *we understand each other*, we know each other's views or are in agreement. **2** to know the ways or workings of, to know how to deal with, *he understands machinery*. **3** to know the explanation and not be offended, *we shall understand if you can't come*. **4** to become aware from information received, to draw as a conclusion, *I understand she is in Melbourne*. **5** to take for granted, *your expenses will be paid, that's understood*. **6** to supply (a word or words) mentally, *before 'coming?' the words 'are you' are understood*.

understandable *adjective* able to be understood. **understandably** *adverb*

understanding *adjective* having or showing insight or good judgment, or sympathy towards others' feelings and points of view. –**understanding** *noun* **1** the power of thought, intelligence. **2** ability to understand. **3** ability to show insight or feel sympathy; kindly tolerance. **4** harmony in opinion or feeling, *a better understanding between nations*. **5** an informal or preliminary agreement, *reached an understanding*.

understate *verb* to state (a thing) in very restrained terms; to represent as being less than it really is. **understatement** *noun*

understudy *noun* a person who studies the part in a play or the duties etc. of another in order to be able to take his or her place at short notice if necessary. –**understudy** *verb* (**understudied**, **understudying**) to act as understudy to; to learn (a part etc.) as understudy.

undertake *verb* (**undertook**, **undertaken**, **undertaking**) **1** to agree or promise to do something, to make oneself responsible for, *undertook the cooking* or *to do the cooking*. **2** to guarantee, *we cannot undertake that you will make a profit*.

undertaker *verb* one whose business is to prepare the dead for burial or cremation and make arrangements for funerals.

undertaking *noun* **1** work etc. undertaken. **2** a promise or guarantee. **3** the business of an undertaker.

undertone *noun* **1** a low or subdued tone; *they spoke in undertones*, spoke quietly. **2** a colour that modifies another, *pink with mauve undertones*. **3** an underlying quality or implication, an undercurrent of feeling, *a threatening undertone*.

undertow (**un**-der-toh) *noun* a current below the surface of the sea, moving in an opposite direction to the surface current.

undervalue *verb* to put too low a value on.

underwater *adjective* situated, used, or done beneath the surface of water. –**underwater** *adverb* beneath the surface of water.

underwear *noun* garments worn under others, next to the skin.

underweight *adjective* weighing less than is normal or required or permissible.

underwent *see* **undergo**.

underworld *noun* **1** (also **Underworld**, in mythology) the abode of spirits of the dead, under the earth. **2** the part of society habitually engaged in crime.

underwrite *verb* (**underwrote, underwritten, underwriting**) **1** to sign and accept liability under (an insurance policy, especially for ships), thus guaranteeing payment in the event of loss or damage. **2** to undertake to finance (an enterprise). **3** to undertake to buy all the stock in (a company etc.) that is not bought by the public. **underwriter** *noun*

undeserved *adjective* not deserved as reward or punishment. **undeservedly** (un-dĕ-**zerv**-ĕd-lee) *adverb*

undesirable *adjective* not desirable, objectionable. **–undesirable** *noun* a person who is undesirable to a community. **undesirably** *adverb*, **undesirability** *noun*

undetermined *adjective* **1** not yet decided. **2** undiscovered.

undeveloped *adjective* not developed.

undies *plural noun* (*informal*) underwear.

undo *verb* (**undid, undone, undoing**) **1** to unfasten; to untie; to unwrap. **2** to annul, to cancel the effect of, *cannot undo the past*.

undoing *noun* bringing or being brought to ruin; a cause of this, *drink was his undoing*.

undone *adjective* **1** unfastened. **2** not done, *left the work undone*. **3** (*old use*) brought to ruin or destruction, *we are undone!*

undoubted *adjective* not regarded as doubtful, not disputed. **undoubtedly** *adverb*

undreamed-of *adjective* (also **undreamt-of**) not imagined, not thought to be possible.

undress *verb* to take off one's clothes or the clothes of (another person). **–undress** *noun* **1** the state of being not clothed or not fully clothed. **2** clothes or a uniform for nonceremonial occasions.

undue *adjective* excessive, disproportionate.

undulate (**un**-dew-layt) *verb* to have or cause to have a wavy movement or appearance. **undulation** *noun*, **undulatory** *adjective* [from Latin *unda* = a wave]

unduly *adjective* excessively, disproportionately.

undying *adjective* everlasting, never-ending, *undying love*.

unearned *adjective* not earned. □ **unearned income** income from interest on investments and similar sources, not wages or salary or fees.

unearth *verb* **1** to uncover or obtain from the ground by digging. **2** to bring to light, to find by searching.

unearthly *adjective* **1** not earthly. **2** supernatural, mysterious and frightening. **3** (*informal*) absurdly early or inconvenient, *getting up at this unearthly hour*. **unearthliness** *noun*

uneasy *adjective* **1** not comfortable, *passed an uneasy night*. **2** not confident, worried. **3** worrying, *they had an uneasy suspicion that all was not well*. **uneasily** *adverb*, **uneasiness** *noun*

uneatable *adjective* not fit to be eaten (because of its condition).

uneconomic *adjective* not profitable; not likely to be profitable.

uneducated *adjective* not educated; ignorant.

unemployable *adjective* unfitted for paid employment, e.g. because of character or lack of abilities.

unemployed *adjective* out of work.

unemployment *noun* **1** the condition of being unemployed. **2** the lack of employment or the extent of this in a country, region, etc. □ **unemployment benefit** a regular government payment made to an unemployed person.

unencumbered *adjective* not encumbered with a burden etc.; (of an estate) having no liabilities on it.

unending *adjective* endless.

unequal *adjective* **1** not equal. **2** (of work or achievements etc.) not of the same quality throughout. **3** not with equal advantage to both sides, not well matched, *unequal bargain* or *contest*. □ **be unequal to** (of a person) to be not strong enough or not clever enough etc. for, *he was unequal to the task*. **unequally** *adverb*

unequalled *adjective* without an equal.

unequivocal (un-ĕ-**kwiv**-ŏ-kăl) *adjective* clear and unmistakable, not ambiguous. **unequivocally** *adverb*

unerring *adjective* making no mistake, *with unerring accuracy*. **unerringly** *adverb*

UNESCO (yoo-**ness**-koh) *abbreviation* (also **Unesco**) United Nations Educational, Scientific, and Cultural Organization.

unethical *adjective* not ethical, unscrupulous in business or professional conduct. **unethically** *adverb*

uneven *adjective* **1** not level or smooth. **2** varying, not uniform. **3** unequal, *an uneven contest*. **unevenly** *adverb*, **unevenness** *noun*

unexampled *adjective* having no precedent or nothing else that can be compared with it, *an unexampled opportunity*.

unexceptionable *adjective* with which no fault can be found. **unexceptionably** *adverb*

unexceptional *adjective* not exceptional, quite ordinary.

unexpected *adjective* not expected. **unexpectedly** *adverb*

unfailing *adjective* never-ending, constant, reliable, *his unfailing good humour*.

unfair *adjective* not impartial, not in accordance with justice. **unfairly** *adverb*, **unfairness** *noun*

unfaithful *adjective* **1** not loyal; not keeping to one's promise. **2** having committed adultery. **unfaithfully** *adverb*, **unfaithfulness** *noun*

unfasten *verb* to make loose, to open the fastening(s) of.

unfeeling *adjective* **1** lacking the power of sensation or sensitivity. **2** unsympathetic, not caring about others' feelings. **unfeelingly** *adverb*, **unfeelingness** *noun*

unfit *adjective* **1** unsuitable. **2** not in perfect health or physical condition. **–unfit** *verb* (**unfitted**, **unfitting**) to make unsuitable.

unflappable *adjective* (*informal*) remaining calm in a crisis, not getting into a flap.

unfold *verb* **1** to open, to spread (a thing) or become spread out. **2** to become visible or known, *as the story unfolds*.

unforeseen *adjective* not foreseen.

unforgettable *adjective* not able to be forgotten.

unformed *adjective* not formed; shapeless.

unfortunate *adjective* **1** having bad luck. **2** unsuitable, regrettable, *a most unfortunate choice of words*. **–unfortunate** *noun* an unfortunate person. **unfortunately** *adverb*

unfounded *adjective* with no foundation of fact(s).

unfreeze *verb* (**unfroze**, **unfrozen**, **unfreezing**) to thaw, to cause to thaw.

unfriend = **defriend**.

unfrock *verb* to dismiss (a priest) from office.

unfurl *verb* to unroll, to spread out.

unfurnished *adverb* without furniture. **unfurnished with** not supplied with.

ungainly *adjective* awkward-looking, clumsy, ungraceful. **ungainliness** *noun* [from *un-*, + *gainly* = graceful]

unget-at-able *adjective* (*informal*) difficult or impossible to reach, inaccessible.

ungodly *adjective* **1** not giving reverence to God, not religious, wicked. **2** (*informal*) outrageous, very inconvenient, *phoning at this ungodly hour*. **ungodliness** *noun*

ungovernable *adjective* uncontrollable, *an ungovernable temper*.

ungracious *adjective* not kindly or courteous. **ungraciously** *adverb*

ungrateful *adjective* feeling no gratitude. **ungratefully** *adverb*

unguarded *adjective* **1** not guarded. **2** thoughtless, incautious, *in an unguarded moment*.

unguent (**ung**-gwĕnt) *noun* an ointment or lubricant. [from Latin *unguere* = to oil or anoint]

ungulate (**ung**-gew-lăt) *adjective* having hooves. **–ungulate** *noun* a hoofed mammal.

unhallowed *adjective* **1** not consecrated. **2** wicked.

unhand *verb* (*literary*) to take one's hands off (a person), to let go of.

unhappy *adjective* (**unhappier**, **unhappiest**) **1** not happy, sad. **2** unfortunate. **3** unsuitable. **unhappily** *adverb*, **unhappiness** *noun*

UNHCR *abbreviation* United Nations High Commissioner for Refugees.

unhealthy *adjective* (**unhealthier**, **unhealthiest**) **1** not having or not showing good health. **2** harmful to health. **3** (*informal*) unwise, dangerous. **unhealthily** *adverb*, **unhealthiness** *noun*

unheard *adjective* not heard. □ **unheard-of** *adjective* not previously known of or done.

unhinge *verb* to cause to become mentally unbalanced, *the shock unhinged his mind*.

unhitch *verb* to release from being hitched or fastened.

unholy *adjective* (**unholier**, **unholiest**) **1** wicked; irreverent. **2** (*informal*) very great, outrageous, *making an unholy row*. **unholiness** *noun*

unhook *verb* **1** to detach from a hook or hooks. **2** to unfasten by releasing the hook(s).

unhoped-for *adjective* not hoped for or expected.

unhorse *verb* to throw or drag (a rider) from a horse.

uni *noun* (*Austral. informal*) a university.

uni- *prefix* one; single (as in *unicorn*). [from Latin *unus* = one]

Uniat *adjective* (also **Uniate**) of the Churches in eastern Europe and the Middle East that acknowledge the Pope's supremacy but retain their own liturgy etc. –**Uniat** *noun* a member of such a Church.

unicameral (yoo-nee-**kam**-ĕ-răl) *adjective* having only one legislative chamber. [from *uni-*, + Latin *camera* = chamber]

UNICEF (**yoo**-nĭ-sef) *abbreviation* United Nations (International) Children's (Emergency) Fund, established to help governments to meet the long-term needs of the welfare of mothers and children.

unicellular (yoo-nee-**sel**-yŭ-ler) *adjective* (of an organism) consisting of one cell.

unicorn *noun* a mythical animal resembling a horse with a single horn projecting from its forehead. [from *uni-*, + Latin *cornu* = horn]

unicycle *noun* a single-wheeled cycle, used especially by acrobats. **unicyclist** *noun*

unidentified *adjective* not identified.

unification *noun* unifying; being unified.

Unification Church a religious and political organisation founded by Sun Myung Moon in Korea in 1954.

unifier *noun* a person or thing that unifies.

uniform *noun* distinctive clothing intended to identify the wearer as a member of a certain organisation or group. –**uniform** *adjective* always the same, not varying, *planks of uniform thickness*. **uniformly** *adverb*, **uniformity** *noun* [from *uni-* + *form*]

uniformed *adjective* wearing a uniform.

unify *verb* (**unified**, **unifying**) to form into a single unit, to unite.

unilateral (yoo-nĭ-**lat**-ĕ-răl) *adjective* one-sided, done by or affecting one person or group or country etc. and not another. **unilaterally** *adverb*, **unilateralism** *noun* [from *uni-* + *lateral*]

unimpeachable *adjective* completely trustworthy, not open to doubt or question, *unimpeachable honesty*. **unimpeachably** *adverb*

unimproved *adjective* **1** not made better; not made use of. **2** (of land) not used for agriculture or building; not developed.

□ **unimproved value** or **capital value** (of land) the value placed on a residential block etc., excluding any improvements, buildings, etc.

uninformed *adjective* not informed, ignorant.

uninspired *adjective* not inspired; commonplace, not outstanding.

unintelligible *adjective* not intelligible, impossible to understand. **unintelligibly** *adverb*

uninterested *adjective* not interested; showing or feeling no concern.

uninviting *adjective* not inviting, not attractive.

union *noun* **1** uniting; being united. **2** a whole formed by uniting parts; an association formed by the uniting of people or groups. **3** a trade union. **4** a coupling for pipes or rods. **5** a fabric with mixed materials, e.g. cotton with linen or jute. **6** (in mathematics) the combination of two or more sets, with repeated elements counted once only. □ **Union Jack** the national flag of the United Kingdom. [from Latin *unio* = unity]

unionise *verb* (also **-ize**) to organise into or cause to join a trade union. **unionisation** *noun*

unionist *noun* **1** a member of a trade union; a supporter of trade unions. **2** (in specific uses **Unionist**) one who favours union or the maintenance of union, e.g. between Great Britain and Northern Ireland. **unionism** *noun*

Union of Soviet Socialist Republics (also **Soviet Union**) a former country extending from eastern Europe to the Pacific, consisting of 15 republics. Formed after the Russian Revolution in 1917, it broke up in 1991.

unique (yoo-**neek**) *adjective* **1** being the only one of its kind, *this vase is unique*. **2** unusual, remarkable, *this makes it even more unique*. **uniquely** *adverb* [from Latin *unus* = one]

Usage Many people regard the use in sense 2 as illogical and incorrect.

unisex (**yoo**-nee-seks) *adjective* (of clothes etc.) designed for people of either sex.

unison *noun* **in unison** sounding or singing together at the same pitch or a corresponding one; in agreement or concord, *all the firms acted in unison*. [from *uni-*, + Latin *sonus* = sound]

unit *noun* 1 an individual thing or person or group regarded for purposes of calculation etc. as single and complete, or as part of a complex whole, *the family as the unit of society*. 2 a quantity chosen as a standard in terms of which other quantities may be expressed, or for which a stated charge is made. 3 a part or group with a specified function within a complex machine or organisation. 4 a piece of furniture for fitting with others like it or made of complementary parts. 5 (also **home unit**) (*Austral*.) a private residence which is one of several in a building. □ **unit matrix** a matrix with 1's in the diagonal from top left to bottom right and 0's in all other positions. **unit pricing** pricing of articles according to a standard unit (e.g. per kilogram or litre). **unit trust** an investment company investing contributions from a number of people in various securities and paying them a dividend in proportion to their holdings. [from Latin *unus* = one]

Unitarian (yoo-nĭ-**tair**-ree-ăn) *noun* a member of a Christian religious body maintaining that God is one person, not a Trinity.

unitary *adjective* of a unit or units.

unite *verb* 1 to join together, to make or become one. 2 to agree or combine or cooperate, *they all united in condemning the action*.

United Arab Emirates a State formed from sheikhdoms lying along the Persian Gulf.

United Kingdom Great Britain and Northern Ireland.

United Nations an organisation of about 190 countries set up in 1945 to promote international peace, security, and cooperation.

United States (of America) a country occupying most of the southern half of North America.

Uniting Church (in full **Uniting Church in Australia**) an Australian Protestant denomination formed in 1977 by the union of the Methodist and Congregational Churches and the majority of the Presbyterian Church.

unity *noun* 1 the state of being one or a unit. 2 a thing forming a complex whole. 3 the number one in mathematics. 4 harmony, agreement in feelings, ideas, or aims etc., *live together in unity*.

univalent (yoo-nee-**vay**-lĕnt) *adjective* having a valence of one. [from *uni-* + *valence*]

univalve (**yoo**-nee-valv) *noun* a shellfish with a shell consisting of only one part (valve).

universal *adjective* of or for or done by all. □ **universal coupling** or **joint** one that connects two shafts in such a way that they can be at any angle to each other. **universal set** (in mathematics) the set containing all the elements under consideration. **universal time** that used for astronomical reckoning at all places. **universally** *adverb*

universe *noun* all existing things, including the earth and its creatures and all the heavenly bodies. [from Latin *universus* = combined into one]

university *noun* an educational institution that provides instruction and facilities for research in many branches of advanced learning and awards degrees. [same origin as *universe*]

unjust *adjective* not just or fair. **unjustly** *adverb*

unkempt *adjective* looking untidy or neglected. [from *un-*, + an old word *kempt* = combed]

unkind *adjective* not kind, harsh. **unkindly** *adverb*, **unkindness** *noun*

unknown *adjective* not known, not identified. – **unknown** *noun* an unknown person or thing. □ **unknown quantity** a person or thing whose nature or significance etc. is unknown. **unknown to** without the knowledge of.

unladen *adjective* not laden.

unleaded *adjective* (of petrol) without added lead.

unlearn *verb* to cause (a thing) to be no longer in one's knowledge or memory.

unleash *verb* 1 to set free from a leash or restraint. 2 to set (a thing) free so that it can attack or pursue something.

unleavened (un-**lev**-ĕnd) *adjective* not leavened; (of bread) made without yeast or other raising agent.

unless *conjunction* if … not, except when, *we shall not move unless we are obliged to*.

unlettered *adjective* illiterate.

unlike *adjective* 1 not like, different from. 2 not characteristic of, *such behaviour is quite unlike him*. – **unlike** *preposition* differently from, *unlike her mother, she enjoys riding*.

unlikely *adjective* 1 not likely to happen or be true, *an unlikely tale*. 2 not likely to be successful, *the most unlikely candidate*.

unlimited *adjective* not limited; very great in number or quantity.

unlined *adjective* **1** without a lining. **2** not marked with lines.

unlisted *adjective* not included in a list; not in a published list of telephone numbers or Stock Exchange prices.

unload *verb* **1** to remove (a load) from (a ship etc.); to remove cargo. **2** to get rid of. **3** to remove the charge from (a gun etc.).

unlock *verb* **1** to release the lock of (a door etc.). **2** to release by or as if by unlocking.

unlooked-for *adjective* unexpected.

unloose *verb* (also **unloosen**) to loose.

unlucky *adjective* not lucky, wretched, having or bringing bad luck. **unluckily** *adverb*

unmade *adjective* not made; (of a bed) not yet arranged ready for use.

unman *verb* (**unmanned**, **unmanning**) to weaken the self-control or courage of (a man).

unmanageable *adjective* not easy to manage or control. **unmanageably** *adverb*

unmanned *adjective* operated without a crew.

unmannerly *adjective* not well-mannered.

unmarked *adjective* **1** not marked; with no mark of identification. **2** not noticed.

unmarried *adjective* not married.

unmask *verb* **1** to remove the mask from; to remove one's mask. **2** to expose the true character of.

unmentionable *adjective* so bad, embarrassing, or shocking that it may not be spoken of. **unmentionables** *plural noun* unmentionable things or people.

unmistakable *adjective* clear and obvious, not able to be mistaken for another. **unmistakably** *adverb*

unmitigated (un-**mit**-ĭ-gayt-ĕd) *adjective* not modified, absolute, *an unmitigated success.*

unmoved *adjective* not moved; not changed in one's purpose; not affected by emotion.

unnatural *adjective* **1** not natural or normal. **2** lacking natural feelings of affection. **3** artificial. **unnaturally** *adverb*

unnecessary *adjective* **1** not necessary. **2** more than is necessary, *with unnecessary care.* **unnecessarily** *adverb*

unnerve *verb* to cause to lose courage or determination.

unnumbered *adjective* **1** not marked with a number. **2** countless.

unobtrusive (un-ŏb-**troo**-siv) *adjective* not obtrusive, not making oneself or itself noticed. **unobtrusively** *adverb*

unoffending *adjective* not offending, harmless, innocent.

unofficial *adjective* not official; *unofficial strike*, one not formally approved by the strikers' trade union. **unofficially** *adverb*

unpack *verb* to open and remove the contents of (luggage etc.); to take out from its packaging or from a suitcase etc.

unpaid *adjective* **1** (of a debt) not yet paid. **2** not receiving payment for work etc.

unparalleled *adjective* not paralleled, never yet equalled, *unparalleled enthusiasm.*

unparliamentary *adjective* contrary to parliamentary custom. □ **unparliamentary language** oaths or abuse.

unperson *noun* a person whose name or existence is ignored or denied.

unpick *verb* to undo the stitching of.

unplaced *adjective* not placed as one of the first three in a race etc.

unplayable *adjective* (of a ball in games) unable to be played or returned etc.

unpleasant *adjective* not pleasant; disagreeable. **unpleasantly** *adverb*, **unpleasantness** *noun*

unplug *verb* (**unplugged**, **unplugging**) **1** to disconnect (an electrical device) by removing its plug from the socket. **2** to unstop.

unplumbed *adjective* **1** not plumbed. **2** not fully investigated or understood.

unpopular *adjective* not popular, not liked or enjoyed by people in general. **unpopularly** *adverb*, **unpopularity** *noun*

unpowered *adjective* not driven by an engine.

unprecedented (un-**press**-ĕ-dent-ĕd *or* un-**pree**-sĕ-dent-ĕd) *adjective* for which there is no precedent, unparalleled.

unpremeditated (un-pree-**med**-ĭ-tayt-ĕd) *adjective* not planned beforehand.

unprepared *adjective* not prepared beforehand; not ready or equipped to do something.

unprepossessing (un-pree-pŏ-**zess**-ing) *adjective* unattractive, not making a good impression.

unpretentious (un-prĕ-**ten**-shŭs) *adjective* not pretentious, not showy or pompous.

unprincipled *adjective* without good moral principles, unscrupulous.

unprintable *adjective* too rude or indecent to be printed.

unprofessional *adjective* 1 not belonging to a profession. 2 contrary to professional standards of behaviour. **unprofessionally** *adverb*

unprofitable *adjective* 1 not producing a profit. 2 serving no useful purpose.

unprompted *adjective* not prompted, spontaneous.

unqualified *adjective* 1 (of a person) not legally or officially qualified to do something. 2 not restricted or modified, *gave it our unqualified approval.*

unquestionable *adjective* not questionable, too clear to be doubted. **unquestionably** *adverb*

unquestioned *adverb* not disputed or doubted.

unquote *verb* (in dictation etc.) end the quotation, close the inverted commas, *Churchill said (quote) 'We shall never surrender' (unquote).*

unravel *verb* (**unravelled, unravelling**) 1 to disentangle. 2 to undo (knitted fabrics). 3 to probe and solve (a mystery etc.). 4 to become unravelled.

unreadable *adjective* not readable.

unreal *adjective* not real, existing in the imagination only. **unreality** (un-ree-**al**-ĭ-tee) *noun*

unreason *noun* lack of reasonable thought or action.

unreasonable *adjective* 1 not reasonable in one's attitude etc. 2 excessive, going beyond the limits of what is reasonable or just. **unreasonably** *adverb*

unrelenting *adjective* not becoming less in intensity or severity.

unrelieved *adjective* not relieved, without anything to give variation, *unrelieved gloom*; *a plain black dress unrelieved by any touches of colour.*

unremitting (un-rĕ-**mit**-ing) *adjective* not relaxing or ceasing, persistent.

unrepeatable *adjective* 1 that cannot be done or offered etc. again, *unrepeatable bargains.* 2 too indecent to be said again.

unrequited (un-rĕ-**kwy**-tĕd) *adjective* (of love) not returned or rewarded. [from *un-* + *requited* = paid back]

unreserved *adjective* 1 not reserved. 2 without reservation or restriction, complete. **unreservedly** (un-rĕ-**zerv**-ĕd-lee) *adverb*

unrest *noun* restlessness, agitation.

unrighteous *adjective* not righteous, wicked.

unripe *adjective* not yet ripe.

unrivalled (un-**ry**-văld) *adjective* having no equal, incomparable.

unroll *verb* to open or become opened after being rolled.

unruly (un-**roo**-lee) *adjective* not easy to control or discipline, disorderly. **unruliness** *noun* [from *un-* + *rule*]

unsaddle *verb* 1 to remove the saddle from (a horse). 2 to unseat (a rider).

unsaid (un-**sed**) *see* unsay. –unsaid *adjective* not spoken or expressed, *many things were left unsaid.*

unsaturated *adjective* (of a substance) able to combine chemically with hydrogen to form a third substance by the joining of molecules.

unsavoury *adjective* 1 disagreeable to the taste or smell. 2 morally unpleasant or disgusting, *an unsavoury reputation.*

unsay *verb* (**unsaid, unsaying**) to take back or retract, *what's said can't be unsaid.*

unscathed (un-**skaythd**) *adjective* without suffering any injury. [from *un-*, + an old word *scathed* = harmed]

unscientific *adjective* not in accordance with scientific principles. **unscientifically** *adverb*

unscramble *verb* to sort out from a scrambled state; to make (a scrambled transmission) intelligible.

unscrew *verb* to loosen (a screw or nut etc.) by turning it; to unfasten by turning or removing screws, or by twisting.

unscripted *adjective* without a prepared script.

unscrupulous (un-**skroo**-pew-lŭs) *adjective* without moral scruples, not prevented from doing wrong by scruples of conscience. **unscrupulously** *adverb*, **unscrupulousness** *noun*

unseal *verb* to open (a sealed letter or receptacle etc.).

unseasonable *adjective* 1 not seasonable. 2 untimely. **unseasonably** *adverb*

unseat *verb* 1 to dislodge (a rider) from horseback or from a bicycle etc. 2 to remove from a parliamentary seat, *was unseated at the last election.*

unseeded *adjective* (of a tennis player etc.) not seeded (*see* seed *verb* sense 4).

unseeing *adjective* not seeing anything.

unseemly *adjective* not seemly, improper. unseemliness *noun*

unseen *adjective* 1 not seen, invisible. 2 (of translation) done without previous preparation. –unseen *noun* a passage in a foreign language for unseen translation.

unselfconscious *adjective* not self-conscious.

unselfish *adjective* not selfish, considering the needs of others before one's own. unselfishly *adverb*, unselfishness *noun*

unsettle *verb* to make uneasy, to disturb the settled calm or stability of.

unsettled *adjective* not settled, liable to change.

unshakeable *adjective* not able to be shaken, firm.

unsheathe *verb* to remove (a knife etc.) from a sheath.

unshockable *adjective* not able to be shocked.

unshrinkable *adjective* not liable to become shrunk.

unsightly *adjective* not pleasant to look at, ugly. unsightliness *noun*

unskilled *adjective* not having or needing skill or special training.

unsociable *adjective* not sociable, withdrawing oneself from others. unsociably *adverb*

unsocial *adjective* 1 not suitable for society. 2 not conforming to standard social practices; *unsocial hours*, hours of work that involve working when most people are free. 3 antisocial. unsocially *adverb*

unsolicited (un-sŏ-**liss**-ĭ-tĕd) *adjective* not asked for, given or done voluntarily.

unsophisticated *adjective* not sophisticated, simple and natural or naive.

unsound *adjective* not sound or strong; not free from defects or mistakes. ☐ **of unsound mind** insane. [from *un-* + *sound²*]

unsparing (un-**spair**-ring) *adjective* giving freely and lavishly, *unsparing in one's efforts*.

unspeakable *adjective* too great or too bad to be described in words, very objectionable.

unstable *adjective* 1 not stable, tending to change suddenly. 2 mentally or emotionally unbalanced. unstably *adverb*

unsteady *adjective* not steady. unsteadily *adverb*, unsteadiness *noun*

unstick *verb* (unstuck, unsticking) to separate (a thing stuck to another).

unstinted *adjective* given freely and lavishly.

unstitch *verb* to undo the stitches of (something sewn).

unstop *verb* (unstopped, unstopping) *verb* 1 to free from an obstruction. 2 to remove the stopper from.

unstoppable *adjective* unable to be stopped or prevented.

unstressed *adjective* not pronounced with a stress.

unstructured *adjective* without a formal structure.

unstuck *adjective* detached after being stuck on or together. ☐ **come unstuck** (*informal*) to suffer disaster, to fail.

unstudied *adjective* natural in manner, not affected, *with unstudied elegance*.

unsubstantial *adjective* not substantial, flimsy; having little or no factual basis.

unsuitable *adjective* not suitable. unsuitably *adverb*

unsuited *adjective* 1 not fit (for a purpose). 2 not adapted (to a specified thing).

unsullied (un-**sul**-eed) *adjective* not sullied, pure.

unsuspecting *adjective* feeling no suspicion.

unswerving *adjective* not turning aside, unchanging, *unswerving loyalty*.

untangle *verb* to free from a tangle, to disentangle.

untapped *adjective* not tapped, not yet made use of, *the country's untapped resources*.

untaught *adjective* 1 not instructed by teaching. 2 not acquired by teaching.

untenable (un-**ten**-ă-bŭl) *adjective* (of a theory) not tenable, not able to be held, because strong arguments can be produced against it.

unthinkable *adjective* incredible, too unlikely or undesirable to be considered.

unthinking *adjective* thoughtless, done or said etc. without consideration. unthinkingly *adverb*

untidy *adjective* (**untidier**, **untidiest**) not tidy. **untidily** *adverb*, **untidiness** *noun*

untie *verb* (**untied**, **untying**) to unfasten; to release from being tied up.

until *preposition* & *conjunction* up to (a specified time or event), *until last year we had never been abroad*; *leave it until his return*.

Usage *Until* is used in preference to *till* when it stands first or in formal contexts.

untimely *adjective* **1** happening at an unsuitable time. **2** happening too soon or sooner than is normal, *his untimely death*. **untimeliness** *noun*

unto *preposition* (*old use*) to.

untold *adjective* **1** not told. **2** not counted; too much or too many to be counted, *untold hardship*.

untouchable *adjective* not able to be touched, not allowed to be touched. **–untouchable** *noun* a member of the lowest Hindu group (non-caste) in India, held to defile members of a higher caste on contact.

Usage Use of the term, and the social restrictions that accompany it, were declared illegal in India in 1949 and in Pakistan in 1953.

untoward (un-tŏ-**wor**'d) *adjective* inconvenient, awkward, *if nothing untoward happens*.

untraceable *adjective* unable to be traced.

untrammelled *adjective* not hampered.

untried *adjective* not yet tried or tested.

untrue *adjective* **1** not true, contrary to facts. **2** not faithful or loyal. **untruly** *adverb*

untruth *noun* **1** an untrue statement, a lie. **2** lack of truth. **untruthful** *adjective*, **untruthfully** *adverb*

unused *adjective* not yet used.

unusual *adjective* not usual, exceptional, remarkable. **unusually** *adverb*

unutterable *adjective* too great or too intense to be expressed in words, *unutterable joy*. **unutterably** *adverb*

unvarnished *adjective* **1** not varnished. **2** (of a statement etc.) plain and straightforward, *the unvarnished truth*.

unveil *verb* **1** to remove a veil from; to remove one's veil. **2** to remove concealing drapery from, as part of a ceremony, *unveiled*

the portrait. **3** to disclose, to make publicly known.

unversed *adjective* not experienced in something, *he was unversed in wedding etiquette*.

unvoiced *adjective* not spoken; not voiced.

unwaged *adjective* not in paid employment.

unwanted *adjective* not wanted.

unwarrantable *adjective* unjustifiable. **unwarrantably** *adverb*

unwarranted *adjective* unauthorised; unjustified.

unwary (un-**wair**-ree) *adjective* not cautious. **unwarily** *adverb*, **unwariness** *noun*

unwearying *adjective* not tiring; persistent.

unwell *adjective* not in good health.

unwholesome *adjective* **1** harmful to health or to moral well-being. **2** unhealthy-looking. **unwholesomeness** *noun*

unwieldy (un-**weel**-dee) *adjective* awkward to move or control because of its size, shape, or weight. **unwieldiness** *noun*

unwilling *adjective* not willing, reluctant, hesitating to do something. **unwillingly** *adverb*

unwind *verb* (**unwound**, **unwinding**) **1** to draw out or become drawn out from being wound. **2** (*informal*) to relax after a period of work or tension.

unwisdom *noun* lack of wisdom.

unwise *adjective* not wise, foolish. **unwisely** *adverb*

unwitting *adjective* **1** unaware. **2** unintentional. **unwittingly** *adverb*

unwonted (un-**wohn**-těd) *adjective* not customary or usual, *spoke with unwonted rudeness*. **unwontedly** *adverb* [from *un-* + *wont*]

unworldly *adjective* not worldly, spiritually-minded. **unworldliness** *noun*

unworn *adjective* not yet worn.

unworthy *adjective* **1** not worthy, lacking worth or excellence. **2** not deserving, *he is unworthy of this honour*. **3** unsuitable to the character of a person or thing, *such conduct is unworthy of a king*. **unworthily** *adverb*, **unworthiness** *noun*

unwrap *verb* (**unwrapped**, **unwrapping**) to open or become opened from being wrapped.

unwritten *adjective* not written; *an unwritten law*, one that rests on custom or tradition, not on statute.

unyielding *adjective* firm, not yielding to pressure or influence.

unzip *verb* (**unzipped**, **unzipping**) to open or become opened by the undoing of a zip.

up *adverb* **1** to an erect or vertical position, *stand up*. **2** to, in, or at a higher place, level, value, or condition; to a larger size; further north; *they are two goals up*, are winning by this amount; *I am $5 up on the transaction*, have gained this amount. **3** so as to be inflated, *pump up the tyres*. **4** at or towards a central place, *went up to town*. **5** to the place, time, or amount etc. in question, *up till now*; *can take up to four passengers*. **6** out of bed; (of a stage curtain) raised at the start of a performance; (of a jockey) in the saddle. **7** into a condition of activity or efficiency or progress, *getting up steam*; *stirred up trouble*; *house is up for sale*. **8** (of a computer system) running and available for use. **9** apart, into pieces, *tore it up*; *the road is up*, with surface broken or removed during repairs. **10** into a compact state, securely, *pack it up*; *tie it up*. **11** to be finished, *your time is up*. **12** (*informal*) happening (especially of something unusual or undesirable), *something is up*. **–up** *preposition* **1** upwards along or through or into; from bottom to top of. **2** at a higher part of, *fix it further up the wall*. **–up** *adjective* directed upwards, *an up stroke*; *the up escalator*. **–up** *noun* a spell of good fortune, *life's ups and downs*. **–up** *verb* (**upped**, **upping**) (*informal*) **1** to begin to do something suddenly or unexpectedly, *he upped and demanded an inquiry*. **2** to raise, to pick up, *he upped with his fists*. **3** they promptly upped *the price*. □ **on the up-and-up** (*informal*) steadily improving. **up against** close to; in or into contact with; (*informal*) faced with, as an opponent or problem; *up against it*, in great difficulties. **up-and-coming** *adjective* (*informal*) enterprising and likely to be successful. **up and down** (*informal*) in varying health or spirits. **up beat** an unaccented beat in music, when the conductor's baton moves upwards. **up-country** *adverb* & *adjective* towards the interior of a country, inland. **up front** (*informal*) in front; in a prominent position; in advance, *paid her fees up front* (see also **upfront**). **up in** (*informal*) knowledgeable about. **up stage** at or towards the back of a theatre stage. **up to** occupied with, doing, *what is he up to?*; required as a duty or obligation from, *it's up to us to help her*; capable of, *don't feel up to a long walk*. **up to date** in current fashion; in accordance

with what is now known or required, *bring the files up to date*. **up-to-date** *adjective* in current fashion, in accordance with what is now known, *up-to-date clothes* or *information*.

Upanishad (oo-**pan**-ĭ-shad) *noun* each of a series of philosophical writings in prose and verse, based on the Vedas and forming the main part of Hindu scriptures.

upas (**yoo**-păs) *noun* (in full **upas tree**) a Javanese tree yielding a poisonous sap. [from Malay *upas* = poison]

upbeat *adjective* cheerful, encouraging.

upbraid *verb* to reproach.

upbringing *noun* training and education during childhood.

upcoming *adjective* about to happen, imminent, *the upcoming elections*.

update *verb* to bring up to date. **–update** *noun* updating; updated information.

up-end *verb* to set or rise up on end.

upfront *adverb see* **up front** (at entry for **up**). **–upfront** *adjective* (*informal*) **1** frank, open. **2** (of payments) made in advance.

upgrade *verb* **1** to raise to a higher grade or rank. **2** to improve (equipment etc.). **–upgrade** *noun* upgrading; an upgraded piece of equipment etc.

upheaval *noun* **1** a sudden heaving upwards. **2** a violent change or disturbance.

uphill *adverb* in an upward direction; further up a slope. **–uphill** *adjective* **1** going or sloping upwards. **2** difficult, *it was uphill work*.

uphold *verb* (**upheld**, **upholding**) **1** to support, to keep from falling. **2** to support a decision, statement, or belief.

upholster *verb* to put a fabric covering, padding, springs, etc. on (furniture). **upholsterer** *noun* [from *uphold* = maintain and repair]

upholstery *noun* **1** the work of upholstering furniture. **2** the material used for this.

upkeep *noun* keeping something in good condition and repair; the cost of this.

upland *noun* higher or inland parts of a country. **–upland** *adjective* of uplands.

uplift (up-**lift**) *verb* to raise. **–uplift** (**up**-lift) *noun* **1** being raised. **2** a mentally or morally elevating influence.

upmarket *adjective* & *adverb* of or towards the more expensive end of the market.

upon *preposition* on, *winter is almost upon us*; *Stratford-upon-Avon*. □ **once upon a time** *see* **once**.

upper *adjective* **1** higher in place or position. **2** situated on higher ground or to the north; *Upper Egypt*, the part furthest from the Nile delta. **3** ranking above others; *the upper class*, people of the highest social class. **4** (of a geological or archaeological period etc.) later in its occurrence. (¶ Called 'upper' because its rock formations or remains lie above those of the period called 'lower'.) **–upper** *noun* the part of a boot or shoe above the sole. □ **on one's uppers** (*informal*) very short of money. **upper case** capital letters for printing-type. **Upper Chamber** or **House** one of the houses in a two-house legislature, usually smaller and functioning as a 'house of review'; the Senate in the Australian Federal Parliament, and the Legislative Council in the States which have a two-house system. **upper crust** (*informal*) the aristocracy. **the upper hand** mastery, dominance, *gained the upper hand*.

uppercut *noun* a blow in boxing, delivered upwards with the arm bent.

uppermost *adjective* highest in place or rank. **–uppermost** *adverb* on or to the top or most prominent position.

uppish *adjective* pert, arrogant.

uppity *adjective* (*informal*) uppish.

upright *adjective* **1** in a vertical position. **2** (of a piano) with the strings mounted vertically. **3** strictly honest or honourable. **–upright** *noun* **1** a post or rod placed upright, especially as a support. **2** an upright piano. **uprightness** *noun*

uprising *noun* a rebellion, a revolt against the authorities.

uproar *noun* an outburst of noise and excitement or anger.

uproarious *adjective* very noisy; with loud laughter. **uproariously** *adverb*

uproot *verb* **1** to pull out of the ground together with its roots. **2** to force to leave a native or established place, *we don't want to uproot ourselves and go to live abroad*.

upset (up-**set**) *verb* (**upset, upsetting**) **1** to overturn; to become overturned. **2** to disrupt, *rain upset our plans*. **3** to distress the mind or feelings of; to disturb the temper or digestion of. **–upset** (**up**-set) *noun* upsetting, being upset, *a stomach upset*.

□ **upset the applecart** to spoil a situation or someone's plans.

upshot *noun* an outcome.

upside down *adverb* & *adjective* **1** with the upper part underneath instead of on top. **2** in great disorder.

upstage *adjective* & *adverb* **1** nearer the back of a theatre stage. **2** snobbish, snobbishly. **–upstage** *verb* **1** to move upstage to make (another actor) face away from the audience. **2** to divert attention from or outshine (a person).

upstairs *adverb* up the stairs, to or on an upper floor. **–upstairs** *adjective* situated upstairs.

upstanding *adjective* **1** standing up. **2** strong and healthy. **3** honest, law-abiding.

upstart *noun* a person who has risen suddenly to a high position, especially one who behaves arrogantly.

upstream *adjective* & *adverb* in the direction from which a stream flows.

upsurge *noun* an upward surge, a rise.

upswept *adjective* (of the hair) combed to the top of the head.

upswing *noun* an upward movement or trend.

uptake *noun* ability to understand what is meant, *quick on the uptake*.

uptight *adjective* (*informal*) **1** nervously tense. **2** annoyed.

upturn (up-**tern**) *verb* to turn upwards; to turn upside down; to turn up (ground, in ploughing etc.). **–upturn** (**up**-tern) *noun* **1** an upheaval. **2** an upward trend in business or fortune etc., an improvement.

upward *adjective* moving, leading, or pointing towards what is higher or more important or earlier. **–upward** *adverb* upwards. **upwards** *adverb* towards what is higher etc.

upwind *adjective* & *adverb* in the direction from which the wind is blowing.

Ur an ancient city in what is now southern Iraq.

Ural Mountains (**yoor**-răl) (also **Urals**) a mountain range forming a natural boundary between Europe and Asia.

Urania (yoo-**ray**-nee-ă) (*Gk*. & *Rom. myth*.) the Muse of astronomy.

uranium (yoo-**ray**-nee-ŭm) *noun* a chemical element (symbol U), a heavy grey metal used as a source of nuclear energy. [named after the planet Uranus]

Uranus (yoo-**ray**-nŭs *or* **yoo**-ră-nŭs) **1** (*Gk. myth.*) the most ancient of the gods, ruler of the universe, overthrown by his son Cronus. **2** a bluish-green gaseous planet in the outer solar system.

urban *adjective* of or situated in a city or town. □ **urban guerrilla** a terrorist operating in an urban area. [from Latin *urbis* = of a city]

urbane (er-**bayn**) *adjective* having manners that are smooth and polite. **urbanely** *adverb*, **urbanity** (er-**ban**-ĭ-tee) *noun* [same origin as *urban*]

urbanise *verb* (also **-ize**) to change (a place) into a townlike area. **urbanisation** *noun*

urchin *noun* **1** a mischievous or needy child. **2** a sea urchin. [from Latin *ericius* = hedgehog]

Urdu (**oor**-doo) *noun* a language related to Hindi, one of the official languages of Pakistan.

urea (yoo-**ree**-ă) *noun* a soluble colourless compound contained especially in urine.

ureter (yoo-**ree**-ter) *noun* either of the two ducts by which urine passes from the kidneys to the bladder.

urethra (yoo-**ree**-thră) *noun* the duct by which urine is discharged from the body.

urge *verb* **1** to drive onward, to encourage to proceed, *urging them on*. **2** to try hard or persistently to persuade, *urged him to accept the job*. **3** to recommend strongly with reasoning or entreaty, *urged on them the importance of keeping to the schedule*. –**urge** *noun* a feeling or desire that urges a person to do something.

urgent *adjective* **1** needing immediate attention, action, or decision. **2** showing that something is urgent, *spoke in an urgent whisper*. **urgently** *adverb*, **urgency** *noun* [from Latin *urgens* = urging]

uric (**yoo**-rik) *adjective* of urine.

urinal (yoo-rĭ-năl *or* yoo-**ry**-năl) *noun* a structure to receive urine in a men's toilet; a room or building containing this.

urinary (**yoo**-rin-ă-ree) *adjective* of urine or its excretion, *urinary organs*.

urinate (**yoo**-rĭ-nayt) *verb* to discharge urine from the body. **urination** *noun*

urine (**yoo**-rĭn *or* **yoo**-ryn) *noun* waste liquid that collects in the bladder and is discharged from the body.

URL *abbreviation* uniform (or universal) resource locator, an address on the World Wide Web.

urn *noun* **1** a vase, usually with a stem and base, especially one used for holding the ashes of a cremated person. **2** a large metal container with a tap, in which tea or coffee is made or from which it is served.

ursine (**er**-syn) *adjective* of or like a bear.

Uruguay (**yoo**-rŭ-gwy) a republic in South America, south of Brazil. **Uruguayan** *adjective* & *noun*

US *abbreviation* (also **USA**) United States (of America).

us *pronoun* **1** the objective case of **we**. **2** (*informal*) = we, *it's us*. **3** (*informal*) me, *give us a hand*.

usable *adjective* able to be used; fit for use.

usage (**yoo**-sij) *noun* **1** the manner of using or treating something, *it was damaged by rough usage*. **2** a habitual or customary practice, especially in the way words are used, *modern English usage*.

USB *abbreviation* universal serial bus, a standard for connecting peripherals to a computer.

use (*pr.* yooz) *verb* **1** to cause to act or serve for a purpose or as an instrument or as material for consumption. **2** to cause oneself to be known or addressed by (a name or title). **3** to treat in a specified way, to behave towards, *they used her shamefully*. **4** to exploit selfishly. –**use** (*pr.* yooss) *noun* **1** using; being used. **2** the right or power of using something, *lost the use of his arm*. **3** the purpose for which something is used; what that a person or thing is able to do. □ **have no use for** to have no purpose for which (a thing) can be used; to refuse to tolerate, to dislike. **make use of** to use, to exploit. **use-by date** a date marked on the packaging of perishable goods to show how long the contents can be used. **use up** to use the whole of (material etc.); to find a use for (remaining material or time).

used¹ (*pr.* yoozd) *adjective* (of clothes or vehicles) second-hand.

used² (*pr.* yoost) *verb* was or were accustomed in the past, *we used to go by train*; *they used not to do this*. –**used** *adjective* having become familiar with (a thing) by practice or habit, *is used to getting up early*.

usedn't (*pr.* **yoos**-nt) (*informal*) = used not.

useful *adjective* able to produce good results, able to be used for some practical purpose.

☐ **make oneself useful** to perform some practical or beneficial service. **usefully** *adverb*, **usefulness** *noun*

useless *adjective* serving no useful purpose, not able to produce good results. **uselessly** *adverb*, **uselessness** *noun*

user *noun* **1** a person who uses a thing. **2** a person who takes drugs. ☐ **user-friendly** *adjective* (of a computer, etc.) easy for the user to understand and operate.

usher *noun* **1** a person who shows people to their seats in a public hall etc. or into someone's presence, or who walks before a person of rank. **2** an official acting as doorkeeper in a lawcourt. –**usher** *verb* to lead in or out; to escort as an usher.

USSR *abbreviation* Union of Soviet Socialist Republics.

usual *adjective* such as happens or is done or used etc. in many or most instances; *the usual* or *my usual*, what I usually have, my usual drink etc. **usually** *adverb* [from Latin *usum* = used]

usurer (**yoo**-*zhŭ*-rer) *noun* a person who lends money at excessively high interest.

usurp (yoo-**zerp**) *verb* to take (power or a position or right) wrongfully or by force. **usurpation** *noun*, **usurper** *noun*

usury (**yoo**-*zhŭ*-ree) *noun* **1** the lending of money at excessively high interest. **2** an excessively high rate of interest.

Utah (**yoo**-tah) a State of the western USA.

ute *noun* (*Austral. informal*) a utility truck.

utensil (yoo-**ten**-sĭl) *noun* an instrument or container, especially for domestic use.

uterine (**yoo**-tĕ-ryn) *adjective* of the uterus.

uterus (**yoo**-tĕ-rŭs) *noun* the womb. [Latin, = womb]

utilise *verb* (also -**ize**) to use, to find a use for. **utilisation** *noun*

utilitarian (yoo-til-ĭ-**tair**-ree-ăn) *adjective* designed to be useful rather than decorative or luxurious, severely practical. [from *utility*]

utilitarianism *noun* **1** the doctrine that actions are right if they benefit or are useful to most people. **2** the doctrine that the greatest happiness of the greatest number should be the guiding principle of conduct.

utility *noun* **1** usefulness. **2** a useful thing; *public utilities*, services such as the supply of water, gas, or electricity etc. **3** (*Austral.*) a utility truck. –**utility** *adjective* severely practical. ☐ **utility truck** (*Austral.*) a car like a small truck with an enclosed cabin and a rear tray for carrying loads. [from Latin *utilis* = useful]

utmost *adjective* furthest, greatest, extreme, *with the utmost care*. –**utmost** *noun* the furthest point or degree etc.
☐ **do one's utmost** to do as much as possible. [from Old English = furthest out]

Utopia (yoo-**toh**-pee-ă) *noun* an imaginary place or state of things where everything is perfect. **Utopian** *adjective* [the title of a book by Sir Thomas More (1516), meaning 'Nowhere']

utter[1] *adjective* complete, absolute, *utter bliss*. **utterly** *adverb*

utter[2] *verb* **1** to make (a sound or words) with the mouth or voice, *uttered a sigh*. **2** to speak, *he didn't utter*. **3** to put (a forged banknote or coin etc.) into circulation. **utterance** *noun*

uttermost *adjective* & *noun* = utmost.

U-turn *noun* **1** the driving of a vehicle in a U-shaped course so as to proceed in an opposite direction. **2** a reversal of policy.

UV *abbreviation* ultraviolet.

uvula (**yoov**-yŭ-lă) *noun* (*plural* **uvulae**) the small fleshy projection hanging from the back of the roof of the mouth above the throat.

uxorious (uks-**or**-ree-ŭs) *adjective* obsessively fond of one's wife. [from Latin *uxor* = wife]

Uzbekistan (uuz-bek-ĭ-**stahn**) a republic in Asia (formerly a republic of the USSR) lying south and south-east of the Aral Sea. **Uzbek** *adjective* & *noun*

Vv

V *abbreviation* volt(s).

v. *abbreviation* **1** versus. **2** (as an instruction in a reference to a passage in a book etc.) see, consult. (¶ Short for Latin *vide*.)

vac *noun* (*informal*) **1** a vacation. **2** a vacuum cleaner.

vacancy *noun* **1** the condition of being vacant, emptiness. **2** an unoccupied position of employment, *we have a vacancy for a typist*. **3** unoccupied accommodation, *this hotel has no vacancies*.

vacant *adjective* **1** empty, not filled or occupied, *a vacant seat; applied for a vacant post*. **2** showing no sign of thought or intelligence, having a blank expression. □ **vacant possession** (of a house etc.) the state of being empty of occupants and available for the purchaser to occupy immediately. **vacantly** *adverb* [from Latin *vacans* = being empty]

vacate (vă-**kayt**) *verb* to cease to occupy (a place or position). [from Latin *vacare* = be empty or free from work]

vacation (vă-**kay**-shŏn) *noun* **1** any of the periods between terms especially in universities and lawcourts. **2** a holiday. **3** vacating, *immediate vacation of the house is essential*. [same origin as *vacate*]

vaccinate (**vak**-sĭ-nayt) *verb* to inoculate with a vaccine. **vaccination** *noun*

vaccine (**vak**-seen) *noun* **1** a preparation of cowpox virus introduced into the bloodstream to immunise a person against smallpox. **2** any preparation injected or administered orally to give immunity against an infection. [from Latin *vacca* = cow (because serum from cows was used to protect people from smallpox)]

vacillate (**vass**-ĭ-layt) *verb* **1** to waver, to keep changing one's mind. **2** to swing or sway unsteadily. **vacillation** *noun*, **vacillator** *noun* [from Latin *vacillare* = sway]

vacuity (vă-**kew**-ĭ-tee) *noun* **1** emptiness. **2** vacuousness.

vacuole (**vak**-yoo-ohl) *noun* a tiny cavity in an organ or cell of the body, containing air or fluid etc. [same origin as *vacuum*]

vacuous (**vak**-yoo-ŭs) *adjective* empty-headed, inane, expressionless, *a vacuous stare*. **vacuously** *adverb*, **vacuousness** *noun* [same origin as *vacuum*]

vacuum *noun* (*plural* **vacuums** *or*, *in science*, **vacua**) **1** space completely empty of matter; space in a container from which the air has been pumped out. **2** absence of normal or previous contents. **3** (*informal*) a vacuum cleaner. **–vacuum** *verb* (*informal*) to clean with a vacuum cleaner. □ **vacuum cleaner** an electrical appliance that takes up dust, dirt, etc. by suction. **vacuum flask** a flask with a double wall that encloses a vacuum, used for keeping liquids hot or cold. **vacuum-packed** *adjective* sealed in a pack from which most of the air has been removed. **vacuum pump** a pump for producing a vacuum. **vacuum tube** a sealed tube with an almost perfect vacuum, allowing free passage of electric current. [from Latin *vacuus* = empty]

vade mecum (vah-dě **may**-kŭm) *noun* a handbook or other small useful work of reference. [Latin, = go with me]

Vaduz (va-**duts**) the capital of Liechtenstein.

vagabond *noun* a wanderer, a vagrant, especially an idle or dishonest one. **–vagabond** *adjective* of or like a vagabond. [from Latin *vagari* = wander]

vagary (**vay**-gă-ree) *noun* a capricious act or idea or fluctuation, *vagaries of fashion*. [from Latin *vagari* = wander]

vagina (vă-**jy**-nă) *noun* the passage leading from the vulva to the womb in women and female animals. **vaginal** *adjective* [from Latin *vagina* = sheath]

vagrant (**vay**-grănt) *noun* a person without a settled home or regular work. **vagrancy** *noun* [from Latin *vagans* = wandering]

vague *adjective* **1** not clearly expressed or perceived or identified. **2** not expressing one's thoughts clearly or precisely. **vaguely** *adverb*, **vagueness** *noun* [from Latin *vagus* = wandering]

vain *adjective* **1** conceited, especially about one's appearance. **2** having no value or significance, *vain triumphs*. **3** useless, futile, *in the vain hope of persuading him.* □ **in vain** with no result, uselessly, *we tried, but in vain.* **take God's name in vain** to use it irreverently. **vainly** *adverb* [from Latin *vanus* = empty]

vainglory *noun* extreme vanity; boastfulness. **vainglorious** *adjective*

Vaisya (**vys**-yă) *noun* a member of the third of the four great Hindu classes, the merchant and farmer class. [from Sanskrit *vaisya* = peasant, labourer]

valance (**val**-ăns) *noun* a short curtain round the frame or canopy of a bedstead, or above a window or under a shelf.

vale *noun* a valley, *McLaren Vale*. [from Latin *vallis* = valley]

valediction (val-ĕ-**dik**-shŏn) *noun* saying farewell; the words used in this. [from Latin *vale* = farewell, + *dicere* = say (compare *benediction*)]

valedictory (val-ĕ-**dik**-tŏ-ree) *adjective* saying farewell, *a valedictory speech*.

valence (**vay**-lĕns) *noun* = **valency**.

valency (**vay**-lĕn-see) *noun* the capacity of an atom to combine with another or others, as compared with that of the hydrogen atom, *carbon has a valency of 4*. [from Latin *valentia* = power]

Valentine, St, an early Italian saint (possibly a Roman priest martyred c. 269), regarded as the patron of lovers. Feast day, 14 February.

valentine *noun* **1** a sweetheart chosen on St Valentine's day (14 February). **2** a card or picture etc. sent on this day (often anonymously) to one's valentine.

valerian (vă-**leer**-ree-ăn) *noun* a strong-smelling herb with pink or white flowers.

valet (**val**-ĕt *or* **val**-ay) *noun* **1** a man's personal attendant who takes care of clothes etc. **2** a hotel employee with similar duties. –**valet** *verb* (**valeted**, **valeting**) to act as valet to.

valetudinarian (val-ĕ-tew-dĭ-**nair**-ree-ăn) *noun* a person who pays excessive attention to preserving health. **valetudinarianism** *noun* [from Latin *valetudo* = health]

Valhalla (val-**hal**-ă) *noun* (*Scand. myth.*) the hall in which the souls of slain heroes feasted with Odin. [from Old Norse *valr* = the slain, + *höll* = hall]

valiant *adjective* brave, courageous. **valiantly** *adverb* [same origin as *value*]

valid (**val**-ĭd) *adjective* **1** having legal force, legally acceptable or usable, *a valid passport*. **2** (of reasoning etc.) sound and to the point, logical. **validly** *adverb*, **validity** (vă-**lid**-ĭ-tee) *noun* [from Latin *validus* = strong]

validate (**val**-ĭ-dayt) *verb* to make valid, to confirm. **validation** *noun*

Valkyrie (**val**-kĭ-ree) *noun* (*Scand. myth.*) any of Odin's twelve handmaidens who hovered over battlefields and carried chosen slain warriors to Valhalla.

Valletta (vă-**let**-ă) the capital of Malta.

valley *noun* (*plural* **valleys**) **1** a long low area between hills. **2** a region drained by a river, *the Hunter valley*. [same origin as *vale*]

valour (**val**-er) *noun* bravery, especially in fighting. **valorous** *adjective* [from Latin *valor* = strength]

valuable *adjective* of great value or price or worth. **valuables** *plural noun* valuable things, especially small personal possessions. **valuably** *adverb*

valuation *noun* estimation of a thing's value (especially by a professional valuer) or of a person's merit; the value decided upon.

value *noun* **1** the amount of money or other commodity or service etc. considered to be equivalent to something else or for which a thing can be exchanged. **2** desirability, usefulness, importance, *he learnt the value of regular exercise*. **3** the ability of a thing to serve a purpose or cause an effect, *nutritional value*; *news value*. **4** the amount or quantity denoted by a figure etc., the duration of a musical sound indicated by a note, the relative importance of each playing card etc. in a game; *tone values in a painting*, the relative lightness and darkness of its parts. –**value** *verb* **1** to estimate the value of. **2** to consider to be of great worth or importance. **values** *plural noun* standards or principles considered valuable or important in life, *moral values*. □ **value added tax** a tax on the amount by which the value of an article has been increased at each stage of its production. **value judgment** a subjective estimate of quality etc. [from Latin *valere* = be strong]

valueless *adjective* having no value.

valuer *noun* a person who estimates values professionally.

valve *noun* **1** a device for controlling the flow of gas or liquid through a pipe. **2** a structure in the heart or in a blood vessel allowing blood to flow in one direction only. **3** a device for varying the length of the tube in a brass wind instrument. **4** each piece of the shell of molluscs such as oysters. **5** a thermionic valve (*see* **thermionic**). [from Latin *valva* = section of a folding door]

valvular (**val**-vew-ler) *adjective* of the valves of the heart or blood vessels.

vamoose *verb* (*informal*) to go away hurriedly. [from Spanish *vamos* = let us go]

vamp¹ *noun* the upper front part of a boot or shoe. –**vamp** *verb* **1** to make from odds and ends, *we'll vamp something up*. **2** to improvise a musical accompaniment to a song or dance tune.

vamp² *noun* (*informal*) a seductive woman who uses her attraction to exploit men.

vampire *noun* **1** a ghost or reanimated body supposed to leave a grave at night and suck the blood of living people. **2** a person who preys on others. ☐ **vampire bat** a tropical bat that bites or is said to bite animals and persons and suck their blood.

van¹ *noun* **1** a covered vehicle for transporting goods etc., or fitted with rows of seats for carrying passengers. **2** a railway carriage for luggage or goods, or for the use of the guard. **3** a caravan. [short for *caravan*]

van² *noun* the vanguard, the forefront.

Van Allen belt *noun* each of two regions of intense radiation partly surrounding the earth at heights of several thousand kilometres. [named after the American physicist J. Van Allen (1914–2006) who discovered them]

vanadium (vă-**nay**-dee-ŭm) *noun* a hard grey metallic element (symbol V) used in certain steels as a hardener.

vandal *noun* a person who wilfully or maliciously damages public or private property or the beauties of nature. **vandalism** *noun* [named after the *Vandals*, a Germanic people who ravaged Gaul, Spain, North Africa, and Rome in the 4th–5th centuries, destroying many books and works of art]

vandalise *verb* (also **-ize**) to damage (property etc.) as a vandal.

van de Velde *see* **Velde**.

Van Diemen's Land the former name of Tasmania given by Tasman to commemorate Anthony van Diemen (1593–1645), Governor of Java. **Vandemonian** *adjective* & *noun*

Van Dyck, Sir Anthony (1599–1641), Flemish painter, best known for his portraits of Charles I and other members of the Royal family.

Vandyke *adjective* in the style of dress etc. common in portraits by Van Dyck. ☐ **Vandyke beard** a neat pointed beard. **Vandyke brown** deep rich brown.

vane *noun* **1** a weathervane. **2** the blade of a propeller, sail of a windmill, or similar device acting on or moved by wind or water.

Van Eyck (*rhymes with* like), Jan (1390–1441), Flemish painter.

Van Gogh (*pr.* gof *or* goh), Vincent Willem (1853–90), Dutch post-impressionist painter, who used colours for their expressive or symbolic values and vigorous swirling brushstrokes.

vanguard *noun* **1** the foremost part of an army or fleet advancing or ready to do so. **2** the leaders of a movement or fashion etc. [from French *avant* = before, + *garde* = guard]

vanilla *noun* **1** a flavouring obtained from the pods of a tropical climbing orchid, or made synthetically. **2** this orchid. [from Spanish *vainilla* = little pod]

vanish *verb* to disappear completely.

vanity *noun* **1** conceit, especially about one's appearance. **2** futility, worthlessness, something vain, *the pomps and vanity of this world*. ☐ **vanity unit** a washbasin set into a flat top with cupboards beneath.

vanquish *verb* to conquer. [from Latin *vincere* = conquer]

vantage *noun* = advantage. ☐ **vantage point** a place from which one has a good view of something.

Vanuatu (van-oo-**ah**-too) a republic consisting of a chain of islands in the SW Pacific north-east of New Caledonia and west of Fiji. Formerly called the *New Hebrides*.

vapid (**vap**-ĭd) *adjective* insipid, uninteresting.

vaporise *verb* (also **-ize**) to convert or be converted into vapour. **vaporisation** *noun*, **vaporiser** *noun*

vapour *noun* **1** moisture or other substance diffused or suspended in air. **2** the air-like substance into which certain liquid or solid substances can be converted by heating (*see* **gas**). **vaporous** *adjective*, **vapoury** *adjective* [from Latin *vapor* = steam]

Varanasi (vă-**rah**-nă-see) (formerly Benares) a Hindu holy city on the Ganges in India.

variable *adjective* varying, changeable; (of a star) periodically varying in brightness. –**variable** *noun* something that varies or can vary, a variable quantity.

☐ **variable costs** costs (e.g. those for raw materials) which vary according to the volume of production. **variably** *adverb*, **variability** *noun*

variance *noun* 1 disagreement. 2 (in mathematics) a quantity equal to the square of the standard deviation.
☐ **at variance** disagreeing, conflicting; (of people) in a state of discord or enmity.

variant *adjective* differing from something or from a standard, *'gaol' is a variant spelling of 'jail'*. –**variant** *noun* a variant form or spelling etc.

variation *noun* 1 varying; the extent to which something varies. 2 a variant; a repetition of a melody in a different (usually more elaborate) form. 3 the difference between individuals of the same family, race, or species. 4 a change in a mathematical function due to small changes in the values of constants etc.

varicoloured (**vair**-ree-kul-erd) *adjective* 1 variegated in colour. 2 of various or different colours.

varicose (**va**-rǐ-kohs) *adjective* (of a vein) permanently swollen or enlarged.

varied *see* vary. –**varied** *adjective* of different sorts, full of variety.

variegated (**vair**-rě-gayt-ěd) *adjective* marked with irregular patches of different colours. **variegation** *noun* [same origin as *various*]

varietal (vă-**ry**-ě-tǎl) *adjective* (of wine) made from a single designated variety of grape.

variety *noun* 1 the quality or state of being the same or of not being the same at all times. 2 a quantity or range of different things, *for a variety of reasons*. 3 a class of things that differ from others in the same general group, a member of such a class, *several varieties of spaniel*. 4 (in biology) a subdivision of a species. 5 an entertainment consisting of a series of short performances of different kinds (e.g. singing, dancing, acrobatics).

various *adjective* 1 of several kinds, unlike one another. 2 more than one, individual and separate, *we met various people*. **variously** *adverb* [from Latin *varius* = changing]

varlet *noun* (*old use*) 1 a menial servant. 2 a rascal.

varna *noun* any of the four great Hindu castes (Brahmin, Kshatriya, Vaisya, Sudra).

varnish *noun* 1 a liquid that dries to form a hard shiny transparent coating, used on wood

or metal etc. 2 nail varnish (*see* nail). –**varnish** *verb* to coat with varnish.

Varuna (vă-**roo**-nă) (in Hinduism) the ancient ruler of the universe, later the god of the waters.

varve *noun* a pair of layers of silt deposited in a lake where a glacier melts, one being of fine silt (deposited in winter, when there is little melting), and one being coarser (deposited in summer, when ice melts more freely).

vary *verb* (**varied, varying**) 1 to make or become different, *you can vary the pressure*; *his temper varies from day to day*. 2 to be different or of different kinds, *opinions vary on this point*.

Vasco da Gama *see* Gama.

vascular (**vas**-kew-ler) *adjective* consisting of vessels or ducts for conveying blood or sap within an organism, *vascular system*. [from Latin *vasculum* = little vessel]

vase (*pr.* vahz) *noun* an open usually tall vessel of glass, pottery, etc. used for holding cut flowers or as an ornament. [from Latin *vas* = vessel]

vasectomy (vă-**sekt**-ŏ-mee) *noun* surgical removal of part of each of the ducts through which semen passes from the testicles, especially as a method of birth control. [from Latin *vas* = vessel, + Greek *ektome* = cutting out]

vaseline (**vas**-ě-leen) *noun* (*trademark*) petroleum jelly used as an ointment or lubricant. [from German *wasser* = water, + Greek *elaion* = oil]

vaso- (vay-soh) *prefix* of or affecting a blood vessel, *vaso-constriction*, *vaso-dilation*. [same origin as *vase*]

vassal *noun* a humble servant or subordinate. **vassalage** *noun*

vast *adjective* 1 immense, very great in area or size, *a vast expanse of water*. 2 (*informal*) very great, *it makes a vast difference*. **vastly** *adverb*, **vastness** *noun* [from Latin *vastus* = unoccupied, desert]

VAT *abbreviation* value added tax.

vat *noun* a tank or other large vessel for holding liquids.

Vatican *noun* 1 the Pope's official residence in Rome. 2 the papal government.
☐ **Vatican City** an independent papal State in Rome, including the Vatican and St Peter's.

vaudeville (**vaw**-dě-vil) *noun* variety entertainment.

Vaughan Williams (*pr.* vawn), Ralph (1872–1958), English composer.

vault *noun* **1** an arched roof. **2** a vaultlike covering; *the vault of heaven*, the sky. **3** a cellar or underground room used as a place of storage. **4** a burial chamber, *the family vault*. **5** an act of vaulting. –**vault** *verb* to jump or leap, especially while resting on the hand(s) or with the help of a pole, *vaulted the gate* or *over the gate*. **vaulter** *noun* [from Latin *volvere* = to roll]

vaulted *adjective* covered with a vault; made in the form of a vault.

vaulting *noun* arched work in a vaulted roof or ceiling. ☐ **vaulting horse** a padded structure for vaulting over in a gymnasium.

vaunt *verb* to boast. –**vaunt** *noun* a boast. [from Latin *vanus* = vain]

VC *abbreviation* Victoria Cross.

VCR *abbreviation* video cassette recorder.

VD *abbreviation* venereal disease.

VDU *abbreviation* visual display unit (*see* visual).

've (*informal*, especially after pronouns) have, *they've finished.*

veal *noun* calf's flesh as food. [from Latin *vitulus* = calf]

vector *noun* **1** (in mathematics) a quantity that has both magnitude and direction (e.g. velocity, = speed in a given direction). **2** the carrier of a disease or infection. **vectorial** *adjective*

Veda (**vay**-dă *or* **vee**-dă) *noun* (also **Vedas**) the most ancient and sacred literature of the Hindus, consisting of the Rig Veda, Sama Veda, Yajur Veda, and Atharda Veda, which codified the ideas and practices of the Vedic religion, and laid down the basis of classical Hinduism. [Sanskrit, = sacred knowledge]

Vedanta (vě-**dahn**-tă) *noun* **1** the Upanishads. **2** a Hindu philosophy founded on these.

Vedic (**vay**-dik *or* **vee**-dik) *adjective* of the Vedas. –**Vedic** *noun* the language of the Vedas, an old form of Sanskrit.

veer *verb* to change direction or course; (of wind) to change gradually in a clockwise direction.

veg (*pr.* vej) *noun* (*informal*) vegetable(s). –**veg** *verb* (*informal*) to relax, to do nothing, *likes to veg out on weekends.*

vegan (**vee**-găn) *noun* a strict vegetarian who eats no animal products (e.g. eggs) at all.

vegetable *noun* **1** a plant of which some part is used (raw or cooked) as food, especially as an accompaniment to meat. **2** a person leading a dull monotonous life. **3** (*informal*) a person who consists of a physical body without mental faculties because of illness, injury, or abnormality. –**vegetable** *adjective* of, from, or relating to plant life.

vegetarian *noun* a person who eats no meat. **vegetarianism** *noun*

vegetate (**vej**-ě-tayt) *verb* to live an uneventful or monotonous life.

vegetation *noun* **1** plants collectively. **2** vegetating.

vegetative (**vej**-ě-tă-tiv) *adjective* **1** of vegetation. **2** of or involving growth and development rather than reproduction by sexual means, as in the propagation of plants from cuttings or runners etc., not from seeds (which involve fusion of male and female cells).

vegie (**vej**-ee) *noun* (*informal*) a vegetable.

vehement (**vee**-ě-měnt) *adjective* showing strong feeling, intense, *a vehement denial.* **vehemently** *adverb*, **vehemence** *noun*

vehicle (**veer**-kŭl) *noun* **1** a conveyance for transporting passengers or goods on land or in space. **2** a means by which something is expressed or displayed, *art can be a vehicle for propaganda; the play was an excellent vehicle for this actor's talents.* [from Latin *vehere* = carry]

vehicular (vě-**hik**-yŭ-ler) *adjective* of vehicles, *vehicular traffic.*

veil *noun* a piece of fine net or other fabric worn as part of a headdress or to protect or conceal the face. –**veil** *verb* to cover with or as if with a veil; *a veiled threat*, partially concealed. ☐ **draw a veil over** to avoid discussing or calling attention to. **take the veil** to become a nun.

vein *noun* **1** any of the tubes carrying blood from all parts of the body to the heart. **2** any of the threadlike structures forming the framework of a leaf or of an insect's wing. **3** a narrow strip or streak of a different colour, e.g. in marble, cheese, etc. **4** a long continuous or branching deposit of mineral or ore, especially in a fissure. **5** a mood or manner, *she spoke in a humorous vein.* [from Latin *vena* = vein]

veined *adjective* filled or marked with veins.

Velázquez (vě-**las**-kwěz), Diego Rodriguez de Silva y (1599–1660), Spanish painter.

velcro *noun* (*trademark*) a fastener for clothes etc. consisting of two strips of fabric that cling together when pressed.

veld (*pr.* velt) *noun* open grassland in South Africa. [Afrikaans, = field]

vellum *noun* **1** a kind of fine parchment. **2** smooth writing paper. [same origin as *veal* (because parchment was made from animals' skins)]

velocity *noun* speed, especially in a given direction. [from Latin *velox* = swift]

velodrome (**vel**-ŏ-drohm) *noun* a place or building with a track for cycle racing.

velour (vĕ-**loor**) *noun* a plush fabric like velvet. [from French *velours* = velvet]

velvet *noun* **1** a woven fabric (especially of silk or nylon) with thick short pile on one side. **2** a furry skin covering a growing antler. □ **on velvet** in an advantageous or prosperous position. **velvet glove** outward gentleness of treatment. **velvety** *adjective* [from Latin *villus* = soft fur]

velveteen *noun* cotton velvet.

Ven. *abbreviation* Venerable (as the title of an archdeacon).

vena cava (vee-nă **kay**-vă) *noun* (*plural* **venae cavae**, *pr.* vee-nee **kay**-vee) each of the two veins carrying deoxygenated blood into the heart. [Latin, = hollow vein]

venal (**vee**-năl) *adjective* **1** able to be bribed. **2** (of conduct) influenced by bribery. **venally** *adverb*, **venality** (vee-**nal**-ĭ-tee) *noun* [from Latin *venalis* = for sale]

vend *verb* to sell or offer for sale. □ **vending machine** a machine that dispenses small articles when a coin is inserted in a slot. [from Latin *vendere* = sell]

vendetta (ven-**det**-ă) *noun* a feud. [Italian, from Latin *vindicta* = vengeance]

vendor *noun* (especially in Law) a person who sells something. [from *vend*]

veneer *noun* **1** a thin layer of finer wood covering the surface of a cheaper wood in furniture etc. **2** a superficial show of some good quality, *a veneer of politeness*. –**veneer** *verb* to cover with a veneer.

venerable (**ven**-ĕ-ră-bŭl) *adjective* **1** worthy of deep respect because of age or associations etc., *these venerable ruins*. **2** the title of an archdeacon in the Anglican Church. **3** (in the RC Church) the title of a deceased person who has attained a certain degree of sanctity, but

is not yet beatified or canonised. **venerably** *adverb*, **venerability** *noun*

venerate *verb* to regard with deep respect, to honour as hallowed or sacred. **veneration** *noun*, **venerator** *noun* [from Latin *venerari* = revere]

venereal (vĕ-**neer**-ree-ăl) *adjective* **1** (of disease or infection) contracted chiefly by sexual intercourse with a person who is already infected. **2** of sexual desire or intercourse. **venereally** *adverb* [from *Venus*, the Roman goddess of love]

Venetian (vĕ-**nee**-shăn) *adjective* of Venice. –**Venetian** *noun* a native or inhabitant of Venice. □ **venetian blind** a window blind consisting of horizontal slats that can be adjusted to let in or exclude light. [from Latin *Venetia* = Venice]

Venezuela (ven-ĕz-**way**-lă) a republic on the north coast of South America. **Venezuelan** *adjective* & *noun*

vengeance *noun* retaliation for hurt or harm done to oneself or to a person etc. whom one supports. □ **take vengeance** to inflict harm in retaliation. **with a vengeance** in an extreme degree. [same origin as *vindictive*]

vengeful *adjective* seeking vengeance. **vengefully** *adverb*, **vengefulness** *noun*

venial (**veen**-ee-ăl) *adjective* (of a sin or fault) pardonable, not serious (contrasts with *mortal*). **venially** *adverb*, **veniality** *noun* [from Latin *venia* = forgiveness]

Usage Distinguish from *venal*, which means 'able to be bribed'.

Venice a city of NE Italy built on numerous islands on a lagoon of the Adriatic Sea.

venison (**ven**-ĭ-sŏn) *noun* deer's flesh as food. [from Latin *venatio* = hunting]

Venn diagram *noun* a diagram using overlapping and intersecting circles etc. to show the relationships between mathematical sets. [named after J. Venn (died 1923), British logician]

venom (**ven**-ŏm) *noun* **1** poisonous fluid secreted by certain snakes, spiders, etc. and injected into a victim by a bite or sting. **2** strong bitter feeling or language; hatred. [from Latin *venenum* = poison]

venomous (**ven**-ŏ-mŭs) *adjective* **1** secreting venom, *venomous snakes*. **2** full of bitter feeling or hatred. **venomously** *adverb*

vent¹ *noun* a slit in a garment (especially a coat or jacket) at the bottom of a back or side seam.

vent² *noun* an opening allowing air, gas, or liquid to pass out of or into a confined space, *a smoke vent*. –**vent** *verb* **1** to make a vent in. **2** to give vent to, *vented his anger on the cat*. □ **give vent to** to give an outlet to (feelings etc.), to express freely, *gave vent to his anger*. **vent light** a small window hinged at the top edge. [from Latin *ventus* = wind]

ventilate *verb* **1** to cause air to enter or circulate freely in (a room etc.). **2** to express (an opinion etc.) publicly so that others may consider and discuss it. **ventilation** *noun* [same origin as *vent*]

ventilator *noun* a device for ventilating a room etc.

ventral *adjective* of or on the abdomen, *this fish has a ventral fin*. **ventrally** *adverb* [from Latin *venter* = abdomen]

ventricle (**ven**-tri-kŭl) *noun* a cavity or chamber in an organ of the body, especially one of the two in the heart that pump blood into the arteries by contracting. [from Latin *ventriculus* = little belly]

ventriloquist (ven-**tril**-ŏ-kwĭst) *noun* an entertainer who produces voice-sounds so that they seem to come from a source other than himself or herself. **ventriloquism** *noun* [from Latin *venter* = abdomen, + *loqui* = speak]

venture *noun* an undertaking that involves risk. –**venture** *verb* **1** to dare, *did not venture to stop him*. **2** to dare to go or do or utter, *did not venture forth*; *ventured an opinion*. **3** to expose to risk; to take risks, *nothing ventured, nothing gained*. □ **venture on** to dare to engage in or make, *venture on a long expedition*. [compare *adventure*]

venturesome *adjective* ready to take risks, daring.

venturi tube *noun* a device consisting of a tube with a narrow section, used to produce suction or in measuring a rate of flow. [named after G. B. Venturi, Italian physicist (died 1822)]

venue (**ven**-yoo) *noun* an appointed place of meeting; a place fixed for a sports match. [from French *venir* = come]

venule *noun* a small blood vessel that unites with others to form a vein. [from Latin *venula* = little vein]

Venus **1** (*Rom. myth.*) the goddess of love, identified with Aphrodite. **2** one of the planets, also known as the morning and evening star. □ **Venus flytrap** a plant with leaves that spring shut on insects and digest them.

veracious (vĕ-**ray**-shŭs) *adjective* **1** truthful. **2** true. **veraciously** *adverb*, **veracity** (vĕ-**rass**-ĭ-tee) *noun* [from Latin *verus* = true]

veranda *noun* (also **verandah**) **1** a roofed terrace along the side of a house. **2** a roof over the pavement in front of a shop etc. [from Hindi *varanda*]

verb *noun* a word indicating action, occurrence, or being, e.g. *bring*, *came*, *exists*. [from Latin *verbum* = word]

verbal *adjective* **1** of or in words, *verbal accuracy*. **2** spoken, not written, *a verbal statement*. **3** of a verb, *verbal inflexions*. □ **verbal noun** a noun (such as *singing*, *drinking*) derived from a verb. **verbally** *adverb* [same origin as *verb*]

verbalise *verb* (also **-ize**) to put into words. **verbalisation** *noun*

verbatim (ver-**bay**-tim) *adverb* & *adjective* in exactly the same words, word for word.

verbena (ver-**been**-ǎ) *noun* a kind of plant with fragrant flowers. □ **lemon verbena** a similar plant with lemon-scented leaves.

verbiage (**verb**-ee-ij) *noun* an excessive number of words used to express an idea.

verbose (ver-**bohs**) *adjective* using more words than are needed. **verbosely** *adverb*, **verbosity** (ver-**boss**-ĭ-tee) *noun*

verdant *adjective* (of grass or fields) green. [compare *verdure*]

Verdi (**vair**-dee), Giuseppe (1813–1901), Italian composer, best known for his operatic works including *La Traviata* and *Aida*, and for his *Requiem*.

verdict *noun* **1** the decision reached by a jury. **2** a decision or opinion given after examining, testing, or experiencing something. [from Latin *verus* = true, + *dictum* = said]

verdigris (**ver**-dĭ-gree *or* -grees) *noun* green rust on copper or brass. [from French, = green (*vert*) of Greece]

verdure *noun* green vegetation; its greenness. [from Old French *verd* = green]

verge *noun* **1** the extreme edge or brink of something. **2** the point beyond which something new begins or occurs, *on the verge of ruin*. **3** the grass edging of a road or flower bed etc. **–verge** *verb* **verge on** to border on, to approach closely.

verger (**ver**-jer) *noun* **1** a person who is caretaker and attendant in a church. **2** an official who carries the mace etc. before a bishop or other dignitary.

verifiable *adjective* able to be verified.

verify *verb* (**verified**, **verifying**) to check the truth or correctness of, *please verify these figures.* **verification** *noun*, **verifier** *noun* [from Latin *verus* = true]

verily *adverb* (*old use*) in truth.

verisimilitude (ve-ree-sĭ-**mil**-ĭ-tewd) *noun* an appearance of being true. [from Latin *verus* = true, + *similis* = like]

veritable *adjective* real, rightly named, *a veritable villain.* **veritably** *adverb* [same origin as *verity*]

verity *noun* (*old use*) the truth of something. [from Latin *veritas* = truth]

Vermeer (ver-**meer**), Jan (1632–75), Dutch painter, famous for his detailed interior scenes.

vermicelli (ver-mĭ-**sel**-ee) *noun* pasta made in long slender threads. [Italian, = little worms]

vermiculture *noun* the cultivation of earthworms, especially in order to use them to convert organic waste into fertiliser.

vermiform (**ver**-mĭ-form) *adjective* wormlike in shape, *the vermiform appendix.* [from Latin *vermis* = worm, + *form*]

vermilion *noun* & *adjective* bright red. [from Latin *vermiculus* = little worm]

vermin *plural noun* **1** common animals and birds of an objectionable kind, especially those (such as foxes, rats, mice) that injure crops, food, or game. **2** unpleasant or parasitic insects (e.g. lice). [from Latin *vermis* = worm]

verminous *adjective* infected with vermin.

Vermont (ver-**mont**) a State of the north-eastern USA.

vermouth (**ver**-mŭth) *noun* white wine flavoured with fragrant herbs.

vernacular (ver-**nak**-yŭ-ler) *noun* **1** the language of a country, district, or group. **2** homely speech. [from Latin *vernaculus* = domestic]

vernal *adjective* of or occurring in the season of spring. **vernally** *adverb* [from Latin *ver* = spring]

Verne (*pr.* vern), Jules (1828–1905), French writer of science fiction, whose novels include

Around the World in Eighty Days and *Twenty Thousand Leagues under the Sea.*

vernier (**ver**-nee-er) *noun* a small movable graduated scale for indicating fractions of the main scale on a measuring device. [named after P. Vernier, French mathematician (died 1637)]

Veronica, St, a woman of Jerusalem said to have offered her headcloth to Christ on the way to his Crucifixion to wipe blood and sweat from his face. The cloth is said to have retained the image of his features.

veronica *noun* a herb often with blue flowers, speedwell.

verruca (vĕ-**roo**-kă) *noun* a wart or wartlike swelling, especially on the foot.

Versailles (vair-**sy**) a town SW of Paris, noted for its royal palace built in the 17th century by Louis XIII and XIV.

versatile (**ver**-să-tyl) *adjective* able to do, or be used for, many different things. **versatility** (ver-să-**til**-ĭ-tee) *noun* [from Latin *versare* = to turn]

verse *noun* **1** a metrical form of composition, poetry as distinct from prose. **2** a metrical composition, a poem. **3** a group of lines forming a unit in a poem or hymn. **4** each of the short numbered divisions of a chapter of the Bible. [from Latin *versus* = line of writing]

versed *adjective* **versed in** experienced or skilled in; having a knowledge of. [from Latin *versatus* = engaged in something]

versicle (**ver**-sĭ-kŭl) *noun* each of the short sentences in the liturgy, said or sung by the priest and alternating with the 'responses' of the congregation. [from Latin *versiculus* = little verse]

versify *verb* (**versified**, **versifying**) to express in verse; to write verse. **versification** *noun*

version *noun* **1** a particular person's account of a matter. **2** a translation into another language, *the Revised Standard Version of the Bible.* **3** a special or variant form of a thing, *the deluxe version of this car.* [from Latin *versum* = turned]

vers libre (vair **leebr**) *noun* verse with no regular metrical pattern. [French, = free verse]

verso *noun* (*plural* **versos**) **1** the left-hand page of an open book. **2** the back of a leaf of a manuscript etc. (¶ the front is the recto).

versus *preposition* against, *Australia versus England at the Adelaide Oval.* [Latin]

vertebra (ver-tĕ-bră) *noun* (*plural* **vertebrae**, *pr.* **ver**-tĕ-bree) any of the individual bones or segments that form the backbone. **vertebral** *adjective*

vertebrate (ver-tĕ-brăt) *noun* an animal that has a backbone. [from *vertebra*]

vertex *noun* (*plural* **vertices**, *pr.* **ver**-tĭ-seez) **1** the highest point of a hill or structure. **2** the meeting point of lines that form an angle, e.g. any point of a triangle or polygon. **3** (in graph theory) any of a set of points that may be joined together by edges. [from Latin *vertex* = top of the head]

vertical *adjective* **1** perpendicular to the horizontal; moving or placed in this way; upright. **2** in the direction from top to bottom of a picture etc. **–vertical** *noun* a vertical line, part, or position. **vertically** *adverb* [from *vertex*]

vertigo (vert-ĭ-goh) *noun* a sensation of dizziness and a feeling of losing one's balance. **vertiginous** (ver-**tij**-ĭ-nŭs) *adjective* [Latin, = whirling (*vertere* = to turn)]

verve (*pr.* verv) *noun* enthusiasm, liveliness, vigour.

very *adverb* **1** in a high degree, extremely, *very good*. **2** in the fullest sense, *drink it to the very last drop*. **3** exactly, *sat in the very same seat*. **–very** *adjective* **1** itself or himself etc. and no other, actual, truly such, *it's the very thing we need!* **2** extreme, utter, *at the very end*. □ **very well!** an expression of consent. [from Latin *verus* = true]

Very light (vair-ree *or* veer-ree) *noun* a flare projected by a pistol for signalling or to give temporary light on a battlefield etc. [named after E.W. Very, American inventor (died 1910)]

vesicle (vess-i-kŭl) *noun* **1** a small fluid-filled sac etc. in an animal body; an air-filled swelling in a water plant. **2** a blister. **3** a small cavity in volcanic rock produced by gas bubbles. **vesicular** (vĕ-**sik**-yŭ-ler) *adjective* [from Latin *vesicula* = little bladder]

vespers *plural noun* a church service held in the evening, evensong. [from Latin *vesper* = evening]

vessel *noun* **1** a hollow structure designed to travel on water and carry people or goods, a ship or boat. **2** a hollow receptacle, especially for liquid. **3** a tubelike structure in the body of an animal or plant, conveying or holding blood or other fluid. [same origin as *vase*]

vest *noun* **1** a waistcoat. **2** a singlet. **3** a sleeveless jumper. **–vest** *verb* **1** to confer as a firm or legal right, *the power of making laws is vested in Parliament*; *Parliament is vested with this power*. **2** (*old use*) to clothe. □ **vested interest** an advantageous right that is securely held by a person or group. [from Latin *vestis* = garment]

Vesta (*Rom. myth.*) the goddess of the hearth and household.

Vestal *adjective* of Vesta. □ **Vestal Virgin** (in ancient Rome) a virgin consecrated to Vesta and vowed to chastity.

vestibule (vest-ĭ-bewl) *noun* an entrance hall or lobby of a building.

vestige *noun* **1** a trace, a small remaining bit of what once existed, *not a vestige of the abbey remains*. **2** a very small amount, *not a vestige of truth in it*. [from Latin *vestigium* = footprint]

vestigial (ves-**tij**-ee-ăl) *adjective* remaining as a vestige of what once existed.

vestment *noun* a ceremonial robe or other garment, especially one worn by clergy or choir at a religious service. [same origin as *vest*]

vestry *noun* a room or building attached to a church, where vestments are kept and where clergy and choir robe themselves.

Vesuvius (vĕ-**soo**-vee-ŭs) an active volcano near Naples in Italy.

vet *noun* a veterinary surgeon. **–vet** *verb* (**vetted**, **vetting**) to examine carefully and critically for faults or errors etc. [short for *veterinary surgeon*]

vetch *noun* a plant of the pea family, used as fodder for cattle.

veteran *noun* a person with long experience, especially in the armed forces. □ **veteran car** a car made before 1916, or (strictly) before 1905. [from Latin *vetus* = old]

veterinarian (vet-ĕ-rĭ-**nair**-ree-ăn) *noun* a veterinary surgeon.

veterinary (**vet**-rĭn-ree) *adjective* of or for the treatment of diseases and disorders of farm and domestic animals. □ **veterinary surgeon** a person who is skilled in such treatment. [from Latin *veterinae* = cattle]

veto (**veet**-oh) *noun* (*plural* **vetoes**) **1** an authoritative rejection or prohibition of something that is proposed. **2** the right to make such a rejection or prohibition. **–veto**

verb (**vetoed, vetoing**) to reject or prohibit authoritatively. [Latin, = I forbid]

vex *verb* to annoy, to irritate, to cause worry to (a person). □ **vexed question** a problem that is difficult and much discussed. [from Latin *vexare* = to shake]

vexation *noun* **1** vexing; being vexed, a state of irritation or worry. **2** something that causes this.

vexatious (veks-**ay**-shŭs) *adjective* causing vexation, annoying. **vexatiously** *adverb*, **vexatiousness** *noun*

VHF *abbreviation* very high frequency, (of radio waves) of frequency 30–300 megahertz.

via (**vy**-ă) *preposition* by way of, through, *from Adelaide to Hobart via Melbourne*. [Latin, = by way]

viable (**vy**-ă-bŭl) *adjective* **1** (of a foetus) sufficiently developed to be able to survive after birth. **2** (of plants) able to live or grow. **3** practicable, able to exist successfully, *a viable plan*; *is the newly-created State viable?* **viably** *adverb*, **viability** *noun* [from French *vie* = life]

viaduct (**vy**-ă-dukt) *noun* a long bridgelike structure (usually with a series of arches) for carrying a road or railway over a valley or dip in the ground. [from Latin *via* = way, + *ducere* = to lead (compare *aqueduct*)]

vial (**vy**-ăl) *noun* a small bottle, especially for liquid medicine. [compare *phial*]

viands (**vy**-ăndz) *plural noun* articles of food.

viaticum (vy-**at**-i-kŭm) *noun* Holy Communion administered to the dying.

vibes (*pr.* vybz) *plural noun* (*informal*) **1** a vibraphone. **2** mental or emotional vibrations.

vibrant (**vy**-brănt) *adjective* vibrating; resonant; thrilling with energy or activity.

vibraphone (**vy**-bră-fohn) *noun* a percussion instrument like a xylophone but with resonators underneath the bars that open and close electronically to give a vibrating effect. [from *vibrate*, + Greek *phone* = voice]

vibrate *verb* **1** to move rapidly and continuously to and fro. **2** to resound; to sound with a rapid slight variation of pitch. [from Latin *vibrare* = to shake]

vibration *noun* a vibrating movement or sensation or sound. **vibrations** *plural noun* mental stimuli thought to be given out by a person or place etc.; the emotional sensations these produce.

vibrato (vĭ-**brah**-toh) *noun* (*plural* **vibratos**) a vibrating effect in music, with rapid slight variation of pitch.

vibrator (vy-**bray**-ter) *noun* a device that vibrates or causes vibration.

vibratory (**vy**-bră-tŏ-ree) *adjective* causing vibration.

viburnum (vy-**ber**-nŭm) *noun* a kind of shrub, usually with white flowers.

Vic. *abbreviation* Victoria (Australia).

vicar *noun* **1** (in the Anglican Church) a member of the clergy in charge of a parish. **2** (in the RC Church) a representative or deputy of a bishop. □ **Vicar of Christ** the Pope.

vicarage *noun* the house of an Anglican vicar.

vicarious (vĭ-**kair**-ree-ŭs) *adjective* (of feelings or emotions) felt through sharing imaginatively in the feelings or activities etc. of another person, *vicarious pleasure*. **vicariously** *adverb*, **vicariousness** *noun* [from Latin *vicarius* = substitute]

vice¹ *noun* **1** evil or grossly immoral conduct, great wickedness. **2** a particular form of this, a fault or bad habit, *smoking isn't one of my vices*. **3** criminal and immoral practices such as prostitution. [from Latin *vitium* = fault]

vice² *noun* an instrument with two jaws that grip a thing securely so as to leave the hands free for working on it, used especially in carpentry and metalworking. [from Latin *vitis* = vine]

vice³ (**vy**-see) *preposition* in place of, *Mr Smith has been appointed as librarian vice Mr Brown, who has retired*. [Latin, = by change]

vice- (*pr.* vys) *prefix* **1** acting as substitute or deputy for (as in *vice-president*). **2** next in rank to (as in *vice admiral*). [from Latin *vice* = by a change]

viceregal (vys-**ree**-găl) *adjective* **1** of a viceroy. **2** of or relating to the Governor-General or a State Governor in Australia.

viceroy *noun* a person governing a colony or province etc. as the sovereign's representative. [from *vice-*, + Old French *roy* = king]

vice versa (vy-see **ver**-să *or* vys **ver**-să) *adverb* the other way round, *we gossip about them and vice versa* (= and they gossip about us).

Vichy (**vee**-shee) a spa town in central France, headquarters of the French government administering southern France during the German occupation in the Second World War.

vicinity (vǐ-**sin**-ǐ-tee) *noun* the surrounding district; *in the vicinity*, near by.

vicious (**vish**-ŭs) *adjective* **1** acting or done with evil intentions, brutal, strongly spiteful. **2** (of animals) savage and dangerous, bad-tempered. **3** severe, *a vicious wind*. ☐ **vicious circle** a situation in which a cause produces an effect which itself produces or intensifies the original cause. **viciously** *adverb*, **viciousness** *noun* [same origin as *vice*[1]]

vicissitude (vǐ-**siss**-ǐ-tewd) *noun* a change of circumstances affecting one's life. [from Latin *vicissim* = in turn]

victim *noun* **1** a person who is injured or killed by another or as the result of an occurrence, *victims of the earthquake*. **2** a person who suffers because of a trick.

victimise *verb* (also **-ize**) to make a victim of, to single out (a person) to suffer ill-treatment. **victimisation** *noun*

victor *noun* the winner in a battle or contest.

Victoria[1] queen of the United Kingdom 1837–1901.

Victoria[2] a State of SE Australia.

Victoria[3], **Lake** (also **Victoria Nyanza**) the largest lake in Africa, in Uganda, Tanzania, and Kenya.

Victoria[4] the capital of the Seychelles.

Victoria Cross *noun* (in the Commonwealth) the highest military decoration, awarded for conspicuous bravery.

Victoria Falls a spectacular waterfall on the River Zambezi at the border of Zimbabwe and Zambia.

Victorian *adjective* **1** of or relating to the State of Victoria. **2** belonging to or characteristic of the reign of Queen Victoria (1837–1901). –**Victorian** *noun* **1** a native or resident of the State of Victoria. **2** a person living at the time of Queen Victoria.

victorious *adjective* having gained the victory.

victory *noun* success in a battle, contest, or game etc. achieved by gaining mastery over one's opponent(s) or achieving the highest score. [from Latin *victum* = conquered]

victuals (**vit**-lz) *plural noun* food, provisions. [from Latin *victus* = food]

vicuña (vǐ-**kew**-nǎ) *noun* **1** a South American animal related to the llama, with fine silky wool. **2** cloth made from its wool; an imitation of this. [Spanish]

vidcast *noun* a video clip that can be downloaded to a computer, mobile phone, etc.

video (**vid**-ee-oh) *noun* **1** recorded or broadcast pictures as distinct from sound. **2** a video recorder or recording. –**video** *verb* to record on videotape. ☐ **video cassette** a cassette of videotape. **video clip** a short film, usually of a pop star or group performing a song. **video game** an electronic computer game played on a television or monitor. **video recorder** (also **video cassette recorder** or **video player**) a device for recording a television program etc. on magnetic tape for playing back later. [Latin, = I see]

videotape *noun* magnetic tape for recording television pictures and sound; a recording on this. –**videotape** *verb* to record on this.

vie *verb* (**vied**, **vying**) to carry on a rivalry, to compete, *vying with each other*.

Vienna the capital of Austria. **Viennese** *adjective* & *noun* (*plural* **Viennese**).

Vientiane (vee-en-tee-**ahn**) the capital of Laos.

Vietcong (vee-et-**kong**) *noun* (*plural* **Vietcong**) a member of the Communist guerrilla forces active in Vietnam 1954–76.

Vietnam a republic in SE Asia bordered on the east and south by the South China Sea. ☐ **Vietnam War** a war between the South Vietnamese Government, aided by the USA (and supported by Australia) and the Communist insurgents (the Vietcong) supported by North Vietnam (1959–75). **Vietnamese** *adjective* & *noun* (*plural* **Vietnamese**).

view *noun* **1** what can be seen from a specified point, fine natural scenery, *the view from the summit*. **2** range of vision, *the ship sailed into view*. **3** visual inspection of something, *we had a private view of the exhibition before it was opened*. **4** a mental survey of a subject etc. **5** a mental attitude, an opinion, *they have strong views about tax reform*. –**view** *verb* **1** to survey with the eyes or mind. **2** to inspect; to look over (a house etc.) with the idea of buying it. **3** to watch television. **4** to regard or consider, *we view the matter seriously*. ☐ **in view of** having regard to, considering, *in view of the excellence of the work, we do not grudge the cost*. **on view** displayed for inspection. **with a view to** with the hope or intention of.

viewer *noun* 1 a person who views something. 2 a person watching a television program. 3 a device used in inspecting photographic slides etc.

viewfinder *noun* a device on a camera by which the user can see the area that will be photographed through the lens.

viewpoint *noun* a point of view, a standpoint.

vigil (**vij**-ĭl) *noun* 1 staying awake to keep watch or to pray; a period of this, *keep vigil*; *a long vigil*. 2 the eve of a religious festival. [from Latin *vigil* = wakeful]

vigilant (**vij**-ĭ-lănt) *adjective* watchful, on the lookout for possible danger etc. **vigilantly** *adverb*, **vigilance** *noun* [from Latin *vigilans* = keeping watch]

vigilante (vij-ĭ-**lan**-tee) *noun* a member of a self-appointed group of people who try to prevent crime and disorder in a community where law enforcement is imperfect or has broken down. [Spanish, = vigilant]

vigneron (**veen**-yĕ-ron) *noun* a grower of vines for wine.

vignette (veen-**yet**) *noun* 1 a photograph or portrait with the edges of the background gradually shaded off. 2 a short description or character sketch. – **vignette** *verb* to shade off in the style of a vignette.

vigoro (**vig**-ŏ-roh) *noun* (*Austral.*) a game adapted from cricket with twelve players in a team.

vigorous *adjective* full of vigour. **vigorously** *adverb*, **vigorousness** *noun*

vigour *noun* 1 active physical or mental strength, energy; flourishing physical condition. 2 forcefulness of language or composition etc. [from Latin *vigor* = strength]

vihara (vi-**har**-ră) *noun* a Buddhist temple or monastery. [Sanskrit]

Viking (**vy**-king) *noun* a Scandinavian trader and pirate of the 8th–10th centuries.

Vila (**vee**-lă) (also **Port Vila**) the capital of Vanuatu.

vile *adjective* 1 extremely disgusting, *a vile smell*. 2 despicable on moral grounds. 3 (*informal*) bad, *vile weather*. **vilely** *adverb*, **vileness** *noun* [from Latin *vilis* = cheap, unworthy]

vilify (**vil**-ĭ-fy) *verb* (**vilified**, **vilifying**) to say evil things about. **vilification** *noun* [same origin as *vile*]

villa *noun* 1 (in ancient Rome) a large country house with an estate. 2 a country house,

especially in Mediterranean countries. 3 a suburban detached house. 4 a home unit. [Latin, = country house]

village *noun* 1 a collection of houses etc. in a country district, a small township. 2 (*Austral.*) a suburban shopping centre. [from *villa*]

villager *noun* an inhabitant of a village.

villain (**vil**-ăn) *noun* 1 a person who is guilty or capable of great wickedness; a wrongdoer, a criminal. 2 a character in a story or play whose evil actions or motives are important in the plot. 3 (*informal*) a rascal. **villainy** *noun*

villainous (**vil**-ă-nŭs) *adjective* 1 wicked, worthy of a villain. 2 (*informal*) abominably bad, *villainous handwriting*. **villainously** *adverb*

villein (**vil**-ĕn) *noun* a serf in the Middle Ages.

villus *noun* (*plural* **villi**) each of the many short narrow finger-like growths of tissue on some membranes of the body, especially the small intestine. [Latin, = shaggy hair]

Vilnius the capital of Lithuania.

vim *noun* (*informal*) vigour, energy.

vina (**vee**-nă) *noun* an Indian musical instrument with four strings and a half-gourd at each end. [Hindi]

vinaigrette (vin-ă-**gret**) *noun* 1 salad dressing made of oil and vinegar. 2 a small ornamental bottle for holding smelling salts.

Vincent de Paul, St (c. 1580–1660), a French priest who devoted his life to work among the poor, the sick, and the oppressed. He founded two religious orders to carry on his work, one of secular priests and the other of nuns. (See also **Saint Vincent de Paul Society**).

Vincentian *adjective* of St Vincent or its people. – **Vincentian** *noun* a native of St Vincent.

vindicate (**vin**-dĭ-kayt) *verb* 1 to clear of blame or suspicion. 2 to justify by evidence or results, to prove (a belief) to be valid. **vindication** *noun*, **vindicator** *noun* [from Latin *vindicare* = to set free]

vindictive (vin-**dik**-tiv) *adjective* having or showing a desire for revenge. **vindictively** *adverb*, **vindictiveness** *noun* [from Latin *vindicta* = vengeance]

vine *noun* 1 a climbing or trailing woody-stemmed plant whose fruit is the grape. 2 a slender climbing or trailing stem. [from Latin *vinum* = wine]

vinegar *noun* a sour liquid made from wine, cider, malt, etc. by fermentation, used in flavouring food and for pickling. [from Latin *vinum* = wine, + *acer* = sour]

vinegary *adjective* 1 like vinegar. 2 sour-tempered.

vineyard (**vin**-yard) *noun* a plantation of vines producing grapes for wine-making.

vintage (**vint**-ij) *noun* 1 the gathering of grapes for wine-making; the season of this. 2 wine made from a particular season's grapes; the date of this as an indication of the wine's quality; *a vintage year*, one in which the wine is of high quality; *vintage wines*, from vintage years. 3 the date or period when something was produced or existed. –vintage *adjective* of high quality, especially from a past period. ☐ vintage car a car made between 1917 and 1930.

vintner (**vint**-ner) *noun* a wine merchant.

vinyl (**vy**-nil) *noun* a kind of plastic, especially polyvinyl chloride; *vinyl recordings*, gramophone records (as distinct from compact discs).

viol (**vy**-ŏl) *noun* a stringed musical instrument popular especially in the 16th–17th centuries, similar to a violin but held vertically.

viola[1] (vee-**oh**-lă) *noun* a stringed musical instrument slightly larger than a violin and of lower pitch.

viola[2] (**vy**-ŏ-lă) *noun* a plant of the genus to which pansies and violets belong, especially a hybrid cultivated variety.

violate *verb* 1 to break or act contrary to (an oath or treaty etc.). 2 to treat (a sacred place) with irreverence or disrespect. 3 to disturb (a person's privacy). 4 to rape. violation *noun*, violator *noun* [from Latin *violare* = treat violently]

violence *noun* being violent; violent acts or conduct etc. ☐ do violence to to act contrary to, to be a breach of.

violent *adjective* 1 involving great force, strength, or intensity. 2 involving the unlawful use of force, *violent crime*; *a violent death*, caused by physical violence, not natural. violently *adverb*

violet *noun* 1 a small wild or garden plant, often with purple flowers. 2 the colour at the opposite end of the spectrum from red, bluish purple. –violet *adjective* bluish-purple.

violin *noun* a musical instrument with four strings of treble pitch, played with a bow.

violinist *noun* a person who plays the violin.

violist (vee-oh-**list**) *noun* a person who plays the viola.

violoncello (vy-ŏ-lŏn-**chel**-oh) *noun* (*plural* violoncellos) a cello.

VIP *abbreviation* very important person.

viper *noun* a small poisonous snake.

virago (vi-**rah**-goh) *noun* (*plural* viragos) a shrewish bullying woman. [Latin, = female soldier]

viral (**vy**-răl) *adjective* of or caused by a virus. ☐ viral video a video that is spread via the Internet, email, etc.

Virgil (**ver**-jil) (70–19 BC), Roman poet, whose most famous work was the *Aeneid*.

virgin *noun* 1 a person (especially a woman) who has never had sexual intercourse. 2 the Virgin the Virgin Mary, mother of Christ. –virgin *adjective* 1 virginal. 2 spotless, undefiled. 3 untouched, in its original state, not yet used; *virgin soil*, not yet dug or used for crops; *virgin wool*, pure new wool. ☐ virgin birth (in Christian teaching) the birth of Christ without a human father. virginity *noun*

virginal *adjective* of, being, or suitable for a virgin. virginals *plural noun* a keyboard instrument of the 16th–17th centuries, the earliest form of harpsichord.

Virginia a State on the Atlantic coast of the USA.

Virgin Islands a group of islands in the Caribbean Sea divided between British and US administration.

Virgo (**ver**-goh) a sign of the zodiac, the Virgin, which the sun enters about 23 August. Virgoan (**ver**-goh-ăn) *adjective* & *noun*

virile (**vi**-ryl) *adjective* having masculine strength or vigour; having procreative power. virility (vi-**ril**-i-tee) *noun* [from Latin *vir* = man]

virology (vy-**rol**-ŏjee) *noun* the scientific study of viruses. virological *adjective*, virologist *noun* [from *virus* + *-logy*]

virtual *adjective* being so in effect though not in name or according to strict definition, *he is the virtual head of the firm*. ☐ virtual image an image (e.g. in a mirror) that appears to exist as a result of reflection or refraction. virtual reality an image or environment generated by computer software with which a user can interact using electronic equipment. virtually *adverb*

virtue *noun* **1** moral excellence, goodness; a particular form of this, *patience is a virtue*. **2** chastity, especially of a woman. **3** a good quality, an advantage, *the seat has the virtue of being adjustable*. ☐ **by** or **in virtue of** by reason of, because of. **make a virtue of necessity** to do with a good grace what one must do anyway. [from Latin *virtus* = worth]

virtuoso (ver-tew-**oh**-soh) *noun* (*plural* **virtuosos** *or* **virtuosi**) a person who excels in the technique of doing something, especially singing or playing music. **virtuosity** (ver-tew-**oss**-ĭ-tee) *noun* [Italian, = skilful]

virtuous *adjective* having or showing moral virtue. **virtuously** *adverb*, **virtuousness** *noun*

virulent (**vi**-rŭ-lĕnt) *adjective* **1** (of poison or disease) extremely strong or violent. **2** strongly and bitterly hostile, *virulent abuse*. **virulence** *noun* [same origin as *virus*]

virus (**vy**-rŭs) *noun* (*plural* **viruses**) **1** a very simple organism (smaller than bacteria) capable of causing disease; such a disease. **2** a hidden code in a computer program, designed to sabotage a computer system or destroy data stored in it. [Latin, = poison]

visa (**vee**-ză) *noun* an official stamp or mark put on a passport by officials of a foreign country to show that the holder may enter their country. [Latin, = things seen]

visage (**viz**-ij) *noun* a person's face. [from Latin *visus* = sight]

vis-à-vis (veez-ah-**vee**) *adverb* & *preposition* **1** in a position facing one another, opposite to. **2** in relation to, as compared with. [French, = face to face]

viscera (**vis**-ĕ-ră) *plural noun* the internal organs of the body, especially the intestines. [Latin, = soft parts]

visceral (**vis**-ĕ-răl) *adjective* **1** of the viscera. **2** of feelings, rather than reason.

viscid (**vis**-ĭd) *adjective* (of liquid) thick and gluey. **viscidity** (vi-**sid**-ĭ-tee) *noun*

viscose (**vis**-kohz) *noun* **1** cellulose in a viscous state, used in the manufacture of rayon etc. **2** fabric made of this.

viscount (**vy**-kownt) *noun* **1** a British nobleman ranking between earl and baron. **2** the courtesy title of an earl's eldest son. **viscountcy** *noun*, **viscountess** *feminine noun* [from *vice-* + *count*]

viscous (**vis**-kŭs) *adjective* thick and gluey, not pouring easily. **viscosity** (vis-**kos**-ĭ-tee) *noun*

Vishnu (**vish**-noo) (in Hinduism) a deity worshipped by his followers as the supreme being and saviour, and by others as the preserver of the cosmos in the triad with Brahma and Siva.

visibility *noun* **1** being visible. **2** the range or possibility of vision as determined by conditions of light and atmosphere, *the aircraft turned back because of poor visibility*.

visible *adjective* able to be seen or noticed. **visibly** *adverb* [same origin as *vision*]

Visigoth *noun* a member of the western branch of the Goths, who invaded the Roman Empire in the 3rd–5th centuries.

vision *noun* **1** the faculty of seeing, sight. **2** something seen in the imagination or in a dream etc. **3** imaginative insight into a subject or problem etc., foresight and wisdom in planning, *a statesman with vision*. **4** a person or sight of unusual beauty. [from Latin *visum* = seen]

visionary *adjective* **1** existing only in the imagination, fanciful, not practical, *visionary schemes*. **2** indulging in fanciful ideas or theories. **–visionary** *noun* a person with visionary ideas.

visit *verb* **1** to go or come to see (a person or place etc.) either socially or on business or for some other purpose. **2** to stay temporarily with (a person) or at (a place). **3** (in the Bible) to inflict punishment for, *visiting the sins of the fathers upon the children*. **–visit** *noun* an act of visiting, a temporary stay. [from Latin *visitare* = go to see]

visitant *noun* **1** a visitor, especially a supernatural one. **2** a migratory bird that is a visitor to an area.

visitation *noun* **1** an official visit, especially of inspection. **2** trouble or disaster looked upon as punishment from God. **3 the Visitation** a Christian festival on 2 July, commemorating the visit of the Virgin Mary to Elizabeth.

visitor *noun* **1** one who visits a person or place. **2** a migratory bird that lives in an area temporarily or at a certain season.

visor (**vy**-zer) *noun* **1** the movable front part of a helmet, covering the face. **2** the projecting front part of a cap. **3** a **sun visor**, a fixed or movable shield at the top of a vehicle windscreen, protecting the eyes from bright sunshine etc. [same origin as *visage*]

vista *noun* **1** a view, especially one seen through a long narrow opening such as an avenue of trees. **2** a mental view of an extensive period or series of past or future events. [Italian, = view]

visual *adjective* of or used in seeing, received through sight. ☐ **visual aids** pictures, models, films, etc. as an aid to teaching. **visual display unit** or **terminal** a device resembling a television screen, connected to a computer or similar apparatus, on which text or images can be displayed. **visually** *adverb* [same origin as *vision*]

visualise *verb* (also **-ize**) to form a mental picture of. **visualisation** *noun*

vital *adjective* **1** connected with life, essential to life, *vital functions*. **2** essential to the existence, success, or operation of something; extremely important. **3** full of vitality, *she's a very vital sort of person*. **vitals** *plural noun* the vital parts of the body (e.g. heart, lungs, brain). ☐ **vital statistics** statistics relating to population figures or births and deaths; (*informal*) the measurement of a woman's bust, waist, and hips. [from Latin *vita* = life]

vitalise *verb* (also **-ize**) to put life or vitality into. **vitalisation** *noun*

vitality (vy-**tal**-ĭ-tee) *noun* liveliness, vigour, persistent energy.

vitally *adverb* in a vital way, essentially.

vitamin (**vy**-tă-mĭn *or* **vit**-ă-mĭn) *noun* any of a number of organic substances present in many foods and essential to human and animal nutrition. [same origin as *vital*]

vitiate (**vish**-ee-ayt) *verb* **1** to make imperfect, to spoil. **2** to weaken the force of, to make ineffective, *this admission vitiates your claim*. **vitiation** *noun* [from Latin *vitium* = fault]

viticulture *noun* the process of growing grapes.

vitreous (**vit**-ree-ŭs) *adjective* having a glasslike texture or finish, *vitreous enamel*. ☐ **vitreous humour** the clear jelly-like material filling the eyeball. [from Latin *vitrum* = glass]

vitrify (**vit**-rĭ-fy) *verb* (**vitrified**, **vitrifying**) to convert or be converted into glass or a glasslike substance, especially by heat. **vitrifaction** *noun*, **vitrification** *noun*

vitriol (**vit**-ree-ol) *noun* **1** sulphuric acid or one of its salts. **2** savagely hostile comments or criticism. **vitriolic** (vit-ree-**ol**-ik) *adjective*

vituperate (vĭ-**tew**-pĕ-rayt *or* vy-) *verb* to use abusive language. **vituperation** *noun*, **vituperative** *adjective*

Vitus (**vy**-tŭs), St (c. 300), a martyr of Roman persecution, invoked against epilepsy, chorea (= St Vitus's dance), and rabies. Feast day, 15 June.

viva (**vy**-vă) *noun* a viva voce examination.

vivace (vĭ-**var**-chay) *adverb* (in music) in a lively brisk manner.

vivacious (vĭ-**vay**-shŭs) *adjective* lively, high-spirited. **vivaciously** *adverb*, **vivacity** (vĭ-**vass**-ĭ-tee) *noun* [from Latin *vivere* = to live]

Vivaldi (vi-**val**-dee), Antonio (1678–1741), Italian composer and violinist, whose compositions include about 500 concertos, as well as operas and motets.

vivarium (vy-**vair**-ree-ŭm) *noun* (*plural* **vivaria**) a place prepared for keeping animals in conditions as similar as possible to their natural environment, for purposes of study etc. [from Latin *vivus* = alive]

viva voce (vy-vă **voh**-chee) *adjective* (of an examination in universities) oral. [Latin, = with the living voice]

vivid *adjective* **1** (of light or colour) bright and strong, intense. **2** producing strong and clear mental pictures, *a vivid description*. **3** (of the imagination) creating ideas etc. in an active and lively way. **vividly** *adverb*, **vividness** *noun* [from Latin *vividus* = full of life]

viviparous (vĭ-**vip**-ă-rŭs) *adjective* producing young in a developed state from the mother's body, not hatching by means of an egg (see **oviparous**). [from Latin *vivus* = alive, + *parere* = bring forth]

vivisection *noun* performance of surgical experiments on living animals. [from Latin *vivus* = alive, + *dissection*]

vixen *noun* a female fox.

viz. *adverb* namely, *the case is made in three sizes, viz. large, medium, and small.*

Usage In reading aloud, the word 'namely' is usually spoken where 'viz.' (short for Latin *videlicet*) is written.

vizier (vĭ-**zeer**) *noun* an official of high rank in certain Muslim countries. [from Arabic *wazir* = chief counsellor]

vlog *noun* a weblog with most of the content in the form of video clips.

V neck *noun* a V-shaped neckline on a pullover etc.

vocabulary *noun* **1** a list of words with their meanings, especially one given in a

reading book etc. of a foreign language.
2 the words known to a person or used in a
particular book or subject etc. [from Latin
vocabulum = name]

vocal (**voh**-kăl) *adjective* **1** of, for, or uttered
by the voice. **2** expressing one's feelings freely
in speech, *he was very vocal about his rights*.
–**vocal** *noun* a piece of sung music. **vocally**
adverb [from Latin *vocis* = of the voice]

vocalise (**voh**-kă-lyz) *verb* (also -**ize**) to utter.

vocalist (**voh**-kă-lĭst) *noun* a singer, especially
in a pop group.

vocation (vŏ-**kay**-shŏn) *noun* **1** a feeling that
one is called by God to a certain career or
occupation. **2** a natural liking for a certain type
of work. **3** a person's trade or profession.
☐ **vocational guidance** advice about suitable
careers. **vocational** *adjective* [from Latin
vocare = to call]

vocative *noun* & *adjective* the **vocative case**,
the grammatical case used in addressing or
invoking a person or thing.

vociferate (vŏ-**sif**-ĕ-rayt) *verb* to say loudly
or noisily, to shout. **vociferation** *noun* [from
Latin *vocis* = of the voice, + *ferre* = carry]

vociferous (vŏ-**sif**-ĕ-rŭs) *adjective* making
a great outcry, expressing one's views
forcibly and insistently. **vociferously** *adverb*,
vociferousness *noun*

vodcast = vidcast.

vodka *noun* alcoholic spirit distilled chiefly
from rye, especially in Russia. [from Russian
voda = water]

vogue *noun* **1** current fashion, *large hats are
the vogue*. **2** popular favour or acceptance, *his
novels had a great vogue ten years ago*.
☐ **in vogue** in fashion.

voice *noun* **1** sounds formed in the larynx
and uttered by the mouth, especially human
utterance in speaking, singing, etc. **2** ability to
produce such sounds, *she has a cold and has
lost her voice*; *she is in good voice*, singing
or speaking well. **3** expression of one's
opinion etc. in spoken or written words, the
opinion itself, the right to express opinion,
gave voice to his indignation; *I have no voice
in the matter*. **4** any of the sets of forms of a
verb that show the relation of the subject to
the action, *active voice*; *passive voice* (see
the entries for *active* and *passive*). –**voice**
verb **1** to put into words, to express, *she voiced
her opinion*. **2** to utter with resonance of the
vocal cords, not only with the breath.

☐ **voice-over** *noun* narration (e.g. in a film) by
a voice not accompanied by a picture of the
speaker. [from Latin *vox* = voice]

void *adjective* **1** empty, vacant. **2** not legally
valid. –**void** *noun* empty space, emptiness.
–**void** *verb* **1** to make legally void, *the
contract was voided by his death*. **2** to excrete
(urine or faeces).

voile (*pr.* voil) *noun* a very thin light dress
material. [French, = veil]

volatile (**vol**-ă-tyl) *adjective* **1** (of a liquid)
evaporating rapidly. **2** (of a person) lively,
changing quickly or easily from one mood or
interest to another. **volatility** (vol-ă-**til**-ĭ-tee)
noun [from Latin *volatilis* = flying]

vol-au-vent (**vol**-oh-vahn) *noun* a round case
of puff pastry with a savoury filling. [French,
= flight in the wind]

volcanic *adjective* of or from a volcano.
volcanically *adverb*

volcano *noun* (*plural* **volcanoes**) a mountain
or hill with openings through which lava,
cinders, gases, etc., from below the earth's
crust are or have been expelled. [from the
name of Vulcan, the ancient Roman god of
fire]

vole (*rhymes with* hole) *noun* a small plant-
eating animal resembling a rat or mouse.

Volga the longest river in Europe, flowing
from western Russia to the Caspian Sea.

volition (vŏ-**lish**-ŏn) *noun* use of one's own
will in choosing or making a decision etc.; *she
did it of her own volition*, voluntarily. [from
Latin *volo* = I wish]

volley *noun* (*plural* **volleys**) **1** simultaneous
discharge of a number of missiles; the
missiles themselves. **2** a number of questions
or curses etc. directed in quick succession at
someone. **3** return of the ball in tennis etc.
before it touches the ground. –**volley** *verb*
1 to discharge or fly or sound in a volley.
2 to return (a ball) by a volley. [from Latin
volare = to fly]

volleyball *noun* a game for two teams of
players who volley a large ball by hand over
a net.

volt *noun* a unit of electromotive force, force
sufficient to carry one ampere of current
against one ohm resistance. [named after
the Italian physicist Count Alessandro Volta
(1745–1827)]

voltage *noun* electromotive force expressed
in volts.

voltaic *adjective* (*old use*) galvanic.

Voltaire (pseudonym of François-Marie Arouet, 1694–1778), author of plays, poetry, and histories, an outspoken critic of the civil and ecclesiastical establishments.

voltameter *noun* an instrument for measuring an electric charge.

volte-face (volt-**fahs**) *noun* a complete change of one's attitude towards something. [French]

voltmeter *noun* an instrument measuring electric potential in volts.

voluble (**vol**-yŭ-bŭl) *adjective* talking very much; speaking or spoken with great fluency. **volubly** *adverb*, **volubility** (vol-yŭ-**bil**-ĭ-tee) *noun* [from Latin *volubilis* = rolling]

volume *noun* 1 a book, especially one of a set. 2 the amount of space (often expressed in cubic units) that a three-dimensional thing occupies or contains. 3 the size or amount of something, a quantity, *the great volume of water pouring over the weir*; *the volume of business has increased*. 4 the strength or power of sound, *the noise had doubled in volume*. [from Latin *volumen* = a roll (because ancient books were made in a rolled form)]

volumetric (vol-yŭ-**met**-rik) *adjective* of or using measurement by volume. □ **volumetric analysis** analysis of solutions by titration. **volumetrically** *adverb* [from *volume* + *metric*]

voluminous (vŏ-**lew**-mĭ-nŭs) *adjective* 1 having great volume, bulky; *voluminous skirts*, large and full. 2 (of writings) great in quantity; (of a writer) producing many works, copious. **voluminously** *adverb*, **voluminousness** *noun*

voluntary *adjective* 1 acting, done, or given etc. of one's own free will and not under compulsion. 2 working or done without payment, *voluntary workers* or *work*. 3 (of an organisation) maintained by voluntary contributions or voluntary workers. 4 (of bodily movements) controlled by the will. –**voluntary** *noun* an organ solo played before, during, or after a church service. **voluntarily** *adverb*, **voluntariness** *noun* [from Latin *voluntas* = the will]

volunteer *noun* 1 a person who offers to do something. 2 a person who enrols for military or other service voluntarily, not as a conscript. –**volunteer** *verb* to undertake or offer voluntarily, to be a volunteer.

voluptuous (vŏ-**lup**-tew-ŭs) *adjective* 1 fond of luxury or sumptuous living. 2 giving a sensation of luxury and pleasure. 3 (of a woman) having a full and attractive figure. **voluptuously** *adverb*, **voluptuousness** *noun* [from Latin *voluptas* = pleasure]

volute (vŏ-**lewt**) *noun* a spiral scroll in stonework. [from Latin *volutum* = rolled]

vomit *verb* (**vomited**, **vomiting**) to eject (matter) from the stomach through the mouth, to be sick. –**vomit** *noun* matter vomited from the stomach.

voodoo *noun* a form of religion based on belief in witchcraft and magical rites, practised by certain Blacks in the West Indies. **voodooism** *noun*, **voodooist** *noun*

voracious (vŏ-**ray**-shŭs) *adjective* 1 greedy in eating, ravenous. 2 desiring much; *a voracious reader*, one who reads much and eagerly. **voraciously** *adverb*, **voracity** (vŏ-**rass**-ĭ-tee) *noun* [from Latin *vorare* = devour]

vortex *noun* (*plural* **vortices**, *pr.* **vor**-tĭ-seez, *or* **vortexes**) a whirling mass of water or air, a whirlpool or whirlwind. [Latin]

vote *noun* 1 a formal expression of one's opinion or choice on a matter under discussion, e.g. by ballot or show of hands. 2 an opinion or choice expressed in this way, *the vote went against accepting the plan*. 3 the total number of votes given by a certain group, *that policy lost them the rural vote*. 4 the right to vote. –**vote** *verb* 1 to express an opinion or choice by a vote. 2 to decide by a majority of votes. 3 (*informal*) to declare by general consent, *the meal was voted excellent*. 4 (*informal*) to suggest, *I vote that we avoid him in future*. □ **vote of thanks** a formal expression of thanks made by a representative of a group. **voter** *noun* [from Latin *votum* = a wish or vow]

votive (**voh**-tiv) *adjective* given in fulfilment of a vow, *votive offerings at the shrine*.

vouch *verb* **vouch for** to guarantee the certainty, accuracy, or reliability etc. of, *I will vouch for his honesty*.

voucher *noun* 1 a document (issued in token of payment made or promised) that can be exchanged for certain goods or services. 2 a document establishing that money has been paid or goods etc. delivered.

vouchsafe *verb* to give or grant, often in a gracious or condescending manner, *they did not vouchsafe a reply* or *to reply*.

vow *noun* a solemn promise or undertaking, especially in the form of an oath to God or a god or a saint. **–vow** *verb* to promise solemnly, *they vowed vengeance against their oppressor*.

vowel *noun* **1** a speech sound made without audible stopping of the breath (as opposed to a *consonant*). **2** a letter or letters representing such a sound, as a, e, i, o, u, ee. [from Latin *vocalis littera* = vocal letter]

voyage *noun* a journey by water or in space, especially a long one. **–voyage** *verb* to make a voyage. **voyager** *noun*

Voyager[1] either of two Australian navy destroyers, one sunk during the Second World War, the other sunk in collision with HMAS *Melbourne* in 1964.

Voyager[2] each of two US space probes launched in 1977 to Jupiter, Saturn, Uranus, and Neptune.

VTO(L) *abbreviation* vertical take-off (and landing).

Vulcan (*Rom. myth.*) the god of fire and metal-working, identified with Hephaestus.

vulcanise *verb* (also **-ize**) to treat (rubber or similar material) with sulphur etc. in order to increase its elasticity and strength. **vulcanisation** *noun* [same origin as *volcano*]

vulcanite *noun* hard black vulcanised rubber.

vulgar *adjective* **1** lacking in refinement or good taste, coarse. **2** commonly used and incorrect (but not coarse; *see* **vulgarism**, sense 1). ☐ **vulgar fraction** a fraction represented by numbers above and below a line (e.g. $\frac{2}{3}$, $\frac{5}{8}$), not a decimal fraction. **vulgarly** *adverb*, **vulgarity** *noun* [from Latin *vulgus* = the ordinary people]

vulgarian (vul-**gair**-ree-ăn) *noun* a vulgar person, especially a rich one.

vulgarise *verb* (also **-ize**) **1** to cause (a person or manners etc.) to become vulgar. **2** to reduce to the level of being usual or ordinary, to spoil by making ordinary or too well known. **vulgarisation** *noun*

vulgarism *noun* **1** a word or phrase used mainly by people who are ignorant of standard usage, *'he is learning her to drive' is a vulgar usage* or *is a vulgarism for 'he is teaching her'*. **2** a coarse word or phrase.

Vulgate (**vul**-gayt) *noun* the 4th-century Latin version of the Bible.

vulnerable (**vul**-nĕ-ră-bŭl) *adjective* **1** able to be hurt or wounded or injured. **2** unprotected, exposed to danger or attack. **vulnerably** *adverb*, **vulnerability** *noun* [from Latin *vulnus* = wound]

vulpine (**vul**-pyn) *adjective* of or like a fox. [from Latin *vulpes* = fox]

vulture *noun* **1** a large bird of prey that lives on the flesh of dead animals. **2** a greedy person seeking to profit from the misfortunes of others.

vulva *noun* the external parts of the female genital organs. [Latin]

vying *see* **vie**.

Ww

W *abbreviation* (also **W.**) **1** watt(s). **2** west; western.

WA *abbreviation* Western Australia.

wad (*pr.* wod) *noun* **1** a lump or bundle of soft material used to keep things apart or in place, stop up a hole, etc. **2** a collection of documents or banknotes placed together; *has wads of money*, is rich. –**wad** *verb* (**wadded**, **wadding**) to line, stuff, or protect with wadding.

wadding *noun* soft fibrous material used for padding, packing, or lining things.

waddle *verb* to walk with short steps and a swaying movement. –**waddle** *noun* a waddling walk.

waddy (**wod**-ee) *noun* (*plural* **waddies**) (*Austral.*) a club formerly used by some Aboriginal peoples; any wooden club. [Dharuk *wadi* tree, stick, club]

wade *verb* **1** to walk through water, mud, or anything that prevents the feet from moving freely; to walk across (a stream etc.) in this way. **2** to make one's way slowly and with difficulty; *wade through a book*, read through it in spite of its dullness, difficulty, or length etc. □ **wade in** (*informal*) to intervene; to make a vigorous attack. **wade into** (*informal*) to attack (a person or task) vigorously. **wading bird** a long-legged waterbird that wades in shallow water.

wader *noun* a wading bird. **waders** *plural noun* high waterproof boots worn in fishing etc.

wadi (**wod**-ee) *noun* (*plural* **wadis**) a rocky watercourse in North Africa and neighbouring countries that is dry except in the rainy season. [Arabic]

wafer *noun* **1** a kind of thin light biscuit. **2** a thin disc of unleavened bread used in the Eucharist. □ **wafer-thin** *adjective* very thin.

waffle¹ (**wof**-ŭl) *noun* (*informal*) vague wordy talk or writing. –**waffle** *verb* to talk or write waffle. [from a dialect word *waff* = yelp]

waffle² (**wof**-ĕl) *noun* a small cake made of batter and eaten hot, cooked in a **waffle-iron** which has two metal pans, usually hinged together, marked with a projecting pattern that presses into the batter when they are closed upon it.

waft (*pr.* woft) *verb* to carry or travel lightly and easily through the air or over water.

wag¹ *verb* (**wagged**, **wagging**) **1** to shake or move briskly to and fro; *tongues are wagging*, talk or gossip is going on. **2** (*informal*) to play truant, especially from school. –**wag** *noun* a single wagging movement.

wag² *noun* a person who is fond of making jokes or playing practical jokes.

wage¹ *verb* to engage in, *wage war*.

wage² *noun* (also **wages** *plural noun*) regular payment to an employee in return for work or services, *he earns a good wage* or *good wages*. □ **wage earner** a person who works for wages. **wage indexation** the adjustment of wages in line with changes in the cost of living based on the consumer price index.

wager (**way**-jer) *noun* a bet. –**wager** *verb* to bet.

wagga (**wog**-ă) *noun* (also **wagga blanket** or **rug**) a covering made from two sacks cut open and sewn together. [from *Wagga Wagga*, a town in NSW]

waggish *adjective* of or like a wag, said or done in a joking way. **waggishly** *adverb*, **waggishness** *noun*

waggle *verb* to wag. –**waggle** *noun* a wagging movement.

waggon *noun* = **wagon**.

Wagner (**vahg**-ner), Richard (1813–83), German composer of operas and music dramas, often based on Germanic myths and legends, including *The Ring*, a series of operas based on the Nibelung saga. **Wagnerian** *adjective*

wagon *noun* (also **waggon**) **1** a four-wheeled vehicle for carrying goods, pulled by horses or oxen. **2** an open railway truck, e.g. for coal. **3** (*informal*) a station wagon. □ **on the wagon** (*informal*) not drinking alcohol; teetotal. **wagoner** *noun*

wagtail *noun* any of several small birds with a long tail that sways from side to side constantly when the bird is standing.

Wagyu *noun* a breed of Japanese cattle; the tender beef obtained from such cattle.

Wahhabi (wǎ-**hah**-bee) *noun* a member of a sect of Muslim puritans following strictly the original words of the Koran. [named after Muhammad ibn Abd-el-*Wahhab*, 18th-c. founder of the sect]

wah-wah *noun* a tremolo device for a musical instrument.

waif *noun* 1 a homeless and helpless person; an abandoned child. 2 a person who appears thin or poorly nourished.

wail *verb* 1 to utter a long sad cry; to lament or complain persistently. 2 (of wind etc.) to make a sound like a person wailing. –**wail** *noun* a wailing cry, sound, or utterance.

wain *noun* (*old use*) a farm wagon.

wainscot *noun* wooden panelling on the wall of a room.

wainscoting *noun* wainscot; material for this.

waist *noun* 1 the part of the human body below the ribs and above the bones of the pelvis, normally narrower than the rest of the body. 2 the part of a garment covering this. 3 a narrow part in the middle of a long object. **waisted** *adjective*

waistband *noun* a band (e.g. at the top of a skirt) that fits round the waist.

waistcoat *noun* a close-fitting waist-length sleeveless collarless garment usually buttoned down the front, worn over a shirt and under a jacket.

waistline *noun* the circumference of the body at the waist.

wait *verb* 1 to stay somewhere or postpone an action for a specified time or until something happens, *we waited until evening*; *wait your turn*, wait until it is your turn. 2 to be postponed, *this question will have to wait until our next meeting*. 3 to wait on people at a meal. –**wait** *noun* an act or period of waiting, *we had a long wait for the train*. □ **waiting game** deliberate delay in taking action so as to act more effectively later. **waiting list** a list of people waiting for a chance to obtain something when it becomes available. **waiting room** a room provided for people to wait in, e.g. at a railway station or a doctor's or dentist's surgery. **wait-list** *verb* to place (a person) on a waiting list, especially for an airline reservation. **wait on** to hand food and drink to (a person or persons) at a meal; to fetch and carry for (a person) as an attendant;

(*formal*) to pay a respectful visit to (a person); (*informal*) to be patient, to wait. **wait up** not go to bed until a person arrives or an event happens.

Waitangi (wy-**tang**-ee) a settlement in New Zealand at which in 1840 the treaty forming the basis of British annexation was negotiated. □ **Waitangi Day** 6 February, celebrated in New Zealand as a public holiday.

waiter, **waitress** *nouns* a person employed to serve food and drink to customers at tables in a hotel or restaurant.

waive *verb* to refrain from using or insisting upon (one's right, claim, or privilege etc.), to forgo or dispense with, *she waived her right to compensation*. [from Old French, = abandon (compare *waif*)]

waiver *noun* the waiving of a legal right; a document recording this.

wake¹ *verb* (**woke**, **woken**, **waking**) 1 = wake up (*see below*). 2 to disturb with noise; to cause to re-echo, *the shout woke echoes in the valley*. –**wake** *noun* a watch by a corpse before burial; lamentations and merrymaking in connection with this. □ **wake up** to cease to sleep; to cause to cease sleeping; to become alert; to cease or cause to cease from inactivity or inattention etc. **wake up to** to realise, *he woke up to the fact that she meant it*.

wake² *noun* 1 the track left on water's surface by a ship etc. 2 air currents left behind an aircraft etc. moving through air. □ **in the wake of** behind; following after.

Wakefield, Edward Gibbon (1792–1862), English social theorist whose views on colonisation influenced settlement in South Australia and in New Zealand.

wakeful *adjective* 1 (of a person) unable to sleep. 2 (of a night etc.) with little sleep.

waken *verb* to wake.

waking *adjective* being awake, *in his waking hours*.

wale *noun* 1 = weal¹ (sense 1). 2 a ridge on corduroy etc. 3 a broad thick timber along a ship's side.

Wales the country forming the western part of Great Britain.

walk *verb* 1 to progress by lifting and setting down each foot in turn so that one foot is on the ground while the other is being lifted; (of quadrupeds) to go with the slowest gait, always having at least two feet on the ground. 2 to travel or go on foot; to take exercise in this way. **3** to go over on foot, *walked the streets in search of her lost dog*. **4** to cause to walk with one; to accompany in walking. **5** to ride or lead (a horse or dog etc.) at a walking pace. **6** (of a ghost) to appear. –**walk** *noun* **1** a journey on foot, especially for pleasure or exercise, *went for a walk*. **2** the manner or style of walking; a walking pace. **3** a place for walking; a route followed in walking. **4** (in graph theory) a sequence through a network of edges and vertices in which a vertex may appear more than once. □ **walk away with** (*informal*) to win easily. **walking frame** a metal frame used as a support by people who have difficulty walking. **walking stick** a stick used as a support when walking. **walk off with** (*informal*) to steal; to win easily, *walked off with the first prize*. **walk of life** social rank, profession or occupation. **walk on air** to walk buoyantly because of happiness. **walk out** to depart suddenly and angrily; to go on strike suddenly. **walk out on** to desert, to leave in the lurch. **walk tall** to feel justifiable pride.

walkabout *noun* **1** (*Austral.*) a journey on foot, as taken by an Aborigine in order to live in the traditional manner. **2** an informal stroll among a crowd by a visiting dignitary. □ **go walkabout** (*Austral.*) to go on a walkabout; to wander around casually; (*informal*) (of a thing) to be lost, *the keys have gone walkabout*.

Walker, Kath *see* **Noonuccal**, Oodgeroo.

walker *noun* **1** a person who walks. **2** a framework in which a baby can walk unaided. **3** a walking frame.

walkie-talkie *noun* a small radio transmitter and receiver that a person can carry while walking about.

walkout *noun* a sudden angry departure, especially as a protest or strike.

walkover *noun* an easy victory or achievement.

walkway *noun* a passage or path for walking along, especially one connecting different sections of a building.

wall *noun* **1** a continuous upright structure forming one of the sides of a building or room, or serving to enclose, protect, or divide an area. **2** something thought of as resembling this in form or function; the outermost part of a hollow structure; tissue surrounding an organ of the body etc. –**wall** *verb* to surround or enclose with a wall, *a walled garden*; *wall up a fireplace*, block it with bricks etc. built as

a wall. □ **drive** or **send a person up the wall** (*informal*) to make him or her crazy or furious. **wall painting** a painting applied directly to the surface of a wall. **wall-to-wall** *adjective* (of a carpet) covering the whole floor of a room.

wallaby (**wol**-ă-bee) *noun* a marsupial similar to but smaller than a kangaroo. □ **on the wallaby** or **wallaby track** travelling as a swagman in search of work. [Dharuk *walabi* or *waliba*]

Wallace, Alfred Russel (1823–1913), British naturalist, who independently formulated a theory of the origin of species that was identical with that of Charles Darwin. □ **Wallace's line** an imaginary line, proposed by Wallace, marking the boundary between countries with Australasian fauna and those with Asian fauna.

wallaroo (wol-ă-**roo**) *noun* a large stocky kangaroo living in rocky or hilly country. [Dharuk *walaru*]

wallet *noun* a small flat folding case for holding banknotes or small documents etc.

wall-eyed *adjective* having a whitish or streaked eye; (of an eye) squinting outwards.

wallflower *noun* **1** a garden plant blooming in spring, with clusters of fragrant flowers. **2** (*informal*) a woman sitting out dances for lack of partners.

Walloon (wol-**loon**) *noun* **1** a member of a people living in southern Belgium and neighbouring parts of France. **2** their language, a French dialect.

wallop *verb* (**walloped**, **walloping**) (*informal*) to thrash, to hit hard, to beat. –**wallop** *noun* (*informal*) a heavy resounding blow.

walloping *adjective* (*informal*) big, thumping, *a walloping lie*. –**walloping** *noun* (*informal*) a beating; a defeat.

wallow *verb* **1** to roll about in water or mud or sand etc. **2** to indulge oneself or take unrestrained pleasure in something, *wallowing in luxury*. –**wallow** *noun* the act of wallowing.

wallpaper *noun* paper for pasting on the interior walls of rooms. –**wallpaper** *verb* to put wallpaper on (a surface).

Wall Street a street in New York City, in or near which the chief American financial institutions are concentrated; the American money market.

wally *noun* (*informal*) a stupid person.

walnut *noun* **1** a nut containing an edible kernel with a wrinkled surface. **2** the tree that bears it. **3** the wood of this tree, used (especially as a veneer) in making furniture.

walrus *noun* a large amphibious animal of Arctic regions, related to the seal and sea lion and having a pair of long tusks. □ **walrus moustache** a long thick moustache that hangs down at the sides.

waltz *noun* **1** a ballroom dance for couples, with a graceful flowing melody in triple time. **2** music for this. –**waltz** *verb* **1** to dance a waltz. **2** to move (a person) in or as if in a waltz. **3** (*informal*) to move gaily or casually, *came waltzing in*. **waltzer** *noun* [from German *walzen* = revolve]

Waltzing Matilda an Australian song with words by A. B. Paterson (1895). A 'Matilda' is a tramp's pack of belongings; to 'waltz Matilda' is to travel with this.

wan (*pr*. wonn) *adjective* pale, especially from illness or exhaustion; *a wan smile*, a faint smile from a person who is ill or tired or unhappy. **wanly** *adverb*, **wanness** *noun*

wand *noun* **1** a slender rod for carrying in the hand, especially one associated with the working of magic. **2** a light pen (*see* light¹) for passing over a bar code.

wander *verb* **1** to go from place to place without a settled route or destination or a special purpose. **2** (of a road or river) to wind, to meander. **3** to leave the right path or direction; to stray from one's group or from a place. **4** to digress from a subject; *his mind is wandering*, he is inattentive or speaking disconnectedly through illness or weakness. –**wander** *noun* an act of wandering.

wanderer *noun* **1** a person who wanders. **2** a monarch butterfly.

wanderlust *noun* strong desire to travel.

wandoo (won-**doo**) *noun* a Western Australian eucalypt with a smooth mottled trunk; its hard, durable wood. [Nyungar *wandu*]

wane *verb* **1** (of the moon) to show a gradually decreasing area of brightness after being full. **2** to decrease in vigour, strength, or importance, *his influence was waning*. –**wane** *noun* **1** the process of waning. **2** a defect in a plank etc. where the bark was. □ **on the wane** waning. **waney** *adjective* [from Old English *wanian* = reduce]

Wangganguru (wung-gă-**ngoo**-roo) *noun* **1** a member of an Aboriginal people of northern SA. **2** their language.

wangle *verb* (*informal*) to obtain or arrange by using trickery, improper influence, or persuasion etc. –**wangle** *noun* (*informal*) an act of wangling.

want *verb* **1** to desire, to wish for. **2** to require or need, *your hair wants cutting*; *that wants some doing*, is hard to do; *you want to be more careful*, ought to be more careful. **3** (*informal*) to desire to come, go, or get, *the cat wants out*. **4** to lack. **5** to be without the necessaries of life, *waste not, want not*; *want for nothing*, not be needy. –**want** *noun* **1** a desire for something, a requirement, *a man of few wants*. **2** lack or need of something, deficiency, *the plants died from want of water*. **3** lack of the necessaries of life, *living in great want*. [same origin as *wane*]

wanted *adjective* (of a suspected criminal) being sought by the police for questioning or arrest.

wanting *adjective* lacking; deficient; not equal to requirements.

wanton (**wonn**-tŏn) *adjective* irresponsible, lacking proper restraint or motives. **wantonly** *adverb*, **wantonness** *noun*

war *noun* **1** strife (especially between countries) involving military, naval, or air attacks. **2** open hostility between people. **3** a strong effort to combat crime or disease or poverty etc. □ **at war** engaged in a war. **have been in the wars** (*humorous*) to show signs of injury or rough usage. **war crime** a crime violating the international laws of war. **war cry** a word or cry shouted in attacking or in rallying one's side; the slogan of a political or other party. **war dance** a dance performed before battle or after a victory. **war game** a game in which models representing troops etc. are moved about on maps; a training exercise in which sets of armed forces participate in mock opposition to each other. **war memorial** a memorial erected to those who died in a war. **war of nerves** an effort to wear down one's opponent by gradually destroying morale. **Wars of the Roses** the English civil wars of the 15th century between Yorkists with the white rose and Lancastrians with the red rose as their emblem.

waratah (**wo**-ră-tah) *noun* an Australian shrub with large bright red flower heads; the floral emblem of NSW. [Dharuk *warrada*]

warble *verb* to sing, especially with a gentle trilling note as certain birds do. –**warble** *noun* a warbling sound.

warbler *noun* any of several small birds usually having a melodic call.

ward (*rhymes with* ford) *noun* **1** a room with beds for a particular group of patients in a hospital. **2** an area (e.g. of a city) electing a councillor to represent it. **3** a person, especially a child, under the care of a guardian or the protection of a lawcourt. **4** each of the notches and projections in a key (or the corresponding parts in a lock) designed to prevent the lock from being opened by a key other than the right one. **–ward** *verb* **ward off** to keep at a distance (a person or thing that threatens danger), to fend off. [from Old English *weard* = guard]

warden *noun* **1** an official with supervisory duties, *traffic warden*. **2** a churchwarden. **3** a governor or president of a college, hospital, youth hostel, etc.

warder *noun* an official in charge of prisoners in a prison.

wardrobe *noun* **1** a large cupboard where clothes are stored, usually with pegs or rails etc. from which they hang. **2** a stock of clothes. **3** a theatrical company's stock of costumes. [from *guard* + *robe*]

wardroom *noun* a room in a warship for the use of commissioned officers.

ware¹ *noun* manufactured goods (especially pottery) of the kind specified, *delftware*. **wares** *plural noun* articles offered for sale, *traders displayed their wares*.

ware² *verb* beware of, look out for, *ware hounds!*

warehouse *noun* a building for storing goods or for storing furniture on behalf of its owners. [from *ware*¹ + *house*]

warfare *noun* making war, fighting; a particular form of this, *guerrilla warfare*.

warhead *noun* the explosive head of a missile or torpedo or similar weapon.

Warhol (**war**-hohl), Andy (1930–87), American painter, graphic artist, and film-maker, prominent in the New York pop art of the 1960s.

warlike *adjective* **1** fond of making war, aggressive, *a warlike people*. **2** of or for war, *warlike preparations*.

warlock *noun* (*old use*) a sorcerer. [from Old English *waer-loga* = traitor]

Warlpiri (**warl**-bree) *noun* **1** a member of an Aboriginal people of the central Northern Territory. **2** their language.

warm *adjective* **1** moderately hot, not cold or cool. **2** (of clothes etc.) keeping the body warm. **3** enthusiastic, hearty, *a warm supporter*; *the speaker got a warm reception*, a vigorous response (either favourable or unfavourable). **4** kindly and affectionate, *she has a warm heart*. **5** (of colours) suggesting warmth, containing reddish shades. **6** (of the scent in hunting) still fairly fresh and strong. **7** (of the seeker in children's games etc.) near the object sought, on the verge of finding it. **–warm** *verb* to make or become warm or warmer. □ **warm-blooded** *adjective* having blood that remains warm (ranging from 36° to 42°C) permanently. **warm-hearted** *adjective* having a kindly and affectionate disposition. **warm to** to become cordial or well-disposed to (a person); to become more animated about (a task). **warm up** to make or become warm; to reheat (food etc.); to prepare for athletic exercise by practice beforehand; to make or become more lively; to put (an audience) into a receptive mood before a performance. **warm-up** *noun*. **warmly** *adverb*, **warmness** *noun*

warmonger (**wor**-mung-ger) *noun* a person who seeks to bring about war.

warmth *noun* warmness, the state of being warm.

warn *verb* to inform (a person) about a present or future danger or about something that must be reckoned with; to advise about action in such circumstances, *we warned them to take umbrellas*. □ **warn off** to tell (a person) to keep away or to avoid (a thing).

warning *noun* something that serves to warn.

warp (*pr.* worp) *verb* **1** to cause (timber etc.) to become bent by uneven shrinkage or expansion; to become bent in this way. **2** to distort (a person's judgment or principles). **–warp** *noun* **1** a warped condition. **2** threads stretched lengthwise in a loom, to be crossed by the weft.

warpaint *noun* **1** paint used to decorate the body before battle. **2** (*informal*) make-up.

warpath *noun* □ **on the warpath** seeking hostile confrontation or revenge.

warrant (**wo**-rănt) *noun* **1** written authorisation to do something, *the police have a warrant for his arrest*. **2** a voucher entitling the holder to receive certain goods or services. **3** a justification or authorisation for an action etc., *he had no warrant for saying this*. **4** a proof or guarantee. **–warrant** *verb* **1** to serve as a warrant for, to justify, *nothing* *can warrant such rudeness.* **2** to prove or guarantee; *he'll be back, I'll warrant you*, I assure you. □ **warrant officer** a member of the armed services ranking between commissioned officers and NCOs.

warrantor (**wo**-răn-ter) *noun* a person who makes a warranty.

warranty (**wo**-răn-tee) *noun* **1** a guarantee, especially one given to the buyer of an article and involving a promise to repair defects that become apparent in it within a specified period. **2** authority or justification for doing something.

warren *noun* **1** a piece of ground in which there are many burrows in which rabbits live and breed. **2** a building or district with many narrow winding passages.

warrigal (**wo**-rĭ-găl) *adjective* wild; untamed. [Dharuk *warrigal* = wild dingo]

warring *adjective* engaged in war.

warrior *noun* a person who fights in battle; a member of any of the armed services.

Warsaw the capital of Poland. □ **Warsaw Pact** a treaty of mutual defence and military aid signed at Warsaw in 1955 by the Communist countries of Europe under Russian leadership.

warship *noun* a ship for use in war.

wart *noun* **1** a small hard roundish abnormal growth on the skin, caused by a virus. **2** a similar growth on a plant. □ **warts and all** without concealment of blemishes, defects, or unattractive features. **warty** *adjective*

warthog *noun* an African wild pig with two large tusks and wartlike growths on its face.

wartime *noun* the period when a war is being waged.

wary (**wair**-ree) *adjective* cautious, in the habit of looking out for possible danger or difficulty. **warily** *adverb*, **wariness** *noun* [compare *aware*]

was *see* **be**.

wash *verb* **1** to cleanse with water or other liquid; *wash the stain away* or *out*, remove it by washing. **2** to wash oneself; to wash clothes etc. **3** to be washable. **4** to flow past or against, to go splashing or flowing, *the sea washes the base of the cliffs*; *waves washed over the deck.* **5** (of moving liquid) to carry in a specified direction, *a wave washed him overboard*; *the meal was washed down with beer*, beer was drunk with or after it. **6** to sift (ore) by the action of water. **7** to coat

with a wash of paint or wall-colouring etc. **8** (*informal*, of reasoning) to be valid, *that argument won't wash.* –**wash** *noun* **1** washing, being washed, *give it a good wash.* **2** the process of laundering. **3** a quantity of clothes etc. that are being washed or to be washed or have just been washed. **4** disturbed water or air behind a moving ship or aircraft etc. **5** liquid food or swill for pigs etc. **6** a thin coating of colour painted over a surface. □ **come out in the wash** (of mistakes etc.) to be revealed or eliminated during the progress of work etc. **wash dirty linen in public** to discuss one's family scandals or quarrels publicly. **washed-out** *adjective* faded by washing; faded-looking; pale, exhausted. **wash-house** *noun* an outbuilding where washing is done. **wash one's hands of** to refuse to take responsibility for. **wash out** to wash (clothes etc.); to make (a game etc.) impossible by heavy rainfall; (*informal*) to cancel. **wash-out** *noun* (*informal*) a complete failure. **wash up** to wash (crockery etc.) after use; to cast up on the shore; (*Amer.*) to wash oneself; *be washed up*, (*informal*) to have failed, to be ruined.

washable *adjective* able to be washed without suffering damage.

washaway *noun* a break in a road or railway line caused by flooding.

washbasin *noun* a basin (usually fixed to a wall) for washing one's hands in.

washboard *noun* a ribbed board formerly used for scrubbing clothes; this used as a percussion instrument.

washer *noun* **1** a machine for washing things. **2** a ring of rubber or metal etc. placed between two surfaces (e.g. under a nut) to give tightness or prevent leakage. **3** (*Austral.*) a cloth for washing the face.

washerwoman *noun* a woman whose occupation is washing clothes etc.

washing *noun* clothes etc. that are being washed or to be washed or have just been washed. □ **washing machine** a machine for washing clothes etc. **washing powder** powder of soap or detergent for washing clothes etc. **washing-up** *noun* the process of washing dishes etc. after use; the dishes etc. for washing.

Washington[1] **1** a State in the north-west of the USA, bordering on the Pacific. **2** the administrative capital of the USA, covering the same area as the District of Columbia.

Washington[2], George (1732–99), American military commander and statesman, 1st President of the USA 1789–96.

washstand *noun* a piece of furniture to hold a basin and jug of water etc. for washing.

wasn't (*informal*) = was not.

wasp *noun* a stinging insect with a black and yellow striped body, especially that introduced into Australia and known as *European wasp*.

waspish *adjective* making sharp or irritable comments. **waspishly** *adverb*, **waspishness** *noun*

wassail (**woss**-ăl) *noun* (*old use*) making merry (especially at Christmas) with much drinking. **–wassail** *verb* (**wassailed**, **wassailing**) to make merry in this way. [from Old Norse *ves heill* = be in good health]

wast (*old use*) the past tense of **be**, used with *thou*.

wastage *noun* loss by waste. □ **natural wastage** loss of employees through retirement or resignation, not through declaring them redundant.

waste *verb* 1 to use extravagantly or needlessly or without an adequate result. 2 to fail to use (an opportunity). 3 to make or become gradually weaker, *wasting away for lack of food*; *a wasting disease*. **–waste** *adjective* 1 left over or thrown away because not wanted; *waste products*, useless by-products of manufacture or of a bodily process. 2 (of land) not used or cultivated or built on, unfit for use. **–waste** *noun* 1 an act of wasting or using something ineffectively, *a waste of time*. 2 waste material or food; waste products. 3 a stretch of waste land. □ **run to waste** (of liquid) to flow away uselessly. **waste breath** or **words** to talk uselessly. **waste pipe** a pipe that carries off water etc. that has been used or is not required. [from Latin *vastus* = empty]

wasteful *adjective* using more than is needed, showing waste. **wastefully** *adverb*, **wastefulness** *noun*

wasteland *noun* an expanse of barren or waste land.

waster (**wayst**-er) *noun* 1 a wasteful person. 2 (*informal*) a wastrel.

wastrel (**wayst**-rĕl) *noun* a good-for-nothing person.

watch *verb* 1 to look at, to keep one's eyes fixed on, to keep under observation. 2 to be on the alert, to take heed, *watch for an opportunity*; *watch your chance*, wait alertly for the right moment. 3 to be careful about. 4 to safeguard, to exercise protective care, *he employed a solicitor to watch his interests* or *watch over them*. **–watch** *noun* 1 the act of watching, especially to see that all is well, constant observation or attention, *keep watch*. 2 a period (usually 4 hours) for which a division of a ship's company remains on duty; a turn of duty; the part (usually half) of a ship's company on duty during a watch. 3 a small portable device indicating the time, usually worn on the wrist or carried in the pocket. □ **on the watch** alert for something.

watch-house *noun* a building, now usually attached to a police station, in which suspected lawbreakers are held under temporary arrest.

watching brief the brief of a barrister who is present during a lawsuit in order to advise a client who is not directly concerned in it.

watch-night service a religious service on the last night of the year. **watch one's step** to be careful not to stumble or fall or do something wrong. **watch out** to be on one's guard. **watcher** *noun*

watchdog *noun* 1 a dog kept to guard property etc. 2 a person who acts as guardian of people's rights etc.

watchful *adjective* watching or observing closely. **watchfully** *adverb*, **watchfulness** *noun*

watchmaker *noun* a person who makes or repairs watches.

watchman *noun* (*plural* **watchmen**) a person employed to look after an empty building etc. at night.

watchtower *noun* a tower from which observation can be kept.

watchword *noun* a word or phrase expressing briefly the principles of a party or group.

water *noun* 1 a colourless odourless tasteless liquid that is a compound of oxygen and hydrogen. 2 a sheet or body of water, e.g. a lake or sea. 3 water as supplied for domestic use. 4 a watery secretion (e.g. sweat or saliva); urine. 5 a watery infusion or other preparation, *lavender water*; *soda water*. 6 the level of the tide, *at high water*. 7 the transparency and lustre of a gem; *a diamond of the first water*, of the finest quality. **–water** *verb* 1 to sprinkle with water. 2 to supply with water; to give drinking water to (an animal). 3 to dilute with water. 4 (of a ship etc.) to take in a supply

of water. **5** to secrete tears or saliva; *make one's mouth water*, arouse desire.
□ **water biscuit** an unsweetened biscuit made from flour and water. **water buffalo** the common domestic buffalo of India, introduced to Australia. **water cannon** a device for shooting a powerful jet of water to disperse a crowd etc. **water chestnut** the corm from a sedge, used in Chinese-cookery. **water closet** a toilet with a pan that is flushed by water. **water colour** artists' paint in which the pigment is diluted with water (not oil); a picture painted with paints of this kind. **water down** to dilute; to make less forceful or vivid. **water glass** a thick liquid used for coating eggs in order to preserve them. **water ice** an edible concoction of frozen flavoured water. **watering hole** a pool from which animals drink; (*informal*) a pub or bar. **watering place** a pool where animals go to drink water; a spa or seaside resort. **water level** the surface of water in a reservoir etc.; the height of this; = water table (*see below*). **water lily** a plant that grows in water, with broad floating leaves and large flowers. **water main** a main pipe in a water-supply system. **water pistol** a toy pistol that shoots a jet of water. **water polo** a game played by teams of swimmers with a ball like a football. **water power** power obtained from flowing or falling water, used to drive machinery or generate electric current. **water rat** a rodent that lives beside a lake or stream. **water rate** the charge made for use of a public water supply. **water softener** a substance or apparatus for softening hard water. **water table** the level below which the ground is saturated with water. **water tower** a tower that holds a water tank at a height to secure pressure for distributing water. **water wings** floats worn on the shoulders by a person learning to swim.

waterbed *noun* a mattress filled with water.

waterbird *noun* a bird that swims on or wades in water.

watercourse *noun* a stream or artificial waterway; its channel.

watercress *noun* a kind of cress that grows in streams or ponds, with strong-tasting leaves, used as salad.

watered *adjective* (of fabric, especially silk) having an irregular wavy marking.

waterfall *noun* a stream that falls from a height.

waterfowl *plural noun* waterbirds, especially game birds that swim.

waterfront *noun* the part of a town that borders on the sea, a river, or lake.

Watergate an incident during the US election campaign of 1972, when the Republican Party supporting President Nixon attempted to bug the offices of the Democratic Party at the Watergate building in Washington, DC. The subsequent scandal forced the resignation of President Nixon.

waterhole *noun* **1** a hole in which water collects, especially in the bed of an otherwise dry river. **2** a pond or pool.

waterless *adjective* without water.

waterline *noun* the line along which the surface of water touches a ship's side.

waterlogged *adjective* **1** (of timber or a ship) saturated or filled with water so that it will barely float. **2** (of ground) so saturated with water that it is useless or unable to be worked.

Waterloo a village in Belgium where in 1815 Napoleon's army was defeated by the British and Prussians. □ **meet one's Waterloo** to lose a decisive contest.

watermark *noun* **1** a mark showing how high a river or tide rises or how low it falls. **2** a manufacturer's design in some kinds of paper, visible when the paper is held against light.

watermelon *noun* a melon with a smooth green skin, red pulp, and watery juice.

watermill *noun* a mill worked by a waterwheel.

waterproof *adjective* unable to be penetrated by water. –**waterproof** *noun* a waterproof coat or cape. –**waterproof** *verb* to make waterproof.

watershed *noun* **1** a line of high land where streams on one side flow into one river or sea and streams on the other side flow into another. **2** a turning point in the course of events. **3** a catchment area.

waterside *noun* the edge of a river, lake, or sea.

waterski *noun* (*plural* **waterskis**) each of a pair of skis for skimming the surface of the water when towed by a motor boat. –**waterski** *verb* (**waterskis**, **waterski'd** or **waterskied**, **waterskiing**) to travel on waterskis.

waterspout *noun* a funnel-shaped column of water between sea and cloud, formed when a whirlwind draws up a whirling mass of water.

watertight *adjective* **1** made or fastened so that water cannot get in or out. **2** (of an excuse or alibi) impossible to set aside or disprove; (of an agreement) leaving no possibility of escape from its provisions.

waterway *noun* **1** a route for travel by water. **2** a navigable channel.

waterwheel *noun* a wheel turned by a flow of water, used to work machinery.

waterworks *noun* an establishment with pumping machinery etc. for supplying water to a district.

watery *adjective* **1** of or like water. **2** made weak or thin by too much water. **3** full of water or moisture, *watery eyes*. **4** (of colours) pale; *a watery moon* or *sky*, looking as if rain will come. □ **watery grave** death by drowning.

Wathawurung (**wut**-ă-wŭ-rung) *noun* **1** a member of an Aboriginal people of Victoria to the west of Melbourne. **2** their language.

Watson¹, **Dr** a doctor who is the companion and assistant of Sherlock Holmes in stories by Sir Arthur Conan Doyle.

Watson², James Dewey (born 1928), American biologist, who together with F.H.C. Crick proposed a structure for the DNA molecule.

Watt (*pr.* wot), James (1736–1819), Scottish engineer, who greatly improved the steam engine.

watt (*pr.* wot) *noun* a unit of electric power. [named after James Watt]

wattage (**wot**-ij) *noun* an amount of electric power, expressed in watts.

wattle¹ (**wot**'l) *noun* **1** a structure of interwoven sticks and twigs used as material for fences, walls, etc. **2** an Australian acacia with long flexible branches, bearing golden flowers adopted as the national emblem.

wattle² (**wot**'l) *noun* a red fleshy fold of skin hanging from the head or throat of certain birds, e.g. the turkey.

waul *verb* to caterwaul.

wave *noun* **1** a ridge of water moving along the surface of the sea etc. or arching and breaking on the shore. **2** something compared to this, e.g. an advancing group of attackers, a temporary increase of an influence or condition (*a wave of anger*), a spell of hot or cold weather (*a heat wave*). **3** a wavelike curve or arrangement of curves, e.g. in a line

or in hair. **4** an act of waving. **5** the wavelike motion by which heat, light, sound, or electricity etc. is spread or carried; a single curve in the course of this, plotted (in a graph) against time. **–wave** *verb* **1** to move loosely to and fro or up and down. **2** to move (one's arm or hand or something held) to and fro as a signal or greeting. **3** to signal or express in this way, *waved him away*; *waved goodbye*. **4** to give a wavy course or appearance to. **5** to be wavy. □ **wave aside** to dismiss (an objection etc.) as unimportant or irrelevant. **wave down** to signal (a vehicle or its driver) to stop, by waving one's hand. **wave front** (in physics) a surface containing all the points affected in the same way by a wave at a given time.

> **Usage** Distinguish *wave* from *waive* meaning 'to refrain from insisting on (one's right etc.)'.

waveband *noun* a range of wavelengths between certain limits.

waveform *noun* a curve showing the shape of a wave at a given time.

wavelength *noun* the distance between corresponding points (e.g. peaks) in a sound wave or an electromagnetic wave.

wavelet *noun* a small wave.

waver *verb* **1** to be or become unsteady, to begin to give way, *the line of troops wavered and then broke*; *his courage wavered*. **2** (of light) to flicker. **3** to show hesitation or uncertainty, *he wavered between two opinions*. **waverer** *noun*

> **Usage** Distinguish *waver* from *waiver*, meaning 'the forgoing of a right etc.'

wavy *adjective* full of waves or wavelike curves. **waviness** *noun*

wax¹ *noun* **1** beeswax. **2** any of various soft sticky substances that melt easily (e.g. obtained from petroleum), used for various purposes such as making candles or polishes. **3** a yellow waxy substance secreted in the ears. **–wax** *verb* **1** to coat, polish, or treat with wax. **2** to remove unwanted hair from (the legs etc.) using wax.

wax² *verb* **1** (of the moon) to show a bright area that is becoming gradually larger until it becomes full. **2** to increase in vigour, strength, or importance, *kingdoms waxed and waned*. **3** to become, *they waxed lyrical*.

waxen *adjective* **1** made of wax. **2** like wax in its paleness or smoothness.

waxwing *noun* any of several small birds with small red tips (like sealing-wax) on some wing-feathers.

waxwork *noun* an object modelled in wax, especially a model of a person with the face etc. made in wax, clothed to look lifelike and to be exhibited.

waxy *adjective* like wax. **waxiness** *noun*

way *noun* **1** a line of communication between places, e.g. a path or road. **2** the best route, the route taken or intended, *asked the way to Ballarat*. **3** a method or style, a person's chosen or desired course of action, *do it my way*; *have one's way*, cause people to do as one wishes. **4** travelling distance, *it's a long way to Tipperary*. **5** the amount of difference between two states or conditions, *his work is a long way from being perfect*. **6** space free of obstacles so that people can pass; *make way*, allow room for others to proceed. **7** the route over which a person or thing is moving or would naturally move, *don't get in the way of the traffic*, *which way is she looking?* **9** a manner, *she spoke in a kindly way*. **10** a habitual manner or course of action or events, *you'll soon get into our ways*. **11** a talent or skill, *she has a way with flowers*. **12** advance in some direction, progress, *we made our way to the front*. **13** a respect, a particular aspect of something, *it's a good plan in some ways*. **14** a condition or state, *things are in a bad way*. **–way** *adverb* (*informal*) far, *the shot was way off target*. ☐ **by the way** incidentally, as a more or less irrelevant comment. **by way of** as a substitute for or a form of, *smiled by way of greeting*. **in a way** to a limited extent; in some respects. **in no way** not at all. **in the way** forming an obstacle or hindrance. **look the other way** deliberately ignore a person or thing. **on one's way** in the process of travelling or approaching. **on the way** on one's way; (of a baby) conceived but not yet born. **under way** *see* **under**. **way back** (*informal*) a long way back. **way-out** *adjective* (*informal*) exaggeratedly unusual in style, exotic; avant-garde.

wayang (**wy**-yung) *noun* (in Indonesia and Malaysia) a theatrical performance employing puppets or human dancers.

waybill *noun* a list of the passengers or goods carried by a vehicle.

wayfarer *noun* a traveller, especially on foot.

waylay *verb* (**waylaid**, **waylaying**) to lie in wait for, especially so as to talk to or rob.

wayside *noun* the side of a road or path; land bordering this.

wayward *adjective* childishly self-willed, not obedient or easily controlled. **waywardness** *noun*

Wb *abbreviation* weber.

WC *abbreviation* water closet.

we *pronoun* **1** used by a person referring to himself or herself and another or others, or speaking on behalf of a nation, group, or firm etc. **2** used instead of 'I' by a royal person in formal proclamations and by the writer of an editorial article in a newspaper etc. **3** (*humorous*) you, *and how are we today?*

weak *adjective* **1** lacking strength, power, or numbers; easily broken, bent, or defeated. **2** lacking vigour, not acting strongly, *weak eyes*; *a weak stomach*, easily upset. **3** not convincing or forceful, *the evidence is weak*. **4** dilute, having little of a certain substance in proportion to the amount of water, *weak tea*; *a weak solution of salt and water*. **5** (of verbs) forming the past tense etc. by adding a suffix (e.g. *walk/walked*, *waste/wasted*) not by changing the vowel (*see* **strong**, sense 6). ☐ **weak-kneed** *adjective* giving way weakly, especially when intimidated. **weak-minded** *adjective* lacking determination.

weaken *verb* to make or become weaker.

weakling *noun* a feeble person or animal.

weakly *adverb* in a weak manner. **–weakly** *adjective* sickly, not robust.

weakness *noun* **1** the state of being weak. **2** a weak point; a defect or fault. **3** inability to resist something, a particular fondness.

weal[1] *noun* a ridge raised on the flesh by a stroke of a rod or whip.

weal[2] *noun* (*literary*) welfare, prosperity, *for the public weal*.

wealth *noun* **1** riches; possession of these. **2** a great quantity, *a book with a wealth of illustrations*. [from *well*[2]]

wealthy *adjective* (**wealthier**, **wealthiest**) having wealth, rich. **wealthiness** *noun*

wean *verb* **1** to accustom (a baby) to take food other than milk. **2** to cause (a person) to give up a habit or interest etc. gradually.

weapon *noun* **1** a thing designed or used as a means of inflicting bodily harm, e.g. a gun or bomb, or a horn or claw. **2** an action or procedure used as a means of getting the better of someone in a conflict, *use the weapon of a general strike*.

weaponry *noun* weapons collectively.

wear¹ *verb* (**wore**, **worn**, **wearing**) **1** to have on the body, e.g. as clothing or ornaments or make-up; *he wears his hair long*, keeps it that way. **2** to have (a certain look) on one's face, *wearing a frown*. **3** (*informal*) to accept or tolerate, *we suggested working shorter hours but the boss wouldn't wear it*. **4** to injure the surface of or become injured by rubbing, stress, or use; to make (a hole etc.) in this way. **5** to exhaust or overcome by persistence, *wore down the opposition*. **6** to endure continued use, *this fabric wears well*. **7** (of time) to pass gradually, *the night wore on*. – **wear** *noun* **1** wearing or being worn as clothing, *choose cotton for summer wear*. **2** clothing, *menswear is on the first floor*. **3** (also **wear and tear**) damage resulting from ordinary use. **4** capacity to endure being used, *there's a lot of wear left in that coat*. □ **wear off** to remove or be removed by wear; to become gradually less intense. **wear one's heart on one's sleeve** to show one's affections quite openly. **wear out** to use or be used until no longer usable. **wear the trousers** (of a wife) to dominate her husband. **wearer** *noun*

wear² *verb* (**wore**, **wearing**) to come or bring (a ship) about by turning its head away from the wind.

wearable *adjective* able to be worn.

wearisome *adjective* causing weariness.

weary *adjective* (**wearier**, **weariest**) **1** very tired, especially from exertion or endurance. **2** tired of something, *weary of war*. **3** tiring; tedious. – **weary** *verb* (**wearied**, **wearying**) to make or become weary. **wearily** *adverb*, **weariness** *noun*

weasel *noun* a small fierce animal with a slender body and reddish-brown fur, living on small animals, birds' eggs, etc. – **weasel** *verb* to default on an obligation. □ **weasel word** a word that is intentionally ambiguous or misleading.

weather *noun* the condition of the atmosphere at a certain place and time, with reference to the presence or absence of sunshine, rain, wind, etc. – **weather** *adjective* windward, *on the weather side*. – **weather** *verb* **1** to dry or season by exposure to the action of the weather. **2** to become dried or discoloured or worn etc. in this way. **3** to sail

to windward of, *the ship weathered the Cape*. **4** to come safely through, *weathered the storm*. □ **keep a weather eye open** to be watchful. **under the weather** feeling unwell or depressed; drunk. **weather-beaten** *adjective* damaged or worn by exposure to weather.

weatherboard *noun* **1** a sloping board for keeping out rain and wind, especially one attached at the bottom of a door. **2** each of a series of overlapping horizontal boards, fixed to the outside wall of buildings. – **weatherboard** *adjective* (of a building) constructed with weatherboards.

weatherproof *adjective* unable to be penetrated by rain or wind.

weathervane *noun* (also **weathercock**) a revolving pointer, often in the shape of a rooster, mounted in a high place and turning easily in the wind to show from which direction the wind is blowing.

weave¹ *verb* (**wove**, **woven**, **weaving**) **1** to make (fabric etc.) by passing crosswise threads or strips under and over lengthwise ones. **2** to form (thread etc.) into fabric in this way. **3** to put together into a connected whole, to compose (a story etc.). – **weave** *noun* a style or pattern of weaving, *a loose weave*. □ **weaver-bird** *noun* a tropical bird that builds a nest of elaborately interwoven twigs etc. **weaver** *noun*

weave² *verb* (**weaved**, **weaving**) to move from side to side in an intricate course, *weaved his way through the crowd*. □ **get weaving** (*informal*) to begin action energetically.

web *noun* **1** the network of fine strands made by a spider etc. **2** a network, *a web of deceit*. **3** skin filling the spaces between the toes of birds such as ducks and animals such as frogs. **4 Web** = World Wide Web. □ **web-footed** *adjective* having the toes joined by webs. **webbed** *adjective*

webbing *noun* strong bands of woven fabric used in upholstery, belts, etc.

webcam *noun* a video camera connected to a computer connected to the Internet, so that its images can be seen by Internet users.

webcast *noun* a live video broadcast of an event transmitted across the Internet.

Weber (**vay**-bă), Max (1864–1920), German economist and sociologist, regarded as one of the founders of modern sociology.

weber (**vay**-ber) *noun* a unit of magnetic flux. [named after the German physicist W. E. Weber (died 1891)]

weblink *noun* 1 = hyperlink. 2 a printed address of a website in a book etc.

weblog *noun* a personal website, on which an individual or groups of users record opinions, links to other sites, etc., on a regular basis.

webpage *noun* a document connected to the World Wide Web.

website *noun* a location connected to the Internet that maintains one or more pages on the World Wide Web.

wed *verb* (**wedded**, **wedding**) 1 to marry. 2 to unite, *if we can wed efficiency to economy.* □ **wedded to** devoted to and unable to abandon (an occupation or opinion etc.).

we'd (*informal*) = we had; we should; we would.

wedding *noun* a marriage ceremony and festivities. □ **wedding ring** a ring worn by a married person.

wedge *noun* 1 a piece of wood or metal etc. thick at one end and tapered to a thin edge at the other, thrust between things to force them apart or prevent free movement etc. 2 a wedge-shaped thing. – **wedge** *verb* 1 to force apart or fix firmly by using a wedge. 2 to thrust or pack tightly between other things or people or in a limited space; to be immovable because of this. □ **wedge-tailed eagle** a large Australian eagle with dark brown plumage and a wedge-shaped tail, also called an *eagle hawk*.

Wedgwood *noun* (*trademark*) a kind of fine pottery named after Josiah Wedgwood, its original 18th-century manufacturer. □ **Wedgwood blue** the blue colour characteristic of this.

wedlock *noun* the married state. [from Old English, = marriage vow]

Wednesday *noun* the day of the week following Tuesday. [from Old English *Wodnesdaeg* = day of (w)odin]

wee *adjective* (*informal*) little, tiny, *it's a wee bit too long.*

weed *noun* 1 a wild plant growing where it is not wanted. 2 (*informal*) marijuana. 3 a thin weak-looking person. – **weed** *verb* to remove weeds from; to uproot weeds. □ **weed out** to remove as inferior or undesirable.

weedkiller *noun* a substance used to destroy weeds.

weeds *plural noun* deep mourning formerly worn by widows.

weedy *adjective* 1 full of weeds. 2 thin and weak-looking.

week *noun* 1 a period of seven successive days, especially one reckoned from midnight at the end of Saturday. 2 the five days other than Saturday and Sunday, *never go there during the week.* 3 the period for which one regularly works during a week, *a 35-hour week.*

weekday *noun* a day other than Saturday or Sunday.

weekend *noun* Saturday and Sunday.

weekender *noun* (*Austral.*) a cottage or shack used for weekend visits.

weekly *adjective* happening, published, or payable etc. once a week. – **weekly** *adverb* once a week. – **weekly** *noun* a weekly newspaper or magazine.

weeny *adjective* (*informal*) tiny.

weep *verb* (**wept**, **weeping**) 1 to shed tears. 2 to shed or ooze moisture in drops. – **weep** *noun* a spell of weeping.

weeping *adjective* (of a tree) having drooping branches, *weeping willow.*

weepy *adjective* (*informal*) inclined to weep, tearful.

weevil *noun* a kind of small beetle that feeds on grain, nuts, bark, etc.

weft *noun* crosswise threads woven under and over the warp to make fabric.

weigh *verb* 1 to measure the weight of, especially by means of scales or a similar instrument. 2 to have a certain weight. 3 to consider carefully the relative importance of value of, *weigh the pros and cons.* 4 to have importance or influence, *this evidence weighed with the jury.* 5 to be burdensome, *the responsibility weighed heavily upon him.* □ **weigh anchor** to raise the anchor and start a voyage. **weigh down** to bring or keep down by its weight; to depress or make troubled, *weighed down with cares.* **weigh in** to be weighed, (of a boxer) before a contest, (of a jockey) after a race. **weigh in with** (*informal*) to contribute (a comment) to a discussion. **weigh one's words** to select carefully those that convey exactly what one means. **weigh up** (*informal*) to assess, to form an estimate of.

weighbridge *noun* a weighing machine with a plate set in a road etc. on to which vehicles can be driven to be weighed.

weight *noun* 1 an object's mass numerically expressed according to a recognised scale of units. 2 the property of heaviness. 3 a unit or system of units by which weight is measured, *tables of weights and measures*; *troy weight*. 4 a piece of metal of known weight used in scales for weighing things. 5 a heavy object, especially one used to bring or keep something down, *the clock is worked by weights*. 6 a load to be supported, *the pillars carry a great weight*. 7 a heavy burden of responsibility or worry. 8 importance, influence, a convincing effect, *the weight of the evidence is against you*. –**weight** *verb* 1 to attach a weight to; to hold down with a weight or weights. 2 to burden with a load. 3 to bias or arrange the balance of, *the test was weighted in favour of candidates with scientific knowledge*. □ **carry weight** to be influential. **throw one's weight about** (*informal*) to use one's influence aggressively. **weight training** a system of physical training using weights in the form of barbells (with adjustable weights) and dumb-bells.

weighting *noun* extra pay or allowances given in special cases.

weightless *adjective* having no weight, or with no weight relative to its surroundings (e.g. in a spacecraft moving under the action of gravity). **weightlessness** *noun*

weightlifting *noun* the athletic sport of lifting heavy weights. **weightlifter** *noun*

weighty *adjective* (**weightier**, **weightiest**) 1 having great weight, heavy. 2 burdensome. 3 showing or deserving earnest thought. 4 important, influential. **weightily** *adverb*, **weightiness** *noun*

Weimar (**vy**-mar) a town in eastern Germany, seat of the National Assembly of Germany 1919–33. □ **Weimar Republic** the German republic of this period.

weir (*pr.* weer) *noun* 1 a small dam built across a river or canal so that water flows over it, serving to regulate the flow or to raise the level of water upstream. 2 the water flowing over it in a waterfall.

weird *adjective* strange and uncanny or bizarre. **weirdly** *adverb*, **weirdness** *noun*

weirdo *noun* (*plural* **weirdos**) (*informal*) an eccentric person.

welcome *adjective* 1 received with pleasure, *a welcome guest* or *gift*; *make a person welcome*, cause him or her to feel welcome. 2 ungrudgingly permitted, *anyone is welcome to try it*; *you're welcome*, a polite phrase replying to thanks for something. –**welcome**

interjection a greeting expressing pleasure at a person's coming. –**welcome** *verb* 1 to greet with pleasure or ceremony. 2 to be glad to receive, *we welcome this opportunity*. –**welcome** *noun* a greeting or reception, especially a glad and kindly one. □ **welcome to country** a welcome to the traditional land of an Aboriginal people by a member of the local Aboriginal community. [from *well²* + *come*]

weld *verb* 1 to unite or fuse (pieces of metal or plastic) by hammering or pressure, usually after softening by heat. 2 to make by welding. 3 to be able to be welded. 4 to unite into a whole. –**weld** *noun* a joint made by welding. **welder** *noun*

welfare *noun* 1 well-being. 2 welfare work. □ **welfare state** a country seeking to ensure the welfare of all its citizens by means of social services operated by the state. **welfare work** organised efforts to secure the welfare of poor or disabled people etc. [from *well²* + *fare*]

welkin *noun* (*poetical*) the sky.

well¹ *noun* 1 a shaft dug in the ground to obtain water or oil etc. from below the earth's surface. 2 a spring serving as a source of water. 3 an enclosed space resembling the shaft of a well; a deep enclosed space containing a staircase or lift in a building. –**well** *verb* to rise or spring, *tears welled up in her eyes*. [from Old English *wella* = spring of water]

well² *adverb* (**better**, **best**) 1 in a good or suitable way, satisfactorily, rightly. 2 thoroughly, carefully, *polish it well*. 3 by a considerable margin, *she is well over forty*. 4 favourably, kindly, *they think well of him*. 5 with good reason, easily, probably, *you may well ask*; *it may well be our last chance*. –**well** *adjective* 1 in good health. 2 in a satisfactory state or position, *all's well*. –**well** *interjection* expressing surprise or relief or resignation etc., or used to introduce a remark when one is hesitating. □ **as well**, **as well as** *see* **as**. **be well away** to have started and made considerable progress. **leave** or **let well alone** to leave things as they are and not meddle unnecessarily. **well-advised** *adjective* showing good sense. **well-being** *noun* good health, happiness, and prosperity. **well-born** *adjective* born of good family. **well-bred** *adjective* showing good breeding, well-mannered; (of a horse etc.) of good breed or stock. **well-connected** *adjective* related to good families. **well-disposed** *adjective* having kindly or favourable feelings (towards a person or plan etc.). **well-favoured** *adjective* good-looking. **well-groomed** *adjective* carefully tended, neat and clean in one's personal appearance. **well-heeled** *adjective* (*informal*) wealthy. **well-intentioned** *adjective* having or showing good intentions. **well-judged** *adjective* (of an action) showing good judgment or tact or aim. **well-knit** *adjective* having a compact body, not ungainly. **well-known** *adjective* known to many; known thoroughly. **well-mannered** *adjective* having or showing good manners. **well-meaning**, **well-meant** *adjectives* acting or done with good intentions but not having a good effect. **well off** in a satisfactory or good situation; fairly rich. **well-read** *adjective* having read much literature. **well-spoken** *adjective* speaking in a polite and correct way. **well-to-do** *adjective* fairly rich. **well-wisher** *noun* a person who wishes another well. **well-worn** *adjective* much worn by use; (of a phrase) much used, hackneyed. [from Old English *wel* = prosperously]

Usage A hyphen is used in combinations of *well-* when used before a noun, as in *a well-groomed woman*, but not when used after the verb, as in *the woman is well groomed*.

---

we'll (*informal*) = we shall; we will.

Wellington¹ the capital of New Zealand, situated in the south of the North Island.

Wellington², Arthur Wellesley, 1st Duke of (1769–1852), British soldier and statesman, victor over Napoleon at the battle of Waterloo (1815).

wellington *noun* a boot of rubber or similar waterproof material, usually reaching almost to the knee. [named after the first Duke of Wellington]

wellnigh *adverb* almost.

Wells, H. G. (Herbert George) (1866–1946), English novelist, an early writer of science fiction.

Welsh *adjective* of Wales or its people or language. **–Welsh** *noun* the Welsh language. **–the Welsh** Welsh people. □ **Welsh rabbit** or **rarebit** melted or toasted cheese on toast. (¶ *Welsh rabbit* is the original name for this dish. The humorous use of *rabbit* was misunderstood and the word was altered to *rarebit* in an attempt to make it sound more understandable, but there is no independent evidence for the word *rarebit*.) **Welshman**, **Welshwoman** *nouns*

welsh *verb* **1** (of a bookmaker at a racecourse) to swindle by leaving without paying out winnings. **2** to avoid paying one's just debts, to break an agreement, *they welshed on us* or *on the agreement*. **welsher** *noun*

welt *noun* **1** a strip of leather etc. sewn round the edge of the upper of a boot or shoe for attaching it to the sole. **2** a ribbed or strengthened border of a knitted garment, e.g. at the waist. **3** a weal, the mark of a heavy blow.

welter *verb* (of a ship etc.) to be tossed to and fro on the waves. **–welter** *noun* **1** a state of turmoil. **2** a disorderly mixture.

welterweight *noun* a boxing weight between lightweight and middleweight, in amateur boxing 63.5–67 kg. [from an old word *welter* = a heavy person]

Wemba-wemba (**wem**-bă-wem-bă) *noun* **1** a member of an Aboriginal people of western Victoria. **2** their language.

wen *noun* a benign tumour on the skin, especially on the head.

Wenceslas, St (907–29), prince of Bohemia and patron saint of the Czech Republic. Feast day, 28 September.

wench *noun* (*old use* or *jocular*) a girl or young woman.

wend *verb* **wend one's way** to go.

went *see* go.

Wentworth, William Charles (1790–1872), Australian lawyer and statesman. In 1813, with Blaxland and Lawson, he made the first crossing of the Blue Mountains.

wept *see* weep.

were *see* be.

weren't (*informal*) = were not.

werewolf (**weer**-wuulf) *noun* (*plural* **werewolves**) (in myths) a person who at times turns into a wolf. [from Old English *wer* = man, + *wolf*]

wert (*old use*) the past subjunctive of be, used with *thou*.

Wesley, John (1703–91), an Anglican priest, who founded the Methodist movement that eventually became an independent denomination. His brother Charles (1707–88) was also a member of the movement and the writer of many well-known hymns.

Wessex the kingdom of the West Saxons, which by the 10th century covered much of southern England.

west *noun* **1** the point of the horizon where the sun sets, opposite east; the direction in which this lies. **2** the western part of something. **3 the West** Europe in contrast to Oriental countries; the States of western Europe and North America. **–west** *adjective & adverb* towards or in the west; *a west wind*, blowing from the west. □ **go west** (*informal*) to be destroyed, lost, or killed. **West Bank** the area on the west side of the River Jordan occupied by Israel in 1967.

westering *adjective* (of the sun) moving towards the west.

westerly *adjective* in or towards the west; *a westerly wind*, blowing from the west (approximately). **–westerly** *noun* a westerly wind.

western *adjective* **1** of or in the west. **2** of westerns. **–western** *noun* a film or story about cowboys in western North America. □ **Western Church** the Churches of western Christendom as distinct from the Eastern or Orthodox Church.

Western Australia the largest State in Australia, comprising the western part of the continent.

Western Desert language the name for a single Aboriginal language (with many dialects) spoken over about one and a quarter million square kilometres of central and western Australia.

westerner *noun* a native or inhabitant of the west.

westernise *verb* (also **-ize**) to make (a person or a country) more like the West in ideas and institutions etc. **westernisation** *noun*

westernmost *adjective* furthest west.

Western Samoa *see* Samoa.

West Indies a chain of islands in the Atlantic Ocean off Central America, enclosing the Caribbean Sea. **West Indian** *adjective & noun*

Westminster *noun* Parliament or the Houses of Parliament in London; *the Westminster system*, a system of parliamentary government as in Britain, involving two houses of parliament, an independent judiciary, and in which the head of state is not the head of government. [named after the district of London where the Houses of Parliament (*Palace of Westminster*) are situated]

Westminster Abbey a church in London, the place of burial of many monarchs.

West Papua another name for Papua.

West Virginia a State of the USA, to the west of Virginia.

westward *adjective & adverb* in or towards the west. **westwards** *adverb*

wet *adjective* (**wetter, wettest**) **1** soaked, covered, or moistened with water or other liquid. **2** rainy, *wet weather*. **3** (of paint or ink etc.) recently applied and not yet dry. **4** allowing the sale of alcohol. **5** (*informal*, of a person) lacking good sense or mental vitality or firmness of purpose, dull. **6** (*informal*) of, or being, a political 'wet'. **–wet** *verb* (**wetted, wetting**) to make wet. **–wet** *noun* **1** moisture, liquid that wets something. **2 the wet** wet weather; the rainy season. **3** (*informal*) a dull or unenterprising person. **4** (*informal*) a socially progressive conservative. □ **wet behind the ears** immature, inexperienced. **wet blanket** a gloomy person who prevents others from enjoying themselves. **wet dock** a dock in which a ship can float. **wet-nurse** *noun* a woman employed to suckle another's child; (*verb*) to act as wet-nurse to; to look after or coddle as if helpless. **wetly** *adverb*, **wetness** *noun*, **wettish** *adjective* [from Old English *waet* = wet]

Usage Distinguish *wet* from *whet*, meaning 'to sharpen' or 'to stimulate', as in *whet the appetite*.

wether *noun* a castrated ram.

wetlands *plural noun* marshy land, swamps.

wetsuit *noun* a close-fitting rubber garment worn for warmth by a diver etc.

we've (*informal*) = we have.

whack *noun* **1** a heavy resounding blow. **2** (*informal*) an attempt, *have a whack at it*. **3** (*informal*) a share, *do one's whack*. **–whack** *verb* **1** to strike or beat vigorously. **2** (*informal*) to put or throw down, *whack your bags in the corner*.

whacked *adjective* (*informal*) tired out.

whacking *adjective* (*informal*) very large. **–whacking** *adverb* (*informal*) very, *a whacking great car*.

whale *noun* any of several very large sea animals some of which are hunted for their oil and flesh. □ **a whale of a** (*informal*) an exceedingly great or good, *had a whale of a time*.

whalebone *noun* a horny springy substance from the upper jaw of some kinds of whale, formerly used as stiffening.

whaler *noun* a person or ship engaged in hunting whales.

whaling *noun* hunting whales.

wham *interjection* & *noun* the sound of a forcible impact.

wharf (*pr.* worf) *noun* (*plural* wharfs or wharves) a landing stage where ships may moor for loading and unloading.

what *adjective* 1 asking for a statement of amount, number, or kind, *what stores have we got?* 2 which, *what languages does he speak?* 3 how great or strange or remarkable, *what a fool you are!* 4 the, any that, or that which, *lend me what money you can spare.* –what *pronoun* 1 what thing or things, *what did you say?*; *this is what I mean.* 2 a request for something to be repeated because one has not heard or understood. –what *adverb* to what extent or degree, *what does it matter?* –what *interjection* an exclamation of surprise. □ what about what is the news about (a subject); what do you think of, how would you deal with; shall we do or have, *what about some tea?* what-d'you-call-it, what's-his- (or its-) name substitutes for a name that one cannot remember. what for? for what reason or purpose?; *give a person what for*, (*informal*) punish or scold him or her. what have you other similar things. what is more as an additional point, moreover. what not other similar things. what's what what things are useful or important etc., *she knows what's what.* what with on account of (various causes), *what with overwork and undernourishment he fell ill.*

whatever *adjective* 1 of any kind or number, *take whatever books you need.* 2 of any kind at all, *there is no doubt whatever.* –whatever *pronoun* anything or everything that, no matter what, *do whatever you like*; *keep calm, whatever happens.* –whatever *interjection* (*informal*) said as a response indicating a reluctance to discuss something, often implying indifference. □ or whatever or anything similar.

whatnot *noun* 1 something trivial or indefinite. 2 a stand with shelves for small objects.

whatsoever *adjective* & *pronoun* = whatever.

wheat *noun* 1 grain from which flour is made. 2 the plant that produces this.

wheaten *adjective* made from wheat.

wheatmeal *noun* wholemeal flour made from wheat.

wheedle *verb* to coax; to persuade or obtain by coaxing.

wheel *noun* 1 a disc or circular frame arranged to revolve on a shaft that passes through its centre. 2 something resembling this. 3 a machine etc. of which a wheel is an essential part. 4 motion like that of a wheel, or of a line of persons that pivots on one end. –wheel *verb* 1 to push or pull (a bicycle or trolley etc. with wheels) along. 2 to turn or cause to turn like a wheel; to change direction and face another way, *he wheeled round in astonishment.* 3 to move in circles or curves. wheels *plural noun* (*informal*) a car. □ at the wheel driving a vehicle or directing a ship's course; in control of affairs. wheel and deal (*informal*) to scheme so as to exert influence. wheels within wheels secret or indirect motives and influences interacting with one another.

wheelbarrow *noun* an open container for moving small loads, with a wheel or ball beneath one end, and two straight handles (by which it is pushed) and legs at the other.

wheelbase *noun* the distance between the front and rear axles of a vehicle.

wheelchair *noun* a chair on wheels, for use by a person who cannot walk.

wheelhouse *noun* a steersman's shelter.

wheelie *noun* (*informal*) 1 the stunt of riding a bicycle or motorcycle for a short distance with the front wheel off the ground. 2 the act of causing a car's drive wheels to spin by heavy acceleration. 3 a person in a wheelchair.

wheeze *verb* to breathe with an audible hoarse whistling sound. –wheeze *noun* 1 the sound of wheezing. 2 (*informal*) a clever scheme or plan. wheezy *adjective*

whelk *noun* any of several sea snails, especially one used as food.

whelp *noun* a young dog, a pup. –whelp *verb* to give birth to (a whelp or whelps).

when *adverb* 1 at what time?; on what occasion? 2 at which time, *there are times when joking is out of place.* –when *conjunction* 1 at the time that, on the occasion that; whenever; as soon as. 2 although; considering that, since, *why risk it when you* *know it's dangerous? –when pronoun* what or which time, *from when does the agreement date?*

whence *adverb & conjunction* from where, from what place or source; from which.

whenever *conjunction & adverb* at whatever time; on whatever occasion; every time that.

whensoever *conjunction & adverb* whenever.

where *adverb & conjunction* 1 at or in what or which place, position, or circumstances. 2 in what respect; from what place, source, or origin. 3 to what place. 4 in or at or to the place in which, *leave it where it is.* –where *pronoun* what place, *where does she come from?*

whereabouts *adverb* in or near what place. –whereabouts *noun & plural noun* a person's or thing's approximate location, *his whereabouts is* or *are uncertain.*

whereas *conjunction* 1 since it is the fact that. 2 but in contrast, *he is English, whereas his wife is French.*

whereby *adverb* by which.

wherefore *adverb (old use)* for what reason; for this reason.

wherein *adverb* in what; in which.

whereof *adverb & conjunction* of what or which.

wheresoever *adverb & conjunction* = wherever.

whereupon *conjunction* after which, and then.

wherever *adverb* at or to whatever place. –wherever *conjunction* in every place that.

wherewithal *noun (informal)* the things (especially money) needed for a purpose.

wherry *noun* 1 a light rowing boat. 2 a large light barge.

whet *verb* (**whetted, whetting**) 1 to sharpen by rubbing against a stone etc. 2 to stimulate, *whet one's appetite* or *interest.* [from Old English *hwettan* = sharpen]

whether *conjunction* introducing an alternative possibility, *we don't know whether she will come or not.*

whetstone *noun* a shaped stone used for sharpening tools. [from *whet* = sharpen, + *stone*]

whew *interjection* an exclamation of astonishment, dismay, or relief.

whey (*pr.* way) *noun* watery liquid left when milk forms curds, e.g. in cheese-making.

which *adjective & pronoun* 1 what particular one or ones of a set of things or people, *which Bob do you mean?* 2 and that, *we invited him to come, which he did very willingly.* –which *relative pronoun* the thing or animal referred to, *the house, which is large, is left to his son.*

Usage As a relative pronoun *which* is used especially for an incidental description rather than one that defines or identifies something. Compare the use of that.

---

whichever *adjective & pronoun* any which, that or those which, *take whichever* or *whichever one you like.*

whiff *noun* a puff of air or smoke or odour.

Whig *noun* a member of the British political party in the 17th–19th centuries opposed to the Tories, succeeded in the 19th century by the Liberal Party. [from *whiggamer*, a Scottish Presbyterian rebel in 1648]

while *noun* a period of time, the time spent in doing something, *a long while ago*; *we've waited all this while*; *worth one's while* = worth while (*see* worth). –while *conjunction* 1 during the time that, as long as, *make hay while the sun shines.* 2 although, *while I admit that he is sincere, I think he is mistaken.* 3 on the other hand, *she is dark, while her sister is fair.* –while *verb* while away to pass (time) in a leisurely or interesting manner.

whilst *conjunction* while.

whim *noun* a sudden fancy, a sudden unreasoning desire or impulse.

whimper *verb* to whine softly, to make feeble frightened or complaining sounds. –whimper *noun* a whimpering sound.

whimsical (**wim**-zi-kǎl) *adjective* 1 impulsive and playful. 2 fanciful, quaint. whimsically *adverb*, whimsicality (wim-zi-**kal**-ĭ-tee) *noun*

whimsy *noun* a whim.

whine *verb* 1 to make a long high complaining cry like that of a child or dog. 2 to make a long high shrill sound resembling this. 3 to complain in a petty or feeble way; to utter complainingly. –whine *noun* a whining cry or sound or complaint. whiner *noun*, whiny *adjective*

whinge *verb* (**whinged, whinging**) to whine, to grumble persistently. –whinge *noun* a whine or grumble.

whinny *noun* a gentle or joyful neigh.
　–whinny *verb* (whinnied, whinnying) to utter a whinny.

whip *noun* 1 a cord or strip of leather fastened to a handle, used for urging animals on or for striking a person or animal in punishment. 2 an official of a political party in parliament with authority to maintain discipline among members of the party, especially to ensure attendance and voting in debates. 3 the action of beating cream, eggs, etc. into a froth. –whip *verb* (whipped, whipping) 1 to strike or urge on with a whip. 2 to beat (cream or eggs etc.) into a froth. 3 to move or take suddenly, *whipped out a knife*. 4 to overcast (an edge). □ **have the whip hand** to be in a controlling position. **whip up** to incite, to stir up, *whip up support for the proposal*.

whipbird *noun* an Australian bird with a cry like the crack of a whip.

whipcord *noun* 1 cord made of tightly twisted strands. 2 a kind of twilled fabric with prominent ridges.

whiplash *noun* 1 the lash of a whip. 2 a neck injury caused by a sudden jerk of the head, especially in a car accident.

whippersnapper *noun* a young and insignificant person who behaves in a presumptuous way.

whippet *noun* a small dog resembling a greyhound, used for racing.

whipping boy *noun* a person who is regularly made to bear the blame and punishment when someone is at fault. [formerly, a boy who was educated with a young prince and whipped in his stead for the prince's faults]

whippy *adjective* flexible, springy.

whipstick *noun* (*Austral.*) a kind of eucalypt with several slim stems.

whirl *verb* 1 to swing or spin round and round; to cause to have this motion. 2 to travel swiftly in a curved course. 3 to convey or go rapidly in a vehicle, *the car whirled them away*. –whirl *noun* 1 a whirling movement. 2 a confused state, *her thoughts were in a whirl*. 3 a bustling activity, *the social whirl*. 4 (*informal*) a try, *give it a whirl*.

whirligig *noun* 1 a spinning or whirling toy. 2 a merry-go-round.

whirlpool *noun* a current of water whirling in a circle, often drawing floating objects towards its centre.

whirlwind *noun* a mass of air whirling rapidly about a central point; *a whirlwind courtship*, a very rapid one.

whirr *verb* to make a continuous buzzing or vibrating sound like that of a wheel etc. turning rapidly. –whirr *noun* this sound.

whisk *verb* 1 to move with a quick light sweeping movement. 2 to convey or go rapidly, *he was whisked off to the doctor*. 3 to brush or sweep lightly from a surface, *whisk away the crumbs*. 4 to beat (eggs etc.) into a froth. –whisk *noun* 1 a whisking movement. 2 an instrument for beating eggs etc. 3 a bunch of strips of straw etc. tied to a handle, used for flicking flies away.

whisker *noun* 1 each of the long hairlike bristles growing near the mouth of a cat and certain other animals. 2 (*informal*) a very small distance, *within a whisker of it*. **whiskers** *plural noun* hair growing on a man's face, especially on the cheek. **whiskered** *adjective*, **whiskery** *adjective*

whisky *noun* (*Amer., Irish* whiskey) 1 spirit distilled from malted grain (especially barley). 2 a drink of this.

whisper *verb* 1 to speak or utter softly, using the breath but not the vocal cords. 2 to converse privately or secretly; to plot or spread (a tale) as a rumour in this way. 3 (of leaves or fabrics etc.) to rustle. –whisper *noun* 1 a whispering sound or remark; whispering speech, *spoke in a whisper*. 2 a rumour. **whisperer** *noun*

whist *noun* a card game usually for two pairs of players.

whistle *noun* 1 a shrill sound made by forcing breath through the lips with these contracted to a narrow opening. 2 a similar sound made by a bird or by something thrown, or produced by a pipe etc. 3 an instrument that produces a shrill sound when air or steam is forced through it against a sharp edge or into a bell. –whistle *verb* to make this sound; to summon or signal or produce a tune in this way. □ **whistle for** (*informal*) to expect in vain, to wish for but have to go without. **whistle-stop** *noun* a brief stop (during a tour made by a politician etc.) e.g. for purposes of electioneering. **whistler** *noun*

whistleblower *noun* a person who exposes an irregularity or a crime, especially from within an organisation.

Whistler, James Abbott McNeill (1843–1903), American-born painter and etcher, noted for his portraits and landscapes.

Whit *adjective* of or including or close to **Whit Sunday**, the seventh Sunday after Easter, commemorating the descent of the Holy Spirit upon the Apostles at Pentecost. [from Old English *hwit* = white, because people used to be baptised on that day and wore white clothes]

whit *noun* the least possible amount, *not a whit better*. [from an old word *wight* = an amount]

White, Patrick Victor Martindale (1912–90), Australian novelist and playwright, whose works include *The Tree of Man* and *Voss*. White was the first Australian writer to be awarded a Nobel Prize (1973).

white *adjective* **1** of the very lightest colour, like snow or common salt. **2** (also **White**) of the human group having a light-coloured skin. **3** pale in the face from illness or fear or other emotion. –**white** *noun* **1** white colour. **2** a white substance or material; white clothes. **3** (also **White**) a white person. **4** the white part of something (e.g. of the eyeball, round the iris). **5** the transparent substance round the yolk of an egg, turning white when cooked. **6** the white men in chess etc.; the player using these. □ **white ant** a termite. **White Australia policy** (*historical*) an unofficial name for the policy that restricted immigration into Australia to white people. **white Christmas** one with snow. **white-collar worker** a worker who is not engaged in manual labour (e.g. an office worker). **white elephant** a useless possession. **white feather** a symbol of cowardice. **white flag** a symbol of surrender. **white gold** any of various silver-coloured alloys of gold used in jewellery. **white goods** large domestic electrical appliances. **white heat** the temperature at which heated metal looks white. **white horses** white-crested waves on sea. **white-hot** *adjective* at white heat, hotter than red-hot. **White House** the official residence (in Washington) of the President of the USA. **white lie** a harmless lie (e.g. one told for the sake of politeness). **white noise** noise containing many frequencies with equal intensities. **White Paper** a government report giving information on a subject. **white pointer** a great white shark. **white sauce** a sauce made of melted butter, flour, and milk or cream. **white slave** a woman who is tricked and sent (usually abroad) into prostitution. **white slavery** this practice or state. **white tie** a man's white bow tie worn with full evening dress. **white water** a shallow or foamy stretch of water. **white wine** amber or golden or pale yellow wine, not red or rosé. **whitely** *adverb*, **whiteness** *noun*, **whitish** *adjective*

whitebait *noun* (*plural* **whitebait**) a small silvery-white fish.

whiteboard *noun* a white plastic board that can be written on with a felt-tipped pen and wiped clean.

Whitehall *noun* the British Government. [from the name of a London street where there are many Government offices]

whiten *verb* to make or become white or whiter.

whitewash *noun* **1** a liquid containing quicklime or powdered chalk used for painting walls, ceilings, etc. **2** a means of glossing over mistakes or faults. **3** a contest in which the losing side has failed to score. –**whitewash** *verb* **1** to paint with whitewash. **2** to clear the reputation of (a person etc.) by glossing over mistakes or faults.

whitewood *noun* a light-coloured wood, especially one prepared for staining etc.

whither *adverb* (*old use*) to what place. –**whither** *conjunction* (*old use*) to the particular place or any place to which.

whiting¹ *noun* (*plural* **whiting**) a small sea fish with white flesh, used as food.

whiting² *noun* ground chalk used in whitewashing, plate-cleaning, etc.

whitlow (**wit**-loh) *noun* a small abscess under or near a nail.

Whitman, Walt (1819–92), American poet.

Whitsun *noun* Whit Sunday and the days close to it (*see* **Whit**). [from *Whit Sunday*]

Whittington, Sir Richard (died 1423), a medieval mayor of London, who inspired the folk tale 'Dick Whittington and his cat'.

whittle *verb* **1** to trim or shape (wood) by cutting thin slices from the surface. **2** to reduce by removing various amounts, *whittled down the cost by cutting out non-essential items*.

whiz (also **whizz**) *verb* (**whizzed**, **whizzing**) **1** to make a sound like that of something moving at great speed through air. **2** to move very quickly. –**whiz** *noun* a whizzing sound. □ **whiz-kid** *noun* (*informal*) an exceptionally brilliant or successful young person.

WHO *abbreviation* World Health Organisation.

who *pronoun* **1** what or which person or persons? **2** the particular person or persons, *this is the man who wanted to see you*.

whoa *interjection* a command to a horse etc. to stop or stand still.

who'd (*informal*) = who had; who would.

whodunit *noun* (*informal*) a detective or mystery story or play etc. [humorous representation of the incorrect phrase 'who done it?']

whoever *pronoun* any or every person who, no matter who.

whole *adjective* **1** with no part removed or left out, *told them the whole story*; *whole wheat*. **2** not injured or broken, *there's not a plate left whole*. –**whole** *noun* **1** the full or complete amount, all the parts or members. **2** a complete system made up of parts. ☐ **on the whole** considering everything; in respect of the whole though some details form exceptions. **a whole lot** (*informal*) a great amount. **whole number** a number consisting of one or more units with no fractions.

wholefood *noun* food that has not been processed or refined more than is necessary.

wholehearted *adjective* without doubts or reservations, *wholehearted approval*. **wholeheartedly** *adverb*

wholemeal *adjective* made from the whole grain of wheat etc.

wholesale *noun* the selling of goods in large quantities to be retailed by others. –**wholesale** *adjective* & *adverb* **1** in the wholesale trade. **2** on a large scale, *wholesale destruction*. –**wholesale** *verb* to sell in the wholesale trade. **wholesaler** *noun*

wholesome *adjective* good for physical or mental health or moral condition; showing a healthy condition. **wholesomeness** *noun*

who'll (*informal*) = who will.

wholly *adverb* entirely, with nothing excepted or removed.

whom *pronoun* the objective case of *who*, as in *Whom did you see?* and *the man whom she married*. **whomever** (*formal*) the objective case of *whoever*, **whomsoever** that of *whosoever*.

Usage In informal speech it is acceptable to use *who* instead of *whom* in questions, as in *Who did you see?*

whoop (*pr.* woop) *verb* to utter a loud cry of excitement. –**whoop** *noun* this cry.

whoopee *interjection* an exclamation of exuberant joy.

whooping cough (**hoop**-ing) *noun* an infectious disease especially of children, with a cough that is followed by a long rasping indrawn breath.

whoops (*pr.* woops) *interjection* (*informal*) an exclamation of surprise or apology.

whopper *noun* (*informal*) something very large.

whopping *adjective* (*informal*) very large or remarkable, *a whopping lie*.

whore (*pr.* hor) *noun* a prostitute; a sexually immoral woman.

whorl *noun* **1** a coiled form; one turn of a spiral. **2** a complete circle formed by ridges in a fingerprint. **3** a ring of leaves or petals round a stem or central point.

who's (*informal*) = who is, who has. ☐ **Who's Who** a reference book containing a list of notable people and facts concerning them.

whose *pronoun* of whom, of which, *the people whose house we admired*; *the house whose owner takes pride in it*.

Usage *Who's* is sometimes confused with *whose*. *Who's* is used where you can substitute 'who is' or 'who has', e.g. *who's coming?* or *who's been there?*

whosoever *pronoun* = whoever.

why *adverb* **1** for what reason or purpose? **2** on account of which, *the reasons why it happened are not clear*. –**why** *interjection* an exclamation of surprised discovery or recognition. –**why** *noun* (*plural* **whys**) a reason. ☐ **whys and wherefores** reasons.

wick *noun* a length of thread in the centre of a candle, oil lamp, or cigarette lighter etc. by which the flame is kept supplied with melted grease or fuel.

wicked *adjective* **1** morally bad, offending against what is right. **2** very bad or formidable, severe. **3** malicious, mischievous, *a wicked grin*. **4** (*informal*) excellent. **wickedly** *adverb*, **wickedness** *noun*

wicker *noun* thin canes or osiers woven together as material for making furniture or baskets etc. **wickerwork** *noun*

wicket *noun* **1** a set of three stumps and two bails used in cricket, defended by the batsman who is 'out' if the bails are knocked off by the ball. **2** the part of a cricket ground between or near the wickets.

wicketkeeper *noun* a fielder in cricket who stands close behind the batsman's wicket.

widdershins *adverb* in a direction contrary to the apparent course of the sun (considered unlucky). [from old German words *wider* = against, + *sin* = direction]

wide *adjective* **1** measuring much from side to side, not narrow, *a wide river*. **2** in width, *one metre wide*. **3** extending far, having great range, *a wide knowledge of art*. **4** open to the full extent, *staring with wide eyes*. **5** at a considerable distance from the point or mark aimed at; *his guess was wide of the mark*, quite incorrect. –**wide** *adverb* widely; to the full extent; far from the target. –**wide** *noun* a bowled ball in cricket that passes the wicket beyond the batsman's reach and counts one point to the batsman's team. □ **give a wide berth to** *see* **berth**. **wide-angle** *adjective* (of a lens) able to include a wider field of vision than a standard lens does. **wide awake** completely awake; (*informal*) fully alert. **wide-eyed** *adjective* with eyes opened widely in amazement or innocent surprise. **wide open** (of a place) exposed to attack; (of a contest) with no contestant who can be predicted as a certain winner. **widely** *adverb*, **wideness** *noun*

widen *verb* to make or become wider.

widespread *adjective* found or distributed over a wide area.

widgeon (**wij**-ŏn) *noun* any of several kinds of wild duck.

widow *noun* a woman whose husband has died and who has not married again. **widowhood** *noun*

widowed *adjective* made a widow or widower.

widower *noun* a man whose wife has died and who has not married again.

width *noun* **1** wideness. **2** distance or measurement from side to side. **3** a piece of material of full width as woven, *use two widths to make this curtain*.

wield (*pr.* weeld) *verb* **1** to hold and use (a weapon or tool etc.) with the hands. **2** to have and use (power).

wife *noun* (*plural* **wives**) a married woman in relation to her husband. **wifely** *adjective*

Wi-Fi *abbreviation* Wireless Fidelity, a group of technical standards enabling the transmission of data over wireless networks.

wig *noun* a covering made of real or artificial hair, worn on the head.

wigging *noun* (*informal*) a lengthy rebuke, a scolding.

wiggle *verb* to move or cause to move repeatedly from side to side, to wriggle. –**wiggle** *noun* a wiggling movement.

wight *noun* (*old use*) a person.

wigwam (**wig**-wom) *noun* a hut or tent made by fastening skins or mats over a framework of poles, as formerly used by some North American indigenous peoples.

Wik *noun* an Aboriginal people of the central-eastern area of the Gulf of Carpentaria. □ **the Wik decision** the judgment handed down in 1996 by the Hight Court of Australia that native title can co-exist with pastoral leases. **Wik-Mungkan** the Aboriginal language spoken by one of the Wik peoples.

wiki *noun* a website or database developed collaboratively by a community of users, allowing any user to add and edit content. [probably from Hawaiian *wiki* = fast, quick]

wilco *interjection* = 'will comply', used in signalling etc. to indicate that directions received will be carried out.

wild *adjective* **1** living or growing in its original natural state, not domesticated or tame or cultivated. **2** not civilised, barbarous, *wild tribes*. **3** (of scenery) looking very desolate; not cultivated. **4** lacking restraint or discipline or control, disorderly. **5** tempestuous, stormy, *a wild night*. **6** full of strong unrestrained feeling; very eager, excited, enthusiastic, or angry etc. **7** extremely foolish or unreasonable, *these wild ideas*. **8** random, *a wild guess*. –**wild** *adverb* in a wild manner, *shooting wild*. □ **run wild** to grow or live without being checked or disciplined or restrained. **the wilds** districts far from civilisation. **wild card** a card having any value chosen by the player holding it; (in computing) a character that will match any character or sequence of characters; an unpredictable person. **wild-goose chase** a useless search, a hopeless quest. **Wild West** the western States of the USA during the period when they were lawless frontier districts. **wildly** *adverb*, **wildness** *noun*

wildcat *adjective* **1** reckless or impracticable, especially in business and finance, *wildcat* *schemes*. **2** (of strikes) unofficial and irresponsible.

Wilde, Oscar Fingal O'Flahertie Wills (1854–1900), Irish-born dramatist and poet, author of *The Importance of Being Earnest*.

wildebeest (**wil**-dĕ-beest) *noun* a gnu.

wilderness *noun* a wild uncultivated area.

wildfire *noun* spread like wildfire (of rumours etc.) to spread very fast.

wildfowl *noun* birds that are hunted as game (e.g. ducks and geese, quail, pheasants).

wildlife *noun* wild animals collectively.

wile *noun* a piece of trickery intended to deceive or attract someone. –**wile** *verb* to lure or entice.

wilful *adjective* **1** done with deliberate intention and not as an accident, *wilful murder*. **2** self-willed, obstinate, *a wilful child*. **wilfully** *adverb*, **wilfulness** *noun* [from *will²* + *full*]

wilga *noun* a small white-flowered drought-resistant Australian tree. [Wiradjuri *wilgarr*]

Wilhelm (**vil**-helm), **Mount** the highest mountain in Papua New Guinea (4509 m).

will¹ *auxiliary verb* (**wilt** is used with *thou*), *see* **shall**.

will² *noun* **1** the mental faculty by which a person decides upon and controls his or her own actions or those of others. **2** willpower. **3** determination; *they set to work with a will*, in a determined and energetic way. **4** that which is desired or determined, *may God's will be done*. **5** a person's attitude in wishing good or bad to others; *good will*; *ill will*; *with the best will in the world*, however good one's intentions are. **6** written directions made by a person for the disposal of his or her property after death. –**will** *verb* **1** to exercise one's willpower; to influence or compel by doing this. **2** to intend unconditionally, *God has willed it*. **3** to bequeath by a will, *she willed her money to a hospital*. □ **at will** whenever one pleases, *he comes and goes at will*.

William the name of two kings of England, one of Great Britain, and one of the United Kingdom, reigning as William I 'the Conqueror' (1066–87), William II 'Rufus' (1087–1100), William III 'of Orange' (1689–1702), William IV (1830–7).

Williams, Tennessee (real name Thomas Lanier Williams, 1911–83), American dramatist whose plays include *A Streetcar Named Desire* and *Cat on a Hot Tin Roof*.

Williamson, David Keith (born 1942), Australian playwright whose works include the plays *The Removalists* and *Don's Party*.

willies *plural noun* the willies (*informal*) nervous discomfort, *that always gives me the willies*.

willing *adjective* **1** doing readily what is required, having no objection. **2** given or performed willingly, *we received willing help*. –**willing** *noun* willingness, *to show willing*. **willingly** *adverb*, **willingness** *noun*

will-o'-the-wisp *noun* a hope or aim that lures a person on but can never be fulfilled.

willow *noun* **1** any of several trees or shrubs with very flexible branches, usually growing near water. **2** its wood. **3** (*informal*) a cricket bat.

willowy *adjective* **1** full of willow trees. **2** slender and supple.

willpower *noun* control exercised by one's will, especially over one's own actions and impulses.

Wills, William John (1834–61), English explorer of Australia (*see* **Burke**).

willy-nilly *adverb* whether one desires it or not.

willy wagtail *noun* a small black and white Australian fantail.

willy willy *noun* (*Austral.*) a whirlwind or dust storm. [from Yindjibarndi *wili-wili* or Wemba-wemba *wilang-wilang*.]

wilt¹ *see* **will¹**.

wilt² *verb* **1** (of plants or flowers) to lose freshness and droop. **2** to cause to do this. **3** (of a person) to become limp from exhaustion. –**wilt** *noun* a plant disease that causes wilting.

wily (**wy**-lee) *adjective* (**wilier**, **wiliest**) full of wiles, crafty, cunning. **wiliness** *noun* [from *wile*]

wimp *noun* (*informal*) a feeble or ineffective person.

wimple *noun* a medieval headdress of linen or silk folded round the head and neck, covering all but the front of the face, still worn by some nuns.

win *verb* (**won**, **winning**) **1** to be victorious in (a battle or game or race etc.); to gain a victory. **2** to obtain or achieve as the result of a battle or contest or bet etc. **3** to obtain as a result of effort or perseverance, *he won their confidence*. **4** to gain the favour or support of, *soon won his audience over*. –**win** *noun* a victory in a game or contest.

wince *verb* to make a slight involuntary movement from pain, distress, or embarrassment etc. –**wince** *noun* a wincing movement.

winceyette *noun* a soft fabric woven of cotton and wool, used for nightclothes etc.

winch *noun* a machine for hoisting or pulling things by means of a cable that winds round a revolving drum or wheel. –**winch** *verb* to hoist or pull with a winch.

wind¹ (*rhymes with* tinned) *noun* **1** a current of air either occurring naturally in the atmosphere or put in motion by the movement of something through the air or produced artificially by bellows etc. **2** a smell carried by the wind, *the deer we were stalking had got our wind*. **3** gas forming in the stomach or intestines and causing discomfort. **4** breath as needed in exertion or speech or for sounding a musical instrument. **5** the wind instruments of an orchestra. **6** useless or boastful talk. –**wind** *verb* **1** to cause to be out of breath, *we were quite winded by the climb*. **2** to make (a baby) bring up wind after feeding. **3** to detect by the presence of a smell, *the hounds had winded the fox*. ☐ **get** or **have the wind up** (*informal*) to feel frightened. **get wind of** to hear a hint or rumour of. **in the wind** happening or about to happen. **like the wind** very swiftly. **put the wind up** (*informal*) to frighten or alarm. **take the wind out of a person's sails** to take away a person's advantage suddenly; to frustrate him or her by anticipating arguments etc. **wind farm** a group of energy producing windmills or wind turbines. **wind instrument** a musical instrument in which sound is produced by the player's breath (e.g. a trumpet or flute). **wind tunnel** a tunnel-like device in which an air stream can be produced past models of aircraft etc. for studying the effects of wind. **wind turbine** a turbine having a large vaned wheel rotated by the wind to generate electricity.

wind² (*rhymes with* find) *verb* (**wound** (*rhymes with* found), **winding**) **1** to go or cause to go in a curving, spiral, or twisting course, *the road winds its way* or *winds through the hills*. **2** to twist or wrap closely round and round upon itself so as to form a ball. **3** to wrap, to encircle, *wound a bandage round his finger*. **4** to haul, hoist, or move by turning a handle or windlass etc., *wind the car window down*. **5** to wind up (a clock

etc.). –**wind** *noun* **1** a bend or turn in a course. **2** a single turn in winding a clock or string etc. ☐ **wind down** to lower by winding; to unwind; to relax; to draw gradually to a close. **winding sheet** a sheet in which a corpse is wrapped for burial. **wind up** to set or keep (a clock etc.) going by tightening its spring or adjusting its weights; to bring or come to an end; to settle and finally close the business and financial transactions of (a company going into liquidation); (*informal*) to arrive finally, *he'll wind up in gaol*; (*informal*) to provoke or tease. **wind-up** *noun* a conclusion. **winder** *noun*

windbag *noun* (*informal*) a person who talks lengthily.

windbreak *noun* a screen or row of trees etc. shielding something from the full force of the wind.

windcheater *noun* a wind-resistant jacket or jumper.

windfall *noun* **1** an apple or pear etc. blown off a tree by the wind. **2** a piece of unexpected good fortune, especially in a sum of money acquired.

Windhoek (**vint**-huuk) the capital of Namibia.

windjammer *noun* a merchant sailing ship.

windlass (**wind**-lăs) *noun* a device for pulling or hoisting things (e.g. a bucket of water from a well) by means of a rope or chain that winds round an axle.

windless *adjective* without wind.

windmill *noun* a mill worked by the action of wind on projecting parts (*sails*) that radiate from a central shaft.

window *noun* **1** an opening in the wall or roof of a building or in a car etc. to admit light and often air, usually filled with glass in a fixed, hinged, or sliding frame. **2** this glass with or without its frame, *broke the window*. **3** a space for the display of goods behind the window of a shop etc. **4** an opening resembling a window, e.g. at a ticket office. **5** an interval during which the positions of planets etc. allow a specified journey by a spacecraft; an opportunity. **6** (in computing) a rectangular area on a computer screen in which text or images can be displayed. ☐ **window box** a trough fixed outside a window, for growing plants and flowers. **window dressing** the displaying of goods attractively in a shop window; presentation of facts so as to create a favourable impression. **window seat** *noun* a seat fixed under a window that is in a recess or bay of a room. **window-shopping** *noun* looking at goods displayed in shop windows etc. without necessarily intending to buy. [from Old Norse *vindauga* = wind-eye]

windpipe *noun* the principal passage by which air reaches the lungs, leading from the throat to the bronchial tubes; the trachea.

windscreen *noun* the glass in the window at the front of a motor vehicle.

windsock *noun* a tube-shaped piece of canvas open at both ends, flown at an airfield etc. to show the direction of the wind.

Windsor the name assumed by the British royal house in 1917.

windsurfing *noun* the sport of surfing on a board to which a sail is fixed (also called *sailboarding*). **windsurf** *verb*, **windsurfer** *noun*

windswept *adjective* exposed to strong winds.

windward *adjective* situated in the direction from which the wind blows. –**windward** *noun* the windward side or region.

Windward Islands a group of islands in the eastern Caribbean Sea, including Dominica, Martinique, St Lucia, and Barbados.

windy *adjective* (**windier**, **windiest**) **1** with much wind, *a windy night*. **2** exposed to high winds. **3** wordy, full of useless talk, *a windy speaker*. **windiness** *noun*

wine *noun* **1** fermented grape juice as an alcoholic drink. **2** a fermented drink made from other fruits or plants, *ginger wine*. **3** dark purplish red. –**wine** *verb* to drink wine; to entertain with wine; *they wined and dined us*, entertained us to a meal with wine. [from Latin *vinum* = wine (compare *vine*)]

wineglass *noun* a glass for drinking wine from.

winepress *noun* a press in which grapes are squeezed in making wine.

winery *noun* an establishment where wine is made.

wineskin *noun* the whole skin of a goat etc. sewn up and used to hold wine.

wing *noun* **1** each of a pair of projecting parts by which a bird, bat, or insect etc. is able to fly. **2** a corresponding part in a non-flying bird or insect. **3** each of the parts projecting widely from the sides of an aircraft and acting upon the air so that the aircraft is supported in flight. **4** something resembling a wing in

appearance or position (e.g. a thin projection on maple and sycamore seeds). **5** a projecting part extending from one end of a building. **6** the part of the bodywork immediately above the wheel of a motor vehicle. **7** either end of an army lined up for battle. **8** either of the side parts of the playing area in various games, e.g. football, hockey; a player stationed in this position. **9** an air force unit of several squadrons. **10** a section of a political party or other group, with more extreme views than those of the majority. –**wing** *verb* **1** to fly, to travel by means of wings, *a bird winging its way home*. **2** to wound slightly in the wing or arm. **wings** *plural noun* **1** the sides of a theatre stage out of sight of the audience; *waiting in the wings*, waiting in readiness. **2** a qualified pilot's badge. □ **on the wing** flying. **take wing** to fly away. **under one's wing** under one's protection. **wing chair** an armchair with projecting side pieces at the top of a high back. **wing commander** an officer of the RAAF, next below group captain. **wing nut** a nut with projections so that the fingers can turn it on a bolt.

winged *adjective* having wings.

winger *noun* a wing player in football etc.

wingless *adjective* without wings.

wink *verb* **1** to close and open one eye deliberately, especially as a private signal to someone. **2** (of a light or star etc.) to shine with a light that flashes quickly on and off or twinkles. –**wink** *noun* **1** an act of winking. **2** a brief period of sleep, *didn't sleep a wink*. □ **wink at** to pretend not to notice something that should be stopped or condemned.

winkle *noun* an edible sea snail. –**winkle** *verb* **winkle out** to extract, to prise out.

winner *noun* **1** a person who wins. **2** something successful, *her latest novel is a winner*.

winning *see* **win**. –**winning** *adjective* charming, persuasive, *a winning smile*. **winnings** *plural noun* money won in betting or at cards etc. □ **winning post** a post marking the end of a race.

winnow *verb* **1** to expose (grain) to a current of air by tossing or fanning it so that the loose dry outer part is blown away; to separate (chaff) in this way. **2** to sift or separate from worthless or inferior elements, *winnow out the truth from the falsehoods*.

winsome *adjective* having an engagingly attractive appearance or manner.

winter *noun* the coldest season of the year, from June to August in the southern hemisphere. – **winter** *verb* to spend the winter, *decided to winter in Cairns*. □ **winter sports** sports on snow or ice (e.g. skiing, skating).

wintertime *noun* the season of winter.

Winton, Tim(othy John) (born 1960), Australian writer, whose works include *Cloudstreet* and *The Riders*.

wintry *adjective* 1 of or like winter, cold, *wintry weather*. 2 (of a smile etc.) chilly, lacking warmth or vivacity. **wintriness** *noun*

wipe *verb* 1 to clean or dry the surface of by rubbing something over it. 2 to spread (a substance) thinly over a surface. 3 to remove by wiping, *wipe your tears away*. 4 to erase (data); to erase data from (a tape etc.). – **wipe** *noun* the act of wiping, *give this plate a wipe*. □ **wipe out** to cancel; to destroy completely, *the whole army was wiped out*. **wipe up** to dry the dishes; to clean up (a spill etc.) by wiping.

wiper *noun* 1 something that wipes or is used for wiping. 2 a rubber strip mechanically moved to and fro across a windscreen to remove rain etc.

Wiradjuri (wĭ-**rad**-jŭ-ree) *noun* 1 a member of an Aboriginal people of southern NSW and northern Victoria. 2 their language.

wire *noun* 1 a strand or slender usually flexible rod of metal. 2 a barrier or framework etc. made from this. 3 a piece of wire used to carry electric current. 4 (*informal*) a telegram. – **wire** *verb* 1 to provide, fasten, or strengthen with wire(s). 2 to install wiring in (a house). 3 (*informal*) to telegraph. □ **get one's wires crossed** to become confused and misunderstand. **wire-haired** *adjective* (of a dog) having stiff wiry hair. **wire-tapping** *noun* the tapping of telephone wires.

wireless *adjective* lacking or not requiring wires – **wireless** *noun* (*old-fashioned*) 1 radio, radio communications. 2 a radio receiver or transmitter.

wireworm *noun* the destructive wormlike larva of a kind of beetle.

wiring *noun* a system of wires for conducting electricity in a building.

wiry *adjective* (**wirier**, **wiriest**) 1 like wire. 2 (of a person) lean but strong. **wiriness** *noun*

Wisconsin (wis-**kon**-sĭn) a State in the northern USA.

wisdom *noun* 1 being wise, soundness of judgment. 2 wise sayings.

□ **Wisdom of Solomon** *see* **Solomon**. **wisdom tooth** the third and hindmost molar tooth on each side of the upper and lower jaws, usually cut (if at all) after the age of 20.

wise[1] *adjective* 1 having or showing soundness of judgment. 2 having knowledge, *where ignorance is bliss, 'tis folly to be wise*. 3 (*informal*) aware, informed, *be* or *get wise to something*; *put him wise to it*, tell him about it. – **wise** *verb* **wise up** (*informal*) to become aware; to inform, *wise him up about it*. □ **be none the wiser** to know no more than before; to be unaware of what has happened. **wise guy** (*informal*) a know-all. **wise man** a wizard; one of the Magi. **wise woman** a woman who is a witch; a fortune-teller. **wisely** *adverb*

wise[2] *noun* (*old use*) way, manner, *in no wise*.

wiseacre (**wyz**-ay-ker) *noun* a person who pretends to have great wisdom, a know-all.

wisecrack *noun* (*informal*) a witty or clever remark. – **wisecrack** *verb* (*informal*) to make a wisecrack.

wish *noun* 1 a desire or mental aim. 2 an expression of desire about another person's welfare, *with best wishes*. – **wish** *verb* 1 to have or express as a wish. 2 to make a wish, *wish when you see a shooting star*. 3 to hope or express hope about another person's welfare, *wish me luck*; *wish her well*, hope that she prospers; *wish him 'good day'*, greet him in this way; *we wish you joy of it*, (used ironically) feel that you will have difficulty in enjoying it. 4 (*informal*) to foist, *the dog was wished on us while its owners were on holiday*.

wishbone *noun* a forked bone between the neck and breast of a bird (pulled in two between two persons, the one who gets the longer part having the supposed right to magic fulfilment of any wish).

wishful *adjective* desiring. □ **wishful thinking** a belief that is founded on what one wishes to be true rather than on fact.

wishy-washy *adjective* weak or feeble in colour, character, etc., lacking strong or positive qualities.

wisp *noun* 1 a small separate bunch or bundle of something, *wisps of hair*. 2 a small streak of smoke or cloud etc. 3 a small thin person. **wispy** *adjective*

wisteria (wis-**teer**-ree-ă) (also **wistaria**, *pr.* wis-**tair**-ree-ă) *noun* a climbing plant with hanging clusters of blue, purple, or white flowers. [named after C. *Wistar* (or *Wister*), American anatomist (died 1818)]

wistful *adjective* full of sad or vague longing. **wistfully** *adverb*, **wistfulness** *noun*

wit¹ *noun* 1 the ability to combine words or ideas etc. ingeniously so as to produce a kind of clever humour that appeals to the intellect. 2 a witty person. 3 intelligence, understanding, *hadn't the wit to see what was needed*; *use your wits*. □ **at one's wits' end** at the end of one's mental resources, not knowing what to do. **have** or **keep one's wits about one** to be or remain mentally alert and intelligent or ready to act. **scared out of one's wits** crazy with fear.

wit² (*old use*) **to wit** that is to say, namely.

witch *noun* 1 a person (especially a woman) who practises witchcraft. 2 a bewitching woman; *old witch*, an ugly woman. □ **witch hazel** (also **wych hazel**) a North American shrub with yellow flowers; an astringent lotion prepared from its leaves and bark. **witch-hunt** *noun* a search to find and destroy or persecute people thought to be witches, or others suspected of holding unorthodox or unpopular views. **witching hour** midnight.

witchcraft *noun* the practice of magic.

witchdoctor *noun* a tribal magician.

witchetty (**wich**-ĕ-tee) *noun* (in full **witchetty grub**) a large edible larva of any of several Australian moths and beetles. [probably from Adnyamathanha *wityu* = hooked stick used to extract grubs, + *varti* = grub, insect]

with *preposition* 1 in the company of, among. 2 having, characterised by, *a man with a sinister expression*. 3 using as an instrument or means, *hit it with a hammer*. 4 on the side of, of the same opinion as, *we're all with you on this matter*. 5 in the care or charge of, *leave a message with the receptionist*. 6 in the employment etc. of, *he is with Telstra*. 7 at the same time as, in the same way or direction or degree as, *rise with the sun*; *swimming with the tide*; *he became more tolerant with age*. 8 because of, *shaking with laughter*. 9 feeling or showing, *heard it with calmness*. 10 under the conditions of, *sleeps with the window open*; *he won with ease*, easily; *with your permission*, if you will allow it. 11 by addition or possession of, *fill it with water*; *laden with baggage*. 12 in regard to, towards, *lost my temper with him*. 13 in opposition to, *he argued with me*. 14 in spite of, *with all his*

roughness, he's very good-natured. 15 so as to be separated from, *we parted with our luggage reluctantly*. □ **be with child** (*old use*) to be pregnant. **I'm not with you** (*informal*) I cannot follow your meaning. **with it** (*informal*) up to date, capable of understanding and appreciating current fashions and ideas; alert.

withal *adverb* (*old use*) in addition; moreover.

withdraw *verb* (**withdrew**, **withdrawn**, **withdrawing**) 1 to take back or away, *withdrew troops from the frontier*. 2 to remove (money deposited) from a bank etc. 3 to cancel (a promise or statement etc.). 4 to go away from company or from a place; *withdraw into oneself*, become unresponsive or unsociable.

withdrawal *noun* 1 withdrawing. 2 the process of ceasing to take drugs to which one is addicted, often with unpleasant reactions, *withdrawal symptoms*.

withdrawn *adjective* (of a person) unresponsive, unsociable.

wither *verb* 1 to make or become shrivelled; to lose or cause to lose freshness and vitality. 2 to subdue or overwhelm by scorn, *withered him with a glance*. [from *weather*]

withers (**with**-erz) *plural noun* the ridge between a horse's shoulder blades.

withhold *verb* (**withheld**, **withholding**) 1 to refuse to give, grant, or allow, *withhold permission*. 2 to hold back, to restrain, *we could not withhold our laughter*. [from *with-* = away, + *hold¹*]

within *preposition* 1 inside, enclosed by. 2 not beyond the limit or scope of, *success was within our grasp*; *he acted within his rights*. 3 in a time no longer than, *we shall finish within an hour*. 4 not further off than, *within two kilometres of the shore*. –**within** *adverb* inside, *seen from within*.

without *preposition* 1 not having or feeling or showing, free from, *without food*; *they are without fear*. 2 in the absence of, *no smoke without fire*. 3 with no action of, *we can't leave without thanking them*. 4 (*old use*) outside, *without a city wall*. –**without** *adverb* outside, *the house as seen from without*; *cleaned within and without*.

withstand *verb* (**withstood**, **withstanding**) to endure successfully.

withy (**with**-ee) *noun* a tough flexible shoot of a willow etc. used for tying bundles etc.

witless *adjective* foolish, unintelligent.

witloof (**wit**-lohf) *noun* a chicory plant; its leaves used as a vegetable or in salad.

witness *noun* **1** a person who sees or hears something, *there were no witnesses to their quarrel.* **2** a person who gives evidence in a lawcourt. **3** a person who is present at an event in order to testify to the fact that it took place; one who confirms that a signature is genuine by adding his or her own signature. **4** something that serves as evidence, *his tattered clothes were a witness to his poverty.* –**witness** *verb* to be a witness at or of; to sign (a document) as a witness. □ **witness box** or **stand** an enclosure from which witnesses give evidence in a lawcourt.

witted *adjective* having wits of a certain kind, *quick-witted.*

witter *verb* (*informal*) to speak at annoying length about trivial matters.

Wittgenstein (**vit**-gĕn-styn), Ludwig Josef Johann (1889–1951), Austrian-born philosopher.

witticism (**wit**-ĭ-sizm) *noun* a witty remark.

wittingly *adverb* knowing what one does, intentionally.

witty *adjective* (**wittier**, **wittiest**) full of wit. **wittily** *adverb*, **wittiness** *noun*

wives *see* **wife.**

wizard *noun* **1** a male witch, a magician. **2** a person with amazing abilities, *a financial wizard.* **wizardry** *noun* [from *wise* (originally = *wise man*)]

wizened (**wiz**-ĕnd) *adjective* full of wrinkles, shrivelled with age, *a wizened face.*

WMD *abbreviation* weapon of mass destruction.

woad *noun* **1** a kind of blue dye formerly obtained from a plant of the mustard family. **2** this plant.

wobbegong (**wob**-ee-gong) *noun* a slow-moving Australian shark with a patterned brown and violet skin, also called a *carpet shark.*

wobble *verb* **1** to stand or move unsteadily; to rock from side to side. **2** (of the voice) to quiver. –**wobble** *noun* a wobbling movement, a quiver. **wobbly** *adjective*

wodge *noun* (*informal*) a chunk, a wedge.

woe *noun* **1** sorrow, distress. **2** trouble causing this, misfortune.

woebegone (**woh**-bĕ-gon) *adjective* looking unhappy.

woeful *adjective* **1** full of woe, sad. **2** deplorable, *woeful ignorance.* **woefully** *adverb*

wog *noun* (*Austral. informal*) a usually minor illness or infection; the germ etc. causing this.

woggle *noun* a leather etc. neckerchief ring used by Scouts and Guides.

wok *noun* a Chinese cooking vessel shaped like a large bowl.

woke, **woken** *see* **wake**[1].

wold *noun* a piece of high open uncultivated land or moor.

wolf *noun* (*plural* **wolves**) **1** a fierce wild animal of the dog family, feeding on the flesh of other animals and often hunting in packs. **2** a greedy or grasping person. –**wolf** *verb* to eat (food) quickly and greedily. □ **cry wolf** to raise false alarms (¶ like the shepherd boy in the fable, so that eventually a genuine alarm is ignored). **keep the wolf from the door** to ward off hunger or starvation. **wolf in sheep's clothing** a person who appears friendly or harmless but is really an enemy. **wolf whistle** a whistle uttered by a man in admiration of a woman's appearance.

wolfhound *noun* any of several large dogs (e.g. a borzoi) of a kind originally used for hunting wolves.

wolfram (**wuul**-frăm) *noun* tungsten (ore).

woman *noun* (*plural* **women**) **1** an adult female person. **2** women in general. □ **women's liberation** or **women's lib** a movement urging the liberation of women from domestic duties and from a subordinate role in society and business etc. **women's refuge** or **shelter** a sanctuary for women threatened by domestic violence. **women's rights** the right of women to have a position of legal and social equality with men.

womanhood *noun* the state of being a woman.

womanish *adjective* like a woman; suitable for women but not for men.

womanly *adjective* having or showing qualities that are characteristic of or suitable for a woman. **womanliness** *noun*

womb (*pr.* woom) *noun* the hollow organ (in woman and other female mammals) in which a child or the young may be conceived and nourished while developing before birth, the uterus.

wombat *noun* a short-legged, burrowing, plant-eating Australian marsupial. [Dharuk *wambad*]

women *see* **woman**.

womenfolk *noun* women in general; the women of one's family.

womma *noun* (also **woma**) an Australian python of arid areas. [Diyari *wama*]

won *see* **win**.

wonder *noun* 1 a feeling of surprise mingled with admiration, curiosity, or bewilderment. 2 something that arouses this, a marvel, a remarkable thing or event. –**wonder** *verb* 1 to feel wonder or surprise, *I wonder that he wasn't killed*. 2 to feel curiosity about, to desire to know; to try to form an opinion or decision about, *we're still wondering what to do next*.

wonderful *adjective* marvellous, surprisingly fine or excellent. **wonderfully** *adverb*

wonderland *noun* a land or place full of marvels or wonderful things.

wonderment *noun* a feeling of wonder, surprise.

wondrous *adjective* (*poetic*) wonderful. **wondrously** *adverb*

wonga-wonga[1] (**wong**-gă-wong-gă) *noun* (in full **wonga wonga pigeon**) a large grey and white pigeon of eastern Australia. [probably Dharuk *wanga-wanga*]

wonga-wonga[2] *noun* (in full **wonga-wonga vine**) an Australian climbing plant with cream and red flowers.

Wongi (**wong**-gy) *noun* an Aboriginal person from central Australia.

Usage see **aborigine**.

---

wonky *adjective* (*informal*) shaky, unsteady.

wont (*pr.* wohnt) *adjective* (*old use*) accustomed, *he was wont to go to bed early*. –**wont** *noun* a habit or custom, *he went to bed early, as was his wont*.

won't (*informal*) = will not.

wonted (**wohn**-tĕd) *adjective* customary, *he listened with his wonted courtesy*.

woo *verb* (**wooed**, **wooing**) 1 (*old use*) to court (a woman). 2 to try to achieve or obtain, *woo fame* or *success*. 3 to seek the favour of, to try to coax or persuade, *wooing customers into the shop*.

wood *noun* 1 the tough fibrous substance of a tree and its branches, enclosed by the bark. 2 this cut for use as timber or fuel etc. 3 (also **woods**) (especially *Brit. & Amer.*) trees growing fairly densely over an area of ground, *woods and forests*. 4 a ball of wood or other material used in the game of bowls. 5 a golf club with a wooden head. □ **can't see the wood for the trees** cannot get a clear view of the whole because of too many details. **out of the wood** or **woods** clear of danger or difficulty.

woodbine *noun* wild honeysuckle.

woodchip *noun* a chip or fragment of wood. –**woodchip** *verb* to reduce felled trees to woodchips for use in papermaking etc.

woodchuck *noun* a reddish-brown and grey North American marmot.

woodcut *noun* 1 an engraving made on wood. 2 a print made from this, especially as an illustration in a book.

wooded *adjective* covered with growing trees.

wooden *adjective* 1 made of wood. 2 stiff and unnatural in manner, showing no expression or animation. **woodenly** *adverb*

woodland *noun* wooded country.

woodlouse *noun* (*plural* **woodlice**) a small wingless creature with seven pairs of legs, living in decaying wood, damp soil, etc.

woodpecker *noun* a bird that clings to tree trunks and taps them with its beak to discover insects.

woodwind *noun* 1 any of the wind instruments of an orchestra that are (or were originally) made of wood, e.g. flute, clarinet, oboe. 2 these collectively.

woodwork *noun* 1 the art or practice of making things from wood. 2 things made from wood, especially the wooden fittings of a house.

woodworm *noun* the larva of a kind of beetle that bores into wooden furniture and fittings.

woody *adjective* 1 like wood, consisting of wood, *the woody parts of a plant*. 2 wooded, *a woody area*. **woodiness** *noun*

woof *noun* the gruff bark of a dog. –**woof** *verb* to bark gruffly.

woofer (**wuuf**-er) *noun* a loudspeaker for reproducing low-frequency signals.

wool *noun* 1 the fine soft hair that forms the fleece of sheep and goats etc. 2 yarn made from this, fabric made from this yarn. **3** something resembling sheep's wool in texture, *cotton wool*. □ **pull the wool over someone's eyes** to deceive him or her. **wool clip** a farmer's or district's etc. (annual) wool production. **wool-gathering** *noun* being in a dreamy or absent-minded state.

Woolf, (Adeline) Virginia (1882–1941), English novelist whose works include *Mrs. Dalloway*, *To the Lighthouse*, and *A Room of One's Own*.

woollen *adjective* made of wool. **woollens** *plural noun* woollen cloth or clothing.

woolly *adjective* **1** covered with wool or wool-like hair. **2** like wool, woollen, *a woolly hat*. **3** not thinking clearly, not clearly expressed or thought out, vague. **– woolly** *noun* (*informal*) a knitted woollen garment, a jumper or cardigan etc. □ **woolly bear** any of several furry larvae of insects; a large hairy caterpillar. **woolliness** *noun*

woolshed *noun* (*Austral.*) a shed for shearing and packing wool.

Woomera a town in central SA, the base for a military testing ground used in the 1950s for British nuclear tests; since 1969 the base for the joint Australian United States Space Communications Station.

woomera (**wuum**-ĕ-rǎ) *noun* an Aboriginal throwing stick used for propelling a spear. [Dharuk *wamara*]

Woop Woop (**wuup** wuup) *noun* a jocular name for any remote outback region of Australia.

woozy *adjective* (*informal*) dizzy; dazed.

Worcestershire sauce (**wuus**-ter-sheer) *noun* (also **Worcester sauce**) a pungent sauce containing vinegar, molasses, and spices. [named after *Worcester* in England where it was first made]

word *noun* **1** a sound or sounds expressing a meaning independently and forming one of the basic elements of speech. **2** this represented by letters or symbols. **3** something said, a remark or statement, *he didn't utter a word*; *too funny for words*, extremely funny. **4** a message, information, *we sent word of our safe arrival*. **5** a promise or assurance; *take my word for it*, accept my assurance that it is true; *a man of his word*, one who keeps his promises. **6** a command or spoken signal, *don't fire till I give you the word*. **7** **the Word** (in the Gospel of St John) the Second Person of the Trinity. **– word** *verb* to phrase, to select

words to express, *word it tactfully*. □ **by word of mouth** in spoken (not written) words. **have a word** to converse briefly. **have words** to quarrel. **word for word** in exactly the same words; *translate it word for word*, literally. **the Word of God** the Bible; = the Word (*see* sense 7). **word of honour** a promise made upon one's honour (*see* honour). **word-perfect** *adjective* having memorised every word perfectly. **word processor** a computer program designed for creating documents, in which text can be entered, stored, and edited before being printed; a computer and printer designed specifically for this purpose.

wording *noun* the way something is worded.

wordless *adjective* without words, not expressed in words, *wordless sympathy*.

Wordsworth, William (1770–1850), English poet.

wordy *adjective* using too many words. **wordily** *adverb*, **wordiness** *noun*

wore *see* wear¹,².

work *noun* **1** use of bodily or mental power in order to do or make something, especially as contrasted with play or recreation. **2** something to be undertaken; the materials for this. **3** a thing done or produced by work; the result of action. **4** a piece of literary or musical composition, *one of Mozart's later works*. **5** what a person does to earn a living, employment. **6** doings or experiences of a certain kind, *nice work!* **7** ornamentation of a specified kind; articles having this; things or parts made of certain materials or with certain tools, *fine filigree work*. **– work** *verb* **1** to perform work, to be engaged in bodily or mental activity. **2** to make efforts, *work for peace*. **3** to be employed, to have a job, *she works in a bank*. **4** to operate, to do this effectively, *it works by electricity*; *a can-opener that really works*; *that method won't work*. **5** to operate (a thing) so as to obtain material or benefit from it, *the mine is still being worked*. **6** to purchase with one's labour, *work one's passage*. **7** to cause to work or function, *he works his staff very hard*; *can you work the lift?* **8** to bring about, to accomplish, *work miracles*. **9** to shape, knead, or hammer etc. into a desired form or consistency, *work the mixture into a paste*. **10** to do or make by needlework or fretwork etc., *work your initials on it*. **11** to excite progressively, *worked them into a frenzy*. **12** to make (a way) or pass or cause to pass slowly or by effort, *the grub works its way into timber*; *work the stick into* *the hole*. **13** to become through repeated stress or pressure, *the screw had worked loose*. **14** to be in motion, *his face worked violently*. **15** to ferment, *the yeast began to work*. **works** *plural noun* **1** operations in building etc., *roadworks*. **2** the operative parts of a machine. **3** a place where industrial or manufacturing processes are carried on, a factory. □ **at work** working; at one's place of employment; operating, having an effect, *there are secret influences at work*. **the works** (*informal*) everything, *a hamburger with the works*; the full treatment, *the hairdresser gave me the works*. **work-hardening** *noun* an increase in the strength of metal, obtained by hammering or shaping it. **work in** to find a place for, to insert. **work of art** a fine picture, building, or composition etc. **work off** to get rid of by work or activity. **work on** to use one's influence on (a person). **work out** to find or solve by calculation; to be calculated, *it works out at $5 each*; to plan the details etc. of, *work out a plan*; to have a specified result, *it worked out very well*; to engage in physical exercise or training. **work over** to examine thoroughly; to treat with violence. **work-shy** *adjective* disinclined to work. **work study** study of people's work and methods, with a view to making them more efficient; ergonomics. **work to rule** to follow the rules of one's occupation with excessive strictness in order to cause delay, as a form of industrial protest. **work-to-rule** *noun* this practice. **work up** to bring gradually to a more developed state; to excite progressively; to advance gradually to a climax.

workable *adjective* able to be worked, used, or acted upon successfully.

workaday *adjective* ordinary, everyday.

workaholic *noun* (*informal*) a person who is addicted to working. **workaholism** *noun* [from *work + alcoholic*]

workbench *noun* a bench for woodwork, metalwork, etc.

worker *noun* **1** a person who works; one who works hard or in a specified way, *a slow worker*. **2** a neuter or undeveloped female bee or ant etc. that does the work of the hive or colony but cannot reproduce. **3** a member of the working class.

workforce *noun* the total number of workers employed or available.

workhouse *noun* a former public institution where people unable to support themselves

were housed and (if able-bodied) made to work.

working *adjective* **1** engaged in work, especially manual labour; working-class, *a working man*. **2** functioning. – **working** *noun* a mine or quarry etc.; a part of this in which work is or has been carried on, *disused mine-workings*. □ **working capital** capital used in the carrying on of business, not invested in its buildings and equipment etc. **working class** the class of people who are employed for wages, especially in manual or industrial work. **working-class** *adjective* of the working class. **working day** a day on which work is regularly done; the portion of the day spent in working. **working knowledge** knowledge adequate for dealing with something. **working order** a condition in which a machine etc. works satisfactorily. **working party** a group of people appointed to investigate and report or advise on something.

workload *noun* the amount of work to be done.

workman *noun* (*plural* **workmen**) **1** a man employed to do manual labour. **2** a person who works in a certain way, *a conscientious workman*.

workmanlike *adjective* showing practised skill.

workmanship *noun* a person's skill in working; the quality of this as seen in something produced.

workmate *noun* a person working with another.

workout *noun* a session of physical exercise.

workplace *noun* a place at which a person works; an office, factory, etc.

worksheet *noun* **1** a paper on which work done is recorded. **2** a paper listing questions or activities etc. for students to work through.

workshop *noun* **1** a room or building in which manual work or manufacture is carried on. **2** a meeting for discussion or group activity, *a writing workshop*.

workstation *noun* **1** a computer terminal and keyboard; a desk or table with this. **2** the location of an individual worker or stage in manufacturing etc.

world *noun* **1** the universe, all that exists. **2** the earth with all its countries and peoples. **3** a heavenly body like it. **4** a section of the earth, *the western world*. **5** a time, state, or scene of human existence; *this world*, this mortal life. **6** the people or things belonging to a certain class or sphere of activity, *the sporting world*; *the insect world*. **7** everything, all people, *felt that the world was against him*. **8** material things and occupations (contrasted with spiritual), *renounced the world and became a nun*. **9** a very great amount, *it will do him a world of good*. □ **for all the world like** precisely like. **man** or **woman of the world** a person who is experienced in the ways of human society. **not for the world** not for anything no matter how great. **think the world of** to have the highest possible opinion of. **world-class** *adjective* of a quality or standard regarded as high throughout the world. **world music** pop or rock music incorporating elements of indigenous traditional music, especially from the developing world. **world power** a country with influence in international politics. **world war** a war involving many important nations; **First World War** that of 1914–18; **Second World War** that of 1939–45. **world-weary** *adjective* bored with human affairs.

World Bank the popular name of the International Bank for Reconstruction and Development, set up by the UN to promote the economic development of member countries.

World Cup 1 any of various international sports competitions or the trophies awarded for these. **2** an international soccer competition, held every fourth year.

World Health Organization a United Nations agency whose aim is to improve health in all countries.

World Heritage list a list kept by UNESCO of those sites, areas, or structures, either natural or man-made, recognised as being of outstanding international importance and therefore deserving special conservation and protection.

worldling *noun* a worldly person.

worldly *adjective* **1** of or belonging to life on earth, not spiritual. **2** devoted to the pursuit of pleasure or material gains or advantages. □ **worldly goods** property. **worldly wisdom** wisdom and shrewdness in dealing with worldly affairs. **worldly-wise** *adjective* **worldliness** *noun*

worldwide *adjective* extending through the whole world.

World Wide Web *noun* (also **Web**) an international computer network incorporating multimedia techniques and using hypertext links to access information.

worm *noun* **1** any of several types of animal with a soft rounded or flattened body and no backbone or limbs. **2** the wormlike larva of certain insects. **3** an insignificant or contemptible person. **4** the spiral part of a screw. **–worm** *verb* **1** to move with a twisting movement like a worm; *worm one's way* or *oneself*, make one's way by wriggling or with slow or patient progress. **2** to obtain by crafty persistence, *wormed the secret out of him*. **3** to rid of parasitic worms. **worms** *plural noun* intestinal or internal parasites. □ **a can of worms** (*informal*) an unmanageable or difficult set of problems. **worm cast** a tubular pile of earth sent up by an earthworm on to the surface of the ground. **worm's-eye view** (*humorous*) a view as seen from below or from a humble position.

wormwood *noun* **1** a woody plant with a bitter flavour. **2** bitter mortification.

worn *see* **wear**[1]. **–worn** *adjective* **1** damaged by use or wear. **2** looking tired and exhausted. **worn-out** *adjective*

worried *adjective* feeling or showing worry.

worrisome *adjective* causing worry.

worry *verb* (**worried**, **worrying**) **1** to be troublesome to, to disturb the peace of mind of. **2** to give way to anxiety. **3** to seize with the teeth and shake or pull about, *the dog was worrying a rat*. **–worry** *noun* **1** a state of worrying, mental uneasiness. **2** something that causes this. □ **not to worry!** (*informal*) there is no need to worry. **no worries!** (*informal*) it's no trouble, it's OK. **worry beads** a string of beads for fiddling with to occupy or calm oneself. **worry out** to obtain (a solution to a problem etc.) by persistent effort. **worrier** *noun* [the verb originally meant 'to strangle']

worse *adjective* & *adverb* **1** more bad, badly; more evil or ill. **2** less good, in or into less good health or condition or circumstances. **–worse** *noun* something worse, *there's worse to come*. □ **the worse for wear** damaged by use; injured or exhausted. **worse luck!** such is my bad fortune. **worse off** in a worse (especially financial) position.

worsen *verb* to make or become worse.

worship *noun* **1** reverence and respect paid to God or a god. **2** acts or ceremonies displaying this. **3** adoration of or devotion to a person or thing. **4** a title of respect used to or of a mayor or certain magistrates, *Your Worship*; *His Worship*; *Her Worship*. **–worship** *verb* (**worshipped**, **worshipping**) **1** to honour as a deity, to pay worship to. **2** to take part in an act of worship. **3** to idolise, to treat with adoration. **worshipper** *noun* [from *worth*]

worst *adjective & adverb* most bad, most badly; most evil or ill, least good. **–worst** *noun* the worst part, feature, state, or event etc., *we are prepared for the worst*. **–worst** *verb* to get the better of, to defeat or outdo. □ **at worst** in the worst possible case. **get the worst of** to be defeated in.

worsted (**wuu**-stĕd) *noun* fine smooth yarn spun from long strands of wool; fabric made from this.

wort (*pr.* wert) *noun* (*old use* except in names of plants) plant, herb, *liverwort*.

worth *adjective* **1** having a specified value, *a book worth $20*. **2** giving or likely to give a satisfactory or rewarding return for, deserving, *the book is worth reading; the scheme is worth a trial*. **3** possessing as wealth, having property to the value of, *he was worth a million dollars when he died*. **–worth** *noun* **1** value, merit, usefulness, *people of great worth to the community*. **2** the amount of something that a specified sum will buy, *a dollar's worth of lollies*. □ **for all one is worth** (*informal*) with all one's energy, making every effort. **worth while** or **worth one's while** worth the time or effort needed, *the scheme isn't worth while*.

Usage *Worth while* is written as *worthwhile* when it comes before the noun it qualifies, e.g. *a worthwhile scheme*. There is also a tendency to write it as one word in other contexts, e.g. *The scheme isn't worthwhile*.

worthless *adjective* having no value or usefulness. **worthlessness** *noun*

worthwhile *adjective* that is worth the time or effort needed, *a worthwhile undertaking*.

worthy *adjective* (**worthier, worthiest**) **1** having great merit, deserving respect or support, *a worthy cause; worthy citizens*. **2** having sufficient worth or merit, *the cause is worthy of support*. **–worthy** *noun* a worthy person. **worthily** *adverb*, **worthiness** *noun*

would *auxiliary verb* used **1** in senses corresponding to **will¹** in the past tense (*we said we would do it*), conditional statements (*you could do it if you would try*), questions (*would they like it?*), and polite requests (*would you come in please?*). **2** expressing something to be expected (*that's just what he would do!*) or something that happens from time to time (*occasionally the machine would*

go wrong). **3** expressing probability, *she would be about 60 when she died*. □ **would-be** *adjective* desiring or pretending to be, *a would-be humorist*.

Usage With the verbs *like*, *prefer*, *be glad*, etc., 'I would' and 'we would' are often used informally, but 'I should' and 'we should' are required in formal written English.

wouldn't (*informal*) = would not. □ **I wouldn't know** (*informal*) I do not know and cannot be expected to know.

wound¹ (*pr.* woond) *noun* **1** injury done to animal or vegetable tissue by a cut, stab, blow, or tear. **2** injury to a person's reputation or feelings etc. **–wound** *verb* to inflict a wound or wounds upon.

wound² (*pr.* wownd) *see* **wind²**.

wove *see* **weave¹**. **–wove** *adjective* (of paper) made on a frame of closely woven wire.

woven *see* **weave¹**.

wow¹ *interjection* an exclamation of astonishment or admiration. **–wow** *noun* (*informal*) a sensational success. **–wow** *verb* (*informal*) to impress or excite greatly.

wow² *noun* a slow fluctuation of pitch in sound reproduction, most perceptible in long notes or piano music.

wowser (**wow**-zer) *noun* (*Austral. informal*) **1** a person with very strict morals who tries to inflict these on others; a spoilsport. **2** a teetotaller.

w.p.m. *abbreviation* words per minute.

wrack *noun* seaweed thrown up on the shore or growing there, used for manure.

wraith (*pr.* rayth) *noun* a ghost; a spectral apparition of a living person, supposed to be a sign that he or she will die soon.

wrangle *verb* to have a noisy angry argument or quarrel. **–wrangle** *noun* an argument or quarrel of this kind. **wrangler** *noun*

wrap *verb* (**wrapped, wrapping**) **1** to enclose in soft or flexible material used as a covering. **2** to arrange (a flexible covering or a garment etc.) round a person or thing, *wrap a scarf round your neck*. **3** (in computing) to cause (text) to be carried over to the next line automatically as the margin is reached. **–wrap** *noun* a shawl, coat, or cloak etc. worn for warmth. □ **under wraps** in concealment or secrecy. **wrap over** (of a garment) to overlap at the edges when worn. **wrapped up in**

with one's attention deeply occupied by, *she is completely wrapped up in her children*; deeply involved in, *the country's prosperity is wrapped up in its mineral trade*. **wrap up** to enclose in wrappings; to put on warm clothing; (*informal*) to finish.

wrapper *noun* a cover of paper etc. wrapped round something.

wrapping *noun* material used to wrap something.

wrasse (*pr.* rass) *noun* a brightly coloured sea fish with thick lips and strong teeth.

wrath (*pr.* roth) *noun* anger, indignation.

wrathful *adjective* full of anger or indignation. **wrathfully** *adverb*

wreak (*pr.* reek) *verb* to inflict, to cause, *wreak vengeance on a person*; *rain wreaked havoc with the painting work*. [from Old English *wrecan* = avenge]

wreath (*pr.* reeth) *noun* (*plural* **wreaths**, *pr.* reethz) **1** flowers or leaves etc. fastened into a ring and used as a decoration or placed on a grave etc. as a mark of respect. **2** a curving line of mist or smoke. [compare *writhe*]

wreathe (*pr.* reeth) *verb* **1** to encircle or decorate with or as if with a wreath. **2** to twist into a wreath; *their faces were wreathed in smiles*, wrinkled with smiling. **3** to wind, *the snake wreathed itself round the branch*. **4** to move in a curving line, *smoke wreathed upwards*.

wreck *noun* **1** the disabling or destruction of something, especially of a ship by storms or accidental damage. **2** a ship that has suffered wreck. **3** the remains of a greatly damaged building or vehicle or thing. **4** a person whose physical or mental health has been damaged or destroyed, *a nervous wreck*. –**wreck** *verb* to cause the wreck of, to involve in shipwreck. [same origin as *wreak*]

wreckage *noun* **1** the remains of something wrecked. **2** wrecking.

wrecker *noun* **1** a person who wrecks something. **2** a person employed in the demolition of vehicles, buildings, etc.

wren *noun* **1** a small usually brown European songbird. **2** (in Australia) a small ground-frequenting bird usually with a long erect tail.

wrench *verb* to twist or pull violently round; to damage or pull by twisting, *wrenched it off*. –**wrench** *noun* **1** a violent twist or twisting pull. **2** pain caused by parting, *leaving home was a great wrench*. **3** an adjustable tool

like a spanner for gripping and turning nuts, bolts, etc.

wrest (*pr.* rest) *verb* **1** to wrench away, *wrested his sword from him*. **2** to obtain by effort or with difficulty, *wrested a confession from him*. **3** to twist or distort.

wrestle *verb* **1** to fight (especially as a sport) by grappling with a person and trying to throw him or her to the ground. **2** to fight with (a person) in this way, *police wrestled him to the ground*. **3** to struggle to deal with or overcome, *wrestled with the problem*. –**wrestle** *noun* **1** a wrestling match. **2** a hard struggle. **wrestler** *noun*

wretch *noun* **1** a very unfortunate or miserable person. **2** a despicable person. **3** (in playful use) a rascal.

wretched (**rech**-ĕd) *adjective* **1** miserable, unhappy. **2** of poor quality, unsatisfactory. **3** causing discomfort or nuisance, confounded, *this wretched car won't start*. **wretchedly** *adverb*, **wretchedness** *noun*

wriggle *verb* to move with short twisting movements. –**wriggle** *noun* a wriggling movement. □ **wriggle out of** to avoid (a task etc.) on some pretext; to escape from (a difficulty) cunningly. **wriggly** *adjective*

Wright[1], Frank Lloyd (1869–1959), American architect, who advocated a close relationship between building and landscape and the nature of the materials used.

Wright[2], Orville (1871–1948) and Wilbur (1867–1912), American brothers, pioneers of powered aeroplane flight.

Wright[3], Judith Arundell (1915–2000), Australian poet and conservationist.

wring *verb* (**wrung**, **wringing**) **1** to twist and squeeze in order to remove liquid. **2** to remove (liquid) in this way. **3** to squeeze firmly or forcibly; *they wrung his hand*, squeezed it warmly or emotionally; *wring one's hands*, squeeze them together emotionally; *wring the bird's neck*, kill it by twisting its neck. **4** to extract or obtain with effort or difficulty, *wrung a promise from him*. –**wring** *noun* a wringing movement, a squeeze or twist. □ **wringing wet** so wet that moisture can be wrung from it.

wringer *noun* a device with a pair of rollers between which clothes etc. are passed so that water is squeezed out.

wrinkle *noun* **1** a small crease; a small furrow or ridge in the skin (especially the kind produced by age). **2** (*informal*) a useful hint about how to do something. **–wrinkle** *verb* to make wrinkles in; to form wrinkles.

wrist *noun* **1** the joint connecting hand and forearm. **2** the part of a garment covering this.

wristlet *noun* a band or bracelet etc. worn round the wrist.

wristwatch *noun* a watch worn on a strap or band etc. round the wrist.

writ¹ (*pr.* rit) *noun* a formal written command issued by a lawcourt or ruling authority directing a person to act or refrain from acting in a certain way. □ **Holy Writ** the Bible.

writ² *adjective* (*old use*) written. □ **writ large** in an emphasised form, clearly recognisable.

write *verb* (**wrote, written, writing**) **1** to make letters or other symbols on a surface, especially with a pen or pencil on paper. **2** to form (letters or words or a message etc.) in this way; *write a cheque*, write the appropriate figures and words and signature etc. to make it valid. **3** to compose in written form for publication, to be an author, *write books* or *music*; *he makes a living by writing*. **4** to write and send a letter, *write to me often*. **5** (*Amer.*) to write to, *I will write you soon*. **6** to indicate clearly, *guilt was written all over her face*. **7** to enter (data) in or on any computer storage device or medium; to transfer from one storage device or medium to another; to output. □ **write down** to put into writing; to write as if for inferiors; to disparage in writing; to reduce the nominal value of. **write off** to cancel; to recognise as lost. **write-off** *noun* something written off as lost; a vehicle too badly damaged to be worth repairing. **write out** to write (a thing) in full or in a finished form. **write up** to write an account of; to write entries in (a diary etc.); to praise in writing. **write-up** *noun* a published written account of something; a review.

writer *noun* **1** a person who writes or has written something; one who writes in a specified way. **2** a person who writes books etc., an author. □ **writer's cramp** cramp in the muscles of the hand.

writhe (*pr.* ry*th*) *verb* **1** to twist one's body about, as in pain. **2** to wriggle, *writhing snakes*. **3** to suffer because of great shame or embarrassment.

writing *noun* **1** handwriting. **2** literary work, a piece of this, *in the writings of Thomas Hardy*. □ **in writing** in written form. **the writing on the wall** an event signifying that something is doomed (¶ after the biblical story of

the writing that appeared on the wall of Belshazzar's palace, foretelling his doom). **writing paper** paper for writing on, especially for writing letters.

written *see* **write.**

wrong *adjective* **1** (of conduct or actions) morally bad, contrary to justice or to what is right. **2** incorrect, not true. **3** not what is required or suitable or most desirable, *backed the wrong horse*; *get hold of the wrong end of the stick*, misunderstand a statement or situation; *wrong side*, (of fabric) the side that is not meant to show. **4** not in a normal condition, not functioning normally, *there's something wrong with the gearbox*. **–wrong** *adverb* in a wrong manner or direction, mistakenly, *you guessed wrong*. **–wrong** *noun* **1** what is morally wrong; a wrong action. **2** injustice, an unjust action or treatment, *they did us a great wrong*. **–wrong** *verb* **1** to do wrong to, to treat unjustly, *a wronged wife*. **2** to attribute bad motives to (a person) mistakenly. □ **get wrong** to misunderstand (a person, statement, etc.). **in the wrong** not having justice or truth on one's side. **on the wrong side of** in disfavour with or not liked by (a person); *on the wrong side of forty*, over 40 years old. **wrong-foot** *verb* to catch (a person) unprepared. **wrong-headed** *adjective* perverse and obstinate. **wrongly** *adverb*, **wrongness** *noun*

wrongdoer *noun* a person who acts contrary to law or to moral standards. **wrongdoing** *noun*

wrongful *adjective* contrary to what is fair or just or legal. **wrongfully** *adverb*

wrote *see* **write.**

wrought (*pr.* rawt) (*old use*) = worked. **–wrought** *adjective* (of metals) beaten out or shaped by hammering. □ **wrought iron** iron made by forging or rolling, not cast.

wrung *see* **wring.**

wry (*pr.* as*rye*) *adjective* (**wryer, wryest**) **1** twisted or bent out of shape. **2** twisted into an expression of disgust or disappointment or mockery, *a wry face*. **3** (of humour) dry and mocking. **wryly** *adverb*, **wryness** *noun*

wt. *abbreviation* weight.

WTO *abbreviation* World Trade Organisation.

wudu *noun* (in Islam) the ritual washing of oneself before prayer.

wurley *noun* (*plural* **wurlies**) an Aboriginal hut or temporary shelter. [Kaurna *warli*]

wuss (*pr.* wuus) *noun* (*informal*) a feeble or inept person, a wimp. **wussy** *adjective*

Wuywurung (**wy**-wŭ-rung) *noun* **1** a member of an Aboriginal people of the Melbourne area and to the north. **2** their language.

wych hazel = witch hazel.

Wyclif (**wik**-lif), John (c. 1330–84), English theologian, a precursor of the Reformation.

Wyoming (wy-**oh**-ming) a State of the western central USA.

WYSIWYG (**wiz**-ee-wig) *adjective* (also wysiwyg) (of a computer system) displaying text and graphics on the screen exactly as they will appear in a printout. [acronym of *w*hat you *s*ee *i*s *w*hat *y*ou *g*et]

wyvern *noun* (in heraldry) a dragon with wings, two legs, and a barbed tail.

Xx

Xanthippe (zan-**thip**-ee) *noun* a shrewish or ill-tempered woman. [the name of Socrates' wife]

Xavier (**zay**-vee-er), St Francis (1506–52), Spanish missionary, one of the original seven Jesuits.

xenon (**zen**-on) *noun* a chemical element (symbol Xe), a colourless odourless gas. [from Greek *xenos* = strange]

xenophobia (zen-ŏ-**foh**-bee-ă) *noun* strong dislike or distrust of foreigners. **xenophobic** *adjective* [from Greek *xenos* = foreigner, + *phobia*]

Xenophon (**zen**-ŏ-fŏn) (c. 428/7–c. 354 BC), Greek general and historian.

xerophytic (zeer-rŏ-**fit**-ik) *adjective* (of plants) adapted to survive drought.

xerox (**zeer**-roks) *noun* (*trademark*) **1** a process for producing photocopies without the use of wet chemicals. **2** a photocopy made in this way. –**xerox** *verb* to photocopy by a process of this kind.

Xerxes (**zerk**-seez) king of Persia 486–465 BC, who led an army against Greece but was eventually defeated on both land and sea.

X factor *noun* (*informal*) a noteworthy special talent or quality.

Xhosa (**koh**-să *or* **kaw**-să) *noun* **1** a member of a Bantu people of Cape Province, South Africa. **2** their language.

Xmas *noun* = Christmas. [the *X* represents the Greek letter chi (= ch), the first letter of *Christos* (the Greek word for *Christ*)]

X-ray *noun* a photograph or examination made by means of a kind of electromagnetic radiation (**X-rays**) that can penetrate solids and make it possible to see into or through them. –**X-ray** *verb* to photograph, examine, or treat by this radiation.

xylem (**zy**-lĕm) *noun* the woody tissue in the stem of a plant, that carries water and dissolved minerals upwards from the ground. [from Greek *xulon* = wood]

xylene (**zy**-leen) *noun* any of three substances derived from benzene by substitution of two methyl groups. [same origin as *xylem*]

xylophone (**zy**-lŏ-fohn) *noun* a musical instrument consisting of flat wooden bars, graduated in length, which produce different notes when struck with hammers. [from Greek *xulon* = wood, + *phone* = sound]

Yy

yabber (*Austral. informal*) *noun* talk, discussion; language. –**yabber** *verb* to talk.

yabby *noun* (*plural* **yabbies**) **1** a small Australian freshwater crayfish, valued as food. **2** (in Queensland) a saltwater prawn used as bait, a nipper. –**yabby** *verb* to fish for yabbies. [Wemba-wemba *yabij*]

yacca *noun* (also **yacka**) (*Austral.*) a grass tree. [probably from Kaurna *yakko* = a kind of gum]

yacht (*pr.* yot) *noun* **1** a light sailing vessel for racing. **2** a vessel used for private pleasure excursions. **3** a light vessel for travel on sand or ice. **yachtsman**, **yachtswoman** *nouns* [from Dutch *jachtschip* = fast pirate ship]

yachting *noun* racing or cruising in a yacht.

yacka *see* **yacca**, **yakka**.

Yagara (**yah**-gă-ră) *noun* **1** a member of an Aboriginal people of the Brisbane area. **2** their language.

yah *interjection* an exclamation of scorn or defiance.

yahoo (**yah**-hoo) *noun* a coarse person; a lout. [the name of an imaginary race in *Gulliver's Travels* by Swift]

Yahweh (**yah**-way) *see* **Jehovah**.

Yajur Veda (**yah**-joor) *noun* one of the four Vedas, based on a collection of sacrificial formulae used in the Vedic religion by the priest in charge of sacrificial ritual. [from Sanskrit *yajus* 'sacrificial formula' + *veda*, '(sacred) knowledge']

yak[1] *noun* a long-haired humped ox of central Asia. [from Tibetan]

yak[2] (*informal*, often *derogatory*) (also **yack**) *noun* a long or trivial conversation. –**yak** *verb* (**yakked**, **yakking**) to engage in this; to chatter.

yakka *noun* (also **yacka** or **yakker**) (*Austral. informal*) work, hard yakka. [Yagara *yaga*]

Yale *noun* (*trademark*) a type of lock for doors etc. [named after Linus Yale (1821–68)]

Yale University an American university of New Haven, Connecticut, named after a notable 18th-century benefactor.

yam *noun* **1** the edible starchy tuber of a tropical or subtropical climbing plant; the plant itself. **2** a sweet potato (*see* **sweet**).

Yama (**yam**-ă) (*Hindu myth.*) the first man to die, who became the guardian, judge, and ruler of the dead.

Yammagi (**ya**-mă-jee) *noun* an Aboriginal person from central Australia. [Watjari *yamaji*]

Usage see **aborigine**.

Yamoussoukro (ya-moo-**sook**-roh) the capital of the Ivory Coast.

Yandruwandha (**yahn**-droo-wahnd-hu) *noun* **1** a member of an Aboriginal people of NE South Australia and SW Queensland. **2** their language.

yandy *noun* **1** a shallow wooden dish used to separate edible seeds from refuse with a shaking motion. **2** a similar iron dish for separating particles of mineral from alluvial material. –**yandy** *verb* to separate seeds or minerals by shaking a yandy; to winnow. [Yindjibarndi *yandi* = winnowing dish]

yang *noun* (in Chinese philosophy) the active principle of the universe (complemented by *yin*).

Yangon (yang-**gon**) the Burmese name for Rangoon, the capital of Myanmar (Burma).

Yangtze River (**yang**-tsee) (formerly **Yangtse-Kiang**) the principal river of China that rises in Tibet and flows through China to the East China Sea.

Yank *noun* (*informal*) a Yankee.

yank *verb* (*informal*) to pull with a sudden sharp tug. –**yank** *noun* (*informal*) a sudden sharp tug.

Yankee *noun* **1** an American. **2** (*Amer.*) an inhabitant of the northern States of the USA.

Yankunytjatjara (**yahn**-kuun-ju-jah-ru) *noun* **1** a member of an Aboriginal people of the desert region around Uluru. **2** their language, a dialect of the Western Desert language.

Yaoundé (ya-**uun**-day) the capital of Cameroon.

yap *noun* a shrill bark. –**yap** *verb* (**yapped**, **yapping**) **1** to bark shrilly. **2** (*informal*) to chatter.

Yaralde (**yu**-răl-dee) *noun* **1** a member of an Aboriginal people of SE South Australia. **2** their language.

yard[1] *noun* **1** a measure of length, = 3 feet or 0.9144 metre. **2** a long pole-like piece of wood stretched horizontally or crosswise from a mast to support a sail.

yard[2] *noun* **1** a piece of enclosed ground, especially one attached to a building or surrounded by buildings or used for a particular kind of work etc., *a timber yard*; *a shipyard*. **2** (*Austral.* & *Amer.*) the garden of a house. **3** (*Austral.*) an enclosure for drafting stock.

yardarm *noun* either end of a yard supporting a sail.

yardstick *noun* a standard of comparison.

Yaren the capital of Nauru.

yarmulke (**yar**-muul-kă) *noun* (also **yarmulka**) a skullcap worn by Jewish men. [Yiddish]

yarn *noun* **1** any spun thread, especially of the kinds prepared for knitting or weaving or rope-making. **2** (*informal*) a tale, especially one that is exaggerated or invented. –**yarn** *verb* (*informal*) to tell yarns.

Yarra a river rising east of Melbourne and flowing through Melbourne to Port Phillip Bay.

Yarralumla the official residence in Canberra of the Governor-General of Australia.

yarraman (**ya**-ră-măn) *noun* (in Australian pidgin) a horse.

yarran (**ya**-răn) *noun* an Australian acacia with rough bark and an unpleasant smell; its dark brown, durable wood. [Kamilaroi *yarraan*]

yarrow (**ya**-roh) *noun* a plant with feathery leaves and strong-smelling white or pinkish flowers.

yashmak *noun* a veil concealing the face except for the eyes, worn in public by Muslim women in certain countries. [Arabic]

yate *noun* a Western Australian eucalypt yielding a strong timber; the timber itself.

yaw *verb* (of a ship or aircraft etc.) to fail to hold a straight course, to turn from side to side. –**yaw** *noun* a yawing movement or course.

yawl *noun* **1** a kind of sailing boat with two masts. **2** a kind of fishing boat.

yawn *verb* **1** to open the mouth wide and draw in breath (often involuntarily), as when sleepy or bored. **2** to have a wide opening, to form a chasm. –**yawn** *noun* **1** the act of yawning. **2** (*informal*) something boring.

yaws *noun* a contagious tropical skin disease causing large red swellings.

ye[1] *pronoun* (*old use*) you (more than one person).

ye[2] *adjective* (*supposed old use*) the, *ye olde tea-shoppe*.

yea (*pr.* yay) *adverb* & *noun* (*old use*) yes.

yeah (*pr.* yair) *adverb* (*informal*) yes.

year *noun* **1** the time taken by the earth to make one complete orbit of the sun, about $365\frac{1}{4}$ days. **2** the period from 1 January to 31 December inclusive. **3** any period of twelve consecutive months. **4** an academic level; a school class or grade, *in year 10 at school*; *in 2nd year at university*. **years** *plural noun* age, time of life, *he looks younger than his years*; a very long time, *we've been waiting for years*.

yearbook *noun* an annual publication containing current information about a particular subject.

yearling (**yeer**-ling) *noun* an animal between 1 and 2 years old.

yearly *adjective* happening, published, or payable etc. once a year, annual. –**yearly** *adverb* annually.

yearn *verb* to be filled with great longing.

yeast *noun* a kind of fungus that causes alcohol and carbon dioxide to be produced while it is developing, used to cause fermentation in making beer and wines and as a raising agent in baking.

yeasty *adjective* frothy like yeast when it is developing. **yeastiness** *noun*

Yeats (*pr.* yayts), William Butler (1865–1939), Irish poet and dramatist.

yell *verb* to give a loud cry, to shout. –**yell** *noun* a loud cry, a shout.

yellow *adjective* **1** of the colour of butter, egg yolks, or ripe lemons, or a colour approaching this. **2** (*informal*) cowardly. –**yellow** *noun* **1** yellow colour. **2** a yellow substance or material, yellow clothes. –**yellow** *verb* to make or become yellow. □ **yellow fever** a tropical disease with fever and jaundice. **yellow peril** (*offensive*) the perceived threat of Asian invasion and takeover of Australia. **yellowish** *adjective*, **yellowness** *noun*

yellowbelly *noun* a large Australian freshwater fish with yellow underparts; a callop or golden perch.

yellowcake *noun* uranium ore, concentrated uranium oxide.

Yellow River (also **Huang He**) the second-largest river in China, so named because of its high silt content.

yellowtail *noun* any of several Australian sea fish with a yellow tail fin; a kingfish.

yelp *noun* a sharp shrill cry or bark. –**yelp** *verb* to utter a yelp.

Yemen (**yem**-ĕn) a republic in the south and south-west of the Arabian peninsula. **Yemeni** (**yem**-ĕ-nee) *adjective* & *noun*, **Yemenite** (**yem**-ĕ-nyt) *adjective* & *noun*

yen[1] *noun* (*plural* **yen**) the unit of money in Japan. [from Chinese *yuan* = round thing]

yen[2] *noun* a longing, a yearning. [Chinese dialect word]

yeoman (**yoh**-măn) *noun* (*plural* **yeomen**) (*Brit. old use*) a man who owns and farms a small estate. □ **Yeoman of the Guard** a member of the British sovereign's bodyguard. **yeoman service** long and useful service. **Yeoman Warder** *see* **beefeater**.

Yerevan (ye-rĕ-**van**) the capital of Armenia.

yes *adverb* **1** it is so, the statement is correct. **2** what you request or command will be done. **3** (as a question) what do you want? **4** (in answer to a summons etc.) I am here. –**yes** *noun* the word or answer 'yes'. □ **yes-man** *noun* a person who always agrees with a superior in a weak or sycophantic way.

yesterday *noun* **1** the day before today. **2** the recent past. –**yesterday** *adverb* on the day before today; in the recent past.

yesteryear *noun* (*literary*) last year; the recent past.

yet *adverb* **1** up to this or that time and continuing, still, *there's life in the old dog yet*. **2** by this or that time, so far, *it hasn't happened yet*. **3** besides, in addition, *heard it yet again*. **4** before the matter is done with, eventually, *I'll be even with you yet*. **5** even, *she became yet more excited*. **6** nevertheless, *strange yet true*. –**yet** *conjunction* nevertheless, but in spite of that, *he worked hard, yet he failed*.

yeti (**yet**-ee) *noun* (*plural* **yetis**) the native (Sherpa) name for the 'Abominable Snowman' (*see* **abominable**).

yew *noun* **1** an evergreen tree with dark green needle-like leaves and red berries. **2** its wood.

Yggdrasil (**ig**-dră-sil) (*Scand. myth.*) the ash tree whose roots and branches connect earth, heaven, and hell.

Yiddish *noun* a language used by Jews of central and eastern Europe, based on a German dialect and with words from Hebrew and various modern languages. [from German *jüdisch* = Jewish]

Yidiny (**yid**-in) *noun* **1** a member of an Aboriginal people of the Cairns region of Queensland. **2** their language.

yield *verb* **1** to give or return as fruit, gain, or result, *the land yields good crops*; *the investment yields 15%*. **2** to surrender, to do what is requested or ordered, *the town yielded*; *he yielded to persuasion*. **3** to be inferior or confess inferiority, *I yield to none in appreciation of his merits*. **4** (of traffic) to allow other traffic to have right of way. **5** to be able to be forced out of the natural or usual shape, e.g. under pressure. –**yield** *noun* the amount yielded or produced; the quantity obtained. [from Old English, = pay]

yin *noun* (in Chinese philosophy) the passive principle of the universe (complemented by *yang*).

Yindjibarndi (yin-jee-**bun**-dee) *noun* **1** a member of an Aboriginal people of western central WA. **2** their language.

yippee *interjection* an exclamation of excitement.

Yirrkala (**yeer**-kul-ă) an Aboriginal settlement on Gove Peninsula in the Northern Territory; a centre for fine bark paintings and wood carvings.

YMCA *abbreviation* Young Men's Christian Association.

yob *noun* (*informal*) a lout, a hooligan. [from *boy*, written backwards]

yobbo *noun* (*plural* **yobbos**) (*informal*) = yob.

yodel (**yoh**-d'l) *verb* (**yodelled**, **yodelling**) to sing, or utter a musical call, so that the voice alternates continually between falsetto and its normal pitch. –**yodel** *noun* a yodelling cry. **yodeller** *noun*

yoga (**yoh**-gă) *noun* a Hindu system of meditation and self-control designed to produce mystical experience and spiritual insight.

yoghurt (**yoh**-gert) *noun* a food prepared from milk that has been thickened by the action of certain bacteria. [Turkish]

yogi (**yoh**-gee) *noun* a devotee of yoga.

yoke *noun* 1 a wooden crosspiece fastened over the necks of two oxen or other animals pulling a cart or plough etc. 2 a piece of timber shaped to fit a person's shoulders and to hold a pail or other load slung from each end. 3 a part of a garment fitting round the shoulders or hips and from which the rest hangs. 4 oppression, burdensome restraint, *throw off the yoke of servitude*. –**yoke** *verb* 1 to put a yoke upon, to harness by means of a yoke, *yoke oxen to the plough*. 2 to unite, *yoked to an unwilling partner*.

yokel (**yoh**-kĕl) *noun* a simple country person, a country bumpkin.

yolk (*pr.* yohk) *noun* the round yellow internal part of an egg.

Yolngu (**yol**-ngoo) *noun* 1 a member of an Aboriginal people of north-east Arnhem Land in the Northern Territory. 2 their language. 3 an Aboriginal person from Arnhem Land.

Usage see **aborigine**.

Yom Kippur (yom ki-**poor**) the Day of Atonement (*see* **atonement**). [Hebrew]

yon *adjective & adverb* (*literary*) yonder.

yonder *adverb* over there. –**yonder** *adjective* situated or able to be seen over there.

yonks *noun* (*informal*) a long time, ages, *I haven't seen him for yonks*.

yore *noun* **of yore** formerly; of long ago.

York the name of the English royal house (descended from the 1st Duke of York) from 1461 (Edward IV) until the death of Richard III (1485).

yorker *noun* a ball bowled in cricket so that it pitches immediately under the bat.

Yorkist *adjective* of the family descended from the 1st Duke of York (died 1402) or of the White Rose party supporting it in the Wars of the Roses. –**Yorkist** *noun* a member or adherent of the Yorkist family.

Yorkshire pudding *noun* a baked batter pudding eaten with roast beef. [from *Yorkshire* in northern England]

you *pronoun* 1 the person(s) addressed. 2 one, anyone, everyone, *you can never tell*.

you'd (*informal*) = you had; you would.

you'll (*informal*) = you will.

young *adjective* 1 having lived or existed for only a short time; *the younger twin*, the second-born. 2 not far advanced in time, *the night is young*. 3 youthful, having little experience. 4 used in speaking of or to a young person, *young man*. –**young** *noun* the offspring of animals, before or soon after birth. **youngish** *adjective*

youngster *noun* a young person, a child.

your *adjective* of or belonging to you.

you're (*informal*) = you are.

yours *possessive pronoun* 1 belonging to you; the thing(s) belonging to you. 2 used in phrases for ending letters: **Yours** or **Yours ever** used casually to friends. **Yours faithfully** used for ending business or formal letters beginning 'Dear Sir' or 'Dear Madam'. **Yours sincerely** used in letters to acquaintances and to friends (other than close friends), and often also in business letters addressing a person by name (e.g. beginning 'Dear Mr Brown'), where it is now more frequently used than *Yours truly*. **Yours truly** used to slight acquaintances and in business letters (less formal than *yours faithfully* but more formal than *yours sincerely*); (*informal*) = me, *the awkward jobs are always left for yours truly*.

Usage It is incorrect to write *your's* (see the note under **its**).

yourself *pronoun* (*plural* **yourselves**) corresponding to *you*, used in the same ways as **himself**.

youth *noun* (*plural* **youths**, *pr.* yoothz) 1 being young. 2 the period between childhood and maturity; the vigour or lack of experience etc. characteristic of this. 3 a young man, *a youth of 16*. 4 young people collectively, *the youth of the country*. □ **youth club** a club where leisure activities are provided for young people. **youth hostel** a hostel providing cheap accommodation where (especially young) people who are hiking or on holiday etc. may stay overnight. **youth hostelling** staying in youth hostels.

youthful *adjective* 1 young; looking or seeming young. 2 characteristic of young people, *youthful impatience*. **youthfully** *adverb*, **youthfulness** *noun*

you've (*informal*) = you have.

yowl *noun* a loud wailing cry, a howl. –**yowl** *verb* utter a yowl.

yo-yo *noun* (*plural* **yo-yos**) a toy consisting of two circular parts with a deep groove between, which can be made to rise and fall on a string (attached to it) when this is jerked by a finger.

yrs. *abbreviation* **1** years. **2** yours.

ytterbium (i-**ter**-bee-ŭm) *noun* a silver-white metallic element of the lanthanide series (symbol Yb).

yttrium (**i**-tree-ŭm) *noun* a grey-white metallic element (symbol Y).

yuan (yoo-**ahn**) *noun* (*plural* **yuan**) the chief unit of money in China.

yucca (**yuk**-ă) *noun* a tall plant with white bell-like flowers and stiff spiky leaves. [Carib]

yuck *interjection* (also **yuk**) (*informal*) an expression of disgust etc.

yucky *adjective* (*informal*) disgusting, repulsive.

yuga (**yoo**-gă) *noun* (in Hinduism) any of the four stages of the life of the world.

Yugoslavia (yoo-gŏ-**slah**-vee-ă) a former country in SE Europe comprising six republics (Bosnia-Herzegovina, Croatia, Macedonia, Montenegro, Serbia, and Slovenia); formed after the First World War, it broke up in 1991 with the secession of Bosnia-Herzegovina, Croatia, Macedonia, and Slovenia. **Yugoslav** (yoo-gŏ-slahv), **Yugoslavian** *adjectives* & *nouns*

Yuin (**yoo**-in) *noun* an Aboriginal person from central Australia.

Usage see **aborigine**.

yule (*pr.* yool) *noun* (also **yuletide**) (*old use*) the Christmas festival.

yummy *adjective* (*informal*) tasty, delicious.

yum-yum *interjection* an exclamation of pleasure at eating or at the thought of eating.

yuppie *noun* (also **yuppy**) (*informal*, *derogatory*) young urban professional person. [from the initials of these words]

Yura (**yoo**-ră) *noun* an Aboriginal person from the Flinders region of South Australia.

Usage see **aborigine**.

Yuwaalaraay (yoo-**wah**-lă-ry) *noun* **1** a member of an Aboriginal people of northern NSW. **2** their language.

YWCA *abbreviation* Young Women's Christian Association.

Zz

Zagreb (**zah**-greb) the capital of Croatia.

Zaïre (zy-**eer**) 1 (also Congo) a major river in central Africa, flowing into the Atlantic Ocean. 2 a former name of the Democratic Republic of Congo. Zaïrean *adjective* & *noun*

zakat (ză-**kaht**) *noun* obligatory payment made annually under Islamic law and used for charitable and religious purposes.

Zambezi (zam-**bee**-zee) a river of Africa forming the border between Zambia and Zimbabwe, flowing into the Indian Ocean.

Zambia a landlocked republic in central Africa. Zambian *adjective* & *noun*

zany *noun* a comical or eccentric person. −**zany** *adjective* (**zanier, zaniest**) crazily funny.

Zanzibar an island off the coast of East Africa, united with Tanganyika to form the republic of Tanzania.

zap *verb* (**zapped, zapping**) (*informal*) 1 to hit; to attack; to knock out, to kill. 2 to exhaust. 3 to move quickly.

Zarathustra (za-ră-**thuus**-tră) the Old Persian name for Zoroaster.

zeal (*pr.* zeel) *noun* enthusiasm; hearty and persistent effort.

zealot (**zel**-ŏt) *noun* a zealous person, a fanatic. **zealotry** *noun*

zealous (**zel**-ŭs) *adjective* full of zeal. **zealously** *adverb*

zebra (**zeb**-ră) *noun* an African animal of the horse family with a body entirely covered by black and white stripes. □ **zebra crossing** a pedestrian crossing where the road is marked with broad white stripes.

zebu (**zee**-boo) *noun* (*plural* **zebu** or **zebus**) a humped ox of India, East Asia, and Africa.

Zechariah (zek-ă-**ry**-ă) 1 a Hebrew minor prophet of the 6th century BC. 2 a book of the Old Testament containing his prophecies.

Zen *noun* a form of Buddhism emphasising the value of meditation and intuition. [Japanese, = meditation]

Zend *noun* an interpretation of the Avesta, each Zend being part of the Zend-Avesta,

Zoroastrian scriptures consisting of Avesta (= text) and Zend (= commentary). [from Persian *zand* = interpretation]

zenith (**zen**-ĭth) 1 the part of the sky that is directly above an observer. 2 the highest point, *his power was at its zenith*. [from Arabic *samt ar-ras* = path over the head]

Zephaniah (zef-ă-**ny**-ă) 1 a Hebrew minor prophet of the 7th century BC. 2 a book of the Old Testament containing his prophecies.

zephyr (**zef**-er) *noun* a soft gentle wind. [from Greek *Zephuros* = god of the west wind]

Zeppelin, Ferdinand, Count von (1838–1917), German airship pioneer, whose airships (known as Zeppelins) were used to bomb England in the First World War.

zero *noun* (*plural* **zeros**) 1 nought, the figure 0. 2 nothing, nil. 3 the point marked 0 on a graduated scale, especially on a thermometer. 4 the temperature corresponding to zero. −**zero** *verb* (**zeroed, zeroing**) to adjust (an instrument etc.) to zero. □ **zero hour** the hour at which something is timed to begin. **zero in on** to focus one's aim on; to go purposefully towards. [from Arabic *sifr* = cipher]

zest *noun* 1 keen enjoyment or interest. 2 a pleasantly stimulating quality, *the risk added zest to the adventure*. 3 the coloured part of the peel of an orange or lemon etc., used as flavouring. **zestful** *adjective*, **zestfully** *adverb*

Zeus (*pr.* zewss) (*Gk. myth.*) the supreme god, identified with Jupiter.

ziff *noun* (*Austral. informal*) a beard.

ziggurat (**zig**-ŭ-rat) *noun* a pyramid-shaped tower in ancient Mesopotamia surmounted by a temple, built in tiers which become smaller in size towards the summit.

zigzag *noun* a line or course that turns right and left alternately at sharp angles. −**zigzag** *adjective* & *adverb* forming or in a zigzag. −**zigzag** *verb* (**zigzagged, zigzagging**) to move in a zigzag course.

zilch *noun* (*informal*) nothing.

zillion *noun* (*informal*) an indefinite large number.

Zimbabwe (zim-**bahb**-wee) a republic in SE Africa. **Zimbabwean** *adjective* & *noun*

zinc *noun* a white metallic element (symbol Zn), used in alloys and to coat iron and steel as a protection against corrosion.

zing *noun* (*informal*) vigour, energy.

zinnia (**zin**-ee-ă) *noun* a daisy-like garden plant with brightly coloured flowers.

Zion (**zy**-ŏn) *noun* **1** the holy hill of ancient Jerusalem, *Mount Zion*. **2** the Jewish people or religion. **3** the Christian Church. **4** the kingdom of heaven.

Zionism (**zy**-ŏ-nizm) *noun* a movement founded in 1897 that has sought and achieved the founding of a Jewish homeland in Palestine. **Zionist** *noun*

zip *noun* **1** a short sharp sound like that of a bullet going through the air. **2** energy, vigour, liveliness. **3** (in full **zip fastener**) a fastening device consisting of two flexible strips of material with projections that interlock when brought together by a sliding tab. **–zip** *verb* (**zipped**, **zipping**) **1** to open or close with a zip fastener. **2** to move with the sound of 'zip' or at high speed. **3** (in computing) compress (a file) so that it takes up less space.

zip code *noun* (*Amer.*) a system of postal codes. [from the initials of *zone improvement plan*]

zipper *noun* a zip fastener.

zippy *adjective* (**zippier**, **zippiest**) lively and vigorous. **zippiness** *noun*

zircon (**zer**-kon) *noun* a bluish-white gem cut from a translucent mineral.

zirconium (zer-**koh**-nee-ŭm) *noun* a hard silver-grey metallic element (symbol Zr).

zit *noun* (*informal*) a pimple.

zither (**zith**-er) *noun* a musical instrument with many strings stretched over a shallow boxlike body, played by plucking with the fingers of both hands.

zloty (**zlot**-ee) *noun* (*plural* **zloty** *or* **zlotys**) the unit of money in Poland.

zodiac (**zoh**-dee-ak) *noun* (in astrology) **1** a band of the sky containing the paths of the sun, moon, and principal planets, divided into twelve equal parts (called **signs of the zodiac**) each named from a constellation that was formerly situated in it (Aries, Taurus, Gemini, Cancer, Leo, Virgo, Libra, Scorpio, Sagittarius, Capricorn, Aquarius, Pisces). **2** a diagram of these signs. **zodiacal** (zŏ-**dy**-ă-kăl) *adjective* [from Greek *zoidion* = image of an animal]

Zola (**zoh**-lă), Émile (1840–1902), French novelist, the leading exponent of naturalism, whose principal work is the series of twenty novels *Les Rougon-Macquart*.

zombie *noun* **1** (in voodoo) a corpse said to have been revived by witchcraft. **2** (*informal*) a person thought to resemble this, one who seems to have no mind or will. [from West African *zumbi* = fetish]

zone *noun* an area that has particular characteristics or a particular purpose or use. **–zone** *verb* **1** to divide into zones. **2** to arrange or distribute into zones; to assign to a particular area. **zonal** *adjective* [Greek, = girdle]

zonked *adjective* (*informal*) exhausted; intoxicated.

zoo *verb* a place where wild animals are kept for exhibition, conservation, and study. [short for *zoological gardens*]

zoological (zoh-ŏ-**loj**-i-kăl *or* zoo-) *adjective* of zoology. □ **zoological gardens** a zoo.

zoology (zoh-**ol**-ŏ-jee *or* zoo-**ol**-ŏ-jee) *noun* the scientific study of animals. **zoologist** *noun* [from Greek *zoion* = animal, + *-logy*]

zoom *verb* **1** to move quickly, especially with a buzzing sound. **2** to rise quickly, *prices had zoomed*. **3** (in photography) to alter the size of the image by means of a zoom lens. □ **zoom lens** a camera lens that can be adjusted from a long shot to a close-up (and vice versa).

zoophyte (**zoh**-ŏ-fyt) *noun* a plantlike animal, especially a coral, sea anemone, or sponge. [from Greek *zoion* = animal, + *phuton* = plant]

zooplankton (zoh-ŏ-**plank**-tŏn) *noun* plankton consisting of tiny animals. [from Greek *zoion* = animal, + *plankton*]

Zoroaster (zo-roh-**ast**-er) the Greek name for the Persian prophet Zarathustra (6th century BC or earlier), founder of Zoroastrianism.

Zoroastrian (zo-roh-**ast**-ree-ăn) *noun* a person who believes in **Zoroastrianism**, the ancient Persian religion based on the teachings of Zoroaster and his followers. **–Zoroastrian** *adjective* of Zoroaster or Zoroastrianism.

zucchini (zoo-**kee**-nee) *noun* (*plural* **zucchini** *or* **zucchinis**) a variety of small vegetable marrow, also called *courgette*. [Italian]

Zulu *noun* (*plural* **Zulus**) **1** a member of a Bantu people of South Africa. **2** their language.

zygospore (**zy**-gŏ-spor) *noun* a thick-walled spore formed by the union of two similar gametes. [from Greek *zugon* = yoke, + *spore*]

zygote (**zy**-goht) *noun* a cell formed by the union of two gametes. [from Greek *zugon* = yoke]

zymase (**zy**-mayz) *noun* an enzyme of a group originally found in yeast, that causes the breakdown of glucose and some other sugars. [from Greek *zume* = leaven]

Appendix 1:
Grammar and reference guide

Contents

Grammar and reference guide

Grammar

Grammar explains how words work together in sentences to create meaningful communication.

The opened door I. (This sentence makes no sense.)

I opened the door. (This arrangement of words makes sense because each word is in its right place.)

Each word in a sentence has a job to do. Its function is called its part of speech.

Parts of speech

There are eight parts of speech: nouns, pronouns, adjectives, verbs, adverbs, prepositions, conjunctions, and interjections.

We need to see a word in a sentence before we can say what part of speech it is. The same word can be a different part of speech depending on its relationship to the other words in the sentence.

water

We need to save **water**. (noun)

We **water** the garden twice a week in summer. (verb)

Nouns

Nouns name people, creatures, places, things, qualities, feelings, and ideas.

Scientist, elephant, lake, monitor, courage, pride, equality

To check if a word in a sentence is a noun, see if it answers the question Who? or What?

Fran plays the **flute**. (Who plays? 'Fran') (Fran plays what? 'the flute')

There are different kinds of nouns:

Proper nouns always begin with a capital letter as they name a particular person, place, or thing.

Tom, Mount Everest, House of Representatives

Common nouns do not begin with a capital letter (unless they begin a sentence).

boy, mountain, dog

Grammar and reference guide

Most common nouns are concrete as they name something that we can see, hear, smell, or touch.

> river, whistle, rose, fur

Some common nouns are abstract as they name something we cannot understand with our senses.

> love, respect, democracy, talent

Collective nouns name groups of people, animals, or things.

> team, flock, bunch

Compound nouns are formed by combining two nouns into one word.

> rain/coat, hair/style, foot/ball, house/boat

Articles

Nouns are often preceded by 'the', 'a' or 'an', known as articles.
'The' is the definite article as it introduces a particular noun.

> **The** car collided with **the** pole.

'A' (or 'an' if the noun begins with a vowel) is an indefinite article as it introduces a general noun.

> **A** car is **an** expensive purchase.

Pronouns

Pronouns replace nouns so that we don't have to repeat the noun.

> The tourists hired a guide. The guide showed the tourists around the town.

> The tourists hired a guide. **She** showed **them** around the town.

Because they replace nouns, pronouns also answer Who?, Whom?, or What?

> Aunt Mary gave **me** a present. **She** said **I** would treasure **it**.

(To whom did Aunt Mary give a present? 'me')
(Who said? 'She')
(She said who would treasure it? 'I')
(What would I treasure? 'it')

The noun that the pronoun stands in for is called the antecedent (meaning the word that comes before). It is important that it is clear which noun the pronoun is replacing.

> Fran told Gemma **she** had won the competition. (Who has won it?)

> Fran boasted to Gemma that **she** had won the competition. (Now it is clear.)

There are several types of pronouns.

Personal pronouns stand in for nouns that name people or things.

> **I, we, me, us, you, he, she, her, him, it, they**

> He asked **her** if **she** would help **him** move the couch.

> **She** said **she** would be happy to help **him** move **it**.

Possessive pronouns show that someone owns something.

> **mine, ours, yours, his, hers, its, theirs**

> The couch was **his**. It was heavier than **hers**.

Reflexive pronouns refer to a noun or pronoun earlier in the sentence.

> **myself, ourselves, yourself, yourselves, itself, herself, himself, themselves**

> Sam taught **himself** to play chess.

> I see **myself** as a comedian.

With personal, possessive, and reflexive pronouns, we can use the first, second, or third person.

> First: **I, me, us, mine, ours, myself, ourselves** (the person or persons speaking)
> Second: **you, yours, yourself, yourselves** (the person or persons spoken to)
> Third person: **he, she, it, they, his, hers, theirs, himself, herself, itself, themselves** (the person or persons spoken about)

> **I** told **you** about **him**.

> The cake is **mine**. That biscuit is **yours** and someone has eaten **hers**.

> **We** must save **ourselves** from starvation.

> **You** can help **yourself** to another biscuit.

> The kitten gave **itself** a fright.

Relative pronouns relate one part of a sentence to another (a subordinate clause to a main clause).

> **who, whom, whose, which, that**

> She was the woman **who** spoke to me.

> I addressed the letter to **whom** it may concern.

> **Whose** is this jumper?

He repeated the joke, **which** I didn't think was funny.

The team **that** wins today goes into the final.

Demonstrative pronouns point to someone or something.

this, that, these, those

'This' and 'these' refer to things close in time and/or place. 'That' and 'those' refer to things further away in time and place.

This is my first job.

These are my favourite shoes.

Who gave you **that**?

Those were the days.

Indefinite pronouns do not refer to anyone or anything in particular.

everyone, something, anybody, each, some, many, all, several

Everyone is coming to the party.

Something is wrong with this situation.

Anybody can enter the competition.

Each of you deserves an award.

Some of the money is missing.

Many of my friends play cricket.

All of the cake was eaten.

I had heard **several** of the songs before.

Adjectives

Adjectives modify (add to the meaning of) nouns.

Usually an adjective precedes the noun that it modifies.

I watched the **happy** children.

She is an **energetic** child.

I bought a pair of **brown** shoelaces.

Sometimes an adjective follows a verb and modifies the subject of the verb.

The children seemed **happy**.

The child is **energetic**.

My shoelaces are **brown**.

Comparison of adjectives

Most adjectives can be used in one of three different forms.

Positive degree (no comparison made):

> Sam is a **tall** girl.

Comparative degree (two people or things compared):

> Sam is **taller** than her mother.

Superlative (more than two people or things compared):

> Sam is the **tallest** person in her family.

If an adjective is a long word, 'more' or 'most', 'less' or 'least' is used.

> My sport is **more dangerous** than yours.
>
> My sport is the **most dangerous** of all.
>
> These shoes are **less expensive** than those ones.
>
> This pair is the **least expensive** of all the shoes in the shop.

Some adjectives are irregular and take different forms.

> **good, better, best**
>
> My brother is a **good** athlete.
>
> My sister is a **better** athlete than he is.
>
> I am the **best** athlete in the family.

> **bad, worse, worst**
>
> This medicine tastes **bad**.
>
> My test result was **worse** than yours.
>
> This is the **worst** day of my life.

Compound adjectives

Two or more words can be joined together to form an adjective. Sometimes the words are joined by hyphens.

> We booked into a **five-star** hotel.
>
> Our house is a **smoke-free** zone.
>
> The plane was hit by a **surface-to-air** missile.

Sometimes they become one word.

> There was **widespread** damage after the cyclone.
>
> Some slang expressions are **overused**.
>
> The steak was **underdone**.

Check the dictionary to see which form to use for a particular word.

Verbs

A verb is the most important word in a sentence. Each sentence must contain at least one verb. A verb says something about a subject by expressing an action or a state of being.

> She **swam** across the pool. (The subject 'she' is performing an action.)
>
> I **understand** grammar now. (The subject 'I' is performing a mental action.)
>
> He **is** a pianist. (The subject 'he' is being a pianist.)
>
> My mum **stays** calm in a crisis. (The subject 'my mum' is in a calm state.)

The form of a verb indicates the time an action or a state of being takes place. We call this aspect of a verb its tense.

Simple tenses show whether the action (or state of being) is in the present, past, or future.

> I **write** in my diary every day. (simple present tense)
>
> I **wrote** a story last week. (simple past tense)
>
> I **will write** a poem next week. (simple future tense, formed by using the auxiliary or helping verb 'will')

To form other tenses we also use auxiliary verbs.

Another aspect of a verb is whether it is in the active or passive voice.

Active voice

A verb is in the active voice if the subject is doing the action of the verb.

> The dog **killed** the snake (The dog is performing the action of killing the snake.)
>
> My brother **kicked** the winning goal.

Passive voice

A verb is in the passive voice if the subject is receiving the action.

> The snake **was killed** by the dog. (The snake is being killed.)
>
> The winning goal **was kicked** by my brother.

It is generally best to write in the active voice as it uses fewer words, is more direct, and makes a stronger statement than the passive voice.

Another aspect of a verb is agreement with its subject. This means that if a subject is singular, the verb must be singular; if the subject is plural, the verb must be plural.

My brother **plays** football. (singular noun 'brother' takes a singular verb)

His friends **play** football. (plural noun 'friends' takes a plural verb)

A collective noun usually takes a singular verb as it names a group.

His football team **is** at the top of the ladder. (The collective noun 'team' takes the singular verb 'is'.)

The fleet of ships **sails** out of the harbour. (The collective noun 'fleet' takes the singular verb 'sails'.)

When an indefinite pronoun is the subject of a verb, it must agree in number.

Everyone **needs** love. (singular subject 'everyone' takes the singular verb 'needs')

Something **is** out there. (singular subject 'something' takes the singular verb 'is')

Both of my parents **are** Italian. (plural subject 'both' takes the plural verb 'are')

Some of my friends **are** Italian. (plural subject 'some' takes the plural verb 'are')

Adverbs

Adverbs modify (add to the meaning of) verbs. They tell us how, when, where, or how often something happens.

He spoke **clearly**. (How did he speak?)

I started a new job **yesterday**. (When did I start the new job?)

Jim rides his bike **everywhere**. (Where does Jim ride his bike?)

Fran **sometimes** walks to work. (How often does Fran walk to work?)

They can also add to the meaning of adjectives and other adverbs.

That was a **very** boring film. (How boring was the film?)

I eat my food **too** quickly. (How quickly do I eat my food?)

Like adjectives, many adverbs can be used in three different forms. Positive degree (no comparison):

It is raining **heavily**.

Comparative degree (two people or things compared):

It rained **more heavily** last week.

Grammar and reference guide

Superlative (more than two people or things compared):

> It rained **most heavily** in June.

Some adverbs are irregular and take different forms.

> **well, better, best**
>
> Sam spoke **well**.
>
> Peter spoke **better** than she did.
>
> Susan spoke the **best** of all.
>
> **badly, worse, worst**
>
> Sam performed **badly** in the test.
>
> Peter performed **worse** than Sam did.
>
> Susan performed the **worst** of all three.

Prepositions

A preposition begins a prepositional phrase. It joins a noun or pronoun (the object of the preposition) to another word in the sentence.

Common prepositions include:

> **above, across, against, among, at, before, below, beside, beyond, down, during, for, from, in, inside, near, of, off, on, opposite, over, through, towards**
>
> We walked **to** the shops. (The preposition 'to' links its object 'shops' to the verb 'walked'.)
>
> She wore a coat with a hood. (The prepositional phrase is 'with a hood'.)
>
> We have been friends since childhood. (The prepositional phrase is 'since childhood'.)
>
> I'll meet you outside the shop. (The prepositional phrase is 'outside the shop'.)

Conjunctions

Conjunctions join words or groups of words.

Coordinating conjunctions

Coordinating conjunctions join two or more words or word groups of the same kind. There are seven of them.

> **and, but, so, yet, or, nor, for**

My cat **and** my dog are great friends. (The conjunction 'and' joins the nouns 'cat' and 'dog'.)

I ran down the stairs **and** out the door. (The conjunction 'and' joins the prepositional phrases 'down the stairs' and 'out the door'.)

I prepared well for the test, **but** I still found it difficult. (The conjunction 'but' joins the main clauses 'I prepared well for the test' and 'I still found it difficult'.)

Subordinating conjunctions

Subordinating conjunctions join unequal parts of a sentence. They begin a subordinate clause (a clause that is dependent on a main clause for complete meaning).

I will speak to you **after** you have eaten your dinner. (The subordinating conjunction 'after' begins the subordinate clause 'after you have eaten your dinner' to the main clause 'I will speak to you'.)

Other subordinating conjunctions include:

before, when, until, unless, although, where, since, while, because

Eat your dinner **before** it gets cold.

When I was your age, my father made me eat my dinner.

I would have to sit at the table **until** I had eaten all my vegetables.

Interjections

Interjections are words or phrases that express emotions (such as surprise, delight, pain).

What?

Wow!

Ouch!

They can also act as 'fillers' that could easily be taken out of a sentence.

Oh, I don't know about that.

You win, **okay**.

It was, **you know**, just a joke.

Well, I didn't mean it.

Sentences

A sentence is a group of words that expresses a complete thought.

A sentence begins with a capital letter and ends with a full stop, question mark, or exclamation mark.

Types of sentences

A statement (ends with a full stop):

> The dog barks all night.

A question (ends with a question mark):

> Is the dog still barking?

A command (ends with a full stop):

> Stop the dog from barking.

An exclamation (ends with an exclamation mark):

> What a loud bark!

Each sentence consists of two parts: a subject and predicate. Every word belongs either to the subject or to the predicate.

The subject is who or what the sentence is about.

The subject will be a noun or a pronoun. To find the subject in a sentence, ask Who? or What? before the verb.

> The dog barks all night. (Who barks all night? The dog.)

The predicate is what is said about the subject. The most important part of the predicate is the verb. (The predicate is 'barks all night'; the verb is 'barks'.)

A subject can consist of more than one noun or pronoun.

> **My aunt and uncle** are coming for a holiday.

A predicate can contain more than one verb.

> My relatives **live and work** interstate.

Sometimes the subject is not at the start of a sentence as in a question or instruction.

> Is the dog still barking? (Who is still barking? 'the dog'.)

Another way to find the subject and predicate is to re-order the words as a statement.

The dog is still barking. ('The dog' is the subject, 'is still barking' is the predicate.)

Stop the dog from barking. (The subject is the unstated 'you' as in 'You stop the dog from barking'.)

Clauses

A clause is a group of words that contains a subject and verb.

A main clause makes sense on its own, so it can be a sentence.

The train was late.

If there is more than one main clause in a sentence, they are joined by a coordinating conjunction.

The train was late, **so** I was also late for school.

I was late for my first class, **but** the teacher accepted my excuse.

A subordinate clause is less important than a main clause. It must be attached to a main clause by a subordinating conjunction or a relative pronoun.

Because the signals had failed. (This subordinate clause beginning with the subordinating conjunction 'because' does not make sense on its own.)

The train was late because the signals had failed. (Now the sentence is complete.)

Who love chocolate. (This subordinate clause beginning with the relative pronoun 'who' does not make sense on its own.)

They are people who love chocolate. (Now the sentence is complete.)

A subordinate clause functions as a single part of speech (an adjective, adverb, or a noun).

We took the road **that follows the coast**. (The subordinate clause 'that follows the coast' functions as an **adjective**, modifying the noun 'road'.)

We lost the match **because we lacked experience**. (The subordinate clause 'because we lacked experience' functions as an **adverb**, modifying the verb 'lost'.)

I know **that you lied**. (The subordinate clause 'that you lied' functions as a **noun**, telling us what I know.)

Phrases

A phrase is a group of words that does not contain a subject and verb. It cannot make sense on its own.

> under the bridge
>
> playing the piano
>
> rushing down the stairs
>
> exhausted by the climb
>
> to keep fit

A phrase must be part of a clause.

> He hid **under the bridge**.
>
> **Playing the piano** is his favourite hobby.
>
> **Rushing down the stairs**, the woman tripped and fell.
>
> **Exhausted by the climb**, she decided not to go ahead.
>
> I jog **to keep fit**.

As with clauses, phrases function as a single part of speech (adjective, adverb or noun).

> That woman **wearing dark glasses** could be a spy. (The phrase 'wearing dark glasses' functions as an **adjective,** modifying the noun 'woman'.)
>
> I will meet you **at nine o'clock**. (The phrase 'at nine o'clock' functions as an **adverb**, modifying the verb 'will meet'.)
>
> I met my friends—**James, Kate and Gino**—and then we had lunch. (The phrase 'James, Kate and Gino' functions as a **noun**, telling us who the friends are.)

Using phrases in a sentence is a useful way to cut down the number of words. A subordinate clause can be reduced to a phrase.

> When you make a curry, you need special spices.
>
> **To make a curry**, you need special spices.

> Because I felt sleepy, I went to bed early.
>
> **Feeling sleepy**, I went to bed early.

> I kept the emails that my friend had sent me.
>
> I kept the emails **sent by my friend**.

When you train a dog, you must have patience and skill.

Training dogs requires patience and skill.

Punctuation

We use various punctuation marks to make the meaning of our written communication clear and to indicate where a reader should stop, slow down, or speed up.

> When we barbecue our neighbour complains about the smoke.
> (No internal punctuation may make us think the neighbour is being barbecued.)
>
> When we barbecue, our neighbour complains about the smoke.
> (Adding a comma after the subordinate clause makes the meaning clear.)

Full stops, question marks, and exclamation marks are used to end sentences.

Full stops (.)

A full stop ends a sentence that is a statement, a command, or an indirect question.

> **The boat sank**. (a statement)
>
> **Save the passengers**. (a command)
>
> **I wonder why the boat sank**. (an indirect question)

Question marks (?)

A question mark ends a sentence that is a direct question:

> **How did the boat sink?**

Exclamation marks (!)

An exclamation mark ends a sentence or an interjection that expresses an emotion.

> **Look out!**
>
> **Oh, no!**

Commas (,)

A comma has many functions.

It precedes a coordinating conjunction joining main clauses.

> I look like my mum, **but** my sister looks more like dad.

It separates additional information from the rest of the sentence.

> The parrot, **which we had only had a week,** fell off its perch.

> Freda, **my friend from Sydney,** is coming to stay.

It separates items in a list. Usage varies as to the inclusion of a comma before *and* in the last item, but its presence often aids clarify:

> I love **chocolate, licorice, and cashew nuts**.

> The flowers are coloured **red, white, yellow, and blue**.

It separates an introductory word, phrase, or subordinate clause from the rest of the sentence:

> **No,** you may not buy a puppy.

> **Laden with parcels,** the woman staggered onto the train.

> **After we had eaten,** the dog ate the leftovers.

It separates spoken words from unspoken words in dialogue.

> '**It began with a pain in my leg,**' said the patient, '**and then I developed an itch.**'

It separates the spoken words from the person being addressed.

> 'What should I do about the itch, **Doctor**?'

Semicolons (;)

A semicolon separates main clauses that are closely connected.

> I was told one-half of the story; the other half remained a mystery.

> The floorboards creaked; someone was coming.

It also separates items in a list if commas are used for other purposes in the sentence.

> Classic science fiction sagas are *Star Trek*, with Mr Spock and his large pointed ears; *Battlestar Galactica*, with its cylon raiders; and *Star Wars*, with Han Solo, Luke Skywalker, and Darth Vader.

Colons (:)

A colon introduces or announces something. It may be followed by a word, a phrase, or a main clause.

A colon can introduce a list.

> Choose from the following flavours: **chocolate, mint, strawberry, or toffee**.

A colon is not needed if the list follows on from the previous word.

> I love chocolate, mint, strawberry, and toffee ice cream.

A colon can introduce more information about what precedes it. This may be a single word, a phrase, or a main clause.

> There is one quality I lack: **modesty**.

> I have a new hobby: **collecting spiders**.

> The crops failed: **the drought had lasted ten years**.

A colon can introduce a quotation.

> The Prime Minister stated: **'This country has never been so prosperous. We have eliminated poverty forever.'**

A colon is used after a character's name in a play script.

> TESS: What shall we do now?

> JAMES: Let's make a run for it.

Apostrophes (')

An apostrophe has two purposes: to show ownership or a contraction of two words.

Possessives are used to show that a noun or pronoun owns or possesses something or someone.

> 'This is my **friend's** house.' (instead of 'The house of my friend')

The apostrophe is always placed after the owner's name.

If the noun is singular, add an apostrophe after the owner's name followed by an 's'.

> My **dog's** coat is curly.

If the singular owner's name ends in 's', add an 's'.

> The **boss's** instructions are confusing.

> Mr **Thomas's** sister is an actor.

If the noun is plural, add an apostrophe after the 's'.

> I was grateful for my **friends'** support.

> The **dogs'** barking kept me awake.

If a plural noun does not end in 's', add the apostrophe and then an 's'.

The **children's** party was great fun.

I respect **people's** feelings.

If more than one person owns something, use an apostrophe in the last name only.

We went to **Beth and David's** wedding.

If each owns something separate, use an apostrophe for each owner.

Beth's dress was new, but **David's** suit was not.

Note that a possessive pronoun does not require an apostrophe as the word already shows possession.

Is this book **your's**? (wrong: no apostrophe needed)

Is this book **yours**? (correct)

The fish swam around **it's** bowl. (wrong: no apostrophe needed)

The fish swam around **its** bowl. (correct)

Contractions are shortened forms of words used in informal writing:

She's (She is) leaving tomorrow.

There's (There is) a sale on.

I'd (I had) tried my best to win the race.

We **should've** (should have) saved our money. (Note there is no such construction as 'should of'.)

It's (It is) going to be a great weekend. (Do not confuse it's with 'its' as in 'The cat licks its paws'.)

Quotation marks (' ')

Direct speech refers to the spoken words of someone.

Quotation marks or inverted commas are used to enclose the spoken words.

The woman said, 'I am knitting a jumper for my grandson.'

Indirect speech refers to reporting what someone has said. There is no need for quotation marks.

The woman said that she was knitting a jumper for her grandson. (Note that the pronoun changes from 'I' to 'she', and the tense changes from the present 'am knitting' to the past 'was knitting'.)

When using direct speech, there are a few points to remember.

Punctuation that is part of the spoken words is placed inside the quotation marks.

> 'Mum!' shouted Dylan. 'Where is my skateboard?'
>
> 'Dylan,' said his mother, 'it's where you left it.'

Punctuation that is part of the sentence as a whole is placed outside the quotation marks.

> Did Dylan's mother hear him shout 'Mum'?

In dialogue, begin a new paragraph every time the speaker changes.

> The teacher handed back the tests. 'I expected a better result,' she said. 'Did you study for the test?'
>
> The student looked a little sheepish. 'A bit,' he said.
>
> 'It shows,' she said.

If a long speech or quotation covers more than one paragraph, open the quotation marks at the start of each paragraph, closing them only at the end of the last paragraph of the quotation.

If a speech contains other quoted words, use double quotation marks to distinguish them.

> 'I heard the woman say "Over my dead body" before she got off the tram.'

Use quotation marks to distinguish special words, phrases, or sentences from the writer's own words.

> The teacher asked, 'What is the capital city of Thailand?'
>
> The judge described the building as a 'hovel'.
>
> My dad always calls me 'petal'.

Use quotation marks to enclose titles of short works such as poems, short stories, essays, articles, songs, works of art, and radio and television programs.

> I wrote a poem called 'View from my Window'.
>
> My dad loves the song 'Hey, Jude' by the Beatles.
>
> 'Blue Poles' is a famous painting.

Hyphens (-)

Hyphens create words by joining two or more words together.

(Do not confuse hyphens with dashes, which are longer and have a different purpose.) There is no space between the hyphen and the words it joins.

> He is a **well-educated** person.

Use hyphens to form compound words (a word formed by joining two or more words). Not all compound words are hyphenated. The dictionary entry will show whether or not hyphens are necessary. Compound words often begin as two separate words. Over time they become hyphenated. Finally they close up.

> table cloth
>
> table-cloth
>
> tablecloth

Compound nouns

> My dog Jessie is a **cross-breed**.
>
> The **editor-in-chief** checked the final draft.

Compound adjectives

> I prefer **home-made** soup.
>
> I owned a cat that was **cross-eyed**.

Compound verbs

> The counsel for the defence **cross-examined** the witness.
>
> The shop **gift-wrapped** the parcel.

Use hyphens in numbers and fractions.

> My grandmother is **ninety-one**.
>
> **Nine-tenths** of those surveyed were overweight.

Use hyphens to join a prefix to a word. (Some prefixes do not require a hyphen. Check your dictionary.)

> The patient had a **pre-existing** condition.
>
> The **post-mortem** revealed that the death was suspicious.
>
> My uncle is an **ex-army** officer.
>
> He works for a **non-profit** organisation.

Use a hyphen if the word after the prefix begins with a capital or if figures are used.

> The article was **anti-American**.
>
> The **pre-Christian** era is fascinating.
>
> Many migrants arrived in Australia **post-1945**.

Use a hyphen to make the meaning clear.

> We had to **re-lay** the carpet after the storm.
>
> Could you relay this message to the director?

He wanted to reform society.

Could we **re-form** the organisation?

There were twenty odd guests at the wedding; everyone else seemed normal.

There were **twenty-odd** guests at the wedding.

Use a hyphen if a vowel is doubled.

We managed to **re-establish** our garden after the drought.

The Historical Society **re-enacted** the battle.

Should we **re-elect** the government?

Note that it is common practice to remove the hyphen from some words.

Will you cooperate or do I have to force you?

I am the coordinator of the program.

Dashes (–)

Dashes have several uses. They are used in pairs unless a full stop, question mark, or exclamation mark ends what follows the dash.

Use dashes instead of a colon in informal writing to introduce a list or an explanation.

Mum says I have too many pets—rabbits, fish, finches, and a ferret.

The man was arrested—he had robbed the bank.

Use dashes to show a change of tone or thought.

The table goes in there—careful!

I bought a new outfit—I just couldn't help myself.

Use dashes instead of brackets or commas to enclose extra information, especially if commas are already present.

The three children—Amy, Tom, and Susan—were found safe and well.

This novel—the latest in the series—is her best.

Use a dash to show that a speaker has been interrupted.

'Come here at once or I'll—'

Round brackets ( ) (or parentheses)

These are always used in pairs. They enclose extra information. The sentence must still make sense without the information in the brackets.

Use brackets to enclose an example, a comment, or an explanation.

> I love mystery novels (*The Case of the Missing Leg,* for example).

> My grandmother has come to stay (not for too long, I hope), and I have to give up my room.

> Your handwriting is illegible (probably through lack of practice), but your typing skills are excellent.

Note that because the information is usually about something mentioned before the first bracket, place any punctuation after the second bracket.

> When I was younger (probably about the age of four), I fell off my bike and broke my collar bone.

If the material in brackets is a sentence, punctuate it appropriately.

> Now I know about punctuation. (The mystery of the semicolon is solved.)

> My mum caught me out. (How did she know I had a ferret in my room?)

> It lurches towards me. (I think it's a dinosaur!)

Use brackets to enclose chapter or page numbers.

> I particularly enjoyed the part about the crocodile hunt (chapter 7).

> Read the second story (page 25).

Square brackets [ ]

Square brackets indicate that someone other than the writer has inserted them.

> 'He came from Perth [Scotland].' (The reader might not know which Perth the writer is referring to.)

> 'They [the gymnasts] won the international competition.' (It may not be clear to the reader who 'they' refers to.)

> 'The possum fell down the chimley [chimney].' (The correct spelling is given.)

Ellipsis points (...)

These are three full stops indicating that words have been left out.
    Use them to show that part of a quotation is missing.

> 'There was movement at the station ... ' (the start of *The Man From Snowy River*)

Use them to show a break in thought or speech (especially in dialogue), or a trailing off at the end of a sentence.

'I don't know what to do … Should I ask her out or not?'

'Let me tell you about my …' 'Yes, fascinating I'm sure, but I'm in a hurry.'

The giant cockroach had something else in mind …

Italics

This slanting typeface is used in printed material for particular purposes.

Use italics for titles of books, plays, musicals, films, newspapers, and magazines.

We are studying *Romeo and Juliet*.

Evita is a musical set in Argentina.

I had a letter published in *The Australian*.

Use italics for the names of ships, aircraft, or trains.

Many people sailed to the UK on the *Fairstar* in the 1960s.

We travelled to Darwin on *The Ghan*.

Use italics for emphasis.

I want to go *today*, not next week.

Use italics for the scientific names of plants and animals.

The red kangaroo, *Macropus rufus*, is a native to Australia.

Abbreviations

An abbreviation is a shortened form of a word or words. They are useful in notes and other informal writing.

Abbreviations ending in the same letter as the full word do not need a full stop.

Qld (Queensland), **dept** (department), **Dr** (Doctor), **Rd** (Road)

Abbreviations that do not end in the same letter as the full word need a full stop.

Tues. (Tuesday), **Oct.** (October), **adj.** (adjective)

Abbreviations consisting of the initial letters of each word are called acronyms and do not require full stops.

> **VIP** (very important person), **BA** (Bachelor of Arts), **PTO** (please turn over)

An acronym is often pronounced as a word.

> **ANZAC** (Australian and New Zealand Army Corps)
>
> **EFTPOS** (Electronic Funds Transfer at Point of Sale)

Some acronyms are written in lower case. Check your dictionary.

> **sonar** (sound navigation and ranging)
>
> **laser** (light amplification by stimulated emission of radiation)

Numbers

Numbers are expressed in figures or words depending on the type of writing and its context.

Use figures in mathematical, scientific, or technical writing.

> Print the document and compare it to Figure **5.14** (Chapter **1**).

Use figures for sums of money, dates, addresses, times of day, and percentages.

> **$4.50, 21** September **2005, 45** Flinders Street, **6.30** a.m., **99** per cent

Use figures for general writing for numbers over ninety-nine.

> I have collected **400** stamps from all over the world.

Use words in general writing for numbers under 100 and for approximations. Always use words if the number begins a sentence.

> There were **forty-six** guests at my party.
>
> The snake was approximately **one** metre long.
>
> **Twenty-two** people were at the auction.

Capital letters

Capital letters (also known as letters in the upper case) have several uses.

Use a capital letter to indicate the start of a sentence (including in direct speech).

Winter is nearly over.

He asked, 'Where are you going for your holidays?'

Use a capital letter to indicate a proper noun. Proper nouns are used to name days of the week, months of the year, holidays and special events, particular people and their titles, organisations, historical events, places, titles of films, books, and plays.

My favourite uncle is Uncle Jim, who is a Member of Parliament.

In March we went to Dreamland on the Gold Coast.

The worst day of the week is Monday, especially in summer.

I have just read a book about the First World War.

My dad recommended I read *The Call of the Wild*. (Capitalise the main words only.)

Use a capital letter for adjectives formed from proper nouns.

Some people want to change the Australian flag.

Some Shakespearean language is difficult to understand.

Use a capital every time the pronoun 'I' is used.

Whenever I feel afraid, I whistle a happy tune.

Check your dictionary if unsure whether a noun is capitalised or not.

Silent letters

Some words contain silent letters which cannot be sounded out. As you meet them, make a list and learn them off by heart.

subtle	psychiatrist	guardian
debt	psalm	vogue
succumb	psychology	dialogue
plumber	pterodactyl	catalogue
indict	receipt	wrangle
victuals	gnaw	wrath
irascible	gnarled	wrench
scissors	campaign	wrinkle
scythe	phlegm	sword
muscle	assign	autumn
scintillate	benign	condemn
mnemonic	consign	hymn
qualm	malign	heir

salmon	align	honour
epistle	resign	rheumatism
mortgage	kneel	aghast
ballet	knowledge	asthma
pneumonia	knave	

Spelling

Some useful rules

To make a noun plural:

Normally, just add -s: skirts, socks, ties, pianos, pieces, stars.

But watch out for some words ending in -o, that need -es:

echoes, heroes, potatoes, tomatoes, volcanoes, etc.

To words ending in -ch, -s, -sh, -x, or -z, add -es:

dress — dresses, box — boxes, stitch — stitches.

To some words ending in -f and -fe, change to -ves:

scarf — scarves, life — lives, half — halves.

But watch out for the exceptions:

beliefs, proofs, roofs, etc.

To words ending in a consonant followed by -y, change the y to i and add -es:

copy — copies, cry — cries, party — parties.

Adding -ing and -ed to verbs

Normally just add -ing or -ed:

load — loading — loaded; open — opening — opened; stay — staying — stayed.

For short words ending in -e, usually leave off the e:

race — raced — racing; blame — blamed — blaming.

For many short words that end with one consonant, double the last consonant:

slam — slamming — slammed; tip — tipping — tipped.

For longer words ending with one consonant and having the stress on the last syllable, double the last consonant:

compel — compelling — compelled;
prefer — preferring — preferred.

For words ending in -y after a consonant, change the y to an i before -ed:

try — trying — tried.

For words ending in -ie, change the ie to y before adding -ing:

lie — lying — lied; tie — tying — tied.

Watch out for these exceptions:

lay — laid; pay — paid; say — said.

Adding -er and -est to adjectives

Normally just add -er and -est, unless the word already ends in -e:

cold — colder — coldest; wide — wider — widest.

For many short words that end with one consonant, change to a double consonant:

wet — wetter — wettest; dim — dimmer — dimmest.

If the word has two syllables and ends in -y, change the y to an i;

dirty — dirtier — dirtiest; happy — happier — happiest.

Adding -ly

Adding -ly to an adjective makes it into an adverb:

slowly, badly, awkwardly.

If the word ends in -ll, just add -y:

full — fully.

For words ending in -y and with more than one syllable, leave off the -y and add -ily:

happy — happily; hungry — hungrily.

For words ending in -le, leave off the e:

idle — idly; simple — simply.

For adjectives ending in ic, you usually add -ally:

basic — basically; drastic — drastically.

But watch out for these special ones:

public — publicly.

Words that are easily confused

These pairs of words can be confused. Check that you know their meaning.

affection/affectation
allowed/aloud
berth/birth
bought/brought
brake/break
cell/sell
cereal/serial
check/cheque
coarse/course
complement/
compliment
confirm/conform
contemptible/
contemptuous
continual/continuous
councillor/counsellor
creak/creek
currant/current
desert/dessert
diseased/deceased
dyeing/dying

emaciated/emancipated
eminent/imminent
except/accept
formally/formerly
gamble/gambol
honourable/honorary
horde/hoard
inedible/indelible
know/no
know/now
lead/led
lightning/lightening
metre/meter
momentary/momentous
moral/morale
officious/official
perpetuate/perpetrate
persecute/prosecute
personal/personnel
piece/peace
plain/plane
political/politic

prey/pray
queue/cue
quite/quiet
recent/resent
respective/respectful
sceptic/septic
seam/seem
sealing/ceiling
site/sight
sole/soul
spacious/specious
stationary/stationery
straight/strait
successful/successive
superficial/superfluous
there/their/they're
threw/through
vocation/vacation
waist/waste
wet/whet
wrap/rap

When words sound alike, learn to use them in their correct context as their meaning will make their spelling clear.

The car stopped when I applied the brake. If I drop this glass it will break.

The food was inedible. She labelled her clothes with an indelible pen.

Some commonly misspelt words

accessible
accommodation
adjournment
administrative
admissible
affectation
aghast
alcoholism
align
allotted
ambiguous
annihilate
asthma
benign
bibliography
biographical
brigadier
bureaucracy
capricious
carnivorous
catalogue
chandelier
cheque
chlorinate
colloquial
condemn
consign
dachshund
desiccated
dialogue
diesel
discernible
disobedient
effervescent
enthusiasm
entrepreneurial
environmentalist
euthanasia
exception
familiarity
fluorescent
fraudulence
freight

fright
gaiety
genealogy
gnarled
gnawed
gracious
guardian
gynaecologist
haemophiliac
haemorrhage
haemorrhoid
hearth
height
heterogeneous
hieroglyphic
idiosyncrasy
ignominious
inadequacy
incoherent
indict
irascible
lascivious
liaison
ludicrous
luscious
malign
miscellaneous
mischievous
moratorium
muscle
noxious
numerous
oblique
occasion
oceanic
omitted
onomatopoeia
paradigm
paralleled
perceive
perspicacious
persuadable
pharmaceutical
phlegm

piece
piteous
pneumonia
psychiatrist
qualm
quarantine
raucous
receive
reconnaissance
rescuing
resign
rheumatism
ricochet
salmon
satisfactorily
sceptic
schism
scintillate
scissors
seize
separate
shield
straight
succumb
supersede
synonymous
technologically
thoroughfare
traumatic
ubiquitous
unequalled
vaccination
vaudeville
ventriloquism
vicissitude
vogue
weight
weird
wrangle
wrath
wrench
wrinkle
yacht

List of prefixes and suffixes

Prefixes

a- not: atypical.

Anglo- English: Anglo-Celtic background.

ante- before: antenatal (= before birth).

anti- against: antisocial.

auto- self: autobiography (= the story of the writer's own life).

bi- two: bicycle, bilingual (= using two languages), bimonthly (= twice a month or every two months).

cent-, centi- hundred: centenary (= the hundredth anniversary), centimetre (= one hundredth of a metre).

circum- around: circumnavigate (= sail around).

co- with; together: copilot, coexist, cooperation.

con- (col-, com-) with; together: context (= the words or sentences that come before and after a particular word or sentence), collide, combine.

contra- against; opposite: contradict (= say the opposite).

counter- against; opposite: counter-revolution, counter-productive (= producing the opposite of the desired effect).

de- taking something away; the opposite: defrost, decentralise.

deci- one tenth: decilitre.

dis- reverse or opposite: displease, disembark, discomfort.

e- electronic; involving electronic communication.

eco- ecology, ecological.

Euro- European: Eurocentric.

ex- former: ex-wife, ex-president.

extra- 1 very; more than usual: extra-thin, extra-special. **2** outside; beyond: extraordinary, extra-terrestrial (= coming from somewhere beyond the earth).

fore- 1 before; in advance: foretell (= say what is going to happen), foreword (= at the beginning of a book). **2** front: foreground (= the front part of a picture), forehead.

in- (il-, im-, ir-) not: incorrect, invalid, illegal, illegible, immoral, impatient, impossible, irregular, irrelevant.

Indo- Indian: Indo-China.

inter- between; from one to another: international, interracial.

kilo- thousand: kilogram, kilowatt.

m- mobile phone; denoting commercial activity conducted by means of mobile phones.

maxi- most; very large: maximum.

mega- million; very large: megabyte, megastar (= a very famous person).
micro- one millionth; very small: microgram, micro-organism.
mid- in the middle of: mid-afternoon, mid-air.
milli- thousandth: milligram, millilitre.
mini- small: miniskirt, minibus.
mis- bad or wrong; not: misunderstand, misbehave, miscalculate.
mono- one; single: monolingual (= using one language), monorail.
multi- many: multinational (= involving many countries).
non- not: nonsense, non-resident, non-smoker.
out- more; to a greater degree: outdo, outrun (= run faster or better than somebody).
over- more than normal; too much: overeat, oversleep (= sleep too long), overestimate (= guess too high).
post- after: postwar.
pre- before: prepaid, preview.
pro- for; in favour of: pro-democracy.
quad- four: quadruple (= multiply by four), quadruplet (= one of four babies born at the same time).
re- again: rewrite, rebuild.
semi- half: semicircle, semitrailer.
Sino- Chinese: Sino-Japanese.
sub- 1 below; less than: subzero, subsonic (= less than the speed of sound). **2** under: subway, subtitles (= translation under the pictures of a film).
super- extremely; more than: superhuman (= having greater power than humans normally have), supersonic (= faster than the speed of sound).
tele- far; over a long distance: telecommunications, television, telephoto lens.
trans- across; through: transatlantic, transcontinental.
tri- three: triangle, tricolour (= a flag with three colours).
ultra- extremely; beyond a certain limit: ultra-modern, ultraviolet (= light that is beyond what we can normally see).
un- not; opposite; taking something away: uncertain, uncomfortable, unsure, undo, undress.
uni- one; single: uniform (= having the same form).

Suffixes

-able, -ible, -ble to make adjectives; possible to: acceptable, noticeable, convertible, divisible (= possible to divide), irresistible (= that you cannot resist).
-age to make nouns; a process or state: shortage, storage.
-al to make adjectives; connected with: experimental, accidental, environmental.

-ance, -ence, (-ancy, -ency) to make nouns; an action, process or state: appearance, performance, elegance, importance, existence, intelligence, patience.

-ant, -ent to make nouns; a person who does something: assistant, immigrant, student.

-ation to make nouns; a state or action: examination, imagination, organisation.

-ble look at **-able**.

-ee to make nouns; a person to whom something is done: employee (= one who is employed), trainee (= one who is being trained).

-en to make verbs; to give something a particular quality; to make something more: shorten, widen, blacken, sharpen, loosen, (but note: lengthen).

-ence (-ency) look at **-ance**.

-ent look at **-ant**.

-er to make nouns; a person who does something: rider, painter, baker, builder, driver, teacher.

-ese to make adjectives; from a place: Japanese, Chinese, Viennese.

-ess to make nouns; a woman who does something as a job: waitress, actress.

-ful to make adjectives; having a particular quality: helpful, useful, thankful, beautiful.

-hood to make nouns; a state, often during a particular period of time: childhood, motherhood.

-ian to make nouns; a person who does something as a job or hobby: historian, comedian, politician.

-ible look at **-able**.

-ical to make adjectives from nouns ending in -y or -ics; connected with: economical, mathematical, physical.

-ify to make verbs; to produce a state or quality: beautify, simplify, purify.

-ise, -ize to make verbs; actions producing a particular state: magnetise, standardise, modernise, generalise.

-ish to make adjectives; **1** describing nationality or language: English, Swedish, Polish. **2** similar to something: babyish, foolish. **3** rather, quite: longish (= fairly long, but not very long), youngish, brownish.

-ist to make nouns; **1** a person who has studied something or does something as a job: artist, scientist, typist. **2** a person who believes in something or belongs to a particular group: capitalist, pacifist, feminist.

-ion to make nouns; a state or process: action, connection, exhibition.

-ive to make adjectives; able to, having a particular quality: attractive, effective.

-less to make adjectives; not having something: hopeless, friendless.

-like to make adjectives; similar to: childlike.

-ly to make adverbs; in a particular way: badly, beautifully, completely.

-ment to make nouns; a state, action or quality: development, arrangement, excitement, achievement.

-ness to make nouns; a state or quality: kindness, sadness, happiness, weakness.

-ology to make nouns; the study of a subject: biology, psychology, zoology.

-or to make nouns; a person who does something, often as a job: actor, conductor, sailor.

-ous to make adjectives; having a particular quality: dangerous, religious, ambitious.

-ship to make nouns; showing status: friendship, membership, citizenship.

-wards to make adverbs; in a particular direction: backwards, upwards.

-wise to make adverbs; in a particular way: clockwise.

-y to make adjectives; having the quality of the thing mentioned: cloudy, rainy, fatty, thirsty, greeny (= similar to green).

Appendix 2:
Countries of the World

Country	Capital	Currency unit	Domain suffix
Afghanistan	Kabul	afghani	af
Albania	Tiranë	lek	al
Algeria	Algiers	dinar	dz
Andorra	Andorra la Vella	euro	ad
Angola	Luanda	kwanza	ao
Antigua and Barbuda	St John's	dollar	ag
Argentina	Buenos Aires	peso	ar
Armenia	Yerevan	dram	am
Australia	Canberra	dollar	au
Austria	Vienna	euro	at
Azerbaijan	Baku	manat	az
Bahamas	Nassau	dollar	bs
Bahrain	Manama	dinar	bh
Bangladesh	Dhaka	taka	bd
Barbados	Bridgetown	dollar	bb
Belarus	Minsk	rouble	by
Belgium	Brussels	euro	be
Belize	Belmopan	dollar	bz
Benin	Porto Novo	franc	bj
Bhutan	Thimphu	ngultrum; Indian rupee	bt
Bolivia	La Paz	boliviano	bo
Bosnia-Herzegovina	Sarajevo	mark	ba
Botswana	Gaborone	pula	bw
Brazil	Brasilia	real	br
Brunei Darussalam	Bandar Seri Begawan	dollar	bn
Bulgaria	Sofia	lev	bg
Burkina	Ouagadougou	franc	bf
Burma (see Myanmar)	Rangoon		
Burundi	Bujumbura	franc	bi
Cambodia	Phnom Penh	riel	kh
Cameroon	Yaoundé	franc	cm
Canada	Ottawa	dollar	ca
Cape Verde Islands	Praia	escudo	cv

Country	Capital	Currency unit	Domain suffix
Central African Republic	Bangui	franc	cf
Chad	N'Djamena	franc	td
Chile	Santiago	peso	cl
China	Beijing	yuan	cn
Colombia	Bogotá	peso	co
Comoros	Moroni	franc	km
Congo	Brazzaville	franc	cg
Congo, Democratic Republic of (Zaire)	Kinshasa	franc	zr
Costa Rica	San José	colón	cr
Croatia	Zagreb	kuna	hr
Cuba	Havana	peso	cu
Cyprus	Nicosia	pound	cy
Czech Republic	Prague	koruna	cz
Denmark	Copenhagen	krone	dk
Djibouti	Djibouti	franc	dj
Dominica	Roseau	dollar	dm
Dominican Republic	Santo Domingo	peso	do
East Timor	Dili	US dollar	tp, tl
Ecuador	Quito	sucre	ec
Egypt	Cairo	pound	eg
El Salvador	San Salvador	colón	sv
Equatorial Guinea	Malabo	franc	gq
Eritrea	Asmara	nafka	er
Estonia	Tallinn	kroon	ee
Ethiopia	Addis Ababa	birr	et
Fiji	Suva	dollar	fj
Finland	Helsinki	euro	fi
France	Paris	euro	fr
Gabon	Libreville	franc	ga
Gambia	Banjul	dalasi	gm
Georgia	Tbilisi	lari	ge
Germany	Berlin	euro	de
Ghana	Accra	cedi	gh
Greece	Athens	euro	gr
Grenada	St George's	dollar	gd
Guatemala	Guatemala City	quetzal	gt
Guinea	Conakry	franc	gn
Guinea-Bissau	Bissau	peso	gw
Guyana	Georgetown	dollar	gy

Countries of the world

Country	Capital	Currency unit	Domain suffix
Haiti	Port-au-Prince	gourde	ht
Honduras	Tegucigalpa	lempira	hn
Hungary	Budapest	forint	hu
Iceland	Reykjavik	krona	is
India	New Delhi	rupee	in
Indonesia	Jakarta	rupiah	id
Iran	Tehran	rial	ir
Iraq	Baghdad	dinar	iq
Ireland, Republic of	Dublin	euro	ie
Israel	Jerusalem	shekel	il
Italy	Rome	euro	it
Ivory Coast	Yamoussoukro	franc	ci
Jamaica	Kingston	dollar	jm
Japan	Tokyo	yen	jp
Jordan	Amman	dinar	jo
Kazakhstan	Astana	tenge	kz
Kenya	Nairobi	shilling	ke
Kiribati	Bairiki	Australian dollar	ki
Kuwait	Kuwait City	dinar	kw
Kyrgyzstan	Bishkek	som	kg
Laos	Vientiane	kip	la
Latvia	Riga	lat	lv
Lebanon	Beirut	pound	lb
Lesotho	Maseru	loti	ls
Liberia	Monrovia	dollar	lr
Libya	Tripoli	dinar	ly
Liechtenstein	Vaduz	franc	li
Lithuania	Vilnius	litas	lt
Luxembourg	Luxembourg	euro	lu
Macedonia	Skopje	denar	mk
Madagascar	Antananarivo	franc	mg
Malawi	Lilongwe	kwacha	mw
Malaysia	Kuala Lumpur	ringgit	my
Maldives	Male	rufiyaa	mv
Mali	Bamako	franc	ml
Malta	Valletta	lira	mt
Marshall Islands	Majuro	US dollar	mh
Mauritania	Nouakchott	ouguiya	mr
Mauritius	Port Louis	rupee	mu
Mexico	Mexico City	peso	mx
Micronesia	Kolonia	US dollar	fm

Country	Capital	Currency unit	Domain suffix
Moldova	Chisinau	leu	md
Monaco		euro	mc
Mongolia	Ulan Bator	tugrik	mn
Montenegro	Podgorica	euro	me
Morocco	Rabat	dirham	ma
Mozambique	Maputo	metical	mz
Myanmar	Yangon	kyat	mm
Namibia	Windhoek	rand	na
Nauru		Australian dollar	nr
Nepal	Kathmandu	rupee	np
Netherlands	Amsterdam	euro	nl
New Zealand	Wellington	dollar	nz
Nicaragua	Managua	cordoba	ni
Niger	Niamey	franc	ne
Nigeria	Abuja	naira	ng
North Korea	Pyongyang	won	kp
Norway	Oslo	krone	no
Oman	Muscat	rial	om
Pakistan	Islamabad	rupee	pk
Panama	Panama City	balboa	pa
Papua New Guinea	Port Moresby	kina	pg
Paraguay	Asunción	guarani	py
Peru	Lima	sol	pe
Philippines	Manila	peso	ph
Poland	Warsaw	zloty	pl
Portugal	Lisbon	euro	pt
Qatar	Doha	riyal	qa
Romania	Bucharest	leu	ro
Russia	Moscow	rouble	ru
Rwanda	Kigali	franc	rw
St Kitts and Nevis	Basseterre	dollar	kn
St Lucia	Castries	dollar	lc
St Vincent and the Grenadines	Kingstown	dollar	vc
Samoa	Apia	tala	ws
San Marino	San Marino	euro	sm
São Tomé and Principe	São Toméan	dobra	st
Saudi Arabia	Riyadh	riyal	sa
Senegal	Dakar	franc	sn
Serbia	Belgrade	dinar	rs
Seychelles	Victoria	rupee	sc

Countries of the world

Country	Capital	Currency unit	Domain suffix
Sierra Leone	Freetown	leone	sl
Singapore	Singapore City	dollar	sg
Slovak Republic	Bratislava	euro	sk
Slovenia	Ljubljana	euro	si
Solomon Islands	Honiara	dollar	sb
Somalia	Mogadishu	shilling	so
South Africa	Pretoria	rand	za
South Korea	Seoul	won	kr
Spain	Madrid	euro	es
Sri Lanka	Colombo	rupee	lk
Sudan	Khartoum	dinar	sd
Suriname	Paramaribo	guilder	sr
Swaziland	Mbabane	lilangeni	sz
Sweden	Stockholm	krona	se
Switzerland	Berne	franc	ch
Syria	Damascus	pound	sy
Taiwan	Taipei	dollar	tw
Tajikistan	Dushanbe	somoni	tj
Tanzania	Dodoma	shilling	tz
Thailand	Bangkok	baht	th
Togo	Lomé	franc	tg
Tonga	Nuku'alofa	pa'anga	to
Trinidad and Tobago	Port-of-Spain	dollar	tt
Tunisia	Tunis	dinar	tn
Turkey	Ankara	lira	tr
Turkmenistan	Ashgabat	manat	tm
Tuvalu	Funafuti	Australian dollar	tv
Uganda	Kampala	shilling	ug
Ukraine	Kiev	hryvna	ua
United Arab Emirates	Abu Dhabi	dirham	ae
United Kingdom	London	pound	uk, gb
United States of America	Washington DC	dollar	us
Uruguay	Montevideo	peso	uy
Uzbekistan	Tashkent	som	uz
Vanuatu	Vila	vatu	vu
Vatican City		euro	va
Venezuela	Caracas	bolivar	ve
Vietnam	Hanoi	dong	vn
Yemen	Sana'a	riyal	ye
Zambia	Lusaka	kwacha	zm
Zimbabwe	Harare	dollar	zw

Appendix 3: Australian leaders

Prime ministers of Australia

1901–03	Sir Edmund Barton	Protectionist
1903–04	Alfred Deakin	Protectionist
1904	John C. Watson	Labor
1904–05	George Houstoun Reid	Free Trade
1905–08	Alfred Deakin	Protectionist
1908–09	Andrew Fisher	Labor
1909–10	Alfred Deakin	Protectionist
1910–13	Andrew Fisher	Labor
1913–14	Joseph Cook	Liberal
1914–15	Andrew Fisher	Labor
1915–23	William M. Hughes	Labor, Nationalist
1923–29	Stanley M. Bruce	Nationalist
1929–31	James H. Scullin	Labor
1932–39	Joseph A. Lyons	United Australia
1939	Sir Earle C. G. Page	Country
1939–41	Robert Gordon Menzies	United Australia
1941	Arthur William Fadden	Country
1941–45	John Curtin	Labor
1945	Francis M. Forde	Labor
1945–49	Joseph Benedict Chifley	Labor
1949–66	Robert Gordon Menzies	Liberal
1966–67	Harold Holt	Liberal
1967–68 (Dec–Jan)	John McEwen	Liberal
1968–71	John Grey Gorton	Liberal
1971–72	William McMahon	Liberal
1972–75	Gough Whitlam	Labor
1975–83	Malcolm Fraser	Liberal
1983–91	Robert J.L. Hawke	Labor
1991–96	Paul Keating	Labor
1996–2007	John Howard	Liberal
2007–10	Kevin Rudd	Labor
2010–	Julia Gillard	Labor

Governors-general of Australia

1901–03	John Adrian Louis Hope, Earl of Hopetoun
1903–04	Hallam Tennyson, Baron Tennyson
1904–08	Henry Stafford Northcote, Baron Northcote
1908–11	William Humble Ward, Earl of Dudley
1911–14	Thomas Denman, Baron Denman
1914–20	Sir Ronald Craufurd Munro-Ferguson
1920–25	Henry William Forster, Baron Forster
1925–31	John Lawrence Baird, Baron Stonehaven
1931–36	Sir Isaac Alfred Isaacs
1936–45	Sir Alexander Gore Arkwright Hore-Ruthven, Baron Gowrie
1945–47	HRH Prince Henry William Frederick Albert, Duke of Gloucester, Earl of Ulster, and Baron Culloden
1947–53	Sir William John McKell
1953–60	Sir William Joseph Slim
1960–61	William Shepherd Morrison, Viscount Dunrossil
1961–65	William Philip Sidney, Viscount de L'Isle
1965–69	Richard Gardiner Casey, Baron Casey
1969–74	Sir Paul Meernaa Caedwalla Hasluck
1974–77	Sir John Robert Kerr
1977–82	Sir Zelman Cowen
1982–89	Sir Ninian Martin Stephen
1989–96	William George Hayden
1996–2001	Sir William Patrick Deane
2001–03	Dr Peter Hollingworth
2003–08	Major General Philip Michael Jeffery
2008–	Quentin Bryce

Chief ministers of the Australian Capital Territory

1989	Rosemary Follett	Labor
1989–91	Trevor Kaine	Liberal
1991–95	Rosemary Follett	Labor
1995–2000	Kate Carnell	Liberal
2000–01	Gary Humphries	Liberal
2001–	Jon Stanhope	Labor

Governors of New South Wales

1788–92	Arthur Phillip
1795–1800	John Hunter

1800–06	Philip Gidley King
1806–08	William Bligh
1810–21	Lachlan Macquarie
1821–25	Sir Thomas Macdougall Brisbane
1825–31	Ralph Darling
1831–37	Sir Richard Bourke
1838–46	Sir George Gipps
1846–55	Sir Charles Augustus FitzRoy
1855–61	Sir William Thomas Denison
1861–67	Sir John Young
1868–72	Sir Somerset Richard Lowry-Corry, Earl of Belmore
1872–79	Sir Hercules George Robert Robinson
1879–85	Lord Augustus William Frederick Spencer Loftus
1885–90	Lord Carrington (Charles Robert Wynn-Carrington)
1891–93	Victor Albert George Child Villiers, Earl of Jersey
1893–95	Sir Robert William Duff
1895–99	Henry Robert Brand, Viscount Hampden
1899–1901	William Lygon, Earl Beauchamp
1901–02	Sir Frederick Matthew Darley
1902–09	Sir Harry Holdsworth Rawson
1909–13	Lord Chelmsford (Frederick John Napier Thesiger)
1913–17	Sir Gerald Strickland
1918–23	Sir Walter Edward Davidson
1924–30	Sir Dudley Rawson Stratford de Chair
1930–35	Sir Philip Woolcott Game
1935–36	Sir Alexander Gore Arkwright Hore-Ruthven, Baron Gowrie
1936	Sir David Murray Anderson
1937–45	Lord Wakehurst (John de Vere Loder)
1946–57	Sir John Northcott
1957–65	Sir Eric Winslow Woodward
1966–81	Sir Arthur Roden Cutler
1981–89	Sir James Anthony Rowland
1989–90	David James Martin
1990–96	Peter Ross Sinclair
1996–2001	Gordon Jacob Samuels
2001–	Professor Marie Bashir

Premiers of New South Wales

1899–01	Sir William John Lyne	
1901–04	John See	Progressive
1904	Thomas Waddell	Ministerialist

1904–07	Joseph Hector McNeil Carruthers	Liberal Reform
1907–10	Charles Gregory Wade	Liberal
1910–13	James Sinclair Taylor McGowen	Labor
1913–20	William Arthur Holman	Labor, Nationalist
1920–21	John Storey	Labor
1921	James Thomas Dooley	Labor
1921	Sir George Warburton Fuller	Nationalist
1921–22	James Thomas Dooley	Labor
1922–25	Sir George Warburton Fuller	Nationalist
1925–27	John Thomas Lang	Labor
1927–30	Thomas Rainsford Bavin	Nationalist
1930–32	John Thomas Lang	Labor
1932–39	Bertram Sydney Barnsdale Stevens	United Australia
1939–41	Alexander Mair	United Australia
1941–47	William John McKell	Labor
1947–52	James McGirr	Labor
1952–59	John Joseph Cahill	Labor
1959–64	Robert James Heffron	Labor
1964–65	John Brophy Renshaw	Labor
1965–75	Sir Robin William Askin	Liberal
1975–76	Thomas Lancelot Lewis	Liberal
1976	Sir Eric Archibald Willis	Liberal
1976–86	Neville Wran	Labor
1986–88	Barrie Unsworth	Labor
1988–92	Nick Greiner	Liberal
1992–95	John Fahey	Liberal
1995–2005	Bob Carr	Labor
2005–08	Morris Iemma	Labor
2008–09	Nathan Rees	Labor
2009–	Kristina Keneally	Labor

Administrators of the Northern Territory

1864–66	Boyle Travers Finniss (Government Resident)
1870–73	William Bloomfield Douglas (Government Resident)
1873–76	George Byng Scott (Government Resident)
1876–83	Edward William Price (Government Resident)
1884–90	John Langdon Parsons (Government Resident)
1890–92	John George Knight (Government Resident)
1892–1906	Charles James Dashwood (Government Resident)
1906–10	Charles Edward Herbert (Government Resident)

1910–12	Samuel James Mitchell (Government Resident)
1912–19	John Anderson Gilruth
1919–21	Henry Ernest Carey (Director)
1921–27	Frederic Charles Urquhart
1927–31	Robert Hunter Weddell (Government Resident for North Australia)
1927–29	John Charles Cawood (Government Resident for Central Australia)
1929–31	Victor George Carrington (Government Resident for Central Australia)
1931–37	Robert Hunter Weddell
1937–46	Charles Lydiard Aubrey Abbott
1946–51	Arthur Robert Driver
1951–56	Frank Joseph Scott Wise
1956–61	James Clarence Archer
1961–64	Roger Bede Nott
1964–70	Roger Levinge Dean
1970–73	Frederick Charles Chaney
1973–76	John Norman Nelson
1976–81	John Armstrong England
1981–89	Eric Eugene Johnston
1989–93	James Henry Muirhead
1993–97	Keith John Austin Asche
1997–2000	Neil Raymond Conn
2000–03	John Christopher Anictomatis
2003–07	Edward Joseph Egan
2007–	Thomas Ian Pauling

Chief ministers of the Northern Territory

1978–84	Paul Everingham	Country Liberal
1984–86	Ian Tuxworth	Country Liberal
1986–88	Stephen Hatton	Country Liberal
1988–95	Marshall Perron	Country Liberal
1995–99	Shane Stone	Country Liberal
1999–2001	Denis Burke	Country Liberal
2001–07	Clare Martin	Labor
2007–	Paul Henderson	Labor

Governors of Queensland

1859–68	Sir George Ferguson Bowen
1868–71	Samuel Wensley Blackall
1871–74	George Augustus Constantine Phipps, Marquess of Normanby

Australian leaders

1875–77	William Wellington Cairns
1877–83	Sir Arthur Edward Kennedy
1883–88	Sir Anthony Musgrave
1889–95	Sir Henry Wylie Norman
1896–1901	Lord Lamington (Charles Wallace Alexander Napier Cochran Baillie)
1902–04	Sir Herbert Charles Chermside
1905–09	Lord Chelmsford (Frederick John Napier Thesiger)
1909–14	Sir William Macgregor
1915–20	Sir Hamilton John Goold-Adams
1920–25	Sir Matthew Nathan
1927–32	Sir Thomas Herbert John Chapman Goodwin
1932–46	Sir Leslie Orme Wilson
1946–57	Sir John Dudley Lavarack
1958–66	Sir Henry Abel Smith
1966–72	Sir Allan James Mansfield
1972–77	Sir Colin Thomas Hannah
1977–85	Sir James Maxwell Ramsay
1985–92	Sir Walter Benjamin Campbell
1992–97	Mary Marguerite Leneen Forde
1997–2003	Peter Maurice Arnison
2003–08	Quentin Bryce
2008–	Penelope Wensley

Premiers of Queensland

1899–1903	Robert Philp	
1903–06	Arthur Morgan	
1906–07	William Kidston	
1907–08	Robert Philp	
1908–11	William Kidston	
1911–15	Digby Frank Denman	Ministerialist
1915–19	Thomas Joseph Ryan	Labor
1919–25	Edward Granville Theodore	Labor
1925	William Neal Gillies	Labor
1925–29	William McCormack	Labor
1929–32	Arthur Edward Moore	Country Progressive National
1932–42	William Forgan Smith	Labor
1942–46	Frank Arthur Cooper	Labor
1946–52	Edward Michael Hanlon	Labor
1952–57	Vincent Clair Gair	Labor
1957–68	George Francis Reuben Nicklin	Country

1968	Jack Charles Allen Pizzey	Country
1968	Sir Gordon William Wesley Chalk	Country
1968–87	Sir Joh Bjelke-Petersen	Country
1987–89	Mike Ahern	National
1989	Russell Cooper	National
1989–96	Wayne Goss	Labor
1996–98	Rob Borbidge	National
1998–2007	Peter Beattie	Labor
2007–	Anna Bligh	Labor

Governors of South Australia

1836–38	John Hindmarsh
1838–41	George Gawler
1841–45	George Grey
1845–48	Frederick Holt Robe
1848–54	Sir Henry Edward Fox Young
1855–62	Sir Richard Graves MacDonnell
1862–68	Sir Dominick Daly
1869–73	Sir James Fergusson
1873–77	Sir Anthony Musgrave
1877–83	Sir William Francis Drummond Jervois
1883–89	Sir William Cleaver Francis Robinson
1889–95	Algernon Hawkins Thomond Keith-Falconer, Earl of Kintore
1895–99	Sir Thomas Fowell Buxton
1899–1902	Hallam Tennyson, Baron Tennyson
1903–09	Sir George Ruthven Le Hunte
1909–14	Sir Day Hort Bosanquet
1914–20	Sir Henry Lionel Galway
1920–22	Sir William Ernest George Archibald Weigall
1922–27	Sir George Tom Molesworth Bridges
1928–34	Sir Alexander Gore Arkwright Hore-Ruthven
1934–39	Sir Winston Joseph Dugan
1939–44	Sir Charles Malcolm Barclay-Harvey
1944–52	Sir Charles Willoughby Moke Norrie
1953–60	Sir Robert Allingham George
1961–68	Sir Edric Montague Bastyan
1968–71	Sir James William Harrison
1971–76	Sir Marcus Laurence Elwin Oliphant
1976–77	Sir Douglas Ralph Nicholls
1977–82	Sir Keith Douglas Seaman
1982–91	Sir Donald Beaumont Dunstan

Australian leaders

1991–96	Dame Roma Flinders Mitchell
1996–2001	Sir Eric James Neal
2001–07	Marjorie Jackson-Nelson
2007–	Kevin Scarce

Premiers of South Australia

1899–1901	Frederic William Holder	Liberal
1901–05	John Greeley Jenkins	Conservative coalition
1905	Richard Butler	Conservative
1905–09	Thomas Price	Labor–Liberal coalition
1909–10	Archibald Henry Peake	Liberal
1910–12	John Verran	Labor
1912–15	Archibald Henry Peake	Liberal
1915–17	Crawford Vaughan	Labor
1917–20	Archibald Henry Peake	Liberal–National coalition
1920–24	Sir Henry Newman Barwell	Liberal
1924–26	John Gunn	Labor
1926–27	Lionel Laughton Hill	Labor
1927–30	Richard Layton Butler	Liberal–Country coalition
1930–33	Lionel Laughton Hill	Labor
1933	Robert Stanley Richards	Labor
1933–38	Richard Layton Butler	Liberal Country League
1938–65	Sir Thomas Playford	Liberal Country League
1965–67	Francis Henry Walsh	Labor
1967–68	Don Dunstan	Labor
1968–70	Steele Hall	Liberal Country League
1970–79	Don Dunstan	Labor
1979	Des Corcoran	Labor
1979–82	David Tonkin	Liberal
1982–92	John Bannon	Labor
1992–93	Lynn Arnold	Labor
1993–96	Dean Brown	Liberal
1996–2001	John Olsen	Liberal
2001–02	Robert Kerin	Liberal
2002–	Mike Rann	Labor

Governors of Tasmania

1803–04	John Bowen (Commandant)
1804–10	David Collins (Lieutenant-Governor)
1810	Edward Lord (Commandant)

1810–12	John Murray (Commandant)
1812–13	Andrew Geils (Commandant)
1813–17	Thomas Davey (Lieutenant-Governor)
1817–24	William Sorrell (Lieutenant-Governor)
1824–36	George Arthur (Lieutenant-Governor)
1836–37	Kenneth Snodgrass (Administrator)
1837–43	Sir John Franklin (Lieutenant-Governor)
1843–46	Sir John Eardley Eardley-Wilmot (Lieutenant–Governor)
1846–47	Charles Joseph La Trobe (Administrator)
1847–55	Sir William Thomas Denison (Lieutenant–Governor)
1855–61	Sir Henry Edward Fox Young
1862–68	Thomas Gore Browne
1869–74	Charles Du Cane
1875–80	Frederick Aloysius Weld
1881–86	Sir George Cumine Strahan
1887–92	Sir Robert George Crookshank Hamilton
1893–1900	Jenico William Joseph Preston, Viscount Gormanston
1901–04	Sir Arthur Elibank Havelock
1904–09	Sir Gerald Strickland
1909–13	Sir Harry Barron
1913–17	Sir William Grey Ellison Macartney
1917–20	Sir Francis Alexander Newdigate Newdegate
1920–22	Sir William Lamond Allardyce
1924–30	Sir James O'Grady
1933–45	Sir Ernest Clark
1945–51	Sir Thomas Hugh Binney
1951–58	Sir Ronald Hibbert Cross
1959–63	Thomas Godfrey Polson Corbett, Baron Rowallan
1963–68	Sir Charles Henry Gairdner
1968–73	Sir Edric Montague Bastyan
1973–82	Sir Stanley Charles Burbury
1982–87	Sir James Plimsoll
1987–95	Sir Phillip Harvey Bennett
1995–2003	Sir Guy Stephen Montague Green
2003–04	Richard William Butler
2004–08	William Cox
2008–	Peter Underwood

Premiers of Tasmania

1899–1903	Neil Elliott Lewis	Conservative
1903–04	William Bispham Propsting	Liberal–Democrat

Australian leaders

1904–09	John William Evans	Liberal
1909	Sir Neil Elliott Lewis	Liberal Fusion
1909	John Earle	Labor
1909–12	Sir Neil Elliott Lewis	Liberal
1912–14	Albert Edgar Solomon	Liberal
1914–16	John Earle	Labor
1916–22	Sir Walter Henry Lee	Liberal, Nationalist
1922–23	John Blyth Hayes	Nationalist–Country coalition
1923	Sir Walter Henry Lee	Nationalist
1923–28	Joseph Aloysius Lyons	Labor
1928–34	John Cameron McPhee	Nationalist
1934	Sir Walter Henry Lee	Nationalist
1934–39	Albert George Ogilvie	Labor
1939	Edmund Dwyer-Gray	Labor
1939–47	Robert Cosgrove	Labor
1947–48	Edward Brooker	Labor
1948–58	Sir Robert Cosgrove	Labor
1958–69	Eric Elliot Reece	Labor
1969–72	Walter Angus Bethune	Liberal
1972–75	Eric Elliot Reece	Labor
1975–77	William Arthur Neilson	Labor
1977–81	Douglas Ackley Lowe	Labor
1981–82	Harry Holgate	Labor
1982–89	Robin Gray	Liberal
1989–92	Michael Field	Labor
1992–96	Ray Groom	Liberal
1996–98	Tony Rundle	Liberal
1998–2004	Jim Bacon	Labor
2004–08	Paul Lennon	Labor
2008–	David Bartlett	Labor

Governers of Victoria

1839–54	Charles Joseph La Trobe
1854–55	Sir Charles Hotham
1856–63	Sir Henry Barkly
1863–66	Sir Charles Henry Darling
1866–73	Sir John Henry Thomas Manners-Sutton
1873–79	Sir George Ferguson-Bowen
1879–84	George Augustus Constantine Phipps, Marquess of Normanby
1884–89	Sir Henry Brougham Loch
1889–95	John Adrian Louis Hope, Earl of Hopetoun

1895–1900	Thomas Brassey, Baron Brassey
1901–03	Sir George Sydenham Clarke
1904–08	Sir Reginald Arthur James Talbot
1908–11	Sir Thomas David Gibson Carmichael
1911–13	Sir John Michael Fleetwood Fuller
1914–20	Sir Arthur Lyulph Stanley
1921–26	George Edward John Mowbray Rous, Earl of Stradbroke
1926–31	Arthur Herbert Tennyson Somers Cocks, Baron Somers
1934–39	William Charles Arcedeckne Vanneck, Baron Huntingfield
1939–49	Sir Winston Joseph Dugan
1949–63	Sir Reginald Alexander Dallas Brooks
1963–74	Sir Rohan Delacombe
1974–82	Sir Henry Arthur Winneke
1982–85	Sir Brian Stewart Murray
1986–92	John Davis McCaughey
1992–97	Richard Elgin McGarvie
1997–2001	Sir James Augustine Gobbo
2001–06	John Landy
2006–	David de Kretser

Premiers of Victoria

1899–1900	Allan McLean	Liberal
1900–01	Sir George Turner	Liberal
1901–02	Alexander James Peacock	Liberal
1902–04	William Hill Irvine	Reform
1904–09	Sir Thomas Bent	Reform
1909–12	John Murray	Liberal
1912–13	William Alexander Watt	Liberal
1913	George Alexander Elmslie	Labor
1913–14	William Alexander Watt	Liberal
1914–17	Sir Alexander James Peacock	Liberal
1917–18	John Bowser	National
1918–23	Henry Sutherland Wightman Lawson	National
1923–24	Henry Sutherland Wightman Lawson	Allan Ministry/ National–Country coalition
1924	Henry Sutherland Wightman Lawson	National
1924	Sir Alexander James Peacock	National
1924	George Michael Prendergast	Labor
1924–27	John Allan	Country–National coalition

1927–28	Edmund John Hogan	Labor
1928–29	Sir William Murray McPherson	National
1929–32	Edmund John Hogan	Labor
1932–35	Sir Stanley Seymour Argyle	United Australia–Country coalition
1935–43	Albert Arthur Dunstan	Country
1943	John Cain	Labor
1943–45	Albert Arthur Dunstan	Country–United Australia coalition
1945	Ian Macfarlan	Liberal
1945–47	John Cain	Labor
1947–48	Thomas Tuke Hollway	Liberal–Country coalition
1948–50	Thomas Tuke Hollway	Liberal
1950–52	John Gladstone Black McDonald	Country
1952	Thomas Tuke Hollway	Electoral Reform
1952	John Gladstone Black McDonald	Country
1952–55	John Cain	Labor
1955–72	Sir Henry Edward Bolte	Liberal–Country coalition
1972–81	Rupert James Hamer	Liberal
1981–82	Lindsay Thompson	Liberal
1982–90	John Cain	Labor
1990–92	Joan Kirner	Labor
1992–99	Jeff Kennett	Liberal
1999–2007	Stephen Bracks	Labor
2007–	John Brumby	Labor

Governors of Western Australia

1828–32	James Stirling
1834–39	Sir James Stirling
1839–46	John Hutt
1846–47	Andrew Clarke
1847–48	Frederick Chidley Irwin
1848–55	Charles Fitzgerald
1855–62	Arthur Edward Kennedy
1862–68	John Stephen Hampton
1869–75	Frederick Aloysius Weld
1875–77	William Cleaver Francis Robinson
1877–80	Sir Harry St George Ord
1880–83	Sir William Cleaver Francis Robinson
1883–89	Sir Frederick Napier Broome
1889–90	Sir Malcolm Fraser

1890–95	Sir William Cleaver Francis Robinson
1895–1900	Sir Gerard Smith
1901–02	Sir Arthur Lawley
1903–09	Sir Frederick George Denham Bedford
1909–13	Sir Gerald Strickland
1913–17	Sir Henry Barron
1917–20	Sir William Grey Ellison Macartney
1920–24	Sir Francis Alexander Newdigate Newdegate
1924–31	Sir William Robert Campion
1931–33	Sir John Alfred Northmore (Administrator, Lieutenant-Governor)
1933–48	Sir James Mitchell (Lieutenant-Governor)
1948–51	Sir James Mitchell
1951–63	Sir Charles Henry Gairdner
1963–73	Sir Douglas Anthony Kendrew
1974–75	Hughie Idwal Edwards
1975–80	Sir Wallace Hart Kyle
1980–83	Sir Richard John Trowbridge
1984–89	Gordon Stanley Reid
1990–93	Sir Francis Theodore Page Burt
1993–2000	Philip Michael Jeffery
2000–06	Lieutenant General John Sanderson
2006–	Ken Michael

Premiers of Western Australia

1890–1901	Sir John Forrest	
1901	George Throssell	
1901	George Leake	
1901	Alfred Edward Morgans	
1901–02	George Leake	
1902–04	Walter Hartwell James	
1904–05	Henry Dalglish	Labor
1905–06	Sir Cornthwaite Hector Rason	Liberal
1906–10	Sir Newton James Moore	Liberal
1910–11	Frank Wilson	Liberal
1911–16	John Scaddan	Labor
1916–17	Frank Wilson	Liberal
1917–19	Sir Henry Bruce Lefroy	Liberal
1919	Sir Harry Pateshall Colebatch	Liberal
1919–24	Sir James Mitchell	National and Country
1924–30	Phillip Collier	Labor
1930–33	Sir James Mitchell	National and Country

Australian leaders

1933–36	Phillip Collier	Labor
1936–45	John Collings Wilcock	Labor
1945–47	Frank Joseph Scott Wise	Labor
1947–53	Sir Duncan Ross McLarty	Liberal Country League and Country
1953–59	Albert Redvers George Hawke	Labor
1959–71	Sir David Brand	Liberal Country League and Country
1971–74	John Trezise Tonkin	Labor
1974–82	Sir Charles Court	Liberal–National Country
1982–83	Ray O'Connor	Liberal–National Country
1983–88	Brian Burke	Labor
1988–90	Peter Dowding	Labor
1990–93	Carmen Lawrence	Labor
1993–2001	Richard Court	Liberal
2001–06	Geoff Gallop	Labor
2006–08	Alan Carpenter	Labor
2008–	Colin Barnett	Liberal

Appendix 4: Presidents, prime ministers, and monarchs

Presidents of the United States of America

1789–97	1	George Washington	Federalist
1797–1801	2	John Adams	Federalist
1801–09	3	Thomas Jefferson	Democratic Republican
1809–17	4	James Madison	Democratic Republican
1817–25	5	James Monroe	Democratic Republican
1825–29	6	John Quincy Adams	Independent
1829–37	7	Andrew Jackson	Democrat
1837–41	8	Martin Van Buren	Democrat
1841	9	William H. Harrison	Whig
1841–45	10	John Tyler	Whig, then Democrat
1845–49	11	James K. Polk	Democrat
1849–50	12	Zachary Taylor	Whig
1850–53	13	Millard Fillmore	Whig
1853–57	14	Franklin Pierce	Democrat
1857–61	15	James Buchanan	Democrat
1861–65	16	Abraham Lincoln	Republican
1865–69	17	Andrew Johnson	Democrat
1869–77	18	Ulysses S. Grant	Republican
1877–81	19	Rutherford B. Hayes	Republican
1881	20	James A. Garfield	Republican
1881–85	21	Chester A. Arthur	Republican
1885–89	22	Grover Cleveland	Democrat
1889–93	23	Benjamin Harrison	Republican
1893–97	24	Grover Cleveland	Democrat
1897–1901	25	William McKinley	Republican
1901–09	26	Theodore Roosevelt	Republican
1909–13	27	William H. Taft	Republican
1913–21	28	Woodrow Wilson	Democrat
1921–23	29	Warren G. Harding	Republican
1923–29	30	Calvin Coolidge	Republican
1929–33	31	Herbert Hoover	Republican

1933–45	32	Franklin D. Roosevelt	Democrat
1945–53	33	Harry S. Truman	Democrat
1953–61	34	Dwight D. Eisenhower	Republican
1961–63	35	John F. Kennedy	Democrat
1963–69	36	Lyndon B. Johnson	Democrat
1969–74	37	Richard M. Nixon	Republican
1974–77	38	Gerald R. Ford	Republican
1977–81	39	James Earl Carter	Democrat
1981–89	40	Ronald W. Reagan	Republican
1989–93	41	George H. W. Bush	Republican
1993–2001	42	William J. Clinton	Democrat
2001–09	43	George W. Bush	Republican
2009–	44	Barack Obama	Democrat

Prime ministers of Great Britain and of the United Kingdom

[1721]–42	Sir Robert Walpole	Whig
1742–43	Earl of Wilmington	Whig
1743–54	Henry Pelham	Whig
1754–56	Duke of Newcastle	Whig
1756–57	Duke of Devonshire	Whig
1757–62	Duke of Newcastle	Whig
1762–63	Earl of Bute	Tory
1763–65	George Grenville	Whig
1765–66	Marquis of Rockingham	Whig
1766–68	Earl of Chatham	Whig
1768–70	Duke of Grafton	Whig
1770–82	Lord North	Tory
1782	Marquis of Rockingham	Whig
1782–83	Earl of Shelburne	Whig
1783	Duke of Portland	coalition
1783–1801	Willliam Pitt	Tory
1801–04	Henry Addington	Tory
1804–06	William Pitt	Tory
1806–07	Lord William Grenville	Whig
1807–09	Duke of Portland	Tory
1809–12	Spencer Perceval	Tory
1812–27	Earl of Liverpool	Tory
1827	George Canning	Tory
1827–28	Viscount Goderich	Tory

1828–30	Duke of Wellington	Tory
1830–34	Earl Grey	Whig
1834	Viscount Melbourne	Whig
1834	Duke of Wellington	Tory
1834–35	Sir Robert Peel	Conservative
1835–41	Viscount Melbourne	Whig
1841–46	Sir Robert Peel	Conservative
1846–52	Lord John Russell	Whig
1852	Earl of Derby	Conservative
1852–55	Earl of Aberdeen	coalition
1855–58	Viscount Palmerston	Liberal
1858–59	Earl of Derby	Conservative
1859–65	Viscount Palmerston	Liberal
1865–66	Earl Russell	Liberal
1866–68	Earl of Derby	Conservative
1868	Benjamin Disraeli	Conservative
1868–74	William Ewart Gladstone	Liberal
1874–80	Benjamin Disraeli	Conservative
1880–85	William Ewart Gladstone	Liberal
1885–86	Marquis of Salisbury	Conservative
1886	William Ewart Gladstone	Liberal
1886–92	Marquis of Salisbury	Conservative
1892–94	William Ewart Gladstone	Liberal
1894–95	Earl of Rosebery	Liberal
1895–1902	Marquis of Salisbury	Conservative
1902–05	Arthur James Balfour	Conservative
1905–08	Sir Henry Campbell-Bannerman	Liberal
1908–16	Herbert Henry Asquith	Liberal
1916–22	David Lloyd George	coalition
1922–23	Andrew Bonar Law	Conservative
1923–24	Stanley Baldwin	Conservative
1924	James Ramsay MacDonald	Labour
1924–29	Stanley Baldwin	Conservative
1929–35	James Ramsay MacDonald	Labour, coalition
1935–37	Stanley Baldwin	coalition
1937–40	Neville Chamberlain	coalition
1940–45	Winston Spencer Churchill	coalition
1945–51	Clement Attlee	Labour
1951–55	Sir Winston Spencer Churchill	Conservative
1955–57	Sir Anthony Eden	Conservative
1957–63	Harold Macmillan	Conservative

1963–64	Sir Alec Douglas-Home	Conservative
1964–70	Harold Wilson	Labour
1970–74	Edward Heath	Conservative
1974–76	Harold Wilson	Labour
1976–79	James Callaghan	Labour
1979–90	Margaret Thatcher	Conservative
1990–97	John Major	Conservative
1997–2007	Tony Blair	Labour
2007–10	Gordon Brown	Labour
2010–	David Cameron	Conservative, coalition

Rulers of England and of the United Kingdom

Saxon line

Edwy	955–59
Edgar	959–75
Edward the Martyr	975–78
Ethelred the Unready	978–1016
Edmund Ironside	1016

Danish line

Canute (Cnut)	1017–35
Harold I	1035–40
Hardicanute (Harthacnut)	1040–42

Saxon line

Edward the Confessor	1042–66
Harold II (Godwinson)	1066

House of Normandy

William I (the Conqueror)	1066–87
William II	1087–1100
Henry I	1100–35
Stephen	1135–54

House of Plantagenet

Henry II	1154–89
Richard I	1189–99
John	1199–1216
Henry III	1216–72

Edward I	1272–1307
Edward II	1307–27
Edward III	1327–77
Richard II	1377–99

House of Lancaster

Henry IV	1399–1413
Henry V	1413–22
Henry VI	1422–61

House of York

Edward IV	1461–83
Edward V	1483
Richard III	1483–85

House of Tudor

Henry VII	1485–1509
Henry VIII	1509–47
Edward VI	1547–53
Mary I	1553–58
Elizabeth I	1558–1603

House of Stuart

James I of England and VI of Scotland	1603–25
Charles I	1625–49

Commonwealth (declared 1649)

Oliver Cromwell, Lord Protector	1653–58
Richard Cromwell	1658–59

House of Stuart

Charles II	1660–85
James II	1685–88
William III and Mary II (Mary d. 1694)	1689–1702
Anne	1702–14

House of Hanover

George I	1714–27

Presidents, prime ministers, and monarchs

George II	1727–60
George III	1760–1820
George IV	1820–30
William IV	1830–37
Victoria	1837–1901

House of Saxe-Coburg-Gotha

Edward VII	1901–10

House of Windsor

George V	1910–36
Edward VIII	1936
George VI	1936–52
Elizabeth II	1952–

Appendix 5:
Weights, Measures and Units

Conversion factors are not exact unless so marked.

1   Metric with imperial equivalents

Linear measure

1 millimetre	= 0.039 inch
1 centimetre = 10 mm	= 0.394 inch
1 decimetre = 10 cm	= 3.94 inches
1 metre = 100 cm	= 1.094 yards
1 kilometre = 1000 m	= 0.6214 mile

Square measure

1 square centimetre	= 0.155 sq. inch
1 square metre = 10,000 sq. cm	= 1.196 sq. yards
1 are = 100 square metres	= 119.6 sq. yards
1 hectare = 100 ares	= 2.471 acres
1 square kilometre = 100 hectares	= 0.386 sq. mile

Cubic measure

1 cubic centimetre	= 0.061 cu. inch
1 cubic metre = 1,000,000 cu. cm	= 1.308 cu. yards

Capacity measure

1 millilitre	= 0.002 pint (British)
1 centilitre = 10 ml	= 0.018 pint
1 decilitre = 10 cl	= 0.176 pint
1 litre = 1000 ml	= 1.75 pints
1 decalitre = 10 litres	= 2.20 gallons
1 hectolitre = 100 litres	= 2.75 bushels
1 kilolitre = 1000 litres	= 3.44 quarters

Weight

1 milligram	= 0.015 grain
1 centigram = 10 mg	= 0.154 grain
1 decigram = 100 mg	= 1.543 grains
1 gram = 1000 mg	= 15.43 grains

1 decagram = 10 g	= 5.64 drams
1 hectogram = 100 g	= 3.527 ounces
1 kilogram = 1000 g	= 2.205 pounds
1 tonne (metric ton) = 1000 kg	= 0.984 (long) ton

2   Temperature

Fahrenheit: water boils (under standard conditions) at 212° and freezes at 32°.
Celsius or Centigrade: water boils at 100° and freezes at 0°.
Kelvin: water boils at 373.15 K and freezes at 273.15 K.
To convert Celsius into Fahrenheit: multiply by 9, divide by 5, and add 32.
To convert Fahrenheit into Celsius: subtract 32, multiply by 5, and divide by 9.
To Convert Celsius into Kelvin: add 273.15.

°F	°C	°C	°F
–40	–40	–40	–40
–10	–23	–10	14
0	–18	0	32
10	–12	10	50
20	–7	20	68
30	–1	30	86
40	4	40	104
50	10	50	122
60	16	60	140
70	21	70	158
80	27	80	176
90	32	90	194
100	38 (approx.)	100	212 (exact)

3   The metric prefixes

Prefix	Abbreviations	Factors
deca-	da	10
hecto-	h	10^2
kilo-	k	10^3
mega-	M	10^6
giga-	G	10^9
tera-	T	10^{12}
peta-	P	10^{15}
exa-	E	10^{18}
deci-	d	10^{-1}

Prefix	Abbreviations	Factors
centi-	c	10^{-2}
milli-	m	10^{-3}
micro-	μ	10^{-4}
nano-	n	10^{-9}
pico-	p	10^{-12}
femto-	f	10^{-15}
atto-	a	10^{-18}

4 SI units

Physical quantity	Name	Abbreviation or symbol
length	metre	m
mass	kilogram	kg
time	second	s
electric current	ampere	A
temperature	kelvin	K
amount of substance	mole	mol
luminous intensity	candela	cd

Supplementary units

Physical quantity	Name	Abbreviation or symbol
plane angle	radian	rad
solid angle	steradian	sr

Derived units with special names

Physical quantity	Name	Abbreviation or symbol
frequency	hertz	Hz
energy	joule	J
force	newton	N
power	watt	W
pressure	pascal	Pa
electric charge	coulomb	C
electromotive force	volt	V
electric resistance	ohm	Ω
electric conductance	siemens	S
electric capacitance	farad	F
magnetic flux	weber	Wb
inductance	henry	H
magnetic flux density	tesla	T
luminous flux	lumen	lm
illumination	lux	lx

Appendix 6:
Elements and periodic table

(In order of atomic number)

Element	Symbol	Atomic no.
hydrogen	H	1
helium	He	2
lithium	Li	3
beryllium	Be	4
boron	B	5
carbon	C	6
nitrogen	N	7
oxygen	O	8
fluorine	F	9
neon	Ne	10
sodium	Na	11
magnesium	Mg	12
aluminium	Al	13
silicon	Si	14
phosphorus	P	15
sulphur	S	16
chlorine	Cl	17
argon	Ar	18
potassium	K	19
calcium	Ca	20
scandium	Sc	21
titanium	Ti	22
vanadium	V	23
chromium	Cr	24
manganese	Mn	25
iron	Fe	26
cobalt	Co	27
nickel	Ni	28
copper	Cu	29
zinc	Zn	30
gallium	Ga	31
germanium	Ge	32
arsenic	As	33

Element	Symbol	Atomic no.
selenium	Se	34
bromine	Br	35
krypton	Kr	36
rubidium	Rb	37
strontium	Sr	38
yttrium	Y	39
zirconium	Zr	40
niobium	Nb	41
molybdenum	Mo	42
technetium	Tc	43
ruthenium	Ru	44
rhodium	Rh	45
palladium	Pd	46
silver	Ag	47
cadmium	Cd	48
indium	In	49
tin	Sn	50
antimony	Sb	51
tellurium	Te	52
iodine	I	53
xenon	Xe	54
caesium	Cs	55
barium	Ba	56
lanthanum	La	57
cerium	Ce	58
praseodymium	Pr	59
neodymium	Nd	60
promethium	Pm	61
samarium	Sm	62
europium	Eu	63
gadolinium	Gd	64
terbium	Tb	65
dysprosium	Dy	66
holmium	Ho	67
erbium	Er	68
thulium	Tm	69
ytterbium	Yb	70
lutetium	Lu	71
hafnium	Hf	72
tantalum	Ta	73

Elements and periodic table

Element	Symbol	Atomic no.
tungsten	W	74
rhenium	Re	75
osmium	Os	76
iridium	Ir	77
platinum	Pt	78
gold	Au	79
mercury	Hg	80
thallium	Tl	81
lead	Pb	82
bismuth	Bi	83
polonium	Po	84
astatine	At	85
radon	Rn	86
francium	Fr	87
radium	Ra	88
actinium	Ac	89
thorium	Th	90
protactinium	Pa	91
uranium	U	92
neptunium	Np	93
plutonium	Pu	94
americium	Am	95
curium	Cm	96
berkelium	Bk	97
californium	Cf	98
einsteinium	Es	99
fermium	Fm	100
mendelevium	Md	101
nobelium	No	102
lawrencium	Lr	103
rutherfordium	Rf	104
dubrium	Dp	105
seaborgium	Sg	106
bohrium	Bh	107
hassium	Hs	108
meitnerium	Mt	109
darmstadtium	Ds	110
roentgenium	Rg	111
copernicium	Cn	112

All the elements heavier than bismuth (no. 83) are radioactive; all those heavier than uranium (no. 92) have only been produced artificially. The names given above for elements up to 112 are in standard use. Names for elements 113 and above are not yet standardised:

Element	Provisional name	Provisional symbol
113	ununtrium	Uut
114	ununquadium	Uuq
115	ununpentium	Uup
116	ununhexium	Uuh
117	ununseptium	Uus
118	ununoctium	Uuo

The IUPAC provisional names are based on the atomic number and are formed from the numerical roots $nil = 0, un = 1, bi = 2$, etc.

Chemical notation

The formula for a compound indicates the number of atoms of each element present in each molecule of the compound: e.g. a molecule of water (H_2O) contains two atoms of hydrogen and one of oxygen. The formula for an ionic compound indicates the proportions of the constituent elements, e.g. common salt (NaCl) contains equal proportions of sodium and chloride ions. Formulae for more complex compounds may indicate the manner of combination of the atoms in a molecule: e.g. ethanol (ethyl alcohol) may be represented as CH_3CH_2OH.

The periodic table of chemical elements

IA	IIA	IIIB	IVB	VB	VIB	VIIB	—	VIII	—	IB	IIB	IIIA	IVA	VA	VIA	VIIA	0
(H)																	He
Li	Be											B	C	N	O	F	Ne
Na	Mg											Al	Si	P	S	Cl	Ar
K	Ca	Sc	Ti	V	Cr	Mn	Fe	Co	Ni	Cu	Zn	Ga	Ge	As	Se	Br	Kr
Rb	Sr	Y	Zr	Nb	Mo	Tc	Ru	Rh	Pd	Ag	Cd	In	Sn	Sb	Te	I	Xe
Cs	Ba	La*	Hf	Ta	W	Re	Os	Ir	Pt	Au	Hg	Tl	Pb	Bi	Po	At	Rn
Fr	Ra	Ac†	Rf	Db	Sg	Bh	Hs	Mt	Ds	Rg	Cn	Uut	Uuq	Uup	Uuh	(Uus)	Uuo
*Lanthanides	La	Ce	Pr	Nd	Pm	Sm	Eu	Gd	Tb	Dy	Ho	Er	Tm	Yb	Lu		
†Actinides	Ac	Th	Pa	U	Np	Pu	Am	Cm	Bk	Cf	Es	Fm	Md	No	Lr		

All these elements are listed alphabetically in the main part of the dictionary.